The Oxford Companion to
Australian Literature

The Oxford Companion to Australian Literature

WILLIAM H. WILDE
JOY HOOTON
BARRY ANDREWS

Melbourne
OXFORD UNIVERSITY PRESS
Oxford Auckland New York

Cover illustration
Julian Ashton, 1851–1942
[The Botanic Gardens, Sydney] *c.* 1880
oil painting 19 x 29.5 cm
In the National Library of Australia

OXFORD UNIVERSITY PRESS

Oxford London New York Toronto
Delhi Bombay Calcutta Madras Karachi
Singapore Hong Kong Tokyo
Nairobi Dar es Salaam Cape Town
Melbourne Auckland
and associates in
Beirut Berlin Ibadan Nicosia

National Library of Australia
Cataloguing-in-Publication data:

Wilde, W.H. (William Henry), 1923–
 The Oxford companion to Australian literature.

ISBN 0 19 554233 9.

1. Australian literature — Dictionaries. I. Hooton, Joy W.
(Joy Wendy), 1935– . II. Andrews, Barry G., 1943– .
III. Title.

A820'.9

Designed by Arthur Stokes
Printed by Impact Printing, Brunswick, Victoria, Australia
Published by Oxford University Press, 7 Bowen Crescent, Melbourne
OXFORD is a trademark of Oxford University Press

Preface

The Oxford Companion to Australian Literature is a reference work which we hope will be of interest to the general reader as well as of use to students of Australian literature and related fields. Central to the book are the alphabetical entries on authors and literary works, and clearly there has been selection and weighting in the preparation of these entries: not every Australian author has been included, and some have been discussed in far greater detail than others. But we have taken a broad definition of 'author' (including entries, for example, on historians, critics and journalists) and of 'literary work', and the varied length of entries is only partly the result of our judgements on relative importances: for example, for some authors information has been difficult to discover, the plots of some novels are more conducive to summary than others, and for contemporary writers we have aimed to be conservative in coverage on the grounds that the output of those writers and the assessment of them is likely to undergo significant change. While we decided very early that to exclude living authors would be absurd in a Companion to as young a national literature as Australia's, we have not included many contemporary critics, except where they are also creative writers (e.g. Michael Wilding) or where their reputation has been established over a significant period of time (e.g. A.A. Phillips). For the author entries our aim has been to supply basic biographical and publishing information (including, with major authors, some critical studies of them) and generally also some measure of description and appreciation. The author entries often include information on literary works which are not the subject of a separate entry, but which are cross-referenced in many cases back to the author. We have been highly selective in our coverage of literary characters, including mainly characters who are of special significance (e.g. Lawson's Joe Wilson) or who can be firmly linked with an historical personage.

The second major group of entries encompasses the literary, historical and other cultural contexts within which Australian authors and their work can be placed. Our notion of literary context has been broad enough to permit entries on literary journals, series, awards, societies and movements; on libraries, publishers and cultural organizations; on aspects of closely associated fields (e.g. cinema, broadcasting, the theatre, Australian English); on overseas writers who either visited Australia (e.g. Trollope, Stevenson) or exercised significant influence in Australian cultural history (e.g. Dickens, Shakespeare); and on other topics. By historical and other cultural contexts is meant those aspects of Australian life and history about which readers unfamiliar with Australia might need basic information (e.g. on the Australian States or the Heidelberg School) or which might be encountered in the reading of Australian literature and need explanation: places, people, events, idioms and so on. Some of these have produced an extensive creative literature of their own (e.g. the phenomenon of bushranging) and most are at least alluded to somewhere in Australian writing. Such entries have been consciously focused towards Australian literature: thus the entry on the Turf deliberately provides only very basic information about the development of horse-racing and associated activities in Australia, and emphasizes instead the kinds of connections between the Turf and Australian literature through information on the poems and stories on the subject, the writers involved in horse-racing, and so on.

In a work of this scope and magnitude it is inevitable that we have been much indebted to the work of others, ranging from standard reference works such as E. Morris Miller's bibliography of Australian literature and the *Australian Dictionary of Biography* to specialist studies of individual authors. It is impossible to list all the works consulted in the preparation of the *Companion*, but we have included entries on many of the standard reference works and mentioned specialist studies in other entries; despite these inclusions, it is essential that we offer a general acknowledgement to all those who have written on Australian literature and its contexts. We are grateful to the writers who are the subject of entries who responded to our request for biographical and publishing information, generously supplying in many cases more information than we were able to use; for additional help over a wide range of inquiries we are also grateful to the staff of the Australian Council for the Arts, the Community Arts Board, the Fellowship of Australian Writers, the Literature Board and the University of Sydney; and to Chris Cunneen, Peter Dennis, Suzanne Edgar, Dorothy Green, Cliff Hanna, J.P. Hardy, Josie Hilliger, Ian Jones, Val Kent, Brian Kiernan, Elaine Lindsay, Roger McDonald, Mungo Ballardie MacCallum, John McQuilton, Brian Matthews, John Meredith, Craig Munro, Margaret O'Hagan, W.S. Ramson, John Robertson, Ken Stewart, Anne Summers, Alrene Sykes, G.P. Walsh and James Wieland. Considerable effort has been made to check the accuracy of the facts included in the *Companion*, although it must be pointed out that in some areas of Australian literature and literary history – Australian theatre history is a case in point – the definitive studies are only now emerging; we welcome any suggestions and corrections for future revisions and editions. The accuracy of this work has been greatly enhanced by the efforts of Sandra Burchill, research assistant in the Department of English at Duntroon throughout the project, who has done much research and performed many routine tasks of checking and filing with enthusiasm and cheerfulness; for other research assistance we are grateful to Patricia Dobrez early in the project and Kay Walsh towards the end. We thank Professor Harry Heseltine, head of the Department of English at Duntroon, for his support and co-operation, and Professor Geoff Wilson, Dean of the Faculty of Military Studies, for making funds available for research assistance. Much of the project was researched at the National Library of Australia, where Margaret Brennan, Jean James and other staff displayed a stunning capacity to produce esoteric material. The bulk of an enormous amount of typing and retyping of entries, lists of headwords and cross-references has been performed by Trish Middleton, without whose efforts the completion of the *Companion* would truly not have been possible; Bev Stuckey also assisted towards the end of the project. Our sincere thanks go to all of these helpers at the Canberra end of the project; at the publishing end we have been fortunate in having Frank Eyre perform the massive task of editing the manuscript. We are grateful to Frank for his endeavours, to Sarah Dawson for her skill and patience as production editor, and to James Hall and David Cunningham for their support and encouragement. Similarly, the support and interest of our colleagues in the Department of English at Duntroon has extended beyond a tolerance of our obsessions to a willingness each to contribute a significant entry. Within the *Companion* these entries have been signed with the initials of the contributors, as follows: Criticism, by Harry Heseltine (H.H.); Katharine Susannah Prichard, *Golden Miles*, *The Roaring Nineties* and *Winged Seeds*, by Sandra Burchill (S.B.); Peter Porter, 'An Exequy' and 'On First Looking into Chapman's *Hesiod*', by Jeff Doyle (J.D.); A.G. Stephens, by Doug Jarvis (D.J.); War Literature, by John Laird (J.L.); *Forefathers*, by Trish Middleton (T.M.); and Aboriginal Song and Narrative in Translation, by Bruce Moore (B.M.). Finally, and still keeping in mind the tolerance of obsessions, we should like to thank our families and friends, notably Ena Wilde, Viv Hooton, and Robyn Andrews.

W.H.W.
J.H.
B.A.

Style

In this work the names of authors (e.g. **BARRY, CLIVE**) and other persons (e.g. **BARRY, DAN**) are printed in bold capitals at the head of articles; the titles of literary works and newspapers in upper and lower case bold italics (e.g. ***Boomerang, Bring Larks and Heroes***); the titles of items within books in bold roman, in quotation marks (e.g. **'Man from Snowy River, The'**); and other entries, including the names of characters, in bold roman (e.g. **Cockatoo, Cabbage Tree, Beck, Martin**). Other aspects of our style should be apparent for such matters as the deletion of the definite article in headwords for newspapers and organizations, or the use of 'Aboriginal' for the singular and 'Aborigines' for the plural noun. There are, however, one or two matters that perhaps need comment or emphasis. Our two most difficult problems were to decide on an effective policy regarding the use of 'q.v.' and the citations of plays. With the former, we have used the cross-reference indicator 'q.v.' selectively rather than automatically, and as a general rule only when a reading of the entry referred to by 'q.v.' will, in our judgement, enhance the entry under consideration; readers are encouraged to use the *Companion* to see if an item not covered by a 'q.v.' is nevertheless the subject of an entry. With plays the problems are whether to give priority to date of performance or publication, and when to italicize the titles of plays, given that plays are not always separately published. Our final decision was to italicize all plays which have been published, whatever the form of publication (e.g. published separately, published as part of a volume of plays, or published within journals), and only to use quotation marks for unpublished plays. For many published plays we have given, where these are known to us, the dates of performance and publication, and we have tried to make clear, where only one date is given, which one it is; where doubt exists, readers are encouraged to turn to the entry on the individual play or its author. Among other decisions of policy, the titles of films and television series have been italicized; known dates of publication which differ from the date on the title page have been preferred for a few works (e.g. *Quintus Servinton*, *The Hermit in Van Diemen's Land* and *The Escape of the Notorious Sir William Heans*, qq.v); titles and subtitles (e.g. those beginning with *Or*) have been standardized so that all words have been capitalized apart generally from articles, conjunctions and prepositions; and better-known pseudonyms have been preferred in the headwords for some authors, although the appropriate cross-references are supplied. The cut-off date for inclusion of material is the end of 1983, although some items published or noticed early in 1984 have been included and some items published during the writing of the work (1979–83) may have escaped our attention.

Abbreviations

The following abbreviations have been generally adopted, but are not used where the full name is of major significance to an entry:

ABC	Australian Broadcasting Commission
AC	Companion of the Order of Australia
ACT	Australian Capital Territory
ADB	*Australian Dictionary of Biography*
AIF	Australian Imperial Force
ALS	Australian Literature Society
ALS	*Australian Literary Studies*
AM	Member of the Order of Australia
ANA	Australian Natives' Association
AO	Officer of the Order of Australia
APG	Australian Performing Group
A&R	Angus and Robertson
ASAL	Association for the Study of Australian Literature
BBC	British Broadcasting Corporation
BEM	British Empire Medal
CAE	College of Advanced Education
CLF	Commonwealth Literary Fund
CMG	Companion of the Order of St Michael and St George
CSIRO	Commonwealth Scientific Industrial and Research Organization
DBE	Dame of the Order of The British Empire
FAW	Fellowship of Australian Writers
FRGS	Fellow of the Royal Geographical Society
MBE	Member of the Order of The British Empire
MHR	Member of the House of Representatives
NSW	New South Wales
NZ	New Zealand
OAM	Medal of the Order of Australia
OBE	Officer of the Order of The British Empire
POW	Prisoner of War
PNG	Papua New Guinea
QC	Queen's Counsel
RAAF	Royal Australian Air Force
RAF	Royal Air Force
RAN	Royal Australian Navy
RN	Royal Navy

RSL	Returned Services League
SA	South Australia
SF	Science Fiction
UN	United Nations
USA	United States of America
VC	Victoria Cross
WA	Western Australia
WAAAF	Women's Auxiliary Australian Air Force

A

ABBOTT, J.H.M. (JOHN HENRY MAC-ARTNEY) (1874–1953), born Haydonton, NSW, was working as a jackeroo when his first contribution was accepted by the *Bulletin* in 1897. He served in the Boer War, an experience which produced both *Tommy Cornstalk* (1902), an early example of Australian war literature which presents the Australian soldier in a way similar to the Anzac (q.v.) legend, and *Plain and Veldt* (1903). In London after the war Abbott worked as a freelance writer and journalist and published *An Outlander in England* (1905) and *Letters from Queer Street* (1908), a moving account of London poverty. Back in Australia, Abbott was a prolific contributor of articles, series and serials to the *Bulletin*, the *Lone Hand* and many other journals. His historical fiction, which presented an influential view of colonial society, included *The Governor's Man* (1919), *Castle Vane* (1920), *Ensign Calder* (1922) and *Sydney Cove* (1923). Other historical works were *The Story of William Dampier* (1911), *Ben Hall* (1934), *The Newcastle Packets and the Hunter Valley* (1943), *Out of the Past* (1944) and *Red O'Shaughnessy* (1946). Historical figures such as Lachlan Macquarie and William Bligh appear in his fiction.

ABC Weekly, the journal of the ABC (q.v.) was published 1939–59, when it was superseded by the *TV Times*. Chiefly a descriptive outline of national and commercial radio programmes (later including television), it also carried articles of broad cultural interest.

ABDULLAH, MENA (1930–), of Indian extraction, was born at Bundarra in northern NSW. She contributed short stories to several of the *Coast to Coast* collections and to Louise Rorabacher's *Two Ways Meet* (1963), and collaborated with Ray Mathew (q.v.) to produce a collection of stories, *The Time of the Peacock* (1965). Most of the twelve stories in the collection are narrated by the small Indian girl, Nimmie, who weaves together the sometimes sad, sometimes happy, strands of a mixed Indian–Australian life. The Indian family, bound together by an intense love, cope with a poignant situation of exile that is tempered by hope for the future and joy in each other in the present. Well-known stories are 'Because of the Ruzilla', in which an Indian lad, insulted by an Australian boy and bereft of his beloved 'rosella', has his happiness restored by the gift

of a kettle that sings like a bird; 'Grandfather Tiger ', in which a little Indian girl creates an *alter ego*, the Tiger, who advises her how to combat the discrimination she meets at her first Australian school; and 'A Long Way', in which a mother walks from her village to Karachi to send a knitted jumper to her student son in Australia. The Abdullah/Mathew stories are examples of the craft of short fiction at its traditional best.

A'BECKETT, Sir WILLIAM (1806–69), born London, had a career in law and literature before coming to Australia in 1837. He was appointed resident judge of Port Phillip in 1845 and chief justice of the newly-created Supreme Court of Victoria in 1852. A'Beckett, who had published a book of verse in England at the age of eighteen, edited the weekly *Literary News* in NSW in 1837, published *Lectures on the Poets and Poetry of Great Britain* in 1839, contributed articles to the *Port Phillip Herald* under the pseudonym 'Malwyn', wrote a poem on Ludwig Leichhardt in that newspaper (later reprinted in Edmund Finn's *The Chronicles of Early Melbourne*, 1888), and published a long verse narrative, *The Earl's Choice*, in 1863. He was the great-grandfather of Martin Boyd (see Boyd Family).

Aboriginal and Islander Identity, see **Identity**

Aboriginal Arts Board, one of the seven arts boards of the Australia Council (q.v.), was founded in 1973. The Board consists solely of Aborigines selected from nominations made mainly by Aboriginal community organizations and is the means by which federal government support is provided to Aboriginal arts. It funds the practice of traditional Aboriginal culture, helps to disseminate knowledge about such culture among both Aboriginal and non-Aboriginal people, and assists Aboriginal people to retain their contact with traditional culture. Unlike the other boards of the Australia Council, the Aboriginal Arts Board offers financial assistance across the spectrum of the arts: theatre, dance, craft, visual arts, music and literature. In the last area its support encompasses recording programmes designed to preserve Aboriginal oral literature, literary groups and individual writers, although individual writers are also assisted by the Literature Board (q.v.).

Aboriginal in Australian Literature. Reflections on the Aborigines in the literature before European settlement in 1788 were mostly unfavourable. William Dampier saw them as 'the miserablest people in the world'; Captain James Cook said they appeared 'to be the most wretched people upon Earth'; Sir Joseph Banks described them as 'naked, treacherous, and armed with Lances, but extremely cowardly'. Governor Arthur Phillip, however, who had a closer and longer acquaintance with them than these earlier commentators, was so impressed by the bearing of some of the Port Jackson Aborigines that he named the cove where he met them, Manly (q.v.) Cove.

David Collins, in *An Account of the English Colony in New South Wales* (1798), indicated that by the end of April 1788 spasmodic violence had broken out between the Aborigines and the settlers. Watkin Tench, in *A Complete Account of the Settlement at Port Jackson in New South Wales* (1793), felt that the attacks by blacks were in retaliation for the convicts having stolen their fishing tackle and weapons. As a result of these early attacks the stereotype of the 'violent savage' soon arose. Aboriginal aggression, whatever its cause, produced an equivalent white response, and the cycle of violence between white and black became established. By the time the Colony's first newspaper, the *Sydney Gazette and New South Wales Advertiser*, appeared in 1803 violent clashes were occurring only on the outskirts of the settlement and the 'civilized' settlement Aboriginal was becoming the butt of colonial ridicule. Early *Gazette* references, reflecting white contempt, lampooned the Aboriginal, thus creating a further stereotype, the 'ignoble savage'; an ugly, comic figure whose image persisted in literature long after the original violent savage stereotype had disappeared. Barron Field, who arrived in Sydney in 1817, noted the growth of a hapless Aboriginal subculture in his *Geographical Memoirs on New South Wales* (1825).

In the earliest poetry emanating from the Colony the Aborigines were portrayed more as objects of curiosity (like the other strange Antipodean fauna) than as individual human beings. The 'sable race' existed in that early poetry as an awestruck backdrop to the energetic scenes of British colonizing. Michael Massey Robinson voiced the conventional evangelizing sentiments of the time by wishing to repair 'their youth neglected and their age untaught'. The only poem with any significant Aboriginal theme was Charles Tompson's 'Black Town', written as a comment on the government's establishment of the hamlet of Black Town for the purpose of civilizing the natives. It expresses platitudinous pity ('poor restless wand'rers of the woody plain') for the savages who lived in ignorance of the benefits of Christianity, but it reveals no understanding at all of the Aboriginal.

With the spread of exploration and settlement, contact between white men and the outlying tribal Aborigines intensified. The development of the overland route from Sydney to Adelaide and the increasing movement of settlers and travellers set off prolonged hostilities with the Aborigines along the Murray River. Reports of these bloody encounters reinforced the stereotype of the violent, treacherous savage. Sir Thomas Mitchell's expeditions had so much trouble with the blacks that he described them as 'implacably hostile and shamelessly dishonest' and his frustration culminated in a concerted attack on them at Mount Dispersion in May 1836, one of several organized white atrocities in the 1830s. Edward John Eyre, however, saw them as human beings, not merely ugly and violent primitives, as his sensitive relationship with his black companion Wylie indicated. In 1838 the Myall Creek massacre (q.v.), following upon the Pinjarra massacre in WA (1834) and the Mount Dispersion incident, brought the Aboriginal into the centre of controversy in Australia. The trial and ultimate hangings of seven white men for the Myall Creek murder of twenty-eight Aborigines was passionately debated in the columns of the colonial newspapers of the day. Much white opinion was outraged at the idea that white men should die for slaughtering Aborigines, who were seen as a threat to white society. The *Sydney Morning Herald* urged the authorities to 'protect the white settler, his wife and children, in remote places, from the filthy, brutal cannibals of New Holland'. Not all newspapers, however, showed the same antagonism. In the Swan River settlement the *Perth Gazette* published a sympathetic account of Aboriginal culture by R. M. Lyon in 1833, entitled 'A Glance at the manners and language of the Aboriginal inhabitants of Western Australia', together with an extensive Aboriginal vocabulary. The *Inquirer* (WA) published a series of articles by William Nairne Clark in 1842 defending the Aboriginal against the accusation of racial inferiority.

One of the earliest novels to feature the Aboriginal was the anonymously-authored *Alfred Dudley: Or, The Australian Settler* (1830). Alfred Dudley, successful in acquiring wealth in the colony, attempts to reconstruct in the Antipodes the lost family estate of Dudley Park in England. Dudley's inclusion of the Aborigines in the transplanted English community reveals an early, and rare, spark of optimism in fiction about the possible union of the two races. In *Tales of the Colonies: Or, The Adventures of an Emigrant* (1843) and *The Bushranger of Van Diemen's Land* (1846), Charles Rowcroft outlines the experiences of the settlers against a backdrop of natural hazards which included bushrangers and Aborigines. The notorious black man, Mosquito, is featured and many instances of butchery are included to confirm the image of the violent savage. Although overly sensational, melodramatic, and inaccurate in his shallow fictional portrait of the blacks, Rowcroft did illustrate some interesting aspects of the Aboriginal, for example his capacity for tracking, his tribal customs and habits and his essentially mild nature in his own environment. *The Bushranger of Van Diemen's Land*, which depicts a white woman in the hands of the Aborigines, guardedly introduces topics such as sexual harassment and miscegenation, topics which were to be exploited more fully by later writers. Thomas McCombie's *Arabin: Or, The Adventures of a Colonist in New South Wales* (1845) contains a separate, concluding section, 'Essay on the Aborigines of Australia'. The two chief fictional works of the 1840s were Alexander Harris's *The Emigrant Family: Or, The Story of an Australian Settler* (1849) and James Tucker's *Ralph Rashleigh*, written in the 1840s but not published in full until 1952. Harris's novel contains stories of depredations by the blacks, including an attack by 'myalls' (a common name for wild natives) on a cottage where a white family is sheltering, and there are some suggestions of cannibalism. Harris discusses black-white relationships at length, and through his protagonist, Reuben Kable, comments that such relationships must, in the isolated pioneer environment, be settled on an individual basis – 'Every man must be his own constable who goes to the extreme verge of civilization, and the retribution enforced must be palpable, prompt and decisive'. His assessment that the aggression of the blacks was the natural result of ill-feeling because of the invasion of their territory is balanced by his typical white settler conviction of his own right to the land in question – 'who will say that the invasion is an improper one?'. Harris's earlier work, *Settlers and Convicts: Or, Recollections of Sixteen Years' Labour in the Australian Backwoods* (1847), essentially non-fiction but not always factual, also deals with black–white relationships and is highly critical of the existing situation. The dilemma in which the sensitive settler found himself is well-portrayed in *Settlers and Convicts*. On the one hand Harris voiced an impassioned plea for the protection of the white settler and for the government to abandon its policy of compelling settlers to take away their workmen's guns, thus encouraging attacks by the Aborigines. On the other hand he acknowledged that the rapaciousness of the squatters and their wholesale appropriation of the land

had led to resentment from the Aborigines, whose own nature was free from avarice. Harris is scornful of the missionary efforts to Christianize the blacks – 'there seems something intrinsically absurd in the nation which is robbing another of its land and its means of subsistence soliciting that other to adopt its religion'. In Tucker's *Ralph Rashleigh*, the relationship between the two 'lowest' elements of Australian society, the escaped convict and the blackfellow, is developed. The convict is despised by the Aboriginal, who sees him as the scum of white society, yet the convict, because he is white, regards the black with contempt. Ralph Rashleigh, the escaped convict of Tucker's novel, spends four years with the Aborigines and the novel provides, especially in its account of Rashleigh entering and leaving the black community, the best contemporary record of Aboriginal society, customs and law.

In conjunction with the increased flow of fiction from the 1840s onwards, there was a constant supply of non-fictional accounts of life in the Australian colonies. Most of those works included descriptive, and sometimes amateurish, ethnographic accounts of the Aborigines. G. H. Haydon's *Five Years' Experience in Australia Felix* (1846) includes some commentary on Benbo, a well-known Melbourne Aboriginal, and his later, more fictional, *The Australian Emigrant* (1854) continues the Benbo story, presenting the 'civilized' Aboriginal as an object of amused, scornful white tolerance, much as Barron Field had done with the Sydney native, Bungaree (q.v.), thirty years earlier. In *A Visit to the Antipodes: with some Reminiscences of a Sojourn in Australia* (1846), E. Lloyd ('A Squatter') wrote of the difficulties of setting up a station. Among the problems he examined was the presence of the Aborigines who, by their adoption of a constant threatening posture, added the psychological burden of fear to the isolated settler's already difficult existence. In WA race relationships became troubled after the opening of pastoral settlements north of the Swan River. There were the same ingredients for violence and hostility that had been present in the eastern colonies, as the Pinjarra massacre of 1834 indicates. A notable WA contemporary account was Edward Landor's satirical *The Bushman: Or, Life in a New Country* (1847). An historical overview of the problems of contact in the west is given in Paul Hasluck's *Black Australians* (1942), which deals with the period from settlement to 1897; and in Peter Biskup's *Not Slaves, Not Citizens* (1973), which carries the investigation from 1898 to 1954.

In the second half of the nineteenth century the Aboriginal presence in literature was much more marked. The poet Charles Harpur, who had viewed with satisfaction the Myall Creek executions of 1838, later wrote 'An Aboriginal Mother's Lament', a poem sympathetic to the Aborigines, based on the massacre. His longer poem, 'Ned Connor', tells of a white stockman wantonly killing an Aboriginal who has led him to safety through the bush. The stockman, Ned Connor, falls victim to a mysterious illness and dies after seeing a vision of the dead Aboriginal. Harpur saw the white stockman's act as a violation of the natural moral order and the poem was his indictment of the practice of casual white brutality towards the Aboriginal. In Harpur's best-known frontier poem, 'The Creek of the Four Graves' (q.v.), where four white men are murdered by tribal Aborigines into whose territory they have come in search of pasture and water for their herds, there is no assessment of guilt or innocence on either side. The event itself is seen only as part of the frontier condition and in the general context of man's inhumanity to man. Henry Kendall's early Aboriginal poems, 'Aboriginal Death Songs' (1862), invest the black man with the charisma of the noble savage. Such songs as 'Kooroora', 'Ulmarra' and 'Urara' dwell on tribal battles, heroic deeds, grief-stricken dusky maidens and desolate landscapes. His much-anthologized 'The Last of His Tribe' (q.v.) pictures the final stages in the destruction of the Aboriginal tribes but avoids the question of culpability. Kendall later joined in the popular literary pastime of lampooning the black-fellow, and his tasteless skits such as 'Black Lizzie', 'Black Kate' and 'Jack the Blackfellow' were typical of the contemptuous and derisive mockery of the Aboriginal that had begun with the *Sydney Gazette* at the turn of the century. Kendall and fellow-poet James Brunton Stephens (q.v.) vied with each other for leadership in this poetry of ridicule – it was Kendall's boast that he could 'out-blackfellow Stephens'. George Gordon McCrae's (q.v.) two poems, 'Mamba ("The Bright Eyed"): An Aboriginal Reminiscence' and 'The Story of Balladeadro' (both 1867), were a significant addition to the poetry on Aboriginal themes, in that they were genuine attempts to understand and represent Aboriginal myth. McCrae's belief that a better understanding of the Aboriginal would come through knowledge and appreciation of Aboriginal myth and legend can be seen, with hindsight, to have been soundly based; in modern times myth and legend have provided a bridge between Aboriginal culture and white consciousness.

The stream of memoirs and reminiscences continued undiminished in the second half of the nineteenth century. The writers, usually erstwhile squatters, government officials and public figures, reflected, often from the height-ened imagination of their twilight years, on the lively colonial times they had lived through. The squatters had the most prolonged and closest contact with the Aborigines, a contact that inevitably entailed dispossession and violence. The constant search for land farther out meant that the far-flung squatter runs kept impinging on hitherto-untouched Aboriginal areas. As Alexander Harris had indicated, the frontier white man's safety lay in constant vigilance and merciless retribution. For him the only absolute solution to the racial problem lay in extermination of the blacks. On established runs, after the frontier had moved on, a changed pattern of relationships developed. The Aborigines who survived became a source of cheap labour; Aboriginal women were available for sexual utilization by the white males; and, in time, a *modus vivendi* evolved, with the Aborigines existing as a dispossessed but patronized minority within the station framework. Squatter literature reveals some close and satisfactory personal relationships between black and white in this secondary stage of settlement, e.g. W. A. Brodribb's *Recollections of an Australian Squatter* (1883) and E. M. Curr's *Recollections of Squatting in Victoria Then Called the Port Phillip District (from 1841 to 1851)* (1883). Along with numerous observations on the Aborigines, Curr included a colourful account of the Crown Lands Commissioners and their methods of settling the 'frequent difference which occurred between the original lords of the soil and the Anglo-Saxon *parvenus*'. One such method was for the Commissioner to appear before the Aborigines 'sabre in hand, surrounded by his troops industriously loading and discharging their carbines'. Not all white justice was so summarily dispensed, but Curr's account indicates the way in which the scales of justice were tipped against the Aboriginal in the outlying areas. Similar reminiscent writings reflecting the racial situation include the works of George Fletcher Moore, the early pioneer settler of WA. His memoirs, *Diary of Ten Years Eventful Life of an Early Settler in Western Australia* (1884), which included an Aboriginal vocabulary, showed a genuine desire to understand the black man. Richard Cannon, a surgeon who visited the remote Cape York area in 1863 in HMS *Salamander*, was horrified, as his *Savage Scenes from Australia* (1885) reveals, by the typical frontier brutality which attached as little significance to the life of an Aboriginal as to that of an animal. Additional reminiscent works include 'Rolf Boldrewood''s *Old Melbourne Memories* (1884), John Phillips's ('A Pioneer') *Reminiscences of Australian Early Life* (1893), James Kirby's *Old Times in the Bush of Australia* (1895), Thomas Bride's edition of *Letters from Victorian Pioneers* (1898) and

Constance Campbell Petrie's *Tom Petrie's Reminiscences of Early Queensland* (1904). Judith Wright's *The Generations of Men* (q.v., 1959), although written in the twentieth century, was compiled from family diaries and letters going back to the nineteenth century. It contains many reflections on the Aborigines, the most illuminating of which are the puzzled ponderings of May Wright (the poet's grandmother) on the possibility of the Aborigines having souls. The story of the Tasmanian Aborigines is related in a series of contemporary semi-historical works by James Bonwick: *Daily Life and Origin of the Tasmanians* (1870), *The Last of the Tasmanians; Or, The Black War of Van Diemen's Land* (1870) and *The Lost Tasmanian Race* (1884). In *Friendly Mission: The Tasmanian Journals and Papers of George Augustus Robinson 1829–1834* (1966, edited by N. J. Plomley), a personal and contemporary account of the destruction of the Tasmanian tribes is given.

The second half of the nineteenth century also brought a number of attempts to document the Aborigines in semi-scientific and ethnographic works. Often the writers were no more than well-intentioned laymen and their observations a mixture of fact, fancy and speculation, but the growing interest in the tribes, even at the informed amateur level, was the forerunner of later substantial sociological inquiries and investigations. With Alfred William Howitt and Lorimer Fison, true anthropological studies of the Aboriginal began. Their joint work, *Kamilaroi and Kurnai* (1880), and Howitt's *Native Tribes of South-East Australia* (1904), constitute the first scientific studies of tribal social relationships. Their successors were W. B. Spencer and F. J. Gillen, whose many published works, such as *The Native Tribes of Central Australia* (1899), *The Northern Tribes of Central Australia* (1904) and a later revision, *The Arunta: A Study of a Stone Age People* (1927), provided the impetus for the extensive ethnological investigation into the Aboriginal that came in the twentieth century.

The fiction of the second half of the nineteenth century included only occasional attempts at a sensitive investigation of racial contact and very little questioning of the accepted Aboriginal stereotypes. In Henry Kingsley's *The Recollections of Geoffry Hamlyn* (1859), the Aborigines are mostly presented as stock figures of savagery, one of the traditional hazards of pioneer life. However, Charles de Boos's novel, *Fifty Years Ago: An Australian Tale* (1867), begins by presenting the customary stereotype of racial contact (violence and counter-violence) but ends with a strong indication that new approaches to the racial problem are possible and desirable. The massacre by the Maroo tribe of the family of the white

settler George Maxwell is followed by vengeance plotted and systematically carried through in the James Fenimore Cooper tradition. Maxwell comes to regret his obsession with vengeance, that way being little better than the way of the myalls who killed his family. The Aboriginal chief, Macomo, comes to understand the atrocity he has committed and moves to an awareness of conventional human and moral values of which he had no comprehension at the beginning. The original violence of the black is seen as the impulsive, semi-instinctive action of the primitive when confronted with the threat of the white man. When not cast in the role of hunter, that is, when surrounded and facing death, the Aboriginal is seen as an heroic though pitiable figure. The novel seems to suggest that the white man is superior to the black only in the lucky accident that he has had the benefit of civilization to develop a higher consciousness. De Boos's close and sympathetic observation, coupled with his imaginative and sensitive analysis, produced an interpretation of the Aboriginal highly unusual for the time. 'Rolf Boldrewood' incorporated all the Aboriginal stereotypes in his fiction. Having experienced, as a squatter in western Victoria in the 1840s, the worst period of racial violence, he clearly found it difficult, even fifty years later, to eliminate from his consciousness the image of the black murderer who himself had to be murdered so that the white man could live free from threat. An attempt to view the racial problems ambivalently occurs in his 'The Squatter's Dream' (1875) where the characters, Guy Waldron and Redgrave, measure the choice between peace through coexistence or peace through extermination. The first alternative is shown to be illusory and moral judgement an irrelevant luxury when, in white opinion, the conflict is inevitable because of the nature of the savage. 'Boldrewood' gave himself the opportunity of presenting a meaningful account of black–white contact by introducing the massacre site of Murdering Lake, but ended, as in *Old Melbourne Memories* (1884), by indulging in nostalgic recreations of the stock, idealized figures of dignified Aboriginal male and winsome Aboriginal girl; Warrigal, the half-caste in *Robbery Under Arms* (1888), embodied much of what 'Boldrewood' innately felt about the black man. Rosa Praed lived as a child in the 1850s in an isolated Queensland environment dominated by the presence of the Aboriginal. She was six years old when the Aboriginal massacre of the Fraser family occurred on nearby Hornet Bank (q.v.) station. That massacre exerted a considerable influence on her fiction, producing an undercurrent of fear and prejudice, some of it sexually based. In many of her novels and in the factual-fictional *My Australian Girlhood: Sketches and Impressions of Bush Life* (1902), she draws on her childhood closeness to and affection for the station blacks, but on the whole she was vague and ill-informed about the Aborigines. In her fictional work *Fugitive Anne* (1902), the Aboriginal, Kombo, is an enigmatic presence, symbolizing the white woman's sexual unease about the black man.

In *Lady Bridget in the Never-Never Land* (1915), the racial problem is at the centre of the confrontation between misguided English philanthropy in the guise of Lady Bridget and hard-headed squatter realism in the form of McKeith, whose family has been massacred by blacks. In Simpson Newland's *Paving the Way* (1893), the inevitability of Aboriginal extinction is envisaged. In spite of their natural virtues of determination, bushcraft and courage (as illustrated in the death of the noble Murray River chieftain) the Aborigines are seen to be unable to withstand the power of the white man. Once physically defeated, detached from their own powerful tribal mores and forced into close contact with white society (rum, tobacco, disease), the Aborigines can only degenerate into the degradation that is summed up in the ignoble savage stereotype. Newland effectively conveys that degradation by his use of pidgin English, the ugly hotchpotch of that language suitably suggesting the new impurity of race.

That the nineteenth century ended with very little prospect for, or progress in, the satisfactory integration of black and white can be gauged from several comments in the press of the day. On 17 December 1887, the radical *Boomerang* made the following racist pronouncement:

The Australian nigger is generally regarded as about the lowest type of human creature about . . . There are some splendid points about the black and one in which he is far ahead of the Chinkie. He'll die out, and the Chinkie won't.

The *Bulletin* (9 June 1883) quoted from the Queensland newspaper, the *Northern Miner*, which deplored the 'holy howling' over the wholesale killing of male Aborigines and the sexual utilization of the females, then went on to offer its own solution to the Aboriginal problem:

Gather them all together on an immense reserve in North–Western Australia . . . Let them have no rum and no religion, but fight and frolic in their own way. And by the time the whites would be closing upon them, they would have reduced their own numbers so much by internal quarrels that the boundary line of their reservation could be shifted inwards far enough to allow four or five 'runs' in the space vacated. So the process of closing in could go on until the last survivors, two or three in number, were frozen out altogether. Some showman by that

time would make a good thing of taking them around the other colonies and exhibiting them as curiosities. This is the way to let the black race die out easily and naturally. The present efforts to ameliorate their conditions only result in killing them out sooner, and making their lives miserable while they do last . . . the relentless logic of the history of all our past dealings with the natives is summed up concisely in the dictum of the *Northern Miner* – 'the nigger must go'.

The turn of the century provided no magic line of demarcation after which the Aboriginal's representation in literature improved dramatically. The nationalism and radicalism of the 1890s, which spilled over enthusiastically into Federation, scarcely bothered to acknowledge the Aboriginal. He was excluded by the Constitution – 'the Aborigine shall not be counted' – and the stories and poems of Henry Lawson and A. B. Paterson, and the novel, *Such Is Life*, of Joseph Furphy paid only the briefest (in the latter case, somewhat vicious) attention to his presence. New attitudes, however, gradually evolved, slowly at first but more rapidly after the Second World War. Protection of the Aborigines against maltreatment and exploitation began to be embodied in parliamentary legislation. Queensland's *Aborigines Protection and Prevention of Sale of Opium Act* (1897) was followed by similar acts in WA (1905), NSW (1909) and SA (1911). Some oppressive legislation such as the *Native Administration Act* of WA and the *Queensland Aborigines and Torres Strait Islanders Act*, which enforced minority status on the Aboriginal, still remained on the statutes but there was a steady progression towards bringing the Aboriginal into the full political and social realities of contemporary Australia. That progress is reflected in the setting up of the Australian Institute of Aboriginal Studies in 1964, the establishment of a Centre for Research into Aboriginal Affairs at Monash University in 1964, the sponsoring in 1964 of the series *Aborigines in Australian Society* by the Social Sciences Research Council of Australia, the referendum to remove discriminating clauses against Aborigines from the Commonwealth Constitution in 1967, the establishment of the federal government's Department of Aboriginal Affairs in 1972, the establishment of the National Aboriginal Conference in 1978, and the Aboriginal Development Commission. On the cultural side there was positive discrimination in favour of Aborigines by the Australia Council and considerable impetus given to Aboriginal art by the establishment of the Aboriginal Arts Board (q.v.). The scientific and anthropological works of the pioneer investigators Howitt and Fison, Spencer and Gillen were followed by numerous other studies, notable among which were A. P.

Elkin's (q.v.) *The Australian Aborigines* (1938), T. G. H. Strehlow's (q.v.) *Aranda Traditions* (1947), J. W. Bleakley's *The Aborigines of Australia* (1961), Ronald and Catherine Berndt's (q.v.) *Aboriginal Man in Australia* (1965) and *The World of the First Australians* (1964, revised edition 1981), Marie Reay's (ed.) *Aborigines Now* (1964), A. R. Pilling and R. A. Waterman's *Diprotodon to Detribalization* (1970) and W. E. H. Stanner's many works on Aboriginal religion. In the light of all this new knowledge the long-held popular image of the Aboriginal as sub-human has gradually faded. Of considerable significance also in this century has been the stimulation of white awareness of the Aboriginal and his culture through Aboriginal myth and legend. The publication of Catherine Langloh Parker's (q.v.) *Australian Legendary Tales* (1896) and *More Australian Legendary Tales* (1898) began a European popularization of Aboriginal tribal stories and songs. In the 1930s the Jindyworobak (q.v.) desire to present Aboriginal lore as an example to white Australians, in the hope that they might establish an equivalent affinity with the Australian landscape, helped inspire the work of Roland Robinson (q.v.) whose numerous volumes include *Legend and Dreaming* (1952), *The Feathered Serpent* (1956) and *Aboriginal Myths and Legends* (1966). Together with many other writers, e.g. W. E. Harney (q.v.), Aboriginal writers such as Kath Walker, Dick Roughsey and David Unaipon (qq.v.) have also participated in the collection and dissemination of tribal stories and legends (see Aboriginal Writing in English). Numerous prestigious volumes of Aboriginal lore have appeared in recent times, e.g. *The Dreamtime Book* (1973), with paintings by Ainslie Roberts and text by Charles P. Mountford; *Australian Dreaming* (1980), compiled and edited by Jennifer Isaacs; and *Dreamtime: The Aboriginal Heritage* (1981), paintings by Ainslie Roberts and text by Melva Jean Roberts.

Fiction writers who included the Aboriginal at the turn of the century were few. Mrs Aeneas Gunn's (q.v.) two stories, *The Little Black Princess* (1905) and *We of the Never-Never* (1908), are classic examples of the patronizing but totally short-sighted approach of many well-intentioned Australians towards the Aboriginal. In her tales of Elsey station and the Never-Never land the Aboriginal is depicted as a cross between a backward but lovable child and an awkward, shambling domestic pet. English biologist E.L. Grant Watson (q.v.) produced the first worthwhile fictional treatment of the Aboriginal in this century. Watson spent most of 1910–11 with fellow biologist Radcliffe Brown and with Daisy Bates (q.v.) among the Kimberley blacks and in the Bernier Island isolation hospital for diseased blacks from the north-west. His story 'Out There', an account of the eternal triangle (white man with black woman and white woman), ends in affirmation of the white–black relationship and the recognition of a harmony and sense of purpose in Aboriginal life. 'Out There' decries the long-lived stigma attached to the white men who decide to 'go black'. In Watson's novels, e.g. *The Desert Horizon* (1923), the problem of white accommodation to the vast isolated north-west is examined, and the relevance and importance of the Aboriginal stressed. In the mid 1920s several major clashes, the Onmalmeri massacre in the Kimberleys (1926) and the Coniston killings (1928) north–west of Alice Springs, led to a concerted demand for new attitudes to the Aboriginal. Against the background of wide national debate on the Aboriginal question two professional writers, Vance Palmer and Katharine Susannah Prichard (q.v.), introduced new dimensions into the particularly sensitive area of black–white sexual relations. Looking back on the 1920s in *Laughter, Not for a Cage* (1956), Miles Franklin (q.v.) stated that 'one of the greatest [literary themes] demanding treatment' was 'black velvet' (q.v.), a major Aboriginal skeleton in the colonization cupboard. The white man's sexual use of Aboriginal women had long been tacitly recognized as an acceptable behaviour pattern in the isolated outback, where white women were few, but that acceptance had always insisted that such miscegenation was merely a casual consorting with no deep underlying emotional attachment. Both Palmer and Prichard presented a much more complicated view of interracial sexuality. In Palmer's *The Man Hamilton* (1928), white man Hamilton chooses life on the station with his half-caste 'wife' and son rather than the love of the white governess; by contrast, in *Men Are Human* the white character Boyd discards the pregnant half-caste Josie and prefers the white woman, Barbara. By some ironic nemesis Boyd is trampled to death by cattle and Josie bears his stillborn son. Between Palmer's two novels came K. S. Prichard's *Coonardoo* (q.v.), after which no return to the simplicity of the original 'black velvet' stereotype was possible. Between station owner Hugh Watt and Aboriginal girl Coonardoo there develops a physical and spiritual affinity, although Watt, unable to reject his white conditioning about miscegenation, tragically rejects Coonardoo and the chance of happiness. Some contemporary opinion was scandalized by *Coonardoo*. S. H. Prior refused to publish Palmer's *Men are Human* in 1929 because 'the disastrous experience with *Coonardoo* shows us that the Australian public will not stand stories based on a white man's relations with an Aborigine'. *Coonardoo* was part of a continuing attempt (which included the short stories 'Happiness' and 'The Cooboo' and the later play, *Brumby Innes*) by Prichard to interpret, often lovingly and always imaginatively, the essence of the Aboriginal, and to present something of the fineness and integrity that she believed to be possible in racial relationships.

In the past fifty years the traditional literary stereotypes of the Aboriginal have faded. Contemporary practice has been to place the Aboriginal in the centre of the literature of social protest, either out of genuine concern for the Aborigines as an underprivileged minority or because the Aboriginal is a ready–made device that writers can use to validate their own particular social or political causes. In recent literature the chief themes have been interracial sexual relationships, contemporary racial prejudice, especially in relation to the part-Aboriginal or half-caste, white guilt about the past, and the territorial rights of today's Aborigines. The theme of interracial sexuality, begun in *Coonardoo*, has been continued by many writers. In Mary Durack's *Keep Him My Country* (q.v., 1955) the young white station owner, Stan Rolt, ultimately achieves serenity through recognizing that his relationship with the native girl, Dalgerie, has linked him indissolubly to the land itself. The primal relationship between the land and the Aboriginal is widened to include the white man, and the union between black and white and the spirit of the land itself is seen as beneficial to all three. In novels such as F. B. Vickers's *The Mirage* (1955), Gavin Casey's *Snowball* (1958), Randolph Stow's *To The Islands* (1958), Donald Stuart's *Yaralie* (1962) and Dymphna Cusack's *Black Lightning* (1964) the problems that follow emotional involvements between black and white are honestly and sensitively examined. The starting point for the modern novel of social protest which features the Aboriginal is Xavier Herbert's *Capricornia* (q.v., 1938), a work which grew out of an earlier unpublished novel, 'Black Velvet'. Although *Capricornia* is not only a novel of social protest (as 'Black Velvet' seems to have been) its opening chapter, 'The Coming of the Dingoes', records the arrival of the white man in Capricornia (the Northern Territory) and his impact on the hitherto-uncorrupted Aboriginal life. *Capricornia* is a devastating indictment of such customary white rationalizations of the treatment of the Aboriginal as the need to civilize and Christianize the black, and the benefits to them of benevolent white despotism. It particularly attacks the white usurpation of Aboriginal territory, the callousness, hypocrisy and cant of official attitudes (both government and religious) and the inhumanity of white attitudes to the half-caste

(the tragic non-person – Naw-Nim – no name) who is alienated from both parent races. The half-caste has continued, since *Capricornia*, to be the centre of a considerable body of fiction, which includes, in addition to the novels mentioned above, T. A. G. Hungerford's war novel, *The Ridge and the River* (1952), Nene Gare's *The Fringe Dwellers* (1961), Leonard Mann's *Venus Half-Caste* (1963), Raymond Aitchison's *The Illegitimates* (1964), Archie Weller's *The Day of the Dog* (1981) and many others. Herbert's criticism of the Christianizing of the Aboriginal has been widely supported by recent writers, who see the substitution of the Dreamtime mythology by Christian beliefs as a weakening of tribal mores leading to the complete demise of the race. The reservation concept, i.e. providing a barrier between black and white races, has also led, in Herbert's opinion, to the degrading and dehumanizing of the Aboriginal who remains, on the reservation, the helpless victim of demeaning patronage and arrogant official ignorance. In his later novel, *Poor Fellow My Country* (q.v., 1975), where the theme of modern Australia as a shiftless, materialistic society is dominant, Herbert returns to his indictment of the nation's shameful treatment of the Aboriginal. His remarkable knowledge of and affinity for Aboriginal customs and language make that massive work a significant expression of protest on their behalf. Other examinations and expressions of white guilt for Australia's history of racialism range from Judith Wright's poetry, e.g. 'Nigger's Leap, New England', 'Bora Ring' and 'At Cooloolah', to Heriot's exorcism of guilt and subsequent spiritual regeneration in Randolph Stow's *To the Islands*. Thomas Keneally's *The Chant of Jimmie Blacksmith* (based on the story of Jimmy Governor, q.v.), a sensational account of tyranny and bigotry finally driving an Aboriginal out of the ignoble into the violent stereotype, has (largely through the impact of the film of the novel) finally awakened many Australians to the reality of Australian racism. In addition to Keneally's novel, Peter Mathers's *Trap* (1966) and David Ireland's *Burn* (1974) illustrate the theme of violence against established society by the 'outsider' of that society. In Australian society there is no more easily-understood and more readily available stereotype of the 'outsider' than the half-caste, and it is in that role and to illustrate his wider theme of social alienation that Patrick White uses the part-Aboriginal Alf Dubbo in *Riders in the Chariot* (1961). Official racism is featured in F. B. Vickers's novel *The Mirage*, where the repressive race laws of WA produce tragedy in the lives of a young half-caste and his bride. Richard Beilby's *The Brown Land Crying* (1975), a novel about an Aboriginal community in WA, indicates how underprivilege in the form of poverty, police brutality and restrictive taboos lead to total social immobility and utter deprivation for the Aborigines involved. Donald Stuart's concern in *The Driven* (1961) and *Yaralie* (1962) is to predict that the final solution to racial conflict lies in racial integration. His belief, expressed in *Yaralie,* is that the combination of the remarkable qualities of both races – the 'forward-thrusting attributes' of the white and the 'wise love of the country' of the black – will produce a people especially suited for the vast outback Australia.

The past two decades have seen the emergence of a strong body of Aboriginal writing in English (q.v.). Not all of this is literature of social protest, but given the long silence during which the Aboriginal people have been unable to speak for themselves it would have been remarkable if their own first utterances had not been highly critical of past attitudes and situations. The main concerns of the new Aboriginal literature have been the spiritual and physical alienation and deprivation of the Aboriginal race throughout colonial and modern times, the modern Aboriginal's search for identity, the insistence on basic human rights for present-day Aborigines, and the particular demand for land rights. Kath Walker (q.v.), a part-Aboriginal poet, indicates by the title of her first volume of poetry, *We Are Going* (1964), the doom of the Aboriginal race if drastic changes are not immediately made in white attitudes. She sees it as her responsibility to record the aspirations and frustrations of the Aboriginal people; her message is that the Aboriginal deserves a place in Australian society equal to that of the white man, but without the forfeiture of his own identity and culture. Jack Davis (q.v.), a part-Aboriginal from WA, poet, playwright and editor of the Aboriginal magazine *Identity* (q.v.) from 1973 to 1979, sees land rights as the key to Aboriginal regeneration. Kevin Gilbert, whose play *The Cherry Pickers* (qq. v.), about Aboriginal seasonal workers was produced in 1971, has published two significant protest works which reflect the Aboriginal crisis through Aboriginal eyes. *Because a White Man'll Never Do It* (1973) advocates Aboriginal land rights and total Aboriginal community development, the latter not through the reservation concept, which produces rapid racial degeneracy, but through the concept of a 'black Israel' which would bring a resurgence of racial pride. His later collection of interviews with Aborigines, *Living Black* (1977), makes clear to contemporary white Australians the sense of injustice and depression felt by Aboriginal people from the slums of Redfern to outback Queensland, and attempts to stimulate white consciences to the acceptance of basic justice for all Australians, black and white. Similar political writings include Cheryl Buchanan's *We Have Bugger All!* (1974) and *Black Power in Australia* (1975), a debate on Aboriginal issues by Aboriginal Senator Neville Bonner and Bobbi Sykes. Gerald Bostock's (q.v.) angry poetry, *Black Man Coming* (1980), has as its theme 'The time has come/to fight the racist scum' and his play *Here Comes the Nigger!* (q.v.) advocates pan-Aboriginal nationalism. Robert Merritt's play *The Cake Man* (1978) (qq. v.) makes its point against condescending paternalism by implying that white Australia cannot salve its conscience for two centuries of Aboriginal deprivation by bribery in the form of seductive handouts. The recent upsurge of both Aboriginal and white protest writing indicates that the near future may well provide an optimistic answer to the frustrated and angry question asked on behalf of all contemporary Aborigines by Gerald Bostock: 'How long must we wait for justice and freedom/To be won?'

From an abundant stream of very recent historical and sociological writing on the Aboriginal, the following are noteworthy: Richard Broome's *Aboriginal Australians: Black Response to White Dominance 1788–1980* (1982), which traces the Aboriginal response to white settlement and domination from initial resistance and destruction to the recent push for 'self-determination'; Noel Loos's *Invasion and Resistance: Aboriginal–European Relations on the North Queensland Frontier 1861–1897* (1982), a carefully-researched regional history; Garth Nettheim's *Victims of the Law: Black Queenslanders Today* (1982), which reviews Queensland's Aborigines Act of 1971 to 1979 and the Torres Strait Islanders Act of 1971 to 1979; Colin Tatz's six essays in *Aborigines and Uranium and Other Essays* (1982), which discusses human rights and race relations; Michael Howard's (ed.) *Aboriginal Power in Australian Society* (1982); Lyndall Ryan's *The Aboriginal Tasmanians* (1981); Judith Wright's *The Cry for the Dead* (1981), which highlights (in part) the contest for the land between black and white in pioneer times; *Race Relations in Australia: A History* (1982) by A. T. Yarwood and M. J. Knowling, which traces the history of racialism (not only towards the Aborigines) in Australia from the beginnings to the present day; and Henry Reynold's *The Other Side of the Frontier* (1981) and other works.

Aboriginal Publications Foundation, established in 1971, produces the quarterly magazine *Identity* (q.v.). Managed by a national committee of Aborigines and Torres Strait Islanders, the Foundation's other functions include the publication of writings by and for Aborigines, the organization of training and the provision of scholarships and financial aid for Aborigines with potential in literature and the creative arts, and the appropriate recognition of distinguished creative achievements by Aborigines.

Aboriginal Song and Narrative in Translation. Aboriginal song and narrative, traditionally oral literature, are much more complex and diverse than one might assume from the evidence of the so-called 'myths and legends' which are often published for the general reading public. These 'myths and legends' have usually been subject to synthetic treatment, and are almost invariably presented in a vacuum – wrenched from and without any account of the cultural contexts in which they were originally performed. Outside the Aboriginal world, songs and narratives in the vernacular have been accessible only to a specialized group of anthropologists, linguists and ethnomusicologists, and although recordings of Aboriginal songs and music are now available it is unlikely that texts in the vernacular will ever become accessible to the wider public in any meaningful ways by such means. The living tradition of oral literature, which is part of the cultural achievement of the people who lived in this land for 40 000 years before being dispossessed by white settlers, is closed to the wider public except through translation. Apart from the usual losses which occur in translation from one language to another, the translation of Aboriginal literature presents special difficulties: in the shift from oral delivery to the written word, aspects of dramatic presentation (such as music, dance, gesture, pace and so on) are inevitably lost; many of the songs are composed in a highly-stylized poetic *koiné* which differs in important ways from the language of common speech (for example, everyday words may have special symbolic associations and even different meanings when used in song, or the songs may include archaic linguistic forms); and the content and the form of the songs and narratives vary according to the cultural and social contexts in which they are performed.

The myths of the Aboriginal religions vary from area to area, but one common factor is the concept of the 'Eternal Dreamtime', which refers in part to that time in the past when mythic heroes or totemic ancestors moved through the country and were responsible for the shaping of the land, the creation of people, the institution of rituals and the establishing of cultural values, but which refers equally to the present, since these mythic beings continue to live on in spiritual form and exert their influence on the people and the environment. The myths enshrine a history, a code of cultural ideals and laws, and an ontology; and central to all these is the sacred bond between the land and everything that exists within it. The literature that embodies these myths is therefore also sacred. There are, however, degrees of sacredness, which depend on such factors as the occasion of the performance, and the sex, age and social status of the performers. For example, songs associated with initiation rites, with fertility and increase rites and with the commemorative re-enactment of events that took place in the Eternal Dreamtime may be limited to certain categories of initiated men and therefore be classified as sacred-secret. Other songs and narratives may be classified as sacred but non-secret, and therefore be known to a wider section of the community. This non-secret material often deals with the same myth that occurs in the sacred-secret songs, or with sections of it, but there are significant differences both in levels of interpretation and in form (including the relative sophistication of the melodic line). At the other end of the scale the distinction between sacred and secular is not always clear-cut: there are narratives of various kinds including 'secular' versions of the sacred myths, children's songs and stories, and songs and stories about contemporary and topical events. Nor is the distinction between song and narrative always clear-cut: there is straightforward narrative, narrative interspersed with songs, forms of narrative whose rhythms so vary from the rhythms of everyday speech that they verge on song, songs with narrative links, song-cycles with narrative links, and songs by individual composers which deal with topical issues. Since the most sacred songs are assumed to have come down from the past unchanged, they are to a large extent 'fixed'; less sacred songs, the songs of individual composers and, of course, narratives, are more susceptible to variation in performance. The style of songs also varies from region to region: for example, in Central Australia and western Arnhem Land the individual songs that make up the song-cycles are typically short, and much of their effect depends on the symbolic and associative significance of key-words which are repeated with variations, whereas in north-eastern Arnhem Land the individual songs are longer and more elaborate, and include rich descriptive detail. These factors (and there are others) suggest why translation without detailed explanatory information (including proper acknowledgement to the owners of the songs and narratives) is an entirely inadequate way of presenting this literature.

Some of the earliest transcriptions and translations of songs appear towards the end of the nineteenth century. G. Taplin, in *The Native Tribes of South Australia*, ed. J. Woods (1879), gives two short songs from the Nirrinjeri tribe, one of which is an exoteric song that compares the smoke and steam which issue from a train with the water that blows from a spouting whale. A. W. Howitt, in *Notes on Songs and Song Makers of Some South Australian Tribes* (1887), gives 'Wenberi's Song', 'Mragula's Song', 'Kurburu's Song' and 'Umbara's Song' (with information about their composers), a short song about elopement, a charm and some children's songs. Howitt stressed the importance of collecting such songs before they are lost, but his warning was not taken up seriously for almost another fifty years, at a time when the cultures which produced them had been even further eroded. In *Oceania* (1933), however, T. G. H. Strehlow, in his 'Ankotarinja, an Aranda Myth', provides a methodological model for the recording and translation of such songs. Strehlow gives the text and translation of the eighteen verses of the 'Song of Ankotarinja', provides a full account of the myth to which the song alludes, and describes in detail the ritual of which the song is an integral part. He also discusses difficulties of translation and explores the complex style of the original, pointing out how, in song, everyday words are often rearranged according to traditional verse patterns, explaining some differences between speech-accent and verse-accent, and noting how the quality and quantity of vowels are often altered in singing. Strehlow continued his study of Aranda songs in *Aranda Traditions* (1947) and in his most important work, *Songs of Central Australia* (1971). Included in this work are transcriptions and translations of over two thousand lines of verse, detailed accounts of the metrical, rhythmic and verbal structures of the originals, full information about the occasions when they were sung and the purposes they were intended to achieve, and discussion of the differences between the song and narrative versions of myth. There are some secular songs of a kind that are sung at camp gatherings (the true 'corroborees'), but Strehlow classifies most of his material as sacred: charms, songs performed during totemic increase ceremonies, songs which commemorate the deeds of totemic ancestors, and initiation songs, songs celebrating the totemic homeland and songs concerned with death. Other important contributions, though not as detailed as Strehlow's, have been made by anthropologists such as N. B. Tindale and E. A. Worms, but the work which ranks in significance with Strehlow's is the combined research of Catherine H. Berndt and Ronald M. Berndt (q.v.). Their account of field work in the Ooldea region of western SA (*Oceania*, 1942–45) includes texts, translations and discussions of a number of short songs, both esoteric and exoteric. A collection of 144 children's songs from the same area (*Mankind*,

1952–54) demonstrates that even these songs have their own highly stylized poetic conventions (for example, the use of words which do not appear in everyday speech), and that they cannot be appreciated or understood without a knowledge of their cultural context. In *Sexual Behaviour in Western Arnhem Land* (1951) there is an interesting collection of eighty-nine 'gossip' songs, the compositions of contemporary songmen, who, while not mentioning names, compose songs about topical issues, especially marital behaviour, which have been gleaned from overheard conversation – although the songmen claim they receive them in dreams. C. H. Berndt (*Oceania*, 1950) gives a selection of songs from Bathurst and Melville Islands, which are sung by women at the death of a husband or near relative. Most important, however, are R. M. Berndt's translations of six song-cycles and a collection of secular songs from the Yirrkalla area in north-eastern Arnhem Land. Although the published material amounts to only about one-fifth of that which Berndt collected in the area (much of it in the period 1946–47), it offers an instructive insight into the function of song in this society and into the beauty and power of the song. *Djanggawul* (1952) is a free poetic translation of the Djanggawul song-cycle (188 songs, 2921 lines in the translation), the most sacred of the song-cycles in this area. There are detailed explanatory notes on the songs, an account of the complete myth and its local variants, and a description of the rituals which the myth sanctions. The song-cycle describes the events which occurred as the Djanggawul (a collective name for three ancestral beings, Two Sisters and a Brother) journeyed from the spirit home of the Bralgu, off the Arnhem Land coast, to the region of Milimgimbi. They brought with them sacred emblems, and the two perpetually-pregnant Sisters created the ancestors of the present-day Aborigines. The major theme is fertility, expressed in the importance of human sexuality and its culmination in childbirth, and in the inextricable relationship between human sexuality and fecundity in the wider natural world. One of the interesting features of the myth is that the Sisters originally possessed the sacred emblems and therefore were the controllers of ritual; but the sacred emblems were stolen by men, thus explaining the contemporary social and ritual roles of men and women, while at the same time emphasizing the fact that woman is the source of the sacred. In *Kunapipi* (1951) Berndt gives an account of a religious cult which is widespread over the Northern Territory, but which is a recent import into the Yirrkalla area, where it has become associated with more established mythology. Kunapipi is one of the sacred names of the Great Mother or Fertility Mother who is responsible for the cycle of reproduction and fertility in the human, animal and natural worlds (in particular the coming of the north-west monsoon). Since the cult is a recently-introduced one, the style of song differs from the Djanggawul song-cycle: the individual songs are short, made up of a few key-words which are suggestive and associative, and which are repeated with variations. The study includes 129 sacred Kunapipi songs, and forty-seven secular songs (which differ in rhythm from the sacred songs, and which are sung, for example, in the main camp before the sacred rituals). Comparisons are made with 118 Kunapipi songs from outside the Yirrkalla area. The 'Wonguri-Mandjikai Song Cycle of the Moon-Bone' (*Oceania*, 1948; see also 'Buladelah-Taree Holiday Song Cycle') made up of thirteen songs (181 lines in Berndt's free translation), is a non-secret sacred cycle which has as its background the myth of the death and rebirth of the moon, which pattern is seen as a reflection of the cyclical process of the seasons and indeed of all life. The 'Wuradilagu Song-Cycle' in *The Anthropologist Looks at Myth*, ed. J. Greenway (1966), is similar in status to the Moon-Bone Cycle, and has as its background the mythical actions of a spirit being (or beings) from the Groote Eylandt area called Wuradilagu, who is not a sacred being although associated with features of the local landscape. It is made up of eighteen songs (166 lines in Berndt's translation), and in common with the other cycles it celebrates the bond between human beings and other living creatures, and between all living things and natural phenomena – in this case, the coming of the south-east wind after the north-west monsoonal season. *Love Songs of Arnhem Land* (1976) contains two song-cycles which are the least sacred of those noted so far (but which nevertheless have sacred overtones), and a collection of secular love songs. The song-cycles are characterized by much sexually frank and erotic imagery, and through association with mythic symbolism they relate human sexuality to fertility in the wider natural world, demonstrating that 'sexual union is an eternal principle in nature which is reflected in universal fertility and natural continuity' (Berndt). The 'Goulburn Island Cycle', made up of twenty-six songs (312 lines in translation), Berndt describes as a manifestation of the 'social face of love': human beings engage in sexual activity, but this activity has significance and meaning primarily in the relationship between it and parallel forces in the natural world, in particular the arrival of the monsoonal rains which revitalize the land. The 'Rose River Cycle' is made up of twenty-six songs (382 lines), and although it shares many features with the 'Goulburn Island Cycle' its

emphasis is on the ritual aspects of sexuality (symbolized in the cycle by the non-local rites of defloration, subincision and ritual coitus), which have their parallels and consequences in the wider natural world – specifically in the coming wet season and more generally in the cyclical pattern of the seasons. The 'Djarada' is a collection of sixty-five self-contained songs (all very short, indicating their non-local origin) which deals with sexual and love matters in a directly personal way, largely divorced from mythological significance. Apart from the work of the Berndts, other significant studies of song include D. H. Turner's *Tradition and Transformation* (1974) which includes a series of mortuary songs from Groote Eylandt; and *Taruru: Aboriginal Song Poetry from the Pilbara* (1974) by C. G. von Brandenstein and A. P. Thomas. The latter work is a collection of eighty tabis (individually-composed songs as distinct from communal songs), from the north-west of WA, with explanatory notes about the songs and information about the composers (where known). The collection includes songs dealing with the honour of dead relatives and the heroic deeds of the past, topical songs dealing with love and other social relationships, and responses to the white man's technology. Although the songs were all composed within the preceding fifty years and usually deal with topical events, they still use the highly-stylized poetic diction which is characteristic of the more traditional songs.

The publications of Aboriginal song in translation have been few in number but in general the songs have been well treated by their translators; Strehlow and Berndt, in addition to illuminating the songs in the light of their specialist knowledge, have produced translations which are in themselves of some poetic quality. Oral narrative has not been so kindly served. Many narrative myths and legends were of course collected by the early anthropologists, but their concern was primarily with content as a springboard to anthropological theorizing rather than with the aesthetic and style of oral narrative. Outside the specialist area, Mrs K. Langloh Parker's (q.v.) *Australian Legendary Tales* (1896) began a tradition of popular retellings of myths, legends and stories by non-Aborigines, which are usually synthetic and non-contextual. This tradition continues up to the present day, with Alan Marshall's (q.v.) *People of the Dreamtime* (1952) and A. W. Reed's (q.v.) *Myths and Legends of Australia* (1965) being representative of it. Closer to the spirit of the oral narratives are Bill Harney's (q.v.) collection of camp-fire stories, *Tales from the Aborigines* (1959), and Roland Robinson's (q.v.) *The Man Who Sold His Dreaming* (1965). A significant early exception to the 'popular-synthetic' approach is the work of Ursula McConnel, who from 1927 onwards collected narratives which treat of the institution of religious cults by totemic ancestors in the Cape York area of northern Queensland. Many of these were published in various numbers of *Oceania* between 1930 and 1950, with transcriptions, literal translations, free translations and accounts of the kinship and totemic systems of the people. These narratives, along with others from the same area, were published in *Myths of the Mungkan* (1957) in their free English versions, where once again McConnel stresses the importance of viewing such narratives in their cultural contexts and discusses the difficulties involved in translating from an oral to a written medium. In this tradition too is A. Capell's collection of ten myths connected with the culture heroes, Gagamara and Gumbar, from the Garadjeri tribe in Western Australia (*Mankind,* 1949); Capell provides transcriptions, interlinear translations, freer translations and interpretative notes. C. H. and R. M. Berndt's report on field work in the Ooldea region (see above) gives many narratives with translations and commentary, including an interesting sampling of women's stories concerned with such topics as hunting, betrothal, initiation, pregnancy, birth and death. C. H. Berndt (*Oceania,* 1952) gives a 'play-story' from the Milingimbi region which is told chiefly to children and young adults; it relates the adventures of two brothers, Balangu and Damburu, in a way that directly and indirectly enforces accepted social values. C. H. Berndt's *The Land of the Rainbow Snake* (1979) gives translations of a number of children's stories collected from women informants in the Gunwinngu language of western Arnhem Land, which provides an insight into the way children are introduced to myths and legends in a relatively simplified form. C. G. von Brandenstein, in *Narratives from the North-West of Western Australia in the Ngarluma and Jindjiparndi Languages* (1970), gives sixty narratives with translations on a variety of subjects ranging from the traditional to the topical. There is no commentary, however, and as with some similar recent publications the emphasis is linguistic rather than literary. Nevertheless, studies of this kind provide valuable source material for a study of the style of oral narrative. The studies outlined above have been published under the names of the compilers and translators, although in general due acknowledgement is given to the informants. Thus in *The Land of the Rainbow Snake* C. H. Berndt gives the names of the main teller after each story (including Mangurug, Ngalmidul, Mareiiga, Hannah Gadjibunda and Dorcas Ngalgindali), and von Brandenstein lists the narratives under the names

of the narrators: R. Churnside, W. King, Waljbira (Bulbul), Cobbin Dale and D. Bobby-Kiagi. More recently, collections of stories by the one narrator have been published in translation, as with *Milbi: Aboriginal Tales from Queensland's Endeavour River* (1980), told by Tulo Gordon and translated by J. B. Haviland. This contains narratives which explain the formation of features of the landscape and the origins of local plant and animal life, and which impart moral lessons; the translations attempt to convey something of the narrative style of the originals.

The studies noted so far have been translations from Aboriginal languages, but the category 'Aboriginal Song and Narrative in Translation' is made more complex by the issue of whether Aboriginal English should be regarded as a bastardized form of Australian English and representative of some of the worst effects of white paternalism, or as a legitimate *lingua franca* in its own right. If the latter, then transcriptions of oral narrative in Aboriginal English such as *Gularabulu* (1983), told by Paddy Roe and transcribed by Stephen Muecke (with the addition of Muecke's comments on various aspects of the style of oral performance), need to be considered in a category such as 'Writing in Aboriginal English'. Until recently, the standard publishing practice has been to edit such Aboriginal English until it conforms more or less to the stylistic conventions of Australian English, so that it really belongs to a category such as 'Aboriginal English in Translation'. *Joe Nangan's Dreaming* (1976), by Joe Nangan and Hugh Edwards, is such a work, and there are many other comparable examples. *My Country of the Pelican Dreaming: The Life of an Australian Aborigine of the Gadjerong, Grant Ngabidj, 1904–1977, as Told to Bruce Shaw* (1981) represents an attempt at compromise. In his introduction, Shaw compares a transcription of Grant Ngabidj's oral narrative with his own edited version and shows how the oral Aboriginal English has its own 'intricate structure' and 'variety of stylistic elements'. Yet the prose in the body of the book has been edited for the benefit of the general reader, although Shaw attempts to retain as many of the dominant features of the oral narrative as possible.

The best surveys of Aboriginal oral song and narrative in their cultural contexts are the relevant chapters in C. H. and R. M. Berndt's *The World of the First Australians* (revised 2nd edn, 1981), and C. H. Berndt's 'Oral Literature' in *The Australian Aboriginal Heritage: An Introduction through the Arts* (2nd edn, 1978), ed. R. M. Berndt and E. S. Phillips. In addition to some examples of songs, there are a good number of narratives in translation in both of these studies, with some useful introductory comments on the style of oral narrative. The music of Arnhem Land songs is examined by A. P. Elkin and T. A. Jones in *Oceania Monographs*, no. 9, and *The Australian Aboriginal Heritage* includes a chapter on 'Music and Dance', with bibliography and discography.

B.M.

Aboriginal Writing in English, a relatively new phenomenon in Australian literature, began with David Unaipon's (q.v.) *Native Legends* (1929), the first book published by an Aboriginal in Australia, but languished until the advent of Kath Walker (q.v.). Her successful first book of poetry, *We Are Going* (1964), has been followed by a profusion of publications by other Aboriginal writers. Aboriginal literature now includes poetry, fiction, drama, biography and autobiography, the collection and interpretation of Aboriginal myth and legend, and political, sociological and educational writing. Significant Aboriginal writers include, in addition to Kath Walker, Jack Davis, Kevin Gilbert, Colin Johnson, Robert Merritt, Dick Roughsey, G. L. Bostock, Bobbi Sykes, Hyllus Maris, Lionel George Fogarty, author of the volumes of poetry *Kargun* (1980) and *Yoogum Yoogum* (1982), Archie Weller, whose novel on the problem of the part-Aboriginal, *The Day of the Dog* (1981) was highly commended in the *Australian*/Vogel Literary Award of 1980, and Raymond Chee, short-story writer. Significant Aboriginal autobiographies include *Moon and Rainbow* (1971) by Dick Roughsey; *Lamilami Speaks* (1974) by the Reverend Lazarus Lamilami; *A Bastard Like Me* (1975) by Charles Perkins; *If Everyone Cared* (1977) by Margaret Tucker; *My People's Life: An Aboriginal's Own Story* (1976) by Jack Mirritji; *There's More to Life* (1979) by Roy Simon (Koorie Dhoulagarle); *My Country of the Pelican Dreaming* (1981) by Grant Ngabidj and *Banggaiyerri* (1983), the story of Jack Sullivan, both of which were told to Bruce Shaw. The biographies of well-known Aborigines, Harold Blair, Sir Douglas Nicholls, Philip Roberts (Waipuldanya), Lionel Rose, Evonne Goolagong, Reg Saunders and Senator Neville Bonner, although not always written by Aborigines, have also been published. Political and social writings by Aborigines are becoming an increasingly significant component of modern Australian literature of protest. Chief of these have been Kevin Gilbert's *Because a White Man'll Never Do It* (1973) and *Living Black* (1977); others include Cheryl Buchanan's *We Have Bugger All! The Kulaluk Story* (1974), *Black Power in Australia* (1975), a debate on Aboriginal issues between Senator Neville Bonner and Bobbi Sykes, and Phillip Pepper's *You Are What You*

Make Yourself to Be (1980). While most Aboriginal writing has been in English, Ngitji Ngitji, Daisy Utemorrah and Titam Tjapangarti have written both in English and in their own Aboriginal language. A white Australian, Colin Tatz, has edited a book of writing by Aborigines, *Black Viewpoints: The Aboriginal Experience* (1975).

The collection and publication of Aboriginal myths and legends have in recent years occupied both white and black writers. The Aboriginal Publications Foundation, which (together with the Aboriginal Arts Board) has helped to maintain the momentum of Aboriginal writing, has also published numerous books of Aboriginal legends. Representative samples of this genre are Wilf Reeves's *The Legends of Moonie Jarl* (1964); Sylvia Cairns's *Uncle Willie Mackenzie's Legends of the Goundirs* (1967); Kath Walker's *Stradbroke Dreamtime* (1972); Dick Roughsey's *The Giant Devil Dingo* (1973) and *The Rainbow Serpent* (1975); Joe Nangan's (and Hugh Edwards), *Joe Nangan's Dreaming: Aboriginal Legends of the North-West* (1976); the Kormilda Community College's (Darwin) *Djugurba: Tales from the Spirit Time* (1980) and *Visions of Mowanjum – Aboriginal Writings from the Kimberley* (1980).

Adam M. Shoemaker produced a survey of Aboriginal Writing in English for the Literature Board of the Australia Council in 1980; it also contains a bibliography of Aboriginal creative writing in English. He also published in *ALS* (October 1983) 'A Checklist of Black Australian Literature'. *Black Australia*, an annotated bibliography compiled and edited by Marji Hill and Alex Barlow in 1978, also provides considerable information on Aboriginal writing up to that point. The first National Aboriginal Writers' Conference was held in Perth in February 1983. See also Aboriginal in Australian Literature; Aboriginal Song and Narrative in Translation.

Aboriginalities was the title of a column which ran in the *Bulletin* from 15 October 1887 until control of the journal passed from the Prior family to Consolidated Press in 1960. For much of its life the column comprised paragraphs about bush life and people supplied by contributors. C. H. Bertie edited *Aboriginalities from the Bulletin* (1913), which was illustrated by Lionel Lindsay.

Acolyte, The, a novel by Thea Astley (q.v.), was published in 1972 and won the 1973 Miles Franklin Award (q.v.). Set mainly in southern Queensland, it is an obliquely-developed study of a blind, egocentric musician, Holberg, seen through the eyes of Paul Vesper, his disciple and factotum. Holberg's blindness, personality and possible genius arouse a mixture of compassion, fascination and dependence in all those drawn into his orbit, including Vesper who has abandoned an engineering career to serve him. A versatile master in the manipulation of others, Holberg manages for the most part to conceal his ruthless self-centredness. Eventually, however, by a slow process of several years' cumulative perceptions, Vesper penetrates the truth and violently rejects him.

Across the Sea Wall, see **KOCH, C. J.**

'Across the Western Plains', see 'Lazy Harry's'

ADAM-SMITH, PATSY (1926–), born Melbourne, grew up in Victorian country districts, where her father worked as a fettler on the railway and her mother was station-mistress-cum-postmistress at numerous small, isolated towns. She served with the VADs in the Second World War; was a radio operator (the first woman to be so articled) on an Australian trading ship, 1954–60; was an Adult Education Officer in Hobart, 1960–67; and was appointed a manuscripts field officer in the State Library of Victoria in 1970. Her autobiographical (to the beginning of the Second World War) *Hear the Train Blow,* adjudged by Kenneth Slessor as 'a minor classic', was published in 1964, an expanded and illustrated edition appearing in 1981. Her long list of other published works includes *Moonbird People* (1965) about the inhabitants of the Furneaux Islands in Bass Strait and their annual harvesting of the migratory shearwater petrels; *There Was a Ship,* the story of her years on the Australian coast (1967, republished in 1977 as *Trader to the Islands* and in a composite volume with *Moonbird People* in 1983); *Tiger Country* (1968); *No Tribesman* (1971); *The Anzacs* (1978), which gives a fresh and vivid account of Australia's participation in the First World War and which shared the 1978 *Age* Book of the Year Award; *Outback Heroes* (1981) which finds heroism in the lives of such diverse personalities as the squatter-explorer, Nat Buchanan, and the Aboriginal's friend, Daisy Bates, and in such types as the mailman and minister of religion in the outback and the workers on the Overland Telegraph Line; and *The Shearers* (1982), a parallel volume to *The Anzacs.* Patsy Adam-Smith's abiding interest, however, stemming from her great affection for her railwayman father and from her childhood experiences when the family's annual fortnight holiday was spent on continuous (and free) train travel, is the Australian railways. In addition to *Hear the Train Blow,* she has written *The Rails Go Westward* (1969), *Across Australia by Indian Pacific* (1971), *The Desert Railway* (1974) and *Romance of Australian Railways* (1973–74); and she has edited *Folklore of Australia's Railwaymen* (1969). Her interest in history is also evident in *Hobart Sketchbook* (1968), *Tasmania Sketchbook* (1971), *Port Arthur Sketchbook* (1971), *Launceston Sketchbook* (1973), *Islands of Bass Strait* (1978) and *Victorian and Edwardian Melbourne from Old Photographs* (1979). She was made OBE in 1980 for her services to literature.

ADAMS, A. H. (ARTHUR HENRY) (1872–1936), born in NZ, graduated from Otago University and tried law and journalism before coming to Australia, where he became secretary to the theatrical entrepreneur J. C. Williamson. In 1900 he left for China to cover the Boxer Rebellion, and after some further visits to London, Australia and NZ returned to Australia and established himself as a leading journalist, editing, in succession, the Red Page of the *Bulletin,* the *Lone Hand* and the Sydney *Sun.* His verse, which includes the collections *Maoriland: And Other Verses* (1899), *London Streets* (1906) and *The Collected Verses of Arthur H. Adams* (1913), avoids the rawness of the contemporary Australian ballads but also lacks their verve and intensity. Of his novels, which include *Tussock Land* (1904), *Galahad Jones* (q.v., 1910), *A Touch of Fantasy* (1911), *The Knight of the Motor Launch* (1913), *Double Bed Dialogues* (1915, under the pseudonym 'Henry James James'), *Grocer Greatheart* (1915), *The Australians* (1920), *Lola of the Chocolates* (1920, under the pseudonym 'James James') and *A Man's Life* (1929), *Galahad Jones* and *The Australians* are the best. Australia, or more often Sydney, frequently figures in his work as a partly-known rather than a fully-felt landscape and although both his fiction and poetry are crafted to a degree, the tone of his work oscillates between romantic sentimentality and cynicism or worldly wisdom. Nevertheless, his fiction is often enlivened by whimsical characterization, gentle irony and a lively writing style. Adams also wrote several full-length plays and a number of one-acters, few of which, though often witty and socially pertinent, achieved commercial production. His most significant published plays include *The Wasters, Galahad Jones* and *Mrs. Pretty and the Premier* (qq. v.), which comprise *Three Plays for the Australian Stage* (1914).

ADAMS, DAVID (1908–), was born at Bringelly, on the outskirts of Sydney in the Camden–Cowpastures area (now Camden), with which his family had long been associated. He became associated with the *Bulletin* in 1927 when he was an assistant to the financial editor

15

on the 'Wild Cat' section of that magazine while completing a diploma in accountancy. He was appointed a director of the *Bulletin* in 1934 and revived and expanded the famous 'Business, Robbery, Etc.' column which had been well-known in the 1930s for its exposure of commercial malpractices, especially in Sydney. In 1948 he became editor of the *Bulletin*, at age thirty–nine the youngest editor since J. F. Archibald, a position he held until 1961. Adams's other notable achievement was the discovery and editing of *The Letters of Rachel Henning* (see Henning, Rachel) which, illustrated by Norman Lindsay, was first serialized in the *Bulletin* 1951–52.

ADAMS, FRANCIS (1862–93), was born at Malta, son of an army surgeon and the well-known novelist, Bertha Jane Grundy Adams. Educated in England, Adams studied languages in Paris with a diplomatic post in mind but was compelled by tuberculosis to come to Australia in 1884. In 1887 he turned to journalism and leader-writing with the *Brisbane Courier* and with William Lane's radical weekly, the *Boomerang*; he also became a prolific contributor of poems, short fiction and critical articles to the *Bulletin*. Although initially enthusiastic about Australia ('a true republic'), in 1890 Adams returned ('mind-sick of Australia') to England where in 1893, with his health much deteriorated, he committed suicide.

Although he spent less than six years in Australia Adams's influence was considerable, for he brought a sophisticated intellect, born partly of his European experiences and background, to contemporary Australian social, cultural and political problems. His major effect was on the developing radicalism of the day. His intensely radical collection of poetry, *Songs of the Army of the Night* (1888), violent in its outbursts against privilege, oppression and exploitation of the poor and lowly, encouraged radicalism in this country by predicting a successful democracy here. The local scene was further scrutinized in the prose works *Australian Essays* (1886) and *The Australians* (1893), the latter contrasting the two Australias, the lush, populated, coastal fringe and the dry sparsely-peopled interior. In a judgement that expressed a belief close to the heart of the developing nationalism of the time Adams assessed the bushman as 'the one powerful and unique national type yet produced in Australia'. Many of the stories in his volume *Australian Life* (1892) take up the theme of outback life, indicating in otherwise ordinary adventure stories, something of its praiseworthy, though idiosyncratic, nature. Of his other fiction, both *John Webb's End* (1891) and *The Melbournians* (1892) indicate the impact of Australia on his

literary creativity, while *A Child of the Age* (1894) is partly autobiographical. Interest in Francis Adams has remained high since the 1890s and continues to increase, a recognition not so much of his own creative writing as of the impact of his intellectual modernity and revolutionary zeal, qualities which helped to sound the death knell of colonialism in this country. Adams is the subject of Clive Turnbull's biographical essay, *These Tears of Fire* (1949), which was included in *Australian Lives* (1965).

ADAMS, GLENDA (1940–), born Sydney, taught Indonesian language and literature at the University of Sydney before going to New York in 1964 to write and study. She has published two collections of short stories, *Lies and Stories* (1976) and *The Hottest Night of the Century* (1979, which includes seven from *Lies and Stories*) and a novel, *Games of the Strong* (1982). Several of the fourteen stories of *The Hottest Night of the Century* concern family and school life in Australia; the later stories are influenced by the experimental form and heavy symbolism of some contemporary American fiction. *Games of the Strong* is a complex novel with strong overtones of the classic Orwellian '1984' personal dilemma that sometimes surfaces in conditions of extremist political identification and group rhetoric.

ADAMS, NANCY (1890–1968), granddaughter of the famous educationalist Alexander Morrison (principal of Scotch College, Melbourne, from 1857 to 1903), was born in Melbourne, grew up in that city and in England, married a well-known Melbourne wine merchant and was, for many years, a noted member of Melbourne's gentility. Her historical novel *Saxon Sheep* (1961) traces the history of the Templeton and Forlong families who brought the first Saxon merino sheep to Australia. Her autobiographical *Family Fresco* (1966) is a remarkably detailed account of a generation that was loyal in its adherence to old British traditions but genuinely proud of its Australian character.

ADAMS, PHILLIP (1939–), born Maryborough, Victoria, has had a wide-ranging career in advertising, television, journalism and the film industry in Australia. Drama critic for the *Bulletin*, columnist of the *Australian*, the Melbourne *Age*, the *Sydney Morning Herald*, the Adelaide *Advertiser* and the Brisbane *Courier-Mail*, and adviser to the Australian government on films and television, Adams has also been a foundation member of the Australia Council and foundation chairman of the Film, Radio and Television Board. He was instrumental in the establishment of the Experimental Film Fund, the Australian Film Development Corporation and the Film School. He has won a *TV Week* Logie and eight Australian Film Festival Awards, including two gold medals in international competition. He has produced such films as *The Adventures of Barry McKenzie, Don's Party, The Getting of Wisdom* and *We of the Never Never*. His publications include *Adams with Added Enzymes* (1975, his observations on the advertising industry), *The Unspeakable Adams* (1977), *More Unspeakable Adams* (1979), *Uncensored Adams* (1981), and *The Inflammable Adams* (1983). He received the Raymond Longford Award for his outstanding contribution to the Australian film industry in 1981; he is currently chairman of the Australian Film Commission.

ADAMSON, BARTLETT (1884–1951), born Ringarooma in north-eastern Tasmania, was a journalist with the *Sunday News* and *Smith's Weekly* in Sydney from 1919 to 1950. His smoothly lyrical poetry includes *Twelve Sonnets* (1918); *These Beautiful Women* (1932); *Bringer of Light: An Allegorical Fantasy* (1945), a long poem on a romantic medieval theme that was judged in the *Bulletin's* Red Page (16 January 1964) to be 'a swoon of romantic nonsense' with versification 'unusually capable'; *Comrades All and Other Poems for the People* (1945), which attests to Adamson's political attitudes (he was a member of the Communist Party); and *For Peace and Friendship* (1952), a posthumous selection from his poetry. His fiction includes *Mystery Gold* (1925), a story of hidden treasure in the South Seas, and *Nice Day for a Murder and Other Stories* (1944), many of which relate to bushranging derring–do.

ADAMSON, ROBERT (1943–), born Sydney, had only a limited formal education and spent periods of his adolescence and young manhood in reform schools and gaols. From about 1965, when his own interest in poetry was awakened, he played a leading role in encouraging, in Sydney, the development of the 'New Australian Poetry' (q.v.) and in transforming the conventional *Poetry Magazine* of the Poetry Society of Australia into the modernistic *New Poetry* (qq. v.). Adamson has been associated with *New Poetry* since its inception, as editor (1970–75), associate editor (1976–80) and since 1980 as editor again. He established and edited (with Ken Quinnell) the Prism Poets and the later Prism Books, of which he is now managing editor, and he has been editor-director (with Dorothy Hewett) of Big Smoke Books which has so far produced Dorothy Hewett's *Greenhouse* and his own *Where I Come From*. Adamson's publications of verse are *Can-*

ticles on the Skin (1970); *The Rumour* (1971); *Swamp Riddles* (1974); *Theatre I-XIX* (1976); *Cross the Border* (1977); *Where I Come From* (1979); *Selected Poems* (1977), for which many of the earlier poems were rewritten, and which won the Grace Leven Prize for Poetry; and *The Law at Heart's Desire* (1983). He has also published *Zimmer's Essay* (1974, in collaboration with Bruce Hanford), an experimental, fictional work which, partly narrative, partly discursive (and with a concluding section of poetry), critically examines the experience of prison.

In Adamson's early, largely autobiographical verse the 'poet as outlaw' predominates, recounting prison experiences ('The Imitator') and drug experiences ('Canticles on the Skin') of his adolescence together with numerous similar headlong attempts to come to grips with life, which the poetry appears to envisage as a highway of dangerous corners to be negotiated at extreme speed on two wheels ('The Big V8') or not bothered with at all. *The Rumour* displays Adamson's imaginative rather than actual experiences. The long title poem, which places the poetic imagination in relation to knowledge as rumour stands in relation to truth, is generally accepted as one of the foundation poems of the new poetry of the day because of its experimental form and its preoccupation with the substance of poetry. It is also seen as 'a manifesto of the new romanticism' (James Tulip) to which Adamson has become increasingly committed. The importance to Adamson of the Hawkesbury River landscape, first evident in 'Jerusalem Bay', is highlighted by many of the 'After Me, Sleep' poems of *Swamp Riddles*. Such poems integrate poet and natural setting into a Romantic synthesis reminiscent of Shelley and Wordsworth. Other poems about fishing, the river, the swamp, mist and mangroves give *Swamp Riddles* its predominant water theme. *Cross the Border*, which Adamson admits to being strongly influenced by Mallarmé and a totally imaginative world, is a beautiful production whose cover carries a reproduction of a diptych ('D. H. Lawrence'), the panels of which were painted by Brett Whiteley and Garry Shead. The latter's lithographs also appear throughout the book. It contains many of the poetic preoccupations of Adamson's earlier volumes but its final section, 'The Grail Poems', Adamson's imaginative interpretation of aspects of the Arthurian legend, confirms his commitment to Romanticism. The poems of *Where I Come From* bring Adamson back to the directly autobiographical approach of the early poetry but although they are, in his words, 'vignettes of remembered experience' of his family and early life, they are not necessarily absolutely factual, for Adamson's poetry as a whole tends to reflect the persona rather than the person. *The Law at Heart's Desire* (the special limited edition is an art object in itself) contains Adamson's most recent work. The poems, in the main, confront the problem of emotional communication in a world that can often be drab and stultifying.

ADAMSON, WALTER (1911-   ), born in Germany, came to Australia in 1939 and has been a full-time freelance writer since 1969. An Australian citizen since 1945, Adamson is best known for his novel *The Institution* (1976). He has also published poetry and short stories, together with two short novels that were published in Germany in 1973-74.

Adelaide, the capital of South Australia (q.v.), is situated in the south-eastern part of the State and lies on the Torrens River several kilometres from the eastern side of the Gulf of St Vincent surveyed first by Matthew Flinders. Named after Queen Adelaide, the wife of King William IV, Adelaide is a city very much with a founder, William Light (q.v.), who selected the site and planned the city after the establishment of SA in 1836. It is the location for Australia's premier cultural festival, the Adelaide Festival, held every even year and including within its programme a Writer's Week, attended by Australian and overseas writers, at which a past Australian writer is commemorated. Among writers identified with SA and Adelaide are Geoffrey Dutton, Ian Mudie, Colin Thiele and Catherine Helen Spence.

Adelaide Observer, see *Observer* (1)

Adelaide Punch, see *Melbourne Punch*

Admella, a steamship, was wrecked on a reef off Cape Northumberland in SA on 6 August 1859. Contemporary accounts of the shipwreck and the ensuing efforts to save the crew and passengers include Samuel Mossman's *Narrative of the Shipwreck of the Admella* (1859), Philip Barry's *The Wreck of the Admella: A Metrical Narrative* (1859), George French Angas's *The Wreck of the Admella and Other Poems* (1874) as well as sundry poems, e.g. Adam Lindsay Gordon's 'From the Wreck' (q.v.). Ian Mudie published *Wreck of the Admella* in 1966; in it he disposes of the legend that Gordon himself took part in the ride described in 'From the Wreck'.

'Advance Australia Fair', see **National Anthem**

Advancement of Spencer Button, The, a novel by 'Brian James' (q.v.), was published in 1950. Spencer Button, the son of a dim-witted struggling farmer of Wombat Creek, NSW, and a mother ambitious for gentility, rises from his inauspicious rural beginnings to be headmaster of Simmons Street (Fort Street), one of Sydney's most important high schools. After education at the nearest town, Selkirk (Mudgee), Spencer begins at fifteen as a pupil-teacher at a Sydney primary school, takes his degree and then alternates between the 'Celestial City' and the necessary 'pilgrim's progress' in the country at such places as Barden (Broken Hill) and Brushwood (Grafton). Dogged by his uncultured relatives and increasingly ashamed of his unfashionable mother, Spencer marries Susie Sparrow, a girl who shares his ambitions but whose life-denying nature becomes increasingly obvious. The well-planned arrival of a son, Carlyle, does little to reanimate their marriage. An earlier romantic relationship with a Selkirk girl, Winnie Ogg, culminates in a nightmarish way after Winnie takes to prostitution and is finally drowned; a later love affair with a member of his staff at Brushwood is prevented from having extensive consequences by Spencer's innate preference for safety. Other potentially destructive experiences, such as the First World War, pass Spencer by, although his brother Graham is a victim. Of his numerous relatives, the most memorable is Aunty May, a little woman of amazing activity, who is obsessed with physical illness and addicted to a comic style of verbal shorthand. Interwoven with Spencer's career are a multitude of minor destinies, from Mr Wren, the part-time farmer and teacher of a small school who battles inspectors and droughts with equal ferocity, to the innocuous Mr Cyril Finger who opts for the Salvation Army, to Mr Foll who dies after his son's disgrace makes his years of sacrificial teaching pointless. The background of the novel consists of a panorama of the general life of NSW from the 1890s to the 1940s and a more detailed picture of the specific life of the State's educational system; particularly striking are 'James''s descriptions of the daily life and characteristics of country and city schools and the perennial trials of the schoolteacher, from angry parents to eccentric headmasters and the rivalries of colleagues.

Adventures in Queensland (1879) by 'Australian' (F.A. Blackman), one of Queensland's most significant early works, is a combination of history, fiction and guidelines for immigrants. Strongly pro-squatter, Blackman describes the settlement of the area west of Maryborough in the 1840s and 1850s; his callous attitude to the Aborigines is typical of the period.

Adventures of a Guardsman, a convict memoir by Charles Cozens, was published in 1848.

One of the few accounts of transportation life by a gentleman convict, it records the early life and adventures of Cozens, his enlistment in the Royal Horse Guards, his court-martial for threatening a superior officer, and his years (1840–46) in NSW when he worked as a constable, clerk and census collector in the Monaro district, Yass, Sydney and elsewhere. *Adventures of a Guardsman* is critical of the convict system but expresses admiration of the governor of the colony, Sir George Gipps.

Adventures on a Journey to New Holland, see **HUBER, THERESE**

Advertiser, the best-known Adelaide morning daily newspaper, began publication in 1858 as the *South Australian Advertiser* (its title until early in 1899). It was founded by John Henry Barrow, editor 1858–73. In 1931 it incorporated its long-standing rival, the *Register.* Sir (John) Langdon Bonython (1848–1939) began the lengthy association of the Bonython family (q.v.) with the *Advertiser* when he gained employment on it in 1864; he bought into the newspaper from the 1870s, became editor in 1884 and proprietor in 1893, and retained personal control until his retirement in 1929. The *Advertiser* then became a public company (although the Bonython family retained an interest) which is now controlled by the Melbourne newspaper group, Herald and Weekly Times Ltd. Editors after Bonython include Sir Frederick Dumas (1929–53). In its early days the *Advertiser* was associated with conservative pastoral interests, but under Bonython identified more with South Australian middle–class and small business interests.

Advocate: A Weekly Catholic Journal, with local and overseas items of Irish–Catholic interest and some literary material, began publication February 1868 and has continued as a general Catholic organ of information and interest.

'AFFERBECK LAUDER', see **MORRISON, A.A.**

AFFORD, MAX (1906–54), born Parkside, Adelaide, was a reporter and feature writer with the Adelaide *News* (1929–34) and then joined the drama staff of the ABC after his play 'William Light the Founder' won the 1936 South Australian Centenary Drama Competition. Between 1932 and 1954 he wrote more than sixty radio and stage plays and radio serials, most of which remain unpublished. Three of his stage plays were published in the posthumous volume, *Mischief in the Air*

(1974); they were the title play, *Mischief in the Air,* which was performed in Sydney in 1944 and later adapted for Broadway presentation; *Lady in Danger* (1944), performed in 1942; and *Awake My Love,* a revised version of 'William Light the Founder', performed in 1947. Two of his radio plays, *Lazy in the Sun,* about Australia's hedonistic unawareness of the problems of the world, and *Consulting Room,* about an attempted suicide by a couple who face the imminent death of the wife from cancer, were also published in the *Mischief in the Air* volume. Afford's radio serials included such popular favourites as 'First Light Fraser' (624 episodes), 'Danger Unlimited' (624 episodes), 'Digger Hale's Daughters' (416 episodes), 'Hagen's Circus' (800 episodes) and 'Stranger Come In' (400 episodes). He adapted Jon Cleary's novel *The Sundowners* (1952) for radio serialization and wrote his own mining town serial, 'Silver Ridge', which ran during 1952–53. His remarkable success as a radio dramatist was due to his exciting plots, realistic characterization and mastery of the technical requirements of radio drama. A successful writer also of detective and 'thriller' fiction, Afford published four novels, *Blood on His Hands* (1936), *Death's Mannikins* (1937) *The Dead are Blind* (1937) and *Owl of Darkness* (1942), which were all republished in White Circle Crime Club editions in London.

AFTERMAN, ALLEN (1941–), born Los Angeles, USA, a graduate in arts and law, was associated with the La Mama (q.v.) poetry workshops and lectured in law at the University of Melbourne before resigning in 1973 to become a full-time writer. Afterman has published two books of poetry, *The Maze Rose* (1974) and *Purple Adam* (1980); much of the latter volume stems from Afterman's reaction to the genocide of the Jews in Europe and the Aborigines in Tasmania.

Age, published in Melbourne since 1854, was a liberal daily of world standard before 1900 and remains today one of Australia's leading newspapers. Founded by John and Henry Cooke, it was run as a co-operative venture, 1854–56; in 1856–57 and 1859–60 it was owned by Ebenezer and David Syme (q.v.), in 1857–59 by Ebenezer, and in 1860–1908 it was under David's control. After his death the *Age* remained within the family until the Syme company became a public one in 1948. In 1983 control of the *Age* passed to the Fairfax (q.v.) chain, which had acquired a fifty per cent interest in the newspaper in 1970. A selection of early *Age* editorials and articles was published as *The Australian Thunderer* (1971); the newspaper's battles with *Argus* (q.v.)

at that time are referred to in Henry Kingsley's *The Hillyars and the Burtons* (1865), where the *Age* becomes the *Mohawk*. A.L. Windsor, a much-admired figure in Australian journalism, was editor 1871–1900, when Alfred Deakin and Charles Henry Pearson were prominent contributors; other editors have included G.H.F. Schuler (1901–26), L.V. Biggs (1926–39), Sir Harold Campbell (1939–59), E.K. Sinclair (1959–66) and Graham Perkin (1966–75). Other staff have included Charles Bright, J.E. Neild, Philip Mennell, Roy Bridges, Benjamin Hoare (leader writer 1890–1914), George Johnston and C.E. Sayers.

Age Book of the Year Awards, two in number, are presented annually, one for a work of imaginative writing, the other for a non-fiction work, which are of outstanding literary merit and express Australia's identity or character. Winners to 1983 have included David Foster's *The Pure Land* and C.M.H. Clark's *A History of Australia*, vol. 3 (both 1974); Thea Astley's *A Kindness Cup* (1975); A.D. Hope's *A Late Picking* and Hugh Stretton's *Capitalism, Socialism and the Environment* (both 1976); Graham Freudenberg's *A Certain Grandeur* (1977); Christopher Koch's *The Year of Living Dangerously* and Patsy Adam-Smith's *The Anzacs* (both 1978); Roger McDonald's *1915* (1979); David Ireland's *A Woman of the Future* and Murray Bail's *Homesickness* (both 1980); Eric Rolls's *A Million Wild Acres* and Blanche d'Alpuget's *Turtle Beach* (both 1981); David Malouf's *Fly Away Peter* and Geoffrey Serle's *John Monash: A Biography* (both 1982); Elizabeth Jolley's *Mr. Scobie's Riddle* and Lloyd Robson's *A History of Tasmania* (both 1983).

AITCHISON, RAY (1923–   ), born Sydney, served with the AIF in the Second World War, and was a journalist with the *Daily Telegraph* (1945–48) and the ABC (1948–70). In 1970 he became executive director of the Australian Confederation of Apparel Manufacturers. He published two novels, *The Illegitimates* (1964), a long and episodic story about the half-caste O'Shannon family which traces their attempts to establish themselves in white Australian society by methods that vary with the personalities of the individuals themselves; and *Contillo* (1966). In 1970 he published *From Bob to Bungles*, a view of the political scene and its personalities in the 1960s, encompassing the period from the retirement of Sir Robert Menzies to the downfall of Sir John Gorton and his succession by Sir William McMahon. Aitchison's fear of foreign investment, especially from America, is contained in *Thanks to the Yanks?* (1972). He edited *Looking at the Liberals* (1974).

AITKIN, DON (1937–   ), born Sydney, capped a distinguished academic career with his appointment as professor of politics at Macquarie University, Sydney (1971–79), and of political science at the Australian National University (since 1980). Aitken has published political works such as *The Country Party in New South Wales* (1972), *Stability and Change in Australian Politics* (1977) and *Australian Political Institutions* (1980, with B.E. Jinks); a biography of Sir Michael Bruxner, *The Colonel* (1969); and a novel, *The Second Chair* (1977), set in 'Phillip' University, Sydney, which combines sexual, political and academic intrigue.

AKHURST, W.M. (WILLIAM MOWER) (1822–78), arrived as a migrant in Adelaide in 1849, with two plays at Cremorne Gardens, London, to his credit. Initially a journalist in Adelaide and Melbourne, he became music and drama critic on the Melbourne *Herald* and a leading figure in Melbourne's theatrical world. From the 1850s until he returned to London in 1871 he wrote numerous stage pieces: dramas, pantomimes, extravaganzas and burlesques. During the 1860s he was the life-force of Melbourne's pantomime productions, devising a piece every year for the Theatre Royal, most of them designed and executed by the scenic artist, John Hennings, and several written specially as a vehicle for George Coppin. His Australian dramatic work, mostly a mixture of traditional English material and colonial topicalities, includes 'Quite Colonial' (1854), 'The Rights of Woman' (1854), 'The Magician's Daughter' (1855), 'Coppin in Cairo' (1858), 'We've Taken Gardiner' (1862), *Gulliver on his Travels* (1866), *King Arthur: or, Launcelot the Loose* (1868), *Paris the Prince and Helen the Fair* (?1868), *Harlequin Robinson Crusoe* (1868), *Harlequin Jack Sheppard* (1869) and *The House That Jack Built* (1869). The last, a pantomime allegory, celebrating and partly satirizing Victoria's sudden prosperity during the gold rush, is his most original work. In London from 1871 to 1877 he produced another sixteen pieces, including nine pantomimes and four dramas. He decided to return to Australia in 1878 but died at sea.

Alcheringa, see **Jindyworobak Movement**

ALDEN, JOHN, see **Shakespeare and Australia**

ALDOUS, ALLAN (1911–   ), born Leederville, Perth, began writing plays in WA before going to England in 1935. There two of his radio plays were produced by the BBC in

1938, 'Timothy Thimble's Boat' and 'Dancing Red Earth'. In the Second World War he served with the AIF in New Guinea and the Solomon Islands as a drama specialist with Army Education. A prolific writer of children's fiction, Aldous was particularly successful with the McGowan series of five novels, beginning with *McGowan Climbs a Mountain* (1945). His other children's fiction included two Colin McKee books (1947, 1948), *Quitters Can't Win* (1946) and *Doctor with Wings* (1960). Other plays by Aldous were 'Westerly Gateway' produced for the 1966 Festival of Perth and the first authentic *son et lumière* presentation in Australia, and 'Cook of the Endeavour', produced in 1970 for the Cook Bicentenary celebrations.

ALDRIDGE, JAMES (1918–), born White Hills, Victoria, worked briefly on the staffs of the Melbourne *Herald* and *Sun* (1937–38) before seeking a journalistic career in England, from where he has only occasionally returned to Australia. A war correspondent in the Second World War, Aldridge has since pursued a successful career in journalism and writing, and is a leading fiction writer. His first three novels, *Signed with Their Honour* (1942), *The Sea Eagle* (1944) and *Of Many Men* (1946), are stories of men in battle in Greece, Crete, Egypt, Finland and Russia. *The Diplomat* (1950), published in some twenty-five languages and a best-seller in Russia, established Aldridge as an important political novelist with Marxist persuasions. A story of the Anglo-American-Russian dispute over Iran and Iranian oil, *The Diplomat* combines a complicated political theme with an analysis of human motives. Other political novels by Aldridge, which are sometimes criticized as being vehicles for their author's political views rather than fiction, include *Heroes of the Empty View* (1954); *The Last Exile* (1961), encompassing the whole story of British rule in Egypt while focusing on the last days of British influence there and the Suez Canal crisis; *A Captive in the Land* (1962); and *The Statesman's Game* (1966). *My Brother Tom* (1966), one of Aldridge's few works concerned with Australia ('I can't escape Australia and don't want to'), concerns religious factions (Protestant and Catholic) in an Australian country town. His other novels include *I Wish He Would Not Die* (1957), a wartime story set in Egypt and the Western Desert; *A Sporting Proposition* (1973); *Mockery in Arms* (1974) and *The Untouchable Juli* (1975). He has also written a book of short stories, *Gold and Sand* (1960); a play 'The 49th State', produced in London in 1946; non-fiction, *Living Egypt* (1969) and *Cairo* (1969); and several books for children.

ALEXANDER, ALAN (1941–), born Strabane, Northern Ireland, migrated to Australia in 1975 and that year won the John Shaw Neilson Prize for his poem, 'Sonnet for C.Y.O. O'Connor'. He has published two volumes of poetry, *In the Sun's Eye* (1977) and *Scarpdancer* (1982), much of which is a response to the writer's new experiences in a new land.

Alfred Dudley, see **Aboriginal in Australian Literature**

Alice Springs, officially known as Stuart until 1933, is situated on the Todd River plain in the heart of the MacDonnell Ranges in the Northern Territory. Named after a waterhole (spring) and in honour of Lady Alice Todd, wife of Sir Charles Todd who was responsible for the construction of the Overland Telegraph Line from Port Augusta in SA to Darwin in 1872, the town is usually referred to as 'The Alice'. The best-known appearance of the town in literature is in Nevil Shute's novel, *A Town Like Alice*, which was made into a film (1956) and into a television series (1980). W.E. ('Bill') Harney, an habitué of the area, wrote a poem 'West of Alice' which describes the impact of modern man (making a new highway) on the ancient, desolate land.

Alien Son, a series of autobiographical sketches of childhood by Judah Waten (q.v.), was first published in 1952 and has been reprinted frequently. The narrator's parents, Russian Jews, settle in a small WA town just before the First World War. The new land appears incomprehensible and alien, especially to the mother, who clings resolutely to the old culture; for the more sanguine father, 'business' projects prove disappointing and he resorts to hawking bottles from a horse-drawn cart. He soon realizes, however, that they 'belong to this new earth. It has sucked us in whether we know it or not', and for his son Australia offers exciting new experiences. As the narratives chronologically develop the story of the family's adjustment, a vivid general picture of immigrant life in Australia emerges. Striking individuals include Hirsch, a lonely old hawker who dreams of settling in Palestine; Mrs Hankin, a formidable Jewish mother in search of a suitable husband for her daughter; Mr Smutkevitch, a severe Jewish father who nevertheless loses his sons to the new culture; Lily Samuels, an Aboriginal girl; and Mr Finnan, a militant waterside worker who becomes a hero to the young narrator. Most memorable of all is the portrait of the strong-willed mother, immersed in 'passionate dreams of the past'. Resigned to her husband's lack of success in this land in which she will always be an alien, she nevertheless

21

fanatically pursues her goal of a good education for her children.

All About Books, originally titled *All About Books for Australian and New Zealand Readers*, was published in Melbourne 1928–38. It resumed publication in 1961 and after August 1963 was incorporated in the journal, *Ideas*. The early series had affiliations with book-publishing interests but devoted a two-page section in each edition to Australian books; that section was conducted by Nettie Palmer and, later, F.T. Macartney.

All That Swagger, a novel by Miles Franklin (q.v.), won the S.H. Prior Memorial Prize for 1936 and was published that year both in book form and serially in the *Bulletin*. The novel's hero, Irish immigrant Danny Delacy, is modelled upon Miles Franklin's paternal grandfather, Joseph Franklin, and the exploits and adventures of four generations of Delacys on the land around the headwaters of the Murrumbidgee River follow roughly the fortunes of the Franklin family from 1833 to 1933. 'Fearless Danny's' story begins in 1833 by the Shannon in County Clare when he and his Johanna elope and take ship for the Antipodes. In Sydney, discovering that land grants had ceased in 1831, Danny sets out as a hired man for Bandalong, one of the most remote stations, far beyond the already-populated Goulburn plains, past Lake George, Gounderu (Gundaroo) and the Limestone Plains. Always the mountains farther south beckon Danny 'as the Lorelei', so after a spell of hired labour to accumulate fifty head of cattle and a dozen horses he finally makes his way to a valley that the blacks called Burrabinga. As the seasons pass, the station, Burrabinga, is carved out of virgin land and Johanna produces sons and daughters who go to school in Sydney and become the second Delacy generation. Significant Australian events dot the narrative, conveying a sense of historical continuity – the gold rushes, the Robertson and Duffy Land Acts, free selection, self-government, the Boer War. From its cohesive opening the narrative falls away (especially after the first generation) into a discursive series of episodes and events, broken only by the favourite Miles Franklin device of 'possuming' or yarning – meandering, conversational reflections on the rapidly-changing scene. Generations merge, each leaving its imprint on the others. Themes become interwoven, the focus of attention shifting easily from one to another. The novel's canvas becomes crowded with more and more participants as the century gradually moves to its ending in the modern day (1933) when the fourth generation Brian Delacy, aviator, lifting

his plane into the Murrumbidgee sky, glimpses in his mind's eye 'the spectral forms of bullock transport and receding Delacys moving against ancient unfamiliar apparitions on the palimpsest of Time'.

All the Green Year, see **CHARLWOOD, DON**

All the Rivers Run (1978), by Nancy Cato (q.v.) was published simultaneously in America, England and Australia as a composite of three earlier novels, *All the Rivers Run* (1958), *Time, Flow Softly* (1959) and *But Still the Stream* (1962). Chosen by the Literary Guild as its first choice for its members (which guaranteed a pre-publication sale of more than 25 000 copies), *All the Rivers Run* was seen by its publishers as a rival to Colleen McCullough's *The Thorn Birds*. Philadelphia (Delie) Gordon, aged thirteen, sole surviving member of her family from the wreck of the *Loch Tay*, joins her Aunt Hester, Uncle Charles and her cousin Adam at the little Snowy Mountains township of Kiandra. From her uncle, a shiftless fossicker for gold, she first learns of the Murray, the great river that carries the Snowy water to the sea. When Uncle Charles has a lucky find the family buys land at Echuca on the Murray and Delie's infatuation with the river begins. With money from her parents' estate she buys a part share in a riverboat owned by the seaman, Tom, her rescuer from the *Loch Tay* disaster. Her cousin Adam, her first love, dies in an accident and Delie goes to live in Echuca, earning a living through her artistic talent. There she meets Brenton Edwards, Tom's partner on the boat *Philadelphia*. Delie goes briefly to Melbourne to study art (her drawing master is Frederick McCubbin) but contracts tuberculosis and returns to Echuca, where she marries Brenton Edwards and accompanies him on the *Philadelphia* on the endless round of riverboat trading. As the years pass Delie has six children, her husband is incapacitated in an accident, and later dies from a stroke. She takes over his role on the *Philadelphia*, raises her family, has lovers, and ends her days living by the river at Goolwa. A mammoth novel, *All the Rivers Run* spans the years 1899 to 1956, encompassing the Boer War and the two world wars, and providing, with the river as the central figure, a romantic and nostalgic view of Australia's pioneer past. A television mini-series of the book was shown in 1983.

ALLAN, J.A. (JAMES ALEXANDER) (1889–1956), born and educated in Melbourne, was a former editor of the *Victorian Historical Magazine* and heraldic adviser to the Royal Australian Navy. He published verse, *A Wineshop Madonna* (1911) and *Revolution* (1940); prose, *The Old Model School* (1934) and *Men and Manners in Australia* (1945); and an historical work, *The History of Camberwell* (1949).

ALLEN, Sir CARLETON KEMP (1877–1966), brother of Leslie Holdsworth Allen (q.v.), born at Carlton, Melbourne, went from the University of Sydney to Oxford, where he studied law and was elected Eldon Law Scholar in 1913. After distinguished service in the First World War he returned to Oxford where, in 1929, he was appointed professor of jurisprudence and, from 1931, second warden of Rhodes House. His chief publications were *Bureaucracy Triumphant* (1931), *Law and Orders* (1945), *The Queen's Peace* (1953), *Law and Disorders* (1954) and *Aspects of Justice* (1958). He also wrote fiction, *The Judgment of Paris* (1924) and *Oh! Mr. Leacock!* (1925).

ALLEN, DAVID (1936–   ), was born in Birmingham, England, spent some years teaching drama in English schools and from 1966 to 1970 worked as an education officer in Uganda where he also helped to found a theatre company. In 1972, after studying under Hugh Hunt, he came to Australia to lecture in drama at the Salisbury College of Advanced Education. Co-founder of Troupe, Adelaide's alternative professional theatre company, for which he has directed and written plays, he has worked as a full-time writer since December 1979. His plays, which have been produced in Australia, England and America, include 'Behold the Gay Marsupial', 'Forests of the Night', 'Buckley's', 'Hat Trick', 'Koala Kapers', 'Pike's Madness', *Gone with Hardy* (published in *Theatre Australia*, 1978), 'Joseph Conrad Goes Ashore', *Don't Listen to Gouger* (published in *Opinion*, 1978), 'Meat', 'Dickinson', 'Down, Down at Dingley Dell', *Karen* (1983), 'Tina's Troupers' and *Upside Down at the Bottom of the World* (1981). This last play, first produced in 1979 by the Nimrod Company and based on D.H. Lawrence's stay in Australia and his novel *Kangaroo*, shared an Awgie in 1979 with David Williamson's *Travelling North*.

ALLEN, L.H. (LESLIE HOLDSWORTH), (1879–1964), was born at Maryborough, Victoria, studied English and classics at the University of Sydney and completed a Ph.D. at the University of Leipzig in 1907. He held lecturing positions at the University of Sydney and Sydney Teachers' College before becoming professor of English at the Royal Military College, Duntroon in 1918. From 1931 to 1951 he was sole lecturer in English and Latin at the Canberra University College, later the Aus-

tralian National University. He became a member of the Commonwealth Book Censorship Advisory Committee in 1933 and was chairman of the Literature Censorship Board from 1937. His poetry, which reflects his classical interests, has a deft lyric touch. It consists of *Phaedra and Other Poems* (1921), *Araby and Other Poems* (1924) and *Patria* (1941). 'Patria', title-poem of the last volume, is a series of nine sonnets which reflect on the future of Australia. Allen also published a book of children's poetry, *Billy-Bubbles* (1920); a volume of prose sketches (with six poems), *Gods and Wood-things* (1913); and translations of three plays by the German dramatist, Friedrich Hebbel.

Alma Mater, a Melbourne University journal, began publication in July 1895, carrying University news, articles of literary interest and original creative material (short fiction and poetry). From April 1899 its subtitle was *An Illustrated Australasian University Newspaper*. It ceased in 1902.

Almanacs were issued in Australia from the early days of European settlement and, in the first half of the nineteenth century in particular, were an important adjunct to newspapers in disseminating information within the colonies as well as overseas (e.g. among intending immigrants). Most almanacs were produced by colonists already associated with publishing, whether mainly as printers (e.g. George Howe), newspaper editors (e.g. Henry Melville), stationers (e.g. John Sands), or booksellers (e.g. James Tegg). Characteristically they comprised not only a calendar of months and days (with ecclesiastical dates, other anniversaries and basic astronomical information noted) but also an increasing amount of miscellaneous material: several statistical tables (tides, weights and measures, ready reckoners); directories of the civil and military establishments, traders and pastoralists; digests of land, police, telegraphic and postal regulations and lists of fees; agricultural reports, rural calendars, and gardening advice; historical reviews, chronologies, and diaries of events; coastal and rural itineraries; and special articles. It was not unusual for a publisher to issue several works with overlapping information. In 1843, for example, James Tegg published *Tegg's Handbook for Emigrants, Tegg's Commercial Sheet Almanac, Tegg's New South Wales Daily Memorandum Book and Pocket Companion,* and *Tegg's New South Wales Pocket Almanac and Remembrancer.*

The first Australian almanac was George Howe's *New South Wales Pocket Almanack and Colonial Remembrancer* (1806), which he issued annually until his death in 1821, when it was continued as the *Australasian Pocket Almanack,*

the *Australian Almanack* and under other titles
(1822–35). The *N.S.W. Calendar and General
Post Office Directory* (1832–46, a publication
from the *Sydney Herald* office) and *Tegg's New
South Wales Pocket Almanac and Remembrancer*
(1836–44) were two other important Sydney
almanacs of the 1830s. In Hobart four prominent newspaper editors or proprietors produced
almanacs in the 1820s and 1830s: Andrew Bent,
who issued the *Van Diemen's Land Pocket Almanack* (later the *Tasmanian Almanack)* in
1824–30; James Ross, whose almanac was issued 1829–36 under various titles, most commonly with the *Hobart Town Almanack* or
(Ross's) Hobart Town Almanack somewhere in
the title, but in 1833–34 as the *Van Diemen's
Land Almanack and Hobart Town Annual;*
William Gore Elliston, who took over from
Ross as government printer and issued *Hobart
Town Almanack*s in 1837–38; and Henry Melville, who issued his almanacs as the *Van
Diemen's Land Almanack* in 1831–33 and as
the *Van Diemen's Land Annual* in 1834–37.
In the other colonies the later appearance of
almanacs reflects their later development: in
Victoria an early printing firm published *Kerr's
Melbourne Almanac, and Port Phillip Directory*
in 1841–42; in South Australia the *Royal South
Australian Almanack and General Directory*
commenced publication in 1839 and was issued
for several decades, sometimes as the *South
Australian Almanac*; in the same State the
Adelaide Almanack (known also as Boothby's
Adelaide Almanack) ran from 1864 to 1883;
in WA two *Western Australian Almanack*s were
published from 1842 until at least the end of
the 1840s; and in Queensland, *Pugh's Almanac*
was published under several titles, 1859–1927.

To varying degrees, the early colonial almanacs combined elements of the calendar, the
diary, the gazetteer, the directory and the yearbook. Although this comprehensiveness of information was retained in later years, consumers
after 1860 were increasingly catered for by publications focused more firmly on one of the
elements; for example, by the business and
postal directories of John Sands and his partners in Melbourne, Sydney and Adelaide; by
specific manuals such as *S.W. Silver & Co.
Australian Grazier's Guide* (1879, 1881), written by 'Rolf Boldrewood'; or by diaries like
the Letts diary for 1883–84, from which Tom
Collins amplifies entries in *Such is Life* (q.v.,
1903). The importance to Australian literature
of almanacs and their offshoots, however, goes
beyond 'Boldrewood''s involvement in the
preparation of a pastoralists' handbook, or Furphy's use of a diary to establish an aleatory
mode of narration. They are important sources
of information about Australian authors and
cultural institutions, and the early almanacs in

particular, prized among collectors of Australiana, are important in publishing history for
the part they played in the activities of pioneering printers and the opportunities they
provided for individual editors and contributors.

Some of the special articles, particularly in
the Tasmanian almanacs of the 1820s and
1830s, are significant both as specimens of early
Australian descriptive and historical prose, and
as sources for subsequent Australian authors;
the *Hobart Town Almanack*s of Ross and Elliston, for example, contain several articles that
were used by Marcus Clarke in *Old Tales of a
Young Country* and *His Natural Life*.

Alphabet Murders, The, see **TRANTER,
JOHN**

Altered I, The, see **HARDING, LEE**; Science Fiction

Alvin Purple, see **BLUNDELL, GRAEME**

Ambrose Kangaroo, a creation of Elisabeth
MacIntyre (q.v.), first appeared in *Ambrose Kangaroo: A Story That Never Ends* (1941). A young
kangaroo (a 'joey') runs away from his mother
and has an enjoyable day's escapading until
returned to his mother by a kindly farmer. His
adventures were continued in *Ambrose Kangaroo
Has a Busy Day* (1944), *Ambrose Kangaroo Goes
to Town* (1964) and *Ambrose Kangaroo Delivers
the Goods* (1978).

Americans, Baby, The, the second prose collection by Frank Moorhouse (q.v.) was published in 1972; reprinted several times since
then, it helped significantly to establish Moorhouse's reputation as a writer of short fiction.
The Americans, Baby reprints one of the stories
in *Futility and Other Animals* (1969) and like
that work is a 'discontinuous narrative', set
mainly within the Sydney alternative subculture
of the late 1960s. The major, but not dominant,
character is Becker, an American Coca-Cola
executive who feels isolated in Australia and
who forms a relationship with the unstable
Terri McDowell, daughter of George McDowell
of *The Electrical Experience* (q.v.); dismissed
from his position as a result of the liaison, he
ends working as a jazz pianist. There are six
Becker stories among the twenty which comprise *The Americans, Baby*; of the remainder,
several focus on the shifting relationships of a
group of university students and fellow radicals.
The fragility of personal relationships (for example, in the failure of sexuality to bond people) and the estrangement and isolation of most
of Moorhouse's characters, are major themes in
the collection, which is also notable for the

satiric portrait of radical movements in stories like 'The American Poet's Visit'.

AMIET, WILLIAM (1890–1959), born near Geelong, Victoria, practised law in various parts of Queensland and from 1920 in Mackay. A contributor of literary articles and reviews over many years to the *Mackay Mercury* (he was spoken of with respect and pleasure by Nettie Palmer), Amiet published numerous works including a book of his newspaper articles, *Scrambled Scrutinies* (1949). In *The Practice of Literary History* (1936) he discusses methods of presenting the history of literature and looks at the relationship of literary history to biography, criticism and history.

AMOS, ROBERT (1920–), Austrian by birth, fled to China when the Nazis took over Austria and was a civilian internee of the Japanese in Shanghai during the Second World War. He came to Australia in 1949, joined CSIRO as a research chemist and then became editor of publications. His play, 'When the Grave Diggers Come' (co-winner of the Sydney Journalists' Club drama competition of 1961), was staged in 1963 at the Emerald Hill Theatre, Melbourne. It concerns a group of emigrants, mostly white Russians, in an Asian city awaiting the communist takeover of the city. Amos wrote numerous plays for television and radio, chief of which are 'A Game of Numbers', 'A Country for Proud People', 'Wind from the Icy Country' and 'Survival in the Service'.

Anapress, see **Australian Natives' Association**

ANCHEN, J.O., see **Criticism**

And the Big Men Fly, see **HOPGOOD, ALAN**

ANDERSON, ETHEL (1883–1958), born Leamington, England, of Australian parents, was educated in Sydney before marrying a British officer serving with the Indian Army. After living for some years in India and England, she returned in 1926 to Australia, where her husband served on the staff of three State governors and the governor-general. Her published works include two volumes of poetry, *Squatter's Luck* (1942) and *Sunday at Yarralumla* (1947); two collections of essays, *Adventures in Appleshire* (1944) and *Timeless Garden* (1945); and three collections of short stories, *Indian Tales* (1948), *At Parramatta* (1956) and *The Little Ghosts* (1959). *The Best of Ethel Anderson,* edited by J.D. Pringle (1973), is a selection from her previous collections. Al-

though she saw herself as primarily a poet, it is her prose work that is most distinctive. *Indian Tales* and *The Little Ghosts,* drawn from her experience of India and its history, illustrate her wry humour, ironic wit, quick observation and spare, precisely-worked style. Although dated in some of their social attitudes, they richly evoke the flavour of Indian life. *At Parramatta* is an even more assured collection; set in the country near Parramatta at the time of the Crimean War, the stories form a sequence with some plot development and recurring characters. In both her short fiction and essays her lyrical power is striking, although in the latter it has more scope. *Adventures in Appleshire,* which draws on her reminiscences of England, and the more varied collection *Timeless Garden,* reflect her diverse interests and distinctive personality.

ANDERSON, HUGH (1927–), born Elenore, Victoria, has had a long teaching career with the Victorian Education Department and has been one of Australia's most prolific writers. He has published some fifty-four titles in Australian history, biography, literary criticism, folklore, folk-song and balladry, and bibliography. His publications include such critical and bibliographical works as *A Guide to Ten Australian Poets* (1953); *Frank Wilmot (Furnley Maurice): A Bibliography and a Criticism* (1955, with Barbara Ramsden); *Shaw Neilson: An Annotated Bibliography and Check List, 1889–1956* (1956); *Christopher John Brennan: A Comprehensive Bibliography with Annotations* (1959, with Walter Stone); *Bernard O'Dowd (1866–1953): An Annotated Bibliography* (1963); *The Singing Roads: A Guide to Australian Children's Authors and Illustrators* (1965, 1969); *The Poet Militant: Bernard O'Dowd* (1969); and *John Shaw Neilson* (1972, with L.J. Blake). Anderson's interest in Australian folk-song and balladry is reflected in his compilation of *Colonial Ballads* (1955, an enlarged and revised edition published in 1970 as *The Story of Australian Folksong*), and in such publications as *Botany Bay Broadsides* (1956), *Songs of Billy Barlow* (1956), *Goldrush Songster* (1958), *Farewell to Old England: A Broadside History of Early Australia* (1964) and *Folk Songs of Australia and the Men and Women Who Sang Them* (1967, with John Meredith). His work on Charles Thatcher (q.v.), *The Colonial Minstrel* (1960), is a detailed biography of Thatcher's Australasian career with liberal quotations from Thatcher's favourite songs. His historical works include *Out of the Shadow: The Career of John Pascoe Fawkner* (1962); *Eureka: Victorian Parliamentary Papers, Votes and Proceedings, 1854–1867* (1969) and *Victoria: From Discovery to Federation* (1974).

ANDERSON, JESSICA, was born in Brisbane but has lived most of her life in Sydney, apart from a few years in London. Although she only began to write novels at the age of forty, she had previously written short stories for newspapers and drama scripts for radio, especially adaptations of novels by Henry James and Charles Dickens. Her novels are *An Ordinary Lunacy* (1963); *The Last Man's Head* (1970); *The Commandant* (1975); *Tirra Lirra by the River* (1978), which won the Miles Franklin Award and the Australian Natives' Association Literary Award; and *The Impersonators* (1980), which also won the Miles Franklin Award and the NSW Premier's Award.

A compressed style, delicate irony, narrative control and dramatic dialogue are characteristics of all Anderson's novels, reflecting her admiration for writers such as Henry James, Evelyn Waugh and, especially, Henry Green. *An Ordinary Lunacy* combines penetrating observation of a sophisticated segment of Sydney society with exploration of an obsessive passion; *The Last Man's Head*, ostensibly a crime novel, has moral and psychological subtleties that lift it out of that category; *The Commandant*, a historical novel based on the life of Captain Patrick Logan, commandant of the Moreton Bay penal settlement 1826–30, is a vivid account given a new, partly-feminist perspective in that it is centred on the experience of Logan's young sister-in-law. But it is in *Tirra Lirra by the River* and *The Impersonators* that Anderson's professed aim of 'poetic brevity' is most fully achieved. *Tirra Lirra by the River* is a retrospective, carefully-structured account of one woman's life. Nora Roche, now in her seventies, returns to her childhood home in Queensland after many years first in Sydney and then in London; confined to bed by a severe illness, she begins to turn her 'globe of memory', rediscovering key incidents and people in her life and attempting, like the Lady of Shallott, to come to terms with her lonely tower. Sociological observation is not the novel's primary concern, but it also presents an intimate picture of life in suburban Australia between the wars. *The Impersonators*, set in Sydney of the 1970s, is a complicated and ambitious study of an Australian family, although once again it deals with the rediscovery of Australia by an expatriate woman; the theme is money and the impersonations that its pursuit imposes on people, especially on women.

ANDERSON, JOHN (1893–1962), born Lanarkshire, Scotland, had a distinguished academic career in Great Britain before occupying the Challis Chair of Philosophy at the University of Sydney, 1927–1958. Instigator of the Sydney Freethought tradition, Anderson exercised great influence over several generations of Sydney students, writers and intellectuals, an influence that continued to be widely expressed into the 1960s in the attitudes of writers and thinkers such as Donald Horne and Peter Coleman and in journals such as the *Observer, Quadrant* and *Nation*. The Sydney Freethought group split radically in the 1950s over attitudes to the Cold War and, apart from small enclaves, Andersonianism is no longer a force in Sydney's intellectual life. Anderson's early publications were *Education and Politics* (1931) and *Some Questions in Aesthetics* (1932); a collection of forty of his major papers was published posthumously in 1962 as *Studies in Empirical Philosophy*. He was for some years editor of the then *Australasian Journal of Psychology and Philosophy* (now the *Australian Journal of Philosophy*) and in its pages appeared several of his most influential essays, 'Art and Morality' (1941), 'The Servile State' (1943) and 'Education for Democracy'. Of importance also was his introduction to W.H.C. Eddy's (ed.) *Prospects of Democracy* (1945). *Art and Reality,* a collection of thirty-five of his essays on aesthetics and literature, was published in 1982, edited by Janet Anderson, Graham Cullen and Kimon Lycos. An analysis of Andersonianism and its influence in Sydney is given in John Docker's *Australian Cultural Elites* (1974); A.J. Baker wrote *Anderson's Social Philosophy* (1979).

ANDERSON, Dame JUDITH (1898–) born Adelaide, made her stage debut at the Theatre Royal, Sydney, in 1915 and her screen debut in 1933 in the film *Blood Money*. Acclaimed in a long career in America, Europe and Australia, Judith Anderson appeared in important stage productions of *Mourning Becomes Electra, Macbeth* and *Medea* and in films such as *Rebecca, Laura* and *Cat on a Hot Tin Roof*. Acknowledged as a fine Shakespearean actress in particular, she was made DBE in 1960.

ANDREONI, GIOVANNI (1935–), born Grosetto, Italy, left Italy in 1962, worked as a teacher in Tasmania (1962–63) and was at the University of WA (1964–68). He worked in NZ, 1968–73, returning to Australia to lecture at the University of New England. Before arriving in Australia Andreoni had published a book of short stories, *Sedici Notti d'Insonnia (Sixteen Nights of Insomnia,* 1962). His later works include the semi-autobiographical novel, *Martin Pescatore (Martin Fisherman,* 1967), set in both Italy and Australia; in the second part of the novel the WA outback makes a considerable impact on the protagonist's spiritual and literary development. He has also written 'Abo Bianco', poems on the Australian outback, published in *Quaderni 4* (1971), and a book of short stories *La Lingua degl'Italiani d'Australia e Alcuni Racconti* (*The Language of Italian-Australians and Some Stories, 1978*).

ANDREWS, J.A. (JOHN ARTHUR) (1865–1903), born Bendigo, was educated in Melbourne and was a public servant for four years before his dismissal for insubordination in 1886. Soon after, he became active in the Melbourne Anarchists Club, and continued espousing the anarchist cause in pamphlets and public platforms after moving to NSW in 1891. Imprisoned twice in 1894–95, he edited *Anarchy* (1891–92) and published a magazine, *The Revolt* (1893–94), before returning to Victoria, although he was in Sydney again in 1897–99 reporting for the *Australian Worker* and the *Australian Workman*; he also wrote for *Melbourne Punch* and the *Bulletin* in the late 1880s, was briefly editor of the *Australian* (1888) and *Tocsin* (1902), and was a reporter for newspapers in Yea (1890) and Mudgee (1894). As 'Sebastian Bach' or under his own name, Andrews published three small volumes of verse, *Temple Mystic* (1888), *Teufelswelt* (1896) and *Poems of Freedom* (?1905); he may also have been the author of a fourth volume, *Apollyon*, suppressed during the 1890s.

'**Andy's Gone With Cattle**', a poem by Henry Lawson (q.v.), laments the departure of a member of a selection family to go overlanding cattle. It was first published in October 1888 in the *Australian Town and Country Journal*, which also published the sequel 'Andy's Return'. Some of the best-known lines of the poem are not Lawson's but are revisions by David McKee Wright when the poem was being prepared for publication in Lawson's *Selected Poems* (1918). The Andy of 'Andy's Gone With Cattle' (which is also in the repertoire of Australian folk-singers) is not the Andy of Lawson's poem, 'Middleton's Rouseabout', which traces the rise to wealth through thrift and hard work of a stolid rouseabout.

ANGAS Family, a notable pioneering family of South Australia, was headed by George Fife Angas (1789–1879), who was born at Newcastle-on-Tyne. He was instrumental in the establishment of the colony of South Australia by providing, through the South Australian Company, several vessels to transport settlers, especially German Lutheran families, to the colony from 1836 onwards. In 1851 he came to South Australia and settled at Angaston, the township site selected by his agent, Charles Flaxman, in the Barossa Valley. Thereafter he

served the new colony industriously, being the Barossa's representative in the Legislative Council from 1851 until his retirement from public life in 1866. George Fife Angas is the subject of a biography by Edwin Hodder (1891). He is prominently treated in Hodder's *The History of South Australia from Its Foundation to the Year of Its Jubilee* (1893) and in A. Grenfell Price's *Founders & Pioneers of South Australia* (1929). George Fife Angas's fourth child and eldest son was George French Angas (1822–86). Born at Newcastle-on-Tyne, George French showed an early interest in natural history; at the age of twenty he published *A Ramble in Malta and Sicily in the Autumn of 1841* (1842). He arrived in Australia in 1844 and toured extensively until 1846 both in that colony and NZ, recording his journeys in watercolour drawings. In 1847 he published *South Australia Illustrated* and *The New Zealanders Illustrated,* together with the illustrated two-volume account of his travels, *Savage Life and Scenes in Australia and New Zealand*. On a second trip to Australia in 1851 he visited the gold diggings at Bathurst, publishing in that year *Six Views of the Gold Field of Ophir* and *Views of the Gold Fields of Australia*. His later publications included *Australia, A Popular Account* (1865). George Fife Angas's fifth child, John Howard Angas (1823–1904), was, like his father, a renowned pastoralist, politician and philanthropist. The family's influence has continued to be exerted in South Australian pastoral and commercial interests to the present time.

Angry Penguins (1940–46), a quarterly journal of literary, artistic, musical and general cultural interest, was sponsored initially by the Adelaide University Arts Association but became an independent enterprise in its third number, published in Melbourne by Reed and Harris. Chiefly edited by Max Harris and John Reed (qq.v.) *Angry Penguins* was a self-consciously modernist magazine which coincided with a radical movement in Australian art and became a rallying point for artists and writers who had otherwise diverse interests; they included the artists Sidney Nolan, Albert Tucker, John Perceval, Danila Vassilieff, Joy Hester and Arthur Boyd and the writers Peter Cowan and Harry Roskolenko. Nolan, Tucker and Roskolenko, in particular, were involved in the magazine's production and publication. Rejecting all political creeds and influenced by the anarchist theories of Sir Herbert Read, *Angry Penguins* and its 1946 monthly supplement, *Angry Penguins Broadsheet*, attempted to present art as an organic whole, producing articles on cinema, jazz, the visual arts and literature. At the same time it attempted to link the Australian writer and artist to the European modernist movement, often publishing work by contemporary overseas writers such as Karl Shapiro and Dylan Thomas. Max Harris, who contributed a large range of material to the magazine, was particularly opposed to the nationalist socialism of such magazines as *Australian New Writing* and attacked what he saw as 'the tired and mediocre nationalism which passed for poetry, the pedestrian bush whackery which gave Australia a novel of unequalled verbal dullness'. Subject to inevitable 'excesses and absurdities', as Harris later admitted, and fatally attracted to any writing which presented itself as *avant garde*, *Angry Penguins* failed to survive the Ern Malley hoax (q.v.).

ANGUS, D.M. (DAVID MACKENZIE) (1851–1901), born Caithness-shire, Scotland, worked in Edinburgh as apprentice to a bookseller before being forced by tuberculosis to come to Australia in 1882. He was employed in the Sydney branch of the Melbourne bookseller and publisher, George Robertson (1) (q.v.) where he met another George Robertson (2) (q.v.) with whom, in 1886, he formed the famous bookselling and publishing firm, Angus & Robertson (q.v.). In 1899 Angus retired through ill-health and returned to Scotland. He, and Angus & Robertson, are discussed in J.R. Tyrrell's (q.v.) *Old Books, Old Friends, Old Sydney* (1952) and in George Ferguson's (q.v.) *Some Early Australian Bookmen* (1978).

Angus & Robertson (A & R), one of Australia's earliest and most important bookselling and book-publishing firms, came into existence in January 1886 as a partnership between David Mackenzie Angus and George Robertson (2) (qq.v.). Angus and Robertson had both arrived in Australia from Scotland in 1882 and worked in the Sydney branch of the Melbourne bookseller and publisher, also named George Robertson (1). In 1884 Angus set up his own bookshop at 110 Market Street, Sydney, later taking George Robertson (2) as partner. The rapid success of its retail bookselling saw the firm expand into the adjoining Market Street premises; in 1890 it moved to 89 Castlereagh Street, where for more than sixty years it was Sydney's best-known bookshop. Angus's chief concern was with the sale of educational books, while Robertson developed a particular interest in the collection and sale of Australiana; one of his main customers was David Scott Mitchell (q.v.), whose collection of Australiana became a major factor in the later establishment of Sydney's Mitchell Library (q.v.). The partnership ended in 1900, Angus returning to England where he died soon after from tuberculosis. The business was converted in 1907 into a public company with George Robertson (2) as

its managing director. After his death in 1933, Walter Cousins became its head; he was succeeded by Robertson's grandson, George Ferguson. In 1970 A & R became a subsidiary of Ipec Insurance and the business was relocated in Pitt Street, Sydney. In 1978 the bookshop division was sold to Gordon and Gotch.

Angus & Robertson's illustrious Australian publishing history, largely inspired by George Robertson (2), began in 1888 with the appearance of two books of verse, *A Crown of Wattle* by H. Peden Steel and *Sun and Cloud on River and Sea* by 'Ishmael Dare' (Arthur Jose), and a reprint of an important piece of Australiana, *Facsimile of a Proposal for a Settlement on the Coast of New South Wales, by Sir George Young* (*1785*). Its halcyon period began in 1895 when it published A.B. Paterson's *The Man from Snowy River and Other Verses*, followed in 1896 by Henry Lawson's *While the Billy Boils* and *In the Days When the World was Wide and Other Verses*. The first catalogue of publications of A & R was circulated in 1895, the first separate catalogue of purely Australian publications ever issued. The long list of Australian writers later published by A & R includes Victor Daley, Will Ogilvie, James Brunton Stephens, Louise Mack, C.J. Dennis, Norman Lindsay, Mary Gilmore, Ion Idriess and Frank Clune. During the First World War Dennis's *The Songs of a Sentimental Bloke* (1915) was one of A & R's major successes. The 1920s saw the publication of *The Australian Encyclopaedia* while the *Official History of Australia in the War of 1914–1918* was distributed by and bore the imprint of A & R. Notable children's books from A & R include Lindsay's *The Magic Pudding* (1918), Dorothy Walls's *Blinky Bill* series, and May Gibbs's *Gumnut Tales*. The firm's natural science list of publications began with Neville Cayley's *What Bird Is That?* in 1931. In 1923 George Robertson (2) took over a small printing house, Eagle Press, which became Halstead Press (q.v.), the chief printing arm of the firm. After the takeover of A & R in 1970 Halstead Press was sold and the publishing division, under Richard Walsh, who became managing director in 1972, was relocated at Cremorne, Sydney. Thereafter, although it maintained some publishing of quality fiction, non-fiction and poetry, it concentrated on the mass market. In 1981 it became part of the News Limited group.

Much of the early history of Angus & Robertson and the men associated with it, such as F.V. Wymark, is included in James Tyrrell's *Old Books, Old Friends, Old Sydney* (1952) and *Postscript: Further Bookselling Reminiscences* (1957), and George Ferguson's *Some Early Australian Bookmen* (1978). In 1910 Henry Lawson wrote a verse tribute to George Robertson (2) and A & R, *The Auld Shop and the New* (1923).

Annabella Boswell's Journal, edited with an introduction by Morton Herman in 1965, was first published under the title *Early Recollections and Gleanings from an Old Journal* (?1916). It records the experiences of Annabella Innes, born near Bathurst in NSW in 1826, her schooling in Sydney and her life from 1843 until her marriage to Patrick Douglas-Boswell in 1856 at Port Macquarie.

Annals of Australian Literature (1970), compiled by Grahame Johnston (q.v.), lists, by yearly entries, noteworthy Australian books from 1789 to 1968 in alphabetical order of authors and with an accompanying abbreviation to indicate genre. Side columns to the yearly entries contain such ancillary information as authors' birth and death dates; the founding and duration of newspapers and periodicals; visits or books by notable writers from overseas; books written in Australia in languages other than English; some books on non-Australian subjects by authors whose own works are in the main column; books written abroad by authors now settled in Australia; and English classics referring to Australia.

Annual Catalogue of Australian Publications, see *Australian National Bibliography*

Anoli the Blind, a psychological melodrama by Sydney Tomholt (q.v.), was published in his collection *Bleak Dawn and Other Plays* (1936) and included in the London anthology *The Best One-Act Plays of 1936*. Set in an isolated part of northern Queensland, the drama, which concentrates on the embittered emotions of three Italians, the blind but powerful Anoli Ferari, his common-law wife Rose and her lover Antonio, moves to a violent conclusion.

'ANSTRUTHER, GILBERT' (RUSSEL S. CLARK) (1909–   ), born Carcoar, NSW, was the author of *An End to Tears* (1946), an account of the war years in Hong Kong, and a successful writer of popular fiction, all published under the pseudonym 'Gilbert Anstruther'. His fiction includes *Three Went West* (1939), *To Hell with Love* (1943), *The Wench Was Wicked* (1944), *Fishes Also Make Love* (1944), *God Glanced Away* (1945), *The Anstruther Three-Story Omnibus* (1946), *The Ladies Came Undressed* (1947), and *Move Over, Honey* (1949).

Anthologies. The earliest attempts to sample Australian writing in anthologies include Isaac Nathan's *The Southern Euphrosyne and Austra-*

lian Miscellany (1848), which contains 'original Anecdote, Poetry and Music'; *The Australian Souvenir for 1851* (1851), which contains stories, essays and poems; and W.H.H. Yarrington's *Prince Alfred's Wreath* (1868) which, with its selections from Henry Kendall, J. Sheridan Moore, W.M. Adams and others, is the first approximation to later verse anthologies. In 1869 William H. Williams introduced a form of anthology with his Christmas 'annuals' for holiday reading; his *Illustrated Australian Annuals* for 1869–70 and 1870–71 contain a medley of verse, short fiction and sketches, mostly by Australian writers. The 'annual' rapidly became a popular anthological device; well-known examples include *The 'Vagabond' Annual* (1877), by John Stanley James; *Hash* (1877) by Garnet Walch; *The Antipodean* (1893, 1895, 1897) by George Essex Evans and others; and *The Golden West* (1906–46) by R.C. Spear. One of the earliest examples of the anthology that comprises selections taken from a newspaper, magazine or journal is *Punch Staff Papers* (1872), a collection of short fiction, sketches and verse by members of the staff of *Sydney Punch*; among the contributors were D.H. Deniehy, Henry Kendall, G.G. McCrae, Garnet Walch and Richmond Thatcher. The first significant anthology to combine selections and criticism was G.B. Barton's *Poets and Prose Writers of New South Wales* (q.v., 1866); Barton used extracts from the writings of Deniehy, W.B. Dalley, W.C. Wentworth, Charles Harpur, Kendall, J.L. Michael and others, to illustrate and substantiate his critical commentary.

The centenary of the colony in 1888 produced two busy anthologists, Douglas Sladen and Arthur Patchett Martin, who took advantage of the historic moment to promote Australian literature; their critical discrimination was, however, somewhat overruled by their enthusiasm and hampered by their lack of awareness of the new spirit of nationalism that was already affecting Australian writing. Sladen's first anthology, *Australian Ballads and Rhymes* (1888), was a selection of 'Poems inspired by Life and Scenery in Australia and New Zealand'; it was reissued in the same year with a critical introduction and in an enlarged edition, titled *A Century of Australian Song*. With the help of contributions and suggestions he gained from canvassing in the press, Sladen published an even wider selection, *Australian Poets, 1788–1888* (1888). In all, he published the work of more than eighty poets; inevitably many were undeserving of recognition and were discarded by later anthologists. Sladen's sins were also of omission. Much of Adam Lindsay Gordon is missing, the *Bulletin* writers are excluded, as also are Ada Cambridge, Victor Daley, Mary Hannay Foott and John Farrell.

Martin, who had edited an earlier anthology, *An Easter Omelette in Prose and Verse* (1879), drew upon Australian writers resident in England for a collection of stories and sketches, *Oak-Bough and Wattle-Blossom* (1888); contributors included Rosa Praed, Sladen, Philip Mennell and Martin himself. His wife, Harriette Anne Martin, compiled similar anthologies, *Under the Gum Tree* (1890) with contributions from Praed, Jessie Couvreur and Hume Nisbet, and *Volcanic Gold* (1890); she also edited the first all-women collection, *Coo-ee: Tales of Australian Life by Australian Ladies* (1891). Philip Mennell added *In Australian Wilds* (1889), a similar collection of largely undistinguished short fiction, and Lala Fisher, a selection of writings by Australians in England, *By Creek and Gully* (1899).

Ignored by Sladen and Martin, the *Bulletin* proceeded to publish its own miscellanies; in 1890 J.F. Archibald in collaboration with F.J. Broomfield compiled *'A Golden Shanty': Australian Stories and Sketches in Prose and Verses by 'Bulletin' Writers*. Those represented include Henry Kendall, Victor Daley, Edward Dyson, A.B. Paterson, John Farrell and Henry Lawson; the fact that only Kendall appears in Sladen and Martin shows how lacking in literary discrimination the earlier anthologies are. Further *Bulletin* collections were *The Bulletin Story Book* and *The Bulletin Reciter*, both edited by A.G. Stephens in 1901; in 1920 Bertram Stevens selected and edited *The 'Bulletin' Book of Humorous Verse and Recitations*.

The first half of the twentieth century brought a continuous stream of anthologies of all kinds, some of which can now be seen as significant landmarks in Australian literary history. Bertram Stevens edited *An Anthology of Australian Verse* in 1906; from it came *The Golden Treasury of Australian Verse* (1909), the first collection that could be said to be truly reflective of Australian sentiment and attitude. Stevens produced other minor anthologies such as *Bush Ballads* (1908), *The Australian Birthday Book* (1908), *A Book of Australian Verse for Boys and Girls* (1915); and he collaborated with George Mackaness to produce *The Children's Treasury of Australian Verse* (1913) and *Selections from Australian Poets* (1913). The selections are characteristically Australian not only in content (Australian life, landscape and events) but also in their simple, direct and sometimes rugged style. Mackaness, an anthologist of other genres also, returned to verse anthologies twenty years later with *The Wide Brown Land* (1934), chosen by himself and his daughter Joan: perhaps the most famous of all Australian verse anthologies, it took its title from Dorothea Mackellar's poem, 'My Country' (q.v.), and was often reprinted. Douglas Stewart continued the title

with his 1971 anthology. A significant milestone was reached in verse anthologies in 1918 when Walter Murdoch (q.v.) edited the first *The Oxford Book of Australasian Verse*; when the second edition was published in 1923 'Oxford' was omitted from the title. Murdoch's original selection did not please all critics but it was more wide-ranging than most of those published earlier and less emphatic on Australian content than the 1913 anthology of Stevens and Mackaness. Murdoch's third edition (1945) was the subject of considerable criticism in *Southerly* (1946); the fourth edition, titled *A Book of Australian and New Zealand Verse* (1950), was edited jointly by Murdoch and Alan Mulgan; Judith Wright's *A Book of Australian Verse* (1956, second edition 1968), ultimately replaced the Murdoch Oxford anthologies. Another well-received verse anthology of the early twentieth century was Percival Serle's *An Australasian Anthology (Australian and New Zealand Poems)* (1927). Serle was assisted by 'Furnley Maurice' and R.H. Croll, both of whom were established critics; the combination produced a comprehensive and well-balanced selection and was accompanied by an account of the development of Australian and NZ poetry. The third edition of Serle's anthology (1946) added a short and rather unsatisfactory section on contemporary verse. Another significant anthologist of this period was J.J. Stable (q.v.), professor of English at the University of Queensland, who compiled *The Bond of Poetry* in 1924. It combines English and Australian poems because Stable felt that poetry provided a bond that might keep nationalistic Australians linked to their British heritage. *The Bond of Poetry* remained a popular school text for many years, more so than Stable's later anthology, *The High Road of Australian Verse* (1929). One of the earliest movements towards the regional collection of verse was Stable's *A Book of Queensland Verse* (1924, with A.E.M. Kirwood), which was published in connection with the Brisbane centenary and illustrated the development of verse in Queensland. A verse anthology that stood deliberately apart from the nationalistic collections of this period was *Poetry in Australia 1923* (1923), edited by Jack Lindsay and Kenneth Slessor with a preface by Norman Lindsay that decried nationalism in literature. Compelled to accept the 'accident' of geographical location and thus label its poetry 'Australian', the anthology is not representatively Australian in a general sense; its contributors were chosen largely to illustrate the Lindsay and *Vision* insistence on internationalism in literature and the importance of language in creative thought. Much of the selected poetry came from Hugh McCrae, Jack Lindsay and Kenneth Slessor, all of whom wrote at that time in accord with *Vision* attitudes. A notable specialized anthology of the period was Louis Lavater's *The Sonnet in Australasia* (1926), a collection of some 225 sonnets by more than 100 Australian poets. The occasional annual selection of the poetry of the period, e.g. *Australian Poetry Annual 1920–21* (1921), chosen from contributions to the magazine *Birth* (q.v.), was the forerunner of the poetry magazines that proliferated after the middle of the century and of such annual selections of verse as *Australian Poetry* (q.v.), published by Angus & Robertson and which ran 1941–73 with a different editor for each volume. Most of *Australian Poetry*'s editors were established poets/critics, e.g. Douglas Stewart, R.D. FitzGerald, Kenneth Slessor and Judith Wright, and the annual selections were, at least until the 1960s, conventional and predictable. Notable among the specialized verse anthologies of the first half of the century were those published by the Jindyworobaks (q.v.). They ran 1938–53, included only poetry that satisfied the Jindyworobak criteria, and were edited by notable poets of the movement, e.g. Rex Ingamells, Flexmore Hudson, W. Hart Smith, Ian Mudie and Roland Robinson.

Although less prolific than verse anthologies, prose collections in the first half of the twentieth century were no less significant. In addition to the *Bulletin* anthologies already mentioned, other early collections of note were the stories reprinted from the *Sydney Mail, Red Kangaroo and Other Stories* (1907); Donald McLachlan's *Austral Garden: An Anthology of Australian Prose* (1922), which contained chapters from novels and extracts of non-fiction as well as short stories; *Australian Short Stories* (1928), edited by Mackaness; *An Australian Story Book* (1928), selected by Nettie Palmer from stories written in this century; and *Adventures in the Bush: Australia's Story* (1931), edited by Herbert Strang. Most prominent in these early anthologies are Barbara Baynton, Henry Lawson, 'Louis' Becke, Edward Dyson, Ernest Favenc, Vance Palmer, Katharine Susannah Prichard and Ethel Turner. In 1941 *Coast to Coast* (q.v.), an anthology of the year's best stories, was first published; it ran annually 1941–48, and biennially 1949–70, with a final issue in 1973. Early collections of Australian essays include *Essays, Imaginative and Critical* (1933), compiled by Mackaness and John D. Holmes, and *Australian Essays* (1935) selected by G.H. Cowling and 'Furnley Maurice'. Notable essayists represented are Marcus Clarke, John le Gay Brereton, Walter Murdoch and Ernest Scott.

Drama and literary criticism also appeared in anthology form in the first part of the century. Collections of one-act plays include *Eight Plays by Australians* (1934) and *Five Plays by Australians* (1936), both published by the Dramatists' Club of Melbourne; *Best Australian One-Act Plays* (1937), edited by William Moore and T. Inglis Moore; and Leslie Rees's *Australian Radio Plays* (1946). In somewhat similar vein to G.B. Barton's critical anthology of the previous century are Colin Roderick's *The Australian Novel* (1945) and *20 Australian Novelists* (1947), where critical and biographical commentary accompany excerpts from such writers as A.H. Adams, 'Rolf Boldrewood', Marcus Clarke, Henry Kingsley, Jessie Couvreur and others of the more modern period.

Since the Second World War poetry anthologies can be categorized in four main types: general anthologies that give a selection from colonial times to the present; those which attempt a periodic update of the contemporary scene prior to 1968; those which specifically illustrate the 'New Australian Poetry' (q.v.) which dates from 1968; and those which reflect sectional interests or illustrate particular types and periods of poetry. The general anthologies, largely a continuation of similar types published earlier in the century, include Judith Wright's *A Book of Australian Verse* (1956, rev. ed. 1968), Geoffrey Dutton's *Australian Verse from 1805* (1976) and Rodney Hall's *The Collins Book of Australian Poetry* (1981). Most of those attempting an up-to-date view of poetry in the period up to 1968 convey their intention by using the word 'modern' in their titles; they include H.M. Green's *Modern Australian Poetry* (1946, rev. ed. 1952); R.G. Howarth, Kenneth Slessor and John Thompson's *The Penguin Book of Australian Verse* (1958, titled . . . *Modern Australian Verse* in 1961) which was replaced by Harry Heseltine's *The Penguin Book of Australian Verse* (1972); Douglas Stewart's *Modern Australian Verse* (1964), which is the second volume of the two-volume *Poetry in Australia*; Rodney Hall and Thomas Shapcott's *New Impulses in Australian Poetry* (q.v., 1968), which concerns itself with the poetry of the 1960s but which appeared before the 'New Australian Poetry' had fully developed; David Campbell's *Modern Australian Poetry* (1970), which was also compiled prior to 1968 and which closes with the work of Geoffrey Lehmann, the only poet in the anthology who was born in the 1940s; Dennis Robinson's *Those Fabled Shores: Six Contemporary Australian Poets* (1972), which contains only the work of the mainstream poets, Slessor, Hope, Wright, James McAuley, Stewart and FitzGerald; and Thomas Shapcott's *Contemporary American and Australian Poetry* (1976), which includes some post-1968 poetry but which continues to emphasize the older representatives of contemporary Australian poetry, i.e. Hope, Wright, McAuley, Campbell, Gwen Harwood, John Blight and others. The 'New Australian Poetry', which came after 1968, has been given almost blanket coverage, chiefly by the myriad of poetry magazines that are a striking phenomenon of the modern literary scene, and to a lesser extent by more formal anthologies. The latter include Shapcott's *Australian Poetry Now* (1970), which is the companion to and extension of David Campbell's *Modern Australian Poetry* and which focuses on the poets who were on the verge of the new movement, e.g. Michael Dransfield, Robert Adamson, John Tranter and Roger McDonald; Robert Kenny and Colin Talbot's *Applestealers* (q.v. 1974), a collection specifically stated to represent the 'renaissance in Australian poetry'; John Tranter's *The New Australian Poetry* (1979), which includes selections from twenty-four poets of 'Australian poetry's most exciting decade', e.g. Bruce Beaver (one of the seminal poets of the 'renaissance'), Dransfield, Adamson, Rae Desmond Jones, Nigel Roberts, Jennifer Maiden, Vicki Viidikas and John Forbes; Heseltine's *The Penguin Book of Modern Australian Verse* (1981), which includes both new and somewhat older writers, e.g. many born in the 1920s and 1930s; and two important attempts to assist the development of contemporary poetry, the Paperback Poets (q.v.) series of Queensland University Press which culminated in two paperback poetry anthologies (1974, 1981) and Angus & Robertson's Poets of the Month (q.v.) series. Robert Gray and Geoffrey Lehmann's *The Younger Australian Poets* (1983) brings the poetry scene up to date, thereby relegating the 1968 revolution into history.

Increasingly in recent years the anthology has been used as a device to espouse causes, highlight philosophies and attitudes, illustrate particular literary movements, types of writing and groups of writers, and draw attention to places and regions. The feminist movement has drawn attention to its cause with such collections as *Mother I'm Rooted* (1975), an anthology of Australian women poets edited by Kate Jennings; *Hecate's Daughters* (1978), verse and prose edited by Carole Ferrier; *Stories of Her Life* (1979) edited by Sandra Zurbo; *The True Life Story of . . .* (1981) and *Frictions* (1982), prose anthologies edited respectively by Jan Ganey and Esther Caldwell and by Anne Gibbs and Alison Tilson; and *The Half-Open Door* (1982), accounts of the lives and careers of sixteen modern Australian women, edited by Patricia Grimshaw and Lynne Strahan. The experience of war had produced earlier anthologies such as C.E.W. Bean's *The Anzac Book* (1916) and Ian Mudie's *Poets at War* (1944). Modern variations on traditional war anthologies include the anti-war collection, *We Took Their Orders and Are Dead* (1971), a protest against the Vietnam War compiled by Shirley Cass, Ros Cheney, David Malouf and Michael Wilding; and Geoff Page's *Shadows from Wire* (1983), which demonstrates, by juxtaposing modern reactions to the First World War with actual war photographs, the irony of the initial response to the war. The reaction to the experience of incarceration is collected in two volumes of poetry, *Poems from Prison* (1973), edited by Rodney Hall, and *Walled Gardens* (1978), poems from NSW prisons, published by the aptly-named Ball & Chain Press. The experiences of the immigrant in Australia are the theme of Louise Rorabacher's group of short stories, *Two Ways Meet* (1963); Nancy Keesing's edition of Jewish stories, *Shalom* (1978), *Voci Nostre (Our Voice)* (1979), an Italo-Australian anthology edited by G.L. Abiuss, M. Geglio and V. Borghese; Manfred Jurgensen's verse and prose anthology, *Ethnic Australia* (1981), the work of twenty-four writers whose native language is not English; and *Tradition* (1982), edited by R.F. Holt. Regionalism provides a constant impulse to anthologizing: recent examples include the WA collections, *Soundings* (1976) edited by Veronica Brady, and *Quarry* (1981) by Fay Zwicky; Graham Rowlands's *Dots Over Lines* (1981), a collection of recent SA poetry; and the various Hunter Valley collections, e.g. Norman Talbot's *Hunter Valley Poets* (1973) and Ross Bennett's *This Place: Poetry of the Hunter Valley* (1980). Typical of specific period anthologies has been the return to colonial poetry in such collections as T. Inglis Moore's *From the Ballads to Brennan* (1964), Brian Elliott and Adrian Mitchell's *Bards in the Wilderness: Australian Colonial Poetry to 1920* (1970), and G.A. Wilkes's *The Colonial Poets* (1974); a similar specialist volume encompassing the twentieth rather than the nineteenth century is James McAuley's *A Map of Australian Verse* (1975); and a narrowing of the focus to inspect a much smaller period of time is seen in Leon Cantrell's *The 1890s* (1977).

Other readily identifiable thematic groups of anthologies include the book of erotic verse, *Within the Hill* (1975), edited by Alan Gould and others; the humorous collections, *Comic Australian Verse* (1972) edited by Geoffrey Lehmann, and *Robust, Ribald and Rude Verse in Australia* (1972) by Bill Wannan; the nationally-oriented Wannan collections, *The Wearing of the Green* (1965) and *The Heather in the South* (1966); Douglas Stewart's *Voyager Poems* (1960); and David Martin's book of left-wing verse, *New World, New Song* (1955).

Literary societies and groups often compile anthologies of the writings of their members:

Wesley Milgate and Imogen Whyse produced the Poetry Society of Australia's first anthology in 1956; Nancy Keesing's *Transition* (1970) is a collection of the ASA; *Square Poets* (1971) groups the work of the Queensland FAW, as does *Breakaway* (1980) for the WA branch of the FAW, Barry Bannister's *Walk a Different Way* (1979) for the Darwin FAW and *Island Authors* (1971) for the Tasmanian Branch. Selections from literary journals and newspapers have been gathered together in periodical collections, e.g. *Austro-verse* (1952) from *Austrovert; An Overland Muster* (1965), selected by Stephen Murray-Smith from *Overland* 1954–64; *On Native Grounds* (1968), selected by C.B. Christesen from *Meanjin; The Vital Decade* (1968), chosen by Geoffrey Dutton and Max Harris from *Australian Letters; Poems from the Age 1967–79* (1979), edited by R.A. Simpson; and *Quadrant: Twenty-Five Years* (1982), selected by Peter Coleman, Lee Shrubb and Vivian Smith. Compatible groups of poets have been brought together in such volumes as Judith Green et al.'s *Four Poets* (1962), Vincent Buckley's *Eight by Eight* (1963), Alexander Craig's *Twelve Poets 1950–1970* (1971), and Michael Dugan's *The Drunken Tram: Six Young Melbourne Poets* (1972). Poetry and short stories submitted to competitions are frequently collected; examples of such anthologies are those associated with the Mattara Spring Festival, the C.J. Dennis and the Harold Kesteven poetry competitions, and the Henry Lawson festivals at Grenfell, NSW.

In the second half of the twentieth century, there has been an intensive gathering of Australian folk-songs and ballads (q.v.), tall tales and folklore; Bill Wannan (q.v.) has been the most assiduous compiler of the last, having published many collections. A.B. Paterson's 1905 edition of *Old Bush Songs* was the forerunner of a host of similar modern collections of ballads and folk-songs by such writers as Vance Palmer, Will Lawson, Douglas Stewart, Nancy Keesing, John Meredith, John Manifold, Russel Ward, Hugh Anderson and Ron Edwards.

The increased attention paid to Australian literature by recent generations of scholars and students has led to a proliferation of critical writing. Notable among the recent collections of important critical statements are *Australian Literary Criticism* (1962) edited by Grahame Johnston; *The Literature of Australia* (q.v., 1964, rev. ed. 1976), edited by Geoffrey Dutton; *Literary Australia* (1966) by Clement Semmler and Derek Whitelock; *Twentieth Century Australian Literary Criticism* (1967) by Semmler; *The Writer in Australia* (1969) by John Barnes; *The Australian Nationalists* (1971) by Chris Wallace-Crabbe; and *Bards, Bohemians, and Bookmen* (1976) by Leon Cantrell.

Antipodean: An Illustrated Annual, The (1893–97), was edited by George Essex Evans and John Tighe Ryan, the third volume being edited by A.B. Paterson although the original editors were named on the title page. In addition to poetry and short fiction by well-known contemporary writers (e.g. Paterson's 'The Geebung Polo Club' and Henry Lawson's 'The Bush Undertaker'), the annuals contained critical and descriptive articles (e.g. 'The Australian Drama' and 'Australian Scenery').

Antipodes, meaning literally 'having feet opposed', emerged in English at the end of the fourteenth century to describe those who dwelt on opposite sides of the globe. It then came to mean the diametrically opposite regions of the earth, as in Shakespeare's *Much Ado About Nothing*, where Benedick, anxious to avoid Beatrice, offers to 'go on the slightest errand now to the Antipodes'. Early references to the Antipodes, which were sometimes imagined as a Utopia, were to the eastern as well as the southern hemispheres, but in 1800 the Antipodes Islands, just over 700 kilometres southeast of NZ, were so named by British seamen because they were diametrically opposite Greenwich; in the nineteenth century 'Antipodes', 'Antipodean' and other derivatives were applied more generally to Australia and NZ, again from a British perspective. The Christmas pantomimes of Australian colonial playwrights sometimes showed a consciousness of the Antipodes, e.g. Garnet Walch's *Hey Diddle Diddle* (1879) has as characters the Longest Day and the Shortest Night, 'subject to reverse in the Antipodes'; *The Antipodean* was an illustrated annual published in Melbourne 1893, 1895, 1897. A popular colloquialism derived from the concept of Antipodes is 'down under' (q.v.); Geoffrey Dutton's book of poems, *Antipodes in Shoes* (1958), derives its title from a line in Andrew Marvell's poetry.

Anzac, originally an acronym, has become one of the words most closely identified with Australia. It originated during the First World War, when the Cairo headquarters of General William Birdwood (later Baron Anzac and Totnes) became cluttered with despatch boxes bearing the words 'Australia and New Zealand Army Corps'; this title was abbreviated to 'A&NZAC' when an administrative stamp was cut which became known as the Anzac stamp. Soon after – and definitely by January 1915 – 'Anzac' was used as a planning code word suggested to, and adopted by, Birdwood to describe the Australasian forces, which he commanded. Early in the Gallipoli (q.v.) campaign, Birdwood named the cove where the first landings of Australian troops took place Anzac Cove; in time any Australian or New Zealand soldier who served at Gallipoli became known as an Anzac, while the Anzacs came to refer, as in Patsy Adam-Smith's *The Anzacs* (1978), to Australian troops serving anywhere in the First World War. The term itself has been widely used in Australian writing. Emily Coungeau's fantasy play, *Princess Mona* (?1916), has Mona wearing a coronet forming the letters Anzac which is a present from her five sons who have died in the war; the last scene has her pronounce Anzac as the name of the new capital city of Australia. Soldier poets and memoirists have frequently adopted Anzac as a pseudonym (e.g. R.W. Jones, J.P. O'Donnell) or used it in the titles of their works (e.g. *An Anzac Areopagus and Other Verses* (1923) by George Black, and *Five Months at Anzac . . .* (1916) by J.L. Beeston). War correspondent and historian C.E.W. Bean (q.v.), who compiled *The Anzac Book: Written and Illustrated in Gallipoli by the Men of Anzac* (1916), titled the first two volumes of the history of Australia's role in the First World War *The Story of Anzac* (1921, 1924) and his one-volume abridgement of that history, *Anzac to Amiens* (1946). The Anzac experience and its treatment form a significant part of Australian war literature (q.v.). Phrases such as the 'Anzac spirit' and the 'Anzac tradition' have become synonymous with courage, loyalty, mateship, and to a lesser degree with the rugged and cheerful insouciance and individualism said to be features of the Australian soldier. By contrast, the recent ironic use (during and since the Second World War) of the phrase 'big, bronzed Anzac' indicates a debunking of the original concept of the physical and mental excellence of the average Australian male. Anzac Day (25 April) has been a public holiday in Australia and New Zealand since about 1920 and falls on the anniversary of the first landing at Gallipoli in 1915; from its unofficial inception in 1916 until the end of the Second World War, its focus was Gallipoli itself and the First World War. It has since become the annual day of remembrance for those who participated in all the conflicts in which Australia has been involved. Anzac Day and its place in the Australian tradition have been examined in Alan Seymour's controversial *The One Day of the Year* (q.v., 1962).

Anzac Muster, An (1915), is a collection of soldiers' tales of the Gallipoli campaign by 'William Baylebridge' (q.v.). Using the Chaucerian device of a band of story-tellers, 'Baylebridge' has nine Gallipoli veterans each tell

three tales, one tale each on three successive Saturday night gatherings on a Queensland cattle station. 'Baylebridge''s tales are markedly different from the usual boisterous Australian 'digger' stories.

Anzac to Amiens, see **BEAN, C.E.W.**

Applestealers (1974), selected and introduced by Robert Kenny and Colin Talbot (qq.v.), is a collection of what is termed the 'New Australian Poetry' (q.v.). In the editors' prefaces the volume is said to represent 'what can be considered a renaissance in Australian poetry, which took place from about 1968'. In addition to the selection of poetry, *Applestealers* includes notes on the Poetry Workshops at La Mama (q.v.); a statement on the origin and development of 'the new poetry in Australia' movement by Kris Hemensley (q.v.); and a chronological check-list of the mini magazines of the period 1968–71, with brief notes on those poetry magazines extant in 1974.

ARABANOO was the first Aboriginal captured by Captain Arthur Phillip as an experiment in learning the language of the Aborigines and ultimately winning their confidence. Taken at Manly (q.v.) Cove on 31 December 1788, Arabanoo grew reconciled to his captivity and became a celebrity in the settlement. He died of smallpox in May 1789. An account of his activities is in Watkin Tench's *A Complete Account of the Settlement at Port Jackson* (1793). He is fictionally represented in Eleanor Dark's *The Timeless Land* (1941).

Arabin: Or, the Adventures of a Colonist in New South Wales (1845), the first novel of Thomas McCombie (q.v.), is a combination of melodramatic romance and moral tale illustrating the rewards of perseverance and patient industry in the pioneering situation. The humble-born, hard-working Godfrey Arabin wins prosperity and a worthy bride, but the highborn, lazy, dissolute Willis meets a violent end. Although fictional, *Arabin* belongs to the emigrant guidebook literature popular at the time. More a treatise on colonization than a novel, it discusses the mysterious grandeur of the bush, the concept of the bushman and the worth of the colonial-bred or currency (q.v.) inhabitant *vis-à-vis* the aristocratic immigrant. Its final chapter, 'An Essay on the Aborigines', mixes description of the lifestyle of the blacks with questions about the morality of their treatment by white society. A stage adaptation of *Arabin* by J.M. McLachlan, titled 'Arabin: Or, the Adventures of a Settler', was presented in Sydney in 1849.

Araluen, in the nineteenth century a gold-mining township, is now a tiny village in southern NSW between Braidwood and Moruya. Charles Harpur was an assistant gold commissioner there in 1859 and Henry Kendall praised the beauty of the tranquil Araluen River scenery in his landscape lyric, 'Araluen'. Kendall's first child, who died in infancy in Melbourne in 1870, was named Araluen, and he wrote a second poem with that title, commemorating her death.

Arcady in Australia, see **LANSBURY, CORAL**

ARCHER Family included the brothers Charles (1813–62), John (1814–57), David (1816–1900), William (1818–96), Archibald (1820–1902), Thomas (1823–1905) and Colin (1832–1921), who were all involved in pioneering pastoral ventures in northern Queensland in the decades 1840–70. Thomas, who was agent-general for the State during most of the period 1872–90, published pamphlets on the history, resources and prospects of Queensland (1881, 1882) and an autobiography, *Recollections of a Rambling Life* (1897), which describes his pioneering experiences in Australia and his adventures on the Californian goldfields. His son was William (1856–1924), a leading London dramatist, critic, and translator of Ibsen's plays.

ARCHER, ROBYN (1948–   ), was born in Adelaide, the daughter of Lykke Smith, a club entertainer and comedian. A television personality at the age of fifteen, Archer graduated from Adelaide University and worked as a secondary schoolteacher before becoming a full-time actress, singer, writer and musician. Well-known as an interpreter of Bertolt Brecht's songs, she has also produced two albums of her own songs, many of which pithily express her strong feminist and political convictions. She has written two plays, 'Il Magnifico', which deals with Lorenzo de Medici, and 'The Conquest of Carmen Miranda', and numerous cabaret shows which she has performed with outstanding success. These include 'Kold Komfort Kaffee', 'Side Show Alley', 'Tonight: Lola Blau', 'Robyn Archer at Large', 'A Star is Torn' and 'A Pack of Women'. 'A Star is Torn' is her best-known show; performed in Australia from 1979 and in London 1982–83, it is a one-woman interpretation of eleven women singers as diverse as Janis Joplin, Bessie Smith, Judy Garland, Billie Holiday and Edith Piaf. She has also published a children's book, *Mrs Bottle Burps* (1983).

ARCHIBALD, J.F. (1856–1919), was born near Geelong, Victoria, the son of an Irish-born policeman; baptized John Feltham Archibald, he adopted the Christian names Jules Francois in the 1870s and revised his family history in accord with his Francophilia. He was educated in Warrnambool, where as a youth he became an apprentice in the printing trade. His first paragraphs were written for the *Hamilton Spectator* and the *Port Fairy Gazette* and in 1875 he left for Melbourne to try journalism. Disappointed in his hopes of securing a position on the *Argus,* he became a public servant from 1876 until he was retrenched early in 1878, when he went to Queensland to a clerkship in an engineering firm. During his time there he had a few months on the Palmer River diggings; it was his 'one real experience of Australian frontier life' (Sylvia Lawson) and imbued him with a deep concern for the bush worker, the 'lone hand' who was central to the bush ethos of the *Bulletin* (q.v.) under his editorship.

In 1879 Archibald went to Sydney where he worked for the *Evening News* and *Hansard.* In 1880, with John Haynes (q.v.), he started the journal which eventually became nationally famous as the radical *Bulletin.* The first issue in January 1880 was dominated by Archibald's account of the hanging of the Wantabadgery bushrangers and established the reformist zeal of the journal. After a stormy first year, in which the *Bulletin's* survival was constantly threatened, Archibald and Haynes lost control of the journal to W.H. Traill (q.v.) although, after spending six weeks in Darlinghurst gaol over a libel action, they returned as salaried staff and from 1883 shared joint ownership with Traill when the Bulletin Newspaper Company was constituted. In the same year Archibald paid his only visit to England, where he struggled for a living after his bank failed. What he saw confirmed the Anglophobia which was the obverse of his republican nationalism and which found expression not only in the *Bulletin's* boycott of the 1888 centenary of settlement, but also in Archibald's willingness – against his natural inclination for the 'boiled-down' contribution – to serialize F.J. Donohue's and 'Price Warung''s revisionist writings about Australia's convict past.

In 1886 Traill left with the *Bulletin* on a sound footing, and thus began the decade and a half in which Archibald put his stamp on the journal. As a journalist he had several great gifts, not the least of which was his ability to recognize talent in other men: through him William Macleod, James Edmond and A.G. Stephens (qq.v.) were enticed on to the staff and given the freedom to make their individual contributions to the *Bulletin's* success. Second, he encouraged writers and artists throughout Australia: although the achievements of Stephens as literary editor cannot be overlooked it was Archibald, a good judge of folk-writing, who 'discovered' Henry Lawson, A.B. Paterson, 'Louis' Becke, 'Price Warung' and others, and who showed in letters, interviews, and in the famous correspondence column that the journal was interested in all *Bulletin* contributors and cared about their welfare. His third great gift was as sub-editor, a 'soler and heeler' of paragraphs who did much to establish the characteristic tone of the *Bulletin*, the brightness and sharpness of its prose in caption, column and leader. As editor Archibald worked obsessively, neglecting his wife Rose, whom he had married in 1885. After 1900 his nervous energy exhausted itself and in 1903 Edmond became editor of the *Bulletin* while Archibald busied himself planning the monthly *Lone Hand*. In 1906 he had a spectacular mental collapse and was admitted to Callan Park Asylum; he was finally discharged, fully recovered, in 1910. He sold his interest in the *Bulletin* in 1914 to S.H. Prior although just before his death in 1919 he returned to journalism to help to establish the fledgling *Smith's Weekly* (q.v.), which had some of the impact on the Australian reading public in the 1920s and 1930s that the *Bulletin* had had in the 1890s. His estate of nearly £90 000 provided Sydney with the Archibald Fountain in Hyde Park; Australian art with the Archibald Prize; and Australian journalism with a massive contribution to the benevolent fund of the Australian Journalists' Association. Sylvia Lawson's incisive study of Archibald and the *Bulletin*, *The Archibald Paradox*, was published in 1983; it won the NSW Premier's Award for non-fiction.

ARDEN, GEORGE (?1820–54) arrived in Australia from England in 1838, settled in Melbourne, and at the age of eighteen launched the weekly *Port Phillip Gazette*. He is credited with having written the first poem on Melbourne and having published (with Thomas Strode) in 1840, *Latest Information with Regard to Australia Felix*, the first book published in Melbourne. In 1843 he also published the short-lived (two monthly issues) *Arden's Sydney Magazine of Politics and General Literature*, with articles on general, local and literary topics.

Arena (1), a small Melbourne weekly magazine carrying short fiction and sketches together with literary theatrical reviews (Catherine Helen Spence was a contributor), was published 1900–04 and was edited by C.H. Chomley. In its final year of publication it was titled *Arena-Sun*.

Arena (2), a Victorian Marxist quarterly journal of criticism and discussion, began publication in 1963. It occasionally publishes articles on literature and aesthetic theory.

ARGLES, THEODORE EMILE ('THE PILGRIM', 'HAROLD GREY') (?1851–86), born London, was well-known in Sydney as both writer and bohemian in the later 1870s and early 1880s. Under several pseudonyms (e.g. 'Harold Grey', 'A (The) Pilgrim', 'The Moocher') he wrote sensational and satiric prose and verse about low-life Sydney and other subjects. In 1877 eight issues of the *Pilgrim*, his satiric periodical pamphlet, were published; it contained a sequence of articles on 'Sydney Cafés after Midnight'. The *Pilgrim* was revived intermittently in 1878 in two series, *Another Pilgrim* (nine issues) and the *Pilgrim* (nine issues, although the first issue was titled *Harold Grey's Sensational Weekly Pamphlet*). The second 1878 series satirized John Stanley James. In 1879 Argles edited *Common Cause* in Adelaide, published one issue of a Melbourne *Pilgrim*, and wrote a reply to an anonymous satire of him, titled the *Pilgrim: A Weakly Sensational Pamphlet*. Among his other publications were *Sum Punkins* (1878), a series of poems and stories ostensibly read by the patients and staff of a Sydney asylum as they gather together over Christmas; the autobiographical *My Unnatural Life* (1878); *Scenes in Sydney by Day and Night* (?1878); and the verse satire, *The Devil in Sydney* (1878), whose targets included several prominent journalists. Employed on the staff of the *Evening News*, Argles contributed spicy society gossip (some of which proved libellous), theatrical criticism and topical verse to the early *Bulletin*. His legendary escapades with Victor Daley included one in which they ran foul of the *Bulletin*'s editor, W.H. Traill, after each appeared in turn in Traill's office to ask for money to pay for the other's funeral.

Argus, a Melbourne daily newspaper published 1846–1957, was described by R.E.N. Twopeny in *Town Life in Australia* (1883) as 'the best daily paper published out of England'. Among the literary identities associated with it were Marcus Clarke, Charles de Boos and John Stanley James ('The Vagabond'), whose *Vagabond Papers*, on Melbourne's social and public life, were first published in the *Argus* in 1876. The great rival of the *Age*, the *Argus* is represented in Henry Kingsley's *The Hillyars and the Burtons* (1865) as the *Palmerston Sentinel*; W.M. Akhurst's 1855 pantomime, *The Magician's Daughter*, has a scene depicting the *Argus* office; and Fergus Hume's *The Mystery of a Hansom Cab* (1886) opens with an *Argus* murder report. Prior to its demise in 1957 the *Argus* carried a literary section as part of its weekend review. John Feely compiled a five-volume index to the *Argus* for 1846–59 (1942–65); the newspaper also published a half-yearly index in 1910–49. Among early proprietors of the *Argus* was Edward Wilson (q.v.); George Higinbotham edited the newspaper 1856–59, as did F.W. Haddon 1867–98 and Sir Edward Cunningham 1906–28. Notable staff or contributors included Julian Howard Ashton, Hugh Buggy, J.F. Hogan, Sir Walter Murdoch, and Frederick Sinnett.

Armidale and District Historical Society Journal and Proceedings began publication in 1961 with R.B. Walker as editor; from 1967 to 1978 it was edited by J.S. Ryan. An annual publication, it carries articles on literature, history and culture, usually from papers presented to the Society at its meetings. It has, for example, produced informative biographical material on 'Rolf Boldrewood' (12, 1970) and Henry Kingsley (19, 1976).

ARMOUR, JOHN (1889–1954), born Warragul, Victoria, served with the Australian Inland Mission (1918–20) and had a long and distinguished career in the Presbyterian ministry in Queensland, Victoria and NSW. His publications include *The Spell of the Inland* (1923), a descriptive narrative of life in Central Australia; *Burning Air* (1928), an adventure story set also in Central Australia; *Century Sandy* (1936, revised in 1938 as *The Road to El Dorado*), and *The Story of Christianity* (1952).

ARMSTRONG, HELEN PORTER, see **MELBA**, Dame **NELLIE**

ARMSTRONG, MILLICENT, born Sydney, served as a nurse in France during the First World War. She began to write and to stage plays during the war. On her return she took up a farming block in the Returned Soldiers' Settlement Scheme. Her play *Drought* (1934), possibly written out of her experience on the land, won a prize in an international drama competition in 1934. *At Dusk* was published in *Best Australian One-Act Plays* (1937). Unpublished plays by her were 'Fire' (1923), which won a *Daily Telegraph* drama competition prize, 'Nina' (1936), 'Windward' (1937) and 'The Moon Sets' (1958); *Thomas* and *Penny Dreadful* were published in 1958 (together with *Drought*) in a volume titled *Plays in One Act*.

'Army of the Rear, The' is, like 'Faces in the Street', one of the early Henry Lawson (q.v.) poems which established his reputation as a radical writer; it was first published in the *Bulletin* in 1888 as 'Song of the Outcasts' and under its better-known title in 1910. 'The Army

of the Rear' is the legion of the poor and the outcasts of society, whom Lawson images marching towards revolution at the end of the poem.

Arna, the journal of the University of Sydney Arts Society, began in 1918 and appeared irregularly; it was incorporated into *New Literature Review* (q.v.) in 1975. Several subsequently well-known writers contributed to *Arna*, including A.D. Hope, Muir Holburn, Charles Higham, Vincent Buckley, Bernard Smith, John Croyston, Bruce Beaver, Donald Horne, Harold Stewart, James McAuley, Geoffrey Lehmann, Les Murray and Clive James.

ARNEIL, STAN, see **War Literature**

Arnhem Land, a large area of north-eastern Northern Territory, was first made known by the discoveries of the Dutch and Portuguese mariners in the sixteenth and seventeenth centuries and by the later English explorers, Matthew Flinders and Phillip Parker King (qq.v.). Its internal exploration began in the 1880s (David Lindsay) and lasted until the 1930s (Donald Thomson). Its history, geography and Aboriginal associations are given in R.M. and Catherine H. Berndt's *Arnhem Land: Its History and Its People* (1954), Colin Simpson's *Adam in Ochre* (1951) and M. Douglas and D. Oldmeadow's *Across the Top* (1972).

ARNOLD, THOMAS (1823–1900), second son of Thomas Arnold, the great English headmaster, and brother of the poet Matthew Arnold, emigrated to New Zealand in 1848 and then went to Hobart in 1850, where he was appointed inspector of schools for Van Diemen's Land. Following considerable and arduous labours for education in that colony (1850–56) he returned to England, ultimately filling the Chair of English Language and Literature at University College, Dublin (1882). Among his many publications was a book of reminiscences, *Passages in a Wandering Life* (1900), which gives a picture of life in the colony of Van Diemen's Land in the 1850s. P.A. Howell published *Thomas Arnold the Younger in Van Diemen's Land* (1964).

ARONSON, LINDA (1950–), born London, has worked in Sydney since 1973 as a professional writer for stage, film, radio and television and as scriptwriting consultant at the Australian Film and Television School. She has written stage plays, 'Lonely for My Garden' (1975), *The Fall Guy* (1976, also published in *Theatre-Australia*, 1977), 'Elegy for a Boy Musician' (1977), 'Endangered Species' (1979), and 'Invitation to Eternity' (1982); radio plays,

'Café in a Side Street' (1980, adapted from 'Lonely for My Garden') and 'Closing Down'; and film scripts, *Kostas* (1978, screened at Cannes in 1980) and *Until It's Over* (1981).

Around the Boree Log and Other Verses (1921) by 'John O'Brien' (q.v.) is a book of ballad-like poems dealing mainly with the vicissitudes of Irish-Australian Catholic rural communities. The characteristics of good nature, obstinacy and religious faith, traditionally associated with the Irish, permeate such well-known and popular verses as 'The Old Bush School', 'Ten Little Steps and Stairs', 'Tangmalangaloo', 'At Casey's after Mass', and 'Said Hanrahan' (q.v.).

Arrow, see ***Dead Bird***

Art in Australia, published quarterly in Sydney from 1916 to 1942, with the exception of 1930 when it was published six times, appeared in four series, 1916–21, 1922, 1922–40, 1941–42. Founded by Sydney Ure Smith and edited initially by him and Bertram Stevens, then Leon Gellert, *Art in Australia* was the leading journal on art, music and literature during its existence, attracting significant contributions from the leading cultural figures of the day, e.g. Norman, Lionel and Jack Lindsay, Kenneth Slessor, A.G. Stephens, Katharine Susannah Prichard, Hugh McCrae, Leslie Rees, Zora Cross and Mary Gilmore. Its numerous special numbers featured the work of, for example, Hans Heysen, Lionel Lindsay, Daryl Lindsay, George Finey, Hugh McCrae and Thea Proctor.

ARTHUR, Sir GEORGE (1784–1854), born Plymouth, England, was an army officer before becoming a colonial administrator, serving as lieutenant-governor of Van Diemen's Land (1824–36) and Upper Canada (1837–41) and as governor of Bombay (1842–46). Highly efficient and authoritarian, Arthur viewed Van Diemen's Land as an 'Extensive Gaol to the Empire' where strict conditions should apply. He established the secondary punishment centre at Port Arthur (q.v.), from which John Rex escapes in *His Natural Life*, refined the system of assignment (see Transportation), and defended his methods in two pamphlets, *Observations upon Secondary Punishment* (1833) and *Defence of Transportation* (1834) (both written in reply to Richard Whately), and in voluminous despatches, some of which are included in the *Historical Records of Australia* (q.v.).

The severity of Arthur's views meant that he had little time for civil liberties and that almost from the day of his arrival he met opposition from some free settlers and most pressmen. He fought strenuously to control the press by prosecution and legislation, introducing licensing provisions in 1827, which were disallowed in England in 1828; among his opponents were Andrew Bent, Robert Murray, Henry Melville, Gilbert Robertson, and Evan Henry Thomas (qq.v.). Apart from the attacks in the contemporary press, there are unflattering portraits of Arthur in David Burn's play *The Bushrangers* (q.v.), which probably for this reason Burn excluded from his *Plays, and Fugitive Pieces* (1842); in Henry Melville's *The History of the Island of Van Diemen's Land* (1835); in 'Price Warung' 's story 'A Day with Governor Arthur' (*Tales of the Old Regime*, 1897); in the broadsides which celebrated Arthur's recall; and in some of the reminiscences of the Canadian exiles transported to Van Diemen's Land after the rebellions of 1837–38 (e.g. Caleb Lyon called him 'the bloody Robespierre of the Revolution'). Other works in which Arthur appears (not always specifically identified) include Roy Bridges's *By His Excellency's Command* (1910); J.B. Cooper's *Leg-Bail* (1918); Horace B. Pithouse's *The Luck of 1825* (1922); *The Hermit in Van Diemen's Land* (1830) and *Quintus Servinton* (1831) by Henry Savery, whose lenient treatment by Arthur was criticized; and Catherine Shepherd's radio play, 'Arthur of Van Diemen's Land', broadcast on ABC radio in the 1940s. Among studies of Arthur, A.G.L. Shaw's *Sir George Arthur* (1980) is a comprehensive biography, and E. Morris Miller's *Pressmen and Governors* (1952), Joan Woodberry's *Andrew Bent and the Freedom of the Press in Tasmania* (1972) and James Bonwick's *Early Struggles of the Australian Press* (1890), discuss his relationship with the press.

Artlook, a monthly newsletter published in 1975 by a Perth (WA) group known as the Nine Club, was intended as a means of disseminating information and opinions on the arts in WA. It contains a 'Poets Profile' and critical reviews and articles. It combined later in 1975 with *Performance*, a publication devoted to theatre in WA.

Arts, the journal of the Sydney University Arts Association, appeared for three issues in 1956. In 1958 it recommenced publication, with the subtitle, *Proceedings of the Sydney University Arts Association*, which was changed to *Journal of the Sydney University Arts Association* in 1967. The inaugural edition contained important articles on 'The Eighteen Nineties in Australia' by G.A. Wilkes and A.G.L. Shaw, developed from a series of lectures delivered under the auspices of the Association in 1956.

Arts Council of Australia is an organization linking nine bodies which operate within the area of the community arts. The six Australian States, the ACT and the Northern Territory each has an autonomous arts council (e.g. the Queensland Arts Council; the Arts Council of Australia, Tasmania Division) which is represented on the board of a federal Arts Council of Australia. This body is also autonomous and in 1978–83 was the largest client of the Community Arts Board (q.v.) of the Australia Council. In those years the Community Arts Board's allocation to the Arts Council of Australia was distributed to the federal division, mainly for national and co-ordinating activities, and to the State and territory organizations, which are also funded from the respective State governments and from private sources. In 1983 a new policy was announced which increases decentralization and provides for direct Community Arts Board allocations to the State and territory organizations. The State Arts Councils have numerous regional branches (248 in 1980).

The various Arts Councils traditionally have helped to provide performing arts experiences for schools and for communities outside metropolitan centres; in recent years exhibitions, festivals, summer schools and workshops have more regularly come within their ambit. The Arts Council movement had its origin in the Council for the Encouragement of Music and the Arts (CEMA), modelled on an equivalent British organization and formed in 1943 by the singer, Dorothy Helmrich; it was centred in NSW, where an arts council, sometimes called the Arts Council of Australia in the 1950s, was established in 1946. Arts Councils were formed soon after in some other States and territories (e.g. SA in 1946, Tasmania in 1951), but lack of adequate funding prevented development until the 1960s. In 1966 the Arts Council of Australia, first proposed in the 1940s, was established, receiving its first funds from the Australian Council of the Arts (q.v.) in 1969. In 1973 the last State or territory arts council, the WA Arts Council, was established, following those in Victoria (1971), the Northern Territory (1967), SA (reformed in 1965 after lapsing in 1952), ACT (reformed 1962 after lapsing in 1952), and Queensland (1961).

ASCHE, OSCAR (1871–1936), the actor, producer, manager and writer, was one of the leading Australian theatrical personalities of the early decades of the twentieth century. Born Geelong, Victoria, Asche studied acting in Norway and London, made his stage debut in London in 1893, became a notable Shakespearean actor and toured Australia on three occasions (1909–10, 1912–13, 1922–24). Two of Asche's greatest successes were *Chu Chin Chow* (1931), his only published play, which ran for a record five-year season, and *The Maid of the*

Mountains, which he produced. He wrote two novels, *The Saga of Hans Hansen* (1930) and *The Joss Sticks of Chung* (1930) and an autobiography (1929).

ASHBOLT, ALLAN (1921–   ), born Melbourne, has had a wide-ranging career in radio, television and political journalism. He came into prominence in 1946 as co-founder, with the actor Peter Finch, of the Mercury Theatre, Sydney. From 1951 to 1957 he was drama critic and book reviewer for the *Sydney Morning Herald*. In his career with the ABC (1954–77) he was a special projects producer and producer of documentary talks, responsible for numerous controversial programmes. His publications include *An American Experience* (1966), an unsparingly critical assessment of such features of American life and government as the segregation of society by race, religion and money, the public scandals, organized crime, imbalance of the American economy, and American foreign policy; and *An Australian Experience* (1974), which is an extended commentary on war and racism, nationalism and imperialism, conscription and conscience, socialism and class consciousness, all in an Australian context.

ASHTON, JULIAN HOWARD (1877–1964), the artist, born in London, son of Julian Rossi Ashton (q.v.), accompanied his parents to Australia in 1878. Following a liberal education in music, art and literature, he turned to journalism as a career although he published short fiction in the *Bulletin* under the pseudonym 'Hassan', from 1904 onwards. Over many years he was a general reporter, music critic and literary and art reviewer on the *Sydney Morning Herald*, *Argus*, Sydney *Sun*, *Sunday Sun and Guardian* and *Art in Australia*, rising eventually to be editor of the *Sun* in 1924. From 1926 he reverted to associate editor, which allowed him to resume his literary and art criticism and leader-writing. He won the Sydney sesquicentenary prize for landscape painting in 1938 and was president of the Royal Art Society, 1940–45.

ASHTON, JULIAN ROSSI (1851–1942), born Surrey, England, came to Australia with his wife Eliza Ann Pugh, and son Julian Howard Ashton (q.v.), in 1878 to work as an illustrator on David Syme's *Illustrated Australian News*. In 1881 he joined the *Australasian Sketcher*; in 1883 he moved to Sydney to work on the *Picturesque Atlas of Australasia* and later on the *Bulletin*. An active professional artist, Ashton was president of the Art Society of New South Wales (1887–92) and president of the Society of Artists (1897–98), the two organizations amalgamating in 1903 to become the Royal Art Society of New South Wales. His own art school, which was variously known as the Sydney Art School and (from 1935) the Julian Ashton Art School, enjoyed a considerable reputation, numbering among its students the later well-known artists Elioth Gruner, J.J. Hilder, Sydney Ure Smith and William Dobell. A gifted teacher and artist, Ashton's achievements included the painting *Evening, Merri Creek* (1882), claimed by him to be the first *plein air* painting done in Australia. He won the Sydney sesquicentenary prize for a watercolour in 1938; painted numerous portraits of prominent Australians (e.g. Sir Henry Parkes); was awarded the Society of Artists' medal for distinguished services to Australian art in 1924; and was made CBE in 1930. He contributed numerous articles to *Art in Australia* and published his reminiscences, *Now Came Still Evening On*, in 1941. *The Julian Ashton Book* was published in his honour in 1920. Ada Cambridge, in *Thirty Years in Australia* (1903), records her visit to the artists' camp which Ashton and others conducted at Balmoral (Sydney) for some years; the hero of her novel, *A Marked Man* (1890), escapes from the restriction of conventional society into an idyllic bush retreat modelled on the camp.

ASLANIDES, TIMOSHENKO (1943–), born Sydney of Greek parents, won the Commonwealth Poetry Prize for 1978 with his first book of poems, *The Greek Connection* (1977). He has also published *Passacaglia and Fugue* (1979).

Aspect: Art and Literature, a Sydney quarterly magazine edited since its inception by Rudi Krausman (q.v.), was first published 1975. It contains interviews, prose, poetry, articles and comments on art and literature.

Aspinall, Arvie, is the central character in Henry Lawson's (q.v.) first major series of stories, written in 1892. The best-known story in the sequence is 'Arvie Aspinall's Alarm Clock', in which Arvie, who has been given an alarm clock so that he can get to work on time at Grinder Brothers railway coach factory, does not hear the alarm go off because he has died of a fever during the night. The other stories in the sequence, which depict the squalor and misery of the urban poor, are 'Two Boys at Grinder Bros', in which friendship grows between the sensitive Arvie and the larrikin of the shed, Bill Anderson, after it is discovered that they have both lived in the tenements of Jones's Alley; 'A Visit of Condolence', in which Bill visits the Aspinall home, discovers Arvie's death and shows a rough humanity to the bereaved mother; and 'Jones's Alley', in which

Bill, meeting Mrs Aspinall some years later after she has lost a court case against her slum landlord, helps her smuggle her possessions at night out of the rented home. Lawson's 'A Fragment of Autobiography' and other sources reveal that the Aspinall stories were largely informed by his experiences at Hudson Brothers coach factory in the 1880s. The name Aspinall, however, came from a family living at New Pipeclay twenty years before: the death of the nine-year-old Thomas Aspinall, who fell down a mine shaft in 1865, was a source for 'His Father's Mate'. In *While the Billy Boils* (1896), which includes three stories from the city sequence, Arvie Aspinall is the first of the children marked present at the bush school in 'An Echo from the Old Bark School'.

Association for Commonwealth Language and Literature Studies (usually known by its acronym, ACLALS) aims to encourage and stimulate the writing, reading and study of what is known as Commonwealth literature (i.e. literatures in English other than English and American literature; therefore it includes Australian literature). An Association whose widespread membership mainly comprises teachers and writers, ACLALS was the brainchild of A.N. Jeffares, professor of English at the University of Adelaide 1951–56 and later at the Universities of Leeds and Stirling; it was formally constituted during a Commonwealth literature conference held at the University of Leeds in 1964. From 1968 the chairmanship of ACLALS and the editorship of the *ACLALS Bulletin* (1965–), which has evolved from a newsletter into primarily a Commonwealth literature critical journal, became rotating offices; since 1971 they have been located for three-year terms in the region hosting the ACLALS conference at the end of that triennial period. The regionalization of ACLALS has been further consolidated by the establishment of branch organizations, the chairman of each having membership of the ACLALS executive. In 1971 the European branch (EACLALS) was established, followed by organizations in Canada (CACLALS) in 1972; the South Pacific (SPACLALS) in 1975; and others in India, the West Indies and elsewhere, each with the appropriate cacophonous acronym. The regional organizations have held regular meetings and conferences and have published bulletins such as EACLALS's *Commonwealth Newsletter*, later the journal *Kunapipi* (1979–) and SPACLALS's *Span* (1975–). The conference volumes and other publications of ACLALS and its constituent organizations represent an impressive body of critical writing in which Australian literature has been placed in a Commonwealth context; ACLALS has also encouraged Commonwealth writers through the provision of visiting fellowships, literary competitions and the like. In 1975–81 SPACLALS was centred at the University of Queensland; other Australian universities with an active interest in Commonwealth literature/new literatures in English include Flinders University, where the Centre for Research in the New Literatures in English (1977–) produces the *CRNLE Reviews Journal* (1980–) and organizes conferences which accommodate Australian topics; and Macquarie University, where a New Literatures in English unit was established in 1982. The *Journal of Commonwealth Literature* arose from the Leeds interest in Commonwealth literature and has been published since 1965; its annual bibliography includes an Australian section which complements the *Australian Literary Studies* bibliography it also regularly publishes criticism on Australian literature. Another overseas new literatures in English journal in which Australian literature is regularly discussed is *World Literature Written in English* (*WLWE*, 1967–).

Association for the Study of Australian Literature (ASAL), was founded in 1977 and formally constituted at its inaugural conference at Monash University in May 1978; its patrons are A.D. Hope and A.A. Phillips (qq.v.) and its life members, to 1983, C.B. Christesen, R.D. FitzGerald, Dorothy Green, Jack Lindsay, Mary Lord, Christina Stead, Douglas Stewart and Judith Wright. The Association, which has a nationwide and overseas membership, includes among its aims the study and encouragement of Australian literature and literary culture, particularly through the interaction of Australian writers with teachers and students. Among its activities are the holding of a yearly conference and the publication of a newsletter, *Notes & Furphies* (q.v.). ASAL has incorporated the Australian Literature Society (q.v.) and now administers the ALS Gold Medal.

ASTLEY, THEA (1925–), born Brisbane, was educated at the University of Queensland and taught in schools in Queensland and NSW until 1967, and at Macquarie University, Sydney, 1968–80. Her published works include the novels, *Girl with a Monkey* (1958), *A Descant for Gossips* (1960, dramatized for ABC television in 1983), *The Well Dressed Explorer* (q.v., 1962), *The Slow Natives* (q.v., 1965), *A Boat Load of Home Folk* (1968), *The Acolyte* (q.v., 1972), *A Kindness Cup* (1974), and *An Item from the Late News* (1982); and the collection of short stories, *Hunting the Wild Pineapple* (1979). She has also published some uncollected verse and short stories, a critical study, *Three Australian Writers* (1979), and

edited an anthology of short stories (1971). She has won several prizes, including the Miles Franklin Award on three occasions. The complexities of her ambivalent relationship with northern Queensland and with Catholicism, both of which are strongly present in her work, colour her original apprehension of the contemporary Australian social environment. Acidulously witty, with a keen eye for egoistic pretension and exploitation and a rich talent for social comedy, she frequently writes from the point of view of the vulnerable misfit, the unspectacular outsider. For the self-conscious hyperperceptive individuals on whom she concentrates, life is necessarily isolated, an unequal, doomed, tragi-comic struggle for identity and integrity. From Elsie Ford of *Girl with a Monkey* to Paul Vesper of *The Acolyte*, she develops related but increasingly complex studies of desperate attempts to preserve the self in the face of disintegration. Occasionally she revives characters from previous novels, so that background characters in one become central in another. Opposed to the hyperperceptive outsiders she presents a vast range of shallow insiders, those who are safely encased in an armour of insensitivity, malice and vanity. The representations of small-town life in *A Descant for Gossips* and *A Kindness Cup* are particularly striking pictures of general malicious stupidity. *The Well Dressed Explorer* and *The Acolyte*, on the other hand, are consummate studies of two very different, voracious egotists who generate a wide destruction by preying on all around them.

ASTON, TILLY (1873–1947), born Carisbrook, Victoria, was blind from the age of six years. She became a teacher of the blind in Melbourne, was a founder of the library of the Victorian Association of Braille Writers (1894) and was, for many years, president of Victoria's Association for the Advancement of the Blind. She wrote nine books of verse and prose, of which *Old Timers* (1938) contains pen pictures of gold-rush characters; *Memoirs of Tilly Aston* (1946) is her autobiography.

At Dawn and Dusk, see **DALEY, VICTOR**

Athenaeum: A Journal Specially Devoted to the Encouragement of Australian Literature, Science and Art, a brief-lived (1875–76) weekly journal, carried short stories, poetry, literary and theatrical reviews; it was edited by H.W.H. Stephen and P.J. Holdsworth, and included Henry Halloran, G.C. McCrae and James Brunton Stephens among its contributors.

Athletic Mad, the shortest Australian play (two and a half pages long), deals with the subject of boxing and was published anonymously in 1886.

ATKINSON, HUGH (?1924–   ), born Parkes, NSW, was educated at the University of Sydney and was both a conscientious objector and an RAAF serviceman during the Second World War. He spent four years in India, the setting for his first novel, *The Pink and the Brown* (1957), before returning to Australia, where he worked in advertising and journalism. In 1963 a Commonwealth Literary Fund fellowship enabled him to move to the Channel Islands; subsequently he lived in London, France, Majorca, Malta and elsewhere before returning again to Australia in 1977. Atkinson has written film scripts and short stories as well as twelve novels: *The Pink and the Brown, Low Company* (1961), *The Reckoning* (1965, also published in 1977 as *Weekend of Shadows,* its film title, and *Weekend to Kill*), *The Games* (1967), *Johnny Horns* (1971), *The Most Savage Animal* (1972), *The Man in the Middle* (1973), *Crack-Up* (1974), *Unscheduled Flight* (1976), *The Manipulators* (1978, released in the USA as *Big Money*), *Billy Two-Toes' Rainbow* (1982) and *The Longest Wire* (1982). His most commercially successful novel, *The Games* (1967), focuses on the seamy politics of the Olympic movement and has as one of its main characters a part-Aboriginal, Sunny Pintubi, who wins an Olympic marathon; the novel was filmed in the USA. Of his other novels, several of which are sensational exposés of the chicanery of governments or multinationals (e.g. *The Most Savage Animal, The Man in the Middle,The Manipulators*), *Low Company* chronicles Sydney bohemian life at the end of the 1950s; *The Reckoning*, which won the Xavier Prize for Literature, is a study of violence in a small mining community in NSW in the 1930s; *Billy Two-Toes' Rainbow* explores multiracial tensions among opal miners at Coober Pedy; and *The Longest Wire* is a fictionalized account of the building of the Overland Telegraph line between Adelaide and Darwin. As 'Hugh Geddes', Atkinson also wrote *The Pyjama Girl Case* (1978), a study of a sensational murder case of the 1930s.

ATKINSON, JAMES (1795–1834), born Oldbury, England, arrived in Australia in 1820 where he became principal clerk in the Colonial Secretary's office and took up 1500 acres of land in the Bong Bong district. Back in England in 1825 he wrote *An Account of the State of Agriculture & Grazing in New South Wales* (1826), one of the first comprehensive accounts of farming in the colony. His daughter was the novelist and naturalist, Louisa Atkinson.

ATKINSON, LOUISA (1834–72), born Oldbury, near Berrima, NSW, was encouraged, as a child, to become an ardent collector and illustrator of botanical specimens. Her articles on flora and fauna, with her own illustrations, appeared in such newspapers as the *Sydney Mail* and the *Sydney Morning Herald*. In addition to four serials published in the *Sydney Mail* and the *Sydney Morning Herald* between 1861 and 1872, she wrote two novels, *Gertrude the Emigrant: A Tale of Colonial Life* (1857), set on a station in outback NSW; and *Cowanda, the Veteran's Grant* (1859), also with a pastoral setting but including a description of the Turon goldfields. One of the earliest writers to find Australian pastoral and bush life a fitting subject for fictional presentation, Louisa Atkinson has been honoured by having several botanical specimens named after her. *Louisa Atkinson, Excursions from Berrima*, introduced by Lionel Gilbert, foreword by Janet Cosh, was published in 1980.

ATKINSON, RUPERT (1881–1961) born Bendigo, Victoria, and educated in Australia and England, was left comfortably off after his father's death and then led a leisurely life as a man of letters. A close friend of poet Hugh McCrae, Atkinson published numerous volumes of lyric, narrative and philosophical verse, including *The Shrine of Desire* (1906), *Wayside Poems* (1913), *A Modern Magdalene* (1913, reprinted as *The Renegades* in 1921), and *A Flagon of Song* (1920), the last being a selection from previously-published work together with some new poems. His series of twenty 'Melbourne Sonnets' gives some local flavour to his verse. Atkinson also wrote several plays including *A Nocturne* (1919), an intriguing two-act verse-drama about a murder committed by a drunken man who can only recollect the incident when under the influence of alcohol, *Each Man a Multitude* (1923), a prose play in three acts, and some one-acters.

Atlas, a weekly journal published in Sydney 1844–48, carried literary reviews, original poetry, articles on literary topics and a considerable dash of satire, especially from William Forster. One of its leading figures was Robert Lowe (q.v.). Liberal in stance, the *Atlas* was originally the organ of the squatting interests against Governor Gipps. Forster's 'The Devil and the Governor' was published in it, 17 May 1845.

'**Atlas, The**', a group of five poems by Kenneth Slessor (q.v.), was published in *Cuckooz Contrey* (1932). The individual poems of the sequence, 'The King of Cuckooz', 'Post-Roads', 'Dutch Seacoast', 'Mermaids' and 'The Seafight', have no continuity or overall theme. Disconnected scraps from Slessor's omnivorous reading interests, they reveal his delight in the odd and exotic.

ATTIWILL, K.A. (KENNETH ANDREW) (1906–60), born Adelaide, was a journalist on the Adelaide *Register*, the *Sun* and *Herald* (both Melbourne) and the *Daily Sketch* (London) before becoming a POW of the Japanese in the Second World War. His novels, which draw on his experiences in journalism, at war and at sea, include *Horizon* (1930), *Steward!* (1932), *Thirteen Sailed Home* (1935, with J.O.C. Orton), *Reporter!* (1933), *Big Ben* (1936), *The Rising Sunset* (1957) and *The Singapore Story* (1959). Resident in England for most of the latter part of his life, Attiwill was also a successful playwright.

AUCHTERLONIE, DOROTHY, see **GREEN, DOROTHY**

AUGHTERSON, W.V., see *Taking Stock*

AUMLA, the journal of the Australasian Universities Language and Literature Association (q.v.), formerly Australasian Universities Modern Languages Association, is a journal of literary criticism, philology and linguistics. *AUMLA* was first published in August 1953 and appeared annually until May 1956, thereafter twice annually. *AUMLA* was edited by R.T. Sussex until 1979.

Aunt's Story, The a novel by Patrick White (q.v.), was published in 1948. In three parts, it narrates the life of Theodora Goodman, an outwardly unattractive spinster, and her solitary quest for ultimate lucidity. The first phase, beginning and ending with her mother's death, deals retrospectively with her life and inner experience till middle age. Brought up on a run-down family property, Meroë, Theodora is surrounded by people who fail to understand her: her pretty but superficial sister Fanny, and Frank Parrott, whom Fanny marries; her mother; her school friend Violet Adams; and her suitor, Huntly Clarkson. Only with her father, her niece Lou, and in a few other fleeting experiences such as those with an old reprobate acquaintance of her father, whom she later calls 'The Man Who Was Given His Dinner' and a Greek cello player, Moraïtis, is Theodora able to experience the fierce intensity she discovers in the natural world. The second section of the novel, titled 'Jardin Exotique', finds Theodora in a dreary European hotel, surrounded by people whose intrusion into her consciousness is expressed in a fragmented, expressionistic way. They include two faded spinsters, the Demoiselles Bloch; Wetherby, a failed Englishman and poet, who is engaged in a passionately destructive affair with the wife of a German count, the decadent Lieselotte; Mrs Rapallo, an American lady whose most prized possession is her fantasy of a titled daughter; Sokolnikov, an exiled Russian general; and Katina Pavlou, a young girl who is ignored by her parents and travels Europe accompanied by an English companion. Through her testing relationships with these people and their fantasies, Theodora achieves a new appreciation of the 'otherness' of others and a fresh perspective on her past relationships. This section ends with a fire at the hotel in which some of the residents die. The brief concluding section finds Theodora on a train in America's Middle West. Unpredictably leaving the train, she makes her way to an isolated farmhouse, where she is briefly cared for by a family, the Johnsons. The end of her quest is achieved the next day in the mountains when she meets Holstius, an emanation from her psyche, who suggests that there is little to choose 'between the reality of illusion and the illusion of reality'. Integration can only be achieved by acceptance of life's irreconcilable dualities, joy and sorrow, illusion and reality, life and death. Theodora is finally led away by the Johnsons and a doctor who remarks that 'lucidity . . . isn't necessarily a perpetual ailment.'

AUROUSSEAU, MARCEL (1891–), born Woollahra, Sydney, of French and Irish parentage, graduated from the University of Sydney with the University Medal in geology and became a lecturer in geology at the University of Western Australia. After distinguished service in the First World War he joined the Carnegie Institute in Washington (1920–23), and later went to Europe to spend time on his growing love of writing. He published *Highway into Spain* (1930), an account of his journey on foot from Paris to Madrid in 1926. A period with the Royal Geographical Society in London led to his compilation of an *Index to Supplements* (1936) to the *Geographical Journal*, an important work of bibliographical reference. During the Second World War he led a small expert group producing numerous gazetteers (the first in 1942) on foreign countries for the Allied forces. A member of the council of the Hakluyt Society, he assisted in the preparation of the indexes to the edition of Captain James Cook's *Journals*, edited by J.C. Beaglehole for the Hakluyt Society, 1955–67. In 1956 he returned to Australia, was president of the Geographical Society of NSW (1959–61) and was a member (1964–68) of the National Committee for Geography of the Australian Academy of Science. Aurousseau's major contribution to Australian writing is his publication of *The Letters of F.W. Ludwig Leichhardt* (1968).

Aussie: The Australian Soldiers' Magazine, originally printed in the field by the AIF printing section in France, began publication in January 1918 and ceased in 1931. Published monthly (but irregularly at times) it changed its title to *Aussie: The Cheerful Monthly* from the April 1920 issue. It contained poetry, short fiction, cartoons, an 'Aussie dictionary', and articles on Australian writers in a series 'Aussie Verse and Verse-Writers' by its long-term editor, Phillip Lawrence Harris. Writers discussed in short articles for general readers included Barcroft Boake, E.J. Brady, John le Gay Brereton, John Farrell, Henry Kendall, Henry Lawson and Roderic Quinn.

Austerica was a derogatory term coined by the Australian architect Robin Boyd (q.v.) and used in his book, *The Australian Ugliness* (1960), to describe the Australian tendency to lionize and imitate American attitudes, opinions and culture.

'Australaise, The' was originally submitted by C.J. Dennis (q.v.) as an entry in a national song competition conducted by the *Bulletin* in 1908. Christened the 'Blanky Australaise' by the judge, because of the many blank spaces for the great Australian adjective 'bloody' to be inserted ('blessed' or 'blooming' were later suggested by Dennis for folk genteel), it won a prize of a guinea and was predicted to 'win its way to every heart in the back-blocks'. In 1913 an expanded version (from four to seven verses) was published in Dennis's *Backblock Ballads and Other Verses*. In 1915 it was reprinted as a leaflet for the Australian soldiers, to whom it was dedicated as a marching song. With a mixture of irony and sincerity typical of him, Dennis suggested that the song be sung to the tune of 'Onward Christian Soldiers'. It was adopted as a recruiting song in 1951 during the Korean War and was selected in 1968 as the official regimental march of the Seventh Battalion of the Royal Australian Regiment.

Australasia (1823), a poem by William Charles Wentworth (q.v.), was an entry in the Chancellor's Gold Medal poetry competition at Cambridge in 1823 on the subject of Australasia. With his opening apostrophe, 'Land of my birth!', Wentworth made clear his special position in relation to the topic. The poem attempts to project a distinctively Australian viewpoint and, with its prophecy of future greatness, is one of the first outbursts in Australian literature of nationalistic pride. Al-

though sometimes marred by the customary inflated rhetoric of the public poem of the day, *Australasia* has been praised for its well-planned structure and its vigorous, eloquent, if rugged, verse.

Australasian, which was formed in 1864 by a merger of three Melbourne weeklies and subsequently incorporated *Bell's Life in Victoria* and the *Australasian Sketcher with Pen and Pencil*, was the weekend companion to the *Argus*; in 1946 it became the popular magazine, the *Australasian Post*. Notable literary features of the *Australasian* were its columns 'Essayist' and 'The Traveller', and Marcus Clarke's 'Lower Bohemia' series of 1869. Marcus Clarke also published, in the *Australasian*, *Old Tales of a Young Country* (intermittently in 1870–71) and *The Peripatetic Philosopher* (1867–70), under the pseudonym 'Q'. Among its other well-known contributors were 'Rolf Boldrewood', Ada Cambridge, Louisa Anne Meredith, J.E. Neild, Catherine Helen Spence, and Jessie Couvreur.

Australasian Anthology, An, see **Anthologies**

Australasian Book News and Library Journal, published monthly 1946–48, and edited by George Farwell with Eve Pownall as children's editor, listed books published in Australia and contained book reviews and other literary articles.

Australasian Book Society, a publishing company with a limited liability incorporated in Victoria and owned by its members, was registered 1952; it was wound up in 1981. Its purpose was to publish 'manuscripts reflecting the life struggles and militant traditions' of the Australian people. Its first publication, with Bill Wannan as secretary-manager, was Ralph de Boissiere's novel of West Indian life, *Crown Jewel* (1952), no suitable Australian manuscript then being available. The Society's political stance was predominantly left, but its relationships with the Communist Party of Australia were never smooth. Some of its notable publications were *The Tracks We Travel* (1953, 1961, 1965), three short-story collections edited successively by Stephen Murray-Smith, Jack Beasley and Leslie Haylen; Judah Waten's novel, *The Australian* (1954); Dorothy Hewett's novel *Bobbin Up* (1959); John Manifold's cultural history, *Who Wrote the Ballads?* (1964); and the memorial tribute to Dame Mary Gilmore in 1965. The Society was active in many fields, e.g. during Ian Turner's period as secretary it commissioned William Dobell's controversial portrait of Dame Mary Gilmore and initiated and participated in the Australian Book Fairs. A full list (to 1977) of the Society's publications is in Jack Beasley's *Red Letter Days* (1979). *Readers and Writers* was the Society's intermittent newsletter.

Australasian Critic: A Monthly Review of Literature, Science and Art, was a short-lived (1890–91) attempt by its editors, Professors T.G. Tucker, W. Baldwin Spencer and E.E. Morris, to institute a regular and systematic review of the arts in Australia.

Australasian Home Reader, which had a wide reading circle during the 1890s and was edited by E.E. Morris and Robert Garran, ran 1892–97 when it was superseded by the *Year Book of the Australasian Home Reading Union*.

Australasian Journal of Psychology and Philosophy, a quarterly journal begun in Sydney in 1923, changed its title to the *Australian Journal of Philosophy* after 1947. It embraced a wide area of interest – psychology, philosophy, education, sociology and literature. Its literary content was especially significant in the 1930s. See also Anderson, John.

Australasian Post, an illustrated weekly published since 1946, is a continuation of the *Australasian* (q.v.). A popular magazine and standard reading material in Australian barbers' shops, it has little literary merit; but, like the early *Bulletin*, its cartoons and other features have helped to consolidate the image of the bush within the Australian consciousness.

Australasian Sketcher with Pen and Pencil, a monthly published in Melbourne 1873–89, had a marked literary content in its early years (short stories, sketches, reviews) but later became an illustrated news magazine with Adelaide and Brisbane editions. It was incorporated into the *Australasian* (q.v.) after 1889.

Australasian Universities Language and Literature Association (AULLA) came into being in 1950 at a congress held in Melbourne, largely through the efforts of A.R. Chisholm and R.H. Samuel. Originally called Australasian Universities Modern Languages Association, which was open to the modern languages staff of Australian universities, it aimed at the advancement of modern languages study and research in Australia. Its journal, which publishes literary criticism and studies in philology and linguistics, is *AUMLA* (q.v.). The Association holds an annual congress, the articles and reports from which are usually published.

Australia (1). The name 'Australia' derives from the Latin word 'australis', meaning 'south-ern', and was originally applied to all regions existing, or thought to exist, south of the equator. The terms 'continens australis' and 'terra australis' were in use from about the sixteenth century to apply to the undiscovered land mass thought to exist in the southern oceans. Pedro Fernandez de Quiros (see *Captain Quiros*) in 1606 named an island of the New Hebrides group (which he believed to be part of the great southern continent) 'Austrialia del Espiritu Santo'. In 1692 Gabriel de Foigny, writing under the pseudonym 'Jacques Sadeur', published a novel in whose title the terms 'la terre Australe' and 'Australiens' occur; the English translation of his novel used the words 'Australia' and 'Australians'. The eighteenth century saw plentiful use of 'Australia' or equivalent terms. Captain James Cook, however, believing that the Australian east coast where he had made landfall in 1770 had no connection with de Quiros's Austrialia continent, called the land New Wales, later New South Wales, and New South Wales was the name applied by the British government to the penal colony established by Captain Arthur Phillip at Botany Bay in 1788. From about 1786 everything east of the 135° meridian of longitude was called New South Wales and everything west of the meridian, New Holland. In James Wilson's *A Missionary Voyage* (1799) the names 'Greater Australia' and 'Lesser Australia' were used; and Matthew Flinders (often erroneously considered to be the first to use 'Australia') spoke in his *A Voyage to Terra Australis* (1814) of his wish to have called the book *Voyage to Australia*, a wish that was thwarted by the influence of Sir Joseph Banks. The charts published in connection with Flinders's voyages used the name 'Australia'; when those charts reached the Colony in 1817 the governor, Lachlan Macquarie, adopted the name for official use, writing in a despatch in December 1817, 'I hope (Australia) will be the name given to this country in future'. When Macquarie was buried in Scotland in 1824, 'Australia' was written on his tomb. Macquarie's 'official' poet, Michael Massey Robinson, had already used the term in his 'Ode for His Majesty's Birthday', published in the *Sydney Gazette* in 1815; and in 1819 Barron Field published *First Fruits of Australian Poetry*, the first book of verse to include 'Australian' in its title. In 1821 a literary magazine titled the *Australian Magazine* appeared, and in the same year the first scientific association formed in the colony was established as the Philosophical Society of Australasia. 'Australia' and 'Australasia' were virtually interchangeable terms; W.C. Wentworth's Cambridge poem of 1823 was titled *Australasia* and it ended with the well-known lines, 'And Australasia float with flag unfurled/A New Britannia in another world!' Wentworth's 1819 history, *A Statistical, Historical and Political Description of the Colony of New South Wales*, was changed in the third edition (1824) to *A Statistical Account of the British Settlements in Australasia*. After Wentworth returned to the Colony from England in 1824 he established with Robert Wardell the newspaper the *Australian*, which was a rival to the *Sydney Gazette* which, incidentally, used 'Advance Australia' on its masthead. The impetus to use 'Australia' thus came almost entirely from the Colony itself and there was noticeable reluctance by the authorities in England to follow the colonial lead. In colonial writing the word was used with increasing regularity from the 1820s onwards, e.g. Phillip Parker King's *Narrative of a Survey of the Intertropical and Western Coasts of Australia* (1827), Robert Dawson's *The Present State of Australia* (1830), Charles Sturt's *Two Expeditions into the Interior of Southern Australia* (1833), R.M. Martin's *History of Australasia* (1836) and W.B. Ullathorne's *The Catholic Mission in Australasia* (1837). Early colonial poet, Charles Harpur, in his poem 'The Emigrant's Vision', portrayed the goddess of the south wearing a helmet on which was engraved the word 'Australia'; in the same poem he proclaimed:

'Tis the Shiloh of freedom expected so long:
'Tis the evergreen land of Australia.

Fellow colonial poet, Henry Kendall, frequently attached to his early verses the initials NAP, 'Native Australian Poet'.

'Australia' was officially used for the new colonies of WA and SA, founded in 1829 and 1836 for free settlers; the Act of 1829 establishing the Swan River colony spoke of 'His Majesty's Settlement in Western Australia'. The Commonwealth of Australia, constituted by an Act of the imperial parliament 9 July 1900, was inaugurated 1 January 1901. 'Australasia' is now used as a joint term for Australia and New Zealand.

Australia (2), an eight-volume descriptive work published 1874–76, was the nineteenth-century equivalent of the modern day coffee-table book. Its text was written by E. Carton Booth and it was illustrated by leading contemporary artists, e.g. J. Skinner Prout and Nicholas Chevalier. Booth also wrote *Another England: Life, Living, Homes and Homemakers in Victoria* (1869), a work describing Victorian society in the post-gold period.

Australia (3), a seminal history by Sir Keith Hancock (q.v.), was first published in 1930. The history, which moves from the efforts of Australia's white settlers to conquer the land to the development of sectional conflict and the growth of democracy and nationalism, prefigures a number of themes taken up by subsequent historians and cultural studies; particularly influential have been Hancock's analyses of the national character and the role of rural values and egalitarianism in Australian society. Writers who have subsequently developed similar themes include Brian Fitzpatrick, Russel Ward, Robin Gollan, Craig McGregor, Vance Palmer, Donald Horne, C. Hartley Grattan, J.D. Pringle and A.A. Phillips.

'Australia' (4), a sonnet by Bernard O'Dowd (q.v.), is the introductory poem to the volume *Dawnward?* (1903). With its well-known opening line, 'Last sea-thing dredged by sailor Time from Space' and its questioning of the destiny of Australia, the sonnet is one of the best-known and most anthologized of O'Dowd's works.

'Australia' (5), a poem written by A.D. Hope (q.v.) in 1939, was first published in 1943 and has frequently been anthologized. In a mood of cool appraisal, the poet dwells on the country's isolation, philistinism and cultural deprivation. In the last two stanzas, however, he accepts this 'Australian desert of human mind' as home in the hope that 'Such savage and scarlet as no green hills dare/Springs in that waste', and that 'still from the deserts the prophets come'. The last quotation provided Geoffrey Serle with the title of his historical study of Australian culture, *From Deserts the Prophets Come* (1973).

Australia & New Zealand Weekly, see *British Australasian*

Australia Council is a statutory authority through which federal government support is provided to the arts. The establishment of such a body to consolidate and extend federal government activity within the arts area was a policy of the government of E.G. Whitlam (q.v.) implemented soon after its election in December 1972, although until the Australia Council Act was passed in 1975 the policy was administered by expanding the structure and activities of the existing Australian Council for the Arts (q.v.). Currently, the Australia Council has a membership of between ten and fourteen and receives an annual grant from the federal government – $37.9 million for the 1983–84 financial year – the bulk of which is distributed to the Council's own programmes in appropriations for the Australian Opera, the Australian Ballet Foundation, and the Australian Elizabethan Theatre Trust orchestras, and to the seven Arts Boards within its jurisdiction: Aboriginal Arts, Community Arts, Craft, Literature, Music, Theatre and Visual Arts. H.C. Coombs, a significant figure in the formation of arts policy in Australia in the 1950s and 1960s, was the first chairman of the Australia Council. His successors have been Peter Karmel, Geoffrey Blainey, Timothy Pascoe (fulltime chairman 1981–84) and Donald Horne. In broad terms the objectives of the Australia Council are to encourage excellence and increased participation in the arts, to project Australia's image in the arts, and to advise the federal government on the arts in general.

Australia Felix was the name given by Major Thomas Mitchell (q.v.), in *Three Expeditions into the Interior of Eastern Australia* (1839), to the land which he discovered on his expedition in 1836 from Portland to the Murray River near Albury, i.e. much of present-day central Victoria. It was frequently used in titles of literary, historical, geographical and biographical works in the nineteenth century, e.g. *Australia Felix Monthly Magazine* (1849) and Richard Howitt's *Impressions of Australia Felix* (1845).

Australia First, an extreme nationalist movement which P.R. Stephensen and W.J. Miles (qq.v.) were instrumental in founding, was formally established in Sydney in October 1941; Stephensen was its foundation president and its membership included C.W. Salier and Ian Mudie. Australia First was isolationist and chauvinist; strongly anti-English, anti-Semitic and anti-communist, it expressed some sympathy for the Japanese and German governments. In March 1942, following the arrest in Perth of four people charged with conspiracy to assist Japan, who had Australia First material in their possession, sixteen people suspected of being Australia First members or sympathizers were arrested in Sydney, including Stephensen, Salier and the poet Harley Matthews. Their internment was criticized at a subsequent inquiry (1944–45) as an infringement of civil liberties; most of the internees were released in 1942, but Stephensen remained in detention until the end of the Second World War. In Xavier Herbert's *Poor Fellow My Country* (q.v., 1975), Australia First is critically portrayed as 'Australia Free'; the movement is also the subject of Bruce Muirden's *The Puzzled Patriots* (1968).

Australia in the War of 1939–45, the official history, edited by Gavin Long (q.v.), consists of twenty-two volumes arranged in five series (Army, Navy, Air, Civil and Medical) published between 1952 and 1977. Volumes I to VII of the first series (Army) include *To Benghazi* (1952) by Gavin Long, *Greece, Crete and Syria* (1953) by Gavin Long, *Tobruk and El Alamein* (1966) by Barton Maughan, *The Japanese Thrust* (1957) by Lionel Wigmore, *South-West Pacific Area – First Year* (1959) by Dudley McCarthy, *The New Guinea Offensives* (1961) by David Dexter, and *The Final Campaigns* (1963) by Gavin Long. G. Hermon Gill wrote the two-volume account of the part played by the Royal Australian Navy (1957 and 1968), which forms the second series. The third series (Air) includes *Royal Australian Air Force 1939–1942* by Douglas Gillison (1962), *Air War against Japan 1943–1945* by George Odgers (1957), *Air War against Germany and Italy 1939–1943* (1954) and *Air Power over Europe 1944–1945* (1963) by John Herington. The fourth series (Civil) includes *The Government and the People 1939–1941* (1952) by S.J. Butlin, *1942–1945* (1970) by Paul Hasluck, *War Economy 1939–1942* (1955) and *1942–1945* (1977) by S.J. Butlin and C.V. Schedvin, and *The Role of Science and Industry* (1958) by D.P. Mellor. Allan S. Walker wrote the four volumes of the fifth series (Medical). A concise one-volume history by Gavin Long, *The Six Years War*, was published in 1973.

Australia in Western Imaginative Prose Writings 1600–1960 (1967), edited by Werner P. Friederich, is a combination of anthology and literary history. It contains commentaries on the works of non-Australian writers about Australia from the time of its discovery to the period after the Second World War. Among those anthologized are the Portuguese-Spanish explorer, Pedro Fernandez de Quiros; the Frenchman, de Brosses; the English writers, Henry Kingsley, Anthony Trollope and D.H. Lawrence; the Italian, Raffaello Carboni; the German, Friedrich Gerstaecker; the Frenchman, Paul Wenz; and the Swiss, Esther Landolt.

'Australia to England', the poem by John Farrell (q.v.) to celebrate Queen Victoria's Diamond Jubilee, was published in the *Daily Telegraph* 22 June 1897, as 'Ave Imperatrix'. With slight alterations and under its new title the poem was reprinted in the same year as a booklet. Highly regarded at the time, the poem is a patriotic expression of hopes for Australia's future and an acknowledgement of the great achievements of the mother country.

Australia Unlimited, see **BRADY, E.J.**

Australia, Visited & Revisited (1853, facsimile 1974), by Samuel Mossman and Thomas Banister, is basically 'a narrative of recent travels and odd experiences in Victoria and New

South Wales', and was intended to lay before the public a work that would be useful to those intending to hazard their fortunes in 'The Australian Gold Colonies' and be interesting to the general reader. The goldfields at Mount Alexander, the Turon, Bathurst, Louisa Creek and Braidwood are described, as are pastoral pursuits and life on sheep and cattle stations. Mossman also wrote *A Voice from Australia* (1852), *The Gold Regions of Australia* (1852), *Railways in Victoria* (1857), *Narrative of the Shipwreck of the 'Admella'* (1859), *Our Australian Colonies* (1866), *Heroes of Discovery* (1868) and *New Japan* (1873); and edited *General Gordon's Private Diary of His Exploits in China* (1885).

Australia Week-End Book, began in 1942 and was published annually until 1946. It was edited by Sydney Ure Smith (q.v.) and Gwen Morton Spencer; and notable among its contributors were Marjorie Barnard, Alan Marshall, D'Arcy Niland, Jon Cleary and Eleanor Dark.

Australian (1), founded by W.C. Wentworth (q.v.) and Robert Wardell, helped produce a free press in NSW. It ran 1824–48 and serialized novels by Charles Dickens and other English authors; its contributors included Henry Halloran, Charles Harpur, Richard Howitt and Charles Tompson. Wardell (1793–1834) was admitted to the Bar in 1821 and came to NSW on the same ship as Wentworth in 1824; he subsequently established a successful law practice.

Australian (2), was established in 1964 by Rupert Murdoch as a national daily newspaper, with Maxwell Newton as foundation editor. Robert Brissenden was its first literary editor and David Campbell its first poetry editor; later Rodney Hall was poetry editor for eleven years from 1967, and Katharine Brisbane its national (1967–74) and Sydney (1978–80) theatre critic. The *Weekend Australian* (the weekend issue of the newspaper) has a literary section.

Australian: a Monthly Magazine, which ran 1878–81, carried short fiction, poetry and serials. Its contributors included Henry Halloran, Richmond (Dick) Thatcher, A. Patchett Martin and John Stanley James ('The Vagabond'); and it professed to be 'national in our views, national in our politics, national in our relations to all public and social questions'.

Australian Academy of the Humanities, a body based in Canberra which replaced the Australian Humanities Research Council (q.v.), was constituted by Letters Patent of Queen Elizabeth II in 1969; it received a royal charter

the same year. Formally 'The Australian Academy of the Humanities for the Advancement of Scholarship in Language, Literature, History, Philosophy and the Fine Arts', the Academy aims to advance scholarship and interest in and understanding of the humanities. It consists of the foundation fellows and honorary fellows (the members and honorary members of the Australian Humanities Research Council at the time of the Academy's creation), together with the fellows and honorary fellows elected by the Academy since then; A.D. Hope was a foundation fellow, and Judith Wright, Jack Lindsay, C.B. Christesen, R.F. Brissenden, James McAuley and Eric Partridge are significant figures in Australian language and literature who have been elected since 1969. Among the long-term projects sponsored by the Academy are language atlases of the Pacific and China, a descriptive catalogue of the art, charts and views of Captain James Cook's voyages of discovery in the South Pacific and the journal, *Australian Cultural History*, which publishes papers from an annual seminar which the Academy co-sponsors. The Academy also assists publications within the humanities (including journals) and publishes on its own account a monograph series, pamphlets and a *Proceedings* (annual 1970–79, biennial 1980–83, triennial 1983–   ).

Australian Accent (1958), by John Douglas Pringle (q.v.), is an impressionistic, sometimes humorous analysis of Australian culture and society, with particular emphasis on the urban environments of Sydney and Melbourne and the political and cultural scenes. The book was illustrated by George Molnar, then cartoonist of the *Sydney Morning Herald*.

Australian Author, the quarterly magazine of the Australian Society of Authors (q.v.), superseded *Broadside* in 1969, the latter having been since 1963 a printed broadsheet of literary news available to members of the Society. Editors of the *Australian Author/Broadside* have included Barrie Ovenden, Nancy Keesing, Gavin Souter, Colin Simpson and Bill Larkins.

Australian Band of Hope Review and Children's Friend, a temperance journal, published short stories, sketches, moral tales and poetry; Charles Harpur and Henry Kendall were contributors. Published fortnightly 1856–61, it was known also as the *Band of Hope Journal and Australian Home Companion* and as the *Australian Home Companion and Band of Hope Journal*.

Australian Bibliography: A Guide to Printed Sources of Information by D.H. Borchardt (q.v.), then chief librarian of La Trobe University, Melbourne, was published first in 1963, with a second edition in 1966, and a rewritten and enlarged edition in 1976. A comprehensive treatment of Australian reference works, the *Bibliography* offers an annotated commentary on libraries and library catalogues, encyclopaedias and general reference works, general and subject bibliographies (the latter divided into the social sciences, the humanities and the pure and applied sciences), bibliographies of geographic regions, sources of biographical information, government publications and the bibliographical scene.

Australian Book Publishers Association (ABPA) was formed in 1949 from a merger of two smaller associations of publishers, the New South Wales Publishers Association and the Victorian Publishers Association. The aims of ABPA include the fostering of original publishing in Australia and encouragement of the highest standards of writing, editing and manufacture of books in Australia. Its chief areas of activity include copyright, the fostering of governmental and public understanding of the book-publishing industry in Australia, the monitoring of members' interests in regard to book bounty, duties, tariffs and taxes, and liaison with other book trade organizations, e.g. the National Book Council, the Australian Society of Authors and the Australian Copyright Council. The initial president of ABPA was W.H. Cousins of Angus & Robertson. George Ferguson (q.v.), largely instrumental in the founding of ABPA, was president 1950–56 and 1959–60. During his term of office ABPA's annual Book Design Awards were inaugurated. Ferguson, Frank Eyre (q.v.) who was president 1961–62, and Harry Weston are ABPA honorary life members.

Australian Book Review (ABR) is the title of two journals. The first, published from Adelaide (1961–74 monthly to 1971, then quarterly), was edited by Max Harris. The second, published from 1978, edited by John McLaren and sponsored (since 1980) by the National Book Council, appears ten times a year. The first series also included an annual children's book and educational supplement (1961–70).

Australian Books in Print, an annual publication, includes (in addition to Australian books in print) lists of literary societies and associations, literary prizes and awards, names and addresses of Australian publishers, their representatives and agents, and those of overseas publishers who have representatives or agents in Australia. It was first published in 1956. It is available also on microfiche and is updated monthly.

Australian Bookseller & Publisher, founded by D.W. Thorpe in 1921, is a monthly publication still emanating from D.W. Thorpe Pty Ltd, publishers of trade journals and reference books. Joyce Nicholson (q.v.), daughter of D.W. Thorpe, has recently been the *Bookseller*'s editor and is now governing director. Originally (1921–25) titled the *Australasian Stationery and Fancy Goods Journal*, and later with other titles, the *Bookseller* split into two in 1971, its other half becoming the *Australian Newsagent and Stationer*. The *Bookseller* contains regular sections such as 'Australian Book Scene', 'Children's Books', 'New Australian Books', and 'A Bookseller's Diary'.

Australian Broadcasting Commission, the national broadcasting service, known also as the 'ABC' and more colloquially as 'Aunty', was established in 1932, nine years after commercial radio broadcasting had begun in Australia with a sealed-set system. Under this system organizations were licensed to broadcast by the Postmaster-General, listeners paid a licence fee to the federal government and a subscription fee to a designated station, and each wireless set was sealed so that it could only operate on the wavelength of the station receiving the subscription. Sealed sets were abandoned in 1924 in favour of A and B class stations, both operating under government licence, with the A class stations (which included 2FC, 2BL and 3LO, all later part of the ABC network) to be financed mainly from licence fees and the B class stations from advertising revenue. The problem with this second system – its concentration of broadcasting services in city areas – led in 1927 to the establishment of a Royal Commission which recommended that the Postmaster-General's department operate the A class stations (at that stage two in Sydney and Melbourne, one each in the other State capitals) but let the programming services out to private companies under contract. In 1929 the contract went to the Australian Broadcasting Company, a combination mainly of theatre and cinema interests. Although in the three years of the Company's operation there were substantial developments in programming, the establishment of stations outside metropolitan areas and the relaying of items between stations, the J.H. Scullin government decided in 1930 that broadcasting should be brought under public control; that decision was implemented in 1932 by the government of Scullin's successor, Joseph Lyons.

Under the first Australian Broadcasting Commission Act, the Commission – originally five members, increased to seven in 1948, nine in 1967, and eleven in 1976 – took over the existing A class stations, with the B class stations continuing to develop commercial radio. The Commission's technical services were to be provided by the Postmaster-General's department (the transmitters remained in the hands of the PMG throughout the history of the ABC, although radio studio services were handled by the ABC from 1964 and by parallel television services from the outset); its funds came from a proportion of the licence fee paid by listeners (although in 1944–45 it received its first supplementary grant and from 1948 a direct government appropriation); it was not allowed to broadcast advertisements (a provision which remains); and it was entrusted to provide adequate and comprehensive programmes and encourage local talent. Initially the Postmaster-General, the minister responsible for the ABC, could 'direct the Commission to broadcast, or refrain from broadcasting, any specified material', although a 1942 Act stipulated notice in writing of intention to use these powers and the reporting of their use in the Commission's annual report. The extent of political interference and related issues of autonomy and bias are themes of some longevity in commentary on the ABC, as also are the extent to which it has been (or should have been) 'highbrow', 'middlebrow' or 'lowbrow', the degree of its neglect of rural listeners, and its relationship (competing with or complementary to) commercial broadcasting. Discussion of some of those issues intensified after the introduction of television to Australia in 1956, which brought profound changes to the operations of the Commission. The enormous developments in communications since the establishment of the ABC, e.g. the improvement of lines to Perth and Hobart in the early days of radio, videotape, coaxial cables and satellites after television was introduced, the introduction of FM radio in 1976, have helped to make the ABC more truly a national broadcasting service, while always maintaining some regionalization. These developments have also made necessary the extensive legislative revision and updating of the early Broadcasting Acts (major Broadcasting Bills were enacted by the federal parliament in 1942, 1948, 1956, 1976 and 1983), the establishment of various broadcasting committees outside of but encompassing the ABC (e.g. the Australian Broadcasting Control Board of 1948–76) and the periodic committees of review of the Commission itself. One such committee, the Dix Committee of 1979–81, produced a report which was the basis of the federal government's decision to dissolve the Australian Broadcasting Commission and establish (on 1 July 1983) the Australian Broad-

casting Corporation in its place.

The main spheres of broadcasting operation of the ABC have been in the areas of music (53 per cent of the ABC's activities in its first year), news, current affairs, sport, drama and other features, education, and youth and rural broadcasts; and in many of these activities Australian writers and critics have been significant. A.B. Paterson expressed interest in being one of the initial commissioners; he was not appointed, but Ernestine Hill (1942–44) and David Williamson (1978–79) served terms on the Commission; Williamson was a contemporary of Dame Leonie Kramer (q.v.), a commissioner in 1977–81 before her appointment as the eleventh (and last) chairman (1982–83). Among long-term employees of the Commission were the critic and biographer Clement Semmler (q.v.), who retired in 1977 after thirty-five years (the last thirteen as deputy general manager); the poet and anthologist John Thompson (q.v.), who joined in 1939 and was associated for many years with the cultural radio programme 'Quality Street', which ran 1946–73 and was narrated in its first year by Peter Finch; the dramatist, novelist and journalist, Mungo MacCallum (q.v.), who produced the ABC's first night of television; and the writer and theatre historian, Leslie Rees (q.v.), who played a significant role in the development of the ABC's tradition of radio drama. Other appointments were held by the poet and critic Dorothy Green, who helped implement the ABC's independent news services; the playwrights Ron Blair, Tony Morphett and Bob Ellis; the novelists Roger McDonald and Christopher Koch; the travel writer Colin Simpson, who prepared the 'Australian Walkabout' series in 1947–49 before leaving to write in the same subject area; and many others. Regular radio broadcasters have included Walter Murdoch, Vance and Nettie Palmer, H.M. Green, A.D. Hope, who was 'Anthony Inkwell' for a time on the famous children's programme 'The Argonauts' (1941–72), and Douglas Stewart, who gave the 1977 Boyer lectures on the *Bulletin*. Frank Hardy and Cyril Pearl have been ABC television panellists.

On the opening nights of both ABC radio and television a play was included in the programme. Although on each occasion the work broadcast was by an English writer (a symptom of the Commission's models and influences), the work of Australian writers has been significantly represented in each medium. In general terms – and leaving aside the countless features and talks programmes such as 'Quality Street' and its successors, 'Sunday Night Radio 2' and 'Radio Helicon', which have all had a significant literary component – Australian writers have been represented in three ways: by dramatic works (single plays and series) written especially for radio or television; by dramatic adaptations (again, single plays or series of already published material – often novels); and by readings rather than dramatic adaptations of already published material (again, often novels, as in the serialization of Miles Franklin's *All That Swagger* in 1942 and the readings on ABC morning radio of Lennie Lower's *Here's Luck* in 1982 and Eve Langley's *The Pea Pickers* in 1983). Two pioneers in the first category were Max Afford (q.v.), whose 'The Flail of God' was the first play by an Australian writer broadcast on Australian radio (19 July 1932), and Edmund Barclay, who wrote the first ABC radio serial, 'As Ye Sow', which ran for nine months (January–September 1937) and like many successors in radio and television took early Australian history as its subject. Both Afford and Barclay were employed on contract by the Commission, although it was more usual for writers to be freelance. Among their contemporaries and successors in the field of radio drama (which was given impetus by several ABC competitions and drama weeks in the 1930s and 1940s) were Alexander Turner, George Landen Dann, Charles Porter, 'Betty Roland', Catherine Shepherd, Gwen Meredith (the creator and writer of two famous long-running serials 'The Lawsons', 1944–49, and 'Blue Hills', 1949–76), Dymphna Cusack, Dulcie Deamer, Catherine Duncan, Colin Thiele, Ruth Park, D'Arcy Niland, Coral Lansbury, Vance Palmer, Jessica Anderson, Oriel Gray, Rex Rienits, George Farwell, Eleanor Witcombe, Peter Kenna, Kay Keavney, Hal Porter, Sumner Locke-Elliott (qq.v.) and Douglas Stewart, whose *The Fire on the Snow* (q.v.), broadcast first in 1941, is a famous Australian radio play, and who also had *Ned Kelly* (1942) and *The Golden Lover* (broadcast 1942, 1943) on the ABC. Several of these writers wrote mainly outside broadcasting, but Dann, Porter, Shepherd, Duncan, Lansbury, Gray and Meredith are among those who established their reputations in radio. Some, like Gray, Keavney, MacCallum and Rienits, who wrote *Stormy Petrel* (1960), the first ABC television serial, made the transition successfully to television; other ABC television playwrights of note have been Locke-Elliott, Peter Yeldham (q.v.), Alan Seymour (q.v.), and Ray Lawler, who were all also successful in television overseas; Colin Free, who wrote for the successful series *Contrabandits, Delta* and *Over There* and *Learned Friends*; Barbara Vernon, who created *Bellbird* (1967–79), television's equivalent of 'Blue Hills'; Pat Flower, Michael Boddy, Phillip Grenville Mann and Tony Morphett.

Some of these writers were responsible for the dramatic adaptations of previously published material, the second major way in which Australian writers have been represented on ABC radio and television. Innumerable Australian poems, plays, stories and novels have been dramatically adapted for or broadcast on ABC radio; to take just one example, on 7 September 1983 an adaptation of Patrick White's *The Tree of Man* was being serialized in the afternoon and a performance of David Williamson's *The Club* was broadcast in the evening. Among notable television series or serials based on Australian novels are George Johnston's *My Brother Jack* in 1965, D'Arcy Niland's *Dead Men Running* in 1971, the Norman Lindsay festival (adaptations of six novels) in 1972, Ethel Turner's *Seven Little Australians* in 1975, Frank Hardy's *Power Without Glory* in 1976, Kylie Tennant's *Ride on Stranger* in 1979, Eleanor Dark's *The Timeless Land* in 1980, Alan Marshall's *I Can Jump Puddles* in 1981, Roger McDonald's *1915* in 1982, and Thea Astley's *A Descant for Gossips* in 1983. Several of these series have been repeated on commercial television, which has also represented the work of Australian writers in its own series, e.g. *His Natural Life* (q.v.) in 1983. Some commentators have criticized the shift from single plays, whether adaptations or not, to series and serials.

The ABC figures prominently in the many studies of Australian communications and the media (e.g. Sandra Hall's *Supertoy: 20 Years of Australian Television*, 1976). More specialist in focus are various memoirs or studies by ex-ABC employees and commissioners, including J.R. Darling's *The ABC and the Community* (1962), M.F. Dixon's *Inside the ABC* (1975), Ellis Blain's *Life with Aunty* (1977), B. McCallum's *Tales Untold: Memoirs of an ABC Publicity Officer* (1978), Richard Harding's *Outside Interference: The Politics of Australian Broadcasting* (1979), Clement Semmler's *The ABC: Aunt Sally and Sacred Cow* (1981), and Ida Elizabeth Jenkins's *Good Rowing!* (1983). There have been two major histories, Alan Thomas's study of the early years, *Broadcast and Be Damned* (1980), and K.S. Inglis's *This is the ABC: The Australian Broadcasting Commission 1932–83* (1983). The ABC has also made its own contribution to Australian literature through publishing activities which range from journals such as the *ABC Weekly* and *24 Hours* to books based on series, including *Australian Writers Speak* (1942), *Current Books Worth Reading* (1941–55), *Todays Books* (1956–63), *Todays Writing* (1963–64), *Books for Comment* (1963–69), John Thompson's *On Lips of Living Men* (1962) and *Five to Remember* (1964), and Douglas Stewart's *Writers of the Bulletin* (1977).

Australian Capers: Or, Christopher Cockle's Colonial Experience, a novel by John Richard Houlding (q.v.), was first published in 1867; it is also known by the title of the 1913 edition, *Christopher Cockle's Australian Experiences*. A cautionary tale of the misadventures of a 'new chum' (q.v.) in the colonies, *Australian Capers* opens with the birth of Christopher Cockle, the son of a wealthy London fishmonger and alderman; the surname–occupation pun is characteristic of Houlding, as is his comic use of dialect and exaggerated metaphor. At twenty, attracted by news of the gold discoveries, Christopher sets sail for Australia but falls victim *en route* to seasickness, drink, tobacco, gambling and his own naivety. On arrival he tours Melbourne, where he is inadvertently left in charge of a runaway cab and is locked up in the watchhouse after a drunken spree, before disembarking at Sydney. He takes rooms in a hotel where he meets Mr Fitz-Chowse Slyver, a swindler who relieves Christopher not only of money but also of the papers by which he can be impersonated. After further difficulties in Sydney, Christopher travels up-country to Kickadingo to stay with his uncle, where his new chum *gaucheries* are revealed when he puts both charges down one barrel of a double-barrelled shotgun; while returning home he meets a young woman, Julia Doveskin, at whose house he takes up lodging and to whom he becomes engaged. On his return from another visit to the country, this time to the kindly Mr Todd, Christopher surprises Julia entertaining a sailor; he goes on a binge, suffers a bout of delirium tremens, and attempts suicide. He is rescued by the support of his uncle Nicholas, Mr Todd and Tim Rafferty, a rough diamond steward on the boat to Australia who has defended Christopher when his family in England, deceived by Slyver's duplicities, had thought the worst of his conduct. Converted to Christianity at the end of the novel, Christopher settles down to become a clerk. The best of Houlding's books, *Australian Capers* is interspersed with homiletic and other tales recounted by the people Christopher meets. A gently satiric picture of the new chum, it contains some shrewd observations of city life and of colonists.

Australian Capital Territory (ACT), comprises an area of 2360 square kilometres in southern NSW, within which is the national capital Canberra (q.v.), together with an area of seventy-two square kilometres at Jervis Bay on the NSW south coast. The constitution which created the Commonwealth of Australia in 1901 stipulated that the seat of the federal government should be not less than 100 miles from Sydney. After the Yass-Canberra district was finally chosen as the site in 1908, the relevant Acts of Surrender were passed by the NSW and Commonwealth parliaments and the ACT became federal territory in 1911 (1915 for the present Jervis Bay portion). Known as the Federal Capital Territory until 1938, the Australian Capital Territory was not formally occupied by government until 1927.

Australian Council for the Arts was established in 1968 to take over from the Australian Elizabethan Theatre Trust the task of advising the federal government and distributing its subsidy in the area of the performing arts. In 1973 its functions were expanded in order to implement the policies of the government of E.G. Whitlam for the enlargement and consolidation of federal government support to the arts. As a consequence, literature and arts other than the performing arts, which had previously attracted separate government support (e.g. through the Commonwealth Literary Fund) were also brought within the jurisdiction of the Australian Council for the Arts, which became the Australia Council (q.v.) after legislation creating that statutory authority was passed in 1975.

Australian Cultural Elites: Intellectual Traditions in Sydney and Melbourne (1974), a provocative study by John Docker, suggests that the different cultural histories of Australia's major cities, Sydney and Melbourne, have produced fundamentally conflicting views of the relationship between Australia's European inheritance of ideas, ideologies and assumptions and the new 'Australian' experience and social environments. Australian culture itself is not unified and monolithic; it contains alternative and varied traditions which are versions, in Australia, of major European cultural arguments, exemplified by Docker as 'social optimism versus social pessimism, varieties of romanticism, pluralism, anarchism, libertarianism, liberal humanism, theories of social intervention, and the role of intellectuals in society'. In two parts, 'A Sydney Literary Tradition', and 'Sydney and Melbourne', *Australian Cultural Elites* discusses, for example, the roles of Christopher Brennan, the Norman Lindsay–Kenneth Slessor Artist-Aristocracy, A.D. Hope, Patrick White, John Anderson and the Sydney Freethought tradition, and the influence of *Meanjin* and *Southerly* in their respective home cities. It concludes by offering a view of the impact of the Vietnam War on Australian cultural life.

Australian Dictionary of Biography (ADB) (1966–), has published nine of a projected twelve volumes. Organized alphabetically within three periods (1788–1850, 1851–1890 and 1891–1939), the *ADB* treats significant Australian identities and personalities, including numerous writers. The *ADB* is based at the Australian National University; its general editors have been Douglas Pike (1-5), Bede Nairn (6) and Bede Nairn/Geoffrey Serle (7-9).

Australian Dream is a phrase that has been used to describe the hopes and anticipations that have been traditionally held by Australians for themselves and their country. Those hopes and anticipations have varied with the changing circumstances and patterns of Australian life from the first settlement in 1788 through the colonial period to nationhood. Components of the dream have included liberty, equality and fraternity (the last given a particular Australian flavour by the creed of mateship), Utopianism, the ethos of the bush, democratic humanism, nationalism and radicalism. Writers who have been significant in the creation of the dream include W.C. Wentworth, Charles Harpur, Henry Kendall, John Dunmore Lang, Daniel Deniehy, William Lane, W.G. Spence, John Farrell, Mary Gilmore, Henry Lawson, A.B. Paterson, Bernard O'Dowd, Miles Franklin, E.J. Brady, Randolph Bedford, Alfred Deakin, Henry Bournes Higgins, R.D. FitzGerald and Brian Penton. Ian Turner compiled an anthology, *The Australian Dream* (1968); T. Inglis Moore traces the chronological variations of the dream in *Social Patterns in Australian Literature* (1971).

'Australian Dream, The', a satirical poem by David Campbell (q.v.), is a humorous account of the unexpected arrival of the Royal Family at Campbell's home. Tucked up in the cottage's only double bed with the Queen and the Queen Mother, the embarrassed poet is made to feel somewhat at ease by the Queen's gracious 'Please call me Ma'am'.

Australian Elizabethan Theatre Trust, first proposed by H.C. Coombs (q.v.), was formed in 1954 to provide assistance to theatre and later the other performing arts. It was funded initially by private sources but subsequently secured increasing government aid and became a combination of private entrepreneur and the agency through which federal government support was dispensed to the performing arts. After the formation of the Australian Council for the Arts in 1968 it continued with its entrepreneurial functions and now administers, through the Australia Council, the orchestras of the Australian Ballet Foundation and the Australian Opera. It played a significant part in establishing performing arts companies in opera, ballet, drama and music; helped to found NIDA

(see National Institute of Dramatic Art) and administered the Elizabethan Theatre in Sydney. Its publications have included *Theatre Spectrum* (1969–71), *Elizabethan Trust News* (1971–76) and *Theatrescope* (1976).

Australian Encyclopaedia, first projected by Angus & Robertson in 1912 as a biographical and historical record of Australia, was published in its inaugural edition in 1925 in two volumes, edited by A.W. Jose and H.J. Carter. A second edition was published in 1958 in ten volumes, edited by A.H. Chisholm and Bruce Pratt. In 1962 Angus & Robertson sold the *Australian Encyclopaedia* to the Grolier Society of Australia. Five reprintings of the 1958 edition, with minor alterations, were made under the editorship of Bruce Pratt between 1962 and 1972. A third edition, edited by Pratt in six volumes, was published in 1977, revised in 1979 and reprinted in 1981. The third edition contains 1700 biographies of notable Australians, many of whom are literary figures and contains many entries on geographical features and historical events that are also significant in Australian literature. An expanded fourth edition of twelve volumes, with new cross-reference and index systems, and produced by an editorial board headed by Sir Harold White with Richard Appleton as editor-in-chief, was published in 1983.

Australian English is a term used to describe the form of English spoken and written in Australia. Like other national varieties of English, it shares much of its vocabulary and pronunciation with the parent form but historical, social and environmental factors mean that it has developed distinctive features of its own. This distinctive component of the English spoken and written in Australia has itself been called Australian English or something similar, as in E.E. Morris's dictionary, *Austral English* (1898), and W.S. Ramson's *Australian English: An Historical Study of the Vocabulary 1788–1898* (1966) where it is suggested that 'For all practical purposes, Australian English consists of the additions to British English'. The narrower usage has declined somewhat, however, and in reference to the vocabulary of Australian English it is now as common to use terms like 'Australianisms' to describe the distinctively Australian component of the lexicon; 'Australianism' was used in this way at least as far back as the 1890s. The spoken English of Australians is referred to by a variety of terms, including Australian pronunciation, Australian speech, the Australian accent and spoken Australian English.

English began to be established in Australia with the arrival of the First Fleet in 1788.

Because of the penal nature of the original British settlement, there existed initially a distinction between the language of the military administrators – what Ramson has called 'polite English' – and the more 'vulgar' language of convicts, e.g. the thieves' slang of James Hardy Vaux (q.v.), and the language of some early immigrants. It was from the latter linguistic group, and well before the end of transportation, that a new speech developed among the Australians born and raised in the colonies, a speech still noted for its homogeneity; in other words, although there is a range of pronunciation in Australia, it is determined by social rather than regional factors. The 'mixing-bowl' theory advanced by A.G. Mitchell, J.R.L. Bernard and some others to account for the evolution of Australian speech has three main ingredients. Firstly, because the earliest settlers came from all parts of Britain, a distinctive speech evolved, initially among colonial children, from the mixture of dialects spoken, with London English the most important influence. Secondly, the urban origins of a significant proportion of the settlers, together with the fact that they were overwhelmingly British, were factors in the standardization of the new speech. Thirdly, regional homogeneity is explained by the recreation of the new speech again and again in 'germinal centres' of the colonies (i.e. in different parts of the colonies, as settlement spread).

That the first distinctively Australian speech derived from the convicts and other humble settlers means that from the outset Australian speech bore, in Bernard's words, a 'halo of attributes which necessarily alienated it from many . . . other speakers of English'. Thus from the 1820s until recently Australian English has been criticized both inside the country (notably among educated Australians adopting as their model, standard English, what is called 'Received Pronunciation' or 'RP') and outside it (notably among RP speakers in England). In 1946 A.G. Mitchell listed as the commonest criticisms that Australian speech was ugly, lazy, slovenly, nasal, drawling, unclear, Cockney, monotonous and flat. Some of the criticisms can be linked with differences between Australian speech and other forms of spoken English – the notion of flatness, for example, derives from the fact that the tonal range of Australian speech is smaller than that of RP – but others (for example, nasality) have no basis in fact; and even the assimilations and elisions which characterize 'Strine' (q.v.) are commonly found in other varieties of English. Fundamentally, spoken Australian English is no worse or no better than other varieties, and the criticisms made of it are substantially value judgements based on taste and association.

Nevertheless, Bernard has suggested that some speakers of Australian English have felt the need to upgrade their speech, and that this is one reason for the evolution of what is recognized as three main styles or types of pronunciation: Broad Australian (the form closest to the distinctive Australian speech which emerged early in the nineteenth century, and the one most commentators have in mind when they are critical of Australian speech); Cultivated Australian (a minority form, the prestige dialect in the minds of its speakers, valued as closer to the prestige dialects of England and the USA and that followed by some broadcasters); and General Australian (the form, spoken by the majority of Australians, which lies between Broad and Cultivated). These varieties share distinctive phonetic and prosodic characteristics but exist on a spectrum, with Cultivated Australian closest to RP and Broad Australian furthest away; Australian speakers have the capacity to use sounds from across the spectrum and to move between categories. It follows that the distinctive features of Australian English are to be found most clearly within the Broad Australian. In general, and in comparison with RP, spoken Australian English is narrower in tonal range, slower in rhythm because of a more even stress pattern, e.g. Australians give more equal weight to their vowels in 'Sunday' than other English speakers. Speech at the Broad Australian end of the spectrum also tends to be marked by assimilation and elision. Apart from these prosodic features, the major differences occur in the vowels and diphthongs: Australian vowels are closer, i.e. made with higher tongue positions, and some are more frontal, i.e. made more towards the front of the mouth. As well as these phonetic differences between Australian English and RP in the quality of what is essentially the same sound, some Australian English vowels and diphthongs are pronounced in such a way that they move towards (and for some Broad Australian speakers become) other sounds; if not become, they are heard as other sounds by other English speakers, hence the numerous stories of Englishmen hearing 'mite' when an Australian has said 'mate'. Among other noticeable features, there is a greater use of the indeterminate or neutral vowel in Australian English than in other varieties; many speakers of Australian English choose quite different vowels or diphthongs from RP speakers in pronouncing words like 'chance'; and Australians make greater use of truncated forms, e.g. 'footy', 'schoolie'.

Like Australian speech, the vocabulary of Australian English is noted for its homogeneity, despite the kind of regional variety that makes it difficult for a New South Welshman when he asks for 'scallops' instead of 'potato cakes' in Melbourne, or for a 'schooner' instead of a 'pint' of beer in Adelaide. That Australians until recently have overwhelmingly used British or American dictionaries is a measure of the extent to which Australian English shares its vocabulary with the parent form and with other national varieties; yet there have been significant additions to British English, particularly in colloquial usage and occupational vocabularies (e.g. shearing) which derive from the unique history of Australia and from other factors. Four historical periods have been identified in the development of the lexicon of Australian English: the colonial period from 1788 to about 1850 (i.e. the end of transportation and the beginning of the gold rushes, when the first settlers were responding to their new environment); the gold-rush period, which is characterized by more diverse immigration which had a consequential effect on the expansion of the vocabulary (for example, in increasing influence from America); the nationalist period from the 1890s (q.v.) until after the First World War, when journals like the *Bulletin* fostered a sense of national identity and some of its most popular writers (e.g. Henry Lawson, 'Steele Rudd') extensively employed Australian idioms; and the modern period, particularly since the Second World War, in which developments in communications have been significant in bringing Australian English closer to other national varieties, at the same time as playwrights such as Jack Hibberd and satirists such as Barry Humphries (qq.v.) have exploited the potential of indigenous idiom. Within and sometimes straddling these chronological boundaries, significant influences on the development of Australian idiom include the convict system, the rural character of nineteenth-century Australia, the war experiences of Australians, and the importance of sport and other leisure activities. In general Australianisms have been created in three main ways: by borrowing from Aboriginal, Australian pidgin, other languages and other national varieties of English (e.g. 'cooee', 'bush', 'squatter', qq.v.); by the extensions and new meanings given to existing English words (e.g. 'wattle', q.v., and the compounds deriving from 'stock'); and by the survival of words, notably slang and dialect words (e.g. 'bowyang', 'larrikin', 'billy', qq.v.), which have had a longer life or more general use in Australia, sometimes to such an extent that they are popularly thought to be Australian creations. The last two processes often overlap.

Throughout the nineteenth century, numerous comments on colonial idiom and pronunciation were made by government officials, visitors and travellers, explorers, newly-arrived settlers and established residents: for example (among many who could be cited), James Backhouse, David Collins, Peter Cunningham, Barron Field, Friedrich Gerstaecker, Richard and William Howitt, David McKenzie, John MacGillivray, Louisa Anne Meredith, T.L. Mitchell, Samuel Mossman, G.C. Mundy, Charles Rudston Read and Alexander Tolmer. The published writings of these observers have been major sources, along with unpublished journals and diaries, contemporary newspapers and the work of early creative writers such as Alexander Harris, for later historians and lexicographers of Australian English. At the end of the century, at a time of increased national awareness, the first studies of Australian pronunciation and the first word lists, glossaries and dictionaries of Australianisms began to appear. The first detailed account of Australasian pronunciation was by Samuel McBurney, a Glasgow-born principal of a Geelong ladies' college who in 1887 travelled extensively in eastern Australia and NZ examining singers in schools; he made extensive notes as he went on his examinees' pronunciation of sample words, and his observations form the basis of the analysis of Australasian pronunciation included in A.J. Ellis's *On Early English Pronunciation* (1887). In the same period were published the anonymous *Sydney Slang Dictionary* (?1882), the German scholar Karl Lentzner's *Dictionary of the Slang-English of Australia and of Some Mixed Languages* (1892), based partly on residence in Australia, and Cornelius Crowe's *The Australian Slang Dictionary* (1895).

These dictionaries are all limited in coverage and reliability, including words that did not have either a currency or a distinctive usage in Australia. Nonetheless, they attest to an interest in collecting Australian idioms, particularly informal idioms, which has continued to the present day; the most important collector until recent times is Sidney Baker (q.v.), whose *The Australian Language* (1945) and other publications remain indispensable reference tools. Apart from his work, there have been many twentieth-century vocabularies and dictionaries, even leaving aside the glossaries of slang and colloquial terms included in dictionaries of folklore, e.g. by Bill Wannan, or literary works which extensively employ Australian popular idiom, from C.J. Dennis's *The Songs of a Sentimental Bloke* (1915) to Hibberd's *A Stretch of the Imagination* (1973). The most important dictionary of informal usage is G.A. Wilkes's scholarly *A Dictionary of Australian Colloquialisms* (1978), an historical dictionary which supplies illustrative quotations taken mainly from printed souces; others include Baker's *A Popular Dictionary of Australian Slang* (1941) and *The Barracker's Bible* (1983) by Jack Hibberd and Garrie Hutchinson, a witty treatment of Australian sporting slang. A second group of works either combines commentary and glossary, e.g. Baker's *The Drum: Australian Character and Slang* (1959), or remains focused on Australian slang and colloquial usage without including any consolidated word list, e.g. Bill Hornadge's *The Australian Slanguage* (1980) and Nancy Keesing's *Lily on the Dustbin: Slang of Australian Women and Families* (1982). These popular publications are all mainly confined to the distinctively Australian informal part of Australian English, the Australianisms; even the Wilkes *Dictionary of Australian Colloquialisms*, by far the most important of those listed, has been renamed a *Dictionary of Colloquial Australianisms* by one of its reviewers. Another group of vocabularies and dictionaries, however, incorporates Australian slang within a wide lexical context. W.H. Downing's *Digger Dialects* (1919), the first record of Australian service slang, includes words current elsewhere in English, and Australian material is incorporated, with Baker as a major source, in the several slang dictionaries of Eric Partridge, notably *Slang To-Day and Yesterday* (1933, 4th edn 1970), *A Dictionary of Slang and Unconventional English* (1937, 7th edn 1970), and *A Dictionary of the Underworld* (1950, 3rd edn 1968).

The most important contribution to the lexicography of Australian English, however, was a work which has been criticized for its scant treatment of colloquial vocabulary: *Austral English: A Dictionary of Australasian Words, Phrases and Usages* (1898, reprinted 1968, 1971, 1972), by E.E. Morris (q.v.), an Indian-born Englishman who came to Australia in 1875 to take up a Melbourne headmastership and was appointed professor of English, French and German in 1883. Begun as a by-product of work for the *Oxford English Dictionary, Austral English* is strongest in its coverage of Aboriginal, Maori and scientific words, particularly in the attention given to flora and fauna, and includes quotations which illustrate the history of the words included. As an historical dictionary of Australianisms it has been complemented by the Wilkes dictionary but has not yet been replaced. An Australian National University team under the direction of W.S. Ramson, however, is preparing on historical principles a comprehensive dictionary of Australianisms, the *Australian National Dictionary*, which is to be published in 1988, the bicentenary of English settlement in Australia.

The preparation of the *Australian National Dictionary* has benefited not only from the attention paid by Baker, Wilkes and others to informal Australian English, but also from a range of other research: more broadly based studies of Australian vocabulary, research into specialist vocabularies, studies of other aspects of Australian English (e.g. phonetics). Historically, the most important centre for research has been the University of Sydney where A.G. Mitchell was both student and professor of English; among his several publications was *The Pronunciation of English in Australia* (1946) the first systematic account of Australian pronunciation. Among later students were Arthur Delbridge, J.R.L. Bernard, R.D. Eagleson, J.S. Gunn, and Ramson, who have all made significant contributions to knowledge about Australian English phonetics and lexicography; all were on the staff and part of the Australian Language Research Centre of the University but several have furthered Australian English research at other institutions, e.g. Delbridge and Bernard at Macquarie University, Ramson at the ANU. The 1960s saw several important studies: Ramson's *Australian English*; revised editions of Baker's *The Australian Language* (1966) and Mitchell's *The Pronunciation of English in Australia* (1966, with Delbridge, who earlier collaborated on *The Speech of Australian Adolescents*, (1965)); *The English Language in Australia and New Zealand* (1966) by G.W. Turner, who like several other scholars of Australian English (Ramson, Baker, Grahame Johnston) was originally from NZ; and studies of migrant varieties of Australian English, e.g. Michael Clyne's *Transference and Triggering* (1967), Aboriginal languages, and Australian place names.

Research has continued in the 1970s and 1980s, although the last decade has been probably more notable for the emergence (as well as the dictionaries of Australianisms already mentioned) of general Australian English dictionaries, i.e. dictionaries which give due weighting both to Australianisms and to the standard English basis of Australian English. Before 1976 general dictionaries used in Australia were predominantly English or American ones such as the various *Oxford* and *Webster's*, although editions with a supplement of Australasian words were published periodically. The first of these was Joshua Lake's dictionary of Australasian words, published in the Australasian edition of *Webster's International Dictionary of the English Language* (1898) and also in the separately published *The Australasian Supplement to Webster's International Dictionary* (1898). Later supplements include Mitchell's 'A Supplement of Australian Words' in a 1952 edition of *Chambers' Shorter English Dictionary*, R.W. Burchfield's 'A Supplement of Australian and New Zealand Words' in the 1969 edition of *The Pocket Oxford Dictionary of Current English*, and George Mackaness's 'A Selective Dictionary of Australian & New Zealand Words and Phrases' in several Collins dictionaries, including *Collins New English Dictionary* (1956), ed. Alexander H. Irvine. Just as Lake's supplement was incorporated into the body of *Webster's*, so many other general dictionaries without Australian supplements have included Australian words, e.g. the *Oxford English Dictionary*. 1976, however, saw the publication of both the *Heinemann Australian Dictionary*, compiled in conjunction with a team at La Trobe University with all words 'written in standard Australian' but limited in its usefulness and the far more important *Australian Pocket Oxford Dictionary*. Edited by Grahame Johnston, the *Australian Pocket Oxford* was based on the 1969 *Pocket Oxford Dictionary of Current English*, but with each entry 'scrutinized for its application to Australian conditions' it went much further than previous English dictionaries of comparable size in covering Australian vocabulary, idiom and, to a lesser extent, pronunciation. In 1979 a new *Collins Dictionary of the English Language* was published in an 'Australian edition', with introductory material on Australian English by G.A. Wilkes. Although it includes Australian words and usages it is an international dictionary, with an identical word list for the Australian, American, English and other editions; its offshoots, however, the *Gem* and the *Pocket* (both 1981, edited by W.A. Krebs) and the *Concise* (1982, edited by Krebs and Wilkes) are 'Australianized' in a comparable way to the *Australian Pocket Oxford*. Finally, there is the monumental *Macquarie Dictionary* (1981), prepared at Macquarie University with Arthur Delbridge as editor-in-chief; modified from the *Encyclopedic World Dictionary* it in turn has been the parent dictionary for the *Concise* (ed. David Blair), *Budget, Pocket* (1982) and *Handy* (1983, ed. Ramson) *Macquarie*. The *Macquarie Dictionary* goes much further than its immediate predecessors in the precedence it gives to Australian pronunciation and definitions. Thus the 'i' and 'y' sounds in 'capacity' are rendered respectively as the neutral vowel and to rhyme with 'sea' in the *Macquarie*; in the *Collins* and the *Australian Pocket Oxford* the international or more standard English 'I' (as in 'sit') is given for both. Similarly, a special Australian usage of a word is given precedence over a special British or American usage, as in 'lay-by' or 'colonial'. Reviews of the *Macquarie* have welcomed the comprehensiveness of its coverage of Australian idiom and vocabulary, although its dropping of such labels as 'Aust.' means, paradoxically, that its readers have no way of knowing which of its words are Australianisms.

Australian Facts and Prospects, see **HORNE, R.H.**

Australian Girl, An, a novel by Catherine Martin (q.v.), was published anonymously in 1890, although the 1894 edition used Martin's pseudonym, 'Mrs Alick MacLeod'. Stella Courtland, an exceptionally well-educated and spirited girl of independent attitudes, is the youngest member of a large, prosperous and happy family. With her deeply-religious widowed mother, she lives on one of the family's properties, Fairacre, in South Australia. Stella's brothers and sisters look forward to marriage as an agreeable destiny, but Stella is far from sanguine about the institution; she has similar, strong ideas about most of the conventional, religious attitudes professed by their neighbours. Fascinated by the life of the Aborigines, sensitive to the sufferings of the rural poor and drawn by the beauties of the bush, she prefers the natural pleasures of station life to the trivial pursuits of the city. Her doubts about marriage are reinforced by the misfortunes of her friend Cicely Mowbray, who has left her alcoholic husband, and contribute to her reluctance to marry Edward Ritchie, a childhood friend who has passionately courted her for several years. Ritchie, a well-connected squatter, has one sister, Laurette, a social climber whose ambitions have been furthered to some extent by her marriage to a dissolute member of the British aristocracy, the Hon. Talbot Tareling. Aware that she feels only a mild affection for Ritchie, Stella is further alienated from him by his inability to share her intellectual interests. At times, however, she feels that it is her inevitable destiny to be his wife. The engagement of her clergyman brother, Cuthbert, appears to threaten one of her closest relationships and to strengthen the likelihood of her own marriage. Meanwhile her aspirations for a real friendship with a member of the opposite sex have been encouraged by a brief meeting with Anselm Langdale, an English doctor with German connections and a man 'devoted to ideas and not jostled up with the meanness of ordinary life'. During a visit to her brother's station in Victoria, she meets Langdale again, and forms a close friendship with him which deepens into love. Langdale is suddenly recalled to England, but before he leaves they become informally engaged. Prevented by circumstances from telling Stella of his previous disastrous marriage and his wife's death, Langdale leaves a letter containing the facts of the past with Laurette in Melbourne. Intent on furthering her brother's desires, since in this way she solves some of her financial difficulties, Laurette conceals the fact of Langdale's visit, partly destroys his letter and inserts a false one implying that his wife is still alive. Anguished by the news Stella agrees to marry Ritchie but discovers shortly afterwards to her horror and disgust that he is an alcoholic. They visit Europe where Stella meets Anselm again and learns the truth. She becomes ill, falling into a mental apathy that is close to insanity, but recovers with Anselm's moral support. Tempted to renounce her marriage, she undergoes a profound religious experience during a service held by Cardinal Newman, which convinces her that she must set aside her personal happiness and find common cause with suffering humanity.

Australian Highway, the monthly journal of the Workers' Educational Association of Australia, was published in Sydney 1919–69; it included literary articles, sketches, short stories and book reviews.

Australian Humanities Research Council, an organization which aimed to promote knowledge in and awareness of the humanities, was formally constituted in 1956, two years after an interim council had been established through, in particular, the efforts of Brian Elliott and A.N. Jeffares of the University of Adelaide. Originally comprising twenty-six members, the Council was enlarged through the regular election of fellows and honorary fellows. One of its first achievements was the survey, *The Humanities in Australia*, published in 1959 under the editorship of A. Grenfell Price. Among its other publications were occasional papers, monographs and a *Report* which was published annually until the Council was replaced by the Australian Academy of the Humanities (q.v.) in 1969.

Australian Journal (weekly 1865–69, monthly 1869–1962), originating in Melbourne and published for much of its life by A.H. Massina & Company, was one of the few Australian magazines to satisfy popular taste for a prolonged period. During the editorship of Marcus Clarke (1870–71) it announced a policy of publishing only original fiction set in the colonies or which treated colonial life or subjects of colonial interest. Best-known for its serialization (1870–72) of the original version of Marcus Clarke's *His Natural Life*, of *Chidiock Tichbourne* (1874–75), and of Charles de Boos's *Fifty Years Ago* (1869–70), it also published works by Charles Harpur, Ada Cambridge, 'Rolf Boldrewood' and James Skipp Borlase. An attractive feature was its profile of 'Australian Characters' such as 'The Shearer', 'The Stockman', 'The Bullock Driver' and so on during the 1860s.

Australian Journalists' Association (AJA) was formed in Melbourne in 1910. Before then there had been organizations of journalists in most capital cities and some provincial centres,

e.g. the Victorian Reporters Association (formed 1889), the Bendigo Press Association (1901), the Melbourne Press Bond (1906), and the NSW Institute of Journalists (1907), but most of these were more social than concerned with bettering the conditions of journalists. The driving force behind the establishment of the AJA was B.S. Baxter Cook (1877–1968) who, as a member of the staff of the *Herald* in Melbourne, had reported the passing of the Commonwealth Conciliation and Arbitration Act (1904). He convened the meeting which formed the AJA in order to seek registration under the Act. In 1911 branches were formed in the other States, in most cases from a nucleus of the existing social organizations, though there was some opposition in NSW from the Writers and Artists Union, which T.D. Mutch had formed in 1910 for a similar industrial purpose; Mutch, however, was later active in the AJA. In 1911 registration was granted and in 1917 the first award was granted, based on a system of grading journalists which survives today. The AJA embraces other newspaper workers such as photographers and artists as well as journalists who work for government and in other places outside newspapers. It is a federal organization with eight districts, one in each of the six States and in the ACT, as well as a NSW provincial district. Among the awards it administers are the Montague Grover Award for cadet journalists and, since 1956, the W.G. Walkley Awards; winners of the Walkley Award have included Craig McGregor, Anne Summers and Keith Willey. Apart from B.S. Baxter Cook, foundation members of the AJA included Benjamin Hoare, Percy Lindsay and Sir Keith Murdoch in Victoria, W.A. Woods (Walter Head) in Tasmania and, in NSW, F.J. Broomfield and H.M. Green who helped in the merging of the NSW Institute of Journalists with the AJA and was a delegate to the first national conference in 1912. Another significant figure in Australian literature to have been involved with the AJA was Brian Penton, who fell foul of the organization's code of ethics while editor of the *Daily Telegraph* in the 1940s.

Australian Left Review, published bi-monthly since 1966, superseded the *Communist Review*. A Marxist journal devoted to promoting socialist ideas, it carries political, economic, historical and literary articles as well as book reviews. Its contributors include literary figures e.g. Dorothy Hewett, Judah Waten and Victor Williams.

Australian Legend, The (1958, 2nd edn 1966 and illustrated edn 1978), is an influential account of the Australian national *mystique*, its origins and development, by Russel Ward (q.v.). Ward's analysis of the national self-image as egalitarian, collectivist, anti-authoritarian and practical, and his thesis that the ethos first grew up among the bush workers of the Australian pastoral industry, have been much debated. Writers who have contributed to the debate include Michael Roe in *Meanjin* (1962 and 1973), J.M. Ward in *The Pattern of Australian Culture* (1963), Coral Lansbury in *Arcady in Australia* (1970), Vincent Buckley in *Prospect* (1959), Sean Glynn in *Urbanisation in Australian History 1788–1900* (1970) , Humphrey McQueen in *A New Britannia* (1970), Ronald Lawson in *Brisbane in the 1890s* (1973) and Graeme Davison in *Historical Studies* (1978). Roe and Lansbury, in particular, have offered alternative theses; Roe argues that the legend was derived from European romantic writers of the eighteenth and nineteenth centuries and transferred to Australia by urban, literary and contemplative men; Lansbury maintains that the legend derives from the rural idyll created in English literature of the 1850s by such writers as Charles Dickens and Bulwer-Lytton, and was transferred to non-industrial Australia, where it was taken up by literary Australians. Ward has frequently replied to his critics and has re-examined his thesis in *Historical Studies* (1978).

Australian Legendary Tales, see **PARKER, CATHERINE LANGLOH**

Australian Letters, a SA quarterly founded by Geoffrey Dutton, Max Harris and Bryn Davies, appeared 1957–68. The editorial team consisted of Dutton and Harris throughout its history, Davies 1957–64 and Rosemary Wighton 1963–68. Cosmopolitan and urbane in tone, the periodical was less consciously political than *Overland*, *Meanjin* or *Quadrant*, less literary and academic than *Southerly* or *Australian Literary Studies* and less regional than *Westerly*. One of its distinctive features, a keen interest in art, was reflected in its covers, which carried reproductions of original drawings or paintings specially executed by Australian artists, and in a series of nineteen artist-poet collaborations. These included such striking partnerships as Russell Drysdale and David Campbell, Donald Friend and Douglas Stewart, Leonard French and James McAuley, and Sidney Nolan and Randolph Stow. Contributors to *Australian Letters* also included Patrick White, Randolph Stow, Judith Wright, Barry Oakley, Peter Mathers and Hal Porter. Many of its best contributions are reprinted in the anthology, *The Vital Decade* (1968), selected by Geoffrey Dutton and Max Harris. The annual verse anthol-

ogy, *Verse in Australia* (1958–61), also appeared under its auspices.

Australian Library Journal, the journal of the Library Association of Australia (formerly the Australian Institute of Librarians), began publication in July 1951. A quarterly, the *Australian Library Journal* is the successor to the much earlier and short-lived *Library Record of Australasia* (1901–02), the organ of the then Library Association of Australasia. Although primarily concerned with Library Association matters, the present journal carries information on recent publications in Australian literature.

Australian Literary Studies (ALS), largely the inspiration of James McAuley who played a significant role in the journal's establishment and maintenance until his death in 1976, began publication in 1963 from the University of Tasmania under the editorship of L.T. Hergenhan (q.v.); in 1975 the journal transferred to the University of Queensland. *ALS*, a journal concerned exclusively with Australian literature, has no particular political affiliation or critical canon. Although devoted to both scholarly and critical studies of Australian literature, its chief interest has lain in the field of literary history; its contribution, for example, to the study of Australian literature of the nineteenth century has been considerable. Two valuable features of *ALS* have been its annual bibliography of Australian literature, compiled in the first years by the arduous research of individuals but maintained later from records of the Fryer Library of the University of Queensland; and the section entitled 'Notes and Documents', where small but significant research discoveries, especially in the biographical and bibliographical fields, are recorded.

Australian Literature: A Reference Guide (1977), by Fred Lock and Alan Lawson, is a guide to the reference sources, both Australian and non-Australian, useful for a study of Australian literature. With the E. Morris Miller and F.T. Macartney (qq.v.) bibliographies of Australian literature and other works as its starting points, it includes sections on bibliographical aids, other reference sources such as encyclopaedias and dictionaries, periodicals and guides to periodicals, literary studies, and Australian libraries holding significant Australian literature material. It also has an authors' section which describes and evaluates bibliographical information on some forty Australian authors. The second edition (1980) revises and updates the original, and includes a new section listing organizations concerned with the study of Australian literature.

Australian Literature from Its Beginnings to 1935: A Descriptive and Bibliographical Survey of Books by Australian Authors in Poetry, Drama, Fiction, Criticism and Anthology with Subsidiary Entries to 1938, was compiled by E. Morris Miller (q.v.) and published in two volumes in 1940. Sir John Quick (q.v.), working in collaboration with such researchers as F.J. Broomfield and Miller, had initiated the bibliographical work but it was left unfinished when Quick died in 1932. Miller undertook to complete the task, although in fact he had to begin the work again and revise its plan and scope. Volume I includes a descriptive, chronological survey of poetry to 1935, arranged by State, and followed by a chronological, extensively-annotated bibliography of poetry, with entries to 1938; a chronological survey of drama for the same period, followed by a similar bibliography; and a descriptive survey of novelists and novels until 1899. Volume II includes a continuation of the fiction survey to 1935, followed by a chronological bibliography of fiction; a historical introduction to Australian criticism, followed by an extensive bibliography, which includes work on classical, modern and English as well as Australian literature, biography, essays, travel writings, philology, anthologies and translation; an appendix listing non-Australian authors of novels associated with Australia; and three exhaustive indexes, a subject index to the fiction entries, a general name-subject index and a general index of Australian authors. Although inaccuracies and critical absurdities can be found in *Miller*, as it is familiarly known, it is still an indispensable reference work, especially for the period from 1850 to 1937, and contains a wealth of detailed, general information in its annotations and indexes. In response to a continuing demand, a facsimile edition was published in 1975. A second edition of *Australian Literature*, condensed, revised and rearranged by Frederick T. Macartney (q.v.), was published in 1956. As the full title *Australian Literature: A Bibliography to 1938 by E. Morris Miller, Extended to 1950, Edited with a Historical Outline and Descriptive Commentaries by Frederick T. Macartney* suggests, Macartney extended the work to 1950, wrote his own descriptive commentaries and included an introductory/historical survey. He also replaced Miller's unwieldy systems of arrangement with an alphabetical order, pruned much of the biographical material, corrected some of the inaccuracies and omitted much information that he regarded as non-literary. When some reviewers of the second edition objected to the narrowed scope, Macartney published a trenchant riposte, titled *An Odious Comparison* (1956), in his Bulldozer Booklets series. Most students of Australian literature would probably agree that although *Miller and Macartney* (as the second edition is known) does not replace *Miller*, it is also an indispensable reference work.

Australian Literature Society (ALS), was founded in 1899 in Melbourne (where it remained based), its twin objects being the study of Australian literature and the encouragement of writers in Australia. The president in 1900 was 'Rolf Boldrewood' whose successors included H.G. Turner, Bernard O'Dowd (whose *Poetry Militant* was delivered as a presidential address in 1909), Percival Serle and Victor Kennedy; other prominent writer/members were F.T. Macartney, 'Furnley Maurice', and Nettie Palmer. The Australian Literature Society's Gold Medal (sometimes called the Crouch Gold Medal after its benefactor, Colonel R.A. Crouch) was originally awarded to the best novel published in the previous year, although from 1937 poetry and other literary forms were entitled to consideration. The first winner, in 1928, was Martin Boyd for *The Montforts*; subsequent winners included 'Henry Handel Richardson' (1929), Vance Palmer (1930), Eleanor Dark (1934, 1936), Xavier Herbert (1939), Patrick White (1941, 1955, 1965), R.D. FitzGerald (1938), Randolph Stow (1959), Herz Bergner (1948), Vincent Buckley (1962), John Morrison (1963), Clem Christesen (1966), Alexander Buzo (1972) and Francis Webb (1973). In 1982 arrangements were completed for the incorporation of the Australian Literature Society within the Association for the Study of Australian Literature (q.v.) which now administers and awards the ALS Gold Medal and the new award, the Dr Walter McRae Russell Award (for an outstanding recent work of literary scholarship by a young or unestablished author) named in honour of the president of the Australian Literature Society during the last quarter century of its existence. In 1983 the Gold Medal was awarded under the new arrangement to David Malouf, winner on the last occasion (1974) on which it was awarded. Among the publications of the Australian Literature Society was the magazine *Corroboree* (1921–22).

Australian Literature to 1900: A Guide to Information Sources (1980), compiled by Barry G. Andrews and William H. Wilde, is a bibliographical guide. The first part offers an annotated list of bibliographies and bibliographic guides, reference works, literary history and criticism, Australian English, nineteenth-century journals and anthologies. The second part provides a bibliographical, biographical and critical guide to sixty-six individual nineteenth-century Australian writers. The third part is a guide to selected non-fiction prose, including writings on exploration, transportation, travel and description, history and biography, and literary and theatrical autobiographies and reminiscences. Its companion volumes are *Modern Australian Poetry, 1920–1970* (1979) by Herbert C. Jaffa and *Modern Australian Prose* (1980) by A. Grove Day.

Australian Little Magazines, 1923–1954 (1964), by John Tregenza, lists forty-nine periodicals with details of their frequency of publication, their usual content, their editors and chief contributors.

Australian Magazine, the first Australian periodical, was published monthly 1821–22. Edited by Ralph Mansfield (q.v.) and published first by George Howe and then by his son Robert, the *Australian Magazine* carried local news, articles on religious topics, fiction and poetry. Other magazines to bear this title appeared in 1835, 1838, 1859 and 1899; the 1899 *Australian Magazine* was edited by A.W. Jose and included among its contributors C.J. Brennan, J. le Gay Brereton and Roderic Quinn.

Australian Mercury was a journal conducted by P.R. Stephensen (q.v.) which ran for one issue, that of July 1935. Over half the issue was devoted to an editorial essay which became the first part of Stephensen's influential *The Foundations of Culture in Australia* (q.v., 1936).

Australian Monthly Magazine was published 1865 to August 1867 under its original title, then changed to the *Colonial Monthly*, its title until its demise in 1870. It was owned for a time, and edited (1867–69), by Marcus Clarke; in its pages are some of Clarke's first contributions to Australian literary journalism. Strongly nationalist in sentiment (although less so than the *Australian Journal*) the *Australian Monthly* carried evaluative articles on Australian writing, e.g. 'Australian Fiction' (March 1866) and 'National Poetry' (August 1867). Contributors included H.G. Turner, G.G. McCrae, Adam Lindsay Gordon and Henry Kendall.

Australian National Bibliography, a publication of the National Library of Australia, Canberra, commenced in January 1961, replacing the *Annual Catalogue of Australian Publications* published 1937–61, covering 1936–60. Its rate of publication has varied, as has its arrangement, but it currently comprises three parts (Classified Sequence; Author, Title and Series Index; and Subject Index) and lists books and pamphlets published in Australia within the preceding year. Overseas publications by Australians or with Australian subject content

are included. It is issued twice monthly as a classified list with an author and title index. The second issue of each month is published as a cumulation with a subject index. Further cumulations are published on microfiche for the periods January-April, January-August and January-December.

Australian Natives' Association, founded in Melbourne in 1871, had the twin aims of promoting the welfare and advancement of Australia and providing mutual aid for its members. It stemmed from the earlier Victorian Natives' Society and branches of the Association now operate in all Australian States. Among its vigorously-pursued causes were Federation, women's suffrage, the one man–one vote principle, a minimum wage, an adequate Australian defence capability, conservation of natural resources, Aboriginal welfare and a policy of 'buy Australian-made'. Well-known members of the Association included Sir Edmund Barton, Alfred Deakin and Sir Robert Menzies. The ANA Literature Award (first awarded 1978) is made annually for a work of sustained quality and distinction with an Australian theme; similar awards are made in art and science and poetry. ANA conducts regular poetry, short-story and essay competitions in the various States. Its publications have included the *Australian Native* (1882–83), the *National Australian* (1885–86), the *Australian* (1887–96) and *Advance Australia* (1897–1919). The *ANA Journal* has been its organ in NSW, *Our Australia* and *Cooee* in Queensland, *Our Australia* in SA, *ANA Advocate* in WA and *Anapress* in Victoria. It shows its interest in Australian writers in many other ways, e.g. it provides for the maintenance of Adam Lindsay Gordon's grave in Brighton Cemetery, Melbourne. Brian Fitzpatrick published *Australian Natives' Association 1871–1961* (1961), B.J. Kelleher, *Australian Natives' Association* (1963) and J.E. Menadue, *A Centenary History of the Australian Natives' Association 1871–1971* (1971).

Australian New Writing, anthologies of prose and verse, were issued annually from 1943 to 1946. Involved in editing the anthologies were Katharine Susannah Prichard, George Farwell, Bernard Smith and Ken Levis.

Australian Outlook, the journal of the Australian Institute of International Affairs, began publication (originally quarterly, then three times a year) in 1947. It superseded the *Austral-Asiatic Bulletin* which had appeared bimonthly 1937–42. Its main focus is socio-political and its area of interest is primarily Australasia and South-East Asia. It carries book reviews and some articles of literary and cultural interest.

Australian Performing Group (APG) was a company formed from actors' workshops at Melbourne's La Mama theatre in the late 1960s. In 1970 the Group established itself at Carlton, an inner suburb of Melbourne, in an old building which had once housed a pram factory and which became known as the Pram Factory theatre. Generally radical and anti-establishment politically and socially, the Group was opposed to 'conventional, conservative and commercial theatre', which it saw as catering for 'middle-brow, middle-class and middle-aged tastes'. Plays which found a ready acceptance by the Group were generally free-wheeling, radical, physically expressive, verbally uninhibited and Australian in origin and content; some contemporary international plays and some classics were, however, also performed. At first an informal grouping, the APG became more structured in a legal sense after 1972, although it continued to be a democratic co-operative in all aspects of administration and production. It later received some sponsorship from the Australia Council and the Victorian Ministry for the Arts. One of the focal points of the 1970s resurgence in Australian drama, the APG gave strong encouragement to the work of such playwrights as Jack Hibberd, Barry Oakley, John Romeril, John Timlin, David Williamson, Barry Dickins and Phil Motherwell, and to such actors as Graeme Blundell, Max Gillies, Bill Garner and Evelyn Krape. Well-known plays which were first produced by the Group include David Williamson's *The Removalists* and *Don's Party*, Jack Hibberd's *White with Wire Wheels* and *A Stretch of the Imagination*, Barry Oakley's *The Feet of Daniel Mannix* and 'Beware of Imitations', John Romeril's 'The Golden Holden Show', *Chicago, Chicago* and *I Don't Know Who to Feel Sorry For*. Several vaudeville-type shows were worked up by the Group as a whole, often focusing on a general theme such as uranium mining, unemployment and the status of women; 'Betty Can Jump' was one of the most striking of the feminist plays produced by the Women's Group and popular entertainments developed by the Group as a whole included 'The Hills Family Show', 'Soapbox Circus', 'Waltzing Matilda', 'Circus Oz' and 'How Grey Was My Nurse'. The Group also freqently played a creative role in workshopping the plays of authors, John Romeril's in particular undergoing numerous adaptations inspired by the actors. In 1980, the Pram Factory was sold by the lessees of the building and the APG disbanded in 1981; its last production was John Blay's 'The Bed Bug Celebration' in September 1981.

Australian Poetry was a series of annual anthologies of Australian poetry published by Angus & Robertson 1941–73. Distinguished writers and critics were invited to edit the anthologies, which contained the individual editor's choice of the outstanding Australian poetry published in the previous year. The series began with *Australian Poetry 1941*, edited by Douglas Stewart. Ensuing volumes were: R.D. FitzGerald (1942), H.M. Green (1943), R.G. Howarth (1944), Kenneth Slessor (1945), T. Inglis Moore (1946), Frederick T. Macartney (1947), Judith Wright (1948), Rosemary Dobson (1949–50), Kenneth Mackenzie (1951–52), Nan MacDonald (1953), Ronald McCuaig (1954), James McAuley (1955), A.A. Phillips (1956), Hal Porter (1957), Vincent Buckley (1958), Nancy Keesing (1959), A.D. Hope (1960), Leonie Kramer (1961), Geoffrey Dutton (1962), G.A. Wilkes (1963), Randolph Stow (1964), John Thompson (1965), David Campbell (1966), Max Harris (1967), Dorothy Auchterlonie (1968), Vivian Smith (1969), Rodney Hall (1970), Chris Wallace-Crabbe (1971), R.F. Brissenden (1972), J.M. Couper (1973).

Australian Poetry Now (1970), an anthology of Australian poetry selected largely from the late 1960s, was edited with an explanatory preface by Thomas Shapcott (q.v.). The anthology is chronologically arranged but since its purpose and emphasis are 'discovery', the older and/or better-known poets, such as Bruce Beaver, Bruce Dawe, Chris Wallace-Crabbe, Les Murray and Geoffrey Lehmann are given only token representation. The anthology is, in the main, representative of 'the New Australian Poetry' (q.v.) and gives a selection of poems that were (at the time of publication) experimental in form and theme.

Australian Public Affairs Information Service: A Subject Index to Current Literature (APAIS) (1945–   ), issued monthly except December and now cumulated annually, lists Australian periodical literature on the social sciences and the humanities, and indexes feature articles in major Australian newspapers.

Australian Quarterly, published since 1935 by the Australian Institute of Political Science, began in March 1929 under the auspices of the Constitutional Association of NSW. It carries a wide range of articles on Australian politics, international relations, literature, education, art and drama.

Australian Rip Van Winkle and Other Pieces, An, a sketch-book imitation of Washington Irving by William Gosse Hay and published in 1921, comprises ten stories; of these, three focus on the explorations of Thomas Livingstone Mitchell, three (including the title story) deal with other Australian subjects, and three deal with significant women in English history, Lady Hamilton, Mary Stuart, and Jonathan Swift's Stella.

Australian Rules, the only football game unique to Australia, is the dominant code in Victoria, Tasmania, SA and WA but takes second place to Rugby League in NSW and Queensland, though it has adherents there as well. A spectacular, fast-moving game played with an oval ball between teams of eighteen men, it features both kicking and handling. If Australian Rules differs from soccer (eleven a side) in allowing the ball to be handled, the essential difference between it and Rugby League (thirteen a side) and Rugby Union (fifteen a side) is that the last are games based on the ball being progressed by being carried by players and passed between them, whereas the ball is mainly progressed in Australian Rules by teammates kicking it to each other. Among other significant differences, apart from scoring methods, is the absence of an 'offside' rule in Australian Rules.

Australian Rules has contributed richly to the lexicon of Australian English (q.v.) and numerous Australian writers have written about the game, notably Bruce Dawe in his poem 'Life-Cycle' (q.v.), Alan Hopgood and David Williamson in their plays *And the Big Men Fly* (1969) and *The Club* (1978), and Barry Oakley in his novel *A Salute to the Great McCarthy* (1970). Leonie Sandercock and Ian Turner have written a study of Australian Rules, *Up Where Cazaly? The Great Australian Game* (1981); the title derives from the phrase, 'Up there Cazaly' which greeted the high leaps to mark (catch) the ball of a famous Australian Rules player, Roy Cazaly. The phrase became a rallying call for Australian soldiers during the Second World War and became entrenched in the idiom of Australian English.

Australian Sketch Book, The see MARTIN, Sir JAMES

Australian Society of Authors (ASA) was founded in 1963 to promote and protect the professional interests of creators of literary, dramatic or musical material, i.e. all those who in Australia or NZ write for publication as opposed to performance. The Society has published *The Australian and New Zealand Writers Handbook* (1975) and *Australian Book Contracts* (1983) by Barbara Jefferis. Its journal is the *Australian Author* (q.v.).

'Australian Sunrise, The', see CUTHBERTSON, JAMES LISTER

Australian Town and Country Journal, also known as the *Town and Country Journal*, was published 1870–1919. Its editors included Samuel Bennett (1870–79), Walter J. Jeffery (1893–1906) and A.B. Paterson (1907–08). The weekly companion of the *Evening News* it provided a constant publication outlet for Australian writers for half a century. Among its best-known contributors were Henry Kendall, 'Louis' Becke, Ethel Turner, Henry Lawson and 'Rolf Boldrewood'.

Australian Tradition, the journal of the Folk Lore Society of Victoria (founded 1955, its first president being Alan Marshall) and the Victorian Bush (later Folk) Music Club, began publication in 1960 as a roneoed bulletin under the title of *Gumsuckers' Gazette*. It became increasingly sophisticated and in 1964 changed its name to *Australian Tradition*; over the next decade it was published mainly three times a year, the final issue (December 1975) consisting of an index to the journal under both titles. Edited by the folklorist Wendy Lowenstein, *Australian Tradition* reflected the revival of interest in Australian folk-song and ballad (q.v.) which gathered pace in the 1950s. It carried the words and music of songs, reports of the activities of folk-music and folklore societies, recitations, reminiscences, book and record reviews, and articles or notes on the provenance and transmission of songs, on Australian idiom, and on other aspects of the Australian folk tradition. Contributors included folklorists such as John Meredith, Bill Wannan, Alan Scott, Edgar Waters and Wendy Lowenstein; among the Australian authors whose lyrics became songs published in *Australian Tradition* are Henry Lawson and Dorothy Hewett.

Australian Tradition: Studies in a Colonial Culture, The (1958, revised 1966) is a significant collection of essays and commentaries, mainly on Australian writing, by A.A. Phillips (q.v.). The 1958 edition includes essays on Henry Lawson and Joseph Furphy as well as Phillips's well-known 'The Cultural Cringe' (q.v.). The revised 1966 edition added 'Lawson Revisited', 'The Short Stories of Vance Palmer', and 'Barbara Baynton and the Dissidence of the Nineties', essays which reflect Phillips's response to some of the new understandings and perspectives of Australian literature that had arisen during the period between the editions. A 1980 reissue of the 1966 edition includes an introduction by H.P. Heseltine, which appraises Phillips's critical stance on Australian literature, especially in the light of the objections that arose from the late 1950s onwards against the nationalist-democratic theories of the origin and development of Australian literature advanced by Phillips, Vance Palmer and others. Such theories are, as Heseltine states, 'based on the translation of the bush ethos into the social-democratic code of mateship, and the effort to express that code in an adequate aesthetic form'.

Australian/Vogel National Literary Award, offered annually since 1980, is awarded to the writer (under 35) of the best original manuscript of fiction, Australian history or biography, each year. Winners of the award have been Paul Radley for *Jack Rivers and Me* in 1980, Tim Winton for *An Open Swimmer* and Chris Matthews for *Al Jazzar* (jointly) in 1981, Brian Castro for 'Solitude' and Nigel Krauth for 'The Jolly Swagman Affair' (jointly) in 1982, and Jenny Summerville for *Shields of Trell* in 1983.

Australian Week-End Review, a fortnightly review of books originating from Melbourne under the editorial direction of G.B. Allan and Bertram Higgins, ran for twenty-one issues 1950–51.

Australian Women's Weekly, the concept of G.W. (George) Warnecke and owned initially by Frank Packer and E.G. Theodore, first appeared 8 June 1933 in Sydney. Warnecke, the *Weekly*'s foundation editor, remained with it until 1939; he was followed by a succession of women editors, Alice Jackson, Esme Fenton, Dorothy Drain, Ita Buttrose and Dawn Swain. Committed to 'an unswerving Australian outlook' so that it would be welcome 'in every Australian home from the outback to the industrial suburbs' the *Weekly* has maintained a remarkably high circulation. It spread to Victoria (September 1933), Queensland (October 1933), SA (March 1934), Tasmania (June 1935) and WA (October 1936). Although the *Weekly* has made some attempt to debate women's issues it has always emphasized the fulfilment to be gained from marriage and motherhood and it was quick to follow government policy on the replacement of women by men in the work-force after the Second World War. Its notable women journalists included (in addition to the editors named) Etta Cowen, Saide Parker, Ruth Preddey, Phyllis Duncan-Brown, Jessie Tait, Louise Mack, Jean Williamson, Kay Keavney, Anne Matheson, Mary Hordern and Adele Shelton Smith. Reg-

ular literary features of the *Weekly* have included book, film and drama reviews, lift-out fiction supplements, short fiction, serials, and poetry. Profusely illustrated, the *Weekly* has been well-served by artists such as W.E. Pidgeon ('WEP'), Virgil Reilly and Wynne W. Davies; its most notable humorists have been L.W. (Lennie) Lower and Ross Campbell; and its most celebrated and enduring comic strip has been 'Mandrake the Magician'. For many years the *Weekly* made no definite attempt to encourage Australian writing; its 'full-length, lift-out' novel supplements (some 250 condensed novels), which were a regular feature from 1934 to 1940, were mostly imported English light romances, as were its regularly-appearing short stories and serials. Frank Dalby Davison's *Forever Morning* and Henrietta Drake-Brockman's *The Disquieting Sex* were two Australian exceptions. Notable among its poetry contributors was Dame Mary Gilmore; she provided the *Weekly* with many poems, two of note during the Second World War being the patriotic pieces 'No Foe Shall Gather Our Harvest' and 'Singapore'. Belatedly recognizing the Australian writer, the *Weekly* conducted a fiction competition in 1942; it received more than 1000 manuscripts. In 1975 the familiar large-size *Weekly* was replaced by a smaller, more conventional size; in 1982 it belied, but kept, its traditional title, becoming a monthly publication. Denis O'Brien compiled the lively biography, *The Weekly*, in 1982.

Australian Worker, the longest-running Australian labour movement newspaper, grew out of the *Hummer*, which was founded in 1891 by Arthur Rae and W.W. Head as the weekly organ of the Wagga branch of the Amalgamated Shearers Union. In 1892 the *Hummer* changed its name to the *Worker* and became the NSW edition of the well-established Brisbane *Worker*. The following year it moved to Sydney and resumed an independent existence; remaining under the control of the Almalgamated Shearers Union (later the Australian Workers' Union), it changed its name to the *Australian Worker* (the present title) in 1913 and incorporated other labour newspapers including the *Australian Workman* in 1897 and the *Westralian Worker* in 1913. A weekly for most of its life, the *Australian Worker* has had a number of prominent Australian writers on its staff: William Lane (1900), E.J. Brady (1904–05), Henry Boote (1914–43) and Frank Moorhouse were all editors; Mary Gilmore ran its women's page from 1908 to 1931; and T.D. Mutch and R.J. Cassidy were prominent staff writers before the Second World War. Its most famous contributor during the 1890s (see Nineties) was Henry Lawson, who had some of his best work published there and moved from contributor to provincial editor and then briefly to salaried writer. Later contributors included Roderic Quinn and John Shaw Neilson.

Australian Workman was a Sydney labour movement newspaper which was established during the great maritime strike of 1890 and ran, mainly as a weekly, until 1897; for most of that time it was the official organ of the Trades and Labour Council. As well as labour news, it published short stories, serial fiction and poetry, sometimes reprinted from other sources (e.g. work by Henry Kendall). E.J. Brady was its editor in 1892, and was succeeded by two other literary figures, 'Price Warung' in 1893 and (Sir) Frank Fox in 1893–95.

Australian Writers (1896), by Desmond Byrne, deplores in its introduction the lack of enthusiasm by readers and critics for colonial writing, and provides analytical essays on Marcus Clarke, Henry Kingsley, Ada Cambridge, Adam Lindsay Gordon, 'Rolf Boldrewood', Rosa Praed and Jessie Couvreur.

Australian Writers and Their Work, a series published by Lansdowne Press until taken over by Oxford University Press in 1966, was initially edited by Geoffrey Dutton and later by Grahame Johnston (qq.v.). The series was designed to offer a concise (some fifty pages) but informative introduction to the main Australian writers.

Australian Writers Guild, founded in Sydney in 1961 as a 'trade union for script writers' of television, radio, screen and stage, publishes a monthly journal, *Viewpoint*, and presents Awgie Awards annually to members for the best scripts for film, stage, radio and television.

Australian Writers Speak (1942) is a booklet of nine scripts prepared for the ABC's series 'Literature and Life in Australia' by the Fellowship of Australian Writers (FAW, q.v.). Topics discussed during this formative period of Australian literary development included 'Our Literature' by Marjorie Barnard, the relationship between author and reader by Vance and Nettie Palmer, the working-class element in Australian literature by Jean Devanny, the difficulties and achievements of Australian dramatists by Leslie Rees, and the impact of Australian writers on the national life by Katharine Susannah Prichard and Gavin Casey. There were also attempts to answer the questions 'What is Literature?' by Frank Dalby Davison and 'Need Australian Writers Write about Australia?' by Norman Bartlett.

Australiana Facsimile Editions (AFE) and **South Australiana Facsimile Editions** (SAFE) were two historical facsimile series published by the Libraries Board of SA. The AFE series included seventy-four titles numbered 1-206 (with many numbers not used) and published 1962–79; among the titles published were journals of explorers (e.g. Matthew Flinders, James Cook, John Oxley, E.J. Eyre, Ludwig Leichhardt), descriptive and historical works (e.g. by David Collins, Raffaello Carboni, W.B. Ullathorne) and some SA titles (e.g. works by George French Angas and Catherine Helen Spence). The SAFE series ran 1962–69, though most of its sixty-five titles (nos 1-91, with numbers not used) were published in 1962; it included works on the foundation and early settlement of SA, exploration, local history, European-Aboriginal contact, almanacs and other SA material.

Australians, The, see ADAMS, FRANCIS

Australia's Writers (1980), by Graeme Kinross Smith, is an illustrated guide to the lives and work of fifty-four Australian or quasi-Australian writers. The book begins with Captain Arthur Phillip and Watkin Tench of the First Fleet and includes the most notable colonial writers, Alexander Harris, Charles Harpur, Adam Lindsay Gordon, Henry Kendall, 'Rolf Boldrewood' and Marcus Clarke. From the nationalist-radical 1890s (*see* Nineties) and later, Joseph Furphy, Henry Lawson, A.B. Paterson and Bernard O'Dowd are included. The twentieth century is represented by Miles Franklin, Martin Boyd, Kenneth Slessor, Xavier Herbert, A.D. Hope, Douglas Stewart, Judith Wright and others.

'AUSTRALIE', see MANNING, EMILY

Austrovert, edited by B.W. Muirden, was published irregularly (ten numbers) 1950–53. Planned as 'a half-way mark' between academic and popular discussion of writers, *Austrovert* ran a series of critical and biographical articles on established Australian authors. A selection of poetry from its pages was published as *Austroverse* (1952).

Awards, see **Literary Awards**

Awful Australian, The (1911), by Valerie Desmond, is an amusing and critical account of Australia from an early twentieth-century perspective. It contains chapters such as 'The Australians at Shirk' and 'The Australian's Parasitical Tendencies'. A response was *The Real Australian* (1912) by Malcolm C. Donald.

Awgie Awards, see **Australian Writers Guild**

Ayers Rock, a giant monolith, orange-brown in colour, rises to a height of 335 metres out of the plains some forty kilometres south of Lake Amadeus in the south-west of the Northern Territory. Sacred to Aborigines who have left rock paintings in its caves, Ayers Rock (named 'Uluru' by the Aborigines) is associated with their legends of the Dreaming. First recorded in 1872 by explorer Ernest Giles but named by William Gosse, the first white man to visit it, in honour of Sir Henry Ayers, then premier of South Australia, the Rock has been more important in Australian art than in literature. W.E. 'Bill' Harney, at one time curator of the Ayers Rock reservation, told the Aboriginal story of the rock in his *Tales from the Aborigines* (1959). C.P. Mountford (q.v.) wrote *Ayers Rock* (1965), which examines the association of the monolith with Aboriginal myth and art. Ayers Rock was officially handed back to the Aborigines by the federal government in 1983.

B

Back o' Bourke, see **Bourke**

Back to Bool Bool, see **'BRENT OF BIN BIN'**

Backblock Ballads, see **DENNIS, C.J.**

'Backblocks Shearer, The' is an Australian folk-song in which a shearer, identified in the last verse as 'Widgigoweera Joe' (an alternative title for the song), first laments that he has never become a 'gun' shearer and then vows to improve his technique until he wins a shearing contest at a country show. The concluding lines of the song,

> 'Instead of Deeming, you will hear
> Of Widgigoweera Joe',

may date the composition of the song to around 1892, when the murderer Frederick Deeming was much in the news. An informant of Russel Ward has suggested that the song was written by a shearer named Bill Tulley at Howlong station in the Riverina.

A similar, but more characteristically confident, shearer's song is 'The Ryebuck Shearer'. In this song the singer demonstrates through several verses his superiority to his fellow shearers and the extent to which he is a 'ryebuck' (i.e. gun or masterful) shearer.

BACKHOUSE, ELIZABETH (1917–), born Northam, WA, served in the WAAAF in the Second World War and then went to England, where she was a scriptwriter with Korda Films. She returned to Australia in 1951. Her publications include the novels, *In Our Hands* (1942), *The Sky Has Its Clouds* (1944), *Leaves in The Wind* (1946), *Day Will Break* (1945), *The Web Of Shadows* (1960) and *The Night Has Eyes* (1961). She has also written stage plays (e.g. 'The Thin Line' produced in 1968, and 'Mirage' produced in 1972), scenarios for ballets, detective novels, and a television feature, 'The Olive Tree', which has been shown in Australia and the USA.

BACKHOUSE, JAMES (1794–1869), born Durham, England, arrived at Hobart Town in 1832 as a Quaker missionary with a particular interest in the welfare of the convicts. From 1832 to 1838, in company with George Washington Walker, he evangelized through Tasmania, NSW and the Moreton Bay district. His experiences are recorded in *A Narrative of a Visit to the Australian Colonies* (1843), a work which contains considerable information on the convicts and Aborigines and on the botany of the colonies. Extracts from his letters from Van Diemen's Land and NSW were published in London in pamphlet form (1838-41) by the Society of Friends. Sarah Backhouse wrote *Memoir of James Backhouse* (1870).

BADHAM, CHARLES (1813–84), born Shropshire, England, and renowned as one of the leading Greek scholars of his day in Europe, became professor of classics at the University of Sydney in 1867. Intensely interested in the problems of tertiary education in the colony, Badham strongly espoused the introduction of evening classes at the University of Sydney. He was the first president of the board of trustees of the Free Public Library, later the Public Library of NSW. An important textual critic, he wrote widely on Plato and Euripides. His

Speeches and Lectures Delivered in Australia were published in 1890 through subscriptions by former students and other admirers.

Bagman's Gazette was an imaginary newspaper circulating among the 'bagmen' of the Australian outback. It was a rich source of rumour and gossip, the expression 'According to the Bagman's Gazette' probably casting doubt on the accuracy of the information being supplied. 'The Drover's Guide' is the equivalent for the droving fraternity. Henry Lawson tends to use the word 'bagman' to mean a commercial traveller, but a bagman was usually a mounted itinerant, with anything from one to a dozen horses. Sometimes shearer, sometimes drover or even general rouseabout, he often concealed a 'cutter' (a racehorse in disguise) among his horses and won an occasional bet from unsuspecting station workers. Tom Ronan's autobiography (1966) is titled *Once There Was a Bagman*.

BAIL, MURRAY (1941–), born Adelaide, has lived in a variety of countries including India (1968–70) and England and Europe (1970–74); in London he wrote for the journals *Transatlantic Review* and the *Times Literary Supplement*. In 1975 he published *Contemporary Portraits and Other Stories,* short fiction that varies between the experimental and the conventional and is, in the main, sardonic and dominated by the strain of absurdity that, for Bail, characterizes contemporary life. His story 'The Drover's Wife', prefaced by an insert of Russell Drysdale's painting of the same name, treads satirically on hallowed Henry Lawson ground; his most effective pieces, however, are the surrealistic 'Cul de Sac' and 'Paradise', and some sections of the 'Heubler' sequence beginning 'At least one person who . . .'. *Homesickness,* a novel published in 1980, won the National Book Council Award and the *Age* Book of the Year Award. It relates the experiences of thirteen Australians who, travelling in that modern phenomenon the 'package tour' (itself a target for satire), visit Africa, England, Ecuador, New York and Moscow. The tourists include a zoologist; an oversexed dentist and his none–too–accommodating wife; a woman and her blind husband; another colourless couple; two fairly thoughtful, unattached males; a youngish male 'ocker'; a wealthy spinster and two actresses, one ageing, the other younger and more naive. There is the usual interaction among individuals within the group – petty jealousies, attempts to impress and an occasional outburst of furtive sex – but the group develops an interesting collective personality that comes to dominate the novel. Tourism, a contemporary mode of perception, compart-

mentalizes the world into a succession of museums. The museums (interpreted satirically or as part of the Absurd) include the Museu (the 'm' had fallen off the sign in a windstorm) of Handicrafts in Africa which contains old lawnmowers, used toothpaste tubes, and a soda-water syphon; the Corrugated Iron Museum of Yorkshire; a Museum of Legs in Quito; and Central Park in New York (a giant zoo) where the tourists watch from a spectator gallery such behavioural patterns as muggings and pack rapes. The group, too, exhibits certain behaviour patterns characteristic of Australians and these are set in ironic contrast with the cosmopolis through which they haphazardly wander. Bail, who is interested in painting and is a trustee of the Australian National Gallery, has written a monograph (1981) on the artist, Ian Fairweather.

BAILEY, BERT (1868–1939), was the actor who became famous for his portrayal of Dad, the patriarch of the Rudd family (q.v.), on stage and screen. Born in Auckland, NZ, Bailey entered vaudeville in the 1880s and had a notable success when he co-authored with Edmund Duggan the bush melodrama, 'The Squatter's Daughter' (staged 1907), in which there is a portrait of Ben Hall and his gang. Versions of the melodrama were filmed in 1910 and 1933; it also forms the basis of a novel by Hilda Bridges in 1922. In 1912 Bailey and Duggan presented 'On Our Selection' (q.v.), their adaptation of the stories of 'Steele Rudd' (q.v.). Remarkably popular, 'On Our Selection' was performed repeatedly until 1929 and was successfully revived in 1979 with additional material by George Whaley. The Bailey-Duggan script of 'On Our Selection' was used in the sound film version of *On Our Selection* (1932), in which Bailey starred. Closely identified with the role of Dad, Bailey was also successful in two plays adapted by 'Steele Rudd' from his books, and made three further films which owed less to 'Rudd' than to Bailey and collaborators such as Duggan and Ken Hall: *Grandad Rudd* (1935), *Dad and Dave Come to Town* (1938) and *Dad Rudd M.P.* (1940). He also produced a stage adaptation of C.J. Dennis's *The Sentimental Bloke* in 1922, taking the part of Ginger Mick.

BAKER, KATE (1861–1953), was born in Ireland, came to Victoria as a child, and was a teacher in the Victorian Department of Education 1881–1913. In 1886 she met Joseph Furphy, with whom she formed a friendship that lasted until Furphy's death in 1912. For the next four decades she was Furphy's 'gallant standard-bearer'; indefatigable in her efforts to promote his works and secure his reputation, she published his poems at her own expense (1916), arranged for the reissue of *Such is Life* (q.v., 1917) and for the first publication in book form of *Rigby's Romance* (1921), addressed literary societies and assembled the material used in Miles Franklin's *Joseph Furphy: The Legend of a Man and His Book* (1944). For her services to Furphy in particular, and to Australian literature in general, she was made OBE in 1937.

BAKER, SIDNEY JAMES (1912–76), born and educated in NZ, became interested in Australasian English when questioned about his own idiom while in England in the late 1930s. Although hampered by multiple sclerosis for most of his last thirty years, he was an enthusiastic pioneer of the study of NZ and Australian English (q.v.), particularly the study of idiom and its relationship to national character and folklore; his several books, which include extensive word lists, have proved invaluable sources for later studies. His major work was *The Australian Language,* first published in 1945 and revised in 1966; a 1953 supplement to the first edition was titled *Australia Speaks.* His other publications include *New Zealand Slang* (1940); *A Popular Dictionary of Australian Slang* (1941); *Australian Pronunciation* (1947); *The Drum: Australian Character and Slang* (1959); a novel, *The Gig* (1958); a study of Matthew Flinders, *My Own Destroyer* (1962); *The Ampol Book of Australiana* (1963); and contributions to encyclopaedias (e.g. the 1958 edition of the *Australian Encyclopaedia),* cultural surveys (e.g. A.L. McLeod's *The Pattern of Australian Culture,* 1963) and dictionaries (e.g. the slang dictionaries of Eric Partridge).

BAKER, 'SNOWY' (REGINALD LESLIE) (1884–1953), born Surry Hills, Sydney, was known as 'Snowy' from childhood because of the colour of his hair. One of Australia's best-known athletes, Baker excelled in swimming, running, Rugby football, cricket, rowing, boxing and horsemanship. He became a film actor, playing roles (1918–20) which featured his athletic prowess, especially his horsemanship. In 1920 he sought to further his film career in America but turned his attention, with conspicuous success, to business ventures in that country. A talented journalist, Baker was a prolific contributor to the Sydney *Evening News* (1908–10), published a book, *General Physical Culture* (1910), and established *Snowy Baker's Magazine,* a monthly that ran 1912–14. In the 1930s he contributed a column to the Sydney sporting paper, the *Referee.*

Balcony, a quarterly journal of literature and the arts, ran for six issues 1965–67. It began under the sponsorship of the Sydney University Arts Seminar Society. Contributors included James McAuley, Rodney Hall, Michael Wilding and Frank Moorhouse. *Balcony* was intended as a counter to the then Leavisite journal, *Melbourne Critical Review.*

BALDERSON, MARGARET (1935–), born Concord, NSW, has interspersed library work with writing children's fiction. Her publications include *When Jays Fly to Barbmo* (1968), which won the Australian Children's Book Council Book of the Year Award, *A Dog Called George* (1975) and *Blue and Gold Day* (1979).

'Ballad of Bloodthirsty Bessie, The', a poem by Ronald McCuaig (q.v.), was first published in the *Bulletin* (19 September 1951) and was later used as the title poem for McCuaig's *The Ballad of Bloodthirsty Bessie and Other Poems* (1961). Sometimes cited as an example of an especially macabre brand of humour, said to be Australian in character, McCuaig's poem tells of the stratagems used by a farmer near Sydney to keep himself in cheap labour and his amorous daughter, Bessie, in lovers. When the exhausted labourers ultimately try to leave, the farmer pushes them off a nearby cliff, at the bottom of which Bessie waits to finish them off with an axe. Some seventeen farmhands end up in graves along the creek. A spying trooper is similarly dispatched and nine investigating soldiers are made drunk by the farmer who pours rum on them and sets them alight. Bessie objects to this wholesale squandering of such valuable amatory material:

> 'Oh, father, I say it is cruel
> Oh, father, I say it's unfair:
> You're using my sweethearts as fuel
> And doing me out of my share.'

She approaches her father menacingly, axe in hand. Thrusting sentimentality sternly behind him, he 'out with a pistol and shot her /Through the heart for the first and last time'.

BALLANTYNE, COLIN (1908–), was born in Adelaide and since the late 1920s has been a strong influence in SA theatre. Actor, producer and playwright, he has produced numerous plays including five major productions for the Adelaide Festival and was instrumental in the establishment of the Adelaide Theatre Group's Sheridan Theatre. Chairman of the SA Theatre Company 1972–78, he has been an active force in the SA division of the Arts Council of Australia and federal president 1974–77. He is also a photographer and has made several documentary films for the federal government. His own plays include *The Ice-*

Cream Cart, a one-act drama about the adjustment of a Turkish couple to Australia, published in *Australian One-Act Plays: Book Two,* ed. Greg Branson (1962); 'Between Gunshots' (1963); 'Harvest'; 'Here Take My Picture'; and 'Pacific Rape', a free verse-drama about Western infiltration into the Pacific, produced in 1970. He was made CMG in 1971.

BALLANTYNE, GINA (1916–), born Adelaide, published several volumes of verse which gave expression to Jindyworobak (q.v.) sentiments, e.g. *Phantom* (1942), *Vision* (1942) and *Vagrant* (1943). She won the C.J. Dennis Memorial Prize in 1942 and edited the 1945 *Jindyworobak Anthology.*

Ballarat, from the Aboriginal 'Balla-arat', meaning 'elbow place', situated some 110 kilometres north-west of Melbourne, is one of Victoria's major provincial cities. The Ballarat area was opened up as a pastoral district in 1837 but, with the influx of population following the discovery of gold in August 1851, a township was surveyed in December of that year. In 1852 the system of deep lead mining exposed 'buried rivers of gold' and Ballarat became Victoria's most active goldfield, with a population of 12 660 miners in 1854. It was on Bakery Hill, Ballarat, that the Eureka Stockade (q.v.) incident occurred, 3 December 1854. Ballarat was prominent in the goldfields literature of the second half of the nineteenth century, e.g. J.A. Patterson's *The Gold Fields of Victoria in 1862* (1862) and W.H. Thomas's *Life at the Gold Mines of Ballarat* (1885), and in the many writings on Eureka. Individual works on Ballarat include the important early history by W.B. Withers, *The History of Ballarat* (1870); *Ballarat and Vicinity* (1894) by W. Kimberly; *History of Ballarat* (1935) by Nathan Spielvogel; *Some Ballarat Pioneers* (1935) by R. Gay; and *One Hundred Years, 1838–1939, Ballarat* (1939), ed. W.H. Rees. The Ballarat goldfields continue to be discussed in more recent works such as Geoffrey Serle's *The Golden Age* (1963); J.H.W. McGeorge's *Buried Rivers of Gold* (1966); H.J. Stacpoole's *Gold at Ballarat* (1971); and Jan Neil and M.C. Sayers's *Ballarat, from Bullion to Begonias* (1973). The most comprehensive history of gold-rush Ballarat is Weston Bate's *Lucky City* (1978). Ballarat and events on the diggings provide an important background in such fictional works as *Australia Felix* (1917) from 'Henry Handel Richardson''s trilogy, *The Fortunes of Richard Mahony* (1930), and Eric Lambert's novel, *Ballarat* (1962). Adam Lindsay Gordon kept a livery stable at Ballarat in 1868 and rode in steeplechase races on its picturesque Dowling Forest course. Norman

Lindsay, who was born at Creswick near Ballarat, based his trilogy, *Saturdee* (1933), *Redheap* (1930), and *Halfway to Anywhere* (1947) on town life of the area; his novel *The Cousin from Fiji* (1945) is also set there.

Ballarat Punch, see **Melbourne Punch**

Balmain, a Sydney suburb, was named after William Balmain (1762–1803), assistant surgeon to John White in the First Fleet and principal surgeon and magistrate at Norfolk Island in 1791 and in Sydney 1795–1801. Balmain was granted 222 hectares of land in the area now bearing his name. The grant was later sold and the land subdivided to become originally a fashionable Sydney suburb (literary patron, N.D. Stenhouse, living there in the 1850s), then a working-class area, and in recent years a gathering-place of writers and artists. The annual Balmain poetry and prose competitions contributed to the rise of the 'New Australian Poetry' (q.v.) in the late 1960s. Frank Moorhouse's *Days of Wine and Rage* (1980) depicts cultural life in Balmain in the 1970s.

Banana-bender, a current colloquialism for a Queenslander, replaced 'bananalander' in the 1970s. Both words derive from the fact that Queensland was, at least from the 1890s, known as 'Bananaland'. The usage survives in, for example, the title of Hugh Lunn's study of Queensland society, *Behind the Banana Curtain* (1979). A play by Barry Dickins, *The Banana Bender,* was produced in 1980 and published 1981.

BANCKS, J.C. (JAMES CHARLES) (1889– 1952), was born at Enmore and brought up at Hornsby amidst a family he remembered as a 'living comic strip'. He became a full-time artist with the *Bulletin,* for which from 1914 he drew cartoons and caricatures; and in 1921 he began drawing 'Us Fellers', a new colour comic strip for the Sydney *Sun.* 'Us Fellers' soon came to centre on the prepubescent larrikin Ginger Meggs (q.v.). The phenomenal success of the strip made Bancks the highest-paid black and white artist of his era. Bancks drew several other strips and panels, collaborated with his first wife, Jessie Nita (Tait), on the musical comedy 'Blue Mountains Melody' (performed 1936), and was also a newspaper columnist.

BANDLER, FAITH (1918–), was born at Tumbulgum, Murwillumbah, NSW, the daughter of Wacvie Mussingkon (Peter Mussing), a Hebridean islander who was brought to Australia by slave traders in 1883 to work on the Queensland canefields. She has written her father's story in the novels, *Wacvie* (1977) and *Marani in Australia* (1980, with Len Fox). She has been strongly identified with the struggle for Aboriginal rights, having served for many years on the executive of the Federal Council for the Advancement of Aboriginals and Torres Strait Islanders, and having been director in NSW of the 1967 referendum campaign which led to equal citizenship for Aborigines under the Australian Constitution.

BANFIELD, E. J. (EDMUND JAMES) (1852–1923), born Liverpool, England, came to Australia as a child; his wide experience as a journalist included a period on the *Townsville Daily Bulletin*, 1882–97. After a severe illness he settled on remote Dunk Island off the Queensland coast, where he remained until his death. His placid but purposeful existence there led to several books about his experiences: *Confessions of a Beachcomber* (1908), *My Tropic Isle* (1911), *Tropic Days* (1918) and *Last Leaves from Dunk Island* (1925). Michael Noonan wrote a biography of Banfield, *A Different Drummer* (1983).

BANISTER, THOMAS, see *Australia, Visited & Revisited*

'BANJO, THE', see **PATERSON, A.B.**

BANKS, Sir **JOSEPH** (1743–1820), who has been called 'the Father of Australia', was born in London and began to devote himself to natural science soon after coming into his inheritance in 1764. In 1766, the year he was elected to the Royal Society, he made his first expedition, collecting specimens from Newfoundland and Labrador, and in 1768 he and a staff of eight joined the *Endeavour* under Captain James Cook on its voyage to the South Seas. The naturalists made collections and observations in South America, Tahiti, NZ and on the eastern coast of Australia (April–August 1770); at Stingray Bay such a variety of specimens was collected that the spot was renamed Botany Bay (q.v.). The expedition returned in 1771; thereafter Banks retained his interest in Australia and became the acknowledged authority on NSW after the Colony was settled in 1788. The correspondent and confidant of governors, immigrants, missionaries, explorers and scientists, all of whom continued to send back specimens to England, he was a famous patron of science, president of the Royal Society (1778–1820) and a principal in the establishment of the Royal Gardens at Kew. He published little in his lifetime, but *The Endeavour Journal of Joseph Banks* edited by J.C. Beaglehole was published in 1962. The Sydney suburb of Bankstown, Cape Banks at Botany Bay, and

the plant genus *Banksia* are among his other memorials. Biographies of Banks were written by J.H. Maiden (1909), Edward Smith (1911), H.C. Cameron (1952) and Charles Lyte (1980).

'Banks of the Condamine, The', one of the few Australian folk-songs (see Folk-Song and Ballad) that take as their subject the relationship between men and women, begins with a shearer's announcement to his love that he is leaving to join 'the Sydney shearers/ On the banks of the Condamine' (River, q.v.). He rejects his girl's request that she accompany him, on the grounds that the squatters have banned women from the shearing sheds and that her constitution would be too delicate. After rejecting her further request that he stay at home and take up a selection, the shearer departs with the promise that he'll return after the season is completed. The version of the folk-song included in some editions of A.B. Paterson's *Old Bush Songs* is entitled 'Banks of the Riverine'; there are other alternatives in which the departing bush worker is a horse-breaker or stockman rather than a shearer. 'The Banks of the Condamine' is an anonymous composition dating from the 1860s (after the passing of the Selection Acts) but clearly derives from 'The Banks of the Nile', an English broadside ballad of the earlier nineteenth century in which the dialogue is between a girl and a soldier departing for the Egyptian front. 'The Banks of the Nile' itself probably borrows from an eighteenth-century song, 'High Germany', which is also in the form of a dialogue between a soldier and his lover, the difference being that it is the girl who refuses the soldier's entreaties that she accompany him.

Banner, Sally, see *Chapel Perilous, The*

'Bannerman of the Dandenong', a popular and much-anthologized ballad by Alice Werner (1859–1935), is a sentimental tale of bush heroism and mateship. Bannerman and his mate are caught in a bushfire while on their way to the latter's wedding. Bannerman insists that his mate takes Bannerman's faster horse. The mate escapes and Bannerman dies in the fire.

BANNING, LEX (1921–65), born Sydney, was, despite the disablement of cerebral palsy, a graduate of the University of Sydney and editor of *Hermes* and *Arna*. He worked as a freelance journalist, writer for film and radio, librarian of the Mosman Spastic Centre (1954–62) and book reviewer for the *Sydney Morning Herald*. His first volume of poems, *Everyman His Own Hamlet* (1951), is a rueful indictment of the disillusioning experiences of life against which the only recourse is the poet's art. *The Instant's Clarity* (1952), as the title suggests, offers a momentary hope but in *Apocalypse in Springtime* (1956) the mood of the title poem is again one of nihilism and despair. Highly regarded by fellow writers, Banning is a poet of intellect and passion, neither of which is concealed by his characteristic sardonic mask.

'BANNISTER, S.F.' is the composite pseudonym of wife and husband Sally and Frank Bannister. Both were born in England, experienced the problems of growing up in poor conditions and developed strong radical attitudes at an early age – attitudes that persisted in their life in Australia – Sally, for example, becoming absorbed in the feminist cause. Their chief works are the novels *God's Own Country* and *Tossed and Blown* (both 1953), which concern an adventurous Australian character named Steve.

BARANGAROO was the wife of the Aboriginal, Bennelong (q.v.). She is mentioned in Watkin Tench's *A Complete Account of the Settlement at Port Jackson* (1793) and is fictionally presented in Eleanor Dark's *The Timeless Land* (1941).

Barcaldine, a town in central Queensland, west of Rockhampton, played an important role in the Shearers' Strike of 1891. The shearers set up an armed camp at Barcaldine, flew the Eureka flag above it and sang Henry Lawson's 'Freedom on the Wallaby' with its well-known threat that if the shearers were denied justice 'blood should stain the wattle'. The strike camp at Barcaldine lasted only a few months, collapsing in June 1891 because of lack of funds.

Barcoo, The, is the name of an outback district and of a river in Queensland. Explorer E.B.C. Kennedy discovered in 1847 that the river named by Sir Thomas Mitchell in 1836 as Victoria River was, in reality, the upper part of Cooper's Creek, and he renamed that part of it the Barcoo River. The Barcoo district was used by A.B. Paterson as the setting for his poem 'The Bush Christening'. 'Barcoo' also became widely used to signify any vague outback malaise; among the variants were Barcoo Rot, Barcoo Spew and Barcoo Vomit. Barcoo Rot indicated a mild type of scurvy brought about by lack of fresh vegetables in the outback diet and by excessive use of tinned meat, damper and tea; a sign of Barcoo Rot (as mentioned in Donald Stuart's novel, *Yaralie*) was a shiny pink patch of skin on the back of the hand. Barcoo Spew and Barcoo Vomit (stomach upsets) were sometimes caused by tainted food and sometimes, in the case of shearers, by excessive sweating and prolonged bending. Phil

Mowbray (the whaler, 'Scotty the Wrinkler') was the *Bulletin*'s expert on Barcoo Rot. Barcoo Rot is a character in Henry Lawson's *Send Round the Hat* sequence of stories.

Bard in Bondage, see O'LEARY, P.I.

Bards in the Wilderness: Australian Colonial Poetry to 1920 (1970), edited (with an introduction) by Brian Elliott and Adrian Mitchell, is an extensive anthology that focuses on the growth of indigenous Australian poetry throughout the colonial period which, the editors suggest, has 'a kind of terminus' about 1920. The wide-ranging selection begins with Aboriginal poetry, extracts from English poets writing about the distant colony and anonymous early balladry, and includes not only the major colonial poets but also lesser-known figures.

Barefooted Bob, see *Buln-Buln and the Brolga, The; Such is Life*

Barjai, a progressive literary magazine for youth, originated in June 1943 from the senior classes of Brisbane High School, edited by Laurence Collinson and Barrett (Barrie) Reid. After the fifth issue its original title, *Senior Tabloid,* was changed to *Barjai*. It ceased publication in 1947.

BARLEE, CHARLES HAYNES, editor of the magazine *Sydney Once a Week* (1878), also published an emigration pamphlet, *Queensland, Australia* (1868), and wrote *Humorous Tales and Sketches of Colonial Life* (1893).

Barlow, Billy, see 'Billy Barlow in Australia'

BARNARD, MARJORIE (1897–), born and educated in Sydney, graduated in 1920 with first class honours in history from the University of Sydney. There she met Flora Eldershaw (q.v.), her future collaborator under the joint pseudonym 'M. Barnard Eldershaw' (q.v.), and was strongly influenced by George Arnold Wood, then professor of history. Later friendships of importance were with Vance and Nettie Palmer, Frank Dalby Davison and Miles Franklin. Unable to take up a graduate Oxford scholarship, Barnard worked as a librarian at Sydney Technical College, resigning in 1935 to write full-time. By 1937 four of the five 'M. Barnard Eldershaw' novels had appeared and Barnard began a series of independent publications, mostly short stories, historical monographs and articles. She also contributed to three historical studies, a collection of critical essays and other work by 'M. Barnard Eldershaw' before returning to librarianship at the CSIRO from 1942 to 1950. Although the publication in 1947 of the novel *Tomorrow and Tomorrow* (q.v.) marked the end of the collaboration with Flora Eldershaw, she remained an active historical and short-story writer, reviewer and literary critic. Her writings, apart from those in collaboration, are *The Ivory Gate* (1920), a group of thirteen children's stories; *The Persimmon Tree and Other Stories* (1943), most of which had first been published in *Home*; two histories, *Macquarie's World* (1941) and *A History of Australia* (1962); five minor historical studies, *Australian Outline* (1943), *The Sydney Book* (1947), *Sydney: The Story of a City* (1956), *Australia's First Architect: Francis Greenway* (1961), and *Lachlan Macquarie* (1964); and a substantial critical study of Miles Franklin (1967). Although it is impossible to assess the relative importance of the contributions by Barnard and Eldershaw to their joint works it seems likely, on the grounds of their differing circumstances, styles and personalities, that Barnard contributed most to the actual writing and Eldershaw most to the organization and shaping.

The ambitious, anti-Utopian novel *Tomorrow and Tomorrow*, however, is essentially Barnard's, described by her in a recent interview as 'the sum of anything I could do or say' and as 'an essay in perspectives . . . a dramatization of the forces at work in our society'. The novel was published in its uncensored form and with its full title, *Tomorrow and Tomorrow and Tomorrow*, in 1983. Barnard's own short stories are ironic, carefully-structured studies of inward, mostly feminine, experience. Their understated effects are seen at their best in such stories as 'The Persimmon Tree' and 'Dry Spell'. As an historian Barnard writes from a wide perspective in a clear, figurative style. *Macquarie's World* is a colourful, convincing picture of Sydney from 1810 to 1821. The more ambitious and substantial *A History of Australia* combines grasp of detail and breadth of vision; although as an academic work it has attracted some criticism, its popularity with the general reader has resulted in a second edition and several reprintings. The same conscious artistry enlivens her minor historical articles and monographs. Her independent contribution as a literary critic, mostly in the pages of *Meanjin* and *Southerly* from the late 1940s to the early 1960s, is a distinguished one. Particularly noteworthy is her review of Patrick White's fiction in *Meanjin* (1956), the first extended appreciation by an Australian critic. Other substantial achievements are her entry on Australian literature for the 1950 edition of *Chambers's Encyclopaedia* and her personally-knowledgeable study of Miles Franklin. She was made AO in 1980 for her services to literature and won the Patrick White Literary Award in 1983.

BARNES, JOHN, see Criticism

Barranugli, one of Patrick White's fictional Australian suburbs and akin to Sarsaparilla, is expressive, as its title suggests, of the suburban ugliness that White deplores. It features in his novels *Riders in the Chariot* (1961) and *The Solid Mandala* (1966), and in several of the short stories collected in *The Burnt Ones* (1964).

BARRETT, CHARLES ('DONALD BARR') (1879–1959), born Hawthorn, Victoria, joined the staff of the Melbourne *Herald* in 1906 and spent much of his life writing on Australian natural history. He was assistant editor of *Emu*, the journal of the Royal Australasian Ornithologists' Union 1910–16, and edited the *Victorian Naturalist* 1925–40. Barrett wrote (sometimes under the pseudonym 'Donald Barr') more than sixty books on the Aborigines, the flora, fauna and landscape of Australia, and on such natural wonders as the Barrier Reef and the Nullarbor Plain, which he frequently visited. He edited anthologies of prose and verse, e.g. *The Swagman's Note-Book* (1943); wrote *Across the Years* (1948), a commentary on early Australian books; and published several collections of essays, e.g. *From a Bush Hut* (1942) and *Wanderer's Rest* (1946).

Barrier Daily Truth, a Broken Hill labour newspaper, commenced publication in 1898 as the *Barrier Truth* and became a daily (the first labour movement daily in Australasia) under its present title in 1908. Joseph Furphy's *Rigby's Romance* was serialized in the newspaper in 1905–06.

BARRINGTON, GEORGE (?1755–1804), was an Irish-born pickpocket of great style and eloquence who fleeced the rich of London in the 1770s and 1780s. Several times acquitted, he was eventually arrested for a racecourse theft in 1790 and transported for seven years to NSW, where by 1792 his good conduct had won him a conditional pardon which was made absolute in 1796, the year of his appointment as chief constable at Parramatta. As well known in his heyday as earlier criminals such as Jonathan Wild and Jack Sheppard had been in theirs, Barrington was the subject of numerous contemporary newspaper articles, pamphlets, broadsides and chapbooks, including *The Genuine Life and Trial of George Barrington* (1790), *Memoirs of George Barrington* (1790) and *The Life of George Barrington* (1792). Barrington wrote neither these nor the subsequent publications associated with his name, including *Barrington's Annals of Suicide* (1803), *Barrington's New London Spy* (1804, 1805, etc.) and several works which incorporated his Australian experiences: e.g. *A Voyage to New South Wales* (1795), *A Voyage to Botany Bay* (1795), *A Sequel to Barrington's Voyage to New South Wales* (1800) and *The History of New South Wales* (1802). *The History of New South Wales* was the first of the Barrington books to contain the 'Barrington Prologue', the lines (long thought to have been spoken at the opening of the first Australian theatre in Sydney in 1796) which begin:

> From distant climes o'er wide-spread seas we come,
> Though not with much eclat or beat of drum,
> True patriots all; for be it understood,
> We left our country for our country's good.

Subsequent research has established, however, that the author of the Prologue was not Barrington but the Englishman Henry Carter, who never visited Australia. As well as the English hack writers who exploited Barrington's name for decades, several Australian authors wrote about his career, including John Lang in *Botany Bay* (1859), Marcus Clarke in *Old Tales of a Young Country* (1871) and Roy Bridges in *Mr. Barrington* (1911).

BARRY, CLIVE (1922–), born Sydney, served in the Second World War, then became a district education officer in Kenya in the mid-1950s. In 1961 he was appointed the United Nations representative in the Congo. Barry has published three novels, two of which, *The Spear Grinner* (1963) and *Fly Jamskoni* (1969), use the same central character, Hector Reed, an Australian, and the same imaginary African state, Jamskoni. In *The Spear Grinner* Jamskoni, prior to independence, is an anarchic state preyed upon by officials such as the Ostrich, the District Commisioner's office boy. In *Fly Jamskoni* Reed returns to the small, newly-independent state as a United Nations officer. Nothing has changed – the Ostrich, now minister of aviation, still controls the country and the chief gangster of *The Spear Grinner* has now become the new superintendent of police. Barry's other novel, *Crumb Borne* (1965), examines the microcosm of a POW camp, drawing to some degree, as do the African novels, on his own experience and background. A vivid stylist with a capacity for dry humour, Barry exploits the bizarre and incongruous to produce interesting, if slight, narratives.

BARRY, DAN (1851–1908), born Dublin, Ireland, as John Ringrose Atkins, was educated in Melbourne where his lawyer father was

friendly with Redmond Barry; the connection may have provided him with the stage name he took from the 1870s. Barry's greatest success as a theatre manager came at the turn of the century. Although his own acting style was understated, he specialized in producing sensational Australian melodramas and adaptations of Shakespeare. His production of 'The Kelly Gang' in 1898 was perhaps among his most popular, although he had a flair for producing topical plays and unacknowledged adaptations of the work of other dramatists. He was best known for his outback tours.

BARRY, J.A. (JOHN ARTHUR) (1850–1911), born Torquay, England, came to Australia in 1870 after an apprenticeship as a seaman, to participate in the Palmer gold rush. He later spent some years in itinerant outback occupations alternating with periods in the coastal trade. While he was in England in 1893 he published *Steve Brown's Bunyip and Other Stories*, a popular collection of tales that had earlier appeared in Australian and English journals. He joined the Sydney *Evening News* in 1896 and also wrote regularly for the *Australian Town and Country Journal*. His other published fiction, based on his adventures at sea and in the outback, included *In the Great Deep* (1896), *The Luck of the Native-Born* (1898), *Against the Tides of Fate* (1899), *A Son of the Sea* (1899, partly autobiographical), *Red Lion and Blue Star with Other Stories* (1902), *Sea Yarns* (1910) and *South Sea Shipmates* (?1914). He also wrote an historical work, *The City of Sydney* (1902).

BARRY, Sir REDMOND (1813–80), was an Irish-born lawyer who settled in Melbourne in 1839 and became a judge of the Supreme Court of Victoria in 1852. During a long career on the Bench he presided over many important trials, including those of the prominent Eureka rebels and of Ellen and Ned Kelly (q.v.). He had a reputation for severity as a judge but was a leading figure in Melbourne intellectual and cultural life and, for 'Garryowen', was 'the most remarkable personage in the annals of Port Phillip'. One of the founders of the University of Melbourne, he was equally important in making the Melbourne Public Library, in the nineteenth century, one of the great libraries of the world. As president of the trustees, Barry was influential in Marcus Clarke's appointment to the Library in 1870. His death just days after Ned Kelly's execution – and after Kelly had promised at the trial to meet Sir Redmond in the beyond – lost Clarke a possible ally in his quest for appointment to the public librarianship in 1881.

BARTLETT, STEPHEN, see 'SLADE, GURNEY'

BARTLEY, NEHEMIAH (1830–94), born London, arrived in Hobart in 1849 and after periods of seafaring, gold digging and over-landing sheep, became a commercial agent and landowner in Queensland. A notable Brisbane eccentric, in his later years he wrote *Opals and Agates* (1892), the reminiscences of his early Queensland experiences, and *Australian Pioneers and Reminiscences* (1896), ed. J.J. Knight.

BARTON, CHARLOTTE, see *Mother's Offering to Her Children, A*

BARTON, Sir EDMUND (1849–1920), brother of G.B. Barton (q.v.), was born and educated in Sydney and was a lawyer before entering the NSW parliament in 1879. Speaker of the Legislative Assembly 1883–87, he was nicknamed 'Toby Tosspot' by the *Bulletin*. He was prominent in the Federation movement in the 1890s and became in 1901 the first prime minister of the Commonwealth of Australia. After his defeat in 1903 he became judge of the High Court of Australia. A biography by John Reynolds was published in 1948.

BARTON, GEORGE BURNETT (1836–1901), born Sydney, elder brother of Sir Edmund Barton, was called to the bar in England in 1860. He became editor of the *Sydney Punch* in 1864 and was reader in English literature at the University of Sydney 1865–68. In 1868 he went to New Zealand to edit the *Otago Daily Times*, then practised law in Dunedin and Christchurch before returning to Sydney in the early 1880s. In 1887 he was appointed to bring out a fifteen–volume edition of the *History of New South Wales from the Records* (q.v.) but lost favour with the government and left the project after completing only one volume, *Governor Phillip, 1783–1789* (1889). A keen federationist and protectionist, Barton wrote 'Historical Sketch of Australian Federation' which appeared in the *Yearbook of Australia, 1896*, and edited, in the year he died, the *Werriwa Times*, a protectionist newspaper published in Goulburn. In a memorial assessment the *Bulletin* described Barton as 'the first purely literary man produced by New South Wales'. The most substantial proof of that commendation lay in his wide-ranging and notable contributions to a variety of journals and newspapers, e.g. 'The Status of Literature in New South Wales', *Centennial Magazine* (1889–90), and in his publication in 1866 of *Literature in New South Wales* and *The Poets and Prose Writers of New South Wales* (qq.v.).

BARTON, ROBERT DARVALL (1843–1924), born Boree, NSW, grazier and grandfather of the poet A.B. Paterson, was the author of *Reminiscences of an Australian Pioneer* (1917).

BASEDOW, HERBERT (1881–1933), born Kent Town, Adelaide, studied anthropology and medicine and became an outstanding contemporary authority on the Aborigines. His publications include *The Australian Aboriginal* (1925) and *Knights of the Boomerang: Episodes from a Life Spent Among the Native Tribes of Australia* (1935).

BASS, GEORGE (1771–1803), born Aswarby, Lincolnshire, joined the Royal Navy as a surgeon's mate at the age of eighteen. With Matthew Flinders (q.v.) he sailed in HMS *Reliance* on its voyage taking Governor Hunter to NSW in 1795. In 1795–96 Bass, Flinders and a boy, William Martin, explored the coastline adjacent to the Port Jackson settlement in two small boats, both named *Tom Thumb*. His major explorations, however, were the 1797–98 voyages down the far south coast of NSW and through the strait (named Bass Strait in his honour by Governor Hunter) that separates the mainland from Tasmania. Bass's journal of the voyage, with its meticulous account of the geology, geography, flora and fauna of the area explored, is quoted in David Collins's *An Account of the English Colony in New South Wales* (1798, 1802). The Bass Strait voyage and the earlier *Tom Thumb* voyages are described in Flinders's *Voyage to Terra Australis* (1814). Bass spent his few remaining years in somewhat fruitless trading ventures to the NSW colony, the Pacific Islands and South America. His ship, *Venus*, disappeared on one such venture in 1803. K.M. Bowden published *George Bass, 1771–1803* in 1952.

BASSETT, MARNIE (Lady FLORA MARJORIE BASSETT) (1890–1980), was born in Melbourne into a distinguished academic family. Her published works include *The Governor's Lady* (1940), the story of Mrs Philip Gidley King, the first woman to come to Australia as a governor's wife; *The Hentys* (1954), an account of the pioneering Henty family (q.v.); *Realms and Islands* (1962), an account of the world voyage of Rose de Freycinet 1817–20; and *Behind the Picture: HMS Rattlesnake's Australia-New Guinea Cruise, 1846–1850* (1966), an account said to have been inspired by a watercolour sketch (hence the title) by marine artist Oswald Brierly, of H.M.S. *Rattlesnake* anchored off Cape York. Lady Bassett uses the *Rattlesnake*'s cruise to unite many slightly related events – the disastrous E.B. Kennedy expedition in the Cape York Peninsula; the rescue of white woman, Barbara Thompson, after her five years as a prisoner of the Prince of Wales Island Aborigines; the career of Benjamin Boyd; and the abortive defence settlement at Port Essington in the now Northern Territory. Lady Bassett also published *Letters from New Guinea 1921* (1969), the letters having been written during a three-months' visit she paid to New Guinea just after the Australian civil administration was established in 1921. They are interesting for the insight they give into the preoccupations of the administrators of the time. Lady Bassett received honorary Doctor of Letters degrees from Monash University (1968) and the University of Melbourne (1974), and was a foundation fellow of the Australian Academy of the Humanities.

Bastard is a word which has several distinctive (though not exclusive) usages in Australia apart from the literal or pejorative (the latter as in 'You bastard' or 'This is a bastard of a book to write'). The word is also used sympathetically (as in 'He's not a bad old bastard') or affectionately (as in 'How are you, you old bastard?') and there are derived forms such as 'bastardry' and 'bastardization' (the Australian equivalent of 'hazing'). Examples of all these usages appear in Australian literature, but the most famous is the Bastard from the Bush, a character so named in some versions of Henry Lawson's 'The Captain of the Push' (q.v.). An example of the use of bastard is Ion Idriess's comment on Gallipoli in *The Desert Column* (1932): 'Of all the bastards of places this is the greatest bastard in the world'.

'Bastard from the Bush, The', see **'Captain of the Push, The'**

Batavia, a Dutch trading vessel under the command of Captain Pelsart (Pelsaert), ran on to the Wallabi reefs of the Abrolhos Islands off the coast of WA in June 1629. In the ensuing weeks some of the crew murdered a number of the survivors and attempted to make off with the *Batavia* to go pirating on the high seas. They were thwarted by the timely arrival of a rescue ship from the East Indies. The crew and passengers of the *Batavia* are the first-known white inhabitants of Australia. The wreck of the *Batavia* and the events which followed are at the centre of Ernest Favenc's novel, *Marooned on Australia* (?1896), Malcolm Uren's narrative *Sailormen's Ghosts* (1940), Douglas Stewart's radio play *Shipwreck* (1947), Henrietta Drake-Brockman's novel *The Wicked and the Fair* (1957) and Robert Close's *The Voyage Continues* (1969). A detailed, factual account of the *Batavia* is in Drake-Brockman's *Voyage*

to Disaster (1963). *Islands of Angry Ghosts* (1966) by Hugh Edwards (q.v.), who led the expedition that discovered the wreck of the *Batavia* and salvaged the remains of her cargo, recounts both sagas, the original story of the *Batavia* and the twentieth-century recovery of the wreck.

BATES, DAISY (1863–1951), the legendary 'Kabbarli' (grandmother/wise woman/friend) of the Aborigines, was born Daisy May O'Dwyer in Tipperary, Ireland. She was sent by her guardians to Australia, probably in 1884 but perhaps earlier, because she was thought to have tuberculosis. On 13 March 1884 at Charters Towers, Queensland, she married an Edwin Henry Murrant, said by Margaret Carnegie and Frank Shields in *In Search of Breaker Morant* (1979) to have been Harry Harbord ('Breaker') Morant; she parted from him almost immediately because of his unstable character. Less than a year later (17 February 1885) she went through a marriage ceremony at Nowra, NSW, with cattleman Jack Bates. She left Bates to return to England in 1894, where she worked as a journalist until she came back to Perth in 1899. By 1901 she was at the Trappist Aboriginal Mission at Beagle Bay near Broome, and in 1904 she was back in Perth, having been appointed by the Western Australian government to study the Bibbulmum tribe of the south–west of the State. During 1910–11 she was with the Radcliffe Brown expedition on the hospital islands, Dorré and Bernier, off Carnarvon in WA. From 1912 to 1945, with brief periods of ill-health intervening, she lived among the Aboriginal tribes but always maintained fastidious, Edwardian standards of dress and decorum at various camps on the fringes of the Nullarbor. She worked assiduously to document Aboriginal customs and lore and to badger governments and authorities into programmes of racial reform. She wrote almost 300 newspaper and journal articles on her experiences and on the Aboriginal situation, publishing her authobiography, 'My Natives and I', as a newspaper serial, and her most important work (written with the help of Ernestine Hill), *The Passing of the Aborigines*, in 1938. In 1940 her vast Aboriginal collection was deposited in the National Library. Her anthropological observations have in modern times received only minimal scientific approval, and her attitude and approach to the Aboriginal question have continued to arouse considerable controversy. Some modern Aboriginal opinion is that in spite of her obvious self-sacrifice and good-will she took a pessimistic and patronizing view of the black man, and that well-intentioned amateurs such as she delayed the development of effective welfare programmes.

Against that view can be set the tremendous affection for her among the tribes, the award of the CBE in 1934, and the widespread approbation of her efforts by the white Australian community, who have placed her among such notable humanitarian women as Caroline Chisholm, Elizabeth Fry and Florence Nightingale. Her biography, *Daisy Bates* by Elizabeth Salter, was published in 1971; an opera *The Young Kabbarli* (1972), written by Lady Maie Casey to music by Margaret Sutherland, celebrates some of her exploits. Aboriginal legends collected by her, *Tales Told to Kabbarli,* and Ernestine Hill's tribute, *Kabbarli: A Personal Memoir of Daisy Bates,* were published respectively in 1972 and 1973. The Sydney Dance Company staged Barry Moreland's dance-drama, *Daisy Bates,* in 1982.

BATESON, CHARLES (1903–75), born Wellington, NZ, came to Australia in 1922. A notable journalist, he was a war correspondent in Europe and Italy during the Second World War and editorial manager of Mirror Newspapers in Australia 1960–66. One of Australia's most prolific maritime historians, Bateson published *The Convict Ships, 1787–1868* (1959), an account of the voyages of the convict ships and the administrative system under which they were selected, manned, provisioned and despatched. His other major published works include *Gold Fleet for California* (1963), *Patrick Logan: Tyrant of Brisbane Town* (1966), *The War with Japan* (1968), *Australian Shipwrecks* (1972), and *Dire Strait: A History of Bass Strait* (1973).

BATEY, PETER (1933–), born Benalla, Victoria, and educated at the University of Melbourne, was a foundation member of the Melbourne Theatre Company, of which he was later associate director. He has also been resident director of the National Theatre of WA, artistic director of the SA Theatre Company, director of the Victorian Arts Council and director/executive producer of Reg Livermore's solo productions. He wrote the popular musical plays, 'The No-Hopers' (1961); 'Adelaide Happening' (1971); 'From Smike to Bulldog', an entertainment based on the letters of Sir Arthur Streeton; 'Ecstasies', a rock opera; and 'Songs My Mother Didn't Teach Me', a dramatic biography for the stage.

Bathurst, one of the major cities of central western NSW, is situated on the Macquarie River some 200 kilometres from Sydney. After the crossing of the Blue Mountains in 1813, Governor Lachlan Macquarie travelled in 1815 to the site of the present city, which he named Bathurst in honour of the secretary of state for the colonies, Earl Bathurst. The town was gazetted in 1833 and boomed from 1851, when gold was discovered at nearby Summer Hill Creek. Significant in bushranging history as a result of the gold discoveries, Bathurst became the headquarters of Cobb & Co. (q.v.) in the 1860s. When the gold rushes subsided it became the centre of a prosperous primary-producing district and, subsequently, a noted educational centre. The history of Bathurst in the gold-rush era is outlined in Geoffrey Blainey, *The Rush That Never Ended* (1963); Bernard Greaves (ed.), *The Story of Bathurst* (1961), covers a wider historical span. Among writers to have lived or worked in Bathurst are William Derrincourt, Nat Gould, George Black, 'Price Warung', and A.W. Jose; several of Gould's sporting novels have Bathurst scenes, as also does 'Grant Hervey's' *An Eden of the Good* (1934), written while 'Hervey' was an inmate of Bathurst gaol. Other literary connections with Bathurst include Gordon Neil Stewart's historical novel, *House of Bondage* (1975), which is focused on Stewart's Bathurst ancestors, and D'Arcy Niland's *Walkabout* article (31, 1965), 'Our First Inland City'.

BATMAN, JOHN (1801–39), born Rose Hill (Parramatta), went to Tasmania in 1821 where he took up a small farming property. He formed an association of fourteen Tasmanian settlers (later the Port Phillip Association) to search for grazing land in the unexplored Port Phillip district, and sailed in the *Rebecca,* landing at Indented Head on the Geelong side of Port Phillip Bay, 29 May 1835. From the Aborigines he purchased almost a quarter of a million hectares of land in return for blankets and other gifts and utensils. At a point on the Yarra River near where Melbourne now stands, Batman's diary of 8 June 1835 noted 'This will be the place for a village'. Although Governor Bourke refused to sanction the land deal, an influx of settlers soon established the first Port Phillip settlement. *The Settlement of John Batman in Port Phillip from His Own Journal* was published posthumously in 1856. James Bonwick's biography *John Batman, the Founder of Victoria* was published in 1867; C.P. Billot wrote a modern biography in 1979. In Xavier Herbert's *Capricornia* (1938), Melbourne is represented as Batman; in Robert Close's novel, *Eliza Callaghan* (1957), Batman's courtship of Eliza is featured.

BATTARBEE, REX (1893–1973), born Warrnambool, Victoria, was severely wounded in the First World War and became a commercial artist (1924–27) before devoting himself to watercolour painting. He travelled and painted extensively in the outback, especially in Central Australia where, in the late 1930s and early 1940s, he worked with some of the Aranda Aborigines at the Hermannsburg mission. He formed the Aranda Art Group, whose best-known representative was Albert Namatjira, and became Namatjira's teacher and mentor, working with him in the documentary film, *Namatjira the Painter*. Battarbee published two works on Aboriginal art, *Modern Australian Aboriginal Art* (1951) and *Modern Aboriginal Paintings* (1971, with Bernice Battarbee).

BATTERSBY, JEAN (1928–), born Drouin, Victoria, graduated from the University of Melbourne. In 1968 she was appointed chief executive officer of what was then called the Australian Council for the Arts. In 1975–82 she occupied the same position with the newly-constituted Australia Council. She was awarded the Henry Lawson Festival of Arts Award in 1976 for the 'best contribution to the arts'.

Battlers, The, a novel by Kylie Tennant (q.v.) first published in 1941, shared the S.H. Prior Memorial Prize, the Australian Literature Society's Gold Medal, and is her most popular work. The 'battlers' are the nomad unemployed, last remnants of the Depression who in 1939 were still tramping the roads. The central characters are Snow, a morose, middle-aged, solitary wanderer who is fleeing the poor 'cocky' life he had known as a boy; and Dancy the Stray, a nineteen-year-old girl waif from Sydney's slums. Dirty, toothless and starving, Dancy is the first and the most remarkable of a group of outcasts who attach themselves to Snow. Although unattractive, frail and beset with terrors, Dancy has sensitivity, spirit, wit and a richly macabre imagination. Other close adherents of the group include Duke, a yodelling busker, and the fat, parasitic, pseudogenteel Miss Phipps. As Snow's 'mob' roams the country in pursuit of the dole stations or work, it becomes absorbed in the larger crowd of nomads who also live aimlessly and desperately at the edge of existence, pushed aside by the rest of 'respectable' society but sustained by a sense of fellowship, dogged will to survive and resilient humour. Individuals who stand out include the Apostle, ex-minister and half-madman, half-saint; the Tyrell family and their companion, Thirty Bob; and the political activists, Burning Angus, Dogger and Snake. Striking and animated as these people are, the immense and indifferent land dwarfs them and defines both the futility and the heroism of their struggle.

BATTYE, J.S. (JAMES SYKES) (1871–1954), born Geelong, Victoria, was appointed chief librarian of the Victoria Public Library in Perth, WA, in 1895 and from 1912 until his death was general secretary of the amalgamated library, museum and art gallery. His keen personal interest in the history of WA is reflected in his establishment in 1923 of the Public Records Committee of WA (later the State Archives Board); his writing and compiling the *Cyclopedia of Western Australia* (1912–13), *The History of the North West of Australia* (1915), and *Western Australia: A History* (1924); and his role in establishing the Royal WA Historical Society in 1926. Pro-chancellor of the University of WA 1931–36 and chancellor 1937–43, Battye is commemorated by the J.S. Battye Library of Western Australian History, established as an adjunct to the State Reference Library of WA in 1956.

BAUME, ERIC (1900–67), born Auckland, NZ, of German–Jewish ancestry, came to Australia in 1924 after a meteoric rise in NZ journalism, having been editor, at the age of twenty–two, of the largest provincial newspaper, the *Timaru Herald*. His successful Australian journalistic career began with a period as news editor of the *Daily Guardian;* he was later editor of the *Sunday Sun*, the *Truth* and *Daily Mirror,* and deputy editor-in-chief of Truth Newspapers Ltd 1949–52. He spent ten years in England (1939–49) representing *Truth* and *Daily Mirror* during the Second World War; he scooped the world press with his forecast of the German invasion of Russia and went as a war correspondent to the Second Front invasion of Europe. It was, however, after the war as a controversial radio and television commentator that he became a household name in NSW. His well-known (loved and hated) radio programmes, ombudsman-like in style and parish-pump in theme, were 'I'm On Your Side' and 'This I Believe'. He chaired, often abrasively, the television discussion programme, 'Beauty and the Beast'. In 1966 he was made OBE for his services to journalism. More the master of the spoken than the written word, Baume was, nevertheless, a prolific writer. He wrote a mixture of fictional, autobiographical and documentary works including *Tragedy Track* (1932), *Half-Caste* (1933), *Burnt Sugar* (1934), *I Lived These Years* (1941), *I've Lived Another Year* (1942), *Sydney Duck* (1944), *Five Graves at Nijmegen* (1945), *Ponty Galler* (1947), *Devil Lord's Daughter* (1948), *Unrehearsed Incident* (1948, short stories) and *The Mortal Sin of Father Grossard* (1953). *Five Graves at Nijmegen* is Baume's only work with some literary claims; the remainder reflect impatience and lack of care. A.E. Manning wrote the biographical account, *Larger Than Life* (1967).

BAXTER, ANNE (1923–), born Indiana, USA, and well-known American film star, married Australian grazier Randolph Galt and lived in Australia for some three years at Galt's property, Giro, in the Barrington Tops area of NSW. Her account of that experience, *Intermission* (1976), is a perceptive look at both the marriage and the Australian environment and is notable for its keen appraisal of Australian customs, manners and landscape.

BAXTER, ANNIE MARIA, see **DAWBIN, ANNIE MARIA**

BAXTER, JOHN (1939–), film historian, biographer and novelist, was publicity director of the Australian Commonwealth Film Unit 1968–70 and lecturer in film and theatre in London 1976–78. Among his numerous publications on the cinema are *The Australian Cinema* (1970) and several books on Hollywood including *Sixty Years of Hollywood* (1973). He edited *The Pacific Book of Australian Science Fiction* (1968) and *The Second Pacific Book of Science Fiction* (1971). He has also written scripts for several films, including the experimental *After Proust,* and was co-editor, until its demise, of the Australian magazine, *Film Digest.*

Bay of Noon, The, a novel by Shirley Hazzard (q.v.), was published in 1970. Time is handled as a series of subtly-linked perspectives on past, present and future so that the following chronological scheme is revealed only in stages. Jenny, the narrator, a girl in her early twenties, born in England, has been deprived of a sense of home by her evacuation to South Africa during the Second World War and by the loss of her mother. When she perceives that her close relationship with her brother Edmund has become part of a convenient triangle after his marriage to a nondescript Englishwoman, Norah, Jenny applies for a clerical position with the NATO establishment at Naples. She finds her occupation sterile and boring but Italy alters her life dramatically. She becomes intimate with a beautiful, sensitive Italian girl, Giaconda, who is involved in a relationship with a middle-aged film-director, Gianni. Giaconda's past has been marked by tragedy; the war visited ostracism and physical suffering on her family, caused the death of her mother and later of her father, a distinguished scholar, and took the life of her artist lover, Gaetano, in a land-mine accident. Gianni has retrieved her from this wreckage and for this reason she clings to him even though he often seems self-centred and cruel. Jenny also becomes friendly with an English scientist, Justin Tulloch, although he prevents their relationship from becoming intimate by keeping it at a humorous level. During the Neapolitan summer, Jenny falls severely ill and only belatedly discovers that Giaconda has left for Spain with Justin. Gianni, in his anguish, turns to Jenny for comfort. They become lovers but it is clear that they both desire the return of Giaconda and, after protecting Jenny on a journey to Genoa, where she is to board a ship for the USA and a new position, Gianni hastens, with Jenny's blessing, to rejoin Giaconda. Justin disappears from their lives until years later Jenny learns of his death in a plane accident. After several years in the USA Jenny revisits Italy, conscious that 'like the dye they had injected into my veins, the country coloured my essence, illuminated my reaction to everything else. Here, literally, I had come to my senses'.

BAYLDON, A.A. (ARTHUR ALBERT DAWSON) (1865–1958), born Leeds, England, arrived in Brisbane in 1889 and contributed to the flood of bush balladry of the 1890s. A typical *Bulletin* poet, Bayldon reflected the ambivalent attitude of the day towards the outback and bush life; sometimes pessimistically depicting the hardships of that life, at other times caught up in the enthusiastic Arcadian vision of A.B. Paterson. His books of poetry include *Poems* (1897), *The Western Track and Other Verses* (1905), *The Eagles: Collected Poems* (1921), a further *Collected Poems* (1932), and *Apollo in Australia and Bush Verses* (1944). His only published work of fiction was *The Tragedy behind the Curtain and Other Stories* (1910); a novel and some various other works remain unpublished.

'BAYLEBRIDGE, WILLIAM' (CHARLES WILLIAM BLOCKSIDGE) (1883–1942), born Brisbane, adopted the name Baylebridge from about 1925. He lived in England 1908–19, publishing numerous limited editions of poetry and working in Intelligence during the First World War. He was assisted financially at this time by his mother's half-sister, Grace Leven (Celia Grace Leven); in her memory he later established the annual Grace Leven Poetry Prize. He returned to Australia in 1919 but became an increasingly isolated figure in the Australian literary scene. Although critics such as H.M. Green and T. Inglis Moore have classed 'Baylebridge' as one of Australia's few philosophical and intellectual poets, others such as F.T. Macartney have seen him as a literary larcenist. He remains one of the more puzzling and enigmatic of Australian writers, the pages of his verse seldom turned by modern readers. In prefaces to several of his works he protested against the philistinism and cultural inertia of contemporary Australian society. His chief works (reprinted under the terms of his will in a memorial edition) include *Love Redeemed* (1934), love sonnets; *This Vital Flesh* (1939), the application of his philosophy of vitalism to Australian nationalism; and *An Anzac Muster* (q.v., 1921), short fiction centred on the Gallipoli campaign of 1915.

BAYNTON, BARBARA (1857–1929), who claimed to have been born in 1862 after the elopement of her mother, Penelope Ewart, with an Indian army officer named Kilpatrick, was actually the daughter of a carpenter, John Lawrence, and his wife Elizabeth, and was born in Scone, NSW. Brought up on the Liverpool Plains, she married a selector, Alexander Frater, in 1880, and bore him three children. In 1887 he ran off with a servant; Barbara moved to Sydney, divorced him in 1890 and the next day married Thomas Baynton, a retired surgeon who moved in literary and academic circles. It was not until the 1890s that she began to write; her first story was published in the *Bulletin* in 1896. In 1902–03 she visited London, where *Bush Studies* (q.v., 1902) was published, and after her husband's death in 1904 she alternated residence between Australia and England, becoming well known as a literary hostess and as a collector of antiques and furniture. In 1921 she married the fifth Lord Headley, a colourful engineer, sportsman and president of the Muslim Society; they separated soon after. As Lady Headley, Baynton continued to divide her time between Australia and England until her death.

Baynton's movement through society obviously led her to distort the facts of her early life and first marriage; yet this part of her past informs her fiction, which depicts the horrors of bush life and confirms Australia as the 'windblown, shimmering, shifting, awful waste, / Fringed by a broken edge of green and grey' that she wrote about in the poem 'To My Country'. The malevolence of the bush is insisted upon throughout her work; so is the suffering of her female characters, who are consistently seen as the victims of predatory, brutal men. In *Bush Studies*, 'Squeaker's Mate' tells of a woman whose back is broken by a falling tree and who is left neglected by the man she has nurtured and protected; in 'Billy Skywonkie' a half-caste woman endures a nightmarish ride from a railway siding to a bush station only to be refused employment as housekeeper because of her colour; and in 'The Chosen Vessel' (q.v.) a young mother left alone in a bush hut is raped and murdered by a passing swagman. Of the other *Bush Studies*, 'Scrammy 'And' and 'A Dreamer' are similar tales of terror and 'Bush Church' presents the inadequacies of religion as a comfort against fear

and loneliness. Baynton's output was small but both in *Bush Studies* and in her short novel, *Human Toll* (q.v., 1907), her grim realism, which is authenticated by the accumulation of detail and by the accuracy of the idiom her characters use, offers a powerful alternative to the romantic pictures of bush life. *Barbara Baynton* in the Portable Australian Authors series was edited by Sally Krimmer and Alan Lawson in 1980.

'Beach Burial', a poem by Kenneth Slessor (q.v.) first published in 1944, is set in the period when Australian soldiers were fighting in the Western Desert near El Alamein. The poem describes the hasty burial of seamen washed ashore from the naval battles of the Mediterranean. A fine poem which reflects the futility of war, it expresses the bewildered pity of battle-hardened troops as they perform rough and ready but deeply-tender last rites over the sodden, nameless corpses.

BEACH, ERIC (1947–), born NZ, came to Australia in 1972 and has written plays, verse and short stories. His published works are *Saint Kilda Meets Hugo Ball* (1974), *In Occupied Territory* (1977) and *A Photo of Some People in a Football Stadium* (1978).

BEADELL, LEN (1923–), born Pennant Hills, NSW, has had a long career in surveying and mapping in outback Australia and Papua-New Guinea. His books are mainly concerned with his surveying life and projects. They include *Too Long in the Bush* (1965), *Blast the Bush* (1967), *Bush Bashers* (1971), *Still in the Bush* (1975), *Beating about the Bush* (1976), *Outback Highways* (1979, a compendium of the five previous books) and *End of an Era* (1983).

BEAGLEHOLE, J.C. (JOHN CAWTE) (1901–71), born Wellington, NZ, became one of his country's foremost historians and a leading figure in its literary, historical and community life. The recipient of numerous awards and honours, Beaglehole was made CMG in 1958 and awarded the Order of Merit in 1970, the latter after the publication of his work on Captain James Cook (q.v.). His most notable historical publications were *Exploration of the Pacific* (1934), *The Journals of Captain James Cook* (1955, 1961, 1967), *The Endeavour Journal of Joseph Banks* (1962) and *The Life of Captain James Cook* (1974).

BEAN, C.E.W. (CHARLES EDWIN WOODROW) (1879–1968), born Bathurst, NSW, was educated in England at Clifton

College and at Oxford, and was called to the bar in 1903. After returning to Australia in 1904 he taught briefly, travelled on the country legal circuit as an assistant (1905–07), and wrote of his impressions in a series of articles published by the *Sydney Morning Herald,* June-July 1907. In 1908 he joined that newspaper as a reporter and was sent in 1909 to western NSW to gather material for a series of articles on the wool industry. Those articles, entitled 'The Wool Land', formed the basis of *On the Wool Track* (1910), one of the classic accounts of outback Australian life. The book traverses the 'red country' – the land of the western rivers (the Namoi, Bogan, Culgoa, Warrego, Paroo and Darling) and the land of the great sheep runs where four stations on the Darling and Paroo made one property of three and a quarter million acres and ran along 280 miles of the winding rivers. Along Bean's wool track passes a procession of squatters, shearers, rouseabouts, boundary-riders, swagmen, bullock teams, flocks of sheep, plagues of rabbits and all varieties of natural and human disasters. Bean's travels also produced his historical and social documentary of the Darling River, *The Dreadnought of the Darling* (1911), an account of his trip down the river on a small paddleboat steamer. From 1910 to 1912 Bean was in London, reporting for his paper on the ships being built for the Royal Australian Navy. Those reports formed the basis of his publication, *Flagships Three* (1913). In the First World War he was appointed official war correspondent with the Australian forces and was at Gallipoli (where he was wounded). In 1916 he edited *The Anzac Book,* a collection of contributions by Australian soldiers on Gallipoli, which includes his own photographs, drawings and verse. His observations on the war in the trenches, *Letters from France,* were published in 1917 and his hopes for the post-war future, *In Your Hands, Australians,* in 1918. In 1919 he began *The Official History of Australia in the War of 1914–1918* (q.v.); the first two volumes, *The Story of Anzac,* were published in 1921 and 1924. He also wrote four other volumes dealing with the war in France and edited the remainder of the *History.* The last of the twelve-volume work was published in 1942; Bean's own single-volume abridgement of the series, *Anzac to Amiens,* was published in 1946. During the Second World War he was occupied in creating the Commonwealth Archives and planning the National War Memorial in Canberra. Bean's later writings include *Here, My Son* (1950), a history of the independent schools of Australia, and *Two Men I Knew* (1957), the two men being 'the founders of the AIF', Sir William Bridges and Sir Cyril Brudenell White. Highly respected as a military historian, Bean

was awarded the Chesney Gold Medal of the Royal United Services Institution in 1930, and honorary doctorates from the University of Melbourne in 1931 and the Australian National University in 1959. Throughout his life an enthusiastic nationalist, Bean did much, through his *Official History,* to establish the Anzac (q.v.) legend. *Gallipoli Correspondent: The Frontline Diary of C.E.W. Bean,* compiled by Kevin Fewster, was published in 1983, as was a biographical account of Bean's war years, *Gallipoli to the Somme* by Dudley McCarthy.

BEASLEY, JACK (1921–), born Merewether, NSW, was an apprentice electrical fitter at the BHP steelworks in Newcastle 1936–41, worked in his trade throughout the war years, part of the time at sea. A functionary of the Communist Party of Australia (1948–51) he became associated with the Australasian Book Society (q.v.) in 1959, spent some fifteen years in retail trade advertising and promotion (1963–77) and in 1977 resumed his interest in the Book Society. His publications include *Socialism and the Novel: A Study of Australian Literature* (1957); a short story anthology, *The Tracks We Travel* (1961); *The Rage for Life: The Work of Katharine Susannah Prichard* (1964); and *Red Letter Days: Notes from Inside an Era* (1979). The latter contains a comprehensive account of the history of the Australasian Book Society and discusses in detail the work and personalities of such Australian writers as Alan Marshall, Frank Hardy, Judah Waten, Mary Gilmore and Leslie Haylen.

BEATTY, BILL (1912–79), born Sydney, was an accomplished pianist who studied at the NSW Conservatorium of Music, worked for the ABC (1941–50) and appeared in public and in radio recitals in Australia and overseas. His chief love, however, was Australiana – folklore, legends, traditions, customs, and oddities of every kind. He ranged the Australian outback garnering material for his profusion of published works which began in 1941 with *This Australia: Strange and Amazing Facts* and include *Amazing Australia* (1943), *Australian Wonders* (1945), *'Come a Waltzing Matilda': Australian Folk Lore and Forgotten Tales* (1954), *A Treasury of Australian Folk Tales and Traditions* (1966), *Around Australia with Bill Beatty* (1966) and *Tales of Old Australia* (1966).

Beaudesart, Maud see *Such is Life*; Buckley Family

BEAVER, BRUCE (1928–), was born Manly, NSW, where he spent much of his youth and where, after many nomadic years, he now lives. Beaver's childhood and adolescence, as revealed by his own frequent comments and in his autobiographical *As It Was* (1979), were unsettled and unhappy. He took refuge as a boy in the fantasy world of comics, radio serials and movies, and later became absorbed in books, the writings of Christopher Brennan in particular making a considerable impact on him. From the age of seventeen he had several periods of psychiatric treatment for manic-depressive psychosis, lived and worked for a time on his uncle's farm on the south coast of NSW, spent six years as chainman for a surveyor in northern NSW and was at various times radio programme arranger, clerk and proof-reader before settling on freelance journalism and writing as a career. He spent six months on Norfolk Island, a place he detested, in 1958 and lived in New Zealand from 1958 to 1962, an experience that he enjoyed. Beaver published his first volume of poetry, *Under the Bridge*, in 1961. His later publications are *Seawall and Shoreline* (1964), *Open at Random* (1967), *Letters to Live Poets* (q.v., 1969), *Lauds and Plaints* (1968–1972) (1974), *Odes and Days* (1975), *Death's Directives* (1978), *As It Was* (1979) and *Selected Poems* (1979). Beaver has also written novels, including *The Hot Spring* (1965) and *You Can't Come Back* (1966). Based on the experiences of a gang of railway fettlers, *You Can't Come Back* takes an abysmal view of the Australian working man's life and of the working man himself.

Throughout his first three volumes of poetry, and with considerable success in individual poems such as 'Camp Shift', 'Seawall and Shoreline', 'Chainman's Diary' (winner of the 1964 *Poetry Magazine* Award), 'The Killers' and 'The Cranes of Auckland', Beaver pursues his search for an understanding of his disturbed life, maintaining a preoccupation with 'the celebration and lamentation of existence' that carries through into his first major collection, *Letters to Live Poets*. Written in 1966 under the spur of an illness that convinced Beaver he had only a couple of months of rationality left, *Letters to Live Poets* represents his attempt 'to make one clear readable statement before I stopped writing altogether'. In the form of the *livre composé*, the thirty-four separate poems piece together the jigsaw of existence and assess the worth of that existence. Influenced by Whitman's *Leaves of Grass* and Brennan's *Poems 1913*, *Letters to Live Poets* ranges over the experiences of Beaver's childhood, his adolescence with its periodic bouts of mental illness, and his present middle-age, attempting a 'spiritual, intellectual and emotional autobiography' set against the striking natural landscape and monotonous suburbia of seaside Manly. *Letters to Live Poets* won the Grace Leven Prize for

Poetry, the Poetry Society of Australia Prize and the Captain Cook Bicentennial Prize for Poetry, all in 1970.

Lauds and Plaints, by contrast with the hasty creation of *Letters to Live Poets,* was slowly (1967–72) and lovingly built. An extension of *Letters to Live Poets* ('the spirit of the body of *Letters*'), *Lauds and Plaints* turns from the poet's self-obsession to an awareness of others, for example, the young man who kills himself jumping from a roof, the old Manly fisherman, Albert Fry, and Arthur Stace (Sydney's 'Mr Eternity'). The technical liberation that Beaver had celebrated in *Letters* ('My thoughts [once] ticked iambically in ten syllables') is complete in *Lauds and Plaints,* where visual and syntactical experimental forms (the shedding of punctuation and the unbridled rhetoric) complement the exultation that Beaver felt as a release from the pessimism of so much of *Letters to Live Poets.* The poems praise ('Lauds') those with largeness of spirit and blame ('Plaints') those lesser spirits whose life vision never transcends the materialism of daily existence. *Odes and Days,* written by Beaver during a period spent at Grace Perry's Berrima house, comprises fifteen odes, eight addressed to himself or the house and seven addressed (as biographical sketches) to the composers Beethoven, Mahler and Delius and to the poets Hölderlin, Brennan, Rilke and Hesse. The 'Days', which form a type of verse-journal, are the forty-seven shorter poems of the second part of the book. Many of them, freed from Beaver's compulsive philosophizing, record and rejoice in natural sights and sounds and contain some of his most attractive lyricism. *Death's Directives,* twenty poems in which Death variously suggests, reminds, advises or lays down directives to the poet about life, are the most relaxed of Beaver's poetry. The near-genial tone and the absence of tension reflect, perhaps for the first time in the whole body of Beaver's poetry, an affirmation of life and a confidence in his own psyche. *As It Was,* the autobiographical prose-poem which Beaver has only in recent times felt able to write, confirms by the fact of its existence that affirmation and confidence. An original and idiosyncratic writer, a fine exponent of the prose-poetry form and one ·of the earliest Australian poets to explore the possibilities of confessional poetry of the life studies genre, Beaver through his own work and in his role as adviser and contributing editor to *Poetry Australia* has been an important influence in the rise of the 'New Australian Poetry' (q.v.). He was awarded the Patrick White Literary Award in 1982 and the Christopher Brennan Award in 1983, both in recognition of the sustained distinction of his work.

Beck, Martin, is the villain and one of the chief characters in Alexander Harris's novel, *The Emigrant Family* (q.v., 1849). The 1852 edition was titled *Martin Beck: Or, the Story of an Australian Settler.* The son of convict partners of black American origin, Beck is an outsider in his native land because of his colour; his avarice is largely an attempt to compensate for his lowly social position. He turns bushranger and is later shot dead.

BECKE, 'LOUIS' (GEORGE LEWIS) (1855–1913), was born Port Macquarie, NSW, and educated in Sydney. At fourteen he sailed for America and began the series of adventures that provided the basis of his writing; for long periods during the next twenty-five years he travelled and traded in the Pacific, numbering among his experiences a spell as supercargo to the legendary 'Bully' Hayes (q.v.), arrest and acquittal for piracy, and several shipwrecks. In 1893, back in Sydney, he met the explorer Ernest Favenc who introduced him to J.F. Archibald; under Archibald's tutelage he began to turn out stories of the Pacific and Australia for the *Bulletin* and other journals. Although some of Becke's best early writings went into 'Rolf Boldrewood's' *A Modern Buccaneer* (q.v.) in 1893, his reputation was established with the publication of *By Reef and Palm* (1894), *His Native Wife* (1895) and *The Ebbing of the Tide* (1896). In 1896 he moved to England, where he enjoyed the patronage of the Earl of Pembroke and was something of a celebrity; he subsequently lived in Ireland and France and visited Jamaica, America and NZ before returning to Sydney in 1909, where he died in poverty four years later. In all Becke wrote thirty-five books, several in collaboration with Walter Jeffery (q.v.). His forte was the short story or sketch in which he drew on his experiences, so that for his readers the Pacific became real as well as romantic. He gave credit for his emergence as a writer to Archibald, who 'taught me the secrets of condensation and simplicity of language' and helped fashion his spare prose style. His departure from Australia and Archibald's influence is part of the reason why his best books are the early collections *By Reef and Palm* and *The Ebbing of the Tide;* like 'Steele Rudd' he became a formula writer. The best of his dozen or so novels are *A First Fleet Family* (1896) and *The Mutineer* (1898), both written in collaboration with Jeffery, and the heavily autobiographical *The Adventures of Louis Blake* (1909); he also wrote descriptive and scientific prose, and was one of the first admirers of Henry Melville. Envied by Joseph Conrad and compared in his lifetime with Rudyard Kipling and Robert Louis Stevenson, Becke is generally catalogued among the *Bulletin* 1890s school by critics of Australian literature but has a considerable reputation overseas. A. Grove Day's study, *Louis Becke,* was published in 1966.

BECKER, LUDWIG (?1808–61), artist, explorer and naturalist, was born in Germany and arrived in Australia in 1851. He established a reputation in artistic and scientific circles in Victoria in the 1850s and in 1860 was appointed artist, naturalist and geologist to the Burke and Wills expedition; left behind at Menindee when Burke divided the party, he was one of the victims of the expedition and died of scurvy and dysentery near Cooper's Creek. His sketchbook and journals (ed. Marjorie Tipping) were published in 1980.

BEDFORD, JEAN (1946–), born Cambridge, England, has been a journalist, teacher and, since 1980, literary editor of the *National Times.* She has written *Country Girl Again* (1979), a short story collection, and *Sister Kate* (1982), a novel based on the life of Kate Kelly.

BEDFORD, RANDOLPH (1868–1941), born Camperdown, Sydney, tramped across outback NSW at sixteen, taking such bush jobs as rabbiter, fencer and Murray River paddle steamer hand. He settled into journalism in the late 1880s, working variously for newspapers in Bourke, Broken Hill, Adelaide and Melbourne. He founded the *Clarion,* a mining and literary journal (1897–1909), and accumulated wealth through gold-mining ventures in WA. In 1901–04 he was in Europe, where his first novels *True Eyes and the Whirlwind* (1903) and *The Snare of Strength* (1905), both largely autobiographical, were published. His *Bulletin* travel notes were published as *Explorations in Civilization* (1914). Bedford's later life was occupied by his writings, his grandiose mining and pastoral speculations, and politics; he was a member of the Queensland Legislative Council 1917–23, and of its Legislative Assembly 1923–41. A prolific and racy writer, Bedford published five novels, countless short stories, poetry, travel, descriptive and autobiographical works, and the play 'White Australia: Or, The Empty North' which was staged in Melbourne in 1909. His short story 'Fourteen Fathoms by Quetta Rock' has been much anthologized but his most significant work is the autobiographical *Naught to Thirty-Three* (q.v., 1944). A man of large appetites, Bedford had a reputation as a raconteur, broadcaster and bohemian, was a celebrated *Bulletin* and *Lone Hand* contributor and was a vocal and militant supporter of an Australia that was white, socialist and republican.

BEDFORD, RUTH (1882–1963), born Petersham, Sydney, published lyric verse e.g. *Sydney at Sunset and Other Verses* (1911) and *The Learner and Other Verses* (1937); fiction (in collaboration with Dorothea Mackellar), e.g. *The Little Blue Devil* (1912) and *Two's Company* (1914); and children's verse e.g. *Rosycheeks & Goldenhead* (1913) and *Hundreds and Thousands* (1934). She also wrote *Think of Stephen, A Family Chronicle* (1954), a delightful account of the family of Sir Alfred Stephen. A minor classic in the social history genre, *Think of Stephen* recreates the life of an upper-middle-class professional family in Sydney in the middle of the nineteenth century. She also wrote several plays including 'At the Inn', 'Fear', 'The Girl from the Marsh Croft', 'Hide the Thimble', 'Murder Next Door', 'Pear's Soap' and 'Postman's Knock'.

BEDFORD, WILLIAM (?1781–1852), was born in England and arrived in Van Diemen's Land in 1823 as that colony's second minister. Popular with successive administrators though not with some settlers and most convicts, Bedford had a reputation for moral earnestness and financial extravagance. He is savagely portrayed as the avaricious hypocrite, Parson Ford, in a dozen or so stories of 'Price Warung' and his practices parallel those of the sanctimonious minister, Meekin, in Marcus Clarke's *His Natural Life*. He is also one of the first colonists Simon Stukeley meets in *The Hermit in Van Diemen's Land* (1830) and is a minor figure in William Gosse Hay's *The Escape of the Notorious Sir William Heans* (1919).

BEEBY, Sir GEORGE (1869–1942), born Sydney, was a pupil teacher, a solicitor, a Labor member of the NSW parliament (1907), and afterwards a State and federal judge. Beeby was editor and manager of the *Bowral Free Press* in 1892 and the *New England Democrat* in 1894. In 1923 he published *Concerning Ordinary People*, a book of six plays, one of which, *Point O'View*, reflected his knowledge of industrial relations and the law. *In Quest of Pan* (1924) is a satiric and somewhat bawdy play; he also wrote the novel, *A Loaded Legacy* (1930), and a number of short stories.

Beechworth, a town in north–eastern Victoria, was once the principal town of the Ovens River goldfields. It was a popular haunt of the Kelly gang.

BEILBY, RICHARD (1918–   ), born in Malacca, Malaysia, of Australian parents, came to WA in 1929. In the Second World War he served in the AIF in the campaigns of North Africa, Greece, Crete and New Guinea. Since then he has worked in the building trades, has been a part-time union organizer, an insurance salesman and a full-time novelist. Two of his novels are set in Greece, *The Sword and the Myrtle* (1968) at the time of Thermopylae, and *No Medals for Aphrodite* (1970) at the time of the German invasion in 1941, when two Australian soldiers attempt to slow the German advance by blowing up a road. *Gunner* (1977, published as *Retreat*), also a war novel, is set in Crete during the German assault. It highlights the unlikely relationship that develops between the Australian digger Gunner Lewis and the young officer ('the boy-bastard') Lieutenant Whiteside. Beilby also published *The Bitter Lotus* (1978). His chief novel, however, is *The Brown Land Crying* (1975) in which he examines the dilemma of the half-caste Aboriginal living in the modern white urban environment (Perth) and torn between the traditional ties of race and tribe and the need for recognition by, and status in, the white community of which he is, perforce, a part.

BELFIELD, FRANCIS one of Australia's earliest playwrights, published *Retribution: Or, the Drunkard's Curse* (1849); it was performed at the Queen's Theatre, Melbourne in 1849 and was later reprinted (?1872) as *The Bottle: Or, the Drunkard's Curse*. He also published *The Rebel Chief* (1850).

'Bell Birds', the much-anthologized Henry Kendall (q.v.) lyric poem, was first published in the *Sydney Morning Herald*, 25 November 1867. The poet hears, in imagination, the chiming notes of the bellbirds of his youth and recreates in rich pictorial phrases the typical bellbird (and Kendall) landscape of 'channels of coolness', 'dim gorges' and 'cool wildernesses'. Like Wordsworth with his 'sensations sweet', Kendall is sustained by his recollections of natural beauty amid the ugliness of later years in the 'city and alleys'.

Bellairs, Cecilia and Ella, see *Cousin from Fiji, The*

Bellarine Peninsula is the neck of land running eastwards from Geelong, Victoria, to Port Phillip Bay and Bass Strait. It was originally claimed by John Batman as a result of his dealings with the Aborigines of the area. William Buckley, who lived with the natives for thirty–two years, was found at Indented Head on the tip of the peninsula in 1835.

Bellbird is the name given to two species of Australian birds: the crested bellbird and the bell-miner. The latter species is responsible for the well-known, persistent chiming sound heard in the cool moist areas along the eastern coast. The bellbird and its bell-like notes have been immortalized in Henry Kendall's poem 'Bell Birds', but other poets have also been fascinated by it: e.g. Charles Harpur, who discusses it in the notes to his poem, 'The Kangaroo Hunt or a Morning in the Bush', and P.J. Holdsworth, who wrote of it in 'The Valley of the Popran'. *Bellbird* (the name of a fictitious country town) was a popular ABC television serial in 1967–79.

'BELLERIVE', see TISHLER, JOSEPH

Bell's Life in Sydney (1845–?71), *Bell's Life in Victoria and Sporting Chronicle* (1857–68) and *Bell's Life in Adelaide and Sporting Chronicle* (1861–62) were sporting journals. They were modelled on *Bell's Life in London and Sporting Chronicle* (1822–86) which in turn exploited the popularity of *Bell's Weekly Messenger*, a London periodical founded by John Bell (1745–1831). The Australian *Bell's* each focused on sport and politics and carried both local and overseas literary material. A distinctive feature of *Bell's Life* was the verse forecast of important races, as exemplified by Adam Lindsay Gordon's 'Hippodromania', originally published in *Bell's Life in Victoria*, which unsuccessfully predicted the results of the 1866 and 1867 Melbourne Cups.

Below and On Top, see DYSON, EDWARD

BENBO, see Aboriginal in Australian Literature

Bendigo, one of the chief cities of central northern Victoria, came into being in 1841 as a goldfields town on a sheep station known as Ravenswood, which had been taken up by Charles Sherratt in 1840. Popularly known as Bendigo (after a Ravenswood Aboriginal stationhand) the town was officially called Sandhurst until 1891. Discontent on the goldfields of Ballarat and Bendigo led to the Eureka Stockade (q.v.); an account of the troubles at Bendigo is given in Geoffrey Serle's *The Golden Age* (1963). The Bendigo goldfields are described in many of the numerous historical and travel books of the period, e.g. George Wathan's *The Golden Colony* (1855), Ellen Clacy's *A Lady's Visit to the Gold Diggings of Australia, in 1852–53* (1853), William Howitt's *Land, Labour and Gold* (1855) and Samuel Mossman's *The Gold Regions of Australia* (1852). Charles Thatcher, the 'Colonial Minstrel', was known as 'The Bard of Bendigo'. Histories of the city include George Mackay's *History of Bendigo* (1891) and *Annals of Bendigo* (1912) and, more recently, Frank Cusack's *Bendigo –*

A History (1973), Jan Neil's *Bendigo, the Golden Age Retraced* (1973), and A.V. Palmer's *The Gold Mines of Bendigo* (1976). James Devaney's novel *Washdirt* (1946) is set in the Bendigo goldfields; the poet William Gay (q.v.) lived and wrote in Bendigo in the late 1890s.

Bengala, see VIDAL, MARY THERESA

BENNELONG (BANNEELON), the second Aboriginal to live in the Port Jackson settlement (Arabanoo was the first), was captured, with another native, Colbee (q.v.), by Lieutenant William Bradley on instructions from Captain Arthur Phillip at the end of 1789. He became a well-known identity of the settlement; Bennelong Point, where the Sydney Opera House now stands, is named after him. In 1792 Bennelong and an Aboriginal boy, Yemmerrawannie, were taken to England by Phillip; Bennelong returned to Australia in 1795 but Yemmerrawannie died in England. An account of Bennelong's activities is in Watkin Tench's *A Complete Account of the Settlement at Port Jackson* (1793) and a fictional portrait of him is given in Eleanor Dark's *The Timeless Land* (1941). Michael Boddy wrote 'The Cradle of Hercules' (1974), a play about Phillip and Bennelong; Joan Phipson's children's story, *Bennelong,* was published in 1975; E.O. Schlunke wrote the poem 'Bennelong Returns to Heaven', in which he portrays Bennelong's later reaction to the white colonization of Australia.

BENNETT, BRUCE, see Criticism

BENNETT, GEORGE (1804–93), born Plymouth, England, wandered the Pacific 1828–35, writing many papers on natural history, as a result of which he was made a fellow of the Linnean Society of London and a member of the Zoological Society. He visited Australia in 1829 and 1832, publishing *Wanderings in New South Wales, Batavia, Pedir Coast, Singapore and China* (1834). Back in Sydney in 1836 he developed a successful medical practice, became a leading figure in the Australian Museum and published *Gatherings of a Naturalist in Australasia* (1860).

BENNETT, ROSS, see Hunter Valley Poets

BENNETT, SAMUEL (1815–78), born Cornwall, England, came to Australia in 1841 to work as a printer on the *Sydney Herald*. In 1859 he resigned to become part-owner of the rival *Empire* (q.v.); he later became proprietor of the *Evening News* and the *Australian Town and Country Journal*. Bennett's *The History of Australian Discovery and Colonisation* (1865) was a significant early history of Australian exploration. His daughter Rose, who later married John Henniker Heaton, is the 'Rose Lorraine' of Henry Kendall's love poetry. Bennett was attacked in the satiric pamphlets of Theodore Argles ('The Pilgrim').

BENNETT, STEFANIE (1945–), born Townsville, Queensland, followed a brief formal education by working as a factory hand, saleswoman, hairdresser, graphic artist, rock musician and reader/editor with various journals. Among her publications are *Blackbirds of Superstition* (1973), *Madam Blackboots* (1974), *Poems from the Paddy Wagon* (1975), *The Medium* (1976, prose and poetry), *Tongues and Pinnacles* (1976), *The Tenth Lady* (1977) and the novel *Stefan* (1978).

Benno and Some of the Push, see **DYSON, EDWARD**

BENT, ANDREW (1790–1851), pioneering Tasmanian printer and publisher, was born in London, convicted of burglary in 1810, and arrived in NSW in 1812 under a sentence of transportation for life. He soon became government printer in Van Diemen's Land and was, in 1816, the first publisher of the *Hobart Town Gazette* (q.v.). In 1824–25 Bent came into conflict with the new lieutenant-governor, George Arthur (q.v.), over leading articles by Evan Henry Thomas in the *Gazette* and letters written for it by Robert Lathropp Murray; eventually he was imprisoned for libel. After Arthur pirated his *Gazette* title, Bent renamed his newspaper the *Colonial Times* and later ran the *Colonial Advocate* (1828) and *Bent's News* (1836–39), which he began in Hobart and continued in Sydney; subsequently he was a hotelier and cedar merchant on the NSW north coast. An important figure in the fight for the freedom of the press in Australia, Bent became known as the 'Tasmanian Franklin' and like Franklin published a series of early almanacs. He also published Thomas Wells's *Michael Howe* (1818), the first private book or pamphlet published in Tasmania, and *The Hermit of Van Diemen's Land* (q.v., 1830), the first volume of Australian essays, for which he was prosecuted for libel. Bent figures largely in most studies (e.g. by E. Morris Miller and James Bonwick) of the earlier Tasmanian press, in biographies and studies of Arthur, and in Joan Woodberry's *Andrew Bent and the Freedom of the Press in Van Diemen's Land* (1972).

BERGNER, HERZ (1907–), born Poland, published a book of short stories, *Houses and Streets,* in Poland in 1935. He migrated to Australia in 1938 and in 1941 published a book of stories, *The New House,* which reflected both the new Australian environment and the difficulties that faced the immigrant Jews. His first novel, written in Yiddish (as were all his books) and translated into English by Judah Waten, was *Between Sky and Sea* (1946); the story of a group of Jewish refugees whose ship is denied landing by the other countries of the world, it won the Australian Literature Society Gold Medal for 1948. In 1950 a further novel, *A City in Poland,* dealing with his Polish experience, was published and in 1955 another collection of short stories, *The House of Jacob Isaacs.* In 1960 his novel, *Light and Shadow,* about the Jewish experience in Australia as seen through the eyes of the migrant Zeling family, won the Zwi-Kessel Prize as one of the world's best Jewish books published in that year; it was translated from the Yiddish by Alec Braizblatt with a foreword by Alan Marshall. *Where the Truth Lies* (1965), a further collection of twenty-two stories on Jewish life in Australia, also won the Zwi-Kessel Prize as well as the Australian Literature Society's Gold Medal Award for the best book of the year.

BERNDT, R.M. (RONALD MURRAY) (1916–) and CATHERINE (1918–). Born Adelaide, R.M. Berndt has had a distinguished career in anthropology. Appointed the foundation professor of anthropology at the University of WA in 1963 he has been, since the 1960s, an influential member of the major Aboriginal welfare and advisory boards. A prolific writer on Aboriginal history, religion, customs, art, song and myth, Berndt has written *Kunapipi* (1951), *Djanggawul* (1952), *Love Stories of Arnhem Land* (1976) and *Three Faces of Love: Traditional Aboriginal Song Poetry* (1976); and has edited *Australian Aboriginal Art* (1964), *Australian Aboriginal Anthropology* (1970), *A Question of Choice* (1971) and (with E.S. Phillips) *The Australian Aboriginal Heritage* (1973). Berndt collaborated with his wife Catherine (born NZ) in writing *The First Australians* (1952, expanded in 1964 as *The World of the First Australians*), *Arnhem Land: Its History and Its People* (1953) and *Man, Land and Myth in North Australia: The Gunwinggu People* (1970). Berndt's translation of the Wonguri-Manjikai Moon-bone Song was used by Les Murray as the basis for the poem, 'The Buladelah-Taree Holiday Song Cycle' (q.v.). Catherine Berndt also published *The Land of the Rainbow Snake* (1979). See Aboriginal Song and Narrative in Translation.

Berrima, some 140 kilometres south-west of Sydney on the Hume Highway, is one of NSW's most historic towns. Sir Thomas Mitchell camped on the site in 1829 and Australia's oldest gaol and oldest licensed inn are both in the town; Starlight and Dick Marston escape from Berrima gaol in 'Rolf Boldrewood''s *Robbery Under Arms* (1888). Berrima has other literary connections: with Louisa Atkinson who was born at nearby Oldbury in 1834; with Grace Perry, who has lived there and has written *Black Swans at Berrima* (1972), a long lyric sequence, and *Berrima Winter* (1974); and with Bruce Beaver, who wrote some of his *Odes and Days* (1975) while living there. Other writers associated with Berrima have been Gwen Meredith, Ronald McKie and Maslyn Williams.

BERTIE, C.H. (CHARLES HENRY) (1875–1952), born Lyonsville on the Clarence River, NSW, joined the Sydney Municipal Council in 1899 as a junior in the city survey office and ultimately rose to be the Council's chief clerk. In 1909 he was appointed first librarian of the new Sydney Municipal Library and later established within it the first public lending library for children in Australia. An indefatigable member of the Royal Australian Historical Society and a regular contributor to its *Journal and Proceedings,* Bertie became one of Sydney's most important collectors of Australiana; his collection is one of the most substantial in the Mitchell Library. Bertie's numerous publications include *The Early History of the Sydney Municipal Council* (1911), *Story of Old George Street* (1920) and *Old Colonial By-Ways* (1928). He did much of the preliminary work for the inaugural edition of the *Australian Encyclopaedia* (1925–26); wrote *The Story of the Royal Hotel & the Theatre Royal, Sydney* (1927); and arranged for the first publication of *Ralph Rashleigh* (1929).

Betty Wayside, see STONE, LOUIS

Between Sea and Sky, see BERGNER, HERZ

Between Two Tides, see FITZGERALD, R.D.

BEYNON, RICHARD (1925–), born Carlton, Melbourne, went to England in 1947 and worked as an actor for stage, film and television, appearing in productions with such well-known artists as Peter Ustinov, Joan Greenwood and Richard Attenborough. On a visit to Australia in 1956 he entered his play, *The Shifting Heart* (q.v., 1960), in the Playwrights' Advisory Board competition and won first prize. First produced in Sydney at the Elizabethan Theatre in 1957, and subsequently produced in New York and London, the play also won third prize in the London *Observer* competition of 1957. A popular text for schools, it has continued to be produced in Australia. Beynon

has subsequently worked mainly for the BBC as script editor and producer, producing such popular television series as *Rebecca, My Cousin Rachel, Madam Bovary* and *Fame is the Spur.* He has also written for television and radio, has published a play, *Epitaph for Two Faces,* in a selection he edited with H.G. Fowler, *Next Act* (1964), and in 1958 won an award for his television play, 'Time and Mr Strachan'. He has written one other stage play which also draws on his memories of working-class Melbourne and which is as yet unproduced, 'Time Me From Now'. One of the group of plays which seemed to herald a renaissance of Australian drama in the 1950s *The Shifting Heart* is, like Ray Lawler's *Summer of the Seventeenth Doll,* a naturalistic study of a tense domestic situation. Concerned with the uneasy relationship between Australians and European migrants, it is perhaps the best-known of a series of plays dealing with cultural conflict which includes Oriel Gray's *Burst of Summer* (1959), J.P. McKinney's 'The Shadows We Cast' (n.d.), Barbara Vernon's *The Multi-Coloured Umbrella* (1961), Anthony Coburn's *The Bastard Country* (1963) and Alexander Buzo's *Norm and Ahmed* (1969). Occasionally criticized on the grounds of ethnic stereotyping and sentimental avoidance of the xenophobic problem it raises, *The Shifting Heart* has strong elements of pathos and humour and several suspenseful situations which ensure its theatrical effectiveness.

Bib and Bub, see GIBBS, MAY

Bibliographies of Australian Writers, a series published by the Libraries Board of SA, began in 1966 with Janette H. Finch's bibliographies of Patrick White and Hal Porter. Other authors covered in the series include Catherine Helen Spence (1967), A.D. Hope (1968), Judith Wright (1968), Randolph Stow (1968), Ian Mudie (1970), R.D. FitzGerald (1970) and C.J. Dennis (1979). After the series was discontinued the bibliographies were updated in *Index to Australian Book Reviews* (q.v.).

Bibliography of Australia, the standard bibliography of printed material relating to Australia and published between 1784 and 1900, was compiled by Sir John Ferguson (q.v.) and published in seven volumes 1941–69. The first four volumes chronologically (and comprehensively) cover the period 1784–1850 and include books, pamphlets, broadsides and periodicals relating to, but not necessarily published in, Australia; the last three volumes alphabetically (and more selectively) cover the period 1851–1900 and exclude certain classes of printed material, notably periodicals and 'belles–lettres as covered by [E] Morris Miller and [F.T.] Macartney'. In 1975 the National Library of Australia (q.v.) acquired the copyright to Ferguson's *Bibliography*, parts of which had become collectors' items. In 1977 it published a facsimile edition which announced plans for further volumes to include addenda and corrigenda (addenda were included in some of the original volumes), more detailed information on the location of items, and indexes. Ferguson's *Bibliography* has been recognized as one of the world's great national bibliographies, an indispensable tool for Australian historians; its usefulness for students of nineteenth-century Australian literature, however, is limited by the omission of poetry, drama and fiction published after 1850.

Biblionews and Australian Notes & Queries, the journal of the Book Collectors' Society of Australia, began publication in 1947 and was edited by Walter Stone until his death in 1981. Originally titled *Biblionews*, it was distributed as a monthly newsletter to members until March 1964. A second, more substantial but irregular series entitled *Biblionews and Australian Notes & Queries,* ran 1966–72; a third series began quarterly publication in 1976. The periodical, which includes much useful miscellaneous bibliographical and biographical material, also publishes lists of important accessions to the Mitchell Library.

Big Fat Tuesday, see CUNNINGTON, VIVIAN

Big Fellow, see Golconda Trilogy

Big Red, see LAMOND, HENRY GEORGE

Big Toys, a play by Patrick White, first produced in 1977, was published in 1978. Set in a luxurious penthouse apartment with a panoramic view of Sydney's skyline, it deals with the brief relationship between Ritchie Bosanquet, a successful Q.C., Mag, his 'utterly chic' wife, originally the daughter of a hawker, and Terry Legge, a working-class Marxist of Irish-Catholic extraction. The Bosanquets, for whom life has become a stylish, sterile game, regard Terry as a welcome diversion. Mag, nostalgically attracted by his working-class cachet, seduces him; Ritchie is partly interested in him for his past connection with his client, Sir Douglas Stannard, and because he arouses his latent homosexuality. The Bosanquets' link with the general corruption in high places, which has some unspecified connection with uranium mining and looks forward to the 'explosion . . . the biggest, gaudiest toy that ever escaped from a child's hand', threatens to involve Terry. But he finally rejects the toy, a Ferrari car, that Ritchie offers him as payment and leaves the Bosanquets to the dull sterility of their possessions and each other.

BIGGE, J.T. (JOHN THOMAS) (1780–1843), born in Northumberland, England, was selected in 1819 as a commissioner to inquire into conditions in the colony of NSW. Bigge's subsequent reports, *Report of the Commissioner of Inquiry into the State of the Colony of New South Wales* (1822), *On the Judicial Establishments of New South Wales and Van Diemen's Land* (1823) and *On the State of Agriculture and Trade in the Colony of New South Wales* (1823), although sometimes inaccurate and received with hostility by Governor Lachlan Macquarie, provide a detailed picture of the Colony at the time. Bigge and his reports are discussed in John Ritchie's *Punishment and Profit* (1970); he also appears as a character in Alexander Buzo's play *Macquarie* (1971).

BIGGS, MAURICE (1915–), born Kadina, SA, served in the Second World War in the Middle East, Greece, Crete, Syria and New Guinea. He published *Poems of War and Peace* (1945), highly regarded at the time.

'BILL BOWYANG', see VENNARD, ALEXANDER VINDEX

'Bill the Bullock Driver', one of Henry Kendall's (q.v.) best-known and most-anthologized poems, published in the *Australian Town and Country Journal* in 1876, is an ironic portrait of one of the stock figures of Australian outback life and literature. While Kendall applauds the sturdy independence and easy-going nature of the teamster, he also subtly criticizes his parochialism and his insensitivity to the natural wonders that surround him.

'Bill, the Ventriloquial Rooster', a humorous story by Henry Lawson, was written in 1893 and included in *On the Track* (1900). One of the Jack Mitchell yarns, the story records the misfortunes of the Mitchell family rooster, Bill, who is unwittingly ventriloquial and believes his own crow is that of a challenging bird. Bill defeats a rooster from the adjoining selection but its owner, Page, borrows another bird, Jim, which Bill believes is the original challenger. In the ensuing fight Bill pursues Jim vigorously until exhausted, whereupon Jim turns on Bill and gives him a hiding; disgusted with himself, Bill dies. The autobiographical bases for part of the story are confirmed by Lawson's 'A Fragment of Autobiography'.

Billabong, a word of Aboriginal origin, means a water-hole which fills in flood time from the overflow of a river or creek and is then cut off from the main stream as the flood waters recede. The word occurs frequently in Australian folk-song and ballad, poetry and fiction; its best-known use is in the song 'Waltzing Matilda' (q.v.) in which the jolly swagman, referred to in other places as a 'billabong whaler', is camped by a billabong when a jumbuck comes there to drink. Charles Fenner's *Bunyips and Billabongs* (1933) and W.E. Bill Harney's *Brimming Billabongs* (1948) reflect the popularity of 'billabong' as a title. Mary Grant Bruce (q.v.) wrote a popular Billabong series of stories for children about station life in north-eastern Victoria.

BILLETER, WALTER (1943–), born Sierre, Switzerland, came to Australia in 1966. He has written *Sediments of Seclusion* (poetry, 1973), *Dreamrobe Embroideries and Asparagus for Dinner* (with John Jenkins, 1974), *Australian Novemberies* (prose, 1978) and *Radiotalk: 10 Pieces for Magnetic Tape* (1979). He has published five books of translations of German writers (e.g. Konrad Bayer and Paul Celan). In 1974 he co-founded with John Jenkins the magazine *Etymspheres*, and in 1977 he co-edited with Kris Hemensley and Robert Kenny the anthology, *3 Blind Mice*.

Billy (Billy-can), a tin can used for making tea, was an essential item of bush equipment, especially for swagmen. 'Boiling the billy' has long been part of Australian bush life and the period spent waiting for it to boil is usually a time for leisurely comradeship and yarning, as Henry Lawson indicates by using *While the Billy Boils* as the title for his 1896 volume of short stories. Suggested origins of 'billy' include the French word 'bouilli', from the French canned soup used on the goldfields; the Aboriginal word 'billa', meaning 'creek' hence water; and the Scottish word, 'billypot', meaning cooking utensil. William Howitt in *Land, Labour and Gold* (1855), Samuel Lemaitre in *Songs of the Goldfields* (1861) and E.S. Sorenson in *Life in the Australian Backblocks* (1911), date the word from the goldfields of the 1850s; but James Lester Burke, in *The Adventures of Martin Cash* (1870), suggests that it was in use in the penal settlement of Norfolk Island in the 1840s. Usually referred to affectionately, as in 'My Old Black Billy' by Edward Harrington, 'To a Billy' by James Lister Cuthbertson, 'The Old Black Billy an' Me' by Louis Esson, and in songs such as 'With My Swag All on My Shoulder', the billy was treated less nostalgically by other writers (of whom Lawson is one) who saw it as the unromantic symbol of hard times, the badge of the out-of-luck, down-at-

heel itinerants of the bush. Billy Tea, the name of a brand of tea that has been popular in Australia for many years, has some links with 'Waltzing Matilda' (q.v.).

'Billy Barlow in Australia' is a folk-song (sometimes called 'Billy Barlow') which recounts the unfortunate experiences of an immigrant from London, who endures most of the hazards of colonial life in both town and bush, e.g. rapacious Sydney merchants who sell him poor stock, attacks by bushrangers and Aborigines when he moves up-country, and eventual arrest for debt. A typical example of new chum literature, 'Billy Barlow in Australia' was written by Benjamin Griffin and first performed by him as a concert piece in Maitland in 1843. In composing the song (which was a source for James Tucker's *Jemmy Green in Australia*, q.v.), Griffin provided an Antipodean context for a character who had been the subject of an earlier series of British street ballads which were so popular that street singers impersonated Billy Barlow in selling their wares. The several sequels to 'Billy Barlow in Australia' are collected with it in Hugh Anderson's *Songs of Billy Barlow* (1956). Billy Barlow was one of George Selth Coppin's (q.v.) most popular stage characters.

'Billy Skywonkie', see **BAYNTON, BARBARA**

BINGHAM, COLIN (1898–), born Townsville, Queensland, had a long and distinguished career as a journalist and administrator in the newspaper world; he was leader-writer on the *Sydney Morning Herald* 1949–57, associate editor 1957–60 and editor 1961–65. His publications include *Marcinelle and Other Verses* (1925), which includes Bingham's University of Queensland Prize poems (1920, 1923, 1924), *A Book of Verse* (1929), *Men and Affairs* (1967), *The Affairs of Women* (1969), *Decline of Innocence and Other Poems* (1970), *National Images and Other Poems* (1979) and *Wit and Wisdom: A Public Affairs Miscellany* (1982). His autobiography, *The Beckoning Horizon*, was published in 1983.

BINGHAM, GEOFFREY (1919–), born Goulburn, NSW, was a POW in Changi during the Second World War and was ordained an Anglican priest in 1953. A regular contributor of short stories to Australian journals (e.g. thirty-four of his stories have been published in the *Bulletin* 1939–83), Bingham has published several collections of short fiction including *To Command the Cats* (1980), *Angel Wings* (1981), *The Translation of Mr. Piffy* (1982), *The Concentration Camp* (1983) and

Three Special Stories (1983). He also wrote *Bright Bird & Shining Sails* (1981), a fantasy illustrated by the artist Pro Hart, and *Harps, Viols and Goodly Guitars* (1981), a collection of verse.

Birds of Passage, see **CASTRO, BRIAN; Chinese in Australian Literature**

Birdsville Track, one of Australia's early and most hazardous overland stock routes, runs for some 500 kilometres between Marree in SA and the outback town of Birdsville in south-western Queensland. The track is featured in Francis Ratcliffe's *Flying Fox and Drifting Sand* (1948) and George Farwell's *Land of Mirage* (1951), and its history is outlined in Jocelyn Burt's *The Birdsville Track* (1971). Douglas Stewart's poem sequence *The Birdsville Track* (1955) describes his experiences on the track in 1954 and celebrates some of its well-known landmarks and identities.

BIRDWOOD, Field Marshall **WILLIAM** (1865–1951), was born in India. After service in India and the Boer War he was appointed general officer commanding the Australian and NZ army corps and led them at Gallipoli and in France; he was involved in the coining of the term Anzac (q.v.). *Khaki and Gown* (1941) and *In My Time* (1946) are his memoirs.

BIRKBECK, HENRY ANGEL (1850–82), born Mexico, came to Queensland as a boy of twelve after a brief schooling in England. He published *Cupid and Psyche* (1875), a classical epic in ten books in the style of *Paradise Lost.*

BIRKETT, WINIFRED (1897–1966), born North Sydney, published poetry, *Edelweiss and Other Poems* (1932), and fiction, *Three Goats on a Bender* (1934), *Earth's Quality* (1935) and *Portrait of Lucy* (1938). *Three Goats on a Bender* is an amusing story of three women living in a house at Camden; *Earth's Quality,* a substantial novel thought of highly by contemporary critics, deals with the influence of an Australian pastoral property on the lives of three generations of the Weldon family; *Portrait of Lucy* tells of the happy outcome of a marriage between a man and his orphaned ward.

BIRNIE, RICHARD (1808–88), born London, arrived in Perth in 1854 as advocate-general and magistrate of territories but after an unsuccessful legal career in WA and Victoria became a columnist ('The Essayist') on the *Australasian* in 1870. A prominent literary figure in Melbourne and a member of the literary society, the Cave of Adullam, Birnie published *Essays: Social, Moral and Political* (1879).

Birth: A Little Journal of Australian Poetry appeared, mostly monthly, 1916–22. A slight journal (usually only four pages), it began as the personal venture of William Mitchell who edited the first few issues, and became the journal of the Melbourne Literary Club. Several well-known Australian poets featured in its pages and two small annuals (1920 and 1921) were published. Other editors of the magazine were, in succession, Gilbert Wallace, Bernard O'Dowd, Nettie Palmer, Frederick Macartney and Frank Wilmot; Louis Lavater was also involved in its production.

BIRTLES, DORA (1904–), born Newcastle, NSW, was a teacher before sailing in 1932 in the cutter, *Gullmarn,* from Newcastle to Singapore; living abroad for the next five years, she visited the Far East, Scandinavia, Russia and most European countries. She has published travel books, short stories and poetry, but is best-known as a writer for children. Her publications include *North-West by North: Journal of a Voyage* (1935), based on the cutter voyage; *The Overlanders* (1946), the book of the Australian film made in that year; *Australia in Colour* (1946); *Pioneer Shack* (1947), a well-known children's novel which, set in Newcastle, uses the well-tried formula of children employing their wits to retrieve family situations that adults have allowed to get out of control; and *Bonza the Bull* (1949), in which a similar retrieval of family fortunes occurs when Bonza wins first prize at the Sydney Show.

BJELKE-PETERSEN, MARIE (1874–1969), born near Copenhagen, Denmark, came to Tasmania with her parents in 1891. Her brother Hans established the Bjelke-Petersen Physical Culture School in Hobart; Marie became an instructor there and taught physical culture in Hobart schools. Forced to abandon that career because of illness, she turned to writing. Three short sketches, religious in tone, were published as *The Mysterious Stranger* (1913), *Before an Eastern Court* (1914) and *Muffled Drums* (1914). Her first novel, *The Captive Singer* (1917), based on a guide who sang at the Marakoopa Caves in Tasmania, was a conspicuous financial success. Her other novels, sentimental, romantic and florid in language, included *The Immortal Flame* (?1919), *Dusk* (1921), *Jewelled Nights* (1924), *The Moon Minstrel* (1927), *Monsoon Music* (1930), *The Rainbow Lute* (1932), *The Silver Knight* (1934) and *Jungle Night* (1937). More appreciated as a novelist in the USA and England than in Australia, she was awarded the King's Jubilee Medal for literature in 1935.

'Black Bonnet', a poem by Henry Lawson (q.v.), was first published in the *Lone Hand* in 1916; one of Lawson's most worked-over compositions, it was extensively revised after a detailed correspondence between Lawson and George Robertson in 1917 and revised again by David McKee Wright (q.v.) for inclusion in his edition of *Selected Poems of Henry Lawson* (1918). A tribute to Australian pioneer women (more specifically bush pioneers in the original version), 'Black Bonnet' pictures an old woman on her walk to church, her memories as she sits through the service, her talk with the local children after the service, and her return home where in dignity and contentment she resumes her domestic routine. Lawson's memories of his own grandmother, Harriet Winn, went into the writing of the poem (just as Robertson's recollection of 'my Mother' stimulated his involvement in the revisions), although he also revealed that his models at the time of composition were a great-aunt and a neighbour at Blues Point, North Sydney.

BLACK, GEORGE MURE (1854–1936), born Edinburgh, migrated to Australia about 1877 to work on a Gippsland station as a bookkeeper. He soon moved to NSW and by 1889 was subeditor on the *Bulletin*. Active in the emerging labour movement of the 1890s, Black edited the *Australian Workman* 1891–92 and was a member of the NSW parliament 1891–98. He then resumed a journalistic career, editing the *Barrier Truth* (1898), the *Australian Worker* (1900–04) and the *National Advocate* (1908) before returning to the NSW Legislative Assembly 1910–17; in 1917–36 he was a member of the Legislative Council. One of the Labor Party's first historians, Black wrote *History of the NSW Labor Party* (1910), expanded 1926–29 into the seven-part *A History of the NSW Political Labor Party*. Among his other publications was *An Anzac Areopagus and Other Verses* (1923).

Black, Simon, see SOUTHALL, IVAN

Black Stump, The, is an expression figuratively denoting the boundary line between civilization and the remote outback. It is most commonly used in the phrase 'this side of the Black Stump', e.g. in Xavier Herbert's *Poor Fellow My Country* there is a reference to 'the biggest mug this side of the Black Stump'. Various suggestions have been made as to the locality of the original Black Stump, e.g. that it once stood on the site of the government stock tank between Gunbar and Crow's Nest Tank in south-western NSW. 'Duke' Tritton in *Time Means Tucker* (1964) states that it had been the name of a wine shanty near Coolah

in north-eastern NSW. The Black Stump is a landmark in 'Rolf Boldrewood's' *Robbery Under Arms* (1888) and it has been suggested that the term may have originated from its use in that novel. *Beyond the Black Stump* (1956) is the title of a novel by Nevil Shute.

Black Velvet is the colloquial term used to indicate the sexual attraction of the Aboriginal female for the white male. Indulgence in black velvet, a common practice in outback areas where white women were often unavailable, was tacitly condoned as an inevitable phenomenon of frontier life. It is featured in such diverse writing as W.A. Cawthorne's *The Kangaroo Islanders: A Story of South Australia before Colonization* (1926), Ernest Favenc's story 'The Parson's Blackboy', Vance Palmer's novel *The Man Hamilton* (1928), Katharine Susannah Prichard's novel *Coonardoo* (1929), Frank Dalby Davison's story 'Further West', G. Herbert Gibson's 'A Ballad of Queensland' (also known as 'Sam Holt'), Mary Durack's novel *Keep Him My Country* (1955), and Henrietta Drake-Brockman's play *Men Without Wives* (1955). The first version of Xavier Herbert's *Capricornia* (1938) was titled 'Black Velvet'. See also Aboriginal in Australian Literature.

'Black Velvet Band, The', also known as 'The Girl With the Black Velvet Band' and 'The Black Ribbon Band', is a folk-song in which a convict recalls the circumstances of his transportation to Van Diemen's Land. As an apprentice in Dublin (Tralee and London in other versions of the song) he meets a young girl whose hair is tied with a black velvet band; she picks a gentleman's pocket but slips the proceeds into the apprentice's hand when the crime is discovered. 'The Black Velvet Band' is claimed as an Australian folk-song and was part of the repertoire of Blind Billy Huntingdon, but clearly derives from Ireland where it is still sung in a longer version than that known in Australia. The brevity of the major Australian version is characteristic of the Irish-to-Australian process of transmission.

Blackbirding was the name given to the practice of kidnapping natives from the Pacific Islands for labour in the sugar-cane industry of Queensland and for pearl diving in the Torres Strait. The first such natives (usually referred to as kanakas) introduced into Australia were 140 Tanna Islanders from the New Hebrides, imported by Benjamin Boyd in 1847. After many notorious blackbirding atrocities, the Pacific Islanders Protection Act was passed in 1872. Other Acts followed and from 1892 stringent regulations were imposed upon the import of Islanders. Recruiting ceased in 1904 and many were repatriated, although those who had married in Australia or had lived here for twenty years were allowed to remain if they so chose. Accounts of blackbirding are given in T. Dunbabin's *Slavers of the South Seas* (1935), Hector Holthouse's *Cannibal Cargoes* (1969) and E.W. Docker's *The Blackbirders* (1970). Faith Bandler has written the story of her father, a New Hebridean Islander who was brought to Australia to work on the Queensland sugar-cane fields in 1883, in *Wacvie* (1977) and *Marani in Australia* (1980). Peter Corris wrote an historical work on blackbirding, *Passage, Port and Plantation* (1973).

Blacksmith, Jimmie, see *Chant of Jimmie Blacksmith, The*

BLADEN, PETER, (1922–), born Subiaco in Perth, WA, published *The Old Ladies at Newington* (1953), a long poem which won first prize in the Commonwealth Jubilee literature competition in 1951. The poem gives a perceptive treatment of Australia's past and present as seen during the visit of a charitable group to the Newington state home for aged women in Sydney. It also develops the theme of human subjection to decay and death and thus a need for sympathy and understanding of those who are nearing that state. As 'L. Bladen' he published *Selected Poems* (1945); he has also written *Masque for a Modern Minstrel* (1962), *Island Trilogy* (1970) and *Adelaide Sonnets: A Biography of the City* (1975).

Blaiklock Memorial Lectures is a series of annual Australian literature lectures inaugurated in 1971 at the University of Sydney as the result of a gift by Lady Gallegan to commemorate both her father, Herbert Blaiklock, and the poet Henry Kendall. The series began with A.D. Hope's 'Henry Kendall: A Dialogue with the Past'. Subsequent lectures (to 1983) have been given by C. Manning Clark, Rosemary Dobson, G.A. Wilkes, James McAuley, Thea Astley, R.F. Brissenden, Peter Quartermaine, Walter Stone, Leonie Kramer, H.P. Heseltine and T.T. Reed. The lectures (except for Walter Stone's) have been printed annually in *Southerly* and those from 1971 to 1980 (except Stone's) have been published as *Blaiklock Memorial Lectures 1971–1981* (1981), edited by Leonie Kramer.

BLAINEY, GEOFFREY (1930–), Ernest Scott professor of history at the University of Melbourne since 1977 and chairman of the Australia Council 1977–81, is one of Australia's most active economic and social historians. His most significant publications (now provided as a trilogy *A Vision of Australian His-*

tory) are *The Tyranny of Distance* (1966), *Triumph of the Nomads* (1975) and *A Land Half Won* (1980). The three books give a comprehensive account of Australian history from the discovery and settlement of the continent by Aborigines some 40 000 years ago to the end of the colonial era, i.e. the end of the nineteenth century. *The Tyranny of Distance* comprises three sections: a study of how Australia's geographic location affected her growth to about 1860; a history of transport since 1850; and a survey of Australia's foreign relations. As the title suggests, distance is proposed as the major influence on both the direction and the scope of Australian development, both the distance of Australia from other parts of the world and distance within Australia itself. *Triumph of the Nomads* reassesses the accepted theories of the humanization of this continent by the Aborigines and speculates on the structure and motivation of Aboriginal society in the distant past. *A Land Half Won* is a history of white settlement in Australia from the early Dutch and Portuguese voyages of discovery and the establishment of the convict colony at Port Jackson to 1900, by which time the struggle was partly over, the 'land half won'. Blainey's other major published works include *The Peaks of Lyell* (1954), a history of the Mount Lyell region and its mining industry; *The Rush That Never Ended* (1963), a general history of Australian mining; and *The Steel Master* (1971), the biography of the industrial magnate Essington Lewis. The ABC produced a sociological and historical series, *The Blainey View*, based on Blainey's interpretation of Australian life and history, in 1982. Blainey's controversial views on modern immigration are contained in *All for Australia* (1984).

BLAIR, DAVID (1820–99), born Ireland, arrived in Australia in 1850 to train under John Dunmore Lang as a Presbyterian minister. After breaking with Lang he settled into radical journalism and politics, mainly in Melbourne; twice member of the Victorian parliament, he wrote for the *Empire* and the *Sydney Morning Herald* and had a long career as leader-writer for the *Age*. Prominent in Melbourne literary and intellectual circles, Blair was the author of an important early history, *The History of Australasia* (1878), and of *Cyclopaedia of Australasia* (1881).

BLAIR, RON (1942–), born Sydney and a graduate of Sydney University, was closely associated with the founding of the Nimrod Street Theatre. He has worked as an actor, producer, writer and play-reader for the ABC, and as an assistant artistic director of the SA Theatre Company. Blair collaborated with Michael Boddy, Marcus Cooney and the actors in writing and producing the entertainment 'Biggles' which marked the opening of Nimrod, and was one of the writers of its Christmas 1971 show, 'Hamlet on Ice'. His first independent dramatic piece, 'Flash Jim Vaux', a ballad-opera dealing with the life of the convict, James Hardy Vaux, was produced in 1971. His other plays include 'Kabul' (1973), *President Wilson in Paris* (first produced 1973, published 1974), *The Christian Brothers* (first produced 1974, published 1976), *Carry On Up the Constitution* (published *Quadrant*, 1977), 'Owning Things' (1975), *Mad, Bad and Dangerous to Know* (published *Quadrant*, 1976), 'Perfect Strangers' (1977), 'The Political Bordello or How Waiters Got the Vote' (1977), 'A Place in the Present' (1977) and *Marx* (1983). He has also collaborated with Nick Enright in 'Servant of Two Masters', and with Michael Cove in 'Too Early to Say'. Blair's work is varied, ranging from the large-scale satirical revue to the free-ranging, chronicle play such as 'Kabul', which centres on the massacre of a British garrison in Kabul in 1841, and to the one-man shows, *Mad, Bad and Dangerous to Know* (a study of Byron) and *The Christian Brothers* (his best-known play, a representative recreation of a day in a 1950s-style, Roman Catholic school). Despite its simple, chronological action and single actor, *The Christian Brothers* is a complex play; an evocation of the old-fashioned authoritarianism, religious paranoia, bigotry, dedication, love, unconscious frustrations and pathos of a representative priest, the play has sounded the same note of familiarity for Australian audiences as Peter Kenna's *A Hard God*, Barry Oakley's *A Lesson in English* and the film *The Devil's Playground* (1976). *President Wilson in Paris*, which shared the Awgie award for the best Australian stageplay in 1973, is part-historical play and part-macabre thriller.

BLAKE, LEILA, born and brought up in England, came to Australia in 1950 and has worked as actress and director in both England and Australia. She is also a playwright. She started the first Australian theatre-in-the-round in Sydney in 1954 (the Intimate Theatre) and was co-founder of the Claremont Theatre. One of her one-act plays, 'Fair Go', was first produced in 1974 and another, *Prey*, first produced in 1973, is included in the collection, *Can't You Hear Me Talking to You?* (1978), ed. Alrene Sykes. Her other plays include 'I Love, You Love (1974), 'The Stirrer' and 'Feminine Plural: The Women of Shakespeare and Wilde', a successessful one-woman show which she has performed in Australia, Asia and the USA.

BLAMEY, Sir **THOMAS** (1884–1951), born Lake Albert near Wagga Wagga, NSW, served with distinction in the First World War (on Gallipoli and in France) and in 1942 became commander-in-chief of the Australian military forces in the Second World War. A controversial figure, extraordinarily unpopular with the Australian troops he commanded but grudgingly admired for his aggressive competence, Blamey has been the subject of several biographical works, including John Hetherington's (ed.) *Blamey, Controversial Soldier* (1973) and *Thomas Blamey* (1974). He is also the subject of Kenneth Slessor's scathing poem 'An Inscription for Dog River', and has parallels with General Starkey in Thomas Keneally's novel, *The Cut-Rate Kingdom* (1980).

Blanche: An Australian Diary 1858–1861 (1980) edited by Edna Hickson and illustrated by Jill Francis, is the diary of Blanche Mitchell, youngest daughter of the surveyor-general, Sir Thomas Mitchell. It tells of the experiences of a modish young lady growing up in Sydney society in the middle of the nineteenth century.

BLAND, WILLIAM (1789–1868), born London, trained in medicine and became a naval surgeon. As a result of a duel Bland was transported for seven years to NSW where he had a stormy career, being sentenced to twelve months' imprisonment (1818–19) for publishing 'pipes' lampooning Governor Lachlan Macquarie. As medical practitioner, philanthropist, political reformer, promoter of education and enthusiastic transportationist, Bland was a considerable force in the colony. He edited the exploration journals of W.H. Hovell and Hamilton Hume (qq.v., 1831).

BLAXLAND, GREGORY (1778–1853), born Kent, England, came to Australia in 1806 as a free settler. Blaxland is remembered for his participation in the expedition with W.C. Wentworth and William Lawson that crossed the Blue Mountains in 1813. His account of the expedition, *A Journal of a Tour of Discovery across the Blue Mountains in New South Wales*, was published in 1823. There were several later editions, some based on variant transcripts of the journal, as is the version included in George Mackaness's *Fourteen Journeys over the Blue Mountains of New South Wales 1813–1841* (1950–51). Blaxland appears as a character in Eleanor Dark's novel, *No Barrier* (1953).

Bleak Dawn, a play by Sydney Tomholt (q.v.), was published in 1936; it probes the twisted relationship between the drunken, bullying Jim

Stanford and his ex-wife Emily, exposing the destructive power of their emotional ties.

BLIGH, Sir **WILLIAM** (1754–1817), born Plymouth, England, sailed under the command of Captain James Cook on the latter's third voyage in 1776, fought against the French in the American Revolutionary War and in 1783–87 served on merchant ships. In 1787 he was given command of HMS *Bounty* to procure breadfruit plants in Tahiti. On 30 April 1789, soon after leaving Tahiti, the crew mutinied under the leadership of Fletcher Christian and cast off Bligh with eighteen of his men in a small open boat. Bligh skilfully navigated the boat 5822 kilometres to Timor in six weeks, charting part of the 'North-East coast of New Holland' *en route*. Although the persistent legend that his tyrannical personality was the major cause of the mutiny immediately established itself, Bligh was acquitted by a court-martial and the general evidence suggests that he was not an excessively harsh commander. An abridged account of his first expedition, *A Voyage to the South Seas*, was published in 1792 and an unabridged version, *Bligh on the Bounty* in 1936. From 1795 to 1802 Bligh fought in several actions, including Copenhagen in 1801, where he earned the praise of Nelson. In 1805 he was appointed, with the influence of Sir Joseph Banks, governor of New South Wales, in succession to Philip G. King; he arrived in Sydney in 1806. His vigorous attempts to control the liquor trade, the currency system and the use of convicts by free settlers, led to strong opposition from interested sections. His arrest of John Macarthur on a charge of sedition led to the Rum Rebellion, an insurrection of the NSW Corps led by Major George Johnston; Bligh was 'arrested' in January 1808, although he appears to have had passive support from a large number of private settlers. Until February 1809, when he agreed to return to England aboard HMS *Porpoise*, Bligh remained in confinement in Sydney. Once on board the *Porpoise*, he took command and sailed instead to Hobart, where he remained until January 1810 and the arrival of Colonel Lachlan Macquarie's regiment in Sydney. Bligh spent the next four months in Sydney gathering evidence for the forthcoming trial of Johnston in London, where the incidental charges against Bligh were investigated and disproved. A courageous and competent naval officer, navigator and cartographer, as an administrator Bligh possessed numerous skills although his quick temper, abusive language and rigid adherence to instructions handicapped him in the last role.

Of the numerous biographies of Bligh and accounts of the *Bounty* mutiny, the most sub-

stantial are Geoffrey Rawson's *Bligh of the Bounty* (1930), Owen Rutter's *Turbulent Journey* (1936), H.V. Evatt's *Rum Rebellion* (1938), George Mackaness's *The Life of Vice-Admiral William Bligh* (1931, 2nd edn 1951), Arthur Hawkey's *Bligh's Other Mutiny* (1975), Kenneth S. Allen's *That Bounty Bastard* (1976) and Glynn Christian's *Fragile Paradise* (1982). Fictional versions of the *Bounty* mutiny have been numerous and are included in *The Mutineer* (1898) by 'Louis' Becke and Walter J. Jeffery, *Joan of the Pilchard* (1930) by Mary Gaunt, and *Man Against the Sea* (1934) and *Mutiny on the Bounty* (1961) by C.B. Nordhoff and J.N. Hall. Other fictional representations of the Bligh story are included in J.H.M. Abbott's *The Governor's Man* (1919), Roy Bridges's *The Fires of Hate* (1915) and Eleanor Dark's *Storm of Time* (1948). J.M. Couper's *The Book of Bligh* (1969) is the major poetic examination of Bligh and his actions although William Beard published a poem on the subject, *Valiant Martinet* (1956). The first stage presentation of Bligh's story was 'The Pirates: Or, the Calamities of Captain Bligh', a 'naval overture' of the late eighteenth century, which has been followed by *Governor Bligh* (1930) by Doris Egerton Jones, *The House That Jack Built* (1950) by George Farwell, 'Governor Bligh' (1955) by Brian Medlin, and 'The Man Who Shot the Albatross' (1971) by Ray Lawler. *Stormy Petrel*, a radio serial of over sixty episodes by Rex Rienits, was popular in the 1940s and 1950s and became the first Australian television series; the Bligh episode in the *Behind the Legend* television series (1973) was written by Thomas Keneally. Films include *The Mutiny of the Bounty* (1916), produced by Raymond Longford; *In the Wake of the Bounty* (1933), produced by Charles Chauvel; and *Mutiny on the Bounty* (1935) by MGM with Charles Laughton as Bligh and Clark Gable as Fletcher Christian.

BLIGHT, JOHN (1913–   ), born Unley, SA, has spent most of his life in Queensland. During the 1930s depression he tramped the Queensland coast in search of work, settling in 1939 to an accountant's job in Bundaberg. After the war he became part-owner of a group of timber mills in the Gympie district but in 1968 he gave up those interests to return to Brisbane where, since 1973, he has been a full-time writer. Blight's first poetry appeared in the *Bulletin* in 1939, his first collection, *The Old Pianist*, being published in 1945. His other volumes of poetry are *The Two Suns Met* (1954), *A Beachcomber's Diary* (1963), *My Beachcombing Days* (1968), *Hart* (1975), *Selected Poems 1939–1975* (1976), *Pageantry for a Lost Empire* (1977) and *New City Poems*

(1980). *A Beachcomber's Diary* won the Myer Award for the best Australian book of verse in 1964, the *Selected Poems* won a National Book Council literary award in 1976, and in the same year he gained the Patrick White Literary Award for the consistently high quality of his poetry. He was awarded the Dame Mary Gilmore Medal in 1965, the Grace Leven Prize for poetry in 1977, and the Christopher Brennan Award in 1980.

The Old Pianist sees Blight, in fellow-poet Bruce Beaver's phrase, 'a reluctant lyrist' celebrating the 'mean, bounteous land' of Queensland, assessing both its landscape and its people. In *The Two Suns Met,* where he continues to explore his own Queensland and more general Australian experiences, Blight's innovations in punctuation and syntax, his staccato, idiomatic phrasing and ironic complexity, produce poetry which diverges considerably from the conventional poetry of the day. With the two 'Beachcomber' volumes (each of ninety sonnets) that explore everything marine 'from the periwinkle to the whale' and search for universal meanings in the everyday life of the sea, Blight established a reputation as Australia's leading poet of the sea. In the sardonic poem 'His Best Poems are About the Sea', in *Hart,* he rejects the inference that he is no other kind of poet. The best of the 'Beachcomber' sonnets include 'Death of a Whale', 'A Child's Essay about the Sea', 'The Beachcomber', 'Mud' and 'The Volutes'. Although not usually regarded as a confessional poet, Blight produces in his substantial volume, *Hart,* some individual and introspective poetry. Many of the brief poems are intensely personal statements, while others ('A Day', 'Racialism', 'Bricks') reflect on the total human condition. Other themes of the collection are urban life, especially the highrise culture ('The New City Series'), female beauty and the sexuality of old men. Similar themes persist in *Pageantry for a Lost Empire* where, in the title poem and in others such as 'Tenant at Number 9', the flight of time, the pathos of age and the disappointment of life itself are highlighted. Blight has long been regarded highly by fellow writers and the Patrick White Literary Award of 1976 is recognition of his sustained contribution to Australian poetry.

Blinky Bill, see WALL, DOROTHY

Bliss (1981), a novel by Peter Carey (q.v.), won the 1981 Miles Franklin Award. Harry Joy, aged thirty-nine and the moderately successful owner of an advertising agency, suffers a severe heart attack and dies for nine minutes. Sure of the love of his wife Bettina and the well-being of his two children, David and Lucy,

Harry has previously insulated himself from pain and anxiety, relying on his natural charm and his talent as a Good Bloke to smooth his way both publicly and privately. He has also had a facile gift for retelling the romantic stories of his globe-trotting father, which have had an unexpected impact on Bettina, who yearns to be part of the sophisticated world of New York; on David, who is determined to be wealthy; and on Lucy, who is attracted to communism. Compelled by his fear of impending heart surgery to contemplate the afterlife, Harry is convinced, once he has survived the operation, that he has entered Hell. He discovers a series of unpleasant truths including David's avarice and involvement with the drug trade; Bettina's infidelity with Joel, his partner; David and Lucy's incestuous relationship; and his agency's connection with carcinogenic products. Disgusted with his family, Harry moves into the Hilton Hotel where he lives in style on credit and meets the woman he is to love passionately, the sexually-generous and vibrantly-alive Honey Barbara. From the rural community of Bog Onion Road, Honey has come to the city to sell the community's crop of marijuana and to make money as a whore. Meanwhile Harry's apparent irresponsibility and his attempts to abandon the profitable account of Krappe Chemicals result in his family's decision to have him committed to an asylum. The authorities at first mistakenly seize Harry's colleague Alex Duval from the Hilton and, once he is also captured and incarcerated, Harry finds that Alex has stolen his identity in order to escape from a disastrous marriage. Eventually reborn as Harry Joy after Alex's ruse has been discovered, Harry buys his way out of the asylum with Bettina's help and looks forward to living with Honey in her community. Bettina, however, has secured her release on condition that he help her in her long-held ambition to design and sell commercials; and both he and Honey join the Joy family at their Palm Avenue home, now also containing Joel and Lucy's lover, Ken. Honey's energy is eventually sapped by the unhealthy aspects of modern city life, by the tangled problems of the Joy family and Harry's rapid moral deterioration, and she leaves for home. Bettina's remarkably successful career is cut short by her discovery that she has fallen victim to the city's cancer epidemic. Her suicide in an explosion that also causes the death of several others, is followed by Joel's suicide and David's departure for Colombia; there he is eventually executed in a style that seems to correlate with the romances of his grandfather. Harry leaves for the Bog Onion community where, after some initial difficulties, he gains acceptance. Rejected by Honey for five years, he finally wins her, fathers two more children, leads a satisfying if obscure life and dies for the third time at seventy-five when a branch of a tree falls on his head.

BLOCKSIDGE, CHARLES WILLIAM, see **'BAYLEBRIDGE, WILLIAM'**

Bloke, The, see **DENNIS, C.J.**; *Songs of a Sentimental Bloke, The*

Blood Red, Sister Rose, see **KENEALLY, THOMAS**

BLOOM, NORMA (1924–), born Melbourne, has lived in England and NZ, but since 1960 has resided in Hobart. Widely represented in NZ and Australian literary journals and poetry anthologies, she has had two books of verse published: *The Larger View* (1972) and *When I See You* (1978). Her play, 'Ruby', was performed in several Victorian country towns in 1973.

Blue Hills, see **MEREDITH, GWEN**; Australian Broadcasting Commission

Blue Lake Leap was one of Adam Lindsay Gordon's (q.v.) celebrated feats of horsemanship. The site, on the MacDonnell Bay Road just outside Mount Gambier, was marked by an obelisk in 1887. Gordon jumped his horse over a four-rail fence on to a small rock ledge some sixty metres above the waters of the Blue Lake. The spectacular jump was so dangerous that none of the party of kangaroo hunters with him attempted to emulate it. The feat is said to have been emulated in more recent time, however, by another legendary Australian horseman, Lance Skuthorpe.

Blue Mountains, a small range about sixty-five kilometres west of Sydney, was first sighted by Governor Arthur Phillip when exploring north of Port Jackson in April 1788. The Blue Mountains proved an impenetrable barrier to the expansion of settlement until the crossing in 1813 by the expedition of Gregory Blaxland, W.C. Wentworth and William Lawson. By 1815 a road had been laid by convict labour across the mountains to Bathurst and pastoral development soon occurred on the western plains. Charles Harpur, born and bred in the Hawkesbury River country near the foothills of the Blue Mountains, celebrated their natural beauty and magnificence in the introductory verses of his narrative, 'The Creek of the Four Graves', and in his descriptive poem, ' A Storm in the Mountains'. Henry Lawson also wrote a short poem, 'The Blue Mountains'. The 1813 crossing is described in Blaxland's *A Journal of*

a Tour of Discovery across the Blue Mountains in New South Wales (1823).

'BLUEBUSH', see **BOURKE, J.P.**

'Bluey and Curley', see **GURNEY, ALEXANDER GEORGE**

BLUNDELL, GRAEME (1945–), born Melbourne, first became involved in student theatre in 1963 at the University of Melbourne while studying to be a teacher. He moved to the Melbourne Theatre Company in 1966, making his first professional appearance in 1967 in 'Private Yuk Objects' by Alan Hopgood. He then became one of the founders of the Australian Performing Group (q.v.). From 1969 onwards he has acted in film and television in such productions as *2,000 Weeks, The Naked Bunyip, The Box, Stork, Mad Dog Morgan, Don's Party, Power Without Glory, The Odd Angry Shot* and *The Best of Friends*. His most spectacular success was, however, in the sex romps, *Alvin Purple* (1973) and *Alvin Rides Again* (1974); *Alvin Purple* appeared also as an ABC series in 1973 but was taken off air by the chairman, Sir Henry Bland. Blundell has also been active as a director (e.g. *Dimboola, Norm and Ahmed, Dad and Dave*) and founder of various productions and companies (e.g. Hoopla Theatre Foundation and Stable Productions, its film-making branch). He has edited *Plays* (1970, early plays by Alexander Buzo, Jack Hibberd and John Romeril) and has written introductions to Romeril's *I Don't Know Who to Feel Sorry For* (1973) and Dorothy Hewett's *Susannah's Dreaming* and *The Golden Oldies* (1981).

BLUNDEN, GODFREY (1906–), born Melbourne, was a journalist in several Australian States before going to America and later to England. He has been a newspaper correspondent in many of the world's capital cities including Moscow, Paris, New York and London. His Second World War despatches were published in the London *Evening Standard* and he was, for some years, an associate editor of *Time* magazine. His chief Australian novel is *No More Reality* (1935); set in the small Australian township, Hobbleton, the novel is an exuberant though sardonic view of the characters and mores of the typical Australian small community. Blunden's other novels include *The Time of the Assassins* (1952), *A Room on the Route* (1947) and *The Looking Glass Conference* (1956). With *Charco Harbour* (1968) he ventured into historical fiction; it deals with the James Cook expedition to observe the transit of Venus at Tahiti in 1768 and particularly the period of seven weeks spent by Cook in Charco

Harbour after the *Endeavour* had run on to a reef. In 1969 Blunden edited *Norman Lindsay Watercolours,* a new edition of the 1939 *The Norman Lindsay Watercolour Book.* In 1954 he compiled *The Land and People of Australia.*

BOAKE, BARCROFT (1866–92), was born in Sydney, son of an immigrant Irish photographer. After a better-than-usual education for the time he decided to work in the bush, first (in 1886) as assistant to a surveyor in the Snowy River country, later as boundary rider and drover. He believed bush life to be 'the only life worth living' and preferred droving to all other occupations, but he felt compelled by difficult family circumstances to return to Sydney in 1891. Taciturn and brooding by nature, and easily disposed to pessimism and depression, Boake failed to cope with the personal and financial difficulties facing him and his family. He disappeared on 2 May 1892 and his body, hanging from a stockwhip, was found eight days later in scrub at Middle Harbour, Sydney. His suicide recalled that of his poetic idol, Adam Lindsay Gordon, twenty-two years earlier. Boake believed that there was 'a romance, though a grim one' in the story of outback life and that belief is well illustrated in his most notable poem, 'Where the Dead Men Lie' (q.v.), the title poem of his only book of poetry, published in 1897 by A.G. Stephens. Boake's attacks on the absentee landlords and ruthless banking systems that exploited the hard-working, long-suffering bushmen were in line with the customary radical complaints of the time, but his obsession with the tragedy and despair associated with bush life set him apart from most contemporary bush balladists, whose stance was more light-hearted and ironic. The grimness of his vision, however, links him with Barbara Baynton and Henry Lawson. Clement Semmler's *Barcroft Boake: Poet of the Stockwhip* was published in 1965.

'BOAKE, CAPEL' (DORIS BOAKE KERR) (1895–1945), born in Sydney, niece of the poet Barcroft Boake, published the novels, *Painted Clay* (1917), *The Romany Mark* (1923), *The Dark Thread* (1936) and *The Twig Is Bent* (1946). Her poetry was published as *Selected Poems of Capel Boake* (1949). Except for *The Romany Mark,* her novels are set in Melbourne; *The Twig Is Bent* recreates such significant events of the 1850s as the gold rushes, the establishment of Victoria as a separate State and the Eureka Stockade.

Bobbin Up, a novel by Dorothy Hewett (q.v.), was first published in 1959 and subsequently translated into several foreign languages. Unified by setting and theme, it describes the disparate experiences, problems and values of a group of fourteen women employed in a Sydney spinning mill. They contend with grinding poverty and are made memorable by their courage, endurance and comradeship.

Bobwirridirridi, see *Poor Fellow My Country*

BODDY, MICHAEL (1934–), born in England and educated at Cambridge University, came to Australia in 1959 and spent three years in Tasmania before joining the Emerald Hill Theatre in Melbourne. Well-known as writer and actor for commercial television and as a children's television personality, Boddy won the Erik Award in 1965 and has also worked as an actor in film, theatre and radio, as a director, a food and wine newspaper columnist and farmer. In 1970 he collaborated with Ron Blair, Marcus Cooney and the actors in writing and producing the entertainment 'Biggles' which marked the opening of the Nimrod Street Theatre, and was one of the writers of Nimrod's 1971 Christmas show, 'Hamlet on Ice'. He also collaborated with Cooney in 'Cash' (1972), a vaudeville musical based on the life of Martin Cash, the bushranger, but is best-known for his collaboration with Bob Ellis in the popular musical play, *The Legend of King O'Malley* (q.v., 1974), which seemed to mark a renaissance in Australian drama. First produced in 1970 by the National Institute of Dramatic Art in a short workshop season at the Jane Street Theatre, and based on the life of an extraordinary Labor politician of the early years of this century, King O'Malley, the play is a series of music-hall sketches linked by song, dance and mime. Boddy has also written 'The Last Supper Show' (1972); 'The Cradle of Hercules' (1974), a chronicle play about Arthur Phillip and Bennelong; 'Lust for Power' (1977), a music-hall melodrama; and 'Crushed by Desire' (1978), an Australian melodrama set on the goldfields. He has also written several books for children. He is married to the artist, Janet Dawson Boddy, who won the 1973 Archibald Prize for her portrait of him.

Bohemia: The All-Australian Literary Magazine, published by the Melbourne Bread and Cheese Club (q.v.), ran in its first series 1939–40; the second series ran 1945–67. Although usually traditional and patriotic in stance, *Bohemia* published the work of such younger writers of the time as Max Harris and Gavin Casey. An earlier journal, also called *Bohemia,* with items of theatrical, social and general interest, was published 1890–92.

Bohemians of the Bulletin (1965) is a collection of reminiscences and drawings by Norman Lindsay (q.v.) of people he knew at the turn of the century. Mostly literary figures connected with the *Bulletin,* they include J.F. Archibald, A.G. Stephens, J.H.M. Abbot, A.B. Paterson, James Edmond, Livingston Hopkins, Bernard O'Dowd, Randolph Bedford, Hugh McCrae and Louis Stone.

'Bold Jack Donahoe', see **DONOHOE, JOHN**

'BOLDREWOOD, ROLF' (THOMAS ALEXANDER BROWNE) (1826–1915), was born in London and arrived in Australia in 1831. His father, Sylvester Brown ('Boldrewood' added the 'e' to his own surname in the 1860s), settled first in Sydney where he engaged in whaling and built the stone mansion after which the suburb of Enmore is named. In 1838 he overlanded cattle to Port Phillip, speculated in land and started a ferry service. He was ruined in the depression of the early 1840s and Thomas saw himself as the means of repairing the family's fortunes. In 1844 he took up a run in western Victoria, where he prospered as a livestock breeder and potato grower over the next fifteen years. The run was named Squattlesea Mere – taken, like his pseudonym, from his favourite author, Sir Walter Scott. In 1862 he sold Squattlesea Mere to buy a sheep station on Lake Boga, near Swan Hill; the move marked the start of a decade of misfortune. In 1863 he was forced to sell the Lake Boga property at a considerable loss, and although he moved in 1864 to another sheep station near Narrandera he was driven off by drought in 1869.

'Boldrewood' moved to Sydney with his family until 1871, when he was appointed police magistrate at Gulgong, a rapidly-expanding gold-mining town in central western NSW. The office of goldfields commissioner, added to his duties in 1872, brought him some unpopularity with local miners and the press although he earned respect for his work on the Bench and became prominent in community affairs; in 1871 he presided over a luncheon for the visiting novelist, Anthony Trollope. In 1881 'Boldrewood' left Gulgong to become police magistrate at Dubbo (where a centenary dinner in 1982 honoured his presence in the town) and from there moved to similar positions in Armidale (1884–85) and Albury (1885–95). After his retirement from the public service he returned with his family to Melbourne, and as a successful author entered the society in which his family had been prominent in the 1830s and 1840s; a stalwart of the Melbourne Club, he did much of his later writing there.

'Boldrewood' had articles published in the *Cornhill Magazine* in 1866 and 1868, but it was not until he was living in Sydney in 1870 and began having contributions accepted by the newly-established *Australian Town and Country Journal* that he began writing seriously; like his hero, Scott, he wrote in part to pay off his debts. An early *Australian Town and Country Journal* series of articles was republished in 1983 as *Shearing in Riverina.* During the 1870s 'Boldrewood' had seven novels serialized in the same journal; the second, 'The Squatter's Dream' (q.v., 1875), was revised and issued as *Ups and Downs* in 1878 and as *The Squatter's Dream* in 1890. By 1881 he was a moderate success, but his reputation was firmly established by the serialization of his bushranging adventure, *Robbery Under Arms* (q.v.), in the *Sydney Mail* in 1882–83. *Robbery Under Arms* was published in London in 1888 and then in revised form by Macmillan in 1889; the great popularity of the 1889 edition made his name in England and the USA as well as in Australia and led Macmillan to publish seventeen more 'Boldrewood' books (1890–1905). Of these, *A Colonial Reformer* (q.v., 1890), *The Miner's Right* (q.v., 1890), *My Run Home* (1897) and *Babes in the Bush* (1900) had been first published as *Australian Town and Country Journal* serials during the Gulgong years; and *A Sydney-Side Saxon* (1891), *Nevermore* (q.v., 1892), *The Crooked Stick* (1895) *The Sphinx of Eaglehawk* (1895), *The Sealskin Cloak* (1896) and *Plain Living* (1898) were first published as serials in other journals in the 1880s. The remaining Macmillan works are *A Modern Buccaneer* (q.v., 1894), which brought 'Boldrewood' a charge of plagiarism from 'Louis' Becke (q.v.); two romances with a pastoral or mining setting, *The Ghost Camp* (1902) and *The Last Chance* (1905); *War to the Knife* (1899), an adventure set in New Zealand; and *A Romance of Canvas Town* (1898) and *In Bad Company* (q.v., 1901), which reprinted some of 'Boldrewood''s shorter contributions to the press. Earlier he had written *Old Melbourne Memories* (1884) and was the anonymous author of two agricultural manuals, each published by a London firm of colonial outfitters as *S.W. Silver & Co's Australian Grazier's Guide* (1879, 1881), the only books not published under his pseudonym. As 'Mrs Rolf Boldrewood' his wife wrote *The Flower Garden in Australia* (1893); as 'Rose Boldrewood' his daughter published the novel, *The Complications at Collaroi* (1911). His pseudonym survives today in the Rolf Boldrewood Short Story Award given by the Eaglehawk Dahlia and Arts Society.

Politically conservative, 'Boldrewood' advocated throughout his life and work a belief in good breeding and education, individual enterprise, and honesty; that many of the heroes of his novels have these qualities in abundance and are also English gentlemen has encouraged some critics to dismiss him as an Anglophile writing for an English audience. In fact he had no small commitment to Australia, where virtually all his work was first published: he recognized the potential of the country and he believed Australians to be the equal of the English in everything save perhaps breeding. Yet equally clearly he looked beyond Australia in his reading, and from Scott he inherited not only a pseudonym but also a literary form. Most of his seventeen novels are romances, some with a pastoral setting, and are characteristically marred by stilted dialogue and self-conscious literariness that plumbs the depths in *A Sealskin Cloak* and *War to the Knife*. 'Boldrewood' wrote best when informed by his experience rather than by his imagination, as in some of the short pieces in *Old Melbourne Memories* and *In Bad Company*, in the strongly autobiographical *The Squatter's Dream*, or in *The Miner's Right* which is rich in the details of mining life which he saw at first hand at Gulgong. His most enduring work, however, is *Robbery Under Arms*, which is often grouped with *His Natural Life* (1874) and *The Recollections of Geoffry Hamlyn* (1859) as the three classics of colonial Australian fiction. Whether by accident or design, 'Boldrewood' chose as his narrator Dick Marston, a poorly-educated colonial worker who tells in the vernacular the story of his and his family's bushranging past as part of Starlight's (q.v.) gang. The colloquial voice establishes in the novel an authentic tone which is confirmed by the historical foundation for most of the major incidents; other virtues of *Robbery Under Arms* are the pace and tightness of its plot and the vivid realization of some of its characters. H.M. Green thought Dick Marston 'perhaps the first thoroughly Australian character in fiction'; certainly the contrast between the Marston and Barnes families on the one hand, and the Byronic hero Starlight and the insufferably responsible George Storefield on the other, helps explain the survival of *Robbery Under Arms* alone of 'Boldrewood''s work. The contrast also points to the ambivalence about Australia and England that characterizes all his writing.

BOLTON, G.C. (GEOFFREY CURGENVEN) (1931–), born Perth, was professor of history at Murdoch University from 1973 until seconded in 1982 to be first head of the Australian Studies Centre at the University of London. His many writings include *Alexander Forrest* (1958); *A Thousand Miles Away: A History of North Queensland to 1920* (1963); *Dick Boyer: An Australian Humanist* (1967), the biography of Sir Richard Boyer; *A Fine Country to Starve In* (1972), a recreation of the 1930s depression years in WA; and *Spoils and Spoilers: Australians Make Their Environment, 1788–1980* (1981), a comprehensive account of the so-called love-hate relationship which Australians have with the land.

BOLTON, KEN (1949–), born Sydney, has been editor of the small magazine, *Magic Sam,* and has published poetry: *Four Poems* (1977), *Blonde & French* (1978), *Christ's Entry into Brussels: Or, Ode to the Three Stooges* (1978), & *Two Sestinas* (1980) and *Talking to You: Poems 1979–81* (1983).

BOND, GRAHAME (1943–), born Sydney, graduated in architecture from the University of Sydney but developed a taste for writing satirical sketches for revues. These sketches appeared in such revues as 'Drip Dry Dreams' (1970) and 'Filth' (1971) and the pantomime, 'Hamlet on Ice' (1971). He created the bizarre pantomime character Aunty Jack, and wrote *The Aunty Jack Show* (1971–72) and *Wollongong the Brave* for ABC television. He also created 'Flash Nick from Jindavick' (1973) and wrote and performed 'Little Big Show' (an Aunty Jack special) for London Weekend TV in 1978. *Boy's Own McBeth* (written in collaboration with Jim Burnett) was produced in Sydney in 1979 and published in 1980.

Bond of Poetry, The, see **Anthologies**

BONWICK, JAMES (1817–1906), born Lingfield, England, was educated in London and began a career in teaching in 1833. In 1841, pledged to the Nonconformist and temperance causes, he arrived in Hobart and ran schools in Tasmania until he left for Adelaide in 1850. In 1852 he was briefly on the Victorian goldfields before moving to Melbourne to become proprietor of the *Australian Gold Digger's Monthly Magazine;* after that he was a lecturer, land agent and schools inspector (1856–59) until a coaching accident caused his retirement in 1859. During the 1860s and 1870s he alternated teaching and writing in Australia with periodic visits to England, where he was a lecturer and emigration agent, and in the early 1880s began searching London for source material relating to early Australia. From 1883 to 1902 he was engaged mainly in transcribing documents for several Australian State governments; most of the material is now in the Mitchell Library and formed the basis, insufficiently acknowledged at the time, for the

Historical Records of New South Wales and the *Historical Records of Australia* (q.v.). After his retirement he completed *An Octogenarian's Reminiscences* (1902).

The 'Bonwick Transcripts', as they came to be known, were a huge endeavour which laid the foundation for later documentation and writing of Australian history, but quite apart from them Bonwick's output was prodigious. He wrote over sixty works covering a wide range of subjects: history, biography, geography, education (in which he was something of a pioneer in teaching practices), anthropology and fiction. Perhaps the most significant, apart from his autobiography and the emigration novel *The Tasmanian Lily* (1873), were the historical works, *Discovery and Settlement of Port Phillip* (1856), *The Bushrangers* (1856), *A Sketch of Boroondara* (1858), *Curious Facts of Old Colonial Days* (1870), *First Twenty Years of Australia* (1882) and *Port Phillip Settlement* (1883); the early biographies of William Buckley (1856) and John Batman (1867); the travel narrative, *Western Victoria: Its Geography, Geology, and Social Condition* (1858); three studies of the Tasmanian Aborigines, *Daily Life and Origin of the Tasmanians* (1870), *The Last of the Tasmanians* (1870) and *The Lost Tasmanian Race* (1884); and a significant sketch of colonial newspapers, *Early Struggles of the Australian Press* (1890). The recent reissue of a number of Bonwick volumes is evidence that several remain useful reference works and others interesting specimens of their genres.

Bony, see UPFIELD, ARTHUR

BONYTHON Family of SA has had among its prominent members Sir (John) Langdon Bonython (1848–1939), who came to SA as a boy of six. At sixteen he joined the Adelaide *Advertiser* (q.v.) as a reporter; by 1879 he was rich enough from mining speculation to buy a share of the newspaper; by 1893 he was sole proprietor. He edited the *Advertiser* 1884–1929, being eighty-one years old when he relinquished control and the paper became a public company. In a wide-ranging public and commercial career that made him one of the wealthiest and most influential figures in SA, one event of literary significance was his part in establishing the Commonwealth Literary Fund and his chairmanship of its central committee 1908–29. His son, Sir (John) Lavington Bonython (1875–1960), an eminent figure in civic affairs and in the commercial world of SA, was associated with his father in the family newspaper empire; he also edited the *Saturday Express* 1912–30. Sir Lavington Bonython's third son, Hugh Reskymer (Kym) Bonython, whose autobiography, *Ladies' Legs and Lemonade,* was

published in 1979, established major commercial art galleries first in Adelaide and later in Sydney. E.G. Bonython has published *History of the Families of Bonython* (1966).

Book Collectors' Society of Australia began as an informal group of bibliophiles who gathered every week in the 1940s in Gilmour's Bond Street Bookshop, Sydney. Regular members were Walter Stone, H.F. Chaplin, F. Malcolm, S.L. Lanarch, D.J. Farrell, E.G. Boreham and C.D. Berckelman. In 1944, at the suggestion of Berckelman, the group established a formal society. Walter Stone was an officebearer of the Society for many years and also edited its journal, *Biblionews and Australian Notes & Queries.*

Book Lover, a monthly literary review, was published by H.H. Champion 1899–1921, although it did not appear between February 1919 and February 1920. The magazine carried creative literature, chiefly poetry, together with book reviews, literary commentaries and reports of the activities of the Melbourne Literary Club and the Melbourne Repertory Society. A notable event was its publication in December 1916 of 'Furnley Maurice's' poem, 'To God: From the Weary Nations'.

Book of Australian Verse, A (1956, rev. ed. 1968), edited by Judith Wright, replaced *The Oxford Book of Australasian Verse* (ed. Walter Murdoch) which was first published in 1918 (later editions with varying titles).

Book of the Bush, The (?1898), by George Dunderdale and illustrated by J. Macfarlane, contains, as its subtitle indicates, 'many truthful sketches of the early colonial life of squatters, whalers, convicts, diggers, and others who left their native land and never returned'. The most remarkable of Dunderdale's stories is that of a Scotsman, Macdonnell of Glengarry, who tries to set up a fiefdom in the remote bush and is known throughout the country as 'Lord Glengarry'.

Bookfellow, planned as early as 1895 by A.G. Stephens (q.v.) as a magazine in which the literary contents of the Red Page could be elaborated, appeared monthly January–May 1899 under the auspices of the *Bulletin;* thereafter until 1906 it was incorporated in the Red Page. In 1907 Stephens, having left the *Bulletin,* briefly revived the *Bookfellow* as a separate weekly, but it lapsed when he became leaderwriter for the *Evening Post* in Wellington, NZ. Back in Australia in 1909, he revived the *Bookfellow* (1911) which led a precarious monthly existence until 1925, apart from the period March 1916–November 1919 when it was suspended because of the war. In addition to being the leading and sometimes the only purely literary magazine of the period, the *Bookfellow* consistently encouraged the Australian book trade, carrying many booksellers' and publishers' advertisements. In its pages was published a wide variety of Australian poetry, together with some of the best literary comment of the day. Under its imprint Stephens published volumes of verse by C.H. Souter, James Hebblethwaite, John Shaw Neilson and others.

Bookman of the Year Award is awarded by the National Book Council to a person who has made a substantial contribution to the promotion of books. Recent winners are printer and publisher, Bob Cudgley (1974); editor, author, printer and publisher, Walter Stone (1975); publisher's editor, Beatrice Davis (1976); bookseller, Cedric Pearce (1977); booksellers, Marcie and Harry Muir (1978); editor, librarian and bibliophile, Austin McCallum (1979). No awards were made in 1980 and 1981.

Books for Comment, scripts of an ABC series of radio talks on Australian and overseas books, ran August 1963–December 1969. Reviewers included contemporary writers and critics, e.g. Flexmore Hudson, Cecil Hadgraft, George Farwell and Leonie Kramer. Similar earlier series were *Current Books Worth Reading* (irregularly 1941–55), *Todays Books* (October 1956–63) and *Todays Writing* (August 1963–January 1964). A.D. Hope and Vance Palmer were regular contributors to the earlier series.

Boomerang, see SIMPSON, HELEN

Boomerang (1887–92) was a radical Brisbane weekly founded by William Lane and Alfred Walker; after Lane's departure at the end of 1890 it was edited by Gresley Lukin. Two notable staff members were Henry Lawson who wrote 'Country Crumbs', a summary of news from the provincial press, and A.G. Stephens. Lawson's attitude towards his retrenchment from the *Boomerang* is recorded in his poem 'The Shame of Going Back'. The demise of the *Boomerang* is often thought to have inspired 'The Cambaroora Star' (q.v.), but although Lawson called his poem 'the *Boomerang*'s own epitaph' he linked 'The Cambaroora Star' more firmly with the *Republican* (q.v.). There were several earlier, less significant journals called the *Boomerang,* (Melbourne, 1861 and 1894; Sydney, 1877).

BOOTE, H.E. (HENRY ERNEST) (1865–1949), born Liverpool, England, became ap

prenticed to a printer after leaving school at the age of ten, and emigrated to Australia in 1889. He soon became involved in the emerging labour movement and edited the *Bundaberg Guardian* (1894–96), the *Gympie Truth* (1896–1902) and the Brisbane *Worker* (1902–11), the last for the Australian Labour Federation, a trade union organization. In 1911 he moved to Sydney to join the *Australian Worker,* which he edited 1914–43, exercising considerable influence in the labour movement. Active in artistic, music, library and literary circles, Boote wrote four volumes of verse, two works of fiction, two books of essays selected from his newspaper articles, and numerous political pamphlets; of these, the most important are his essays, *A Fool's Talk on Various Subjects* (1915) and *Tea with the Devil and Other Diversions* (1928); the political novel, *The Human Ladder* (1920); and the satiric allegory, *The Land of Wherisit* (1919).

BOOTHBY, GUY (1867–1905), born Adelaide and educated in Australia and England, became private secretary to the mayor of Adelaide before returning to live in England in 1894. He became a highly successful novelist creating a character, Dr Nikola a magician, around whom he wove a popular fictional series. Australian settings are frequently used in his fiction, mainly to add colour to his exciting romance and adventure stories. Between 1894 and 1907 some fifty books of fiction by Boothby were published; of them *In Strange Company* (1894), *A Lost Endeavour* (1895), *The Marriage of Esther* (1895), *Sheilah McLeod: A Heroine of the Backblocks* (1897), *The Curse of the Snake* (1902), *Connie Burt* (1903) and *The Race of Life* (1906) have a significant Australian connection. Boothby's travels in Australia prior to his return to England are recorded in *On the Wallaby: Or, Through the East and Across Australia* (1894). Paul Depasquale wrote *Guy Boothby: His Life and Work* (1982).

'Bora Ring', see Corroboree

BORCHARDT, D.H. (DIETRICH HANS) (1916–), born Hanover, Germany, went to NZ in 1939 where he was a university librarian. He moved to the University of Tasmania in 1950 as deputy librarian and was later librarian (1953–64). From 1965 until his retirement he was chief librarian at La Trobe University, Melbourne. A compiler of many bibliographical works and check-lists, Borchardt published *Australian Bibliography: A Guide to Printed Sources of Information* (1963, with subsequent editions 1966 and 1976, the latter considerably revised and enlarged) and edited *Seven Essays on Australian Subject Bibliography* (1977). He has been editor, since 1970, of the professional journal, *Australian Academic and Research Libraries.*

BORG, SONIA (1931–), born Vienna, Austria, has been an actress, scriptwriter, script editor and associate producer for cinema and television in Australia since 1962. As scriptwriter for Crawford Productions she was involved in the beginnings of Australian television drama. Her screenplays include *Storm Boy* (1976), for which she received an Awgie, and *Blue Fin* (1979); her television dramas include episodes of *Rush, Homicide, Division 4* and *Matlock,* and adaptations of *Power Without Glory* and *I Can Jump Puddles.* She collaborated with Hyllus Maris in *Women of the Sun* (q.v.), a television series about the Aborigines.

Borker, Billy is the humorous 'bar-fly' and spinner of tall yarns in three collections written by Frank Hardy (q.v.). The yarns formed a popular television series in 1964.

BOSTOCK, GERALD (1942–), born Grafton, NSW, was a seasonal worker before joining the army and serving in Malaya and Borneo. After leaving the army he became interested in the history and welfare of his Aboriginal people. In 1972 he helped establish the Black Theatre in Sydney and has since been involved in various aspects of drama and film production. His important play 'Here Comes the Nigger' (q.v.) was performed in Sydney in 1976. He has also published poetry, *Black Man Coming* (1980, see Aboriginal in Australian Literature), and co-produced in 1983, with Alex Morgan, the film *Lousy Little Sixpence,* a documentary about the lives of the Aboriginal people in NSW in the early part of this century. The film's title comes from the amount that an Aboriginal girl house-servant was entitled to receive as her week's wages from the white family for whom she worked.

Botany Bay, an inlet on the eastern coast of Australia just south of Sydney, was the site of the first landing by Captain James Cook 29 April 1770; originally Stingray Bay, it was renamed because of the profusion of specimens collected there by Sir Joseph Banks and his assistants. Botany Bay figured on the London stage even before the arrival of the First Fleet, and although in January 1788 Governor Phillip found Botany Bay unsuitable for settlement and moved the First Fleet to Port Jackson (Sydney Harbour), Botany Bay became, particularly in the nineteenth century, a term referring to the penal colony of NSW in particular, as in the folk-song 'Botany Bay' (q.v.), and to the Aus-

tralian colonies in general, as in the title of John Lang's collection of stories, *Botany Bay* (1859), in many cartoons, and later in Mary Gilmore's poem 'Old Botany Bay'. A number of related phrases derived from 'Botany Bay', including 'Botany Bay Dozen' (a punishment of twenty-five lashes), 'Botany Bay Disease' (insanity, from its prevalence among prominent early colonists of NSW) and 'Botany Bay Rothschild' (Samuel Terry, an early colonial capitalist). Barron Field's poem, 'Botany Bay Flowers', was included in his *First Fruits of Australian Poetry* (1819).

'Botany Bay' is, along with 'Click Go the Shears' and 'The Wild Colonial Boy', one of the most popular Australian folk-songs. Several songs bearing the title 'Botany Bay' have survived; the best-known one (which begins 'Farewell to Old England for ever') is the lament of a male convict who has been transported to Botany Bay, although the warning embodied in the text is made less sombre by the jauntiness of the melody. The words in this version of 'Botany Bay' owe much to an early nineteenth-century English broadside about transportation, 'Farewell to Judges and Juries', but the song derives directly from a comic song in the burlesque drama *Little Jack Shepherd,* which was performed in London in 1885 and in Melbourne a year later. The origins of the song are discussed in Hugh Anderson's *Farewell to Old England* (1964).

BOULT, JENNY (1951–), born England, came to Australia in 1966. Co-editor with Kate Veitch of *Pearls: Writing by South Australian Women* (1979–80), she has published three volumes of verse: *The Hotel Anonymous* (1980), *Handbaggery* (1982) and *The White Rose and the Bath* (1984), and a play, *Can't Help Dreaming* (1981). *The Hotel Anonymous* shared the Anne Elder Poetry Award for 1981.

***Bounty,* HMS,** see **BLIGH,** Sir **WILLIAM**

Bourke, one of the chief towns of northwestern NSW, is situated on the Darling River. The Bourke region was explored by Charles Sturt in 1829 and in 1835 Thomas Mitchell erected a stockade which he named Fort Bourke (after Sir Richard Bourke, then governor of NSW) as a protection against the Aborigines. The present township was laid out in 1862 about eleven kilometres south-west of Mitchell's fort. Bourke has legendary associations with the outback. Henry Lawson set out from Bourke in 1892 on his tramp around the outback, an experience that led to a number of his best-known stories and poems. Stories like 'Send Round the Hat', and the poem 'Bourke', emphasize how central to Lawson's perception of mateship and outback life were his experiences at the back o' Bourke. The phrase 'Back o' Bourke', indicating extreme remoteness, occurs in Will Ogilvie's poem 'At the Back o' Bourke', which concludes nostalgically,

> It's the bitterest land of sweat and sorrow
> But if I were free I'd be off tomorrow
> Out at the Back o' Bourke.

The phrase, still in general use, occurs also in Alexander Buzo's play, *The Front Room Boys* (1970). Noted folklorist Bill Wannan has published *Tales from Back o' Bourke* (1957). Bourke has also lent its name to other picturesque phrases, e.g. a 'Bourke shower' which indicates not a welcome shower of rain but a dust storm.

BOURKE, JOHN PHILIP ('BLUEBUSH') (1860–1914), born Peel River diggings, NSW, was a schoolteacher who turned gold-digger and in 1894 went off to the WA diggings. Under the pseudonym 'Bluebush' (a WA desert mallee) he wrote ballads and lyric poems that were published in such WA newspapers as the Kalgoorlie *Sun* and the Perth *Sunday Times*. One of a group of popular versifiers writing in the west in the 1890s and at the turn of the century – others were E.G. Murphy ('Dryblower'), Julian Stuart ('Saladin') and Francis Ophel ('Prospect Good') – Bourke recorded, with vigour and realism, experiences in the outback and in the mines. His poems were collected into a volume, *Off the Bluebush: Verses for Australians, West and East*, edited by A.G. Stephens in 1915; Stephens had already, in a *Bulletin* review 'The Manly Poetry of Western Australia' (1910), praised Bourke and his contemporaries for writing 'the most virile' poetry in Australia at the time.

Bowyang is a piece of string or a strap tied around the trouser leg below the knee to allow freedom of movement, to prevent the bottom of the trouser from dragging, or to keep the full weight of the trouser off the belt or braces. Bowyangs were popular on the goldfields and among selectors in the second half of the nineteenth century; the term was thought to have derived from the two words 'bowie' and 'Yankee' (American miners on the diggings often wore a bowie knife strapped to their legs), although the derivation accepted now is from the English dialect word 'bowy-yanks', for the leather leggings worn by agricultural labourers. Bowyangs are seldom now worn in Australia, but the term has survived in twentieth-century Australian English, usually to indicate rustic naivety. This usage probably derived from C.J. Dennis's 'Letters from the Bush', a series of misspelt letters in the Melbourne *Herald* purporting to be written by the 'Dad and Dave' type farmer, Ben Bowyang, to his son in the city; 'Ben Bowyang' subsequently became a popular comic strip (sometimes known as 'Gunn's Gully') which was drawn by Daryl Lindsay, Alex Gurney and others. The connection between bowyangs and rural life was consolidated by the recitation booklets brought out by 'Bill Bowyang' (q.v.) in the 1930s, although the contemporary journal *Bowyang* (1979–   ) is more general in focus and publishes articles on politics, history, literature, art and other subjects.

Boy in the Bush, The (1924), a novel written by D.H. Lawrence and Mollie Skinner (qq.v.) in collaboration, recounts the adventures of Jack Grant, a young English immigrant who establishes a life for himself on the land in the WA outback in the 1880s. Lawrence, who met Mollie Skinner while he was in Australia in 1922, took her unpublished novel 'The House of Ellis', transformed it ('the only thing was to write it all out again, following your MS almost exactly, but giving a unity, a rhythm, and a little more psychic development than you have done'), and had it published. In particular, he dramatically modified the character of Jack and totally altered the last two chapters. Accounts of the collaboration are given in Frieda Lawrence's autobiography, *Not I, But the Wind* (1935) and in Mollie Skinner's autobiography, *The Fifth Sparrow* (1972).

BOYD, A.J. (WILLIAM ALEXANDER JENYNS) (1842–1928), born in France of Scottish parents, came to Australia in 1860 and took up a small selection at Oxley Creek in southern Queensland. From 1866 to 1897 Boyd was mainly a farmer and schoolteacher; he then became editor of the *Queensland Agricultural Journal*, a position he held for the next twenty-five years. Boyd's minor publications included *Queensland* (1882), an immigration handbook; *The Earth's History for Boys* (1889), a poetic *aide-memoire* for schoolboys studying geology; and *Some Fragments of Old Sydney* (1898). His major work was *Old Colonials* (1882), a collection of shrewd observations of life in northern Queensland in the latter half of the nineteenth century. *Old Colonials* contains thirty-five anecdotal sketches; some describe familiar bush characters such as the stockman, the shepherd, the drover, the cockatoo farmer and the swagman; others offer insight into contemporary events such as the gold discoveries, into contentious issues such as the presence of the Chinese on the diggings, and into the relationships between the white settlers and the Aborigines. Many of the sketches had appeared under Boyd's pseudonym 'Old Chum' in the *Queenslander* in 1875–76.

BOYD, ARTHUR (1920–   ), the son of the potter and sculptor Merric Boyd and a nephew of the novelist Martin Boyd, was born at Murrumbeena, Victoria. He studied at the National Gallery School in Melbourne but was chiefly taught by his parents and grandfather, Arthur Merric Boyd. In the pre-war years he painted numerous landscapes, but by 1941 was producing his first distinctive figurative works. Closely associated with Sidney Nolan, Albert Tucker and John Perceval, he was greatly influenced by the ideas of John Reed (q.v.). Boyd's first retrospective exhibition was held in Sydney in 1950 and in the same year he visited Central Australia, which resulted in his famous 'Love, Marriage and Death of a Half-Caste' series. He has since drawn on biblical stories, Aboriginal ballads, Shakespearean drama, the Australian landscape and religious legend. He lived in London 1959–78, establishing an international reputation as painter, ceramicist and theatrical set designer, but returned to Australia in 1978 to live near the Shoalhaven River in NSW. Boyd has collaborated with the poet Peter Porter in two works, *Jonah* (1973) and *The Lady and the Unicorn* (1975), and has illustrated a collection of poetry by A.D. Hope, *The Drifting Continent* (1979).

BOYD, BENJAMIN (?1803–51), born London, became a stockbroker and successful businessman. Convinced that the use of steamships on regular coastal runs would be both profitable to himself and of benefit to the Australian colonies, he sought in 1840 the use of numerous harbours on the Australian coast and the right to buy land adjacent to them. He arrived at Port Jackson in his schooner, *Wanderer,* in July 1842, having been preceded by four steamships carrying the supplies for his operations. His coastal steamers were soon engaged on regular schedules to Twofold Bay on the NSW south coast and to Hobart Town. Within a few years Boyd and his business associates controlled or owned more than three million acres in the Port Phillip, Monaro and Riverina areas. Twofold Bay became established as the port through which the agricultural and pastoral products of the Monaro district were shipped to Sydney and Boyd Town, of which some buildings still exist, became its township; at East Boyd a whaling station was established. Boyd, having overreached himself financially, unsuccessfully sought to repair his fortunes on the Californian goldfields. In 1851 he set out in *Wanderer* to cruise the Pacific and establish, if the opportunity arose, a 'Papuan Republic

or Confederation'. In October 1851 at Guadalcanal in the Solomon Islands he went ashore to shoot game and was never seen again. The captain of the *Oberon,* one of the two ships sent to search for Boyd in 1854, returned with a skull which was finally proved to be that of a native. An account of Boyd and his varied activities is given in Francis Webb's poem, *A Drum for Ben Boyd* (q.v., 1948). He is also mentioned in Hugh McCrae's edition of *Georgiana's Journal* (1934). J. Webster published *The Last Cruise of the 'Wanderer'* (?1863) and H.P Wellings wrote *Benjamin Boyd in Australia, 1842–1849* (1936).

BOYD Family has a distinguished history in the arts both in Australia and Europe. The family was founded in Australia by Captain John Theodore Boyd (1825–91), military secretary to an early governor of Victoria, who migrated from Ireland in 1860 and had earlier eloped with Lucy Martin, an heiress of Spanish ancestry. One of their sons, Arthur Merric Boyd (1862–1940), became well-known as a painter, mainly in watercolour, and three of the children of his marriage to Emma Minnie à Beckett (also a talented painter and granddaughter of Sir William à Beckett, q.v.) had distinguished careers. They were the potter (William) Merric Boyd (1888–1959), the landscape artist (Theodore) Penleigh Boyd (1890–1923) and the novelist Martin Boyd (q.v.). Of Merric's children three sons have also become prominent in the arts: the painter Arthur Boyd (q.v., 1920–   ), who has established an international reputation in figurative painting; the sculptor Guy Boyd (1923–   ), who has compiled several large mural reliefs for public display; and the potter and painter David Boyd (1924–   ), who has exhibited widely in Australia and overseas. Another distinguished member of the family was the architect and writer, Robin Boyd (q.v.), the son of Penleigh above. Contemporary members who are continuing the family tradition include Robin's son Penleigh, who is an architect, and Arthur's son Jamie, who is a painter.

BOYD, MARTIN (1893–1972), was born Lucerne, Switzerland, but his early years were spent in Victoria. The Boyd family (q.v.), a distinguished one with a long history in Australia and roots in England, Ireland and Spain, has in the past conferred on its members an inheritance which transcends country and owes as much to European cultural tradition as to Australia. In Martin Boyd's fiction this inheritance was to emerge in an independence of thought and aristocratic, anti–bourgeois values, a strong sense of the past and tradition, an interest in heredity, and a complex, dual allegiance to Australia and Europe. In response to an interest in 'poetic religion', Boyd first studied theology but later turned to architecture. In the First World War he joined an English regiment and served in France 1915–18, first in the infantry and then in the flying corps. The experience had a permanent effect on his attitudes to war and Britain's governing classes, determining his anti-authoritarianism and commitment to a 'qualified pacifism'. His privately published verse collection, *Retrospect* (1920), expresses his post-war restlessness and alienation. After a stay in Australia he returned to Europe in 1921, where he did some newspaper work, made another unsuccessful attempt at a religious vocation by joining a Franciscan community in the Church of England, and began his career as a fiction writer. His first three novels, *Love Gods* (1925), *Brangane: A Memoir* (1926) and *The Montforts* (1928) appeared under a pseudonym, 'Martin Mills'. They were followed by *Dearest Idol* (1929), under the pseudonym 'Walter Beckett'), *Scandal of Spring* (1934), *The Lemon Farm* (1935), *The Painted Princess* (1936), *The Picnic* (1937), *Night of the Party* (1938), *Nuns in Jeopardy* (1940), *Lucinda Brayford* (q.v., 1946), and *Such Pleasure* (1949). In 1948 he returned to Australia to restore his grandfather's house near Berwick but ill-health and other difficulties intervened and he left for England in 1951, finally settling in Rome in 1958. There he completed his best-known work, the series of novels now referred to as the Langton tetralogy: *The Cardboard Crown* (1952), *A Difficult Young Man* (1955), *Outbreak of Love* (1957) and *When Blackbirds Sing* (1962) (qq.v.). His other works include a lighter novel, *The Tea-Time of Love* (1969); two autobiographies, *A Single Flame* (1939) and *Day of My Delight* (1965); and a 'subjective travel book', *Much Else in Italy* (1958). A week before his death in Rome after a long illness he was received into the Roman Catholic Church.

Boyd's first major work was *The Montforts*, winner of the first Australian Literature Society's Gold Medal and an ambitious attempt to chronicle the history of his mother's family in Victoria from the 1850s to the end of the First World War. The novel's emphasis on heredity, the reflection of social change, the ironically-detached juxtaposition of English and Australian attitudes as well as some characters and incidents anticipate his later works. In his next five novels, which are lighter works, he turns away from his Australian experience. *Nuns in Jeopardy*, which approaches religious allegory with its typed characters and metaphysical theme, is in form an anomaly in his fiction although characteristic in its preoccupation with the nature of man and the place of evil. *Lucinda Brayford*, which made a strong impres-

sion overseas, returns to his family's history but in a more leisurely and expansive manner. Although the novel is interesting as social history, Boyd's main concern is with the individual and the possibility of spiritual fulfilment. Lucinda, who is the novel's focus (although the destiny of her son Stephen dominates in the latter part), embodies Boyd's conception of the aristocratic principle in her natural pleasure-seeking response to life and beauty. The four movements of the novel which trace the consecutive stages of Lucinda's outward tragic defeat by circumstance, also describe her spiritual growth and final victory. Contrasting with Lucinda and the saintly Stephen is a diverse array of individuals, many of whom have lost touch with real civilization in their pursuit of power, money or position.

Boyd's most striking achievement is the Langton tetralogy in which he again takes up the Australian material, although now more obviously influenced by his renewed contact with the Graeco-Christian tradition in Italy. The subject of the four novels is the history of the Langton family over more than eighty years, narrated mainly by one of its mature members, Guy Langton, and illuminated by the lives of three main characters: Alice, Guy's grandmother; Diana, his aunt; and Dominic, his brother. Guy is involved as both narrator and character; his birth is a determining event in *The Cardboard Crown* although most of the action occurs before it; *A Difficult Young Man* spans his childhood and youth, and he is a self-preoccupied young man in *Outbreak of Love*. In the first two novels particularly, this narrative perspective contributes to the complexity of Boyd's recreation of the past. The external destinies of Alice in *The Cardboard Crown* and Diana in *Outbreak of Love* reflect the processess of disintegration within the family as new bourgeois, materialist forces make themselves felt. Nevertheless both women remain exceptional figures of steadfast integrity. Dominic, the troubled young man who is the subject of *A Difficult Young Man* and *When Blackbirds Sing*, reflects even more acutely the disparity between personal and social morality. Boyd sees all three central characters as aristocrats, in that they try to live by natural, inner ideals rather than by external valuations. Contrasting with them are individuals like Aunt Baba, Cousin Sarah and Colonel Rodgers who follow only the dictates of their misguided society, whether English or Australian. The detached social satire of Boyd's representation of Australian and English life before 1914, his evocation of place and of time passing are generally admired, although his narrowness of social range has also been criticized.

Boyd's remaining non-fiction works illuminate his preoccupations and fictional method. *Much Else in Italy* develops his religious and aesthetic ideas in a lively and idiosyncratic manner. His two autobiographies are remarkably similar and demonstrate his fiction's dependence on fact. Both reveal Boyd as a religious man without a calling, a lover of order who disliked institutionalized authority and an admirer of the aristocratic way who rejected the Establishment of his day.

BOYD, ROBIN (1919–71), born Melbourne, became a leading figure in Australian architecture as professional practitioner, writer, critic and lecturer. During his distinguished career he was awarded the Gold Medal of the Royal Australian Institute of Architects (1969) and the honorary degree of Litt.D. from the University of New England (1967); he was made CBE in 1971. He published twelve books, the most important of which were *Australia's Home* (1952), *The Australian Ugliness* (1960), *The Walls Around Us* (1962) and *Living in Australia* (1970). He was the editor of *Architect* in 1969 and delivered the Boyer Lectures in 1967.

Boyer Lectures were inaugurated in 1959 under the title ABC Lectures, but the series was renamed the Boyer Lectures in 1961 as a memorial to Sir Richard Boyer who, as chairman of the ABC, had been largely responsible for the introduction of the original series. Since 1959 the ABC has each year invited a prominent Australian to present the results of his work and thinking on major social, scientific or cultural issues in a series of radio talks; these talks are published by the ABC. The series includes Robin Boyd's *Artificial Australia* (1967), W.E.H. Stanner's *After the Dreaming: Black and White Australians – An Anthropologist's View* (1968), Sir Keith Hancock's *Today, Yesterday and Tomorrow* (1973), C.H. Manning Clark's *A Discovery of Australia* (1976), Douglas Stewart's *Writers of the Bulletin* (1977), and Bernard Smith's *The Spectre of Truganini* (1980).

Boys in the Island, The, a novel by Christopher Koch (q.v.), was published in 1958 (revised 1974). Set mainly in Tasmania it deals with the childhood and adolescence of a boy, Francis Cullen. From the age of six the boy has a dream of a 'web of horizons', of a paradisal future that will somehow enlarge his being. He pursues the dream through his experiences at school, through his relationship with his larrikin mates, Lewie Mathews and Jake Brodie, and through his love affair with a country girl, Heather Miles. After this last relationship crumbles he responds to the lure of Melbourne, whence Lewie and Jake have

already gravitated. Their anarchic life in the city culminates in a car crash after a three-day drinking bout. One man is killed, Francis is injured and returns to Tasmania having finally abandoned his dream. Another friend, Shane Noonan, who also runs away to Melbourne with similar aspirations, commits suicide rather than face the death of his romantic vision.

Boys Who Stole the Funeral, The (1980) by Les Murray (q.v.) is subtitled 'a novel sequence' and has been variously described by Murray as 'a novel in poetry', 'a verse play' and 'a verse movie . . . because of its filmic construction'. Essentially it is a narrative in verse made up of 140 separate sonnets, some formal Petrarchan, others irregular in form and structure; some serious, even portentous in tone, others ironic, even tongue-in-cheek. The narrative tells how two young city men, Kevin Stace Forbutt, 'unemployed for speaking proudly under pressure', and former university student Cameron Reeby, 'nicknamed Ratchet, for his prospects', steal the body of Kevin's great-uncle, Clarrie Dunn, from a city funeral parlour and take it by car for burial to the isolated farming community of Dark's Plain on the north coast of NSW where Clarrie was born. Throughout the drive north and later in 'Dunn's country', snatches of conversations and flashbacks reveal many facets of the characters' lives and attitudes – Cameron Reeby's violent altercation with feminists at the university and his later fracas with one of them, Noeline Kampff; Clarrie Dunn's nostalgia for his birthplace; the unbridgeable gap in attitudes and values between Kevin and his father, Stacey Forbutt; Stacey's infidelity to Kevin's mother, which the son has discovered; Kevin's dissatisfaction with city life ('Sydney? It's a building site now') and his yearning for a meaningful life and occupation, 'not just employment'. After they arrive at the farm of Athol Dunn, Clarrie's nephew, the corpse is placed in the smoke-house ('he'll be on the turn to-night') then prepared ('rock salt and bagging needles and sheets') for the burial. Organization of the funeral passes to the matter-of-fact ('It must not be let grow dramatic') postmistress, Beryl Murchison, and the district, now accessory to the fact, seethes with a conspiratorial sense of community. As the funeral ceremony ends the police arrive and the two funeral-stealers escape into the bush. They hide out in a shack on the postmistress's farm and take a job driving a truck loaded with beef for illegal sale in Newcastle. Cameron Reeby is shot and killed by a policeman who stops their meat run and recognizes them as the funeral-stealers. Kevin wanders into the bush and, dazed with shock and grief at his mate's death, falls into a coma. He is confronted by a vision of two figures from Aboriginal legend, Njimbin and Birroogun, the latter's name varying from the pure Aboriginal to the Irish–Australian 'Berrigan', illustrating the blend of both black and white in early Australia. Kevin is put through a series of initiations and instructions and (in echoes of Aboriginal ritual) his soul is renewed by the 'crystal of Crystals'. He listens to 'the blood-history of the continent' and eats from the Common Dish carried by the spirit of Clarrie Dunn. Kevin is free to choose whether he eats or not from this dish but he is not free (nor is anyone) to merely taste in theory the 'work, agony, laughter' in it. It has to be 'body and soul'. As Kevin eats, his reaction deepens: 'It's – ordinary. It's – subtle. It is – serious.' He wakes from the coma with the vision's final injunction in his mind:

'Go back now, find your true work,
Now you can be trusted with it.
Go back. Keep faith with the battlers' food.'

Kevin, 'reborn' after the vision, makes his life with the rural 'battlers' of Dark's Plain on a part of Beryl Murchison's farm that was to have been Clarrie Dunn's. *The Boys Who Stole the Funeral* is notable for its absorbing narrative, intricate symbolism, and innovatory technique. It expresses Murray's admiration for the mores and values of both legendary rural Australia and earlier Aboriginal culture.

BOZIC, SRETEN, see 'WONGAR, B.'

Bracton Family, see *Emigrant Family, The*

BRADDON, RUSSELL (1921–   ), born Sydney, was posted to Singapore in 1942 with the Australian army shortly after graduating from the University of Sydney. For four years he was a prisoner of the Japanese in Changi and on the notorious Burma–Thailand railway. He vividly describes his experiences in his controversial best-selling book, *The Naked Island* (1952); rewritten later as a three-act play (published in 1961), *The Naked Island* was produced in Australia and Britain. *End of a Hate* (1958) describes some of Braddon's experiences after his release from Changi and his initiation into the profession of writing via scriptwriting for a friend's telepathic act produced by the BBC. From 1949 Braddon has been resident in Britain. He has written numerous novels, including *When the Enemy Is Tired* (1968), *End Play* (1972), produced as a film with an Australian setting in 1976, and *The Finalists* (1977). Novels which draw on his Australian experience are *Out of the Storm* (1956), *The Year of the Angry Rabbit* (1964), produced as a film titled *Night of the Lepus, When the Enemy Is Tired* and *The Finalists*. He has also written

documentary accounts and biographies, including *Cheshire, V.C.* (1954), *Nancy Wake* (1956) and *Joan Sutherland* (1962).

BRADLEY, JOHN (1944–   ), born and educated in Brisbane, lived for some years in Canada but returned in 1972 to Queensland, where he teaches English. He has written several plays one of which, *Irish Stew,* first performed in 1979, is included in *Three Political Plays* (1980) ed. Alrene Sykes.

BRADLEY, WILLIAM (1757–1833), came to Australia in the First Fleet as first lieutenant of HMS *Sirius* and surveyed, with Captain John Hunter, the Port Jackson and Broken Bay areas; Bradley's Head on the northern shore of Sydney Harbour is named after him. In 1790 he surveyed Norfolk Island while compelled to remain there because of the wreck of the *Sirius*. Considerable information on the Aborigines and on the flora and fauna of the colony is contained in his journal, *A Voyage to New South Wales,* which was first published in 1969 from the original manuscript.

BRADSHAW, JACK (1846–1937), born Dublin, arrived in Australia in 1860 and was a swagman and small-time confidence man in the outback before graduating to bank robbery. Arrested after a Quirindi robbery in 1880, he spent most of the next twenty years in prison. Released at the turn of the century he became known as a topical balladeer, a Domain orator and a sensational chronicler of crime. Bradshaw's first publications were the autobiographical *The Quirindi Bank Robbery* (?1899) and *Twenty Years' Experience of Prison Life in . . . New South Wales* (?1899), but his best-known work was *The True History of the Australian Bushrangers* (?1924), in which he claimed personal acquaintance with Dan Morgan, Ned Kelly and others. A bitter opponent of the prison system, Bradshaw hawked his broadsheet poems and paperback books, which had several, sometimes combined, editions on the streets of Sydney and in the larger country towns of NSW.

BRADSHAW, RICHARD (1938–   ), born and educated in Sydney, began to tour as a puppeteer in 1969 working with shadow puppets. Well-known overseas, he has performed at puppet theatres and international festivals throughout Europe and America. In 1976 he was appointed artistic director of the Marionette Theatre of Australia. *Bananas* and *The Fourth Wall* (1976), his first plays for actors, were produced in 1975. He is married to drama historian, Margaret Williams.

BRADY, E.J. (EDWIN JAMES) (1869–1952), born Carcoar, NSW, was the son of an Irishman who came to Australia from America, where he had fought in the Civil War. Brady first worked as a shipping clerk on the Sydney wharves, thereby forming that strong link with ships and sailors that inspired his taste for sea shanties and ballads of the days of sail. Thereafter he followed, for brief periods, a variety of occupations in many places. As journalist, feature-writer, dramatic reporter and editor he was connected with the *Australian Workman,* the *Australian Worker,* the *Bull-Ant,* the *Arrow,* the *Native Companion* and the *Grip.* Accounts of his wanderings are contained in two travel books: *The King's Caravan: Across Australia in a Wagon* (1911), the story of his journey from Parramatta to Townsville in 1899–1900; and *River Rovers* (1911), the story of his trip in an open boat down the Murray River from Albury. The impressions gathered from his many experiences are contained in *Australia Unlimited* (1918), a survey of Australia's resources and potential. Brady settled finally on the Victorian east coast at Mallacoota (where Henry Lawson spent some time with him) and while living a simple outdoor life there continued to write, invent and plan prodigiously. Much of this can be gleaned from his entertaining autobiography, 'Life's Highway', published in instalments in *Southerly* 1952–55. Brady's poetry, which first appeared in the *Bulletin* in 1891, was published in four main collections, *The Ways of Many Waters* (q.v., 1899), *Bush-land Ballads* (1910), *Bells and Hobbles* (1911) and *Wardens of the Seas* (1933). It is as a writer of sea ballads that Brady has his particular niche in Australian literary history, but his literary talents were varied: he also wrote children's books, economic treatises, a biography, many short stories and a semi-fictional book on his father's adventures.

BRADY, MATTHEW (1799–1826), was a celebrated early Tasmanian bushranger who had been sentenced to transportation for stealing in 1820. In 1823 he was sent to the newly-established penal settlement at Macquarie Harbour, from where he escaped in 1824. He remained free for two years, staging a daring capture of the township of Sorell and at one stage posting his own reward for the apprehension of the lieutenant-governor of the colony, George Arthur. Popular legend has Brady using violence only in self-defence, and he was treated sympathetically by contemporary writers: e.g. by David Burn (q.v.) in *The Bushrangers* (performed 1829) and *Vindication of Van Diemen's Land* (1840), and by 'Pindar Juvenal' in *The Van Diemen's Land Warriors* (1827) in which Brady captures his would-be captors and sends

them home to Launceston. Richard Butler's biographical novel, *And Wretches Hang,* was published in 1977.

BRAHE, WILLIAM, see **BURKE and WILLS**

BRAIM, T.H. (THOMAS HENRY) (1814–91), born Doncaster, Yorkshire, studied divinity at Cambridge and went to Tasmania in 1835. He was a headmaster in Hobart and Sydney prior to his ordination to the Anglican priesthood in 1849; he returned to England in 1865. Braim edited the *New South Wales Magazine* in 1843 and published two significant works, *A History of New South Wales* (1846) and the emigrant guidebook, *New Homes* (1870).

BRAND, MONA (1915–   ), born Sydney, worked during the Second World War as an industrial social-welfare worker. She was a research officer with the Department of Labour and National Service 1945–48, travelled and worked in Europe 1948–54 and lived in Hanoi 1956–57, where she assisted with the teaching of English. In 1958 she returned to Sydney. Her plays, which deal frequently with controversial, political topics and which reflect her dedication to socialism, appeared from 1948, mainly before left-wing New Theatre audiences, until in 1963 *Our 'Dear' Relations* won first prize in the New South Wales Arts Council drama festival. Since then her revues and more conventional dramas for adults and children have found a wider audience. Her two-act satire 'Going, Going, Gone' (1968), in particular, found the same sort of popular acceptance as Bob Ellis's and Michael Boddy's *The Legend of King O'Malley* (1970). Much of her early dramatic work gained a wider popularity overseas (especially in socialist countries) than in Australia. Her published writing includes three collections of poetry, *Wheel and Bobbin* (1938), *Silver Singing* (1940) and *Lass in Love* (1946); *Daughters of Vietnam,* a collection of five novellas and five poems published in Vietnam in 1958; *Strangers in the Land* in *Two Plays about Malaya* (1954); *Mona Brand: Plays* (1965), published in Moscow and comprising *Strangers in the Land, No Strings Attached* and *Better a Millstone; Here Under Heaven* (1969), comprising *Barbara, Our 'Dear' Relations* and *Here Under Heaven; Flying Saucery* (1971), a children's play; and *Here Comes Kisch* (1983). Her unpublished plays and revues include 'First Aid' (1940), 'Out of Commission' (1955), 'Hold the Line' (1960), 'Come All Ye Valiant Miners' (1965), 'On Stage Vietnam' (1967), 'Going, Going, Gone' (1968), 'And a Happy New Year' (1976) and 'The Pirates of

Pal Mal' (1977). Brand has also written educational books for schools, and scripts for television and radio. She is married to the poet and writer, Len Fox.

BRAY, J.J. (JOHN JEFFERSON) (1912–), born Adelaide and admitted to the bar in 1933, was chief justice of South Australia (1967–78) and has been chancellor of the University of Adelaide since 1968. He has published three volumes of verse, *Poems* (1962), *Poems 1961–1971* (1972) and *Poems 1972–1979* (1979).

Brayford Family, see *Lucinda Brayford*

Bread and Cheese Club was an all-male society formed in Melbourne in 1938 with twelve original members to foster a knowledge and love of Australian literature, art and music and to cultivate an Australian sentiment. Its co-founder and first president was J.K. Moir (q.v.); its monthly journal was *Bohemia* (q.v.). It published the work of Australian writers e.g. Christina Mawdesley's *The Corroboree Tree: and Twelve Shorter Poems of Melbourne's Early Days of Settlement* (1944) and Kathleen Dalziel's *Known and Not Held* (1941). P.I. O'Leary compiled the anthology, *The Bread and Cheese Book* (1939), containing poems by Australian writers, e.g. Roderic Quinn, E.J. Brady, J. Shaw Neilson, Mary Gilmore and others. Henry William Malloch, foundation member and secretary of the Club and first editor of *Bohemia,* published *A Brief History of the Bread and Cheese Club* (1940) and *Fellows All: The Chronicles of the Bread and Cheese Club* (1943).

Bread and Wine, see **SLESSOR, KENNETH**

'BREAKER, THE', see **MORANT, HARRY HARBORD**

Breaking of the Drought, The, see **HOLT, BLAND**

'BREE NARRAN' see **WILLIS, WILLIAM NICHOLAS**

BREEN, B.A. (BARRY ANDREW) (1938–), born St Arnaud, Victoria, has been a teacher since 1960 with the Victorian Education Department. He has published poetry, *Behind My Eyes* (1968), and *Interim* (1973); and short stories, *Flop & Mick & John & Me* (1976). He edited five anthologies for schools between 1969 and 1975.

BRENNAN, C.J. (CHRISTOPHER JOHN) (1870–1932) was born in Sydney, eldest son of Irish Catholic immigrants. He was educated at St Ignatius College (Riverview) and at the University of Sydney where he studied classics and philosophy and graduated in 1892. In that year he won a travelling scholarship to the University of Berlin where he intended to study philosophy. He was distracted from his original intention to obtain a doctorate, by a love affair with Anna Werth (daughter of his German landlady), by the cultural life and institutions of Berlin and by the attraction of French symbolist writers, particularly Mallarmé. Returning to Sydney in 1894 Brennan gained a position in the Public Library and began to write poetry that differed markedly from the prevailing balladry and nationalist–radical verse of the day. He married Anna Werth in Sydney in 1897. During the next decade Brennan was disappointed many times in his efforts to secure an academic appointment at the University of Sydney. His jibes about the conservative reactions of some University senate members to the sexual nature of his poetry, his anti-British attitude in the Boer War controversy and his reputation for intemperate habits and behaviour led to his being passed over for numerous lecturing positions. In 1909 he was finally given a permanent lecturing position in modern literature and in 1920, in spite of a stormy career studded with many differences of opinion between himself and the University authorities, he was appointed associate professor in German and comparative literature. His contemporary and friend, John le Gay Brereton, then professor of English, underlined the brilliant scholarship and intellectual capacity of Brennan by indicating that he could have filled with distinction any of the University chairs in philosophy, classics, literature or languages. Some contemporary opinions stress Brennan's remarkable charisma and unpredictability as a teacher and his contribution to the intellectual life of the University. His domestic life, however, grew increasingly strained, especially after the addition to his household of his German mother-in-law, and after the birth of his children, of whom there were four by 1907. With the gradual failure of the marriage that had begun with such romantic expectations on his part, Brennan turned to Sydney café society where, e.g. in the Casuals Club (q.v.) and in the group known as 'les Compliqués' (q.v.), he became a notorious figure. His ebullience, wit and dominating personality made him a legend in the city's bohemian circles but to his wife and children he was often a ranting, drunken bully. In 1922 he formed a tender relationship with Violet Singer ('Vie'), a lively, fun-loving woman nearly twenty years his junior, with whom he lived until she was killed by a tram in 1925. The open scandal surrounding his affair with

Violet Singer and the University's dissatisfaction with what they saw as his degenerate behaviour and irresponsible conduct led to his dismissal in June of that year. The alcoholism and poverty of his remaining years were occasionally alleviated by the attempts of friends and former students to rehabilitate him. In 1931 he was awarded a Commonwealth Literary Fund pension of £1 a week. Following a period of ill-health he gave up alcohol and returned before his death to his Catholic faith, which he had neglected since his early University days.

Brennan's first collection of verse was a booklet stereographed by himself (eight copies), entitled *XVIII Poems: Being the First Collection of Verse and Prose by Christopher Brennan* (1897). In the same year he also published *XXI Poems: (1893-1897) Towards the Source*. This booklet met a mixed critical reception: praise from friendly reviewers in *Freeman's Journal* and *Hermes* and from A.G. Stephens in the *Bulletin* Red Page, but contemptuous dismissal (e.g., 'musical, meaningless words to an accompaniment of equally futile and meretricious pessimism') from other critics. In 1903, with the help of John le Gay Brereton, he prepared several copies of a manuscript edition of poems written in response to the Boer War. Entitled *XV Poems* it was not published until Harry F. Chaplin's 1953 edition, *The Burden of Tyre: Fifteen Poems by C.J. Brennan*. Brennan was opposed to the Boer War and Australia's role in it; in common with many, he felt sympathy for the Boers and saw Britain ('Tyre') as an overbearing, imperial power, prostituting herself to commerce. He denounced Christianity, which sanctioned the conquest and exploitation of the Boers, as the immoral, ideological support of the imperialist system. It was probably because of its stringent attack on Great Britain that the poems remained unpublished during Brennan's lifetime. Brennan's chief volume, entitled *Poems* but usually referred to as *Poems (1913)*, was published in December 1914. It incorporates revisions of material published in both of the 1897 booklets and many earlier poems. It is made up of three major sections – 'Towards the Source', 1894-7; 'The Forest of Night', 1898-1902; 'The Wanderer', 1902 – and two concluding segments, 'Pauca Mea' and 'Epilogues'. *Poems (1913)*, although long a source of bewilderment to readers, has been largely interpreted and explained by the analysis and commentary of such writers as A.R. Chisholm and G.A. Wilkes (qq.v.). Wilkes was responsible for the interpretation of the poems as corresponding to Mallarmé's concept of the *livre composé* (i.e. the book of verse which, although made up of many separate individual pieces, is conceived

and executed as a whole). With the publication in 1980 of Axel Clark's biography of Brennan, much of *Poems (1913)* can be seen to be biographically based. *Poems (1913)* has the overall theme of man's search for Eden, a paradisal state. The opening section, a mainly lyrical prelude, 'Towards the Source', has thirty individual poems that recall the courtship of Brennan and Anna Werth in Berlin and reveal him as the impatient, expectant lover who is confident that the consummation of their love in marriage will achieve his Eden. Extravagantly expressed and highly embellished, these lyrical attempts (e.g. 'A Prelude', 'We Sat Entwined', 'Autumn', 'Deep Mists of Longing') to invest his love with an ethereal, paradisal quality are not highly regarded. In the second section, 'The Forest of Night' (originally conceived as 'The Book of Lilith'), the search for Eden, apparently unsuccessful in the love affair of 'Towards the Source' (as the linking poem 'Luminary', written only four months after his marriage, clearly shows), is pursued into the deepest regions of the poet's innermost self and into myth and legend where other searches for the paradisal state are recorded. The second cycle opens with the twelve-poem series 'The Twilight of Disquietude', and reveals the poet tormented by his 'vast and impotent' dreams. 'The Quest of Silence', which follows, explores the mythology and legendry of the past. At the centre of 'The Forest of Night' is the figure of Lilith, in Hebrew tradition 'Lady of Night', an ambivalent figure who is both the source of man's longing yet a source also of malignity which brings apprehension and horror. In Jewish legend, Lilith is Adam's mate before Eve but is forsaken by Adam. Her revenge on Adam is to destroy his capacity for contentment in his new life and to instil in him a torturing vision of a lost paradise, which she represents, for which he is fated to yearn eternally but never attain. The essence of Lilith, a powerful concept containing within it Brennan's recognition of the dualistic view of man's divided nature, is conveyed in the thirteenth part with the lines beginning 'She is the night'. 'The Shadow of Lilith' section ends also in failure of the quest for the paradisal state. The concluding lines of 'The Wanderer' (the last of the major sections of *Poems (1913)*) sum up Brennan's life more aptly than any complex appraisal could do:

> I am the wanderer of many years
> Who cannot tell if ever he was king
> Or if ever kingdoms were.

'The Wanderer' abandons the quest for Eden through the Absolute and with an air of resolution turns to the Actual, the life–experience of the material world. 'Disabused of illusory hopes' (Clark) he appears to accept that Eden, as he dreamed it, is unattainable. With that acceptance comes the calm of resignation.

I feel a peace fall in the heart of the winds
and a clear dusk settle, somewhere, far in me.

Such a peace never really settled on Brennan's life but 'The Wanderer' does signal the poetic, if not the actual, end of his exhaustive search.

Brennan's only other collection of poetry was *A Chant of Doom and Other Verses* (1918), the title poem, a violent denunciation of Germany's role in the First World War, having been published in the *Lone Hand* 1 August 1916. He wrote some love lyrics during the period he lived with Violet Singer. The tenderness and certainty of poems such as 'Midnight' and 'Because She Would Ask Me Why I Loved Her', indicate how important that relationship was to him. His critical works include 'German Romanticism: A Progressive Definition', which appeared in the *Modern Language Review of New South Wales* in January 1920; 'Studies in French Poetry', a planned series of sixteen articles for the *Bookfellow* in 1920, only six of which were completed; and 'Symbolism in Nineteenth Century Literature', a series of University Extension lectures, later published in *The Prose of Christopher Brennan* (1962), edited by A.R. Chisholm and J.J. Quinn. For a long time only dimly understood, yet reverenced the more because of that inaccessibility, Brennan is one of the first legendary figures in Australian literature. Unresponsive to, and seemingly uninfluenced by, the forces of nationalism and radicalism that dominated the contemporary Australian scene, he was a literary enigma standing apart from his own social and literary milieu, finding instead an intellectual affinity with European interest in philosophy and human psychology, and a literary affinity with the French symbolist writers. Although virtually unkown and unrecognized outside Australia, he is clearly part of the international mainstream of writing that gave rise to poets such as T.S. Eliot and William Butler Yeats. Axel Clark's 1980 study is the definitive Brennan biography; other important works on Brennan include A.R. Chisholm's *Christopher Brennan: The Man and His Poetry* (1946) and G.A Wilkes's *New Perspectives on Brennan's Poetry* (1953).

'BRENNAN, D.' see **LAMBERT, ERIC**

BRENNAN, NIALL (1918–   ), born Melbourne, has published numerous works on politics, moral philosophy and biography as well as several small volumes of verse. His two chief biographies are those on Archbishop Daniel Mannix (1964) and John Wren (1971). His

other works include *The Ballad of a Government Man* (1944, a satire on public servants), *The Making of a Moron* (1953, social philosophy), *A Hoax Called Jones* (1962, memoirs), *The Politics of Catholics* (1972, historical and political issues), *Vice Versa* (1975, poetry) and *Tales from the Australian Mountains* (1979, tales, history and memoirs). 'A Man Upon His Mountain' won the 1976 prize of the FAW for a manuscript novel but has not yet been published because of a dispute over copyright.

'BRENT OF BIN BIN' was the pseudonym under which Miles Franklin (q.v.) wrote a series of six novels dealing with Australian station and rural life from the 1850s to the 1920s. The opening novel of the series, *Up the Country* (1928), roughly dated about the year of the great floods, 1852, is a saga of several squatting families whose complicated interrelationships, set against the backdrop of the Monaro (q.v.) region of southern NSW, produces a confused, almost chaotic narrative. The novel's narrative is aptly described by the author's own term 'possuming', a word used to describe the seemingly frenzied and unco-ordinated movements of possums in the branches of a tree. *Ten Creeks Run* (1930), which moves the stories a generation further on (1880s–90s), has an ambivalence to sex that leads to improbabilities of plot and character, marring an otherwise compelling story and evocation of the loveliness of the countryside. Chronologically, *Cockatoos* (1954) follows, set in the period 1890s–1900. It concerns the lives of the small farmers and selectors, descendants of the earlier squatters, and in particular the destiny of Ignez Milford who, dissatisfied with the sterility of a future life at Oswald's Ridges, follows Miles Franklin's own example of escape into a larger, more satisfying world through her writing and emigration to America. *Gentlemen at Gyang Gyang* (1956) reverses the story of *Cockatoos*; Bernice Gaylord, a successful artist, returns disillusioned to Australia, marries Peter Poole (great grandson of James Poole of the first novel) and finds happiness. The final novel of the series (published third in 1931), *Back to Bool Bool*, completes the cycle, returning far-flung descendants of the original families to Bool Bool for reunion celebrations. In spite of its web of intricate human relationships and rather repetitive plot the closing novel provides a strong value judgement in favour of Australia from those who have sought their fulfilment in a variety of ways in a variety of places. The remaining novel *Prelude to Waking* (1950) is, according to its title and its prefatory comment, intended as a prelude to the series but has little real connection with the chronicle novels.

The pseudonym (originally 'Brand of the

Bin Bin' but changed by a typing error to 'Brent') was said to represent a kindly, elderly gentleman (perhaps a composite of Miles's father, John Franklin, and the novelist Joseph Furphy) writing from his experience of Australian bush life. The identity of 'Brent of Bin Bin' caused lively speculation in the early 1930s and was not completely established until the 1950s. Her motive in using the pseudonym is usually attributed to the embarrassment she had experienced from the publication of *My Brilliant Career* (q.v.) in her own name, while her correspondence with Mary Fullerton about the pseudonym indicates her overwhelming fear of intrusions upon her privacy.

Brentwood Family, see *Recollections of Geoffry Hamlyn, The*

BRERETON, JOHN LE GAY (1) (1827–86), born Yorkshire, came to Australia in 1859 as a doctor and practised in Sydney. Father of John le Gay Brereton (q.v.), he published the volumes of poetry, *The Travels of Prince Legion* (1857), *Poems* (1865), *The Goal of Time* (1883) and *Beyond* (1886). His prose works included *One Teacher: One Law* (1883) and *Genesis and the Beatitudes* (1887).

BRERETON, JOHN LE GAY (2) (1871–1933), born Sydney, son of Englishman John le Gay Brereton (q.v.) had a long association with the University of Sydney as student, librarian and, finally, professor of English literature. Well-known for his charm and his interest in the writers who sought his advice (he was a close friend of Henry Lawson, q.v.) he was an unusual academic for the time, never divorcing himself from the world of men outside the University. His own scholarship is evident in such a work as *Writings on Elizabethan Drama* (1948), collected by R.G.Howarth. His charming though slight lyric poetry includes *The Song of Brotherhood* (1896), *Sea and Sky* (1908) and *Swags Up!* (1928). He published two whimsical collections of essays and reminiscences: *Landlopers* (1899), which records his wanderings along the coast and in the mountains near Sydney, and *Knocking Round* (1930), which contains anecdotal reminiscences and occasional references to writers like Christopher Brennan and Henry Lawson. With Brennan and under the direction of Louisa MacDonald, the first principal of the Women's College of Sydney University, Brereton composed *A Mask* in 1913 to celebrate the twenty-first anniversary of the Women's College. The *Mask*, a pageant of famous women, was presented again in 1932 and in 1982, the centenary of the College. R.D. FitzGerald (Brereton's nephew) has an account of Brereton in *Of Places and Poetry* (1976);

H.P. Heseltine wrote *John le Gay Brereton* (1965).

BRICKHILL, PAUL (1916–   ), born Melbourne, began work as a copy boy with the Sydney *Sun* and became one of its feature writers before serving in the RAAF during the Second World War. He was a prisoner of war in Germany for two years; his wartime experiences provided the material for his first book, *Escape to Danger* (1946). After the war he was an Australian newspaper correspondent in England, Europe and the USA, returning to Australia in 1948. Other war books followed: *The Great Escape* (1950), the story of 'X organization', the escape network in the camp, Stalag Luft III; *The Dam Busters* (1951), the story of 617 Squadron and its attacks on the German network of dams in the Ruhr valley; *Escape – or Die* (1952); and *Reach for the Sky* (1954), the story of Douglas Bader. *The Dam Busters* became a world best-seller, a radio feature and was made into a film; *The Great Escape* and *Reach for the Sky* were also filmed. Brickhill has also written *The Deadline* (1962), a novel about a young Australian who becomes involved in a murder campaign conducted by Algerian terrorists.

BRIDE, T.F. (THOMAS FRANCIS) (1849–1927), born Cork, Ireland, came to Australia as an infant, had a brilliant career as a law student and became librarian of the Public Library in Melbourne in 1881; one of his rivals for the position was Marcus Clarke. In 1895 he became curator of estates of deceased persons, retiring to private life in 1909. During his term as librarian he edited *Letters from Victorian Pioneers*, a collection of colonial reminiscences presented to Lieutenant-Governor Charles La Trobe for his own proposed book of reminiscences which was never published. La Trobe returned the letters to Victoria in 1872; they were finally published in 1898.

Bridge, a magazine published quarterly by the Australian Jewish Quarterly Foundation, began in 1964 and ceased in 1972. It contained Jewish history, creative writing and book reviews; its contributors included David Martin, Herz Bergner, Walter Stone, Frank Moorhouse, C.B. Christesen, Randolph Stow and Leslie Rees.

BRIDGES, HILDA (1881–1971), sister of Roy Bridges (q.v.), was born at Hobart. She wrote some twenty books of light fiction 1922–50. They include *The Squatter's Daughter* (1922, a novel adapted from the play by Bert Bailey and Edmund Duggan), *House of Storms* (1931), *Chinese Jade* (1933), *Distant Fields* (1936) and *Men Must Live* (1938). She also wrote children's books, e.g. *Bobby's First Term* (1924) and *The House of Make Believe* (1928).

BRIDGES, ROY (1885–1952), born Hobart, joined the staff of the Melbourne *Age* in 1909 and was associated with that newspaper for almost twenty years before retiring to Tasmania to live with his sister Hilda Bridges (q.v.) on the old family property, Wood's Farm, in the Sorell district. Most of Bridges's books are connected with the early history of Tasmania although some are set in Victoria. He wrote some forty adventure novels 1909–50, which have contrived plots and stereotyped characters. Among the best-known are *The Barb of an Arrow* (1909); *Mr. Barrington* (1911), which gives a fictional account of well-known convict, George Barrington, in London; *The Immortal Dawn* (1917), a series of Anzac character sketches; *These Were Thy Merchants* (1935), *The House of Fendon* (1936) and *Sullivan's Bay* (1937), three novels dealing with the early Port Phillip settlement; *Green Butterflies* (1923), which begins a series of books about the Richmond-Sorell district of Tasmania from the convict period, e.g. *Negrohead* (1930), *Trinity* (1931), *Cloud* (1932) and *The League of the Lord* (1950). Bridges also wrote *That Yesterday Was Home* (1948), which is partly autobiographical and contains some of the history of Wood's Farm. D.H. Borchardt and B. Tilley compiled *The Roy Bridges Collection in the University of Tasmania* (1956).

BRIGGS, ERNEST (1905–), born Sydney, became music and art critic for the Brisbane *Courier-Mail*. He published two volumes of meditative lyrics, *The Merciless Beauty* (1943) and *The Secret Listener* (1949). The 'merciless beauty' is that of the pure mind; the seven metaphysical-style poems of the volume emphasize the permanence of the mind of man in contrast with the transience of material things. The poems of a third volume, *The Timeless Flowers* (1952), are chiefly translations or derivations from the Chinese.

BRIGHT, CHARLES (1832–1903), born probably Liverpool, England, came to Australia to join the Victorian gold rush at Ballarat but was soon back in Melbourne, where he joined the *Argus* as a reporter and later wrote for the *Herald*. Significant in Melbourne intellectual life in the second half of the nineteenth century, he was editor (1859–64) of the *Examiner and Melbourne Weekly News* and of *Melbourne Punch* (1863–66). He contributed also to the *Spectator*, a free-trade journal; to Marcus Clarke's *Humbug*; and in later life to the *Age*. He edited (1856–59) the popular literary weekly, *My Note Book*, his contributors including R.H. Horne and J.E. Neild.

'Brighten's Sister-in-Law' is both a poem and a story by Henry Lawson (q.v.) in which the narrator's sick son is nursed through a fever by the sister-in-law of a shanty keeper, to whom the narrator has been guided by the vision of a woman he sees in the branches of a tree. When the poem was published in 1889 the narrator was a carrier and his son Harry a schoolboy with seven brothers and sisters; in the prose version, which forms part of the Joe Wilson (q.v.) sequence, the narrator is Joe and his son Jim is an only child of three years.

Brindabella, see **FRANKLIN, MILES**

Bring Larks and Heroes, Thomas Keneally's (q.v.) third novel, was published in 1967 and won the Miles Franklin Award for that year. Its protagonist is Phelim Halloran, a corporal in the marine detachment guarding the prisoners in a penal colony at 'the world's worse end'; the novel records the effect on the individual conscience of a repressive and authoritarian society. Although an Irish Catholic dragooned into the military service of the Protestant English, Halloran feels bound to live within a society to which he has given an oath of allegiance, until a series of incidents reveals the brutality and corruption of the 'System' and makes moral evasion impossible; these incidents include the flogging to the point of death of a convict on suspicion of his involvement in an Irish uprising, the execution of a convict artist wrongly accused of rape, the bureaucratic bungling which victimizes a convict at the end of his sentence, and the savage quelling of an uprising. Under the influence of the convict Robert Hearn, who presents the view of an alternative society informed by the ideas of the Enlightenment and the French and American revolutions, Halloran steals the stores of the starving colony to help victual an American whaler; he is assisted by Ann Rush, a convict servant with whom, in the absence of a priest, he has contracted a secret marriage validated by their oaths to each other. Betrayed by an accomplice, Terry Byrne, Halloran and Ann are executed.

BRINSMEAD, HESBA (1922–), born near Bilpin in the Blue Mountains, NSW, trained as a teacher but worked during the Second World War as a governess before marrying and moving to the Mallee. After the war she returned with her family to Melbourne, where she worked as a kindergarten teacher, acted in repertory and from the mid-1960s onwards became a prolific writer of books for children and young adolescents. Her first book, *Pastures of the Blue Crane* (1964), winner of the 1963 Mary Gilmore Award and the 1965 Children's Book of the Year Award, is set in the coastal NSW-Queensland border area; a story of tangled personal relationships and racial prejudices, it also proved to be a successful television series in 1971. Her other works include *Season of the Briar* (1965), a story of a girl lost in the mountains of Tasmania; *Beat of the City* (1966), set against a background of adolescent, urban violence; *A Sapphire for September* (1967); *Isle of the Sea Horse* (1969); *Listen to the Wind* (1970); *Who Calls from Afar* (1971); *Longtime Passing* (1971), which won the Children's Book of the Year Award for 1972; *Echo in the Wilderness* (1972); *The Ballad of Benny Perhaps* (1977); *The Honey Forest* (1979); *Once There Was a Swagman* (1979); *Time for Tarquinia* (1981) and *Longtime Dreaming* (1982). Although much of Hesba Brinsmead's fiction is adolescent romance, it is also concerned with the pressures that a fast-moving and confusing modern society exert on the young.

Brisbane, named after Sir Thomas Brisbane, governor of NSW 1825–31, is the capital city of Queensland and is situated in the south-east of the State on the Brisbane River, which flows into Moreton Bay (q.v.); the centre of the city is some thirty kilometres from the mouth of the river. The Brisbane River was discovered by John Oxley in 1823 and settlement began with the establishment of the Moreton Bay penal settlement the following year. In 1842 the Moreton Bay district was opened up for settlement and in 1859 Brisbane was designated the capital of Queensland, newly-proclaimed after separation from NSW; it became a city in 1902. Brian Penton in *Landtakers* (1934) and Rosa Praed in several of her novels document its colonial past, and David Malouf's novel *Johnno* (1975) captures the texture of Brisbane life in the 1940s and beyond.

Brisbane Courier, the oldest Queensland newspaper, began publication as a weekly, the *Moreton Bay Courier,* in 1846; its founder, Arthur Sydney Lyon, established other early Queensland newspapers including the *Moreton Bay Free Press,* the *North Australian* and the *Darling Downs Gazette.* James Swan, an early partner of Lyon, became proprietor of the *Moreton Bay Courier* in 1848; subsequent owners included Theophilus Pugh (1859–63), under whom the newspaper became a daily titled the *Courier* in 1861, Thomas Blackett Stephens (1864–73), Gresley Lukin (1873–80) and Charles Hardie Buzacott. The *Courier* became the *Brisbane Courier* in 1864 and ran until 1933, when it merged with the *Daily Mail*

(1903–33) to form the *Courier-Mail.* This newspaper was under the control of Sir Keith Murdoch and John Wren until sold to the Herald and Weekly Times group after Murdoch's death in 1952. Among editors of the *Brisbane Courier* were William Wilkes (1848–56), Charles Lilley, Lukin, F.W. Ward (1894–98), C. Brunsdon Fletcher (1898–1903) and J.J. Knight (1906–16); staff or contributors significant in Australian literature include W.H. Traill in the 1870s and Nettie Palmer and Brian Penton in the 1920s. David Rowbotham became literary editor of the *Courier-Mail* in 1980.

BRISBANE, KATHARINE (1932–), born Singapore, was educated in WA, where she worked on the *West Australian* as reporter and theatre critic (1954–59). She was national theatre critic 1967–74 and Sydney theatre critic 1978–80 for the *Australian* and has written extensively on Australian drama in books and periodicals. With her husband Philip Parsons she founded Currency Press (q.v.) in 1971 for the publication of the work of Australian playwrights.

Brisbane Water, the north-east arm of Broken Bay about forty kilometres north of Sydney, was explored by Governor Arthur Phillip in 1788 and was named after Governor Sir Thomas Brisbane in 1825; on it is situated such well-known resorts as Gosford, Woy Woy and Ettalong Beach. Henry Kendall (q.v.) recuperated there from alcoholism in 1872 and wrote a long description of the area, 'Arcadia in Our Midst', for the *Australian Town and Country Journal,* 27 February and 6 March 1875. Three of his poems are set against the Brisbane Water background, 'The Voice in the Wild Oak', 'Narrara Creek' and 'Mooni', the last two using well-known Brisbane Water place names. Charles Swancott wrote *The Brisbane Water Story* (1953–55).

BRISSENDEN, R.F. (ROBERT FRANCIS) (1928–), born Wentworthville, Sydney, was educated at the Universities of Sydney and Leeds. He has held teaching and research positions at several Australian and overseas universities and is reader in English at the Australian National University. In 1977–78 he was a member of the Literature Board of the Australia Council and was its chairman 1978–81. Associate editor of *Meanjin Quarterly* 1959–64 and literary editor of the *Australian* 1964–65, Brissenden edited the anthologies *Southern Harvest* (1964, short stories) and *Australian Poetry 1972* (1972). In addition to critical work on English and Australian literature he has written several books of poetry, *Winter*

Matins (1971), *Elegies* (1974), *Building a Terrace* (1975) and *The Whale in Darkness* (1980). A sensitive observer of both nature and human nature, Brissenden is most effective in his poetic descriptions of seascapes and in his presentation of the mellow side of life associated with the past.

Britannica–Australia Award, see Encyclopaedia Britannica Award

British Australasian, an Anglo–Australian weekly which catered for expatriates living in England and for investors, intending immigrants and others interested in the Australian colonies and New Zealand, began publication in London in 1884. In 1924–40 it was known as the *British Australian and New Zealander*, but reverted to its original title in 1941, and in 1948 became the *Australia & New Zealand Weekly*; from 1943 until it ceased publication in 1969 it was a magazine. For most of its life the *British Australasian* carried Australian business, political and sporting news as well as information about Australasian visitors to the United Kingdom and reports of activities in the United Kingdom (e.g. meetings of the Royal Colonial Institute) of relevance to Australasia. Two important editors were Philip Mennell (1892–1905) and Charles Henry Chomley (1908–42); Chomley published literary supplements in which he included the work of his circle of ex–Australian writers and artists, among them his nephew, Martin Boyd.

Broad Arrow, The, a novel written by Caroline Leakey (q.v.) under the pseudonym 'Oline Keese', was first published in 1859; there were several later editions, including one in 1886 revised by Mrs Townshend Mayer which omitted three chapters of the original. Subtitled *Some Passages in the History of Maida Gwynnham, A Lifer, The Broad Arrow* opens with the innocent Maida in prison, having been seduced and then tricked into forgery by the caddish Henry Norwell. Wrongly convicted also of infanticide, she is transported to Van Diemen's Land where she becomes a servant in the Evelyn household and struggles to reconcile her pride and sense of worth with the degradation she endures. At the end of the novel she is converted to a Christian's acceptance of her situation, but dies soon after. Her death is discovered by Norwell, who has come repentant to the colony after the revelation of his perfidy has led to his wife's death in England. Broken by his sins, Norwell ends his days in a local asylum.

Within this melodramatic frame *The Broad Arrow* is a social and domestic novel offering a picture of Tasmanian society during transportation, based on Leakey's experiences in the colony between 1848 and 1853 and centred on the household of George Evelyn, his wife, his brother the Reverend Herbert Evelyn, and the minister's daughter Emmeline and visiting niece Blanche D'Urban. The paradoxes of colonial attitudes towards 'Home' are shrewdly observed, but the main focus of the narrative is on the convict system; in particular, on the contrast between the Christian fortitude advocated by Herbert Evelyn and the harsh realities of convict life which he recognizes and which lead George Evelyn to temper his humane instincts with a rational, hard-headed approach to the management of convict servants. The emphasis in *The Board Arrow* is on the humiliations of convict life rather than on the horrors; an anti-System novel which was read by Marcus Clarke, it played its part in creating the legend that the convicts were more sinned against than sinning.

Broad Stream, The, see **STEWART, DOUGLAS**

Broadcaster, a WA weekly published 1934-55, included items of literary and historical significance (e.g. articles on bushrangers and the goldfields) and fiction serials (e.g. Katharine Susannah Prichard's *Black Opal*).

Broadsides or, as they were sometimes called, broadsheets, were a popular way of spreading the news in Australian towns and cities in the period prior to the widespread circulation of the daily newspapers. Hawkers of broadsides, often referred to as 'chapmen', 'ballad singers', 'flying stationers' or 'patterers', would carry their supply of printed sheets through the streets, attracting the crowds by their lively 'spiel' about the subject of the broadside – the latest murder, horror, tragedy, war, battle, death or remarkable event. Broadsides were also used to carry the words of ballads or songs and for the issue of proclamations and government orders. Printed on only one side of the paper, the broadsides could be posted on fences and walls for better communication of their contents; they thus anticipated the modern poster. Geoffrey C. Ingleton's *True Patriots All* (1952) includes typical Australian broadsides from the first half of the nineteenth century.

BRODERICK, DAMIEN (1944–), born Melbourne, graduated in 1966 from Monash University where he had been co-editor of the student newspaper, *Lot's Wife* (q.v.). He had a brief but varied career in journalism before becoming a full-time writer, chiefly of science fiction (q.v.). Now one of the leading Australian exponents of SF, although antagonistic to the limiting nature of such a label, Broderick has been widely represented in Australian and overseas SF anthologies and has published a book of short science fiction, *A Man Returned* (1965), as well as several science fiction novels, *Sorcerer's World* (1970), *The Dreaming Dragons* (1980), *The Judas Mandala* (1982) and *Transmitters* (1984). *The Dreaming Dragons* was runner-up in the worldwide John W. Campbell Memorial Prize for science fiction. With Rory Barnes, a colleague from Monash student days, Broderick wrote the SF novel *Valencies* (1983). In 1977 he edited *The Zeitgeist Machine,* an anthology of Australian science fiction.

'BRODNEY, SPENCER' (LEON BRODZKY) (1883–1973), born Melbourne, spent most of his life abroad working as editor and journalist under his well-known pseudonym. In 1904 he founded the Australian Theatre Society in Melbourne with the object of producing Australian plays of merit; after his departure for London the Society, renamed the Playgoers' Club, dwindled into a playreading social gathering and around 1909 ceased to exist. Inspired by the efforts of Louis Esson and the Pioneer Players, Brodzky later completed a provocative and spirited three-act play, *Rebel Smith,* published in New York in 1925 but not produced by the Pioneer Group.

BRODRIBB, W.A. (WILLIAM ADAMS) (1809–86), born London, went to Hobart in 1818 but from 1835 was a squatter in southwestern NSW (one homestead being on the present site of Gundagai), in the Gippsland area, in the Monaro district, and then on huge runs (up to 1165 square kilometres) in outback NSW. His reminiscences of a long and successful career on the land are contained in his *Recollections of an Australian Squatter* (1883).

BRODZKY, LEON, see **'BRODNEY, SPENCER'**

BRODZKY, MAURICE (1847–1919), born in East Prussia, migrated to Australia in 1871 after service in the French army during the Franco-Prussian War. He taught for some years after his arrival, then became a journalist with the Sydney *Evening News,* the Melbourne *Age* and the Melbourne *Herald.* In 1885 he began his own journal, *Table Talk,* a weekly compendium of literature, the arts, political and social affairs. Brodzky was sued for libel in 1902 and lost *Table Talk,* which continued (under the aegis of the Melbourne *Herald*) until 1939. He went to San Francisco where he became editor of a weekly, the *Wasp,* and later worked as a

journalist in London and New York. He published two small books, *Genius, Lunacy and Knavery* (1876), the story of an unprincipled doctor, and *Historical Sketch of the Two Melbourne Synagogues* (1877).

BROINOWSKI, ROBERT (1877–1959), born Balwyn, Victoria, became a Commonwealth public servant, rising to be Clerk of the Senate 1939-42. Active in Melbourne literary circles, he was secretary of the Repertory Theatre Club and a member of the Melbourne Literary Club. He was editor of the poetry page in *Stead's Review* and launched the *Spinner* (1924-27), which published Australian poetry. After his retirement in 1942 he was a reviewer for the *Sydney Morning Herald.*

'Broken-Down Squatter, The', see **FLOWER, CHARLES AUGUSTUS**

Broken Hill, a mining city situated almost on the western border of NSW, is much closer to Adelaide than to Sydney and has been linked more closely, both commercially and culturally, with SA than with NSW. Charles Sturt discovered the Barrier region in 1844; noting a break in the range at one point, he named the area 'Broken Hill'. Charles Rasp, a boundary rider, discovered outcrops of ironstone in the area in 1883; from his discoveries emanated the Broken Hill Proprietary Company (BHP) in 1885 to exploit the rich silver, lead and zinc deposits later found there. BHP remains one of Australia's most important industrial giants; the city of Broken Hill, one of Australia's most colourful mining and frontier communities. The nearby township of Silverton (silver town) grew up in 1880s on the site of a rich silver field, Umberumberka. Mary Gilmore was a young schoolteacher there 1887–89; her association with the working-class people of the area stimulated her radical attitudes. The *Silver Age,* a newspaper that originated from Silverton in 1884, published some of her early poetry. Other literary personalities associated with Broken Hill include A.A.G. ('Smiler') Hales, who was a journalist with the *Broken Hill Times* and the *Barrier Miner* (1886–90); C.J. Dennis, who worked at odd jobs in the mines and wrote a poem 'A Ballad of the Barrier'; Ion Idriess, who attended the Broken Hill School of Mines and worked in an assay office there; and Joseph Furphy, whose novel *Rigby's Romance* (1946) was serialized in the Broken Hill newspaper, the *Barrier Truth,* 1905–06. R.H.B Kearns, who rose to be chief accountant of North Broken Hill Ltd, wrote an historical series beginning with *Broken Hill 1883–1893* (1973), followed by three other volumes, 1974, 1975, 1976. Geoffrey Blainey wrote *The Rise of Bro-*

ken Hill (1968), Brian Kennedy *Silver, Sun and Sixpenny Ale: A Social History of Broken Hill 1883–1921* (1978) and Barry Ellis *Broken Hill 1883–1983* (1983). Kenneth Cook's novel *Wake in Fright* (1961) appears to be set in Broken Hill.

Typical of the anecdotes about fortunes won and lost in the early days of Broken Hill is the story of cattleman Sidney Kidman, who sold four steers to James Poole, one of the original members of the Broken Hill syndicate, for a fourteenth share of the initial lease. Kidman, unimpressed by the area's prospects, sold the share for £150; within three years it was worth one and a quarter million pounds.

Broken Melody, The, F.J. Thwaites's (q.v.) first novel, was published in 1930 and has been reprinted many times. The novel chronicles the misadventures and eventual triumph of Ted Jenkins, a member of a pioneer Riverina family who is expelled for drug addiction from his school in Sydney. He returns to the family station, Nullabean, where he restores himself to health until ordered from home by his father when the truth emerges about his expulsion. Back in Sydney under an assumed name and again a drug addict Ted is rescued from despair by a young woman, Carmol Blythe, who towards the end of the novel leaves him a substantial legacy after she is accidentally killed. With Carmol's assistance he again breaks his addiction, secures a job as a club celloist, and after moving to Thursday Island because of his health is discovered by a visiting concert pianist, Fay Le Bretton; she sponsors him to England, where he makes a billiant debut at the Albert Hall playing 'The Broken Melody' on a stage festooned with gum trees and wearing a white silk shirt, breeches, leather leggings and riding boots. After further success in Europe and the USA he returns to Australia, purchases drought-stricken Nullabean and is reconciled with his father and Nibs, the girl from the adjoining property.

Thwaites's most successful novel, *The Broken Melody* was followed in 1935 by *The Melody Lingers,* which takes the story of the Jenkins family into the next generation. Dale Jenkins, the son of Ted and Nibs, is sent down from Sydney University for desecrating the Cenotaph in a drunken spree and has to endure privation in London and Colombo before being rescued by an old friend and restored to his family. The epigraph to *The Melody Lingers* dedicates the novel to the first Riverina Jenkins, Francis, 'my great-great grandfather'; this places Thwaites in the next generation after Dale Jenkins, although *The Melody Lingers* also carries an assurance that the characters in the novel are fictitious.

BROOKE, G.V. (GUSTAVUS VAUGHAN) (1818–66), born Dublin, had established himself on the British and American stage when he was engaged by George Selth Coppin early in 1855 for an Australasian tour. He arrived with a company which included Fanny Cathcart, and played major Shakespearean roles in Melbourne and Sydney and on provincial tours both before and after going into partnership with Coppin in 1856. In 1859 he broke with Coppin but failed on his own account as manager and entrepreneur, partly through the drinking problem which was also an important factor in his deterioration as an actor when he returned to England in 1861. He made numerous farewell appearances both in Australia in the 1850s and England in the 1860s, and was *en route* back to Australia under engagement again to Coppin when he was drowned in the Bay of Biscay. Several contemporary accounts of the shipwreck were published in Australia.

BROOKES, HERBERT (1867–1963), born Sandhurst (Bendigo), Victoria, played a leading role for many years in Victorian cultural and community affairs. Brookes held appointments with the Commonwealth Board of Trade (1918–28) and the Tariff Board (1922–28) and was Australian commissioner-general to the United States. He was a foundation commissioner of the ABC (1932–39), edited *Liberal* (1911–14), the journal of the People's Liberal Party, and actively promoted the Protestant newspaper *Vigilant*. He also edited *The Federal Story* (1944) by Alfred Deakin, his father-in-law. His son-in-law, Rohan Rivett, published *Australian Citizen: Herbert Brookes* (1955).

BROOKES, Dame **MABEL** (1890–1975), born Melbourne, won esteem for a lifetime of patriotic, social and charitable work. She was made CBE in 1933 and DBE in 1955 and was awarded an honorary LLD by Monash University in 1967. She published fiction, *Broken Idols* (1917), *On the Knees of the Gods* (1918) and *Old Desires* (1922), as well as historical, documentary and autobiographical works, e.g. *Crowded Galleries* (1956), *St. Helena Story* (1960), *Riders of Time* (1967) and *Memoirs* (1974).

BROOKS, DAVID (1953–), born Canberra, was founding editor of the Open Door Press (Canberra and Toronto, Canada) and North American editor of *New Poetry* 1976–80. He compiled *New South* (1980), an anthology of Australian poetry of the late 1970s; his own published work includes *Five Poems* (1981) and *The Cold Front* (1983).

BROOKSBANK, ANNE (1943–), born Melbourne, has written television documentaries and dramas, stage plays and film scripts. With her husband Bob Ellis (q.v.), she wrote the stage play *Down Under* (1977), first produced in 1975. She also wrote *Green Room* (1976), performed in Perth in 1976 and was co-author of the feature film *Maybe This Time* (1980). She has won five Awgies.

Broome, situated on Roebuck Bay some 2000 kilometres north of Perth, is the chief port of north-west WA. First settled in 1865 in an abortive sheep-farming endeavour, the area turned to pearling in the 1880s; at its peak the port of Broome had a pearling fleet of 400 luggers and a polyglot population of more than 5000 people. It was designated as a township in 1883 and named after Sir Frederick Napier Broome (1842–96), who was governor of WA 1883–90 and whose wife was the writer Lady Broome (q.v.). Although the pearling industry has declined in recent years, Broome is now a centre for processing meat from the Kimberley cattle stations and for offshore drilling for oil and gas. The pearling industry offered a romantic and mysterious background for many novels of adventure and intrigue; works which feature Broome are Henrietta Drake-Brockman's *Blue North* (1934) and *Sheba Lane* (1936); Ion Idriess's *Forty Fathoms Deep* (1937); Katharine Susannah Prichard's *Moon of Desire* (1941); John Harcourt's *The Pearlers* (1943); Arthur Upfield's (q.v.) *The Widows of Broome* (1951); Colin Simpson's *Come Away, Pearler* (1952); and Tom Ronan's *The Pearling Master* (1959).

BROOME, Lady **MARY ANNE** (MARY ANNE BARKER) (1831–1911), born Spanish Town, Jamaica, was educated in England and, after marrying for the second time in 1865, went to New Zealand where her first book, *Station Life in New Zealand* (1870), won praise for its vivid account of pioneering life. In 1882 her husband, after whom the port of Broome is named, became governor of WA; her account of their experiences in that colony was published as *Letters to Guy* (1885), her elder son Guy having remained at school in London. Her final work (she had earlier written novels, children's books, cookery books and edited travel books) was *Colonial Memories* (1904). *Remembered with Affection,* edited by Alexandra Hasluck (1963), is a new edition of *Letters to Guy*.

BROOMFIELD, F.J. (FREDERICK JOHN) (1860–1941), born Hampshire, England, was brought to Australia in 1868. For more than three decades from the 1880s he had wide experience as a journalist. As subeditor on the *Bulletin* Broomfield reputedly accepted Henry

Lawson's first contribution and helped prepare the *Bulletin's* famous anthology, *A Golden Shanty* (q.v., 1890). He also wrote for the *Freeman's Journal,* the *Sydney Mail,* the *Brisbane Courier* and the *Australian Worker,* edited the *Centennial Magazine,* the *Elector* and the *Golden Fleece,* and was employed on the *Picturesque Atlas of Australia* and as a government journalist. His creative work included several published songs and contributions to anthologies of prose and verse, but his major contributions to Australian literature were his encouragement of contemporaries like Lawson, John Farrell and Victor Daley, and his great assistance to Sir John Quick and later E. Morris Miller in the compilation of the pioneering bibliographical work, *Australian Literature From Its Beginnings to 1935* (q.v., 1940). Broomfield was a flamboyant *Bulletin* bohemian and a central figure in the Dawn and Dusk Club (q.v.).

Brown, Arthur and Waldo, see *Solid Mandala, The*

'BROWN, CARTER' (ALAN GEOFFREY YATES) (1923–), born London, served in the Royal Navy in the Second World War and came in 1948 to Australia where he began, almost immediately, to write for the thriving pulp fiction market, turning out an endless stream (six books a year) of mystery stories, westerns, romances, science fiction and horror stories under a variety of pseudonyms including 'Paul Valdez' and 'Tex Conrad'. As 'Peter Carter Brown' (later 'Carter Brown' because it suited the American market) he began in 1950 a series of mystery stories, which by his own vague count stands at upward of 150 titles, many of which have sold 200 000 copies in the USA alone. 'Carter Brown's' staple is a combination of mystery, violence, sex and snappy dialogue. His fictional hard-drinking heroes are Al Wheeler, Rick Holman and Danny Boyd; typical titles are *Tomorrow Is Murder, Ice-Cold Nude, Blonde on the Rocks, No Blonde is an Island* and *Lady is Available.* 'The Carter Brown Mystery Theatre', an Australian radio series 1956–58, was devoted to his works, and an Australian musical, 'The Stripper', based on his book, was performed by the Sydney Theatre Company in 1982. His autobiography *Ready When You Are, CB,* was published in 1983.

BROWN, ELIZA and **THOMAS** arrived in the Swan River colony in 1841 and took up land at York, Grassdale. Eliza Brown's letters to her father William Bussey back in Oxfordshire, during the period 1840–51, offer one of the most comprehensive accounts of life in the colony. Their descendant Peter Cowan edited

A Faithful Picture: The Letters of Eliza and Thomas Brown at York in the Swan River Colony 1841–1852 (1977).

BROWN, LYN (1918–), born Fairfield, NSW, graduated from the University of Sydney in 1946. Editor, librarian and teacher, she has also published poetry: *Late Summer* (1970), *Jacaranda and Illawarra Flame* (1973) and *Going Home at Night* (1979).

BROWN, MAX (1916–), born Invercargill, NZ, was educated in Melbourne and has worked as a journalist there and in Sydney, Perth and country towns in NSW and WA; he has also worked as a teacher, labourer and film publicist. He served in the RAAF during the Second World War and used his severance pay to write *Australian Son* (1948), a highly-regarded and sympathetic biography of Ned Kelly. He has subsequently published two novels, *Wild Turkey* (1958), which focuses on making a film about Australia by a Hollywood company, and *The Jimberi Track* (1966), as well as *The Black Eureka* (1976), which focuses on the 1946 strike by Aboriginal station hands in the Pilbara region of WA fictionalized in Donald Stuart's *Yandy* (q.v., 1959).

BROWN, PAMELA (1948–), born Seymour, Victoria, has published poetry, *Sureblock* (1972), *Cocabola's Funny Picture Book* (1973), *Automatic Sad* (1974), *Correspondences* (1979, with Joanne Burns) and *Café Sport* (1979); and a book of poetry and prose, *Country and Eastern* (1980).

BROWNE, THOMAS ALEXANDER, see 'BOLDREWOOD, ROLF'

BRUCE, MARY GRANT (1878–1958), was born and educated at Sale in the Gippsland district of Victoria, and began writing as a young child. After thrice winning the essay competition of the Melbourne Shakespeare Society she settled into journalism in Melbourne. Employed on the staff of the *Age* to run, as 'Cinderella', the children's page of the *Leader* (q.v.), she contributed short stories, articles on a wide variety of subjects, and serials not only to the *Age* and the *Leader* but also to *Woman's World, Woman* (both of which she temporarily edited), *Lone Hand, Pastoralist's Review, Table Talk* and other journals. In 1905–07 *A Little Bush Maid* was serialized in the *Leader;* published as a book in 1910, it inaugurated the Billabong series of children's books, which ran until 1942 and made Bruce one of the best-known Australian authors of her time. Sales of her work have been estimated at two million copies. Bruce went to England in 1913 and

wrote for the *Daily Mail;* in 1914 she married her second cousin, George Bruce, who wrote two novels and many angling pieces. They spent most of the war in Ireland before returning to Victoria, where Mary resumed journalism in Melbourne and renewed contacts there with other women writers. In 1927 the Bruces settled in Ireland but following the accidental death of one of their two sons lived on the Continent and at Bexhill-on-Sea in Sussex until 1939, when they again settled in Victoria. In 1949 George Bruce died, and in 1954 Mary, visiting England for the centenary of her publisher, Ward, Lock and Company (whose 'stable' had also included her contemporary and competitor, Ethel Turner) moved once more to Bexhill, where her last years were spent.

In all, Mary Grant Bruce published thirty-seven children's novels 1910–42, usually at the rate of one a year; a book of Aboriginal legends, *The Stone Age of Burkamukk* (1922); a collection of radio talks, *The Power Within* (1940); and an enormous amount of journalism, short fiction and poetry, most of it uncollected. The special subject of her fiction was the re-entered bush world of her childhood, most memorably recreated for her readers in the Utopian portrait of Billabong, a fictional station in northern Victoria, home of David Linton, his two children Jim and Norah (Mrs Linton has died after Norah's birth), Jim's friend Wally Meadows (who comes on holidays soon after the series starts and stays on to marry Norah), the homestead staff, various hired hands and periodically-appearing Linton relatives. In *A Little Bush Maid,* the first of the fifteen Billabong books, David Linton is about forty and his children about fifteen and eleven respectively. They remain so in the next two novels but the First World War forces a change in the timeless, static nature of existence at Billabong: Jim and Wally go to the Front *(From Billabong to London,* 1915; *Jim and Wally,* 1916; *Captain Jim,* 1919), and after the war the courtship of Wally and Norah *(Billabong's Daughter,* 1924) is followed by their marriage *(Billabong Adventures,* 1927) and first child *(Bill of Billabong,* 1931). In contrast to the feminine, urban world created by Ethel Turner, Bruce's Billabong is masculine, emphasizing such virtues as independence, resourcefulness, a love of adventure (Billabong is both a sanctuary and the centre of many crises), hard work, honesty and mateship, mateship encompassing even the relationship between Wally and Norah. Although Bruce drew on other traditions (e.g. Jim is the schoolboy-brother hero familiar in children's domestic fiction), she also meant her small stock of characters to be seen as typical bush Australians. Her popularity made Jim and Norah Linton as significant in the development of an Australian mythology as the Little Boy from Manly, Ginger Meggs, Dad and Dave, and the characters in Gwen Meredith's *Blue Hills*. Brenda Niall's *Seven Little Billabongs* (1979) compares the fictional worlds of Bruce and Ethel Turner; Alison Alexander's *Billabong's Author* (1979) is a biography.

Brumby is a term of uncertain origin. It may have derived from a Major James Brumby, who reputedly left behind a number of horses when he returned to England in the early years of the settlement; they ran wild and became known as Brumby's horses. Another possible source was from a Major William Brumby, who was a noted horse-breaker in the nineteenth century. A.B. Paterson, who wrote a poem 'Brumby's Run', believed it sprang from the Aboriginal word 'booramby' meaning 'wild'. The *Bulletin*, 21 March 1896, suggested it came from Baramba, the name of a property in the Burnett district of Queensland. Will Ogilvie wrote a poem 'The Brumby Stallion' and Katharine Susannah Prichard created a rather wild character, Brumby Innes, in her play of that name.

Brumby Innes, see **PRICHARD, KATHARINE SUSANNAH**

BRYANT, WILLIAM (1757–91) and **MARY** (1765–?), convicts in the First Fleet, married at Port Jackson, 10 February 1788. On 28 March 1791 the Bryants and seven other convicts escaped in a small boat, making a hazardous voyage to Koepang in Timor, some 5200 kilometres in ten weeks. Taken back into custody, they were being returned to England when William died. Mary was pardoned in 1793. Literature on the William and Mary Bryant saga includes 'Louis' Becke and Walter Jeffery, *A First Fleet Family* (1896); Geoffrey Rawson, *The Strange Case of Mary Bryant* (1938); C.H. Currey, *The Transportation, Escape and Pardoning of Mary Bryant* (1963); and Anthony Scott Veitch, *Spindrift: The Mary Bryant Story* (1980).

BRYNING, FRANK, see Science Fiction

BRYSON, JOHN (1935–), born Melbourne, is a lawyer who also carried on the family motor-car business after his father's death in 1971. He has been secretary of the Australian Performing Group (APG) and member and acting chairman of the Literature Board. He published a collection of short fiction, *Whoring Around* (1981); subtitled 'Stories of a world where scruples are a fair exchange for fortunes'. *Whoring Around* examines, ironically, the moral consciousness of contemporary middle-class life.

His story 'The Routine' won the 1979 Patricia Hackett Award.

BUCHANAN, A.J. (ALFRED JOHNSON) (1874–1941), journalist and lawyer, was on the staff of the Melbourne *Age* and was editor of the Brisbane *Daily Mail*. His publications include the novels, *Bubble Reputation* (1906), *She Loved Much* (1907), *Where Day Begins* (1911) and *The Modern Heloise* (1912). *Where Day Begins* is a fictionalized version of the Harry Harbord Morant ('The Breaker') saga. Buchanan also wrote *The Real Australia* (1907), which contains chapters on the literary figures Adam Lindsay Gordon, Victor Daley, Henry Lawson and Louise Mack.

BUCHANAN, NAT (1826–1901), born Dublin, arrived in Australia in 1837. One of the early overlanders, he joined William Landsborough in 1859 in establishing vast runs in the Thomson River country of western Queensland. He made a succession of overlanding trips: in 1878 to stock the Glencoe station in the Northern Territory; in 1880 with 20 000 cattle, again to Glencoe; and in 1883 with 4000 cattle to the Ord River in the Kimberleys. He died owning only a small farm on Dungowan Creek near Tamworth, NSW. Buchanan's feats as bushman and overlander are recorded in C. Featherstonhaugh's *After Many Days* (1918), G. Buchanan's *Packhorse and Waterhole* (1933), Ernestine Hill's *The Territory* (1951), Mary Durack's *Kings in Grass Castles* (1959) and D.S. McMillan (ed.) *Bowen Downs, 1863–1963* (1963).

BUCKLEY, SAMUEL ('FRANK BLAIR') (1886–1950), born Strathpine, Queensland, served in the AIF in the First World War and taught in Queensland. His published poetry includes *They Shall Not Pass and Other Poems* (1943) and *'Neath Sunny Skies* (1944); he also wrote a novel, *Digger Sea Mates* (1929), under the pseudonym 'Frank Blair'.

Buckley Family, comprising the Waterloo veteran, Major James Buckley, his wife Agnes and their son Sam, is one of the three families whose fortunes are chronicled in Henry Kingsley's *The Recollections of Geoffry Hamlyn* (q.v., 1859). Distinguished but impoverished members of the English gentry, the Buckleys succeed gloriously as pastoralists in Australia and eventually return to the ancestral home of Clere. Sam's comment towards the end of the novel, 'I don't want to be young Sam Buckley of Baroona. I want to be the Buckley of Clere', is often quoted as evidence of Kingsley's Anglocentrism, which led Joseph Furphy to object to the unrealistic portrayal of Australia in *Geof-*

frey Hamlyn and to present an alternative history of the Buckley fortunes in Chapter VI of his novel *Such is Life*. There it is reported that 'Hungry Buckley' has lost his property, Baroona, to the banks and has died, his son has gone to gaol for embezzlement, and his daughter Maud, after three husbands, has become housekeeper at Runnymede station.

BUCKLEY, VINCENT (1925–), was born in Romsey, a small Victorian country town. Of Irish Catholic lineage (seven of his great-grandparents were Irish) he has a strong sense of identity with Irish culture, as is demonstrated by his long involvement in Australian Catholic intellectual life, his interest in Irish Republican politics and his love for Ireland itself, where he has spent considerable time in recent years. He was educated at a Jesuit college in Melbourne and at the Universities of Melbourne and Cambridge. He was Lockie Fellow at the University of Melbourne 1958–60, and subsequently professor of English there. As poet, critic, academic and editor, Buckley was influential (especially in Melbourne) in the late 1950s and 1960s, when he was the central figure of a group of University poets and intellectuals with a distinctive philosophy of literature.

Buckley's volumes of poetry are *The World's Flesh* (1954), *Masters in Israel* (1961), *Arcady and Other Places* (1966), *Golden Builders* (q.v., 1976), *The Pattern* (1979), *Late-Winter Child* (1979) and *Selected Poems* (1982). He has also published the critical works, *Essays in Poetry: Mainly Australian* (1957), *Poetry and Morality* (1959), *Henry Handel Richardson* (1961) and *Poetry and the Sacred* (1968). He has edited *Australian Poetry 1958*, *The Campion Paintings, by Leonard French* (1962), and *Eight by Eight* (q.v., 1963), the last a poetry anthology. In 1958–64 he edited the magazine *Prospect*, and in 1961–63 he was poetry editor of the *Bulletin*, during which period (but not, according to Buckley, through his own editorial prejudices) the domination of the *Bulletin's* pages by the then 'mainstream' poets was broken and a new set of poets came into prominence.

The poems of Buckley's first volume, *The World's Flesh*, the title referring to the body of Christ which sustains and nourishes the world, are essentially, if sometimes subtly and ambivalently so, poems of love – religious love, familial love and love of nature and of places. The complex ten-poem sequence 'Land of No Fathers' takes up, in its links with de Quiros, the voyager theme, relating it to Buckley's people, celebrating them and their pioneer endeavours. The second volume, *Masters in Israel*, the title from the Gospel of St John, contains better-known Buckley poems: 'Late Tutorial',

'Reading to My Sick Daughter' and 'Impromptu for Francis Webb' – all of which reflect largely on the poetic process – and 'In Time of the Hungarian Martyrdom' and 'Sinn Fein: 1957', which are Buckley's personal views of past and contemporary political and historical events. Buckley later judged the poetry of these first two volumes as glib, falsely spontaneous and couched in smooth, soft rhythms, 'not fit to express the things I was groping to express'. Other critics saw it as over-rhetorical, extrovert and too obviously didactic in stance. *Arcady and Other Places,* more moderate in tone and flexible in style, saw Buckley achieve some measure of the 'hardness in phrasing' that he desired so long as it was not inconsistent with the 'rhythmic impulse' that he believed to be the essence of poetry. The volume begins with the seven-part 'Stroke' (q.v., perhaps the earliest illustration of the influence on Buckley of the 'life studies' genre then popular in American poetry), which reveals, behind its terse language and often brutally frank description, the pathos of the final encounter between a father and son who have never in the course of their lives really 'learned to touch'. *Arcady and Other Places* has five other sections: poems with the familiar religious and family backgrounds; eight translations from Catullus; and 'Eleven Political Poems', satirical verses on the expediency of politics and certain of its practitioners. Ten years later Buckley published *Golden Builders*. Its opening sequence, 'Northern Circle', is a series of seven 'postcard' poems recording his experiences in Canada. They illustrate the other side of modern globetrotting, the boredom and loneliness that engulf the single traveller who spends hours and days on planes and trains. 'Gunsynd', 'Jumps Jockey' and 'Kilmore Races' reflect Buckley's well-known fascination with the turf. A twenty-seven poem sequence set in Melbourne, 'Golden Builders' (q.v.), examines the problems that modern city life poses for the human spirit. Despite the constant assault of the din, squalor and ugliness of the city, human resilience is seen to triumph. Buckley's innovations in the shape and spacing of the verses on the page, in the use of lower-case lettering and in the free-running speech rhythms, make *Golden Builders* his most technically adventurous work. *The Pattern* (1979) begins with a series of poems on Ireland which merge long-past historical events, such as the massacre at Smerwick in 1580 (Edmund Spenser and Sir Walter Raleigh were reputedly present), and more recent happenings (such as the internment of Patrick Shivers in the present 'trouble') with contemporary Irish life, with the vividly-evoked Irish landscape and with the reflections of the visiting Irish-Australian poet who seeks that part of himself that has its roots in Ireland. Ireland, 'the source country', flows imperceptibly into Australia, the Irish poems giving way to those with Australian settings – and the 'pattern' is demonstrated. While in Ireland writing these poems Buckley was awarded the 1977 Dublin Prize, a quinquennial award by the University of Melbourne for an outstanding contribution to art, music, literature or science. *Late-Winter Child* (1979) moves back to the personal world of man and wife, celebrating the birth to Buckley and his younger second wife of a daughter. *Late-Winter Child* reinforces the impression from his early poetry that Buckley, although sometimes accused of a certain academic detachment and lack of commitment, is a sensitive love poet.

Buckley's published critical works began with *Essays in Poetry: Mainly Australian* (1957), a collection drawn from lectures given at the Universities of Sydney and Melbourne under the auspices of the Commonwealth Literary Fund and from articles contributed to Australian journals. The essays encompass individual poets (Kenneth Slessor, R.D. FitzGerald, A.D. Hope, Judith Wright and James McAuley), contemporary left-wing Australian poetry (especially John Manifold, John Thompson and Laurence Collinson), and the new generation of poets who were emerging in the *Bulletin*. By dismissing, or at least devaluating, such traditionally-accepted influences as nationalism, radicalism and vitalism on the development of Australian literature, Buckley set up an alternative canon which, though controversial, has proved to be significant and influential. Buckley was awarded the FAW Christopher Brennan Award in 1982. His memoirs *Cutting Green Hay* (1983) tell of his involvement with the Catholic movements of the 1950s and 1960s, and celebrate his friendships with such writers as Hope, McAuley and Francis Webb.

BUCKLEY, WILLIAM (1780–1856), born Cheshire, England, was sentenced to transportation for life for having received a stolen roll of cloth. He was taken with David Collins's colonizing expedition to Port Phillip in 1803 and there absconded with two fellow convicts who were never heard of again. Buckley was befriended by the Watourong tribe of Aborigines who believed him to be 'Murrangurk', a reincarnation of a dead chieftain of the tribe, and he lived with them until 1835. On his return to white civilization he was pardoned and became a government interpreter. Accounts of his life as a 'white blackfellow' have been given by John Morgan in *The Life and Adventures of William Buckley* (1852), by James Bonwick in *William Buckley, the Wild White Man, and His Port Phillip Black Friends* (1856) and

by W.T. Pyke in *Buckley, the Wild White Man* (1889). Craig Robertson published the biographical *Buckley's Hope* (1980), the title stemming from the phrase 'Buckley's Hope' (sometimes 'Buckley's Chance'), meaning little or no hope and reflecting the pessimistic view of Buckley's prospects of survival. The phrase is, however, linked by some to the Melbourne store of Buckley and Nunn.

BUCKMASTER, CHARLES (1951–72), born Gruyere, Victoria, was closely involved in his brief life with the drug subculture of the 1960s and with the hostility of his generation towards the materialism and sterility that it believed pervaded Australian life. A strong supporter of the 'New Australian Poetry' movement, Buckmaster participated in the poetry workshops of La Mama and edited the small magazine, *The Great Auk,* which helped to disseminate the new poetry. He published two volumes of poetry, *Deep Blue and Green* (1970) and *The Lost Forest* (1971); prior to his suicide he burned his unpublished manuscripts. Buckmaster's poetry reflects both his enthusiasm for the traditional Australian Arcadia under threat and his repugnance for the shallow artificiality of some modern values. With an output of only some forty-five poems it is difficult to be certain of Buckmaster's talent, but in poems such as 'A History of the Father', 'Willochra', 'Vanzetti' and 'The Beginning' there is evidence of a significant poetic voice.

BUDDEE, PAUL (1913–   ), born WA, was a concert flautist by the age of fourteen and while teaching in WA conducted a large choir (1935–40) and organized singing broadcasts for schools (1946–50). He served in the AIF in the Second World War, publishing *Stand To and Other Poems* in 1943. After the war he combined a successful teaching career with active participation in civil and community affairs; he was president of the WA branch of FAW (1947–49). A prolific writer of children's books and historical fiction, Buddee created the Air Patrol series, the Ann Rankin Pony stories, the Peter Devlin Outback series and the Jim Meredith series. He also wrote *The Escape of the Fenians* (1972), a story of the journey in 1876 by Irish patriots from the USA to rescue Irish political prisoners from the Fremantle gaol. His *The Escape of John O'Reilly* (1973) is a companion volume. Buddee's other writings include *Airways: The Call of the Sky* (1978), the story of Australian civil aviation, and *The Fate of the Artful Dodger* (1983), the story of boy convicts sent to Australia and NZ.

BUGGY, HUGH (1896–1974), born Seymour, Victoria, joined the Melbourne *Argus* in

1917 and in a career extending over half a century became one of Australia's best-known reporter-journalists, covering many of the nation's major (and sometimes bizarre) criminal, sporting and political events. He is said, for example, to have coined the word 'bodyline' to describe the intimidatory bowling that caused a furore in the 1930s. He was a journalist with the *Argus,* the Melbourne *Sun News-Pictorial,* the *Evening Sun,* the Sydney *Sun,* the Melbourne *Herald* and the *Truth.* He 'ghosted' *Story of the Southern Cross Trans-Pacific Flight* (1928) for the aviators Charles Kingsford-Smith and Charles Ulm; wrote *Pacific Victory* (1946), a history of Australia's part in the war against Japan; compiled *Hugh Buggy's Murder Book* (?1953), a selection from the murder trials he had covered as a reporter; and wrote *The Real John Wren* (1977), a rebuttal of Frank Hardy's *Power Without Glory* (1950).

'Buladelah – Taree Holiday Song Cycle, The', a long poem in thirteen sections by Les Murray (q.v.), published in his volume of poetry, *Ethnic Radio* (1977), won the C.J. Dennis Memorial poetry competition for 1976. The 'Holiday Song Cycle', claimed by Murray to be the first poem written by a white man in an Australian Aboriginal metre (derived essentially from music – clapsticks and didgeridoo – and dance), is based thematically and structurally on R.M. Berndt's translation of the Wonguri-Mandjikai song, 'The Moon-bone Song', from north-eastern Arnhem Land. Murray uses as his 'spirit country' the mid-north-coast countryside of NSW between Buladelah and Taree, renowned for its coastal strip of popular beaches and seaside resorts and its lush hinterland of dairy farms. To accord with the Aboriginal Moon-bone song, which illustrates harmony and total communication between all living creatures in an intimately-known and coherent environment, Murray introduces into his north-coast world the annual migration of holiday-makers at Christmas time, many of whom are families returning to their ancestral places – the farms, rural villages and seaside towns from which they sprang a generation or so ago. There they recover or, in the case of the younger ones, discover by communion with the bush, the mountains, the sea and by contact with their parents and grandparents, the origins of their being. The first section describes the pleasurable preparations in the country for the annual influx of visitors. In the second section the holiday-crammed Pacific Highway, which runs through the district, is described (ironically according to Murray but with inspired effect) as the 'great fiery but all-giving Rainbow Snake, writhing over the country and throwing out deadly little offshoots of excitement into

the districts up back roads'. After their arrival in 'that country of the Holiday' the returnees rediscover many half-forgotten things, the poem's capitalizing of seemingly-commonplace things ('Wood Duck's Nest', 'Cattlecamp') bestowing on them a totemic significance. The cycle goes on to celebrate holiday activities and the animals, birds, topography, and events of the 'spirit country'. Murray's belief that place names are an essential way for people to encapsulate the spirit of place and to link themselves with that spirit is manifested in the song cycle's numerous place names; some come from the Aboriginal ('Kiwarric', 'Bucca Wauka', Krambach'), others are associated with the white inhabitants and events of the district ('the place of Bingham's ghost', 'the place of the Plough Handles'). Murray sees the latter nomenclature as the white equivalent of the Aboriginal habit of naming from the spirit of place. The eleventh section describes the children establishing affinity with ancestral things: they bite into the old-fashioned summer fruits (china pear, quince and persimmon) of the abandoned 'fruit trees of the grandmothers' and absorb 'the taste of former lives, of sawdust and parlour song, the tang of manners'. In the final section the whole holiday experience is crystallized and evaluated; having gazed for a week or two 'at their year's worth of stars', the holiday-makers prepare to return to their ordinary concerns.

BULCOCK, EMILY (1877–1969), born Tinana near Maryborough, Queensland, was an older sister of the novelist, Vance Palmer. A schoolteacher and later a regular writer for Brisbane and southern newspapers, she was a life member of the Queensland Authors' and Artists' Association. She wrote several books of verse, *Jacaranda Blooms* (1923), *From Quenchless Springs* (1945) and *From Australia to Britain* (1961). Remembered particularly for her verses celebrating important national occasions, she remains somewhat underrated as a poet. At her best she displays a sensitive perception of life and nature, imaginative imagery and a firm control of poetic form and structure.

Bull-Ant, a Melbourne literary weekly containing short fiction, poetry, sketches, theatrical reviews and cartoons, was edited by its part-owner, Edward George Dyson, and ran 1890–92, although its title was changed to *Ant* from April 1891 to June 1892. Dyson wrote material for it under the pseudonym 'Silas Snell'.

BULL, J.W. (JOHN WRATHALL) (1804–86), born Kent, England, arrived in Australia with his family in 1838. After he took up farming he invented a mechanical means of harvesting wheat. His book of reminiscences,

Early Experiences of Colonial Life in South Australia (1878), first appeared in the South Australian *Chronicle;* a revised, expanded edition was published in 1884.

Bulletin, the most famous and most significant Australian literary journal, was founded 31 January 1880 by J.F. Archibald and John Haynes (qq.v.); it took its title from the San Francisco *Bulletin.* In the first year it suffered crises over printing, advertising revenue and libel actions, and in January 1881 published a leader by W.H. Traill (q.v.) on larrikinism at the Clontarf picnic grounds. The proprietors of the picnic grounds wrote protesting their innocence, Haynes composed a cheeky rejoinder, and a libel action ensued which led to the imprisonment of Archibald and Haynes for failure to pay legal costs. By then Traill had control of the *Bulletin*; although he allowed Archibald and Haynes each to purchase a quarter share when the Bulletin Newspaper Company was constituted in 1883, he remained editor and proprietor until he sold out in 1886. In 1887 Archibald and William Macleod (q.v.) became joint owners, Archibald as editor and Macleod as business manager and later managing director. In subsequent years principal members of the literary and artist staff of the *Bulletin* such as Livingston Hopkins (q.v.) were permitted to buy shares but Macleod remained in financial control until 1927, when he sold out to the family headed by S.H. Prior (q.v.), who had purchased Archibald's holding in 1914. Prior edited the *Bulletin* 1915–33, following Archibald (1886–1903) and James Edmond (q.v., 1903–15). Subsequent editors included John Webb (1933–48), David Adams (1948–61) and, after the *Bulletin* was sold in 1960 by the Prior family to Australian Consolidated Press and changed direction towards a news magazine format, Donald Horne (1961–62, 1967–72). From an initial circulation of 3000 it now sells in excess of 80 000 copies, its estimated circulation during the 1890s.

Traill played a significant part in consolidating the *Bulletin* by improving its appearance, by developing its political and economic policy, and by securing the services of Hopkins and Phil May (q.v.) who did much to establish the *Bulletin*'s reputation in the field of black and white art. Prominent among subsequent cartoonists and illustrators were Norman and Lionel Lindsay, Will and Ambrose Dyson, David Low, D.H. Souter, Alf Vincent, Frank Mahony, George Lambert, Percy Leason and Ted Scorefield. The heyday of the journal is traditionally reckoned as the Archibald years and particularly the 1890s (see Nineties), when Archibald had the assistance of A.G. Stephens (q.v.) as editor (1896–1906) of the Red Page (q.v.) and

Edmond as expert financial journalist as well as Macleod's sound business sense. Just as Archibald needed the support of the varied talents of these men, so the key to the *Bulletin*'s success was not its innovations so much as its blend of ingredients: neither the first radical or humorous weekly in Australia, nor the first to seek an Australian audience and contributors, it was the first to combine these elements into an attractive whole. During the early days the *Bulletin* had a somewhat negative creed, economically and racially isolationist, politically and culturally anti-British; it was, in Vance Palmer's words, a 'waspish little guerilla', striking out at antiquated values. But by the 1890s it had positive attitudes as well, promoting itself as the 'premier literary journal' with an 'Australian national policy'. It advocated republicanism, a democratic franchise, land taxation, State education, penal reform and 'A United Australia and Protection against the World.' It denounced sectarianism, foreign titles, the Chinese, and Imperial Federation.

A significant part of the programme was the cultural chauvinism fostered among its writers and artists, who confronted readers with villains (John Bull, Fatman, Johnny Chow) and heroes (The Little Boy from Manly, q.v., the idealized bushman) stereotyped according to the *Bulletin* philosophy. The bushman appeared in many costumes – one week as the Lone Hand fighting Fatman in a 'Hop' cartoon; on another page as the Man from Snowy River or the Man from Ironbark in an A.B. Paterson poem; next as Steelman or Mitchell in a Henry Lawson story; later as one of 'Steele Rudd's' selection battlers. Whatever the guise, he was a distinctive 'Australian', a product of the bush environment to which Archibald encouraged his writers to turn, urging them all the while to write in an equally distinctive 'no nonsense' way. 'Shun superfluous adjectives', Archibald advised a contributor in 1894, 'stick to sturdy nouns'. The results included hard-bitten paragraphs about up-country life packed into such columns as 'Plain English' and 'Aboriginalities' (q.v.); the bush ballads which were often strikingly illustrated; and the famous *Bulletin* yarn, with its emphasis on originality, brevity, realism and dramatic force.

That the *Bulletin* cultivated the bush did not necessarily guarantee enduring literature or mean that there was a consensus about what the 'bush' itself meant, as the famous *Bulletin* debate (q.v.) shows. Similarly, the *Bulletin*'s bush ethos and its contribution to the emergence of literary nationalism has sometimes been over-emphasized, with the result that the diversity of interests, attitudes and opinions expressed in the journal has been underestimated; Stephens, for example, was as much an internationalist as a nationalist critic. Similarly, the endeavours of earlier colonial writers and journals have been somewhat undervalued. But it remains true that the *Bulletin* did great service for Australian literature by encouraging local writers and artists, providing a regular outlet for their work. Backing up its policies with practical help, it paid its contributors, advised them in the correspondence column and instituted a publishing programme which included the anthologies 'A *Golden Shanty*' (1890), *The Bulletin Reciter* (1901) and *The Bulletin Story Book* (1901); 'Steele Rudd''s *On Our Selection* (1899) and Joseph Furphy's *Such is Life* (1903); and, in subsequent years, novels by Louis Stone, Norman Lindsay, Kylie Tennant and Brian Penton. The literary contributors to the *Bulletin* comprise a roll-call of Australian poets and writers of fiction since 1880. Some of them, notably G.A. Taylor, A.W. Jose, Randolph Bedford (qq.v.) and Norman Lindsay, left reminiscences which either established or confirmed the reputation of the journal before the First World War. Equally significant are the writings of *Bulletin* staff members or their families: Archibald's and Traill's 'The Genesis of the *Bulletin*' (*Lone Hand*, May-December 1907), Haynes's 'Early *Bulletin* Memories' (*Newsletter*, April-December 1905), Dorothy June Hopkins's *Hop of the 'Bulletin'* (1929), A.C. Macleod's *Macleod of 'The Bulletin'* (1931), Douglas Stewart's (q.v.) *Writers of the Bulletin* (1977), and the commemorative numbers of the *Bulletin* in 1930, 1950 and 1980. Patricia Rolfe has written a history of the *Bulletin*, *The Journalistic Javelin* (1980) and Sylvia Lawson *The Archibald Paradox* (1983).

The *Bulletin*'s contribution to Australian literature did not end with the departure of Archibald and Stephens early in the twentieth century. Under Edmond, Mary Gilmore, Louis Esson, C.J. Dennis and 'John O'Brien' first appeared in its pages; under Prior there were contributions by the youthful Kenneth Slessor, Jack Lindsay and Vance and Nettie Palmer; under Webb the S.H. Prior Memorial Prize for fiction was awarded 1935-45; under Adams, assisted by Stewart as editor of the Red Page (1940-61), its writers included Judith Wright, Rosemary Dobson, Ronald McCuaig, 'Brian James', Hal Porter and David Campbell. But there was more than a measure of truth in Archibald's prediction, when the *Bulletin* was a 'clever youth', that it would become a 'dull old man'. Part of the reason may be that many of its prominent staff stayed so long: W.H. East, the *Bulletin*'s printer, was there for forty-nine years, Macleod for forty-one, Adams for thirty-four, Prior for thirty, Edmond for twenty-nine, Webb for twenty-eight. The *Bulletin* became increasingly conservative and its policies,

some of which had not changed since the turn of the century, increasingly anachronistic. The slogan 'Australia for the White Man', which replaced 'Australia for the Australians' in 1908, was only removed from the masthead in 1960. After a brief resurgence during the Second World War, sales dropped steadily until the format was changed under the new proprietors. As a news magazine the *Bulletin* has made an insignificant contribution to Australian literature in the last two decades, although in 1980 it instituted a quarterly literary supplement edited by Geoffrey Dutton, after the success of the centenary issue, 29 January 1980.

Bulletin **Debate** began as a rather contrived argument in verse between Henry Lawson and A.B. Paterson and then widened into a full-scale controversy that involved numerous well-known writers, including John le Gay Brereton, Francis Kenna, Edward Dyson, A.G. Stephens, Henry Cargill ('The Dipso'), Joseph Furphy and James Brunton Stephens. At issue was the real nature of Australian life (at first in the outback, but ultimately in the whole country) and the responsibility of writers to interpret it truthfully. In literary terms it was the traditional argument between romance and realism. The debate began with Lawson's poem 'Borderland', later titled 'Up the Country', published in the *Bulletin* (9 July 1892). Lawson's outback was not a landscape of shining rivers and sunlit plains peopled by folk heroes living gay, carefree lives. It was a callous land, inhabited by gaunt, haggard men and women, broken by the never-ending battle against natural disaster, voracious banking systems and unsympathetic absentee landlords. Paterson replied with 'In Defence of the Bush' (23 July 1892). He evaded Lawson's issue of literary honesty and dismissed his criticism with the jibe that Lawson had better stick to the city for he would 'never suit the bush'. Then followed (6 August 1892) Lawson's 'In Answer to "Banjo" and Otherwise', later titled 'The City Bushman', and Paterson's 'Defence of the Bush' (1 October 1892), later titled 'An Answer to Various Bards'. Lawson's 'Poets of the Tomb' (8 October 1892) widened the discussion to include the role of literature in reforming the total Australian society and was followed (18 November 1893) by 'Some Popular Australian Mistakes', a list of romantic fallacies concluding with a rough handling of the mythical Australian outback folk hero ('the real native outback bushman is narrow-minded, densely ignorant, invulnerably thick-headed'). Lawson's twenty-three facts and concluding summary are now recognized as an important early statement on Australian literary realism. Three years later Lawson began his crusade again. In the *Bulletin*

(27 February 1897) he declared the 'bush bard' to be 'blinded to the Real', and in further articles ' "Pursuing Literature" in Australia', 'Crime in the Bush' and 'If I Could Paint' continued, often in the face of considerable hostility and in spite of personal attacks on his integrity, to insist on truth. The weakness of Lawson's attitude lay in his failure to recognize, or at least to admit, that literary nationalism, with its idealization of the outback life, had helped to usher Australia out of colonialism and had made a significant contribution to the development of a national pride, a fact made evident by the staggering sales of Paterson's *The Man from Snowy River and Other Verses*. What is obvious now, with the benefit of almost a century's hindsight, is that Lawson's insistence on realism instead of romance was, in the light of literary movements then in full force throughout the world, an inevitable step forward in Australian literature. What is equally clear is that his own stories of outback life settled the issue far more decisively than the doggerel verses of the 'Debate' and the angry outbursts in the *Bulletin* columns.

'Bullocky', a poem by Judith Wright (q.v.), links the bullock driver in his pioneer role of unlocking the land with Moses, leading his people into the promised land. In a dramatic switch to the present, the poem shows the long-dead bullocky and his teams continuing to nourish the land – 'the plough strikes bone beneath the grass'. The poem indicates that the continuing fruitfulness and progress of the country depend upon the past as much as the present; that Australia of the future will be shaped by its traditions and history.

Bullocky was the term applied to the drivers of the bullock wagons that were for many years the sole means of transporting supplies and essentials between the settlements and the outback. Usually of dour or phlegmatic disposition but capable of legendary powers of imprecation when his beasts faltered, the bullocky was a vital factor in the opening of the country. His pioneering role is emphasized in Judith Wright's fine poem 'Bullocky' (q.v.) and in the anecdotes of Mary Gilmore's *Old Days, Old Ways* (1934). Joseph Furphy's novel *Such is Life* (q.v., 1903) is centred on bullock drivers and the way of life that they represented. The bullocky is featured by many other writers, e.g. Alexander Harris, Henry Kendall, Henry Lawson, Will Ogilvie, C.J. Dennis and Katharine Susannah Prichard, usually in affectionate but occasionally in critical tones. Charles Thatcher revealed the disasters that could happen when the bullocky had to curb his language in the song 'The Lady and the Bullock Driver' (1861).

Well-known traditional bullocky songs include 'Bullocky-Oh', 'The Bullockies' Ball', 'The Old Bullock Dray' and 'Holy Dan'. It is in the bullocky's song 'Nine Miles from Gundagai' that the famous dog on the tuckerbox has its origin. After a procession of woes ('the team got bogged, the axle snapped in two') the final indignity is added when 'the dog sat (?) on the tuckerbox, nine [five] miles from Gundagai'. L.G. Braden wrote *Bullockies*, an illustrated history, in 1968; Arthur Cannon's *Bullocks, Bullockies and Other Blokes* (1983) is a lively account of ten years' bullock driving in the Gippsland and Mallee areas between the wars; Olaf Ruhen wrote the documentary work *Bullock Teams* (1980).

Buln-Buln and the Brolga, The, is a long story by Joseph Furphy (q.v.) which formed part of the original version of *Such is Life* (q.v., 1903); it was deleted during the revision of *Such is Life,* and was itself revised and elaborated by Furphy in 1904-05. First published in 1948, it was republished with other Furphy stories in 1971 as *The Buln-Buln and the Brolga and Other Stories*.

The narrator of *The Buln-Buln and the Brolga*, Tom Collins (q.v.), is in Echuca to meet a representative of the Melbourne firm for which he works when he receives a telegram announcing the arrival of his childhood friend Fred Falkland-Prichard and his family; Fred is the buln-buln or lyre-bird (pheasant-type bird native to Australia) of the title, so called because he is an inveterate liar, as Tom demonstrates when he reminisces about his childhood. *En route* to the station to meet the Falkland-Prichards Tom meets Barefooted Bob, the brolga or 'native companion' (a species of crane also native to Australia) of the title, so called because of his physique and rough manners. Barefooted Bob strikes up a friendship with Fred and the bulk of *The Buln-Buln and the Brolga* consists of the yarns each swaps with the other during that day and night; Fred's stories get taller and taller but Bob accepts them as truth. *The Buln-Buln and the Brolga* is much slighter than *Such is Life* but raises some of the same issues, particularly the significance of the individual's perception of reality. It also contains a humorous account of Bob's visit to a performance of *Hamlet* in Melbourne which is similar to the better-known visit by the Sentimental Bloke and Doreen to a performance of *Romeo and Juliet*. In the discussion of Fred's English background Furphy parodies 'Rolf Boldrewood''s *The Miner's Right* (q.v., 1890).

BULWER-LYTTON, EDWARD (Baron Lytton of Knebworth) (1803-73), born London, had as parliamentarian and popular novelist several connections with Australia. As secretary for the colonies 1858–59 he presided over the separation of Queensland from NSW in 1859. His novel, *The Caxtons* (1850), first published pseudonymously, was popular in Australia and depicted Pisastratus Caxton's recuperation of his fortunes in an Arcadian Australia; in writing the novel Bulwer-Lytton was informed by the work of Samuel Sidney (q.v.). Dramatic adaptations of his work were also staged in Australia.

Bunch of Rathags, A, see DICK, WILLIAM

BUNGAREE (BONGAREE, BOUNGAREE), of the Broken Bay tribe, was one of the first Aborigines (Arabanoo was the first) to have extended contact with the white settlement at Port Jackson. A well-known figure in the colony for over thirty years, he accompanied many expeditions and voyages of discovery (e.g. Matthew Flinders in HMS *Norfolk*) acting as intermediary with other Aborigines. Accounts of Bungaree and other Aborigines whose characters disintegrated after prolonged exposure to white influence are in Barron Field's *Geographical Memoirs on New South Wales* (1825), Robert Dawson's *The Present State of Australia* (1830), and Richard Sadleir's *Aborigines of Australia* (1883). John Lang wrote 'Bungaree, King of the Blacks', a story in *All the Year Round*, 21 May 1859, published also in *Australian Home Companion* of that year. Ernestine Hill mentions him in *My Love Must Wait* (1941). A portrait of him (c. 1826) by Augustus Earle is in the Australian National Gallery.

Bunyip, a monster of Aboriginal mythology with a huge body covered with fur, is said to live in swamps, lagoons and billabongs from which it emerges on moonlit nights to prey on humans, especially women and children. Zoologists believe the Aboriginal legend may have originated in the occasional appearances of seals in coastal and inland streams and rivers. Numerous accounts of the bunyip are given in nineteenth-century literature of travel and description, e.g. in E. Lloyd's *A Visit to the Antipodes* (1846), William Westgarth's *Australia Felix* (1848) and G.C. Mundy's *Our Antipodes* (1852). It is mentioned also in Joseph Furphy's *Such is Life* and 'Steele Rudd''s *On Our Selection* and is the subject of a well-known title story of J.A. Barry's collection, *Steve Brown's Bunyip* (1893); Ella Airlie's pantomime, 'The Bunyip' was staged in Sydney in 1916. The bunyip has persisted in modern Australian writing, e.g. in Charles Fenner's *Bunyips and Billabongs* (1933), Charles Barrett's *The Bunyip and Other Mythical Monsters and Legends* (1946) and in 'Brian James's' short story 'The

Bunyip of Barney's Elbow' (q.v., 1946). One of the best-known of the 'species' is the Dynevor Bunyip (mentioned in Ernestine Hill's writings) which was said to inhabit the Dynevor Lakes in the Thargomindah district of south-western Queensland. A notable use of the word 'bunyip' was in 'Bunyip Aristocracy', used derisively in 1853 by Daniel Deniehy to ridicule W.C. Wentworth's suggested colonial peerage. Norman Lindsay created a koala character Bunyip Bluegum in his famous book for children, *The Magic Pudding* (1918).

'Bunyip Aristocracy' see DENIEHY, D.H.; Squatter; WENTWORTH, W.C.

'Bunyip of Barney's Elbow, The', a short story by 'Brian James' and set in the Henry Lawson country near Mudgee, was first published in the *Bulletin* (15 May 1946) and reprinted in 'James''s collections *The Bunyip of Barney's Elbow* (1956) and *The Big Burn* (1965). Mick Cullen's Wild Cat Hotel (named after his first wife), at the foot of Barney's Elbow in the Sandy Ridges close to the NSW township of Summerlea (Mudgee), acquires a brief interstate fame after spine-chilling cries of unknown origin are heard in the surrounding hills. A party of Summerlea 'sports', which includes Mr Simpson Butler, the local Member, 'a sprinkling of young fellows from the Grey Box and beyond – Doolans, Ryans, Rosens, Wenns, Wotts', van-loads of hunters and a representative from the *Western Argus*, sets out in unsuccessful pursuit of the bunyip-like monster. Reunited at the hotel that evening and miraculously unharmed by their own indiscriminate shooting, they hear once again the terrifying cry of the 'yahoo' but fail to respond to its challenge. Although the failure of their expedition continues to be a jest in the neighbourhood, 'the Yahoo was never heard again . . . gone to join the Bunyip and other impossible terrors'.

BURCHETT, WILFRED (1911–83), born Melbourne, left Australia in 1936 and became involved in negotiating the release of Jews from Germany in the immediate pre-war years. Returning from Europe early in 1939, he was sent by a group of Australian newspapers to report on war preparations in South-East Asia and the Far East. He joined the staff of the London *Daily Express* in Chungking in 1941 and spent the war reporting on the Asian–Pacific area. One of his greatest journalistic 'scoops' was 'The Atomic Plague', the first eye-witness account by a Western journalist of the aftermath of the Hiroshima atom bomb. After the war he worked for the *Daily Express* in Berlin and returned to Australia in 1950, lecturing for the campaign against nuclear armaments and against the proposed banning of the Communist Party in Australia. He went to China as a correspondent, thence to Korea to cover the cease-fire talks; his visit to an Allied POW camp in North Korea led to a furore in Australia, charges of treachery, a court case for defamation (which he lost) and the withdrawal of his Australian passport (returned in 1972 by the Whitlam Labor government). Later in Moscow, Hanoi, Phnom Penh, Paris and Bulgaria, Burchett consolidated his links with the communist world, always maintaining his lack of interest in communist ideology as such, while avowing a lifelong interest in and support of national independence movements. One of Australia's most controversial and most experienced international journalists, Burchett wrote more than twenty books, *At the Barricades* (1981) being his autobiography. His published works include *Pacific Treasure Island* (1941), *Bombs over Burma* (1944), *China's Feet Unbound* (1952), *This Monstrous War* (1953), *North of the 17th Parallel* (1955), *Come East, Young Man* (1962), *The Furtive War* (1963), *Vietnam North* (1966), *Again Korea* (1968), *Vietnam Will Win!* (1968), *Passport* (1969), *China: The Quality of Life* (1976) and *Catapult to Freedom* (1978).

Burden of Tyre, The, see **BRENNAN, C.J.**

BURKE AND WILLS. The Burke and Wills expedition, the most costly exploration of its time in terms of money spent (£60 000) and lives lost (seven), originated when the Royal Society of Victoria, supported by the Victorian government, decided to snatch from J. McDouall Stuart and the colony of South Australia the honour of making the first south-north crossing of the Australian continent. Abundantly provisioned, the expedition left Melbourne in August 1860 under the leadership of the inexperienced Robert O'Hara Burke (1821–61), an Irish-born superintendent of police; others in the party included the German naturalist Ludwig Becker (q.v.) and the surveyor and meteorologist William John Wills (1834–61), who was promoted to second-in-command after Burke fell out with the camel master. Burke reached Menindee on the Darling River in October and Cooper's Creek six weeks later; in both places he divided his party, taking Wills, John King (1841–72) and Charles Gray with him on the final haul to the Gulf of Carpentaria, which was reached in February 1861. On 21 April Burke, Wills and King staggered back into Camp LXV at Cooper's Creek on the very day the party left behind there under the command of William Brahe

had departed for Menindee. Burke decided to try for Mount Hopeless, north-west of Menindee, leaving a message of his plans at Camp LXV in case Brahe returned. Brahe did so but did not find the message and departed again for Menindee; Burke, Wills and King were too weak to get beyond the reaches of Cooper's Creek, and by the time A.W. Howitt's search party arrived in September 1861 only King had survived. The remains of Burke and Wills were returned to Melbourne for burial in January 1863; a monument to them, one of the many memorials in Victoria and overseas, was later erected outside the Victorian parliament house. The royal commission appointed to enquire into the disaster apportioned blame among the death-or-glory Burke, those commanding his back-up parties, and the expedition's organizing committee; none was attached to Wills, whose journal formed the basis of *A Successful Exploration through the Interior of Australia* (1863), prepared for publication by his father. Although successful in completing a south-north crossing, Burke's expedition was virtually worthless as exploration; the search parties led by McKinlay, Landsborough and Howitt were much more useful in advancing geographical knowledge. Burke and Wills have long been enshrined in Australian folklore, and have captured the imagination of a number of Australian artists and writers. Becker and William Strutt left contemporary sketches of the early parts of the expedition; later artists attracted to the story include Sir John Longstaff, whose famous painting of the return to Camp LXV is familiar to generations of Australian schoolchildren, and Sidney Nolan. Frank Clune's *Dig* (1937), often reprinted, did much to publicize the Burke and Wills legend in the twentieth century although it has been superseded as the standard popular account by Alan Moorehead's *Cooper's Creek* (1963). The poets Henry Kendall in 'The Fate of the Explorers, Burke and Wills' (1861), R.H. Horne in 'Australian Explorers' (1863), Adam Lindsay Gordon in 'Gone' (1867), Catherine Martin in 'The Explorers' (1874), Margaret Thomas in 'Death in the Bush' (1888) and Ken Barratt in 'Burke and Wills' (1946), helped to develop an heroic dimension to the disaster. In the 1940s Colin Thiele's 'Burke and Wills', a radio verse-play, uses King as narrator; Bill Reed's (q.v.) later play, *Burke's Company* (1969), takes up the question of Brahe's responsibility, while Burke's culpability is addressed in Philip Mead's poem, 'W.J. Wills to R. O'Hara Burke 1861' (1980). Tom Bergin, a zoologist and veterinarian who retraced the Burke and Wills expedition in a modern-day attempt to discover the reasons for the disaster, wrote *In the Steps of Burke & Wills* (1981).

BURKE, COLLEEN (1943–   ), born Sydney, has published several volumes of verse: *Go Down Singing* (1974); *Hags, Rags & Scriptures* (1976), a combined work with two other women poets; and *The Incurable Romantic* (1979). Active in workshops and concerts on poetry and folk music, she was editor (1974–75) of the *Cornstalk Gazette,* magazine of the NSW Folk Federation, and was involved in establishing the Australian National Folk Trust 1974–75.

BURKE, JAMES LESTER (c.1820–79), was born in Ireland and served as a soldier in India before his conviction there of insubordination in 1847; sentenced to transportation, he arrived in Hobart in 1848 and eventually received a conditional pardon in 1859. Burke was the author, although only acknowledged as the editor, of *The Adventures of Martin Cash* (1870), one of the best-selling studies of the Tasmanian bushranger; he may also have 'ghosted' *A Burglar's Life* (1893), the memoir of a well-known convict, Mark Jeffrey.

Burke, Red, see **PRICHARD, KATHARINE SUSANNAH**

Burn, see **IRELAND, DAVID**

BURN, DAVID (?1799–1875), was born in Scotland and followed his mother, the first woman to be granted land in Van Diemen's Land, to Hobart in 1826. Until 1845 he combined residence in Hobart with visits to Britain, participated in colonial affairs, and wrote widely on colonial life and politics. In 1845 he left Tasmania for NSW and in 1847 went to New Zealand where he edited several newpapers. His travel and descriptive accounts include *A Picture of Van Diemen's Land* (first published 1840–41), *Vindication of Van Diemen's Land* (1840), *An Excursion to Port Arthur in 1842* (first published 1842) and *Narrative of the Overland Journey of Sir John and Lady Franklin and Party from Hobart Town to Macquarie Harbour 1842* (first published 1843). Burn is chiefly remembered for his play *The Bushrangers* (q.v.). Staged at the Caledonian Theatre, Edinburgh, in 1829 with his nautical farce, *Our First Lieutenant,* the play was not published or performed in Australia until 1971. His other plays include *Sydney Delivered* (q.v., 1845) and several literary–historical dramas, mainly in verse with European settings, published in his *Plays, and Fugitive Pieces, in Verse* (1842).

BURNELL, F.S. (FREDERICK SPENCER) (1880–?), born Sydney, was special correspondent for the *Sydney Morning Herald* with the New Guinea expedition in 1914 and compiled an illustrated account of that action, *How Australia Took German New Guinea* (1914), and an expanded version of the same, *Australia versus Germany: The Story of the Taking of German New Guinea* (1915). He also wrote several travel books and two volumes of verse, *Before Dawn and Other Poems* (1912) and *A Sallet of Songs* (1920).

BURNS, D.R. (DAVID ROBERT) (1925–   ), teaches English at the University of NSW and has written two novels, *Mr Brain Knows Best* (1959) and *Early Promise* (1975); and a critical study, *The Directions of Australian Fiction 1920–1974* (1975).

BURNS, JOANNE (1945–   ), born Sydney, and a teacher, has published four volumes of verse, *Snatch* (1972), *Ratz* (1973), *Adrenalin Flicknife* (1976), *Radio City 2AM* (1976); two books of prose, *Correspondences* (1979), with Pamela Brown) and *Ventriloquy* (1981); and a book of children's stories, *Alphabatics* (1976).

Burnt Ones, The, see **WHITE, PATRICK**

BURSTALL, BETTY, see **La Mama**

BURSTALL, TIM (1929–   ), born Stockton-on-Tees, England, went to school in England and to universities in Australia and the USA. Formerly a film officer with the National Film Library, then publications officer with the Australian Antarctic expedition, in the 1970s he became one of Australia's most prolific and best-known film directors. His successes as director and producer include *Stork* (1971), *Alvin Purple* (1973), *Petersen* (1974), *Eliza Fraser* (1976) and *The Last of the Knucklemen* (1979). He wrote the scripts for the films *2,000 Weeks* (1969), *Alvin Rides Again* (1974) and *The Last of the Knucklemen* (1979). He has also written and directed documentary and short films. His wife, Betty Burstall, was associated with La Mama.

Burton Family, see *Hillyars and the Burtons, The*

BURY, THOMAS ('TOM TOUCHSTONE') (1838–1900), born Dublin, came to Australia in 1854 during the gold rushes. He wrote under his pseudonym for the *Ballarat Courier* from the late 1870s until his death. His weekly column, 'Cornerisms', touched on most of the moral, philosophical, artistic and social questions of the day. He was a significant influence on the poet Bernard O'Dowd.

Bush is a term which probably derives from the Dutch word 'bosch' and was used as early as 1800. By the 1820s it was in common use to denote the unsettled areas of the Colony and, more specifically, as the Australian equivalent of the English words 'woods' or 'forest'. Although many early settlers disliked and feared the bush, it did not go completely unpraised. Barron Field's *First Fruits of Australian Poetry* (1819) and *Geographical Memoirs on New South Wales* (1825) are enthusiastic about the flora of the bush. Charles Tompson, born in the colony, spent much of his youth in the bush settlements around Windsor and Penrith and sees the bush, in his *Wild Notes, from the Lyre of a Native Minstrel* (1826), through the sympathetic eyes of a 'currency lad'. Early complaints about the sombreness of the bush were strengthened by the many tragedies that befell the explorers and pioneers in their efforts to chart and settle it. Charles Harpur and Henry Kendall write of such tragedies in 'The Creek of the Four Graves' and 'The Glen of the Whiteman's Grave'. Harpur, also a 'currency lad' bred in the spectacular Hawkesbury valley, writes of the bush with affectionate awe in 'Lost in the Bush', 'A Bush Fire' and 'Dawn and Sunrise in the Snowy Mountains'. Kendall suggests both the loneliness and the loveliness of the bush in poems such as 'Death in the Bush', 'Morning in the Bush', 'September in Australia', 'Bellbirds' and 'Arcadia in Our Midst', the last a prose description of the Brisbane Water area. The bush was also the background for many of the journals, reminiscences and memoirs of early colonial life. Typical of a host of such works ranging over more than half a century are H.W. Haygarth's *Recollections of Bush Life in Australia* (1848), James Armour's *The Diggings, the Bush and Melbourne* (1864), Mrs James Foott's *Sketches of Life in the Bush* (1872), James Kirby's *Old Times in the Bush of Australia* (1895) and George Dunderdale's *The Book of the Bush* (1898). Similarly, much of the fiction of early colonial times is set in the bush, e.g. Charles Rowcroft's *Tales of the Colonies* (1843), Alexander Harris's *The Emigrant Family* (1849), Louisa Atkinson's *Gertrude the Emigrant* (1857), William Howitt's *Tallangetta* (1857), Henry Kingsley's *The Recollections of Geoffry Hamlyn* (1859), Rosa Praed's *The Head Station* (1885) and 'Rolf Boldrewood''s *Robbery Under Arms* (1888), the last subtitled 'A Story of Life and Adventure in the Bush and in the Goldfields of Australia'. In her autobiographical *My Australian Girlhood: Sketches and Impressions of Bush Life* (1902), Rosa Praed reminisces, 'I never smell the pungent aromatic scent [of gum trees] . . . without falling again under the grim spell of the bush'. When Marcus Clarke, in his preface in the 1876 edition of Adam Lindsay Gordon's *Sea Spray and Smoke Drift,* describes the dominant note of the Australian bush as one of 'weird melancholy' and the bush itself as 'funereal, secret, stern', he is

reflecting the view that persisted for most of the first century of white settlement; that view persists, half a century further on, in D.H. Lawrence's *Kangaroo* (1923), whose keynote is 'the terror of the bush'. With the 1890s and the upsurge of nationalism and through the influence of the *Bulletin* and the works of A.B. Paterson, Henry Lawson, Joseph Furphy, 'Steele Rudd', Bernard O'Dowd and Miles Franklin (to name only the major figures) the bush (now often capitalized, The Bush) comes to be viewed as a major shaping instrument of the Australian national spirit and outlook. The bulk of the literature 1890–1914 is bush-inspired, and bush values as illustrated in that literature are accepted as Australian values. Observers who recognize this particular significance of the bush include Francis Adams, who finds 'all that is genuinely characteristic in Australia and Australians springing from this heart of the land [the bush]' (*The Australians,* 1893); French writer, Emile Saillens, who believes that 'the bush has its history which is that of Australia – the bush is not a fixed place, it is a state of things' ('Le Bush Australien et Son Poete', 1910); and C.E.W. Bean, who is sure that in the bush is 'the core of Australia' (*On the Wool Track,* 1909). An almost inevitable extension of this assessment of the bush was the development of the mystique of the bush, a sense that it was a sacred, inspiriting power, influencing for good, both individual and nation. Voiced earlier in Kendall's 'To a Mountain', which echoes the pantheism of Wordsworth, this mystique is expressed by O'Dowd in *The Bush* (1912) but is present also in 'Furnley Maurice''s poem 'The Gully' and to some degree in the poetry of John Shaw Neilson, Douglas Stewart and Roland Robinson. It exists also in the Jindyworobak (q.v.) movement and is expressed in such works as 'Henry Handel Richardson''s *The Fortunes of Richard Mahony* (1930), Eleanor Dark's *The Timeless Land* (1941), Mary Durack's *Keep Him My Country* (1955), Patrick White's *Voss* (1957) and Randolph Stow's *To the Islands* (1958) and in more recent times in Les Murray's *The Boys Who Stole the Funeral* (1980) and Geoffrey Lehmann's *Ross' Poems* (1978). Not that the bush is glorified by all writers, as the *Bulletin* Debate (q.v.) on literary realism in the early 1890s reveals. While there are contrary views on the merits of the bush and bush life, there is, with the exception of Barbara Baynton, reasonable unanimity on the qualities of the bush people. There were, of course, examples in the bush of the flotsam and jetsam of humanity (Lawson's Sweeney and Jimmy Woods) but the bushman stereotype emerges as a rugged, versatile individualist, cheerful, laconic, philosophical in the face of hardship, independent in his own troubles but generous and loyal to his mates and others who need help. Such a stereotype is partly glimpsed as early as Adam Lindsay Gordon's 'The Sick Stockrider' and in Gordon's philosophy of 'kindness in another's trouble, courage in your own'. The literature of the nationalist 1890s has many such figures; typical in some or all respects are Lawson's Joe Wilson, 'Steele Rudd''s Dad, and Miles Franklin's Danny Delacy.

In a less complex fashion than O'Dowd and the Jindyworobaks, a host of other Australian writers used the bush (and bush life) as the theme or as the setting in their work, e.g. Katharine Susannah Prichard, Miles Franklin as 'Brent of Bin Bin', Vance Palmer, Frank Dalby Davison, Kylie Tennant, Jon Cleary, Tom Ronan, D'Arcy Niland and, at times, Patrick White. The travel and descriptive works of Ion L. Idriess, following on from earlier writers such as Mrs Aeneas Gunn and C.E.W. Bean, popularized the bush and were, in turn, followed by others such as Myrtle Rose White, William Hatfield and Ernestine Hill. Louis Esson, seeking a valid indigenous drama in the early twentieth century, went as W.B. Yeats had suggested to a particularly Australian source – the bush. His plays Dead Timber (1920), The Drovers (1923) and Mother and Son (1923) employ bush settings and laconic bush idiom. The tragic aspects of the bush, developed in Esson, reappear in Vance Palmer's The Black Horse (1924), Sydney Tomholt's Anoli the Blind (1936), Millicent Armstrong's Drought (1932) and 'Betty Roland''s The Touch of Silk (1942).

There has been a significant correlation between the visual and literary interpretations of the bush. Artist J.W. Lewin (1770–1819) accompanied Governor Macquarie over the Blue Mountains to Bathurst, the first major breaching of the bush's inviolability. In his watercolours (e.g. Cox's River and Springwood) the bush is freed from the artificiality of both earlier writers and painters. Artists of the mid-century, e.g. William Strutt (1825–1915), with their grim interpretations of the bush provide suitable parallels to the melancholy poetry of Adam Lindsay Gordon and the equally melancholy stories of Marcus Clarke. Of the later Heidelberg School, Frederick McCubbin's The Lost Child (1886) and Bush Burial (1890) retain much of the elemental sense of doom and tragedy associated with Marcus Clarke's view of the bush but Tom Roberts's Shearing the Rams (1890) and The Breakaway (1891) convey the dynamic energy of bush life and activities associated with the 1890s. Russell Drysdale's 1941 Riverina paintings contain the same realistic appraisal of the bush as is seen in the Henry Lawson stories: 'I have left out the wattle – because it wasn't there'.

From the bush has come a multitude of expressions, several of which reflect the townsman's patronizing attitude towards his bush cousin, e.g. 'bushwhacker', a naive, country type; 'bush carpenter', one who builds in a rough and ready fashion; 'bush week', the time of the year when the bush cousin comes to town and is ripe for plucking; 'bush baptist', one who is of very doubtful religious persuasion; and 'bush lawyer', one who will argue his rights in any and every situation. 'Bushed', which originated about the 1850s, meant 'lost in the bush' but now is used as a general colloquial expression to indicate a state of perplexed indecision. 'The Bushman's Bible' was the Bulletin and 'the Bushman's Clock' was, according to C.E.W. Bean in On the Wool Track, the kookaburra, the noisiest bird in the bush. 'Sydney [Melbourne] or the Bush' indicates an 'all or nothing' decision, which results in the 'big time' (Sydney or Melbourne) or obscurity (the bush).

Bush Ballads and Galloping Rhymes (1870), is the second and more important of the collections of poetry of Adam Lindsay Gordon (q.v.). Best-known peoms are the opening verses 'A Dedication' (q.v.); narratives such as 'From the Wreck' (q.v.), 'How We Beat the Favourite' and 'The Romance of Britomarte'; the character sketch 'The Rhyme of Joyous Garde' (q.v.); and Gordon's most significant poem, 'The Sick Stockrider' (q.v.). The contents scarcely substantiate the impression given by the title of an overwhelming Australian flavour to this Gordon collection.

'Bush Christening, A', published by A.B. Paterson in The Man from Snowy River and Other Verses (1895), is a rollicking account of how the traditional Irish preoccupations – whisky and religion – come together in the unique christening ceremony of the lad, Maginnis Magee. Paterson used the Irish Catholic community as the basis of many similar bush verses, e.g. 'Father Riley's Horse', 'Gilhooley's Estate' and 'Mulligan's Mare'.

Bush Studies, a collection of six stories by Barbara Baynton (q.v.), was published in 1902; it included Baynton's best-known stories, 'Squeaker's Mate', 'Scrammy 'And', 'Billy Skywonkie' and 'The Chosen Vessel'. The collection was issued in another edition in 1917 under the title Cobbers, with two new stories added and the others revised.

Bush, The (1912), by Bernard O'Dowd (q.v.), is one of the most important expressions of nationalist–radical sentiment in Australian literature. O'Dowd's most attractive poem, it forecasts future greatness for Australia once the ideals of radicalism are transplanted from the 'grottos of decrepitude' of the Old World into the eagerly waiting green sanctuary of the Australian bush.

'BUSHMAN, A', see SIDNEY, SAMUEL

Bushman's Bible, was a common nickname of the *Bulletin* before the First World War. It is used, for example, in Randolph Bedford's autobiographical *Naught to Thirty-Three* (1944).

Bushranger in Australian Literature. The term 'bushranger', which is still used in Australia to describe a manipulative or exploitative person (e.g. a club golfer who arranges his form in such a way as to gain maximum advantage of his handicap is called a 'bushranger' or 'burglar'), originally meant someone with an official task in the bush; thus it was a compound of 'bush' and 'ranger'. From this origin the word broadened to cover anyone skilled in bushcraft (i.e. a 'bushman'); deteriorated to describe a runaway convict attempting to survive in the bush; and then acquired its most common meaning, a person who evaded the law by living in the bush and committing robbery and related crimes (e.g. arson, murder, the stealing of horses), usually in partnership with others in a bushranging 'gang'. As well as 'bushranging' and other derivatives, the bushranging phenomenon introduced into or consolidated within Australian English such words and phrases as 'duffing', 'bush telegraph', 'bail up', 'stick up' and 'game as Ned Kelly'.

Bushrangers operated periodically from 1789, when Black Caesar, a First Fleet convict, first took to the bush, until 1880 when Ned Kelly (q.v.), the most famous Australian bushranger, was hanged in Melbourne. Apart from isolated instances such as the activities of 'Moondyne Joe' (q.v.) in WA and Alpin McPherson (q.v.), 'The Wild Scotchman', in Queensland, bushranging was confined to the south-eastern part of Australia – to the colonies of NSW, Tasmania and Victoria. Three main periods of activity are usually identified; the first, longest but most intermittent, encompasses the convict bushrangers up to 1850, particularly in the period 1820–50. The most prominent mainland bushranger in this period was John Donohoe (q.v.), an early Australian folk hero whose exploits near Sydney in the late 1820s are the subject of the 'Bold Jack Donahoe' cycle of ballads and inspired Charles Harpur's early

play, *The Bushrangers* (q.v., 1853). In the same decade that Donohoe operated near Sydney, Matthew Brady (q.v.) in Tasmania staged several daring attacks on property before his death in 1826. Brady was treated sympathetically by early writers, notably David Burn in his play *The Bushrangers* (q.v., performed 1829) and 'Pindar Juvenal' in *The Van Diemen's Land Warriors* (q.v., 1827), but some other Tasmanian bushrangers had deserved reputations for violence. They included Michael Howe (q.v.); the cannibal Alexander Pearce or Pierce, a convict escapee from Macquarie Harbour who was the model for Gabbett (q.v.) in Marcus Clarke's *His Natural Life* (1874); and, at least for part of his career, Martin Cash (q.v.).

The defiance of authority which marked the careers of Donohoe, Brady and Howe was met by intermittent government legislation, beginning in 1800 with the outlawing of robbers and stock thieves and culminating in this period in a harsh Bushranging Act of 1830, which gave the authorities in NSW wide powers of seizure and arrest. This Act, bitterly resented by many settlers and discussed in Alexander Harris's *Settlers and Convicts* (1847), was still in force at the start of the second wave of bushranging activity, the twenty years following the discovery of gold in 1851. The increase in activity was caused by a combination of factors, including the isolation of the various goldfields and the inadequacy of the police force. Perhaps the best-known bushrangers of the 1860s were Ben Hall, Frank Gardiner and Johnny Gilbert (qq.v.), who several times operated together in western NSW and had sympathizers beyond their immediate circle. Among other well-known bushrangers whose careers broadly coincided with theirs were the Clarke brothers, the evil Dan Morgan and the exotically-named 'Captain Thunderbolt', 'Captain Moonlite' and 'Captain Starlight' (qq.v.); earlier 'Captain Melville' had had brief notoriety in Victoria before his death in detention in 1857. Despite some spectacular successes – e.g. the Eugowra gold robbery which was used by 'Rolf Boldrewood' in *Robbery Under Arms* (1888) and *The Miner's Right* (1890) – most of the bushrangers, in this period as in others, died young and violently: Morgan, Gilbert and Hall were all killed in 1865, and by 1870, when Thunderbolt was hanged, bushranging had been more or less brought under control. The 1870s were quiet until near the end of the decade, when in 1878 the Kelly gang was outlawed and began its defiance of governments on both sides of the Murray River which lasted until the siege of Glenrowan in 1880.

Kelly's convict connections, like those of Hall and Melville and all the bushrangers before 1850, indicate that to insist upon a firm division of bushranging history into distinct periods can disguise important links between many of the bushrangers. For example, bushranging was very often a response by those affected directly by the cruelty, weakness or corruption of government and other forms of authority. Thus in the early period most convict bushrangers were escaping from cruel masters or gaolers; after the discovery of gold the encouragement offered by an incompetent or corrupt police force (attested to by as respectable a writer and citizen as Louisa Anne Meredith) to a 'wild colonial boy' like Frank Gardiner was compounded by the injustice some settlers, including the Kellys and the Halls, felt at the unequal distribution of land. The Kellys and the Halls were from selection (q.v.) stock and their activities have something of the dimension of social banditry and agrarian protest. Again, despite the cold-blooded murderousness of such as 'Mad Dog' Morgan, others had deserved reputations for bravery (e.g. Donohoe), dash and pluck (e.g. Kelly), chivalry (e.g. Hall), bravado (e.g. Gardiner) or cheek (e.g. Brady) which consolidated support from some settlers and confirmed their placement within a larger highwayman/outlaw, Robin Hood/Dick Turpin/Jesse James tradition. The preponderance of bushrangers by the name of 'Captain' is evidence that some agreed with this romantic image of themselves.

The extent of the sympathy for many bushrangers has made them important figures in Australian folklore who are sometimes seen to embody national characteristics, e.g. in enacting deeply-ingrained antagonisms towards authority and the police. Although some commentators have viewed them less favourably, seeing in the cockiness and flashness of bushrangers early manifestations of larrikin and ocker behaviour, favourable entries on bushranging figure prominently in Australian folklore compendiums. There is a bushranging section in most Australian folklore and ballad anthologies; virtually all the bushranging songs and ballads (e.g. 'The Death of Ben Hall', 'How Gilbert Died', 'The Streets of Forbes') are sympathetic to their subjects. Among general bushranging histories, the best-known are Frank Clune's *Wild Colonial Boys* (1948) and *A Pictorial History of Australian Bushranging* (1966) by Tom Prior, Bill Wannan and Harry Nunn, who have each also written separately on the subject; earlier studies include Charles White's *History of Australian Bushranging* (1902), George Boxall's *The Story of the Australian Bushrangers* (1899) and Jack Bradshaw's (q.v.) *The True History of the Australian Bushrangers* (?1924). Most of these works have been written for a popular market, although Russel Ward's *The Australian Legend* (1958) is one of several works

which place bushranging within the Australian tradition.

For all the importance of the bushranger in Australian folklore and in studies of the Australian tradition, the bushranging phenomenon has produced a creative literature significant as much for its quantity as its quality. The bushranging plays of Burn, Harpur and Henry Melville (q.v.) have historical importance as early Australian plays; drawing on the stage tradition of the outlaw protagonist, they are also significant in confirming the links between bushranging and convict literature evident in folksongs like 'Jim Jones at Botany Bay' and novels like *Ralph Rashleigh* (written in the 1840s). In addition, Harpur's play displays an ambivalence about the bushranger which characterizes stage portrayals later in the nineteenth century; the ambivalence derives from the intersection of the melodrama (which demanded the triumph of virtue over vice) with the folklore tradition (overwhelmingly sympathetic), and was partly resolved by the emergence of both good and bad bushrangers and police. The government licensing of plays in NSW meant few bushranging plays in the period 1840-70, but the bushranger emerged again in the 1870s as one of the heroes – despite condemnation by some newspaper critics – of the Australian melodrama which flourished into the twentieth century. The most popular of all bushranging plays was the Alfred Dampier and Garnet Walch adaptation of *Robbery Under Arms* (q.v., 1888), first staged in 1890 with 'Rolf Boldrewood' in the audience, but its success was rivalled by some of the numerous Kelly plays staged during the gang's activities and after Ned's execution. Other bushranging plays focused on Midnight, Thunderbolt, Gardiner, Hall and Gilbert; apart from these, the bushranger was a stock character in more broadly-based plays such as George Darrell's *The Sunny South* (first staged 1884).

Beyond the colonial stage, the nineteenth-century bushranging plays can be placed within what one commentator on Kelly has called the 'media tradition' treatment of bushrangers, which remains ambivalent towards the bushranger, because, although influenced by folklore, it is concerned also to harness the abundant potential for sensation, excitement, adventure or romance. Within the media tradition can be placed some of the films made before a ban on the making of bushranging films was instituted in the NSW police department in 1912 – seven such films had been made the previous year – and a clutch of novels centred on individual outlaws, fictitious and real. Examples of the former include Charles Rowcroft's Mark Brandon, E.W. Hornung's Captain Stingaree and Gavin Holt's Captain Scarlet; examples of the latter include novels by Hume Nisbet, Nat Gould, Thomas Walker and Roy Bridges about Howe, and by Carlton Dawe, Ambrose Pratt, Hilda Bridges and Launcelot Booth about Hall or the Hall/Gardiner gang. Ambivalence is also to be found in the most famous bushranging novel of all, 'Boldrewood''s *Robbery Under Arms,* which is both a cautionary tale about how crime doesn't pay and a novel which enjoys the dash of Captain Starlight, the efficiency of Ben Marston and the discomfort of Sir Ferdinand Morringer, Starlight's police opponent. Part of the appeal of *Robbery Under Arms* stemmed from 'Boldrewood''s ability to incorporate familiar elements from the experiences of several bushrangers, e.g. the easy identification of Wall, Hulbert, Moran and Lardner with Hall, Gilbert, Morgan and Gardiner. Wall and Lardner reappear in 'Boldrewood''s *The Miner's Right* (1890). The contrast between this novel, in which bushranging is an incidental ingredient to provide colour or excitement in a goldfields romance, and *Robbery Under Arms,* which can be catalogued more accurately as a bushranging novel, is similar to the contrast not only between *The Sunny South* and the stage adaptation of *Robbery Under Arms,* but also between other bushranging novels (e.g. the works by the media tradition novelists already mentioned) and a larger body of fiction with a bushranging element. The latter include Alexander Harris's *The Emigrant Family* (1849), John Lang's *The Forger's Wife* (1855), Henry Kingsley's *The Recollections of Geoffry Hamlyn* (1859), William Gosse Hay's *Strabane of the Mulberry Hills* (1929), several of the sporting (as distinct from bushranging) novels of Nat Gould and Arthur Wright, and an even larger number of children's novels. There are some children's novels, however, which deal explicitly with bushrangers, including William Howitt's *A Boy's Adventures in the Wilds of Australia* (1854) and Judith Wright's *Range the Mountains High* (1962).

The fact that Australian creative writers have been concerned to exploit rather than to explore the phenomenon of bushranging has produced a lot of plays and novels which have mainly historical interest, one or two exciting adventures of which *Robbery Under Arms* is justifiably the best-known, and a handful of fine ballads and later poems (e.g. Francis Webb's 'Morgan'); these can be put alongside the paintings of Tom Roberts and Sidney Nolan. To these works should be added the novels by David Martin and Randolph Stow, *The Hero of Too* and *Midnite* (qq.v., both 1967), which satirize the bushranging legend, and Douglas Stewart's 1941 play *Ned Kelly* (q.v.), which explores the 'deep national significance' Stewart felt was embedded in the Kelly story.

Bushranger of Van Diemen's Land, The, see Aboriginal in Australian Literature; ROWCROFT, CHARLES

Bushrangers, A Play in Five Acts, and Other Poems, The (1853), was one of the two major works published by Charles Harpur (q.v.) in his lifetime. Although *The Bushrangers* first appeared in full in 1853, Harpur worked on the melodrama intermittently, publishing part of it in 1835 with the title 'The Tragedy of Donohoe' (*Sydney Monitor*) and leaving a final manuscript version entitled 'Stalwart the Bushranger' (dated 1867). Incongruously dependent on Elizabethan models and weakly constructed, the play nevertheless has some dramatic and literary merit and is interesting for Harpur's ambivalent treatment of the bushranger hero/ villain.

Bushrangers: Or, Norwood Vale, The, a play by Henry Melville (q.v.) staged in Tasmania in 1834 and published in the *Hobart Town Magazine* in the same year, was the first dramatic piece with an Australian theme presented and published by an author resident in Australia. A melodrama of little literary merit, it consists of thirteen tableaux and deals with an attack by bushrangers on a settler's home.

Bushrangers, The, a three-act play in prose by David Burn (q.v.), was presented at the Caledonian Theatre, Edinburgh, in 1829 and was the first Australian drama to be performed on stage. It remained unpublished and unperformed in Australia until 1971. Although of little literary merit, the play has action and colour and is interesting for its innovative treatment of a familiar theme in Australian literature, the romanticizing of the rebel (in this case the bushranger Matthew Brady, q.v.) and for its incidental revelation of life in colonial Tasmania.

But the Dead Are Many, a novel by Frank Hardy (q.v.), was published in 1975. The story of John Morel, born in 1917 and a leading member of the Communist Party of Australia after a dedicated Catholic youth, the novel has a complex structure, explicitly analogous to a musical fugue. Subjects, incidents, individuals, themes, relationships and experiences are constantly counterpointed so that past and present merge and time proceeds vertically rather than chronologically. Morel's story emerges from several chapters of autobiography and a note that he bequeaths after his suicide at the age of fifty to his close friend and *alter ego,* Jack. Convinced that an understanding of Morel's suicide will uncover personal, psychological and general ideological truths, Jack combines Morel's notes with his own extensive researches, interviews and recollections. As Morel's history gathers shape, personal crises such as the death of his father, his decision to leave the Catholic seminary and his hunger strike in the 1940s merge with public events, and private relationships are tainted with the tense, unresolved ambivalences of the political movement. Morel's story becomes not just an individual history but a reflection of the conflicts within the international communist movement from the 1930s to the 1960s and of the ever-widening gap between ideal and real. Morel's relationship with his wife Penelope, his Russian mistress Anna, his colleagues such as the party hack Trevor Duncan, his best friend Jack and, above all, with his memory of the old Bolshevik Buratakov, whose Stalinist trial he witnessed, reflect his futile quest for harmony and integrity in an increasingly tangled, baffling environment. Afflicted with an acute sense of duality and inadequacy, Morel seeks to find a final transcendence in suicide, which he hopes will transform his memory and resolve the inevitable dichotomy in life between ideal and blemished selves; suicide becomes an act 'not of self-destruction but of self-preservation, an attempt to confront the meaning of death by making it part of life, an attempt to synthesise the unresolvable paradox of life and death by thwarting the life-denying forces which make actual living impossible . . . suicide is an attempt to equate the identity of the self as experienced by the self and the self as experienced by others, an attempt to establish the interconnection between the living and the dead'.

Butcher Shop, The (1926), a novel by Jean Devanny (q.v.), was published in England and went through six printings by 1931, after which it was not republished until 1981, when it reappeared with an introduction and notes by Heather Roberts and an account by Bill Pearson of its banning in NZ in 1926 and Australia in 1929. Grounds for its censorship were its emphasis on sexuality, its depiction of the brutality of life in rural NZ and its expressions of socialism in a country that in the 1920s would have been appalled by the idea of a socialist form of government and society. Feminism and socialism are central to the novel. Devanny sees in the family situation the bondage of the woman; it is because the males in the story (husband and lover) both conform, albeit unconsciously, to the view that the married woman is her husband's property, that the final tragedy occurs. Set on Maunganui station in the King Country of the North Island of NZ, the novel advances placidly through the first ten years of married life of Margaret and Barry Messenger,

owners of the station. Physically beautiful, intellectually aware and comfortably situated, they appear to be a perfect match. However, with the arrival of the Scot overseer, Glengarry, Margaret realizes the full impact of her sexuality and while Barry is away the two become lovers. The three then live for some time in a precarious relationship. Barry, who notes the attraction between Margaret and Glengarry, does not suspect the extent of the affair, while Glengarry, who is at first torn with jealousy, comes to like and respect Barry so much that he finally decides not to continue the affair because Margaret is his friend's wife. He thus denies Margaret the very individuality she seeks and confirms her sense of herself as merely property. Threatened by Glengarry's decision, Margaret reveals their full liaison to Barry, who drowns himself in a dam. The now-unbalanced Margaret cuts the throat of the sleeping Glengarry, claiming that she has revenged 'the Margarets of the world' and that 'never again shall man claim property rights in me'. A couple from England, Ian and Miette Longstair, have been a contributing factor to the tragedy, both with their disturbing socialist attitudes and Miette's sexual approaches to Glengarry which have inflamed Margaret's jealousy. The violence of NZ rural life, objected to by the censors, is characterized by such things as lamb killing, the killing of cats for their skins, the mutilation of a dog, the decapitation of a drunken rabbiter by his mate and the oral castration of lambs. Devanny explains the novel's title by affirming that it is the woman who is butchered in life.

BUTLER, RICHARD (1925–), born and educated in Liverpool, England, served in the RAF and then taught in England and Australia (1963–74) before becoming a full-time writer. His novels include *Fingernail Beach* (1964), *South of Hell's Gates* (1967), *Sharkbait* (1970), *The Buffalo Hook* (1974), *Lift-Off at Satan* (1978) and several based on Australian historical subjects: *The Men That God Forgot* (1975), *And Wretches Hang* (1977, on Matthew Brady), *A Blood-Red Sun at Noon* (1980) and *The Devil's Coachman* (1981). He has also written television and film scripts, historical texts for schools, and novels associated with TV series, e.g. *Against the Wind* (1978), *The Sullivans* (1980) and *Eureka Stockade* (1983).

Button, Spencer, see ***Advancement of Spencer Button, The***

BUTTROSE, LARRY (1952–), born Adelaide, was a journalist with the ABC 1970–75 and has since been a freelance writer. In 1971 he founded *Dharma* with Stephen Measday; he was co-editor of *Real Poetry* 1977–78, and of

Number Three Friendly Street Poetry Reader. He has published two books of verse, *One Steps Across the Rainbow* (1974) and *Random Leaves* (1976), and a more substantial collection, *The Leichhardt Heater Journey* (1982), a work which illustrates his capacity to combine thematic depth and subtlety with colloquial idiom. He has also written fiction and science fiction.

BUZO, ALEXANDER, born Sydney in 1944, the son of an Albanian civil engineer and an Australian mother, was brought up and educated in Armidale, NSW, and at the International School in Geneva. He graduated from the University of NSW in 1965. The play which first brought Buzo to national notice was *Norm and Ahmed* (first produced in 1968, published 1969), largely because of the prosecutions for obscenity that followed its productions in Brisbane and Melbourne. 'The Revolt' (1967), his first play remains unpublished. *Norm and Ahmed* was followed by the comedy *Rooted* (q.v., 1969; published 1973), the first of his plays to receive overseas productions, *The Front Room Boys* (q.v., 1969; published 1970), and *The Roy Murphy Show* (1971, published 1973), a farce which draws on the clichés and familiar rituals of a television football panel for its hilarious effects. In 1972–73 Buzo was resident playwright with the Melbourne Theatre Company and during this time produced *Macquarie* (1972, published 1971), his first historical drama and his first serious study of a complex individual; *Tom* (1972, published 1975); and 'Batman's Beach Head' (1973), a free adaptation of Ibsen's *An Enemy of the People.* He was awarded the Australian Literature Society's Gold Medal in 1972 for *Tom* and *Macquarie*. His next play, *Coralie Lansdowne Says No* (q.v., 1974), was followed by *Martello Towers* (1976), *Makassar Reef* (1978, published 1979), 'Vicki Madison Clocks Out' (1979), 'Big River' (1980) and 'Duff' (1981). He has also written screenplays and three books of general interest, *Tautology* (1981), *Meet the New Class* (1981) and *Tautology Too* (1982).

Buzo's plays were first seen as similar to those of David Williamson in their satiric treatment of Australian society, although concentrating on Sydney's mores rather than Melbourne's. In his early work the focus is more on the dehumanizing characteristics of the society that oppresses its individuals, than on the individuals themselves, whether it is general Australian society as in *Norm and Ahmed* or the world of a large corporation as in *The Front Room Boys.* In plays such as *Rooted, Tom, Coralie Lansdowne Says No* and *Martello Towers,* he has been seen as wittily exposing the hollowness of the new generation of educated, prosperous and permissive Australians. Buzo has frequently stressed, however, that his plays are fiction not documentary sociology, and his later work in particular reveals a concern with the human predicament that is universal and existential, and only incidentally Australian. Nearly all his main characters, however witty their dialogue and comic their situation, are engaged in a serious stuggle to find purpose, value and stability in an alien, amoral and meaningless world. *Macquarie,* which centres on Macquarie's career as governor of NSW from 1810 to 1822, explores the impact of a corrupt society on the ideals of a liberal humanist; *Martello Towers,* ostensibly a light, witty comedy of manners, describes the renewed marital commitment of Edward and Jennifer Martello in the face of generally fragmented, 'free' and tenuous relationships; *Makassar Reef,* set in the torpid, tropical port of Ujung Padang, explores the search for stability in love, the ennui, shifting bonds and compromises that life forces on an odd but representative assortment of people. Often admired for their verbal brilliance and their satiric wit, Buzo's plays also depend heavily on a more serious subtext, which is both romantic and sad and demands sensitive skills on the part of actor and producer. A subtle stylist with a strong sense of structural balance, he is both traditional and innovative in his approach, a mix which some of his critics have found difficult to accept.

By Reef and Palm, see BECKE, 'LOUIS'

'By the Banks of the Murrumbidgee', see GORDON, J.W.; LAWSON, HENRY

By the Walls of Old Kyoto, see STEWART, HAROLD

BYRNE, DESMOND, see *Australian Writers*

BYRNE, JOE, see *Ned Kelly*

C

Cabbage-lander (Cabbage-patcher) was a colloquial name to denote a resident of Victoria, which was known as the 'Cabbage Patch' – possibly because of its size in comparison with the other States, possibly because of the large market-garden industry around Melbourne. Victoria is referred to as the 'Cabbage Patch' in Thomas Wood's *Cobbers* (1934) and as the 'Cabbage Garden' in Joseph Furphy's *Such is Life* (1903).

Cabbage Tree, a tall palm with large leaves, is found in the coastal areas of eastern Australia. In early colonial times its leaves were used to make the cabbage-tree hat, which came to be something of a symbol of nationalistic feeling. A well-known song, 'The Cabbage Tree Hat', allegedly written by C.A. Flower, was popular from the 1880s. The so-called Cabbage Tree Mobs, the precursors of the later larrikin pushes, were gangs of young rowdies, usually native-born and wearing cabbage-tree hats, who roamed the streets of Sydney in the 1840s and 1850s. They are described in G.C. Mundy's *Our Antipodes* (1852) and are mentioned in many of the reminiscences of the period, e.g. James T. Ryan's *Reminiscences* (1894) and Charles MacAlister's *Old Pioneering Days in the Sunny South* (1907).

Cabell Family, see *Landtakers*

Caddie, a Sydney Barmaid (1953), an autobiographical work published anonymously but edited by Dymphna Cusack (q.v.) is the poignant story of a young woman (identified in some catalogues as Mrs Henry Elliott) who leaves her adulterous husband and attempts to fend for herself and her two small children in the 1930s depression. The book pays tribute also to the generous-hearted slum dwellers of inner Sydney, whose kindness and charity help her in her struggle. Both the book and the Australian film *Caddie,* produced in 1976 with Helen Morse in the title role, effectively recreate the inner Sydney environment of the time.

CAFFYN, KATHLEEN ('IOTA') (1853–1926), wife of Stephen Mannington Caffyn (q.v.), usually wrote under the pseudonym 'Iota'. Of her seventeen novels, mainly written after the death of her husband in 1896, only the first, *A Yellow Aster* (1894), was written in Australia and only two, *A Comedy in Spasms* (1895) and *Dorinda and Her Daughter* (1910), have any connection with Australia. Her success as a novelist was due to the strong romantic and sexual element in her books and to her skill in characterization.

CAFFYN, STEPHEN MANNINGTON (1850–96), born Sussex, England, migrated with his wife Kathleen Caffyn (q.v.) to Australia in 1880, where he worked as government health officer in Sydney and Wollongong before moving in 1883 to private medical practice in Melbourne. In addition to numerous medical pamphlets, he wrote for the *Bulletin, Centennial Magazine* and other journals. He published two novels, *Miss Milne and I* (1889) and *Poppy's Tears* (1890).

Cake Man, The (1978), a play by Aboriginal dramatist Robert Merritt (q.v.), was performed at the National Black Theatre, Redfern, Sydney in 1975 and at the World Theatre Festival in Colorado, USA, in 1982. A television version of the play was produced by the ABC in 1977. The play's title has its origin in the story told by Ruby, the Aboriginal mother on the mission at Cowra, NSW, to her son Pumpkinhead, about the mythical half-blind cake man who will one day be able to see little black boys as clearly as he seems to see little white boys and will give the black boys their overdue rewards. The white man's salving of his conscience for Aboriginal mistreatment is suggested by the play's white character, the Civilian, who offers cakes and goodies to the poverty-stricken black family. The more important themes of the play lie in the presentation of the poor conditions suffered by mission Aborigines, the warm affection existing within the Aboriginal family, and the male Aborigines' loss of self-respect and dignity. Brian Syron has been associated with Merritt in the success of *The Cake Man;* he has co-directed the play and has played the role of the Aboriginal husband, Sweet William.

CALDER, JAMES ERSKINE (1808–82), born Buckinghamshire, England, arrived in Van Diemen's Land at the age of twenty-one as an assistant surveyor. His appointment as surveyor-general in 1859 reflected his achievements in opening up and surveying the island. In addition to many articles on the early history of the colony and numerous official reports, Calder published *The Woodlands . . . of Tasmania* (1874), *Some Accounts of the Wars, Extirpation, Habits &c of the Native Tribes of Tasmania*

(1875) and a parliamentary paper in 1901 on the Aboriginal languages of Tasmania.

CALDWELL, ROBERT ('ANDREW COCHRANE') (1843–1909), born near Ardrossan, Scotland, came to Australia in 1849 and was a farmer and Methodist lay preacher. In 1884 he became a member of the SA House of Assembly. He published nine volumes of verse 1874–1908, including *A Vision of Toil* (1875), *The Australian Year* (1876), *In Our Great North-West* (1894), *The Pioneers* (1898) and *Adam Gowrie: Or, the Australian Farmer* (1903).

Calloway Family, see *Passage, The*

CALTHORPE, MENA (1905–), born Goulburn, NSW, taught in small country schools and later did secretarial and clerical work. She published two novels, *The Dye House* (1961), which was translated into German and Czechoslovakian, and *The Defectors* (1969). *The Dye House* creates the atmosphere of a seedy Sydney factory where the workers' lives follow the tedious humdrum enjoined in earning a living in an oppressive environment. *The Defectors* exposes the power struggle in the world of trade unions.

Calverton, Archie, a character in George Johnston's novel *Clean Straw for Nothing* (q.v., 1969), is a fictionalized study of the actor, Peter Finch (q.v.).

'Cambaroora Star, The', a poem by Henry Lawson (q.v.) about the rise and fall of a goldfields newspaper, was first published in the *Boomerang* in 1891. As the result of a reference in ' "Pursuing Literature" in Australia' (q.v.) the *Cambaroora Star* has usually been identified as the *Boomerang* itself, which ceased publication four months later, but Lawson's 'A Fragment of Autobiography' specifies the *Republican* (q.v., 1887–88), which he contributed to and nominally edited while it was under the management of his mother, Louisa Lawson.

CAMBRIDGE, ADA (1844–1926), born and raised in Norfolk, England, had published moral tales and verse which reflected her strong religious feelings by the time she married a young curate, George Frederick Cross, in 1870. They soon left for Victoria, where Cross served as an Anglican minister at Wangaratta, Yackandandah, Ballan, Coleraine, Sandhurst (Bendigo) and Beechworth before moving to Williamstown in 1893. Ada Cambridge's colonial experience is chronicled in her perceptive autobiography, *Thirty Years in Australia* (q.v., 1903); a companion volume, *The Retrospect*

(1912), deals mainly with her early years and her reactions to England during her first return visit in 1908. In 1913 she returned again to England after her husband's retirement, but following his death in 1917 moved back to Victoria.

Cambridge's first book of poems, *The Manor House and Other Poems,* was published 1875; she began to contribute fiction to the *Australasian* in the same year, ostensibly to supplement the family finances. In 1875–86 the *Australasian* published nine of her serials; three of them, *In Two Years' Time* (1879), *A Mere Chance* (1880) and *The Three Miss Kings* (q.v., 1882), were subsequently published as novels (1879, 1882, 1891 respectively). In 1886–87 Cambridge suffered a physical and emotional crisis. Her second book of poems, *Unspoken Thoughts* (q.v., 1887), which reveals religious uncertainty, deals frankly with sexuality and marriage, and expresses strong concern for the socially disadvantaged, was published anonymously but almost immediately suppressed. Following hospitalization and a Sydney convalescence, where she delighted in the artistic contacts she made, she resumed her literary career with the novel, *A Marked Man* (1890), her first significant financial success. Her other novels, some of which established an English as well as Australian reputation, were *My Guardian* (1878), *Not All in Vain* (1892), *A Little Minx* (1893), *A Marriage Ceremony* (1894), *Fidelis* (1895), *A Humble Enterprise* (1896), *Materfamilias* (q.v., 1898), *Path and Goal* (1900), *The Devastators* (1901), *Sisters* (1904), *A Platonic Friendship* (1905), *A Happy Marriage* (1906), *The Eternal Feminine* (1907) and *The Making of Rachel Rowe* (1914). She also wrote *At Midnight and Other Stories* (1897) and a final volume of poetry, *The Hand in The Dark* (1913), which reprints some of the uncontroversial material from *Unspoken Thoughts*.

Ada Cambridge has been traditionally bracketed with Jessie Couvreur and Rosa Praed (qq.v.) as a writer of romance fiction – tales of courtship and marriage – and despite her contemporary popularity has been criticized for the contrivances and trivialities of her plots, her narrow social focus (many of her novels are set among the pastoral aristocracy or within Toorak society), and her Anglo-Australian biases which permit many of her heroines to marry Englishmen of good breeding. Such an assessment not only ignores the importance of marriage and its organization for colonial women, but also does less than justice to the delight Cambridge sometimes found in the Australian landscape, to the realistic and sometimes satiric view which she offers of colonial society and to her informed and sometimes radical treatment of courtship, romantic love, marriage and parenting. The heroines of her *Australasian* serials are characteristically sensitive newcomers who come into conflict as Cambridge herself did, particularly when she began to write fiction, with the middle-class guardians of respectability, among them materialistic matriarchs and defenders of country town hierarchies; her later more substantial novels continue to explore the proper bases for marital choice although the exploration is combined with such other themes as exile, the nature of sexual passion, and the alternatives to organized religion. Her major novels include *A Marked Man,* in which the hero, Richard Delavel, periodically escapes from the consequences of a disastrous marital choice to a bush retreat modelled on the artists' camp Cambridge visited during her Sydney sojourn; *The Three Miss Kings,* where the contrivances of a conventional romantic plot (three sisters acquiring suitable husbands) are relieved by Cambridge's sardonic view of *nouveau riche* vulgarity and her acute presentation of Melbourne during the Great Exhibition of 1880; *Not All in Vain,* in which the heroine defies convention to wait for her fiancé, imprisoned for defending her honour, only to find on his release that he no longer loves her; *A Marriage Ceremony* and *Fidelis,* which both include as major characters a disfigured and isolated artist; *A Little Minx,* which shows the provincialism and religious bigotry in a small town; and *Materfamilias,* a grandmother's chronicle of her first marriage, widowhood and remarriage, in which Cambridge's ironic representation of her narrator permits a satiric exposé of traditional feminine roles. *Unspoken Thoughts* gives Cambridge some claims to being a significant poet, and *Thirty Years in Australia* is an incisive and moving autobiography.

Camden, an historical township on the western outskirts of Sydney, had its origin in one of John Macarthur's properties, Camden Park, named in honour of Lord Camden, secretary of state for the colonies, who authorized the grant of land to Macarthur in 1805. The district in general, one of the Colony's finest, had been known as the Cowpastures after the discovery in 1795 of a herd of wild cattle, descendants of the government herd that had earlier strayed from the Port Jackson settlement. The Camden area, and the Macarthur properties in particular, were important in the early pastoral development of the colony, especially in the rise of the merino wool industry. Hugh McCrae, who lived in the then-small township for many years from 1931, wrote the poems 'Camden' and 'Camden Magpie', indicating his affection for the place. S. Macarthur Onslow edited *Some Early Records of the Macarthurs of Camden* (1914) and Wil-

liam Hardy Wilson wrote *The Cow Pasture Road* (1920), an illustrated work on the Camden district. Winifred Birkett's amusing novel, *Three Goats on a Bender* (1934), is set in the Camden area.

CAMERON, J.A. (JOHN ALEXANDER) (1869–1949), born Cowabbie near Wagga, NSW, was the younger brother of Dame Mary Gilmore. He was a journalist on the *Coolgardie Miner* and *Clare's Weekly* in WA, a war correspondent in the Boer War and First World War, and then a member of the British diplomatic service at Schaffhausen, Detroit and Danzig. He wrote *The Spell of the Bush* (1909), a story of the Riverina.

CAMPBELL, DAVID (1915–79) born Ellerslie, the family property near Adelong in the Monaro district of NSW, was educated in Australia and at Cambridge, where his tutor was the well-known scholar, E.M.W. Tillyard. In the Second World War he served with distinction in the RAAF; after the war he lived on various properties in the Canberra area, dividing his time between a farming life and a career as a poet. In 1964 he became poetry editor of the *Australian;* he edited *Australian Poetry 1966* and *Modern Australian Poetry* (1970).

His first volume of poetry, *Speak with the Sun* (1949), is strongly Australian in tone. The poem 'Harry Pearce' forms a triptych with two other celebrated 'teamster' poems, Henry Kendall's 'Bill the Bullock Driver' and Judith Wright's 'Bullocky'; 'The Stockman' catches the easy-going, nonchalant air which Campbell believed was and always would be the mark of the outback breed. The first volume also contains his well-known war poem, 'Men in Green' (q.v.). *The Miracle of Mullion Hill* (1956), with 'The Speewah Picnics', 'The Westing Emu' and the title poem itself, shows Campbell's continued interest in balladry and the tall tale but the meditative lyrist is evident in two of his best poems, 'Night Sowing' and 'Who Points the Swallow?'. In *Poems* (1962) his characters and poetic landscapes are still Australian but have lost much of their parochial quality, taking on a universality that provides the basis for more mature, philosophical meditations. 'On Frosty Days', 'Winter Hills', 'Pallid Cuckoo' and 'Bindweed and Yellowtails', all from 'Cocky's Calendar', the twelve-poem sequence devoted to the countryman's life, are fresh and original nature lyrics with roots in the pastoral tradition. *The Branch of Dodona and Other Poems, 1969–1970* (1970) uses the Jason and Medea legend to offer a biting commentary on modern life and attitudes. *Devil's Rock and Other Poems, 1970–*

1972 (1974) begins with the biographical sequence *Starting from Central Station* (published separately in 1973), includes a tribute to Kenneth Slessor and contains 'Letters to a Friend', memories of pleasant activities shared with Douglas Stewart. The title poem, 'Devil's Rock and Other Carvings', is a series of brief, imaginative glimpses into the Aboriginal past. After the colloquial narrative and dramatic sequence entitled *Deaths and Pretty Cousins* (1975) came the collection, *Words with a Black Orpington* (1978); its cameo nature lyrics, seriocomic travel verses, fragments from Sappho, and love poetry (whether the lusty 'Portrait of a Lady' or the tender 'Soundings') reveal Campbell adopting the free-ranging attitudes and experimental techniques characteristic of the poetry of the 1970s. In his final volume *The Man in the Honeysuckle* (1979) he insists, as Leonie Kramer has indicated, on the relationship between physical science and poetry. The taut lines, pointed language and uncluttered statements of poems from that volume (e.g. 'Cicadas', 'A Yellow Rose' and 'August') represent Campbell's attempt to capture the quintessential nature of lyricism itself.

Campbell published two volumes of short stories: *Evening under Lamplight* (1959), childhood impressions of homestead life on a sheep station, and *Flame and Shadow* (1976). With Rosemary Dobson he published *Moscow Trefoil* (1975) and *Seven Russian Poets* (1979), translations of Russian poetry; and with artist Keith Looby he produced *The History of Australia* (1976). Campbell received numerous awards in recognition of his poetry – the Henry Lawson Australian Arts Award in 1970, the Patrick White Literary Award in 1975, the NSW Premier's Prize in 1980 for *The Man in the Honeysuckle* and FAW's Christopher Brennan Award in 1980. *Poetry Australia* (December 1981), edited by Leonie Kramer, is a special David Campbell edition; it contains, in addition to numerous eulogies for one of the most respected and popular of modern Australian poets, some unpublished poems and significant biographical material.

Campbell Howard Collection of Australian Plays in Manuscript is held at the Dixson Library at the University of New England, Armidale, NSW. The collection was made by A.C.M. (Campbell) Howard (1906–84) who was lecturer in music at the Armidale Teachers' College (1928–47), inspector of schools (1947–54), assistant director of adult education at the University of New England (1955–70), and acting director of University Extension (1970–72). For his service to education he was awarded BEM. The Campbell Howard Collection contains upwards of 300 manuscripts of plays by both well-known and lesser-known Australian writers and covers the period from 1920 to the present.

CAMPBELL, JEAN (1906–), born Melbourne, is a prolific writer of light novels, the first of which was *Brass and Cymbals* (1933), set in Melbourne in the first two decades of the twentieth century. It deals with a Jewish family which faces disintegration as the children gradually relinquish their Jewish background. *Greek Key Pattern* (1935) deals with a Greek family in Melbourne in a somewhat similar vein. Other novels, many of which have tangled personal relationships, include *Lest We Lose Our Edens* (1935), *The Red Sweet Wine* (1937) and *The Babe Is Wise* (1939).

CAMPBELL, ROSS (1910–82), born Kalgoorlie, WA, was educated in Victoria. From Melbourne University he won a Rhodes Scholarship to Oxford. Back in Australia he joined the staff of the Sydney *Daily Telegraph,* staying with that paper until the Second World War in which he served in the RAAF. After the war he joined the *Sydney Morning Herald* as a feature writer then transferred to Consolidated Press, writing articles and reviews for its stable of publications, the *Daily Telegraph, Sunday Telegraph, Australian Women's Weekly* and *Bulletin.* A selection of those articles was published by Campbell in two small books, *Daddy Are You Married?* (1962) and *Mummy, Who Is Your Husband?* (1964); a further selection of longer, more sophisticated articles from his *Bulletin* writings appeared as *She Can't Play My Bagpipes* (1970). The first two books tell of the vicissitudes of Campbell, Mrs Campbell, Theodora, Lancelot, Little Nell and Baby Pip in Oxalis Cottage. Intent after his Oxford days on being a 'dag' (an Australian humorist), Campbell became part of a long line of ironic Australian writers. Through his writings, and those of contemporaries such as Leon Gellert, Alexander Macdonald and Cyril Pearl, the Australian newspaper-reading public came to appreciate a particular type of humour, one in which a keen intelligence provided a sophisticated and lively set of ideas combined with a satirical scrutiny of contemporary Australian society. Campbell's autobiography, *An Urge to Laugh,* was published in 1981.

CAMPION, EDMUND (1933–), born Sydney, graduated from the Universities of Sydney and Cambridge before being ordained as a priest in 1961. After a curacy in several Sydney parishes he became a lecturer in history at St Patrick's College, Manly, NSW. He edited *Lord Acton and the First Vatican Council* (1975) and published *John Henry Newman*

(1980) and *Rockchoppers: Growing up Catholic in Australia* (1982). He has, since 1975, been editor of *Studies in the Christian Movement*. Regarded as one of the most important recent contributions to Australian religious literature – and certainly one of the most lucidly-written – *Rockchoppers*, often personal in tone and occasionally autobiographical, is largely a series of essays about the state of Catholic culture in Australia, and the history of Catholicism locally and internationally. The title, a derivation from the initials RC, is also a derogatory Protestant reference to Irish-Australian Catholic convict origins.

'CAMPION, SARAH' (MARY ROSE ALPERS) (1906–   ), born Eastbourne, England, was a teacher who married NZ writer Antony Alpers and had only a brief association with Australia, 1938–40. Her fiction contains an Australian-based trilogy, *Mo Burdekin* (1941), *Bonanza* (1942) and *The Pommy Cow* (1944). The trilogy tells the story of Moses Burdekin, only survivor of a pioneer family drowned in the Burdekin River in Queensland. He is found floating in a wooden cradle and is adopted by storekeeper Reuben Abraham. The quest for gold becomes Mo's lifelong obsession; that he is sometimes successful is indicated by the title, *Bonanza*, but in that book he suffers several personal tragedies including the death of an illegitimate son. The final volume finds Mo in South Africa fighting the Boers and meeting Kate, an English girl, the 'pommy cow' of the title. After the war he brings her to Australia where they marry, and the story ends with Mo's death on another prospecting venture. The Mo Burdekin stories contain many fresh intuitions about the Australian landscape. Several of 'Sarah Campion''s other novels, e.g. *Turn Away No More* (1940), *Makeshift* (1940) and *Dr. Golightly* (1946), have slight Australian connections.

Canadian Exiles is a name given to a group of about 200 men, also known as the Canadian Patriots, transported to Australia after the failure of rebellions in Canada in 1837–38. The Canadian Exiles comprised in fact two distinct groups: the rebels from Upper Canada (now the province of Ontario, then under the governorship of Sir George Arthur) consisted mainly of British Canadians and Americans and were sent to Tasman's Peninsula in Van Diemen's Land; the rebels from Lower Canada (now the province of Quebec) were French Canadians and were sent to Sydney. Some of the patriots were harshly treated and all felt their exile keenly, although within five years of their arrival most had won pardons or effected escapes. Like earlier political prisoners they were rela-

tively well-educated convicts and several left memoirs of their Canadian and Australian experiences which form part of Australian convict literature (see Convict in Australian Literature). William Gates's *Recollections of Life in Van Dieman's* [sic] *Land* (1850), Daniel D. Heustis's *A Narrative of the Adventures and Suffering of Captain Daniel D. Heustis and His Companions* (1847), Caleb Lyon's *Narrative and Recollections of Van Dieman's* [sic] *Land, during a Three Years' Captivity of Stephen S. Wright* (1844), Robert Marsh's *Seven Years of My Life* (1847), Linus W. Miller's *Notes of an Exile to Van Dieman's* [sic] *Land* (1846), Samuel Snow's *The Exile's Return* (1846) and Benjamin Wait's *Letters from Van Dieman's* [sic] *Land* (1843) are reminiscences of convicts from Upper Canada; the prison diary of one of the Lower Canadian prisoners is translated by F.M. Greenwood in *Land of a Thousand Sorrows* (1980).

Canberra, the capital of Australia, lies on the edge of the Monaro (q.v.) within the Australian Capital Territory (q.v.) some 300 kilometres from Sydney. The Canberra area, first explored in 1820, figures in Barron Field's *Geographical Memoirs on New South Wales* (1825) and was settled as a pastoral district from the 1830s; other variants of the name, which is of Aboriginal origin, include 'Canbury', 'Canberry', 'Kamberra' and 'Caamberra'. Chosen in 1908 as the site of the national capital after federal parliamentarians had earlier selected Bombala, Tumut and Dalgety, Canberra was officially named in 1913 at a ceremony at which Lady Denman placed the emphasis on the first syllable, the accepted pronunciation. The city of Canberra, designed by Walter Burley Griffin (1876–1937), began to be occupied after the federal parliamentary building was opened in 1927. Among several studies of Canberra are Warren Denning's *Capital City* (1938), Lionel Wigmore's *The Long View* (1963) and Roger Pegrum's *The Bush Capital* (1983), which chronicles its selection as the capital; John Gale's *Canberra* (1927) and the reminiscences of Samuel Shumack, *An Autobiography: Or, Tales and Legends of Canberra Pioneers* (1967), focus on its earlier history. The magazine *Canberra Poetry* began in 1973 to encourage ACT writers, and published a collection of erotic verse, *Within the Hill* (1975).

Canberra Times, founded by Thomas Mitchell Shakespeare (1873–1938), published its first issue 3 September 1926; in 1928 it became a daily. It was controlled by T.M. Shakespeare and his sons A.T., C.J. and J.W. Shakespeare, until it was sold to John Fairfax and Sons Ltd in 1964. It carries regular literary columns, organizes an annual National Short Story competition sponsored by the Commonwealth Bank, and publishes prize-winning entries from each year's competiton. In 1983 it co-sponsored the first National Word Festival.

CANNON, MICHAEL (1929–   ), born Brisbane, has spent his working life as a journalist and historian in Melbourne, Sydney and London and is at present chief editor of the *Historical Records of Victoria* (q.v.). He has written *The Land Boomers* (1966, 2nd edn titled *Land Boom and Bust* 1972); the best-selling series *Australia in the Victorian Age,* comprising three volumes, *Who's Master? Who's Man?* (1971), *Life in the Country* (1973) and *Life in Cities* (1975); *An Australian Camera 1851–1914* (1973); *That Damned Democrat: John Norton, An Australian Populist, 1858–1916* (1981); and *Australia: A History in Photography* (1983). Cannon's wide historical interest in Australia is also reflected in his editing of e.g. *The Vagabond Papers* (1969), *Victoria's Representative Men at Home* (1977), *Vagabond Country: Australian Bush and Town Life in the Victorian Age* (1981), and *The Victorian Goldfields, 1852–3: An Original Album (S.T. Gill)* (1982), and the first three volumes of *Historical Records of Victoria.*

'Canticle, The', a poem in four parts by Francis Webb (q.v.), was published in Webb's volume *Birthday* (1953). In notes to the poem, Webb said that St Francis of Assisi had provided, in his *Canticle to the Sun* written at Assisi in the garden of the Minoresses of San Damiano shortly before his death, 'a great hymn of devotion, a rewarding personal document, and fine poetry'; excerpts from *Canticle to the Sun* are used in Webb's poem. Webb builds up the character of St Francis by observations from those in contact with him and by indicating the changes wrought in them through his influence. The first such observer is the leper, whose bitter sense of rejection by God and society is transformed to joy and peace through St Francis's loving embrace and cure of his putrefying body. St Francis's father (the cloth merchant, Pietro di Bernadone), the Jongleur, the Wolf of Gubbio whom St Francis called 'brother', and the Knight and the Serf, are others regenerated through the saint's influence. The fourth part emphasizes the veneration in which St Francis, the 'second Christ', is held by his devoted followers and concludes with a reference to the stigmata of Christ, which are said to have appeared on St Francis's body in the latter part of his life.

Canticles on the Skin, see **ADAMSON, ROBERT**

CAPPIELLO, ROSA, see *Paesa Fortunata*

Capricornia, a novel by Xavier Herbert (q.v.), was published in 1938, when it won both the Commonwealth sesquicentenary literary competition and the Australian Literature Society's Gold Medal. The story of the writing, editing and publication of the novel is a celebrated and, so far as the editing is concerned, controversial episode in Australian literary history. In a talk given at the Adelaide Festival in 1962, Herbert recalled that *en route* to England in 1930 he wrote a 'tough little book' called 'Black Velvet', seemingly focused on sexual relations between European men and Aboriginal women, which he failed to place with publishers. Disenchanted with England and about to leave for Africa he was persuaded by Sadie Norden, later his wife, to remain and rewrite 'Black Velvet'. What emerged over the next two years was a much longer work in which the toughness of 'Black Velvet' was softened by Herbert's sense of 'the loveliness of the land I'd left' and his feeling that the people 'were really comical, not so bad as mad, as aren't we all?'. Herbert returned to Australia with the first draft of *Capricornia;* in 1933 he met P.R. Stephensen (q.v.), who urged him to revise the novel and acted as adviser during the revision in which its half-million words were reduced by half. The extent of Stephensen's assistance was the subject of some dispute between the two men, but it seems clear that even if Stephensen did not actually write any part of the novel he made suggestions which Herbert adopted. Stephensen started typesetting in 1934 but his company went into liquidation before *Capricornia* could be published. After three years, during which time Herbert had tried to place the novel with other publishers, Stephensen accepted *Capricornia* for publication with the press of the *Publicist* (q.v.) and not only completed printing in time to enter it in the sesquicentenary competition but also promoted it enthusiastically. Angus & Robertson, which had twice rejected *Capricornia,* accepted it finally in 1938 and has published the many editions and reprints since then which attest to its popularity.

In 1933 Stephensen urged Herbert 'to keep the story of *Capricornia* strictly to Norman's life, deleting everything extraneous'. Although in its final form the novel retains a large cast of characters (more than a hundred) and a broad chronological sweep (from the mid-1880s to about 1930), the story of Norman Shillingsworth and his family occupies an important part of the foreground. Arriving in Capricornia, a fictional name for the Northern Territory, in 1904 with his brother Oscar, Mark Shillingsworth soon becomes part of the flotsam and jetsam of Port Zodiac (Darwin) society. Dismissed from the public service for drunkenness, Mark fathers a half-caste son whom he deserts and who acquires the name of Naw-Nim (No-Name), later Norman, and after killing a Chinese storekeeper, disappears from view until the second half of the novel. Oscar, the respectable contrast to Mark, marries and tries to establish himself on a Capricornian cattle station, Red Ochre, but is deserted by his wife and eventually returns for a time to Batman (Melbourne) accompanied by his daughter Marigold and foster son Norman, who has been sent to him after Mark's desertion. Before their departure Oscar rejects the plea of a former employee, Peter Differ, to see to the welfare of his half-caste daughter Constance; Constance Differ is placed under the 'protection' of Humbolt Lace, a Protector of Aborigines, who seduces her and then marries her off to another half-caste. Forced into prostitution, Constance is dying of consumption when discovered by a railway fitter, Tim O'Cannon, one of the few inhabitants of Capricornia who treat the Aborigines with humanity and compassion. After Connie's death, Tim takes her daughter Tocky into his household; after Tim's own death in a railway accident she is sent to the native compound at Port Zodiac and then to a mission station.

Hearing news in 1928 of an economic boom in Capricornia, Oscar returns to his station where he is joined by Marigold and Norman, who has grown to manhood believing himself to be the son of a Javanese princess and a soldier killed in the First World War. Soon after he discovers part of the truth about his identity – that his mother was Aboriginal – Norman meets his father, now a railway construction boss working under the name of Jack Ramble. Their reconciliation is not completed until after Ramble disappears again and Heather Shay, Norman's aunt and Mark's former lover, reveals Ramble's secret. The discovery of the truth about his past is the first stage of Norman's education in *Capricornia;* in response to his discoveries he embarks on a series of journeys to discover his true, part-Aboriginal self. On his second journey, which takes place after Oscar has died, he meets and wanders in the wilderness with Tocky, who has escaped from the mission station. Their interlude is interrupted when Tocky, while separated from Norman, shoots Frank McLash, a fugitive from the police, in self-defence. Tocky does not tell Norman of the killing and after their return to civilization Norman is arrested and stands trial for Frank's murder. Mark, too, once his identity becomes known beyond his own circle, stands trial for the original murder of the Chinese storekeeper. At the end of the novel both are

acquitted, Heather and Mark are married, and Norman returns to Red Ochre where he finds the body of Tocky and their child in a water tank in which she had taken refuge from the authorities.

Like *Poor Fellow My Country,* Herbert's later novel about the Northern Territory, *Capricornia* is a sprawling, swashbuckling work teeming with incident and with 'mad' characters. A major focus is the indictment of civilization in this part of Australia, particularly the violent treatment meted out to the Aborigines (as well as the Chinese) by the pioneering Europeans, whose racism is responsible for the tragedies of Connie Differ and Tocky O'Cannon and for the ambivalent status in society of half-castes such as Norman. In exposing the institutions of white society (e.g. religion, the law, civil administration) as hypocritical, corrupt and inefficient, Herbert has recourse to heavy irony, e.g. in the capitals which signal the clichés of his Dickensian and satirically-named characters: thus the legal profession is represented by Judge Caesar Bightit, the prosecutor is Thumscrough and the solicitors Nawratt and Nibblesom. Yet it does an injustice to the vitality of *Capricornia* to see it as simply a novel of social protest that encompasses class as well as race. Herbert has written that 'the greatest feeling expressed' in the novel is 'my love of this good earth'. The abundance of nature is emphasized but so is its fickleness and the danger it holds for the isolated Europeans who fail to adapt to its changing moods and demands. Although the element of chance in human affairs is an important ingredient in Capricornian life, so is human culpability for the disasters that befall characters like Tim O'Cannon. The rhythm of the seasons is one of the ways *Capricornia* is shaped; others are the search for identity and the quest to belong, which encompass not only individuals like Norman and Tocky but also whole societies. The journey (hence the importance of trains) is a dominant motif in a novel that combines comedy and tragedy and, like many other saga-chronicles of the 1920s and 1930s (e.g. *Landtakers* and *All That Swagger*), offers a radical view of Australia's development.

'Captain Dobbin', a poem by Kenneth Slessor (q.v.) in *Cuckooz Contrey* (1932), is based partly on a Captain Bayldon, retired sea captain and uncle of Slessor's first wife, Noela, and owes some of its picturesque detail to Herman Melville's *Omoo.* The poem describes an eccentric old seaman who has enshrined in his cottage by the harbour the treasures of his seafaring days. Slessor's colourful description of the exotic places and incidents that live in the old captain's memory and his contrast of those with the cold, unfeeling contemporary scene point to his own commitment to the romantic past. A fine piece of characterization with the Slessor penchant for lavish and colourful imagery, 'Captain Dobbin' is one of his major poems.

'Captain of the Push, The', Henry Lawson's (q.v.) poem about a stranger from the country (called 'The Bastard from the Bush' in some versions) who wins membership of a larrikin (q.v.) gang or 'push' in the Rocks area of Sydney and then disappears after he has 'taken down' the Captain of the Push, was first published in the *Bulletin* in 1892. Obscene versions of the poem, titled 'The Bastard from the Bush', are extant; the one closest to 'The Captain of the Push' emphasizes the bravado of the bushman Foreskin Fred, chronicles a physical beating he gives to each member of the Push and concludes with the long, inventive curse which the battered Captain heaps upon Fred's head. There have been periodic suggestions that Lawson wrote this 'The Bastard from the Bush' as well as 'The Captain of the Push'; the association explains why Robin Ramsay's one-man show on Lawson, which has been successful in Australia and overseas from 1979, is titled 'The Bastard from the Bush'. The Bastard from the Bush has passed into folklore as the epitome of the aggressive country 'tough'.

Captain Quadring (1912), William Gosse Hay's (q.v.) third novel, is set in Manalia (Hay's name for Australia in his early novels) where the ex-convict Henry Fairservice, whose aliases in the novel are first Mr Meadstone and then Captain Quadring, comes to restore order at a quarry worked by convicts, which is near land held by his brother Andrew. The brothers have become bitter enemies in England and, after believing he has killed Henry Fairservice in a fight at Quadring quarry, Andrew has fled to Tasmania. The brothers are eventually reconciled (although Henry is killed at the end of the novel by vengeful convicts) through the endeavours of the saintly Elizabeth Beckworth, who has taken over the Fairservice family home.

Captain Quiros (1964), James McAuley's (q.v.) narrative poem describing the expeditions of the Portuguese explorer Pedro Fernandez de Quiros (1563–1614) in his search for the Great South Land, is an important contribution to the voyager theme in Australian literature. In 'The Inception of the Poem' the long-held fascination of the theme for McAuley is revealed:

> Then suddenly, unbidden, the theme returns
> That visited my youth; over the vast
> Pacific with white wake at their sterns,
> The ships of Quiros on their great concerns
> Ride in upon the present from the past!

The first part of the poem, 'Where Solomon was Wanting', records through the narrator Belmonte the voyage of Alvaro de Mendana in 1595 to Santa Cruz Island near the Solomon Islands with Quiros as navigator; the establishment of the abortive settlement at Graciosa Bay; the murder of the native chieftain, Malope; and the forced withdrawal of the expedition. The second part, 'The Quest for the South Land', recounts Quiros's own expedition to establish the New Jerusalem in the South Seas. He comes to an island in the New Hebrides which he names La Austrialia del Espiritu Santo (Southern Land of the Holy Spirit). A river to the west of the anchorage is named Jordan and a site is selected for a city to be called New Jerusalem. Quiros's great plan fails not because of any defect on his part but because no man can bring about the millennium – 'The New Jerusalem . . . shall never be Christ's bride save in eternity'. The third part, 'The Times of the Nations', presents Quiros's dying vision of the unveiling of the Great South Land (Australia) by the Dutch explorers and Bougainville and Cook; the formation of the initial colony 'under the shadow of harsh penal law'; and its growth to nationhood 'fortunate and free'. De Quiros is also the subject of a play, 'The Quest', by Louis Esson and of a television opera by Peter Sculthorpe in 1982.

Captain Swift, a play with slight Australian content by Charles Haddon Chambers (q.v.), was first produced in London in 1888 with Herbert Beerbohm Tree in the name role and published in 1902. It is chiefly memorable for originating the phrase 'the long arm of coincidence', used by the title character, a bushranger.

CARBONI, RAFFAELLO (1820–75) was born Urbino, Italy, and after a restless youth in which he studied for the priesthood attempted a commercial career, joined the Young Italy movement and was wounded in the rebellion of 1849, he arrived on the Ballarat goldfields in 1853. He became a member of the miners' central committee supervising the events leading to the Eureka Stockade (q.v.) but was a spectator when the stockade was attacked, 3 December 1854. He was charged with treason for his role in the Eureka incident but was acquitted with the other participants. His account of the revolt, *The Eureka Stockade*, was published as by 'Carboni Raffaello' late in 1855 and was sold personally by Carboni at the site of Eureka on the first anniversary of the attack. A modern edition (1942) has an introduction by H.V. Evatt, who asserts that 'it is impossible to deny him greatness as writer and historian'. Although that is excessive praise

Carboni's book has become recognized, in spite of its eccentric structure and florid style, as a vivid and reliable account of the Eureka events as well as a remarkably sound analysis of the underlying causes of those events. Carboni left Australia in January 1856 and travelled widely for several years. He returned to Italy to participate in the Risorgimento, and in later years was a busy but unacknowledged dramatist and composer. Carboni's long allegorical poem 'Gilburnia', dealing with Eureka and the diggings, was discovered in 1980 by A.D. Pagiaro in Rome. Carboni and the Eureka Stockade are the subjects of John Romeril's play, 'Carboni' (1980). He appears in other literature about Eureka, e.g. in Louis Esson's play *The Southern Cross* (1946) and in E.V. Timm's juvenile novel, *The Red Mask* (1927).

Cardboard Crown, The, a novel by Martin Boyd (q.v.) published in 1952, is the opening work of a tetralogy in which Boyd depicts the fortunes of the Langton family, living between two hemispheres and two cultures. With the aid of her diaries and a relative's reminiscences Guy Langton reconstructs the history of his grandmother Alice from the 1850s to the turn of the century, her marriage to Austin Langton and their life in Australia and England. The narrative centres on Austin's adultery with a cousin, Hetty Mayhew, who bears him four sons, and on Alice's friendship with Aubrey Tunstall, a cultured Italianate Englishman living in Rome. Alice invests her favourite daughter, Diana, with her aspirations towards European civilization although Diana's marriage to an impecunious Australian musician and the financial crash of the 1890s erode the family's aristocratic expectations and way of life.

Careful, He Might Hear You, a semi-autobiographical novel by Sumner Locke Elliott (q.v.), was published in 1963 and won the Miles Franklin Award that year. Immediately successful, it was translated into six languages and selected by *Reader's Digest* Book Club; produced as a film in 1983 directed by Carl Schultz, it won the award for best Australian film. Set in 1930s Sydney, the novel traces the relationship between a small boy (nicknamed 'PS' by his mother, the writer Sinden Marriott, who had died at his birth) and his aunt Vanessa. Brought up from birth by his impoverished but loving Aunt Lila and her husband George, PS has been impressed with the legend of his talented and charming mother, referred to as 'Dear One' by Lila. He has never met his father, Logan Marriott, an alcoholic ex-journalist who is incapable of affecting his destiny. Two other aunts, the perennially girlish

Vere, and Agnes who suffers from a religious mania, care for him intermittently. The stability of his childhood is threatened when Vanessa, the aunt who has lived with the family's wealthy Cousin Ettie for many years, arrives from England and attempts to gain sole custody. PS is sent to an expensive but unpleasant school, instructed in good manners and provided with an elegant home, clothes and friends. His instinctive resistance to Vanessa's attempts to appropriate him, heightened by a visit from his father, culminates in his refusal to return after a weekend with Lila. Meanwhile the grounds of Vanessa's prickly insecurity, the inadequacies of her relationship with her parents and sisters and with Logan Marriott, are suggested. After a protracted legal battle, PS is assigned to Vanessa by an insensitive judge. Incarcerated once again in her unfriendly house, he engages in an effective game of passive resistance. Vanessa's confidence is progressively undermined and finally crumbles when she witnesses his cruelly accurate imitation of her at a children's party. She decides to give him up, experiences a new sense of peace and freedom, but is drowned in a ferry accident on her way to Lila. After her funeral, PS is reconciled to her memory and determines to follow her last advice to him, to be himself. Refusing to be categorized any longer as a postscript, he demands to be known by his real name, Bill.

CAREW, ELSIE (1895–1971), born Auckland, NZ, had by her account a Cinderella-type existence as a child before setting out at nineteen for an independent life in Australia. In her lonely and rather unusual life she spent long periods at the Sydney People's Palace, where she died; she had a failed marriage, occasional bouts of travel including a trip to Moscow, and a penchant for writing esoteric verse and prose which she kept in tattered notebooks. Made known to Australian readers through the interest of Nancy Keesing, who wrote *Elsie Carew: Australian Primitive Poet* (1965), she still remains something of an enigma; her visionary experiences and dry perceptions on the follies of modern humanity are conveyed in direct and aphoristic verse. *The Passing Pageant: Poems and Prose by Elsie Carew* was published in 1970.

CAREY, PETER (1943–), born Bacchus Marsh, Victoria, was educated at Monash University. At Monash, where he met Barry Oakley and Morris Lurie, he studied science but became interested in writing. After leaving university he worked for advertising agencies in Melbourne and London (the latter 1968–70), moved to Sydney in 1974 and now divides his time between his own advertising agency and writing.

His first three novels are unpublished although part of an early book, titled *Contacts*, appeared in the anthology *Under Twenty Five* (1966). His short stories, some of which first appeared in such periodicals as *Overland, Tabloid Story, Stand, Nation Review* and *Meanjin,* have been published in two collections *The Fat Man in History* (1974) and *War Crimes* (1979), which won the NSW Premier's Literary Award in 1980. A collection published in London in 1980 and titled *The Fat Man in History* contains some stories from both collections. He has also published a novel, *Bliss* (q.v., 1981), which won the Miles Franklin Award in 1982.

An accessible writer, Carey has been described as a fabulist similar to such overseas writers as Jorge Luis Borges and Donald Barthelme, although his fiction is distinctive and not derivative. He sees himself as an Australian writer but is not indebted to any tradition. Surrealism and realism blend in most of his stories to create a compelling, often nightmarish world which is mysterious and serious, fantastic yet real. Common to most of his stories are a sardonic sense of comedy and a relish for the macabre, a matter-of-fact tone, a controlled treatment of suggestive, seemingly-bizarre detail and a narrator whose character is as ambiguous and shadowy as his experience is immediate and compelling. Underlying Carey's surrealism is a keen sense of what he sees as the absurd paradoxes and contradictions of contemporary life, of the problematic nature of ordinary reality. Many of his characters are social failures, such as the unemployed man in 'Peeling'; or dispossessed, as the young man Crabs is dispossessed of physical stature and car parts in the story of that title; or victims of insane institutions, such as the soldier in 'Windmill in the West', who is ordered at all costs to guard an indeterminate area for an indeterminate reason, or the shepherd class 3 in 'Life and Death in the South Side Pavilion', who is futilely employed by his faceless 'Company' to prevent horses from falling into an unenclosed tank. Most of his individuals are powerless against an exterior force of some kind, whether it is small-town prejudice as in 'American Dreams', the 'Committee' ruling the world in 'The Fat Man in History', or the new dictators, the corrupt and corrupting Fastalogians in 'The Chance'. Occasionally, as in the brilliantly suggestive story 'War Crimes', the victim forces himself to rise above his degrading status only to be irretrievably debased by the vicious means he chooses. Carey has described his characters as 'victims of a way of living', people who have 'come to accept their nightmares', embodiments of his own 'faint-hearted optimism and strong pessimism'. Frequently their absurd experiences are a metaphor of the mindless destructiveness of contemporary, technological society. Stories such as 'Crabs', which starts with the realistic setting of a drive-in cinema and ends with the transformation of an inadequate young man into a perfectly-functioning machine (a tow-truck), and 'The Fat Man in History' which deals with the dilemma of a fat man after the revolution has declared obesity to be subversive, satirize recognizable, reductive trends in modern society. Others such as 'War Crimes', 'Conversations with Unicorns' and 'The Chance' suggest the conditions that combine to create alienation and frustration. *Bliss,* Carey's schematically-conceived novel which deals with the life of Harry Joy, an advertising man who dies three times and is resurrected on each occasion to new hellish or heavenly experience, combines light comedy, incisive social satire and a poetic, futuristic vision.

CARLETON, CAROLINE (?1820–74), migrated from England to Australia in 1839. She wrote 'The Song of Australia' (1858) and *South Australian Lyrics* (?1860), the latter the first recorded book of verse published by a woman in SA.

'CARMICHAEL, JENNINGS' (1868–1904), born Ballarat, spent her childhood in the Gippsland area – there is a plaque to her memory in Orbost – and then trained as a nurse in Melbourne. She published prose sketches, *Hospital Children* (1891), and *Poems* (1895). After a tragic marriage she was left destitute in London, where she died in a workhouse in 1904.

CARNEGIE, D.W. (DAVID WYNFORD) (1871–1900), born London, came to WA and worked on the Coolgardie goldfields. His prospecting for gold and his interest in exploring the country led him on a memorable expedition across the desert; the journey is described in his *Spinifex and Sand* (1898).

Carringbush, the setting of Frank Hardy's novel, *Power Without Glory* (q.v., 1950), is the Melbourne suburb of Collingwood. The fictitious name was subsequently adopted by the Collingwood council for the local library.

CARRINGTON, TOM (1843–1918), born London, is reputed to have taken drawing lessons from the caricaturist George Cruikshank; his early work imitated John Tenniel, the illustrator of Lewis Carroll. He came as a gold-seeker to Australia in the 1860s and in 1866 began a long association as a cartoonist with *Melbourne Punch,* in which he virulently satirized the politician Graham Berry in the late 1870s. He also drew for *Adelaide Punch* and produced a notable series on the capture of Ned Kelly (q.v.) for the *Australasian Sketcher* in 1880. He was on the staff of the *Australasian* and the *Argus* after his departure from *Melbourne Punch* in 1887. A founder of the Yorick Club, Carrington was the best political cartoonist in Australia before the advent of the *Bulletin;* he developed his own line and successfully bridged the transition from wood to process engraving. With the journalist John Eville, he published the pantomime *Adaptation and Localization of Humpty Dumpty: Or, Harlequin King Arthur* (1874).

CARRON, WILLIAM, see **KENNEDY, E.B.**

Cartload of Clay, A, see **JOHNSTON, GEORGE;** *Clean Straw for Nothing*

CASEY, GAVIN (1907–64), born Kalgoorlie, WA, grew up in a gold-mining environment from which he drew in his later writings. During the 1930s depression he worked in the Kalgoorlie mines and began his long experience as a journalist by reporting the Kalgoorlie news for the Perth *Mirror*. By 1936 he was publishing short stories in the *Australian Journal* and the *Bulletin*. He won the *Bulletin* short-story prize in successive years with 'Rich Stew' and 'Mail Run East'. In 1942 and 1943 he published his two chief collections of short stories, *It's Harder for Girls* (which won the S.H. Prior Memorial Prize and was republished in 1973 as *Short Shift Saturday and Other Stories*) and *Birds of a Feather*. Short story fiction was Casey's forte; such stories as 'A Job in the Mill', 'That Day at Brown Lakes', 'It's Harder for Girls' and 'Short Shift Saturday' (q.v.) are accepted as among the finest Australian examples of the genre. As a short-story writer he has often been compared with Henry Lawson. In his stories of the goldfields (as with Lawson's of the bush) there is, beneath the easy yarning style and gently melancholy tone, a consistent emphasis on hardship that is tempered, for the male at least, by the conviviality ('beery goodfellowship' in the eyes of one critic) of mates. In 1945 Casey went to New York to administer the Australian News and Information Service; later he was with the Australian News and Information Bureau in Canberra and Sydney. A gregarious personality, Casey became a popular member of Sydney's journalistic scene. His novels include *Downhill Is Easier* (1945), which illustrates the fatal ease with which the gradual slide into crime occurs; *The Wits Are Out* (1947), a light-hearted but perceptive and occasionally critical account of a beer party and its participants; *City of Men* (1950), which

records the saga of two generations of the Willard family on the goldfields; *Snowball* (1958), a study of a group of half-caste Aborigines and their interaction with the white community in the country town of Gibberton; *Amid the Plenty* (1962), an account of the Mayhew family who struggle through adverse times; and *The Man Whose Name Was Mud* (1963), which returns to the goldfields setting and is one of Casey's most interesting character studies. With Ted Mayman he wrote a documentary about Kalgoorlie, *The Mile That Midas Touched* (1964). An interesting alternative view of the ethos of mateship that pervaded both Casey's life and his fiction is that given by his first wife, Dorothy Casey-Congdon, in *Casey's Wife* (1982); her account of their marriage would seem to vindicate the theory that in the male-dominated Australian environment it was certainly 'harder for girls'.

CASEY, Lady MAIE (1892–1983), born Melbourne, was the wife of Baron Casey of Berwick. She published three autobiographical accounts, *An Australian Story 1837–1907* (1962), a history of four generations of her family in Australia; *Tides and Eddies* (1966), an account of her early married life; and *Rare Encounters* (1980), her reminiscences of several distinguished individuals; an account of Nellie Melba's life, *Melba Revisited* (1975); and two volumes of verse, *Verses* (1963) and *From the Night* (1976). She also edited, with others, *Early Melbourne Architecture 1840 to 1888* (1953).

CASEY, RICHARD GARDINER (Baron Casey of Berwick, Victoria and of The City of Westminster) (1890–1976), a distinguished Australian soldier, politician and statesman, was governor of Bengal, India, 1944–46. Created a life peer, the first outside the United Kingdom, Lord Casey was governor-general of Australia 1965–69. His writings include *An Australian in India* (1947), *Friends and Neighbours* (1955), the autobiographical *Personal Experience, 1939–46* (1962), and *The Future of the Commonwealth* (1963). In *Australian Father and Son* (1966) he writes about his grandfather, Cornelius Gavan Casey (1811–96), and his father, Richard Gardiner Casey (1846–1913). T.B. Millar edited *Australian Foreign Minister: The Diaries of R.G. Casey 1951–60* (1972). His wife, Lady Maie Casey (q.v.), tells of her husband and their life together in *Tides and Eddies* (1966). W.J. Hudson and Jane North edited *My Dear P.M.: R.G. Casey's Letters to S.M. Bruce 1924–1929* (1980).

CASH, MARTIN (1808–77), born Enniscorthy, Ireland, was transported to NSW in 1827 for housebreaking. He worked out his seven-year sentence in assignment in the Hunter valley before going to Van Diemen's Land in 1837 to avoid charges of cattle duffing. In 1839 he was convicted of larceny and sentenced to seven years' imprisonment; over the next five years he made several escapes from Port Arthur, and in 1843 was the leader of a bushranging gang sometimes called 'Cash and Co.'. After his arrest Cash was sentenced to death, but his sentence was commuted to transportation for life. He spent 1844–54 on Norfolk Island, a reformed character, and soon after his return to Tasmania received a ticket of leave; conditionally pardoned in 1856, he lived in NZ for four years before returning to Tasmania, where he was a farmer and an affectionately-regarded old identity. In 1870 his autobiography, *The Adventures of Martin Cash,* edited and also probably written by James Lester Burke, was published; it went through several editions and was a source used by Marcus Clarke in his account of John Rex's escape from Port Arthur in *His Natural Life* (1874). Discussed in most histories of bushranging in Australia, Cash is the subject of Frank Clune's *Martin Cash* (1955) and of 'Cash', a play by Michael Boddy and Marcus Cooney which inaugurated the Tasmanian Theatre Company in 1972. Cash and his gang are also a threat in William Hay's novel, *Strabane of the Mulberry Hills* (1929).

'Cassidy Album, The', see KENNA, PETER

Cassidy, Joey, see DAWE, BRUCE

CASSIDY, ROBERT JOHN ('GILROONEY') (1880–1948), born Coolac, NSW, worked in various bush occupations before joining the *Australian Worker,* then the *Barrier Truth* and the *Worker* again in 1912. Under the pseudonym 'Gilrooney' he published bush ballads, *The Land of the Starry Cross and Other Verses* (1911); a novel, *Chandler of Corralinga* (1912); and *The Gipsy Road and Other Fancies* (1919), a book of humorous prose sketches and verse.

Casterton, a farming town in western Victoria on the Glenelg River, was associated with the Henty brothers one of whom, Francis, took up land in the area in 1837. The town is also associated with Dame Mary Gilmore, who lived in the district 1902–12 after her return from the New Australia venture. The novelist-journalist and somewhat extraordinary character, 'Grant Hervey' (q.v.), was born at Casterton in 1880.

'Cast-Iron Canvasser, The', a short story by A.B. Paterson (q.v.), was published in *Three*

Elephant Power and Other Stories (1917). One of the most humorous Australian stories, it tells of a mechanical book-seller devised to counter the treatment bush folk mete out to travelling salesmen, and its attempt to sell an atlas to the giant Scot, Macpherson.

Castlemaine, see 'Wild Colonial Boy, The'

Castlereagh River, discovered by George Evans, a member of John Oxley's 1818 expedition, and explored by Charles Sturt in 1829 to its junction with the Darling River, was named after Lord Castlereagh, then secretary of state for the colonies. It flows through the wool country of central northern NSW, its course marked by such outback towns as Coonabarabran, Gilgandra, Gulargambone and Coonamble. The Castlereagh is A.B. Paterson country, his famous 'land of lots of time along the Castlereagh': in his poem 'The Travelling Post Office' an old man sends a letter addressed to his drover son, 'care of Conroy's sheep along the Castlereagh'; and in his 'Shearing at Castlereagh' the quality of the wool grown on the Castlereagh is stressed. Not everything remains idyllic, however, on Paterson's Castlereagh, for his poem 'A Bushman's Song', which later became a popular bush song with the title 'Travellin' down the Castlereagh', expresses the radical and racist sentiments typical of the bushman's philosophy in the 1890s. In the poem the true bushman is forced 'further out' once the Castlereagh pastoral idyll has been corrupted by 'scab' Chinese labour and 'the little landlord god'.

CASTRO, BRIAN (1950–), born Hong Kong, taught English and French in Australia and France 1972–79 before becoming a full-time writer. In addition to short stories in various journals he has published a novel, *Birds of Passage* (1983), which was the joint winner of the *Australian*/Vogel Literary Award of 1982. The novel, set in both the mid-nineteenth century and the present day, links the experiences of two characters – Shan, a Chinese who takes part in the Australian gold rushes, and Seamus, his mixed-race descendant.

Castro's Last Sacrament, see DORRINGTON, ALBERT

Casuals Club, an informal association of literary figures, artists and *bons vivants* founded in Sydney in 1906 by R.F. Irvine, lasted until 1922. Its members met fortnightly for conversation, convivial company and at times rowdy entertainment. Among its notable members were Christopher Brennan, Arthur H. Adams, John

147

le Gay Brereton, Lionel Lindsay, Julian Ashton and Bertram Stevens. It was in the Casuals Club that Christopher Brennan gained the reputation for bohemianism that made him the leading figure of the Sydney café society of the day. Brennan came, in time, to dominate the Casuals Club, which afforded a group of disciples to admire his oratory, scholarship, wit and outrageous behaviour.

CATALANO, GARY (1947–), born Brisbane, has published two books of poetry, *Remembering the Rural Life* (1978) and *Heaven of Rags: 40 Poems 1978–1981* (1982); and two works on Australian art, *The Years of Hope: Australian Art and Criticism 1959–1968* (1981) and *The Bandaged Image: A Story of Australian Artists' Books* (1983). 'Remembering the Rural Life', a long personal poem from the first volume, and the prose poems 'The Vortex', 'A Voyage' and 'A Geography' from *Heaven of Rags* are typical of Catalano's talent for precise, elegant phrasing and provocative ideas. He has also published a book of short fiction, *The Woman Who Lives Here and Other Stories* (1983).

'Catalpa, The', also known as 'The Escape of the *Catalpa*' and 'The Ballad of the *Catalpa*', is an Australian folk-song which celebrates the daring escape of several Irish political prisoners from WA in 1876. A triumph for the Fenian movement, the escape was organized in America by John Boyle O'Reilly (q.v.) and others, who purchased the *Catalpa*, a New Bedford whaler used to transport the prisoners back to America. The escape, during which the *Catalpa* had to hoist the American flag to avoid being boarded off Fremantle, is the subject of Z.W. Pease's *The Catalpa Expedition* (1897), Sean O. Luing's *Fremantle Mission* (1965) and Paul Buddee's *The Escape of the Fenians* (1971), and is discussed in most studies of O'Reilly. There was sympathy for the prisoners among the citizens of Perth at the time of the escape and the song which celebrated it became popular enough to be banned by the embarrassed authorities.

CATCHPOLE, MARGARET (1762–1819), born Suffolk, England, arrived in Australia in 1801 under a life sentence after having been twice sentenced to death, for horse-stealing and then for escaping from Ipswich gaol. In the Colony she led an industrious and productive life; pardoned in 1814 she remained in Australia, keeping a small store at Richmond and becoming a well-known and much-appreciated citizen of that district. Her letters (now in the Mitchell Library) to her uncle and aunt in Suffolk and to her former mistress Mrs John

Cobbold are an excellent account, in somewhat erratic spelling and syntax, of contemporary colonial life and events. The letters, distorted and rewritten, were used by Richard Cobbold as the basis of his *The History of Margaret Catchpole* (1845). *The True Story of Margaret Catchpole* by G.B. Barton, was published in 1924 and a novel, *Margaret Catchpole*, by G.G. Carter in 1949.

CATHCART, FANNY (1833–80), arrived in Australia (where she reached her professional maturity as an actress) in 1855 with G.V. Brooke. During the next decade she was the leading legitimate actress in Australia, with Joseph Jefferson and Barry Sullivan as well as with Brooke. In 1855 she married Robert James Heir, a juvenile lead in Brooke's company, and after his death married George Darrell in England, with whom she toured extensively in Australasia and America in the 1870s. Her brother James Faucitt Cathcart (1828–1902) was an actor who was discovered by Charles Kean and worked with him throughout the 1850s and 1860s. He accompanied Charles and Ellen Kean on their Australian tour of 1863–64; in Melbourne they played in opposition to Barry Sullivan whose leading lady was Fanny. After Charles Kean retired in 1867, James played supporting roles to Sullivan for some years in London and America. He returned to Australia in 1879, where he performed in Shakespearean and other roles for George Musgrove, George Rignold and J.C. Williamson.

CATHELS, WILLIAM, see **FURPHY, JOSEPH**

Catholic Magazine, published quarterly 1888–91 and monthly 1892–1920, had various titles. As a quarterly it was the *Catholic Magazine;* as a monthly both *Austral Light and Sword of St. Michael* (1892–99) and *Austral Light: A Catholic Magazine* (1900–1920). In addition to Irish Catholic news and information it carried fiction, poetry, sketches and articles on literary topics.

CATO, NANCY (1917–), born Adelaide, was a cadet journalist on the Adelaide *News* 1936–41 and an art critic on the same newspaper 1957–58; since then she has been a freelance writer. Active in literary affairs, she edited the 1950 *Jindyworobak Anthology*, co-edited *Southern Festival* (1960), and has been involved in the SA branch of the FAW (1956–64) and ASA (1963–64). Her most important work is her trilogy of historical novels set against the background of the Murray River, *All the Rivers Run* (1958), *Time, Flow Softly* (1959) and *But Still the Stream* (1962). These were rewritten and combined into a single bestseller, *All the Rivers Run* (q.v., 1978). She has also published *Forefathers* (q.v., 1983), another long historical novel which traces the fortunes of three Australian families through seven generations. Her other prose works include *Green Grows the Vine* (1960), a novel about an irrigation settlement on the banks of the Murray but not linked with the trilogy; *The Sea Ants, and Other Stories* (1964); *North-West by South* (1965); *Brown Sugar* (1974); and *Mister Maloga* (1976), about the Aboriginal mission of Daniel Matthews on the Murray River. The Murray has a place also in her poems; 'Paddle Steamer', for example, emphasizes the majesty of 'the endless river' in comparison with the humans who exploit it. Her two volumes of poetry, *The Darkened Window* (1950) and *The Dancing Bough* (1957), show her to be a lyrist with a capacity for serious, sometimes sombre, themes; *The Dancing Bough*, for example, is concerned with the twin forces that threaten existence – nuclear weapons that can destroy the world's order and loveliness, and the more persistent enemy, Time. She was made AM in 1984.

Cattle Camp, see **HARDIE, J.J.**

'CATTLE KING, THE', see **KIDMAN,** Sir **SIDNEY**

CATTS, DOROTHY (1896–1961), born Beecroft, NSW, was the second wife of union secretary, politician and businessman James Howard Catts (1877–1951). She edited and published (with her husband) the *Australian Home Budget;* published fiction, including *Dawn to Destiny* (1946) and *Cornerstone* (1947); and wrote biographies, *James Howard Catts MHR* (1953) and *King O'Malley* (1957).

Cave and the Spring, The, see **HOPE, A.D.**

Cave of Adullam was an eccentric, bohemian literary society founded by Marcus Clarke in Melbourne in 1869. It took its name from the Old Testament (I Samuel XXII: 1-2), 'David therefore departed thence, and escaped to the cave, Adullam . . . And every one that was in distress, and every one that was in debt, and every one that was discontented gathered themselves unto him'. The word 'Adullamites' had been applied in 1866 in England to a group of Liberal members of the House of Commons who were opposing certain aspects of franchise reform then being canvassed in the Franchise Bill. The club appears in fictional guise, 'the honourable and exclusive Society of Native Companions', in Clarke's *'Twixt Shadow and Shine* (1875).

CAVENAGH, GEORGE (1808–69), born India, arrived in Australia in 1825 and after various ventures joined the staff of the *Sydney Gazette* in 1833 and became its editor in 1836. By 1840 he was in Melbourne, where he founded the *Port Phillip Herald*. He also printed the first Melbourne almanac (1841–42).

CAWTHORNE, W.A. (WILLIAM ANDERSON) (1825–97), born England, came to SA in 1841. He wrote 'The Islanders' in 1854; a significant account of black-white relationships in SA, it was published first in the *Illustrated Adelaide Post*, which Cawthorne published 1867-74, and then in 1926 as *The Kangaroo Islanders: A Story of South Australia before Colonization 1823*. Cawthorne also wrote *The Legend of Kupirri, or the Red Kangaroo: An Aboriginal Tradition of the Port Lincoln Tribe* (1858), a work that concerned the customs, tradition and lore of that tribal group. His biographical sketch of SA's first mineralogist, Johann Menge (1788–1852), was published in 1859.

CECIL, Lord **ROBERT (ARTHUR TALBOT GASCOYNE)** (1830–1903), third Marquis of Salisbury, travelled throughout the colonies recording in his diaries many pertinent and lively comments about life in Australia. A portion of his diaries was edited by Sir Ernest Scott as *Lord Robert Cecil's Gold Fields' Diary* (1935, 1945). He was prime minister of England at the time of Australian federation.

'Cell, The', a play by Robert Wales set in a convent of an order that cares for delinquent girls, was produced in Adelaide and Sydney in 1966 and subsequently on ABC and BBC television. Part naturalistic drama and part thriller, 'The Cell' explores the tensions, frustrations, conflicting ambitions and internal politics of a claustrophobic community. 'The Grotto' (1962), another play by Wales, who came to Australia in 1946 and subsequently worked for the ABC, focuses on the feuds of a southern European family living in Sydney.

Celtic Twilight, see **DALEY, Victor**

Centennial Magazine, a magazine largely devoted to literary topics and carrying original fiction, poetry and literary criticism, ran monthly 1888–90. Its contributors included most of the well-known contemporary writers, e.g. Francis Adams, 'Rolf Boldrewood', G.B. Barton, George Gordon McCrae, Louisa Meredith and Catherine Helen Spence.

Centre, The, or the Red Centre, the Heart, the Red Heart and the Dead Heart, are terms used to denote the central portion of Australia, an area roughly centred on Alice Springs and radiating from that township for almost 800 kilometres. J.W. Gregory wrote *The Dead Heart of Australia* (1906) and H.H. Finlayson *The Red Centre* (1953). See Dead Heart.

CHABRILLAN, CELESTE DE (1824–1909), born Paris, had a colourful career as a dancer ('La Mogador') and courtesan before marrying the impecunious Lionel, Comte de Chabrillan, who vainly tried his luck on the Victorian goldfields in 1852 and later returned to Australia in a semi-official consular post in Melbourne. Celeste's scarlet diary-memoirs, *Adieux au Monde,* were published just before the Chabrillans reached Australia. Of her other numerous writings, the main one with an Australian background is the novel *Les Voleurs d'Or* (1857), a violent story set in Victoria in the gold-rush days. It was translated by Lucy and Caroline Moorehead and published in 1970 as *The Gold Robbers.* An account of her life, *Daughter of Paris* by Charlotte Haldane, was published in 1961.

CHAMBERS, CHARLES HADDON (1860 –1921), born and educated in Sydney, left Australia to live in England in 1882. He achieved substantial success in the light drama of high-society manners then popular in London, writing fourteen full-length plays of which only one, *Captain Swift* (q.v., 1902), first produced in 1888, has any Australian content. *Thumbnail Sketches of Australian Life* (1891) is his only other publication of Australian interest.

'Champion Bullock Driver, The', see **SKUTHORPE, LANCE**

CHAMPION, HENRY (1859–1928), born Poona, India, first came to Australia in 1890, an established socialist with a background of militancy and an amply-demonstrated capacity for the organization and motivation of the radical forces in society through his public speeches and writings. On a second visit, which extended from 1894 until his death, he set out to lead the socialist movement in Australia. He helped found the Fabian Society and formed the Social Democratic Federation of Victoria and the National Anti-Sweating League. He was prominent in the Victorian Socialist Party 1906–09 and was actively involved in co-operative socialist business and farming ventures. By 1909 prolonged illness and bitter factional disputes had forced him out of politics. His literary activities were mainly allied to his politics. He published *The Root of the Matter: Being a Series of Dialogues on Social Questions* (1895); conducted the *Champion* (1895–97), a

weekly propagandist journal; and edited the *Socialist* (1908). With his wife he conducted the Book Lovers' Library for over thirty years and in 1899 founded the monthly literary journal, *Book Lover,* which ran until 1921. He also founded the Australian Authors' Agency in 1906 and published numerous works by Australian writers, e.g. Dorothea Mackellar, Martin Boyd and Marjorie Barnard.

CHANDLER, A. BERTRAM, see **Science Fiction**

CHANDLER, ALFRED ('SPINIFEX') (1852–1941), born Geelong, was a journalist with the Hamilton *Spectator* and the *Register* in Adelaide where he established *Quiz,* a satirical weekly, and published two books of verse, *A Bush Idyl* (1886) and *Songs of the Sunland* (1889). In 1894 he went to the goldfields of WA, where he played an important role in the rapidly-developing newspaper scene; he edited the *Goldfield Courier,* the first newspaper in Coolgardie, the *Golden Age,* the *Coolgardie Miner* and the Perth *Sunday Times,* and was associated with the monthly magazine, *Leeuwin.* With William Siebenhaar, he published *Sentinel Sonnets* (1919), a book of war poetry; his other volume of verse, published in 1935, is *'Beauty' and Other Poems: A Selective Anthology from the Author's Previous Books and Manuscripts.*

Channel Country, a large area of south-western Queensland extending into the corners of SA and NSW, is drained by the Georgina and Diamantina Rivers and Cooper's Creek. Important in the pastoral expansion of Australia in the latter part of the nineteenth century, the Channel Country was the scene of the pastoral exploits of Sir Sidney Kidman (q.v.) and the Durack family. Burke and Wills (q.v.) perished at Cooper's Creek in 1861. It is featured in Ion Idriess's *The Cattle King* (1936), Mary Durack's *Kings in Grass Castles* (1959), Frank Clune's *Dig* (1937) and Alan Moorehead's *Cooper's Creek* (1963).

Chant of Jimmie Blacksmith, The, Thomas Keneally's (q.v.) fifth novel, was published in 1972 and filmed in 1978. A fictional recreation of the experiences of Jimmy Governor (q.v.), the novel chronicles the rejection by the half-caste Jimmie Blacksmith of his Aboriginal heritage and his attempt to become part of European society by embracing its institutions, including marriage to the white girl, Gilda. The indignities and injustices Jimmie suffers at the hands of a succession of white employers culminate in his mistreatment by the Newby family, who try to break up his marriage and use Gilda's refusal to leave Jimmie and the arrival at their property of Jimmie's uncle Tabidgi Jackie Smolders and brother Mort as an excuse to cut off rations. Assisted by Tabidgi, Jimmie murders the Newby women and their governess and the party flees the district. The second half of the novel records the pursuit of Jimmie and Mort, who leave the others, by police and vigilantes; during the pursuit further murders are committed, a schoolteacher McCreadie is taken hostage, Mort is shot and Jimmie taken prisoner. The context of Jimmie's execution in May 1901, just after Federation and during the Boer War, gives an historical dimension to the racism which Jimmie has tragically confronted.

Chantic Bird, The, a novel by David Ireland (q.v.) published in 1968, won the Adelaide *Advertiser's* literary competition in 1966. The novel focuses on the narrator, an anonymous teenage boy and extreme anarchist who oscillates between murderous violence and protective care for his 'family', especially his 'brother' Stevo and the girl, Bee, who cares for them. Despite the savagery of his behaviour, his perspective as outsider illuminates the suffocating drabness of ordinary, adult, law-abiding, suburban life.

Chapel Perilous, The, a play by Dorothy Hewett (q.v.), was first performed in Perth in 1971 arousing a storm of protest and approval, and was published in 1972. The life of Sally Banner from age fifteen to sixty-one is the play's subject. A self-absorbed heroine in constant search for a commitment that will bring 'a sense of immortality', she confronts the conventions and taboos of her society as boldly and hazardously as Sir Lancelot confronts the knights guarding the Chapel Perilous in Malory's *The Tale of King Arthur.* Persistently judged and condemned by her contemporaries and a series of older authority figures, and frequently betrayed by her lovers, Sally makes a tormented journey finally back to 'that lonely place/where I began'. Fast-moving and expressionistic, with diverse effects and moods, the play ranges from burlesque to lyrical to satirical, evoking Hewett's ambivalent attitude to her heroine.

CHARLWOOD, DON (1915–), born Hawthorn, Melbourne, worked on the land at Nareen in western Victoria during the 1930s depression years and served in the RAAF during the Second World War. After the war he worked for thirty years in air traffic control. His published works include *No Moon Tonight* (1956), memoirs of thirty bombing operations over Germany in 1942–43; *All the Green Year* (1965), a novel of adolescence set in the Vic-

torian town of Frankston where Charlwood spent much of his boyhood; *An Afternoon of Time* (1966), a book of ten short stories tracing the experiences of growing up, and based to some degree on Charlwood's time at Nareen; *Take-Off to Touchdown* (1967), the story of air traffic control in Australia; *Wrecks and Reputations* (1977), an account of the loss of the sailing ships *Schomberg* and *Loch Ard* off the Victorian coast; *Settlers Under Sail* (1978), which depicts shipboard life on the early sailing vessels; *Flight and Time* (1979), another small volume of eleven short stories most of which are autobiographically-based, seven being stories of wartime or civil flying; and *The Long Farewell* (1981), largely based on diaries that early nineteenth-century emigrants kept on their long sea voyage to Australia. The latter won the 1982 NSW Premier's Ethnic Literary Award.

CHAUNCY, NAN (1900–70), born Northwood, England, went to Tasmania as a child, was educated there and trained as an industrial welfare worker. Her books for children are based mainly on her affectionate observations of rural Tasmania and the people who lived there. Three of her novels, *Tiger in the Bush* (1957), *Devils' Hill* (1958), and *Tangara* (1960), won Children's Book of the Year Awards. Among her other children's books are *They Found a Cave* (1948), *World's End Was Home* (1952), *A Fortune for the Brave* (1954), *Half a World Away* (1962), *Mathinna's People* (1967) and *The Lighthouse Keeper's Son* (1969).

CHAUVEL, CHARLES (1897–1959), born Warwick, Queensland, formed his own film company in 1923, producing two silent films. In 1928 he and his wife Elsa (1898–1983), actress and scriptwriter, went to America to study the making of sound films. His first sound film, *In the Wake of the Bounty* (1933), began the career of Errol Flynn. Chauvel's later successes include *Heritage* (1935), a generalized view of Australian history; *Forty Thousand Horsemen* (1940), starring Chips Rafferty and based on the campaigns of the Australian Light Horse in the First World War; *The Rats of Tobruk* (1944), about the famous siege of the Second World War; *Jedda* (1955), the tragic story of a young Aboriginal girl. The Chauvels, a successful husband and wife team, also made the notable television series *Walkabout* for the BBC. Elsa Chauvel wrote the autobiographical *My Life with Charles Chauvel* (1973).

CHAUVEL, Sir HARRY (1865–1945), uncle of Charles Chauvel and father of writer Elyne Mitchell, was born Tabulam, NSW, and spent most of his adult life as a soldier, rising to the rank of general in 1929, the first Australian to attain that rank. He served in both the Boer War and the First World War; in the latter he was at Gallipoli and in 1917 commanded the Desert Mounted Corps. His biography, *Chauvel of the Light Horse* (1978), was written by A.J. Hill. Elyne Mitchell's *Chauvel Country* (1983) gives details of her father's childhood on the Clarence River at Tabulam.

Cheery Soul, A, is the title of a short story and a play by Patrick White (q.v.). The short story, first published in 1962, is included in his collection *The Burnt Ones* (1964); the play, first produced in 1963, is included in his collection *Four Plays* (1965). Miss Docker, a tactless, destructive but invincible and even pathetic do-gooder, is the central figure of both.

Cheon, see *We of the Never-Never*

'Cherry Pickers, The', a play by Kevin Gilbert (q.v.), staged in Sydney 1971, deals with a group of Aboriginal fruit-pickers preparing to work on the year's cherry crop. They are delayed by the non-appearance of Johnollo, one of their number who turns out to have been killed in an accident, and by a disease that has affected the cherry trees. The delay is the device which allows the play's themes to be presented; these include the close relationship that exists between the Aborigines and nature, the white man's lack of affinity with and his despoiling of nature, the Aborigines' concern for tribal traditions but their inability to incorporate those traditions into their lives, and the white man's inability to understand Aboriginal life.

CHEVALIER, NICHOLAS (1828–1902), was a Russian-born artist who studied in Switzerland and worked in London before arriving in Australia in 1855. He became the first prominent cartoonist for the newly-established *Melbourne Punch,* for which he drew for six years; he later worked for the *Illustrated Australian News* and continued as a landscape painter in oils and watercolour. Chevalier married in Australia and his home was a centre of cultural and intellectual life in Melbourne until his departure in 1869 for London.

CHIDLEY, WILLIAM JAMES (?1860–1916), was an eccentric whose sexual and social theories brought him into trouble with the authorities, particularly in the period 1911–16. A proponent of vegetarianism, the open air, unrestrictive clothing, and sexual intercourse 'in the Spring . . . between true lovers only', Chidley ran foul of the Melbourne police when he began to sell copies of his work, *The Answer* (1911), which was regularly revised and reprinted and is included in Bill Hornadge's *Chidley's Answer to the Sex Problem* (1971). He

moved to Sydney where, characteristically clad only in a short white tunic, he was regularly fined for offensive behaviour and several times committed to mental asylums. His case was debated in the NSW parliament and a Chidley Defence Committee was formed in 1916; his supporters included J. le Gay Brereton, H.H. Champion, T.D. Mutch and Dowell O'Reilly. In 1899 Chidley sent the manuscript of his autobiography, 'The Confessions of William James Chidley', to Havelock Ellis who including extracts in *Studies in the Psychology of Sex* (1897–1910); the autobiography was published in full in 1977 as *The Confessions of William James Chidley,* ed. Sally McInerney. The Chidley case raised issues of personal freedom and the power of legal authorities to commit people to asylums, issues which are the focus of the plays by Alma de Groen, 'Chidley' (1976), and George Hutchinson, 'No Room for Dreamers' (1980).

CHIFLEY, J.B. (JOSEPH BENEDICT) (1885–1951), born Bathurst, NSW, was a locomotive driver before entering federal parliament as the member for Macquarie in 1928. He lost the seat in 1931, regained it in 1940 and became treasurer in the 1941 Labor government; in 1945 he became prime minister of Australia. Vance Palmer has a chapter, 'The Labour Leader', on Chifley in *National Portraits* (1949 edition). A.W. Stargardt edited *Things Worth Fighting For: Speeches by J.B. Chifley* (1953) and L.F. Crisp wrote the biography, *Ben Chifley* (1960).

'Child in the Dark, and a Foreign Father, A', a story by Henry Lawson (q.v.), was written in 1902 and included in *Triangles of Life* (1913). The story records the return home to his farm on New Year's Eve of a poor carpenter, who discovers that his three children and the household chores have been neglected by his neurotic and slatternly wife; after cleaning up and attending to his family during the night, the workman returns to his trade next morning. The setting of the story (Pipeclay), the fact that the 'foreign father''s name is Nils, and the tension between the parents, suggest that the story is autobiographical.

CHILDE, VERE GORDON (1892–1957), born Sydney, had a brilliant scholastic record at the Universities of Sydney and Oxford but his strongly-held socialist, pacifist and anti-conscription beliefs prevented his securing an academic appointment in the conservative universities of Australia after his return from England in 1917. In 1918 he taught briefly in Maryborough, Queensland, where P.R. Stephensen was a pupil, and in 1919–21 was private secretary to the NSW Labor politician, John Storey; he returned to England as a research officer in the NSW agent-general's office, but was dismissed in 1922 after a change of government. The following year *How Labor Governs,* a pessimistic view of the difficulties faced by working-class politicians working within a parliamentary system, was published; thereafter Childe's attention was focused on the fields of archaeology, prehistory and anthropology. In a career that saw him librarian of the Royal Anthropological Institute (1925–27) and professor of archaeology at the Universities of Edinburgh (1927–46) and London (1946–57), he published some twenty books and many papers; the best known were his much revised and republished *The Dawn of European Civilization* (1925) and two works written primarily for the general public, *Man Makes Himself* (1936) and *What Happened in History* (1942).

Childhood at Brindabella, see **FRANKLIN, MILES**

Children of the Bush, a collection of twenty-three stories and sketches by Henry Lawson (q.v.), was first published in London in 1902; most of the stories date from the late 1890s and early 1900s, although some were written as early as 1894. In 1907 the first part of *Children of the Bush,* including 'Send Round the Hat', other Bourke stories and several more in which Jack Mitchell is the dominant character, was published as *Send Round the Hat;* the second part, including several Eurunderee stories and three in which the central character is Peter McLaughlin, 'Christ of the Never Never', was published, also in 1907, as *The Romance of the Swag.*

Children of the Dark People, a popular children's novel with adult appeal by Frank Dalby Davison (q.v.), was first published in 1936, illustrated by Pixie O'Harris. It narrates the adventures of two Aboriginal children, Nimmitybelle and Jackadgery, separated from their tribe by the evil purposes of a witch-doctor, but saved by the spirits of the bush, especially Old Mr Bunyip, guardian spirit of the land. Although the story's fantastic elements make no pretensions to represent tribal lore, it is true to the Aboriginal way of life and reflects Davison's understanding of outback Australia.

Children's Book Council of Australia came into being in 1958 largely through the efforts of an earlier Children's Book Council, established in Sydney in 1947. The Council presents annual Children's Book of the Year (q.v.), Picture Book of the Year and Junior Book awards.

Its quarterly publication is *Reading Time;* it published a booklet in 1980, *The Children's Book Council in Australia 1945–1980.*

Children's Book of the Year Award was first presented by the Australian Book Society in 1946 but from 1950 has been administered by the Children's Book Council of Australia (q.v.). The winners to 1983 have been: 1946, *Karrawingi the Emu* by Leslie Rees; 1948, *Shackleton's Argonauts* by Frank Hurley; 1949, *Whalers of the Midnight Sun* by Alan Villiers; 1951, *Verity of Sydney Town* by Ruth C. Williams; 1952, *The Australia Book* by Eve Pownall; 1953, shared by *Good Luck to the Rider* by Joan Phipson and *Aircraft of Today and Tomorrow* by J.H. and W.D. Martin; 1954, *Australian Legendary Tales* by C. Langloh Parker; 1955, *The First Walkabout* by Norman B. Tindale and H.A. Lindsay; 1956, shared by *The Crooked Snake* by Patricia Wrightson and *Wish and the Magic Nut* by Peggy Barnard; 1957, *The Boomerang Book of Legendary Tales* edited by Enid Moodie Heddle; 1958, *Tiger in the Bush* by Nan Chauncy; 1959, shared by *Devils' Hill* by Chauncy and *Sea Menace* by John Gunn; 1960, *All the Proud Tribesmen* by Kylie Tennant; 1961, *Tangara* by Chauncy; 1962, shared by *The Racketty Street Gang* by L.H. Evers and *Rafferty Rides a Winner* by Joan Woodberry; 1963, *The Family Conspiracy* by Phipson; 1964, *The Green Laurel* by Eleanor Spence; 1965, *Pastures of the Blue Crane* by H.F. Brinsmead; 1966, *Ash Road* by Ivan Southall; 1967, *The Min-Min* by Mavis Thorpe Clark; 1968, *To the Wild Sky* by Southall; 1969, *When Jays Fly to Barbmo* by Margaret Balderson; 1970, *Uhu* by Annette Macarthur-Onslow; 1971, *Bread and Honey* by Southall; 1972, *Longtime Passing* by Brinsmead; 1973, *Family at the Lookout* by Noreen Shelley; 1974, *The Nargun and the Stars* by Wrightson; 1976, *Fly West* by Southall; 1977, *The October Child* by Eleanor Spence; 1978, *The Ice Is Coming* by Wrightson; 1979, *The Plum-Rain Scroll* by Ruth Manley; 1980, *Displaced Person* by Lee Harding; 1981, *Playing Beattie Bow* by Ruth Park; 1982, *The Valley Between* by Colin Thiele; and 1983, *Master of the Grove* by Victor Kelleher. There were no awards in 1947, 1950 and 1975.

Children's Literature, see **Anthologies; Children's Book Council of Australia; Children's Book of the Year Award;** *History of Australian Children's Literature, A*

Child's Play, see **MALOUF, DAVID**

Chinese in Australian Literature. The idea of introducing Chinese coolie labour into Australia can be found as early as Edward Gibbon Wakefield's *A Letter from Sydney* (1829); in 1848, less than a decade after transportation of convicts to NSW ceased, the first consignment of Chinese workers (all males) arrived. The establishment in 1854 of a select committee on Asiatic labour in NSW reflected the rapidly-growing unpopularity of the Chinese presence. With the development of the goldfields, however, Chinese numbers increased dramatically: 10 000 on the Victorian diggings in 1855, 25 000 by 1857; 1700 at the newly-discovered Palmer River goldfields in Queensland in 1875, 17 000 (compared with 1400 Europeans) by 1877. The earliest agitation against the Chinese gold-miners was at Bendigo in July 1854, a disturbance that resulted in Victorian legislation imposing a tax of £10 on every Chinese immigrant. Shipping owners, unwilling to lose their profitable cargo, evaded the Victorian tax by landing the Chinese at Twofold Bay in southern NSW or at Guichen Bay in SA. From those points the hapless immigrants trekked to the diggings; an account of them in a procession two miles long, each one with a pole and two baskets 'winding across the plain like a long black mark', is given in J. Chandler's *Forty Years in the Wilderness* (1893).

Anti-Chinese riots occurred on the Buckland River goldfield in eastern Victoria, 4 July 1857. The anonymous song 'Dick the Digger: A Tale of the Buckland', published in J. Small's *The Colonial Songster* (?1884), reflects the white digger's hostility:

> For pick, pick it made him sick
> To think that he was getting daily, a
> Heap of these accursed Chinese
> And he cried 'They'll ruin Australia'.

A similar song is Charles Thatcher's 'The Chinamen'. The Lambing Flat riots of June 1861, described in George E. Boxall's *The History of the Australian Bushrangers* (1899) and Frank Clune's *Wild Colonial Boys* (1948), are the subject of Mary Gilmore's poem, 'Fourteen Men', with its lines:

> Fourteen men
> Chinamen they were
> Hanging on the trees
> In their pig-tailed hair.

After Lambing Flat with its alleged 'lynchings' denied by official reports, the NSW government in 1861 enacted the Chinese Immigration Bill; the jubilant response of the white diggers was:

> Rule Britannia! Britannia rules the waves
> No more Chinamen will enter New South Wales

In September 1873 the Clunes (Victoria) riots

occurred when cheap Chinese labour was brought in to break strikes. This practice, later used in the shearing troubles of the 1890s as A.B. Paterson's poem 'A Bushman's Song' suggests, led to the use of the contemptuous words 'leprosy' and 'scab' to indicate Chinese and later all strike-breakers; both words were linked to the white man's irrational fear that the Chinese harboured exotic infectious diseases. A light-hearted evocation of the Chinese on the Victorian goldfields is Edward Dyson's story, 'A Golden Shanty' (q.v.), in which Michael Doyle and his 'strongly anti-Chinese' mongrel dog finally outwit the Chinese fossickers who are attempting to demolish his Shamrock Hotel for the rich gold bricks with which it was built. Henry Lawson, who frequently included Chinese in his stories, was less inclined to be critical of them, as his opening remarks in the story 'Ah Soon', published in *Lone Hand*, 1911, indicate: 'I never knew or heard of a Chinaman who neglected to pay his debts, who did a dishonest action, or who forgot a kindness to him or his, or was not charitable when he had the opportunity.'

When it was possible to obtain gold only by the costly quartz-crushing process, those Chinese miners who did not return to their own country were absorbed peaceably into the life of the Australian community, mainly as market gardeners, fruit hawkers, laundry operators, storekeepers and bush cooks. Cheon in Mrs Aeneas Gunn's *We of the Never-Never* (1908), and James Brunton Stephens's 'My Chinee Cook' and 'My Other Chinee Cook', are examples of the patronizing and sometimes racist perceptions of the Chinese in later literature.

Anti-Chinese legislation was periodically enforced and periodically allowed to lapse in all States, but in 1880–81 an intercolonial conference resulted in uniformly-based legislation in all the eastern States. An immigration Act of 1901, incorporating the so-called White Australia Policy, almost entirely debarred Asiatics from entering Australia. Despite this apparent safeguard, white fear of the 'yellow peril' continued, finding literary expression in such plays as Randolph Bedford's 'White Australia: Or, the Empty North' (1909), which pointed to the danger of foreign occupation; and F.R.C. Hopkins's *Reaping the Whirlwind* (1909), 'an Australian patriotic drama for Australian people'. Similar works, both factual and fictional, that incorporate the presence of the Chinese include James Murdoch's *Felix Holt Secundus* (1892), William Craig's *My Adventures on the Australian Goldfields* (1903), Joyce Vincent's *The Celestial Hand* (1903), R.A. Kent's *A Chinese Vengeance* (1909), Hilda Bridges's *Our Neighbours* (1922) and H. Haverstock Hill's

Golden Harvest (1919). The Chinese presence is also obvious in David Martin's fiction, *The Hero of Too* (1960) and *The Chinese Boy* (1973), and in Helen Heney's *The Chinese Camellia* (1953). Brian Castro's novel *Birds of Passage* (1983) records some of the experiences of a Chinese gold-miner in Australia in the gold-rush days. After the restrictions imposed in the 1901 Act, Chinese numbers declined markedly, from 50 000 in 1888 to less than 10 000 in 1934. Important sociological and historical works on the Chinese in Australia include Persia Campbell's *Chinese Coolie Emigration to Countries within the British Empire* (1923), Arthur Huck's *The Chinese in Australia* (1967), C.Y. Choi's *Chinese Migration and Settlement in Australia* (1975), Jean Gittins's *The Diggers from China* (1981) and Kathryn Cronin's *Colonial Casualties: Chinese in Early Victoria* (1982).

CHISHOLM, A.R. (ALAN ROWLAND) (1888–1981), born Bathurst, NSW, who had a distinguished academic career in Australia, France and Germany, was head of the school of French at the University of Melbourne 1921–56 and gained an international reputation as a critic of French poetry. He edited the brief-lived *Modern Language Review of New South Wales*, 1920–21. A strong supporter of Australian literature, Chisholm was chiefly interested in the poetry of Christopher Brennan. His lectures on Brennan were published as *Christopher Brennan: The Man and His Poetry* (1946); he published, with J.J. Quinn, the first comprehensive editions of Brennan's verse and prose (1960, 1962); edited the *Selected Poems of Christopher Brennan* (1966); and wrote *A Study of Christopher Brennan's 'The Forest of Night'* (1970). He also edited the poems of John Shaw Neilson in 1965 and 1973, and wrote two autobiographical books, *Men Were My Milestones* (1958) and *The Familiar Presence* (1966), which helped to document Australian cultural history. Long associated with *Meanjin* as a member of its editorial committee, Chisholm was honoured in May 1959 in a special number of *AUMLA*.

CHISHOLM, A.H. (ALEXANDER HUGH) (1890–1977), born Maryborough, Victoria, worked on the staff of the Maryborough *Advertiser* before transferring to the Brisbane *Daily Mail* in 1915. His subsequent experience as a newspaper man included editorship of the Melbourne *Argus*, the *Australasian* and the Sydney *Sunday Pictorial*. A keen naturalist – he gave his recreation as 'idling in green places' – he edited the *Victorian Naturalist* (1939–48) and wrote numerous naturalist works including *Bird Wonders of Australia* (1934), *Australian Wild*

Life (1966) and *The Joy of the Earth* (1969). He was editor of *Who's Who in Australia* (1947); editor-in-chief of the *Australian Encyclopaedia* (1958); and wrote *The Making of a Sentimental Bloke: A Sketch of the Remarkable Career of C.J. Dennis* (1946). He edited *Selected Verse of C.J. Dennis* (1950); E.J. Banfield's *The Confessions of a Beachcomber* and *Last Leaves from Dunk Island* (first published 1908, 1925); and John White's *Journal of a Voyage to New South Wales* (first published 1790).

CHISHOLM, CAROLINE (1808–77), born near Northampton, England, arrived in Australia in 1838 with her husband and family, settling at Windsor. Deeply concerned at the plight of immigrants who could find no employment because of the rural depression, she convinced Governor Gipps to support her establishment of a Female Immigrants' Home and her scheme to disperse the immigrants into employment in the interior of the Colony. The report of her first year's activities was published as *Female Immigration Considered, in a Brief Account of the Sydney Immigrants' Home* (1842). She travelled to England in 1846 to promote her colonization scheme, which she furthered by publishing *Emigration and Transportation Relatively Considered* (1847). *The ABC of Colonization* (1850) explains her Family Colonization Loan Society, formed in 1849, and criticizes existing colonization schemes. By the time Chisholm returned to Australia in 1854 the Society had sent out more than 3000 immigrants. Her humanitarian interests continued in spite of ill-health and needy circumstances. She returned to England in 1866; her grave at Northampton bears the inscription 'The emigrant's friend!'. Robert Lowe wrote a poem 'To Mrs. Chisholm and Henry Kendall wrote 'Caroline Chisholm'; George Landen Dann published a play, *Caroline Chisholm*, in 1943. Biographical works on her include Eneäs Mackenzie's *Memoirs of Mrs Caroline Chisholm* (1852), Margaret Kiddle's *Caroline Chisholm* (1950), and Mary Hoban's *Fifty-One Pieces of Wedding Cake* (1973).

CHOMLEY, C.H. (CHARLES HENRY) (1868–1942), born Sale, Victoria, uncle of Martin Boyd, graduated in law in 1891 but settled on the land in 1893 with a group of friends and relatives in the King River valley in north-east Victoria. Ill-health took him back to Melbourne in 1900, where he edited *Arena*, an illustrated weekly, until its demise in 1904. Chomley published fiction including *Tales of Old Times: Early Australian Incident and Adventure* (1903), *The Flight of the Black Swan* (1903), *Mark Meredith: A Tale of Socialism* (1905) and, with R.L. Outhwaite, *The Wisdom* *of Esau* (1910). He also wrote *The True Story of the Kelly Gang of Bushrangers* (1900) and a number of works on economics, trade and law. From 1908 until his death, Chomley edited the *British Australasian* (q.v.) in England.

'Chosen Vessel, The', Barbara Baynton's (q.v.) first story, was published in the *Bulletin* in 1896 as 'The Tramp'; it was revised and included in *Bush Studies* (1902) and *Cobbers* (1917) under the title 'The Chosen Vessel'. Reminiscent of Henry Lawson's 'The Drover's Wife', it tells of the terror of a young wife left with her baby in a bush hut as she awaits attack by a swagman who has called there during the day. The sound of hoofbeats causes her to flee the house for assistance but the horseman is a young Catholic who is on his way to record an election vote against the wishes of his mother and the local priest. He interprets the 'white-robed figure' crying 'For Christ's sake!' as a vision from God and gallops madly away, leaving the woman to be raped and murdered by the swagman.

CHRISTESEN, C.B. (CLEMENT BYRNE) (1911–), born Townsville, was educated at the University of Queensland, then became a publicity officer for the Queensland government and later a journalist on the *Brisbane Courier* and the *Telegraph*. He worked briefly for the London *Times* and the *New York Times* before returning to Brisbane, where in 1940 he founded the literary magazine *Meanjin* (q.v.), moving with it to Melbourne early in 1945. Christesen's first publication was a tourist guide, *Queensland Journey* (1937). Subsequently he published four volumes of verse, *North Coast* (1943), *South Coast* (1944), *Dirge and Lyrics* (1945) and *Having Loved* (1979); edited the anthologies *Australian Heritage* (1949), *Coast to Coast 1953–54* (1955) and *On Native Grounds* (1967), a selection from *Meanjin*'s first twenty-five years; and edited *The Gallery on Eastern Hill* (1970). A selection of his own short fiction and poetry, *The Hand of Memory*, was published in 1970. Although his lyrical verse and spare short stories have a modest reputation, Christesen is best known for his tireless promotion and encouragement of Australian writing, particularly as editor for thirty-five years of *Meanjin*, which he transformed from the little poetry magazine of 1940 into a major Australian cultural journal significant in the development of Australian literary criticism. Active also as broadcaster, writer of radio features and University Extension and CLF lecturer, he has been honoured by the Britannica-Australia Award (1970) and an honorary doctorate from Monash University (1975). He was made OBE in 1962.

Christian Brothers, The, see **BLAIR, RON**

CHRISTISON, ROBERT (1837–1915), born Berwickshire, Scotland, came to Australia in 1852. Before returning to Scotland in 1910 he made an outstanding contribution to the expansion of the pastoral industry in southern Queensland, where he established the properties of Lammermoor and Cameron Downs in the 1860s. His daughter M.M. Bennett wrote his biography, *Christison of Lammermoor* (1927), and Vance Palmer included him in *National Portraits* (1940).

'Christmas Creek', see *Songs from the Mountain*

Christopher Brennan Award, formerly known as the Robert Frost Award, is given by FAW to a poet whose sustained work achieves distinction. Recipients of the Award have included R.D. FitzGerald, Judith Wright, A.D. Hope, Douglas Stewart, Gwen Harwood, Rosemary Dobson, Vincent Buckley and Bruce Beaver. It was also awarded poshumously to Francis Webb, James McAuley and David Campbell.

Christopher Columbus (1948), by William Hart-Smith (q.v.), is part of the voyager (q.v.) theme in Australian poetry. The sequence of forty-two poems begins in antiquity with its comfortable certainty that 'The world is flat/ And that's that' but moves rapidly to the late medieval world and 'the Brothers Columbus, Mapmakers of Lisbon'. The series encompasses Columbus's first voyage to the New World, his triumphant return to Spain, his second voyage and the discovery of the tragedy of the colony he left at La Navidad, the initial enchantment of the New World spoiled by the European taints of disease and greed, the founding of the city of Isabella, his final voyages and the decay of his great dream.

Chronicle, the weekly companion of the *Advertiser*, was published in Adelaide 1858–1975. Originally titled the *South Australian Weekly Chronicle*, it became the *South Australian Chronicle* (sometimes the *South Australian Chronicle and Weekly Mail*) in 1868 and the *Chronicle* in 1895; in 1931 it incorporated the *Observer*. A literary supplement titled the *Wallet* was published in the *Chronicle* in 1864–65.

Chu Chin Chow, see **ASCHE, OSCAR**

CHURCH, HUBERT (1857–1932), born Hobart, Tasmania, spent lengthy periods in both England and NZ before settling in 1923 in Melbourne, where he was well-known in literary circles. A poet of elegance and restraint, Church published *The West Wind* (1902), a *Bulletin* booklet republished in the anthology *A Southern Garland* (1904); *Poems* (1904); *Egmont* (1908); and *Poems* (1912), a selection from the earlier volumes with ten additional poems. He also wrote a novel, *Tonks: A New Zealand Yarn* (1916).

CILENTO Family includes Sir Raphael West Cilento (1893–), Lady Phyllis Dorothy Cilento (1894–) and their daughter, actress and writer Diane Cilento (1934–). Lady Cilento has published numerous books on nutrition, child care and birth control and was medical columnist of the Brisbane *Courier-Mail*. Diane Cilento has followed a successful career on stage and in films since 1953, has been a television film producer and has published two novels, *The Manipulator* (1968) and *The Hybrid* (1970).

Cinema and Australian Literature. The first film made in Australia was of the Melbourne Cup of 1896, and just over a decade later a feature-film industry had evolved before equivalent developments in England and the USA. Claims have been advanced for considering *Soldiers of the Cross* (1900) as the first full-length film made in the world and for *The Story of the Kelly Gang* (1906), one of the six Ned Kelly films, as the first feature film. The most productive and the most nationalistic period for the Australian cinema was 1906–14, when films about convicts and bushrangers were particularly popular. In 1911, for example, films which focused on the exploits of Captains Midnight and Starlight, Frank Gardiner and Dan Morgan were screened and Ben Hall was the subject of no fewer than three treatments. Since those early days the Australian cinema has had to fight overseas competition and distribution domination, particularly from Hollywood, but has intermittently flourished. There have been three significant periods: the years just after the First World War when Raymond Longford (q.v.), at the height of his powers, made naturalistic adaptations of *The Sentimental Bloke* and *On Our Selection* which are regarded as classics of film-making and consolidated myths about Australian larrikins and pioneers embodied in those works; the 1930s, when Ken Hall's (q.v.) Cinesound Company had a number of commercial successes including a far different *On Our Selection* (1932) which, with three Rudd family spin-offs, helped to popularize Dad and Dave as rural hayseeds; and the years from 1970 when, after three decades in the doldrums, the Australian cinema has undergone a renaissance and films like *Picnic at Hanging Rock* (1975), *Breaker Morant* (1980) and *Gallipoli* (1981) have won critical acclaim both in Australia and overseas.

Almost from its inception the Australian cinema established firm links with Australian writing and writers. *On Our Selection* is not the only Australian literary work to have been filmed more than once: so also were *Robbery Under Arms* (1907, 1920, 1957; Alfred Dampier's stage adaptation of the novel was also filmed in 1911 as *Captain Starlight*); *For the Term of His Natural Life* (1908, 1927; another treatment in 1911 was titled *The Life of Rufus Dawes* and starred Longford as the convict, Gabbett); *The Mystery of a Hansom Cab* (1911, 1924); *The Pioneers* (1916, 1926); *The Sentimental Bloke* (1919, 1932); and adaptations of the stories of Henry Lawson (1921, 1924, 1957). Among other well-known literary works to have been filmed are *The Double Event* (1911), *The Sick Stockrider* (1913), *Moondyne* (1913), *The Sunny South* (1913), *Struck Oil* (1919), *How McDougall Topped the Score* (1924), *Around the Boree Log* (1925), *Seven Little Australians* (1929), *Red Sky at Morning* (1944), *The Summer of the Seventeenth Doll* (1959), *Age of Consent* (1969), *Wake in Fright* (1971), *Picnic at Hanging Rock* (1975), *The Great McCarthy* (1975), *The Getting of Wisdom* (1977), *The Mango Tree* (1977), *Dot and the Kangaroo* (1977), *The Chant of Jimmie Blacksmith* (1978), *Monkey Grip* (1981), *We of the Never-Never* (1982), *The Year of Living Dangerously* (1982) and *Careful, He Might Hear You* (1983). Popular novelists to have attracted the attention of film-makers include Ambrose Pratt, Marie Bjelke-Petersen, Beatrice Grimshaw, Dorothy Cottrell, 'Gurney Slade', F.J. Thwaites, Ion Idriess, Jon Cleary, D'Arcy Niland, Frank Hardy and John O'Grady. In general it is only recently that Australian writers established outside the cinema have become involved in that medium, though Hugh McCrae played Adam Lindsay Gordon in *The Life's Romance of Adam Lindsay Gordon* (1916), Arthur Wright had several of his racing and mining novels filmed and wrote the scripts for several others, and E.V. Timms and Douglas Stewart wrote briefly for films. In the last decade Frank Moorhouse (*Between Wars*, 1974), Hal Porter (*Libido*, 1973), Thomas Keneally (*Libido*, 1973, *The Chant of Jimmie Blacksmith*, 1978), Jack Hibberd (*Dimboola*, 1978), and John Romeril (*The Naked Bunyip*, 1970; *Bonjour Balwyn*, 1971; and *The Great McCarthy*, 1975) are examples of the many Australian writers who have written film scripts, but David Williamson's involvement has been perhaps the most extensive. Four of his plays, *Stork* (1971), *The Removalists* (1975), *Don's Party* (1976), and *The Club* (1980), have been filmed and he has written or collaborated on the screenplays not only for these but also for

Peterson (1974), *Eliza Fraser* (1976), *Gallipoli* (1981) and *The Year of Living Dangerously* (1982). Williamson, Romeril and Keneally have played 'bit' parts in films, continuing the tradition of Marion Marcus Clarke who played Lady Devine in the 1927 version of her father's *For the Term of His Natural Life*, having earlier prevented *His Convict Bride* (1919) being titled *For the Term of Her Natural Life*! Henry Lawson also made a brief appearance as a bushman yarning around a campfire at the start of the film of *While the Billy Boils* in 1921. Among studies of the Australian cinema, John Baxter's *The Australian Cinema* (1970), Hal Porter's *Stars of Australian Stage and Screen* (1965), Eric Reade's *The Australian Screen* (1976) and *History and Heartburn: The Saga of Australian Film 1896–1978* (1979), Andrew Pike's and Ross Cooper's *Australian Film 1900–1977* (1980), John Tulloch's *Legends of the Australian Screen* (1980), and *The New Australian Cinema*, ed. Scott Murray (1980) all discuss the relationship between Australian literary works and Australian films, a subject which is the focus of Brian McFarlane's *Words and Images* (1983).

Civilization Without Delusion, see **CLARKE, MARCUS**

CLACY, ELLEN, see *Lady's Visit to the Gold Diggings of Australia 1852–53*, A

Clanalder Sennachie, (1963–75), originated by John J. Alderson, was the journal (monthly, then quarterly) of the Clanalder Archives. The Clanalder Archives house material of local history, anthropology and folklore interest from an area of Victoria bounded on the south by Ballarat, on the north by Inglewood, on the east by Bendigo and on the west by St Arnaud. The Archives date back into the nineteenth century but serious collection began from 1942. 'Sennachie' is an old Scottish word meaning 'historian'.

CLANCY, LAURIE (1942–), born Melbourne, had a Catholic education and has since taught in the English departments at Melbourne and La Trobe Universities. In 1975 he published his first novel, *A Collapsible Man*, which traces the life of the narrator Paul O'Donohue through his Catholic education to university and on to a bohemian existence which culminates in a period in a sanatorium; the novel shared the National Book Council Award for fiction in 1975. Clancy also published *The Wife Specialist* (1979), a book of ironic short stories some of which are set among academics in the inner-city Carlton area of Melbourne. His most recent novel is *Perfect Love* (1983),

another chronicle of the lower middle-class Catholic milieu.

'Clancy of the Overflow', a poem by A.B. Paterson (q.v.), was first published in the Christmas 1889 number of the *Bulletin* under the pseudonym 'The Banjo'. A great favourite with Australians, the poem established Clancy as one of Australia's best-known folk heroes. The poem records the writer's distaste for city life as well as hymning the great outdoors; it pictures Clancy's carefree existence amid the 'vision splendid' of 'the sunlit plains extended' and 'the everlasting stars'. A phrase from the poem, 'a thumbnail dipped in tar', has come to be used in modern times as a derogatory label for both the bush ballad genre and the unsophisticated, bucolic view of Australia which produced and encouraged it.

Clara Morison (1854), a novel written by Catherine Helen Spence (q.v.) and subtitled *A Tale of South Australia during the Gold Fever*, was one of the first novels about the Australian colonies written by a woman. Catherine Helen Spence sent the manuscript to England with a letter to the publishers indicating the authenticity of its characters, events and backgrounds – 'the domestic life represented in my tale is the sort of life I have led – the people are such as I have come in contact with – the letters from the diggings are like those I have seen – . . . so that it may be considered a faithful transcript of life in the Colony'.

The heroine, Clara Morison, and her sister Susan, left orphaned by the death of their father, come under the care of their uncle in Edinburgh. Nineteen-year-old Clara is sent to the colony of SA, supposedly to be taken into the family of a merchant, Mr Campbell, prior to gaining a position as governess. She arrives in Adelaide to find Mr Campbell's wife has died and the merchant neither able nor especially anxious to do much about her welfare. After unsuccessful attempts to become a governess she goes into service, surviving such a shock to her fragile, well-bred system by her determination and courage. Her situation is ameliorated somewhat when she is taken into the home of a relative where she falls in love with Charles Reginald, an up-country squatter whom she meets on her arrival in Adelaide. Reginald is engaged to a girl in England who has no intention of coming to live in the colonies. After many vicissitudes the engagement is broken and Charles and Clara marry.

Highly thought of by early critic, Frederick Sinnett, *Clara Morison* is an important Australian literary landmark rather than a notable work of literature. It is a domestic novel with considerable soul-searching by its heroine and many wrong turnings and culs-de-sac which a word of explanation could have set right. Particular Australian interest is provided by the novel's portrayal of the conditions on the diggings and the effects of gold fever in the Colony.

CLARE, BILLY (1863–1940), pioneer journalist and printer in WA, was founder and owner of the *Coolgardie Miner* and was associated with later newspapers and publishing ventures (e.g. *Clare's Weekly,* Clare Printery) in Perth, Bunbury and Fremantle.

Clarence River, see **Grafton**

Clarion, a Melbourne monthly mining and literary journal launched by Randolph Bedford (q.v.), ran 1897–1909. An ardent Australian nationalist, Bedford used the *Clarion* to carry his message of white Australian, socialist republicanism. The magazine's notable contributors included the writers Hugh McCrae, John Shaw Neilson, Edward Dyson and Louis Esson, and the artists Will Dyson and Norman Lindsay. Dyson's multicoloured political cartoons were a feature of the *Clarion's* covers in its last years.

CLARK, J.H. (JOHN HOWARD) (1830–78), born Birmingham, England, came to Adelaide in 1850 and in 1865 bought the *Register,* which he edited 1870–78 and to which he contributed under the pseudonyms 'Geoffrey Crabthorn' and 'Pleeceman X'. He published a selection of his burlesques as *Echoes from the Bush* (n.d.).

CLARK, MANNING (1915–), was born in Sydney and was educated at the Universities of Melbourne and Oxford. He taught at Geelong Grammar School (1940–43) before joining the staff of the University of Melbourne; in 1949 he was appointed professor of history at Canberra University College, later part of the Australian National University. Clark's first articles were on French topics but increasingly he came to focus his attention on Australian history and culture; a 1943 contribution to the 'Letters to Tom Collins' (q.v.) series in *Meanjin* was his first publication in this area. Clark established a scholarly reputation in the 1950s with his collections of documents (*Select Documents in Australian History,* 2 vols, 1950–55; *Sources of Australian History,* 1957) and with his contribution to the dismantling of the convict legend (see Transportation), but it was the publication of his multi-volumed *A History of Australia* which made him Australia's most widely-read but also most controversial historian. Five volumes of his *History* have so far been published (1962, 1968, 1973, 1978, 1981), taking the story of Australia from the days before European settlement to the experience of Gallipoli. The interplay of the forces of Protestantism, Catholicism and the Enlightenment in nineteenth-century Australia is an important theme in the *History,* which is informed by Clark's idealism and by a pessimism about Australian society influenced in part by the extended years of conservative political rule since the Second World War and by the dismissal of the Whitlam government in 1975. Clark has been criticized, sometimes savagely, for his pessimism as well as for factual inaccuracies in the *History,* the state of 'moral hypertension' in which many of his historical personages operate, and his 'apocalyptic' prose style. A strong defence has been mounted in which Clark's imagination, vision and the magnitude of his achievement have been emphasized and his detractors reminded of his insistence that his is a personal view of Australia's development.

Although Clark's reputation derives primarily from his historical writing, which includes the popular *A Short History of Australia* (1963), his other works have attracted attention; in particular the sombre biographical portrait *In Search of Henry Lawson* (1978) provoked vigorous criticism, notably by Colin Roderick, and spirited defences of Clark by Patrick White, Xavier Herbert and others. The view that Australia is Lawson 'writ large' is restated in the fifth volume of *A History of Australia,* in which Lawson is a central character; among other creative writers significantly to have shaped Clark's response to Australian history are Joseph Furphy, 'Henry Handel Richardson', James McAuley, Martin Boyd, Bernard O'Dowd and Douglas Stewart. Clark's own contribution to Australian literature includes not only the study of Lawson but also a volume of short stories, *Disquiet and Other Stories* (1969), which is strongly autobiographical, and an edition of *Settlers and Convicts* (1953) which encouraged a renewed interest in its then-unknown author, Alexander Harris. In addition Clark has written *Meeting Soviet Man* (1960), the product of a 1958-59 visit to Russia by a FAW delegation comprising Clark, James Devaney and Judah Waten; *A Discovery of Australia* (1976), which reprints Clark's ABC Boyer Lectures for that year; and *Occasional Writings and Speeches* (1980), which reprints the 'Letter to Tom Collins', essays on Ned Kelly and Barry Humphries, and a tribute to David Campbell. Stephen Holt's *Manning Clark and Australian History* (1982) traces Clark's life and intellectual evolution between 1915 and 1963.

CLARK, MAVIS THORPE (?1912–), was born in Melbourne where, after a somewhat itinerant childhood, she settled to a successful career as a writer of children's and educational books. The most notable of her many books are *The Brown Land Was Green* (1956), which was adapted by the author into a fifty-two episodes serial for the ABC; *The Min-Min* (1966), which won the 1967 Children's Book of the Year Award and was published in America, Germany and Japan; and *Pastor Doug* (1965), the biography of Pastor Doug Nicholls. Her other children's books, often translated into several languages and into Braille for blind children, include *Gully of Gold* (1958), *Pony from Tarella* (1959), *They Came South* (1963, serialized by the ABC), *Blue above the Trees* (1967), *Spark of Opal* (1968), *Iron Mountain* (1970), *Wildfire* (1973), *The Sky is Free* (1974), *The Boy from Cumeroogunga* (1979), the children's version of the Nicholls biography, and *Solomon's Child* (1981).

CLARK, RALPH (?–1794), an officer in the marines, volunteered for duty at Botany Bay in an attempt to gain promotion and sailed in HMS *Friendship* in the First Fleet. Clark's detailed and frank diary, kept assiduously 1787–92, is a source of information about shipboard life during the voyage to Botany Bay and the daily routine of the Colony, especially the convict settlement at Norfolk Island where Clark was stationed 1790–91. *The Journals and Letters of Lt. Ralph Clark 1787–1792*, edited by Paul G. Fidlon and R. J. Ryan, was published in 1981.

CLARK, ROBERT (1911–), born Darjeeling, India, came to Australia as a boy and was educated in Adelaide, where he has practised as a solicitor. He won the 1956 *Sydney Morning Herald* prize for poetry for the poem 'The Dogman' and has been widely represented in Australian anthologies. Co-editor of *Verse in Australia* 1958–61 he wrote the significant introduction on Max Harris in Harris's poems, *A Window at Night* (1967). His own publications of verse are *The Dogman and Other Poems* (1962), *Segments of the Bowl* (1968) and *Thrusting into Darkness* (1978). A traditional poet concerned especially with language, he has written lyrical and meditative poetry.

CLARK, WILLIAM NAIRNE (1804–54), born Perthshire, Scotland, emigrated to WA in 1830, where he practised as a lawyer, edited the *Inquisitor* in 1833 and established the *Swan River Guardian* in 1836. His accomplishments include the killing of a Major George Johnson, an associate on the *Inquisitor*, in a duel in 1831 - Clark was acquitted of murder - and

the publication of the first book in the Swan River Colony. In many newspaper articles Clark defended the Aboriginal people. He later left WA for Tasmania.

CLARKE, CORALIE (1909–72), was born in Perth and educated at the University of WA. There she subedited the student magazine, the *Black Swan*, which was edited by her future husband Leslie Rees. Some of her one-act plays were printed in the *Black Swan*, including 'Shielded Eyes', produced in 1930 with Paul Hasluck in the main role. In 1931 she and Rees were married in London, where they lived until 1936. During this time she contributed numerous articles to the *West Australian* under the pseudonym 'Boronia'. After their return to Australia, she wrote extensively for radio and was an occasional broadcaster. As well as short stories for children and travel articles, she wrote a verse-elegy, *Silent His Wings* (1946), for her brother who was killed in the Second World War, and four travel books in collaboration with Leslie Rees, *Spinifex Walkabout* (1953), *Westward from Cocos* (1956), *Coasts of Cape York* (1960) and *People of the Big Sky Country* (1970). Her play for children, *Wait Till We Grow Up*, is included in *Australian Youth Plays* (1948) edited by Leslie Rees.

CLARKE, DONOVAN (1907–), born Bristol, England, has had a long career as schoolmaster and academic, poet and literary critic. Particularly interested in Australian colonial poetry he has written on the Henry Kendall–Charles Harpur relationship and edited a selection of Harpur's poetry in 1963. He has also published two volumes of poetry, *Ritual Dance* (1940) and *Blue Prints* (1942).

CLARKE, DOREEN (1928–), born Manchester, England, came to Australia in 1958. Since the production of her first play, *Roses in Due Season* (performed 1978, published 1982), she has worked in the theatre or in projects connected with the theatre. Her other published plays include *Bleedin' Butterflies* (1982) and *Farewell Brisbane Ladies* (1982). Unpublished but performed plays include 'Missis Queen' (1979), 'The Sad Songs of Annie Sando' (1981) and 'Salt and Vinegar' (1982), plays dealing with life in the South Australian satellite city of Elizabeth.

CLARKE, MARCUS (1846–81), born Kensington, London, was educated at Highgate, where Gerard Manley Hopkins and his brother Cyril were contemporaries and close friends. He had expectations of a substantial inheritance and a Foreign Office career but these hopes were dashed at sixteen by the sudden illness of his father, a Chancery lawyer, and the discovery that his financial affairs were in disarray. One of Clarke's uncles had been governor of WA, another was a judge in Ararat, and a cousin, Captain Andrew Clarke, had been Victorian surveyor-general and a member of parliament, and had recently returned to England; it was Andrew who arranged Clarke's emigration to Australia in 1863 armed with some £800 and several letters of introduction.

Clarke began to write for the Australian press soon after arrival in Melbourne, but his first employment was in the Bank of Australasia; in 1856 he left Melbourne to spend two years working on sheep stations in the Wimmera district of Victoria. During his time there he contributed to the *Australian Monthly Magazine* under the pseudonyms 'Mark Scrivener' and 'Q'; later it became the *Colonial Monthly* (q.v.) and serialized his first novel, *Long Odds* (q.v.), in 1868–69. In 1867 he returned to Melbourne and was soon writing for the *Argus* and the *Australasian,* where the popular series 'The Peripatetic Philospher' (q.v.) was published 1867–70; together with the 'Lower Bohemia' (q.v.) sketches, theatre criticism and other writings, 'The Peripatetic Philosopher' helped to establish Clarke as a leading Melbourne journalist, a reputation he held till his death. His efforts as an editor and publisher were less successful: brief periods with the *Colonial Monthly* (1868–69), the *Humbug* (q.v., 1869–70) and the *Australian Journal* (q.v., 1870–71) were unprofitable and contributed to the first of his bankruptcies in 1874. This period also established Clarke's reputation as a bohemian, a leading member of Melbourne's café society: witty, urbane, brilliant, he was one of the founders of the Yorick Club in 1868 and moved easily in theatrical circles. His published plays include the pantomimes, *Goody Two Shoes* (1870) and *Twinkle, Twinkle Little Star* (1873); the comedy, *Reverses* (1876); the operetta, *Alfred the Great* (1879); and the satire, *The Happy Land* (q.v., 1880). In 1869 he married the actress Marian Dunn.

In 1870 Clarke was sent by the *Argus* management to Tasmania to research the convict past. The immediate literary consequences were the series of historical articles published in the *Australasian* (1870–71) as 'Old Stories Retold' by 'Q', and collected in 1871 as *Old Tales of a Young Country* (q.v.); and Clarke's most famous work, *His Natural Life* (q.v.), which was serialized in the *Australian Journal* in 1870–72 and revised for its first publication in book form in 1874. Soon after his return from Tasmania he found employment at the Public Library in Melbourne, first as secretary to the trustees and then from September 1873 as sub-librarian. Two months later his association with

the *Argus* group ceased after a squabble over Clarke's report in the rival *Herald* of the 1873 Melbourne Cup. As well as *The Peripatetic Philosopher* and *Old Tales of a Young Country,* the *Argus* and *Australasian* years had resulted in three newspaper columns and in the short stories published 1870–73 and included in *Holiday Peak and Other Tales* (1873) and *Four Stories High* (q.v., 1877).

In comparison with the immensely-productive years 1869–74 Clarke was subsequently less prolific, partly because of his work at the Public Library and partly because he was involved in the management of a country property for his cousin. But he still found time to write for the theatre; to publish two novels, *Chidiock Tichbourne* (1893, serialized 1874–75) which traded on the Tichborne controversy but is not about Australia, and *'Twixt Shadow and Shine* (1875), and begin a third ('Felix and Felicitas'); to prepare the commentary accompanying *Photographs of Pictures in the National Gallery, Melbourne* (1875), part of which became a famous preface to the 1876 edition of Adam Lindsay Gordon's *Sea Spray and Smoke Drift;* to write the pamphlet, *The Future Australian Race* (1877); and to contribute to a variety of newspapers and periodicals including the *Age,* the *Leader,* the *Melbourne Review* and *Victorian Review* in Melbourne, and the *Daily Telegraph* and *Notes and Queries* in London. A *Victorian Review* article in 1879 by Clarke on the role of the Church in society led to a reply by the Bishop of Melbourne; Clarke wrote a rejoinder and the controversy was collected and published as *Civilization Without Delusion* (1880). His resulting unpopularity with officialdom, increased by his involvement in *The Happy Land,* a satire on the Berry government of the day, was instrumental in his failure to become public librarian in 1881. He had fallen into financial difficulties again; when he was not appointed he was pressed for payment, made bankrupt a second time, collapsed amidst the strain and died within a week, leaving his wife and six children destitute. His friend Hamilton Mackinnon prepared *The Marcus Clarke Memorial Volume* (1884) to help the family, and *The Austral Edition of the Selected Works of Marcus Clarke* (1890); parts of the latter were reissued as *Stories of Australia in the Early Days* (1897), *Australian Tales* (1896) and *Australian Tales of the Bush* (1897). Other Clarke volumes published soon after his death include the two stories, *The Mystery of Major Molineux and Human Repetends* (1881) and *Sensational Tales* (1886). Significant recent publications on Clarke include Brian Elliott's biography, *Marcus Clarke* (1958); L.T. Hergenhan's selection of journalism, *A Colonial City* (1973); the bibliography by Samuel Rowe Simmons (1975, ed. Hergenhan); and the volume on Clarke in the Portable Australian Authors Series (1976), ed. Michael Wilding who has also edited a collection of Clarke's short stories (1983) and written a monograph revaluing Clarke's achievements (1977).

For years Clarke was remembered as the popular author of one major work, *His Natural Life*, a convict novel of immense proportions and power although regarded as somewhat flawed by melodramatic excesses. Since Clarke's death it has been reprinted frequently, reserialized, dramatized, filmed, abridged, anthologized and translated. However, modern scholarship and criticism and the increasing availability of Clarke's other writings have resulted not only in a reconsideration of *His Natural Life* itself – Michael Wilding, for example, sees the plot coincidences less as naturalistic absurdities than as a mechanism for exploring psychological levels of character – but also in a revaluation of Clarke's achievement. Although *His Natural Life* remains his most important work, he was amazingly versatile and made significant contributions to colonial literary culture as novelist, short-story writer, historian, critic, journalist, dramatist, poet and editor. As an historian, particularly in *Old Tales of a Young Country,* he helped to create the romance of the Australian past, as had Cooper and Hawthorne for American literature and Scott for English literature. As a short-story writer he ranged from realism to the Gothic to fantasy and preceded Henry Lawson in opening up the bush to Australian readers. As a critic he took part, as *Civilization Without Delusion* shows, in the great questions of the day and wrote perceptively about American, English and European literature (Balzac was his favourite author and a major influence) as well as about his contemporaries. As a journalist he continued, in the 'Lower Bohemia' sketches, the investigative tradition of Henry Mayhew, while *The Peripatetic Philosopher* and his other series derived their success from the skilful blend of satire, irony and characterization which created the Clarke style.

CLARKE, PEG, see Feminism and Australian Literature

CLARKE, W.B. (WILLIAM BRANWHITE) (1798–1878), born Suffolk, England, was an Anglican clergyman, schoolteacher, experienced geologist and published poet before he arrived in Australia in 1839. He was headmaster of the King's School at Parramatta before his appointment to a North Sydney ministry in 1846. His geological explorations revealed gold in the Colony as early as 1841 but Governor Gipps, alarmed at the specimen of gold shown

him in 1844, is reported to have said 'Put it away, Mr Clarke, or we shall all have our throats cut'. After the discovery of gold by Edward Hammond Hargraves in 1851, Clarke became the government's scientific adviser on the goldfields. His publication *Plain Statements and Practical Hints Respecting the Discovery and Working of Gold in Australia* (1851) became known as 'The Prospector's Bible'; he also published *Researches in the Southern Gold Fields of New South Wales* (1860). A tireless contributor of scientific articles to newspapers and journals, Clarke deserved the title 'Father of Australian Geology', as in James Jervis's biography (1944).

CLAY, H.E. (HENRY EBENEZER) (1844–96), born Cheshire, England, migrated in 1858 to WA, where he worked as a government clerk. His volume of verse, *Two and Two: A Story of the Australian Forest, with Minor Poems of Colonial Interest* (1873), was the first separate publication of poetry in WA. His other works include *Westralian Poems* (1907), *Poems* (1910) and the proclamation song, *Rouse Thee Westralia* (1890). Although he wrote in a conventional English poetic style, Clay included such colonial ingredients as kangaroos, sheep, wild dogs, bushfires, and life on the diggings.

Clean Straw for Nothing, a novel by George Johnston (q.v.), was published in 1969 and won the Miles Franklin Award. The middle volume of Johnston's semi-autobiographical trilogy, which includes *My Brother Jack* (q.v., 1964) and *A Cartload of Clay* (1971), it narrates the experience of David Meredith from 1945 to the 1960s. Looking back at the kaleidoscope of the past, Meredith searches for the reasons for his sense of failure. After leaving his first wife to marry Cressida Morley, he abandons Melbourne for Sydney, then Sydney for London, and finally London and his career as a journalist for life as a creative writer on a Greek island. Freedom, however, proves elusive: his hopes of writing a great novel disintegrate, his health is ruined and material worries threaten his hopes for his children. His relationship with Cressida, deteriorating even in London, almost collapses after her affair with an American, Jim Galloway, in 1959. Although they are helped by their friends, especially Tom Kiernan (a study of Sidney Nolan) and Archie Calverton (a study of Peter Finch), Meredith returns to Australia in 1964 with the sense that he will always be an alien 'because there is no-one you will ever really know, not even yourself'.

CLEARY, JON (1917–), born Sydney, the eldest of seven children, left school at fifteen.

He worked at various occupations − · in the textile industry, as a film cartoonist, salesman, laundryman, bushworker and commercial artist. He served in the Australian army 1940–45 in the Middle East and New Guinea. From 1945 he has been a full-time writer apart from two periods as a journalist with the Australian News and Information Bureau. In 1946 he married Joy Lucas who as Joy Cleary wrote *Strike Me Lucky* (1959). Cleary has lived abroad for extensive periods in the USA, England, Spain, Italy and Austria and has travelled widely to research his novels. His books, published in numerous foreign countries, have a wide overseas audience and have been produced as films on several occasions. Cleary's novels are *You Can't See Round Corners* (q.v., 1947), *The Long Shadow* (1949), *Just Let Me Be* (1950), *The Sundowners* (q.v., 1952), *The Climate of Courage* (1954, also titled *Naked in the Night*), *Justin Bayard* (1955, also titled *Dust in the Sun*), *The Green Helmet* (1957), *Back of Sunset* (1959), *North from Thursday* (1960), *The Country of Marriage* (1962), *Forests of the Night* (1963), *A Flight of Chariots* (1963), *The Fall of an Eagle* (1964), *The Pulse of Danger* (1966), *The High Commissioner* (1966), *The Long Pursuit* (1967), *Season of Doubt* (1968), *Remember Jack Hoxie* (1969), *Helga's Web* (1970), *Mask of the Andes* (1971, also titled *The Liberators*), *Man's Estate* (1972, also titled *The Ninth Marquess*), *Ransom* (1973), *Peter's Pence* (1974), *The Safe House* (1975), *A Sound of Lightning* (1976), *Vortex* (1977), *High Road to China* (1977), *The Beaufort Sisters* (1979), *A Very Private War* (1980), *The Faraway Drums* (1981), *The Golden Sabre* (1981) and *Spearfield's Daughter* (1982). He has also published two collections of short stories, *These Small Glories* (1946), and *Pillar of Salt* (1963). He has written scripts for television, radio and film for production in Australia, the USA and England, and has had stories published in several of the world's leading magazines. Novels which have been filmed include *You Can't See Round Corners*, *The Sundowners*, *Justin Bayard*, *The Green Helmet*, *The High Commissioner*, *Helga's Web* (as Scobie Malone) and *High Road to China*. Cleary won first prize in the ABC's 1944 competition for radio drama, second prize in the *Sydney Morning Herald's* novel competiton of 1946, the Australian section prize in the World Short Story contest of the *New York Herald Tribune* in 1950, the Gold Medal of the Australian Literature Society for the best Australian novel of 1966 (*The High Commissioner*) and the Mystery Writers Edgar Award of 1975.

Although Cleary's novels have varied settings, ranging from Bhutan to the USA to New Guinea, several of them are set in Australia, most notably *You Can't See Round Cor-*

ners, *The Long Shadow*, *The Sundowners*, *Justin Bayard*, *Back of Sunset* and *Helga's Web*. In others, Australian characters frequently appear and with Scobie Malone, the Sydney detective who figures in *Helga's Web*, *The High Commissioner* and *Ransom*, Cleary has come close to creating the Australian Maigret. A popular adventure writer with a talent for gripping action, atmosphere and convincing dialogue, Cleary frequently evokes the psychological subtleties and moral complexities of personal relationships.

CLEMENS, SAMUEL LANGHORNE, see **'TWAIN, MARK'**

'Click Go the Shears', one of the best-known Australian folk-songs, was probably written in the early years of the twentieth century and derives from the English song, 'Ring the Bell, Watchman'. It offers a picture of shearing life in the days of the blade shears, and each of its several verses focuses on a typical inhabitant of the shearing shed and his activities: the old shearer, the boss, the new chum, the boy supplying tar to seal a wound caused by the shears, the spree after the shearing season is over. The chorus,

> Click go the shears boys, click, click, click
> Wide is his blow and his hands move quick
> The ringer looks around and is beaten by a blow
> And curses the old snagger with the bare [blue]-bellied 'joe'

refers to the sound of the shears, the shearing style of the ringer or fastest shearer, and his chagrin when his tally is bettered by a snagger, a shearer who works roughly.

CLIFT, CHARMIAN (1923–69), was born Kiama, NSW. During the Second World War she served in the Australian Women's Army Service as an anti-aircraft gunner and edited a magazine for the Army Ordnance Corps. On demobilization she worked as a journalist for the Melbourne *Argus*. She married George Johnston (q.v.) in 1947 and accompanied him to London in 1950 and to Greece in 1954. After the Johnstons returned to Australia in 1964, Charmian Clift turned to freelance journalism. She contributed a popular weekly column to the *Sydney Morning Herald* and also wrote regularly for the Melbourne *Herald* and for various other magazines and newspapers. She wrote three novels with George Johnston: *High Valley* (1949), which won first prize in the 1948 literary competition of the *Sydney Morning Herald*, *The Big Chariot* (1953) and *The Sponge Divers* (1955), the last published in the USA with the title *The Sea and The*

Stone (1955); two other novels, *Walk to the Paradise Gardens* (1960) and *Honour's Mimic* (1964); and two accounts of the Johnston family's experiences in Greece, *Mermaid Singing* (1956) and *Peel Me a Lotus* (1959). Some of her essays are collected in *Images in Aspic* (1965) and *The World of Charmian Clift* (1970, both edited by George Johnston). She also adapted Johnston's novel *My Brother Jack* (q.v.) for televison. His study of Cressida Morley in that novel and in *Clean Straw for Nothing* (q.v., 1969) and *A Cartload of Clay* (1971) is loosely based on her life and his reactions to her early death. Her son is the poet, Martin Johnston. A fluent writer with a range of tones and a congenial wit, Charmian Clift found her natural bent in the essay, where she moves easily from concerned discussion of national issues to nostalgic, personal reminiscence of people or places, to humorous reflection on social practices or everyday experiences.

CLOSE, ROBERT (1903–) born Camberwell, Victoria, became an apprentice at the age of fourteen on a sailing ship and after six years' exuberant adventures gave up the sea when he failed his second mate's ticket because of colour-blindness. With his one career ambition lost, Close drifted through a series of unsatisfactory occupations such as shipping clerk, vacuum-cleaner salesman and accounts collector with the Melbourne *Truth*. Developing tuberculosis, employment difficulties during the Depression, and an unhappy marriage also contributed to his bleak view of life at the time. After six months of sanatorium care in 1936 his tuberculosis was cured and he was successful in having short stories published. In 1945 he published his first novel, *Love Me, Sailor* (q.v.). It deals with the voyage of a windjammer and the chaos caused on board ship by its sole passenger, a neurotic nymphomaniac. The first edition sold out in a few weeks but the novel was then banned and Close and his publishers, Georgian House, were charged with 'obscene libel'. After a second trial and in a blaze of publicity and controversy, Close was found guilty and sentenced to three months' gaol and a fine of £100. The gaol sentence was quashed on appeal but the fine increased to £150. In 1950 Close, divorced and 'tired of living in an atmosphere of parochial suburbanism', left Australia to live in France, where the French edition, *Prends-moi, Matelot*, was a best-seller. Close's second novel, *The Dupe* (1948), written to prove that he did not have to rely on sex to win literary acclaim, is also set on a windjammer but contains no female characters and no sexuality. *The Dupe* is the story of a young seaman apprentice who loses his indentures by missing his ship because of a drunken spree

and attempts to regain his lost prestige by pretending responsibility for the murder of the ship's brutal first mate. As with *Love Me, Sailor,* Close's knowledge of the sea and sailing ships is impressive; his portrait of the young man, Carson, is also superior to that of Ella, the central figure in the earlier novel. After *The Dupe,* Close published an autobiographical account of his seafaring days, *Morn of Youth* (1948), and after arriving in Europe, wrote an autobiographical novel 'Not of Salt Nor Earth', but withdrew it before publication. In 1977, his autobiography up to the point of his gaol sentence was published as *Of Salt and Earth.* His next novel, *Eliza Callaghan* (1957), described by the *New York Times* as 'a realistic historical novel, replete with sex, booze, violence and malevolence', is based on the courtship of John Batman and the young Irish girl of the title. Later less significant novels by Close are *With Hooves of Brass* (1961), set in the Victorian timber country; *She's My Lovely* (1962), with an American setting; and *The Voyage Continues* (1969), a fictional reconstruction of the wreck of the *Batavia* off the west coast of Australia in 1629, with the events leading up to it and its tragic sequel. Close's significance in Australian literary history is largely due to the extraordinary events attached to *Love Me, Sailor,* but his ability to construct a realistic narrative set against the background of life on a sailing ship is considerable.

CLOUSTON, BRIAN, see Jacaranda Press

CLOW, ROBITT JON (1877–?), born Melbourne, was a minister of the Christian Church in Victoria, SA and Queensland in the early part of this century. He published two plays, *The Cause of Kelly* (1919) and *The Dewmah* subtitled *The Collected Literature of the Australian Aborigine as Told in Native Drama* (1949); fiction, *The Pillar of Salt: A Story of Station Life* (1903); verse, *Vive la Australe* (1910) and *Australie . . . Three Poems* (1910); and miscellaneous works including *Among the Chief Colonials* (1921), *The Pacific Empire: An Authentic History of the Venerable James Clow* (1929), *The Book of the Ages: A Centennial Story of Melbourne and Adelaide* (1937) and *The Royal Charter* (1938).

Club, The, a play by David Williamson (q.v.), first performed in 1977, was published in 1978 and produced as a film in 1980. Set in the committee room of a top Melbourne Australian Rules football club (perceived as Collingwood by many) and surveyed by the ranged photographs of the Club's past heroes, it comically enacts familiar competing tensions between six of its members. The personal rivalries between Ted Parker (the president), Jock Riley (the vice-president, ex-player and ex-coach) and Laurie Holden (ex-player and dedicated coach) have their roots in the Club's past history and are exacerbated by the current pressure to revive its declining fortunes. They are manipulated by Gerry Cooper, the new-breed administrator who ignores tradition and practises the 'logic of pragmatism'. Players are no longer men but marketable commodities, and committee members and coaches are equally subject to the demands of football as an entertainment industry. Danny Rowe, the player who lives for the game but is almost expendable, and Geoff Hayward, the brilliant but uncommitted new 'purchase', watch and barrack the game of power politics from the sidelines.

CLUNE, FRANK (1893–1971), born and educated in Sydney, got his first job, selling newspapers, at the age of seven. At fifteen he left home and for the next five years led an adventurous life on sea and land in Australia, France, Belgium, the USA and Canada. He returned to Australia in 1913, enlisted in the AIF and was wounded at Gallipoli; invalided home, he resumed a vagabond's existence and was in turn a fireman, recruiting sergeant, concert balladist, steward, vaudevillian and mousetrap salesman before settling into the practice of accountancy around the time of his marriage in 1923. A decade later, while convalescing from an ulcer attack, he wrote an account of his earlier wanderings. Published as *Try Anything Once* (1933), the book launched Clune on a writing career that produced over sixty books 1934–71. During much of this period, when he was one of Australia's best-selling authors, he had the services of P.R. Stephensen (q.v.) as collaborator; Stephensen is acknowledged as co-author of *The Viking of Van Diemen's Land* (1954) and *The Pirates of the Brig 'Cyprus'* (1962), and as 'literary collaborator' in other volumes (e.g. in the preface to *Wild Colonial Boys*, 1948). On the evidence, Clune provided the travel diaries, historical research and other raw material for his books which were mostly written by Stephensen, especially in the 1940s and 1950s.

Clune regularly catalogued his works under several headings: autobiography (*Try Anything Once*; *Pacific Parade*, 1945; *Try Nothing Twice*, 1946; *Korean Diary*, 1955); biography, (some dozen titles including studies of varying length on the bushrangers 'Captain Melville', 'Captain Starlight' and Martin Cash; the adventurers Edward Hammond Hargraves, 'Bully' Hayes, Jorgen Jorgenson, 'Chinese' Morrison and Louis de Rougemont; and the mass murderer, Deeming); history (a similar number of titles including *Wild Colonial Boys*; *Bound for Botany Bay*,

1964; *The Norfolk Island Story*, 1967; and *The Scottish Martyrs*, ?1969); exploration (notably *Dig*, 1937, a narrative of the Burke and Wills expedition); historical novels (*Dark Outlaw*, 1945, a study of the bushranger Frank Gardiner reprinted as *Gunman Gardiner*, 1951, and *King of the Road*, 1967; and *Ben Hall the Bushranger*, 1947); adventure (e.g. *The Red Heart*, 1944); and travel (more than two dozen volumes including *Rolling down the Lachlan*, 1935; *Roaming Round the Darling*, 1936; *Prowling Through Papua*, 1942; *Tobruk to Turkey*, 1943; *High-ho to London*, 1948; *Somewhere in New Guinea*, 1951; *Roaming Round Europe*, 1954; *Flight to Formosa*, 1958; *Journey to Kosciusko*, 1964; *Journey to Pitcairn*, 1966). Such distinctions, however, camouflage important overlaps in Clune's work: for example, there is little difference apart from scale between his historic novels, histories, biographies and exploration studies, which all focus on sensational personalities or historical incidents and in which Clune characteristically takes liberties with the evidence, as in the reporting of invented conversations. Clune's prose is racy, journalistic and immediate, an appealing amalgam of alliteration, cliché, colourful image and title which has its parallel in the writing of journalists such as John Norton and Cyril Pearl. Although Clune's Cold War travel books are politically conservative, his historical writing reflects his Irish Catholic background and shows sympathy for some Australian underdogs, notably bushrangers such as Ben Hall and Ned Kelly or the Scottish martyr, Thomas Muir. Apart from the personal appeal of *Try Anything Once*, which went through several editions in its first decade, his importance in Australian literature is mainly as an historical popularizer – on radio as well as in books – who introduced successive generations to some of the legendary figures of Australia's past, notably in the often-reprinted *Dig*, *King of the Road*, *Wild Colonial Boys*, and *The Kelly Hunters* (1954). One such reader was the novelist Thomas Keneally, whose interest in the Jimmy Governor story, aroused by Clune's 1959 volume on the Aboriginal mass-murderer, led eventually to the novel, *The Chant of Jimmie Blacksmith* (1972).

Coast to Coast, an anthology of Australian short stories, was published annually 1941–48 and biennially 1949–70. The final anthology in the series appeared in 1973. The editors of the individual volumes were: Cecil Mann (1941), Beatrice Davis (1942), Frank Dalby Davison (1943), Vance Palmer (1944), Douglas Stewart (1945), 'M. Barnard Eldershaw' (1946), Don Edwards (1947), Brian Elliott (1948), Nettie Palmer (1949–50), Ken Levis (1951–52), C.B. Christesen (1953–54), H. Drake-

Brockman (1955–56), Dal Stivens (1957–58), Cecil Hadgraft (1959–60), Hal Porter (1961–62), Leonie Kramer (1963–64), Clement Semmler (1965–66), A.A. Phillips (1967–68), Thea Astley (1969–70), Frank Moorhouse (1973).

Cobb & Co. The first mention of public road transport in Australia was a notice in the *Sydney Gazette,* May 1803, by one Henry Cable that he proposed 'to run a Common Stage Machine from Sydney to Parramatta and Hawkesbury'. By 1814 regular weekly services by 'Common Stage Cart' ran for passengers from Sydney to Parramatta, Windsor and Richmond; in 1821 the Colony's first regular coach service began along the road to Parramatta and extended in the 1830s across the Blue Mountains to Bathurst, with an overnight stay at the present township of Wentworth Falls. Prior to the gold-rush period there were few coach services in the Port Phillip district but an overland service for mail and passengers existed between Sydney and Melbourne, following roughly the route of the present Hume Highway. With the discovery of gold in 1851 in both NSW and Victoria an army of 'diggers', many from overseas, surged to the goldfields; their demands – and those of eager entrepreneurs, tourists, and harassed governments who had to set up administrations on the fields – for fast, reliable transport led to the emergence of Australia's most famous pioneering transport company, Cobb & Co. In 1853 American-built Concord coaches, well-tested on the Californian goldfields in 1850, arrived in Australia; with them came four young Americans, Freeman Cobb, John Murray Peck, James Swanton and John B. Lamber, the first two of whom had been employees of the well-known American express companies, Adams & Co and Wells, Fargo & Co. One version of the origin of Cobb & Co suggests that the four formed a small carrying company (named Cobb & Co) plying between Melbourne and Sandhurst (Bendigo) which, after a very wet 1853 Victorian winter, they converted to a coaching service. A different account suggests they began the carrying service in the names of the two American express companies, but after their suggestion of a change to coach service had been rejected by the parent companies they resigned to start their own service between Melbourne and the goldfields at Forest Creek (now Castlemaine) and Bendigo. They were financially assisted by American entrepreneur, George Francis Train (q.v.), who had also arrived in Australia in 1853. By 1856 Freeman Cobb had sold his coaching interests and returned to America; the name Cobb & Co, however, was retained by the new owners and came in time to be used by num-

erous other coaching firms, many of whom had little or no connection with the original Cobb & Co. The impression thus gained of a massive network of coaching routes which by the 1880s traversed the whole country, all part of a single Cobb & Co empire, is somewhat erroneous. By 1861 the name of Cobb & Co had become a legend in Victoria. In 1862, then owned by a syndicate headed by another American, James Rutherford, Cobb & Co extended into NSW, running first between Bathurst and Sydney and later opening up numerous other routes. A factory was established at Bathurst to build the company's coaches and Rutherford lived there until his death in 1911; he helped to establish the Bathurst *National Advocate* in 1889. In 1865 the Cobb & Co Queensland services were inaugurated; the Cobb & Co tradition of serving the frontier was maintained by its pioneering of the service to the Gympie goldfields. In 1866 Cobb & Co coaches were running in SA. By 1883 it was possible to travel on a coach named Cobb & Co (but not necessarily part of the original company) from the Gulf of Carpentaria to SA, the most extensive system of coach routes in the world. At its peak Cobb & Co itself harnessed in excess of 6000 horses a day and served more than a hundred separate routes in NSW and Victoria alone. Cobb & Co coaches were 'bailed up' by bushrangers on thirty-six separate occasions; and it gave to Australian legend such famous driver-figures as 'Cabbage Tree Ned' Devine (1833–1908), who was paid £1000 a year, and George Adams, later the founder of Tattersall's lottery. By the turn of the century, with the advent of the railway, and later with the coming of the motor car, Cobb & Co lost its importance as the country's chief source of transport. By 1913 Cobb & Co coaches had ceased running in NSW, and in 1924 in Queensland the last commercial Cobb & Co coach journey was made.

Although newspapers and journals of the 1850s gave considerable publicity to the advent of the coaching days, the first clear signs of a Cobb & Co legend were in Thomas McCombie's *Australian Sketches* (1861). Anthony Trollope's *Australia and New Zealand* (1873) added to that growing legend by describing the coach journeys of his Australian tour and expressing his admiration for the Cobb & Co drivers. Some old bush songs dating from as early as the 1870s (e.g. 'The German Girls') have direct reference to Cobb & Co. From the 1890s, however, the ubiquitous Cobb & Co coach featured widely in verse and story that celebrated the final conquest of 'the tryanny of distance' and the opening of the land. Will Ogilvie's poem 'Cobb & Co' and Henry Lawson's 'The Lights of Cobb & Co' appeared in the *Bulletin* in 1895 and 1897 respectively, Lawson's poem conveying the excitement of travelling by coach to the goldfields in those halcyon times. Other Lawson poems, nostalgic and sentimental like 'The Roaring Days', 'The Last Review' and 'The Old Bark School', describe coaching incidents and mention Cobb & Co by name; there are also references to the firm in such Lawson stories as 'The Shanty Keeper's Wife', 'Payable Gold', 'Brighten's Sister-in-Law', 'The Buck Jumper', 'The House That Was Never Built', 'Getting Back on Dave Regan' and 'The Horses'. Other poems and stories to celebrate coaching exploits are 'Salt' (A.S. Allison), 'The Braidwood Coach' (Guy Eden), and 'The Coachman's Yarn' and 'The Western Road' (both by E.J. Brady). Will Lawson's novel *When Cobb & Co. Was King* (1936) deals with the adventures of a youth who became a coach driver in the 1860s. 'Rolf Boldrewood''s *Robbery Under Arms* (1888) expresses the impact of Cobb & Co with the comment 'the Yankee came and showed us what cross-country coaching was'. Australian artists Tom Roberts and Sir Lionel Lindsay have immortalized Cobb & Co in their work, Roberts with his famous oil painting *Bailed Up,* and Lindsay with an etching of a Cobb & Co coach which was used on the Cobb & Co commemorative stamp issued in 1955. The Cobb & Co history and legend have inspired such works as William Lees's *A History of the Coaching Firm of Cobb & Co.* (1917), E.J. Aisbett's *Men of Cobb & Co.* (1940), N. Rutherford's *A Brief Account of Cobb & Co.* (1963), Joan E.L. Rutherford's *Cobb & Co.* (1971), Margaret Jean Jennings's *Cobb & Co.* (1972) and K.A. Austin's *The Lights of Cobb & Co.* (1967, republished in 1977 as *A Pictorial History of Cobb & Co.*).

COBB, CHESTER (1899–1943), born and educated in Sydney, was a journalist until he came into an inheritance in 1921 and left for England. He published two novels, *Mr Moffatt* (1925) and *Days of Disillusion* (1926); in both he drew on his Australian experiences. He is significant as the first Australian-born novelist to employ the 'stream of consciousness' technique in his work.

Cobbers (1), see *Bush Studies*

Cobbers (2), see **WOOD, THOMAS**

COBLEY, JOHN (1914–   ), is the author of a series of books relating to the First Fleet and the early days of British settlement in Sydney, including *Sydney Cove 1788* (1962), *Sydney Cove 1789–90* (1963), *The Convicts 1788–1792* (1964), *Sydney Cove 1791–92* (1965), *The Crimes*

of the First Fleet Convicts (1970) and *Sydney Cove 1793–1795* (1983). The *Sydney Cove* series aims to chronicle events up to the publication in 1803 of the first Australian newspaper, the *Sydney Gazette.*

COCHRANE, GEORGE HENRY, see **'HERVEY, GRANT'**

'Cock Crow', a poem by Rosemary Dobson (q.v.) published in the *Bulletin* (29 August 1953), is the title poem of her first volume of poetry (1965). Walking alone at night, the poet attempts to resolve a common problem of adult life – the conflict between responsibility to people in one's life and the demands of one's individuality. Linked by its title to Peter's denial of Christ, the poem anticipates on this occasion the triumph of loyalty over self-respect.

Cockatoo is a word of Malay origin for a crested parrot, of which there are several varieties distinctive to Australia; but the word has two additional Australian usages and once had a third, meaning a convict from Cockatoo Island in Sydney Harbour, which is now obsolete. A cockatoo, firstly, is a sentinel keeping watch for people engaged in an unlawful activity, e.g. convicts in road gangs in the nineteenth century who wanted to sleep rather than work, and two-up players in the twentieth century seeking to avoid the police; the usage derives from the long-held belief that feeding cockatoos post a sentry to warn of approaching danger. The second meaning of cockatoo, a small farmer, emerged around 1850, was pejorative in the nineteenth century and probably derived from the small farmer's practice, particularly after the Selection (q.v.) Acts, of settling or perching on parts of a squatter's run. Other suggested derivations relate to the 'scratching' of the land by selectors, their departure to a new district after a few years, their (enforced) thrift and their meagre harvests because of the ravages of the cockatoos themselves. A number of compounds have developed from cockatoo (which has also been used as a verb) or from the diminutive 'cocky' (commonly used from the 1880s): 'stringybark cockatoo' (the poorest small farmer of all, whose soil was so thin it could only nourish the stringybark gum tree), 'cockatoo fence' and 'cockatoo gate' (both improvised from rough materials), 'cocky's friend' and 'cocky's string' (fencing wire), 'cocky's joy' (golden syrup, a popular Australian treacle), 'boss cocky' (someone usually assertive and enjoying the exercise of authority), and 'cow cocky' or 'spud cocky' (referring to the main source of income). There is some evidence that cocky is undergoing elevation, e.g. in the fact that the word is now often used to mean any kind of farmer, not necessarily one with a small holding. There are numerous folk-songs and ballads about the trials of the cocky (e.g. the anonymous 'The Stringybark Cockatoo', 'Cockies of Bungaree' and 'The New England Cocky'), but the most extensive treatment in Australian literature is in 'Steele Rudd''s famous *On Our Selection* (q.v.) series.

Cockatoos, see '**BRENT OF BIN BIN**'

Cockatoos, The, see **WHITE, PATRICK**

COCKERILL, GEORGE (1871–1943), born Bendigo, Victoria, spent a lifetime in journalism culminating in his editorship of the Sydney *Daily Telegraph* 1926–28. His memoirs were published in 1944 as *Scribblers and Statesmen*. He also wrote fiction: *Down and Out: A Story of Australia's Early History* (1912), *The Convict Pugilist* (1912) and *In Days of Gold* (1926).

COLBEE (COLEBEE), an Aboriginal captured with Bennelong as part of Captain Arthur Phillip's plan to win the confidence of the Aborigines, escaped from captivity within a week but became a well-known identity around the First Fleet settlement. An account of his activities is in Watkin Tench's *A Complete Account of the Settlement at Port Jackson* (1793) and he appears as a character in Eleanor Dark's *The Timeless Land* (1941).

COLE, E.W. (EDWARD WILLIAM) (1832–1918), the most amazing bookseller in the history of Australian publishing, was born Kent, England, and arrived as a gold-rush immigrant to Australia in 1852. He sold lemonade and speculated in land on the goldfields, rowed down the Murray River taking photographs and ran a piestall in Melbourne before the refusal of publishers to handle the manuscript of his *The Real Place in History of Jesus and Paul* (1865) led him to open his own bookshop in the Eastern Market, Melbourne, in 1865. The business flourished and in 1873 he opened the first Cole's Book Arcade; in 1883 it found a permanent base in Bourke Street, where it eventually ran through to Little Collins Street. Cole's Book Arcade was as much bazaar as bookshop, with a huge rainbow over the door and such features inside as funny mirrors, slot machines, live monkeys, talking birds and brightly-dressed staff; the public was encouraged to browse as long as they liked without being pressed to buy. The arcade was phenomenally successful, allowing Cole to establish more orthodox branches interstate and to publish pamphlets on public questions and mis-

cellanies such as *Cole's Funny Picture Book* (1879– c), *Cole's Fun Doctor* (1886), and *Cole's Intellect Sharpener* (?1890); the miscellanies sold widely, the *Funny Picture Book* achieving more than a million sales to 1984. A prominent Book Arcade employee was 'Furnley Maurice' (q.v.), who rose from messenger boy to manager before the business, which needed Cole's entrepreneurial ingenuity and good will, was wound up in 1929. Cole Turnley's affectionate pictorial biography, *Cole of the Book Arcade*, was published in 1974. Cole also published C.J. Dennis's first book of verse, *Backblock Ballads*, in 1913.

COLEBATCH, HAL (1945–), born Perth, WA, has published three volumes of verse, *Spectators on the Shore* (1975), *In Breaking Waves* (1979) and *Coastal Knot* (1980). A traditionalist, Colebatch has a strong regard for poetic values such as clarity and coherence. One of his notable poems is 'Crowhurst', the story of lone yachtsman Donald Crowhurst, lost at sea in a round-the-world yacht race. He is the son of Sir Hal Colebatch (1872–1953), a prominent WA newspaper proprietor and politician.

COLEMAN, PETER (1928–), born Melbourne, has combined careers in politics, public administration and literature. One-time leader of the parliamentary Liberal Party in NSW, he is presently federal member for Wentworth. He was editor of the *Bulletin* 1964–67 and has been co-editor of *Quadrant* since 1967. With Lee Shrubb and Vivian Smith he edited *Quadrant: Twenty Five Years* (1982). His publications include *Obscenity, Blasphemy, Sedition: Censorship in Australia* (1962); *Cartoons of Australian History* (1967, compiled with Les Tanner); and *The Heart of James McAuley* (1980). He also edited the collection of essays, *Australian Civilization* (1962).

COLLIER, JAMES (1846–1925), born Dunfermline, Scotland, became a leader-writer and reviewer for the *Scotsman* and spent a decade working with Herbert Spencer on his sociological works. He came to Australia in 1895 from NZ, where he was parliamentary librarian at Wellington (1885–95) and where he compiled the bibliography, *The Literature Relating to New Zealand* (1890). In Australia he published widely in journals on sociological and colonization subjects but his main works were *Sir George Grey* (1909) and *The Pastoral Age in Australasia* (1911), which discusses some of the books written on bush life.

COLLINGRIDGE, GEORGE (1847–1931), born Oxfordshire, England, and educated in France in architecture, painting and wood engraving, came to Australia in 1879 to join the *Illustrated Sydney News* and later the *Australian Town and Country Journal* and the *Sydney Mail*. With his brother Arthur (1853–1907) he launched the short-lived *Australian Art* in 1888, the first such journal in Australia. His chief passion was the history of maritime discovery involving Australia; his major work was *The Discovery of Australia* (1895, revised 1906 as *The First Discovery of Australia and New Guinea*) based on the so-called Dieppe maps, in which he espoused the Portuguese claim to have charted most of Australia by 1530. Among his other published works are children's books, *Alice in One Dear Land* (1922) and *Through the Joke in Class* (1923); and travel reminiscences, *Round and Round the World* (1925) and *Pacifika, the Antediluvian World* (1928), which places the lost civilization of Atlantis in the Pacific.

COLLINS, DALE (1897–1956), born Balmain, Sydney, became a reporter with the Melbourne *Herald* and contributed stories to *Table Talk* and the *Bulletin*. In 1922 he acccompanied American millionaire, A.Y. Gowen, on a world tour in his yacht *Speejacks,* an experience that provided Collins with the material for his travel book, *Sea-Tracks of the Speejacks Round the World* (1923) and the novel *Ordeal* (1924) which became a best-seller and later a film, *The Ship from Shanghai*. In the period 1923–48 Collins lived in England but travelled widely gathering material for the many romantic novels about shipboard life and Oceanian places, including Australia, that appeared under his own name or under his pseudonyms 'Michael Copeland' and 'Stephen Fennimore'; the latter was also used in his books for children. He returned to Australia to live in 1948. In addition to *Ordeal* his novels included *The Haven* (1925), *The Sentimentalists* (1927), *Vanity under the Sun* (1928), *Idolaters* (1929), *Rich and Strange* (1930), *Jungle Maid* (1932), *Lost* (1933), *Vulnerable* (1933) and *The Mutiny of Madam Yes* (1935). *Race the Sun* (1936) is set in the new medium of air travel while *The Fifth Victim* (1930) is, like his first novel *Stolen or Strayed* (1922), a crime novel. *Bright Vista* (1946) and *Victoria's My Home Ground* (1951) are autobiograpically-based.

COLLINS, DAVID (1756–1810), born London, joined the Marine Corps at fourteen. After an active service life in which he participated in the War of American Independence, he was retired in 1783 but accepted appointment in 1786 as deputy judge-advocate of the impending expedition to Botany Bay. On his arrival with the First Fleet Collins became responsible to the governor for the Colony's entire legal establishment; in June 1788 he was also made secretary to the governor. So keen was his sense of duty to the new colony that it was not until 1797 that he returned to England. Because of his exceptional knowledge of colonial affairs he was appointed lieutenant-governor of the proposed new settlement to be established at Port Phillip. Unimpressed by the prospects in that area, which he reached in October 1803, he transferred his expedition to Van Diemen's Land where he established Hobart Town. After six frustrating years of trying to make the settlement flourish in the face of appalling local conditions and neglect from the Colonial Office in London, he died in Hobart.

Collins's *An Account of the English Colony in New South Wales* (1798, 1802) was the most complete and optimistic account of the settlement to emerge in its first decade. Although he had indicated in his private correspondence that he saw the Colony as 'a Place of Banishment for the Outcasts of Society', he claimed that the object of his long and detailed *Account* was to dissuade Englishmen from viewing the Colony with 'odium and disgust'. He revealed a humanitarian interest in the Aborigines, blaming the convicts rather than the natives for the violent racial clashes that occurred in the early months of the settlement.

C.R. Collins wrote *Saga of Settlement: A Brief Account of the Life and Times of Lieutenant-Colonel David Collins* (1957). The house where Collins died forms part of the setting of William Hay's novel, *The Escape of the Notorious Sir William Heans* (1919).

COLLINS, PAUL, see Science Fiction

Collins, Tom, was, at the end of the nineteenth century, a slang term for a mythical bush rumour-monger. The expression was obviously known to Joseph Furphy (q.v.), who adopted 'Tom Collins' as his pseudonym from 1892 and also made Collins an important character in *Such is Life* (1903), *Rigby's Romance* (1946), and *The Buln-Buln and the Brolga* (1948, qq.v.). By coincidence the term 'Tom Collins' was replaced by 'furphy' (q.v.), not because of Joseph Furphy's adoption of the pseudonym but because his brother's water carts came to be known as 'furphies' and gossip was exchanged around them during the First World War.

COLLINSON, LAURENCE (1925–), born Yorkshire, England, was brought to Australia in infancy and returned to England to live in 1964. He worked as a freelance writer for radio, newspapers and magazines; as a secondary teacher; and as actor, director and writer for Australian little theatres. He has published four collections of verse, *Poet's Dozen* (1953), *The*

Moods of Love (1957), *Who Is Wheeling Grandma?* (1967) and *Hovering Narcissus* (1977); a novel, *Cupid's Crescent* (1973); three plays, *Friday Night at the Schrammers* in *Australian One-Act Plays Book Two*, ed. Greg Branson (1962), *A Slice of Birthday Cake* in *Eight Short Plays* (1965) and *Thinking Straight* in *Homosexual Acts* (1975); and a children's book (1968). Of his numerous unpublished plays for stage, radio and television the best-known in Australia is the stage play, 'The Zelda Trio', produced in Melbourne in 1961 and London in 1974. Collinson also contributed to the poetry collection *Eight by Eight* (1963) and was one of the editors of the magazine, *Barjai*.

Although Collinson, a Marxist, was criticized on publication of *The Moods of Love* for his treatment of social and political issues, he has always been more concerned with love and its disappointments, and with what he terms 'the self-destruction that pervades our personal and social lives', than with political themes. His interest in the formal aspects of poetry is especially reflected in his later verse, which is compressed and tightly-structured. The same concern with love, the limitations of conventional morality and the 'admass' culture can be found in his plays.

Colonial is a word which in Australia refers to the period between 1788, when the first British colony, NSW, was established, and 1901, when NSW and the other five colonies were federated to form the Commonwealth of Australia; thus a 'colonial' was an inhabitant of one of those colonies (particularly one whose allegiance was to the colony rather than Britain), and 'colonial architecture' is the architecture of the period. Compounds derived from 'colonial' include 'colonial goose (duck)', a boned and stuffed shoulder or leg of mutton, from the prevalence of mutton in the colonial period; 'my colonial oath', where 'colonial' is a euphemism for 'bloody', the Great Australian Adjective; and 'colonial experience(r)' (q.v.).

Colonial Experiencer was a phrase particularly used in the nineteenth century to describe a young, well-connected Englishman sent out to gain work experience in Australia. Enough colonial experiencers proved themselves new chums (q.v.) for the terms to be almost synonymous. The new chum's colonial experience is an important feature of nineteenth-century Australian drama, as in W.M. Akhurst's 'Colonial Experience' (1854) and Walter Cooper's *Colonial Experience* (1979, first performed 1868).

Colonial Literary Journal and Weekly Miscellany of Useful Information, edited by

James Reading and Francis Sandoe, appeared weekly in Sydney 1844–45. One of the earliest magazines to use illustrations, it included poetry, short stories, sketches and literary reviews and notices. Among its contributors were Charles Harpur and Daniel Deniehy.

Colonial Monthly, successor to the *Australian Monthly Magazine,* was published 1867–70. For its first year it was edited by Marcus Clarke, whose novel *Long Odds* (two monthly instalments of which were written by G.A. Walstab) was serialized in it 1868–69. Three significant critical articles on Australian literature (a general account of the relationships between literature and national character, and separate analyses of Henry Kendall and Charles Harpur) appeared in the issues December 1868–February 1869. Contributors included David Blair, J.E. Neild, Adam Lindsay Gordon, R.H. Horne, Henry Kendall, James Smith and Julian Tenison Woods.

Colonial Reformer, A (1896), a novel by 'Rolf Boldrewood' (q.v.), was first published as a serial in the *Australian Town and Country Journal,* 1876–77. It chronicles the experience in Australia of the Buckinghamshire gentleman new chum (q.v.) Ernest Neuchamp, who is guided to success by a banker, Paul Frankston, and a squatter, Abstinens Levison, whom 'Boldrewood' modelled on James Tyson. Another character in the novel, the Reverend Herbert Heatherstone, is based on Cuthbert Fetherstonhaugh (q.v.).

Colonial Times and Tasmanian Advertiser was a journal that grew out of the battle for the freedom of the press in Tasmania, which was centred on the disputes between Andrew Bent and the lieutenant-governor of Van Diemen's Land, George Arthur (qq.v.). Incensed by criticism of his administration in Bent's *Hobart Town Gazette* in 1824–25, Arthur pirated Bent's title for his own newspaper, so that from June until August 1825 there were two *Hobart Town Gazettes* published in Hobart. Bent then changed the title of his journal to the *Colonial Times and Tasmanian Advertiser,* which he ran until 1830 although publication was briefly suspended after Bent was refused a licence under Arthur's new press legislation in 1827. In 1829 the *Colonial Times* serialized *The Hermit in Van Diemen's Land,* for which Bent was prosecuted for libel. The following year he sold the newspaper to Henry Melville; other prominent journalists associated with the proprietorship or editorship of the paper were John Macdougall, R.L. Murray, Thomas Richards and Henry Savery. The *Colonial Times* incorporated the *Tasmanian and Austral-Asiatic Re-*

view (see *Tasmanian*) in 1845 and was itself incorporated into the *Mercury* in 1857.

Colonist, a Sydney weekly journal with some literary content, was published 1835–40; a regular contributor was John Dunmore Lang. A more general Launceston journal also named the *Colonist*, subtitled *A Weekly Journal for Town and Country*, ran 1888–91.

'Colonist, A', see MURRAY, R.W.F.L.

Columbus Goes West, see HART-SMITH, WILLIAM

Come In Spinner, a novel by Dymphna Cusack (q.v.) and Florence James, was published in 1951. Set in Sydney during the Second World War, the novel gives a vivid picture of the impact of American forces on the city and traces the fortunes of a group of girls, most of whom work in the beauty salon of the Hotel South-Pacific. They include Deborah Forrest, a masseuse whose husband Jack is with the Australian forces in New Guinea, and whose daughter Luen lives with Deborah's motherly sister, Nolly. For Deborah the war has presented new opportunities in the form of remarriage with the wealthy, but considerably older, Angus McFarland. Resentful of Jack's decision to resume their life of poverty in the country after the war and of his assumption that she will automatically follow where he leads, she eventually accepts Angus. Claire, the manageress of the salon, has a long-standing relationship with a weak but good-looking Englishman, Nigel, and looks forward to the time when they will have saved enough to marry. When Nigel loses their savings by gambling, she considers ending their relationship, but soon realizes that he is necessary to her happiness. The most lively, self-sufficient girl of the group, Guinea Malone, breezily circumvents all sexist and class barriers although her deep feeling for her first love, Kim, is at first frustrated by his immature chauvinism. Guinea eventually gains love on her terms and Nolly appears to have found fulfilment in her large family. Dallas MacIntyre, a surgeon whose professional life has flourished in the absence of men, is another who finds life satisfying. But others succumb to the emotional and physical dangers of wartime Sydney; they include Guinea's younger sister Monnie, who is trapped into a brief life in a brothel, and Mary Parker, an AWAS and the mistress of an American soldier, who dies as the result of an abortion. The more conventional losses of war are reflected in the life of Val, whose husband is posted as missing shortly after their marriage. Contrasting with these destinies are the aimless,

exploitative existences of several wealthy women such as Mrs D'Arcy-Twyning and her obnoxious daughter Denise, and the overweight society matron, Mrs Dalgety.

Comic Australian Verse (1972), edited by Geoffrey Lehmann, contains 220 poems or extracts of poems, beginning with an anonymous epitaph on a headstone at St Matthews cemetery, Windsor, NSW, and concluding with three poems by Bruce Dawe. Lehmann notes the importance of humorous verse as a literary form in the nineteenth century and its relative demise in modern times. The *Bulletin* is the chief source of his nineteenth-century selections; A.B. Paterson, W.T. Goodge and Joseph Tishler ('Bellerive') are his chief representatives from the early twentieth century; later poets represented are A.D. Hope, Douglas Stewart, Kenneth Slessor, Ronald McCuaig and Bruce Dawe.

Coming of Stork, The, see WILLIAMSON, DAVID

Comment, A, a magazine devoted to experimental writing, was published irregularly in Melbourne 1940–47. Australian contributors included Max Harris, Alister Kershaw, Muir Holburn and Arthur Ashworth; the work of prominent overseas avant-garde writers, e.g. Harry Roskolenko and Karl Shapiro, was also featured.

Commonwealth: An Annual of Australian Art & Literature, The, was published 1901–02 by A.C. Rowlandson. George Essex Evans's acrostic poem 'The Commonwealth' was used on the opening page of the first edition. The magazine made a brief reappearance in 1907–08 as *Rowlandson's Success*.

Commonwealth Literary Fund, the first systematic federal government initiative in support of the arts, was established by the Alfred Deakin government in 1908; its model was the Royal Literary Fund (UK) and its original allocation was £500. For its first thirty years the CLF, as it came to be known, was administered by a central committee comprising representatives from NSW, SA and Victoria with advisers in the other States, and awarded pensions to sick and distressed authors and their families, the families of authors who had died poor, and literary men doing good work but 'unable on account of poverty to persist in that work'. In 1939, after agitation by the former prime minister J.H Scullin and by the FAW, the budget of the Fund, then £1500, was trebled and this enabled the Fund eventually to embrace four additional activities: the award of annual fellowships and other grants to writers; assistance to publishers through a guarantee against loss on Australian literary works approved by the Fund; assistance to literary journals such as *Meanjin, Southerly, Overland* and *Quadrant;* and the promotion of Australian literature, notably through annual lectures in the universities (1940–64) and lectures in regional centres. The broadening in scope of the CLF was accompanied by a change in administrative structure: the central committee was replaced by a parliamentary committee comprising initially the prime minister, R.G. Menzies, the leader of the Opposition, John Curtin, and Scullin, and eventually a representative of the three major political parties in the federal parliament; and by an advisory board which included writers, academics and, later, publishing interests. Sir Langdon Bonython, Sir Mungo MacCallum, (qq.v.), Sir A. Grenfell Price, Vance Palmer, T. Inglis Moore, Douglas Stewart and Geoffrey Blainey had significant terms in the administrations of the CLF, which had increased its budget to $300 000 by the time its functions were taken over by the Literature Board (q.v.) in 1973. In its first thirty years the CLF could do little more than ameliorate the lot of writers and their dependants who had fallen on hard times; in its second phase it played a significant part in the development of Australian literature through its scheme of fellowships and through its publishing and promotional activities. A brief history of the CLF by Grenfell Price, *Helping Literature in Australia,* was published in 1967.

Commonwealth Poetry Prize, an annual award, is administered jointly by the Commonwealth Institute and the National Book League. It is awarded for a first published book of poetry in English from a country other than the United Kingdom. Australian winners of the prize, first awarded in 1972, were Timoshenko Aslanides (1978), Phillip Salom (1981) and Peter Goldsworthy (1982).

Community Arts Board, one of the seven arts boards of the Australia Council (q.v.), was established in 1977; before that community arts came within the ambit of the Council's own programmes. The Board's annual allocation is distributed in support of multi-arts programmes (including literature) implemented by community arts organizations; in 1978–83 its largest grant went to the Arts Council of Australia (q.v.) but it has also supported organizations and individuals catering for the needs of regional, ethnic, suburban and disadvantaged communities.

Compass, the journal of the Melbourne University literature club, was published irregularly 1956–63. Originally intended as a workshop journal publishing experimental undergraduate creative writing, *Compass* included among its early contributors now-established figures such as Chris Wallace-Crabbe and Bruce Dawe. Among its editors have been the poets Wallace-Crabbe, Clive Faust and Andrew Taylor.

Compliqués, Les, a club for literati and intellectuals, originated in Sydney during the First World War. It met for lunch and French conversation at Paris House in Phillip Street, a well-known Sydney restaurant of the day. A notable member of the group was Christopher Brennan.

COMPTON, JENNIFER (1949–), born NZ, came to Australia in 1973. Her play *Crossfire,* also produced as 'No Man's Land' (1976), shared first place with John Romeril's *The Floating World* in a 1974 Newcastle playwriting competition and was first produced in 1975. Another play, *They're Playing Our Song,* first produced in 1975, is included in the collection *Can't You Hear Me Talking to You?* (1978) ed. Alrene Sykes. Her other plays include 'Adolf', 'All Good Children Go to Heaven' and 'Stream of Consciousness'; she has also written for television and radio.

Concrete Poetry conceives of the poem as ideogram, as an instantly assimilable, visually-ordered text in which the word stands both as physical spatial object and as a plurality of simultaneous meanings. Said to have originated with the publication of *Konstellationen* in 1953 by the Bolivian-born Swiss poet, Eugen Gomringer, concrete poetry was evident in Australia in the 1960s but became more widespread in the 1970s with the growth of the little magazines. The all-concrete magazine *Born to Concrete* (q.v.) evolved in 1975 from *Fitzrete,* which was an all-concrete issue of *Fitzrot* (1975–77), which itself had developed as an outlet for concrete poetry under the leadership of Peter Oustabasidis ('Pi O', q.v.). Other modernist magazines and journals, e.g. *Dharma, Magic Sam, New Poetry, The Saturday Club Book of Poetry, SCOPP* and *Your Friendly Fascist,* have published concrete poetry. Australian poets, e.g. Oustabasidis, Peter Murphy, Garrie Hutchinson, B.A. Breen, Alex Selenitsch and Peter Taylor, have published concrete poetry volumes or sections of volumes.

Condamine River, discovered by Allan Cunningham in 1827 and named after T. de la Condamine, aide-de-camp to Governor Darling, flows through south-eastern Queensland. It is linked in the traditional song, 'The Banks of the Condamine' (q.v.), with male-oriented outback life. Cattle- and horse-bells made at the township of Condamine were hung around the necks of stock; the expression 'to lay the Condamine on' thus meant to put the bell on stock inclined to wander. Mary Gilmore, in *The Tilted Cart* (1925), indicated that it was a cruel practice for the note of the Condamine bell was so penetrating that it often made the animal deaf. The drover-poet Jack Sorenson wrote a poem 'Condamine Bells'; the bells are also mentioned in Vance Palmer's *Men Are Human* (1930). John Joseph Jones compiled '*Condamine Bells': Songs and Stories of the Australian Outback* (1961). K. Emmerson wrote *A History of the Condamine 1856–1963* (1963).

CONDER, CHARLES (1868–1909), born London, came to Australia in 1883. In 1885 he obtained a position on the *Illustrated Sydney News*. In 1888 with Tom Roberts, Frederick McCubbin and Arthur Streeton, Conder formed the well-known Heidelberg School (q.v.) of Australian painting. Biographical works on Conder include Frank Givson's *Charles Conder* (1914), J.K.M. Rothenstein's *Life and Death of Conder* (1938) and Ursula Hoff's *Charles Conder: His Australian Years* (1960). Charles Brydon, the painter in Kathleen Caffyn's novel *A Yellow Aster* (1894), is based on Conder.

Conditional Culture, see INGAMELLS, REX; Jindyworobak movement

Condolences of the Season (1971), the first selected volume of Bruce Dawe's (q.v.) poetry, was chosen by the author from the four earlier volumes, *No Fixed Address* (1962), *A Need of Similar Name* (1965), *An Eye for a Tooth* (1968) and *Beyond the Subdivisions* (1969); it also contains nineteen new poems. An extraordinarily popular collection, *Condolences of the Season* was reprinted annually 1971–80, except in 1974.

It contains many of Dawe's best-known poems: 'Public Library, Melbourne', 'Enter without So Much as Knocking', 'Happiness Is the Art of Being Broken', 'Any Shorter and I'd Have Missed It Altogether', 'The Not-so-good Earth', 'Life-Cycle', 'A Victorian Hangman Tells His Love', 'Homecoming', 'Homo Suburbiensis' and 'Weapons Training'.

Confederates, see KENEALLY, THOMAS

Conference-ville, a novella by Frank Moorhouse (q.v.), was published in 1976. A work which reflects Moorhouse's interest in the social dynamics of the conference, *Conference-ville* explores the Australian intellectual subculture as it chronicles the personal and group experiences

of the narrator (characteristically self-doubting yet self-aware) when he attends and presents a paper on the mass media at a conference early in 1976. Among the other participants are James McAuley, Frank Hardy and Stephen Murray-Smith.

Confessions of a Beachcomber, see BANFIELD, E.J.

Congewoi Correspondence, The (1874), purports to be the letters of a Hawkesbury farmer, John Smith, 'edited' by Charles de Boos (q.v.); in fact Smith was a character created in the Sydney press by de Boos in 1862. *The Congewoi Correspondence* comprises three series of letters, the first two satirizing members of the NSW parliament in office in 1862 and 1870, and the last consisting of Smith's impressions of the Duke of Edinburgh's visit to Sydney in 1868. The letters were originally published in the *Sydney Mail* and the *Sydney Morning Herald*. The humour of the volume derives from Smith's uneducated dialect and comic misspellings, which have been seen as an early form of 'Strine' (q.v.). Possible models for Smith are Sam Slick, a Nova Scotian character created in 1835 by the Canadian writer T.C. Haliburton, and the 1860s American frontier humoristphilosopher 'Artemus Ward' (C.F. Browne).

CONNOLLY, ROY (1896–1966), born Queensland, wrote an important pastoral novel, *Southern Saga* (1940). It traces the history of station life in the 1850s in the Burnett district of Queensland, and portrays the difficulty that a city-bred girl of fashion has in adapting to the harsh, unglamorous outback life. As it works towards a conventional happy ending, *Southern Saga* gives a full account of the activities and vicissitudes of pioneer pastoral life.

CONRAD, JOSEPH (1857–1924), the Polish-born English novelist, made several brief visits to Australia (1879, 1880, 1887 and 1892). In *Mirror of the Sea* (1906) he records his impressions of Sydney – its people, pleasures, personalities and especially its harbour ('one of the finest, most beautiful, vast and safe bays the sun ever shone upon'). Scattered throughout his novels and in his short story 'Because of the Dollars' are Australian references, usually expressing his 'affection for that young continent'. From his third voyage to Australia (1887) came the experiences which gave rise to the story *The Shadow Line* (1917) and which are echoed in 'The Secret Sharer' (1910) and 'The Planter of Malata' (1914). David Allen has written a play, 'Joseph Conrad goes Ashore'.

Contempa, a Melbourne illustrated magazine of poetry and prose, was published in two series. The first series of ten undated issues (1972–75) aimed 'to publish and encourage nascent writers, and where possible present them alongside more accomplished writers' and was edited by Phillip Edmonds and Robert Kenny. The second series (1975–   ) is also edited by Edmonds, who has written fiction, *Scientists Discover* (1977) and *Big Boys* (1978). Contempa Publications, also founded in 1972 by Kenny, Edmonds and Michael Dugan, has published works by contemporary writers such as Dugan, Colin Talbot, B.A. Breen, Walter Billeter, John Jenkins and Ken Taylor.

Contemporary American & Australian Poetry (1976), an anthology edited by Thomas Shapcott (q.v.), intersperses, mostly chronologically, the work of Australian and American poets; the Australian selection emphasizes the work of the younger writers. Shapcott's reasons for juxtaposing modern American and Australian poets in an anthology are that they are the product of English language cultures and originate from backgrounds with striking historical similarities despite important divergences.

Convict in Australian Literature. Transportation (q.v.) of convicts to the Australian colonies began in 1787 when the First Fleet (q.v.) left England for NSW, and continued until 1868 when the *Hougoumont* arrived in WA, numbering among its convict passengers John Boyle O'Reilly (q.v.), first WA novelist. In the eighty-one years of transportation approximately 160 000 convicts were sent to Australia, eighty per cent after 1820. They dominated the demography of the colonial settlements for more than fifty years, and although it was clear well before the discovery of gold in 1851 that Australia had a future other than as a giant gaol, the convict experience was crucial in the development of the Australian consciousness and has been of major significance to Australian historians and creative writers.

Transportation has also been of interest to writers overseas, which is not surprising given the British and Irish origins of the convicts, the decline in the eighteenth and nineteenth centuries of punishment as spectacle, and the corresponding rise of punishment through imprisonment; thus Marcus Clarke's *His Natural Life* (q.v., 1874) the most famous novel about the 'System', as it came to be called, is the product of a century which produced *Crime and Punishment, Little Dorrit* and *Les Misérables*. The famous lines,

True patriots all; for be it understood
We left our country for our country's good,

were written to amuse an English coterie by the journalist Henry Carter, who never set foot in Australia. Nor did Robert Southey, the author of 'Botany Bay Eclogues' (1794); 'William Thomas Moncrieff', the author of the play *Van Diemen's Land* (q.v., performed in London 1830); or Charles Dickens, who has convict characters in some of his novels. Southey's poem is significant both for the use of the 'Botany Bay' (q.v.) tag for NSW, and for the lamentation of the convict, Elinor, at her exile from England. The elegiac mood and the sense of exile are important ingredients in a street literature written for an English, Irish and Scottish audience throughout the transportation period; some of the songs, ballads, broadsides and later music-hall adaptations reached Australia to become part of local folk-song and ballad (q.v.). Other overseas writers who became interested in the Australian convicts include penal reformers such as Charles Reade (q.v.), investigators of the plight of the urban poor such as Henry Mayhew, and journalists seemingly interested only in the sensational potential of the transportation material, such as George Augustus Sala (q.v.). The willingness of Reade and Mayhew to include Australian material even though their main interest was in reforming English prisons or in exposing the condition of the London working class is complemented by such novels as *Ralph Rashleigh* (q.v., 1952) and *The Broad Arrow* (q.v., 1859), which for significant parts of their narratives are set in the streets of London or in the prisons and hulks preceding transportation. The voyage to the penal settlement produced a body of writing that establishes a link between convict literature and the voyager theme in Australian poetry and prose. There are voyage sections in most memoirs of convicts (who kept collective journals on some ships), and in many convict novels (e.g. *His Natural Life*). In addition, the voyage is the focus of reminiscences of officials employed aboard the ships (e.g. the surgeon Colin Arrott Browning, author of *The Convict Ship, and England's Exiles*, 1847); several strongly-worded complaints by convicts about their treatment by those officials (see Scottish Martyrs); and several novels and plays written after the cessation of transportation (e.g. William Gosse Hay's *Stifled Laughter*, 1901; Jill Shearer's play, *Catherine*, 1977; Thomas Keneally's *Passenger*, q.v., 1979).

Despite the overseas interest in transportation, the Australian contribution to convict literature remains dominant; and given transportation as the major reason for the First Fleet settlement, all early Australian writing in a broad sense forms part of convict literature: the diaries, annals and journals kept by the officers of the NSW Corps; official documents such as the *New South Wales General Standing Orders* (q.v., 1802), the first Australian 'book'; the despatches and enclosures forwarded by successive governors to the Colonial Office and included in the *Historical Records of New South Wales* and the *Historical Records of Australia* (qq.v.); and the early newspapers and other publications printed and edited by convicts and emancipists such as George Howe and Andrew Bent. Studded throughout this historical material, which was a source for later writers such as 'Price Warung' (q.v.), are references to some convicts (e.g. Michael Massey Robinson, Edward Geoghegan, Henry Savery and James Tucker) who became known in Australian literature.

In the narrower sense, however, convict literature begins with the convict memoirs, which were sometimes 'ghosted' or invented (e.g. the publications associated with George Barrington, q.v.) and start to trickle from colonial and English presses after 1810. The end of transportation did not mean the end of these memoirs, for Mark Jeffrey's *A Burglar's Life* was published in 1893 and there have been recent publications (e.g. Thomas Cook's horrendous *The Exile's Lamentations*, 1978) in the historically-conscious 1970s and 1980s. The memoirs usually conform to three sometimes overlapping formulae. The rogue's picaresque adventure is exemplified by the *Memoirs* of the sleazy entertainer, James Hardy Vaux (q.v.), who is significant as probably the only convict thrice transported to Australia and whose autobiography, the first full-length one written in the Colony, includes a slang vocabulary which is an important source for the study of Australian English. The second and largest group of memoirs, but the least distinguished as literature, comprises the moral tales, sometimes mere pamphlets, of the child of respectable parents who is led astray by bad companions, suffers great physical hardship and emotional anguish during transportation, but returns to the native land to issue a suitable warning to recalcitrant youth. Thirdly, there are the memoirs written by the political prisoners despatched by an offended English government through its legal system to Australia from Scotland, Ireland, Wales and even England itself (e.g. the Scottish Martyrs, John Mitchel, John Frost, the Canadian Exiles, George Loveless, qq.v.). The political prisoners were largely literate, well-educated men and their memoirs are significant because of their disproportionate number – only about a thousand political prisoners were transported to Australia – and because they form part of other national literatures.

Whether for motives of sensation, instruction or protest, the memoirs characteristically assert the innocence or underplay the culpability of the writer, as well as accentuating his suffering in Australia. The guiltless, suffering convicts of the memoirs helped to establish the legend, which has much credence still, that the convicts were 'more sinn'd against than sinning'. Another influence on the development of this legend was the transportation songs and ballads which reached Australia or were modified or composed here. Where the cause of transportation is stated, the most common offence is poaching (e.g. 'Jim Jones at Botany Bay', q.v.) and even when the offenders are from the cities they have often been tricked into crime (e.g. 'The Black Velvet Band', q.v.). In Australia the dismal experiences of the convict are highlighted so that the songs become protest songs, lamentations of the downtrodden (e.g. 'Van Diemen's Land'), occasionally mixed with the threat of revolt (e.g. 'Jim Jones at Botany Bay' and 'Moreton Bay', q.v.). In fact there were not many acts of open rebellion by convicts in Australia, although Vinegar Hill (q.v.) has produced a literature and 'A Convict's Tour to Hell' (q.v.) stands as a form of literary revenge for all downtrodden convicts. The fact that 'Bold Jack Donahoe' is one of the heroes of 'A Convict's Tour to Hell' and of 'Jim Jones at Botany Bay' confirms the link in much early Australian literature between the convict and the bushranger (see Bushranger in Australian Literature). For example, in the first Australian play performed overseas, David Burn's *The Bushrangers* (q.v., performed 1829, published 1971), Matthew Brady and his associates are designated 'Convicts and Bushrangers' and Burn bitterly attacks the penal administration of Governor Arthur (q.v.); Mark Brandon, the protagonist of Charles Rowcroft's *The Bushranger of Van Diemen's Land* (1843), is an escaped convict (like most early bushrangers); and *Ralph Rashleigh* has an important interlude in which Ralph is the unwilling member of a bushranging gang of escaped convicts. These works were all written before 1850, yet the links between convict and bushranging literature continued to be forged after the cessation of transportation, e.g. in Ned Kelly's reference to 'Moreton Bay' in the Jerilderie Letter (q.v.).

Ralph Rashleigh, almost certainly written in 1845–50 by the convict James Tucker, is a text which links not only convict and bushranging literature but also convict fiction and the convict memoirs; indeed it was presented as a convict memoir when first published in abridged form in 1929. Two other major novels which are informed by their authors' experiences as convicts are Savery's *Quintus Servinton* (q.v., 1831), and O'Reilly's *Moondyne* (q.v., 1879). Although in structure each corresponds to a different memoir formula – *Ralph Rashleigh* to the picaresque, *Quintus Servinton* to the moral tale and *Moondyne* to the socio-political protest – they are alike in that each is a kind of 'literary wish fulfilment': *Ralph Rashleigh,* in that it projects a convict's attempt to come to terms with and free himself physically and spiritually of the effects of transportation; *Quintus Servinton,* in the loyalty offered to the recalcitrant Quintus by his wife Emily, which contrasts with the desertion of Savery by his wife after she saw at first hand his real situation in Australia; and *Moondyne* in the idealized portrait of the convict-turned-gentleman, Wyville, who succeeds in reforming a system about which O'Reilly felt so strongly.

The confrontation with the issue of penal reform which occurs in *Moondyne,* a major theme also in Caroline Leakey's *The Broad Arrow,* looks back to the great debates about transportation in the years after 1820. Among the issues were the question of whether the labourers of the Colony should be convicts or freemen and, particularly in the 1830s, whether transportation, which had become more 'systematized' following the reports of J.T. Bigge (q.v.), should itself be abolished. In a period which also saw fundamental press liberties secured in NSW and Van Diemen's Land, a polemical prose literature emerged in which the convicts became ambivalent figures. At one extreme, they were 'branches lopp'd for their rottenness from the tree of British freedom', as James Mudie called them in *The Felonry of New South Wales* (1837); at the other, they were innocent exiles undergoing *The Horrors of Transportation* (1838), as William Bede Ullathorne titled his anti-System treatise. Stern defences of transportation were offered by some writers (e.g. George Arthur) but a seemingly greater proportion of writers either opposed the continuation of transportation or desired its reformation. Some writers (e.g. John Dunmore Lang, q.v.) argued for the abolition of transportation mainly from a concern for the moral welfare of free settlers or from a belief in the future of the colonies, but most abolitionists or reformers were sympathetic to convict suffering, including James Backhouse, Alexander Maconochie, Henry Melville, W.B. Ullathorne (qq.v.) and, perhaps most influential of all the opponents of transportation, Richard Whately (q.v.), whose writings provoked replies not only from Arthur but also from Arthur's own critic, David Burn. The significant proportion of antitransportation material published in 1837–38 is linked with the exhaustive review of transportation undertaken in those years by a select committee of the British parliament. The committee's report and minutes of evidence, usually called the Molesworth Report after its chairman, Sir William Molesworth (1810–55), is a famous specimen of convict literature which

confirms the brutalities which the System perpetrated at its worst. Like other parliamentary papers concerned with transportation, and the polemical writings of crusaders such as Whately, these publications became sources to be tapped by later writers, e.g. Marcus Clarke in *His Natural Life* or 'Price Warung', who used Whately's reference to Norfolk Island as an 'Isle of Death' as the title for his last series of stories. The Molesworth Report helped to abolish transportation to NSW; subsequent attempts to revive it provided the occasions for such writings as Charles Harpur's 'The Proposed Recurrence of Transportation', William Forster's satire 'The Genius and the Ghost', and other poems. Transportation continued, however, and led to the swamping of Tasmania with convicts in the 1840s and in the same period to the use of Norfolk Island and Port Arthur (q.v.) as penitentiaries for long-term or colonially-reconvicted prisoners. The high proportion of Tasmanian convicts helps to explain why the island is the setting for much of the literature written about the convicts. The use of Port Arthur and Norfolk Island led to the worst excesses of transportation, particularly after the recall of Maconochie from Norfolk Island and his replacement by Joseph Childs (the model for 'Warung''s arch-villain, Commandant Scragge) and John Price (q.v.), the model for Maurice Frere in *His Natural Life*. Norfolk Island and Tasman's Peninsula as natural paradises turned into man-made Hells, and the desire of many convicts to commit capital crimes in order to earn their freedom from a 'worse than death' existence (as Dawes seeks to do under Frere), became literary commonplaces from the 1840s.

The 'prose of controversy', as H.M. Green termed the polemical literature about transportation, largely ended with the cessation of transportation to the eastern colonies. In ensuing decades, the first important colonial histories were written by G.B. Barton, David Blair, William Howitt, Thomas McCombie, George Rusden, John West, William Westgarth (qq.v.) and others. With the notable exception of West's *History of Tasmania* (1852), which contains a savage indictment of transportation, the convicts are conspicuously absent from these histories; the desire to avoid embarrassing those of convict or gaoler descent, and the desire to emphasize colonial progress have been advanced as the reasons. It was in – and partly because of – this climate of silence that convict literature became more and more the province of the creative writer, particularly in fiction and drama. Most importantly, it was the period which saw the publication of the major anti-System novels and stories – *The Broad Arrow, His Natural Life, Moondyne* and 'Warung''s *Tales of the Convict System* (1892), *Tales of the*

Early Days (1894), *Tales of the Old Regime* (1897), and *Tales of the Isle of Death* (1898) – which by their popularity helped to consolidate the convict legend within the Australian consciousness. *His Natural Life,* it has been claimed, was to be found in every cottage in Australia; *The Broad Arrow* and *Moondyne* each went through several editions (*Moondyne* at the rate of one a year in its first dozen years), and 'Warung' was the most prolific contributor of stories to the *Bulletin* in the 1890s. These works are in part the fictional equivalents of the contributions to the prose of controversy by the abolitionists of the 1830s. Whatever questions they explore beyond transportation, they are texts which explicitly confront the System and condemn it; as Clarke writes in his preface to *His Natural Life,* the novel is intended to demonstrate the 'inexpediency of again allowing offenders against the law to be herded together in places remote from the wholesome influence of public opinion'. 'Warung' went further than Clarke in insisting on the accuracy of his historical interpretation of convictism to strengthen the political message of his stories, which were written in support of the republican anti-English stance of the *Bulletin* and its editor, J.F. Archibald. For Archibald, as much as for 'Warung', the legacy of the past could be detected in the sustained brutality of the penal code and in the corruption endemic in politics and business life in the 1880s and 1890s. A second group of novels published 1850–1900 focuses on but exploits rather than confronts or condemns transportation. In this tradition of fiction, which encompasses John Lang's (q.v.) *Botany Bay* (1855) and *The Forger's Wife* (1859), James Hebblethwaite's *Castle Hill* (1895), and E.W. Hornung's *The Rogue's March* (1896), the interpretation offered of the System seems less important to a reader than the author's desire to harness the potential for excitement, romance or adventure inherent in the subject.

In drama, convicts gave the first theatrical performance in Australia (*The Recruiting Officer,* 1789), briefly ran the first theatre in 1796, and conducted the activities of the Emu Plains theatre from the 1820s to the 1840s (as *Ralph Rashleigh* depicts). The government licensing of plays in NSW resulted in few convict as well as bushranging plays in the first decades after the cessation of transportation, but in the 1870s the convict emerged in the Anglo-Australian melodramas of George Darrell and later in the repertoires of Alfred Dampier and Dan Barry (qq.v.); in 1882 Barry was arrested in Sale as a prison escapee when he dressed up as a convict to advertise a performance. The melodrama tradition emphasized the triumph of virtue over vice; the necessity to reconcile this

tradition with the emerging convict legend probably explains why the convict as villain is increasingly replaced on the stage from the 1870s onwards by the convict who has been wrongly convicted or transported, as in Darrell's first Australian play, 'Transported for Life' (performed 1877), and in the many stage adaptations of *His Natural Life,* an outstanding theatrical success from the 1880s into the 1920s. As well, in many melodramas not specifically about transportation, the convict or ex-convict became one of the stock characters alongside his cousin the bushranger, the new chum (q.v.) and the remittance man. This second use of the convict, as a character who is an incidental part of the fabric of colonial society and history, can be placed within a literary tradition stretching back to the fiction of Charles Rowcroft and Alexander Harris. Both authors have convict characters or explicitly discuss the issue of transportation, e.g. Rowcroft in *Tales of the Colonies* (1843), Harris in *Settlers and Convicts* (1847) and *The Emigrant Family* (1849), the last dedicated to Maconochie in admiration of his work in penal reform. Yet both are also catalogued as 'guide-book' novelists interested more in the emigrant's total experience than specifically in any one of those experiences; indeed, *Tales of the Colonies* is less significant in convict literature than in the study of the Aboriginal in Australian literature. If Harris and Rowcroft can be said to have inaugurated a tradition, then between 1850 and 1900 it is continued in other fictional works. These works include emigration novels (e.g. Henry Kingsley's *The Hillyars and the Burtons,* 1865); the first generation of historical novels and romances to look back on the early period of Australian history and embrace the convict experience as part of a broader historical sweep (e.g. Mary Vidal's *Bengala: Or Some Time Ago,* 1860; Charles de Boos's *Fifty Years Ago,* 1867; Eliza Winstanley's *Twenty Straws,* 1864); and an increasing number of popular works in which convictism is only one of a number of staple or sensational ingredients (e.g. Carlton Dawe's *The Golden Lake,* 1891). There are also novels which make use of ex-convict characters for the purposes of plot construction (e.g. Hume Nisbet's sensational *Dr Bernard St. Vincent,* 1889); or character motivation (as in *Robbery Under Arms,* 1888, where Ben Marston, an old lag, is naturally inclined towards cattle-duffing); or to distinguish between English and Australian types (as in *The Recollections of Geoffry Hamlyn,* 1859).

The inevitable overlap between these traditions of convict fiction is demonstrated by the fact that to a significant extent they all embrace the melodramatic, a consequence of the System's concern with the extremes of human behaviour. Yet for all the blurring of distinctions, it is possible to consider the convict in Australian literature after 1900 in terms of the three major traditions. Thus the Lang tradition (the literary works which focus on the convict experience but which are less concerned with interpreting that experience than in mining its narrative, dramatic, sensational or other literary potential) is continued in literally dozens of novels, many intended for a popular market. These include William Hay's early romances (*Stifled Laughter*, 1901; *Herridge of Reality Swamp*, q.v., 1907) and even, arguably, *The Escape of the Notorious Sir William Heans* (q.v.,1919); several of the New South Wales Bookstall Company's 'pulps' (e.g. Roy Bridges's *The Barb of an Arrow*, 1909, and *Mr. Barrington*, 1911; J.B. Cooper's *Leg-Bail*, 1916; Ambrose Pratt's *Her Assigned Husband*, 1916; and James Devaney's *The Currency Lass*, 1927); and several recent works among them Richard Butler's *The Men That God Forgot* (1975) and *Against the Wind* (1978), Colin Free's *Vinegar Hill* (1978), Yoram Gross's children's book *The Little Convict* (1979), and Frank Baron Kreffl's projected trilogy *Con, Vic* and *Ted* (1979) (equals 'convicted'). The tradition incorporates some of the radio plays of the 1940s and is paralleled by many of the early silent films including adaptations of *His Natural Life* (1908, 1911, 1927), *It Is Never Too Late to Mend* (1911) and *Moondyne* (1913), and by some of the film and television series of the 1970s and 1980s (*Journey Among Women, Against the Wind, For the Term of His Natural Life*).

If the Lang tradition has continued, the Rowcroft-Harris tradition (in which the convict experience forms only an intrinsic or incidental part of the subject matter or themes of the work) has positively flourished. The novels that form part of such a tradition can be numbered not in dozens but in hundreds, and include several multivolume historical sagas which embrace the transportation period. A notable example, and one of the major achievements in Australian historical fiction, is Eleanor Dark's trilogy, *The Timeless Land* (q.v., 1941), *Storm of Time* (1948) and *No Barrier* (1953), which has been greatly admired for the imaginative entrance it permits into the early days of settlement. Among other series are the Hobart-Richmond series of Roy Bridges, a group of six novels published 1927–33 which offer an interpretation of Tasmanian society from the 1830s to the 1850s, Doris Chadwick's children's triology *John of the 'Sirius'* (1955), *John of Sydney Cove* (1957) and *John and Nanbaree* (1962); and Vivian Stuart's recent romances. The single-volume novels which encompass the transportation period range from the more 'respectable' historical novels such as J.H.M. Ab-

bot's *The Governor's Man* (1919), *Castle Vane* (1920), *Ensign Calder* (1922) and *Sydney Cove* (1923), 'M. Barnard Eldershaw''s *A House Is Built* (1929), Helen Simpson's *Under Capricorn* (1937), 'G.B. Lancaster''s *Pageant* (1933), Nancy Cato's *North-West by South* (1965), and Patrick White's *A Fringe of Leaves* (1976) and *Voss* (1957); to the historical romances such as Catherine Gaskin's *Sara Dane* (1954) and Ernestine Hill's *My Love Must Wait* (1941); down to the followers of Carlton Dawe using convictism as an ingredient for a mass market concoction (e.g. Nat Gould in *King of the Ranges*, 1902). The Rowcroft-Harris tradition has also lived on in several radio plays and in the historical costume-dramas seen so often on Australian television (e.g. Rex Rienits's *Stormy Petrel* in 1960).

The third and most important tradition, the Clarke tradition (comprising the major literary works which in 1850–1900 explicitly confronted the System), has undergone an interesting modification in the twentieth century. As the convict period has receded further into the past, twentieth-century writers have focused their attention less on an indictment of the System (although that is one of the purposes of David Hennessey in his 1913 novel, *The Outlaw*, and Stuart Macky in his convict plays) than on the exploration of its meaning for and beyond contemporary Australian society. The general direction to be taken was signposted in the stories of 'Warung', who in the 1890s was preoccupied with the legacy of the past. Similarly preoccupied, though in the 1930s, was Brian Penton (q.v.), whose polemical *Think or Be Damned* (1941) set out to dispel some national myths, and who in *Landtakers* (q.v., 1934) and *Inheritors* (1936) embarked on a revaluation of Australian history in which the convict experience is seen as significant in the development of the national psyche. In another historically-conscious age, the 1970s, Ron Blair's 'Flash Jim Vaux' stands as one of the earliest plays in which the local melodramatic tradition of the late nineteenth century was revived, but with a difference: plays like 'Flash Jim Vaux' are satiric slices of history designed not merely to return their audience to the past but also to look sideways at the contemporary political scene. If the tone of 'Flash Jim Vaux' is consistently light-hearted, that mood is conspicuously absent from R.D. FitzGerald's poem, 'The Wind at Your Door' (q.v., 1958). The poem explores FitzGerald's response to his discovery that an ancestor, Martin Mason, was a penal official in attendance at a particularly brutal flogging of a convict who shared the poet's surname. The conclusion he reaches is to accept that the convict and the ancestor, the brutalized and the brutalizer, are both victims of the System. FitzGerald's major source, the 1838 memoirs of Joseph Holt, was used for a similar purpose by Thomas Keneally in *Passenger*. Holt, 'the one who would not watch' the flogging in 'The Wind at Your Door', is also one of the 'gentry from the aft cabins' on board the *Minerva* in Keneally's novel. The journey of the *Minerva* to Australia provides Keneally with an important metaphoric parallel for the modern journey of his main passenger, Sal FitzGerald's foetus-narrator, towards birth. The foetus identifies himself with another passenger on the *Minerva*, Maurice FitzGerald, who is not only the victim of 'The Wind at Your Door' but also the ancestor of Sal's husband. Through the foetus/FitzGerald identification, Keneally establishes the same kind of link between the present and the past that is explored in 'The Wind at Your Door' and also in his more explicitly convict novel, *Bring Larks and Heroes* (1967), which Keneally has described as a 'parable for the present'. The protagonist of *Bring Larks and Heroes*, Phelim Halloran, is an outsider destroyed by a society whose 'systems' – civil, military and religious – do not adequately serve the needs of the individual. The point of the parable, several commentators have suggested, is the spiritual emptiness of Australian society, which has developed an effective machinery for crushing individual initiative.

Although it might be tempting to see as evolutionary the process by which writers like Penton, Blair, FitzGerald and Keneally have moved Australian literature away from a confrontation with the historical phenomenon of transportation and towards an appropriation of its symbolic or metaphoric possibilities, the symbolic and metaphoric possibilities of the System have always been present. *His Natural Life* does more than merely confront and condemn the System: it also, and more broadly, explores man's capacity for evil. Similarly, one reason why some convict novels are difficult to classify according to any single tradition is partly because such classifications do not accommodate their thematic, metaphoric and stylistic complexity; Hal Porter's richly-textured *The Tilted Cross* (q.v., 1961) and the mixture of contrived romance, historical costumery and subtle exploration of evil that comprises *The Escape of the Notorious Sir William Heans*, are two such texts. Among more recent novels, Patrick White's *A Fringe of Leaves* is surprisingly considered as a convict novel even though White in his own way is as opportunistic in his use of the convict experience as any New South Wales Bookstall novelist. The convicts in the novel, in the words of L.T. Hergenhan (*Unnatural Lives: Studies in Australian Fiction about the Convicts*, 1983) provide an 'ambience

of imprisonment' and are a reference point in relation to which Ellen Roxburgh's attempt to effect a spiritual escape are measured. Similarly, the convict system is recalled in a novel about modern Systems, David Ireland's *The Unknown Industrial Prisoner* (1971), in which the workers have marks on their legs where the irons have chafed their ancestors.

Finally, it is impossible either to say how Australian literature would have been different without the convict experience, or to quantify the effect of that experience on the Australian creative imagination. What can be said is that alienation, exile, imprisonment, the search for freedom and the legacy of the past are all recurring themes in convict literature and perhaps, partly because of this, important themes in Australian literature generally.

Convict Oath is the oath of allegiance between convicts which begins

> Hand to hand
> On Earth, in Hell,
> Sick or Well
> On Sea on Land
> On the Square, ever.

Much quoted by historians as evidence of mateship, it first appeared in 'Price Warung''s (q.v.) story, 'The Liberation of the First Three', in which three convicts kill three other convicts with whom they have been chained; in the sequel, 'The Liberation of the Other Three', the irony is completed when the three survivors kill each other. Although the Convict Oath may have been 'Warung''s invention, there is evidence to suggest that it came to him through oral tradition.

Convict Once (1871) is a long narrative poem by James Brunton Stephens (q.v.). It has an intricate, melodramatic plot which revolves around a beautiful *femme fatale* – a 'convict once' but now a governess – who becomes romantically involved with several men but dies before disaster overtakes all concerned. Heavily ornate, and outmoded in its elevated literary tone, the poem at times conveys an impressive air of gravity and grace. Highly valued by contemporary critics, who regarded it as Stephens's most significant literary work, it has been largely ignored in recent years.

'Convict's Lament on the Death of Captain Logan, A', see 'Moreton Bay'

'Convict's Tour to Hell, A', a witty long poem in rhyming couplets, was written by 'Frank the Poet' (see MacNamara, Francis) probably in 1839 at Stroud, NSW. Modelled on the satires of Jonathan Swift, who attended school in Kilkenny (where MacNamara committed the offence which led to his transportation), 'A Convict's Tour to Hell' chronicles Frank's tour of the underworld, where he discovers that notorious penal administrators such as Captain Logan and Governor Darling are suffering the kind of hellish punishments that they inflicted on the convicts. At the end of the poem, just after Frank is admitted into Heaven, he awakens to find that he has been dreaming. There is evidence that 'A Convict's Tour to Hell', which is also known as 'The Convict's Dream' and 'Frank's Tour of Hell', was popular among the more incorrigible convicts. Parts of the poem are quoted in 'Price Warung''s (q.v.) story of the chain gangs, 'The Ross Gang 'Yarner'-Ship'.

CONWAY, RONALD VICTOR (1927–), psychologist and journalist, published *The Great Australian Stupor* (1971) and *Land of the Long Weekend* (1978), controversial views of the Australian character and environment.

Coo-ee, a penetrating shout used by those in the bush to denote their own whereabouts or to seek an indication of the whereabouts of others, has become a recognized feature of Australian bush life. Daniel Southwell, an officer in the First Fleet, in a letter 27 July 1790, referred to an expression 'coe' used by the Aborigines meaning 'come hither'. Governor Hunter in the vocabulary of the Port Jackson Aborigines given in his *An Historical Journal of the Transactions at Port Jackson* (1793) spells the word 'cowee'. The Aborigines appear to have derived the expression from the call of the koel cuckoo, sometimes termed the 'cooee bird'. Peter Cunningham in *Two Years in New South Wales* (1827) indicates that the call was then in general use among the white settlers. The word has been used in the titles of numerous Australian books and anthologies in order to indicate an Australian flavour, e.g. *Cooee: Tales of Australian Life by Australian Ladies* (1891) by Harriette Anne Martin; *Coo-oo-ee: A Tale of Bushmen from Australia to Anzac* (1916) by J.B. Cooper; and *The Coo-ee Call: Dedicated to the Men in Khaki* (1917) by M.W. James. 'Cooee: Or, Wild Days in the Bush Forty Years Ago' (1906) was a popular stage melodrama by E.W. O'Sullivan. Henry Lawson uses 'coo-ee' to superb effect in the opening verse of his poem 'Jack Cornstalk':

I met with Jack Cornstalk in London today,
He saw me and coo-eed from over the way.
The solemn-faced Londoners stared at Long Jack,
At his hat, and his height, and the breadth of his back.

Then he coo-eed again (and his voice was not low)
And – there's not room to coo-ee in London, you know.

Although the expression 'within cooee' meant literally to be within shouting distance (upwards of three kilometres on a still night) of the place or person desired and is used in that sense in Lawson's poem 'The Shanty on the Rise' and in 'Henry Handel Richardson''s *The End of a Childhood* (1934), it also has a metaphorical meaning, i.e. close to but not exactly on the mark; its rather derisory antithesis 'not within cooee' means to be widely astray in judgement.

Coo-ee: Tales of Australian Life by Australian Ladies (c. 1891), an Anglo-Australian anthology edited in England by Harriette Anne Martin (Mrs Patchett Martin), includes fiction by Jessie Couvreur, Kathleen Caffyn, Rosa Praed and the editor.

Cook, Alf, see *One Day of the Year, The*

COOK, Captain JAMES (1728–79), born at Marton-in-Cleveland, near Middlesbrough, Yorkshire, lived much of his young life at Staithes and Whitby, in close proximity to the sea. Briefly an apprentice shopkeeper, he became indentured at fifteen on the coal ships of John Walker of Whitby. He entered the Royal Navy as an able seaman in 1755, served in the Seven Years' War and, as master of HMS *Pembroke*, participated in the siege of Louisburg and the survey of the St Lawrence River that facilitated General Wolfe's capture of Quebec. Promoted to lieutenant in 1768, he was given command of HMS *Endeavour* in an expedition to Tahiti to observe the transit of the planet Venus and then to search for the Great South Land, the unknown continent (see Terra Australis) of the southern seas. Between October 1769 and March 1770, Cook chartered the coast of NZ. His decision to sail westward from NZ led to landfall at Point Hicks (now Cape Everard) on the Australian coast. Sailing northward, he reached Botany Bay (28 April 1770) and on 22 August 1770 at Possession Island, off the northern tip of Cape York Peninsula, named the whole of the east coast 'New South Wales' and took possession of it for Britain. Promoted to captain, Cook returned to search for the Great South Land in a second voyage (1772–75) with the ships *Resolution* and *Adventure* and by circumnavigating the globe at high southern latitudes confirmed that no southern continent other than New Holland existed. On his third voyage (1776–80), again in the *Resolution*, while attempting to find a passage from the Pacific to the Atlantic, Cook was killed by natives at Kealakekua Bay in the Hawaiian Islands. Contemporary accounts of Cook's voyages include John Hawkesworth's *An Account of the Voyages Undertaken by the Order of His Present Majesty for Making Discoveries in the Southern Hemisphere* (1773), Sydney Parkinson's *A Journal of a Voyage to the South Seas, in His Majesty's Ship, the Endeavour* (1773), G. Forster's *A Voyage Round the World in His Britannic Majesty's Sloop, Resolution, Commanded by Captain James Cook, During the Years 1772,3,4 and 5* (1777). Cook is the subject of numerous studies including Arthur Kitson's *Captain James Cook* (1907), G. Arnold Wood's *The Voyage of the Endeavour* (1926), R.T. Gould's *Captain Cook* (1935), Hugh Carrington's *Life of Captain Cook* (1939), John R. Muir's *The Life and Achievements of Captain James Cook* (1939), C. Lloyd's *Captain Cook* (1952), G.M. Badger's *Captain Cook* (1970), J.V.S. Megaw's (ed.) *Employ'd As a Discoverer* (1971), Gavin Kennedy's *The Death of Captain Cook* (1978) and Jillian Robertson's *The Captain Cook Myth* (1981). The most substantial work on Cook is, however, that of J.C. Beaglehole, who edited *The Journals of Captain Cook* in three volumes (1955, 1961, 1967) and wrote *Cook the Writer* (1970) and the definitive biography, *The Life of Captain James Cook* (1974).

Popular with poets, Cook was the subject of two sonnets by Barron Field in the *Sydney Gazette*, 22 March 1822, celebrating the unveiling of a tablet to commemorate the landing at Botany Bay in 1770, and he is mentioned in W.C. Wentworth's *Australasia* (1823). The newly-established University of Sydney selected 'Cook, Meditating on Australia's Future' as the subject for a prize poem in 1859 (won by William Yarrington and published 1908). Henry Kendall wrote four sonnets about Cook at Botany Bay, including the poetic recreation of the first landing, 'The Spot Where Cook Landed'. Roland Robinson ('Captain Cook') and Alan Frost ('Elizabeth to James Cook, August 1770') have also written poems on Cook, but the most important is Kenneth Slessor's 'Five Visions of Captain Cook' (q.v.). K.J. Prunty published *On a Picture of Captain James Cook R.N.: Selected Poems* (1979) and Lance Banbury *Captain James Cook: A Poetical Drama* (1981). Fictional treatments of Cook include Godfrey Blunden's *Charco Harbour* (1968), while in Henry Kingsley's *The Hillyars and the Burtons* (1865) part of the narrative is set in the Australian colony of Cooksland. A Cook tableau was included in Garnet Walch's pantomime *Hey Diddle Diddle* (1878), and in 1888 Alfred Dampier staged John Petry's 'The Life and Death of Captain Cook', a winner of a drama prize to celebrate the centenary. The

imaginative impact of Cook's voyages is the subject of the collection of essays edited by Walter Veit, *Captain James Cook, Image and Impact* (1972). Cook is commemorated in Australia by numerous places bearing his name – mountains, rivers, towns, streets, lighthouses – by a variety of statuary, by having his father's Yorkshire cottage transferred to Melbourne's Fitzroy Gardens, and by James Cook University at Townsville. He was also honoured in 1970 by the Cook Bicentenary literary competitions in Australia.

COOK, KENNETH (1929–), born Sydney, worked at first as a journalist but turned to full-time writing in 1960, shortly before the publication of his best-known novel, *Wake in Fright* (1961). A gripping account of a young teacher's nightmarish experience in an outback town of NSW, *Wake in Fright* was produced as a film in 1971. His musical stage play, *Stockade*, which centres on the Eureka Stockade, was first produced in 1971 and published in 1975. Fast-moving and interspersed with songs, *Stockade* is more sombre in mood and less of a spectacular entertainment than similar productions, e.g. *The Legend of King O'Malley*; central to the play is an extended debate on the question of the rule of law versus individual rights and the validity of violence. *Stockade* was produced as a film in 1971 and has been shown on television. Cook has published numerous novels, television plays, film scripts, documentaries and short stories, and as director of his own company has produced, written and appeared in numerous films, mostly for children's television.

Cook, Nellie, see *Cotters' England*

COOK, B.S. BAXTER, see **Australian Journalists' Association**

Cooley, Benjamin, see **LAWRENCE, D.H.**; *Kangaroo*

Coolgardie, a town in WA some 600 kilometres west of Perth, was the scene of a rich gold discovery in September 1892. It is featured in David Carnegie's *Spinifex and Sand* (1898) and its part in the gold rushes is described in Malcolm Uren's *Glint of Gold* (1948). Coolgardie is the leaping-off point for M.J. O'Reilly ('Mulga Mick') in his poem 'The Adams River Rush'; E.G. Murphy ('Dryblower'), one of the first employees of William Clare's newspaper, the *Coolgardie Miner*, tells of the conditions on the Coolgardie field, especially the presence of so many 'faceless' men, in the poem 'The Smiths'; and Dorham Doolette ('The Prodigal') wrote the ballad, 'The Old Coolgardie Road'.

In J. Arthur Barry's *The Luck of the Native Born* (1899), Coolgardie is the background for the adventures of his hero, Ned Linton. Richard Donald Lane wrote *The Romance of Old Coolgardie* (1929), a novel which is a mixture of historical fact and fiction; Norma King wrote the historical *Early Days around Coolgardie* (1975). The 'Coolgardie Safe' was standard equipment of the prospector in the desert; it used percolating water to keep food cool.

Coolgardie Miner, see **CLARE, BILLY**

Coolibah (also spelt coolabah, koolibah and coolybar) is the Aboriginal name for a eucalypt tree common in the Australian inland. It was on a coolibah that Brahe carved the word 'Dig' to inform Burke and Wills that their stores were buried there. It was under the shade of a coolibah in A.B. Paterson's 'Waltzing Matilda' that the 'Jolly Swagman' camped, and 'in the shade where the coolibahs grow' that the Dying Stockman wished to be buried.

COOMBS, H.C. (HERBERT COLE) (1906–) born Kalamunda, WA, had a distinguished career as an economist, culminating in his appointments as governor of the Reserve Bank of Australia (1960–68) and chairman of the Reserve Bank Board (1960–68). Active in Aboriginal affairs and the arts, he founded the Australian Elizabethan Theatre Trust (q.v.), was chairman of the Australian Council of the Arts (1968–74) and of the Australian Council of Aboriginal Affairs (1968–76). His publications include *Other People's Money* (1971), *The Fragile Pattern* (1970, the Boyer Lectures for that year), and *Kulinma – Listening to Aboriginal Australians* (1978). His autobiography, *Trial Balance* (1981), records Coombs's commitment to public service over four decades. He was voted Australian of the Year, 1972.

Coonardoo (1929), a novel by Katharine Susannah Prichard (q.v.), deals with the deep emotional relationship that exists between white man Hugh Watt and Aboriginal girl Coonardoo who have been friends since childhood. Raised by his mother, Bessie Watt, on Wytaliba, a cattle station in north-west WA, Hugh is sent south to be educated before returning to manage Wytaliba. After the death of his mother he is rescued from his obsessive grief by the love of Coonardoo, who ultimately bears his son. Repelled by the ugly, casual attitude of white males towards sexual relationships with Aboriginal women, Hugh cannot bring himself to allow the natural feelings that he and Coonardoo share for each other to develop to their mutual satisfaction. In an attempt to solve his moral dilemma he marries a white

girl from the south but several years later she discovers the secret of Coonardoo's son, Winni, and uses it as an excuse to leave the outback life she loathes. Coonardoo's tribal husband Warieda dies, and, partly out of his still-strong desire for her and partly to save her from other tribal husbands, Hugh acknowledges Coonardoo as his woman. His white 'morality', however, continues to prevent him living with her. After the white man Sam Geary forces himself upon Coonardoo while Hugh is away, Hugh, furiously jealous, beats Coonardoo and banishes her from Wytaliba. As the years pass, she drifts into a life of shame among the boats of the pearling fleet around Broome. The seasons go from bad to worse and Hugh loses Wytaliba to his enemy, Sam Geary. Coonardoo, soiled by the white man's ill-use and wasted by disease, returns to the deserted Wytaliba to die. Highly controversial and offensive to many in the 1930s, *Coonardoo* threw new light on the taboo subject of black–white sexual relationships.

COOPER, WALTER (1842–80), born Liverpool, NSW, was actor, journalist, playwright, lawyer and, briefly, member of parliament. Although handicapped by an unstable temperament, financial problems and scandal, Cooper was a popular playwright who successfully exploited the colonial perspective, especially in his comedy, *Colonial Experience* (1868, first published 1979). In 1870 his first sensation drama, 'Sun and Shadow', was staged, followed by 'Foiled: Or Australia Twenty Years Ago' (1871), *Hazard* (1872) and 'Fuss' (1880), all enjoying longer than usual runs. Cooper also presented some of these plays successfully in American cities in 1872–73.

Cooper's Creek, which skirts the eastern side of Queensland's Channel Country (q.v.), runs through south-western Queensland into SA and on infrequent occasions (e.g. 1949–50, 1973) its flood waters have reached Lake Eyre. Cooper's Creek was discovered by Charles Sturt in 1845 and named after Charles Cooper, SA's first chief justice. Extraordinary confusion surrounded the original identification of the much-interrupted stream but north from its junction with the Thomson River it is now known as the Barcoo (q.v.) and south from the junction, Cooper's Creek. Linked in the history of Australian exploration with the Burke and Wills (q.v.) expedition, the Cooper is featured in such accounts as Frank Clune's *Dig* (1937) and Alan Moorehead's *Cooper's Creek* (1963). The Cooper's Creek area was also important in Australia's pastoral expansion in the mid-nineteenth century. The account of its opening by the Durack and Costello families in the 1870s is given in

Mary Durack's *Kings in Grass Castles* (q.v., 1959). After Burke and Wills and the Duracks, the Cooper's most celebrated personality is probably A.B. Paterson's Clancy of the Overflow (q.v.), whose romanticized life as a drover 'down the Cooper where the western drovers go' has stirred nostalgia and envy in many an Australian heart.

Coorong, The, a national park comprising a salt-water lagoon and adjacent sandhills along the SA coastline near Lake Alexandrina, was the setting for Colin Thiele's children's novel, *Storm Boy* (1963), and the 1976 film of the book. A natural wonderland, the Coorong is also the subject of Thiele and McKelvey's illustrated work, *Coorong* (1972) and B.J. Noye's *The Coorong* (1973). Max Harris published a book of verse, *The Coorong and Other Poems* (1955).

COPPEL, ALEC, an actor and writer for stage and radio, published three plays, *I Killed the Count* (1938), *The Captain's Paradise* (1961) and *The Gazebo* (1962); and four books of light fiction, *A Man about a Dog* (1947), *Mr Denning Drives North* (1950), *The Last Parade* (1953), and *Tweedledum and Tweedledee* (1967). His other plays include 'Believe It or Not', 'Cadenza', 'The Joshua Tree' and 'Mr Smart Guy'.

COPPIN, GEORGE SELTH (1819–1906), born Sussex, England, was one of the earliest significant figures of the nineteenth-century Australian stage to have had extensive theatrical experience before coming to Australia. The son of itinerant English performers, Coppin made his deput as an infant and performed mainly in the English provinces and Ireland before emigrating to Australia in 1843, performing first in Sydney. In 1845–46 he toured Hobart, Launceston, Melbourne and Adelaide, where he was based 1846–51 and expanded his interests into hotels, racehorses and other business. Insolvent in 1851, Coppin repaired his fortunes as a theatrical performer on the Victorian goldfields; after repaying his creditors in full in Adelaide he left for England, where he had some success as a comedian – Billy Barlow (q.v.) was one of his notable roles – and engaged G.V. Brooke (q.v.) for an Australian tour. Later performers who toured under Coppin's management were Joseph Jefferson, Charles and Ellen Kean (q.v.), and J.C. Williamson (q.v.). Back in Melbourne in 1854, Coppin was in partnership with Brooke 1856–59 and 1860–61 and despite another financial crisis in 1863 remained one of the major figures of the Melbourne and Australian stage until his retirement early in the 1880s. He had many other

business interests and was also active in politics as a member of the Victorian Legislative Council or Legislative Assembly for much of the period 1858–95.

Coralie Lansdowne Says No, a play by Alexander Buzo (q.v.) first produced in 1974, was published the same year. Set in a large modern house perched high above the sea in the Bilgola-Palm Beach area north of Sydney, the action turns on the predicament of Coralie Lansdowne, a vibrant, satirically-witty former art-teacher now looking after the house of a wealthy American ex-lover. Daunted by her approaching thirtieth year, Coralie ponders her future and the three different men who pursue her, none of whom seems to offer the 'high-flying' role that she had always anticipated would be hers. Unpredictably, she finally compromises by marrying the outsider, the outwardly unprepossessing Stuart Morgan, since with him she has a better chance of retaining her authentic self.

Cornstalk was originally used early in the nineteenth century to denote a colonial-born white Australian, as opposed to those born overseas; the word derived from the physique of the colonial-born, who were thought to be taller and fairer than the European-born and had thus flourished like the Indian corn brought to Australia. With the spread of settlement 'cornstalk' narrowed in meaning to apply to someone born in NSW as distinct from the other colonies (c.f. 'croweater', 'sandgroper'), as in Henry Lawson's poem 'Jack Cornstalk'. Synonyms for 'cornstalk' in its original sense included 'currency' and 'native' (qq.v.). There was a 'Jack Cornstalk' series in the *Australian Star* in 1899, and the word itself was sometimes used in titles and for pseudonyms, e.g. *Land of Australia: Songs and Verses by Samuel Cornstalk* (1913) by F.S. Walker. Daniel Healey ('Whaks Li Kell') wrote *'The Cornstalk' His Habits and Habitat* (1893), a mixture of satirical prose and verse, and J.H.M. Abbott, in *Tommy Cornstalk* (1902), related some of the Australian soldiers' experiences in the Boer War. Many Australian stage characters in the nineteenth century bore the name Cornstalk.

CORRIS, PETER (1942–), born Stawell, Victoria, has been an academic historian, literary editor of the *National Times* (1978–80) and full-time writer. His boyhood reading of Raymond Chandler and other American 'thriller' writers led him into detective fiction writing and he has, especially with his recent novel *The Empty Beach*, become one of Australia's most popular exponents of the thriller genre. His private detective, Cliff Hardy, is an Australian version of Chandler's Phillip Marlowe. *The Empty Beach* was serialized on ABC radio in 1983. Corris's published works include *The Dying Trade* (1980), *Lords of the Ring* (1980), *White Meat* (1981), *The Marvellous Boy* (1982) and *The Empty Beach* (1983).

Corroboree, see **Australian Literature Society**

Corroboree is the term for an Aboriginal ceremonial dance accompanied by song. The dancers are usually painted with clay in traditional designs. Music is provided by clapping sticks and the didgeridoo. The circle of dancers in the corroboree is known as the bora ring; Judith Wright's poem 'Bora Ring' regrets the loss of the corroboree in modern times. One of the earliest instances of the corroboree in Australian literature is in David Burn's play *The Bushrangers* (performed 1829), where a 'corobbora' is mentioned.

Cosme, see **New Australia**

Cosmos Magazine, which contained a considerable amount of literary material, both creative writing (stories, sketches, poetry) and review articles, ran monthly in Sydney 1894–99, after which it was incorporated into the monthly *Southern Cross* 1898–1900. Its contributors included G.B. Barton, Edward Dyson, Ernest Favenc and 'Price Warung'.

Cost of Seriousness, The, see **PORTER, PETER**

Cotters' England, a novel by Christina Stead (q.v.), was published in London in 1967 and in New York in 1966 with the title *Dark Places of the Heart*. The two titles reflect the novel's dual political–personal theme. Set in working- and middle-class England of the early 1950s and written almost wholly in dialogue with a cumulative rather than a chronological plot form, the story centres on Nellie Cook, née Cotter, a domineering woman from the industrial north. Loquacious, excitable, histrionic, Nellie is a compelling study of unconscious corruption, a coarse-grained egoist who manipulates the emotions of her relatives and friends. A vociferous champion of the underdog, she works for a socialist newspaper and is married to a trade union organizer although, like her husband, she is a political charlatan. The past effects of her influence, apparent in the stunted lives of her sister Peggy and brother Tom, are dramatically acted out in a grotesque scene in a Palace of Mirrors. It is clear that she has a stifled incestuous relationship with Tom and lesbian undercurrents also affect her connections with the various women who are drawn to her Islington house. They reach a tragic culmination in the suicide of her protegee, Caroline.

COTTON, JOHN (1801–49), born London, arrived in Australia in 1843. His account of the voyage was published as *Journal of a Voyage in the Barque, 'Parkfield'* (1845). Cotton soon became a substantial squatter, occupying some sixty square miles by 1846. His correspondence with his brother William in England is of historical significance and was published by George Mackaness in 1953. His great-grand-daughter, Lady Maie Casey, has written of him in *An Australian Story 1837–1907* (1962).

COTTRELL, DOROTHY (1902–57), born Picton, NSW, contracted infantile paralysis as a child and was thereafter confined to a wheelchair. The separation of her parents led to a rather chaotic girlhood, part of which she spent on stations in Queensland. She attended classes at the Royal Art Society of NSW and became a competent black-and-white artist. At eighteen she went to live at Ularunda station near Morven, Queensland, and married the station bookkeeper in 1922. Her first novel, *The Singing Gold*, serialized in the American *Ladies Home Journal* in 1927 and in the *Sydney Mail* in 1928, was published in book form in 1928. Set in pastoral Queensland and on a small island of the Family group off the Queensland coast, *The Singing Gold* is a warm, unsophisticated story of young love. It takes its title from the ground lark, an attractive, small, golden bird which flourishes in the open Queensland grasslands. Royalties from *The Singing Gold* enabled the Cottrells to go to America; they returned to Australia only briefly 1954–56. In the USA Dorothy became a successful journalist and writer, especially of short fiction on Australian themes. She published *Earth Battle* (1930, titled *Tharlane* in America); less charming and less successful than *The Singing Gold*, *Earth Battle* draws a grim picture of the struggle between man and the environment in western Queensland. A later novel, *The Silent Reefs* (1953), a tale of mystery and adventure set in the Caribbean, was serialized in the *Saturday Evening Post* and filmed in 1959. She also published two children's books, *Winks: His Book* (1934) and *Wilderness Orphan* (1936).

COUANI, ANNA (1948–   ), born Sydney of Greek and Polish extraction, is a qualified architect and teacher and an experienced painter. She has been active as editor, feminist and poet, and is a writer of contemporary prose; her publications include *Italy: Short Stories* (1977), *Were All Women Sex Mad?* (1982) and

The Train (1983). She is a founding member of Sea Cruise Books which publishes new and experimental writing of the Sydney Women Writers' Workshop.

COUNGEAU, EMILY (1860–1936), born London, came to Australia in 1887. She published several books of verse, including *Stella Australis* (1914), *Rustling Leaves* (1920), *Palm Fronds* (1927) and *Fern Leaves* (1934). Her verse drama, *Princess Mona* (1916), is a fantasy in which a pageant of Anzac is featured.

COUNIHAN, NOEL (1913–), born Albert Park, Melbourne, went to the National Gallery Drawing School at night while working by day in a Flinders Lane warehouse. Counihan exhibited his first drawings in a Melbourne restaurant in 1933, as a result of which he gained a job as a newspaper caricaturist with the Melbourne *Argus*. His caricatures of the 1930s depression, in which he often used the nude human figure to depict social injustice, are among his best-known. Following a career as a political cartoonist for newspapers, mostly those with radical tendencies, he turned in 1941 to painting, winning the major prize in 1945 in the 'Australia at War' art competition exhibited at the National Gallery of Victoria. A socialist-realist painter, Counihan deplores through his art the Vietnam war, urban poverty, racism and human suffering. Two literary personalities depicted by him are Henry Lawson and Alan Marshall.

Count Your Dead (1968), subtitled *A Novel of Vietnam*, was written by professional Australian soldier, John Rowe (q.v.), who served for a year in the Vietnam War. The novel, centred on the village of Dong Tuy earmarked for destruction because it is suspected of harbouring Viet Cong, presents a realistic picture of the jungle war and concerns the relationship between two officers who disagree on the pacification programme of the area.

Country I Come From, The, see **LAWSON, HENRY**

'Country Press', a frequently-anthologized poem by Rosemary Dobson (q.v.) was first published in the *Bulletin* (15 January 1947). It tells of the *Western Star*, newspaper of the 'Nyngle' District, which with its record of births, deaths, marriages, council reports, wool prices, river heights, Baptist socials and euchre drives encapsulates the history of and catches the characteristic flavour of the life in an Australian country town.

COUPER, J.M. (JOHN MILL) (1914–), born Dundee, Scotland, came in 1951 to Australia where he lectured in education and English at the Universities of Queensland and New South Wales and Macquarie University. Couper has published four volumes of verse, *East of Living* (1967), *The Book of Bligh* (1969), *In From the Sea* (1974) and *The Lee Shore* (1979); he also published two children's books, *The Thundering Good To-Day* (1970) and *Looking for a Wave* (1973). *East of Living* has four sections: 'Cape Catastrophe', which tells of the drowning in the Great Australian Bight of the master and several of the crew of Matthew Flinders's ship the *Investigator*, a series of sonnets addressed to Mark Alexander Boyd (1563–1601), a Scottish poet with whom Couper, exiled in Australia, feels he shares experiences of love, life and nostalgia for home; 'Catterline', in which a born loner ultimately achieves self-respect and a resolution of his place in the scheme of things; and 'East of Living', which reflects Couper's own intellectual, cultural and spiritual estrangement in Australia and his attempt to come to terms with the situation. *The Book of Bligh*, a contribution to the voyager theme in Australian writing, recounts the mutiny on the *Bounty* and the epic voyage of Bligh and his crew in a small boat to Timor. It also makes moral and psychological judgements on the Bligh story, contrasting the integrity and selfless sense of service displayed in those events with the hedonism of modern man. *In from the Sea* is more emphatically personal, with the values instilled in Couper's early life and upbringing in Scotland in obvious collision with the new Australian attitudes and environment.

Courier-Mail, see *Brisbane Courier*

Courland Penders, an old derelict family estate, is the setting for a sequence of poems by Michael Dransfield (q.v.). The imaginary house, introduced in Dransfield's *Streets of the Long Voyage* (1970) in the poem 'Portrait of the Artist as an Old Man', is further described in 'Courland Penders: Going Home', 'Tapestry at Courland Penders', 'Library, Courland Penders', 'Birch Trees, Courland Penders' and the unpublished 'Courland Penders: Reminiscences'. The obsession with vanished glory indicates the romantic strain in Dransfield.

Courtland, Stella, see *Australian Girl, An*

Cousin from Fiji, The, a novel by Norman Lindsay (q.v.), was first published in 1945. Set in Ballarat, Victoria, in the 1890s, it describes the comically-unsettling effects of Cecilia Bellairs and her eighteen-year-old daughter Ella, recently arrived from Fiji to live with their relations the Domkins. The romantic adventures of Cecilia and Ella as they successfully elude Ballarat's straitlaced conventions structure the story, although there is a range of memorable characters. These include the outwardly respectable Uncle George, torn between two mistresses and threatened with financial ruin; the indomitable Grandma Domkin, who combines senility and licence to farcical effect; and her intimate, old Miss Biddlecombe, still manically obsessed with romantic pursuit. By means of these and other characters, Lindsay presents a vivid contrast between the surface tedium of small-town religiosity and the comic excitement of its secret sexual life.

COUVREUR, JESSIE ('TASMA') (1848–97), was born Jessie Huybers at Highgate, London, and came to Australia when her family migrated to Tasmania in the early 1850s. In 1867 she married Charles Fraser; they settled on the land in the Kyneton district in Victoria, but the marriage was a failure and after long periods of separation – Jessie spent much of 1873–83 in England and Europe – they were divorced in 1883. Returning to Europe, Jessie married in 1885 Auguste Couvreur, a Belgian journalist and politician. She was thereafter based in Brussels, succeeding her husband as Brussels correspondent of the London *Times* after his death in 1894. She also lectured on Australian life and commerce in France and Belgium.

Writing usually as 'Tasma', Couvreur began her literary career in 1877 with a contribution to *The 'Vagabond' Annual* and over the next few years had short stories, travel articles and other pieces published in the *Australasian*, the *Melbourne Review* and other annuals; before her divorce she helped to support herself in Europe by freelance journalism. Her major fiction, however, was written after 1885. *Uncle Piper of Piper's Hill* (q.v., 1889), her first and best novel, portrays middle-class society in colonial Melbourne; its characterization, humour, and analysis of the interaction between the genteel but impoverished Cavendish family newly arrived from England, and their hosts the Pipers, won praise in England as well as Australia. Couvreur's later novels – *In Her Earliest Youth* (1890), *The Penance of Portia James* (1891), *A Knight of the White Feather* (1892), *Not Counting the Cost* (1895), and *A Fiery Ordeal* (1897) – may reflect contemporary interest in the problems of sexuality and marriage but are also informed by her experience of Charles Fraser: they characteristically portray heroines in Australia or England who are the victims of husbands who to varying degrees are weak, boorish,

egotistical, alcoholic, brutal and dishonest. Couvreur also wrote *A Sydney Sovereign and Other Tales* (1889), which reprints stories originally published in the *Australasian* in the 1880s, and had work included in the Anglo-Australian anthologies of A.P. Martin and others. She is often grouped with another contributor to these anthologies, Rosa Praed (q.v.), and with Ada Cambridge (q.v.) in studies of colonial fiction.

COVE, MICHAEL (1946–), born London, came in 1971 to Australia, where he has written for film, radio, stage and television. His stage plays include 'Fields of Offerings', 'Gingerbread House', 'Running Away', *Dazzle*, 'Duckling', 'Convict Cakewalk', 'Kookaburra', 'Jesters', 'Mariner', *The Gift* (published in *Biala*, 1977), 'Happy Landings', *Family Lore* (published in *Theatre-Australia*, 1976) and, with Ron Blair, 'Too Early to Say'. His play, *Dazzle*, is published in the collection *Can't You Hear Me Talking to You?* (1978), ed. Alrene Sykes.

COWAN, PETER (1914–), born into a family long established in WA, was educated at the University of WA where he later taught. He is best known for his short-story collections which include *Drift* (1944), *The Unploughed Land* (1958), *The Empty Street* (1965), *The Tins* (1973) and *Mobiles* (1979). He has also written two novels, *Summer* (1964) and *Seed* (1966), and edited several collections of short stories. Interested in his family's history, he has published a biography of his grandmother, Edith Cowan, the first woman member of an Australian parliament (1978), as well as editions of writings by his earlier ancestors, *A Colonial Experience* (1978) and *A Faithful Picture* (1977). Cowan is also co-editor of *Westerly*.

Both in his short stories and novels, Cowan's central theme is isolation. The physical isolation imposed by the WA bush dominates his early work, although in *Seed* and his later stories he also contemplates the frustration and boredom of suburbia, the emotionally impoverished and fragmentary lives of mundane, middle-class Australians. His concern with the spiritual emptiness of Australian life is similar to Patrick White's, but he lacks White's satire and range. A writer of understated prose, he is mostly content to express the pathos, tedium and alienation of normal daily experience, whether rural or urban. Some of his most striking stories, however, such as 'The Empty Street' and 'The Tins', explore abnormally isolated states of mind. Other consistent characteristics of his work are a keen interest in the natural environment and a dislike of urban growth.

COWLING, G.H. (GEORGE HERBERT) (1881–1946), born Leeds, England, was professor of English at the University of Melbourne 1928–43. An authority on Shakespeare, Milton and Blake, whose texts he edited, Cowling also wrote on other English literary figures. With Victorian poet 'Furnley Maurice' he compiled the significant anthology, *Australian Essays* (1935). It was Cowling's critical article on Australian literature in the *Age* 16 February 1935 that partly led to Rex Ingamell's statement of Jindyworobak attitudes, *Conditional Culture* (1938), and it was also criticized by P.R. Stephensen.

COX, ERLE (1873–1950), born Melbourne, was one of Melbourne's best-known journalists, working on the staff of the Melbourne *Argus*, the *Australasian* and later the *Age*. He published three novels: *Out of the Silence* (1925), a fantasy in which an Australian station owner finds on his property an underground treasure house of remarkable works of art, craft and machinery which indicate the existence here of an older, superior civilization; *Fool's Harvest* (1939), in which Cox, picturing Australia invaded by an oriental power, attempts to shake the country out of its lethargy as the Second World War approaches; and *The Missing Angel* (1947), which records the transformation, with the help of the Devil, of the straitlaced, sober young Melbourne wowser, Tydvil Jones, into a boisterous hedonist.

COX, WILLIAM (1764–1837), born Dorset, England, arrived in NSW in 1800 and succeeded John Macarthur as paymaster of the NSW Corps. Cox was commissioned by Governor Lachlan Macquarie in 1814 to make the road across the Blue Mountains; the journal that he kept while making the road was published as *A Narrative of Proceedings of William Cox* (1888). His memoirs were published in 1901 from the Cox collections in the Mitchell Library, Sydney.

COZENS, CHARLES, see *Adventures of a Guardsman*

'Crabs', see **CAREY, PETER**

CRAIG, ALEXANDER (1923–), born Malvern, Victoria, studied at the Universities of Melbourne and Iowa and served with the AIF in New Guinea, before teaching English at Macquarie University. He has published three volumes of verse, *Far-Back Country* (1954), *The Living Sky* (1964) and *When No-One is Looking* (1977); and edited *Twelve Poets 1950–1970* (1971). Craig's poetry is included in the anthology, *Eight by Eight* (q.v, 1963).

Cranky Jack, a character who occasionally appears in the Rudd family books, is a bush 'hatter' whose arrival at the selection is narrated in 'Cranky Jack', a story in *On Our Selection* (1899). Engaged by Dad Rudd at no wages, Cranky Jack is a willing worker but subject to delusions of paranoia; on one occasion when chasing a snake that he is convinced is the Devil, he recoils in horror from his own image, which he sees in a mirror and thinks is his father. Locked away because he terrifies Mother Rudd, Jack escapes, smashes the mirror and becomes a docile worker for the family again. The story has been seen as a dramatic and psychologically-coherent comment on the decline in familial relationships because of the rigours of selection life, although the incident of the snake and the smashing of the mirror were not part of the story when originally published in the *Bulletin* in 1897.

CRAWFORD, R.M. (RAYMOND MAXWELL) (1906–), born Grenfell, NSW, was Professor of History at the University of Melbourne 1937–71 and chairman of the Australian Humanities Research Council 1966–68. An influential teacher, he is recognised in a special edition of *Historical Studies* (1971) for his contribution to Australia's intellectual life. His published works include *The Study of History* (1939), *Ourselves and the Pacific* (1941), *Australia* (1952), *An Australian Perspective* (1960) and *'A Bit of a Rebel': The Life and Work of George Arnold Wood* (1975). He was made OBE in 1971.

Creative Effort, see **LINDSAY, NORMAN**

Creative Writing in Australia, see **EWERS, J.K**

'Creek of the Four Graves, The', one of Australia's earliest narrative poems, was published by Charles Harpur (q.v.) in *The Bushrangers, A Play in Five Acts, and Other Poems* (1853). Its story of a group of settlers murdered by natives is presented with individuality and force. Set in the Hawkesbury district and the Blue Mountains, the poem combines a realistic narrative with effective description of the local Australian scene.

Creeve Roe (1947), a collection of Victor Daley's (q.v.) radical and satiric verse, was edited by Muir Holburn and Marjorie Pizer. The title (also Daley's pseudonym) is taken from the Red Branch Knights of Conchubar, one-time kings of Ulster. Most of the poems had earlier been published in the *Bulletin* and the *Tocsin*, a labour weekly which was edited in the 1890s by fellow-radical, Bernard O'Dowd. One of

Daley's best-known satirical poems (mainly on A.G. Stephens) is 'Narcissus and Some Tadpoles', published in the *Bulletin* (19 April 1899).

CRICK, DONALD (1916–), born Sydney, has combined creative writing with such occupations as farm and factory worker, clerk, insurance representative, publisher and book reviewer for the *Australian* and the *Sydney Morning Herald*. He has published five novels, *Bikini Girl* (1963), *Martin Place* (1963), *Period of Adjustment* (1966), *A Different Drummer* (1972) and *A Moon to Play With* (1981). *Period of Adjustment,* the first Australian novel, in the opinion of its author, to deal specifically with class distinctions and values in Australian society, won the Dame Mary Gilmore Centenary Prize in 1965. *The Moon to Play With,* a satirical comedy, won the Rigby 1980 Anniversary Award.

Critic (1), an Adelaide weekly which ran 1897–1924 when it was succeeded by the *Gossip,* carried, especially in its later years, literary articles, poetry and news of books and authors. C.J. Dennis was briefly its editor (c.1904). Various other journals entitled *Critic* were published earlier, e.g. 1843 (Sydney), 1862–63 (Adelaide), 1873 (Sydney), 1883 (Melbourne), 1889 (Windsor, NSW) and 1892–93 (Hobart).

Critic (2), a mainly monthly journal published by the Literary Society of the University of WA in Perth, ran 1961–70. Its contributors included many significant literary personalities of WA, e.g Gavin Casey, Henrietta Drake-Brockman, Mary Durack, J.K. Ewers, Dorothy Hewett and Randolph Stow.

Critical Review, known 1958–64 as the *Melbourne Critical Review,* was first published in 1958, jointly by the Department of English at the University of Melbourne and the Melbourne University Literary Club. Some issues were later edited at the University of Sydney but it has been published since 1977 by the History of Ideas Unit of the Research School of Social Sciences at the Australian National University. Its long-standing editor is S.L. Goldberg.

Criticism. The beginnings of literary criticism in Australia are inextricably bound up with the early history of magazine publishing in the colonies. As Frank S. Greenop's *History of Magazine Publishing in Australia* (1947) makes clear, the early decades of the nineteenth century are strewn with short-lived journals, some of which at least made a gesture towards disseminating literary views and information. The

first magazine published in NSW, the *Australian Magazine,* appeared in 1821 under the editorship of the Rev. Ralph Mansfield as *A Compendium of Religious, Literary, and Miscellaneous Intelligence*; it laid greater stress, however, on religious than on literary matters. The *Australian Quarterly Journal* paid equally slight attention to literature from its inception in Sydney in 1828; the *Hobart Town Magazine,* produced 1833–34 by Henry Melville, was rather livelier in tone and content. Meagre as it was, most of the literary material that found its way into the early colonial magazines was largely derived from and concerned with English writing; a good deal of it, indeed, was reprinted from English sources.

As early as 1838 James Martin, then only eighteen, published his *Australian Sketch Book,* a collection of essays one of which, 'The Pseudo-Poets', was an unflattering account of some Australian versifiers. In spite of Martin's *Sketch Book* most of the still rudimentary criticism of colonial writers appeared in magazines or newspapers of the day. In 1855–56 the *Month* caused some stir in Sydney largely by virtue of the controversial style of Frank Fowler (q.v.), a young visitor to the colony, and by the contributions of 'Peter Possum' (Richard Rowe). In 1856 the *Leader* began publication as the weekly companion of the *Age,* to be followed in 1864 by the *Australasian* produced in the office of the *Argus.* These were early examples of the close connection between criticism and journalism which continued in Australia to the end of the nineteenth century and beyond. A Sydney counterpart to the *Australasian* was the *Sydney Mail,* which had a close association with the *Sydney Morning Herald.* Almost contemporaneously with these ventures, there were attempts to reproduce in Australia the success of the London *Punch. Melbourne Punch* appeared in 1855, the first Sydney *Punch* in 1856, and for the rest of the century there were sporadic attempts to emulate the British journal.

In the 1860s much of the liveliest literary discussion was centred in Melbourne, and especially on such groups as the Yorick Club and the Cave of Adullam, some of whose leading members are recollected in Hugh McCrae's *My Father and My Father's Friends* (1935). *Melbourne Punch,* for instance, included among its founding writers R.H. Horne, Marcus Clarke and Frederick Sinnett. Sinnett is especially notable for his essay *The Fiction Fields of Australia* (q.v., 1966), first published in two instalments in the *Journal of Australasia* in 1856. This early conspectus of the Australian novel included comments on *Clara Morison* (1854), *The Emigrant Family* (1849) and *Tales of the Colonies* (1843), as well as taking up the general problem of developing a native literature in a derivative culture, an issue which has continued to exercise Australian criticism ever since. Some of Sinnett's remarks about the thinness of the social materials on which fiction might be based quite remarkably foreshadow Henry James's more celebrated remarks in his *Hawthorne* (1879) of more than twenty years later.

While Melbourne was developing a lively literary community, Sydney was also discovering new ways of supporting cultural activity. The University of Sydney was founded in 1852, and soon began to help the fostering of the arts which, prior to that time, had rested largely on the efforts of individual patrons like Nicol Drysdale Stenhouse. In the 1850s, furthermore, a revived Mechanics' School of Arts provided another forum for literary discussion and debate. Yet it was not until 1864 that there appeared what Cecil Hadgraft (q.v.) has described as the 'first piece of literary criticism published in Australia as a separate work'. William Walker's *Australian Literature* was first given as a public lecture in the Windsor School of Arts, 20 July 1864. Restricting his survey to NSW, Walker argued that, while no great Australian author had yet appeared, 'Australia certainly has a literature, though it is a circumscribed one'. In support of his case, he gave some account of magazine publication in the colony as well as of historical writing and verse.

Two years later G.B. Barton produced *The Poets and Prose Writers of New South Wales* (q.v., 1866), among the first examples of a kind of work – the chronological review of the national achievement in creative literature – that has consistently attracted the attention of Australian critics. In association with his survey, Barton compiled a companion work, *Literature in New South Wales* (q.v., 1866). By the late 1860s, too, the time was ripe for the appearance of another mode of criticism by which to interpret a literary tradition already more than half a century old. J. Sheridan Moore's *Life and Genius of J.L. Michael* (1868), in its own right a minor study of a minor poetaster, nevertheless initiated a kind of critical activity important to the repertoire of any culture. Sheridan Moore began contributing to literary journalism in Sydney at much the same time as Marcus Clarke was writing for the Melbourne newspapers. Clarke collected some of his journalistic pieces in *The Peripatetic Philosopher* (1869); several of his more explicitly critical essays, e.g. on 'Balzac and Modern French Literature' and 'Charles Dickens', are included in *A Colonial City, High and Low Life: Selected Journalism of Marcus Clarke* (1972), edited by L.T. Hergenhan.

Probably the best-known single piece of Clarke's critical prose is, however, his introduction to the posthumous edition of A.L. Gordon's *Sea Spray and Smoke Drift* (1876). In spite of propagating much misinformation about Australia's 'trees without shade' and 'flowers without perfume', Clarke's essay made three significant contributions to the stock of critical ideas about Australian writing: it stressed the gothic element in the Australian literary imagination, identified the response to landscape as an abiding issue, and lavished high praise on Gordon. From the year of Gordon's death (1870) at least until the end of the nineteenth century, Australian critics consistently placed him at the head of their country's roll of poets. Arthur Patchett Martin, for example, included some highly laudatory remarks about Gordon in his *Fernshawe* (1882), as did Francis Adams in *The Australians: A Social Sketch* (1893). Gordon was the only poet allotted a complete chapter in Desmond Byrne's *Australian Writers* (q.v., 1896), while Martin repeated his praise in *The Beginnings of Australian Literature* (1898) at the same time as he assigned Marcus Clarke an equivalent place in fiction. *The Beginnings of Australian Literature* was originally delivered as a lecture in London, 27 March 1898, and in their *The Development of Australian Literature* (1898) H.G. Turner and Alexander Sutherland identify Martin and Douglas Sladen as prime movers in developing a London awareness of Australian writing. By 1898, however, significant forces were generating a critical response to Australian writing on its own soil. The best known of these was the Sydney weekly, the *Bulletin*, founded in 1880. From 1894 to 1906 the literary voice of the *Bulletin* was A.G. Stephens (q.v.), who instituted the paper's famous Red Page on 29 August 1896. Stephens's personal self-confidence, critical astuteness and wide knowledge of literature gave the *Bulletin* an influence and importance in literary matters probably unmatched by any Australian weekly before or since. Stephens himself was arguably the first great critic to have been produced by Australian society. He certainly assisted the careers of virtually every important writer of his generation, e.g. Joseph Furphy through the acceptance of *Such is Life* (1903), as well as providing a forum for wide ranging, often competing, critical ideas and attitudes. The writers of the 1890s did not, nevertheless, have to depend entirely on the *Bulletin* for periodical publication. The latter years of the century were as rich in ephemeral magazines as any earlier decade. 1888 was an appropriate year for the *Centennial Magazine* to appear in Sydney; it was followed two years later by the *Australasian Critic* (1890); in 1899 the *Australian Magazine* carried work by Christopher Brennan and John le Gay Brereton among others; the *Antipodean* appeared in Melbourne 1893–97.

During the 1890s also, several collections of essays appeared, some carrying pieces on Australian writers and writing. In 1893 C.H. Pearson published *National Life and Character* and in 1896 *Reviews and Critical Essays*. A.H. Carney's *Land of the Dawning* (1894) combined *belles lettres* with some critical comment, while A.G. Stephens rounded out his years with the *Bulletin* with *The Red Pagan* (1906). The closing years of the century were also marked by some efforts to provide reliable texts of major writers. Charles Harpur had been poorly served by the posthumous edition of his *Poems* (1883), but in 1886 Alexander Sutherland made a more successful attempt to present an accurate text of Henry Kendall's verse. Douglas Sladen's anthology, *A Century of Australian Song* (1888), offered a practical signpost to achievement in poetry, but among the most characteristic critical work of the 1890s were historical surveys of the kind exemplified by Barton's earlier studies. Among these, Desmond Byrne's *Australian Writers* offers a sensible and moderate account of Australian literary achievement up to the time of its publication. Turner and Sutherland's *The Development of Australian Literature* is a better-known work of the same kind. Nearly all the nineteenth-century historians of Australian literature, however, pick out the same writers for praise and attention: among the poets, Harpur, Kendall, Gordon, J. Brunton Stephens; among the novelists, Clarke, 'Rolf Boldrewood', Henry Kinglsey. If any theoretical theme pervades their judgements, it is likely to be that voiced by Barton in 1866 in the opening pages of his *Literature of New South Wales*: 'What *is* Australian Literature?' Variations on the same question have continued to dominate a large proportion of Australian criticism up to the present time.

During the 1890s questions about the nature and limits of truly Australian writing were answered largely but not entirely in nationalistic terms: genuinely Australian work was that which, written by the native-born, expressed a recognizably Australian subject matter in an essentially Australian way. There were, to be sure, countervailing views. Christopher Brennan expressed some of his personal enthusiasms in a series of seven *Bulletin* articles on 'The Newer French Poetry' (1899), while A.G. Stephens himself had an impressive acquaintance with contemporary English and European writing. Recent scholarship, furthermore, has suggested that European theories about fictional realism, among others, were quite deeply assimilated into the critical ideas and literary expression of the time.

Brennan was a classical scholar as well as a student of contemporary French and German literature, and his years as associate professor of German and comparative literature at the University of Sydney (1920–25) gave him a platform for the exercise of his scholarship. The University of Sydney has enabled a number of scholar-critics to develop areas and kinds of interest which might otherwise have been difficult to cultivate in Australia. The Sydney tradition of English Renaissance scholarship and criticism is especially noteworthy; it is exemplified by such figures as Mungo MacCallum, J. le Gay Brereton, A.J.A. Waldock, R.G. Howarth, Wesley Milgate, H.J. Oliver and G.A Wilkes. Similar traditions of scholarly and critical specialization can be associated with the other Australian universities, of which the excellence in French studies in the University of Melbourne, fostered by A.R. Chisholm's long occupancy of the chair (1921–57), is a good example.

Balancing the growing cosmopolitan awareness of Australian criticism at the end of the nineteenth century was an understandable and necessary concern for some of the grass-roots elements of the indigenous literary culture. A.B. Paterson's collection of *Old Bush Songs* (1905) was an important recognition that since 1788 Australia had developed a rich folk literature which needed to be incorporated into critical interpretation of the country's culture. In the twentieth century the need met by Paterson's collection has been served by Bill Wannan's several anthologies, by Douglas Stewart and Nancy Keesing's *Australian Bush Ballads* (1955) and *Old Bush Songs* (1957), as well as by collections and historical research by writers like John Manifold, Hugh Anderson and John Meredith (see also Folk-Song and Ballad).

It is often said that Australian literature and culture generally went through a kind of trough in the period between Federation and the First World War. The same point might be made of literary criticism. Several phenomena, however, can be noted which indicate that critical activity was not completely stagnant. After breaking with the *Bulletin*, Stephens edited *The Bookfellow*. Another important magazine, the *Lone Hand*, was joined in 1915 by the *Triad* which had originated in NZ and which appeared, under a variety of editors and towards the end of its existence as the *New Triad*, until 1928. In the years after 1901 Stephens also wrote a number of brief lives of poets with whom, for the most part, he had been personally acquainted. Even in 1897 he had contributed a memoir to Barcroft Boake's posthumous *Where the Dead Men Lie*. His later work in this vein include *Victor Daley* (1905), *Henry Kendall* (1928) and *Chris. Brennan* (1933).

During the post-Federation period the mode of belle lettristic criticism was maintained in T.G. Tucker's *The Cultivation of Literature in*

Australia (1902) and Archibald T. Strong's *Per-adventure* (1911). Probably Australia's best-known practitioner of the graceful essay, not uncommonly applied to literary appreciations, was Walter Murdoch (q.v.), whose *Collected Essays* came out in 1938. Bertram Stevens's *An Anthology of Australian Verse* (1906) added to the list of representative selections, while in 1909 Bernard O'Dowd produced *Poetry Militant*, an example of a kind of criticism comparatively rare in Australian writing: the practitioner's manifesto of what should be the aims and methods of his art. O'Dowd, who had corresponded with Walt Whitman in his youth, argues for a set of democratic, egalitarian values in large measure derived from the American poet, and demands a deliberately didactic poetry to put them into effect. Norman Lindsay's *Creative Effort* (1920) resembles *Poetry Militant* in being an artist's passionate statement of the nature and purposes of his art, but in almost nothing else. Where O'Dowd had promulgated the values of a democratic literature, Lindsay was unashamedly élitist, taking his stand on the special value of the artist's energy, talent, will. *Creative Effort* was the first full-scale expression of that Nietzschean element in Australian literary thought which has subsequently attracted a good deal of attention, most thoroughly in Noel Macainsh's *Nietzsche in Australia* (1970). Lindsay's ideas did not have to wait fifty years, however, before they filtered into many areas of Australian culture. The force of his personality had an enormous effect on poets like R.D. FitzGerald, Kenneth Slessor, Douglas Stewart and 'Seaforth' Mackenzie. It was an obvious element in the best-known literary magazine of the 1920s, the short-lived *Vision* (1923–24) edited by Frank C. Johnson, Kenneth Slessor and Jack Lindsay, Norman's son. In spite of its notoriety, *Vision* was only one among many 'little magazines' which appeared and disappeared in the years between the two world wars. The magazines most important to the history of criticism in that period and beyond are dealt with in John Tregenza's *Australian Little Magazines 1923–1954* (1964).

Book-length criticism during the 1920s continued to serve much the same ends as those established in the 1890s: the provision of a coherent historical account of Australian writing within the framework of nationalist democratic values. Zora Cross's *Introduction to the Study of Australian Literature* (1922) conforms to this pattern, as does Nettie Palmer's (q.v.) *Modern Australian Literature* (1924). Of particular interest to this article are those figures whom Nettie Palmer considers to have made a genuine contribution to Australian criticism. They include Arthur Adams, Hilary Lofting,

David McKee Wright, Frank Morton, T.G. Tucker and Walter Murdoch. Throughout her life Nettie, along with her husband Vance Palmer (q.v.), spared no effort in advancing the cause of Australian writing and Australian writers, especially those who, like Joseph Furphy and 'Henry Handel Richardson', had been unjustly neglected. Even by the end of the 1920s the Palmers were established as the leading partnership in Australian writing, critical as well as creative. For them and their contemporaries the generation of the 1890s was far enough in the past to be susceptible of idealization as the fountainhead of all that was best in the Australian literary tradition. This historiographical enterprise was reinforced by such works of first-hand reminiscence as George Taylor's *Those Were the Days* (1918) and A.W. Jose's *The Romantic Nineties* (1933). By 1930 one of the most significant results of this trend in criticism was the general acceptance of Henry Lawson as the representative Australian writer, *par excellence*.

In a number of ways 1930 proved to be a fulcrum year in the history of Australian literary criticism. In that year, for instance, J. le Gay Brereton published *Knocking Round*, combining *belles-lettres* with personal recollection. In the same year F.J. Broomfield consolidated Lawson's reputation with his *Henry Lawson and His Critics*, which was followed in 1931 by a work in similar vein, the set of essays edited by Brereton and Bertha Lawson under the title of *Henry Lawson by His Mates*. 1930 also saw the appearance of H.A. Kellow's *Queensland Poets*. A shrewd critic, and headmaster of Rockhampton Grammar School, Kellow made a substantial addition to the regional study of Australian writing. Since Kellow's book, it is possible to discern something like a tradition of such studies, including Cecil Hadgraft's *Queensland and Its Writers* (1959), Paul Depasquale's *A Critical History of South Australian Literature 1836–1930* (1978) and Bruce Bennett's *The Literature of Western Australia* (1979). If, on the one hand, 1930 witnessed the consolidation of a tradition of critical interpretation and assessment going back something like half a century, it also saw the rise of some new elements in Australian critical thought. John Anderson, professor of philosophy at the University of Sydney, had strong interests in literature and criticism as well as in philosophy. He expressed some of the former in a series of talks given to the Sydney University English Society. His topics in 1930 included 'Realism and Some of Its Critics' and 'Ulysses'. Anderson's concern for modernism in literature was certainly not unique, but it is worth noting that his defence of James Joyce in particular relates him to several distinguished Joycean commentators who came to prominence much later; S.L. Goldberg in *The Classical Temper* (1961), Clement Semmler in *For the Uncanny Man* (1963) and Clive Hart with his *Concordance to Finnegans Wake* (1963).

Even in the 1930s, however, native-born Australian critics as well as the Scot, John Anderson, were keenly aware of literary movements overseas. Although a committed nationalist, Vance Palmer was nevertheless widely acquainted with contemporary English, European and American writing. Randolph Hughes's 1935 monograph, *Christopher Brennan: An Essay in Values*, makes an analysis of the Australian poet the occasion for an attack on Australian provincialism. P.R. Stephensen was an enthusiast, at first hand, for D.H. Lawrence, his books and ideas. After returning home from Europe in 1932, Stephensen made a contribution of a somewhat different kind to Australian critical attitudes. *The Foundations of Culture in Australia* (q.v., 1936) argues the necessity of building a local culture out of local experience rather than materials derived at second hand from England and Europe. Two years later Rex Ingamells and Ian Tilbrook extended Stephensen's thesis in *Conditional Culture* (1938) which provided, in turn, the basic doctrines of the Jindyworobak movement (q.v.). The Jindyworobaks never commanded the allegiance of more than a section of the literary community. Yet they crystallized much of the critical feeling of the 1930s, especially the steady advance in the belief that a national literature could and should be created out of indigenous experience expressed in that form of the English language which had grown up through a hundred and fifty years of Antipodean usage. Out of that ambience came several important surveys, among them 'M. Barnard Eldershaw''s *Essays in Australian Fiction* (q.v., 1938), which included among its subjects Frank Dalby Davison, Leonard Mann, Christina Stead and Eleanor Dark. Another overview of fiction was J.O. Anchen's *The Australian Novel: A Critical Survey* (1940). Anchen's study opens with a brief history of Australian criticism, selecting for particular praise Barton, Byrne, Turner and Sutherland and Tucker from the nineteenth century; Zora Cross, Nettie Palmer, H.M. Green (q.v.), P.R. Stephensen and 'M. Barnard Eldershaw' in the twentieth. A book of rather greater importance than Anchen's also appeared in 1940: E. Morris Miller's *Australian Literature* (q.v.). A bibliographic compilation, it was revised and extended by F.T. Macartney in 1956 and remains a fundamental reference work.

The wartime years of the 1940s produced in criticism, as in so much of Australian life, a heightened and vigorous activity. Some of it represented an implicit acknowledgement of the message of Miller's bibliography: that there was a need to consolidate the factual bases of interpretation and judgement. The need was in part met by a series of literary biographies: Vance Palmer's *A.G. Stephens: His Life and Work* (1941) and *Frank Wilmot* (1942), Miles Franklin and Kate Baker's *Joseph Furphy* (1944), James Devaney's *Shaw Neilson* (1944) and Nettie Palmer's *Henry Handel Richardson* (1950). At the same time, other commentators continued the process of assessment. Tom Inglis Moore's *Six Australian Poets* (1942) offered accounts of Hugh McCrae, Shaw Neilson, Bernard O'Dowd, 'William Baylebridge', Christopher Brennan and R.D. FitzGerald. Brian Elliott collected a number of his essays in *Singing to the Cattle* (1947). Douglas Stewart, literary editor of the *Bulletin* 1939–61, published *The Flesh and the Spirit* (1948), the lead essay clearly announcing Stewart's affinity with Norman Lindsay. In 1944 H.M. Green's *Fourteen Minutes* put into print a series of radio talks on Australian poets, recognizing the possibilities of a further medium for critical discourse which was most fully exploited by Vance Palmer in his regular book reviews for the ABC. C.B. Christesen's (q.v.) anthology, *Australian Heritage* (1949), indicated through its title its emphases and principles of selection. Christesen's contribution to and influence on Australian literary criticism began in Brisbane in 1940 when he founded *Meanjin Papers*. Later to shift to Melbourne and to change its name to *Meanjin Quarterly, Meanjin* soon became a major force in the literary life of the country. With a democratic temper and a bias distinctly Australian, the journal not only maintained its own point of view; it offered a forum for some of the most sophisticated and professional criticism to have been written in Australia. By his unfailing commitment to the development of Australian literature and culture, together with his flair for discovering writers of major talent, Christesen proved himself to be the most gifted literary editor in Australia since A.G. Stephens. In 1967 he published some of the most distinguished contributions to *Meanjin* under his editorship in *On Native Grounds. Southerly* (q.v.), the other leading journal of the 1940s, was born a little earlier than *Meanjin* – in 1939 as the organ of the Sydney branch of the English Association. Not so exclusively concerned with indigenous writing as *Meanjin, Southerly* nevertheless regularly found space for local creative and critical work. First edited by R.G. Howarth and later by Kenneth Slessor and G.A. Wilkes, it remains an important arena for literary discussion. One other well-known magazine came into existence in the early years of the Second World War: Max Harris's (q.v.) *Angry Penguins*, first issued in Adelaide in 1941, was rendered notorious in 1944 as host to the Ern Malley (q.v.) hoax poems. Where *Southerly* was eclectic and *Meanjin* vigorously Australian, *Angry Penguins* was modernistic and cosmopolitan. Between them, the three magazines exemplify the range, spirit and variety of Australian literary culture in the 1940s. During the 1940s Colin Roderick began his long career as critic, historian and editor. *In Mortal Bondage* (1948) is a biography of Rosa Praed, but Roderick's most substantial contribution to Australian literary scholarship has been as an editor of Henry Lawson.

The kind of historical research demonstrated in these volumes runs through the 1950s, sometimes intersecting with critical evaluation, sometimes remaining parallel and separate. The concern for research, furthermore, was intensified by the noticeable growth in academic attention to Australian literary studies. Before the 1950s isolated individuals in university English departments, Hadgraft in Brisbane, Elliott in Adelaide, Inglis Moore in Canberra, had taken a serious professional interest in Australian writing. It was not until the middle of the century, however, that a major institutional commitment became apparent in the universities. An early manifestation of this phenomenon was G.A. Wilkes's *New Perspectives on Brennan's Poetry* (1952). The product of post-graduate research, *New Perspectives* was a very thorough exegesis of a body of verse whose symbolic difficulties had hitherto largely defied penetration. Wilkes's unravelling of *Poems (1913)* pointed the way to a wide-ranging academic enquiry into the sources, materials, affinities and techniques of Australian literature. The universities provided only one part of the critical effort of the 1950s. Major metropolitan dailies like the *Sydney Morning Herald* and the Melbourne *Age*, joined later by the national daily the *Australian*, continued through their literary pages to disseminate information and opinion. An independent writer like Hugh Anderson added to the growing story of bibliographical information with his *Guide to Australian Poets* (1953) and *Frank Wilmot* (1955). The bibliophile Walter Stone maintained publication of his *Biblionews*. Many established writers expressed their views in books of criticism, among them James Devaney's *Poetry in Our Time* (1952), Miles Franklin's *Laughter, Not for a Cage* (1956) and Frederick T. Macartney's *Australian Literary Essays* (1957). Leslie Rees, for many years a leading producer of radio drama with the ABC, wrote in *Towards an Australian Drama* (1953) one of the first books on the subject. Later revised and expanded as *A History of Australian Drama* (1973, 1978) it remains an important reference work. The 1950s were further marked by the

entry into the field of some new literary journals which soon made their mark. *Australian Letters*, edited by Max Harris, Geoffrey Dutton and Bryn Davies, was devoted more to creative than critical work. A selection of some of its best material was brought out in 1968 under the title of *The Vital Decade*. *Overland* (q.v.), first issued in 1954 under the editorship of Stephen Murray-Smith, was radical on social and political issues, more catholic in the range of fiction, verse and criticism it accepted. A sampling from its first ten years of publication appeared in 1965 as *An Overland Muster*. *Quadrant* (q.v.), founded in 1956 by James McAuley, adopted a political attitude almost the exact opposite of *Overland*'s, although it was similarly willing to print a wide range of literary material. 1958 was an especially important year for Australian criticism, bringing with it at least three books of major consequence. Russel Ward's *The Australian Legend*, although essentially a work of history, illustrated, through its heavy dependence on bush songs and ballads, the close nexus between historical and literary studies in Australia. *The Penguin Book of Australian Verse*, edited by John Thompson, Kenneth Slessor and R.G. Howarth, was one of the several collections of poetry which have helped to form Australian taste. This Penguin anthology was replaced in 1972 by a new selection made by Harry Heseltine. Finally in 1958 A.A. Phillips published *The Australian Tradition* (qq.v.). The essays brought together in this volume were drawn from the best Phillips had written in the previous ten years or so, many of them for *Meanjin*. They included close analyses like 'The Craft of Lawson' and 'The Craft of Furphy', along with more general commentaries such as 'The Democratic Theme' and a piece which has given Australian criticism some of its permanent currency, 'The Cultural Cringe' (q.v.). Printed within the covers of a single book, work of this calibre established Phillips as one of the major critics of the mid-century. In the year following *The Australian Tradition* Vincent Buckley (q.v.) brought out his *Essays in Poetry, Mainly Australian* (1959), which views its material from a quite different standpoint from Phillips. Suspicious of both the democratic account of Australian writing and what he termed the 'vitalism' of the Lindsay school, Buckley, in pieces like 'The Image of Man in Australian Poetry', looked for a spiritual dimension to his culture. Cecil Hadgraft's *Australian Literature: A Critical Account to 1958* (1960), on the other hand, falls more readily into the ambience of Phillips and Ward. For many years a member of the English department of the University of Queensland, Hadgraft carried out much pioneering work in

Australian literary history. His own historical overview is commonsensical, engaging and free of distorting dogma. His large contribution to Australian literary scholarship was recognized on the occasion of his retirement when a collection of essays, *Bards, Bohemians, and Bookmen* (1976), was edited by Leon Cantrell.

The permanent commitment of the universities to Australian literary studies was marked by the appointment in 1962 of G.A. Wilkes to the chair of Australian literature at Sydney University, the first in the country. He was succeeded in 1968 by Leonie Kramer, editor of *The Oxford History of Australian Literature* (1981) and the author of several studies on 'Henry Handel Richardson'. A further indication of the increasing professionalization of Australian criticism was the establishment in 1963 of *Australian Literary Studies* (q.v.), a journal devoted, under the editorship of L.T. Hergenhan, exclusively to the scholarly and critical study of Australian writing. Its annual bibliographies and reports on research in progress, along with its wide-ranging articles and reviews, offer a useful index to the state of the discipline. In the 1960s and 1970s the growth of a body of professional criticism was further assisted by the activities of a number of publishing houses: the Australian Writers and their Work series, for instance, initiated by Lansdowne Press and taken over by Oxford University Press; the University of Queensland Press's Portable Australian Authors series; the Australian Literary Reprints, facsimile texts of nineteenth-century works from Sydney University Press; or the many play texts from Currency Press. The increased availability of previously inaccessible titles was matched by the provision of fuller and more reliable texts of major authors, e.g. T.T. Reed's edition of Kendall (1966) or the editions of Brennan's *Verse* (1960) and *Prose* (1962) by A.R. Chisholm and J.J. Quinn. Comprehensive interpretations of various aspects of literary history were offered by Brian Elliott in *The Landscape of Australian Poetry* (1967) and Tom Inglis Moore in *Social Patterns in Australian Literature* (1971). Other important reference works came from Grahame Johnston and John Barnes. Johnston's *Annals of Australian Literature* (1970) followed his earlier selection, *Australian Literary Criticism* (1962); Barnes collated some major literary documents in *The Writer in Australia*, ranging from Sinnett's *The Fiction Fields of Australia* to Judith Wright's 'The Upside-down Hut'. The flow of literary biographies was maintained by Clement Semmler's *The Banjo of the Bush* (1966), James Normington-Rawling's *Charles Harpur: An Australian* (1962), Hugh Anderson's *Poet Militant: Bernard O'Dowd* (1968) and Jack Beasley's account of Katharine Susan-

nah Prichard, *The Rage for Life* (1964). Two general histories were especially characteristic of the critical achievement of the 1960s. In 1964 Geoffrey Dutton edited *The Literature of Australia* (q.v.), recruiting a panel of writers to provide broad surveys of the chief literary genres, together with specialist studies of leading individual figures. Three years earlier (1961) a quite different kind of conspectus had appeared in H.M. Green's two volume *History of Australian Literature* (q.v.). Unlike Dutton's co-operative venture, this was the culmination of a lifetime's effort of an individual who had been intimately involved in many of the episodes he chronicled. Green's two volumes encompass an extraordinarily comprehensive survey of every department and level of literary activity, including criticism. His thoroughness, sympathetic commonsense and unique relation to his material make Green's *History* a major work unlikely ever to be duplicated. R.F. Brissenden's 1966 study, *Patrick White*, was characteristic of its time in a different way, in its response to a writer who had imposed himself as the giant of contemporary Australian writing. From the early 1960s on, Australian criticism responded with markedly increased understanding and frequency to the body of White's creative literature, especially his fiction. Brissenden is a poet as well as an academic critic, and the 1960s saw the production of several important critical works by leading creative writers. The tradition of the artist-critic goes back in Australia through figures like Stewart, Slessor and FitzGerald to Lindsay and Brennan, even to Kendall and Harpur. In the 1960s it was notably represented by Judith Wright's *Preoccupations in Australian Poetry* (1965) and A.D. Hope's *Australian Literature 1950–62* (1963). Hope had taken part in some of the livelier polemical debates of the 1940s, conducting skirmishes with Arthur Phillips and Max Harris among others. It was not, however, until comparatively late in his career that he brought together his critical writings into a number of substantial volumes: *The Cave and the Spring* (1965), *Native Companions* (1974), *The Pack of Autolycus* (1978) and *The New Cratylus* (1979). Especially in *The New Cratylus* he embarks on a kind of consideration quite rare in Australian critical prose, speculation by a creative artist about the sources and processes of his own imagination. The uniquely stimulating and personal brand of criticism sometimes commanded by the practising writer is further exemplified in Les A. Murray's *The Peasant Mandarin* (1974) and in many of the judgements of Chris Wallace-Crabbe, whose *Melbourne or the Bush* (1974) is a representative work. D.R. Burns, a novelist and university teacher, combines the strengths of both callings in his lively *The Directions of Australian Fiction 1920–1974* (1975), while Nancy Keesing brings together the work of several hands in *Australian Postwar Novelists* (1975). Her title reflects the widely-held view that the most challenging Australian literature is increasingly to be found towards the more recent end of its time span, leaving the work of the colonial writers as the domain of research scholars and cultural historians.

In the last decade the established modes of critical discourse have continued to find major expression. Dorothy Green's *Ulysses Bound* (1973) and Axel Clark's *Christopher Brennan* (1980) are splendid examples of analytical biography. Brian Kiernan's *Images of Society and Nature* (1971) focuses on the canon of classic Australian novelists like Joseph Furphy, 'Henry Handel Richardson', Christina Stead, Xavier Herbert and Patrick White, while his *Criticism* (1974) provides a brief but comparatively rare account of how the discipline has been practised in Australia. Jack Beasley's *Red Letter Days* (1979) sets down personal memoirs of the postwar radical movement in literature. Nevertheless, if there was any definable new tendency in Australian criticism during the 1970s it was towards the interpretation of literature along sociological lines, as culturally symptomatic rather than for its own intrinsic achievement. Australian criticism in the past has conspicuously failed to generate its own systems of literary analysis; in turning to contemporary European and American theorists, it maintained a deeply-ingrained habit. Characteristic products of the 1970s were John Docker's *Australian Cultural Elites* (q.v., 1974), Humphrey McQueen's *A New Britannia* (1975) and David Walker's *Dream and Disillusion* (q.v., 1976) which placed figures influential earlier in the century such as Palmer, 'Furnley Maurice' and Louis Esson into a new framework of interpretation. J.J. Healy's *Literature and the Aborigines in Australia 1770–1975* (1978) mirrored changing attitudes to the continent's indigenous peoples, while Drusilla Modjeska's *Exiles at Home: Australian Women Writers 1925–1945* (1981) further reflected the impingement of new social attitudes upon the understanding of literature. G.A. Wilkes's *The Stockyard and the Croquet Lawn* (1981) demonstrated that even an established and fairly conservative critic could be responsive to the challenge of newer methodologies. However, perhaps the most telling evidence of the status of literary criticism in Australia in the last quarter of the twentieth century was the establishment in 1977 of a professional organization, the Association for the Study of Australian Literature (q.v.). Within a few years ASAL had achieved a membership of some three hundred, published its own journal, *Notes & Furphies* (q.v.), and held regular conferences. Its existence and success were a decisive demonstration of how far literary criticism in Australia had travelled from its tentative beginnings as an adjunct to *belles-lettres* and journalism towards a fully-professional, self-sustaining discipline.

H.H.

CRNLE Reviews Journal, see Association for Commonwealth Language and Literature Studies.

CROLL, R.H. (ROBERT HENDERSON) (1869–1947), born Stawell, Victoria, combined a long career on the administrative staff of the Victorian Education Department with an unusually active participation in literary, artistic, travel and educational organizations. One of Melbourne's best-known men of letters and a prolific contributor of verse and prose to Australian newspapers and journals, Croll published numerous works including *By-products: A Book of Verses* (1932), *The Open Road in Victoria* (1928), *Along the Track* (?1930), *Tom Roberts* (1935), *Wide Horizons: Wanderings in Central Australia* (1937) and *I Recall: Collections and Recollections* (1939). He edited *Collected Poems of John Shaw Neilson* (1934), *Smike to Bulldog* (1946, letters of Sir Arthur Streeton to Tom Roberts), and he collaborated with Percival Serle and 'Furnley Maurice' to produce *An Australasian Anthology* (1927).

CRONIN, BERNARD (1884–1968), born Middlesex, England, came to Australia as a child in 1890 and was later a jackeroo in Gippsland, northern Victoria and Tasmania. He worked briefly as a government clerk in Melbourne, then freelanced as a journalist before joining the *Herald* in the 1930s. During the Second World War he was a publicity censor in Victoria and WA and later taught creative writing at the Melbourne Technical College as well as contributing regular items to the Melbourne *Sun*. In 1920 Cronin helped found the Old Derelicts Club for indigent authors and artists. He also founded the Quill Club in 1933 and was made a life member in 1961 of the International PEN Club. A prolific writer of light fiction, Cronin wrote some thirty novels; several one-act plays including the radio play *Stampede*, represented in *Best Australian One-Act Plays* (1937); short fiction, and poetry. Two of his best novels are *Bracken* (1931) and *The Sow's Ear* (1933), in both of which aspects of Australian life are critically examined. His other novels include *The Coastlanders* (1918), *Timber Wolves* (1920), *Bluff Stakes* (1922), *Salvage* (1923) and *Red Dawson* (1927), all of which are derived from Cronin's rural experi-

195

ences in Tasmania, as is *The Sow's Ear*. The northern areas of Australia are the setting for *White Gold* (1927), *Dragonfly* (1928) and *The Treasure of the Tropics* (1928). Cronin used various pseudonyms, 'Wallace Dixon', 'Hugh Bohun', 'Eric North' and 'Denis Adair'.

Crooked Mick, see Speewah

CROSS, STAN (1888–1977), was the artist responsible for a 1930s cartoon famous in Australia, 'For gorsake stop laughing – this is serious!' (q.v.). Born Los Angeles, Cross arrived in Australia with his parents in 1892 and was well-known for his work on *Smith's Weekly*, which published his comic strips, 'You and Me' (renamed 'The Potts' when taken over by another artist) and later 'Dad and Dave' (q.v.), a visual adaptation of the radio serial of that name. A superb draughtsman, Cross was also responsible for 'Wally and the Major' which, with 'Bluey and Curley', was tremendously popular during the Second World War. 'Wally and the Major' began as 'The Winks' in the Melbourne *Herald* in 1940 but later that year, to give the strip a wartime flavour, Cross took Mr Winks and Wally Higgins into the army, Mr Winks becoming Major Winks in July 1940; later Pudden Benson was added to 'Wally and the Major' as the major's batman and often stole the scene. The major has been compared in attitude, temperament and efficiency with Captain Mainwaring of the British television series, *Dad's Army*. After Cross's retirement in 1970, 'Wally and the Major' was continued by Carl Lyon.

Cross the Border, see **ADAMSON, ROBERT**

CROSS, ZORA (1890–1964), born Brisbane, was for much of her life a freelance journalist. A remarkable woman much in advance of her time, she had a rather chaotic personal life, her long *de facto* relationship with David McKee Wright scandalizing the Sydney literary Establishment of the day. She published several volumes of frank love poetry in which she explored her reactions to the experience of love, sexuality and motherhood. They were *A Song of Mother Love* (1916), *Songs of Love and Life* (1917) and *The Lilt of Life* (1918). She also wrote *The City of Riddle-me-ree* (1918), children's verses which illustrate her lyric gift, and *Elegy on an Australian Schoolboy* (1921), an impressive poem in which she mourns the death of her young brother, John Skyring Cross, in the First World War. She published several works of fiction: *Daughters of the Seven Mile: The Love Story of an Australian Woman* (1924), a romance set against the background of the Queensland bush; *The Lute Girl of Rainyvale:*

A Story of Love, Mystery and Adventure in North Queensland (1925), accurately described by the subtitle; and *This Hectic Age* (1944), in which a country girl has problems coping with the sophisticated milieu of Sydney. Zora Cross also wrote a pamphlet, *An Introduction to the Study of Australian Literature* (1922), now dated and superficial but valuable at the time. Another novel, *The Victor*, was serialized in the *Sydney Morning Herald* in 1933.

Crouch Gold Medal, see Australian Literature Society

Crow, of which there are several varieties, is a large bird of the genus *Corvus* with black plumage and a mournful, monotonous call. It is native to the bushlands of eastern, western and southern Australia. An omnivorous feeder and skilful scavenger, it prefers a meat diet, usually of small bush animals but it also preys on helpless livestock, especially sheep and lambs, a practice that makes it unpopular with farmers. Its sombre appearance, doleful cry and repulsive habit of feeding on carrion have combined to represent it in Australian literature as a harbinger of tragedy and death, an integral part of the 'weird melancholy' that Marcus Clarke saw as the distinctive feature of the Australian bush. So marked a feature is the crow of the lonely outback enviroment that G. Herbert Gibson ('Ironbark'), in his advice 'How to Write an Australian Novel', stressed the need for its presence,

> Have a drawin' of a station
> And another illustration
> Of a carcass, with a crow upon a fence.
> There is nothing so expressive
> Of the sadness of our solitude immense
> . . . As a carcass and a crow upon a fence.

The ceaseless conflict between crow and man has been widely illustrated in Australian writing. In Henry Lawson's 'The Drover's Wife', the crow is seen as one of the numerous predators against which the hard-pressed people of the outback have to battle. In Lawson's story 'A Hero in Dingo Scrubs' and Mary Gilmore's poem 'The Crows Kept Flyin' Up', helpless human beings are targets for the cruel but cowardly bird. Barcroft Boake sees the crow as an omen of disaster:

> Crows are flying, hoarsely crying
> Burial service o'er the dying -
> Four Harbingers of Death.

A.B. Paterson refers to them as 'grim sextons of the Overland'. Barbara Baynton's tragic story 'The Chosen Vessel' sees them thwarted in their attempt to inflict the final indignity on the raped and murdered woman. The well-known folk-song 'The Dying Stockman' (q.v.) reiterates in its chorus the bushman's last wish to be buried out of their reach. Stories of crows preying upon helpless livestock are equally commonplace. In Barbara Baynton's 'Billie Skywonkie' the infuriated rouseabout tells of their 'scoffin' out' the eyes of the tottering, drought-weakened sheep. Dowell O'Reilly's story 'Crows' depicts a young ewe with one eye picked out and her dead lamb with both eyes gone and kidneys torn out. Countryman and poet David Campbell has a similar grisly scene in 'The Kidney and the Wren'. In E.G. Moll's poem 'During Drouth' there is a sense of the perverse irony of nature in the Australian environment where drought, an enemy to most living things, is a benefactor to the carrion-eating crows, providing them with a feast in the midst of famine. Dislike of the crow has led to derogatory use of its name, e.g 'crow' is a slang term for a female, especially if ugly or old, and was also used contemptuously for female Aborigines. To 'cop the crow' or 'draw the crow' is to get the poorest or least attractive of a set of alternatives. 'Stone the crows!' is an exclamation of exasperation or disgust, largely because stoning the crows was the ultimate exercise in futility. The term 'croweater' is used as a derisory comment on the imagined primitivism of the inhabitants of SA. An area of extreme remoteness, heat, aridity and general unattractiveness can be described as a place where 'the crows fly backwards' to keep the dust, the wind or the sun out of their eyes. The eternal, exasperating presence of the crows is reflected in such jokes as: Horseman to Cocky: 'How far is it to Bilga, mate – as the crow flies?' Cocky: 'Struth I dunno! The flamin' crows never leave here.'

CROYSTON, JOHN (1933–), born Enfield, Sydney, has spent most of his career with the ABC; from 1957 in the radio drama and features department, where he instituted the poetry anthology series, 'A First Hearing'; from 1965 with television drama as a producer; and since 1983 as head of forward planning. His own work includes *23 Poems* (1953, with Julian Woods); a verse drama, 'The Hills Shall Fly'; several plays including *The Runaway*, published in Brian Fitzsimmons (ed.) collection *Sight and Sound* (1969); numerous scripts for the series 'Certain Women' and 'Behind the Legend'; and translations and adaptions of *Lysistrata* and *Medea*.

Crucible, see MCKINNEY, JACK

Cry in the Jungle Bar, A, see DREWE, ROBERT

'CULOTTA, NINO', see O'GRADY, JOHN

Cultural Cringe was an expression first used by A.A. Phillips (q.v.) as the title of an essay in *Meanjin* (1950) and subsequently included in his *The Australian Tradition* (1958). The expression implies Australian cultural self-depreciation and subservience to European culture.

CUMPSTON, AMY (1921–), born Melbourne, has been a writer for television and director of the International Theatre Forum. She has published poetry, *Human My Race* (1955), *Borrow the Spring* (1961), *The Towers of Earth: Poems of the Blue Mountains* (1969); and drama, *This Fatal Island* (1973) and *Woodrow Wilson* (1973). Her other plays include 'Chinese Gordon', 'The Dragon Throne', 'Crusade', 'Kublai Khan', 'Sir Walter Raleigh' and 'The Swagman'.

CUNNINGHAM, PETER (1789–1864), born Dumfries, Scotland, became a surgeon in the Royal Navy; between 1819 and 1828 he made five voyages to NSW as surgeon-superintendent in convict transports. In 1825 he took up land on the Hunter River and in 1827 published *Two Years in New South Wales*, a combination of memoirs, experiences and information for intending immigrants. In 1830 he returned to England and in 1841 published a further work, *Hints for Australian Emigrants*, in which he urged the use of irrigation for farming in dry areas, he himself having been driven from his Hunter River property in 1830 by a severe drought.

CUNNINGTON, VIVIAN (1921–), born Toowoomba, Queensland, served with the AIF in the Second World War, conducted an electroplating business 1946–67 and has since been a freelance writer. A prolific writer of short fiction, Cunnington has published *Big Fat Tuesday* (1963, short stories), *A Change of Key* (1975, verse and short stories), *Naked at the Typewriter* (1977, poems and prose pieces) and a novel, *Jack Bones* (1978). At his best in brief humorous sketches of people, Cunnington made a considerable impression with *Big Fat Tuesday* (a literal translation of 'Mardi Gras') the stories of which are unpretentious and illustrate Cunnington's talent as a raconteur.

Cupboard under the Stairs, The, see Treelake Series

Curate in Bohemia, A, see LINDSAY, NORMAN

Cure, The, see KOCAN, PETER

CURLEWIS, JEAN (1899–1930), collaborated with her mother, Ethel Turner (q.v.), in

The Sunshine Family: A Book of Nonsense for Girls and Boys (1923); she also wrote five books for children and edited the children's column of the *Daily Telegraph* before her early death from tuberculosis. A more romantic and less humorous writer than her mother, she made Sydney's beaches and waterways the setting of several of her novels. In *The Ship That Never Set Sail* (1921), a representative Curlewis novel, Sydney Harbour suggests to the heroine the romance and adventure she yearns for but fails to find in real life; *Drowning Maze* (1922) describes the adventures of high-school boys on Pittwater; and *Beach Beyond* (1923) which deals partly with the thrills and perils of surfing, has an imaginary beach as an idyllic background.

CURR, E.M. (EDWARD MICKLETHWAITE) (1820–89), was born Hobart, son of Edward Curr (1798–1850), merchant and landowner who wrote *An Account of the Colony of Van Diemen's Land* (1824); he was educated in England and returned to Australia at the age of nineteen. He managed a series of runs in Victoria, many of them in tribal Aboriginal areas. His later life, mostly connected with pastoral activities, alternated between Victoria, NZ and Queensland and he wrote voluminously on matters pertaining to the land. His chief work was *Recollections of Squatting in Victoria* (1883), which contained his reminiscences of squatting life and reflected his keen and unusually humanitarian interest in the Aborigines. He also compiled and partly wrote a four-volume collection of observations entitled *The Australian Race* (1886–87).

Currency, a word with special Australian meanings during the nineteenth century, was first used thus in Governor Macquarie's time to denote the promissory notes issued by Sydney merchants at a time when sterling coinage was in short supply; its usage was soon extended also to include those born in the Australian colonies, as in 'currency lads' and 'currency lasses', to distinguish them from 'sterling', those born in England. The latter distinction was originally something of an insult (given that the currency notes had been valued at less than their sterling equivalents) but became more and more a jest between European Australians, and in the 1830s sporting contests were regularly held in NSW between 'currency' and 'sterling'. 'Cornstalk' and 'native' (qq.v.) were contemporary synonyms for 'currency'; it is used also in the *Currency Lad*, a newspaper which articulated the interests of the 'Cornstalks' in 1832–33, and in *The Currency Lass*, the title both of a play (performed 1844) by

Edward Geoghegan and of a novel (1927) by James Devaney.

Currency Lass, The, a musical comedy by Edward Geoghegan (q.v.), probably the earliest with a local setting, was first performed in Sydney in 1844 and published in 1976. Although flawed by stilted mannerisms and typed characters, the play has colour and is interesting for its reflection of the division in colonial society between expatriate and native-born, and for its idealization of the latter.

Currency Press, initiated in 1971 by wife and husband team Katharine Brisbane (q.v.) and Philip Parsons, has by its publication and promotion of Australian dramatists contributed greatly to the 1970s renaissance of Australian drama. Currency Press is or has been responsible for producing several separate drama series: *Modern Drama*, edited by Katharine Brisbane, which makes available the newest work of established playwrights such as David Williamson, Patrick White, Alexander Buzo, John Romeril, Louis Nowra and Peter Kenna, as well as the work of newer writers; *National Theatre*, edited by Philip Parsons, which presents important older plays in well-annotated texts with critical biographical and social comment; *Double Bills*, edited by Frank Bladwell, which comprise short plays in pairs (e.g. *The Christian Brothers* by Ron Blair and *A Lesson in English* by Barry Oakley) designed to capture aspects of Australian life; *Australian Screen*, edited by Sylvia Lawson, which comprises critical and historical studies of aspects of film and television in Australia, published in joint imprint with the Australian Film Institute; and the *Current Theatre*, devoted exclusively to modern Australian drama.

CURREY, C.H. (CHARLES HERBERT) (1890–1970), born Ulmarra, near Grafton, NSW, was long associated with history and the teaching of it in NSW, and was president of the Royal Australian Historical Society 1954–58. His publications include *Modern British History* (1931), *The Story of Man* (1947), *The British Commonwealth since 1815* (1951), *The Irish at Eureka* (1954), *The Transportation, Escape, and Pardoning of Mary Bryant* (1963), *Sir Francis Forbes* (1968) and *The Brothers Bent* (1968).

CURTIN, JOHN (1885–1945), prime minister of Australia 1941–45, is the subject of Alan Chester's *John Curtin* (1943), Irene Dowsing's *Curtin of Australia* (1969), Lloyd Ross's *John Curtin for Labor and for Australia* (1971), Kim E. Beazley's *John Curtin: An Atypical Labor Leader* (1972), Ross's fuller biography, *John Curtin* (1977), and Norman E.

Lee's *John Curtin, Saviour of Australia* (1983). The past history of Johnny Mulhall in Thomas Keneally's novel, *The Cut-Rate Kingdom* (1980), parallels that of Curtin.

CUSACK, DYMPHNA (1902–81), born Wyalong, NSW, was educated at the University of Sydney and worked as a teacher until 1944 when chronic illness forced her to retire. Her published writings include twelve novels, *Jungfrau* (1936), *Pioneers on Parade* (1939) written in collaboration with Miles Franklin, *Come In Spinner* (q.v., 1951) written in collaboration with Florence James and winner of the 1948 *Daily Telegraph* (Sydney) competition, *Say No to Death* (1951), *Southern Steel* (1953), *The Sun in Exile* (1955), *Heatwave in Berlin* (1961), *Picnic Races* (1962), *Black Lightning* (1964), *The Sun is Not Enough* (1967), *The Half-Burnt Tree* (1969) and *A Bough in Hell* (1971); eight plays, *Red Sky at Morning* (q.v., 1942), *Morning Sacrifice* (1943), *Three Australian Three-Act Plays (Comets Soon Pass, Shoulder the Sky, Morning Sacrifice)* (1950), *The Golden Girls* (1955), *Shallow Cups* in *Eight Plays by Australians* (1934) and *Pacific Paradise* in *Theatregoer* (1963); three travel books, *Chinese Women Speak* (1958), *Holidays Among the Russians* (1964) and *Illyria Reborn* (1966); and two children's books, *Four Winds and a Family*, with Florence James (1947), and *Kanga-Bee and Kanga-Bo* (1945). In 1953 she edited and introduced *Caddie, the Story of a Barmaid*, produced as a film, *Caddie*, in 1976. Cusack was awarded the Elizabeth II Coronation Medal (1953) and was made AM in 1981 for her contribution to Australian literature. Translated into numerous languages and especially popular with the socialist bloc, her books have been published in thirty-four countries. Her biography, *Dymphna* (1975), was written by her husband, Norman Freehill, with her co-operation.

Although Cusack never belonged to a political party, she was preoccupied with social injustice of all forms: *Jungfrau*, runner up in the 1935 *Bulletin* competition, deals frankly with sexual matters; *Come In Spinner* is an unillusioned study of wartime Sydney; *The Sun in Exile* is a bitter denunciation of racism; *Picnic Races* gives a light-hearted but critical picture of Australia's rural background; *The Half-Burnt Tree* deals partly with the Vietnam War and partly with Aboriginal problems; *Heatwave in Berlin* treats of the survival of fascism in post-war Germany; and *A Bough in Hell* focuses on the problems of alcoholism. Similar preoccupations inform her published and unpublished plays, many of which have been produced on stage, radio and television both in Australia and overseas. *Pacific Paradise*,

a particularly popular play which deals with the issue of nuclear weapons, has been published and performed in China and in numerous overseas countries; 'Eternal Now', which won a prize in the 1946 Playwrights Advisory Board (q.v.) competition, was televised by the BBC in 1954 with the title 'Stand Still Time'; *The Golden Girls*, produced several times by the ABC, was staged in England and won a British Arts Council grant in 1955; a dramatized version of *Heatwave in Berlin* was produced in Moscow and several other socialist countries; *Red Sky at Morning* was produced as a film in 1944.

CUTHBERTSON, JAMES LISTER (1851–1910), born Glasgow, Scotland, came to Australia in 1875 and taught at Geelong Grammar School for most of the period 1875–97. His *Grammar School Verses* appeared in 1879 and his chief book of poetry, *Barwon Ballads*, in 1893; a memorial edition *Barwon Ballads and School Verses*, edited by E.T. Williams, was published in 1912. His poem 'The Australian Sunrise' has been frequently anthologized.

CUTLACK, F.M. (FREDERICK MORLEY) (1886–1967), born Sussex, England, came to SA in 1891. After some early journalistic experience in Australia he served in France in the First World War, then became an assistant to C.E.W. Bean on *The Official History of Australia in the War of 1914–1918*. He returned to Australia, joined the *Sydney Morning Herald* in 1920 and wrote volume eight of the official history, *The Australian Flying Corps in the Western and Eastern Theatres of War, 1914–1918* (1923). He was associate editor of the *Sydney Morning Herald* 1937–47. His other publications include *The Manchurian Arena* (1934), *War Letters of General Monash* (1934) and *Breaker Morant* (1962), an attempted vindication of Harry Harbord Morant, whom he met in 1899 and whose execution in South Africa in 1902 he believed to be a miscarriage of justice.

Cyprus, The, a Government brig carrying convicts from Hobart Town to Macquarie Harbour, was seized by the convicts in Recherche Bay, Tasmania, in August 1829. One of the more dramatic events in Australia's convict history, the seizure of the *Cyprus* was dramatized on the London stage and a ballad sympathetic to the convicts, 'Seizure of the *Cyprus* Brig in Recherche Bay', was written by Frank MacNamara (q.v.). The full story of the incident is in Frank Clune and P.R. Stephensen, *The Pirates of the Brig Cyprus* (1962), and it is represented fictionally in Marcus Clarke's *His Natural Life* (1874).

D

Dad and Dave, two of Australia's most famous rural inhabitants, began life in the *Bulletin* in 1895 as father and son of the Rudd family in the first of 'Steele Rudd''s (qq.v.) selection sketches. In *On Our Selection* (q.v.) and other early 'Rudd' books, the Rudds were battlers, the harshness of their pioneering life emphasized rather than its humour. A younger son Joe, rather than Dave, was the 'galoot' of the family. In time, however, Dad and Dave emerged as comic characters and were finally transformed into generic Australian hayseeds – laconic, unsophisticated and slow-witted, occasionally putting one over a new chum but more usually the victims of their own dullness or of the sharp practices of 'city slickers' when they came to town.

The transformation of Dad and Dave was due partly to 'Rudd', who responded to the popularity of his work by making the Rudd family more farcical in his later sketches. But equally responsible were 'Rudd''s illustrators, who may in turn have influenced his change of direction: e.g. a drawing of Dave as a yokel by Norman Lindsay, first published in *Our New Selection* in 1903, clearly influenced the portrayal of Dave by Fred McDonald in the stage (1912) and sound film (1932) adaptations of *On Our Selection*, and also the portrayal by Tal Ordell in Raymond Longford's (q.v.) silent film version (1920), which was closer in mood to the original. A third factor was 'Rudd''s loss of control over what he had created. He had no part either in the stage adaptation of *On Our Selection*, which was phenomenally successful, or in the four Rudd films made in 1932–40 which starred McDonald and Bert Bailey (q.v.); and he died before the commencement of 'Dad and Dave', the radio serial produced by George Edwards which ran for over two thousand episodes 1937–51. The popularity of the radio serial consolidated the phrase 'Dad and Dave' in Australian idiom and confirmed the characters as bush stereotypes. The serial also introduced Mabel as Dave's sweetheart, placed Snake Gully on the map of mythical Australia alongside the Black Stump, and spawned yet another metamorphosis, the comic strip 'Dad and Dave' drawn by Stan Cross in *Smith's Weekly*. For their part the proprietors of *Smith's Weekly* encouraged a backblocks theme (sometimes called 'Dad and Dave' humour) for its single panel cartoons.

The heyday of Dad and Dave was in the 1930s and 1940s: *Smith's Weekly* ceased publication in 1950 and the radio serial a year later, although it had a number of repeats and there was a 'Dad and Dave' television series (1972) scripted by Ralph Peterson. The stereotypes survive in such comic strips as 'Gunn's Gully', and Dad and Dave survive in countless bar-room jokes, in which Dave rather than Dad is the rural idiot and Mabel alternates between being as slow-witted as her sweetheart and sexually more sophisticated. The fact that recent reprints of *On Our Selection* and *Our New Selection* have themselves been titled *Dad and Dave* illustrates the extent of the transformation of 'Rudd''s original creations.

Dad in Politics and Other Stories, a series of sketches by 'Steele Rudd' (q.v.), was published in 1908. In the chronicle of the Rudd family (q.v.), *Dad in Politics* precedes *Back at Our Selection* (1906). Dad is persuaded to stand for parliament, unexpectedly wins, is soon embroiled in feuds and suspensions when he takes his seat, and resigns in disgust to return to the selection. *Dad in Politics*, which resulted in 'Rudd' being barred from the Queensland parliamentary press gallery, is a key volume in the movement towards a farcical presentation of Dad, which characterized the later Rudd volumes and stage and screen adaptations of them; it obviously influenced the film *Dad Rudd M.P.* (1940), starring Bert Bailey (q.v.) and made after 'Rudd''s death. The other stories in the volume include two of particular biographical interest, 'The Selection Where I Was Reared' and 'How I Wrote *On Our Selection*'.

Daily Mail, see ***Brisbane Courier***

Daily Telegraph, a morning daily newspaper, began publication as the *Sydney Daily Telegraph* on 1 July 1879, struggled in its first years but survived to become – as it remains – the great rival of the *Sydney Morning Herald*. A supporter of free trade, political democracy and private property, the *Daily Telegraph* 'scooped' the world in 1884 with its announcement of the German annexation of northern New Guinea, but is probably best remembered before 1900 for its opposition to Federation in the referenda of 1898–99; in the twentieth century it has had a long tradition of opposition to the Labor Party. Notable editors of the newspaper have included Frederick Ward (1884–90, 1903–14), John Farrell (1890), Lachlan Brient (1890–1901), Thomas Heney (1924–26) and Brian Penton

(1941–51); Farrell and Penton also occupied other staff positions, as did Lennie Lower, Frank Moorhouse and Kenneth Slessor among other prominent Australian authors. A *Daily Telegraph* company ran the newspaper for over forty years from 1884, but by 1927 it had been taken over by Sun Newspapers, later Sir Hugh Denison's (q.v.) Associated Newspapers; subsequently the *Telegraph* was rejuvenated when brought under the control (1936–72) of Frank Packer and E.G. Theodore of Consolidated Press, and since 1972 it has been owned by Rupert Murdoch's News Limited. The *Tribune* (1882–89), a weekly 'companion' of the *Daily Telegraph*, was less successful in this role than the *Sydney Mail* and the *Australian Town and Country Journal* with their parent dailies (the *Sydney Morning Herald* and *Evening News* respectively), but the *Tribune*'s twentieth-century equivalent, the *World's News* (1901–?55) and the *Sunday Telegraph* (1939–), have had longer and more prosperous lives.

DALEY, VICTOR ('CREEVE ROE') (1858–1905), born County Meath, Ireland, came to Australia at the age of twenty. For several years he roamed southern Australia as an itinerant journalist, but from 1882 began to establish himself as a popular lyric poet, contributing to *Punch, Freeman's Journal* and the *Bulletin*. In 1898 he published his first book of verse, *At Dawn and Dusk*; the Sydney literary coterie used the title for their bohemian Dawn and Dusk Club (q.v.). With fellow poet Roderic Quinn, he was part of the so-called 'Celtic Twilight', a small enclave of lyrical romanticism amid the intense nationalistic-radical writing and the noisy bush balladry that dominated the literary scene of the day. Although he, too, was a radical poet his chief poetic love was 'the shining shallows' of the lyric. After his early death from tuberculosis, several further volumes of his poetry were published – *Poems* (1908, a miniature edition), *Wine and Roses* (1911, ed. Bertram Stevens) and *Creeve Roe* (q.v., 1947), a selection of his radical verse edited by Muir Holburn and Majorie Pizer. A.G. Stephens wrote the biographical, *Victor Daley* (1905).

Dalgerie, see *Keep Him My Country*

DALLEY, J.B. (JOHN BEDE) (1876–1935), born Rose Bay, Sydney, son of William Bede Dalley, was called to the Bar in England in 1901. After an accident caused deafness, Dalley became a journalist, editing the Bathurst *National Advocate* 1906–07, then joining the *Bulletin* where by 1911 he was a leader-writer and a contributor of short stories, verse, and witty, ironic paragraphs. After the First World War,

during which he contributed to *Aussie*, he rejoined the *Bulletin*, edited *Melbourne Punch* in 1924 and was then representative of the Melbourne *Herald* in London. As a novelist Dalley perceptively satirized the upper-class life of Sydney of the 1920s. His novels are *No Armour* (1928), *Max Flambard* (1928) and *Only the Morning* (1930).

DALLEY, W.B. (WILLIAM BEDE) (1831–88), born Sydney, the son of convict parents, attended Sydney College, was admitted to the bar in 1856 and capped a long parliamentary career by being the first Australian to become a member of the Privy Council (1887). In 1865 he became editor and part-proprietor of the *Freeman's Journal* and wrote for the *Sydney Morning Herald* and Sydney *Punch* to which he contributed a number of satirical biographical sketches of notable contemporary political figures. Although a successful barrister, Dalley lost two important cases – his defence of the bushranger, Frank Gardiner, in 1864 and of H.J. O'Farrell for the shooting in 1868 of the Duke of Edinburgh. In 1884 he published *Speeches on the Proposed Federal Council for Australasia*. His contemporary literary reputation is indicated by his presence in G.B. Barton's *The Poets and Prose Writers of New South Wales* (1866).

D'ALPUGET, BLANCHE (1944–), born Sydney, daughter of Lou d'Alpuget, former well-known Sydney journalist, worked as a journalist prior to her marriage which took her overseas for nine years. She spent four years in Indonesia and one in Malaysia. Her first novel, *Monkeys in the Dark* (1980), is set in Indonesia in 1966 and centres on Alexandra Wheatfield, a young journalist attached to the Australian Embassy at Djakarta, and her ambivalent reactions to the problems of life in Indonesia. *Turtle Beach* (1981), which won the *Age* Book of the Year Award, the SA government's biennial award for literature and the PEN Golden Jubilee award for fiction in Sydney, also concerns an Australian journalist, Judith Wilkes. In spite of her husband's displeasure, Judith obtains an assignment to Malaysia to cover the arrival in that country of Chinese refugees from Vietnam. Although the novel is primarily concerned with Judith Wilkes's own emotional problems culminating in her separation from her patronizing, selfish husband, other characters to create interest are Minou, said to have been a Saigon bar-girl but now Lady Hobday, second wife of the Australian High Commissioner to Malaysia, and Ralph Hamilton, Australian immigration officer in Kuala Lumpur. The novel's long-delayed climax comes with the disclosure of the horrors of the refugee island of Bidong and Minou's suicide so that her refugee relatives may reach safety. Blanche d'Alpuget also wrote *Mediator* (1977), a biography of Sir Richard Kirby, who was the chief judge of the Conciliation and Arbitration Commission for seventeen years. In researching *Mediator* she became interested in one of its background figures, Robert (Bob) Hawke, then president of the Australian Council of Trade Unions and currently prime minister of Australia. In 1982 she published the biographical work, *Robert J. Hawke*, which won the NSW Premier's Award for non-fiction. Based extensively on interviews, the work is a frank psychobiography.

'DALY, RANN', see PALMER, VANCE

Dam Busters, The, see **BRICKHILL, PAUL**

Damned Whores and God's Police, see **SUMMERS, ANNE; Feminism and Australian Literature**

DAMPIER, ALFRED (?1848–1908), born London, acted in a provincial company headed by Henry Irving before coming to Australia in 1873; in 1877 he formed his own company which included his wife, Katherine Russell, and his daughters, Lily and Rose. He specialized in producing the spectacular, nationalistic melodramas that were the staple of colonial audiences and provided a fruitful field for local playwrights. Dampier wrote several melodramas himself including 'The Nihilists' (1880, with 'Julian Thomas'), 'Marvellous Melbourne' (q.v., 1889, with J.H. Wrangham and possibly others), 'This Great City' and 'The Scout' (both 1891, with Garnet Walch) and 'To the West' (1896, with Kenneth Mackay). He also presented popular versions of Australian novels, adapting Marcus Clarke's *His Natural Life* in 1886 with 'Thomas Somers' as collaborator; and, with Walch, 'Rolf Boldrewood''s *The Miner's Right* in 1891. The most popular was his 1890 adaptation with Walch of 'Boldrewood''s *Robbery Under Arms*, which he took to London in 1894.

DAMPIER, WILLIAM (1652–1715), born Somerset, England, spent his early manhood trading and privateering in both the Atlantic and Pacific Oceans. In 1688 he spent about three months on the north-western coast of Australia (New Holland) in the area of King Sound. His account of his voyages in the Pacific (1686–91), published in 1697 as *A New Voyage Round the World*, led to his commanding an English naval expedition in 1699 to explore further in New Holland and New Guinea. He cruised the WA coast from Shark Bay to Roe-

buck Bay (named after his ship), before going on to discover New Britain. His later voyages included one in 1702 in which Alexander Selkirk (Daniel Defoe's Robinson Crusoe) was marooned on Juan Fernandez from one of Dampier's ships. Dampier's writing created a new vogue in travel literature at the time; his publications, in addition to the 1697 work, being *A Supplement to the Voyage Round the World* (1699), *A Voyage to New Holland in the Year 1699* (1703, 1709) and *Captain Dampier's Vindication of His Voyage to the South Seas in the Ship St. George* (1707). Dampier's narratives of his voyages were edited by John Masefield in 1906, and biographical studies of him were written by J.M.H. Abbott (1911), W.H. Bonner (1934), Joseph C. Shipman (1962) and Christopher Lloyd (1966).

Dandaloo, a small country town some fifty kilometres due west of Narromine, NSW, is presented in two A.B. Paterson (q.v.) poems, 'An Idyll of Dandaloo' and 'An Evening in Dandaloo', as the archetypal bush town where 'life's total sum' is 'sleep, diversified with rum'. Dandaloo's chief pride is its annual race meeting, where a combination of extraordinary decisions by the race judge and tampered weighing scales usually results in Dandaloo money staying in local pockets rather than filling the pockets of the city slickers who deem the Dandaloonies to be easy pickings.

DANN, GEORGE LANDEN (1904–77), born Sandgate, Queensland, wrote numerous plays for stage, radio and television. Two of his full-length plays have been published, *Caroline Chisholm* (1943) and *Fountains Beyond* (1944); the latter deals in an enlightened and sympathetic way with the problems faced by Aborigines in Australian society, as did Dann's earlier, controversial drama, 'In Beauty It Is Finished' (1931). His other plays include 'Days of Roses', 'The Giant', 'The Green Trees', 'Monday Morning', 'Oh, The Brave Music', 'Rainbows Die at Sunset', 'Resurrection at Matthewtown', 'No Incense Rising' which won first place in two play-writing competitions in 1937, 'Wild Bells', 'The Orange Grove', 'Funerals for Fieldmice' and 'Ha Ha, Among the Trumpets'.

D'ARCY-IRVINE, GERARD ADDINGTON (1862–1932), born London, went with his family to NZ before moving to Goulburn, NSW, where his father conducted a school. He entered the Anglican ministry and was consecrated coadjutor bishop of Sydney in 1926. In 1899 he published his first verse collection, *Poems*, followed by *Additional Poems* in 1901 and a further collection, *Poems*, in 1903. In 1905 an illustrated edition of his work was produced and it was later reprinted and enlarged. His final volume, *Analects*, appeared in 1923. D'Arcy-Irvine preached at Henry Lawson's funeral.

DARCY, LES (1895–1917), born Stradbroke, near Maitland, NSW, became a boxing champion in Australia but went to the USA in 1916 at the time of the conscription controversy in Australia and in circumstances that led to his being branded as a shirker of his duty to his country. Unable to gain an opportunity to establish himself as a boxer in America, Darcy fell ill and died. Darcy's undoubted boxing prowess and his untimely death have established him, like Phar Lap, as an Australian folk hero. A number of sentimental verse tributes to Darcy (e.g. by Jack Bradshaw) were composed soon after his death. W. Lawless wrote the contemporary *The Darcy Story* (1919) and Raymond Swanwick the later biographical study, *Les Darcy: Australia's Golden Boy of Boxing* (1965). Darcy is portrayed in Frank Hardy's *Power Without Glory* (1950) as Lou Darby; Monk O'Neill reminisces about him in Jack Hibberd's play, *A Stretch of the Imagination* (1973); and Hibberd's celebration of him, *The Les Darcy Show* (published 1976), was first performed in 1974. The Darcy myth also had a great influence on D'Arcy Niland, who was working on a Darcy biography when he died.

'DARE, ISHMAEL', see JOSE, ARTHUR WILBERFORCE

DARK, ELEANOR (1901–), the only daughter of the writer Dowell O'Reilly (q.v.), was born and educated in Sydney. After a brief period of employment as a stenographer, in 1922 she married Dr Eric Payten Dark, a general practitioner and writer on physiotherapy and sociological medicine. In 1923 the Darks moved to the Blue Mountains town of Katoomba, where they have remained, apart from lengthy visits 1951–57 to their citrus and nut farm in Queensland. They also made an extended visit to the USA in 1937. Eleanor Dark's earliest writings, short stories and verse, were contributed from 1921 to a range of magazines including the *Bulletin*, *Home* and *Triad*, mostly under the pseudonym 'Patricia O'Rane' or 'P. O'R.'. *Slow Dawning*, her first novel, was completed in 1923 though it failed to find a publisher until 1932. Her other novels are *Prelude to Christopher* (1934), *Return to Coolami* (1936), *Sun across the Sky* (1937), *Waterway* (1938), *The Little Company* (q.v., 1945), *Lantana Lane* (1959) and the historical trilogy, *The Timeless Land* (q.v., 1941), *Storm of Time* (1948) and *No Barrier* (1953). Dark's short stories, as yet uncollected, continued to appear until 1946

and she has also contributed some historical and travel articles to journals and anthologies. Most of the latter reflect her keen appreciation and knowledge of the Australian landscape. She was awarded the Australian Literature Society's Gold Medal in 1934 and 1936, and in 1978 received the Australian Society of Women Writers' Alice Award. In 1977 she was made AO. Some of her later novels have been translated into other languages and in October 1941 *The Timeless Land* was selected as Book of the Month in the USA. One of Australia's best-selling serious novelists for twenty years, Dark has received little attention in recent times, although a dramatized version of her historical trilogy was produced by the ABC in 1980.

A writer of formidable intellectual powers and technical subtlety, Dark has distinctive skills which find their fullest scope in her novels. Stylistically influenced by major European writers of the 1920s and 1930s, especially in her psychological focus and use of timeshifts, she rapidly developed a characteristic narrative technique. Concerned always to represent the inward experience of reality as well as its objective shape, she most characteristically uses the interior monologue. A novelist of ideas, particularly receptive to the power of cultural myths, she is personally committed to a socialist philosophy that stops short of ideological dogma. Striking features of her novels include her deep love of the land, her insight into the needs of women, her respectful understanding of Aboriginal culture and her awareness of the destructive effects of Western civilization.

Her feminist concerns are already apparent in *Slow Dawning*; the story of a young woman doctor's search for happiness in both personal life and career, the novel is remarkable for its technical control and authentic representation of life in an Australian country town. *Prelude to Christopher*, a more complex work, reveals a deep interest in heredity and abnormal psychology; the action, compressed into four days, is the critical culmination of a series of events in the past which are gradually and suspensefully revealed to explain the motives of the main characters. This is the first of her novels in which Dark's expressed concern to record life 'as an endless present moment, moving snail-wise through time, carrying the past and future on its back' rather than as a 'steady onward march', finds full expression. *Return to Coolami*, which deals mainly with the interrelationship of four people on a three-hundred mile journey by car through NSW, is a dramatic unfolding of the dynamic emotions of ordinary, likeable people. In *Sun across the Sky* the action is restricted to a single day of crisis and turns upon the relationship between three different men: Gormley, a philistine, power-hungry capitalist; Denning, a humane, vitalist doctor; and Kavanagh, a craggy, poetic genius whose spirit dominates the book and who is based on Dark's memory of C.J. Brennan. Unobtrusively but deftly structured, the novel is shaped by opposing ideas of life and sterility. *Waterway*, a lengthy novel which features a number of the characters from *Sun across the Sky* and is similarly restricted to a single day culminating in violent tragedy, includes a broader statement of Dark's general ideas. A densely-characterized novel distinguished by descriptions of its Sydney harbour setting, its action consists mainly of a diverse, inward drama. With *The Little Company*, Dark returned to a more conventional novel form. Darker and more pessimistically determinist than her earlier work, it is concerned with various forms of failure and deals with a number of broad issues such as war and pacifism, education, feminism and religious and political attitudes. *Lantana Lane*, more a light-hearted collection of loosely-united short stories and essays than a novel, was inspired by the Darks' experience of farming in Queensland. Humorously affectionate in tone, it offers some memorable pictures of Queensland rural life.

Dark is best known, however, for her historical trilogy which traces the development of the European settlement in Australia 1788–1814. Based on extensive research, the trilogy is true to the events of history, although enlivened by the novelist's imaginative treatment of the inward life of the participants. As its title suggests, the underlying theme of *The Timeless Land*, which deals with the first five years of white settlement, is the spiritual dichotomy between the age-old, relatively timeless continent of Australia and the time-governed, new 'civilization' of Europe. The experiences of and the relationship between Bennelong and Governor Phillip, both representative of and yet distanced from their respective cultures, contain the central conflict. Striking features of the novel include a wide range of well-realized individuals, both white and black, convict and free; a consistently sympathetic presentation of the culture of the Aborigines; lyrical descriptions of the Australian landscape; and a style that moves easily from epic to comic and graphic. Unillusioned in its attitude to Western civilization, the novel has been praised as a landmark in Australian historical fiction and an important work for all students of the first period in Australian history or of general ethnic conflict. There is no reduction in tone in the massive, solidly-detailed *Storm of Time*, which covers the governorships of Hunter, King and Bligh; the novel is also an incisive analysis of the dynamic interplay of interests in the new society. The same flair for

description, characterization and detail enlivens *No Barrier*, which takes the story up to the crossing of the Blue Mountains.

Dark Moon, see HENEY, HELEN

Dark Places of the Heart, see *Cotters' England*; STEAD, CHRISTINA

Dark Windows, see 'ERCOLE, VELIA'

Darkening Ecliptic, The, see Ern Malley Hoax

Darling Downs, one of Queensland's most fertile pastoral and agricultural areas, watered by the Condamine River and its tributaries, is situated about 160 kilometres west of Brisbane. Discovered in 1827 by explorer and botanist Allan Cunningham and named after Sir Ralph Darling, then governor of NSW, the Darling Downs district was settled in the 1840s by squatters such as the Leslie brothers who established the Canning Downs station near the present township of Warwick, one of the chief urban centres of the area. The regional capital of the Darling Downs is Toowoomba; it grew into a township in the 1840s because it was on the wagon route to Brisbane. Toowoomba's famous literary sons include A.G. Stephens, 'Steele Rudd', George Essex Evans (q.v.) and, in more recent times, Bruce Dawe (q.v.). *Downs Images*, a selection of essays, stories and poems by some twenty-one Downs writers, was published in 1981. D.B. Waterson wrote *Squatter, Selector and Storekeeper: A History of the Darling Downs 1859–93* (1968).

DARLING, Sir **JAMES** (1899–), born Tonbridge, England, became headmaster of Geelong Grammar School in Victoria in 1929. He served on the Universities Commission 1942–51, was foundation president of the Australian College of Education in 1959 and chairman of the ABC 1961–67. His reflections, *The Education of a Civilized Man*, appeared in 1962.

DARLING, Sir **RALPH** (1772–1858), was governor of NSW 1825–31. He introduced extensive financial and administrative reforms in the Colony and encouraged exploration, but had a reputation for autocracy in a time of change. Darling tried unsuccessfully to legislate to control the press and was criticized in verse and editorials published in the *Australian* and the *Sydney Monitor*; he also prevented Barnett Levey's (q.v.) attempts to establish a colonial theatre and banned the singing of the John Donohoe (q.v.) ballads. The Darling River and the Darling Downs, which were discovered during his term of office, were named after him; so was the 'Darling necklace', an iron collar which imprisoned two soldiers, Sudds and Thompson, in a controversial punishment in 1826. Darling appears briefly in 'Price Warung''s story of 1820s Sydney society, 'Marie Antoinette's Fandango' (1891).

Darling River, named after Sir Ralph Darling, governor of NSW 1825-31, is a major part of the great inland river system that runs from Queensland through NSW to Victoria and SA. The Darling has its source near Stanthorpe in Queensland, where it it known as the Severn, and flows under various names – the Dumaresque, the Macintyre, the Barwon – until, from the junction of the Barwon and Culgoa Rivers, it flows as the Darling, joining the Murray River at Wentworth in south-western NSW. Exploration of the Darling basin began with Allan Cunningham in 1827 and in 1828 Charles Sturt and Hamilton Hume reached the spot on the river where Bourke now stands. Settlement followed in the wake of exploration and by the latter decades of the century the Darling region had been carved up into gigantic runs. The pastoral occupation of the Darling is described in C.E.W. Bean's *On the Wool Track* (1909). The use of the river for transport and commerce is discussed in Bean's *The Dreadnought of the Darling* (1911) and Ian Mudie's *Riverboats* (1961). F.M. Browne's poem, 'The Last of the Darling Dreadnoughts' captures the atmosphere of the riverboat era. Henry Lawson, sent by J.F. Archibald of the *Bulletin* to Bourke in 1892 to collect material for outback stories, spent laborious months tramping the environs of the Darling; his poems 'Song of the Darling River' and 'Bourke', together with his story 'The Darling River', capture much of the area's atmosphere. The Darling has given its name to the toxic plant, the Darling pea, which poisons cattle, and the phrase is applied to humans who, exhibiting strange symptoms of moodiness or eccentricity, are said to 'have the Darling pea'. The river's name is also used in such outback humourisms as a 'Darling shower', i.e. a clap of thunder, two drops of rain and a dust storm; a 'Darling sandwich', i.e. a goanna between two layers of bark; and a 'Darling pie', i.e. baked rabbit and bindi-eyes.

DARRELL, GEORGE (1841–1921), born Bath, England, with the name George Frederick Price, came to Australia in 1865 and joined the NZ gold rush in the same year. He spent little time as a digger, having quickly discovered his interest in the theatre, and achieved some success as an actor at Dunedin. He returned to Melbourne in 1868 to act at the Theatre Royal and at the same time changed his name to Darrell. In 1870 he married the well-known actress Fanny Cathcart (q.v.), who had already influenced his career, and for the next ten years toured with her in NZ, Australia and the USA. During this time he also formed his own company, for which he wrote numerous plays, and acquired a reputation as an actor, playwright, manager, producer and entrepreneur. After the death of Fanny in 1880, he continued to tour extensively in Australia and overseas, often accompanied by his second wife, the young actress Christine Peachey, whom he married in 1886 and who died in 1892. In addition to these personal tragedies, his career was curbed by an accident in 1884 and by illness in 1887, but was not severely checked until the 1890s when the growth of the J.C. Williamson company offered strong competition and the economic depression affected the size of audiences. By 1905 his career was virtually over, his later productions having failed and his acting skills finding few openings, and in 1921 he committed suicide. Of the numerous plays written by Darrell, possibly as many as fifty-eight, most retained the traditional elements of melodrama, although they had a distinctive topical and lively Australian flavour including a range of stock colonial types and featuring both expatriate nostalgia and robust good humour. Apart from *The Sunny South* (q.v., 1883), his only extant work, his most popular productions were 'Man and Wife' (1871), 'The Trump Card' (1874), 'Transported for Life' (1876), 'Back from the Grave' (1878), 'The Forlorn Hope' (1879) and 'The Naked Truth' (1883). Most of these were original, although Darrell occasionally wrote adaptations of English and Australian novels, including one of Fergus Hume's *The Mystery of a Hansom Cab*, produced in 1888. Darrell's career is the subject of Eric Irvin's *Gentleman George* (1980).

DARWIN, CHARLES (1809–92), the famous English naturalist and evolutionary theorist, visited Australia briefly in HMS *Beagle* in 1836. His *Journal of Researches into the Geology and Natural History of the Various Countries Visited by H.M.S. Beagle* (1839) includes his impressions of that brief visit. J. Lort Stokes published *Discoveries in Australia: With an Account of the Coast and Rivers Explored and Surveyed during the Voyage of H.M.S. Beagle* (1846). He appears in 'Price Warung''s story, 'Absalom Day's Promotion', and in 'Grant Hervey''s novel, *An Eden of the Good* (1934).

DAVEY, JACK (1910–59), one of Australia's earliest and best-known radio and television entertainers, was born in Auckland, NZ, and came to Australia in 1934. His book *Hi, Ho! Everybody!*, the title being the famous opening remark of his programmes, was published in 1945. Lew Wright published *The Jack Davey Story* (1961).

DAVIDSON, JIM, see *Meanjin*

DAVIES, ALAN FRASER (1924–), born Wangaratta, Victoria, and professor of politics at the University of Melbourne since 1968, has published numerous sociological and political works including *Policies for Progress* (1954), *Australian Democracy* (1958), *Private Politics* (1961), *Australian Society* (1965, edited with Sol Encel), *Images of Class* (1967) and *Skills, Outlooks and Passions* (1981); the last is a psychoanalytic contribution to the study of poli-·tics.

DAVIES, JOHN (1813–72), born London, came to Australia at the age of eighteen, having been sentenced to transportation for seven years for fraud. An audacious and energetic character, Davies became a reporter for the *Port Phillip Gazette* in 1842 and in 1852 in Hobart, in partnership with George Auber Jones, published the *Hobarton Guardian*, which was incorporated in 1854 with the *Hobarton Mercury*. Davies became its sole proprietor, absorbing several other Tasmanian newspapers and establishing it as a daily by 1858. The *Mercury* was taken over by his sons, John George Davies and Charles Ellis Davies, in 1871. John Davies, an amateur actor, was also part-proprietor of the Theatre Royal, Hobart.

DAVIS, ARTHUR HOEY, see 'RUDD, STEELE'

DAVIS, BEATRICE (1909–), born Bendigo, Victoria, had a distinguished career as an editor with Angus & Robertson 1937–73. She edited *Coast to Coast* in 1942, and compiled *Short Stories of Australia: The Moderns* (1967). Her contribution to Australian publishing was recognized when she was made MBE in 1965 and AM in 1981. She was elected as Bookman of the Year in 1976.

DAVIS, JACK (1918–) is a member of the Aboriginal Bibbulmun tribe and son of part-Aboriginal parents from north-west WA. After some years of work on cattle stations in the north, where he saw at first hand the injustice with which the tribal Aborigines were treated, he returned to Perth to write and to take up the Aboriginal cause. Following a period as a government transport driver he was manager of the Perth Aboriginal Centre (1967), director of the Aboriginal Advancement Council in WA (1969) and joint editor of the Aboriginal magazine, *Identity*, 1973–79. In 1976 he was

awarded the BEM for services to the Aborigines and for his writings; in 1980 he received the Patricia Weickhardt Award for an Aboriginal writer.

His first book of poetry, *The First-Born and Other Poems* (1970), contains an introductory autobiographical sketch and an appendix of Bibbulmun tribal words. The title poem, a nostalgic *cri de coeur* for the 'dark proud race', indicates in its opening line, 'Where are my first-born said the brown land, sighing', the innate Aboriginal gentleness and melancholy. Other poems that reveal Davis's yearning for the past include 'The Drifters' and 'Desolation', the latter echoing the sense of loss so predominant in Aboriginal verse. His strongest protest poem 'Whither?' portrays the typical Aboriginal life from optimistic youth to disillusioned age, a life characterized by a succession of withheld or withdrawn basic human rights. His best-known individual poem is possibly 'Yadabooka', the story of a tribal Aboriginal who was sentenced by white law to life imprisonment for a ritual killing that was sanctioned by Aboriginal law. 'Integration', with its message 'This is ours together/This nation', is a plea for black-white union in attempting to resolve racial problems. Davis's second volume of poems, *Jagardoo: Poems from Aboriginal Australia*, was published in 1978. A play by Davis, *The Dreamers* (1982), dealing with the problems of Aboriginal people in an urban setting, was first performed as a one-act play in 1973. It was rewritten as a two-act play and adapted to suit the changing Aboriginal scene in 1982. His other play, *Kullark* (1979), written to mark the sesquicentenary celebrations in WA and successfully staged there, focuses upon three episodes in the race-relations history of that state – the Nungar (Nyoongah) tribe during the years 1829–30, a black family in the Moore River district of the 1930s, and a contemporary Aboriginal family. The same treatment of the Aboriginal by white society, repeated at the three intervals during a century and a half, creates a cyclical effect of injustice that leads to a fatalistic pessimism. That pessimism and despondency can only be broken, the play indicates, by a change in the Aboriginal view of itself as a race.

DAVISON, FRANK DALBY (1893–1970), born Glenferrie, Victoria, was christened Frederick Douglas but began to use the names Frank Dalby after 1931 to distinguish himself from his father, Frederick Davison (q.v.). After leaving school at twelve, he worked on farms in Victoria, acquiring a wealth of rural experience that he later used in his short stories. In 1908 the Davison family moved to the USA, where Frank was apprenticed to the printing trade, worked for some time in New York and tried his hand at writing. He travelled widely in North America and in the West Indies, the latter experience proving useful for his travel book, *Caribbean Interlude* (1936). He enlisted enthusiastically in the First World War and served with the British cavalry in France, returning to Australia in 1919. Throughout these years of travel his nostalgia for home quickened his appreciation of the Australian bush. There followed four years of hard farming in southern Queensland, brought to a close by drought and debt, a period of working in his father's real estate business in Sydney and involvement in his father's journal, the *Australian*, later *Australia*, 1923–25. The *Australian* published several of his short stories and serialized versions of his two novels, *Man-shy* (q.v.) and *Forever Morning*. In 1931 both novels were published separately in cheap editions by Frederick Davison, *Man-shy* winning the Australian Literature Society Award. *The Wells of Beersheba* (q.v.), an account of the Australian Light Horse in Palestine 1914–18, appeared in 1933; *Blue Coast Caravan*, a travel book, in 1935, *Children of the Dark People* (q.v.) and *Caribbean Interlude* in 1936. He was also writing short stories, many of them published first in the *Bulletin* and revised for his collection, *The Woman at the Mill* (1940). In 1944 he married for the second time and in 1951 bought a small farm north of Melbourne, 'Folding Hills', where he lived for his last two decades. *Dusty* (q.v., 1946) and his collection of shorter works in one volume, titled *The Road to Yesterday* (1964), seemed to set the seal on his reputation as a writer of animal stories and a sensitive interpreter of Australian bush life in the tradition of Henry Lawson, Joseph Furphy and Vance Palmer. The publication of the massive novel *The White Thorntree* (q.v., 1968), however, a book that had taken twenty-two years to write, seemed a major change in direction, requiring a new, more difficult assimilation of his talent.

Apart from the novels *Man-shy* and *Dusty*, Davison's most popular works are his short stories. The fourteen stories grouped under the heading 'Queensland' in *The Road to Yesterday* are an imaginatively-coherent whole, evoking a way of life that is particular in time and place but universal in its reflection of human motives, frustrations, hopes and disillusionments. The theme of sexuality as a subterranean, potentially destructive force, a continuing preoccupation for Davison, as *The White Thorntree* shows, runs through several of the stories including 'The Woman at the Mill', 'Return of the Hunter', 'Further West' and 'Blood Will Tell'. Others such as 'Tank-Sinkers', 'Nobody's Kelpie' and 'Soldier of Fortune' deal sensitively with the important minutiae of human rela-

tionships in a landscape where relationships are sparse. 'The Good Herdsman' and 'A Letter from Colleen' express unsentimentally the pathos of old age. Throughout the stories the common implication of all things animate in a tragic, endless recurrence is indirectly probed. Hume Dow has published an account of Davison's work (1971) and Owen Webster in *The Outward Journey* (1978) deals with his early life and writing. Davison appears as Knarf in 'M. Barnard Eldershaw''s novel, *Tomorrow and Tomorrow* (1947).

DAVISON, FRED (1868–1942), born Mount Buninyong near Ballarat, was printer, publisher, editor, journalist, fiction writer and the father of Frank Dalby Davison (q.v.). His energetic nationalism, which included a keen interest in Australian literature, found expression in the organ of the Australian Natives' Association, *Advance Australia*, which he edited 1897–99. After an unsuccessful sojourn in the USA (1908–17) and service with the First AIF in France, he continued his efforts in two journals which he founded, the *Australian Post* (1920–21) and the *Australian*, later *Australia* (1923–25). These depended heavily on contributions from his son Frank and other members of the Davison family. During the 1930s depression, he turned the family's energies to publishing and produced cheap editions of Frank Davison's novels, *Man-shy* and *Forever Morning*, in 1931. He also wrote several works of fiction, including *Storm Bradley – Australian* (1932) and *Duck Williams and His Cobbers* (1939).

DAWBIN, ANNIE MARIA (ANNIE MARIA BAXTER) (1816–1905), born Devon, England, came to Australia as the seventeen-year-old bride of Lieutenant Andrew Baxter, whose regiment was stationed in Van Diemen's Land. From 1834 to 1851, in a steadily-deteriorating marriage, she accompanied Baxter over much of the colony – to Sydney and Port Macquarie as a soldier's wife, to the Macleay River in NSW and the Port Fairy district in western Victoria as a pastoralist's wife. A second marriage, after her husband's suicide in 1855, to Robert Dawbin was marked by further disappointments and unsuccessful ventures in Victoria, England and NZ. In 1873 she published *Memories of the Past by a Lady in Australia*, memories drawn from the diaries which she had maintained over thirty-two years and which gave not only a revealing picture of the society of the colony in the years, 1834–65, but also a remarkable self-portrait of one of Australia's pioneer women. Lucy Frost included a selection of the diaries in *No Place for a Nervous Lady* (1984).

DAWE, BRUCE (1930–), born Geelong, Victoria, left high school at sixteen, a dissatisfied and uninterested student. A variety of briefly-held jobs followed until he completed adult matriculation at night classes in 1953 and began a university course in 1954. Although he left the University of Melbourne after a year, his developing literary talent benefited by the advice of Melbourne University writers Chris Wallace-Crabbe and Vincent Buckley, and by his association with *MUM* (*Melbourne University Magazine*), *Compass* and *Farrago*, in the last of which he published the 'Joey Cassidy' stories. After a period as factory worker in Sydney and postman in Melbourne he joined the RAAF. During his airforce service (1959–68) he published two volumes of poetry, married a Toowoomba girl and completed his first degree (he now holds a Ph.D.) at the University of Queensland. In 1971 he became a teacher at Downlands College, Toowoomba, and in 1972 a lecturer at the Darling Downs Institute of Advanced Education. Dawe's volumes of verse are *No Fixed Address* (1962); *A Need of Similar Name* (1965, the Myer Award for poetry); *An Eye for a Tooth* (1968, the Sidney Myer Charity Trust Award for poetry); *Beyond the Subdivisions* (1969); *Heat-Wave* (1970); *Condolences of the Season* (q.v. 1971); *Just a Dugong at Twilight* (1975); and *Sometimes Gladness: Collected Poems 1954–1978* (q.v. Grace Leven Prize for poetry; a new edition 1954–1982 in 1983). *Bruce Dawe Reads from His Own Work*, in the Poets on Record series, was published in 1971. Dawe edited the poetry anthology, *Dimensions*, in 1975. *Over Here Harv'*, a collection of the 'Joey Cassidy' and other early stories by Dawe, was published in 1983. He was awarded the Ampol Arts Award for creative literature in 1967, the Dame Mary Gilmore Medal of the Australian Literature Society in 1973 and the Patrick White Literary Award in 1980.

In a CLF lecture in 1964 Dawe regretted the lack of 'social awareness' in contemporary Australian poetry. His own poetry, by contrast, is one of unremitting critical concern; the criticism is of governments, régimes, institutions and modes of life which oppress and deprive; the concern is for individuals, 'the lost people in our midst for whom no one speaks', and for modern man in general, 'homo suburbiensis', for whom happiness and meaning in life are mostly withheld. There is criticism of totalitarianism in the poems 'Only the Beards are Different' and 'The Not-so-good Earth'; of the Church (Dawe was a convert to Roman Catholicism) in 'The Decay of Preaching'; and of the self-centred insularity and nationalism of Australia in '"A" is for Asia' and 'Burial Ceremony. Hungary 1956–62'. Dawe's chief

criticism, however, is for the oppressive force of modern life – 'one of the main things I would say ... about this awkward proposition known as Life, is that it can be a bit of a bastard'. Life's brevity and meaninglessness are at the heart of 'Enter Without So Much As Knocking' and 'Any Shorter and I'd Have Missed It Altogether'; its pettiness is illustrated in 'Two Ways of Considering the Fog', 'Beatitudes' and in the masterly evocation of Melbourne football mania, 'Life-Cycle' (q.v.); its unrelenting pressure is exposed in 'Slow Coach' and 'Leasehold'; and its victims are categorized in 'No Fixed Address' (alcoholics), 'Happiness Is the Art of Being Broken' (the aged), 'Good Sport' (the ugly), 'Homecoming' (q.v., the casualties of war) and 'The Family Man' (the casualty of domesticity). The totality of man's bondage, and Dawe's somewhat rueful recognition that it is a situation beyond mending, are illustrated in the closing words of 'Homo Suburbiensis'. Man's offering to the insatiability of life is all that he has to give: 'time, pain, love, hate, age, war, death, laughter, fever'.

Paradoxically Dawe's poetry is neither sombre nor pessimistic. Humour, usually satirical, introduces a lightness of tone and the resultant mixture of the serious and the droll is one of the most attractive features of his verse. His poems are invariably brief, succinct and pertinent, 'one-shot' poems that say only as much as they need to. Sometimes they end without the ultimate confrontation, but with a poetic shrug of the shoulders that, in characteristically Australian fashion, implies a laconic acceptance of things as they are. His articulate and readily-understood response to situations and themes is expressed in speech cadences that combine the brashly colloquial of the spoken Australian language (and 'slanguage') with subtle and deftly-placed lyricism. His success in blending these apparent incongruities of language is his most remarkable technical achievement.

DAWE, CARLTON (1865–1935), born Adelaide, published three volumes of verse and two works of fiction including *The Golden Lake* (1891), an adventure story based on the search for a cave of gold in Australia, before settling permanently in England from 1892. He then became a prolific writer of popular fiction (romance, mystery, crime) with more than seventy books published over a period of forty years. His experience of Australia is drawn on mainly in his earlier novels, which include *Mount Desolation* (1892), where he uses a bank robbery based on an incident from the exploits of the Kelly gang; *The History of Godfrey Kinge* (1893), a story of English disinheritance and colonial rehabilitation; *The Emu's Head* (1893), a search for treasure hidden by a bushranger;

The Pilgrims (1894), set in a gold-mining town in Victoria; and *The Confessions of a Currency Girl* (1894), a transportation story.

Dawes, Rufus, see *His Natural Life*

Dawn, the first Australian journal for women, was edited by Louisa Lawson (q.v.) and ran as a monthly 1888–1905. Boycotted by male printers in its early days because of Lawson's policy of employing women where possible, *Dawn* had a reformist and feminist outlook, and contained articles on social issues such as divorce reform and women's suffrage as well as news items, fiction and poetry. Significant contributors included Lawson herself, sometimes writing as 'Dora Falconer', and the self-titled 'female bachelor', Rose Soley.

Dawn and Dusk Club, a convivial society of artists and writers, was established in Sydney after the publication of Victor Daley's (q.v.) first book of verse, *At Dawn and Dusk* (1898), and named in honour of that work. The 'Symposiarch' or chief Dawn and Dusker was Daley himself; other notable members of the club of *bon vivants* were F.J. Broomfield, Norman Lindsay, Henry Lawson, Bertram Stevens and Randolph Bedford. The rules of the club were allegedly printed in Chinese; the only person allowed to interpret them was supposedly Jim Philp, who could not read Chinese. G.A. Taylor's *'Those Were the Days'* (1918) contains details of the club's membership.

Dawnward? (1903), Bernard O'Dowd's (q.v.) first volume of poetry, speculates on the prospects of freedom, equality and fraternity in Australia and ponders the nation's future direction – 'To Failure's midnight sea or Dawnward?'. The numerous inflammatory personified poems, e.g. 'Prosperity', 'Hate', 'Compromise' and 'Proletaria', heap abuse upon such enemies of society as 'Vested Rights', 'Mammon', 'Bacchantic Trade' and 'Lamias of Caste'. *Dawnward?* satisfied the radical tenets of O'Dowd's *Poetry Militant* (q.v.) but with its baffling maze of personification and allusion and its mesmerizing 'fourteener' stanza it met a puzzled and unsympathetic reception from readers and literary critics of the day.

DAWSON, A.J. (ALEC JOHN) (1872–?) born England, came to Australia as an apprentice on a sailing ship. He deserted his ship in Melbourne and remained in Australia for several years before returning to England. Author of more than twenty fictional works and numerous works of non-fiction including war memoirs, Dawson drew only incidentally on his Australian experiences. In his book of short stories,

Mere Sentiment (1897), four of the twelve pieces have Australian settings. *The Record of Nicholas Freydon* (1914), purporting to be the autobiography of an Englishman who was brought to Australia as a boy, captures something of the atmosphere of the bush.

Dawson, Mum, see **LOCKE, SUMNER; Rudd Family**

DAY, A. GROVE, see *Modern Australian Prose, 1901–75*

Day of My Delight, see **BOYD, MARTIN**

'DAY, WILLIAM', see **DERRINCOURT, WILLIAM**

Daybreak, a novel by Vance Palmer (q.v.), was published in 1932. Set in a small Victorian town in the 1920s, its action is compressed into twelve hours. The central figure, a fruit farmer Bob Rossiter, has reached a turning point in his close relationship with Harry Sievright, another farmer and his ex-commanding officer. Sievright, who is suffering from severe psychological stress induced by the war and is subject to jealous fantasies about his wife Jean and Rick Lennard, the district doctor, wants Rossiter to abandon his farm and join him in a search for gold. Meanwhile Rossiter's wife Mary is in hospital expecting the baby they have long hoped for. In addition, there has been a lock-out at the local sawmill and Lysaght, a labour agitator, is anxious for Rossiter to persuade the local orchard workers to support the mill hands in their claims. Although the novel centres on Rossiter's self-liberation from a tangle of conflicting loyalties, it includes a wide range of distinctive, dramatically-conceived personalities and is a convincing, socio-political study of small town life. The action culminates in the death of Sievright in an apparent shooting accident, the birth of Rossiter's son, the ending of the lock-out and the completion of Rossiter's moral growth to full self-acceptance.

Dead Bird: A Journal Devoted to Sport and the Drama, a sensational weekly journal containing short fiction and verse together with sporting and theatrical news, ran 1889–91. It continued under the title *Bird o' Freedom* 1891–96, then as *Arrow: Sport and Play* 1896–1912 and as *Saturday Referee and Arrow* 1912–16; it was then incorporated into the *Referee* (q.v.).

Dead Heart, The, is a phrase coined by J.W. Gregory in his book, *The Dead Heart of Australia* (1906), to describe the desolate region between Lake Eyre and the Simpson Desert.

The term was retained by C.T. Madigan in *Crossing the Dead Heart* (1946), his account of the first scientific expedition across the Simpson Desert in 1939. Madigan's earlier book, *Central Australia* (1936), gives an account of expeditions in the area in the 1930s. The phrase is still in general use to describe the most arid areas of the centre of the continent.

Dead Men Rising, a novel by Kenneth Mackenzie (q.v.), was first published in London in 1951 under his pseudonym 'Seaforth Mackenzie'. Based on an outbreak of Japanese prisoners-of-war from a camp at Cowra, NSW, in 1944, which Mackenzie witnessed, the novel was not published in Australia until 1969 and copies of the London publication were withheld from circulation in Australia. Rather than attempting to probe the psychology of the Japanese, the novel concentrates on the general boredom of garrison life and the individual experiences of some of those who are involuntarily involved, from the camp commandant to the half-Japanese interpreter, Orloff. The love story of Corporal Sargent and his girl, Cathie, which comes to a tragic end when Sargent is killed in the outbreak, takes up a large proportion of the story.

Dead Men Running, see NILAND, D'ARCY

Dead Timber, a play by Louis Esson (q.v.) which was first produced in 1911 and published in the same year, gives a grim but starkly-impressive picture of Australian rural life. The action takes place on a Gippsland selection and deals with a family plagued by a range of farming disasters and personal bitternesses, culminating in the suicide of the father.

DEAKIN, ALFRED (1856–1919), one of the important figures in Australian political history, was born and educated in Melbourne, where he was admitted to the bar in 1877. After experience as a teacher and as a journalist for the *Age*, as well as in the law, he entered politics in 1879. A member of the Victorian State parliament for over twenty years, he was a minister in 1883–86 and joint leader of the coalition government in 1886–90. Active in the Federation (q.v.) movement during the 1890s, he moved to the federal (national) parliament in 1901 and was Australian prime minister in 1903–04, 1905–08 and 1909–10. Throughout his term in the federal parliament (1901–13) he wrote a regular letter on Australian subjects which was published anonymously in the London *Morning Post*; a selection of the million or so words he sent to the *Morning Post* was published in 1968 as *Federated Australia*, ed. J.A. La Nauze.

Deakin had wide literary interests and wrote prolifically on English poetry and drama in the 1870s. He subsequently destroyed many of his early manuscripts, which included verse dramas, dramatic narratives and studies of Shakespeare and Wordsworth, although he had occasional poems published; his verse drama, *Quentin Massys* (q.v., 1875), is credited as the first volume of verse by a native Victorian, and *A New Pilgrim's Progress* (1877) is an allegory written in some forty-nine sittings at a time when Deakin believed himself to be a medium. In the 1880s and 1890s Deakin wrote several reports on irrigation which were published separately; later narratives of his early involvement in Victorian politics and in the Federation movement were published after his death as *The Crisis in Victorian Politics, 1879–1881*, ed. J.A. La Nauze and R.M. Crawford (1957), and *The Federal Story* (1944, ed. H. Brookes; 1963, ed. J.A. La Nauze). Even more important for Australian literature was his understanding of and sympathy for the problems of Australian writers. During his career in State politics he was active on behalf of writers and their families in need (e.g. he helped to provide for Marcus Clarke's widow), and as prime minister he responded to the call of Henry Bournes Higgins and was instrumental in the foundation of the CLF in 1906–08. A long-standing friend of later years was the essayist Walter Murdoch; letters between the two, many of them on literary topics, were published in 1974 as *Walter Murdoch and Alfred Deakin on Books and Men*, ed. J.A. La Nauze and Elizabeth Nurser. Murdoch's *Alfred Deakin* (1923) was the standard account of Deakin before the appearance of La Nauze's comprehensive biography, *Alfred Deakin* (1965). Deakin is also the subject of Kylie Tennant's radio play, *Tether a Dragon* (performed and published 1952).

DEAMER, DULCIE (1890–1972), born Christchurch, NZ, actress, freelance journalist, dramatist and writer of fiction, was a well-known figure in Sydney bohemian and literary society in the 1920s and 1930s. She published a book of short stories, *In the Beginning: Six Studies of the Stone Age and Other Stories* (1909), the title story of which won a *Lone Hand* short fiction competition in 1907. Her novels include *The Suttee of Safa: A Hindoo Romance* (1913), *Revelation* (1921, set in Jerusalem during the life of Jesus), *The Street of the Gazelle* (1922), *The Devil's Saint* (1924), and *Holiday* (1940) which deals with the persecution of the early Christians. Her two volumes of poetry are *Messalina* (1932), the first section, 'Nine Women', comprising portraits of classical or historically-significant women; and *The Silver Branch* (1948), elaborately-phrased verses. Deamer also wrote plays performed in Sydney, including 'That by Which Men Live' (1936) and 'Victory' (1938). She is represented in *Best Australian One-Act Plays* (1937) by *Easter*, a morality play dealing with death.

Dean Case, also known as the Lemon Syrup Case, was a legal sensation in 1895 when a Sydney ferryboat captain, George Dean, was convicted of poisoning his wife with intent to murder and sentenced to life imprisonment. Public opinion forced a royal commission to be established which led to a pardon but after revelations in parliament that Dean's solicitor, R.D. Meagher, had earlier tricked him into a confession, the chemist who supplied the poison came forward and Dean was gaoled for perjury. A.G. Stephens wrote a special *Bulletin* pamphlet on the Dean case (1895), which is also discussed by Cyril Pearl in his *Wild Men of Sydney* (1958). A dramatization of the case was televised in 1983.

DE BOISSIERE, RALPH (1907–), born Trinidad in the West Indies, emigrated to Australia in 1948 after experiencing persecution in Trinidad for his political activities. He has since worked in various capacities, e.g. salesman, car assembler and clerk, while writing novels and plays. *Crown Jewel* (1952), the first book published by the Australasian Book Society is de Boissiere's story of the Trinidadians' struggle to establish trade unionism and culminates in the island's riots of 1936. Its sequel *Rum and Coco Cola* (1957), set during the American presence in the island in the Second World War, enlarges on the urban proletariat's struggle for their rights in that period. *No Saddles for Kangaroos* (1964) is set in a Melbourne car-manufacturing firm and continues the theme that trade union action is the remedy for social and economic injustice.

DE BOOS, CHARLES (1819–1900), born London, came to Australia in 1839 and tried farming in the Hunter district of NSW before turning to journalism. He worked on the *Monitor* and the *Sydney Gazette* before joining the *Argus* to write about the Victorian goldfields. In 1856 he was the *Sydney Morning Herald*'s correspondent on the NSW goldfields and later its parliamentary reporter; his weekly column, 'The Collective Wisdom of New South Wales' (1867–73), is a lively and informative account of political affairs in the days before Hansard. In 1862 he created for the *Sydney Morning Herald* the character 'John Smith', whose satirical 'letters' became *The Congewoi Correspondence* (q.v., 1874). In 1870 de Boos' evidence to the royal commission on the goldfields led to his appointment as mining warden and po-

lice magistrate (posts in which he was considerably criticized) on the NSW diggings. His chief literary work was the novel, *Fifty Years Ago: An Australian Tale* (q.v., 1867). Although somewhat overlooked by critics, *Fifty Years Ago* successfully brings together several strands of early Australian life – convicts, settlers, bushrangers and Aborigines.

DE BRUNE, AIDAN (1879–?1944), born Montreal, Canada, was a journalist in London but wandered the world prior to coming to Australia. His many popular novels of mystery and adventure include *The Carson Loan Mystery* (1926), *The Dagger and Cord* (1927) and *The Shadow Crook* (1930). Involved in the establishment of the FAW in Sydney in 1928, de Brune also wrote *Fifty Years of Progress in Australia 1878–1928* (1929).

'Dedication, A', is the opening poem of Adam Lindsay Gordon's (q.v.) final volume, *Bush Ballads and Galloping Rhymes* (1870). The dedication was to English novelist G.J. Whyte–Melville, whose popular adventure novels appealed to Gordon. The chief interest in Gordon's lines is his reluctant admission that Australia, to which he had been exiled, had helped to inspire his verse. Despite his well-known but inaccurate claim that Australia is a land 'where bright blossoms are scentless/ And songless bright birds', Gordon makes, in the lines beginning 'In the Spring, when the wattle gold trembles', one of his rare acknowledgements of the land's natural beauty.

DEEBLE, R.J. (RUSSELL JOHN) (1944–), born Melbourne, has published several books of verse including *War Babies and Other Poems* (1965), *A Trip to Light Blue* (1968), *High on a Horse with Wax Wings* (1969), *You* (1970), *Changelings* (1978), *Just Before Eyelight* (1979), *In a Poem That Wants to Be Painted* (1979) and *Aqualine and Other Poems* (1980).

DEEMING, FREDERICK (1853–92), born Leicestershire, England, was a bigamist, petty thief and swindler who lived in Australia 1881–87 and 1891–92. In 1891 he murdered his first wife and four children at Rainhill, Lancashire, and cemented their bodies under the kitchen floor. At Christmas 1891 in Windsor, Melbourne, he murdered his second wife and repeated his burial practice; the discovery of this murder led to the discovery of the first murders. Deeming's arrest in WA and subsequent trial in Melbourne, where he was defended by Alfred Deakin but convicted and hanged, caused a contemporary sensation. Alfred Dampier staged 'Wilful Murder' in Melbourne during his trial, and the outback melodramatist Dan Barry characteristically also made capital out of the sensation with his 'Deeming: Or, The Rainhill Horrors and the Cemented Hearth'. Frank Clune wrote *The 'Demon' Killer* (1948) and J.S. O'Sullivan *A Most Unique Ruffian* (1968).

DE GARIS, C.J. (CLEMENT JOHN) (1884–1926), born North Melbourne, was one of Australia's most flamboyant entrepreneurs. He was associated with the dried-fruit industry at Mildura, land ventures in WA, oil exploration, the theatre, the publishing industry and land subdivisions in outer Melbourne. He made and lost several fortunes, faked one suicide but carried out the real thing when he gassed himself in his home in 1926. The proprietor and founder of the provincial newspaper, the *Sunraysia Daily*, for which he often wrote articles and stories, de Garis was also the author of a war drama, *Ambition Run Man* (1914), an autogiographical novel, *Victories of Failure* (1925), and a musical comedy 'F.F.F.', staged in Perth and Melbourne. In 1920 he founded the C.J. de Garis publishing house which ran a literary competition 1920–21 and published eight books before its demise in 1922. *Rigby's Romance*, submitted in the 1921 competition by Kate Baker as part of her plan to resurrect the writings of Joseph Furphy, was published by de Garis in an abridged edition in 1921.

DE GROEN, ALMA (1941–), born NZ, came to live in Australia in 1964, spent some years in Europe and Canada, and returned here in 1973. Her plays include *The Joss Adams Show* (first produced in 1970), 'The Sweatproof Boy' (1972), *Perfectly All Right* (produced 1973), 'The After-Life of Arthur Cravan' (1973), *Going Home* (produced 1976), *Chidley* (published in *Theatre-Australia*, 1977) and 'Vocations' (1982). *Going Home*, her best-known play, which concentrates on the problems of a group of alienated Australians living in Canada, was published in 1977 with the two one-act dramas, *Perfectly All Right* and *The Joss Adams Show*. De Groen has dealt with a range of subjects, from marital relationships (*Going Home*) to the battered-baby syndrome (*The Joss Adams Show*) to the social challenges posed by eccentric individuals such as William James Chidley, a propagandist on the subjects of food, dress and sex, and 'Arthur Cravan', nephew of Oscar Wilde.

Delacy, Danny and **Johanna**, see *All That Swagger*

Delacy, Jeremy, see *Poor Fellow My Country*

'DE LOGHE, SYDNEY', see LOCK, FREDERICK SYDNEY

'Demon Bowler, The', see STIVENS, DAL

DENIEHY, D.H. (DANIEL HENRY) (1828–65), was born in Sydney of emancipist Irish parents. His intellectual potential was recognized in childhood by his parents and teachers and he was well educated by colonial standards. In adolescence he visited England and the Continent with his parents to further his education and after his return to Australia in 1844 was articled to solicitor and literary patron, N.D. Stenhouse, being admitted as a solicitor in 1851. His growing literary and political interests at this time are indicated by the lectures he gave on literary subjects in 1851–53 at the Sydney Mechanics' School of Arts and by his radical speeches at public meetings on the political controversies of the day. One of his memorable satirical speeches was his ridicule in 1853 of W.C. Wentworth's suggestion of a colonial peerage, dubbed by Deniehy a 'bunyip aristocracy'. As a member of parliament in 1857–60 he made effective parliamentary speeches on land and immigration matters and on electoral reform. Disillusioned by politics and lacking a clear purpose in life, he began drinking heavily. In 1862 he went to Melbourne, where he edited the *Victorian*, but returned to Sydney to resume his legal practice after the paper closed in 1864. He died from head injuries following a fall in Bathurst 22 October 1865. His death was widely mourned, more so because it was felt that his enormous promise had not been adequately fulfilled.

Deniehy's creative writing was meagre. He published a brief adolescent novel, 'Love at First Sight', in the *Colonial Literary Journal* in 1844 and some youthful verses in *Heads of the People*. He later contributed verse to the *Empire* and the *Freeman's Journal*. The best evidence of his wit and intellect lies in his wide-ranging speeches, lectures, critical articles and essays. A selection of these is included in Elvera A. Martin's *The Life and Speeches of Daniel Henry Deniehy* (1884). The only widely-known Deniehy creation is the prose satire, *How I Became Attorney–General of New Barataria* (1860), written to ridicule the appointment of L.H. Bailey as attorney-general in the second Cowper ministry of 1859, and first published that year in the *Southern Cross*, which Deniehy had established. Although rather dated by modern standards, the *New Barataria* piece is a good example of the literary satire popular in mid-nineteenth century in the colony. Because of the sparse nature of his published literary works any modern judgement of Deniehy must take account of the golden opinions he won from such contemporaries as Stenhouse, Dalley, Charles Harpur, G.B. Barton and R.H. Horne. A biography of Deniehy by Cyril Pearl, *Brilliant Dan Deniehy: A Forgotten Genius*, was published in 1972.

DENISON, Sir HUGH (1865–1940), born Forbes, NSW, was a cousin of the collector of Australiana, Sir William Dixson. He was born Hugh Robert Dixson but changed his surname in 1907 to avoid confusion with his uncle, Sir Hugh Dixson, with whom he established a tobacco business partnership in 1902. In 1910 he formed Sun Newspapers Ltd, which later took over publication of the *Sunday Sun* and the *Sun*, formerly the *Australian Star*. In 1927 Denison acquired the *Daily Telegraph Pictorial*, formerly the *Daily Telegraph*, and when in 1929 he combined with the Samuel Bennett (q.v.) group to form Associated Newspapers and also bought the *Daily Guardian* and *Sunday Guardian*, he controlled eight Sydney newspapers. A programme of rationalization over the next two years saw the eight become three, one morning daily, one afternoon daily and one Sunday newspaper: the *Sunday News*, *Sunday Guardian* and *Sunday Pictorial* were incorporated into the *Sunday Sun*, the *Daily Guardian* and the *Daily Pictorial* were amalgamated into a revamped *Daily Telegraph*, and the *Evening News* (q.v.) ceased publication to avoid competition with the *Sun*. Denison's managing director of the *Daily Telegraph* in 1931–33 was R.C. Packer, whose son Frank Packer gained control of the newspaper in 1936. One of the significant figures in Australian newspaper proprietorship between the wars, Denison was also interested in developments in radio and was the founder in 1938 of Macquarie Broadcasting Services.

DENNIS, C.J. (CLARENCE MICHAEL JAMES) (1876–1936), born Auburn, SA, spent much of his boyhood in the care of four maiden aunts. He worked briefly as a solicitor's clerk, was a journalist on the Adelaide weekly, the *Critic* (q.v.), filled in as barman at his father's hotel in Laura and then drifted off to become an odd-jobs man about the mines of Broken Hill. Returning to Adelaide, he later became editor of the *Critic* and in 1906 commenced the short-lived, satirical journal, the *Gadfly* (q.v.). In 1908 after a miserable period in Melbourne as a freelance journalist, he went with Hal Waugh, the artist, to Toolangi, an isolated timber-settlement not far from Healesville north-east of Melbourne. At Toolangi, living in a tent and later in a timber-getter's hut, he worked hard at his writing mainly, in his own words, 'to fend off the blues'. In 1913 he published through Cole's Book Arcade of Melbourne his first book of verse, *Backblock Ballads and Other Verses*, with a cover designed by the cartoonist David Low. The book was not successful so Dennis went off on a spree to Sydney, working there on the union journal, the *Labour Call*, but was back in Melbourne

early in 1915. From four verse stories of 'The Sentimental Bloke' in the *Backblock Ballads* he conceived the idea of a separate series and late in 1915 *The Songs of a Sentimental Bloke* (q.v.) was published. Dennis's story of the young larrikin Bill, who is enticed from his life with the 'push' to domestic bliss on a berry farm with his 'ideal bit o'skirt', Doreen, rapidly became popular, bringing fame and affluence to its creator. A sequel dealing with the adventures of Ginger Mick, the 'Bloke''s friend and 'best man', titled *The Moods of Ginger Mick*, was published in October 1916. In an inspired move Dennis had Ginger Mick answer the 'Call of the Stoush' and go off to 'the flamin' war' as so many young Australians had done. The book, and Mick, went straight to the hearts of the Australian soldiers serving overseas and the pocket editions of both *The Sentimental Bloke* and *Ginger Mick* were treasured possessions of many homesick diggers. In 1917, the year that Dennis married Olive Herron, he published the very different work, *The Glugs of Gosh*, a satire on such pretentious community figures as lord mayors, councillors and petty government officials.

Dennis tried to repeat the Bloke and Ginger Mick formula with *Doreen* (1917), which looked at the lovers of *The Sentimental Bloke* in their married roles; and with *Digger Smith* (1918), the adventures of one of Mick's mates on Gallipoli who returned to Australia, not to the slums of Collingwood where he had been born but to the freshness and beauty of the Australian bush. But the public's love affair with the racy, vernacular verse was over. An attempt in 1924 to revive the passion with *Rose of Spadgers*, the saga of Ginger Mick's girl friend of bygone days, also failed. Dennis's other works include the 'Australiaise' (q.v.), a marching song (1908); the verse narrative, *Jim of the Hills* (1919), a timber-getter's story told with only a smattering of exaggerated colloquialisms; a revised and enlarged *Backblock Ballads and Later Verses* (1918); *A Book for Kids* (1921), a whimsical mixture of verse and prose; and *The Singing Garden* (1935), prose and verse which reflect Dennis's long-sustained devotion to the landscape around Arden, his home at Toolangi. From 1922 until his death he held the highly unusual position of staff poet with the Melbourne *Herald*. His many contributions of prose and verse to the *Herald* include 'Epistles to Ab', a series of letters from a farmer to his son in the city; the 'Ben Bowyang' series; and the 'Miss Mix' series, snippets from the gossipy but deadly accurate pen of a country-town seamstress.

After Dennis's death enthusiastic eulogies saluted him as Australia's national poet, one who had captured much of the essential Australian spirit. Prime Minister Joseph Lyons referred to him as the 'Robbie Burns of Australia'. Much of that adulation evaporated as the years passed and Dennis's ingenious verse came to be looked on as a literary curiosity, an extreme and idiosyncratic expression of the intense nationalism that gripped Australia from the 1890s until after the First World War. Some Australians found the Bloke and Ginger Mick nationally embarrassing and thus ignored them, while even well-disposed readers were puzzled by the extraordinary and exaggerated idiom and were doubtful about the authenticity of the central characters, larrikins with hearts of gold. The well-publicized Dennis centenary (1976), which was accompanied by a successful musical version of *The Sentimental Bloke* for television, and the later stage performances of John Derum, 'More Than a Sentimental Bloke', have sparked a revival of interest in his work. Its ability to convey the quality of 'wit' in down-to-earth Australian humour makes it an integral part of this country's folk literature. But there is more to it than that. Beneath its apparent trite and banal surface there is at times a pathos, an appreciation of the foibles of human nature and a sophistication of thought that explores some of the complex issues of life. Henry Lawson, well-qualified to judge talent and achievement in this area of literature, paid Dennis a significant tribute in the foreword to the first edition of *The Songs of a Sentimental Bloke*, when he echoed the Bloke's own words – 'I dips me lid'. Dennis is commemorated by the C.J. Dennis Award, an annual award (since 1976) provided by the Victorian government and administered by the Victorian branch of the FAW for a book about Australian flora and/or fauna. A.H. Chisholm published the biography, *The Making of a Sentimental Bloke* (1946); 'Margaret Herron' (Dennis's wife, Olive), *Down the Years* (1953); I.F. MacLaren, *C.J. Dennis* (1961); and G.W. Hutton, *C.J. Dennis, the Sentimental Bloke* (1976). Barry Watts edited *The World of the Sentimental Bloke* (1976), which contains A.H. Chisholm's 'The Remarkable Career of C.J. Dennis' and articles by such associates of Dennis as David Low and R.H. Croll, together with excerpts from *The Sentimental Bloke* and *The Moods of Ginger Mick*.

Department, The, a play by David Williamson (q.v.), was first performed in 1974 and published in 1975. Set in the engineering department of a college of advanced education, the play consists of a staff meeting called by the head of the department, Robby, a consummate power-broker. The characters, instantly recognizable as types of any institution, include Hans, the departmental clown; Peter, its kept radical; the vindictive, prickly Al; Myra, the intruder from humanities; the irrelevant, apologetic Bobby, who can only teach one outdated course; and the independent, indispensable mechanic, Gordon. Overhanging the familiar frictions, power struggles and rituals is a scandal about a costly water tank, erected by mistake on the mezzanine floor, that no one dares fill. As the academics wrangle, Gordon fills the tank without disaster and the play ends as Robby reassesses his tactical position.

DEPASQUALE, PAUL (1938–), born Lockleys, Adelaide, was a teacher 1959–70 and since 1974 has been a bookseller and publisher. He has published short stories, *In the Land of the Devil's Promise* (1962) and *Angelo* (1979); and verse, *The Will to Dream* (1968, with Janeen Samuel), *A Lonely, Venturesome Outgoing* (1969), *The Mad Priest Meditates* (1982) and *The Dying Dago's Dance of Death* (1982). His historical/critical publications include *The Writing of Plays in South Australia to 1950* (1977); *A Critical History of South Australian Literature 1836–1930* (1978); *Guy Boothby* (1982); and *Sherlock Holmes and Doctor Nikola* (1982), Nikola being the magician created by Guy Boothby. He also published the critical pamphlets, *Patrick Eiffe* (1980) and *Flexmore Hudson* (1981).

DERHAM, ENID (1882–1941), born Hawthorn, Melbourne, was educated at the Universities of Melbourne and Oxford and held lecturing appointments in the department of English at Melbourne. A lyric poet, she published *The Mountain Road and Other Verses* (1912) and a posthumous selection, *Poems* (1958), the latter revealing her to be a poet of considerable – hitherto unsuspected – emotional intensity.

DERRINCOURT, WILLIAM (1819–?), born King's Norton, England, was a convict whose reminiscences, 'Old Convict Times to Gold-Digging Days', were serialized under the pseudonym 'William Day' in the Sydney newspaper, the *Evening News*, in 1891. Prepared for publication by 'Louis' Becke, the reminiscences were then published in book form as *Old Convict Days* (1899). *Old Convict Days* vividly chronicles Derrincourt's experiences as a convict at Port Arthur and elsewhere, as well as his life following the completion of his sentence: bushworker, gold digger, bushranger, prisoner again and finally selector near Bathurst, where he was still living when 'Old Convict Times to Gold-Digging Days' completed its run in the *Evening News*.

Descant, see **Drylight**

Desiderata, subtitled *A Guide to Good Books*, was an SA magazine of book reviews published by the bookselling firm of F.W. Preece; it ran for a decade, 1929–39. Almost entirely confined to critical reviews and articles by named contributors, *Desiderata* was a useful guide to current Australian and world literature. Contributors included Randolph Bedford, Norman and Lionel Lindsay, 'M. Barnard Eldershaw', Mary Gilmore, Hugh McCrae, Rex Ingamells, Kylie Tennant and 'Seaforth Mackenzie'.

Design: An Australian Review of Critical Thought, edited by Patrick I. O'Leary (q.v.) and published in Melbourne, appeared for three issues in 1940. Writers who contributed to the journal included James Devaney, P.R. Stephensen, Martin Haley, Rex Ingamells, Mary Finnin and Max Harris.

DESMOND, ARTHUR (?1859–?1926), born NZ, came to Sydney in 1892 after being an active radical in NZ. In Sydney he became a leading figure in socialist and radical circles, publishing the magazine *Hard Cash* in 1893–94, attacking capitalism. In 1893–94 he also published the vitriolic journal the *Standard Bearer* and contributed poetry in 1894 to the socialist magazine, *New Order*. He left Australia for the USA in 1895 and later published, as 'Ragnar Redbeard', *Survival of the Fittest* (1896). Desmond is purported to have been a strong influence on the radicalism of Henry Lawson.

DESMOND, VALERIE, see *Awful Australian, The*

DEVANEY, JAMES (1890–1976), born Bendigo, Victoria, and educated in Sydney, was a teacher in several Australian States and NZ and a tutor on outback stations before incipient tuberculosis sent him permanently to Queensland to full-time writing and journalism. For more than twenty years he published a weekly column of nature notes for the Brisbane *Courier-Mail* under the pseudonym 'Fabian'; in it and in his numerous books, his knowledge and love of the Australian bush found full expression. For years a leading literary figure in Queensland, he was president of the Queensland Authors' and Artists' Association (later the FAW) and gave CLF lectures on Australian literature in 1947.

Devaney's unpretentious, traditional lyric poetry, well regarded by contemporary critics, began with the volume *Fabian* (1923), written during a period of ill-health and religious doubts. The chief poem, 'The Lost Love', reflects his mood of the time, personal disquiet and a loss of delight in the natural world.

Earth Kindred (1931) reveals the delight regained, the disquiet gone. *Dark Road* (1938), a privately-printed edition of twenty-five copies which is now extremely rare, consists of six deeply-personal poems written in tribute to his wife, his nurse during his tubercular illness in Diamantina hospital. From his later volumes, *Debutantes* (1939), *Where the Wind Goes* (1939) and *Freight of Dreams* (1946), Devaney selected the bulk of the verses chosen for his *Poems* (1950), a volume of wistful, melodious lyrics. Devaney also wrote fiction, *The Currency Lass* (1927), *The Vanished Tribes* (1929), a collection of short stories focusing on Aboriginal myths and tribal adventures, and *Washdirt* (1946), a novel of the Bendigo goldfields. He wrote a play, *The New Law* (1955), his version of the Gospel story. His critical credo, *Poetry in Our Time* (1952), with its emphasis on the maintenance of recognizable form and rhythm and the need for beauty and lucidity, was seen by some as reactionary but it embodied all that Devaney stood for. A friend and mentor of John Shaw Neilson (q.v.) in his final years, Devaney wrote the biographical *Shaw Neilson* (1944) and edited *Unpublished Poems of Shaw Neilson* (1947).

DEVANNY, JEAN (1894–1962), born Jane Crook at Ferntown in the South Island of NZ, married miner and radical, Hal Devanny, when she was seventeen. She and her husband were active in the NZ labour movement before coming to Australia in 1929 and joining the Communist Party of Australia. Although expelled from the organization during 1940–44 for reasons unspecified, but possibly connected with her feminist attitudes and forthright personality, she was prominent in the party as agitator and orator until she left it in 1950. She spent most of her Australian life in north Queensland, where she played a leading role in Popular Front activities and helped to form the Writers' League (later the Writers' Association) and the Queensland branch of the FAW. Ill-health and an increasing desire to develop her craft as a writer led her, in her last years, away from political activities into journalism and writing on Queensland local and natural history.

Before leaving NZ she published four novels, *The Butcher Shop* (q.v., 1926), *Lenore Divine* (1926), *Dawn Beloved* (1928) and *Riven* (1929); and a book of short fiction, *Old Savage and Other Stories* (1927). *The Butcher Shop* (published in Germany as *Die Herrin*) was banned in NZ, Australia, Boston and Nazi Germany; it was objected to because of its feminist and socialist attitudes, its emphasis on sexuality and its depiction of violence and brutality in rural NZ life. Sensational, undisciplined and highly-coloured, *The Butcher Shop* is nevertheless a remarkable novel for its time, especially for its feminist examination of the role of women in the family situation. Three other novels with NZ settings are *Bushman Burke* (1930), *Devil Made Saint* (1930) and *Poor Swine* (1932). After her arrival in Australia, Devanny wrote a further fourteen novels, four of which remain unpublished, and several works of non-fiction: *By Tropic Sea and Jungle* (1944), *Bird of Paradise* (1945) and *Travels in North Queensland* (1951). Her first novel set in Australia is *Out of Such Fires* (1934), based on her experiences as a domestic on a sheep station in western NSW. *Sugar Heaven* (1936), which was translated into Russian, deals with the 1935 strike on the Queensland canefields. Dulcie, the novel's heroine, begins as a naive, passive girl but develops into an ardent political activist. The novel contains some interesting details of the 1935 strike, in particular the part that Weil's Disease, a plague spread by rats, played in the discontent of the cane-cutting communities. Something of a literary curio, the novel is now being suggested as one of the earliest and most significant of the socialist–realist Australian novels. Devanny's other literary projects include an uncompleted trilogy about the sugar industry, of which only the first volume, *Cindie* (1949), was published, and an autobiography which is expected to be published. *Cindie* opens in the 1890s on the Queensland canefields and deals largely with the changes that occur as kanaka labour is repatriated. Among her other novels are *All for Love* (1932), *The Virtuous Courtesan* (1935), *The Ghost Wife* (1935), *Paradise Flow* (1938), *The Killing of Jacqueline Love* (1942) and *Roll Back the Night* (1945). In most of her fiction Devanny draws attention to the need for women to struggle against sexual and class oppression.

Development of Australian Literature, The (1898), by Henry Gyles Turner and Alexander Sutherland, is one of the pioneering works of Australian literary criticism. Biographical essays on colonial literary figures, Adam Lindsay Gordon, Henry Kendall and Marcus Clarke, are prefaced by Turner's essay 'A General Sketch of Australian Literature', said by its author to be an attempt to define the growth and current position of Australian literature.

'Devil and the Angel, The', a sequence of short, anecdotal poems by Rosemary Dobson (q.v.), was published in the *Bulletin* 1945–46. The whimsical series, with its blend of humour and irony, is based on the idea that the Angel and the Devil, jointly responsible for everybody's transition from this life to the next, offer each dying person the choice of Heaven or Hell. Three of the anecdotes are especially ef-

fective – the explanation that Methusaleh's great age was caused by the forgetfulness of the pair as they indulged in a gambling match on their way to collect him; the story of the poet who peremptorily orders them from his door so that he may complete his unfinished ode; and the decision of the scarecrow in the fields to resist their blandishments and choose instead the simple joys of rural existence.

'Devil and the Governor, The', see FORSTER, WILLIAM

DEVINE, NED, see Cobb & Co.

DIAMOND, DICK, the author of *Reedy River* (q.v., 1970), the popular Australian musical based on the shearers' strike of 1891, has also written sketches for vaudeville, plays for radio and television, and a novel about the war between Vietnam and France, *The Walls Are Down*, published in Hanoi in 1958. *Reedy River* was first produced by the New Theatre, Melbourne, in 1953 and has had frequent revivals.

Diary of a New Chum, by Paul Wenz (q.v.), was published under his pseudonym 'Paul Warrego' in 1908. A largely humorous account of some of Wenz's first experiences in Australia, it describes his reactions to the climatic extremes and hardships of the outback; to the varied activities he engages in as jackeroo, from boundary-riding to cutting Bathurst burrs; to the various bush characters he meets, such as swagmen, itinerant salesmen, rabbiters, selectors, Aborigines and Chinese cooks; and to the practical jokes that are inevitably visited on the new chum. The account is enlivened by the narrator's vivid descriptions of the bush landscape, by his feeling for the animals of the outback, and by his fiction of flight from a recklessly-incurred engagement back home. The narrative concludes with ten points of advice, which include the recommendations to 'keep an angelic temper and a live imagination, for you will have to see jokes' and, when hearing a snake or Murray cod yarn, to 'multiply the breadth by the length and divide by ten'.

DICK, CHARLOTTE ISABEL, born Tasmania, published several novels set there: *The Veil of Discretion* (1920), which has the well-tried plot of governess marrying squatter; *Huon Belle* (1930), which is also concerned with the vicissitudes of an orphaned girl immigrant in Tasmania; *Wild Orchard* (1945), a story of early Tasmania; and *Country Heart* (1946). Her volume *Garden Peace and Christmas Tales* (1927) combines verse and prose.

DICK, WILLIAM (1937–), born Yarraville, Victoria, grew up in the Melbourne suburb of Footscray (Goodway in *A Bunch of Ratbags*). He worked first as a furniture upholsterer, then in a variety of temporary occupations while pursuing a career as a writer, part of which has been as a television scriptwriter (e.g. *Bellbird*). His first published work, the semi-autobiographical novel, *A Bunch of Ratbags* (1965), is set in the slum world of Melbourne; it conveys a realistic picture of the harsh poverty and aimless violence of that environment and depicts the gradual movement away from it of the central character, Terry Cooke, who is saved by a decent girl and a brush with the law. A successful musical adaptation of the novel, with lyrics and music by Don Battye and Peter Pinne, was staged in Melbourne in 1966. Dick also wrote the novels, *Naked Prodigal* (1969) and *The Pope and the President* (1972).

DICKENS, CHARLES (1812–70), had several connections with Australia and Australian literature. He established his reputation with *The Posthumous Papers of the Pickwick Club* (1837) which, like *Nicholas Nickelby* (1839), has a character who is transported to Australia. The *Papers* proved widely popular in colonial Australia, where Pickwick parties were held, an Australian imitation was advertised (*Tobias Twickenham*) and the first pirated edition of the original was published in Hobart in 1838. Although in later works Dickens continued to transport occasional characters to Australia (e.g. Uriah Heep in *David Copperfield*) he increasingly came to regard the colonies as a land of opportunity both for convicts and for immigrants. Thus in *David Copperfield* the Micawbers, Peggotty, Emily and others emigrate and succeed in Port Middlebray (Melbourne), and in *Great Expectations* Pip's benefactor, the convicted felon Magwitch, makes his fortune on the land. An Australian tradition that Miss Havisham in *Great Expectations* is based on the Sydney eccentric, Eliza Emily Donnithorne (?1826–86), who was jilted in 1856 and thereafter never left her house at Newtown in Sydney, is impossible to verify. Dickens's view of Australia, discussed in Coral Lansbury's (q.v.) controversial *Arcady in Australia* (1970), seems to have developed as a result of his meetings with Caroline Chisholm and his awareness of Samuel Sidney's (q.v.) encouraging writings about the colonies. The first issue in 1850 of the Dickens journal, *Household Words*, carried an approving exposition of Chisholm's emigration schemes, and subsequent numbers of the journal carried contributions by J.G. Lang (q.v.) as well as Sidney, who dedicated his *Gallops and Gossips in the Bush of Australia* (1854) to Dickens. Extracts from both *Household Words* and the later journal, *All the Year Round*, were regularly printed in Australian newspapers; similarly, Dickens's novels were not only widely sold and serialized in Australia but also dramatized. In 1841 Dickens, wearying of English society, thought that he might emigrate to Australia. Two of his sons, Alfred D'Orsay Tennyson Dickens (1845–1912) and Edward Bulwer Lytton Dickens (1852–1902), in fact did so, the latter becoming a member of the NSW parliament in 1889–94; their careers are discussed in Mary Lazarus's *A Tale of Two Brothers* (1973). Henry Lawson, in 'A Fragment of Autobiography' and in the long poem 'With Dickens' (*When I Was King*, 1905), expresses his love for and wide knowledge of Dickens. Among modern authors, Barry Oakley in *The Ship's Whistle* (1979) portrays the relationship between Dickens and Kate Horne, the wife of R.H. Horne, during Horne's absence in Australia.

DICKINS, BARRY (1949–), born Reservoir, Victoria, was a member of the La Mama theatre and poetry group of the early 1970s; his first play, 'Ghosts', was produced at La Mama in 1974. Dickins is now a full-time writer, a contributing cartoonist to the *Age* and an occasional poet. His published plays are *The Banana Bender* (1981), *The Death of Minnie* (1981) and *Lennie Lower* (1982). His unpublished plays include 'Only an Old Kit Bag' (1976), 'The Rotten Teeth Show' (1977), 'The Fools' Shoe Hotel' (1978), 'The Bridal Suite' (1979), 'The Ken Wright Show' (1980), 'The Golden Goldenbergs' (1981), 'The Interrogation of Angel' (1981) and 'A Couple of Broken Hearts' (1983). He also wrote and illustrated a book of autobiographical short stories, *The Gift of the Gab* (1981).

Dictionary of Australian Biography, see **SERLE, PERCIVAL**

Dictionary of Australian Colloquialisms, A, see **Australian English**

DIESENDORF, MARGARET (1912–), born Vienna, Austria, came to Australia in 1939. A gifted linguist, educationist and creative writer, she has played an active role in the Sydney literary scene for more than two decades; she became associate editor of *Poetry Australia* in 1967. Widely featured in anthologies and journals, she has also published *Light: Poems by Margaret Diesendorf* (1981). Poems in tribute to her are included in Gwen Harwood's volume, *The Lion's Bride* (1981).

Difficult Young Man, A, a novel by Martin Boyd (q.v.), the second in a tetralogy dealing with the Langton family, was published in 1955. The narrator, Guy Langton, recounts the history of his family during the turn-of-the-century period, concentrating on his elder brother Dominic. A passionate individual, invested with a dark inheritance from the Spanish side of the family, Dominic frequently finds it impossible to reconcile his personal sense of honour with the prevailing social morality. A series of incidents reveals his 'difficult' nature: he is expelled from school; walks naked at night and allegedly seduces his Aunt Baba's maids; rides his horse to death; and is found worshipping in an Hellenic mood his half-dressed cousin, Helena Craig. His behaviour causes his parents, Steven and Laura, to uproot their family and move to England. There Dominic experiences two curious relationships, one with a retired Colonel Rodgers and the other with Sylvia Tunstall, the daughter of Lord Dilton. His engagement to Sylvia, seen by some as a brilliant match, is broken off because of Sylvia's snobbery. Once again in Australia, Dominic elopes with his childhood sweetheart, Helena, on the eve of her wedding to a wealthy grazier.

Dig, see **BURKE and WILLS**

Digger was in use as a term in Australia before 1850 but it came to prominence with the gold discoveries, the 'diggers' being those who rushed to 'the diggings' (the goldfields) to make their fortune. The term is encountered in the titles of such early works as David Mackenzie's *The Gold Digger* (1852) and James Bonwick's *Notes of a Gold Digger, and Gold Diggers' Guide* (1852); in the words of songs such as 'The Broken-Down Digger', a fragment of which is in Charles MacAlister's *Old Pioneering Days in the Sunny South* (1907, but including reminiscences from the 1830s on), and 'The Palmer Days' with its refrain 'I see the diggers as they go with dreams of wealth untold'; and in the sketch-book of contemporary artist S.T. Gill, published as *Sketches of the Victorian Gold Diggings and Diggers as They Are* (1852). The rebellious miners at Ballarat were also referred to as the 'diggers' in contemporary official and unofficial reports of Eureka. In George Dunderdale's *The Book of the Bush* (1898), 'diggers' is used in the subtitle with such other Australian types as 'squatters' and 'convicts'. Although there is some indication that the term persisted in bush life from the goldfields period until the First World War, it did not return to prominence until the Gallipoli campaign of 1915. The Australian and NZ soldiers adopted 'digger' because it described their lifestyle on the Gallipoli cliffs (to the ironic question of

'What's your present occupation?' the reply in unison by the troops was 'Digging, digging, always bloody well digging') and because it carried with it the rebellious flavour of Eureka, defiance of authority being seen as part of the Anzac's character. War historian C.E.W. Bean, however, suggests that it originated among members of the Anzac Corps on the Somme front, June–August 1917; as on Gallipoli, the word 'digger' carried so rich an implication of the Anzac infantryman's own view of his functions and character that it spread like wildfire through the AIF. 'The Digger's Song', written during the First World War, carries typical 'digger' sentiments – contempt of the frontline soldier for the pompous, regulation-bound headquarters' soldier ('brave men are dying for bastards like you' and 'Lord Gort awarded the digger a V.C. and two bars/ For giving the corporal a kick in the a. . .).

'Digger' or 'A Digger' was adopted as a pseudonym by several minor war memoirists; C.J. Dennis published *Digger Smith* (1918), the experiences of a Gallipoli veteran; and the soldiers' magazine, *Aussie*, published a selection of sketches by soldiers as *Digger Aussieosities* (192?). Politician W.M. Hughes, who often wore the Australian soldier's slouch hat during the patriotic public occasions of the war, was popularly known as 'The Little Digger'. Since the First World War, 'digger' has continued as the regular synonym for the Australian soldier and is widely used to apply colloquially to the Australian male in general; the friendly, colloquial diminutive 'dig' still retains the flavour of 'mate'.

Digit Dick, see **REES, LESLIE**

Dimboola, an outstandingly popular play by Jack Hibberd (q.v.), was first produced by the Australian Performing Group in 1969 and published in 1974. Subtitled *A Wedding–Reception Play*, it has proved popular with theatre-restaurants, has been more widely produced than any other play in Australia and has also been staged in London, in the USA and in several European countries. Dimboola, a small town in western Victoria, has also produced and welcomed the play, although Hibberd denies that it is based on any particular reception there. The wedding reception of Morris (Morrie) and Maureen (Reen) McAdam has all the familiar, if exaggerated, attributes of a country ritual. Held in the church hall, which has been decorated 'beaut' in green and orange, the reception is provided with music by Lionel Driftwood and the Pile Drivers and is enlivened by several scheduled entertainments such as a tapdance by Astrid, the flower girl, to the tune of 'Animal Crackers in My Soup', and the traditional speeches. For the audience, however, a variety of unscheduled entertainments proves more comic, such as a strident quarrel between Shirl, the 'experienced' bridesmaid, and Dangles, the best man; the irreverent, scatological clowning of two uninvited local drunks, Mutton and Bayonet; an outbreak of Protestant/ Catholic animosity; the total alcoholic collapse of the Catholic priest, Father O'Shea; and several brief, amicable fights between both male and female guests. The disapproval of Leonardo Radish, a reporter from the *Mildura Trumpet* (and a caricature of a well-known theatre critic, Leonard Radic) is quenched by his physical removal from the scene.

Dingo was an Aboriginal name (see also Warrigal) for the wild dog which roamed the Australian bush and which was believed to have originated from domesticated dogs that accompanied the first Aborigines to the Australian continent. Recorded by such early voyagers as Jan Carstensz and William Dampier, the dingo is described as 'the dog of New South Wales' in *The Voyage of Governor Phillip to Botany Bay* (1789) and in John White's *Journal of a Voyage to New South Wales* (1790). Colonial poets such as Charles Harpur and Henry Kendall saw the dingo as part of the hazardous pioneer environment. It and its 'blood polluted dens' form the backdrop to the murder of the settlers in Harpur's 'The Creek of the Four Graves' and Kendall's 'The Glen of Arrawatta', and it is hunted down in Adam Lindsay Gordon's 'The Sick Stockrider'. Because the dingo's attacks on the pioneers' precious sheep and cattle were perpetrated with cunning and stealth, the word 'dingo' came into colloquial use also as a term of contempt to denote cowardice and treachery in humans. The dingo has had a more attractive presence in children's literature, being featured in such stories as H.G. Lamond's *White Ears the Outlaw: The Story of a Dingo* (1949), John Kiddell's *The Day of the Dingo* (1955) and Elyne Mitchell's *Jinki, Dingo of the Snows* (1970).

Diogenes, the journal of the Literary Society of the University of Tasmania, was published annually 1955–65. It carried original poetry and short fiction as well as critical articles and expositions.

Direction, published in four issues 1952–55, 'devoted exclusively to the encouragement of a youthful and vigorous literature in Australia, honest criticism and discussion', was edited by L.H. Davison. Contributors included Max Harris, Judith Wright, James McAuley, A.D. Hope, Vivian Smith, Brian Elliott, Vincent Buckley, Barry Oakley, Bruce Dawe and Evan Jones.

Dis-Honourable, The, see **HENNESSEY, JOHN DAVID**

Displaced Person, The, see **HARDING, LEE; Science Fiction**

Dissent, a quarterly emanating from the University of Melbourne Students' Representative Council and Dissent Publications, began in 1961 with an editorial committee that included Chris Wallace-Crabbe and Brian Buckley. Radical in attitude, *Dissent* sees itself as an independent forum for the discussion of social, cultural, economic and political issues. It publishes book reviews, some poetry and short fiction. Its special-subject editions have included topics such as education, women in Australia and abortion.

Disturbing Element, see **HERBERT, XAVIER**

DIXSON, MIRIAM (1930–), born Melbourne and at present associate professor of history at the University of New England, Armidale, NSW, is a well-known feminist writer. She has published *The Real Matilda* (1976), a work on 'woman and identity in Australia, 1788 to 1975' and *Greater than Lenin?: Lang and Labor 1916–1932* (1977), which reflects her interest in the Australian labour movement.

DIXSON, Sir WILLIAM (1870–1952), born Sydney, was an engineer in Scotland 1889–96, then returned to Australia where, while making a business fortune, he became a keen collector of Australian rare books, manuscripts and art works. He donated his collection to the State of NSW and the government of the day built the Dixson wing of the NSW Public Library to house it in 1929. He donated the great bronze doors of the library's main entrance, dedicating them to the memory of David Scott Mitchell. He also set up the William Dixson Foundation to reproduce and translate manuscripts and rare books relating to Australia and the Pacific. The Dixson Library of the University of New England was named after him to recognize his generosity in helping its establishment 1937–39. *The Great South Land* (1979) by Suzanne Mourot and Paulette Jones describes the treasures of the Dixson and Mitchell Libraries and the Dixson Galleries.

'Djin Djin', see **WILLIAMSON, J.C.**

DOBELL, Sir WILLIAM (1899–1970), born Newcastle, NSW, into a poor family, studied art in Sydney before leaving for London and Europe in 1929. In London he developed his particular forte, the genre painting which epitomizes a common trait or tendency. Paintings which belong to his London period include *The Charlady*, *Mrs South Kensington*, *Irish Youth*, *The Red Lady* and *Boy at the Basin*. In 1939 he returned to Australia and became established as a leader of a vigorous wartime Sydney movement, painting such celebrated portraits as *The Billy Boy*, *The Strapper*, *Scotty Allan*, *The Cypriot* and *Cement Worker*. He won the 1943 Archibald Prize with a controversial portrait of his colleague, Joshua Smith, which led to a celebrated trial. Dobell, who subsequently won the Archibald Prize in 1948 and 1959 and the Wynne Prize in 1948, painted several well-known portraits of Australian writers including Brian Penton, Frank Clune and Mary Gilmore. His story of an experience in London, embodied in his painting *The Dead Landlord* (1936), was the starting point of Patrick White's play, *The Ham Funeral* (1965). Dobell's life and work is described in James Gleeson's *William Dobell* (1964) and in Brian Adams's *Portrait of an Artist* (1983).

DOBSON, ROSEMARY (1920–), born Sydney, is the granddaughter of Austin Dobson, English poet and essayist. During the Second World War she joined the publishing firm Angus & Robertson, where she worked with Douglas Stewart, Beatrice Davis and Nan McDonald. Her first collection of poems, *In a Convex Mirror*, was published in 1944. In 1946 'The Ship of Ice' (q.v.), later the title-poem of her second volume (1948), won the *Sydney Morning Herald* prize for poetry. She published her third collection, *Child with a Cockatoo*, in 1955, a further volume, *Cock Crow* (q.v.), appearing in 1965. From 1966 to 1971, while her husband A.T. Bolton was London editor for Angus & Robertson, she was in England and Europe, visiting the places and studying the artistic masterpieces that strongly influence her poetry. Since 1972 she has lived in Canberra, where she renewed her association with fellow poet, the late David Campbell; Dobson, Campbell and Natalie Staples produced *Moscow Trefoil* (1975) and Dobson and Campbell *Seven Russian Poets* (1978), translations of Russian poetry. Her own later poetry includes two volumes of selected verse (1973, 1980) and *Over the Frontier* (1978). From her husband's Brindabella Press she has published *Three Poems on Water-Springs* (1973) and *Greek Coins: A Sequence of Poems* (1977); the latter comprises twenty four-line poems, each of which sets out 'a visual idea which could be contained within the circle – that is, within the coin-sized four-line stanza'. The poems, accompanied by her own line drawings, reflect her attachment to Greek themes, her general love of antiquity and her admiration for the wisdom

and perception of the Greek traveller, Pausanias, who wrote a guide to Greece in the second century AD. *Over the Frontier* contains a section, 'Poems from Pausanias', that includes the *Greek Coin* poems.

Throughout the early volumes Dobson is concerned with the problem of transience and is plainly obsessed with the Renaissance masterpieces; in *Child with a Cockatoo*, e.g. there is a group of fifteen 'Poems from Paintings'. She believes that in those celebrated paintings, where suspended moments of life are eternally captured, lies the triumph of art over time. Her response to the actual experience of those works of art is well conveyed in the wonder expressed in the lines from 'Landscape in Italy':

> but five steps from where we lay
> Drowsing upon the short-cropped grass
> Lightly, with all her springtime flowers,
> Did Botticelli's Flora pass.

Some of her poems, e.g. 'Still Life' (q.v.), 'Over the Hill', 'Young Girl at a Window' and 'In a Convex Mirror', capture in similar fashion and somewhat in the style of a Robert Browning dramatic lyric, images of existence frozen in time. She turns to more personal themes in the third section of *Child with a Cockatoo* and in *Cock Crow* where, in the title poem and in 'Child of Our Time', 'Annunciations', 'Into Winter' and 'Out of Winter', she explores her roles as mother, wife, individual and artist. In the sequence 'The Devil and the Angel' (q.v.) she displays a deft touch for whimsy and fantasy. Overall her approach is restrained and decorous and her poetry characterized by simplicity, lucidity and cool, elegant grace. Rosemary Dobson edited *Songs for All Seasons: 100 Poems for Young People* (1967), *Australian Voices, Poetry and Prose of the 1970s* (1975) and *Sisters Poets* (1979), the feminist anthology. In 1979 she was awarded the Robert Frost Award, now known as the Christopher Brennan Award, by FAW for the consistently distinguished quality of her work.

DOCKER, JOHN, see *Australian Cultural Elites*; Criticism

Docker, Miss, see *Cheery Soul, A*

Dog on the Tuckerbox, see **Gundagai**

Doll, The, see *Summer of the Seventeenth Doll*

DONOHOE, JOHN (?1806–30), born Dublin, Ireland, was convicted in 1823 of intention to commit a felony, sentenced to transportation and arrived in NSW in 1825. At the end of 1927 he committed his first robberies on the roads outside Sydney, was captured and sentenced to death, but escaped from custody and for over two years headed a bushranging gang that operated mainly in the Nepean area. In September 1830 he was killed in a shoot-out with soldiers and police near Campbelltown.

Donohoe's defiance of authority, his sympathy for the convict and emancipist poor (who helped to protect him) and his personal courage in urging the police to fire on him during the exchange which led to his death, won him many admirers: in 'Jim Jones at Botany Bay' the convict narrator announces his intention of taking to the bush and joining the 'brave bushrangers . . . Jack Donohoo and Co.', and in 'A Convict's Tour to Hell' (q.v.) a knowledge of Donohoe helps 'Frank the Poet' gain admission to Heaven. 'Bold Jack Donahoe' (sometimes spelt 'Donahue', 'Donohue', 'Donohoo' and 'Donahoo' as well as the original 'Donohoe') became one of the first bushrangers (q.v.) depicted in Australian literature, notably in Charles Harpur's play *The Bushrangers* (q.v., 1853), titled 'The Tragedy of Donohoe' when extracts were first published in the *Sydney Monitor* in 1835. Donohoe was also an early hero of Australian folklore, his exploits celebrated in several songs and ballads, one of which he may have written himself. Texts of the Donohoe cycle of ballads, which were banned as treason songs by the penal authorities in the 1830s and are known in Ireland, are provided in John Meredith's *The Wild Colonial Boy: Bushranger Jack Donahoe, 1806–30* (1982), which also discusses the links between the 'Bold Jack Donahoe' songs and 'The Wild Colonial Boy' (q.v.) songs. John Manifold's poem, 'The Afterlife of Bold Jack Donahue', pictures Donohoe as a president of the company of folk heroes enjoying an idyllic afterlife until he is ready to lead an attack on the corrupt rich of Australia.

DONOHUE, FRANK ('ARTHUR GAYLL') (?–1908) published fiction, *A Sheaf of Stories for the Centenary Year* (1888) and *The History of Botany Bay* (1888), which originally appeared in the *Bulletin*. He also published *Stray Leaves* (1883), relating to Henry Kendall and Daniel Deniehy.

Donovan, Macy, is the central character of Vance Palmer's *Golconda* trilogy (q.v.) of novels. His career has affinities with that of Edward G. Theodore (q.v.).

Don's Party, a popular play by David Williamson (q.v.), was first performed in 1971 by the Australian Performing Group, published in 1973 and later made into a film. A group of eleven people, mostly in their early thirties, materially well-established although mostly committed Labor-voters, attends a party on the night of the 1969 federal election. As the evening progresses, the various sexual expectations of the participants are frustrated, usually farcically. As the party degenerates into drunkeness, the couples scrutinize their tired marriages and the discrepancy between youthful aspirations and present bourgeois reality. The fortunes of the Labor Party simultaneously decline, although virtually unnoticed by the party-goers.

Dorchester Labourers, see **LOVELESS, GEORGE**

Doreen, see **DENNIS, C.J.**; *Songs of a Sentimental Bloke, The*

DORRINGTON, ALBERT ('AD', 'ALBA DORIAN') (?1874–1953), born London, came to Australia in his youth and travelled widely until 1895 when he settled in Sydney. A frequent contributor to the *Bulletin* in the 1890s, often under the pseudonyms 'AD' and 'Alba Dorian', he published a book of short stories, *Castro's Last Sacrament and Other Stories* (1900), then collaborated with A.G. Stephens in a romantic novel, *The Lady Calphurnia Royal*, which was serialized in the *Bookfellow* in 1907 and published in book form in 1909. Disgruntled with his lack of recognition from local critics, Dorrington returned to England in 1907 and thereafter published a further thirteen works of fiction, some of which have an Australian background. They include *And the Day Came* (1908); *Children of the Cloven Hoof* (1911), a novel of pastoral life; *A South Sea Buccaneer* (1911), in which Bully Hayes figures; and *Our Lady of the Leopards* (1911). *The Lady Calphurnia Royal* deals with an exotic female character whose bizarre career extends from Paris to the French penal colony of Noumea and into outback Australia. His best-known short story is 'A Bush Tanqueray'. A popular novelist whose pen was guided mainly by commercial opportunism, Dorrington relied chiefly on sensational plots filled with mystery and romance.

Dot and the Kangaroo, see **PEDLEY, ETHEL C.**

'Double Buggy at Lahey's Creek, A', see **Wilson, Joe**

Double Event, The, see **GOULD, NAT**

Double X, see **Feminism and Australian Literature**

Down Under or 'down-under', a colloquial term for Australia and sometimes applied also to NZ, was in existence at least by the end of the nineteenth century. The term, seldom used by Australians themselves, implies a northern-hemisphere perspective of Australia and clearly derives from the notion of the Antipodes (q.v.). The popular song 'Down Under', sung during the successful challenge for the America's Cup in 1983, is an example of a modern usage.

DOYLE, MARY, see **HARPUR, CHARLES**

DRAKE-BROCKMAN, HENRIETTA (1901–68), born Perth, spent considerable time with her husband, Geoffrey Drake-Brockman in outback WA. Her impressions of those colourful pioneering times are recorded in articles she wrote under the pseudonym 'Henry Drake' for the *West Australian*. A considerable force in the literary community of WA over many years, she played a major role in the establishment of the State branch of FAW in 1938 and was also a long-serving member of the advisory committee of *Westerly*. Her novels are *Blue North* (1934), set against the background of the pearling industry at Broome; *Sheba Lane* (1936), also in Broome, but no longer the raw frontier town; *Younger Sons* (1937), an historical novel, which portrays the development of the colony and the struggles of the early settlers; *The Fatal Days* (1947), set during the American servicemen invasion of Australia during the Second World War; and *The Wicked and the Fair* (1957), a fictional account of the events surrounding the wreck of the *Batavia*, which she explores more fully and authentically in *Voyage to Disaster: The Life of Francisco Pelsaert* (1963). Her short fiction is represented in her collection of stories, *Sydney or the Bush* (1948). Henrietta Drake-Brockman also wrote with success for the theatre in the late 1930s and 1940s. Her first play, *The Man from the Bush* (1934, published in *Eight Plays by Australians*) examines the contrasting ethics of the privileged and the poor during the depression years; her chief dramatic work, however is *Men Without Wives and Other Plays* (1955), which contains *Men Without Wives, Hot Gold, Dampier's Ghost* and *The Blister*. The title play, which won the NSW sesquicentenary competition of 1938, is set in the remote north-west of WA and is concerned with the difficulties of a white bride in adjusting to life in the harsh environment of an outback station. The interaction of character and environment (the favourite device of both Drake-Brockman's fiction and drama) leads in the end to a mood of optimism, expressed by the play's strongest character, Ma Bates – 'the land looks after those who love it'. *Hot Gold* uses the contemporary Kalgoorlie scene (gold, gambling, romance) to depict interplay and complexity of character. *The Lion Tamer* (1948) is a comedy about expatriate

Australians successfully using their Antipodean wit in a London society situation. Drake-Brockman was co-editor, with Walter Murdoch, of *Australian Short Stories* (1951) and she edited the 1957 edition of *Coast to Coast* as well as *West Coast Stories* (1959). She also edited *Australian Legendary Tales* (1953) by Mrs K. Langloh Parker and wrote the critical monograph, *Katherine Susannah Prichard* (1967). Her husband gives much of the background to her life and work in his autobiographical *The Turning Wheel* (1960).

DRANSFIELD, MICHAEL (1948–73), born Sydney, dropped out of his university studies, worked intermittently on several newspapers and was for a time a government clerk. His short, restless, adult life was spent largely in bohemian areas of Sydney (Balmain, Paddington, Darlinghurst), in the country at Cobargo and Candelo, NSW, or wandering over eastern Australia from Queensland to Tasmania. Failing to discover a meaningful role for himself in conventional society, Dransfield vainly sought an alternative in the drug culture. After a motor-cycle accident in April 1972 his health deteriorated and he died, aged twenty-four. Dransfield published three volumes of poetry, *Streets of the Long Voyage* (1970), *The Inspector of Tides* (1972) and *Drug Poems* (q.v., 1972). A further collection largely prepared by him, *Memoirs of a Velvet Urinal*, was published posthumously in 1975. Some 600 other poems, collated and edited by Rodney Hall, were brought together in two volumes, *Voyage into Solitude* (1978, poems from the period 1969–71) and *The Second Month of Spring* (1980, poems from 1972). First published in the late 1960s in the underground magazines that arose in criticism of the conservative nature of Australian poetry, Dransfield's talented verse soon became a regular feature of more established newspapers and journals. The consistent themes of his poetry include protest against the quality of modern Australian life, especially the monotony and regimentation of an urban existence; the drug culture and the addiction process; the fragility of life itself; the loneliness of the individual; the importance of human relationships; and the clash between the innate romantic spirit and the ugliness of modern life. *Streets of the Long Voyage*, his first and perhaps his most effective body of verse, won the University of Newcastle special award for a work of literature by an Australian writer under thirty. It contains the 'Courland Penders' (q.v.) group of poems; important drug poems such as 'Overdose', 'Fix' and 'Bum's Rush' (see *Drug Poems*); protest poems such as 'Lamentations' and 'That Which We Call a Rose'; and love poems such as 'Parthenogenesis', 'July with

Her' and 'Dread Was'. In *The Inspector of Tides* his attempts to resolve the technical and language problems raised by his complex, radical, poetic aspirations led to contrived and somewhat gimmicky innovations in punctuation and typography. In protest poems such as 'Endsong' and 'Prosperity', the 'enemies' are specified – pollution, commerce, urban ugliness, insensitive governments and conservative 'Official Poets' who merely chide in 'genteel iambics'. *Drug Poems*, which contains poems from earlier volumes, is both an insight into the process of addiction and an acknowledgement of the isolation and despair that face the addict. *Memoirs of a Velvet Urinal*, extreme in content, obscure in meaning and overly-experimental in technique, lacks the richness and appeal of the earlier works. The final volume, *The Second Month of Spring*, consists mainly of poems written in the last few months of his life. They are angry and tragic expressions of his desperate attempts to survive the forces engulfing him. After his death Dransfield rapidly became a cult-hero among people who shared his criticism of modern society and his preference for an alternative life-style. Although that personal adulation may only be temporary, his poetry, brilliant at its best, is likely to survive.

Dream and Disillusion: A Search for Australian Cultural Identity (1976) by David Walker, examines the lives and times of Vance Palmer, Louis Esson, 'Furnley Maurice' and Frederick Sinclaire, and their efforts to establish both a distinctively Australian culture and a national literature.

Dreamers, The, see DAVIS, JACK

Dreamtime, see Aboriginal Song and Narrative in Translation; Jindyworobak movement

DREWE, ROBERT (1943–), born Melbourne and educated in WA, began a journalistic career with the *West Australian* in 1961. He was literary editor of the *Australian* (1971–74) and has also written for the *Age* and the *Bulletin*. He won the Walkley Award for journalism in 1976 and 1981. Drewe has published two successful novels, *The Savage Crows* (1976) and *A Cry in the Jungle Bar* (1979). *The Savage Crows* (its title being a colonial term for the Aborigines) carries two stories in tandem: that of the complex nineteenth-century figure, George Augustus Robinson, who was involved in the oppression of the Tasmanian blacks; and that of the present-day Stephen Crisp who, in danger of losing control of his own personal existence, vainly attempts to es-

cape his immediate dilemma by investigating the demise of the race of 'King Billy' and Truganini. *A Cry in the Jungle Bar* is based on the experiences of a beefy, ex-footballer Australian, the tragi-comic Dick Cullen who is working in Manila as an agricultural scientist for the UN. Well-meaning and earnest, Cullen is inept and unsuccessful in both his personal and his professional lives; he typifies especially the blundering Australian caught in an Asian experience he is totally unequipped to either understand or handle. Drewe has also published a book of short stories, *The Body Surfers* (1983), in which the beach and its associated life-style, so strongly a feature of Australian life, provides the background.

DREYER, MARIEN (1911–80), born Mornington, Victoria, lived mainly in Kings Cross, Sydney, where she became a well-known figure in bohemian circles and an effective activist on local issues. Deprived of the chance of becoming an actress by the loss of a leg, she worked as a stenographer before turning to full-time, freelance journalism in the 1940s. She wrote short stories, plays and radio scripts as well as numerous articles for magazines and newspapers, and a column, 'Marien's Day', for the magazine *New Idea*. One of her plays, 'Bandicoot on a Burnt Ridge', produced in 1965, won the 1962–63 Journalists' Club Award. Her other plays include 'Coffee for Sixpence', 'Don't Forget Barney', 'Hangover', 'No Need for Tinkers', 'A Touch of the Dark', 'Wish No More', 'Return of the Tinker' and 'Marien Dreyer's World' which includes three short plays, 'Charles Was There', 'The Power of a Woman' and 'Too of a Kind'.

Driven, The, (1961), a novel by Donald Stuart (q.v.), describes a marathon cattle drive across the north-west of WA. The tough, taciturn drover boss, John Napier, a young drover, Tom, and three Aborigines, Charlie (Yahndrangoo), Kicker (Bahnidjarroo) and Youngbill (Koodrah), all build up a relationship of mutual trust and respect as they endure the hazards of the long trek. John Napier, at first pictured as cantankerous and uncommunicative, is shown by the end of the novel to be a humane character who carries with him the scars of a difficult past. Stuart's knowledge and love of the tough north-west, its people and their attitudes, bring a satisfying realism to both incident and character.

'Drought', see HUDSON, FLEXMORE

Drover (see also Overlander) is a Middle English noun stemming from an Old English verb 'to drove', i.e. to drive herds of cattle or flocks of sheep to market. The drover is the less glamorous cousin of the overlander; droving was the mundane, day-to-day process of moving mainly small groups of sheep and cattle over relatively short distances; overlanding was on a more epic scale, often vast distances were traversed and stock by the thousands moved. The occupations are to some extent interchangeable and both could be included under the more general heading of 'stockman', the latter term involving the overall handling rather than the mere moving of stock. The most famous literary drover is A.B. Paterson's Clancy of the Overflow, whose 'vision splendid' of the droving life confirmed the idyll, first envisioned in Adam Lindsay Gordon's 'The Sick Stockrider', of carefree stockmen 'sitting loosely in the saddle all the while'. Paterson's Saltbush Bill poems present the other version of the drover, the grass-stealer, whose ruses to allow his travelling sheep to graze on the squatters' best runs confirmed him as the outback's most skilled artist in sharp practices. Henry Lawson created two well-known drovers, the unfortunate Harry Dale of 'The Ballad of the Drover', and Andy who went with cattle and came safely home in 'Andy's Return'. Lawson also wrote the poem, 'The Drover's Sweetheart' and the stories, 'A Droving Yarn' and 'The Drover's Wife', the latter a famous Australian short story. Paterson further contributed to the droving legend with his nostalgic poems, 'In the Droving Days', 'The Travelling Post Office' and 'With the Cattle'. Other well-known droving verses are Harry Morant's 'West by North Again', Will Ogilvie's 'The Last Muster' and 'From the Gulf', G.H. Gibson's 'A Ballad of Queensland', Roland Robinson's 'The Drovers', David Campbell's 'Droving' and Thea Astley's 'Droving Man'. Donald Stuart's novel *The Driven* (1961) and Louis Esson's play *The Drovers* (1920) are also notable representations of the droving theme. Droving and stockman songs and ballads are plentiful. Douglas Stewart and Nancy Keesing include a section 'The Stockmen of Australia' in their volume, *Old Bush Songs* (1957). Best-known of the droving-stockman songs are 'The Sandy Maranoa' and 'The Dying Stockman'. Documentary and historical works on droving include Mary Durack's *Kings in Grass Castles* (1959), H.M. Barker's *Droving Days* (1966) and Keith Willey's *The Drovers* (1981). P.R. Gordon compiled *A Drover's Guide* in 1893; from it stemmed the colloquial expression 'The Drover's Guide', to indicate an anonymous source of outback rumours. An early Australian film, *The Drover's Sweetheart*, was produced in 1911.

Drover's Guide, see **Bagman's Gazette**

Drovers, The, a one-act play by Louis Esson (q.v.) first produced in 1923 by the Pioneer Players (q.v.), was published in 1920 and is often described as an Australian classic. The simple plot, which relates the death of Briglow Bill, a drover injured in a stampede and left to die by his mates who are bound to drive the cattle on to water, has an austere and terse inevitability, reflecting the grimness of life in the bush.

'Drover's Wife, The', one of Henry Lawson's (q.v.) best-known stories, was first published in the *Bulletin* in 1892. It recounts the experiences of an outback woman left alone with her four children in an isolated hut; her husband has been away droving for six months. Near sunset one day a snake disappears under the house; the woman puts her children to bed in the kitchen, and as she awaits its reappearance she recalls incidents which confirm the drabness, tragedy and struggle of her life. As dawn approaches the snake emerges and is killed by the woman with the assistance of Alligator, the family dog.

'The Drover's Wife' has been justly admired for its ruthlessly-realistic portrayal of pioneering life, although the courage and stoicism of the unnamed woman temper Lawson's pessimism. Much anthologized and also filmed, it inspired a famous painting by Sir Russell Drysdale (q.v.). That both the story and the painting have become classic responses of Australian artists to the bush is confirmed by the recent publication of three other stories called 'The Drover's Wife'. Murray Bail's (q.v.) story, published in 1975 in *Contemporary Portraits*, is centred on the painting and is ostensibly narrated by the drover's wife's first husband, a dentist, who outlines the circumstances of her desertion of him and questions the 'reality' of Drysdale's interpretation. Frank Moorhouse's (q.v.) hilarious 'The Drover's "Wife" ', published in 1980 in the centenary *Bulletin*, is narrated by an Italian student of Australian literature and satirizes both the bush ethos of writers like Lawson and the responses of academics to those writers. Barbara Jefferis's 'The Drover's Wife', also published in the *Bulletin* in 1980, is narrated by the woman herself and offers a feminist answer not only to males like Lawson, Drysdale, Bail and Moorhouse, whose 'errors' she corrects, but also to journals like the *Bulletin* which during the 1890s only told 'how half the world lives'.

Drug Poems (1972), a collection by Michael Dransfield (q.v.), gives an insight into the drug culture. Poems such as 'Bum's Rush', 'Fix', 'Overdose', 'Jam' and 'Getting Out' comment upon many aspects of the drug experience –

the isolation of the addict, the need for the 'fix', the terror of withdrawal and the difficulty of returning to normality.

Drum for Ben Boyd, A, a major poem in fifteen sections by Francis Webb (q.v.), was published in the *Bulletin* in three weekly segments in July 1946, then as a separate publication with illustrations by Norman Lindsay in 1948, when it was awarded the Grace Leven Prize for poetry. Indebted in its form and structure to Kenneth Slessor's 'Five Visions of Captain Cook', Webb's poem attempts a composite picture of Benjamin Boyd (q.v.), the enterprising Scottish merchant-entrepreneur who sought his fortune in maritime and pastoral activities in NSW in the 1840s. Boyd's arrival at Port Jackson in his yacht, *Wanderer*, in 1842 is pictured in the third part of the sequence. In turn, Boyd is assessed by the Norwegian boat-builder, Jan Strinberg; by an envious journalist, who bewails the fact that Boyd will 'grind out a fortune, rule this blasted colony/ While I sit here rotting slowly between editions'; by Sir Oswald Brierly, who accompanied him to Australia in the *Wanderer*; by a disgruntled whaler at Twofold Bay, who ruefully reflects on 'Mr Blasted Boyd . . . [who] owns us all'; by a Papuan, who becomes a victim of Boyd's blackbirding activities; by a colonial politician, who likes the aura of power and aristocratic tradition that surrounds Boyd; by a Monaro squatter who deplores Boyd's misuse of the land; by the captain of the *Oberon*, who is sent to unravel the mystery of Boyd's death at Guadalcanal in the Solomon Islands; and, finally by John Webster, who accompanies Boyd on his last voyage of self-aggrandizement around the Pacific.

'DRYBLOWER', see **MURPHY, E.G.**

Drylight, a literary journal published by the Students Representative Council of the Sydney Teachers' College, appeared annually 1955–67 and in 1971 and 1974. Integrating literature, music and art, *Drylight* was a lively and informative journal in whose pages appeared items from many well-known Australian literary personalities of the day. *Descant*, the annual of the Sydney Teachers' College Literary Club, appeared 1948–50.

DRYSDALE, Sir RUSSELL (1912–81), one of Australia's best-known artists, was born Bognor Regis, England, and settled in Australia in 1923. His paintings are notable for their depiction of the harshness of the outback landscape and for their interpretation of the difficult lives of the settlers and Aborigines of the area. He won the Wynne Prize in 1947, the Melrose

Prize in 1949 and the Britannica Australia Award in 1965. In 1957 he toured central Australia and WA, an experience that was rich in artistic results and which led to the publication, in collaboration with A.J. Marshall, of *Journey Among Men* (1962). Joseph Burke introduced *The Paintings of Russell Drysdale* (1951), Geoffrey Dutton wrote *Russell Drysdale* (1964) and Lou Klepac wrote *The Life and Work of Russell Drysdale* (1984). Drysdale was knighted in 1969.

Dubbo, Alf, see ***Riders in the Chariot***

Duffield, Hurtle, see ***Vivisector, The***

Duffing, a slang Australian term for livestock stealing, probably derives from an English slang word, 'duff', which meant to fake old things for new, e.g. clothes, jewellery. A cattle duffer either stole unbranded cattle (a practice referred to as 'poddy-dodging' when calves were involved) and put his own brand upon them or changed the brands already there. Livestock duffing gave rise to an extended vocabulary dealing with the practice, e.g. 'duffing yard', a secluded corral in the bush where stolen cattle were yarded and branded; and 'plant', the secluded spot itself, where the cattle were hidden. The practice of duffing was especially rife in squatting times before the use of fencing wire; it is often mentioned in nineteenth-century Australian fiction, e.g. in Alexander Harris's *The Emigrant Family* (1849) and 'Rolf Boldrewood''s *Robbery Under Arms* (1888), the latter using the famous Harry Redford duffing incident in 1870, as well as in later semi-historical writing such as S.H. Robert's *The Squatting Age in Australia 1835–1847* (1935) and Margaret Kiddle's *Men of Yesterday* (1961). Cattle duffing has been immortalized in one of Australia's best-known folk-songs, 'The Eumerella Shore' (q.v.). The Redford incident and its use by 'Boldrewood' is discussed in P.H. McCarthy's *Starlight: The Man and the Myth* (1972).

Dufrayer, Louise, see ***Maurice Guest***

DUFFY, Sir CHARLES GAVAN (1816–1903), born Monaghan, Ireland, migrated to Melbourne in 1855 after a stormy political career in Ireland. He was soon involved in colonial politics, where he was active in land reform and was premier of Victoria briefly in 1871. He helped found the Catholic journal the *Advocate* in 1868, having been involved with an earlier Irish Catholic weekly, the *Victorian* (1862–64). After his retirement from politics in 1880 he lived in France. In addition to numerous important works on Irish history, the most popular of which was *Young Ireland* (1880), he wrote *My Life in Two Hemispheres* (1898), which includes a record of his activities in Victoria. He was knighted in 1873 and made KCMG in 1877. Leon O'Broin wrote *Charles Gavan Duffy, Patriot and Statesman* (1967). Members of Sir Charles Gavan Duffy's family, e.g. his son, Sir Frank Gavan Duffy (1852–1936) and his grandson, Sir Charles Leonard Gavan Duffy (1882–1961), achieved distinction in Australian legal and political life. Duffy appears briefly as Dempsey in Henry Kingsley's novel, *The Hillyars and the Burtons* (1865).

DUGAN, MICHAEL GRAY (1947–   ), born Melbourne, was closely associated with the rise of the 'New Australian Poetry' (q.v.). Dugan produced the small magazine, *Crosscurrents*, was involved in Contempa (q.v.) Publications with Robert Kenny and Phillip Edmonds, and edited *The Drunken Tram: Six Young Melbourne Poets* (1972) and with John Jenkins *The Outback Reader* (1975), a collection of contemporary and experimental Australian short fiction. He has also edited a number of books for children, has been the children's books reviewer for the *Age* and editor of the children's magazine, *Puffinalia*. He has written considerable nonsense verse e.g. *Stuff and Nonsense* (1974), *Nonsense Places* (1976), and has publishd three volumes of verse, *Missing People* (1970), *Returning from the Prophet* (1972) and *Clouds* (1975).

DUGGAN, EDMUND (?1862–1938), born County Waterford, Ireland, came to Australia as a child and became a professional actor in his early twenties. He was known as a comedian but is more significant for his stage adaptation in 1891 of *For the Term of His Natural Life* and for his collaborations, sometimes under the joint pseudonym of 'Albert Edmunds', with Bert Bailey (q.v.). Their successes included 'The Squatter's Daughter' (1907), 'The Man from Out Back' (1909), 'On Our Selection' (q.v., 1912) and 'The Native Born' (1913). Duggan's work on his own account included 'The Democrat' (1891), a Eureka play later staged as 'Eureka Stockade' (1897), and 'My Mate' (1911), in which there are excerpts from the writings of Adam Lindsay Gordon. He also played Dad in a stage version of *The Rudd Family* in 1928.

DUGGAN, LAURIE (1949–   ), born South Melbourne, won the Anne Elder Poetry Award for his book *East: Poems 1970–74* (1976), the title poem of which won the Poetry Society of Australia Award in 1971. Associated with the magazines *New Poetry*, *Surfers Paradise* and

Three Blind Mice, Duggan has also published verse, *Under the Weather* (1978).

Dummying, see **Selection**

Dunbar, a ship bound for Sydney from Plymouth, was wrecked near South Head, Sydney Harbour, on 20 August 1857 with the loss of 120 lives; an able seaman, James Johnson, was the sole survivor. In September 1887 the playwright Alfred Dampier (q.v.) staged an unsuccessful melodrama, 'The Wreck of the Dunbar', in Sydney. Henry Kendall's poem 'The Merchant Ship', about the wrecking of the *Dunbar*, was published in the *Empire* in 1860.

DUNCAN, CATHERINE (1915–   ), born Launceston, Tasmania, was a well-known stage and radio actress of the 1930s and 1940s, as well as a playwright. She later worked as a film-maker and in 1945 joined the Australian National Film Board. Her plays include 'The Sword Sung', winner of the Sydney New Theatre League competition in 1937; *Sons of the Morning* (1946), which won the 1945 Playwrights' Advisory Board competition; *Some New Moon* (1961) in the Derwent series of one-act plays which she edited; and 'We the Living'. She also wrote, for radio, her verse-play *Path of the Eagle* which is included in *Australian Radio Plays* (1946, ed. Leslie Rees), winning an ABC award in 1943.

DUNCAN, W.A. (WILLIAM AUGUSTINE) (1811–85), born Aberdeenshire, Scotland, was a bookseller and publisher in Aberdeen before emigrating to NSW in 1837. In 1839 he founded the Catholic newspaper, the *Australasian* (later *Sydney*) *Chronicle*, and after losing control of it established *Duncan's Weekly Register* (1843–45); Charles Harpur and Henry Parkes contributed to both journals and Duncan published Harpur's first major collection, *Thoughts, A Series of Sonnets* (1845). In 1846 Duncan became a public servant, working in the customs service in Moreton Bay 1846–59 and Sydney 1859–81. He wrote a number of pamphlets and other works on religion, education, politics and history.

Dunciad Minor, a lengthy, mock-heroic satire in the eighteenth-century manner by A.D. Hope (q.v.) published in 1970, is based on an earlier, mainly unpublished work of 1950 titled 'Dunciad Minimus'. In 1950 when both Hope and A.A. Phillips took part in a series of radio broadcasts titled 'Standard Works I'd Like to Burn', Phillips's denunciation of Alexander Pope presented Hope with an ideal opportunity to write a modern *Dunciad*. Arthur Phillips, presented by Hope as descended from the infamous Ambrose Philips, is only nominally the butt of the satire, the main brunt of which is directed at modern literary criticism in general. Witty and lively and equipped with the required superstructure of footnotes, the poem is both an amusing *jeu d'esprit* and a serious criticism of academic pedantry. In 1978 Hope and Phillips became joint patrons of the Association for the Study of Australian Literature.

DUNDERDALE, GEORGE (1822–1903), born Lancashire, England, worked as a schoolteacher in the USA before joining the gold rush to Australia in 1853. He was later a clerk of courts and a customs officer in the Victorian western districts and Gippsland. His experiences of early colonial life, especially in the Gippsland district, are related in *The Book of the Bush* (q.v., 1898). He also wrote *Prairie and Bush* (1891), the title reflecting his interest in the two continents, North America and Australia.

Dungaree Men were poor settlers in the early part of the colonial period in Australia, the forerunners of the 'stringybark cockatoos' (see Cockatoo). The term was used, for example, in Alexander Harris's *Settlers and Convicts* (1847).

DUNN, MAX (1895–1963), born Dublin and educated in Scotland, France and America, came to Australia in 1924 having served in the First World War. A mysterious sophisticate and impressive intellectual with a somewhat obscure background, Dunn played numerous roles in the Melbourne scene in the years before and during the Second World War. He was a psychotherapist, a journalist with the *Argus*, *Smith's Weekly* and other papers and magazines, a publisher and a poet. His books of poetry include *Random Elements* (1943), *No Asterisks* (1944), *Time of Arrival* (1947), *Portrait of a Country* (1951), *The Journey of Diornos* (1953) and *The Mirror and the Rose* (1954). The poem 'The Journey of John Donne', which had appeared in *Time of Arrival*, was republished in 1952. A collection of his translations from the Chinese, *The City of Wide Streets by the Friendly River: Leaves of Jade: Poems from Dragon Land*, was also published in 1952. The best of his poetry is in *Portrait of a Country* and *The Mirror and the Rose*. The former, which reflects Dunn's views of the Australian environment, has been described as a kind of Australian *Waste Land*; the latter is a collection of eleven poems ('Reflections') concerned with love, life and death, the rose and the mirror being the key symbols. His work is represented in the anthology *Eight by Eight* (1963). In 1955 Dunn became a Buddhist priest; he celebrated his ordination

with the publication of the booklet *Into the Radiance*, which consisted of one short poem, one line of which was printed on each page of the booklet.

DUNSTAN, KEITH (1925–), born Melbourne, served in the RAAF before becoming a journalist in 1946; a columnist with the *Courier-Mail* in Brisbane 1954–58 and the *Sun News-Pictorial* in Melbourne 1958–78, he has worked as a correspondent in London, New York and on the west coast of America 1979–82. Dunstan has written nine books; his second, *Supporting a Column* (1966), amusingly reflects on his life as a daily columnist. Since then he has confirmed his reputation as a witty and perceptive analyst of Australian life, his observations assisted by the research of Philip Garrett in such works as *Wowsers* (1968) and *Knockers* (1972), which are accounts of those traditions in Australia; *Sports* (1973), which discusses the sporting obsessions of Australians; *Ratbags* (1979), which chronicles the careers of two dozen Australian eccentrics including Barry Humphries, E.W. Cole, H.D. McIntosh and Xavier Herbert; and *Saint Ned* (1980), a contribution to the literature of the Ned Kelly centenary.

DURACK, Dame **MARY** (1913–), of the pastoralist Durack family (see *Kings in Grass Castles*), was born in Adelaide and spent her very early life in the Kimberley region of WA. She was educated in Perth, then returned to the Kimberleys where she and her younger sister, Elizabeth (1915–), helped to run the family company properties during the 1930s depression. The sisters collaborated in publishing *All-About: The Story of a Black Community on Argyle Station, Kimberley* (1935), Mary supplying the text and Elizabeth the illustrations. Mary and Elizabeth produced a number of books for children: *Chunuma* (1936), *Son of Djaro* (1940), *The Way of the Whirlwind* (1941), *The Magic Trumpet* (1946), *Kookanoo & Kangaroo* (1963) and *To Ride a Fine Horse* (1963). Mary was on the staff of WA Newspapers Ltd 1937–38, where as columnist 'Virgilia' she wrote for country women and children. Since 1938 she has been a prolific freelance writer. Her most significant literary works are the novel *Keep Him My Country* (q.v., 1955), the story of an idyllic relationship between white stationowner, Stan Rolt, and native girl, Dalgerie, which brings Rolt into a spiritual union with the land itself; *Kings in Grass Castles* (1959), which traces the saga of the Durack family from their emigration from Ireland in the middle of the nineteenth century to the death of Mary's grandfather, the legendary pastoralist,

Patsy Durack, in 1898; and *Sons in the Saddle* (1983), the sequel to *Kings in Grass Castles*, which continues the Durack family saga through to the time of her father, Michael ('MP') Durack. Mary Durack's other writings include further children's books, e.g. *The Courteous Savage: Yagan of Swan River* (1964), *An Australian Settler* (1964, in Australia titled *A Pastoral Emigrant*), *The Ship of Dreams* (1968, a two-act play) and *Tjakamarra: Boy Between Two Worlds* (1977). Her other historical writings include *The Rock and the Sand* (1969), which deals with missionary activities in WA; *Swan River Saga* (1975), a play about the experiences of pioneer WA woman, Eliza Shaw; *To Be Heirs Forever* (1976), Eliza Shaw's biography; and *The Aborigines in Australian Literature* (1978). In recognition of her achievements Mary Durack was made OBE in 1966 and DBE in 1978. Elizabeth Durack CMG, internationally-recognized for her artistic representation of the WA outback and its Aboriginal people, is the subject of *The Art of Elizabeth Durack* (1981) with introduction by Patrick Hutchings.

Dusty, a novel by Frank Dalby Davison (q.v.), first published in 1946 and winner of the *Argus* novel competition, is second only to his *Manshy* (q.v.) in popularity. The main protagonist is a half-breed dog, offspring of a wild dingo bitch and a red kelpie working dog. The dog's divided personality, reflected in his response to the call of the wild coupled with his yearning for the quiet domestic life of the farm, creates tensions that finally destroy him. No simple animal story, the novel has human relevance, illustrating the unity of all nature in cyclical change and the universal tension between conformism and rebellion. An Australian film, *Dusty*, was screened in 1983.

Dutiful Daughter, A, a novel by Thomas Keneally (q.v.) published in 1971, has been described variously as a fable or parable about human nature, familial relationships, power, pride and authority. Set mainly on a dairy farm at Campbell's Reach in northern NSW, it focuses on the Glover family in which the parents were transformed into dairy cattle from the waist down the day after their daughter Barbara began to menstruate; she has stayed at home to minister to their needs. The fourth member of the family, Barbara's younger brother Damian, acts as narrator for part of *A Dutiful Daughter* and returns, in its opening pages, on vacation from university. The action of the novel covers the three days after his return to the district, although the history of the Glovers, notably the change in the parents and Barbara's guilt and her power (which extends to her

incestuous relationship with Damian), is told retrospectively. After spending the night in town with his girlfriend Helen, Damian returns to the farm to find his parents' condition worsening. He is visited by Helen, who wants their relationship to be resolved. Helen realizes the hold of Barbara and the family over Damian and departs, but has to be rescued from the rising floodwaters first by Damian and then by Barbara and her new lover, Frederic (who, from some suggestions in the novel, might also be Damian). Her experience with Frederic convinces Barbara that she cannot escape the impulses that have literally transformed her parents. At the end of *A Dutiful Daughter* she leads them to suicide amidst the flood that engulfs the region, leaving Damian in the 'awful tower of his freedom'.

DUTTON, GEOFFREY (1922–), was born at Kapunda, SA, where his great-grandfather founded that State's first stud sheep station in 1838. He was educated at the University of Adelaide before enlisting in the RAAF in 1941 as a flying instructor. During the 1940s Dutton was associated with the *Angry Penguins* (q.v.) group. Close friends included the poets Donald Kerr, Paul Pfeiffer, Max Harris and Alister Kershaw, and the painters Arthur Boyd and Sidney Nolan. The cover of his first book of poetry was designed by Sidney Nolan and he has continued to work closely with artists. He studied at Oxford 1946–49. After spending the early 1950s travelling extensively, he lectured in English at the University of Adelaide 1955–62. He was editor of Penguin Australia 1961–65 and in 1965 founded, with Brian Stonier, the paperback publishing firm Sun Books, of which he is still editorial director. He was joint founder and editor of the periodicals, *Australian Letters* and *Australian Book Review*; was one of the editors of the annual poetry anthology, *Verse in Australia* (1958–61); and edited the Australian Writers and Their Work series 1962–66. He is currently editor of the *Bulletin*'s quarterly literary supplement, inaugurated in January 1980. Active in the Australian Council for the Arts 1968–70, and in other cultural organizations, he was made AO in 1976.

A versatile writer, Dutton has published seven collections of verse, *Night Flight and Sunrise* (1944), *Antipodes in Shoes* (1958), which was awarded the Grace Leven Prize, *Flowers and Fury* (1962), *Poems Soft and Loud* (1967), *Findings and Keepings* (1970), which is mainly a substantial collection from the preceding volumes, *New Poems to 1972* (1972) and *A Body of Words* (1977); four novels, *The Mortal and the Marble* (1950), *Andy* (1968), *Tamara* (1970) and *Queen Emma of the South Seas* (1976);

a collection of short stories, *The Wedge-Tailed Eagle* (1980); two critical studies, *Patrick White* (1961) and *Walt Whitman* (1961); three substantial historical biographies, *Founder of a City* (1960), *The Hero as Murderer: The Life of Edward John Eyre* (1967) and *Australia's Last Explorer: Ernest Giles* (1970); three works of art appreciation, *The Paintings of S.T. Gill* (1962), *Russell Drysdale* (1964) and *White on Black* (1974); three travel books, *A Long Way South* (1953), *Africa in Black and White* (1956), and *States of the Union* (1958); three novels for children, *Seal Bay* (1966), *Tisi and the Yabby* (1965) and *Tisi and the Pageant* (1968); and a book of verse for young people, *On My Island* (1967). His work as an editor has been equally varied and includes the influential collection of critical essays, *The Literature of Australia* (1964, 2nd edn 1976); two anthologies of verse, *Australian Poetry 1962* (1962) and *Australian Verse from 1805* (1975), and two of verse and prose, *Modern Australian Writing* (1966) and, with Max Harris, *The Vital Decade* (1968); two collections of essays on republicanism, *Australia and the Monarchy* (1966) and *Republican Australia?* (1977), and one on censorship in Australia (1970); and a collection of photographs 1901–14 in the *Australia Since the Camera* series. He has also written numerous uncollected critical essays, articles and reviews and published translations of the Russian poets, Yevgeny Yevtushenko and Bella Akhmadulina. His less ambitious publications include several 'coffee-table' books of which the most significant are *A Taste of History* (1978) and *Patterns of Australia* (1980).

Dutton's early poetry, self-consciously modernist and experimental, has given way to an easy reflective lyricism marked by a strong visual element. He has written some topical and satiric poems but his most characteristic are those celebrating the joys of love, the beauties of the natural scene or the pleasures of friendship. Some of his best work is found in his more sustained autobiographical poems such as 'The Smallest Sprout' and 'Abandoned Airstrip, Northern Territory', where the tone is part-elegiac and part-humorous. An urbane and uninhibited prose writer, Dutton is a versatile novelist. *The Mortal and the Marble*, an Anglo–Australian novel, is partly the story of a young marriage and partly a study of national differences. *Andy* is a lively, picaresque tale of a wartime flying instructor; *Tamara* is a deeply-felt love story set mainly in Russia; *Queen Emma of the South Seas* is an exotic, historical tale based on the life of an extraordinary Samoan–American woman, who built a vast trading empire in the Pacific.

DUWELL, MARTIN, see *Makar*

DWIGHT, HENRY TOLMAN (?1823–71), born London, migrated to Melbourne in 1855 with a large stock of second-hand books which enabled him to open a bookshop in 1857 in Bourke Street of that city. By 1862 his stock had grown to 60 000 volumes. Dwight's shop became a regular meeting place of the Melbourne literary coterie that included Adam Lindsay Gordon, Henry Kendall, Marcus Clarke, George Gordon McCrae and R.H. Horne. Dwight published works by Horne, McCrae, Thomas McCombie and others.

DWYER, J.F. (JAMES FRANCIS) (1874–1952), born Camden Park, NSW, became a contributor of verse and short fiction to the *Bulletin* under J.F. Archibald while serving a prison sentence 1899–1902. He left Australia in 1906 and became a prolific short-story writer and novelist in the USA and France. Of his ten novels, most of which are tales of mystery and adventure, *The White Waterfall* (1912) and *O Splendid Sorcery* (1930) have some connection with Australia. He also published a collection of short stories, *Breath of the Jungle* (1915), and an autobiographical work, *Leg Irons on Wings* (1949).

Dye House, The, see **CALTHORPE, MENA**

'Dying Stockman, The' is a lugubrious Australian folk-song (q.v.) which chronicles the last wishes of a stockman as he lies dying, his head supported by a saddle. His requests, communicated to his two mates, begin with the words of the chorus:

> Wrap me up with my stockwhip and blanket,
> And bury me deep down below,
> Where the dingoes and crows can't molest me,
> In the shade where the coolibahs grow.

The song was included as an anonymous composition in A.B. Paterson's pioneering collection, *Old Bush Songs* (1905), but claims have been made (*Australian Tradition*, September 1968) for Horace Alfred Flower's authorship while he was a bank manager in Queensland in 1892. More certainly the song derives, as Hugh Anderson has explained in *The Dying Stockman* (1954), from the English sentimental song 'The Tarpaulin Jacket'; Anderson traces parallels between 'The Tarpaulin Jacket' and an earlier English song, 'Rosin the Beau', although American melodies have also been associated with 'The Dying Stockman'. The popularity of 'The Dying Stockman' is attested to by the many close parallels and parodies about dying shearers, bagmen, aviators, gunners, bargehands, fettlers and so on. Part of the reason for its popularity may well lie in its parallels with Adam Lindsay Gordon's earlier literary ballad, 'The Sick Stockrider', although it is also one of the relatively few traditional Australian songs given currency in the twentieth century by hillbilly singers such as Tex Morton. More recently, Rolf Harris's popular song 'Tie Me Kangaroo Down Sport' clearly belongs to the 'Dying Stockman' tradition, despite the unsentimental response to the last request of Harris's stockman:

'Tan me hide when I'm dead, Fred,
Tan me hide when I'm dead;'
So we tanned his hide when he died, Clyde,
And that's it hangin' in the shed!

DYMOCK, WILLIAM (1861–1900), born North Melbourne, came to Sydney as a boy and began in the book trade in 1878 working for, among others, George Robertson (1), (q.v.). He established his own bookshop in the early 1880s; it was known as Dymock's Book Arcade by 1884 when situated in Pitt Street, Sydney. In 1890 he moved to 428 George Street, where the business still operates. In 1896 he took over William Maddock's circulating library with Maddock as manager and advertised his shop as 'the largest Book shop in the world', with upwards of a million books. A bookseller rather than a publisher, William Dymock was the first native-born Australian to launch and maintain a succesful bookselling venture. He is among the personalities discussed in George Ferguson's *Some Early Australian Bookmen* (1978).

DYSON, EDWARD (1865–1931) was born at Morrison near Ballarat, Victoria, son of a mining engineer. He moved with his family about the goldfields during childhood and grew up familiar with life both in the bush and on the diggings. In adolescence he worked in odd jobs about the Victorian mines, then was a miner in Tasmania and a factory worker in Melbourne before turning to journalism and free-lance writing. Throughout a long career as a writer he contributed short stories and novels of bush life, the diggings and Melbourne slums to journals and newspapers such as the *Bulletin*, the *Age* and *Melbourne Punch* under a variety of pseudonyms. His *métier* was the short story, his novels being little more than a series of simply-connected sequential events. His best-known story, a classic among Australian gold-fields tales, was 'A Golden Shanty' (q.v.). In the *Fact'ry 'Ands* (q.v., 1906) stories he departs from the traditional 'slum' literature portrayal of human misery to emphasize the bizarre and comic side of slum life. His large output of

fiction included the short-story collections, *Below and On Top* (1898), *Benno and Some of the Push* (1911), and *Spats' Fact'ry* (1914), and the novels, *The Gold-Stealers: A Story of Waddy* (1901) and *In the Roaring Fifties* (1906). Dyson's collection of verse, *Rhymes from the Mines and Other Lines* (1896), although very much the balladist's usual concoction of irony and humour, pathos and comedy, is singular in that it reflects the life and environment of the underground miner.

DYSON, WILL (1880–1938), born Alfredton near Ballarat, Victoria, was a younger brother of the writer, Edward Dyson (q.v.). In 1903 he became a caricaturist with the Adelaide *Critic* and in 1906 illustrated his brother's book of stories, *Fact'ry 'Ands*. In 1908 he drew coloured cartoons for the covers of Randolph Bedford's journal, *Clarion*. In 1912 he was appointed chief cartoonist of the *Daily Herald* in London and became extremely popular through his championing of the working man and his satirical tilts at pomposity and greed. His most famous cartoon depicted Woodrow Wilson, Lloyd George and Orlando of Italy leaving the Versailles peace treaty in a self-congratulatory mood while in the background was a child (labelled '1940 Class') weeping. By 1925 Dyson was back in Australia, his cartoons appearing in the Melbourne *Herald*, *Punch* and *Table Talk*. On the termination of his contract with the *Herald* he returned to England, where he died while working again for the *Daily Herald*. Australia's most trenchant satirical cartoonist, Dyson published *Cartoons* (1914), *Kultur Cartoons* (1915) and a volume, *Australia at War*, the last from his work as an Australian official war artist (he was twice wounded) in the First World War. He also published a small volume, *Poems: In Memory of a Wife* (1919), after his wife Ruby, sister of Norman Lindsay and a talented black-and-white artist, died in the influenza epidemic of 1919. In 1933 he published *Artist among the Bankers*, a hostile commentary on the commercial world. Will Dyson's elder brother, Ambrose Arthur Dyson (1876–1913), was a cartoonist for the Adelaide *Critic* 1898–1903, was similarly employed on the *Bulletin* 1903–06, and contributed drawings to numerous other newspapers and journals including the *Gadfly*, the *Clarion*, *Table Talk* and the Sydney *Worker*. Ambrose is credited with the first artistic portrayal of the Australian larrikin. Ross McMullin wrote *Will Dyson: Cartoonist, Etcher and Australia's First War Artist* (1984).

E

Eaglehawk Neck, see Arthur, Port

Ear in a Wheatfield, a poetry magazine edited by Kris Hemensley (q.v.) 1972–76, began as an extension of *Earth Ship*, a small literary journal that Hemensley had produced in England in 1970–72. It was succeeded by *The Merri Creek, or Nero* (1977–), a section of which is entitled 'H/Ear'.

Earth-Visitors, see SLESSOR, KENNETH

'EAST, MICHAEL', see WEST, MORRIS

Echo, see FAIRFAX, JOHN

Echuca, a town on the Murray River, was an important railhead from Melbourne and the focal point of the paddle-steamer trade along the Murray 1880–1900. It is the setting for Joseph Furphy's *The Buln-Buln and the Brolga* (1948), the opening of *Rigby's Romance* (1946), and for several of 'Price Warung''s *Tales of the Riverine* (1898) and J.A. Barry's stories. Nancy Cato's *All the Rivers Run* (1978) is largely set at Echuca in its riverboat heyday.

EDEN, CHARLES HENRY (1839–1900), born England, came to Moreton Bay in 1863 and tried various occupations, including digging for gold, before being appointed a police magistrate and subcollector of customs in 1868. He was dismissed from those posts in 1870 and returned to England where he later wrote sixteen novels and numerous travel books; two of the latter, *Australia's Heroes* (1875) and *The Fifth Continent* (1877), relate to Australia. His chief Australian work was the autobiographical *My Wife and I in Queensland* (1872), a disenchanted and highly-coloured account of his altogether-undistinguished Australian experience.

EDEN, GUY E. MORTON (?1864–1954), elder son of Charles Henry Eden (q.v.), wrote numerous works of fiction of which *The Cry of the Curlew: A Yarn of the Bush* (1892) and *He Went Out with the Tide* (1896) are set in Australia. He also wrote *Bush Ballads and Other Verses* (1907).

Eden of the Good, An, see 'HERVEY, GRANT'

EDMOND, JAMES (1859–1933), born Glasgow, Scotland, migrated in 1878 to NZ and to Australia in 1884. While on the staff of the Rockhampton *Morning Bulletin* he contributed financial comments to the Sydney *Bulletin* and in 1886 joined the latter, becoming associate editor in 1890, financial editor in 1892, and initiator of the well-known 'Wild Cat' column dealing with financial matters. He also contributed short stories, sketches, dramatic criticism and a column titled 'The Brickbat'; his pseudonym for some of this writing was 'Titus Salt'. He was editor 1903–14; under his influence the *Bulletin* retained and even expanded its nationalistic outlook but dropped much of its earlier republican emphasis. Edmond exercised some influence on the shaping of the Australian constitution and Australian federal politics through his *Bulletin* editorials advocating protectionism, immigration control and centralist control of education and transport. His *Bulletin* leaders were published as *A Policy for the Commonwealth* (1900) and some of his humorous writings were collected as *A Journalist and Two Bears* (1913), illustrated by Norman Lindsay.

EDMONDS, PHILLIP, see *Contempa*

'EDMUNDS, ALBERT', see DUGGAN, EDMUND

Education of Young Donald, The, an autobiography by Donald Horne (q.v.), was published in 1967. The first section, titled 'Primary, 1927–1933', deals with his early life in Muswellbrook, a small town in NSW, and compellingly evokes the general flavour of Australian life between the wars. Horne records the town's clearly-defined social system, ranging from the 'Old Families' to the scroungers and outcasts, and his own family's niche in the lower-middle ranks (his father was a schoolteacher). Also memorable are his descriptions of the town's religious divisions and varied social activities which engaged everyone in a 'demanding bustle of pleasure'. Nostalgic descriptions of frequent visits to Sydney, where his maternal grandparents lived, heighten the impression of a golden age. In the second section, titled 'Secondary, 1934–1938', which deals with his experiences at high school and the family's move to Sydney, the mood darkens. In the city the family lives in a withdrawn way, threatened by the father's growing mental disorder which culminates in a breakdown. Horne, unable to identify himself with his family, school or suburb, takes refuge partly in fantasy and partly in his intellectual growth. The last section, titled 'Tertiary, 1939–1941', covers Horne's experiences at the University of Sydney and his association with such figures as John Anderson, A.D. Hope, James McAuley, Oliver Somerville, Harold Stewart and Ronald Dunlop. This section is both an effective realization of an important intellectual milieu and a frank study of a young man's reaction to heady new influences.

EDWARDS, DON (1905–63), born Sydney, became a teacher and from 1945 was also literary critic for the *Sydney Morning Herald*. He published a book of short stories, *High Hill at Midnight* (1944), with recurring themes of marital problems and unemployment during the 1930s depression. His novel, *The Woman at Jingera* (1948) is an expansion of his short story 'The Woman from the Bend', about the narrator's fascination for a strange woman of the bush.

EDWARDS, GEORGE (1886–1953), was born Harold Parks in SA and had a career as a comic actor and dancer in vaudeville and films before moving into radio in 1931, when he changed his name. For two decades he dominated the production of comic and dramatic serials, which were popular on commercial radio during that period. Perhaps the best-known was 'Dad and Dave' (q.v.), which ran for over two thousand episodes 1937–51 and was one of the last metamorphoses of *On Our Selection* (q.v.). *Ralph Rashleigh*, Edwards's last serial (1953), was another work of Australian literature to attract his attention. A man of wide ventriloquial gifts, Edwards played upwards of six characters in a single scene, sometimes doubling that number in an episode, and was widely known as 'The Man with a Thousand Voices'. His fourth and last wife was Coral Lansbury.

EDWARDS, HUGH (1933–), born Perth and educated in Victoria, was a journalist with the *West Australian* 1953–68 and has since been a full-time writer. His best-known books are those dealing with wrecks of Dutch ships off the Australian coast, e.g. the *Batavia* (q.v.), the *Zeewyk* and the *Gilt Dragon*. His *Islands of Angry Ghosts* (1966) is an important addition to the large body of literature about the ill-fated *Batavia; The Wreck on the Half-Moon Reef* (1970) is the story of the *Zeewyk*, wrecked in 1727. A skilled diver, Edwards carried out much of the hazardous exploratory work for both books. His interest in wrecks led to the compilation of *Australian and New Zealand Shipwrecks and Sea Tragedies* (1978); his interest in sharks to the editing of *Sharks and Shipwrecks* (1975), a collection of seventeen stories. His other books, including books for adolescents, are *Captain William Bligh R.N.* (1972), *The Triumphs and Tragedies of Pearl Divers of Australia* (1972), *Skin Diving* (1975), *Tiger Shark* (1976), *Sea Lion Island* (1977), *The Pearl Pirates* (1977), *Sim, the Sea Lion* (1981) and *The Crocodile God* (1982). With Aboriginal writer Joe Nangan, he compiled *Joe Nangan's Dreaming* (1976), a collection of twenty illustrated Aboriginal legends.

EDWARDS, RON (1930–), born Geelong, Victoria, is an artist, writer and publisher who has been active for many years in the field of Australian folklore. In 1952 he established the Rams Skull Press, which published the series *Bandicoot Ballads* (1951–55) and *Black Bull Chapbooks* (1954–57), illustrated by Edwards and including John Manifold and Hugh Anderson as authors. Edwards's major folk-song collections are *The Overlander Songbook* (1971) and *The Big Book of Australian Folk Song* (1976), which both incorporate material published in smaller compilations. He has also written or compiled *The Australian Yarn* (1977), *Yarns and Ballads* (1981), *Australian Traditional Bush Crafts* (1975), *Skills of the Australian Bushman* (1979); other publications include sketch-books, some of which reflect his recent interest in Eastern calligraphy, and chapbooks on Australian folklore topics.

1890s, see **Nineties**

Eisenbart, Professor, an enigmatic creation of the poet Gwen Harwood (q.v.), has been interpreted as a 'mask' through which the poet expresses certain anarchic or anti-Establishment views, and as a persona which allows her to reflect ironically on the human condition. Eight Professor Eisenbart poems form the second part of Gwen Harwood's *Poems* (1963), although several of them had appeared earlier in *Meanjin* (1956, 1959). In 'Prize-Giving', the first poem in the series, Eisenbart, an ageing nuclear physicist, attends a girls' school speech night to present the prizes and is there bewitched by a girl pianist with titian hair who plays Mozart with extraordinary passion and skill. The remaining poems, in which she has become his mistress, demonstrate such facets of their relationship as her maturity and wisdom compared with his erratic megalomania and his gradual acquisition, largely through her influence, of self-knowledge.

'EK DUM', see **ELLIS, M.H.**

ELDER, ANNE (1918–76), born Auckland, NZ, lived in Australia from the age of three.

As Anne MacKintosh she was a noted ballet-dancer with the Borovansky Ballet Company. She published her first book of poetry, *For the Record*, in 1972; a second volume, *Crazy Woman and Other Poems*, highly commended in the National Book Council awards for 1977, was published posthumously in 1976. *For the Record* contains some fine individual poems, especially those with deep personal associations for the poet, e.g. 'Midnight' which concerns her mother, and 'Journey to the North' with its immense joy in homecoming after an absence; and the sequence, 'Four Elegies for the Death of Women'. The Anne Elder Trust Fund Award for poetry is administered by the Victorian branch of FAW and is awarded annually to the best first book of poetry published. First awarded in 1977 it was won by Laurie Duggan for *East* and Graeme Curtis for *At Last No Reply*. The 1978 award went to Lee Cataldi for *Invitation to a Marxist Lesbian Party*; 1979 to Les Harrop for *The Hum of the Old Suit*; 1980 to Richard Lunn for *Pompeii Deep Fry*; 1981 to Jenny Boult for *The Hotel Anonymous* and Gig Ryan for *The Division of Anger*; 1982 to Kate Llewellyn for *Trader Kate and the Elephants* and Peter Goldsworthy for *Reading from Ecclesiastes*.

ELDERSHAW, FLORA (1897–1956), born Sydney and brought up on a sheep station in the Riverina, graduated in 1918 from the University of Sydney where she met Marjorie Barnard (q.v.). Their collaboration under the pseudonym 'M. Barnard Eldershaw' (q.v.) produced five novels and various other writings. After teaching in Sydney 1921–40 she joined the Department of Reconstruction in Canberra, then transferred to Melbourne in 1943 to the Department of Labour and National Service. In 1948 she entered private practice as an industrial consultant. Active in the Sydney branch of FAW, she was president in 1935 and 1943. With Frank Dalby Davison she was significant in the expansion of the CLF and was an active member of its Advisory Board 1939–53. She was also a member of the Women's Advisory Council. Some of her most important friendships were with Vance, Nettie and Aileen Palmer, Katharine Susannah Prichard, Frank Dalby Davison and T. Inglis Moore. More active in public life than Barnard, she achieved fewer independent publications. Two of her addresses to the English Association were published in 1931 and 1935; the first, titled *Contemporary Australian Women Writers*, is the more significant. In 1936 she edited the *Australian Writers' Annual* for the FAW and in 1938 *The Peaceful Army*, an anthology of essays and poems by women in honour of Australia's sesquicentenary in which prominent women writers such as Mary Gilmore, Miles Franklin, Eleanor Dark, Kylie Tennant and Helen Simpson are represented.

'ELDERSHAW, M. BARNARD', was the pseudonym adopted by Flora Eldershaw and Marjorie Barnard (qq.v.) for their works of collaboration, published 1929–47. Although it is impossible to assess the relative importance of their contributions, it seems likely that the lion's share of the writing fell to Barnard but that Eldershaw played an important role in the conceptual and shaping stages. The last novel published under the joint pseudonym, *Tomorrow and Tomorrow* (q.v.), seems to have been almost entirely Barnard's work. Writings published by 'M. Barnard Eldershaw' are five novels, *A House is Built* (q.v. 1929), *Green Memory* (1931), *The Glasshouse* (1936), *Plaque with Laurel* (1937) and *Tomorrow and Tomorrow* (1947) republished in its full, uncensored version as *Tomorrow and Tomorrow and Tomorrow* in 1983; three histories, *Phillip of Australia* (1938), *The Life and Times of Captain John Piper* (1939) and *My Australia* (1939); and a significant collection of critical essays, *Essays in Australian Fiction* (q.v. 1938). They also wrote several short stories, other general critical and historical essays, a radio drama, *The Watch on the Headland*, published in *Australian Radio Plays* (1946), and edited a collection of short stories, *Coast to Coast 1946* (1947).

The novels of the collaboration have met varying receptions. *A House is Built*, a study of one family's fortunes in nineteenth-century Sydney, shared first prize in the 1928 *Bulletin's* novel competition. The combination of a well-realized historical background and varied individual characters assured the novel an immediate and lasting popularity in England and Australia. *Green Memory*, also set in nineteenth-century Sydney, has been less popular; with *The Glasshouse* the novelists moved to contemporary times and life aboard an ocean vessel. *Plaque with Laurel*, a more complex novel, has the unusual background of a three-day conference of the Australian Writers' Guild in Canberra.

Electrical Experience, The, Frank Moorhouse's (q.v.) third 'discontinuous narrative', was published in 1975 and won the National Book Council Award for fiction for that year. Comprising nineteen stories which are interspersed with more than twenty fragments, *The Electrical Experience* focuses on T. George McDowell, a manufacturer of soft drinks in a NSW south-coast town; most of the stories recount significant moments in his life though not in chronological order. Although McDowell becomes a successful businessman partly because he is able to adapt to change, symbolized by his acceptance of electricity, *The Electrical Experience* establishes the gulf between his generation and that of his unstable daughter Terri, an important character in *The Americans, Baby* (q.v., 1972). Among the other inhabitants of his town are Irving Bow, the central character in the 'Pacific City' section of *The Everlasting Secret Family and Other Secrets* (q.v. 1980), and Dr Trenbow, the protagonist of the film *Between Wars* (1974). The ironic detachment with which a past ethos is established, partly by the fragments of 1930s folklore and history, is balanced by Moorhouse's sympathy towards and understanding of the central character.

ELISHA, RON (1951–), born Jerusalem, Israel, came to Melbourne with his family in 1953. He graduated in medicine from the University of Melbourne and has worked as a general practitioner. His earliest play, *In Duty Bound* (1983), was first produced in Melbourne in 1978. Its story of a young Jewish doctor prevented from marrying a Gentile by family opposition, and its criticism of the obstructive barriers of racial and religious prejudice aroused considerable controversy, especially in Jewish circles. His play 'Einstein', produced in 1981, won Awgies for best stage play and most outstanding script; it was taken by the Melbourne Theatre Company on its tour of the USA in 1982. Another play by Elisha, 'Two', was performed in 1983.

Elizabethan Theatre Trust, see **Australian Elizabethan Theatre Trust**

ELKIN, ADOLPHUS PETER (1891–1979), born West Maitland, NSW, was professor of anthropology at the University of Sydney 1934–56. A Fellow of the Social Science Research Council of Australia and a member of the Australian Institute of Aboriginal Studies, Elkin was a much-honoured anthropologist, receiving the Royal Society of NSW, James Cook, Mueller and H.E. Gregory medals. He was made CMG in 1966. His publications include *The Australian Aborigines* (1938), *Aboriginal Men of High Degree* (1946) and *The Aboriginal Australians* (1961). His son Peter Kingsley Elkin (1924–), who edited *Australian Poems in Perspective* (1978), became professor of English at the University of New England in 1972.

ELLIOTT, BRIAN (1910–), born and educated in Adelaide, was on the staff of the University of Adelaide 1940–75, first as lecturer in English and then as reader in Australian literary studies 1961–75. Instrumental in the founding of the Humanities Research Council

of Australia, he was made AM in 1976. Elliott is the author of the novel, *Leviathan's Inch* (1946), but his major contribution to Australian literature has been as essayist (*James Hardy Vaux*, 1944; *Singing to the Cattle*, 1947); critic (*The Landscape of Australian Poetry*, 1967); biographer (*Marcus Clarke*, 1958); and editor (*Coast to Coast*, 1948; *Bards in the Wilderness*, 1970; *Adam Lindsay Gordon*, 1973; *The Jindyworobaks*, 1979).

ELLIOTT, SUMNER LOCKE (1917–), the son of the writer Sumner Locke (q.v.), who died soon after his birth, and Henry Logan Elliott, a freelance journalist, was born in Sydney. Brought up by several aunts he was the subject of a fierce battle for custody that was determined when he was ten. On leaving school he became an actor and writer for radio and joined the Independent Theatre, which produced seven of his plays: *Interval* (produced in 1939, published in 1942), 'The Cow Jumped Over the Moon' (1939), 'The Little Sheep Run Fast' (1940), 'Goodbye to the Music' (1942), 'Your Obedient Servant' (1943), 'The Invisible Circus' (1946) and *Rusty Bugles* (q.v. 1948). *Buy Me Blue Ribbons*, produced at the Empire Theatre, New York, in 1951 and published in 1952, was also produced by the Independent in 1953. During the Second World War Locke Elliott served in the Australian army, spending six months at a remote ordnance camp at Mataranka in the Northern Territory, an experience which he drew on for *Rusty Bugles*. In 1948 he left for the USA before the first production of *Rusty Bugles* and missed both the play's outstanding success and the public storm over the censorship of its language. In the USA he worked for CBS and NBC, eventually becoming one of the best-known writers for television. Of the fifty or more plays that he wrote for television at least one, 'The Grey Nurse Said Nothing' (1959), has acquired the status of a classic. Two plays for theatre, both produced on Broadway, *Buy Me Blue Ribbons* and 'John Murray Anderson's Almanac' (1953), were less successful. In 1955 he became an American citizen.

Apart from a brief visit in 1950, Locke Elliott did not return to Australia until 1974. The visit stirred memories of his youth, which he had already drawn on for his successful autobiographical novel, *Careful, He Might Hear You* (q.v. 1963), and resulted in a further two novels with Australian settings, *Edens Lost* (1969) and *Water under the Bridge* (q.v. 1977). *Careful, He Might Hear You* won the Miles Franklin Award, was subsequently translated into six languages, was selected by the *Readers Digest* Book Club and was filmed in 1983. *Water Under the Bridge* was produced as an

Australian television serial in 1980. Locke Elliott's other novels, apart from *Going* (1975), a work of science fiction, are set in the USA; they are *Some Doves and Pythons* (1966), *The Man Who Got Away* (1972) and *Signs of Life* (1981). In 1977 he won the Patrick White Literary Award.

For Australian readers the outstanding feature of Locke Elliott's work is his ability to reproduce the distinctive flavour of the national life of the 1930s and 1940s. *Rusty Bugles*, which he later described as a documentary rather than a play, was the most popular production with Australian audiences since *On Our Selection* (1912). A mirror of the unspectacular daily life of the ordinary soldier, it represents the deprivation, boredom, irritations, loneliness, disappointments, loves and griefs of wartime, familiar to many of its first audiences. At the same time, Elliott's exploitation of the comic possibilities of the vernacular and his critical attitude to aspects of the Australian legend foreshadowed what was to be a continuing preoccupation in Australian drama and was to shortly emerge in Lawler's *Summer of the Seventeenth Doll* (1957) and Seymour's *The One Day of the Year* (1962).

His Australian novels illustrate even more fully his powers of authentic sociological recreation, his psychological insight and diversity of range from comedy to pathos. *Careful, He Might Hear You*, a carefully-structured novel with an intricate time-scheme, is presented to a large extent from a child's perspective. As the boy's unusual emotional experience propels him rapidly to a precocious maturity, he becomes increasingly aware of life's ambivalences. *Edens Lost* turns on the theme of sophisticated corruption versus guileless innocence, which is also one of the themes of his more ambitious novel, *Water under the Bridge*. Set mainly in mid-1930s Sydney, it deals with several interrelated but diverse destinies, some of which are drawn from Elliott's memories of news stories of the period. Of the book's numerous memorable characters, the most striking and the most illustrative of Elliott's simultaneous detachment and sympathy is the central character's aunt and surrogate mother, the ageing ex-chorus-girl, Shasta Davies. But Sydney itself it also a loved and hated protagonist; in this stagnant, blandly suburban environment which constantly exalts the mediocre at the expense of the talented and the idealistic, the Harbour Bridge images the unachieved possibilities of creativity and communication.

ELLIS, BOB (1942–), born Lismore, NSW, has worked as a writer and production assistant for the ABC and has written plays for stage, television and film. His published plays include the musical extravaganza *The Legend of King O'Malley* (q.v. 1974), which he wrote with Michael Boddy and which was first produced with great success in 1970; and a more naturalistic play, *Down Under* (1977), written with his wife, Anne Brooksbank (q.v.), and first produced in 1975. He has also written 'The James Dossier' (1975), a musical based on the life of Francis James (1918–), the controversial Australian editor and journalist who was a prisoner in China 1969–72; with Dick Hall, 'The Duke of Edinburgh Assassinated: Or, the Vindication of Henry Parkes' (1971); and, with Chris McGill, the film script for *Fatty Finn*, the 1980 version of the classic silent film about Fatty Finn (q.v.), *The Kid Stakes*. Ellis also wrote a children's tie-in to the film, *Fatty Finn* (1980). He has won four Awgies.

ELLIS, HAVELOCK (1859–1939), born Surrey, England, spent three years teaching in Australia 1875–78; some of that time was spent in small schools at Sparkes and Junction Creeks near Scone, NSW. His later career in England saw the publication of his major works, *Studies in the Psychology of Sex* (1897–1910), and *Impressions and Comments* (1914–24). Ellis's brief novel, *Kanga Creek: An Australian Idyll* (1922), is based largely on his experiences in Australia. His autobiography, *My Life*, which also recounts his time in Australia, was published in 1940. Houston Peterson wrote the biography, *Havelock Ellis: Philosopher of Love* (1928) which also contains the most complete bibliography of Ellis's writings. He corresponded with the eccentric, William Chidley (q.v.).

ELLIS, M.H (MALCOLM HENRY) (1890–1969), born Narine, Queensland, grew up in the Queensland bush; his account of those early times and experiences was published in the *Bulletin* in 1965. He entered journalism in Brisbane and later joined the Sydney *Daily Telegraph*. Aged forty-two he joined the *Bulletin* where, in a career of thirty-three years, he became well-known as a feature writer on historical and political affairs, usually under the pseudonym 'Ek Dum'. During the Second World War 'Ek Dum' published accounts of battles and campaigns in which Australian troops were involved, remarkably accurate considering they were written at second hand. Ellis is best-known for his writing on early Australian history, e.g. the biographies *Lachlan Macquarie* (1947), for which he won the Harbison-Higinbotham Award in 1948, *Francis Greenway* (1949) and *John Macarthur* (1955). His interest in colonial literature is reflected in his exchanges with Colin Roderick in the *Bulletin* (1952–53), about the authorship of the convict novel *Ralph Rashleigh* (q.v.). He was involved in planning the ADB. Recognition of his journalistic and historical writings came when he was made CMG in 1956 and when he later received an honorary doctorate from the University of Newcastle.

ELLISTON, W.G. (WILLIAM GORE) (1798–1872), born Bath, England, was the son of the English actor and theatre manager, Robert Wiliam Elliston (1774–1831), who in 1828 composed an ode for his son's projected departure for Australia and after his arrival had the playwright, 'William Moncrieff', write the extravaganza, *Van Diemen's Land* (q.v. performed 1830). Briefly engaged in business pursuits, Elliston was a schoolmaster in 1833–37 before taking over from James Ross as government printer and proprietor of the *Hobart Town Courier* and publisher of the *Hobart Town Almanack*; after his retirement from the press in 1848 he was prominent in civic affairs.

Elocution of Benjamin Franklin, The, a one-actor play by Steve J. Spears (q.v.), was first produced in 1976, has been widely staged in Australia, and was produced in London in 1978 and in New York and San Francisco in 1979. Gordon Chater, a well-known Australian actor, appeared in all productions. The play was published in 1977 in *Drag Show* with Peter Kenna's *Mates*. The protagonist of the play, a middle-aged transvestite and speech therapist, Robert O'Brien, reveals in a private monologue and in his telephone conversations both the ordinary human nature of his life and his reciprocated feelings for one of his pupils, the dissolute twelve-year old Benjamin Franklin. The relationship remains innocent but O'Brien is harassed by his Toorak neighbours and by Act III, which takes place eight years later, has become the helpless, tormented inmate of a mental hospital.

Elsey Station, see GUNN, JEANNIE; *We of the Never-Never*

'ELZEVIR', see MURDOCH, Sir WALTER

Emancipist is a word regularly used in nineteenth-century Australia and by modern historians to designate an ex-convict, both one who completed his term of sentence and one whose good conduct earned a conditional or absolute pardon. The emancipists formed a significant group in a colonial society and their struggles with the 'pure merinos' (free settlers), particularly in the period 1810–50, is a significant theme in the history of NSW and Tasmania. George Howe, the first Australian printer, sentenced to transportation for life in 1799 but conditionally pardoned in 1803, is an example of an emancipist; others include Michael Massey Robinson, Mary Reibey and Francis Greenway. 'Price Warung''s 'The Pure Merinoes' Ball' and 'Marie Antoinette's Fandango' humorously recreate the emancipist/pure-merino tensions of the 1820s.

EMERSON, ERNEST SANDO ('MILKY WHITE') (1870–1919), whose father was a first cousin of American poet Ralph Waldo Emerson, was born Ballarat, Victoria, and became a journalist with the *Brisbane Courier* and a freelance writer and journalist. He published *A Shanty Entertainment* (1904, bush stories and poems) and *An Australian Bird Calendar* (1909, illustrated by Norman Lindsay).

EMERY, JOHN (1947–), born Cairns and educated in SA where he now lives, has had a variety of occupations including college lecturing and writing for films and television. His film scripts include *Caravan Park* (1973), *Backroads* (1977), *The Coming* (1980) and *Freedom* (1982). His publications are the collection of short stories, *Summer Ends Now* (1980) and the novels, *Freedom* (1982) and *The Sky People* (1984). *Summer Ends Now* includes the story 'Rape', which won the 1974 Commonwealth Bank National Short Story of the Year Award.

Emigrant Family: Or, The Story of an Australian Settler, The (1849), a novel by Alexander Harris (q.v.) but ascribed on the title page to 'the author of *Settlers and Convicts*', was titled in an 1852 edition *Martin Beck: Or, The Story of an Australian Settler*. Although it is a fictional account of the adventures of the Bracton family in the Australian colony, Harris stresses in his preface the authenticity of the events narrated and the background to them. The novel has several major plots, all reasonably successfully interwoven; they include the experiences of the Bracton family in establishing themselves on the land in the Colony, the adventures of the 'Australian', Reuben Kable, and the machinations of the American negro, Martin Beck (q.v.). Harris's elevation of Beck to the title of the second edition indicates the importance he attached to that malign, and maligned, outsider, who seeks to gain wealth and power in order to compensate for the inferior position his colour creates for him in colonial society. Numerous subplots include the exploits of Willoughby Bracton, who strikes out for himself in the new land; the affairs of John Thomas, the stubborn ticket-of-leave bullock-driver; the fortunes of the Moses family, Jewish storekeepers at Ghiagong; and the development of various romantic relationships, Reuben Kable–Catherine Bracton, Willoughby Bracton–Mary Kable and Mr Hurley–

Marianna Bracton. As a background to the sometimes repetitive plot and the meanderings of the romances there is much compensatory colonial colour. Harris provides many interesting local details, e.g. Australian eating habits (steak and damper), the ceremony of boiling the billy, and includes descriptions of bush huts, bullock-driving, cattle-stealing, an Australian Christmas, bushfires, scabby sheep, depredations of bushrangers and attacks by blacks. At various points the narrative pauses to discuss such colonial problems as land reform, the brutalities of the convict system, and the inadequacy of the official attitudes towards the Aborigines. Although marred by its melodramatic events, *The Emigrant Family* is an important work of early colonial fiction.

'EMIGRANT MECHANIC, AN', see HARRIS, ALEXANDER

Emigrant's Guide to Australia, The (1853), by John Capper, was typical of the many guide-books written in England for sale to intending migrants to the Australian colonies. Capper's *Emigrant's Guide* was an enlarged version of a work published in 1852 as *Philips' Emigrants' Guide*. The guide-books and handbooks informed the migrants about the geography and climate of Australia, prospects of employment and how to win a living on the land or on the goldfields. Full of well-meaning advice, sometimes based on the briefest personal experience of the writer (and occasionally on none at all) the guide-books were a lucrative source of revenue for English publishers.

Empire, a liberal–radical newspaper, was founded by Henry Parkes (q.v.) in 1850; it began as a weekly, but soon became a daily and was the main rival of the *Sydney Morning Herald* between the death of the *Australian* in 1848 and the birth of the *Daily Telegraph* in 1879. Publication of the *Empire* was suspended in 1858 after Parkes ran into financial difficulties; the newspaper was revived the following year by Samuel Bennett and was incorporated into the *Evening News* in 1875. Significant contributors included Daniel Deniehy, William Forster, Frank Fowler, Henry Kendall and Charles Harpur.

Emu Creek, see 'RUDD, STEELE'

Encyclopaedia Britannica Australia Awards, also known as the Britannica Australia Awards, were given 1964–73 to recognize outstanding achievement in Australia and to recognize Australian–American links. Sponsored by the *Encyclopaedia Britannica* company, the awards were presented in the fields of the arts, education,

literature, medicine and science 1964–67, and in the arts, science and humanities 1968–73. Winners in the literature or humanities area included Judith Wright (1964), R.D. Fitz-Gerald and A.D. Hope (1965), Hal Porter and Randolph Stow (1966), Douglas Stewart (1968), C.B. Christesen (1970) and James McAuley (1972). No award was made for literature in 1967, when Christina Stead was rejected on the grounds that she had ceased to be Australian.

***Endeavour* HMS, see COOK, Captain JAMES**

ENGLAND, E.M. (EDITH MARY) (1899–1979), born Townsville, Queensland, was a prolific contributor of verse and prose to a variety of Australian and overseas journals. Her publications include fiction, *The Sealed Temple* (1933), *Tornado and Other Stories* (1945), *Where the Turtles Dance* (1950); and verse, *The Happy Monarch and Other Verses* (1927) and *Queensland Days* (1944).

English Association (Sydney Branch), which is affiliated with the parent English Association (London, 1906–), was founded in 1923 and until 1944 was known as the Australian English Association. It has aimed since its inauguration to foster the recognition, study and teaching of English language and literature, with the additional objective since 1949 of encouraging the study of Australian literature. Prominent among its activities are the annual public lectures for matriculation students and the sponsorship of the journals *Southerly* (q.v.) and *Sydney Studies in English* (1975–). There have been other Australian branches of the English Association, e.g. in Melbourne, Adelaide and Townsville. The last-named published *North* (1963–68).

ENRIGHT, NICK (1950–), born Maitland, NSW, was educated at the University of Sydney after which he spent a year with the Nimrod Street Theatre before joining the Melbourne Theatre Company in 1973 as their first trainee director. He gained a master of fine arts degree at New York University School of Arts; from 1978 to 1981 he was assistant director at the SA State Theatre Company and in 1983 became head of acting at NIDA. In addition to being director, actor and musician he has published *The Maitland and Morpeth String Quartet* (1980), a long humorous poem, and *On the Wallaby* (1982), a play about the 1930s depression. His other performed plays include 'Variations' (1982 , winner of the NSW Premier's Award) about the changing roles of women within the family; 'First Class Women', about the treatment of women convicts in the days of the first settlement; and 'Summer Rain' (1983), about an acting troupe stranded in a small bush town at Christmas. He has also translated and adapted the work of Molière, Goldoni, Beaumarchais and Sophocles for the theatre in Adelaide, Melbourne and Sydney.

'ERCOLE, VELIA' (MARGARET GREGORY) (1910–), born White Cliffs, NSW, daughter of Italian parents, experienced life in a country town (Grenfell, NSW) before becoming a journalist with the Sydney *Sun*. Her first novel, *No Escape* (1932), winner of the *Bulletin* novel competition, concerns the experiences of an Italian family in a small NSW country town in 1905. Leo Gherardi, an Italian political emigrant, takes up a medical practice in Banton with his wife Teresa and son Dino, intending to return to Italy as soon as practicable. Teresa, unable to accommodate to her new and hated environment, commits suicide and Leo ultimately marries an Australian, Olwen Ferrars, has another son and participates in the First World War as an army doctor; these events conspire to turn him into an Australian in spite of himself. In a second novel, *Dark Windows* (1934), Julie Purvis, daughter of an Australian father and French mother, goes to France to live after her father's death. Ultimately convinced of her inability to bridge the gulf between the two worlds with their widely-differing traditions, manners and cultures, she returns to the familiarity of Australia. As Margaret Gregory (her married name) and living in England, 'Velia Ercole' has published numerous popular romances, e.g. *Marriage Made on Earth* (1939), *Marriage by Ordeal* (1941) and *This Life to Live* (1944).

ERICKSEN, RAY (1919–), born Springvale, Victoria, graduated from the University of Melbourne and served with the Australian army in the Second World War. Following a career as a historian at the University of Melbourne 1947–69, he became a full-time writer. His publications include the travel book *West of Centre* (1972) and *Cape Solitary* (1975, winner of the National Book Council's Australian Book of the Year); the latter is his account of an attempt to live alone in an isolated environment. His biography of the explorer Ernest Giles (q.v.), published in 1978, also won a National Book Council award.

Ern Malley Hoax. The Autumn 1944 issue of *Angry Penguins* (q.v.) contained *The Darkening Ecliptic*, sixteen poems supposedly written by a recently-deceased mechanic/insurancesalesman named Ern Malley and sent to Max Harris (q.v.), co-editor of *Angry Penguins*, by Ethel Malley, the sister of Ern Malley. On 5 June

1944 the Sydney *Sun* magazine section, 'Fact' carried the news that the Ern Malley poems were a hoax, written by James McAuley and Harold Stewart (qq.v.). A statement by the coauthors in 'Fact' explained that their action stemmed from their anxiety over what they saw as 'the gradual decay of meaning and craftsmanship in poetry'. McAuley and Stewart believed that the avant-garde poetry of the day was 'insensible of absurdity and incapable of ordinary discrimination'. To put that belief to the test they compiled Ern Malley's 'life-work' in an afternoon with the aid of any books that lay within reach: the *Concise Oxford Dictionary*, a collection of Shakespeare's plays, a *Dictionary of Quotations*, Ripman's *Rhyming Dictionary* and an American report on the drainage of swamps where mosquitoes bred. In their words, 'We opened books at random, choosing a word or a phrase haphazardly. We made lists of these and wove them into nonsensical sentences. We misquoted and made false allusions.' The Ern Malley hoax was featured in the world press and a lively discussion ensued as to the literary merit of the concocted verses which had been highly acclaimed by many literary experts of the day, e.g. Herbert Read. The discussion was temporarily silenced by the action of the SA police in prosecuting Harris for the publication of 'indecent advertisements' in the form of some of the Ern Malley poems. A marathon trial followed and Harris was fined £5. More important than the hoax itself was the effect that it had on the development of Australian poetry. The vigorous and legitimate movement for modernism in Australian writing, espoused by many writers and critics in addition to the members of the Angry Penguins group, received a severe setback and the conservative element was undoubtedly strengthened. The Ern Malley controversy continued throughout the following two decades; Harris's views on it are given in the introduction to *Ern Malley's Poems* (1960), and in 'Angry Penguins and After', *Quadrant* (1963); James McAuley's attitude is given in 'The Ferment of the Forties' in *A Map of Australian Verse* (1975).

Ern Malley's Journal, a journal of six numbers (1952–55) edited in Adelaide by Max Harris, John Reed (qq.v.) and Barrie Reed (q.v.), took its name from the 'poet' Ern Malley (q.v.). Less extreme than the earlier *Angry Penguins* (q.v.), *Ern Malley's Journal* reflected the editors' continuing interest in modernist literature and art.

Escape of the Notorious Sir William Heans and the Mystery of Mr. Daunt, The, William Gosse Hay's (q.v.) best-known novel, was published in 1919 although 1918 is the date given on the title page of the first edition. First published in England, where it was well received, it was republished in Australia in 1955 in an edition which stimulated renewed interest in Hay, although his mannered, dense style and melodramatic plots have been savagely attacked by some critics. *The Escape of the Notorious Sir William Heans* is an historical romance focused on Tasmania in the late 1830s and early 1840s. Its protagonist, an Irish baronet who has been transported for abduction, is befriended by a distant cousin, Matilda Hyde-Shaxton, and her husband. Despite his privileges as a gentleman convict and the efforts of the Hyde-Shaxtons to assist him, the proud Heans feels his reduced position in society keenly, frequents tavern society and plans to escape the island on board a ship he has purchased. He enlists the assistance of Matilda, with whom he has fallen in love, but although Matilda acts as a go-between before the escape is attempted she refuses Heans's entreaty that she elope with him. Their conversation is overheard both by Captain Paul Hyde-Shaxton and by Heans's nemesis, the penal official, Mr Daunt, whose own attachment to Matilda is one of the reasons for his relentless surveillance of the baronet.

The second of the novel's three books opens a year later with Heans, his escape detected, now the assigned servant of an ex-convict, Charles Oughtryn, whose house was formerly the residence of the first governor, David Collins. Heans's fall is reflected not only in his lowly position as a groom who is teaching Oughtryn's half-blind daughter Abelia to ride but also in the sinister people among whom he is forced to work, notably the tormented soldier, Joseph Spafield. As Heans unravels Spafield's past and the secrets of the house, he learns that Spafield, a 'murderer's murderer', was responsible for the death of the young stone-cutter Walter Surridge, whose narrative confessing to the murder of Collins (a Hay invention) and implicating Spafield in his own death, Heans finds in the caves near the house. Heans, still watched carefully by Daunt, plans again to escape, but this time is thwarted by his concern for Abelia, who he believes is under threat from Spafield; in a fight in the caves, Spafield is killed. Heans's selflessness in protecting Abelia is a significant stage in his moral rehabilitation, although equally significant in this section of the novel has been his defence of Matilda's honour against the scandalmongering of Daunt, who has perpetrated the rumour that Matilda used her husband's money to help Heans's first escape attempt. During a theatrical entertainment at Oughtryn's house on the day of the fight between Heans and Spafield, Captain Hyde-Shaxton challenges Daunt to a duel but Daunt dies of a heart attack just before revealing to Heans information 'deeply to his advantage'. The nature of this information is part of the mystery surrounding Daunt as signalled in the title, although the extent and nature of his evil and the exact reasons why he relentlessly pursues Heans are equally mysterious. Having achieved moral freedom through his defence of Matilda and Abelia, Heans achieves physical freedom in the brief final part of the novel when he is assisted to escape from Port Arthur to Dieppe in France by Hyde-Shaxton and by Conapanny, the Aboriginal lover of Walter Surridge.

The Escape of the Notorious Sir William Heans is an elaborately patterned, carefully written novel, influenced by Sir Walter Scott in its exploration of the romance of the past; reminiscent of Nathaniel Hawthorne in its exploration of Heans's fall and regeneration; and demanding of its readers as a consequence of Hay's abdication of authorial omniscience and the piecemeal way evidence is presented. R.G. Howarth called it Australian literature's 'most successful period novel'. Although some commentators dispute that conclusion, the novel does introduce historical personages such as Sir John Franklin, William Bedford and Henry Savery, and captures the texture of Tasmanian society during Franklin's rule as lieutenant-governor, e.g. in its depiction of the machinery of patronage in a penal colony, the aftermath of the destruction of Tasmanian Aboriginal society and in the presentation of the faction fights between Franklin and his colonial secretary, John Montagu.

'Essay on Memory', a long, meditative poem by R.D. FitzGerald (q.v.) , was published in the *Sydney Morning Herald* 9 April 1938, having won that newspaper's Australian sesquicentenary prize for poetry. It was also published in FitzGerald's *Moonlight Acre* (1938) and later in *Forty Years' Poems* (1965). The intellectual content of the poem stems in part from the writings of the philosopher, A.N. Whitehead. Rain images, FitzGerald's symbol for memory, dominate the poem, which was conceived while he was surveying the mountains of Veivatuloa in Fiji. He sees memory as the total past — more than the past of an individual, or a people, or a nation, or a civilization. The poem insists that the past should activate the life of the present; the past influences the present and the present individual, for every individual is a composite of everyone and everything that has gone before him — 'we are the substance of their thought'. It also suggests (FitzGerald's abiding principle) that individual lives, perishable though they are, are made meaningful both in themselves and for the future by action. The themes of the poem, the continuing core of existence and meaning in the universe and the implications of this for individual lives, are solidly held in the logical structure of the poem and illuminated by effective, if complex, imagery.

Essays in Poetry: Mainly Australian, see BUCKLEY, VINCENT

Essays on Australian Fiction, a group of seven critical essays by 'M. Barnard Eldershaw' (q.v.), was published in 1938. One of the earliest extended pieces of modern criticism and written when publishing opportunities were meagre, it is still fresh and mostly valid. The collection includes one essay on Katharine Susannah Prichard and 'Henry Handel Richardson' and individual essays on Frank Dalby Davison, Vance Palmer, Leonard Mann, Martin Boyd, Christina Stead and Eleanor Dark. The essay on Boyd, although still valuable, restricts itself to *The Montforts*, and time has made others less comprehensive, expecially those on Dark and Mann.

ESSON, LOUIS (1879–1943), born Edinburgh, Scotland, was brought to Australia in childhood. For most of his working life he was a freelance journalist, writing for such periodicals as the *Bulletin*, the *Socialist*, *Table Talk* and the *Lone Hand*, where he was able to give vent to his artistic–socialist ideals and iconoclastic wit. He travelled widely 1915–21 and became deeply impressed by the work of the Irish dramatists at the Abbey Theatre, Dublin, especially by his meetings and correspondence with W.B. Yeats. His second wife was Dr Hilda Bull, who continued to promote his theatrical aims after his death and who was the financial mainstay of the family after Esson was afflicted with a nervous illness in the 1930s.

Esson's plays were published in several collections: *Three Short Plays*, which includes *The Woman Tamer*, *Dead Timber* and *The Sacred Place* (1911); *The Time is Not Yet Ripe* (1912); *Dead Timber and Other Plays*, which includes *The Drovers* (q.v. 1920); *The Southern Cross and Other Plays*, which includes *The Southern Cross*, *Mother and Son* and *The Bride of Gospel Place* (1946, ed. Hilda Bull); and *The Woman Tamer* (1976). *Andeganora* is included in *Best Australian One-Act Plays* (1937), and an anthology of Esson's writing edited by Hugh Anderson, *Ballads of Old Bohemia* (1980), includes *The Sacred Place*, *Dead Timber*, *The Woman Tamer* and *Vagabond Camp* as well as verse, stories and articles. His unpublished plays include 'The Battler' (1922), 'Australia Felix' (1926), 'The Quest' and 'Shipwreck' (1928). Vance Palmer published a volume of reminiscences

and some of Esson's letters in *Louis Esson and the Australian Theatre* (1948). Esson also published two collections of poetry, *Bells and Bees* (1910) and *Red Gums* (1912), as well as numerous uncollected short stories. Often described as the first Australian playwright to achieve distinction for plays with Australian settings, Esson was in fact a naturally cosmopolitan, urbane and witty writer. He suppressed this gift in favour of nationalistic folk themes and poetic realism. Although his more extended efforts are flawed by weak construction and confused characterization, he produced some fine, short 'bush' plays of which *The Drovers* is the best.

'Euabalong Ball, The', is an Australian folksong which celebrates a dance at the bush hamlet of Euabalong on the Lachlan River in NSW. The humour of the song derives from the parallels drawn between the appearance and activities of the bucolic participants and the sheep and cattle with which they normally work; thus the shearers are 'stringy old wethers', the 'sheilas' are 'weaners' or 'two-tooths', and during the dancing

> There was bucking and gliding,
>   pigrooting and sliding,
> When they varied the gait,
>   there was couples colliding.

'The Euabalong Ball' was possibly adapted by A.L. Lloyd from an earlier song, 'The Wooyeo Ball', written by 'Vox Silvis' (?Rob Webster) and published in a history of Temora in 1888. The printed original reports a lively but not uproarious dance focused on the squatters and jackeroos rather than the pastoral workers. John Manifold, in *Who Wrote the Ballads?* (1964), speculates that the 'Euabalong Ball' adaptation represents not only an oral-transmission improvement of the original but also a proletarianization by bush workers of a jackeroo homestead song.

'EULO QUEEN' was the nickname of Isabel Robinson, mistress of the Royal Mail Hotel at Eulo in south-western Queensland at the turn of the century. A handsome woman with red hair and generous *décolletage*, she appears in Barcroft Boake's poems 'A Wayside Queen' and 'Skeeta', and in Harry Harbord Morant's story 'West by North Again'.

'Eumerella Shore, The', is a well-known folk-song about the 'duffing' (q.v.) of cattle; there are a number of variant texts and titles including 'The Eumeralla Shore', 'The Neumerella Shore' and 'The Numerella Shore'. The references to free selection and Sir John Robertson make it clear that the 'Eumerella' district referred to is that in the NSW Monaro region, where there is a river known as the Numerella, and not the Eumerella River in south-eastern Victoria. It is less certain whether the song is the sarcastic lament of a squatter who feels his cattle will be stolen as a result of the Robertson Lands Acts or the boasts of a selector at the increased opportunities for 'duffing' as a result of the same Acts. 'Cockatoo Jack' is sometimes given as the author of the song, which was in print in the early 1860s.

Eureka Stockade is the title given to the clash that occurred on Bakery Hill, Ballarat (q.v.), 3 December 1854, between rebellious miners, mainly from the Ballarat diggings, and soldiers and police of the Victorian government. Contributing factors to the Eureka incident were the discriminatory arrogance of the goldfields authorities towards the miners, the licence-fee system and the notorious licence hunts, the corruption and ineptitude of the Ballarat goldfields administration, the lack of political rights for the miners, and the presence on the diggings of considerable numbers of disaffected Irish and American nationals. On 29 November 1854 the rebel Eureka flag, The Southern Cross, was raised on Bakery Hill; on 30 November Peter Lalor (q.v.) and 500 miners swore on that flag of independence to fight for their rights; on 1 December the miners' 'Declaration of Independence' was publicly proclaimed on Bakery Hill; on 2 December the Stockade, enclosing an acre of ground, was completed; on 3 December a force of 270 soldiers and police attacked the stockade and dispersed its 150 defenders. Within ten minutes, five soldiers and thirty miners were dead or dying and the incident itself was over, but its repercussions have continued to be felt in Australian politics, history and literature. The official version of Eureka is contained in Sir Charles Hotham's 'Despatches to the Secretary of State for the Colonies, 1851–54'. Contemporary accounts of Eureka by the participants include Raffaello Carboni's (q.v.) *The Eureka Stockade* (1855), Peter Lalor's 'Statement on the Ballarat Rebellion' (*Age* and *Argus*, 10 April 1855) and Frederick Vern's 'Colonel Vern's Narrative' (*Age*, 15 January 1855). Later personal reminiscences include J. Lynch's 'The Story of the Eureka Stockade' (*Austral Light*, October 1893 – March 1894); H.R. Nicholls's 'Reminiscences of the Eureka Stockade' (*Centennial Magazine*, May 1890); and Frank Skurray's 'Some Memories of the Eureka Stockade' (*Steele Rudd's Magazine*, January 1905). In almost every general study of the Australian goldfields the past century writers have described, analysed, pondered over and pontificated on Eureka. Studies of particular

significance include W.B. Withers's *The History of Ballarat* (1870), H.G. Turner's *Our Own Little Rebellion – the Story of Eureka* (1913), R.S. Ross's *Eureka! Freedom's Fight of '54* (1914), Clive Turnbull's *Eureka: The Story of Peter Lalor* (1946), C.H. Currey's *The Irish at Eureka* (1954), Robin Gollan's *Radical and Working Class Politics* (1960), Geoffrey Serle's *The Golden Age* (1963), Geoffrey Blainey's *The Rush That Never Ended* (1963) and Richard Butler's *Eureka Stockade* (1983); the last-named researched the event for the television series.

Eureka, with its colour and drama, has also provided a rich lode for creative writers to mine but no great work of fiction, poetry or drama has so far been produced. The first fictional account of Eureka appeared in 1870–72 in the original serial version in the *Australian Journal* of Marcus Clarke's *His Natural Life* but the goldfields section was omitted from the novel when it was published in 1874. Clarke's account owes much to Raffaello Carboni's earlier eye-witness version and to W.B. Withers's *The History of Ballarat*, which had just been published. Edward Dyson's novel *In the Roaring Fifties* (1906), is centred on Eureka and gives a faithful if melodramatic version of the incident. In *Australia Felix* (1917), the first part of 'Henry Handel Richardson''s trilogy *The Fortunes of Richard Mahony* (1930), the rebellion is assessed by Dr Mahony, who tends the wounded and dying on Bakery Hill, as futile 'straws against the wind' but the novel brings out the united determination of the diggers to oppose the oppressive administration. Leonard Mann's novel, *Human Drift* (1935), portrays the conflicts that occurred within the ranks of the participants and examines the roles of the various national groups. Eric Lambert wrote two Eureka novels, *The Five Bright Stars* (1954) and *Ballarat* (1962). Other fictional works which include Eureka are J.M. MacDonald's *Roll-Up: A Tale of the Eureka Riots* (1901), John Sanders's *The Call of the Southern Cross* (1915), Mollie Skinner's *Black Swans* (1925), George Cockerill's *In Days of Gold* (1926), E.V. Timmo's *Red Mask* (1927), and Nathan Spielvogel's *An Affair at Eureka* (1930).

The outburst of egalitarianism, republicanism and democratic fervour that characterized the 1890s had some of its roots in Eureka. The radical nationalists of that decade were scarcely more than a generation removed from their counterparts, the Stockade diggers, as is indicated by Henry Lawson's story, 'An Old Mate [i.e. a Eureka mate] of Your Father's'; by his words 'It is thirty-six years this December' in his poem 'The Fight at Eureka Stockade'; by his 'Eureka (A Fragment)', which was inspired by Peter Lalor's death in 1889; by Mary Gilmore's childhood reminiscence 'Here comes a Eureka man!', and her poem 'The Men of Eureka'; and by Victor Daley's 'A Ballad of Eureka'. Anti-imperialist Francis Adams brought the Eureka flag to the centre of national attention in the 1880s with his poem 'Fling out the Flag', written for the newly-formed Australian Labour Federation. There it has certainly stayed. It was raised in 1891 by the striking shearers at Barcaldine, Queensland, and Lawson was moved to applaud that gesture with his lines from 'Freedom on the Wallaby', 'So we must fly a rebel flag/As others did before us'. He had in 1887 expressed much the same sentiments in his 'Flag of the Southern Cross' and E.J. Brady had also taken up the flag of independence in his poem 'The Flag of the South', as Helen Palmer later did in her 'Ballad of Eureka'. In modern times the Eureka flag and Billy Bluegum have become rallying symbols for those Australians of republican persuasion and for those who feel, with H.V. Evatt, that 'Australian Democracy was born at Eureka'. Len Fox wrote *Eureka and Its Flag* (1973).

Playwrights have attempted, with limited success, to present the chaos of Eureka in drama and on stage. Edmund Duggan's 'Eureka Stockade' (staged in 1891 as 'The Democrat') was performed at the Adelaide Theatre Royal in 1897. Duggan follows the Eureka events accurately but includes nationalist sentiments ('This flag is destined to wave over free and united Australia') more typical of the 1890s than of mid-century on the goldfields. E.W. O'Sullivan's 'The Eureka Rebellion' (1907) also echoes the sentiment of the author's own times rather than of Eureka's by having Peter Lalor quote 'a new Britannia in another world' from W.C. Wentworth's *Australasia*. Of many other Eureka plays, those of significance are Louis Esson's *The Southern Cross* (1946); Leslie Rees's 'Lalor of Eureka' which won a Melbourne New Theatre Prize in 1939; Leslie Haylen's *Blood on the Wattle* (1948), a crowded and confused drama; Richard Lane's radio play in free verse, 'Eureka Stockade'; Kenneth Cook's *Stockade* (1975), one of the more successful theatre attempts on the subject; and John Romeril's 1980 production, 'Carboni'. Films of Eureka include *The Loyal Rebel* (1915), *Eureka Stockade* (1949) and *Stockade* (1971). A television series was shown in 1984. An extensive bibliography of Eureka literature is contained in *Historical Studies: Eureka Supplement* (1954).

Eurunderee, located some six kilometres north of Mudgee in central western NSW, was called New Pipeclay at the time gold was discovered there in 1863; its name was changed to Eurunderee around the time a school was estab-lished in 1876 for the children of the selectors who had remained in the area after the diggings petered out. The most celebrated inhabitant of Eurunderee was Henry Lawson, who lived there for most of his first fifteen years (1867–82).

Lawson's experiences in and recollections of Eurunderee, both as a 'Roaring Days' gold community and as the home of struggling selectors, was an important source for numerous poems, e.g. 'Eurunderee', 'The Free Selector's Daughter', 'The Shanty on the Rise', and stories, e.g. 'His Father's Mate' and the school stories in *While the Billy Boils* (1896).

EVANS, GEORGE ESSEX (1863–1909), born London, came to Australia in 1881. He tried farming then turned briefly to teaching, and later journalism as agricultural editor of the *Queenslander*. In 1888 he joined the public service, ultimately becoming district registrar at Toowoomba. His first volume of poetry, *The Repentance of Magdalene Despar*, was published in 1891. Two other volumes are *Loraine and Other Verses* (1898) and *The Secret Key and Other Verses* (1906). In 1901 he won £50 for his 'Ode for Commonwealth Day'. The *Collected Verse of George Essex Evans* was published as a memorable edition in 1928. His best-known individual poem, a great favourite in the first half of this century and frequently anthologized, is 'The Women of the West', a tribute to the women of the outback. His 'An Australian Symphony' is still considered highly as a patriotic poem but in his other verse romantic themes predominate. More highly thought of in Queensland than elsewhere, Evans was undoubtedly a better poetic craftsman than many of his contemporaries among the bush balladists but he failed to win the popularity achieved by them. His major narrative works, e.g. 'Magdalene Despar', although competent and enthusiastic have lapsed into obscurity. In Toowoomba, where he worked and died, there is a monument to him and an annual George Essex Evans pilgrimage is held. Henry A. Tardent wrote *The Life and Poetry of George Essex Evans* (1913).

EVANS, GEORGE WILLIAM (1775–1852), born Warwickshire, England, came to Australia in 1802 and after the crossing of the Blue Mountains (q.v.) in 1813 was employed by Governor Lachlan Macquarie to extend and exploit the crossing. He guided the governor's party on its tour to the Bathurst plains in 1815 and accompanied John Oxley on his explorations in 1817–18. From 1818 until his resignation in 1825 Evans was a government surveyor in Tasmania. He published *A Geographical, Historical and Topographical Description of Van Diemen's Land* (1822). Sketches by

Evans of early Sydney and Hobart are in the Dixson Gallery of the State Library of NSW. A.K. Weatherburn wrote *George William Evans, Explorer* (1966).

EVANS, MATILDA JANE ('MAUD JEANNE FRANC') (1827–86), born Surrey, England, came to Australia with her family in 1852. At first a governess, she later opened her own school at Mount Barker and continued as a teacher until 1868, when she became a deaconess in the Baptist Church and devoted herself to writing. She published fourteen novels and numerous short stories and articles. Her fiction, with its ringing moral message and its inspiration from the scriptures, was mainly for young people, with whom it was highly popular. Her first novel, *Marian: Or, The Light of Some One's Home* (1861), deals with bush life, as do many others, e.g. *Emily's Choice* (1867) and *John's Wife* (1874). A collected edition of her Australian tales was published in 1888. Her two sons were Henry Congreve Evans (1861–99), who became chief of staff of the Adelaide *Advertiser* and the creator of *Quiz*, a social and political weekly; and William James Evans (1863–1904), who collaborated with her in the volume of short stories, *Christmas Bells* (1882), and who wrote *Rhymes without Reason* (1898).

EVATT, H.V. (HERBERT VERE) (1894–1965), born East Maitland, NSW, capped a brilliant university record in law at the University of Sydney with the award of doctor of laws in 1924. Made KC in 1929, he was appointed justice of the High Court in 1930. He resigned in 1940 to win the federal seat of Barton for the Labor Party. In the wartime Curtin ministry he was attorney-general and minister for external affairs; in the Chifley ministry he became deputy prime minister. He was Australia's chief representative at the newly-formed United Nations Organization and was the first president of the General Assembly 1948–49; he left politics in 1960 to become chief justice of NSW. Evatt published books on Australian history, politics and law; they included *Rum Rebellion* (1938) and *Australian Labor Leader* (1940) whose subject was W.A. Holman. Allan Dalziel wrote *Evatt, the Enigma* (1967); Kylie Tennant, *Evatt: Politics and Justice* (1970); and Alan Renouf, *Let Justice Be Done* (1983). Evatt is Dr Bert Effort in Barry Oakley's play, *The Feet of Daniel Mannix* (1975).

Evening News, the first penny newspaper in NSW, was established by Samuel Bennett (q.v.) in 1867; it incorporated the *Empire* in 1875, and remained under the control of the Bennett

family until the public company Samuel Bennett Ltd was formed in 1918. In 1929 this company merged with that of Sir Hugh Denison (q.v.) to form Associated Newspapers, which controlled both the *Sun* and the *Evening News* as afternoon dailies until the latter ceased publication in 1931. Although periodically ridiculed as the *Snooze* and the *Noose* by the *Bulletin* and other competitors, the *Evening News* was a technically-innovative, middlebrow newspaper which outsold other metropolitan dailies for significant periods of its life, e.g. the 1880s and 1890s. Its editors included William Ridley (1873–78), James Alexander Hogue (1884–94) and A.B. Paterson (1903–06); Walter Jeffery was manager and editor 1906–22. Among notable staff were Theodore Argles ('The Pilgrim'), whose dismissal by Samuel Bennett led to *The Devil in Sydney* (1878), in which Argles caricatured the Bennetts; John Haynes, a sub-editor in 1879, when he secured J.F. Archibald a position as reporter before they founded the *Bulletin*; John Norton, a star reporter in the 1880s; and J.D. FitzGerald, Alex Montgomery and Will Lawson. *The Evening News 1867–1926* (1926) is a company history.

Everage, Edna, a character created by Barry Humphries (q.v.), made her stage debut in 1955 and became a central persona in Humphries's satiric presentation of Australian life. An 'average' (hence 'Everage') housewife from Moonee Ponds in Victoria, married to Norm ('normal') Everage and the mother of three children, Edna originally articulated the prejudices and pretensions of the suburban middle class. In 1965, in the show 'Excuse I', she first induced her audiences to wave gladioli at the end of the performance – an Edna trademark, as Norm's troublesome prostate also became – which signalled that the audience as well as Edna herself was becoming the target of Humphries's satire. In the 1970s, after her creation as DBE in the film *Barry McKenzie Holds His Own* (1974), and possibly as a consequence of Humphries's domicile overseas, Edna became an international jet-setter. Although dubbed 'Suburbia's La Stupenda' and the 'Moonee Ponds Megastar', she is increasingly a celebrity in her own right, a cult figure rather than a satiric portrait of suburban momism. She is the 'author' of *Dame Edna's Coffee Table Book* (1976) and *Dame Edna's Bedside Companion* (1982) and has 'made' many gramophone records.

Everlasting Secret Family and Other Secrets, The, a collection of stories and notes by Frank Moorhouse (q.v.), was published in 1980. It consists of four sequences linked by an association in each between sexuality and secrecy. The first, 'Pacific City', focuses on the secret world of Irving Bow, a cinema proprietor in the township where T. George McDowell, the central character of *The Electrical Experience* (q.v. 1975), has his soft-drink business; the sequence records Bow's sexual dalliances with the children of the town and his association with its other outsiders who, like Bow, are spiritual exiles. 'The Dutch Letters', the second sequence, consists mainly of the Second World War letters of a Dutch family, discovered and divulged by the narrator when he occupies a student's room during a conference; it emerges at the end of the sequence that the student is the child Dirk, whose castration is recorded in the letters between his parents. The third sequence, 'Imogene Continued', is set at the time of the same conference, during which an academic, Cindy (a recurring character in Moorhouse's fiction), is raped by an Aboriginal delegation; the sequence records her reaction to this and that of the narrator, her former lover. The final, title sequence is the erotic memoir of a homosexual.

EVERS, L.H., see *Racketty Street Gang, The*

EWART, ERNEST ANDREW ('BOYD CABLE') (1878–1943), born India, served in the Boer War, migrated to Australia where he lived a nomadic existence, contributing to the *Bulletin* and *Lone Hand*, and was a newspaper correspondent in the First World War. His numerous fictional works include some that arose out of his war experiences, e.g. *Between the Lines* (1915), *Action Front* (1916), *Front Lines* (1918) and *The Old Contemptibles* (1919); in the last he claims to have originated the phrase 'Old Contemptibles' and explains its derivation. He also wrote books for children, including *Mates* (1929) and *The Wrist Watch Castaways* (1929).

EWERS, J.K. (JOHN KEITH) (1904–78), born Subiaco, WA, was a schoolteacher in WA 1924–47, thereafter living by his writing. Foundation president of the WA branch of the FAW (1938–39), he was made a life member in 1967. Ewers published poetry, fiction, history and works of literary criticism and social analysis. His two books of verse were *Boy and Silver* (1929), the narrative of a boy and a kangaroo, and *I Came Naked* (1976), philosophical comments on life. His novels began with *Money Street* (1933), moulded from a series of short stories; his second novel, *Fire on the Wind* (1935), is based on the experiences of the Ewers family in the Gippsland bushfire in 1898. *Men Against the Earth* (1946) and *For Heroes to Live In* (1948) are set in the WA wheat belt. His short stories include the children's works, *Tales from the Dead Heart*

(1944), about the life and legends of the Aborigines, and *Written in Sand* (1947), as well as the whimsical adult collection, *Harvest and Other Stories* (1949). *With the Sun on My Back* (1953), an autobiographical account of Ewers's travels in northern Australia, won a prize in the Commonwealth Jubilee literary competition. His general works include *The Story of the Pipe Line* (to Coolgardie) (1935) and *The Western Gateway* (1948), about the city of Fremantle. His books of social commentary and literary criticism include *The Great Australian Paradox* (1939), a patriotic address he gave to the FAW in Perth at the beginning of the Second World War; *Tell the People!* (1944), an application of the social philosophy of Joseph Furphy to Australia's problems of the day; and *Creative Writing in Australia* (1945), an early survey of Australian literature. His biography of the explorer Charles Sturt, *Who Rides on the River?*, was published in 1956. He edited *Modern Australian Short Stories* (1965) and, with Deirdre Watson, *Take 23: Short Stories round the World* (1971). Very much a favourite son of his home State and one of its first writers to gain Australia-wide recognition, Ewers is the subject of *The Ultimate Honesty: Recollections of John K. Ewers 1904–1978* (1982), published by the WA branch of the FAW and edited by Peter Bibby.

Examiner and Weekly Melbourne News, published 1857–64, contained a wide selection of literary articles including serials. Its drama critic was J.E. Neild writing as 'Christopher Sly'. In 1864 it was incorporated into the *Australasian*.

'**Exequy, An**' by Peter Porter (q.v.) from *The Coast of Seriousness* (1978), forms, with 'The Delegate', the crux of the volume. It displays his ability to blend artistic and deeply-personal responses, the traditional and the contemporary. 'An Exequy' is modelled in metrics and theme on Bishop King's poem on the untimely death of his young wife. In 'An Exequy' and 'The Delegate' Porter explores new avenues of the art of poetry. The poem states that the 'cost of seriousness' is death, implying at once that it is his pursuit of poetry, his seriousness, which has robbed both him and his wife of her life, and moreover that his art is insufficiently alive to console the feelings aroused, feelings not only of loss but of guilt. In 'The Delegate' the wife's ghost is speaking to the poet; it seems she has been sent ahead and is reluctantly reporting and advising him on the afterlife. The images she uses are not comforting and disrupt his attempted consolings, leaving him with more shame and guilt and the 'punishment of remembrance'. In these poems as in others in the volume, Porter's preoccupations with the landscape of the mind turns to the inability of art, particularly his, to offer any more than a public expression of feeling. The paradox is that in poetry which is so private in its source of feeling Porter is able, by earnestly questioning in language textured with artistic allusions, to convince the reader while he himself is left unconvinced.

J.D.

Extra, The, see **PORTER, HAL**

Eye of the Storm, The, a novel by Patrick White (q.v.), was published in 1973 and awarded the Nobel Prize for Literature. The last days of Elizabeth Hunter, a wealthy, dominant and once-beautiful socialite, are the novel's subject. Now in her eighties, bed-ridden and half-blind, Mrs Hunter lies in her opulent Sydney mansion, still profoundly affecting all those around her. As her memories of the past and the memories of others are counterpointed with present events, both at her bedside and in the outer world, a comprehensive picture of Mrs Hunter's quest for transcendent meaning emerges. Crucial experiences in her life include her relationship with her husband Alfred, especially during his last illness, and a vision of 'glistening peace' fifteen years earlier when she lived through a cyclone on a tropical island. Her perception of her inclusion in the unity of being, perhaps as 'a flaw at the centre of this jewel of light', has shaped both her subsequent life and her act of dying. Those who are most affected by her intense authenticity of being include Arnold Wyburd, her lawyer; two of her nurses, as antithetical as their names suggest, Sister de Santis and Sister Manhood; and her cook, Lotte Lippmann, an ex-cabaret performer from Berlin. The psychological drama is heightened and unified by the return of her two middle-aged children, Dorothy and Basil, from Europe, their co-operation in an effort to accelerate their inheritance and their re-discovery of past experiences. Dorothy, the Princess de Lascabanes, ex-wife of a French nobleman and a Catholic convert, never casts off her resentful jealousy of her mother's beauty and dominance. Basil, now Sir Basil Hunter, an eminent but tired West End actor, has a keener perception of the alienating gulf between acted selves and authentic selves. Mrs Hunter's eventual death re-frames the lives of others: Sister de Santis finds in her next 'case' an even more rigorous testing of her powers of selfless love; Sister Manhood abandons nursing for marriage with Col Pardoe, a future she had attempted to avoid; Dorothy returns to the comforts of her religion and European society; Sir Basil leaves with a renewed hope that he will be able to play a great tragic role with authenticity. For two individuals her death has a curtailing effect: Lotte Lippmann cuts her wrists in the bath, and Arnold Wyburd continues a drab existence, lit only by the brilliance of Mrs Hunter's sapphire that he keeps as an object of contemplation.

'Eyre All Alone', a poem in fourteen parts by Francis Webb (q.v.), was first published in its entirety in Webb's volume *Socrates* (1961), although parts of it (3, 10, 14) were published in the *Bulletin* in 1959. In Webb's *Collected Poems* (1969), 'Eyre All Alone' was printed as a separate section. The poem begins with the SA settler's 'dream of a stock-route' to WA. The explorer Edward John Eyre (q.v.), who had failed in an alternative attempt to open up the north of SA, sets out to chart a stock-route to the west by way of the Great Australian Bight. The last stanza of the first part, beginning

> Walk, walk. From dubious footfall one
> At Fowler's Bay, the chosen must push on

which refers to the departure of Eyre, John Baxter, Wylie (q.v.) and two other Aborigines from Fowler's Bay to the distant goal of King George Sound, is repeated several times as a sonorous, almost biblical, refrain throughout the poem. The third part tells of Baxter's murder by the two Aborigines; the fifth part reflects Eyre's uncertainty about Wylie's loyalty; the eighth part dwells on the ever-present menace of the Aborigines who shadow them. In the tenth part, 'Banksia', virtually the climax to the sequence, Wylie sights the banksia tree in flower and their hazardous journey across the desert is almost over. Webb's use in this part of the dramatic technique of question and answer to further the narrative ('Wylie, what can you see?/I see a flower') is particularly effective. Later at Thistle Cove they are given supplies and companionship by the French whaler *Mississippi* and the sequence ends with Wylie reunited with his tribesmen and Eyre about to make his dramatic entrance into Albany on King George Sound. In his notes to the poem Webb suggests that this journey, in which the hero's greatest discovery is not a stock-route but himself, might be symbolically interpreted: 'My insistence upon Eyre's aloneness is not an overlooking of Wylie, but comes from my seeing such a journey of discovery as suggestive of another which is common to us all'. The poem re-emphasizes Webb's interest, reflected in the earlier 'A Drum for Ben Boyd' and 'Leichhardt in Theatre', not so much in the heroic events of Australia's past as in the characters of the men who shaped and were shaped by those events.

EYRE, EDWARD JOHN (1815–1901), born Bedfordshire, England, arrived as an emigrant in Sydney in 1833. After experience on a sheep station and in overlanding cattle to Port Phillip and Adelaide, he embarked in 1840 on an epic journey of exploration into central Australia and overland around the Great Australian Bight to King George Sound in WA. In 1841–44 he was a magistrate and protector of Aborigines at Moorundie on the Murray River. He then left Australia to serve as a colonial administrator in NZ (1846–53), St Vincent (1854–60), Leeward Islands (1860–61) and Jamaica (1861–65); in Jamaica he was responsible, as governor-in-chief, for the vigorous and controversial suppression of a Negro uprising that led to his recall and to a royal commission in London. Eyre's *Journals of Expeditions of Discovery into Central Australia and Overland from Adelaide to King George's Sound, in the Years 1840–1*, a classic of exploration literature, were published in 1845; almost a century later the seeds for *Voss* (1957) were sown when Patrick White read the journals during the London 'blitz'. Other writers attracted to the Eyre story include Henry Kingsley in his story 'Eyre's March' and Francis Webb in his poem sequence 'Eyre All Alone' (q.v.). Lake Eyre, Eyre Peninsula, Eyre Creek and other geographical features are named after Eyre, who is the subject of Geoffrey Dutton's biographical studies *The Hero as Murderer* (1967) and *In Search of Edward John Eyre* (1982), and Malcolm Uren and Robert Stephens's *Waterless Horizons* (1941).

EYRE, FRANK (1910–), born Manchester, England, came to Australia in 1949. While in England he published *The Naiad and Other Poems* (1935), *Poems by Frank Eyre & Peter Lagger* (1936), *Selected Poems* (1941), *Loving in Truth* (1942) and *English Rivers and Canals* (1945), and also edited several anthologies including *The Quiet Spirit* (1946). After the war Eyre joined the editorial staff of Oxford University Press, became managing editor of Oxford children's book publishing and in 1952 published *Twentieth Century Children's Books*. As editorial manager of Oxford University Press in Australia from 1950 to 1975 he, advised by Grahame Johnston (q.v.), made an important contribution to the study of Australian literature by publishing a new series of Australian Writers and their Work, and books of Australian literary criticism. He also published important books by Australian writers at a time when other Australian publishers were rejecting them, e.g. *The Generations of Men*, *The Australian Legend*. With George Ferguson and others he helped to establish the Australian Book Publishers Association, of which he was president 1961–63. He was a member of the committee which was responsible for the *Commonwealth Style Manual*, and chairman of the one which produced the Victorian government's *Plain English*, and he was also a member of the final board of the CLF before its dissolution. His later publications include *Ian Clunies Ross* (1961), *British Children's Books in the Twentieth Century* (1971), *Scholarly Publishing* (1976) and *Oxford in Australia* (1978).

F

FABINYI, ANDREW (1908–78), born Budapest, Hungary, came to Australia in 1939. He joined the publishing firm of F.W. Cheshire, of which he ultimately became publishing director. President of the Australian Book Publishers Association 1965–66, Fabinyi was made OBE in 1960 and was given the Redmond Barry Award in 1974 for his work with the Library Association of Australia. In some forty years of publishing in Australia, Fabinyi produced over one thousand titles by Australian authors; they include works by Xavier Herbert, Alan Marshall, Brian Fitzpatrick, Cyril Pearl, Judah Waten and Bruce Dawe. In 1983 *A Nation Apart: Essays in Honour of Andrew Fa-*binyi was edited by John McLaren; it contains a memoir of Fabinyi by John Hooker and views of Australia in the 1980s by writers such as McLaren, Leonie Sandercock, Gwyneth Dow, Laurie Clancy, Ronald Millar, Sol Encel and Belinda Vaughan.

'Face of the Waters, The', a long poem whose title comes from Genesis,'And the spirit of God moved upon the face of the waters', was first published by R.D. FitzGerald (q.v.) in the *Bulletin* (1944). FitzGerald explained that the poem, in free verse with occasional use of rhyme, was a 'pantheistic view of the universe modified by the recognition of a dualism somehow integral with it'. The poem is an expansion of the lines occurring in 'The Hidden Bole', 'the Nothing (contracted to some blackened point)/Where wakes the dream, the brooding ultimate'. The poem attempts an account of Creation. The 'utter nothingness' of pre-existence is so inconceivable that a creator – God or some consciousness – is a necessity. But the creator so envisaged is given a duality that assists, and mockingly frustrates, the attempts of life to burst forth from the nothingness. The poem is also seen as a reworking, using terms and concepts of modern physics and metaphysics, of the myth of Creation, with the Nothing (or Chaos) transformed or even hatched (the 'egg' imagery of the poem) by the 'brooding Ultimate' (the spirit). The most puzzling and complex of FitzGerald's poetry, yet accepted as one of his most impressive works, 'The Face of the Waters' has been described by Judith Wright as 'a meditation on no less a subject than Creation, and on the impossibility of meditating on Creation'.

'Faces in the Street', one of the best-known protest poems of Henry Lawson (q.v.), was first published in 1888 in the *Bulletin*; it was revised during the preparation of *Selected Poems of Henry Lawson* (1918). Written in a stirring rhythm from the perspective of a person whose 'window-sill is level with the faces in the street', the poem focuses on the flotsam and jetsam of the city who pass by from before dawn until after midnight. It concludes with the vision of a revolution which will do away with poverty and the other 'terrors of the street'.

FACEY, A.B. (ALBERT BARNETT) (1894–1982), born in Maidstone, Victoria, grew up on the Coolgardie goldfields and in outback WA. His autobiography, *A Fortunate Life* (1981), which won the NSW Premier's Award for non-fiction for 1981 and which relates his remarkable survival of a series of severe misfortunes, has been described as a microcosm of the earlier life of Australia. After his father died, before he was two, and he was deserted by his mother, he, a sister and two brothers were looked after by his impoverished grandmother. He began his working life at the age of eight and suffered periods of extreme hardship and exploitation; his numerous occupations included general station work, droving, railway 'dogging' and boxing in a travelling troupe. During the First World War he served at Gallipoli before injuries incapacitated him; his brother Joseph, who was also at Gallipoli, was killed. Back in Perth in 1915, he married and joined the Perth tramways for a time, before becoming a farmer in the Soldier Settlement Scheme in 1922. By 1934 the depression and Facey's war injuries

led to his return to the city with his family. Re-employed by Perth tramways, he became active in the Tramways Union. Three of his sons served in the Second World War and one was killed in the fall of Singapore. Facey, who had no formal education, taught himself to read and write and began to compile notes on his life soon after the First World War. *A Fortunate Life* was dramatized by Clem Gorman in 1985.

FAHEY, WARREN (1946–), born and educated in Sydney, established in 1974 the Larrikin record label which specializes in Australian folk-song (q.v.), contemporary, ethnic and children's music. An accomplished performer of Australian traditional music who has made several records, he has also conducted folklore research with the support of the Australia Council and other organizations. His publications include *Joe Watson – Traditional Singer* (1975), *Pint, Pot and Billy* (1977) and *While the Billy Boils* (1982).

Fair Girls and Gray Horses, see OGILVIE, WILL

FAIRBAIRNS, ZOE, see Feminism and Australian Literature

FAIRBRIDGE, WOLFE (1918–50), born Cottesloe, WA, was a research officer with the CSIRO. He died from poliomyelitis at the early age of thirty-one; his poetry was posthumously collected as *Poems* (1953). Notable poems include 'Denial and Riposte', which won second prize in the *Sydney Morning Herald* competition in 1947; 'The Man Who Caught the Wind', an Aboriginal tale; and 'Consecration of the House', the poignant expression of the poet's quiet expectation of delight in a future that, tragically, was not to be.

FAIRFAX, JAMES GRIFFYTH (1886–1976), born Sydney into the *Sydney Morning Herald* Fairfax family, grew up in England and was largely an expatriate, visiting Australia only for brief periods. A poet of both lyric grace and intellectual subtlety, Fairfax published numerous volumes of verse including *The Gates of Sleep and Other Poems* (1906), *Poems* (1908), *The Troubled Pool and Other Poems* (1911), *The Horns of Taurus* (1914), *Side Slips: A Collection of Unposted Postscripts, Admissions and Asides* (1914), *The Temple of Janus: A Sonnet Sequence* (1917), *Mesopotamia: Sonnets and Lyrics at Home and Abroad, 1914–1919* (1919), *Carmina Rapta* (1919) and *The Fifth Element* (1937). Fairfax served in the First World War; four of his 'Mesopotamia' poems were included in *Valour* *and Vision: Poems of the War, 1914–18* (1920), ed. J.T. Trotter.

FAIRFAX, JOHN (1805–77), born Warwickshire, England, was apprenticed to the printing trade in 1817. He worked on the London *Morning Chronicle* and was proprietor of the *Leamington Spa Courier* and the *Leamington Chronicle* before a libel suit forced him to the insolvency court and to a decision to emigrate to Australia, where he arrived with his family in 1838. In 1841, in partnership with Charles Kemp, he bought the daily *Sydney Herald;* in 1842 it became the *Sydney Morning Herald* (q.v.). Fairfax bought out Kemp in 1853 and brought his sons into the management; the *Echo* (1875–93), a penny evening newspaper, and the *Sydney Mail* (q.v.) were added to the *Sydney Morning Herald* stable in his lifetime. Since Fairfax's death his descendants have carried on John Fairfax and Sons, which was formed in 1856 and remained a family company (limited in 1916, proprietary in 1937) until the public company, John Fairfax Ltd, was formed in 1956.

'FALCONER, DORA', see **LAWSON, LOUISA**

FALLAW, LANCE (1876–1958), born Gateshead, England, joined the staff of the Rockhampton *Daily Record* in 1908 after a period as a newspaperman in South Africa. He was later editor of the *Charters Towers Telegraph, Cairns Post, Geelong Advertiser* and associate editor of the *Sydney Morning Herald*. He published a collection of verse, *Silverleaf and Oak* (1906), before he arrived in Queensland; later volumes of poetry were *The Ampler Sky* (1909), *Unending Ways* (1926) and *Hostage and Survival* (1939).

Fanfrolico Press, a fine publishing company, was first established by Jack Lindsay (q.v.) and John Kirtley, a stock-exchange employee with an interest in printing. Kirtley had earlier (1923) printed and published Lindsay's *Fauns and Ladies*, with three woodcuts by Norman Lindsay. In 1925 the Kirtley-Norman and Jack Lindsay collaboration produced in Sydney *Lysistrata*, the first book to carry the imprint of Fanfrolico Press. The unbound issue of *The Passionate Neatherd* by Jack Lindsay followed in 1926 and in the same year Jack Lindsay and Kirtley went to London to establish and expand their publishing activities and to attempt to export to Europe the philosophy propounded by Norman Lindsay in his *Creative Effort* (1920). Fanfrolico's publications included works by Australian, European and English writers, produced on hand-made paper, painstakingly edited or translated and often sumptuously illustrated. After Kirtley's early departure from the Press his place was taken first by P.R. Stephensen (q.v.) and then by Brian Penton. Philip Lindsay was also involved in its management. P.R. Stephensen's account of his involvement in Fanfrolico Press is in *Kookaburras and Satyrs* (1954). Jack Lindsay wrote *Fanfrolico and After* (1962) and Harry Chaplin, *The Fanfrolico Press* (1976).

FARJEON, BENJAMIN (1838–1903), born London, broke away from his family's Jewish faith as a youth and came penniless to Australia in 1854. From sixteen to twenty-three he roamed the Victorian goldfields, sometimes digging, sometimes caught up in attempts to establish a modest type of newspaper. He went to NZ in 1861, settled in Dunedin and worked on the *Otago Daily Times*. In 1865 he published his first book, *Shadows on the Snow: A Christmas Story*, which he dedicated and sent to Charles Dickens, his literary idol. Dickens responded kindly and Farjeon returned to England, hoping to make a reputation as a writer. In 1866 he published *Grif: A Story of Australian Life*. Between *Grif* and his death, some fifty other novels were written, some concerned with the urban poor, others more straightforward stories of mystery and crime. Farjeon's Australian experiences, especially on the goldfields, are reflected in such works as *Joshua Marvel* (1871), *At the Sign of the Silver Flagon* (1876), *The Sacred Nugget* (1885), *While Golden Sleep Doth Reign* (1887), *Basil and Annette* (1890) and *The Betrayal of John Fordham* (1896).

FARMER, BEVERLEY (1941–), born Melbourne and educated at the University of Melbourne, has had a variety of occupations and spent three years in Greece. She has written a novel, *Alone* (1980), which deals in part with lesbian love and incidentally provides a vivid picture of Melbourne's inner suburb, Carlton; and a collection of highly-acclaimed short stories, *Milk* (1983). *Milk* won the 1984 NSW Premier's Award for fiction.

FARRELL, JOHN (1851–1904), was born Buenos Aires, son of Irish gold rush immigrants who came to Australia in 1852 from South America. After a limited education, he worked mainly as a brewer until he turned to journalism. A radical, he contributed frequently to the *Boomerang* and the *Worker* and enthusiastically shared William Lane's vision of an Australian Utopia. In the 1880s he contributed verse satires and narratives to numerous newspapers and journals, including the *Bulletin*, writing one of its earliest Australian stories,

'One Christmas Day' (1884); his first major book of verse, *How He Died and Other Poems* (q.v.), was published in 1887. Farrell became involved with Henry George of the Single Tax movement, editing two of that movement's Australian journals, but worked mainly for the *Daily Telegraph*, briefly as editor but mostly as columnist, leader-writer and book-reviewer. Two of his minor verse successes were 'Australia to England' (q.v.), a poem written for Queen Victoria's Jubilee in 1897, widely-esteemed and publicly praised by Kipling; and 'Hymn of the Commonwealth', sung by massed choirs at the Sydney Commonwealth celebrations. The main collection of his poetry, *My Sundowner and Other Poems*, published posthumously in 1904, was edited by Bertram Stevens. Although Farrell's was a minor poetic voice in the nationalistic-radicalism of the 1890s, in his person and character he represented the best of that movement. Mary Gilmore's tribute that he most influenced her life and work is characteristic of contemporary sentiments about him.

FARWELL, GEORGE (1911–76), born in Bath, England, came to Australia in 1936. He travelled widely in Australia and New Guinea and worked in a variety of occupations, as goldminer, wharf labourer, radio broadcaster, actor and freelance journalist. He edited *Australian Book News* 1946–48, and was public relations officer for the Adelaide Festival 1959–64. A prolific author, Farwell wrote short stories, biographies, plays, documentary features for radio and television and travel accounts. His study of the Philippines, *Mask of Asia* (1966), won the Moomba-Rothman Award of 1967 but his best-known books are those which reflect his extensive knowledge of Australia. They include *Land of Mirage* (1950), an account of the Birdsville Track; *Vanishing Australians* (1961); *Riders to an Unknown Sea* (1963), a biography of Charles Sturt for young readers; *Ghost Towns of Australia* (1965); *Ned Kelly* (1970); *Requiem for Woolloomooloo* (1971); and *Squatter's Castle* (1973), a biography of a nineteenth-century pastoralist, Edward Ogilvie. *Farwell Country* (1977) is a selection of his writings 1946–76. He also published a collection of short stories, *Surf Music* (1950); memoirs, *Rejoice in Freedom* (1976); and two plays, *The House that Jack Built* (1970), which focuses on the Rum Rebellion and won an award in the Commonwealth Jubilee State play competition of 1951, and *Portrait of a Gentleman*, an award-winning radio play on the subject of Thomas Griffiths Wainewright, first produced in 1940 and included in *Australian Radio Plays* (1946, ed. Leslie Rees). Another play, 'Sons of the South', is set in outback Queensland and deals with the shearers' strike of 1891.

Fat Man in History, The, see **CAREY, PETER**

FATCHEN, MAX (1921–), born near Adelaide, served in the Second World War then became a journalist with the Adelaide *News* and later the *Advertiser*, where he was literary editor. He has visited most of the remote parts of Australia; the outback, the rivers and the sea form the background to many of his books for children. These include *The River Kings* (1966) and *Conquest of the River* (1970), anecdotes about the personalities of the riverboat trade along the Murray; *The Spirit Wind* (1973); *Chase through the Night* (1976, televised by the BBC in 1980 on *Jackanory*); *The Time Wave* (1978); *Songs for My Dog and Other People* (1980); and *Closer to the Stars* (1981).

'Father Riley's Horse', published in *Rio Grande's Last Race and Other Verses* (1902), is a typical A.B. Paterson (q.v.) story of horse-racing in the bush. Andy Regan, horse thief, stage-manages his own 'death', leaving his horse, 'king of all the leppers' (leapers) in the care of Father Riley. When the races come to Kiley's Crossing, Father Riley's horse, well supported at lucrative odds by the Irish Catholics of the district, and ridden by a jockey who all declare is 'Andy Regan's ghost', easily wins the steeplechase. The jockey disappears, the bookies are fleeced and the poor of the parish have an unexpected Christmas feast.

Fatty Finn, the comic-strip creation of Syd Nicholls (q.v.), began life in 1923 in the Sydney *Sunday News* and appeared intermittently in several formats until 1977. The great rival of Ginger Meggs (q.v.), the Fatty Finn strip was better drawn but less humorous and ultimately less successful. The adventures of Fatty formed the subject of the classic Australian film *The Kid Stakes* (1927); a modern version of the film, titled *Fatty Finn* and scripted by Bob Ellis and Chris McGill, was made in 1980.

FAUCHERY, ANTOINE (?1827–61), born Paris, came to Melbourne in 1852 and worked on the Victorian goldfields both as a digger and a storekeeper until he left Australia in 1856. His *Lettres d'un Mineur en Australie* were published first in *Le Moniteur Universel* in fifteen instalments and also separately (1857). The letters were translated from the French by A.R. Chisholm and published with drawings by Ron Edwards as *Letters from a Miner in Australia* (1965). Full of radical sympathies, even for the Chinese diggers, the letters give a vivid impression of the goldfields and early Melbourne life. In a later visit to Australia in 1858–59, Fauchery conducted a photographic studio in Melbourne. His photographic studies, with those of English geologist Richard Daintree, have been collected with text by Dianne Reilly and Jennifer Carew as *Sun Pictures of Victoria: The Fauchery-Daintree Collection – 1858* (1983). The collection includes photos of Le Comte Lionel de Chabrillan, husband of Celeste de Chabrillan, Sir John O'Shanassy, Sir Henry Barkly, after whom the Barkly Tablelands were named, and Fauchery himself, as well as numerous gold-mining scenes and Aboriginal studies.

FAUST, CLIVE (1932–   ), born Melbourne, graduated in philosophy from the University of Melbourne, lived in Japan for seven years and became a lecturer at Bendigo College of Advanced Education. Featured in the American magazine, *Origin* (July 1978), he was included as a representative of the new wave of Australian poetry in John Tranter's anthology, *The New Australian Poetry* (1979). Faust has published two books of verse, *Metamorphosed from the Adjacent Cold* and *Token and Trace* (both 1980).

FAVENC, ERNEST (1845–1908), born Surrey, England, came to Australia in 1864 and worked for fourteen years on stations in north Queensland. He led the 1877 expedition, financed by the *Queenslander*, for which he sometimes wrote under the pseudonym 'Dramingo', to investigate the feasibility of a railway linking Queensland to Darwin. His reputation as an explorer established, Favenc spent several years working for pastoral interests opening up the country along the south-western coast of the Gulf of Carpentaria and across into WA. He then joined the staff of the Sydney *Evening News* and began to turn his adventurous past as an explorer into a lucrative source of fiction and non-fiction. His pastoral and geographic works include *The Great Austral Plain* (1881), *Western Australia* (1887), *The History of Australian Exploration from 1788 to 1888* (1888), *A Century of Progress, 1788–1888* (1902) and *The Explorers of Australia and Their Lifework* (1908). His short fiction includes 'The Last of Six': *Tales of the Austral Tropics* (1893), the title story relating the macabre finale on Australian soil of an escape from a French penal island in the Pacific; *Tales of the Austral Tropics* (1894), which includes the stories of the earlier work and an additional two tales; and *My Only Murder and Other Tales* (1899), stories also set in Oceania and north Queensland. His novels are *The Secret of the Australian Desert* (1896), which concerns the fate of the explorer Ludwig Leichhardt; *Marooned on Australia* (?1896), based on the wreck of the *Batavia* in 1629; and *The Moccasins of Silence* (1896), an adven-

turous romance which takes its title from the footwear used by some Queensland Aborigines in the story. Favenc's only volume of poetry, *Voices of the Desert* (1905), attempts to evoke something of the emptiness and silence of the inland. Cheryl Frost wrote *The Last Explorer: The Life and Work of Ernest Favenc* (1983).

FAWKNER, JOHN PASCOE (1792–1869), born London, accompanied his father and family to Van Diemen's Land in 1803, his father having been sentenced to fourteen years' transportation for receiving stolen goods. As a young man in Van Diemen's Land, Fawkner was in constant trouble with the authorities; for aiding and abetting the escape of seven convicts he was given 500 lashes and three years' hard labour. Ever the speculator, he organized an expedition across Bass Strait to Port Phillip in 1835, gained large landholdings and was an influential figure in that colony's rapid development to statehood. On the introduction of responsible government he was returned for the Central Province of Victoria, holding the seat until his death. Fawkner saw the press as an instrument of reform. In 1828 he commenced the *Launceston Advertiser*, was its editor for two years and used the paper as 'the active and avowed friend of the emancipist class in Van Diemen's Land'. In 1838 in Port Phillip, he commenced the *Melbourne Advertiser*, which was suppressed because Fawkner had no licence; in 1839, with a licence, he began the *Port Phillip Patriot and Melbourne Advertiser* (1839–48). Strongly opposed to the squatting interests, he published a pamphlet, *Squatting Orders* (1854). Hugh Anderson wrote *Out of the Shadow: The Career of John Pascoe Fawkner* (1962). Fawkner appears as a minor character in Eric Lambert's novel, *The Five Bright Stars* (1954).

FEARN-WANNAN, WILLIAM, see WANNAN, BILL

Federation was the movement which promoted the union of the six Australian colonies, NSW, Victoria, Queensland, SA, Tasmania and WA. The idea of a federal union was proposed in the 1840s and 1850s but did not gather momentum until the 1880s and 1890s. Perhaps the most decisive steps were taken at federal conventions held in 1897–98, when a constitution was drafted which, after amendments, was approved at a referendum held in 1899 in all colonies except WA. While an Australian delegation was discussing the constitution with the British government in London, WA voted to join the federal system and the inauguration of the Commonwealth of Australia took place on 1 January 1901. A number of 'writer politicians' were involved in the Federation movement, notably Alfred Deakin and Sir Henry Parkes (qq.v.); 'Price Warung' was active as publicist throughout the 1890s. Federation also attracted the interest of many Australian poets, including John Farrell, whose 'Hymn to the Commonwealth' was sung by massed choirs at the inauguration in Sydney; George Essex Evans, who wrote the patriotic 'An Ode for Commonwealth Day' (1901); Edward Dyson; Mary Hannay Foott; William Gay; A.B. Paterson; Roderic Quinn; and A.G. and J. Brunton Stephens. Two pantomimes with Federation themes staged at the time of the inauguration ceremonies were an updated version of J.C. Williamson's 'Djin Djin' and 'Australis', set in Sydney in 2001.

Feet of Daniel Mannix, The, see OAKLEY, BARRY

Fellowship (1914–22), a monthly Melbourne journal and the organ of the Free Religious Fellowship, a group dedicated to an undogmatic religion, was edited by Frederick Sinclaire. Mainly concerned with socialist and pacifist ideas, the journal included some poetry and comment on Australian literature. Sinclaire was a major contributor but others included Vance and Nettie Palmer, 'Furnley Maurice', Bernard O'Dowd, J. le Gay Brereton and Frederick Macartney.

Fellowship of Australian Writers, known also as the FAW, was formally inaugurated in Sydney on 23 November 1928. Claims have been advanced for both Roderic Quinn and Mary Gilmore as its founder but it seems that Gilmore, prompted by Quinn and assisted by Lucy Cassidy, wife of the poet R.J. Cassidy, arranged the meeting at which J. le Gay Brereton was elected first president. At first the FAW was a Sydney-based organization but, as membership spread, branches were set up in the other States, Victoria and WA being the first. Membership has waxed and waned in some areas but at present there is an autonomous Fellowship in each State and the Northern Territory, with numerous regional branches in the larger States. In 1955 a federal council was formed and since then the national presidency has been held on a rotating basis by State presidents. The FAW exists to bring writers together and to promote their interests, and although this has been characteristically done through regular meetings, lectures, newsletters and anthologies there have also been activities associated with each of the individual organizations. For example, in NSW, a pilgrimage to Henry Lawson's statue in the Domain was for long an annual event; the WA branch has

its headquarters in Tom Collins House, bequeathed to it by Joseph Furphy's (q.v.) son in 1948; in Victoria the FAW administers a large number of literary awards (q.v.). Periodically the FAW has incorporated other writers' organizations, such as the Writers' Club in Sydney (amalgamated with the FAW in 1938) and the Queensland Authors' and Artists' Association, which was founded in 1921 and became the FAW Queensland branch in 1959. As well as providing 'fellowship' among writers, the organization has many times advanced the interest of writers in specifically practical ways, notably in the proposals it put forward in the late 1930s which widened the charter of the CLF (q.v.). For over a decade Vance Palmer and Flora Eldershaw represented the FAW on the advisory board of the CLF. The FAW was also heavily involved in the formation of the ASA in 1963. Among the many prominent Australian writers and publishers who have been associated with the FAW are (apart from those already cited) George Mackaness, T. Inglis Moore, Leslie Haylen, Frank Dalby Davison and Walter Stone in NSW; Nettie Palmer and 'Furnley Maurice' in Victoria; Paul Buddee, Gavin Casey, Henrietta Drake-Brockman, J.K. Ewers, Katharine Susannah Prichard and Donald Stuart in WA; Joan Woodberry and E. Morris Miller in Tasmania; Madelaine Brunato in SA; and James Devaney, R.S. Byrnes, Martin Haley and Maureen Freer in Queensland.

Female Eunuch, The, a feminist analysis of female, sexual stereotypes by Germaine Greer (q.v.), was first published in Britain in 1970 and became outstandingly popular after publication in the USA in 1971. Subsequently translated into eleven languages, the book became almost a sacred text for the international women's liberation movement of the 1970s, notwithstanding sporadic criticisms of aspects of its ideology from some feminists. Designed to question 'the most basic assumptions about female normality in order to re-open the possibilities for development which have been successively locked off by conditioning', the book begins with a study of the female body. Confined by male, historically-determined definitions of female sexuality, women's perceptions of themselves have stressed passivity and elements which belong to the castrate, such as plumpness, languor, delicacy and timidity. In a section titled 'Soul', Greer next examines ways in which the female stereotype is processed in our consumer society and presented to succeeding generations, perpetually suppressing energy or diverting it from a public, powerful sphere to a private, powerless one. In the third section, titled 'Love', a range of distorted perceptions are examined from 'Romance' to the 'Middle-Class Myth of Love and Marriage', and the nuclear family in particular is subjected to stringent criticism. The fourth section, titled 'Hate', discusses negative aspects of the inevitable estrangement of the sexes, given their mutually destructive, predominantly sado-masochistic perceptions of each other. In her last section, 'Revolution', Greer tentatively suggests some sexual alternatives which might free both sexes from their imprisoning stereotypes and from 'building symbiotic, economically-determined' relationships.

Female Factory was the name given, during the early years of settlement in NSW, to an institution at Parramatta for the detention and employment of female convicts; there were similar institutions in Hobart and Launceston. The expression is used in the *Sydney Gazette*, in Peter Cunningham's *Two Years in New South Wales* (1827) and in John Lang's *The Forger's Wife* (1855). A song, 'Australian Courtship', from the *Sydney Gazette* 14 July 1832, with its lines 'But the lass I adore, the lass for me/Is a lass in the female factory', indicates that male convicts and other colonial males saw the factory as a marriage market. 'Price Warung''s story 'Parson Ford's Confessional' (1892) climaxes in a scene at the Hobart Female Factory in which the inmates revenge themselves on Ford by confessing to some visiting matrons that he is the father of their children. The Female Factory is also referred to in Frank Clune's *Wild Colonial Boys* (1948) when Sam Clift tells Benjamin Hall, father of the bushranger Ben Hall, to avoid 'the flash molls in Sydney Town' and select his bride from the Female Factory. J.H.M. Abbott in *Out of the Past* (1944) says that Australia owes much to the women from the Female Factory, many of whom 'valiantly pioneered the new wild country with their men, and played their parts nobly'. Anne Summers in her feminist history, *Dammed Whores and God's Police* (1975), suggests that one of the alternative roles available to Australian women, especially in the nineteenth century, derived in part from the Female Factory. Annette Salt wrote *These Outcast Women* (1984), a history of, and commentary on, the Parramatta Female Factory.

Feminism and Australian Literature. In 1902 Australian women were granted, several years before their European and American sisters, the right to vote in federal elections, an event which seemed to justify J.S. Mill's earlier impression, recorded in his letter to Archibald Michie in 1868, of Australia as an enlightened country. It is an impression that is not supported, however, by feminists and some modern historians and sociologists. Feminist reinterpretations of Australian history, in particular, see women as inevitably reduced to the margins of the national life by the nature of the nation's pioneering and convict beginnings; forced into such opposed but equally crippling stereotypes as Anne Summers describes in her history, *Damned Whores and God's Police* (1975), women are seen as having been implicitly excluded from the nineteenth century's shaping of the national consciousness. The exclusive masculinity of the historical self-image has been indirectly described by Russel Ward, for instance, in a well-known passage of his seminal cultural history, *The Australian Legend* (1958); according to Ward, the chief elements of the 'typically Australian outlook', an ethos which he sees as deriving from convict, working-class, Irish and native-born Australian sources, are 'a comradely independence based on a group solidarity and relative economic plenty, a rough and ready capacity for "stringybark and green-hide" improvisation, a light-hearted intolerance of respectable or conventional manners, a reckless improvidence, and a conviction that the working bushman was the "true Australian" whose privilege it was to despise "new chums" and city folk'. Whatever the historical validity of this implicitly-sexist perception of the national character, feminists argue that it was an inevitable part of the cultural baggage of the Australian writer, male or female, from at least the 1890s until the 1950s. Similarly, the masculine, patriarchal, acquisitive and anti-intellectual nature of Australian society, both in actuality and in myth, has been a commonplace of many cultural and general histories, and a dominant theme of feminist accounts. Norman Mackenzie expressed what he saw as the actualities of the situation in his pioneering sociological study, *Women in Australia* (1962, assisted by Enid Campbell): 'Australia is more "a man's country" than other industrial democracies', and Miriam Dixson has energetically attacked the traditional myths in *The Real Matilda: Women and Identity in Australia, 1788–1975* (1976): 'there are . . . no women in the pantheon of Australian gods . . . there is an animal, a horse called Phar Lap. The rest tend to be males under all-male and danger-fraught conditions'.

Women writers of the nineteenth and early twentieth centuries formed a variety of responses to the national ethos. Miles Franklin, hailed in her own lifetime as a proponent of bush values, was in fact highly ambivalent, recording her bitter alienation in *My Brilliant Career* (1901) even as she celebrated the Australian landscape. Ada Cambridge, Rosa Praed and Jessie Couvreur have traditionally been thought to have escaped into the world of the genteel romance reserved for women although Cambridge, in her volume of poetry *Unspoken Thoughts* (1887), expressed strikingly strong feminist concerns, and all three document the importance of the marriage question for women and offer critical comment on the Australian male ethos. Catherine Spence realistically tackled a range of female issues, including the problem of work and patriarchal, religious doctrines although her most radical novels, *Gathered In* (serialized 1881–82) and *Handfasted* were not published in book form during her lifetime and she eventually abandoned fiction for more direct means. Catherine Martin in *An Australian Girl* (1890) retained the stock ingredients of the romance but included remarkably frank considerations of marriage, the limitations of the typical Australian male and of conventional religious, Anglo-Saxon pieties. Barbara Baynton's short stories were a dramatic and bitterly incisive confrontation of the myths of mateship and romantic bush life. 'Henry Handel Richardson' is seen by feminists as demonstrating her implicit hostility to national values in various ways: by her departure from Australia; personal avoidance of domestic encumbrances; cultivation of a romantic, European conception of the artist; use of a male pseudonym; and persistent representation of female characters whose destinies depend on men. One of the most interesting products of the women's liberation movement in Australia which dates from the early 1970s has been a re-examination of central literary texts and previous perceptions of them. A number of provocative essays by such commentators as Jill Roe, Anne Summers, Frances McInherny, Coral Lansbury, Carole Ferrier, Jane Sunderland, Delys Bird, Shirley Walker and Helen Thomson have appeared in both feminist and literary journals. At the same time the lives, problems and attitudes of a range of women writers, some of whom were formerly dismissed as minor, or untypically Australian, have been reassessed from a modern perspective and the political and personal aspirations, cultural, sexual and racial assumptions in the work of such writers as Katharine Susannah Prichard, Nettie Palmer, Miles Franklin, Marjorie Barnard, Christina Stead, Jean Devanny, Elizabeth Harrower, Shirley Hazzard, Kylie Tennant, Eleanor Dark, Dymphna Cusack, 'Betty Roland', Eve Langley and Mary Gilmore are now being extensively and illuminatingly explored. Similarly, assumptions and attitudes of certain male writers such as Henry Lawson, Joseph Furphy, Christopher Brennan, Patrick White, David Ireland, Martin Boyd and Thomas Keneally have also been subjected to a feminist reassessment, with revealing results. A collection of

essays, titled *Who is She?* (1983, ed. Shirley Walker), explores the image of women implicitly held by both male and female writers and Drusilla Modjeska in *Exiles at Home* (1981) examines the work and problems of women writers 1925–45.

Re-examination of literary texts has been accompanied by a reassessment of the standard texts of Australian historiography, such as those by Russel Ward, Manning Clark, Geoffrey Serle, Alan Shaw and C.E.W. Bean, and analyses of their limitations from a feminist point of view. Ann Curthoys in *Arena* 22 (1970), and Kay Daniels in *New History: Studying Australia Today* (1982, eds G. Osborne and W.F. Mandle), outline the gaps in Australian historiography although as yet only two histories, those by Dixson and Summers, have made pioneering attempts to grapple with the issues and in both historiography and literary criticism the problems of methodology are still hotly debated. Beverley Kingston's *The World Moves Slowly* (1977) is a documentary history illustrating many of the attitudes described by Summers and Dixson and Ruth Teale's *Colonial Eve* (1978), serves the same purpose.

Norman Mackenzie's *Women in Australia* (1962), updated by S. Encel and Margaret Tebbutt (1974), is the only comprehensive interpretation of the contemporary position of women, although several collections confront a range of women's problems in such areas as education, law, work and family. These include Barbara Thiering ed., *Created Second?* (1973); Jan Mercer ed., *The Other Half* (1975); Elizabeth Windschuttle ed., *Women, Class and History* (1980); Norma Grieve and Pat Grimshaw eds, *Australian Women* (1981); Rosalie Stephenson ed., *Women in Australian Society* (1970); and Julie Rigg ed., *In Her Own Right* (1969). Others which concentrate more on the problems of work, both now and in the past, include Beverley Kingston's *My Wife, My Daughter and Poor Mary Ann* (1975); Ann Curthoys, Susan Eade and Peter Spearitt eds, *Women at Work* (1975); Janice Brownfoot and Dianne Scott eds, *The Unequal Half* (1976); Edna Ryan and Anne Conlon eds, *Gentle Invaders* (1975); Margaret Bevege ed., *Worth Her Salt* (1982); Ann Game and Rosemary Pringle, *Gender at Work* (1983); Kay Daniels, *Uphill All The Way* (1980); and Joan Clarke and Zoe O'Leary, *Girl Fridays in Revolt* (1969). *The Half-Open Door*, eds Patricia Grimshaw and Lynne Strahan (1982), is a collection of autobiographical essays, including some from such women writers as Joyce Nicholson, Therese Radic, Lynne Strahan and Kathleen Fitzpatrick, which discuss the problems faced by women in their professional and personal lives. *Women Academics: Why So Few?* (1983), a report based on a survey of the Universities of Sydney and NSW, provides a mass of data on the experience of women in the field of tertiary education. Several essays on the specific problems faced by Aboriginal women, both now and in the past and in both white and Aboriginal society, have been published as well as a collection edited by Fay Gale, *Women's Role in Aboriginal Society* (1970). Feminist concerns have also helped to illuminate the migrant experience in Australia.

As yet there is no comprehensive history of the feminist movement, although some research into the work of such women as Louisa Lawson, Rose Scott, Vida Goldstein, Alice Henry, Catherine Helen Spence, Adela Pankhurst Walsh, Jean Devanny, Jessie Street and Bessie Rischbieth has been published. Dianne Scott in *Royal Australian Historical Society Journal* (1967) provides one of the few accounts of the women's suffrage movement. Contemporary accounts of the first wave of the feminist movement include Jessie Ackermann's *Australia From a Woman's Point of View* (1913) and Mrs F. Anderson's 'Women in Australia' in *Australia: Economic and Political Studies* (1920, eds M. Atkinson and Alice Henry). Jessie Street in her memoirs, *Truth or Repose* (1966), provides an account of feminism in Australia in the 1940s. General and individual biographies of women abound although some of these, which tend to cultivate the 'God's Police' stereotype or which exclusively foster the worthy, pioneering image, are regarded critically by feminists. General collections of biographies include Eve Pownall's *Mary of Maranoa* (1959), 'Denton Prout' and Fred Feely's *Petticoat Parade* (1965), Flora Eldershaw ed., *The Peaceful Army* (1938), *A Book of South Australia: Women in the First Hundred Years* (1936, ed. Louise Brown and others), Helen Heney's *Australia's Founding Mothers* (1978), Barbara Jefferis's *Three of a Kind* (1982), and *The Changemakers* (1983, eds Suzanne Fabian and Morag Loh). A *Who's Who of Australian Women* was published in 1982. Several bibliographies on women's affairs have appeared, of which the most comprehensive and best organized is *Her Story* (1980) by Margaret Bettison and Anne Summers. Others include *Women in Australia: An Annotated Guide to Records* (q.v., 1977), *Women in Australian Society* (1977) by Janet Reed and Kathleen Oakes, *Australian Women 1952-1975* (1975) by M.J. Gepp, as well as a range of bibliographies on specific items published in magazines and in some of the collections listed.

Since the early 1970s feminist magazines, newsletters and newspapers have proliferated, their variety and their often brief existence reflecting the increasingly pluralistic nature of the women's movement. Several, such as *Refractory Girl* and *Hecate* (qq.v.), deal occasion-

ally with women writers. They include *Mejane* (1971-74), *Hussy* (1972–), *Vashti's Voice* (1972–), *Mabel* (1975-77), *Womanspeak* (1975–), *Scarlet Woman* (1975–), *Working Papers in Sex, Science and Culture* (1976–), *Luna* (1976–), *Lip* (1976–), *Join Hands* (1972–), *Women's News Service* (1975–), *Double X* (1974–) and *Rouge* (1979–). A series of well-publicized and influential Women and Labour Conferences (1978, 1980 and 1982) sponsored by departments of Macquarie University and the Australian Society for the Study of Labour History have resulted in the publication of papers, many of which are literary, and in the *Women and Labour Conference Bulletin*. Conversely, the reductive value system of the *Australian Women's Weekly* (q.v.) in the 1940s and 1950s is analysed by Bill Bonney and Helen Wilson in *Australia's Commercial Media* (1983) and by Helen Wilson in *Glamour and Chauvinism* (1982). Meanwhile the increasing awareness of women's problems at a government level, the growth of women's studies at universities and colleges, the establishment of Women's Electoral Lobby in 1972, and the proliferation of organizations, groups and movements concerned with the multitudinous aspects of women's affairs, have resulted in a mass of published material since 1970 from the politically radical to the sexually deviant, to the mildly polemical or the official. Radio series concentrating on women's issues and several television programmes and films have been produced. Publishing, also seen as traditionally a male, white, middle-class hegemony, has seen the advent of several feminist presses, including Everywoman Press (Sydney), Sybylla Press (Melbourne) and Sisters (Melbourne). Another well-established feminist publishing enterprise is Melbourne's Women's Movement Children's Literature Co-operative Ltd, which produces non-sexist materials.

Links between women's movements and women writers have always existed, but it was not until the advent of the women's liberation movement in the 1970s, roughly coinciding with Germaine Greer's *The Female Eunuch* (q.v.), that a large, specific body of self-conscious, feminist literature emerged. Writers who contributed to or had some links with early women's movements include Mary Gilmore, Jean Devanny, Dymphna Cusack, Mona Brand, Miles Franklin, Katharine Susannah Prichard and 'Betty Roland'. Some writers with implicit feminist perceptions, such as Kylie Tennant, Thea Astley, Marjorie Barnard and Gwen Harwood, and others with spiritedly explicit attitudes, such as Dorothy Hewett, Mona Brand and Dymphna Cusack, continued to write during the relatively stagnant period 1940–70. Unlike their predecessors, feminist writers from

1970 have been greatly sustained by ideas stemming from the international women's movement. Another distinction between the two periods is that for some second-wave feminists at least, marxism and other intellectual systems have combined more easily with feminist issues, especially at the level of methodology. For such writers as Prichard, Devanny and 'Roland', party and feminist aspirations were frequently at odds. Working-class women have also had some role in the second period although the movement is still mainly a middle-class one. Novelists of the post-1970 period who have written on feminist or semi-feminist themes include Helen Hodgman, Elizabeth Jolley, Christine Townend, Suzanne Holly Jones, Glen Tomasetti, Barbara Hanrahan, Jessica Anderson, Stefanie Bennett and Helen Garner (qq.v.). Zoe Fairbairns, the English feminist who visited Australia in 1971 and 1983, draws on her Australian experiences in her novels *Benefits* (1979) and most extensively in *Stand We At Last* (1983). Lesbian novels include Elizabeth Riley's *All That False Instruction* (1975) and Beverley Farmer's *Alone* (1980). K. Lette and G. Carey in *Puberty Blues* (1979), which was also produced as a film in 1983, have written an important exploration of an adolescent, male-dominated subculture of the 1970s. A relatively large body of short fiction has emerged, mostly published in feminist and literary journals, and several anthologies have appeared: *Stories of Her Life* (1979) ed. Sandra Zurbo, *Frictions* (1982) ed. Anna Gibbs and Alison Tilson, and *The True Life Story Of...* (1981) ed. Jan Craney and Esther Caldwell are prose anthologies, the last two of which include contributions from such well-known writers as Elizabeth Jolley, Mona Brand, Finola Moorhead, Christine Townend, Kate Llewellyn and Anna Couani. *Hecate's Daughters* (1978) ed. Carole Ferrier, includes verse and prose from such writers as Judith Rodriguez, Jennifer Maiden and Dorothy Hewett. Several autobiographical accounts of feminist experience have also appeared including Zelda D'Aprano's *Zelda: The Becoming of a Woman* (1977) and the anthologies, *Brian's Wife, Jenny's Mum* (1975) ed. Gwen Wesson, and *A Book About Australian Women* (1974) ed. Carol Jerrems and Virginia Fraser. *For Love Or Money* (1983), compiled by Megan McMurchy, Margot Oliver and Jeni Thornley, is a companion work to an influential feature film of the same title, which depends partly on interviews and autobiographical accounts.

From the time of Ada Cambridge, poetry has consistently attracted women writers. Dorothy Hewett, Rosemary Dobson, Marie Pitt, Lesbia Harford and Gwen Harwood are examples of older writers who have written some memorable feminist poems but since 1970 the form appears to have been regarded as the most accessible as a means of expression. Kate Jennings in her anthology *Mother I'm Rooted* (1975) brings together some of the more recent poets including Stefanie Bennett, Lee Cataldi, Anne Elder, Helen Garner, Jill Hellyer, Sylvia Kantarizis, Peg Clarke, Antigone Kefala, Jennifer Maiden, Carol Novack, Marjorie Pizer, Jennifer Rankin, Judith Rodriguez and Vicki Viidikas. Fay Zwicky has emerged as a significant figure in both short fiction and poetry; Stefanie Bennett, one of the most prolific of feminist poets, is editor and publisher of the Cochon poetry series, which includes several of her own volumes, and of joint collections such as *Hags, Rags & Scriptures* (1976). Rosemary Dobson in *Sisters Poets, 1* (1979) has brought together the work of Anne Lloyd, Kate Llewellyn, Joyce Lee and Susan Hampton.

Several women writers such as Dymphna Cusack, Mona Brand, 'Betty Roland' and, outstandingly, Dorothy Hewett, have contributed feminist or semi-feminist plays throughout their careers stretching from the 1940s. And several of the plays of the 1950s renaissance of Australian drama, including Ray Lawler's *Summer of the Seventeenth Doll* (qq.v., 1957) and Alan Seymour's *The One Day of the Year* (qq.v. 1962), were critical of traditional male values, if they were not otherwise especially feminist. The 1970s renaissance of Australian drama, however, produced a wide range of feminist plays from both male and female playwrights. The Women's Group and later the Women's Theatre Group of Melbourne's Pram Factory company, created several co-operative productions of which 'Betty Can Jump' (1971) is probably the best known. Playwrights whose work was produced by the Australian Performing Group during the 1970s and who showed a high level of feminist awareness include Jack Hibberd, John Romeril, Alex Buzo and David Williamson. Outstanding in this area are Hibberd's *White with Wire Wheels* (q.v., 1970) and Williamson's *The Coming of Stork* (1974) and *The Removalists* (1972). Other plays from these writers which deal, at least in part, with the situation of women are Hibberd's 'Peggy Sue' (1974) and *A Toast to Melba* (1976), Romeril's 'Mrs. Thally F' (1971), Williamson's *Don's Party* (1973) and *The Perfectionist* (1983), Buzo's *Rooted* (1973) and *Coralie Lansdowne Says No* (1974). Ron Blair in 'Perfect Strangers' (1971) and Robin Thurston in 'Sisters' (1974) contribute diverse perspectives on so-called normal and abnormal feminine experience. Therese and Leonard Radic have combined in dramatizing a selection of women's writing, *Some of My Best Friends Are Women* (1983). Dorothy Hewett has been a dominant figure whose most influential play has been *The Chapel Perilous*

(1972), followed by *Bon-Bons and Roses for Dolly* (1976), *The Tatty Hollow Story* (1976) and 'Joan' (1975). Other contemporary feminist playwrights include Alma de Groen, Doreen Clarke, Jennifer Rankin, Suzanne Spunner, Gilly Fraser, Jennifer Compton, Mary Gage, Jill Shearer, Alison Lyssa, Gillian Jones and Oriel Gray. A feature of the feminist theatre has been the establishment of women's theatre groups such as Fool's Gallery, Footfall Theatre and the Home Cooking Company, which have occasionally staged co-operative group productions. Better known to the general public are the cabaret artists, Robyn Archer and Barry Humphries; whereas Archer has directly confronted the problems of Australian women in several of her shows, Humphries indirectly reflects them in his creation of a range of 'ocker' types and development of Dame Edna's overcompensating superhuman efforts towards the significance of stardom.

FENTON, JAMES (1820–1901), born Dunlavin, Ireland, came to Van Diemen's Land in 1834 and in 1840 began farming on the Forth River in thickly forested country deemed unsuitable for settlement. He was the first to apply the technique of ring-barking to clear forest land. Becoming aware of the need of the growing colony of Victoria for housing, he then turned to exploiting his land for its timber; as the land was cleared some of Tasmania's best farm land emerged. After his retirement from farming in 1879 he wrote *A History of Tasmania* (1884) and a book of memoirs, *Bush Life in Tasmania Fifty Years Ago* (1891).

FERGUSON, G.A. (GEORGE ADIE) (1910–), born Sydney, is the son of noted bibliographer and collector of Australiana, Sir John Alexander Ferguson, and grandson of George Robertson (2). While he was a director of Angus & Robertson 1936–70 and its publishing director 1949–70, he consolidated the reputation that the firm had gained as one of Australia's greatest publishing houses. In 1949 he was instrumental in the founding of the Australian Book Publishers Association; the Association's annual book-design awards were inaugurated during his ten year period as president; he was director of the Association 1971–75. A member of the ABPA committee, the Australian Book Trade Advisory Committee and the Joint Publishers Committee, Ferguson was also involved in the Spicer Committee on copyright revision. An advisor to the Australian government on matters such as the CLF and the Commonwealth Printing Office, Ferguson was also, from its inception, a member of the Book Printing Bounty Advisory Panel; he was made CBE in 1956. He wrote *Some Early*

Australian Bookmen (1978); it discusses such identities as the two George Robertsons, D.M. Angus, Samuel Mullen, F.V. Wymark, Sir William Dixson and David Scott Mitchell.

FERGUSON, Sir JOHN ALEXANDER (1881–1969), born Invercargill, NZ, trained as a lawyer in Sydney, where in 1936–53 he was a judge on the Industrial Commission. Ferguson was involved over many years with the Presbyterian Church, the Royal Australian Historical Society, the Public (later State) Library of NSW and the Unversity of Sydney; a member of its Senate, he supported C.J. Brennan at the time of his dismissal. His marriage in 1906 to the daughter of the Sydney bookseller, George Robertson (2), stimulated and facilitated his interest in bibliography and bookcollecting. Ferguson submitted an article on Henry Kendall to the *Bulletin* in 1900 which was reprinted in 1963 in *Foreshadowings*, and contributed several bibliographical, biographical and historical essays to the Royal Australian Historical Society's *Journal* 1917–31. His major endeavours, however, went into the monumental *Bibliography of Australia* (q.v.), published in seven volumes 1941–69, a pioneering work of scholarship which remains a basic reference work in Australian studies. Ferguson's other lasting memorials are his collection of Australiana, presented to the National Library of Australia after his death, and the John Alexander Ferguson Memorial lecture, a public lecture on Australian history, bibliography or literature, held at intervals of not less than two years in Sydney and Canberra. The inaugural lecture by G.D. Richardson, *The Instruction and Good of His Country: Sir John Ferguson, Libraries, and the Historical Record* (1977), includes a survey of Ferguson's career. George Adie Ferguson (q.v.) is his son.

'FERRES, ARTHUR' (JOHN WILLIAM KEVIN), NSW teacher and school inspector, was best known for his stories for boys. His fiction includes *My Centennial Gift: Or, Australian Stories for Children* (1887), the contents of which had originally appeared in the *Sydney Mail* under the title 'Bush Stories for Children'; *His Cousin the Wallaby and Three Other Australian Stories* (1896); *His First Kangaroo: An Australian Story for Boys* (1896), which depicts life and adventure on a Lachlan River station; and *The Ploughboy Premier: A Story for Boys* (1916), which captures school life in the bush. 'Ferres' also published verse, *The Free Selector and Other Verses* (1901), and edited *Poetic Selections* (1894).

FERRIER, CAROLE, see **Feminism and Australian Literature**

o

FETHERSTONHAUGH, CUTHBERT (1837–1925), born County Westmeath, Ireland, came to Australia in 1853 and for the following twenty years was active as jackeroo, explorer and squatter in the developing north Queensland pastoral areas. He was briefly an Anglican minister (1873–75) before resuming his pastoral career; he helped organize the meat-export industry and mined successfully in the Gulf country. The character the Rev. Herbert Heatherstone in 'Rolf Boldrewood''s *A Colonial Reformer* (1890) is based on him, and his supposed encounter with the bushranger Bluecap is recalled in Barcroft Boake's poem 'Fetherstonhaugh' in *Where the Dead Men Lie and Other Poems* (1897). Fetherstonhaugh's lively career is outlined in his autobiographical *After Many Days* (1918).

Fiction Fields of Australia, The, an essay by Frederick Sinnett (q.v.), was published in the *Journal of Australasia* in 1856. It was republished in 1966, ed. Cecil Hadgraft. The first critical essay to deal solely with Australian literature, *The Fiction Fields of Australia* has more than historical significance. It raised questions that are still relevant about an Australian literary voice and the ways of representing 'local manners and customs' in fiction, and concluded with useful comments on works by Catherine Helen Spence, Alexander Harris and Charles Rowcroft.

FIELD, BARRON, (1786–1846), an unsuccessful legal practioner in England, came to Sydney in 1817 as a judge of the Supreme Court of NSW. In 1819 George Howe, the government printer, published Field's *First Fruits of Australian Poetry* (q.v.). The Colony's unfamiliar flora and fauna attracted him but he disliked the uninviting terrain, the reversed seasons and the penal nature of the settlement. He saw it as a 'prose-dull land', a land without associations, and left it gladly in 1824. Back in England he edited *Geographical Memoirs on New South Wales* (1825), then went to Gibraltar as chief justice. Although Field's claim to be the first 'Austral Harmonist' is presumptuous, 'Botany Bay Flowers' and 'The Kangaroo', in spite of some ridiculing of the colonial scene, are among the first poems to evoke the Australian environment.

FIELDING, SYDNEY GLANVILLE (1856–1930), born Parramatta, went to sea as a boy but gave up the seafaring life at the age of twenty-four to join the Anglican ministry, serving for half a century in various parishes in the Bathurst and Sydney dioceses. He published fiction, *The Southern Light* (1895) and

Down to the Sea in Ships (1900), both of which deal with the adventurous times at sea and ashore of their young heroes; *The New Vicar of Wakefield* (1902), which is based on the vicissitudes of a minister of religion in western NSW and takes in the Boer War; and the futuristic *Australia A.D. 2000: Or, the Great Referendum* (1917). Fielding also published verse, *The Castaway and Other Poems* (1884), as well as several religious tracts.

XV Poems, see **BRENNAN, C.J.**

'Fifth Day', see **FITZGERALD, R.D.**

Fifty Years Ago: An Australian Tale, a novel by Charles de Boos (q.v.), first published in fourteen booklets (1866–67) and then in a single volume in 1867, was also serialized in the *Australian Journal* (1869–70). It was reprinted as *Settler and Savage* in 1906 by A.C. Rowlandson in the NSW Bookstall series. The novel opens with the massacre of the wife and family of settler George Maxwell by a group of marauding Aborigines from the Maroo tribe led by chieftains Macomo, Atara and Opara. Maxwell and his son Jamie, who survive the attack, swear vengeance on the blacks and the novel follows, with numerous sub-plots, the hunt for the guilty tribe and its leaders. The Maroo are exterminated, leaving Macomo alone to be hunted down. Jamie, victim of his own obsession for vengeance, is slain by the blacks but George Maxwell, when confronted with the suffering and nobility of Macomo, regrets his hatred and comes to a new understanding of the Aboriginal psyche. The novel has sometimes been linked with J. Fenimore Cooper's writing, with Macomo as the Magua figure and Maxwell as a white Deerslayer. The novel successfully captures both the physical environment and the psychological ambience of those colonial times; its somewhat revolutionary conclusion in favour of the Aborigines contrasts greatly, however, with the disparagement of them so widely aired in other colonial literature.

Film see Cinema and Australian Literature

FINCH, PETER (1916–77), born England, the legal son of an Australian-born soldier, mountaineer and scientist, George Ingle-Finch, was brought up by a variety of relatives and friends in Paris, India and Australia. After leaving school in Sydney he worked as a journalist, artist's model, waiter and straight-man in a vaudeville act before becoming an actor for stage and radio. His first successful part in film was as Bill Ryan in *Dad and Dave Come to Town* (1938). In the Second World War he served as a gunner, interrupting his service for the production of films including *The Rats of Tobruk* (1944). After the success of the British–Australian film, *Eureka Stockade* (1949), he moved to England where he established an outstanding reputation as a film actor. Films in which he appeared include *The Miniver Story* (1950), *The Wooden Horse* (1950), *The Heart of the Matter* (1953), *A Town Like Alice* (1956), *Robbery Under Arms* (1957), *The Shiralee* (1957), *Far from the Madding Crowd* (1967), *Sunday Bloody Sunday* (1971), *Network* (1976) and *Raid on Entebbe* (1977). He was particularly noted for his portrayal of vulnerable public figures such as Lord Nelson in *Bequest to the Nation* (1973) and Oscar Wilde in *The Trials of Oscar Wilde* (1960). Finch appears as the character Archie Calverton in George Johnston's novel, *Clean Straw for Nothing* (1969).

FINEY, GEORGE (1895–), born Auckland, NZ, sold his first drawings to local newspapers at the age of fourteen. In the First World War he served in France with the NZ forces both as infantry soldier and war artist, and studied briefly at art school in London before settling in Australia in 1919. His first cartoons were published in the *Bulletin*, but in 1921 he began a decade's association with *Smith's Weekly* and won a reputation as a superb caricaturist. Subsequently he worked as a political cartoonist and strip artist for the *Labour Daily*, *Truth*, the *Sunday Sun*, the *Daily Telegraph* and other journals, although he often ran foul of editors and proprietors. A notable Sydney bohemian, Finey worked in many media including pen and ink, brush drawing, ceramics, enamel paint and collage, and was judged by his contemporary, Stan Cross, to be the finest of the *Smith's Weekly* artists. His simple verse is included in *Poems* (1975) and *Book of Finey* (1976) as well as in his entertaining autobiography, *The Mangle Wheel* (1981).

FINLAYSON, H.H., see **Dead Heart**

FINN, EDMUND ('GARRYOWEN') (1819–98), born Tipperary, Ireland, settled in the infant city of Melbourne in 1841 and worked on the *Port Phillip Herald* for thirteen years before becoming a public servant in 1858. As 'An Old Colonist', Finn published *The Garryowen Sketches* (1880), which was followed by 'Garryowen''s two-volume *The Chronicles of Early Melbourne 1835 to 1852* (1888); both are significant accounts of colonial Melbourne life based on Finn's wide exprience and extensive records. A selection from the *Chronicles* was

published as *Garryowen's Melbourne*, ed. Margaret Weidenhofer (1967). Finn's son, also Edmund, wrote pantomimes.

FINNIN, MARY (1906–), born Kildare near Geelong, Victoria, trained as an artist, held successful exhibitions of paintings, and has been an art teacher, critic and businesswoman. Her major literary interest has been poetry; her six volumes of verse include *A Beggar's Opera* (1938), *Look Down, Olympians* (1939), *Royal* (1941), *Alms for Oblivion* (1947), *The Shield of Place* (1957) and a collected volume, *Off Shears* (1958–1978) (1979). *The Shield of Place* (the title refers to her commitment to Victoria) includes the ballad, 'The Ride of Richard Illidge', which commemorates an epic horse ride of 160 kilometres in a night to save a condemned prisoner from execution. Other poems with local Victorian flavour are 'Bacchus in the Marsh' and 'Rain in Glenrowan'. Mary Finnin also wrote and illustrated the children's book, *The Book of Bauble* (1945).

Fire on the Snow, The, a verse-drama by Douglas Stewart (q.v.), was written in 1939, and published in part in the *Bulletin* (13 December 1939). Produced as a radio play by the ABC, 6 June 1941, it was published with *The Golden Lover* in 1944. The play traces Captain Robert Scott's Antarctic expedition from 4 January 1912, when Scott and his four companions, Wilson, Bowers, Oates and Evans, set out on the final dash to the South Pole, to the last entry in Scott's diary on 29 March 1912. At the Pole they find the flag of the Norwegian party led by Amundsen. Disconsolate, exhausted and short of supplies, they set out on the return journey. Evans dies from concussion as a result of a fall. Oates, with his famous words, 'I am just going outside. I may be some time', is next. Then, after the death of Bowers, Scott and Wilson die together in their tent only eleven miles from the sanctuary of their One Ton Camp. As the tragedy unfolds, the omniscient announcer traces the historic journey, the glory of which only the participants themselves are fated never to know. *The Fire on the Snow* is remarkable for its radio drama technique and for its skilful verse variations, which range from the colloquialism of the blindly-struggling mortals to the solemn tones of the announcer reporting the progress of their fate.

First Boke of Fowle Ayres, The, a collection of unattributed scurrilous and bawdy verse by such poets as A.D. Hope, James McAuley, O.M. Somerville and Harold Stewart, was published in a limited edition in 1944. Epigrams from it and some verse by Somerville and Hope are included in *Comic Australian Verse* (1972) ed. Geoffrey Lehmann.

First-Born and Other Poems, The, see DAVIS, JACK

First Fleet is the name given to the ships which carried the first convicts to Australia; it is also applied more generally to the passengers of those ships, both during their time on board and in the early years of settlement. The First Fleet comprised two warships (the *Sirius* and the *Supply*), six chartered transports to carry the convicts, and three supply vessels, none of them as big as, for example, a Sydney harbour ferry of the twentieth century. The Fleet left England on 13 May 1787, sighted Van Diemen's Land on 5 January 1788 and arrived at Botany Bay on 18–20 January; just over 1000 people disembarked to form the first settlement. Among the naval and military officers and other personnel who sailed with the convicts were Arthur Phillip, William Bradley, Watkin Tench, David Collins, John White and John Hunter, all of whom published contemporary accounts of the voyage or the early years of settlement. Later fictional accounts were written by 'Louis' Becke and Walter Jeffery, J.H. Abbott and Eleanor Dark (qq.v.). In recent years the term 'First Fleeter' has emerged to describe those Australians who can trace part of their family back to a passenger on the First Fleet. One was Miles Franklin; another, Jonathon King, has written *The First Fleet* (1982), an account of the voyage. Other recent publications include the First Fleet journals of Arthur Bowes Smyth, Philip Gidley King and Ralph Clark, each edited by P.G. Fidlon and R.J. Ryan (1979, 1980, 1981); Victor Crittenden's *The Voyage of the First Fleet* (1981) and *A Bibliography of the First Fleet* (1981); Don Chapman's *1788 – The People of the First Fleet* (1981); and John Cobley's (q.v.) *The Crimes of the First Fleet Convicts* (1970).

First Fruits of Australian Poetry (1819), by Barron Field (q.v.), contains two poems, 'Botany Bay Flowers' and 'The Kangaroo'. On the title page, the lines 'I first adventure; follow me who list/ And be Australia's second harmonist' indicate Field's claim to be Australia's first poetic voice, and his book is, in fact, the first book of poems published in Australia. With 'Botany Bay Flowers' Field provides the first poetic description of wildflowers and native shrubs of the Sydney bush. 'The Kangaroo' depicts that animal as an Antipodean oddity, an anomaly of the animal world yet typical of the equally strange Australian landscape. In spite of Field's amazement and amusement at

colonial oddities of flora and fauna there is, in both poems, a sincere note of interest.

FISHER, LALA (1872–1929), born Rockhampton, Queensland, spent the years 1897–1901 in England where she published poetry, *A Twilight Teaching* (1898), and edited *By Creek and Gully* (1899), a mainly prose anthology of Australian writers then in England. Back in Australia she lived first in Charters Towers and wrote for various journals and newspapers, including *Steele Rudd's Magazine*. In 1909 in Sydney, she bought the *Theatre Magazine* which she edited until 1918. Her later books of verse were *Grass Flowering* (1915) and *Earth Spiritual* (1918). A remarkably progressive and liberated woman for her time, Lala Fisher expressed in her poetry some of the sentiments that the restricting conventions of the day were prone to stifle.

Fisher Library, the University of Sydney, was named in honour of Thomas Fisher (1820–84), boot- and shoe-shop proprietor of Pitt Street, Sydney, who left the bulk of his large fortune to the University for establishing and maintaining a library. In 1909 the library building was opened and the Fisher bequest was used to stock it with books. Substantial additions were made to the original library building after the Second World War. H.M. Green (q.v.) was Fisher librarian 1921–46; he is largely responsible for its extensive holdings of Australiana.

Fisher's Ghost is Australia's best-known and most-discussed apparition. Frederick Fisher, a ticket-of-leave convict and farmer of the Campbelltown area, disappeared 16 June 1826 from the house of a neighbour, George Worrall. More than four months later, following a supposed sighting by a John Farley of Fisher's Ghost sitting upon the rail of a fence or bridge and pointing to a nearby creek, the body was found and Worrall was hanged for Fisher's murder, 5 February 1827. The story of Fisher's Ghost is outlined in R. Montgomery Martin's *History of the British Colonies* (1835); in 'Fisher's Ghost: A Legend of Campbelltown' by W. Kerr in *Tegg's Monthly Magazine* (March 1836), reprinted in Geoffrey C. Ingleton's *True Patriots All* (1952); in 'Fisher's Ghost' (probably by John Lang) in Charles Dickens's *Household Words* (1853); and in John Lang's story, 'The Ghost upon the Rail', from his book of stories, *Botany Bay* (1859). A poetic version of Fisher's Ghost, 'The Sprite of the Creek!', by an unknown author (Lang has again been suggested), occurs in an early newspaper, *Hill's Life in New South Wales*, 14 September 1832. Fisher's Ghost has been the subject of many other stories, articles, tall tales, a film by Raymond Longford in 1924, and a play by Douglas Stewart in 1960. The creek near which the body was found now bears the name Fisher's Ghost Creek.

FISON, LORIMER, see **Aboriginal in Australian Literature**

FITCHETT, WILLIAM HENRY ('VE-DETTE'), (1842–1928), born Lincolnshire, England, came to Australia in 1854 and worked as a jackeroo in Queensland before entering the Methodist ministry in 1866. He was principal for forty-six years of the Methodist Ladies' College, Melbourne; columnist of the Methodist church paper, the *Spectator*, and editor of a Sunday family magazine, the *Southern Cross*, and the *Review of Reviews*. Fitchett published, in the Melbourne *Argus*, a series of articles that were collected in 1895 as *Deeds That Won the Empire*, a book that ran to thirty-five printings. Other popular historical narratives by Fitchett, under the pseudonym 'Vedette', include *Wellington's Men* (1900), *The Tale of the Great Mutiny* (1901), *Nelson and His Captains* (1902), *The New World of the South: Australia in the Making* (1903) and *The Romance of Australian History* (1913). Fitchett also wrote fiction, *The Commander of the Hirondelle* (1904), *Ithuriel's Spear* (1906), *A Pawn in the Game* (1908) and *The Adventures of an Ensign* (1917).

FITTON, Dame DORIS (1897–), born Manila of an English father and an Australian mother, was brought to Sydney at the age of five. She worked as a secretary before training as an actress with Gregan McMahon and subsequently acting with the Melbourne and Sydney Repertory Societies and in numerous J.C. Williamson productions. In 1930 she founded the Independent Theatre in Sydney, formed from the Turret Theatre repertory company. An important part of the Australian theatrical scene for almost half a century, the Independent provided both actors and playwrights with stage opportunities, producing plays by such authors as Sumner Locke Elliott, Sydney Tomholt, Catherine Shepherd, Gwen Meredith, Max Afford, Coral Lansbury, Douglas Stewart, Peter Kenna, Jack Hibberd, Richard Beynon, Alan Seymour and 'Betty Roland'. The staging of Sumner Locke Elliott's *Rusty Bugles* (q.v.) in 1948 was the Independent's most controversial production, resulting in the play's temporary banning by the NSW government. The Independent also produced a range of international plays and fostered the careers of numerous Australian actors, including Ruth Cracknell, John Meillon, Leonard Teale and Helen Morse. In 1977 lack of funds caused the Theatre's closure. Director of the Independent during its lifetime, Fitton also frequently produced plays or acted in its productions; she was made DBE in 1981. Her autobiography, *Not Without Dust & Heat* (1981), is also a history of the Independent.

FITZGERALD, JOHN DANIEL (1862–1922), born Shellharbour, NSW, was an apprentice printer in Bathurst, NSW, before joining the Sydney *Evening News* and later (1890–91) travelling to England and Europe as secretary of the Trades and Labour Council, seeking strike funds. He was editor of *Freeman's Journal* (1899–1904), was called to the Bar in 1900 and, as an alderman of the Sydney City Council (1900–04), was particularly concerned with town planning, housing and municipal reform. His close but stormy relationship with the Labor Party ended in 1916 with his expulsion over the conscription issue. His parliamentary career, which began in 1891, continued until 1920. In addition to publications such as *Greater Sydney and Greater Newcastle* (1906) and *The Rise of the Australian Labor Party* (1915), FitzGerald wrote fiction, *The Ring Valley* (1922) set in rural NSW in the 1860s and 1870s, and *Children of the Sunlight: Stories of Australian Circus Life* (1923). He also wrote *Studies in Australian Crime* (1924), a reference work on Australian crime fiction.

FITZGERALD, R.D. (ROBERT DAVID) (1902–), nephew of John le Gay Brereton (q.v.), was born at Hunters Hill, Sydney, where he has lived for much of his life. He attended the University of Sydney in 1920–21 but abandoned a science course for surveying. Like many young writers of the early 1920s, FitzGerald came under the influence of Norman Lindsay, and participated, with Hugh McCrae, Kenneth Slessor and Jack Lindsay, in the production of the journal, *Vision*, in which several of his early poems were published. In 1931–36 he was mostly in Fiji, surveying the vague, traditional boundaries of the tribal lands for the Native Lands Commission. In 1936–40 he was a private surveyor in Sydney, then municipal surveyor to the suburban councils of Manly and Ryde. Late in 1940 he joined the Commonwealth Department of the Interior, surveying sites for wartime aerodromes. He remained with the Department of the Interior after the war, ultimately becoming supervising surveyor of the NSW branch of the department prior to his retirement in 1965 . In 1951 he was made OBE; in 1965 he shared the Encyclopaedia Britannica Award; in 1982 he was made AM and a life member of ASAL. He gave public lectures in Australian literature at the Universities of Melbourne and Queensland in 1959 and 1961 respectively, published in 1963 as *The Elements of Poetry*, and in 1963 spent a semester as a visiting lecturer in poetry at the University of Texas. Best-known as a poet, FitzGerald has also been a prolific reviewer of, and influential commentator on, modern Australian writing.

His first collection of verse, *The Greater Apollo: Seven Metaphysical Songs* (1927), consists of short, meditative poems that reveal the predicament of man torn between the opposing attractions of the transcendent reality ('the Greater Apollo') and the material world. Although he recognizes its transience, FitzGerald chooses the visible world with its obvious delights – 'It is enough that trees are trees/ That earth is earth and stone is stone.' His comment in the fourth part of 'The Greater Apollo', 'I look no more for gods among the lace-like ferns and twisted boughs', while further emphasizing his decision in favour of the actual, might also be taken to indicate the end of his relationship with the exotic fantasies of the *Vision* group. *To Meet the Sun* (1929), a collection of thirty-three poems including 'The Greater Apollo' series, won recognition in England where it was awarded, before it was published in Australia, the Bronze Medal of the Festival of Arts and Letters sponsored by the Panton Arts club. *Moonlight Acre* (1938), which contains two groups of short poems, 'Moonlight Acre' (the phrase occuring in the poem 'Invasion') and 'Copernicus', and two long poems, 'The Hidden Bole' and 'Essay on Memory' (qq.v.), won the Australian Literature Society's Gold Medal in 1938. It established FitzGerald, in the eyes of many, as the major Australian poet of the 1930s. 'The Hidden Bole', using as examples the banyan tree and the famous ballerina, Pavlova, examines the nature of Beauty, while 'Essay on Memory', which won the *Sydney Morning Herald*'s sesquicentenary prize for poetry in 1938, insists, in the complex and knotty manner of FitzGerald's long, speculative verse, on the vital influence of the past upon the present.

Heemskerck Shoals (1949) incorporates some shorter poems with the long dramatic monologue of that title, one of several works by FitzGerald with a Fijian background. The poem consists of the angry meditations of the Dutch seaman and explorer, Abel Tasman, after the near disaster of his expedition on the reef which he named Heemskerck Shoals, near Nanuku Island, Fiji, in 1643. *Between Two Tides* (1952), drawn from *An Account of the Natives of the Tongan Islands* by J.M. Martin (1817), is a very long poem on which FitzGerald had worked spasmodically over many years. It was awarded the Grace Leven Prize for poetry in 1952. In five parts, the poem relates and discusses the life and exploits of Will Mariner, a young sailor on the privateer, *Port au Prince*, which was attacked and burned by Tongan natives in 1806. Mariner survived the massacre of the crew and was adopted by the Tongan chief, Finau. The poem focuses on both Mariner and Finau, guiding the reader to an assessment of the two men and their achievements. Well-constructed and impressively written, the poem urges 'the necessity for advance in action', for it is only by 'acts of resolution' that any man can fashion himself a recognizable identity. At the same time it recognizes the fragility of individual human existence, which lasts only 'between two tides', the new, incoming tide washing away all traces of the individual's efforts and achievements. *This Night's Orbit* (1953) reprinted two of FitzGerald's most important poems, 'The Face of the Waters' (q.v.), which meditates on the Creation, and 'Fifth Day', an incident from the trial of Warren Hastings. 'The Wind at Your Door' (q.v.), a poem based on a convict-flogging incident which involved FitzGerald's ancestor, Martin Mason, was published in the *Bulletin* (1958) and published separately in 1959. *South-most Twelve* (1962), incorporating the poems written after *This Night's Orbit*, includes the series 'Eleven Compositions: Roadside' and the well-known 'Bog and Candle', published in *Meanjin* (1960). 'The Wind at Your Door' and *South-most Twelve* won the Grace Leven Prize for poetry in 1959 and 1962 respectively. Fitz-Gerald's Australian Poets selection and his American volume *Of Some Country*, published by the University of Texas, both appeared in 1963 and were followed in 1965 by *Forty Years' Poems*. It contains most of his later work and an opening section, 'Salvage', which reprints, with revisions, all the poems that FitzGerald wished to retain from the earliest period of his writing, 1922–30. The salvaged poems deal mainly with the alienation of the artist, e.g. 'Passed By', and romantic love, e.g. 'The Wall' and 'Black Woods'. After a considerable break he published *Product: Later Verses by Robert D. FitzGerald* (1977), its appearance a further proof of his lifetime principle of 'advance in action', of his Carlylean belief that 'Were it but the pitifullest infinitesimal fraction of a Product, produce it, in God's name!'. Some of the poems express his protest at Australia's participation in the Vietnam War, others recreate early colonial times in Australia. In 'Just Once', his judgement of the present ('This age of shoddy') seems out of keeping with his normally-optimistic view of life and humanity. *Of Places and Poetry*, a collection of FitzGerald's prose, appeared in 1976. He edited a volume of Mary Gilmore's verse in 1963 and the letters of Hugh McCrae in 1970.

FitzGerald has never been a popular or fashionable poet. His use of poetry for the carriage of complex, philosophical ideas and for the examination of abstract, intellectual concepts has made him inaccessible to all but the most persevering and dedicated of readers. Even expert literary opinions of his work have varied widely and the prestige he enjoyed from the late 1930s to the 1960s has lately diminished. Some fellow poets and critics have judged his work, in spite of its integrity and painstaking conscientiousness, as ungainly, lacking in lyricism, grace and spontaneity: Vincent Buckley, for example, has said that 'Essay on Memory' moves with 'an arthritic goosestep'. Even when the qualities of wisdom, humanity, courage and sturdy optimism are admitted in his poetry, the poetry itself is seen as uninspiring and unmemorable. Opinions to the contrary are also widely held. He continues to be praised as a true and even great poet and has been judged, with Kenneth Slessor, as the major inflence that compelled modern Australian poetry to address itself, in a professional manner, to a range of intellectual, philosophical and metaphysical themes that it had rarely attempted before. *R.D. FitzGerald* in the Portable Australian Authors series, was published in 1985, edited by Julian Croft.

FITZPATRICK, BRIAN (1905–65), born Cudgee near Koroit, Victoria, embraced radical socialism when he became a philosophy student at the University of Melbourne in 1921. He began a career of journalism in 1927 but resigned from the Melbourne *Herald* in 1935. During the Second World War he worked for the Labor government and was subsequently a writer and freelance journalist. A regular columnist for *Smith's Weekly* during the 1940s, he began in 1947 publishing the journal, *Australian Democrat*, which was replaced by *Australian News Review* in 1951; from 1958 until his death he edited *Labor Newsletter*. He became general secretary in 1937 for the Australian Council for Civil Liberties and his name has become synonymous with that organization and its aims. Fitzpatrick published *British Imperialism and Australia* (1939), a work which set Australia's beginnings in the context of social and economic changes then occurring in England, and which won the Harbison-Higinbotham scholarship of the University of Melbourne. Its sequel was *The British Empire in Australia: An Economic History 1834–1939* (1941). His other works were *A Short History of the Australian Labor Movement* (1940), *The Australian People* (1946), *The Australian Commonwealth* (1956) and, with E.L. Wheelwright, *The Highest Bidder* (1965). Fitzpatrick's writings reflect his ideology: his economic works are radical reinterpretations of Australian economic history, his idiosyncratic social histories

are based upon his radical socialist ideals. Don Watson published the biography, *Brian Fitzpatrick: A Radical Life* (1979).

FITZPATRICK, JOHN CHARLES (1862–1932), born Moama, NSW, served a printing apprenticeship then worked on the *Melbourne Punch* (1880) before becoming a journalist on country newspapers in Goulburn, Gunnedah, Narrabri and Parramatta. In 1888 he established the *Windsor and Richmond Gazette*, controlling it until 1899; subsequently he owned the *Molong Argus*, 1904–07. A long-time member of the NSW Legislative Assembly (1895–1930), Fitzpatrick was also the author of several local histories and travel books including *Good Old Days of Windsor* (1900), *Eastward Ho* (1905), *Jaunt to Java* (1908) and *Good Old Days of Molong* (1913).

FITZPATRICK, KATHLEEN ELIZABETH (1905–), born Omeo, Victoria, became associate professor in the department of history, University of Melbourne, where she taught 1930–62. She wrote the biography, *Sir John Franklin in Tasmania, 1837–1843* (1949), and edited *Australian Explorers* (1958), one of the first anthologies of the writings of such explorers as Gregory Blaxland, John Oxley, Hamilton Hume, William Hovell, Alan Cunningham, Charles Sturt, T.L. Mitchell, Edward John Eyre, Ludwig Leichhardt, John McDouall Stuart, Robert O'Hara Burke, William John Wills and Ernest Giles. Her monograph, *Martin Boyd* (1963), provoked a response, 'Dubious Cartography', by Boyd in *Meanjin Quarterly* (1964). She also published a history of Presbyterian Ladies College, Melbourne, in 1975 and *Solid Bluestone Foundations* (1983), which encompasses the years 1908–28 and recalls her childhood in Melbourne and her student years in Australia and at Oxford.

Fitzrot, a Victorian anarchic poetry magazine edited by Peter Oustabasidis ('Pi O') (q.v.), was published 1975–77. *Fitzrot* was originally intended to publish poetry from the varied ethnic groups of inner Melbourne, especially Fitzroy. *Fitzrete* was an issue of *Fitzrot* devoted to concrete poetry (q.v.) and *Period* an issue devoted to women's poetry, both in 1975. Fitzrot Publications produced several volumes of contemporary poetry.

'Five Bells', the title poem of Kenneth Slessor's (q.v.) volume of poetry published in 1939 and acknowledged as his major work, is a meditation, compressed into memory's own time scale as a ship's bell rings five bells in Sydney Harbour, on Slessor's drowned friend, Joe Lynch. Able to recapture only disconnected, trivial scraps of the dead man's past existence and unsuccessful in his attempt to understand the significance of Joe Lynch's life, or to decide what purpose gave him life at all, Slessor is forced to an admission of the futility of human existence. Although the emphasis is on the impermanence of all human relationships and thus the triumph of time (moved by 'little fidget wheels') over life, the affection expressed for the scruffy, unruly, unimportant Irishman gives the poem a tender and human character.

'Five Days Old', a poem by Francis Webb (q.v.), was first published in the *Bulletin* 30 April 1958. The background to the poem, according to Webb's friend, Sister M. Francisca Fitz–Walter, was that a kindly doctor, hoping to renew Webb's interest in life and to restore his desire to write, placed a five-day old baby named Christopher John in Webb's arms. His response,

> I am launched upon sacred seas
> Humbly and utterly lost,
> In the mystery of creation,

has made the brief lyric one of Webb's most poignant poems.

'Five Visions of Captain Cook', first published in *Trio* (1931) by Kenneth Slessor (q.v.), builds the character of Captain James Cook (q.v.) from the reactions of those who sailed with him on his three major voyages. Based on Cook's journals and other contemporary writings, the poem is an important contribution to the voyager theme in Australian literature. The first section, focusing on the first *Endeavour* voyage of 1768–71, recounts Cook's historic decision to sail 'westabout' to Australia. The final section, the most attractive part of the poem, reviews the golden days with Cook through the nostalgic memories of retired sea-captain, Alexander Home. Full of memorable lines that attest to Slessor's delight in language, the poem is distinguished by its characterization of Cook and Captain Home and demonstrates that men who change the face of the world inevitably change the lives of those who associate with them.

'FLACK, JAMES', see LINDSAY, NORMAN

FLANAGAN, RODERICK (1826–62), born County Roscommon, Ireland, came to Australia in 1840 and worked with the *People's Advocate* and the Melbourne *Daily News* before founding the brief-lived weekly, *Chronicle*, in Sydney in 1851. He joined the *Empire* in 1852 and published in it a series of articles in 1853 on the Aborigines, later published as *The Aborigines*

of Australia (1888). In 1854 he joined the *Sydney Morning Herald*; in 1862 his *History of New South Wales with an Account of Van Diemen's Land, New Zealand, Port Phillip, Moreton Bay and Other Australasian Settlements* was published. A collection of his verse, *Australian and Other Poems*, was published in 1887.

'Flash Jack from Gundagai' is an Australian folk-song in which a shearer, the self-proclaimed Flash Jack from Gundagai, sings of the shearing sheds and practices he has experienced. Several times in the song Flash Jack pays tribute to 'Old Tom Patterson on the One Tree Plain'. Patterson was a pastoralist who took up Ulong station in the Riverina in 1871 and added to his holding until it measured more than 120 000 hectares and took in the whole of the One Tree Plain.

'Flash Jim Vaux', see BLAIR, RON; VAUX, JAMES HARDY

Flaunted Banners, see KENNEDY, VICTOR

Flaws in the Glass, by Patrick White (q.v.), was published in 1981. A collage of his memories of himself from an early age, significant emotional experiences, artistic and religious growth and relationships with family, friends and enemies, *Flaws in the Glass* is a remarkably frank study which has numerous links with his fiction. White's early memories of parents, relatives, servants and nannies are dominated by a sense of difference; born to extrovert, unimaginative parents who are leisured, wealthy and philistine, he is aware of emotions, gifts and interests which are alien to their experience and expectations. Sent at fourteen to an English boarding school, which he hates, he nourishes his creative gifts and memories of the Australian landscape: 'Till well into my life, houses, places, landscape meant more to me than people . . . It was landscape which made me long to return to Australia while at school in England'. During the grazier's son's compulsory spell as a jackeroo, in the Monaro and at Walgett, NSW, he writes three 'immature' novels. After taking his degree in modern languages at Cambridge, he decides to try a writing career in London, supported by an allowance from his father. In London he mingles in bohemian and artistic circles and meets the painter, Roy de Maistre, who influences his attitudes to art, music, writing and sex. He is in the USA negotiating the publishing of *Happy Valley* when the Second World War breaks out, but he returns to London and later joins the RAF as an Intelligence Officer. Posted to the Middle East he experiences the tedium, futility and occasional danger of war in the desert and in 1941 meets Manoly Lascaris, his future life-companion. A year in Palestine provides him with a highly-varied human experience and an insight into the Jewish consciousness. A year in Greece is such a fundamentally important experience that he contemplates remaining there, although he fears becoming 'the beachcomber all foreigners become when they settle in Greece – tolerated, but never much more than a joke'. He is demobbed in London, begins to write *The Aunt's Story* and returns to Australia to prepare for Manoly's arrival. Reunited with his mother, Ruth, and his old nurse, Lizzie, he re-experiences feelings of ambivalence towards the first and of empathy with the second. After Manoly's arrival in Australia, they settle on a small holding at Castle Hill on the outskirts of Sydney, where White writes his novels *The Tree of Man* and *The Solid Mandala*. In 1963 they move to more congenial surroundings near Centennial Park, Sydney. The last two sections of *Flaws in the Glass* are titled 'Journeys' and 'Episodes and Epitaphs'; 'Journeys' describes White and Lascaris's travels in Greece, interspersed with White's individual journeys into the recesses of the unknown self: 'The masks I put on in my fictions are very different from those which strangers try to force on me, or to use another metaphor, the characters of whom I am composed cannot include those not yet revealed to me. At the age of sixty-nine I am still embarking on voyages of exploration which I hope may lead to discovery'. 'Episodes and Epitaphs' deals with some significant incidents in White's life, including his late involvement in political issues and his relationships with other writers and artists.

FLEMING, W.M. (WILLIAM MONTGOM-ERIE) (1874–1961), born Avon Plains in the Wimmera district of Victoria, spent much of his life as a State and federal parliamentarian. His literary achievements lie mainly in the field of children's literature, e.g. *Bunyip Says So* (1922) and *The Hunted Piccaninnies* (1927), highly-imaginative short stories based on the Aboriginal understanding of animals and nature. A regular contributor of verse and prose to the *Sydney Morning Herald* and the *Bulletin*, Fleming also wrote a novel, *Broad Acres* (1939), which was made into a radio serial for the ABC in 1940.

Flesh and the Spirit, The, see STEWART, DOUGLAS

Flesheaters, The, see IRELAND, DAVID

Flesh in Armour (1932), the first novel by Leonard Mann (q.v.), is a fictional account,

based to some degree on Mann's own experiences, of the AIF in action on the Western Front in France in the First World War. Unable to find a publisher for the novel in England or Australia, Mann published it himself. The novel's central character is the ex-schoolteacher, now corporal, Frank Jeffreys, a nervous, introverted and sensitive soldier who spends his time at the Front in an agony of fear. On leave in London he meets Mary Hatton, who has already had a brief wartime intimacy with Jeffreys's fellow Australian, a rather callow youth, Charley Bentley. Frank and Mary write to each other, fall in love and plan to marry. Frank, however, learns of her affair with Bentley and kills himself with a grenade. Although the Mary–Frank romance runs throughout the novel, most of the book is set in France where the Australian division acquits itself superbly, especially in the opinion of the author, in the battles of the Somme, Ancre, Villers Bretto-neux, Ypres and Mont St Quentin. Jim Blount is the novel's archetypal Australian digger, irreverent of authority, competent and coldly effective in hand-to-hand combat with the enemy but warm-hearted and generous with his Australian mates. He dies charging the enemy trenches single-handed. The battle scenes and characterization lose little by comparison with Frederic Manning's *Her Privates We* (1930), but the novel has attracted some criticism because of Mann's excessive praise of the Australian fighting soldier.

FLETCHER, CHARLES BRUNSDON (1859–1946), born Somerset, England, came to Sydney as a boy of thirteen with his parents, who had earlier emigrated to NZ. Trained as a surveyor, Fletcher turned to journalism in 1893, joined the *Brisbane Courier* as a leader-writer and became its editor in 1898. In 1903 he returned to Sydney as associate editor of the *Sydney Morning Herald* and was its editor 1918–37. One of Fletcher's prime concerns, on which he wrote three books, was the security of the Pacific and the need for Australian interest in its development. His book *The Black Knight of the Pacific* (1944) was a biography of the Pacific Methodist missionary, Dr George Brown. Among his Australian works was *Water Magic: Australia and the Future* (1945) on water conservation. His autobiography, *The Great Wheel: An Editor's Adventures* (1940), is an illuminating account of the newspaper world.

FLETCHER, HENRY (1856–1932), born London, came to Australia in 1872, and lived an itinerant life in Australia, NZ, France and England. He published six works of fiction, including four which chronicled the fortunes of the Wayback (q.v.) family: *The Waybacks* in *Town and at Home* (1902), *Dads Wayback: His Work* (1904), *Dads and Dan: Between Smokes* (1908) and *The Waybacks Again: Or, Love at Dingo Flat* (1909). An unsophisticated rural family, the Waybacks, who were also the subject of a 1918 film, were modelled on the Rudd family (q.v.) of 'Steele Rudd'.

'Flight of Wild Geese, A', a highly-regarded poem by Harold Stewart (q.v.) published in his first volume of verse, *Phoenix Wings* (1948), depicts an imaginary incident concerning Wu Tao-tzu, the great Chinese artist who was commissioned by the Emperor Ming Huang of the T'ang Dynasty to paint a landscape roll. The poem's opening gloss indicates that Wu so enters into the spirit of the scene that he can walk about in the picture at will. One day he wanders over a distant mountain in the roll and is never seen again. During his wanderings Wu meets Chang Chih-ho, 'the Old Fisherman of the Waters and the Mists'. Their ensuing conversation is conducted with traditional Oriental decorum. Wu believes the old man to be evading life by his self-imposed exile; Chang responds that he 'fled not from the world but into it'. The conversation, charged with subtleties and innuendos that range deep into Oriental religious philosophies, is interrupted and illuminated by the sudden arrival and abrupt departure of a flight of geese.

FLINDERS, MATTHEW (1774–1814), born Lincolnshire, England, entered the Royal Navy at the age of fifteen, sailed as a midshipman with Vice-Admiral William Bligh to Tahiti in 1791, and was at the naval battle the 'Glorious First of June'. He went to Port Jackson in 1795 in HMS *Reliance* in which George Bass was ship's surgeon, explored the coast around Sydney with Bass in the *Tom Thumb*, circumnavigated Van Diemen's Land with Bass in 1798–99 and returned to England where he published *Observations on the Coasts of Van Diemen's Land, on Bass's Strait and Its Islands, and on Part of the Coasts of New South Wales* (1801). From January to May 1802 Flinders, in command of HMS *Investigator*, mapped the coastline from Fowler's Bay on the Great Australian Bight to Port Jackson, then charted north along the Queensland coast, through Torres Strait and the Gulf of Carpentaria, and completed the circumnavigation of the continent, returning to Port Jackson in June 1803. That momentous voyage proved that Australia was 'Terra Australis', the Great South Land. On his way back to England later that year, Flinders put into Port Louis, Mauritius, seeking water and provisions. He was arrested and held on the island by the French governor, de Caen, until 1810, when he was allowed to return to

England. From 1810 until his death Flinders worked on the memorable account of his experiences and explorations, *A Voyage to Terra Australis*, which he wished to title *A Voyage to Australia* but was dissuaded by Sir Joseph Banks. After the publication of *A Voyage to Terra Australis* (1814), in which Flinders writes 'Had I permitted myself any innovation upon the original term, it would have been to convert it into "Australia", as being more agreeable to the ear, and an assimilation of the names of the other great parts of the earth', the name 'Australia' began to be generally used. Flinders has been widely recognized in Australia; his name has been given to streets in towns and cities, to bays, islands, national parks, rivers, reefs and mountain ranges, to Australia's main naval base and to a university in Adelaide. His statues are in several Australian cities but the Mitchell Library in Sydney holds his manuscript collection, donated by his grandson, Sir William Matthew Flinders Petrie, because Sydney was the first city to erect a statue in his memory. Biographical works on Flinders include Ernest Scott's *The Life of Captain Matthew Flinders, R.N.* (1914), James D. Mack's *Matthew Flinders 1774–1814* (1966) and Ernestine Hill's fictional *My Love Must Wait* (q.v. 1941). In addition to his own *A Voyage to Terra Australis*, his explorations are described and assessed in K.A. Austin's *The Voyage of the Investigator 1801–1803* (1964) and Max Colwell's *The Voyages of Matthew Flinders* (1970). The poems 'Flinders' Map' by John Blight and 'Cape Catastrophe' by J.M. Couper recreate incidents from Flinders's career.

Floating World, The, a play by John Romeril (q.v.), was first performed by the Australian Performing Group in 1974 and published in 1975. Les Harding, a member of the AIF during the Second World War and a survivor of the Burma–Thailand railway, has embarked on an *Australian Women's Weekly* 'Cherry Blossom' cruise to Japan with his wife Irene. Les displays what Romeril regards as the worst characteristics of his generation – philistinism, xenophobia, racism and an aggressive masculinity that manifests itself in crude sexual jokes and gargantuan feats of beer consumption. Irene's natural habitat is lower-middle-class suburbia, with its mindless materialism, processed entertainment and false gentility. Unknown to Les the journey to Japan is about to bring him face to face with his inner, more sensitive self, which has been unable to forget the war, the deaths and sufferings of his mates, his hatred of the Japanese and his guilt that he survived. The blandness of current Australian–Japanese relations, meanwhile, is typified by the useless Dippy-Birds, mechanical drinking storks which are set in motion by the steward according to quaintly-phrased Japanese instructions. Against the impressionistically presented background of a pleasure cruise with its third-rate entertainment, pseudo-romance and familiar rituals, Romeril imposes Les's anguished hallucinations; a passenger, Williams, becomes McLeod, an old digger mate; the Malay steward, a Japanese soldier; and Robinson, an ex-RN officer, a spy from the RSL. As he retreats into the unreality of madness Les discovers his true reality, his floating world, where his paranoid identity is at least given coherent meaning by real enemies.

FLOWER, CEDRIC (1920–), born Sydney and best-known as a painter, has also written several studies of Australia's cultural life, including *Duck & Cabbage Tree: A Pictorial History of Clothes in Australia 1788–1914* (1968, 2nd edn 1984), *The Antipodes Observed: Prints and Printmakers of Australia 1788–1850* (1975), and *Illustrated History of New South Wales* (1981). He has also collaborated with his wife, Pat Flower, in writing for television, including a play, 'Love Returns to Umbrizi', and an award-winning film script, *From the Tropics to the Snow* (1963).

FLOWER, CHARLES AUGUSTUS (?1856–1948), born Port Fairy, Victoria, worked as a jackeroo in Victoria before settling in Queensland, where he overlanded sheep and was employed as an accountant for a firm of railway contractors; he was later a pastoralist for many years in the Roma district of central Queensland. He is credited by some folklorists with the authorship of the overlanding song, 'A Thousand Miles Away' (q.v.), which mentions the Roma railway, and 'The Broken-down Squatter', the lament of a pastoralist who has been forced by drought and high rents to give up his run. Similarly, Horace Alfred Flower, the elder brother of Charles (uncle in some less reliable accounts), is claimed as the author of another well-known Australian folk-song, 'The Dying Stockman' (q.v.).

FLOWER, PAT (1914–77), born Kent, England, came to Australia at the age of fourteen. A prolific writer of radio and television plays, she also wrote satirical sketches for Sydney's New Theatre and numerous crime novels, most of which were published in the Collins Crime Club series and translated into French, German and Italian. One of her television plays, 'The Tape-Recorder', the first play to be produced in colour by BBC 2, was also produced in Australia, Canada and the USA and was published in *The Best Short Plays 1969* (1970); another, 'Fiends of the Family', is included in

Take One (1972), ed. Richard Lane. In 1967 she won the Mary Gilmore Award for a one-hour television play, 'Tilley Landed on Our Shores'. With her husband, Cedric Flower, she wrote the award-winning film script, *From the Tropics to the Snow* (1963). Her novels include *A Wreath of Water-Lilies* (1960), *One Rose Less* (1961), *Cat's Cradle* (1973) and *Crisscross* (1976).

Fly Away Peter, see **MALOUF, DAVID**

Flying Doctor, see **FLYNN, JOHN**

Flying Fox and Drifting Sand (1938), by Francis Ratcliffe, is an account of inland Australia following two surveys Ratcliff undertook for the CSIRO: in 1929–31 when he investigated the flying foxes of Queensland, and in 1935 when he studied soil erosion from SA to Queensland. Ratcliffe's lively description of the wildlife of mangrove swamps and deserts and his anecdotes of outback personalities and incidents have made the book perennially popular.

FLYNN, ERROL (1909–59), the swashbuckling Hollywood film hero, was born in Hobart; his father, Theodore (1883–1968), was a prominent zoologist and his mother a descendant of a *Bounty* mutineer. After a rebellious childhood, mainly in Australia, Flynn spent several years adventuring in New Guinea before going into films. His heyday was 1935–42, when he played such roles as Captain Blood and Robin Hood. Flynn was a notorious playboy, thrice married and addicted in his later years to drugs, alcohol and young girls; his amorous adventures are said by some to have inspired the current colloquial Australianism, 'in like Flynn' (or 'in like Errol'), meaning to take advantage of a situation, particularly a sexual opportunity. Flynn wrote New Guinea columns for the *Bulletin*; a travel book, *Beam Ends* (1937); a novel, *Showdown* (1946); and the autobiographical *My Wicked, Wicked Ways* (1960). He is the subject of two biographical studies, J.H. Moore's *The Young Errol* (1975) and Charles Higham's *Errol Flynn* (1980); his abilities as an actor are analysed in *The Films of Errol Flynn* (1969) by T. Thomas, R. Behlmer and C. McCarty; and he is celebrated in Rob George's play, 'Errol Flynn's Big Adventure Book for Boys' (1979) and in Australian Crawl's popular song, 'Oh Errol'. Grahame Bond starred in the Flynn musical, 'Captain Bloody', in 1984.

FLYNN, JOHN (1880–1951), born Moliagul, Victoria, joined the Home Mission staff of the

Presbyterian Church of Victoria in 1902 and was ordained in 1911. In 1912 he was appointed superintendent of the Northern Territory mission area, a position he held for almost forty years. In 1928 he founded the Australian Inland Mission Aerial Service at Cloncurry, Queensland, later known as the Royal Flying Doctor Service. Made OBE in 1933, he was moderator–general of the Presbyterian Church of Australia 1939–42. Flynn published *The Bushman's Companion* (1910) and was editor of the *Outback Battler*, a quarterly magazine (1911–12), and of *Inlander*, another bush magazine (1913–29). He is the subject of Ion L. Idriess's *Flynn of the Inland* (1932) and W.S. McPheat's *John Flynn, Apostle to the Inland* (1963). He is also featured in Ernestine Hill's *Flying Doctor Calling* (1947) and H. Hudson's *Flynn's Flying Doctors* (1956).

Folk-Song and Ballad. In Australia the terms 'folk-song' and 'ballad' describe a body of songs, often but by no means always of anonymous authorship, which tell stories of or depict Australian life and which have had currency among ordinary Australian people as a result of oral performance, particularly between the early days of European settlement and the advent of recordings and the radio. The terms are generally used with others indicating the subject, period, type or audience of the songs, e.g. 'sung ballads', 'traditional songs', '(traditional) bush ballads', '(old) bush songs', 'popular ballads' and 'colonial ballads'. There are different views concerning the most important influences on Australian folk-songs, the major ways in which they were created, and the significance of oral transmission, dismissed by one folklorist as the 'Trench Mouth School of Folklore'. Commentators place little emphasis on the collective composition of the 'folk' (a process satirized as 'composition in committee' and 'immaculate conception'), but most accept that Australian folk-songs are part of popular culture; that they therefore articulate communal values, establishing the Australianness of the singer and the audience; and that the effects of oral transmission can be detected in the textual refinements over time of many songs, in the variants that exist for others (e.g. 'The Wild Colonial Boy', q.v.) and in the transfer of tunes between songs (e.g. 'A Thousand Miles Away', q.v.). No formal census of Australian folk-songs has been undertaken, and estimates vary from seventy to 1500 as to the number which have survived. Most folklorists, however, agree with a central canon of 250–400; among modern collections and indexes, Douglas Stewart's and Nancy Keesing's *Old Bush Songs* (1957) has the words of 216 songs, Hugh Anderson's (q.v.) *Australian Song Index 1828–1956* (1957) lists

375 titles and Ron Edwards's (q.v.) *The Big Book of Australian Folk Song* (1976) has the words and music of 308 songs as well as an index of 1800 published songs and recitations. Some of the folk-songs included in these tallies have as much right to be regarded as part of the folk culture of other countries; this is particularly true of transportation songs such as 'The Black Velvet Band' (q.v.) and 'Van Diemen's Land', which are set for a significant part of their narratives in the convicts' country of origin. These songs clearly originated overseas and were brought to Australia; recent research suggests that there were many similar songs (and many more than has been realized) which have an Australian content but have never had an Australian currency.

The three nineteenth-century experiences of European Australians which contributed most to the creation of Australian folk–song were transportation, the discovery of gold, and pastoral expansion in the period 1860–90. Transportation was the first, although very few of the earliest Australian songs and ballads dealing with the subject have survived; indeed the transportation song best known to modern Australians, 'Botany Bay'(q.v.), was not performed until the 1880s, well after the last convicts had arrived in eastern Australia. In that the popular version of 'Botany Bay' was originally a London parody 'transported' to Australia, it illustrates a common way Australian folk-songs have been created: by the parody, imitation, adaptation and other forms of borrowing from existing English, Irish and, later, American songs; sometimes the words, as in 'Sam Holt' (q.v.); sometimes the tunes, as in the widespread use of 'The Wearing of the Green'; and sometimes both, as in 'The Dying Stockman' (q.v.) which is the Australian remake of an English popular song sometimes set to an American melody, and a song which has itself been subsequently parodied. In that 'Botany Bay' is a music-hall parody of an 1820s broadside, it also illustrates two important influences on Australian folk-songs: the nineteenth-century popular theatre, and the street ballad which until about 1850 was as popular among certain classes as the modern tabloid newspaper and was thus a major source of news for the urban poor who comprised the bulk of the convicts. The traditional rural folk-ballad of the British Isles was less influential on Australian folk-song than either of these influences.

Most transportation songs are cautionary tales of poachers (e.g. 'Van Diemen's Land') or petty criminals tricked into crime (e.g. 'The Black Velvet Band'), usually told in the first person by the offenders themselves, by their victims (e.g. 'Maggie May') and occasionally by the loved ones they have left behind (e.g. 'A Thousand Miles Away'). The narrative element dominates most in the songs which seem to have emerged, like 'Botany Bay', after the cessation of transportation and are normally sung to jaunty, lilting or rollicking tunes. The most rollicking are 'Ten Thousand Miles Away' and 'Maggie May', partly because they are songs of seamen as well as of convicts. In contrast, the folk-songs which can be more firmly dated to the time of transportation (e.g. 'Van Diemen's Land', 'The Convict Maid', 'The Exile of Erin', 'Jim Jones at Botany Bay', q.v.) and the compositions associated with Francis MacNamara (q.v., 'Frank the Poet') notably 'Labouring with the Hoe' and 'Moreton Bay' (q.v.), are descriptive rather than narrative, focusing on the dismal experiences of the convicts once they have arrived in Australia. In general, the protagonists in these songs lament their lives as felons but are relatively compliant towards the social systems which led to their transportation. This is not the case, however, with 'Moreton Bay' and 'Jim Jones at Botany Bay', among the most haunting of all Australian songs, which both strike a defiant note at the end. The exhilaration of the convict in 'Moreton Bay' at the death of the tyrannical commandant, Patrick Logan, and the vow of Jim Jones to join the bushranger 'Bold Jack Donahoo' (see Donohoe, John) in order to 'shoot the floggers down', provide the kind of evidence supporting speculations that the reason more of the songs sung by the convicts have not survived is that as treason songs they were banned by the penal authorities. Certainly in later decades it could be dangerous to sing 'The *Catalpa*' (q.v.) in front of the authorities in Fremantle and the Ned Kelly (q.v.) songs to bush policemen in Victoria; certainly also 'Moreton Bay' and 'Jim Jones at Botany Bay' are among the first Australian protest songs, helping to inaugurate a tradition of anti-authoritarian sentiment, often thought to be a national virtue, which accommodates the best-known Australian song of any description, 'Waltzing Matilda' (q.v.). In tone, the tradition ranges from the lightly mocking irreverence of 'The *Catalpa*' to the revolutionary calls of some shearers ballads of the 1890s. In time, it ranges from convict songs like 'Moreton Bay' through the convict-bushranger songs centred on Bold Jack Donahoe, who is linked with his legendary descendant, 'The Wild Colonial Boy', because both 'scorn to live in slavery/bound down by iron chains'; then through the bushrangers, themselves part of a wider highwayman-Robin Hood tradition, of the 1860s and 1870s, notably Ben Hall (q.v.) and Ned Kelly, who sang 'The Wild Colonial Boy' at Glenrowan and quoted 'Moreton Bay' in the Jerilderie Letter; next through the songs of the pastoral workers, which have been called

'democratic in the extreme'; and reaching finally into modern times in such songs as Frank Hardy's 'Sydney Town' and in the work of Eric Bogle and the band, Redgum, among contemporary 'folk' commentators. The strong Irish connection in the convict and bushranger songs gives an anti-English dimension to the protest tradition.

By the time transportation to eastern Australia ceased in 1853, the first official discoveries of gold had been made, stimulating the immigration of 'new chum' diggers who, like Billy Barlow and Paddy Malone (qq.v.) of earlier days and the new chum jackeroos of the subsequent pastoral expansion, were the targets for the 'old hands'. Collectively the experiences of the new chums make up one of the categories into which collections of Australian folk-songs are normally arranged; that apart, the goldfields are significant in Australian folk-song less for the intrinsic quality of the surviving songs than for the fact that the kaleidoscopic nature of goldfields society meant the introduction of new musical influences and instruments. With the exception of a song like 'The Old Palmer Song', which grew out of and is almost a variant of 'Ten Thousand Miles Away', the songs of the goldfields were seldom anonymous and clearly identifiable folk-songs. This is mainly because the gold rushes attracted to Australia a wide range of professional entertainers, including the notorious Lola Montez, Shakespearean actors such as G.V. Brooke, and troubadours who entertained their audiences by adopting the ditties they had learnt and played in the music-halls of England to the new conditions of Ballarat and elsewhere. The best was the inimitable Charles Thatcher (q.v.), the 'Bard of Bendigo', whose compositions smack of the concert-hall but gained currency beyond it because they were published in one of his series of songsters. When in time, as with songs like 'Look Out Below', they gained through oral transmission a currency beyond both the composer and his songster, they became part of Australian folk-song. In a similar way, other folk-songs which began life as literary compositions have passed from print into oral circulation and thus into the mainstream of Australian folk-song: the songs which derive from the literary balladists of the 1880s and 1890s came into this category, as also do such well-known songs as 'The Eumerella Shore' and 'Ladies of Brisbane' (qq.v.).

Thatcher, it is said, earned far more singing than he ever did puddling or panning. His lack of success paralleled that of the diggers at large, many of whom became itinerants like the miner turned pastoral worker in 'With My Swag All on My Shoulder':

With my swag all on my shoulder
Black billy in my hand
I've travelled the bush of Australia
Like a true-born native man.

The half-century or so after the gold rushes, roughly from 1860 to the outbreak of the First World War, are years covering the decades of major pastoral expansion. They are also the years in which the bush became the dominant subject of Australian folk-song; hence, given also that the bulk of Australian folk-songs dates from this period, the generalized use of terms like 'bush songs' and 'bush ballads'. Songs such as 'The Cocky Farmer' and 'The New England Cocky' chronicle the experiences of the small-scale, 'cockatoo' farmer who tried to grub a living from the land after the passing of the Selection Acts in the 1860s. His erstwhile enemy on the pastoral frontier was the squatter, whose own struggle is recorded in 'The Broken-down Squatter' and 'The Eumeralla Shore'. Allied with the squatter was the 'cadet' jackeroo, whose songs alternated from wonderment at the novelty of bush life to despair at its harshness (e.g. 'The Dying Stockman'). The greatest proportion of Australian folk-songs from this period, however, focus on the men who serviced, albeit grudgingly, e.g. 'Cockies of Bungaree', 'Goorianawa', both selector and squatter: the bush workers, the drovers (although some of the drovers were intending selectors or failed squatters), bullockies, swagmen, shearers and other pastoral nomads of Russel Ward's *The Australian Legend* (q.v., 1958). Mostly isolated on the one hand from the homestead culture of those settled on the land, and on the other from the centres of popular entertainment in the towns and cities, these itinerant bucolics, particularly the shearers, constituted a ballad community which made its own entertainment, often in ways that expressed their collectivist ethic. Their heroes were the bushrangers and others who snubbed their noses at authority. They enjoyed their freedom, had an ambivalent attitude towards 'flashness', admired daring and despised cockies and new chum jackeroos, whose verses they took over and refined in a hard-bitten way, as is shown by a comparison between 'The Wooyeo Ball' and 'The Euabalong Ball' (q.v.). The songs of the bush workers reflect this ethos. Although there are inevitable differences, e.g. the songs of the drovers are action songs and tend to be longer, possibly because they were sung in the saddle, the differences are not as significant as the similarities. Most bush songs are celebrations rather than narratives; they describe aspects of pioneering life in the first person while preserving communal values, and name individual places and people while retaining the essential impersonality of the music of the

'folk'. Many of them come into the category of work or occupational songs (e.g. 'The Overlander', 'The Sandy Maranoa', 'Click Go the Shears', 'The Lime-juice Tub', Flash Jack From Gundagai', qq.v., 'The Old Bullock Dray'), in some cases asserting (e.g. 'The Ryebuck Shearer') or implying (e.g. 'The Overlander') the superiority of the singer to others in his occupation or the superiority of the occupation itself. The dominant mood of the work songs is an acceptance of the occupation bordering on swaggering cheerfulness, although there are some songs (e.g. 'The Backblocks Shearer', q.v.) in which these attitudes are satirized and others still which are rueful (e.g. the shanty songs 'Lazy Harrys'' q.v., 'All for Me Grog' and 'The Wild Rover'); sentimental (e.g. 'The Banks of the Condamine', q.v.) or lugubrious (e.g. 'The Dying Stockman' and other jackeroo songs, and most swagmen's songs). Despite the sentimental and the lugubrious, humour which is self-mocking and sardonic, as in most pioneering communities, is an important ingredient.

The Australian bush song seldom reflects, either in theme or melody, the earlier rural folk-ballads of England and Scotland. For example, very few of the bush songs are love songs, and those which are (e.g. 'The Bush Girl', 'The Banks of the Condamine', 'Ladies of Brisbane') characteristically depict the desertion of the female by the male worker using peripatetic necessity as an excuse; equally, very few of the bush songs have the wild, haunting melodies of the traditional rural ballads. Nevertheless, there remained, as in earlier periods, a strong influence from overseas which can be seen in the genre parallels with America (bushranger/outlaw, swagman/hobo, stockman/cowboy); in the links between individual songs and their parent songs in England, Ireland and America; in the imported dances; and in the accompanying instrumentation, although some singing was done unaccompanied and it was common to learn both words and tune from the acknowledged singer of a district.

The influence in the area of instrumentation is conveniently recorded in 'The Drovers's Dream', in which a stockman on watch at night falls asleep and dreams that the fauna put on a concert for him. Early on in the entertainment,

Three frogs from out the swamp where the
    atmosphere was damp,
Came out and gently sat upon a stone.
They unrolled their little swags, took from out
    their dilly bags,
The violin, the banjo and the bones.

The last line forms the title of John Manifold's (q.v.) brief study of bush music (1957); and what is significant about the instruments named is that the popularity of the violin as a folk instrument derived from the popularity of tavern and street fiddlers in eighteenth-century England and Ireland, and that the introduction of the banjo and the bones reflects the spread of the Christy and Negro minstrel culture beyond America. Among other instruments used, particularly for dancing, were the concertina and the accordion, a German instrument which provides the music at 'Steele Rudd''s story, 'Kate's Wedding'; the Jew's harp and the tin whistle; and a variety of 'indigenous' instruments such as the gum leaf, bullock bells, the bush bass (traditionally constructed of a tea chest body, a neck of hide or sapling wood, and a rawhide bow), and the lagerphone (beer bottle tops nailed to an upright). The popularity of the indigenous instruments, however, like that of the guitar and the mouth organ which are common instruments in modern bush bands, is a comparatively recent phenomenon; the emergence of the lagerphone, for example, can be linked specifically with the success of the 1950s bush musical *Reedy River* (q.v.). The instruments that were used in the nineteenth century have been seen as influential in the process of melodic erosion .of many Australian folk-song tunes. Roger Covell refers in *Australia's Music* (1967) to the 'slack-jawed gumminess' of much Australian folk-song, in part because of the unfortunate musical influence of the popular theatre but in part also because most of the songs were collected in a terminal form, after the Industrial Revolution and at 'the fag end of a tradition'

Beyond an acknowledgement of their 'vigour', 'vitality','immediacy' and 'authenticity', terms often used in tandem with others like 'rough', 'robust' and 'raw', very few claims have been made for the bush songs as poetry despite the occasional literary flourishes (e.g. the internal rhymes of 'The Drover's Dream') which are apparent also in the folk-songs of earlier times: e.g. in 'Frank the Poet''s ballad 'The Seizure of the *Cyprus Brig* in Recherche Bay' and 'Moreton Bay', which was originally a recitation piece rather than a song. More substantial claims have been made, though the genre is still regarded more as 'popular verse' or 'folk literature' than as 'literary poetry', for what is generally called the 'literary ballad': a set of rhyming verses written in a ballad metre, usually with an eye to publication (and thus more often of known authorship than the majority of folk-songs, and less often subject to refinement or erosion through oral transmission). From the beginning, the bush was a dominant subject of the literary ballad, although the form subsequently accommodated nautical and military subjects as well as occupying an urban landscape. Henry Kendall's

'Jim the Splitter' (1880), a satiric portrait of a bush woodcutter, is regarded by some commentators as an early Australian literary ballad. Ten years earlier Adam Lindsay Gordon, himself a dashing horseman and generally accepted as the first literary balladist, wrote 'The Sick Stockrider', 'From the Wreck', 'Wolf and Hound' and the other ballads that went into his *Bush Ballads and Galloping Rhymes* (1870). 'Jim the Splitter' is unlike much of Kendall's verse, and Gordon was a derivative writer who modelled himself on Tennyson, Swinburne and Browning. Yet descended from Gordon are the literary balladists clustered around the *Bulletin* (q.v.), who in the decades either side of 1900 helped liberate Australian literature by promoting, as much by the quantity as by the quality of their work, a distinctive, nationalist bush ethos. A.B. Paterson (q.v.) is by common consent the best of the balladists; among others who established a reputation in the *Bulletin* and elsewhere were his fellow 'equestrians', Barcroft Boake, Will Ogilvie and 'Breaker' Morant (qq.v.); the mining balladists, notably Edward Dyson (q.v.); bush humourists such as W.T. Goodge and Thomas E. Spencer (qq.v.); those who focused on farming communities, such as Charles Henry Souter and 'John O'Brien' (qq.v.); others whose range was eclectic, including Henry Lawson, G.H. Gibson ('Ironbark') and E.G. Murphy ('Dryblower') (qq.v.); and others still who went beyond the bush, notably E.J. Brady and later C.J. Dennis (qq.v.).

Although Gordon 'showed the way', in the words of one commentator, there were other influences operating on the literary balladists. That they were read so avidly is in part an effect of the spread of literacy in the latter part of the nineteenth century. At the same time they were part of a widespread movement towards ballad poetry, particularly among frontier communities. The popularity of Paterson, for example, paralleled the popularity of John Hay and Bret Harte in America, Robert Service in Canada, and Rudyard Kipling throughout the British Empire. Thirdly, and perhaps most important, the literary ballads were influenced by the existing folk-songs, despite differences between the two: principally, in the literary ballads, a greater emphasis on third-person action narratives (e.g. 'The Man from Snowy River', 'How McDougall Topped the Score', qq.v.); a more wide-ranging sympathy towards the inhabitants of the bush (thus the literary ballads less single-mindedly articulate the prejudices of the pastoral nomads); a greater empathy with and idealization of the land itself as well as of its inhabitants (e.g. 'Clancy of the Overflow', q.v.); and a greater attention to the rudiments of verse technique. Yet the differences are differences of degree rather than kind, and against them must be set the similarities in subject matter, in the importance of humour, in attitude (e.g. the admiration of the daring, albeit in different circumstances, of the Wild Colonial Boy and the Man from Snowy River), and in the unself-conscious use of the vernacular which is symptomatic both of a shared, positive response to 'Australianness' and of a common folk origin of the literary ballads and the bush songs. There is clear evidence also of cross-pollination. On the one hand, Paterson acknowledged that he had heard songs such as 'The Wild Colonial Boy' and 'The Old Bark Hut' in his youth (both are recalled also in Lawson's story, 'The Songs They Used to Sing'), and specific parallels exist between a song like 'The Dying Stockman' and a poem like 'The Sick Stockrider'. On the other, many of the literary ballads became recitation pieces which formed part of the repertoire of bush singers and entertainers such as Jack Moses (q.v.), and were printed side by side with folk-songs in the popular outback songsters; some of them (e.g. 'Andy's Gone with Cattle', 'The Bush Girl', 'Reedy River', 'The Shearer's Dream', 'The Streets of Forbes', 'Travelling down the Castlereagh') became folk-songs because they had tunes put to them and passed into oral circulation – a process which has continued, to judge by the popularity in 1980 of a musical version of 'Clancy of the Overflow'.

Perhaps the most significant link between the folk-songs and the literary ballads was forged in 1898, when Paterson began assembling the first collection of Australian folk-songs. Published in 1905 as The Old Bush Songs (q.v.), the collection sold widely and went through several editions between 1905 and 1932, in which songs additional to the original fifty-five were included; it introduced the bush song to many Australians, including important modern folklorists (e.g. John Meredith, q.v.). In the 1930s, the recitation booklets of 'Bill Bowyang' (see Vennard, Alexander Vindex), which continued a publishing tradition established on the goldfields and consolidated by the Bulletin Reciter, kept some of the Paterson texts in circulation.

Neither Paterson nor 'Bill Bowyang' included musical scores in their collections; the first collectors firmly to focus on this aspect of Australian folk-song were musicologists such as Percy Jones (q.v.) and folklorists such as A.L. Lloyd (q.v.), although some of Lloyd's reconstructions have been criticized by some Australian folklorists. In 1951 Vance Palmer's selection of Old Australian Bush Ballads was published, the first to include the music of the songs, restored by Margaret Sutherland. It appeared in the same year as the first of Ron Edwards and John Manifold's Bandicoot Ballads (1951–

55), a series of broadsheets which made available some of the convict songs; the convict songs had been largely ignored by Paterson, although the text of 'Moreton Bay' had been included in Will Lawson's Australian Bush Songs and Ballads (1944). In 1953 Dick Diamond's Reedy River, which incorporated several traditional songs and introduced urban audiences to the music and instruments of the bush, was successfully staged; it came at the beginning of a decade of intense activity, in collection and research as well as in performance, which confirmed the revival of interest in Australian folk-song. The revival subsequently accommodated folklorists such as Ron Edwards, Bill and Alan Scott, Hugh Anderson, Wendy Lowenstein and John Meredith; scholars with university connections, including Russel Ward (q.v.) and Edgar Waters; and established writers such as John Manifold (q.v.), Douglas Stewart and Nancy Keesing. Working sometimes in isolation and sometimes in partnership, they substantially enlarged the corpus of Australian folksong by fieldwork among the surviving traditional singers (e.g. Simon McDonald, Duke Tritton, qq.v.; Sally Sloane, Joseph Cashmere and 'Hoop-Iron' Jack Lee) and by research in the libraries which unearthed important sources such as the early newspapers and songsters, and the reminiscences of Jack Bradshaw and Charles MacAlister (qq.v.).

In time, these research workers published collections or studies which reflected their individual emphases; often the collections were cumulative in that they incorporated or consolidated material previously published in broadsheets, chapbooks, pamphlets and journals, or were subsequently revised and expanded. Hugh Anderson's The Story of Australian Folksong (1970), an expansion of his earlier Colonial Ballads (1955, 1962), and Ron Edwards's The Big Book of Australian Folk Song (1976), which incorporates material from successive editions of his The Overlander Song Book (first published in 1956) as well as from his Black Bull Chapbooks (1954–57), Bandicoot Ballads and other compilations, are examples of cumulative collections. Among other anthologies the most important are Stewart and Keesing's Old Bush Songs (1957), which takes the Paterson text as its basis, and Australian Bush Ballads (1955), both reprinted under their original and other titles; John Manifold's The Penguin Australian Song Book (1964); Bill Scott's The Second Penguin Australian Song Book (1976); and Russel Ward's The Penguin Book of Australian Ballads (1964). These anthologies usually have important introductions or notes on the groupings, origins, significance or transmission of Australian folk-songs. These subjects are also addressed in specialist studies (e.g.

Anderson's study of Thatcher, *The Colonial Minstrel*, 1960); in Manifold's imaginative, speculative left-wing interpretation, *Who Wrote the Ballads? Notes on Australian Folk Song* (1964) and Anderson's *Farewell to Old England* (1964); in more broadly-based works, e.g. Ward's *The Australian Legend*, H.M. Green's *A History of Australian Literature* (1961) and several folklore compilations; in anthology-commentary combinations (e.g. Anderson's and Meredith's *Folk Songs of Australia and the Men and Women Who Sang Them*, 1967); and in journals ranging from the literary-cultural (e.g. *Meanjin*) to the specialist folklore magazines (e.g. *Singabout, Gumsucker's Gazette, Australian Tradition*, q.v.; *National Folk*) which were issued by the Sydney Bush Music Club, the Australian Folklore Society, the Folk Lore Society of Victoria and other emerging bush music and folklore societies.

As the dates of some of these works indicate, the revival of interest in Australian folk-song continued into the 1960s, attracting the interest of coffee-shop proprietors and corporation recording companies whose executives probably noted the success of some of the Wattle Records (1954–62). The coffee shops no longer employed folk-singers by the end of the 1960s, but in the 1970s and 1980s interest had periodically been renewed: Anderson, Meredith, Manifold, Edwards and others have continued research and publication, folklore festivals have continued to be held, and in Sydney a successful business in recording and publishing has been established by Warren Fahey (q.v.). Given the major contribution of the bush to Australian folk-song, it is ironic that the modern folk-song movement is essentially an urban phenomenon, centred in the universities and in the trade unions; hence the attraction of the old protest songs and their influence on contemporary songwriters like John Dengate and Eric Bogle. In general, Australian country-dwellers have long forsaken traditional music in favour of travelling country-western shows featuring such singers as Buddy Williams, Reg Lindsay, Slim Dusty and Chad Morgan. Although in some of their songs they draw on an indigenous tradition (Morgan's 'The Fatal Wedding' has parallels with 'The Dying Stockman', and Rolf Harris's 'Tie Me Kangaroo Down Sport' is even more firmly linked), their models are overwhelmingly American: the rural city of Tamworth, NSW, promoted as the home of Australian country music, copies Nashville, Tennessee. Country-western singers such as Lindsay and Morgan are often dismissed as derivative 'hillbillies' by Australian folklorists yet it was an Australian, John Edwards, who provided the impetus for the scholarly study of country-western music. After the death of

Edwards in 1960, his collections formed the basis of the John Edwards Memorial Foundation, established in 1962 at the University of California at Los Angeles, where there is a folklore centre. There is no equivalent centre for the study of Australian folk-song.

FOOTT, MARY HANNAY (1846–1918), born Glasgow, Scotland, came to Australia in 1853 and went in 1887 with her husband, Thomas Wade Foott, to take up land in southwest Queensland. After her husband's death in 1884 she went to Brisbane, where she opened a private school and contributed to the *Queenslander* and *Brisbane Courier*; she joined the staff of the *Queenslander* in 1887 and was its literary editor for about a decade, writing verse and stories, sometimes under the pseudonym 'La Quenouille'. She published two books of verse, *Where the Pelican Builds and Other Poems* (1885), expanded as *Morna Lee and Other Poems* (1890). Her best-known poem, frequently anthologized, is 'Where the Pelican Builds'; it records, from the viewpoint of the waiting women, the tragedy that so frequently struck the pioneer families – the loss of loved ones who were drawn by the lure of the land further out.

'For gorsake stop laughing – this is serious!' was the title of a famous cartoon by Stan Cross (q.v.), first published in *Smith's Weekly* in 1933. The cartoon depicts a workman hanging precariously from a girder on top of a building as he remonstrates in the words of the punch line with a second workman; the second workman has fallen and in seizing the other's trousers has yanked them down over the ankles and is now convulsed with laughter. The cartoon was reprinted and distributed widely, becoming a standard adornment of barbers' shops and hotel bars. It has been seen as an assault on dignity, archetypal of humour in general and of Australian humour in particular.

For Love Alone, a novel by Christina Stead (q.v.), was published in 1944. Set in Sydney and London in the 1930s, it is the story of Teresa Hawkins, an intelligent, ardent young woman, and her search for the ideal passion of love. She attempts to engage the feelings of the unworthy Jonathan Crow, an intellectual young man and advocate of free love, and follows him to London after four years of severe self-sacrifice. In London the mediocrity, corruption and egoistic shallowness of Crow gradually becomes obvious. With the help of James Quick, however, a devoted older man who takes Teresa to live with him, she is able to abandon her idealized vision. After a brief interlude with Quick's friend, Harry Girton,

Teresa advances to new, more detached appreciation of passion and renews her commitment to Quick in full awareness of the compromises that love imposes.

For the Term of His Natural Life, see *His Natural Life*

FORBES, 'ALEXANDER' (WILLIAM ANDERSON) (1839–79), born Banffshire, Scotland, was sent down from King's College, Aberdeen, for a youthful misdemeanour ('either snowballing or lampooning a professor') and came to Australia in 1862, wandering outback Queensland in a variety of menial jobs. His early Australian poems express resentment at his exile and disgust with the colonial environment. Gradually inured to the hardships of colonial life by alcohol, tobacco and the adoption of a rueful, ironic pose, Forbes, known widely as 'Alick the Poet', recovered from his nostalgia for Scotland and began to sing the praises of bush life. He published, as 'Alexander' Forbes, *Voices from the Bush* (1869); one of the earliest bush balladists, he caught in his verse the humour and tragedy of the bush experience.

FORBES, JOHN (1950–), born Melbourne, lived much of his early life in New Guinea, Malaya and Sydney. He won the Poetry Society of Australia award in 1972; the H.M. Butterley–F. Earle-Hooper *Southerly* Award for a young writer in 1976 for the poem, 'Breakfast'; and was granted a travelling fellowship in 1975. He has co-edited the journal *Leatherjacket*; edits the magazine, *Surfers Paradise*; and has published three volumes of poetry, *Tropical Skiing* (1976), *On the Beach* (1977) and *Stalin's Holidays* (1980).

Forefathers (1983) by Nancy Cato (q.v.), described by one reviewer as Australia's *Roots*, is an epic of Australian life covering the period 1824–1969. Tracing the fluctuating fortunes of three families, the Forbes, the Kings and the Browns, over seven generations, as their lives cross and re-cross, it links them with almost every important event in Australia in that period. The first book (1824–94) introduces a Tasmanian squatting family, the Forbes, and Canadian patriot–convict Jamie Brown and his family, and ends on a sheep station in Victoria. The second book (1870–1930) follows members of the Brown family through the shearing sheds of NSW and Queensland, through the beginnings of unionism with the shearers, and into the cane-cutting area of Queensland, where the kanaka people enter the story. The second book ends with Chukka, grandson of Jamie, too old for cane-cutting, becoming 'a swagman,

"Waltzing Matilda" over the dusty roads and camping beside the dry watercourses of inland Australia'. The third book (1853–1933) introduces the King family and its search for gold in SA, WA, South Africa and even in the Klondike of the new territories of Canada. It includes a world trip for the family when the fortunes are high and a side-track to India for engineering and medical missionary work and for William King to meet Elaine Hamilton Forbes. The fourth book (1933–49) follows playboy, amateur racing-driver, Vincent King, through his early life and his marriage to Maggie Pinjarra, who is the great-great-granddaughter of Jamie Brown. Vincent meets an early death in a motor-racing accident. The fifth book (1949–69) tells almost exclusively of the life of Joseph Forbes King, son of Maggie Pinjarra and Vincent King. Born in Queensland and mistakenly believing he is part-Aboriginal, Joseph Forbes King grows up in Adelaide. Visits north awaken his feelings for the coloured people and attending University in Canberra in the 1960s he becomes involved in demonstrations. In Brisbane he physically attacks the Minister for Aboriginal Affairs and the experience of seven days in gaol means, when conscripted for Vietnam, he cannot face either the army or further prison. He goes to the Blue Mountains intending to take his life at Govett's Leap. Unable to jump, he heads for Sydney and the Harbour Bridge and dies on the train involved in the Granville railway disaster.

T.M.

'Forest of Night, The', see BRENNAN, C.J.

Forever Morning, see DAVISON, FRANK DALBY

Forger's Wife, The, alternatively titled *Emily Orford*, a short novel by John George Lang (q.v.), was published first in the English journal *Fraser's Magazine* while Lang was in England in 1853, and appeared in book form in 1855. It later appeared under various titles, two of which, *Assigned to His Wife* and *The Convict's Wife*, reflect something of its plot. The Forger's Wife is Emily Orford, a naive young beauty from an established English family, who succumbs to the practised wiles of an opportunist, Charles Roberts, masquerading as Captain Reginald Harcourt. Not long after their elopement and marriage at Gretna Green, Roberts is arrested for forgery and transported for life to NSW. Emily follows him and succeeds with the help of George Flower, a renowned Sydney 'thief-taker', probably a fictional version of the Sydney identity, Israel Chapman, in having Roberts assigned to her as a servant. While

Flower is away at Bathurst apprehending some bushrangers, police magistrate Brade, probably a fictional version of the well-known and unscrupulous magistrate, Ernest Augustus Slade, attempts, with the connivance of Roberts who has returned to his old villainous ways, to 'have his way' with Emily. Flower returns in time to save Emily and later kills Roberts, who has turned bushranger. Emily and Flower return to England, where it is revealed that they are half-brother and sister. Emily succeeds to the family estate, marries a faithful suitor of old, and Flower returns to Australia where his particular qualities are more appreciated. From there he apparently attempts to denude the colony of its fauna for he 'frequently' sends to Emily and her father 'Australian curiosities such as kangaroos, emus, flying squirrels, parrots and cockatoos'. Although marred by sentimentality, by a 'fate worse than death' morality and by a dependence on coincidence, *The Forger's Wife* has literary potential which its author seems not to have perceived. Its strengths lie in its picture of convict Sydney in which Lang grew up; in its casual depiction of violence and death in an era and locale in which the value of individual human life seemed almost negligible; in its portrayal of capricious and callous authoritarianism; and in its author's skill in conveying the speech rhythms of the various levels of colonial society.

'FORREST, DAVID' (DAVID DENHOLM) (1924–), born Maryborough, Queensland, saw service as a militiaman in New Guinea in the Second World War. After the war he worked as a bank officer until 1964, when he undertook full-time academic study; he now teaches at the Riverina College of Advanced Education, Wagga Wagga. His first novel, *The Last Blue Sea* (1959), one of the best fictional accounts by an Australian of the jungle campaigns of New Guinea, records the attempt by the 83rd Battalion, a battalion of conscript soldiers (chocolate soldiers or 'chockos' as opposed to the volunteer soldiers of the AIF) to advance along the Missim trail towards Salamaua in New Guinea to assist in the ultimate capture of that port. An authentic account of the horrors of jungle fighting and an excellent portrayal of the young Australian soldier, *The Last Blue Sea* won the inaugural Dame Mary Gilmore Award in 1959. 'Forrest''s second novel, *The Hollow Woodheap* (1962), combines light social satire with restrained humour. It uses the institution of banking and its conventions as a metaphor of middle-class respectability; the 'hollow woodheap' is the bank, a shaky edifice even though it prides itself upon solid values. Of 'Forrest''s

short stories, which deal mainly with life in small-town and outback Queensland, the best known are 'That Barambah Mob' and 'The Keeper of the Night'. The former, a humorous cricket classic, turns on the feats of the Aboriginal fast-bowler, Eddie Gilbert; the latter reveals 'Forrest''s gift for evoking both the understated compassion of the Australian 'battler' and his laconic wit. Connected with the Realist Writers group, 'Forrest' holds forthright views on the role of the writer and has expressed these in an essay, 'The Split-Level Culture' in *Literary Australia*, eds Clement Semmler and Derek Whitelock (1966), and in the 1962 CLF lecture on Patrick White. Under his own name, David Denholm, he has also written an individual interpretation of aspects of nineteenth-century life in Australia, *The Colonial Australians* (1979). It won the ANA Literature Award for 1979.

FORREST, Sir JOHN (Baron Forrest of Bunbury) (1847–1918), born Bunbury, WA, led an expedition to search for Ludwig Leichhardt's party in 1869. In 1870 he explored the south-coast route from WA to Adelaide, and was awarded 5000 acres of land in WA and the gold medal of the Royal Geographical Society. A further expedition to SA by way of the Murchison River and the overland telegraph line in 1874 was also successful. His chief work, an account of his journeys, *Explorations in Australia*, was published in 1875. His later career as surveyor–general, then politician (he was WA's first premier), coincided with the boom in WA development. He entered the first federal parliament, becoming treasurer and, briefly, acting prime minister. Two of his chief successes were the supplying of the WA goldfields with water and the building of the transcontinental railway. F.K. Crowley published in 1971 the first part of a projected two-volume biography of Forrest. Forrest's younger brother, Alexander (1849–1901), also an explorer and politician, discovered and explored the Kimberley area of north-west Australia, helping to open that area for pastoral expansion; he wrote *Journal of Expedition from De Grey to Port Darwin* (1880). G.C. Bolton wrote *Alexander Forrest: His Life and Times* (1958).

FORREST, MABEL (1872–1935), born near Yandilla, Queensland, was a versatile writer of short fiction, novels and verse. Her first book, *The Rose of Forgiveness and Other Stories*, was published in 1904; a volume of verse, *Alpha Centauri*, followed in 1909 and a novel, *A Bachelor's Wife*, in 1914. Her other publications include a prose and verse collection, *The Green Harper* (1915); a book of verse, *Streets and*

Gardens (1922); and a series of novels, *The Wild Moth* (1924), *Gaming Gods* (1926), *Hibiscus Heart* (1927), *Reaping Roses* (1928) and *White Witches* (1929). A collection of her poems submitted to journals in various countries was published as *Poems* in 1927.

FORSHAW, THELMA (1923–), born Glebe Point, Sydney, served with the WAAAF in the Second World War. She has since been a secretary, advertising writer, freelance writer and book reviewer for such journals and newspapers as the *Bulletin*, *Nation*, the *Sydney Morning Herald*, the *Age* and the *Australian*. Her short stories, published in many Australian journals, were collected as *An Affair of Clowns* (1967); of these the best regarded is the section, 'Some Customs of My Clan', a series of unsentimental, autobiographical sketches of the Hallorans, her mother's Irish-Australian family. She describes this rumbustious family environment with irony and verve.

FORSTER, WILLIAM (1818–82), grandson of the explorer Gregory Blaxland, was born Madras, India, and in 1829 came to Australia. In 1840–67 he acquired land throughout northern NSW and Queensland, becoming one of the most successful squatters in the pastoral boom of the mid-nineteenth century. Elected to the NSW parliament when it was first constituted in 1856, Forster served almost continuously until his death and held many important offices, including that of premier briefly, 1859–60. A prolific writer of satirical, political and social essays and a sound literary critic with a wide awareness of the developing colonial literary scene, Forster contributed frequently to Robert Lowe's *Atlas* and Daniel Deniehy's *Southern Cross*. In the *Atlas* appeared two of his significant verse satires, 'The Devil and the Governor', directed against Governor Sir George Gipps, and 'The Genius and the Ghost', an attack on the proposals for the renewal of transportation. His perceptive, if somewhat trenchant, literary criticism is evident in his attack on Francis Fowler, then the darling of Sydney literary society, in the *Empire* 25 May 1857. Forster published other poetry and verse plays: *The Weirwolf* (1876), which included, in addition to the title work, sonnets on the Crimean War and other poems; *The Brothers* (1877); and *Midas* (1884).

Fortunate Life, A, see FACEY, A.B.; War Literature

Fortunes of Richard Mahony, The, a novel trilogy by 'Henry Handel Richardson' (q.v.), was first published as a sequence. *Australia Felix*, the first volume, which covers twelve years of Richard Mahony's life from the early 1850s, was published in 1917; *The Way Home*, which deals with his subsequent eight years, appeared in 1925; and *Ultima Thule*, the final volume covering his last four years, in 1929. The novel was first published as a trilogy in 1930.

Australia Felix, which is divided into four parts, opens with a 'Proem' describing the death of a miner on the Ballarat gold diggings and the despair of Long Jim, an English lamplighter turned miner, at his own living burial in an alien, harsh and ugly land. The first part begins the story of Richard Mahony, a twenty-eight year old medical graduate of Edinburgh University and now the keeper of a general store in Ballarat. Against a dense picture of life in Ballarat, Melbourne and Geelong, 'Richardson' gives several individuals prominence; these include Henry Ocock, a shrewd, unscrupulous lawyer emotionally involved with the wife of a squatter, Agnes Glendinning; the volatile and impressionable Purdy Smith, Mahony's childhood friend from Dublin; John Turnham, Mahony's brother-in-law, a political opportunist and typical Victorian family man; John's younger brother, the irresponsible pursuer of gold, Ned Turnham; the chemist Tangye who, like Mahony, is alienated from Australia; the Beamish girls (especially Tilly Beamish), English lower-class migrants in search of husbands; and the ineffective, pretentious old maid Sarah (later Sara and then Zara) Turnham. Although Mahony does not make friends easily, his marriage to sixteen-year-old Polly (later Mary) Turnham draws him into the life of others. The first part follows Mahony's career until his marriage; the second part deals with the Eureka Stockade, the growth of the varied society of Ballarat and a legal hearing in Melbourne of a claim by Mahony in which Ocock's dubious practices prevail. It concludes with Mahony's decision to start a practice in Ballarat instead of returning to England, a decision which indicates Polly's growing influence. In the third and fourth parts 'Richardson' extends her panoramic picture of a dynamic colonial society in which individuals are subject to great reversals or advances of fortune. Although the Mahonys eventually prosper, financial and family worries beset them. Others, like John Turnham or like Old Devine who rises from gardener to parliamentary candidate, succeed in their ambitions; or, like Tilly Beamish who enters into a marriage of convenience with Henry Ocock's father, make compromises; or, like Ned Turnham, Tangye and the Beamish parents, suffer degrees of failure. Some, like Glendinning who dies of alcoholic poisoning, are destroyed by Australian conditions. At the same time relationships undergo change; Mahony quarrels with Purdy after he believes his friend has compromised Mary, and Henry Ocock becomes alienated after Mahony is frank about the alcoholism of Agnes, now his wife. The most profound change of all, however, is in the relationship between the Mahonys themselves, in which Mary plays more and more of a maternal role towards her husband. The fourth part concludes with their return to England, Mahony having become thoroughly dissatisfied with life in Australia.

The Way Home begins with his arrival in England and concludes with his final, second return to Australia, a ruined man. In the intervening years he grows disillusioned with English society, returns to Australia to find his investments have made him suddenly rich, attempts to settle into the wealthy community of Melbourne and becomes the father of three children. Eventually afflicted with his old restlessness, he takes his family on a grand tour of Europe that is abruptly terminated when he learns that his investments have failed. During his years as a general practitioner in England, Mahony first attempts to practise at Leicester but finds that the dominance of industry makes life as limited as on the Ballarat gold diggings. In his next practice at the pretty seaside resort of Buddlecombe, he finds the English social hierarchy offensive and cramping. Nor does he find himself at home in his old 'homes'; in Dublin he discovers that his relatives 'had made giant strides along the road to decay', lavishing the last remnants of vitality on their religious passions; in Edinburgh, on the other hand, Mahony himself feels like a ghost 're-turning for a glimpse of the scenes of his youth', displaced by a new generation of hopeful, active students. His experience as a member of Melbourne's plutocracy also proves less than satisfying, notwithstanding his purchase of a well-appointed home, Ultima Thule; the unexpected arrival of children, a son Cuffy and twin daughters Lallie and Lucie; and his growing interest in spiritualism. His sense of loneliness is deepened by the gulf in temperament between himself and Mary: 'had they, between them, a single idea in common? . . . Did they share an interest, a liking, a point of view? – with the one exception of an innate sobriety and honesty of purpose', he asks himself. Meanwhile his sense of transience is heightened by the suffering and death of John Turnham. Some months later Mahony decides to sell Ultima Thule and take his family to Europe; circumstances and Richard's haste to depart result in his choice of an unscrupulous agent to handle his affairs and, in Italy after an extremely busy period of travelling, the family learns suddenly of his ruin. Two days later Richard leaves alone by the Overland Mail for Egypt, bound thence for Australia.

Ultima Thule takes up his story on his return to Australia, his attempts to establish himself as a medical practitioner, first in Melbourne and then at Barambogie, a small town in northern Victoria. The family's life in Melbourne proves tolerable, although financial worries dominate; these are compounded by a visit from Agnes Ocock, now a pathetic alcoholic, on her way to South Africa, where her husband believes she will be less a subject of scandal. At her death, soon afterwards, only Mary of all her family and friends seems to feel any sorrow. At Barambogie, a place of heat, dust and isolation, the Mahonys' troubles reach crisis-point. The practice fails to prosper, Lallie dies of dysentery, and Richard begins to show clear signs of physical and mental deterioration. After Lallie's death, Mary takes the children to the cooler climate of the coast and the practice dwindles to nothing as Richard's increasing strangeness alarms the townsfolk. Although on her return Mary attempts with some success to re-establish good relations at Barambogie, Richard's rapidly deteriorating condition defeats her; when he fails to set a patient's leg properly, he is threatened with a horse-whipping and a lawsuit. He contemplates suicide but resists the temptation and experiences a brief but intense vision of unity of suffering with his fellow men. The family leaves Barambogie and settles briefly at Shortlands' Bluff on the coast, where Richard gets the post of acting health officer. Here his condition rapidly worsens and culminates in total insanity; the crossing of the Rubicon is signalled by his burning of his deeds, mortgages and share scripts. With Henry Ocock's help Mary secures a position as postmistress at Gymgurra, a small settlement in western Victoria, and Richard is placed first in a private nursing home and then, when money has run out, in the government asylum. When Mary visits him there she is appalled at his treatment and engages in an heroic fight to have him released. In this crisis, only Henry Ocock's help is of any avail. Following his release, Richard lives contentedly at Gymgurra, devotedly cared for by Mary, until paralysis incapacitates his body. After his death he is buried in the local cemetery, within sound of the sea.

Forty-Two Faces (1962) by John Hetherington (q.v.) is a collection of biographical studies of Australian writers including Katharine Susannah Prichard, Frank Dalby Davison, Xavier Herbert, Alan Marshall, John Morrison, Gavin Casey, Judah Waten, Kylie Tennant, Patrick White, David Martin, Morris West, Hal Porter, Frank Hardy, 'David Forrest', Elizabeth Harrower and Randolph Stow.

Forty Years' Poems, see FITZGERALD, R.D.

FOSTER, DAVID (1944–), born Sydney, graduated from the University of Sydney and the Australian National University, and was a research scientist who worked in the USA and Sydney before resigning in 1972 to become a full-time writer. His first major publication was a collection of three novellas, *North South West* (1973). Since then he has published a book of verse, *The Fleeing Atalanta* (1975); a second collection of short fiction, *Escape to Reality* (1977); and four novels: *The Pure Land* (1974), which shared the *Age* Book of the Year Award, *The Empathy Experiment* (1977, science fiction with D.J. Lyell), *Moonlite* (1981), which won a National Book Council Award, and *Plumbum* (1983). *The Pure Land* traces in three parts the experience of Albert Manwaring, a Katoomba photographer who departs from Australia for America seeking a fuller life; secondly, those of his daughter in England; and thirdly, his grandson, who at the end of the novel returns to Katoomba to try and piece together his past. *Moonlite*, rich in historical and literary allusions, parody and comedy, has been variously described as a satire, myth and allegory about imperialism and colonialism. It begins in the Hebridean isle of Mugg, ruled by MacIshmael, who dispossesses his people and forces them to emigrate to the even more remote and pagan island of Hiphoray, where Finbar MacDuffie, an albino later to be called Moonlite, is born. When Christianity comes to Hiphoray, disrupting its patterns and rhythms, Finbar emerges as the minister's protégé and zealot. Sent to another island to further his education, he eventually finds his way first to Newbridge (Cambridge) and then to the North West Highlands (Australia), a colony in the grip of material obsessions where bottles form the currency and where Finbar is about to become premier before his death at the end of the novel.

FOSTER, LYNN (1913–), born Rose Bay, Sydney, was active in the 1930s and 1940s, adapting plays for radio and writing her own plays; she was in England 1948–58, where she wrote for radio and television. Best-known of her plays is *There Is No Armour* (1945), which uses the living-room of the homestead on Minnabooka station to trace the domination of the land over its people over eighty years. Her 1946 play 'And the Moon Will Shine', which shared the Playwrights Advisory Board Prize, deals with the problems of the generation between the two world wars. She also wrote the novels, *The Exiles* (1960) and *Blow the Wind Southerly* (1969).

Foundation for Australian Literary Studies, which is funded by membership subscriptions and by donations, was established in 1966 within the department of English, University College of Townsville (later James Cook University of North Queensland). As part of its aim to foster the study of Australian literature within the University and the wider community, it has sponsored since 1966 an annual series of lectures, now titled the Colin Roderick Lectures, by a distinguished author (e.g. James McAuley in 1966, Thea Astley in 1978, Les A. Murray in 1982) or scholar (e.g. G.A. Wilkes in 1967, L.T. Hergenhan in 1973, H.P. Heseltine in 1975). Several of the lectures have been included in the Foundation's monograph series (e.g. G.A. Wilkes's lectures on 'Novelists of Australia' were revised and published as *Australian Literature: A Conspectus* in 1969). The Foundation has also supported occasional seminars, has made since 1967 an annual award which carries a cash prize, and from 1980 the award of the H.T. Priestley Memorial Medal for the best book published in Australia on any aspect of Australian life. The journalist and historian Gavin Souter has won the award three times (1968, 1976, 1981); among creative writers who have been successful are Douglas Stewart, the inaugural winner, Francis Webb (1969), David Malouf (1974), Alan Marshall (1977) and Thea Astley (1979)

Foundations of Culture in Australia, The, was written by P.R. Stephensen (q.v.) and published in 1936; the first and most important of its three parts had been published the previous year as an editorial essay in the *Australian Mercury*. Subtitled *An Essay towards National Self-Respect*, *The Foundations of Culture in Australia* posits that '*Art and Literature are at first nationally created, but become internationally appreciated*' (Stephensen's italics) and argues that while the English basis of European Australian culture should be recognized, English elements should not be allowed to dominate Australian culture; the contribution of culture to nationalism is the part it plays in a nation's self-definition. Among many targets in the essay were the emphasis on convicts and bushranging in Australian writing, which Stephensen thought confirmed English notions of a colonial Australia; the *Bulletin*, which was attacked for producing a larrikin literature that overstated the national life; the Anglo-centrism of curricula in Australian schools and of literature professors in Australia, such as G.H. Cowling; the 'brain drain' of Australian artists and scholars to Europe; and the failure to develop independent economic, business, political and cultural policies in Australia. Chauvinist and iconoclastic, Stephensen's essay most directly influenced the Jindyworobak writers, although it shares, ironically, some of the views and assumptions about literature and humanities espoused by the *Bulletin* in the 1890s, and some of the issues it canvassed about Eurocentricism in university teaching of literature were still being discussed in the 1970s by John Docker and other writers. *The Foundations of Culture in Australia* also expresses many of the political views (e.g. isolationism) which Stephensen took into the Australia First (q.v.) movement.

Four Stories High (1877), by Marcus Clarke (q.v.), comprises in fact five stories: four are told on a Melbourne verandah by the host and by each of his three friends, and the last is told by the host to his son after his friends have left. All five stories originally appeared as unrelated contributions to the *Australasian* in 1870–73; the most significant is 'La Béguine', which has autobiographical relevance.

Fourteen Men (1954), Dame Mary Gilmore's (q.v.) final volume of poems, was published when she was approaching her ninetieth year. The title poem recalls the massacre of the Chinese at Lambing Flat. The volume also contains the well-known poems, 'Nationality' (q.v.) and 'The Pear Tree'.

Fourteen Years: Extracts from a Private Journal 1925–1939, by Nettie Palmer (q.v.), was published in 1948. Although the journal extracts are structured according to the author's movements (Caloundra 1925–29, Melbourne 1929–32, Green Island 1932, Kalorama 1932–35, Paris 1935, London 1935–36, Barcelona 1936, Melbourne 1936–39), the unity of the whole is immediately striking. Moving easily among diverse places, cultural milieux, and individuals, the prose passes from humorous personal reflection to incisive social comment, to observation of the natural scene and to meditation on current and past writing. Like the letters of Madame de Sévigné, with which it has been compared, the journal has the same historical value as the reflection of a generation and the same clear perceptions of personalities, places and things. Some of the well-known individuals captured by the journal are John Masefield, F.R. Leavis, Ruth Pitter, Rebecca West, André Gide; and the writers, 'Henry Handel Richardson', Christina Stead, Havelock Ellis, Stewart Macky, Will Dyson, Leonard Mann, Louis Esson, Paul Wenz, Frank Dalby Davison, A.G. Stephens, Flora Eldershaw and Marjorie Barnard.

FOWLER, FRANK (1833–63), born London, came to Australia for health reasons in 1855. He made a living, in his own words, 'as a journalist and bookseller's hack', writing initially for the *Empire* and the *Sydney Morning Herald*. Under the pseudonym 'Cosmopolitan', he wrote a series, 'Sketches in Parliament', in the *Empire* in 1856; as 'A Literary Vagabond' he contributed the series, 'Home Senators', to the *Sydney Morning Herald* in 1857; and as editor of the *Month*, which began publication in July 1857, he contributed significantly to literary, political and social discussion of the contemporary colonial scene. He wrote a play, 'Eva', which was performed in Sydney in 1856. By March or April 1858 he was on his way back to England, having stood unsuccessfully in January 1858 as a candidate in the Legislative Assembly elections. It was on the return voyage that he wrote his chief work, *Southern Lights and Shadows*, published in London in 1859, a work in which he gave his observations and impressions of life in the colony. Fowler also published a book of his sketches contributed to the *Weekly Mail* (London), titled *Dottings of a Lounger* (1859), and *Texts for Talkers* (1860). A posthumous collection of his writings, *Last Gleanings* (1864), which indicates his talent in *belles-lettres*, was compiled by his Australian friend, Richard Rowe.

FOX, Sir **FRANK ('FRANK RENAR')** (1874–1960), born Adelaide, was educated in Hobart and edited the *Australian Workman* in 1893 and the Bathurst *National Advocate* in 1895, before becoming chief of the *Age* reporting staff. In 1901 he joined the *Bulletin* and was first editor of the *Lone Hand* 1907–09. In 1909 Fox went to England to pursue the career in conservative journalism for which he was knighted in 1926. He wrote several books based on his activities as a war correspondent and soldier, but his most significant Australian works were the study of Harry Harbord Morant titled *Bushman and Buccaneer* (1902); the political essays, *From the Old Dog* (1908); the descriptive work, *Australia* (1910); and the novel, *Beneath an Ardent Sun* (1923).

FOX, LEN (1905–), born Melbourne, was a teacher at Scotch College, Melbourne, 1928–32. In 1935 he became Victorian state secretary of the Movement against War and Fascism; in 1939 he went to Sydney where he worked on the Labor Party newspaper *Progress* (1940–45) and on the communist newspaper, *Tribune* (1946–55). Fox and his wife Mona Brand lived in Hanoi 1956–57; on their return journey to Sydney in 1958 he joined the Miners' Federation paper, *Common Cause*, and was its editor 1965–70. A prolific writer of socio-political pamphlets, Fox has also published verse, short fiction and dramatic works. His verse, which includes *Chung of Vietnam* (1957, children's verse), *Gumleaves and Bamboo* (1959), *Vietnam Neighbours* (1966), *Gumleaves and People* (1967) and *Gumleaves and Dreaming* (1978), clearly reflects his interest in the people of Vietnam and the Australian Aborigines. He also wrote *The Aboriginals* (1978). He was co-editor with Faith Bandler of *The Time Was Ripe* (1938), the history of the Aboriginal–Australian Fellowship, and collaborated with her in the story of her father, *Marani in Australia* (1980). His plays include 'Never No More', 'Stay Down Miner', 'Jim's Secret Weapon', 'They Shall Not Pass' and 'We're Bringing Our Singing to Sydney'.

'Fragment of Autobiography, A' is a long, autobiographical essay by Henry Lawson (q.v.) covering the years up to his father's death on New Years Eve 1888. It was written between 1903 and 1908 but not published in full until its appearance in modern collections of Lawson's prose. Some of the same incidents are mentioned in two shorter pieces by Lawson: 'From Mudgee Hills to London Town', which has information on his early poems; and ' "Pursuing Literature" in Australia', which focuses more directly on his literary career up to the end of the 1890s and contains his famous advice to any young Australian writer: 'go steerage, stow away, swim, and seek London, Yankeeland or Timbuctoo – rather than stay in Australia until [your] genius [turns] to gall, or beer'. ' "Succeeding" ', a sequel to ' "Pursuing Literature" in Australia' and focusing on Lawson's experiences when he went to England, is among recently-discovered Lawson material included in Brian Kiernan's selection, *The Essential Henry Lawson* (1982).

'FRANC, MAUD JEANNE', see **EVANS, MATILDA JANE**

'FRANK THE POET', see **MACNAMARA, FRANCIS**

FRANKLIN, Sir JOHN (1786–1847), the naval officer and Arctic explorer famous for his death while searching for the North–West Passage, was a nephew of Matthew Flinders (q.v.) and served under him on the *Investigator* in 1801–04. In 1837–43 he was lieutenant-governor of Van Diemen's Land (Tasmania) in succession to Sir George Arthur (q.v.); it was a period of great difficulty because of the faction fighting within Tasmanian politics, which had carried over from Arthur's regime, the economic climate and the uncertainty over Tasmania's future as a gaol or as a free colony. Franklin's disputes with the colonial secretary, John Montagu, an Arthur protégé, erupted in

1842 when Montagu was suspended from office; the Colonial Office disapproved of this action and both censured and recalled Franklin. Franklin's *Narrative of Some Passages in the History of Van Diemen's Land, during the Last Three Years of Sir John Franklin's Administration of Its Government* (1845) is a vindication of his government in which he was supported by his wife, Lady Jane Franklin (1791–1875), who was active in the development of Tasmania's intellectual life. The Franklins made several explorations and excursions during their term of office; David Burn (q.v.) reported one in *Narrative of the Overland Journey of Sir John and Lady Franklin and Party from Hobart Town to Macquarie Harbour*, which was first published serially in *Colburn's United Services Journal* in London in 1843. Franklin's career in the Arctic and Tasmania is chronicled in Nancy Cato's novel, *North-West by South* (1965) and his relationship with his wife is portrayed in Catherine Shepherd's play, 'Jane, My Love' (1951); he also appears as a character in William Gosse Hay's *The Escape of the Notorious Sir William Heans* (1919), in which the Franklin–Montagu dispute is mentioned. George Mackaness published *Some Private Correspondence of Sir John and Lady Jane Franklin (Tasmania, 1837–1845)* (1947) and Kathleen Fitzpatrick the biographical study, *Sir John Franklin in Tasmania, 1837–1843* (1949).

FRANKLIN, MILES ('BRENT OF BIN BIN') (1879–1954), known to her family as Stella, was born at Talbingo, the grazing property then held by her maternal grandmother, Sarah Lampe, near Tumut, NSW. On that side of the family, Miles Franklin was a fifth-generation Australian, her great-great-grandfather, Edward Miles, having been a convict in the First Fleet. Her Franklin grandparents, of whom there is a fictionalized account in *All That Swagger* (q.v.), arrived as Irish immigrants in 1839. Both sides of the family 'squatted' in the 1840s in the isolated and sparsely-settled Monaro region of NSW; the Franklin home station, Brindabella, and the neighbouring run, Bin Bin, have now become familiar names in Australian literature through Franklin's novels. The eldest of seven children, Miles Franklin spent her first ten years at Brindabella. In 1889 the family moved to a smaller, poorer property – Possum Gully of her autobiographical novel *My Brilliant Career* (q.v., 1901) – at Bangalore near Goulburn, NSW. After some years of arduous and monotonous dairy farming, which Franklin loathed, the family moved in 1903 to a small holding near Penrith and finally in 1914 to the Sydney suburb of Carlton. Between the publication of *My Brilliant Career* in 1901 and her departure for the USA in

1906, she made a brief attempt at a nursing career; spent almost two years in a 'Mary-Anne' housemaid role in Sydney and in Melbourne, where she met Joseph Furphy and began a lifetime infatuation with *Such is Life* (1903); developed literary contacts with A.G. Stephens, Norman Lindsay and Henry Lawson, who wrote the preface to *My Brilliant Career*; worked as a freelance journalist for the *Daily Telegraph* and *Sydney Morning Herald* under the pseudonyms 'An Old Bachelor' and 'Vernacular'; and became involved in the Australian feminist movement through friendship with Rose Scott and Vida Goldstein. In the USA she was associated with Alice Henry, another prominent Australian feminist, in the National Women's Trade Union League, for whom she did secretarial and editorial work in 1908–15. In England in 1915, in spite of a life-long detestation of war (the 'lunacy' of the male), she was impelled by the deep ties of sentiment and lineage to help in the war effort, serving with the Scottish Women's Hospital at Ostrovo in the Serbian campaigns of 1917–18. In 1919–25 she was assistant secretary with the National Housing and Town Planning Council in London. She visited Australia for three months in 1923–24, an episode which linked her new awareness of County Clare, Ireland, the birthplace of her grandfather Joseph Franklin, with her old memories of the Monaro uplands. The visit formulated within her that sense of historical perspective that produced the chronicle novels of 'Brent of Bin Bin' (q.v.) and the family saga, *All That Swagger*. She returned to Australia 1927–31; in that time the 'Brent of Bin Bin' series, beginning with *Up the Country* (1928), began to be published and the identity of their pseudonymous author became the subject of prolonged speculation. After spending 1931 and most of 1932 in England she returned permanently to Sydney to an increasingly eventful literary life. She was awarded the S.H. Prior Memorial Prize for *All That Swagger* (1936), winning it again in 1939 for her collaboration with Kate Baker in an unpublished Furphy biography. *All That Swagger* and novels of the Bin Bin series were broadcast serially over national radio stations and she herself broadcast to schools on 'My Life and My Books'; she was involved in the nationalism of the 1930s; she played a leading role in the promotion of Mary Fullerton's (q.v.) poetry; and she delivered the CLF lectures in Perth in 1950, afterwards publishing them as *Laughter, Not for a Cage* (1956). By 1948 the sole survivor of her family she bequeathed her estate to establish annual literary awards, now known as the Miles Franklin Awards (q.v.).

The chief novels published by Miles Franklin in her own name were *My Brilliant Career* (1901); *Some Everyday Folk and Dawn* (1909), an inferior work reflecting the drabness of life in an Australian town (Penrith) and carrying overtones of female suffrage; *Old Blastus of Bandicoot* (q.v., 1931); *Bring the Monkey* (1933); *All That Swagger* (1936); and *My Career Goes Bung* (1946), written shortly after the turn of the century as a sequel to *My Brilliant Career* but rejected as early as 1910 by publishers because it was too audacious. Under the pseudonym 'Brent of Bin Bin' she published six novels, *Up the Country* (1928), *Ten Creeks Run* (1930), *Back to Bool Bool* (1931), *Prelude to Waking* (1950), *Cockatoos* (1954) and *Gentlemen at Gyang Gyang* (1956), the last two appearing after her death. In collaboration with Dymphna Cusack she wrote the satirical *Pioneers on Parade* (1939), a tilt at the pretentiousness and snobbery of established Australian society. Following the 1939 collaboration with Kate Baker she wrote *Joseph Furphy: The Legend of a Man and His Book* (1944), much more her own individual work although acknowledging her debt to the original collaborator. In 1963 the autobiographical *Childhood at Brindabella* was published. *On Dearborn Street*, similar in attitude to *My Brilliant Career* but set in Chicago in 1914, was first published in 1981, edited by Roy Duncan. There are some twenty unpublished Miles Franklin novels and plays.

Miles Franklin was one of a small group of Australian women who, born into a colonial society in the ultra-conservative Victorian era, attempted to fulfil themselves according to their own lights and in defiance of the accepted conventions of the day. She exhibited attitudes regarded as psychological aberrations at the time: sexual ambivalence, with attraction and repulsion both present; hostility to the traditional role of women in marriage and childbearing, the latter being seen as the 'most cruelly agonizing of human duties'; and rejection of the idea of a male-dominated society. She had a fetish for privacy and sought refuge from painful confrontations by absenting herself for twenty years from family, friends and country and by adopting literary disguises such as 'Brent of Bin Bin'. She became famous, even notorious, for *My Brilliant Career* but the long literary silence between it and the advent of the Bin Bin series and *All That Swagger*, combined with her long absence from Australia, meant that the later novels when published in the 1930s were virtually out of date and seen to be part of the old-fashioned nostalgic nationalism that was then passing into Australian literary history. They were out of phase with the bulk of contemporary Australian literary opinion which, rejecting the vociferous outburst of Jindyworobak nationalism, was rapidly becoming international in outlook. But the Bin Bin novels and *All That Swagger*, although never a popular success and often validly criticized as clumsily-written, ill-constructed, trivial in incident and vague in characterization, form part of the chronicle of Australian pioneer life. More recently her work has attracted attention in the feminist revaluation of Australian literature.

Marjorie Barnard wrote the biographical study, *Miles Franklin* (1967); Verna Coleman filled in the biographical gaps with *Miles Franklin in America* (1981); Colin Roderick also published a biography in 1982; he discovered that Miles Franklin was the author of *The Net of Circumstance* (1915), a novel published under the pseudonym 'Mrs Ogniblat l'Artsau' (i.e. Talbingo, Australia).

'FRANKLYN, ROSS' is a pseudonym used by Frank Hardy (q.v.) in his early writing and is also the name of the central character of his novel, *Who Shot George Kirkland?* (1980).

FRASER, ELIZA (?1798–1858), was the wife of James Fraser, captain of the *Stirling Castle*, a ship that was wrecked on Swain Reef near Rockhampton, Queensland, in May 1836. The survivors of the wreck, including Eliza and her husband, landed on the then Great Sandy Island and were captured by Aborigines; several, including James Fraser, were later murdered. After six weeks of captivity, Eliza and the remaining survivors were rescued by a detachment of the 14th Regiment sent from Moreton Bay. Great Sandy Island was later renamed Fraser Island in memory of Captain James Fraser. An account of the shipwreck and rescue is given in John Curtis, *Shipwreck of the Stirling Castle* (1838). Eliza Fraser's experiences are recounted in Robert Gibbings's *John Graham, Convict* (1937), in Charles Barrett's *White Blackfellows* (1948) and in Michael Alexander's *Mrs. Fraser on the Fatal Shore* (1971). Patrick White's novel *A Fringe of Leaves* (1976) is substantially based on her adventures; the dustjacket of the original edition featured one of the Eliza Fraser paintings of Sidney Nolan, which also inspired the South African Andre Brink's novel, *An Instant in the Wind* (1976). *Eliza Fraser*, an Australian film scripted by David Williamson was made in 1976. The history of Fraser Island itself is contained in Fred Williams's illustrated *Written in Sand* (1982).

FRASER, GILLY, see Feminism and Australian Literature

Frearson's Weekly Illustrated: A Journal for the People, published in Adelaide 1878–84,

was incorporated in 1884 into *Frearson's Monthly Illustrated Adelaide News* and continued 1885–95 as the *Pictorial Australian*. It contained original sketches, poetry and fiction.

FREE, COLIN (1925–), a prolific writer for television, has also written dramas and features for radio, stage plays, short stories and novels. His published plays include the stage play, *Cannonade of Bells* (1968), a television episode from the serial *Contrabandits; Cage a Tame Tiger* in *Take One*, ed. Richard Lane (1972); and two radio plays, *Nightmares of the Old Obscenity Master* and *A Walk among the Wheeneys* in *Five Plays for Radio*, ed. Alrene Sykes (1975). Several of his stage plays have been produced, including *Cannonade of Bells*, 'Where Did Vortex Go', *A Walk among the Wheeneys* and a duo of two-act plays titled 'Unspeakable Acts'. His novels are *Carbon Copy* (1972), *The Soft Kill* (1973), *Ironbark* (1976) based on the life of the bushranger Frank Gardiner (q.v.), *Vinegar Hill* (1978) and *Bay of Shadows* (1980). Free has written both serials and single episodes for television and radio, has contributed to such popular television serials as *Rush*, *Ben Hall* and *Over There*, and has won several awards for his work.

'Freedom on the Wallaby', a poem by Henry Lawson (q.v.), exists in two versions. The first, which has also become a well-known folk-song, is the poem as originally published in the Brisbane *Worker* May 1891, when it contained a much-quoted reference to Eureka (q.v.) in the last verse:

> So we must fly a rebel flag
> As others did before us,
> And we must sing a rebel song
> And join in rebel chorus;
> We'll make the tyrants feel the sting
> O' those that they would throttle;
> They needn't say the fault is ours
> If blood should stain the wattle.

There were minor changes (e.g. 'bankers' replaced 'tyrants') when the poem was published in the Sydney *Worker* in 1894, and a major revision (including the deletion of the Eureka reference) for publication in *For Australia* (1913), which provides the text of the poem printed in most Lawson collections. Lawson's original poem was inspired by the 1891 shearing strikes in western Queensland; both the title and the last line have become familiar in the rhetoric of social protest, e.g. in Leslie Haylen's Eureka novel, *Blood on the Wattle* (1948). The publication of the poem led to its being quoted in the Queensland parliament during a motion voting thanks to the strike-breakers, to which Lawson derisively replied in two further contributions to the Brisbane *Worker*, 'The Vote of Thanks Debate' and 'The Labour Agitator'.

Freeman's Journal, one of the most substantial of the nineteenth-century Australian journals, catered mainly for the Irish Catholic population but appealed to a wide reading public with its literary articles. Published twice weekly 1850–65, thereafter weekly, it retained its title until 1932 when it became the *Catholic Freeman's Journal* and in 1942 was incorporated into the *Catholic Weekly*. Notable literary figures such as W.B. Dalley, Daniel Deniehy, William Forster, Frank Fowler, J. Sheridan Moore and Victor Daley were associated with it. A frequent contributor was Henry Kendall who conducted a regular feature on Irish writers, 'The Harp of Erin' (1871), and wrote a series of articles titled 'Men and Books' (1871). His controversial poem 'The Gagging Bill' appeared in the *Freeman's Journal* (1879), as did his well-known 'Jim the Splitter' (1880).

Fremantle, named in honour of Sir Charles Howe Fremantle (1800–69), who claimed British possession of the western area of the Australian continent at the mouth of the Swan River in 1829, is a city within the Perth metropolitan area and the principal seaport of WA. The *Diary and Letters of Admiral Sir C.H. Fremantle*, edited by Lord Cottesloe in 1928, record Fremantle's impressions of the area. The first newspaper of the Swan River colony was the *Fremantle Journal and General Advertiser* (1830). Fremantle was associated with the famous *Catalpa* incident in that the Fenian prisoners escaped from the Fremantle gaol. The present-day Fremantle Arts Centre, one of Australia's most progressive literary bodies, is an important publisher of WA writing. John E.V. Birch compiled *The City of Fremantle, Western Australia* (1962) and J.K. Ewers wrote *The Western Gateway* (1948).

Fremantle Arts Centre, whose director is Ian Templeman, is active in contemporary WA literature. It has published the contemporary anthologies, *Soundings* (1976), *Quarry* (1981) and *Decade* (1982), and individual works in the Shoreline Poetry series. It has published works by Nicholas Hasluck, Philip Salom, Wendy Jenkins, T.A.G. Hungerford, A.B. Facey, Alan Alexander, Caroline Caddy, John Catlin, Alec Choate, Philip Collier, Elizabeth Jolley, Lee Knowles, Andrew Lansdown, Justina Williams, Elizabeth Lawson Marsh and others.

Fremantle Herald, which ran weekly 1867–86, was owned and produced by three ex-convicts, William Beresford, James Pearce and James Roe. Written specifically for the working man, it championed democracy and campaigned for land, education and social reform. It published verse, short fiction and serials, but its major literary feature was a weekly column by Beresford, 'Chips by a Sandalwood Cutter'. Through the character of the unsophisticated sandalwood-cutter Beresford was able to expose pomposity and privilege and to extol the virtues of the simple working man's morality.

Frere, Maurice, see *His Natural Life*; PRICE, JOHN

FRIEDERICH, WERNER PAUL, see *Australia in Western Imaginative Prose Writings*

FRIEND, DONALD (1915–), born Moree, NSW, lived and painted in England, France and West Africa before the Second World War, in which he served in the artillery and as an official war artist 1945–46, visiting New Guinea and Borneo. Since the war he has lived in Sri Lanka and Bali as well as Australia, where he won the Blake Prize in 1965. His first books, *Gunner's Diary* (1943) and *Painter's Journal* (1946), are selections from the illustrated diaries he kept before his appointment as a war artist; his official work is collected in Gavin and Colleen Fry's *Donald Friend: Australian War Artist 1945* (1982). Friend's other publications include an historical miscellany, *A Collection of Hillendiana* (1956); *Donald Friend in Bali* (1972); a loosely-autobiographical novel, *Save Me from the Shark* (1973); limited art editions, *The Cosmic Turtle* (1976), *Birds from the Magic Mountains* (1977, Balinese folk stories), *An Alphabet of Owls Et Cetera* (1981) and *Songs of the Vagabond Scholars* (1982); an illustrated satire on bushranging and other pioneering traditions, *Coogan's Gully* (1979); and *Bumbooziana* (1979), a limited edition portfolio of pictures and text which ranges beyond its immediate satiric target – scientific and anthropological expeditions and nineteenth-century books of reminiscences – to embrace sexuality and art styles. Friend has also illustrated a nineteenth-century story, *The Surprising Adventures of Blue-Eyed Patty* (1979) and a licentious play of Rochester, *The Farce of Sodom* (1980).

Friendly Street, a regular series of public poetry readings, began in Adelaide in late 1975, largely as the result of efforts by Ian Reid, Andrew Taylor and Richard Tipping. The name 'Friendly Street' was chosen to indicate the feeling of community which was generated by the meetings. Originally held fortnightly in an old fireworks factory, the meetings are now monthly at the Box Factory, Regent Street, Adelaide. An annual *Friendly Street Poetry Reader*, selected from the work read at the meetings, is published; the first was edited by Richard Tipping in 1976, the eighth (in 1984) by Robert Clark and Jeri Kroll. The annual readers and separate books of verse by Friendly Street regulars are published by Friendly Street Poets, a small collaborative which is doing for SA poets what the Fremantle Arts Centre Press is doing for WA writers. Writers whose work has been published by Friendly Street Poets include Larry Buttrose, Kate Llewellyn, Graham Rowlands, Jeri Kroll, Rory Harris, Mike Ladd, K.F. Pearson, Jenny Boult, Rob Johnson and Jeff Guess.

Fringe Dwellers, The (1961), a novel by Nene Gare (q.v.), highlights the problem of the part-Aborigines who live on the fringes of white society. Noonah and Trilby Comeaway, two part-Aboriginal girls, leave the Murchison Mission, where they have been educated, to rejoin their parents in the squalid half-caste enviroment of 'Nigger Hill' on the outskirts of Geraldton, WA. Under pressure from the two girls, the Comeaways move into a housing development where an experiment in assimilation is being tried by the Department of Native Welfare. But the family is unable to escape its background. The new house is invaded by relatives, Trilby becomes pregnant by a half-caste boy, the baby is killed by its mother in a more or less deliberate accident, Mr Comeaway goes 'walkabout', the rent is unpaid, the family is evicted and returns to a one-roomed house on a native reservation. Trilby, the rebel against the old life, is finally resigned to the squalid card-playing, wine-drinking emptiness that the novel characterizes as the existence of the fringe-dweller.

Fringe of Leaves, A, a novel by Patrick White (q.v.) based on the adventures of Mrs Eliza Fraser, was published in 1976. In the autumn of 1836 Ellen Roxburgh, previously Ellen Gluyas, and her husband Austin set out from Sydney on the *Bristol Maid* on their return voyage to England after visiting Austin's reprobate brother, Garnet, in Van Diemen's Land. In describing the early days of the voyage, White also establishes the inhibited relationship of the Roxburghs, Ellen's past life as a simple farm girl in Cornwall, her marriage to the invalid gentleman, Austin, the early years of their marriage and her education in gentility, and the more recent past in Australia. Among Ellen's uneasy memories is her surrender on one occasion to Garnet, a man she thoroughly

dislikes. The voyage is disrupted when the ship founders on a reef and the subsequent, lengthy ordeal in unseaworthy long boats arouses the unexpected in both crew and passengers. The captain turns rapidly into an ineffective old man whereas others, such as the mate Pilcher and even Austin, discover strong instincts of survival. The cabin boy, Oswald Dignam, who is devoted to Ellen, and Spurgeon the steward, who becomes Austin's friend, both die and Ellen is delivered of a still-born child. When they finally make land they are attacked by Aborigines and most of them killed, Austin dying from a spear in his neck. Ellen is captured by the tribe, stripped of her clothes apart from a girdle of convolvulus in which she hides her wedding ring, and treated as a slave. Her privations and indignities arouse her sympathy for the Aborigines and grant her an insight into the unity of being and her inevitable implication in the eternal duality of good and evil. Later, when she is rescued by an escaped convict Jack Chance, she experiences rare moments of passionate or tender communion although both their pasts strain the relationship. When they finally reach civilization, Chance flees back into the wilderness, wary of colonial justice. Ellen, stripped even of her fringe of leaves and her wedding ring, is discovered by the Oakes family outside their farm and cared for by them until her journey to the prison settlement at Moreton Bay. Her renewed confrontation with society, especially with its authority figures, is embued with her singular spiritual experience. Peace of mind comes when she visits the rude chapel at Moreton Bay built by Pilcher, the only other survivor of the wreck, and rediscovers what her experiences have taught her, the painful complexity of the religious phrase above its altar, 'God is Love'.

From Selection to City (1909), the seventh in 'Steele Rudd' 's (q.v.) series of sketches of the Rudd family (q.v.), was the first in which Steele Rudd appears as a character. The volume centres on Steele who, in a sequence of four stories, goes shearing with his brother Dave before moving to Brisbane to a clerkship in the public service, as narrated in the story 'My First Day in a Government Office'. The work experiences of Steele in *From Selection to City* closely parallel those of 'Rudd' himself 1880–85.

'From the Wreck', a narrative poem by Adam Lindsay Gordon (q.v.) published in *Bush Ballads and Galloping Rhymes* (1870), concerns the wreck of the steamship *Admella* (q.v.) near Cape Northumberland, SA, 6 August 1859, and the subsequent ride by two station-hands to carry the news to the nearest telegraph station so that help might be brought to the crew and passengers. The poem is strongly reminiscent of Robert Browning's 'How They Brought the Good News from Ghent to Aix'.

Front Room Boys, The, a play by Alexander Buzo (q.v.), was first performed in 1969 and published in 1970. The Front Room Boys are clerks who work for a large corporation headed by the executives, the Back Room Boys, unseen except for the silent Hendo who emerges from time to time to exert authority. Two women, Sundra, a typist in search of extra-marital diversion, and Pammy, the nubile junior and office mascot, complete the group. Set in twelve scenes to accord with the months of the year, the play explores motives for subservience to established, unjust powers; the acceptance of stereotyped roles and meaningless functions; and the willing complicity of the oppressed in their oppression. In its conformity to rituals and ceremonies, its submission to strong, unseen powers and its need to propitiate those powers with sacrificial scapegoats, this modern urban group follows timeless, primitive tribal practices. Only Jacko, who finally sees the absurdity of their situation, challenges the system and is consequently attacked and ejected by his mates.

FROST, JOHN (1784–1877), was a Chartist who in 1839 led an abortive attack on his birthplace of Newport, Wales; he was sentenced to be hanged, drawn and quartered for this treasonous offence but the sentence was commuted to transportation for life. Frost arrived in Tasmania in 1840, served part of his sentence at Port Arthur and after securing a conditional pardon in 1854 went to America. He returned to England from exile in 1856 after hearing news of a free pardon, and gave lectures on his experiences which were published as *The Horrors of Convict Life* (1856) and *A Letter to the People of Great Britain and Ireland on Transportation* (1857). Several contemporary accounts of Frost's trial were published. David Williams's *John Frost: A Study in Chartism*, and James Davies's *The Chartist Movement in Monmouthshire* both appeared in 1939, the centenary year of the Newport attack.

Fryer Memorial Library, part of the University of Queensland library, is named after J.D. Fryer, an ex-serviceman who died in 1924 from injuries sustained in the First World War; its establishment in 1927 owed much to F.W. Robinson of the University. The Fryer Library is a significant repository of Australian literature material, including papers of many writers with strong Queensland affiliations, e.g. Thea Astley, John Blight, James Devaney, George Essex Evans, Mary Hannay Foott, Xavier Herbert,

Ernestine Hill, David Malouf and Thomas Shapcott. It also has papers of many other writers, e.g. A.G. Stephens, E.G. Moll, Martin Boyd, Mary Gilmore, and has a strong drama collection centred on the Eunice Hanger (q.v.) collection of unpublished play scripts but also including Brisbane theatre records and papers of G.L. Dann and Nat Phillips, the straightman for Roy Rene. The Fryer Library is publishing on microfiche the checklist of Australian plays being prepared at the University of Queensland, and maintains the index which is the basis of the annual bibliography of Australian literature included in *Australian Literary Studies*.

FULLERTON, MARY ELIZA ('E') (1868–1946), born in a bark hut in Glenmaggie, Victoria, became, in young womanhood, a devotee of literature and a strong campaigner for feminist issues. As 'Alpenstock', she wrote poetry and short fiction for newspapers and journals. She published poetry, *Moods and Melodies* (1908), *The Breaking Furrow* (1921) and *Bark House Days* (1921), the last containing her childhood reminiscences. She also wrote fiction, e.g. *Two Women* (1923), *The People of the Timber Belt* (1925) and *A Juno of the Bush* (1930) as well as a descriptive work, *The Australian Bush* (1928). Her friendship with Miles Franklin (q.v.) led to that writer arranging publication of Fullerton's poetry in the 1940s under the pseudonym 'E'. The identity of 'E', the author of *Moles Do So Little With Their Privacy* (1942) and *The Wonder and the Apple* (1946), was one of the major literary talking-points of the time; it was revealed after her death. Her adoption of the pseudonym was linked with her belief that being a woman prejudiced the recognition of her work.

Furphy, a word still used in Australia for a rumour or false report, seems to have originated during the First World War from the gossip around the water-carts (also known as 'furphies') made by the Furphy foundry at Shepparton in Victoria. Ironically, the phrase 'Tom Collins', the pen-name of Joseph Furphy who wrote *Such is Life* (1903) while employed at the foundry from 1883 to 1905, carried the meaning that furphy has now.

FURPHY, JOSEPH (1843–1912), was born at Yering in the upper Yarra valley in Victoria, the son of Protestant Irish bounty emigrants who arrived in Australia in 1841 and from whom he inherited a capacity for hard work and a love of literature. His elder brother John, who inherited their dourness and religious zeal, was the inventor of the Furphy water-cart and thus directly responsible for the introduction of 'furphy' into Australian English. Furphy completed his schooling at Kyneton, where he first worked on his father's farm before brief stints on the goldfields and as a threshing-machine operator in the Daylesford district; in 1867 he married a young French girl, Leonie Germaine, and took over her mother's farm and vineyard. The following year he selected land in the Lake Cooper district but was driven off after five years and forced to work as a labourer and to return to the gold diggings. Around the end of 1877 he moved with his family to the Riverina in NSW to set himself up with a bullock team; based in Hay, he carted wool and other goods on both sides of the Murray River and to stations further north. The life was particularly hard on Furphy and his family, and after his team was virtually wiped out in the 1883 drought he moved to Shepparton in Victoria to work at his brother's foundry. The move lost Furphy his independence but provided his family with security and gave him the opportunity to read at the local mechanics institute and to write. In 1889 he began contributing short items and sketches to the *Bulletin*, first as 'Warrigal Jack' and from 1893 as 'Tom Collins' (q.v.). By 1897 he had finished a 'full-sized novel, title, "Such is Life"; scene, Riverina and northern Vic.; temper, democratic; bias, offensively Australian', which he tentatively sent to the *Bulletin*'s editor, J.F. Archibald, for an opinion. Archibald passed the manuscript of 1125 pages over to his literary editor, A.G. Stephens (q.v.), who recognized its originality but suggested revisions which Furphy doggedly worked on before *Such is Life: Being Certain Extracts from the Diary of Tom Collins* (q.v.) was eventually published in 1903. His euphoria at seeing the novel in print stimulated Furphy into making two books, *The Buln-Buln and the Brolga* and *Rigby's Romance* (qq.v.), out of the excised portions of the original manuscript but because of the slow sale and lukewarm reception of *Such is Life* neither was published in book form during his lifetime. In 1905 he moved to WA to join his sons, who had established an iron foundry; he died there seven years later. The house that Furphy built at Swanbourne, a Perth suburb, is now the house of the WA branch of the FAW and is described in Justina Williams's *Tom Collins & His House* (1973).

Although Furphy's death in 1912 attracted little attention, the eventual recognition of his stature is an important episode in Australian literary history. At Shepparton he had met a young schoolteacher, Kate Baker (q.v.), who along with Furphy's Melbourne friend, William Cathels, provided encouragement and assistance during the writing and revision of *Such is Life*. Furphy's death coincided with Kate Baker's retirement from teaching. For the next four decades, she devoted herself to promoting Furphy by collecting Furphiana and by arranging for the publication of his works including *The Poems of Joseph Furphy* (1916), a reissue in 1917 of *Such is Life* and a severely edited version in 1921 of *Rigby's Romance*. The efforts of Baker and other admirers of Furphy such as Vance Palmer and A.G. Stephens were rewarded during the 1940s, when his reputation was secured; towards the end of the decade Douglas Stewart was writing that 'An amiable, an estimable madness is abroad in the land. Namely, the deification of Joseph Furphy, *alias* Tom Collins', and protesting with tongue-in-cheek that 'at a conservative estimate, fifteen thousand articles' on him had been contributed to *Southerly* alone. Furphy texts became available again with the republication of *Such is Life* (1944) and the first full publication of *Rigby's Romance* (1946) and *The Buln-Buln and the Brolga* (1948); together with the release of Baker's material in Miles Franklin's (q.v.) *Joseph Furphy: The Legend of a Man and His Book* (1944), they stimulated the increased interest in Furphy already apparent in the 'Letters to Tom Collins' (q.v.) series in *Meanjin* and confirmed by the Furphy special numbers in both *Meanjin* and *Southerly* (1943, 1945). Considerable attention then was devoted to Furphy's social and political ideas, which made him a central figure in the legend of the Nineties (q.v.). The democratic temper of, and the egalitarianism, nationalism and Christian socialism embedded in, his work was explicated by J.K. Ewers among others in *Tell the People!* (1943) and a decade later Furphy's 1897 description of his novel was adopted as the motto for the radical *Overland*. The second major thrust of Furphy commentary in the 1940s was directed towards unravelling the mysteries of *Such is Life*, which had confused most earlier commentators despite the clues offered by Furphy himself in an anonymous review of the novel published in the *Bulletin* in 1903. Most importantly, commentators demonstrated that *Such is Life* is not as structurally formless as its narrator, Tom Collins, would have readers believe; that the relationship between Furphy and his narrator is an ambivalent and ironic one in which, for example, Collins reveals things to the reader which are hidden from himself; that it is an experimental work which in form and design explores the relationship between fiction and reality; and that these complexities of structure and theme provide evidence that *Such is Life* is judged wrongly if judged simply as a rich portrait of bush life in the 1880s. The structure, form and themes of *Such is Life* have continued to detain literary critics and historians since the 1940s. There has been further exploration of the unities of its plot and of the role and morality of its narrator, which has involved discussions of *Rigby's Romance* and *The Buln-Buln and the Brolga*. Attention has also been focused on the philosophy of the novel, e.g. whether life as a mixture of pre-destination and free will is its central theme; on its balance of comedy and moral seriousness; on its ironic modes; on its romance and pica-resque elements; and on Furphy's language and style. John Barnes has written a critical mon-ograph (revised edition, 1979) and edited a Furphy volume in the Portable Australian Authors series (1981).

Furphy once described himself as 'half bush-man and half bookworm'. Just as his wide experience of bush life gave him the knowledge which informed his writing and made *Such is Life* an important and realistic portrayal of rural Australia, so his wide reading helped fashion the form of the novel and make it an important

and original exploration of the relationship be-tween literature and life. The isolation in which Furphy worked is the probable reason why, for all the cleverness and appropriateness of his literary allusions to Shakespeare, the Bible, Sterne and other authors, there remains a cer-tain self-consciousness about his literary style; the effect, when the ponderousness and pom-posity natural to the character of Tom Collins are added, is to make *Such is Life* difficult to read, if increasingly enjoyable to reread. The irony, then, is that an Australian classic by an author of strong nationalistic sentiments (de-spite recent suggestions that parts of *Such is Life* attest to hierarchies of class in rural Aus-tralia) is inaccessible to ordinary Australians. Nonetheless, *Such is Life* is significant for the part it played in turning Australian fiction away from the colonial romance, and Furphy remains one of the most significant writers of Australian fiction before the First World War.

G

Gabbett, the convict cannibal in Marcus Clarke's novel, *His Natural Life* (q.v., 1874), is based on the Tasmanian convict, Alexander Pearce or Pierce (c. 1790–1824), who twice es-caped with other convicts from Macquarie Har-bour, was the sole survivor on each occasion, and was hanged for cannibalism. Clarke read about Pearce in the Molesworth Report on transportation (1837–38); so did 'Price Wa-rung', who used the source for two gruesome stories about convict cannibalism, 'In Shoes of Death: The Tanning of the Hide' and 'The Wearing of the "Shoes of Death" ' (1892). Pearce, whose skull is now at the University of Pennsylvania, is the subject of Dan Sprod's *Alexander Pearce of Macquarie Harbour* (1977), which includes information on the other writ-ers, e.g. David Burn, T.G. Ford, Patsy Adam-Smith, who have written up the Pearce story.

Gadfly, a provocative Adelaide weekly founded by C.J. Dennis (q.v.), was published 1906–09. It aimed to encourage Australian literature and art, support nationalistic attitudes such as pro-tection and restricted immigration, and lam-poon pomposity and hypocrisy. Its contributors included writers Dennis, Edward Dyson, 'Grant Hervey', and artists Hal Gye, Will and Am-brose Dyson and Ruby Lindsay.

GAGE, MARY (1940–   ), born England, where she worked as a freelance journalist and for the London *Times*, settled in WA in 1972. She has written short stories, some of which have been published in *Argosy* and broadcast by the BBC; an unusual book about life in a chicken run, *Praise the Egg* (1981), which won the 1980 Angus & Robertson Writers' Fellow-ship; and several plays. These include 'The Catalyst' (1972), 'Supermarket' (1975), 'Every-one's a General' (1976), *The New Life* (1977), 'Gas' (1977), 'The Same Square of Dust' (1979) based on the life of Charles Kings-ford–Smith and co-winner of WA's 150th an-niversary play competition, 'The Price of Pearls' (1980) and 'My Name is Pablo Picasso' (1981). Her best-known play, *The New Life*, a one-act study of the experience of a British immigrant family, was first produced in 1974.

Galah, a word of Aboriginal origin, is the name applied to the rose-breasted, grey-backed species of cockatoo found in considerable num-bers in inland Australia. Like most types of cockatoo, the galah is a pest to farmers because of its attacks on crops. Its noisy and rather stupid behaviour has led to the word being used colloquially to denote noisy, foolish peo-ple who lack common sense. Popular expressions are 'as mad as a galah' or 'as mad as a gumtree full of galahs'. This derogatory use of galah is widespread in Australian writing, e.g. in Sumner Locke Elliot's *Rusty Bugles* (1948), D'Arcy Niland's *Call Me When the Cross Turns Over* (1957) and David Ireland's *The Unknown Industrial Prisoner* (1971). A 'galah session' is the phrase used to denote a gossip session on the Flying Doctor radio network.

Galahad Jones, a novel by Arthur Henry Adams (q.v.), was pubished in 1910. The hero, a middle-aged bank clerk with a chivalric spirit, intervenes in the life of a young girl dying of consumption in an effort to bring her happiness. The novel, which successfully combines realism, romance, humour and melodrama, was subsequently reworked by Adams as a play and published in 1914.

GALLAGHER, KATHERINE (1935–), born Maldon, Victoria, was a teacher in Victoria 1964–68 and in Paris 1971–78. She has written two books of poetry, *The Eye's Circle* (1975) and *Tributaries of the Love-Song* (1978); a second edition of *The Eye's Circle* in 1978 contains a significant new poem, 'Winterfalls'.

Gallipoli, a word of legendary significance to Australians, is a town (spelt 'Gelibolu' on some modern, international maps) in Turkey, which is at the neck of and gives its name to a peninsula bounded on one side by the Gulf of Saros and the Aegean Sea, and on the other by the Dardanelles Straits connecting the Aegean Sea and the Sea of Marmora, which in turn is connected to the Black Sea by the Bosporus. The peninsula was the scene of a campaign, known as the Gallipoli or Dardanelles campaign, in the First World War. Early in 1915, after Russia had asked Britain to help relieve Russian troops fighting the Turks by mounting their own attack on the Turkish forces, it was decided that an attempt should be made to force the Dardanelles, thus opening the way for an attack on Constantinople (Istanbul). After naval bombardments in the Straits, the Allies attempted an amphibious landing on the Aegean side of the Gallipoli peninsula with the objective of crossing overland to capture the Turkish emplacements protecting the Dardanelles. Australian and NZ troops formed part of the Allied forces and from 25 April 1915 the Anzacs (q.v.) were put ashore at what came to be known as Anzac Cove. They established a toehold on the ridges above the beach but were unable to make much progress towards winning the summit which commanded the Straits; a stalemate developed in which the impact of troops was reduced by indecision and sometimes incompetent planning, by the threat of disease, and by the unfavourable terrain. The campaign itself foundered and in December 1915 it was decided to evacuate the peninsula. By one estimate almost half a million Allied troops were landed on the Gallipoli peninsula; of those up to a quarter of a million were casualties in one form or another, Australasian casualties numbering 27,594.

The commemoration of Anzac Day, as the anniversary of the first landing at Anzac Cove came to be known, began in 1916 and in time the Gallipoli experience came to be seen as an event of national significance: in broad terms, as the occasion when Australia underwent its baptism of fire and came of age through the heroic sacrifice of its young men, who demonstrated the ideals of Australian manhood. That the sacrifice was made in an imperial rather than national cause illustrates the paradoxes of Gallipoli in particular and Australian nationalism in general. The mythic significance of Gallipoli was firmly established in the writings of the war historian C.E.W. Bean (q.v.), particularly in his *The Story of Anzac*. C.J. Dennis, known as the 'Anzac Laureate', in *The Moods of Ginger Mick* (1916) and *Digger Smith* (1918), and Henry Lawson in 'Song of the Dardanelles' also paid contemporary tribute to the distinctive qualities of the Australian soldier. David McKee Wright's poem 'Gallipoli' celebrates the Australian achievement there; Mary Gilmore's 'Gallipoli' grieves for those who died there. Although in its generalised aspects the myth has been much scrutinised, e.g. by Alan Seymour in *The One Day of the Year* (q.v., 1962), Australian writers have continued to be detained by Gallipoli. A number of them, e.g. Leon Gellert, Ion L. Idriess, Frank Clune, Harley Matthews, were at Gallipoli and recorded their experiences. More recently, Peter Weir's film *Gallipoli* (1981; screenplay by David Williamson, novelization by Jack Bennett) was a major success in Australia and overseas; Roger McDonald's *1915* (q.v., 1979) won several major literary awards before its adaptation into a successful television series in 1982; and Albert Facey's memoirs, *A Fortunate Life* (1981), cover the First World War. Although the events of Gallipoli form only part of Weir's film, McDonald's novel and Facey's autobiography, the success of all three illustrates how firm a hold the Gallipoli experience retains on the imagination of Anglo-Saxon Australians. Sidney Nolan painted a notable Gallipoli series; among recent books on Gallipoli, Bill Gammage's *The Broken Years* (1974) is based on diaries and personal accounts. Gammage also published, with Peter Weir and David Williamson, *The Story of Gallipoli* (1981).

Galmahra, a University of Queensland magazine, was published three times a year 1921–

65. Two of its notable editors were P.R. Stephensen and Cecil Hadgraft. It published, in addition to university news, literary articles, reviews, short fiction and verse.

GAMAS, Citizen, was author of an early play concerned with Australia, *Les Emigrés aux Terres Australes, ou Le Dernier Chapitre d'une Grande Révolution* (1794), performed in Paris in 1792. Other early plays were performed on the English stage including 'Botany Bay' (1787), before the First Fleet reached Australia.

GAMMAGE, W.L., see **Gallipoli**

Gap, The, a famous Sydney landmark in the suburb of Watson's Bay, is a precipitous cliff face which has been a regular site for accidents and suicides. It first appeared in Australian literature in the melodrama *Forged* (1873) by Arthur Murray; the heroine, Diana, is saved from the Gap by Charlie Woolley, 'a Riverina squatter', an early example in Australia drama of the bush hero. The *Dunbar* (q.v.) was wrecked not far from the Gap in 1857.

GARDINER, FRANK (FRANCIS CHRISTIE) (?1830–1903), born near Goulburn, NSW, was the son of a Scottish free settler named Christie and an Irish-Aboriginal servant girl; he took the name Frank Gardiner around 1860. From 1861 until his capture in 1864 he took part in several daring robberies in central western NSW, often teamed with Ben Hall and Johnny Gilbert (qq.v.). One of the few bushrangers to escape death during capture or execution after it, he was eventually released in 1874 subject to his exile, a controversial decision which brought down the government of Sir Henry Parkes. The bushranger Lardner in 'Rolf Boldrewood''s *Robbery Under Arms* (1888) and *The Miner's Right* (1890) is modelled on Gardiner, who is also the subject of an extensive ballad literature, e.g. 'Frank Gardiner He Is Caught at Last' and 'The Fierce and Bloody Battle of the Weddin Mountains'. Colin Free wrote *Ironbark* (1976), a novel about Gardiner and his exploits.

GARE, NENE (1919–), born Adelaide, was educated at the Adelaide Art School and Perth Technical School. Her publications include the significant novel *The Fringe Dwellers* (q.v., 1961), which concerns the plight of part-Aborigines who fail in their effort to integrate with white society; *Green Gold* (1963), a novel loosely based on the author's banana-growing experiences at Carnarvon, with a backdrop of the natural hazards of that area of Australia; *Bend to the Wind* (1978), short stories about her friends, the Aborigines of WA; and *A House*

With Verandahs (1980), an autobiographical account of her family life as a girl in Adelaide, together with a sequel, *An Island Away* (1981), dealing with her experiences when her husband was a patrol officer in Papua New Guinea.

Gargoyle Poets, see **Makar**

GARNER, HELEN (1942–), born Helen Ford at Geelong, graduated from the University of Melbourne in 1965 and taught in Melbourne secondary schools until her controversial dismissal in 1972 for answering students' questions about sexual matters. She later worked as a journalist, in 1973 with *Digger* and since then as a freelance reviewer and feature writer; she has also written rock lyrics, acted on stage and film, and lived in Paris (1978–79). She has written *Monkey Grip* (1977), a widely-acclaimed novel which won a National Book Award and was filmed (1981), and two novellas published together, *Honour and Other People's Children* (1980). Set against a background of inner city communal life in Melbourne, *Monkey Grip* focuses on the fluctuating relationship between Javo, a heroin addict, and the narrator, Nora.

GARRAN, ANDREW (1825–1901), born and educated in London, came to Australia in 1851 because of ill-health. He was co-editor of the *Register* 1853–55 then became assistant editor of the *Sydney Morning Herald* in 1856 and editor 1873–85. He edited the *Picturesque Atlas of Australia* (1886–88) and was a member of the NSW Legislative Council 1887–92. His son was Sir Robert Garran (q.v.).

GARRAN, Sir **ROBERT** (1867–1957), son of Andrew Garran (q.v.), was born in Sydney and was called to the Bar in 1890. Private secretary to Edmund Barton in the Federation movement, he published *The Coming Commonwealth* (1897) and collaborated with John Quick in the *Annotated Constitution of the Australian Commonwealth* (1901). A foundation member of the Commonwealth public service, Garran became solicitor-general in 1916 and played a leading role in many undertakings including the establishment of the Australian National University. He was made GCMG in 1937 and received numerous other honours. Garran's memoirs, *Prosper the Commonwealth*, were published in 1958. *The Gifted Knight* (1983), by Noel Francis, collects Garran's poetry.

'GARRYOWEN', see **FINN, EDMUND**

GARTNER, JACK, see **Hawthorn Press**

GASK, ARTHUR CECIL (1872–1951), born London, practised as a dental surgeon for more than forty years in England and Australia and wrote upwards of thirty crime and mystery novels, some of which involve the detective Larose and are set in SA, where Gask lived. Gask's first novel was *The Secret of the Sandhills* (1921). The scope and nature of Gask's fiction are indicated by their titles e.g. *The Red Paste Murders* (1923), *The Shadow of Larose* (1931), *Gentlemen of Crime* (1932) and *The Hangman's Knot* (1936).

GASKIN, CATHERINE (1929–), born County Louth, Ireland, came to Australia as a child. At sixteen she startled the Australian reading public by having a successful novel, *This Other Eden*, published. After her second novel, *With Every Year* (1947), she went to England and has since lived in the USA, Ireland and the Isle of Man. Her most successful novel, *Sara Dane* (1954), the story of a convict girl who goes on to make a successful life in Australia, is based partly on the life of Mary Reibey. It sold over two million copies and was made into a television series in Australia in 1982. She produced a stream of other bestsellers, including *Blake's Reach* (1958), *Corporation Wife* (1960), *The Tilsit Inheritance* (1963), *The File on Devlin* (1965), *Edge of Glass* (1967), *Fiona* (1970), *A Falcon for a Queen* (1972), *The Property of a Gentleman* (1974), *The Summer of the Spanish Woman* (1977), *Family Affairs* (1980) and *Promises* (1982). Although she has not attracted the interest of literary critics, she is one of the most successful contemporary exponents of the popular romance. Her plots, carefully-crafted and woven into a solidly-researched background, are the strength of her fiction; her characters, predictable figures who vary little from book to book, are less effective.

Gateway, The (1953), the third volume of poetry by Judith Wright (q.v.), shows the poet moving away from the familiar world of the senses which characterize the earlier volumes, *The Moving Image* (1946) and *Woman to Man* (1949), to begin a quest for self-knowledge. The title poem speaks of 'the traveller' (the poet herself) passing through 'the gateway' to new perceptions. In addition to poems about other searchers for knowledge, e.g. 'The Journey' and 'The Cicadas', the volume contains poems such as 'Old House', 'Train Journey' and 'Eroded Hills', which reflect Wright's long-established interest in her ancestry and the New England environment.

Gathered In, a novel by Catherine Helen Spence (q.v.), was published as a serial in the Adelaide *Observer* 1881–82 and in book form in 1977. Although broadly typical of the nineteenth-century romantic novel, *Gathered In* presents an unusual view of illegitimacy and the moral and philosophical problems that confront those involved. Spence shows that illegitimacy can sometimes involve the father as an unwilling victim and a sufferer, and that an illegitimate child can be anxious, not for revenge for himself and his betrayed mother, but for his father's good reputation and for the welfare of his half-brothers and sisters. Kenneth Oswald, illegitimate son of Scottish gentleman, Norman McDiarmid, loses his mother when he is ten years old and unknowingly makes the acquaintance of his father, who wishes to provide for his future without upsetting the present McDiarmid family relationship, which full recognition of the boy would entail. Kenneth later joins another benefactor, his uncle George Oswald, on his large Australian property, Tingalpa, an occasion which allows the author to enlarge on the low-born Australian immigrant who has grown to a graceless colonial prosperity on the sheep's back and by ruthlessly grasping enormous tracts of land. Most of the remainder of the novel is set in the colony in the 1860s, where, by a series of remarkable coincidences, Kenneth meets and rescues his half-sister, Sybil, from a villainous husband; meets, loves and finally marries Edith Gray, daughter of a nearby English gentleman squatter; becomes so firmly entrenched in the favour of his rough and ready, but essentially good-hearted, Uncle George, that the latter makes him heir to his colonial wealth; and is wrongfully arrested for the murder of Uncle George's wastrel son Jim, a 'currency lad', but is acquitted when Sybil's husband, the murderer, flees to America. The last scenes occur in England and Scotland, where Edith agrees to marry Kenneth on condition he first restore his mother's reputation and claim justice from his father. Kenneth reverses the usual course of the illegitimacy novel by refusing but Edith withdraws her condition when Norman McDiarmid is able to show that his own anguish about the situation has over many years made abundant recompense for his early lack of judgement. Thus Kenneth is left illegitimate, but, in view of his being finally 'gathered in' to the bosom of his real family, his marriage to Edith, and his inheritance from his uncle, scarcely lamenting.

In spite of its elaborate, circuitous and melodramatic plot, *Gathered In* is not altogether a failure. Some of the Australian station scenes, e.g. the men's hut at Gray's property, are effectively described although there is the usual implication that to be colonial is to be uncouth and crude, whereas to be English is to be instinctively fine and elegant. Spence's own religious doubts, evident in *An Agnostic's Progress* (1884), are solved in the novel. Religion, especially as exemplified in the itinerant bush missionary, David Henderson, is shown to be no grim Calvinistic scheme of rewards and punishments but a process where love of God is expressed through a religion of humanity.

GAUNT, MARY (1861–1942), born Chiltern, Victoria, was one of the first two women admitted to the University of Melbourne. After the death of her husband in 1900 she lived in England and later in Italy. An indefatigable traveller, she wrote numerous travel books but her forte was fiction; of some twenty published works, six novels and a book of stories concern Australia. Her first novel, *Dave's Sweetheart* (1894) and *Deadman's: An Australian Story* (1898) are set in the Victorian goldfields; *Kirkham's Find* (1897) is a story of prospecting in the Northern Territory; *As the Whirlwind Passeth* (1923) is set in NSW in Governor John Hunter's time; and *Joan of the Pilchard* (1930) is linked to Bligh's voyage to Tahiti in the *Bounty*. *The Moving Finger* (1895) is a book of Australian short stories and *The Ends of the Earth* (1915) also contains Australian tales.

'GAVAH THE BLACKSMITH', see **O'DOWD, BERNARD;** *Tocsin*

GAY, WILLIAM (1865–97), born Bridge of Weir, Scotland, emigrated to NZ in 1885 and then to Victoria in 1888 in a vain attempt to ward off tuberculosis. He taught briefly at Scotch College, Melbourne, and was a tutor on a Riverina station and later in Melbourne. He spent the last four years of his life in a Bendigo hospital but maintained his keen interest in writing poetry and helped foster literature in the Bendigo area. He published *Sonnets and Other Verses* (1894), *Sonnets* (1896) and *Christ on Olympus and Other Poems* (1896). A miniature edition of his poems was published posthumously in 1910; *The Complete Poetical Works of William Gay*, edited with a memoir by J. Glen Oliphant, appeared in 1911. His best-known individual poems are those which appeal for the establishment of the Australian Commonwealth, i.e. 'Australia 1894', 'Australian Federation' and 'Australia Infelix'. 'Christ on Olympus', a long poem in blank verse, shows the Olympian dieties relinquishing their power to the greater God.

GELLERT, LEON (1892–1977), born Walkerville, SA, was a schoolteacher before he was wounded at Gallipoli. In 1917 he published *Songs of a Campaign* (see War Literature), which won the University of Adelaide's Bundey prize for poetry and established Gellert as the sol-

dier-poet of the day. In eloquent poems such as 'Through a Porthole', 'Patience', 'The Burial', 'The Diggers' and 'Attack at Dawn', Gellert recorded the dignity and courage of the soldier caught haplessly in the futility of war. In 1919 he published *The Isle of San*, a long allegorical poem divided into six dreams with a prologue and an epilogue and numerous songs and sonnets that are used as interludes between the dreams. In 1928 he included the connecting pieces of *The Isle of San* in a booklet *Desperate Measures*, which is largely concerned with the vicissitudes of domesticity, Gellert having married in 1918. He taught in Sydney after the War before his friendship with Norman Lindsay, Sydney Ure Smith and Bert Stevens led him into journalism, initially with *Art in Australia*, then with *Home* and later as literary editor, columnist and book reviewer with the *Sydney Morning Herald* and the *Daily Telegraph*. His later publications included the satirical *These Beastly Australians* (1944), *Week after Week* (1953) and *Year after Year* (1956).

Generations of Men, The (1959), an imaginative blend of history and fiction by Judith Wright (q.v.), tells the story of her grandparents, Albert and May Wright, and May Wright's parents and grandparents, early pioneers of the Hunter Valley district of NSW. The book is based largely on diaries of Albert Wright and on letters and personal reminiscences.

'Genius and the Ghost, The', see **FORSTER, WILLIAM**

GEOGHEGAN, EDWARD, (?1813–?), born Dublin, arrived in Sydney in 1840. A medical student convicted of obtaining goods on false pretences, he was transported for seven years. He became associated with Francis Nesbitt and within a few years produced ten plays, some of which were adaptations. They include 'Ravenswood' (1843), 'The Last Days of Pompeii' (1844), 'A Christmas Carol' (1844), *The Currency Lass* (q.v., 1844), 'The Hibernian Father' (q.v., 1844), 'Captain Kyd' (1845), 'Lafitte the Pirate' (1845) and 'The Royal Masquer' (1845). As a convict subject to prohibitions in the theatre, Geoghegan was inhibited from publicly claiming authorship of his plays and, in addition, was accused of plagiarism in 'The Hibernian Father'. After 1852 nothing further is known of his life.

'Geological Spieler, The', a humorous story by Henry Lawson (q.v.), was written in 1895 and published in *While the Billy Boils* (1896). One of the Steelman (q.v.) sequence, the story records the experiences of Steelman and his offsider, Smith, after they come across a railway construction party while travelling in NZ. By posing as a geologist Stoneleigh with, Smith as his assistant, Steelman is able to impress the boss of the gang and secure food and accommodation for three days. On the fourth morning Steelman talks with one of the party, who tells him that the boss is a university-educated mineralogist; in fact, as Steelman later learns, it is the informant who has the geological knowledge, a discovery which leads Steelman to decide that it is time he and Smith moved on.

Georgiana's Journal, see McCRAE, GEORGIANA HUNTLY

Geraldton Express, a weekly newspaper, began publication in WA in 1878 as the *Victorian Express*; in 1894 it became the *Geraldton Express and Murchison Goldfields News* and in 1897 the *Geraldton Express and Murchison and Yalgoo Goldfields Chronicler*. Usually referred to as the *Geraldton Express*, or the *Express*, it became in the 1890s one of the most important goldfields newspapers, identifying with the working man and aggressively championing the cause of the miners. Its solid core of literary content was largely due to its energetic and progressive editors and journalists, among whom were Alfred Carson, John Drew, C. Andrée Hayward and F.C.B Vosper. In 1880 the *Express* introduced a regular literary supplement which reprinted literary material from the newspapers of the eastern states and overseas. In an editorial in January 1896 Hayward assessed Australian literature, especially the work of the *Bulletin* writers; he also held regular literary competitions for local writers, the material from which was printed in the *Express*'s Christmas numbers.

GERARD, EDWIN FIELD ('GERARDY'; 'TROOPER GERARDY') (1891–1965), born Yunta, SA, worked on the WA goldfields and later served with the AIF at Gallipoli and in the campaigns in the desert. Under the pseudonyms 'Gerardy' and 'Trooper Gerardy' (see War Literature), he contributed poems about the war to journals such as the *Bulletin* and published two volumes of poetry, *The Road to Palestine and Other Verses* (1918) and *Australian Light Horse Ballads and Rhymes* (1919). Sometimes dubbed 'the laureate of the Light Horsemen', Gerard produced in poems such as 'The Horse That Died for Me', 'El Maghara', 'South of Gaza' and 'Riding Song' his most vigorous and effective verse. After the war he was a journalist, then a farmer, and wrote prolifically for the *Bulletin* in verses that reflected nostalgically on the vanished rural life of his youth.

GERSTAECKER, FRIEDRICH (1816–72), born Hamburg, Germany, came to Australia in 1851 by way of the Californian goldfields and various South Sea islands with an established reputation as a novelist and writer of travel books. His stay of less than a year in Australia was hectic; it included an unsuccessful attempt to travel down the Murray River in a home-made canoe, a tramp of 700 miles across country to Adelaide, and a visit to the Bathurst goldfields in NSW. His writings on Australia include a handbook for German immigrants, *Nord-und-Sud Australien: Ein Handbuch fur Auswanderer* (1849); *Narrative of a Journey round the World* (1853), a vivid description of his activities here; *The Two Convicts* (1857), the romantic story of a bushranger which was serialized in the *Examiner and Melbourne Weekly News* (1859–60); and *Im Busch* (1864), a story of the goldfields. An Australian background was also used in several of his other novels. He translated into German, Charles Rowcroft's *Tales of the Colonies* (1843).

Getting of Wisdom, The, a novel by 'Henry Handel Richardson' (q.v.), was first published in 1910 and was produced as a film in 1977. Based on 'Richardson''s personal experience as a boarder at the Presbyterian Ladies' College, Melbourne, 1883–87, the novel consists of a series of graphically-realized scenes which present the various stages of Laura Rambotham's growth in self and worldly knowledge. At the same time she is unconsciously developing a theory of fiction that she will later use as a writer. At home with her hard-working, widowed mother, her sister Pin and her two little brothers, Laura is used to being dominant, but at school she is immediately subjected to ridicule and hostility both because of her name and her unusual clothes. Although the chilly reception of Mrs Gurley, the awesome Lady Superintendent, and of the teachers adds to the load of misery she feels in the first six weeks, Laura begins to value life at school for its indirect lessons in experience. One of the first she learns, after an unseemly display of her musical virtuosity, is that 'the unpardonable sin is to vary from the common mould'. Her sense of inner difference is accentuated by her reaction to the public expulsion of Annie Johns, a classmate, for stealing; Laura, who understands Annie's motive better than 'nice-minded girls', is less shocked by the crime than by its punishment and her own thrilled response to its drama. Sex appears to be another area in which she differs from her schoolmates, Laura having no talent for and little real interest in attracting masculine admirers. Anxious to enhance her prestige, however, she invents a romance with the curate, Mr Shepherd. Invited to spend a week-end at his home, she discovers the pedestrian facts about Mr Shepherd, that he is bad-tempered and unattractive, but is unable to resist further opportunities to embellish her passionate tale. Eventually exposed when another girl also visits the Shepherds' home, Laura is completely ostracized and endures a period of intense misery. A seaside holiday is a healing experience but back at school Laura disciplines herself in socially-acceptable behaviour, now bitterly aware that 'the majority is always in the right'. Entry to the prestigious literary society develops her awareness of the differences between literal truth and the truth of fiction, and a deep friendship with an older girl, Evelyn Soultar, who soon leaves school, convinces Laura of the eternal 'fleetingness of things'. Her final lesson is about God; unprepared for her final examinations she fervently seeks His help and is rewarded by being given an opportunity to cheat, which she takes. Deep resentment of God as a pitiless Being succeeds this experience. Laura leaves school for the last time with the 'uncomfortable sense of being a square peg which fitted into none of the round holes of her world', although the narrator hints that she will ultimately find the right one. Her immediate response, however, is to celebrate her freedom by running with complete abandon down the avenue of a public park until she is lost to sight.

Ghost of the Cock, The see **WEBB, FRANCIS**

'Ghost upon the Rail, The', see **LANG, JOHN GEORGE**; Fisher's Ghost

GIBBS, MAY (1876–1969), born Surrey, England, came to WA as a child but returned to England in 1896 to study graphic art. Back in Australia again, she settled in Sydney, publishing her first Australian children's book, *Gumnut Babies*, in 1916. The Gumnut Babies, from whom sprang her later famous creations, Bib and Bub and Snugglepot and Cuddlepie, were bush creatures of her imagination, naked cherubs crowned with gumnut hats and adorned with long gum-blossom eyelashes. Other bush creatures made famous in her stories were Mrs Kookaburra, Mr & Mrs Bear and the less likeable Mrs Snake and the Banksia Men. Her later publications include *Gum Blossom Babies* (1916), *Boronia Babies* (1917), *Flannel Flowers and Other Bush Babies* (1917), *Wattle Babies* (1918), *Snugglepot and Cuddlepie* (1918), *Little Ragged Blossom* (1920), *Bib and Bub, Their Adventures* (1925), *Mr. & Mrs. Bear and Friends* (1943) and *The Complete Adventures of Snugglepot and Cuddlepie* (1940). 'Bib and Bub', her longest running comic strip, first appeared

in the *Sunday News* in 1924 and apart from a brief period in 1932 ran in various newspapers until 1967, absorbing another of her strips, 'Tiggy Touchwood', a sow with magical powers. May Gibbs's strength as a writer and illustrator lay in her ability to interpret animal behaviour in human terms suitable for children and in her craftsmanship, which loses little by comparison with such famous exponents of the art as Beatrix Potter.

GIBSON, G.H. (GEORGE HERBERT) ('IRONBARK') (1846–1921) born Plymouth, England, was a solicitor when he migrated to NZ in 1869 and thence in 1874 to Sydney, where in 1876 he joined the Department of Lands. His work as an inspector in that department took him to many outback stations, where he gained the knowledge of the bush that informs the light-hearted and lively ballads he published under the pseudonym 'Ironbark'. His books of verse are *Southerly Busters* (1878), *Ironbark Chips and Stockwhip Cracks* (1893) and *Ironbark Splinters from the Australian Bush* (1912), the last containing some of the poems from the earlier volumes. He is also the author of *Old Friends under New Aspects* (1883), an unusual depiction of characters from the Old Testament.

GILBERT, JOHN (?1842–65), was a bushranger who took part in some forty armed holdups and robberies in NSW 1862–65, often working with Frank Gardiner and Ben Hall (qq.v.). Gilbert was the model for Hulbert in 'Rolf Boldrewood''s *Robbery Under Arms* (1888); his career is the subject of the anonymous satire, 'The Diverting History of John Gilbert', and his death is romanticized in A.B. Paterson's ballad, 'How Gilbert Died'. Edgar F. Penzig published *A Real Flash Cove: The Story of the Bushranger John Gilbert* (1983).

GILBERT, KEVIN (1933–), born Condoblin, NSW, to an Irish father and part-Aboriginal mother, who both died when he was seven, was brought up in welfare homes and by relatives. After a limited education he worked through his teens as an itinerant labourer in towns of western NSW. Married at an early age, and with two children, Gilbert was found guilty at the age of twenty-three of the murder of his wife after a domestic argument and was sentenced to life imprisonment. In prison Gilbert, until then almost illiterate, became interested in art and literature. He soon showed a considerable talent for both lino cuts and painting and his work from prison was exhibited in 1970 by the Australian Council for the Arts. In 1971, after fourteen years in prison, Gilbert was paroled. His play 'The Cherry Pickers' (q.v.), a story of Aboriginal seasonal workers, written while he was in prison and staged in Sydney in 1971, earned Gilbert the distinction of being the first Aboriginal playwright to have a play performed in Australia. In 1972 he became associated with the Purfleet Aboriginal Reserve near Taree, NSW, where he instituted community aid projects and worked as a community developer. He also established the Kalari Aboriginal Art Gallery, an experiment in the training of young Aboriginal artists. Gilbert rapidly became active in the wider Aboriginal cause, editing periodicals such as *Alchuringa* and *Black Australian News*, canvassing the federal government for a national inquiry into Aboriginal education, and working for the Centre for Continuing Research into Aboriginal Affairs at Monash University, Melbourne. In addition to 'The Cherry Pickers' he has published two volumes of poetry, *End of Dreamtime* (1971) and *People Are Legends* (1978). His poetry is protest verse, displaying his anger against white society in 'People Are Legends' and 'Cock Robin'; the indifferent treatment of the black in 'Trying to Save Joan Ella'; the degradation brought into the Aboriginal's life by the hopelessness of his future in 'Goomee Jack'; the need for violence in order to gain basic land rights in 'Land Claims', and the tragedy of the part-Aboriginal in 'Inhabitants of the Third World'. His contentious poem, 'To My Cousin, Evonne Cawley', in the *Bulletin* (30 September 1980) attacks what he sees as her lack of involvement in Aboriginal problems. Gilbert's chief political tract is the prose work, *Because a White Man'll Never Do It* (1973), the chief purpose of which was to procure land rights for the Aborigines so that dignity and self-esteem could be restored and a total Aboriginal community re-established. *Living Black* (1977), a collection of interviews by Gilbert with Aborigines from all parts of Australia, won a National Book Council Award. In *Living Black*, which attempts to give an authentic view of what it means to be an Aboriginal, Gilbert incorporates his conversations with Aborigines of all types, urban, reserve, tribal and fringe dwellers. He proposes a programme of physical and spiritual compensation to the Aborigines for two hundred years of deprivation, a programme based on the granting of land rights and a regeneration of Aboriginal culture.

GILES, BARBARA (1912–), born Manchester, England, came to Australia in 1923 and later taught in Victoria. She has also been involved in migrant education and has written about migrants in her poetry. Editor of the magazine *Luna*, she has published two books of poetry, *Eve Rejects Apple* (1978) and *Earth*

and Solitude (1983). She has largely concerned herself with children's literature, having edited, with Michael Dugan and J.S. Hamilton, *Messages in a Bottle: Poetry by Young Australians* (1978), *Of Human Beings and Chestnut Trees: Poetry by Young Australians* (1980) and *The Hat Trick: Australian Short Stories* (1981). She has also written and selected numerous books of verse and stories for children, e.g. *My Animal Friends* (1981), *People and Places* (1981) and *Bicycles Don't Fly* (1982).

GILES, ERNEST (1835–97), born Bristol, England, came to Australia in 1850 and was on the Victorian goldfields in 1852. In the early 1860s he explored the pastoral potential of the western areas of NSW beyond the Darling River, but his chief ambition was to make an overland crossing to WA. In spite of several failures in the early 1870s to find a route from Central Australia to the coast of WA, Giles ultimately crossed from SA to WA in 1875. His expeditions added greatly to the knowledge of the western half of the continent and his journals and published works are among the most perceptive and literary of the writings of the explorers. He published *Geographic Travels in Central Australia from 1872 to 1874* (1875), *The Journal of a Forgotten Expedition* (1880), and *Australia Twice Traversed* (1889). Geoffrey Dutton wrote *Australia's Last Explorer: Ernest Giles* (1970) and extracts from Giles's journals are included in Kathleen Fitzpatrick's selection, *Australian Explorers* (1958). Ray Ericksen's *Ernest Giles: Explorer and Traveller 1835–1897* (1978) won a National Book Council Award.

GILL, S.T. (SAMUEL THOMAS) (1818–80), born Somerset, England, came to SA in 1839 and established a portrait studio in Adelaide. In 1846 he accompanied J.A. Horrocks's expedition to Spencer Gulf; his diary of that journey was published in the *South Australian Gazette and Colonial Register* (1846), and many of his drawings from the expedition remain in the National Gallery of SA. Gill is represented in George French Angas's *South Australia Illustrated* (1847) by a scene in Hindley Street, Adelaide, and by a scene of the departure of Charles Sturt on his 1844 expedition. In 1852 Gill visited the Victorian goldfields: twenty-four lithographed sketches by him comprise *Victoria Gold Diggings and Diggers As They Are* (1853); many were included as illustrations in John Sherer's *The Gold-Finder of Australia* (1853). Gill's *Scenery in and around Sydney* was published in 1856; he also published *The Australian Sketchbook* (1865), a popular book of lithographed views depicting aspects of Australian rural life (see Overlander). In 1869 he was commissioned by the Melbourne Public Library to do forty sketches of the Victorian goldfields of 1852–53 (see Gold). Selections of his work include Geoffrey Dutton's *The Paintings of S.T. Gill* (1962) and J.E.B. Curry's *The Goldfields Illustrated: The Sketches of S.T. Gill* (1972). K.M. Bowden published the biographical *Samuel Thomas Gill, Artist* (1971).

GILLEN, FRANCIS JAMES, see **SPENCER, Sir WALTER**

GILLESPIE, BRUCE, see **Science Fiction**

GILMORE, Dame **MARY** (1864–1962) was born Mary Jean Cameron at Cotta Walla near Goulburn, NSW. After a bush childhood with sporadic formal schooling she completed her education by assisting in small schools in the Cootamundra, Wagga and Albury districts of NSW. In 1888–89 she taught in the mining town of Silverton, near Broken Hill, where close contact with the militant, working-class community aroused her life-long interest in the labour movement. In 1890–95 she taught at Neutral Bay and Stanmore in Sydney and became involved in the developing radicalism of the day by supporting the maritime and shearers' strikes of the early 1890s. In those years her friendship with Henry Lawson began and she was influenced by three men, William Lane, John Farrell and A.G. Stephens, who, she said, 'shaped my heart and my life'. In 1896 she joined Lane's New Australia venture in Paraguay and in May 1897, at the Cosme settlement, married a Victorian shearer, William Alexander Gilmore. They returned to Australia in 1902 and settled to an isolated farming existence in the Casterton district of western Victoria. In October 1903 her poetry was featured by A.G. Stephens in the Red Page of the *Bulletin*, and in 1908 she began to edit the Women's Page of the Sydney *Worker*, a task which occupied her until 1931. In 1910 her first volume of poetry, *Marri'd and Other Verses* was published, and in 1912, when her husband joined his brother on the land in north Queensland, she and her son went back to Sydney. Her campaigns for the welfare of the young and old, sick and helpless, depressed and under-privileged, and her irate and constantly-expressed disgust with privilege and corruption in high places filled the pages of the *Worker* and other newspapers for many years. In the two decades 1920–40, she published six volumes of poetry and three of prose. In 1937, in recognition of her literary achievement and her community and social activities, and as a tribute to her growing national status, she was made DBE, an honour which she cherished. During the tense months of 1942 after Singapore fell and the Japanese island-

hopped towards Australia, her defiant and well-publicized poem, 'No Foe Shall Gather Our Harvest' (q.v.) was a timely booster to public morale. In her remaining years, perched in her tiny flat in the heart of Sydney's bohemian Kings Cross, she continued her writing and her encouragement of other writers, her social crusading, and her gathering of the diminishing store of pioneer lore and legend. William Dobell's controversial portrait of her was unveiled for her ninety-second birthday in 1957. Her last years passed amid growing public acclaim; her death was mourned by a ceremonial state funeral through the streets of Sydney.

Mary Gilmore's earliest poems *Marri'd and Other Verses* are mainly spontaneous reactions, in a colloquial style, to the joys and sorrows of life's daily round; the short, lively lyrics are interspersed with occasional outbursts against injustice and inhumanity. *The Passionate Heart* (q.v., 1918), with its emphasis on the desolation of war, is more mature verse. In *The Tilted Cart* (1925), *The Wild Swan* (q.v., 1930) and *Under the Wilgas* (1932), and in her prose anecdotes and reminiscences, *Old Days: Old Ways* (q.v., 1934) and *More Recollections* (1935), her interest in recreating pioneer times and her concern with the despoiling of the land and destruction of the Aboriginal tribes are paramount. *Battlefields* (1939) contains her most strongly radical verse. 'The Baying Hounds' depicts the customary Gilmore stance, 'There was no hunted one/With whom I did not run', while 'Contest I Ask' affirms her life-long belief, 'Better to wounded lie/Than undeclared to die'. In the inscription to her final volume, *Fourteen Men* (q.v., 1954), published when she was almost ninety, she faces life's final encounter with the calm judgement that death is 'the last thing left to defeat'. Mary Gilmore's best poetry insists on love, courage and selflessness, and enshrines those values in some fine lyrics. Dymphna Cusack, T. Inglis Moore, Barrie Ovenden and Walter Stone compiled *Mary Gilmore: A Tribute* (1965); W.H. Wilde and T. Inglis Moore edited *Letters of Mary Gilmore* (1980).

One-woman dramatic interpretations of the life and work of Mary Gilmore include Theatre ACT's production 'When Butter Was Sixpence a Pound' (Joan Murray, 1983) and Melbourne Theatre Company's 'To Botany Bay on a Bondi Tram' (Beverley Dunn, 1984).

Gimme the Boats! see **MACDONNELL, J.E.**

Ginger Meggs, Australia's most famous 'boy' from the 1920s to the 1960s, was the comic strip creation of J.C. Bancks (q.v.). A small, red-headed boy in a black waistcoat, he began life in November 1921 as a googly bowler in the first episode of the strip 'Us Fellers'; by the time he became Ginger Meggs in April 1922 he was the central character; had acquired a girl friend, Minnie Peters, and a rival for her affections, Eddie Coogan; and had gathered about him a gang of mates including Benny and Ocker Stevens. For the next thirty years, weekly in the Sydney Sunday *Sun* and other newspapers and annually in *The Sunbeams Book, Adventures of Ginger Meggs* (1924–59), he experienced under Bancks both joy and tribulation. The joys include cricket, football, fishing, fighting, billy-cart derbies, 'wagging' school and toughening up curly-headed 'sooks' named Clarence, Cuthbert and Gerald. The tribulations included having to run messages (and the gauntlet of Tiger Kelly), brushes with the law over broken windows, with schoolteachers named Flogger and Canehard over his absence from school, and with his parents, John and Sarah Meggs, over almost any issue. Although the basic ingredients were established in its first year, the success of the strip was consolidated by its visual improvement over the years. Throughout all his adventures Ginger remained sturdily optimistic, self-confident, cunning and quick-thinking, a combination of larrikin, battler, philosopher and humorist. 'Us Fellers' changed its name to 'Ginger Meggs' in 1939, by which time the strip had become the first Australian one to be syndicated overseas. After Bancks's death in 1952 it was drawn by Ron Vivian (1953–74) and after Vivian by Lloyd Piper. Ginger has been the subject of several children's books, a pantomime written by Ray Lawler in the 1950s, the play 'Ginge's Last Stand' by Ken Horler (1975) and an Australian film (1982). A selection from the Bancks years was published as *The Golden Years of Ginger Meggs 1921–1952* (1978).

Ginger Mick, see **DENNIS, C.J.**

GIPPS, Sir **GEORGE** (1791–1847), after whom the region of Gippsland in Victoria is named, was born in Kent, England, entered the British army in 1809, and was appointed the ninth Governor of NSW in 1837. During his eight years in office, 1838–46, he presided over great changes in the colony: the cessation of transporation to NSW in 1840 and Alexander Maconochie's penal experiments at Norfolk Island; an increase in migration which almost doubled the population and made more urgent the need to establish a satisfactory education system; demands for separation by the colonists at Port Phillip; the beginnings of self-government through the establishment of a partly-elected Legislative Council, which increased tensions between Gipps and the colonists; and turmoil over relationships between the colonists and the Aborigines, most dramatically illustrated by the Myall Creek massacre of 1838. A governor whose contemporary unpopularity during difficult times influenced subsequent judgements of him, Gipps had most trouble with the squatters, who sought security of tenure for their runs and objected to Gipps's attempts to recover land rents in order to provide funds to assist immigration. In 1844, after the announcement of proposals which would implement Gipps's policies, the *Atlas* (q.v.) began publication in Sydney in the squatting interest; as part of the campaign the *Atlas* published the verse satires of Robert Lowe, notably 'Songs of the Squatter', and William Forster. Forster's 'The Devil and the Governor', published in the *Atlas* on 17 May 1845, depicts a visit by the Devil to his friend Gipps and their discussion of contemporary problems. Samuel Prout Hill published *Monody on the Death of Sir George Gipps* (1847).

Giraffe, The, see **'Send Round the Hat'**

Gladstone Colony was a short-lived attempt to settle the east coast of Queensland in 1847. Initiated by William Ewart Gladstone (later prime minister of England) it was to be a semi-penal colony, carrying emancipists, those whose terms of transportation had expired, and well-behaved prisoners from England who would be pardoned on arrival; it lasted only a few months. Contemporary satires on the ill-fated colony were written by Robert Lowe in the *Atlas*. Lowe's biographer, J.F. Hogan, wrote *The Gladstone Colony* (1898).

GLASKIN, GERALD MARCUS (1923–), born Perth, WA, served in the Second World War with both the RAN and the RAAF. He commenced writing short fiction while in hospital during the war; after the war he combined motor merchandising and stockbroking with writing, but became a full-time writer from 1958, spending considerable periods travelling and living outside Australia. Glaskin's first novel, *A World of Our Own* (1955), examines the attempts by a number of ex-servicemen to cope with the post-war world; praised in England and a best-seller in Norway, neither it nor any of Glaskin's equally successful later novels aroused significant literary interest in Australia. His other novels include *A Minor Portrait* (1957); *A Change of Mind* (1959); *A Lion in the Sun* (1960), which he considers his first important novel; *The Beach of Passionate Love* (1961), set in Malaysia; *A Waltz through the Hills* (1961); *Flight to Landfall* (1963); *O Love, O Loneliness* (1964); *No End to the Way* (1965), under the pseudonym 'Neville Jackson'; and *The Man Who Didn't Count* (1965). He has

Glaskin, Gerald Marcus

also published short stories, *A Small Selection* (1962) and *The Road to Nowhere* (1967); non-fiction, *Windows of the Mind: The Christos Experience* (1974), *Worlds Within: Probing the Christos Experience* (1976) and *A Door to Eternity: Proving the Christos Experience* (1979); and autobiographical works, *A Bird in My Hands* (1967), *Two Women*, comprising *Turn on the Heat* and *The Eaves of Night* (1975), and *One Way to Wonderland: Letters to a Pen-Friend* (1981). He has also written screenplays of several of his novels and a factual book, *The Land That Sleeps* (1961), on Australia's empty North.

Glass Canoe, The, a novel by David Ireland (q.v.), was first published in 1976 and won the Miles Franklin award for that year. Narrated by a young golf-course greenkeeper, nicknamed Meat Man because he is sexually well-endowed, *The Glass Canoe* describes the customs of an urban tribe of drinkers, who regularly congregate at their watering hole, the Southern Cross pub in an outer area of Sydney, referred to as The Mead. The characters, whose stories or random experiences form much of the kaleidoscopic structure of the novel, including Ernie, who first suffers excessive grief when his mother dies and then horribly murders a girl who appears to be threatening his job; the Great Lover, who combines a prodigious, indiscriminate sexual appetite and submissive domesticity; Aussie Bob, the ex-Englishman who ultimately loses all his four children in car accidents; Serge, the Russian pub fighter of unerring aim and unpredictable anger, who has been barred from the pub although no one has been game enough to tell him; Eh, a Queenslander who never got over it and has had a wandering but complicated life; and Alky Jack, Meat Man's surrogate father, whose bitterly wise pronouncements on modern life find a willing but uncomprehending audience at the Southern Cross. Alternating with their individual experiences is the communal life of the pub, a solid shelter against the so-called life outside of jobs, weddings, dismissals, babies, hunger and defeat. The pub offers 'A sort of past solidified in masonry. The traffic tried to run by all the faster to stay in the present or the past might grab them. But to us, our tomb was where life was: outside was a world fit only to die in.'

Meat Man perceives his tribe as the exploited, hunted victims of an urban world, whose only escape is the glass canoe, the schooner of beer: 'wage and small enterprise sheep and cattle amongst the unattainable riches of civilization; among tall, unfamiliar buildings, unimaginable processes, incomprehensible aims, scratching a living on the edge of the educated world'. Contrasting with his perspec-

tive is that of Sibley, his old schoolfriend, who earnestly documents the anti-social attitudes of the drinkers for his Ph.D. thesis in social psychology. As the narrative progresses, it is clear that much of life at the Southern Cross and outside is mysterious to the stoically acquiescent and perhaps wilfully blind Meat Man. Sibley suddenly disappears, the link between his continued absence and a malodorous beer keg apparently unperceived by Meat Man; a stranger, Vivian, hangs himself in an outer shed for love; Liz the Large is declared dead by her doctor but survives long enough to have the child she did not know she was carrying; Meat Man's girlfriend, whom he calls My Darling, appears to have another life from which he is divided; the brain-damaged victim of a savage mugging leaps on the roof of the Southern Cross and tries to drive the pub like a car; women unexpectedly demand feats of sexual prowess or casually offer themselves in payment for trivial favours; a pub widow hurls her husband's ashes into the bar. Alky Jack's pronouncements on the 'modern cult of animalism and violence' and the hopelessness of attempting to cast off 'the monster on our backs . . . absurd, gross, degrading' appear more and more justified by the pattern of events, which culminate in an extended, epic brawl with all the attributes of a ritualistic, tribal blood-letting.

'Glass on the Bar, The', see **Mateship**

GLASSOP, LAWSON (1913–66), born Lawson in the Blue Mountains, NSW, began a career in journalism with the *Newcastle Morning Herald*. In 1940 he joined the AIF serving in the Middle East, where he worked on an army newspaper. After the war he joined the *Sydney Morning Herald* and was a war correspondent in Korea 1950–51. From 1951 to 1960 he was with the Sydney *Daily Mirror*, Sydney *Truth* and Adelaide *Truth* and from 1960 was a columnist and feature writer for the Adelaide *Advertiser*. Glassop's chief literary work was the novel, *We Were the Rats* (1944, see War Literature); he also published a children's book, *Susan and the Bogeywomp* (1947), *Lucky Palmer* (1949), a novel about a gambler, and *The Rats in New Guinea* (1963), a sequel to the earlier novel. *We Were the Rats* was banned as obscene by the NSW government in 1946; a modified verson of the book was published in 1961. The hero of the novel, a cricketer and furniture salesman, enlists in the Australian army and after initial training in Australia goes to the Middle East, where he participates in the siege of Tobruk. Later he has a period in Cairo, returns to Australia, marries, and resumes his soldiering in the island campaigns of the Pacific War. A factual account of army life in wartime and an accurate reflection of army language and attitudes, *We Were the Rats* is reportage rather than a creative novel. The crude language, the repellent details of army life, and the blatant sexuality of the book led the appeals judge to describe much of it as 'just plain filthy', an assessment hotly contested by its numerous defenders, including the American writer John Dos Passos. The novel's realistic characterization and tracing of the extraordinary experiences that came to so many Australian volunteer soldiers make *We Were the Rats* a significant addition to Australian war literature.

'Glen of the Whiteman's Grave, The', a narrative poem, was first published by Henry Kendall (q.v.) in an undated booklet (?1865); it was later published in *Leaves from Australian Forests* (1869) as 'The Glen of Arrawatta' and republished with minor variations as 'Orara' in 1881. The tale of a lone settler murdered by natives, Kendall's poem is similar to the earlier Charles Harpur narrative, 'The Creek of the Four Graves' (q.v.).

Glugs of Gosh, The, see **DENNIS, C.J.**

Godbold, Ruth, see *Riders in the Chariot*

GODDARD, FRANCIS, see **MACNA-MARA, FRANCIS**

Godolphin Arabian: The Story of a Horse, The (1873), by James Brunton Stephens (q.v.), is a narrative about a famous Arab stallion, Scham. A gift from an Arabian sultan to the King of France, the horse languishes in obscurity pulling a cart in Paris, but is ultimately rescued and mated with the mare Roxana to found the modern line of thoroughbred racehorses.

Going Home, see **DE GROEN, ALMA**

Golconda trilogy is a series of novels by Vance Palmer (q.v.) which centres on the history of Macy Donovan, who has affinities with the politician E.G. Theodore (q.v.), and his rise from small union organizer to premier of Queensland. The series comprises *Golconda* (1948), *Seedtime* (1957) and *The Big Fellow* (1959). *Golconda*, set in a new mining settlement in the Queensland outback just after the First World War, traces the beginnings of Donovan's career. Brought up in the Maranoa district, Donovan has come to Golconda as a water-carter but a chance meeting with Frank Mahony, a union organiser, changes the direction of his life. In his new role of local union official, Donovan soon becomes dominant on the mining field but is less fortunate in his private life, especially in his inability to establish a relationship with the girl who most strongly attracts him, Neda Varnek. Neda, a sculptress with unconventional attitudes stemming partly from her childhood association with Aborigines, is more powerfully drawn by the primitive landscape, especially by the huge mountain Golconda, than by its inhabitants. Donovan passes through a period of depression when he discovers that Mahony has been dismissed from his union office for embezzling funds, and when his brief liaison with Carita Keighley, the wife of one of the company managers, comes to an end. Neda's mother, May Varnek, dies and Neda leaves for the interior with Farelli, an Italian bird-catcher, but soon returns disillusioned. Mahony also returns to Golconda, where he falls desperately ill with pneumonia and is nursed back to health by a schoolteacher, Dora Venn, whom he subsequently marries. Donovan wins pre-selection as the Labor Party candidate in the forthcoming State election and gains the seat. On the plane that takes him to Brisbane is Neda Varnek, bound for Sydney to pursue a career in art. The novel is distinguished by Palmer's evocation of the brooding, dominating mountain, and by the well-realized panorama of diverse individuals who live round its foot. One of the most striking of these is Christy Baugham, an old gouger who has been with William Lane in the New Australia venture.

Seedtime picks up Donovan's history after a gap of two years. He appears to be a failure in Brisbane, given to wild drinking sprees and has been stabbed in a brawl with an Italian he took to be Farelli. He is admitted to a hospital where he meets Dr Hugh McCoy and his sister-in-law, Nurse Judy Hegarty. Judy's fast-developing love for Donovan fails to move him, although her influence, together with his involvement with the McCoy and Hegarty families, has the effect of widening his aspirations. Meanwhile his political career reaches a crisis when he challenges his party chief and premier, Lambert, over a strike in the sugar industry and is soundly defeated. He returns to Golconda to ensure preselection for the next election; is warmly welcomed by the mining community, especially by Frank and Dora Mahony who now have a son, Peter; wins the seat with an increased majority; is reconciled with Lambert; and becomes engaged to Kitty, Judy's elder sister. Judy leaves to join the Flying Doctor Service and Frank Mahony dies of pneumonia.

The Big Fellow opens twenty years later just after the Second World War. Donovan is now at the height of his power, premier of his State and temporary leader of his party, but he is under threat both in his private and his public life. Neda Varnek comes back from a successful stay abroad and asks Donovan to help Leo, her son by Farelli, who is in a reformatory. His revived feeling for Neda makes Donovan more aware of the flaws in his family life. His sense of disappointment is deepened by the decision of Peter Mahony, whom he has virtually adopted and who has been working as his secretary, to study medicine. At the same time his political career is threatened by a scandal about the sale of government mines. Although a Royal Commission later clears him, he loses preselection for the *Golconda* seat. A peaceful interlude with Neda is disrupted by the return of Leo and their relationship is later shattered by Leo's violent confrontation with Donovan and subsequent death in a car smash. Neda leaves Queensland. Donovan's tired marriage is patched up and he leaves Golconda for a new career in federal politics.

Gold was officially discovered in NSW in April 1851, in Victoria in July of the same year and in Queensland in 1867. The rush to the Kimberley district of WA began in 1886 and in 1892–93 the rich Coolgardie and Kalgoorlie fields of that State were discovered. The mass movements to the various goldfields were known as the gold rushes, the alluvial goldfields were known as 'the diggings', and the gold seekers, 'diggers', a word which has carried into this century as a colloquialism for Australian soldiers of two World Wars. Gold mania fundamentally affected the nature of Australian society: the traditional dominance of the pastoralist was thrown off; an enhanced sense of egalitarianism ('Jack's as good as his master') disturbed the existing class strata; the colony's traditional ethnic balance was upset by the polyglot population that swarmed on to the goldfields; an upsurge of republican nationalism sprang from the new population mix and from the possibility of national independence offered by the country's new-found wealth; respect for the traditional values of education, industry and integrity wavered before the onslaught of greed, materialism and sharp practices; and public morality, law and order were threatened by the corruption and licentiousness that thrived on the diggings. The ultimate decline of gold fever produced further change, leading to a renewed interest in pastoral pursuits, a consequent demand to 'unlock the land' and the most significant pastoral reform, the Selection Acts. Gold brought into Australian life a new personality, the bearded, flannel-shirted, cabbage-tree hatted, Chinese-hating digger; a new language, the slangy jargon of alluvial mining; and a new set of legends, Ophir, the Turon, Bendigo Mac, the Welcome

Stranger, the 'inimitable' Thatcher, Eureka and the Southern Cross, the Palmer, Paddy Hannan and the Golden Mile, Harold Lasseter and his lost reef. It brought to a land that had known only convictism and the arduous tedium of pioneering a stimulating wave of excitement, glamour and optimism.

Although the profound social and economic changes that gold brought aroused sustained and serious literary comment in the second half of the nineteenth century, contemporary writers sought mainly to capture the spectacular nature of the gold rushes and the dramatic character of life on the diggings. Oral composition (balladry, song and the tall tale) was first in the field. Charles Robert Thatcher (q.v.), balladist and song-writer, was typical of the many itinerant entertainers, whose songs such as 'Who Wouldn't Be a Digger?', 'Where's Your Licence?', 'The Song of the Trap' and 'The Rising Generation' capture much of the colour and controversy of the goldfields life. Thatcher's compositions, which are included in his various songsters, celebrate contemporary goldfields events and personages and were enormously popular with the digger audiences. Commentaries such as James Bonwick's *Notes of a Gold Digger, and Gold Diggers' Guide* (1852), Samuel Mossman's *The Gold Regions of Australia* (1852), John Capper's *The Emigrant's Guide to Australia* (1853), and John and Samuel Sidney's *The Three Colonies of Australia* (1852), are a *pot-pourri* of history, geography, description and advice in the guide-book genre. Mrs Charles Clacy's *A Lady's Visit to the Gold Diggings of Australia, in 1852–53* (1853) is a lively personal account of the Victorian goldfields. Similarly spontaneous and informative are David Mackenzie's *The Gold Digger* (1853), which gives an account of a visit to the goldfields in February 1852; C. Rudston Read's *What I Heard, Saw and Did at the Australian Goldfields* (1853), a colourful and humorous account by a goldfields administrator; and *The Gold-Finder of Australia* (1853), ed. John Sherer, an entertaining but fictitious account of a tour of the goldfields, supplemented by stories and articles. Edward Hammond Hargreaves (q.v.), popularly but inaccurately accepted as the discoverer of gold in Australia, wrote *Australia and Its Gold Fields* (1855). William Howitt's *Land, Labour and Gold* (1855) forecast that from the melting pot of the goldfields would emerge 'a go-ahead, self-confident, Yankee sort of people'. The discovery and development of the Victorian goldfields is recorded in George Wathen's *The Golden Colony* (1855) and William Kelly's *Life in Victoria* (1859). Somewhat later reflections include James Armour's *The Diggings, the Bush, and Melbourne* (1864); W.J. Barry's *Up and Down* (1879); Charles D. Ferguson's *The Experiences of a Forty-Niner, During Thirty-Four Years' Residence in California and Australia* (1888), which includes a discussion of the Eureka uprising; and G.A. Preshaw's *Banking Under Difficulties* (1888), an account of a journey on foot from Melbourne to the Ballarat diggings by a lad of thirteen, who makes his 'pile' and then turns to the more secure occupation of banking.

Fictional representation of the goldfields is similarly abundant. 'Rolf Boldrewood', himself a Gulgong gold commissioner, wrote several novels with goldfields themes, including *The Miner's Right* (q.v., 1890) which is set in the NSW diggings and contains such ingredients as a successful gold strike, claim jumping, an attack by bushrangers on a gold escort, anti-Chinese riots, and the hero's return to England to a comfortable existence on the proceeds of Australian gold. Henry Lawson, son of an inveterate optimist whose life was ruled (and ruined) by the golden lure, grew up around the primitive alluvial goldfields of Gulgong and Pipeclay (Eurunderee) in western NSW. He records the colour and squalor, hope and despair, of the diggings in his 'A Fragment of Autobiography', in stories such as 'The Golden Graveyard', 'Payable Gold' and 'An Old Mate of Your Father''s, and in poems such as 'The Roaring Days' and 'Eureka'. Edward Dyson (q.v.), the son of a mining engineer, tells graphically of the deep mines in *Below and On Top* (1898) and *Rhymes from the Mines and Other Lines* (1896), while his classic story, 'A Profitable Pub' (1887), better-known as 'A Golden Shanty' (q.v.), has echoes of the goldfields with its golden bricks and anti-Chinese sentiments. 'Henry Handel Richardson''s *The Fortunes of Richard Mahony* (1930) opens with descriptions of goldfields life; Katharine Susannah Prichard (q.v.) wrote a trilogy, *The Roaring Nineties* (1946), *Golden Miles* (1948) and *Winged Seeds* (1950) set in the WA goldfields. The WA goldfields also provided the setting for John Arthur Barry's *The Luck of the Native Born* (1898), Hume Nisbet's *The Swampers: A Romance of the Westralian Goldfields* (1897), Hubert Stewart's *Ungodly Man* (1904), a moral tale about the ignobility of striving for material riches, Nat Gould's *The Miner's Cup: A Coolgardie Romance* (1896), and Helen Helga Wilson's several anecdotal accounts of the era, e.g. *Gateways to Gold* (1969) and *The Golden Miles* (1977). Australian melodrama of the late nineteenth century was obsessed with the theatrical possibilities offered by the gold era. George Darrell's *The Sunny South* (1883), with its theme of fortune won, lost and regained, was one of Australia's most popular and successful plays. Drury Lane Theatre in London had a long-running success in 1896, *The Duchess of Cool-*

gardie, by two English writers, Euston Leigh and Cyril Clare, while the rush to Kalgoorlie and Coolgardie is also depicted in 'To the West' (1896) by Alfred Dampier and Kenneth McKay. In 1921 the Pioneer Players staged Louis Esson's 'The Battler', which deals with the chanciness of the prospecting life. Later writers have continued to describe, record, explain and analyse every aspect of the golden revolution. Among such works are Malcolm Uren's *Glint of Gold* (1948); Geoffrey Serle's *The Golden Age* (1963); Nancy Keesing's *Gold Fever: The Australian Goldfields 1851 to the 1890s* (1967). They, and others like them, illustrate the truth of the title of Geoffrey Blainey's comprehensive account of mining in Australia, *The Rush That Never Ended* (1963).

Equally as authentically as in literature, the atmosphere of the gold rush era was captured and preserved in sketches and on canvas. S.T. Gill (q.v.) joined the gold rush to Victoria in 1852 and spent several years sketching scenes of goldfields life. In 1869 he was commissioned by the Melbourne Public Library to prepare watercolour paintings based on those sketches. Four of his most famous paintings, featured on Australian stamps in 1981, of the goldfields were *Puddling, Quality of Washing Stuff, Licence Inspected* and *On Route to Deposit Gold*. His original album, *The Victorian Goldfields 1852–53*, was edited in 1982 by Michael Cannon. The diary and drawings of another noted artist of the period, Eugene von Guerard (q.v.), were published as *The Artist on the Goldfields* (1982) with an introduction and annotations by Marjorie Tipping. A television series, 'Peach's Gold' by Bill Peach, was screened by the ABC in 1983 and the book of the series, *Gold*, was published simultaneously.

Gold-Finder of Australia, The, see **SHERER, JOHN**

GOLDBERG, S.L., see **Criticism**

'Golden Builders', which takes its title from William Blake's 'Jerusalem', is a twenty-seven poem sequence by Vincent Buckley (q.v.) forming the second half of *Golden Builders and Other Poems* (1976). The sequence emphasises the oppressive impact on the individual human consciousness of an urban environment, in this case the inner Melbourne suburbs where the university sits cheek by jowl with slums, highrise flats, factories, hospitals and a cemetery. The oppression of noise 'piped up like muzak' from the eternal jack-hammers and ceaseless traffic is the constant accompaniment to the ugliness and sordidness of the city, the 'crouched brick houses', the garbage and rats, the graffiti, a woman seeking an abortion, a self-immolation, and doomed dogs howling in the cages of medical laboratories. Although the overwhelming impression of the poem is of an environment deeply depressing to the human spirit, the underlying theme, as indicated by the introductory reference to Blake and by the 'Practising Not Dying' sequences and other areas of the poem, is that the human spirit can find within itself the strength and resilience to survive.

Golden Lover, The, see **STEWART, DOUGLAS**

Golden Mile is the name given to the goldbearing reef that forms the basis of the Kalgoorlie goldfield of WA. It was discovered by Paddy Hannan (q.v.) in 1893. Gavin Casey and Ted Mayman wrote *The Mile That Midas Touched* (1964); Stuart Gore's novel, *Down the Golden Mile* (1962), has some of its action set in the WA goldfields.

Golden Miles (1948), a novel in Katharine Susannah Prichard's (q.v.) goldfields trilogy, continues the story of Sally Gough, her friend Dinny Quin and her descendants, while depicting the period of the mining industry 1914–27. It moves on from *The Roaring Nineties* (q.v., 1946), which juxtaposes man against the natural elements, to a concentration on the dehumanizing world of machines, whose oppressive and evil energy dominates not only the slave-like lives of the mining community but also the Aborigines who come in contact with its corruption. A more didactic work, *Golden Miles* traces the democratic impulses which lead to trade unionism, the miners' strikes and the opposition to war with anti-conscription campaigns. Sally, now a mother of four sons, although hesistant at becoming involved in politics, finds that she is more responsive as both the war and the mines deprive her of her sons. The capitalist villain of the piece, Sir Paddy Cavan, who has evolved from the impish but ambitious young rogue in the previous novel, frames her son Tom, a political activist, and her husband on charges of gold-stealing; is implicated in the murder of her Aboriginal friend, Maritana; and elopes with her eldest son's wife, Amy. Sally's romantic attraction to Frisco, the charming blackguard, reaches its climax in this novel after the death of her husband and as a consequence of Frisco's debilitating blindness. See *Roaring Nineties, The* and *Winged Seeds*.

S.B.

'Golden Shanty, A', one of Australia's most famous goldfields short stories, written by Edward Dyson (q.v.), was published originally as 'A Profitable Pub' in the *Bulletin*'s Christmas issue, 1887. J.F. Archibald used Dyson's story as the title of the *Bulletin*'s first anthology (1890). On an old abandoned goldfield near Ballarat stands the Shamrock Hotel, owned by Irish-Australian Michael Doyle. Doyle's only neighbours are Chinese fossickers who appear intent on dismantling his hotel brick by brick. Doyle's running battle with the Chinese culminates in their offering him £50 for the building. The elated Doyle family are celebrating this handsome offer when, sharpening his carving knife on one of the hotel's bricks, Doyle discovers the reason for the Chinese enthusiasm for his pub – the bricks are made of goldbearing clay. Chasing off the 'thavin' hathins' Doyle takes the pub apart himself, collects nearly £2,000 in gold, goes off to Melbourne and becomes a Justice of the Peace, where it is his greatest delight to sentence any Chinaman who comes under his jurisdiction to 'foive pound or a month'. Despite its humour, 'A Golden Shanty' reflects the hostility that existed between white men and the Chinese on the goldfields.

Golden Treasury of Australian Verse, The, see **Anthologies; STEVENS, BERTRAM**

Golden West, an annual journal emanating from WA, was founded by R.C. Spear, former editor of the weekly newspaper, the *Spectator*, and was published 1906–46, edited by Spear for the whole of its existence. Begun largely as a survey of the State, and characterized by its strong pro-WA attitudes, it was soon expanded to carry short stories, sketches and verse, much of which was nostalgic in tone. Well-known WA literary figures who regularly contributed to the *Golden West* were 'Dryblower' (E.G. Murphy), John Drayton, 'Crosscut' (T.H. Wilson), Julian Stuart, Billy Clare and Spear himself.

GOLDHAR, PINKUS (1901–47), a Polishborn Jew, migrated to Australia in 1928. His book, *Short Stories of Australia* (1939), written in Yiddish, paints a pessimistic picture of the weakening of traditional Jewish family and religious ties in the Australian environment. He also published *Two Short Stories* (1968), the stories being 'Drummond Street' and 'Newcomers'. Among his other notable stories are 'The Pioneer', published in the *First Jewish Almanack* (1937), 'The Circumcision' and 'The Last Minyan', published in *Short Stories of Australia*, and 'The Funeral', published in *Coast to Coast* (1944).

GOLDSTEIN, VIDA (1869–1949), born Portland, Victoria, the daughter of progressive

Melbourne parents, was educated at first privately and then at the Presbyterian Ladies' College and the University of Melbourne. With her sister Bella, who married the British socialist H.H. Champion, she opened a school at St Kilda, which she ran until she became a full-time worker for the women's suffrage movement in 1899. President of the Women's Political Association of Victoria, and keenly interested in the rights and needs of women and children, she stood as an independent candidate for the Senate in the federal election of 1903, becoming the first woman parliamentary candidate in the British Empire. Although unsuccessful, she polled well and stood again for the Senate in 1910 and 1917, and for the House of Representatives in 1913 and 1914. In 1899 she founded a feminist newspaper, *Woman's Sphere*, which she continued to edit until its demise in 1905, and in 1909 she launched another, the *Woman Voter*. She also contributed to journals in Australia and overseas, and published in London *Woman Suffrage in Australia* (n.d.). In 1919 she retired from politics to devote herself to Christian Science.

GOLDSWORTHY, PETER (1951–), born Minlaton, SA, grew up in various SA towns and in Darwin and graduated in medicine from the University of Adelaide in 1974. His first published collections of poetry, *Readings from Ecclesiastes* (1982), was awarded the 1982 Commonwealth Poetry Prize. His poetry is characterized by crisp contemporary idiom and keen powers of observation. Most of the nineteen stories in his *Archipelagoes* (1982) have an SA background, range from serious to farcical in theme, and are vivid and original in their imagery. 'Memoirs of a small "m" marxist' was joint winner of the 1979 WA sesquicentenary literary competition and 'Before the Day Goes' won the 1980 Premio Bancarella Literary Award from the Italian Festival of Victoria.

GOODE, ARTHUR RUSSELL, ('ARTHUR RUSSELL') (1889–1937), born Wedderburn, Victoria, worked as a telegraphist for eighteen years before taking up journalism and ultimately becoming technical editor of *Listener In,* a Melbourne radio journal. A prolific writer of books for boys, usually under the pseudonym 'Arthur Russell', Goode published such successful novels as *Ginger for Pluck* (1926), *Storm Child* (1932), *Snowy for Luck* (1934), *The Sky Pirates* (1946) and *Mason's Circus* (1947). He also published *Twenty-Six Radio Stories* (1931), *Twenty-Six Australian Stories* (1934), *Twenty-Six South Sea Stories* (1936), and, with Bernard Cronin, *Bushranging Silhouettes* (1932).

GOODGE, W.T. (WILLIAM THOMAS) (1862–1909), born London, went to sea as a steward but left his ship in Sydney in 1882 to go 'on the wallaby' for twelve years in outback NSW. In later life Goodge was a journalist, becoming editor of the Orange *Leader* and for the last nine years of his life contributing a weekly account to the Sydney *Truth* of the happenings of an imaginary club of boozers, the Gimcrack Club. Goodge's comic journalism is part of the long line of notable Australian writing in that genre which includes the work of Lennie Lower, Alex Macdonald, Ross Campbell and Ron Saw. A popular *Bulletin* poet and assessed by Norman Lindsay as one of Australia's best writers of light verse, Goodge published *Hits! Skits! and Jingles!* (1899). His poems are filled with bush identities such as Temora Mat, Slippery Bill, Brandy Jack and The Melodious Bullocky, and with tall tales of the bush such as the story of Jock McPherson who rode the Oozlum Bird from the Centre to Sydney and back, and of Pat Ahearne who exhibited lobsters at outback shows as 'monster Sydney fleas'. Goodge's best-known poem is 'The Great Australian Adjective' (q.v.), which is also the title of a volume of his verse (1965).

GOODING, TIM (1950–), born Melbourne, has written for television, especially for the popular series, *The Aunty Jack Show*, and for the stage. His stage plays include 'The Great Australian Play', 'A Bent Repose', 'Tent Show Pagliacci', 'Drums along the Diamantina', 'Paradise Depression Style', and 'Rockola', a surrealistic celebration of the rock and roll era produced in Sydney, Melbourne and Adelaide in 1978.

Goodman, Theodora, see *Aunt's Story, The*

GORDON, ADAM LINDSAY (1833–70), was born at Fayal in the Azores where his mother's father had a plantation. On his father's retirement from a commission with the Bengal cavalry, he completed his education in England. After numerous youthful escapades, Gordon was in 1853 banished by his parents to SA, where he enlisted in the mounted police. Resigning from the constabulary after two years service he drifted about SA dealing in horses and riding in steeplechases. With a sizable legacy from his parents' estate he purchased several properties, married, and lived in Dingley Dell, a small stone cottage still lovingly preserved near the seaside settlement of Port MacDonnell, not far from Mount Gambier. From those years come many stories of Gordon's daring feats of horsemanship, most notably the Blue Lake Leap (q.v.). He had a brief and unspectacular parliamentary career in 1864–66, an abortive grazing venture in WA in 1866–67, and then conducted a livery stable in Ballarat in 1867–68. After a severe head injury in a riding accident, bankruptcy caused by a fire in the livery stable, and the death of his infant daughter, he left Ballarat for Melbourne. There he lived an unhappy and aimless existence, working spasmodically at his writing and suffering from depression, insomnia and pain from his numerous riding injuries. When an attempt to claim heirship to the ancestral Gordon lands in Scotland failed, he faced financial disaster. On 24 June 1870, the day following the publication of his poems, *Bush Ballads and Galloping Rhymes* (q.v.), he committed suicide on Brighton Beach, Melbourne.

Gordon's published works began with *The Feud* (1864), a ballad inspired by Noel Paton's engravings of scenes from the ballad, 'The Dowie Dens o'Yarrow'. *Ashtaroth* (1867), his second publication, a long dramatic poem indebted to the Faust theme, has failed down the years to arouse any critical enthusiasm. The two main volumes upon which his poetic reputation rests are *Sea Spray and Smoke Drift* (q.v., 1867) and *Bush Ballads and Galloping Rhymes*. In 1934 a bust of Gordon was unveiled in the Poets' Corner of Westminster Abbey, making him the only Australian poet to have been thus honoured. That mark of recognition reflects the adulation for him after his death and through the first decades of the twentieth century. His popularity sprang partly from the romantic aura of his life, his aristocratic background, his exile in the colony, his reckless riding exploits, and the pathos of his death. It sprang, too, from the gratitude of Australian nationalists for Gordon's acclaim in his poetry of the outback way of life. His verses were loved and recited around camp fires and in the homesteads and shearing sheds of the backblocks. Yet very little of Gordon's poetry reflects the fragrance of the wattle blossom, the blue of Australian skies, or the camaraderie of Australian mateship. Such Australian flavour is present only in 'The Sick Stockrider', 'A Dedication' (qq.v.) and some parts of 'Ye Wearie Wayfarer'. Most of his poetry is modelled upon the conventional verse which his English education and background had instilled in him. Apart from the occasional narrative, notably 'The Rhyme of Joyous Garde' (q.v.), that poetry has little significance. The small Australian segment does, however, have undoubted historical importance and 'The Sick Stockrider', in particular, is recognized as the poem which sketched in broad outline the territory which later balladists filled with profuse and picturesque detail; it thus pointed literature in a new and more characteristically Australian direction. Poems to Gordon and his

memory include Henry Kendall's 'The Late Mr A.L. Gordon: In Memoriam' and Will Ogilvie's 'Adam Lindsay Gordon'. Edith Humpris wrote *The Life of Adam Lindsay Gordon* (1934), C.F. MacRae, *Adam Lindsay Gordon* (1968) and W.H. Wilde, the monograph *Adam Lindsay Gordon* (1972).

Gordon and Gotch was established in 1854 in Melbourne as a partnership between Alexander Gordon and John Speechley Gotch to act as news and advertising agents and to distribute newspapers and periodicals from Britain. In 1859 Gordon sold his interest in the business to Gotch and returned to Scotland. Gotch was joined by his brother William in 1860 and brother-in-law Alfred Jones in 1861. Branches were opened in Sydney (1861), London (1867), Brisbane (1875), Perth (1894), Wellington (NZ) (1899) and Launceston (1903). In 1885 Gordon and Gotch became a public company. Chiefly a distributor of periodicals to newsagents and booksellers, Gordon and Gotch is also well-known for its publication, *Australian Handbook,* a comprehensive volume of facts and information about Australia, published 1870–1906. *Years to Remember: The Story of Gordon and Gotch* was published in 1953.

GORDON, J.W. (JAMES WILLIAM) ('JIM GRAHAME') (1874–1949), born Creswick, Victoria, was a mate of Henry Lawson and a possible model for Mitchell (q.v.), one of Lawson's most important fictional characters. The two met in 1892 at Bourke during Lawson's celebrated outback trek, worked together for several months and then parted, to meet again when Lawson went to Leeton in 1916. They remained friends from then until Lawson's death. Gordon wrote under the pseudonym 'Jim Grahame', a name reputedly given to him by Lawson. After 1903 he was a regular contributor of bush verse to the *Bulletin* and other journals, and published three volumes of verse: *Call of the Bush* (1940), *Home Leave and Departing* (1944) and *Under Wide Skies: Collected Verse* (1947). Gordon's recollections of Lawson form part of *Henry Lawson by His Mates* (1931); Lawson's recollections of Gordon form part of his articles on Yanco contributed to the *Bulletin* in 1916–17.

GORE, STUART (1905–), born Portsmouth, England, came to Australia in 1910. A jack-of-all-trades, he finally settled on cinematography for a living, touring Australia making films and bringing them to the public in a show called 'See Australia First'. After war service in the RAAF Gore made industrial and public relations films in England and in recent years has divided his time between writing and lecturing, much of the latter on behalf of the Commonwealth Institute in London. Gore's travel books include *Overlanding with Annabel* (1956), which relates the experiences of Gore and his wife as they travelled in an old Chrysler car through outback Australia. Gore's other publications include the humorous *Holy Smoke* (1968), Saltbush Bill's (q.v.) version of the scriptures, and a novel, *Down the Golden Mile* (1962), set in the goldfields and outback of WA.

GORMAN, CLEM (1942–), born Perth, WA, was educated at the University of Sydney, was a freelance stage manager and administrator in Sydney 1967–68, founded the Australian Free Theatre Group and co-founded the theatre magazine *Masque*. He spent some years in England as an arts administrator before returning to Australia to work in the same field. His plays include 'Let Me In, I'm a Friend of the Band', performed in London 1978; *A Manual of Trench Warfare* (1980, performed 1978); *A Night in the Arms of Raeleen* (1983, performed 1981); *The Harding Women* (1983, performed 1981); and *Motivators* (1983). He adapted A.B. Facey's *A Fortunate Life* for performance in 1985.

Gossip from the Forest, see **KENEALLY, THOMAS**

GOUGER, ROBERT (1802–46), born London, visited Edward Gibbon Wakefield in Newgate prison to discuss their mutual interest in the colonizing of Australia. His *Sketch of a Proposal for Colonizing Australasia* was published in 1829, the year he edited Wakefield's *A Letter from Sydney*. Gouger's efforts were largely responsible for the formation in 1830 of the National Colonization Society, whose object was to assist pauper emigration to the colonies, especially SA. At first unsuccessful, Gouger finally prevailed when the SA Colonization Commission was gazetted in 1835 with himself as colonial secretary. He arrived in SA in 1836 but was involved in faction fighting which negated much of his usefulness to the new colony which he had so long championed. In ill-health he returned to England in 1845. He published *South Australia in 1837* (1838). His journals were used by Edwin Hodder in the compilation of *The Founding of South Australia* (1898).

Goulburn, an important railway town and commercial centre for the surrounding pastoral and agricultural area, is situated at the junction of the Wollondilly and Mulwaree Rivers, a little more than 200 kilometres from Sydney on the southern tableland of NSW. John Oxley in 1820 was the first white man to cross the site of the present city, which was named after Henry Goulburn, undersecretary for the colonies; it was gazetted as a township in 1833 and declared a city in 1885. An early garrison town, Goulburn was the centre for the pursuit of bushrangers from the 1830s. Daniel Deniehy lived there in 1854 and was member for Argyle in the NSW Legislative Assembly 1857–59; poet and journalist John Farrell was a brewer there in the 1880s; Mary Gilmore, born in the district, spent a period there in the 1920s recuperating from illness and dedicated her book of verse, *The Rue Tree* (1931), to the Sisters of the Convent of Mercy, Goulburn, who nursed her; Miles Franklin's grim experiences on the unrewarding small holding of Stillwater near Goulburn are included in *My Brilliant Career* (1901). One of the Colony's first country newspapers was the *Goulburn Herald*, begun in 1848; it was later incorporated in the *Goulburn Evening Post*, which is still published. Charles MacAlister's reminiscences, *Old Pioneering Days in the Sunny South*, was published in 1907. Histories of Goulburn include R.T. Wyatt's *The History of Goulburn, NSW* (1941) and W.A. Bayley's *Lilac City* (1954).

GOULD, ALAN (1949–), born London of Icelandic forebears, graduated from the Australian National University in 1971. He has published three books of verse, *Icelandic Solitaries* (1978), *Astral Sea* (1981), which won the NSW Premier's Poetry Award for 1981, and *The Pausing of the Hours* (1984). *Astral Sea* has two sequences derived from Icelandic legend, 'The Vinlanders' and 'The Songs of Ymir'. His first novel, *The Man Who Stayed Below* (1983), won the 1982 Angus & Robertson award.

GOULD, JOHN (1804–81), born Dorset, England, had published two significant ornithological works, *A Century of Birds from the Himalaya Mountains* (1831–32) and *The Birds of Europe* (1837), before coming to Australia in 1838. He remained in the colonies until 1840 working in Van Diemen's Land, SA and NSW. *The Birds of Australia*, in thirty-six parts and bound in seven volumes, was published 1840–48; a supplementary volume was completed in 1869. The total work includes 681 coloured plates. In addition to many other works he also published *The Mammals of Australia* (1845–63) and *Handbook to the Birds of Australia* (1865); he was at work upon *The Birds of New Guinea and the Adjacent Papuan Islands* at the time of his death, the work being completed by R.B. Sharpe. His name has been honoured in Australia by the establishment of the Gould League of Bird Lovers. C.L. Barrett

303

wrote the biographical *The Bird Man* (1938). Elizabeth (1804–41), John Gould's wife and a talented artist, supplied many of the drawings for the colour plates of her husband's books. Her letters from Australia admirably reflect the contemporary colonial scene; A.H. Chisholm wrote her biography, *The Story of Elizabeth Gould* (1944).

GOULD, NAT (1857–1919), who wrote sometimes under the pseudonym 'Verax', was born in Manchester, England, served as a reporter on the *Newark Advertiser*, and arrived in Australia in 1884. He worked on newspapers in Brisbane, Bathurst and Sydney, where 'With the Tide' was serialised in the *Referee*. Published as a novel, *The Double Event* (1891), it was staged in 1893 and established Gould's reputation. Subsequently he wrote well over a hundred readable, exciting and popular novels, mostly about the turf and other sports; in many of these, published under such titles as *Jockey Jack* (1892), *The Doctor's Double* (1896), *The Miners' Cup* (1896), *King of the Ranges* (1902), *Bred in the Bush* (1903), *A Sporting Squatter* (1906) and *A Chestnut Champion* (1920), he continued to draw on his Australian experiences even though he returned to England in 1895. Gould's success derived from his clever blending of the mystery story with a sporting subject. Although seldom regarded as a significant Australian novelist, he inaugurated the Australian sporting novel and is still beloved by *aficionadoes* of sporting fiction. His volumes of reminiscences, *On and Off the Turf in Australia* (1895), *Town and Bush: Stray Notes on Australia* (1896) and *The Magic of Sport Mainly Autobiographical* (1909), are useful for their information about Australian journalism and theatre as well as about the turf (q.v.) and other sports.

GOVERNOR, JIMMY (1875–1901), a part-Aboriginal born Talbragar River, NSW, achieved notoriety in 1900 when with his brother Joe he committed several murders and eluded capture in northern NSW. He was captured and hanged early in 1901. Frank Clune's *Jimmy Governor* (1959) introduced Thomas Keneally (q.v.) to the story of the Governors, which forms the historical basis of *The Chant of Jimmie Blacksmith* (q.v., 1972), Keneally's novel about Aboriginal dispossession and white racism. Sympathy for Governor is also displayed in Les Murray's poem, 'The Ballad of Jimmy Governor'. Brian Davies wrote *The Life of Jimmy Governor* (1979).

Grace Leven Prize for Poetry, an annual award in memory of Grace Leven, who died in 1922, was established by her friend and admirer, 'William Baylebridge' (q.v.); she was his mother's half-sister. The award, first made in 1947 to Nan McDonald's *Pacific Sea*, is for the best volume of poetry published in the preceding twelve months by a writer either Australian-born and writing as an Australian, or naturalized in Australia and resident in Australia for not less than ten years. In 1948 the second award was made to Francis Webb's *A Drum for Ben Boyd*. Some of the notable recipients have been Judith Wright, R.D. FitzGerald, A.D. Hope, James McAuley, Geoffrey Dutton, Thomas Shapcott, Douglas Stewart, David Campbell, Rodney Hall, Gwen Harwood and John Blight.

Grafton, situated on the Clarence River in NSW, almost 700 kilometres north of Sydney, was opened up as a timber-cutting area in the 1830s and was named by Governor Fitz Roy after his grandfather, the Duke of Grafton. It was declared a city in 1885. Henry Kendall was associated with Grafton as a boy and later as a clerk and companion to James Lionel Michael, the poet-lawyer who had a law practice there and who died in somewhat mysterious circumstances by drowning in the Clarence River. E.J. Brady (q.v.) was part-owner and editor of the Grafton *Grip* 1901–03. Bert Beros wrote the nostalgic poem, 'When it's Springtime on the Clarence', while serving in the Second World War.

'GRAHAME, JIM', see **GORDON, J.W.**

GRAHAM, JOHN (1822–79), born County Tyrone, Ireland, and minister of the Pitt Street Congregational Church, Sydney, in the 1860s and 1870s, published a book of poetry, *Poems: Sacred, Didactic and Descriptive* (1861) and the fictional narrative, *Laurence Struilby: Or, Observations and Experiences during Twenty-Five Years of Bush Life in Australia* (1863); the latter gives an account of early life in the colony, some of it in narrative form, other parts including extracts from journals and letters. Most of the story is set in the Bathurst district with a period in the 1830s in Van Diemen's Land. His brother, Charles Graham, published *Memoir of the Rev. John Graham* in 1880.

GRANO, PAUL (1894–1975), born Ararat, Victoria, graduated in law from the University of Melbourne but practised only briefly, working as an insurance salesman, advertising writer, commercial traveller and journalist. He went to Queensland in 1932 and worked in the Main Roads Commission until his retirement. Grano founded the Catholic Poetry Society in Brisbane in 1934 and the Catholic Readers' and Writers' Society in 1943. In 1946 he edited *Witness to* *the Stars*, an anthology of Catholic poetry of Australia and NZ. A Keatsian dedication to the ideals of truth and beauty, a wistful tone and skilful imagery are the hallmarks of his best verse. His volumes of poetry are *The Roads and Other Poems* (1934), *Quest* (1940), *Poet's Holiday* (1941), *Poems, New and Old* (1945) and *Selected Verse*, published posthumously in 1976.

GRANT WATSON, ELLIOTT LOVE-GOOD, see **WATSON, GRANT**

GRATTAN, C. (CLINTON) **HARTLEY** (1902–80), born Massachusetts, USA, was a journalist and freelance writer in New York 1926–64 and professor of history 1964–74 at the University of Texas, where the Grattan collection of Australian and Pacific material is housed. Grattan made the first of several visits to Australia in 1927, becoming friendly with Percival Serle and 'Furnley Maurice'. That visit resulted in the booklet *Literature Australia* (1929), with a foreword by Nettie Palmer. In 1936 the Carnegie Corporation of New York commissioned him to produce a political, economic and cultural synthesis of Australia. The result was the 1942 publication, *Introducing Australia*, a work which he described as a non-academic investigation of Australian society but which helped publicise Australia in America. In 1947 he edited *Australia*, a symposium of specialist articles on Australian society. Having been introduced to Joseph Furphy's writings by 'Furnley Maurice', Grattan published an American edition of *Such is Life* in 1948. Grattan's interest extended during the Second World War to NZ and the South Pacific. His subsequent publications include the massive work in two volumes, in two volumes, *The Southwest Pacific to 1900* and *The Southwest Pacific to 1900* and *The Southwest Pacific Since 1900* (both 1963).

GRAY, ORIEL (1921–), born Sydney, has written numerous plays for stage, radio and television. A member of the Communist Party of Australia until 1950, she was originally closely associated as actor and writer with Sydney's New Theatre. Her political interests are reflected in her stage plays, nearly all of which deal with oppression, exploitation and discrimination, especially racial discrimination. She was married for a time to the journalist, John Hepworth.

Gray's first full-length stage play, 'Lawson', a dramatization of some of the short stories of Henry Lawson, produced in 1943 and included in extract in *Australian One-Act Plays, Book II*, ed. Greg Branson (1962), was followed by 'Western Limit'; 'Had We but World Enough';

'Sky Without Birds'; 'Royal Tour'; 'Belle and the Bushranger'; 'The King Who Wouldn't'; 'Let's be Offensive'; 'Marx of Time'; 'Milestones'; 'Antarctic Four'; 'The Torrents', which shared first prize with *Summer of the Seventeenth Doll* in the Playwrights Advisory Board competition of 1955; and 'Burst of Summer', which was produced in 1960 and won the playwriting competition of the Little Theatre Guild of Melbourne in 1959. She had also written two one-act plays, 'My Life is My Affair' and *Drive a Hard Bargain* (1958), and contributed to the popular television serial of the 1970s, *Bellbird*. Her other plays for television include 'Antarctic Four' and 'The Brass Guitar'.

GRAY, ROBERT (1945–), born Coffs Harbour, NSW, was a cadet journalist on a country newspaper before coming to Sydney, where he has been a bookshop assistant, an advertising copywriter and a reviewer of poetry for the *Sydney Morning Herald* and the ABC. Gray has published four books of poetry, *Introspect, Retrospect* (1970), *Creekwater Journal* (1974), *Grass Script* (1978) and *The Skylight* (1983); with Geoffrey Lehmann he edited the anthology, *The Younger Australian Poets* (1983). Gray has been commended for the brilliance of his imagery, the economy of his diction and the clarity of his ideas.

Great Australian Adjective, ('Bloody'), was observed to be flourishing in the colony as early as 1859, Frank Fowler noting, in *Southern Lights and Shadows*, that the cornstalk (q.v.) was prone 'to interlard his diction with the crimsonest of adjectives'. In 1894 the *Bulletin* explained the Australian appropriation of 'bloody' thus – 'we call it the *Australian* adjective simply because it is more used and used more exclusively by Australians than by any other allegedly civilized nation'. The three best-known literary examples of the crimson adjective's use are C.J. Dennis's 'The Australaise' (q.v.); Joseph Furphy's *Such is Life* (q.v., 1903); and W.T. Goodge's poem, 'The Great Australian Adjective', about 'the sunburnt – stockman' (for –, mostly read 'bloody') whose attempted crossing of a flooded creek on horseback ended thus:

> He plunged into the – creek
> The – horse was – weak
> The stockman's face was a – study
> And though the – horse was drowned
> The – rider reached the ground
> Ejaculating ' – !'
> ' – !'

In his anthology *Verse in Australia* (1959), Ian Mudie included 'The Man from Tumbarumba' by J. Wolfe. That worthy's pastime was 'shootin' kanga-bloody-roos/At Tumba-bloodyrumba'. In *They're a Weird Mob* (1957), Nino Culotta, as a new arrival to Australia, tries to make his way to 'Kings-bloody-Cross'.

Great Australian Loneliness, The, see HILL, ERNESTINE

Great Escape, The, see BRICKHILL, PAUL

Great South Land, The, see INGAMELLS, REX

Greek Coins, see DOBSON, ROSEMARY

GREEN, CLIFF (1934–), born Melbourne, was in the printing trade before becoming a primary school teacher in Victoria. He resigned in 1969 to become a staff writer with Crawford Productions, contributing to such television series as *Rush, Power Without Glory* and *Against the Wind*. Green's major contribution to television writing, however, has been *Marion* (1974), which won an Awgie Award and the Television Society Award; *End of Summer* which also won an Awgie, and *Summerfield*, both of which were published in *Four Scripts* (1978). Green also wrote the screenplay for the film *Picnic at Hanging Rock* (1975), and two original screenplays, 'Break of Day' and 'Burn the Butterflies'. His first stage play, 'Cop Out', was performed by the Melbourne Theatre Company in 1977. He has also written a novel, *Break of Day* (1976), based on the screenplay; a collection of short stories, *The Sun is Up* (1978); and the Riverboat Bill books for children (1975, 1981). Among his adaptations for television are the series, *Lawson's Mates* (1978), *Lucinda Brayford* (1980) and *I Can Jump Puddles* (1981).

GREEN, DOROTHY (DOROTHY AUCHTERLONIE) (1915–), was born County Durham, England, and educated there and at the University of Sydney. She worked as a reader, journalist and news editor with the news service of the ABC 1942–49 and was co-principal of a large girls' school in Warwick, Queensland, 1955–60. She has subsequently lectured in English at Monash University, at the Australian National University, and at the Royal Military College, Duntroon. In 1944 she married H.M. Green. Well-known as an essayist and reviewer, she is a regular contributor to Australian literary magazines and has published significant essays on Martin Boyd, E.L. Grant Watson, 'Henry Handel Richardson', Patrick White, C.J. Brennan, Christina Stead and Kylie Tennant. In 1950 she revised her husband's collection of radio talks, *Fourteen Minutes,* but her most substantial work is her extensively-researched biography and critical study of 'Henry Handel Richardson', *Ulysses Bound* (1973). A witty and eloquent critic, she is noted for her memorably trenchant comments. Her poetry, under the name Dorothy Auchterlonie, has appeared regularly in literary magazines and in two collections, *Kaleidoscope* (1940) and *The Dolphin* (1967). Although she has written some satiric verse reflecting her involvement in contemporary issues, her work consists mainly of intensely reflective, concentrated lyrics that are traditional in form and theme. A collection of her literary essays, *The Music of Love*, with bibliography by Sandra Burchill and Joy Hooton, was published in 1984. She was awarded the OAM in 1984.

GREEN, H.M. (HENRY MACKENZIE) (1881–1962), born Sydney, was educated in arts and law at the University of Sydney. After travelling in Europe for a year he returned to Sydney in 1907 and spent two years on the staff of the *Sydney Morning Herald*, followed by eleven years with the *Daily Telegraph*. He was librarian at the Fisher Library, University of Sydney, 1921–46. Green was an active member of the Casuals Club and had close personal associations with most of Sydney's leading writers, artists, academics and publishers. Green was married twice, on the second occasion to Dorothy Auchterlonie. Well known as a lecturer, he participated regularly in the arts courses at the University. He also lectured to the WEA and other groups, gave the first lectures in Sydney sponsored by the CLF, and was a familiar broadcaster on Australian literature for the ABC. Evidence of his considerable influence on writers and students of Australian literature survives in his publications and in the Fisher Library's extensive holdings of Australiana.

Apart from numerous essays and reviews, including annual surveys of Australian literature in *Southerly* 1939–51, Green's published writings are *The Story of Printing* (1929) and, with J.A. Ferguson and Mrs A.G. Foster, *The Howes and Their Press* (1936); five lectures, *Australian Literature: A Summary* (1928), *The Poetry of W.B. Yeats* (1931), *Midsummer Night's Dream* (1933), *Kendall* (1933) and *Wentworth as Orator* (1935); a significant study of Brennan which he originally delivered as two lectures for the English Association, *Christopher Brennan* (1939); *An Outline of Australian Literature* (1930), which, although preceded by Nettie Palmer's *Modern Australian Literature* (1924), was the first comprehensive critical survey to 1928; a further more cursory survey, *Australian Literature 1900–1950* (1951) and *Fourteen Minutes* (1944), a series of radio talks on Australian poetry, revised by Dorothy Green in 1950. Green also published two books of poetry, *The Happy Valley* (1925) and *The Book of Beauty*

(1929), and edited *Australian Poetry 1943* (1944) and the influential collection, *Modern Australian Poetry* (1946). A writer of short fiction, he is represented in *Australian Short Stories* (1928), ed. George Mackaness. But Green's most important work is his two-volume *A History of Australian Literature* (q.v., 1961). A work of wide scope, thoroughness and painstaking scholarship, it is a mine of information, culled partly from Green's own unique knowledge of Australian writing.

GREEN, JAMES (1864–1948), born Newcastle-on-Tyne, England, was ordained a Methodist minister in 1893 and served as a chaplain with the Australian Bushmen's contingents in the Boer War and later with the Australian forces in the First World War. His published works include books of verse, *The Story of the Australian Bushmen* (1903), *News from No Man's Land* (1917), *Angel of Mons* (1921) and a collection of religious meditations, *From My Hospital Window* (1934). His works of fiction include *The Selector* (1907) and *The Lost Echo* (1910).

GREEN, JUDITH, see RODRIGUEZ, JUDITH

Green Mountains, see O'REILLY, BERNARD

GREENWAY, FRANCIS (1777–1837), born near Bristol, England, was an architect when transported to NSW in 1814 for forgery. Appointed a government architect in 1816, he was emancipated on the completion of his first assignment, the lighthouse known as Macquarie Tower on South Head, Sydney Harbour. Greenway's many architectural achievements include St James's Church and the Supreme Court in King Street, Sydney; St Luke's Church, Liverpool; St Matthew's Church, Windsor; and the Court House, Windsor. Greenway's reminiscences in the *Australian Almanack* of 1835 provide considerable information about colonial life of the time. M.H. Ellis wrote the biography, *Francis Greenway* (1949).

GREER, GERMAINE (1939–), born Melbourne and educated at the Universities of Melbourne, Cambridge and Sydney, lectured in English at the University of Warwick 1967–72. Co-founder of the controversial magazine *Sunk*, she was a columnist for the *Sunday Times* 1971–73 and contributed to such periodicals as *Listener, Spectator, Oz, Rolling Stone* and *Esquire*. She also appeared in a British television series and had contacts with rock musicians and other members of the pop culture but did not become a well-known media personality until the American publication of her influenal feminist work, *The Female Eunuch* (q.v.) in 1971. Attacked by some hard-line feminists, the book was nevertheless hailed generally as a landmark in the women's liberation movement, achieved enormous sales and was subsequently translated into twelve languages. In 1971 Greer toured the USA to promote the book, appearing on numerous television and radio shows and debating feminist issues with various well-known figures, including Norman Mailer. In Australia reviews were mixed and Greer has continued to have an ambivalent relationship with her homeland, visiting it only fleetingly and spending most of her time in Southern Tuscany. She was director of the Tulsa (Oklahoma) Center for the Study of Women's Literature 1979–82. She has also written an historical account of obstacles to female achievement in the field of painting, *The Obstacle Race* (1979); and, under the pseudonym, 'Rose Blight', a parodic work, *The Revolting Garden* (1979).

GREGORY, Sir AUGUSTUS CHARLES (1819–1905), born Nottinghamshire, England, arrived in the Swan River colony in 1829 and became a surveyor. In 1855 he led a major exploration and scientific expedition across northern Australia from the Victoria River to Brisbane; his last major expedition was to search for Ludwig Leichhardt in 1858. Thereafter he was Queensland's surveyor-general and its first commissioner for Crown Lands. In addition to numerous pamphlets and reports on various aspects of his administration, his collected papers and records, together with those of his brother and fellow surveyor-explorer, Francis Thomas Gregory (1821–88), were published in 1884 as *Journals of Australian Explorations*. Wendy Birman and Geoffrey Bolton published *Augustus Charles Gregory* (1972); J.H.L. Cumpston wrote *Augustus Gregory and the Inland Sea* (1972).

'GREIG, MAYSIE' (JENNIFER AMES) (?1901–71), born Jennifer Greig Smith, Sydney, won a literary competition at fifteen, worked as a journalist with the Sydney *Sun* 1919–20, and then went to England where she published *Peggy of Beacon Hill* (1920) which was serialized and later filmed. Permanently resident in England, except for a brief period in Australia in the 1950s, 'Maysie Greig' went on to write some 200 popular romantic novels, few of which have any connection with Australia.

'Gretel', a short story by Hal Porter (q.v.), was first published in the American periodical *Literary Review* (1963–64), and is included in his collection, *The Cats of Venice* (1965). A forty-five year old man, smugly conscious that he is *dégagé* and safe from life, is recalled to his mother's funeral in the provincial Victorian town where he was born and relives an important emotional incident of his youth. At the age of twelve he had flouted his mother's prohibitions to encounter a beautiful young girl, Gretel, who was briefly staying in a secluded part of the house. The most exquisite creature he had ever seen, or was ever to see, she had 'the hair of Rapunzel, of all immolated princesses, of all the children lost in the snow or woods of ballads'. Entranced, he gave her a white china necklace. Now, thirty-three years later, he is appalled to learn that Gretel is still in the town, incarcerated in the mental asylum where she has always had to live; now aged beyond her years and hideous, she grimly clings to the china necklace.

GREY, Sir GEORGE (1812–98), born Lisbon, Portugal, was an army officer before being attracted to the Australian colonies through the publicity associated with the explorations of Charles Sturt. In 1837–39 he led two abortive expeditions to establish a settlement in north-western Australia; in 1839 he was resident magistrate at King George Sound; and in 1840–45 he was governor of SA. In 1845 he went to NZ as governor. His published works in Australia include his compilation of *A Vocabulary of the Dialects of South Western Australia* (1840) and the account of his explorations, *Journal of Two Expeditions of Discovery in North-West and Western Australia during the Years 1837, 38, and 39* (1841). John Rutherford and G.C. Henderson published biographies of Grey in 1961 and 1967; he was the subject of a television series, *The Governor*, in 1979.

'GREY, HAROLD', see **ARGLES, THEODORE EMILE**

GREY, ZANE (1872–1939), born Ohio, USA, was a prolific writer of novels about the American west and big game fishing. He visited Australia in 1936 and 1939, mainly for big game fishing off the NSW south coast. He wrote *An American Angler in Australia* (1937) which helped create world interest in Australian game fishing, and *Wilderness Trek* (1944), a novel about inland Australia.

Grif, see **FARJEON, BENJAMIN**

GRIFFITHS, BRYN (1933–   ), born Swansea, Wales, was a seaman in the British merchant navy (1951–58) and a full-time writer (1962–76), before becoming cultural adviser and arts co-ordinator for industry with the Trades and Labour Council of WA. His inter-

ests lie in community arts, theatre, modern poetry and Celtic history; his books of poetry include *The Mask of Pity* (1966), *The Stones Remember* (1967), *Scars* (1969), *At the Airport* (1971), *The Survivors* (1971), *Beasthoods* (1972), *Starboard Green* (1973), *Dark Convoy* (1974), *Love Poems* (1980) and *The Shadow Beasts* (1981). His radio plays, 'The Sailor' (1967) and 'The Dream of Arthur' (1968), were broadcast by the BBC.

GRIMSHAW, BEATRICE (1870–1953), born County Antrim, Ireland, travelled widely in the South Pacific as a tourist publicity agent. She ultimately settled in New Guinea, where she wrote numerous pamphlets on commission from the Australian government to publicise the region and its needs. Her experiences yielded such works as a novel, *Vaiti of the Islands* (1907); and the travel books, *From Fiji to the Cannibal Islands* (1907), *In the Strange South Seas* (1907) and *The New New Guinea* (1910). She also wrote some forty books of romance and adventure set in the South Seas. Best-known of these is *When the Red Gods Call* (1911); others include *Guinea Gold* (1912), *The Sorcerer's Stone* (1914), *Kris Girl* (1917) and *The Coral Queen* (1919).

GRIMSTONE, MARY LEMAN (c.1800–?), born Hamburg, Germany, was the daughter of Leman Thomas Rede, an English expatriate known in literary circles. In 1826 she came to the colony of Van Diemen's Land for her health and during her three years there wrote most of *Woman's Love* (q.v., 1832), which although set in England was probably the first novel written in Australia. There are passing references to the penal system in *Woman's Love* and in Grimstone's other novels, *Louisa Egerton* (1830) and *Cleone* (1834). She also wrote several short stories based on her Tasmanian experiences, and a letter about the colony which attracted replies in Hobart after it was published in London in 1829.

GRIN, HENRI LOUIS (1847–1921), was the Swiss-born hoaxer 'Louis de Rougemont' whose sensational account of his adventures during thirty-odd years as a castaway among the Aborigines of north-west and Central Australia was published in London in the *Wide World* magazine, 1898–99. 'De Rougemont' was supported by his publishers and by the explorer John Moresby, and lectured to the British Association for the Advancement of Science, but his claims were disputed by 'Louis' Becke and David Wynford Carnegie. He was exposed by the London *Daily Chronicle*, which provided in *Grien on Rougemont: Or, The Story of a Modern Robinson Crusoe* (1898) the information on Grin's life and Australian experiences from which subsequent accounts derive. 'De Rougemont' was satirized by E.J. Brady in 'Rougemont Outdone' (*Arrow*, 1898–99) and was the subject of a play by Geoffrey Maslen included in *Five Plays for Radio*, ed. Alrene Sykes (1975).

Grogan, Dick, see *Hero of Too, The*; 'Wild Colonial Boy, The'

'GROVER, MARSHALL' (L.F. MEARES) (1921–   ), born Merrylands, NSW, has published a handful of crime and romance stories but has gained a reputation as Australia's most prolific writer of western stories, having published 600 titles in that genre in a career extending over forty years.

GROVER, MONTY (1870–1943) born Melbourne, had an extensive career in journalism. He was the foundation editor of the Sydney *Sun* (1910–16), editor of the *Sunday Sun* (1917) and its representative in London (1918–21), and foundation editor of *Sun-News Pictorial* (1922) and the *Evening Sun* (1923). He was magazine editor of the Melbourne *Herald* (1929–30) and first editor of the Sydney labour daily, the *World* (1931–32). His writings include the dramas, *The Sleeping Beauty and the Beast* (1903), *The Minus Quantity and Other Short Plays* (1914), *Judah and the Giant* (1915) and *The Time is Now Ripe* (1937), a socialist work. Verses by Grover are included in *The 'Bulletin' Book of Humorous Verses and Recitations* (1920) under the title 'The Man Who Writes *The Bulletin*', and in W.T. Pyke's *The Australian Favourite Reciter* (1907).

Guardian, The, see MURRAY, ANNA MARIA

Gulgong a town in NSW, 341 kilometres north-west of Sydney, was established following a gold rush which began in the area in 1870. In 1871 two people significant in Australian literature came to the goldfields: the youthful Henry Lawson, whose parents joined the rush and remained for two years before returning to the Mudgee district; and 'Rolf Boldrewood', a police magistrate and gold commissioner there for most of the 1870s, who drew on his experiences when writing *The Miner's Right* (1890). Significant in Australian photography because of the Bernhardt Holtermann collection of plates, Gulgong also became known as the 'town on the $10 note' after early photographs of the town were used to form the background to a representation of Lawson during the introduction of decimal currency in 1965.

GULLETT, HENRY (1837–1914), born Devonshire, England, came to Australia in 1853 and worked on the Victorian goldfields. Although he returned to England in 1861, he came back to Melbourne to join the staff of the *Argus*. He later edited the *Australasian* (1872–85), was associate editor of the Sydney *Daily Telegraph* and editor of the weekly *Tribune*. He was acting editor of the *Sydney Morning Herald* in the federal referendum period (1898), federalism being a cause he supported wholeheartedly. After a period as editor of the *Daily Telegraph* (1901–03) he retired from active journalism; from 1908 until his death he was a member of the NSW Legislative Council. Gullett made the *Australasian* the outstanding colonial literary journal of the day; his editorship of three of the major daily newspapers of the time attests also to his status as an Australian newspaperman. A scholarly man, Gullett was president of the Shakespeare Society of NSW 1904–11. He was uncle of Sir Henry Somer Gullett (q.v.) and his mother, Isabella, was a cousin of the poet John Keats.

GULLETT, Sir HENRY SOMER (1878–1940), born Toolamba West, Victoria, was a member of the literary staff of the *Sydney Morning Herald*, of which his uncle, Henry Gullett (q.v.) had been editor. He later became a war correspondent in the First World War. Director of Immigration (1920–22), an area in which he had long been interested, and then a member of the House of Representatives (1928–40), Gullett was killed in the Canberra air crash 13 August 1940. Gullett was related to fiction writer, Barbara Baynton, through marriage to her daughter; his son, Henry Baynton Somer ('Jo') Gullett, wrote a biographical memoir to the 1965 edition of Baynton's *Bush Studies*. Sir Henry Gullett's own writings include the immigration booklets, *The Opportunity in Australia* (1914), *Unguarded Australia* (1919) and a volume of the official history of Australia in the First World War, titled *The Australian Imperial Force in Sinai and Palestine, 1914–1918* (1923).

Gumsucker was a colloquialism, now largely obsolete, for a resident of Victoria. The term is used in William Howitt's *Land, Labour and Gold* (1855), Frank Fowler's *Southern Lights and Shadows* (1859) and Nathan Spielvogel's books of reminiscences, *A Gumsucker on the Tramp* (1905) and *The Gumsucker at Home* (1913). Joseph Furphy uses the abbreviation 'sucker' in *Such is Life* (1903). The folklore journal, *Gumsuckers' Gazette* (later *Australian Tradition*) is an example of the partial revival of the term.

309

Gumsuckers' Gazette, see *Australian Tradition*

Gundagai, a town on the Murrumbidgee River in southern NSW and on the main inland highway between Sydney and Melbourne, has long been a natural meeting-place for travellers. Before the advent of the automobile it was a gathering spot for teamsters, drovers, shearers and all varieties of bush travellers. It is best-known as the spot where the bullocky's dog fouled the tuckerbox, an act commemorated in the teamster song, 'Nine (Five) Miles from Gundagai'; in later poems (e.g. by Jack Moses, q.v.), in which the dog guards the tucker box; and in recent times by a bronze statue of a dog on a tuckerbox by the Italian sculptor Rosconi, whose 'Marble Masterpiece' is one of Gundagai's tourist attractions. 'The Road to Gundagai', with its well-known chorus beginning 'There's a track, winding back to an old-fashioned shack', was composed by Jack O'Hagan and included in the repertoire of Australian baritone, Peter Dawson. The traditional shearers' song, 'Lazy Harry's' (q.v.) celebrates the legendary 'lambing down' pub on the road to Gundagai. A.B. Paterson and R.J. Cassidy ('Gilroony') both wrote poems titled 'The Road to Gundagai'.

GUNN, JEANNIE (1870–1961), was born Jeannie Taylor in Melbourne, daughter of a journalist. She established a private school with her sister at Hawthorn, a Melbourne suburb, then in 1901 married Aeneas Gunn and went with him to Elsey station on the Roper River in the Northern Territory. She returned to Melbourne after his death in 1903. She published two books, *The Little Black Princess* (1905) and *We of the Never-Never* (q.v., 1908) (see Aboriginal in Australian Literature). The latter, which has sold over half a million copies, is an extended anecdote of the vicissitudes of life in the Territory and it has given Australian literature such characters as the Maluka (the boss), Cheon (the Chinese cook) and the Fizzer (the mailman), as well as the Little Missus, Jeannie Gunn herself. An Australian film of *We of the Never-Never* was screened in 1982.

GURNEY, ALEX (1902–55), born Portsmouth, England, studied art at Hobart Technical School. In 1926 he published a book of caricatures of leading Tasmanian citizens, *Tasmanians Today*. A cartoonist with numerous newspapers, Gurney was the creator of the comic strip, 'Bluey and Curley', which appeared in 1940 and rapidly became one of Australia's most popular strips. It depicted the vicissitudes of army life as seen through the eyes of Bluey, the hard-bitten veteran of the First World War and his mate Curley, the ingenuous young recruit. Other cartoonists to draw the strip after Gurney's death were Norm Rice and Les Dixon; the latter carried it through until his retirement in 1975, when 'Bluey and Curley' was also retired from the Melbourne *Sun-News Pictorial* where it had first appeared.

GURR, ROBIN (1934–), born Sydney, wrote and illustrated *Red Pepper* (1954), the story of a horse, while she was still a schoolgirl; a special edition of the story was printed for the NSW Department of Education. She has also written two other stories for children, *Music in the Grass* (1971) and *A House of Carols* (1975), and a book of verse, *Song is a Mirror* (1963).

GWYNNE, AGNES M. published several romantic novels with Australian settings, e.g. *The Mistress of Windfells* (1921), a station romance of the Victorian western districts; *The Mystery of Lakeside House* (1925), set in a Victorian north-west country town in the period after the First World War; *An Emergency Husband* (?1926), which related the vicissitudes of a young woman compelled to marry to satisfy the terms of an inheritance; and *High Dawn* (1935), a sentimental account of the convict period with a hero badly used by fate. Agnes Gwynne published two plays, *A Social Experiment* (1908) which won an exhibition of women's work in Melbourne, and *The Capitalist* (1931).

Gwynnham, Maida, see *Broad Arrow, The*

GYE, HAL ('JAMES HACKSTON', 'HACKO') (1888–1967), born Ryde, Sydney, worked as a law clerk before pursuing three separate careers in Australian art and letters: as Hal Gye, illustrator of the original 1915 edition of C.J. Dennis's *The Songs of a Sentimental Bloke* and illustrator for Angus & Robertson and for the *Bulletin*, the *Melbourne Punch* and other papers; as short story writer 'James Hackston', who from 1936 wrote the 'Father' series of stories for the *Bulletin* and published two collections of short fiction, *Father Clears Out* (1966) and *The Hole in the Bedroom Floor* (1969); and as the *Bulletin* poet 'Hacko', whose pithy and often amusing verses appeared through the 1940s and 1950s on the 'Aboriginalities' page of the *Bulletin*. A competent short fiction writer, somewhat in the 'Steele Rudd' and the later Eric Schlunke manner, Gye combines the comic and the tragic of rural life in amusing and frequently moving stories.

Gympie Miner, see STEPHENS, A.G.

H

HACKETT, PATRICIA (1908–63), daughter of Sir Winthrop Hackett, benefactor of the University of WA, graduated in law in London and practised in Adelaide. Her interest in drama led to her acquiring her own little theatre, the Torch, in Adelaide in 1934 where, in the 1930s and later in the 1950s, she produced, designed the sets for and acted in many plays. In 1938 she published *These Little Things*, a volume of forty-one poems set in Adelaide and in the Solomon Islands where she lived on the island M'bangai, which she owned just before the outbreak of the Pacific War in 1941. The Patricia Hackett prize was endowed in her memory in 1965 for the best original creative contribution published in *Westerly* (q.v.) each year.

'HACKSTON, JAMES', see GYE, HAL

HADDON, F.W. (FREDERICK WILLIAM) (1839–1906), born Surrey, England, came to Australia in 1863 to work for the Melbourne *Argus*. He was co-editor of the *Australasian* when it began publication in 1864 as the weekend journal of the *Argus*, and in 1865 became its editor. In 1867 he became editor of the *Argus*; his thirty-one years in that position were not without criticism, especially from the opponents of free trade which Haddon espoused, but they were the heyday of the *Argus*. Haddon, a friend of Marcus Clarke's, was instrumental in the founding of the Yorick Club in 1868.

HADGRAFT, C.H. (CECIL HUDDLE-STONE) (1904–), born Melbourne, studied at the Universities of Queensland and Manchester and in 1956–57 studied and lectured at the University of Omaha and Louisiana State University. In Australia he taught at the University of Queensland, ultimately becoming a reader in its department of English. Hadgraft's critical writings include *Queensland and Its Writers* (1959), *Australian Literature: A Critical Account to 1955* (1960), and the biography of James Brunton Stephens in 1969. He edited new editions in 1962 and 1964 of Henry Savery's early works *The Hermit in Van Diemen's Land* and *Quintus Servinton* (first published 1830 and 1831); a new edition in 1969 with Ray Beilby of Jessie Couvreur's novel, *Uncle Piper of Piper's Hill* (first published 1889); *Coast to Coast* (1961); with Richard Wilson, *A Century of Australian Short Stories* (1963); and

in 1966 Frederick Sinnett's *The Fiction Fields of Australia* (first published 1856). See Criticism.

HADOW, LYNDALL (1903–76), born Kalgoorlie, was the sister of the novelist, Donald Stuart, and daughter of Julian Stuart, 1891 shearers' strike prisoner, and Florence Collings, one of WA's first women journalists. Long-time editor of the magazine, *Our Women*, she was a prolific writer of short stories, reviews and critical articles. Her collection of short fiction, *Full Cycle and Other Stories* (1969), deals with the State's wheat belt, its far north-west and the assimilation of non-British migrants into its more settled south-west. She edited a book of her father's writings, *Part of the Glory* (1967). The WA branch of the FAW created the Lyndall Hadow award for short stories in 1977; it also published *She too Is Part of the Glory: Lyndall Hadow 1903–1976* (1976).

HAENKE, HELEN (1916–78), published two volumes of poetry, *The Good Company* (1977) and *Prophets and Honour* (1979), both characterized by wit, compassion, perceptive awareness of people and fine control of language. She also published a play, *The Bottom of a Birdcage* (performed 1976, published 1978). Her unpublished plays include 'Golden Sword' (1961), 'The Passage' (1978), 'Black Out' (1967) and 'Truth to Tell', which won an award in the Ipswich drama competition for 1960.

Hail Tomorrow, see PALMER, VANCE; New Australia

HAILES, NATHANIEL (1802–79), born London, claimed to have enjoyed the acquaintance of such prominent English literary figures as Sir Walter Scott and Thomas de Quincey. He published *The Emigrant and Other Poems* (1833) in England prior to his departure for SA in 1839. In 1856 he published *The Soul's Journey: A Metrical Fantasy*; as 'Timothy Short' he edited the brief-lived literary magazine *The Wanderer* (1853), in which several of his own poems on Australian subjects were published. His autobiographical 'Personal Recollections of a Septuagenarian' were published serially in the *Observer Miscellany* in 1877.

HALES, A.A.G. (ALFRED ARTHUR GREENWOOD) (1860–1936), nicknamed 'Smiler', was born Kent Town, SA, and wandered the outback working at a variety of jobs and contributing to country newspapers stories of his experiences, many of which were published in *The Wanderings of a Simple Child* (1890). He was a war correspondent in the Boer War, in which he was taken prisoner, a participant in the rebellion against the Turks in Macedonia in 1903, and a war correspondent in the Russo-Japanese war and the First World War. He then lived in England, where he continued to write a long line of adventure novels, which had begun with *Driscoll, King of Scouts* (1901), a story of the Boer War. His best-known creation is McGlusky, an Australian of Scots descent, who is the hero in 1902 of *McGlusky: Being a Compilation from the Diary of Trooper McWiddy of Remington's Scouts* and who appears in a further eighteen novels. He also wrote a series of sporting novels, and often set his fiction in countries other than Australia. In his Australian period his interest in newspapers is reflected in his founding of the *Coolgardie Mining Review* and the Boulder *Evening Star*. He published a volume of poetry in the bush ballad tradition, *Poems and Ballads* (1909). His autobiographical works are *My Life of Adventure* (1918) and *Broken Trails* (1931).

HALEY, MARTIN (1905–80), born Brisbane, was a teacher in Queensland. He was, with Paul Grano, a foundation member of the Queensland Catholic Poetry Society and was president of the Catholic Readers' and Writers' Society. Haley published numerous books of verse and translations including *Poems and a Preface* (1936), *More Poems and Another Preface* (1938), *Translations (Mostly)* (1941), *Good Measure: A Century of Epigrams* (1950), *Middle Kingdom* (1952), *Asphodel and Wistaria* (1955, poems from Chinese and Greek), *Preciosa* (1962, poems from Spanish), *Beatrice, Being the Sonnets of Louis Labé 1525–66* (1963), *Lucretia and the Banks of the Anio* (1965), *The Central Splendour (Chung Hua): An Anthology from the Chinese* (1969), and *Trophies: Taken Mostly from the French of Jose Maria de Heredia* (1972).

Half-Crown Bob and Tales of the Riverine, see 'WARUNG, PRICE'

Half Open Door, The, see Anthologies; Feminism and Australian Literature

HALL, BEN (1837–65), born Breeza, near Tamworth, NSW, was a bushranger who operated in central western NSW in the early 1860s, often in partnership with Frank Gardiner, Johnny Gilbert and others. The exploits of the Hall-Gardiner-Gilbert gang are the subject of Ambrose Pratt's *The Outlaws of Weddin Range*

(1911) and Launcelot Booth's *The Devil's Nightcap* (1912), and figure prominently in 'Rolf Boldrewoods''s *Robbery Under Arms* (1888), where Hall becomes Wall, Gardiner, Lardner and Gilbert, Hulbert. Two famous bushranging incidents involving the gang, the Eugowra gold escort robbery in 1862 and the raid on Henry Keightley's homestead at Dunn's Plains a year later, are recreated in *Robbery Under Arms*, although 'Boldrewood' transposed the events to the 1850s and made the evil Dan Moran/Dan Morgan (with whom Hall, Gardiner and Gilbert had no contact) leader of the gang. Wall, Lardner and the Eugowra robbery reappear in 'Boldrewood''s *The Miner's Right* (1890). Hall also appears as a character in the novel by Hilda Bridges, *The Squatter's Daughter* (1922), which is based on the successful play (1907) and film (1910) by Edmund Duggan and Bert Bailey. He is the subject of several ballads, including the anonymous 'Brave Ben Hall', 'Ballad of Ben Hall' and 'Ballad of Ben Hall's Gang', John McGuire's bitter 'The Streets of Forbes' and W.H. Ogilvie's 'The Death of Ben Hall'. A television series based on Ben Hall's career was produced by the ABC in 1975; D.J. Shiel published *Ben Hall* (1983), a detailed reconstruction of Hall's life.

HALL, EDWARD SMITH (1786–1860), born London, came to Australia in 1811 intending to be a gentleman farmer. Unsuccessful on the land, he became active in the commercial life of Sydney, being in 1817 the first cashier and secretary of the newly-formed Bank of NSW. In 1826 he established with Arthur Hill the *Monitor*, a newspaper which took up the settlers' causes and attacked administrative abuses and incompetence, especially in the rule of Governor Darling. Hall was imprisoned for libel but continued to conduct his campaigns through the *Monitor*, eventually having the pleasure of seeing Darling recalled. From 1838, when he sold the *Monitor*, until 1848 he edited the *Australian*, then worked on Henry Parkes's *Empire*, and finally became a public servant. Hall's struggles for such democratic freedoms as representative government, trial by jury, and freedom of the press and his support of the rights of the native-born led to him being dubbed the 'Colonial Cobbett'. The disputes between the press and Governor Darling are treated in C.H. Currey's *Sir Francis Forbes* (1968). An editorial by Hall figures prominently in 'Price Warung''s story, 'Mr Slyde's Auction'.

HALL, JAMES NORMAN (1887–1951), American novelist and short story writer, was born in Iowa, served in France in the Lafayette Flying Corps during the First World War and spent some time as a POW in Germany. In 1920 he moved to Tahiti with Charles Nordhoff (q.v.), with whom he collaborated in a series of popular novels, mostly about the South Seas. As well as the novels he published with Nordhoff, the most famous of which are the three dealing with the mutiny against Sir William Bligh, *Mutiny on the Bounty* (1932), *Men against the Sea* (1934) and *Pitcairn's Island* (1934), Hall published verse, novels for adults and children, and an autobiography *My Island Home* (1952). He also contributed verse, short stories and essays to such periodicals as *Atlantic Monthly, Harper's Magazine* and *Saturday Evening Post*. The Bounty trilogy was published in one volume in 1936, *Mutiny on the Bounty*, and was a major source for the film treatments. Another novel with Australian content, *Botany Bay* (1941), was also produced as a film in 1953.

HALL, KEN G. (1901–), born Sydney, was one of Australia's most successful film producers of the 1930s. He made a series of films starring Bert Bailey, the first of which was *On Our Selection* (1932). Other films of Hall's were *The Silence of Dean Maitland* (1934), *Tall Timbers* (1937) and *Smithy* (1946, about Sir Charles Kingsford-Smith). *Autobiography of an Australian Filmmaker* appeared in 1977, updated in 1980 as *Australian Film: The Inside Story*.

HALL, RODNEY (1935–), born England, came to Australia after the Second World War. He graduated from the University of Queensland in 1971 and has worked as a freelance script-writer for television and radio, as an actor, as film critic for the ABC, as a youth officer for the Australian Council for the Arts, and as a tutor and lecturer in music and creative writing. Poetry editor of the *Australian* 1967–78, he was poetry adviser to the publishers, Angus & Robertson, 1972–75. He has travelled extensively in Europe, Asia and the USA, and for a long period has been actively involved in Aboriginal affairs.

A prolific writer, Hall contributed to *Four Poets* (1962) and has published the following volumes of poetry, *Penniless till Doomsday* (1962), *Forty Beads on a Hangman's Rope* (1963), *Eyewitness* (1967), *The Autobiography of a Gorgon* (1968), *The Law of Karma* (1968), *Heaven, In a Way* (1970), *Romulus and Remus* (1971), *A Soapbox Omnibus* (1973), *Selected Poems* (1975), *Black Bagatelles* (1978) and *The Most Beautiful World* (1981); three novels, *The Ship on the Coin* (1972), *A Place Among People* (1975) and *Just Relations* (1982); and studies of the artist Andrew Sibley in 1968, and of the writer who has influenced him most, John

Manifold, in 1978. He has also edited several significant collections of Australian verse *New Impulses in Australian Poetry* (q.v., 1968, with Thomas Shapcott) *Australian Poetry 1970* (1970), *Poems from Prison* (1973), and *The Collins Book of Australian Poetry* (1981); a collection of Australian poems and paintings, *Australians Aware* (1975); and two collections of Michael Dransfield's poetry, *Voyage into Solitude* (1978) and *The Second Month of Spring* (1980). He has also written the text of the photographic collection, *Australia – Image of a Nation 1850–1950* (1983). Hall's poetry, ironically detached and frequently witty, is characterized by economy of form and diction, a wide range of tone and a familiarity with myth and legend. His concern with technical virtuosity, especially his use of free, flexible verse-forms and associated patterns of imagery, was evident from the first. Particularly striking is his development of the form he has termed a 'Progression', which consists of a series of short poems, sometimes as many as sixty, each of which is capable of standing alone, but which together form a tightly-related unity resembling a single, long poem.

Hall's novels emphasize the range of his interests, each one developing a different idea of the novel. *The Ship on the Coin* is a satiric allegory that attacks the apathy, crudity and blindness of bourgeois society; *A Place Among People* is a more conventional 'imagist' novel, that is deliberately open-ended and suggestive. In *Just Relations*, Hall's most ambitious novel, and winner of the 1982 Miles Franklin Award, he has created a white mythology around an Australian country landscape that is almost as pervasive and substantial as Aboriginal mythology. Set in Whitey's Fall, a small, decaying town with a gold-mining past and peopled by a remarkable group of elderly eccentrics, the novel gradually develops a dense web of relations that persuasively knits past, present and future into a pattern of meaning. Other awards won by Hall include the Grace Leven Prize (1973) and the Poetry Society Prize (1975).

HALLORAN, HENRY (1811–93), born Cape Town, South Africa, son of L.H. Halloran (q.v.), came to Sydney in 1822, had a successful career in the public service, becoming chief clerk in the Survey Department, under-secretary of the Colonial Secretary's Department and a justice of the peace. He was made a CMG after his retirement in 1878. A well-known member of the Sydney literary society of the day and a frequent contributor to the *Month, Sydney Morning Herald* and *Sydney Gazette,* he also assisted young writers, e.g., Henry Kendall, for whom he obtained civil service employment. A minor poet himself, he published *Poems,*

313

Odes, Songs (1887) and *A Few Love Rhymes of a Married Life* (1890); made translations from the Greek poems of Anacreon; and wrote numerous commemorative poems for the 1888 centenary.

HALLORAN, L.H. (LAURENCE HYNES) (1765–1831), born County Meath, Ireland, father of Henry Halloran (q.v.), ruined a career as a chaplain and schoolmaster by indulgence in libellous verse and other acts. Indicted on a minor forging charge in 1818, he was transported for seven years. In 1819 he was given a ticket-of-leave by Governor Lachlan Macquarie, opened a private school in 1820, and in 1825 became principal of the Sydney Free Public Grammar School. His unpredictable behaviour, which led to constant litigation, finally deprived him of his schoolmastering career and he then published a journal, the *Gleaner* (1827), a voice for the emancipist cause. Governor Darling, in a kindly gesture, appointed him the Sydney coroner in 1828 but his last years were spent drawing up memorials for people with grievances – his own situation for much of his later life. His numerous publications prior to his transportation were minor poetry and drama. They included, under the pseudonym 'Philo-nauticus', *Odes, Poems and Translations* (1790) and *Newgate: Or, Desultory Sketches in a Prison* (?1819).

Halloran, Phelim see *Bring Larks and Heroes*

'Halloran's Little Boat', see *Bring Larks and Heroes*

Halstead Press, Angus & Robertson's (q.v.) book printing department, grew from Eagle Press, established in 1923. Known originally as Halstead Printing Company, its first manager was W. Kirwan; he was succeeded by W.G. Cousins, who was chief of Angus & Robertson's publishing department throughout the 1930s. The Press was named Halstead in honour of the town in Essex where George Robertson (2) was born in 1860.

Ham Funeral, The, a play by Patrick White (q.v.), written in 1947, was published in *Four Plays* (1965). Rejected in 1961 by the governors of the Adelaide Festival as too abstract for the general public, a decision that aroused some acrimony, it was produced that year by the Adelaide University Theatre Guild and in 1962 by the Australian Elizabethan Theatre Trust in Sydney. It is an expressionistic play, in which the characters, the two-storey set and the language combine to suggest the conflict in a young artist's emerging consciousness. For the introspective Young Man, life is a struggle between ideality, represented by the Girl, his anima in the upstairs room, and hearty but repellent and frightening reality. The latter is represented by his Landlord, Will Lusty, and his wife, the part-seductive, part-motherly Alma, who inhabit the basement. After a series of incidents ranging from the horrific to the macabre and the comic, the Young Man is able to reconcile ideality and lusty reality and moves out into the world.

HAMILTON, GEORGE (c.1812–83), whose diverse experience included a period as a police commissioner, was one of the first to overland cattle between Port Phillip and Adelaide. He wrote a lively account of his adventures, *Experiences of a Colonist Forty Years Ago* (1879), and two entertaining brief discussions of the role of the horse in Australia, *The Horse: Its Treatment in Australia* (1864) and *An Appeal for the Horse* (1866). A man of many talents, Hamilton also illustrated his own work and some of Sir George Grey's publications.

Hamlyn, Geoffrey, see *Recollections of Geoffry Hamlyn, The*

HAMMIAL, PHILIP (1937–), born Michigan, USA, came to Australia in 1972. He published several books of esoteric and complex poetry that is notable for its considerable technical skill. They include *Foot Falls & Notes* (1976), *Chemical Cart* (1977), *Mastication Poems* (1977), *Hear Me Eating* (1977) and *More Bath, Less Water* (1978).

HAMPTON, SUSAN, see Feminism and Australian Literature

HANCOCK, Sir KEITH (1898–), born Melbourne, was educated at the Universities of Melbourne and Oxford. He was professor of history at the Universities of Adelaide, 1926–33, and Birmingham, 1934–41. In 1941 he was appointed to the British War Cabinet as supervisor of civil histories. He became professor of economic history at Oxford in 1944 and was director of the Institute of Commonwealth Studies at London University 1949–57. In 1957 he was appointed director and professor of history at the Research School of Social Sciences at the Australian National University, which he had helped to found. Generally recognized as one of Australia's most distinguished historians, he has received many awards and honorary degrees, including the Britannica–Australia Award in 1969. He was knighted in 1953 and made KBE in 1965.

Hancock's most influential cultural study is *Australia* (q.v., 1930), although that account is by no means as substantial as some of his later works. His other most significant writings are *Ricasoli and the Risorgimento in Tuscany* (1926); the three-volume *Survey of British Commonwealth Affairs* (1937–42); *Argument of Empire* (1943); *Politics in Pitcairn* (1947); *British War Economy* (1949); *Four Studies of War and Peace in This Century* (1961); a two-volume biography of Jan Smuts (1962, 1968); *Discovering Monaro* (1972); and *Today, Yesterday and Tomorrow* (1973). He also co-edited the Smuts papers in 1966 and has written two volumes of autobiography, *Country and Calling* (1954) and *Professing History* (1976).

Handfasted, see **SPENCE, CATHERINE HELEN**

HANDFORD, NOURMA (1911–), born Queensland, edited the *Australian Women's Digest* for three years, wrote four novels for adults, *High River* (1947), *Murder for Tea* (1949), *Coward's Kiss* (1954), and *Fools of Time* (1958), and several books for adolescent girls.

Handful of Friends, A, a play by David Williamson (q.v.), was first performed in 1976 and published the same year. It is an obliquely-developed study of betrayal, in marriage, in friendship and in love. The relationships between the five friends involved range over thirty years, although the action of the play, divided into eight scenes, spans only a week. A libellous film script by one of the group is the action's catalyst, but the play's interest centres on the intricately convoluted relations that gradually develop and establish a composite picture of egoism and isolation.

HANGER, EUNICE (1911–72), born Rockhampton, Queensland, was educated at the University of Queensland, where she taught from 1955. An enthusiastic proponent of Australian drama, she was active as writer, director and producer in theatre in Brisbane and began the Hanger Collection of unpublished play scripts, which is now held by the University's Fryer Library (q.v.) Her own published plays are *Upstage* (1952), *An Actor Prepares* in *Never Kill a Dolphin* (1959), and *2D and Other Plays* (includes *The Frogs* and *Flood*) ed. Alrene Sykes (1978). Her unpublished plays include 'Tragedy' (1948), 'The Dolls' (1952), 'Well, Well!' (1954), 'For Love or Money', 'Foundations' (1961), 'Short Street' (1962), 'The Lawn Mower', 'Ring the Changelings', 'A Sandwich for the Teacher' (1976), and an adaptation of 'M. Barnard Eldershaw''s *A House Is Built* (1954). She also edited *Australian One-Act Plays Book I* (1962), *Khaki, Bush and Bigotry* (1968),

Six One-Act Plays (1970) and *Drama for High Schools* (1971).

HANNAN, PADDY (1843–1925), born County Clare, Ireland, migrated to Australia in 1862 and worked on the Ballarat and Bendigo goldfields. In 1893 in company with two other Irishmen, Thomas Flanigan and Dan Shea, Hannan found gold at Mount Charlotte, north–east of the established goldfield of Coolgardie in WA. The resultant gold rush led to the establishment of Kalgoorlie, one of Australia's richest goldfields and long referred to as Hannan's town; its main street is named after him and his statue stands near the town hall. Clive Turnbull wrote *Frontier: The Story of Paddy Hannan* (1949).

HANRAHAN, BARBARA (1939–), was born in Adelaide. After her father's early death her mother worked as a commercial artist and her solitary childhood was supervised mainly by her grandmother and other women relatives. She spent three years at SA School of Art, taught briefly and then left for London in 1963 to continue her art studies. She has since spent extensive periods in England, although she is now settled in Adelaide. A painter and printmaker with an international reputation, she has lectured at the SA School of Art and at art colleges in England, and has had numerous exhibitions in Australian cities and in London. Her initiation into authorship was relatively late, stimulated by the death of her grandmother, which released powerful childhood memories of Adelaide. She has written a memoir of her childhood, *The Scent of Eucalyptus* (1973), and six novels, *Sea Green* (1974), *The Albatross, Muff* (1977), *Where the Queens All Strayed* (1978), *The Peach Groves* (q.v., 1979), *The Frangipani Gardens* (1980) and *Dove* (1982). A writer with a plain but suggestive prose style, Hanrahan is a brilliant creator of atmosphere. She is particularly preoccupied with the contrast between the prim respectability of nineteenth-century society, especially Adelaide society, and its seamy or horrific underside. She has described Adelaide as a 'terribly sinister place', and sees her novels as 'concerned with contrasts, contradictions: beauty and horror, love and death, frivolity and menace; the precisely-detailed world of substance, the darker world of instinct; the queerness of mind split from body, the absurd fantasy of the "ordinary" '. These contrasts are already present in *The Scent of Eucalyptus*, a vivid evocation of childhood experience, and in *Sea Green*, the story of a young Adelaide artist who goes to London. In *The Albatross Muff*, however, Hanrahan's gift for Gothic romance is given full scope. Set mainly in the middle years of nineteenth-century London, it mingles fairy-tale fantasy and baroque horror. In *Where the Queens All Strayed* Hanrahan turns her attention to Edwardian Adelaide and, in *The Peach Groves* to NZ and Adelaide in the 1880s. Both are suggestive, delicately-woven blends of frivolity and menace, pretension and primitivism, quaint old-world charm and coarse, unnatural passion. *The Frangipani Gardens*, set in Adelaide of the 1920s, is a compelling exploration of the horror and mystery that lie below the brittle surface of respectable high society. *Dove*, which ranges over three SA generations from the late nineteenth century to the 1930s, focuses mainly on the diverse experiences of a mother and daughter.

Hansard, the official record of parliamentary debates, is named after T.C. Hansard, who began to print reports from the British parliament in 1803. There is now a *Hansard* for all the Australian parliaments, but the dates of commencement vary, as do the frequency of publication (daily, weekly, by session) and the dates from which the parliamentary debates were formally titled *Hansard*. The first Australian *Hansard* was established in Victoria in 1856 by the *Argus*; it received financial support from the Victorian parliament in 1861 and became independent of the newspaper in 1866. In SA *Hansard* was contracted to the *Register* or the *Advertiser* from its inception in the 1857–58 session of parliament until 1914, when it came formally under the control of the government. Elsewhere, *Hansard* commenced in 1864 in Queensland, 1879 in NSW, 1876 in WA, 1901 for the Commonwealth parliament, 1948 in the Northern Territory and 1979 in Tasmania; the last two use a sound recording system, all others a shorthand reporting staff. Among *Hansard* reporters, J.F. Archibald worked on the NSW staff in 1879 immediately before establishing the *Bulletin*, Ernest Scott on the Victorian *Hansard* 1895–1901 and the Commonwealth 1901–13; and Fred Johns worked in SA from 1914. Before *Hansard*, parliamentary debates and topics were extensively reported in major colonial newspapers; the novelist, Charles de Boos, was parliamentary reporter for the *Sydney Morning Herald* in the 1860s and his weekly column, 'The Collective Wisdom of New South Wales' (1867–73), remains a useful source for historians.

Happy Dispatches, see PATERSON, A.B.

Happy Land, The, a theatrical satire by Marcus Clarke (q.v.), was performed in Melbourne in 1880. Adapted from an 1873 London burlesque of the same title which had lampooned Gladstone and been banned by the Lord Chamberlain, *The Happy Land* satirized the government of Graham Berry, which took steps to ban the piece; it had two performances in Melbourne and was played also in Sydney and Wellington, NZ. Berry's actions aroused controversy in the Victorian press and parliament, where he was attacked by the rebellious politician, David Gaunson, who later in 1880 defended Ned Kelly.

Happy Valley, see WHITE, PATRICK

Harbinger of Light, a monthly journal published in Melbourne, began in 1870 and ran until 1956, after which it was known as *Psychic Science News Magazine*. In addition to articles on psychic and literary topics, it featured fiction serials and poetry. Contributors included Charles Bright and James Smith.

HARCOURT, J.M. (JOHN MEWTON) (1902–71), born Melbourne, worked for a time in the pearling industry at Broome, and as a journalist 1926–47, on newspapers in Perth and Melbourne and for the Australian government. He wrote three novels, *The Pearlers* (1933), *Upsurge* (1934) and *It Never Fails* (1937). *The Pearlers* is a lively story with the pearling industry as background; *Upsurge*, an account of Perth during the depression of the early 1930s, is an attack on social injustice; *It Never Fails*, an improbable account of the adventures of a young English immigrant, is a satire on Australian social attitudes.

HARDIE, J.J. (JOHN JACKSON) (1894–1951), born Scotland, migrated to Australia in 1911, served in the First World War and spent much of his later life on sheep and cattle stations in northern NSW. He wrote three station romances, *Cattle Camp* (1932, winner of the *Bulletin* prize), *Lantana* (1933), and *The Bridle Track* (1936). Another novel, *Pastoral Symphony* (1939), is an account of the breeding of cattle and sheep by two escaped convicts and their descendants in northern NSW.

HARDING, LEE (1937–), born Colac, Victoria, is both a science fiction writer and children's author; the two interests often merge, as in his remarkably successful novel, *The Displaced Person* (1979, see Science Fiction), a first-person narrative by an alienated adolescent, which won both the Children's Book of the Year Award for 1980 and the Alan Marshall Award for a manuscript novel in 1978. His other works include *The Fallen Spaceman* (1973), *The Frozen Sky* (1976), *The Children of Atlantis* (1976), *Return to Tomorrow* (1976), *The Weeping Sky* (1977, see Science Fiction),

Journey into Time (1978) and *Waiting for the End of the World* (1983). Dramatizations of *The Frozen Sky* and *Journey into Time* were broadcast on ABC radio in 1978. Harding has also edited several significant anthologies of modern science fiction, including *Beyond Tomorrow* (1975); *The Altered I: An Encounter with Science Fiction* (1976, with Ursula Le Guin and others); and *Rooms of Paradise* (1978).

Hardy, Cliff, see **CORRIS, PETER**

HARDY, FRANK (1917–   ), born into a large Roman Catholic family, was brought up at Bacchus Marsh, Victoria, the 'Benson's Valley' of several of his short stories. He left school at thirteen and worked as a fruit-picker, road-construction worker, seaman, grocer and cartoonist. Deeply impressed by the sufferings of the 1930s depression, he joined the Communist Party of Australia in 1939 and later became a member of the Realist Writers' group. He joined the army in 1942, was posted to Mataranka, Northern Territory, and there established a camp newspaper, the *Troppo Tribune*, providing the illustrations and most of the written work himself. In 1944 he joined the staff of the Army magazine, *Salt*. After leaving the army in 1946, he worked part-time as a journalist in Melbourne, meanwhile assiduously gathering information for his novel *Power Without Glory* (q.v., 1950), a semi-fictional account of the millionaire, John Wren. Because of the book's controversial nature, Hardy published and distributed the first issues himself. In September 1950 he was charged with libel of Mrs Ellen Wren, allegedly the Nellie West of the novel who has a child as a result of an extra-marital love affair. After a criminal trial that lasted nine months and aroused keen national interest, he was acquitted; in *The Hard Way* (1961) he gives an account of the writing of the novel and the subsequent trial. *Power Without Glory* has since been translated into several languages, frequently reprinted, and produced as a successful television serial in 1976. His other novels are *The Four-Legged Lottery* (1958), a study of the tragedy caused by gambling; *The Outcasts of Foolgarah* (1971), a slapstick comedy about garbage collectors; *But the Dead Are Many* (q.v., 1975), his most ambitious work and a reconstruction of the personal and political predicaments of a Marxist intellectual after his suicide; and *Who Shot George Kirkland?* (1980, co-winner of the ANA Literature Award) and an extension of one of the incidents in *Power Without Glory*; and *The Obsession of Oscar Oswald* (1983), an attack on the role of lawyers, financial companies and debt collectors in modern society, which is accompanied by a booklet ostensibly written

by Oscar Oswald, *Warrant of Distress* (1983). Clement Semmler edited *A Frank Hardy Swag* (1982), a collage of Hardy's works. Hardy is now well known as a television personality, playwright, songwriter, journalist, lecturer, and writer for radio and television. He has also written travel books and an account of a strike by Aboriginal stockmen in the Northern Territory, *The Unlucky Australians* (1968). Apart from *Power Without Glory* which, with all its formal defects, is a coherent and convincing study of a corrupt and corrupting individual, Hardy's most significant achievement lies in the short story. His main short story collections are *The Man from Clinkapella* (1951), *Legends from Benson's Valley* (1963), republished with one addition in *It's Moments Like These* (1972), *The Yarns of Billy Borker* (1965) (see Borker, Billy) and *Billy Borker Yarns Again* (1967), republished with some additions in *The Great Australian Lover* (1972). His most carefully structured stories, the studies of the depression years in rural Victoria in *Legends from Benson's Valley*, illustrate his sympathy with the battler's sufferings, stoicism and humour, and his ear for the laconic Australian idiom. The Billy Borker stories are lighter pieces, tall stories casually narrated by Borker, the ever-thirsty, ubiquitous bar-dweller and folksy humorist.

Hare, Mary, see *Riders in the Chariot*

HARFORD, LESBIA (1891–1927), was born Lesbia Keogh in Melbourne. From an early age she was subject to ill-health but possessed a charismatic, eccentric and outspoken personality. After graduating in law and philosophy from the University of Melbourne in 1916, she worked as an art teacher, a confidential clerk in a business office and a freelance social researcher. This last role led her to work for some time in a clothing factory in order to understand women's working conditions. She was a prolific writer of lyrical poetry, some of which was collected after her death by Nettie Palmer and published as *The Poems of Lesbia Harford* (1941); apparently artless and even casual, her slender, remarkably frank lyrics focus on a variety of subjects from love to factory life.

HARGRAVES, EDWARD HAMMOND (1816–91), born Gosport, England, came to Australia in 1834, worked on the Californian goldfields in 1849–50, and returned to Australia in 1851; he began prospecting for gold in the Bathurst–Orange region of NSW, largely because the topography there resembled that of the gold-bearing areas of California. His discovery of gold at Summer Hill Creek and Ophir began the Australian gold rushes. In 1855 he published *Australia and Its Gold-*

fields. His exploits are recorded in Frank Clune's *Golden Goliath* (1946), Jay Monaghan's *Australians and the Gold Rush* (1966) and in most of the historical works associated with the Australian goldfields era, e.g. Geoffrey Serle's *The Golden Age* (1963) and Nancy Keesing's *Gold Fever* (1967).

HARNEY, BILL (1895–1962), born Charters Towers, Queensland, was a drover, bushman, soldier in the First World War, lugger captain, patrol officer in the Native Affairs Branch of the Northern Territory, member of several UN expeditions into Arnhem Land, curator of Ayers Rock reservation, and an ardent supporter of the cause of the Aborigines, to whom he was known as 'Bilarni'. His numerous popular books about the Northern Territory, the Aborigines and his own life include *Taboo* (1943), *North of 23°* (1946), *Brimming Billabongs* (1947), *Life Among the Aborigines* (1957), *Content to Lie in the Sun* (1958), and *Grief, Gaiety and Aborigines* (1961). With A.P. Elkin he wrote *Tales from the Aborigines* (1959). A skilful raconteur, Harney colours his writings with a wealth of bush lore and bush humour. *Bill Harney's War* (1983), introduced by Manning Clark, is adapted from a radio programme, 'Harney's War', by John Thompson in the 1950s.

Harp in the South, The, a novel by Ruth Park (q.v.), won first prize in the 1946 *Sydney Morning Herald* novel competition and was published in 1948. Dramatized by Park and Leslie Rees, it was staged in 1949. Set in the slums of Surry Hills, Sydney, it deals with the fortunes of an Irish–Australian family, the Darcys. Hughie Darcy, the feckless, boisterous father, dominates the household which includes his wife Mumma and two daughters, nineteen-year old Roie and Dolour, who is still a schoolgirl. The Darcys' son Thady has mysteriously disappeared at the age of six. Their dilapidated house is shared by three tenants, Patrick Diamond, a solitary Irishman whose patriotic fervour reaches boiling-point every St Patrick's Day, and Miss Sheily, a lady who has come down in the world and is forced to live with the illegitimate, handicapped son, Johnny, whom she detests. Later, Johnny is killed by a truck and Miss Sheily remorsefully and secretly punishes herself. Life for the Darcys grows more exciting after their Irish-born, maliciously-humorous grandmother comes to live with them. Meanwhile their lives are affected both by the general teeming life of Surry Hills and by several of their neighbours, such as the Siciliano family and Licky Jim, the Chinese greengrocer. Roie's dull life as a factory hand is temporarily lightened by her love affair with Tommy Mendel, an inarticulate Jewish boy,

but after the romance fades she finds that she is pregnant. She is unable to face up to an abortion but loses her baby when she is beaten up in a drunken mêlée. After the accident she is severely ill for several months and meanwhile Grandmother, now eighty-six, weakens and dies. Hughie believes for one halcyon day that he has won a lottery prize but is disappointed, Miss Sheily leaves after her marriage to a barrel-organ grinder, Mr Gunnarson, and Roie finds a new lover, Charlie Rothe, marries and has a daughter. The fortunes of the Darcys are continued in Park's next novel, *Poor Man's Orange* (1949).

HARPUR, CHARLES (1813–68), born Windsor of emancipist parents, was raised in the Hawkesbury River (q.v.) district; his later use of the pseudonym 'A Hawkesbury Lad', indicates his affection for that area. In young manhood his abrasive and radical personality led to erratic and unsatisfactory employment. His long courtship of Mary Doyle ('Rosa' of his love sonnets) culminated in their marriage in 1850. After a period as an unwilling sheep farmer in the Hunter valley, Harpur in 1859 was appointed assistant gold commissioner at Araluen. In 1866 the goldfields position was retrenched; in 1867 his farm at Nerrigundah near Eurobodalla was ruined by floods, and his son Charles was killed in a shooting accident. These personal setbacks, combined with the lack of recognition of his literary efforts, made his final years bitter and frustrated.

Harpur's published works include *Thoughts: A Series of Sonnets* (1845), *The Bushrangers, A Play in Five Acts, and Other Poems* (q.v., 1853), *The Tower of the Dream* (q.v., 1865), and several smaller works: a broadsheet, *Songs of Australia, First Series* (1850); a pamphlet containing two poems, titled *A Poet's Home* (1862); and a four page booklet, *A Rhyme* (1864). The first Harpur collected edition was the posthumous *Poems,* edited by H.M. Martin in 1883. Relied on for some years as the definitive edition of Harpur, it has now been largely discredited because of Martin's arbitrary handling of the text, excising whatever he felt was controversial or radical in Harpur and leaving him as little more than a descriptive nature poet. In 1948 *'Rosa': Love Sonnets to Mary Doyle* was published, edited by C.W. Salier; K.H. Gifford and D.F. Hall edited *Selected Poems of Charles Harpur* (1944).

In the early years of settlement, when colonial poetry was largely ignored or derided, Harpur's ambition was to be Australia's first authentic poetic voice. He believed that Australian poetry should be modelled upon traditional English verse before seeking its own individuality. Thus his own poetry relies heavily on traditional poetic techniques such as ornamental diction, wide use of personification and metaphor, solemnity of tone and ponderous movement, while attempting on some occasions at least to describe and interpret the colonial Australian scene. Such attempts include his nature poems, 'A Mid-Summer Noon in the Australian Forest' (q.v.), 'Dawn and Sunrise in the Snowy Mountains', 'The Bush Fire' and 'A Storm in the Mountains', which describe some of the typical though more dramatic components of the Australian landscape, and convey a sense of vast distance and wide horizons.

Ignored or badly mutilated in the 1883 collection were several substantial philosophical poems, The Tower of the Dream, 'The Witch of Hebron', 'Genius Lost', 'The World and the Soul' and 'The Temple of Infamy'. The long blank verse dissertation, 'The World and the Soul', combines the Darwinian theory of evolution with a highly unorthodox, religious view of the universe and its purpose. The subject itself is so complicated and Harpur's treatment of it so unconventional that his editor, Martin, probably at a loss how to handle it, omitted it altogether. Only a few lyrics and choruses of the 2300 lines of 'Genius Lost', a series of poems on the death of Thomas Chatterton, appeared in the 1883 edition. 'Genius Lost', one of the most ambitious of colonial poetic efforts, demonstrates Harpur's grasp of technique and his intellectual capacity. 'The Witch of Hebron' was printed in the 1883 collection with some 400 lines, vital to the understanding of the poem, excised. The best-known Harpur narrative poem, 'The Creek of the Four Graves' (q.v.), the story of settlers murdered by Aborigines, was altered by Martin to highlight the descriptive rather than the narrative areas. The deficiencies of the 1883 collection resulted, for many years, in an undervaluing of Harpur's poetic achievements. Research and scholarship in recent times, however, have increased his reputation, and modern critical opinion sees him as the most substantial of the colonial poets. In spite of his own unfulfilled dream to be acknowledged as 'the Muse of Australia', Harpur was an influential figure in the mid-century colony.

Journals and newspapers such as the Weekly Register, the People's Advocate, the Empire, and the Sydney Morning Herald, carried his wide-ranging political, social and literary commentary, including outbursts against injustice and inequality, satirical tilts at squattocracy and snobbery, defence of the Aborigines, and literary articles and essays. With other currency lads such as Daniel Deniehy, Harpur attempted to direct the colony along the path of egalitarianism and democracy. J. Normington-Rawling published the biography, Charles Harpur, An

Australian (1962) and Judith Wright, a strong advocate of Harpur's talent, the monograph, Charles Harpur (1963). Elizabeth Perkins published The Poetical Works of Charles Harpur (1984), the most complete edition to date of Harpur's poetry; it is accompanied by critical and bibliographical apparatus.

HARRINGTON, EDWARD PHILLIP (1896–1966), born Colbinabbin near Shepparton, Victoria, served in the First World War in Palestine with the Australian Light Horse. Those experiences are recorded in his first book of verse, Songs of War and Peace (1920). He later wandered through the Victorian outback as rouseabout, drover and farmer, saturating himself in the atmosphere of the bush ('Oh the careless, droving, roving life is the finest life of all'). The last of the bush balladists, Harrington enshrines in his poetry such attitudes as mateship, egalitarianism and love of the bush. He lived for a time at Swan Hill in Victoria and later in Melbourne, where he was instrumental in founding the Bread and Cheese Club. His bush balladry is represented in his volumes, Boundary Bend and Other Ballads (1936), My Old Black Billy and Other Songs of the Australian Outback (1940), The Kerrigan Boys (1944) and The Swagless Swaggie and Other Ballads (1957), which includes some verse from earlier books.

HARRIS, ALEXANDER ('AN EMIGRANT MECHANIC') (1805–74), born London, spent his childhood at Windsor in Berkshire, and then returned to London at the age of eighteen to work in the printing trade. Dissolute living led to his being secretly sent out to Australia by his parents and friends in 1825. Until his return to England in 1840 he worked as a cedar getter, an occupation described at length in his Australian writings, and established himself on the land. In London he became involved in city missionary work (an indication of his reformed character) and wrote widely on life in the colonies. In 1851 he went to America, where he made a living from teaching and writing. He ultimately became an American citizen and died in Canada. Harris's first book, Settlers and Convicts: Or, Recollections of Sixteen Years' Labour in the Australian Backwoods (q.v., 1847), was published under the pseudonym 'An Emigrant Mechanic'. His fictional work, The Emigrant Family: Or, the Story of an Australian Settler (q.v., 1849) and ascribed to 'the author of Settlers and Convicts', a mixture of romantic novel and social history, belongs as does his first book to the emigrant literature genre so popular at the time, when interest in the colonies was stimulated by difficult economic conditions in the home countries. Between these two Australian works Harris published, also anonymously, an autobiographical account of his religious conversion, *Testimony to the Truth: Or, the Autobiography of an Atheist* (1848). In its fourth edition Harris was named as the author and *Settlers and Convicts* was also credited to him. An emigrant handbook, *A Guide to Port Stephens in New South Wales, the Colony of the Australian Agricultural Company* (1849), also linked his name to *The Emigrant Family*. Harris's original anonymity confused modern literary researchers, who were not convinced of his authorship, but the controversy was largely settled by Harris's grandson, Grant Carr Harris, producing corroborative biographical information and an autobiographical work, 'Religio Christi', which was published by Harris in serial form in the *Saturday Evening Post* in 1858. An updated account of Harris's life and career is in A.H. Chisholm's *The Secrets of Alexander Harris* (1961), but there still remain some unauthenticated biographical details, especially about his time in Australia, and some inconsistencies in Harris's autobiographical writings. With *Settlers and Convicts* and *The Emigrant Family*, Harris provides the most realistic and comprehensive accounts of early colonial life in Australia. They have been a valuable reference source for social historians, who have found in them informed and accurate comment on such features of the colonial scene as the convict system, the Aborigines, land reform, modes of transport, bushrangers, urban and outback lifestyles. Nor are they negligible as literature. *The Emigrant Family*, in spite of its length and its conventional, romantic subplots, is one of the major works of fiction of the period.

HARRIS, MAX (1921–   ), born Adelaide, grew up in Mount Gambier. He went from school in Adelaide to journalism to the University of Adelaide, where he obtained a degree in economics. During the Second World War he worked as a government economist and published two volumes of verse and a novel. He also co-edited the literary and artistic journal, *Angry Penguins* (q.v.), which gave expression to the noisy revolutionary modernism in literature and the arts of a group of avant-garde young intellectuals known as the Angry Penguins. The failure of Harris and his co-editors to detect the deliberately-concocted nonsense of the Ern Malley hoax (q.v.) and the publication of 'The Darkening Ecliptic' in the Autumn 1944 issue of *Angry Penguins* resulted in ridicule and prosecution for publishing indecent material. Harris's own career in literature, however, suffered little more than a minor setback from the Ern Malley affair. After the

war he was involved in many successful literary projects, including the establishment of the Mary Martin bookshop chain; the creation and editing of *Ern Malley's Journal* (1952–55); the publication of *Ern Malley's Poems* (1961); the founding and editing, with Geoffrey Dutton, of *Australian Letters* (q.v., 1957–68) and *Australian Book Review* (q.v., 1961–74); the publication with Dutton of *The Vital Decade* (1968); the compilation, with Alison Forbes, of a pictorial history of Australia titled *The Land That Waited* (1967); and a criticism of present-day Australian values, *Ockers: Essays on the Bad Old New Australia* (1974). His creative work began with *The Gift of Blood* (1940) and *Dramas from the Sky* (1942), two slight volumes of verse. The poems are love lyrics, responses to the local scene, and reflections on the Spanish Civil War. *The Coorong and Other Poems* (1955) is more noteworthy. Poems such as 'Incident at the Alice', 'Martin Buber in the Pub', 'Apollo Bay to Kingston', 'Allegory of Dante and the Apes' and 'On Throwing a Copy of the New Statesman into the Coorong' led readers and critics to hope that Harris would publish more frequently. But the next volume, *A Window at Night*, selected by Robert Clark, who wrote a valuable introduction discussing Harris as a poet, did not appear until 1967 and more than half the poems it contains had been published earlier. Harris had insisted in 'The Faded Years' in *Direction* (May 1952) that there was no room for 'posturing' in poetry and that poetry should establish a real relationship between the poet and the reader. The new poems attract the reader, often in quite different ways: 'A Window at Night' with its intricate intimacy and 'The Death of Bert Sassenowsky' with its ironic narrative of Bert and his oxen disappearing into a volcanic hole in the Mount Gambier district. After another twelve years came the tiny volume *Poetic Gems* (1979), sarcastically titled and puzzlingly ambivalent. Many of the brief poems exhibit both an arrogant contempt for life and a strong fear of death, Harris treating life to the scornful 'Sirrah' which he claims to prefer that life direct at him but the *enfant terrible* of the Angry Penguin days is still seen in such poems as 'I'm Shagging in the Wagon'. There are some 'gems' nevertheless, e.g. 'Love Poems for the Thompson Children'. Harris's early experimental novel, *The Vegetative Eye* (1943), was not a success; he later published a section of another novel, provisionally titled 'Biography of a No-Hoper' in a 1960 anthology, *Southern Festival*. As drama, art and literary critic, belletrist and, in his own description, 'socio-cultural diagnostician', Harris has been for the past forty years one of Australia's most controversial figures. Some of the fruits of those years of acting as irritant of the political, social, literary and artistic establishment are preserved in *The Angry Eye* (1973), the aptly-named collection of Harris's writing from the *Australian* and *Nation*. He also published *The Unknown Great Australian and Other Psychobiographical Portraits* (1983), a collection of pen pictures of various Australian outsiders and eccentrics.

HARRIS, PHILLIP LAWRENCE, see *Aussie: The Australian Soldiers' Magazine*

HARRIS, ROBERT (1951–), born Melbourne, has published *Localities: Poems* (1973), *Translations from the Albatross* (1976) and *The Abandoned* (1979). He was awarded the Harri Jones Prize for poetry in 1975.

HARRIS, ROLF (1930–), born Perth, studied art in London before becoming a stage and television entertainer; along with Dame Edna Everage and Clive James, he is one of the best-known Australians in England. He wrote *Rolf Goes Bush* (1975) but is more commonly associated with 'Tie Me Kangaroo Down Sport', a comic song in the 'Dying Stockman' (q.v.) tradition.

HARRISON, KEITH (1932–), born Melbourne, taught in Victoria and England before taking up an academic career in North America. Represented in numerous Australian, English and American anthologies, Harrison has achieved a considerable international reputation as poet, editor, academic and critic. His poetry publications include *Points in a Journey* (1966); *Songs from the Drifting House* (1972), which won a British Arts Council award; *The Basho Poems* (1975), built around a central figure, Basho, whom Harrison describes as 'a kind of trickster figure ... the kind of figure you see occurring in Red Indian mythology, who essentially upsets the expected order of things', and through whom Harrison deflates the ridiculous, stupid and pompous; *A Town and Country Suite* (1980); and *The Sense of Falling* (1980).

HARROP, LES (1948–), born Blackburn, England, and educated in England and Canada, taught in America before coming to Australia in 1977; he was poetry editor of *Overland* and later founding editor of *Helix*. Awarded the Greenwood Prize of the Poetry Society of Great Britain in 1976, the Stroud Festival Poetry Prize in 1977 and the Anne Elder Award in 1980, he has published, in Australia, *The Hum of the Old Suit* (1979).

HARROWER, ELIZABETH (1928–), born Sydney, spent her first eleven years in the industrial town of Newcastle, the model for Ballowra in her novel *The Long Prospect* (q.v.). After leaving school she worked as a clerk and studied psychology before discovering her bent as a writer. She lived in London 1951–59; returning to Sydney she worked for the ABC, as a reviewer for the *Sydney Morning Herald*, and for a publishing firm. Harrower has written four novels, *Down in the City* (1957), *The Long Prospect* (1958), *The Catherine Wheel* (1960) and *The Watch Tower* (q.v., 1966), and short stories.

At the centre of all Harrower's novels is an intense psychological drama, a struggle between the strong (as far as position is concerned) and the weak, although the nature and the terms of the struggle vary widely. She has a keen understanding of the motivating forces of selfishness, envy, ignorance, malice, pride, pity and fear and of the way these forces can work within a small, familiar group to produce misery for the innocent or defenceless. At a deeper level, her fiction tentatively and searchingly explores the ambivalent problems of responsibility and freedom, guilt and innocence, naivety and experience. *Down in the City* traces the disillusionment of an upper-class woman, Esther Prescott, with the working-class businessman Stan Peterson, whom she marries after an acquaintanceship of two weeks. Apparently easygoing and fun-loving, Stan turns out to be a racketeer and a paranoid bully. A weak man, unable to abandon either old habits or his old mistress, he finds in Esther a new object on which to vent his grudge against the system. *The Long Prospect* is a more complex exploration of the banality of evil. Here the adult world, seen partly through the consciousness of a child, Emily, reveals itself as both seedy and dangerous, vulgar and destructive. In her progression to a finer moral awareness and a new condition of isolation, Emily is typical of Harrower's heroines. *The Catherine Wheel*, a subtle study of an exceptional and complicated relationship, is her least popular novel. Set in London, it traces the struggle between a young Australian girl, Clemency James, and a penniless, handsome, enigmatic young man, Christian Roland. Christian's self-indulgence, unpredictable moods, manufactured charm and exhibitionism are convincingly presented but the struggle between Clem's passive integrity and his uncompromising selfishness becomes somewhat unequal. *The Watch Tower* is a darker exploration of anarchic evil, made more compelling by the novel's ordinary suburban setting. Felix Shaw, a domestic tyrant who lives only to gratify his need for power, is chillingly presented, as is the gradual collusion of his chief victim, his wife Laura. For Clare, Laura's sister, suffering is morally rewarding, however, an illuminating experience both of the enfeebling force of pity and the indomitable power of the self to resist appropriation.

HARRY, J.S. (1939–   ), born Adelaide, was awarded the Harri Jones Prize in 1971 for her first volume of poetry, *The Deer Under the Skin*, which was highly regarded for its sensitivity and control of language. Her second volume, *Hold for a Little While and Turn Gently*, appeared in 1979.

Hart, see BLIGHT, JOHN

HART, ALFRED, see Shakespeare and Australia

HART, GERTRUDE, born Melbourne, published *The Dream Girl* (1912), an unusually-told love story, *The Laughter Lady* (1914), an interpretation of the Christmas message, and *Chubby* (1937). In co-operation with Bernard Cronin, Gertrude Hart founded the Derelicts, a club that later became the Melbourne Society of Australian Authors. She contributed poems to *The Little Track and Other Verses* (1922).

HART, KEVIN (1954–   ), born London, was educated at the Australian National University and has taught at Geelong College, Victoria, and also Deakin University. Hart has published two books of elegant and contemplative verse, *The Departure* (1978) and *The Lines of the Hand* (1981).

HART-SMITH, WILLIAM (1911–   ), born Tunbridge Wells, England, went to NZ as a boy and came to Australia in 1936. He worked in radio in Sydney before enlisting in the Australian army in 1940. After the war he returned to NZ, where he was involved in adult education and advertising. He was back in Sydney in 1962 as an advertising manager, then radio technician, but went to Perth in 1970. He was president of the Poetry Society of Australia 1963–64. His poetry includes *Columbus Goes West* (1943), *Harvest* (1945), *The Unceasing Ground* (1946), *Christopher Columbus* (q.v., 1948), *On the Level: Mostly Canterbury (NZ) Poems* (1950), *Poems of Discovery* (1959, which includes *Columbus Goes West* and *Christopher Columbus* and which won the Australian Literature Society Gold Medal), *The Talking-Clothes* (1966, which shared the Grace Leven Prize for poetry); *Minipoems* (1974), brief verses based on Maori legends and proverbs, and evocations of the WA landscape. Soon after his arrival in Australia, Hart-Smith became involved with the growing Jindyworobak movement, largely because of his delight in the

Australian spirit of place and his fascination with the primitive animism of the Aborigines and the romantic mysticism of their legends. From 1940 his poems were regularly featured in the Jindyworobak anthologies and he edited the 1944 volume. Traces of Jindyworobak subjects and sentiment persist in his later poetry. Notable among his numerous Jindyworobak verses were 'The Pleiades', a poem based on Aboriginal legend; 'Moondeen', a character-study of 'the oldest man of the river tribe'; and 'Nullarbor', his account of a brief meeting with a young Aboriginal in the desert and his consequent conviction of his own white grotesqueness. Hart-Smith's poetic talents are too considerable, however, to be limited to an expression of Jindyworobak philosophy. His major poetic work is *Christopher Columbus*. With the incisive, delicately-constructed, sometimes sombre, sometimes ironic, poems of personal observation, it has assured him a small but enthusiastic following among discerning readers who are impressed by the clarity, exactness and sensitivity of his observations and by his capacity for communicating those observations in distinctive and often startling imagery.

HARTIGAN, PATRICK JOSEPH, see 'O'BRIEN, JOHN'

HARWOOD, GWEN ('FRANCIS GEYER', 'WALTER LEHMANN', 'T.F. KLINE', 'MIRIAM STONE') (1920–   ), was born at Taringa, Brisbane. She studied music, which she later taught, and was organist at All Saints' Church in Brisbane. In 1945 she married William Harwood, a linguist, and moved to Tasmania. Her first volume, *Poems*, was published in 1963; *Poems: Volume Two* in 1968; *Selected Poems* in 1975; and *The Lion's Bride* in 1981. She has written librettos for Larry Sitsky's operas, e.g. *Fall of the House of Usher* (1974), and has also written for the composers James Penberthy and Ian Cugley. In 1961 she achieved some notoriety with two acrostic sonnets which hoaxed the *Bulletin*. Her usually wide use of pseudonyms has been variously ascribed to her fear of publishers discriminating against her as a woman writer, her wish not to trade upon her established reputation, and her reticence when publishing poetry of an intimate, personal nature.

It was not until her late thirties, when she was in hospital, that Gwen Harwood allowed herself to satisfy her 'deep inner necessity' to write poetry, which, she said, was 'an attempt to realise in words the moments that gave my life its meaning'. Many of the poems of her first volume tell of pain, direct physical pain as in 'The Wound', 'In Hospital' and 'Ad Orientem', and the more oblique but equally damaging pain of life which brings with its passing no real sense of fulfilment, either physically ('The Wine is Drunk') or spiritually ('The Old Wife's Tale'). The self-scrutiny of this early poetry, sometimes thinly disguised by masking or impersonalization, is at its most perturbed in 'Triste, Triste', and at its most confident in 'O Could One Write As One Makes Love'. She creates two distinctive figures who are regarded to some extent as ironic projections of herself. They are Professor Eisenbart (q.v.), whose eight poems constitute the second part of *Poems*, and Professor Kröte (q.v.), who appears intermittently throughout *Poems: Volume Two*, in 'New Poems' of the *Selected Poems*, and in three poems of *The Lion's Bride*, e.g. 'A Music Lesson', 'The Silver Swan' and 'A Scattering of Ashes'. These two tragi-comic figures, the first an ageing nuclear physicist with a young mistress, the second a frustrated, alcoholic European musician, set down in the 'philistinia' of Australian suburbia, are used by the poet to present a veiled criticism of established conventions and attitudes and some forthright views on life, truth and the human condition. In the third part of the first volume, all ten poems of which had been contributed to the *Bulletin* under the pseudonym 'Walter Lehmann', is her well-known 'In the Park'; with several other poems from the second volume, e.g. 'Suburban Sonnet: Boxing Day', 'Suburban Sonnet' and 'Burning Sappho', it is a *cri de coeur* for women whose lives are eaten away by the cares of motherhood and domesticity.

Poems: Volume Two reiterates her preference for the conventional devices of rhyme, metre and stanzaic regularity and illustrates her continuing preoccupation with personal fulfilment, especially the dilemma of the individual caught between newly-glimpsed freedom and long-practised restraint. In numerous poems in the second volume, the ubiquitous Kröte agonizes and riots his self-pitying way through an oblivious and imperceptive world; whether Kröte or the world is the anti-hero is sometimes difficult to judge. The effects of new experiences in the poet's own life are evident in the dedication of many of the second volume's poems to people important in her life at the time, e.g. Rex Hobcroft, Larry Sitsky, and A.D. Hope. The first and second parts of the *Selected Poems* contain her choice from the two earlier volumes. The third part consists of twenty-seven finely-crafted new poems. Many of the latter, e.g. 'Dust to Dust', 'The Violets', 'Iris', 'David's Harp', 'Father and Child' and 'Night Flight', are intensely personal and deeply moving, but not, as has sometimes been said of her poetry in general, despondent and sad. In these 'New Poems' she continues to contemplate the frus-

tration of personal fulfilment by such inevitabilities as separation, loss, the passing of time, and the demands made by the ordinary process of life. The compromise that she makes in the face of this frustration is to incorporate, in David Moody's words, 'the intolerable within the accepted order of things'. *The Lion's Bride* combines her already apparent consciousness of death and pain with her strong affirmation of life. The title sonnet tells of an unusual relationship between a lion and its keeper's daughter, a relationship ended or only properly begun when the girl in her wedding finery is devoured by the lion. Many of the poems are set in Tasmania, e.g. memorial pieces to the poet James McAuley, while Truganini and the Tasmanian Aborigines are also recalled.

The great extent to which Gwen Harwood's thought and poetry have been influenced by the philosopher Wittgenstein is reflected in her own comments and in critical analyses, where the bases of such poems as 'I Am the Captain of My Soul' (one of her own favourites) and 'Night Thoughts: Baby and Demon' have been traced to Wittgenstein's propositions about the value of the aesthetic insight; Harwood, too, came to believe in the 'power of poetry to infuse experience with value'. The distinctive and impressive poetry which has emerged from that belief has led to widespread popular and critical acclaim of her talent. She was awarded the *Meanjin* Poetry Prize in 1958 and 1959, the Grace Leven Poetry Prize in 1975 for her *Selected Poems*, the Robert Frost Award in 1977 and the Patrick White Literary Award in 1978.

HASLUCK, Dame **ALEXANDRA** (1908–), was born in Perth with the name Darker, into a family which had been established in WA for four generations. After graduating from the University of WA, she taught before her marriage in 1932 to Sir Paul Hasluck (q.v.). Although the latter's subsequent role as a federal politician, prominent minister and governor-general involved her in a busy public life, she has written numerous substantial historical and biographical studies. They include *Portrait with Background* (1955), the biography of Georgiana Molloy, a pioneer botanist of WA; *Unwilling Emigrants* (1959), a social study of the convict period in WA; *Evelyn Hill* (1963), a memoir of her mother; *Thomas Peel of Swan River* (1965); and *Royal Engineer: A Life of Sir Edmund DuCane* (1973). She has also edited the Australian letters (1899–1903) of Lady Audrey Tennyson (1978) and, with the title *Remembered With Affection* (1963), some of the letters of Lady Broome (1831–1911). She has also written short stories, *Of Ladies Dead* (1970), and an autobiography, *Portrait in a*

Mirror (1981). In 1970 she was granted an honorary D. Litt., by the University of WA and in 1978 was made a Dame of the Order of Australia.

HASLUCK, NICHOLAS (1942–), born Canberra, son of Sir Paul and Dame Alexandra Hasluck, graduated from the Universities of WA in 1963 and Oxford in 1966. A lawyer and versatile writer, Hasluck has published two volumes of verse, *Anchor and Other Poems* (1976) and *On the Edge* (1980, with William Grono); three novels, *Quarantine* (1978), *The Blue Guitar* (1980) and *The Hand That Feeds You* (1982); and a volume of short stories, *The Hat on the Letter 'O' and Other Stories* (1978). His poetry is quietly discursive and mildly satirical; the whimsical 'Islands' and the holiday sequence 'Rottnest Island', both from *On the Edge*, are notable pieces. His first novel, *Quarantine*, which tells of a group of passengers held in seemingly purposeless isolation when their ship is detained in a small deserted port on the Suez Canal, combines the suspense of the 'thriller' with considerable skill in characterization and a talent for amusing satire. *The Blue Guitar*, which concerns the marketing of a newly-invented transistorized guitar, enters the slippery commercial world of entrepreneurial double-dealing. *The Hand That Feeds You* is a satire on contemporary Australian society, with its preoccupations of tax evasion, defrauding the welfare system and watching cricket. In 1984 published *The Bellarmine Jug* which won the *Age* Book of the Year Award for fiction in that year.

HASLUCK, Sir PAUL (1905–), was born in Perth into a Salvation Army family. He graduated from the University of WA, where he taught history (1939–40, 1947–48). He served on the staff of the *West Australian* 1922–38, and in 1932 married Alexandra Darker (see Alexandra Hasluck). In 1941 he joined the Department of External Affairs and served on numerous missions to the UN. He entered federal politics in 1949, serving as minister for territories (1951–63), for defence (1963–64) and for external affairs (1964–69).

He was governor-general of Australia 1969–74. As well as receiving numerous awards he was made GCMG in 1969, GCVO in 1970, and KG in 1979. Hasluck has published numerous papers on historical and political subjects and public administration as well as two collections of verse, *Into the Desert* (1939) and *Collected Verse* (1969), and a 'discursive essay', *The Poet in Australia* (1975); two volumes of autobiography, *Mucking About* (1977) and *Diplomatic Witness* (1980); accounts of government policy towards Aborigines, *Our Southern Half-Caste Natives* (1938) and the influential *Black Australians* (1942); *Native Welfare in Australia* (1953); an account of the Australian administration in Papua and New Guinea 1951-63, *A Time for Building* (1976); a collection of speeches, *An Open Go* (1971); an account of the work of the UN Security Council, *Workshop of Security* (1948); and two volumes in the official history of Australia in the Second World War, *The Government and the People 1939–41* (1952) and *1942–45* (1970).

HATFIELD, WILLIAM (1892–1969), born Nottingham, England, son of Joseph Chapman, used his mother's maiden name for his writing, adopting it by deed poll in 1938. He abandoned law studies to come to Australia in 1911, intent on experiencing and writing about outback life. After ten years of bush experience on sheep and cattle stations in the north of SA, in Queensland and in the Northern Territory, he began to write of his adventures. He first published a semi-autobiographical novel, *Sheepmates* (1931), about a young English immigrant, Atherton, who becomes a boundary-rider on a remote sheep property, Borella, in Central Australia. *Desert Saga* (1933) is the story of an Aboriginal boy of the Arunta tribe; its realistic glimpses of Aboriginal life and its awareness of Aboriginal attitudes were gleaned from Hatfield's study of the Aboriginal in his tribal environment. His other fiction, mostly popular romances and boys' books, includes *Ginger Murdoch* (1932) and *Buffalo Jim* (1938), while his descriptive and documentary works include *Australia through the Windscreen* (1936), *I Find Australia* (1937), *Into the Great Unfenced* (1940), *This Land of Ours* (1940), *Australia Reclaimed* (1944), *Barrier Reef Days* (1948) and *Wild Dog Frontier* (1951).

Hatter was a word formerly applied to the lonely eccentrics of the bush, e.g. the solitary shepherd, the gold fossicker and the boundary rider. The isolated bush existence often led to the development of strange behaviour patterns, colourfully described as 'kangaroos in the top paddock', in those compelled to endure its monotony, hence the term may have derived from the earlier expression 'mad as a hatter'. Another theory sees it as a corruption of 'hutter', a term describing the solitary shepherd who lived in a makeshift hut. The term 'hatter' is widely met in literature, e.g. in 'Rolf Boldrewood''s *A Romance of Canvas Town* (1898); George Darrell's play, *The Sunny South*, performed in 1883; several of Henry Lawson's stories e.g. ' "Rats" ' and 'The Bush Undertaker'; C.E.W. Bean's *On the Wool Track* (1910) and *The Dreadnought of the Darling* (1911); Vance Palmer's *The Man Hamilton*

(1928); and Katharine Susannah Prichard's *The Roaring Nineties* (1946).

HAWDON, JOSEPH (1813–71), born County Durham, England, was one of Australia's first overlanders (q.v.). He drove cattle from the Murrumbidgee area of NSW to the Port Phillip district in 1836, and in 1838 with Charles Bonney made the first overland journey from Howlong, near Albury on the Murray river, to Adelaide. After Hawdon's journey, the overland trail to Adelaide was followed by hundreds of settlers in the following decade. That overlanding epic is recorded in Hawdon's *The Journal of a Journey from New South Wales to Adelaide*, first published in book form in 1952.

Hawk, published weekly in Melbourne, began in 1892 and from 1895 until its demise in 1931 had the title, *Hawklet: Sport and Stage.* It contained serial fiction and cartoons by Norman Lindsay.

Hawker, George, see *Recollections of Geoffry Hamlyn, The*

Hawkesbury River, one of NSW's most scenic waterways, flows into Broken Bay to the north of Sydney. Important from the earliest days of settlement, when farms were established on its fertile flats, the Hawkesbury was discovered by Governor Arthur Phillip in June 1789 while he was examining Broken Bay and he named it after the then Earl of Liverpool, Baron Hawkesbury. The Hawkesbury area was the home of many early colonial identities, e.g. Samuel Marsden, James Ruse, Charles Tompson and Charles Harpur, the last sometimes signing his writings 'A Hawkesbury Lad'. Descriptions of the Hawkesbury landscape, with its background of the Blue Mountains, are frequent in the early colonial writing, e.g. W.C. Wentworth's *Australasia*, Charles Harpur's 'A Storm in the Mountains' and Alexander Harris's *The Emigrant Family*. Charles de Boos's *The Congewoi Correspondence* (q.v., 1874) supposedly emanates from the Hawkesbury region; the area is also important in the poetry of Robert Adamson (q.v.). Histories of the area include Charles Swancott's *Hawkesbury River Saga* (1967) and D.G. Bowd's *Historic Hawkesbury* (1964). The township of Windsor, established 1794, was one of the earliest settlements on the Hawkesbury; it was one of Governor Macquarie's Five Towns (Richmond, Wilberforce, Castlereagh and Pitt Town were the others) that were planned to be built above the Hawkesbury flood level.

Hawkins, Ned, see *Workingman's Paradise, The*

'HAWTHORN, J.R.H.', see **HOULDING, JOHN RICHARD**

Hawthorn Press, begun by Jack Gartner in the 1930s, became a general publishing and printing house in 1945 and by the late 1960s was publishing exclusive commercial books and some private press books. In 1970 it commenced the series, Hawthorn Poets; it played a pioneering role in publishing the works of Australian migrant poets and in producing local histories and other aspects of Australiana. It closed down in the 1970s, after a disastrous fire.

Haxby's Circus, see **PRICHARD, KATHARINE SUSANNAH**

HAY, AGNES GRANT ('ANGLO-AUSTRALIAN') (1838-1910), born London, was the mother of novelist William Gosse Hay (q.v.). She published several small books of memoirs and fiction, e.g. *After-Glow Memories* (1905), *Malcolm Canmore's Pearl* (1907) and *Footprints: A Memoir of the Late Alexander Hay* (1899). The Gosse and Hay families are discussed in Fayette Gosse's *The Gosses: An Anglo-Australian Family* (1981).

'Hay and Hell and Booligal', a poem by A.B. Paterson (q.v.), was published in *Rio Grande's Last Race and Other Verses* (1902). Hay and Booligal, two towns in the remote parts of south-western NSW with their snakes and mosquitoes, heat and drought, 'sand, and dust, and stacks of flies', are rated in Paterson's poems on a par with Hell. The phrase, abbreviated to 'Hay, Hell and Booligal', denoting the unattractive nature of the isolated towns of the outback, has become a part of Australian idiom.

HAY, WILLIAM GOSSE (1875–1945) was born into a successful Adelaide family with literary connections; his self-made father was an early SA colonist and his novelist mother, Agnes Grant Hay, was related to Edmund Gosse. Hay was educated at the University of Cambridge, where he decided to become a writer. In 1901 his first novel, *Stifled Laughter*, was published; it was set in Manalia, a fictional name for Australia, as were his next two novels, *Herridge of Reality Swamp* (q.v., 1907) and *Captain Quadring* (q.v., 1912). On his return to Australia in 1901 he settled near Adelaide and was able, because of independent means, to concentrate on his literary work. In 1909 the family home burnt down, an incident which was possibly recalled during the writing of *Strabane of the Mulberry Hills* (q.v.) and which prompted Hay's mother and sister to embark on a visit to Europe; their ship vanished off the African coast. Their deaths deeply disturbed Hay, and while recuperating in Tasmania he became more deeply interested in that State's history. The interest is reflected in *Captain Quadring*, which has some Tasmanian scenes, and in his subsequent novels, *The Escape of the Notorious Sir William Heans* (q.v., 1919), *Strabane of the Mulberry Hills* (1929) and *The Mystery of Alfred Doubt* (1937) which are all focused on Tasmania. A painstaking writer, Hay only completed one other book, *An Australian Rip Van Winkle* (q.v., 1921).

In a statement about his work Hay recalled that 'When I began writing, just before the beginning of this century, Australian novels had relapsed entirely into fifth-rate tales of the "paddock and stockyard variety", in spurious imitation of Rolf Boldrewood's distinguished work [*Robbery Under Arms*, 1888]. I felt it was necessary to try and raise Australian literature out of that desolate bog, and turned to her tragic and ballad-like history and its proper costumes'. The particular period he chose, and researched carefully, was the decade from the early 1830s, a decade in which his six novels and some of the stories in *An Australian Rip Van Winkle* are set. It was a period of flux in Australia, especially in Tasmania, where the mix of convicts, ex-convicts and free settlers made the future of the colony uncertain. It also had an heroic, romantic quality which attracted Hay, a devotee of Sir Walter Scott, and provided a suitable setting for him to explore such themes as the conflict between good and evil within individuals, the discovery of moral identity, the education towards spiritual freedom through trial and suffering, and the balance between suffering and sin. Such themes are central to Hay's novels, which are characterized by the tribulations faced by the hero or heroine, who are pursued by malicious forces, sometimes associated with a system such as the convict system, and who are tested in hazardous circumstances, often at the climax to the novel; good is detected in courage, endurance and constancy, evil emerges in hatred and jealousy.

The gothic and romance elements in Hay's fiction are demonstrated in his predilection for exotic names (Sligo Quibb, Homely O'Crone, Abelia Oughtryn, Haylin Talmash); in the extreme incidents (fights, fires, escapes); and in the mystery surrounding many of his characters, which partly arises because Hay's narrators seldom know more than his readers at a particular point in the novels and the truth is often presented piecemeal. Balancing these qualities are the careful way Hay builds up a sense of period by his elaborate attention to detail and costume, and his use of the techniques of the historical novelist to establish verisimilitude:

for example, the footnotes which admit invention or discuss sources, or the clear indication that his novels are based on the evidence of witnesses, as in the authorial reminders that *The Escape of the Notorious Sir William Heans* is informed by Heans's own letters after his escape. The last technique is employed also in *Herridge of Reality Swamp*, *Captain Quadring*, and *Strabane of the Mulberry Hills*. There is strong division among commentators on Hay's work. Although his novels have been dismissed as obtuse, overwritten, poorly resolved, stagey, and melodramatic, *The Escape of the Notorious Sir William Heans*, which in some ways recalls Henry Savery's *Quintus Servinton* (1831) and in others anticipates Hal Porter's *The Tower* (1963) and *The Tilted Cross* (1961), is both a successful historical novel and a significant contribution to convict literature. Fayette Gosse published the monograph *William Gosse Hay* (1965) and discusses Hay in her *The Gosses: An Anglo–Australian Family* (1981).

HAYBALL, DORIS, a Melbourne writer, wrote several plays as well as recollections of mainly British personages whom she met during her travels, *Strawberries in the Jam* (1940). Her published plays are *Blue Willow Pattern* (1944), *Opening Movement: Two Comedies from Australia's Beginnings* (1944), *The Grotesque* in *Eight Plays by Australians* (1934) and *Out of a Clear Sky* in *The Playbill* (1935). Her other plays are 'The Mirror' and 'Old Mr Wintersapple'.

HAYDON, G.H. (GEORGE HENRY) (1822–91), born Devon, England, emigrated to Australia in 1840 in search of fortune. He became one of Melbourne's earliest commercial sketchers, his work appearing in both Sydney and Melbourne newspapers. Haydon, who studied the Aboriginal way of life and defended the blacks against the charge of racial inferiority, was especially friendly with Benbo, a well-known Aboriginal of the Werribee tribe. After his return to England he published *Five Years' Experience in Australia Felix* (1846), which brought him recognition as an authority on Australian life. A later novel, *The Australian Emigrant* (1854), with illustrations based on his sketches, gives a short account of the settlement of the Port Phillip District, stressing the egalitarian nature of the Australian pioneering life.

HAYES, 'BULLY' (WILLIAM HENRY) (?1829–77), born in America, was a notorious and legendary South Seas adventurer and blackbirder. His colourful career has been documented by several Australian writers, most notably 'Louis' Becke, who sailed with him and supplied most of the material that 'Rolf Boldrewood' used in *A Modern Buccaneer* (q.v., 1894). *Tom Wallis* (1900), *The Strange Adventure of James Shervinton* (1902), *The Adventures of Louis Blake* (1909), and *Bully Hayes, Buccaneer* (1913) are other Becke books in which Hayes appears or is discussed. Hayes is also the main character in Albert Dorrington's *A South Sea Buccaneer* and *Our Lady of the Leopards* (both 1911) and he appears in Beatrice Grimshaw's *Victorian Family Robinson* (1934), and Will Lawson's *The Laughing Buccaneer* (1935).

HAYGARTH, H.W., see Bush, The

HAYLEN, LESLIE CLEMENT (1899–1977), was born near Canberra into a large Catholic farming family. After serving in the First World War, he worked as a journalist in Sydney and Wagga; later he joined the staff of the *Australian Women's Weekly* in Sydney. He was the Labor member for the federal seat of Parkes 1943–64 and gained a reputation as a witty debater and an eloquent proponent of Australian literature; his maiden speech was a plea for the establishment of a national theatre. As well as numerous articles, pamphlets, occasional verse and short stories, Haylen wrote plays and novels. His published plays are *Two Minutes' Silence* (1933), a well-received, antiwar drama first produced in 1930 and also produced as a film in 1933, and *Blood on the Wattle* (1948), a stirring treatment of the Eureka rebellion which requires a cast of over fifty. His other plays are 'Change of Policy' (1934), 'Freedom has a Beard' (1937), and 'The Stormy Blast' (1966). His first three novels, *The Game Darrells* (1933), *The Brierley Rose* (1935) and *Brown Boy Singing* (1940), were first serialised in the *Australian Women's Weekly* and later produced as radio serials. They were followed by *New Guinea Newsreel* (1945), *A for Artemis* (1960, under the pseudonym 'Sutton Woodfield'), and *Big Red* (1965). Most of his novels, especially *Big Red* and *The Game Darrells*, draw on his experience of country life and of the labour movement. Haylen also wrote an account of his second visit to China in 1957, *Chinese Journey* (1959), memoirs of his years in parliament, *Twenty Years' Hard Labor* (1969), and edited the third and fourth short story collections in the series titled *The Tracks We Travel* (1965 and 1976).

HAYNES, JOHN (1850–1917), born Singleton, NSW, began a career in journalism in Morpeth. He moved to Sydney in 1873 and worked on the *Empire*, the *Australian Town and Country Journal* and the *Evening News*; while sub-editor on the *Evening News* he met J.F. Archibald, with whom he founded the *Bulletin* in 1880. Haynes made a significant contribution to the establishment and early success of the *Bulletin*, but his free trade economic beliefs clashed with the protectionism of W.H. Traill and by 1885 he had severed his connection with the journal. Haynes was a controversial member of the NSW parliament 1887–1904 and 1915–17. He ran *Haynes Weekly* 1885–87, the *Weekly News* 1890–91, and the *Elector*, later the *Newsletter*, 1895–1917. His version of the early *Bulletin* days was serialised in the *Newsletter* in 1905.

HAYTER, HENRY HEYLYN (1821–95), born Eden Vale, England, came to Victoria in 1852 and became government statist of Victoria in 1874; his statistical methods were adopted for the whole of Australia. An eager travel author, he published *Notes of a Tour in New Zealand* (1874), *Notes on the Colony of Victoria* (1875), and *A Handbook to the Colony of Victoria* (1884). He also wrote poetry, *Carboona, A Chapter from the Early History of Victoria* (1885) and *My Christmas Adventure, Carboona and Other Poems* (1887). Hayter's chief creation, however, was the *Victorian Year Book,* published in twenty volumes from 1874; in his yearbooks, commended throughout the world, Hayter made statistics interesting and understandable for the ordinary reader.

HAYWARD, CHARLES W. ANDRÉE (1866–1950), born Herefordshire, England, was a lawyer in England and South Africa prior to his arrival in WA in 1894. He joined the *Geraldton Express*, expanding that newspaper's literary interests by examining in January 1896 the achievements of the flourishing *Bulletin* school of writers. His own contributions to the *Geraldton Express* include satire, sonnets, ballads and lyric verse; some of his poems, usually written under the pseudonym 'Viator', were published in 1897 as *Along the Road to Cue and Other Verses*. He left the *Geraldton Express* in 1898 to edit the *Murchison Advocate* at Cue; thereafter he worked on the Kalgoorlie *Sun*, the Perth *Sunday Times* and again the *Geraldton Express*. From 1922 until his death Hayward worked on the staff of the *Bulletin*, contributing copious light and topical verse under various pseudonyms, e.g. 'Thomas the Rhymer'.

HAZZARD, SHIRLEY (1931–), was born and educated in Sydney. From 1947 she has lived overseas, in Hong Kong, NZ, Europe and the USA. She is now an American citizen, married to Francis Steegmuller, the American litterateur, and divides her time between New York and Capri. In 1966 she was awarded a grant by the United States National Institute of Arts and Letters, and in 1980 won the National Book Critics Circle Award. She revisited Australia in 1976 and wrote a lengthy, influential account of her impressions for the *New Yorker* (January 1977). She worked as a clerical employee of the UN 1952–62, and became a passionate opponent of that institution. Her one non-fiction work, *Defeat of an Ideal* (1973), is a well-documented analysis of its weaknesses.

Hazzard has written numerous short stories, mainly for the *New Yorker*. Some are collected in *Cliffs of Fall* (1963), and she has also written four novels: *The Evening of the Holiday* (1966), *People in Glass Houses* (1967), *The Bay of Noon* (q.v., 1970) and *The Transit of Venus* (q.v., 1980). An admirer of Flaubert and Turgenev, Hazzard writes with poise and restraint. Her novels and short stories are centrally concerned with the poignant experience of love, its discovery, loss and recollection. She is sensitive to the nuances and minutiae of feelings and to the distinctive flavours of different places and relationships, writing lucid prose that can be evocative, reflective or ironic, but is always compressed in its effects. Apart from one short story, 'Woollahra Road', *New Yorker* (1961), Hazzard has not drawn heavily on her experience of Australia, although the heroines of *The Transit of Venus* are expatriate Australians. The short stories in *Cliffs of Fall* are set in Italy, Switzerland and America; Florence is the setting for *The Evening of the Holiday* and Naples for *The Bay of Noon*; the sterile atmosphere of the UN building in New York is the background of *People in Glass Houses*; and *The Transit of Venus* moves between Sydney, London, New York and Stockholm. A sense of geographical, national and social dislocation is common to Hazzard's very different heroines and their quest for love is also a quest for a sense of belonging and knowledge of the self. At the beginning of her career the short story provided the perfect form for her concern with love as a general experience and for her gifts of psychological insight, suggestive symbolism and creation of atmosphere. Several, such as 'A Place in the Country' and 'The Picnic' in *Cliffs of Fall*, and 'A Long Short Story' and 'A Crush on Doctor Dance', *New Yorker* (1976 and 1977), are interconnected narratives. *People in Glass Houses* is also a series of portraits connected by the participants' common experience of working for the UN. Both *The Evening of the Holiday* and *The Bay of Noon* are close to the novella in their measured approach, and both are nostalgic treatments of the fragility of unaccountable love. Italy, colourful and passionate but also unpredictable and insecure, provides the suggestive background. *People in Glass Houses*, a witty, satirical work, pillories

the suffocating stupidity of organization life. Underlying the acute sketches of people and incongruous situations is an awareness of the dehumanising effect of a large organisation that exists only for itself, using jargon as its servant of destruction. *The Transit of Venus*, more elaborate, ambitious and extended than her previous work, has established Hazzard as a major novelist. The novel's mannered quality has led to comparisons with Jane Austen and Henry James, but in atmosphere it is thoroughly modern. Although the theme once again is love, the chronological and geographical range is wide, extending from the First World War to the time of Richard Nixon. A self-conscious work of art, its complex ambiguity is heightened by an equivocal narrative technique, discreet but resonant symbolism and an elaborately-sculpted structure. Wit and verbal play, psychological insight and a wide-ranging literary allusiveness are other striking aspects.

HEAD, WALTER WILLIAM (1861–1939), born Oakleigh, Victoria, came to prominence as founder and editor, with Arthur Rae, of the labour movement newspaper, the *Hummer*, 1891–92. After the newspaper became the *Worker*, Head moved with it to Sydney, where he continued his involvement in the New Australia movement as secretary, later treasurer and trustee, of the New Australia Co-operative Settlement Association and editor of its monthly journal, *New Australia*, 1892–94; Mary Cameron, late Dame Mary Gilmore, helped with the latter. Head resigned as editor of the *Worker* in November 1893 preparatory to leaving for Paraguay, but the death of his son, who became lost in the bush in Victoria, prevented his departure. Henry Lawson, who was disappointed in his hopes of succeeding Head as editor of the *Worker*, wrote a poem and a story, both titled 'The Babies in the Bush', based on the tragedy. The major Australian point of contact for the New Australia settlers, Head became embroiled in its internecine disputes in 1894; although probably not guilty of financial impropriety, he was personally liable for its debts and disappeared from view to avoid imprisonment. He surfaced again in Tasmania in 1895, probably via NZ, and as Walter Alan Woods, William Ashe Woods and other combinations of the Christian names, he made a new start in the labour movement. Editor of the *Tasmanian Democrat* (1895–96), owner (1898–99) and editor (?1900–1909) of the *Clipper*, and involved in the *Clipper*'s successors, the *Daily Post* and the *World*, Woods was a member of the Tasmanian parliament 1906–17 and 1925–31 and Speaker of the House of Assembly, 1925–31. The author of several ballads under the pseudonym 'John Drayman', he retained contact with Lawson after his departure from Sydney.

Headlocks Other Stories, see **HILL, BARRY**

Heads of the People, subtitled *An Illustrated Journal of Literature, Whims and Oddities,* was published weekly in Sydney 1847–48; it contained serials, poetry and short fiction. *Heads of the People* serialized Charles Dickens's *Dombey and Son* in 1847 before its publication in book form and carried illustrations by J. Skinner Prout. A notable contributor was D.H. Deniehy.

HEALEY, DANIEL see **Cornstalk**

Heans, Sir William see *Escape of the Notorious Sir William Heans, The*

Heart of Spring (1919), containing fifty seven poems, was the first published collection of John Shaw Neilson (q.v.). It met a mixed critical reception: A.G. Stephens in the book's preface called Neilson 'first of Australian poets'; Hubert Church described the poems as 'marvellous songs'; David McKee Wright in the *Bulletin* believed the poet to be 'a whispering person, not likely to be heard of again'.

HEATON, Sir JOHN HENNIKER (1848–1914), born Rochester, England, came to NSW in 1864, working first as a jackeroo, then as a journalist on the *Cumberland Mercury, Goulburn Evening Penny Post, Cumberland Times* and *Australian Town and Country Journal.* He married Rose Bennett, daughter of Samuel Bennett of the *Empire* and often presumed to be the 'Rose Lorraine' of Henry Kendall's love poetry. In 1879 Heaton published the pioneer reference work, *Australian Dictionary of Dates and Men of the Time.* From 1883 he lived in England, where he represented Australian interests, especially in the campaign for cheaper postal, telegraphic and freight charges between England and the Australian colonies. A keen collector of Australiana, he once owned the *Endeavour* journals of Sir Joseph Banks. R. Porter wrote *The Life and Letters of Sir John Henniker Heaton* (1916).

Heavy Odds, see *Long Odds*

HEBBLETHWAITE, JAMES (1857–1921), born Preston, England, was a teacher in England before migrating to Tasmania in 1892 for health reasons and gaining a teaching position at the Friends' School, Hobart. He was later a minister of religion, initially with the Congregational Church, then the Church of England.

A scholar and a graceful if limited lyric poet, Hebblethwaite published five books of poetry: *Verse* (1896); *A Rose of Regret* (1900); *Meadow and Bush* (1911); a collected edition, *The Poems of James Hebblethwaite* (1920); and *New Poems of James Hebblethwaite* (1921). His only novel, *Castlehill* (1895), is a romance associated with the convict period.

Hecate, a women's journal named after 'the goddess invoked by women who desired freedom from male tyranny', is published from the University of Queensland. First published in 1975, it gives expression to the creative writing of women and covers many other aspects of feminist experience. Contributors include Carole Ferrier (editor), Eric Beach, Dorothy Hewett, Kate Jennings, Judith Rodriguez, Jenny Boult, Dymphna Cusack and Kath Walker.

Heemskerck Shoals, see **FITZGERALD, R.D.**

Heidelberg School, the first distinctive school of Australian painting, originated in the period 1885–90 after the artist Tom Roberts (q.v.) returned to Australian from Europe, where he had become acquainted with the work of the French Impressionists. Roberts and Frederick McCubbin (q.v.) established an artists' camp in 1885 at Box Hill, Melbourne, and used it as a centre for a modified form of *plein-air* and impressionist painting. Emphasizing brightness, light and colour, Roberts and McCubbin sought, in Bernard Smith's words, 'to produce a naturalistic interpretation of the Australian sunlit landscape'. In 1888 Roberts was joined by Arthur Streeton and Charles Conder (qq.v.); they moved to a house at Eaglemont, Heidelberg, and established another artists' camp; in 1889 they opened the now-famous '9 x 5' exhibition of Australian Impressionism comprising some 180 oil sketches on cigar box lids. A second Heidelberg camp, with which Norman Lindsay (q.v.) was connected, was established in 1890 at a house, Charterisville, near Eaglemont, and in the period up to the end of the century the new painting philosophy spread rapidly.

Like the writers of the 1890s, the Heidelberg artists became increasingly nationalistic, seeking out subjects of national interest and significance. Although they were not concerned exclusively with the bush (Roberts and Conder, for example, also produced some remarkable urban paintings) the Australian Impressionists forged their closest links with literature when they emphasized the bush and incidents from bush life. McCubbin's *The Lost Child* (1886), for example, illustrates an incident that had already found literary expression in Henry Kingsley's novel, *The Recollections of Geoffry Hamlyn* (1859) and Marcus Clarke's story, 'Pretty Dick.' His canvas, *Down on his Luck* (1889), illustrates the type of unfortunate swagman portrayed in Henry Lawson's stories and poems, and in the verse of A.B. Paterson and Barcroft Boake; his *Bush Burial* (1890) reflects to some extent a scene in Henry Kendall's poem, 'A Death in the Bush', and has been used on the dust jacket of *Leaves from Australian Forests: Poetical Works of Henry Kendall* (1970) in the Australian Classics series. Roberts's paintings associated with outback life, e.g. *Bailed Up* (1888), *Shearing the Rams* (1889), *The Breakaway* (1891), and *The Golden Fleece* (1894), reflect a host of similar incidents from the writings of 'Rolf Boldrewood', Lawson, Paterson, 'Breaker' Morant, Will Ogilvie and others, while the idealization of the landscape evident in some of the Heidelberg school paintings echoes the attitudes taken by writers such as Bernard O'Dowd, Roderic Quinn and John le Gay Brereton. The relationship between the work of the Heidelberg school and literature is discussed in Bernard Smith's *Australian Painting : 1788–1970* (1961).

Helix, a literary journal founded in Canberra by Les Harrop in 1978, later transferred with him to Victoria. Dedicated to publishing Australian and overseas writing in the same journal, *Helix* produced an Ezra Pound special issue in 1982. A book review supplement to *Helix* (9, 10) was published as a separate issue, *Fresh Flounder* (1981).

HELLYER, JILL (1925–), born North Sydney, has been a consistent contributor of poetry to literary magazines such as *Westerly* and *Overland* over many years. Instrumental in founding the Australian Society of Authors (ASA), she was its first executive secretary 1963–71. She has published verse, *The Exile* (1969) and *Song of the Humpback Whales* (1981); a novel, *Not Enough Savages* (1975); and edited a biographical work, *Fifty Years in Psychiatry: D.W.H. Arnott* (1980).

HEMENSLEY, KRIS (1946–), born on the Isle of Wight, came to Australia in 1966 and quickly settled into the Melbourne literary scene, orginally with the Melbourne New Theatre, then at La Mama, where in 1968–70 he helped to produce the poetry workshops that played a significant role in the rise of what has been termed the 'New Australian Poetry' (q.v.). To publish that poetry Hemensley created the mini-magazine, *Our Glass*. While in England in 1969–72 Hemensley edited the magazine, *Earth Ship* (1970–72), and after his return to Australia continued his literary interests through poetry,

prose and editorial activities. He edited a second series of *Earth Ship*, titled *The Ear in a Wheatfield* (q.v., 1972–76), a third series, *The Merri Creek or Nero* (1977), and other associated journals; became an advisory editor to *New Poetry* 1973–74; and was poetry editor of *Meanjin* 1976–78. His own publications of poetry and prose have been prolific; they include *Two Poets* (1968, with Ken Taylor), *The Going* (1969), *Dreams* (1971), *No Word – No Worry* (1971), *The Soft Poems* (1971), *Mimi* (1973), *Rocky Mountains & Tired Indians* (1973), *Domestications* (1974), *Love's Voyages* (1974), *Here We Are* (1975), *The Rooms and Other Prose Pieces* (1975), *The Poem of the Clear Eye* (1975), *Sulking in the Seventies* (1975), *The Moths* (1978, prose/poetry), *Beginning Again* (1978, prose/poetry), *Down Under* (1978, a comic novel), *Games: An Exhibition 1970–72* (1978, prose), *The Miro Poems* (1979) and *A Mile from Poetry* (1979). One of Hemensley's plays, 'Stephany' which was produced, as were several others, at La Mama, was made into a short film in 1972.

Hemensley's literary range is considerable: brief, enigmatic and personal poems such as those in *Domestications*; a long, complex examination of contemporary poetic attitudes in *The Poem of the Clear Eye*; and the poetry–prose compositions, such as those in *Here We Are*, where fantasy and realism meet in a startling mix. An indefatigable Utopian and campaigner for world peace, an active and dedicated literary internationalist, and a vociferous commentator on Australian writing, Hemensley was a colourful figure in the Australian literary scene of the 1970s.

Hemisphere: An Asian–Australian Magazine, began publication as a monthly in 1957 and was then issued by the federal government six times a year 1979–84. Edited from 1969 by Ken Henderson, it was intended initially as an extension of the Colombo Plan programme but broadened to reflect a deeper interest in the Asian region. In addition to its variety of historical, sociological and cultural articles, *Hemisphere* had a wide-ranging survey of Australian and Asian writing and a selection of the poetry and short fiction of contemporary writers in both areas, e.g. the 1981–82 numbers feature work by Alan Gould, Ken Hart, Andrew Lansdown, Mark O'Connor, Graham Rowlands, Geraldine Heng, Ou–Yang Hsiu, Kamola Kant Lenka, Du Mu and Russell Soaba. *Hemisphere* produced four annuals and three anthologies, one on Indonesia (1976), two on the Australian Aborigines (1978, 1981).

HENDERSON, JAMES (1926–), born Perth, WA, was a sixteen-year-old copy boy with the Perth *Daily News* when he falsified his age, enlisted in the AIF and served in New Guinea. He has since been a journalist. His book *Marooned* (1982) is the story of the *Gilt Dragon*, a Dutch East India Company ship wrecked off the WA coast in 1656. The book challenges some preconceptions about early Australian history, e.g. that William de Vlaming, not Dirk Hartog, was the first white man to land on that part of Australia.

HENDERSON, W.G. (WALTER GORDON [GEORGE]) (1870–1957), born Roslyn, near Goulburn, NSW, became a lawyer and lived at Albury but always maintained a keen interest in the bush and bush life. His first volume of fiction, *Midnight's Daughter and Other Stories* (1907), comprises bush tales, including bush-ranging stories of the 1840s to 1860s. His other fiction includes the novels, *Norah Conough* (1908), which deals with the conflict between large and small landowners of the 1890s; *The Bathers* (1911), which shows the impact of the wholesome attitudes of country life on urban and religious conservatism; *Bush Bred* (1922), a romantic tale which is complicated by the impact of the Chinese immigrants on the lives of the protagonists; and *Nelligang* (1945), a tale of family problems and life in the bush.

HENEY, HELEN (1907–), born Sydney, the daughter of Thomas William Heney, was educated at the University of Sydney and lived. mainly in Poland 1929–35, working as a translator and a teacher of English. During the war she worked with the Red Cross and was a social worker with UNRRA in various European countries 1945–47. She has published five novels, *The Chinese Camellia* (1950), *The Proud Lady* (1951), *Dark Moon* (1953), *This Quiet Dust* (1956) and *The Leaping Blaze* (1962); a substantial biography of the explorer Sir Paul Strzelecki, *In a Dark Glass* (1961); and a well-researched study of Australian women between 1788 and 1822, *Australia's Founding Mothers* (1978). Apart from *The Proud Lady*, which traces the destiny of a woman set against the dramatic background of Polish history between 1885 and 1939, all Heney's novels have Australian settings. Although some have intricate plots and well-realised historical backgrounds, they are less memorable for their action than for their psychological studies. *Dark Moon*, which deals with the case of a white woman, presumed dead, who is discovered to be living with an Aboriginal tribe and the effects of the discovery on those involved, and *The Chinese Camellia*, which focuses on the impact of a Chinese concubine on an Australian settlement, express most effectively her insight into the relationship between outsider and social group.

This Quiet Dust and *The Leaping Blaze* both contain striking portraits of egoistic, dominating women.

HENEY, THOMAS WILLIAM (1862–1928), born Sydney, father of Helen Heney, spent a lifetime in journalism. He was editor of the *Sydney Morning Herald* (1903–18), the *Brisbane Telegraph* (1920–23), and the Sydney *Daily Telegraph* (1924–25). He published two novels with outback settings, *The Girl at Birrell's* (1896) and *A Station Courtship* (1899), and two collections of verse, *Fortunate Days* (1886), and *In Middle Harbour and Other Verse, Chiefly Australian* (1890).

HENNESSEY, JOHN DAVID (1847–1935), born London, came to Australia in 1875, lived in Queensland, NSW and Victoria, and combined service as a Methodist and Congregational minister with religious journalism and general editing and publishing. He founded and edited the *Australian Christian World* 1886–91 and in 1894 the *Australian Field*, a weekly agricultural paper. He also tried pineapple farming in the 1890s and became active in political affairs, working for Edmund Barton and the *Federalist*. As well as several short stories in magazines in Australia and England, he published several novels including *The Dis-Honourable* (1895), *An Australian Bush Track* (1896), *Wynnum* (1896), *A Lost Identity* (1897), *The Outlaw* (1913), *A Tail of Gold* (1914), *The Caves of Shend* (1915) and *The Cords of Vanity* (1920). He also wrote a book of advice for farmers, *The New Chum Farmer* (1897). Hennessey's novels are characterized by graphic descriptions of the Australian scene, both contemporary and past; sensational, melodramatic plots; and romantically-happy conclusions. Particularly striking are *The Dis-Honourable*, which draws on conditions and events in Brisbane of the 1890s, especially on the catastrophic flood of 1893, and *The Outlaw*, which deals with the adventures of an assigned convict forced to turn bushranger by the injustice of his master.

HENNING, RACHEL (1826–1914), born Bristol, England, joined her brother, Biddulph, in Australia in 1854 but returned to England in 1856, homesick and disillusioned by the colony. She came back to Australia in 1861 and, although settling much better on the second occasion and increasingly sensitive to the beauty of the land, never completely overcame her antipathy to what she saw as the crudeness of the colonial environment. In 1862 she and her sister Annie joined Biddulph on his run, inland from Rockhampton in Queensland. In 1866 she married Deighton Taylor, one of her brother's overseers, and settled in NSW, ultimately on a farming property near Wollongong. The popular collection, *The Letters of Rachel Henning* (1969), edited by David Adams and illustrated by pen drawings by Norman Lindsay, ranges in time from 1853, when Biddulph left England, to 1882 and were mainly written to her sisters Etty and Amy, the former in England and the latter in Australia. A sensitive account of the delights, difficulties and drawbacks involved in the process of migration to, and acclimatization in, an alien environment, the Rachel Henning letters reveal as much about the personality of the writer as they do about the colony of Australia in the nineteenth century. Of particular interest is the information offered about squatting life in Queensland.

HENRY, ALICE (1857–1943), born Richmond, Victoria, was a journalist with the Melbourne *Argus* and the *Australasian* in the 1890s. In 1905 she visited England, then the USA, to lecture on women's suffrage, later becoming secretary of the Chicago branch of the National Women's Trade Union League and editor in 1910–19 of the League's journal, *Life and Labor*. She returned to Australia in 1933. She published *The Trade Union Woman* (1915) and *Women and the Labor Movement* (1923). Nettie Palmer edited *Memoirs of Alice Henry* (1944).

Henry Lawson by His Mates, edited by J. le Gay Brereton and Lawson's daughter, Bertha, was published in 1931. A collection of verse tributes, reminiscences, anecdotes and assessments, most of them first published as journal contributions, it offers an affectionate and somewhat sentimental portrait of Lawson. The contributors include Arthur Adams, H.E. Boote, E.J. Brady, F.J. Broomfield, R.J. Cassidy, Ernest O'Ferrall, W.E. Fitz Henry, 'Jim Grahame', Mary Gilmore, T.D. Mutch, Roderic Quinn and Lawson's wife, Bertha.

Henry Lawson Literary and Memorial Society, which incorporated the Australian Poetry Lovers' Society in 1973, grew out of the annual commemorative meetings held since 1923 at Footscray Park, Melbourne, where there is now a memorial bust of Lawson, a Lawson tree, and a plaque; Joseph Jones has recorded his impressions of one of the annual gatherings in the pamphlet, *The Union Honours Its Dead: Henry Lawson Commemorative Gathering Number Thirty Nine* (1966). The society meets in Melbourne once a month to discuss Australian literature in general as well as Lawson in particular, and since 1960 has published a newsletter, the *Lawsonian*. In Sydney, the Henry Lawson Literary

Society was organized in 1928 but is now in abeyance.

Henslowe's Annual, published in Sydney 1900–04, was both an artistic and literary annual, written by Australian authors and illustrated by Australian artists. Its publisher, Leonard Henslowe, was also connected with the brief-lived theatrical weekly, the *Dramatic Critic* (1903).

HENTY Family. The Henty family was a pioneering family headed by Thomas Henty (1775–1839), whose wife, seven sons and a daughter all came to Australia. In 1828 Thomas, a Sussex farmer and banker dissatisfied with prospects in England, decided to emigrate to the colonies. The first party, headed by the eldest son James (1800–82), went to the new settlement of WA in 1829 and to Van Diemen's Land, which became their base, in 1831; Thomas joined them with the rest of the family a year later. Dissatisfied with their failure to secure land in Van Diemen's Land, the Hentys turned their attention across Bass Strait to the unoccupied and virgin territory of the Port Phillip District. Starting initially as whalers at Portland Bay on the south-western coast of what became the colony of Victoria, they moved inland to establish themselves as squatters in the 'Australia Felix' territory explored by Thomas Mitchell.

The pioneers of the pastoral industry in Victoria, the Hentys only secured title to their land after protracted wrangling with the NSW governors and the British Colonial Office. Edward (1810–78) and Stephen (1811–72) Henty were central to the Port Phillip operations; of the other sons, Francis (1815–89) succeeded on the station in WA, earlier mismanaged by his brother John (1813–68), the black sheep of the family; Charles (1807–64) and William (1808–81) settled in Tasmania and, like Edward, Stephen and James, became active in politics; and James became a successful merchant in Melbourne after earlier setbacks in Launceston. The early days at Portland Bay are recorded in *Australiana; Or, My Early Life* (1886) by Richmond Henty, son of Stephen; Marnie Bassett's *The Hentys* (1954) is the standard account of the family, which is commemorated by the naming of towns in NSW and Victoria and by a highway linking Horsham and Warracknabeal in the Wimmera district of Victoria. Charles Gee composed the folk-song, 'The Henty Song', while *en route* with the first party to WA.

HEPBURN, EDITH see 'WICKHAM, ANNA'

HEPWORTH, JOHN (1921–), born Pinjarra, WA, has worked mainly as a journalist and with the ABC. Well-known for his column, Outsight, in *Nation Review*, which he helped establish and of which he was editor for several years, Hepworth is an outstanding if controversial essayist and raconteur. *John Hepworth . . . His Book* (1978), edited by Morris Lurie and illustrated by Michael Leunig, is a collection of his Outsight writings. His other numerous works include several performed plays, 'The Last of the Rainbow' (1963) which won the Lady Manifold competition in 1961, 'The Beast in View' (1959) and 'My Aunt the Unicorn'. With John Hindle he wrote the pub-crawl guide, *Boozing Out in Melbourne Town* (1980), and *Around the Bend* (1983), an account of a forty-nine-day raft trip down the Murray River by 'three middle-aged eccentrics' (Hepworth, Hindle and ABC producer, Patrick Amer); it is said to have been 'an excursion kept afloat by rum, Scotch whisky, egotism and the presence of an ABC camera crew'.

Her Privates We, see MANNING, FREDERIC; *Middle Parts of Fortune, The*; War Literature

Herald, one of the oldest Australian daily newspapers, began publication in Melbourne as the *Port Phillip Herald* (1840–48); in 1849–55 it was known as the *Melbourne Morning Herald* and from 1855 by the present title. The *Herald* was originally a morning newspaper but was converted into an evening publication by David Syme, who took it over briefly in 1868; under Sir Keith Murdoch it had a reputation between the First and Second World Wars as one of the leading evening newspapers of the British Empire. Edmund Finn worked for the *Herald* 1845–58; later contributors included Marcus Clarke, A.T. Strong, C.J. Dennis, and Will Dyson.

HERBERT, BOB (1923–), born Yea, Victoria, has worked in pantomime, vaudeville, radio, television and little theatre as actor, stage hand, stage manager and director, and has written numerous plays. From 1971 he has been theatres manager at the University of New England. His plays include 'Mr Jones', 'New England Honeymoon', *A Man of Respect* (published in *Biala* 1977), 'Don't Let the Title Put You Off', 'An Isolated Case of Heterochromia', which won second prize in the drama section of the 1970 Captain Cook literary competition, and *No Names . . . No Pack Drill* (1980). The last, which deals with a relationship between a young widow and an American deserter, shared

first prize in the WA sesquicentenary playwriting competition and has been extensively staged in Australia.

HERBERT, XAVIER (1901–84), born Port Hedland, WA, was educated there and at Fremantle, where he moved with his family at the age of twelve. Two years later he began work in a chemist shop but continued schooling in order to qualify as a pharmacist. He remained in Fremantle during the First World War, but after passing his pharmaceutical exams moved to Melbourne to work as a dispenser in a hospital. In 1926 his first story was published in the *Australian Journal* under the pseudonym 'Herbert Astor'. By this time he had left Melbourne and gone to Sydney, staying there for a year before his wandering took him northwards. In 1927 he reached Darwin, worked as a railway fettler in the Rum Jungle area, and visited the South Pacific. The experiences Herbert gathered in the late 1920s helped to inform his first and last novels, *Capricornia* (q.v., 1938) and *Poor Fellow My Country* (q.v., 1975).

In 1930 Herbert left Darwin for England; during his two years there the Anglophobia most apparent in *Poor Fellow My Country* was confirmed but he managed before his return to Australia at the end of 1932 to complete, with the support of Sadie Norden, later his wife, the first draft of *Capricornia*, a long novel about the Northern Territory. In 1933 he wrote stories for the *Australian Journal* and the Sydney *Sun* to help bring Sadie to Australia; then, with the encouragement and advice of P.R. Stephensen (q.v.), also recently returned from England, he settled to the task of revising and reducing *Capricornia*. In 1934 the novel was set in type, but the collapse of Stephensen's publishing company meant that publication did not resume until in 1937 Stephensen accepted it for a new press with which he had become associated. *Capricornia* was officially published in 1938, and in March won the sesquicentenary novel competition. It soon became a best-seller and remains one of the best-known novels of its type and period.

In 1940 Herbert was awarded the first of several CLF fellowships to work on 'The King and the Kurrawaddi'; like several other works given titles and mentioned in Herbert's letters, it was never published. He served in the Second World War, mainly in the Northern Territory and the Pacific; following his discharge in 1946 he left Sydney and finally settled with his wife at Redlynch, near Cairns, in northern Queensland. Alternating writing with a variety of casual occupations and with validating the concluding words of *Disturbing Element*, 'the main thing in life is Living!', he wrote prolifically but published little until the end of the 1950s. The appearance in 1959 of *Seven Emus*, a novella significant mainly for an eccentric system of punctuation which was subsequently abandoned, was the start of a period in which Herbert had four books published in as many years. The others were *Soldiers' Women* (1961), a novel about wartime Sydney originally punctuated in the same form as *Seven Emus* but rewritten after the critical disapproval of that work; *Larger than Life* (1963), a collection of short stories; and *Disturbing Element* (1963), an unsparing autobiography of his first twenty-four years, which some commentators see with *Capricornia* as containing his best work. Then, in 1975 after a decade of preparation and amidst much publicity, Herbert's *Poor Fellow My Country* was published. A massive work of some 850 000 words, a third longer than *War and Peace* and the longest novel ever published in Australia, it is Herbert's final statement about Australia in general and the Northern Territory in particular. It won the Miles Franklin Award in 1975, an award which was soon followed by honorary doctorates from the Universities of Queensland and Newcastle and by other tributes.

One of the legendary figures of Australian literary culture in the twentieth century, justifiably included in Keith Dunstan's affectionate gallery, *Ratbags* (1979) Herbert was a man about whom anecdotes abound and who periodically emerged from the isolation of Redlynch to promote the publication of his books as well as to deliver strongly-held opinions about life in Australia. Perhaps influenced by the chronological span of *Disturbing Element*, commentators have discovered in his early experiences some of the crucial influences on the subject matter and thematic concerns of his fiction. The title and substance of the autobiography attested to the difficult relationship Herbert had with his family: terrorised by his father and rejected by his mother, he felt himself the 'disturbing element' in their lives. There are many travellers among the hundreds of characters who inhabit Herbert's fictional work, and most of these are embarked on a search for security, for familial, social or national identity; in particular, the figure of the half-caste, caught between European and Aboriginal society, is a dominant one in *Capricornia, Seven Emus, Larger than Life* and *Poor Fellow My Country*. A second and connected influence to emerge from Herbert's early years was his contact at Port Hedland with Aborigines and with pioneering European Australians like his engine-driver father. These contacts, together with a strong feeling of both his own and Aboriginal attachment to the land, were consolidated by his wanderings after he left Melbourne, and

shaped the outback settings and discussion of man's relationship to the environment that figure prominently in his fiction with the exception of *Soldiers' Women*. The matriarchal world of that novel, however, was itself partly shaped by Herbert's experience of his mother's dominance of his childhood household and by his father's absence on active service in the First World War.

Herbert's literary career was marked by a succession of false starts, multiple drafts, and much revision, and also by the influence the success of his first novel, *Capricornia*, had on his subsequent work. A saga which encompasses the 1880s to the 1930s, *Capricornia* won renown when first published as a savage indictment of the treatment of Aboriginal Australians by European Australians. Without minimizing the significance of the indictment, subsequent commentators have directed attention to other aspects of Herbert's achievement: the narrative momentum retained throughout the work; the tight control exerted over what appears to be a sprawling canvas of incident and character; the richness with which Herbert establishes his isolated, frontier, fictional territory of Capricornia; the exploration in the novel of human culpability and man's response to the land; the range of its characterization; and its mixture of comedy, satire and tragedy. The fictional works which have been published since *Capricornia* have been unfavourably compared with it. *Seven Emus*, the plot of which has been summarized by Harry Heseltine as a 'tall story of two confidence tricksters who succeed in the end in outsmarting themselves', is not only flawed by the failed experiment in punctuation but also by the hectoring tone of its sneers at academics and the other familiar Herbert targets, and by the ponderous prose style. *Larger than Life* is a collection of traditionally plotted stories new from the 1930s, 1940s and 1950s. It encompasses familiar territory (northern Australia) and themes (the mistreatment and alienation of racial and ethnic minorities), although several stories attest to the development of Herbert's interest in flying. *Soldiers' Women*, the most uncharacteristic of Herbert's work in its urban setting, which has been equated with Sydney during the Second World War, is a richly-textured portrait of women in wartime, which explores through symbol and narrative the themes of destiny in human lives and the nature of sexuality. Some critics, however, have suggested that Herbert's own, sometimes idiosyncratic, views on female sexuality have intruded too much into the novel, in which all sexual relationships outside heterosexual monogamy are condemned. Finally, there is *Poor Fellow My Country*, which has been praised as Herbert's *magnum opus* and condemned by Laurie Clancy as a kind of literary brontosaurus, *Poor Bugger My Book*. In the novel Herbert carries the story of life in northern Australia forward from 1936, the time at which *Capricornia* ends, to 1942. One of its two central characters is Prindy, the half-caste who, unlike Norman Shillingsworth, acquires his Aboriginal identity in the opening chapter and retains it, in the face of white oppression, until his death at the end, a death which represents the wholesale destruction of Aboriginal society. The second major figure is Jeremy Delacy, a hard-bitten pioneer who articulates where Australia has gone wrong, e.g., in letting its citizens become involved in the imperialist wars of 1914–18 and 1939–45; his experience embodies the national tragedy which culminates in the 'Day of Shame', the title of the last section, when Australians flee Darwin in fear of Japanese bombs. Although Prindy's tragedy is realized and Herbert has characteristically exerted some control over his material, *Poor Fellow My Country* clearly suffers from authorial intrusions thinly disguised as Jeremy's lectures to a series of listeners; from the failure of Jeremy to emerge as a moral model and his emergence instead as a self-righteous, quirky, intolerant, paternalistic, sexist bore; from the chauvinist attitudes expressed to all non-Australians; and from the prolixity of the writing. Harry Heseltine and Laurie Clancy have published studies of Herbert (1973, 1981).

'**Here Comes the Nigger!**', a play by Gerald Bostock, was performed in the Black Theatre, Sydney, in 1976. It concerns a blind Aboriginal poet, Sam Matthews, and a white woman, Odette O'Brien, who is tutoring him for his Higher School Certificate. A loving relationship develops between them but is strongly opposed by racist relatives on both sides. Billy, Sam's brother, warns him that white women 'can screw you up'; Neil, Odette's brother, accuses her of being 'partial to the taste of licorice sticks'. The play, with its distinctive modern urban idiom, is a powerful and violent statement on modern racism.

Here's Luck, a comic novel by Lennie Lower (q.v.), was first published in 1930. It chronicles the misadventures of Jack Gudgeon, a forty-eight-year-old Sydneysider, after the departure of his wife Agatha gives him new freedoms. In company with his sleazy son, Stanley, and later his brother-in-law, George, Gudgeon embarks on a series of drunken escapades which give full rein to Lower's talent for slapstick and his satiric observations of domestic strife and city lowlife. At the climax to the novel, a riotous party is held at the family home, which is burnt down. The party is the occasion also of the reconciliation between Jack and Agatha, although the last page of *Here's Luck* suggests that Jack's decision to settle down may be only a temporary one.

HERGENHAN, L.T. (LAURENCE THOMAS) (1931–), born Bega, NSW, was educated at the Universities of Sydney and London, and has taught at the Universities of Tasmania and Queensland, where he was director of the Australian Studies Centre 1979–82. Foundation editor of *Australian Literary Studies* (q.v.) in 1963, he has also edited the Portable Australian Authors series since 1976 and written widely on Australian and English literature; his editorship of *Australian Literary Studies* over more than two decades has significantly advanced Australian literary scholarship. Hergenhan's major Australian publications include an edition of the journalism of Marcus Clarke, *A Colonial City* (1972), a Clarke bibliography (1975), and a critical study of fiction about the convicts, *Unnatural Lives* (1983).

Heriot, see *To The Islands*

Hermes began in 1886 as an undergraduates' magazine sponsored by the Students' Representative Council of the University of Sydney. Published monthly it ran until 1894; in 1895 a new series began, published twice a term, which continued until 1969 although the magazine failed to appear in 1953, 1955, 1964, 1967 and 1968. In addition to university news, *Hermes* published original verse and literary articles. A special Jubilee number was issued in 1902 to commemorate the fiftieth year of the university; it included a history of the university and an article by Christopher Brennan on 'The University and Australian Literature'. Numerous other subsequently well-known writers either edited or contributed to *Hermes*, including J. le Gay Brereton and A.D. Hope.

Hermit in Van Diemen's Land, The, is a series of thirty prose sketches which first appeared under the pseudonym 'Simon Stukeley' in weekly parts in Andrew Bent's *Colonial Times* June–December 1829. The sketches were then collected in book form by Bent, and the resulting volume, released in 1830 although 1829 appears on the title page, constitutes the first book of essays published in Australia. The acknowledged model for *The Hermit in Van Diemen's Land* was *The Hermit in London*, a series of didactic, anecdotal and descriptive sketches of London life which forms part of a larger series of *Hermit* books, e.g. *The Hermit in the Country*, *The Hermit Abroad*, *The Hermit in Edinburgh*, generally attributed to Felix

McDonough or Macdonogh. The technique, however, of employing as narrator a wide-eyed visitor (Simon announces himself a native of Yorkshire coming to 'look over' the colony and inhabitants of Van Diemen's Land) not only owes something to a long-established prose genre which accommodates some of the essays of Montesquieu and Goldsmith but also establishes Simon, at least for part of *The Hermit in Van Diemen's Land*, as an early specimen of the new chum type. Characteristically the sketches combine authorial contemplation, satiric description, and narration. They follow Simon from his arrival in Van Diemen's Land, through his meetings with prominent citizens and his peripatetic visits to courts, parties, weddings, schools, farms, and so on in Hobart and the surrounding countryside. Some characters appear in several sketches; two recurring themes are the confusion over Simon's identity, and the rapacity and incompetence of lawyers. Although individual colonists are not named, the precise descriptions of dress, speech and mannerism made identification easy for contemporary audiences, and led to Bent's prosecution for libel by one disgruntled target, the advocate Galmiel Butler. The case delayed release of the book.

The Hermit of Van Diemen's Land is generally agreed to have been written by Henry Savery (q.v.), the author of the first Australian novel, *Quintus Servinton* (1831); the two works are complementary in their attitude towards the legal system, although *The Hermit* is more openly antagonistic. If Savery was the author he wrote it while in gaol for debt in 1829; the use of a pseudonym is understandable, not least because the convicts were banned by a government order of 1828 from writing for the press. The identification of Savery was first firmly made by Henry Melville in a copy of *The Hermit in Van Diemen's Land* now in the British Library, London; Melville stated that Savery was wholly responsible for the work and that Thomas Wells (q.v.), a fellow debtor in prison, acted as an amanuensis, preparing the copy for the printer. Other contemporaries, however, identified Wells as the author, as also did later writers such as James Bonwick. The only modern text, edited by Cecil Hadgraft (1964), accepts Melville's view and assigns the work to Savery. Also included in this edition are notes on the Hobart citizens, e.g. Sir George Arthur, William Bedford, Andrew Bent, whose identities are confirmed by a contemporary key now held in the Mitchell Library, Sydney.

Hero of Too, The, a novel by David Martin (q.v.), was first published in 1965. It is both a sustained, hilarious comedy and a mild satire on the bushranging (q.v.) tradition and small-

town life and politics. Tooramit, a tiny Victorian town faced with the problem of how best to celebrate its founding day, gradually discovers a series of embarrassing truths about its most famous son, the bushranger Dick Grogan. Although many of the Tooramites are aware that Grogan's heroic image is paper-thin and have private reasons for not perpetuating his memory, others have equally good reasons for raising his ghost. Neighbouring Boobyalla, with which Tooramit is locked in traditional rivalry, also yearns to celebrate the Grogan legend. The arrival of a Grogan devotee from Melbourne, a young schoolteacher, Steve Turner, acts as a catalyst to the involved political situation, setting a chain of events in inevitable motion. Not only is Grogan revealed as a feeble and unwilling hero, but unsuspected intricacies of relationships also come to light that link the family of Jack Bollman, shire president and supposedly grandson of the man who shot Grogan in the buttocks in the 'Affair at Tooramit Bridge' in 1874, and that of Klep Quinn, the local nightcart man and an amiable kleptomaniac. The past events, brought fully into light by two of the oldest inhabitants, Pongo Quinn and Lam the Chinese herbalist, prove benign for the younger generation, rearranging George Bollman and Lacy Quinn, and Steve Turner and Clare Lovelett, in more appropriate relationships. They also have a liberating impact on the lives of the middle-aged, such as Jack Bollman, his sister Alison, and his low-pulsed wife Norma.

Herridge of Reality Swamp (1907), William Gosse Hay's (q.v.) second novel, is focused on the experiences of a minister, John Sydenham, who comes to Manalia (Australia) to escape from a romantic scandal in which he is the innocent party. He changes his name to Herridge, goes to work among the convicts, and rescues a would-be suicide who turns out to be the woman who ruined his reputation; in time she marries Sir Ralph Eardley and manages to reduce him to alcoholism, to drive his heiress daughter Ellen towards madness, and to have Herridge imprisoned. Herridge is sent to the isolated penal settlement of Reality Swamp, where Sir Ralph is in charge and Herridge and Ellen fall in love. When the settlement runs short of food, the dominant Lady Eardley plans to remove herself and the officers, leaving the prisoners to starve. Hay himself planned to have Lady Eardley's boat attacked by Aborigines and the only survivor, Ellen, return it to the starving settlement; but at the insistence of Hay's publishers, Herridge leads the party back to civilization, is pardoned, and settles down with Ellen as his wife in a country vicarage.

'HERVEY, GRANT' (GEORGE HENRY COCHRANE) (1880–1933), born Casterton, Victoria, as George Henry Cochrane, was a blacksmith before becoming a journalist, working on newspapers in both eastern and western Australia. He contributed ballads and other verse to the *Bulletin*, and published *Australians Yet, and Other Verses* in 1913. Acquitted in 1905 of attempted murder, 'Hervey' was arrested in 1914 after he offered to provide John Norton with divorce evidence against his wife. Convicted of forgery, he was sentenced to four years' imprisonment; his open letter about prison conditions to the NSW Premier, W.A. Holman, was printed in Vance Marshall's *The World of the Living Dead* (1919). In 1919, posing as an American, 'Madison Harvey', 'Hervey' appeared in Mildura to drum up financial support for a new state; he was exposed by C.J. de Garis and after seeking his revenge through the editorship of the *Mildura and Merbein Sun* was tarred and feathered by de Garis's supporters in 1921. After another gaol sentence for forgery he was, in 1929, briefly editor of the salacious Sydney weekly, *Beckett's Budget*; in 1931 he was convicted on a third charge of forgery. At Bathurst gaol he wrote *An Eden of the Good* (1934), a bizarre historical novel set in Tasmania and Sydney in the 1830s. Peopled by historical characters such as Charles Darwin, John Dunmore Lang and William Charles Wentworth as well as by the exotically-named governor, Sir Dratsum Sneek (the well-known 'Keens Mustard' spelt backwards), the madame, Venus Colossal, and the newspaper editor, Ebenezer Weaselfidjetts, *An Eden of the Good* focuses on the rise to prosperity of the poet, Randolph Cochrane, and his brother, Walter. At the end of the novel both have married well and depart the 'poisonous convict-minded village of Sydney', Randolph to a new settlement to be named after his wife Mildura, and Walter to Moreton Bay. Although his central characters share his real name, 'Hervey' begins the novel with the convict experiences of his 'grandfather', George Hervey; another convict in *An Eden of the Good*, the Irish baronet, Sir Terence Hayes, bears some resemblance to the title character of William Gosse Hay's *The Escape of the Notorious Sir William Heans* (1919).

HESELTINE, H.P. (HARRY PAYNE) (1931–), born Fremantle, WA, was educated at the University of WA and at Louisiana State University. He returned to Australia in 1956 and has taught at the Universities of New England and NSW (1959–77) before becoming professor of English at the James Cook University of North Queensland; in 1982 he became professor of English in the faculty of Military Studies, Royal Military College, Duntroon. The essays Heseltine has contributed to literary journals such as *Meanjin* since the early 1960s have included important assessments of Henry Lawson, A.B. Paterson, Francis Webb and other Australian writers as well as studies of the Australian literary tradition. He edited *Australian Idiom* (1963) and, with Stanley Tick, *The Writer in the Modern World* (1962); his other publications include monographs on J. le Gay Brereton (1965) and Xavier Herbert (1973); a biographical and critical study of Vance Palmer (1970) and *Intimate Portraits and Other Pieces* (1969), a selection of Palmer's prose; editions of *The Penguin Book of Australian Verse* (1972), *The Penguin Book of Australian Short Stories* (1976), and *The Penguin Book of Modern Australian Verse* (1981); and *Acquainted with the Night: Studies in Classic Australian Fiction* (1979).

HESLING, BERNARD (1905–), born Yorkshire, England, came to Australia in 1928. A well-known painter and cartoonist whose work has been a familiar feature of the Sydney *Daily Telegraph*, he has also written and drawn for a variety of newspapers and magazines, including *Meanjin*, the *Bulletin*, the *Sydney Morning Herald*, *Smith's Weekly*, *Quadrant*, *Nation*, the *New Yorker* and the *Listener*. Art critic for the Sydney *Observer* 1950–55, he lived in Sydney for thirty years before moving to Adelaide. He has published a collection of his drawings, *Cartoons* (1945); an illustrated account of Sydney, *Sydney Observed* (1953); and several humorous, illustrated autobiographies, *Little and Orphan* (1954), *The Dinkumization and Depommification of an Artful English Immigrant* (1963), later published with the title *The Dinkum Pommie*), *Stir Up This Stew* (1966), *My Picture Book* (1971) and *Art Ruined My Career in Crime* (1977). One of his plays, 'My Life with an Interval with Asprin', was performed in 1972.

HETHERINGTON, JOHN (1907–75), born near Melbourne, worked for several Melbourne newspapers until the Second World War, during which he served in Greece as war correspondent for the London *Times*, the *Manchester Guardian* and the Melbourne *Herald* group of newspapers. He was editor of the Adelaide *News* 1945–49, deputy editor of the *Argus* 1952–54, and a feature–writer for the *Age* 1954–67. His publications based on his war experience included *Airborne Invasion* (1943), an account of the battle of Crete; *The Australian Soldier* (1943); and *The Winds Are Still* (1947), winner of the *Sydney Morning Herald* war-novel competition. He also wrote several biographies of famous Australians, including two of Sir Thomas Blamey, *Blamey* (1954) and the more substantial *Blamey: Controversial Soldier* (1973); *Melba* (1967); and a monograph on Norman Lindsay (1961) and the authorized account, *Norman Lindsay: The Embattled Olympian* (1973). He published several collective biographical studies, *Australians: Nine Profiles* (1960), *Forty-Two Faces* (q.v. 1962), *Australian Painters* (1963) and *Uncommon Men* (1965). Interested in Victorian architecture and social history, he wrote a history of some Victorian buildings, *Witness to Things Past* (1964), and a history of churches and churchmen in early Victoria, *Pillars of the Faith* (1966). In addition to some uncollected short stories and verse he wrote an account of his childhood at Sandringham, *The Morning Was Shining* (1971). A painstaking, balanced and self-effacing biographer, with a lucid style, Hetherington had unusual ability to appreciate and realize the diverse personalities and interests of his subjects.

HEWETT, DOROTHY (1923–), was born and brought up in WA on her father's isolated wheat farm. Until the age of twelve she was educated by correspondence. At seventeen her first poetry appeared in *Meanjin*, and by twenty-two she had won a drama competition and a national poetry competition. Her personal life at this time was turbulent: she failed her university course and attempted suicide. At nineteen she joined the Communist Party. Marriage in 1944 to the lawyer and Communist writer, Lloyd Davies, and the birth of a son provided a brief stability, but her son died, the marriage failed and Hewett left for Sydney in 1948. There she lived in the poorer areas and worked in a variety of factory jobs. For nine years she lived with Les Flood, boiler-maker and Communist, by whom she had three sons. She became deeply involved in Party activities during the turbulent anti-Communist period of the 1950s, but wrote little. In 1959 her novel, *Bobbin Up* (q.v.), based on her factory experiences, appeared and won immediate popularity. Her relationship with Flood having come to an end, she resumed her university studies in Perth in 1960 and married Merv Lilley (q.v.), merchant seaman and Communist, in the same year. In 1968, disillusioned by Soviet treatment of dissidents, she left the Communist Party. After some years of tutoring at the University of WA, she moved again to Sydney.

Her poetry, a continued preoccupation, has appeared in five collections: *What about the People!* (1961, with Merv Lilley), *Windmill Country* (1968), *Rapunzel in Suburbia* (1975), *Greenhouse* (1979) and *Journeys* (1982). But she is best known for her recent drama. Her published plays are *This Old Man Comes Rolling Home* (q.v., 1976), *The Chapel Perilous* (q.v., 1972), *Bon–Bons and Roses for Dolly* [and] *The Tatty Hollow Story* (1976), *The Golden Oldies* (in *Hecate* 1976, and with a radio play, *Susannah's Dreaming*, in 1981), *The Beautiful Mrs. Portland* (*Theatre Australia* 1976), and *The Man from Mukinupin* (1979). Other plays, produced but unpublished, are 'Time Flits Away, Lady' (1941), 'Mrs. Porter and the Angel' (1970), the musicals 'Catspaw' (1974), 'Joan' (1975) and 'Miss Hewett's Shenanigans' (1975), and 'Pandora's Cross' (1978). She has also written radio plays, numerous short stories and edited a collection of WA literature, *Sandgropers* (1973).

A romantic quest for the intrinsic but elusive self lies at the heart of Hewett's poetry and drama. It determines the emotional range and impact of her work, its vigour and frankness. Critics of her work also claim that her romantic commitment leads to structural weakness, thematic confusion and self-indulgence. After the naturalism of her first professionally-produced play, *This Old Man Comes Rolling Home*, Hewett turned to a more expressionistic, free-wheeling theatre, that mixes diverse styles and moods and uses a wide range of effects, visual, verbal and musical. The mixture of black comedy and absurdist allegory in 'Mrs. Porter and the Angel' prefigures the later plays, although the theme of division between dream and reality is dealt with more purposefully in her next, most-produced play, *The Chapel Perilous*. Reactions to the formidable heroine have ranged from delight to disgust, but the play's vigorous momentum and abrasive variety have made it memorable theatre. The bitch-goddess figure also features in the next three plays: *Bon–Bons and Roses for Dolly* is a part-nostalgic, part-satiric look at the dream-world created by the cinema of the 1930s, in which the heroine, Dolly Garden, is both victim and creator of the dream; *The Tatty Hollow Story* is a more controlled study of the resistance between authentic self and perceived and conditioned selves; *The Golden Oldies* explores the tedium and frustrations of petit-bourgeois, 'respectable' femininity. The musicals 'Catspaw' and 'Joan' are more schematic elaborations of the previous themes via knock-about vaudeville, but *The Beautiful Mrs. Portland* is a return to a more naturalistic, Ibsenesque theatre. Another change is registered in her most unified and objective play so far, *The Man from Mukinupin*. Many of Hewett's dramatic themes, incidents and images are present in her poetry. Apart from some proletarian ballads, her verse is confessional and romantic in theme, wryly humorous, frankly bawdy, varied in tone and rich in imagery. Sexuality is her main subject, seen as both liberation and imprisonment, although increasingly she writes of the fear and attraction of death.

'Hey Blue, It's Raining', see **MUDIE, IAN**

HIBBERD, JACK (1940–), born Warracknabeal, Victoria, studied medicine at the University of Melbourne, graduated in 1964 and practised as a doctor until 1973 when he began to work for the theatre full-time. At the beginning of his career he was closely associated, both as writer and director, with the Australian Performing Group, which performed ten of his early plays. In 1976 he left the group although, unlike Barry Oakley and David Williamson, he has remained in Melbourne. Active in public discussion of the arts, he has served a term on the Theatre Board. His first play, *White with Wire Wheels* (q.v. published in *Plays*, ed. Graeme Blundell, 1970) was followed by 'Three Old Friends' (1967) and in 1968 by a sequence of short plays which include 'Brainrot', *Just Before the Honeymoon* (published in *Komos*, 1969), 'O', *One of Nature's Gentlemen* (1976), 'This Great Gap of Time', *Who?* (also published in Blundell's edition of *Plays*), 'No Time Like the Present', and a musical drama, 'Jack Juan'. 'Commitment' also appeared in 1968 and the following year he was commissioned by the University of NSW Drama Foundation to write 'The Last Days of Epic J. Remorse'. *Dimboola* (q.v., 1974), his best-known play, was first produced by the Australian Performing Group in 1969, but only became successful after David Williamson directed it in 1973. In 1970 the musical extravaganza he wrote with John Romeril, *Marvellous Melbourne* (*Theatre-Australia*, 1977) was produced by the Group, followed by 'Klag' and 'Customs and Excise' (later 'Proud Flesh'); 'Aorta' was produced in 1971 and 'Women!' and *Captain Midnight V.C.* in 1972. *A Stretch of the Imagination* (1973), regarded by some critics as his most important play to date, was also first produced in 1972. His remaining plays include 'The Architect and the Emperor of Assyria' (1973–74), *The Les Darcy Show* (performed 1974), *Peggy Sue* (performed 1974), *A Toast to Melba* (performed 1975), 'Goodbye Ted' (1975, with John Timlin), 'Memories of a Carlton Bohemian' (1977), *The Overcoat* (*Theatre-Australia*, 1977), *Sin* (in *Meanjin* 1978, and with *The Overcoat*, 1981) an opera libretto performed by the Victorian State Opera in 1978, 'A Man of Many Parts' (1980), *Mothballs* (*Meanjin*, 1980), *Breakfast at the Windsor* (*Meanjin*, 1981), *Glycerine Tears* (*Meanjin*, 1982), *Lavender Bags* (*Aspect*, 1982) and 'Liquid Amber' (1982). Hibberd's collection *Three Popular Plays* (1976) includes *One of Nature's Gentlemen*, *A Toast to Melba* and *The Les Darcy Show*. He has also published translations of poems by Baudelaire, *Le Vin des Amants* (1977), and, with Garrie Hutchinson, *The Barracker's Bible: A Dictionary of Sporting Slang* (1983).

Hibberd's early plays favour a rough, aggressive, cabaret style that is abrasive and disconcerting in impact. He was the first of the new dramatists to explore the contemporary 'ocker' stereotype and the limitations of prevalent Australian male attitudes and rituals from the point of view of both sexes. *White with Wire Wheels* concentrates on male conformity, *One of Nature's Gentlemen* on the exploitative relationships between 'mates', *Peggy Sue* on varieties of female experience of male domination.

Some of his plays, like those of David Williamson, which crystallize and satirize familiar attitudes or myths, engage the audience in the shock of recognition. *Dimboola*, a send-up of the Australian country wedding that is more comic and affectionate than satiric, has become part of the national folklore, and is the most performed of any Australian play; *A Toast to Melba*, *The Les Darcy Show* and *Captain Midnight V.C.* are part comic parody, part affirmative celebration of legendary national figures. But Hibberd is more interested in the possibilities of popular theatre than in sociology. Influenced by Pinter, Beckett and Brecht, Elizabethan and Jacobean theatre, the expressionists from Buchner to Wedekind and nineteenth-century Australian theatre, he draws on a wide range of theatrical modes for his own experimental effects. A loose, episodic structure, broadly-drawn characters, scatalogical humour, songs and other musical effects, and a general, absurdist tenor are recurrent characteristics of his diverse theatre. In his introduction to *Three Popular Plays*, Hibberd develops his concept of a popular, accessible theatre that intermingles 'celebration with satire, fun with gravity, fiction with information, ignorance with politics, slang with poetry'; such a theatre offers no political messages or psychological explanations, but is nevertheless able to 'jolt and agitate within a context of sheer local enjoyment, a whirl of community, and an awareness of a shared heritage and its absurdities'. Especially fascinated by language, he uses the Australian idiom not as a sociological reflector, but in an attempt to reanimate and recolour the English language. This reinvigorating effect is particularly obvious in his adaptation of Gogol's story, *The Overcoat*, a part-comic, part-sombre evocation of a crazy, absurdist world, and in his monodrama, *A Stretch of the Imagination*. In this play, a recreation over one day of his life by an old man, Monk O'Neill, as he faces death (both literally and in imagination), Hibberd draws heavily on the variety of the vernacular, especially on its ironic capacities. Monk O'Neill is simultaneously a complex individual, an archetypal Australian and an Everyman figure. Once a man-about-town, scholar, and world traveller, Monk as pioneer, fossicker, explorer, sporting hero and womanizer also embodies ideal aspects of the Australian legend as well as some of its exploitative and destructive aspects. Although death and alienation are the play's starting-points, the underlying mood is strongly positive and life-affirming. Pathetic and dignified, comic and tragic, callous and humane, self-centred and selfless, Monk emerges as an unnaturalistic figure of elastic dimensions, a fusion of myth, type and caricature.

'Hibernian Father, The', a popular melodrama by Edward Geoghegan (q.v.), was presented anonymously in Sydney in 1844; it is set in fifteenth century Ireland. The author was accused of plagiarism by some spectators, who claimed the play borrowed heavily from *The Warden of Galway* by a Rev. Groves, performed in Dublin and published in 1832. Geoghegan refuted the charge and the controversy subsided since the earlier play could not be produced for comparison. Opinion is still divided about the validity of the charge although free adaptations were then common practice.

'Hidden Bole, The', a complex, philosophical poem by R.D. FitzGerald (q.v.), was written in 1935 in Sydney while FitzGerald was convalescing from a severe operation. It was published in *Moonlight Acre* (1938). Highly valued by FitzGerald ('my chief claim to be a poet at all'), the poem reflects on the death of the ballerina Pavlova in 1931, moving from that event to a contemplation of the nature and essence of beauty and the relationship between beauty and time. The banyan tree, which puts out aerial roots to reinforce the original sapling, thus producing a maze of trunks, is taken as a natural example of continuous survival, that survival stemming from the original core, the 'hidden bole' itself. The individual blossoms of the tree, coming in profusion from the many trunks, have only a momentary existence and glory but that glory (beauty) continues with the new blossoms that quickly replace the old. Beauty thus persists because, paradoxically, it is transient. Although the beauty of Pavlova's actual dance seems to die with her, it survives in the memory of those who witness it.

Hidden Tide, The, see QUINN, RODERIC

HIDES, JACK (1906–38), born Port Moresby, Papua, was a patrol officer and later assistant resident magistrate and gold prospector. His books, *Through Wildest Papua* (1935), *Papuan Wonderland* (1936), *Savages in Serge* (1938) and *Beyond the Kubea* (1939), are a combination of adventure fiction, description and ethnographical studies. J.P. Sinclair wrote *The Outside Man: Jack Hides of Papua* (1969).

HIGGINS, BERTRAM (1901–74), born Malvern, Melbourne, went to Oxford in 1919 and remained in England until 1930 as a literary journalist, being assistant editor of the *Calendar of Modern Letters* and a reviewer for the *Times Literary Supplement*, the *Spectator*, the *New Statesman*, and the *Sunday Times*. After a brief period in Australia (1930–33), part of which time he worked on Cyril Pearl's short-lived magazine, *Stream*, he returned to England, where he served in the RAF in the Second World War. In 1946 he returned to Australia. Higgins published *Mordecaius Overture* (1933), a complex work that saw him recognized by a small coterie as the intellectual and poetic equal of T.S. Eliot, but which remained only dimly understood. Mordecaius, a witness to both the crucifixion of Christ and the destruction of Pompeii, attempts to fit both events into a frame of reference which has some relevance to the confusion of his own life. Higgins's lack of other published works, deplored by his devotees, has been somewhat compensated for by the recent posthumous edition, *The Haunted Rendezvous: Selected Poems* (1980), a selection made by Higgins, in collaboration with Robert King, in the year before his death. In addition to Higgins's best poems, *The Haunted Rendezvous* contains a selection of the sparse critical commentary available on Higgins, most of it written about the time *Mordecaius Overture* was published.

HIGGINS, HENRY BOURNES (1851–1929), born Ireland, came to Australia in 1870 and graduated from the University of Melbourne with degrees in arts and law in 1875. In 1901 he entered the first Commonwealth parliament and although not a member of the Labor Party became attorney-general in 1904 in J.C. Watson's Labor ministry. As a federal parliamentarian he was influential in the establishment of the CLF. He was made a justice of the High Court in 1906 and president of the Federal Court of Conciliation and Arbitration, in which capacity he was largely responsible for the establishment of the principle of a basic wage for workers. His biography *Henry Bournes Higgins* (1931) was written by his niece, Nettie Palmer. His own publications include *Essays and Addresses on the Australian Commonwealth Bill* (1900) and *A New Province for Law and Order* (1922).

High Commissioner, The, see **CLEARY, JON**

High Valley, see **CLIFT, CHARMIAN**

HIGHAM, CHARLES (1931–), born London, became a book reviewer for the *Sydney Morning Herald* in 1956 and was literary editor of the *Bulletin* 1964–67 before moving to the USA. His first two volumes of poetry, *A Distant Star* (1951) and *Spring and Death* (1953), were published in England. His Australian publications are *The Earthbound and Other Poems* (1959), *Noonday Country* (1966), sub-titled *Poems 1954–1965* and *The Voyage to Brindisi, and Other Poems* (1970). He edited *Australian Writing Today* (1968), *They Came to Australia* (1961, with Alan Brissenden) and *Australians Abroad* (1967, with Michael Wilding). He published a controversial biography of Errol Flynn in 1980.

HIGINBOTHAM, GEORGE (1826–92), born Dublin, came to Australia in 1854 after being called to the Bar in England. He combined journalism and law in Australia, writing initially for the Melbourne *Herald*; in 1856–59 he was editor of the *Argus*. Following an interrupted political career during which he campaigned assiduously for extreme secularism in state education, he was appointed to the Supreme Court in 1880, becoming chief justice in 1886. Throughout his political and judicial career Higinbotham was concerned with the conditions of the working man and the rights of women. E.E. Morris wrote *A Memoir of George Higinbotham* (1895), Gwyneth M. Dow *George Higinbotham: Church and State* (1964) and Vance Palmer included a biographical sketch of him in *National Portraits* (1940).

HILL, BARRY (1943–), born Melbourne, graduated from the University of Melbourne and was a teacher and psychologist in Victoria and London. In 1972 he returned to Melbourne as founding editor of the education page of the *Age* but has been a full-time fiction writer since 1975. His documentary of contemporary Australian educational practice, *The Schools* (1977), won a National Book Council Award. Hill has published two books of short fiction, *A Rim of Blue* (1978) and *Headlocks & Other Stories* (1983) and a novella, *Near the Refinery* (1980). His complex and disturbing short stories written, in Nancy Keesing's phrase, in prose 'as clear as rainwater', reflect on social themes and probe the raw areas of individual experience. 'A Bold Headline' from *A Rim of Blue*, the story of watchmaker–turned–teacher, Charles Bristol, is painfully poignant; 'Headlocks', in which a visitor is battered to death and his body burned by his erstwhile friends, is casually macabre. *Near the Refinery* deals with the relationship between a dying man and his middle–aged son; it subtly explores the discrepancy between reality and what passes for observable facts.

HILL, ERNESTINE (1900–72), born Rockhampton, Queensland, worked briefly as a public servant before her marriage. A wanderer by nature, she began to indulge her love of travel as early as 1930 and after the death of her husband in 1933 embarked on a life of almost continuous travel and writing. Apart from an adolescent book of verse, *Peter Pan Land* (1916), her first publication was *The Great Australian Loneliness* (1937), an account of five years' travel over outback Australia from Adelaide to Darwin via the Birdsville Track, the Red Centre and Arnhem Land. *Water into Gold*, a history of the Murray River irrigation areas, was published in the same year. Her only novel, *My Love Must Wait* (q.v., 1941), based on the life of Matthew Flinders (q.v.) and published also in England and the USA, sold more than 10 000 copies in Australia, a remarkable achievement in the austerity of wartime. In 1947, in *Flying Doctor Calling*, she gives an absorbing account, spiced with extraordinary anecdotes, of the foundation of the Australian Inland Mission, of the dedication and courage of John Flynn and others, and of the ultimate spread of airborne medical care over two million square miles of inland Australia. By the time she had published the best-known of her works, *The Territory* (q.v., 1951), she had been, in her own words, 'twice round Australia by land, clockwise and anti–clockwise . . . three times across it from south to north, many times east and west, and once on the diagonal'. *The Territory* is a book that J.K. Ewers believed 'ought to be in the swag of every Australian'. In addition to her numerous contributions to newspapers and journals about her experiences, especially to *Walkabout*, Ernestine Hill also published posthumously in 1973 *Kabbarli: A Personal Memoir of Daisy Bates*, in which she claims that she was largely responsible for the writing of Daisy Bates's book, *The Passing of the Aborigines* (1938). She was a commissioner of the ABC, 1942–44.

HILL, FIDELIA S.T. (?1790–1854), born Pontefract, Yorkshire, published *Poems and Recollections of the Past* (1840), suggested as the first book of verse written by a woman to be published in Australia.

Hill of Content is the name given to three Melbourne literary ventures: a bookshop, an archive series and a publishing company. The

Hill of Content antique and rare book bookshop was established by A.H. Spencer in Bourke Street, Melbourne, in 1922 and was owned by him until after a brief period of ownership by Angus & Robertson in 1951 it was bought by Collins Book Depot. Spencer's autobiographical work, *The Hill of Content* (1959), highlights the Sydney and Melbourne literary worlds from the turn of the century to the end of the Second World War. The Hill of Content Archive series was launched in 1966 to gather historical documents for educational purposes on various topics, e.g. Hugh Anderson's *Australia in the Depression* (1972) and Margaret Jennings's *Australian Explorers* (1969) and *Australia in the Great War* (1970). The Hill of Content publishing company, formed by a group of employees of the Collins Book Depot in Melbourne in 1965, presents the Archive series and has also published a wide range of Australian writing, e.g. Marjorie Barnard's *Miles Franklin* (1967) and Hugh Anderson's *The Poet Militant: Bernard O'Dowd* (1969).

HILL, SAMUEL PROUT (1812–61), born Devonshire, England, came to Australia in 1841. He alternated residence between NSW and Tasmania in various clerical occupations but made more of a reputation as a man of letters than of business. He published *Tarquin the Proud and Other Poems* (1843) and *Monody on the Death of Sir George Gipps* (1847). Hill was also a respected political writer with the Hobart *Mercury* in the late 1850s.

Hillyars and the Burtons, The, Henry Kingsley's (q.v.) fourth novel, was serialized in *Macmillan's Magazine* 1863–65 and revised for publication in book form in 1865. The novel is sub-titled, *A Story of Two Families*; these are the Hillyars, English gentry whose story is told contemporaneously with the events depicted by the author-narrator; and the Burtons, a family of Chelsea blacksmiths whose history is chronicled in part by the author but mainly by the retrospective narration of one of the Burton children, James. The narratives, which concentrate on events in England and Australia in the middle and late 1850s, alternate in the early part of the novel but increasingly overlap as the affairs of the several Hillyars become entangled with those of the Burtons. The prehistory of the novel accommodates one such Hillyar-Burton relationship, that between George Hillyar, son of the baronet, and his former servant Samuel Burton, James's uncle. A reckless youth, George has eventually been despatched as a 'remittance man' to Australia, where Samuel is transported after robbing the Hillyar family home. George's reputation follows him to the colonies but he joins the police

and becomes a hero by quelling an attack by bushrangers, thus overcoming the objections to his marriage to Gertie Neville, sister-in-law of the colonial secretary of the colony of Cooksland. The Hillyars return to England, where George hopes to regain the respect of his father and to supplant his favoured and protected younger half-brother, Erne. Erne, meanwhile, has become friendly with the Burton family, particularly the children, James, Joe and Emma and their cousin Reuben, Samuel's putative son but the child of George Hillyar's secret early marriage, as is eventually revealed. Sir George Hillyar is on the point of changing his will to make it more equitable to his elder son when he suddenly dies; but as the will cannot be found George is able to take over the family seat and to turn out Erne Hillyar, who seeks refuge with the Burtons. *The Hillyars and the Burtons* continues to chronicle the decline of the Hillyars: George's discovery that the will is held by a vengeful Samuel; his desertion of Gertie; Gertie's departure for Australia; her overland walk back to her sister's place; her descent into harmless madness; the eventual death of the dissipated George; and Reuben's succession to the baronetcy. It also focuses increasingly on the Burtons. After the collapse of the blacksmith's business in London, they emigrate to Cooksland accompanied by Erne, and achieve prosperity: Burton senior becomes part-owner of a copper mine while James and Joseph enter politics. The family's success is tempered at the end of the novel, however, by the death of the saintly Emma just after she has been released from her vow of service to her crippled brother Joe and is free to marry her devoted suitor, Erne. This ironic but sensational climax to *The Hillyars and the Burtons* is characteristic of a novel spoilt also by its contrived plot and by its melodramatic set pieces. Yet the Chelsea scenes of Kingsley's own youth are evoked by James Burton, and the depiction of Cooksland is notable for the way Kingsley captures the complexities of colonial politics. Parallels can be seen between some Cooksland politicians and newspapers, e.g. Dempsey, the *Palmerston Sentinel* and the *Mohawk*, and their Victorian equivalents in the 1850s, e.g. respectively Charles Gavan Duffy, the *Argus* and the *Age*. The success story of the Burtons, who remain in Australia, and the critical view Kingsley seems to take of English gentlemen contrasts with the exploitation of Australia and the celebration of the virtues of the Buckleys and Brentwoods in *The Recollections of Geoffry Hamlyn* (1859), which so offended Joseph Furphy.

Himmelfarb, Mordecai, see *Riders in the Chariot*

'His Father's Mate', Henry Lawson's first story, was published in the *Bulletin*'s Christmas issue in 1888 and later revised for inclusion in *While the Billy Boils* (1896); the original in particular shows the influence of Bret Harte, with whom Lawson was often compared. 'His Father's Mate' is the name given to Isley Mason, who is working an abandoned goldfield with his father, Tom, and is killed when the soil collapses around a mineshaft. Isley's death is the final tragedy in Tom's life, for his wife had died of a broken heart after Isley's elder brother had been convicted of bushranging. In the melodramatic climax to the story, the elder son, presumably released from prison, comes to the goldfield to become, like Isley, his father's 'mate' only to discover that his father has died.

His Natural Life, a novel by Marcus Clarke (q.v.), was first published in the *Australian Journal* 1870–72 and revised for first publication in book form in 1874; the alternative title *For the Term of His Natural Life* was first used in an 1882 edition of the revised version. The revised version has been regularly reprinted, usually under the long title and often from an 1885 reprint of the 1882 edition; the original serial version, which the *Australian Journal* ran again in 1881–83, 1886–88 and 1913–15, was published in 1970, edited by Stephen Murray-Smith. *His Natural Life* has been translated into German, Dutch, Swedish and Russian; several dramatizations were made in 1886–90, film versions were screened in 1907, 1917 and 1926, and a television series in 1983.

Influenced by Charles Reade's *It Is Never Too Late to Mend* (1856), Victor Hugo's *Les Misérables* (1862) and by other fictional treatments of convict life, *His Natural Life* was also informed by Clarke's researches into transportation at the Public Library in Melbourne and by his visit to the Tasmanian penal settlements in 1870. Its protagonist is Richard Devine, alias Rufus Dawes; in the prologue to the revised version he is exposed as the bastard son of Lady Devine and her cousin, Lord Bellasis, and is ordered from home by Sir Richard Devine, who threatens to make his nephew, Maurice Frere, his heir. That night Richard discovers the body of Lord Bellasis on Hampstead Heath; supposing his putative father to have been the murderer, he takes the name Rufus Dawes when apprehended and is transported for the robbery of Lord Bellasis. One of his guards on the voyage to Australia is Frere, whose hopes for the inheritance have been thwarted by Sir Richard's death. Typhus breaks out and a mutiny is planned by the convicts Gabbett, Vetch and John Rex, assisted by Sarah Purfoy, Rex's lover and nurse to Sylvia Vickers, the daughter of a military officer. Dawes thwarts the mutiny

but is one of those tried for it and is sent on arrival to the penal settlement of Macquarie Harbour.

The subsequent sections of *His Natural Life* comprise the bulk of the novel and focus on Dawes's suffering under Frere at Macquarie Harbour and two other famous secondary punishment centres, Port Arthur and Norfolk Island (qq.v.) The Macquarie Harbour scenes open with Dawes in solitary confinement on Grummet Island; after failing to escape overland, he returns to Macquarie Harbour to find another mutiny has been engineered by Rex and that Frere, Sylvia and her mother are among those marooned there. Dawes asserts his natural role to become leader of the group's escape back to Hobart, but on the journey Mrs Vickers dies, Sylvia loses her memory and Frere takes the credit for their survival and Sylvia's hand in marriage. In despair at Sylvia's failure to recognize his contribution at Macquarie Harbour Dawes is sent to Port Arthur for the original escape; in the Port Arthur chapters the most dismal aspects of transportation life are presented, including the homosexual rape and flogging to death of the young convict, Kirkland, the human tramway and the cannibalism practised by Gabbett, Vetch and others after they escape from Port Arthur. Another escapee is John Rex, who has recognized Dawes's identity and returns to England to impersonate Richard Devine, supposedly lost at sea; the impersonation owes something to the contemporary Tichborne case. The action of the last book of *His Natural Life* is centred on Norfolk Island, where the final stages of Dawes's decline are presented through extracts from the diary of the Reverend James North (q.v.), an alcoholic chaplain whose kindnesses Dawes had experienced at Port Arthur. The determination of North to save Dawes is paralleled by Sylvia's pity for him and by her resolve to leave her husband because of his continued brutality. Dawes discovers from North that Sir Richard Devine had not murdered Lord Bellasis, and that North had committed the robbery for which Dawes was transported; the real murderer turns out to be Rex, who is pursued to England by Sarah and when exposed by Lady Devine reveals unwittingly that he has killed his own father and is therefore Dawes's half–brother. Rex has a stroke and spends the rest of his life in a kind of living death similar to the one that Dawes has experienced; but the final irony is that when Dawes and Sylvia escape from Norfolk Island, the ship is hit by a cyclone and they are drowned at the moment when Sylvia's memory returns and she and Dawes have been reunited. In the serial version of the novel, which is almost twice as long, the ending is different: Sylvia (called Dora) is

343

drowned, but Dawes and Dora's daughter Dorcas survive to prosper on the mainland and return to England. Some of the dramatic film and television adaptations preserve the lives of Dawes and Sylvia. The other major but not only revision is the prologue, reduced from 40 000 to just over 2000 words; in the serial version Dawes is transported for the murder of a business associate, Hans Blinzler, in which neither North nor Rex is involved.

His Natural Life is the most significant and most famous nineteenth-century Australian novel, the major contribution of colonial fiction to the English novel. Profoundly pessimistic, it has been criticized for its melodramatic scenes and unrealistic coincidences, e.g. Sylvia's loss of memory, but its power continues to move modern readers. Although it moves beyond a documentary treatment of the convict system to explore fundamental questions concerning man's capacity for evil, its treatment of transportation played a significant part, along with the works of Caroline Leakey, 'Price Warung' (qq.v.) and others, in consolidating the legend that the convicts were more 'sinn'd against than sinning'.

Historical Journal of the Transactions at Port Jackson and Norfolk Island, An, by John Hunter (q.v.), was published in 1793 in London, where a year later Hunter was selected as successor to Governor Arthur Phillip. One of the first examples of Australian exploration literature, it chronicles the voyage of the First Fleet to Australia, the early days of the colony of NSW, and Hunter's subsequent voyages, including visits to the Cape of Good Hope for provisions (during which his ship, the *Sirius*, circumnavigated the globe) and to Norfolk Island, where the *Sirius* was wrecked. *An Historical Journal of the Transactions at Port Jackson and Norfolk Island* incorporates material from the journals of Phillip and Philip Gidley King.

Historical Records of Australia (HRA), a series of volumes of documents covering several areas of the history of the Australian colonies before 1850, was published in thirty-three volumes 1914–25. When the publication programme for the *Historical Records of New South Wales* (q.v.) terminated in 1902, the Commonwealth government in 1907 took over the task of completing the collection and publication of the early documentary record of Australia. Material already collected, notably the official documents transcribed by James Bonwick (q.v.) and assistants in London, was arranged and indexed 1907–11 and in 1912 Frederick Watson was appointed editor of the *Historical Records of Australia*. As originally envisaged, the project was to take the documentary record from 1811, the year at which the coverage of the *Historical Records of New South Wales* ended, to 1837, later revised to 1856. This plan was found to be impractical, partly because some important pre-1811 documents had not been published in the *Historical Records of New South Wales*, a series which as well had excluded documents relating to the other colonies. Watson then suggested that the *Historical Records of Australia* should comprise seven series of volumes: the despatches between the governors of NSW and the Colonial Office; administrative papers; papers relating to early settlement (including in areas then part of NSW, later of other colonies); legal papers; exploration papers; scientific papers; and ecclesiastical, naval and military papers. Of the thirty-three volumes published, twenty-six belong to the first series (taking the historical record up to 1848), six to the third series (to 1830), and one to the fourth series (to 1827). The *Historical Records of New South Wales* and the *Historical Records of Australia* (known to historians as *HRA*) have documents in common; the main difference between the series, apart from the different chronological coverage, is that the latter is more strictly an official record, excluding the newspaper extracts and other material included in the former. Both series, however, are valuable compilations of the early prose written in Australia; in addition, the *Historical Records of Australia*, which unlike its predecessor includes the names of convicts, yields references to early convicts who became significant in Australian literature, e.g. Henry Savery. The cessation of the *HRA* project accelerated the creation of the Australian Archives.

Historical Records of New South Wales, a documentary record of the discovery and early years of British settlement in NSW, was published in seven volumes, the first in two parts, making eight books in all, 1892–1901. Their publication grew out of the collecting of documents for a multi-volume history of NSW, which began under G.B. Barton as a contribution to the 1888 centenary but was abandoned in 1894 with only two volumes published. Volume one, part one, of the *Historical Records of New South Wales* comprises mainly extracts from the logs of Captain James Cook and his subordinates relating to the discovery and exploration of the eastern coast of Australia in 1770. Succeeding volumes comprise governors' despatches, many of them transcribed by James Bonwick (q.v.), other official and personal documents, and extracts from newspapers and other sources, arranged chronologically 1783–1811 and covering plans for the establishment of the colony of NSW and the first decades of settlement. The *Historical Records of New South Wales*, like the later *Historical Records of Australia*, have been important sources for Australian historians of the twentieth century and are significant in Australian literature as records of early prose written in Australia and as historical sources used by later creative writers. The *Records* were annotated by their editors, Alexander Britton (for the volumes on Phillip published in 1892) and F.M. Bladen (for the succeeding volumes).

Historical Records of Victoria, of which the foundation series has been commissioned by the Victorian government, has Michael Cannon (q.v.) as editor-in-chief. The foundation series covering 1835–39 comprises a projected seven volumes, of which Volume 1, *The Beginnings of Permanent Government* (1981), and Volumes 2A and 2B, *The Aborigines of Port Phillip* (1982, 1983) have been published so far.

Historical Societies. In each Australian State there now exists an historical society which focuses attention on the history, including literary history, of that State. The oldest is the Royal Australian Historical Society, founded in 1901 as the Australian Historical Society; it received its royal charter in 1918 and has published a journal since 1906 (now quarterly, from 1965 the *Journal of the Royal Australian Historical Society*, known also as *JRAHS*). In the other States, the Historical Society of Victoria was founded in 1909, became the Royal Historical Society of Victoria when it received a royal charter in 1952 and has published the quarterly *Victorian Historical Journal* from 1911 (from 1983 as the *Royal Historical Society of Victoria Journal*); the Queensland Historical Society was founded in 1913, became the Royal Historical Society of Queensland when it received a royal charter in 1963 and has published a journal, mainly quarterly, since 1920; the Royal Western Australian Historical Society, founded in 1926, received its royal charter in 1962 and publishes an annual, *Early Days*; the Tasmanian Historical Research Association founded in 1951, publishes quarterly papers and proceedings; and the Historical Society of South Australia, founded in 1974, publishes an annual journal. With the exception of Tasmania, each of these historical societies is an umbrella organization to which a number of the local and special interest historical societies within the State is affiliated with varying degrees of formality, e.g. in 1983 191 historical societies within NSW were affiliated with the Royal Australian Historical Society; at the start of 1984 170 similar societies within Victoria were affiliated with the Royal Victorian Historical Society. These societies publish newsletters and other material; similarly, the umbrella organizations publish regular bulletins as well as journals and in some cases other publications of historical interest, e.g. the Royal Australian Historical Society has published the early journals of David Collins, John Hunter and Watkin Tench. Apart from the State historical societies, there are history teachers' associations in most States and an academic organization, the Australian Historical Association, which was formed in 1973.

Although State and professional historical associations were not established until the twentieth century, their *de facto* predecessors were a number of nineteenth-century cultural and scientific bodies with historical interests, e.g. the activity of the SA branch of the Royal Geographical Society of Australasia partly explains the late formation of the Historical Society of South Australia. There have been many figures significant in Australian history associated with the State historical societies; among figures significant in Australia literature and literary history are David Scott Mitchell, Sir John Ferguson, Malcolm Ellis, Colin Roderick and George Mackaness in NSW, Alfred Deakin and Geoffrey Blainey in Victoria, Thomas Welsby in Queenland, Sir Paul Hasluck in WA and E. Morris Miller in Tasmania.

History of Australian Children's Literature, A, by H.M. Saxby, was published in two volumes, (1841–1941) in 1969 and (1941–1970) in 1971. The history surveys dominant themes in Australian books for children, attitudes towards the family, fantasy, responses to nature, the Aboriginal culture and Australian myths and historical events. A section is included on children's library services, publishing, editing and reviewing, and the work of the Children's Book Council. The second volume includes supplementary chapters by Marjorie Cotton on books for very young children.

History of Australian Drama, A, by Leslie Rees (q.v.) published in two volumes, is an expansion of his earlier work, *Towards an Australian Drama* (1953). The first volume, originally titled *The Making of Australian Drama: A Historical and Critical Survey from the 1830s to the 1970s*, appeared in 1973 and in a revised edition in 1978 when the second volume, titled *Australian Drama in the 1970s: A Historical and Critical Survey*, was published. The standard history, it covers stage, radio and television drama, commercial and little theatres, repertory groups, theatrical societies, and the role of the universities, government subsidization and censorship, as well as critical appraisals of the work of individual playwrights. Both volumes contain informative appendices.

History of Australian Literature, A, by H.M.
Green (q.v.), was published in two volumes in
1961. Apart from a few anomalies and a final
chapter which summarizes 'The Last Ten Years',
the history covers work from 1789 to 1950.
Divided into four periods ending roughly in
1850, 1890, 1923 and 1950, the work is further
divided within each period into 'pure literature'
and 'applied literature'. In the first category
Green discusses verse, fiction, drama, essays,
criticism, scholarship, oratory and magazines;
in the second he discusses, less intensively,
histories, descriptive and biographical works,
works on law, science, economics, politics, anthropology, psychology, philosophy, geography,
education and religion and finally newspapers.
In his preface Green stresses that 'a double
standard has been definitely and deliberately
maintained', works that are of 'value ... to
Australian literature' having been included that
a history of world literature would have ignored.

Hits! Skits! and Jingles! see **GOODGE, W.T.**

HOARE, BENJAMIN (1842–1932), born
Buckinghamshire, England, arrived in Australia
in 1856. After founding and editing the *Evening Times* and *Evening Star* in Geelong (1871,
1879) he joined the editorial staff of the
Melbourne *Daily Telegraph* in 1886; he was
leader-writer for the *Age* 1890–1914. Active in
Catholic affairs, he helped found the *Catholic
Magazine* in 1888. He published poetry including *The Maori* (1869) and *Figures of Fancy*
(1869); essays on political and economic subjects, e.g. *Preferential Trade* (1904) and the
pro-British *War Things That Matter* (1918);
literary essays and reminiscences, e.g. *Looking
Back Gaily* (1927); and a political drama, *Poll-
ing Day: Or, Wooed and Won* (1883). His work
reflects sincere if naive ideas and strong religious convictions.

Hobart, the capital of Tasmania (q.v.), was
settled in 1804 when a party under David
Collins established a camp on the Derwent river
estuary some twenty kilometres from the open
sea and across the Derwent from Risdon, where
the first British settlement had been made in
September 1803. The primary motive for a
British presence in Tasmania, then Van Diemen's Land, was to establish sovereignty over
the island and to protect the sea routes through
Bass Strait, which separates Tasmania from con-
tinental Australia. Hobart Town, as Hobart was
originally called ('Hobarton' was another nineteenth-century usage) was proclaimed a city in
1842, when the ecclesiastical diocese of Tasmania was established, was granted municipal

government in 1852, and was incorporated in
1857; in 1881 its name was officially changed
to Hobart. Peter Bolger's *Hobart Town* (1973)
discusses the development and character of the
city in the nineteenth century.

Hobart Town Courier was a newspaper
founded by James Ross (q.v.) in 1827; it supported the lieutenant–governor of Van Diemen's Land, George Arthur (q.v.), and was
thus in opposition to the anti-Arthur journals,
notably the *Colonial Times* (q.v.). The *Hobart
Town Courier*, which began publication after
the pro-Arthur *Hobart Town Gazette* (q.v.)
ceased to function as a newspaper, was edited
by Ross until 1837, when it was taken over
by William Gore Elliston. In 1859 the *Hobart
Town Courier* was incorporated in the *Mercury*.

Hobart Town Gazette was founded by Andrew Bent (q.v.) in 1816 and for some years
was the official newspaper of the colony of Van
Diemen's Land. In 1824 and 1825 it carried
criticisms of Lieutenant–Governor George Arthur by R.L. Murray and Evan Thomas which
led to Bent's prosecution for libel. Arthur pirated the title of Bent's newspaper for his own
government organ, which was run conjointly
by James Ross and George Terry Howe (q.v.),
so from June to August 1825 two *Hobart Town
Gazettes* were published with the same volume
and serial numbers. Bent changed his *Gazette*
to the *Colonial Times and Tasmanian Advertiser*
(q.v.) 19 August 1825; Arthur's *Gazette* ceased
to function in newspaper form in October
1827, when it became the Tasmanian government gazette.

Hobart Town Magazine was the first Tasmanian literary journal and ran for eighteen
monthly issues, the first titled the *Hobart Town
Monthly Magazine*, in 1833–34. It was edited
by Henry Melville assisted by Thomas Richards, who were also its most prolific and important contributors. Richards's fiction sketches
contributed to the *Hobart Town Magazine* were
among the first short stories published in Australia.

Hobart Town Punch, see ***Melbourne Punch***

HODGMAN, HELEN (1945–), born Tasmania, left school at fifteen, has worked at a
variety of occupations and has lived in London
and Vancouver. She has written two novels,
Blue Skies (1976) and *Jack and Jill* (1978),
both of which have been praised as incisively-
expressive reflections of contemporary female
experience of Australia. *Jack and Jill* won the
1979 Somerset Maugham Prize.

HODGSON, C.P. (CHRISTOPHER PEMBERTON) (1821–65), born Hertfordshire, England, was in Australia 1839–45 when he engaged in squatting and pastoral activities in southern Queensland and was briefly involved with Ludwig Leichhardt's 1844–45 expedition to Port Essington. On his return to England he published *Reminiscences of Australia with Hints on the Squatter's Life* (1846) and in 1849 a book of verse, *The Wanderer*, and a travel book, *El Ydaiour*, in both of which there are references to Australia.

HOGAN, J.F. (JAMES FRANCIS) (1855–1924), born County Tipperary, Ireland, came to Australia in 1856. He became a teacher then turned to journalism, being sub-editor of the *Victorian Review* before joining the *Argus*. In 1887 he went to England, became a member of the House of Commons, and returned to Australia for only a brief visit in 1901. Hogan's publications include *An Australian Christmas Collection* (1886), a selection of his own stories; *The Irish in Australia* (1887), his assessment of the Irish contribution to the development of Australia; *The Australian in London and America* (1889); *The Lost Explorer* (1890, on Ludwig Leichhardt); *The Convict King* (1891, on Jorgen Jorgenson); *Robert Lowe, Viscount Sherbrooke* (1893); *The Sister Dominions* (1896); and *The Gladstone Colony* (q.v., 1898).

HOGUE, OLIVER ('TROOPER BLUEGUM') (1880–1919), born Sydney, was a journalist with the *Sydney Morning Herald* before enlisting as a trooper in the Sixth Light Horse regiment. He soon gained a commission and served at Gallipoli and in the desert campaigns; he survived the war only to die in the influenza epidemic in England in 1919. As 'Trooper Bluegum' he wrote articles for the *Sydney Morning Herald* which were collected in two books, both published in 1916, *Love Letters of an Anzac* and *Trooper Bluegum at the Dardanelles*. He also wrote *The Home-Sick Anzac and Other Verses* (1918) and a work of fiction, *The Cameliers* (1919).

HOLBURN, MUIR (1920–60), born Sydney, was a journalist with the NSW public service 1947–59; he was president of the NSW branch of the FAW in 1948–50. Although well known as a poet, he did not publish a volume of poetry; with his wife Marjorie Pizer, he edited *Creeve Roe* (q.v., 1947).

HOLDSWORTH, PHILIP (1851–1902), born Sydney, was a public servant and member of the literary coterie of Sydney in the second half of the nineteenth century. He was editor of the *Illustrated Sydney News* in the 1880s, a con-

tributor to the *Bulletin, Freeman's Journal* and *Athenaeum*, and a founding member of the Athenaeum Club. His only published work was *Station Hunting on the Warrego* (1885), the first poem a long account of a search by two pioneers for pastures for their flocks. He wrote a biographical note to *Poems of Henry Kendall* (1886), edited by Alexander Sutherland.

Hollow Woodheap, The, see 'FORREST, DAVID'

HOLMAN, ADA (1869–1949), born Ballarat, Victoria, as Ada Kidgell, entered journalism in the 1890s, contributing as 'Myee' a Sydney letter to *Melbourne Punch*; she also wrote for the *Sydney Mail* and *Sydney Morning Herald* under her own name and as 'Marcus Malcolm' and 'Nardoo'. In 1901 she married the politician, W.A. Holman (q.v.), but continued to write, sometimes ghosting for her husband. Her publications include travel articles for the *Daily Telegraph* later published as *My Wander Year* (1912); the political novel, *Sport of the Gods* (1921): children's fiction, *Little Miss Anzac* (1917), *The Adventures of Woodeny* (1923) and *Elka Reva-Ree* (1928); several plays, including 'Annabel Goes to a Party', 'Mrs Milligan Seeks Her Ideal', 'The Premier's Wife' (1936), 'The Six Queens' and 'The Three Little Dears' (1932); and an autobiography, *Memoirs of a Premier's Wife* (1947). Her strong feminist beliefs are present in 'The Premier's Wife'.

HOLMAN, W.A. (WILLIAM ARTHUR) (1871–1934), born London, came to Australia in 1888. He soon interested himself in the organization of the NSW Labor Party, and was elected to parliament in 1898 as the member for Grenfell. In a State political career that lasted to 1920, he was premier for nearly seven years, 1913–16 as leader of the Labor Party and 1916–20 as leader of the Nationalist Party. A lawyer, Holman delivered the Macrossan lectures at the University of Queensland, published as *Three Lectures on the Australian Constitution: Its Interpretation and Amendment* (1928). His biography, *Australian Labor Leader* by H.V. Evatt, was published in 1940.

HOLT, BLAND (1851–1942), born Norwich, England, as Joseph Thomas Holt, was the son of Clarence Holt, a theatre-manager and actor who had successful seasons in Australia in the 1850s and 1860s. Bland Holt became a professional actor at the age of fourteen and returned to Sydney in 1876 to become one of Australia's foremost actor-managers, leasing the Lyceum Theatre in Sydney and the Theatre Royal in Melbourne. Known as the 'King of Melodrama', he presented mainly English melodramas, rewritten for Australia with sensational effects such as live animals on stage and stunts such as balloon ascents and diving scenes. The most famous melodrama staged by Holt, written for him by Arthur Shirley, was 'The Breaking of the Drought' (1902), which included a realistic bushfire and a drought scene in which crows picked at the bones of dead cattle. One of the first plays to have a contemporary setting, 'The Breaking of the Drought' is also remarkable as an early treatment of the theme of bush versus city life. Other melodramas staged by Holt, many of which he enhanced with his own versatile skills as an actor, included 'Riding to Win' (1901), 'A Desperate Game' (1903), 'The War of Wealth' (1903), 'Beseiged at Port Arthur' (1905) and 'The Great Rescue' (1907).

HOLT, EDGAR (1904–), born England, had a wide-ranging career as a journalist in Brisbane, Sydney and Melbourne before becoming editor of *Smith's Weekly* 1947–50. He published poetry, *Lilacs out of the Dead Land* (1932) and a book of memoirs, *Politics is People* (1969).

'HOLT, GAVIN', see RODDA, PERCIVAL CHARLES

HOLT, JOSEPH (1756–1826), was an Irish Protestant farmer who became embroiled in the rebellion of the United Irishmen in 1798. As a 'general' of the rebels, he led a successful guerilla campaign and only surrendered on condition that he be exiled without trial to NSW. He arrived in Sydney in 1800 and although rearrested in 1800 and 1804 at a time of unrest among the Irish prisoners, he eventually secured a pardon in 1809 and returned to Ireland in 1812. His self-vindicating *Memoirs* (1838), which are a contribution to Australian convict literature (q.v.), include an account of his voyage to Australia on board the *Minerva* and his presence at a celebrated and brutal flogging of two convicts at Toongabbie near Sydney in 1800. The former incident is used by Thomas Keneally in *Passenger* (1979), the latter is recreated by R.D. FitzGerald in his poem 'The Wind at Your Door' (q.v.).

Home is a term, now largely obsolescent, used by Australians of British descent to refer to Great Britain in general and England in particular; it was most prevalent between the discovery of gold and the First World War and reflected, like the term 'Mother Country', which also referred to Great Britain or England and has had a greater longevity, the colonial mentality of many Australians in those times. 'Rolf

Boldrewood''s account of his visit to Britain, *My Run Home* (1897), is one of many examples of its usage.

Home was published as a quarterly, 1920-42. Its art editor was Sydney Ure Smith, its literary editor, Bertram Stevens. Literary contributions included interviews, critical articles, poetry and short fiction.

'Homecoming', a poem by Bruce Dawe (q.v.), published in *Beyond the Subdivisions* (1969), tells of the return to their homelands (both Australia and the USA are suggested) of the bodies of soldiers who died in the Vietnam war. With its deliberate air of casual inhumanity ('they're zipping them up in green plastic bags . . . they're rolling them out of the deep-freeze lockers') the poem brings out the dehumanising effect and wastefulness of war. Its final line, 'they're bringing them home, now, too late, too early', hints at the bitterness and controversy that the Vietnam war engendered.

Homesickness, see **BAIL, MURRAY**

Homestead History, A, see **JOYCE, ALFRED; Shearer in Australian Literature**

Honi Soit, the students' journal of the University of Sydney, began publication in 1929. It carries university news, political, social and literary articles. It has had several significant periods when its influence in the university has been considerable; its editorial staff and contributors include many names that have been significant in Australian literary, political and sporting life. James McAuley wrote for it, 1937–38; Donald Horne was its editor 1941; Neville Wran contributed a column 'Flotsam and Jetsam' in 1946 and was dubbed 'Beachcomber' for his pains; Craig McGregor wrote film and book reviews in 1954; Robert Hughes contributed illustrations in 1956; Clive James wrote prolifically in 1958, including a long (and unfinished) serial, 'The Hand beneath the Table'; Geoffrey Havers wrote an anti-Anzac Day article in 1958 which is said to have inspired Alan Seymour's *The One Day of the Year* (1962). Others associated with *Honi Soit* include A.D. Hope, Bob Ellis, Ken Horler, Mungo MacCallum, Bruce Beresford, Ron Blair, Richard Walsh, Patrick Cook, Nick Enright, Les Murray, Geffrey Lehmann, Geraldine Pascall and Sally McInerney.

HOOKER, PATRICIA was at one time employed in the ABC programme department; she left Australia in the late 1960s to write in

London. Her plays include 'A Season in Hell' (1965), which recreates the personal relationship between the poets Rimbaud and Verlaine; 'Socrates', where the force of truth is ranged against that of malevolence; 'Concord of Sweet Sounds', a study of an ageing concert pianist; 'Twilight of a Hero', about the Biblical father–son pair, David and Absalom; 'The Lotus Eaters' (1964), a drama of industrial relationships on the Queensland wharves; 'George; and 'The Little Woman'.

HOOTON, HARRY (1908–61), born Hampstead, London, migrated to Australia in 1926. Unable to get employment, he wandered widely in Australia, finally settling in Sydney, where he worked for a time as a journalist and became connected with the libertarian group dominated by the philosopher John Anderson (q.v.). An iconoclast who developed a philosophy he called Anarcho-Technocracy, Power Over Things or the Dictatorship of Art, Hooton appears to have had more influence as a witty raconteur than as philosopher or poet, although he had become a minor cult figure in Sydney by the time of his death. He published three collections of poetry, These Poets (1941), Things You See When You Haven't Got a Gun (1943), which includes some prose, and It Is Great To Be Alive (1961); and with A.D. Hope, Garry Lyle and O.M. Somerville contributed to the booklets of verse, No. 1, Number Two and Number Three (1943–48). A film on Hooton's life was made by Arthur and Corinne Cantrill in 1972 and he appears as the poet Mulcahy in Hugh Atkinson's novel, Low Company (1961).

HOPE, A.D. (ALEC DERWENT) (1907–), born Cooma, NSW, the son of a Presbyterian minister, spent most of his childhood in rural NSW and Tasmania. He graduated in 1928 from the University of Sydney, and took up a scholarship at Oxford the same year. Returning to a depressed Australia in 1931, he tried various occupations before becoming lecturer in education at Sydney Teachers' College in 1937, lecturer in English there 1938–44, moved to the University of Melbourne in 1945 and in 1951 was appointed to the chair of English at Canberra University College, later part of the Australian National University. He retired in 1968 to devote himself to poetry, but has continued to lecture and retains a close association with the university as emeritus professor.

Although Hope recognised his poetic vocation early, his work appeared only fugitively until 1955 when his first collection The Wandering Islands (q.v.) was published. His subsequent collections include Poems (1960), A.D. Hope (1963), Collected Poems 1930–1965 (1966,

republished in an expanded form 1972), Selected Poems (1973), A Late Picking (1975), A Book of Answers (1978), The Drifting Continent (1979), Antechinus (1981) and The Tragical History of Dr Faustus (1982). He has also contributed a volume to the Poets on Record series (1972) and a lengthy mock-heroic poem, Dunciad Minor (q.v., 1970). A selection of his verse has been translated into Italian by G. Distesano, titled Tre Volti Dell'Amore (1983). A major figure in Australian critical work since the late 1940s, he has published several collections of essays: The Cave and the Spring (1965), Native Companions (1974), The Pack of Autolycus (1978) and The New Cratylus (1979); a study of Judith Wright (1975); a brief survey of Australian literature from 1950–62 (1963); a scholarly, imaginative study of a sixteenth-century poem by William Dunbar, A Midsummer Eve's Dream (1970); and a variety of smaller monographs on aspects of literature. The international recognition that Hope's poetry has won is reflected in the diversity of his awards which include, among others, the Britannica–Australia Award (1965), the Myer Award (1967), the Levinson prize for poetry (Chicago, 1968), the Ingram Merrill Award, New York (1969), and the Robert Frost Award (1976). He was made OBE in 1972 and AC in 1981.

The distinctive note of Hope's poetry, authoritative, measured, rich in literary, biblical and mythological allusion and adhering to traditional rhythms and forms, led to his being classed at first as 'classic', 'academic' or 'intellectual'. The lack of any identifiable Australian experience, the satiric dismissal of much of modern life, the diversity of his interests and the emphasis on sexual experience bewildered most early readers. Many saw him as principally a satirist, opposed to the cowardice of technocratic man in preferring tame, vicarious, standardized experience. Certainly, rejection of conforming rituals which stifle life's resources of heroism and energy was, and is, a characteristic theme of Hope's verse. Poems such as 'Private Dick', 'The Brides', 'The House of God' and 'Conquistador' are hilarious treatments of the subject; others such as 'A Commination', 'Easter Hymn' and 'Toast for a Golden Age' are more bitter. But, as The Wandering Islands and the later collections reveal, satire is secondary in Hope's work and springs from his persistent concern with the nature of poetry and the serious, even sacred role that he accords it. As his fine poem 'William Butler Yeats' illustrates, he shares Yeats's romantic, heroic conception of the artist. In 'Invocation' he unequivocally describes the poet as one who 'alone' defends 'That darkness out of which our light is won' and celebrates the working of 'the spirit elect' in his own poetry; and in several other poems he has dealt explicitly with the elect role of the poet. Poetry's complementary communal role emerges in his perception of it as 'Celebration', meaning not just 'admiration and delight' but 'an intellectual assent to the causes that make the natural world an order and a system, and an imaginative grasp of the necessity of its processes'. In essays and poems he has described the poet as one with the gift of night-time vision in a world where others see only by day, and as 'a man continually obsessed with a passion for a synoptic view', concerned always to present his subject, 'man in all aspects', 'under the aspect of eternity'. The poem, 'Conversation with Calliope', and the essay, 'The Three Faces of Love', define his conception of the poet's distinctive 'creative way of life', bringing 'new objects of desire into being'.

Hope also sees mythology as playing an indispensable part in this creative reinterpretation; myths embody 'the great commonplaces' that define man's place in the universal order. Yet, as 'An Epistle from Holofernes' affirms, 'myths will not fit us ready made' and 'It is the meaning of the poet's trade/To recreate the fables and revive/In men the energies by which they live'. Frequently he refashions myth for his own purposes: 'Imperial Adam' (q.v.) and 'Paradise Saved' deal playfully with the Edenic myth; 'The End of a Journey' casts a new, bleak light on Ulysses's homecoming; 'The Return of Persephone' elicits sympathy for Dis; and in the 'Coup de Grace' even the story of Red Riding Hood is given an unexpected twist.

If Hope confidently sees the poet's task as sacred, he also presents it as hazardous, painful and even terrifying. In much of his verse regularity of form contrasts with strong emotional content, sensuality with intellectual detachment, but within some poems there is a struggle between opposites that is left unreconciled. Poems such as 'Flower Poem' and 'The Watcher', expressive of the terrors and pain of poetic vision, are balanced by others such as 'Pseudodoxia Epidemica' and 'As Well as They Can', which establish an emotional poise between suffering and achieved insight. Similarly, poems such as 'X-Ray Photograph', 'The Dinner' and 'Rawhead and Bloody Bones', testifying to the horrors of the mind's imaginings, are balanced by others such as 'Argolis', 'The Trophy' and 'On an Engraving by Casserius', which express a more harmonious acceptance of life's dualities. In his essays Hope has expressed his conviction of the poet's negative capability, and some of his finest poems are also his most impersonal: 'The Death of the Bird', 'Man Friday', 'Meditation on a Bone', 'Moschus Moschiferus' and 'On an Engraving by Casserius'. Other striking achievements include 'The Double Looking Glass', a complex, ornate, richly sensual poem, and the simpler 'Ode on the Death of Pius the Twelfth' which celebrates his mature, joyful intuition of a harmonious natural order.

The characteristic duality of his perceptions, both in terms of harmony and ambivalence, is particularly evident in his love poetry. Love is central to his work, and he has not only frequently drawn analogies between the transcending, creative experience of love and that of poetry but also expressed their inter-dependence. 'Chorale', 'The Gateway' and 'The Lamp and the Jar' are his most explicit celebrations of this dependence. Others such as 'Pygmalion', 'The Coasts of Cerigo', 'Fafnir', 'The Damnation of Byron' and 'The Dinner' are more ambivalent expressions of the conflicting pull of delight and revulsion, surrender and freedom.

Most of Hope's discursive critical work reflects his preoccupations as a poet. Witty, original and incisive, his essays in *The Cave and The Spring*, *The New Cratylus* and *The Pack of Autolycus* develop his ideas on the nature and forms of poetry, including an energetic defence of rhyme and poetic modes that have fallen into disuse. Regarding poetry as a damaged 'ecology' of forms, he particularly laments the passing of that 'middle form of poetry' successfully resurrected in much of his own verse. As a trenchant, individual, witty reviewer and unrelenting enemy of the second-rate, he has had a strong influence on Australian critical standards and has often been notoriously and valuably unsettling. *Native Companions* reprints some of his essays and reviews written over four decades.

HOPEGOOD, PETER (1891–1967), born Essex, England, came to Australia in 1924 after serving in the First World War. He worked as a hand on a pearling lugger in Broome and a jackeroo on north-west cattle stations; he then became a journalist and freelance writer. A man-of-action turned mystic, Hopegood became obsessed with myth, attempting to indicate in his verse and in several essays that there are correspondences between the myths of diverse races. In the title poem of his first book of verse, *Austral Pan and Other Verses* (1932), the subject is the eternal, ubiquitous spirit of Pan, known to 'Ovid's ancient rustic clan' in rural Italy two thousand years ago and equally present in the Australian bush today – 'his steps outback with glee are bent/He sniffs the saltbush with content'. Hopegood's echo of the vitalism of the time, and his link with the contemporary vision of poets such as Hugh McCrae, Kenneth Slessor and the Lindsays are evident. His second book of verse,

Thirteen from Oahu (1940), sees him chiefly in the role of myth interpreter. Oahu is the Hawaiian Place of the Setting Forth for Hawaiki, the Isles of the Blessed. Regeneration is the central theme and the poems are accompanied by copious explanatory notes, the notes often being more effective and interesting than the poems they illustrate. His chief poetic work, *Circus at World's End* (1947), is prefaced by an essay which sets out his poetic/philosophic theory; at the heart of all the myths of the diverse races of the world and of all literature and psychoanalytic theory there is a single underlying concept of earth consciousness, the union of earth and man. Hopegood said that his poems in *Circus at World's End* were 'written in emulation of the skill of the mythmakers' and especially the makers of the traditional ballads. That Hopegood can write effectively in the medieval ballad style is illustrated in 'Swastika Stepmother' which echoes the Scottish 'Lord Randal' but is translated from the German traditional ballad, 'Die Stiefmutter'. By adding the word 'swastika' to the title, Hopegood allows the poem to become a reflection on the contemporary German people. *Snake's-eye View of a Serial Story* (1964), Hopegood's first collection for seventeen years, sees him still using myth, from Australian ballad to Maori legend and Scots pibroch. As always, it is the simplest and least pretentious of his verse that is the most effective. Acknowledged by his contemporaries as a significant poet, Hopegood has been roundly attacked for the obscurity of his major poetry; friend and fellow poet, R.D. FitzGerald, believes that he sacrifices his artistic integrity to his mystical preoccupations. Hopegood published the autobiographical *Peter Lecky by Himself* in 1935, 'Lecky' being the pseudonym he adopted in an earlier literary competition.

Hopeton High, see 'JAMES, BRIAN'

HOPGOOD, ALAN (1934–), born Launceston, is a well-known stage and television actor, and has written several plays: *And the Big Men Fly* (1969), a popular comedy about Australian Rules football first produced in 1963; *The Golden Legion of Cleaning Women* (1979), first produced in 1964; 'Private Yuk Objects', a play about the impact of the Vietnam war on Australian society, first produced in 1966; 'Terribly, Terribly' (1968), a black comedy first produced in Los Angeles in 1967 and in Australia in 1979; and *And Here Comes Bucknuckle* (1980), a sequel to *And the Big Men Fly* and a television serial. Hopgood has also written film scripts and plays for television, one of which, 'The Cheerful Cuckold', won an Awgie award in 1968.

HOPKINS, F.R.C. (FRANCIS RAWDON CHESNEY) (1849–1916), born Bombay and educated in England, came in 1865 to Victoria, where he managed various stations, eventually purchasing his own. His plays, all adapted from European works, were very successful, largely due to their production by Alfred Dampier. They include 'Good for Evil' (first performed 1876, published 1875 with the title *Clay and Porcelain*), 'All for Gold' (first performed 1877), 'Only a Fool' (first performed 1880), '£ S D' (first performed 1882) and 'Michael Strogoff', later titled 'Russia As It Is' (first performed 1882). He also edited the *Australian Ladies Annual* (1878); wrote a book of verse *Gum Leaves Old and Gum Leaves New* (1902); and published two collections of short stories with Australian settings (1908, 1909). His later play, *Reaping the Whirlwind*, published anonymously in 1909, was intended to alert Australians to what he saw as the Asiatic menace.

HOPKINS, LIVINGSTON YORK ('HOP') (1846–1927), born Ohio, USA, was best known as the cartoonist, 'Hop', for the *Bulletin* (q.v.). He served in the American Civil War, and worked mainly in New York as a freelance designer and cartoonist until 1882, when his services were secured for the *Bulletin* by W.H. Traill. He arrived in Australia soon after and was joined by Phil May with whom he contributed much to the spread of the *Bulletin's* popularity and prosperity. Hopkins remained with the *Bulletin* and eventually became a director; his prodigious output has been estimated at 19 000 drawings. His best-known cartoons include those on the Sudan War and Federation and the caricatures of Sir Henry Parkes, Sir George Reid and other public figures. His interpretation of the politicians and the regular appearance of his symbolic figures such as The Little Boy from Manly (q.v.) and a host of allegorical animals did much to explain the economic, political, racial and cultural policies of the *Bulletin*, particularly before Federation. In 1880 he prepared *A Comic History of the United States* and in 1904 published *On the Hop*, a selection of his Australian work. In 1929 his daughter, Dorothy, published the biographical tribute, *Hop of the 'Bulletin'*.

HORNE, DONALD (1921–), born Muswellbrook, NSW, was educated at the University of Sydney, where he was strongly influenced by John Anderson (q.v.), became friendly with A.D. Hope, Harold Stewart, Oliver Somerville and James McAuley, and edited *Honi Soit* for a brief period. He served in the AIF 1941–44, was a cadet in the diplomatic service 1944–45 and a reporter for the Sydney *Daily Telegraph* 1945–49. After visiting Britain 1950–54, he returned to become involved in a variety of editorial work. He edited *Weekend* (1954–61), the *Observer* (1958–61), *Everybody's* (1961–62), and the *Bulletin* (1961–62 and 1967–72). He was also co-editor of *Quadrant* (1963–66) and contributing editor to *Newsweek International* (1973–76). In 1973 he began an academic career at the University of NSW.

In the 1960s Horne was in the forefront of the politically-conservative polemicists and was a member of the executive of the Australian Association for Cultural Freedom 1962–66. In 1972 he became an ardent supporter of the Labor government, however, and has been one of the most outspoken critics of its dismissal in 1975. As well as innumerable essays, reviews and articles he has written several works of social and political comment: *The Lucky Country* (q.v., 1964, 2nd revised edn 1968); *God Is an Englishman* (1969), a study of British society; *Money Made Us* (1976), an analysis of materialist propensities in Australian society; *The Next Australia* (1970), an examination of changes in social and cultural attitudes, in the economy, the political system and foreign policy; *Death of the Lucky Country* (1976), an account of the 1975 political crisis from a Labor perspective; *Time of Hope* (1980), a study of changes in Australian society 1966–72; and *Winner Take All?* (1981), an examination of the issues facing Australia after the 1980 election. He has also written a social history, *The Australian People* (1972); a portrait of W.M. Hughes, *In Search of Billy Hughes* (1979) which won the Con Weickhardt Award for 1979; three novels, *The Permit* (1965), *But What If There Are No Pelicans?* (1971) and *His Excellency's Pleasure* (1977); an account of his travels in Australia, *Right Way, Don't Go Back* (1978); and an autobiography, *The Education of Young Donald* (q.v., 1967). He also provided the text for *Southern Exposure* (1967), a collection of unusual Australian photographs by David Beal. Already familiar to readers of the *Bulletin* and the *Observer* as a writer of witty, provocative articles, Horne sprang into general prominence with the publication of *The Lucky Country*. One of the first of a series of critiques of Australian society in the 1960s, it aroused so much interest that its title has become familiar usage, frequently adopted by politicians and others without regard to Horne's intended ironies. Central to the book and a continuing preoccupation in Horne's work is the thesis that Australia is a derivative and provincial society, obsessed with material pursuits at the expense of excellence in any field except sport. In his later books, and especially in *The Next Australia*, Horne has extended and changed some of the opinions and conclusions of *The Lucky Country*. His novels reveal a versatile talent;

The Permit, a slapstick comedy, deals with the absurdities of officialdom, the political sphere and the press; *His Excellency's Pleasure* satirizes the institution of the governor-general in Australia; *But What If There Are No Pelicans?*, part-allegory, part-fantasy, explores human nature and the possibilities of faith in humanity. Horne's most striking literary achievement, however, is his autobiography. A dispassionately honest study of the artist as child and young man, and an authentic representation of Australian lower middle-class society in the 1930s, it is important both as a social document and a work of literature. In 1982 he was made AO.

HORNE, R.H. (RICHARD HENRY) (1802–84), who in 1867 substituted 'Hengist' for his second name, was born Edmonton, near London, and became devoted to the idea of a poetic career after reading Shelley's *Queen Mab*. He became a literary celebrity through his successful editorship of the *Monthly Repository*, and the triumph of his epic poem *Orion* (1843), which ran to six printings in its first year, causing him to be later dubbed 'Orion' Horne. In 1852 he came to Australia, partly to escape a dramatic decline in his personal situation, partly to restore his fortunes on the Australian goldfields. He held and lost minor administrative positions on the Victorian diggings, failed to win election to the Victorian parliament, was briefly and unsuccessfully a commissioner for Melbourne's sewerage and water supply, and drifted, often unemployed, until 1863 when he was made warden of the Blue Mountain goldfield near Trentham in Victoria. There he returned to serious writing. In 1864 *Prometheus the Fire-Bringer*, a lyrical drama, was published and in 1866 he wrote, for the Intercolonial Exhibition of Australasia, *The South Sea Sisters, A Lyric Masque*, which contains his poetic version of an Aboriginal corroboree. Restored to literary prestige and influence he was an important member of the Melbourne literary circle, centred on the Yorick Club. He returned to England in 1869, continuing to write profusely but unprofitably. Horne's Australian writings, except for his prose work *Australian Facts and Prospects* (1859), were of little significance in themselves but the presence in the colony of such an established literary figure as he did much to bolster the respectability of the literary profession in the hitherto sceptical colonial mind and acted as a stimulus to such rising literary talents as Henry Kendall, Adam Lindsay Gordon and Marcus Clarke. Biographical works include Cyril Pearl's *Always Morning: The Life of Richard Henry 'Orion' Horne* (1960) and Anne Blainey's *The*

Farthing Poet (1968). Barry Oakley's play, *The Ship's Whistle* (1979) focuses on Horne.

Hornet Bank Massacre, in which the Fraser family was murdered by Aborigines, occurred at Hornet Bank station on the Dawson River in the Burnett district of Queensland in October 1857. The event has echoes in some of the writings of Rosa Praed, especially in *Australian Life: Black and White* (1885), *My Australian Girlhood* (1902) and *Fugitive Anne* (1902). *The Cry for the Dead* (1981) by Judith Wright deals in detail with the invasion of the north by the white man's cattle stations which provoked the massacre and includes an account of it. *A Nest of Hornets* (1982) by Gordon Reid is the first full account of the massacre itself, its causes and consequences.

HORNUNG, E.W. (ERNEST WILLIAM) (1866–1921), born Middlesborough, England, was in Australia 1884–86. He spent most of his life in England and France, where he became a well-known literary figure, a prolific writer of popular romance, crime and mystery fiction. His brief Australian experience is reflected in a number of his novels: *A Bride from the Bush* (1890), said to have been begun while he was a tutor at Mossgiel station in the Riverina, reflects the contrast between the cold formality of upper-class English life and the warm open-heartedness of outback Australian life; *Tiny Luttrell* (1893) is similarly in favour of the colonial environment; *Denis Dent* (1903) is partly set on the diggings at Ballarat; and *The Boss of Taroomba* (1894) contains incidents of station life and bushranging. Other bushranging figures are in *Irralie's Bushranger* (1896) and *The Belle of Toorak* (1900); *The Rogue's March* (1896) is set in the convict period. Hornung is also well known as the creator of Raffles, the polished gentleman burglar whose exploits begin in Australia and fill many of his tales, and were carried on by Barry Perowne after Hornung's death. Of particular interest to Australian readers is Hornung's love of cricket, evident especially in his short stories, major collections of which are *Under Two Skies* (1892), *Some Persons Unknown* (1898) and *Old Offenders and a Few Old Scores* (1923).

Horse of Air, A, see STIVENS, DAL

Horseracing, see Turf

Hostages, see ZWICKY, FAY

HOULDING, J.R. (JOHN RICHARD) (1822–1918), born Essex, England, worked in a lawyer's office both in London, where he was supposed to have met Charles Dickens, and in Sydney where he arrived in 1839. A country storekeeper for most of the 1840s, he sold out in 1852 and visited England in 1854. The loss of his modest fortune on his return to Sydney in 1855 led to a nervous collapse and to the commencement, while convalescing, of a writing career which lasted until his retirement in the 1890s. Houlding's first novel, *Australian Capers* (q.v., 1867) published under the pseudonym 'Old Boomerang', chronicles the colonial experiences of a new chum (q.v.), Christopher Cockle. Informed by Houlding's own experiences of sharp Sydney businessmen, *Australian Capers* also reflects his Methodist and temperance beliefs, and benefited in the preparation from the advice of the Sydney literary patron, N.D. Stenhouse. As 'Old Boomerang' or as 'J.R.H. Hawthorn', the most popular of his several pseudonyms, Houlding published six further novels, *Rural and City Life* (1870), *Investing Uncle Ben's Legacy* (1876), *The Pioneer of a Family* (1881), *Launching Away* (1882), *In the Depths of the Sea* (1885), *A Flood That Led on to Fortune* (1886), and *Australian Tales, and Sketches from Real Life* (1868), a selection of his contributions to the *Sydney Mail*. Strongly moralist in tone, his instructional tales became popular as Sunday school prizes but *Australian Capers* in particular is redeemed by its interest as an example of the guide book genre of fiction; by the vividness of some of its scenes based on Houlding's perceptive observation of Australian life; and by its humour, in which exaggerated metaphor, the use of dialect and puns, and the presentation of immigrant and colonial types are important ingredients.

House Is Built, A, a novel by 'M. Barnard Eldershaw' (q.v.), shared first prize in the *Bulletin*'s novel competition of 1928. After serialization in the *Bulletin* as 'The Quartermaster' it was published in London in 1929, was produced as a play in 1954 after dramatization by Eunice Hanger and has continued to be popular in England, the USA and Australia. Set in Sydney from the 1830s to the 1880s, it deals with the fortunes of the family of James Hyde. A quartermaster in the Royal Navy, Hyde decides at the age of fifty to set up in the supply business on Sydney's waterfront. He is joined by his two daughters, Fanny, practical, energetic and serious-minded, and Maud, vivacious, beautiful and gregarious, and by his son William, conventional, reserved and priggish. Thanks to the indomitable and innovative energies of the quartermaster and the growing business sense of William, the family's fortunes thrive. Fanny is disappointed in her love for a whaling captain, Hildebrand, but Maud elopes with the son of one of Sydney's wealthiest families, the Gillams, and is soon happily absorbed in her role of wife and mother. William is eventually joined by his English fiancée of five years, Adela Gage, and becomes the father of two temperamentally-different sons, James, an apparent replica of his grandfather, and Lionel, less robust and artistic. Adela, who has been keenly disappointed in her romantic expectations of William, has more affinity with Lionel than with James. When the gold rushes of the 1850s provide even greater opportunities for the supply business, the quartermaster sets out for the diggings himself and Fanny finds her true vocation in administration of the waterfront store. Later, only Adela's near-death from scarlet fever takes Fanny away from her work, and William's conventional notions prevent her from returning. Embittered, she finds a partial refuge in genteel charity work. Established as one of Sydney's prominent families, the Hydes move to a mansion at Hunter's Hill and James prepares for his role as head of the business. At twenty he falls in love with the volatile Laurel Franklin, the daughter of a business rival. Trapped by Laurel into betraying a business secret and unable to confess his crime to Adela, he takes to his small boat and is drowned in a storm. His death, following closely on private news of his disloyalty, causes the immediate collapse of the quartermaster and he dies after two years of mute paralysis. Although Adela is able to keep the fact of James's betrayal from William, the loss of his son contributes to his early death. Lionel loyally but unenthusiastically takes up the business and after the death of Adela marries the quiet, undemanding Mary Bardon.

HOVELL, W.H. (WILLIAM HILTON) (1786–1875), born Yarmouth, England, was captain of a vessel trading to South America before settling on the land in Australia after 1813. His explorations in 1824 with Hamilton Hume (q.v.) from the Goulburn district of NSW to Corio Bay in Port Phillip led to the discovery of the Murray River and the pastoral expansion of the Colony. In an ensuing public controversy between the two explorers over the 1824 expedition, Hovell's point of view is given in *Reply to 'A Brief Statement of Facts'* (1855). A character, Captain Travers, in Edward Maitland's novel *The Pilgrim and the Shrine* (1867), is based on Hovell.

'How He Died', the title poem of John Farrell's (q.v., 1887) volume of bush ballads, is a sentimental tale of the station boozer Nabbage, who gives his life to save his 'little mate', the squatter's boy Freddie. It was published first in the *Bulletin*, 1883.

'How McDougall Topped the Score', the title poem of T.E. Spencer's (q.v.) 1906 collection of verse, is the story of the historic cricket match between Piper's Flat and Molongo. When challenged by Molongo to a single-innings match, the loser to pay for a slap-up lunch at McGinnis's pub, Piper's Flat can only muster ten players. They reluctantly recruit the old Scotsman, McDougall, from nearby Cooper's Creek to make up the number. Molongo are dismissed for sixty-six and when Piper's Flat in reply are nine wickets down for seventeen, McDougall marches to the crease. He hits the first ball gently back towards the bowler and in response to his command, 'Fetch It', his aptly-named old sheep-dog Pincher seizes the ball and makes off, with the whole Molongo team in wrathful but vain pursuit ('brain the mongrel with a bat'). McDougall, meanwhile, begins his initially swift but eventually ponderous and painful but successful pursuit of the fifty runs needed for victory:

> Then Pincher dropped the ball, and, as instinctively he knew
> Discretion was the wiser plan, he disappeared from view
> And as Molongo's beaten men exhausted lay around
> We raised McDougall shoulder high, and bore him from the ground.

Both sides then repair to McGinnis's to celebrate with 'whisky-punch' the historic occasion when 'McDougall topped the score'. Spencer's poem celebrates the bushman's talents for devising ingenious but essentially harmless methods of besting a rival; it takes its place alongside A.B. Paterson's accounts of the stratagems of drovers to outwit squatters and of racehorse owners and jockeys to outwit bookmakers.

How I Became Attorney General of New Barataria, see DENIEHY, D.H.

HOWARD, CAMPBELL, see Campbell Howard Collection of Australia's Plays in Manuscript

HOWARD, FREDERICK (1904–), born London, came to Australia in 1920, entered journalism and was a member of the Melbourne *Herald* staff before and after the First World War. He edited *Stead's Review* 1929–31; his published novels include *The Emigrant* (1928) and *Return Ticket* (1929), which have a romantic theme and an Australian setting.

HOWARTH, R.G. (ROBERT GUY) (1906–74), born Tenterfield, NSW, graduated from the Universities of Sydney and Oxford before being appointed to the English department at the University of Sydney in 1933. In

1955–71 he was professor of English literature at the University of Cape Town, South Africa. Widely acknowledged by contemporaries as one of Australia's finest literary scholars and regarded as an inspiring and encouraging teacher by a generation of literature students at Sydney, Howarth early in his academic career produced several important works on English literature, e.g. *The Letters of George Gordon, Sixth Lord Byron* (1933). He was an active member of the English Association (q.v.) in Sydney and was foundation editor (1939–56) of *Southerly* (q.v.). He served on the advisory board of the CLF 1950–55, was a foundation member of the Australian Humanities Research Council, and in 1952 was elected a fellow of the Royal Society of Literature. An enthusiastic advocate of Australian literature, he edited Hugh McCrae's *Forests of Pan* (1944) and *The Best Poems of Hugh McCrae* (1961), and collaborated with John Thompson and Kenneth Slessor in *The Penguin Book of Australian Verse* (1958). His editing of the letters of Norman Lindsay was completed after his death by A.W. Barker, who published them in 1979. Howarth's poetry appeared in the collection *Spright and Geist* (1944), a series of epigrammatic love poems, *Involuntaries* (1948) and *Nardoo and Pituri* (1959); many of his essays on literature are included in his *Literary Particles* (1946).

HOWE, GEORGE (1769–1821), the first important government printer in Australia, was born in the West Indies and apprenticed there to the printing trade. He went to London in 1790, worked on the *Times* and other newspapers, and was transported for shoplifting in 1799. He became government printer soon after his arrival in Sydney in 1800 and 1802 issued the first book printed in Australia, *New South Wales General Standing Orders*. In 1803 he began publication of the *Sydney Gazette* (q.v.); other publishing initiatives in which he was involved were the natural history and art book, *Birds of New South Wales*, (1813), Barron Field's *First Fruits of Australian Poetry* (1819) and a series of early almanacs (q.v.). Conditionally pardoned in 1803 and fully emancipated in 1806, Howe was successful in commerce. Two of his sons, Robert and George Terry Howe (qq.v.), followed him into printing and publishing.

HOWE, GEORGE TERRY (1806–63), born Sydney, a son of the pioneer Sydney pressman George Howe, came to Van Diemen's Land in 1821 and in 1825 founded the first newspaper in Launceston, the *Tasmanian and Port Dalrymple Advertiser*. Later that year he moved his press to Hobart to join James Ross in produc-

ing the *Hobart Town Gazette* (q.v.). After the partnership was dissolved in 1827, Howe re-established the *Tasmanian* in Hobart before returning to Sydney.

HOWE, JACK (?1861–1920), born Killarney near Warwick in Queensland, began work as a shearer in the 1870s. In 1892 he established a world record tally when he shore 321 sheep in eight hours with blade shears; he was equally expert with machine shears when they gained a wider usage. He retired from shearing to become a publican in 1900, and was active also in the union movement. A man with huge hands whose shearing feats were legendary, Howe is mentioned in several shearers' songs (e.g. 'Goorianawa') as well as in poems such as Ian Mudie's 'They'll Tell You About Me'. Howe's fame also explains why a 'Jacky (ie) Howe' became established as an Australian colloquialism for a sleeveless flannel shirt of the type worn by shearers and other bush workers.

HOWE, MICHAEL (1787–1818), was a notorious early Tasmanian bushranger (q.v.) who was convicted of highway robbery in York, England in 1811 and transported for seven years. In 1813 he absconded and took to the bush at the head of a gang of desperadoes which terrorised the pioneer settlers of Van Diemen's Land. An amnesty in 1814 led most of the gang to report to the authorities, but by early 1815 Howe had again gathered about him a new well-armed band; martial law was declared and Howe styled himself 'Lieutenant-Governor of the Woods'. In 1817 negotiations between Howe and the *de jure* lieutenant-governor, William Sorell, broke down and he again took to the bush; a year later he was betrayed and clubbed to death near his hut at Shannon River. Cunning, callous, vicious and probably deranged, Howe was the subject of the first non-official book or pamphlet published in Tasmania, Thomas Wells's *Michael Howe, the Last and Worst of the Bush Rangers of Van Diemen's Land*, published in the year of his death. Other early responses to his sensational exploits are a play by J. Amherst advertised in London in 1821 (no copy has survived), and *Van Diemen's Land* (q.v., 1830), 'W.T. Moncrieff''s extravaganza in which the gang is captured at the end of the play and Howe led away to execution. James Bonwick wrote the biographical *Mike Howe, the Bushranger of Van Diemen's Land* (1873), while Hume Nisbet's *The Savage Queen* (1891), Nat Gould's *King of the Ranges* (1902), and Roy Bridges's *On His Majesty's Service* (1914) are works of popular fiction in which Howe appears.

HOWE, ROBERT (1795–1829), born England, was the eldest son of George Howe (q.v.), whom he accompanied to Australia in 1800. From boyhood he assisted in his father's printing office and carried on the business after George Howe's death in 1821. He continued to produce the *Sydney Gazette* and the *New South Wales Pocket Almanack*, renamed the *Austral(as)ian Almanack*, as well as publishing the *Australian Magazine*, the first Australian periodical, and Charles Tompson's *Wild Notes, from the Lyre of a Native Minstrel* (1826), the first book of poems by a native-born poet. After Robert's death, the production of the *Gazette* and the *Almanack* was carried on by his widow, Ann.

HOWITT, ALFRED WILLIAM (1830–1908), the son of William Howitt (q.v.), was born in Nottingham, England, and went with his father to the Victorian goldfields in 1852. In 1859 he explored the Lake Eyre region, and in 1861 he was sent by the Royal Society of Victoria to search for Burke and Wills; he arrived only in time to save King, and returned to Cooper's Creek to bring the bodies of Burke and Wills back to Melbourne for burial. One of the few explorers not to publish his journal, he later wrote prolifically in the fields of natural science and anthropology, e.g. *The Native Tribes of South-East Australia* (1904). His biography, *Come Wind, Come Weather* (1971), was written by his granddaughter, Mary Howitt Walker.

HOWITT, WILLIAM (1792–1879), born Derbyshire, England, was in Australia 1852–54, accompanied by his sons, Alfred and Charlton, exploring the colony and seeking a fortune on the goldfields. The literary results of those experiences were *A Boy's Adventures in the Wilds of Australia* (1854), *Land, Labour and Gold: Or, Two Years in Victoria* (1855), *Tallangetta, the Squatter's Home* (1857), and *The History of Discovery in Australia, Tasmania, and New Zealand* (1865). *Land, Labour and Gold* is one of the most accurate and comprehensive in the popular contemporary travel book genre. Based on Howitt's diaries and a series of forty letters written by him at various places in his two year stay, the book possesses the colour and immediacy of fiction. Howitt was not content, however, with highlighting only the more dramatic aspects of colonial life at the time – cities and towns deserted by the gold fever, raging inflation, the eccentricities of colonial flora, fauna and climate, and the excitement and interest of the Bendigo and Ballarat diggings. He saw it as his duty, at a time when the English parliament was attempting to frame constitutions for NSW and Victoria, to give also a candid and honest exposition of the social and political state of the colonies. After his return to England in 1854 (he ultimately made his home in Rome), Howitt continued an active literary life, he and his wife Mary Botham being credited with some 180 published works; a biography of them, *Laurels & Rosemary* (1955), was written by Howitt's great-niece, Amice Lee. Of less significance in Australian literature was William's younger brother, Richard (1799–1870), who came to Australia in 1840 with a still younger brother, Godfrey, who remained in Australia until his death in 1873, by which time he had become a noted physician, botanist and entomologist. Richard returned to England in 1844 and published, in prose and verse, an account of the colony and his experiences, *Impressions of Australia Felix during Four Years' Residence in That Colony* (1845).

'How's Andy Going?', see **MARSHALL, ALAN**

HUBER, THERESE (1764–1829), born Gottingen, Germany, married Georg Forster who at eighteen had accompanied his father, the naturalist, Johann Reinhold Forster (1729–98), on Captain James Cook's second voyage around the world (1772–75). She later divorced Forster and married Ludwig Ferdinand Huber (1764–1804). Her novel, *Adventures on a Journey to New Holland*, was published in 1801 although it was probably completed in 1793; if so it is perhaps the first novel in world literature that has the Australian penal settlement as its background. *The Lonely Deathbed* (1810) is a continuation of *Adventures on a Journey to New Holland*. German translations of the journals of Arthur Phillip (1789), John White (1790) and John Hunter (1793) by Huber's first father-in-law, Johann Reinhold Forster, and Ludwig Huber's 'New Holland and the British Colony in Botany Bay' (Berlin's *Historical Almanac for the Year 1787*), were the sources for her novel. Basically a story about people caught up in the aftermath of the French Revolution (with a Welsh rebel miner, Henry Belton, giving a British touch to the penal settlement), *Adventures on a Journey to New Holland* gives only a vague picture of the Australian colony. The characteristic features of Australian fauna and flora, staples in early English novels about the colony, are seldom mentioned; the colony itself appears to have been chosen solely because it provided a contrast between the natural virgin setting and its depraved convict inhabitants and was a suitable site for the confrontation between the protagonists, Rudolph, the French ex-revolutionary, and Belton, the Welsh ex-revolutionary, over the whole question of revolution itself.

In her later years Therese Huber attained considerable status in German literary life and was recognized as one of the first professional women writers in German literature. She published numerous short stories and novels, and was editor of the widely-read German newspaper, the *Morgenblatt für gebildete Stände* in Stuttgart. *Adventures on a Journey to New Holland* and *The Lonely Deathbed*, translated by Rodney Livingstone and edited by Leslie Bodi, were republished in one volume in 1966.

HUDSON, FLEXMORE (1913–), born Charters Towers, Queensland, graduated from the University of Adelaide and was a teacher, freelance writer and seaman in the Australian coastal trade. His published poetry includes *Ashes and Sparks* (1937), *In the Wind's Teeth* (1940), *With the First Soft Rain* (1943), *Indelible Voices* (1943), *As Iron Hills* (1944), and *Pools of the Cinnabar Range* (1959). He edited *Poetry*, a quarterly, 1941–47, and the 1943 *Jindyworobak Anthology*; contributed numerous short stories to various periodicals and anthologies; and wrote a book of aesthetics, *The Child Discovers Poetry* (1941).

Involved in the Jindyworobak movement almost from its beginning, Hudson was strongly committed to the unique Australian spirit of place. Unlike Rex Ingamells, however, the Jindyworobak founder, Hudson wished to interpret the Australian environment, firstly in his own individual way, then in more universal terms. He was not willing to visualize the Australian landscape specifically through a pattern of Aboriginal legend ('a good many of us find the Alcheringa myth unpalatable and unprofitable'). His love for the Australian countryside embraced everything from the harshness of the Mallee environment, which produced his much-anthologized 'Drought', to the softer beauty of a Murray River sunrise. That intense affection gives his landscape lyrics warmth and sincerity. Less effective are his Jindyworobakish radical and political homilies, which are prominent in *Indelible Voices* and which mar the effect of individual poems such as 'To a Boy on His Eleventh Birthday'.

HUGHES, BILLY (WILLIAM MORRIS) (1862–1952), born in London of Welsh parents, migrated to Australia in 1884. Following the maritime strike of 1890 he became secretary of the Wharf Labourers' Union, then established and became president of the Waterside Workers' Federation. Elected to the first federal parliament, Hughes later became attorney-general and, in 1915, prime minister. His advocacy of conscription, rejected in national referenda in 1916–17, led to his break with

the Labor Party but he saw the war through as leader of several coalition governments and, from May 1917, as leader of the National Party and prime minister. He forcefully represented Australian interests at the Versailles Peace Conference of 1919, and although his parliamentary fortunes gradually declined thereafter he remained involved in politics until his death. Nicknamed 'The Little Digger' and known widely as 'Billy', Hughes was both idolized and detested in the Australian community. In the heat of the conscription controversies he was the target of derisive songs ('No use for Billy' and 'Billy Hughes's Army'). He was more literally the target for the famous 'Warwick Egg', a putrid missile aimed at him in 1917 in a conscription meeting at Warwick in Queensland. Angered by the local constabulary's refusal to arrest the culprit, Hughes established the Commonwealth police force. With his diminutive stature and aquiline features, Hughes was also the constant target of cartoonists, notably David Low (q.v.). He is the subject of biographies by W. Farmer Whyte (1957), L.F. Fitzhardinge (1964, 1979, two volumes), and Donald Horne (1979 and 1983). Hughes published the autobiographical *Crusts and Crusades* (1947) and *Policies and Potentates* (1950). He appears as a character in the play by Michael Boddy and Bob Ellis, *The Legend of King O'Malley* (1974). Douglas Sladen edited *From Boundary Rider to Prime Minister* (1916), a book of Hughes's speeches.

HUGHES, E.F. (EDWARD FRANCIS) (1814–79), born Kidderminster, England, and who sometimes wrote under the pseudonym 'Frederick Gundase Shaw', published drama, *Bernard: A Drama of the Year 1848* (1859) and poetry, *Portland Bay: A Poem* (1864); *The Millennium: An Epic Poem* (1873), a ten-book work which encompasses the whole scope of biblical history; and *Lays for Thoughtful Workers* (1875). Hughes had earlier (1846) published in London *The Benighted Traveller: A Tale and Other Poems*. He established the Portland *Chronicle* which he edited from its inception in 1855.

HUGHES, ROBERT (1938–), born Sydney, gave up painting at the age of twenty-six 'to write about art authoritatively'. He has since then established an international reputation as art critic and associate editor of *Time* magazine and as television and newspaper commentator on art throughout Europe. His published works include the controversial *The Art of Australia* (1966), *Heaven and Hell in Western Art* (1968), monographs on Caravaggio, Brueghel and the Van Eyck brothers, a biography of

Leonardo da Vinci and a book on Donald Friend. *The Shock of the New* (1980) is based on his successful BBC television series.

Human Toll, a novel by Barbara Baynton (q.v.) published in 1907, depicts the struggles of a bush girl, Ursula Ewart, after she is orphaned and then taken away from the care of Boshy, her father's station hand. She is raised in town by an unloving Mrs Irvine whose nephew, Andrew Cameron, for a time befriends and protects her; after the death of Mrs Irvine, who has married the rapacious minister, Mr Civil, Boshy returns and is nursed by Ursula through his final illness. Afterwards Ursula returns to her bush home with Mina, a German neighbour who has tricked Andrew into marriage and who has a child by Andrew's partner; appalled by Mina's treatment of the baby, Ursula flees with it into the bush. The child dies, and Ursula becomes both lost and delirious; although in the last ambiguous paragraphs of the novel she seems to be rescued by Andrew, another possibility is that she experiences her final hallucination.

Humbug, a satiric illustrated weekly, was published in Melbourne 1869–70; it was edited by Marcus Clarke (q.v.), whose co-proprietor was Garnet Walch. Other contributors included Charles Bright and James Edward Neild.

HUME, FERGUS (1859–1932), born in England, trained as a lawyer in NZ and came to Melbourne in 1885. His ambitions to become a dramatist led him to write a novel to attract the attention of theatre managers. The result was the detective story, *The Mystery of a Hansom Cab* (q.v., 1886), which was an instant success in Australia and a continuing one in England. Hume, however, sold his rights to *The Mystery of a Hansom Cab* soon after publication of the first edition and did not reap any benefit from the many printings of the novel associated with the Hansom Cab Publishing Company in England. In 1888 Hume settled in England, where he published more than 130 additional novels; of these, only *Madame Midas* (1888), its sequel *Miss Mephistopheles* (1890), *Whom God Hath Joined* (1891) and *High Water Mark* (1911) can be classified as Australian in setting, although several others have Australian associations.

HUME, HAMILTON (1797–1873), born Toongabbie near Parramatta, NSW, made several significant journeys of exploration in early colonial times: in 1824 with W.H. Hovell (q.v.) from the Goulburn area of NSW to Corio Bay in Port Phillip, during which they discovered the Murray river, naming it the Hume; and in 1828 with Charles Sturt to the interior of NSW, during which they discovered the Darling river. A controversy between Hume and Hovell over their respective roles in the 1824 expedition led to Hume publishing *A Brief Statement of Facts in Connection with an Overland Expedition from Lake George to Port Phillip in 1824* (1855). William Bland compiled *Journey of Discovery to Port Phillip, New South Wales: By Messrs. W.H. Hovell and Hamilton Hume: in 1824 and 1825* (1831). Jean Prest wrote *Hamilton Hume and William Hovell* (1963) and Alan E.J. Andrews edited *Hume and Hovell 1824* (1981), much of which is devoted to the acrimonious public argument between the two men over their exploits. In 1860 Hume was elected FRGS and spent the latter part of his life as a grazier and magistrate in the Yass district. Joyce Nicholson wrote a fictional account, mainly for children, of Hamilton Hume's explorations, *Our First Overlander* (1956). Hume is commemorated by the Hume highway linking Sydney and Melbourne. Frank O'Grady's novel, *No Boundary Fence* (1964), is based on the life of Hume.

Hummer, see Australian Worker

HUMPHRIES, BARRY (1934–), born Melbourne, was educated at the University of Melbourne, where he appeared in revues. After leaving university he toured Victoria in *Twelfth Night* with Ray Lawler and others, entertaining the company with a party turn in which he impersonated a suburban housewife. Lawler suggested that Humphries incorporate the act into the Melbourne Union Theatre's Christmas revue, and thus in December 1955 Edna Everage (q.v.) made her stage debut in Melbourne. Humphries moved to Sydney, where he established himself as a revue artist with the Phillip Street Theatre. In 1959 he went to England, but before leaving released *Wild Life in Suburbia*, two records of the monologues of Edna and Sandy Stone, the latter a 'decent humdrum little old man' whose character Humphries first created on stage in 1958. Through Edna and Sandy, he satirized the philistinism, emptiness, materialism and pretensions of the Australian suburban middle class.

In England Humphries worked as a theatre and television actor, and in 1962 toured Australia in 'A Nice Night's Entertainment', the first of the one-man shows for which he has become famous. In this, two later shows and several gramophone records of the 1960s Sandy and Edna remained central to Humphries's presentation of national life, but the introduction of other characters widened the satiric coverage of Australian types: for example, Debbie Thwaite, who spends her entire working holiday in England meeting other Australians; Neil Singleton, whose monologues reveal him as a trendy and manipulative academic; Martin Agrippa, a film-maker who has won the coveted Bronze Scrotum at the Helsinki International Experimental Film Biennale; and Buster Thompson, an ex-public school slob who is pub-crawling his way around Europe. Although their social backgrounds are different, Buster is the prototype of Barry (Bazza) McKenzie (q.v.), a character in a comic strip written by Humphries and drawn by Nicholas Garland which was published for over a decade in the English satiric magazine, *Private Eye*. The strip, which focuses on the innocent Bazza's search for sexual satisfaction and his gargantuan capacity for alcohol, cleverly exploits mutual English–Australian prejudices, with the Poms characteristically portrayed as unwashed and avaricious and the Ockers, like Bazza, as unsophisticated vulgarians. Selections from the strip were published in 1968, 1971 and 1979 as well as *The Adventures of Barry McKenzie* (?1973) and *Barry McKenzie Holds His Own* (1974), in which are published the scripts written by Humphries and Bruce Beresford for two McKenzie films (1972, 1974).

By the end of the 1960s Humphries's reputation was firmly established in Australia and abroad; in the next decade that reputation was consolidated, particularly in England, with a further series of one-man shows. In 1971 Sandy 'died' while his wife Beryl was overseas, although he reappeared in Limbo in 1974 and in 1978, reporting on the response to his death. New characters of the 1970s include Lance Boyle, a wheeler-dealing union official, and Sir Les Patterson (q.v.), Australia's cultural ambassador at the Court of St James whose view of the 'Yartz', a common Humphries target, is presented in *Les Patterson's Australia* (1978). Despite these later creations, Humphries has been increasingly identified with Edna Everage, who has evolved from the pretentious, self-opinionated, suburban housewife of 1955 into an outrageous, international superstar. A 'gladdimaniac', made DBE by Gough Whitlam in the second McKenzie film in 1974, eight years before Humphries's own award of AO, she assails her television and stage audiences in two hemispheres, dispenses advice in the *Australian Women's Weekly* and is the author of two books, *Dame Edna's Coffee Table Book* (1976) and *Dame Edna's Bedside Companion* (1982). Under his own name, Humphries has compiled a controversial anthology, *Bizarre* (1965); *The Barry Humphries Book of Innocent Austral Verse* (1968), a collection of 'bad' verse which includes poems of Barcroft Boake, E.J. Brady

and Louise Mack as well as more thoroughly primitive poets; *Barry Humphries' Treasury of Australian Kitsch* (1980); and the important retrospective, *A Nice Night's Entertainment: Sketches and Monologues 1956–1981* (1981). A member of *Quadrant*'s editorial board since 1975, he has conducted 'Pseud's Corner' in that journal.

Much admired by writers such as Patrick White, whose suburban characters have often employed a similar idiom, Humphries has been identified as 'Australia's only true Augustan' and his material described as 'Joyce Grenfell rewritten by Jonathan Swift'. On stage he has been part-satirist, part-caricaturist, and part-music-hall entertainer, sometimes in league with, sometimes antagonistic to, his audience. His creations are defined and exposed by their names, their dress, their possessions and obsessions, and by their argot. As well as finding the precise identifying phrase, e.g. Sandy having a 'bit of strife parking the vehicle', Sir Les nudging his audience 'Ya with me?', Humphries brings a creative imagination to bear on Australian idiom, and probably influenced later playwrights such as Alexander Buzo and David Williamson. In particular some of his phrases, notably the alliterative euphemisms for urination which characterize the speech of Barry McKenzie, have become part of the Australian lexicon. For much of his career Humphries has attacked, with an ambivalent mixture of cruelty and affection, the pretension, self-centredness, prejudices and vulgarity of his imaginary Australian characters, 'accurately based on real people who have never lived'. The most affectionate portrait has been that of Sandy Stone, in whose making Humphries was influenced by Gertrude Stein's *Three Lives* and Samuel Beckett's *Watt*; Sandy's popularity has been attributed to the depth and sympathy of Humphries's characterization, which has helped him tap a rich vein of nostalgia in his audiences.

The cruellest portraits, e.g. Singleton, Boyle, Patterson, the film makers Agrippa and his 1970s descendant, Phil Philby, have led to criticisms that Humphries has become not only increasingly malevolent, e.g. in his jibing at the disadvantaged in society, but also increasingly the misanthropic reactionary, railing against arts grants racketeers (even though he himself was awarded a CLF fellowship in 1970) and deeply suspicious of any progressive movement in Australian politics or culture. Other criticisms include charges that he gives Australians a poor reputation overseas; that Dame Edna's megastar status evinces Humphries's megalomania; that his material has become dated as he has lost touch with Australia, an issue raised in Jack Hibberd's brief sketch, *Breakfast at the Windsor* (*Meanjin*, 1981); and that such definitions

as 'AUSTRALIAN-BASED, a person of diminished aspiration who has been successfully
bribed with grants and awards to resist the lure
of expatriation', reveal him to be the victim of
his own 'cultural cringe'. Nevertheless there is
little doubt about his popularity over more
than two decades with Australian audiences, a
popularity which increased self-awareness among
those audiences, and that abroad he is one of
the best-known Australian figures in the arts.

Humping My Bluey, see McINNES, GRA-
HAM

'Hungerford', a sketch by Henry Lawson, was
published in *While the Billy Boils* (1896) and
later volumes. Informed by Lawson's tramp
from Bourke to Hungerford and back in the
summer of 1892-93, as were other stories such
as 'The Lost Soul's Hotel' and 'Baldy Thompson', 'Hungerford' offers a laconic view of a
desolate town on the NSW-Queensland border, which has an 'interprovincial rabbit-proof
fence - with rabbits on both sides of it'.

HUNGERFORD, T.A.G. (THOMAS AR-
THUR GUY) (1915-), born Perth, WA,
grew up in that city during the 1930s depression and served in the commandos in the Second World War in New Guinea, New Britain
and Bougainville. After the war he went with
the occupation forces to Japan where his novel,
Sowers of the Wind, is set. Back in Australia he
edited the Australian War Memorial's *Stand
Easy* series, writing six of the stories himself.
He then freelanced, writing for the *Bulletin*
and in 1954 joined the Australian News and
Information Bureau, accompanying the Australian Antarctic expedition in 1954-55. He spent
a period as press officer in the New York office
of the Australian Consul-General. After his
resignation from the Bureau in 1967 he travelled in the Far East, then returned to WA,
where he compiled a book on that State titled
A Million Square: Western Australia (1969). In
recent years Hungerford has been a public relations officer for the WA government.

His first book published (third written) is
the war novel, *The Ridge and the River* (1952)
(see War Literature). Based on the Australian
commandos' campaign in Bougainville in the
Solomon Islands, the novel captures the horror,
not only of man fighting against man, which
it does with stark bestiality, but also of man
attempting to survive the intolerable jungle.
Sowers of the Wind (1954) grew out of his
concern for the mistreatment of the Japanese
by the Australian occupying forces after the
war. He believed that they were 'sowing a wind
of hatred for the future'. Their exploitations of

the conquered Japanese, economically and sexually, reveal such a distasteful side to the
character of the young Australian troops that
Hungerford's publishers, Angus & Robertson,
kept *Sowers of the Wind*, written in the late
1940s, back until 1954. Hungerford's two other
novels are *Riverslake* (1953), set in a Canberra
post-war immigration camp and concerned with
the deplorable conditions experienced by European migrants, and *Shake the Golden Bough*
(1963), in which the central character, Charlie
Dangerfield, a handsome drifter loosely modelled on Australian boxer, Tony Madigan,
plays upon his physical charms to win a niche
for himself in the brittle Manhattan society.
Hungerford has also written a collection of
short stories, *Wong Chu and the Queen's Letter-
box* (1977); *Stories from Suburban Road* (1984),
autobiographical fiction based on his childhood
and adolesence; and several radio plays, e.g.
'Help Me Cut Up a Cat' (1972) and 'Looking
After Bert' (1976).

HUNT, HUGH (1911-), born Surrey, England, was educated at Oxford and the Sor-
bonne. Director of the Abbey theatre in Dublin
1935-38, of the Bristol Old Vic 1938-48, and
the London Old Vic 1950-53, he came to
Australia in 1955 as the first executive director
of the Australian Elizabethan Theatre Trust, a
position he held until 1960. In 1961 he became
the first professor of drama at the University
of Manchester. Instrumental in the founding of
the National Institute of Dramatic Art, he also
did much to encourage professional theatre
companies and the staging of Australian plays.
Some of his ideas on drama are expressed in
the second series of Kathleen Robinson lectures
on drama and the theatre at the University of
Sydney, published in 1960 and titled *The Making of Australian Theatre*.

Hunter, Elizabeth, see *Eye of the Storm,
The*

HUNTER, JOHN (1737-1821), born Leith,
Scotland, the son of a shipmaster, went to sea
in 1754. After extensive experience with the
Royal Navy in North America and the West
Indies, he was appointed second-in-command
of the First Fleet and was in command of the
main convoy for part of the journey to Botany
Bay. Following the establishment of the settlement at Port Jackson, Hunter was engaged on
surveying and magisterial duties, and undertook journeys for Governor Arthur Phillip to
the Cape of Good Hope and Norfolk Island,
where he was stranded for almost twelve months
in 1790 after his ship was wrecked. He returned
to England in 1792, published *An Historical*

Journal of the Transactions at Port Jackson and Norfolk Island (q.v.) in 1793 and a year later was appointed as Phillip's replacement. He assumed office in September 1795. During his five years as governor he struggled to retain control of the Colony against the power of the NSW Corps and John Macarthur. Recalled in 1799, he handed over to his successor, Philip Gidley King, in 1800 and returned to England, where he vindicated his conduct in *Governor Hunter's Remarks on the Causes of the Colonial Expense of the Establishment of New South Wales* (1802). Hunter is commemorated by the Hunter River; he appears as a character in Eleanor Dark's *The Timeless Land* (1941) and *Storm of Time* (1948), in Mary Gaunt's *As the Whirlwind Passeth* (1923) and in Catherine Gaskin's *Sara Dane* (1954). B.R. Blaze wrote the biography of Hunter, *Great Scot* (1982).

Hunter River, discovered in 1797 by Lieutenant John Shortland and named after the then governor of NSW, John Hunter, rises in the Mount Royal Range and after flowing south west, then south east, for 470 kilometres, enters the Pacific Ocean at Newcastle. Associated with sheep and cattle raising, thoroughbred horse breeding, coal mining and wine making, the Hunter has also some literary associations. Judith Wright's original ancestor in Australia, George Wyndham, established the homestead Dalwood there, as she indicates in her book, *The Generations of Men* (1962), and in her poem, 'Old House', both of which describe the Hunter environment in pioneer times. Charles Harpur was associated with the Hunter, living at Patrick's Plains (now Singleton) and the village of Jerry's Plains. Much of the early history of the Hunter is in the papers (University of New England) of Henry and Grace Dangar, who established the estate of Neotsfield at Patrick's Plains and were the district's chief pioneering family. See Hunter Valley Poets.

Hunter Valley Poets first emerged as an identifiable literary group with the publishing by Norman Talbot of *XI Hunter Valley Poets + VII* (1966) and the anthology *Hunter Valley Poets* (1973), which presents not only the work of established and lesser-known writers of the region but also a sampling of poetry from schoolchildren. *IV Hunter Valley Poets* (1975) was a first collection from each of four poets of the region, T.H. Naisby, Maureen Bonomini, Denis King and Ross Bennett. T.H. Naisby, more than a poet of a particular place, has also published *The Fabulous Dross* (1979), a second and more expanded collection of verse. Ross Bennett, in addition to publishing another work, *River* (1980), a long poem set mainly in the Upper Allyn, a rainforest area near the Bar-

rington Tops, edited *This Place: Poetry of the Hunter Valley* (1980), an anthology of the prose and poetry of thirty-three writers. Bennett's anthology was accompanied by *The Companion to This Place: Studies in Hunter Valley Poetry and Glossary of Poetic Terms* (1980), which was intended for the valley's secondary school students. *V Hunter Valley Poets* (1978) presents another five first collections, those of Jean Talbot, Christopher Pollnitz, David McQualter, Jess Dyce and Tim McGee. Jean Talbot has also edited *Huntress: Women Poets of the Hunter Valley* (1981) and Norman Talbot and Zeny Giles have edited *Contrast and Relief: Short Stories of the Hunter Valley* (1981). *Riverrun*, a little magazine produced by Keith Russell and Brian Musgrove, published some of the more experimental of the Hunter Valley poets. Ken Stone published *Hunter* (1980), a collection of poems which expresses his affection for the landscape and people of the region.

HUNTINGDON, 'BLIND BILLY', a notable ballad singer in the late 1870s in Sydney, where his favourite position was in George Street on Gowing's Corner, a spot that took its name from the department store of 'Gone to Gowing''s fame. He is mentioned in James Tyrrell's *Old Books, Old Friends, Old Sydney* (1952) and in Randolph Bedford's *Naught to Thirty–Three* (1944).

HURLEY, FRANK (1885–1962), born Sydney, was official photographer to the first Australasian Antarctic Expedition led by Douglas Mawson 1911–13 and in 1914–16 was photographer to the Imperial Trans-Antarctic Expedition. He accompanied the AIF in France in the First World War as an official war photographer with the rank of captain; thereafter he was known as Captain Frank Hurley. He was with Ross and Keith Smith on the Australian section of their England–Australia flight; in 1920 he produced the film of this journey, *The Ross Smith Flight*. Between the wars he filmed in New Guinea and was chief cameraman for Cinesound Productions Limited 1932–36, filming such productions as *The Squatter's Daughter* (1933). In the Second World War he was an official photographer for the AIF. His photographic books on Australia include *Sydney* (1948), *The Blue Mountains and Jenolan Caves* (1952), *Sydney from the Sky* (1952), *Tasmania* (1953), *Western Australia* (1953) and *Australia* (1955). Frank Legg and Toni Hurley wrote the biographical *Once More on My Adventure* (1966).

Hussy, see **Feminism and Australian Literature**

HUTCHINSON, GARRIE (1949–), born Melbourne, was involved with the La Mama writers' workshops and is a freelance journalist and writer. His published poetry includes *Dart Objets: Poured Concrete, 1967–71* (1971), *Nothing Unsayable Said Right: 50 Poems, 1968–72* (1974) and *Terror Australis: Poems* (1975). He has also written several works on sport, including *The Barracker's Bible* (1983, with Jack Hibberd).

HUTCHINSON, GEORGE (1930–), born Sydney, has had several plays produced, e.g.

'My Shadow and Me' (1974), 'Island on the Rocks' (1977) and *No Room for Dreamers*, produced in 1979 and published in 1981. *No Room for Dreamers* received acclaim as the best Fringe play at the 1980 Edinburgh Festival.

Hyde Family, see *House Is Built, A*

Hyde–Shaxton, Paul and Matilda, see *Escape of the Notorious Sir William Heans, The*

I

I Can Jump Puddles, a childhood autobiography by Alan Marshall (q.v.), was first published in 1955. Outstandingly popular both in Australia and overseas, the book has been translated into several languages and was produced as an award-winning film in Czechoslovakia in 1970 and as a television series in Australia in 1981. The story of a young boy's adjustment to paralysis of the legs after contracting polio at the age of six, it is also a vivid picture of Victorian country life between the wars. Particularly memorable are Marshall's portraits of a range of individuals, from the men whom the boy encounters in hospital to the swagmen who pass through the little settlement of Turalla; to Mrs Carruthers, who is rich enough to own an Abbot buggy; to the school children who are both a challenge and a help in his adjustment. These include the stalwart Maggie Mulligan, who on one occasion carries him home in a fireman's lift; Joe Carmichael, with whom Alan hunts for rabbits, and his inconvenient smaller brother, Andy (both also figure in Marshall's short stories); and Freddie Hawk, who is a champion at marbles. Determined that his crutches will not be a hindrance, Alan proves himself at fighting, hunting, climbing and swimming, and even teaches himself to ride a horse. Entranced by his father's tales of the bush, he goes on a week-long trip with a teamster, Peter McLeod, and is impressed by the examples of bush mateship that he witnesses. Most striking of all is Marshall's portrait of his father, a horse-breaker, who represents to the boy all that is self-reliant, forthright and compassionate about the Australian rural tradition. The narrative closes as the family pre-

pares to move to Melbourne, cars having begun to replace horses and Alan having won an accountancy scholarship.

Identity, also titled *Aboriginal and Islander Identity* and *Aboriginal and Thursday Islander Identity*, was established in 1971. Its original editor was Barrie Ovenden; later editors have included Jack Davis, Michael Anderson, John Newfong and Les Malezer. Its stance has been strongly aggressive and it has reported widely on significant political and social issues affecting Aborigines. It has also done much to foster Aboriginal talent in the creative arts, consistently publishing Aboriginal poetry, short stories, and myths, publicizing Aboriginal artists and reviewing Aboriginal literature. Its funding was withdrawn in 1982 as a result of what was considered its over-political stance.

IDRIESS, ION (1889–1979), was born at Waverley, Sydney, but educated in several NSW country towns. He attended the Broken Hill School of Mines, started work in an assay office, and around the age of sixteen began a nomadic existence which lasted for a quarter of a century and provided him with the experience which informs his writing. Following a spell as a seaman on coastal ships around Newcastle he worked as a rabbit exterminator, boundary rider, rouseabout and drover in western NSW, then mined for opals at Lightning Ridge; while there he began contributing paragraphs to the *Bulletin*'s 'Aboriginalities' column and other journals under such pseudonyms as 'Gouger', 'Up North' and 'Emucrest'. After further experience as gold fossicker, pearler and station hand in northern Queensland, the Northern Territory, the Torres Strait Islands, Papua and the Great Barrier Reef, he served in the First World War with the Australian Light Horse. Idriess claimed to have 'encircled' Australia in the 1920s, travelling from Central Australia through south-west Queensland to the Gulf country and then across to the Northern Territory and WA; among other occupations he was explorer, surveyor, and hunter of buffalos and crocodiles. In 1927, while on a trip to Sydney, he was encouraged by Alec Chisholm to write up a diary he had kept while marooned on an island off the Queensland coast. The resulting work, *Madman's Island* (1927), was a failure, principally because of the love story which George Robertson (2) had insisted Idriess incorporate in the plot and which was excised from the second successful edition (1938).

After the publication of *Madman's Island* Idriess returned to the outback, but around 1930 settled in Sydney and was a freelance contributor to the *Sunday Pictorial* and other Sydney journals when his mining manual, *Prospecting for Gold*, was published in 1931. In the same year came his first great success, *Lasseter's Last Ride*, an account of the expedition which searched for the rich gold lead which Harold Lasseter (q.v.) claimed to have found some years before. Over the next four decades, writing mainly in the Angus & Robertson office, Idriess became a household name, with more than forty books published; many of them went through several reprints. The best-known are *Flynn of the Island* (1932), *The Desert Column* (1932), *Gold-Dust and Ashes* (1933), *Drums of Mer* (1933), *The Cattle King* (1936), *Forty Fathoms Deep* (1937), *Headhunters of the Coral Sea* (1940), *Nemarluk: King of the Wilds* (1941), a series of six military handbooks in the *Australian Guerrilla* series (1942), *Horrie the Wog-Dog* (1945), *Outlaws of the Leopolds* (1952) and *The Red Chief* (1953). With the exception of 1943 he published at least a book a year 1931–64, and was made OBE in 1968. Although he kept writing until the end of the 1960s, his heyday was the period from the 1930s depression until the end of the Second World War.

Several of Idriess's books are novels, e.g. *Drums of Mer*, *Forty Fathoms Deep*, but in the main he wrote basically factual stories, imaginatively recreated, with the invented conversations that are a feature also of the works of Frank Clune. The major territory of his writing is outback and coastal Australia, the Torres Strait Islands and Papua. His subjects include mining, pearling, outback pioneers such as John Flynn and Sidney Kidman, Aboriginal freedom fighters such as Pidgin and Nemarluk, and the war experiences of Australians; *The Desert Col-*

umn, based on Idriess's Gallipoli diary, is the first view of the First World War from the point of view of the ordinary soldier. Idriess wrote best when informed by his own experience, combining this with romantic portrayals of heroic individuals from Australia's adventurous past, a snappy prose style which effectively employs Australian idiom, and an optimism about the future of the country; several of his works argue for the development of the resources of inland Australia, and several Onward Australia Leagues were established after his *Onward Australia* was published in 1944. His portraits of Aboriginal Australians reflect the prejudices of the time, although he admires their courage and acumen, notes the cohesion of Aboriginal culture, and documents the effects of the Aboriginal–European culture clash. As well as informing an Australian audience about little-known parts of the continent and its near neighbours, he carried on the *Bulletin's* bush ethos and played a significant part in fashioning the legends surrounding the Australian Light Horse and such individuals as Flynn, Kidman and Lasseter.

IGGULDEN, JOHN (1917–), born Brighton, Victoria, entered the family's Melbourne engineering business as a youth but has been able to give substantial periods to writing. His published works include *Breakthrough* (1960), a futuristic novel which is partly thriller and partly science fiction; *The Storms of Summer* (1960), a novel set on the Australian east coast fishing grounds and concerned with the struggle between migrant and Australian fishermen; *The Clouded Sky* (1965), a complex novel in which he examines the proposition that a man needs relationships with various women – passionate, romantic and domestic. In *The Clouded Sky* the sport of gliding provides a background drawn from Iggulden's personal experience; he was Australian national gliding champion 1959–60. *Dark Stranger* (1965) is a race relations novel in which Iggulden attempts to illustrate the need of the white to accept the black on his own merits, and the need of the black to take pride in himself and not to seek to imitate the white.

IKIN, VAN, see **Science Fiction**

Illawarra, a picturesque south coast district of NSW, has the city of Wollongong as its centre. Discovered by Bass and Flinders in 1796 on one of their *Tom Thumb* voyages, it was originally known as the Five Islands; Illawarra is a corruption of the Aboriginal name of the area, Illowra (Alowrie), meaning a pleasant place. Coal was discovered there in 1797 and cedar milling began about 1812. The pastoral and dairying industries began after Charles Throsby discovered a route by land to the area in 1815; the Illawarra Shorthorn breed of cattle was developed there. The area has long been an important coal mining and steel producing area with Port Kembla its chief industrial town. Frequently mentioned in early colonial literature, e.g. Alexander Harris's *The Emigrant Family* (1849), the Illawarra is closely associated with the poetry of Henry Kendall, who spent some of his adolescence there and who wrote of its beauty in poems such as 'Wollongong', 'Bellambi's Maid', 'Kiama' and 'The Maid of Gerringong'. Coral Lansbury wrote the play, *Krubi of the Illawarra*, published in *Hermes* in 1949. Albert McFarland wrote *Illawarra and the Manaro Districts of New South Wales* (1872) and Frank McCaffrey, *History of Illawarra, and Its Pioneers* (1922). Robyn Rowland's *Three Illawarra Poets* (1978) includes her own verse and that of Don Diespecker and Trevour Q Irwin.

Illustrated Adelaide Post, see **CAWTHORNE, W.A.**

Illustrated Australian Magazine (Ham's Illustrated Australian Magazine), the first Australian illustrated journal, was published monthly in Melbourne 1850–52; it included creative writing and reviews, and its contributors included William àBeckett, William Westgarth and editor Thomas Ham (1821–70), a lithographer and engraver. The *Illustrated Australian Magazine* followed eight years after the establishment of the *Illustrated London News*, of which there was an Australian edition in 1888–91 published by W.J. Akhurst 1888–90, and was itself succeeded by several other journals of similar title in the second half of the nineteenth century. They include the *Illustrated Australian Mail* (1861–62), which had Eugene von Guérard and William Strutt as artists; the *Illustrated Australian News*, a Melbourne monthly 1862–96, which incorporated the *Illustrated Melbourne Post* (1862–68); the *Illustrated Adelaide Post* (1867–74); the *Illustrated Adelaide News*, a monthly which was published 1875–80, became *Frearson's Monthly Illustrated Adelaide News* 1880–84 and the *Pictorial Australian* 1885–95, and the *Illustrated Sydney News*, published in two series, 1853–55 (weekly), 1864–94 (monthly 1864–?88, fortnightly ?1888–93, weekly 1893–94), edited in the 1880s by P.J. Holdsworth. These journals generally carried literary contributions.

Image in the Clay, see **IRELAND, DAVID**

'Imperial Adam', a poem by A.D. Hope (q.v.), was first published in 1951. A fresh, sensuous look at the Edenic myth, the poem describes Adam's discovery of Eve, 'Man's counterpart/In tender parody', their joyous lovemaking and Eve's subsequent travail in childbirth, aided by the 'first gentle midwives of mankind', the 'gravid elephant', the 'calving hind', the 'she-ape big with young' and the 'teeming lioness'. The poem's final comment on the birth of 'the first murderer' and other possible ambivalences are the subject of influential essays by James McAuley, Vincent Buckley and S.L. Goldberg, to which Hope has replied in his essay, 'The Practical Critic', in *The Cave and the Spring* (1965).

In Bad Company and Other Stories (1901), a collection of tales and essays by 'Rolf Boldrewood' (q.v.) includes some of his pieces written in the 1860s, the informative 'How I Began to Write' and the title story, a fictionalized account of the conflicts between the shearers and the squatters in the 1890s, in which 'Boldrewood''s conservative political views are revealed.

In Strange Company, see **BOOTHBY, GUY**

In the Days When the World Was Wide, Henry Lawson's (q.v.) first major book of verse, was published in 1896; dedicated to J.F. Archibald, it carried on the title page a sketch by Frank Mahony of Lawson humping his bluey. *In the Days When the World Was Wide* contains many of the best Lawson poems, including famous bush verses such as 'The Roaring Days', 'The Free-Selector's Daughter', 'Andy's Gone with Cattle' and 'Middleton's Rouseabout'; several important poems of political and social protest, including 'Faces in the Street', 'The *Cambaroora Star*' and 'The Star of Australasia'; and the pick of Lawson's contributions to the *Bulletin* debate (q.v.). *In the Days When the World Was Wide* went into a revised edition in 1900, when new poems such as 'Past Carin'' were added.

'In the Park', see **HARWOOD, GWEN**

Independent Theatre, see **FITTON, DORIS**

Index to Australian Book Reviews, published quarterly with an annual cumulation in the fourth number each year, began in 1965 through the auspices of the Libraries Board of SA. In recent years the entries have been supplied by the University of Queensland library staff. The *Index* includes reviews of books by Australians originating in Australia or of Australian interest. It was suspended in 1980 but one *Index* was issued in 1981.

INGAMELLS, REX (1913–55), poet and founder of the Jindyworobak movement (q.v.), was born at Ororoo, a small town in outback SA. Educated at the University of Adelaide, he was a high school teacher, freelance journalist, then a representative of a Melbourne publishing firm. His first book of verse, *Gumtops* (1935), carried a foreword by L.F. Giblin stressing the need for Australian poets to give 'their first-hand, direct reaction to nature and man as they find them in Australia'. This directive, P.R. Stephensen's *The Foundations of Culture in Australia* (1936) and Ingamells's irritation with G.H. Cowling's article on Australian literature in the *Age*, 16 February 1935, led to his own prose manifesto, *Conditional Culture* (1938), and the formation of the Jindyworobak movement in 1938. In 1941 Ingamells joined the Australia First movement, whose political aims were to some extent complementary to the literary ambitions of the Jindyworobaks. Ingamells's own political attitudes and his thwarted hopes for a massive takeover of the literary scene by the Jindyworobaks (see the controversy in the *Southerly* editorials of 1941–42) are summed up in his poem 'The Gangrened People', published in *At a Boundary* (1941). In 1951 he was appointed a judge of the Commonwealth Jubilee literary competition and he lectured in Australian literature at the Melbourne Technical College.

Ingamells's publications of poetry include *Gumtops* (1935), *Forgotten People* (1936), *Sun-Freedom* (1938), *Memory of Hills* (1940), *At a Boundary* (1941), *Content Are the Quiet Ranges* (1943), and *The Great South Land* (1951), which won the Grace Leven Prize for poetry. He wrote a novel, *Of Us Now Living* (1952) and a children's story, *Aranda Boy* (1952). He was general editor of the *Jindyworobak Anthologies*, published annually 1938–53, compiled *The Jindyworobak Review 1938–1948* (1948) and edited an anthology for schools, *New Song in an Old Land: Australian Verse* (1944). Although Ingamells's own poetic talent was inadequate for the task of carrying the Jindyworobaks to the eminence he desired for them, he was a competent craftsman with a capacity for graceful imagery and picturesque description. These qualities are particularly evident in poems such as 'Forlorn Beauty', 'Sun-Freedom' and 'Memory of Hills', which are filled also with his love for the Australian spirit of place, and in 'The Forgotten People' and 'Uluru', where his emotional affinity with the Aboriginal race lifts the verse above the ordinary.

INGLIS, ROB (1933–), has worked as actor, writer, journalist, critic and producer in Australia and England. His plays include 'Voy-age of the Endeavour' (1965), which is based on the journal of Captain James Cook; 'Canterbury Tales' (1968), dramatized readings from Chaucer; 'Erf' (1971), a one-actor play about the twenty-first century, presented in Australia and in the USA; 'A Rum Do' (1970), a musical based on the governorship of Lachlan Macquarie; and 'Men Who Shaped Australia, for Better or for Worse' (1968), a one-actor play dealing with significant historical figures.

Inner Voices, see **NOWRA, LOUIS**

'INNES, MICHAEL' (JOHN INNES MACKINTOSH STEWART) (1906–), born Edinburgh, Scotland, was professor of English at the University of Adelaide 1935–45. A distinguished literary scholar and well-known novelist, Stewart used the pseudonym 'Michael Innes' mainly for his detective fiction; novels written or published during his period in Australia, some of which have Australian references, include *Death at the President's Lodging* (1936), *Hamlet, Revenge!* (1937), *Lament for a Maker* (1938), *The Spider Strikes Back* (1939), *The Secret Vanguard* (1940), *A Comedy of Errors* (1940), *Appleby on Ararat* (1941), *The Daffodil Affair* (1942), *The Weight of the Evidence* (1943) and *Appleby's End* (1945).

inprint, a short story magazine, was published quarterly 1977–83 from the Mitchell College of Advanced Education. Its policy was to encourage new writers; some of those originally published in *inprint* have gone on to establish literary reputations, e.g. James McQueen, Peter Goldsworthy, as has one of its editors, Nigel Krauth.

Inquirer, a weekly WA journal of politics and literature, was established in 1840 under the editorship of Edmund Lochée. More lively in outlook and more alert to literature than its rival, the *Perth Gazette*, the *Inquirer* advocated in 1841 the establishment of a literary society in WA, encouraged local writers and presented a regular series of book reviews. Its enlightened racial attitudes are reflected by the series of articles by William Nairne Clark in 1842 defending the Aborigines against charges of racial and intellectual inferiority. In 1851–55 the *Inquirer* published a Saturday supplement, which began with a literary flourish but quickly faded. After 1857 the *Inquirer* (which had incorporated the *Commercial News* in 1855) was also an agent for the purchase of books, a common practice in those times. It ceased publication in 1901.

Inspector of Tides, The, see **DRANSFIELD, MICHAEL**

Inwards to the Sun, see **SHAPCOTT, THOMAS**

IRELAND, DAVID (1927–), born Lakemba, NSW, has had a variety of occupations, including greenkeeping, factory work and a lengthy period in an oil refinery. Since 1973 he has been a full-time writer. He first came to notice in 1958 when his play *Image in the Clay* (1964) shared third prize in a competition. He has written some poetry and another play, 'The Virgin of Treadmill Street' (1959), but is best known for his novels, *The Chantic Bird* (q.v., 1968), *The Unknown Industrial Prisoner* (q.v., 1971), *The Flesheaters* (1972), *Burn* (an adaptation of his play *Image in the Clay*) (1974), *The Glass Canoe* (q.v., 1976), *A Woman of the Future* (q.v. 1979), and *City of Women* (1981). He won the Miles Franklin Award in 1971, 1976 and 1979 and was made AO in 1981.

Ireland uses the novel form in diverse, innovatory and non-representational ways to embody his explorations of the contemporary human condition. His use of fragmented scenes rather than formally-constructed chapters and his often opaque narrators are reminiscent of Laurence Sterne, a debt he acknowledges. Like the Brazilian writer Machado de Assis, who has also influenced him, he is concerned with the indifference of the human environment to the individual and with self-betrayal. Pessimistic but not nihilistic, his indictment of the futility of contemporary industrialized existence is satiric and compassionate, humorous and bitter, detached and committed. Underlying his representations of meaningless activity is a philosophical questioning of man's true function and purpose, as distinct from his arbitrary functions and stop-gap purposes. *The Chantic Bird*, narrated by an anonymous, underground youth, committed to equalizing things by acts of violence, is set in a dehumanizing, materialistic and predatory world. The narrator yearns for some transforming magic that will invest life with inherent meaning, but is left with the bleak conviction that it is 'a tale told by nobody'. His next, more ambitious novel, *The Unknown Industrial Prisoner*, concentrates on the collective experience of workers in an oil refinery owned by a multi-national company Puroil. In this huge industrial complex, man is but another resource, a prisoner of institutionalized incompetence and avarice and of his own weaknesses. This comprehensively-worked picture of an inane economic structure, a vast 'termitary' in which everyone consciously or unconsciously is subservient, transcends political solutions. *The Flesheaters*, a more absurdist novel which combines social reality and surrealist fantasy, deals once again with an anarchic, predatory

world. A tight unity is provided by the growth in self-awareness of the narrator, Lee Mallory, who writes from within Merry Lands, a home for outcasts and incurables. *Burn*, a more modest novel in a realistic mode, describes one day of crisis in the life of a part Aboriginal family; concerned less with the conflict between society and outsiders, it probes the grounds of the outcast's inner inertia that partly determines his defeat. *The Glass Canoe*, Ireland's most comic novel, evokes the lost tribal community of the public bar, the last outpost of such traditional male values as mateship, sexual prowess, sport, anti-authoritarianism and support of the underdog. The glass canoe (a schooner of beer) supports the tribe in its escape from the suffocating demands of their otherwise unnatural, industrialized life. *A Woman of the Future* is a complete contrast: partly surrealist allegory, it embodies Ireland's hopes and fears for Australia, presenting the future as offering both Arcadian potential and the possibility of further social degradation. *City of Women*, a novel without a male character, traces the inner journey of Billie Shockley, a retired water engineer and lesbian separatist. Helen Daniel has published a critical account of Ireland's work, *Double Agent* (1982).

Irishman, The see **'O'CONNER, ELIZABETH'**

'IRONBARK', see **GIBSON, G.H.**

IRVIN, ERIC (1908–), born Newtown, Sydney, left school at fifteen becoming, in his words, 'one of the drop-outs of the 1920s'. After a succession of occasional jobs he became a journalist, served with the AIF in the Second World War and was on the editorial staff of the *Sydney Morning Herald* 1962–73, when he retired. Irvin published two volumes of poetry, *A Soldier's Miscellany* (1945) and *A Suit for Everyman* (1968). An expert on the Australian theatre in the nineteenth century, he has published numerous articles in scholarly journals in Australia, England and the USA, and the following books: *Theatre Comes to Australia* (1971); *Sydney As It Might Have Been* (1974); *Gentleman George* (1980), a biography of the actor-dramatist George Darrell; *Australian Melodrama* (1981); and a *Dictionary of the Australian Theatre 1788–1914* (1984). He also edited Walter Cooper's play *Colonial Experience*, with a valuable historical introduction, in 1979.

Island Magazine, a quarterly journal of literature, the arts and allied disciplines, is produced in Tasmania largely to promote the work of Tasmanian artists and writers. It began as the *Tasmanian Review* in 1979 but became *Island Magazine* in 1981. Edited by Michael Denholm, it carries contributions by prominent poets as well as critical articles and fiction.

It Is Never Too Late To Mend, see **READE, CHARLES**

'It's Harder for Girls', a short story by Gavin Casey, is the title story of Casey's first book of short fiction, which was published in 1942 and won the S.H. Prior Memorial Prize. It is the story of the impoverished Dawson family who live in one of the tumbledown houses that dot the old mining leases on the edge of Kalgoorlie. The father is a loafer and boozer, the mother frail and long-suffering. The older boy, Monk, has a spell in a reformatory, returns without 'any sting left' and settles to the grind of life in the mines, a wife and kids. Johnny, the youngest, narrowly escapes the reform school, takes a job in a local store and attempts to break out of his social class by courting the daughter of one of the staff men at the mines. His efforts come to nothing when the girl is frightened off by the loose reputation of his sister Molly. A fiery, beautiful girl, Molly has basically good instincts but indulges in spells of wildness, usually as a gesture of revolt against the feeling that her future is restricted by her family background. A bank clerk, Sid Polson, visits Kalgoorlie briefly and falls in love with Molly. Before he has time to know much about her he returns to Perth, and when she goes there to work they marry and are extremely happy. Ironically, and tragically, the bank later transfers Sid to Kalgoorlie, where his friends soon enlighten him about Molly's past. Broken-hearted, he leaves Molly and equally as devastated, she bitterly resumes the life she had known earlier. As Casey indicates in this story and in much of his fiction, life in the lower social order is circumscribed and frustrated: 'it was tough being any sort of a Dawson [but] it was harder for girls'.

J

Jacaranda Press, which took its name from Queensland's famous flowering jacaranda tree, was founded in 1952 by Brian Clouston to produce material by Australian writers, initially for Queensland schools but later for the whole Australian educational network. Jacaranda has produced a wide range of Australian poetry, fiction, natural history, politics and conservation titles; its authors have included Judith Wright, Douglas Stewart, Nancy Cato, Kath Walker, Bill Scott and Russel Ward. Control and ownership of Jacaranda has changed frequently (eight owners in twenty-five years); since 1977 it has been known as Jacaranda Wiley but retains the Jacaranda Press imprint for school and general books.

Jack Rivers and Me, see **RADLEY, PAUL**

Jacka's Mob, see **War Literature**

Jackeroo (also 'Jackaroo') was a term originally used to describe a young man, usually with good family connections and often directly from England, working as a station hand, sometimes paying for the privilege, in order to gain experience prior to taking over his own station. A similar term was 'colonial experiencer' (q.v.) and, although it chiefly emphasized the young man's inexperience, 'new chum' (q.v.). Suggestions of the origin of 'jackeroo' include the Aboriginal word, 'tchaceroo', to describe a chattering, garrulous bird; a corruption of 'Jack Carew', said to be the name of one actual young gentleman engaged as a station-hand; and a corruption of the term 'Johnny Raw', meaning 'new chum' to 'Jacky Raw' then euphonically to 'Jackeroo'. Widely used in literature, the term is found e.g. in 'Rolf Boldrewood', Henry Lawson, A.B. Paterson and G.H. Gibson. In his *Old Bush Songs* Paterson includes an anonymous song, 'Jim Sago, Jackeroo', and explains that a jackeroo 'occupies a position much like an apprentice . . . has to work with the men though supposed to be above them in social status'. The song carries the traditional contempt of the experienced bushman for the aristocratic and useless new chum. Still a widely used term to denote a young man gaining experience of the cattle and sheep industry by working on outback properties, 'jackeroo' is now complemented by 'jilleroo' ('jillaroo') the female of the species, the latter dating from the Second World War when female station hands were used in times of manpower shortage. Many Australian writers have worked as jackeroos; a notable example is Patrick White, who draws extensively on his experiences in *The Twyborn Affair* (1979).

JACKMAN, WILLIAM (1821–?), born near Dartmouth, England, lived with the Aborigines for almost two years in 1837–39 after his ship, the *Carib*, was wrecked off Nuyts Archipelago. He published a somewhat fanciful account of his experiences in *The Australian Captive: Or, An Authentic Narrative of Fifteen Years in the Life of William Jackman* (1853). The book tells also of Jackman's further adventures in whalers, slavers and merchantmen around the world and contains an appendix with information on Van Diemen's Land and the Australian goldfields.

JACKY JACKY (JACKEY JACKEY), an Aboriginal guide (tribal name Galmahra), accompanied the explorer E.B.C. Kennedy (q.v.) in 1848 on an expedition to explore the north-eastern coast of NSW, as it was then still known, from Rockingham Bay to the Cape York Peninsula and through the Gulf country earlier traversed by Sir Thomas Mitchell and Ludwig Leichhardt. When Kennedy was killed by the Aborigines in December 1848, Jacky Jacky found his way back to civilization. His loyalty and courage went largely unrewarded and he was burned to death in a campfire in 1854. His exploits are recorded in William Carron's *Narrative of an Expedition, Undertaken under the Direction of the Late Mr Assistant Surveyor E.B. Kennedy* (1849) and he is, with Kennedy, the subject of Judith Wright's poem, 'Two Sides of a Story'. The widespread derogatory use of 'Jacky' or 'Jacky Jacky' as a name for male Aborigines probably derives from the fame of Jacky Jacky.

'JACQUES', see **NEILD, J.E.**

JAFFA, HERBERT C., see *Modern Australian Poetry, 1920–70*

'JAMES, BRIAN' (JOHN TIERNEY) (1892–1972), was born at Eurundaree, NSW, the son of a schoolteacher, who taught Henry Lawson and whom Lawson commemorated in his poem 'Eurunderee'. 'Brian James' also became a pupil teacher on leaving school, and taught mainly English for thirty-seven years in state high schools in many parts of NSW and in Sydney. He later combined teaching and farming, both of which occupations colour his fiction, before retiring from teaching in 1951. He did not publish any of his writing until 1942, when he sent his first short story to the *Bulletin* and received strong encouragement from

the editor of its Red Page, Douglas Stewart, and from Norman Lindsay.

Under his pseudonym he published four collections of short stories, *First Furrow* (1944), *Cookabundy Bridge* (1946), *The Bunyip of Barney's Elbow* (1956) and *The Big Burn* (1965); two novels, *The Advancement of Spencer Button* (q.v., 1950) and *Hopeton High* (1963). He also edited two collections of short stories, *Selected Australian Stories* (1959) and *Australian Short Stories – Second Series* (1963). Norman Lindsay, who regarded 'Brian James' as one of the two best short-story writers Australia has produced, edited, with introductions, *The Bunyip of Barney's Elbow* and *The Big Burn*.

Strongly influenced by Lawson and owing an allegiance to the Lawson country, 'Brian James' writes in the same *Bulletin* tradition that fostered such writers as 'Steele Rudd', Frank Dalby Davison and E.O. Schlunke. Similarly a regionalist, recreating the life of the hinterland of NSW, 'Brian James' shares with these writers a wry, sardonic sense of humour and a capacity for sharp satire, understated realism and stylistic economy. Distinctive features of his short stories are his eloquent evocations of rich rural landscapes and the joys and hardships of farming, as in 'Bungaly' and 'First Furrow'; his acute insight into the workings of the collective rural or small-town mind, as in 'Shots in the Orchard' (q.v.) and 'Cookabundy Bridge'; and his varied range of bush and town characters. An unsentimental writer, with a sure, satiric eye for the significant social or psychological detail, 'Brian James' creates a wide range of effects, from light family comedy, as in 'Grandfather Celebrates'; to macabre farce, as in 'Dorf', which relates a botched attempt to kill a pig; to terse pathos, as in 'Brosie', which deals with the death of a child. Particularly striking are his philosophical, fatalistic sense of humour which accepts defeat and even death as part of life's comic inevitability; his combination of detachment and acute observation; and his relish for the absurd rituals of social life from school speech days to political meetings. Although 'Brian James' is probably best known for such comically-extended tales as 'The Bunyip of Barney's Elbow' (q.v.) and 'Hawkins' Pigs', some of his most distinctive stories, such as 'Jacob's Escape' and 'Doolan's Devotions', are subtle explorations of inner, reflective experience.

In his novels 'James' draws on his wide experience of teaching in the NSW system. *Hopeton High*, narrower in scope than *The Advancement of Spencer Button*, is a comic extension of one episode in the life of a typical Australian high school – the acquisition of a 'Warwick Peerless' sound system with loudspeakers in every room, funded by the Parents' and Citizens' Association. He deftly exploits the human comedy of the incident, creating a wide range of characters from the inadequate but aspiring headmaster, Mr Mullett ('Dead Fish'), to the cynical strategies of the more astute teachers, to the political manoeuverings of ambitious parents. Meanwhile, irreverent but acute observations on the part of both teachers and students on the inane activities inspired by the advent of the sound system provide a constant ironic background. *The Advancement of Spencer Button*, 'James''s most significant achievement and the biography of a NSW high-school teacher is also a broad picture of life in the State from the 1890s to the 1940s, and an ironical presentation of the working of its educational system. As Spencer Button, the efficient but unexciting hero of the novel, advances from rural Wombat Creek, his birthplace, to the pinnacle of teaching achievement, headmastership of one of Sydney's big high schools, successfully avoiding the hazards posed by malevolent inspectors, aggressive parents, eccentric colleagues and manic headmasters, a richly-detailed human comedy unfolds.

JAMES, CLIVE (1939–), born and educated in Sydney, edited *Honi Soit*, wrote for university magazines such as *Arena* and worked briefly for the *Sydney Morning Herald* before settling in England in 1962. After completing a second degree at the University of Cambridge, he became a freelance literary journalist and critic and has written for the *New Statesman, Punch*, the *Listener*, the *Times Literary Supplement* and other publications in England and the USA; in 1972–82 he was the highly respected television critic for the *Observer*, and he is well known as a television broadcaster. James's eclectic interests range from high culture to mass entertainment and embrace literature, television, films and popular music. Apart from four mock-heroic epics, e.g. *The Improved Version of Peregrine Prykke's Pilgrimage through the London Literary World* (1976) he has written rock lyrics; two books of literary criticism, *The Metropolitan Critic* (1974), *At the Pillar of Hercules* (1979); three selections of his television journalism, *Visions Before Midnight* (1977), *From the Land of Shadows* (1982), *Glued to the Box* (1983); *Fan-mail: Seven Verse Letters* (1977); a fictionalized autobiography, *Unreliable Memoirs* (1980), an hilarious account of his experiences growing up in and leaving Australia; and a novel, *Brilliant Creatures* (1983), the experiences of a publishing executive who conquers literary London. James's work is distinguished by a delight in the resources of language which fuels his exuberant wit. Although very much an expatriate metropolitian critic, his style and humour have been recog-

nized as essentially Australian and have led him to be described, not necessarily unkindly, as 'the highbrow coming on as Chips Rafferty'.

JAMES, FLORENCE (1904–), born Gisborne, NZ, graduated from the University of Sydney and co-authored with Dymphna Cusack the novel, *Come In Spinner* (1951, qq.v.), and the children's book, *Four Winds and a Family* (1947).

JAMES, JOHN STANLEY ('THE VAGABOND', 'JULIAN THOMAS') (1843–96), led a vagabond's life that began in Walsall, England, where he was born, educated and began work in his father's legal office. From there he moved to London, where he got his start as a freelance journalist, and then worked in Wales as a railway clerk and station master before returning to journalism. Around 1872 he went to America, changed his name to 'Julian Thomas', and married, so he later claimed, the widow of a Virginian planter; in 1875 he arrived in Australia. In April 1876 the *Argus* published, under the pseudonym 'A Vagabond', the first of a long series of articles on high and low life and their institutions. The series was extremely popular, partly because of the mystery surrounding its author, and was republished in four parts as *The Vagabond Papers* (1877). A fifth part, with the same main title, was published in 1878 and sketched life in Sydney and Queensland, where James travelled in 1877–78. Thereafter James was mainly occupied in visiting the Pacific, the Orient and Europe writing for the *Argus*. He returned periodically to Victoria, where at his death in Melbourne he was remembered for his humanitarianism; his true identity was not publicly known until 1912. Apart from *The Vagabond Papers*, he compiled *The 'Vagabond' Annual* (1877); published eight other descriptive works, including *South Sea Massacres* (1881), *Occident and Orient* (1882) and *Cannibals and Convicts* (1886); wrote two plays, 'No Mercy' (first performed 1882) and, with Alfred Dampier, 'The Nihilists' (first performed 1880 and revised as 'England and Russia', 1885); and was portrayed in Francis Hopkins's play, 'Michael Strogoff' (1882). Michael Cannon has edited two selections of James's journalism, *The Vagabond Papers* (1969) and *Vagabond Country* (1981).

JAMES, WINIFRED (1876–1941), born Prahran, Melbourne, was a journalist in Melbourne before going in 1905 to England, where she became a successful novelist, essayist and writer of travel books. She returned to Australia to live in 1940. Her most successful novel was *Letters to My Son* (1910) which in less than a decade went through eighteen reprintings. Her other novels include *Bachelor Betty* (1907), *Patricia Baring* (1908), *Saturday's Children* (1910) and *The Gods Arrive* (1941). Her travel books include *The Mulberry Tree* (1913), *A Woman in the Wilderness* (1915), *Out of the Shadows* (1924) and *Gangways and Corridors* (1936).

Jane Street Theatre, founded by the Old Tote Theatre Company in a small church building in Jane Street in the Sydney suburb of Randwick in 1966, was the venue for numerous productions by the National Institute of Dramatic Art. At a time when Australian drama was generally neglected by theatres, Jane Street produced numerous contemporary plays, providing a Sydney impetus to the 1970s renaissance. Plays staged include Edward Geoghegan's *The Currency Lass*, James Searle's *The Lucky Streak*, Rodney Milgate's *A Refined Look at Existence*, Thomas Keneally's *Halloran's Little Boat* and 'An Awful Rose' and William Marshall's 'King Edward'. Particularly popular and influential was the theatre's 1970 production of *The Legend of King O'Malley*. In 1980 the theatre closed, having proved too small for many productions.

JARDINE Family, including John Jardine (1807–74) and his two elder sons, Francis Lascelles Jardine (1841–1919) and Alexander William Jardine (1843–1920), was an important pioneering family in northern Queensland. John Jardine was appointed superintendent of the settlement to be established at Cape York in 1863; his sons, in a ten months trek of some 2000 kilometres, overlanded the stock that was to form the nucleus of the settlement. F.J. Byerley edited *Narrative of the Overland Expedition of the Messrs. Jardine from Rockhampton to Cape York, Queensland* (1867) and A.J. Richardson published the *Private Journal of the Surveyor . . . Jardine's Overland Expedition to Cape York* (1867).

JEFFERIS, BARBARA (1917–), born Adelaide, has been a journalist and has written dramas and documentaries for the ABC. She has also written popular fiction, characterized by gripping plots and subtle psychological insights, which has been published outside Australia; her novels include *Contango Day* (1954), *Beloved Lady* (1955), *Half Angel* (1959), *Solo for Several Players* (1961), *The Wild Grapes* (1963), *One Black Summer* (1967), *Time of the Unicorn* (1974), and *The Tall One* (1977). She has also published *Three of a Kind* (1982), a biographical work on the mother and daughter actresses, Susan and Harriet Wooldridge, personalities of the Victorian goldfields and needleworker Mary Carol of the 1910–40 pe-

riod. President of the ASA 1973–76, Barbara Jefferis played a part in the establishment of the Public Lending Right scheme and has published, for the society, *Australian Book Contracts* (1983).

JEFFERY, WALTER JAMES (1861–1922), born into a naval family at Portsmouth, England, went to sea at fifteen. He served in the Royal Navy and the merchant navy before settling in Australia in 1886. In 1887 he joined the staff of the *Evening News*, moved from there in 1891 to become sub-editor and later editor of the *Australian Town and Country Journal* and returned to the *Evening News* in 1906 as managing editor. Highly respected in the newspaper world, Jeffery was also an enthusiastic student of maritime history. He published *A Century of Our Sea Story* (1900) and a novel, *The King's Yard* (1903), but of more significance are the fruits of his harmonious collaboration with 'Louis' Becke: three novels, *A First Fleet Family* (1896), *The Mystery of the Laughlin Islands* (1896), and an admired *Bounty* story, *The Mutineer* (1898), which was the first novel published by Angus & Robertson; a history, *The Naval Pioneers of Australia* (1899); a biography, *Admiral Phillip* (1899); and a miscellany, *The Tapu of Banderah* (1901). In general, Jeffery did the research and rough drafts of these works, Becke did the polishing and negotiated with publishers.

Jemmy Green in Australia, a play by James Tucker (q.v.), was probably written in 1845, although not published until 1952; publicly performed on radio in the same year, it was staged at the Adelaide Festival in 1966. A slight three-act comedy, each act consisting of five short scenes, *Jemmy Green in Australia* records the experiences in Australia of the 'new chum' (q.v.) Londoner, Jemmy Green, who soon after his arrival is duped into the purchase of a squatting run in the back country stocked by diseased sheep and wild cattle. During his journey there he is robbed by bushrangers and mistaken for an escaped convict; after his arrival, his huts are burned by Aborigines, he learns that his sheep have catarrh, and he is served with writs from his employees, his neighbours and Sydney businessmen. He takes advice, declares himself bankrupt, and is released under a new government act in time to save his London sweetheart, Priscilla Peasblossom, from marriage into a rapacious merchant family. Priscilla has inherited a sizable fortune, followed Jemmy to Sydney, and been told that he is dead. The most likely direct source for Tucker when he wrote *Jemmy Green in Australia* was 'Billy Barlow in Australia', a Billy Barlow song first performed in 1843 in Maitland, where

Tucker was working. The character of Jemmy Green, however, was by then already well-established on the stage. In 1821 'W.T. Moncreiff' (q.v.) had introduced Jemmy into his popular *Tom and Jerry: Or, Life in London*, which spawned many adaptations, imitations and sequels, including 'Life in Sydney: Or, The Ran Dan Club' (1843); in both plays, as in *Jemmy Green in Australia*, Jemmy's rawness ('greenness') leads to his unwise bidding at an auction.

JENKINS, JOHN (1949–), born Melbourne, was associated with the rise of the 'New Australian Poetry' and the small magazines that accompanied it. He edited the brief-lived *A* and *Aardvark* in 1970, and was co-editor, with Walter Billeter, of *Etymspheres: The Journal of the Paper Castle* in 1974–75 and, with Rudi Krausman, of *Aspect* in 1976–77. He has also been involved with Billeter in Paper Castle Publications, with Robert Kenny in Rigmarole Publications, and co-edited with Michael Dugan *The Outback Reader* (1975). His own poetry includes *Zone of the White Wolf and Other Landscapes* (1974, partly prose) and *Blindspot* (1977).

JENNINGS, KATE (1948–), born near Griffith, NSW, has edited a well-known collection of feminist verse, *Mother I'm Rooted* (1975), and has published a collection of her own poetry, *Come to Me My Melancholy Baby* (1975).

JEPHCOTT, SYDNEY (1864–1951), born Nariong, Upper Murray, Victoria, lived most of his life in the Mount Kosciusko area, whose beauty and grandeur he claimed influenced his literary imagination. He published two books of poetry, *The Secrets of the South* (1892) and *Penetralia* (1912), which contained some verses from the earlier volume. The short, meditative lyrics are frequently solemn and stately in tone; 'Thredbo River', for example, conveys well the atmosphere of the snow country.

Jerilderie Letter was the letter vindicating his conduct which Ned Kelly (q.v.) attempted to get published in Jerilderie during the raid of the Kelly gang in 1879. When it was discovered that the local printer had fled in fear of his life, Kelly gave the letter to a teller of the bank the gang had robbed. The letter, which contains echoes of the convict song, 'Moreton Bay', and is a classic outlaw manifesto, was published in Max Brown's *Australian Son* (1956), and in Graham Seal's *Ned Kelly in Popular Tradition* (1980). The Jerilderie Letter is a reworking of an earlier letter, now known as the Cameron Letter, which Kelly left to be

posted to the Victorian politician, Donald Cameron, when leaving the scene of an earlier bank robbery at Euroa.

'Jim Jones at Botany Bay', one of the best early Australian folk-songs (q.v.) is the bitter lament of an English convict who has been transported for poaching and who at the end of the song vows defiantly that he will join Jack Donohoe's bushranging gang and take revenge on the 'tyrants' who have illtreated him at Botany Bay. The reference to Donohoe suggests that the ballad was written around 1830, although it was not collected until 1907, when it was published as a 'typical song of the convict days' in Charles MacAlister's *Old Pioneering Days in the Sunny South* (1907). Usually sung to the tune 'Irish Mollie, Oh!', 'Jim Jones at Botany Bay' has features which link it with the English street ballad tradition; it is one of the few treason songs, reputedly banned by the authorities, to have survived from the penal days.

'Jim the Splitter', a poem by Henry Kendall (q.v.) first published in the *Freeman's Journal* in 1880, illustrates the poet's belief that 'your bushman is one of the most finished rogues out'. Kendall exposes, and lightly satirizes, Jim's roguery in business matters, admires his mastery of his sawyer's and splitter's art, but is critical of Jim's assumption of superiority over the world at large merely because of his talent with timber.

***Jimmy Brockett*, see STIVENS, DAL**

Jimmy Woods/Woodser is a colloquial expression which denoted a person who drank alone in a bar, a practice shunned by the Australian male who traditionally only drank in public when accompanied by his mates. The expression may derive from one James Wood, a shearer on the Darling River in the 1880s, who spent the 'off season' in Bourke drinking alone in the pubs and thus not 'shouting' or buying a round of drinks for other people. The practice of drinking alone has also been described as 'drinking with the flies'. In the *Bulletin* (1892) Barcroft Boake wrote a poem, 'Jimmy Wood', about 'a solitary Briton' who has a mission 'to end the "shouting" mania' so common in Australian drinking circles. Boake's Jimmy Wood, drinking alone – and often – fast develops into a 'soaker', dying an alcoholic. Henry Lawson also commemorates the lonely alcoholic of the bush in his poem, 'The Old Jimmy Woodser'.

Jindyworobak Movement, the most extreme expression of the revival of nationalism in Australia in the 1930s, arose partly as a reaction against the colonialism still present at the time and partly as a counter to the international influences that had made steady inroads into Australia's isolation throughout the 1920s. It came into being in 1938 when Rex Ingamells (q.v.) founded the Jindyworobak club in Adelaide, published *Conditional Culture*, a prose manifesto explaining the aims and methods of the movement, and produced the first *Jindyworobak Anthology* of poetry. The anthologies were continued annually until 1953, and in 1948 an historical account of the movement, *Jindyworobak Review (1938–48)*, was compiled by Ingamells. *The Jindyworobaks* (1979), edited by Brian Elliott in the Portable Australian Authors series, is a comprehensive historical and critical account of the movement. Many writers were associated, with varying degrees of commitment, with the Jindyworobaks. In addition to Ingamells those most closely involved, although briefly in some cases, included Ian Tilbrook, Flexmore Hudson, Max Harris, Ian Mudie, William Hart-Smith, Victor Kennedy, Paul Grano, Roland Robinson, Gina Ballantyne and Nancy Cato. Considerable as the Jindyworobak body of literary talent was, it contained no outstanding Australian poet. By the mid 1950s the movement had lost much of its impetus but has not disappeared entirely: Elliott sees evidence of a Jindyworobak continuation or a new phase beginning, in the work of Xavier Herbert, Les Murray and Peter Porter.

The word 'Jindyworobak' was adapted by Ingamells from 'Jindy-worabak', a term used in the glossary of James Devaney's *The Vanished Tribes* (1929) with the meaning 'to annex, to join'. Ingamells chose the word as the name for the movement because it was 'aboriginal', 'outlandish', i.e. likely to arrest attention, and 'symbolic', i.e. directing Australian writers to what should be their distinctive material. Major stimuli to the creation of the movement were P.R. Stephensen's *The Foundations of Culture in Australia* (1936), an aggressively nationalistic demand for a distinctive Australian culture based largely on the spirit of place, and D.H. Lawrence's sensitive reaction to the bush in his novel, *Kangaroo* (1923). Ingamells's first exposition of Jindyworobak philosophy came with *On Environmental Values*, an address delivered in 1937, later expanded into *Conditional Culture*. He applied the term 'Jindyworobak' to 'those individuals who are endeavouring to free Australian art from whatever alien influences trammel it, that is, to bring it into proper contact with its material'. Ingamells insisted that the national culture depended on a clear recognition of 'environment values' and an understanding of Australian history and traditions, primaeval, colonial and modern. Aust-

ralian writers were urged to express their distinctive environment, not in conventional terms suited to other countries but in language indicating its own primal essence. Ingamells concluded *Conditional Culture* with the celebrated and much ridiculed linking of the Jindyworobak philosophy with Aboriginal culture. He believed that 'the laws, the customs, and the art of the Australian Aboriginals went to make a culture which was closely bound in every way with their environment'. The inference was that the Jindyworobak culture could best develop by assimilating the spirit of Aboriginal culture and by identifying with it. From Aboriginal art and song modern Australian culture could learn the necessary techniques and from Aboriginal legend ('sublimated through our thought') would come the required 'pristine outlook on life'. The Jindyworobaks, or some of them, came to see a fitting symbol in the Aboriginal 'Dreamtime' (more properly 'Alchera' or 'Alcheringa') the myth of the 'first time', the time of creation itself, the root of all Aboriginal lore. They felt that the order and spiritual wholeness implanted in Aboriginal life through the concept of Alcheringa could be taken as a symbol or image which might provide a key for a larger Australian 'Dreamtime'. Contrary to popular opinion, they had no intention of peddling Aboriginal culture for its own sake. It seemed to them to offer a suitable example of environmental values in action. Misconception of their emphasis on Aboriginal culture, exacerbated by the infrequent but much publicized Jindyworobak habit of using Aboriginal words in poetry, led to misrepresentation, even ridicule of the movement as a whole. R.H. Morrison's coining of the term 'Jindyworobakwardness' reflected the reaction of many people to the idea of basing modern literary culture on an Aboriginal one. In that the movement was symptomatic of a deeply-felt need to perceive and express a sense of national identity, it met with some encouragement and support. In that it attempted to force Australia's literary development into narrow nationalistic channels it failed, both because it was too idiosyncratic and backward-looking and because it was parochial and isolationist. In the final outcome it was simply swept aside by the inevitable movement of Australia after the Second World War into the wider international arena, where the simplicity, perhaps naivety, of the Jindyworobak dream appeared to have no real relevance.

Joe Wilson and His Mates, Henry Lawson's (q.v.) fifth prose collection, was first published in 1901 while Lawson was in England. It contains two sections, sometimes published separately: *Joe Wilson*, which comprises the four major parts of the Joe Wilson (q.v.) sequence; and *Joe Wilson's Mates*, fourteen stories which include the famous 'The Loaded Dog'. The popularity of the *Joe Wilson's Mates* title is confirmed by 'Joe Wilson's Mate', a poem by David Campbell, and *Joe Wilson's Mates*, the title both of modern Lawson selections and of a 1957 film of Lawson's story, 'The Union Buries its Dead', in which Joe Wilson is named as the drowned unionist whose funeral is attended.

Johnno, a novel by David Malouf, was published in 1975 and traces the childhood and early adult life of the narrator, who has returned to Brisbane at the age of thirty on the death of his father. During the Second World War the placid life of the Brisbane seaside suburb of Scarborough, where the child's family is settled, is only mildly disturbed and little happens to alter his perception of Australia as 'familiar and boring' or his acceptance of the rituals of his conventional upbringing. At the age of thirteen, however, when his friendship with the school rebel, Johnno, suddenly ripens, his world widens. Johnno, whose father has been posted as missing, is a wiry, reckless, tearaway of precocious sexuality, wide-ranging vituperative powers and impressive mendacity. He exerts a strong influence on a small group of would-be disciples but appears, at times, to place most value on his relationship with the narrator, whom he nicknames 'Dante'. At university, after a period of separation, Dante and Johnno take to roaming around the town, frequenting fights and brothels, where Johnno delights in disturbing the domestic calm. Dante's relationship with Johnno is as ambivalent as his relationship with Australia; cut off from Johnno because of his inability to be romantic enough and his unwillingness to share fully in his fantasies, he is also cut off from Brisbane, 'a place where poetry could never occur'. Johnno eventually leaves for the Congo to work in a copper mine; Dante stubbornly hangs on in Brisbane in a routine occupation, surprised at his own lack of ambition but determined 'to make life reveal whatever it had to reveal *here*, on home ground, where I could recognize the terms'. Later he visits Johnno in Paris, where he witnesses his bizzare, underworld lifestyle before leaving for England, where he settles in the north as a teacher. After three years he is treated by fellow Australians as an expatriate, although he reflects: 'I had once found it odd, gratuitous even, that I should be an Australian. I found it even odder, more accidental, that I should be anything else'. Meanwhile Johnno has moved to Athens, where Dante eventually visits him, discovering that some of his life force has now been sapped and

that his style of life is more mysterious than ever. Back in Brisbane some time later, he runs into Johnno again; now massive and dishevelled, Johnno is working on an oil survey on the Condamine. His sudden, mysterious death by drowning forces Dante to re-examine their relationship, including Johnno's expectations of himself and of Australia. Johnno, he realises, had aimed at 'some dimension in which the hundred possibilities a situation contains may be more significant than the occurrence of any one of them, and a metaphor truer in the long run than mere fact'.

JOHNS, FRED (1868–1932), born Michigan, USA, of Cornish descent, came in 1884 to SA where he found employment on the *Register*; in 1914 he left to become a Hansard reporter in the SA parliament, and in 1920–25 he was editor of the *South Australian Freemason*. Johns wrote a small volume of patriotic verse, *In Remembrance* (1920), as well as *A Journalist's Jottings* (1922), but is best remembered for his pioneering, meticulous biographical research. *Johns's Notable Australians* (1906), a volume of biographies of living Australians, was revised and updated in 1908 under the original title; in 1912–14 as *Fred Johns's Annual*; in 1922 as *Who's Who in the Commonwealth of Australia*; and in 1927 as *Who's Who in Australia* (q.v.), a title which continued after his death. Johns was also the author of *An Australian Biographical Dictionary* (1934); he endowed the University of Adelaide scholarship for biography which bears his name.

JOHNSON, COLIN (1939–), part-Aboriginal novelist, born Beverley, WA, was educated in a Roman Catholic orphanage, had minor brushes with the law as a young man, and then went to Melbourne, where he began writing, and worked in the Victorian public service. He published *Wild Cat Falling* in 1965, the first novel to be published by an Aboriginal writer. Since then he has travelled widely, remaining for about six years in India, where he spent time as a Buddhist monk. At intervals since 1975 he has been in Australia working on fiction, Aboriginal histories and documentaries. His second novel, *Long Live Sandawara*, was published in 1979.

Wild Cat Falling outlines the search of a young part-Aboriginal for a meaningful existence in a white world which excludes him, because of his colour and background, from its rewards and privileges. As an outcast on the fringes of white society, his instinctive reaction is to attack that society, fruitlessly, as the novel indicates. Near the end of the novel, as he awaits capture on an attempted murder charge, he is given a new sense of identity and purpose when he meets and talks with an old Noongar, a tribal elder turned rabbiter. *Long Live Sandawara* is the story of a part-Aboriginal youth, Alan, who, inspired by the heroic fight of Sandawara (based on the legendary Pidgin) against his race's oppressors, attempts to establish his own modern Aboriginal resistance group in the slums of Perth. Although the result is inevitable failure, mainly because of the ironies and contradictions of human nature and the human situation, the heroic archetype of Sandawara set up in the novel remains undiminished. A highly-regarded novelist, Johnson interweaves character and incident with ironic adroitness; he was awarded the 1979 Patricia Weickhardt Award for an Aboriginal writer.

JOHNSON, FRANK C., was an employee of Dymock's, the Sydney booksellers, when he joined with Norman Lindsay and Kenneth Slessor to found *Vision* (q.v.) magazine. He subsequently published Slessor's *Darlinghurst Nights* (1933) and, particularly in the 1940s, a wide range of popular material, e.g. magazines, children's books, comic books and popular fiction.

JOHNSON, J.C.F. (JOSEPH COLIN FRANCIS) (1848–1904), born Adelaide, and widely-known as 'Alphabetical' Johnson, became experienced and knowledgable in mining operations, on which he wrote the successful handbooks, *Practical Mining* (1889) and *Getting Gold* (1897). A journalist with the SA *Register*, subsequently proprietor and editor of *Adelaide Punch*, and contributor of bush verse to the *Savage Club Annual* and the *Observer Miscellany*, Johnson published several collections of fiction and verse that caught, with considerable affection, the atmosphere of bush and mining life and mirrored typical characters from those environments. His published works were *On the Wallaby: Or, Tales from the Men's Hut* (1872), *Christmas on Carringa* (1873), *Over the Island* (1873) and *An Austral Christmas* (1888).

JOHNSON, RICHARD (1753–1827), born Yorkshire, England, came to Australia with the First Fleet as Australia's first clergyman. He conducted the first religious service in the colony on 3 February 1788. Johnson's chief interest apart from religion was farming; Watkin Tench judged him 'the best farmer in the colony'. He returned to England in 1800. Johnson wrote *An Address to the Inhabitants of the Colonies Established in New South Wales and Norfolk Island* (1794), the first book published with the intention of being distributed throughout the Colony. George Mackaness edited *Some Letters of Rev. Richard Johnson* (1954); biographical studies include James

Bonwick's *Australia's First Preacher* (1898), W.H. Rainey's *The Real Richard Johnson* (1947), and Neil K. Macintosh's *Richard Johnson* (1978); the last-named is the most comprehensive.

JOHNSTON, GEORGE HENRY (1912–70), was born in Malvern, Melbourne, the son of a tramway sheds foreman. After education at state schools he became an apprentice lithographer in a commercial art studio, meanwhile studying art at the National Gallery School. A series of imaginative articles about sailing ships gained him a start as a journalist on the staff of the *Argus* and during the Second World War his syndicated despatches from battle zones in New Guinea, China, Burma, India, Italy and the north Atlantic appeared regularly in national and overseas newspapers. He also wrote two accounts of the war at sea, *Grey Gladiator* (1941) and *Battle of the Seaways* (1941); a graphic description of his experiences in New Guinea, *New Guinea Diary* (1943); a contemporary and historical account of the Australian army, *Australia at War* (1942); and a description of the Australian war effort for American readers, *Pacific Partner* (1944). Brought up on the myth of Anzac he turned finally towards pacifism as a result of his experiences of war and disillusionment with Western policies in China in 1945. After the failure of his first marriage he married Charmian Clift (q.v.) in 1947 and joined the staff of the Sydney *Sun*, which sent him to London in 1950 as its European editor. He resigned from the position in 1954, having decided to rely solely on his writing for support, and with his wife and three children spent the next ten years on the Greek islands of Kalymnos and Hydra. The difficulties and joys of their years there are described in his novel, *Clean Straw for Nothing* (q.v., 1969) and in Charmian Clift's *Mermaid Singing* (1956) and *Peel Me a Lotus* (1959). In 1964, when his novel *My Brother Jack* (q.v., 1964) won the Miles Franklin Award, he returned to Australia and lived in Sydney until his death from tuberculosis, a disease that had threatened his life for several years.

A prolific writer, Johnston produced a range of novels, short stories and plays for radio and television. Although many of his books are 'potboilers', such as the series of thrillers published under the pseudonym 'Shane Martin', several of his novels achieve distinction. Among the most notable are *Moon at Perigee* (1948), published in London with the title *Monsoon* (1951), *The Cyprian Woman* (1955), *The Darkness Outside* (1959), *Closer to the Sun* (1960), *The Far Road* (1962) and *The Far Face of the Moon* (1964). But his outstanding achievement is his semi-autobiographical trilogy, *My Brother*

Jack (1964), *Clean Straw for Nothing* (1969) and *A Cartload of Clay* (1971). His other writings include *Journey Through Tomorrow* (1947), a description of his travels in India, China, Tibet, Burma and Japan; *Skyscrapers in the Mist* (1946), an account of a wartime visit to New York; three novels with Charmian Clift, *High Valley* (1949), which won first prize in the 1948 literary competition of the *Sydney Morning Herald*, *The Big Chariot* (1953) and *The Sponge Divers* (1955), published in the USA with the title *The Sea and the Stone* (1955); and a popular collection of essays, *The Australians* (1966), lavishly illustrated with photographs by Robert B. Goodman. He also edited two collections of essays by Charmian Clift. Other awards won by Johnston include the Miles Franklin Award for *Clean Straw for Nothing* and the Literary Guild Award of the USA for *Closer to the Sun*. There are two well-known portraits of Johnston, by Russell Drysdale and Ray Crooke. His son, Martin Johnston (q.v.), is a poet.

A victim of his natural fluency and the necessity of writing to make a living, Johnston did not achieve a work of major importance until *My Brother Jack*. An absorbing, frank study of early experience, the novel is also a remarkable social document, a densely-textured recreation of life in Melbourne between the wars. The semi-autobiographical narrator, David Meredith, appears in both *Closer to the Sun* and in *The Far Road*, although neither develops his Odysseus qualities. *My Brother Jack*, which deals with David's youth and early manhood, begins the story of his journeyings in quest of meaning. Doomed to be an expartriate, David never inwardly conforms to accepted patterns but constantly seeks to find and assert his own. Rejecting first his family, then his own false values, his marriage and finally his country, he seems to find at the end of the novel authentic freedom in his union with Cressida Morley. *Clean Straw for Nothing* has a kaleidoscopic structure, criss-crossing time from 1945 to 1968 and covering Meredith's experiences in Melbourne, Sydney, London and Greece. The mood of the novel, heavy with creative, emotional and material failure, is darkened even further by Meredith's inability to grasp the promised freedom. His voyaging has resulted in a baffled awareness of unfulfilled dreams and the near-collapse of his marriage. In the unfinished novel, *A Cartload of Clay*, Meredith, now deprived of a future, ceaselessly probes the past to discover a meaning. Left with 'only the brittle present, fragmenting at a touch, and the long accumulated mucked-up obscurity of the past, with all its unlearned lessons', he concludes that the only pattern to life is the search itself.

JOHNSTON, GRAHAME (1929–76), born Wellington, NZ, was educated at Victoria University, Wellington, and at the University of Oxford. He came to Australia in 1954 and taught at the University of Queensland and the Australian National University, and was professor of English at the University of Melbourne (1963–65) and at the Royal Military College, Duntroon (1968–76). Originally a medievalist, Johnston later worked in American literature and particularly in Australian language and literature, where he won a reputation as critic, editor, bibliographer and lexicographer. His *Australian Literary Criticism* (1962) was an early critical anthology devoted to Australian literature and the beginning of a successful relationship with the Australian branch of Oxford University Press. Adviser on Australian literature to the Press from the early 1960s, he became an active general editor of its Australian Writers and Their Work and Australian Bibliographies series, compiled *Annals of Australian Literature* (q.v., 1970), and edited the *Australian Pocket Oxford Dictionary* (1976), a major contribution to the study of Australian English (q.v.).

JOHNSTON, MARTIN, (1947–), born Sydney, the son of George Johnston and Charmian Clift, has published two collections of poetry, *Shadowmass* (1971) and *The Sea-Cucumber* (1978), and a series of translations of modern Greek poetry, *Ithaka* (1973). He has also written an introduction to a reprint of Charmian Clift's essays, *The World of Charmian Clift* (1983). His first novel, *Cicada Gambit* (1984), concerns a young Greek chess player who earns a precarious living in bohemian Sydney. Experimental in form, the novel is notable for its central character and its city setting.

JOLLEY, ELIZABETH (1923–), born Birmingham, England, was educated in England and Europe, served as a nurse in the Second World War and came in 1959 to WA, where she taught prior to her emergence as a significant contemporary writer. She has published short fiction, *Five Acre Virgin and Other Stories* (1976), *The Travelling Entertainer* (1979) and *Woman in a Lampshade* (1983); and novels, *Palomino* (1980, which shared the Con Weickhardt Award for an unpublished novel in 1975), *The Newspaper of Claremont Street* (1981), *Mr. Scobie's Riddle* (1982, which won the *Age* Book of the Year Award), and *Miss Peabody's Inheritance* (1983). A successful radio dramatist she has had numerous plays produced on ABC radio, e.g. 'Night Report' (1975), which won a special award in the Sound-Stage competition of 1975–76; 'The Performance' (1976); 'The Shepherd on the Roof' (1977); 'Woman in a Lampshade'; and 'Two Men Running' (1981), which was awarded an Awgie in 1982. Jolley combines farce and an unerring eye for the eccentric and incongruous with an underlying seriousness and a subtle prodding of the community's moral conscience.

JOLLIFFE, ERIC (1907–), born Portsmouth, England, came to Australia in 1914 and spent his late teens as a bush worker. He studied art in Sydney and in the late 1930s became a regular contributor of cartoons to the *Bulletin*. He worked briefly for *Smith's Weekly* after the Second World War but established his reputation with his cartoon series, 'Saltbush Bill' and 'Witchetty's Tribe' in *Pix*, and 'Sandy Blight' in the *Sun-Herald*; in 1973 he established his own magazine, *Jolliffe's Outback*. Saltbush Bill and Sandy Blight are farmers whose experiences form part of the Dad and Dave (q.v.) tradition of rural humour. 'Witchetty's Tribe', a series dominated by busty Aboriginal women in tribal 'suburbia', has been criticized for its patronizing Eurocentricism, although Jolliffe has often protested his deep love and respect for the Aborigines whom he has regularly visited in outback Australia. Upwards of a hundred books of Jolliffe's cartoons have been published; he also illustrated *Corroboree* (1946), which includes poems and stories by other authors.

Jonah, a novel by Louis Stone (q.v.), was first published in 1911. Set in Sydney's working-class districts in the early years of the twentieth century, it is the story of a larrikin, Joe Jones or Jonah, leader of a street 'push'. A hunchbacked outsider rejected as a child by his family, Jonah leads a fierce existence that acknowledges only the solidarity of the gang. His discovery of his love for his son, offspring of his liaison with the unattractive Ada Yabsley, revolutionizes his life, turning him into a successful capitalist, owner of a large shoe shop. Ada's mother, Mrs Yabsley, a washerwoman of generous proportions and instincts, helps his early rise. Happiness eludes the ruthless Jonah, however; Ada lapses into alcoholism and is killed in a fall that has been partly caused by the intervention of Clara Grimes, a refined music teacher to whom Jonah is attracted. He ends by forming a marriage of convenience with his saleswoman, Miss Giltinan. The destiny of his old friend Chook, another larrikin, contrasts with that of Jonah. Chook marries the courageous Pinkey and finds happiness through feeling rather than possessions. *Jonah* was made into a television series by the ABC in 1982.

JONES, DORIS EGERTON (1889–1973), born Adelaide, turned to fiction writing after her plans for a career in law were abandoned because of ill health. Her novels are *Peter Piper* (1913), *Time O'Day* (1915), *Green Eyes* (1915), *The Coconut Planter* (1916) and *The Year Between* (1918). *Peter Piper* was well received at the time; A.G. Stephens in the *Bookfellow* saw it as 'the most Australian story since Stella Franklin's *My Brilliant Career*'. Romantic stories with some feminist elements, the later novels attracted only minor critical interest. Doris Jones also wrote the play *Governor Bligh* (1930), which was performed in Sydney and Melbourne and collaborated with Emelie Polini in the play 'The Flaw', produced in Sydney in 1923.

JONES, EVAN (1931–), born Preston, Victoria, was educated at the University of Melbourne and Stanford University in the USA. Jones has taught history and English at the University of Melbourne and the Australian National University. He has published four volumes of poetry, *Inside the Whale* (1960), *Understandings* (1967), *Recognitions* (1978) and *Left at the Post* (1982). He edited, with Geoffrey Little, *The Poems of Kenneth Mackenzie* (1972) and wrote the monograph, *Kenneth Mackenzie* (1969). In the 1950s Jones was one of a group of writers at the University of Melbourne which included Vincent Buckley and Chris Wallace-Crabbe. His early poetry is seen as being in a 'rigidly imitation Classical manner'; his later poetry, although more modern in both technique and language, retains its emphasis on traditional values. Strongly personal in tone, Jones's poetry subjects life, himself and human relationships to a close and mildly sardonic scrutiny.

JONES, JOHN JOSEPH (1930–), born London, migrated to Australia in 1948 and has been a teacher of English in WA. Singer, musician, poet and playwright, Jones is a well-known WA identity. As a folksinger he compered and sang at the first Winthrop folk festival for the ABC. From his 1964 recitals at the Adelaide Festival of Arts sprang his five records and ballads, *Five Australian Ballads*, *Songs and Ballads of Australia*, *Songs of John Shaw Neilson*, *Australian Songs and Ballads* and *Ballads of Durack and Sorensen*. His performed plays include 'Wildflowers', 'Tea Towels and Earrings', 'Harvest', *The Undivided* (1965), *Sturt* (1972), 'Loving Lady' (on Caroline Chisholm), 'Bitter Grapes' and 'The Hamburger Man'. He has also published an opera, *My New-Found Country* (1963), *Love* (1983, sonnets and paintings) and *A Day at Hiroshima, Parkerville and Other Poems* (1983).

JONES, JOSEPH JAY (1908–), taught at the University of Texas for over forty years until his retirement in 1975. An enthusiastic promoter of Australian and Commonwealth literature studies in the USA, he first visited Australia in 1953. He is the author of *Radical Cousins* (1976), a comparative study of nine-teenth-century Australian and American writers; edited the Australian section of the Twayne's World Authors series and the special Australian number of the *Texas Quarterly* reprinted as *Image of Australia* (1962); and co-authored with his wife, Johanna Jones, pamphlets on Henry Lawson and authors and areas of Australia.

JONES, PERCY (1914–), born Geelong, was educated at the University of Melbourne and overseas and was vice-director of the Melbourne University Conservatorium of Music 1950–72. A member of the Catholic clergy, he has been mainly interested in church music, although he was an early modern collector of Australian folk-songs (q.v.) and ballads.

JONES, RAE DESMOND (1941–), born Broken Hill, graduated in 1976 from the University of Sydney. After a succession of casual positions he joined the Commonwealth Employment Service. Jones has published four books of verse, *Orpheus with a Tuba* (1973), *The Mad Vibe* (1975), *Shakti* (1977), and *The Palace of Art* (1982). He has also published the short-story collection, *Walking the Line* (1979), and one side of the poetry record, *Two Voluminous Gentlemen* (1977). He was the founding editor of the modern poetry journal, *Your Friendly Fascist*. Jones's early poetry, personal in tone, modernistic in language and theme, and violent in attitude, reflected his own individual 'mad vibe', a term that he adopted to indicate the anti-social, self-destructive characteristic present in most people but dominant in some. His later poetry focuses more on the external world.

JONES, SUZANNE HOLLY (1945–), has written two novels, *Harry's Child* (1964), a study of a relationship between a teenage girl and her middle-aged guardian, and *Crying in the Garden* (1974), narrated by a patient in a psychiatric clinic. Distinguished by a striking, impressionistic style, both novels explore elusive elements in human relationships.

JONES, T. HARRI (1921–65), born Llanafan, Wales, served in the Royal Navy during the Second World War and graduated from the University of Wales in 1947. In 1951–59 he taught English at the naval dockyard in Portsmouth before his appointment as lecturer in English at Newcastle University College. He published three books of poems: *The Enemy in the Heart* (1957), *Songs of a Mad Prince* (1960) and *The Beast at the Door* (1963). An active and popular member of the Newcastle community who did much to foster poetry in the Hunter River district, Harri Jones died by drowning 29 January 1965. A posthumous volume, *The Colour of Cockcrowing*, was published in 1966 and *The Collected Poems of T. Harri Jones*, bringing together all four volumes and some uncollected poems, was edited by Julian Croft and Don Dale-Jones in 1977.

In Jones's unpublished poem, 'Thinking to Write an Ode', are the lines, 'Thinking to write an ode, I thought of my country' and 'Thinking to write an ode, I thought of love!' Wales and love are the constant subjects of Jones's mostly elegiac poetry. The poems written in Australia about his sense of exile from his country are mainly collected in the second section, 'Hiraeth', of *The Beast at the Door*; typical of them is 'The Welshman in Exile Speaks'. The progress of love is recorded almost chronologically in his published verse; the early sensuous enjoyment and the 'impatient debonair' love of 'The Bridegroom' gives way to a bewilderment about the loss of personal identity in love, to a state of disillusionment and hostility, and finally, in the 'Eros' poems of *The Beast at the Door*, to a resigned acceptance of disappointment and futility. A deeply personal poet, Jones had scarcely time to achieve the potential that his verse seemed to promise. His long poem, 'Cotton Mather Remembers the Trial of Elizabeth How: Salem, Massachusetts, 30th June 1692', reconstructs the thoughts of the Calvinist preacher and judge as he writes of the Salem witch trials; it is notable for its evocation of character and its subtly ambivalent exploration of the nature of good and evil. Julian Croft's study, *T.H. Jones* (1976) has a brief biography and a sensitive and detailed commentary on the poet's work; Croft had been a student of Jones.

JORGENSON, JORGEN (1780–1841), was an adventurer born Jorgen Jorgensen in Copenhagen; he changed his surname in 1817. At fifteen he went to sea, and was in Australian waters in 1801–05, first at Port Jackson, later at Port Phillip and Van Diemen's Land. In 1809 he was involved in proclaiming Iceland independent of Denmark, and subsequently styled himself 'ex-King of Iceland'. In 1826, after years of adventure, debauchery and some ill-fortune, he returned to Australia under sentence of transportation for life. He spent most of his time in Tasmania, where he was a minor explorer and where he eked out a living in the 1830s as an exterminator of Aborigines, as a convict constable, and as a contributor to the press. Jorgenson's 'A Shred of Autobiography' was published in the *Hobart Town Almanack* in 1835 and 1838, and his stormy career detailed by J.F. Hogan in *The Convict King* (1891); by Marcus Clarke in *Old Tales of a Young Country* (1871); and by Frank Clune and P.R. Stephensen in *The Viking of Van Diemen's Land* (1954). Jorgenson appears as a character in several historical novels about Tasmania, e.g. Roy Bridges's *The Cards of Fortune* (1922) and William Hay's *The Escape of the Notorious Sir William Heans* (1919).

JOSE, A.W. (ARTHUR WILBERFORCE) (1863–1934), who has been described as 'one of the best Australians ever born and educated in England', was born in Gloucestershire, England, and at nineteen emigrated to Australia for his health. In 1885–99, after experience in the bush, he worked mainly as a teacher and university extension lecturer; after a five-year interlude spent in South Africa, India and England, he returned to Australia as correspondent for the London *Times* (1904–15). Jose's first publication was *Sun and Cloud on River and Sea* (1888), an early Angus & Robertson collection of verse written under the pseudonym 'Ishmael Dare'; later he made substantial contributions to Australian writing as an historian, editor, essayist. His *A Short History of Australasia* (1899), expanded as *History of Australasia*, went through fifteen editions by 1929. Among other works, he wrote the naval volume in the *Official History of Australia in the War of 1914–1918* (1928), two volumes of essays, *Two Awheel and Some Others Afoot in Australia* (1903) and *Builders and Pioneers of Australia* (1928), and was editor-in-chief of the first edition of the *Australian Encyclopaedia* (1925–26). Jose's most significant work, however, was *The Romantic Nineties* (q.v., 1933), which played an influential part in the development of the legend of the Nineties (q.v.). A publisher's reader for many years, he edited major collections of Henry Lawson and A.B. Paterson.

Journal of Australasia, (1856–58), also known as the *Illustrated Journal of Australasia* for part of 1857–58, was a Melbourne monthly which contained serial and short fiction, poetry and literary articles. Thomas McCombie and Henry Gyles Turner contributed to the journal, which is best known as the original place of publication for *The Fiction Fields of Australia* (q.v., 1856) by Frederick Sinnett, editor in 1857.

Journal of Commonwealth Literature, see **Association for Commonwealth Language and Literature Studies**

Journalist and Two Bears, A, see **EDMOND, JAMES**

JOYCE, ALFRED (1821–1901) born London, England, came to Australia in 1843. He and his older brother George, who had arrived in 1840, paid £50 for a run of some 10 000 acres in the Loddon River district of Victoria, which they named Plaistow after the family home in Essex. After his marriage in 1853 Alfred took over Norwood, a 37 000 acre property nearby, but after a period of prosperity he was driven into the hands of the banks and by 1887 had lost the property. In 1896–98 he set down his reminiscences but they remained unpublished until 1942 when G.F. James (a significant figure in Australian publishing) edited *A Homestead History*, which comprises two sections: 'The Reminiscences, 1843–51', which relate the establishment of Plaistow and experiences in the Port Phillip District up to the Joyce brothers' purchase of Norwood in 1851; and 'The Letters, 1851–64', most of which were written at Norwood and recount the development of the station during the gold rush period and up to the building of the permanent homestead in 1864.

Jugglers Three, see **WILLIAMSON, DAVID**

JURGENSEN, MANFRED (1940–   ), born Flensburg, then in Denmark now in West Germany, came to Australia in 1961 after living in Germany, Switzerland and the USA. He was educated at the Universities of Melbourne and Zurich and now holds a personal chair in German literature at the University of Queensland. Interested in the study of comparative literature and bilingualism in poetry, Jurgensen has written more than thirty books, including the first history of Australian literature in German. His poetry collections in English (he has also published three in German) are *Signs and Voices* (1973), *A Kind of Dying* (1977), *A Winter's Journey* (1979), which records details of a return visit to Flensburg, *South African Transit* (1979), and *The Skin Trade* (1983). In 1979 his novel, *Wehrersatz*, about a Flensburg man trying to escape national service, was made into a television film in Germany; his first novel in English was *Break Out* (1979). He edited *Ethnic Australia* (1981), an anthology of short stories and poetry by twenty-four authors whose first language is not English.

JURY, C.R. (CHARLES RISCHBIETH) (1893–1958), born Glenelg, SA, was educated at Oxford, served with the British army in the First World War and became a lecturer in English at the University of Adelaide in 1933. In 1946–49 he was professor of English at the

University; the chair was later named in his honour. A considerable contemporary influence on the SA literary scene, he held strictly classical and traditional concepts of poetry. Represented in *Lamps and Vine Leaves* (1919) with Vernon Knowles and E.J. Morgan, he also published *Love and the Virgins* (1929, a verse play), *Galahad, Selenemia, and Poems* (1939), *Icarius* (1955, a Greek drama), *The Sun in Servitude and Other Plays* (1961) and *Well Measur'd Song* (1968); the last is an essay on prosody, in particular on his own use of quantitative and quasi-quantitative verse, edited by Barbara Wall and D.C. Muecke.

K

'KABBARLI', see BATES, DAISY

Kable, Reuben and Mary, see *Emigrant Family, The*

'Kaddish', see ZWICKY, FAY

KAHAN, LOUIS (1905–   ), born Vienna, Austria, was a clothes designer and illustrator in Paris before enlisting in the French Foreign Legion and serving for a time as a war artist with the Allied armies in North Africa. In 1947 he came to Australia and worked as a full-time artist; his work is represented in all the major galleries. In 1960 he began a series of portrait sketches of important literary figures in *Meanjin*; many of these are included in Kahan's *Australian Writers: The Face of Literature* (1981). In 1962 he won the Archibald Prize with a portrait of novelist Patrick White.

KALESKI, ROBERT (1877–1961), born Burwood, Sydney, was a dog owner from the age of six and became during his life an expert on Australian dogs, including the dingo. In 1893 he began improving the blue heeler strain of cattle dog; he also established breeding standards for the kelpie and barb varieties of sheepdog. Under various pseudonyms, including 'Falder', he wrote articles on dogs, other animals and rural topics for the *Sydney Mail*, *Sydney Morning Herald*, *Bulletin* and *Bookfellow*. Some of his articles and stories appeared in book form as *Australian Barkers and Biters* (1914). He also compiled *The Australian Settler's Complete Guide* (1909).

Kalgoorlie, the chief town in the south-eastern mining area of WA, is some 600 kilometres east of Perth. Both Kalgoorlie and the adjoining town of Boulder owe their existence to the Golden Mile (q.v.), a rich gold-bearing reef. Gold was first discovered in the Kalgoorlie area by Paddy Hannan (q.v.) in 1893 and the settlement that sprang up in the gold rush that followed has continued to flourish to the present time. Represented in most books on the history of the Australian goldfields, Kalgoorlie is the particular subject of Gavin Casey and Ted Mayman's *The Mile That Midas Touched* (1964). Popular novelist Arthur Wright wrote the adventure story *Keane of Kalgoorlie* (1907); it was produced as a film in 1911. Katharine Susannah Prichard's goldfields trilogy, *The Roaring Nineties* (1946), *Golden Miles* (1948) and *Winged Seeds* (1950), is set partly in the Kalgoorlie–Coolgardie area.

Kanga Creek, see ELLIS, HAVELOCK

Kangaroo is an animal of the Macropodidae ('great-footed') family; other members of the family of over sixty species include wallaroos, wallabies, rat and tree kangaroos. The name was first met with by Captain James Cook when he encountered Aborigines near the site of present Cooktown in northern Queensland. Readily adopted by the early colonists, the name occurs frequently in colonial writing: Watkin Tench, Charles Harpur, Henry Kendall and Alexander Harris, for example, all record their surprise at the unfamiliar animal. Barron Field (q.v.) in his poem 'The Kangaroo' sees the bounding marsupial as an almost malicious afterthought of the Creator, made in defiance of all zoological propriety. The identification of the kangaroo with Australia (Field called it 'thou spirit of Australia') is seen in its presence on the Australian coat-of-arms; as the symbol, the 'Flying Kangaroo', of Australia's international airline Qantas; as the nickname, the Kangaroos, of Australia's representative Rugby League football team; and as the symbol, Matilda, at the Commonwealth Games, 1982.

Writers of children's fiction have used the kangaroo family to considerable effect; notable examples are Ethel Pedley's *Dot and the Kangaroo* (1899), Elizabeth MacIntyre's Ambrose Kangaroo books (1941, 1944, 1968), Mavis Mallinson's *The Magic Kangaroo* (1944), C.K. Thompson's *King of the Ranges: The Saga of the Grey Kangaroo* (1945), Ian Mudie's *The Christmas Kangaroo* (1946), Leslie Rees's *The Story of Shadow the Rock Wallaby* (1948), Lydia Eliott's *Kangaroo Coolaroo* (1950) and Dennis Clarke's *Boomer: The Life of a Kangaroo* (1955). J.K. Ewers wrote a verse narrative about a boy and a kangaroo, *Boy and Silver* (1929). The most successful literary kangaroo, however, is undoubtedly *Skippy the Bush Kangaroo* (1968) by Victor Barnes and filmed as an Australian television series. By the end of 1969 eighty countries had bought the *Skippy* series. A feature film was screened in 1969. The English novelist, D.H. Lawrence, used *Kangaroo* as the title of his Australian novel, published in 1923.

'Kangaroo, The', see *First Fruits of Australian Poetry*

Kangaroo (1923), a novel by D.H. Lawrence (q.v.) based on his experiences in Australia May–August 1922, is set in the same period. The writer and poet Richard Lovat Somers, Lawrence's self-portrait, and his wife Harriet, a picture of Frieda Lawrence, arrive in Sydney, where they rent a small suburban bungalow, Torestin. Convinced that in Europe 'everything was done for, played out, finished', Somers has come to the 'newest country' to 'start a new life and flutter with a new hope'. In Sydney the Somers become friendly with their neighbour, a returned digger, Jack Callcott, his wife Victoria, and his brother-in-law William James ('Jaz') Trewhella. Jack Callcott attempts to draw Somers into connection with a secret right-wing political movement, made up mainly of returned soldiers and committed to the aim of eventually seizing power. Although Somers does not really care about politics, which he sees as no more than a 'country's housekeeping', he is intrigued by his meetings with Kangaroo, the charismatic Jewish leader of the movement and in public life Benjamin Cooley, an eminent lawyer. Nevertheless he remains uncommitted, dedicated to his instinctive need to keep his individuality isolated. After a few weeks in Sydney, the Somers rent a cottage, Cooee, at Mullumbimby (Thirroul), a coastal mining town south of Sydney. There Somers continues his unsuccessful struggle to direct his marriage into the 'Pacific Ocean . . . [of] lord-and-masterdom', while Harriet attempts to reach 'the Atlantic of pure companionship'. Meanwhile at Canberra Hall in Sydney Somers also meets Willie Struthers, the labour movement leader,

although he is as unattracted by the 'generalized love' of socialism as he is by Kangaroo's 'great general emotion'. His ultimate rejection of Kangaroo, which is accompanied by feelings of terror and repulsion, recalls Lawrence's wartime experiences in England when he was persecuted for his refusal to subscribe to the 'wave of criminal lust' that possessed the nation from 1916 to 1919. Before leaving Australia for the USA, Somers has a last terrifying contact with the digger movement when it disrupts a labour meeting in Sydney, causing extensive casualties; Jack Callcott derives a passionate satisfaction from the violence but Kangaroo is shot and later dies of his wounds.

KANTARIZIS, SYLVIA, see **Feminism and Australian Literature**

KAVANAGH, PAUL (1941–), born Sydney, teaches English at the University of Newcastle, where he has edited *The Members of the Orchestra* (1981) and *Instructions for Honey Ants* (1983), anthologies of poems submitted for the 1981 and 1983 Mattara Spring Festival poetry prizes. His own books of verse are *Wild Honey* (1974) and *The Summerhouse* (1978).

'KAYE, LOUIS' (**NOEL WILSON NORMAN**) (1901–), born Claremont, Tasmania, spent considerable time as a young man on outback stations, where he assimilated the atmosphere that characterizes his novels. A successful contributor of short fiction to overseas magazines, 'Kaye' is best known in Australia as a writer of popular fiction. His first novel, *Tybal Men* (1931), is the story of a WA sheep station founded by the pioneer Maclean family and the difficulties of maintaining the heritage; an additional virtue of the book is its authentic presentation of the Aborigines. His other novels include *Trail of Plunder* (1931), a reflective work on the passing of the bushranging days; *The End of the Trail* (1933), which takes the author to the 'real Australia', the desert lands where pastoralists attempt to survive in a battle against the elemental forces of nature; *The Desert Boss* (1934), which emphasizes the brutalizing effect of the arid-land environment on certain types of men; *Tightened Belts* (1934), in which an old prospector strikes a rich opal field; *Pathways of Free Men* (1935), which underlines the allure of far horizons to the stockman; and *Tracks of Levask* (1938) which has, as do several of 'Kaye''s later novels, the basic ingredients of the American western.

KEAN, CHARLES (1811–68) and **ELLEN** (1805–80), were actors who toured Australia under contract to George Coppin 1863–64. Charles Kean was the son of Edmund Kean, the celebrated tragedian. Although their career in England had been successful, crowned by Charles Kean's appointment as director of Queen Victoria's private theatricals in 1848, it had not been lucrative and the colonial tour was designed to finance their anticipated retirement. Their stay was plagued by a series of illnesses and managerial problems but was not unsuccessful and helped to foster Australian interest in serious theatre. J.M.D. Hardwick edited *Emigrant in Motley: The Journey of Charles and Ellen Kean in Quest of a Theatrical Fortune in Australia and America, as Told in Their Hitherto Unpublished Letters* (1954).

Keep Him My Country (1955), a novel by Mary Durack (q.v.), is set in the 1950s on a cattle station in the Kimberleys of WA, where the author's parents and grandparents settled in the late nineteenth century. The manager of Trafalgar station, and central character in the novel, is Stan Rolt, grandson of the original pioneer. Stan takes over the running of the station on a temporary basis, expecting to stay only two years then to return to his university studies. He has a brief, idyllic love affair with the native girl, Dalgerie, but she is reclaimed by tribal law and returns to her own people. Depression and the war compel Stan Rolt to stay on at Trafalgar, and when after fifteen years the opportunity to depart finally comes, he finds himself unable to go. Through his love for Dalgerie, his understanding of her affinity with the land and his own long and close association with it, a bond has been forged which he is unable to break. Mary Durack gives an account in the novel of the varied and demanding activities of an outback cattle station, and also presents the dilemma of the Aborigines, faced with conflicting attachments to old tribal and new white environments. Her main concern, however, is to convince the white people of the outback that they must grow into the same spiritual harmony with the land that the Aborigines have achieved by generations of patient and loving understanding of it.

KEESING, NANCY (1923–), born Sydney, graduated from the University of Sydney and was a social worker at the Royal Alexandra Hospital for Children 1947–51. She has since been a freelance writer and active in numerous literary organizations, e.g. the English Association (committee member 1940–73); ASA, whose journal, the *Australian Author*, she edited 1971–74; the Literature Board (member, 1973–74 and chairman 1974–77); and the National Book Council. Her published works include criticism, *Elsie Carew* (1965) and *Douglas Stewart* (1965); she has edited *Australian Post-war Novelists* (1975) and, with Douglas Stew-

art, the important anthologies, *Australian Bush Ballads* (1955) and *Old Bush Songs* (1957). She has compiled *Gold Fever* (1967), *Transition* (1970, an ASA anthology), *The Kelly Gang* (1975), *The White Crysanthemum* (1977), *Henry Lawson: Favourite Verse* (1978), *Shalom* (1978, Australian Jewish short stories) and *Lily on the Dustbin: Slang of Australian Women and Families* (1982). She has also written children's novels, *By Gravel and Gum* (1963) and *The Golden Dream* (1974); a book of memoirs, *Garden Island People* (1975), and a biographical work, *John Lang and 'The Forger's Wife'* (1979). Her volumes of poetry are *Imminent Summer* (1951), *Three Men and Sydney* (1955), *Showgrounds Sketchbook* (1968) and *Hails and Farewells* (1977).

KEFALA, ANTIGONE (1935–), born in Braila, Romania, of Greek parents, has lived in Romania, Greece, NZ and Australia. She graduated from Victoria University, Wellington, in 1960 and has worked as a librarian, migrant English teacher and as an arts administrator. She has published two books of poetry, *The Alien* (1973) and *Thirsty Weather* (1978), and two short novels, *The First Journey* and *The Boarding House*, under the title *The First Journey* (1975).

KELLAWAY, FRANK (1922–), born London of Australian parents, graduated from the University of Melbourne in 1948 and worked as a librarian and as a lecturer at the Preston Institute of Technology in Melbourne. His volumes of poetry are *Beanstalk* (1973) and *Mare's Nest* (1978). He has also written fiction, *A Straight Furrow* (1960), *The Quest for Golden Dan* (1962) and *Golden Dan* (1976), and verse libretti for the music of George Dreyfus in operas performed in Australia and abroad.

KELLEHER, VICTOR (1939–), born London, completed his university education in South Africa and has been an academic at universities in South Africa, NZ and Australia. A successful writer of novels for children, e.g. *Forbidden Paths of Thual* (1979) and *The Hunting of Shadroth* (1981), he won the 1983 Australian Children's Book of the Year Award for *Master of the Grove* (1982). His adult fiction includes a volume of short stories, *Africa and After* (1983), and the two novels, *Voices from the River* (1979) and *The Beast of Heaven* (1984).

KELLOW, H.A. (HENRY ARTHUR) (1881–1935), born Fifeshire, Scotland, was educated at the University of Glasgow and was a schoolmaster in Airdrie and Glasgow before accepting the headmastership of Rockhampton Grammar School in 1912. He remained there until his death; the critic, Cecil Hadgraft, was a pupil and returned to teach at the school. Before leaving Scotland, Kellow had written a study of Robert Burns, compiled an anthology of Scottish verse and had published *A Practical Training in English* (1911). In Rockhampton he wrote *Queensland Poets* (1930), a pioneering critical study. He is the subject of a monograph by Lorna McDonald (1981).

KELLY, GWEN (1922–), born Gwen Smith at Thornleigh, an outer Sydney suburb, is a distinguished graduate of the University of Sydney who has combined a career in secondary and tertiary teaching with the writing of several novels, *There Is No Refuge* (1961), *The Red Boat* (1968), *The Middle-Aged Maidens* (1976) and *Always Afternoon* (1981). In 1980 she published, with A.J. Bennett, a volume of selected poems, *Fossils and Stray Cats*. A successful short story writer with wide representation in Australian journals and periodicals, she has won four Henry Lawson prose awards. In 1981 she was presented by the Society of Women Writers with the first Hilarie Lindsay Award for achievement by a woman writer.

KELLY, JOHN EDWARD, see *Stockwhip*

KELLY, KATE (1862–98), Ned Kelly's sister, was a supporter of the Kelly gang although she neither played as active a role as is attributed to her in Australian folklore, nor became after Ned's death a disgrace to the family by trading on the notoriety of its name. Present at the siege of Glenrowan, she pleaded his case with the governor of Victoria and with Melbourne theatre audiences on the night of his execution. Following the release of her mother from prison in 1881, she worked in Adelaide, toured as an equestrienne, worked on a central western station in NSW, and moved in 1886 to Forbes, where she married in 1888 and was drowned a decade later; she is buried near Ben Hall in Forbes cemetery. Frank Hatherley's play 'Ned Kelly's Sister's Travelling Circus', later titled 'Kate Kelly's Roadshow', was first performed in 1980; Jean Bedford's novel, *Sister Kate*, was published in 1982.

KELLY, NED (1855–80), was the eldest son of an Irish ex-convict, John 'Red' Kelly (1820–66), who was transported to Van Diemen's Land in 1842, went to the mainland when his sentence expired, and married Ellen Quinn in 1850; he appears as a character in Eric Lambert's Eureka novel, *The Five Bright Stars* (1954). After his death, Ellen moved with the children to a small selection between Greta and Glenrowan in north-eastern Victoria, the 'Kelly country' as it has become known. Along with the Lloyds and the Quinns, relatives with whom they sometimes feuded, the Kellys formed part of the rural poor, suspected of duffing cattle and other crimes but also persecuted by the police. In 1870, after a previous acquittal for robbery under arms, Ned was sentenced to six months' hard labour for assault and offensive behaviour, and in 1871 to three years' gaol for receiving a stolen horse. Following his release he stayed out of trouble for several years but eventually became involved again in the theft of stock, partly because he was provoked, like others of the clan, by the actions of the local squatters in impounding the cattle of the selectors. In April 1878 a trooper named Fitzpatrick went to the Kelly shanty to arrest Dan Kelly (1861–80), Ned's brother, for stealing horses. What happened there has never been completely established but Fitzpatrick, later dismissed from the police force, claimed he had been shot by Ned, who was almost certainly not present. Dan went into hiding in the Wombat Ranges, where he was joined by Ned. In October, Ellen Kelly received three years' hard labour for her part in the attempted murder of Fitzpartick; later that month the Kellys, together with Joe Byrne, Steve Hart and a fifth man, Tom Lloyd Jnr., who was never identified as a member of the Kelly gang, surprised a police camp at Stringybark Creek, where according to one account Constable Lonigan was reading a copy of *The Vagabond Papers*. In the ensuing affray Lonigan, his fellow constable Scanlon and Sergeant Kennedy were killed, but the fourth policeman, McIntyre, escaped to give evidence at Ned Kelly's trial.

Within a week the gang had been outlawed, but avoided capture for nearly two years, not least because of the 'bush telegraph' operated by sympathizers. In December 1878 the bushrangers 'stuck up' a bank at Euroa, and in February 1879 made a similar raid at Jerilderie in NSW. On both occasions they cleared more than £2000 and gallantly entertained their victims; at Jerilderie, Ned produced a written vindication of his conduct which has become known as the Jerilderie Letter (q.v.). The climax to the gang's adventures came at the end of June 1880, when the Kellys, Hart and Byrne ensconced themselves in a hotel at Glenrowan, planning to derail a special police train sent up from Melbourne; it is probable that they hoped to spark off a wider rebellion in the area. (A Bertram Chandler fantasy novel, *Kelly Country* (1983), shows what might have happened if the Kellys had won at Glenrowan.) The plan was foiled when the local schoolmaster, Curnow, receiving permission to leave the hotel to go home, warned the train crew. In the battle between police and the gang,

Byrne, Hart and Dan Kelly died in the hotel and Ned, clad in metal armour, was wounded and captured. Tried in October 1880 for one of the Stringybark Creek murders, he was convicted, sentenced to death and executed on 11 November; by one account his last words were 'Such is Life'. The anniversary of his death falls on the same day as two other events of significance to Australians: the Armistice ending the First World War, and the dismissal of the Whitlam government in 1975.

The Kelly gang was the last of the famous bushranging gangs and for many colonists in 1880 the capture of Ned meant safety from a cold-blooded killer. Such was the view of most of his pursuers, among whom John Sadleir, in *Memoirs of a Victorian Police Officer* (1913), left the best-known account from the law-and-order side, and more recently of George Farwell in *Ned Kelly, What a Life!* (1970). Yet 32000 people petitioned for Ned's reprieve, and since his execution the Kelly legend in Australian folklore has grown and been celebrated in song and dance, verse and prose, paint and film. The legend's sympathy for the Kellys has its origin in the several factors which made them underdogs: they were of the selector class, disadvantaged by the inequitable distribution of land by urban legislators in favour of the squatters; they were of Irish and convict origins; and were subject to a legal system which showed its severity in Sir Redmond Barry's sentencing of Ellen and Ned Kelly and which was administered by a force of police whose incompetence was satirized during the long pursuit of the gang and whose shortcomings were exposed in a subsequent Royal Commission (1881–83). Added to this, Ned was brave (to be as 'game as Ned Kelly' is to show the same kind of pluck that helped him survive multiple wounds received at Glenrowan), a superb bushman loyal to his mates and, although something of a 'larrikin', possessed the kind of daring and gallantry both at Euroa and Jerilderie that place him within a wider outlaw-highwayman folk tradition. Most of the Kelly folk-songs (q.v.) and ballads, including the anonymous 'The Kelly Gang', 'The Kellys, Byrne and Hart', 'Kelly was Their Captain' and 'Farewell to My Home in Greta', express this view of Ned and his circle. Three works in the same tradition are J.J. Keneally's influential *The Complete Inner History of the Kelly Gang and Their Pursuers* (1929), which carries a testimonial by Ned's brother Jim and was a major source for Frank Clune's best-selling *The Kelly Hunters* (1954); Max Brown's fine biography, *Australian Son* (1948), which first published some of the Kelly songs and the Jerilderie Letter; and Eric Lambert's novel *Kelly* (1964), which presents Ned as an 'underground saint'.

A second view of the Kellys has emerged through what Graham Seal (*Ned Kelly in Popular Tradition*, 1980) has called the 'media tradition', which has exploited the sensational aspects of the story. From the start, the exploits of the Kelly gang were media events, as evidenced by the contemporary booklet, *The Kelly Gang: Or, The Outlaws of the Wombat Ranges* (1879); the popularity of Thomas Carrington's sketches for the Melbourne press; the photographs taken at Glenrowan and sold later as postcards; and the several Kelly plays performed before Ned's capture, during his trial, and immediately following his execution. Within the same tradition can be placed J.J.G. Bradley's serialized story, *Ned Kelly: The Ironclad Australian Bushranger* (1881), Nat Gould's novel, *Stuck Up* (1894), Ambrose Pratt's *Dan Kelly* (1911), which exploits the rumours of Dan's escape from Glenrowan (the rumour-mongering is satirized in Nettie Palmer's ballad, 'The Mystery Man'), Roy Bridges's romance, *The Fenceless Ranges* (1920), the Kelly stage melodramas of Dan Barry and Arnold Denham (1898–99), and the six Kelly films made 1906–70. Some of these works, influenced by the oral tradition, offer unashamedly sympathetic portrayals of the Kellys but a more characteristic note is one of ambivalence towards Ned and his fellow hero-criminals. Something of the same ambivalence is to be found in Douglas Stewart's play *Ned Kelly* (q.v., 1943) and in the two series (1946–55) of Kelly paintings by Sidney Nolan; both Stewart and Nolan explore Ned's symbolic significance. Like David Campbell's Kelly poems in *Devil's Rock and Other Poems 1970–72* (1974) and the Kelly comics and modern songs, Stewart and Nolan have done much to keep the legend alive.

Thirdly, Ned Kelly has loomed large in Australian historical writing, including the general histories of Australia such as Manning Clark's *A History of Australia*; studies in the Australian tradition such as Russel Ward's *The Australian Legend* (1958); the early bushranging histories of James Bonwick, Charles White, George Boxall and Jack Bradshaw; and a number of specific studies. The centenary of Ned's capture and execution saw moves for a retrospective pardon; the screening of the television series *The Last Outlaw*; and the publication or reprinting of numerous Kelly books, including studies of the Kelly legend by Graham Seal (*Ned Kelly in Popular Tradition*) and Keith Dunstan (*Saint Ned*), the biographical interpretation by John Molony (*I Am Ned Kelly*), *Ned Kelly, after a Century of Acrimony*, by the folklorists John Meredith and Bill Scott, and Gary Langford's black comedy, *The Adventures of Dreaded Ned*. Of the many other works published earlier the most important are perhaps David Martin's satiric novel debunking the bushranging legend, *The Hero of Too* (1965), the collection of papers edited by Colin Cave as *Ned Kelly: Man and Myth* (1968), Charles Osborne's *Ned Kelly* (1970), Brian Carroll's *Ned Kelly, Bushranger* (1976), and especially John McQuilton's *The Kelly Outbreak 1879–1880* (1979), which places the exploits of the Kelly gang within the phenomenon of agrarian protest and social banditry. Despite its central character and the brief appearance of policemen named Kennedy and Scanlon, Thomas Keneally's children's fantasy, *Ned Kelly and the City of the Bees* (1978), is of little significance to the Kelly story beyond demonstrating that Ned's name still sells books. Jean Bedford's *Sister Kate* (1982) loosely reconstructs the life of Ned's sister Kate Kelly.

KEMP, EDWARD (1822–?), born near Hobart, was the author of the early political satire, *A Voice from Tasmania* (q.v., 1846). He was the son of the pioneer settler Anthony Fenn Kemp (1773–1868), who was involved in the Rum Rebellion and who makes a brief appearance in 'Price Warung''s story, 'The Evolution of Convict Hendy', and in Henry Savery's *The Hermit in Van Diemen's Land* (1830).

KENDALL, HENRY (1839–82), born near Milton on the NSW south coast, spent his impressionable boyhood in the coastal districts of Illawarra in the south and the Clarence river in the north. Their cool moist rainforests, deep-shadowed gullies and lush pastures became the centrepieces of Kendall's best-known poetry, the landscape lyrics such as 'Bell Birds', 'September in Australia', 'Araluen' (qq.v.) and 'Narrara Creek'. After a difficult childhood with loving but impractical parents, and a stint of two years at sea in a whaler, Kendall settled into the literary coterie of Sydney, making his mark with poems in Sydney journals and newspapers from 1859 onwards. His first volume, *Poems and Songs* (q.v.), was published in 1862 with the assistance of J. Sheridan Moore. Although generously received by local and some English critics, the volume failed to sell its first edition of 500 copies. Beset by debts and personal problems, including a growing dependence on both literary patronage and alcohol, Kendall sought a new life in Melbourne after his marriage in 1868; his second volume, *Leaves from Australian Forests* (q.v.), was published there in 1869. The failure of the Melbourne venture which led to increasing poverty, alcoholism and the death of his daughter Araluen, brought his return to Sydney in 1870, where the rapid disintegration of his personal and literary life continued. This painful period, described by him as 'The Shadow of 1872', brought alienation from his wife and periods of treatment for addiction in the Gladesville asylum. He was restored to health and sanity, and cured of alcoholism, by the extraordinary kindness of the Fagan family, timber merchants of Gosford and Sydney, who for two years, 1873–75, supervised his rehabilitation in their home near Gosford. In 1876 Kendall was reunited with his wife and family when he began a new life at the Fagan timber mill at Camden Haven on the north coast of NSW. His return to writing was signalled by his winning the *Sydney Morning Herald*'s International Exhibition poetry competition in 1879 and by the publication of his final volume, *Songs from the Mountains* (q.v.), in 1880. In 1881 he was appointed inspector of forests by Sir Henry Parkes, the long-time patron whom Kendall offended many times down the years but never more deeply than with his satire, 'The Gagging Bill', in 1879. Kendall's health deteriorated under the strain of the travelling and work associated with his new position; he died in Sydney of phthisis when only forty three.

Kendall's literary reputation, extraordinarily high in his own lifetime and immediately after his death but never at the same peak in this century, still rests chiefly on his lyric poetry. 'Bell Birds', 'September in Australia' and 'The Song of the Cattle Hunters', with their elaborate word pictures, extravagant melody and haunting melancholy, endeared themselves to succeeding generations of Australian readers and established Kendall as a favourite schoolroom poet. Some modern critical opinion, while not denying the importance of these popular lyrics in the total Kendall canon, has drawn attention to the many-sided nature of Kendall's poetic talent, ignored when the nationalistic fervour of the 1890s and the early decades of this century dismissed his work as derivative. Kendall's neglected narrative poems, whether with an Australian setting such as 'The Glen of Arrawatta' or 'A Death in the Bush', or with biblical backgrounds such as 'King Saul at Gilboa' and 'Manasseh', or based on the Homeric legends of Ulysses such as 'The Voyage of Telegonus', now attract attention because of their significant themes and their controlled narrative skill. Kendall's affectionate though tart commentaries on the colonial outback types, e.g. 'Bill the Bullock Driver' and 'Jim the Splitter' (qq.v.) are now seen to have anticipated Henry Lawson and A.B. Paterson portraits of similar bush characters. In the role of literary hatchetman, as in the satires 'The Gagging Bill' and 'The Song of Ninian Melville', and to a lesser extent, 'The Bronze Trumpet', he reveals a vindictiveness that does not surprise those who know the correspondence of his early manhood. His love poetry, especially 'Rose Lorraine' and 'At Nightfall', which tell of his lost love for Rose Bennett, and the poignant 'Araluen' and 'On a Street', which reflect his guilt over the broken years 1869–72, are powerful statements of the problems of his troubled life. His patriotic verse, such as 'The Far Future', which attempts to create new loyalties and new hopes; his public poems, written for important occasions such as the 1879 International Exhibition in Sydney; his memorial verses for Charles Harpur, James Lionel Michael and Adam Lindsay Gordon; and his attempt in the fragmentary 'The Australian Shepherd' to begin the first Australian rural epic, all support the claim that Kendall was the most substantial poet of the colonial period. T.T. Reed compiled the definitive edition of Kendall, *The Poetical Works of Henry Kendall* (1966) and wrote *Henry Kendall: A Critical Appreciation* (1960). W.H. Wilde published the biographical and critical account *Henry Kendall* (1976).

KENEALLY, THOMAS (1935–   ), was born in Sydney, where he completed his schooling after some years at Kempsey, Wauchope and Taree on the NSW north coast. At seventeen he commenced study for the Catholic priesthood, a vocation he abandoned in 1960 before ordination; the experience informed his early fiction, e.g. *Three Cheers for the Paraclete*, which focuses on a young priest's conflict with his superiors. He worked as a schoolteacher and clerk before the publication of his first novel, *The Place at Whitton*, in 1964. Since then he has been mainly a full-time writer, although in 1969–70 he lectured in drama at the University of New England; he has travelled widely in Australia and overseas, and has lived abroad for extended periods, in 1975–77 mainly in the USA. *The Place at Whitton* and Keneally's second novel, *The Fear* (1965), won some praise among reviewers, but his first major success was *Bring Larks and Heroes* (q.v., 1967), which won the Miles Franklin Award. His subsequent novels are *Three Cheers for the Paraclete* (1968), which also won the Miles Franklin Award; *The Survivor* (1969), which shared the Cook Bicentenary Award in 1970 and was filmed for television (1971); *A Dutiful Daughter* (q.v., 1971); *The Chant of Jimmie Blacksmith* (q.v., 1972), which won awards from the *Sydney Morning Herald* and the Royal Society of Literature and was filmed in 1978; *Blood Red, Sister Rose* (1974); *Gossip from the Forest* (1975), which was filmed for television (1978); *Season in Purgatory* (1976); *A Victim of the Aurora* (1977); *Passenger* (1979); *Confederates* (1979); *The Cut-Rate Kingdom* (1980), a magazine novel with modern advertisements and

photography contemporary with its setting, Australia and New Guinea during the Second World War; and *Schindler's Ark* (q.v., 1982), which won the prestigious Booker McConnell prize in the UK, for which Keneally had previously been shortlisted with *The Chant of Jimmie Blacksmith*, *Gossip from the Forest* and *Confederates*. Apart from involvement in the television and film adaptations of his fiction, Keneally has written stage adaptations of *Bring Larks and Heroes* (*Halloran's Little Boat*, first performed 1966, published 1975), and *Gossip from the Forest* (first performed 1983); three other plays, 'Childermas' (1968), 'An Awful Rose' (1972) and 'Bullie's House' (1980); scripts for television (e.g. the Bligh episode in *Behind the Legend* series, 1974) and film (e.g. *Libido*, 1973); a children's fantasy, *Ned Kelly and the City of the Bees* (1978); *Moses the Lawgiver* (1975), a book written to complement an English television series; and a lavishly-illustrated travel book, *Outback* (1983). A Fellow of the Royal Society of Literature, Keneally was made AO in 1983.

A fluent writer who has on several occasions expressed his contempt for academic critics and stated that he writes for a middlebrow audience, Keneally is a novelist who is both popular – overseas as well as in Australia – and serious. The range of his fiction is apparent in his prose, which moves from the idiomatic and vernacular to the symbolic and rhetorical; in his choice of subject matter, which is mainly Australian up to *The Chant of Jimmie Blacksmith* and has since included France, England, America, Antarctica, Yugoslavia and Poland; and in his diverse use of fable (e.g. *A Dutiful Daughter*), fantasy (e.g. *Passenger*), parable (e.g. *Bring Larks and Heroes*) suspense (e.g. *The Survivor*, *A Victim of the Aurora*) and other modes. Many of his novels have a starting point either in Keneally's experience (e.g. the importance of Catholicism in *The Place of Whitton*, *The Fear* and *Three Cheers for the Paraclete*) or in history. *Bring Larks and Heroes*, set in early NSW, is informed by Watkin Tench's writings and by Keneally's knowledge of the Vinegar Hill (q.v.) uprising by Irish convicts in 1804. *The Chant of Jimmie Blacksmith* is a fictional recreation of the Jimmy Governor (q.v.) episode in the history of European–Aboriginal relationships in Australia. The subject of *Blood Red, Sister Rose* is Joan of Arc, a figure who recurs in other Keneally novels, notably *A Place at Whitton* and *A Dutiful Daughter*. The setting of *Gossip from the Forest* is the Armistice negotiations at the end of the First World War. *Season in Purgatory*, in which Tito makes an appearance, focuses on the Yugoslav partisans during the Second World War and *Confederates* on the 1862 campaigns of Stonewall Jackson in the

American Civil War. *Schindler's Ark* uses 'the texture and devices of a novel to tell a true story', that of the German industrialist, Oskar Schindler, who saved more than a thousand Jews from the gas chambers during the Holocaust. On more than one occasion the links between history and Keneally's fiction have caused controversy, e.g. in the parallels drawn between *Season in Purgatory* and an earlier work on the same subject, Bill Strutton's *Island of Terrible Friends* (1961), and in the objections raised when *Schindler's Ark* was awarded the Booker Prize that the novel was less fiction than 'faction'.

Yet despite Keneally's ability to capture the authentic texture of history, notably in *Gossip from the Forest*, *Schindler's Ark* and *Confederates*, his novels are not simply historical reconstructions, nor is his imagination enslaved by the past. Several of his works, e.g. *Three Cheers for the Paraclete*, *A Dutiful Daughter*, *Passenger*, 'An Awful Rose', are contemporary in setting or in the issues they address, e.g. religious belief, abortion, familial relationships. Those works that are 'historical' remain also, as Keneally suggested of *Bring Larks and Heroes*, 'essentially contemporary', forging linkages between the past and the present. *Bring Larks and Heroes*, described by him as 'a parable for the present', was written during the Australian experience of Vietnam, an experience influential in 'Childermas', an anti-war play commissioned by the Australian Committee of Responsibility for Children in Vietnam. The historical framework so overtly established in *The Chant of Jimmie Blacksmith* offers an implicit explanation for the current state of Black/White relationships in Australia. *Blood Red, Sister Rose*, to take a third example, is in part a novel about how myths are established. A recurring theme in Keneally's work is the predicament of the ordinary individual, vulnerable in the midst of a hostile world. This preoccupation is reflected in the extreme situations that his characters find themselves in, e.g. in times of war (eight of the novels); the sense of fragility and absurdity of the body and of life itself; and the prevalence of violence, e.g. the murders, hangings, sacrifices, butchery, blood and witchcraft that commentators have noticed as staples in his fiction. The attempts of Keneally's protagonists to act with integrity, decency or honour are characteristically at odds with the demands of the systems of authority that mankind constructs: religious systems (as in *Three Cheers for the Paraclete*); political systems of various forms (e.g. communism in *The Fear*, Nazism in *Schindler's Ark*); systems of kinship (e.g. the family in 'An Awful Rose' and *A Dutiful Daughter*, race in *The Chant of Jimmie Blacksmith*). In some Keneally novels the individual

is oppressed by the combinations of authority (e.g. Halloran by both Church and State in *Bring Larks and Heroes*), in others by their conflict (e.g. *Confederates* and the other war novels). The irony is that humanity constructs and codifies authority, and that individuals (e.g. Halloran, Erzberger in *Gossip from the Forest*) are drawn to seek moral protection or justification for their conduct within the systems. Thus humanity is collectively responsible for what has been made of the world, although some critics (e.g. Shirley Walker in *Who Is She?*, 1983) have argued persuasively that it is Keneally's women (e.g. Ettie Bumphass in *Confederates*, Barbara Glover in *A Dutiful Daughter*) who are made to bear the moral burden. That issue apart, the recognition of collective complicity and guilt, and Keneally's mixing of comedy and tragedy, offer what little hope there is in his fictional worlds.

KENNA, FRANCIS (1865–1932), born Maryborough, Queensland, worked in a post office, was a teacher, member of the Queensland parliament and a newspaperman. He was editor of the Queensland *Worker*, the *Clarion*, the Brisbane *Sun* and the Charters Towers *Telegraph*, and owned and edited the Bangalow *Herald* and the *Logan and Albert Bulletin*, now the *Gold Coast Bulletin*. A regular *Bulletin* poet, Kenna often used the pseudonym 'K'; he contributed to the *Bulletin* debate in the 1890s, siding with Henry Lawson and satirizing A.B. Paterson with his parody, 'Banjo of the Overflow'. Kenna published two volumes of verse, *Songs of a Season* (1895) and *Phases* (1915), which range from the easy vernacular of the bush ballad to elegiac poetry of considerable intensity. A devoted Labor Party man, Kenna shared the sentiments of poets such as Lawson and Barcroft Boake, fulminating against the 'Lords of the Money' and their oppression of the working class.

KENNA, PETER (1930–   ), was born in Sydney into a large Irish-Catholic family and at the age of ten began to work with a concert party entertaining troops. After leaving school at fourteen, he worked in a variety of jobs, meanwhile performing with amateur theatre groups. By the 1950s he was an established radio actor and joined the Australian Elizabethan Theatre Trust on its formation in 1954. In 1959 his play, *The Slaughter of St. Teresa's Day*, won the General Motors–Holden national playwrights' competition, was subsequently widely performed in Australia and was produced on radio and television in Australia and Britain. Between 1960 and 1971 Kenna lived mainly in London, where his play, *Talk to the Moon* (1977), was first produced in 1963, although he visited Australia briefly to direct his farce, 'Muriel's Virtues', at the Independent Theatre in 1966. In 1971 he returned to live permanently in Sydney, where he re-established his name with a number of productions. His published plays are *The Slaughter of St. Teresa's Day* (1972), *A Hard God* (q.v., 1974), *Three Plays* (*Talk to the Moon, Listen Closely* and *Trespassers Will Be Prosecuted*) (1977), *Mates* in *Drag Show* (1977), and *Furtive Love* (1980).

The Slaughter of St. Teresa's Day, set in Sydney's inner suburb Paddington in the 1950s, deals with the criminal underworld of the city and one of its prominent female individuals. It effectively combines naturalism, sensational events, comedy and sentiment, and touches on one of Kenna's characteristic themes, the difficulty of establishing and maintaining intimate human relationships. This theme is more obvious in his working-class family drama, *Talk to the Moon*, and in his play for two actors, *Trespassers Will Be Prosecuted*; set in a culvert beneath a railway line, the latter is a territorial battle between an aging alcoholic tramp and an adolescent boy, in which the corruption and innocence, aggressions and needs of both are laid bare. *Listen Closely*, a farce which turns on a country father's attempt to impose a ritual of initiation on his son and the reactions of the various women involved, is also an effective satire of Australian middle-class mores. Kenna's best-known play, *A Hard God*, which draws heavily on his Irish-Catholic boyhood and has aroused memories of familiar experiences in many of his audiences, is concerned with the difficulties and comforts of the Catholic religion, the effects of time and the experience of loss. The play's structure, and its division between the experience of the older members of the Cassidy family and Joe Cassidy's adolescent relationship with another boy, reflect Kenna's interest in combining an expressionistic, thematically-developed form with representational realism. Kenna conceived *A Hard God* originally as part of a trilogy and has since completed it with the further two plays, *Furtive Love* and 'An Eager Hope' to form 'The Cassidy Album'. The trilogy was first performed at the Adelaide Festival in 1978. *Furtive Love*, which takes up the story of Joe Cassidy, now an actor and author, a decade later, centres on the conflict between his homosexuality and his religion; 'An Eager Hope' returns to the home of the Cassidy family, where Joe, now in his thirties, unsuccessfully fights kidney disease, whereas his brother Francis evades suffering by means of his facile charm. Kenna's short play, *Mates*, a confrontation between Sylvia, a transvestite homosexual and a night-club performer, and Perce, an old shearer who is firmly heterosexual, is a further exploration of the theme

of the absence of intimacy in modern life and the inadequacy of relationships, including sexual ones.

KENNEDY, E.B.C. (EDMUND BESLEY COURT) (1818–48), born Guernsey, arrived in Australia in 1840 and was almost immediately appointed a government assistant surveyor. After an initial period of exploration and surveying in the Portland Bay area in 1841, he joined Sir Thomas Mitchell's 1845 expedition to find an overland route to the Gulf of Carpentaria. In 1847 Kennedy led a further expedition that corrected Mitchell's errors about the Cooper's Creek (q.v.)/Barcoo River system. In an 1848 expedition to traverse Cape York Peninsula he was killed by Aborigines; from that tragedy came the story of the devotion of his native servant, Jacky Jacky (q.v.). William Carron wrote *Narrative of an Expedition, Undertaken under the Direction of the Late Mr. Assistant Surveyor E.B. Kennedy* (1849) and Judith Wright wrote about Kennedy and Jacky Jacky in the poem, 'Two Sides of a Story'. William Beard wrote of Kennedy's last expedition in *Heroic Journey* (1952); Edgar Beale published the biography, *Kennedy of Cape York* (1970)

KENNEDY, VICTOR (1895–1952), born Eaglehawk, Victoria, spent a lifetime in journalism and freelance writing in WA, Queensland and Victoria. A Jindyworobak in outlook, he wrote *Flaunted Banners* (1941), an essay in defence of the Jindyworobak movement and edited the Jindyworobak anthology of verse for 1942. His poetry includes *The Unknown Anzac and Other Poems* (1917), *Farthest North and Other Verses* (1928), *Light of Earth* (1938) and *Cyclone: Selected Poems* (1949). With Nettie Palmer he wrote the biographical and critical work, *Bernard O'Dowd* (1954).

KENNY, ROBERT (1950–), born Melbourne, was co-founder and co-editor until 1974 of *Contempa* magazine and publications. In 1974 he founded the Rigmarole of the Hours (q.v.) series of publications. He co-edited with Colin Talbot the verse anthology, *Applestealers* (1974) and has published two volumes of poetry, *Dead Ocean Poems* and '*Poem*' (both 1975); fiction, *A Book of Detection* (1978) and *The Last Adventures of Christian Doom: Private I* (1982); and prose, *Etcetera* (1978).

KENTISH, N.L. (NATHANIEL LIPSCOMB) (1797–1867), born Hampshire, England, arrived in NSW in 1830 to take up a government surveying appointment. He lost his job in 1833 and in 1834–38 ran the *Sydney*

387

Times, a pro-emancipist newspaper with a strong verse content which was published irregularly but sold strongly in competition with the *Sydney*, later *Sydney Morning, Herald*. Briefly an emigration agent, Kentish returned to surveying and spent most of the 1840s in Van Diemen's Land; in 1849 he went to Port Phillip, where he was gaoled for horsewhipping a newspaper editor, then returned to Sydney, where his last years were spent. A self-promoting controversialist, Kentish became embroiled with officialdom wherever he went and published several pamphlets in which he justified his conduct. Besides these, he wrote two descriptive works, *The Present State of New South Wales* (1835) and *The Political Economy of New South Wales* (1838), and several verse essays and miscellanies including *Essay on Capital Punishment* (1835); *The Bush in South Australia* (1836); the bibliographical curiosity, *Work in the Bush, Thoughts in the Bush, and Life in the Bush, of Van Diemen's Land* (1846); and *The Question of Questions* (1855), which reprints the broadsheet verse anthems with which Kentish, self-styled 'Amateur Poet Laureate' of Victoria, celebrated the separation in 1851 of that colony from NSW.

KEOGH, LESBIA, see **HARFORD, LESBIA**

KERR, D.B. (DONALD BEVIS) (1920–42), killed in air operations in New Guinea in the Second World War, was a poet whose talent was recognized by critics such as Max Harris and Geoffrey Dutton. A founder of the Angry Penguins journal and a leading figure in the avant-garde poetry movement of the early 1940s, Kerr is represented by the small posthumous collection, *Death Be Not Proud* (1944).

KERSHAW, ALISTER (1921–), born Melbourne, was for some years the ABC's radio correspondent in Paris, where he has spent much of his life. He published three books of poetry in the 1940s, *The Lonely Verge* (1943), *Excellent Stranger* (1944) and *Defeat by Time Past* (1947). He also wrote *History of the Guillotine* (1958), which is to some extent also a study of the French character. Kershaw's poetry, lucid, precise, almost austere in style but without significant substance, was well received at the time.

Kid Stakes, see **LAWLER, RAY**

KIDDLE, MARGARET (1914–58), born South Yarra, Melbourne, graduated in 1947 from the University of Melbourne, where she later taught history. She wrote two children's books, *Moonbeam Stairs* (1945) and *West of*

Sunset (1949), and a biography, *Caroline Chisholm* (1950), but her chief work was *Men of Yesterday: A Social History of the Western District of Victoria 1834–1890* (1961). Based largely on the family records of the early pioneers, *Men of Yesterday* begins with a prologue that describes Australia Felix and its Aboriginal inhabitants prior to white settlement and examines the conditions in Scotland and Ireland that led to large-scale emigration in the 1830s and 1840s. The first part depicts the pioneering ventures in Australia Felix from Van Diemen's land and overland from NSW. The second part has a chapter on the Victorian goldfields and outlines the problems associated with the land Acts. The third part sees the squatter dynasties firmly entrenched on magnificent merino studs with elaborate but practical rural homesteads and alternative mansions in Melbourne.

KIDMAN, Sir **SIDNEY** (1857–1935), born Athelstone, SA, became known throughout Australia as the 'Cattle King' because of his vast pastoral empire of more than a hundred properties. At twenty-three he bought his first property, Owen Springs station south-west of Alice Springs, and gradually extended his holdings into many parts of outback Queensland and NSW. The north-west of NSW was known as 'Kidman's Corner'. His exploits are recorded in E.J. Brady's *Australia Unlimited* (1918) and Ion L. Idriess's *The Cattle King* (1936). An Australian television film, *The Cattle King*, written and produced by Bill Bennett, was screened in 1984.

KIERNAN, BRIAN, see **Criticism**

Kiernan, Tom, a character in George Johnston's novel *Clean Straw for Nothing* (1969), is a fictionalized study of Sidney Nolan.

Kiley's Run, from the poem 'On Kiley's Run' by A.B. Paterson (q.v.) published in *The Man from Snowy River and Other Verses* (1895), is usually identified with the station, Narambla, where Paterson was born and spent many happy boyhood times. In its opening verses the poem presents an attractive glimpse, in the usual Paterson manner, of the carefree existence and camaraderie of bush life. But with droughts and unpaid overdrafts, Kiley's Run is eventually lost and passes through the bank to an absentee landlord in England. As Chandos Park Estate, it becomes merely an investment. Paterson had in 1888 written a pamphlet, 'Australia for Australians' urging land reform; 'On Kiley's Run' is a further attack on the evils of the land grant system, made more personal by its echoes of a situation that had occurred in the poet's own family years earlier.

Kimberleys, or more properly the Kimberley, a vast, sparsely-settled area of tropical north-western Australia, was named after the Earl of Kimberley, a former colonial secretary. Settlement of the Kimberleys followed Alexander Forrest's (q.v.) explorations in 1879; sheep were introduced into the western part of the region by Julius Brockman in 1879; the southern area began to be settled in 1881; by 1885 cattlemen from western Queensland, the Duracks, Nat Buchanan and others, had overlanded stock to the eastern area. Gold, discovered at Hall's Creek, led to an influx of settlement and the establishment of the port of Wyndham. The history and physical geography of the Kimberleys are recounted in such works as Alexander Forrest's *Journal of Expedition from De Grey to Port Darwin* (1880), Gordon Buchanan's *Packhorse and Waterhole: With The First Overlanders to the Kimberleys* (1933), Ion L. Idriess's *Over the Range* (1937), *One Wet Season* (1949) and *Outlaws of the Leopolds* (1952), J.K. Ewers's *With the Sun on My Back* (1953), Leslie and Coralie Rees's *Spinifex Walkabout* (1953) and Mary Durack's *Kings in Grass Castles* (q.v., 1959) and *Sons in the Saddle* (1983). The Kimberley region is now a major contributor to Australia's export of beef and iron ore.

KING, PHILIP GIDLEY (1758–1808), born Cornwall, England, was second lieutenant of the *Sirius* in the First Fleet and superintendent of the Norfolk Island settlement established in March 1788; he was its lieutenant-governor 1789–96. King succeeded Governor John Hunter at Port Jackson in 1800. An energetic administrator, he tried to eliminate the rum trade and other malpractices, developed agriculture and coal mining, extended exploration by land and sea, expanded the Colony's public works programme and improved the lot of convicts and emancipists. The journal of his experiences was published as an appendix to Hunter's *An Historical Journal of the Transactions at Port Jackson and Norfolk Island* (1793) and separately in 1980. King was the subject of some of the 'pipes' (q.v.) circulating in the Colony at the time; during his governorship the *Sydney Gazette* began publication. He is featured in H.V. Evatt's *Rum Rebellion* (1938); his wife, the first governor's wife to live in Australia, is the subject of Marnie Bassett's *The Governor's Lady* (1940); and the biography by his decendants, Jonathan King and John King, was published in 1981.

KING, PHILLIP PARKER (1791–1856), son of Governor Philip Gidley King, was born at Norfolk Island, where his father was lieutenant–governor. Trained as a surveyor, King was given command of the cutter, *Mermaid*, in

1817 to explore the north-western coast of Australia, the first of four such voyages he made between then and 1821. In 1826 he published *Narrative of a Survey of the Intertropical and Western Coasts of Australia*, partly illustrated by his own sketches. His connection with Australia was resumed in 1832 when he returned to the colony as a substantial landowner; in 1834 he became resident commissioner of the Australian Agricultural Company, which he had joined as a shareholder in 1824. King's exploits are discussed in G.C. Ingleton's *Charting a Continent* (1944) and G.S. Ritchie's *The Admiralty Chart: British Naval Hydrography in the Nineteenth Century* (1967). Dorothy Walsh edited *The Admiral's Wife: Mrs. Phillip Parker King* (1967).

Kings Cross, known colloquially as 'the Cross', and a byword throughout Australia for bohemianism, is a small area of the inner Sydney suburb of Darlinghurst. With a long-established reputation for its colourful citizenry, its cosmopolitan lifestyle and its exciting night life, Kings Cross has always been regarded as the 'sin centre' of Sydney, a constant allure to those escaping from the tedium of the bush on their annual jaunt to the city or to those city dwellers who want to escape, usually on a Saturday night, from the respectable monotony of the suburbs. It was beloved by writers such as the bohemian Marien Dreyer (q.v.), the impeccably moral Dame Mary Gilmore, who lived for over thirty years at 99 Darlinghurst Road in a comfortable – and at times, delighted – propinquity with strip joints, brothels and nightclubs, and *bon vivant* Kenneth Slessor (q.v.), an habitué of the area for even longer. The Cross has often been prominent in the literature of Sydney. Slessor's poems about Kings Cross, best-known of which is 'William Street' (q.v.), have been published separately as *Darlinghurst Nights* (1981) with the original *Smith's Weekly* illustrations by Virgil Reilly. Slessor and Robert Walker published *Life at the Cross* (1965); other personal reminiscences include Robin Eakin's *Aunts up the Cross* (1965); Rennie Ellis's *Kings Cross Sydney: A Personal Look at the Cross* (1971); and Ricki Francis's *96 Kings Cross* (1972) and *Kings Cross Hooker* (1974). Historical accounts of the Cross include Freda MacDonnell's *Before Kings Cross* (1967) and the nostalgic recall of the war years by the Kings Cross Community Aid and Information Service, *Kings Cross 1936–1946* (1981). The phrase, 'Kings-bloody-Cross' in 'Nino Culotta''s *They're a Weird Mob* (1957), aptly illustrates the combined impact of that unique part of the Sydney environment and the colloquial Australian language on the migrant consciousness.

Kings in Grass Castles (1959), an account of the Durack family's part in the saga of the pastoral expansion in Australia in the period 1853–98, was written by Mary Durack (q.v.). Patrick (Patsy) Durack, the author's grandfather, born in County Galway, Ireland, in 1834, arrives in Australia with his family in 1853. Three months later, after the death of his father in an accident, he is left at the age of nineteen as the provider for his mother and seven other children. He takes a cartload of merchandise (on credit) to the Ovens diggings in Victoria, sells it profitably and digs for gold until he has accumulated £1000. In 1867 he settles the family on a small property at Dixon's Creek near Goulburn. In 1862 he marries Mary Costello from a neighbouring Irish family and with her brother John, 100 horses and 400 cattle heads north of Bourke, believing that 'out there between the Warrego and the Paroo are kingdoms waiting to be claimed'. In the drought-stricken outback, Durack and Costello lose their stock and are themselves saved from death only by the intervention of Aborigines, who escort them to safety. In 1867 both families leave their Goulburn properties and set off north. In 1868 they reach the Cooper's Creek (q.v.) area where they settle at the now famous stations, Thylungra (Durack) and Kyabra (Costello). In 1869–73 the registered holdings of the two families in the vast plain watered by the Cooper, the Diamantina and the Georgina Rivers total eleven million acres. In the good years that follow (1874–77) they see the Channel country and the Cooper's Creek district opened up to closer settlement and cattle grazing over the spot where Burke and Wills had died only fifteen years earlier. The urge to 'poke along up North', which continues to grip both Patsy Durack and John Costello, then quite wealthy men, is probably a symptom of the consuming land hunger that stems from their deprived Irish background. Costello sells Kyabra for £60 000 and later moves off into the Gulf Country. In 1882 Stumpy Michael, Patsy's brother, sails from Brisbane to Darwin thence to the mouth of the Ord River in the Kimberleys (q.v.) and explores the country with a view to the Duracks moving there. Following his favourable report the decision is made to leave Thylungra and in June 1883 in probably the greatest droving epic in Australian pastoral history, 7250 cattle leave Cooper's Creek on the 3000 miles trek to the Ord. The journey takes two years and three months; less than half the stock survive and the total cost is £70 000. The Duracks' arrival coincides with the Kimberley gold rushes but the development of the properties – Argyle, Rosewood, Ivanhoe – goes on largely under the control of M.P. (Michael) Durack, Patsy's eldest son and the father of the author. The economic collapse of 1890–91 brings financial ruin to Patsy Durack, bearing out the truth of the statement he made back in the 1878 heyday, 'We are kings in grass castles that may be blown away upon a puff of wind'. In 1893 Mary Durack, Patsy's wife, dies and in 1896 he visits Ireland. He dies in Fremantle in 1898, melancholy and dispirited at the collapse, as he sees it, of his life's work. In the book's epilogue Mary Durack briefly traces later events in the family history, including her brother Kim's role in the Ord River irrigation project and the disposal by her father of the Kimberley empire in 1950.

Kings in Grass Castles is not simply the story of a family. It is a wide-ranging social history in which the family's exploits are seen in the wider context of pastoral expansion in the second half of the nineteenth century. As well as analysing the colonial problem of land rights, it describes the lifestyle of outback communities; examines the role of the Irish immigrant in the pioneering days; assesses, without rancour or prejudice, religious divisions in colonial Australia; portrays, with fairness to both sides, the conflict between the frontier settlers and the Aborigines; and describes, with considerable flair and expertise, the constantly changing natural wonders of the country from southern NSW to the Kimberleys. The sequel, *Sons in the Saddle* (1983), continues the Durack story during the lifetime of Mary Durack's father, M.P. (Michael) Durack.

KINGSFORD-SMITH, Sir CHARLES (1897–1935), born Hamilton, Queensland, flew in the Royal Flying Corps in the First World War, and then pioneered a mail route between Geraldton and Derby for the WA Airways; he later formed a transport company with fellow-aviator, Keith Anderson. In 1927 Kingsford-Smith, known nationally as 'Smithy' in later years, and Charles Ulm made a record flight around Australia and in 1928 in their Fokker aircraft, *Southern Cross*, they became the first men to fly across the Pacific Ocean from America to Australia. Numerous other significant flights followed: to England in record time; the first east to west crossing of the Atlantic Ocean; the first aerial circumnavigation of the globe. Smithy and Ulm established the first Australian National Airways in 1930 and made abortive attempts to establish air mail services between Australia and England. In 1935 Smithy and T. Pethybridge were lost off the coast of Burma. A national hero after whom the Sydney airport at Mascot has been named, he has been the subject of numerous biographies, including Ward McNally's *Smithy: The Kingsford-Smith Story* (1966), Pedr Davis's *Charles Kingsford-*

Smith: The World's Greatest Aviator (1977) and John Pickering's *The Routes of the Valkyries* (1977, which also deals with Charles Ulm). Two plays about Kingsford-Smith are Mary Gage's 'The Same Square of Dust', co-winner of the WA 150th anniversary play competition in 1979 and Richard Lane's 'Boy on an Old Bus'. His career has some parallels with that of Roy Hilman in Roger McDonald's novel, *Slipstream* (1982).

KINGSLEY, HENRY (1830–76), the younger brother of the English novelist Charles Kingsley (1819–75), was born in Northhamptonshire, England. His early life was spent in Devon, where parts of *The Recollections of Geoffry Hamlyn* (q.v.) and *Ravenshoe* are set, and in Chelsea, which is recalled in *The Hillyars and the Burtons* (q.v.). In 1850 he matriculated to Oxford where he was more interested in sport than in his studies; although he did not row in the boat race against Cambridge, he won an event at the 1852 Henley regatta. In 1853 he left without a degree and migrated to Australia. He spent 1854 on the Victorian goldfields, e.g. Bendigo and Beechworth, visited NSW in 1855 and returned to Victoria in 1856 by way of the Monaro; he also spent some time at Langi Willi station near Skipton, where a start was made on *The Recollections of Geoffry Hamlyn*. The novel was completed on his return to England, published in 1859 and met with some success. His next novel, *Ravenshoe* (1862), was also well received and encouraged Kingsley to make writing his career, but thereafter he struggled to support himself and his wife and in 1869 accepted the editorship of the Edinburgh *Daily Review*. He covered the Franco-Prussian War as correspondent for the *Review* in 1870, and then settled in London in 1871. Three years later he moved to Cuckfield, Sussex, where he died.

In all Kingsley published some twenty works, most of them novels. There is Australian material in *Tales of Old Travel Re-Narrated* (1869), a bushranging story, 'The Two Cadets', in *Hetty and Other Stories* (1871), essays on the explorers Charles Sturt and Edward John Eyre in *Hornby Mills and Other Stories* (1872), and some Australian scenes in *The Boy in Grey* (1871) and *Reginald Hetherege* (1874), but Kingsley's two major contributions to Australian literature are his family chronicles, *The Recollections of Geoffry Hamlyn* and *The Hillyars and the Burtons* (1865). They are both emigrant success stories in the line initiated by Charles Rowcroft, Alexander Harris and others, but whereas, ironically, *The Hillyars and the Burtons* is the more Australian in allegiance, *The Recollections of Geoffry Hamlyn* was more significant for the development of Australian lit-

erature. A celebration of pastoral Australia 'before the Gold', it inaugurated the colonial romance continued by 'Rolf Boldrewood' and others. In describing it as 'that immortal work, the best Australian novel', 'Boldrewood' echoed Marcus Clarke's judgement, 'the best Australian novel that has been, and probably will be written'. In contrast, Joseph Furphy (q.v.) objected to its unrealistic picture of bush life in nineteenth-century Australia and dismissed it as 'exceedingly trashy and misleading' in *Such is Life* (1903), in which he purports to tell the real story of the Buckleys (q.v.) of Baroona. The twentieth-century decline in popularity of *The Recollections of Geoffry Hamlyn* paralleled Kingsley's status in English literature, which led S.M. Ellis to write *Henry Kingsley 1830–1876: Towards a Vindication* (1931). Recent studies include W.H. Scheuerle's *The Neglected Brother: A Study of Henry Kingsley* (1971), John Barnes's *Henry Kingsley and Colonial Fiction* (1971), and J.S.D. Mellick's comprehensive biography, *The Passing Guest: A Life of Henry Kingsley* (1983). Mellick also edited the Kingsley volume in the Portable Australian Authors series (1982). 'Rolf Boldrewood' recollected Kingsley in his *Old Melbourne Memories* (1884) and portrayed him in his pastoral romance *Babes in the Bush* (1900).

KINGSTON, BEVERLEY (1941–), born Sydney, was educated at the University of Queensland and Monash University, Melbourne. Associate professor of history at the University of NSW since 1980, she has published the pioneering feminist history, *My Wife, My Daughter, and Poor Mary Ann: Woman and Work in Australia* (1975) and has edited *The World Moves Slowly: A Documentary History of Australian Women* (1977).

KIRBY, JAMES, see *Old Times in the Bush of Australia*

KIRBY, REGINALD (1901–?50), born Buckinghamshire, England, became a minister in the Baptist Church and arrived in Australia in 1936, serving as a padre in the RAAF in the Second World War. A prolific writer of adventure and romance fiction, Kirby published such books as *Basing House* (1943), *Beaufighter* (1943), on the war in New Guinea), *Pearl Harbour Pilot* (1944, about American pilots in the New Guinea campaign), *So Lovers Dream* (1945), *Girl of the Sierras* (1946) and *Wind of the Morning* (1950).

KIRKPATRICK, JOHN SIMPSON (Private JACK SIMPSON) (1892–1915), known affectionately as 'The Man with the Donkey', was born in England, jumped ship in Australia in

1910, carried his swag to northern Queensland and then worked on coastal shipping before enlisting in the AIF. On 25 April 1915, the day of the landing on Gallipoli, he obtained a donkey and from then on worked day and night carrying the wounded from the front lines to the beach. Three weeks later, he and the donkey were killed by shrapnel. Although no award for valour was made to Simpson, such awards then being given only for single acts of valour, his name became legendary for qualities of self-sacrifice and bravery. There is a statue of The Man with the Donkey at the Melbourne Shrine of Remembrance and a bronze by W. Leslie Bowles in the Gallipoli galleries at the Australian War Memorial, Canberra. T. Walsh wrote *The Man and the Donkey* (1948) and Sir Irving Benson, *The Man with the Donkey* (1965).

KIRWAN, Sir JOHN (1869–1949), born Liverpool, England, came to Australia in 1890 and worked as a journalist in Brisbane, Melbourne and Adelaide before becoming editor-in-chief of the *Kalgoorlie Miner* and the *Western Argus*, where he remained until 1926. A long-time member of parliament and a member of the Senate of the University of WA 1912–34, he was knighted in 1930. In addition to numerous articles on the history of WA he published *An Empty Land: Pioneers and Pioneering in Australia* (1934) and the autobiographical *My Life's Adventure* (1936).

Knocking Round, see **BRERETON, J. LE GAY** (2)

KNOPWOOD, ROBERT (1763–1838), born Norfolk, England, went to Port Phillip with the expedition of David Collins in 1803 as chaplain. When the projected settlement at Port Phillip was abandoned he went on to Hobart, where he was clergyman and magistrate. Knopwood kept a diary of his thirty or more years in Tasmania; an extraordinary document with eccentric spelling it gives an enlightening account of the early days of the Tasmanian colony. Parts of it were published in *Historical Records of Port Phillip* (1879) and *Proceedings of the Royal Society of Tasmania* (1946–47). Mabel Hookey edited *Bobby Knopwood and His Times* (1929) and wrote the biographical *The Chaplain* (1970). Mary Nicholls edited *The Diary of the Reverend Robert Knopwood 1803–1838* (1977). He appears as a benevolent figure in 'Price Warung''s story, 'The Procession of the Buttercup'.

KNOWLES, CONRAD (1810–44), born England, the son of a Wesleyan minister, was well educated and came to Tasmania as a tutor in 1830. A scandal seems to have cut short his appointment and he moved to Sydney, where he soon became one of the leading actors at Barnett Levey's Theatre Royal when it opened in 1832. He was a versatile, popular but heavily overworked actor, often playing several parts at one performance, presenting many Shakespearean roles including Australia's first Hamlet and Othello, and becoming involved in management at the Theatre Royal and later at the Victoria Theatre and others. The strain of overwork, however, frequently showed in his acting. In 1837 he left for England with the actress, Mrs Harriet Jones, but by 1838 they were back in Sydney. In his absence, other actors had replaced him in popularity, a situation that worsened with the arrival of Francis Nesbitt in 1842, and although he tried a series of acting-managing positions at theatres in Sydney and Melbourne, none was successful and he died of overwork. He is also the author of *Salathiel: Or, the Jewish Chieftain*, performed and published in 1842, a pseudo-historical 'literary' drama with a turgid plot.

KNOWLES, MARION MILLER (1865–1949), born Wood's Point, Victoria, was as a young woman a teacher in Victorian schools. She was a prolific writer of simple poetry and fiction dealing with experiences of Australian bush life, often filtered through devout Roman Catholic attitudes. Her poetry includes *Song from the Hills* (1898), *Fronds from the Blacks' Spur* (1911), *Roses on the Window Sill* (1913), *Songs from the Land of the Wattle* (1916), *Love, Luck and Lavender* (1919) and *Ferns and Fancies* (1923). Her *Selected Poems* was published in 1935. Her fiction includes *Country Tales and Sketches* (1896), *Barbara Halliday* (1896, partly autobiographical), *Shamrock and Wattle Bloom* (1900), *The Little Doctor* (1919), *Meg of Minadong* (1926) and *Pretty Nan* (1928). She is featured in J.R. Stevens's *Adam Lindsay Gordon and Other Australian Writers* (1937).

KNOWLES, VERNON (1899–?), born Adelaide, worked on the Adelaide *Register* then went to England to continue a journalistic and writing career; he remained an expatriate but the influence of his Australian boyhood frequently surfaces in his work. His partly autobiographical novel, *Eternity in an Hour* (1932), contains memories of childhood events in Adelaide and descriptions of the bush setting of creeks and gullies. His other works of fiction include *Bypaths* (1921), which combines prose and verse; *The Street of Queer Houses and Other Tales* (1925); *Here and Otherwhere* (1926, short stories); *Pitiful Dust* (1931); and *Two and Two Make Five* (1935). His poetry includes *Songs and Preludes* (1917), *Poems* (1925) and *The*

Ripening Years (1927). He is represented with C.R. Jury and E.J.R. Morgan, in *Lamps and Vine Leaves* (1919). He wrote a critical work, *The Experience of Poetry* (1935).

KNOX, JAMES (?1810–65), arrived in Hobart from England about 1832. An indefatigable contributor to journals and newspapers, he published *Poetic Trifles* (1838), a small book of simple immigrant lyrics which he claimed as the first book of poetry published in Tasmania.

KOCAN, PETER (1947–), born Newcastle, NSW, was sentenced to life imprisonment in 1966 for the attempted murder of Labor Party leader, Arthur Calwell. He served ten years in prison, where he became interested in writing. He has written two partly autobiographical novels, *The Treatment* (1980) and *The Cure* (1982), which won the NSW Premier's Award for fiction. They are based on Kocan's experiences as an inmate of the Morissett Mental Hospital, *The Treatment* being set in the maximum security wing of that establishment, *The Cure* in the more open refractory ward. The protagonist of the novels, Len Tarbutt, is largely Kocan himself. His two collections of poetry are *The Other Side of the Fence* (1975) and *Armistice* (1980). His plays, 'The Card Players' (1979), 'Who Do You Think You Are?' (1980) and 'The Walking Stick of the Desert' (1980), have been performed but not published. He won the 1982 Mattara Spring Festival poetry prize for 'From the Private Poems of Governor Caulfield'.

KOCH, C.J. (CHRISTOPHER JOHN) (1932–), born Hobart, has lived for extensive periods in Europe and America and has travelled in Asia. He worked for more than ten years as a producer for the ABC, becoming federal supervisor of school broadcasts, but resigned in 1973 to write full time. Apart from some striking, uncollected poetry, some of it anthologized, he has written three novels: *The Boys in the Island* (q.v., 1958, extensively revised in 1974), *Across the Sea Wall* (1965, a heavily revised version in 1982), and *The Year of Living Dangerously* (q.v., 1978). *The Year of Living Dangerously* won the 1978 *Age* Book of the Year Award and a National Book Council award in 1979; it was made into a film of the same title by Peter Weir in 1982, the screenplay being written by Weir, David Williamson and Koch.

The Boys in the Island, an unsentimental account of a boy's childhood and adolescence in Tasmania and Melbourne, received wide acclaim. Although the boy's experiences are captured with immediacy, it is his fresh openness

to experience as he restlessly pursues his dream of a paradisal, illimitable state that is memorable. Striking aspects of the book are the youth's disillusioning love affair, described with lucid honesty, and his excited response to the magical lure of the big city. *Across the Sea Wall*, written entirely in the present tense, spans six years and is set partly in India, partly in Australia. It deals with the strange, obsessive relationship between a young Australian and a Latvian showgirl and traces a similar pattern of dream and disillusionment. Koch's concentration on visionaries had led earlier to his being classed with Patrick White and Randolph Stow, but the reception of this novel was very mixed. *The Year of Living Dangerously* revived Koch's reputation. More of a mainstream novel, set in Indonesia in 1965 just before the fall of Sukarno, it is an engrossing narrative. Diverse yet unified, it convincingly meshes public and private worlds, setting the unpredictable political events against a spiritual and cultural background.

'KODAK', see **O'FERRALL, ERNEST FRANCIS**

Komos, published quarterly 1967–73 from the Monash University English department, contained articles and discussions on drama and theatre. Some playscripts were issued as supplements. An index was published in 1973.

Kookaburra, sometimes referred to as the Laughing Jackass, is an Australian member of the kingfisher family of birds. It makes a loud, harsh noise resembling raucous human laughter, that was often regarded as fiendish and mocking by the early pioneers. Specimens of the kookaburra were taken to England by Sir Joseph Banks from Captain James Cook's first visit to Australia in 1770. In Captain Arthur Phillip's *The Voyage of Governor Phillip to Botany Bay* (1789) and in Surgeon–General John White's *Journal of a Voyage to New South Wales* (1790) there are engravings of a kookaburra, labelled the Great Brown Kingfisher, although Phillip notes the Aboriginal name 'kookaburra'. The term 'laughing jackass' is recorded as early as 1797 in the notes of the ex-convict, Thomas Watling. Later writers, such as Henry Kendall, used the term 'gooburra', a version of which ('goburra') is found in Mary Anne FitzGerald's *Australian Fur and Feathers* (1889). Forty-five variations of the name are listed by A.H. Chisholm in *Bird Wonders of Australia* (1934). Like its compatriots, the kangaroo and the emu, the kookaburra has often been used as an Australian symbol, e.g. as trademarks for Australian products, on badges of Australian military units, as a laughing motif on the Australian version of Movietone news in cinemas during the 1930s–50s, and as striking dust jacket illustrations on specifically Australian books. The bird is widely and variably featured in Australian children's literature, e.g. May Gibbs portrays the kookaburras as 'goodies' in the struggle against Mrs Snake and the evil Banksia men in *Snugglepot and Cuddlepie*, while Norman Lindsay's kookaburra in *The Magic Pudding* (1918), is the complete larrikin. Other writers such as Leslie Rees and Ida Rentoul Outhwaite have created well-known fictional kookaburras, e.g. Kurri Kurri and Johnny Kookaburra. Well adapted to illustration because of its striking features, the kookaburra has been immortalized in the paintings of Neville Cayley (senior) and in the illustrations of Hal Gye. The kookaburra's habit of making its first loud outburst at dawn led to it being known as 'the settler's clock' or 'the bushman's clock'. Two significant works on the kookaburra are the ornithological investigation, *Kookaburras* (1970), by Veronica Parry and the profusely illustrated, anecdotal *The Laughing Australian* (1982) by Toby and Juliana Hooper.

KRAMER, Dame **LEONIE** (1924–), born Melbourne, was educated at the Universities of Melbourne and Oxford. She has been professor of Australian literature at the University of Sydney since 1968 and has been a member of numerous community and educational boards and committees. She was chairman of the ABC 1982–83. Editor of *The Oxford History of Australian Literature* (1981), she has also written extensively on 'Henry Handel Richardson' including *Henry Handel Richardson and Some of Her Sources* (1954), *A Companion to Australia Felix* (1962, a guide to 'Richardson''s work), and *Myself When Laura* (1966, on 'Richardson''s novel, *The Getting of Wisdom*). She edited the 1961 volume of *Australian Poetry* and the 1963 volume of *Coast to Coast*. With A.D. Hope she edited *Henry Kendall* (1973) and with R.D. Eagleson wrote *Language and Literature: A Synthesis* (1976) and *A Guide to Language and Literature* (1978). She was made OBE in 1976 and DBE in 1983.

KRAUSMAN, RUDI (1933–), born Mauerkirchen, Austria, came to Australia in 1958. He worked as a journalist in Salzburg, as a language teacher in Sydney and Melbourne, and is now a freelance writer and editor. In 1975 he founded *Aspect: Art and Literature*, a magazine which he still edits. He also edited the collection, *Recent German Poetry* (1977). His own published works include *From Another Shore* (1975, prose), *The Water Lily and Other Poems* (1977), and *Flowers of Emptiness* (1982, poetry). His plays include *Everyman: A Sentence*

Situation (1978), 'The Leader', based on the diaries of the German architect, Albert Speer, and 'Life Is Never New', based on the work of the Russian revolutionary poet, Mayakowsky.

KRAUTH, NIGEL (1949–), born North Sydney, graduated from the University of Queensland and has taught English at the University of Papua New Guinea, the Mitchell College of Advanced Education at Bathurst, where he helped to found *inprint*, and the Northern Rivers College of Advanced Education at Lismore, NSW. With Elton Brash he edited *Modern Poetry from Papua New Guinea* (1972) and *Traditional Poems, Chants and Songs of Papua New Guinea* (1973). He also edited *New Guinea Images in Australian Literature* (1982) in the Portable Australian Authors series. His 'The Jolly Swagman Affair' was co-winner of the *Australian*/Vogel Award for 1982; it was published in 1983 as *Matilda, My Darling*, and is a fictional investigation of events surrounding the composition of 'Waltzing Matilda' (q.v.) in 1895.

Kröte, Professor, a creation of the poet Gwen Harwood (q.v.), is a European musician who finds himself alienated in a materialistic Australian environment, where he must keep body and soul together by teaching music and giving performances. Most of the Kröte poems were published in Gwen Harwood's second collection, *Poems: Volume Two* (1968), but her continued interest in him is indicated by his reappearance in several of the 'New Poems' of her *Selected Poems* (1975) and in 'A Music Lesson', 'A Scattering of Ashes' and 'The Silver Swan' of *The Lion's Bride* (1981). Sympathetically portrayed by her ('I should think I like Kröte'), the professor of music, with his vagaries of behaviour and unfulfilled dreams and expectations, is in constant conflict with, but never defeated by, the unsympathetic and stuffily-conventional society which surrounds him.

Kunapipi, see **Association for Commonwealth Language and Literature Studies**

KYNASTON, EDWARD (1924–), born Aberystwyth, Wales, came to Australia in 1957 and taught in high schools before becoming education columnist and correspondent for the Perth *Independent* (1969–71) and literary editor of *Nation Review* (1972–75). His published works are *Australian Voices* (1974), a collection of verse and pictures; *The Penguin Book of the Bush* (1977) which, in the guidebook mode, tells of such bush activities as 'Practical Camping' and 'Orienteering' and of such bush hazards as 'Getting Lost and Other

Emergencies' and 'Bush Beasts'; *A Man on Edge* (1981), a biography of Baron Sir Ferdinand von Mueller which won the Con Weickhardt Award

for 1982; and, with Richard Bates as co-editor, *Thinking Aloud: Interviews with Australian Educators* (1983).

L

LABILLIERE, FRANCIS PETER (1840–95), born Melbourne, went to England in 1859 and was called to the bar in 1863. An advocate of imperial federation, he was made secretary of the Imperial Federation League in 1884. In 1878 he published the two-volume *Early History of the Colony of Victoria*, which includes personal reminiscences and makes detailed use of documentary material. In 1894 he published *Federal Britain: Or, Unity and Federation of the Empire*.

Lachlan River, see **Riverina**

LACK, CLEM (1901–72), a well-known Queensland journalist and historian, began his career on the *Gympie Times* in 1918. He was subsequently on the staff of the *Courier-Mail* (1920–40), the *Telegraph* (1940–44) and the Melbourne *Age* (1944–48), and in 1948 returned to Brisbane to work for the State's Public Relations Bureau. He retired in 1966 but continued as a freelance writer. Fellow and later vice-president of the Royal Historical Society of Queensland, he edited the Society's journal, wrote numerous articles on Queensland's history, edited the Queensland centenary book, *Queensland, Daughter of the Sun* (1959), co-authored other books on Queensland's history with Sir Raphael Cilento and Harry Stafford, and wrote an independent history, *Three Decades of Queensland Political History 1929–1960* (1962). He also published a volume of verse, *The Fields of Amaranth and Other Poems* (1936), and a collection of essays on Celtic legends and sagas, *A Bookman's Essays* (1969).

'**Ladies of Brisbane**', an Australian folk-song which exists in several versions and is also known as 'Farewell and Adieu to You, Brisbane Ladies', 'The Drovers', 'The New Chum's First Trip', 'Brisbane Ladies' and 'Augathella Station', is an overlanders' (q.v.) song of farewell to the ladies of Brisbane as they depart up-country. The destination of the overlanders in most versions, Augathella, is in central Queensland but most of the places (Caboolture, Kil-

roy, Yarraman, Nanango, and so on) named are on the main route between Brisbane and Kingaroy. 'Ladies of Brisbane' is a parody of the English shanty song 'Ladies of Spain' and was first published in the *Boomerang* in February 1891, under the title 'The Drover's Song'. Saul Mendelsohn, a Nanango storekeeper, has been identified by some folklorists as the original author.

Lady's Visit to the Gold Diggings of Australia, 1852–53, **A** (1853), by Ellen (Mrs Charles) Clacy, is one of the best-known and most graphic accounts of the goldfields. Ellen Clacy arrived in Victoria a year after gold was discovered and returned home to England within a year. She also wrote *Lights and Shadows of Australian Life* (1854), comprising four novelettes and some short stories, all set in the colonies and dealing with such staples of colonial times as station life, bushrangers, convicts, the diggings and the emigration experience.

LAKE, DAVID (1929–   ), born India, spent his childhood in Calcutta. A graduate of the University of Cambridge, he taught in English schools until 1959 and at tertiary level in Vietnam, Thailand and India 1959–67; in 1967 he joined the University of Queensland. He has contributed verse to such periodicals as *Westerly*, *Southerly* and *Makar* and has published one collection, *Hornpipes & Funerals* (1973), and a satiric poem, *The Portnoyad* (1980). He has also written academic studies of renaissance literature, as well as five science-fiction (q.v.) novels which form a series culminating in *The Fourth Hemisphere* (1980), and a continuation of *The Time Machine* by H.G. Wells, *The Man Who Loved Morlocks* (1981).

LAKE, JOSHUA (1848–1908), born Sussex, England, a graduate of the University of Oxford and a schoolmaster, was friendly with Alexander Leeper, whom he assisted in the founding of the *Melburnian*. He contributed to *Cassell's Picturesque Australasia* (1887–89) and to the Australasian supplement to *Webster's International Dictionary* (1898). Editor of the anthology, *Childhood in Bud and Blossom* (1900), which includes contributions from A.B. Paterson, Ada Cambridge, John Sands and E.E. Morris, he also wrote a libretto, *Vercingetorix: Or, Love and Passion* (1881), and contributed sonnets to the anthology, *Town Halle, Melbourne* (1881).

LALOR, PETER (1827–89), Irish-born leader of the Eureka Stockade (q.v.), migrated to Victoria in the 1852 gold rushes. Elected commander-in-chief of the diggers on Bakery Hill, Lalor was wounded in the attack on the Stockade. From 1855 until his death he was an elected member of the Legislative Council, then a member of the Victorian parliament. Lalor's account of Eureka is in his 'Statement on the Ballarat Rebellion', *Age* and *Argus* 10 April 1855, and in further statements in the *Ballarat Star* 12 January 1857 and the *Geelong Advertiser* 21 September 1864 and 3 March 1874. Raffaello Carboni's (q.v.) account of Lalor's activities at Eureka is in *The Eureka Stockade* (1855). All the significant historical accounts of Eureka emphasize Lalor's role; those which particularize him include Clive Turnbull's *Eureka: The Story of Peter Lalor* (1946) and C.H. Currey's *The Irish at Eureka* (1954). Lalor has been celebrated in such fictional accounts of Eureka as Edward Dyson's *In The Roaring Fifties* (1906) and Jack Lindsay's *Rebels of the Goldfields* (1936); in poems such as Henry Lawson's 'Eureka (A Fragment)', written as a eulogy after Lalor's death, and 'The Fight at Eureka Stockade'; and in the several plays relating to Eureka but particularly in Leslie Rees's 'Lalor of Eureka' (1939).

La Mama, one of the most important influences in the 1970s 'new wave' of Australian theatre, originated in 1967 as a 'coffee-house' or 'café' theatre through the enthusiasm of Betty Burstall, wife of film director and producer Tim Burstall. In an abandoned shirt factory behind a vacant lot in Faraday Street, Carlton, an inner Melbourne suburb popular with students, academics, artists and writers, Betty Burstall established the intimate, non-commerical type of theatre she had experienced in New York in 1965. Such writer-oriented theatres worked with few of the trappings of traditional theatre – props, make-up, large casts, elaborate stages and plush auditoriums. Writers such as Jack Hibberd, David Williamson, Barry Oakley and John Romeril all had plays performed at La Mama in its first years. An actors' workshop was established there; from it developed the Australian Performing Group which based itself at the nearby Pram Factory in

Carlton. Poetry workshops inspired by Kris Hemensley (q.v.) and others also used La Mama for their meetings; from them came a considerable impetus to the 'New Australian Poetry' (q.v.) movement of the late 1960s and early 1970s.

LAMB, CHARLES (1775–1834), the English essayist, was a friend of Barron Field. In one of his essays, titled 'To Distant Correspondents' and addressed to 'B.F. Esq. at Sydney', Lamb sarcastically asks Field about the state of literature in the colony: 'Have you poets among you? Damn'd plagiarists, I fancy, if you have any. I would not trust an idea or a pocket-handkerchief of mine, among 'em'.

LAMBERT, ELISABETH (1918–), whose married name is Terpening, contributed verse in the 1940s to such periodicals as *Meanjin, Southerly* and *Angry Penguins,* and edited with Harry Roskolenko the September 1944 issue of the American magazine, *Voices,* which was devoted to Australian poetry. She also published three collections of verse, *Insurgence* (1939), *The Map* (1940) and *Poems* (1943), and a novel, *The Sleeping House Party* (1951).

LAMBERT, ERIC (1918–66), born Stamford, England, and educated in Sydney, served in the Second World War in the Middle East, New Guinea and Singapore. He began writing stories in the late 1940s and in 1951 published *The Twenty Thousand Thieves* (q.v.), a novel based on his war experiences. Lambert became a member of the Communist Party in 1947 and was active in left-wing literary circles for almost a decade after the war; he joined the Realist Writers and was a member of the first editorial board of *Overland.* In 1955 he was an Australian delegate to the Helsinki peace conference; he stayed on in England after the conference, alienating the Australian literary left with his 'on-the-spot' despatches, the first of them possibly written in London, which reported the Hungary uprising of 1956 and, more significantly, were published in the conservative Sydney newspaper, the *Daily Telegraph.* In all, Lambert wrote some seventeen novels under his own name and a number of novelizations of films under the pseudonym 'D. Brennan'. His most successful work was *The Twenty Thousand Thieves* which has had numerous editions and reprintings and has become a paperback classic of war literature. Informed both by Lambert's abhorrence of war and his admiration of the ordinary Australian soldier, the novel exhibits its contempt for the officer class and it was attacked in the 1950s by some ex-officers for its unflattering portrait of the Australian army. Lambert's other war novels include *The Veterans* (1954), *Glory Thrown In* (1959) and *MacDougal's Farm* (1965), the last based on a visit to the notorious Changi POW camp at the end of the war. He also wrote a biography of Oscar Wilde's parents, *Mad with Much Heart* (1967); and two Eureka novels, *The Five Bright Stars* (1954) and *Ballarat* (1962) which, like his Ned Kelly novel *Kelly* (1964), are strongly anti-authoritarian and introduce as characters historical personages such as Raffaello Carboni, John Pascoe Fawkner, Charles Thatcher and Lola Montez. Zoe O'Leary's biography of Lambert, *The Desolate Market* (1974), focuses on his literary and political activities both before and after his break with the Australian Left.

LAMBERT, GEORGE WASHINGTON (1873–1930), born St Petersburg, Russia, of American–English parentage, was educated in England and arrived in Australia in 1887. A station hand, clerk and shop assistant before establishing himself as an artist, Lambert was a cartoonist and illustrator of poems for the *Bulletin* from 1895. In 1900 he was awarded a travelling scholarship and went to England, where he lived mainly as a portait painter. In 1917–20 he was an AIF war artist, visiting Palestine, France and Gallipoli; he returned in 1921 to Australia, where he was active in the Society of Arts and the Contemporary Arts group. Lambert's earliest extant portrait is of A.W. Jose, whose work he illustrated and with whom he was involved in the *Australian Magazine*. Apart from his war paintings, he is best known for *Across the Black Soil Plains* (Art Gallery of NSW), a tribute to the Australian pioneering spirit; it won the 1899 Wynne Prize but was subsequently criticized by Joseph Furphy for the inaccuracy of detail. Lambert sculpted the Sydney memorial to Henry Lawson, using Lawson's children as models. Featured in *Art in Australia* in 1924 and 1930, Lambert is the subject of J.S. MacDonald's *The Art and Life of George W. Lambert* (1920) and Amy Lambert's *Thirty Years of an Artist's Life* (1938).

'Lambing Down', see Gundagai; 'Lazy Harry''s

Lambing Flat, see Chinese in Australian Literature

Lame Dog Man, The, see Treelake Series

'Lament for St. Maria Goretti', probably the last poem written by Francis Webb (q.v.), was published in *Poetry Australia* in 1973. The poem reconstructs the dying moments of Maria Goretti (1890–1902), who died at Nettuno,

Italy, in defence of her chastity and was canonized as a martyr for the Christian life. The poignant account of the young girl's death is sometimes said to reflect Webb's premonition of his own death, which followed shortly after the poem was written.

LAMOND, HECTOR (1865–1947), born Broughton Creek on the NSW south coast, entered journalism after a printing apprenticeship. In 1890–95 he was editor of the *Chronicle* in Carcoar before moving to Sydney, where for over two decades he was associated as manager and editor with the *Worker*, later *Australian Worker*. He resigned in 1916 over the conscription issue, which split the Labor Party, and was a Nationalist member of the federal parliament 1917–22; in later life he was a country newspaper proprietor. A son-in-law of the pioneer unionist W.G. Spence, he helped Spence in the writing of *Australia's Awakening* (1909) and other work. It was Lamond who persuaded Mary Gilmore (q.v.) to write the women's page in the *Worker*.

LAMOND, HENRY GEORGE (1885–1969), born Carlo Creek in northern Queensland, was educated in Brisbane and worked on stations in Queensland. He used this experience in sketches and stories contributed to journals in Australia and overseas; his speciality was the animal tale. The best-known of his books was *Big Red* (1953, published in the USA as *Kangaroo*). His other publications include *Tooth and Talon* (1934), *An Aviary on the Plains* (1934), *Amathea* (1937, published in the USA as *Kilgour's Mare* 1943), *Brindle Royalist* (1946), *Dingo* (1945, published in Australia as *White Ears the Outlaw*, 1949), *The Manx Star* (1954), *Towser, Sheep Dog* (1955), *The Red Ruin Mare* (1958) and *Sheep Station* (1959).

LA NAUZE, J.A., see **DEAKIN, ALFRED; MURDOCH, Sir WALTER**

'**LANCASTER, G.B.**' (EDITH JOAN LYTTLETON) (1874–1945), born Tasmania into a pioneering family, spent part of her childhood in NZ. She subsequently travelled widely but lived for some time in Australia. As 'G.B. Lancaster' she contributed stories to the *Bulletin* and the *Lone Hand* and published thirteen works of fiction: *Sons O' Men* (1904), *A Spur to Smite* (1905), *The Tracks We Tread* (1907), *The Altar Stairs* (1908), *Jim of the Ranges* (1910), *The Honourable Peggy* (1911), *The Law-Bringers* (1913), *Fool Divine* (1917), *The Savignys* (1918), *Pageant* (1933), *The World Is Yours* (1934), *Promenade* (1938) and *Grand Parade* (1943). Of these only *A Spur to Smite*, *Jim of the Ranges* and *Pageant* have Australian settings. *Pageant*, 'Lancaster''s best Australian novel and winner of the Australian Literature Society's Gold Medal, draws on the records of 'Lancaster''s own family in its presentation of the fortunes of a Tasmanian family from 1826 to the twentieth century. The novel's attempts to present Tasmanian history as a colourful pageant result in woodenness and contrived effects, although some of the characters have vitality.

Land, Labour, and Gold, see HOWITT, WILLIAM

Land of the Rainbow Snake, see Aboriginal Song and Narrative in Translation

LANDOLT, ESTHER (1893–1943), born Switzerland, was the author of two novels of Swiss life written in German, *Das Opfer* (1937) and *Delfine* (1939) which was awarded the Schiller Prize. In 1937 she accompanied her husband, Dr Moritz Meyer, to Australia and wrote a further two novels in German but with Australian settings, *Ewige Herde* (*Eternal Flock*) (1942), and *Namenlos* (*Nameless*) (1947). *Ewige Herde* gives a finely-detailed, unsentimental picture of life on a Victorian sheep station; drought, bushfire, rats, rain and frost prove to be implacable enemies to all human endeavour, although the novel also celebrates human resilience and courage. *Namenlos*, the story of a Swiss who settles in Melbourne, is distinguished more by its psychological insight into the dual consciousness of the migrant than by its presentation of Australian life.

LANDOR, EDWARD WILLSON (1811–78), a WA poet and essayist, wrote a satirical account of early WA life, *The Bushman: Or, Life in a New Country* (1847).

LANDSBOROUGH, WILLIAM (1825–86), was the Scots-born son of a clergyman who emigrated to NSW in 1841 and became an expert bushman. In 1861–62 he led a search party for Burke and Wills; although unsuccessful in the search, he completed the first north-south crossing of the continent, discovering good grazing land in the process. His *Journal of Landsborough's Expedition from Carpentaria, in Search of Burke and Wills* and *Landsborough's Exploration of Australia from Carpentaria to Melbourne* ed. J.S. Laurie were published in 1862 and 1866 respectively. They stirred pastoral interest in the Gulf country, as is evidenced in *Kings in Grass Castles* (1959) by Mary Durack. His pioneering role is recalled in *Bowen Downs, 1863–1963* (1963) ed. D.S. Macmillan and is commemorated by townships in Queensland and Victoria.

Landtakers, a novel by Brian Penton (q.v.), published in 1934 as the first of a projected trilogy, was followed only by *Inheritors* (1936). The chief 'landtaker' of the novel, Derek Cabell, is an informant of its unnamed narrator, who is piecing together from letters, gossip and memoirs an account of Queensland's pioneering days in order to understand the roots of the national psyche. Arriving in Australia in 1842 intending only to make his fortune before returning to his native Dorset, Cabell takes a job as an overseer on Murrumburra station, some forty miles from the penal settlement of Moreton Bay. The convict experience is important in *Landtakers* because its legacy of conflict and hatred characterizes Cabell's experience of pioneering life and most of his personal relationships. At Murrumburra Cabell is bullied by the brutal lessee, Bob McGovern, but during a flood manages to engineer his escape and that of the convict, Joe Gurney. Together they overland a mob of cattle and sheep into the hinterland of Queensland where, threatened by Aborigines whom Cabell massacres and by a succession of natural and man-made hazards, e.g. fire, flood, drought, loneliness and threats to his security by later settlers, he struggles over the next seventeen years to establish himself as a squatter. Recovering from a nightmarish journey in which he gets lost while taking his wool clip down to Brisbane, Cabell encounters Emma Surface, an ex-convict, whose degraded past he does not discover until after their marriage. Their relationship becomes a paradoxical one: Cabell is repelled by his knowledge of Emma's history but released from his selfishness by his passion for her; Emma loathes Cabell's brutality towards her but sees in the marriage, and in her children, the focus of *Inheritors*, her chance to achieve respectability. At the climax to *Landtakers* Gurney, who has been ordered by Cabell to leave the station when it emerges that he knows of Emma's past, is allowed to return. During his absence he has met McGovern, who arrives in the district to take up an overseer's position on an adjoining property; McGovern is seemingly much changed in character but later returns to his bullying ways. Gurney, long fearing McGovern's power to return him to imprisonment for his original escape from Murrumburra, hopes Cabell will kill McGovern. It is Emma, however, who kills him while he is fighting with Cabell. The novel concludes with Cabell's renunciation of his long-held plans to return to England. *Inheritors*, the sequel to *Landtakers*, brings the story of the Cabell family forward to the end of the century, and explores the destructive relationship between Cabell and his children.

Like other novels of the 1930s, *Landtakers*

offers an iconoclastic revaluation of Australia's past. Influenced by 'Henry Handel Richardson''s *The Fortunes of Richard Mahony* (1930), it powerfully portrays the revenge of the environment on those who try to 'take' from the land. The world of the novel, characterized by violence and cruelty, peopled by characters who, if not broken, are brutalized by their experience and only survive because of their vitality, doggedness and courage (qualities admired in Penton the journalist), is a sobering contrast to more romantic accounts of pioneering life.

LANE, LAURA M., see **LUFFMANN, LAURA BOGUE**

LANE, RICHARD, born Sydney, began writing plays for radio in the 1930s and is one of the most prolific of writers for television and radio. He spent eight years with Macquarie Broadcasting as writer and producer, and later worked as a freelance writer for commercial radio in Sydney and for the ABC. Author of Australia's first television serial, *Autumn Affair* for ATN 7, he also worked on the television serial, *Motel*. His *The Remittance Man* is included in *Australian Radio Plays*, ed. Leslie Rees (1946), and his adaptation for television of Jon Cleary's novel, *You Can't See Round Corners*, is included in the collection he edited, *Take One: A Selection of Award-Winning Australian Radio and Television Scripts* (1972). His other plays for radio and television include 'Pointless Design', 'Eureka Stockade', 'Boy on an Old Bus' (about Charles Kingsford-Smith), 'Gods in Wedlock', 'The Purple Jacaranda' and 'What About Next Year?'.

LANE, WILLIAM ('JOHN MILLER', 'TO-HUNGA'), (1861–1917), born Bristol, England, of Irish–English parentage, worked his passage to America at the age of sixteen. After a series of casual jobs he turned to the printing trade as a compositor, then journalist, on a Detroit newspaper. His American experience developed his radical interests; his socialist thinking was moulded by the Americans, Henry George and Edward Bellamy, and later in Australia by Karl Marx. His strong racist attitudes, especially his implacable hostility towards the Chinese, also date from his American period. Lane returned to England briefly in 1885 with a wife and daughter but in the same year came to Australia to join other members of the family already in Queensland. He became a journalist in Brisbane, where in 1887 he founded a branch of the Bellamy Society and established, with Alfred Walker, the weekly newspaper, the *Boomerang*. He became deeply involved with the 'New Unionism' and with the planning of the Queensland Australian Labour Federation, a federal organization of unions. In 1890 he became editor of the Brisbane *Worker* in which he advocated full-scale socialism, supported the maritime strike of 1890 and the shearers' strike of 1891, campaigned for the rights of women in letters under the pseudonym 'Lucinda Sharpe' and persistently mooted the idea of a 'Co-operative Commune' either in Australia or abroad. Disappointed in the prospects for socialism/communism in Australia after the failure of the strikes in 1890–91, he established in 1891, and became chairman of, the New Australia Settlement Association with the object of organizing a communist colony in South America which would be the vanguard of world communism. Lane led the New Australia (q.v.) expedition to Paraguay in the *Royal Tar* in 1893 but when the original settlement broke up in discord, he and his followers formed another settlement, Colonia Cosme. He visited England in 1896 on an unsuccessful recruiting trip for the Cosme settlement, returned to Cosme in February 1898 and left permanently in August 1899. After three months as editor of the Sydney *Worker* he became in 1900 the leader-writer of the *New Zealand Herald* in Auckland (1900), ultimately becoming its editor in 1913. As 'Tohunga' (Maori for 'prophet') he wrote voluminously on social and political topics, but his stance grew increasingly conservative. After his death he was praised in the NZ press as a great editor and imperialist, but the radical Australian press, apart from some sporadic recriminations about his change to conservatism, contented itself with remembering the intense idealism of his younger years. Lane's first novel, 'White or Yellow? A Story of the Race War of A.D. 1908', was serialized in the *Boomerang* in twelve episodes in 1888 under the pseudonym 'Sketcher', but his chief literary work was the novel, *The Workingman's Paradise* (q.v., 1892), written under the pseudonym 'John Miller' to raise funds to help the unionists gaoled for conspiracy in the shearers' strike of 1891. His writings for the *New Zealand Herald* were published as *Selections from the Writings of 'Tohunga'* in Auckland in 1917. Lane is the subject of Lloyd Ross's *William Lane and the Australian Labor Movement* (1937), and he and his philosophies are analysed in Michael Wilding's introduction to the 1980 facsimile of *The Workingman's Paradise*. He features in Vance Palmer's play about the shearers' strike of 1891, *Hail Tomorrow* (1947), and his work for New Australia is comprehensively examined in Gavin Souter's *A Peculiar People: The Australians in Paraguay* (1968). Hume Nisbet's *A Dream of Freedom* (1902) deals unfavourably with New Australia.

LANG, JOHN DUNMORE (1799–1878), born Greenock, Scotland, arrived in Sydney in 1823 as the city's first Presbyterian minister. For the next fifty years he was an energetic and controversial figure in the colony's religious and political scene. He established the Scots Church and the Australian College in Sydney; was a member of the Legislative Council; was dismissed from his ministry by the Australian synod but retained his own congregation based on the Scots Church; and campaigned assiduously for the abolition of transportation, Protestant immigration, the separation of Victoria and Queensland from NSW, a system of national education, republicanism and federation. Lang wrote numerous historical, political and religious books and pamphlets, lectured widely, addressed countless meetings, and wrote public letters on every possible topic of colonial interest. His main published works are *An Historial and Statistical Account of New South Wales both as a Penal Settlement and As a British Colony* (1834), referred to by the *Westminster Review* as 'The History of Doctor Lang, to which is added the History of New South Wales'; *Transportation and Colonization* (1837); *The Coming Event: Or, the United Provinces of Australia* (1850); and *Freedom and Independence for the Golden Lands of Australia* (1852). His several volumes of poetry are consolidated in *Poems: Sacred and Secular* (1872), which is chiefly religious in tone but contains some satire, humour and translations from Greek and German. Lang was also closely associated with the newspapers, the *Colonist* (1835–40), the *Colonial Observer* (1841–44) and the *Press* (1851). A valuable picture of Lang is given in *John Dunmore Lang – Chiefly Autobiographical, 1799 to 1878* (1952), ed. Archibald Gilchrist. Lang is the 'Scotch parson' the title character meets in Henry Savery's novel, *Quintus Servinton* (1831); he also appears briefly in James Tucker's *Ralph Rashleigh* (1952) and other historical fiction as well as in contemporary polemical verse.

LANG, JOHN GEORGE (1816–64), born Parramatta, was the second son of sea captain and land-owner Walter Lang and Elizabeth Harris who was the daughter of convict parents. Lang was educated at William Cape's school in King Street, Sydney, and at Sydney College from which he received the first gold medal awarded 'in approbation of his talents, acquirements and general good conduct'. In 1837 he went to England to study law at Cambridge but was sent down for unspecified indiscretions ('Botany Bay tricks, not gentlemanly tricks') and completed his legal training at the Middle Temple, proceeding to the bar in May 1841. Lang returned to Australia with a wife and child in 1841 but early in 1842 left for India where his wife's brother was a successful barrister. His brief stay in Australia and his sudden departure have been attributed to his Jewish and emancipist backgrounds, a combination not well accepted in the exclusive Sydney society of the day, and to some injudicious public statements about representative government and colonial law which made him unpopular with, and ridiculed by, the colony's political and legal circles. In 1843–45 he practised law in Calcutta then moved, for his health's sake, to the hill city of Meerut. He became editor and ultimately owner of the *Mofussilite* ('up-country man'), an English-language newspaper. Financial success from his legal and newspaper pursuits enabled Lang to spend most of 1853–59 in England and Europe, where he was a well-known and popular literary figure, contributing to many leading journals and newspapers, especially *Fraser's Magazine* and Charles Dickens's *Household Words*. He returned to India in 1859, remarried in 1861 and died, according to the *Madras Times*, 'a melancholy example of wasted talents and degraded abilities'. The enigma surrounding the life and personality of John Lang has not, even a century later and in spite of considerable literary research, been completely solved. Lang published nine novels, a volume of short stories and a travel book, *Wanderings in India* (1859), first published serially in *Household Words*. It appears probable that he was also the author of *Legends of Australia*, an anonymous work of fiction published in four parts, of a projected twelve, in 1842. Titled 'Frederick Charles Howard', it is a romance about an aristocratic transportee who is followed to the colony by his beautiful wife and ultimately finds happiness, and bears some resemblance to *The Forger's Wife* (q.v., 1855), one of Lang's later novels with an Australian setting. Authorship of *Legends of Australia* would entitle Lang to the distinction of being the first Australian-born novelist. Lang's most significant Australian work was *Botany Bay: Or, True Tales of Early Australia* (1859), a fictional but factually-based series of stories about early Sydney, some parts of which were published initially in *Household Words*. The best-known of the tales is 'The Ghost upon the Rail', the story of Fisher's Ghost (q.v.). Lang's Indian novels are also significant in their field for they aptly convey, in gentle satire, English social life in India in the period before the Mutiny. *John Lang & 'The Forger's Wife'* (1979), edited by Nancy Keesing, contains a facsimile of the novel and a biographical outline.

LANG, JOHN THOMAS (1876–1975), born Sydney, was Labor premier of NSW 1925–27 and 1930–32 and became a legendary figure in Australian history during the 1930s depression. The controversy surrounding him was at its most acute after February 1931, when he instituted the 'Lang Plan', a scheme devised to withhold interest payments on British loans and reduce the interest on private ones. The plan caused a deep split between the NSW and federal branches of the Labor Party. Dismissed by the State governor in May 1932, Lang was soundly defeated at the election held shortly afterwards. A populist and an effective orator who was both passionately loved and hated, Lang was known as the 'Big Fella' by his supporters and often received popular endorsement for his course at political meetings in the familiarly-chanted phrase, 'Lang is right!'. He continued to have a strong hold over the State party machine until 1939 and attracted a large following for even longer. Expelled from the party in 1943, he served as an independent member in the federal parliament 1946–49. In 1971 he was readmitted to the party through the efforts of younger members. Editor of the weekly newspaper, the *Century*, until his death, Lang wrote three autobiographical accounts, *I Remember* (1956), *The Great Bust* (1962) and *The Turbulent Years* (1970). His political career has been the subject of numerous studies, including Bethia Foott's *Dismissal of a Premier* (1968), Robert Cooksey's *Lang and Socialism* (1971) and *Jack Lang* (1977), a collection of essays edited by Heather Radi and Peter Spearritt. Miriam Dixson wrote *Greater than Lenin: Lang and Labor 1916–1932* (1977). He was a brother-in-law of Henry Lawson.

LANG, W.H. (WILLIAM HENRY) (1859–1923), born Selkirk, Scotland, a medical practitioner and brother of the Scottish scholar and poet, Andrew Lang, was editor of the *Pastoralists' Review* for a time. He published a descriptive account, *Australia* (1908), with drawings by G.W. Lambert; and a novel, *The Thunder of the Hoofs* (1909), which is set partly in Scotland and partly in the Riverina and deals extensively with such sports as cricket, racing and hunting. He also edited *Racehorses in Australia* (1922) with K. Austin and S. McKay.

LANGFORD, GARY (1947–), born NZ, moved to Sydney in 1974. A versatile writer, he has contributed to numerous NZ and Australian anthologies and periodicals, and has written for television and stage. He has published two volumes of poetry, *The Family* (1973) and *Four Ships* (1982); a collection of short stories, *The Death of James Dean* (1978), of which one, 'The Dying Man', shared the Patricia Hackett Prize in 1975; and three novels, *Death of the Early Morning Hero*

(1976), which won second prize in an Angus & Robertson literary award, *Players in the Ballgame* (1979) and *The Adventures of Dreaded Ned* (1980), a black comedy on the Ned Kelly legend. Lively, witty and unpredictable, with a taste for the macabre and the bizarre, Langford's picaresque heroes have often been compared with those of J.P. Donleavy.

LANGLEY, EVE (1908–74), born Forbes, NSW, went to NZ in 1932, married artist and art teacher, Hilary Clark, had three children and later returned to Australia, where at first she played an active role in the Sydney literary scene but spent the latter part of her life as a recluse in her shack, Iona-Lympus, in the bush near Katoomba in the Blue Mountains. Few other details of Eve Langley's later life are publicly known but her eccentricities have often been stressed; she dressed in mannish clothes, wore a white topi, carried a sheath knife in her belt, was obsessed with guns, had Oscar Wilde as an *alter ego*, and lived as an isolate. Her twin novels, *The Pea Pickers* (q.v., 1942) and *White Topee* (1954), are considered by many to contain clues to the enigma of her life. *The Pea Pickers* was acclaimed by Douglas Stewart as 'the most delightful novel' to have been written by an Australian; by Norman Lindsay as 'a sport of genius'; and by Hal Porter as 'a superb and haunting work'. Such early enthusiasm has largely faded; some modern critics see it as an extreme example of the *passé* nationalist tradition of Joseph Furphy and Miles Franklin, while others are critical of the elaborate prose style that often obliterates the narrative itself. *White Topee* is an extension of *The Pea Pickers*, both novels being centred on the narrator, Steve, who attempts to reconcile the twin demands of her female nature: the intellectual, with its need for expression in thought, poetry and art, and the emotional, which seeks fulfilment in personal love. The conflict in the novels is often expressed sardonically; Steve alternates between poet and clown, ecstatic and sublime at one moment, wryly self-deprecatory the next. *The Pea Pickers* concludes with Steve not fully in command of her turbulent nature; *White Topee* brings a greater measure of self-understanding: 'I really didn't want to be loved . . . What I really wanted was to be a man, and free for ever to write and think and dream'. In the fictional tug-of-war Steve's psyche is stretched to breaking-point but survives; it would seem that in the real world Eve Langley's did not.

Langton Tetralogy, see **BOYD, MARTIN**

LANSBURY, CORAL, who has taught in the USA for a decade, was born in Sydney and started work early as an actress on ABC radio. Educated at the University of Sydney, where she frequently contributed to *Hermes*, she wrote numerous plays for radio in the 1940s and 1950s, one of which, *Krubi of the Illawarra*, won the Henry Lawson Prize for poetry and was published in *Hermes* (1949). Her other plays for radio and television include 'The Bronze Plain', 'Mockery Bend', 'The Bombora', 'The Gate of the Sea', 'The Living Rock', 'Court of Angels' and 'Account Rendered at Ringarra'. She has also written some verse and several works on nineteenth-century English fiction as well as the polemical *Arcady in Australia* (1970), a study of perceptions of Australia in nineteenth-century English literature. Developing the thesis that the Australian bush ethos was a literary importation rather than of native, folk origin, Lansbury draws illustrations from such writers as Charles Dickens, Bulwer-Lytton and Charles Reade and explores the influence of such emigration publicists as Samuel Sidney.

LANSDOWN, ANDREW (1954–), born Pingelly, WA, and a graduate of Murdoch University, has published two books of poetry, *Homecoming* (1979) and *Counterpoise* (1982), together with *A Ball of Gold: Poems for Children* (1981). *Counterpoise* has been praised for its imagery, metrical variety and unconventionality.

LA PEROUSE, JEAN-FRANCOIS DE GA-LAUP, Comte de (1741–88), born Albi, France, joined the navy at fifteen, developed interests in navigation and oceanography and was made a captain in 1780. In 1785 he was selected by Louis XVI to lead an exploratory expedition into the north and south Pacific, to complete the unfinished work of Captain James Cook. The expedition, made up of two ships, *La Boussole* and *L'Astrolabe*, sailed to South America, rounded Cape Horn, and sailed to the Sandwich Islands and Alaska, turning south to explore the coast as far as California. La Perouse then sailed across the Pacific and surveyed the coasts north of Korea; in September 1787 he put in to Kamchatka and sent an account of his voyage thus far back to Paris. Published in 1797 in four volumes titled *Voyage de La Perouse autour du Monde*, the account includes much valuable cartographic and scientific information. From Kamchatka La Perouse's expedition set course south for New Holland and in December at Samoa encountered a major setback when natives attacked some of the crew of the *L'Astrolabe*, killing the commander and eleven men. La Perouse left without taking reprisals and reached Botany Bay 24 January 1788, six days after the arrival of the First Fleet, although bad weather prevented his

landing for some days. Governor Phillip, who had left for Port Jackson, did not meet La Perouse but cordial relations were established with the remaining British officers and the French established a camp on the north shore of Botany Bay. Six weeks later La Perouse sailed from Botany Bay and was never heard from again. Not until 1828 was it discovered that the expedition had been wrecked at Vanikoro, Santa Cruz, north of the New Hebrides. Apart from La Perouse's own account, the only remaining record of the expedition is an anonymous pamphlet, *Fragmens du dernier voyage de La Perouse* (1797), which may have been written by Pere Receveur, a scientist on the expedition who died at Botany Bay. Biographies of La Perouse include Sir Ernest Scott's *Laperouse* (1911).

Larger Than Life, see **HERBERT, XAVIER**

Larrikin in Australian Literature. Although the term 'larrikin' did not emerge in Australia until the 1860s, and was widely-used only in the period 1870–1910, the symptoms of larrikinism were evident in the behaviour of 'currency' lads who, as early as 1819, were accused of rowdy behaviour such as drinking, brawling, profanity and gambling. The *Sydney Gazette* reported critically on the activities of 'larky boys' in 1825. The cabbage-tree mobs, young native-born men whose name came from their wearing of the broad-brimmed hats woven from cabbage tree palms, were also forerunners of the larrikin pushes, in that they roamed the Sydney streets of the 1830s and 1840s abusing and assaulting the citizenry. Their activities are criticized in G.C. Mundy's *Our Antipodes* (1852) and Charles MacAlister's *Old Pioneering Days in the Sunny South* (1907). Larrikinism, in the shape of hooliganism and loutish behaviour, appears to have originated in the Colony in the Sydney Rocks area but it soon came to be a common phenomenon in the inner city and poorer, crowded areas of both Sydney and Melbourne. Suggestions for the origin of the term 'larrikin' include a rolling Irish pronunciation of 'larking' by a police sergeant (both a Jack Staunton and a Sergeant Dalton have been named) in the courts of the day; a diminution ('Larry') of the Irish name Lawrence, together with 'kin'; an existing Cornish word which meant 'larker'; a corruption of the two words 'leary kinchen', meaning a knowing or cunning fellow; and a Worcestershire and Warwickshire dialect word meaning mischievous fellow. As described by Sidney J. Baker, the larrikin's distinguishing features were that he was young, between the ages of fifteen and twenty-five, was a city dweller, dressed with exaggerated precision, extracted comfort from being a member of a gang, looked upon refinement in social conduct as a form of weakness, spoke in a weird jargon which it seemed only his kind could understand, and was given to spasms of violence. Larrikin dress ran to a surprising neatness, described in *Jonah* (q.v.) as 'tight-fitting suits of dark cloth, soft black felt hats, and soft white shirts with new black mufflers round their neck in place of collars'. Their ornamented, pointed and heavy boots, known as 'Romeos', were lethal weapons in street brawls. The larrikin's violent behaviour is described in Marcus Clarke's *A Colonial City* (1972), T.E. Argles's *Pilgrim* (1877), R.E.N. Twopeny's *Town Life in Australia* (1883), J.A. Froude's *Oceana* (1886) and with some gusto in a poem, 'Kicking Their Livers Out', in the seamy Sydney weekly, the *Dead Bird*. The linguistic innovations of the larrikin have been, in the main, a passing phenomenon, as a modern reading of W.T. Goodge's contemporary slang poem, 'The Great Australian Slanguage' (1897), and of the works of Louis Stone, Edward Dyson and C.J. Dennis verifies. Certain larrikin expressions, however, e.g. 'king hit', 'blue' and 'stoush' from street fighting; 'tart', 'sheila' and 'good sort' from the larrikin's assessment of the female; 'bludger', 'queen' and 'poof' from his abhorrence of effeminacy, have made a definite impact on the vernacular language. That the larrikin's push (mob) was a recognizable feature of city life at the turn of the century is reflected in the notoriety of such street gangs as Sydney's the Livers Push of Glebe, the Waterloo Push, the Blues Point Mob and Melbourne's Bouverie Street Push, the Fitzroy Murderers and the Richmond Dirty Dozen. In literature the push is prominent in the fiction of Louis Stone and Edward Dyson, and in Henry Lawson's poem, 'The Captain of the Push' (q.v.). Two minor novels by Ambrose Pratt, *King of the Rocks* (1900) and *The Great 'Push' Experiment* (1902), give an authentic picture of Sydney larrikinsim but the classic larrikin works, in a relatively small literary field, are Louis Stone's *Jonah* (1911), Edward Dyson's *Fact'ry 'Ands* (1906), *Benno and Some of the Push* (1911) and *Spats' Fact'ry* (1914); and C.J. Dennis's chief works, *The Songs of a Sentimental Bloke* (q.v., 1915) and *The Moods of Ginger Mick* (1916). In those works the larrikin's viciousness, his lovesick sentimentality and his twisted sense of mateship (an inverted *noblesse oblige* which compels him to join in kicking a common enemy into insensibility) are all demonstrated. His less reprehensible qualities are also demonstrated, e.g. jauntiness of spirit even in adversity, cheery optimism, amused contempt for pompous and incompetent authority, and a strong streak of vulgarity. These latter characteristics, which are important in modern usages of 'larrikin' and 'larrikinism', have led to the larrikin being regarded with affectionate tolerance rather than with animosity. James Murray's *Larrikins: 19th Century Outrage* (1973) is a comprehensive account of the larrikin phenomenon in Australia and contains both an extensive bibliography of larrikin literature and a glossary of larrikin terms.

LARSEN, NIELS HERTZBERG, see **LAWSON, HENRY**

LASERON, CHARLES FRANCIS (1887–1959), collector at Sydney's Technological Museum 1909–29 and a fellow of the Royal Zoological Society of NSW, was born Wisconsin, USA, and brought to Australia as a child. He served at Gallipoli during the First World War and published a small volume of reminiscences and extracts from his diary, *From Australia to the Dardanelles* (1916). Assistant biologist to Sir Douglas Mawson on the first Australasian Antarctic expedition 1911–14, he wrote an account of his experiences, *South with Mawson* (1947), which graphically relates the nature of the hazards encountered by the group and the personalities and qualities of the individual men. He also wrote two popular geological accounts of Australia, *The Face of Australia* (1953) and *Ancient Australia* (1954).

LASSETER, 'HAROLD BELL' (LEWIS HUBERT) (1880–1931), born Bamganie near Meredith, Victoria; left behind, following his death in the Petermann Range in 1931, one of Australia's greatest enigmas – the existence or not of a gold reef of extraordinary size and richness ('Lasseter's Lost Reef'). The true facts of Lasseter and his reef appear to have been finally settled by the research of Gerald Walsh for the *ADB* (1983). Lasseter was in America from 1901 to 1908, then returned to Australia where he took up a small farm at Tabulam on the Clarence River, NSW. He saw some service in the AIF in the First World War in Australia but the military authorities kept him only briefly, discharging him twice as unfit for service. In 1925–30 Lasseter worked as a carpenter in Canberra and on the Sydney Harbour Bridge, of which he claimed, unsuccessfully, to be the original designer. In 1929 he claimed that he had, in about 1911, discovered 'a vast gold-bearing reef in Central Australia'. Government authorities, having interviewed Lasseter, lost interest in his claim. In 1930 Lasseter repeated his story to a John Bailey, president of the AWU central branch in Sydney (dating the find this time about 1897) and a well-equipped expedition led by Fred Blakeley and guided by Lasseter, left Alice Springs on 21 July 1930 to search for the reef. In September the expedition abandoned the search but Lasseter carried on, at first with Paul Johns, an Englishman, but later alone. A search party led by Bob Buck claimed to have found Lasseter's body and buried it at Shaw Creek in the Petermann Range in March 1931. Walsh argues that Lasseter had never before been in central Australia and had not discovered any reef. The existence of such a reef had been suggested in earlier literature, e.g. Simpson Newland's *Blood Tracks of the Bush* (1900), J.D. Hennessey's *The Bush Track* (1896) and Conrad Sayce's *Golden Buckles* (1920), while the American, Harold Bell Wright, whose Christian names were used by Lasseter, wrote *The Mine with the Iron Door* (1923), a work on the same theme. Versions of Lasseter's story have been told in Ion Idriess's popular *Lasseter's Last Ride* (1931, seventeen printings in four years), in Errol Coote's *Hell's Airport* (1934, republished in 1981 as *Hell's Airport and Lasseter's Lost Legacy*), in Edward Harrington's poem, 'Lasseter's Last Ride', in Fred Blakeley's *Dream Millions* (1972) and in A. Stapleton's *Lasseter Did Not Lie!* (1981). Ivan and Jocelyn Smith published *The Die-Hard* (1979), an illustrated poem about Lasseter.

Last Blue Sea, The, see 'FORREST, DAVID'

'Last of His Tribe, The' a widely-anthologized poem by Henry Kendall (q.v.), was first published in the *Sydney Morning Herald*, 1864. In it Kendall captures the attractive nature of Aboriginal life and sentimentally mourns its passing.

'Last of Six, The', see FAVENC, ERNEST

LA TROBE, CHARLES JOSEPH (1801–75), born London and educated in Switzerland, was tutor to the family of the Swiss Count de Poutales (1824–27) and accompanied him on a tour of America (1832–34). Washington Irving, who accompanied them on a tour of the prairies, published an account of the journey and La Trobe also published *The Rambler in North America: 1832–1833* (1835) and *The Rambler in Mexico 1834* (1836). Appointed superintendent of the Port Phillip District in 1839, he was on excellent terms with his senior, Governor Gipps, but had constant problems with the Melbourne colonists, who frequently resented economic and political aspects of the link with NSW; he won some popularity, however, in 1849 when he took a bold stand on transportation. In 1851–54 La Trobe was lieutenant-governor of Victoria after the colony gained representative government. After gold was discovered at Ballarat in 1851, La Trobe faced a chaotic period of government, made

worse by his decision to wrest a revenue from the goldfields in the form of monthly licence fees. A cultured and religious gentleman, La Trobe gave his support to the establishment of numerous cultural, educational and charitable institutions. He left Australia in 1854. An extensive collection of his letters and papers is held by the State Library of Victoria, which has named its Australiana collections after him. Victoria's third university is also named in his honour. His career is described in a biography by A. Gross (1956) and in Geoffrey Serle's *The Golden Age* (1963). La Trobe's brother, John Antes La Trobe, an English clergyman, published a collection of sacred lyrics (1850) and other books on church music as well as a collection of verse, *The Solace of Song* (1837), which has been wrongly attributed to Charles La Trobe.

La Trobe Library, the section of the State Library of Victoria which holds the Library's special collections of Australiana, has several important manuscript collections relating to such authors as Mary Grant Bruce, Rex Ingamells, Victor Kennedy, Louis Lavater, Percival Serle, Henry Gyles Turner and R.H. Croll. It also holds the substantial J.K. Moir collection, as well as papers relating to Melbourne's literary associations and journals. Information about the collections is contained in the *Catalogue of the Manuscripts, Letters, Documents, etc. in the Private Collection of the State Library of Victoria* (1961). The twice-yearly *La Trobe Library Journal*, which has been published since 1968, lists recent acquisitions as well as including bibliographical and other articles of relevance to Australian literature.

'LAUDER, AFFERBECK', see MORRISON, A.A.

Lauds and Plaints, see BEAVER, BRUCE

LAVATER, LOUIS (1867–1953), born Melbourne of a Swiss father who came to Victoria during the 1851 gold rush, was educated at Wesley College and began a medical course at the University of Melbourne which he soon abandoned for music. Subsequently prominent in Melbourne's musical circles, he was at various times president of the Association of Music Teachers of Victoria, music critic for several Melbourne newspapers, frequent adjudicator of musical competitions and founder of the Guild of Australian Composers. Also a well-known literary figure, he contributed verse and short stories to numerous anthologies and to such journals as the *Lone Hand* and the *Bulletin*, and edited the little magazine, *Verse* (1929–33). He also published three collections of verse,

Blue Days and Grey Days (1915), *A Lover's Ephemeris* (1917) and *This Green Mortality* (1922); and edited a popular anthology, *The Sonnet in Australasia* (1926), revised in a second edition edited by Frederick Macartney (1956). Among his musical compositions were *Swagman's Treasure: Five Camp-fire Ditties* (1937).

Law at Heart's Desire, The, see **ADAMSON, ROBERT**

LAWLER, RAY (1921–), born Footscray, Melbourne, left school at thirteen to work in a foundry. Ten years later a growing interest in amateur dramatics and playwriting led to his leaving the foundry to act in variety shows in Brisbane. He subsequently worked as actor and producer with the National Theatre company, Melbourne, and as director of the Melbourne Union Theatre repertory company. One of his plays, 'Cradle of Thunder', was produced in Melbourne in 1949. In 1955 his outstandingly successful play, *Summer of the Seventeenth Doll* (q.v.) shared first prize with Oriel Gray's *The Torrents* in a competition organized by the Playwrights Advisory Board. *The Doll*, as it is familiarly called, was first staged by the Union Theatre of Melbourne University with Lawler in the role of Barney in 1955, and in 1956 in Sydney by the Australian Elizabethan Theatre Trust. John Sumner produced both productions, as well as a subsequent revival in 1977 by the Melbourne Theatre Company. After extensive touring in Australia, *The Doll* was produced in 1957 in London at the New Theatre, where it enjoyed a highly successful long run. A production in New York in 1958 failed to attract audiences, but it was produced as a film in 1960 starring Ernest Borgnine and Anne Baxter and was included in *Ten Best Plays of the American Season 1957–58*, edited by Louis Kronenberger. *The Doll*, which has been produced in numerous European countries and frequently restaged in Australia, was first published in 1957 and is now studied in schools as a classic of the national theatre. With Richard Beynon's *The Shifting Heart* (1958) and Alan Seymour's *The One Day of the Year* (1962), *The Doll* seemed to herald a flowering of Australian theatre that in fact failed to sustain itself, unlike the renaissance of the 1970s. After the success of *The Doll* Lawler lived in Denmark, England and (most extensively) in Ireland. He visited Australia in 1970 for a production of his play, 'The Man Who Shot the Albatross', and returned in 1975 to work as deputy artistic director, literary adviser and subsequently actor with the Melbourne Theatre Company. Apart from some adaptations of works by other authors, produced by

the BBC, other plays by Lawler which have been staged include *The Piccadilly Bushman* (first produced 1959, published 1961), 'The Unshaven Cheek' (1963), 'A Breach in the Wall' (1967) and two framing plays to *The Doll, Kid Stakes* (first produced 1975) and *Other Times* (first produced 1976). All three plays were produced together in two day-long performances in 1977 by the Melbourne Theatre Company and published as *The Doll Trilogy* in 1978. In 1958 Lawler won the London *Evening Standard* Award. Lawler's latest play, 'Godsend' (1982), has an English background and reflects his religious beliefs. He was made OBE in 1980.

Although the contemporary popularity of *The Doll* coincides with a national nostalgia for the recent past, the play had a more revolutionary impact in 1955. Concerned with the terminal stage of an unconventional relationship between two cane-cutters and their Melbourne girlfriends, a relationship that depends on conventional national assumptions, it was the first successful play to examine critically Australian myths and attitudes. Some of the underlying themes of the play, such as the limitations of mateship and of received Australian stereotypes of masculinity and the outback, have become familiar in contemporary drama. All three of Lawler's affectionately-realized characters are attracted to vitalist, ennobling and supposedly free aspects of the Australian legend, but the legend's inadequacies, which they experience rather than acknowledge, finally impose tragic, life-denying consequences. *Kid Stakes* and *Other Times*, the first dealing with the beginning of the relationship and the second with a critical later stage, complement *The Doll* but add nothing to its dramatic urgency. *The Piccadilly Bushman*, which deals with the ambivalences of Australian/English loyalties, especially those experienced by the artist, is much less universal in its effects and has been less sympathetically received. With 'The Man Who Shot the Albatross', his remaining Australian play, Lawler turned his attention to history and the fate of Governor William Bligh. Impressionistic in structure and setting, the play is a powerful exploration of an enigmatic figure, combining imaginative psychological penetration with authentic historical fact.

LAWLOR, ADRIAN (1890–1969), painter and art critic, was born London and arrived in Australia in 1910. He served with the AIF in the First World War, studied art for a short period at the National Gallery School in Melbourne, but did not begin painting seriously until 1930. His provocative, modernist works made an immediate impact, although by 1940 he had given up painting for art criticism for the *Sun* newspaper and literary magazines, and for radio broadcasting. Lawlor also wrote some verse, some of which appeared in *Vision* and in *Poetry in Australia 1923* (1923), ed. Jack Lindsay and Kenneth Slessor, and a novel, *Horned Capon* (1949). A witty polemicist and one of the boldest proponents of modernism, Lawlor deals with the controversial issues of the Australian art world of the time in his *Arquebus* (1937).

LAWRENCE, D.H. (DAVID HERBERT) (1885–1930), the English novelist, came to Australia from Ceylon in 1922, arriving with his wife Frieda at Fremantle on 4 May. In Perth, where he stayed for two weeks, he met some of the local literati and the Quaker nurse, Mollie Skinner (q.v.), with whom he collaborated in a novel, *The Boy in the Bush* (q.v., 1924). Katharine Susannah Prichard, who missed meeting him, later corresponded with him and attempted to interest him in Australian literature. After leaving Perth, the Lawrences arrived in Sydney on 27 May. They spent a brief time in the city and then rented a house, Wyewurk, at Thirroul, a mining village on the NSW coast, where they remained until their departure for San Francisco on 11 August. In eastern Australia Lawrence appears to have led a deliberately isolated life, mainly devoted to the writing of his novel *Kangaroo* (q.v., 1923). The extent of his involvement in and knowledge of Australian political life is uncertain; although Lawrence's letters, Frieda Lawrence's autobiography, '*Not I, But the Wind*' (1935), and his numerous biographers, suggest that his involvement was minimal, recent researches have tentatively suggested that he may have had personal knowledge of a secret political organization. Of these, the most substantial is Robert Darroch's *D.H. Lawrence in Australia* (1981).

In his letters Lawrence describes Australia as 'a weird country – fascinating – but humanly non-existent' and in both *The Boy in the Bush* and *Kangaroo* he vividly expresses his response to the 'subtle, remote, *formless* beauty' of the bush, its indifference to humanity, its 'fern-world' aura and separation from history. Almost equally evocative are his descriptions of Australian suburbia and the ramshackle impermanence of small coastal settlements. In *Kangaroo* the inability of the land's white inhabitants to relate to each other or to Australia is a dominant theme; in *The Boy in the Bush* the bush becomes a shaping force, a source of mysterious vitality and freedom. Lawrence's perceptive descriptions of the Australian landscape have been frequently praised, but his interpretation of the national character has aroused some fierce dissent. Describing Aus-

tralia in *Kangaroo* as a land where 'nobody felt *better* than anybody else, or higher; only better off', where 'Demos was . . . his own master, undisputed, and therefore quite calm about it' and as a 'vast continent . . . really void of speech', Lawrence was critical of what he saw as intellectual and spiritual lethargy, a lack of individuality and a general exaltation of the average. In Jack Callcott, his prototypical Australian, drawn from the Australians he met on board ship and from the pages of the *Bulletin*, which he read avidly, he develops his idea that the Australian indifference is not stoic but is based on recklessness and an unpredictable propensity for violence.

Written in six weeks, although he later revised the manuscript in Mexico, *Kangaroo* is strongly autobiographical, reflecting the almost daily flow of Lawrence's thoughts and impressions while in Australia. Richard Somers, the restless hero, is a barely-disguised picture of Lawrence, as Harriet his wife is of Frieda, and many of the domestic incidents are drawn directly from their Australian experience. Described by Lawrence as a 'thought-adventure', the novel's apparent formlessness expresses the flow of Somers's inner life; his attraction to and withdrawal from politics; his European memories; his concern with the fundamental question of authority in marriage, society and politics and with the attractions and dangers of democracy, fascism and socialism. For Somers/Lawrence the practical aims of political parties are far less important than their potential for the spiritual regeneration that his wartime experiences, described at length in *Kangaroo*, had convinced him was humanity's only hope: 'What Richard wanted was some sort of new show: a new recognition of the life-mystery, a departure from the dreariness of money-making, money-having and money-spending'. In *Kangaroo*, Lawrence appears to be searching for the same religious answer, 'The Great God who stands dark on the threshold of the phallic me', that was to concern him in *The Plumed Serpent* (1926) and *Lady Chatterley's Lover* (1928). It is probable that in Somers's ambivalent relationship to the figure of Kangaroo, alias Benjamin Cooley, a charismatic lawyer and leader of a secret right-wing group, Lawrence develops his response to Whitman's idea of generalized love, an issue he also deals with in his 'Essay on Democracy' which he was revising in 1922. Some readers have assumed, however, that Lawrence was transferring his observations of incipient Italian fascism to Australia and others have suggested a range of 'originals' of Kangaroo, including Lawrence's friend, S. Koteliansky, and Sir John Monash. Lawrence's description of NSW politics and the digger movement, once regarded as pure fabrication but which surprisingly foreshadows the formation of the New Guard of Colonel Eric Campbell in Sydney in 1931–32, has been defended as close to fact, based on local observation and reading of the *Bulletin*, even if not, as Darroch suggests, on personal involvement.

Lawrence's concern with the dark gods and the growth of an inner life also shapes the WA adventure story, *The Boy in the Bush*, affecting particularly the novel's conclusion which is totally different from the original written by Mollie Skinner. Largely neglected by Lawrence critics as a collaboration, the novel is, however, distinctly Lawrencean in atmosphere and preoccupations.

Other Australians whom Lawrence knew in Europe included Jack Lindsay and P.R. Stephensen; the latter's Mandrake Press was responsible for the publication of reproductions of some of Lawrence's controversial paintings in 1929 and for his essay, *A Propos of Lady Chatterley's Lover* (1930). Lawrence's Australian experience has recently been made the subject of a play by David Allen, *Upside Down at the Bottom of the World* (1981).

LAWSON, ALAN, see *Australian Literature: A Reference Guide*

LAWSON, BERTHA (1876–1957), born Bertha Bredt in Bairnsdale, Victoria, was working as a nurse when she met Henry Lawson (q.v.) in 1895. She married him the following year; they had two children, lived in WA, NZ, Sydney and England, but Bertha won a judicial separation in 1903. Lawson claimed that the portrait of Mary in the Joe Wilson stories was informed by his marriage to Bertha, who is also the subject of 'To Bertha', the dedicatory poem of *Children of the Bush* (1901); the bitterness between them after the separation, when Lawson spent time in gaol for arrears of maintenance, emerges in several poems, e.g. 'The Separated Woman', included in *For Australia and Other Poems* (1913). Bertha's account of the 1896–1902 period is included in *Henry Lawson by His Mates* (1931) and *My Henry Lawson* (1943), which was ghosted by Will Lawson.

LAWSON, HENRY (1867–1922), was born on the goldfields at Grenfell, NSW, the eldest son of Niels Hertzberg Larsen (Peter Lawson, 1832–88), a Norwegian ex-sailor, and his wife Louisa (see Lawson, Louisa); his surname was registered as Lawson, which became the family one. Peter and Louisa had been living near Mudgee at New Pipeclay, later called Eurunderee (q.v.), and returned there soon after Lawson's birth. They moved to the Gulgong

goldfields in 1871, but settled back at New Pipeclay on a selection in 1873. In 1883 they separated, Louisa moving to Sydney to become active in publishing and the women's movement.

Henry's early life was difficult: the family was poor, the tensions between his parents have some parallels in the short stories, particularly in 'A Child in the Dark, and a Foreign Father' (q.v.), and from the age of nine he was afflicted by deafness. He attended several schools at Eurunderee and Mudgee – John Tierney, one of his teachers, was the father of the comic novelist and short-story writer 'Brian James' – and then worked with his father on building contracts until 1883, when he joined Louisa. Over the next few years he was based in Sydney, worked mainly as a coach-painter and, influenced by his mother's radical friends, became interested in the republican movement. In 1887 his first published prose piece appeared in the *Republican*, of which he became nominal publisher, and his first poem, 'A Song of the Republic' (q.v.), in the *Bulletin*. The *Bulletin* also published his first short story, 'His Father's Mate' (q.v.), several days before his father's death on New Year's Eve 1888. In 1890 he left Sydney to find work in Albany, WA, where he wrote for the *Albany Observer*. He returned in September 1890 before accepting early in 1891 an offer of employment on the radical Brisbane newspaper, the *Boomerang*, to write a digest of news from the provincial press. After six months he was retrenched and returned to Sydney, then in the grip of the depression of the Nineties (q.v.). To this point Lawson had established himself primarily as a writer of verse: some of his enduring poems of bush life, e.g. 'The Teams', 'Andy's Gone With Cattle', 'The Roaring Days' (qq.v.), date from before 1892; so do the major poems of social and political protest, e.g. 'The Watch on the Kerb', 'Faces in the Street', 'Freedom on the Wallaby', 'The Army of the Rear', which made him the obvious model for Arty, the People's Poet, in William Lane's *The Workingman's Paradise* (1892). But from the time of his return to Sydney after working with the *Boomerang*, his talent as a writer of short stories began to emerge as he drew more and more on his own observation to supplement his past experiences and the experiences of his family. In 1892, despite the diversion of the *Bulletin* debate (q.v.) which he conducted with A.B. Paterson about the right way to represent bush life, he wrote the Arvie Aspinall (q.v.) series, his first major fiction sequence, and a series of bush stories including 'A Day on a Selection', 'The Drover's Wife' (q.v.) and 'The Bush Undertaker'. Later that year, unable to find regular work, he was funded by J.F. Archibald and went on a celebrated trip to Bourke, where he worked as a house painter for some months before tramping with his swag to Hungerford and back in the midst of a fierce drought. The experience, his first of the real outback, was crucial for Lawson in several ways: it confirmed the horrors of bush life; it not only provided him with the immediate copy for such stories as 'Hungerford' and 'The Union Buries Its Dead' (qq.v.) but also by its intensity enslaved his imagination to the point where his fiction subsequently became repetitive; and it gave him in J.W. Gordon (q.v.) one of the models for Mitchell (q.v.), his most important fictional character, as well as the models for the bush workers whose mateship (q.v.) he celebrates in 'Send Round the Hat' and other stories.

In 1893 Lawson wrote up his outback trip in stories and sketches contributed to the *Bulletin*, the Sydney *Worker* and *Truth*; the influence of journalism on his fiction is an important one, particularly in the links between his brief sketches and the paragraphs of journals like the *Bulletin*. With the depression at its worst, he went to NZ for seven months, travelling part of the time with the original of another of his fictional characters – the 'sharper', Steelman (q.v.). He returned on the expectation of a position with the *Worker*, which had become a daily; when this venture failed and the *Worker* reverted to a weekly he continued with it, first as provincial editor and then as a prolific salaried contributor. At the end of 1894 his first collection, *Short Stories in Prose and Verse*, was published. It was a poor production, but nevertheless confirmed his growing reputation, which was consolidated by the appearance in 1896 of the first two volumes in a long publishing partnership between Lawson and Angus & Robertson: *While the Billy Boils* (q.v.), generally considered as his best prose collection, and *In the Days When the World Was Wide* (q.v.), a collection of verse. By now he had met Bertha Bredt (see Lawson, Bertha), the stepdaughter of W.H. McNamara, a radical Sydney bookseller; her sister married the politician, J.T. Lang. Soon after their marriage in 1896 the Lawsons went to WA then continued their itinerant life by travelling in 1897 to New Zealand, where they taught at a Maori school at Mangamaunu, near Kaikoura. Although he eventually became frustrated by the isolation of Mangamaunu, Lawson wrote steadily and was relatively free of his weakness with alcohol, which had emerged a decade before. His drinking problem surfaced again on their return to Sydney in 1898, especially during his membership of the bohemian Dawn and Dusk Club, but he managed to complete contracts with Angus & Robertson which resulted in the publication in 1900 of two more collections of

prose, *On the Track* and *Over the Sliprails*, and a collection of verse, *Verses Popular and Humorous* (q.v.). Like many of his books they consisted largely of material first published in Australian periodicals and subsequently revised. An essay, ' "Pursuing Literature" in Australia' (q.v.), published in the *Bulletin* in 1899, shows his dissatisfaction at this time with Australia and his wish for wider recognition for his work. In 1900 Lawson left with his wife and two children for England, assisted in the endeavour by the Governor of NSW, Earl Beauchamp, the bibliophile, David Scott Mitchell, and the publisher, George Robertson. In England he wrote some of his finest stories and published *The Country I Come From* (1901), a selection of his previous work; *Joe Wilson and His Mates* (q.v., 1901), which is dominated by the Joe Wilson (q.v.) sequence; and *Children of the Bush* (q.v., 1902), which contains the material subsequently published as *Send Round the Hat* (1907) and *The Romance of the Swag* (1907). By 1902 the climate, poverty, illness and perhaps other unexplained reasons caused the Lawsons to leave England, the marriage failing. Thereafter, with the exception of a few weeks immediately following their return to Sydney, Lawson lived apart from Bertha and the children, with increasing bitterness on both sides.

Lawson's best work was now behind him, and the remaining twenty years of his life were years of spasmodic literary output in which he produced more verse than prose, and of steady personal disintegration. He was in and out of prison, particularly 1905–10, for drunkenness and arrears of maintenance, spent some time in mental and 'convalescent' hospitals and became a familiar sight on the streets of Sydney, a dishevelled, cadging drunk. That he survived so long was the result of the devotion of friends, old literary colleagues such as J. le Gay Brereton and E.J. Brady but in particular George Robertson, who assisted him financially, and Mrs Isabel Byers, a woman twenty years his senior who regularly provided care and lodging for him after 1904. There were political friends as well, including T.D. Mutch (q.v.) and W.A. Holman, which led to his being granted a sinecure in 1916 to live in Leeton, a prohibition area, in order to write material advertising the Murrumbidgee Irrigation Area; during his year or so there he met J.W. Gordon from the Bourke days. The interest of parliamentarians in him was also in evidence in 1920–22, when he was awarded a CLF pension and negotiations were conducted between the federal and NSW governments over a supplement to the pension.

The ostensible reason for Lawson's deterioration was his collapse into alcoholism and mental illness although several commentators, viewing his dependence on alcohol more as a symptom than as a cause, have suggested other sources for his decline: the failure of his marriage; the death of close friend, Hannah Thornburn (q.v.), just before his arrival from London; and, perhaps more significantly for his reputation as a prose writer, an artistic crisis in the same period deriving from his realization of, and anguish at, the failure of his inspiration, which led him eventually to rely more and more for effect on melodrama, contrivance and romance, features of some of his very first stories. Brian Matthews's *The Receding Wave* (1972) is the most important study of Lawson's achievement and decline; signs of the decline can be detected in the prose collections, the Joe Wilson sequence apart, immediately following *While the Billy Boils*; they are more in evidence in the two new collections published after his return from England, *The Rising of the Court* (1910) and *Triangles of Life* (1913). That Lawson had little new to say explains the return to the past which is characteristic of his later prose. In 1912–20 he essayed a new and flabby city series, 'Elder Man's Lane', published in the *Bulletin*; but more typical of his work were the autobiographical pieces, in particular the long 'A Fragment of Autobiography' (q.v.), begun in 1903 and recalling his life up to 1888, and the stories such as 'Grandfather's Courtship' which went back even further. To some extent this nostalgia was stimulated by visits with Mutch to Eurunderee in 1914 and by the memories evoked after the reunion with Gordon in Leeton, as the 1916 *Bulletin* sketch, 'By the Banks of the Murrumbidgee', reveals.

Lawson's decline after 1902 did not mean, however, that he lost his appeal for the Australian public. In part this was because his verse, in such volumes as *When I Was King* (1905), *The Skyline Riders* (1910), *For Australia* (1913), *My Army, O, My Army* (q.v., 1915) and *Song of the Dardanelles* (1916), continued to strike a popular chord. Some of his best-known poems, e.g. 'One-Hundred-and-Three' and 'Black Bonnet' (qq.v.), date from this period; he was particularly prolific during the First World War, when his poetic affirmation of the imperial link was such as to see him later accused of jingoism and apostasy of his socialism and republicanism of the 1880s. A second reason for his continuing appeal was the publishing programme of George Robertson (2), who republished Lawson's earlier prose and verse, often in series bearing such titles as While the Billy Boils, as well as arranging for the first collection of poetry, *Selected Poems of Henry Lawson* (q.v., 1918). Also involved in the preparation of *Selected Poems* was David McKee Wright (q.v.), who edited Lawson extensively while working on the much-criticized *Poetical Works of Henry Lawson* (q.v., 1925).

Notwithstanding the scholarly edition of Colin Roderick, *Poetical Works of Henry Lawson* has been the most popular collection of Lawson's verse and has remained in print under various titles.

In 1921 Lawson suffered a cerebral haemorrhage, from which he recovered sufficiently to be still writing reminiscences of his visit to London when he died at Abbotsford on 2 September 1922. The extent of the Lawson legend in his lifetime can be measured by the fact that he was the first Australian writer granted a State funeral. Since his death, he has remained Australian literature's most famous son, commemorated by a statue in the Sydney Domain, sculpted by George Lambert using Lawson's children as models, and by memorials elsewhere, as well as by his appearance on the Australian ten-dollar note when decimal currency was introduced in 1965. He has been the subject of one-man shows by Leonard Teale and Robin Ramsay, and of numerous plays, films, stories, readings and television series. In Melbourne there is a Henry Lawson Memorial and Literary Society (q.v.), which publishes the *Lawsonian* and conducts an annual gathering at the 'Lawson Tree' at Footscray. In Sydney, apart from the Domain statue, there is a Henry Lawson Bookshop and a Henry Lawson Literary Society, and the FAW conducted for some years annual pilgrimages to his grave at Waverley cemetery and to the Domain statue. In Grenfell, the local school and a festival are named after him; in Mudgee and Eurunderee there are memorial shelters. The Lawson publishing industry has not remained confined to reprints deriving from the earlier Angus & Robertson collections. The same publishers issued *The Stories of Henry Lawson*, edited by Cecil Mann (q.v.) in 1964, which was trenchantly criticized. Not until the appearance in 1972 of *Henry Lawson: Short Stories and Sketches 1888–1922* and *Henry Lawson: Autobiographical and Other Writings 1887–1922*, the first two of Colin Roderick's projected three-volume edition of Lawson's prose, was a reliable text established. Roderick had earlier edited several Lawson selections: in 1967–69 he edited the three-volume *Henry Lawson: Collected Verse*, which provided an authoritative text of the poetry, and subsequently *Henry Lawson: Letters 1890–1922* (1970) and the anthology *Henry Lawson Criticism 1894–1971* (1972). Recent Lawson selections include Brian Kiernan's *The Essential Henry Lawson* (1982), which includes recently-discovered material. Important biographical studies, some of them anecdotal, include his daughter Bertha Lawson and J. le Gay Brereton's collection of tributes, *Henry Lawson by His Mates* (q.v., 1931); his wife Bertha's *My Henry Lawson* (1943); 'Denton Prout''s *Henry*

Lawson: The Grey Dreamer (1963); W.H. Pearson's Henry Lawson Among Maoris (1968); the controversial In Search of Henry Lawson (1978) by Manning Clark; and Colin Roderick's The Real Henry Lawson (1982). The definitive biography remains to be written, however, and some of the most interesting commentary on Lawson's life has appeared in significant critical studies, among them A.A. Phillips's The Australian Tradition (1958) and Henry Lawson (1970), Stephen Murray-Smith's monograph, Henry Lawson (1975), and Brian Matthews's The Receding Wave. These works represent only a fraction of the published material on Lawson, much of which remains in periodicals or is to be found in collections of essays and critical anthologies.

In general, there have been two schools of Lawson criticism: a popular one which has seen many of Lawson's short stories as artless yarns and regards him as the poet of the people, a folk writer whose galloping rhythms and facility for rhyme articulate the voice and attitudes of Australians; and a professional one, which sees mainly historical interest now in the poetry and finds enduring virtues in the prose. Despite the continuing appeal of the stirring calls for social change in 'Faces in the Street' or 'Freedom on the Wallaby', the lyricism of 'Andy's Gone With Cattle' or 'Black Bonnet', the sardonic sharpness of 'The Uncultured Rhymer to his Cultured Critics' or 'The Captain of the Push' (q.v.), and the robust balladry of 'The Roaring Days', only Roderick among recent critical writers has argued for more than a handful of Lawson's poems. Far more attention, particularly among literary critics, has been focused on the quality of the prose. Lawson's well-plotted, humorous magazine stories, notably 'The Loaded Dog' and 'Bill the Ventriloquial Rooster' (qq.v.), continue to be admired and anthologized but more and more the apparent artlessness of Lawson's stories has been recognized as the work of a conscious craftsman seeking the effect of naturalness. The peak of Lawson's achievement is now usually seen to be in While the Billy Boils and Joe Wilson and His Mates. These fifty or sixty stories and sketches include the best of Mitchell and Steelman, e.g. 'Enter Mitchell', 'Shooting the Moon' and 'The Geological Spieler' (q.v.); sketches such as 'The Drover's Wife', 'An Old Mate of Your Father''s, ' ''Rats'' ', 'In a Wet Season', 'The Union Buries Its Dead' and 'Going Blind', in which he drew most effectively on his early life, the Bourke trip and his experiences in the city; and the emerging alienation and isolation of Joe and Mary Wilson in ' ''Water Them Geraniums'' 'and 'Brighten's Sister-in-Law' (q.v.). In stories like these Lawson's fundamentally pessimistic fictional bush world is memorably

authentic and dramatically realized. Central to the presentation are the sharpness and selection of detail, Lawson's documentary quality; the use of an involved narrator, sometimes a character like Mitchell or Wilson, sometimes ostensibly Lawson himself, to establish a natural colloquial voice and an ironic tone, an important ingredient in Lawson's humour; immense sympathy for the victims or survivors of the bush in his characterizations; and a deceptively lucid, understated prose style. Together, these qualities mean that Lawson did more than write the Australia of the 1890s: at his best he has few superiors anywhere in the field of the short story.

LAWSON, LOUISA (1848–1920), the mother of Henry Lawson (q.v.) but an important figure in her own right in the history of Australian radicalism, feminism and publishing, was born near Mudgee, NSW, the daughter of Henry Albury and his wife, Harriet Wynn; a version of Henry's wooing of Harriet is presented in Lawson's 'Grandfather's Courtship'. In 1866 Louisa married Niels Hertzberg (Peter) Larsen, a Norwegian ex-sailor some years her senior; they moved soon after to the Grenfell goldfields – where Henry, the first of their five children, was born – before returning to New Pipeclay, near Mudgee, where they were based until 1883, apart from a stint at Gulgong. The marriage had its periods of tension, with Larsen usually characterized as gentle with his children but somewhat stolid, and Louisa as strongwilled, temperamental and increasingly frustrated with the poverty of selection life. Henry Lawson's 'A Child in the Dark, and a Foreign Father' (q.v.), in presenting substantially this view of the parents, is somewhat unfair to Louisa, who had married Peter under pressure. Her radicalism and sensitivity could find no outlet at New Pipeclay and in 1883 she moved to Sydney, where she was quickly in contact with leading figures in the spiritualist, republican and women's movements. By 1885 her house was a meeting-place for reformists, and in 1887 she took over the radical monthly, the Republican (q.v.). The following year she founded Dawn (q.v.), the first Australian feminist journal, and the Dawn Club; active also in the women's suffrage movement, she established the Association of Women in 1889, merging her activites with those of Rose Scott and the Womanhood Suffrage League in 1891. In 1894 Louisa brought out Henry's first collection, Short Stories in Prose and Verse; it was poorly produced and contributed to the estrangement between mother and son. Louisa's own published work includes a novel, Dert and Do (189?), and a book of poems, The Lonely Crossing (1905). She invented a new buckle for post-office mailbags but the piracy of the invention and the subsequent litigation contributed to her failing health and the closure of *Dawn* in 1905. The subject of Lorna Ollif's *Louisa Lawson: Henry Lawson's Crusading Mother* (1978), Louisa was featured on an Australian ten-cent postage stamp during International Women's Year (1975).

LAWSON, SYLVIA (1932–), born Sydney, a great-granddaughter of Louisa Lawson, has written a biography of J.F. Archibald, *The Archibald Paradox* (1983), and has edited David Williamson's play, *The Removalists* (1972). A journalist before her appointment as lecturer in film at Griffith University, she edits the Australian Screen series for Currency Press.

LAWSON, WILL (1876–1957), born Durham, England, was brought to Australia as a child and educated in Brisbane. In the 1890s his family moved to Wellington, NZ, where Lawson worked as a clerk for an insurance company. In 1912, after contributing some verse to the *Bulletin*, he came to Sydney where he joined the staff of the *Evening News* and later worked as a freelance writer for newspapers and magazines, including the *Bulletin* and *Smith's Weekly*. A familiar figure in Sydney's bohemian circles, he was friendly with such writers and artists as Roderic Quinn, Edward and Will Dyson, Percy Lindsay, Randolph Bedford and Livingston Hopkins. Enthusiastic about Australia's sailing and coaching past, especially the coaching days, Lawson wrote numerous ballads, publishing five collections, *The Red West Road* (1903), *Between the Lights* (1906), *Stokin' and Other Verses* (1908), *The Three Kings* (1914), *Bush Verses* (1943) and *Bill the Whaler* (1944). He also drew on the same sort of material for several novels, including *The Laughing Buccaneer* (1935), *When Cobb and Co. Was King* (1936), *Old Man Murray* (1937), *In Ben Boyd's Day* (1939), *Red Morgan Rides* (1940), *Bound for Callao* (1942), *Black Diamonds* (1945), *The Lady of the Heather* (1945), *Forbidden Gold* (1945), *Paddle-Wheels Away* (1947) and, with Tom Hickey, *Galloping Wheels* (1947) and *Moira of Green Hills* (1950). He also edited an anthology, *Australian Bush Songs and Ballads* (1944); and wrote several descriptive and historical works about Australia and NZ, of which the best-known are *Harpoons Ahoy* (1938) and *Blue Gum Clippers and Whale Ships of Tasmania* (1949). Although not related to Henry Lawson he was a friend of Bertha Lawson and collaborated in her reminiscences of her husband, *My Henry Lawson* (1943).

Lawsons, The, see **MEREDITH, GWEN**

Lawton, Nellie, see *Workingman's Paradise, The*

LAZAR, JOHN (1801–79), the first entrepreneur of serious theatre in Adelaide, was born in Edinburgh and arrived in Sydney in 1837. Adopting the name Lazarus, he claimed to have appeared in well-known London theatres and began his Australian dramatic career by playing Shylock at Sydney's Theatre Royal. Manager of the Theatre Royal December 1837–March 1838, and actor and stage manager at the Victoria Theatre until late 1840, he appears to have had more talent as an administrator than an actor. In 1841 Lazar leased the newly-established Queen's Theatre in Adelaide and with the help of his daughter Rachel, who appeared as both actress and dancer, he presented Adelaide audiences with Shakespearean plays, burlettas, farces and operas. A depressed economy contributed to the lack of interest in his entertainments and he was forced to abandon his lease in November 1842 and return to Sydney, where he again managed the Victoria Theatre (1842–44 and 1846). In 1848 he returned to Adelaide as an associate of George Selth Coppin and on this occasion enjoyed some popularity as a comedian and manager. In the 1850s he abandoned the theatre for a jeweller's and silversmith's business in Adelaide, became an alderman of the city council in 1853 and was mayor of Adelaide 1855–58. In 1859 he retired from the council, and in 1863 settled in NZ where he worked in local government as an administrator.

'Lazy Harry''s is perhaps the best-known Australian folk-song to chronicle the notorious 'lambing down' of shearers by shanty-keepers. In the song two shearers travel through the Riverina towards Sydney but go on a spree at Lazy Harry's shanty on the road to Gundagai and are relieved of their shearing cheques. The rueful tone of 'Lazy Harry''s is repeated in other Australian folk-songs about bush workers in shanties, e.g. 'The Wild Rover' and 'Across the Western Plains' (also known as 'The Jolly Jolly Grog'). Both songs are included in A.B. Paterson's *Old Bush Songs* (1905). In each the protagonist has spent his money on drink and is about to depart, the former to return like the prodigal son to his parents, the latter to resume as an itinerant bush worker on the Riverina's western plains.

LEA, SHELTON (1946–), born Melbourne, left school aged twelve and has spent extensive periods in gaols in Victoria, NSW and Queensland. He has contributed verse to such periodicals as *Bogus*, *Fitzrot* and *New Poetry* and has published several collections including *Cor-*

411

ners in Cans (1969), *The Paradise Poems* (1973), *Chockablock with Dawn* (1975) and *Palantine Madonna* (1978).

Leader, the weekly companion of the *Age* (q.v.), began publication in 1856 as the *Melbourne Leader* and changed title to the *Leader* in 1862; it ceased publication in 1957. It contained a literary section which included serials, short stories, and news and information on books and writers. James Smith and Marcus Clarke were prominent early contributors to the *Leader*; at the turn of the century Mary Grant Bruce began her literary career when she took over the *Leader*'s children's page.

LEAKEY, CAROLINE WOOLMER ('OLINE KEESE') (1827–81), born and educated in Exeter, England, returned there after spending five years (1848–53) in Tasmania with her sister. Her life was dominated by ill-health and a strong Christian faith. The former limited her schooling, made her an invalid for most of her time in Australia, caused her return to England and severely restricted her activities after 1871; the latter led her, when able, to become involved in a variety of charitable works and to write for the Religious Tract Society and the *Girls' Own Paper*. Religion and the problems of sickness and death are major themes in her collection of poems, *Lyra Australis*, published under her own name in 1854, and important ingredients also of *The Broad Arrow* (q.v., 1859), a novel about the convict system which was informed by her Tasmanian experiences and published under her pseudonym in 1859. *Clear Shining Light*, a memoir of Leakey by her sister Emily, was published in 1882.

LEASON, PERCY (1889–1959), born Kaniva, Victoria, served an apprenticeship as a lithographer in Melbourne, and then moved in 1917 to Sydney, where he established himself as a cartoonist on the *Bulletin*. Lured back to Melbourne to work on the *Melbourne Punch* and its successor, *Table Talk*, he eventually renewed his association with the *Bulletin* before settling in America in 1939. A precise draughtsman with a fine sense of detail, Leason won a reputation not only for his cartoons, notably the series on the country town, Wiregrass, but also for his illustrations of the works of Australian authors, notably for the drawings included in the *Selected Poems of Henry Lawson* (1918). He published a series of articles on his boyhood in the magazine, *Pandemonium*, in 1934.

Leaves from Australian Forests, the second volume of verse published by Henry Kendall (q.v.) in 1869, contains the well-known lyrics, 'Bell Birds' and 'September in Australia'; the important narratives, 'The Glen of Arrawatta' and 'King Saul at Gilboa'; the love poem, 'Rose Lorraine'; and memorial poems to Charles Harpur, James Lionel Michael and Adam Lindsay Gordon.

'LECKIE, PETER', see **HOPEGOOD, PETER**

LEE, GERARD (1951–), born Melbourne, grew up in Melbourne and Brisbane, and graduated from the University of Queensland in 1974. He has worked as a teacher, clerk, journalist and house-painter and has contributed verse and short stories to a range of periodicals including *Ear in a Wheatfield*, *Meanjin*, *Riverrun*, *Magic Sam*, *Semper Floreat* and *Makar*. Lee has published a collection of prose poems, *Manual for a Garden Mechanic* (1976); a collection of short stories, *Pieces for a Glass Piano* (1978); and a novel, *True Love and How to Get It* (1981). A witty writer with a deceptively naive narrative style, Lee frequently satirizes contemporary Queensland lifestyles, from numerous varieties of the alternative to the mainstream. *True Love and How to Get It*, set in Coolangatta and suburban Brisbane, has been praised as an authentic representation of contemporary southern Queensland; the episodic story of the sexual and other adventures of a picaresque hero, narrated by an omniscient author in a wryly comic style that is reminiscent of Fielding, the novel presents a range of social scenes from the bizarre to the bourgeois.

LEE, IDA (c.1875–1943), born Kelso, NSW, into one of the earliest pioneering families, married Charles Marriott and is occasionally referred to as Ida Marriott. She wrote several historical accounts, some of which contain extracts from previously unpublished journals, including *The Coming of the British to Australia, 1788–1829* (1906), *Commodore Sir John Hayes* (1912), *The Logbooks of the 'Lady Nelson'* (1915), *Captain Bligh's Second Voyage to the South Sea* (1920), *Early Explorers of Australia* (1925); and edited *The Voyage of the 'Caroline' from England to Van Diemen's Land and Batavia in 1827–28* by R. Hare (1927). She also published a collection of verse, *The Bush Fire and Other Verses* (1897).

LEETE, HENRY BENJAMIN, see **RICKARDS, HARRY**

Leeuwin, an occasional journal published in WA in five issues 1910–11, was edited by Alfred Chandler ('Spinifex') and A.G. Plate. Its most noteworthy literary articles were four contributions by A.G. Stephens on 'The Manly Poetry of Western Australia.'

Legend for Sanderson, see **PALMER, VANCE**

Legend of King O'Malley, The (1974), a popular musical play by Bob Ellis and Michael Boddy (qq.v.), was first produced in 1970 by the National Institute of Dramatic Art (NIDA) at Sydney's Jane Street Theatre. Frequently re-staged since 1970 and often compared to Ray Lawler's *Summer of the Seventeenth Doll* (1957) in its stimulating effect on Australian drama, the play won a first prize in the Captain Cook Bicentenary competition of 1970, an Awgie Award and the Producers' and Directors' Guild Award, both in 1971. Based on the life of an eccentric, larrikin hero of the Australian labour movement, King O'Malley (q.v.), the play opens in the form of a meeting of the revivalist Waterlily Rockbound Church, according to O'Malley founded by him in Texas, and fol-lows his career until his arrival in Queensland. Hounded by his *alter ego*, Angel, who appears in various disguises, e.g. as a devil wearing army boots and bloomers, a swagman, Long John Silver and a fortune-telling beggar, O'Malley eventually makes his way to the first federal parliament, which transpires to be a troupe of tired vaudeville artists led by W.M. (Billy) Hughes. Alienated from Hughes over the conscription issue, O'Malley dies shortly after him and is taken off to the next world in a truck, accompanied by a rousing hymn from the chorus. A fast-moving series of comic, mu-sic-hall sketches linked by song, dance and mime, the play also makes some serious state-ments about Australian political life.

Legend of the Nineties, The, an influential work of cultural criticism by Vance Palmer (q.v.), was published in 1954. It attempts to take dispassionate stock of the nineties (q.v.), a decade that became invested with mythic significance for many Australians by the end of the Second World War. After opening with a generalized description of the period, 'which turned the eyes of Australians inward and im-pelled them to discover themselves and their country', Palmer moves on to chapters on the composition of the population, on the period's oral literature and its myth-making, on Uto-pian aspirations and ventures, the role of the *Bulletin*, the literature of Henry Lawson, A.B. Paterson, Bernard O'Dowd, Joseph Furphy and others, and on the political ferment of the time and its resolution. In his last chapter, 'A Lost Tradition', he speculates on the continuing sig-nificance of the decade for the national con-sciousness of Australia.

Legends of Australia, see **LANG, JOHN GEORGE**

LEGG, FRANK (1906–66), born England, came to Australia in 1927. After working as a freelance journalist in Sydney, Melbourne and Adelaide, he joined the staff of the Adelaide *News* in 1937. He also began to establish a reputation as a broadcaster on ABC radio. In 1940 he joined the AIF and served in the Middle East, sending back a series of articles, 'Tales of Tobruk', to the *ABC Weekly*. In Jan-uary 1944 he went to New Guinea as an ABC war correspondent and covered the retreat of the Japanese to the ultimate surrender in Tokyo Bay. After the war he became one of the best-known commentators on ABC radio and tele-vision. He published the biographies, *The Eyes of Damien Parer* (1963), *The Gordon Bennett Story* (1965), *Once More on My Adventure* (1966, on Frank Hurley); an account of his and others' war experiences based on diaries, recorded talks and official reports to the ABC, *War Correspondent* (1964); and a collection of reminiscences of his cats, *Cats on Velvet* (1966).

LEHMANN, GEOFFREY (1940–), born Sydney, graduated with degrees in arts and law from the University of Sydney, where he was associated with fellow-poet Les Murray and co-edited the magazines *Arna* and *Hermes*. Leh-mann has practised as a solicitor and now lectures in law at the University of NSW. His published verse consists of *The Ilex Tree* (1965, a shared volume with Les Murray); *A Voyage of Lions and Other Poems* (1968); *Conversation with a Rider* (1972); *From an Australian Coun-try Sequence* (1973); *Extracts from Ross' Poems* (1976); *Ross' Poems* (q.v., 1978); and *Nero's Poems* (1981). His *Selected Poems* was published in 1976. Lehmann has also written a novel, *A Spring Day in Autumn* (1974), edited *Comic Australian Verse* (1972), an anthology, *The Younger Australian Poets* (1983, with Robert Gray), and *Australian Primitive Painters* (1977) which is a selection of the work of such painters as Irvine Homer, Charles Callins, James Far-doulys, Sam Bryne and Harry Bastin.

In *The Ilex Tree* Lehmann's predilection for family poetry is shown in the four 'Pieces for My Father' and the long, seven-part poem, 'For William Rainer, My Grandfather'. *A Voyage of Lions and Other Poems* is dominated by the much-admired historical series, 'Monologues for Marcus Furius Camillus, Governor of Africa', and other shorter poems with an ancient Ro-man setting. As a background to the observa-tions and meditations of the ageing Camillus there is a passing parade of Roman decadence – victory marches, lavish banquets, slave girls, gladiators, ornate villas, lush vineyards and

413

olive groves. The monologues, which are also included as the opening section of Lehmann's later *Selected Poems*, convey well the fatal combination of opulence and ennui that marks a civilization near collapse. The highlights of the series are the dolphin and lion poems. The capture and transshipping of the African lions to the Colosseum ('A Voyage of Lions') are taken up by the following poem, 'Colosseum', and in a later volume, 'Colosseum at a Distance'. The lion sequence pinpoints the ultimate barbarity of Roman civilization, the charnel-house of the Colosseum where the burial pits were 'So foul that workmen digging two thousand years later/Sickened by the smell will lay down their spades'. *Conversation with a Rider* combines poems on historical personages such as 'Pope Alexander VI' and 'Cellini' with those on family and friends. The sequence of eleven poems, which recalls experiences from the life and death of Lehmann's father, lovingly and good-humouredly charts the close relationship between the two. The 'Roses' sequence, with its patterning of natural beauty and grace against man's destructiveness, is more complex, both technically and thematically, than Lehmann's usual lucid, undemonstrative compositions.

Ross' Poems, Lehmann's most popular and impressive work, is a long poem segmented into seventy-five separate pieces. It has as its persona Lehmann's then father-in-law, Ross McInerney, and describes his experiences as a farmer in central-western NSW. Partly memoirs, partly anecdotes and partly reflections, the poems build up a composite of close-knit family life in a typically Australian rural community. *Ross' Poems* form part of the Australian 'vernacular republic' of Lehmann's fellow-poet, Les Murray, and are an important illustration of the modern resurgence of interest in the bush and its people. In *Nero's Poems* Lehmann returns to the ancient world which had so intrigued him in *A Voyage of Lions*. He resumes the successful dramatic monologue of the Camillus poems to explore the enigma of Nero and to examine and even account for that strange ruler's bizarre character and conduct. The poems are accompanied by Lehmann's introductory comments on Nero.

LEICHHARDT, LUDWIG (1813–?48), born Trebatsch, Prussia, studied philosophy, languages, natural science and medicine in Germany, England and France before coming to Australia in 1842 to study natural science in a hitherto unexplored environment. In 1844–45 he led an overland expedition from Brisbane to Port Essington, a journey of almost 5000 kilometres. After an abortive attempt in 1846–47 to cross the continent east-west from the Darling Downs to the coast of WA, Leichhardt tried again in March 1848, setting out from the Condamine River near the present township of Roma, but the expedition disappeared virtually without trace. In spite of nine major searches over a period of almost a century the disappearance of Leichhardt's expedition still remains one of the great mysteries of the Australian bush.

Leichhardt's own records of his explorations are contained in diaries, notebooks, sketch-books and letters, many of which are in the Mitchell Library. He published *Journal of an Overland Expedition in Australia from Moreton Bay to Port Essington* (1847). Marcel Aurousseau collected, translated and published *The Letters of F.W. Ludwig Leichhardt* (1968). The Leichhardt saga and the controversial character of the man himself have inspired a large body of writing, chief of which are the descriptive and biographical works of A.H. Chisholm, *Strange New World: The Adventures of John Gilbert and Ludwig Leichhardt* (1941, republished 1973 as *Strange Journey*); E.M. Webster, *Whirlwinds in the Plain* (1980), the most complete analysis of the man and his achievement; and Gordon Connell, *The Mystery of Ludwig Leichhardt* (1980). Leichhardt and his fate have also inspired poets such as Henry Kendall, who wrote the long poem 'Leichhardt' and whose first published verses were four stanzas ('Oh, Tell Me Ye Breezes') pondering the explorer's disappearance. A.B. Paterson wrote 'The Lost Leichhardt' and Francis Webb examines the enigma of Leichhardt's character in 'Leichhardt in Theatre'. The most celebrated fictional representation of him is in Patrick White's novel, *Voss* (1957). Rosa Praed in several of her novels portrays Queensland and Brisbane respectively as 'Leichardt's [sic] Land' and 'Leichardt's [sic] Town'.

'Leichhardt in Theatre', a poem by Francis Webb (q.v.), was published as 'Leichhardt Pantomime' in the *Bulletin*, 1947. In 1952 it was published with other poems in a revised form with a new title, 'Leichhardt in Theatre', in a volume of that name. The opening section of the original poem, 'Introduction in a Waxworks', was replaced by a segment titled 'Advertisement', and the 'Epilogue' of the original poem was omitted. The poem's central figure is the explorer, Ludwig Leichhardt (q.v.). The poem opens with a vision of the earlier explorer Charles Sturt who, thwarted in his several attempts to establish the existence of an inland sea, left an 'Impasse at the Centre'. The solving of that 'Impasse' provided much of the lure for Leichhardt. Webb's portrait of Leichhardt begins by emphasizing the visionary side of his nature ('This is a land where man becomes a myth'), then, by introducing a clown and by the use of a type of music-hall doggerel, he pictures Leichhardt as a buffoon who does not know 'north from south' but who is clever at 'playing with windmills in the Never Never'. Glimpses of Leichhardt's expeditions follow: the first triumphant journey of fifteen months and 5000 kilometres to the Gulf of Carpentaria, marred only by the death of botanist, John Gilbert; and the second journey, a farcical failure led by the equally-farcical figure of Leichhardt. In the interval between the second and third expeditions Leichhardt is forced to confront the painful realization of the conflicting duality of his nature. The third expedition, although only briefly exposed in the poem, sees purpose and significance restored. The outcome is seen as uncertain, but that is unimportant – the venture is everything ('Where they will go, how perish – this is nothing'). In its use of psychological analysis and self-analysis for characterization rather than the simple observer technique employed in 'A Drum for Ben Boyd', 'Leichhardt in Theatre' is more skilful and subtle than the earlier Webb poem. It builds up a fascinating and deeply-unified vision of the enigmatic and contradictory character of the Prussian explorer. Douglas Stewart included 'Leichhardt in Theatre' in his anthology, *Voyager Poems*, in 1960.

LENTZNER, KARL, see **Australian English**

Les Darcy Show, The, see **DARCY, LES**

LETT, LEWIS (1878–1966), born Waddingham, England, came to Australia in 1910. Shortly afterwards, he settled in Papua as superintendent engineer of a large development company. In 1911 he and his partner, G.H. Thomas, found petroleum in the Gulf of Papua and prospected an extensive area of jungle for further indications, Thomas dying in the attempt. Lett travelled extensively in Papua before settling in Port Moresby, where he acted as Reuters' correspondent, contributing to the London *Times*, the *Manchester Guardian* and other overseas and Australian newspapers. He published a biography of Sir Hubert Murray (1949); several accounts of Papua including *Knights Errant of Papua* (1935), *The Papuan Achievement* (1942), *Papuan Gold* (1943) and *Papua: Its People and Its Promise* (1944); and a collection of short stories of Papuan life, *Savage Tales* (1946).

Let's Hear It For Prendergast, see **OAKLEY, BARRY**

Letter from Sydney, A, see **WAKEFIELD, EDWARD GIBBON**

LETTERS, F.J. (FRANCIS JOSEPH HENRY) (1897–1964), born Queensland, graduated from the University of Sydney in 1918 and practised as a barrister 1927–37 before joining the staff of the New England University College in 1938. He published several works of academic criticism on classical and European literature; a collection of general essays, *In a Shaft of Sunlight* (1948); and two volumes of poetry, *Darkness and Light* (1934) and *The Great Attainder* (1943). A collection of essays on classic literature, *For Service to Classical Studies*, was published in 1966 in his honour.

Letters from Victorian Pioneers, see **BRIDE, T.F.**

Letters to Live Poets (1969), the major work of Bruce Beaver (q.v.), comprises thirty-four confessional-type poems in a *livre composé*. It was influenced by the NZ poet James K. Baxter's *Pig Island Letters*, *Life Studies* by Robert Lowell and *Letters from Darkness* by Lawrence Durrell; in its turn *Letters to Live Poets* influenced the style and direction of much Australian poetry of the 1970s. Written with obsessional purpose and speed (forty-nine poems in as many days in 1966) because Beaver believed he was losing his rationality, the *Letters* are directed to the 'not-impossible creative reader, a live poet in his or her own sense'. They begin with a letter to the American poet, Frank O'Hara, recently killed in a bizarre fashion when crushed by a beach buggy while sunbathing. The opening letters despairingly catch certain appalling aspects of contemporary life: the Vietnam war ('infants blistered and skinned alive by napalm'); international complicity in corruption ('your country's president ... among us like a formidable virus'); the rank commercialism of modern society ('keyed to obsolescence'); the vegetable existence and mindless passivity of today's people who demand only the material trivia of life, none of its beauty and fullness. Other letters recall painful episodes of Beaver's early life ('damn my childhood') and the ever-present threat of mental illness ('so it's one day at a time spent checking the menagerie of self'). From Letter XIX, whose self-revelations are taken up more fully in Beaver's later work, *As It Was*, the tone changes. Its comfortable opening, 'I welcome the anonymity of the middle years', reflects a growing note of self-confidence born out of an ironic acceptance of himself as he is and of the achievement of a limited kind of working arrangement with his environment. Although the early despair subsides, the sense of futility does not completely disappear and the *Letters*, 'never to be posted', close with the recognition of at least one supreme saving gift – that of the 'living word'.

'Letter[s] to Tom Collins' is a series of letters supposedly addressed to Joseph Furphy through 'Tom Collins' (q.v.), which discuss either Furphy's works and their reception, or Australian literature and society in the 1940s in the light of Furphy's critical and social attitudes. The series was published in *Meanjin*, commencing with 'Brian Vrepont''s 'Letter to Tom Collins: "New" Verse – and *Meanjin* Trends' in 1941 and concluding with Sidney Baker's 'Letter to Tom Collins: Demise of the *Bulletin*' in 1946; other contributors include James Devaney, Kylie Tennant, Nettie Palmer, Miles Franklin, Manning Clark and A.A. Phillips. The device of addressing Collins or the deceased Furphy himself as a way of commenting, usually critically, on contemporary Australian society has been periodically revived, e.g. in *Overland* in 1957.

Lettres d'un Mineur en Australie, see FAUCHERY, ANTOINE

LEVEY, BARNETT (1798–1837), born London, arrived in Sydney in 1821 to join his brother Solomon, who had been transported in 1815 but had become a prosperous merchant. Barnett Levey worked for his brother for about four years, before going into business as merchant and auctioneer with an interest in banking. He achieved some financial success but was temperamentally unsuited to commercial life. A man of impulse and unrealistic ambitions, he opened his own retail and wholesale warehouse, established one of the first lending libraries, and built a flour-mill, wheat store and windmill on the site of his warehouse between Colchester and George Streets. A great lover of the theatre, he nourished grandiose, entrepreneurial projections, took a prominent part in Sydney's cultural events, performing as a singer at concerts, and from 1826 was actively engaged in establishing the first permanent theatre in Australia. In November 1827 he founded a company to finance the theatre, which was to be included in his Colchester Street property. Hindered by acrimonious disputes with Governor Darling and the colonial secretary over his mill, by financial worries, by his own mercurial, irascible nature, and by the unwillingness of others to finance the theatre, Levey mortgaged his property to do so. Meanwhile he faced great opposition from the government and clergy in his repeated bids to gain a theatrical licence. To acquire more money he converted the front of his building into the Royal

Hotel and in July 1829 obtained a licence to present balls and suppers and, later, concerts in his hotel. In August he held a vocal and instrumental concert ostensibly in the Royal Hotel, referred to as the Assembly Rooms, but which was in fact held in his Theatre Royal, designed by Francis Greenway to accommodate 700 people. The first concert was succeeded by others, at all of which Levey himself performed. In November he performed in a one-man show titled 'At Home', which proved highly popular with the audience but incurred the wrath of the colonial secretary. By December 1830 Levey, still unable to obtain a theatrical licence, was forced to sell his hotel, store, granary and mill and to turn to working as an auctioneer, watchmaker and estate agent. Governor Darling's replacement by Governor Burke, however, resulted in a more relaxed attitude to theatrical performances and in April 1832 Levey was granted a licence. Levey's original Theatre Royal, now owned by Cooper and Levey, was redesigned and enlarged by John Verge. While the theatre was being adapted, Levey and his company presented entertainments and plays on a temporary stage in the converted saloon of the Royal Hotel. The company opened their first season on 26 December 1832 with Douglas Jerrold's *Black-Eyed Susan*. Enormously popular, Levey's company presented performances of a variety of plays from melodrama to farce to Shakespearean drama three nights a week in its first season, which ran to July 1833. The expanded Theatre Royal, capable of seating at least 1200, was opened in October 1833. To the end of its turbulent life the Theatre Royal company experienced more lows than peaks, due to perennial disputes between Levey and his players, unruly audiences, some careless performances and some poor houses. Charles Harpur, who was briefly an actor, took Levey to court to recover money from him and legal actions between Levey and other players were a constant phenomenon. Actors of some note who performed with the company included Conrad Knowles, John Meredith, George Buckingham, Joseph Simmons, Eliza Winstanley and John Lazar. John Simmons joined Levey as partner in 1834. In 1835, worn out by the difficulties of running the company, Levey lost control of the theatre to other lessees although in 1836 he briefly resumed management. In April 1837 he staged his last great entertainment, the spectacle *Napoleon Buonaparte*. He died in October, leaving his widow and four children in poverty. Mrs Levey, assisted by others including Joseph Simmons, continued to run the theatre until March 1838, when the opening of the Royal Victoria under the directorship of Joseph Wyatt ensured the demise of the company. In October 1838 Wyatt bought the Royal Hotel and the Theatre Royal to house his own company. Barnett Levey's life and achievements are described by Eric Irvin in *Theatre Comes to Australia* (1971).

LEVY, JULIA ETHEL, who frequently used the pseudonym 'Juliet', published several light-weight and conventional one-act plays, novels and volumes of poetry in the 1920s. Her plays include *The Way Out* (1925), *The Snob* (1925), *The Proposal* (1926), *Woman Disposes* (1927) and the three-act piece, *The Choice* (1928). Her novels include a *A Soul of Sincerity* (1923), *God's Good Woman* (1926), *Devotion* (1927) and *The Snob and the Lady* (1929); her collections of verse are *Songs of Solace* (1922) and *Signposts on Life's Highway* (1926).

LEWIN, J.W. (JOHN WILLIAM) (1770–1819), born England, arrived in Sydney in 1800. His *Birds of New Holland with Their Natural History* was published in London in 1808; the 1813 edition issued in Sydney with the title *Birds of New South Wales* was the first illustrated book published in Australia and was printed by George Howe.

LHOTSKY, JOHN (1795–?), born Galicia (now part of Poland) of Czechoslovakian parents, was a trained naturalist and doctor who arrived in Sydney in 1832. In 1834 he explored the Argyle and Monaro districts in NSW, publishing on his return *A Journey from Sydney to the Australian Alps*; this lively, somewhat eccentric, and incomplete work was first issued in sixteen-page parts to subscribers (1834–36) and then bound in book form (dated 1835). After failing to secure a scientific post in NSW, Lhotsky went in 1836 to Van Diemen's Land, where he worked as a scientist, lecturer and journalist before leaving for England in 1838; the last reference to him overseas is in 1865. A controversial colonist during his six years in Australia, Lhotsky was an important early natural historian, explorer and geologist; his *A Song of the Women of the Menero Tribe* (1835) is the first arrangement of Aboriginal music. He contributed widely to scientific journals overseas as well as writing political and scientific articles for the *Sydney Gazette*, the *Sydney Monitor* and the *Sydney Herald* in Sydney and the *Hobart Town Courier*, *Colonial Times* and *Tasmanian and Austral-Asiatic Review* in Hobart. In Sydney Lhotsky also helped edit the *New South Wales Magazine* (1833), edited the *Reformer* (1836) and wrote all of the *New South Wales Literary, Political and Commercial Advertiser*, a short-lived periodical (1835–36), some of the issues published with part of *Illustrations of the Present State and Future Prospects of the Colony of New South Wales* (1835); the *Illus-*

trations parts were published anonymously but were written by Lhotsky and were bound together (1836), like the earlier *A Journey to the Australian Alps*. In Hobart he wrote the three weekly numbers of *Information for the People* (1837), which included a description of Tasman's Peninsula. Lech Paszkowski edited *Dr. John Lhotsky: The Turbulent Australian Writer Naturalist and Explorer* (1977), which includes biographical information on Lhotsky's birth (previously reckoned as 1800), and a year later appeared Alan E.J. Andrews's edition of Lhotsky's *Journey* which includes material recently discovered at the British Museum.

Libraries Board of South Australia has made a major contribution to Australian literature, history and biography, with its Australian Facsimile Editions, Bibliographies of Australian Writers and other series.

Life, a popular monthly magazine published in Melbourne 1904–38, was edited by J.S. and W.H. Fitchett and was concerned with local and international affairs. W.H. Fitchett wrote much of the material until his death in 1927. The magazine published some articles and verse by Australian writers and reprinted poetry and prose from overseas sources. In 1938 it was superseded by *Life Digest*, which ran until 1961, becoming increasingly journalistic and less literary.

'Life-Cycle', one of Bruce Dawe's (q.v.) best-known poems, was published in his volume, *An Eye for a Tooth* (1968). Both a satire on, and a celebration of, the Victorian obsession with Australian Rules football, the poem presents the ingredients of the Saturday afternoon football ritual – the wearing of the club colours and the shouting of club nicknames ('Tigers', 'Demons', 'Saints'); the barracking chant ('Carn . . . carn'); the abuse of umpires ('ooohh you bludger'); and the football spectator's fare ('hot pies and potato-crisps'). Like some mass opiate, Aussie Rules adds meaning to otherwise meaningless lives. Old-timers by boundary fences 'dream of resurgent lions and centaur-figures from the past' and visualize present salvation 'in the six-foot recruit from Eaglehawk'. With his parody of the threnody 'For the Fallen', Dawe catches, in serio-comic fashion, the analogy between the football game and life itself.

> They will not grow old as those from more
> northern States grow old,
> for them it will always be three-quarter time
> with the scores level and the wind advantage
> in the final term.

'Life in Sydney: Or, the Ran Dan Club', an anonymous adaptation of *Tom and Jerry: Or,*

417

Life in London (1821) by 'W.T. Moncrieff' (q.v.), was written in 1843 but refused a performance licence by the colonial secretary on the grounds that it was libellous. The adaptation uses the same names for its principal characters as well as the Jemmy Green who is also the subject of James Tucker's *Jemmy Green in Australia* (q.v., 1845). The script of the play is by various authors, including H.C. O'Flaherty who also seems to have been prominent in its promotion.

Life Rarely Tells, see LINDSAY, JACK

LIGHT, WILLIAM (1786–1839), born Malaya, served in the British army and travelled widely in Europe before his appointment in 1836 as surveyor-general of the new colony of SA. In 1836–37 he selected the site, surveyed and laid out the plan of Adelaide and is generally recognized as the founder of that city. He also explored the SA coast and surveyed part of the hinterland of the colony before conflicts with his superiors caused his resignation. Light wrote *A Brief Journal of the Proceedings of William Light* (1839), a vindication of his activities in SA; an accomplished artist, he also published *Sicilian Scenery* (1823) and *Views of Pompeii* (1828). The Lighthouse Theatre Company of SA is named after him; among several biographical studies is Geoffrey Dutton's *Founder of a City* (1960). Max Afford's play *Awake My Love*, first titled 'William Light the Founder', won the SA centenary competition in 1936 and was published in 1960; it centres on the conflicts between Light and the SA governor, John Hindmarsh. Early settlers who wrote commemorative poems on Light include Caroline Carleton in *South Australian Lyrics* (?1860) and Fidelia Hill in *Poems and Recollections of the Past* (1840).

Lilith, see BRENNAN, C.J.

LILLEY, MERV (1919–), born Rockhampton, left school early, served in the army 1941–44, and has worked as drover, cane-cutter, seaman and wharf-labourer. He has contributed verse and songs to numerous periodicals and is represented in several well-known anthologies. He collaborated with Dorothy Hewett, whom he married in 1960, in a volume of verse with a socialist theme, *What About the People?* (1962), has published an independent collection, *Cautious Birds* (1973), and a collection of stories, reminiscences, poems and bush cookery ideas titled *Git Away Back! A Knockabout Life* (1983).

Lilley's Magazine was founded and edited by Norman Lilley (1876–1941), who was familiar with many of Sydney's writers and for some years conducted the literary page of the Sydney *Worker*. The magazine appeared monthly June–October 1911 and provided a much needed outlet for several artists and writers, including Hugh McCrae, C.J. Brennan, Mary Gilmore and Lionel Lindsay.

'Lime-Juice Tub, The' is a shearers' work song which pokes fun at the new chum (q.v.) working in the shearing shed; it was collected around 1930 by A.L. Lloyd (q.v.) while he was a bush worker in NSW, and was one of the Australian folk-songs actually sung during shearing. The title of the song establishes the new chums as English ('limeys') who will be sent home by ship (a 'tub') if their work doesn't improve. An earlier song, 'The Whaler's Rhyme', printed in the *Bulletin* in 1898, may be one of the originals of the song Lloyd heard despite the fact that it carries no reference to a 'lime-juice tub'.

'LINDALL, EDWARD' (EDWARD ERNEST SMITH) (1915–), born Adelaide, worked as a journalist for many years and during the Second World War served in the Middle East and New Guinea. He started writing in 1948 during an extended stay in England, sold his first fiction, a short story, in 1949, and subsequently contributed several stories to the *Saturday Evening Post*. He has since become a popular author in the USA, Australia and Britain, having written numerous adventure novels mostly set in outback, northern Australia. They include *No Place to Hide* (1959), *Untamed Land* (1961), *The Killers of Karawala* (1961), *Stranger Among Friends* (1956), *A Kind of Justice* (1964), *Northward the Coast* (1966), *A Time Too Soon* (1967), *The Fires of Kiwai* (1968), *Roar of the Lion* (1969), *A Gathering of Eagles* (1970), *The Last Refuge* (1972) and *Season of Discovery* (1978).

LINDESAY, VANE (1920–), the cartoonist 'Vane', was born in Sydney, became senior artist on *Salt* during the Second World War and since then has worked for the Melbourne *Herald*, the *Argus* and the *Australasian Post* where he has illustrated the Australiana feature, 'Come in Spinner', by Bill Wannan. A book illustrator and theatrical designer as well as a cartoonist, Lindesay has conducted extensive research into the history of Australian comic art. He has written *The Inked-In Image* (1970), *The Way We Were* on Australian popular magazines (1983), and has contributed numerous articles to *The World Encyclopedia of Cartoons* (1980).

LINDSAY, Sir **DARYL** (1890–1976), born Creswick, Victoria, was the brother of Percy,

Lionel, Norman and Ruby Lindsay. After some experience on sheep and cattle stations he enlisted in the AIF in 1915 and served in France. After his return to Australia in 1919 he became known for his landscapes and equestrian studies, but is most widely known as a gallery director and art adviser. He was director of the National Gallery of Victoria 1942–55; helped to establish the National Trust of Australia; from 1953 was a member of the Commonwealth Art Advisory Board and its chairman 1960–69; and was chairman of the interim council for the Australian National Gallery 1968–71. He was knighted in 1956. In 1922 he married Joan à Beckett Weigall (Joan Lindsay). His only work of literary interest is *The Leafy Tree* (1965), an account of the Lindsay family.

LINDSAY, HAROLD ARTHUR (1900–69), born Adelaide, travelled extensively in Australia before starting work as a commercial beekeeper in 1928 and as a farmer in 1933. In 1940 he joined the army as a special instructor in bushcraft, teaching survival techniques to Australian and American servicemen in Australia, New Guinea and New Britain. His *The Bushman's Handbook* (1948), one of his most popular books, was published in three editions. After the war he became a full-time writer and broadcaster, contributing a weekly 'Naturalist's Diary' column to the *Age* for several years, as well as numerous articles to geographical and naturalist magazines. He published five novels for adults, *The Red Bull* (1959), *Sweeps the Wide Earth* (1960), *Janię McLachlan* (1961), *Faraway Hill* (1963) and *And Gifts Misspent* (1964); *The Red Bull*, drawing on his knowledge of forestry and bushfire, has been the most acclaimed. He wrote the juvenile novel, *The Arnhem Treasure* (1952) and, with Norman Tindale, three books for children: *The First Walkabout* (1954, winner of the 1955 Children's Book of the Year Award), *Rangatira* (1959) and *Aboriginal Australians* (1963).

LINDSAY, JACK (1900–   ), son of Norman Lindsay (q.v.), was born Melbourne and brought up in Brisbane. He graduated from the University of Queensland in 1921. Although hardly aware of his father during his childhood after his parents separated, he came strongly under Norman's influence from 1919 and in 1921–26 was a part of the lively cultural life of Sydney that he has described in *The Roaring Twenties* (q.v., 1960). Profoundly impressed by his father's ideas, especially as expressed in *Creative Effort* (1920), he was the major force behind the establishment of the journal *Vision* (q.v.). He also edited with Kenneth Slessor the anthology *Poetry in Australia 1923* (1923). His first book of verse, *Fauns and Ladies* (1923), was illustrated by Norman Lindsay's woodcuts. In 1926 he left for England with the object of establishing himself as a poet and disseminating the Lindsay aesthetic via the Fanfrolico Press (q.v.), which he founded and ran with Jack Kirtley and P.R. Stephensen. The same motives prompted his establishment of the journal, the *London Aphrodite* (q.v., 1928–29). By 1930 Lindsay's contact with a wider culture and international political issues had counteracted the influence of his father's ideas and by 1936 he had moved from Nietzscheanism to Marxism, a commitment that has persisted. His importance to the Soviet cause was recognized in 1968 when he was awared the Soviet Badge of Honour, but he remained a philosophical adherent rather than a political activist. During the war he worked as a private in the signals corps and then in the War Office as script writer for army drama groups. Since then he has supported himself by his prodigious writing. Poet, dramatist, editor, historian, translator, classical scholar, biographer, novelist and critic, he has a formidable international reputation, especially in the last five fields. Author of over a hundred books, he has also contributed to many of the better-known journals in Australia and England. Although he has never returned to Australia, he has retained a lively interest in its culture and has frequently contributed to Australian literary debates. His autobiographical trilogy, *Life Rarely Tells* (1958), *The Roaring Twenties* (1960) and *Fanfrolico and After* (1962), is particularly valuable as sociocultural history. A recent collection, *Decay and Renewal* (1976), brings together some of his essays on Australian and international literature. In 1968 his services to Australian literature were recognized by a D.Litt. from the University of Queensland. In 1980 he was elected a life member of the Association for the Study of Australian Literature; in 1981 he was made AM. *Culture and History: Essays Presented to Jack Lindsay*, edited by Bernard Smith, was published in 1984.

LINDSAY, JANE (1920–   ), is the daughter of Norman and Rose Lindsay (qq.v.). She has written a novel, *Kurrajong* (1945), a humorous, realistic story of rural folk, and *Portrait of Pa* (1973), reminiscences of her father, particularly of his latter years at Springwood.

LINDSAY, Lady JOAN (1896–1984), born Joan à Beckett Weigall, was related to the Boyd family and became a member of the Lindsay family when she married Sir Daryl Lindsay (q.v.) in 1922. She was born in Melbourne and educated at the Clyde Girls Grammar School, the basis for the Appleyard College of *Picnic at Hanging Rock* (q.v., 1967). Although she studied art at the National Gallery School in Melbourne, writing became her main interest. Her first book, written under the pseudonym 'Serena Livingstone-Stanley' and titled *Through Darkest Pondelayo* (1936), parodies, among other things, feminine literature of the genteel variety, British colonialism and accounts of exploration; complete with photographs and 'Appendicites' the book purports to be edited by 'Barnaby Whitecorn D.D.'. Its humour has been compared to that of the Marx brothers. Her next two books, *Time Without Clocks* (1962) and *Facts Soft and Hard* (1964), are autobiographical. The former is a series of reminiscences of her married life before the outbreak of the Second World War; the latter describes her impressions of a visit to the USA. Her best-known book, *Picnic at Hanging Rock*, was made into an internationally-successful film in 1975. A carefully crafted, suggestive and intriguing work with mythic overtones, it is shaped by her characteristically-penetrating insights into human behaviour. Also prominent in the novel is her preoccupation with the ambiguities of time, especially the disparities between man-made time, natural time and time of the mind. She also wrote a children's book, *Syd Sixpence* (1982).

LINDSAY, Sir LIONEL (1874–1961), born Creswick, Victoria, etcher, watercolour painter, wood-engraver, black-and-white artist, book illustrator, and art critic, was the brother of Percy, Norman, Daryl and Ruby Lindsay. After a period of work as a pupil-assistant at the Melbourne Observatory and some training in drawing at the National Gallery School in Melbourne, he worked as a freelance artist and journalist for weeklies in Melbourne and Sydney including the *Hawk* (later the *Hawklet*), the *Free Lance* and the *Bulletin*. He taught himself the techniques of etching and engraving, in which he became a master, and pioneered local interest in them. After a visit to Spain 1901–02 he settled in Sydney, working as a cartoonist on the *Evening News* and meanwhile establishing his reputation as an artist in Australia and overseas. In 1903 he married Jane Dyson, the sister of Will Dyson. He travelled extensively, visiting Spain, France, Italy, North Africa and India 1926–35, and continued to work and exhibit after his return to Australia in 1935. His work is held extensively by Australian and overseas galleries. He was knighted in 1941 for his services to art and was a trustee of the Art Gallery of NSW 1919–29 and 1934–49.

In addition to several collections of his art work, Lindsay produced numerous works of art criticism including an entry on Arthur Streeton's Australian paintings 'The Art of Arthur Streeton' in a special edition of *Art in Australia* (1919), *Conrad Martens* (1920), *The Art of Hans Heysen* (1920) and *Charles Keene* (1934). An outspoken and articulate critic of modernism in art, he expressed his views most provocatively in *Addled Art* (1942). His autobiography, *Comedy of Life* (1967), includes reminiscences of other members of the Lindsay family and of the artists, writers, musicians and well-known figures with whom he was familiar. Although he worked closely with his brother Norman in his early years their ideas eventually diverged and the relationship was severed in 1922.

LINDSAY, NORMAN (1879–1969) was born Creswick, Victoria, the fourth son of Robert Lindsay, an Irish-born doctor; of Robert Lindsay's family of ten children, five were to become prominent artists. Norman Lindsay's work spans various fields: painter, etcher, illustrator, cartoonist, sculptor and model-maker. He also wrote numerous works of fiction, philosophical, polemical and autobiographical essays, literary criticism, art appreciations, reviews and reminiscences. Although he classed himself primarily as an artist, he was more significant in the literary sphere, where his positive aesthetic credo and charismatic personality had a profound influence. Educated at Creswick Grammar School after a delicate childhood, Lindsay left home at sixteen to join his brother Lionel in Melbourne and earn his living as an artist. His first novel, *A Curate in Bohemia* (1913), describes his lively, precarious student life in Melbourne, supported mainly by the topical drawings for a local weekly, the *Hawklet*, that he 'ghosted' for Lionel. In 1901 he attracted the attention of J.F. Archibald and moved to Sydney, where he joined the staff of the *Bulletin* as a black-and-white artist. His association with the *Bulletin*, later expanded to reviewer, essayist and fiction writer, lasted until two years before his death. From the first his work attracted controversy: his characteristic bacchanalian paintings were often condemned as immoral or irreligious; during the First World War his war cartoons aroused protests; and two of his novels, *Redheap* (q.v.) and *The Cautious Amorist*, were banned for a period within Australia. In 1931, after a police prosecution was launched against an issue of *Art in Australia* devoted to his work, he left for America, but soon returned. Apart from another earlier stay in Europe 1909–10, he remained firm in his conviction that an artist worked best within his own country. Lindsay was married twice. By his first marriage to Kate Parkinson he had three sons Jack, Raymond and Philip; by his second wife, Rose Soady (Rose Lindsay) he had two daughters Jane and Helen. He bequeathed a large part of his work to the University of Melbourne and the remainder to the National Trust of Australia on condition that it was preserved in the house at Springwood, NSW, where he lived for more than fifty years.

Lindsay's novels are *A Curate in Bohemia* (1913), *Redheap* (1930, banned in Australia until 1958 but published in the USA as *Every Mother's Son*), *Miracles by Arrangement* (1932, published in the USA as *Mr. Gresham and Olympus*), *The Cautious Amorist* (1932, banned in Australia 1934–58), *Saturdee* (q.v., 1933), *Pan in the Parlour* (1933), *Age of Consent* (1938), *The Cousin from Fiji* (q.v., 1945), *Halfway to Anywhere* (1947), *Dust or Polish?* (1950) and *Rooms and Houses* (1968). His children's novels are *The Magic Pudding* (q.v., 1918) and *The Flyaway Highway* (1936). Three works develop his aesthetic ideas: *Creative Effort* (1920), *Hyperborea* (1928) and *Madam Life's Lovers* (1929). *My Mask* (1970) is an autobiographical work, *The Scribblings of an Idle Mind* (1966) is a collection of philosophical essays, and *Bohemians of the Bulletin* (1965) describes some of the well-known personalities with whom Lindsay worked. Two anthologies, *Norman Lindsay's Book, No. I* (1912) and *Norman Lindsay's Book, No. II* (1915), contain some of his sketches and stories. Numerous selections of his artwork have been published and Lindsay also illustrated many of his own books and those of other Australian authors, including Hugh McCrae, Leon Gellert, A.B. Paterson, Jack Lindsay, Kenneth Slessor, Dulcie Deamer, Kenneth Mackenzie and Douglas Stewart. There is as yet no collection of Lindsay's prolific writings for the *Bulletin*, *Art in Australia*, the *Lone Hand* and other journals. His involvement with various publishing ventures, such as the Fanfrolico Press and the Endeavour Press, is well documented, however.

Writers who have been directly influenced by Lindsay's aesthetic credo include R.D. FitzGerald, Hugh McCrae, Kenneth Slessor, Kenneth Mackenzie, Douglas Stewart and, of course, Jack Lindsay, although his indirect influence, coinciding with a traditional, vitalist strain in Australian literature, is inestimable. His ideas probably achieved their most concentrated effect in the 1920s, especially during the existence of the journal *Vision* established by Jack Lindsay and himself. An ardent admirer of Nietzsche, Rabelais and Plato, Lindsay saw aesthetic values as the only values in a disordered world and 'creative effort' as the 'one enduring element in man's life'. By perpetual self-discovery and self-expression the great creative artist was seen as gifted with the power to penetrate contingent reality to life's eternal, natural essence. Key values in his credo were

beauty, passion, youth, vitality, sexuality and courage. The artist's mission, inevitably separating him from the passionless, materialistic majority, naturally involved a continual resistance to all outwardly-imposed restrictions. For the wowser and all kinds of humbug and pretension, Lindsay had an invincible contempt. His admiration for the ancients and the Italian Renaissance, and his conviction that true art was life-affirming and a quest for joy, were deepened by his hatred of 'modernism'. The First World War confirmed his intuition that modern civilization was anti-life. Although social, political and religious issues failed to interest him, the implications of his attitudes were élitist, reactionary and anti-religious.

Lindsay's ideas are prominent in his novels, especially his conviction of the importance of sexual self-expression. *A Curate in Bohemia* is a vivid picture of Melbourne bohemian life in the 1890s, enlivened by Lindsay's liking for Dickensian oddities. But his talent for keen social observation and comedy is at its height in the trilogy on small-town life based on his memories of Creswick, *Saturdee*, *Redheap* and *Halfway to Anywhere*. Lindsay brilliantly captures both the pretentious adult life of a sleepy country town at the turn of the century and the spontaneous, if undercover, sexual energy of his youthful heroes and heroines. *Pan in the Parlour*, also set in a fictional country town, is a more schematized presentation of his ideas on the connection between sexuality and creativity; although lively and witty, it is less substantial than *Redheap* and *The Cousin from Fiji*. Both *Age of Consent* and *The Cautious Amorist* are popular comic novels but limited by Lindsay's preference for adolescent sexuality. *Miracles by Arrangement*, set in Sydney between the wars and concerned with the marital dilemma of a middle-aged couple, is his most successful and balanced attempt to deal with the world of his adult life. *Dust or Polish?* and *Rooms and Houses* are slacker works: the former, an attempt at a conventional novel, lacks Lindsay's distinctive satiric energy and the latter, ostensibly set in Melbourne in 1899, is an assortment of his diverse reminiscences and attitudes. Both Lindsay's children's novels are remarkable achievements: *The Magic Pudding*, a versatile blend of fantasy, droll humour, satire and comic verse, is probably Australia's favourite children's book; *The Flyaway Highway*, though less popular, has the same elements and both are enhanced by Lindsay's distinctive illustrations.

The centenary of Lindsay's birth was marked by the publication of his fantasy, *Micomicana* (1979), ed. Jane Lindsay; by a collection of his letters (1979), ed. R.G. Howarth and A.W. Baxter; and by *The World of Norman Lindsay* (1979), ed. Lin Bloomfield. A collection of his war cartoons 1914–18 was published in 1983, ed. Peter Fullerton. Accounts of Lindsay's life and work include Douglas Stewart's personal memoir (1975), John Hetherington's authorized biography *Norman Lindsay: The Embattled Olympian* (1973), and Jane Lindsay's *Portrait of Pa* (1973).

LINDSAY, PERCY (1870–1952), born Creswick, Victoria, was the eldest son of Robert Lindsay and brother of Norman, Lionel, Daryl and Ruby Lindsay. He studied art at Ballarat and Melbourne and later became a well-known landscape painter, particularly noted for his use of light and for tranquil paintings of trees. He was also a proficient black-and-white artist. From 1918 he lived in Sydney, but during the 1890s he was prominent in Melbourne's intellectual bohemian circles which included his brothers, Norman and Lionel, and such figures as Max Meldrum, Ernest Moffitt and Will Dyson. Renowned for his ebullient, gregarious and genial personality, Percy Lindsay remained a bohemian all his life. His son Peter also became a painter.

LINDSAY, PHILIP (1906–58), born Sydney, son of Norman Lindsay and brother of Jack Lindsay, was a prolific writer of historical fiction. He tried journalism in Australia before leaving in 1929 for England, where he remained. His first printed book was a collection of verse in a limited edition, *An Affair of Philip Lindsay's* (1924), illustrated by his brother Raymond. A writer for film and an acknowledged specialist on medieval England, he wrote over forty historical novels and numerous works of non-fiction, mainly historical biographies. His autobiography, *I'd Live the Same Life Over* (1941), includes reminiscences of other members of the Lindsay family and of several Australian writers such as R.D. FitzGerald, Kenneth Slessor and P. R. Stephensen. Philip Lindsay's daughter by his first marriage, Cressida Lindsay, is also a novelist.

LINDSAY, ROSE (1885–1978), born Sydney as Rose Soady, was the second wife of Norman Lindsay. After a childhood of some hardship, she began work as an artist's model at the age of eighteen and later modelled for many of Lindsay's paintings. They had two children, Jane and Helen. Rose Lindsay wrote two books: *Ma and Pa* (1963), which recounts her childhood experiences as one of a large family, is also a lively picture of Sydney in the 1890s; and *Model Wife* (1967), a collection of reminiscences which includes descriptions of many of the well-known personalities who gathered at the Lindsays' home at Springwood.

LINDSAY, RUBY (1887–1919), born Creswick, Victoria, painter and illustrator also known as 'Ruby Lind', was the sister of Percy, Lionel, Norman and Daryl Lindsay. For several years before her marriage to Will Dyson in 1909, she studied art in Melbourne, meanwhile contributing drawings and cartoons to the *Hawklet*, the *Lone Hand* and other journals. She left for England with her husband and brother Norman in 1909, and continued to work as a pen-and-ink artist until her death in the influenza epidemic. Her daughter Betty also became a talented artist. Will Dyson's *Poems in Memory of a Wife* (1919) commemorates her personality, as does an introduction to a collection of her drawings published in 1920.

LiNQ (Literature in North Queensland), a quarterly literary journal emanating from James Cook University in Townsville, Queensland, was first published in 1971. Among its contributors have been Judith Wright, John Blight and Noel Macainsh.

Linton Family, see **BRUCE, MARY GRANT**

Lion's Bride, The, see **HARWOOD, GWEN**

Lip, see **Feminism and Australian Literature**

'LISLE, MARY' (1897–1973), born in the Riverina, NSW, lived and farmed at Coonamble after her marriage to D.M. Cornish in 1925. She contributed verse to such periodicals as *Country Life*, the *Bulletin*, *Poetry*, *Southerly Prism* and *Vision*; and published two collections, *The Secret Fire* (1947) and *The Inlander* (n.d.).

LITCHFIELD, JESSIE (1883–1956), born Sydney as Jessie Phillips, was a pupil of Mary Gilmore. In 1908 she married a tin-miner, Valentine Litchfield, and travelled with him in many parts of the Northern Territory until 1917, meanwhile raising seven children. Her reminiscences of ten years of wandering, *Far-North Memories*, were published in 1930. She also contributed poems and short stories to the *Bulletin*, *Age* and *Woman's Mirror*, and was editor of the *Northern Territory Times* in Darwin 1930–42 until the family was evacuated after enemy bombing. She returned to Darwin in 1946 to work as a librarian and in 1951 unsuccessfully contested the Territory's federal seat in parliament as an independent candidate. The Jessie Litchfield Award, administered by the Melbourne Bread and Cheese Club, is presented annually to a new and unknown writer. Her biography, which also includes several of her poems, *Jessie Litchfield – Grand Old Lady of the Territory* (1982), was written by her granddaughter, Janet Dickinson.

Literary Awards. The rewarding of Australian writers began soon after the establishment of the first colony when in 1818 Lachlan Macquarie, governor of NSW, awarded Michael Massey Robinson two cows from the government herd for his services as an Antipodean 'poet laureate'. Macquarie's decision inaugurated government patronage of Australian literature, and throughout the nineteenth century and even later there are similar instances of support for writers, notably through the creation of employment opportunities in government departments: Henry Kendall, for example, was appointed a government inspector of forests in NSW in 1881, his widow was appointed superintendent of cleaners in a government office in 1884, and Henry Lawson was one of several *Bulletin* authors who found employment in the office of the NSW government statistician, which became known as the *'Bulletin* Bards' Refuge'. But such public or semi-public assistance was at best intermittent and depended upon the personal sympathies of individual politicians or public servants; it was not until the twentieth century that Australian writers began to receive prizes and awards on a regular basis.

There are now more than fifty literary prizes, or types of prizes, awarded regularly (usually annually) in Australia, each falling into one or two main categories. The first and smaller category comprises the awards which *sustain* creative activity, in the sense of supporting a writer during the creation of a work. These awards include some which are available in several fields including literature and journalism, e.g. the Churchill Fellowships awarded by the Winston Churchill Memorial Trust, or the Anzac Fellowships awarded by the New Zealand government, and others which are restricted to literature. Notable among the latter are the fellowships ($25 000 per annum in 1984) and other writing grants awarded annually by the Literature Board (q.v.) of the Australia Council. Like its predecessor, the CLF (q.v.), the Literature Board spends a significant amount of its budget on direct assistance to writers, including the provision of pensions and emeritus fellowships and the support of writers-in-residence programmes; it also funds such prizes as the Children's Book of the Year Award and the National Book Council (qq.v.) awards.

The second award category comprises those prizes and awards which *reward* the writer for a completed, and usually published, literary work, and includes awards funded or sponsored by governments, e.g. the SA government's Biennial Literature Prizes awarded in conjunction with the Adelaide Festival; by business corporations, e.g. the Shell Book of the Year Award; by newspapers, e.g. the *Age* Book of the Year (q.v.); by publishers, e.g. the Australian Book Publishers' Association Book Design Awards; by writers' groups, e.g. the FAW which administers and/or funds more than a dozen awards; by educational institutions, e.g. the Foundation for Australian Literary Studies; by miscellaneous organizations, e.g. the ANA's Award, the Winton Tourist Promotion Association's Bronze Swagman Award; and by individuals, e.g. the Grace Leven Poetry Prize (q.v.) awarded under the will of 'William Baylebridge'. A third category which could be established comprises the awards or prizes received by Australian writers from overseas sources, including the Booker McConnell Prize awarded to Thomas Keneally in 1982 for *Schindler's Ark*, but even more importantly the Nobel Prize awarded to Patrick White for *The Eye of the Storm* in 1973. White used the Nobel Prize money to establish a trust which administers the Patrick White Award, usually given to an older writer of distinction. Other writers to have funded awards are Miles Franklin and 'Baylebridge'. Among writers to have awards named after them are 'Rolf Boldrewood', Alan Marshall, Anne Elder, Mary Gilmore, A.B. Paterson, C.J. Dennis, Christopher Brennan, and John Shaw Neilson (qq.v.). There are also a number of defunct awards, e.g. the S.H. Prior (q.v.) Memorial Prize and the Encyclopaedia Britannica Awards, and others which have been awarded intermittently, e.g. by the *Sydney Morning Herald*.

Although the direct assistance provided by the Literature Board covers all forms of creative literature, most Australian awards and prizes carry more specific restrictions, which range from those which demand an Australian subject or theme, e.g. *Age* Book of the Year; to those which are restricted within genre, e.g. the Miles Franklin Award (q.v.) for a published novel, the Bronze Swagman Award for bush verse; to those which carry age, occupational or other restrictions, e.g. the Patrick White Award. Similarly, there is a wide range in value of the prizes regularly awarded for individual works. The richest in 1983 was the *Australian*/Vogel National Literary Award; the most prestigious include the *Age* Book of the Year, the Children's Book of the Year, the Miles Franklin Award, the National Book Council Awards, the NSW Premier's Literary Award, the SA government's Biennial Literature Prizes and the Gold Medal of the Australian Literature Society now awarded by ASAL. Some of the most important literary awards are described elsewhere in this volume, usually under their titles.

e.g. the Miles Franklin Award; a comprehensive, if not complete, listing is provided annually in *Australian Books in Print*, and information on new awards and the winners of existing ones is provided regularly in such journals as *Australian Author*, *Notes & Furphies* and *Southerly*.

Literary Criterion, a prominent Indian quarterly journal of English studies edited by C.D. Narasimhaiah, has on two occasions been devoted exclusively to Australian literature (1964 and 1980). On both occasions the issues were reprinted as *An Introduction to Australian Literature* (1965, 1982) edited by Narasimhaiah.

Literary News (1) was an early Sydney weekly journal which was published for six months 1837–38 and included sketches and poetry. Its proprietor, James Tegg, edited the journal in conjunction with William à Beckett.

Literary News (2) was a Melbourne weekly journal which ran for just over a year 1882–83. Avoiding politics, it focused on literature, theatre, art and science, and included reviews of books and theatrical productions, poetry, short stories, serials and literary news from Australia and overseas. Two notable contributors were 'Australie' (Emily Manning) and 'Australienne' (Frances Holden), the latter a contributor to other literary journals and active in social reform and women's rights.

Literature Board, one of the seven arts boards which form part of, and are responsible to, the Australia Council (q.v.), was established in 1973; it comprises eight members including a chairman, who normally serve for four years and include representatives from different regions within Australia and of a variety of literary interests. The Literature Board dispenses federal government support to literature and took over the functions of the CLF (q.v.) but with a greatly increased budget: the first full allocation of the Literature Board was four times that of the final budget ($300 000) of the CLF, and the 1983–84 allocation was $2.1 million. With increased funding, the Literature Board has been able, particularly in its early years, to broaden the support to Australian literature provided by the CLF, although assistance is offered in the same four areas: direct assistance to writers through the provision of pensions, now replaced by emeritus fellowships, and several types of fellowships and grants to established and developing writers; assistance to publishers through a per-page subsidy for approved titles; assistance to literary journals; and assistance in a wide variety of promotional activities including grants to festivals, associations and educational institutions. The Board is committed to the pursuit of excellence and to the fostering of creative literature, although it also supports non-fiction. The greatest proportion of its allocation goes in direct assistance to writers, and its innovations in this area include longer-term fellowships (of up to three years), general writing grants, special-purpose grants and grants to educational institutions for writer-in-residence programmes. Other notable aspects of its activities have been the promotion of Australian literature overseas and the development of the Public Lending Right scheme.

Literature in New South Wales (1866), by G.B. Barton (q.v.), is one of the first substantial assessments of the development of literature in the colony. Although Barton states that Australia is too young to possess a national literature he attempts a detailed account and critical assessment of the whole body of indigenous writing. He finds that in every field of letters the colony has produced something of value and in many instances there is evidence of 'undoubted genius'. In some areas, especially poetry, fiction and exploration narrative, he sees the 'rough groundwork' of a national literature laid. The remarkably wide-ranging and perceptive survey covers newspapers, periodicals, poetry, fiction, oratory, history, biography, travel writings, philology, physical science, geography, law and theology. Both *Literature in New South Wales* and its companion volume, *The Poets and Prose Writers of New South Wales* (q.v., 1866), were commissioned for the Paris Exhibition of 1867.

Literature of Australia, The, an influential collection of critical essays edited by Geoffrey Dutton, was published by Penguin Books in 1964 and in a second edition in 1976. The collections include general essays on such topics as the social setting, poetry, fiction and drama; essays on selected individual writers; and detailed bibliographies.

Literature of Western Australia, The (1979), edited by Bruce Bennett, is a volume in the Western Australian Sesquicentenary Celebrations series. It contains descriptive rather than definitive discussions of diaries, letters, journals, fiction, poetry, drama, children's books, newspapers and literary journalism. Its contributors include Peter Cowan, Veronica Brady, Nicholas Hasluck, Fay Zwicky, Bill Dunstone, Barbara Buick, Maxine Walker, Bill Bunbury and Don Grant.

Little Black Princess, The, see GUNN, JEANNIE; Aboriginal in Australian Literature

Little Boy from Manly, The, a sailor-suited personification of NSW and, after Federation, Australia, was the cartoon creation of Livingston Hopkins (q.v.) in the 1885 *Bulletin*; other artists to draw him included David Low and Norman Lindsay.

Little Bush Maid, A, see **BRUCE, MARY GRANT**

Little Company, The, a novel by Eleanor Dark (q.v.), was published in 1945. Set in wartime Sydney it deals mainly with the experience of Gilbert Massey, a middle-aged bookseller and author of leftist political inclination. After an unhappy childhood dominated by his father William Massey, a sanctimonious religious hypocrite, Gilbert has drifted into marriage with their housekeeper's daughter, Phyllis Miller, a similarly sanctimonious self-martyr. Gilbert's now-hearty dislike of Phyllis is shared by Marty, his vehemently feminist sister who is also an author, and by Nick his younger brother, a voluble Marxist. Of the Masseys' two daughters, Virginia and Prue, Gilbert is closer to Prue, the flippant Virginia having slipped into a life of promiscuity. An important relationship in both Gilbert's and Marty's youth has been that with the now-dead Scott Laughlin, an unsuccessful Labor candidate. Deserted by his wife Denny for Jerrold Kay, a celebrated cartoonist, Laughlin had died early, as had his daughter Janet, Marty's close friend. For the daughter of Denny and Jerrold, Elsa Kay, who becomes involved in an unsatisfactory love affair with Gilbert, the memory of the Laughlin family, nourished by her mother, had been a destructive influence. Against the background of national insecurity, Gilbert and Marty, both afflicted with a 'creative paralysis', struggle with their individual insecurities. Although the affair with Elsa soon comes to an end, Gilbert finds it releases his creative block and he begins a novel about Scott Laughlin. His relationship with Phyllis, which deteriorates still further after the death of Virginia from a complicated pregnancy, reaches its nadir when Phyllis unsuccessfully attempts suicide. At the close of the novel she is temporarily confined to a nursing home, and life for the Masseys resumes what normality it can in abnormal times.

Little Minx, A, see **CAMBRIDGE, ADA**

Little Missus, The, see **GUNN, JEANNIE**

LITTLE, WILLIAM, (1839–?), born Cumberland, England, arrived in the Colony in 1851. He was mayor of Ballarat in the 1890s; he used the pseudonym 'Lambda' for two works of fiction, *The Trinity of Man* (1896) and *Visit to Topos* (1897), and numerous booklets of verse including *Reveries* (1896), *A Dream of Paradise* (1904) and *Sonnets by Lambda* (1908).

LITTLEJOHN, AGNES, a regular contributor of short stories and verse to the *Sydney Mail* and the *Sydney Morning Herald* from before the First World War until the 1930s, published several works of fiction and collections of verse 1907–39. Described in reviews of the time as graceful, charming, spontaneous and fluent, her work has now more historical than literary value, reflecting in its willed floweriness very conventional, imported notions of beauty. Her fiction includes *The Daughter of a Soldier* (1907), *A Lapse of Memory* (1909), *Mirage of the Desert* (1910), *The Breath of India* (1914), *The Silver Road* (1915), *Star Dust and Sea Spray* (1918), *Rainbow Dreams* (1919), *The Sleeping Sea-Nymph* (1921), *The Lost Emerald* (1924) and *The Pipes o' Pan* (1939). Her verse was published under the following titles: *Verses* (1914), *Poems* (1915), *Patriotic Poems* (1915), *Lyrics and Lyrical Prose* (1927), *Lyrics and Mystic Sketches* (1928), *The Lady of the Doves* (1929), *The Guardian of the Gate* (1933), *The Unforgotten Watch* (1935), *Drowsy Hours* (1936) and *Lighthouse Keepers* (1938).

LIVERANI, MARY ROSE (1939–), born Glasgow, the daughter of a ship's rigger, came to Australia at the age of thirteen when her family migrated to Wollongong, NSW. In *The Winter Sparrows: Growing Up in Scotland and Australia* (1975), she vividly recreates her early years in the Glasgow slums and her experiences in Australia until the time she left school. The book has been acclaimed as a landmark in Australia's migrant literature.

LIVERMORE, REG (1938–), born Parramatta, is a well-known actor, singer, dancer and female impersonator. After collaborating in the writing of such musical shows as 'The Good Ship Walter Raleigh' (1962), 'West of the Black Stump' (1965), 'Gone Potty' (1969) and 'Lasseter' (1971), and independently writing the rock musical 'Ned Kelly' (1978), Livermore devised a series of one-man shows which have given scope to his individual, abrasive, energetic style. They include 'Betty Blokkbuster Follies', 'Wonder Woman', 'Sacred Cow', 'Son of Betty' and 'Firing Squad'. Occasionally compared to Barry Humphries in the range of persona that he presents and his interpretation of female identities, Livermore is a less specifically Australian satirist.

Living and the Dead, The, see **WHITE, PATRICK**

LLEWELLYN, KATE, see Feminism and Australian Literature

LLOYD, A.L. (ALBERT LANCASTER) (1908–), born London, was the son of folk-singers who had died by the time he came to Australia in the middle 1920s. Over the next eight or nine years Lloyd worked mainly in the bush in NSW, learning a number of folk-songs and ballads in the years before the revival of interest in Australian folk music after the Second World War. From 1950 Lloyd worked as a freelance folklorist and ethno-musicologist, paying a return visit to Australia in 1970 to lecture and perform. His major interest and writing was in British and European music, but he made a number of albums of Australian folk-songs, including *Across the Western Plains* (1958), and helped establish songs like 'Flash Jack from Gundagai', 'The Euabalong Ball' and 'The Lime-Juice Tub' within the canon of Australian folk-song and ballad.

LLOYD, ANNE, see Feminism and Australian Literature

LLOYD, JESSIE (1843–85), born near Launceston, lived on stations near Gunnedah and Coonamble after her marriage to George A. Lloyd, later a NSW politician. Jessie Lloyd, using the pseudonym 'Silverleaf', began writing short stories, essays and poems in 1878 for such periodicals as the *Echo*, the *Illustrated Sydney News* and the *Sydney Mail*. She also published three novels, *The Wheel of Life* (1880); 'All Aboard', which was serialized in the *Echo* in 1879; and 'Retribution', serialized in the *Illustrated Sydney News* 1884–85. In 1881–82 she contributed a regular series on various aspects of bush and station life, titled the 'Silverleaf Papers', to the *Illustrated Sydney News*. The mother of four children, two of whom received a boarding-school education on the proceeds of her writing, Jessie Lloyd wrote in an easy, graceful way on the aspects of outback life which were likely to have a general appeal.

'Loaded Dog, The', by Henry Lawson (q.v.), is probably the best-known short story in Australian literature, a standard children's favourite and anthology piece. One of the Dave Regan (q.v.) sequence, it chronicles the misadventures of Dave and his mates, Andy Page and Jim Bently, after they make a cartridge in order to blast fish from a waterhole. Their dog Tommy retrieves the cartridge, accidentally sets the fuse alight at their campfire, and then follows them in turn as they desperately try to escape his attentions. Eventually Tommy pursues Dave to a nearby shanty and drops the cartridge when molested by the resident cattledog, which is

blown to pieces. The story was written in 1900 and published in *Joe Wilson and His Mates* (1901).

'Lobster and the Lioness, The', see O'FER-RALL, ERNEST FRANCIS

LOCH, FREDERICK (1889–1954), who worked as a farmer in Gippsland in his early years, served at Gallipoli in the First World War and wrote a novel about his experiences, under the pseudonym 'Sydney de Loghe', *The Straits Impregnable* (1916). After marrying Joice Nankivell (q.v.) he spent eighteen months in Ireland 1920–21 as a freelance journalist before volunteering to serve with Quaker relief units in Poland. The Lochs settled in Greece 1923–39, combining work for refugees with writing, worked for Polish refugees in Bulgaria and Rumania 1939–44, and returned to Greece after the war. Loch wrote two further novels under his pseudonym, *Pelican Pool* (1917) and *One Crowded Hour* (1918), and another under his real name, *Three Predatory Women* (1925). With his wife he wrote two descriptive books, *Ireland in Travail* (1922) and *The River of a Hundred Ways* (1924). Some of his experiences are described in Joice Nankivell's autobiography, *A Fringe of Blue* (1968).

LOCK, ARNOLD CHARLES COOPER, an Adelaide author and an officer of the PMG who subsequently transferred to Queensland, wrote seven novels under the pseudonym 'Charles Cooper'. They include *The Turkish Spy* (1932) and *Reflected Glory* (1934), both of which are war novels, the first dealing with Australians in the Middle East and the second set in France; *Satan's Mercy* (1934), *The Soul of Tak-Ming* (1935), *By Command of Yee-Shing* (1937), *Hong Kong Mystery* (1938) and *West in the East* (1941). Under his real name, Lock wrote three books which reflect his extensive travels in Australia, *Tropics and Topics* (1949), *People We Met* (1950) and *Travels Across Australia* (1952).

LOCKE, SUMNER (HELENA SUMNER LOCKE ELLIOTT) (1881–1917), born Sandgate, Brisbane, who died the day after the birth of her son, the playwright and novelist Sumner Locke Elliott, was herself a playwright and novelist. In 1908 her play, 'The Vicissitudes of Vivienne', was produced in Melbourne but her reputation was more firmly established with the popular Mum Dawson books sketching selection life: *Mum Dawson, Boss* (1911), staged by Bert Bailey in 1917, and *The Dawsons' Uncle George* (1912). In both, Mum is a female version of 'Steele Rudd''s Dad Rudd (see Rudd Family) and presides as matriarch over a family of yokels whose misadventures are humorously portrayed. The success of the Dawson books prompted another selection volume, *Skeeter Farm Takes a Spell* (1915), although Locke's last novel, *Samaritan Mary* (1916), is set in the USA where she lived during part of the First World War. *In Memoriam Sumner Locke* (1921) contains poems by Sumner Locke and verse tributes which attest to her popularity. As Sinden Marriott, 'Dear One', she is an important presence in her son's novel, *Careful, He Might Hear You* (q.v., 1963).

LOCKWOOD, DOUGLAS (1918–80), born Natimuk, Victoria, joined the Melbourne *Herald* in 1940. Sent to Darwin in 1942, he witnessed the bombing of the city before serving with the AIF in New Guinea and the Solomons and as a war correspondent in the South Pacific. In 1946 he returned to Darwin, where he remained until 1968 apart from a two-year stay in London. Managing editor of the *Herald*-owned *South Pacific Post* in Port Moresby 1968–71, he was editorial manager and then manager of the *Herald* in Melbourne 1971–73 and managing editor of the *Bendigo Advertiser* from 1975. He wrote numerous books on Darwin and the people and way of life of the Northern Territory, including *Crocodiles and Other People* (1959); *Fair Dinkum* (1960); *Life on the Daly River* (1961, with Nancy Polishuk); *I, the Aboriginal* (1962), a biography of a Northern Territory Aboriginal, which won the *Advertiser* Prize; *We, the Aborigines* (1963); *The Shady Tree* (1963, with Bill Harney); *Up the Track* (1964); *The Lizard Eaters* (1964); *Australia's Pearl Harbour: Darwin 1942* (1966); *Northern Territory Sketchbook* (1968, with Ainslie Roberts); *The Front Door* (1968), a history of Darwin 1869–1969; and *My Old Mates and I* (1979). Lockwood also won the London *Evening News* Award in 1957 and the Walkley Award in 1958.

LOGAN, PATRICK (1791–1830), was a Scots-born soldier and explorer who came to NSW in 1825 and was appointed later that year as commandant of the penal station at Moreton Bay; he was harsh in his treatment of the convicts, and is presented as a tyrant in the folk-song 'Moreton Bay' (q.v.). Killed by Aborigines possibly encouraged by the Moreton Bay convicts, Logan is the subject of Charles Bateson's biography, *Patrick Logan* (1966), Jessica Anderson's novel, *The Commandant* (1975) and Thomas Shapcott's poem, 'Portait of Captain Logan'.

London Aphrodite, a periodical edited by Jack Lindsay and P.R. Stephensen and published in London by the Fanfrolico Press, ran for a planned six issues 1928–29. Named as a rebuttal of the conservatism of J.C. Squire's *London Mercury*, it was committed to the same aesthetic attitudes as *Vision*. Some prominent English authors, including Aldous Huxley, contributed although the majority were Australian. Jack Lindsay, the dominant force, used the pseudonym 'Peter Meadows' for several articles. Other Australian contributors were Norman Lindsay, Hugh McCrae, Kenneth Slessor, Philip Lindsay, Brian Penton, P.R. Stephensen, Les Robinson, W.J. Turner, Bertram Higgins, E.J. Rupert Atkinson and Edith Hepburn ('Anna Wickham').

Lone Hand, an illustrated monthly modelled on the London *Strand* magazine, was published in two series in unbroken sequence 1907–21. A journal which remained under the control of the *Bulletin* for most of its life, the *Lone Hand* was planned by J.F. Archibald who gave it the name he had originally wished to confer on the *Bulletin*. After Archibald's mental collapse in 1906 delayed publication of the first issue, Frank Fox took over as editor 1907–09; he was followed by A.H. Adams (1909–11), Bertram Stevens (1912–19) and Walter Jago (1919–21). Major contributors included Randolph Bedford, Will and Edward Dyson, Mabel Forrest, Norman Lindsay, Ernest O'Ferrall, Rod Quinn and Adams himself. The *Lone Hand* was a success in its early years (its first issue of 50 000 sold out in three days, and its second in one) and was responsible for such innovations in journalism as the beauty contest and columns by famous people. Its decline is attributed to increasing competition after the First World War, evidenced by the departure of Jago to edit the rival, *Aussie*. Cyril Hannaford compiled an index to the *Lone Hand* for the period 1907–13 in 1967, and Kit Taylor *A History with Indexes of the Lone Hand, the Australian Monthly* (1977).

Long Farewell, The, see **CHARLWOOD, DON**

LONG, GAVIN (1901–68), born Foster, Victoria, was the son of George Long, Bishop of Bathurst and later Newcastle, and the founder of the Australian army's education service. Educated at the University of Sydney, Gavin Long worked first as a teacher and then as a journalist for the Sydney *Daily Guardian*, the *Argus* and the *Sydney Morning Herald*. Attached to the British expeditionary force in France as correspondent for Australian morning newspapers, he also covered the war in Libya and Greece as officially-accredited correspondent for the AIF. He was recalled to Australia in 1941 and made two visits to New Guinea. In 1943 he was appointed general editor of the official history, *Australia in the War of 1939–45* (q.v.). Of the twenty-two volume history, Long wrote three himself, *To Benghazi* (1952), *Greece, Crete and Syria* (1953) and *The Final Campaigns* (1963), and his wartime diaries and notes were widely used in the writing of the Service volumes of the history. In 1963 Long resigned as general editor to become a research fellow at the Australian National University. He also wrote a one-volume history of Australian participation in the Second World War, *The Six Years War* (1973), and a study of General Douglas Macarthur as military commander (1969). An unpretentious but painstaking historian, Long presented a systematic, balanced account of events in a factual, fluent style.

Long Odds, Marcus Clarke's (q.v.) first novel, was serialized in the *Colonial Monthly* 1868–69 and revised for publication in book form (1869); the serial version, which was issued as *Heavy Odds* in 1896, includes two instalments written by G.A. Walstab. Set almost entirely in England, *Long Odds* recounts the tragedy of Cyril Chatteris, who makes an unfortunate marriage with Carry Manton while in disfavour with his father, Saville Chatteris. After the death of his elder brother, Cyril becomes the family heir, conceals the marriage and becomes engaged to his cousin Kate Ffrench, but the truth is discovered by Rupert Dacre. Cyril plots to rid himself of Carry by compromising her with Dacre, but their planned elopement enrages him and he murders Dacre after Dacre's victory in a House of Commons election for which they are both candidates. With the truth revealed to Kate and Saville, Kate marries Bob Calverley, a member of the squattocracy who is visiting England, loses money gambling and is duped by Dacre into buying a poorly-performed racehorse against which Dacre and his cronies bet heavily. Bob hears of the plot and foils it, wins a race at 'long odds' which recovers his fortune, and takes Kate back to Australia to his new station, where Cyril turns up in the last chapter as a dying swagman.

Long Prospect, The, a novel by Elizabeth Harrower (q.v.), was published in 1958. Emily Lawrence, on the edge of adolescence, has lived with her twice-widowed grandmother, Lilian, at Ballowra since she was four. Her parents, both colourless, unimaginative individuals, have drifted apart, Harry to manage in the outback, Paula to run a hat shop in Sydney. An eventual reconciliation is likely, however, as they share a Hollywood concept of marriage. Lilian, a vulgar, insensitive, domineering woman, is more interested in her own complicated love life than in her granddaughter and Emily is conscious

that her life is as bleak and featureless as the industrial town of Ballowra. The one previous bright period in her experience, stemming from her relationship with one of Lilian's boarders, a young woman, Thea, had ended with Thea's departure. Emily, aware of being inwardly alienated from her parents, her grandmother and her grandmother's friends, particularly dislikes Mr Rosen, her grandmother's sycophantic suitor. Neither her school friends nor Dotty, the kindly 'daily help', can provide the stimulating companionship she seeks. When Lilian takes in another boarder, Max, a scientist who also happens to be Thea's old lover, Emily's life changes dramatically. Max treats her as an individual, introduces her to books and music and provides her with someone to love. Although Max grows increasingly and uneasily aware that he cannot stay in Ballowra, their relationship is terminated unpleasantly and abruptly. Disaster ensues when Rosen and another of Lilian's friends, Billie Duncan, both of whom have suffered recent humiliations, find gratification in implying that there is a sexual relationship between Max and Emily. Lilian is privately unconvinced but their innuendoes coincide with her desire to exert her supremacy. She calls in Paula and Harry as reinforcements, and Max leaves after an unpleasant scene. The experience ironically unites the parents and three months later Emily, still mourning her loss of Max, moves to live with them in their sterile, new flat in Sydney. Later, however, she realizes that the experience has been valuable: 'she was responsible for her actions. What had been amorphous and unreliable in her seemed, now, to be solid'.

LONG, RICHARD (1874–1948), born in England, was brought to Australia at the age of five and settled at Sandringham, Melbourne. A ship's carpenter and joiner, he was a member of the Socialist Party of Victoria, the Free Religious Fellowship and the Australian Peace Alliance and was familiar with such prominent individuals as John Cain, Adela Pankhurst, Marie Pitt, Bernard O'Dowd and Frederick Sinclaire. From 1911 he began contributing verse and articles to the *Socialist* and later verse to *Fellowship* and *Birth*, some of which was reprinted in his one collection, *Verses* (1917), with a foreword by Sinclaire.

LONGFORD, RAYMOND (1878–1959), born Melbourne as John Walter Longford, later adopted the name Raymond Hollis. He went to sea and served in the Boer War before becoming an actor with various companies in Australia and NZ. After acting in three films produced by Charles Cozens Spencer in 1911, he directed several films for Spencer, beginning with *The Fatal Wedding* (1911), and became one of the most innovative of Australian film directors. Although he found it difficult to get continuity of work, he directed more than thirty silent films, including *The Romantic Story of Margaret Catchpole* (1911), *Sweet Nell of Old Drury* (1911), *Australia Calls* (1913), *The Silence of Dean Maitland* (1914), *The Mutiny of the Bounty* (1916), *The Sentimental Bloke* (1919), *On Our Selection* (1920), *The Blue Mountains Mystery* (1921) and *The Dinkum Bloke* (1923), of which only *The Sentimental Bloke* and *On Our Selection* have survived as complete copies. After reaching his peak in the 1920s, Longford was employed only in minor productions as associate director or actor by the 1930s and finally broke with the film industry, spending his last years as a night watchman. During his most creative years he was closely associated with Lottie Lyell (1890–1925), who worked variously as actress, writer, co-director and co-producer. The Australian film industry now presents an annual award in Longford's name for outstanding work in cinema.

Longleat, Thomas and Honoria, see *Policy and Passion*

LONGSTAFF, Sir **JOHN** (1862–1941), born Clunes, Victoria, studied art in Paris from 1887, returning to Australia in 1894 where he became a leading portrait-artist. He won the Archibald Prize in 1925, 1928, 1929, 1931 and 1935, the last for a portrait of A.B. Paterson. Well known among his paintings are the portrait of Henry Lawson in the NSW Art Gallery, *Burke and Wills* in the National Gallery of Victoria and *Breaking the News* in the WA Art Gallery. The April 1931 number of *Art in Australia* was given over to his work; Nina Murdoch published *Portrait in Youth of Sir John Longstaff* (1948).

' "Lord Douglas" ', see 'Send Round the Hat'

LORIMER, PHILIP DURHAM (1843–97), born Madras, India, was a Scotsman who migrated to Sydney in 1861, worked mainly as an overlander in Queensland in the 1860s, and in the 1870s became a swagman poet known to many as 'Old Phil the Poet'. He spent much of his time wandering in outback NSW and Victoria, repaying the hospitality of diggers, bush workers, station owners and newspaper editors with extempore verse. His *Songs and Verses* (1901), mainly descriptive and lyrical verse, contains an appreciation by E.A. Petherick and incorporates material published in two earlier selections.

Lot's Wife, a weekly student newspaper published at Monash University, began fortnightly publication in 1961 titled *Chaos*, changing its name in June 1964. Concerned mainly with politics, student news, educational issues and the cultural life of the university, the newspaper has occasionally published original contributions from well-known writers, as well as substantial interviews.

LOUKAKIS, ANGELO (1951–), an Australian of Greek parentage, has written screenplays and short stories, some of which have been published in a collection titled *For the Patriarch* (1981). His stories deal with the diverse experience of first- and second-generation Greeks and Italians in Australia, as well as with the Australian rediscovery of European roots.

Love Me Sailor (1945), by Robert Close (q.v.), is the story of a voyage of the windjammer *Annabella* with a cargo of Chilean nitrate from Mejillones to San Francisco. The voyage is complicated by the presence on the ship of a lone female passenger, Ella Miller, whose past history and present conduct show her to be a nymphomaniac on the verge of insanity. Her effect on the crew is catastrophic; their lust for her produces sexual rivalries and jealousies that lead to arguments, fights, knifings, accidents, insanity and death. Although the captain appropriates her for his own sexual use, some of the crew, especially the second mate, Bill Hawkins, Christenson, Spider Lukes and the steward, Catspaw, vainly attempt to satisfy their own passion for her. The young apprentice, Ernie, sees her in an idealistic, romantic light and constantly defends her against his shipmates' foul-mouthed talk. After the captain is hurt in an accident Bill Hawkins takes over the ship and is about to satisfy his desire for Ella when they are caught in a hurricane and he is forced to employ all his seamanship skill to save the ship. When the danger has almost passed Ella is swept overboard by a huge wave and Ernie sets out to rescue her in a rowing boat. He gets the naked girl into the boat but she believes him to be the devil and pushes him overboard to his death. Soon after, she is taken back aboard the *Annabella* but the crew, looking upon her now with contempt, put her aboard a passing steamer.

Love Songs of Arnhem Land, see **Aboriginal Song and Narrative in Translation**

'LOVEGOOD, JOHN', see **WATSON, GRANT**

LOVELESS, GEORGE (1797–1874), born Tolpuddle near Dorchester, England, became the best-known of the famous Tolpuddle Martyrs, the six agricultural workers also called the Dorchester Labourers, who were victimized when they attempted in 1833 to protect their livelihood against the rapacious local landowners by forming a rural trade union, the Friendly Society of Agricultural Labourers. Convicted in 1834 of administering unlawful oaths, the Martyrs were sentenced to seven years' transportation; Loveless was separated from his colleagues and sent to Van Diemen's Land where he impressed the lieutenant-governor, George Arthur, with his integrity and character. Early in 1837, after pardons had been issued in London to the prisoners, Loveless left Australia and he later migrated from England to Canada. His book, *The Victims of Whiggery* (1837), an account of his arrest and trial and his experiences in Australia, is a contribution to convict literature. In 1982 'Tolpuddle', a radio play by Alan Plater and Vince Hill highly sympathetic to Loveless, was broadcast in London; H.V. Evatt wrote *Injustice within the Law* (1937) about the Tolpuddle Martyrs.

'Love's Coming', a brief lyric poem by John Shaw Neilson (q.v.), was published in the Sydney *Sun* in 1911. It was later set to music by Dr W.G. Whitaker of the London College of Music. Acknowledged as one of Neilson's most attractive lyrics, there is a perfect harmony between the poem's simple but artistic form and its delicate imagery.

LOW, Sir DAVID (1891–1963), the creator of Colonel Blimp and as 'Low' one of the most significant cartoonists of the twentieth century, was born NZ and came to Australia at the age of twenty to become a staff artist on the *Bulletin*. With an early style which showed the influence of his *Bulletin* predecessor, Phil May, Low made his reputation with *The Billy Book* (1918), in which he caricatured the Australian prime minister, W.M. 'Billy' Hughes. In 1919 he moved to England, where he became famous as a political cartoonist with the *Star*, the *Evening Standard*, the *Daily Herald* and the *Manchester Guardian*. Apart from *The Billy Book*, he published *Low's Annual* (1908) and *Caricatures* (1915) before his departure for England; his caricatures include a celebrated portrayal of Henry Lawson. Among his later publications was *Low's Autobiography* (1956), which includes reminiscences of his work with the *Bulletin*.

LOWE, ERIC (1889–1963), born Birriwa, NSW, into a well-known pioneering family, was a pastoralist before the First World War in which he served in the Australian Light Horse. He subsequently worked at numerous rural occupations, travelled for a time, spending some years in Denmark, and trained as an engineer and accountant. He wrote a trilogy dealing with station life, *Salute to Freedom* (1938), *Beyond the Nineteen Counties* (1948) and *O Willing Hearts* (1951). *Beyond the Nineteen Counties*, chronologically the first volume of the series, recounts the early history of the pioneering Stewart family; adapted for radio by Colin Roderick, it was serialized in 1949. Lowe's major achievement, however, is his study of a single complex individual, Robin Stewart, in *Salute to Freedom*, which covers the period 1902–36. *Framed in Hardwood* (1940), Lowe's remaining novel, also draws on his rural experience.

LOWE, ROBERT (1811–92), from 1880 Viscount Sherbrooke, was born in Nottinghamshire, England, and was a successful scholar at Oxford, where in the late 1830s he was a private tutor whose pupils included Charles Reade. An albino, he came to NSW to seek his fortune in 1842 after being warned of impending blindness, and in his eight years in the colony won renown but not always popularity as a politician, orator, journalist and satirist. In 1843 Lowe was appointed to the Legislative Council by Governor Gipps, although he soon fell out with Gipps over his proposed squatting regulations. Lowe was a leading contributor of satiric poems, e.g. 'Songs of the Squatters', poems attacking the Gladstone Colony and pungent articles to the *Atlas* (q.v.), but by 1847 he had broken with the squatting interest, whose land monopoly he opposed. Active also in the development of educational policies and in the opposition to the resumption of transportation, Lowe left Australia in 1850; subsequently he was a leader writer for the London *Times* and a long time Liberal member of the British parliament, serving as Gladstone's chancellor of the exchequer (1869–73) and home secretary (1873–74). Lowe's Australian poems are included in his *Poems of a Life* (1885); several of his Australian speeches were published in Sydney during the 1840s. Lowe has been the subject of biographies by A.P. Martin, *Life and Letters of the Right Hon. Robert Lowe, Viscount Sherbrooke* (1883), J.F. Hogan, *Robert Lowe, Viscount Sherbrooke* (1893), and Ruth Knight, *Illiberal Liberal: Robert Lowe in New South Wales 1842–50* (1966).

'Lower Bohemia' was a series of six sketches by Marcus Clarke (q.v.), published in the *Australasian* in 1869. With the earlier 'Night Scenes in Melbourne' in the *Argus* (1868) and

'A Melbourne Alsatia' in *Colonial Monthly* (1869), the 'Lower Bohemia' sketches show Clarke to be an important predecessor of 'The Vagabond' (John Stanley James) in depicting Melbourne low life.

LOWER, LENNIE (1903–47), born Dubbo, NSW, was educated in Sydney. After leaving school, he served briefly in the army and navy and carried his swag in Queensland and NSW before settling into journalism. At twenty-three his first piece was published in *Beckett's Budget*, a Sydney scandal sheet; soon after, he joined the *Labor Daily* as a humorous columnist, and moved from there to the *Daily Guardian* and *Smith's Weekly*. In 1930 his widely-acclaimed comic novel, *Here's Luck* (q.v.) was published; a sardonic record of the tribulations of Jack Gudgeon, suburban battler, it established Lower's reputation beyond Sydney. From *Smith's Weekly* Lower moved to the *Daily Telegraph*, the *Sunday Telegraph* and the *Australian Women's Weekly*, but after being dismissed by Sir Frank Packer, allegedly for insulting Noel Coward, returned to *Smith's Weekly* in 1940. The books following *Here's Luck* comprise sketches mostly selected from his regular newspaper contributions; they include *Here's Another* (1932), *Life and Things* (1936), *The Bachelor's Guide to the Care of the Young and Other Stories* (1941), *Loweritis* (1940) and *Lennie Lower's Annual* (1941). A well-known character in Sydney journalistic circles, whose periods of depression were punctuated by absurdist escapades that are a feature also of his writing, Lower was widely mourned after his early death. Two of his Sydney friends, Cyril Pearl and the artist 'Wep' (W.E.) Pidgeon, prepared the selection of his work, *The Best of Lennie Lower* (1963); Tom Thompson introduced the 1983 selection, *Here's Lower*. Barry Dickins's play, 'The Sadness of Lennie Lower' (1981), was published as *Lennie Lower* (1982).

Lower's humour, primarily verbal, has the flavour of the 1930s and 1940s which is reflected in the idiom employed, with its sprinkling of words like 'whacko', 'mug', 'galoot' and 'lair' and in its preoccupation with six o'clock hotel closing and meals of steak and eggs in 'greasy spoon' cafes. Both in the titles of his pieces, e.g. an article on chess titled 'By Rook or by Crook', and within the body of the text, e.g. in the report of a Lower character who dies of a cold as a result of shoeing draught horses, he had habitual recourse to punning; the danger of tiring his readers by repetition was minimized by the piecemeal method of publishing his work and by a self-mocking authorial voice. The Lower scripts characteristically focus on domestic life or place a subject, usually male, in chauvinist, outra-

geous fantasy situations which allow full play to Lower's talent for the one-line gag, his cynicism and his sense of the slapstick dimension to life. Among regular satiric targets are the conformism of suburban life, nagging wives, wowsers of any kind, and those who make life difficult for the ordinary people with whom he sympathized.

LOYAU, GEORGE ETIENNE (1835–98), born London, arrived in Sydney in 1853 and spent seven years travelling extensively in Australia and working at a range of occupations from gold digger to private tutor. From the 1860s to the 1880s he had extensive experience in journalism and as a newspaper editor in Queensland, NSW, Victoria and SA, editing the *Maryborough Chronicle* (1861–62), the Gawler *Bunyip* (1878–79) and the *Illustrated Adelaide News* (1880–81). He also published three volumes of verse, *The Australian Seasons* (1871), *Australian Wild Flowers* (1871) and *Colonial Lyrics* (1872); an autobiographical account titled *The Personal Adventures of George E. Loyau* (1883); and two collections of biographical studies, *The Representative Men of South Australia* (1883) and *Notable South Australians* (1885). Founder and editor of the short-lived Adelaide magazine, the *Australian Family Herald* (1877), he also edited *The South Australian Annual: Australian Tales by Well Known Writers* (1877).

Lucinda Brayford, a novel by Martin Boyd (q.v.), was published in 1946. The novel comprises four parts, the early section dealing in a leisurely way with Lucinda's antecedents and her Australian childhood at the turn of the century. Descended from two very different English grandfathers, her nature reconciles the daredevil energies of the one with the aesthetic, religious sense of the other. After a period of struggle, her parents become wealthy and her expected brilliant future seems to be assured when she marries a well-connected Englishman, Hugo Brayford, aide-de-camp to the governor of Victoria. Their return to Hugo's English home, Crittenden House, begins both the outward decline of Lucinda's fortunes and her spiritual growth. After the birth of a son, Stephen, she discovers her husband's infidelity, although his severe wounding in the war prevents her from seeking a divorce. An affair with one of her husband's friends, Pat Lanfranc, proves equally disillusioning. Meanwhile the ideals of her brother-in-law, Paul Brayford, who pursues his concept of a civilized existence at his villa in Provence, strengthen her instinctive belief in the goodness of the natural world. This belief is put to the test of sorrow when her son becomes a martyr to the pacifist cause during the Second World War.

Lucky Country, The, by Donald Horne, a critique of Australian society in the 1960s, was published in 1964 and won unprecedented popularity. Frequently reprinted, and published in a second revised edition in 1968, its title has become a common idiom for Australia, although not always with the sense that Horne intended. Horne defines Australia as 'a lucky country run mainly by second-rate people who share its luck'. Provincial and derivative, content with the second-rate but fortuitously prosperous, 'it lives on other people's ideas, and, although its ordinary people are adaptable, most of its leaders (in all fields) . . . lack curiosity about the events that surround them'. Taking for his image of Australia 'a man in an open-necked shirt, solemnly enjoying an ice-cream' at the beach, his 'kiddy . . . beside him', Horne defines the Australian dream and what it is to be an Australian. He analyses what he sees as the country's social, cultural, political and religious attitudes, as well as attitudes to work and leisure, the place of women, migrants, Aborigines and intellectuals, the relationship with Britain, America, Asia and Oceania, the political and educational systems, industry and the unions, the bureaucracy and the press. In his last chapter he examines the possibilities of the nation's continuing to live on its luck. Underlying his criticisms is an enthusiasm for the ordinariness and for what he defines as the 'innocent happiness' of Australian life.

LUFFMANN, LAURA BOGUE (1846–1929), born Laura Lane in England, was educated in France and married a Melbourne horticulturist, Carl Bogue Luffmann. As Laura M. Lane and before her arrival in Australia, she wrote several books for children as well as a biography of Alexander Vinet (1890) and an adult novel, *Gentleman Verschoyle* (1875). In Australia she was prominent in women's movements, wrote numerous articles for the Australian, South African and American press, edited the *Woman's Voice* and as 'Una' contributed to the Sydney *Daily Telegraph*. She also wrote an Australian novel for children, *Will Aylmer* (1909), and an adult novel, *A Question of Latitude* (?1912). The Laura Bogue Luffmann literary competition was established in her memory.

LUKIN, GRESLEY (1840–1916), born Launceston, Tasmania, was an actor before becoming a public servant in Queensland, where he drafted Selection Acts for the Lands Department. In 1873 he became editor of the *Brisbane Courier* and the *Queenslander* and was associated on

both journals with Ernest Favenc and W.H. Traill. His other major connection with Australian journalism was with the *Boomerang*, which he bought from William Lane in 1890; soon after its collapse in 1892 he left Australia for NZ. During his long career (1896–1916) as editor of the Wellington *Evening Post*, he employed Arthur Adams as a reporter.

Luna, a general literary magazine, began in 1975 as a publication edited by women and published by the FAW. Although *Luna* emphasizes women's issues and the work of women, its editorial criteria are based on the quality of the work to be published; thus the work of men as well as women has been represented in its pages. Its editorial collective has been led by Barbara Giles.

LURIE, MORRIS (1938–   ), born in Melbourne of Jewish parents from Poland, studied architecture and worked for a time in advertising before becoming a full-time writer. He lived overseas, in Greece, Denmark, Morocco and England with frequent visits to New York, 1965–73. His stories have been widely published in Australia and in such overseas magazines and newspapers as the London *Daily Telegraph*, *Esquire*, the *Transatlantic Review*, *Argosy*, the *New Yorker*, *Punch*, the London *Times*, *Antaeus* and *Penthouse*. He has published four novels, *Rappaport* (1966), *The London Jungle Adventures of Charlie Hope* (1968), *Rappaport's Revenge* (1973) and *Flying Home* (1978); four collections of short stories, *Happy Times* (1969), *Inside the Wardrobe* (1975), *Running Nicely* (1979) and *Dirty Friends* (1981); three collections of prose pieces which he refers to as 'reportage', *The English in Heat* (1972), *Hackwork* (1977) and *Public Secrets* (1981); three plays in the collection *Waterman* (1979), which includes *Jangle, Jangle* and *A Visit to the Uncle* as well as the title play; and several children's books, *The Twenty-Seventh Annual African Hippopotamus Race* (1969), *Arlo the Dandy Lion* (1971), *Toby's Millions* (1982), and *The Story of Imelda Who Was Small* (1984). His stories are also represented in several anthologies and in the collection *The Most Beautiful Lies*, ed. Brian Kiernan (1977).

Lurie's Jewish qualities, especially his humour, are often described as reminiscent of such American writers as Isaac Singer, Saul Bellow and Phillip Roth, although other characteristics such as his preoccupation with loneliness in an empty land and the cult of taciturnity mark him as distinctively Australian. Describing himself as having grown up 'in a strange bubble of isolation' as a result of his parents' double alienation, from contemporary Poland and from Australia, Lurie is interested in all types of cultural displacement. The comic protagonists of his novels and stories are all solitary, homeless figures, misfits, romantic dreamers, hapless shlemiels, perpetual tourists or bewildered expatriates. Rappaport, the hero of his first novel, of *Rappaport's Revenge* and of several short stories, is a self-centred, overweight, aspiring antique dealer with a less-than-keen nose for a bargain, cursed with a suffocating Jewish mother, a surly father and an innate incapacity to lead a normal existence. In London in *Rappaport's Revenge* he stands out as even more of an oddity, becoming a part-comic, part-painful test of friendship for Friedlander, the more conventional narrator. Leo Axelrod of *Flying Home*, Lurie's most complex novel, leaves Australia, his birthplace, for Israel, the emotional 'home' of his parents and grandfather, and gradually discovers that a relationship has more human substance than a place. Charlie Hope of *The London Jungle Adventures of Charlie Hope* is another outrageously comic figure, even more larger-than-life than Rappaport, who operates in the surreal world of advertising, fascinating the rather immature narrator with his capacity for grandiose near-successes and massive failures.

Lurie's inventive talents are best suited to the short story. In several he explores the mysteries, frustrations, comedy and pathos of family relationships, concentrating especially on outwardly prickly but inwardly anguished father/son relations. Observant of nuances in human relationships, Lurie often combines delight in a farcical, outrageous situation with an understanding of its poignant relevance to universal experience. In the same way his gift for comic dialogue, for the devastating quip or the brilliant aphorism, is joined by a Pinteresque awareness of the way language both masks and reveals meaning. Generally in his stories a wry, self-deprecating humour forestalls sentimentality or self-indulgence, the verbal and situational comedy effectively distancing pain and nostalgia. Nevertheless, the general aura of loneliness, rootlessness and emptiness persists; as Lurie has commented, 'It's funny on the surface, but what I'm talking about is not really funny.'

LYCETT, JOSEPH (?1774–?), born Staffordshire, England, was a professional portrait and miniature painter who was convicted of forgery in 1811 and sentenced to transportation for fourteen years. After arriving in Sydney in 1814, he worked as a clerk in the police office but was convicted of forgery again in 1815 and sent to Newcastle. His work on the plans of a Newcastle church led to a conditional pardon and in 1819–20 he travelled extensively in NSW and Van Diemen's Land, completing a series of drawings of Australian life. Three of his drawings sent by Governor Macquarie to Lord Bathurst are believed to have won him an absolute pardon in 1821. Lycett returned to England in 1822 and in 1824–25 published his *Views in Australia: Or, New South Wales, and Van Diemen's Land Delineated* in thirteen parts, reissued in a single volume in 1825. Nothing is known of the rest of Lycett's life, although a pencilled note in a copy of his *Views* held by the Mitchell Library states that he committed suicide after being charged again with forgery. A delicate and perceptive artist at his best, Lycett was not averse in his *Views* to presenting a Europeanized version of the Australian landscape to suit London tastes.

Lyceum Miniature, a monthly paper published in Melbourne 1878–79, circulated among members of the Melbourne and Sydney Progressive Lyceums. The paper published news of the society and original contributions from members consisting of articles on general topics, short stories and verse. Alfred Deakin was editor from January 1878 to January 1879.

LYLE, GARRY, a Melbourne poet, founder and publisher of the untitled booklets of verse, *Number One*, *Number Two* and *Number Three* (1943–48), contributed verse to such periodicals as *Bohemia* and *Venture*, and published one collection, *Eighteen Poems* (1940). His verse is also represented in the anthology, *Dawnfire* (1941), ed. John Cremin.

LYNCH, ARTHUR ALFRED (1861–1934), born near Ballarat of an Irish father who had taken part in the Eureka rebellion and of a Scottish mother, graduated from the University of Melbourne in 1887, and also trained as a civil engineer. He later studied science, psychology and electrical engineering in Europe, qualified as a doctor in London, worked for a time as a journalist and in 1892 tried unsuccessfully to enter the House of Commons as a Parnellite candidate. He served with the Boers during the Boer War. In 1901 he was elected to the House of Commons as Nationalist candidate for Galway but was imprisoned and tried for treason in 1902. Convicted in 1903, he was sentenced to life imprisonment but was released on licence a year later and subsequently won a free pardon. A prominent Irish member of parliament until 1918, he was active in British interests during the First World War. The author of numerous books on a range of subjects including science, psychology, ethics and the Irish problem, Lynch also published an autobiography, *My Life Story* (1924); five volumes of verse, some of which shows a satirical wit, *A Koran of Love* (1894), *Our Poets!* (1894), *Religio Athletae* (1895), *Prince Azreel*

(1911) and *Sonnets of the Banner and the Star* (1914); and two works of fiction, *Poppy Meadows* (1915) and *O'Rourke the Great* (1921). A man of wide-ranging interests and talents, Lynch in his combination of an affection for Australia and a fierce love of Ireland is an extreme representative of a common political phenomenon in Australia before 1918.

LYNCH, JOE, see 'Five Bells'

LYNG, JENS SORENSEN (1868–1941), born Hasle, Denmark, came to Australia in 1891, was for a time secretary to the botanist, Baron von Mueller, and served with the Australian forces in New Guinea 1914–18. He edited the *New Guinea Government Gazette* and later founded the *Rabaul Record*. On his return to Australia he worked for the Commonwealth Bureau of Census and Statistics until his retirement in 1933. Editor of the Melbourne Scandinavian journal, *Norden*, for ten years, he wrote several fiction works in Danish and a novel in English, *Teddy Wilkins' Trials* (1910), the story of a Danish printer in Melbourne. He also wrote several general books in English including *Non-Britishers in Australia* (1927), which won the Harbison-Higinbotham Prize, *The Road to Canberra* (1931) and *The Scandinavians in Australia, New Zealand and the Western Pacific* (1939). Lyng also founded the *Australian National Review*.

LYONS, Dame ENID (1897–1981), born Smithton, Tasmania, married the future prime minister, J.A. Lyons, in 1915 and became the mother of twelve children. After her husband's death, she became the first female member of the federal parliament in 1943, and later the first woman to hold ministerial office. She retired from politics in 1951 but was a commissioner of the ABC 1951–62. She wrote an account of her early life and marriage, *So We Take Comfort* (1965); a volume of political reminiscences, *Among the Carrion Crows* (1972); and a series of short essays and sketches on aspects of daily life, *The Old Haggis* (1969).

LYSTER, WILLIAM SAURIN (1828–80), operatic entrepreneur, was born Dublin. He first came to Australia in 1842, and after various overseas military adventures formed an opera troupe in San Francisco with his brother Frederick. In 1861 the troupe travelled to Australia and, after beginning a successful season in Melbourne, which was to become Lyster's base, continued to tour Australasia for the next six years. After an unsuccessful season in San Francisco in 1868, followed by dispersal of the troupe, Lyster formed another company which he brought to Australia in 1870 and continued to present both English and Italian operas successfully in Australia until his death. His career is described by Harold Love in *The Golden Age of Australian Opera* (1981).

Mabel, see Feminism and Australian Literature

MACAINSH, NOEL, see Criticism

MACALISTER, CHARLES (1830–1908), born Scotland, came to Australia in 1833 and spent much of his life in the Goulburn district of NSW. His book of reminiscences, *Old Pioneering Days in the Sunny South* (1907), vividly recalls aspects of colonial life, e.g. the effects of transportation, overlanding experiences, the gold discoveries, the selection experiment and the bushranging phenomenon, and presents MacAlister's recollections of Daniel Deniehy, Robert Lowe and other nineteenth-century notables. A significant source book for Australian folklorists, *Old Pioneering Days in the Sunny*

South includes a number of early folk-songs (q.v.).

MACARTHUR Family exercised a considerable influence on the growth of the merino wool industry and on the political affairs of NSW during the Colony's first fifty years. John Macarthur (1767–1834), a lieutenant in the NSW Corps, and his wife Elizabeth (1769–1850), came to Australia in June 1790. By 1794 they had established Elizabeth Farm House on a grant of forty hectares in the Parramatta district. Macarthur's appointment in 1793 as inspector of public works and his position as paymaster of the NSW Corps placed him in such advantageous circumstances that he rapidly became one of the most powerful men in the Colony. After quarrels with successive governors John Hunter and Philip Gidley King, and a duel with his commanding officer, William Paterson, Macarthur was sent to England for court martial. He returned in 1805 with a grant of 2000 hectares of land of his own choosing and with plans to promote the fine-wool industry in the Colony; he took up his grant in the Cowpastures area, establishing the historic property, Camden Park. In 1808 he played a leading role in deposing Governor William Bligh and he returned to England in 1809, again to answer for his actions. Although threatened with arrest if he returned to the colonies, in 1817 he was back in Australia where he exercised considerable influence on the enquiry of Commissioner J.T. Bigge in 1819, quarrelled with Governor Lachlan Macquarie, continued on bad terms with Macquarie's successor, Sir Ralph Darling, helped to found the Australian Agricultural Company, the Australian Bank and the Australian and Sydney Colleges and energetically promoted his pastoral interests. Macarthur was survived by his wife Elizabeth, a woman of great resource and initiative who managed the growing pastoral empire with skill and success in Macarthur's absence from Australia of more than thirteen years. Macarthur was also survived by his sons, Edward (1789–1872) and James (1798–1867); the latter published *New South Wales: Its Present State and Future Prospects* (1837), ghosted by Edward Edwards. James, a leading figure in NSW politics prior to self-government, was the father of Elizabeth, who in 1867 married Captain A.A.W. Onslow, thus originating the Macarthur-Onslow family. Macarthur is the subject of M.H. Ellis's biography, *John Macarthur* (1955), and is included in Vance Palmer's *National Portraits* (1940). Sibella Macarthur-Onslow edited *Some Early Records of the Macarthurs of Camden* (1914). Differing versions of some of the events of the Macarthur period are given in Ellis's biography and in H.V. Evatt's *Rum Rebellion* (1938). J.M. Ward wrote *James Macarthur: Colonial Conservative 1798–1867* (1981).

MACARTNEY, F.T. (FREDERICK THOMAS) (1887–1980), born and educated in Melbourne, left school at twelve and followed a variety of occupations including stints as a clerk, a bookkeeper on a Riverina station, a shorthand reporter, a freelance journalist and a Victorian government employee, until his appointment in 1921 to the Northern Territory public service. Macartney returned to Melbourne in 1933 and, apart from 1942–47 when he was employed as a public servant and 1948–54 when most of his energies were devoted to the revision of E. Morris Miller's bibliography, *Australian Literature* (q.v., 1940),

he worked as a freelance broadcaster, reviewer (in 1935–38 for *All About Books*) and university extension and CLF lecturer.

Active in Melbourne literary circles from his early twenties, Macartney helped to found the Melbourne Literary Club in 1916 and was editor of its journal, *Birth*, in 1920; he was prominent in the Australian Literature Society, PEN and the FAW. Although he contributed short stories to periodicals and anthologies and illustrated some of his books with lino-cuts, his main creative activity was as a writer of cool and crafted verse which ranges from the densely philosophical to the lightly satiric. His major volumes were *Preferences* (1941) and *Selected Poems* (1961), which both include material from earlier volumes, e.g. *Dewed Petals* (1912), *Earthern Vessels* (1913), *Commercium* (1917), *In War Time* (1918), *Poems* (1920), *Something for Tokens* (1922), *A Sweep of Lute-Strings* (1929), *Hard Light* (1933), *Ode of Our Times* (1944), *Gaily the Troubadour* (1946) and *Tripod for Homeward Incense* (1947). He is better known, however, for the abridgement and rearrangement of the Miller bibliography, published in 1956 under their joint names as *Australian Literature: A Bibliography to 1938... Extended to 1950*. 'Miller and Macartney', as *Australian Literature* has become known, remains an indispensable tool for students of Australian literature, although contemporary criticism of the work led Macartney to publish *An Odious Comparison Considered in Its Relation to Australian Literature* (1956). His other work includes *A Historical Outline of Australian Literature* (1957) which comprises the historical introduction to 'Miller and Macartney'; *Australian Literary Essays* (1957); an autobiography, *Proof Against Failure* (1967); a biography, *Furnley Maurice (Frank Wilmot)* (1955); a revision of Louis Lavater's 1926 anthology, *The Sonnet in Australasia* (1956); and the 1947 number of *Australian Poetry* (1948).

McAULEY, JAMES (1917–76), born Lakemba, NSW, was educated at the University of Sydney where he gained his MA in 1940 with the thesis, 'Symbolism: An Essay in Poetics', a topic which foreshadows the classical stance he later adopted in his poetry. Although he was regarded by some as an arch-conservative in later life, McAuley's university days were filled with the usual dalliances with atheism, anarchism, radicalism and idealism. Drafted for military service in 1942, he was appointed to the Australian Army Directorate of Research and Civil Affairs under A.A. Conlon where he helped to train the personnel of the Australian New Guinea Administration Unit (ANGAU), whose post-war task was to re-establish civil administration in the island. Thereafter New

Guinea was a major factor in McAuley's life. In 1946–60 he was a member of the instructional staff of the Australian School of Pacific Administration in Sydney. He visited New Guinea frequently, becoming deeply interested in the problems facing its primitive society and fascinated by its exotic landscape. His writings on New Guinea, published throughout the 1940s and 1950s in the journal, *South Pacific*, won him an international reputation among scholars of Oceania. In 1956 he became editor of the literary and current affairs journal, *Quadrant* (q.v.); in 1961 he was appointed reader in poetry at the University of Tasmania, Hobart, then professor of English, occupying the chair until his death. McAuley was instrumental in establishing *Australian Literary Studies*, and was president of the Australian Association for the Teaching of English 1970–75. In 1972 he won the Britannica–Australia Award; in 1975 he was made AM.

McAuley's first collection of verse was *Under Aldebaran* (q.v., 1946). In 1947–49 he wrote 'Prometheus', 'The Death of Chiron', 'The Ascent of Heracles' and 'The Tomb of Heracles', the four poems which make up his important work 'The Hero and the Hydra', first published together in his second volume, *A Vision of Ceremony* (q.v., 1956). Using the Greek tales based on the Prometheus legend, McAuley comments adversely on modern civilization and affirms traditional moral and spiritual values. His *Selected Poems* appeared in 1963. The epic narrative, *Captain Quiros* (q.v.), was published in 1964. *Surprises of the Sun* (1969), a series of mainly autobiographical lyrics, disappointed critics who felt that after *Captain Quiros* McAuley would continue to write public poetry with substantial themes. Two of the poems, 'In the Huon Valley' and 'St. John's Park, New Town', reflect McAuley's reaction to his new Tasmanian environment, a reaction more fully explored in the posthumous collection *A World of Its Own* (1977), where his handwritten poems in praise of the Tasmanian east coast area near Coles Bay are combined with paintings and drawings by Patricia Giles. *Collected Poems 1936–1970* appeared in 1971, and in the year he died *Music Late at Night: Poems 1970–1973* and *Time Given: Poems 1970–1974* were published; both titles reflect his awareness of approaching death. McAuley's chief prose works are *The End of Modernity* (1959), essays on modern literature, art and culture in general, written mainly from a traditional religious viewpoint; *The Personal Element in Australian Poetry* (1970), the texts of his 1968 lectures for the Foundation for Australian Literary Studies; and *The Grammar of the Real* (1975), essays and literary criticism. *A Map of Australian Verse: The Twentieth Century* (1975) combines samples of the work of Australian poets with critical commentary, biographical and bibliographical information.

One of the so-called 'University' poets of the 1950s, McAuley was considered a classicist because of his belief, expressed in 'The Magian Heresy' (*Quadrant*, September 1957), that in the 'high world of Virgil and Chaucer and Dante and Shakespeare . . . the true proportions of things are recognized' and because of his stance, taken in 'An Art of Poetry' (*A Vision of Ceremony*), that 'only the simplest forms can hold/A vast complexity'. McAuley eschewed 'individual, arbitrary/And self-expressive art', demanding (and providing in his own writing) traditional control and order, grace and precision. Such attitudes explain his impatience with what he saw as the self-indulgent, 'immense deviation' of the avant-garde verse of the 1940s and the resultant Ern Malley hoax (q.v.). Those opposed to his viewpoint saw his stance as arch-conservative and his attitudes as reactionary. To some of his admirers the graceful autobiographical lyrics of his later volumes represent his best poetry, but they do little to enhance the reputation and prestige he gained from *Under Aldebaran, A Vision of Ceremony* and *Captain Quiros*. His final years, however, brought an increasing recognition of his stature as critic and intellectual. Peter Coleman wrote *The Heart of James McAuley: Life and Work of the Australian Poet* (1980).

McBURNEY, SAMUEL, see **Australian English**

MACCALLUM, MUNGO BALLARDIE, (1913–), grandson of Sir Mungo William MacCallum (q.v.) was born Sydney, educated at the University of Sydney and began work as a journalist and as writer and producer for ABC radio. During the Second World War he edited the army education journal, *Salt*. After studying television in Britain and Europe, he was involved as producer, announcer and interviewer in ABC television for several years, producing its opening night of television in 1956. He has since worked as a freelance radio and television broadcaster, film and arts critic, and playwright. In 1966 his radio play, 'Five Days', was entered for the Italia Prize, and he has written documentary film scripts, poetry and two novels, *A Voyage in Love* (1956) and *Son of Mars* (1963). Television and book critic for *Nation*, he is also a well-known contributor to journals and newspapers. In 1968 he edited a collection of essays, *Ten Years of Television*.

MACCALLUM, Sir MUNGO WILLIAM (1854–1942), born Scotland, was educated at the Universities of Glasgow, Leipzig and Berlin before his appointment in 1879 as professor of English, University College of Wales at Bangor. In 1887 he was selected by a committee that included Matthew Arnold, Leslie Stephen and Max Muller to a new chair of modern literature at the University of Sydney; after his retirement in 1920 he was successively acting warden and warden (1923–24), vice-chancellor (1925–27, during the time Christopher Brennan was dismissed from the university), deputy chancellor (1928–34) and chancellor (1935–36). He was knighted for his services to education in 1926 and honoured by doctorates from the Universities of Glasgow and Oxford.

MacCallum's first major publication was in the field of German philology, but his international reputation in English studies was established with the expository *Tennyson's Idylls of the King* (1894), and particularly with *Shakespeare's Roman Plays and Their Background* (1910) which remains a significant study. A man of massive learning who found his colonial appointment some hindrance to his scholarly endeavours, he was enormously influential, not only in the University of Sydney, where he developed the tradition of Elizabethan scholarship in its English department, but also in the intellectual and cultural life of NSW. He was chairman of trustees of the Public Library of NSW 1906–12, during which time the Mitchell Library opened, helped to found the CLF, was NSW representative on its central committee 1917–29, and was instrumental in the formation of the Shakespeare Society and the Australian English Association; foundation and life president of the latter 1923–42, he gave several lectures on English literary topics which were published as pamphlets, and was the subject of a special number of *Southerly* in 1944. His other publications include a biblical verse-drama, *Queen Jezebel* (1930), a biography of the Sydney headmaster, A.B. Weigall (1913), and *The Dramatic Monologue in the Victorian Period* (1925). His son, Mungo Lorenz MacCallum (1883–1932), was a lecturer in law at the University of Sydney, edited several plays of Shakespeare, and was leader writer for the *Sydney Morning Herald* 1919–32; his grandson, Mungo Ballardie MacCallum (q.v.), is a journalist and writer; and his great-grandson, Mungo Wentworth MacCallum (1941–   ), a journalist and satirist, is the author of *Mungo's Canberra* (1977) and *Mungo on the Zoo Plane* (1979).

McCOMBIE, THOMAS (1819–69), born Aberdeenshire, Scotland, arrived in Melbourne in 1841, where he briefly tried squatting before becoming editor and part-proprietor of the *Port Phillip Gazette* 1844–51. He was a member of the Port Phillip Legislative Council in 1856–59, then returned to England where he gave auth-oritative opinions on such colonial matters as the Aborigines, gold and the convict system, and reflected publicly on various methods of colonization. He returned to Australia in 1866 but, discovering he was terminally ill, went back to England to die. His two main novels are *Arabin: Or, The Adventures of a Colonist in New South Wales* (q.v., 1845) and *Frank Henly: Or, Honest Industry Will Conquer* (1867), unexceptional works of literature but worthwhile because of their enthusiasm for, and realistic account of, life in Australia. He also published historical and descriptive prose which includes *Australian Sketches* (1847), *Essays on Colonization* (1850) and *The History of the Colony Of Victoria from Its Settlement to the Death of Sir Charles Hotham* (1858).

McCONNEL, URSULA, see **Aboriginal Song and Narrative in Translation**

McCRAE, GEORGE GORDON (1833–1927), born Leith, Scotland, son of Andrew Murison McCrae and Georgiana Huntly McCrae (q.v.) and father of the poet, Hugh McCrae (q.v.), came to Australia in 1841. The family settled in 1843 at Arthur's Seat on the Mornington Peninsula, an area later described in his mother's journal. McCrae entered the civil service in Melbourne in 1854, ultimately rising to the post of deputy registrar-general. Artistic in temperament, he became an important member of the Melbourne cultural and literary scene, being one of the founders of the Yorick Club and an associate of such literary figures as Marcus Clarke, Henry Kendall, Adam Lindsay Gordon and R.H. Horne. Two of McCrae's poems, *Mamba ('The Bright-Eyed') : An Aboriginal Reminscence* and *The Story of Balladeadro* (both 1867) are among the earliest Australian poems on Aboriginal themes. They found favour with contemporaries like Henry Kendall, who judged McCrae 'the highest poet in Australia' whose voice was for 'scholars and thinkers only', but they soon came to be considered too romanticized and unrealistic in their treatment of the Aboriginal. *The Man in the Iron Mask* (1873), a long poem in blank verse, was enlivened, like all McCrae's work, by some graceful passages but its story of the imprisonment of a mysterious royal Frenchman held little attraction for Australian readers. A further collection, *The Fleet and Convoy and Other Verses*, was published in 1915, and his only novel, *John Rous*, in 1918.

McCRAE, GEORGIANA HUNTLY (1804–90), the mother of George Gordon McCrae and grandmother of Hugh McCrae (qq.v.) was the natural daughter of George, Marquis of Huntly, later fifth Duke of Gordon. Educated in London at a convent school run by aristo-cratic refugees from the French Revolution, she became an accomplished linguist and talented musician. Her forte, however, was painting, especially portraiture, a talent that was nour-ished by several distinguished teachers. After leaving school, she lived for seven years at Gordon Castle, followed by a period in Edin-burgh where she attempted to earn her living from portrait painting. In 1830 she married a lawyer, Andrew McCrae, who migrated to Aus-tralia in 1839. Georgiana followed in 1841 and the family lived in various areas of Victoria, including Arthur's Seat near Frankston, Mel-bourne, where Andrew farmed. She painted some portraits and miniatures in Australia, but was better known during her lifetime as a cultured, witty and resourceful woman, the friend of most of the colony's political and cultural figures. Some of her journals covering the period 1838–65, supplemented by George Gordon McCrae's diary 1846–47, were edited by Hugh McCrae and were first published in 1934 titled *Georgiana's Journal*. One of the most valuable records of Melbourne life in the 1840s, the journal is also remarkable as the reflection of a distinctive, lively personality. Extracts from some of Georgiana McCrae's English notebooks (1804–29) were also pub-lished in *Southerly* (1946, 1947), and some of her letters and drawings are listed in H.F. Chaplin's bibliography, *A McCrae Miscellany* (1967).

McCRAE, HUGH (1876–1958), born Mel-bourne, son of George Gordon McCrae and grandson of Georgiana Huntly McCrae (qq.v.), was initially articled to a Melbourne architect but, influenced by the Norman Lindsay set that included Randolph Bedford, Lionel Lindsay, Edward and Will Dyson, sought a living by freelance writing and illustration. In 1904 he moved to Sydney where he became involved with J.F. Archibald, A.G. Stephens and Frank Fox. In 1914–17 he was in the USA attempting a living as an artist and actor; he later played Adam Lindsay Gordon in an Australian film. In 1917–29 he lived in Melbourne, where he edited the *New Triad* (1927–28), then moved again to Sydney and in 1931 to Camden (q.v.) where he wrote poetry, prose, drama and letters, gave radio talks and public lectures, wrote for newspapers and compiled and edited personal and family memoirs. In 1953 he was made OBE.

McCrae's first collection of poetry is *Satyrs and Sunlight* (q.v., 1909), illustrated by Nor-man Lindsay; the title was also given to a 1928 collection of his poetry. McCrae's other volumes of poetry include *Colombine* (1920); *Idyllia* (1922) which contains a short extract

from an unfinished verse-drama, 'Joan of Arc', a further extract being included in the 1928 *Satyrs and Sunlight; The Mimshi Maiden* (1938); *Poems* (1939), a selected volume; *Forests of Pan* (1944), containing a number of earlier poems which were not reprinted in *Poems* (1939); and *Voice of the Forest* (1945). R.G. Howarth, who edited *Forests of Pan* and ar-ranged and introduced *Voice of the Forest*, also edited *The Best Poems of Hugh McCrae* (1961). McCrae wrote a musical fantasy, *The Ship of Heaven* (1951); a prose work, *The Du Poissey Anecdotes* (1922); and a prose collection, *Story-book Only* (1948), which includes the *Du Poissey* pieces and his reminiscences of his father and his times, *My Father and My Father's Friends*, first published in 1935. He edited *Georgiana's Journal* (1934), the diaries of his grandmother. McCrae also wrote an endless stream of letters to friends and acquaintances, each beautifully hand-written letter illustrated with figures and scenes and often accompanied by a verse com-posed for the occasion. A selection of his letters was edited by R.D. FitzGerald in 1970. A Hugh McCrae number of *Southerly* appeared in 1956.

McCrae's poetry has consistently attracted a small band of devotees: fellow-Rabelaisian Kenneth Slessor, who believed that *Satyrs and Sunlight* (1909) ushered modern Australian po-etry into being; Mary Gilmore, who was de-lighted by McCrae's verbal artistry and regarded him as Australia's finest poet; literary historian, H.M. Green, who saw him as 'a prince of lyrists' with 'as near an approach to pure beauty as can be made by means of the purely phys-ical'; and Judith Wright, who found in him 'a poet to love and admire and be proud of'. With the gradual disappearance of the gener-ation who knew McCrae personally, much of that ardour has evaporated. Recent judgements tend, in the main, to reject the whimsy, the exotica and the seductive carnival of colour and sound that characterize his verse, finding in-stead incoherence of thought and lack of control over imagery and syntax; in effect, little more than imaginative chaos. He remains, however, of importance in Australian literary history, both because he anticipated the *Vision* school and because he offered, with other lyrists, an alternative to the balladry that had dominated Australian poetry in the preceding generation.

McCRONE, FRANCIS NESBITT, see **NES-BITT, FRANCIS**

McCUAIG, RONALD (1908–), born Newcastle, NSW, began writing for radio in 1927 and was employed by *Wireless Weekly* 1928–38. During the Second World War he worked for the ABC and for *Smith's Weekly*.

He was a special writer and occasional literary critic for the *Sydney Morning Herald* 1945–46, and *Smith's Weekly* 1947. In 1949 he joined the editorial staff of the *Bulletin* where, as 'Swilliam', he wrote much topical verse and numerous literary and theatre reviews. McCuaig's poetry publications include *Vaudeville* (1938), *Wanton Goldfish* (1941) and the cumulative collections, *Quod Ronald McCuaig* (1946) and *The Ballad of Bloodthirsty Bessie and Other Poems* (1961). He has also written *Tales out of Bed* (1944, essays and short stories) and *Australia and the Arts* (1972). He edited the 1954 edition of *Australian Poetry* and has published the children's books, *Gangles* (1972) and *Tobolino and the Amazing Football Boots* (1974). With his shrewd, and sometimes crude, satirical observations of life, his talent for dry and witty cynicism, and his delicately-humorous love lyrics, McCuaig seemed likely to occupy an important place in the post-war poetry scene; however, the success of 'The Ballad of Bloodthirsty Bessie' (q.v.), a rollicking fantasy which combines greed, lust, religious mania and superbly-portrayed indifference to human life, has been followed by virtual poetic silence.

McCUBBIN, FREDERICK (1855–1917), born West Melbourne, studied at the Melbourne National Gallery School, later becoming its master. A prime mover in the development of the nationalistic Heidelberg School (q.v.), McCubbin began his interpretation of the local scene with *The Lost Child* (1886), a typical colonial tragedy that had already found literary expression in Henry Kingsley's novel, *The Recollections of Geoffry Hamlyn* (1859), and Marcus Clarke's story, 'Pretty Dick'. Other McCubbin paintings to illustrate the hardship and melancholy of pioneer life so consistently emphasized in colonial writing are *Down on His Luck* (1889), *Bush Burial* (1890), *On the Wallaby Track* (1896) and *The Pioneers* (1904). McCubbin is the art teacher of heroine Delie Gordon in Nancy Cato's novel, *All the Rivers Run* (1958). The opening chapters of Katharine Susannah Prichard's novel, *The Pioneers* (1915), are an imaginative interpretation of McCubbin's painting of that title; the same painting is discussed in Mary Marlowe's novel, *The Ghost Girl* (1921). J.S. MacDonald edited *The Art of Frederick McCubbin* (1916). Okko Boer compiled *Frederick McCubbin: The Man and His Art* (1980), a folio of reproductions of McCubbin's paintings with commentary; Ann Galbally wrote the biographical *Frederick McCubbin* (1981).

McCULLOUGH, COLLEEN (1937–), born Wellington, NSW, of Irish Catholic stock, was educated at the University of Sydney. After brief periods as schoolteacher, library assistant and journalist, she worked as neurophysiologist in Sydney and England and at the Yale University's School of International Medicine 1967–76. Her first novel, *Tim*, published in the USA in 1974, depicts the relationship between Tim Melville, an unskilled labourer with the mind of a child and the body of an Adonis, and Mary Horton, a plain spinster in her forties. Although *Tim* met with some commercial success and was made into a film, its critical reception has been unenthusiastic. Her second novel, *The Thorn Birds* (q.v., 1977), a colourful and sometimes bizarre story that chronicles the fortunes of several generations of the Cleary family on Drogheda station in northern NSW, was selected from a proof copy by the United States Literary Guild. As a result it became a best-seller in both hardback and paperback; a television series was screened in 1983. Her next novel, *An Indecent Obsession* (1981), is set in the psychiatric ward of a small military hospital in the South Pacific soon after the end of the Second World War. A novel about duty (the 'indecent obsession'), it has the prescribed mix of best-selling ingredients, romance, sex, violence and paranoia.

MACDONALD, ALEXANDER (1) (1878–1917), born Scotland, spent some time in WA and Queensland, and served with the Australian contingent in the Boer War. A keen traveller and prospector, he wrote several accounts of his adventures, including *In Search of El Dorado* (1905), *In the Land of Pearl and Gold* (1907) and *Through the Heart of Tibet* (1909), the first two of which deal partly with Australia. He also wrote adventure stories, mostly addressed to the young, male reader and extolling the active life and traditional public-school virtues; several of them draw upon his Australian experience. They include *The Lost Explorers* (1906), *The Pearl Seekers* (1907), *The Quest of the Black Opals* (1907), *The Island Traders* (1908), *The White Trail* (1908), *The Hidden Nugget* (1909) and *The Invisible Island* (1910).

MACDONALD, ALEXANDER (2) (1915–73), a well-known Sydney journalist, was born Sydney but spent most of his boyhood in a Catholic seminary in Scotland. At sixteen he was reunited with his father, who was mining for gold in north Queensland, before joining the ABC in Sydney as a continuity writer. He later became a gag-writer for such comedians as Jack Davey and Roy Rene, moved to commercial radio and wrote a weekly column of radio reviews for *Smith's Weekly*. He also contributed feature articles and humorous columns, radio and television reviews to a range

439

of newspapers including the *Daily Telegraph*, *Sydney Morning Herald*, *Sun*, *Daily Mirror* and the *Sunday Telegraph*. Some of his pieces for the *Daily Telegraph* and *Sunday Telegraph* are reprinted in his collection, *Don't Frighten the Horses* (1961). He also wrote a humorous autobiography, *The Ukelele Player under the Red Lamp* (1972), which includes vivid pictures of bohemian life in Sydney in the 1930s and 1940s, as well as reminiscences of Peter Finch, Roy Rene and Kenneth Slessor.

MACDONALD, DONALD ALISTER (1857–1932), born Melbourne, worked on the staff of the *Argus* from 1881 until his death. Its correspondent during the Boer War, he wrote a well-received account of the siege of Ladysmith, *How We Kept the Flag Flying* (1900). Also well known as a naturalist, contributing essays and the column 'Nature Notes' to the *Argus* and other articles to the *Australasian* under the pseudonym 'Gnuyang', he published two collections of reprinted essays which represent his fluid style, enthusiastic response to nature and feeling for childhood experience, *Gum Boughs and Wattle Bloom Gathered on Australian Hills and Plains* (1887) and *Sweet-Scented Flowers and Fragrant Leaves* (1897). Another collection of his essays on a range of subjects was published after his death, titled *The Brooks of Morning* (1933). His cricket and football commentaries established a new trend in sports writing and were a popular, regular feature of the *Argus*. He also wrote two books for children, *The Bush Boys' Book* (1911), based on his column 'Notes for Boys' in the *Argus*, and *At the End of the Moonpath* (1922); and, with J.F. Edgar, a novel, *The Warrigal's Well* (1901).

McDONALD, NAN (1921–74), born Eastwood, Sydney, was educated at the University of Sydney. As publishing editor for Angus & Robertson she made a considerable contribution to the publication of Australian literature in the decades following the Second World War. She edited the annual anthology, *Australian Poetry*, in 1953. Her own volumes of poetry are *Pacific Sea* (1947), which won the inaugural Grace Leven Prize for poetry, *The Lonely Fire* (1954) and *The Lighthouse and Other Poems* (1959). Her *Selected Poems* was published in 1969. *Pacific Sea* captures in smooth, attractive verse the beauty of the Sydney bushlands, the grandeur of the Hawkesbury district and the pleasant seascapes of the NSW south coast. In philosophic poems such as 'The Ship' and 'The Tollgate Islands' she probes the future, wondering 'what dark fee, what cruel payment' life may exact from her. *The Lonely Fire*, more powerful and at times quite sombre, uses a

series of masks, like the old tramp in the title poem, to lay bare the human condition. 'The Lighthouse' is a long, dramatic study of a lighthouse-keeper who spends three days of terror fighting to regain his self-control after discovering the dead body of his companion.

MACDONALD, ROBERT MACLAUCHLAN (1874–?), wrote a series of boys' adventure stories set in New Guinea, the South Pacific and Australia, which are now mainly remarkable for their improbable plots, shallow characters and frank expressions of racist prejudice and imperial pride. They include *The Great White Chief* (1907), *Rival Treasure Hunters* (1909), *Chillagoe Charlie* (1909), *The Secret of the Sargasso* (1909), *The Gold Seekers* (1910), *The Moon God's Secret* (1910), *Danger Mountain* (1911), *The Opal Hunters* (1912) and *The Pearl Lagoons* (1911). Macdonald also wrote an account of his travels as a prospector, *Opals and Gold* (1928).

McDONALD, ROGER (1941–), the son of local historian, Lorna McDonald, was born and educated in Sydney and was a high-school-teacher and a radio and television producer with the ABC before becoming, in 1969, a professional editor with the University of Queensland Press, which published his two volumes of poetry, *Citizens of Mist* (1968) and *Airship* (1975). In his seven years with the Press, McDonald was responsible for the Paperback Poets series which both reflected and stimulated the 'New Australian Poetry' (q.v.); his selection from the first series was published in 1974 as *Paperback Poets Anthology*. In 1976 he moved to Canberra to work on *1915* (q.v.), a novel about the Gallipoli experience. Published in 1979, *1915* proved an outstanding success, winning the *Age* Book of the Year Award and the SA government's Biennial Literature Award; Peter Yeldham adapted it into a seven-part television series which was shown in 1982. After completing *1915*, McDonald moved to the country near Braidwood, NSW, where he now lives with his wife, Rhyll McMaster (q.v.). In 1981 he was awarded the Canada–Australia Literary Prize; in 1982 his second novel, *Slipstream*, was published.

In the intensely political world of Australian poetry since the 1960s McDonald has been much admired for his editorial activities, which helped significantly to establish or consolidate the reputation of a number of (mainly younger) Australian poets. His own poetry occupies a corner of Les Murray's 'Vernacular Republic' and is distinguished by a selection of detail and by metaphoric observations which give freshness and resonance to his metaphysical exploration of experience. His fiction also reflects his intention to 'write out of the Australian character and in the Australian accent': in practice this has often meant the exploration of the Australian character within an historical framework, as in *Citizens of Mist* which includes poems on Adam Lindsay Gordon and other historical subjects; in *1915*, which, although explicitly described by McDonald as 'a work of the imagination', embodies also considerable research; and in *Slipstream,* a novel about a pioneer aviator of the 1920s and 1930s whose career loosely resembles that of Charles Kingsford-Smith. The interpretation offered of Gallipoli has preoccupied reviewers of *1915*, often to the distortion of the novel, in which the domestic scenes set in Australia are as important as the war scenes in establishing its major theme, the search of the four central characters for a coherent shape to their existence. A second point of discussion concerning *1915* has been the evaluation of McDonald's transformation from poet into novelist, which perhaps influenced him to jettison some of the lyricism in *1915* in the preparation of *Slipstream,* written in plainer, understated, allusive prose in keeping with the elusiveness of its central character, Roy Hilman.

McDONALD, SIMON (1907–68), one of the finest Australian traditional singers in the twentieth century, was born and lived most of his life near Creswick, Victoria, where he worked mainly as a gold fossicker, labourer and woodcutter. He was a folk poet and fiddler as well as a bush singer whose repertoire included material learnt from the earlier singers in his family. He is the subject of Hugh Anderson's *Time out of Mind* (1974).

MACDONNELL, J.E. (JAMES EDMOND) ('MACNELL') (1917–), born Mackay, Queensland, joined the RAN as an ordinary seaman at the age of seventeen. He spent fourteen years in the navy, saw action in the Second World War and finished his career as a commissioned gunner. A contributor of stories and articles to the *Bulletin* under the pseudonym 'Macnell', he joined the *Bulletin* in 1948 to write the weekly 'Personal Items' page. He also contributed articles on naval actions in the war which were subsequently published as a book, *Valiant Occasions* (1952), and supplemented his previous, non-fictional naval account, *Fleet Destroyer* (1945). His first novel, *Gimme the Boats,* was published in 1953. MacDonnell left the *Bulletin* in 1956 to write full-time for Horwitz publications, for whom he has subsequently written an average of twelve, wide-selling paperback novels a year. Almost all set against a naval background, several are series focusing on the exploits of individual sea warriors, the most popular of whom is Jim Brady. Horwitz has also published a series of reprints under the general title *The J.E. MacDonnell Classic Library.* MacDonnell has also written several books for boys under the pseudonym 'James Macnell'.

McFADYEN, ELLA MAY, born near Sydney, worked as a freelance journalist and was on the staff of the *Sydney Mail* 1918–38. A contributor of verse to the *Lone Hand, Sydney Morning Herald* and *Sydney Mail,* she published two collections, *Outland Born and Other Verses* (1911) and *Songs of the Last Crusade* (1917). She is better known as a writer of children's books, which include *Pegmen Tales* (1946), *Pegmen Go Walkabout* (1947), *Little Dragons of the Never Never* (1948), *The Wishing Star* (1956) and *The Big Book of Pegmen Tales* (1959). She also wrote a collection of verse for children, *Here's Fun for You* (1938). Her Pegmen series, which focuses on a family of peg toys and its re-enactment of the story of Noah's Ark, originated as a newspaper serial and was later broadcast on radio.

McGARVIE, WILLIAM (1810–41), born Glasgow, had some journalistic experience on the *Glasgow Herald* before coming to Sydney in 1828 where, through his involvement in the Australian Stationery Warehouse and its attached circulating library run by Robert Howe, he became one of Australia's earliest booksellers. McGarvie's *Catalogue of Books* (1829) of the library was the first catalogue of books issued in Australia. With Alfred Ward Stephens and Frederick Michael Stokes as partners, McGarvie imported a printing press and began publication of the *Sydney Herald* (q.v.) in 1831. McGarvie sold out to the other two after only a month, and later returned to bookselling.

MACGILLIVRAY, JOHN (1821–67), born Aberdeen, Scotland, studied medicine and zoology before accepting, in 1842, an appointment as assistant naturalist in HMS *Fly* on a surveying voyage to Australia and New Guinea. He spent three years with the *Fly,* assiduously collecting specimens whenever the ship anchored off the coast. He joined as naturalist, assisted by T.H. Huxley and James Fowler Wilson, another surveying voyage to Australia in HMS *Rattlesnake* 1847–50. His work in the natural history and exploration of Australia is recorded in his *Narrative of the Voyage of H.M.S. Rattlesnake* (1852). In 1853 he again visited Australia and the Pacific as naturalist on HMS *Herald* and subsequently spent some years in Sydney before in 1864 settling at Grafton, where he continued his work in natural science.

McGlusky, see HALES, A.A.G.

McGRATH, RAYMOND HERBERT (1903–77), born Sydney, studied arts and architecture at the University of Sydney, where he was art director of *Hermes*. He also studied painting under Julian Ashton and won a reputation as a wood-cut artist. Well known in literary circles, he contributed short stories to *Art in Australia* and other journals and anthologies, and published a collection of verse, illustrated, bound and printed by himself on J.T. Kirtley's private press, *Seven Songs of Meadow Lane* (1924). At the age of twenty-three he won the Wentworth Travelling Scholarship to London, and later settled in Dublin; he became one of the leading architects of the modern movement. He is one of the poets recalled by J. le Gay Brereton in his reminiscences of Sydney's literary life in *Knocking Round* (1930).

McGREGOR, CRAIG (1933–), born Jamberoo, NSW, left school at sixteen to join the *Sydney Morning Herald*. He studied part-time at the University of Sydney in the 1950s, meanwhile establishing a reputation as a journalist. In the 1960s he spent four years in England, working partly as a freelance journalist, and then lived for several years in the USA on a Harkness Fellowship. He is most widely-known for his analysis of Australia's culture, history, social mores and political attitudes, *Profile of Australia* (1966), revised and published in 1980 titled *The Australian People*. He has also written two novels, *Don't Talk to me about Love* (1971), winner of the Xavier Society Prize, and *The See-Through Revolver* (1977); numerous short stories, which have appeared in Australian and overseas magazines and newspapers; the texts of several photographic studies of Australia, *The High Country* (1967), *To Sydney with Love* (1968), *Life in Australia* (1968) and *The Great Barrier Reef* (1974); and an account of the 1983 Australian federal election, *Time of Testing: The Bob Hawke Victory* (1983). His interest in popular culture and music is reflected in the essays he has written for such newspapers as the *New York Times*, *Observer*, *Spectator* and *New Statesman*; in his anthology of essays on Bob Dylan (1972); and in his collections of essays on Australian society in the 1960s, *People, Politics and Pop* (1968); on American society, *Up Against the Wall, America* (1973); and on Western society in general and Australian society in particular, *Soundtrack for the Eighties* (1983). He has also written scripts for films and for a rock-opera, *Hero*, and has edited an original collection of interviews with Australian writers and artists, *In the Making*

(1969). In 1977 he won the Walkley Award for journalism.

McGUIRE, FRANCES (1900–), born Glenelg, SA, as Frances Cheadle, was educated at the University of Adelaide and later worked as a biochemist on insulin research. In 1927 she married Paul McGuire (q.v.) and subsequently lived in Europe, Asia and the USA. Well known as a freelance journalist, she has published two novels, *September Comes In* (1961) and *Time in the End* (1963); a history of the RAN (1948); an account, with Paul McGuire, of the war service of HMAS *Parramatta*, *The Price of Admiralty* (1944); a novel for children, *Three and Ma Kelpie* (1964); a series of part-satiric, part-pious fairy-tales, *Twelve Tales of the Life and Adventures of Saint Imaginus* (1946); a history of the Australian theatre (1948) with Paul McGuire and Betty Arnott; and an account of her childhood in SA, which is also a social history, *Bright Morning: The Story of an Australian Family before 1914* (1975). She has also translated the autobiography of John Gerard, *The Flight of the Falcon* (1954). Co-founder of the Dante Alighieri Society of SA, she has won cultural awards from the Italian government.

McGUIRE, PAUL (1903–78), born Peterborough, SA, was educated at the University of Adelaide and in 1927 married Frances Cheadle (see Frances McGuire) with whom he collaborated in two books. He was special overseas correspondent for various newspapers before serving in the RAN Volunteer Reserve during the Second World War. European correspondent for the *Argus* from 1945, he was appointed Australian delegate to the General Assembly of the United Nations in 1953 and was Australia's first ambassador to Italy 1954–59. He was decorated by both the Italian and the Australian governments. A well-known lecturer on international politics, McGuire published four influential books on current affairs, *Australia: Her Heritage, Her Future* (1939), subsequently revised and reprinted several times with the title, *Australian Journey; Westward the Course* (1942), a survey of Asian and Pacific countries, which went to press the month Pearl Harbour was bombed and became a best-seller; *The Three Corners of the World* (1948); and *There's Freedom for the Brave* (1949). He also published a booklet of poems, *The Two Men and Other Poems* (1932); and a series of popular crime novels which were subsequently translated into several languages. These include *Murder in Bostall* (1931), *Three Dead Men* (1931), *The Tower Mystery* (1932), *Murder by the Law* (1932), *There Sits Death* (1933), *Death Fugue* (1933), *Murder in Haste* (1934), *Day-*

light Murder (1934), 7.30 *Victoria* (1935), *Born to be Hanged* (1935), *Prologue to the Gallows* (1936), *Threepence to Marble Arch* (1936), *Cry Aloud for Murder* (1937), *W.I.* (1938), *Burial Service* (1938) and *The Spanish Steps* (1940).

MACILWAINE, HERBERT C. born in England, spent some years in Australia before returning to London, where he worked as a publisher's reader. He published two books of short tales which draw upon his Australian experience, *The Twilight Reef* (1897) and *The Undersong* (1903), and three novels which describe Australian bush life from the point of view of an English migrant, *Dinkinbar* (1898), *Fate the Fiddler* (1900) and *Anthony Britten* (1906).

McINNES, COLIN (1914–), son of the novelist Angela Thirkell (q.v.) and her first husband, James Campbell McInnes, and brother of the writer Graham McInnes (q.v.), was brought to Australia in 1920 after his mother married George Thirkell (q.v.). After an education in Melbourne he returned to England in 1930. During the Second World War he served in an intelligence unit and based his first book, *To the Victors the Spoils* (1950), on his experiences. He has since written nine novels, of which two, *June in Her Spring* (1952) and *All Day Saturday* (1966), are set in Australia. Some of his essays, contributed to such British periodicals as *Encounter*, *New Left Review* and *Twentieth Century*, are reprinted in the collection *England, Half English* (1961). He has also written a monograph on the painter, Sidney Nolan (1961), and a pictorial account, *Australia and New Zealand* (1964). His biography by Tony Gould, *Inside Outsider*, was published in 1983.

McINNES, GRAHAM (1912–70), was the son of the novelist Angela Thirkell (q.v.) and her first husband, James Campbell McInnes, and the brother of the novelist, Colin McInnes (q.v.). Brought to Australia in 1920 after his mother married George Thirkell (q.v.), he was educated in Melbourne; in 1934 he left for Canada, which subsequently became his permanent home. He worked as a university lecturer, art editor of a Toronto newspaper and producer for the Canadian Film Board before joining the Canadian diplomatic service in 1948. As well as numerous film scripts and articles on art, he wrote two books on Canadian art (1939 and 1950), but he is best known in Australia for his autobiographical sequence, *The Road to Gundagai* (q.v., 1965), *Humping My Bluey* (1966), *Finding a Father* (1967) and *Goodbye, Melbourne Town* (1968).

The Road to Gundagai, which deals mainly

with his schooldays and culminates with his mother's permanent departure for England in 1930, is both a sociological study of Melbourne in the 1920s and a vivid recreation of the joys and fears, humiliations and enthusiasms of childhood. Particularly striking are his portraits of his mother and stepfather, and the intimate, detailed picture of the family's daily life in suburban Malvern. *Humping My Bluey*, less integrated than the earlier volume but still an effective recreation of youthful life in Melbourne of the 1930s, retraces the events of his last year at school and his years at the University of Melbourne; it ends with his departure for Canada in search of his father. *Finding a Father* deals with his experiences in Canada and London and closes with his marriage and return to Canada in 1938. In *Goodbye, Melbourne Town*, which he described as a coda to his autobiographical sequence, McInnes explores further youthful memories of Melbourne.

McINTOSH, HUGH DONALD (1876–1942), born and educated in Sydney, reputedly began work at eight years of age. He established a flamboyant reputation as a catering entrepreneur and sporting promoter; he built the first Sydney Stadium, where in 1908 he staged the famous Tommy Burns–Jack Johnson world title heavyweight boxing bout, which attracted reporters such as Jack London. McIntosh sold his interest in Sydney Stadium in 1912, around the time that he became a theatre entrepreneur with the purchase of the Tivoli theatre circuit after the death of Harry Rickards (q.v.); he also became a newspaper proprietor with control, by 1916, of the *Sunday Times* and the *Referee* (qq.v.). Known as 'Huge Deal', McIntosh was a member of the NSW Legislative Council 1917–32 and entertained lavishly in society, but his financial empire began to collapse in 1927 and he was declared bankrupt in 1932.

MACINTYRE, ELISABETH (1916–), born Sydney, has worked as a freelance artist and feature writer for the *Age*, *Sunday Telegraph* and *Australian Women's Weekly*, as a designer for an advertising agency, and as a television cartoonist for the ABC. A well-known writer for children, she concentrated at first on visual realization of character, as in her books for pre-school children focusing on a humanized kangaroo, *Ambrose Kangaroo* (1941), *Ambrose Kangaroo Has a Busy Day* (1944), *Ambrose Kangaroo Goes to Town* (1964) and *Ambrose Kangaroo Delivers the Goods* (1978). Her lively drawings are also the main feature of her four books of animal stories, published in 1944, her verse-stories, *Susan, Who Lives in Australia* (1944, published in Australia as *Katherine*,

1946), and *Mr Koala Bear* (1954). *Willie's Woollies* (1951), *Jane Likes Pictures* (1959), *Hugh's Zoo* (1964) and *The Affable, Amiable, Bulldozer Man* (1965) combine in both text and drawing light-hearted fun and serious social comment. MacIntyre's later books, *Ninji's Magic* (1966), *The Purple Mouse* (1975) and *It Looks Different When You Get There* (1978), have been written for successively older age groups and are concerned with urgent, complex social problems. She has also written radio serials and has illustrated the work of other children's authors. In 1965 she won the Australian Children's Book Council Picture Book of the Year Award.

MACK, AMY (c.1877–1939), the sister of Louise Mack (q.v.), was born Port Adelaide. She edited the women's page of the *Sydney Morning Herald* 1907–14 and served in the ministry of munitions, London, 1916–17. Between 1909 and 1928, she published fourteen collections of bushland stories for children. Her major collections are *A Bush Calendar* (1909), *Bushland Stories for Children* (1910), *Birdland Stories* (1910), *Waterside Stories* (1910), *Bush Days* (1911), *Scribbling Sue and Other Stories* (1913), *Tomtit's Nest and Other Stories* (1914) and *The Wilderness* (1922). Anthropomorphic animals and plants feature in her stories, although Mack implicitly includes much natural science and history. Her gifts for drama and realism, her sensitive recording of the natural world and avoidance, on the whole, of an overly didactic tone, make her stories still accessible.

MACK, LOUISE (1874–1935), born Hobart, was the daughter of a Wesleyan minister whose career took the family later to Adelaide and then to Sydney. She was educated at Sydney High School, which she drew on for her popular children's books, *Teens* (1897), *Girls Together* (1898) and *Teens Triumphant* (1933), and where she edited the *High School Magazine*. From 1896 until 1901, when she left for London, she was a member of the *Bulletin's* staff and author of its 'A Woman's Letter'. From 1901 she lived for some years in England and Italy, edited a newspaper for the English residents of Florence for a period, and was in Belgium at the outbreak of war in 1914. She recorded her intrepid adventures in Antwerp and Brussels in *A Woman's Experiences in the Great War* (1915).   Married twice, to J.P. Creed and Allen I. Leyland, Mack published several novels for adults, most of which are light romances and draw on her impressions of Europe and Australia: *The Red Rose of a Summer* (1909), *In a White Palace* (1910), *Theodora's Husband* (1909), *The Romance of a Woman of Thirty* (1911), *Wife to Peter* (1911), *The Mar-*

riage of Edward (1913), *Attraction* (1913), *The Music Makers* (1914) and *The House of Daffodils* (1915). *An Australian Girl in London* (1902) records her impressions of Britain. Her books for girls include those mentioned above and *The World Is Round* (1896), *Children of the Sun* (1904) and *The Maiden's Prayer* (1934). She also published a volume of poetry, *Dreams in Flower* (1901, reprinted in *A Southern Garland*, 1904), and several short stories, some of which were reprinted in *The Bulletin Story Book* (1901). Mack's breathless style, described as 'ecstatic' by a contemporary reviewer, and her concentration on a conventional version of love, have tended to date her novels although her perceptions are often fresh and her vitality undeniable. She is at her best and her least conventional in her writing for children, especially in the school trilogy, *Teens*, *Girls Together* and *Teens Triumphant*, which is lively, realistic and unpretentious. She was the sister of Amy Mack (q.v.).

MACKANESS, GEORGE (1882–1968), born Sydney, graduated from the University of Sydney in 1907 and was head of the department of English at Sydney Teachers' College 1924–46. In a long and distinguished career as educationist, historian, author, bibliographer and bibliophile, Mackaness received honorary degrees from the Universities of Sydney and Melbourne, was president and fellow of the Royal Australian Historical Society, president of the FAW, a member of the CLF advisory board, and a trustee of the Public Library of NSW; he was made OBE in 1938.

Mackaness excelled in editorial and anthologist roles. Between 1935 and 1962 he edited, and sometimes translated from their original languages, forty-six small volumes dealing with such diverse subjects as Robert Louis Stevenson's association with Australia, the goldfields, the correspondence of Samuel Marsden, Richard Johnson and John Cotton, early Tasmanian history, and the discovery and exploration of the Moreton Bay District. The series, reduced to forty-four volumes titled *Australian Historical Monographs*, was reprinted in 1981. Mackaness's most significant works are the biographies, *The Life of Vice-Admiral William Bligh, R.N., F.R.S.* (1931), *Sir Joseph Banks: His Relations with Australia* (1936) and *Admiral Arthur Phillip, R.N.* (1937). His poetry anthologies began in 1913 with *Selections from the Australian Poets* and *The Children's Treasury of Australian Verse*, both in collaboration with Bertram Stevens (q.v.). In 1934 he edited the famous anthology, *The Wide Brown Land* in collaboration with his daughter Joan. His other anthologies include *Australian Short Stories* (1928), *Essays, Imaginative and Critical, From*

Australian Writers (1933, with J.D. Holmes) and *Poets of Australia* (1946). Other Mackaness publications of interest are *The Art of Book-Collecting in Australia* (1956), in which he records his experiences as a bibliophile; *The Books of the Bulletin: An Annotated Bibliography* (1955, in collaboration with Walter Stone), a record of the *Bulletin* books 1888–1952; and *Bibliomania: An Australian Book Collector's Essays* (1965).

MACKAY, ANGUS (1824–86), born Aberdeen, Scotland, was educated in Sydney and began a varied career as a journalist when he succeeded James Martin as editor of the *Atlas* in 1847. Subsequently he worked on the *People's Advocate* in Sydney, was a goldfields' correspondent for the *Empire* and the *Argus*, edited the *Bendigo Advertiser*, was proprietor of the *Riverine Herald*, foundation editor of the *Queenslander* and helped to found the Sydney *Daily Telegraph*. In 1868–77 and 1883–86 he was a member of the Victorian parliament, serving several terms as a minister. He was the author of *The Great Gold Field* (1853) and *A Visit to Sydney and the Cudgegong Diamond Mines* (1870).

McKAY, CLAUDE (1878–1972), was born at Kilmore, Victoria, where he began his journalistic career on the *Kilmore Advertiser*. In the next decade he was a journalist in Seymour, Melbourne, Warrnambool, Bendigo, Brisbane and Sydney before he became a publicist for a circus and, in 1908, a press agent, talent scout and house author for the theatrical entrepreneur, J.C. Williamson. In 1918, while seconded as a government war-loan publicist, he met Sir James Joynton Smith. With Smith and R.C. Packer, McKay founded *Smith's Weekly* (q.v.) and was its editor or editor-in-chief 1919–27 and 1939–50; he was also involved in the management of the *Daily Guardian*, which ran the first Miss Australia contest in 1926–27, and was managing director of *Smith's Weekly* briefly in the 1930s. With Harry Julius, McKay published *Theatrical Caricatures* (1912); he also wrote a book of memoirs, *This is the Life* (1961) and ghosted Joynton Smith's autobiography, *My Life Story* (1927).

MACKAY, JAMES ALEXANDER KENNETH (1850–1935), born Wallendbeen, NSW, was a member of the NSW Legislative Council and vice-president of the Executive Council 1899–1900, and a distinguished military officer, rising to the rank of major-general. He raised the Camden Light Horse in 1885, the first Australian volunteer horse regiment in 1897, commanded a contingent in the Boer War and served in several significant official

capacities during the First World War. He frequently contributed articles and verse to Australian newspapers; and published two novels, *Out Back* (1893) and *The Yellow Wave: A Romance of the Asiatic Invasion of Australia* (1895), and three collections of verse, *Stirrup Jingles from the Bush and the Turf* (1887), *A Bush Idyl* (1888) and *Songs of a Sunlit Land* (1908).

MACKELLAR, DOROTHEA (1885–1968), was born in Sydney into a well-established and wealthy family, and was educated privately and at the University of Sydney, acquiring a facility for languages which proved useful during her wide-ranging travel in Australia and overseas. At nineteen she wrote a poem (the second verse of which is probably the best-known stanza in Australian poetry) which was published in 1908 in the London *Spectator* as 'Core of My Heart'. When revised and published in her first book, *The Closed Door* (1911), it carried the title 'My Country' (q.v.), familiar to generations of Australian schoolchildren. Mackellar published three further volumes of poetry, *The Witch-Maid* (1914), *Dreamharbour* (1923) and *Fancy Dress* (1926), which confirm her delight in nature as well as her facility at verse translations, but for many Australians she remains the author of one famous poem. Before prolonged ill-health forced her largely to abandon writing in the middle 1920s she also wrote three novels, *The Little Blue Devil* (1912), *Outlaws' Luck* (1913), and *Two's Company* (1914), the first and last in collaboration with Ruth Bedford. Made OBE in 1968, she was for some years active in and patron of the English Association. A collection of her poetry was published in 1971 as *The Poems of Dorothea Mackellar*.

McKELLAR, JOHN (1881–?), born Greenock, Scotland, settled in Melbourne, where he worked as a journalist and developed connections with the Jindyworobak poets. He contributed to *Merringek*, and published a series of pamphlets 1946–54 to express his strong views on a range of subjects including conscription, evolution, Christianity and politics. He also published two novels, *Sheep without a Shepherd* (1937) and *Tree by the Creek* (1961), an imaginative account of the Burke and Wills' expedition of 1860–61 narrated by John King, the sole survivor, and originally an award-winning radio script. In 1951 some of McKellar's essays were collected as *Digging at Roots*.

McKELLAR, J.A.R. (JOHN ALEXANDER ROSS) (1904–32), born Dulwich Hill, Sydney, left school at fifteen to work in a bank. At a time when he was regarded as a poet of some potential, encouraged by such writers as Kenneth Slessor, Hugh McCrae and H.M. Green, and was also establishing a reputation as an athlete, McKellar died suddenly of pneumonia. He contributed poetry to the *New Triad* and published one collection in his lifetime, *Twenty-Six* (1932), selected by Kenneth Slessor. Some of his poems have appeared in anthologies but it was not until 1946 that his *Collected Poems* was published, edited by J.W. Gibbes; *Southerly* published a commemorative issue in 1944. A keen classical student, McKellar expressed his admiration for Greek literature in his choice of subject and style.

McKenzie, Barry, a film and comic-strip character created by Barry Humphries (q.v.) and the artist, Nicholas Garland, embarked on a series of adventures in the English satiric magazine, *Private Eye*, in 1963. An Australian innocent abroad, Barry, or 'Bazza' to his mates, was the stereotyped, uncultivated Australian in London, perpetually failing in his quest for 'sheilas' who would 'come across', but finding recompense in alcohol. Selections from the *Private Eye* strip, which ran until 1974, were published in 1968, 1971 and 1979, as were the scripts (?1973) of two McKenzie films, *The Adventures of Barry McKenzie* (1972) and *Barry McKenzie Holds His Own* (1974), written by Humphries and the film director, Bruce Beresford; both comic strip and film satirize the English as much as the Australians. The popularity of Barry McKenzie, which can be measured by the number of his phrases which have become part of Australian English (q.v.), helped focus attention on and discussion of the 'ocker' (q.v.) stereotype during the 1970s, when 'Bazza' was a generic term for such stereotypes. 'Bazzaland' also had a brief currency as a synonym for Australia.

MACKENZIE, DAVID a clergyman who visited Australia 1835–45 and 1848–52, published an account of his experiences, *Ten Years in Australia* (1851), which was an expansion of his *The Emigrant's Guide: Or, Ten Years' Practical Experience in Australia* (1845) and which proved popular with English readers especially after the discovery of gold. Mackenzie deals with a range of aspects of colonial life including the 'Literature of Botany Bay'. He also wrote *The Gold Digger: A Visit to the Goldfields of Australia in February 1852,* which was first published with the third edition of *Ten Years in Australia* in 1852.

MACKENZIE, KENNETH ('SEAFORTH') (1913–55), born Perth, was educated at Guildford Grammar School, Muresk Agricultural College and the University of WA. His periods of education were all incomplete: at sixteen he ran away from school and never returned, his stay at Muresk lasted a year, and he left university without taking a degree. After moving to Sydney in 1934 at the suggestion of Norman Lindsay, he tried journalism but his dislike of routine, combined with an increasing addiction to alcohol, made him an unreliable employee. He married Kathleen Bartlett, an art teacher, in 1934 and they had two children. In 1942 he was drafted into the army and served as a corporal attached to a compound of Italian prisoners at the POW camp at Cowra. A mass outbreak of Japanese prisoners there in 1944 was used by Mackenzie as the subject of his novel, *Dead Men Rising* (q.v.). After some time in an army hospital in 1945, he attempted to rejoin the civilian work-force but his handicaps persisted and the family was eventually forced to separate. During his last few years, Mackenzie lived on a very small property at Kurrajong owned by his wife, while she supported their children in Sydney by teaching sculpture. In 1955, during a visit to a friend at Goulburn, he drowned in a creek.

His novels, all first published under the pseudonym 'Seaforth' Mackenzie, include *The Young Desire It* (q.v., 1937), which won the Australian Literature Society's Gold Medal, *Chosen People* (1938), *Dead Men Rising* (1951) and *The Refuge* (1954). Two collections of poetry under the name Kenneth Mackenzie were published in his lifetime and two posthumously. They include *Our Earth* (1937, illustrated by Norman Lindsay), *The Moonlit Doorway* (1944), *Selected Poems* (1961, ed. Douglas Stewart) and *The Poems of Kenneth Mackenzie* (1972, ed. Evan Jones and Geoffrey Little). Several uncollected short stories were also published and he left manuscripts of others as well as radio plays and an uncompleted novel.

Preoccupations that persist in Mackenzie's distinctive fiction include alienation, discontinuity and obsessive parent–child relationships, although the success of his treatment of them varies. *The Young Desire It*, based on his experiences at school, attempts themes previously unexplored in Australian fiction. An intensely introspective account of a boy's experience of love, both homosexual and heterosexual, it shows a poet's sensitivity to experience and language. *Chosen People*, which includes two of the characters of the earlier novel though with a different narrative focus, is sophisticated and technically assured but lacks depth and authenticity of feeling. Although *Dead Men Rising* is a well-realized and varied work, it is uneven in tone and unequal to its potentially interesting subject. In *The Refuge*, narrator and protagonist are combined in the figure of the crime reporter, Lloyd Fitzherbert, who relives his relationship with his secret wife Irma and his eventual murder of her. Carefully crafted, the novel has a well-controlled narrative although there are some absurdities of plot and character.

Mackenzie's early poetry, with its penchant for romantic melodrama and vitalist themes, shows the influence of Norman Lindsay and Hugh McCrae. His second collection is marked by an unusually frank exploration of sexual relationships. Later, he began to write a more austere poetry which turns on the themes of pain, isolation, time, family relationships and death and which achieves, at its best, a controlled tranquillity and compassion. Among his finest pieces are those he wrote about his experiences in hospital, published for the first time in full in the 1972 collection.

McKERN, LEO (1920–), one of Australia's best-known actors, was born in Sydney and trained at first as an electrical engineer. A spell of two years in the army introduced him to amateur acting and in 1946 he left for London to try his luck on the West End stage. He has since appeared with many of the world's finest theatre companies, including the Old Vic and the Royal Shakespeare Company, playing a range of serious and comic parts. He has also acted in several outstanding films, including *Ryan's Daughter*, *A Man for All Seasons*, *Moll Flanders* and *The Mouse That Roared*, and as Rumpole in the popular BBC television series, *Rumpole of the Bailey*. In 1970–72 he spent twenty months in Australia and has appeared in numerous Australian stage productions. His autobiography, *Just Resting*, was published in 1983. He was made AO in 1983.

McKIE, RONALD (1909–), born Toowoomba, Queensland, was educated at the University of Queensland and worked as a journalist on various newspapers in Australia, Singapore and China. He served with the AIF in the Second World War before becoming a war correspondent in Burma and Italy; he later reported the Potsdam Conference in Berlin and the Quisling trial in Norway. As a journalist-writer he has published prolifically, e.g. documentary works such as *This Was Singapore* (1942), written after the Japanese capture of the city, *Malaysia in Focus* (1963), *The Company of Animals* (1965), *Bali* (1969) and *Singapore* (1972). His war writings include *Proud Echo* (1953), the story of the exploits of HMAS *Perth*; *The Heroes* (1960), the story of the little-known Rimau party, a group of twenty Australian and British servicemen who were beheaded by the Japanese for their raid on Japanese shipping in Singapore harbour; and

Echoes from Forgotten Wars (1980). His novels include *The Mango Tree* (1974, which won both the Miles Franklin and the Barbara Ramsden Awards), *The Crushing* (1977) and *Bitter Bread* (1978).

McKINLAY, JOHN (1819–72), born Sandbank, Scotland, emigrated to Australia in 1836. He was chosen by the SA parliament to lead a relief expedition in search of Burke and Wills in 1861 but did not leave until after the explorers had died at Cooper's Creek. In his expedition he completed the second south-north crossing of the continent and charted new territory. His *McKinlay's Journal of Exploration in the Interior of Australia (Burke Relief Expedition)* was published in 1862.

McKINNEY, JACK (1891–1966), born Melbourne, spent a large part of his life working as a freelance journalist and on the land as farmer, drover, shearer and jackeroo. He wrote short stories for the *Australian Journal* and other periodicals; a novel, *Crucible* (1935), which drew on his experiences of the First World War and won first prize for a work of fiction by a member of the armed forces; and several plays. Of these, *The Well*, published in *Khaki, Bush and Bigotry* (1968, ed. Eunice Hanger), was first produced in 1960 and won a minor play-writing prize; *Next Door*, included in *Australian One-Act Plays*, *Book I* (1962, ed. Eunice Hanger), is an adaptation of Act I of *The Well*. An experimental playwright, McKinney attempts to enliven the naturalistic, rural Australian play with expressionistic elements and an innovative approach to language. Interested also in philosophy, he published a brief exposition of his thinking, *The Challenge of Reason* (1950), which has been superseded by his longer work, *The Structure of Modern Thought* (1971). He was the husband of Judith Wright.

MACKLIN, ROBERT (1941–), born Brisbane, left school at sixteen to work as a jackeroo before joining the *Courier-Mail* as a cadet journalist. In 1964 he joined the *Age* and in 1967 became press secretary to the deputy prime minister, John McEwen. His next position as an information officer in Manila led to his directing, editing and narrating several documentary films on Asian countries. He published four popular novels, *The Queenslander* (1975), *The Paper Castle* (1977), *Newsfront* (1978) based on a screenplay by Bob Ellis, *The Journalist* (1979) adapted from a screenplay by Edna Wilson and Michael Thornhill; and has collaborated with Frank Galbally, a prominent lawyer, in a murder mystery, *Juryman* (1982). *The Queenslander* traces the history of a young man as he progresses from youth in suburban

447

Brisbane to life as a jackeroo in the Queensland outback and subsequently as a journalist and writer in Brisbane; *The Paper Castle*, set partly in Canberra, Queensland and Asia, deals with the world of politics and international affairs.

MACKY, STEWART brought up in NZ, graduated in medicine from the University of Melbourne and subsequently practised his profession in SA and Melbourne. A keen amateur actor, producer and playwright he was a friend of Vance Palmer and Louis Esson and an active member of the Pioneer Players, although his disillusionment with audience reactions and the demands of his profession made his contribution short-lived. His plays, 'John Blake' and *The Trap*, were produced in Melbourne in 1922 by the Players. Both draw upon Australia's convict past, *The Trap*, which is included in *Best Australian One-Act Plays* (1937) ed. William Moore and Tom Inglis Moore, being a dramatized version of a short story by 'Price Warung'. In the 1930s Macky spent some time in London. A cousin of W.J. Turner, he was friendly with Aldous Huxley, James Stephens and S.L. Koteliansky. His work with the Pioneer Players is described by Vance Palmer in his *Louis Esson and the Australian Theatre* (1948).

McLAREN, JACK (1887–1954), born Melbourne, the son of a puritanical Presbyterian clergyman, ran away from home at sixteen. After a year's wandering in the bush he became a cabin boy on a sailing vessel bound for South Africa. These early, severe experiences are graphically described in *Blood on the Deck* (1933), revised in 1947 with the title *My First Voyage*. He was subsequently mate on a timber schooner trading along the Queensland coast and tried a variety of occupations in the Pacific, northern Australia and New Guinea, before in 1911 settling on the west coast of the Cape York Peninsula where he established a coconut plantation. His account of his eight years on Cape York, *My Crowded Solitude* (1926), distinguished by his detailed observations of the area's natural life and including succinct descriptions of his hardships and achievements and more extended accounts of Aboriginal life, was popular both in England and overseas. During these years McLaren also began to contribute prose sketches to the *Bulletin*, often using the pseudonym 'Jack McNorth'. He moved to Melbourne in 1919 to work as a freelance writer, and subsequently settled in London where he eventually established a reputation. A familiar radio broadcaster in England, McLaren contributed articles and short stories to English, American and Australian magazines. He published three other autobio-

graphical travel books, *My Odyssey* (1923), which describes his experiences in Papua, Thursday Island and the Solomons, *My South Seas Adventures* (1936), and *My Civilized Adventure* (1952). He also wrote numerous short stories and novels, which are competent if undistinguished adventure stories or romances based on his experiences in northern Australia, the Pacific Islands and New Guinea. Generally sympathetic, if occasionally paternalistic, towards the indigenous peoples of these areas, McLaren interprets their way of life in his travel writings with sensitivity and even deference. His novels and short-story collections include *Red Mountain* (1919), *The White Witch* (1919), *The Skipper of the Roaring Meg* (1919), *The Savagery of Margaret Nestor* (1920), *The Oil Seekers* (1921), *Feathers of Heaven* (1921), *Fagaloa's Daughter* (1923), *Spear-Eye* (1925), *The Hidden Lagoon* (1926), *Isle of Escape* (1926), *The Sun Man* (1928), *A Diver Went Down* (1929), *The Money Stones* (1933), *The Devil of the Depths* (1935), *The Crystal Skull* (1936), *Their Isle of Desire* (1941), *The Marriage of Sandra* (1946), *Stories of Fear* (1946), *Stories of the South Seas* (1946) and *New Love for Old* (1948). Of these one of the most distinctive is *The Sun Man*, a romance set on Thursday Island, which includes some graphically-described diving scenes. McLaren's knowledge of diving also animates one of his best short stories 'A Diver Went Down'. In addition, he published a volume of verse, *Songs of a Fuzzy-top* (1926), the love story of a South Sea Islander; and *Gentlemen of the Empire* (1940), an account of the work of district commissioners, patrol officers and other officials in some of 'the British Empire's tropical outposts'.

MACLEAN, DONALD FINDLAY (1874–1937), born Hotspur, Victoria, left school at twelve and became a bush missionary at twenty, later entering the Baptist ministry. After serving as a padre in the First World War he travelled extensively, meanwhile contributing frequently to Australian magazines and newspapers. In 1927 he returned to Melbourne, where he worked in radio. Maclean published three novels, *The Man from Curdie's River* (1907), which deals with the career of a bush missionary in western Victoria; *John Scarlett, Ganger* (1912), an account of the adventures of a welfare worker among railway labourers; and *The Luck of the Gold Moidore* (1920), an adventure story concerning quests for gold in the sixteenth century, which was originally published as a serial in England with the title 'The Mahogany Ship'.

McLEAN, DONALD JAMES (1905–75), born Broken Hill, trained at Sydney Teachers' College and became one of Australia's foremost educationists. Headmaster of several government schools, he published three influential books on education, *The Education of the Personality* (1952), *Nature's Second Son* (1954), and *Children in Need* (1956), and edited a collection of essays on Australian educational policies, *It's People That Matter* (1969). Editor of all the publications of the NSW Department of Education in the 1960s, he was also educational correspondent for the *Sydney Morning Herald*, and one of the initiators of the ASA. Mclean also wrote three novels which draw upon his own and his family's experiences at Broken Hill and in outback NSW, *No Man Is An Island* (1955), *The Roaring Days* (1960), and *The World Turned Upside Down* (1962).

McLEOD, ALAN LINDSAY (1928–), born Sydney, was educated at the University of Sydney, where he edited the magazines, *Vesperis* and *Descant,* and has taught for many years in the USA. The author of numerous articles on Australian literature and of three collections of poetry, *The Change of Light* (1953), *Beyond the Cresting Surf* (1959) and *Chautauqua Canticles* (1962), he has also edited, with Richard Preston, *The Lincoln Anthology 1951* (1951), a selection of writing by young Australians including Lex Banning, Sylvia Lawson and Reba Ginsburg, and the essay collections, *The Commonwealth Pen* (1961) and *The Pattern of Australian Culture* (1963). McLeod has also edited *Australia Speaks* (1969), a selection of speeches, and an account of Walt Whitman's reputation in Australia and NZ (1964).

'MACLEOD, FIONA' see SHARP, WILLIAM

McLEOD, MARJORIE (1893–), was born Dimboola, Victoria. Founder of the Swan Hill National Theatre, of which she was director and producer for many years, she worked as a teacher of speech and as an actress and writer for ABC radio before moving to Swan Hill in 1946. Two of her plays were published in anthologies, *Travail* in *Eight Plays by Australians* (1934) and *Moonshine* in *Five Plays by Australians* (1936), and she also published *Within These Walls* (1948), a four-act historical play first produced in Melbourne in 1936, and *Four Period Plays* (1958). The last-named collection comprises *Within These Walls; Mine a Sad One*, which is based on an imaginary incident in the life of the explorer Robert O'Hara Burke and was first produced in 1956; *A Shillingsworth*, a study of a Melbourne family in the Depression, which was first produced in 1931 and won first prize in the Australian Literature Society competition; and *Horizons*, a study of the experience of New Australians in

the Murray River district, which was first produced in 1952. She has also published a poetry collection, *Verses from Swan Hill* (1946), which includes a verse-drama, 'The Enchanted Tryst'; and an account of her experience with the Swan Hill National Theatre, *All the World's a Stage* (1980).

MACLEOD, WILLIAM (1850–1929), born London of Scots descent, arrived in Australia in 1855. Like his stepfather, James Anderson, he became an artist, and established a reputation as a portrait painter, designer of stained glass, and illustrator for such journals as the *Sydney Mail* and the *Illustrated Sydney News*. He was a regular contributor to the *Bulletin* (q.v.) from its inception in 1880. Following the departure of W.H. Traill from the management of the journal in 1886, Macleod withdrew from his involvement with the *Picturesque Atlas of Australasia* and became managing director in 1887; he remained in that position until his retirement in 1927, retaining financial control of the *Bulletin* throughout the editorship of J.F. Archibald and his successors. The Archibald–Macleod partnership (1886–1903) presided over the most successful years of the *Bulletin*, and clearly Archibald benefited from Macleod's sound business sense. 'Without Archibald after Traill left there would have been no *Bulletin*', suggested A.G. Stephens, 'without Macleod, or some similar manager, there would have been no *Bulletin* long'. Macleod's career both as artist and *Bulletin* proprietor were enthusiastically sketched by his widow, Agnes Conor Macleod, in *Macleod of 'the Bulletin'* (1931).

McMAHON, GREGAN (1874–1941), actor and theatrical producer, was born in Sydney and in 1896 graduated from the University of Sydney. A member of the Sydney University Dramatic Society, McMahon also performed in amateur theatre, and in 1900 decided to leave the firm of solicitors for which he was working to join Robert Brough's comedy company. In 1911 he established the Melbourne Repertory Theatre Society, formed mainly of well-trained amateurs. Notwithstanding its lack of a permanent theatre, the Society produced a range of avant-garde international plays, as well as plays by Australian writers such as Louis Esson, William Moore, Blamire Young, Arthur Adams, Helen Simpson and Alfred Buchanan. In 1917, when the effects of the war were clearly restricting the activities of the Society, McMahon accepted a professional engagement in Sydney with the Tait brothers, who had taken over the J.C. Williamson firm. Still committed to the idea of an alternative theatre, McMahon was able to use his position with J.C. Williamson's to establish, with the backing of the Tait brothers, the Sydney Repertory Theatre Society. Australian playwrights were inactive during this period and McMahon, though sympathetic to Australian drama, produced only four Australian plays between 1920 and 1927 and these were by obscure playwrights. In 1926, after the Taits purchased the Comedy Theatre in Melbourne, it was agreed that McMahon should produce three months of repertory theatre there each year with the Melbourne Society. Financial losses in 1928, however, led the Taits to impose economic restrictions on the societies, which both failed to accept. McMahon continued to produce plays for the Taits as director of a semi-professional society in both Sydney and Melbourne and in 1930 formed the group known as the Gregan McMahon Players. Backed by a series of theatrical entrepreneurs, the group included some able actors, the most brilliant being Coral Browne, and continued to stage at least eight productions a year until McMahon's death. Producing plays by such writers as Shaw, Chekhov, Ibsen, Galsworthy and Pirandello, McMahon provided an alternative, serious theatre for thirty years at a time when Australia was culturally isolated and its entertainment industry was dominated by foreign stars and commercially successful, internationally popular productions. He was made CBE in 1938. His personality and work have been recorded by two of his ex-students, Doris Fitton in her autobiography, *Not Without Dust & Heat* (1981), and Hal Porter in *The Watcher on the Cast-Iron Balcony* (1963).

McMASTER, RHYLL (1947–), born Brisbane, has published some short stories but is best known as a poet. Her verse, which appeared in anthologies and in most Australian newspapers and literary magazines, has also been published in *The Brineshrimp* (1972). In 1971 she was awarded the Harri Jones Memorial Prize by the University of Newcastle. A poet who frequently experiments with language to gain her individual effects, McMaster combines close observation of external detail with an ability to express its strangeness and mystery. She is married to the writer, Roger McDonald (q.v.).

McMILLAN, ROBERT (1862–1929), born Edinburgh, came to Australia in 1893 and worked as a freelance journalist before editing the *Stock and Station Journal* until 1917, when he was appointed editor of the *Grazier*. One of the foundation members of the New South Wales Institute of Journalists, he was its first secretary. His column 'Science Gossip', under the pseudonym 'Gossip', was very popular with country readers and was partly republished in

his *Science Gossip for Young and Old* (1907). He also wrote a series of popular books on such subjects as philosophy, religion and science, including *Origin of the World* (1913), *The Story of a Microscope* (1914), *No Breakfast* (1905) and *Why We Do It* (1919); an account of his travels, *There and Back* (1903); a novel for young people, *The Voyage of the Monsoon* (1900); and three collections of prose pieces, *Australian Gossip and Story* by 'Globetrotter' (1895), *Unsuccessful Competitors* (1897) and *Cities of the War* (1917).

McNALLY, WARD (1917–), born NZ as Clifford Douglas Keane, had an exceptionally deprived childhood. After running away from home at thirteen, he had some success as a boxer before he was convicted of housebreaking and sentenced to imprisonment. In 1950 he came to Australia, where he has travelled widely, working mainly as a journalist. Editor of the *Centralian Advocate* in Alice Springs and some Queensland newspapers in the late 1960s, he also spent some time in Fiji, where he edited the *Fiji Times* and the *Herald*. A passionate advocate of the Aboriginal cause, McNally has written two books about their treatment by white society, *Goodbye Dreamtime* (1973) and *The Angry Australians* (1974). He has also written two descriptive accounts of Australia, *Australia, the Challenging Land* (1965) and *Australia, the Waking Giant* (1969); two biographies of Sir Charles Kingsford-Smith, *Smithy* (1966) and *The Man on the Twenty-dollar Note* (1976); an account of mining in Broken Hill, *To Broken Hill and Back* (1975); two frank autobiographies which have aroused the interest of sociologists and social historians, *Cry of a Man Running* (1968) and *Man from Zero* (1973); a pseudo-autobiographical novel for the late teenager about a boy's depressed childhood in Sydney, *Supper at Happy Harry's* (1982); and a biography of T.G. Strehlow, *Aborigines, Artefacts and Anguish* (1981).

MACNAMARA, FRANCIS (1811–?), a convict who was probably the writer best known as 'Frank the Poet' and also as Francis Goddard, was born in Ireland and transported to NSW in 1832. His original offence was stealing but he may, in addition, have been a political agitator. Certainly he was a recalcitrant during his first decade in Australia: he absconded several times, suffered numerous floggings and other punishments, and served extended terms as a member of a chain gang. In 1839, while employed as a shepherd with the Australian Agricultural Company, he composed 'A Convict's Tour to Hell' (q.v.), an anti-authoritarian satire which passed into oral tradition. In 1842 MacNamara was sent to Port Arthur, where his conduct improved to the point where he was given a ticket-of-leave in 1847 and his freedom in 1849. Known as a composer of cheeky extempore verse, he reputedly farewelled the audience which had come to see him off at Launceston with the verse, which exists in several versions:

Land of Lags and Kangaroo,
Of 'possum and the scarce Emu,
The farmer's pride but the prisoner's Hell
Land of Buggers [Bums] Fare-thee-well!

MacNamara's movements after leaving Tasmania are largely unknown, although John Meredith and Rex Whalan in *Frank the Poet* (1979), who first linked 'Frank the Poet' with the Francis MacNamara transported in 1832, suggest he may have been 'the Poet', a balladeer living in a Melbourne doss-house whom Marcus Clarke wrote about in 1868. Among the other poems associated with 'Frank the Poet', who appears as a character in Michael Boddy's play 'Cash' (1972), are a ballad about Bold Jack Donohoe and the convict laments, 'Labouring with the Hoe', which shows the influence of Robert Burns, and 'The Convict's Arrival', known also as 'Moreton Bay' (q.v.).

McNEIL, JIM (1935–82), born Melbourne, began to write plays while in Parramatta gaol where, since 1967, he had been serving a lengthy sentence for armed robbery and wounding a policeman. A member of the Resurgents Discussion and Debating Society at Parramatta, McNeil took part in weekly drama workshops. One of his first plays, *The Chocolate Frog* (1973), written to communicate the realities of prison life to outsiders, was first publicly performed in 1971 and has been frequently staged since. Another, originally titled, 'The Last Cuppa', was reworked by McNeil, was first given a professional performance in 1972 with the title *The Old Familiar Juice* and was published in 1973 with *The Chocolate Frog*. In 1974, while still imprisoned, McNeil won a grant from the Australian Council for the Arts. He was released in 1975, married for the second time (to the actress, Robyn Nevin), but was unable to cope with the pressures of outside life and died of alcoholism. His third play, *How Does Your Garden Grow* (1974), is his most complex and won the Awgie Award for the best script of 1975; 'Jack' (1977), his last, is a less coherently-developed piece.

McNeil's plays, especially 'Jack', deal realistically with the violent, sordid aspects of prison life, but a quiet form of comedy, both verbal and situational, is their most memorable quality. Particularly striking is his ability to give his claustrophobic, unnatural world a universal, natural dimension and to recreate the monotonous triviality of prison existence while investing it with significance, humour and even tenderness.

McNICOL, DAVID (1914–   ), born Geelong, Victoria, and one of Australia's best-known journalists, began his career as a cadet on the staff of the *Sydney Morning Herald*. A war correspondent during the Second World War, he covered the campaigns in the Middle East and the invasion of Normandy. He was special correspondent 1945–54 for the Sydney *Daily Telegraph* to which he contributed the front-page column 'Town Talk', and was editor-in-chief of Sir Frank Packer's newspaper empire 1953–72. He has published two volumes of verse, *Air Mail Palestine* (1943, see War Literature) and *The Round Dozen* (1947); and a volume of memoirs, *Luck's a Fortune* (1979), in which he draws on his familiarity with prominent politicians and his memories of Packer.

'McNORTH, JACK', see **McLAREN, JACK**

Macomo, see **Aboriginal in Australian Literature; *Fifty Years Ago***

MACONOCHIE, ALEXANDER (1787–1860), born Edinburgh, Scotland, had a career in the Royal Navy and was the first professor of geography at the University of London before going to Hobart Town in 1836 as private secretary to the lieutenant-governor, Sir John Franklin. In 1838 he wrote a condemnation of the convict system, *Report on the State of Prison Discipline in Van Diemen's Land*, as a result of which he was dismissed from his position but was later appointed superintendent of the Norfolk Island penal settlement in 1840. In his four-year period of office he implemented enlightened penal theories which are expounded in *Crime and Punishment* (1846), which led to his recall by Governor Gipps; subsequently he was governor of Birmingham prison and is presented sympathetically in this role as O'Connor in Charles Reade's novel, *It Is Never Too Late to Mend* (1856). Alexander Harris's novel, *The Emigrant Family,* published in 1849 just after Maconochie's period on Norfolk Island, was dedicated to him 'in testimony of the soundness of the principles he has endeavoured to introduce into penal discipline'. He is the subject of J.V. Barry's *Alexander Maconochie of Norfolk Island* (1958) and appears in several 'Price Warung' stories, notably 'Captain Maconochie's "Bounty for Crime"' and 'Secret Society of the Ring'.

McPHERSON, ALPIN (1842–95), better known as the bushranger (q.v.) 'The Wild

Scotchman', was born in Inverness-shire, Scotland, and emigrated with his family to Moreton Bay in 1855. The only Queensland bushranger of note, he was active in 1865–66 before his imprisonment on St Helena Island, Moreton Bay. After his release in 1874 he worked as a stockman and station overseer and came into contact with Sylvester Browne, who is alleged to have passed on McPherson's story, which he was fond of telling, to his brother 'Rolf Boldrewood' (q.v.) for use in the celebrated bushranging novel, *Robbery Under Arms* (1888); the bushranging incidents in the novel, however, are drawn from the careers of several other bushrangers. An ineffective lawbreaker, one of the few bushrangers to have been actually wounded by the notoriously incompetent policeman, Sir Frederick Pottinger, and first captured while reading quietly by the Lachlan River, McPherson is the subject of P.W. McNally's *The Life and Adventures of the Wild Scotchman* (1899) and P.H. McCarthy's *The Wild Scotsman* (1975).

MACQUARIE, ELIZABETH (1778–1835), the daughter of John Campbell of Airds, Scotland, was the second wife of Governor Lachlan Macquarie, and accompanied him to the colony of NSW in 1809. The journey is recorded in her lively journal, 'Diary of Journey from England to New South Wales 1809'. A loyal supporter of her husband in the various faction fights into which he was drawn, she also took an interest in the welfare of women convicts and the Aborigines. Her knowledge of architecture was also of use to her husband's architect, Francis Greenway. After leaving Australia in 1822, she and her husband settled in England on the Macquarie estate at Jarvisfield, although Macquarie had not long to live. His last days in 1824 are recorded in Elizabeth's letters to her friends in NSW (1825). Her life is described in Marjorie Barnard's *Macquarie's World* (1941), Malcolm Ellis's *Lachlan Macquarie* (1947) and in Lysbeth Cohen's *Elizabeth Macquarie* (1979). She also appears as a character in Eleanor Dark's historical novel, *No Barrier* (1953). Her name has been applied to various natural and man-made features of Sydney, one of which is Mrs Macquarie's Chair overlooking Sydney Harbour.

MACQUARIE, LACHLAN (1762–1824), born Ulva in the Scottish Hebrides, had, prior to his appointment as governor of the colony of NSW, seen army service in Canada, America, India and Egypt. One of the Colony's longest serving (1809–21) and most successful governors, Macquarie largely healed the rift caused by the John Macarthur–Governor William Bligh disputes, expanded the settlement by

systematic exploration, instituted an energetic public works programme, promoted cultural and civil amenities, developed education, treated the Aborigines humanely and introduced a policy of enlightened treatment of the emancipists. The last policy produced friction with the 'exclusives' ('pure merinos') of the Colony and was a significant cause of the Bigge (q.v.) enquiry. True to his own prediction that 'my name will not be readily forgotten' Macquarie has been commemorated in Australia by streets, towns, ports, harbours, islands, rivers, lakes and a university named in his honour. M.H. Ellis wrote the biography, *Lachlan Macquarie: His Life, Adventures and Times* (1947). Marjorie Barnard wrote *Macquarie's World* (1941) and Anthony Hewison edited *The Macquarie Decade* (1972). Macquarie's *Journals of His Tours in New South Wales and Van Diemen's Land 1810–1822* was published in 1956. He is the major character in Alexander Buzo's play, *Macquarie* (1971) and also appears as a character in the novels, *The Rebel of the Bush* (1914) by John Sandes, *Sally: The Tale of a Currency Lass* (1918) by J.H.M. Abbott and *No Barrier* (1953) by Eleanor Dark.

Macquarie, see **BUZO, ALEXANDER**

Macquarie Harbour, on Tasmania's west coast, was named after Governor Lachlan Macquarie and was the site of a notorious penal settlement 1822–33. It figures prominently in much convict literature, e.g. *His Natural Life* (1874), and is the subject of Rex Ingamells's poem 'Macquarie Harbour'.

McQUEEN, HUMPHREY (1942–), born and educated in Queensland, has taught history at secondary and tertiary level. A member of the Labor Party early in his career, he became disillusioned with parliamentary socialism and in 1968 was appointed chairman of the Revolutionary Socialists in Melbourne. His *A New Britannia : An Argument Concerning the Social Origins of Australian Radicalism and Nationalism* (1970), is a 'new left' history, an analysis of the effects of the Protestant-capitalist ethos on Australian society. Particularly critical of the myths of egalitarianism and mateship, the history drew a series of strong reviews including responses from other interpreters of Australia's cultural history, such as Arthur Phillips and Russel Ward. McQueen has also published an account of racism in Australian society, *Aborigines, Race and Racism* (1974); a provocative assessment of the media, *Australia's Media Monopolies* (1977); an alternative social history from the 1890s, which includes accounts of the treatment of the Aborigines, migrants, the unemployed and women, *Social Sketches of Australia 1888–1975* (1977); an account of the emergence of modernist painting in Australia, which also deals with the Ern Malley hoax and the links between modernist art and literature, *The Black Swan of Trespass* (1979); and a study of Australia's economic past and its implications for the future, *Gone Tomorrow : Australia in the 80s* (1982).

McQUEEN, JAMES (1934–   ), born Tasmania, has worked at a variety of occupations including ship's cook, fruit-picker, weatherman on Macquarie Island and window-dresser. He studied at the National Art School, Sydney, and completed a four-year course in accountancy, but at the age of forty returned to Tasmania to grow orchids. Although he did not begin writing until 1974, he has won several awards and short story competitions. He has published two novels, *A Just Equinox* (1980), the story of an artist divided by the demands of art and alcohol; and *Hook's Mountain* (1982), a study of a man's destruction by conflicting passions, by the need to preserve the mountain wilderness which is his home and by homicidal impulses deriving from his military past. He has also published three collections of short fiction which vary widely in subject and tone, *The Electric Beach* (1978) *The Escape Machine* (1981) and *Uphill Runner* (1984).

MADIGAN, C.T. (CECIL THOMAS) (1889–1947), geologist and explorer, was born at Renmark, SA, and educated at the University of Adelaide where he won distinction. After accompanying Douglas Mawson on the Australasian Antarctic Expedition 1911–14, Madigan served in the Royal Engineers in the First World War, pursued further study in natural science at Oxford as a Rhodes scholar and served in the Sudan civil service 1920–22. In 1922 he was appointed senior lecturer in geology at the University of Adelaide. He began geological investigations of Central Australia in 1927, making various expeditions into the area in the 1930s, and in 1939 led the first scientific expedition across the Simpson Desert. His account of the expedition, *Crossing the Dead Heart* (1946), understated, deliberately unsensational but nevertheless vivid and enlivened by his knowledge of human nature, has maintained its popularity. An earlier book, *Central Australia* (1936), includes accounts of his journeys up to 1932. President of the Royal Society of South Australia in 1936 and of the geographical section of ANZAAS in 1937, Madison received the Murchison Grant of the Royal Geographical Society in 1941. He served in the Second World War 1940–42.

Magic Pudding, The, an outstandingly popular novel for children by Norman Lindsay (q.v.), was first published in 1918 and is frequently compared in its appeal to Lewis Carroll's *Alice in Wonderland*. The plot relates to misadventures of three friends, Bunyip Bluegum, Bill Barnacle and Sam Sawnoff, in their efforts to save their magic pudding from two professional Puddin' thieves, Watkin Wombat and Possum. The pudding, which plays a vocal but passive part in the story, has a variety of flavours and an endless life. After a series of comic encounters, the friends elude their enemies by coming to the end of the story and settle down at the home of Benjamin Brandysnap, an elderly dog and market-gardener. The narrative is enlivened by Lindsay's distinctive illustrations and comic verse; the verse was separately published as *Puddin' Poems* (1977).

MAGOFFIN, RICHARD (1937–   ), known as 'The Boredrain Balladist', is a writer of bush verse, songs and yarns and is well known in outback Queensland for his recitations. He is the author of the often-reprinted *We Bushies* (1968); *Chops and Gravy* (1972), *Fair Dinkum Matilda* (1973), which is an important contribution to Waltzing Matilda (q.v.) literature, *Down Another Track* (1983) and *Waltzing Matilda : Song of Australia* (1983).

Magpie, one of Australia's best-known and most prolific birds, belongs to the crowshrike family. It is especially notable for its melodious carolling, particularly at dawn and dusk, and for its aggression, dive-bombing or swooping on unsuspecting humans in the nesting season. Its name has been adopted by football teams that wear the bird's black and white colours, e.g. Collingwood in Melbourne. The bird's sturdy personality is well expressed in James McAuley's poem 'Magpie' and Judith Wright's 'Magpies'. As part of the typical Australian scene it is mentioned in Judith Wright's poem 'Old House' and James Lister Cuthbertson's 'The Australian Sunrise'. *Magpie* is the title of the short-lived weekly periodical published in Melbourne 1865–66.

Mahony Family, see 'RICHARDSON, HENRY HANDEL'; *Fortunes of Richard Mahony, The*

MAHONY, FRANK (1862–1916), born Melbourne, went with his parents to Sydney at the age of ten. He worked in an architect's office after leaving school, but in the 1890s became established as a black-and-white illustrator and watercolour artist for the *Bulletin*, the *Sydney Mail*, the *Antipodean* and other journals. He gained a reputation for his bush subjects, notably horses and swagmen; his portrait of Henry Lawson 'on the wallaby' became the frontispiece of Lawson's *In the Days When the World Was Wide* (1896). Mahony also illustrated Lawson's *While the Billy Boils* (1896), the works of A.B. Paterson and Ethel Pedley's *Dot and the Kangaroo* (1899); he was one of the Heptarchs of the Dawn and Dusk Club, his job being to predict, through paint, the winner of the Melbourne Cup. He was an instructor for the Art Society of NSW before his departure for England in 1904; in later years he was a contributor to the *Lone Hand*.

MAIDEN, JENNIFER (1949–), born Penrith, NSW, left school in her early teens and worked in a variety of casual jobs before returning to private study to obtain matriculation. She graduated in 1974 from Macquarie University, Sydney, and has since been a professional writer and a tutor in creative writing. She has published six collections of poetry: *Tactics* (1974); *The Problem of Evil* (1975), the long title-work a protest against the idea that poetry and prose are mutually exclusive in theme; *The Occupying Forces* (1975), a series of poems integrated by the normal experiences and preoccupations of life; *Birthstones* (1978), structurally based on introductory poems related to each month's particular precious or semi-precious stone; *The Border Loss* (1979), more personal in tone and attitude than her earlier works; and *For the Left Hand*, which comprised a special issue in 1981 of *Poetry Australia*. She has also published *Mortal Details* (1977), a collection of poetry and two short stories; *The Terms* (1982), a novel; and a major collection of poetry and prose, *The Warm Thing* (1983). Much of Jennifer Maiden's poetry is an attempt to analyse life and self in language stretched to its shadowiest subtleties and complicated by obscure and sometimes inscrutable associations. At its best, however, her remarkable sensitivity to language enables her to explore the deepest core of experience. Her prolific output in less than a decade has taken her from one of a coterie of promising literary *ingénues* to an assured and mature writer who moves with skill and certainty in both prose and verse.

MAITLAND, EDWARD (1824–97), born Ipswich, England, was educated at Cambridge and destined for the church, but suffered a crisis of faith and left England for Mexico, California and Australia in 1849. Appointed commissioner of crown lands and police magistrate at Wellington, NSW, in 1854, he married a year later the granddaughter of the explorer, W.H. Hovell. President of the Goul-

burn School of Arts, which he helped to found, Maitland propounded the casting off of colonial ties and attitudes in his lectures. In 1858 he left for England after delivering a lecture published as *The Meaning of the Age* (1858). In England he wrote several novels which draw partly on his Australian experience. *The Pilgrim and the Shrine* (1867?) gives vent to his political and spiritual ideas as well as providing pictures of life on the Australian goldfields. One of the novel's characters, Captain Travers, is based on Hovell, and another, Mary, on Mary Woolley, the wife of John Woolley; John Woolley is also mentioned by name. Mary Woolley is also the basis of the heroine of his next novel, *The Higher Law* (1870). His subsequent fiction was more mystical and psychological, anticipating in some respects the views of C.G. Jung. *By and By* (1873) is particularly speculative, expressive of Maitland's radical ideas on a range of social institutions. Although Maitland acquired a reputation as a writer, mainly for the *Spectator* and the *Examiner*, his friendship with the feminist and spiritualist Dr Anna Kingsford and his own spiritualist ideas aroused suspicion, hostility and ridicule. His reputation was irretrievably damaged by his book, *England and Islam* (1877), a passionate attempt to expose the dangers of materialism in politics and science. In (?1896) he published a two-volume work, *Anna Kingsford*, which was to have an important influence on C.J. Brennan. Other works which were influential amongst those sympathetic to his views were *The Keys of the Creeds* (1875), *The Soul and How It Found Me* (1877) and, with Anna Kingsford, *The Perfect Way* (1882). Maitland's exploration of spiritualism and psychic phenomena stimulated or coincided with similar explorations in Australia, reflected particularly in the linked interests of such figures as C.J. Brennan, Alfred Deakin, John le Gay Brereton, Dowell O'Reilly and John Woolley.

Makar, a magazine of new writing published by Makar Press, ran 1960–80, edited successively by Graham Rowlands, Martin Duwell and Rodney Wissler. It began as the quarterly magazine of the English Society of the University of Queensland, its title using the Middle Scots form of the word 'maker', meaning poet. In 1972 one of the quarterly editions was replaced by three small books of verse which inaugurated the Gargoyle Poets series, the name deriving from the University of Queensland's gargoyles, four of which had been depicted on *Makar*'s covers. With Martin Duwell as general editor, the Gargoyle Poets series included works by Graham Rowlands, Alan Wearne, Richard Packer, Peter Annand, Antigone Kefala, Rae Desmond Jones, Kris Hemensley, Graeme Curtis, John Griffin, Stephanie Bennett, Eric Beach, Carol Novack, John Tranter, Shelton Lea, Philip Neilsen and Jennifer Maiden. *Makar* also conducted a series of interviews with significant contemporary writers; some of those interviews (and others unpublished in the journal) were incorporated into *A Possible Contemporary Poetry* (1982) edited by Duwell.

Mallee, an Aboriginal term, is applied to scrub and certain low-growing eucalypts which are found in low-rainfall areas of southern Australia, especially in north-western Victoria. The term, which seems to have come into use in the late 1840s, was given official sanction in 1883 in the *Mallee Pastoral Leases Act of Victoria.* Certain animals and birds natural to this sort of environment have also acquired the name, e.g. mallee fowl, mallee hen and mallee kangaroo. The term 'mallee' is used colloquially to denote an area far from civilization, as in the expression 'take to the mallee', i.e. go out into the remote areas of the bush; 'fit as a mallee bull' is a common expression denoting good health and virility, usually through hard physical work and tough conditions. The best-known part of the mallee scrub is its large underground root system, renowned for its burning qualities in an open fireplace; C.H. Souter's poem, 'The Mallee Fire' praises these qualities.

The mallee country is the setting of several novels, including Patricia Stonehouse's *The Years of Forgetting* (1914), John Truran's *Green Mallee* (1932), Benjamin Cozens's *The Princess of the Mallee* (1903), Roy Bridges's *Merchandise* (1918) and Catherine Martin's *An Australian Girl* (1890), but the life of the area is best commemorated in the ballads of C.H. Souter, one of whose collections is titled *The Mallee Fire* (1923). The poet John Shaw Neilson spent his early manhood in the Mallee; in his autobiography he tells of an existence of poverty and misery accentuated by the severe climate, dust storms, rabbit plagues, droughts and the long desperate wait for a cash crop.

Malone, Scobie, see **CLEARY, JON**

MALOUF, DAVID (1934–), born Brisbane of Lebanese and English parents, was educated at the University of Queensland. He lived in Europe 1959–68, and worked for a time as a relief teacher in London before taking up a permanent teaching position at Birkenhead. He taught English at the University of Sydney 1968–77, but now devotes himself to full-time writing, living partly in Australia and partly in southern Tuscany. Well known as a poet, Malouf has published six volumes of

verse, *Bicycle and Other Poems* (1970), published in New York with the title, *The Year of the Foxes and Other Poems* (1979), *Neighbours in a Thicket* (1974), *Poems 1975–76* (1976), *Wild Lemons* (1980), *First Things Last* (1980) and *Selected Poems* (1980). He has also written two novels, *Johnno* (q.v., 1975) and *An Imaginary Life* (q.v., 1978); and four novellas, *Child's Play*, which was first published in 1981 with *Fly Away Peter* (titled here *The Bread of Time to Come*) and republished in 1982 with two other novellas, *The Prowler* and *Eustace.* The retitled *Fly Away Peter* was also published separately in 1982. Malouf also contributed verse to the collection *Four Poets* (1962) and has edited an anthology of Australian verse, *Gesture of a Hand* (1975) and, with others, *We Took Their Orders and Are Dead* (1975). He has also contributed to the collection *New Currents in Australian Writing* (1978), and is the author of the libretto of Richard Meale's opera, *Voss*, which is based on Patrick White's novel.

An exceptionally diverse writer, Malouf is concerned with certain fundamental, consistent and unifying themes: the relationships between past and present, continuity and change, animal and human, and the role of language as a mediator of experience. Drawn by the force of his own early experience, and regional in his preoccupations in that much of his poetry and fiction recreates his childhood in Brisbane, Malouf is nevertheless thoroughly European in his interests and attitudes. *Johnno*, his most outwardly autobiographical novel, which has been much praised as a realistic presentation of wartime Brisbane, has been followed by the ostensibly different *An Imaginary Life*. A meditative book close to a prose poem and dealing with the last years of Ovid, the Roman poet, in exile on the shores of the Black Sea and his strangely-maturing relationship with a wolf-child, *An Imaginary Life* narrates an inner history whereas *Johnno* is ostensibly more concerned with outer change. In *An Imaginary Life* Roman sophistication is confronted with primitive animality and for Ovid the confrontation results in a subtle dying into life. *Child's Play,* an apparently factual and even documentary account of the experience of an Italian terrorist bent on perfecting his assassin's task, has again an inward, poetically-suggestive direction. As the assassin meticulously studies his victim, a great writer, he gradually comes to see himself as mysteriously linked to his victim, an organic part of the great man's work and the inevitable agent of his life's conclusion. Personal time is overtaken by an objective, impersonally-shaping time, which finally rushes both assassin and victim towards their predestined 'event'. *The Prowler* is a comically-orchestrated foray into the sexual repressions and fantasies of the suburbs; *Eustace* is a more chilling account of innocence confronted with a dangerous stranger. *Fly Away Peter*, set in Queensland before the First World War, is the compressed but subtly-worked account of crucial events in the life of Jim Saddler, a dedicated bird-watcher, who becomes drawn into the war. In Queensland, Saddler's life enriches those of Ashley Crowther, his employer, and Imogen Harcourt, an eccentric English photographer. The idyllic, life-affirming landscape of a Queensland swampland contrasts with the nightmarish, destructive horror of the trenches, and both experiences are present in Imogen's final transcendent vision of all life, anonymous or notable, as having integrity, dignity and a unique presence. Malouf's verse has an individual, polished style, distinguished by arresting images and an urbane, dispassionate tone. As in his prose work, childhood experience and the rediscovery of European roots are revealed as powerful creative forces. He has won several awards, including the Grace Leven Prize, the Foundation for Australian Literary Studies Award and the Australian Literature Society's Gold Medal for *Neighbours in a Thicket;* the NSW Premier's Literary Award for *An Imaginary Life;* the *Age* Book of the Year Award for 1982 for *Fly Away Peter;* and the Australian Literature Society's (now ASAL's) Gold Medal in 1983 for *Child's Play* and *Fly Away Peter.*

Maluka, The see *We of the Never-Never*

Man, a monthly magazine which was published in Sydney but circulated widely in Australia, began publication in 1936; modelled on *Esquire*, its arrival reflected the increasing Americanization of Australian society. In its early years it had a strong literary component: as 'Gilbert Anstruther', Russel Clarke was its literary editor, Ion Idriess edited its 'Australiana' section, and its contributors included J.H.M. Abbott, Frank Clune, Vance Palmer, Ruth Park, P.R. Stephensen, Dal Stivens and E.V. Timms. After the Second World War and particularly from the 1950s, it became primarily a 'girlie' magazine but failed to withstand the competition from more explicit magazines such as *Playboy* and *Penthouse* and ceased publication in 1974.

'Man from Ironbark, The' one of A.B. Paterson's most humorous ballads, was published in the *Bulletin* (December 1892). A city barber, who pretends to cut the throat of the man from Ironbark, gets more than he bargains for when the bushman, holding his throat to 'save his vital spark', wrecks the barber's shop. In Ironbark the oft-told story reinforces traditional bush suspicion of the city and leads to a pronounced fashion in beards.

'Man from Snowy River, The', first published in the *Bulletin* (April 1890), is the title poem of A.B. Paterson's (q.v.) first collection, *The Man from Snowy River and Other Verses* (1895), the most successful volume of poetry ever published in Australia. Other well-known Paterson poems in the collection include 'Clancy of the Overflow', 'The Man from Ironbark', 'A Bush Christening' and 'The Travelling Post Office'. Paterson's story of the Snowy River poem's origin is that it was not based on a specific event but was written to describe the cleaning up of wild horses in his district. Wanting to create a character who could ride better than anybody else he 'naturally' chose a man from the Snowy mounted on a typical horse of the district, a half-thoroughbred mountain pony. Various names have been suggested down the years in an attempt to identify the original Man from Snowy River; they include Jim Troy, Jack Riley, whose grave in the Corryong cemetery has a tablet naming him as Paterson's character, Owen Cummins, Jim Spencer, Jack Clarke and Lachie Cochrane. Probably Australia's most famous poem, 'The Man from Snowy River' tells of a hectic chase after the valuable colt from 'Old Regret' who had broken out of his station yard and joined the wild bush horses. A select band of horsemen gather at the homestead to take part in the chase; among them is 'a stripling on a small and weedy beast' who is at first excluded but is finally allowed to join the hunt because Clancy of the Overflow indicates that he and his horse come from the Snowy River country, a sure sign of courage and skill. The wild horses flee to the shelter of the mountains and when the pursuing riders fail to turn them before they reach the summit of the first mountain, the colt's owner angrily stops the chase, declaring 'We may bid the mob good day/No man can hold them down the other side'. The Man from Snowy River has other ideas. At breakneck speed he gallops his horse down the steep mountain side, runs the mob relentlessly until 'cowed and beaten' they are brought back singlehandedly by him to the station. Around the hills of Kosciusko the ride becomes a legend; with its combination of courage, daredevilry and horsemanship, qualities much prized in rural Australia from pioneer times, the ride has also become part of Australian legend. A highly-successful Australian film was shown in 1982.

Man Hamilton, The, see **PALMER, VANCE; Aboriginal in Australian Literature**

Man in the Silo, The, see SCHLUNKE, E.O.

Man-shy, a novel by Frank Dalby Davison (q.v.), first serialized in *Australia* 1923–25 and published in a cheap, home-bound edition by his father, Frederick Davison, in 1931, won the Australian Literature Society's Gold Medal and has been frequently republished. Written from the perspective of a wild red heifer, the novel describes her life and that of outback 'scrubber' cattle in general. Although the heifer successfully and courageously resists several attempts to take or kill her, the fast approach of civilization spells doom for her kind and at the end freedom for her also means death. The simple story, told with restrained lyricism, reflects Davison's belief in the power of the spirit to surmount physical defeat.

Man Who Loved Children, The, a novel by Christina Stead (q.v.), was published in 1940. Set in Baltimore and Annapolis in the USA of the 1930s, the novel nevertheless draws on the author's childhood memories of Sydney. The title ironically refers to Sam Pollit, a compelling portrait of a complacent, egocentric, infantile adult, whose optimistic humanitarianism and cheerful *bonhomie* mask his tyrannical, self-righteous, self-deceptive motives. Opposed to him are his second wife Henrietta or Henny and, increasingly as the novel develops, his daughter by his first marriage, Louisa. The other members of the Pollit family include six younger children and, in the background, a diverse group of relatives. As Henny and Sam (temperamental opposites in that she lives in the real as much as he in the ideal) foster their mutual hatred, the children tenaciously survive as uneasy subjects and shifting allies in the struggle. The development of Louisa's understanding of the situation and her final rejection of Sam provides the story's main movement, although the family's external fortunes also progressively decline. Sam, who has depended on his father-in-law's support in the Conservation Bureau where he works, is beset with enemies when he dies. In addition the family is forced to leave their spacious home, Tahoga House, which Henny fails to inherit, and they move to a run-down part of Annapolis. There Sam, suspended from work, devotes his manic energies to his family's activities at the same time as he neglects to provide for their material welfare, and Henny sinks deeper and deeper into despair. Her threats of suicide inspire Louisa with the idea of winning freedom for the children by killing both parents, but her attempt results in Henny's actual suicide through cyanide poisoning. Louisa's confession is disbelieved by her wilfully sanguine father, and the novel closes as she leaves home to find her own destiny.

Man with the Donkey, see KIRKPATRICK, JOHN SIMPSON

Mandrake Press was formed in London by P.R. Stephensen and bookseller Edward Goldston, in 1929. It developed out of the Fanfrolico Press (q.v.) and produced some Fanfrolico-type publications as well as a volume of reproductions of D.H. Lawrence's paintings and his essay, *A Propos of Lady Chatterley's Lover*, and works by Liam O'Flaherty and Aleister Crowley. By late 1930, economic circumstances and meddling by the controversial Crowley contributed to the demise of the Press.

Mango Tree, The, see McKIE, RONALD

MANIFOLD, J.S. (JOHN STREETER) (1915–   ), was born Melbourne into one of the oldest and richest rural families of western Victoria. After an education at the University of Cambridge, where he joined the Communist Party, he was employed as editor-translator by a German publishing firm in the Rhineland. During the Second World War he was in the British army intelligence corps. By 1949, when he returned with his wife to Australia, he was recognized in England and the USA as a rising literary star. His Communist Party allegiance caused family difficulties, so Manifold left Victoria to live in Brisbane. He has since been occupied with freelance writing, the composition and teaching of music, the collection and recording of bush songs and ballads and the establishment of the Realist Writers group. Manifold's early books of poetry are *Verses 1930–1933* (1933), *The Death of Ned Kelly and Other Ballads* (1941), *Trident* (1944, with David Martin and Hubert Nicholson) and *Selected Verse* (1946). After his return to Australia he produced *Nightmares and Sunhorses* (1961) and *Op. 8: Poems 1961–69* (1971). His *Collected Verse* was published simultaneously in 1978 with Rodney Hall's *J.S. Manifold: An Introduction to the Man and His Work;* his volume *On My Selection* (1983), includes his old favourites and a number of new poems. His interest in bush ballads and songs led to *Bandicoot Ballads* (1953), broadside forms of Australian folk-songs which were set to music and sung at the weekly music nights at Manifold's house; *The Violin, the Banjo & the Bones: An Essay on the Instruments of Bush Music* (1957); *The Queensland Centenary Songbook* (1959), of which he was chief editor; and the popular, much-reprinted *The Penguin Australian Song Book* (1964) which includes musical scores and notes on provenance. In 1964 he published *Who Wrote the Ballads? Notes on Australian Folksong*, an important book on the origins of Australian folk-song and balladry. Two of his works on music which reflect Manifold's early academic background, *The Music in English Drama (from Shakespeare to Purcell)* (1956) and *Music of the Elizabethan Stage* (1964), although highly acclaimed overseas, have been surprisingly ignored in Australia. Manifold is an important but neglected poet. His preference is for the lyric, especially in the style of the seventeenth century; for satire, often aggressive and violent; for lively, swaggering verse set, with touches of a Byronic romanticism, in an Australian Arcadia; and for war poetry. His elegy, 'The Tomb of Lt. John Learmonth A.I.F.' (q.v.), is perhaps his best-known poem.

Manly, originally Manly Cove, was visited by Captain Arthur Phillip 22 January 1788 when he was examining Port Jackson as an alternative site to Botany Bay for a settlement. In his report to Lord Sydney, he commented on the natives he met at the spot: 'their confidence and manly behaviour made me give the name of Manly Cove to this place'. In September 1790 Phillip was speared in the shoulder at Manly while trying to persuade the native, Bennilong, to return to Sydney Cove. Well-known as a popular Sydney seaside resort, Manly has been immortalized in the cartoon creation of Livingston Hopkins in the *Bulletin*, The Little Boy from Manly (q.v.).

MANN, CECIL (1896–1967) born Cudgen, NSW, served with the AIF at Gallipoli and in France in the First World War and was on active service also in the Second World War. In 1923–25 he was a journalist with the *Sydney Morning Herald*, then spent the rest of his working life with the *Bulletin*, as editor of the Red Page and later associate editor of the journal. His publications of well-crafted fiction include the volumes of short stories, *The River and Other Stories* (1945) and *Three Stories* (1963), as well as a novel, *Light in the Valley* (1947). He edited the first series of *Coast to Coast* (1941), *The Stories of Henry Lawson* (1964), *Henry Lawson's Best Stories* (1966) and *Henry Lawson's Humorous Stories* (1967).

MANN, DAVID DICKINSON (?1775–?), born England, was convicted of forgery in 1798 and sentenced to transportation, arriving in Sydney in 1799; he prospered in the Colony and was granted an absolute pardon in 1802. Involved in the Rum Rebellion he accompanied George Johnston to England in 1809 and gave evidence at his court martial. In 1811 he published *The Present Picture of New South Wales*,

an important early descriptive work about the Colony and specially significant as it includes a statistical survey.

MANN, LEONARD (1895–1981), born Toorak, Melbourne, worked as a clerk in the public service before serving in France in the First World War. After the war he graduated in law from the University of Melbourne and in the 1930s was secretary of the Victorian Employers' Federation. In that period he published *Flesh in Armour* (q.v., 1932), and two other works of fiction, *Human Drift* (1935) and *A Murder in Sydney* (1937), as well as his first book of verse, *The Plumed Voice* (1938). In the 1940s and 1950s he was a senior public servant; after his retirement he farmed at Macclesfield in the Dandenong Ranges. In 1960 he moved to Olinda, also in the Dandenongs, and later to Inverloch in South Gippsland, locales which allowed him the privacy to write. His later novels are *Mountain Flat* (1939), *The Go-Getter* (1942), *Andrea Caslin* (1959) and *Venus Half-Caste* (1963); his other volumes of poetry are *The Delectable Mountains* (1944) and *Elegiac and Other Poems* (1957). Less regarded as a poet than a novelist, Mann exhibits much the same attitudes in all his writing: criticism of a world order which sanctions the barbarity of war and the social and economic strictures that depress the lives of ordinary people, yet a sense of optimism about the innate worth of life itself in spite of the difficulties that accompany it. Rugged, prosy and careless as it sometimes is, his poetry is often strikingly effective. His novel, *Flesh and Armour*, is particularly effective in battle narrative, character portrayal and dialogue, but tends to overemphasize the remarkable qualities of the Australian 'digger'. *Human Drift* is a story of the Victorian goldfields in their halcyon days and climaxes in the Eureka Stockade. *A Murder in Sydney*, set in contemporary urban life, has a complicated psychological family framework in which a daughter murders her father's fiancée, partly to vindicate her dead mother's memory, partly as an act of self-indulgence. *Mountain Flat* combines the fierce lust of land ownership with a somewhat tangled romantic interest. *Venus Half-Caste*, an important novel in the saga of the part-Aboriginal attempting to find a meaningful role in a white-dominated society, is about a beautiful and intelligent girl's fight to be accepted in that society and the impact on her life of three men, two of whom are white and one part-Aboriginal. The young white lawyer, Phillip Roke, takes possession of Beatrice in order to satisfy his own bizarre lust and then murders the elderly white surgeon Mr Panner who, he believes, has stolen her from him. Beatrice ultimately finds happiness with Vic

Pegram, himself the result of a liaison between a white station owner and an Aboriginal girl.

MANN, PHILLIP GRENVILLE, born Sydney, was educated at the University of Sydney, and served in the Second World War. He drew on his war experiences for his first radio play, 'The Seas Between', which won the Lux Radio Theatre competition of 1946. After some years of freelance writing for radio, he spent seven years in London, where he wrote for radio, television and stage, becoming well-known after the success of his television series, *Pentecost Road*. Mann returned to Sydney in the 1960s to work as a television drama editor for the ABC. In 1961 his television play, 'The Attorney General', won the Sydney Journalists' Club drama competition, was subsequently produced overseas, and as a stage production by the Melbourne Theatre Company with the title, 'Day of Glory'. Another play produced on radio and television in Australia and overseas, 'The Sergeant from Burralee', was also produced by the Melbourne Theatre Company in 1970. Mann's other stage plays include 'Sky High', *Eight Days a Week* (1972) and *How Sleep the Brave* (1982). He has also published two novels, *The Keys of Heaven* (1966), based on his historical series for television, *The Patriots*, and *Candles in the Sun* (1978).

MANNING, EMILY (1845–90), was born and educated in Sydney. As 'Australie' she contributed to the *Sydney Morning Herald* and the *Australian Town and Country Journal* and was briefly on the staff of the *Illustrated Sydney News* and the *Sydney Mail*. She wrote on art and literature as well as on the public questions of the day but is most significant as a poet; her book, *The Balance of Pain and Other Poems*, by 'E.M.A. Heron' was published in 1877. A well-known member of Sydney society, she is featured in Ruth Bedford's *Think of Stephen* (1954) and was linked romantically with David Scott Mitchell.

MANNING, FREDERIC (1882–1935), born Sydney, had a limited formal education, largely because he suffered from bronchial asthma. He went to England at the age of fifteen with Arthur Galton, former private secretary to Sir Robert Duff, governor of NSW, and lived with Galton in Lincolnshire near the town of Bourne, whose name he gave to the protagonist, Private Bourne, of *The Middle Parts of Fortune* (q.v.). Through Galton, who acted as mentor, educator and friend, Manning became devoted to a scholastic, recluse-like existence, steeping himself in literature and the classics. Before the First World War Manning published *The Vigil of Brunhild* (1907, poetry), *Scenes and Portraits*

(1909, prose) and *Poems* (1910), and was a reviewer for the *Spectator*. At the outset of the war Manning took the unexpected step of joining the King's Shropshire Light Infantry Regiment as a private. He served, as did Private Bourne of his novel, on the Somme front in August 1916 and on the Ancre front in November, being back in England by the end of the year. During 1917 he was a subaltern in Ireland, where the British army had been sent to quell disturbances. Personality clashes with his fellow officers, a dislike of the pretensions of the officer class and continuing poor health led to his resigning his commission in 1918. Manning's post-war life was uneventful. He returned to an isolated existence, with study and writing his twin pursuits. He published *Eidola* (poetry) in 1917 and wrote the *Life of Sir William White* (1923), White being the designer of the first dreadnought; he also edited Walter Charleton's *Epicurus's Morals* (1926). In 1929 *The Middle Parts of Fortune: Somme and Ancre 1916* was published anonymously, an expurgated edition appearing in 1930 as *Her Privates We* by 'Private 19022'. Manning died of pneumonia in 1935, virtually unknown in Australia and largely neglected by critics in England after the initial surge of excitement about his novel. *The Middle Parts of Fortune*, whose autobiographical basis has been traced by L.T. Hergenhan, is now internationally acknowledged as one of the most comprehensive and authentic documents of the First World War. *Scenes and Portraits*, a series of dialogues and discussions rather than stories, deals with the problems of transience, the anguish of human existence and the reconciliation of the burdens of mankind with a belief in a merciful, benevolent deity.

Mannion Family, see *Timeless Land, The*

MANNIX, DANIEL (1864–1963), Roman Catholic Archbishop of Melbourne, was the son of a tenant farmer in County Cork, Ireland. Educated at Maynooth College, he became its president in 1903. In 1913 he joined Archbishop T.J. Carr of Melbourne as coadjutor and became archbishop in 1917. An extremely influential and forceful figure, he was prominent in several controversies which affected Irish and Catholic Australians. Strongly opposed to the suppression of the 1916 Irish rebellion, he campaigned against conscription during the 1916 and 1917 referenda and was an equally dominant protagonist in the recurrent debate about state aid to non-government schools. Energetic in the field of education, he helped to found numerous Catholic schools, and in 1923 established the Corpus Christi seminary at Werribee. His opposition to both capitalism and communism sharpened and often polarized political and religious debate in Victoria and led to the formation in 1937 of the National Secretariat of Catholic Action by the Catholic bishops in Australia and the emergence of the Catholic Social Movement, presided over by B.A. Santamaria. Several biographies have been written of Mannix, including those by Cyril Bryan (1918), Frank Murphy (1948), Niall Brennan (1964) and Michael Gilchrist (1983). He appears as the character, Archbishop Malone, in Frank Hardy's novel, *Power Without Glory* (1950) and in Barry Oakley's (q.v.) play, *The Feet of Daniel Mannix* (1975).

MANSFIELD, KATHERINE (1888–1928), the NZ writer of Australian descent, published her first professional writing in Australia. Encouraged by a NZ journalist, Tom L. Mills, she contributed four prose pieces to the *Native Companion* (1907), edited by E.J. Brady. Brady's acceptance strengthening her resolve to pursue a writing career. They are 'Vignettes', 'Silhouettes', 'In a Cafe' and 'In the Botanical Gardens' (signed 'Julian Mark'). Mansfield also made one contribution to the *Triad* in 1908 and one to the *Lone Hand* in 1909. In 1977 her contributions to the *Native Companion* were republished in Jean E. Stone's bibliographical study, *Katherine Mansfield: Publications in Australia 1907–09*.

MANSFIELD, RALPH (1799–1880), Methodist missionary and newspaper editor, was born Liverpool, England. He arrived at Sydney in 1820 and soon became prominent in the activities of the Colony's Methodists, as well as editing the *Australian Magazine*. After difficulties had developed in his relationship with the British Committee, he resigned as a missionary in 1828 and in 1829 became joint editor with Robert Howe of the *Sydney Gazette*, and sole editor after Howe's death, a position he held until 1832. Subsequently he was a businessman and bookseller and in 1840–54 he was leader-writer and unofficial editor of the *Sydney Morning Herald*. An early demographer, Mansfield published *Analytical View of the Census of New South Wales for the Year 1841* (1841) and a similar work for 1846.

MANT, GILBERT (1902–   ), born Sydney, was a journalist with the *Daily Telegraph* 1925–30 and subsequently worked for Reuters in Australia, Britain and Canada. He joined the AIF in 1940 and went to Malaya with the first contingent of Australian troops in 1941. After serving for fourteen months he rejoined Reuters as its Australian news editor and returned to Malaya as a war correspondent after the outbreak of war with Japan, eventually escaping from Singapore in a British destroyer. His account of the Malayan campaign, *Grim Glory* (1942), went to eight printings. Mant also published another descriptive war account, *You'll Be Sorry* (1944); two novels, *Glamour Brat* (1941), the story of a male Shirley Temple who comes to Australia and is kidnapped in the Blue Mountains, and *Gone Tomorrow* (1948); a collection of verse and stories, most of which were previously contributed to the *Australasian* and the *Bulletin*, *Holy Terror and Other Stories and Verse* (1923); and a book for children, *Buttercup* (1969).

Manuscripts: A Miscellany of Art and Letters, a Victorian magazine, ran, mainly quarterly, 1931–35. A vehicle for moderately advanced literary and art criticism, *Manuscripts* also became, especially in its later years, the publisher of avant-garde poetry. A contemporary section on European literature was included in its final two issues. Contributors included Hugh McCrae, Nettie Palmer, K.S. Prichard, Blamire Young and Clive Turnbull; it was edited by Harry Tatlock Miller and others.

MAQUARIE, ARTHUR (1874–1955), born Dubbo, NSW, as Arthur Frank Macquarie Mullens, later changed his name by deed poll. After graduating from the University of Sydney in 1895 he worked in England as a freelance writer, in Italy as a teacher of English, and also lived in France and Spain; he was active in the Royal Society of Literature and organized the British committee which promoted intellectual harmony among the Allies in the First World War. He wrote several plays on medieval subjects and several volumes of lyrical verse, but is most significant for the assistance he provided to Henry Lawson in London in 1900–01; as well as writing articles about Lawson which helped introduce him to literary London, Maquarie arranged meetings with editors, publishers and literary agents, and lived with Lawson while part of the Joe Wilson sequence was being written. Lawson's poignant portrait of Maquarie's struggle as a hack writer in London forms part of recently discovered material and is included in Brian Kiernan's *The Essential Henry Lawson* (1982).

Maranoa River, see 'Sandy Maranoa, The'

MARIN LA MESLÉE, EDMOND MARIE (1852–93), born France, settled in Australia in 1876 and was private secretary to the French consul-general before becoming a public servant. Instrumental in the foundation of the Geographical Society of Australasia, he travelled extensively in eastern Australia and wrote an account of his impressions which was published in France in 1883 as *L'Australie Nouvelle;* an English edition, edited and translated by Russel Ward, appeared in 1973. A committed Austrophile, Marin la Meslée was a propagandist for Australia in France, was interested in Federation and did research for Sir Henry Parkes.

MARIS, HYLLUS see *Women of the Sun*

Marked Man, A, see **CAMBRIDGE, ADA**

MARKS, HARRY (1923–77), born Melbourne, worked for a Melbourne advertising agency, was president of the Victorian FAW, and was one of the first Australian novelists to write about the experience of migrants. The main protagonists of both his novels are Jews, *The Heart Is Where the Hurt Is* (1966) dealing with a German-Jewish girl who comes to live with her Melbourne relatives a few years before the Second World War, and *Unicorn among the Wattles* (1979) describing the experience of a young Jewish man at Gallipoli and in Australia. Marks also edited, with Oscar Mendelsohn, an anthology of contemporary prose, *Australian New Writing* (1973) and wrote a biography of Alan Marshall, *I Can Jump Oceans: The World of Alan Marshall* (1976).

MARLOWE, MARY (?1892–1958), born St Kilda, Melbourne, a granddaughter of Sir John O'Shanassy, premier of Victoria, began her career as an actress although she came from a middle-class, Catholic family which regarded the profession as disreputable. After acquiring some minor roles in Australia, she went to London in 1910, and eventually achieved moderate success in Britain, the USA and Canada. Returning to England she published two novels, *Kangaroos in King's Land* (1917), which draws on her early experience of London, and *The Women Who Wait* (1918), a war novel intended to impress British women with the need to produce children. In 1920 she returned to Australia and joined the staff of the Sydney *Sun,* eventually writing a weekly theatre column for the newspaper, signed 'Puck'. She retired from journalism in 1946 but continued as a part-time writer of Dorothy Dix letters 1953–57. During the 1930s depression she began to supplement her income by radio broadcasting and by 1935 had become an established interviewer of stage and film celebrities, and a regular commentator on a range of topics from household hints to world events. Her subsequent novels, all of them written to the romantic, escapist formula popular with such magazines as the *Australian Woman's Mirror,* which serialized several of them, include *The Ghost Girl* (1921), *Gypsy Royal* (1923), *An Unofficial Rose* (1927), *Said the Spider* (1929), *Psal-*

mist of the Dawn (1934) and *Island Calm* (1940).

Marriage Ceremony, A see **CAMBRIDGE, ADA**

Marri'd, see **GILMORE, MARY**

MARSDEN, SAMUEL (1765–1838), born Yorkshire, England, was a blacksmith and a lay preacher when he attracted the attention of an Evangelical society within the Church of England, which sent him in his twenties to the University of Cambridge. In 1794 he arrived in NSW to take up a chaplaincy to which he had been recommended by William Wilberforce. Although he revisited England in 1807–09 and made several missionary voyages to NZ, he was based mainly at Parramatta, where he engaged in farming and was a magistrate as well as a minister. A controversial colonist, Marsden argued with Lachlan Macquarie, W.C. Wentworth and John Dunmore Lang among others, and published several vindications of his conduct; he retained a correspondence with Barron Field after Field's return to England in 1824. Known as the 'Flogging Parson', he was much criticized for his severity to the convicts, and appears in this light in 'Price Warung''s story 'Mr Slyde's Auction'; he also figures in several historical novels and plays. A.T. Yarwood wrote the biography, *Samuel Marsden: The Great Survivor* (1977).

MARSHALL, ALAN (1902–84), was born Noorat in western Victoria. At the age of six he contracted infantile paralysis, which left his legs permanently crippled. After his family moved to Melbourne when he was sixteen, he attended business college and later worked as an accountant for a struggling shoe company. His main interest, however, was writing and he won several short-story competitions, although publication eluded him. In 1935, when the shoe company closed down, he turned to freelance writing. He contributed numerous topical, whimsical sketches to newspapers in Melbourne, Brisbane and Adelaide, and for many years contributed a 'lonely hearts' column to the women's magazine, *Woman.* Another similar column, titled 'Alan Marshall's Casebook', was a regular feature of the *Argus* until that newspaper's demise in 1957; he also collaborated in a regular cartoon strip for the *Argus,* titled 'Speewa Jack'. Several of his short stories, meanwhile, were published in such periodicals as *Smith's Weekly,* the *Bulletin, ABC Weekly, Bohemia* and *Meanjin.* During the war Marshall travelled Australia by horse-drawn and motorized caravan, gathering messages from servicemen's families to be published in *A.I.F.*

News; he also lectured for the army education service. Enthusiastic about the outback, he continued to travel widely in Australia after the war and spent some time in Hong Kong and China.

Although Marshall's reputation as a writer was slow to gain ground, it increased dramatically after the publication of his childhood autobiography, *I Can Jump Puddles* (q.v., 1955). The book has sold over three million copies, has been translated and published in numerous overseas countries, proving particularly popular in the Soviet Union and eastern Europe, and was produced as an award-winning film in Czechoslovakia in 1970, and as a television series in Australia in 1981. Marshall himself also became a familiar national figure, particularly well-known to schoolchildren. He was made OBE in 1972, AM in 1981 and received the Soviet Order of Friendship in 1977.

Marshall published six collections of short stories, *Tell Us About the Turkey, Jo* (1946), *How's Andy Going?* (1956), *Short Stories* (1973), later published as *Four Sunday Suits* (1975), *Hammers over the Anvil* (1975), *Festival and Other Stories* (1975), and *The Complete Stories of Alan Marshall* (1977); an autobiographical trilogy, *I Can Jump Puddles* (1955), *This Is the Grass* (1962) and *In Mine Own Heart* (1963); an account of a visit to Arnhem Land, *Ourselves Writ Strange* (1948), later published with the title, *These Were My Tribesmen* (1965); a description of his travels in Australia, *These Are My People* (1944); two collections of his newspaper sketches, *Pull Down the Blind* (1949) and *Bumping into Friends* (1950); a novel, *How Beautiful Are Thy Feet* (1949); an interpretation of Aboriginal myths, *People of the Dreamtime* (1952); two books for children, *Whispering in the Wind* (1969) and *Fight for Life* (1972); and a series of sketches of Australian country life originally contributed to *Permewan's Review* and *Australasian Post*, *Alan Marshall's Australia* (1981). *Alan Marshall Talking* (1978) records his yarns and Harry Marks has written an account of his life, *I Can Jump Oceans* (1976).

Underlying all Marshall's writing is a simple code, grounded in an optimistic faith in humanity, that values social solidarity, tenacity, work and physical courage. Distinctive features of his work include an open response to both the natural world and the world of children, an ability to describe graphically scene, character and incident, and to reproduce the Australian idiom. His most-loved stories are those which centre on the instinctive life of animals, such as 'The Grey Kangaroo', 'My Bird', 'The Three-Legged Bitch' and 'The Gentleman'; or which recreate the world of early childhood,

such as 'Tell Us about the Turkey, Jo' (q.v.), 'Little Girl', 'Crossing the Road' and 'How's Andy Going?'; or which recall personalities and minor incidents from his early life in rural Victoria as in the *Hammers over the Anvil* collection; or which rely on the broadly-humorous effects of the outback tall story, such as 'They Were Tough Men on the Speewah'. Rapidly-sketched characters, a simple story line culminating in a moment of revelation, a boy observer who is often crippled, and the impression of a speaking-voice narrating events, are recurrent characteristics of his short fiction. 'Trees Can Speak', perhaps his most technically-accomplished story, is archetypal in its use of these ingredients to achieve a simple but striking effect. His autobiographies, like his novel, consist of loosely-connected anecdotes or reminiscences which combine to form a vivid social history of rural Victoria in the early years of this century and of Melbourne in the 1920s and 1930s. The Alan Marshall Award for literature which contains a strong narrative element and whose purpose is to entertain the reading public is awarded annually through the Victorian branch of the FAW.

MARSHALL, ALAN JOHN (1911–67), zoologist and explorer known familiarly as 'Jock' Marshall, grew up in Penshurst, NSW. He lost an arm in a shooting accident at the age of sixteen but was nevertheless a keen sportsman. Educated at the Universities of Oxford and Sydney, where he supported himself by part-time journalism, he took part in explorations of the New Hebrides, New Guinea and the Arctic and led the Oxford University expedition to Jan Mayen in 1937. He taught anatomy and zoology at the Universities of Oxford, Yale, California, and London, before his appointment in 1960 as professor of zoology and comparative physiology at Monash University. During the Second World War he served in army intelligence leading a special force ('Jock Force') behind Japanese lines in New Guinea. He published numerous scientific papers, and books on natural history, zoology and the conservation of wildlife, e.g. *The Men and Birds of Paradise* (1938), for which he was an active campaigner; *The Black Musketeers* (1937), an account of his experiences in the New Hebrides; an account of the work of Charles Darwin and T.H. Huxley in Australia (1970); and, with Russell Drysdale, a lively and popular description of a journey in north-western Australia in 1958, *Journey Among Men* (1962). His *Australia Limited,* first published in 1942, went to six printings by 1945; a deeply critical account of the Australian character, it echoed the sentiments of many at the time. Marshall is given a chapter in John Hetherington's *Uncommon Men* (1965).

MARSHALL, JAMES VANCE (1887–1964), born Casino, NSW, was an inveterate traveller, working at a range of occupations from bank clerk to railway ganger to purser on a banana ship. A prominent member of the Labor Party and union organizer, he was active also in British labour politics. An ardent campaigner against conscription in the First World War, he was imprisoned under the government of W.M. Hughes. He wrote two pamphlets relating to his prison experiences, *Jail from Within* (1918), a series of autobiographical sketches, and *The World of the Living Dead* (1919), a collection of poems and sketches of similar context, which includes a preface by Henry Lawson with whom Marshall was friendly. He also wrote *Timely Tips for New Australians* (1926) under the pseudonym, 'Jice Doone'. A subsequent tale, *The Children* (1959), republished in 1961 with the title *Walkabout*, which describes the experiences of two white children, sole survivors of a plane crash in the outback, and an Aboriginal boy, was apparently written by an English author who collaborated with Marshall in that he used, with his consent, his notes on outback life deriving from his period as a sandalwood cutter in the Northern Territory. Some subsequent books, similarly reliant on his notes, have been published under his name, including *A River Ran Out of Eden* (1962), *My Boy John That Went to Sea* (1966) and *A Walk to the Hills of the Dreamtime* (1970). *The Children* proved popular at the time of its publication and was also produced as a film, but it has subsequently been described as 'a good record of white Australian folk-lore about Aborigines'.

MARSHALL, WILLIAM LEONARD (1944–), born Sydney, has worked as a proof-reader, mortuary attendant, schoolteacher, postman, chemical worker and storeman, and now lives in Europe. His first novel, *The Fire Circle*, a concentrated tale of guilt and violence set in a construction camp in the WA desert, was published in 1969. He has also written two novels of a projected trilogy which deal with the historical inheritance of the twentieth century, *The Age of Death* (1970) and *The Middle Kingdom* (1971); three mystery novels, *Yellowthread Street* (1975), *The Hatchet Man* (1976) and *Gelignite* (1976); and a play, 'King Edward', based on the abdication of Edward VIII, which was produced in Sydney in 1971.

MARSHALL-HALL, G.W.L. (GEORGE WILLIAM LOUIS) (1862–1915), was born in London, where he studied at the Royal College of Music. In 1888 he was appointed conductor of the choral and orchestral societies of the London Organ School, and in 1891 Ormond professor of music at the University of Melbourne. A charismatic but impetuous and volatile personality, he was frequently involved in acrimonious debates with music critics in Melbourne's newspapers. He also became well-known as a conductor and in 1895 established, with W.A. Laver, the University's Conservatorium of Music. In 1897 he published two booklets of verse, *Hymn to Sydney* and *A Book of Canticles*, neither of which attained a circulation of fifty copies, but which succeeded in offending by their alleged eroticism large numbers of citizens. His next collection, *Hymns, Ancient and Modern* (1898), aroused ill-founded claims of irreverence and lasciviousness, and prompted the University council to dismiss him, an action which sparked an intense controversy. He subsequently established a private conservatorium in East Melbourne, the Marshall-Hall Conservatorium. In 1914 he was again appointed to the Ormond Chair but died shortly afterwards. He also published two historical tragedies, *Aristodemus* (1900) and *Bianca Capello* (1906); another collection of verse, *To Irene* (1896); and wrote both music and libretti for two operas. At his death, Sir Herbert Brookes published a part-prose, part-verse elegy in his memory, *At the Graveside*. Therese Radic published *G.W.L. Marshall-Hall: Portrait of a Lost Crusader* (1982).

Marston Family, see *Robbery Under Arms*

MARTENS, CONRAD (1801–78), prominent colonial artist, was born London and joined HMS *Beagle* in 1833 on its scientific cruise to Patagonia and Tierra del Fuego, becoming a close friend of Charles Darwin. In 1835 Martens came to Sydney; he sketched and painted the Port Jackson, Illawarra and Blue Mountains areas and later the New England and Darling Downs districts. Lionel Lindsay wrote *Conrad Martens: The Man and His Art* (1920).

MARTIN, A.E. (ARCHIBALD EDWARD) (1885–?), worked for a time with C.J. Dennis on the *Gadfly* and as publishing agent for the J.C. Williamson firm. He wrote radio serials, four books on place names in Australia and six novels, several of which were serialized in the *Australian Women's Weekly*. They include *Common People* (1944), which won the *Weekly's* novel prize in 1943, *Sinners Never Die* (1944), *The Misplaced Corpse* (n.d.), *Death in the Limelight* (1946) and *The Chinese Bed Mysteries* (1955). His last novel, *The Hive of Glass* (1962), a study of small-town life in NSW, was completed after his death by his son, J.T. Martin.

MARTIN, A.P. (ARTHUR PATCHETT) (1851–1902), born Kent, England, was brought to Australia in 1852. A member of the Victorian public service, he took an active role in Melbourne's literary life and was editor of the *Melbourne Review* from its inception in 1876 until he left for London in 1882 to work as a journalist. Martin edited three anthologies which included contributions from prominent Australian writers, *An Easter Omelette* (1879), *Oakbough and Wattle-blossom* (1888) and *Over the Sea* (1891); wrote one of the earliest surveys of Australian literature, *The Beginnings of an Australian Literature* (1898); the historical accounts, *Australia and the Empire* (1889) and *True Stories from Australasian History* (1893), and a biography of Robert Lowe (1893). A composer of conventional, romantic verse, he contributed to various anthologies such as *Hash* (1877), *The 'Vagabond' Annual* (1877) and *Under the Gum Tree* (1890); and published three collections, *Lays of Today* (1878), *Fernshawe* (1882), and *The Withered Jester* (1895). *Fernshawe*, which includes some prose sketches, reprints material from the *Melbourne Review* and other journals, e.g. 'Two Australian Poets' (on Adam Lindsay Gordon and J.B. Stephens). He also wrote a book of verse and fiction, *Sweet Girl Graduate* (1876). His wife was Harriette Anne Martin (q.v.).

MARTIN, C.E.M. (CATHERINE EDITH MACAULEY) (1847–1937), born Catherine Mackay on the Isle of Skye, was brought to SA by her parents. It is known that she lived for a time at Naracoorte and Mount Gambier, worked as a journalist in Adelaide and as a clerk in the education department and married Frederick Martin, but little further biographical information has come to light. Extremely reticent, she published almost all her work anonymously or under a pseudonym. No manuscript material relating to her life or work is held by Australian libraries and almost the only specific, contemporary biographical reference is that of Catherine Spence, who describes meeting Martin after the publication of *An Australian Girl* (q.v.) in her *Autobiography* (1910). Spence's conclusion that she was outstanding as a novelist appears to have been shared by readers of the 1890s, although her work has received little subsequent attention. She published four novels and a serial, 'Bohemian Born', which was never published in book form: *An Australian Girl* (1890), published anonymously; *The Silent Sea* (1892), published under the pseudonym, 'Mrs Alick Macleod'; *The Old Roof-Tree: Letters of Ishbel to Her Half-brother, Mark Latimer* (1906), published anonymously; and *The Incredible Journey* (1923), under C.E.M. Martin. She also published a collection of verse, *The*

Explorers and Other Poems (1874), under the initials M.C.

An advanced writer for her time, and unusual in that she has no interest in the bush ethos, Martin is concerned with social issues, religion and philosophy, anticipating several of the themes of such writers as Martin Boyd, 'Henry Handel Richardson' and, in her few realistic images of bush life, Barbara Baynton. *An Australian Girl* presents a perceptive, intellectually alive and idealistic heroine, whose sceptical view of marriage proves tragically well-founded. Out of print for many years and often described as a conventional, nineteenth-century, genteel romance with the standard preoccupation with love and courtship, *An Australian Girl* is more the account of one woman's spiritual pilgrimage in which personal loss is finally transcended by the discovery of a religious humanism that is reminiscent of George Eliot's. Martin's originality emerges in her realistic but sympathetic treatment of her well-rounded characters and her imaginative penetration of their inner life; in her transcendence of an ostensibly conventional plot; and in her treatment of such large themes as religion, the realities of marriage, the pursuit of happiness and the nature of civilization. Particularly striking are her finely-detailed descriptions of the Mallee country, which is the background of the early part of the novel. The final scenes, set partly in Berlin and dominated by intense anguish, doomed love, and music, anticipate some of the atmosphere of 'Henry Handel Richardson''s *Maurice Guest* (1908). *The Incredible Journey* is a sympathetic and knowledgeable story of the journey of two Aboriginal women, Iliapo and Polde, over hundreds of miles of desert country to retrieve a little boy who had been kidnapped by a white man. *The Old Roof-Tree*, supposedly made up of letters written from England, Holland, Germany and Italy, ranges over a large span of subjects from religion and philosophy to painting and visions of an ideal, social future, and reflects Martin's horror of the poverty and inequalities of English life as well as her witty, colonial perception of English manners at the turn of the century. Her verse collection includes a long narrative poem, 'The Explorers', on the Burke and Wills' story, which includes an idyllic vision of the Australian future, as well as some ballads and lyrics and translations from Herder, Goethe, Schiller and other European poets.

MARTIN, DAVID (1915–), was born Ludwig Detsinyi into a Jewish family in Hungary and subsequently changed his name by deed poll. He was brought up in Germany, a country for which he has ambivalent feelings and which he left at seventeen. After some time in Holland, where he worked on the reclamation of the Zuider Zee, and a year in Palestine where he lived on a kibbutz, he served as a first-aid orderly in the International Brigade in Spain 1937–38. In 1938 he settled in London, where he worked for the *Daily Express* and later for the European service of the BBC. He married Richenda Powell, a schoolteacher and writer, in 1941. He was literary editor of *Reynolds News* 1945–47, and foreign correspondent in India for the *Daily Express* 1948–49. In 1949 he visited Australia, was impressed by the peaceful, extrovert life, and decided to stay. For many years a member of the Communist Party, Martin left it in 1956 but retains his left-wing sympathies.

Although German is his native language, Martin began writing verse in English in the 1940s and had established a reputation as a poet, short-story writer, novelist and playwright before his arrival in Australia. He has published eight collections of verse, *Battlefields and Girls* (1942), *Trident* (1944, with Hubert Nicholson and John Manifold), *From Life* (1953), *Rob the Robber* (1954, under the pseudonym 'Spinifex'), *Poems of David Martin 1938–1958* (1958), *Spiegel the Cat* (1961), *The Gift* (1966) and *The Idealist* (1968). His verse has also appeared in numerous anthologies including *Eight by Eight* (1963) and *Modern Australian Writing* (1966). He has written seven novels, *Tiger Bay* (1946), *The Stones of Bombay* (1949), *The Young Wife* (q.v., 1962), *The Hero of Too* (q.v., 1965, published in New York as *The Hero of the Town*), *The King Between* (1966, published in New York as *The Littlest Neutral*) and *Where a Man Belongs* (1969); two collections of short stories, *The Shoes Men Walk In* (1946) and *Foreigners* (1982); numerous books for children, including *Hughie* (1971), *Frank and Francesca* (1972), *Gary* (1972), *The Chinese Boy* (1973), *The Cabby's Daughter* (1974), *Katie* (1974, with Richenda Martin), *Mister P and His Remarkable Flight* (1975), *The Devilish Mystery of the Flying Mum* (1977), *The Man in the Red Turban* (1978) and *The Mermaid Attack* (1978); and a collection of verse for children, *I Rhyme My Time* (1980). Two of his plays, 'The Young Wife' and *The Shepherd and The Hunter*, have been produced, and the latter published in 1946; *Tiger Bay* has been produced as a film and *Frank and Francesca* as a serial on ABC television. As well as numerous essays and reviews, he has edited two collections of verse, *Rhyme and Reason* (1944) and *New World, New Song* (1955); written a travel book, *On the Road to Sydney* (1970); provided the text for a collection of photographs on migrant life in Australia, *I'll Take Australia* (1978).

Martin's novels have diverse settings and themes, ranging from the Cardiff dockside area of *Tiger Bay* or the tiny Indo-Chinese kingdom of Lhaodia of *The King Between* to the small Australian country town of Tooramit of *The Hero of Too*. Variety of tone is also a marked feature of his work. *The Young Wife*, a powerful and sombre domestic drama played by Greek migrants in contemporary Melbourne, sensitively explores an archetypal theme; the Rabelaisian *The Hero of Too* wittily but affectionately explodes a number of Australian myths; *Where a Man Belongs*, Martin's most autobiographical and ambitious novel, is both complex and searching; *The King Between*, a comic fantasy on the theme of neutrality, is a virtuoso display of his satiric skills.

Martin's writing for children, directed mainly at teenagers, shows the same verve and, for the most part, the same uncompromising realism. Several of his novels concentrate on the struggle of the outsider: *Frank and Francesca* deals with migrants, *Hughie* with an Aboriginal boy, *The Chinese Boy* with Chinese experience on the Australian goldfields of the 1860s. Particularly notable are *The Cabby's Daughter*, the story of the experience of a motherless girl in 1903 as she confronts adult realities for the first time, and *Mister P and His Remarkable Flight*, an account of a lonely boy and his racing pigeon, written from the perspectives of both the boy and his bird.

Martin's verse has moved from simple and stirring revolutionary themes that address 'all who love life and peace above war and death' *(From Life)* to the more personal, lyrical and complex. His predilection for humorous satire emerges in some shorter poems and in *The Idealist*, a narrative about a Reverend Eric Green who chooses to live literally as a Christian. His comic versatility is seen at its best in *Spiegel the Cat*, a narrative poem based on a tale by the nineteenth-century Swiss writer, Gottfried Keller.

MARTIN, HARRIETTE ANNE, born Queensland as Harriette Cookesley, married Arthur Patchett Martin. She edited three anthologies, *Under the Gum Tree* (1890), which includes contributions from Mrs Campbell Praed and Hume Nisbet; *Coo-ee : Tales of Australian Life by Australian Ladies* (1891), which includes contributions from Jessie Couvreur and Mrs Campbell Praed; and *Volcanic Gold and Other Tales* (1890), to which Victor Daley contributed.

MARTIN, Sir **JAMES** (1820–86), born County Cork, Ireland, was brought to Sydney as an infant by his parents and was educated at W.T. Cape's academy. In 1838 his *The Australian Sketch Book*, a collection of fifteen essays imitative of Washington Irving, was published;

with the possible exception of Henry Savery's *The Hermit of Van Diemen's Land* (1830) it was the first book of essays published in Australia and included 'The Pseudo-Poets', which criticized Charles Harpur, Charles Tompson and others. Martin contributed to the *Australian* after leaving school and was its acting editor in 1839; in 1845–47 he was editor and manager of the *Atlas*. He qualified as a solicitor in 1845 and in 1848 began a long career in conservative politics which culminated in the premiership of NSW (1863–64, 1866–68, 1870–72). Knighted in 1869, Martin was a distinguished chief justice of the colony in 1873–86. He gave his name to Martin Place in the central business district of Sydney and is the subject of Elena Grainger's *Martin of Martin Place* (1970). Anthony Trollope regarded him as the best Australian speaker he heard in his time in Australia.

MARTIN, PHILIP (1931–   ), born Richmond, Victoria, graduated from the University of Melbourne in 1958 and has taught at Monash University, Melbourne. A script-writer of literary programmes for radio and television for the ABC, Martin has also published several volumes of verse, *Voice Unaccompanied* (1970), *A Bone Flute* (1974), *From Sweden: Translations and Poems* (1979) and *A Flag for the Wind* (1982).

Marvellous Melbourne, a phrase commonly applied to Melbourne in the nineteenth century to describe its growth in prosperity from the 1850s to the late 1880s, derived from an account of the city written by the English journalist, George Augustus Sala, following a visit in 1885, and published in the *Argus*, the *Australasian*, the *Sydney Morning Herald* and the London *Daily Telegraph*. The phrase immediately stuck in the popular imagination and summed up for Melburnians their long-established confidence in their city's material progress, its thriving commercial, social and cultural life, and its dominance over Sydney. This pride was reflected in the popular press, in the statements of political, business and church leaders, and in the work of the city's chroniclers such as Alexander Sutherland's *Victoria and Its Metropolis* (1888) and H. Perkins's *Melbourne Illustrated and Victoria Described* (1880). Alfred Dampier used the phrase as the title for one of his popular melodramas (staged 1889), written in collaboration with J.H. Wrangham and possibly others; but the myth received its most ornate literary treatment in the public poems produced by Victorian poets on appropriate occasions, from R.H. Horne's 'Lyric Masque', commissioned for Melbourne's Intercolonial Exhibition of 1866, to Reverend William Al-

len's *The Centennial Cantata* (1888), written for Melbourne's Centennial International Exhibition. The phrase was also frequently adjusted to express less attractive aspects of the city; the deficiencies of its sanitation led to the title 'Murderous Melbourne', celebrated in the Sydney *Bulletin* in 1889 in the following terms:

> Sing hey! for the City that's Queen
> Of the continent known as Australia
> Where the gutters are slimy and green
> And all sorts of terrors assail yer. . .

Four years later, the city's financial scandals gave the *Bulletin*'s cartoonists plenty of material for their theme of 'Marvellous Smellboom'. Another familiar theme was the contrast between Melbourne's prosperity and its seamier underside; John Stanley James's *The Vagabond Papers* (1876–77) presents authentic descriptions of the city's slums; John Freeman's *Lights and Shadows of Melbourne Life* (1888) exploits the sensational aspects of the same topic; and Fergus Hume's novel, *The Mystery of a Hansom Cab* (1886), paints a dramatic contrast between the two sides of Melbourne's life. After the severe depression of the 1890s, Melbourne began to attract the adjective 'Miserable' in the popular press and the theme was a common one with contemporary historians and literary figures. Both Alfred Deakin and Charles H. Pearson wrote of the disadvantages and social evils of the city; George Essex Evans's poem, 'In Collins Street' (1898) reflects a familiar feeling of unease and disillusionment; and the theme of the evil city is treated with particularly incisive bitterness by Bernard O'Dowd in his poem, 'The City' (1901). The myth of 'Marvellous Melbourne' has been thoroughly explored by Graeme Davison in *The Rise and Fall of Marvellous Melbourne* (1978). It has also given rise to a popular extravaganza by John Romeril and Jack Hibberd, *Marvellous Melbourne* (1970), which presents a dense, lively picture of nineteenth-century Melbourne with Alfred Dampier at the centre of the action, and explores political and social analogies with modern Victoria.

Mary Poppins, see **TRAVERS, PAMELA**

MAS, JOAN (1926–74), born Sydney as Joan Morgan, was a freelance writer for the ABC and was for a time editor of *Poetry Magazine*. She contributed verse to numerous Australian anthologies and periodicals as well as to overseas journals, and published two collections *Isis in Search* (1966) and *The Fear and the Flowering* (1975).

Masque, a review of the performing arts, was published six times a year in Sydney 1967–

71. Edited by John Allen, it included contributions from playwrights, producers and drama critics such as Roger Covell, Robert Helpmann, Alan Seymour and John Tasker.

MASS, NURI (1918–), born Melbourne, spent some years in Argentina as a child, returning to Australia at the age of twelve. After graduating from the University of Sydney she was an editor with Angus & Robertson, Consolidated Press and the Sydney *Sun*, and established her own private press, the Writers Press. Her books for children include *Australian Wild Flower Fairies* (1937), *The Little Grammar People* (1942), *Magic Australia* (1943), *The Wizard of Jenolan* (1946), *The Wonderland of Nature* (1964), *Many Paths, One Heaven* (1965), *China – The Waking Giant* (1966), and *Australian Wildflower Magic* (1967). She has also written five novels for adults, *Randy Blair* (1955), *The Gift* (1969), *Donna Roon* (1970), *As Much Right to Live* (1971), and *Don't Kill It – It's Me* (1972).

MASSINA, A.H. (ALFRED HENRY) (1834–1917), born London, arrived in Melbourne in 1855. After an unsuccessful stint on the Victorian goldfields he returned to his former trade of printing, and in 1859 he helped form Clarson, Shallard & Co, which became Clarson, Massina & Co in 1868 and A.H. Massina & Co, the present name, in 1876. Among the firm's publications were the *Colonial Monthly* and the *Australian Journal; His Natural Life* was serialized in the latter 1870–72, Massina allegedly locking Clarke in an office so that instalments could be completed. Massina also published Adam Lindsay Gordon's *Bush Ballads and Galloping Rhymes* (1870), presenting Gordon with the account the day before Gordon's suicide. He was chairman of the Melbourne *Herald* board 1902–09.

Master of the Grove, see KELLEHER, VICTOR

Materfamilias, a novel by Ada Cambridge (q.v.), was published in 1898. The retrospective narration of incidents in the life of a Melbourne matron, Polly Braye, the novel opens with her leaving home, almost immediately to marry, after her father takes a second wife. Although Polly's marriage is unsuccessful, she voyages to Melbourne when she hears her husband is ill there; *en route* she falls in love with the captain of the ship, Tom Braye, whom she marries when it is discovered that her first husband has died. The bulk of *Materfamilias* chronicles significant events in the marriage of Polly and Tom: the birth of their four children, although Polly's favourite son, Bobby, is later killed in

a shooting accident; the struggle to establish themselves, which is alleviated by a legacy from Polly's aunt; Tom's retirement from the sea to take up pig-farming outside Melbourne; the education and courtship of their eldest children, Harry and Phyllis; the silver wedding anniversary of Polly and Tom; and at the end of the novel, the birth of the first grandchild and the marriage of Harry to Emily Blount, whom Polly has long resisted. The most fully-drawn of Cambridge's characters, Polly, despite her vitality and exuberance, reveals herself as wilful, possessive, self-deceiving, inconsistent and increasingly jealous; through her, the novel makes ironic comment on contemporary feminine roles.

Mateship, a much-discussed term in Australian literary, historical and cultural commentary, emerged in the second half of the nineteenth century; it derives from the word 'mate' used in Australian English as a synonym for 'cobber', which denotes an habitual companion, associate, friend or partner. 'Mate' has also been used as a mode of address, which is often friendly and implies equality, as in the famous "'ow yer goin' mate, orright?' in *They're a Weird Mob*, (1957); sometimes neutral, as in the common reply, 'Sorry, mate, haven't got a clue', to a request for information; and sometimes hostile, as in the threatening 'Watch it, *mate*'. The comradeship and mutual support which form part of 'mateship', and the fact that it is an almost exclusively male phenomenon, an 'informal male-bonding institution involving powerful, sublimated homosexuality' in the words of polemicist, Miriam Dixson, were noticed by Alexander Harris in the 1840s. In *The Emigrant Family* (1849) Harris noted that 'The Australians . . . are growing up a race by themselves; fellowship of country has already begun to distinguish them and bind them together'; in *Settlers and Convicts* (1847) he expressed surprise at the extent of the 'exertions bushmen of new countries, especially mates, will make for one another, beyond people of the old countries'. Mateship has also been discovered in the following decade among the Eureka rebels, but as a term it gained a wider currency in the 1890s. In part this was an indirect consequence of the late nineteenth-century interest in the 'Coming Man', a question addressed by such writers as Marcus Clarke, Francis Adams and 'Rolf Boldrewood', but more important were the propagandists for the emerging union movement (the group loyalties and brotherhood of 'mates' were contrasted by W.G. Spence with the treachery of 'scabs') and the numerous, if varied, references to mateship in the writings of Henry Lawson. Mateship also figures in the work of C.E.W. Bean and others writing about Australian soldiers in the First World War. Its importance in the Anzac tradition, celebrated in Leonard Mann's novel, *Flesh in Armour* (q.v., 1932) and scrutinized in Alan Seymour's play, *The One Day of the Year* (1962), is reinforced by the 1983 survey which showed that mateship is regarded by the participants as the main reason for the higher survival rate of Australians in Japanese POW camps in 1942–45.

The several social, political and military contexts in which mateship has been used in the 1890s and later has contributed to the semantic extension of the term beyond a collection of qualities such as comradeship and mutual support among males towards its status almost as a creed, certainly a term around which have clustered a number of associations, values, practices or ideals: associations such as the link with the bush and with Australianness, noticed by Harris, consolidated by Lawson and present in other writers, e.g. 'Duke' Tritton, Alan Marshall and even Mary Grant Bruce; male values and practices such as manliness and drinking beer; ideals such as egalitarianism, democratic political and social reform, and Utopianism. In the hands of some writers mateship has become a synonym for these associations, practices, values or ideals. For example, in H.G. Oxley's *Mateship in Local Organization* (1974), the term is largely dispensed with after the title in favour of the egalitarianism which is the focus of the book. Similarly, mateship in the narrow sense is only one of the ingredients which make up the stereotype of the typical Australian in Russel Ward's *The Australian Legend* (q.v., 1958), a stereotype which Ward sees as a national self-image, also partly a myth, which originated with the convicts, developed through the character and experience of the itinerant bush workers in the second half of the nineteenth century and was publicized by such journals as the *Bulletin* (q.v.). Yet because Ward's typical Australians exhibit not only mateship but also the characteristics associated with it, phrases like 'the Australian ideal of mateship' and 'one huge myth of mateship' have become the shorthand of commentators on, and critics of, Ward's Australian legend (e.g. Humphrey McQueen, q.v.) and the other myths, e.g. the Anzac tradition, about national character with which it has been linked. To take a third example, mateship and other manifestations of 'maleness' such as 'ockerism', 'larrikinism' and male chauvinism have been used interchangeably in critiques, particularly those by feminists and journalists, of Australian society and historiography.

It is largely because of the flexibility with which the term has been used that discussions of, and attacks on, mateship have paralleled the discussions of the Australian legends into which it so centrally fits. Broadly, commentators have focused on four issues: the extent to which mateship is uniquely or even distinctively Australian (although it is doubtful whether in any other country would an all-male club like the Melbourne Bread and Cheese Club (q.v.) specify that its journal, *Bohemia*, was published in the interest of Mateship, Art and Letters; or a journal like *Realist Writer*, in its first issue, use the word 'mateship' as a code word for the radical tradition it was asserting); the extent to which it is a true description of Australian (male) behaviour; whether, even if not a true description, it forms part of the Australian self-image of (male) Australians, at least at one stage in Australian history, or whether instead it is a myth created by historians and others; and finally, its value as an ideal or a mode of behaviour. In most of these discussions, Australian literature has been one of the major sources of evidence to which commentators have turned. As well as citing some of the numerous examples which can be found within Australian folk-song and ballad attesting to the ideal or practice of comradeship and mutual support among Australian males, e.g. 'How Gilbert Died', 'The Dying Stockman', 'Sam Holt', 'The Sick Stockrider', Ward adduces evidence from Harris, Lawson and the writings of Marcus Clarke, 'Price Warung', Anthony Trollope, Friedrich Gerstaecker and Joseph Furphy. Although the evidence of these authors is seen as positive about the existence and value of mateship, some of it at least is open to different interpretation, even in the case of 'Warung' who had strong egalitarian beliefs and whose story 'Secret Society of the Ring' climaxes in the self-sacrifice and mateship of the convict, Felix. The famous Convict Oath (q.v.) in 'Warung''s story, 'The Liberation of the First Three', is cited by Ward and several other writers as evidence of the freemasonry of the convicts, an early form of mateship. The story, however, recounts how three convicts kill three other convicts with whom they are chained and have sworn the oath, and in the sequel ('The Liberation of the Other Three') two survivors murder the third and then kill each other, making an ironic mockery of the oath. Similarly, the work of other Australian writers has been cited as evidence of the darker side of mateship. To take a few examples among many, some cited in T. Inglis Moore's chapter on mateship in *Social Patterns in Australian Literature* (1971), the theme of men as predators in Barbara Baynton's (q.v.) fiction finds bitter expression in the ironically titled 'Squeaker's Mate', a story which chronicles the desertion of the morally stronger female by her male partner after she has her back broken in an accident. The exclusiveness, hostility and even violence towards outsiders such as women, class traitors and different racial or ethnic groups finds expression in Gavin Casey's (q.v.) *It's Harder for Girls* (1942), in some of John Morrison's stories, e.g. 'Bo Abbott', in the crucifixion of Himmelfarb in Patrick White's *Riders in the Chariot* (1961), in the brutality of the larrikins (q.v.) in Louis Stone's *Jonah* (1911), and in the murder of Sibley in David Ireland's *The Glass Canoe* (1976). Among dramatists, Ray Lawler's *Summer of the Seventeenth Doll* (1957) shows the fragility even of a long-term mateship and Jack Hibberd, one of a number of more recent Australian playwrights to scrutinize national myths, exposes the ethic as insular and imprisoning in *White with Wire Wheels* (q.v., 1970).

Something of the darker side of mateship is also seen in the work of the writer most closely identified with its celebration, Henry Lawson. According to J. le Gay Brereton in *Henry Lawson by His Mates* (1931), 'More than any other writer who ever dipped a pen, [Lawson] has made clear to all men an ideal that has always been cherished in the bush, and in our growing towns, and has helped to fix it as a national inspiration. In his life and in his writings he exalted the idea of "mateship" – an ideal of personal devotion, trust and generosity, irrespective of class or creed'. The ideal to which Brereton refers, implied in the numerous titles of stories (the first, 'His Father's Mate', as well as 'An Old Mate of Your Fathers', 'His Mother's Mate', 'Macquarie's Mate', 'Meeting Old Mates', 'A Sketch of Mateship', 'Mateship', 'The Stranger's Friend', 'Their Mate's Honour', and so on) finds perhaps its fullest expression in poems like 'The Glass on the Bar' in *Children of the Bush* (1902), which is prefaced by the moving verse tribute to 'The Shearers',

No church-bell rings them from the Track,
No pulpit lights their blindness —
'Tis hardship, drought and homelessness
That teach those bushmen kindness;
The mateship born of barren lands,
Of toil and thirst and danger —
The camp-fare for the stranger set,
The first place to the stranger

and includes stories such as 'That Pretty Girl in the Army', ' "Lord Douglas" ', 'A Sketch of Mateship', 'His Brother's Keeper' and the much-anthologized 'Send Round the Hat' (q.v.) which chronicles the fellowship and practical support which 'The Giraffe', Bob Brothers, offers to all those in need. Yet several qualifications need to be made to the impression Brereton leaves of Lawson as a celebrant of mateship. Firstly, *Children of the Bush* is seen as the start of Lawson's decline as a writer, his succumbing to the sentimentality and contriv-

ance that marked his first work; his sentimentalizing of mateship in the volume is both a symptom of this and a contrast to the more critical appraisal found in his other writings. For example, in 'The Cant and Dirt of Labour Literature' published in the *Worker* in 1894, Lawson suggests that mateship 'is an egotistic word' implying a state of things 'too angelic to exist among mortals'; the mortals we encounter in Lawson's stories include Steelman and Smith, who are given to sharp practices in their conduct with other human beings, and other groups of men whose mateship is seen by H.P. Heseltine, in an ironically titled article, 'Saint Henry – Our Apostle of Mateship' (*Quadrant*, 1961), to be a combination of 'cruel practical joking, irresponsible behaviour, and, occasionally, even dishonesty'. Secondly, as even 'The Shearers' makes clear in ' "Tis hardness, drought, and homelessness/ That teach those bushmen kindness', mateship is commonly presented by Lawson as a defensive tactic rather than as an ideal, a code of conduct which is one of the protections against poverty, as in the Arvie Aspinall stories, notably 'A Visit of Condolence' where mateship unites the urban poor against rapacious capitalists; illness, as in ' "Going Blind" '; or the terrible conditions of bush existence, as in 'Hungerford' or the best of the Mitchell stories, where mateship is implicit and not always confined to the itinerant workers rather than bosses like Baldy Thompson. Even then, what remains finally memorable about Lawson's fiction is not the partnerships which in sum attest to the triumph of mateship, but the gallery of loners, hatters, and battlers, who at best survive ('The Drover's Wife', Mitchell, the bushman in ' "Going Blind" ') and at worst are defeated (Mrs Spicer). The relentless realism which is a major source of Lawson's fictional achievement finds no better expression than in 'The Union Buries Its Dead', in which the emptiness of the ritual in which a group of bushmen bury an unknown unionist (therefore 'mate') is confirmed by a consistently ironic nihilism. After noting the hard, dry Darling River clods rebounding on the coffin, the narrator explains:

I have left out the wattle – because it wasn't there. I have also neglected to mention the heart-broken old mate, with his grizzled head bowed and great pearly drops streaming down his rugged cheeks. He was absent – He was probably 'Out Back'. For similar reasons I have omitted reference to the suspicious moisture in the eyes of a bearded bush ruffian named Bill. Bill failed to turn up – and the only moisture was that induced by the heat.

MATHERS, PETER (1931–), born Fulham, England, was brought to Australia in infancy. He left school at sixteen to undertake an agricultural course and has had numerous occupations which have taken him all over Australia and which include farming, labouring, wool-classing, work in a brewery and in the Victorian public service. He lived in Britain and Europe, mainly in London 1964-67, where he combined research for stockbrokers and literary scholars with writing. The literary research led to a year in the USA attached to the University of Pittsburgh as adviser to students studying theatre; he has comically described this experience in his article 'Pittsburgh Identity: 0000000621' in *Overland* (1968). He has published two novels, *Trap* (1966), which won the Miles Franklin Award, and *The Wort Papers* (1972); and a collection of short stories, *A Change for the Better* (1984).

An ebulliently comic, innovative and inventive writer, Mathers is exceptional in his variety and range. He sees the writer's role as one of preaching and practising subversion, holding up 'authoritative' claims to ridicule and analysis, reflecting the reality of disorder rather than the myth of order; as he has commented in an interview: 'Pattern and order can be pleasant. But ... If we feel that disorder is necessary, it's to be disorder'. His novels are deliberately negligent of novelistic rules, shaped not in orderly chronological form, but fluid, digressive and web-like. Both *Trap* and *The Wort Papers* are dislocated but connected jumbles of episodes, yarns, individual histories and reflective meanderings that fuse fact and fiction, past and present, cultural myth and private reality, the order of external history and the chaos of inner experience. Both novels offer a varied number of perspectives on contemporary and past Australian society, mediated by numerous narrative voices, tones and styles. While vivid comic incident and incisive social satire dominate the foreground, time sequences are constantly dislocated, localities abruptly change, narrators overtake each other and even blur. Gradually a pattern emerges that presents actual history as a complex dynamic movement, simultaneously chaotic and integrated, chronological, continuous and circular.

Trap is to some extent the diary of a young, conformist social worker, David David, who is hired by a group of people belonging to the Establishment, to interrogate, analyse and subdue Trap, a part-Aboriginal iconoclast. The entries in David's diary, covering one year, but extending as far back as the early nineteenth century and to places as dissimilar as Tierra del Fuego and Hobart, are mainly in flashback and record the insidious growth of his doubt under Trap's subversive influence. As the tale approaches its climax – David's almost total lapse into an outlaw-consciousness – the digres-sions are less extensive and the voices of Trap and David merge. Trap's casual but devastating power stems, as his name suggests, from his stubborn singularity, his resistance to categories, his genius for unpredictable independence in a materialistic, secular society that prizes categorized order at the expense of imagination and poetry. Trap denies validity to established mores in various ways: by simply existing as a charismatic embodiment of anarchy; by violating accepted standards in the most comically outrageous way possible as when, gaoled for infringing a township's embargo on Aborigines in swimming pools, he kills (police-)man's best friend, his dog; or by exaggerated over-com-mitment to the System, such as his ingenious 'improvement' to the hangman's trap during his period of working for Vulcan and Trap Scaffoldwrights. Eventually, the full threat of Trapism, the blurring of black and white uncovered by David's investigations, emerges: Trap is revealed as sharing ancestry with prominent capitalists and aristocrats, the Australian historical myth is reversed and the subservient, fringe figure of the Aboriginal is presented as a central, disturbing power.

The Wort Papers, also written in semi-diary form and covering an even wider social and historical spectrum, purports to be the jumbled manuscript of the Wort family history, compiled by the iconoclastic, anarchic Percy Wort and threatening the security of his bourgeois brother, Thomas. Although in both novels rebellion and political action are presented as comically ineffective, the anarchic characters in *The Wort Papers* are more passive and accidentally anti-social in their effects than in *Trap*; in both novels, however, they retain such an invincible, inalienable freedom that the outward severity of their various persecutions and hardships becomes more of a comic fantasy. The pattern, meanwhile, of their impacts on society, reinforced and mirrored by Mathers's flexible form, creates an impression of Australian history as an intricate maze of contingent but involuntarily significant destinies. In both novels Mathers's energetic, resourceful use of language, his powers of verbal slapstick, comic exaggeration, witty parody and incisive satire, contribute markedly to the overall destructive effect.

MATHEW, RAY (1929–   ), born Sydney, was a NSW schoolteacher (1949-51), a freelance journalist (1951-52), a member of the CSIRO (1952-54) and a tutor and lecturer with the University of Sydney (1955-60). In 1961 he left Australia and has subsequently lived in London, Italy and New York. One of Australia's most enterprising playwrights of the 1950s, Mathew wrote a series of experimental dramas which anticipate a number of themes and modes used by writers of the late 1960s renaissance. His published plays include *We Find the Bunyip* in *Khaki, Bush and Bigotry* (1968, ed. Eunice Hanger), a satirical rural comedy first produced in 1955; *The Bones of My Toe* in *Australian One-Act Plays, Book One* (1962, ed. Eunice Hanger); and *A Spring Song* (1961), the story of a young male schoolteacher and his involvement in the crises and relationships of a country family, first produced in 1958. His unpublished plays include 'The Boomerang and the Bantam' (n.d.); 'Church Sunday' (1950) and 'Lonely Without You' (1957), both of which are one-act plays set in the bush; 'Sing for St. Ned' (1960), a comic musical satire on the Ned Kelly myth, which anticipates the rough style of *The Legend of King O'Malley*; and 'The Life of the Party' (1961), a sophisticated comedy set against the bohemian background of Kings Cross, which was produced in London in 1961 but has been neglected by Australian theatres. He has also written two radio plays, 'The Love of Gotama' (1952), and an adaptation of Euripides' *Medea* (1954). Mathew's attempts to achieve a new, suggestive realism by means of unusual verbal techniques and indeterminate, even circular plots which deliberately avoid the expected climaxes of the 'well-made play', were not fully appreciated by Australian audiences of the 1950s. It was his misfortune to be writing ahead of his time and he is now often classed with Peter Kenna and Jack McKinney as one of the 'lonely playwrights'. Mathew also published three volumes of verse which demonstrate his unusual verbal techniques and ability to create a well-defined regional identity, *With Cypress Pine* (1951), *Song and Dance* (1956) and *South of the Equator* (1961); and a collection of short stories, most of which draw on his experiences of rural NSW and Sydney and were previously published in the *Bulletin* and *Southerly*, *A Bohemian Affair* (1961). He also contributed stories to another collection with Mena Abdullah, *The Time of the Peacock* (1965) and is represented in numerous anthologies. His other publications include a novel, *The Joys of Possession* (1967), which is partly autobiographical and draws on his talent as social comedian, and studies of Miles Franklin (1955) and Charles Blackman (1965).

Matilda, the colloquial term for a swag (q.v.) or bed-roll, probably derives from the German word *mathilde*, meaning a female travelling-companion, probably imported into the vernacular during the gold rushes from the speech of SA German immigrants visiting the goldfields. The phrase, 'to waltz matilda', meaning to carry one's swag or live as a swagman, has received its most famous usage in 'Waltzing Matilda' (q.v.). In Henry Lawson's short story ' "Rats" ', the matilda reverts to its human origins in the crazed antics of an old bushman.

Mattara Spring Festival Poetry Prize, sponsored by the Hunter District Water Board and under the administration of the department of English, the University of Newcastle, has been awarded annually since 1981. In 1981 the prize was shared by Les Murray and Kevin Hart; in 1982 it was won by Peter Kocan for 'From the Private Poems of Governor Caulfield'; in 1983 it was won by Craig Powell for 'Five Pieces for a Homecoming'. Selected entries for the prize have been incorporated into anthologies: *The Members of the Orchestra and Other Poems* (1981), edited by Paul Kavanagh; *Lines from the Horizon and Other Poems* (1982), edited by Christopher Pollnitz; *Instructions for Honey Ants and Other Poems* (1983), edited by Paul Kavanagh.

MATTHEWS, BRIAN, see **LAWSON, HENRY**

MATTHEWS, CHRISTOPHER, see *Australian*/Vogel **National Literary Award**

MATTHEWS, HARLEY (1889–1968), born Harry Matthews, at St Leonards, Sydney, served in the First World War at Gallipoli and in Egypt and France. Although he was qualified as a solicitor and had experience as a journalist, he became a vigneron at Moorebank near Sydney in 1922; his vineyard was a popular gathering place for writers in the 1930s. Suspected of being a member of the Australia First movement, Matthews was imprisoned for six months in 1942; cleared by the Royal Commission into the movement in 1945, he was awarded £700 compensation. He spent the remainder of his life on a small farm at Ingleburn on the outskirts of Sydney.

Matthews published several books of verse, the first two of which (1912, 1916) had the same title, *Under the Open Sky*, but contained mostly different poems. To *Trio* (1931), which he shared with Kenneth Slessor and Colin Simpson, he contributed the Gallipoli narrative poem 'Two Brothers'. One of his best early poems *The Breaking of the Drought* was published as a separate pamphlet in 1940. *Vintage* (1938), a group of four war poems and four lyrics, also contained 'Two Brothers'. His best book of mostly lyrical verse, *Patriot's Progress* (1965), reflects Matthews's independent spirit, love of the rural scene and scorn for convention and materialism. His two books of short stories are *Saints and Sinners* (1918), which captures much of the character of the Australian soldier, and

Wet Canteen (1939), which contains a mixture of previously published and new tales. He also wrote a three-act play, *We Are the People* (1940), and edited an anthology of short stories, *Pillar to Post* (1944).

'MAURICE, FURNLEY' (FRANK WILMOT) (1881–1942), born Collingwood, Melbourne, published most of his work under the pseudonym 'Furnley Maurice', a combination of the names of two of his favourite Melbourne haunts, Ferntree Gully and Beaumaris. Inclined to nationalism and radicalism by his background, 'Furnley Maurice' published his first verses in Bernard O'Dowd's radical journal *Tocsin*. He worked for thirty-five years, from errand boy to manager, in Cole's Book Arcade in Melbourne, was active in the Melbourne Literary Club which sponsored the magazine *Birth*, printed on his own treadle press, was a member of Louis Esson's Pioneer Players, became the successful manager of Melbourne University Press, helped to establish the Victorian branch of the FAW, was on the advisory board of the CLF and presented the Fund's inaugural lectures on Australian literature at the University of Melbourne. 'Maurice''s early poetry, *Some Verses* (1903) and *Some More Verses* (1904), are home-made booklets produced on an old hand printing press which also produced his small and short-lived monthly magazine the *Microbe*. After *Unconditioned Songs* (1913) came some of 'Maurice''s most significant work, the poetry which contains his reaction to the First World War. In the poem 'To God: From the Warring Nations' (q.v.), and in the volume *Eyes of Vigilance* (1920) he expresses his disgust at the glamorizing of war, at the pressures on young men to enlist and at the criminality of war itself. His radical-nationalist views are evident in his condemnation of Australia for departing from the nationalist dream of moulding her destiny to follow the European pattern of ancient hatreds between nations. During the war he also wrote, for his two small sons, some excellent children's verse, *The Bay and Padie Book* (1917). *Arrows of Longing* (1921) with its preface by Bernard O'Dowd, also reflects 'Maurice''s deep concern, with the memory of war still fresh, for the future of Australia and of the human race in general. 'Maurice' was fundamentally a townsman but he loved the bushland of the Dandenong Ranges, as his poem 'The Gully' (1925), which has been equated with Bernard O'Dowd's 'The Bush', indicates. 'Maurice''s most significant literary achievement is *Melbourne Odes* (q.v., 1934). In the preface to the odes 'Maurice' expounds the principles of modern European and American poetry and stresses the need for new methods, techniques and objectives for Australian poetry.

In the *Odes* 'Maurice' seeks to employ the best features of the modern movement in verse; the work is thus experimental and educational and its impact upon the development of modern Australian verse, though long and perhaps still underestimated, is undoubted. Vance Palmer wrote *Frank Wilmot (Furnley Maurice)* (1942); Hugh Anderson, *Frank Wilmot (Furnley Maurice) : A Bibliography and a Criticism* (1955); and F.T. Macartney, *Furnley Maurice (Frank Wilmot)* (1955). The impact of his life is also discussed in David Walker's *Dream and Disillusion* (1976).

Maurice Guest, a novel by 'Henry Handel Richardson' (q.v.) was first published in 1908. Set in Leipzig at the turn of the century, it deals with the fatal passion of an idealistic, young English student of music, Maurice Guest, for an Australian woman, Louise Dufrayer. Louise, several years older than Maurice but disturbingly attractive, is deeply involved in an unequal relationship with a Polish musician of genius, Schilsky. Maurice, who has grown up in a cheerless, middle-class home, totally bereft 'of the great gladness, the ideal beauty of life', romanticizes both his passion for music and his passion for Louise. In his sentimental idealism he differs from his friends, Madeleine Ware, a purposeful, realistic, sympathetic girl who repeatedly attempts to rescue Maurice from his self-destructive path, and Dove, a shallow egoist who is easily able to adapt to his disappointments in love and whose busy concern for others satisfies his mild lust for power. The enigmatic, unpredictable Heinz Krafft, another talented student, who also seems to have been sexually involved with both Schilsky and Louise, appears to be inspired with a more malevolent urge to manipulate others. Ephie Cayhill, on the other hand, a child-like American, is completely vulnerable in this milieu, especially after she falls in love with Schilsky. The latter, who casually encourages her passion while attempting to disentangle himself from Louise, is making plans to leave Leipzig and further his career with the financial help of yet another admirer. Maurice quarrels violently with Schilsky after he discovers these facts at a drunken party. Although Louise has barely noticed Maurice up to this point, he shows his devotion to her in the crisis following Schilsky's sudden departure, by taking Ephie to her apartment. The American girl, in despair at her enlightenment about Schilsky and Louise, is removed from Leipzig by her family. Two months later, Maurice, who has attempted to subdue his passion for Louise, discovers that she is living in a state of apathetic withdrawal, and takes over the management of her practical affairs. After their relationship becomes one of close companionship, Maurice proposes marriage and is rejected, Louise realizing that 'there is something irreconcileable in their two natures'. Shortly after, however, she suddenly consents to accept him as a lover, hoping perhaps to escape from her ennui in this way. In July they spend an idyllic two weeks in the country. Back in Leipzig, Maurice throws himself into his work, which he has previously neglected, but becomes increasingly uneasy about Louise's uninterest in everything except sensual passion. By October Louise is aware that for her 'the whole affair had been no more than an episode' and Maurice is made to realize that 'to him the gradual unfolding of their love had been a wonderful revelation; to her, a repetition, and a paler and fainter one, of a tale she already knew by heart'. Their relationship rapidly degenerates: Maurice, maddened by her inconstancy and his discovery of her relationship with Krafft, beats her in despair. Krafft suddenly disappears from Leipzig, although he continues to write to Maurice denigrating Louise. His departure is also followed by the suicide of his inscrutable but devoted mistress, Avery Hill. Maurice, now aware that Louise is indifferent to him and will return to Schilsky but powerless to surmount his feelings, which he now recognizes have passed beyond 'tenderness, faithfulness, respect' to become simply 'the morbid possession by a woman's face', commits suicide. The novel concludes with a glimpse of Schilsky and Louise, now married, two years later; Schilsky, now *Konzertmeister* in a large south German town, is firmly set in his career and Louise, of whom it is said that 'an English chap shot himself on her account', is still exerting her power over other men. In 1954 the novel was produced as a film titled *Rhapsody* and starring Elizabeth Taylor.

Mavis Bramston Show, The, a satirical television series produced by Sydney's Channel 7, ran 1964–68. A revue-type show, which lightly satirized national attitudes, surburban living, contemporary politics and media personalities, and hosted by 'Mavis', a symbol of every disastrous English import, it anticipated the liberal mood of the drama of the late 1960s. Scripted by a team of writers, it provided employment for such well-known actors as Gordon Chater, Barry Creyton, Noelene Brown and Carol Raye.

MAWSON, Sir DOUGLAS (1882–1958), born Bradford, Yorkshire, was brought to Australia as a child. He graduated in engineering and science at the University of Sydney and in 1907 accompanied Shackleton's expedition to Antarctica; he was knighted for his exploits on both that and the 1911–14 Australasian Ant-

arctic expedition and was awarded many honours, including the King's Polar medal, the Founder's Medal of the Royal Geographical Society and the first David Livingstone Centenary Medal of the American Geographical Society. Professor of geology at the University of Adelaide from 1920, Mawson was also responsible for setting up the first Australian National Antarctic research expedition in 1947 and for establishing an Antarctic division of the Department of External Affairs in 1948. One of the Australian Antarctic bases is named after him, as is the Mawson Institute in Adelaide, established in 1961 to further Antarctic research. Mawson published *The Home of the Blizzard* in 1915, acknowledged as one of the finest books on the polar areas. His solitary journey back to base after the disappearance of his two companions down a crevasse is told in Lennard Bickel's *This Accursed Land* (1977). C.F. Laseron, assistant biologist on the 1911–14 expedition, wrote *South with Mawson* (1947); Geoffrey Dutton wrote a valedictory sonnet, 'On the Death of Sir Douglas Mawson'. Paquita Mawson, the explorer's wife, published the biography, *Mawson of the Antarctic* (1964). In 1982 the ABC produced a television documentary, 'Douglas Mawson – The Survivor' (which reconstructs the ill-fated 1912 expedition), to mark the centenary of his birth.

MAY, PHIL (1864–1903), born and educated in Leeds, England, was becoming known as a cartoonist in London when he was lured to Australia by W.H. Traill in 1885 to work for the *Bulletin*. He remained with the *Bulletin* for three years, produced some 800 drawings, and helped Livingston Hopkins to establish the journal's reputation in the field of black-and-white art. In Australia May developed his characteristic economy of line although it is doubtful whether, as is commonly thought, the *Bulletin*'s inadequate printing facilities were the cause. On his return to England he became famous on *Punch* and other journals; his best-known Australian drawings were the caricatures of politicians such as Sir Henry Parkes and Sir John Robertson and the series, 'Things We See When We Go Out Without Our Gun'. A.G. Stephens edited *Phil May in Australia* (1904), a collection of May's *Bulletin* cartoons.

MAYMAN, TED, see **Kalgoorlie**

Meanjin, a journal known as *Meanjin Papers* (1940–47), *Meanjin* (1947–60, 1977–) and *Meanjin Quarterly* (1961–76), began in Brisbane in December 1940 with an eight-page edition of eight poems, two each by Clem Christesen (q.v.), the editor, James Picot, Brian Vrepont and Paul Grano. Bimonthly in 1940–

42, *Meanjin* has been quarterly since 1943. It takes its name from the Aboriginal word for Brisbane, combined from the words 'migon' (spike) and 'chagun' (earth, place, land), the composite word 'meanjin' ('mianjin') referring to the spike or finger of land on which Brisbane is built. In 1945 *Meanjin* moved with Christesen to Melbourne, where the University of Melbourne gave it the home it has occupied to the present time. The constant battle for financial viability has seen *Meanjin* supported from Christesen's own resources then assisted by grants-in-aid from the Lockie Bequest, University of Melbourne (since 1949), from the CLF and the Literature Board, and the Ministry for the Arts, Victoria. *Meanjin* owed its survival to its long-standing (1940–74) editor, Clem Christesen. He was succeeded by Jim Davidson (1974–82), who changed the appearance of the magazine and introduced new features such as the regular interviews with contemporary writers, and in 1982 by Judith Brett. Dorothy Green, Harry Heseltine, A.A. Phillips, Humphrey McQueen, and Geoffrey Serle have been among its advisers or consultants. Opinions of *Meanjin's* political leanings range from a 'fellow-travelling publication', the description of James McAuley, editor of *Meanjin's* right-wing rival *Quadrant*, to Christesen's own phrase, 'democratic left of centre', which more accurately describes its liberal humanist stance. *Meanjin's* task, according to Christesen in his 1951 commentary, 'The Wound as the Bow', on the magazine's first decade of existence, was to offer 'disinterested criticism that is interested in all pertinent ideas', to be 'flexible because of its inflexible sincerity' and 'as a matter of principle' to be 'unattached to any one principle'. Although *Meanjin* has regularly published or focused on overseas writing, its major literary importance has been in its publication of Australian poetry and short fiction and its establishment of a body of seminal criticism (q.v.) on a wide range of Australian writers. A review of arts and letters for much of its life, it has also paid attention to music, cinema and the other arts, and has periodically investigated contemporary Australian society, as in its 'Austerica' and 'Godzone' series in the 1960s and its 'State of the Nation' articles in the 1970s. Important new work by established writers such as A.D. Hope, James McAuley, Douglas Stewart, Judith Wright, Patrick White, Randolph Stow, and by younger writers such as Frank Moorhouse, Les Murray and others has been published in *Meanjin*. Special numbers of *Meanjin* have been devoted to writers, e.g. Joseph Furphy (3, 1943) and Vance Palmer (2, 1959); genres, e.g. Australian theatre and drama (3, 1964); Aboriginal writing (4, 1977); and traditions, e.g. the 'St Petersburg or Tinsel Town' issue on cultural traditions in Sydney and in Melbourne (1, 1981) and A.A. Phillip's notable essay, 'The Cultural Cringe (4, 1950). *On Native Grounds* (1968), edited by Christesen, and *Sideways from the Page* (1983), a selection of Davidson's interviews with writers, are both volumes which reprint material first published in *Meanjin*. The Meanjin Press, also associated with the journal, published several volumes in the 1940s, e.g. Judith Wright's *The Moving Image* (1948) and Nettie Palmer's *Fourteen Years* (1948). Lynne Strahan's *Just City and the Mirrors: Meanjin Quarterly and the Intellectual Front, 1940–65* was published in 1984.

Meat Man, see *Glass Canoe, The*

Meeting Pool, The, see SKIPPER, MERVYN

Mejane, see Feminism and Australian Literature

MELBA, Dame **NELLIE** (HELEN PORTER ARMSTRONG) (1861–1931), was born Helen Mitchell in Melbourne and studied music with Pietro Cecchi, an Italian tenor. In 1882 she accompanied her father, a building contractor, to northern Queensland, where she married Charles Armstrong, manager of a sugar plantation, the same year. Although a son was born in 1883, the marriage soon failed and Melba returned to Melbourne to begin her singing career. In 1886 she sailed for London with ambitions of making a name in opera, but was at first unsuccessful and moved to Paris, where the well-known teacher, Madame Marchesi, undertook to make 'something extraordinary' of her. She appeared for the first time as Madame Melba, the title deriving from her native city, late in 1886 and made a triumphant debut in *Rigoletto* in Brussels in 1887. Her career thereafter progressed with few setbacks and for many years she sang at Covent Garden, was equally successful in Europe and the USA and regarded as unrivalled in many of her twenty-five operas. She toured Australia 1902–03 and from 1909 lived partly in Europe and partly in Australia. Actively associated with the Melbourne University Conservatorium of Music and a highly successful fund-raiser for the Australian Red Cross during the First World War, she was made DBE in 1918 and GBE in 1927. She made her final appearance at Covent Garden in June 1926 and her last Australian appearance at Geelong in November 1928. In May 1927 she sang the national anthem at the opening of Parliament House, Canberra. Her reminiscences, *Melodies and Memories*, appeared in 1925 and she also contributed to a substantial anthology of Australian writing, *Melba's Gift Book of Australian Art and Literature* (1915), and to the *Australian Soldiers' Gift Book* (1918), edited by Ethel Turner and Bertram Stevens. Of the numerous biographies of Melba, Agnes G. Murphy's *Melba* (1909), Percy Colson's *Melba: An Unconventional Biography* (1932), Joseph Wechsberg's *Red Plush and Black Velvet* (1961), Geoffrey W. Hutton's *Melba* (1962), and John Hetherington's *Melba* (1967), Hetherington's is the most substantial. Maie Casey has offered a reassessment in *Melba Revisited* (1975) and her life has been the subject of two plays, *Melba* (1976) by Paul Sherman and *A Toast to Melba* (1976) by Jack Hibberd. The phrase 'to do a Melba' derives from her many 'retirements'.

Melbourne, the capital of Victoria (q.v.), is situated in the southern part of the State, along the lower reaches of the Yarra River; at the mouth of the Yarra is Port Phillip Bay, beyond which is Bass Strait, separating Victoria from Tasmania. Intending pastoralists were the first to settle in the Melbourne area. In 1835 John Batman, acting for the Port Phillip Association from Van Diemen's Land, explored parts of the area and claimed to have purchased land from the Aborigines; later that year John Pascoe Fawkner camped along the Yarra. After any purchases from the Aborigines were declared null and void by the colonial government in New South Wales, settlement began in earnest in Melbourne and other parts of the Port Phillip District (q.v.), as Victoria was called until separated from New South Wales in 1851. Incorporated as a town in 1842 and proclaimed a city in 1847, Melbourne underwent a boom following the discovery of gold; an impression of the boom city is given in 'Henry Handel Richardson''s *The Fortunes of Richard Mahony* (1930). Named after the prime minister of England, Melbourne was designated 'Marvellous Melbourne' in the 1880s; its character then is analysed in Graeme Davison's *The Rise and Fall of Marvellous Melbourne* (1978). John Arnold edited *The Imagined City: Melbourne in the Minds of Its Writers* (1983), which includes extracts from more than two dozen writers. Dame Nellie Melba took her stage name from Melbourne.

Melbourne Advertiser published at Port Phillip by John Pascoe Fawkner from 1 January – 23 April 1838, began as a handwritten sheet carrying classified advertisements, shipping and travel notices and a 'Poet's Corner'. From 5 March – 23 April the sheet appeared in printed form, thus becoming the first printed publication in Melbourne. Suppressed because of failure to comply with the Newspaper Act, it

was re-established as the *Port Phillip Patriot and Melbourne Advertiser* (1839–48).

'Melbourne Alsatia, A', see **'Lower Bohemia'**

Melbourne Bulletin a weekly paper, was published 1880–86 and was owned and produced by Edmund Finn, Alex McKinley, John Booth and others. Subsequently absorbed into *Melbourne Punch*, the paper contained general articles on socio-political, religious and business matters, as well as theatrical notices and some fiction and light verse.

Melbourne Critical Review, see ***Critical Review***

Melbourne Cup is a handicap horse race run over 3200 metres (formerly two miles) on the first Tuesday in November at Flemington racecourse in Melbourne. First run in 1861, it soon became an event of national significance and was commented on by visitors such as 'Mark Twain' and prominent journalists such as 'Garryowen' and 'The Vagabond'. Numerous nineteenth-century plays have Melbourne Cup scenes e.g. *Marvellous Melbourne* (1889); in Alfred Dampier's adaptation of Nat Gould's *The Double Event* (staged 1893) and William Anderson and Temple Harrison's 'Winning Ticket' (1900) the Cup race was staged with live horses. Other writers to have used 'the Cup' and its rituals in their work include Adam Lindsay Gordon, Ada Cambridge, Marcus Clarke, Victor Daley, Jessie Couvreur, Douglas Sladen, Arthur Wright, Nat Gould, Ambrose Pratt, A.B. Paterson, C.J. Dennis, Rosa Praed and Alexander Buzo. Among Australian artists, Charles Nuttall published a series of humorous sketches, *Peter Wayback Visits the Melbourne Cup* (1902), and Frank Mahony's Dawn and Dusk Club colleagues required him to predict, through paint, the Melbourne Cup winner.

Melbourne Journal: Australian Serial Tales, Short Stories, and the Literature of the Day, an illustrated fortnightly newspaper, appeared 1894–1927. Advertising 'Thrilling Tales of Romance and Adventure: Interesting, Instructive, and Amusing Home Reading', the newspaper included serials and original and reprinted short stories, as well as articles on local and overseas news.

Melbourne Morning Herald, see ***Herald***

Melbourne Odes (1934) are among the most important poems of 'Furnley Maurice' (q.v.). The opening ode, 'Melbourne and Memory', won the Melbourne centenary poetry competition. Other odes in the volume deal with places and events familiar in the life of the city: the Victoria Markets, the annual agricultural show and orchestral concerts in the Melbourne Town Hall. Together they represent the first attempt by an Australian poet to depict life in the modern city. 'Upon a Row of Old Boots and Shoes in a Pawnbroker's Window', with its grim account of the plight of the unemployed of the 1930s depression and its macabre description of the ghostly march of the boot-pawners, is a powerful radical commentary on the economic misery and injustice of the time.

Melbourne Punch, the best, most famous and longest-running of the colonial imitations of London *Punch*, was founded in 1855 by Edgar Ray and Frederick Sinnett. An illustrated humorous weekly which included articles on society and politics, satirical verse and prose and cartoons, it merged with *Table Talk* (1885–1939) in 1929. Sinnett was succeeded as editor by James Smith (1857–63) and Charles Bright (1863–66). Prominent early contributors included Butler Cole Aspinall, Charles Gavan Duffy, R.H. Horne, and the cartoonists Thomas Carrington and Nicholas Chevalier. *Melbourne Punch* was a significant colonial literary magazine but was even more important for the part it played in the development of an Australian tradition of political caricature. Of the other Australian imitations of *Punch*, three separate magazines carried the title *Sydney Punch* (1856, 1857, 1864–88), the third of them founded also by Ray and numbering Daniel Deniehy, Garnet Walch and later William Macleod among its contributors; *Adelaide Punch,* like its Melbourne counterpart, carried cartoons by Carrington and ran intermittently 1868–84, when it was incorporated into the *Lantern; Tasmanian Punch* ran 1866–68 (1867–68 as *Hobart Town Punch*) and was revived in 1870; *Queensland Punch* (1868–85) published work by Ernest Favenc, Henry Halloran, and J. Brunton Stephens before it was incorporated into *Queensland Figaro*; and there were even two versions of *Ballarat Punch* (1857, 1867–70). The best study of *Melbourne Punch* and other colonial equivalents of London *Punch*, which include humorous weeklies such as *Humbug* and *Touchstone*, is Marguerite Mahood's *The Loaded Line* (1973).

Melbourne Review, a quarterly magazine which ran 1876–85, was modelled on the English magazines, *Contemporary Review* and *Fortnightly Review*. Edited by H.G. Turner, later assisted by A.P. Martin and Alexander Sutherland, the magazine attracted contributions from such writers as G.B. Barton, Marcus Clarke, Sir

Henry Parkes, Catherine Spence, David Syme, Ethel Turner and Jessie Couvreur.

Melbourne Theatre Company was established in 1953 under the auspices of the University of Melbourne, administered by John Sumner and located in the Union Theatre on the campus. In 1959 the Australian Elizabethan Theatre Trust came into association with the Company, although it was not until 1966 that the MTC left the Union Theatre and established a permanent theatre in the city at Russell Street. In 1977 the MTC expanded further, to the Athenaeum theatre in one of Melbourne's oldest buildings, and in 1979 established its third venue, Athenaeum 2, a small theatre appropriate for more intimate plays. The largest and most prestigious repertory company in Australia, the MTC has dominated Melbourne theatre for the last three decades. As well as producing a wide range of international plays, the Company has frequently produced Australian plays, often supporting a playwright in residence. Outstanding plays staged for the first time by the MTC include Ray Lawler's *Summer of the Seventeenth Doll*, Vance Palmer's *Prisoner's Country*, Patrick White's *A Cheery Soul*, Alan Hopgood's *And the Big Men Fly*, Alexander Buzo's *Macquarie*, and David Williamson's *Jugglers Three*.

Melbourne University Magazine, a student magazine known familiarly as MUM and published annually since 1907, started as a review of the university year with contributions in prose and verse, photographs, and notes on the activities of colleges, societies and sporting clubs. Eventually expanded into more of a literary publication, with a strong interest in political, philosophical and social issues, the magazine has often included original contributions from Australian writers as well as significant interviews. Contributors have included Vincent Buckley, Tim Burstall, Max Harris, A.D. Hope, Bruce Dawe and R.G. Menzies.

Melbourne University Press, see **University Presses**

'MELVILLE, CAPTAIN', see **Bushranger in Australian Literature**

MELVILLE, HENRY SAXELBY MELVILLE WINTLE (1799–1873), born England, always used the name Henry Melville and probably arrived in Hobart late in 1827. In 1830 he bought the *Colonial Times* from Andrew Bent and published Henry Savery's *Quintus Servinton* (1831), the first Australian novel: three years later he founded the first literary monthly in Tasmania, the *Hobart Town*

Magazine (q.v.). During the 1830s he was involved in the running, not only of the *Colonial Times*, which passed out of his hands in 1839, but also of the *Tasmanian*, its offshoot, the *Tasmanian and Austral-Asiatic Review* and the *Trumpeter*, an advertising paper. In the *Tasmanian* ventures he combined forces with Robert Lathropp Murray (q.v.) and was critical of Governor Arthur's administration. While in prison for contempt of court in 1835 he wrote 'A Few Words on Prison Discipline', which formed part of the pioneering *The History of the Island of Van Diemen's Land, from the Year 1824 to 1835 Inclusive* (1835); like his anti-government pamphlet, *Two Letters Written in Van Diemen's Land* (1834), it was published anonymously. In the 1840s Melville engaged primarily in agricultural pursuits and in the study of the occult and freemasonry, on which he published several later works. After leaving Tasmania in 1849, he settled in England, where he published in 1851 the work known in different editions as *Australasia and Prison Discipline* and *The Present State of Australia*. His activities as a journalist, editor and publisher are discussed in E. Morris Miller's *Pressmen and Governors* (1952).

Melvyn, Sybylla, see *My Brilliant Career*

Memoirs of a Velvet Urinal, see **DRANS-FIELD, MICHAEL**

Men Are Human, see **PALMER, VANCE**

'Men in Green', a notable war poem by David Campbell (q.v.), was published in the *Bulletin* in 1943. The poem's narrator, an RAAF pilot in New Guinea, flies fifteen infantry reinforcements to the jungle frontline in 1942. The cool detachment of the pilot is contrasted with the impact that their first real glimpse of the war has on the raw, young soldiers. Their noisy, nervous confidence ('the green men laughed aloud') fades into apprehensive silence as they come face to face with the sick and wounded they have come to replace.

Men of Yesterday, see **KIDDLE, MARGARET**

MENNELL, PHILIP (1851–1905), born Newcastle, England, qualified as a solicitor before coming to Australia in the middle 1870s. He founded and edited the *Bairnsdale Advertiser*, 1877–82, and wrote for the *Age* in Melbourne, 1882–83, before returning to London as the *Age*'s representative 1883–91, and later as editor of the *British Australasian*, 1892–1905. Active within the London Anglo-Australian community (called the 'AAs' by Marcus Clarke),

Mennell edited *In Australian Wilds* (1889), which carried contributions by B.L. Farjeon, C. Haddon Chambers, 'Tasma' and others; contributed to similar anthologies, e.g. A.P. Martin's, *Oak-bough and Wattle-blossom* (1888), and wrote a descriptive travel work and emigrants' guide on WA, *The Coming Colony* (1892), which derived from a return visit to Australia in 1891. He paid later visits in 1895 and 1900 as correspondent for the London *Times* and *Morning Post*, respectively. His most important work, however, was *The Dictionary of Australasian Biography (1855–1892)* (1892), which includes historical material as well as biographies of colonial worthies.

MENZIES, Sir **ROBERT** (1894–1978), prime minister of Australia 1939–41 and 1949–66, was born at Jeparit, Victoria, and worked as a lawyer before entering federal politics in 1934. His published works include *Rule of Law during War* (1917), *Studies in the Australian Constitution* (1933), *Speech Is of Time* (1958), *Central Power in the Australian Commonwealth* (1962), and two volumes of reminiscences, *Afternoon Light* (1967) and *The Measure of the Years* (1970). Appointed a Knight of the Thistle in 1963, he was also made Lord Warden of the Cinque Ports on his retirement in 1966. Numerous biographies of Menzies have been published, including Kevin Perkins, *Menzies : Last of the Queen's Men* (1968), Cameron Hazlehurst, *Menzies Observed* (1979) and Sir Percy Joske, *Menzies 1894–1978* (1978); a collection of his witticisms, compiled by Ray Robinson, was published in 1966. Known familiarly as 'Ming the Merciless' and 'Pig-iron Bob', Menzies was frequently the butt of satirists and cartoonists. He is the subject of a long satirical poem, *Rob the Robber* (1954), by 'Spinifex' (David Martin), and appears in an extensive role in Barry Oakley's play, 'Beware of Imitations' (1973).

MERCER, HAROLD (1882–?), born Brisbane, served in the First World War, studied law before becoming an actor, and was also an active unionist. A contributor of verse and short stories or prose sketches to the *Bulletin* and other journals, often under the pseudonym 'Hamer', he published four collections of short stories, *Search for the Bonzer Tart* (1920), *The Lady Who Was French* (1929), *The Adventures of Mrs. Parsley* (1942) and *Romances in Real Life* (1944); a romance of the Pacific, *Amazon Island* (1933); and a collection of verse, *The Frequent Lover* (1928).

MERCIER, EMILE (1901–81), born Noumea, New Caledonia, of French parentage, came to Australia as a young man (1919 and 1923 have both been suggested) and was a clerk and translator while studying art under Julian Ashton. He had his first cartoons and joke drawings published in the early 1920s but was forced to work at many part-time jobs, including those of 'spruiker' and music-hall actor, while making freelance contributions to the *Bulletin*, *Melbourne Punch*, *Smith's Weekly*, and other journals. From 1940 he obtained more regular work as the illustrator of Lennie Lower's *Smith's Weekly* column; as political cartoonist for *Truth*, for which he also created two comic strips, and the *Daily Mirror*; and as writer-illustrator of comics for Frank Johnson; in 1949–68 he was a full-time cartoonist with the Sydney *Sun*. Mercier published more than twenty comic books and books of cartoons; many of his comic book protagonists, e.g. Mudrake the Magician, Tripalong Hoppity, Speed Umplestroop, were the satiric equivalents of the heroes of cinema serials and other strips, e.g. Mandrake, Hopalong Cassidy, Speed Gordon. His *Sun* cartoons, now affectionately remembered, were irreverently topical, contemptuous of pretension, and characterized by oddball characters, e.g. an old gent with a long white beard who often appeared on stilts, numerous stray animals such as yaks and cats with immodestly raised tails; by zany details, e.g. the springs on which the cartoon often sat; and by absurd alliterations and repetitions, e.g. phrases like 'Post no Gravy' and words like 'shrdlu', which confirm the verbal-visual mix of his work. Mercier's humour, although intensely Australian in content and target, has its parallel overseas in the humour of the Goons and the Goodies.

Mercury, the major Tasmanian newspaper, was founded in 1854 by John Davies and George Aubey Jones, who incorporated the *Hobarton Guardian*, which they had taken over in 1852, into their new newspaper, which was named the *Hobarton Mercury* 1854–58, and the *Hobart Town Daily Mercury*, 1858–60. A morning daily from 1858, the *Mercury* incorporated a number of other Hobart newspapers, including the *Colonial Times* in 1857, the *Tasmanian Daily News* in 1858, the *Hobart Town Courier* in 1859, and the *Illustrated Tasmanian Mail* in 1935. The Davies family retained control of the *Mercury* until 1895, when a public company was formed, in which the Herald and Weekly Times company of Melbourne has a significant interest.

MEREDITH, GWEN (1907–), born Orange, NSW, was educated at the University of Sydney where she began writing plays, two of which were staged. In 1939 she contributed to a long-running radio serial, *Fred and Maggie*.

Blue Hills, her outstandingly popular radio serial which was broadcast four days a week 1949–76, was preceded by another serial with a farming background, *The Lawsons*, which ran 1943–49. Both drew on the Australian nostalgia for the bush and were sustained by Meredith's gift for developing a drama of slowly-unfolding human relationships and for creating ordinary characters faced with problems such as romantic love, business difficulties, or the onset of old age. Sensitive to some extent to changing social mores and frequently topical in its public concerns, *Blue Hills* never succumbed to permissive sexual standards. The series provided regular employment for a range of well-known actors including John Meillon, John McCallum, Queenie Ashton, Nellie Lamport, June Salter, Rod Taylor, Madge Ryan and Ray Barrett. Meredith also wrote other plays for radio and stage, including a three-act comedy, *Wives Have Their Uses* (1944); *Great Inheritance* in *Australian Radio Plays* (1946, ed. Leslie Rees) and *Modern Short Plays* (1951); and 'Cornerstone', a stage-play produced in 1955; several novels based on the radio serials, *The Lawsons* (1948), *Blue Hills* (1950), *Beyond Blue Hills* (1953), and *Into the Sun* (1961); and, with her husband, Ainsworth Harrison, a travel book, *Inns and Outs* (1955). In 1967 she was made MBE.

Meredith Family, see *My Brother Jack*; *Clean Straw for Nothing*

MEREDITH, JOHN (1920–) born and educated at Holbrook, NSW, worked in the pharmaceutical industry before becoming a full-time writer in 1978. At fourteen he bought a copy of A.B. Paterson's *Old Bush Songs* (q.v.), which inspired his long-term interest in Australian folk-song (q.v.) and folklore. A founding member of the Sydney Bush Music Club, he was first editor of its journal, *Singabout*. With Hugh Anderson, Meredith wrote *Folk Songs of Australia and the Men and Women Who Sang Them* (1967); he also compiled other song books, e.g. *Reedy River Song Book* (1953), *Songs from the Kelly Country* (1955), and several *Bushwhacker Broadsides* (1955–60). His other publications include important studies of Bold Jack Donahue, *The Wild Colonial Boy* (rev. ed. 1982); Francis MacNamara, *Frank the Poet* (1979, with Rex Whalan); Ned Kelly, *Ned Kelly, After a Century of Acrimony* (1980, with Bill Scott); 'Duke' Tritton, *Duke of the Outback* (1983); and *The Coo-ee March* (1981). With Joan Clarke, Meredith wrote a ballad opera, 'The Wild Colonial Boy', first produced in 1955; a second ballad opera, 'How Many Miles from Gundagai', has also been produced.

MEREDITH, LOUISA ANNE (1812–95), born Birmingham, England, married her cousin, Charles Meredith, in 1839 and went with him to NSW, where he had pastoral interests. In 1840 they moved to Tasmania, where Charles was a successful member of parliament 1860–79. An energetic, talented and strongly independent woman, Louisa compiled and illustrated several books on colonial life and society and native flora and fauna, including *Notes and Sketches of New South Wales* (1844) and *My Home in Tasmania* (1852). She also wrote a travel book, *Over the Straits; A Visit to Victoria* (1861) and published numerous illustrated books of poetry, e.g. *Some of My Bush Friends in Tasmania* (1860), *Our Island Home* (1879) and *Bush Friends in Tasmania, Native Flowers, Fruits and Insects* (1891). She also wrote p\ etry for children, e.g. *Waratah Rhymes for Young Australia* (1891). Of her several books of fiction, *Tasmanian Friends and Foes, Feathered, Furred, and Finned: A Family Chronicle of Country Life* (1880) is of most relevance to Australia and includes coloured plates from her own drawings. It has been said of her that she was 'a poet in feeling, an artist by instinct, a naturalist by force of circumstances, a keen botanist, and an ardent lover of landscape scenery'. Vivienne Rae Ellis wrote the biography, *Louisa Anne Meredith: A Tigress in Exile* (1979).

MERRITT, R.J. (ROBERT JAMES) (1945–), born Cowra, NSW, one of nine children of an Aboriginal labourer, was brought up on Erambie Mission. He attended Cowra primary and high schools, where he was an outstanding student, but was later unable to find any work other than seasonal manual labour. He has since spent long periods in prison. His play *The Cake Man* (q.v., 1978), the first play by an Aboriginal playwright to be performed in Australia, recalls his childhood experiences of Erambie Mission.

Merry-Go-Round in the Sea, The, a novel by Randolph Stow (q.v.), was published in 1965. Set in Geraldton, WA, 1941–49, the novel is a semi-autobiographical, nostalgic recreation of an Australian childhood. The story concentrates on the growth of a boy, Rob Coram, who is six when the novel opens, and less extensively on the experience of his much-loved, older cousin, Rick Maplestead. During the years covered by the first section of the novel, when Rick is away at war, Rob's experiences within his extensive family reinforce his yearning vision of life as familiar and circular, as safe in its movement as the merry-go-round he rode as a child. The second section of the novel, which deals with the years after Rick's return,

ends with the destruction of this comfortable vision of circularity and the realization of life as linear, transient, and lonely.

Michael Howe: The Last and the Worst of the Bushrangers of Van Diemen's Land, see **WELLS, THOMAS**

MICHAEL, JAMES LIONEL (1824–68), born London, was educated in languages and the arts and entered the legal profession in England. He came to Australia in the gold rush period but preferred the more comfortable existence of the Sydney legal world to a stint on the goldfields. He became a member of the Sydney literary coterie of the day, contributing verse, essays and literary criticism to the *Month* edited by James Sheridan Moore, and the *Southern Cross* edited by D.H. Deniehy. He extended patronage to the fledgling poet, Henry Kendall, allowing him access to his ample library and employing him as a clerk. Near bankruptcy, Michael went to Grafton in 1861 to open a legal practice but died there by drowning. He published a collection of lyric poems, *Songs Without Music* (1857) and a semi-autobiographical narrative poem, *John Cumberland* (1850). His poetry is pleasantly smooth and graceful but devoid of originality or significant theme. Kendall wrote two poems in tribute to Michael after his death, 'James Lionel Michael' and 'Lines to J.L. Michael'. Sheridan Moore published *The Life and Genius of James Lionel Michael* (1868). Geoff Page wrote a series of short poems reflecting on Michael's life and character and pondering on the puzzle of his death. Titled 'From the Life and Death of James Lionel Michael' the poems were published in *Instructions for Honey Ants*, the 1983 Mattara Spring Festival anthology.

MICHELL, KEITH (1928–), born Adelaide, taught art before leaving Australia in 1949 to work with the Old Vic Theatre school. He made his first West End appearance in 1951 and has since become a well-known actor, particularly renowned for his role in the BBC series, *The Six Wives of Henry VIII*. Formerly artistic director of the Chichester Festival Theatre, he also established a reputation as a painter, an illustrator of children's books, and a singer whose novelty song, 'Captain Beaky and his Band', rose to the top of the pop charts in 1980. He has toured Australia on several occasions, and in 1981 appeared in his own play produced by the Melbourne Theatre Company 'Peter McGynty and the Dreamtime', an Australian version of Ibsen's *Peer Gynt*.

MICKLE, ALAN (1883–1969), born Melbourne, lived mostly as a full-time writer, although he developed an interest in painting late in life. His publications include eight collections of philosophical essays 1910–47; two volumes of reminiscences, *Of Many Things* (1941) and *Many a Mickle* (1953); a book for children, *The Trio from Rio* (1942); two novels, *The Pilgrimage of Peer* (1938) and *The Execution of Newcome Bowles* (1948); a book of sporting reminiscences, *After the Ball* (1959); and six collections of poetry, of which only the juvenile verse has continued to receive attention, *The Poor Poet and the Beautiful Lady* (1931), *Pemmican Pete and Other Verses* (1934), *The Great City* (1935), *The Loony Cove* (1940), *Mine Own Land* (1944) and *The Ballad of Flatfoot Fred* (1944).

Middle Parts of Fortune : Somme and Ancre 1916, The, a novel by Frederic Manning (q.v.), was published anonymously in 1929 and was not published again in its original form until 1977. An expurgated edition was published in 1930 under the title *Her Privates We*, with the author's identity partly revealed by the pseudonym 'Private 19022' (Manning's army number). It was not until the 1943 reprint of *Her Privates We* that the author was clearly revealed as Manning, an Australian-born writer, who had served with the British army in France in the First World War. The novel covers parts of the Somme and Ancre fighting in the latter part of 1916 and revolves around a small group of British soldiers, chief of whom is Private Bourne, a shadowy, enigmatic character who is so obviously superior in background and potential to his fellow soldiers in the ranks that he is vainly badgered by his commanding officers to seek a commission. Bourne's two closest comrades are Shem and Martlow. Martlow and Bourne both die in action and Shem is wounded. Other characters pass in and out of the narrative, including the fine officer, Captain Malet, the deserter, Miller, and the soldier, 'Weeper' Smart, whose behaviour patterns and nickname reveal his precarious hold on sanity. The novel seldom describes the actual fighting, concerning itself more with the repetitive trivia of the soldiering life behind the lines: moving in and out of billets, drilling, scrounging, gossiping, quarrelling, getting mail from home, searching perfunctorily in one despondent French village after another for the elusive 'bon time!'. The few battle scenes are, however, intensely dramatic and Bourne's death at the end of the novel deeply moving. In spite of the novel's recreation of the horror of war and the spiritual ennui that swamps men's souls in such protracted, hopeless situations, it also emphasizes such positives as pride in themselves as soldiers ('we're a fuckin' fine mob'), their deep involvement in the comradeship of the trenches, and

their almost perverse determination to endure the unendurable. Although it records, with undoubted authenticity, monotonous blasphemous soldier talk, the novel fails to capture the ironic, earthy wit emphasized by other Australian war writers.

'Middleton's Rouseabout', see 'Andy's Gone with Cattle'

'MIDNITE (MIDNIGHT), CAPTAIN' was the name under which Thomas Smith, alias Harry Wilson, alias George Gibson, operated as a bushranger (q.v.) in western NSW before he was shot in 1878. In 1881 'Rolf Boldrewood' was appointed police magistrate at Dubbo, in the area of Midnite's activities, and is said to have partly modelled his character Captain Starlight on him. This Midnite should not be confused with the title character of Randolph Stow's *Midnite* (1967), which satirizes the bushranging ethos in general but is based in part on the activities of the only WA bushranger of note, 'Moondyne Joe'.

Midnite: The Story of a Wild Colonial Boy, an outstandingly popular children's novel by Randolph Stow (q.v.), was published in 1967 and later translated into several languages. Midnite is a good-natured, almost handsome, not very clever boy of seventeen who, on the advice of his shrewd Siamese cat, Khat, becomes a famous bushranger. His gang consists of his animals: Red Ned, a noble horse; Gyp, a sheep dog; Dora, a silly cow; and Major, an irascible cockatoo. Midnite's adventures land him in gaol several times, incite the anger of Queen Victoria, and engage him in contests with the charming but disreputable Trooper O'Grady. Midnite eventually makes good as the law-abiding gold-discoverer, Mr Daybrake. For the older reader *Midnite* is also delightful satire which has fun with familiar aspects of the Australian romantic tradition from bushrangers to explorers.

'Midsummer Noon in the Australian Forest, A', published in the *Empire*, 1858, is Charles Harpur's (q.v.) best-known and most-anthologized descriptive poem. Although often praised for its creation of the hushed somnolent atmosphere of the summer noonday in the Australian bush, the poem lacks Australian definition.

Miles Franklin Award is made annually from the estate of Miles Franklin (q.v.) for a published novel portraying some aspects of Australian life. If the judges consider that there is no novel of sufficient merit, a radio or television play may be considered for the award. The list of awards is as follows: 1957, *Voss* by Patrick White; 1958, *To The Islands* by Randolph Stow; 1959, *The Big Fellow* by Vance Palmer; 1960, *The Irishman* by 'Elizabeth O'Conner'; 1961, *Riders in the Chariot* by Patrick White; 1962, *The Well-Dressed Explorer* by Thea Astley and *The Cupboard under the Stairs* by George Turner; 1963, *Careful, He Might Hear You* by Sumner Locke Elliot; 1964, *My Brother Jack* by George Johnston; 1965, *The Slow Natives* by Thea Astley; 1966, *Trap* by Peter Mathers; 1967, *Bring Larks and Heroes* by Thomas Keneally; 1968, *Three Cheers for the Paraclete* by Thomas Keneally; 1969, *Clean Straw for Nothing* by George Johnston; 1970, *A Horse of Air* by Dal Stivens; 1971, *The Unknown Industrial Prisoner* by David Ireland; 1972, *The Acolyte* by Thea Astley; 1973, no award; 1974, *The Mango Tree* by Ronald McKie; 1975, *Poor Fellow My Country* by Xavier Herbert; 1976, *The Glass Canoe* by David Ireland; 1977, *Swords and Crown and Rings* by Ruth Park; 1978, *Tirra Lirra by the River* by Jessica Anderson; 1979, *A Woman of the Future* by David Ireland; 1980, *The Impersonators* by Jessica Anderson; 1981, *Bliss* by Peter Carey; 1982, *Just Relations* by Rodney Hall.

MILES, WILLIAM JOHN (1871–1942), was a Sydney businessman who met P.R. Stephensen (q.v.) in 1935 and employed him as his assistant to conduct the *Publicist*, a monthly dominated by Miles's rationalist, isolationist political views. Miles published Stephensen's *The Foundations of Culture in Australia* and financed the publication of Xavier Herbert's *Capricornia* (1938). Influenced in his last years by the biological theories of Morley Roberts, Miles was the father of the famous Sydney eccentric, Bea Miles (1901–73), who was well-known for her evasion of taxi and bus fares and for her recitations of Shakespeare and other writers.

MILGATE, RODNEY (1934–   ), born Kyogle, NSW, is a well-known painter as well as a playwright and has worked as an art teacher and as an actor in stage productions and on radio and television. He has had numerous exhibitions of his paintings, both in Australia and overseas, and has won several prizes including the prestigious Blake prize on three occasions. He has published some poetry and one play, *A Refined Look at Existence* (1968), which was staged during the first Jane Street theatre season in 1966. Fast moving, free-wheeling, impressionistic and satiric, the play is a mock-heroic portrayal of the impact of a pop singer on contemporary society; the most popular of the 1966 season, it heralded the arrival of a new kind of 'total' or 'rough'

theatre in Australia. Milgate's other plays include 'Joshua's Dilemma', 'At Least You Get Something Out of That' (1968) and 'Golden Pathway Through Europe' (1980).

MILLER, E. (EDMUND) MORRIS (1881–1964), born Natal, South Africa, was brought to Melbourne in infancy. Educated at the University of Melbourne, he worked for the Public Library of Victoria 1900–13. In Melbourne he was active in both library and public affairs; secretary of the Imperial Federation League, he published two pamphlets (1911,12) in support of its aims. He also published a pioneering book on librarianship in Australia, *Libraries and Education* (1912). In 1913 Morris Miller was appointed lecturer in mental and moral science at the University of Tasmania, where he subsequently held the positions of professor of philosophy and psychology (1922–51) and vice-chancellor (1933–46). In Hobart his activities were remarkably diverse; as well as running the department of philosophy and psychology without an assistant until 1950 he became prominent in the field of mental health; in 1920 he drafted a Mental Deficiency Act which became a blueprint for other States. One outcome of his activities in this area was his psychological study, *Brain Capacity and Intelligence* (1926). He was also active in the general educational field, helping to found the WEA in Tasmania. He held the post of honorary librarian of the University of Tasmania 1919–45 and was responsible for extensively building up the holdings of the library, which is now named after him; he also helped to form the Australian Library Association in 1928 and was chairman of the board of trustees of the Public Library of Tasmania 1922–43. For the last three decades of his life Morris Miller devoted himself to the bibliography of Australian literature and in 1932 began the eight years' research leading to his monumental work, *Australian Literature from Its Beginnings to 1935 ... with Subsidiary Entries to 1938* (q.v., 1940). Created emeritus professor on his retirement and made CBE in 1963, he received numerous other awards, including the Gold Medal of the Australian Literature Society. Apart from the works already mentioned and numerous essays, reviews and pamphlets Morris Miller published four studies of Kant's philosophy, (1911, 1913, 1924, 1928); a brief study of Henry Savery and Mary L. Grimstone, *Australia's First Two Novels* (1958); and an exhaustive account of early journalism in Tasmania, *Pressmen and Governors* (1952). Morris Miller is now probably best known for his two-volume descriptive and bibliographical survey of Australian literature. A fundamental reference work, it is full of detailed information that is unavailable elsewhere and is particularly useful for the period from 1850, when J.A. Ferguson's *Bibliography of Australia* (1941–69) ceases to cover literature, until 1937, when the National Library's *Annual Catalogue of Australian Publications* began publication. Although a second edition of *Australian Literature* appeared in 1956, revised and updated by Frederick T. Macartney, it by no means replaced the 1940 publication.

'MILLER, JOHN', see **LANE, WILLIAM**

MILLETT, JOHN (1928–), served as a RAAF air gunner in Britain during the Second World War, and subsequently practised as a lawyer in Sydney and on the Gold Coast. He has contributed poetry to numerous Australian periodicals and to some American ones and has published five collections, *Calendar Adam* (1971), *The Silences* (1973), *Love Tree of the Coomera* (1975), *West of the Cunderang* (1977) and *Tail Arse Charlie* in *Poetry Australia* (1982). He has also written a play with Grace Perry, *Last Bride at Longsleep* (1981). An elusive and strikingly individual poet, Millett has a strong sense of place and a fascination with language, which he uses with zest and dexterity. His gift for sharp imagery and his pronounced, self-conscious use of a persona add power and colour to such spiritually-autobiographical sequences as *Calendar Adam* and *Love Tree of the Coomera*. *Tail Arse Charlie*, his simplest work, which was broadcast on radio in a dramatized version, is a powerful anti-war sequence, bolstered by photographs and records from the Australian War Memorial. Partly based on his memories of the air war, it is also evocative of the experience of all the 'old-young men', involved in the Battle of Britain.

'MILLS, MARTIN' see **BOYD, MARTIN**

Mimshi Maiden, The, see **McCRAE, HUGH**

Miner's Right, The, a novel by 'Rolf Boldrewood' (q.v.), was serialized in the *Australian Town and Country Journal* in 1880, published in book form in 1890, and adapted for the stage in 1891. The hero of the novel is Hereward Pole, an Englishman of good breeding who emigrates to Australia to seek on the Turon goldfields of NSW the fortune that will allow him to marry Ruth Allerton, a squire's daughter. After four years he and his three partners are successful, but their claim is jumped; they win the case before the goldfields commissioner, William Blake, but a court appeal is lodged and Pole goes to the Oxley goldfields while awaiting the decision. There he again strikes a rich lead, which he leaves to

visit Sydney with the gold escort to help an old friend, Jane Morsley, escape her villainous husband, Ned. The escort is attacked *en route* by bushrangers and the wounded Pole nursed back to health by Jane; he returns to Oxley, where an anti-Chinese riot is quelled. With the appeal dismissed and both claims flourishing, Pole looks forward to selling up and returning to England, but he receives a letter from Ruth's father breaking off the relationship because of a libellous report that Jane has become Pole's mistress. Jane herself is murdered, and Hereward accused of the crime. Acquitted following Ned's arrest, he is honoured by a dinner on his departure from the goldfields and goes to Sydney to be reunited with Ruth, who has travelled with her family to Australia for her health. After a final tour of the goldfields Hereward returns with his bride to England to establish his own estate.

A typical 'Boldrewood' success story of an English gentleman, *The Miner's Right* has weaknesses of plot, style and characterization that led Joseph Furphy to parody it in *The Buln-Buln and the Brolga* (1948); a comparison between Hereward Pole and Dick Marston, the narrator of *Robbery Under Arms* (1888) explains why *Robbery Under Arms* is the more successful novel. That *The Miner's Right* has endured at all derives from the strength of the minor characters, together with the fact that 'Boldrewood' drew extensively on his Gulgong experiences of the 1870s and transferred them to a story, set in the 1850s and 1860s, in which he was able to recreate other historical incidents such as the Lambing Flat riots.

Mirage, The (1955), a novel by F. Bert Vickers (q.v.), has also been published in Russia and in East Germany, resulting in considerable correspondence between Vickers and European students about the Aboriginal situation in Australia. The novel's principal characters are two Aborigines, Freddie Adams and the girl, Nona. Freddie Adams, growing up as a half-caste, is alien to both the tribal life of the Aborigines and to white society, and the discrimination he suffers ultimately brings about his destruction. A well-planned novel with warm and realistic characters, *The Mirage* convincingly argues for greater racial tolerance by white Australians.

Miss Jacobsen's Chance, see **PRAED, ROSA**

Miss Peabody's Inheritance, see **JOLLEY, ELIZABETH**

MITCHEL, JOHN (1815–75), born Derry, Ireland, was an Irish lawyer and nationalist who became actively involved in the Young Ireland movement in 1845. Assistant editor of the *Nation* under Charles Gavan Duffy, later premier of Victoria, he launched the *United Irishman* in 1848 and was soon arrested for sedition. He was sentenced to transportation, and arrived in Hobart in 1850; in 1853 he escaped to America, where he became a controversial journalist. Mitchell's *Jail Journal* (1854) includes an account of his Australian experiences, which were also written up by Marcus Clarke in *Old Tales of a Young Country* (1871). Several of his Young Ireland colleagues were also transported to Australia, where they briefly ran the journal, the *Irish Exile* (1850–51).

MITCHELL, DAVID SCOTT (1836–1907), book collector, was born in Sydney, the son of Dr James Mitchell (1792–1869), a prominent colonial surgeon and businessman from whom he inherited estates. Educated at the University of Sydney, Mitchell was admitted to the bar in 1858 but never practised; after a broken romance with Emily Manning in 1864 and the death of his parents in 1869 and 1871, he lived in increasing seclusion to pursue his interest in books. For twenty years from the 1860s he collected mainly English literary works, but from about 1886 devoted himself to the aim of collecting every document relating to Australia, the Pacific, the East Indies, and Antarctica. He bequeathed to the trustees of the Public, now State, Library of NSW his collection and an endowment of £70 000; the collection of some 60 000 volumes and other material formed the basis of the collection of the Mitchell Library (q.v.), which was opened in 1910.

MITCHELL, ELYNE (1913–), born Melbourne, the daughter of the military commander, Sir Harry Chauvel, married Thomas Mitchell in 1935 and has subsequently lived on a station on the upper Murray in the foothills of the Victorian Alps. She has drawn on this alpine landscape and its wild horses for many of her popular children's books, which have been translated into several languages and published in Britain and the USA. They include the popular Silver Brumby series beginning with *The Silver Brumby* (1958). She has also written two novels for adults, *Flow River, Blow Wind* (1953) and *Black Cockatoos Mean Snow* (1956); a collection of descriptive essays that deal with aspects of the snow country, *Images in Water* (1947); reminiscences of skiing and climbing experiences, which reflect her prowess as a champion skier and her sensitive response to the alpine landscape, *Australia's Alps* (1942); a detailed, often lyrically-expressed chronicle of her work on the family station during the Second World War, *Speak to the*

Earth (1945); a history of the Australian Light Horse (1978); and an account of her parents and her early life, *Chauvel Country* (1983).

Mitchell, Jack, is a major character in the fiction of Henry Lawson (q.v.), appearing in about forty sketches and stories; he is an important figure in *While the Billy Boils* (1896), although there are Mitchell stories in later Lawson volumes, including *On the Track* (1900) *Over the Sliprails* (1900), and *Children of the Bush* (1902). Described in 'Enter Mitchell' as 'short, and stout, and bow-legged, and freckled, and sandy', Mitchell, as he is usually called, reveals at the end of that story that he was once a cab-driver for five years in Sydney; more characteristically he appears as a bushman who has been on the track for several years carrying his swag. Mitchell is an evolving, complex character in his own right but is most significant as a narrator, particularly in *While the Billy Boils*, where his understated, laconic yarns help establish the authenticity of Lawson's fictional world. A number of bushmen whom Lawson met have been suggested as models for Mitchell, including Arthur Parker, with whom he worked in the Blue Mountains in 1887; Bill Louisson, a foreman in NZ; and J.W. Gordon (q.v.), also known as 'Jim Grahame', with whom Lawson travelled during his outback trek in 1892–93. In 'By the Banks of the Murrumbidgee' Lawson states that in 1892–93 he travelled as Joe Swallow (one of his literary pseudonyms) and Gordon as Jack Mitchell; but it is also clear that Mitchell is a composite character, independent of any model, and that in the Mitchell stories Lawson drew on a wide range of experiences, including those of his family, rather than simply on his experiences with Gordon.

Mitchell Library, which is housed in a wing of the State Library of NSW in Sydney, was opened in 1910 as a result of the bequest of the bibliophile, David Scott Mitchell (q.v.). The Mitchell collection, one of the world's significant national collections, includes not only the most extensive and important collection of Australiana but also material relating to New Zealand, the Pacific and other regions near Australia. The Mitchell Library's *Dictionary Catalog of Printed Books* was published in 1968, with a first supplement appearing in 1970; part of its manuscript catalogue has been published (1967, 1969), as well as an index to periodicals covering 1944–63 (1950–67). Phyllis Mander-Jones, long time member of the Mitchell library staff, published *Sources of Australian Literature in the Mitchell Library, Sydney* (1962) and contributed a chapter on the library to Charles Barrett's anthology, *Across* *the Years* (1948). *The Great South Land* (1979) is an outline of the treasures of the Mitchell and Dixson Libraries and Dixson Galleries, written by Suzanne Mourot and Paulette Jones.

MITCHELL, MARY (1892–1973), born Melbourne, was educated in Australia and Europe. In 1923 she returned to Australia, and until 1932 worked with the Victorian Junior Red Cross. She published some twenty popular novels, many of them with romantic, even fantastic plots. They include *A Warning to Wantons* (1934), *Pendulum Swing* (1935), *Viper's Progress* (1939), *Dark Tapestry* (1942), *Prelude to Jesting* (1950) and *Birth of a Legend* (1956). Her best-known novel, *A Warning to Wantons*, was translated into several languages and produced as a film in 1948. Afflicted with blindness in her later years, Mitchell also wrote a well-received account of the experience of the blind, designed to improve relations between them and the sighted, *Uncharted Country* (1963).

MITCHELL, Sir THOMAS (1792–1855), born Craigend, Scotland, went to NSW in 1827 as assistant surveyor-general, succeeding to the main position in 1828 on the death of John Oxley. In 1831–36 Mitchell made three exploratory expeditions: to northern NSW in the Namoi, Gwydir and Barwon River areas; to the Darling River from the point where Charles Sturt had explored in 1828 down to its junction with the Murray River; and finally along the Lachlan, Murrumbidgee and Murray Rivers and up the Darling River towards Menindee, then back to the Murray and into what is now Victoria, which he called Australia Felix, thence south and west until he came across the Henty brothers near Portland. As a result of the third expedition rapid settlement of Victoria followed. Mitchell's account of his explorations is contained in *Three Expeditions into the Interior of Eastern Australia* (1838). Following further explorations in 1845–46 to find an overland route to Port Essington and/or a great north-flowing river, he published *Journal of an Expedition into the Interior of Tropical Australia* (1848). The experiences of his final years, including a prolonged visit to England (1852–54) during which he sought to interest the Admiralty in a propeller for steamships modelled on the Aboriginal boomerang, are contained in J.H.L. Cumpston's biography (1954). The best literary stylist of the Australian explorers, Mitchell is featured in William Hay's book of sketches, *An Australian Rip Van Winkle* (1921).

'MO', see **RENE, ROY**

Mo Burdekin, see 'CAMPION, SARAH'

Modern Australian Literature (1900–1923), a brief but comprehensive account by Nettie Palmer (q.v.), was published in 1924 and won the Lothian Prize for an essay in Australian literature since 1900. Although preceded by *An Introduction to the Study of Australian Literature* (1922) by Zora Cross, it is the first systematically critical survey to be published in book form. Written in an agreeable, readable style, enlivened by frequently striking epithets and analogies, the book makes many judgements which are still fresh. The conclusion presents a bleak picture of the Australian writer's isolation in the 1920s and the absence of 'facilities for ordinary publishing'. The monograph incidentally led to Nettie Palmer's discovery of 'Henry Handel Richardson': Mrs Mary Kernot, an acquaintance of both Nettie Palmer and the novelist, surprised to find no mention of 'Richardson', lent Nettie Palmer her books and thus initiated the intense interest that led to her *Henry Handel Richardson* (1950), the first full-length study of that writer.

Modern Australian Poetry, 1920–70: A Guide to Information Sources (1979) by Herbert C. Jaffa, is a bibliographical guide covering Australian poetry from Kenneth Slessor to the new Australian poets of the late 1960s and early 1970s. Sections annotating bibliographies, bibliographic guides, background reference material, critical studies and anthologies precede author checklists which cover the author's work and an annotated selection of bibliographical and critical material. The author sections are organized within the categories of major poets (Slessor, R.D. FitzGerald, A.D. Hope, Douglas Stewart, Judith Wright, James McAuley), important and established poets (e.g. David Campbell, Francis Webb, Les Murray), Jindyworobak poets, Angry Penguins poets, expatriate poets, other poets of the 1940s–1960s, and younger poets. The companion volumes to *Modern Australian Poetry* are *Modern Australian Prose* by A. Grove Day and *Australian Literature to 1900* by Barry Andrews and William H. Wilde (qq.v.).

Modern Australian Prose, 1901–75: A Guide to Information Sources (1980) by A. Grove Day, is mainly a reference guide to twentieth-century Australian prose, although the last of its four sections lists critical material on modern Australian drama. The first part is an annotated listing of bibliographies and bibliographical guides, background reference works, literary history and criticism, materials on Australian English, periodicals and anthologies. The second part provides a bibliographical and critical guide to fifty-four authors; the third annotates selected non-fiction titles, including material on

Aborigines. The companion volumes to *Modern Australian Prose* are Herbert Jaffa's *Modern Australian Poetry* and Barry Andrews and William H. Wilde's *Australian Literature to 1900* (qq.v.).

Modern Buccaneer, A (1894), a fictionalized account of the career of 'Bully' Hayes, was published by 'Rolf Boldrewood', but roughly two-thirds was the work of 'Louis' Becke (q.v.). As a fledgling author, Becke sent a narrative about Hayes to 'Boldrewood' in 1893 and was paid, expecting that it would form only the framework for a work. When Becke protested about the use of the material, 'Boldrewood' publicly acknowledged his indebtedness.

Modern Language Review of New South Wales, see CHISHOLM, A.R.

MOFFITT, IAN (1929–), born Sydney, has worked for several Australian newspapers, including the Sydney *Mirror*, the *Australian* and the *Bulletin*, after beginning his career in Hong Kong on the staff of the *South China Morning Post*. He spent some years in New York as head of the News Ltd bureau, but gave up journalism in 1978 to write full-time. He has written a critique of Australian attitudes to conservation, the arts, the press, sport, foreign policy, migrants and racism, *The U-Jack Society* (1972); the text of an illustrated work, *The Australian Outback* (1976); and two novels which have been well-received, *The Retreat of Radiance* (1982) and *The Colour Man* (1983). *The Retreat of Radiance*, which draws on his experiences in China during the civil war, deals with a nineteen-year-old Australian journalist, Quinn, who witnesses a Nationalist massacre and returns to the Far East thirty years later to seek vengeance. Frequently compared in style, pace and tone to the work of 'John le Carré', the novel has been praised for its depth of characterization and authentic background. *The Colour Man* is a psychological thriller with Gothic characteristics.

MOIR, J.K. (JOHN KINMONT) (1893–1958), born Normanton, Queensland, was brought up in Queensland, but spent his adult life in Melbourne. A businessman, he was, in his spare time, an avid collector of Australiana, his home in Richmond becoming well known to students of Australian literature, authors and bibliophiles. In 1957 his large collection of books, photographs, prints and other memorabilia was donated to the La Trobe Library. An ardent devotee of Australian literature, particularly interested in Adam Lindsay Gordon, he was co-founder and Knight Grand Cheese (president) of the Bread and Cheese Club and editor of its monthly bulletin, *Bohemia*; patron of the Gordon Lovers' society; life member of the Australian Literature Society and of the Henry Lawson society; and member of the Poetry Lovers' society and of the C.J. Dennis Memorial Committee. His only published work was a history of Australia's first electric tram (1940), but he also wrote biographies of Gordon and of Edward Devine, coach-driver for Cobb & Co. He was made OBE in 1952.

MOLL, E.G. (ERNEST GEORGE) (1900–), born Murtoo, Victoria, was educated at schools in NSW and at Harvard University. He left Australia for the USA in the 1920s and was professor of English at the University of Oregon 1928–66, but has retained his Australian citizenship and has frequently revisited Australia. Moll's verse, which is represented in numerous Australian anthologies, has appeared in several collections, including *Sedge Fire* (1927), *Native Moments* (1931), *Campus Sonnets* (1934), *Blue Interval* (1935), *Cut from Mulga* (1940), *Brief Waters* (1945), *Beware the Cuckoo* (1947), *The Waterhole* (1948), *The Lifted Spear* (1953), *Poems 1940-1955* (1957), *The Rainbow Serpent* (1962), *Briseis* (1965), and *The Road to Cactusland* (1971). He has also written a critical study, *The Appreciation of Poetry* (1933); and *Below These Hills: The Story of a Riverina Farm* (1957), an account of his family's farm, established in 1910. Strongly indebted to his rural Australian experience, Moll has often been classed as a regionalist. Using a variety of genres, he writes an amiable, technically proficient, but unremarkable poetry.

Monaro is the name of the geographical district that now extends from south of the Australian Capital Territory to the Victorian border and eastward from the alpine area of the Great Dividing Range to the escarpment that abuts on to the far-south coastal plain of NSW. Discovered in 1823 by Captain M.J. Currie it has been known by a variety of names, Monaroo, Manaroo, Moneiro, Monera, all of which are said to derive from the Aboriginal word 'manaroo' meaning woman's breast, the name denoting the rounded nature of the hills of the original district. The 1840 Moneroo Squattage District, much larger than the present Monaro, extended from north of the present NSW city of Goulburn well down into the modern State of Victoria; Henry Kingsley's *The Recollections of Geoffry Hamlyn* (1859) is partly set in this extended area. The Monaro soon figured in Australian writing. John Lhotsky records his travels through it in *A Journey from Sydney to the Australian Alps* (1835); Paul de Strzelecki explored it, giving a Polish name, Kosciusko, to Australia's loftiest peak; Henry W. Haygarth records details of squatting life in the area in his *Recollections of Bush Life in Australia during a Residence of Eight Years in the Interior* (1848); W.A. Brodribb does the same in retrospect in *Recollections of an Australian Squatter* (1883); and Charles Cozens records his experiences as a convict constable in the Monaro in *Adventures of a Guardsman* (1848). Mentioned in fiction as early as 1849 in the novel, *The Emigrant Family*, the Monaro is assessed by Alexander Harris as 'the best grazing grounds for horned cattle within the Australian colonies'. Harris describes it as 'far above the sea, and utterly bare of forest over its main expanse; its winter is piercing and desolate. Its extent is such that in some parts a rider may tire a good horse two days in succession in passing across from bush to bush'. In more recent Australian literature it has featured as the home of A.B. Paterson's legendary Man from Snowy River; as the birthplace of Miles Franklin and the setting of many of her novels; and as the well-loved country of poet, David Campbell, sometimes referred to as 'The Man from the Monaro'. The chief study of the district is W.K. Hancock's *Discovering Monaro* (1972).

MONASH, Sir JOHN (1865–1931), born Melbourne of Prussian–Jewish extraction, graduated in arts, law and engineering from the University of Melbourne. Before the First World War he practised successfully as an engineer, pioneering construction in reinforced concrete. A citizen soldier, he was commissioned in 1908, became colonel of an infantry brigade in 1913, and commanded the 4th Infantry Brigade at Gallipoli. He quickly established his reputation as a commander in France 1917–18 and succeeded General Birdwood in command of the Australian Corps in March 1918. At the close of the war his reputation exceeded that of any other Australian general; he was described by Sir Basil Liddell Hart as having 'probably the greatest capacity for command in modern war among all those who held command'. Monash subsequently gave an account of the main action in which he was involved in *The Australian Victories in France in 1918* (1920). His *War Letters*, edited by F.M. Cutlack, were published in 1934 and both publications reveal his wide-ranging intellect and interests, humanity, administrative capability, and shrewd, psychological insight. After the war he was prominent in the development of electrical power in Victoria. He was vice-chancellor of the University of Melbourne and received numerous other honours; in 1958 Victoria's second university was named after him. Monash's military achievement is described in C.E.W. Bean's official history of the First World War and several biographies have

been published, although the definitive account has been written by Geoffrey Serle, in his award-winning *John Monash* (1982).

'MONCRIEFF, WILLIAM THOMAS' (WILLIAM GEORGE THOMAS) (1794–1857), was theatre manager, critic, editor of play texts and dramatist and wrote well over one hundred plays for the English stage in the 1820s and 1830s; two of them, the burletta *Tom and Jerry: Or, Life in London* (produced 1821, performed Sydney 1834) and the extravaganza, *Van Diemen's Land: Or, Tasmania in 1818* (q.v.) (produced 1830, published 1831) are significant in Australian literature. In adapting for the stage Pierce Egan's (1772–1849) enormously popular series of sketches of London life, 'Moncrieff' introduced into *Tom and Jerry* the character of Jemmy Green, a raw ('green') East-Ender. His popularity was such that he survived in the similar figure of the 'new chum' (q.v.) in the plays, *Jemmy Green in Australia* (q.v.) by James Tucker and 'Life in Sydney: Or, the Ran Dan Club' (q.v.), an adaptation of *Life in London* possibly by H.C. O'Flaherty. *Van Diemen's Land* was one of the earliest plays about Australia produced in England and owed its writing to the desire of 'Moncrieff '' 's colleague, the actor and theatre manager, Robert Elliston (1774–1831), to celebrate the arrival of his two sons, William and Henry, in Van Diemen's Land. 'Moncrieff''s propensity to respond to the theatrical fashion of the day and adapt the novels of writers like Sir Walter Scott and Charles Dickens led the latter to present him satirically in *Nicholas Nickleby*.

Monitor, see *Sydney Monitor*

Monkey Grip, see **GARNER, HELEN**

MONTEZ, LOLA (MARIA DOLORES ELIZA ROSANNA GILBERT) (1818–61), born Limerick, Ireland, eloped with a young army officer, Thomas James, in 1837 but was deserted by him in India. She returned to England in 1841, trained as a dancer in Spain and as Donna Lola Montez made her London theatre debut in 1843. Hissed off the stage when her identity became known (her hypocritical husband had earlier won a separation because of her adultery aboard ship returning from India), she reappeared in Europe, where she became the mistress of Franz Liszt, Alexandre Dumas, and King Ludwig 1 of Bavaria, among others. Created Countess Marie von Landsfeld by Ludwig she exercised political influence until the riots which broke out against her in 1848 caused the King to abdicate. By 1849 Lola was back in London, where she bigamously married a second young army officer; after his death in

1850 she returned to the stage and toured Europe and America, where in goldrush California she first performed her lascivious Spider Dance. Another bigamous and broken marriage later she toured Australia for almost a year (1855–56), opening on most occasions in the farrago, 'Lola Montez in Bavaria'. In Sydney she avoided arrest for debt by undressing and daring a sheriff to arrest her, in Melbourne the Spider Dance appalled some respectable citizens and was parodied by George Coppin, notably in his role of Scrumptious Katunka, Egyptian Professor of the Spider Dance in 'Coppin in Cairo' (1858); Montez, however, had successful if scandalous seasons in Adelaide and on the goldfields. After leaving Australia she returned to America, where, in San Francisco, William Robertson satirized her in the play, 'A Trip to Australia, or Lola Montez on the Fanny Major'. In later years her physical decline was paralleled by her moral reformation, and she became known on the lecture platform.

A number of historical and fictional accounts of goldfields life mention Lola Montez, including Eric Lambert's novel *Ballarat* (1962); in 1958 the musical 'Lola Montez' by Alan Burke, Peter Benjamin and Peter Stannard was performed in Sydney. Among recent accounts of her life are Doris Foley's *The Divine Eccentric: Lola Montez and the Newspapers* (1969), which includes her autobiography and American reports of her Australian experiences, Ishbel Ross's *The Uncrowned Queen* (1972), and the anonymous *Lola Montez: The Tragic Story of a 'Liberated Woman'* (1973).

Montforts, The, see BOYD, MARTIN

MONTGOMERY, ALEXANDER (1847–1922), was born in Londonderry, Ireland. In 1870, in the course of extensive travels, he visited Melbourne, where he worked for a time as a journalist. After further travel in the Malay archipelago, he arrived in Sydney, where he worked for the *Evening News* and the *Echo*, and contributed to the *Bulletin*, directing the 'Aboriginalities' page. He wrote several serials for the *Australasian* and other newspapers, using such pseudonyms as 'Montalex', 'Sardonyx' and 'Heretic', as well as an historical novel with a European setting, *The Sword of a Sin* (1898) and a collection of short stories, *Five Skull Island and Other Tales of the Malay Archipelago* (1897).

Month, a monthly literary and critical journal established in Sydney by Frank Fowler, was edited by him July 1857 – April 1858 and then by J. Sheridan Moore until its demise in December 1858. Its contributors included R.H. Horne, Richard Rowe and J.L. Michael. Fowler's stated aims for the *Month* included a denunciation of Australian philistinism and the creation of a national literature based on the highest standards of European excellence. Among his own contributions to the *Month* was a series of nine travel essays on 'Sydney and Its Suburbs'. Much of the magazine's material was not particularly Australian in character, although it did offer reviews of Australian books and occasional serials on bush life; its highlight was the series, 'The World of Books'. Under Moore's editorship, the *Month* became less substantial as a literary journal and perished through financial difficulties. An account of the journal's foundation and fortunes is included in Ann-Mari Jordens's *The Stenhouse Circle* (1979).

Month in the Bush of Australia, A, see WALKER, THOMAS

MOODIE HEDDLE, ENID (1904–   ), born Elsternwick, Victoria, was educated at the University of Melbourne and taught in Australia and England 1927–34. In 1935–46 she was educational adviser in Australia to Longmans Green and to William Collins and in 1947–60 educational manager for Longmans in Australia. The author or editor of more than thirty books, Enid Moodie Heddle wrote two books of verse, *Solitude* (1937) and *Sagitta Says* (1943); and *Boy on a Horse* (1957, with H.J. Samuel), the story of Adam Lindsay Gordon. She published *Australian Literature Now* (1949) and *How Australian Literature Grew* (1962) but is best known as editor of the Boomerang Books series, which includes *The Boomerang Book of Australian Poetry* (1956) and *The Boomerang Book of Legendary Tales* (1957), which both won Children's Book Council Awards. Moodie Heddle edited the Australian editions of *The Poets' Way* (1942, 1943, 1944), *Discovering Poetry* (1956, 1957) and *A Galaxy of Poems Old and New* (1962).

Moomba Festival, Melbourne's popular autumn festival was established in 1955 and extends over eleven days in March. Initiated by a special committee of the Melbourne City Council and titled Moomba from an Aboriginal word meaning 'get together and have fun', the festival was granted a permanent administration in 1963. It includes a wide range of sporting events, art shows, popular and classical concerts, dramatic performances, dances and displays, as well as a special literary programme organized by the FAW, and a system of book awards. Keith Dunstan has written a history of the festival, *Moomba: The First 25 Years*

(1979). John Romeril's play, *Mickey's Moomba* (1978), criticizes the festival's crowning of Mickey Mouse as King of Moomba in 1977.

Moondyne, a novel by John Boyle O'Reilly (q.v.), was published in America in 1879 and in Australia a year later; originally a serial in the Boston *Pilot*, which O'Reilly edited after his escape from WA in 1869, it began publication in November 1878 as 'Moondyne Joe', the title of one of the three or more American editions published in 1879, but the title was changed to 'Moondyne' the following February. Although only the first and last of its five sections are set in WA, it is generally accepted as the State's first novel. It was filmed in 1913. The first part of *Moondyne* focuses on the title character, a convict of heroic stature who has effected several escapes in the colony, originally from the cruel ex-convict, Isaac Bowman, to whom he has been assigned. He takes to the bush and joins an Aboriginal tribe, which christens him Moondyne and leads him to the gold-mine of which there have long been rumours in the colony. Recaptured by Bowman, now an officer in the penal service, Moondyne offers to lead him to the gold-mine in return for his freedom. Bowman predictably reneges on the bargain, escapes with the gold to return to civilization, but is pursued by Moondyne and eventually dies in the desert; Moondyne himself escapes, to reappear later in the novel as the compelling penal reformer, Mr Wyville. The focus now shifts to Will Sheridan, a Lancashire seaman whose love for Alice Walmsley is thwarted by the evil Sam Draper and who deserts his ship in Singapore and becomes successful in the sandalwood trade in WA. After nine years, he returns to England to find that Alice is in prison for murdering the child she bore in an unwittingly bigamous marriage to Draper. While in London he meets Wyville, who has interested himself in Alice's case, believed her innocent, saved her from despair, and is eventually to discover the real murderer, Draper's original wife. Having persuaded the English authorities of the efficacy of his penal theories which, like those of Alexander Maconochie, are based on the reformation rather than the punishment of the offenders, Wyville returns to Australia as comptroller-general of convicts; also on the ship, the *Hougoumont* (on which O'Reilly was transported to Australia), are Sheridan, Alice, Sister Cecilia, who has befriended Alice in prison, Draper and his wife Harriet, who confesses her crime. In Australia Wyville successfully puts his theories into practice, Will and Alice are reunited and take over Wyville's estate, and Wyville dies heroically (he drowns in a bushfire!) trying to save Sam and Harriet Draper.

Moondyne is a poorly constructed novel, perhaps because of its weekly publication in the *Pilot*, with more than its share of cliché-ridden melodramatic set pieces. It has more than historical interest, however, for the way O'Reilly integrates the legendary experiences of the convict bushranger, 'Moondyne Joe' (q.v.), e.g. the early scenes of the novel, with his own experiences, e.g. the scenes on board the convict ship, and ideas, e.g. those articulated by the idealized Wyville and his sympathizers on the noble savages, freedom, politics and religion. In addition, *Moondyne* is remarkably prescient in its prediction about the importance of gold in WA's history and its presentation of WA as a cinderella State anticipates some later thinking in that State.

'MOONDYNE JOE' (JOSEPH BOLITHO JONES) (?1827–1900), was a WA convict bushranger (q.v.), who was born in Wales, sentenced to transportation in 1848 and arrived at Fremantle in 1853. He established his reputation in the period 1860–73, when he made several daring escapes from gaol, remaining at large for long periods; on one occasion the authorities were forced to confine him to a specially reinforced cell, from which he escaped when allowed out for medical treatment. John Boyle O'Reilly's novel, *Moondyne* (1879), titled *Moondyne Joe* in some editions, traded on the reputation of Jones and probably helped perpetuate his reputation for gallantry. More recently, Ian Elliot's *Moondyne Joe* (1978) has separated the man and the myth, and Roger Montgomery's folk musical, 'Moondyne Joe', was presented at the Perth Festival in 1982.

Moonlight Acre, see **FITZGERALD, R.D.**

Moonlite, see **FOSTER, DAVID**

'MOONLITE (MOONLIGHT), CAPTAIN' (ANDREW GEORGE SCOTT) (1842–80), was an Irish-born bushranger (q.v.), who had a brief career in crime in the late 1860s and early 1870s. A recalcitrant prisoner until his release in 1879, Scott was almost immediately active again, and was hanged early in 1880 after a notorious attack on Wantabadgery station in the Riverina; the execution of the Wantabadgery bushrangers was highlighted in the first issue of the *Bulletin*. The activities of 'Captain Moonlite' have been thought by some writers to have contributed to the portrait of Starlight in *Robbery Under Arms* (1888) although 'Rolf Boldrewood' denied any connection. 'Moonlite''s early career was noticed by 'The Vagabond' and is discussed in G.A. Calderwood's *Captain Moonlite* (1971).

MOORE, GEORGE FLETCHER (1798–1886), born County Tyrone, Ireland, practised as a lawyer in that country before emigrating to the Swan River settlement in 1830. His accounts of the vicissitudes of life in the colony were published in *Extracts from the Letters and Journals of George Fletcher Moore* (1834) edited by Martin Doyle, and *Diary of Ten Years' Eventful Life of an Early Settler in Western Australia* (1884), Moore's own expanded version. Sympathetic to the Aboriginal cause he also published an Aboriginal vocabulary in 1842.

MOORE, JOSEPH SHERIDAN (1828–91), born Dublin, migrated in 1847 to Sydney and became a Benedictine monk and headmaster of Lyndhurst College, Glebe. After many disagreements with his superiors, including Archbishop Polding, he left Lyndhurst in 1856 and only rejoined the church in 1872, although he edited the Catholic magazine, *Freeman's Journal*, 1856–57. Well known, if not universally popular, in Sydney's literary milieu, Moore was familiar with such men as N.D. Stenhouse, Richard Rowe, James Lionel Michael, Daniel Deniehy, W.B. Dalley, Henry Kendall, John Woolley and Frank Fowler, and edited the *Month* (q.v.). An energetic teacher, he claimed proficiency in a range of subjects, including classics, languages, geography and science, meanwhile bolstering his precarious financial fortunes by literary journalism and lecturing. His publications include a collection of poetry, *Spring Life Lyrics* (1864); a collection of essays which also includes some verse and professes to initiate Irish-Australians into Irish history and customs, *The Ethics of the Irish under the Pentarchy* (1872); and a biography of Michael (1868). Aspects of his career are discussed in *The Stenhouse Circle* (1979), by Ann-Mari Jordens.

MOORE, MAGGIE (1851–1926), born Margaret O'Sullivan in San Francisco, came to Australia with her husband, J.C. Williamson (q.v.), in 1874. She starred with him in the long-running, commercially successful play, *Struck Oil* (q.v.), before touring in England, Ireland and the USA. In 1879 the Williamsons returned to Australia, where Moore became a versatile and outstandingly popular actress and singer, playing numerous roles in light opera, including Josephine in the first authorized performance of *HMS Pinafore* by Gilbert and Sullivan. She divorced Williamson in 1899 and in 1901 married H.R. Roberts, continuing to appear as an actress until 1924, when the fiftieth anniversary of her arrival in Australia was marked by large concerts. She died in San Francisco.

MOORE, TOM INGLIS (1901–79), born Camden, NSW, was educated at the Universities of Sydney and Oxford and taught in the USA and at the University of the Philippines (1928–31). In 1934–40 he was on the staff of the *Sydney Morning Herald* as reviewer and leader-writer. After service in the Second World War he joined the Canberra University College, later the Australian National University, where he remained until his retirement in 1966. He was a long-serving member of the CLF advisory board and active in the FAW, the ASA and the English Association. His creative writing includes a novel, *The Half Way Sun: A Tale of the Philippine Islands* (1935); a radio play in verse, *We're Going Through* (1945), broadcast by the ABC; and three books of verse, *Adagio in Blue* (1938), *Emu Parade: Poems from Camp* (1941) and *Bayonet and Grass* (1957). As an editor he published *Best Australian One-Act Plays* (1937, with William Moore); *Australia Writes: An Anthology* (1953); *Henry Kendall* (1957), the introduction to which contained a major scholarly reappraisal of Kendall's work; *Poetry in Australia* (1964, in collaboration with Douglas Stewart); and *Letters of Mary Gilmore* (1980, in collaboration with W.H. Wilde). His critical writing includes *Modern American Poetry* (1935), *Six Australian Poets* (1942), *The Misfortunes of Henry Handel Richardson* (1957), *Mary Gilmore: A Tribute* (1965, with others), and *Social Patterns in Australian Literature* (1971).

Moore's poetry, largely of love and war, appeals because of its attractive imagery, its spontaneity of feeling, whether of joy in loving or anger at the plight of a war-torn world, and its sprinkling of Australian symbols to explain and illustrate universal attitudes. His valuable contribution as a pioneer teacher of Australian literature and as one of its earliest scholarly critics, was recognized when he was made OBE in 1958.

MOORE, WILLIAM (1868–1937), born Bendigo, Victoria, was art and drama critic for the Melbourne *Herald* and later for the Sydney *Daily Telegraph*. His interest in the theatre led to the presentation of four 'Australian drama nights' which ran in Melbourne 1909–12. During these informal drama sessions Moore staged several one-acters of his own as well as plays by Louis Esson, Katharine Susannah Prichard and others. He combined with the Melbourne Repertory Theatre for the third drama night in 1911 and this group continued the staging of Australian plays after Moore's drama nights ceased. One of Moore's one-act plays, *The Tea-Room Girl*, was published in 1910 and he also edited with T. Inglis Moore *Best Australian One-Act Plays* (1937). His major achievement was *The Story of Australian Art* (1934); he also published two semi-fictional works, *City Sketches* (1905) and *Studio Sketches* (1906). He was married to Dora Wilcox.

MOOREHEAD, ALAN (1910–83), born Melbourne, was educated at the University of Melbourne, where he edited the *Melbourne University Magazine*. He subsequently worked for five years for the Melbourne *Herald*, before leaving Australia for Europe in 1936. In London he joined the *Daily Express*, was sent to Gibraltar in 1937 and in 1940 to the Middle East, where he soon established himself as the outstanding correspondent of the North African war. His three books about the war in Africa, *Mediterranean Front* (1941), *A Year of Battle* (1943) and *The End in Africa* (1943), republished together titled *African Trilogy* in 1944, proved highly popular; the trilogy was also published in an abridged version, *The Desert War* (1965). His other significant war book is *Eclipse* (1945). In 1946 Moorehead retired from active journalism to write full-time and lived mainly in Italy. His other books include biographies of Winston Churchill (1955 and 1960) and General Montgomery (1946); historical narratives, *The Traitors* (1952), *Gallipoli* (1956), *The Russian Revolution* (1958), *The White Nile* (1960), *The Blue Nile* (1962), *Cooper's Creek* (1963), *The Fatal Impact: An Account of the Invasion of the South Pacific 1767–1840* (1966) and *Darwin and the Beagle* (1969); travel documentaries, *Rum Jungle* (1953), *The Villa Diana* (1951) and *No Room in the Ark* (1959); two novels, *The Rage of the Vulture* (1948), which was produced as an American film titled *Thunder in the East*, and *A Summer Night* (1954); and an autobiography, *A Late Education* (1970). Awards won by Moorehead include the 1956 *Sunday Times* Book Prize and the Duff Cooper Memorial Award (for *Gallipoli*) and the Royal Society of Literature Award (for *Cooper's Creek*). He was made CBE in 1968 and AO in 1978.

MOORHEAD, FINOLA, see **Feminism and Australian Literature**

MOORHOUSE, FRANK (1938–   ), born Nowra on the south coast of NSW, was a cadet journalist on the Sydney *Daily Telegraph* and then worked on country newspapers before returning to Sydney to edit the *Australian Worker* in 1963 and to become an organizer for the WEA. Subsequently he edited *City Voices*, an inner city newspaper modelled on New York's *Village Voice*, and was a union organizer for the AJA; his active interest in the welfare of writers in Australia has also included

a stint as president of the ASA and involvement in a test case aimed at winning income for authors whose work had been photocopied in educational institutions. In 1957 Moorhouse's first story was published in *Southerly*, but in the 1960s he found it difficult, partly because of the explicitness of his fiction, to have work accepted by the established literary quarterlies. He found his outlets instead in smaller publications, often on the radical fringe, and in men's magazines; a publisher of the latter brought out his first collection of stories, *Futility and Other Animals* (1969). The appearance in 1972 of *The Americans, Baby* (q.v.) established Moorhouse's reputation as a leading exponent of short fiction in Australia, a reputation that has been confirmed by four later collections, *The Electrical Experience* (q.v., 1974), *Conference-ville* (q.v.,1976), *Tales of Mystery and Romance* (1977), and *The Everlasting Secret Family and Other Secrets* (q.v., 1980); a selection from these works was published in 1982. Co-founder in 1972 of the alternative fiction magazine, *Tabloid Story* (q.v.), Moorhouse edited the last issue of *Coast to Coast* (1973) and in 1983 an anthology of contemporary short fiction, *The State of the Art*. His other work includes screenplays, for the film, *Between Wars* (1974), and for short films of two stories from *The Americans, Baby, The Girl from the Family of Man* (1969) and *The Machine Gun* (1971); and columns and contributions written for the *Bulletin*. Some of the *Bulletin* material is included in *Days of Wine and Rage* (1980), a 1970s retrospective edited and dominated by Moorhouse. The influence of journalism in his fiction can be seen not only in the catchy titles and clipped prose style of the stories, but also in the use of some of the techniques of American 'new journalism', notably a scene by scene method of construction and an extensive use of realistic dialogue. Another influence which emerges in his fiction is the Andersonianism (see Anderson, John) of the Libertarian Society circles in which Moorhouse moved in Sydney, the belief in enquiry, the rejection of absolutes, and the suspicion of political and other enclosing systems which emerge throughout his fiction.

Moorhouse has been widely identified as a Balmain (q.v.) writer; the label derives from the congregation of intellectually-oriented, politically radical, sexually-experimental writers, artists and academics who gathered there from the late 1960s. The link with Balmain is strongest in *The Americans, Baby* and *Tales of Mystery and Romance* and evocatively recalled in *Days of Wine and Rage*, but is not as important as his innovative narrative method: the 'discontinuous narrative', a phrase which forms the subtitle of *Futility and Other Ani-*

mals, The Americans, Baby and *The Electrical Experience* and remains an important element in the later collections. As Moorhouse has described it, once he got beyond the apprentice stage 'and was starting to write stories which (looking back on it) were departures from the essentially social realist type story of the time, I found. . .that the stories were clustering. I wasn't writing a novel, but one story suggested the next. I was writing about one locality or one group of people, and even though the connections were often oblique, tangential, and at first not altogether perceived by me, they were real and growing'. The tension between connection and fragmentation, implied in the paradoxical word 'discontinuous', is a distinctive feature of the narrative form, which has its parallels, although Moorhouse was not specifically influenced by these writers, in the stories of Henry Lawson, Judah Waten and J.D. Salinger. Although individual Moorhouse volumes focus on particular localities and groups, e.g. the 'urban tribe' of *Futility and Other Animals*, T. George McDowell's country town world in *The Electrical Experience*, and the 'academic rodeo' of *Conference-ville*, there are enriching connections within and between the collections, e.g. incidents alluded to in one story become the focus of another, or characters appear and reappear. Thus Cindy Braughtin ages from a university student in *Futility and Other Animals* to a history lecturer in *The Everlasting Secret Family*, and is a character in *The Americans, Baby* and *Conference-ville*. Yet the links between Moorhouse's narratives have been recognized as molecular rather than linear and the sense of elusiveness and fragmentation is reinforced by the piecemeal way a reader is forced, as a result of the organization of the stories and the variation in point of view, to put together the history of individual characters who flit in and out of focus. It is also reinforced by the astringent prose style, with its emphasis on discrete paragraphs; by the inclusion of fragments as well as stories in some collections; and even by the physical makeup of the books.

The effect of discontinuity is to sharpen the reader's awareness of uncertainty and ambiguity, an ambiguity which encompasses not only the formal characteristics of the stories but also the extent to which they are autobiographical and historical, and the links between Moorhouse himself and his various and increasingly self-conscious authorial voices. Moorhouse's *raison d'etre* for his choice of form is that it corresponds to experience. Much of his fiction, focused on subcultural, submerged groups, emphasizes change and the resulting social and personal tensions. Thus, the 'central dilemma' of the members of the urban tribe in *Futility and Other Animals* is 'of giving birth, of cre-

ating new life': they leave home, move to the city, experience sexual liberation, try to overcome the sense of futility that accompanies their loss of equilibrium. *The Americans, Baby*, which like *Futility and Other Animals* is rapidly acquiring the status of an historical chronicle of the late 1960s and early 1970s, explores the ineffectiveness of political activism and the way sex can act as a destabilizing force, fragmenting personality. The title of *The Americans, Baby* is a reference to the Americanization of Australian society that many commentators have noticed. The American influence is important also in *The Electrical Experience*, which focuses on the generation gap between T. George McDowell, a south coast soft drinks manufacturer who, influenced by his visit to a Rotary convention in America, has tried to create order and shape to his existence, and his neurotic daugher Terri, who emerges in *The Americans, Baby* as 'unstable as jazz'. The ironized family motif recurs in *Tales of Mystery and Romance*, which contrasts the narrator's past conventional, coherent world with his present unattained hopes centred on Milton, the academic friend who has rejected him; and in *The Everlasting Secret Family*, in which the four sections are linked by the secrets, most of them relating to sexuality, which are shared with the reader in each.

The process of living can be seen to produce uncertainty, ambiguity, even chaos in the lives of Moorhouse's characters; freedom, it seems to be increasingly implied, comes from spontaneity and impulse, from accepting the fragmentations and discontinuities of a changing world. Not to do so is to risk becoming as lifeless as Hugo and the unnamed history lecturer in *The Americans, Baby*. Both pride themselves on the order and shape to their existence, yet Hugo's relentless self-sufficiency (he even makes his own soap) becomes terrifyingly claustrophobic for anyone he comes in contact with, and the history lecturer, who tries to arrive at a formula for living in the story 'Will power + natural sex-drive + intelligence + personal organization + aggression = sexual success' (*Futility and Other Animals*) is reduced in 'Letters to Twiggy' (*The Americans, Baby*) to pouring out obscenities when his obsession with forming a relationship with the pop star, Twiggy, is thwarted by the response of a series of identical form letters. The emphasis on a flexible attitude towards life's ambiguities has led some commentators to see Moorhouse's fictional world as profoundly pessimistic and fundamentally pointless. Despite this, he is generally regarded as one of the finest contemporary prose stylists, an original writer whose characters are delineated by their language, and whose observation of Australian society is characterized by a reverberating realism and by a sharp satiric wit.

'MOPOKE', see **POLLARD, JAMES**

MORAN, HERBERT MICHAEL (1885–1945), a distinguished cancer specialist and outstanding rugby union player, was born in Sydney, educated at the Universities of Sydney and Edinburgh and served in the First World War. He subsequently worked in Italy, Abyssinia and England, occasionally returning to Australia. He published three mainly autobiographical books, *Viewless Winds* (1939), *Beyond the Hill Lies China* (1945) and *In My Fashion* (1946). The first and last of them demonstrate his keen but sardonic wit and his strong, trenchant opinions, especially on such topics as the medical, academic and religious professions. *Beyond the Hill Lies China*, the most fictionalized of his books, includes a portrait of C.J. Brennan as Charles Maginn.

MORAN, PATRICK FRANCIS (1830–1911), born Ireland and educated at the Irish College in Rome, was ordained in 1853, established a distinguished reputation as academic and ecclesiastic and became archbishop of Sydney in 1884; he was created cardinal in 1885. In Australia he established several orphanages, hospitals, schools and churches, as well as two seminaries and was particularly active in the field of education. In secular affairs he proved to be a strong supporter of the Labor Party and a powerful advocate of Federation. He published a *History of the Catholic Church in Australasia* (1895), a work of extensive research. Vance Palmer includes an account of Moran in his *National Portraits* (1940) and his career is also described in J.G. Murtagh's *Australia, the Catholic Chapter* (1946), Patrick Ford's *Cardinal Moran and the A.L.P.* (1966) and Patrick O'Farrell's *The Catholic Church and Community in Australia* (1977).

MORANT, HARRY HARBORD (? EDWIN HENRY MURRANT) (?1864–1902) whose death by firing squad at Pretoria, South Africa, 27 February 1902 provoked one of the most-prolonged controversies in Australian military history, was a minor balladist of the 1890s. His origins are somewhat uncertain. By his own account he was born at Bideford, Devon in 1865, son of Admiral Sir Digby Morant. Recent research (*In Search of Breaker Morant, Balladist, and Bushveldt Carbineer* by Margaret Carnegie and Frank Shields, 1979) strongly suggests that he was Edwin Henry Murrant, born at Bridgwater, Somerset, 9 December 1864, son of Edwin Murrant and his wife Catherine, née Riely; that he sailed for

Australia from Plymouth 1 April 1883; that he landed in Townsville in northern Queensland in June 1883; that he took a job with a travelling rodeo and ended up in Charters Towers where, on 13 March 1884 he married a Daisy May O'Dwyer who was later to become the well-known Australian identity, Daisy Bates. The marriage supposedly lasted a few brief weeks, Morant, by which name he was known in April 1884 according to Charters Towers court records, taking off on a nomadic life of droving and horse-breaking. His skill and daring as a horse-breaker and rider led to the nickname, 'The Breaker', being bestowed on him. He developed a widespread reputation for riotous and unpredictable behaviour but his horsemanship, swagger, poetry, and cheerful nature generally won him more friends than enemies. He enlisted in the SA Mounted Rifles to get to the Boer War and ultimately joined the Bushveldt Carbineers, dubbed 'the Buccaneers', a horse regiment especially formed to combat the Boer commandos. Following the death and mutilation of his close friend, Captain Hunt, at the hands of the Boers, Morant was court-martialled with several others for the murder of some Boer prisoners and a German missionary, and executed with another Australian, P.J. Handcock. Morant and his associates, although amost certainly guilty of the charges against them, came to be regarded by many as pawns in the game of war and politics sacrificed by Kitchener to appease the German government or expended in an effort to secure a cease-fire in the war.

Although Morant's literary talent was meagre, the bizarre circumstances of his life and death have added piquancy to the public image of him as a poet. His first verses, 'A Night Thought', signed by 'The Breaker', were published in the *Bulletin* in 1891. During the next ten years he wrote some sixty poems for the *Bulletin* with occasional contributions to the Sydney *World News* and the *Windsor and Richmond Gazette*. Best known of his verses are 'Since the Country Carried Sheep', 'West by North Again', 'Who's Riding Old Harlequin Now?', 'Stewed' and 'Beyond His Jurisdiction'; 'Butchered to Make a Dutchman's Holiday', written in Pretoria gaol on the eve of his execution, was featured on the *Bulletin* Red Page 19 April 1902. He did not publish a volume of verse but selections of his work are included in some of the books that have been written about him. Morant was one of the multitude of 'back-block bards' of the 1890s; his verse is lively, breezy, and entertaining, and conveys in an ebullient, rough and ready fashion both the flavour of outback life and the laconically humorous, devil-may-care attitude of the Australian bushman of legend. A notable Australian film, *Breaker Morant*, focusing on the events in South Africa, was released in 1980. Pro Hart paintings illustrated a Breaker Morant series which was compiled by Dawn Ross and published in 1981. Kit Denton, who wrote *The Breaker* (1973), a fictionalized account of Morant's exploits, has reversed his attitude to his subject in *Closed File* (1983), where Morant is assessed as a vicious, amoral type. Other works on Morant include F.M. Cutlack's *Breaker Morant* (1962), Frank Fox's *Bushman and Buccaneer, Harry Morant* (1902) and George R. Witton's *Scapegoats of the Empire* (1907), Witton being one of the Bushveldt Carbineers who was imprisoned with Morant and later released from an English prison.

'MORDAUNT, ELINOR' (EVELYN MARY CLOWES) (?1872–1942), born Nottinghamshire, England, came to Australia in 1902 and remained for nine years. Some of her contributions to the *Bulletin* and *Lone Hand* were published as *Rosemary, That's for Remembrance* (1909); her first fictional work, *The Garden of Contentment* was published in 1902. Her impressions of Victoria are recorded in *On the Wallaby through Victoria* (1911). In later years she wrote prolifically: some forty novels and books of short fiction, several accounts of her extensive travels in many out-of-the-way places, and an autobiographical work, *Sinabada* (1937). Of her novels, *A Ship of Solace* (1911), which describes her voyage to Melbourne in 1902, *Lu of the Ranges* (1913), *The Rose of Youth* (1915) and *The Real Sally* (1925) have some Australian background.

MORELL, MUSETTE (MOYRA MARTIN) (1898–1950), wrote various plays for radio, including *Webs of Our Weaving, The Better Road* and *Even the Birds of the Air*, published in 1948 under the title, *Three Radio Plays*. Her other plays include 'His Gentle Art of Making Enemies' (a study of James Whistler), 'The World His Oyster' (about Alexandre Dumas), 'Brolgah the Beautiful'; and *The Quick and the Dead* (in *Australian Writers' Annual*, 1936). Two popular animal serials for children, broadcast on ABC radio, were published as books, *The Antics of Algy* (1946) and *Bush Cobbers* (1948); she also published two collections of plays for children, *Australian Youth Plays* (1948) and *Ten Puppet Plays* (1950).

Moreton Bay, a body of water in south-eastern corner of Queensland into the centre of which the Brisbane River runs, was discovered in 1770 by Captain James Cook (q.v.). It was a penal settlement, 1824–39 (hence the title of one of the best-known convict folk-songs) and until 1859 what became the State of Queensland (q.v.) was known as the Moreton Bay District. A dedicated historian of the Moreton Bay district was Thomas Welsby (1858–1941), born and educated at Ipswich. He published several books on Moreton Bay, e.g. *Early Moreton Bay* (1907), *Sport and Pastime in Moreton Bay* (1931), and his extensive library is now located at the University of Queensland. His *Collected Works*, ed. A.K. Thomson, were published in 1962.

'Moreton Bay' a famous Australian folk-song (q.v.), is the bitter lament of an ex-Irish convict who has been a prisoner at several notorious penal establishments. His most severe strictures are reserved for the 'excessive tyranny' prevailing at the Moreton Bay settlement under Captain Patrick Logan, at whose death the convict rejoices. The best-known version of 'Moreton Bay', played to the Irish tune 'Youghal Harbour', was arranged by John Manifold, and appeared in his *Bandicoot Ballads* (1953). There are, however, two earlier versions, which are as much recitation pieces as folk-songs, and are titled 'The Convict's Arrival' and 'The Convict's Lament'; later 'A Convict's Lament on the Death of Captain Logan'; literary tradition has the Irishman, 'Frank the Poet' (Francis MacNamara) as the author of 'The Convict's Arrival'. The echoes of 'Moreton Bay' in Ned Kelly's Jerilderie Letter have led to suggestions that the Kellys acquired their knowledge of the song during the 1840s, when both Ned's father, 'Red' Kelly, and 'Frank the Poet' were prisoners in Van Diemen's Land.

Moreton Bay Courier, see *Brisbane Courier*

MORGAN, DANIEL (1830–65), born Campbelltown, NSW, a bushranger who took the name of the pirate Morgan, was the son of Sydney prostitute, Kate Owen, and cabbage-seller, 'Gypsy' Fuller. Notoriously cruel and probably insane, Morgan was the model for the evil, snake-eyed Moran in 'Rolf Boldrewood''s *Robbery Under Arms* (1888) and is the subject of Edward Harrington's ballad, 'Morgan', Francis Webb's poem, 'Morgan's Country', and the Australian film, *Mad Dog Morgan* (1976).

MORGAN, JOHN (?1792–1866), born near Portsmouth, England, served with the royal marines before coming to the Swan River settlement in 1828. At Perth he served as magistrate, justice of the peace and barracks master and in 1834 took up a police magistracy in Van Diemen's Land. Three years later he tried farming and then journalism. Foundation editor of the *Hobart Town Advertiser* (1839), he also established the *Tasmanian Weekly Dispatch*

Morgan, John

(1839–41) and edited the *Morning Advertiser* (1841) and the *Britannia and Trades' Advocate* (1846–51). Before coming to Australia, Morgan published in 1824 *The Emigrant's Note Book and Guide*; he also collaborated with William Buckley in *The Life and Adventures of William Buckley* (1852).

Morley, Cressida, see **CLIFT, CHARMIAN;**: *My Brother Jack*; *Clean Straw for Nothing*

MORPHETT, TONY (1938–), born Sydney, worked for the ABC as an interviewer and reporter, before he became a freelance writer for radio and television. One of the best-known writers for ABC television, and the author of the popular series, *Dynasty*, he originated the series, *Certain Women*, and contributed to *The Sullivans*, *Ben Hall*, *Against the Wind* and *Seven Ages*. He has won several television awards. He has also written stage plays, one of which, *I've Come about the Assassination*, is included in Eunice Hanger's anthology, *Six One-Act Plays* (1970); and three novels, *Mayor's Nest* (1964), a lively satire in which the mayor of Parramatta becomes dictator of Australia; *Dynasty* (1967), a family board-room drama which became the basis of his television series; and *Thorskald* (1969), a multi-faceted study of an Australian artist.

Morringer, Ferdinand, see **POTTINGER, Sir FREDERICK WILLIAM**

MORRIS, E.E. (EDWARD ELLIS) (1843–1902), born Madras, India, was educated at Rugby and Oxford, and in 1875 came to Australia to take up the position of headmaster of the Melbourne Church of England Grammar School. In 1883 he was appointed professor of English, French and German languages and literature at the University of Melbourne, a position he held until his death. He published an important, pioneering work on Australian English (q.v.), *Austral English* (1898), and a biography of his father-in-law, George Higinbotham, Chief Justice of Victoria (1895). He also edited *Cassell's Picturesque Australasia* (1887–89).

'MORRIS, JULIAN', see **WEST, MORRIS**

MORRIS, MYRA (1893–1966), born Boort, Victoria, was brought up in the Mallee district. A freelance writer, she published verse, short stories and articles in newspapers and magazines. Her collections of verse include *England and Other Verses* (1918) and *White Magic* (1929). She also published a collection of short stories, *The Township* (1947); two novels, *The*

Wind on the Water (1938) and *Dark Tumult* (1939); and a novel for children, *Us Five* (1922). Morris's simple, rhythmic, ballad-style verses, which exuberantly reflect her love of the outdoor life, found a ready acceptance in the 1920s and 1930s. As a novelist she competently handles narrative and character, revealing a keen insight into the difficulties faced by women in inadequate marital relationships. But her talents for domestic realism and naturalistic description, especially of rural environments, are best suited to the short story.

MORRISON, A.A. (ALISTAIR ARDOCH) (1911–), born Melbourne, has worked as an artist and graphic designer, mainly in Sydney. As Professor 'Afferbeck Lauder', Professor of Strine (q.v.) studies at the University of Sinny, he published several 'papers' on strine in the *Sydney Morning Herald* in 1965. Some of these were subsequently republished in his books *Let Stalk Strine* (1965) and *Nose Tone Unturned* (1966), both illustrated by 'Al Terego'. He has also published compilations of Knightsbridge English for the uninitiated, *Fraffly Well Spoken* (1968) and *Fraffly Suite* (1969); a compendium, *Fraffly Strine Everything* (1969); and, under the name, Alistair Morrison, a comic miscellany, *The Scrambled Egghead* (1971).

MORRISON, G.E. (GEORGE ERNEST) (1862–1920), journalist, doctor and expert on Chinese affairs, often referred to as 'Chinese Morrison', was born at Geelong College, where his father was principal. He began a medical course at the University of Melbourne but failed his exams and travelled for a period in the South Seas, contributing influential articles to the *Age* on the evils of the kanaka trade. Sent to New Guinea as correspondent for the *Age* in 1883, he succeeded in penetrating well into the hinterland but was seriously wounded by natives. He went to Edinburgh for treatment and continued his medical studies there, graduating in 1887. After some further travel, he left for China in 1893. In *An Australian in China* (1895) he describes his 100 day journey from Shanghai to Rangoon in 1894, made with very little money and little knowledge of Chinese. Appointed special correspondent for the London *Times* in the Far East in 1896, he travelled widely in China, Thailand and Manchuria, providing the *Times* with accurate and often anticipatory reports of the country's troubled affairs and relations with Russia and Japan. He resigned from the *Times* in 1912 to become political adviser to the new Chinese government. Several biographies have been written, including Frank Clune's *Chinese Morrison* (1941), W.A. Morrison's *Ernest Morrison* (1962) and Cyril Pearl's *Morrison of Peking*

(1967); A.B. Paterson included an account of his life in *Happy Dispatches* (1934). A two-volume edition of his correspondence, edited by Lo Hui-Min, was published 1976–78.

MORRISON, JOHN (1904–), born Sunderland, England, migrated to Australia in 1923. A member of the Realist Writers Group, Morrison first published his short stories in trade union magazines. His published works include novels, *The Creeping City* (1949) and *Port of Call* (1950); collections of short stories, *Sailors Belong Ships* (1947), *Black Cargo* (1955), *Twenty-Three* (1962), *John Morrison, Selected Stories* (1972, selected by Ian Reid) and *North Wind* (1982); and a collection of memoirs and reflective essays, *Australian By Choice* (1973). Two translated collections of his short stories were published in Budapest (1957 and 1959), one in Warsaw (1955) and two in Moscow (1961 and 1962). He was awarded the Gold Medal of the Australian Literature Society for *Twenty-Three*. Although Morrison's socialist convictions are reflected in his choice of subjects and his naturalistic mode, he is an undogmatic, sensitive observer. Restricted to a narrow span of action and unexceptional individuals, his short stories characteristically record a particular, frequently undramatic, human situation, such as a family argument, a chance meeting in the bush, an interchange between passengers in a halted railway carriage, a conflict between a worker and his employer. Recurrent themes include isolation, whether imposed by psychological or physical conditions, and the destructive power of possessions or possessive attitudes. 'The Man on the 'Bidgee', 'Pioneers' and 'Goyai' are particularly striking studies of the former, 'It Opens Your Eyes', 'This Freedom' and 'Morning Glory' of the latter. Of his more extended narratives, 'The Battle of Flowers' describes an absurd but implacable and destructive struggle between two sisters to worst each other at their hobby of gardening; 'To Margaret' is a delicate study of young love opposed to middle-aged possessiveness; 'Black Night in Collingwood', a particularly popular story, deals with the impact of football on a typical Melbourne family. Morrison's range is wide but his attitude is consistent and is revealed implicitly in his novels and short stories as a belief in the simple virtues of work, loyalty and self-discipline. Although he avoids the experimental, usually preferring an uncomplicated linear progression and first-person narration by a reliable narrator, in his best narratives, such as 'Pioneers' and 'Goyai', Morrison achieves a powerful, cumulative suggestiveness. His revealing stories of waterfront workers, mostly more documentary than fictional, are frankly partisan in their sympathies, although 'The

Drunk' explores the ambivalences of the creed of mateship in a working situation. His novels, episodic in form, concentrate on a small number of characters set against a restricted environment.

MORRISON, R.H. (ROBERT HAY) (1915–), born South Yarra, Melbourne, studied modern languages at the University of Melbourne and was an army translator in Italian during the Second World War. A poet, verse translator and literary reviewer, Morrison has published the volumes of poetry *Lyric Images* (1954), *Opus 4* (1971), *Leaf-fall* (1974), *In the Ear of Dusk* (1977), *The Secret Greenness and Other Poems* (1978) and *For the Weeks of the Year* (1981). His other publications include *Australia's Russian Poets* (1971), *Australia's Ukrainian Poets* (1973), *Australia's Italian Poets* (1976), *One Hundred Russian Poems* (1979), *Ancient Chinese Odes* (1979) and *Sonnets from the Spanish* (1980).

MORTLOCK, J.F. (JOHN FREDERICK) (1809–82), born Cambridge, England, was convicted in 1843 of attempting to murder his uncle, who he believed had defrauded him of his inheritance. He was transported for twenty-one years, arrived in Australia in 1844, and served the first part of his sentence on Norfolk Island, where he was tutor to the family of ex-Tasmanian journalist, Gilbert Robertson. In 1857 he returned to England but was arrested and transported again in 1858 to complete his sentence; he settled finally in England in 1864. Mortlock wrote more than a dozen pamphlets in which he pursued vigorously the claims to his inheritance, but his major work is the memoir, *Experiences of a Convict*, which reflects Mortlock's wide knowledge of the Australian penal settlements. It was published in five parts in 1864–65 and republished in 1965, edited by G.A. Wilkes and A.G. Mitchell.

MORTON, WILLIAM LOCKHART (1820–98), born Cambusnethan, Scotland, studied engineering before migrating to Australia in 1841. A hard-working and innovative pastoralist who invented the sheep dip and the swing gate for drafting sheep, Morton was handicapped by adverse circumstances and personal tragedy, as well as by his inflexible, hypersensitive and censorious personality. He was also a keen and effective explorer, who meticulously recorded his observations on his trips in northern Queensland and the Mallee and Gippsland districts of Victoria, publishing *Notes of a Recent Personal Visit to the Unoccupied Portions of Northern Queensland* (1860) and *Suggestions for the Formation of a New Settlement in Australia* (1861). Morton published a series of accounts of his experiences in *Once A Month*, including his encounter with the bushranger, Frank Gardiner, 1884–86. In 1978 the accounts were published as *Adventures of a Pioneer*, edited by J.O. Randell.

MOSES, JACK (1860–1945), born Sydney, spent most of his working life as a commercial traveller in wine, and became known on the agricultural show circuit of NSW and other States both as a salesman and as a reciter of Australian ballads; *The Bulletin Book of Humorous Verses and Recitations* (1920) was dedicated to him as a 'good Australian' who was 'for many years a *Bulletin* reciter in the bush'. One of his favourite authors was Henry Lawson, who in the poem, *Joseph's Dreams* (1923), refers to Moses in stating, 'my best friend was a Yid'; Moses recalled their friendship in *Henry Lawson by His Mates* (1931). A long-time contributor to the *Bulletin*, the *Sydney Mail*, *Smith's Weekly* and other journals, Moses wrote *Beyond the City Gates* (1923), a volume of sketches and poems in which he celebrates bush life as the 'matrix of our Australian nation', and *Nine Miles from Gundagai* (1938), a volume of verse; the title piece is the well-known poem about the dog on the tucker box at Gundagai (q.v.). After his retirement Moses settled again in Sydney, where he was an affectionately-regarded street character who distributed postcards of his poems.

MOSSMAN, SAMUEL, see *Australia, Visited & Revisited*

Mother and Son, a three-act play by Louis Esson (q.v.), was first produced in 1923 by the Pioneer Players and was published in 1946. Set in Gippsland, it deals mainly with the relationship between a young man, Harry Lind, and his possessive mother. Harry rejects the girl his mother prefers, brings home a barmaid of dubious reputation, is rejected in turn for a rival squatter, and finally killed in a riding accident.

Mother's Offering to Her Children, A, written anonymously by 'A Lady Long Resident in New South Wales' and published in 1841, was an early Australian book written especially for children. In the form of a dialogue it contains naive and trivialized anecdotes of the Aborigines and their customs as well as stories of shipwrecks on the Australian coasts. It has been suggested by Marcie Muir in *Charlotte Barton: Australia's First Children's Author* (1980) that its author was Charlotte Barton (1797–1862) mother of the first Australian-born woman novelist, Louisa Atkinson. It was previously attributed to Lady Gordon Bremer.

MOUBRAY, (MOWBRAY), PHILIP (?–1903) who died at Narrandera, was well-known in the 1890s as a *Bulletin* writer under the pseudonym 'Scotty the Wrinkler'; he adopted the name for his contributions after meeting in the Riverina a Scottish shepherd who claimed to be an expert on wrinkles. Of Scots descent himself, Moubray seems to have been a British army officer who served in India and Abyssinia before travelling to America and then Australia where, among other occupations, he was miner, drover, tutor, cook, and whaler. His gently cynical, often humorous *Bulletin* contributions consist mainly of paragraphs published in such columns as 'Aboriginalities'; he celebrates the freedoms of bush life and attacks cant and humbug. His death prompted Henry Lawson's poem, 'The Passing of Scotty', published in the *Bulletin*, 12 November 1903. A collection of his writings was published as *The Swag* around 1900.

MOUNTFORD, C.P. (CHARLES PEARCY) (1890–1977), one of Australia's best-known ethnologists, was born in the SA outback settlement of Hallett. A post office mechanic in the 1920s, he was sent to the Northern Territory where his contacts with the Aboriginal tribes of the area stimulated his life-long interest in their culture and resulted in a series of books on Aboriginal art, myths, rituals and music, many of them illustrated with his own photographs. The best-known are *Brown and Red Sand* (1948), *The Art, Myth and Symbolism of Arnhem Land* (1956), *The Tiwi, Their Art, Myth and Ceremony* (1958), *Winbaraku and the Myth of Jarapiri* (1968), and *Ayers Rock* (1965). Three of his most popular interpretations of Aboriginal music, *The Dreamtime* (1965), *The Dawn of Time* (1969) and *The First Sunrise* (1971), illustrated by Ainslie Roberts, were published together in 1973 titled *The Dreamtime Book*. Although he was removed from the conventional areas of teaching and research, Mountford established a significant reputation as an ethnologist and led two National Geographic expeditions, one to Arnhem Land and the other to Melville Island, as well as eight expeditions to inland Australia for the University of Adelaide. He received numerous awards for his skills as anthropologist and photographer. His biography *Monty*, by Max Lamshed, was published in 1972.

Moving Image, The, (1946), the first volume of poetry by Judith Wright (q.v.), takes its title from Plato's 'Time is a moving image of eternity'. The title poem is a philosophical meditation on the metaphysical role of the poet as interpreter of the processes of change wrought by time. The volume includes poems celebrating her affection for New England, e.g. 'South of My Days' and others which present figures and themes from Australia's past, e.g. 'Bullocky', 'Bora Ring' and 'Remittance Man'.

'Mr. Butterfry', the title story of Hal Porter's (q.v.) collection, *Mr. Butterfry and Other Tales of New Japan* (1970), was first published in the *Bulletin* in 1968. In a Tokyo bar frequented by expatriate Australians, the narrator encounters Blue, a man with whom he had been friendly eighteen years earlier during the postwar occupation of Japan. When he had first known him, Blue had been a cheeky, self-confident if boring individual in love with his major's housegirl. Now a commercial traveller, he seems strangely embittered and his cheekiness has degenerated into foul-mouthed brashness. He is known to the Japanese bar hostesses in the many bars that he visits, as 'Mr. Butterfry', the loathsome, uncouth barbarian. For the narrator the source of his bitterness is not clear, although it transpires he has lost the fortune he made on the black market, until he is invited to visit his home. There he meets his now-detested, ex-housegirl wife; she has contracted her husband's brand of verbal abuse and forcefully returns his hatred, notwithstanding the presence of a stranger. It becomes clear that she has used her husband's fortune to buy modelling careers for their Eurasian daughters, Lana and Shirley. Aware that there is no way back for 'Mr. Butterfry' and that his abuse of the bar-hostesses is a kind of blind revenge, the narrator leaves this 'ageing terrier of a spiv snarling and sniffing in the daily darker corners of [his] prison'.

Mrs. Pretty and the Premier, a play by Arthur Henry Adams (q.v.), was first produced in Sydney in 1914, published the same year and produced in London two years later. A light comedy, the play ironically mixes up the male world of politics and the female one of marriage, to the detriment of the former. The central character, William Power, a Labor State premier with little social finesse, finds himself in a political and personal dilemma when a reporter from an opposition paper sees him with a veiled lady, Mrs Pretty, in compromising circumstances. The situation is complicated by Mrs Pretty's engagement to the leader of the opposition and her position as one of the landholders threatened by Power's new Bill to reclaim large estates. To extricate himself, Power claims that the lady is his secret wife and the action turns upon Mrs Pretty's reactions to the situation.

Mrs. Tregaskiss, see **PRAED, ROSA**

Muddle-Headed Wombat, see **PARK, RUTH**

MUDIE, IAN (1911–76), born Hawthorn, SA, was a freelance writer who also worked as a publisher's editor and lecturer in creative writing. Active in literary affairs, he was federal president of the FAW, regularly conducted the Writers' School held in conjunction with the Adelaide Festival and frequently addressed school and adult groups on Australian literature. In 1978 the SA FAW instituted the annual Ian Mudie Award for poetry with an Australian theme.

A prolific poet, Mudie published nine volumes of verse, including *Corroboree to the Sun* (1940), *This Is Australia* (1941), *The Australian Dream* (1943), *The Blue Crane* (1959), *The North-Bound Rider* (1963), winner of the Grace Leven Prize for poetry, *Look, The Kingfisher* (1970) and *Selected Poems 1934–1974* (1976), which contains some forty uncollected poems written while he was in his early sixties. He edited numerous works and anthologies, including *Poets at War: An Anthology of Verse by Australian Servicemen* (1944) and the *Jindyworobak Anthology* (1946). He wrote several histories, chief of which are *Riverboats* (1961), an account of the paddle steamers that plied the Darling-Murray waterways, and *The Heroic Journey of John McDouall Stuart* (1968).

A member of the Australia First movement and attracted to Rex Ingamells's Jindyworobak movement through his patriotism, affinity with the landscape, and concern and respect for the Aborigines and their lore, Mudie was a strident champion of the 'good old days' of pioneer Australia. Aggressively conservationist, much of his early poetry tells of a once-lovely land 'turned to barrenness, made dead by the lust of men', and of once-proud tribesmen, dispossessed so that their lands 'cut up and divided by Torrens title' could be given to the white man for his 'five-roomed coffins'. 'This Land' and 'This is Australia' are representative of Mudie, the ardent nationalist, the Jindyworobak proselytizer. Sensitive also to the paradox of 'a harsh land . . . that scorches its flowers of spring', Mudie sought to employ a poetic language that captured the spirit and character of the land and the people who survived in it. He settled in the main for spare, laconic and often colloquial style. At its best that style produced poetic flashes, at its worst it was prosaic and slangy. His most popular successes were the colloquial 'They'll Tell You About Me' (q.v.), 'Hey Blue, It's Raining', and 'I Wouldn't Be Lord Mayor'. Mudie's poetry is, however, not confined to Jindyworobak and nationalist preoccupations. *The North Bound Rider*, the prize-winning collection of 1961, has numerous reflections on city and suburban life. Personal lyrics are plentiful in *The Blue Crane* (1959), *Look, The Kingfisher* (1970) and *Selected Poems 1934-1974* (1976). One of the most likeable men, full of camaraderie, yarns and good nature, Mudie embodied much of the best and most characteristic features of the traditional Australian bush ethos.

MUDIE, JAMES, see **Convict in Australian Literature**

MUELLER, Sir FERDINAND VON (1825-96), botanist and explorer, was born in Germany and arrived in Australia in 1847. In 1853 he was appointed foundation government botanist of Victoria and carried out extensive explorations of the Victorian hinterland, greatly extending the knowledge of Australian plant species. He also later accompanied or conducted expeditions in the Northern Territory, Queensland, WA and Tasmania. Appointed director of the Melbourne Botanical Gardens in 1857, he established what is now the National Herbarium but was deprived of his directorship in 1873 because of a demand that more attention be paid to the gardens' aesthetic appeal. One of the founders of the Royal Society of Victoria and the University of Melbourne, von Mueller received numerous awards and honours, including election as FRS (1861) and as president of the Australasian Association for the Advancement of Science (1890). His numerous publications on Australian plants include the twelve-volume *Fragmenta Phytographiae Australiae* (1858-82); with George J. Bentham, the seven-volume *Flora Australiensis* (1863-78); and the two-part study, *Systematic Census of Australian Plants* (1882 and 1889). His work is described in the biographies by Margaret Willis, *By Their Fruits* (1949) and Edward Kynaston, *A Man on Edge* (1981).

MUIR, MARCIE (1919-), born Perth, has worked for many years on Australian children's literature. She has compiled an extensive two-volume bibliography of children's books published in Australia (1970, 1976); edited a collection of tales for children, *Strike-a-Light the Bushranger* (1972); written an account of Charlotte Barton (q.v.), Australia's first children's author (1980); and a *History of Australian Children's Book Illustration* (1982), which supersedes her earlier *Australian Children's Book Illustrators* (1977), and which records the image of Australia presented to children from the early romanticized misconceptions of overseas publishers to the realism of such contemporary artists as Dick Roughsey. She has also published an edition of C. Langloh Parker's *My Bush Book* (1982), which includes a discussion of Mrs Parker's life and her literary contribution; and *Anthony Trollope in Australia* (1949). In 1978 Marcie Muir shared with her husband, Harry Muir, an Adelaide bookshop proprietor and founder of the Wakefield Press, the National Book Council's Bookman of the Year Award.

MUIR, THOMAS, see **Scottish Martyrs**

MUIRDEN, BRUCE, see **Australia First Movement**; *Austrovert*

Mulga Bill, the central figure in A.B. Paterson's (q.v.) poem, 'Mulga Bill's Bicycle' published in *Rio Grande's Last Race and Other Verses* (1902) is one of Paterson's well-known comic folk characters. Concerned to keep abreast of progress, Bill turned away 'the good old horse that served him many days' and 'caught the cycling craze'. After a brief but spectacular encounter with the 'two-wheeled outlaw', Bill ended up, with the cycle, in Dead Man's Creek. There he left it, the lesson learned: 'a horse's back is good enough, henceforth for Mulga Bill'. Mulga Bill takes his name from his habitat, the mulga, which in colloquial speech denotes the remote bush or outback. Will Ogilvie's poem, 'The Mulga Mail', demonstrates how news travels through the outback via the bush telegraph (see Bush).

MULLEN, SAMUEL (1828-90), born Dublin, was apprenticed to bookseller, William Curry, in whose shop he met fellow apprentice, George Robertson (1) and emigrated with him to Australia in 1852. After five months working as a station-hand at Mount Bute, he joined Robertson as an assistant in the latter's bookshop in Melbourne. He travelled to London to take up the position of manager of Robertson's London branch in 1857 but when Robertson appointed his brother, William Robertson, in his stead the two men fell out and never spoke to each other again. Mullen returned to Melbourne in 1859 and opened up his own bookshop and a successful library. He retired in 1889 and his brother William, a bookseller and stationer of Ballarat, joined with A.G. Melville and Leonard Slade to acquire Samuel's business. They traded as Melville, Mullen & Slade and in 1900 became Melville and Mullen, and in 1921 merged with George Robertson & Co to become Robertson & Mullen, the well-known Melbourne bookshop and publishing firm.

MUM, see *Melbourne University Magazine*

MURDOCH Family is significant in the history of the twentieth-century Australian, and latterly British and American, newspaper industry. Sir Keith Murdoch (1885–1952), the nephew of Sir Walter Murdoch, was born in Melbourne, began his career in journalism in 1903 as a district correspondent for the *Age*, had a brief and unsuccessful sojourn in England 1908–09 before returning to the *Age* as a reporter. He was a Melbourne correspondent of the *Sun* from 1912 to 1915, when he was narrowly defeated by C.E.W. Bean in an AJA ballot to be Australian war correspondent. The same year he left for England to become manager of a cable service; *en route* he visited Gallipoli, and his subsequent report of conditions there to the Australian and British governments was significant in the recall of Sir Ian Hamilton and the evacuation of Gallipoli. Murdoch remained in England until his appointment as editor of the Melbourne *Herald* in 1921. Fighting off Sir Hugh Denison's attempt to enter Melbourne journalism, Murdoch, as managing director and chairman of the Herald and Weekly Times company, proceeded to build the company into a position of prominence in Australian journalism, with interests in the *Advertiser* and *News* in Adelaide, the *West Australian* in Perth, and the *Courier-Mail* in Brisbane. He was also a significant figure in the establishment of the Australian newsprint industry and the development of cable services, and during the Second World War was director-general of information. He is the subject of Desmond Zwar's *In Search of Keith Murdoch* (1980).

Murdoch's sudden death in 1952, three years after his retirement from the Herald and Weekly Times, left his family with a controlling interest only in News Limited, which ran the *News* and the *Sunday Mail* in Adelaide. Rupert Murdoch (1931–   ), born Melbourne and educated at the University of Oxford, worked briefly in London on the *Daily Express* before returning to Australia to join News Limited. He was based in Adelaide for the rest of the 1950s; in 1960 he expanded into NSW with the purchase by News Limited of the *Daily* and *Sunday Mirror* and a chain of Sydney suburban newspapers. In 1964 Murdoch founded the *Australian* and launched his assault on Fleet Street in 1969 with the purchase of *News of the World* and the *Sun*. In the 1970s and 1980s News Limited and its associated companies have continued expansion – in Australia with the purchase of the Sydney *Daily* and *Sunday Telegraph* (1972) but also into NZ, USA and elsewhere in the UK. Apart from interests in television, records, magazines and numerous other areas, Murdoch's companies founded the *National Star*, later the *Star*, in 1974 in New York; purchased the *San Antonio Express* (1973), the New York *Post* (1976) and *Village Voice*

(1977), the *Boston Herald* (1982) and *Chicago Sun-Times* (1983) in the USA; and the *Times* and *Sunday Times* (1980) in the UK; by 1984 he controlled over eighty significant newspapers and magazines. A controversial figure who has been admired for his business acumen and criticized for lowering newspaper standards, he is the subject of Simon Regan's *Rupert Murdoch: A Business Biography* (1976) and Michael Leapman's *Barefaced Cheek: The Apotheosis of Rupert Murdoch* (1983).

MURDOCH, NINA (1890–1976), born Melbourne, worked first as a schoolteacher. A contributor of verse to the *Bulletin*, she won a prize for a sonnet on Canberra and subsequently published two collections, *Songs of the Open Air* (1915) and *More Songs of the Open Air* (1922). In 1914 she joined the staff of the Sydney *Sun* and transferred to the Melbourne *Sun* in 1922; in 1930 she gave up journalism for radio broadcasting. Founder of the children's programme, 'The Argonauts', she became a familiar voice to many Australian children. She also published three novelettes, which have been popular with both adults and children, *Miss Emily in Black Lace* (1930), *Portrait of Miss Emily* (1931) and *Exit Miss Emily* (1937); a biographical account of Sir John Longstaff, *Portrait in Youth* (1948); and four books which reflected her keen interest in travel.

MURDOCH, Sir WALTER (1874–1970), born Aberdeenshire, Scotland, came to Melbourne in 1884. Educated at the University of Melbourne, Murdoch worked as a private tutor and as a country schoolmaster before starting a school in Camberwell in 1897. He ran another school in Warrnambool 1901–03, but in 1904 was appointed to a lecturing position in English at the University of Melbourne. A familiar figure in literary and academic circles in Melbourne, a member of various literary societies and founder and editor of *Trident*, Murdoch was friendly with many prominent individuals; one of his students and a lifelong friend was Nettie Palmer. Murdoch was widely known for his contributions to the *Argus*. His weekly column, titled 'Books and Men' and signed 'Elzevir', ran 1905–13 and in a second series, 1919–38. One of his first ventures as a critic, an essay on Australian poets of the 1890s, published in the *Argus* in 1899, drew trenchant reactions from such writers as Edward Dyson, 'Rolf Boldrewood' and A.G. Stephens. During his years in Melbourne Murdoch also contributed leaders and anonymous book reviews to the *Argus*, and contributed to many other newspapers and periodicals under such pseudonyms as 'Aden', 'Nick O'Teen', 'W.L. Forbes' and 'Diogenes T. Moxhaye'.

When in 1911 he was not appointed to the Chair of English, which had been left vacant since the death of E.E. Morris in 1902, Murdoch took a full-time position on the literary staff of the *Argus*. In 1912, however, he was appointed to the Chair of English at the newly-founded University of WA and moved to Perth. During his years in WA his reputation as a public figure grew, both because of his regular contributions to the *Argus* and the *West Australian* and because of his regular radio talks which were particularly influential in the 1930s and 1940s and continued until the 1960s. The publication in 1930 of *Speaking Personally*, a collection of some of his pieces for the *Argus*, followed by other collections, made his name familiar throughout Australia. In 1939 he retired from the teaching staff of the university but was re-elected to the Senate 1941–43, and served as chancellor 1943–48. His writing career meanwhile continued unabated. After his association with the *Argus* ceased in 1938, he began a regular syndicated column for the Melbourne *Herald*. In 1945 his journalism took a new turn when he began a weekly series of much briefer essays titled 'Answers', which took the form of responses to readers' questions; this series, which appeared for varying periods in all States of Australia and NZ, ceased in 1964. His last journalistic venture was a series titled 'Afterthoughts', which appeared in the *Australian* 1965–68. Murdoch was made CBE in 1939 and knighted in 1964; in 1970, WA's second university was named after him. His daughter, Catherine, also a well-known broadcaster, married the poet and critic, Alec King; the newspaper proprietor, Sir Keith Murdoch, was his nephew and Rupert Murdoch is his grand-nephew.

Although Murdoch wrote some verse and short stories, his natural medium was the essay. He published several collections of essays which had previously only appeared in newspapers, *Loose Leaves* (1910), *Speaking Personally* (1930), *Saturday Mornings* (1931), *Moreover* (1932), *The Wild Planet* (1934) and *Lucid Intervals* (1936); the last five of these are brought together in his *Collected Essays* (1938); another subsequent collection, *The Spur of the Moment* (1939), is included in the second edition of *Collected Essays* (1940); *Steadfast* (1941) is his last collection of new essays. Other selections, which are all reprinted from the above collections, include *The Two Laughters* (1934), *Selections from Walter Murdoch* (1941), *72 Essays* (1947), *Selected Essays* (1956) and *The Best of Walter Murdoch* (1964). *Answers* (1953), largely reprinted in *My 100 Answers* (1960), is selected from the *Herald* series of essays in miniature. He also wrote a biography of Alfred Deakin (1923) and edited two well-known anthologies, *The Oxford*

Book of Australasian Verse (q.v.,1918), and, with Henrietta Drake-Brockman, *Australian Short Stories* (1951). Of his many school editions and textbooks, *The Struggle for Freedom* (1903) and *The Australian Citizen* (1912) are interesting both as records of social and political attitudes of the time and as reflections of Murdoch's personal philosophy. J.A. La Nauze has published an account of Murdoch's life (1977) and has edited, with Elizabeth Nurser, *Walter Murdoch and Alfred Deakin on Books and Men: Letters and Comments 1900–1918* (1974).

As Murdoch himself commented, he only wrote one 'real' book, that is, his biography of Deakin, but probably no other Australian writer has enjoyed so wide and sympathetic an audience, especially from the 1930s to the late 1950s. His essays and his radio talks shared the same characteristics: whimsical, often shrewd humour, an easy, conversational but economical style and a disarming, persuasive, personal flavour. Writing or talking urbanely on a wide range of subjects, from tripe and onions and tin-openers to the nature of man and the meaning of life, he frequently dealt, in a light and original way, with familiar, ordinary ideas. *Loose Leaves* consists entirely of literary essays but Murdoch turned more and more to the general, topical essay, although his wide reading and enthusiasm for literature were always manifest. A liberal humanist, he professed a traditional morality which derived from his Presbyterian background and his years in the distinctive cultural milieu that was Melbourne's from the 1890s to 1914. A courageous and often effective critic of pretension, and an enemy of the 'suburban spirit', he deliberately encouraged his readers in what he saw as the healthy habit of scepticism and his faith in 'the sacred duty of growling'. Occasionally, and particularly in the 1930s, his independent attitudes involved him in economic, educational, political, and even religious controversy. He was also, on occasion, the centre of literary controversy; his survey of Australian literature for a special supplement of the London *Times*, published in 1938, aroused the anger of several Australian writers for its excessive concentration on the nineteenth century. A protest from the FAW resulted in a letter of apology from the *Times*. Equally acrimonious was the response in *Southerly* and elsewhere to the 1945 edition of the *Oxford Book of Australasian Verse* which, it was claimed, was totally unrepresentative and out-of-date. Although Murdoch showed some interest in Australian writing during his career, his real literary affinities were with nineteenth-century English literature.

As an essayist, however, Murdoch eluded criticism for the most part by keeping to general, uncontroversial topics. Some of his essays are purely fanciful; others touch on his travels; others on his literary interests; and others deal with his detestation of pretension and jargon. A great number use an apparently trivial topic to introduce consideration of some universal subject, such as patriotism, tolerance, true democracy, civilization or education. In his later series, 'Answers', the topics became even more general, covering such questions as 'Can One Be a Snob and a Christian?', 'What Is a Perfect Day?', or 'Does It Ever Rain Cats and Dogs?'.

MURNANE, GERALD (1939–), born Melbourne where he now lives, spent part of his childhood in rural Victoria. He has written three novels, *Tamarisk Row* (1974), which describes an Australian Catholic childhood in the 1940s; *A Lifetime on Clouds* (1976), a tragicomic exploration of the experiences of a Catholic youth in the 1950s; and *The Plains* (1982), an original and suggestive work described by Murnane as 'a sort of . . . mirror reflection or a photographic negative of some of my experiences, and the experiences of people I know in the past twenty years in Australia'.

MURPHY, EDWIN GREENSLADE (1861–1939), was born in Victoria but joined in the great gold rush to Coolgardie in WA in 1893. From prospecting he turned to journalism and the writing of topical verses, becoming, as 'Dryblower', one of the best-known and most colourful identities of the west. For forty years he wrote a column of jingles, 'Verse and Worse', for the Perth *Sunday Times*. Two collections of his verses were published, *Jarrahland Jingles* (1908) and *Dryblower's Verses 1894–1926* (1926). Unpretentious in style, his poems are humorous and full of affection for the ordinary toilers of the world; his pseudonym 'Dryblower' was the name given to the rudimentary apparatus used by miners in the waterless west to separate the gold from dirt and gravel.

MURPHY, PETER (1945–), born Melbourne, works as a teacher and has published three collections of verse, *Escape Victim and Other Poems* (1974), *Seen & Unseen* (1975), and *Glass Doors and Other Poems* (1977); and one collection of short stories, *Black Light* (1979).

MURRAY, ANNA MARIA (1808–89), born Balliston, Ireland, came to Sydney in 1827 and married Captain George Bunn, a shipowner, whaler and sealer. Widowed early, she wrote a melodramatic novel under the pseudonym 'An Australian' and titled *The Guardian* (1838), the first novel to be printed and published on the mainland of Australia, Henry Savery's *Quintus Servinton* (1831) having been published in Hobart Town.

MURRAY, LES (1938–), born at Nabiac, a rural village on the north coast of NSW, spent his childhood and adolescence on his father's dairy farm in the nearby Bunyah district, a remote, dairying community. Murray left the University of Sydney in 1960 without a degree but with an abiding love for the old Fisher Library and some editorial experience with the University's literary magazines, *Hermes* and *Arna*, and its newspaper, *Honi Soit*. In 1963 he took a position as a translator of foreign scholarly and technical material at the Australian National University; in 1965 he attended the British Commonwealth Arts Festival Poetry Conference at Cardiff; in 1967 he gave up his translator position and lived for more than a year in England and Europe. Back in Australia he resumed his university course, graduating in 1969. In recent years Murray has pursued a full-time writing career as a book-reviewer, contributor to newspapers and journals, editor (in part) of *Poetry Australia* and for Angus & Robertson and has written several volumes of poetry. A leading figure in Sydney's literary society, Murray maintains his rural ties, from which he derives so much of his poetic inspiration, by alternating between a working city life and bush holidays on a sixteen-hectare Bunyah farm only a kilometre or so away from the old weatherboard house where he lived as a boy.

Murray's volumes of poetry are *The Ilex Tree* (1965, with Geoffrey Lehmann), *The Weatherboard Cathedral* (1969), *Poems Against Economics* (1972), *Lunch & Counter Lunch* (1974), *Selected Poems: The Vernacular Republic* (1976), *Ethnic Radio* (1977), *The Boys Who Stole the Funeral* (q.v., 1980), *Equanimities* (1982), *The Vernacular Republic: Poems 1961–1981* (1982), and *The People's Otherworld* (1983), the last-named winning the Australian Literature Society's Gold Medal in 1984. He has also published a selection of his prose, *The Peasant Mandarin* (1978). An important statement by Murray on his work and thought is 'The Human Hair-Thread', *Meanjin* (1977).

The Ilex Tree, whose middle title from Virgil's *Eclogues* concerns 'two youths in their prime, Arcadian singers both of them', won the 1965 Grace Leven Prize for poetry. The best of these early Murray poems, 'Spring Hail', 'The Widower in the Country', 'Driving through Sawmill Towns', and 'Noonday Axeman', with their sensitive awareness of the humanity that exists in situations that might seem too banal for poetry, all stem from personal experience. In them he celebrates his farming boyhood, his ancestors, and the rural life and people he intuitively understands. In 'The Widower in the Country' with its description of the meaningless, mechanical daily round, and in 'Driving through Sawmill Towns' where the close-knit tedium of isolated village life surfaces in the gestures and movements of the characters, Murray achieves, in James Tulip's words, a remarkable 'anecdotal sense of people'. These early poems also illustrate Murray's flair for fresh, original and brilliantly-inventive language and imagery. His second collection, *The Weatherboard Cathedral* (1969), containing forty-five poems, indicates, in the apparent contradiction of its title, Murray's chief philosophic stance, an almost Jindyworobakish insistence on the worth, even the sanctity, of Australian rural uniqueness, its landscape, lifestyles and value. The opening sequence of seven poems, 'Evening Alone at Bunyah', contains 'two weatherboard cathedrals', the shabby country house in which he lived as a boy, and his grandfather's derelict house on whose walls hang generations of dead relatives. Both are hallowed places, as is the simple rural scene,

> The road itself's not paved, and there's no town
> In the valley yet at all.

Two of the best-known poems of this collection, 'Blood', which probes beneath the apparent primitivism of the pig-killing to the natural rural order that requires it, and 'An Absolutely Ordinary Rainbow', which emphasizes the wholesome regeneration of 'the gift of weeping', have been frequently anthologized. In 'The Fire Autumn' Murray, deploring the materialism of the civilized European world, catalogues such ingredients of the 'cesspools of maturity' as 'the chain saw, junked beercans, newsprint, the torrents of birth', and calls for an appreciation of 'the kingdom of the living' (Australia) where simpler appetites and sounder values prevail. *Poems Against Economics* (1972) is a composite of three sequences, 'Seven Points for an Imperilled Star', which won the Captain Cook Bicentenary literary competition of 1970, 'Juggernaut's Little Scrapbook' (minor satirical squibs) and 'Walking to the Cattle-Place' (q.v.). The 'Imperilled Star' sequence contains several important poems: 'Toward the Imminent Days', an epithalamium for his friends Geoff Lehmann and Sally McInerney; 'The Conquest' and 'The Ballad of Jimmy Governor', commentaries on racial issues; and 'SMLE', a countryman's reflections on guns. 'Walking to the Cattle-Place', an ambitious meditation sequence of sixteen 'cow' poems is given its framework by Murray's own comment: 'I set out to follow a cow and I found a whole world, a spacious, town-despising grassland

where Celt and Zulu and Verdic Aryan were one in their concerns'. The obscurity of some of the poems in the 'cow' sequence is brought about by masses of incomprehensible allusions and, in Roger McDonald's words, by a 'corner-of-the-mouth speech that has the effect of under-explanation rather than concentration'. *Lunch & Counter Lunch* (1974), although full of Murray's extraordinary verbal inventiveness, moves back to a plainer poetic diction and a more dramatic technique. 'The Police: Seven Voices', Murray's most thematically structured sequence, deals with the problem of law and order and the image of police authoritarianism in Australian society; it is also a rare example of his success with satire. In 'The Mitchells', titled originally 'Dedication, Written Last: For the Vernacular Republic', Murray captures, in the voices of the speakers ('Like trying to farm the road') and in the verse itself ('Water boils in a prune tin'), the laconic ritual of rural Australian language. *Ethnic Radio* (1977) includes 'Five Gaelic Poems' and 'The Figures in Quoniam', which illustrate the Gaelic influence that is ever-present in Murray's poetry, and 'The Euchre Game', 'The Returnees' and 'The Powerline Incantation', the last a remarkable poetic illustration of the effects of an electric shock; its broken verse patterns and 'electrified' language match the chaotic flashes of thought and agonized visions of the victim. The most substantial poem of *Ethnic Radio* is, however, 'The Buladelah–Taree Holiday Song Cycle' (q.v.), a group of thirteen poems (songs) in the style and metre of R.M. Berndt's translation of 'The Moon-bone Song' from the Wonguri linguistic group of the Aboriginal Mandjigai (Manjikai) tribe of north-eastern Arnhem Land. A remarkable fusing of ancient Aboriginal and modern white Australian urban and rural cultures (for example, the Pacific Highway in peak holiday time is described in terms of the all-giving Rainbow Snake) the 'Holiday Song Cycle' is an imaginative poetic statement of the Jindyworobak dream that white Australians should have the same affinity as the Aborigines with the environment.

The Boys Who Stole the Funeral (q.v., 1980), a sequence of 140 sonnets, is an attempt at a novel in verse. Two young men, Kevin Forbutt and Cameron Reeby, steal the body of a First World War veteran, Clarrie Dunn (Kevin's great-uncle) from a Sydney funeral parlour and carry it by car to the old man's native place, an isolated spot named Dark's Plain on the north coast of NSW. Although they do this because they want to carry out the old man's dying wish they are also attempting to find their own fulfilment. *The Boys Who Stole the Funeral* brings together such passionate Murray attitudes as devotion to the Australian rural scene, respect and affection for the ordinary country man, and a conviction that modern society relinquishes, at its peril, the values that are enshrined in the land and in the lives of those who live in intimacy with it.

Murray River, more than 2500 kilometres long, rises in the Australian Alps just south of Mt Kosciusko, flows for much of its distance as the border between NSW and Victoria, then enters SA and reaches the ocean through the waters of Lake Alexandrina. The Murray was discovered in 1824 by Hamilton Hume and William Hovell who named it the Hume, and was charted by Charles Sturt who renamed it after Sir George Murray, then secretary of state for the colonies. Sturt travelled by boat in 1830 from Gundagai, on the Murrumbidgee River to Lake Alexandrina and back again. Following the tracks of these early explorers, and others such as Sir Thomas Mitchell, overlanders and pastoralists soon occupied the river and its environs. The Murray exploration literature includes Hume and Hovell's *Journey of Discovery to Port Phillip* (1831) compiled by William Bland, Charles Sturt's *Two Expeditions into the Interior of Southern Australia* (1833), and T.L. Mitchell's *Three Expeditions into the Interior of Eastern Australia* (1838). Settlement literature of the Murray region includes travellers' and pastoralists' memoirs and reminiscences such as T.F. Bride's *Letters from Victorian Pioneers* (1898); R.V. Billis and A.S. Kenyon's *Pastures New* (1930) and *Pastoral Pioneers of Port Phillip* (1932); and Joseph Hawdon's *The Journal of a Journey from New South Wales to Adelaide* (first published 1952). Allan Morris's *Rich River* (1953) is an historical account of the Murray riverboat trade, based on the McCulloch Carrying Company papers; Ian Mudie's *Riverboats* (1961) also highlights the colour and excitement of the river trade; Charles Shaw's poem 'Murray Memory', is a nostalgic re-creation of the riverboat days. G.W. Broughton wrote *Men of the Murray* (1966) and John Larkins and Steve Parish published *Australia's Greatest River* (1982). The major fictional work in which the Murray and its riverboats are the central characters is Nancy Cato's trilogy, *All the Rivers Run* (1958), *Time, Flow Softly* (1959) and *But Still the Stream* (1962). A rewritten combination of the three volumes was published as a single volume, *All the Rivers Run* (1979) and a television series was screened in 1983. Max Fatchen published two books about the river for children, *The River Kings* (1966) and *Conquest of the River* (1970). Tom Collins in *Such is Life* (1903) loses his trousers trying to cross the Murray, which also figures prominently in *Rigby's Romance* (1948).

MURRAY, ROBERT WILLIAM FELTON LATHROP(P) (1777–1850), born Shropshire, England, was baptized Robert Felton Lathropp but took the additional surname of Murray, claiming connection with a baronetcy, after coming of age; there have also been suggestions, usually discarded, that he was a natural son of George III. Commissioned in the army in 1797, Murray served in the Peninsular Wars, and may have met Napoleon in exile at Elba; the meeting, although never confirmed, has been taken by some as evidence either that Murray was acting as emissary for the royal family and was indeed of royal parentage, or that he was engaged in undercover work for the government. As a consequence, his conviction for bigamy in 1815 has been interpreted as a trumped-up charge designed to remove an embarrassing witness from England. Murray fought vigorously in petitions, e.g. *An Appeal to the British Nation* (1815), and broadsides, e.g. *The Case of Captain Murray* (1842) to overturn the conviction, but was transported to Australia. He served his sentence in Sydney before moving to the developing colony of Van Diemen's Land, where for over two decades he was a prominent polemicist and newspaper editor. Under the pseudonym 'A Colonist', Murray wrote a series of letters in the *Hobart Town Gazette* in 1824–25 attacking the administration of Lieutenant-Governor George Arthur. Briefly editor of the *Hobart Town Gazette* (1825) and its successor the *Colonial Times* (1825–26), Murray founded *Murray's Austral-Asiatic Review* in 1828. Founded as a monthly magazine rather than as a newspaper in order to circumvent Arthur's licensing provisions, the *Austral-Asiatic Review* ran until 1845; it underwent several changes of name and was intermittently amalgamated with the *Tasmanian*. After 1828 Murray was more kindly disposed towards Arthur but remained a firm defender of press freedom and wrote vigorously from a humanitarian stance on transportation and press freedom.

Murray's Austral-Asiatic Review, see *Tasmanian*

MURRAY-SMITH, STEPHEN (1922–), born Melbourne, was educated at the University of Melbourne and served with the AIF in New Guinea during the Second World War. He lived in London and Prague 1948–51. A member of the Communist Party of Australia for thirteen years, he became organizing secretary of the Australian Peace Council, and a prominent member of the Melbourne Realist Writers Group. Editor of the *Realist Writer*, 1952– 54, in 1954 he founded the magazine, *Overland* (q.v.), which he has since continued to edit. A reader in education at the University of Melbourne, and editor of the series *Melbourne Studies in Education* to 1982, he has also been chairman of the National Book Council. Murray-Smith has edited a range of books including two collections of short stories, *The Tracks We Travel* (1953) and, with Judah Waten, *Classic Australian Short Stories* (1974); a collection of writing from *Overland*, *An Overland Muster* (1965); an edition of Marcus Clarke's *For the Term of His Natural Life* (1970); with Leonie Sandercock, a selection of Ian Turner's writing, *Room for Manoeuvre* (1982); and the journals of the missionary voyages of Canon Marcus Brownrigg, 1872–85, *Mission to the Islands* (1979). With Edgar Waters he compiled the collection, *Rebel Songs* (1947) and, with John Thompson, *Bass Strait Bibliography* (1981). He has written a short study of Henry Lawson (1962, 2nd edn 1975); and an autobiography based on a series of lectures delivered at James Cook University in 1979, *Indirections* (1981). Under the pseudonym 'Simon Ffuckes', he compiled with Ken Gott ('Sebastian Hogbotel') a collection of bawdy songs, *Snatches and Lays* (1973), which includes verse from such writers as A.D. Hope, James McAuley and Robert Brissenden. In 1981 he was made AM.

MUSGROVE, GEORGE (1854–1916), born Surbiton, England, into a theatrical family, came to Victoria at the age of twelve, and later worked for W.S. Lyster. In 1880 he had his first entrepreneurial success with Offenbach's *Tambour Major* at the Melbourne Opera House; in 1882 he entered into partnership with George Garner and J.C. Williamson, and with one interruption continued to work as Williamson's partner until 1899. Musgrove energetically and imaginatively produced shows until 1914, with varying degrees of commercial success, and fostered the careers of several successful stars, including Nellie Stewart, with whom he formed an alliance, and Dame Nellie Melba.

Music Late at Night, see McAULEY, JAMES

MUSPRATT, ERIC (1899–1949), born in England, led an extremely colourful life as a traveller or professional tramp, and a womanizer. His travels, which took him around the world four times and included several visits to Australia, were interspersed by brief periods in prison in South Africa and England. He served in the AIF in both world wars and subsequently settled in Victoria. He published four autobiographical accounts, *My South Sea Island* (1931), his most popular book, which sold particularly well in America, *Wild Oats* (1932), *The Journey Home* (1933), and *Greek Seas* (1933); and three

novels which draw heavily on his unusual experiences, *Ambition* (1934), *Going Native* (1936) and *Time is a Cheat* (1946).

MUTCH, T.D. (THOMAS DAVIES) (1885–1958), born London and educated in Sydney, became a rural worker before joining the staff of the labour newspaper, the *Worker*. In 1902 he met Henry Lawson (q.v.) to whom he offered friendship and practical assistance during the long years of Lawson's decline. Active in local government and newspaper unionism, he held office in the AJA and entered politics in 1917, distributing a broadsheet testimonial from Lawson to his Botany electors during his first campaign. He served in the New South Wales parliament 1917–30 and 1938–41, and as minister for education was the subject of Lawson's satiric poem, 'The Parsin for Edgerkashun', published in the *Lone Hand* in February 1921; later that year Lawson retracted this 'cowardly attack on an old friend and mate' in a poem titled 'A Song of Mutch and Little', which was reprinted as *Henry Lawson's Message to the Electors of Botany* in Mutch's 1925 election campaign. For over forty years a trustee of the Public Library of NSW, Mutch was active also in the Royal Australian Historical Society and the Society of Australian Genealogists, which named an annual lecture after him; he conducted extensive research into early Australian history and genealogy and his indexes to historical material are now in the Mitchell Library. His writings include important biographical articles and reminiscences about Lawson, an edition of the journals of Lachlan Macquarie (1956), and historical material used in radio scripts.

Mutiny on the *Bounty*, see **BLIGH,** Sir **WILLIAM**

My Army, O, My Army! and Other Songs, the book of poems which briefly re-established Henry Lawson (q.v.) as a leading verse commentator on public events, was published in 1915; the following year the contents of the volume were reassembled and published as *Song of the Dardanelles.* The poems in *My Army, O, My Army!,* which were mostly written in 1914–15 and first published in the *Bulletin,* reflect Lawson's reaction to the outbreak of the First World War. His early enthusiasm for the war as good for national character is apparent in *My Army, O, My Army!;* so also is the imperial fervour which stands in contrast to his socialist republicanism of the 1880s. The title poem, however, in which the army referred to is the same army of the poor as in 'The Army of the Rear', is remarkably prophetic of the Russian Revolution.

My Australian Girlhood, see **PRAED, ROSA**

My Beachcombing Days, see **BLIGHT, JOHN**

My Brilliant Career (1901), the first of the novels published by Miles Franklin (q.v.) in her own name, was written and revised in the period September 1898 – November 1899, when the author was nineteen. Henry Lawson wrote the preface for it, offered the opinion that it 'beats *Jane Eyre* or the *African Farm*' and helped to have it published in England by Blackwoods. The novel's heroine, Sybylla Melvyn, a girl of sixteen, rebels against the stagnant life on her parents' dairy farm at Possum Gully and against the inevitable fate of teaching or marriage that awaits her; both forms of 'slavery' are distasteful to her but she sees marriage as particularly degrading. Rescued temporarily by a period with her affluent grandmother at the congenial station homestead, Caddagat, she faces interwoven problems – her sexual ambivalence which is characterized by strong physical attraction to eligible young squatter, Harold Beecham, and an equally strong physical revulsion which causes her to slash his face with a whip when he attempts to kiss her; and her fierce insistence on retaining her independence. The ultimate disqualification of Harold Beecham is that 'he offered me everything – but control'. The novel's setting in the picturesque Monaro district, its close description of station and farming life, its poignant assessment of the barren existence in the bush for a sensitive girl or woman, and its love of the Australian landscape led Lawson to declare it 'true to Australia – the truest I ever read'. With its strong autobiographical links, the novel brought both fame and distress to its author. She later claimed that friends and relatives were hurt by the book's personal disclosures and that she was embarrassed by the publicity and by their reaction. Sale of the book was stopped by her in 1910 and she refused permission on many occasions for its reprinting. An Australian film of the book was made in 1979.

My Brother Jack (1964), a novel by George Johnston and the first of his semi-autobiographical trilogy, was succeeded by *Clean Straw for Nothing* (q.v., 1969) and *A Cartload of Clay* (1971). It won the Miles Franklin Award and was adapted for television by Charmian Clift. Set in lower-class Melbourne, mainly between the wars, it deals with the different histories of the narrator, David Meredith, and his brother Jack. Beginning in 1919, when both Meredith parents return from the First World War to resume the care of their four children, the story describes first the effect on the Meredith family of the war's aftermath, brought home most

forcibly to the two boys by the disabled soldiers their mother brings home to nurse, then the gradual reduction to humdrum normality and later the social upheaval of the 1930s depression. Jack, straightforward, frankly virile, the epitome of the mythical Australian, engages in an uninhibited pursuit of adventure, whereas David, introverted and escapist, becomes absorbed in a private world of writing. As Jack attempts to wrest a living from the bush, undergoes severe suffering during the depression and takes on family responsibilities, David, while ostensibly committed to his apprenticeship to a printing firm, establishes himself as a correspondent for the *Morning Post* under the benevolent patronage of its editor, Mr Brewster. Released by the Depression from this ambiguous situation, and his career as a reporter on the ascendant, he becomes involved with, and subsequently marries, Helen Midgely. But he soon recognizes that his marriage is artificial and sterile, largely because of his friendship with a colleague, Gavin Turley, and he quickly escapes from it with the outbreak of war. As David becomes increasingly aware of his growing, but unmerited reputation as the courageous war correspondent, Jack's genuine heroic potential is frustrated by an accident and he never sees action. The novel ends as the war comes to a close and David embarks on a serious relationship with Cressida Morley, a girl who represents the freedom and vitality he has always sought.

My Career Goes Bung, see **FRANKLIN, MILES**

'My Country', a poem by Dorothea Mackellar (q.v.), was first published as 'Core of My Heart' in the London *Spectator* 5 September 1908, but was published in the *Sydney Mail* 21 October 1908 as 'My Country', by which it has become famous in Australian literature. A recitation and anthology favourite, 'My Country' is a poem of six eight-line stanzas which contrasts a love of the English landscape,

> The love of field and coppice,
> Of green and shaded lanes,

with the poet's love of Australia represented, for example, in its famous second stanza:

> I love a sunburnt country
> A land of sweeping plains,
> Of ragged mountain ranges,
> Of droughts and flooding rains.
> I love her far horizons,
> I love her jewel-sea
> Her beauty and her terror –
> The wide brown land for me!

Most versions of the poem print 'rugged' in the third line, although Mackellar is recorded as having intended 'ragged'. Similarly, there are several versions about the origins of the poem: by one account it was written in response to the 'anti-Australianism . . . of many Australians we knew', by another it was inspired by the breaking of the drought on the Mackellar property of Torryburn, near Maitland in NSW. The popularity of 'My Country' is evidenced in the way some of its phrases have been appropriated: *The Wide Brown Land* is the title of anthologies of Australian verse edited by Joan S. and George Mackaness (1934), one of the best-known anthologies, and by Douglas Stewart (1971), and several publications have adopted or adapted the phrase, 'a sunburnt country'.

Despite the preference for 'a sunburnt country' in her most famous poem, Mackellar was attracted in other moods to other landscapes. For example, in 'Merry England' (*Dreamharbour*, 1923) she writes that

England wrapped me in her cloak
Silvery-grey, silvery-gold,
Silvery-grey and gold and green,
Whose touch can heal the sorest stroke –
Mother and Priestess, Nurse and Queen.

My Crowded Solitude, see **McLAREN, JACK**

My Father and My Father's Friends, see **McCRAE, HUGH**

My Love Must Wait (1941), a novel by Ernestine Hill (q.v.), is based upon the life of Matthew Flinders. Carefully researched from Flinders's manuscripts and given additional atmosphere and colour by her own retracing of his circumnavigation of the continent, sometimes using a copy of the charts that he had made more than a hundred years earlier, Ernestine Hill's novel is an imaginative and highly sympathetic portrait of the celebrated navigator. In addition to her detailed accounts of his voyages culminating in his proof, by circumnavigation in 1802–3, that Australia was indeed 'Terra Australis', Ernestine Hill provides many interesting biographical details of Flinders: his daydreams of Robinson Crusoe islands during his boyhood in the Lincolnshire village of Donington; his youthful friendship with George Bass, the apothecary's apprentice in the nearby town of Boston; his opinion of Bligh of the *Bounty* with whom he sailed to the Pacific as a midshipman; his adventures with Bass in *Tom Thumb*; his marriage to Ann Chappell in 1801; his long imprisonment 1803–10 on Mauritius because of the vindictiveness of the French governor, General de Caen; his reunion with his wife in 1810 after nine years' separation; his arduous work of preparing the monumental text of his explorations, *A Voyage to*

Terra Australis (1814), and his claim to be recognized as the first user of the name 'Australia'. In an unusual concluding chapter to the novel, Ernestine Hill abandons the fictional mode to reveal the remarkable emotional affinity that developed between her and Flinders: 'Matthew Flinders, long dead, became to me as a friend'. The final chapter, a resumé of the achievements of Flinders, also adds some later family history and outlines the various ways in which the navigator's exploits have since been recognized in Australia.

My Note Book, a weekly literary journal published in Melbourne 1856–59, edited by Thomas Lockyer Bright, Charles Bright and J.E. Neild, included verse, theatrical notices, prose sketches, serials and book reviews as well as articles on current affairs. Contributors included David Blair, R.H. Horne, George Gordon McCrae and James Smith.

My Run Home, see **'BOLDREWOOD, ROLF'**

My Sundowner and Other Poems, see **FARRELL, JOHN**

Myall Creek Massacre, 9 June 1838, was a highly-publicized atrocity in which twenty-eight Aborigines were shot and their bodies burned by twelve white men, eleven of them convicts, on the Myall Creek run of squatter, Henry Dangar, in the northern tablelands of NSW, north-west of the present township of Guyra. Governor George Gipps, in spite of the widely-held view in the Colony that it was absurd to punish white men for the extermination of the Aborigines, and in the face of outraged editorial comment of such newspapers as the *Sydney Morning Herald*, proceeded to charge eleven of the white men with murder. Although they were acquitted on the first charge of murdering two Aboriginal adult males, seven were found guilty of a subsequent charge of murdering an Aboriginal child and were executed 18 December 1838. The massacre and trial were prominently featured in many later accounts of the Aboriginal problem in the Colony, e.g. in Alexander Harris's *Settlers and Convicts* (1847), R. Therry's *Reminiscences of Thirty Years' Residence in New South Wales and Victoria* (1863) and T.F. Bride's *Letters from Victorian Pioneers* (1898). 'Myall' ('myal') an Aboriginal word meaning 'wild' or 'savage' came to be used generally to denote the hostile native of the less settled areas. There is a sympathetic poem by Mary Gilmore titled 'The Myall in Prison' and Charles Harpur, who witnessed the Myall Creek executions, wrote a poem, 'An Aboriginal Mother's Lament', based on the massacre.

The massacre is also described in *The Walla-badah Manuscript* (1981).

Mystery of a Hansom Cab, The, a novel by Fergus Hume (q.v.), was first published in Melbourne in 1886; a significant early example of detective fiction, it was a huge success both there and in England, where the Hansom Cab Publishing Company, in which Hume had no financial interest, was formed. A stage adaptation of the novel, first staged in Australia by George Darrell in 1888, later had a long run in London; Barry Pree wrote a later adaptation (1961). Written in the style of Emile Gaboriau (1832–73), the father of the detective novel in France, *The Mystery of a Hansom Cab* opens with the *Argus* report of the murder of an unknown man in a Melbourne cab. Detective Gorby, assigned to the case, pieces together the identity of the man, Oliver Whyte, a rake recently arrived from England who has been paying court to a Melbourne beauty, Madge Frettlby. Gorby's suspicions fall on Madge's fiancé, Brian Fitzgerald, who is tried for the murder but acquitted when a missing witness, Sal Rawlins, turns up at the last moment to testify that Fitzgerald had been visiting a dying woman in a Melbourne slum at the time of the murder. The second part of the novel unravels the mystery of both the murder and Fitzgerald's hostility since his arrest towards his prospective father-in-law, Mark Frettlby. The dying woman, a former actress named Rosanna Moore, has revealed to Brian that she is Mark Frettlby's wife, long thought dead, that Sal is their daughter and that Madge is therefore illegitimate. As Rosanna and Whyte have been blackmailing Mark Frettlby, Brian is convinced that Frettlby is the murderer; however, Frettlby's confession to the marriage, discovered after his death from a heart attack, states that the murderer is Whyte's companion, Roger Moreland, who hopes also to blackmail Frettlby. Moreland's suicide after his arrest allows the secret of Madge's illegitimacy to be preserved and she and Brian leave Australia after their marriage for a new life overseas. A parody of *The Mystery of a Hansom Cab*, titled *The Mystery of a Wheelbarrow, or Gaboriam Gaborooed* (by 'W. Humer Ferguson') was published in 1888.

N

NAGEL, CHARLES, see Shakespeare and Australia

NAGLE, WILLIAM, see War Literature

NAISBY, T.H., see Hunter Valley Poets

NAISH, JOHN (1923–63), born Wales, served in the British army during the Second World War and came to Australia in 1950. He worked as a cane-cutter, labourer, miner, barman, clerk and fruit-picker, spent some time in Fiji and returned to Australia in 1958. He published two novels, *The Cruel Field* (1962), which deals with life on the canefields, and *That Men Should Fear* (1963), a study of an affluent Australian farming family and its struggle with an incurable, inherited disease, and an autobiography *The Clean Breast* (1961). His plays include *The Claw* in *Australian One-Act Plays Book II*, ed. Greg Branson (1962), *Deuteronomy* in the Derwent Series of *Australian One-Act Plays*, 2nd series (1961), 'The First Mrs Peters' and 'The Maoris'.

Naked Island, The, see **BRADDON, RUSSELL**

Naked Under Capricorn, see **RUHEN, OLAF**

NAMATJIRA, ALBERT (1902–59), the Aboriginal artist, was born at Hermannsburg Lutheran Mission near Alice Springs, where he received some education; a member of the Aranda tribe, he was also initiated into tribal life. He became acquainted with Rex Battarbee, an Australian artist, who taught and encouraged him in the 1930s and held several exhibitions of his landscape paintings from the late 1930s to the 1950s. Divided by the conflicting claims of two different cultures, he became addicted to alcohol in his later years and suffered a variety of misfortunes. His work is represented in all the major Australian galleries, and is described by Rex Battarbee in his *Modern Australian Aboriginal Art* (1951). Accounts of his life and work include C.P. Mountford's *The Art of Albert Namatjira* (1944), Victor Hall's *Namatjira of the Aranda* (1962) and Joyce D.

Batty's *Namatjira: Wanderer Between Two Worlds* (1963).

NANKIVELL, JOICE, born Queensland and brought up partly in Gippsland, published a collection of prose and verse for children, *The Cobweb Ladder* (1916); a collection of sketches of bush and city life, *The Solitary Pedestrian* (1918); and an account of life in Moscow from 1923 to the death of Lenin, *The Fourteen Thumbs of St Peter* (1926). With her husband, Frederick Sydney Loch (q.v.), she also published an account of a visit to Ireland 1920–21, *Ireland in Travail* (1922); and of life in Eastern Poland after the First World War, *The River of a Hundred Ways* (1924). The Lochs settled in Greece 1923–29, combining work for refugees with writing, worked for Polish refugees in Bulgaria and Romania, 1939–44, and returned to Greece after the war. Their experiences are described in Joice Nankivell's autobiography, *A Fringe of Blue* (1968), which she published under her married name.

NAPIER, SYDNEY ELLIOTT (1870–1947), born Sydney, trained as a solicitor. He served with the AIF during the First World War and returned in 1919 to Australia, where he worked as a legal officer and freelance journalist; in 1925 he joined the *Sydney Morning Herald*. Subsequently assistant editor of the *Sydney Mail* and leader writer of the *Sydney Morning Herald*, he compiled, with P.S. Allen, *A Century of Journalism: The Sydney Morning Herald and Its Record of Australian Life 1831–1931* (1931). He contributed prose and verse to numerous English and Australian journals and newspapers, and published a collection of essays, *The Magic Carpet* (1932); a collection of biographical sketches, *Great Lovers* (1934); and two collections of verse, *Potted Biographies* (1930) and *Underneath the Bough* (1937). He also wrote a history of the Sydney Repertory Theatre Society (1923); a series of travel accounts, *On The Barrier Reef* (1928), *Walks Abroad* (1929), *Men and Cities* (1938) and *This Roundabout* (1938); and edited *The Book of the Anzac Memorial* (1934).

Narrative of a Visit to the Australian Colonies, A, see **BACKHOUSE, JAMES**

NATHAN, ISAAC (1790–1864), musician and musical librarian to George IV, was born in Kent of Polish-Jewish parents. A friend of Lord Byron, he persuaded him in 1814 to write a series of poems on Hebrew subjects, which he set to adaptations of ancient Jewish chants and titled *Hebrew Melodies* (1815). Deprived of patronage by Byron's flight from England in 1816 and the death of his pupil, Princess Char-

lotte, Nathan composed musical comedies and operatic pieces such as *Sweethearts and Wives* (1823) and *The Alcaid* (1827). His *An Essay on the History and Theory of Music* (1823) acquired a European reputation and in 1829 he edited *Fugitive Pieces and Reminiscences of Lord Byron*. By 1837 Nathan's financial state was precarious and, unable to obtain payment for secret services he had rendered William IV before his death, he left for Australia. In Sydney he rapidly acquired the status of leading musician and composed several odes to mark public events, including 'Australia the Wide and Free' (1842), 'Currency Lasses' (1846) and 'Leichhardt's Grave' (1846). In May 1847 his romantic opera, *Don John of Austria*, the first opera to be composed and produced in Australia, was performed in the Victoria Theatre. Another Australian achievement of note is his miscellany, *The Southern Euphrosyne and Australian Miscellany* (1848), which includes sections on Aboriginal music. Studies of Nathan include those by C.H. Bertie (1922) and O.S. Phillips (1940) and Catherine Mackerras's *The Hebrew Melodist* (1963).

Nation, a weekly newspaper published in Sydney and subtitled *An Independent Journal of Opinion*, ran 1958–72, when it merged with the *Review* to form *Nation Review* (qq.v.). Mainly representing the views of the liberal left, the newspaper attracted a range of regular contributors, including Cyril Pearl, Manning Clark, Charles Higham and Sylvia Lawson. As well as general articles on political and international affairs, the newspaper published book reviews, articles of literary interest and theatrical notices. An earlier weekly of the same name ran in Sydney 1887–90; it contained news and social and political commentaries of interest to Irish Catholics and carried some short stories and verse.

Nation Review, a weekly newspaper published in Melbourne, ran 1972–81 and was formed by the merger of the Sydney *Nation* (q.v.) and the Melbourne *Review* (q.v.). Radical and provocative, in accordance with its self-adopted nickname, 'The Ferret', *Nation Review* frequently published controversial articles on Australian writers, pugnacious literary debates and outspoken book reviews and theatrical notices. Michael Leunig frequently contributed cartoons expressive of the spirit of the newspaper.

National Anthem. Until 1974 'God Save the King' or 'God Save the Queen' was the Australian national anthem, before 1901 because the Australian colonies 'belonged' to Great Britain and after 1901 because it became the national anthem of the Commonwealth of Australia. There has, however, been a long history of dissatisfaction in some quarters with 'God Save the King/Queen' and many Australian writers or composers have attempted to compose an alternative anthem. Among them were the republican, John Dunmore Lang, who included an 'Australian Anthem' and an 'Australian Hymn' in his *Aurora Australis* (1826); Nathaniel Kentish, who was one of several writers who composed national songs in the 1850s, around the time of the separation of Victoria from NSW; James Brunton Stephens, who wrote a new national anthem in 1902 to the music of 'God Save the King'; A.H. Adams, whose 'Fling Out the Flag' won first prize in an anthem competition sponsored by the Musical Association of NSW in 1913; and Marie Pitt, who won an ABC competition in 1945 with 'Ave Australia'. Neither these compositions nor the many others submitted at the several competitions organized since Federation, e.g. one run by the Australian Council for the Arts in 1973 which attracted 2500 verse entries, won any popular support to replace 'God Save the Queen/King', but three songs have had their champions: 'Advance Australia Fair', composed about 1878 by Peter Dodds McCormick; 'Song of Australia', composed by Carl Linger in 1860; and 'Waltzing Matilda' (q.v.), Australia's most famous song and the one most closely identified with the country by non-Australians. In 1974, after a sample poll of these three songs at which 'Advance Australia Fair' received just over half the vote, the then prime minister, E.G. Whitlam, announced that 'Advance Australia Fair' would supersede 'God Save the Queen' as the national tune (i.e. its words were not then officially recognized), except during the presence of the Queen or when it was necessary to acknowledge Australian links with the royal family, when both would be played; in 1975–76 the governor-general's salute combined the first six bars of 'God Save the Queen' and the last few bars of 'Advance Australia Fair.' This decision was modified in 1976 by the then prime minister, Malcolm Fraser, whose government reinstated 'God Save the Queen' for royal, vice-regal and defence occasions and for others left optional the choice between 'God Save the Queen' and 'Advance Australia Fair'. Thus at the 1980 Olympic Games 'God Save the Queen' was played when Australian swimmers won gold medals, but for the equivalent ceremonies at the 1982 Commonwealth Games the choice was 'Advance Australia Fair'. These guidelines, laid down formally in 1978 after a national poll at which the figures were approximately 43 per cent for 'Advance Australia Fair', 28 per cent for 'Waltzing Matilda', 18 per cent for 'God Save the Queen' and 10 per cent for 'Song of

Australia', remained in force until April 1984, when the federal government announced that 'Advance Australia Fair' (with some words modernized or made non-sexist) would become the national anthem except during the presence of the Queen, when 'God Save the Queen' would be played.

National Book Council was created in 1973 to promote books and book use and to bring together a variety of organizations and individuals who had an interest in, or concern for, books. Foundation members of the Council, which has rapidly expanded since its inception, included the ASA, the Australian Book Publishers' Association, the Library Association of Australia, the FAW, the Australian Booksellers' Association, the Australian Library Promotion Council, the Book Trade Group, the Children's Book Council and the National Library. Managed by a governing council which draws representatives from professional and trade organizations, the National Book Council has instituted a system of annual literary awards, sponsored book fairs and Australian Book Week, and publishes material relevant to the book trade, as well as the revived monthly, *Australian Book Review* (1978–).

National Institute of Dramatic Art (NIDA) was founded in 1958 under the auspices of the University of NSW, the Australian Elizabethan Theatre Trust and in association with the ABC 'to encourage the knowledge and appreciation of drama, opera, music and all the arts of the theatre, and in particular to provide training for young people who wish to enter the profession of theatre as actors, directors, designers and stage-managers'. Located on the campus of the University, NIDA offers courses in acting, technical production, design and directing to a small group of stringently-selected students. Professor Robert Quentin, head of the University's department of drama and a member of the University of NSW Drama Foundation (q.v.), was founder and first director of NIDA (1958–63); Tom Brown (1963–68) and John Clark (1968–) were subsequent directors. Financially supported in turn by the Australia Council, the University of NSW, the Tertiary Education Commission and the Department of Home Affairs, NIDA has useful affiliations in subsidized theatre throughout Australia and has been particularly supportive of Australian drama, especially following its establishment in 1966 of the Jane Street Theatre (q.v.). Well-known actors who have been trained at NIDA include Denis Olsen, Kate Fitzpatrick, Gary McDonald, Helen Morse, Judy Davis, Mel Gibson and Robyn Nevin.

National Library of Australia, which has, after the Mitchell Library, the largest collection of Australian literature, was known as the Commonwealth National Library from 1923–60. Developed from 1901 from the parliamentary library, it was finally established as an autonomous corporate body by the *National Library Act* of 1960. The *Petherick Collection Act* of 1911 secured for the library the extensive collection related to Australasia and the Pacific assembled by E.A. Petherick (q.v.) and the inclusion of legal deposit provision in the *Copyright Act* of 1912 enabled the library to claim one copy of Australian publications free of charge. Other important collections acquired by the library were those of Sir John Ferguson and Rex de C. Nan Kivell. Dispersed in various buildings in Canberra from its early years, the several collections were brought together in one building in 1968. C.A. Burmester has compiled *National Library of Australia: Guide to the Collections* (1974, 1977, 1980 and 1982). The bibliographical services of the library are reflected in a range of regular publications including *Australian National Bibliography*, *Australian Government Publications*, *Current Australian Serials*, *Australian Books*, *Australian Public Affairs Information Service*, *Serials in Australian Libraries: Social Sciences and Humanities*, *Scientific Serials in Australian Libraries*, and *Acquisitions Newsletter*. One of the most important bibliographical achievements has been the publication of the *National Union Catalogue of Monographs* (*NUCOM*) on microfilm. *NUCOM* is now supplemented by the Australian Bibliographical Network (ABN) a data base which allows member libraries throughout Australia on-line access to details of Australian and overseas publications.

In the 1940s the library began to develop major archival collections, leading to its establishment as the Commonwealth Archival Authority; the archives division was reconstituted separately in 1961, becoming the Commonwealth Archives Office (now Australian Archives), taking responsibility for federal government archives from the library, which continued to develop its collection of non-public records and manuscripts. These include numerous significant collections of literary manuscripts, and large collections relating to exploration and the early years of settlement and to the political history of the Commonwealth of Australia. Many of these are listed in *Principal Manuscript Collections in the National Library of Australia* (1973 2nd edn 1978) and *Guide to Collections of Manuscripts Relating to Australia* (1965–). There are descriptive guides to the collections of the Poetry Society of Australia, Kate Baker, Mary Gilmore, Henry Kendall, Vance and Nettie Palmer, 'Henry Handel Richardson', Kenneth Slessor, Judah Waten, and others. The Library also maintains a publishing department which has published numerous Australian literary texts, bibliographies and studies of Australian writers.

National Portraits, a collection of twenty-five brief biographical studies of significant figures in Australian history by Vance Palmer (q.v.), was first published in 1940. Palmer chose his figures either 'because of their representative character' or 'because they seemed . . . true pioneers, originating ideas and tapping springs that were later to enrich the national life'. Most of the figures are drawn from the 1850s or, more substantially, from the 1890s. Each portrait includes an outline of the individual's career and character and an assessment of his contribution to Australian life, especially to what Palmer sees as its distinctive democratic substance. As history the collection is oversimplified, but as a cultural document it has value in the light it sheds on the general myth of the 1890s and on Palmer's particular credo.

National Times, a weekly newspaper published in Sydney from February 1971, generally addresses itself to an educated, affluent, middle-class reader and deals with current political, social and economic issues. The newspaper also includes substantial critical and biographical articles on Australian literature, interviews with writers, short stories, book reviews and theatrical notices from all the major cities.

'Nationality', is a brief poem published in *Fourteen Men* (1954) in which Dame Mary Gilmore (q.v.), while conceding the need for internationalism, acknowledges the pre-eminent claims of race and blood:

> All men at God's round table sit
> And all men must be fed;
> But this loaf in my hand,
> This loaf is my son's bread.

Native was a term used from the 1830s, like 'currency' (q.v.), to indicate a white man born in the Australian colonies. The expression was commonly used in fictional and factual literature of the middle nineteenth century, e.g. Alexander Harris's *The Emigrant Family* (1849). Compound words were formed to indicate indigenous flora and fauna as contrasted with the English species, e.g. 'native dog', 'native pear'.

Native Companion, a monthly magazine published in Melbourne, appeared from January to June and August to November 1907. Edited by Bertram Stevens for its first six issues, the magazine included verse, short stories, literary notes and articles, and book reviews. E.J. Brady took over the editorship from August 1907 and the magazine's contents became more substantial, varied and representative of Australian literature. Contributors included Mary Gilmore, Hugh McCrae, Sumner Locke, Randolph Bedford, Louis Esson, 'Furnley Maurice' and Roderic Quinn. Katherine Mansfield contributed prose sketches to the last two issues.

Native Companions, see **HOPE, A.D.**

Naught to Thirty-Three, published posthumously in 1944, is Randolph Bedford's (q.v.) racy and nostalgic autobiography covering the years between his birth in 1868 and his departure overseas in 1901. Like the volumes of reminiscences by G.A. Taylor, A.W. Jose and Norman Lindsay, *Naught to Thirty-three* pays tribute to the *Bulletin's* encouragement of Australian writers and helped to foster the legend of the Nineties (q.v.) as a golden decade.

Ned Kelly, a play by Douglas Stewart (q.v.), partly in verse, was written during 1940 for stage production and won an ABC prize for drama in 1942, when it was produced as a radio play. The play has been staged many times, and was chosen for a special performance during the Olympic Games in Melbourne in 1956. The four-act, three-hour drama begins with the four members of the bushranger gang, Ned Kelly (q.v.), Joe Byrne, Dan Kelly and Steve Hart, holding up the bank at Jerilderie, NSW. Later, in a long, drawn-out scene in the Jerilderie hotel, the outlaws proclaim, often in verse, their justification of past depredations and their romantic, cavalier view of themselves. Opposed to their braggadocio is the stubborn insistence of the Reverend Gribble on their ultimate downfall. Act Two, sixteen months later, is set in the gang's hideout in the ranges. The tension of men living on their nerves pervades the scene. Isolated from the outside world by the vastness of the bush and apprehensive of every noise, they are driven to desperate measures: the killing of the informer, Aaron Sherritt, and the decision to carry the war to the police by setting a trap at Glenrowan. After Sherritt's death, they take over the hotel and township of Glenrowan and await the wrecking of the train carrying the pursuing police. Following Curnow's treachery and Joe Byrne's assessment that the Kelly legend is 'a bitch legend – wrong from the start', the play ends with the death of three members of the gang and Ned's dramatic but vain onslaught on the police in his legendary armour.

The play's strengths are its characterization, its background and its functional use of poetry. Joe Byrne, with his imaginative intelligence, exemplifies the futility of the outlaws' crusade

against law and order. Ned, the central figure in spite of the importance of Joe Byrne, conveys a chilling sense of neurotic instability that inevitably brings about the gang's undoing. The historical explanation of the bushranging ethos in Australia and the attraction it has always held for the Australian temperament and nature are convincingly explored. The play's poetry is used to convey the epic quality that Stewart sees in the bushranger story. Successful though the poetry is in a literary sense it has sometimes provided an obstacle to the play's stage presentation for it has proved difficult to create the suspension of disbelief that allows an audience to accept the startling change in the bushrangers' language from the casually colloquial to the elevated and solemn.

NEILD, J.E. (JAMES EDWARD) (1824–1906), born Doncaster, Yorkshire, was interested in music and the theatre from an early age, but trained as a medical practitioner. Politically radical, he was a personal friend of John Bright and was active in the movement for repeal of the Corn Laws. He came to Australia in 1853, spent some time at the Castlemaine diggings and later worked as a chemist in Melbourne. In 1855 he joined the staff of the *Age*, meanwhile trading in the pharmaceutical business. Between 1855 and 1861 he was theatrical critic of *My Note Book* (which he also edited for a period), the *Examiner* and the *Argus*, writing under the name 'Christopher Sly'. A prominent member of Melbourne's cultural life, he was friendly with Marcus Clarke, G.G. McCrae, Patrick Moloney, R.H. Horne, J.J. Shillinglaw, Henry Kendall and Adam Lindsay Gordon. He began medical practice in Melbourne in 1861, soon became an influential member and office-bearer of the Medical Society of Victoria and edited the *Australian Medical Journal* 1862–79. He was lecturer in forensic medicine at the University of Melbourne, 1865–1904, was acting coroner and city medical officer of health for a time, and was prominent in a wide range of professional societies and institutions connected with public health. He was theatre critic for the *Australasian* 1865–80, writing as 'Jacques' or 'Tahite', and acquiring a reputation for forthright views. He contributed numerous articles to the *Herald*, the *Melbourne Punch*, the *Weekly Review* and the *Victorian*, published a critical essay, *On Literature and the Fine Arts in Victoria* (1889) and a theatrical novel under the pseudonym 'Cleofas', *A Bird in a Golden Cage* (1867). He also wrote for the stage and had two of his comediettas produced.

NEILSEN, PHILIP (1949–), born Brisbane, was educated at the University of

Queensland, where he has also taught. He has published some short stories, but his main interest has been verse, which he has contributed to various periodicals, newspapers and anthologies, including *Poet's Choice*. He has also published three collections of verse, *Faces of a Sitting Man* (1975), *The Art of Lying* (1979) and *Life Movies* (1981). Flexible and accessible, Neilsen's verse frequently mingles an easy wit and a sinister surrealism with unpredictable effects. Several, such as 'Veronica Lake', 'The Poet Imagines Himself an SS Officer', 'Superman in Our Town', 'Son of Dracula' and 'The Bushranger Comes Home', take a fresh, humorously-disturbing look at familiar myths and cultural heroes.

NEILSON, JOHN (1844–1922), the father of John Shaw Neilson (q.v.), was born in Scotland and came to Australia at the age of nine. Proficient at a variety of bush trades, he worked at shearing, sheep-herding and roadmaking, married in 1871 and settled at Penola. In 1881 he took up land at Minimay in the southwest of Victoria, but was severely handicapped by lack of capital and in 1889 moved to Nhill, where he was forced to rely on roadmaking for a living. Another move in 1895 to Sea Lake in the central Mallee proved disastrous and again he had to turn to manual work. At the turn of the century he took up land at Eureka, where he lived by wheat-growing. The father of nine children, he was married twice. Although he was entirely self-educated, he acquired a reputation as a bush poet, contributing verse from his early thirties to the Mt Gambier newspapers and the *Adelaide Punch*, and later to the *Australasian* and other journals, and winning two prizes (in 1893 and 1897). Much of his verse has been lost but three volumes have been published, *Poem for Recitation: Love's Summer in the Snow* (1893), *The Men of the Fifties* (1938) and *The Song of the Shearer* (1960). His life is described in James Devaney's *Shaw Neilson* (1944); in *John Shaw Neilson* (1972) by Hugh Anderson and L.J. Blake; and in *The Autobiography of John Shaw Neilson* (1978).

NEILSON, JOHN SHAW (1872–1942), born Penola, SA, was the eldest son of Scottish-born parents, John Neilson (q.v.) and Margaret McKinnon. Beset by debts the Neilson family moved in 1881 to a selection at Minimay in the Wimmera region of western Victoria. Poor as the county was, it proved rich in associations and experiences for the young poet. He revelled in the limitless space of the inland and was fascinated by the bird and animal life. Recollections of life at Minimay are seen in his poem 'The Poor, Poor Country', where his own attitude is made clear – 'in that poor country no pauper was I'. Neilson's formal education lasted only two and a half years, including a final year at Minimay when he was thirteen. In 1889 the family moved north to Dow Well, near the new township of Nhill. By 1895 had taken up blocks in the Mallee country, where life continued to be difficult and unproductive. The clearing of the scrub, the severe climate, the terrible dust storms, the rabbit plagues, the drought years 1895–1903, and the long despairing wait for a cash crop all made for an existence of poverty and misery. In 1896 Neilson's poem, 'Polly and Dad and the Spring Cart', was published in the *Bulletin*, thus beginning a relationship with A.G. Stephens, his literary adviser, editor and financial mentor, that spanned almost forty years. Stephens's influence on Neilson's literary career was not wholly beneficial and his editorial liberties with the poetry were excessive, but without his guidance and promotion the inexperienced bush poet would have made little or no impact. Neilson's eye trouble began in 1905 and his resultant inability over the years to read anything but large print was a great hindrance to his writing. Until 1928 Neilson was an itinerant labourer, clearing land, navvying in quarries, on roads and railways, fencing, potato-digging, fruit-picking – work that seemed incompatible with the delicate poetry he produced. In 1901, J.F. Archibald of the *Bulletin* published 'Sheedy was Dying' (q.v.) and asked for more. In 1905 Stephens bought three poems (for £1), including 'The Land Where I Was Born'. The *Bookfellow* (1907) published 'Old Granny Sullivan' (q.v.) with a full page illustration by Dagmar Ross. In 1909 twenty-eight of Neilson's poems were published in Randolph Bedford's *Clarion*. 'Love's Coming' (q.v.) was published in the Sydney *Sun* in 1911, and in October 1912, Stephens used it and 'You and Yellow Air' to illustrate an article on him. The first proposed volume of his poetry, *Green Days and Cherries*, remained unpublished except for three proof copies. His first published volume, *Heart of Spring* (q.v., 1919), was followed in 1923 by *Ballad and Lyrical Poems* and by *New Poems* in 1927. In 1928 a position was secured for him as messenger with the Country Roads Board in Melbourne. This supposedly congenial position with a guaranteed weekly wage was expected to lead to increased writing but the city environment lowered his poetic impulse. His *Collected Poems*, edited by R.H. Croll, was published in 1934 and *Beauty Imposes* in 1938. In 1941, his health failing, he went to Queensland to visit James Devaney (q.v.), who had replaced Stephens as his friend and adviser, and he died soon after in Melbourne of heart trouble. After his death Devaney edited *Unpublished Poems* (1947); in 1970 *Witnesses of Spring: Unpublished Poems* was edited by Judith Wright, Val Vallis and Ruth Harrison; in 1981 *Green Days and Cherries* finally appeared, edited by Hugh Anderson and L.J. Blake. Most of the Australian poetry written in the 1890s and the first two decades of this century is now thought less of than when it was written. But the best work of Neilson, who felt that 'five shillings seems a good deal for people to pay for my verses', has so grown in esteem that he is now claimed by some to be pre-eminent among Australian lyrists. The incongruity between the grace, delicacy and subtlety of his poetry and his hard life and rough background have also made him Australia's chief literary enigma, but those who knew him well have never subscribed to the popular theory that he was merely a literary fluke. Victor Kennedy found him remarkably well-informed and intellectually aware, 'steeped in the current philosophies – rationalism, evolution, the labour movement and Australian poets and poetry'. The immediate impression his poetry gives, with its spareness, brevity and uncomplicated structure, is that of simplicity, even naivety. Some of it is naive, even trivial and banal. But in his finest work the combination of disturbing mysticism and haunting language, well exemplified in the enigmatic 'The Orange Tree' (q.v.), shows him to be a sensitive and unusually-gifted poet. The Victorian branch of the FAW annually honours his memory with the John Shaw Neilson Award for poetry.

NELSON, JEREMY LOCKHART (1933–), born Sydney, grew up in Cessnock and was educated at the University of Sydney. A secondary schoolteacher in Sydney, he has lived in India, Greece and England. He has published three collections of verse, *Images of Living and of Dying* (1977), *Images of Innocence* (1978) and *City of Man* (1983).

Nepean River, part of the Hawkesbury River system which with the Pacific Ocean encloses the metropolitan area of Sydney, rises near Wollongong, passing Camden to join with the Warragamba near Wallacia. At this point it becomes part of the main Hawkesbury but retains its name until, flowing through Penrith, it meets the Grose. Discovered by Watkin Tench in 1789 and named by Governor Phillip after Evan Nepean (1751–1822), under-secretary of state, the Nepean marks the start of the Blue Mountains and its catchment area is an important part of Sydney's water supply. The bushranger Bold Jack Donahue operated in the Nepean, and one of his hiding places is on the river. Writers to focus on the area include

James Tucker in the convict novel *Ralph Rashleigh* (q.v.); Mary Theresa Vidal (q.v.) in *Cabramatta, and Woodleigh Farm* (1850) and *Bengala* (1860); Miles Franklin, whose novel *Some Everyday Folk and Dawn* (1909) gives an unflattering portrait of Penrith; and James Tobias Ryan, member for Nepean in the NSW parliament, 1860–72, whose *Reminiscences of Australia* (1895) includes an entertaining account of pioneering times. The *Nepean Review*, a literary journal, began publication in 1975.

Nero's Poems, see **LEHMANN, GEOFFREY**

NESBITT, FRANCIS (?1810–53), born England as Francis Nesbitt McCrone, came to Sydney in 1842 and soon established himself at the Victoria Theatre as a highly popular tragedian, even described by some critics as 'the best actor in the Southern hemisphere'. In 1843–44 he was instrumental in staging the plays of the convict-writer, Edward Geoghegan, including 'Ravenswood' (1843), which he presented as his own. His career underwent several vicissitudes in Sydney and in Hobart and Launceston where he played for some time, partly due to his occasional drunkenness and partly to the fading popularity of his declamatory style.

Never Never is the vast, remote, inland area of northern Australia, in particular north-west Queensland and the Northern Territory. Frederic de Brébant Cooper in *Wild Adventures in Australia* (1857) suggests that the term's origin lies in the Aboriginal expression, 'nievah vahs', meaning unoccupied land. Many writers, e.g. 'Rolf Boldrewood' in *A Colonial Reformer* (1890) and A.J. Boyd in *Old Colonials* (1882), use the term without indicating its source. Jeannie Gunn, whose popular work, *We of the Never-Never* (q.v., 1908), gave the expression widespread currency, romantically asserted that the farthest outback was called the Never Never 'because they who have lived in it and loved it never never voluntarily leave it'. By contrast, many believe that it is so called because those who succeed in getting out of it swear that they will 'never never' return to it. The best description of the Never Never and the lifestyle that goes with it is in Henry Lawson's poem, 'The Never-Never Land'. Lawson sees it as a land of 'wide wastes of scrub and plain', of blazing and hopeless deserts, where man has named its few distinctive features Mount Desolation, Mount Dreadful and Mount Despair, but a land where mateship flourishes. Laura Palmer-Archer wrote the fictional *Racing in the Never Never* (1899) and 'Gurney Slade', a travel book, *Through the Never Never* (1935).

Nevermore (1892), a novel by 'Rolf Boldre-wood' (q.v.), was first published as a serial in the *Centennial Magazine* 1889-90. One of the few 'Boldrewood' novels in which an English-born hero meets tragedy, *Nevermore* recounts the adventures of Lance Trevanion, who leaves his Cornwall home to seek fortune on the Australian goldfields. He succeeds at Ballarat but is seduced into crime by the Lawless family and is gaoled, then sent to the Williamstown hulks. He escapes and moves to the Omeo goldfields, but again falls into crime and is murdered by his evil partner, Caleb Coke, and Lawrence Trevenna, Lance's double, with whom he has quarrelled on the voyage to Australia. Trevenna impersonates Lance to his fiancée, Estelle, when she visits Australia but both the impersonation and the murder are exposed at the altar; after her return to England, Estelle discovers that Trevenna is Lance's natural half-brother, a device which owes something to *His Natural Life* (1874). The Lawless family, mo-delled on the family of Ned Kelly, recurs in two later 'Boldrewood' novels, *The Last Chance* (1905) and *The Ghost Camp* (1902). *Nevermore* is a melodramatic work but there are some effective goldfields scenes, in which 'Boldre-wood' draws on experiences that are also put to good use in *The Miner's Right* (1890).

NEVILLE, RICHARD (1941–), editor of the student magazines *Tharunka* and *Noise*, was joint founder with Richard Walsh and Martin Sharp, a graphic artist, of the controversial Sydney magazine, *Oz*, in 1963. Given a six-months' prison sentence (which was later quashed) on the grounds of obscenity, Neville went to London in 1966 and re-established *Oz* with Felix Dennis and Jim Anderson as co-editors. In 1971 the editors were subjected to a sensational trial on a charge of issuing a publication likely 'to corrupt public morals', were sentenced to fifteen months' imprison-ment, but were freed on appeal. Neville also defeated a deportation order which was issued after the trial. In 1973 *Oz*, grown familiar if not respectable, expired. Neville has since trav-elled extensively, worked as a journalist and broadcaster in Sydney, London and New York, and returned in 1979 to Australia, where he has worked in television. He has published two books, *Play Power* (1970), an analysis of the Youth Movement and the antagonistic alliance between the 'new left' and the 'Underground of hippies, beats, mystics, madmen, freaks, yip-pies, crazies, crackpots, communards etc.'; and, with Julie Clarke, an account of the mass murderer, Charles Sobhraj (1979).

New Australia was the name of the co-operative socialist settlement established origi-nally by William Lane (q.v.) in Paraguay in 1893. The abortive shearers' and maritime strikes of 1891, the severe drought of 1892, and the economic depression of 1892-93 con-firmed for many working-class people their be-lief that a true socialist existence was not possible in Australia. In 1891 William Lane established the New Australia Co-operative Settlement As-sociation and sent Alfred Walker to negotiate a land grant for such a settlement from the government of Argentina. The New Australia Office was opened at Elizabeth Street, Sydney, and a monthly journal, *New Australia*, com-menced publication in November 1892 under the editorship of Walter Head. The Association purchased a 598 ton sailing ship, the *Royal Tar*, which left Sydney, carrying 220 colonists and their children, 16 July 1893, arriving off Montevideo 11 September 1893. By small boat and train the settlers were transhipped to Las Ovegas, the site for the New Australia settle-ment. Within a few months the settlement had broken into irreconcilable factions. By July 1894 Cosme, a breakaway settlement of Lane's staunchest followers, had been established. The original New Australia gradually disintegrated, its assets being sold and divided in 1897, but vestiges of it survive even today in the district known as Nueva Australia. Cosme prospered until 1898 but after Lane's return to live in NZ in 1899 it, too, gradually broke up and by 1909 had ceased to exist as a separate society, being absorbed into the Paraguayan community. The journals *New Australia, Cosme Monthly*, and *Cosme Evening Notes*, the last two edited by Mary Gilmore (q.v.), then Mary Cameron, contain much of the history of the New Australia movement and a bibliography of material held in the Mitchell and National libraries was published as *New Australia and Cosme* (1965). A full account of New Australia is in Gavin Souter's (q.v.) *A Peculiar People: The Australians in Paraguay* (1968).

Vance Palmer's play, *Hail Tomorrow* (1947), concerns Lane's Utopian dream, while numer-ous songs and verses sing the settlement's praises, e.g. 'The Men of the New Australia' by Mary Gilmore, 'Over There in Paraguay' by 'A Bush-man', 'It's Nice to Live in Paraguay' by 'The Doctor' and 'The Man from Bogantungan' by Hilda Lane, William Lane's niece, who was born at Cosme in 1899. Hume Nisbet wrote an unfavourable account of New Australia, *A Dream of Freedom* (1902).

New Australian, a term for migrant, gained currency during the period of accelerated im-migration after the Second World War to pro-mote assimilation and to replace less desirable terms, such as 'reffo', 'Balt', 'boong', 'wop' and 'pommy'. It has largely been confined to non-English speaking migrants.

New Australian Poetry was the vague and somewhat grandiloquent title bestowed by its proponents on the wave of poetry, mainly from young poets of the so-called 'Generation of '68', which found expression in poetry readings and in the small and often briefly-lived magazines which sprang into existence in the late 1960s and 1970s. Although the practitioners of the new poetry held various, and sometimes opposing, views as to its character, attitude, and limits, they felt a common antagonism to the mainstream of Australian poetry as represented by the work, for example, of A.D. Hope, R.D. FitzGerald, Judith Wright and James McAuley, who had dominated Australian poetry for the previous quarter of a century. The new poets judged the established poetry to be, in its form and content, traditional and conservative to the point of atrophy. The new poetry movement took much of its inspiration from contemporary American poetry as represented in, for example, Donald Allen's *The New American Poetry* (1960) and Donald Hall's *Contemporary American Poetry* (1962), both of which were having an impact in Australia in the mid-1960s. The movement sought to have contemporary Australian poetry reflect a similar modernity of attitude and technique. The genesis of the movement is difficult to be exact about but the obvious originating forces were, in Melbourne, the poetry readings held at Monash University 1967–69, and the poetry workshops 1968–69 at the La Mama (q.v.) Theatre and other venues; and, in Sydney, the 1964 birth of Grace Perry's *Poetry Australia* (q.v.), the annual Balmain poetry and prose competitions, the poetry readings run by Robert Adamson (q.v.), and the 1971 rise of the journal, *New Poetry*, from the ashes of *Poetry Magazine* (qq.v.). The movement's growth was spurred by the rise of a myriad of little magazines that carried the poetry and the message. Magazines such as *Our Glass, Mok, Crosscurrents, The Great Auk* and *Free Poetry* flourished briefly and disappeared but were replaced by others almost immediately, some, such as *Parachute Poems* and *Flagstones*, being equally short-lived, others, such as *The Saturday Club Book of Poetry* and *Contempa*, proving more durable. Such magazines, and the rapid development of printing technology, allowed the new poets easy access to the publication both of their individual poems and small inexpensive volumes of their work, access which had previously been available only to poets with an established reputation. These publication opportunities were augmented in the 1970s by the emergence of such printing houses as South Head Press,

Outback Press, Wild and Woolley and Rigmarole of the Hours; by the increased activity of the University of Queensland Press, which catered for the new poetry in its Paperback Poets series and anthologies; and by the traditional publisher, Angus & Robertson, which introduced an innovatory Poets of the Month series. In addition to the dissatisfaction with existing poetry and the impact of contemporary international writing, other causes of the rise of the new poetry are said to have been the influence of the 1950s decade in which the new poets grew up; the ready availability of tertiary education to their generation; the influence of the new rock music; the impact of drugs; the sense of outrage that accompanied the Vietnam war and Australia's participation in it; conscription; the belief in poetry as part of the weaponry in the struggle for wider freedom; and the impact of such poets as Francis Webb and Bruce Beaver (q.v.). Although many poets who published during the period were involved in the movement to some degree, the more important figures were Beaver, Thomas Shapcott, Rodney Hall, Robert Adamson, John Tranter, Kris Hemensley, Bruce Dawe, Les Murray, Michael Dransfield, Charles Buckmaster, Ken Taylor, Robert Kenny, Garrie Hutchinson, Walter Billeter, Vicki Viidikas and John A. Scott (qq.v.). Many of these worked independently of the literary cliques that developed and many were not in agreement with each other or even with the theory of a 'New Australian Poetry'. The new poetry is represented in the anthologies *Australian Poetry Now* (1970) and *Contemporary American & Australian Poetry* (q.v., 1976), both edited by Shapcott, *Applestealers* (1974) edited by Kenny and Colin Talbot, *The New Australian Poetry* (1979) edited by Tranter and *The Younger Australian Poets* (1983) edited by Robert Gray and Geoffrey Lehmann. *New Impulses in Australian Poetry* (q.v., 1968), edited by Hall and Shapcott, is not properly descriptive or illustrative of the movement, although it indicates the changes that were then emerging.

That the 'New Australian Poetry' is likely to be supplanted by a similar movement, and that the 'Generation of '68' has become the anti-establishment establishment, to be replaced by a further anti-establishment force, is foreshadowed by the October 1977 special issue of *Australian Literary Studies* titled 'New Writing in Australia'. The new poetry is subjected to considerable criticism in Richard Packer's 'Against the Epigones', *Quadrant* (1975) and Mark O'Connor's 'The Graying of the Underground', *Overland* (1979). The explosion of poetry in the decade 1970–80, and the resultant confusion over standards, is well exemplified in the article by Thomas Shapcott,

Australian Poetry 1970–1980: Some Statistical Observations', *Australian Literary Studies* (1983). The extent to which the then contemporary American poets had an influence on the New Australian Poetry is investigated in *The American Model: Influence and Independence in Australian Poetry* (1983), edited by Joan Kirkby.

New Britannia, A, see McQUEEN, HUMPHREY

New Chum was a phrase, derived from prison slang, which was originally used in Australia to describe a newly-arrived convict, a usage which occurs in James Tucker's novel, *Ralph Rashleigh*. From about 1840 it had come to mean any new arrival but particularly one, e.g. a well-connected young Englishman sent out to gain 'colonial experience' (q.v.), who betrayed his ignorance and inexperience in the colonies. A number of anonymous Australian folk-songs record the experiences of the new chum, including 'I've Been to Australia-Oh' and 'The Settler's Lament', which both tell of new chums being 'taken down'; 'A New Chum in the Country', in which the reverse happens; and 'The New Chum's Farewell to Queensland', a long, inventive curse which concludes

> To stay in thee, O land of Mutton!
> I would not give a single button,
> But bid thee now a long farewell,
> Thou scorching sunburnt land of Hell!

Another folk-song new chum is Billy Barlow (q.v.) who, as a stage character in his own right and as a source for James Tucker's 1840s play, *Jemmy Green in Australia* (q.v.), helped to inaugurate the long tradition of the new chum on the nineteenth-century Australian stage; a famous later example of this stock character is Charles Harold Vane Cholmondeley Vane Somers Golightly in Alfred Dampier and J.H. Wrangham's *Marvellous Melbourne* (first performed 1889), a role played by Dampier himself.

The term 'new chum' was most often used in a derogatory way, with 'old hand' its antonym. Henry Lawson, however, provides a spirited defence of the type in his poem, 'The New Chum Jackaroos', and some new chums themselves, e.g. Percy Clarke in his reminiscences, *The New Chum in Australia* (1886) and Paul Wenz in his *Diary of a New Chum* (1908), exploited the currency of the phrase without discomfort. Among prominent fictional new chums are Christopher Cockle in J.R. Houlding's *Australian Capers: Or, Christopher Cockle's Colonial Experience* (q.v., 1867) and Ernest Neuchamp, the hero of 'Rolf Boldrewood''s *A Colonial Reformer* (1890).

New England. The New England district of NSW, of which Armidale is the main city, is a high plateau covering some 27 000 square kilometres of fine grazing land. The history of New England dates from 1818, when John Oxley crossed its southern areas; its occupation began in 1832 when H.C. Sempill moved north from the Hunter valley to occupy a station which he named Wolka (now Walcha). The name 'New England' came into use about 1836. Armidale took its name from G.J. MacDonald, commissioner of crown lands, who established a station in the area in 1839 and named it after his father's estate in Scotland. New England has many historical and literary associations. The Myall Creek massacre (q.v.) of Aborigines took place there in 1838; a similar but later massacre is recalled in Judith Wright's 'Nigger's Leap, New England'. Judith Wright, who grew up in New England, has celebrated its history and landscape in her poems, 'South of My Days' and 'For New England', and in her historical works, *The Generations of Men* (q.v., 1959) and *The Cry for the Dead* (1981). The bushranger Thunderbolt was active in the New England area in the 1860s and was killed near Uralla in May 1870. 'Rolf Boldrewood' was a goldfields commissioner stationed at Armidale 1884–85. The privations of the poor selector, especially in New England's severe winters, are recalled in the anonymous ballad, 'The New England Cocky'. The colour and excitement of the district's history are captured in Robin B. Walker's *Old New England* (1966) and in E.C. Sommerlad's *The Land of 'the Beardies'* (1922), published to mark the jubilee of the town of Glen Innes. *The Wallabadah Manuscript* (1980), edited by Roger Milliss, also contributes to the historical coverage of the district. The Armidale & District Historical Society has done much to record the district's pioneer past.

New Holland, the name given by Dutch explorers in the seventeenth century to that part of the Australian continent west of the meridian passing through Torres Strait, was occasionally subsequently applied to the continent as a whole. By the 1820s the name Australia had established itself. W.J. Gordon in 1888 published *The Captain General: Being the Story of the Attempt of the Dutch to Colonize New Holland*, one of a number of works which investigated, fictionally and otherwise, the attempts by the Dutch to anticipate British colonization of the continent. Two popular modern historical novels about the establishment of settlement in WA, the scene of the early Dutch discoveries, are Rix Weaver's *Behold, New Holland* (1940) and *New Holland Heritage* (1941).

New Impulses in Australian Poetry (1968), an anthology of Australian poetry of the 1960s, was edited, with an introduction, by Rodney Hall and Thomas W. Shapcott (qq.v.). The keynote of these 'new impulses' is 'a suspicion of idealism, and an inbred awareness of the consequences of totalitarian beliefs'. Authoritarianism in religion and politics is eschewed, as is the concept of national and international aggression. Major established poets such as Kenneth Slessor, Judith Wright and A.D. Hope are not represented because the editors felt that their poetry of the decade added little to their already defined stances. Their contemporaries, however, Gwen Harwood and Francis Webb, are given considerable space because they are important influences on younger poets.

New Literature Review began publication in 1975 as the successor to *Arna*; its first issue contained poetry, e.g. by Vivian Smith and Chris Wallace-Crabbe, short fiction e.g. by Frank Moorhouse and Michael Wilding, critical articles, and a *Tabloid Story* supplement. Since the second issue in 1977 it has been published twice yearly and has been a solely critical journal which has focused on new literatures in English, including Australian literature, and literary theory. Periodically, national literatures in English are the special subject of an issue, e.g. No.6 (1979), devoted to new directions in Australian literary studies.

New Pilgrim's Progress, A, see **DEAKIN, ALFRED**

New Poetry is the magazine of the Poetry Society of Australia (q.v.). It replaced *Poetry Magazine* in 1971, which earlier replaced *Prism* (q.v.) in 1961, as a result of a dispute among the Society's members over the amount of non-Australian writing that the magazine should contain. Edited initially by Robert Adamson and Carl Harrison-Ford and later, mostly by Adamson alone, *New Poetry* has been published bi-monthly, quarterly and sometimes irregularly. One of Australia's major poetry magazines, *New Poetry* played an important role in the rise of the 'New Australian Poetry' (q.v.) during the 1970s and has, by publishing contemporary American poetry in particular, kept Australian poets and readers abreast of modern developments in poetic form and content. It now publishes an extensive range of contemporary poetry from well-known Australian and overseas poets, as well as lesser-known writers and previously unpublished writers. It also contains critical articles, reviews, notes and comments.

New South Wales was the name given to part of the eastern coast of New Holland (q.v.), as Australia was then called, when Lieutenant James Cook claimed British sovereignty over it on 22 August 1770. By a commission of 1786 proclaimed at Sydney Cove on 7 February 1788, soon after the arrival of the First Fleet, Governor Phillip extended New South Wales so that it encompassed the whole of New Holland east of the 135th meridian, although the island of Tasmania was not known to be separate from the mainland until the explorations of George Bass and Matthew Flinders in 1798. In 1824 the boundary of New South Wales was extended further west to the 129th meridian, which meant that the name now encompassed the whole of the Australian continent and the island of Tasmania except what is now the State of Western Australia. From this time New South Wales gradually shrank in size as the other colonies and territories were separated from it: Van Diemen's Land in 1825, South Australia in 1836, although it was not until 1842 that it comprised all the area of the present State, Victoria in 1851, and Queensland in 1859. When the Northern Territory came under the jurisdiction of South Australia in 1863, New South Wales had diminished to its present size excluding the small area within it which became the Australian Capital Territory after Federation, and remained a British colony, self-governing from 1856, until it became part of the Commonwealth of Australia in 1901. Bordered in the north by Queensland, in the west by South Australia and in the south by Victoria, New South Wales is the second smallest mainland State but the most populous.

New South Wales Bookstall Company, see **ROWLANDSON, A.C.**

New South Wales General Standing Orders, a selection of governors' orders, was, when published in 1802, the first book printed in Australia.

New South Wales Magazine, owned and edited by Ralph Mansfield, was published monthly in Sydney, August 1833 – March 1834. The magazine included general news items, religious material, serials, short stories, poetry and literary reviews. Henry Halloran and John Lhotsky were contributors. A second monthly *New South Wales Magazine* was published in Sydney in 1843.

New Theatre (Australia), a federal organization which has affinities with the American New Theatre movement and sponsors a 'committed', broadly socialist theatre, was formed in the early 1950s to link various New Theatres or workers' theatre groups which had formed in Sydney, Melbourne, Brisbane, Perth, and later Newcastle. The Sydney and Melbourne groups, formed in 1932 and 1936 respectively, were the first to establish themselves as serious theatres, adopting the name New Theatre League in 1936, shortened to New Theatre in 1945. Some of the other State groups enjoyed periods of intense activity, but only the Melbourne and Sydney New Theatres are now operational. Although New Theatre has been seen as a predominantly left-wing organization, subject at times to mild attempts at censorship on the part of State governments, the theatres have staged a range of international and classical plays and have presented the work of numerous Australian playwrights, including Louis Esson, Leslie Rees, 'Betty Roland', Katharine Susannah Prichard, Oriel Gray, Dymphna Cusack, Barry Oakley, John Romeril, Sumner Locke Elliott and Mona Brand. *Reedy River*, first performed in 1953, was New Theatre's most popular and widely-staged production.

New Triad, edited by Hugh McCrae and Ernest Watt and published in Sydney, appeared monthly April 1927 – July 1928. The magazine included short stories, articles, verse and theatrical notices and attracted such contributors as Louis Esson, R.D. FitzGerald, H.M. Green, Vance Palmer, Dora Wilcox, David McKee Wright and Les Robinson.

NEWLAND, SIMPSON (1835–1925), born Staffordshire, England, came to Australia as a small child, settling with his parents in the Encounter Bay area of SA. As a young man he travelled the outback, ultimately becoming a squatter along the Darling River. He returned to Adelaide in 1876 and spent the remainder of his life as a member of the SA parliament, where he was a constant advocate of the development of the Murray River district and the Northern Territory, on which subjects he wrote numerous pamphlets. His chief literary work was the novel, *Paving the Way* (1893), the title a tribute to the pioneers who had 'paved the way' for the development of the country. The novel's long, loose and rather melodramatic narrative incorporates many features of pioneering life including squatting, the Aborigines and the outback woman. A less effective novel, *Blood Tracks of the Bush*, was published in 1900. Newland's *Memoirs* (1926), written when he was nearly ninety years of age, gives a vivid account of the early days of SA settlement and considerable details of Aboriginal life and customs.

Newsfront, a film directed by Phil Noyce and dealing with the Australian newspaper world of the 1940s, was released in 1978. Bob Ellis wrote the screenplay and Robert Macklin published a book based on the film in 1978. One of the most popular and influential productions of the 1970s renaissance in Australian film, *Newsfront* is also one of the more intelligent recreations of the 1940s decade, which found favour with Australian audiences in the late 1970s.

Newspapers in Australian Libraries: A Union List (1959–60, 3rd edn 1973–75) published by the National Library of Australia, is published in two parts, the first listing overseas newspapers and the second listing Australian newspapers. The standard guide to the location of newspapers in Australia, it is arranged by place of publication, with an index of titles.

NICHOLLS, CHARLES FREDERICK (1826–?) and **HENRY RICHARD** (1830–1912), born London, were brothers who became Chartists in 1848 and emigrated to Australia in the early 1850s. They were both members of the Eureka Stockade, but left before the attack and were afterwards active in the campaign to secure release of the rebels. In later years Charles was a mining investor, prospector, explorer and promoter, owned and edited the Melbourne *Evening Star* (1867–69) and wrote *Democracy and Representation* (1871). Henry pursued mainly a career in journalism, as writer for the *Ballarat Times*, editor and proprietor (1875–83) of the *Ballarat Star*, editor of the *Mercury* in Hobart (1883–1912), and contributor under the pseudonym 'Henricus' to the *Argus* and *Australasian*. He also wrote a brief satiric pamphlet, *An Essay on Politics in Verse* (1867).

NICHOLLS, SYD (1896–1977), born Tasmania, studied art at the Royal Art Society in Sydney, and was a prominent cartoonist for the *Bulletin* and the left-wing journal, *Direct Action*, during the First World War. During the 1930s he pioneered the Australian adventure comic strip with pirate, 'Middy Malone', but his best-loved creation was Fatty Finn (q.v.); *Fatty Finn's Weekly* (1934–35) was the first Australian comic book.

NICHOLSON, JOHN HENRY (1838–1923), born England, was a close friend of Ludwig Leichhardt and came to Australia in 1854. He tried various occupations, including prospector, theatre manager, bird-collector and schoolteacher, finally settling in Queensland. In his later years he suffered periodic bouts of mental illness. He wrote verse, plays and prose sketches, acquired a temporary and local reputation for his patriotic song, 'Rouse Australians!', in the late 1880s, but is now best known for his moral and religious allegory, *The Adventures of Halek* (1882) and its sequel, *Almoni* (1904). The autobiography of a pilgrim from the sensual level of existence to the intellectual to the spiritual, *Halek* is greatly inferior but obviously indebted to such books as *The Pilgrim's Progress, Erewhon* and *Gulliver's Travels.* Nicholson also published two volumes of humorous prose sketches, *The Mysterious Cooks* (1867) and *My Little Book* (1873); a volume of prose and verse, *The Opal Fever* (1878); two collections of verse, *Hubert and Other Poems* (1879) and *A Book of Verses* (1916); the dramas *Moike: Or, Melbourne in a Muddle* (1886), *The Spanish Coachman* (1888) and *Hubert* in the 1879 verse collection; and *Recreations of a Registrar* (1904).

NICHOLSON, JOYCE (1919–), born Melbourne, daughter of D.W. Thorpe, publisher, is herself managing director and proprietor of the family publishing firm. She was also cofounder and is director of Sisters Publishing. She has edited *Australian Booksellers and Publisher* and *Australian Books in Print* and has written some twenty-six books, many for children and many based on actual events and people. They include *Our First Overlander* (1956), *Man Against Mutiny* (1961), *A Goldseeker* (1970), *Freedom for Priscilla* (1974, first published in 1963 as *A Mortarboard for Priscilla*) and *The Convict's Daughter* (1976). A feminist, she has published a study of sex-role conditioning, *What Society Does to Girls* (1975); has been an active participant in the Women's Electoral Lobby, for whom she edited the *WEL Broadsheet* for three years; and has published *The Heartache of Motherhood* (1983).

'Night-Ride, The', a brief poem by Kenneth Slessor (q.v.) published in *Earth Visitors* (1926), captures the chaotic atmosphere of the arrival of a train at a country railway station late at night. The poem, which is sometimes symbolically interpreted to represent the journey through life, also marks the beginning of Slessor's use of his descriptive talent in realistic themes.

'Night Scenes in Melbourne', see 'Lower Bohemia'

Night the Prowler, The, a novella by Patrick White (q.v.), is included in his collection *The Cockatoos* (1974). It was also adapted for film in 1976 and was published in its dramatized form in 1978.

'Night We Watched for Wallabies, The', one of the best-known stories by 'Steele Rudd' (q.v.), appears in *On Our Selection* (1899). The story sketches the annoyance of the sons of Dad Rudd when they are forced to spend a cold and windy night helping their father prevent the wallabies from ravaging the wheat crop. The next morning they learn the real reason for their outdoors vigil – their mother has given birth again.

NILAND, D'ARCY (1919–67), was born at Glen Innes, NSW, into a large Irish-Catholic family. After leaving school at fourteen he worked in a woolshed, then at sixteen went to Sydney, where he was a copy boy for the Sydney *Sun* but soon lost his job because of the depression. He then 'went bush' for several years, working at a variety of occupations, opal gouger, blacksmith's striker, shearer, circus hand, fencer, fruit-picker, rouseabout and member of a travelling boxing troupe. In 1942 he married the writer, Ruth Park (q.v.), and after a period of travelling in country areas they settled in Surry Hills, Sydney. Their joint autobiography, *The Drums Go Bang!* (1956), describes the early years of their marriage and their various attempts to wrest a living from writing. Niland, already well-known for his short stories in *Smith's Weekly* and other magazines, won international fame after the publication of his best-selling novel, *The Shiralee* (1955). Later filmed with Peter Finch in the main part, it was selected by many book clubs and as book of the month by newspapers in Australia and overseas. As well as articles, plays for radio and television, ballads and hundreds of uncollected short stories, Niland wrote six novels, *The Shiralee* (1955), *Call Me When the Cross Turns Over* (1957), *Gold in the Streets* (1959), *The Big Smoke* (1959), *The Apprentices* (1965) and *Dead Men Running* (1969). He also published four collections of short stories, *The Ballad of the Fat Bushranger* (1961), *Logan's Girl* (1961), *Dadda Jumped Over Two Elephants* (1961) and *Pairs and Loners* (1966); with Leslie Raphael, a collection of ballads, *Travelling Songs of Old Australia* (1966); and a book on the writer's craft, *Make Your Stories Sell* (1955). He worked for many years on a biography of Les Darcy the boxer, after whom he was christened, but died before it was completed. Many of his short stories and several of his novels have been translated into other languages and have appeared in international anthologies. Niland won several minor. literary prizes for his work including second prize in the 1948 *Sydney Morning Herald*'s short story competition and third prize in the novel section with *Gold in the Streets.* In 1961 he won, with Ruth Park, a British award for their television play, 'No

Decision'; and *Dead Men Running* also proved popular when it was produced as an ABC television serial. Of the Nilands' five children, their twin daughters Kilmeny and Deborah are well-known as illustrators.

Niland's Irish Catholic childhood and his experiences as a bush-worker in the 1930s depression were seminal. Strongly influenced by the realist writers of the 1890s, his own work is a rich source of social history, capturing the life of both rural and urban Australia from the 1930s to the 1950s. A versatile and lively writer, he has a gift for graphically evoking atmosphere, incident and memorable characters, as well as an ability to create suspense. Uninhibited in his use of language, he is particularly adept at producing the rhythm and flavour of colloquial idiom. As far as characterization and plot development are concerned, his approach tends to the picaresque and is more suited to the short story than the novel. His occasional tendency to sentimentality, especially in his creation of feminine characters, is avoided for the most part in *Dead Men Running*, which is held together by a well-controlled, retrospective design and by the predominance of its complex main character.

Nimrod Street Theatre was founded in 1970 by John Bell and Ken Horler and was an attempt to offer an alternative, younger, more radical and generally appealing theatre than was then available to Sydney audiences. First located in a former stable and gymnasium in Nimrod Street, Kings Cross, the theatre moved in 1974 to a more capacious building, an old tomato-sauce factory in Surry Hills. In the new venue the intimate atmosphere between cast and audience was maintained and extended to a downstairs theatre, which was subsequently added. From its first production of 'Biggles' by Ron Blair, Michael Boddy and Marcus Cooney, the Nimrod has continued to foster Australian drama, producing the work of such playwrights as Ron Blair, Dorothy Hewett, David Williamson, Alma de Groen, Steve Spears and Louis Nowra as well as, increasingly, international playwrights. Subsidized in part by the Australia Council and the NSW government, the Nimrod Theatre became the Nimrod National Theatre in 1982.

1915, a novel by Roger McDonald (q.v.) was first published in 1979, and won the *Age* Book of the Year and the South Australian biennial literature awards; in 1982 a seven-part adaptation by Peter Yeldham was shown on Australian television. The narrative of *1915* is told primarily from three alternating perspectives, those of Walter Gilchrist, Billy McKenzie and Frances Reilly. Walter, sensitive, uncertain, from a relatively well-off farming family and Billy, confident, knowing, something of a larrikin, are two boys from the bush in NSW, whose ambivalent relationship, a mixture of friendship and rivalry, is established in the opening pages of the novel. As they grow up in the period immediately preceding the First World War, their rivalry is focused on their desultory pursuit of the unsettled and flirtatious Frances, whom Billy meets on a visit to Forbes and introduces to Walter. As 1913 turns into 1914 the shadows of war settle over the country town of Parkes, disrupting the texture of life there. When war is declared, Billy and Walter soon join up, Billy making the more comfortable transition into service life. The war affects their relationship with Frances: just before their departure for the Front, Walter establishes an intimate relationship with Frances, and Billy one with Diana Benedetto, Frances's best friend.

The second half of the novel is concerned primarily with the experiences of Walter and Billy as Anzacs at Gallipoli, but there are both temporal and geographical shifts in the narrative. For example, while at Gallipoli, Walter recollects his last days in Sydney before embarkation and his experiences while training in Egypt, and there are chapters which chronicle Frances's betrayal of Walter by her pursuit of the rich landowner, Robert Gillen, and the death of Diana, who is drowned while carrying Billy's child. At the Front, as in the early days of recruitment, Billy settles more comfortably into the experiences of war, winning repute as a sniper. Wally, on the other hand, experiences most of the awfulness of war: its carnage, the appalling confrontations with and randomness of death, the omnipresent and drugging fear of extinction which makes comrades out of soldiers because of a lust for remembrance. At the end of the novel, however, Wally is captured and presumably preserved but Billy is destroyed. Wounded while on sniping patrol in an attempt to save Walter, whom he sights under threat in a trench, Billy is invalided back to Australia and placed in an asylum after he visits and physically attacks Frances, whom he blames for Diana's death.

1915 has elements of the war novel and the historical novel but its major focus is the evolution of its central characters and their search for a meaning and shape to their existence. The view the novel offers of Gallipoli has attracted the attention of reviewers, yet the war scenes are integrated with and paralleled by the Australian and Egyptian scenes. Walter, Billy and Frances are seeking throughout the novel to create a mosaic out of the fragments of experience but what war does for Frances and Diana, no less than for Walter and Billy, is make them aware of the forces for disintegration.

Nineties is a word used to describe the 1890s, a significant and even legendary decade in Australian history and Australian literature. Historically, it was a period in which the labour movement gained representation in parliament (the first Labor government in the world was formed briefly in Queensland in 1899); progressive social welfare legislation and political reforms were implemented; and a national self-awareness found expression in the Federation movement, climaxed by the proclamation of the Commonwealth of Australia on 1 January 1901. But countering these achievements were an economic depression, the worst experienced in the colonial period, which began in 1889 and peaked in 1892; a severe financial crisis the following year, characterized by the collapse of a number of banks; the end of the land boom; a decline in the pastoral industry, exacerbated by the long drought from 1895 to 1903; industrial conflict, notably in the shearing and maritime industries, in which the unions lost more disputes than they won; and massive unemployment of up to thirty per cent. As well, the beginning of a new technological age was signalled by the arrival of the motor car, electric street lighting and cinema, and by improvements in transport and communication which made Australia less isolated from Europe.

These momentous and contradictory events have produced fluctuating responses among commentators. Several volumes of reminiscences published from the end of the First World War, e.g. G.A. Taylor's *Those Were the Days* (1918), A.W. Jose's *The Romantic Nineties* (1933), Randolph Bedford's *Naught to Thirty-Three* (1944), Norman Lindsay's *Bohemians of the Bulletin* (1965), looked back nostalgically and helped foster the legend of the nineties as a 'golden' decade in the development of Australia; in which, specifically, Australian writers and artists looked inwards and found an authentic identity distinct from the cultural models of Great Britain. As articulated by the memoirists and in the writings of later radical nationalist commentators such as Vance Palmer in *The Legend of the Nineties* (1954), A.A. Phillips, Russel Ward and H.M. Green, Australian literature was finally born in the 1890s. The midwife was the *Bulletin* (q.v.), which under J.F. Archibald and A.G. Stephens encouraged writers and illustrators to discover a 'real' Australia in which the importance of the bush was stressed, and to affirm in short sketches and ballads written in a natural idiom, certain distinctive values: national pride, egalitarianism, republicanism, collectivism, Utopianism, scepticism. A major symbol in this version of the nineties is the pastoral worker; the major creative publicists are Henry Lawson,

'Banjo' Paterson and Joseph Furphy. Furphy's famous, though tongue-in-cheek, description of his novel, *Such is Life* (1903), 'temper, democratic; bias, offensively Australian', has been taken as a motto for the spirit of the age.

Since the Second World War, and more particularly from the 1960s, the nineties has undergone revaluation. Literary historians and critics, noting the darker side to the history, have made several corrections to the legend: for example, in suggesting that the *Bulletin* was xenophobic, racist, provincial, sexist and bourgeois as well as (or perhaps rather than) radical, nationalist and youthfully zestful; that the bush ethos it promoted was in some senses a romantic escape from the disillusionment with and despair of the realities of urban life; that the accepted model of the *Bulletin* writer does not accommodate some of its notable contributors, e.g. the Celtic Twilight lyricists, or more significantly a writer such as Christopher Brennan, whose concerns were moral and metaphysical and whose literary heritage was European; and that literary nationalism and the promotion of an Australian identity were not *Bulletin* inventions, but had been a concern of many colonial writers in the century before 1890. The extent to which the glow surrounding the nineties has been dissipated is measured by the 'sense of alienation and loss' which Leon Cantrell, the editor of *The 1890s* (1977), the most recent anthology devoted to the period, sees as its 'principal literary hallmark'. Some commentators have warned of the danger of replacing an old orthodoxy, the golden nineties, with a new one, the gloomy nineties, but the revaluation has at least contributed to an acceptance of the complexities and contradictions that emerged in the literature of the period. Just as, for example, nationalism itself was an amalgam of allegiances to an emerging Australia, an individual colony like NSW, and even Britain itself, so Australian literature was both inward-looking *and* influenced by international movements such as Utopianism, feminism and the growth of literary journalism. Similarly, there has been an increasing acceptance of an ambivalence towards the bush and city in many nineties writers, and of the inadequacy of a simplistic response to writers like Lawson and Furphy. The vitality and variety of nineties writing, including critical writing, have survived; less so the uniqueness of the decade, particularly as more attention is directed to earlier Australian literature.

NISBET, HUME (1849–1921), a Scottish artist who was an associate of John Ruskin, taught art at Edinburgh and exhibited at the Royal Scottish Academy, visited Australia 1865–72, 1886 and 1895. On his first visit he travelled extensively in eastern Australia and tried acting in Melbourne. He published more than forty books of fiction (many of which draw on his Australian experience), plays, verse, works on art and painting and accounts of his travels. Novels and short story collections which are set in or refer to Australia include *The Land of the Hibiscus Blossom* (1888); *Doctor Bernard St Vincent* (1889); *Bail Up!* (1890); *The Savage Queen* (1891), which includes Truganini, Michael Howe and G.A. Robinson as characters; *The Black Drop* (1891); *The Bushranger's Sweetheart* (1892); *The Divers* (1892); *A Bush Girl's Romance* (1894); *A Sweet Sinner* (1897); *The Swampers* (1897), which was banned because of scurrilous references to public figures in NSW; *In Sheep's Clothing* (1900); *Children of Hermes* (1901); *A Losing Game* (1901); *Mistletoe Manor* (1902); *Wasted Fires* (1902); and *A Dream of Freedom* (1902), which deals unfavourably with William Lane's founding of New Australia in Paraguay. Several of his novels and short stories focus on one of his most individual characters, an Australian-born Chinese detective, Wung-Ti, based on an individual whom Nisbet met in Melbourne. Nisbet's travel writings which have reference to Australia are *My Illustrated Diary of a Voyage from London to Australia* (1890) and *A Colonial Tramp* (1891). His verse, some of which is Australian in context, was published in several collections, *Memories of the Months* (1889), *The Matador and Other Recitative Pieces* (1893), and *Hathor and Other Poems* (1905). Hackneyed as far as plots and characters are concerned and crammed with the stock ingredients of bushrangers, convicts, squatters and Aborigines, Nisbet's novels have more historical than literary interest, although his anachronistic and outspoken comments and prefaces on such topics as racial prejudice in Australia and especially the treatment of the Aborigines enliven his turgid narratives.

No Escape, see 'ERCOLE, VELIA'

'No Foe Shall Gather Our Harvest', a stirring poem written by Dame Mary Gilmore (q.v.) in 1941, proved a remarkable morale booster in the tense days of the Japanese threat to Australia in 1942. The poem, with its refrain 'No foe shall gather our harvest/ Or sit on our stockyard rail' was at the time considered as a possible battle hymn, even national anthem.

No Moon Tonight, see CHARLWOOD, DON

No Roads Go By, see WHITE, MYRTLE ROSE

NOLAN, CYNTHIA (?1913–76), was born in Tasmania into a wealthy, pastoral family. A sister of John Reed (q.v.), she had connections with the Angry Penguins group of writers and artists in the 1940s. Several Australian writers, including George Johnston and Patrick White, have recorded their impressions of her personality. As Cynthia Reed, she published two novels, *Lucky Alphonse* (1944) and *Daddy Sowed a Wind!* (1947), although after her marriage to Sidney Nolan (q.v.) in 1948 she published under her married name. She wrote another novel, *A Bride for St Thomas* (1970), which draws heavily on her experiences as a student nurse, and several travel books, *Outback* (1962), *One Traveller's Africa* (1965), *Open Negative* (1967), *A Sight of China* (1969) and *Paradise, and Yet* (1971). *Open Negative*, her most sympathetically-received book, describes a visit to the USA and her experiences in a New York hospital while undergoing treatment for tuberculosis.

NOLAN, Sir **SIDNEY** (1917–   ), born Melbourne into a working-class family, left school at fifteen and two years later enrolled in the Art School of the National Gallery of Victoria. In 1940 he held his first exhibition of abstract paintings, which aroused some controversy and even a destructive attack by one enraged viewer armed with a can of green paint. He served in the army 1942–45 and was stationed in the Wimmera, which gave him his first taste of the Australian open landscape and determined the form of his interest in the Ned Kelly legend. A visit to Central Australia in 1949 resulted in a series of paintings on the explorations of Burke and Wills, which won him the Dunlop Art Prize in 1950. In the 1940s he was encouraged by John Reed, president of the Contemporary Art Society and brother of Cynthia Reed (see Cynthia Nolan), whom Nolan married in 1948. A member for a time of the publishing firm, Reed and Harris, Nolan also became friendly with Max Harris and was one of the editors of *Angry Penguins Broadsheet*. In 1952 he met George Johnston, spent an extended period with him on the island of Hydra in 1955, and was subsequently portrayed by Johnston as Tom Kiernan in his novel, *Clean Straw for Nothing* (1969). From 1950 Nolan has lived abroad, and has gained the most outstanding international reputation of any Australian artist; he has returned to Australia at regular intervals. His two Ned Kelly series are perhaps his most famous paintings; inspired partly by the stories of his grandfather, a trooper in the Kelly era, they illustrate his Irish-Australian temperament, his literary streak and his strong feel for the strange individuality of the Australian landscape. Nolan has also drawn on other Australian myths for series of paintings on the story of Eliza Fraser and on Gallipoli (qq.v.). His Gallipoli series, consisting of 252 paintings, produced over thirty years, were donated to the nation in 1977. Another series, 'Ern Malley', comments on the Ern Malley poems and includes portraits of members of the Angry Penguins group. He has illustrated the work of Randolph Stow, Patrick White, Alan Moorehead, Colin McInnes, George Johnston, Robert Lowell and Charles Osborne and has designed the dust-covers of C.P. Snow's novels, many of which allude to his work. A selection of Nolan's own verse, *Paradise Garden*, illustrated by his paintings, was published in 1971. In 1972 he produced a film, *Kelly Country*, and has co-operated in several films and television programmes on his life and work, including *The Dreaming, Spinning Thing* (1967) and *Nolan at Sixty* (1977). He was awarded the Britannica-Australia Award in 1969 and knighted in 1981. Several biographical and critical accounts of Nolan have been published, including *Sidney Nolan* (1961), by Kenneth Clark, Colin McInnes and Bryan Robertson and Elwyn Lynn's *Sidney Nolan: Myth and Imagery* (1967).

NORDHOFF, CHARLES (1887–1947), an American citizen, was born in London but lived in the USA from the age of three. Educated at Harvard University, he served in the First World War in France, where he met his future collaborator, James Norman Hall (q.v.). In 1920 they visited Tahiti, where Nordhoff remained until 1941. He independently published several South Seas novels 1919–29. With Hall he published some non-fiction works and the following novels, many using glamorous incidents of South Seas history: *Falcons of France* (1929), *Mutiny on the Bounty* (1932), *Men against the Sea* (1934), *Pitcairn's Island* (1934), *The Hurricane* (1936), *The Dark River* (1938), *No More Gas* (1940), *Botany Bay* (1941), *Men Without Country* (1942) and *The High Barbaree* (1945). Their best known books, the trilogy (1932–34) dealing with the Bligh (q.v.) mutiny and the subsequent settlement on Pitcairn Island, were published together in 1936, titled *The Bounty Trilogy*; several of Nordhoff and Hall's books met Hollywood's formula for romantic-adventure films. The Nordhoff-Hall collaboration has been described by Paul L. Briand in *In Search of Paradise* (1966).

Norfolk Island, situated about 1500 kilometres east-north-east of Sydney, was discovered by James Cook on 10 October 1774 and was used as a prison settlement 1788–1814 and 1825–56. In 1856 the penal settlement was finally abolished and descendants of the *Bounty*

mutineers were transferred from Pitcairn Island. Settlers from Australia and NZ, known locally as 'mainlanders', have since joined the 'islanders', and in 1914 the island became an external territory under the administration of the Australian government.

First settled by Philip Gidley King with a small group of convicts and some free men on the orders of Governor Phillip, the island's first period as convict settlement 1788–1814, was relatively unremarkable. Some disturbances between troops and convicts arose, especially under the administration of Major Robert Ross, and there were some abortive convict rebellions and periods of near-famine. When the penal settlement was re-established in 1824, however, following the report of Commissioner J.T. Bigge, the object was to segregate there the worst type of convict, Norfolk becoming in the words of Governor Ralph Darling 'the place of extremest punishment short of death'. For the next twenty-five years the island, which held an average of 1500 to 2000 desperate convicts, had a reputation as a natural paradise turned into hell, and was administered with great severity; the only relative respite occurred under the administration of Alexander Maconochie (q.v.) (1840–44). Mutinies and insurrections were frequent, especially under the infamously repressive administration of Joseph Childs (1844–46), the model for 'Price Warung''s (q.v.) Commandant Scragge, and John Price (1846–50), the model for Marcus Clarke's (q.v.) Maurice Frere. Norfolk's years as a convict settlement have been frequently commemorated in Australian fiction, most notably in Clarke's *His Natural Life* (1874), 'Price Warung''s short stories including *Tales of the Isle of Death (Norfolk Island)* (1898), but also in Eliza Winstanley's *Twenty Straws* (1864), Mark Jeffrey's *A Burglar's Life* (1893), Roy Bridges's *The Fires of Hate* (1915) and Thomas Gillard Ford's short stories, *Inhumanity* (1935).

Norm and Ahmed, a one-act play by Alexander Buzo (q.v.) was first produced in 1968 and first published in 1969. The play's action, which consists simply of a midnight conversation between Norm Gallagher, a middle-aged, average Australian, and Ahmed, a young Pakistani student, probes the inadequacy of the 'Aussie' self-image. Norm, the typical beer-drinking, rough and ready good mate and family man, supporter of the 'fair go', the RSL, the Leagues Club, sport and law and order, the unthinking cog in the industrial system, unwittingly reveals his inner anxiety and unconscious insufficiency as he talks to the politely formal student. The suspense aroused by his ambivalent behaviour, varying from the threatening to the friendly, culminates in his physical attack on the student and the succinct phrase 'Fucking boong'. The final line of the play led to prosecutions for obscenity when it was performed in Melbourne and Brisbane, although in the latter case the prosecution was quashed.

NORMAN, LILITH (1927–), born Sydney, has worked as a library assistant, research officer, nurse and children's librarian. Since 1976 she has been editor of *School Magazine*, published by the NSW Department of Education and widely used in primary schools. She has published local histories of inner areas of Sydney and plays for children, several of which have been published in *School Magazine*, but is best known for her novels for children, *Climb a Lonely Hill* (1970), *The Shape of Three* (1971), *The Flame Takers* (1973), *A Dream of Seas* (1978) and *My Simple Little Brother* (1979). A keen and often humorous observer of family relationships, Norman has dealt with a diverse range of personalities and environments, from the deprived, alcoholic family of *Climb a Lonely Hill* to the affluent, artistic one of *The Flame Seekers*. In *A Dream of Seas* she interweaves fantasy and realism with unpredictable, powerful effects.

North, James, an important character in Marcus Clarke's *His Natural Life* (1874), was loosely modelled on Thomas Rogers (1806–1903), a chaplain at the Norfolk Island penal settlement 1845–47.

Northern Territory is the middle section of the northern half of Australia; originally part of NSW, then SA, it became the Northern Territory of Australia in 1911 and was administered by the federal government until self-government in 1978. Its history, geography, character and legendry have been dealt with in such works as A. Grenfell Price's *The History and Problems of the Northern Territory, Australia* (1930), W.E. ('Bill') Harney's *North of 23°* (1946), *Australia's Frontier Province* (1950) by C.L. Abbott, for nine years the administrator of the Northern Territory, Ernestine Hill's *The Territory* (q.v., 1951), Douglas Lockwood's *Up the Track* (1964), J.H. Kelly's *Struggle for the North* (1966), Glenville Pike's *Frontier Territory* (1972) and Alan Powell's *Far Country: A Short History of the Northern Territory* (1982). The Northern Territory is depicted as Capricornia in Xavier Herbert's (q.v.) novel, *Capricornia* (1938) and figures largely in his *Poor Fellow My Country* (1975).

NORTON, EZRA, see **NORTON, JOHN**; *Truth*

NORTON, JOHN (1858–1916), a colourful Sydney newspaper editor at the turn of the century, was born in Brighton, England, and brought up in unhappy circumstances in which he was maltreated by his stepfather. He was a private secretary to an architect before entering journalism. In 1884 he arrived in Australia and soon established himself as a reporter on the *Evening News* and as a publicist for the labour movement; among the works he wrote at that time were *The Australian Labour Market* (1886) and the Australian material in *The History of Capital and Labour* (1886). In 1890, after a stint as editor of the *Newcastle Morning Herald*, he joined the recently-established radical weekly, *Truth* (q.v.), which he edited in 1891–92 and 1896–1905; he bought into the journal in 1896 and owned it outright from 1899 until his death. Under Norton, *Truth* was notorious for its focus on political, sexual and domestic scandal (e.g. during the Dean case) some of it relating to Norton's own violent private life. After his death, *Truth* came under the control of his son Ezra (1897–1967), who subsequently established the tabloid *Daily Mirror*; in 1958, when Cyril Pearl's sensational exposé of John Norton and his milieu, *Wild Men of Sydney*, was being published, Ezra threatened legal action for libel and is often credited with influencing the passing of stricter defamation laws in that year. A later study of Norton, Michael Cannon's *That Damned Democrat* (1981), reprints a selection of Norton's alliterative editorials and has information on his political activities, which saw him several times elected to parliament (where he was several times ejected for disorderly conduct), as well as on his crusades in *Truth* on behalf of the underprivileged.

Nosey Alf is the disfigured boundary rider in Joseph Furphy's *Such is Life* (1903) who turns out to be a woman, Molly Cooper, in disguise. Furphy's idea for the characterization came from his awareness of the double life led by Johanna Jorgensen (1843–93), who had also been kicked in the face by a horse as a young woman.

Notes & Furphies, published by the Association for the Study of Australian Literature (q.v.) since 1978, includes short articles, reports of Australian and overseas conferences, information about work-in-progress, awards and competitions, biographical notes on Australian writers, lists of theses on Australian literature since 1976 and miscellaneous news.

NOVACK, CAROL, see **Feminism and Australian Literature**.

NOWRA, LOUIS (1950–) was born in Melbourne and studied English at La Trobe University without taking a degree. Best known as a playwright, he has published *Albert Names Edward* in *Five Plays for Radio* (1975), ed. Alrene Sykes, *Inner Voices* (1977), *Visions* (1979) and two plays published together, *Inside the Island* and *The Precious Woman* (1981). Other plays include 'The Death of Joe Orton', 'The Girl', 'Kiss the One-Eyed Priest', 'Prince of Hamburg', 'Royal Show', 'Strange Words', 'Sunrise' and 'The Song Room'. He has also published a novel, *The Misery of Beauty* (1976), which won the fourth Angus & Robertson fellowship, and a collection of newspaper reports of personal catastrophies or tragedies, *The Cheated* (1979). Interested also in music, he has collaborated as lyricist with his wife, the composer Sarah De Jong. An innovative and individual playwright, Nowra is concerned more with exploring timeless questions about human motivation, aspirations and interdependence, than with recreating a specific Australian environment. Only *Inside the Island* has a recognizable Australian setting; *Inner Voices* takes place in Russia of 1794, *Visions* in Paraguay of the 1860s, *The Precious Woman* in China of the 1920s. In all his plays, however, the external setting is less important than the inner one, 'the landscape of the mind'. The structure of his stage-plays, usually composed of succinct, visually-striking, emblematic scenes, partly determines his characteristic Brechtian effect of simultaneous engagement and detachment. Both *Albert Names Edward* and *Inner Voices* deal with the experiences of abnormally isolated and unformed young men: Edward, who suffers from total amnesia, presents himself as a *tabula rasa* to an older man, Albert, and becomes finally Albert's mental replica; the central protagonist of *Inner Voices* is Ivan, the twenty-four-year-old claimant to the Russian throne, whom Catherine II has kept imprisoned since infancy and who, at the beginning of the play, knows only his own name. In both plays Nowra is preoccupied with the power of language as an instrument of domination and as a means of interpreting and defining the world. For Ivan, the search for subjective and objective knowledge is fatally conditioned by the warped structure of his 'education' at the hands of his tyrannical instructor and 'liberator', Mirovich. The close of the play sees him in almost the same situation that he was in at the beginning; trapped in his palace/prison, he is surrounded by the indecipherable voices of his followers, whose tongues he has had removed. *Visions*, where the scope of the action is social and national, dealing with the fates of President Lopez of Paraguay and his wife, Eliza Lynch, a one-time Paris courtesan, concentrates more on the inner lives of the dominators than of the victims. Both, however, emerge as fatally corruptible by half-truths masquerading as absolutes. *The Misery of Beauty*, narrated by a physical grotesque, christened Frogman, and assistant to a magician, Earl, who is both dominating and dependent, deals with the unique experience of the excluded, isolated individual.

'Nullarbor', see **HART-SMITH, WILLIAM**

Nullarbor Plain is an arid limestone plateau extending between SA and WA about 320 kilometres west and 240 kilometres east from the WA border and 240 kilometres inland from the coast. As the average rainfall is less than 250 mm, the plain is virtually treeless (hence its name), the only vegetation being saltbush and bluebush. A.G. Bolam wrote *The Trans-Australian Wonderland* (1923) and Basil Fuller, *The Nullarbor Story* (1970).

No. 1 (1943), a deliberately unnamed magazine, was founded and published by Garry Lyle in 1943 with the aim of presenting poetry that was neither self-consciously nationalistic nor a meretricious imitation of current European trends. Two further issues appeared, *Number Two* (1944) and *Number Three* (1948). Of the four contributors to the magazine, Garry Lyle, O.M. Somerville, Harry Hooton and A.D. Hope, Hope was to have the most lasting reputation, several of his early satiric poems appearing there for the first time.

NUTTALL, CHARLES (1872–1934), born Melbourne, began his education in art at that city's National Gallery School and contributed drawings to the *Bulletin*. In 1902 he painted *Opening of the First Commonwealth Parliament* and published *Representative Australians*, a series of portrait sketches as well as *Peter Wayback Visits the Melbourne Cup* (1902), a series of humorous sketches. He became a cartoonist with *Table Talk* in 1904; in 1905 he joined the *New York Herald*. Back in Australia in 1910 he had regular exhibitions of drawings and sketches, illustrated *Pals*, a boys' weekly, wrote stories and articles, and in 1933, published *Melbourne Town* with reproductions of Melbourne drawings.

O

OAKES, RUSSELL (1910–52), was an officer in the Australian army and served in New Guinea during the Second World War. He wrote verse, short stories (one of which, 'No-one Spoke', won an award) and plays for radio and stage. His published plays include the one-act *Judgment* (?1951), which is set in wartime Papua, and *Enduring as the Camphor Tree* (1967), which is based on a Chinese love story and was first produced in Melbourne in 1946. His other plays include 'Invisible Circus', 'The Alchemist', 'The Arrival of Arthur', 'Carry On, Sergeant', 'The Egg', 'The Embarrassing Proviso', 'In Puris Naturalibus', 'The Substantial Phantom', 'These Little Pigs', 'The Voice of Jerome Keddle' and 'Wool Gathering'.

OAKLEY, BARRY (1931–), was born in Melbourne and educated at the Christian Brothers College, St Kilda, and at the University of Melbourne. He taught at secondary schools in central Victoria and in Melbourne 1955–62, meanwhile writing copiously, although publication eluded him. In 1963 he lectured in humanities at the Royal Melbourne Institute of Technology, worked as an advertising copywriter 1964–65 and as a journalist for the federal Department of Trade and Industry 1966–73. During these years he lived mainly in the inner suburbs of Melbourne, with his wife and six children. He now lives in Sydney. Oakley has published three novels, *A Wild Ass of a Man* (1967), *A Salute to the Great McCarthy* (1970), which was produced as a film, *The Great McCarthy*, in 1976, and *Let's Hear It for Prendergast* (1970); a collection of short stories, *Walking Through Tigerland* (1977), which reprints only some of his stories that have appeared in magazines and newspapers since 1955; and numerous plays, *Witzenhausen, Where Are You?* in *Meanjin* (1967) and *Six One-Act Plays* (1970), ed. Eunice Hanger; *A Lesson in English* which first appeared in *English in Australia* (1968) and was published with Ron Blair's *The Christian Brothers* (1976); *The Feet of Daniel Mannix* (1975); *Bedfellows* (1975); *Buck Privates in Nation Review* (1977); *Scanlan* in *Meanjin* (1978); *The Ship's Whistle* (1979); *The Great God Mogadon and Other Plays* (1980), which includes *Witzenhausen, Where Are You?*, *The Hollow Tombola*, *Buck Privates*, *Eugene Flockhart's Desk* and *Scanlan*; and *Marsupials and Politics: Two Comedies* (1981). Two plays have been produced but not published, 'Beware of Imitations' (1973) and 'It's a Chocolate World' (1968). He has also written two books for children, *How They Caught Kevin Farrelly* (1972) and *A Letter from Hospital* (1975). In 1970 Oakley shared the Captain Cook Bicentenary Award with Thomas Keneally.

Oakley's three novels are picaresque comedies in which the hero/victim pits his manic energies against an absurd but conformist world. Oakley, who sees himself as refracting rather than recording reality, is interested in the riddle of 'Middle Australia', the enigma of 'Glen Waverley Man, *homo suburbiensis*, forever patrolling and mowing his front lawn'. Satiric and iconoclastic, but also sympathetic and affirmative, his fiction attacks many targets in a free-wheeling, amiable way including religion, sport, suburbia, academia, publishers, avant garde artists, public servants, schoolteachers and advertising executives. Two of his most potent topics are Catholicism, especially Catholic education, and the norms of life in Melbourne, which he presents with penetrating irony. *A Wild Ass of a Man*, his most exuberant and inventive novel, traces the progress of a luckless, innocent young man called Muldoon, who perpetually strives but always fails to make an imprint on his society and who ends by suffering a revolving crucifixion on a ferris wheel at Luna Park. *A Salute to the Great McCarthy*, which restricts itself to Australian Rules football and the doomed rise of a young, star player from the country, has almost the same satiric impact and frenetic pace, if not the same episodic variety, as *A Wild Ass of a Man*. In *Let's Hear It for Prendergast*, Prendergast, the tallest poet in the world, with a mission to destroy all Melbourne's sacred cows, is granted an unwilling, 'normal' interpreter, Morley; as Prendergast chaotically progresses to his fate of self-immolation in fires that consume Melbourne's Exhibition building, he exposes indirectly the equally chaotic absurdity of the city's pretensions and social conventions. Oakley's gifts for satire and for evoking the absurd are seen at their best in his short stories. Frequently using the epistolary form, he interprets various experiences of failure and isolation – discarded husbands, restive priests, failed writers, jaded public servants, tired academics, bored housewives; immediate, ironic, witty and often hilariously comic, they have an underlying seriousness that seems to regard failure as the universal price of being human.

Oakley is probably best known for his drama, however, and for his associations with other new dramatists such as John Romeril, David Williamson, Jack Hibberd and Alexander Buzo. His earliest plays were performed at the La Mama theatre, although his non-partisan stance and ironic subtleties are often at odds with the approach of doctrinaire 'rough' theatre. His first play to be produced was *From the Desk of Eugene Flockhart* (its original title) at the Emerald Hill Theatre in Melbourne in 1967; set in a Canberra public service office, it is an uproarious attack on the deadening absurdities of office life which has similarities with Buzo's more intricate play, *The Front Room Boys* (1969). The subject of *Witzenhausen, Where Are You?*, one of the first plays to be produced at La Mama (in 1968), is a mystic messenger in a large car company who causes a disruption by locking himself in the lavatory, passing subversive messages on toilet paper under the door to the dismayed staff, and finally disappearing in a flash of light. 'It's A Chocolate World' is a comic but compassionate treatment of the problems of an unhappily-married research officer in a large international firm, Candy Bar Inc. A later play which deals similarly with the effects of power on people and with the incongruities between public facades and private realities, and which has affinities with Oakley's short story 'Malvolio', is the radio play, *The Great God Mogadon*. Two plays which were highly successful at La Mama and are more in keeping with the Pram Factory's 'rough' theatre are *The Feet of Daniel Mannix* and 'Beware of Imitations'; the former, a vaudevillean-style production, draws on the life of the Roman Catholic Archbishop, Daniel Mannix, and moves from his descent on Melbourne from heaven, clutching a wrench and a tube of Tarzan's Grip, to his Western-style shoot-out with W.M. Hughes over conscription, to his association with John Wren and 'Greensleeves' (B.A. Santamaria) and his conflict with 'Dr Bert Effort' (H.V. Evatt). 'Beware of Imitations' centres on the life of ex-prime minister, 'Sir Wilfred McLuckie' (R.G. Menzies), Warden of the Ports and Brandies, the Garters and the Privy Seal, who is spending his last days in a private nursing home, tended by Roy, his valet, a former digger and staunch member of the RSL, now sustained by whisky and visits to the TAB. In dreams and re-enactments the pair play out the highs and lows, the aspirations and the disappointments of the Prime Minister's career. Two later plays, the farce *Politics*, which has a more general theme, and *The Ship's Whistle*, which focuses on the life of the nineteenth-century poet, R.H. Horne, show the same flair for comic exaggeration, verbal display and serious buffoonery.

Three plays which reflect Oakley's literary interests are *The Hollow Tombola*, a sharp satire on Patrick White's novel *The Solid Mandala* (1966), *Scanlan*, a part-comic, part-pathetic parody of a conference paper delivered by a middle-aged paranoid, nervously-debilitated academic on the poet, Henry Kendall, and *A Lesson in English*. The last, performed at La Mama in 1969, deals comically at first with a teacher's unlucky efforts to interpret Marvell's poem 'To His Coy Mistress' to rowdy schoolboys, and ends in a moment of rare communication between teacher and boys on the real nature of sexuality. Oakley's other more naturalistic plays include *Buck Privates*, a subtle exploration of the private yearnings of Lovelock, a Dried Fruits publicity officer, and his old school rival, Daley, now a middle-aged priest; *Marsupials*, a study of the complexities and paradoxes of one man's relationship with his wife, her ex-lover, his work, his role as a father and, with the greatest paradox of all, Australia; and *Bedfellows*. The last named is Oakley's most extended treatment of relationships, a funny/sad look at a tired marriage between a university lecturer, editor of a literary magazine and Carlton resident, Paul Cummins, and his wife Carol, part-time student and mother of two. Shaken out of their usual boredom by a mutual disclosure of extra-marital affairs, especially Carol's with Bill Butler, rising writer and Paul's best friend, the couple re-examine their feelings in a way that mixes the mundane, the farcical and the anguished.

O'BRIEN, ERIS (1895–1974), Archbishop of Canberra and Goulburn 1953–67, was born at Condobolin, NSW, and entered the priesthood in 1918. He studied overseas 1934–38, gaining a doctorate from the University of Louvain, Belgium, for his work, *The Foundation of Australia (1786–1800)* (1937). O'Brien also published the *Life and Letters of Archpriest John Joseph Therry* (1922), *The Dawn of Catholicism in Australia* (1928) and *The Establishment of the Hierarchy in Australia* (1942). He is the author of a three-act play, *The Hostage* (1928), dealing with the life of Father Jeremiah O'Flynn, an Irish priest who was expelled by Governor Macquarie; Michael Massey Robinson appears as a character. O'Brien was made CMG in 1957.

'O'BRIEN, JOHN' (PATRICK JOSEPH HARTIGAN) (1878–1952), born Yass, was ordained as a Roman Catholic priest in 1903. In 1910, after a curacy of seven years at Albury, he was appointed inspector of Catholic schools in the Goulburn diocese. He administered the last rites in 1911 to Jack Riley of Brigenbrong, who had some claims to having been A.B.

527

Paterson's 'The Man from Snowy River'. He was priest-in-charge at Berrigan in 1916 and parish priest at Narrandera 1917–44. He published two volumes of verse under the pseudonym 'John O'Brien', *Around the Boree Log and Other Verses* (1921) and *The Parish of St Mel's* (1954), the latter a tribute to his Narrandera parish. A selection of his poems, illustrated by the paintings of Patrick Carroll, was published in 1978 as *Around the Boree Log*. He also wrote *On Darlinghurst Hill* (1952), the centenary volume of the Sacred Heart parish, Darlinghurst, and a series of articles, 'In Diebus Illis', recording the achievement of the pioneer clergy in Australia, published originally in the *Australasian Catholic Record* and later in book form, *The Men of '38 and other Pioneer Priests* (1975). The 'John O'Brien' poetry is simple, homely balladry centred on the Irish-Australian, Catholic, rural communities. Its great successes are 'Said Hanrahan' (q.v.), 'The Old Bush School', 'At Casey's, After Mass' and 'Tangmalangaloo'. The *Around the Boree Log* poems were made popular by the recitations of John Byrne ('The Joker'); they were made into a film in 1925; twenty of them were set to music by Dom. S. Moreno of New Norcia, WA, in 1933. His nephew, Frank Mecham, published the biography, *'John O'Brien' and the Boree Log* in 1981.

Observer (1) was an Adelaide weekly associated with the *South Australian Register*. Absorbing the *Adelaide Examiner* (1841–43), it began publication in 1843 as the *Adelaide Observer*, its title until 1905, and ran until 1931, when it was itself incorporated into the *Chronicle*. Catherine Helen Spence's novels, *The Author's Daughter* and *Gathered In* were first published as serials in the *Observer* in 1867 (as 'Hugh Lindsay's Guest') and in 1881–82 respectively. Her work was also included in the *Observer Miscellany* (1875–79), an annual literary selection from the *Observer*.

Observer (2), a fortnightly newspaper published in Sydney and edited by Donald Horne, ran 1958–61, when it merged with the *Bulletin*. A liberal-conservative, polemical newspaper concerned with local political and international affairs, the *Observer* also published substantial literary articles, book reviews, short stories, verse and theatrical notices. Many of Australia's leading writers either contributed to or were reviewed by the newspaper. Regular contributors included Chris Wallace-Crabbe and Desmond O'Grady. Peter Coleman was on the editorial staff.

Ocker is a word in current usage denoting someone uncouth, boorish or uncultivated, us-

ually an Australian male. The origin of the word is uncertain, although it existed innocently from at least the 1920s until the end of the 1960s, best known as a nickname for people with the Christian name of Horace or Oscar, as in 'Ocker' Stevens, a character in the comic strip 'Ginger Meggs', or with the surnames O'Connor and O'Connell. In its present sense it seems to have superseded 'Alf' during the 1970s, possibly as a result of the television portrayal by the actor Ron Frazer of the beer-swilling philistine Ocker in the television series, *The Mavis Bramston Show*; other famous stage Ockers include Barry Humphries's 'Bazza' McKenzie and Les Patterson, and Paul Hogan. For some social commentators the Ocker is an Australian national type, as in Max Harris's *Ockers* (1974); the stereotype is explored in such recent plays as Alexander Buzo's *Norm and Ahmed* (1969) and John Romeril's *The Floating World* (1975). Recent neologisms include 'Ockerina' for the female of the species, 'Ockerdom' and 'Ockerism', although there is some evidence that 'Ocker' is now under threat from 'Norm'.

'O'CONNER, ELIZABETH' (BARBARA McNAMARA) (1913–), the daughter of Eric Lowe, was born at Dunedoo, NSW, and studied art at Adelaide and Sydney before teaching at a Brisbane girls' boarding school. After marrying a cattle-station manager, she spent many years in outback areas of northern Australia and now lives in Cairns. She has written two autobiographical accounts of life on large cattle stations, which have proved perennially popular, *Steak for Breakfast* (1958) and *A Second Helping* (1969), and three novels, all of which are set in northern Queensland, *The Irishman* (1960), *Find a Woman* (1963) and *Spirit Man* (1980). Of these, *The Irishman*, which deals with the experiences of an Irish teamster, Paddy Doolan, and his two sons against a colourful panorama of Gulf country life, has received most attention. Produced as a film in 1978, the novel also won the Miles Franklin Award in 1960. *Find a Woman* is a family comedy which describes the revolutionary impact of a new wife on the masculine idyll of two middle-aged brothers; *Spirit Man*, set in the mid-1930s, is a tense racial drama. 'O'Conner' has also written a book for children, *The Chinese Bird* (1966).

O'CONNOR, MARK (1945–), born Melbourne, graduated from the University of Melbourne in English and classics and has taught English literature. Editor of *Canberra Poetry*, 1973–75, O'Connor won a travelling scholarship in 1976 and spent four years in Europe. He has written plays, several of which, e.g.

'Overture' and 'Cure of the Ring', have been produced, and short stories but is best known as an award-winning poet; he has published three collections, *Reef Poems* (1976), *The Eating Tree* (1980) and *The Fiesta of Men* (1983). His long poem, *Batavia*, was published in broadsheet form in 1977 and in *Seven Poets* (1977). He has also published three lectures on verse and drama, *Modern Australian Styles* (1982). A sensitive and accurate observer of nature, O'Connor has recorded his impressions of Barrier Reef life in *Reef Poems*; his last two collections extend his naturalist concerns and deal in part with his European travels. A proponent of phonetically-accurate spelling, he writes a rhythmic verse that is well suited to oral delivery.

Odes and Days, see **BEAVER, BRUCE**

O'DOHERTY, EVA (1826–1910), born in Ireland as Mary Eva Kelly, was an early contributor of nationalistic ballads and poems to Charles Gavan Duffy's the *Nation*, earning for herself the name 'Eva of the *Nation*'. She became engaged to Kevin Izod O'Doherty, a medical practitioner and political activist who was sentenced to transportation in 1848. After O'Doherty was set free in 1854, the two married, lived for a time in Paris and Dublin and finally settled in Brisbane, where O'Doherty practised medicine and had some success as a politician. In 1886 they returned to Ireland, where O'Doherty joined the Irish National Party and was briefly a member of the House of Commons, before returning to Queensland. Eva O'Doherty published two collections of verse, *Poems* (1877) and *Poems* (1880). Popular as O'Doherty's verse was in her lifetime both in Ireland and Queensland, her predictable themes, images and rhymes are now only of historical interest.

O'DONOHUE, BARRY (1947–), born Innisfail, Queensland, was conscripted into the Australian army in 1967 and spent a year on active service in Vietnam. He now lives in Brisbane and edits the magazine, *Image*, and the annual, *The Border Issue*. His verse has been published in two collections, *From the Edge of the World* (1979) and *Addiction to False Landscapes* (1981). He has also edited a volume of competition entries from young writers, *Queensland Youth Festival Young Writers 1979* (1980).

O'DOWD, BERNARD (1866–1953) born Beaufort, Victoria, the son of Ulster immigrants, grew up in Ballarat, strongly compelled by his Irish background and the events of the recent Eureka Stockade to radical socialism. He had both arts and law degrees before he was thirty, a considerable achievement for those times. After periods of teaching, O'Dowd moved to Melbourne, entered the State public service by way of the Crown Solicitor's office, and ultimately became chief parliamentary draftsman in 1931. He married Eva Fryer in 1889 but later left her for the socialist poet, Marie E.J. Pitt, with whom he lived from 1919. O'Dowd's strong radical tendencies found full expression in Melbourne at the turn of the century. He was a member of the Progressive Lyceum, edited its manual, the *Lyceum Tutor*, until his views became too vehement even for that coterie of radicals, and he attended Charles Strong's Australian Church, which was renowned for its radical sermons and debates and its emphasis on intellectual freedom. His first writings of note appeared in the *Bulletin* and in the *Tocsin* (q.v.), a journal which he produced and edited. His *Tocsin* column, 'The Forge', under the pseudonym 'Gavah the Blacksmith', consistently attacked the Establishment and the injustices of the contemporary social system. His belief, which he shared with Walt Whitman, that the poet's true socialist role was to further the best interests of mankind was contained in his 1909 address, *Poetry Militant* (q.v.). His first volume of poetry, *Dawnward?* (q.v., 1903), indicated by its question mark O'Dowd's uncertainty about Australia's future direction. The sonnet 'Australia' (q.v.) is the volume's best-known poem. *The Silent Land* (1906) speculates about a mystic world which exists beyond the physical world, influencing and being influenced by it. *Dominions of the Boundary* (1907) examines the nature and purpose of the deities such as Hermes, Vulcan and Bacchus and attempts to bestow contemporary significance on them. *The Seven Deadly Sins* (1909), a series of sonnets on those sins, contains some unusually fine imagery. *The Bush* (q.v.), O'Dowd's most substantial and worthwhile poem, envisages a future in which Australia occupies a place of glory similar to that occupied by Greece and Rome in antiquity. O'Dowd's last major composition was *Alma Venus* (1921), a remarkable but largely-ignored poetic exploration of the mystery of sex. From 1921 until his death in 1953 O'Dowd maintained an almost complete poetic silence. Apart from radical verse like *Dawnward?* and *The Bush*, in which he assumed the role of standard-bearer of the nationalist radical movement, O'Dowd's poetry made little impact. His concern with 'Poetry Militant' made his verse too obviously didactic for general taste and his predilection for classical allusions made it largely incomprehensible to the ordinary reader. But he attempted to make a meaningful examination of Australian life and not simply describe, as the balladists had done, its more picturesque aspects. He also wrote a book of essays, *Fantasies* (1942). Victor Kennedy and Nettie Palmer wrote *Bernard O'Dowd* (1954) and Hugh Anderson, *Bernard O'Dowd* (1968).

O'FARRELL, HENRY JAMES (1833–68), born Arran Quay, Dublin, arrived in Melbourne in 1841. An epileptic, alcoholic, paranoid Fenian, O'Farrell shot and wounded the visiting Duke of Edinburgh at Clontarf, 12 March 1868. He was hanged 21 April 1868. The incident accentuated sectarianism in a colony that was already strongly divided on Protestant and Roman Catholic lines. Henry Kendall wrote two poems about the incident, 'In Hyde Park' and 'Australia Vindex', both published in the *Sydney Morning Herald*, 26 March 1868; they echo Australian shame at the assassination attempt and anger at O'Farrell, whose name, Kendall believed, was sure to become 'a byword for hisses and hate'. The events are recorded in Brian McKinlay's *The First Royal Tour 1867–1868* (1970).

O'FERRALL, ERNEST FRANCIS (1881–1925), born Melbourne, joined the staff of the *Bulletin* in 1907. A popular writer of short stories and sketches for the *Bulletin* and the *Lone Hand*, often under the pseudonym 'Kodak', O'Ferrall is represented in numerous anthologies. He published two collections of stories, *Bodger and the Boarders* (1921) and *Stories by 'Kodak'* (1933), and a collection of verse, *Odd Jobs* (1928). O'Ferrall's stories have mainly urban settings. Lightly satiric, they rely heavily on situational comedy, especially on bizarre but credible incidents arising from boarding-house life, on the predictable but originally-handled collisions between shrewish, unattractive landladies and drunken male boarders. His most famous story, 'The Lobster and the Lioness', which has affinities with Henry Lawson's 'The Loaded Dog', recounts an encounter between a drunken boarding-house inmate and an escaped lioness which he mistakes for a dog.

Official History of Australia in the War of 1914–1918, The, begun in 1919 when C.E.W. Bean (q.v.) was appointed official historian, was completed in 1942. The three-volume *The Official History of the Australian Army Medical Services in the War of 1914–1918*, (1930, 1940, 1943) by A.G. Butler was also under Bean's general editorship. Bean wrote the first six volumes of the general history, *The Story of Anzac* (1921, 1924) and *The Australian Imperial Force in France* (1929, 1933, 1937, 1942). Volume 7, *The Australian Imperial Force in Sinai and Palestine, 1914–1918* (1923) was written by Sir

Henry Gullett; 8, *The Australian Flying Corps in the Western and Eastern Theatres of War, 1914–1918* (1923) by F.M. Cutlack; 9, *The Royal Australian Navy, 1914–1918* (1928) by A.W. Jose; 10, *The Australians at Rabaul* (1927) by S.S. Mackenzie; 11, *Australia during the War* (1936), by Ernest Scott; 12 *Photographic Record of the War* (1939), annotated by C.E.W. Bean and H.S. Gullett. Bean's single volume abridgement, *Anzac to Amiens*, was published in 1946. One of Australia's most impressive and massive historical works, the *Official History* has elicited great praise from military historians all over the world. It is an absorbing amalgam of military, social and political history; it offers a lively analysis, frequently by anecdote and inference, of the Australian character, especially of the Australian fighting men; and it is a sustained illustration of Bean's view of the democratic basis of Australian life and society. The *Official History* is being republished by the University of Queensland Press (1981–).

O'FLAHERTY, H.C. (HENRY CHARLES) (?–?1854) was theatre musician, actor and playwright. Little is known of his life apart from his marriage to the actress, Eliza Winstanley, in 1841. He was possibly the author of the burletta, 'Life in Sydney : Or, The Ran Dan Club' (1843), and he also wrote a play as a vehicle for his wife, 'Isabel of Valois : Or, The Tyrant Queen', produced in 1842. Between 1841 and 1846 when they left for England, the O'Flahertys played at all three of Sydney's theatres, with visits to Tasmania and Melbourne. After they left Australia Eliza's career eclipsed his and he sank into oblivion, Eliza reverting to her maiden name in 1847.

OGILVIE, WILL (1869–1963), born near Kelso, Scotland, arrived in Australia at the age of twenty, drawn to the colony by his love of horses and adventure, and in addition to this by his admiration for the poet Adam Lindsay Gordon, whose tragic story had captured his imagination. He spent twelve years in a nomadic existence on far-flung stations like Belalie on the Warrego and Maroupe in SA, droving, mustering, breaking in horses and capturing in hastily-scribbled, buoyant, romantic verses the many experiences of outback life. A prolific contributor to the *Bulletin* and popular also with readers of the *Australasian* and the Mount Gambier *Border Watch*, he published his popular and best-known volume of verse, *Fair Girls and Gray Horses* (1898), prior to his return to Scotland in 1901. The poems, a mixture of ballads and lyrics, celebrated 'all Fair Girls' and 'all Gray Horses', for Ogilvie believed that 'Golden and Gray are the loves to hold'. The classic droving poem 'From the Gulf', with its nostalgic refrain, 'Store cattle from Nelanjie', the sentimental, horsebreaker poem, 'The Riding of the Rebel', and the poem that celebrated the courage and endurance of the teamsters, 'How the Fire Queen crossed the Swamp', are examples of Australian balladry at its best. But it is in lyrics such as 'A Tell-tale Tryst' and 'The Bush, My Lover', where the loveliness of fair girls blends with the shimmering Australian moonlight, that Ogilvie's singular contribution to the verse of the period lies. In the mostly pragmatic and masculine world of bush verse, his was virtually the only, and certainly the best, romantic voice. His later volumes, *Hearts of Gold* (1903) and *The Australian* (1916), were both published in Sydney although Ogilvie did not return to this country. The story of his Australian adventures is in his autobiographical *My Life in the Open* (1908).

O'GRADY, DESMOND (1929–   ), born Melbourne, has worked as literary editor of the *Bulletin* and since 1962 has lived as a freelance journalist in Rome. His short stories have been collected in *A Long Way from Home* (1966) and *Valid for All Countries* (1979). He has also published a novel, *Deschooling Kevin Carew* (1974), and a play, produced in Melbourne, 'Heart of the Wise'. A skilful raconteur, with a plain but expressive style and a keen eye for the odd and the eccentric, O'Grady gives his stories diverse settings, ranging from Europe to Asia to Australia. Frequently his central character is an outsider, a misfit, an exile or a returned expatriate; an Australian in Rome or a Hungarian in Melbourne, the O'Grady hero is afflicted with a divided consciousness and a vague sense of displacement and dispossession, although his predicament is interpreted as comic or even farcical. As the hero reluctantly absorbs his unpredictable experience and the perverse irony of his circumstances, he 'progresses' from a state of fragile certainty to one of total bewilderment. O'Grady's Irish Catholic childhood has provided him with much of his absurd material. Several of his short stories, including the trio, 'Memoirs of Catholic Boyhoods', in *Valid for All Countries*, draw on the comic, discomforting collisions between the simple rigidities of an Irish Catholic education and the complex actualities of modern adult life. *Deschooling Kevin Carew*, which draws heavily on this material, relates Carew's excessive but uncertain efforts to come to terms with his Catholic conditioning.

O'GRADY, FRANK (1910–   ), was working as an employee of the Sydney City Council when he wrote his first novel, *The Golden Valley* (1955). The story of a pioneering family in NSW in the 1830s, *The Golden Valley* was followed by five similar historical novels: *Goonoo Goonoo* (1956), *Hanging Rock* (1957), *No Boundary Fence* (1960), which is based on the life of Hamilton Hume, *Wild Honey* (1961), which includes the bushranger Fred Ward as a character, and *The Sun Breaks Through* (1964). O'Grady has also written a biography of Francis James McGarry, *Francis of Central Australia* (1977).

O'GRADY, JOHN PATRICK (1907–81) born Sydney, the eldest of eight children, spent most of his childhood on a remote New England farm and had no formal education until the age of twelve. He qualified as a chemist but never found the profession satisfying and in 1936 began work as a commercial traveller selling medical goods, meanwhile writing short stories, plays and poems, some of which were published in the *Bulletin*. During the Second World War he served in New Guinea and Borneo, left the army in 1950 and worked successively as a pharmacist, a builder's labourer, a teacher of pharmacy for the NZ government in Samoa, and a fisherman. In 1957 his novel, *They're a Weird Mob* supposedly written by an Italian migrant journalist turned Sydney builder's labourer, Nino Culotta, was an instant and continuing success. Nino Culotta's bewildered but sympathetic perceptions of Australian habits and language and his progress from outsider to insider provided a perspective on national attitudes that many Australians found fresh and congenial. The book was produced as a film in 1966. O'Grady subsequently wrote two more Nino Culotta books, *Cop This Lot* (1960) and *Gone Fishin'* (1962) and sixteen books under his own name, none of which proved as popular. They include *No Kava for Johnny* (1961), a novel based on his Samoan experience; *Aussie English* (1965); *Gone Troppo* (1968); *O'Grady Sez* (1969), a collection of short stories and verse; *Are You Irish or Normal?* (1970); *Aussie Etiket* (1971); *Gone Gougin'* (1975); and *There Was a Kid* (1977), an account of his New England childhood. O'Grady, occasionally described as the Rolf Harris of Australian literature, had a keen ear for the Australian idiom, especially of the 1950s, but he overworked his material.

O'Halloran, Mary, is the young daughter of Rory O'Halloran in Joseph Furphy's *Such is Life* (1903). Her tragic death half an hour before search parties reach her is narrated by Steve Thompson in the novel. Although Thompson's story has links with the rest of the novel, it has been judged a fine short story in its own right and has several times been included in anthologies of Australian short stories.

O'HARA, J.B. (JOHN BERNARD) (1862–1927), born Bendigo, was educated at the University of Melbourne, where he achieved distinction, and became lecturer in mathematics and physics at Ormond College in 1886. In 1889 he established a girls' school, South Melbourne College, of which he was headmaster until 1917. Katharine Susannah Prichard and Elsie Cole were two of his pupils and protegées. A respected poet in his lifetime, he won a prize in a competition connected with the Melbourne Exhibition of 1880, although his bland, meditative verse, reminiscent of the late Victorians, has now dated. He published nine collections of verse, mostly short lyrics, although his second volume, *Songs of the South Second Series: The Wild White Man and Other Poems* (1895), includes a narrative poem relating the adventures of William Buckley. His other volumes are *Songs of the South* (1891), *Lyrics of Nature* (1899), *A Book of Sonnets* (1902), *Odes and Lyrics* (1906), *Calypso and Other Poems* (1912), *The Poems of John Bernard O'Hara* (1918), *At Eventide* (1922) and *Sonnets and Rondels* (1925).

'O'HARRIS, PIXIE' (RONA OLIVE PRATT) (1903–), born Cardiff, Wales, came to WA in 1920. Wife of Bruce Pratt, aunt of Rolf Harris and close friend of Miles Franklin, she has written and illustrated some twenty books for children, and had acquired a considerable reputation as an illustrator by the mid-1920s. Some of her most popular books are the fairytales, *Pearl Pinkie and Sea Greenie* (1935), *The 'Pixie O'Harris Fairy Book'* (?1925), *Marmaduke the Possum* (1943) and *Marmaduke and Margaret* (1953), in which her conventionally-pretty art work complements the fantasy. She has also written a series of romantic stories for girls, beginning with *The Fortunes of Poppy Treloar* (1941), and has recently produced new stories and verse, such as *Cavalcade of Cats* (1981) and *The Little Grey Mouse* (1982). As well as illustrating the work of other children's authors, she has illustrated work by C.J. Dennis, Frank Dalby Davison and Ruth Bedford. Her autobiography, *Was It Yesterday?*, illustrated by herself, was published in 1983.

'Old Bark Hut, The', is an anonymous Australian folk-song which exists in several versions; the best-known one introduces the singer as Bob the Swagman, who chronicles the misfortunes he experiences while living on rations in an old bark hut, poorly furnished and open to the elements. The song was one of the most popular of Australian folk-songs in the nineteenth century. Its jaunty melody, simple four line verse stanza, and chorus which repeats the last line of each verse, permit the kind of extension which gave rise to the legend that a party of shearers once started singing the song as their train pulled out of Bourke, and finished it as the train arrived at Central railway station in Sydney.

Old Blastus of Bandicoot, a novel by Miles Franklin (q.v.), was originally published in 1931 in England but many copies of that edition were destroyed in a fire. Set in the Murrumbidgee ranges, the novel traces the course of a feud between the rival pioneer families, the Lindseys and the Barrys. William Barry, nicknamed 'Old Blastus' because of his fondness for that mild expletive, has two daughters: Mabel, seduced by a Lindsey boy, with a resultant illegitimate son; and the younger Dora who, ignorant of the family 'shame', is compelled to a cloistered existence by her overprotective father. The original Lindsey-Barry romance is in time repeated with Dora and Ross Lindsey, although not with the same result. All comes to a happy conclusion when Old Blastus heroically saves the Lindsey estate from a bushfire, thus clearing up the old feud. Mabel marries and leaves the district taking her 'shame' with her and Dora marries young Ross Lindsey. The novel's routine plot and outdated moral attitudes are its weaknesses; its strength lies in the character of Old Blastus, at times a figure of fun and the butt of Miles Franklin's feminism, at other times something of a hero in spite of himself.

'OLD BOOMERANG', see HOULDING, J.R.

'Old Bush School, The', see 'O'BRIEN, JOHN'

Old Bush Songs Composed and Sung in the Bushranging, Digging and Overlanding Days, The, was compiled and edited by A.B. Paterson (q.v.) in 1905. The first major collection of Australian folk-songs (q.v.), it rescued from oblivion many old ballads and songs which had existed precariously by being sung or recited around the camp-fires and in the shearing sheds of the outback. The first edition contained some fifty songs; by 1926 the fifth edition contained more than seventy, some with choruses, many with footnotes and identification of the tunes to which they were sung. Among the well-known inclusions were 'The Wild Colonial Boy', 'The Eumerella Shore', 'The Stringy Bark Cockatoo', 'The Dying Stockman'. 'The Old Bark Hut' and the Paddy Malone songs.

Old Colonials, see **BOYD, A.J.**

Old Convict Days, see **DERRINCOURT, WILLIAM**

Old Days: Old Ways (1934) are reminiscences and anecdotes of the pioneering days by Mary Gilmore (q.v.). A companion volume, *More Recollections*, was published in 1935. In vivid and lyrical prose she tells of the struggle to survive the hazards and discomfort of bush life, of the epic feats of the teamsters in the servicing of the outback, of the Aborigines and their lore, and of the beauty of the land before its ravage by the onward march of civilization.

'Old Granny Sullivan', a sentimental poem by John Shaw Neilson (q.v.), was published in the *Bookfellow* in 1907; A.G. Stephens published it again in 1916 as a leaflet and it was also used in school publications. Based, according to Neilson, on an old lady who lived in Penola when he was a boy, the poem recounts the typically sad story of a woman in early colonial times.

Old Pioneering Days in the Sunny South, see **MACALISTER, CHARLES**

Old Tales of a Young Country, a series of fifteen historical tales by Marcus Clarke (q.v.), was published in 1871; all but one of the series had appeared in 'Old Stories Retold' in the *Australasian* 1870–71. A by-product of the research for *His Natural Life* (1874), *Old Tales of a Young Country* reveals a similar opposition to the effect of authority on individual freedom and focuses on romantic incidents and individuals of Australian history; subjects include George Barrington, William Buckley, Jorgen Jorgenson, John Mitchel, the Rum Rebellion and Macquarie Harbour.

Old Times in the Bush of Australia (1895) is James Kirby's account of the trials and experiences of bush life in Victoria during the 1840s. Kirby came to Australia from Northampshire in 1839 and went to the Swan Hill area of Victoria in 1846. One of Victoria's earliest pioneers, he was encouraged in 1894 by the then Governor of Victoria, Lord Hopetoun, to compile his memoirs. *Old Times* has much information about the Aborigines, the bushrangers and life on the goldfields in the 1840s–1860s period.

Old Tote Theatre Company, founded in 1963 by the University of NSW in association with the Australian Elizabethan Theatre Trust, derived its name from its first home, an old racecourse totalizator in the grounds of the University. Robert Quentin, one of the founders of the Company and head of the University's Drama department, was co-director with Tom Brown 1963–65; he was succeeded by Robin Lovejoy, who became director in 1969 after Brown's resignation. In 1978 Sir Robert Helpmann was appointed artistic director. Originally closely associated with the National Institute of Dramatic Art, the Old Tote became an independent company in 1969 and moved to a larger building on the University campus, the Parade Theatre. A professional company of high standing, the Old Tote staged mainly international, lavishly-produced plays which catered for an affluent, middle-aged audience. In 1968, however, the company produced with scant success a series of Australian plays: Thomas Keneally's 'Childermas', Rodney Milgate's *A Refined Look at Existence* and *At Least You Get Something Out of That*, Dorothy Hewett's *This Old Man Comes Rolling Home*, Alexander Buzo's *Norm and Ahmed*, and Douglas Stewart's *The Fire on the Snow*. Funding for the company transferred to the Australian Council for the Arts in 1968, but in 1978 the Theatre Board decided to discontinue the Old Tote's subsidy and the company consequently dissolved. Its history is given in Josephine South's *Ten on the Tote* (1973).

O'LEARY, P.I. (PATRICK IGNATIUS) (1888–1944), born Adelaide, was an organizer for the SA labour movement in his early years. He later worked as a journalist for newspapers in Broken Hill, Adelaide and Melbourne. Editor of *Design*, he was also editor in Melbourne of the *Advocate* 1920–44, dominating the literary page and contributing poetry, political comment and leading articles. Connected with the Pioneer Players, he was also a member of the Bread and Cheese club. Pseudonyms he used included 'M', 'Historicus', 'Francis Davitt' and 'P.I.O.L.'. Some of his essays, which include several studies of Australian writers, were published in 1954, edited by Joseph O'Dwyer and titled *Bard in Bondage*. Although O'Leary tends to be prolix and even declamatory, when his Irish nationalism is aroused as in 'The Heroes of Easter Week' his judgements are often sound. He also edited an anthology, which includes verse by Roderic Quinn, E.J. Brady, John Shaw Neilson, Edward Harrington and others, *The Bread and Cheese Book* (1939), and published a volume of his own verse, *Romance and Other Verses* (1921).

OLIVER, HAROLD JAMES, see **Criticism; Shakespeare and Australia**

'On First Looking Into Chapman's Hesiod', by Peter Porter (q.v.), published in *Living in a Calm Country* (1975), is one of his central poems and vital to the understanding of his relationship with Australia. The vehicle of the poem is the purchase at a village fête of a copy of Chapman's *Hesiod* and Porter's recognition of the similarity of the attitudes of Boeotian poetry to Australian life; both are robust and innocent, essentially physical and direct in their emotions. Porter identifies his own preference as the European 'Athenian' culture of 'precept and the Pleiades'. The evocation of Australia is sharp in visual and aural detail but the irony is tender and amused rather than scabrous, as in his earlier satires on human folly; his admiration for Australian modes is also made clear. In view of Porter's self-avowed lack of simple and direct response, the poem's tone even suggests partial envy of such Australian modes. His exile from Australia is explained as a feeling of homelessness, a seeking for the 'permanently upright city' which is not London, but the 'new land', the world of ideas which dominates his poetry, especially the later volumes, *The Cost of Seriousness* (1978) and *English Subtitles* (1981). In an interview with Bruce Bennett (*Westerly*, 1982) Porter spoke of the 'new land' as the republic of the imagination 'where everyone is as gifted as the great men of the past and where you are made welcome as a confrère'. His preference is personal, imposing no clear-cut advocacy of the exiled over the native, more a resignation to the difference between his attitude and the Australian.

J.D.

On Our Selection, 'Steele Rudd''s (q.v.) first book, is a series of sketches of selection life on the Queensland Darling Downs; it was first published in 1899 and contained twenty-six stories. In 1909, when 'Rudd' sold the rights of *On Our Selection* and its immediate sequel, *Our New Selection*, to A.C. Rowlandson of the New South Wales Bookstall Company, the last ten chapters, deleted from subsequent editions, were included in *Stocking Our Selection*.

As originally contributed to the *Bulletin* the *On Our Selection* sketches were about different families, but on the suggestion of A.G. Stephens, 'Rudd' reworked them for the book so that they focused on the experiences of the Rudd family (q.v.), although Steele himself does not emerge as a character until *From Selection to City* (1909). 'Starting the Selection', the first story, depicts the family's arrival at Shingle Hut from Stanthorpe and Dad's first attempt at sowing a crop; subsequent sketches, of which 'The Night We Watched for Wallabies', 'Cranky Jack' (qq.v.) and 'Kate's Wedding' the best-known and most-anthologized, chronicle the struggle of the family to survive

a harsh and fickle climate, the poorness of the soil, and the exploitation of cockatoo farmers like Dad Rudd by storekeeper and squatter alike. There are moments of comedy and indeed high farce in *On Our Selection*, but the book emphasizes the harshness of pioneering life; it was not until *Our New Selection* and subsequent volumes that the family became relatively comfortable. *On Our Selection* was a major publishing success; one estimate put its sales to 1940 at 250 000. The sale of the rights to Rowlandson meant, however, that 'Rudd' did not reap the benefits of its popularity, except in higher fees for the rights to his other books. Similarly, the agreement he reached with Bert Bailey and Julius Grant for the stage adaptation of *On Our Selection* worked to the entrepreneurs' rather than to 'Rudd''s advantage. 'Rudd' had no involvement in the dramatization of *On Our Selection*, which was also highly popular for many years after its first production in 1912; a sound film of the play was screened in 1932 and led to three further films starring Bailey as Dad. Both the play and the film were influential in the transformation of Dad and his second son, Dave, into stereotypes of the rural hayseed, although 'Rudd' himself, in resorting primarily to farce in his later work, was also partly responsible. Raymond Longford's classic silent film version (1920) of *On Our Selection*, with a print of which 'Rudd' toured Australia in 1922, is closer in spirit to the 1899 book.

On the Beach, see 'SHUTE, NEVIL'

On the Track, see LAWSON, HENRY

On the Wool Track, see BEAN, C.E.W.; Shearer in Australian Literature

Once a Month : A Magazine for Australasia, a monthly magazine published in Melbourne 1884–86, included articles on literary topics, short stories and verse, much of which was reprinted.

Once a Week, see *Saturday Night*

One Day of the Year, The, a play by Alan Seymour (q.v.), was first produced in 1960 and published in 1962. The 'One Day' is Anzac Day, the servicemen's day of commemoration, commemorated by Alf Cook, a Sydney working-class man who served in the Second World War, as the most sacred day of the year. Anzac Day, for Alf, is bound up with his strong but otherwise undefined faith in mateship, his masculinity, his pride in Australia and his contempt for other races, nations and classes. In other years his participation in the Dawn Service had been reverently witnessed by his son Hughie, now a university student, but for Hughie Anzac Day has become a symbol of bigoted and ignorant working-class attitudes from which he seeks to free himself. His disaffection has been encouraged by his friendship with another student, Jan Castle, a girl from Sydney's upper-class North Shore; they determine to produce an article and pictures for the university newspaper, exposing the national day of mourning as a national day of 'boozing'. Hughie, who soon realizes that for him the issue is far from clear-cut, is torn by conflicting feelings of loyalty and love, anger, disgust and pity as his embattled father strives to redefine what the day means for him; that for one day he is not just an insignificant lift-driver but a man of status: 'They make a fuss of y' for once. The speeches and the march ... and y're all mates. Y're mates an' everythin' seems all right'. The conflict between father and son is watched helplessly but sympathetically by Hughie's mum, Dot, and by Wacka Dawson, an old friend of the family and an original Anzac, whose own response to the 'Day' is far more muted than Alf's. By Act III, which takes place some days after Anzac Day, Hughie's friendship with Jan is at an end and he has decided to remain at home for the time being, having reached an uncomfortable truce with his father.

'One-Hundred-and-Three', a robust ballad about prison life by Henry Lawson (q.v.), was written in secret in 1908, while Lawson was in Darlinghurst gaol ('Starvinghurst' in the poem) for arrears of maintenance to his wife, Bertha Lawson; smuggled out of prison, it was published in 1910 in *The Rising of the Court*, and revised substantially for inclusion in *Selected Poems of Henry Lawson* (1918). The title refers to the number of a prisoner addressed periodically throughout the poem. Although Lawson cannot be identified as 'One-Hundred-and-Three', the poem reflects his horror at the drudgery and dehumanization of prison life, his misogynic bitterness at his incarceration, and his belief that

> The clever scoundrels are all outside,
> and the moneyless mugs in gaol –
> Men do twelve months for a mad wife's lies
> or Life for a strumpet's tale.

O'Neill, Monk, see HIBBERD, JACK

Opinion, a monthly magazine published in Sydney, which included verse, literary essays, notes on literary societies and appreciations of past and contemporary Australian writers, appeared from May to October 1935. Its first issue included a highly sympathetic review of Patrick White's volume of verse, *The Ploughman* (1935).

'O'RANE, PATRICIA', see DARK, ELEANOR

'Orange Tree, The', one of John Shaw Neilson's (q.v.) best-known poems, was inspired by the beauty of the orange groves at Merbein near Mildura in the Murray River irrigation area, where Neilson was fruit picking in 1917. The poem was completed in 1919 and published in his *Ballad and Lyrical Poems* (1923). Neilson's comments, 'I was struck with the very beautiful light there is in May ... the dark green of the orange trees and beautiful sunlight give them enchantment hard to describe', explain the genesis of the poem. He partly attributes the mysticism of the poem to his reaction to a print of Botticelli's *Spring*. In the poem the young girl's instinctive response to the beautiful light that glows within the orange tree has sometimes been interpreted as youth's innate understanding of the natural beauty of life, an understanding that requires none of the hapless and complex explanations offered by the experience of age.

O'REILLY, BERNARD (1903–75), born Hartley, NSW, was a member of a pioneering family which opened up the McPherson Ranges on the border of NSW and Queensland. He became a national hero in 1937 when he single-handedly searched for and discovered a crashed plane on the Lamington Plateau and rescued the two survivors. He served in New Guinea and Borneo during the war, and subsequently ran a well-known tourist lodge in the Lamington National Park. He published a popular account of the exploits of his family and a record of the 1937 rescue, *Green Mountains* (1940), which was later produced as a film, *Sons of Matthew*; a collection of memories, *Cullenbong* (1944), which was later republished with *Green Mountains*; a collection of verse, *Over the Hills* (1963); and a book for children, *Wild River* (1949). A television documentary of his life was made in 1975.

O'REILLY, DOWELL (1865–1923), born Sydney, was in 1894 elected to the NSW parliament. He later taught at his old school, Sydney Grammar, and then became a public servant in Sydney. In 1914 his first wife died and in 1917 he married his cousin, Marie Miles. The correspondence of their courtship, *Dowell O'Reilly From His Letters* (1927), edited by his wife, reveals much of his personality and character. The contemporary and friend of Henry Lawson, John le Gay Brereton, and Mary Gilmore, O'Reilly was active in the Sydney literary scene. Because he was such a rigorous critic of his own writing, O'Reilly's output was small but impressive. His verse includes *Australian Poems* (1884) and *A Pedlar's Pack* (1888), both published under the pseudonym 'D'. His fiction includes the novel, *Tears and Triumph*, (1913), and *Five Corners* (1920), short stories of excellent quality. *The Prose and Verse of Dowell O'Reilly* (1924) is a composite selection of his work. His daughter is Eleanor Dark, the novelist.

O'REILLY, JOHN BOYLE (1844–90), born Drogheda, Ireland, was a printer and reporter in Ireland and England before becoming a Fenian. In 1863 he enlisted as a trooper in the British army for the express purpose of winning his fellow soldiers to the cause but was arrested in 1866. After stints in prisons at Millbank, Portsmouth and Dartmoor – there are Millbank scenes in his novel *Moondyne* (q.v., 1879) and the Dartmoor experiences are presented fictionally in *The King's Men* (1884) – O'Reilly was transported to WA in 1868 on the *Hougoumont*, the last convict ship to be sent to the Australian colonies; he helped edit the *Wild Goose*, a journal produced on board the ship. In 1869 he staged an extraordinary escape to America, where he became prominent in Boston as editor of the *Pilot* and as a publicist and lecturer on Irish affairs. In 1875 he was part of the daring plan organized by the Clan na Gael to rescue six Irish prisoners from Fremantle gaol. The plan was successfully carried out in 1876 and is celebrated in the Australian folk-song, 'The *Catalpa*'. O'Reilly's sudden death in 1890, from an accidental overdose of chloral, stunned the Irish community in Boston, where a memorial to him was erected as well as in his native Drogheda. The heroic dimension of his life is captured in J.J. Roche's hagiographic *Life of John Boyle O'Reilly* (1891), a work which incorporates his poems and speeches; in W.G. Schofield's anecdotal *Seek for a Hero: The Story of John Boyle O'Reilly* (1956) and in Paul Buddee's children's book, *The Escape of John O'Reilly* (1973). He was the model for Morres Blake in Rosa Praed's novel *Outlaw and Lawmaker* (1893). Like other transported political prisoners, including George Loveless, Thomas Muir and John Mitchel (q.v.), O'Reilly had a relatively brief sojourn in Australia and has a larger reputation overseas. In Ireland he is remembered as a folk hero, his poetry is included in standard anthologies of Irish political verse, and he himself edited an anthology, *The Poetry and Song of Ireland* (1887); in the USA he is remembered additionally as a fine sportsman who composed the important sporting treatise, *Ethics of Boxing and Manly Sport* (1888). He wrote several volumes of verse, including *Songs from*

the Southern Seas (1873), *Songs, Legends and Ballads* (1878), *The Statues in the Block* (1881), and *In Bohemia* (1886); in each there are poems relating to Australia, notably several verse narratives. His major contribution to Australian literature, however, was *Moondyne*, generally recognized as the first WA novel and significant in convict literature (q.v.). Although clumsily constructed and melodramatic, *Moondyne*, the story of a convict who escapes with the help of Aborigines and eventually returns in disguise to WA as a penal reformer, is of interest for the way O'Reilly meshes his own experiences with those of the convict bushranger 'Moondyne Joe' (q.v.), and for the views it offers on transportation from the point of view of an idealistic ex-convict.

Orford, Emily, see *Forger's Wife, The*

'ORION', see **HORNE, R.H.**

O'SHAUGHNESSY, EDWARD (1801–40), born Ireland, was transported for false pretences in 1824. In Sydney he worked out his sentence as a reporter on the pro-convict *Sydney Gazette*, which he edited 1833–35; subsequently he wrote for its rival, the *Sydney Herald*. During his time with the *Gazette* he wrote lyrical and satiric verse as well as some of the first Australian theatre reviews.

O'SHAUGHNESSY, PETER (1923–   ), actor and producer, has produced numerous Australian plays, including John Courtney's 'Off to the Diggings' and James Tucker's *Jemmy Green in Australia* at the Adelaide Festival in 1966. He has played the major Shakespearean tragic roles both in Australia and overseas and is well known for his one-act show, 'Diary of a Madman', an adaptation of Gogol's short story. In 1968 he collaborated with Graeme Inson and Russel Ward in *The Restless Years*; a lavishly-illustrated anthology of documents, ballads, poems, letters, extracts from journals, newspaper reports and advertisements, *The Restless Years* ranges from 1770 to 1901 and is based on an award-winning television programme, produced by O'Shaughnessy. In the 1950s he also wrote and produced with Jeff Underhill a popular children's play, 'The Bunyip and the Satellite'.

O'SULLIVAN, EDWARD WILLIAM (1846–1910), journalist, trade unionist and politician, was born at Launceston and was apprenticed to the printing trade with the Hobart *Mercury* at an early age. He subsequently became a reporter, moved to Sydney in 1869, and returned to Hobart in 1871 to found the *Tasmanian Tribune*. In 1874 he sold out to work as a journalist on the mainland. Editor of the *Evening Tribune-City News* (1874), *St Arnaud Mercury* (1875–78), *Democrat* (1884) and *Freeman's Journal* (1896–99), he also worked for the *Argus*, Sydney *Daily Telegraph* and *Australian Star*. He was a member of the NSW parliament 1885–1910. One of the creators of the Protectionist Party of the 1880s, O'Sullivan was Minister for Public Works 1899–1904 and was responsible for significant development of the railways and tramway systems. The author of two melodramas, 'The Eureka Rebellion' (1907) and 'Cooee' (1906), both of which drew on his earlier play, 'Eureka Stockade' (1898), and co-author with Arthur Wright of another, 'Keane of Kalgoorlie' (1908), O'Sullivan also published a novel in the 1890s, *Esperanza: A Tale of Three Colonies*, and a collection of sketches, stories and speeches, *Under the Southern Cross* (1906). Bruce Mansfield has written his biography, *Australian Democrat* (1965).

Other Times, see **LAWLER, RAY**

OTTLEY, REGINALD LESLIE (1909–), born London, came to Australia at the age of fifteen. He has travelled widely in Australia and the Pacific and has worked as a seaman, farm-worker, cattle-drover, horse-breaker, racehorse trainer and property manager. He has written several books for children, of which the most notable is his trilogy dealing with the effects of isolation and the harsh outback environment on a sensitive boy, *By the Sandhills of Yamboorah* (1965), *The Roan Colt of Yamboorah* (1966) and *Rain Comes to Yamboorah* (1967). The first volume won a *New York Herald Tribune* prize in 1966. His other children's books are *Giselle* (1968), *The Bates Family* (1969), *Jim Grey of Moonbah* (1970), *The War on William Street* (1971), *No More Tomorrow* (1971), *A Word About Horses* (1973) and *Mum's Place* (1974). He has also written short stories for children, *Brumbie Dust* (1969); an adult novel, *Stampede* (1961); and a radio play, 'The Feather Shoes' (1964).

Our Glass, a Melbourne magazine associated with the rise of the 'New Australian Poetry', was edited by Kris Hemensley. It contains a selection of the poetry from the La Mama poetry workshops and was published 1968–69.

Our New Selection, the second 'Steele Rudd' (q.v.) volume sketching selection life, was published in 1903. The sequel to *On Our Selection* (1899), *Our New Selection* recounts the improvement in fortunes of the Rudd family (q.v.), reflected in the sale of Shingle Hut and the move to the larger holding of Saddletop. Dad's increasing prosperity does not, however,

prevent him from continuing to fall victim to predatory neighbours and storekeepers. The tone of *Our New Selection* is more consistently comic than that of *On Our Selection*, but it was not until later sketches of the Rudd family that the transformation of Dad and Dave into figures of farce was consolidated, although Norman Lindsay's drawing of Dave published in *Our New Selection* influenced the depiction of Dave as a country bumpkin in later stage and film presentations of the original *On Our Selection*.

Out of the Silence, see **COX, ERLE; Science Fiction**

Outback denotes the remote and sparsely-settled inland districts of Australia but does not indicate such extreme remoteness as is implied in a similar expression, the 'Never Never' (q.v.). The noun 'Outback' and the adverb or adjective 'outback' occur frequently in Australian writing in the latter part of the nineteenth century, e.g. in 'Rolf Boldrewood''s novel, *Ups and Downs* (1878) and in Henry Lawson's celebrated poem, 'Out Back', but are much more commonplace in this century; the original, semi-colloquial expression is now an orthodox term. Although the Outback has been widely romanticized in Australian writing, especially by such bush balladists as A.B. Paterson and Will Ogilvie, the other side of the picture is forcibly given by Lawson, who concludes his 'Some Popular Australian Mistakes' with the wish 'that Australian writers would leave off trying to make a paradise out of the Outback Hell'. Thomas Keneally's *Outback* (1983) records his impressions of the Northern Territory, its people and legends.

Outback Marriage, An, see **PATERSON, A.B.**

Outback Press was formed in Melbourne in 1973 by Colin Talbot, Morris Schwarz, Mark Gillespie and Alfred Milgrom. Intent on publishing books of interest to young, thinking people it has produced e.g. *Applestealers*, *Mother I'm Rooted* (q.v.), *The Collapsible Man* (see Laurie Clancy) and *The Outback Reader: A Collection of Australian Contemporary and Experimental Short Fiction*. An associate company is Dingo Books.

Outbreak of Love, a novel by Martin Boyd (q.v.), was published in 1957. The third in a tetralogy dealing with the Langton family, the narrative is mainly concerned with Diana von Flugel, aunt to Guy Langton, the novel's occasional narrator, and daughter to Alice of *The Cardboard Crown* (1952). Diana's twenty-three-year marriage to a feckless musical genius, Wolfgang ('Wolfie') von Flugel, is at a point of crisis, firstly because she has discovered that her husband has a vulgar mistress, and secondly because she is attracted to Russell Lockwood, an agreeable, cultivated dilettante. Diana's plans to leave for Europe with Russell are frustrated by Wolfie's continuing dependence on her, by her unwillingness to embarrass her recently-married daughter Josie, and by the declaration of war in 1914.

OUTHWAITE, IDA RENTOUL (1889–1960), born Melbourne, daughter of John Laurence Rentoul and sister of Annie Rattray Rentoul, became well known as an illustrator of children's books, especially fairy stories. She illustrated her mother's (Annie Isobel Rentoul) collection of verse, *Mollie's Staircase* (1906), contributed to *At the Sign of the Sword* (1915) with her father, mother and sister, and illustrated numerous books by her sister, Annie Rentoul, as well as some of those of Tarella Quin. Three sumptuously-produced books in particular gave scope to her delicate work, *Fairyland of Ida Rentoul Outhwaite* (1926), which included verses and stories by Annie Rentoul and stories by Grenbry Outhwaite, Ida's husband; *The Enchanted Forest* (1921), to which Grenbry Outhwaite contributed the text; and *Elves and Fairies* (1916), which included verses by Annie Rentoul. She also published and illustrated a collection of her own verse for children, *A Bunch of Wild Flowers* (1933), and a story, *Sixpence to Spend* (1935). Her paintings are represented in galleries in Melbourne and Hobart. Although Ida Outhwaite's illustrations are now dated to some extent by their commitment to the sentimental, conventional standards of their day, they are finely executed, detailed and imaginative and have a definite period charm.

Outlaw and Lawmaker, see **PRAED, ROSA**

Outlook, a bi-monthly socialist journal edited by Helen Palmer (q.v.), ran 1957–70. Although the magazine's main concerns were political, it included some theatrical notices and reviews of cultural studies as well as attracting such writers as Russel Ward, Merv Lilley, Jack Lindsay, Len Fox and Ian Turner. Some of Helen Palmer's writing for the journal was reprinted in *Helen Palmer's Outlook* (1982), edited by Doreen Bridges.

Over the Sliprails, a collection of seventeen stories by Henry Lawson (q.v.), was published in 1900; in the same year it was combined with *On the Track*. Lawson's fourth collection of stories and sketches, *Over the Sliprails* in-

cludes material written in the early 1890s as well as at the end of the decade. Its range encompasses an Arvie Aspinall story; 'The Hero of Redclay', one of Lawson's longest stories, which grew out of his attempt to write a play for Bland Holt; stories which focus on the experiences of well-known Lawson characters, e.g. Mitchell, Steelman, Stiffner; and stories which reflect his travels to Bourke, NZ and WA.

Overland, one of Australia's major contemporary literary magazines, began publication in Melbourne in 1954. It originally incorporated the *Realist Writer*, a left-wing journal which had begun publication under editor, Bill Wannan, in 1952 but it severed its connection with the Realist Writers groups after the Hungarian uprisings of 1956. The original role of *Overland* was, in Ian Turner's words, 'to develop a radical tradition, including within that the Marxist tradition; to encourage a working-class audience and working-class writers . . . and to take part in polemics against the Right'. *Overland*'s successful struggle to survive the factional difficulties and lack of government patronage in its early years was largely due to the energy and devotion of its original and long-standing editor, Stephen Murray-Smith (q.v.) and Ian Turner. Others involved in its continued existence have been John McLaren, Barrie Reid, Nancy Keesing, Leonie Sandercock, Ken Gott, Gwen Harwood and Martin Duwell. *Overland* gives expression to a diversity of literary and social attitudes and opinions but its overall tone and spirit reflect its motto, 'Temper democratic, bias Australian', derived from Joseph Furphy's description of *Such is Life* (1903). *An Overland Muster* (1965), an anthology of writing from the pages of *Overland* between 1954 and 1964, was edited by Murray-Smith.

Overlander, a parallel term to drover (q.v.), derives from 'overland', an English word meaning simply 'over the land', and is a term peculiar to Australia. An 'overlander' is defined in H.W. Haygarth's *Recollections of Bush Life in Australia* (1848) as 'one who makes long expeditions from one colony to another with stock, either for the purpose of finding new pasture land on which to establish himself, or to take advantage of a favourable market'. The earliest overlanders, notably Charles Bonney, Joseph Hawdon and Alexander Mollison, who followed in the tracks of the explorers had, by the early 1830s, reached the Murray and Monaro regions and, by the late 1830s, the Port Phillip and Adelaide districts. In the second half of the nineteenth century the real sagas of the overlanders occurred with the stocking of the vast runs in the Cooper's Creek area, northern Queensland, the Gulf country and the Kimberley region of north-west WA. Among these élite and intrepid stockmen were D'Arcy Uhr, Sydney and Alfred Prout (commemorated in Mary Hannay Foott's ballad, 'Where the Pelican Builds Her Nest'), Nat Buchanan (q.v.), Sam Croaker, John Costello and the Duracks. In addition to Haygarth's book the overlander is discussed in such memoirs and historical writings as Sir George Grey's *Journals of Two Expeditions of Discovery* (1841), Frederic de Brebant Cooper's *Wild Adventures in Australia* (1857), C. Wade Browne's *Overlanding in Australia* (1868), Gordon Buchanan's *Packhorse and Waterhole* (1933), Ernestine Hill's *The Territory* (1951), Joseph Hawdon's *The Journal of a Journey from New South Wales to Adelaide* (first published 1952), Mary Durack's *Kings in Grass Castles* (q.v., 1959), Garry Hogg's *The Overlanders* (1961), H.M. Barker's *Droving Days* (1966), Eleanor Smith's *The Beckoning West: The Story of H.S. Trotman and the Canning Stock Route* (1966), Margaret Ford's *Beyond the Furtherest Fences* (1966), Jeff Carter's *In the Tracks of the Cattle* (1968), and Alexander Fullerton Mollison's *An Overlanding Diary* (first published 1980), from the original manuscript presented to the State Library of Victoria in 1886. The overlander is represented in many works of fiction including Alexander Harris's *The Emigrant Family* (1849), Marcus Clarke's *Old Tales of a Young Country* (1871), Vance Palmer's *The World of Men* (1915), and Donald Stuart's *The Driven* (q.v., 1961). He is also depicted in Australian short stories and poetry, including A.B. Paterson's 'With the Cattle', Will Ogilvie's 'From the Gulf' and Roland Robinson's 'The Drovers'. Traditional overlanding ballads and folk-songs include 'A Thousand Miles Away' and 'The Overlander'; the latter celebrates the overlander's free life and probably dates from the 1840s. Ron Edwards published *The Overlander Song Book* (1971), not all the songs of which are concerned with the overlanders. An Australian film, *The Overlanders* (1946), featured the driving of 85 000 head of cattle from the north of WA to the Queensland coast in 1942 as part of the wartime scorched earth policy. One of S.T. Gill's famous water-colours, *Overlanders* (1865) depicts two men on horseback moving across a great flat stretch of semi-arid country with their dogs and packhorses behind them. 'The Overland' is a term that has come to be applied generally to the vast outback districts through which the stock routes ran, and to the stock routes themselves, e.g. the Canning, the Great North Road and the Georgina. *Overland* is one of Australia's distinguished literary journals.

Oxalis Cottage, see **CAMPBELL, ROSS**

Oxford Book of Australasian Verse The, see **Anthologies**

Oxford History of Australian Literature, The, edited by Leonie Kramer, was published in 1981. The history comprises an introduction by Kramer, surveys of fiction (by Adrian Mitchell), drama (by Terry Sturm) and poetry (by Vivian Smith) and includes a descriptive bibliography (by Joy Hooton).

Oxford University Press, see **University Presses**

OXLEY, JOHN (?1783–1828), born Yorkshire, England, entered the Royal Navy as a midshipman and travelled to Australia in HMS *Buffalo* in 1802. He was appointed surveyor-general of NSW in 1812 and undertook in 1817–18 a series of exploratory journeys in the Lachlan, Macquarie, Castlereagh, Peel and Hastings Rivers regions of NSW. Unable to trace fully the Macquarie and Lachlan Rivers, Oxley subscribed to the theory of a vast inland sea, a theory later disproved by the journeys of Charles Sturt. Oxley's *Journals of Two Expeditions into the Interior of New South Wales* (1820), with its detailed description of the colony's interior, was the forerunner of the large body of later exploration literature. His further expeditions led to the discovery of the Tweed and Brisbane Rivers and the establishment of a penal settlement at Moreton Bay. His name is commemorated in the township Oxley near the junction of the Lachlan and Murrumbidgee Rivers and in the Oxley highway, which runs from Nevertire to Port Macquarie. A contemporary account of Oxley's exploration achievements was in Barron Field's *Geographical Memoirs on New South Wales* (1825).

Oz, see **NEVILLE, RICHARD**

P

Pacific Highway, see **WILDING, MICHAEL**

PACKER, Sir **FRANK** (1906–74), born Sydney, a well-known and influential media proprietor, was the son of Robert Clyde Packer (1879–1934), managing director of *Smith's Weekly*, 1919–33, and general manager of Associated Newspapers, 1931–33. Frank Packer began his career as a cadet reporter on his father's newspaper, the *Daily Guardian*, in 1923. He had become general advertising manager by 1927 and in 1933, with E.G. Theodore, founded Australia's best-known women's magazine, the *Australian Women's Weekly*. Packer was managing director of Consolidated Press from 1936 and chairman from 1957. The group, now Australian Consolidated Press, publishes a range of popular magazines such as the *Bulletin, Cleo,* the *Australian Home Journal* and the *Australian Women's Weekly*, as well as a number of suburban and country newspapers, and holds large interests in radio stations in Victoria and WA. The group also owned the Sydney *Daily Telegraph* (q.v.), and the *Sunday Telegraph*, although these were sold to Rupert Murdoch's News Ltd in 1972. Chairman of television corporations in Melbourne and Sydney and credited with great right-wing political influence, Packer was also well known in racing and yachting circles. An authorized biography by Richard Whitington was published in 1971. Sir Frank Packer's two sons, Clyde Packer (1935–), and Kerry Packer (1937–), have also become well-known figures. Clyde Packer was a member of the NSW Legislative Council, 1964–76, and from 1959 was involved as administrator and part-owner of his father's publishing empire. From 1970 he was joint manager of the television corporations but resigned from all his positions in the Packer industries 1972–73. He now lives in Los Angeles, where he owns an entertainment agency and a magazine, *New Times*. Owner and founder of the Sydney magazine, *Forum*, he has also been a major supporter of *Quadrant*. Kerry Packer has succeeded to his father's publishing and television empire, and has extended the group's interests into mining, real estate, film production and leisure industries. In 1977 he became a controversial figure in his own right when he launched World Series cricket.

PACKER, RICHARD (1935–), was born NZ, where he worked mostly as a journalist. Since his arrival in Australia in 1966 he has worked in advertising. He has published two collections of poetry, *Prince of the Plague Country* (1964) and *Being out of Order* (1972), which included his verse play for radio, 'The Uncommercial Traveller'. He has also written two other plays, *The Powerhouse* (1972) and 'The Applicant'.

Paddy Malone is a 'new chum' Irishman who in several Australian folk-songs (q.v.) and ballads chronicles his misfortunes after emigrating to Australia; like Billy Barlow and Jemmy Green, he probably originated as a stage character. Two of the Paddy Malone songs, 'Paddy Malone in Australia' and 'Paddy's Letter, 1857', were included in A.B. Paterson's *Old Bush Songs* (1905) and date from the second half of the nineteenth century.

Paesa Fortunata (1981, published in English 1985), a novel in Italian by Rosa Cappiello who was born in Naples and came to Australia as a migrant in 1971, won the 1982 Italian literary prize, the Premio Calabria. The novel, whose title means 'Lucky Country', a phrase often used ironically of Australia by migrants, gives a realistic, even grim, picture of the migrant experience, especially for women. It traces the lives of the narrator, Rosa, and a group of migrant women whom she meets in a hostel on her arrival in Sydney in the early 1970s.

PAGE, GEOFF (1940–), born Grafton, NSW, was educated in Canberra. He has published several volumes of poetry, *The Question in Two Poets* (1971 with Philip Roberts), *Smalltown Memorials* (1975), *Collecting the Weather* (1978), *Cassandra Paddocks* (1980) and *Clairvoyant in Autumn* (1983). He has a dry, spare, unpretentious style, often made striking by vivid imagery. Page also edited *Shadows from Wire* 1983, an anthology of recent poetry about the First World War and illustrated by original photographs from the Australian War Memorial collections.

Pageant, see **'LANCASTER, G.B.'**

Palmer, one of Australia's most notable goldfields, was opened up after the discovery of gold in 1873 by prospector James Venture Mulligan on the banks of the Palmer River in the hinterland of Cooktown in northern Queensland. The wildest of all Australian diggings, the Palmer was especially notable for the large number of Chinese who gathered there and for the depredations on them by the white diggers. The history of the Palmer is recorded in Hector Holthouse's *River of Gold* (1967) but much of its atmosphere is caught in such traditional songs as 'The Old Palmer Song', 'The Golden Gullies of the Palmer' and 'The Palmer Days'.

PALMER, AILEEN (1915–), daughter of Vance and Nettie Palmer and sister of Helen Palmer, was born in London and educated at the University of Melbourne. She served with the British medical unit and medical service of the International Brigade in Spain 1936–38 and with the London Auxiliary Ambulance Service, 1939–43. She has contributed verse to such journals as *Overland, Meanjin, Southerly, Vietnam Advances* and *Realist Writer* and has published one collection, *World Without Strangers?* (1964).

PALMER-ARCHER, LAURA (1864–1929), who also used the pseudonym 'Bushwoman', was the sister of E.F. O'Ferrall and the wife of a station-owner. She contributed short stories to the *Australasian* and the *Australian Town and Country Journal* and published two works of fiction, *A Bush Honeymoon and Other Stories* (1904) and *Racing in the Never Never* (1899). Lively, humorous and written in a direct, unpretentious style, her stories vividly convey the dramas and hazards, tedium and deprivations, personalities, idioms and social convention of bush life in the 1890s.

PALMER, HELEN (1917–79), daughter of Vance and Nettie Palmer and sister of Aileen Palmer, graduated from the University of Melbourne and was a high-schoolteacher and writer. During the Second World War she was in charge of education services by WAAAF personnel throughout Australia. Her published writings are *Australian Teacher in China* (1953), which records a visit to China in 1952; *Beneath the Southern Cross* (1954), a story about Eureka that was later serialized on ABC radio's children's session; and, with Jessie MacLeod, a series of Australian historical texts directed mainly at schools (1954, 1956, 1961, 1964). Other school texts that she wrote independently are *Our Sugar* (1949), *Fencing Australia* (1961) and *'Banjo' Paterson* (1966). Her poem, 'Ballad of 1891', became a highlight of the musical, *Reedy River* (1953). She also founded and edited the journal, *Outlook: An Australian Socialist Review;* some of her writing for the journal is collected in *Helen Palmer's Outlook* (1982) ed. Doreen Bridges. She was a member of the Communist Party of Australia until expelled in 1957.

PALMER, NETTIE (1885–1964), was born Janet Gertrude Higgins at Bendigo, Victoria, the daughter of John Higgins, an accountant. She graduated from the University of Melbourne in 1909 and in 1910 left for Europe to study languages, first in London, then in Marburg and Paris. She returned to Australia in 1911, completed her MA degree at the University of Melbourne in 1912 and left again for London in 1914 to marry Vance Palmer (q.v.). Their marriage was to be a remarkable literary partnership, of great importance to Australia's cultural life. Although Nettie Palmer's life centred mainly on her husband and her two daughters, Aileen and Helen, she made an independent contribution and there were important distinctions between her work and her husband's. At a personal level she seems to have been at least as influential as Vance Palmer and in particular her relationship with 'Henry Handel Richardson' was important. Her prolific literary journalism, especially during the 1920s and 1930s, when Vance Palmer was concentrating on creative work and when Australian publishing and literary debate were at a low ebb, was of inestimable significance. She moved easily in international literary circles and in 1935 she attended the Writers' Congress in Paris. There she made contact with the Australian writer, Christina Stead (q.v.), and with many international writers, including André Gide, Paul Elvard, André Malraux and E.M. Forster. Only a few of her penetrating impressions there are recorded in her published journal extracts, *Fourteen Years* (q.v., 1948), although others survive in manuscript form. Nettie Palmer was also in the forefront of the Palmers' practical work for refugees and immigrants, especially during the Spanish Civil War; two pamphlets express her urgent concern, *Spanish Struggle* (1936) and *Australians in Spain* (?1937). In addition, she frequently worked closely with Vance Palmer in research for his novels and in particular on the 1937 abridgement of Joseph Furphy's *Such is Life*. Like her husband, she was a familiar broadcaster on ABC radio in the 1940s and 1950s and on several occasions lectured in Australian literature for the CLF. After her husband's death in 1959, she continued to write, concentrating on her projected autobiography, but rapid deterioration of her health prevented its completion.

Her published work consists of two volumes of poetry, *The South Wind* (1914) and *Shadowy Paths* (1915); a critical appreciation, *Modern Australian Literature 1900–1923* (q.v., 1924); a collection of essays, *Talking It Over* (1932); a memoir of her uncle, Henry Bournes Higgins (1931); *Fourteen Years : Extracts from a Private Journal, 1925–1939* (1948); a study of 'Henry Handel Richardson' (1950) and, with Victor

Kennedy, one of Bernard O'Dowd (1954); and an unusual account of the Dandenong country near Melbourne which mingles personal reminiscence and history, *The Dandenongs* (1952). Another account, of Green Island, Queensland, that she worked on in 1932 and that has been described as 'a minor Australian *Walden'*, was never published. She also edited two collections of short stories, *An Australian Story Book* (1928) and *Coast to Coast* (1950) and, with Frances Fraser, a collection of women's writings, *Centenary Gift Book* (1934). In addition, she edited or introduced several other works by Australian writers. In 1953 letters she received from 'Henry Handel Richardson' were published, and in 1977 Vivian Smith edited a selection of her and Vance Palmer's letters, 1915–63. She was also editor of the periodical *Birth* for a short time. In 1959 when *Meanjin* published an issue in tribute to the Palmers, some attempts were made to assess her contribution, and Drusilla Modjeska has written extensively on her difficulties and achievements in *Exiles at Home* (1981).

Nettie Palmer's creativity found its fullest scope in her prose work; her poems, mainly simple lyrics, are now interesting mainly as period pieces. Apart from *Talking It Over* and the pioneer study, *Modern Australian Literature 1900–1923*, little of her criticism has appeared in book form. Papers that she contributed articles to in the 1920s included the *Brisbane Courier, Argus,* Brisbane *Telegraph, Bulletin, Woman's Mirror* and Brisbane *Sunday Mail*. Her personal column, entitled 'A Reader's Notebook', appeared in *All About Books,* 1928–38, but many of her most extended pieces were published in the *Illustrated Tasmanian Mail,* 1927–33. Written with ease, humour and perception on contemporary as on classical literature, on international and on Australian writers, her notices display a fine sense of proportion, independence and integrity. A keen student of comparative literature, she knew French, German and Greek, and later studied Spanish to have access to South American literature. A vigorous proponent of Australian writing, she contributed five articles on 'Henry Handel Richardson'; other writers who received substantial appreciations, some for the first time, include Miles Franklin, Katharine Susannah Prichard, Paul Wenz, Joseph Furphy, 'Price Warung', Barbara Baynton, Shaw Neilson, Bernard O'Dowd, Henry Tate, 'M. Barnard Eldershaw', Martin Boyd, Frank Dalby Davison, R.D. FitzGerald and Dowell O'Reilly. Her collection, *An Australian Story Book,* brings together work by well-known and lesser-known writers and reflects her desire to foster interest in disparate Australian writing. The commissioned study of Henry Bournes Higgins reflects

her personal piety for his memory and her sense of shared values. Her *Henry Handel Richardson* (1950), which was the first full-length study of the novelist, written after an association of twenty-five years, is revealing as biography and deals with issues that are still central. The account of Bernard O'Dowd's life and work, a reshaping of the incomplete manuscript left by Victor Kennedy, is an invaluable one, especially of his origins and influences. Perhaps her most enduring work is *Fourteen Years,* a unique document in Australian literature that moves easily from personal reminiscence to accounts of literary and personal meetings in Australia and overseas. Striking features of the work are the easy, conversational tone and graphic, individual portraits, the revealing presentation of varying cultural milieux and the impression throughout of a distinguished, illuminating mind.

PALMER, VANCE (1885–1959), was born at Bundaberg, Queensland, the youngest in a family of eight. His father was a schoolmaster with diverse literary interests and his childhood was spent in a succession of Queensland country towns. He rejected the idea of a university education, spent some time as a private secretary, and in 1905 left for London, where he stayed for two years earning his living as a 'Grub Street hack'. He returned to Australia by way of Finland, Russia and Japan, tried salesmanship and schoolteaching, and spent some time as tutor, book-keeper and drover in north-west Queensland. Five of his early novels and many of his short stories reflect these experiences. In 1910 he revisited London, this time making contact with several British writers, most importantly with A.R. Orage, the editor of the *New Age,* who encouraged his writing and influenced his social philosophy. He returned briefly to Australia in 1912, travelling through the USA and Mexico, which was at that time in revolution. In 1914 he married Janet Higgins (see Palmer, Nettie) in London. Before their return to Australia in September 1915, Palmer had begun his literary career with collections of poetry, *The Forerunners* (1915), and short stories, *The World of Men* (1915), and with numerous articles for the *New Age,* the *Manchester Guardian Fortnightly,* and the *British Review*. His return to Australia at the height of imperialist fervour generated by the war quickened his commitment to his own culture and his concern for the development and preservation of its distinctive identity. A vigorous opponent of conscription, he nevertheless enlisted in the AIF in 1918 and was sent overseas, but was too late to see action. For the next decade, spent at Emerald, Palmer was actively engaged in the cause of Australian literary nationalism as an essayist and reviewer and as a leading member of the Pioneer Players (q.v.). This period also saw the publication of another collection of poetry, *The Camp* (1920), a collection of plays, *The Black Horse and Other Plays* (1924), and five novels: *The Shantykeeper's Daughter* (1920), *The Boss of Killara* (1922), *The Enchanted Island* (1923), *The Outpost* (1924) and *Cronulla* (1924). Both *The Enchanted Island* and *The Outpost* were published under the pseudonym, 'Rann Daly' and *The Outpost* was rewritten and re-published as *Hurricane* in 1934. Palmer later dropped his first four novels from his list of publications. In 1925 the Palmers left for Cal-oundra, a small fishing port in Queensland. Freelance literary journalism, largely under-taken by Nettie Palmer, provided a living, while Vance l'almer worked on a group of novels: *The Man Hamilton* (1928), *Men are Human* (1930), *The Passage* (q.v., 1930), *Day-break* (q.v., 1932) and *The Swayne Family* (1934). In order to educate their daughters, Aileen and Helen, the family returned to Mel-bourne, 1929–32, spent some time at Green Island, Queensland, in 1932 and then at Ka-lorama, Victoria, 1932–35, before revisiting Europe in 1935–36, where they witnessed the beginning of the Spanish Civil War. Apart from another visit to Europe in 1955 and winter holidays in Queensland, Palmer lived in Melbourne for the rest of his life. By the 1940s his reputation as Australia's pre-eminent cul-tural figure was well-established, reinforced by his regular talks and reviews for the ABC. He served on the CLF, 1942–53. His other publi-cations are the novels, *Legend for Sanderson* (1937), *Cyclone* (1947) and the trilogy, *Gol-conda* (1948), *Seedtime* (1957) and *The Big Fellow* (1959) (see *Golconda* trilogy); the col-lections of short stories, *Separate Lives* (1931), *Sea and Spinifex* (1934), *Let the Birds Fly* (1955) and the reprinted selection, *The Rainbow-Bird and Other Stories* (1957); the plays, *Ances-tors*, in *Best Australian One-Act Plays* (1937) and *Hail Tomorrow* (1947); and the essays and studies, *National Portraits* (q.v., 1940), *A.G. Stephens: His Life and Work* (1941), *Frank Wilmot (Furnley Maurice)* (1942), *Louis Esson and the Australian Theatre* (1948) and *The Legend of the Nineties* (q.v., 1954). He also edited a collection of short stories, *Coast to Coast* (1945); was instrumental in both the re-issue of Joseph Furphy's *Such is Life* in 1917 and the abridged edition (1937); and compiled a collection of bush ballads, *Old Australian Bush Ballads* (1951). *Intimate Portraits* (1969), ed. H.P. Heseltine, is a selection of his essays and talks, and a selection of his and Nettie Palmer's letters, edited by Vivian Smith, was published in 1977. Apart from Heseltine's small

selection, no attempt has been made to collect or select from his vast number of essays for such journals as *Fellowship,* the *Bulletin,* the *ABC Weekly, Birth,* the *New Triad* and *Mean-jin,* or from his talks and reviews broadcast for the ABC, 1941–59. In 1959, when *Meanjin* published a special issue in tribute to Vance and Nettie Palmer, many of the writers for whom Palmer had been an important influence expressed their appreciation. His preoccupa-tions and achievements are explored in Harry Heseltine's *Vance Palmer* (1970), Vivian Smith's *Vance and Nettie Palmer* (1975) and David Walker's *Dream and Disillusion* (1976).

The pervading theme of all Palmer's work is his firm belief in an 'Australia of the spirit' and in literature as its influential and lasting expression. For Palmer, Australian literature was, or should be, an integral part of the fabric of national life, an expression of its inner spirit and values, its distinctive 'undertones'. As he asserted in an early essay, writers 'must be at one with the purposes and aspirations of the people and their hearts must beat in unison with them'. A profound admirer of Henry Lawson, Barbara Baynton, Bernard O'Dowd and Joseph Furphy, he saw the 1890s as the period in which their national identity was first revealed to Australians, primarily through the work of the *Bulletin* writers. He perceived this revealed national consciousness as robust, mas-culine, close to nature and physical work, dem-ocratic, taciturn, sardonic, frugal, unsentimental and communal; he rapidly saw the communal concept as a threatened ideal, subject to erosion by the materialism of the expanding cities. These values inform his own work. Five of his first novels, *The Shanty Keeper's Daughter, The Boss of Killara, Cronulla, The Man Hamilton* and *Men Are Human*, are station novels, set in the Queensland outback, although only the last two seriously engage with his subject. These begin to develop the elements of Palmer's best work: controlled narrative technique, unpreten-tious prose style, lyrical evocation of place, and preference for psychological rather than physical action, all of which combine to form an un-derstated realism. *The Passage,* set in a small Queensland fishing port similar to Caloundra, brings these elements to full realization; his best-known novel, it is distinguished by the gradual lyrical development of the numinous relationship between the central figure, Lew Calloway, and his natural surroundings. *Day-break* has the dramatic unity and achieved insights of the best of Palmer's short stories. The complexities of family relationships which figure in *The Passage,* are also the subject of *The Swayne Family,* Palmer's one novel with an urban setting, although explored here more thoroughly and subtly. *Legend for Sanderson* and

Cyclone are less assured works, but in the *Golconda* trilogy Palmer attacks his socio-cultural themes from a panoramic conspectus and with renewed, shaping purpose. Palmer's talent is most at home in his short stories. 'The Foal', 'The Rainbow Bird', 'The Red Truck', 'Mathieson's Wife', 'The Birthday' and 'Greta' provide ideal scope for his characteristic style of ironic detachment and controlled tone. They achieve a muted realism and deceptively artless effect which is similar to Henry Lawson's. Several of his most effective stories concentrate on a crucial childhood initiation into the complex adult world. His verse, characterized by simple forms and generalized emotions, clearly fails as a means of giving rein to his keenest concerns, although 'The Farmer Remembers the Somme' is one of Australia's most effective war poems. His plays, mostly set in the outback, are marred by obviously manipulated plots and stilted dialogue; his most ambitious, *Hail Tomorrow,* is an attempt to express the meaning of William Lane's career and the 1890s. Palmer's wide-ranging literary journalism displays tact, discrimination and practical, intuitive evaluations rather than critical theories or strikingly original perceptions. His series of books on key national figures written between 1940 and 1954, and especially his seminal *The Legend of the Nineties,* reflect his preoccupation with the inner life of Australia and his concern to preserve its distinctive democratic quality.

Pandemonium, a monthly magazine published in Melbourne and edited anonymously by Mervyn Skipper (q.v.), ran 1934–35. A response to the unstable world situation of the time, *Pandemonium* satirized a wide range of contemporary topics from capitalism and imperialism to Australian censorship and communist peace movements. Striking features of the journal are Skipper's bold cartoons and the prominence given to the views of such controversial figures as the psychologist, G.W.R. Southern, and the economist, Major Douglas. *Pandemonium* also included book reviews, theatrical notices, articles on Australian literature and short stories by Skipper, Percy Leason and Vance and Nettie Palmer.

PANKHURST, ADELA (1888–1961), the daughter of Emmeline Pankhurst, was born in England and became prominent in the suffragette movement and in socialist agitation before leaving for Australia in 1914. One of the most formidable leaders of the feminist movement in Australia and a prominent socialist, Pankhurst threw her energies into the organization of the Women's Political Association, renamed the Women's Peace Army, and the fight against conscription. In 1917 she left the Army to join the Victorian Socialist Party, wrote frequently for the *Socialist* and edited *Dawn,* a socialist newspaper for children. In the same year she married Tom Walsh, a militant trade-unionist. The founding of the Communist Party of Australia engaged the energies of Pankhurst and Walsh for a time, but they were soon alienated by the Party's ideological disputes and subsequently became staunchly anti-communist. Pankhurst's ideas found their widest scope during her association with the Australian Women's Guild of Empire, a middle-class organization whose newspaper, the *Empire Gazette,* she edited. She visited Japan in 1939 with her husband, joined with him in urging closer ties between Australia and Japan, and was interned during the Second World War. No stranger to imprisonment, having spent time in Strangeways and Pentridge, she was released when she went on a hunger strike. Pankhurst published a play, *Betrayed* (1917), which is a propagandist, anti-conscription piece; and four political pamphlets, *Put up the Sword* (1915), *After the War, What?* (1917), *Conditions in Japan* (1940) and *What We Should Know about the Orient* (1940). Her life and achievements are described by David Mitchell in *The Fighting Pankhursts* (1967).

Paper Chase, The, see **PORTER, HAL**

Paperback Poets, a series initiated by the University of Queensland Press in 1970, presented a wide range of contemporary Australian poetry. The first series of eighteen books, mostly edited by Roger McDonald, was published 1970–73, and comprised David Malouf's *Bicycle and Other Poems* (1970), Michael Dransfield's *Streets of the Long Voyage* (1970), Rodney Hall's *Heaven, in a Way* (1970), Andrew Taylor's *The Cool Change* (1970), Geoff Page and Philip Roberts's *Two Poets: The Question and Single Eye* (1971), J.S. Harry's *The Deer under the Skin* (1971), R.A. Simpson's *Diver* (1972), Dransfield's *The Inspector of Tides* (1972), Rhyll McMaster's *The Brineshrimp* (1972), Richard Tipping's *Soft Riots* (1972), Thomas Shapcott's *Begin with Walking* (1972), Leon Slade's *Slade's Anatomy of the Horse* (1972), David Lake's *Hornpipes & Funerals* (1973), Judith Rodriguez's *Nu-Plastik Fanfare Red and Other Poems* (1973), Andrew Taylor's *Ice Fishing* (1973), Rodney Hall's *A Soapbox Omnibus* (1973), Manfred Jurgensen's *Signs and Voices* (1973), and Vicki Viidikas's *Condition Red* (1973). *The First Paperback Poets Anthology,* edited by McDonald, was published in 1974.

The second series of nineteen books was published 1974–81 and comprised Jennifer Maiden's *Tactics* (1974), Paul Kavanagh's *Wild Honey* (1974), Robert Gray's *Creekwater Jour-*

nal (1974), McDonald's *Airship* (1975), Page's *Smalltown Memorials* (1975), Graeme Kinross Smith and Jamie Grant's *Turn Left at Any Time with Care* (1975), Robin Thurston's *Believed Dangerous* (1975), Peter Skrzynecki's *Immigrant Chronicle* (1975), Tipping's *Domestic Hardcore* (1975), Roberts's *Will's Dream* (1975), Peter Kocan's *The Other Side of the Fence* (1975), Simpson's *Poems from Murrumbeena* (1976), Andrew McDonald's *Absence in Strange Countries* (1976), Alan Wearne's *New Devil, New Parish* (1976), Martin Johnston's *The Sea-Cucumber* (1978), Alan Gould's *Icelandic Solitaries* (1978), Kevin Hart's *The Departure* (1978), Gary Catalano's *Remembering the Rural Life* (1978), and Susan Whiting's *Between Breaths* (1981). *Consolidation : The Second Paperback Poets Anthology* comprising selected poems from the second series, edited by Shapcott, was published in 1981.

Paraguay, see **New Australia; NOWRA, LOUIS**

PARER, DAMIEN (1912–44), born Malvern, Victoria, was the youngest of a large family of Spanish-Irish heritage, and spent his early years on King Island in Bass Strait. In 1933 he was employed by Charles Chauvel on the camera crew making the film *Heritage,* and he worked on further films with Chauvel 1935–36, including *Forty Thousand Horsemen.* He joined a Commonwealth film unit in 1939 and in 1940 accompanied the AIF to the Middle East. Documentaries he produced of Australian troops in action in Greece and Syria and at Tobruk include *The Fall of Bardia* (1941), *The Relief of Tobruk* (1941) and *The RAAF in the Western Desert* (1942). In 1942 he joined the Australian forces in New Guinea and produced numerous documentaries, several of which were to become internationally well-known; one, *Jungle Warfare on the Kokoda Front,* was awarded an Oscar in 1943. Late in 1943 Parer joined the American forces to cover the invasion of the Pacific and was killed at the landing on Peleliu. Probably Australia's best-known photographer, Parer also became legendary for his courage, unswerving dedication to the camera and unpretentious, if eccentric, personality. His career is described by Frank Legg in *The Eyes of Damien Parer* (1963) and by John Hetherington in *Australians: Nine Profiles* (1960).

PARK, RUTH (?1923–), was born in Auckland, NZ, and educated at the University of Auckland. She spent her early childhood in isolated areas of NZ and in several of her books has drawn on her memories of the NZ bush and the Maori culture. After some experience as a journalist, she came to Australia in 1942 and married the writer, D'Arcy Niland (q.v.). Wartime conditions resulted in the Nilands leading a wandering life in the outback for a time but they eventually settled in the slum area of Surry Hills, Sydney, and turned to full-time writing. They wrote at first a variety of material, 'radio copy, paragraphs, jingles, short-stories, articles . . . advertising copy' and even gag scripts for a local comedian. Two of Park's novels, *The Harp in the South* (q.v.) and *Poor Man's Orange,* are based on their experience in Surry Hills and the Nilands' joint autobiography, *The Drums Go Bang!* (1956), also covers this period. By the mid-1950s the Nilands had become known as a successful writing couple, who managed to combine full-time careers and parenthood. After D'Arcy Niland died in 1967, Park visited London but soon returned to Sydney. In 1973 she moved to Norfolk Island. Park has written eight novels for adults, *The Harp in the South* (1948), which won the 1946 *Sydney Morning Herald* novel competition, *Poor Man's Orange* (1949), published in the USA as *12½ Plymouth Street* (1951), *The Witch's Thorn* (1951), *A Power of Roses* (1953), *Pink Flannel* (1955), *One-a-Pecker, Two-a-Pecker* (1957), published in London as *The Frost and the Fire* (1958), *The Good Looking Women* (1961), published in 1962 as *Serpent's Delight,* and *Swords and Crowns and Rings* (q.v., 1977), which won that year's Miles Franklin Award. She has also written a guide to Sydney (1973); a factual book about Australia for German readers, *Der Goldene Bumerang (The Golden Boomerang)* (1955); and plays for radio and television, including, with Leslie Rees, a dramatized version of *The Harp in the South* and, with D'Arcy Niland, a television play, 'No Decision', which won a British award in 1961. Many of her books, but especially *The Harp in the South, The Witch's Thorn* and *Swords and Crowns and Rings,* have been best-sellers in Australia and overseas and have been frequently selected by book clubs. She has won distinction as a prolific writer of children's fiction and is well-known to younger children as the creator of the Muddle-Headed Wombat series. The series, which originated as a radio drama sequence on the ABC children's session, has resulted in fourteen books, published 1962–81, all illustrated by Noela Young's lively drawings. Of her numerous other children's books, the most notable are *The Hole in the Hill* (1961), *The Road under the Sea* (1962), *Uncle Matt's Mountain* (1962), *The Ship's Cat* (1961), *The Sixpenny Island* (1968), *Callie's Castle* (1974), *Come Danger, Come Darkness* (1978), *Playing Beatie Bow* (1980), which won the Children's Book of the Year Award for 1981, and *When the Wind Changed* (1980) which won the 1981 NSW Premier's Award. She has also written short stories and plays for young readers, including *The Uninvited Guest*, published in 1978 in the Australian Youth Plays series.

Park's gifts for dramatic action and credible, graphically-drawn characters are apparent in her first two novels, dealing with the hardships of a poverty-stricken Irish-Australian family and their Surry Hills neighbours. The sordid actuality, pathos and ebullient humour of slum life are sympathetically realized in both. In *The Witch's Thorn* and *Pink Flannel*, both of which draw on her memories of NZ, she brings to life a wide range of eccentric characters, as well as the peculiar world of childhood. *A Power of Roses* and *Good-Looking Women* are family dramas, set once again in the inner suburbs of Sydney, but in *Swords and Crowns and Rings* Park breaks new ground. The novel is a sensitive recreation of social change in Australia 1907–30 and a fable-like odyssey whose hero is a social misfit, a dwarf. The same vigorous characteristics enliven Park's fiction for children. In the Muddle-Headed Wombat series her enjoyment of zany dialogue, comic nonsense and absurdly-human animal characters finds full scope. Her books for teenage children, such as *Callie's Castle, Come Danger, Come Darkness* and *Playing Beatie Bow*, show a perceptive understanding of adolescence, which, in the last two, combines with gripping recreations of nineteenth-century Australia.

Parker, Amy and **Stan**, see *Tree of Man, The*

PARKER, CATHERINE LANGLOH (?1855–1940), born Catherine Field at Encounter Bay, SA, spent much of her childhood on her father's stations on the Darling Downs, Queensland, where Aboriginal children were her companions. In 1879 she went with her husband, K. Langloh Parker, to pastoral properties in northern NSW and Queensland where she collected native legends and stories. After her first husband's death she married Percival Stowe and returned to SA. Her *Australian Legendary Tales* (1896), under the name Mrs K. Langloh Parker, was the first substantial collection of Aboriginal legends and tales. Although not regarded as a scholarly treatise on, or penetration of, the complex mysteries of Aboriginal custom and tradition, Catherine Parker's tales capture such features of Aboriginal lore as the belief in Baiame, the All-Father; the wanderings of Wurrunna, the culture-hero; and the significance attached to Mullee Mullees, Doowis, Yowis and Mingga, or spirit trees. Her other Aboriginal legend publications are *More Australian Legendary Tales* (1898), The

Walkabouts of Wurrunnah (1918) and *Woggheeguy* (1930). She also wrote the factual *The Euahlayi Tribe: A Study of Aboriginal Life in Australia* (1905). A selection from her earlier volumes of tales, titled *Australian Legendary Tales*, selected and edited with an introduction by Henrietta Drake-Brockman and illustrated by Elizabeth Durack, was published in 1953 and won the Children's Book of the Year Award for 1954. In 1982 one of her unpublished manuscripts was produced, together with a background and biography by Marcie Muir, as *My Bush Book: K. Langloh Parker's 1890s Story of Outback Station Life*.

'PARKER, LESLIE', see **THIRKELL, ANGELA**

PARKES, Sir **HENRY** (1815–96), born Warwickshire, England, grew up in Birmingham, where he received only a meagre education. Unsuccessful business ventures as a young man led to his departure from England in 1839, a situation which he deplored in some verses, 'A Poet's Farewell'. In Australia he tried a variety of jobs, agricultural labourer, clerk, ivory and bone turner, before turning to politics, supporting the causes of liberalism and anti-transportation. He was assisted financially, in 1850, to become an editor of the newspaper, the *Empire* (q.v.), an important voice in the developing democracy of the day. He was elected to the Legislative Council in 1854 and the first Legislative Assembly in 1856. Years of political and commercial crises followed, his fortunes in both arenas fluctuating wildly, but Parkes, a natural survivor, became premier in 1872, a position he was to hold on five subsequent occasions. His major administrative achievement was the Public Instruction Act of 1880 which ensured 'free, secular and compulsory' education in NSW. Often called the 'Father of Federation', Parkes played a key role in the Federation conventions of 1890–91. The *Bulletin's* famous cartoon after his death, which shows 'The Little Boy from Manly' closing a huge volume, titled simply 'Parkes', indicates the scope of his achievements and the impact of his personality throughout half a century of public life. He is portrayed in George Darrell's play, 'The Lucky Lot' (1890). An important figure also in the colonial literary milieu, he was a friend of Charles Harpur and the long-suffering patron of Henry Kendall. His own publications include the volumes of verse, *Stolen Moments* (1842), *Murmurs of the Stream* (1857), *Studies in Rhyme* (1870), *The Beauteous Terrorist and Other Poems* (1885), *Fragmentary Thoughts* (1889) and *Sonnets and Other Verse* (1895). His chief prose work is the autobiographical *Fifty Years in the Making of Austra-*

lian History (1892). He wrote *Australian Views of England* (1869) as well as numerous political pamphlets. A collection of letters to his family, *An Emigrant's Home Letters,* was edited in 1896 by his daughter, Annie. Biographies of Parkes include C.E. Lyne, *Life of Sir Henry Parkes* (1896) and Sir Thomas Bavin, *Sir Henry Parkes* (1941), but the outstanding account of his life and work is A.W. Martin's *Henry Parkes* (1980) which won the Barbara Ramsden Award. Martin also edited *Letters from Menie: Sir Henry Parkes and His Daughter* (1983).

PARKIN, RAY (1910–   ), born Melbourne, served with the RAN, 1928–46, and has written three accounts of his experiences in the Second World War. *Out of the Smoke* (1960) narrates the sinking of the cruiser HMAS *Perth* in the Sunda Strait; *Into the Smother* (1963) records the experiences of Australian servicemen on the Burma–Siam railway; *The Sword and the Blossom* (1968) continues the author's experiences in Japan until the end of the war. Quietly narrated, reflective and balanced, Parkin's accounts, which he has illustrated with his own drawings, have been internationally acclaimed.

PARKINSON, SYDNEY (?1745–71), born Edinburgh, Scotland, went as botanical draughtsman with Sir Joseph Banks in the *Endeavour.* During the voyage he made upwards of a thousand drawings and sketches and compiled vocabularies of the natives of Tahiti and New Holland. He died of dysentery on the voyage. His drawings were later used, with scant acknowledgement, in John Hawkesworth's *An Account of the Voyages Undertaken by the Order of His Present Majesty for Making Discoveries in the Southern Hemisphere* (1773); Stanfield Parkinson compiled his brother's book, *A Journal of a Voyage to the South Seas, in His Majesty's Ship, the Endeavour,* in the same year. D.J. Carr edited *Sydney Parkinson: Artist of Cook's Endeavour Voyage* (1983).

Parramatta, after Sydney the oldest settlement in Australia, is located twenty-four kilometres west of Sydney at the head of the Parramatta River and is a city within the metropolitan area of Sydney. The site, discovered by Governor Phillip on 23 April 1788, was settled in November that year. Until 1792 Parramatta was the major settlement, Sydney being reserved as a depot for stores, and it retained social importance as the seat of the governor, even after Sydney became the commercial centre. The first land grant issued in Australia was made at Parramatta to James Ruse (1760–1837), who was the Colony's first successful

farmer; many other notable pioneers settled in the area, including John Macarthur, whose home, Elizabeth House, is still standing. The area has figured frequently in Australian historical fiction and is the background to Mary Gaunt's novel, *As the Whirlwind Passeth* (1923), Ethel Turner's novel, *Seven Little Australians* (1894), Ethel Anderson's short stories, *At Parramatta* (1956), David Ireland's novel, *The Glass Canoe* (1976), and part of Donald Horne's autobiography, *The Education of Young Donald* (1967). James Jervis wrote *The Cradle City of Australia: A History of Parramatta 1788–1961* (1961).

PARSONS, PHILIP, see **Currency Press**

PARTRIDGE,   ERIC   HONEYWOOD (1894–1979), born NZ, was brought to Australia in 1907 and after service in the AIF, 1915–19, completed a degree at the University of Queensland. In 1921 he went to Oxford and after graduation taught at the Universities of Manchester and London. In 1927 he founded the Scholartis Press, which he directed for the next four years, publishing a wide range of books with a bias towards younger writers. *Glimpses* (1927), Partridge's volume of short stories under the pseudonym, 'Corrie Denison', was published by the press as was his first slang lexicography, *Songs and Slang of the British Soldier 1914–1918* (1930), compiled with John Brophy. After the Scholartis Press foundered in 1935, Partridge began a career as a lexicographer of unconventional English, which continued until his death. His major dictionaries, which include Australian slang, are *A Dictionary of Slang and Unconventional English* (1937), *A Dictionary of the Underworld* (1949) and *Origins: A Short Etymological Dictionary of Modern English* (1958). All have been repeatedly revised and enlarged. Partridge's other outstanding achievements include *Usage and Abusage* (1942), *Shakespeare's Bawdy* (1947) and *English: A Course for Human Beings* (1949). An indefatigable researcher and compiler, Partridge also produced dictionaries of abbreviations, etymological dictionaries, guides to punctuation, collections of quotations and several anthologies of essays on language and literature. Of these the best known are *A Dictionary of Clichés* (1940), *A Dictionary of Catch Phrases* (1977) and *A Charm of Words* (1960). He also edited numerous collections of prose and verse, and early in his career published several studies of European literature. An unpretentious scholar whose main object was to be readable, Partridge was also not averse to publishing potboilers such as *The 'Shaggy Dog' Story* (1953) and *Comic Alphabets* (1961). His autobiographical writing includes

The First Three Years (1930), an account of the Scholartis Press; *A Covey of Partridge* (1937) and *The Gentle Art of Lexicography* (1963). His reminiscences of the First World War include 'Frank Honeywood, Private' in *Three Personal Records of the War* (1929) and 'A Mere Private' in *Glimpses*. Partridge received two academic honours, both Australian: an honorary doctorate of letters from the University of Queensland and an honorary fellowship of the Australian Academy of the Humanities.

'PARTRIGE, SYDNEY' (KATE MARGARET STONE) (1871–1953) was the wife of Hal Stone (1872–1956), whose private Wayside Press produced numerous publications by Australian writers and who edited the magazines, the *Red Ant, Ye Kangaroo* and *Ye Wayside Goose*. She published two collections of verse, *The Lie and Other Lines* (1913) and *The One Life and Other Verses* (1936); two novels, *Rocky Section* (1907) and *The Mystery of Wall's Hill* (1921, with Cecil Raworth); and a collection of short stories reprinted from the *Bulletin,* the *Australasian* and other magazines, *Life's Wallaby* (1908).

Passage, The, a novel by Vance Palmer (q.v.), was published in 1930 and won first prize in the *Bulletin's* 1929 novel competition and the Gold Medal of the Australian Literature Society. Set in a small Queensland fishing port, it deals mainly with the life of a fisherman, Lew Calloway, the eldest son and breadwinner of the Calloway family of five children, and incidentally with that of their neighbours. Lew has an attachment to the slow rhythms of life at The Passage which is deep, instinctive, inarticulate and tenacious, unlike his brother Hughie and sister Marnie, who yearn for the bustling activity of the city. Anna Calloway, their mother, anxious that her children should have wider opportunities than those of their relations, Tony and Rachel Calloway, only belatedly understands the meaning of Lew's organic bond to The Passage. Although the novel's action moves quietly and undramatically, the Calloways undergo various vicissitudes in its course: Hughie, whose charm and quick energy seemed to augur success, eventually fails in the city and returns to The Passage to take up his old job of managing the local store; Lew allows his first chance of a relationship with Clem McNair to pass him by, makes a disastrous marriage with Lena Christensen, suffers the death of his son, Peter, loses Lena to her previous lover, Craig, and is finally reunited with Clem. The ebb and flow in individual lives is also mirrored in the difference between the changing fortunes of Lavinia, a neighbouring tourist resort, and the stability of life at The Passage.

Passionate Heart, The (1918), a volume of poems by Dame Mary Gilmore (q.v.), was dedicated to 'The Fellowing Men', the soldiers of the First World War. Poems such as 'The Measure', 'The Satin of the Bee', 'Corn' and 'Gallipoli' tell of the loss and heartache of war as seen through a woman's eyes and reflect the general disenchantment with war that followed the Allied victory in 1918. Other poems, such as 'Life-Song', 'Life at Autumn' and the title poem, carry the typical Mary Gilmore affirmation of life.

'Past Carin' ', a poem by Henry Lawson (q.v.) which records the lament of a bush woman whom hardship and tragedy have made 'past carin' ', was published in 1899. It subsequently became the title of the second part of ' "Water them Geraniums" ', a story in the Joe Wilson (q.v.) sequence, which chronicles the spiritual disintegration and death of the bush woman, Mrs Spicer.

Pastures of the Blue Crane, The, see BRINSMEAD, HESBA

PATCHETT, MARY (1897–), who also writes under the names Mary Patchett and M.E. Patchett, was brought up on a cattle station near the town of Texas in northern NSW. She became a feature writer for the *Sun* group of newspapers in 1926. She left Australia in 1931, spent some time in England as a freelance writer, travelled extensively in Europe and eventually ran a beauty salon in Mayfair. She married Stanser Patchett, an Australian journalist, and during their stay in Gibraltar and Bermuda was responsible for setting up a system of press censorship. After the war she settled in London. Her first book for children, *Ajax the Warrior* (1953), set the pattern for a long series of adventure stories with bush settings and animal characters. She has also written stories about interplanetary flight and undersea exploration, but her forte is wild animal life. Of her forty-seven books for children, the most significant are *Wild Brother* (1954), *Tiger in the Dark* (1964) and *The Brumby* (1958). She has also written several novels for adults.

PATERSON, A.B. (ANDREW BARTON) (1864–1941), widely known as 'Banjo' Paterson from the pseudonym 'The Banjo' that he adopted for his early contributions to the *Bulletin,* was born at Narambla Station, near Orange, NSW. Growing up in the bush on Illalong Station near Yass, NSW, he had an early acquaintance with identities such as drovers, teamsters and even bushrangers, with occasions such as picnic race meetings, and with relationships such as the animosity between squatters and drovers. Those early experiences provided him with a fund of incidents, characters and scenes, which his later writings turned into legend. After early schooling in the small town of Binalong he completed his education in Sydney, then entered a lawyer's office as clerk, ultimately being admitted as a solicitor. A literary celebrity after the rapturous reception of *The Man from Snowy River and Other Verses* in 1895, the handsome, well-bred, athletic Paterson rapidly became the toast of the country; he is portrayed as such in Nigel Krauth's novel, *Matilda, My Darling* (1983). His later life was full of glamour and adventure. He went crocodile-hunting and buffalo-shooting in the Northern Territory, dived for pearls with the Japanese at Broome, was a war correspondent in the Boer War, and travelled to China to cover the Boxer Rebellion. Back in Australia he was successively editor of the Sydney *Evening News* and the *Australian Town and Country Journal*. In the First World War he was initially a war correspondent but, dissatisfied with his inability to get to the front in France, returned to Australia and enlisted in the Remount Service which provided horses for the Australian cavalry in the Middle East. After the war he returned to journalism, edited the *Sydney Sportsman,* continued to indulge his love for all sports, especially the turf (q.v.), and wrote further verse and fiction as well as scripts for radio. He had lived periodically in the country on the property, Coodravale, on the upper Murrumbidgee, fulfilling the dream he had expressed years earlier in 'A Mountain Station', but from 1919 he lived in Sydney.

Paterson's books of verse are *The Man from Snowy River and Other Verses* (1895), *Rio Grande's Last Race and Other Verses* (1902), *Saltbush Bill J.P. and Other Verses* (1917), and the children's book, *The Animals Noah Forgot* (1933). *A Collected Verse* was published in 1923. His fiction comprised two novels, *An Outback Marriage* (1906) and *The Shearer's Colt* (1936); and short stories, *Three Elephant Power and Other Stories* (q.v., 1917). Reminiscences of his travels and adventures were brought together in the semi-autobiographical *Happy Dispatches* (1934). He also compiled the seminal anthology, *Old Bush Songs* (q.v., 1905). Paterson left several unpublished works, including 'Racehorses and Racing' and 'Illalong Children', both of which have since been published in his complete works collected and introduced by his granddaughters, Rosamund Campbell and Phillipa Harvie in 1983 in two volumes, *Singer of the Bush* (writings 1885–1900) and *Song of the Pen* (writings 1901–41).

Paterson is the chief folk-poet of Australia. 'Waltzing Matilda' (q.v.), Australia's national song, and 'The Man from Snowy River' (q.v.), Australia's national narrative poem, substantiate that claim. Add such folk figures as 'Clancy of the Overflow', 'Saltbush Bill', 'The Man from Ironbark' and 'Mulga Bill' (qq.v.), set them 'On Kiley's Run', at 'Conroy's Gap', along 'The Road to Gundagai' or 'By the Grey Gulf Water', and have them sing 'A Bushman's Song', dream 'A Dream of the Melbourne Cup', swap old yarns of 'Father Riley's Horse' and 'The Geebung Polo Club', or ruefully recount 'How the Favourite Beat Us', and the outlines of the map of Australian folklore are broadly drawn. That mythical map's outlines merge with actual geographical boundaries. It begins in the western plains of NSW, takes in the Murrumbidgee and the Monaro, heads north to the Queensland Downs and the Northern Territory, encompassing the whole limitless outback. It is 'the land of lots o' time', signposted with fabled names, the Overflow, the Castlereagh, the Snowy, Dandaloo, Gundaroo, Come-by-Chance, Hogan's Gap, Hay and Hell and Booligal. It is Australian Arcadia, created by all the bush balladists and in his more optimistic moods contributed to by Henry Lawson himself, but it is indisputably Paterson country. Whether Australian Arcadia ever existed in the way Paterson pictured it is problematical but the general Australian populace has long been beguiled by his vision. The first edition of *The Man from Snowy River* sold out in the week of publication; it went through four editions in six months and it still outsells any other volume of Australian poetry ever published. The Arcadian view was strongly challenged in the *Bulletin* debate (q.v.) with Lawson in 1892–93, but Paterson did not, in his own opinion, ignore those aspects of the outback which coloured Lawson's attitude — the minor irritants like dust, heat and flies, or the darker calamities like droughts, floods, despair and tragedy. His Arcadians simply accepted their lot, good or bad, with cheerful, laconic patience.

Paterson is the supreme balladist of the horse. In bushman fashion he viewed the horse as an animal trained for and useful in specific tasks and he admired it for its excellence in those tasks, one of which is racing. Racing involves feats of speed, courage and endurance and there is plenty of human drama associated with it. 'Rio Grande's Last Race', 'Father Riley's Horse', 'The Old Timer's Steeplechase', 'Mulligan's Mare' and 'In the Droving Days' are notable Paterson stories of the horse, but 'The Man from Snowy River' is the undisputed classic of that genre. Paterson belongs also to the stream of nationalist-radical writers that the 1890s nurtured. In 'A Bushman's Song' he is the radical, putting the case for the ordinary drover and shearer against the squatter and the absentee landlord, while 'Song of Federation', 'Song of the Future' and 'Old Australian Ways' express nationalist sentiments.

Paterson is commemorated in the Banjo Paterson Award made biennially by the Orange Festival of Arts Committee for one-act plays and poetry. The major biographical and critical study is Clement Semmler's *The Banjo of the Bush: The Work, Life and Times of A.B. Paterson* (1966).

Patrick White Literary Award is an annual award established by Patrick White (q.v.) in 1973 with the proceeds of the Nobel Prize for Literature which he won that year. It is awarded to an older Australian writer whose work, in the opinion of the administrators of the fund, has not received the critical acclaim or the financial rewards it deserves. The following writers have won the award: Christina Stead (1974), David Campbell (1975), John Blight (1976), Sumner Locke-Elliott (1977), Gwen Harwood (1978), Randolph Stow (1979), Bruce Dawe (1980), Dal Stivens (1981) and Bruce Beaver (1982).

PATTERSON, HENRY (1867– ?), born Scotland, came to Australia in 1878 and acquired ownership of several country newspapers in Victoria. A prolific, conventional and flowery poet who specialized in elevated, patriotic themes, Patterson published nine volumes of verse. They are *The Litany of Liberty* (1918), *Song of the Anzacs* (1918), *Sunrise Hymns and The Litany of Liberty* (1919), *Morning Songs* (1922), *More Morning Songs* (1924), *Joan of Domremy* (1925), *The King's Chamberlain* (1939), *Armageddon* (1940) and *Kingdom Come* (1944). Both *The King's Chamberlain* and *Armageddon* were published under the pseudonym, 'Bartimaeus'.

Patterson, Sir Les, a character created by Barry Humphries (q.v.) in 1974, was originally presented as the entertainments officer of a well-known Sydney licensed club, the St George Leagues' Club, but developed into an Australian cultural attaché abroad; from 1978 the recently knighted Australian cultural attaché at the Court of St James. A chauvinistic, obscene, vulgar, ex-politician, who has survived the fall of E.G. Whitlam's government, Sir Les is part larrikin and part ocker (q.v.), the means whereby Humphries can attack both Australian philistinism and government support for the arts. The views of Sir Les on Australian cultural life are presented in *Les Patterson's Australia* (1978).

PAULL, RAYMOND ALLAN, see War Literature

Paving the Way, see NEWLAND, SIMPSON; Aboriginal in Australian Literature

Pea Pickers, The (1942), a novel by Eve Langley (q.v.), is a story of two sisters, aged eighteen and nineteen, who leave their Dandenong home to taste the free and wandering life. Dressed as boys, a half-hearted disguise that only partly conceals their sex, and answering to the names Blue and Steve, they journey to Gippsland, their soul country, where their ancestors had first gone by bullock dray. They work as apple packers and Steve, whose feverish preoccupations are an obsession to be loved and a counter conviction that her beloved land 'loved me for my virginity and would be with me while I kept it', meets her first love, Kelly Wilson, 'bow-legged, booted and spurred'; he demonstrates his gallantry in Gippsland male fashion by taking her rabbit-shooting. Kelly, who feels 'like a bottle of yeast that must soon explode', ultimately loses interest as Steve clings to 'the cold but happy ideal of the virgin'. Steve and Blue become mates with another Gippslander, Jim. Estimable in most respects, Jim is an embarrassment to them on social occasions such as Sunday tea at the boss's house because of his rapid and unerring plunder of the tea table. After apple-packing and trips to the vineyards at Rutherglen on the Murray and the maize fields at Tumut in NSW, they rejoin Jim for the pea-picking at Metung on the Gippsland lakes. The grand passion of Steve's life appears in the person of Macca Mackinnon, 'a short fair bloke with a slow voice', and she becomes, again, tortured by conflicting desires. She reads the *Aeneid* to Macca in the moonlight and they lie, afterwards, decorously on (not in) her bed. While Steve agonizes the night away, the puzzled but equable Macca finally falls asleep. A pragmatic Gippslander, Macca ultimately sidesteps the complexities of Steve; proclaiming to her his satisfaction with 'the uncloying cleanliness' of her passion he indulges, on the side, in less complicated frolics with the local girls. At Metung the itinerant Italian workers enter the narrative: Peppino, who always wears green socks ('Dese me mudder makes') and avows distraught, unintelligible love for Blue by letter; Domenic Gatto ('Tomcatto'), who is prone to drawing the Australian coat-of-arms and hollowly crying 'Viva l'Owstralia'; and the amorous Puglisi ('Rudolph Valentino . . . he not dead while I alive'). Later, while hop-picking in the Australian Alps, they encounter more such characters: another Italian, 'The Little Black Flea', whose continual wail of despair at Steve's indifference to him, 'no luna ancora' (no moon yet), becomes her own cry for Macca; and another Australian mate, the lisping Charlie Wallaby and his mare, Blothum. After a winter of near starvation in the Alps, relieved only by their adroitness in stealing food from the Italians and pumpkins from nearby fields, they return in the spring with renewed optimism to another pea-picking season at Metung. Her idyll over, Blue finally returns to normality by going home to Dandenong to marry her patient suitor, but Steve, still virginal, still obsessed by love, vows to stay on in Gippsland in 'pure and poetic solitude', a reminder to the errant Macca, now comfortably 'sweet on a cattleman's daughter', of 'flawless love' and 'ideal faithfulness'.

Peach Groves, The, a novel by Barbara Hanrahan (q.v.), was published in 1979. Although Adelaide of 1884 is the opening setting, the scene soon shifts to North Island, NZ. Blanche Dean, bored with her genteel existence and her respectable husband, George, decides to visit her brother, Harry, in NZ. She is accompanied by her two small daughters, Ida and Maud. For the perceptive Ida and later for the more superficial Maud, NZ reveals itself as a place of mystery, danger and corruption. Not only does Uncle Harry have an illicit relationship with his wife's half-Maori sister, Tempe, but Tempe also proves to have witch-like powers. The dangers surrounding the Deans multiply when they visit the Peach Groves, the property of Mr Maufe, Harry's apparently kindly friend. Mr Maufe's strange family includes his wife, Zillah, who takes refuge in obsessive sketching, and his shy son, Oc, who is afflicted with an outsize head. But it is Mr Maufe who turns out to be the most frightening, a pederast with murderous designs on Maud. Blanche, unaware of these undercurrents, succumbs to her own form of corruption in a recurrence of her incestuous relationship with Harry, an incident that the children witness. The family returns to Harry's residence, Harry repents his sin of incest, the revengeful Tempe, after attempting to poison Blanche and corrupt Maud, is drowned, and Mr Maufe suffers a stroke when his attempt to strangle Maud is intercepted by Oc. Chastened, and looking forward to the dull respectability of Adelaide and George, Blanche sails for Australia. Maud has emerged from the experience unchanged but Ida has grown up and away from the influence of her mother.

PEARCE, HARRY HASTINGS (1897–), born Creswick, Victoria, worked as a goldminer and farm labourer and lived in NZ for fourteen years before settling in Melbourne. A professed atheist and rationalist, he published several pamphlets in support of his views. A member of the Melbourne Bread and Cheese Club, treasurer and secretary of the Australian Poetry Lovers' Society from 1948 until its demise in 1973, and editor of its little magazine, the *Poetry Lover,* 1955–73, he was also active in the Henry Lawson Memorial and Literary Society, and the Folklore Society of Victoria. He published two collections of poetry, *The Song of Nature* (1948) and *Dreams and Arrows* (1969); a narrative poem, *Thomas Kennedy's March from Creswick's Creek* (1954), written to commemorate the centenary of Eureka; and a detailed argument concerning the origins of 'Waltzing Matilda' (q.v., 1971).

PEARL, CYRIL (1906–), born Fitzroy, Melbourne, graduated from the University of Melbourne where he was editor of *Stream,* and subsequently became a well-known Sydney journalist; he edited the *Sunday Telegraph* 1939–49, *A.M.* 1949–54 and the *Sunday Mirror* 1960–61. A prolific social historian and biographer, he has written an influential account of some of Sydney's controversial figures such as John Norton, *Wild Men of Sydney* (1958); biographies of R.H. Horne, *Always Morning* (1960), George Ernest Morrison, *Morrison of Peking* (1967), Dan Deniehy, *Brilliant Dan Deniehy* (1972) and Charles Gavan Duffy, *The Three Lives of Gavan Duffy* (1979); studies of nineteenth century and sexual mores, *The Girl with the Swansdown Seat* (1955) and *Victorian Patchwork* (1972); accounts of curious incidents in Australian history, *Rebel Down Under* (1970), *Five Men Vanished* (1978) and *The Dunera Scandal* (1983); satiric studies of Australian attitudes, *So, You Want to Be an Australian* (1959) and *So, You Want to Buy a House and Live in It!* (1961); a novel, *Pantaloons and Antics* (1964); a history of beer in Australia, *Beer, Glorious Beer* (1969); an account of Hardy Wilson's work (1970), of James Joyce's Dublin (1969) and of Robert Burns (1958); and has edited a selection of the work of Lennie Lower, *The Best of Lennie Lower* (1963). Pearl has also been a well-known television personality.

PEARSON, C.H. (CHARLES HENRY) (1830–94), born London, studied history at Oxford and was professor of modern history at King's College, 1855–65, and lecturer in modern history at Trinity College, Cambridge, 1869–71. Editor of the *National Review* in 1862, he also contributed to the *Saturday Review* and the *Spectator.* In 1871 Pearson migrated to SA where he had bought a farm, but in 1874 accepted a post at the University of Melbourne. In Melbourne he became friendly with such prominent individuals as Alfred Deakin and George Higinbotham. A strong advocate of education for women, he was headmaster of the Presbyterian Ladies' College 1875–77, and presented an influential report on public education in Victoria in 1878. Leader-writer for the *Age*, 1874–85, and the *Leader*, 1880–84, Pearson entered Victorian politics in 1878 and held various ministerial positions, 1886–90. In 1892 he left for England, where he was made permanent secretary to the Victorian Agent-General's office, but was retired two years later. Pearson published *History of England during the Early and Middle Ages* in 1868, and other historical works, but his main achievement was *National Life and Character* (1893). The most influential contentions of the book included predictions of the growth of the power of the state, and the rise of the working classes and of undeveloped nations such as China. This last influenced Australia's subsequent immigration policies. A memoir of Pearson drawn from his own writings and recollections of his family and friends was published in 1900; some of his reviews and critical essays were collected in 1896, edited by H.A. Strong; and John Tregenza has written an account of his life, *Professor of Democracy* (1968).

Peasant Mandarin, The, see **MURRAY, LES**

Peculiar People, A, see **SOUTER, GAVIN; New Australia**

PEDLEY, ETHEL C. (c.1860–98), born London, was a teacher of music in Sydney, and wrote a book for children that has proved to be a perennial, *Dot and the Kangaroo* (1899). Dot, small daughter of an outback settler, becomes lost in the bush. She befriends a red kangaroo, who carries her, after meeting with such bush creatures as a platypus, a koala and a kookaburra, back to safety in her pouch. Delicately illustrated by Frank Mahony, the novel's humanized animals, fantasy and comedy owe something to Lewis Carroll's *Alice in Wonderland*, although Pedley includes a plea for the conservation of Australia's wildlife. The novel was adapted for the stage by Stella Chapman and Douglas Ancelon in 1924, and made into a film in 1977.

PELL, OLIVE (1903–), born Kalgoorlie, has worked as a secretary and librarian. She has written numerous radio features, short stories, plays for radio and television, and has published two collections of poetry, *Gold to Win* (1964) and *I'd Rather Be a Fig!* (1977).

PENN-SMITH, FRANK (1863–1935), born Lancashire, came to Tasmania in 1880 and worked as a farmer and prospector. He lived on the mainland 1900–05, when he left to

travel in South Africa and other countries, revisited Tasmania briefly in 1922 and finally settled in England. *The Unexpected* (1933) is an account of his travels. He also published *Hang!* (1925), a collection of short stories and animal fables, and a collection of verse, *Austral Lyrics and Fugitive Pieces* (189?).

Penola, a town near the south-eastern border of SA and Victoria, has literary connections with poets Adam Lindsay Gordon and John Shaw Neilson (qq.v.). Gordon was stationed there for two years (1853–54) while a trooper in the SA Mounted Police, rode in steeplechase races there and bought a small property in the district. Julian Tenison-Woods began his friendship with Adam Lindsay Gordon while Woods was a priest at Penola in 1857. John Shaw Neilson was born there in 1872; his father (and poet) John Neilson, had a property there. John Shaw Neilson's 'Old Granny Sullivan' is based on an old lady who lived at Penola.

PENTON, BRIAN (1904–51), born and educated in Brisbane, began a long career in journalism with a brief spell on the *Brisbane Courier*; at nineteen he went to England to freelance for eighteen months before returning to Australia to join the *Sydney Morning Herald*. As its 'Special Correspondent', Penton contributed a daily column, 'From the Gallery', reporting on the events and personalities of the new federal parliament in Canberra. Its irreverent tone led to complaints from politicians, to Penton's recall to Sydney at the end of 1927, and his resignation from the *Herald* soon after. He spent most of the depression years in England, where in 1929–30 he was P.R. Stephensen's successor as business manager of the Fanfrolico Press, which published Jack Lindsay's translation, *The Mimiambs of Herondas* (1929), with an introduction by Penton, and in 1930–32 was a reporter on the *Daily Express*. While in England Penton also contributed to the *London Aphrodite* and helped to place Norman Lindsay's *Redheap* with publishers. In 1933 he began a long association with the Sydney *Daily Telegraph* which culminated in his successful editorship of the newspaper from 1941 until his death. Aggressively anti-Labor, Penton campaigned vigorously during the Second World War years to limit the amount of government censorship imposed on Australian newspapers. The dispute, the subject of Penton's *Censored!* (1947), flared most seriously in 1944, when issues of the *Telegraph* and the *Sydney Morning Herald* were suppressed.

Penton was a flamboyant and fearless journalist who has been ranked alongside J.F. Archibald as an outstanding editor, although some of his staff, e.g. Don Whitington in *Strive To*

Be Fair (1977), have recorded their resentment of his aggression and authoritarianism. The crusading spirit which informed countless editorials and columns is evident also in two polemical works, *Advance Australia — Where?* (1943) and *Think — Or Be Damned* (1941), iconoclastic discussions of contemporary society, which have their parallel in works like Donald Horne's *The Lucky Country* (1964) and Ronald Conway's *The Great Australian Stupor* (1971) a generation later. *Think — Or Be Damned,* in particular, offers sardonic comments on some of the myths about Australia's historical development; on a larger scale, Penton's two novels *Landtakers* (q.v. 1934) and *Inheritors* (1936), parts of a projected trilogy that was never completed, explore the same territory. Generally described as a 'saga' novel, a term which perhaps does less than justice to the inner life of the characters, *Landtakers* chronicles pioneering life in Queensland in the period 1842–64. Its focus is Derek Cabell, an innocent immigrant who arrives in Australia intending only to make his fortune and return to England, but who stays and is changed dramatically by the rigours he is forced to endure. *Inheritors,* the sequel to *Landtakers,* takes the story of the Cabells forward to the 1880s and 1890s, and explores the destructive relationship between the successful but brutalized Cabell and his four children. Although the plots of Penton's novels are sometimes clumsy in construction and melodramatic, *Landtakers* in particular offers a powerful vision of the colonial experience and its legacies.

'Peripatetic Philosopher, The', was a weekly column written by Marcus Clarke (q.v.) under the pseudonym 'Q', for the *Australasian,* 1867–70; a selection from the series was published as *The Peripatetic Philosopher* in 1869 and was Clarke's first book. 'The Peripatetic Philosopher' was also a Clarke pseudonym, most notably for his 'Lower Bohemia' sketches in the *Australasian* and *Argus* in 1869.

PERKINS, ELIZABETH, see **HARPUR, CHARLES**

PERRY, GRACE (1927–), born Sydney, was educated in England, then graduated in medicine from the University of Sydney in 1951. She has, since then, combined a family life with a professional career as a paediatrician and an extremely energetic involvement in contemporary literary affairs as poet, editor, publisher, founder member of the ASA and convener/organizer of numerous Sydney poetry workshops and writing schools. She was editor of *Poetry Magazine* (q.v.), 1961–64; in 1964 she inaugurated, and has since then been editor of, *Poetry Australia* (q.v.). She founded South Head Press in 1964. Her own published poetry began with teenage volumes *Staring at the Stars* (1942) and *I Live a Life of Dreams* (1943). Her first mature volume, *Red Scarf* (1963), is in two sections: 'Where the Wind Moves', love poems in which natural scenery, usually seascapes, is used to reflect personal emotions; and 'Red Scarf', striking poems born out of her experiences as a doctor, which express the horror and fascination of disease and death. *Frozen Section* (1967), notable also for its considerable medical sequence, reflects the problem that is nearly always present in Grace Perry's writing, the accommodation of the clinical detachment of the physician with the sensitive involvement of the poet. *Two Houses* (1969) contains the sequence, 'Notes on a Journey', small intense landscape images of the picturesque Warrumbungles and western NSW, and poems of contemporary events such as President Lyndon B. Johnson's Australian visit. *Black Swans at Berrima* (1972), an ambitious sequence of more than 100 individual lyric pieces, is set in the historic township of Berrima (q.v.) in southern NSW. The sequence begins with the building of the historic magistrate's house at Berrima, describes a journey from Sydney to Berrima, and explores the passing of time and the approach of age and death. Following *Berrima Winter* (1974), Grace Perry published *Journal of a Surgeon's Wife and Other Poems* (1976), the title poem a long verse-diary of the experiences of an immigrant doctor's wife in early colonial Australia. The poem captures the sense of exile that so oppressed the early settlers. Another book of poetry, *Snow in Summer* (1980), was followed in 1981 by a play, with John Millett, *Last Bride at Longsleep.*

Perth, the capital of Western Australia (q.v.), is situated in the south-west corner of the State on the banks of the Swan River; the centre of the city is some sixteen kilometres from the mouth of the Swan, where the port of Fremantle (q.v.) is located. The site for Perth was discovered in 1697 and the city, named after Perth in Scotland, was founded in 1829 by Captain James Stirling with the establishment of the Swan River Colony (q.v.). Very much a convict settlement in its early years, Perth was proclaimed a city in 1856 and incorporated in 1871. It underwent great changes during the gold rush era of the 1890s.

Perth Gazette, see *West Australian*

Peter Possum's Portfolio, see **ROWE, RICHARD**

PETERSON, RALPH (1921–), born Adelaide, served in the army during the Second World War and became a radio actor and scriptwriter for such comedians as Roy Rene, Dick Bentley and Jack Davey. He also wrote radio serials for the ABC and two verse plays for radio, one of which, 'The Problem of Jonny Flourcake', led to his departure for England in 1949 to work for the BBC. In London he scripted work for Tony Hancock and Benny Hill and had two stage plays produced, 'The Square Ring' (1951) and 'The Night of the Ding Dong' (1954). 'The Square Ring', which deals with a boxer's comeback, was also produced in Melbourne the same year and in the USA. Ealing Studios produced it as a film starring Jack Warner, Kay Kendall and Sid James and Peterson re-wrote it in the form of a novel, published in 1954. 'The Night of the Ding Dong', a historical drama set in Adelaide of 1870, was produced in Britain and the USA in 1954 and toured Australia in 1966. Peterson returned in 1954 to Australia where he has remained, apart from a period overseas 1959–64, becoming well-known as a writer for film, radio and television. Award-winning television serials he has written include *My Name's McGooley, What's Yours?* (1966–69), *Rita and Wally,* and *Dad and Dave* (1972). Other stage plays by Peterson that have been produced are 'The Mating of Ulick Dooley' (1965), 'The Big Boat' (1965), winner of the *Australian*'s playwriting competition, and *The Third Secretary* (1972). A naturalistic political play, *The Third Secretary* deals with the defection of a Russian diplomat and has been linked with the celebrated defection of Vladimir Petrov in 1954, although the link is extremely tenuous. Peterson has also written another novel, *Greater the Truth* (1956), a study of a journalist's crisis of conscience.

PETHERICK, E.A. (EDWARD AUGUSTUS) (1847–1917), born Somerset, arrived in Melbourne at the age of six and joined the bookselling and publishing firm of George Robertson (1) in 1862. In 1870 Robertson chose him to reorganize the London branch of the firm, a position Petherick held until Robertson's retirement in 1887, when he set up his own business, Colonial Booksellers' Agency. Bankrupted in 1894, Petherick lost most of his book stocks to E.W. Cole of Melbourne, but his magnificent collection of Australiana, begun in 1865, was saved. After unsuccessful efforts to present the collection to the nation, he brought it to Australia in 1908 and in 1909 it was acquired by the library committee of federal parliament, Petherick obtaining an annuity of £500 a year in consideration. The Petherick Collection Act was passed in 1911. Appointed

government archivist in 1911, Petherick worked at the task of collecting titles for an all-embracing Australian bibliography. Although some sections were published in the *Victorian Historical Magazine* in 1911 and 1912 it remains in manuscript in the National Library of Australia, where the Petherick Collection is housed. Petherick won renown as a bibliographer in 1882 with his *Catalogue of the York Gate Geographical and Colonial Library* (1882) and *Catalogue of Books Relating to Australasia* (1899). As a publisher he issued the *Colonial Book Circular and Bibliographical Record* (1888), later the *Torch,* and *Collection of Favourite and Approved Authors* (1889).

Phar Lap, Australia's most famous racehorse, was actually foaled in NZ in 1926. He created a sensation on the Australian turf, 1929–31, when he won thirty-six races, including the major classics in NSW and Victoria and the Melbourne Cup in 1930. His death in mysterious circumstances in California in 1932 added to his legend and occasioned many sentimental verse tributes; since then he has been the subject of Peter Porter's poem, 'Phar Lap in the Melbourne Museum', Isabel Carter's chronicle, *Phar Lap* (1964), Stephen Mastare's play, 'Phar Lap, It's Cingalese for Lightning, Y'Know', produced in Melbourne in 1977, and Michael Wilkinson's *The Phar Lap Story* (1980). An Australian film, *Phar Lap: Hero to a Nation,* was screened in 1983; Helen Townsend wrote a novel, *Phar Lap* (1983), based on the film.

PHELAN, NANCY (1913–), born and educated in Sydney, lived in England for several years and has travelled widely in the Pacific Islands, Europe, Asia and the Middle East. She has written three novels, 'The Voice beyond the Trees', winner of third prize in the *Sydney Morning Herald*'s 1950 novel competition, *The River and the Brook* (1962) and *Serpents in Paradise* (1967); an account of her childhood in Sydney, *A Kingdom by the Sea* (1969); and six travel books, of which the most popular are *Some Came Early, Some Came Late* (1970), which describes the various people she has met in different parts of Australia, and *The Swift Foot of Time* (1983), which deals with her experiences in England in the 1930s.

'PHIL THE POET', see **LORIMER, PHILIP**

PHILLIP, ARTHUR (1738–1814), born London, joined the Royal Navy as midshipman in 1755; by 1781 he had gained the rank of captain. In 1786 he was appointed captain-general of the proposed expedition to NSW and governor of the projected convict settlement. On 13 May 1787 the First Fleet sailed from Portsmouth and Phillip, in HMS *Supply,* reached Botany Bay 18 January 1788. Disappointed in Botany Bay as a place for the settlement, he explored the Port Jackson district, finally selecting a suitable cove that he named Sydney Cove. On 26 January 1788, now celebrated as Australia Day, a party was landed at Sydney Cove and a ceremony marked the founding of the British settlement. A humane, decisive, energetic and determined governor, Phillip was sustained by a positive vision of the Colony's future, as many of his memoranda and letters preserved in the *Historical Records of New South Wales* reveal. The official account of the expedition to NSW and the founding of the settlement, titled *The Voyage of Governor Phillip to Botany Bay* and first published in 1789, is a compilation from the official dispatches of Phillip and from accounts by several of his officers; it contained detailed appendices and was illustrated with maps, plans and drawings of native flora and fauna. Frequently reprinted, the most accessible edition is that edited by J.J. Auchmuty (1970); also important are the accounts by Watkin Tench, John White, John Hunter and David Collins. Of the accounts of Phillip's life those by G.D. Milford (1935), George Mackaness (1937), and 'M. Barnard Eldershaw' (1938) are the most substantial. He appears in J.H.M. Abbott's novel, *Sydney Cove* (1923), but the most extensive fictional interpretation of his governorship is in Eleanor Dark's *The Timeless Land* (1941).

PHILLIPS, A.A. (ARTHUR ANGELL) (1900–), was born in Melbourne of Jewish ancestors who had arrived in Australia from England in the 1820s, and of parents who were strongly nationalistic in sentiment; his father was president of the ANA. Phillips studied at the Universities of Melbourne and Oxford before becoming a schoolmaster at Wesley College, 1925–71. While on the committee of the English Association, his interest in Australian literature was aroused by a request from England for a list of Australian poets for inclusion in a British Empire anthology. His own publications began with an anthology of Australian and English poetry, *In Fealty to Apollo* (1932, with Ian Maxwell) and a prose anthology, *An Australian Muster* (1946). Phillips's first major impact on the Australian literary scene came with his article, 'The Cultural Cringe' (q.v.) in *Meanjin* (1950), in which he expresses his dissatisfaction with the prevailing Australian attitude of cultural servility. He published *Thinkers At Work,* a book on logical writing (1946, with A. Boyce Gibson); edited *Five Radio Plays* (1949), which includes Douglas Stewart's *The Fire on the Snow, Ten Tales : A Collection of Short Stories* (1951), *Presenting Ideas*

(1952, with Mary Phillips), and *Australian Poetry* (1956). A selection of his critical articles from *Meanjin* and *Overland* was published as *The Australian Tradition* (q.v., 1958) a work which emphasizes the importance of the democratic theme in the development of a distinctive Australian literary tradition. *The Australian Tradition* established him as one of Australia's leading critics and the book itself has become an integral part of the literary heritage it posits. Phillips edited, with valuable introductions, *Bernard O'Dowd* (1963) and Barbara Baynton's *Bush Studies* (1965), and compiled *Coast to Coast* (1968), which emphasizes rural and country town stories and reflects Phillips's belief in the importance of the Henry Lawson–Joseph Furphy tradition. His chief critical work, *Henry Lawson* (1970), although directed towards an American reading public, adds to the contribution he made to Lawson studies with his earlier articles, 'The Craftsmanship of Lawson' and 'Henry Lawson Revisited', included in the 1966 edition of *The Australian Tradition. Responses* (1979), edited by Brian Kiernan, is a selection of Phillips's literary journalism in his characteristic lucid, fresh and pugnacious style. A.A. Phillips, long associated with the FAW and with *Meanjin,* was awarded the honorary degree of Doctor of Letters from the University of Melbourne in 1975 and was made foundation patron of ASAL in 1978.

PHILLIPS, CHARLES WALTER ('DENTON PROUT') (1910–), born Broadford, Victoria, spent most of his working life as a public servant, ending his career as chief electoral officer of Victoria. He has written an important biography of Henry Lawson, *Henry Lawson: The Grey Dreamer* (1963) and two books with Fred Feely, *Petticoat Parade* (1965), a collection of biographies of colonial women, and *50 Years Hard : The Story of Pentridge Gaol from 1850 to 1900* (1967).

PHILP, J.A. (JAMES ALEXANDER) (1861–1935), born Stirling, Scotland, was a journalist in Queensland and sub-editor of the *Bulletin,* to which he also contributed short stories. He published two collections of verse, *Jingles That Jangle* (1918) and *Songs of the Australian Fascisti* (1923). His short stories, several of which are set in NZ, where he was educated, were collected in 1916, titled *Some Bulletin Stories.*

PHIPSON, JOAN (1912–), born Warrawee, NSW, was educated in Australia and overseas, and worked as a secretary, librarian and script-writer for radio before her marriage in 1944. Subsequently she lived on stations in western NSW. A well-known writer of fiction for the younger adolescent, Phipson has published numerous novels which include *Good Luck to the Rider* (1953), *Six and Silver* (1954), *It Happened One Summer* (1957), *The Boundary Riders* (1962), *The Family Conspiracy* (1962), *Threat to the Barkers* (1963), *Birkin* (1965), *A Lamb in the Family* (1966), *The Crew of the Merlin* (1966), *Peter and Butch* (1969), *The Haunted Night* (1970), *Bass & Billy Martin* (1972), *The Way Home* (1973), *Polly's Tiger* (1973), *The Cats* (1976), *Keep Calm* (1978), *Mr. Pringle and the Prince* (1979) and *A Tide Flowing* (1981). She has twice won the Children's Book of the Year Award (for *Good Luck to the Rider* and *A Family Conspiracy*). Phipson's first novels were bush adventures or family stories dealing with the familiar routines of station life, but she has subsequently explored a range of genres from surrealist fantasy, as in *The Way Home*, to historical fiction, as in *Bass & Billy Martin*, to sea adventure, as in *The Crew of the Merlin*. Sensitive to the need of the young individual to find acceptance, she has increasingly turned her attention to social problems such as delinquency, the generation gap, the limitations of modern urban life, destruction of the environment and even drug abuse.

Phoenix, the literary annual of the University of Adelaide Union, was published irregularly 1935–50 and included verse, short stories and book reviews. Contributors included Rex Ingamells, Clement Semmler, C.R. Jury, Max Harris, Ian Mudie, Flexmore Hudson, Hal Porter and Brian Elliott.

'PI O' is the pseudonym of Peter Oustabasidis, who was born in Greece but has been resident in Australia since infancy. A draughtsman in the Victorian public service, he is well-known out of working hours as an anarchist and a reader and writer of concrete verse. He has been editor of such underground poetry magazines as *Fitzrot, Born to Concrete, Free, Free Too, Free Read, i's and e's* and 9.2.5 and is a familiar contributor to such magazines as *Ploughman, Contempa, Magic Sam, Luna* and *Your Friendly Fascist*. An enthusiastic supporter of poetry readings in schools, prisons, universities, at political demonstrations and on radio, Pi O has also attempted to interpret and represent the views of Melbourne's migrant community. He has published seven collections of verse, *Fitzroy Brothel* (1974), *Shade* (1974, with Stephanie Bennett), *Emotions in Concrete* (1975), *Street Singe* (1976), *Pi O Revisited* (1976), *Panash* (1979) and *Re: The National Neurosis : Ockers* (1983).

Piccadilly Bushman, The, see LAWLER, RAY

Picnic at Hanging Rock, a novel by Joan Lindsay (q.v.), was first published in 1967 and made into an internationally successful film in 1975. On St Valentine's Day 1900, a party of nineteen schoolgirls and two mistresses from the fashionable Appleyard College picnic at Hanging Rock, a volcanic mass in the Mt Macedon area of Victoria. A tragedy strangely disfigures the idyllic outing: three girls, Miranda, Irma Leopold and Marion Quade, and their teacher, Greta McCraw, mysteriously disappear from the face of the rock. The incident has profound, progressive effects on numerous lives, most notably on a young Englishman, Michael Fitzhubert, who is drawn by his single vision of the beautiful Miranda and later succeeds in finding one of the girls, Irma Leopold. Four other deaths eventually flow from the initial tragedy, including that of the headmistress of the College, the evil Mrs Appleyard.

PICOT, JAMES (1906–44), born England, came to Australia in 1923 and graduated from the University of Queensland. In 1941 he enlisted in the AIF and died as a POW on the Burma–Siam railway. He was one of the four contributors of verse to the first issue of *Meanjin*, which published a selection of letters, personal recollections and critical appreciations of his work in 1954. His extant poems were collected after his death, titled *With a Hawk's Quill* (1953). Influenced by such poets as Robert Browning, T.S. Eliot and Gerard Manley Hopkins, Picot wrote mainly conventional, contemplative verse.

Picturesque Atlas of Australasia, a lavishly-illustrated descriptive work which also covers the history, geography and development of the Australian colonies, NZ, and parts of the Pacific (e.g. New Guinea, Fiji), was a publishing enterprise initiated by American book salesman, Silas Lyon Moffett, and J.W. Lyon, who had worked on the successful *Picturesque Canada* (1882–85). They interested a number of Australian journalists and artists in an equivalent Australian project, and the Picturesque Atlas Publishing Company was formed with William Macleod as chairman. The *Picturesque Atlas* was published in parts (?1883–86) and as a three volume set in 1886; it was several times reprinted and updated, e.g. in 1892 as *Australasia Unlimited,* but the publishing venture was unsuccessful and the methods used to promote the work led to changes to the law to protect consumers. Andrew Garran was nominal editor with F.J. Broomfield and F.J. Donohue as assistant editors. Literary contributors included Broomfield, Donohue, G.B. Barton, James Smith, W.H. Traill, Baron von Mueller, and Ada Cambridge (writing as Ada Cross). Artists whose work was featured in the *Atlas,* which was significant not only for the quality of its wood-engravings but also because the project brought artists and engravers to Australia who had experience with recently-developed techniques, were F.B. Schell, Macleod, Frank Mahony, A.H. Fullwood, Tom Roberts, and Julian Rossi Ashton.

PIDDINGTON, W.R. (WILLIAM RICHMAN) (1815–87), born London, was brought up in the book trade. He migrated to NSW in 1838 and in 1848 formed a partnership with a Sydney bookseller, W.A. Colman. When the partnership foundered fourteen months later, Piddington went into business on his own and published Charles Harpur's collection, *The Bushrangers* (1853). A prominent figure in public affairs, Piddington opposed transportation and campaigned for constitutional reform. Elected to the NSW parliament in 1856, he served in several governments and was treasurer in two ministries headed by Henry Parkes, with whom he was friendly. Appointed to the Legislative Council in 1879, on Parkes's recommendation, he was chairman of committees 1885–87.

PIDGEON, WILLIAM EDWIN (1909–81), the cartoonist, 'Wep', was born in Paddington, Sydney, and began an art cadetship with the *Evening News* in 1925; the following year he had his first comic strip published in the *Sunday News*. For more than two decades with the Sydney press he worked, in a style which shows the influence of Phil May, for the *Daily Guardian,* the *Sun,* the *Daily Telegraph,* and, most importantly, the *Australian Women's Weekly,* where he formed a partnership with Lennie Lower and drew 'In and Out of Society', a domestic strip which gently focuses on marital discord. Although best known for his comic strips and cartoons, Pidgeon illustrated many books, e.g. John O'Grady's *They're a Weird Mob* (1957), and won the Archibald Prize for portraiture in 1958, 1961 and 1968, after he gave up newspaper work in 1949.

PIKE, DOUGLAS HENRY (1908–74), born China, the son of a missionary, came to Australia in 1924 and was manager of a pastoral property and a minister of religion before becoming a lecturer in history at the University of Adelaide. He was appointed professor of history at the University of Tasmania in 1961 and general editor of the *Australian Dictionary of Biography* (q.v.) in 1964. He published two influential histories, *Paradise of Dissent : South Australia 1829–1857* (1957), an encyclopaedic account of the settlement of SA and the role of dissenting religious attitudes, and *Australia:*

The Quiet Continent (1962), a general history of Australia. General editor of the first five volumes of the *Australian Dictionary of Biography,* he won the Encyclopaedia Britannica Award in 1971. He was also advisory editor of the Great Australians Series (1955–75) in which Oxford University Press, with Pike's assistance, published some sixty small monographs, the majority of which at that time had to be written from primary sources. Many of the scholarly authors recommended by Pike have since published major biographies of the subjects of their Great Australians monographs.

'PILGRIM, A (THE)', see **ARGLES, THEODORE EMILE**

Pinchgut Press, see **PIZER, MARJORIE**

'PINDAR JUVENAL', see *Van Diemen's Land Warriors, The*

PINNEY, PETER (1922–   ), born Sydney, and grandson of the colonial administrator Sir Hubert Murray, was educated in Sydney and served in New Guinea during the Second World War. He has worked as an opal-digger, wharf-labourer and seaman, but his main interest has been travel. An eccentric traveller, who has often moved round the world without money or passport, he has written several vivid accounts of his travels: *Dust on My Shoes* (1951), his best-known book, a description of a journey on foot in the Middle East and Asia; *Who Wanders Alone* (1954); *Anywhere But Here* (1956); *The Lawless and the Lotus* (1963); and *Restless Men* (1966), dealing with his travels in northern Australia. He has also written two novels, *Road in the Wilderness* (1952) and *Ride the Volcano* (1960), the first of which draws on his war experiences; an account of a crocodile-shooting expedition, *To Catch a Crocodile* (1976); and, with Estelle Runcie, *Too Many Spears* (1978), the biography of Frank Jardine, government resident and police magistrate in the Cape York Peninsula in the 1860s.

Pioneer Players was a company formed in 1921–22 in Melbourne by Louis Esson, Vance Palmer and Stewart Macky (qq.v.). Although financially limited and composed of amateur players, apart from the actor, George Dawe, the company aimed at producing simple plays expressive of the life of ordinary Australians and as nationally inspiring as those staged by the Abbey Theatre in Ireland. The first season in 1922 saw the production of Esson's 'The Battler' and *The Woman Tamer,* Stewart Macky's 'John Blake' and *The Trap,* and plays by Gerald Byrne and Vance Palmer. The following year the company produced *Mother and Son* and *The*

Drovers by Louis Esson, *Travellers* and *The Black Horse* by Vance Palmer, and plays by Katharine Susannah Prichard, Alan Mulgan, Frank Wilmot and Ernest O'Ferrall. To Esson's deep disappointment, the plays failed to arouse a popular following and although he managed to organize a single night's performance of his play, *The Bride of Gospel Place*, in 1926, the death of George Dawe and the departure of the Palmers saw the end of the project.

Pioneers, The, see **PRICHARD, KATHARINE SUSANNAH**

Pipes were anonymous, scurrilous verses, which were occasionally circulated in NSW during the early years of settlement and which lampooned those in authority from the governor down. The name may derive from the verb, to pipe, meaning to observe and victimize an individual, or from the habit of folding the lampoon in the shape of a pipe. The first pipes, directed against Governor King, were written in 1803 and others to suffer from the lampoons were Samuel Marsden and Lieutenant-Colonel George Molle. W.C. Wentworth is known to be author of some pipes and other alleged authors are Michael Massey Robinson and some officers of the NSW Corps.

PITT, MARIE (1869–1948), was born in a mining town in Gippsland as Marie McKeown. She married William Pitt, a Tasmanian gold miner, in 1893 and subsequently lived in mining and farming areas of Tasmania, moving to Melbourne in 1902 after her husband contracted a lung disease. A familiar figure in feminist and socialist circles, a member of the Victorian Socialist Party, and editor for a time of the *Socialist,* she wrote several ballads which have an underlying note of social protest. Friendly with such writers as Vance and Nettie Palmer and Louis Esson, she was particularly influenced by Bernard O'Dowd, with whom she lived from 1919. Her verse, which first began to appear in the *Bulletin* in 1900, was published in four collections, *The Horses of the Hills* (1911), *Bairnsdale and Other Poems* (1922), *The Poems of Marie E.J. Pitt* (1925) and *Selected Poems* (1944). Pitt's best-known work is contained in her studies of landscape, her most radical verse being omitted from the 1944 selection.

PIZER, MARJORIE (1920–), born Melbourne and educated at the University of Melbourne, lives in Sydney where she works as a psychotherapist. She has published several collections of poetry, *Thou and I* (1967), *To Life* (1969), *Tides Flow* (1972), *Seasons of Love* (1975), *Full Summer* (1977), *Gifts and Remembrances* (1979), *To You, the Living* (1981), *The*

Sixtieth Spring (1982), and with Anne Spencer Parry, *Below the Surface* (1982). She has also edited an anthology of poetry, *Freedom on the Wallaby* (1953); a selection of stories and poems by Henry Lawson, *The Men Who Made Australia* (1957); and with her husband, Muir Holburn, a collection of verse by Victor Daley, *Creeve Roe* (1947). Pizer and Holburn were founders of the Pinchgut Press in 1947, which published *Creeve Roe* and *Freedom on the Wallaby* and which was revived in 1975 to publish Pizer's poetry and Anne Spencer Parry's first novel, *The Land behind the World* (1976).

Playwrights Advisory Board was founded in 1938 by Leslie Rees, Rex Rienits and Doris Fitton, with the object of fostering Australian theatre. Although the Board had no production capacity, it negotiated productions with both professional and amateur theatres, acted as an intermediary in the nomination and collection of royalties, and advised both theatres and playwrights on scripts. Rees was chairman of the Board during its existence; Fitton and Rienits soon withdrew, but numerous others worked for the Board for varying periods, including Dymphna Cusack, Sumner Locke-Elliot, May Hollinworth, Sydney Tomholt, Gwen Harrison, Alrene Sykes, George Farwell, Alan Ashbolt and Richard Lane. The Board was instrumental in securing publication of Australian plays, and was active in opposing censorship and in the running and judging of play competitions. One of the most important competitions, held in 1955, yielded two first-prize winners, *Summer of the Seventeenth Doll* by Ray Lawler, and *The Torrents* by Oriel Gray; the Board was later active in securing professional production of Lawler's internationally-successful play. Other significant competitions in which the Board was involved were those of 1956, when first prize was awarded to Richard Beynon's *The Shifting Heart,* and 1961, when first prize was shared by Hal Porter's *The Tower* and Robert Amos's *When the Gravediggers Come.* After 1963 the Board ceased operations, its functions having been taken over by various commercial agencies and by the Australian Elizabethan Theatre Trust.

Ploughman, and Other Poems, The, see **WHITE, PATRICK**

Pluralist, a magazine which described itself as 'of the non-popularist left' and adopted the subtitle, *A Journal of Social and Literary Criticism,* from its third issue, was published irregularly in Sydney 1962–69. Edited by Richard Appleton, W. Maidment and others, it included articles of general literary or philosophical interest and some verse and short stories. Contributors included Bruce Beaver, Norman

Talbot, Frank Moorhouse, John Tranter and Clive James.

Poems (1913), see **BRENNAN, C.J.**

Poems and Songs, Henry Kendall's (q.v.) first volume of verse, was published in 1862. Many of these early Kendall poems attempt, however imperfectly, to reflect the spirit and character of Australian life and to picture the beauty of the Australian coastal landscape. Kendall, the sentimental young romantic, is also evident in them. Well-known poems include 'The Muse of Australia', 'Wild Kangaroo', 'The Curlew Song' and 'Morning in the Bush'.

Poems from Prison, see Anthologies

Poetical Works of Henry Lawson, the first major edition of Henry Lawson's (q.v.) verse published after his death, was edited by David McKee Wright (q.v.) and appeared in 1925. It contained Wright's preface to the 1918 *Selected Poems of Henry Lawson* (q.v.), a new introduction, and the text of three Lawson selections published in 1924: *Winnowed Verse, Popular Verses* and *Humorous Verses. Poetical Works of Henry Lawson,* which contains virtually all of Lawson's most famous poems, is the Lawson volume best-known to Australians, sometimes under other titles. The text, however, is unreliable: Wright, who persuaded Lawson to make many changes to the poems included in the 1918 *Selected Poems of Henry Lawson,* continued 'editing' Lawson's work after his death with the assistance also of A.W. Jose and George Robertson (2). The fruits of their labour were the three 1924 selections and then the *Poetical Works of Henry Lawson;* but it was not until the appearance of Colin Roderick's three-volume *Collected Verse* (1967–69) that an authoritative text was established.

Poetry: A Quarterly of Australian and New Zealand Verse, founded and edited by Flexmore Hudson, was published in Adelaide, 1941–47. Uncommitted to any particular ideology, the magazine published a mixture of notable and negligible talents; it changed its subtitle in 1946 to the *Australian International Quarterly of Verse* to reflect the subsequent inclusion of British, Irish and American poets. Contributors included Judith Wright, 'Brian Vrepont', Gina Ballantyne, Rex Ingamells and A.D. Hope.

Poetry Australia, a quarterly poetry magazine founded, managed and edited by Grace Perry (q.v.), was first published in 1964 when Perry led a movement away from the Poetry Society of Australia (q.v.) and its journal, *Poetry Mag-* *azine,* later *New Poetry* (q.v.). *Poetry Australia,* aided by editorial advice and assistance from poets such as Bruce Beaver and Les Murray and from critics and academics such as Ronald Dunlop, James Tulip and Leonie Kramer, publishes both new and established Australian writers, as well as modern overseas poetry. It has published issues of NZ, Canadian, Italian, Japanese, Dutch and Flemish, American, Gaelic and Papua-New Guinean poetry; commemorative issues on Francis Webb and David Campbell; two Young Poets issues; and poetry of the various Australian States. Based in Sydney, *Poetry Australia* has also played a leading part in poetry readings and workshops, in literary seminars, and in visits by overseas writers of distinction. A comprehensive account of the *raison d'être* of *Poetry Australia* and of its history is given by Les Murray, its acting-editor 1973–79, in 'Inside *Poetry Australia', Quadrant* (1983).

Poetry Magazine, see **Poetry Society of Australia**

Poetry Militant is the name given to the poetic credo expressed by Bernard O'Dowd (q.v.) in a presidential address to the Australian Literature Society in 1909. The poet is to be 'the ferment who alters for the better, the ordered, natural, inert sequence of things'; his role is to accelerate the process of intellectual and moral evolution. Poetry Militant stresses the need for the poet to concern himself with worthy themes, e.g. politics, religion, sex, science, social reform, and with simple forms. It eschews 'Poetry Triumphant', the poetry of beauty and ornamentation, until the proper social order has been achieved.

Poetry Society of Australia was founded in Sydney in 1954 to encourage the study of poetry and to establish an active fellowship with a love of poetry as a common bond. In addition to performances by members of the Society (Shelley's *The Cenci* was produced in its first year), lectures and poetry competitions, the Society commenced publication in July 1954 of a journal, *Prism. Prism* was superseded in 1961 by *Poetry Magazine,* a bi-monthly publication edited, until 1964, by Grace Perry, assisted by Roland Robinson and others. *Poetry Magazine* ran until 1970 when a dispute as to the question of how much space should be devoted to American and English writers saw its disappearance and replacement by *New Poetry* (q.v.) in February 1971.

Poets and Prose Writers of New South Wales, The (1866), edited by G.B. Barton (q.v.), is a supplementary volume to *Literature in New South Wales* (q.v.), published earlier the same year. Whereas the earlier volume is a comprehensive account of the literature of the colony, the supplement concentrates on important writers. The writers discussed are W.C. Wentworth, John Dunmore Lang, Charles Harpur, William Forster, James Martin, Henry Parkes, D.H. Deniehy, Robert Sealy, W.B. Dalley, Henry Kendall, Henry Halloran, T.L. Mitchell, J.L. Michael and G.R. Morton. Both volumes were compiled for the Paris Exhibition of 1867.

Poet's Choice, see **ROBERTS, PHILIP**

Poets of the Month was a series of slim booklets of verse, published monthly by Angus & Robertson, each booklet featuring the work of a single poet. The booklets were consolidated in several series, 1976–80.

Poets on Record, a series of recordings of well-known Australian poets reading from their own works, was published by the University of Queensland Press and edited by Thomas Shapcott. The series ran 1970–75.

POIGNANT, AXEL (1906–   ), born in England of Anglo-Swedish parentage, was educated partly in Sweden. He arrived in Australia in 1926 and began to pursue an interest in photography when he moved to Perth in 1930. By the mid-1930s he had extended the range of his work to include press photographs, and began to experiment with the photo-story. Fascinated by the Australian landscape, wildlife and outback personalities, Poignant also photographed several Australian writers and artists. He developed a strong affinity with the Aborigines, which is reflected in his highly popular book for children, *Piccaninny Walkabout* (1957), redesigned and retitled *Bush Walkabout* in 1972. In 1956 Poignant left Australia and settled in London, where he worked as a freelance photo-journalist for such newspapers as the *Observer* and the London *Times*. His other books on Australia are *Bush Animals of Australia* (1949) and *The Improbable Kangaroo and Other Australian Animals* (1965). A selection of his photographs was published in 1982, titled *Axel Poignant: Photographs 1922–1980*.

Pole, Hereward, see *Miner's Right, The*

Policy and Passion, a novel by Rosa Praed (q.v.), was published in 1881, adapted for the stage by Edward Reeve (q.v.) in 1884, and republished in 1887 as *Longleat of Kooralbyn;* like other Praed novels, it is set in Leichardt's (sic.) Land (Queensland) and informed by

Praed's experience of her family's property, Maroon (Kooralbyn in the novel), and of political activities in Brisbane (Leichardt's Town). *Policy and Passion* centres on the passions of Thomas Longleat, self-made premier of Leichardt's Land, his daughter, Honoria, and the people with whom they become emotionally involved: Thomas with Constance Vallancy, the wife of a politician opposed to Longleat, Honoria with Hardress Barrington, the dissolute second son of an English baronet who has been sent to the colonies by a disappointed mother and who turns Honoria away from her long-term and faithful suitor Dyson Maddox. Meeting Constance in his electorate early in the novel, Longleat travels back to Leichardt's Town with her, and as their relationship develops he is persuaded to appoint her husband to a police magistracy in the country. This action, together with a controversy about railway extension, contributes to the fall of his government, although he is successful at the polls. Barrington, meanwhile, pays a series of visits to Kooralbyn while staying with friends nearby, and attracts the interest not only of the strong-willed Honoria, whose need for excitement has caused her to reject the stolid Dyson's appeal, but also of Angela Ferris, the delicate artistic daughter of Anthony Ferris, storekeeper at Kooralbyn, who is jealous of Longleat's success. Barrington, motivated partly by Honoria's wealth, declares his love; when Honoria escapes to Leichardt's Town fearing his growing mastery, he follows and is eventually successful in his proposal, although the match is violently opposed by Longleat, who wishes her husband to be an Australian such as Maddox. Longleat's opposition leads to his estrangement from his daughter and to her meeting Barrington in secret.

The third volume of the novel opens with the death of Angela from a fever; her father, blaming Barrington and Honoria for her decline, revenges himself on the Longleats by informing Vallancy of the affair between Constance and the premier. Vallancy's return to Leichardt's Town, confirmation of the liaison, and subsequent scene with Constance results in her decision to leave the colony, and Longleat's problems are compounded by the fact that Barrington has compromised Honoria when their secret night-time meeting becomes public, although Dyson Maddox saves her reputation by pretending that he and Honoria are engaged. The reconciliation of Honoria and her father is, however, short-lived; on information originating from Ferris, the leader of the parliamentary opposition exposes Longleat's ex-convict past. He commits suicide, although at the end of the novel Dyson, whose engagement has become reality, has married Honoria and succeeded in politics.

POLITZER, LUDWIG, editor of the *Centenary Journal 1934–35* (1935) and the author of two volumes of verse, *Autumn Leaves* (1934) and *In Introspective Mood* (1944), compiled several useful bibliographies of French, German and Dutch writing on the subject of Australia (1952, 1953). He also compiled a bibliography of Leichhardt literature (1953), translated some of Leichhardt's letters (1932) and Stefan Kotze's *Australian Sketches* (1945).

POLLARD, JAMES ('MOPOKE') (1900–), born Yorkshire, England, migrated to WA at the age of fourteen. After the First World War, in which he served with the AIF and was severely wounded, Pollard took up land under the soldier settlement scheme but soon abandoned farming for writing. A well-known writer on natural history, a frequent contributor to *Walkabout* and, as 'Mopoke', the author of a column on natural history in the *West Australian*, Pollard also contributed short stories to such newspapers as the *Australasian* and the *Western Mail*. Some of these were collected in 1948, titled *Twenty-Eight Tales*. He wrote two novels for children and three for adults; his adult novels, *The Bushland Man* (1926), *Rose of the Bushlands* (1927) and *Bushland Vagabonds* (1928), are distinguished more by their incidental naturalist descriptions than by any literary features.

Pollit Family, see *Man Who Loved Children, The*

Pom, Pommy, are Australian words denoting an English immigrant or national, and are often used derogatively, as in 'pommy bastard'. The origin of 'pommy' is uncertain: derivations from the acronym POME (Prisoner of Mother England), from 'pomegranate', and from rhyming slang (from 'immigrant' via 'pommygrant') have been suggested. H.J. Rumsey uses the expression in his novel, *The Pommies* (1920).

Poor Fellow My Country, a novel by Xavier Herbert (q.v.), was published in 1975 and won the Miles Franklin Award for that year; some 850 000 words, it is the longest Australian novel ever published. Set mainly in and around the Northern Territory, like Herbert's earlier novel, *Capricornia* (q.v., 1938), *Poor Fellow My Country* shares many of *Capricornia's* themes, techniques and concerns, e.g. the majesty of the land, the motif of the journey, the destruction of Aboriginal society. Chronologically it follows *Capricornia* in depicting the tragic effects of white settlement in Australia, although its time span is much more concentrated, covering the years from 1936 to 1942. Among the several dozen characters whose histories are nar-

rated, the most important are Jeremy Delacy, a hard-bitten, idealized pioneer, at odds with many of his fellow whites, whose talents, prejudices and passions find some parallels in Herbert himself; the women whom Jeremy influences, notably his half-caste second wife, Nanango, the aristocratic Lydia Lyndbrooke-Esk, the idealistic Alfie Candlemass, and the Jewish refugee, Rifkah; Jeremy's grandson, Prindy, who is of Irish, English and Aboriginal descent, responds to Jewish and Indian as well as Aboriginal culture in the novel and whose death signals the end of hopes of an integration of culture and belief in Australia; Bobwirridirridi, 'Cock-Eye Bob' to the whites, and perhaps the finest piece of characterization in the novel, an Aboriginal wise man who meets Prindy and adopts him as tribal protégé in the opening scene; representatives of the institution of white society, e.g. the police sergeant, Dinny Cahoon, who believes Prindy to be his son, anthropologist Fabian Cootes, protector of Aborigines, Eddie McCuskey, and British military commander of the Australian Army, Sir Mark Esk, Lydia's father; and numerous railway workers, pioneering families and outback types.

'Terra Australis', the first of *Poor Fellow My Country's* three books, covers 1936–37 and is summarized by Herbert as 'Blackman's Idyll Despoiled by White Bullies, Thieves and Hypocrites'. That summary is elaborated, for the first but not the last time, early in 'Terra Australis' by Jeremy to a stock inspector visiting his property, Lily Lagoons, a sanctuary where Jeremy tries to live in harmony with the environment and its original inhabitants. In contrast, the disruption and attempted control of Aboriginal practices twice results in violence in 'Terra Australis': first, the pursuit of Prindy after he leaves Lily Lagoons with Bobwirridirridi to undergo the first stage of his initiation culminates in the death of Willy Ah Loy, his adoptive father; later, the deaths of Nelyerri, Prindy's mother, and Njorjinga, his tribal uncle, have their origins in the attempted separation of Prindy and Nelyerri by the authorities at Port Palmerston (Darwin), where they are brought after Willy's murder. The other major focus of 'Terra Australis' is Jeremy's relationships with Lydia Lyndbrooke-Esk and Alfie Candlemass. He meets Lydia, the fiancée of the land baron, Lord Vaisey, at the Beatrice River races, an annual Territory occasion and a recurring event in *Poor Fellow My Country;* she falls in love with him but is rejected, along with her fascist philosophy, during a tour of Lily Lagoons and surrounding areas, in which she is shown the realities of outback life. Similarly, Alfie Candlemass, who has come to the Territory imbued with idealism and been disillusioned by the corruption and insensitivity of government, falls in love with Jeremy when they meet at the Beatrice River races the following year; although Jeremy rejects her advances also, he rekindles her desire to effect social and political change. She returns south to write and become involved in Australia Free, a nationalist movement modelled on Australia First (q.v.).

The second book of *Poor Fellow My Country*, sardonically titled 'Australia Felix — Whiteman's Ideal Sold Out by Rogues and Fools', covers the period from 1937 to 1939, when the Beatrice River races are postponed because of the onset of the Second World War. Against a background of the worsening international situation, much of the action of 'Australia Felix' is centred on Lily Lagoons, where Prindy finds temporary refuge from representatives of authority such as Cahoon and McCuskey, into whose hands he has fallen after witnessing the deaths of his mother and uncle following their escape from Port Palmerston. Two new visitors to Lily Lagoons are Sir Mark Esk, who is sufficiently impressed by Jeremy's beliefs and integrity to eventually ask him to take over military command of the northern region, and Rifkah, a Jewish refugee who finds in Lily Lagoons and in her experience with Prindy of Aboriginal culture an inner harmony that radiates to others around her; her understanding of the land and its inhabitants is in contrast to the lack of perception of the government anthropologist, Fabian Cootes. The outside world, however, threatens Rifkah when she is arrested and faces deportation on the grounds that she is a communist, although she finds refuge, after barely escaping death while on the run from the security police, at Leopold Catholic mission off the coast, which she has already visited with a party from Lily Lagoons. Prindy joins her there under the guardianship of the church after himself escaping from Dinny Cahoon, whose death he engineers in the process. Jeremy, meanwhile, has become involved in Australia Free and journeys to Sydney and Melbourne to help Alfie inaugurate it as a political party, cleanse it of its fascist and anti-semitic elements, and direct it towards fulfilling its responsibilities to the Aborigines. He fails in the attempt, and returns to Lily Lagoons at the end of 'Australia Felix' to live on his old individualistic terms.

The title of the final book, 'Day of Shame — A Rabble Fled the Test of Nationhood', refers to the mass exodus from Darwin in 1942 in the face of the Japanese attack. The progress of the war again forms part of the background, and again Jeremy journeys south, this time at the request of Mark Esk that he join his staff and report on conditions in Malaya. A meeting with the officer who led his

brother to death at Gallipoli convinces Jeremy that the sacrifice of the Australian Army to imperial rather than nationalist ends is being repeated; he resigns his commission but before leaving Sydney is badly beaten up with Alfie during a political meeting in the Domain. She loses the child Jeremy has fathered during the Australia Free interlude, and becomes disillusioned with Jeremy when in her eyes he fails to act with spirit when they are unfairly detained for security reasons after the fracas. Soon after his return to the Territory, Jeremy discovers that Lily Lagoons is to be commandeered by the army; with his sanctuary there invaded, he creates another one further away from civilization, where he is joined briefly by Prindy and Rifkah before they return to the Leopold mission, where they have spent much of the time during Jeremy's absence. At the mission Rifkah, who has been pursued by several men since her arrival in Australia, finds fulfilment in her relationship with a priest; Prindy, too, has become attached to Savitra, the daughter of an Indian hawker who has several times sheltered him. The idyll of Rifkah, Prindy and their lovers is interrupted by their enforced evacuation for military reasons, but their arrival in Port Palmerston coincides with the Japanese bombing, and they escape back to Jeremy's camp in company with Bobwirridirridi, who has retained his Aboriginal claim on Prindy despite Prindy's ability to accommodate other cultures. It is in the region of Jeremy's camp that the final tragedies of *Poor Fellow My Country* occur: when Prindy's initiation is interrupted by Savitra's search for him, she is brutally murdered for her intrusion; Jeremy's pursuit of her results only in Prindy's death, in that Prindy's attention, distracted by Jeremy's cry during the trial by ordeal Savitra's intrusion has forced upon him, means that he is speared; and Jeremy too, having caused Prindy's death, is speared by Bobwirridirridi. The final chapter of the novel is an epilogue set some years after the war, in which the profound pessimism of the novel is confirmed by the description of how post-war development of the Northern Territory has completed the destruction of Aboriginal society; for example, the Rainbow Pool and the Painted Caves, central to the novel's presentation of Aboriginal belief, have been despoiled by mining and tourism.

Poor Man's Orange, see **PARK, RUTH**

Port Arthur, some 160 kilometres from Hobart on the south-eastern coast of Tasmania, was a notorious penal settlement, 1830–77. A natural penitentiary because of its situation on Tasman peninsula and of the narrowness of Eaglehawk Neck, a narrow isthmus joining

Tasman and Forestier peninsulas, Port Arthur is described in detail in Marcus Clarke's novel, *His Natural Life* (1874), and figures prominently in much other convict literature. Among many works on Port Arthur is Margaret Weidenhofer's *Port Arthur : A Place of Misery* (1981).

Port Phillip District, which became the State of Victoria (q.v.), has its origin in Governor Philip King's naming of the large inlet on the central Victorian coast on which the major cities of Melbourne and Geelong now stand, Port Phillip Bay. The earliest attempt to establish a settlement at Port Phillip was by David Collins; J.H. Tuckey's account of that expedition, *An Account of a Voyage to Establish a Colony at Port Phillip in Bass's Strait* was published in 1805. The Port Phillip Association was formed in Hobart early in 1835 to attempt again to establish a settlement at Port Phillip where, soon after, John Batman (q.v.) established himself. The first successful overland expedition from NSW into the Port Phillip District was that of W.H. Hovell and Hamilton Hume in 1824–25. The titles of most early Melbourne newspapers, e.g. the *Port Phillip Herald, Port Phillip Gazette, Port Phillip Patriot,* confirm the currency of the term in the 1830s and 1840s. Descriptive and historical writings on the Port Phillip District include J.B. Clutterbuck's *Port Phillip in 1849* (1850), E.M. Curr's *Recollections of Squatting in Victoria, Then Called the Port Phillip District* (1883) and T.F. Bride (ed.) *Letters from Victorian Pioneers* (1898). Early settlers of the Port Phillip District include the McCraes, the Furphys and the family of 'Rolf Boldrewood'. Early Port Phillip society is described in Paul de Serville's *Port Phillip Gentlemen* (1980) and in the contemporary reminiscences, *Georgiana's Journal* (1934).

Port Phillip Gazette, one of Victoria's earliest newspapers, was published in Melbourne, sometimes daily and sometimes weekly, 1838–51; in 1844–51 it was edited by Thomas McCombie (q.v.). A modern *Port Phillip Gazette* was published in Melbourne, 1952–56, edited by Desmond Fennessy.

Port Phillip Herald, see *Herald*

Port Phillip Patriot and Melbourne Advertiser, see **FAWKNER, JOHN PASCOE**

Portable Australian Authors, a series of editions of Australian authors and literary movements, has been published by the University of Queensland Press since 1976 under the general editorship of L.T. Hergenhan. The series so far encompasses Barbara Baynton, 'Rolf

Boldrewood', Marcus Clarke, Joseph Furphy, Henry Kingsley, Henry Lawson, Hal Porter, the 1890s, the Jindyworobaks, science fiction, *New Guinea Images in Australian Literature* and *Five Plays for Stage, Radio and T.V.*

PORTEOUS, R.S. (RICHARD SYDNEY) (1897–1963), born Melbourne, served in the Australian Light Horse in the First World War and subsequently worked on a cattle station in central Queensland and on Australian coastal vessels. During the Second World War he served in the navy, before working as mate on cargo ships on the Queensland and New Guinea coasts. His experiences led to a series of sea stories contributed to the *Bulletin,* often under the pseudonym, 'Standby'. As 'Standby' he published a novel, *Sailing Orders* (1949), and two collections of short stories, *Little Known of These Waters* (1945) and *Close to the Wind* (1955). As R.S. Porteous, he published another collection of short stories, *Salvage* (1963); two novels of cattle station life, *Brigalow* (1957) and *Cattleman* (1960), which won the *Courier-Mail's* centenary novel competition; and three novels for young readers, *Tambai Island* (1955), *The Tambai Treasure* (1958) and *The Silent Isles* (1963).

PORTER, HAL (1911–84), the eldest of six children, was born in Melbourne, and educated mainly at Bairnsdale in Gippsland, where his family moved when he was six. He began writing early and had a number of short stories and poems published in school magazines. After leaving school he worked briefly as a cub reporter on the *Bairnsdale Advertiser* but then turned to schoolteaching, living in Williamstown 1927–37. In 1929 the death of his mother, who is lovingly recalled in the first volume of his autobiography, *The Watcher on the Cast-Iron Balcony* (q.v., 1963), was a severe blow. Although he was writing steadily in the 1930s and 1940s, he published little. He married in 1939 and in the same year suffered a severe traffic accident which kept him in hospital for twelve months and prevented him, to his regret, from taking part in the Second World War. Divorced in 1943, he has never remarried. He spent the rest of the war in Adelaide, where he taught at private schools, and resumed his writing. In 1942 fourteen of his stories were published in a limited edition, titled *Short Stories.* After the war Porter had numerous occupations, including cook, actor, hotel manager, hospital orderly, theatrical producer, schoolteacher and librarian. He was attached as a teacher to the Occupation Forces in Japan 1949–50, an experience which has proved seminal; his last appointment was as a librarian at Bairnsdale and Shepparton, 1953–61, after which he became a full-time writer. By that time he had published two novels and a collection of poetry, as well as numerous uncollected short stories, but his reputation was not firmly established until the mid-1960s. He has won most major literary awards in Australia, some of them more than once. In 1967 he received, with Randolph Stow, the Britannica-Australia Award; in 1982 he was made AM.

A prolific and versatile writer, Porter has published three novels, *A Handful of Pennies* (1958), *The Tilted Cross* (q.v., 1961) and *The Right Thing* (1971); three collections of poetry, *The Hexagon* (1956), *Elijah's Ravens* (1968) and *In an Australian Country Graveyard* (1974), which includes his own drawings; seven collections of short fiction, *Short Stories* (1942), *A Bachelor's Children* (1962), *The Cats of Venice* (1965), *Mr. Butterfry and Other Tales of New Japan* (1970), *Selected Stories* (1971), *Fredo Fuss Love Life* (1974) and *The Clairvoyant Goat* (1981); three autobiographical works, *The Watcher on the Cast-Iron Balcony* (1963), *The Paper Chase* (1966) and *The Extra* (1975); and three plays, *The Tower* in *Three Australian Plays* (1963), *The Professor* (1966) and *Eden House* (1969). Another play, 'Parker', was produced in 1972. He has also written an account of modern Japanese life and culture, *The Actors* (1968), and a history of his home town, *Bairnsdale: Portrait of an Australian Country Town* (1977), both of which are illustrated by his own drawings, the latter extensively; and a book of theatrical biography, *Stars of Australian Stage and Screen* (1965). *Hal Porter* (1980), edited by Mary Lord, is an extensive selection of his writing. In addition, he has written numerous magazine articles and some uncollected short stories and poems, and has edited two collections of short stories, *Coast to Coast* (1962) and *It Could Be You* (1972), and one of poetry, *Australian Poetry* (1957).

The most immediately striking aspect of Porter's short fiction is his style, which is markedly different from that of earlier Australian short-story writers. A self-conscious stylist, he writes an intricate, densely-woven prose that is studiedly extravagant, crammed with spectacular, and often idiosyncratic, images. Exuberantly witty but controlled and precise in its effects, his style is not just concerned with verbal display but is a conscious attempt to capture the complex texture of experience. Porter has said that his main aim is 'to write with many-planed clarity, to achieve an incandescence', and describes himself as constantly 'burnishing' and 'pruning' his prose. Although he has been occasionally accused of excessive decoration and inappropriate 'baroque' effects, and of an obsessive interest in the grotesque, the violent and the melodramatic, he has steadily

won more sympathetic appreciations. His short stories have a variety of settings ranging from Earl's Court, London, to a typical Australian country town, to Venice and to Japan, but he is essentially a regional writer, interested in the actuality of Australian life, past and present. This interest is apparent in the thirty stories of *A Bachelor's Children,* where Porter's remarkable ability to evoke atmosphere and to re-create time and place in full solidity of detail has wide scope. Many of his stories are nostalgic in that they deal with the loss of innocence, the death of illusion or past happiness, and the destruction of love. Stories such as 'At Aunt Sophia's', 'Miss Rodda' and 'The Cuckoo' deal with varieties of violent initiation from the safe familiarity of childhood into the unpredictable realities of the adult world; others such as 'Fiend and Friend', 'Uncle Foss and Big Bogga' and 'Country Town' explore the changed quality of the past from the perspective of the present. Violent events, suicides, deaths, disfigurements and monstrosities are common to many, although their plots are less memorable than the authentic evocation of character, situation and place. Porter's gift for pungent satire is more noticeable in *The Cats of Venice* collection, in such stories as 'Vulgar's the Word' and 'Party Forty-Two and Mrs. Brewer'; in others, such as 'Great Aunt Fanny's Picnic', 'Say to Me Ronald!' (q.v.) and 'The Cats of Venice', satire fades imperceptibly into social commentary. Others, such as 'Francis Silver' or 'Gretel' (q.v.), return to the familiar themes of lost innocence and the changed past. The seven stories in *Mr. Butterfry and Other Tales of New Japan* are extended character studies, centring on aspects of cultural opposition and based, like *The Actors,* on Porter's disillusionment with Japan after a return visit in 1967. The title-story, 'Mr. Butterfry' (q.v.), is archetypal in its finely-modulated effects and cumulative impact. The nine stories of the *Fredo Fuss Love Life* collection are similarly extended accounts of past incidents and diverse personalities; deceptively artless, they are virtuoso displays of his wide range of effects. Throughout Porter's short fiction the pressure of personally remembered experience can be felt, reinforced by his frequent use of an older, semi-autobiographical narrator, and by numerous similarities between characters and incidents in the short stories and his autobiographies.

Porter's novels have had a less sympathetic reception. *A Handful of Pennies,* which is set in post-war Japan and deals, often satirically, with tragi-comic aspects of East–West opposition, is an episodic work with a heavily-encrusted style. *The Tilted Cross,* however, is more successfully integrated; set in colonial Hobart Town, it is a concentrated and compelling recreation of a society that is fundamentally anti-Christian. *The Right Thing,* set in contemporary Australia, explores the power of a calcified social code; schematic and didactic, it has brilliant moments and some vividly-realized characters, but is finally more memorable for its parts than as a whole.

But Porter is best known for his three autobiographies, especially *The Watcher on the Cast-Iron Balcony.* A work of sustained imaginative power, it is a remarkably authentic recreation of childhood and youthful experience that fully extends Porter's ability to present the past as an immediate, almost tangible, present. Particularly striking are his acute awareness of the effects of time and the unique phenomenon of memory, and his frank, retrospective self-analysis; the latter is made more compelling by the constant impression of an older narrator who, from his experienced perspective, watches the child who is also a watcher, an analyst both of the inner self and of the external changes in his widening world. *The Watcher* takes Porter to the age of eighteen and the death of his mother; *The Paper Chase* covers the period between 1929 and 1949. More lighthearted in mood, less nostalgic and structurally coherent, and less of an immediate social record, its main theme concerns the narrator's growing awareness of schism between the needs of the creative artist and of the man. *The Extra,* which takes Porter to the 1970s, takes its title from one of his poems and emphasizes his stance as observer rather than as participant. Concerned more with events and people than with the self, this volume contains numerous portraits of Australian writers.

Porter regards his plays less seriously than his other work, and both *The Tower* and *Eden House* are frank entertainments; the former is a satiric melodrama set in colonial Hobart Town and the latter, set in contemporary Melbourne, is a satirical family comedy. Although both have two-dimensional characters and a stylized action, they are sustained by Porter's practical knowledge of stagecraft. *The Tower* was first produced in 1964, *Eden House* in 1969, on television in 1970, and as a stage play in London with the title *Home on the Pig's Back* in 1972. *The Professor,* which turns once again to the gulf between occidental and oriental culture, is a far more serious work; subtle and perceptive, it is a compelling study of love and lust and the degrees between them. It was first produced, with the title *Toda-San,* in Adelaide in 1965 and in London in 1966.

Porter's verse is both less abundant and less original than his prose work. Framed in traditional forms, his poems dwell in a brief way on many of the same general themes as his fiction: the passage of time, the fact of death,

the anguish of disillusionment and the paradoxes of personality.

PORTER, PETER (1929–), born Brisbane, worked in 1947–48 as a cadet journalist for the *Courier-Mail.* In 1951 he left for England where, apart from a brief period in Australia in 1954, he remained until 1974 when he returned at the invitation of the Adelaide Festival. Since then he has visited Australia more frequently but still lives in London. Porter has worked as a bookseller, journalist, clerk and advertising copywriter. He is now a freelance writer reviewing for such journals as the *New Statesman, London Magazine,* the *Observer, TLS, Encounter* and the *New Review* and he is also a regular BBC broadcaster. Porter is the author of nine major volumes of poetry, two collaborations with Arthur Boyd, and three unpublished radio plays broadcast by the BBC. His early poetry, *Once Bitten, Twice Bitten* (1961), *Poems Ancient and Modern* (1964) and A. Alvarez's selection for *Penguin Modern Poets 2* (1962) displays an ironic wit tinged with melancholy, formal structural control, wide variety of subject matter and skilful use of aphorisms. Such poems as 'Story from a Time of Disturbance' and 'An Anthropologist's Confession', with their acute verbal play and lurid, even scabrous, details, highlight a variety of social follies. Some of the early poetry, e.g. 'Your Attention Please', 'Soliloquy at Potsdam' and 'The Frankenstein Report', reveals the influence of Browning's dramatic monologues. In 'Beast and the Beauty' and 'Made in Heaven' the persona of the self-deprecating outsider scathingly attacking English folly comes close at times to self-pity and envy. But alongside the satire and melancholy Porter, through his constant and knowledgeable allusions to art, literature and music, displays an equally strong attachment to European culture. The affirmation of human capacity afforded by art balances modern life's artlessness in poems such as 'John Marston Advises Anger' or 'Homage to Gaetano Donizetti', while doubt about fictional deferral of real experience, a theme of great centrality in later volumes, is already present in 'What a Lying Lot the Writers Are'. Through its sheer enjoyment of ideas, Porter's early poetry affirms art's ability to make palatable the essential difficulty and hopelessness of life, while qualifying the confrontations of art with mortality by irony and paradox.

In this early verse the ambivalent adoption of European civilization counters an uneasy, often mistrustful, attitude to Australia. Porter expresses (*TLS,* 1971) his self-exile as an aversion to Australian bluntness and physicality, and to its national lack of sophistication in response to complexity in life and art. This aversion is reflected, though less harshly, in such early verse as 'Sydney Cove, 1788' and 'The Recipe' from *A Porter Folio* (1969), while the poems of bitter-sweet boyhood, 'A Christmas Recalled' and 'Two Merits of Sunshine', are melancholy rather than antagonistic.

Two small volumes, *Words without Music* (1968) and *Solemn Adultery at Breakfast Creek: An Australian Ballad* (1968), the latter a collaboration with musician, Michael Jessett, were followed by *A Porter Folio* (1969) and *The Last of England* (1970), which consolidated his reputation as a difficult but valuable poet. These volumes continue his use of witty personas ('The Return of Inspector Christopher Smart', 'A Consumer's Report'), widen the range of formal experiments ('The Sanitized Sonnets', 'The Widow's Story'), and develop a more personal voice which, though still involved with complex analysis of art confronting experience, often laments the poet's inability to feel except through the mediation of art.

Two volumes of translations, *Epigrams by Martial* (1971) and *After Martial* (1972), show the same wide range and increasing confidence and maturity evident in one of his finest volumes, *Preaching to the Converted* (1972). 'Le Deploration sur la Mort D'Igor Stravinsky', 'Fossil Gathering', 'May 1945' and several other poems, continue the exploration of aesthetic immortality and physical death, each poem twisting the focus of inquiry as Porter's discrimination of all graduations of meaning becomes a moral pursuit, a way of living in and through the world of ideas.

A Share of the Market (1973) and two collaborations with Arthur Boyd, *Jonah* (1973) and *The Lady and the Unicorn* (1975), precede *Living in a Calm Country* (1975); all confirm the growing trend of urbane complexity in his work. Not regarded as one of his finest books, *Living in a Calm Country* contains, nevertheless, a number of excellent poems, two of which are central to an understanding of Porter. In 'The Story of My Conversion' he laments that having been converted to the seriousness and difficulty of 'the new land of disappointment' of the over-40s, looking forward only to death, he will never be able to learn simplicity. The second central poem, 'On First Looking into Chapman's *Hesiod*' (q.v.), presents a similar view presented in terms of Porter's differences with Australia.

The small volume, *The Tres Riches Heures* (1978), was published before his best volume, *The Cost of Seriousness* (1978). Although he is praised by critics for a new maturity in approach to the darker sides of love in *The Cost of Seriousness,* his lack of experience, lamented in earlier volumes, finds tragic expression in the central poems which were occasioned by the untimely death of his wife in 1974. In *The Cost of Seriousness* the sufficiency of art's consolation in the face of deeply-felt grief is questioned and art, itself, is often found to be unable to 'alter human circumstance or alleviate human distress'. In two of his finest and most significant poems, 'An Exequy' (q.v.) and 'The Delegate', the refuge in art is shown to leave the poet even more isolated although, paradoxically, the poems bring profoundly moving consolation to the reader.

The next volume, *English Subtitles* (1981), takes up the theme of loss in 'Alcestis and the Poet' and 'Good Ghost, Gaunt Ghost'. The theme of ageing also reappears in some outstanding pieces, 'The Werther Level', 'What I Have Written I Have Written', 'The Unfortunate Isles' and 'At Lake Massaciuccoli'. In this volume, complexity of feelings and ideas are effectively handled and the value of seriousness, of art, reaffirmed. The final poem, 'Landscape with Orpheus', a composite of tradition and innovation, explores the adequacy of art as a complex response to the seriousness of living.

The *Collected Poems* (1983) has revitalized interest in the satiric material and formal variations of Porter's earlier work, reinforced the impression of the gifted aphorist, and consolidated his poetic status both overseas and in Australia.

J.D.

Portraits. The will of J.F. Archibald (q.v.) specified that the Archibald Prize be given annually 'for the best portrait preferentially of some man or woman distinguished in Art Letters Science or Politics'. Several prominent Australian writers have been the subject of Archibald Prize-winning paintings, including Ambrose Pratt (1933, artist C. Wheeler); A.B. Paterson (1935, John Longstaff); Patrick White (1962, Louis Kahan); James McAuley (1963, J. Carrington Smith); George Johnston (1969, Ray Crooke); Michael Boddy (1973, Janet Dawson); and Philip Adams (1979, Wes Walter). Of these artists, Longstaff painted Henry Lawson just prior to Lawson's departure from England in 1900, George Lambert's 1890s portrait of A.W. Jose is his first extant portrait, and Kahan published *Australian Writers: The Face of Literature* (1981), a selection of his *Meanjin* portraits. Among other well-known paintings of Australian writers are William Dobell's portraits of Frank Clune, Brian Penton and Mary Gilmore, the last causing controversy when it was exhibited in 1957.

POTTINGER, Sir **FREDERICK** (1831–65), born India, was an Eton-educated guards officer who succeeded to a baronetcy in 1856 but dissipated his inheritance and was forced to emigrate to Australia. He was a mounted trooper in NSW until the discovery of his title led to rapid promotion. During 1862–65 he was an inspector of police in central western NSW, a persistent, unlucky and sometimes incompetent hunter of such bushrangers as Ben Hall, Frank Gardiner and John Gilbert; like most of them he died young, when he accidentally shot himself jumping on board a coach. An earlier incident, in which his pistol failed to discharge and Gardiner escaped, was recorded in the anonymous ballad, 'The Bloody Field of Wheogo', and may have given rise to the phrase, 'even blind Freddie couldn't miss it'. As Sir Ferdinand Morringer, Pottinger is sympathetically portrayed in 'Rolf Boldrewood''s *Robbery Under Arms* (1888).

POWELL, CRAIG (1940–), born Wollongong, graduated in medicine from the University of Sydney in 1964 and now works as a psychiatrist. In 1972 he left Australia to spend ten years in Canada. His verse has appeared in numerous anthologies and magazines and in five collections, *A Different Kind of Breathing* (1966), *I Learn by Going* (1968), *A Country without Exiles* (1972), *Selected Poems* (1978), and *Rehearsal for Dancers* (1978). He received the *Poetry Magazine* Award in 1964, the Henry Lawson Festival Award in 1969, and the 1983 Mattara Spring Festival Poetry Prize for 'Five Pieces for a Homecoming'. He writes a forceful, concise, direct and tightly-structured poetry, which draws sometimes on his experiences as a psychiatrist, but also on such subjects as love, the experiences of parent and child, grief and death. A friend of Francis Webb, he has recorded his memories of him in *Poetry Australia* (1975) and in his poems, 'Francis Webb in Plenty' and 'Spring Thaw'.

POWELL, S.W. (**SYDNEY WALTER**) (1878– ?), born England and educated partly in South Africa, served in the Boer War before coming to Australia in 1904. He joined the army and was drafted to Thursday Island, where he began writing for the *Bulletin* under the pseudonym, 'Wyben'. He left Australia in 1908, spent some time in NZ and Tahiti but returned in time to enlist in the AIF. A participant in the landing at Gallipoli, he was wounded and invalided back to Sydney in 1916. His war poem, 'Gallipoli', was awarded first prize in the John Masefield competition, 1932, and included in his collection, *One-Way Street and Other Poems* (1934). Powell subsequently traded in the Paumotu archipelago before joining the Commonwealth public service; in 1925 he returned to England. Powell wrote seventeen romances and novels, 1920–37. Those

which have Australian characters or associations include *The Maker of Pearls* (1920), *The Great Jade Seal* (1922), *The Game* (1925) and *Noah's Ark* (1935). He also published a volume of short stories, *Tales from Tahiti* (1928) and an account of his travels, *Adventures of a Wanderer* (1928).

POWER, HELEN (1870–1957), was born at Campbell Town, Tasmania, the granddaughter of the first surveyor-general of Tasmania. A distinguished member of Hobart's literary community, she contributed verse to the *Bulletin, the Australasian* and numerous poetry magazines, especially during the years 1912–32. Her work, which is represented in several anthologies, appeared in two collections, *Poems* (1934) and *A Lute with Three Strings* (1964), introduced by Clive Sansom. Conventional and simple, Power's lyrics dwell on such themes as death, love, growing old, the loss of friends and the persistence of the past in the present.

Power Without Glory, a novel by Frank Hardy (q.v.), was first published in Melbourne in 1950 and led to his trial for criminal libel. After proceedings that lasted nine months and aroused keen public interest, Hardy was acquitted. He has described the writing of the book and subsequent trial in *The Hard Way* (1961). *Power Without Glory* has since been translated into several languages and was produced as a successful television serial by the ABC in 1976. Divided into three sections which span the years 1890–1950, the novel narrates the fortunes of its anti-hero, John West (q.v.).

Born into one of the poorest working-class families of Carringbush, Melbourne's inner suburb of Collingwood, West takes his first step on the road to wealth and power when he rigs a pigeon race, and quickly progresses to running an illegal and crooked totalizator disguised as a tea-shop. Accomplices in his rapid rise include his brother Joe and his cronies, Sugar Renfrey, Barney Robinson, Piggy, Flash Alec, Cauliflower Dick and Mick O'Connell; some of these have been identified as contemporary Melbourne figures, as have other characters in the novel. West's older brother, Arthur, who becomes a member of the West machine on his release from a long prison term for rape, is more of a liability that West doggedly endures for the sake of their mother. Apart from Sugar Renfrey, few of his early cronies survive to share his later life of respectability, and some, such as Barney Robinson, die violent deaths. Meanwhile West's relationship with David Garside, a brilliant lawyer, furthers his early career most effectively. By the time of the First World War, West has a reputation as a wealthy philanthropist, an important friend of the Roman Catholic Archbishop Daniel Malone (see Mannix, Daniel), and of others in high places, but his secret career is studded with infamous incidents. He is involved in three murders and in the attempted murder of a detective; bribes police, magistrates and police witnesses; he attempts to bribe the judiciary; strives, with only limited success, to manipulate politicians, in particular the idealistic Labor member, Frank Ashton (Frank Anstey); and in all his gambling enterprises consistently cheats his customers. Inadequate in his personal relationships, West finds that his private life deteriorates as surely as his public one flourishes. His wife, Nellie, has a child in mid-life after a one-sided affair with a young labourer and subsequently lives a disabled, reclusive existence; his talented elder daughter, Marjorie, alienated from him by her choice of a foreign husband, dies subsequently in a German concentration camp; his son, John, becomes an alcoholic and eventually commits suicide; his younger daughter, Mary, defiantly leads her own life as a member of the Communist Party, then leaves Australia and dies before West's longed-for reconciliation can take place. Public affairs also soon pass beyond West's influence and he comes to be valued only as a convenient source of funds for the projects of others. At the end of the novel West faces death, an embittered, lonely and frustrated old man, an unconscious victim of the cash nexus. The novel is overcrowded and untidy, but is a compelling study of one man's single-minded pursuit of powerful forces which he fails to understand and which finally overtake him, as well as a vivid representation of Melbourne life, especially before the First World War.

POWERS, JOHN (1935–), born Melbourne, spent his early years as a jackeroo and labourer, travelling around Australia, and has since worked as a freelance journalist and public servant. His one-act play, 'The Hot Centre of the World' (1971), subsequently produced as a film by Tim Burstall, won two film awards, and he has written two further full-length plays, *The Last of the Knucklemen* (1974) and 'Shindig' (1975). *The Last of the Knucklemen*, Powers's most popular play, focuses on the tense relationship between nine miners in a mining camp of north-western Australia and effectively displays his gifts for rumbustious action and an earthy vernacular. It was produced as a film in 1974. 'Shindig', set in the opal mining town of Lightning Ridge, complicates a similar situation with the presence of numerous women. Powers has also written *The Coach* (1978), a study of the famous Melbourne footballer, Ron Barassi, and *Australian Sports Heroes* (1982).

POWNALL, EVE (? –1982), born Sydney, published several novels for children, including *Cousins-Come-Lately* (1952), *Squik the Squirrel Possum* (1949) and *Binty the Bandicoot* (1957); and for adults *Mary of Maranoa* (1959), a popular account of Australian pioneer women. She also wrote several non-fiction books for children, one of which, *The Australia Book* (1952), won the Children's Book of the Year Award.

PRAED, ROSA (1851–1935), born in Bromelton, near Beaudesert, Queensland, was the daughter of Thomas Murray-Prior, a pastoralist and later a public servant and politician. Brought up on stations in the Burnett River district, which Murray-Prior left in 1858 after the Hornet Bank (q.v.) massacre, and at Maroon, near Bromelton, she also experienced political and social life in Brisbane before her marriage in 1872 to Arthur Campbell Praed. They lived at Praed's station at Port Curtis, near Gladstone, for three years; the isolation and appalling conditions are recalled in Rosa's first novel, *An Australian Heroine* (1880), and particularly in the ironically-titled *The Romance of a Station* (1889). In 1875 they sold up and settled in England where, as Mrs Campbell Praed, Rosa established herself as a popular novelist and dramatist; her play, *Ariane*, adapted from the novel, *The Bond of Wedlock* (1887), was a controversial production in 1888 in its portrayal of the limitations of marriages. Among her acquaintances were Oscar Wilde, who is portrayed in *Affinities* (1885); the politician, Justin McCarthy, with whom she collaborated on three novels and whose letters she edited and amplified as *Our Book of Memories* (1912); and J.B. O'Reilly, whom she met on a visit to America and who was the model for the politician bushranger, Morres Blake, in *Outlaw and Lawmaker* (1893). Of Praed's forty-odd works of fiction, almost half have Australian settings or associations; as well as *An Australian Heroine*, *The Romance of a Station* and *Outlaw and Lawmaker*, they include *Policy and Passion* (q.v., 1881), *The Head Station* (1885), *Miss Jacobsen's Chance* (1886), *Mrs. Tregaskiss* (1895), *Nulma* (1897), *Dwellers by the River* (1902), *Fugitive Anne* (1903), *The Ghost* (1903), *The Maid of the River* (1905), *The Lost Earl of Ellan* (1906), *The Luck of the Leura* (1907), *A Summer Wreath* (1909), *Opal Fire* (1910), *Lady Bridget in the Never-Never Land* (1915) and *Sister Sorrow* (1916). Her other works include contributions to the Anglo-Australian anthologies by Arthur Patchett Martin and others; reminiscences of her Australian experiences (which included a return visit in 1894), *My Australian Girlhood* (1902), in which J. Brunton Stephens is portrayed, and *Australian Life:*

Black and White (1885); and a number of novels, particularly from *As a Watch in the Night* (1900) onwards, which reflect her interest in spiritualism and the occult. Among other beliefs she embraced astral bodies, telepathic communication and reincarnation; after separating from her husband she lived with Nancy Harward, 1899–1927, and believed Nancy to be the reincarnation of a Roman slave girl. Praed's story of this, *Nyria*, caused something of a sensation when published in 1904, and was succeeded by *Soul of Nyria* (1931) after Nancy's death. Praed also believed that her family tragedies were a consequence of her own past, as a priestess in classical times. Her daughter, born deaf, died in a mental asylum, and of her three sons, one died in a car accident, one was gored to death by a rhinoceros, and the third committed suicide. Praed's philosophical interests and her relationship with Nancy Harward are discussed in Colin Roderick's *In Mortal Bondage: The Strange Life of Rosa Praed* (1948).

Praed has often been bracketed with Ada Cambridge and Jessie Couvreur (qq.v.), e.g. in Raymond Beilby and Cecil Hadgraft's monograph on the three writers (1979), and has been categorized as a writer of women's formula romance fiction who succumbed to the cultural cringe (q.v.) both in writing of colonial life for a 'Home' market and in her admiration of English breeding. Yet despite the exotic set pieces in some of her novels, the melodramatic resolutions of some of her plots, and her observation of the crudities of colonial society, she was responsive to her Australian experience, even to the mystery and power of the bush, despite its harshness. Several of her novels apart from *An Australian Heroine* and *The Romance of a Station* are informed by her knowledge, and that of her family, of pastoral and political life in Queensland, designated in her fiction as Leichardt's (sic) Land: her memories of Naraigin station in the Burnett district are drawn on in *Mrs. Tregaskiss*, and of Maroon in *Policy and Passion*, *The Head Station* and *Outlaw and Lawmaker; Policy and Passion, Nulma* and *Miss Jacobsen's Chance* reflect her acute awareness of colonial politics in the years after Queensland's separation from NSW; and *The Lost Earl of Ellan* and *Lady Bridget of the Never-Never Land* utilize the experiences of her brother and sister elsewhere in Queensland. Although many of Praed's heroines are victims of 'Anglomania', and seem to prefer the English gentleman to the Australian suitor who characteristically completes the love triangle, that preference often ends in the kind of disillusionment that Honoria Longleat experiences in her relationship with Hardress Barrington in *Policy and Passion,* generally believed to be her best work. Austra-

lian men, despite their subjugation of colonial women, are admired for their bluff honesty, endurance and steadfastness. The limitations of marriage and the idealizations of love can be set against the failure of her own marriage and are prominent themes throughout her work.

Pram Factory, see **Australian Performing Group**

PRATT, AMBROSE (1874–1944), born Forbes, NSW, was for some time a solicitor, but turned to journalism and was on the staff of the *Age* from 1906 and the *Industrial Australian and Mining Standard* from 1917. His novels, which deal with such facets of Australian life as the convict and bushranger eras and the mining and larrikin periods, include *The Great "Push" Experiment* (1902), a story of the larrikin gangs; *Three Years with Thunderbolt* (1905), the narrative of William Monckton, who accompanied Thunderbolt; *The Remittance Man* (1907); *The Outlaws of Weddin Range* (1911), on the Ben Hall gang; *Her Assigned Husband* (1916); and *Lift up Your Eyes* (1935). Of his many other publications, several with Australian interest include *David Syme: The Father of Protection in Australia* (1908) and *The Handbook of Australia's Industries* (1934).

Preaching to the Converted, see **PORTER, PETER**

PREE, BARRY see *Mystery of a Hansom Cab, The*

Prelude to Waking, see **'BRENT OF BIN BIN'**

Prentice Family, see *Timeless Land, The*

Pressmen and Governors, see **MILLER, E. MORRIS**

PRICE, GEORGE FREDERICK, see **DARRELL, GEORGE**

PRICE, JOHN (1808–57), born Cornwall, England, was a notorious commandant of the Norfolk Island penal settlement in the 1840s and the model for Maurice Frere in Marcus Clarke's *His Natural Life* (1874). The links between Frere and Price are discussed in J.V. Barry's *The Life and Death of John Price* (1964). Price also appears in 'Price Warung''s story, 'John Price's Bar of Steel'.

PRICHARD, KATHARINE SUSANNAH (1883–1969), born Levuka, Fiji, was the daughter of Tom Prichard, editor of the *Fiji Times*. Her childhood, vividly recreated in her children's book *The Wild Oats of Han* (1928), was spent initially in Tasmania, and then in Melbourne. On matriculating from South Melbourne College, where she came under the influence of poet and teacher, J.B. O'Hara, she spent a couple of years as a governess at Yarram in South Gippsland and then at Turella sheep station in the far west of NSW. Returning to Melbourne to teach, she attended night lectures in English literature under the auspices of Walter Murdoch.

In 1908 Prichard made her first trip to London as a freelance journalist for the Melbourne *Herald* and on her return accepted a position with the newspaper as social editor of the women's page for two years. In 1912 she again left for England to pursue her career as a writer. Her first novel, *The Pioneers* (1915), won the colonial section of the Hodder and Stoughton novel competition and was made into an Australian film in 1916 (and re-made in 1926). Drawn from her memories of Gippsland, the novel was a romantic, period tale of escaped convicts, cattle-duffing and people in the act of creating a new and better life. Although seen as a germinal work containing both stylistic and thematic aspects later to be developed by the author, *The Pioneers* has much in common, in terms of contrived plot and characterization, with its successor, *Windlestraws* (1916), a melodramatic romance involving an impoverished Russian prince, a female dancer and the London theatrical scene; the latter was written before *The Pioneers,* but published after it.

In 1916 Prichard returned to Australia. She married Hugo Throssell (VC winner) in 1919, went to live in WA and immersed herself in both politics and writing; the first, some critics say, to the detriment of the second. In 1920 she became a founding member of the Communist Party of Australia and served for a period on its central committee. She wrote a few simple political pamphlets such as *The New Order* (1919), and later a book, *The Real Russia* (1934), which reported on her experiences and observations as a traveller in the Soviet Union the previous year. She founded, with Cecilia Shelley, the Unemployed Women and Girls' Association in Perth and, after the Labor Party's decision to exclude women from the movement against war and fascism, she established the Modern Women's Club in 1938. She was elected, in 1935, federal president of the Australian Writers' League (an organization she had helped to establish the previous year) and three years later became a founding member of the WA branch of the FAW which later nominated her for a Nobel Prize.

Her initial attempt to embody political concepts in her novels came with the publication in 1921 of *Black Opal,* a study of an opal-mining community of Fallen Star Ridge which seeks to maintain the ethos of independent ownership of mines and to stave off the threat to its way of life from capitalism. Although her next novel, *Working Bullocks* (1926), stressed the political nature of work in the Karri timber industry of WA and the alienation of man's labour implicit in its title, its primary focus was far more aesthetic. Regarded as rich in literary merit, it sought to explore the elemental attraction existing between man and his environment through the central characters of Red Burke, as powerful as the bullock teams he drives, and Deb Colburn, the primitive child of nature. The more polished *Coonardoo* (q.v.), which shared the 1928 *Bulletin* novel prize and was praised as the first realistic and detailed portrayal of an Aboriginal, and *Working Bullocks* are regarded as the basis for Katharine Susannah Prichard's literary reputation.

Her other novels include *Haxby's Circus* (1930), which traces the struggles of Gina Haxby, deformed as a result of a circus accident, and her counterpart, the hunchback clown Roca, who together attempt to maintain both the circus and their self-respect; *Intimate Strangers* (1937), a psychological study of the marital breakdown of Greg and Elodie Blackwood, with a not very credible reconciliation through their joint work for a new social order; the poorly constructed *Moon of Desire* (1941), a flimsy and unbelievable adventure story transporting its protagonists from Broome to Singapore in search of a fabulous pearl; and her most contentious work, the WA goldfields trilogy, published separately as *The Roaring Nineties* (q.v., 1946), *Golden Miles* (q.v., 1948) and *Winged Seeds* (q.v., 1950). This trilogy, with its mass of historical detail, is a dynamic 'story of an industry' seen through the lives of the central heroine, Sally Gough, and the archetypal prospector, Dinny Quin. In *The Roaring Nineties,* Prichard traces the period of early pioneering and prospecting and the growth of companies; in *Golden Miles,* the impact of the First World War and conscription, and the industrial strife of the 1920s. In *Winged Seeds,* its name taken from the novel's last image of a Kalgoorluh nut breaking over the grave of an Aboriginal woman and symbolizing the renewal of life and hope, she completes the trilogy through the economic depression to 1946. The trilogy, on the one hand, has been criticized for its didacticism, its subordination of character to propaganda and its overwhelming historical documentation; on the other, it has been praised for its political concerns by such people as Jack Lindsay in *Meanjin Quarterly* (1961) and Jack Beasley in his analysis of her work, *The Rage for Life* (1964). Her last novel, *Subtle Flame* (1967), was a manifestation of her increasing desire for world peace and centred on a middle-aged newspaper editor who suffers a personal and political crisis during the era of the Korean War which causes him to leave both family and job to crusade for peace and nuclear disarmament.

Numerous short stories of uneven quality have been collected and published in *Kiss on the Lips* (1932), *Potch and Colour* (1944), *N'Goola* (1959), *On Strenuous Wings* (edited by Joan Williams, 1965) and *Happiness* (1967). One story, 'The Grey Horse', which cleverly juxtaposes the virility of a stallion with the frustration of a farmer, won the 1924 *Art in Australia* Award and, with symbolic sketches like 'The Cow' and 'The Cooboo', has been a popular choice for anthologies.

Prichard published two volumes of poetry, *Clovelly Verses* (1913) and *The Earth Lover* (1932). Her several plays include *Brumby Innes* (1940, which won the 1927 *Triad* Award for the best Australian three-act play) and *Bid Me to Love* (published posthumously in 1974). Two seminal books on her writing are Jack Beasley's *The Rage for Life* and Henrietta Drake-Brockman's monograph, *Katharine Susannah Prichard* (1967), while information on her life is to be found in her autobiography, *Child of the Hurricane* (1963) and a biography by her son, Ric Throssell (q.v.), *Wild Weeds and Wind Flowers* (1975). Throssell has also collected many of her articles and polemics in one volume, *Straight Left* (1982). Her books have been translated into many languages and in 1983 *The Roaring Nineties*, previously out of print, was re-issued to commemorate the centenary of her birth.

S.B.

Prindy, see *Poor Fellow My Country*

PRINGLE, J.M.D. (JOHN MARTIN DOUGLAS) (1912–), born Scotland, was educated at Oxford and was on the editorial staff of the *Manchester Guardian*, 1934–39, assistant editor, 1944–48, special writer for the London *Times*, 1948–52, and deputy editor of the *Observer*, 1957–62. In 1952 he came to Australia, where he was editor of the *Sydney Morning Herald*, 1952–57, 1965–70, and managing editor of the *Canberra Times*, 1964–65. *Australian Accent* (1958), a frank discussion of Australian attitudes, politics, culture and social mores, is Pringle's best-known and most influential book. He has also written a collection of essays on aspects of Australian life, some of them literary, *On Second Thoughts* (1971); an account of Australian art, *Australian Painting Today* (1963); and reminiscences of his career in journalism, *Have Pen: Will Travel* (1973). He has made a selection of Ethel Anderson's

stories, *The Best of Ethel Anderson* (1973), and written *The Last Shenachie* (1976), a biography of Angus John Macdonald (1900–75), oral historian of Scotland who lived in Australia for forty-seven years.

PRIOR, S.H. (SAMUEL HENRY) (1869–1933), born Brighton, SA, was educated at Glenelg and Bendigo, and at twenty-one became editor of the *Barrier Miner* in Broken Hill. He moved to the *Bulletin* in 1903, becoming assistant editor in 1912 and editor 1915–33; his family held a controlling interest in the *Bulletin*, 1927–60. Under Prior, the *Bulletin* became less oriented towards the bush and more conservative, but continued to encourage Australian writers; novel-writing contests initiated by him in 1928 and 1929 drew a large response, including such entries as *A House Is Built* (1929), *Coonardoo* (1929) and *The Passage* (1930). The S.H. Prior Memorial Prize of £100 was instituted by the *Bulletin* after Prior's death, and was awarded, 1935–46; winning entries later published include *Tiburon* (1935), *All That Swagger* (1936), *Joseph Furphy: The Legend of a Man and His Book* (1944) and *The Battlers* (1941).

Prism, the journal of the Poetry Society of Australia (q.v.), appeared in July 1954, edited by Peter Daventry, and was thereafter published, usually monthly, until it was succeeded in 1961 by *Poetry Magazine* (q.v.). *The Poetry Society of Australia: First Anthology* (1956), edited by Wesley Milgate and Imogen Whyse in 1957, was a selection of verse from the pages of *Prism*.

Prizes, see Literary Awards

Profile of Australia, see McGREGOR, CRAIG

Prometheus, intended as the annual student magazine of the Canberra University College and subsequently of the Australian National University, has appeared irregularly since 1933. The magazine has attracted verse and literary articles from a range of contributors associated with the University, including T. Inglis Moore, L.H. Allen, A.D. Hope, R.F. Brissenden, Manning Clark, Alan Gould, Nick Jose, Mark O'Connor and David Campbell.

Prospect, a journal published by a group of Catholic laymen from the University of Melbourne, appeared quarterly 1958–64. The journal, which published literary articles, verse and book reviews, attracted a range of contributors including Vincent Buckley, A.D. Hope, Evan

Jones, James McAuley, Francis Webb and Chris Wallace-Crabbe.

'PROUT, DENTON', see **PHILLIPS, CHARLES WALTER**

PROUT, J.S. (JOHN SKINNER) (1806–76), born Plymouth, England, came to Australia in 1840 and lectured on art in Sydney. An artist and lithographer, he organized in Hobart the first art exhibition held in Australia, and followed it with other successful exhibitions. He returned to England in the early 1850s but may have paid a subsequent visit to Australia. During his stay he published *Sydney Illustrated* (1842–44), with letterpress by John Rae, *Tasmania Illustrated* (1844–46) and *Views of Melbourne and Geelong* (1847). He also provided illustrations for the journal *Heads of the People*. After his return he published two popular works, *An Illustrated Handbook of the Voyage to Australia* (1852) and *A Magical Trip to the Gold Regions* (1853). His drawings were also used to illustrate E.C. Booth's *Another England: Life, Living, Homes and Homemakers in Victoria* (1869).

Public Lending Right, a federal government scheme which compensates authors and publishers for the multiple use of books in public lending libraries, was instituted in July 1975; the Literature Board and writers' organizations such as the ASA were instrumental in its implementation. Under the provisions of Public Lending Right, authors in 1984 were paid sixty-six cents and publishers sixteen and a half cents for each estimated copy of a book held in public lending libraries in Australia, the amount of payment being calculated after annual surveys of library bookstocks. The scheme was administered by the Australia Council, 1976–80, when it passed back to the federal government.

Publicist was a monthly founded and edited by W.J. Miles (q.v.) and conducted with the assistance of P.R. Stephensen (q.v.) from July 1936 until Stephensen was interned in March 1942. Miles died in January 1942, and Stephensen edited the last few issues of the journal. Apart from Miles and Stephensen, contributors to the *Publicist* included George Farwell, Xavier Herbert, Rex Ingamells, Alister Kershaw, John Manifold, Harley Matthews, Ian Mudie and C.W. Salier, although not all of these writers were sympathetic with the chauvinist, isolationist, anti-Semitic, pro-Japanese political views increasingly espoused by the journal. The Publicist Publishing Company was also responsible for the publication of the first edition of Xavier Herbert's *Capricornia* (1938).

PULVERS, ROGER (1944–), born New York into a Jewish–American family, studied political science, Polish and Russian at the Universities of California, Harvard and Warsaw. He taught at Kyoto Sangyo University in Japan, 1967–71, before moving in 1972 to Australia to teach Japanese at the Australian National University. In 1979–82 Pulvers was director and writer-in-residence at the Playbox Theatre Company and now lives in Japan. Some of his plays were performed by the Australian Theatre Workshop in Canberra, La Mama and the Playbox Theatre Company. They include 'Bones' (1973), 'The Fat Lady' (1973), 'The Senator from California' (1974), 'Ice' (1974), 'The Covenant of the Rainbow' (1974), 'Fair Go', later titled 'Joe' (1975), 'Drop Drill' (1976), *Yamashita* (1977, published in Japanese in 1970 and in English in 1981), 'Cedoona' (1978), 'Witold Gombrowicz in Buenos Aires' (1978), *Bertolt Brecht Leaves Los Angeles* (1979, published 1982), 'Australia Majestic' (1980), and a radio play, 'Coma Berenices' (1980). He has also translated plays by European authors, some of which have been staged; has published two other plays, *The Perfect Crime of Mrs Garigari* (1970), and *General MacArthur in Australia* (1978); and a book of short stories, *On the Edge of Kyoto* (1969) and a novel, *The Death of Urashima Taro* (1981). Pulvers's theatre, which is expressionistic, experimental and highly unconventional, notwithstanding traces of Japanese traditional drama, has occasionally been described as inaccessible to the general audience. His themes are shaped by his opposition to American policies and social mores and his admiration for Japanese culture; few of his plays deal with Australian subjects, although 'Australia Majestic' concerns Americans in Australia during the Second World War and his novel, a self-conscious anti-thriller, centres on the outbreak of Japanese POWs from a camp at Cowra in 1944.

Punch, see *Melbourne Punch*

Purfoy, Sarah, see *His Natural Life*

' "Pursuing Literature" in Australia', see **'Fragment of Autobiography, A'**

PUSELEY, DANIEL ('FRANK FOSTER') (1814–82), born Devon, England, was a commercial traveller and a hosier and silk merchant. He acquired a distinguished reputation as a public speaker on literary and political subjects. In 1854 he visited Australia, and after his return published a general description, titled *The Rise and Progress of Australia, Tasmania, and New Zealand* (1857) under the pseudonym 'An Englishman'. He revisited

Australia in 1857 before settling in England, where he devoted himself to literature and philanthropic works. Puseley published several novels under the pseudonym 'Frank Foster', 1872–76; he also published drama, poetry and essays on contemporary issues.

Push, see **Larrikin in Australian Literature**

PYKE, LILLIAN (?–1927), born Victoria as Lillian Heath, published sixteen novels for children 1916–27. She also compiled *Cole's Happy Time Picture and Nursery Rhyme Book* (1920); edited a miscellany, *The Southern Seas Story Book* (1920); and wrote three novels for adults, *The Harp of Life* (1924), *Clem* (1925) and *A Wife by Proxy* (1926), the last two under the pseudonym, 'Erica Maxwell'. Several of her

stories, such as *Max the Sport* (1916) and *Jack of St. Virgil's* (1917), are school stories set in Wesley College, Melbourne (called St Virgil's); others, such as *Sheila at Happy Hills* (1922), deal with a school for girls. With their stress on fair play and honourable sporting behaviour, these novels reflect the code of the contemporary scouting and guiding movements; other dominant features are improbable, melodramatic plots and repetitious expressions of high-flown sentiment. Of more interest is her group of novels set in railway-construction camps in North Queensland, *Phyl of the Camp* (1918), *Bruce at Boonderong Camp* (1920) and *Camp Kiddies* (1919), where the unusual environment allows Pyke's gift for authentic detail more scope.

Q

'**Q**', see **CLARKE, MARCUS**

Quadrant, the magazine of the Australian Association for Cultural Freedom, an offshoot of the International Congress for Cultural Freedom set up in 1950 to counter what was seen as the threat of communism to intellectual and cultural freedom throughout the world, commenced publication as a composite political, social and literary journal in 1956. Its foundation editor was James McAuley and while he was its sole editor (1956–63) it bore the McAuley stamp of conservatism and traditionalism in culture and literature. It changed from a quarterly to a bi-monthly in 1964 and was co-edited by McAuley and Donald Horne 1964–67, by McAuley and Peter Coleman (q.v.), 1967–75, and since 1975, when it became a monthly, by various editors, including Coleman, Elwyn Lynn and H.W. Arndt. Partly through McAuley's influence and partly through the influence of its long-standing literary editor, Vivian Smith, *Quadrant* has been especially notable for the high quality of its poetry and some significant criticism. *Quadrant: Twenty Five Years*, edited by Peter Coleman, Lee Shrubb and Vivian Smith, an anthology from the journal's first quarter century, was published in 1982.

Quartermaster, The, see *House Is Built, A*

Queensland, the second largest Australian State (over 1 727 000 square kilometres), comprises the north-eastern part of the Australian continent and is bordered by New South Wales in the south, by the Northern Territory and South Australia in the west, and for much of its coastline by the Great Barrier Reef. Originally part of New South Wales, Queensland was largely unexplored until the 1840s, when settlement began on the Darling Downs, except for the Moreton Bay district in the south where the present capital, Brisbane (q.v.), is situated, which was a penal settlement 1824–39. Queensland achieved separation from New South Wales in 1859, and remained a British colony until incorporated into the Commonwealth of Australia in 1901.

Queensland Writers' and Artists' Association, see **Fellowship of Australian Writers**

Queenslander, a weekly newspaper published in Brisbane, was the companion of the *Brisbane Courier* and appeared 1866–1939. Edited first by Angus Mackay and in the 1870s by W.H. Traill, the newspaper numbered Alexander Boyd and Ernest Favenc among its contributors, serializing Boyd's *Old Colonials* 1875–76 and financing a Favenc expedition in 1878–79. As well as news summaries and items of topical interest, the *Queenslander* included short stories and verse. Mary Hannay Foott was its literary editor in the 1890s.

Quentin Massys is a didactic verse play about a fifteenth-century Dutch painter by Alfred Deakin (q.v.). It was written in his teens and published in 1875 though never produced. Although Deakin later burned all but a few copies, the play has survived and shows energy, vitality and mature perception.

QUICK, Sir JOHN (1852–1932), born Cornwall, was brought to Australia in infancy and left school at the age of ten to work in an iron foundry. Later he worked as a journalist and in 1874 gained a scholarship to the University of Melbourne, where he studied law. He gained his doctorate in 1882. He was a member of the Victorian parliament 1880–89 and became a prominent figure in the Federation movement. He was a member for Bendigo for twelve years in the federal parliament, was chairman of the first Tariff Commission 1905–07 and Postmaster–General 1909–10. After electoral defeat in 1913 he returned for a time to legal practice. He was deputy president of the Federal Arbitration Court 1922–30. Quick wrote several legal works and combined with Sir Robert Garran in *The Annotated Constitution of the Australian Commonwealth* (1901), which includes a valuable historical account of the Federation movement. He spent his last years working on a series of bibliographies of Australian writing, in co-operation with F.J. Broomfield, Firmin McKinnon, Bernard Cronin, E. Morris Miller and others. After his death Miller continued his work, which resulted in *Australian Literature from Its Beginnings to 1935* (q.v., 1940). L.E. Fredman edited *Sir John Quick's Notebook* (1965).

Quiet Stockman, The, see *We of the Never-Never*

QUIN, TARELLA, (? –1934), born Tarella station, near Wilcannia, NSW, also wrote under her married name, Daskein, and was one of Australia's most successful writers of fairy stories for children. Humour, irony, a fluent, dramatic style and fantasy reminiscent of Lewis Carroll enliven her stories, several of which were illustrated by Ida Outhwaite. They include *Gum Tree Brownie* (1910, later enlarged with changed title), *Freckles* (1910), *Before the Lamps are Lit* (1911), *The Other Side of Nowhere* (1934) and *Chimney Town* (1934). She also wrote the novels for adults, *A Desert Rose* (1912), *Kerno* (1914) and *Paying Guests* (1917).

QUINLAN, LUCILLE MARY see War Literature

QUINN, PATRICK (1862–1926), born Sydney, was the brother of Roderic Quinn and father of Marjorie Quinn (1889–1972), who wrote poems and short stories. He was a member of the NSW parliament 1898–1904, was deputy commissioner of trade for NSW in San Francisco for six years, returned to Australia in 1917 and subsequently worked on the staff of the Sydney *Daily Telegraph*. He published a musical drama, *Captain Cook* (1891); a detective novel, *The Jewelled Belt* (1896); and a collection of short stories, *The Australian Storyteller for an Idle Afternoon* (n.d.). After his death some of his poems were collected and edited by Marjorie Quinn, titled *Selected Poems* (1970).

QUINN, RODERIC (1867–1949), was born in Sydney of Irish parents who had come to Australia about 1853. He was educated in Sydney with his lifelong friends, E.J. Brady and C.J. Brennan, studied law briefly, was a country schoolteacher, then returned to Sydney as a freelance journalist. His chief publications are the romantic novel, *Mostyn Stayne* (1897), and three books of verse, *The Hidden Tide* (1899) *The Circling Hearths* (1901) and *Poems* (1920), his major volume. Although linked with Victor Daley (q.v.) as poets of the so-called Celtic Twilight, Quinn lacked Daley's easy, lyric artistry. He often attempted more, however, for in addition to capturing the spirit and atmosphere of the Australian outdoors he sought a hidden meaning beneath the externals of life and nature.

Quintus Servinton, a novel by Henry Savery (q.v.), was written in 1829 or 1830 in Hobart, where early in 1831, despite the 1830 date on the title page, it was published by Henry Melville. It is generally regarded as the first Australian novel by reason of its place and date of publication and its author's residence, although several earlier works of fiction contain Australian scenes and *Quintus Servinton* itself was printed expressly for sale in England, where the first and second of its three volumes are set, giving it status also as a regional English novel of manners. It may not, however, have been the first novel written in Australia, for Mary Leman Grimstone wrote most of *Woman's Love* (1832) while resident in Hobart in 1826–29. *Quintus Servinton* was published anonymously, but the identification of Savery as author is readily made possible by the close parallels between Savery's experiences and those of his protagonist and by the extensive use of the name Servinton, within the Savery family. The major difference between the experiences of Savery and those of Quintus Servinton is the devotion to Quintus of the idealized Emily, whose spiritual superiority to her husband has been seen by some critics as inaugurating a significant theme in Australian literature.

A moral tale with elements of the picaresque and the allegory, *Quintus Servinton* demonstrates the virtues of moderation, discipline, prudence and humility, the dangers of selfishness, ambition and wilfulness, and the need to recognize the ways of Providence as inscrutable but wise. The novel purports to be a fictionalized biography written by an unnamed author who meets the sixty-year-old subject, Quintus, in the first chapter, when he is laid up at the Servinton home in Devonshire with an ankle dislocated in a walking accident. In the course of his convalescence, he is given a manuscript which details the experiences of Quintus during the first forty years of his life. He secures permission to use the manuscript as the basis of a fictionalized biography, subsequently published in Hobart rather than in London because of the author's posting to Australia; the story of Quintus occupies all but the last few pages of the rest of the book. It begins in 1772 just before Quintus's birth, with a gypsy's prophecy made to his father that in the fourth decade of his life his fifth son would thrice be in danger of his life, would undergo great reverses of fortune, but would thereafter live happily and peacefully. Determined to strengthen his son's character in case the prophecy should come true, Servinton sends Quintus away to boarding school. He remains there for over five years, becoming captain of the school but exhibiting also some of the petulance and overweening self-confidence that are to bring about his downfall. Leaving school for a clerkship in London, Quintus has early success both in business and society, and has several flirtations before falling in love with the beautiful Emily Clifton, whom he courts and marries. Emily is a model of moral balance, virtue and loyalty against which the immature, erratic but basically decent Quintus is measured. After experiencing both the peaks and troughs of business life, the former the reward of his intelligence and acumen, the latter resulting sometimes from providential bad luck but more often from his dangerous self-confidence, Quintus arrives at his thirty-first year in partnership in business in the west of England. His downfall commences when, having extended the credit of his firm beyond its resources, he starts signing fictitious bills of exchange. Discovering that this activity constitutes forgery punishable by death, Quintus panics and decides to flee to America; his boat is delayed by unfavourable winds and when he sees his partner arriving on board with a constable he throws himself into the sea but is rescued and brought back to face trial. His second brush with death comes when he takes legal advice to plead guilty. Condemned to death, he is reprieved at the last moment and transported to Australia, where the last quarter of the novel is set.

Resolving to be a model prisoner, Quintus is treated well in the prison hulks and on the voyage out, during which he finds congenial company in a Scottish minister modelled on John Dunmore Lang. On arrival he is at first given a comfortable government billet in Sydney and the freedom to dabble in business, but this leniency is resented and the secretary of state in England is persuaded to order that his privileges be denied. The decline in his fortunes affects his relationship with Emily when, after several years, she follows Quintus to Australia with their son Olivant. Persuaded by Alverney Malmers to whom she had been entrusted for protection by her family, Emily temporarily leaves Quintus, who attempts suicide. He is saved by one of his remaining friends and reconciled with Emily, who returns to England and eventually secures his pardon. Meanwhile Quintus has learnt moderation; he waits patiently for his release, which comes as the gypsy foretold in his forty-first year. With Emily and Olivant he voyages back to England to a congenial retirement in Devonshire.

QUIROS, PEDRO FERNANDEZ, DE, see *Captain Quiros*

Quiz, a satirical, social and sporting journal published in Adelaide, appeared weekly 1889–1930. Edited by Alfred C. Chandler and H. Congreve Evans, among others, the journal included short stories, verse and theatrical notices.

R

Racing, see Turf, The

Racketty Street Gang, The (1961) by L.H. Evers, an adventure story for children set in the city, shared the Australian Children's Book of the Year Award in 1962 and was made into a BBC television serial.

RADIC, LEONARD (1935–), born Melbourne, studied English at the University of Melbourne, where he also edited the student magazine, *Farrago*; he later became theatre critic for the *Age*. He has written several plays which include 'Side-Show' (1971), *The General* (1974), 'Ordeal by Fire' (1972), *The Particular* (1972), *Cody versus Cody* (1980), 'A Clean Sweep' (1979), 'Ground Rules' (1979) and 'Now and Then' (1982). With his wife, Therese Radic, he has written *Some of My Best Friends Are Women* (1983), a compilation of songs and readings on the theme of Australian women. Radic is caricatured as Leonardo Radish in Jack Hibberd's play, *Dimboola* (1974).

RADIC, THERESE (1935–), born Footscray, Melbourne, graduated with a doctorate in music from the University of Melbourne. She has been music critic, reviewer and feature writer for *Finance Week*, the *Age* and *Australian Book Review*; assistant archivist at the Grainger Museum at the University of Melbourne; and adviser in 1982 to the Percy Grainger centenary celebrations at the University of Melbourne. Her published works include *G.W.L. Marshall-Hall: Portrait of a Lost Crusader* (1982) and a biography, *Sir Bernard Heinze* (1984, in collaboration with Barry Jones). She has also written plays; *Some of My Best Friends Are Women* (1983), co-authored with her husband, Leonard Radic, was produced by the Melbourne Theatre Company in 1976. Her unpublished plays include '40 Watt' (1977), 'A Whip Round for Percy Grainger' (1982) and 'Cinders' (1983). She compiled *A Treasury of Favourite Australian Songs* (1983).

RADLEY, PAUL (1962–), born Waratah, NSW, left school at sixteen to work as a storeman. He has published two novels, *Jack Rivers and Me* (1981), winner of the 1980 *Australian*–Vogel Award, and *My Blue-Checker Corker and Me* (1982). Radley, who explores the territory of boyhood and family life, has set both his novels in a fictional country town of the 1950s, Boomeroo. *Jack Rivers and Me*,

narrated by a perceptive five-year-old, James Oxford 'Peanut' Delarue, recounts the history of the boy's relationship with his invisible but charismatic friend, Jack Rivers. *My Blue-Checker Corker and Me* deals with the progress to maturity of a twelve-year-old boy after the death of his beloved racing pigeon, the prized blue-checker that he named Corker. Both novels are sensitive to the ebb and flow of family experience and to the colourful texture of country existence. Particularly striking is Radley's verbal energy and his ear for the idiosyncrasies of the regional idiom of the Boomeroosters as well as for the more individual private language of siblings, friends, parents and grandparents.

RAFFERTY, CHIPS (1909–71), the film and television actor whose lanky build and weathered features made him the popular conception of the archetypal Australian, was born John Goffage, the son of a Broken Hill miner. He tried a range of occupations including stationhand, cane-cutter, shearer, drover, pearl-diver and miner before he was selected by Cinesound Productions for two small parts in the local films *Come Up Smiling* (*Ants in His Pants*, 1938), and *Dad Rudd, M.P.* (1940). His first major part was in *Forty Thousand Thieves* (1941), produced by Charles Chauvel. Although he had no formal training, he became a well-known, international actor, particularly in demand for character parts. He starred in such films as *Mutiny on the Bounty, Eureka Stockade, The Overlanders, Bitter Springs, The Desert Rats, The Sundowners* and *Kangaroo*. He also starred in popular television serials in Britain, the USA and Australia, including *Gunsmoke, Big Valley* and *Dead Men Running*. During the Second World War he served in the RAAF, apart from a brief period when he was released to make *Rats of Tobruk* with Peter Finch and Grant Taylor. During the 1950s he also founded a film company which produced several successful films such as *The Phantom Stockman* and *King of the Coral Sea*; the business collapsed after the advent of television.

'RAGNAR REDBEARD', see DESMOND, ARTHUR

Rainbow Serpent, The, see ROUGHSEY, DICK

Ralph Rashleigh, a novel generally assigned to the convict, James Tucker (q.v.), was probably written in 1844–45, although the later date of 1850 has been suggested. It was first published in severely edited form in 1929 as a convict memoir by an unknown author. In 1952 the original text was published, edited by Colin Roderick, whose research uncovered the links between Tucker and the novel. Subtitled *The Life of an Exile*, *Ralph Rashleigh* purports to be a squatter's record of the reminiscences of a convict who is given the name of Rashleigh (because he acts rashly); this narrative frame, established in the preface, is of no significance to the rest of the novel, although it parallels the device used in another early convict novel, *Quintus Servinton* (1831).

In structure, *Ralph Rashleigh* is a picaresque novel with elements of the cautionary tale, the prisoner's memoir, the Robinson Crusoe castaway novel and the guide book genre made popular by Tucker's contemporaries, Alexander Harris and Charles Rowcroft. It records the adventures and experiences of Ralph from his descent into crime before 1820 until his death at the hands of Aborigines in 1844, although the last three quarters of the novel concentrate on the eight or nine years following his arrival in the colony of NSW in the middle 1820s. The first part is set in England, where Ralph, the son of a London shopkeeper, is apprenticed to a conveyancer. After two years he is allowed to occupy lodgings and begins his life of crime by passing counterfeit coins. Eventually arrested and imprisoned for twelve months, he leaves gaol wise in criminal ways and successfully carries out several daring burglaries. To his dismay he loses the proceeds of a bank robbery in a disastrous fire, and soon after is arrested for a burglary he did not commit. Ralph's sentence of death is commuted to transportation.

On arrival in Australia he is sent to Emu Plains, where the rigours of work in a government gang are relieved only by opportunities to take part in theatrical entertainments or to work for free settlers during harvest. Ralph spends two years at Emu Plains and then travels to the Campbelltown district to be assigned to an emancipist farmer; on the journey there he enjoys the revels of an Irish family and the hospitality offered by Bob Marshall, a model yeoman farmer. Ill-treated at his place of assignment, he complains to the local constable and is held in custody pending the resolution of his case; the gaol is attacked by bushrangers and Ralph taken prisoner by the murderous Foxley and his companions. The gang, of which Ralph is an unwilling member, commits several atrocities, including the capture of an overseer, who is pegged out on an anthill and eaten alive by soldier ants, and an attack on the home of a settler, whose daughters are raped.

Eventually the gang is caught, and Ralph and the remaining survivor are convicted and condemned. Reprieved for the second time, on this occasion on the gallows, Ralph is sent to Newcastle, where he is forced to endure several floggings and the privations of work in a gang. In company with seven other convicts, he escapes northwards, where the party is racked by internal feuding and attacked by Aborigines. The sole survivor of a flash flood while he is building a canoe to escape Australian waters, Ralph becomes a member of an Aboriginal tribe, whose ceremonies and lifestyle are briefly described. He spends a peaceful four years in its company, but hostility towards him increases following the death of his protector; in the company of two Aboriginal women, he reaches the northern tip of Australia, where he rescues two women from a shipwreck. He accompanies them to Sydney and after a period of assignment to the father of one of the women, he becomes a free settler in the New England district.

Partly because of the circumstances of its composition and discovery, *Ralph Rashleigh* has attracted the attention of commentators on Australian fiction. If Tucker's authorship is assumed, it is one of the few, and undeniably the best, fictional treatment of transportation written by a convict and provides a link between the memoirs of Tucker's fellow prisoners and the novels about the System written in the second half of the nineteenth century. Although the brutality of the penal officials is not ignored in *Ralph Rashleigh*, notably in the Emu Plains and Newcastle scenes, neither is the brutality of the convicts and ex-convicts themselves, which has led to suggestions that the protest against the System in the novel is undercut by Tucker's desire to come to terms with his experience by embracing it. Other approaches to the novel have focused on its contribution to the depiction of the bushranger and the Aboriginal in Australian literature, the comparative brutalities of civilized and savage society, and the search for freedom implicit in Ralph's journeys in the novel.

Rambotham, Laura, see 'RICHARDSON, HENRY HANDEL'; *Getting of Wisdom, The*

RAMSON, W.S., see **Australian English**

RANKEN, GEORGE (1827–95), born Ayrshire, Scotland, trained as a surveyor and emigrated to Australia in 1851. He pursued various occupations in Queensland and became commissioner for crown lands in 1868; following a violent incident with his ex-partner, William Rea, Ranken was charged with attempted murder in 1869, but was acquitted and moved to Sydney, where he became an estate agent, alderman and, in 1886, mayor. He wrote for the *Sydney Morning Herald* on land questions under the pseudonym 'Capricornus' and in 1879 was a member of a royal commission into the Lands Department, whose report subsequently provided the basis for important legislation. Ranken also published two novels, *The Invasion* (1877), under the pseudonym 'W.H. Walker'; and *Windabyne* (1895), previously serialized in the *Australian Magazine* (1878–79); *Bush Essays* (1872); and *The Federal Geography of British Australasia* (1891). A digressive, discursive narrative of station life in NSW, *Windabyne* is his most significant literary achievement.

RANKIN, JENNIFER (1941–79), born Sydney, graduated from the University of Sydney and worked both in England and Australia in the social sciences and education. Her poetry, which was published widely in magazines in Australia, England and the USA, appeared in two collections, *Ritual Shift* (1976) and *Earth Hold* (1978), illustrated by John Olsen. She also wrote plays for stage and radio, one of which, *Bees*, was published in *Theatre Australia* (1976). *Bees* treats a feminist theme in an unusual, undogmatic and part-surrealistic way. Rankin's poetry, unpretentious and quietly lyrical, reveals a strong, open response to the natural and human world.

RATCLIFFE, FRANCIS, see *Flying Fox and Drifting Sand*

Rapunzel in Suburbia, see **HEWETT, DOROTHY**

RAYMENT, TARLTON (1882–1964), born Reading, England, came to Australia at the turn of the century and worked as a professional beekeeper and commercial artist. A Fellow of the Royal Zoological Society, he published several books and numerous articles as a result of his research into Australian native bees, and was a regular contributor to *Walkabout* 1939–50, writing under his own name and under the pseudonyms 'Ralph Darling', 'Kavai', 'Johan Moorst' and 'Moroko'. He also wrote *The Prince of the Totem* (1933), a collection of Aboriginal legends and fairy tales previously broadcast on radio; *The Valley of the Sky* (1937), winner of an award in a 1935 world novel competition, which was based on Angus McMillan's discovery of Gippsland and was subsequently translated into several European languages; and *Eagles and Earthlings* (1945), a collection of verse commemorating the Allied air crews of the Second World War. He also contributed short stories to several leading newspapers. His biography, *The Melody Lingers On*, by Lynette Young, was published in 1967.

READE, CHARLES (1814–84), the nineteenth-century English novelist and dramatist popular in his own time and remembered chiefly for the medieval romance, *The Cloister and the Hearth* (1861), had several literary connections with Australia although he never visited the colonies. After education at the University of Oxford, where he studied privately for a time with Robert Lowe, Reade was called to the bar but pursued instead a career as a dramatist. In 1853 his sixth play, *Gold*, was performed successfully in London; a five-act melodrama, the third and fourth acts set in Australia, the play exploited the current interest aroused by the discovery of gold. It focuses on the experiences of a poor English farmer, George Sandford, who emigrates to Australia and earns the thousand pounds which allows him to marry his sweetheart, Susan Merton, thus thwarting the plans of another suitor. Over the next three years Reade, his experience of Australia enlarged by the descriptive writing of Peter Cunningham, William Howitt and others, reworked the *Gold* material into a novel, published in 1856 as *It Is Never Too Late to Mend*. Reade developed his celebrated documentary method in writing *It is Never Too Late to Mend*. He retained the success story of George Sandford changing his name to George Fielding but the novel became famous for its other major plot, the story of a thief, Thomas Robinson, a minor character in *Gold*, who goes to Australia with Sandford. Influenced by *Uncle Tom's Cabin* and by his visit to Birmingham and Reading gaols and other institutions, Reade made his story of Robinson's experiences before his transportation a savage indictment of the English prison system. The novel impressed Marcus Clarke, who adapted Reade's novel, *Foul Play*, for the stage and referred to Reade in the preface of *His Natural Life* (1874). Dramatizations of *It Is Never Too Late to Mend* were popular on the Australian stage and formed part of the repertoire of Alfred Dampier.

Real Matilda, The, see **DIXSON, MIRIAM**

Realist Writer, the journal of the Melbourne branch of the left-wing Realist Writers group, appeared quarterly March 1952–April 1954, when it was incorporated in *Overland* (q.v.). Bill Wannan edited the first two issues and Stephen Murray-Smith the subsequent seven; contributors included David Martin, Frank Hardy, Laurence Collinson, John Manifold, John Morrison, Eric Lambert and Katharine Susannah Prichard. A second *Realist Writer*, journal of the Sydney branch of the Realist Writers group, began publication in July 1958, edited by Frank Hardy. From 1962 to 1970, when it ceased publication, Ray Williams was its editor; it included verse, stories, articles and occasional plays. In 1964 the title changed to the *Realist*. Contributors included Prichard, Morrison, Manifold, Dorothy Hewett, Len Fox, Wilma Hedley, Judah Waten and Ron Tullipan.

Recollections of Geoffry Hamlyn, The, a novel by Henry Kingsley (q.v.) was first published in 1859. A chronicle of three families, the Buckleys (q.v.), the Thorntons and the Brentwoods, it covers the period from the 1780s to 1858, focusing on the period after 1820. The novel is narrated by the bumbling bachelor, Geoffry Hamlyn; ostensibly the story is read aloud to Major and Agnes Buckley and Captain Brentwood at Baroona station in 1857, where the first chapter is set, but in the last pages of the novel it is revealed that Hamlyn has revised and enlarged the oral version. The first part of *Geoffry Hamlyn* is set mainly at Drumston in Devon, England, where Major Buckley has settled with his wife after being forced to sell the family seat of Clere; other inhabitants of the village include the Rev. John Thornton, his daughter Mary, his sister and his nephew, Thomas Troubridge, Mary's suitors James Stockridge and George Hawker, the German Dr Mulhaus, and Hamlyn himself. Rejected by Mary, Stockridge emigrates to Australia with Hamlyn; Mary elopes with the wild and ignoble George, which causes her father to have a stroke and the couple to be pursued by Major Buckley to London, where they are married. George falls into bad company and eventually into crime. After he is arrested for forgery, Mary struggles home with her baby to be reunited with her father on his deathbed. The second part of the novel is set in Australia, where the Buckleys and Thorntons emigrate to join Stockridge and Hamlyn as pastoralists in the Monaro region; they are followed out by Dr Mulhaus. Mary settles on Toonarbin in partnership with Thomas Troubridge, the Buckleys on Baroona near the station of Captain Brentwood and Mrs Mayford; despite such hazards as bushfires and attacks by Aborigines, which result in the death of Stockridge, their breeding makes success inevitable. Much of the focus of the Australian scenes, however, is on the affairs of the next generation: Sam Buckley, Alice and Jim Brentwood, Charles Hawker, Cecil Mayford. The conflict between Cecil and Sam over their love for Alice is resolved by her acceptance of Sam, whose heroic qualities are tested when bushrangers enter the district and he rescues Alice just before her house is besieged. During the attacks both Cecil and Charles are killed, Charles by the notorious bushranger, Captain Touan, who turns out to be his father, George Hawker. George is hanged for the murder, which allows Mary to find happiness at the end of the novel by her marriage to Thomas Troubridge. They remain in Australia; Sam and Alice, however, return to England rich enough to reclaim Clere, where they are eventually joined by their parents and Hamlyn himself. They are visited by the successful soldier, Jim Brentwood, and by Dr Mulhaus, who has been revealed to be a baron wounded at the battle of Jena.

An emigrant success story which presented Australia largely as a pastoral Eden, *The Recollections of Geoffry Hamlyn* influenced the direction of Australian fiction by providing a romance model for later successful writers such as 'Rolf Boldrewood'. The Anglocentric attitudes revealed in the novel and its lack of realism led to its dismissal by Joseph Furphy in *Such is Life* (q.v., 1903), and for much of the twentieth century its historical importance was solely emphasized. Recent commentators have stressed its mythic qualities as well as Kingsley's abilities to depict landscape.

Recruiting Officer, The, a play by George Farquhar and staged by a group of convicts in honour of the King's birthday, was the first play performed in the colony of NSW (4 June 1789).

Red Letter Days, see **BEASLEY, JACK**

Red Page, the major literary section of the *Bulletin* (q.v.) 1896–1961, was so named because it appeared on the inside of the journal's distinctive red cover. The Red Page was the innovation of A.G. Stephens (q.v.), who developed it from 'Books of the Day' and 'The *Bulletin* Book Exchange', the lists of new literature with occasional editorial comment that replaced advertisements in the *Bulletin* 1894–96. Stephens, satirized as the Red Page Rhadamanthus in Victor Daley's poem, 'Narcissus and Some Tadpoles' (1899), was editor of the Red Page until 1906 and was succeeded by A.H. Adams, Bertram Stevens, David McKee Wright, Cecil Mann and most importantly Douglas Stewart (1940–61). A selection of Stephens's Red Page criticism was published as *The Red Pagan* (1902); some of Stewart's criticism is included in *The Flesh and the Spirit* (1948) and *The Broad Stream* (1975).

Red Sky at Morning, a play in three acts by Dymphna Cusack (q.v.), was first produced in 1935 and published in 1942. Set in 1812, the action takes place at an inn at Parramatta. Alicia, a well-born lady who has been trapped into an illicit relationship with a sadistic officer of the NSW Corps and who is now fleeing from him, renews her acquaintance with Michael, an Irish convict, at the inn, where she has taken refuge from a fierce storm. Three years earlier Michael had suffered a flogging after Alicia had been seen speaking to him. Michael and Alicia agree to escape together by ship but the officer, in pursuit of Alicia, arrives at the inn and, recognizing Michael and intent on subjecting him to further humiliation, buys him as a servant from the landlord. Meanwhile he disregards the pleas of Emma, the landlord's daughter, who is engaged to Michael. While the officer sleeps, heavily sedated by the alcohol Michael has given him, Michael makes plans for their escape. Next day, the collapse of a bridge under flood water appears to have frustrated his hope of escape with Alicia. Convinced that they love each other, however, and that their only hope is to go forward, they decide to brave the swollen river and are drowned.

Redheap, a novel by Norman Lindsay (q.v.), was published in the USA in 1930 with the title *Every Mother's Son*; banned in Australia until 1958, it was published in 1959. Part of Lindsay's trilogy on small-town life in the 1890s that includes *Saturdee* (q.v., 1933) and *Halfway to Anywhere* (1947), it relates the amatory adventures of Robert Piper, aged nineteen, and his sister Ethel, aged twenty. Robert's reckless love affair with Millie Kneebone, the daughter of a local parson and an alcoholic mother, almost terminates in parenthood and matrimony. Ethel, however, adroitly manages her indiscretions, eventually depriving her sister Hetty of the eligible Dr Niven. Against the background of Redheap's torpor and repressive pretensions is ranged an array of memorable characters, from the senile but libidinous Grandpa Piper to the grandiloquent, irreverent tutor, Mr Bandparts, dogged by his partiality for beer.

REED, A.W. (ALEXANDER WYCLIF) (1908–), formerly chairman of the NZ publishing firm, A.H. & A.W. Reed, and a nephew of Sir Alfred Hamish Reed, who established the firm in Dunedin in 1911, has written numerous accounts of Aboriginal legends, several of them for young readers. They include *Aboriginal Fables* (1965), *Myths and Legends of Australia* (1965), *The Mischievous Crow* (1969) and *Aboriginal Fables and Legendary Tales* (1977). He has written on Australian place names, *Aboriginal Place Names and Their Meanings* (1967), and *Place Names of Australia* (1973); compiled *An Illustrated Encyclopedia of Aboriginal Life* (1969); edited extracts from

Captain James Cook's journals, *Captain Cook in Australia* (1969); and written recollections of Sir A.H. Reed, *Young Kauri 1875–1975* (1975). He has also written several Australian educational books and books for children. The publishing house of A.H. & A.W. Reed, which extended to Sydney in 1963, has published numerous works of Australian literature and history.

REED, BILL (1939–), born Perth but educated in Adelaide, has worked as a book editor and journalist since the early 1960s in Canada, England and Australia and as publishing director for A.H. & A.W. Reed. Best-known as a playwright, he has published several plays, *Burke's Company* (1969), *Mr Siggie Morrison with His Comb and Paper* (1972), *Cass Butcher Bunting* (1977) and *Truganini* (1977, a series of three plays, *White Exercises*, *Pantagruel In-Between* and *King Billy's Bones*). His other plays include 'The Pecking Order', 'The Old Pig Rat', 'Jack Charles Is Up and Fighting', 'Just Out of Your Ground', 'You Want It, Don't You Billy?', 'Paddlesteamer', 'Bullsh', 'More Bullsh', 'I Don't Know What to Do with You', 'Hit and Run' and 'English Expression'. He has also published five novels, *Dogod* (1977), *The Pipwink Papers* (1978), *Me, the Old Man* (1979), *Stigmata* (1980, winner of the ANA Literature Award) and *IHE* (1982). *Burke's Company*, focusing on the last days of the Burke and Wills expedition, interweaves experiences of Burke, Wills and King on the trek, of William Brahe as he waits at Cooper's Creek, and the proceedings of the subsequent court of enquiry, to form an intense, but necessarily inconclusive study of respective guilt. Both *Cass Butcher Bunting*, which explores the feelings of three trapped miners just before the final cave-in, and *Mr Siggie Morrison with His Comb and Paper*, a goon-like, vaudevillean production, have dying as a central theme. The three plays based on the life of Truganini are studies of fear, violence and racism, ranging from mime to farce-melodrama to tragedy. Nearly all Reed's plays are distinguished by his innovative treatment of language to create a disturbing atmosphere verging on the surreal.

REED, JOHN (1901–81), born Tasmania into a wealthy pastoral family, trained as a lawyer although he later abandoned law for art. President of the Contemporary Art Society, Melbourne, 1940–43, 1953–58, he was founder and director of the Museum of Modern Art and Design of Australia in Melbourne 1958–65, and with his wife Sunday was one of the most influential proponents of modernism in Australian art. Artists whose work was fostered by the Reeds include Sidney Nolan, John Perceval,

Arthur Boyd, Albert Tucker, Joy Hester, Danila Vassilieff and Charles Blackman. Part-owner with Max Harris of the publishing firm, Reed & Harris, which published work by numerous Australian authors including Peter Cowan, Dal Stivens, Alister Kershaw, Geoffrey Dutton and Max Harris, Reed was a prominent member of the Angry Penguins group and joint editor and publisher of *Angry Penguins*. A brother of Cynthia Nolan and an energetic patron of Sidney Nolan, Reed was instrumental in gaining international recognition of Nolan's Ned Kelly series of paintings. The work of John and Sunday Reed is commemorated in the Heide Park and Art Gallery, Heidelberg, Melbourne, and described by Richard Haese in his *Rebels and Precursors* (1981).

REED, SUNDAY, see **REED, JOHN**

Reedy River, a musical play with a script by Dick Diamond (q.v.), was first produced by the Melbourne New Theatre in 1953, was published in 1970 and has since been regularly revived. The rather sketchy plot concerns a group of shearers who in spite of the failure of the strikes of the 1890s continue to oppose the use of scab labour. The play's real attractiveness lies in its combination of ballads and folksongs (q.v.) sung to the accompaniment of a bush band. The title song comes from Henry Lawson's poem, 'Reedy River'; other well-known pieces include 'Click Go the Shears', 'The Eumerella Shore', 'Flash Jack from Gundagai' and 'The Old Black Billy', most of which carry nostalgic echoes of the nationalist and radical sentiments of the 1890s and continue to appeal to urban audiences.

REES, ARTHUR J. (1877–1942), born Melbourne, was for a time on the staff of the *Age*, then joined the *New Zealand Herald* and, while still in his twenties, left for England. He lived for some time as a freelance journalist but soon acquired a reputation as a prolific writer of detective stories, none of which reflect his Australian experience. Several of his novels were translated into other languages.

REES, CORALIE CLARKE, see **CLARKE, CORALIE**

REES, LESLIE (1905–   ), was born in Perth and educated at the University of WA, where he edited the student magazine, the *Black Swan*. He spent some time on the staff of the *West Australian*, before winning a scholarship to study in London in 1929. In London in 1931 he married Coralie Clarke (q.v.). He was a senior drama critic on the London weekly, *Era*, 1931–35, and met many prominent British and

European writers. He returned in 1936 to Sydney, where he reviewed plays and films for the *Sydney Morning Herald* before being appointed federal drama editor for the ABC, a position from which he retired in 1966. Well-known as a playwright and a drama critic with international interests, Rees has had a strong influence on Australian drama through his work with the ABC and his twenty-five years chairmanship of the Playwrights Advisory Board. His wide-ranging experience is recorded in his autobiography, *Hold Fast to Dreams* (1982). In 1981 he was made AM. Rees has written two histories of Australian drama, *Towards an Australian Drama* (1953) and the more ambitious *A History of Australian Drama* (q.v., 1973, 1978) which won the 1978 Townsville Foundation for Australian Literary Studies Award; and has edited four collections of plays, *Australian Radio Plays* (1946), *Australian Youth Plays* (1948), *Modern Short Plays* (1951) and *Mask and Microphone* (1963). Of his own plays, *Sub-Editor's Room*, the first Australian play to be televised, is included in *Best Australian One-Act Plays* (1937), edited by William Moore and T. Inglis Moore, and *Mother's Day* in *Six Australian One-Act Plays* (1944). He also collaborated with Ruth Park in a dramatization of her novel, *The Harp in the South*, produced in 1949. His other plays include 'On the Edge of the Future' (1934) and 'Lalor of Eureka' (1935).

As well as numerous articles, memoirs and critical essays, Rees has written four travel books in collaboration with his wife, *Spinifex Walkabout* (1953), *Westward from Cocos* (1956), *Coasts of Cape York* (1960) and *People of the Big Sky Country* (1970). He is also one of Australia's best-known and most prolific children's writers. He has written four adventure stories, *Quokka Island* (1951), *Danger Patrol* (1954), *Boy Lost on Tropic Coast* (1968) and *Panic in the Cattle Country* (1974); an animal fantasy, *Mates of the Kurlalong* (1948); a series of popular stories centering on a local Tom Thumb called Digit Dick (1942–82); and an extensive and informative series of nature stories dealing with Australian fauna. Of these the most popular are *The Story of Shy the Platypus* (1944), *Two-Thumbs: The Story of a Koala* (1953), *The Story of Sarli the Barrier Reef Turtle* (1947), *The Story of Aroora the Red Kangaroo* (1952) and *The Story of Karrawingi the Emu* (1946), which won the 1946 Children's Book of the Year Award. Several of the tales have been reprinted in two collections (1958, 1974) and others have also been translated and published in the Soviet Union and other countries. Rees has recently broken new ground in *Here's to Shane* (1977), a story of a deaf boy's battle with his handicap.

581

REEVE, EDWARD (1822–89), born England, arrived in Sydney in 1840, and after some years as a teacher and then clerk, joined the staff of the *Sydney Morning Herald* in 1857. He contributed articles on various subjects to contemporary journals, was associated with the literary group which included Frank Fowler, Joseph Sheridan Moore and Nicol Drysdale Stenhouse and with their founding of the *Month*. He became the first curator of the Nicholson Museum at the University of Sydney in 1860 and, in 1871, a founder and honorary secretary of the NSW Academy of Art. His blank verse tragedy, *Raymond, Lord of Milan* (1851), first produced for a four-night run in Sydney in 1863, was revived in 1950. The play has some good verse and incidental scenes but lacks unity and direction. In 1882 in the *Sydney Mail* he also published a long, well-written and tightly constructed romance, 'Friends and Foes'; Or, The Bride of Bernback', and in 1884 'Passion', his adaptation of Rosa Praed's novel, *Policy and Passion* (q.v., 1881), was staged in Sydney.

Referee, a Sydney weekly newspaper was launched in 1886 to compete with the Melbourne *Sportsman* and later the *Arrow* and *Sydney Sportsman* for the attention of a burgeoning sporting public. During its fifty-odd years existence it was dominated by W.F. Corbett and his son Claude but in earlier days Nat Gould and 'Smiler' Hailes were prominent contributors. Its demise in 1939 resulted less from the competition of rival sporting journals than from the increasing popularity of evening newspapers such as the *Sun*.

Regan, Dave, is a bush worker who appears in some of Henry Lawson's (q.v.) most famous humorous stories, including 'The Loaded Dog' and 'The Ironbark Chip'; in both he is characteristically presented as ironic victim. The major Regan stories involve Regan and his mates Andy Page and Jack Bently, and were published in *On the Track* (1900), *Joe Wilson and His Mates* (1901) and *Children of the Bush* (1902). Lawson's 'A Fragment of Autobiography' suggests that Regan was modelled on a drover he knew in childhood; several of the stories in which he participates are based on incidents Lawson heard about while working with his father in the Mudgee district and elsewhere in the early 1880s.

Register, the first SA newspaper and for most of its life the great rival of the *Advertiser*, began publication in 1836; its first issue was produced by George Stevenson (q.v.) and was published in England, as were other publications relating to early SA, but it resumed in Adelaide in 1837. Titled the *South Australian Gazette and Colonial Register* (1836–39), the *South Australian Register* (1839–1900) and the *Register News-Pictorial* (1929–31), the *Register* became a daily in 1850 and was absorbed by the *Advertiser* in 1931. A major contributor both to the *Register* and its weekly companion, the *Adelaide Observer*, was Catherine Helen Spence.

REIBEY, MARY (1777–1855), born Mary Haydock, Lancashire, England, was convicted of horse stealing in 1790 while masquerading as a young lad and was transported to NSW in 1792. In 1794 she married Thomas Reibey (1769–1811), a young Irishman who became one of the Colony's most successful traders and merchants. When Reibey died, Mary, then the mother of seven children, took over his business interests and became one of the leading members of the new emancipist society favoured by Governor Lachlan Macquarie. An enterprising and successful businesswoman, she eventually owned several ships, substantial properties in the heart of Sydney and in Tasmania and established the Reibey dynasty, which included her grandson, Thomas, a member of the Tasmanian State parliament for twenty-five years and, briefly, premier of that State. Her biography, *Mary Reibey – Molly Incognita* (1982), by Nancy Irvine, was launched at Mary Reibey's Coffee Palace in the Rocks, Sydney, at a 1982 reunion of the Reibey family.

REID, Sir GEORGE HOUSTON (1845–1918), premier of NSW (1894–99) and prime minister of Australia (1904–05), was born in Scotland and came to Australia in 1852. He began his working life in 1858 as clerk to a Sydney merchant, but subsequently gained a position in the colonial treasury and studied law, which he began to practise in 1879. Elected to the NSW parliament in 1880, he proved to be an active, skilful politician and a colourful debater with a gift for witty repartee. His vacillation over Federation led to him becoming known as 'Yes–No' Reid in a series of cartoons by Livingston Hopkins. He retired from politics in 1908, was Australian High Commissioner in London 1910–16, and held the seat of Hanover Square in the House of Commons 1916–18 as an independent imperialist. Reid's publications include a collection of five essays on free trade (1875), which won him honorary membership of the Cobden Club; an account of his own colony, *An Essay on New South Wales, the Mother Colony of the Australias* (1876); a volume of autobiography, *My Reminiscences* (1917); and a poem, *Lines Addressed to New South Wales on the Opening of the First Australian International Exhibition* (1879). He also wrote the foreword to Barbara Baynton's *Cobbers* (1917). Extracts from his London notebooks and letters, illustrative of Australia's role in the planning and execution of the Gallipoli campaign, and selected by his granddaughter, Anne Fairbairn, were published in the *Australian* (1981). Some of the most trenchant criticisms of Reid are contained in Alfred Deakin's *The Federal Story* (1944).

Remittance Man was usually the black sheep of the family, sent out to the colonies from England so that he would no longer be an embarrassment at home. He was usually sustained by regular remittances of money from the family in England. Often an inebriate or isolate, the remittance man was recognized by his faded aristocratic air and his inability to cope with the rough and ready colonial life. Well-known portraits of the type are in Henry Lawson's 'The Story of "Gentleman-Once"' in *Children of the Bush* (1902), Ambrose Pratt's *The Remittance Man* (1907) and Judith Wright's poem, 'Remittance Man' in *The Moving Image* (1946). References to remittance man, usually in derogatory terms, are widespread in writing of the late nineteenth century, e.g. in Nat Gould's *On and Off the Turf in Australia* (1895) and 'Mark Twain''s *Following the Equator* (1897).

Removalists, The, a play by David Williamson (q.v.) first performed in 1971 at the La Mama Theatre, has been widely performed in Australia and in London and New York. It was published in 1972, was co-winner of the 1971 British George Devine Award and also won two Awgies. Set partly in a small police station and partly in a suburban home, the cast includes the authoritarian, pontificating Sergeant Simmonds; Ross, his impressionable junior; Fiona Carter, a young housewife who reluctantly makes a complaint about her physically abusive husband, Kenny; her socially pretentious sister, Kate; and a removalist. After Fiona's complaint, orchestrated by her domineering sister and exploited for its sexual possibilities by Simmonds, the two policemen offer to help Fiona move out. The sexually frustrated Simmonds aspires, fruitlessly, to a liaison with Kate. In Act Two Kenny arrives home early and immediately engages aggressively with Simmonds. Both men are committed to a tough self-image which stresses sexual and fighting ability. First Simmonds methodically bashes Kenny and then Ross, who has been ceaselessly humiliated all day, explodes into violence at Kenny's taunts. Kenny appears to die, recovers, matily discusses a call-girl racket with Simmonds, and then collapses with a cerebral haemorrhage. After some panic-stricken recriminations, Simmonds and Ross fall to blows in

an attempt to claim that Kenny died while resisting arrest.

'RENAR, FRANK', see **FOX**, Sir **FRANK**

RENE, ROY (1892–1954), born Adelaide as Henry Van der Sluys, was also known as Harry Sluice but took the stage name of Roy Rene. Initially a boy soprano, Roy Boy, Rene in 1914 formed with Nat Phillips a comedy partnership, Stiffy and Mo, which delighted Australian vaudeville audiences until the end of the 1920s. Phillips was Stiffy, the straight man who fed lines to Mo, characteristically made up with chalk white face and black beard as he leered and lisped catch-phrases like 'Strike me lucky'. A city-oriented clown who remained enormously popular on the Australian stage after the breaking of the Stiffy and Mo partnership, Rene had success also on radio in the late 1940s; as Mo McCackie he presided over *McCackie Mansions*, an establishment also inhabited by Mo's stupid son, Young Harry, his layabout relative, 'Orrible 'Erbie, next-door neighbour, Lasho, and the sweetly spoken visitor, Spencer the Garbage Man. *Mo's Memoirs*, ghosted by Max Harris and Elisabeth Lambert, was published in 1945; John Thompson included Rene in his *Time to Remember* (1962) and his scriptwriter, Fred Parsons, wrote the biographical tribute, *A Man Called Mo* (1973). Rene has also been the subject of a musical tribute, 'Mo', by George Dreyfus (performed 1972), and of Steve J. Spears's play, *Young Mo* (first performed 1976, published 1977).

RENTOUL, ANNIE RATTRAY, the daughter of notable Presbyterian clergyman and minor poet, John Laurence Rentoul (1846–1926), and sister of Ida Rentoul Outhwaite, wrote stories and verse for children which Ida illustrated. Her stories include *Mollie's Bunyip* (1904), *The Lady of the Blue Beads* (1908), and *The Little Green Road to Fairyland* (1922); her verse, *Australian Songs for Young and Old* (1907), *Bush Songs of Australia for Young and Old* (1910), *More Australian Songs for Young and Old* (1914) and *Australian Bush Songs* (1937). She contributed verses and stories to the sumptuous production, *Fairyland* (1926), and verses to *Elves and Fairies of Ida Rentoul Outhwaite* (1916), and was also a contributor, with her sister, father, and mother, Annie Isobel Rentoul, to *At the Sign of the Sword* (1915). Less well-known than her sister, whose delicate illustrations complemented her ethereal transformation of the Australian landscape into a traditional fairy land, Annie was a more productive writer.

Republican, a Sydney radical journal, ran for ten issues 1887–88; for part of the time, when it was under the management of Louisa Lawson, her son Henry was nominal publisher and had his first prose articles published there. The *Republican* is the subject of Lawson's poem, 'The Cambaroora Star'.

Retrospect, The, see *Thirty Years in Australia*

Review, a weekly newspaper published in Melbourne 1970–72, was titled *Sunday Review* until July 1971 and in March 1971 incorporated the *Sunday Observer*. In July 1972 the newspaper merged with the Sydney *Nation* to form *Nation Review*.

Review of Reviews for Australasia, was published monthly in Melbourne 1892–1914, when its title changed to *Stead's Review of Reviews*. From 1931 to 1934, when it ceased publication, the magazine was titled *Today*. *Review of Reviews* included some material from the parent British edition, reprinted extracts and cartoons from Australian periodicals to give a general survey of affairs, and included reviews of Australian books and articles on Australian artists and writers. One of the most useful surveys of contemporary Australian newspapers appeared as a series from July 1892 to September 1893.

Rex, John, see *His Natural Life*

REYNOLDS, HENRY, see Aboriginal in Australian Literature

'Rhyme of Joyous Garde, The', published in *Bush Ballads and Galloping Rhymes* (1870) by Adam Lindsay Gordon (q.v.), portrays the love affair between Sir Lancelot and Queen Guinevere in the Arthurian legend. In presenting the affair through the eyes of the guilty lovers, Gordon gives a perceptive analysis of human frailty without passing conventional moral judgement on that frailty. With its substantial theme and sustained control of rhythm and imagery (unusual for Gordon) it is one of his best poems.

Rhymes from the Mines and Other Lines, see DYSON, EDWARD

RICHARDS, JAMES, a Ballarat clergyman, who also used the pseudonyms 'Frank Dripstone' and 'J.R.R.', published at least three works of fiction and four volumes of verse. The novels that have survived are *Fern Glen* (188–), *Edwin Randolph* (n.d.) and *Under a*

Face (n.d.); another titled *Ada Maitland*, and apparently much prized by the author, has not been traced. His collections of verse are *Poems* (1867), *Ada and Other Australian Poems* (1888), *Ada: An Australian Poem* (1890) and *The Poetical Works of the Rev. J. Richards* (1890). Sentimental, conventional and derivative, Richards's work is more English than Australian in tone.

RICHARDS, THOMAS (1800–77), born Wales, trained as a doctor in London and moved in literary and journalistic circles before he came to Australia in 1832 as surgeon on an emigrant ship. He settled in Van Diemen's Land where, in 1833, he edited the *Tasmanian* and collaborated with Henry Melville in the production of the *Hobart Town Magazine*; after it ceased publication in 1834 he ran a correspondence agency to assist the poor and illiterate to communicate with the government. In 1837 he was editor of the *Hobart Town Courier* and for about a decade from 1837 was associated with the *Colonial Times*; in the 1850s he returned full-time to medicine but in his later years was active on the *Mercury*. Richards was a talented journalist whose varied output included polemical and descriptive essays and dramatic criticism; his fictional sketches contributed to the *Hobart Town Magazine* make him one of the pioneers of the short story in Australia.

'RICHARDSON, HENRY HANDEL' (ETHEL FLORENCE LINDSAY ROBERTSON) (1870–1946), was born in Melbourne, the eldest daughter of a physician, Walter Lindsay Richardson, who had emigrated to Australia in 1852. Strikingly dependent on autobiographical and family experience for her creative writing, 'Richardson' drew heavily on her father's life for the central character of her novel trilogy, *The Fortunes of Richard Mahony* (q.v.), although she made several significant changes. Like Mahony, Walter Richardson was born in Dublin, trained at the University of Edinburgh, came to Australia during the gold rushes of the 1850s in an attempt to recoup his family's fortunes, worked first as a storekeeper and then as a general practitioner and in 1855 married a much younger girl, also recently arrived from England, Mary Bailey. By the time of Ethel's birth fifteen years later, Walter Richardson was a prosperous, prominent figure in Melbourne society and had retired from general practice in 1869 when his investments in stocks returned him a small fortune. Four years later he took his wife and two daughters on a grand tour of Europe but his visit was cut short by the sudden failure of his investments and his abrupt return to Australia to rebuild his practice. The next four years were dominated by the family's frequent changes of home in Victoria as Walter Richardson vainly attempted to re-establish himself, meanwhile contending with rapidly increasing symptoms of what was probably syphilis. In 1878 he was admitted to a private asylum in Melbourne and later spent some time in the government asylum. He died in 1879 after some months in the care of his family at Koroit, a remote village in western Victoria where Mary Richardson had been appointed postmistress. Ethel Richardson's memories of Koroit were distasteful although she was happier at Maldon after the family moved there in 1880. From the age of thirteen to seventeen she was a boarder at the Presbyterian Ladies' College, Melbourne, an experience she drew on for her novel, *The Getting of Wisdom* (q.v.), although, unlike its heroine, Laura Rambotham, she won distinction there, especially as a musician. In other respects, however, her experience was close to Laura's, especially in her strong attachment to another, older girl. In 1888 her mother resigned from the postal service and took her two daughters to Europe so that Ethel could continue her musical studies at Leipzig Conservatorium. 'Richardson''s childhood in Australia left her with strong memories of the Australian landscape, a precocious but lasting awareness of the dark side of human experience and a conviction of her own distinctive apartness.

Life in Germany proved to be liberating and intellectually stimulating; she discovered European literature, in which she read widely, and began to concentrate on her own creative talent, ultimately abandoning music for writing. She also met her future husband, J.G. Robertson, a Scotsman and a doctoral student in German literature, who had a profound influence on the direction of her cultural interests. A year after her marriage in 1895 'Richardson' published translations from the German J.P. Jacobsen's Danish novel, *Niels Lyhne*, which she titled *Siren Voices* and afterwards described as having 'stirred [her] as few books have ever done either before or since', and B. Björnson's *The Fisher Lass*. She began her own first novel, *Maurice Guest* (q.v.), in 1897 in Strasbourg, where her husband had been appointed as lecturer at the university. The death of her mother that year, which was a severe blow, gave rise to a short story, 'Death', published in 1911, later titled 'Mary Christina' and included in *Two Studies* (1931). As at Leipzig, 'Richardson' led an active social life at Strasbourg. After 1903 however, when she moved to London with her husband who had been appointed to a chair of German at the University of London, 'Richardson''s life quickly set into the solitary

pattern that was to continue until her death. Common to nearly all the reminiscences of 'Richardson' is the picture of a deliberately-isolated figure, hard at work in an upper-storey, sound-proof study, devotedly attended by first her husband and then her companion-secretary, Olga Roncoroni.

Maurice Guest, published by Heinemann in 1908 under the pseudonym that she later described as deriving from the Irish side of her family, received varying reviews although it was praised by several prominent writers of the time, including Hugh Walpole and Somerset Maugham. *The Getting of Wisdom*, written as a light relief from *Maurice Guest*, appeared in 1910 but failed to attract immediate attention. In London 'Richardson' began the painstaking research for *Australia Felix*, the first volume of the trilogy, *The Fortunes of Richard Mahony*, which was to occupy her for twenty years. In 1912 she visited Australia for two months to check details for the trilogy then remained in England for the rest of her life. *Australia Felix*, completed in 1915, was published in 1917 and sold reasonably well although it was neglected in Australia. *The Way Home*, the middle volume of the trilogy and 'Richardson''s favourite, was published in 1925 but sold so poorly that Heinemann refused in 1928 to publish the last volume, *Ultima Thule*. Published in 1929 at J.G. Robertson's expense, it was an immediate success and was quickly reprinted by Heinemann and by Norton in the USA. The trilogy, published as one volume for the first time in 1930, has been frequently reprinted and translated into Swedish and Danish. Well-known in England, Europe, the USA and Australia by the mid-1930s, 'Richardson' was nominated for the Nobel Prize in 1932 and was awarded the Australian Literature Society's Gold Medal (1929) for *Ultima Thule*. As well as two collections of short stories, *Two Studies* (1931) and *The End of a Childhood* (1934), some other short stories, which have been recently collected in *The Adventures of Cuffy Mahony* (1979), several uncollected articles and a volume of unfinished autobiography, *Myself When Young* (1948), 'Richardson' produced one other major piece of fiction, *The Young Cosima* (1939). Some of her letters to Nettie Palmer were published in the latter's study of 'Richardson' (1950) and in a separate edition in 1953. The death of 'Richardson''s husband in 1933 was an irreparable loss, after which she moved to Sussex, and the Second World War proved to be even more of a personal ordeal than the First. As one of her critics has commented, all three countries in which she lived, Australia, Germany and England, offered 'Richardson' distinctive experiences and gifts, but 'it is open to question whether any . . . gave her a home'.

At Leipzig 'Richardson' became interested in German romanticism and in French, Russian and Scandinavian writers of the nineteenth century. She read both Dostoevsky and Freud some years before English translations of their work were available and was also particularly influenced by Swedenborg, Goethe, Ibsen, and Flaubert as well as Jacobsen. Swedenborg's work probably reinforced the interest in spiritualism that she shared with her father (she was a lifelong member of the Society for Psychical Research); and she found much in the German world-view of the time to confirm her own pessimistic perception of the human condition as inevitably limited and subject to constant change. Although 'Richardson' owes much to the European tradition of scientific realism, especially so far as a concern for accurate documentation, psychological veracity and narrative impartiality is concerned, she is also preoccupied with romantic themes such as love and spiritual and artistic fulfilment. In *Maurice Guest* realism and romanticism combine in the study of an aspiring artist who lacks the talent to achieve his ambition and who becomes the victim of an obsessive love, leading finally to his suicide. Against the vividly-realized background of Leipzig's musical world 'Richardson' carefully and objectively traces the successive stages of Maurice's corrosive passion, his failure in everything except acceptance of his fate. Some readers have uncovered a debt to Nietzsche in its theme, especially in 'Richardson''s treatment of Maurice's opposite, the genius and free spirit, Schilsky; others, however, have stressed the novel's ironic undercurrents that imply an objective attitude to the concept of the artist-hero. *The Getting of Wisdom*, described by 'Richardson' as a 'merry little book', is comically ironic in tone, but has a serious subject, the story of an artist's painful inner growth during her impressionable adolescent years. The freshness, clarity and honesty of 'Richardson''s presentation of youthful experience has often been praised, although at the time some regarded the book as a satire on education, and in 1912 'Richardson' was denied admittance to the Presbyterian Ladies' College. In her picture of Laura, her 'odd and unaccountable' heroine, she undoubtedly drew heavily on her own experience, but Laura differs from herself in certain respects, most importantly in her outward failure. The wisdom that Laura acquires takes various forms, none of which derives from her formal education, but all of which concern the nature of truth and honesty, the force and forms of passion, and the ambivalent need to be individual and conform. Like Mahony, Laura learns that nothing is permanent and that life inevitably involves loneliness, disillusionment and loss.

If *The Getting of Wisdom* has acquired the status of a classic in the genre of childhood autobiography, it is *The Fortunes of Richard Mahony* that is generally judged to be 'Richardson''s major achievement and one of the showpieces of Australian literature. The trilogy has been variously defined as an emigrant novel, a chronicle of colonialism in Australia, a study of failure or of an ill-matched marriage, an analysis of the 'complex fate' of dual nationality, or, simply, as 'a book about money'. The central subject, however, is Mahony himself, in accordance with 'Richardson''s view of the importance of character: 'I never cease to believe that character-drawing is [the novel's] main end and object, the conflict of personalities its drama'. In *Australia Felix*, which presents a varied, densely-packed picture of Victorian colonial life, Mahony gradually emerges as a man suffering from cultural alienation; *The Way Home* records, from a narrower perspective, his successive failures to find 'home' in any sense; *Ultima Thule* places him firmly in the foreground and traces the final stages of his self-destruction. Lack of unity, an excessive and cramping attention to detail and stylistic clumsiness have been some of the charges levelled at the trilogy although some critics have found that 'Richardson' shapes and illuminates her material in minutely detailed ways. Some of these include her use of recurrent images, especially of confinement and burial, age and youth, of recurrent incidents, scenes and objects and of contrasting or parallel characters, so that the work is held together by a pattern of interlocking ironies and reveals several layers of meaning. Although *Ultima Thule* is generally regarded as the most assured and moving volume of the trilogy, the whole has been described as similar to a symphony, of which the 'Proem' to *Australia Felix* is the overture. In her portrait of Mahony, 'Richardson' undoubtedly invested the facts of her father's life with her own personality traits and emotional experience. Afflicted with a romantic dilemma, an awareness that there is no permanence, coupled with an ineradicable yearning for an ideal point of rest, Mahony pursues his fate as relentlessly as Maurice Guest. His relationship with his wife, the practical, common-sense Mary, defines both the absurdity and the magnificence of his search, as 'Richardson''s use of a third observer in *Ultima Thule*, the child, Cuffy, emphasizes its poignance and suffering. Ultimately Mahony emerges as an Everyman figure, as the epigraph to *Australia Felix* suggests, an illustration of the universal human vulnerability to pain and loss.

With the trilogy and the four stories dealing with Cuffy Mahony in *The End of a Childhood*, 'Richardson' exhausted her family experience and attempted in *The Young Cosima* a different sort of historical novel, a study of the relationships between Wagner, Liszt, Hans von Bülow and Cosima von Bülow. Within the framework of this familiar story of genius and passion 'Richardson' attempts to re-examine some of the problems of art and life that had preoccupied her in *Maurice Guest*. In this last novel, however, her prose lacks energy and she fails to achieve that impression of felt life which is, for the most part, a marked feature of her work. Studies of 'Richardson' include Leonie Kramer's *Henry Handel Richardson and Some of Her Stories* (1954) and *Myself When Laura* (1966); Vincent Buckley's monograph, *Henry Handel Richardson* (1961); and Dorothy Green's extensive biographical and critical analysis, *Ulysses Bound* (1973).

RICHARDSON, WALTER LINDESAY, see 'RICHARDSON, HENRY HANDEL'

RICKARDS, HARRY (1845–1911), born Henry Benjamin Leete in London, took the stage name of Harry Rickards and established a reputation as a singer of music-hall comic songs. On his first visit to Australia beginning in 1871, Marcus Clarke wrote vaudeville sketches for him; Rickards made subsequent tours in 1885–87, 1888 and 1892–93, and in 1893 took a lease on the Garrick Theatre in Sydney. He renamed it the Tivoli and established himself as a successful vaudeville entrepreneur, with theatres in Melbourne, Adelaide, Perth, and other places. Visiting England every year, Rickards was responsible in the decades either side of 1900 for the Australian engagement of many overseas variety entertainers. One of his few failures was a lecture tour by the hoaxer, 'Louis de Rougemont', in 1904.

RIDDELL, ALAN (1927–77), born Townsville, Queensland, was educated in Scotland and lived in Greece, Spain and France, as well as Australia, where he worked as a journalist for the *Age*, *Daily Telegraph* and *Sydney Morning Herald*. Founder of the Scottish poetry review, *Lines*, which he edited 1952–55 and 1962–67, he contributed verse to Australian and overseas journals and anthologies and published four collections, *Beneath the Summer* (1952), *Majorcan Interlude* (1960), *The Stopped Landscape* (1968) and *Eclipse* (1972). Editor of the Scottish section of *Young Commonwealth Poets '65* (1965), he also edited the anthology, *Typewriter Art* (1975). In 1956 Riddell won the Heinemann Lyric Prize and a Scottish Arts Council Prize in 1968. Originally a traditional poet, he became interested in concrete and visual poetry in the 1960s, *Eclipse* being the first one-author volume of concrete poetry published in England.

RIDDELL, ELIZABETH (1910–), born Napier, NZ, settled in Australia shortly after leaving school. A distinguished journalist, she has travelled widely in Europe, USA and South-East Asia and is now a special writer with the *Australian* and News Limited Group. Her poetry, which has appeared in three collections, *The Untrammelled* (1940), *Poems* (1948) and *Forbears* (1961), is controlled, spare, frequently witty and lightly lyrical.

Ride On Stranger, a novel by Kylie Tennant (q.v.), was published in 1943. Shannon Hicks, an intelligent, independent girl in search of a role that will add meaning to her life, restlessly tries and discards a series of occupations and relationships. Although she works desperately hard in each succeeding missionary venture, whether it is in radio or in the United Council for the Defence of Labour, her keen awareness of the egoism that underlies human motive inevitably undermines her commitment. Her ultimate marriage to John Terrill, a young unambitious farmer, seems an achievement of happiness but even this is disrupted by the war and Terrill's unexpected enlistment and death. By the end Shannon has found through suffering that her only home is her own stoic independence and acceptance of the claims of others.

Riders in the Chariot, a novel by Patrick White (q.v.), was published in 1961 and won the Miles Franklin Award. Set mainly in the Sydney suburbs of Sarsaparilla and Barranugli (qq.v.), it deals with the lives and final spiritual meeting of four 'illuminates': Mary Hare, an elderly spinster; Mordecai Himmelfarb, a Jewish refugee from Germany; Ruth Godbold, a housewife; and Alf Dubbo, a tubercular part-Aboriginal. Miss Hare, the small, unattractive and unloved daughter of incompatible parents, lives on in the crumbling mansion, Xanadu, built by her half-mad father, Norbert Hare. Tortured by her memories of her father's violent death, which she had witnessed, and uneasy in most human relationships, she has a natural affinity with birds and animals and an instinct for spiritual truth. The latter quickly alienates her from her newly-engaged housekeeper, Mrs Jolley, whose vulgar materialism and capacity for evil is only surpassed by her more sinister friend, Mrs Flack. Both ladies have annihilated their husbands with their versions of 'married love'. The most important event in Miss Hare's later life is her friendship with Mordecai Himmelfarb. The brilliant son of a devoutly orthodox mother and a shallow, worldly father, Himmelfarb discovers his faith belatedly, although he is early recognized as a *zaddik* by others. After studying at Oxford and service in the First World War, he becomes a professor of English in Germany and marries the devout Reha Liebmann. The growing force of anti-Semitism eventually disturbs the quiet of their devoted marriage. Himmelfarb loses his post and Reha is seized by police one night when he is absent. After a period of hiding, protected by his friends the Stauffers, Himmelfarb gives himself up, is transported to a concentration camp in Poland and escapes during an uprising. He briefly visits Israel but decides to settle in Australia, where he finds employment in Harry Rosetree's Brighta Bicycle Lamps factory. Harry Rosetree, formerly Haim Rosenbaum, now assimilated and living with his wife Shirl and 'the kids' in their textured-brick house in Paradise East, finds Himmelfarb's orthodoxy disturbing. Others who are impressed by his spirituality are Miss Hare, Ruth Godbold and Alf Dubbo. After a childhood in rural England, Ruth Godbold had settled in Australia where she had gone into service. Her spiritual superiority, amounting to saintliness, had reluctantly impressed one of her employers, the frivolous Mrs Chalmers-Robinson. Now the mother of a large family, married to a violent, alcoholic husband, Ruth lives in a temporary shed and takes in washing. Her genius for love touches Miss Hare, Himmelfarb and, briefly, Alf Dubbo, and on one occasion even extends to retrieving her husband from the local brothel. Alf Dubbo, the fourth 'illuminate', lives on the margins of their lives. Born on a reserve to an old Aboriginal and an indeterminate father, he had been adopted by the Reverend Timothy Calderon, Anglican rector of Numburra, and his widowed sister, Mrs Pask. Before he is forced to flee by the Reverend's homosexual advances, Alf discovers the joy of painting. He lives for a while with the degenerate Mrs Spicer, mistress of a humpy set on a rubbish dump, and later with Hannah, a city prostitute, and her homosexual friend, Norm Fussell. He contracts syphilis, of which he is cured, and tuberculosis, which rapidly worsens. Picking up work when he needs it to support his obsession of painting, Dubbo encounters Himmelfarb at Rosetree's factory, where he works as a sweeper. The forces of good and evil clash when Himmelfarb, long the object of Mrs Flack's venom, is half-lynched or crucified by her secret son, Blue, and his mates at the factory. Later the same day Himmelfarb's house is burned, although he has been previously rescued by Mrs Godbold. Nursed by Mrs Godbold and Miss Hare and watched over by Alf Dubbo, he dies on Good Friday. Harry Rosetree, unhinged by the incident, commits suicide; Alf Dubbo finds expression in paint

for the elusive vision of the chariot of fire that all four 'illuminates' have in common but dies once it is completed. Miss Hare disappears and Xanadu is destroyed to make way for fibro homes. Mrs Jolley and Mrs Flack remain locked in a mutually destructive relationship. Only Mrs Godbold, now widowed and a grandmother, remains to testify to the divine mystery realized by the visionaries.

Ridge and the River, The, see HUNGERFORD, T.A.G.; War Literature

RIDLEY, WILLIAM, see Aboriginal in Australian Literature

Rigby's Romance, a novel by Joseph Furphy (q.v.), was in its original form the fifth chapter of Furphy's major work, *Such is Life* (1903), but was excised from that novel during revision. Serialized in the Broken Hill newspaper, the *Barrier Truth*, in 1905–06, *Rigby's Romance* was published in truncated form in 1921 and in full in 1946.

As in *Such is Life* and *The Buln-Buln and the Brolga* (1948), the latter also created out of material deleted from the former, the narrator of *Rigby's Romance* is Tom Collins (q.v.), who at the opening of the novel (April 1884, soon after the events of *Such is Life*) is on his leisurely way to fulfil a contract to clear a Riverina run of cattle. Between Echuca and Yooringa, where he expects to cross the path of an old friend, the American, Jefferson Rigby, he meets two women also in search of Rigby; one of them, Kate Vanderdecken, is Rigby's former sweetheart. After reaching Yooringa and helping to facilitate the reunion between Rigby and Kate, Collins repairs to the banks of the nearby Murray River to fish for a thirty-pound cod known to be in the area. He is joined by the bullock drivers, Robert Dixon and Steve Thompson, both of whom appear in *Such is Life*; Rigby himself; the kangaroo hunter, Smith; a trapper named Furlong; the farmer, Binney and his brother-in-law, the Methodist minister, Harold Lushington. The bulk of the novel comprises the yarns swapped among these men and their discussions and arguments about politics, religion and ethics, and the law, until Furlong eventually catches the fish and the party breaks up. Thompson, Dixon, Rigby, Furlong and Smith all tell stories of love affairs that end in unhappiness or failure, an important theme in *Such is Life*, although as the night wears on the socialist Rigby, despite the efforts of Tom and Steve to deflect him, increasingly dominates the conversation as he expounds his political ideas. In doing so, he forgets the appointment he has made with Kate and returns to her hotel next morning to discover that she has left Yooringa.

At one stage in his career Furphy preferred *Rigby's Romance* of all his writing, although most commentators see it as slighter than and much inferior to *Such is Life*. *Rigby's Romance* is the less complex and less subtle work, although Rigby articulates many of Furphy's views on state socialism. The novel also contains similar surprises of plot to *Such is Life*, e.g. the revelation that Thompson is the man in Furlong's story who provided assistance when the trapper needed desperately to go to his dying wife; enlarges our understanding of some of the characters of *Such is Life*, e.g. in the extra information which confirms Thompson's pessimistic view of life; and explores some of the same themes. Just as, in the long work, Tom's obsession with theory contrasts with his inability to interpret experience, so Rigby's idealistic concern that one should be responsible for one's fellows contrasts with his inability to keep his appointments in life. The ironic contrasts between theory and practice and between belief and experience are emphasized throughout *Rigby's Romance* and provide some of the novel's best moments, notably in Dixon's account of a courtship that fails because he is influenced by his reading of *Jane Eyre* into 'bullyragging' his girl. Dixon's earthy narrative of the story of Moses, the 'knowledge ill-inhabited' which causes him to mistranslate the Latin phrases he has acquired, and the elaborate code by which his profanities are recorded and satirized, are among the other comic highlights of the novel.

Rigmarole of the Hours, based in Melbourne, was a small press which operated 1974–79, published seventeen titles of new writings in Australia. Initially it was a magazine, *Rigmarole of the Hours*, which intended to publish books as special issues; after the first number in August 1974, edited by Robert Kenny, the magazine disappeared and the press began publishing books by writers such as Katherine Gallagher, Walter Billeter, Kris Hemensley, Robert Kenny, Laurie Duggan and Jennifer Maiden. Rigmarole of the Hours stopped publishing in 1980 but resumed in 1982 as Rigmarole Books when John Jenkins joined Kenny. It has since published works by Anna Couani, Philip Jenkins and Ken Bolton.

RIGNOLD, GEORGE, see Shakespeare and Australia

RILEY, ELIZABETH, see Feminism and Australian Literature

Rim of Blue, A, see HILL, BARRY

Ring, see 'Secret Society of the Ring'

Ringer, a term used to denote a stockman or a champion shearer, as in the famous ballad, 'Click Go the Shears, Boys', or more recently any individual of exceptional ability, occurs frequently in Australian literature. See also Shearer in Australian Literature.

'Rio Grande's Last Race', one of A.B. Paterson's (q.v.) favourite ballads, is the title poem of his second collection of verse, *Rio Grande's Last Race and Other Verses* (1902). The poem's theme, a jockey's premonition of death, is unusual in Paterson who prefers to applaud the deeds of racehorses and riders or to depict the humour and irony associated with the turf. Jack Macpherson's dream of his last fatal ride on Rio Grande is a traditional rather than a bush ballad. The language, which matches the sombre theme, is lifted above the usual colloquial style of the bush poem and the narrative moves with impressive urgency towards its fatal climax.

Rising of the Court, The, see LAWSON, HENRY

Riverina is a district in south-western NSW. Its borders have never been formally established but are generally taken to be the Lachlan and Murrumbidgee Rivers in the north and west, although sometimes the country beyond the Lachlan-Murrumbidgee towards the Darling River is counted; the Murray River in the south; and in the east an imaginary line from Albury northwards through the city of Wagga Wagga to the town of Condobolin. The Riverina, which is divided roughly in two (north and south) by the Murrumbidgee after it separates from the Lachlan, is a predominantly rural district, wheat producing to the east and more suitable for wool further west; there are many arid parts, notably the Old Man Plain and the country between Hay and Booligal celebrated in A.B. Paterson's poem, 'Hay and Hell and Booligal'. The Murrumbidgee Irrigation Area, in the centre of the Riverina produces citrus, cereals and wine, although it was an area of prohibition when Henry Lawson was sent there to 'dry out' in 1913. Within the borders of the Riverina are, as well as the cities of Albury, Wagga Wagga and Griffith, smaller towns such as Jerilderie, where Ned Kelly staged a daring raid in 1879 and is said to have composed the Jerilderie Letter, and Deniliquin, near where 'Rolf Boldrewood' was living in 1865, when he wrote one of his first sketches, *Shearing in Riverina*.

The Riverina rivers were explored by John Oxley, Thomas Livingstone Mitchell and Charles

Sturt, who all left journals of their expeditions. Pastoral settlement began in the 1830s, and other principal towns grew up around points on the various rivers across which stock was ferried southwards in the 1840s and 1850s; selectors first took up land in the 1860s. There are Riverina scenes or characters in a number of station romances and other works of fiction, including Randolph Bedford's *True Eyes and the Whirlwind* (1903), Carlton Dawe's *Love, the Conqueror* (1925), Mary Gaunt's *The Moving Finger* (1894), Nat Gould's *Racing Rivals* (1922), Thomas Heney's *The Girl at Birrell's* (1896), E.W. Hornung's *Irralie's Bushranger* (1896), Jessie Couvreur's *In Her Earliest Youth* (1890), F.J. Thwaites's *The Broken Melody* (q.v., 1930), Lilian Turner's *April Girls* (1911), and Arthur Wright's *A Rogue's Luck* (1910), *Gambler's Gold* (1911) and *The Outlaw's Daughter* (1919) and E.O. Schlunke's *Stories of the Riverina* (1965). Among visitors to the area who recorded their impressions was Morley Roberts in *Land-travel and Sea-faring* (1891). The two Australian writers most closely associated with the Riverina, however, are Joseph Furphy, who worked as a bullocky in the Riverina for ten years and whose *Such is Life* (1903) depicts life there in the early 1880s; and Miles Franklin, who as 'Brent of Bin Bin' published three volumes of a station saga set in the Murrumbidgee area: *Up the Country* (1928), *Ten Creeks Run* (1930) and *Back to Bool Bool* (1951). A derivation from, and possible early alternative to 'Riverina' is 'Riverine', as in the folk-song, 'Banks of the Riverine', and in 'Price Warung''s *Tales of the Riverine* (1898), where it refers to the Murray River, its reaches, and foreshores.

Riverrun, see **Hunter Valley Poets**

RIVETT, ROHAN (1917–77), born Melbourne, a grandson of Alfred Deakin and son of the eminent scientist, Sir David Rivett, was educated at the Universities of Melbourne and Oxford. He joined the *Argus* in 1939, was a war correspondent in Malaya and was taken prisoner by the Japanese. *Behind Bamboo* (1946), his best-known book, is a detailed account of his experiences in prison camps and on the Burma-Siam railway. In 1951 Rivett became editor-in-chief of Adelaide *News* and later a director of News Ltd, and was director of the International Press Institute at Zurich, 1961–64. He returned to Melbourne in 1964 and worked as a freelance journalist and as a radio and television commentator on international affairs. As well as contributing to numerous books about Australia, he wrote a biography of Herbert Brookes, *Australian Citizen* (1965); a short history, *Australia* (1968);

a series of lectures delivered for the Foundation for Australian Studies, *Writing about Australia* (1969); and a biography of his father, *David Rivett* (1972).

Road to Gundagai, The, a childhood autobiography by Graham McInnes (q.v.), the son of Angela Thirkell (q.v.), was published in 1965. The narrative opens in 1920 at Fremantle, where the Thirkell family, comprising Angela, her new husband, George Thirkell ('Thirk'), her sons Graham and Colin, aged eight and six, and her 'lady-help', Mabel Baden, land on their way to Melbourne after a difficult seven-weeks' voyage aboard a troop ship, S.S. *Friedrichsruh*. After a six-months' visit to Tasmania, where they stay with Thirk's parents, they settle in the Melbourne suburb of Malvern. McInnes vividly describes both the general life of Melbourne in the 1920s, the city's sights, sounds and seasons, rituals, celebrations and social attitudes, and his individual experiences. The last include his education at Scotch College, holiday visits to country properties owned by their friends, Basil and Nell Hall, his brief career in the scouts, relationships with a varied sequence of 'lady-helps', with Thirk's relatives, and his maternal grandparents, and his brief associations with eminent friends of his mother such as the classical scholar Alexander Leeper, the artists Thea Proctor and Arthur Streeton, General Sir John Monash and the Papuan administrator Sir Hubert Murray. Most compelling of all is his picture of life at 4 Grace Street, Malvern dominated by his literary mother, who remains doggedly committed to her Oxbridge values despite her imprisonment in a country which she considers fit only 'for Warrant Officers'.

The contrast between the parents' worlds ('With mother everything was sharp and tight and on schedule. Bells rang, cannons boomed, gongs clanged, flags were run up and the form was more important than the substance. With Dad it was a world of laissez-faire, sudden impulses, timeless cheerful whistling, odd tasks begun and never finished') gradually widens into an unbridgeable gulf; as Angela devotes herself to writing and broadcasting, Thirk retreats into his passions of stamp-collecting and standard roses, his small engineering firm TAMECO and the Naval and Military Club, where the Anzac dream is ever fresh. After Thirk is eased off the board of TAMECO following the crash of 1929 and Graham wins a scholarship to the University of Melbourne, Angela leaves permanently for England with Colin and her youngest son, Lance. *The Road to Gundagai* was followed by three further autobiographies, *Humping My Bluey* (1966), *Finding a Father* (1967) and *Goodbye, Melbourne Town* (1968).

Road to Yesterday, The, see **DAVISON, FRANK DALBY**

Roaring Days, The, is a phrase referring nostalgically to the gold rushes. Its best-known literary use is in Henry Lawson's poem, 'The Roaring Days', written from Lawson's boyhood memories of Gulgong and Pipeclay. The poem was first published in the *Bulletin* in 1889.

Roaring Nineties, The (1946), a novel by Katharine Susannah Prichard (q.v.), is the first part of a socialist realist trilogy intended to document the history of the WA goldfields and tell the story of the development of the State's gold industry. *The Roaring Nineties* explores the early prospecting days, the wild rushes to the new fields of the Cross, Coolgardie and Kalgoorlie, the diggers' struggle for alluvial rights, and exploitation by wealthy foreign companies. Against this broad historical tableau is set the life and experiences of Sally Gough, the protagonist. The daughter of an Australian pioneer, Sally is married to an English gentleman who, caught in the madness of goldfever, chases the 'yellow siren'. The novel follows Sally's attempts at financial independence as she cooks and runs boarding houses for the miners, offending the aristocratic prejudices of her husband Morris, who feels she is abrogating her dignity, breeding in deference to his wishes. Yet she is a dutiful wife and devoted mother who believes implicitly in marriage as a contract and so she repels the emotional attraction which draws her to Frisco, a prospecting partner of Morris. Attuned to the fundamental principles of life on the goldfields, Sally encompasses the loyalty and egalitarian impulses of the workers and is responsive to the hardships and injustices suffered by the ordinary people and her Aboriginal friends. See *Golden Miles* and *Winged Seeds*.

S.B.

Roaring Twenties, The (1960), the middle volume of Jack Lindsay's autobiographical trilogy, describes his life in Sydney 1921–26. A vivid picture of Sydney's cultural life at that time, it includes reminiscences of members of the Lindsay family, especially of Jack Lindsay's father, Norman, and his brothers, Raymond and Philip. As well as profiles of important literary figures such as Chris Brennan, Hugh McCrae, Kenneth Slessor and R.D. FitzGerald, Lindsay gives an account of the establishment of the journal, *Vision*, and of the Fanfrolico Press.

Robbery Under Arms, a novel by 'Rolf Boldrewood' (q.v.), was first published as a serial in the *Sydney Mail* 1882–83. With minor revisions, it was published in book form in 1888 and again in a one-volume edition, with further deletions which reduced the 269 000 words of the original to 231 000 in 1889. The 1889 edition proved very popular and was reprinted over thirty times in the next fifty years. An adaptation by Alfred Dampier and Garnet Walch was first staged in 1890 and became part of Dampier's repertoire. *Robbery Under Arms* has been filmed three times (1907, 1920, 1957) and seralized on radio both in England and Australia.

The narrator, Dick Marston, awaiting execution at the start of the novel, decides to tell the cautionary tale of his life as a bushranger. Led into crime by their father, Ben Marston, Dick and his brother Jim join Ben and the aristocrat, Captain Starlight (q.v.) in driving a mob of stolen cattle overland from NSW to SA. With the proceeds Dick and Jim holiday in Melbourne, where they take up with the sisters, Kate and Jeannie Morrison, and then work their way back to the family selection at Rocky Flat, where Dick is captured and sentenced, along with Starlight, to Berrima gaol. After an escape is effected by Jim and Starlight's half-caste assistant, Warrigal, the gang turns from cattle-stealing to bushranging; they elude capture through the assistance of the Barnes family and because they have a secret hideout, Terrible Hollow, which has recently been linked with Horse-stealer's Gully in the Gwydir district near Inverell, NSW. The news of the discovery of gold eventually seduces Dick, Jim and Starlight to the Turon fields, where they have some success as miners and Jim brings Jeannie from Melbourne to be married. Kate, however, has married unhappily and runs a hotel on the goldfields; when she discovers Dick's love for Grace Storefield, who lives on the next farm at Rocky Flat, she betrays the brothers and Starlight. Jim is captured but rescued by Dick, and Starlight also eludes capture; back at Terrible Hollow, they embark on a second series of bushranging adventures, the gang now enlarged by the inclusion of Moran, Wall, Hulbert, Lardner and others. Moran, Wall, Hulbert and Lardner are based on the bushrangers, Daniel Morgan, Ben Hall, John Gilbert and Frank Gardiner. Similarly, some of the subsequent exploits of the gang, including the robbing of the gold escort, Starlight's appearance at the Turon races while the police under Sir Ferdinand Morringer are looking for him elsewhere, and the raid on a squatter's homestead, are based on the exploits in the 1860s of the Hall–Gardiner–Gilbert gang. Starlight, Dick and Jim plan to go to America but en route to Queensland and escape they are again betrayed by Kate and also by Warrigal;

in the ensuing battle with police, Starlight and Jim are killed. At the end of the novel, Dick's death sentence is commuted through the intervention of George Storefield, the former neighbour of the Marstons, whose respectability and progress to wealth and position are contrasted throughout the novel with Dick's wildness and decline. When he leaves gaol twelve years later he marries Grace and settles in Queensland.

ROBERTS, BARNEY (1920–   ), born Flowerdale, Tasmania, where he lives on a farm, was a POW in the Second World War. He has published two books of verse, *The Phantom Boy* (1976) and *Stones in the Cephissus* (1979), and a novel, *The Penalty of Adam* (1980).

ROBERTS, MORLEY (1857–1942), the English writer who published over eighty books including stories of the sea, travel and other adventures, historical romances and novels and studies dealing with psychological, medical and literary topics, came to Australia early in 1877. He worked in Melbourne and on stations in the Riverina, returned to England at the end of 1879 and subsequently revisited the country in the course of other travels, recording his experiences in *Land-travel and Sea-faring* (1891) and *A Tramp's Notebook* (1904). Several of his short stories have Australian settings, the best-known being 'King Billy' of *King Billy of Ballarat and Other Stories* (1892), the story of a Ballarat Aboriginal with a taste for fine clothes. Other Australian sketches are in *The Reputation of George Saxon and Other Stories* (1892), *Bianca's Caprice* (1904), *The Grinder's Wheel* (1917) and *The Madonna of the Beech Wood* (1918). He also wrote several Australian romances and included some Australian material in others. Novels which are wholly or partly set in Australia are *The Adventures of a Ship's Doctor* (1895), *The Adventures of the Broad Arrow* (1897), a romance about the discovery of a lost tribe descended from escaped convicts which anticipates the tale of 'Louis de Rougemont', *The Flying Cloud* (1907), *Hearts of Women* (1919) and *Women and Ships* (1932). In *The Private Life of Henry Maitland* (1912), based on the life of his friend, George Gissing, Roberts includes thinly veiled references to his own travels in Australia.

ROBERTS, NIGEL (1941–   ), born Wellington, NZ, has lived in Australia for over twenty years and has been an art teacher. A leading member of the Balmain poetry group 1970–76 and associated with *Free Poetry* (1968) and *Living Daylights* (1974), Roberts has published *In Casablanca for the Waters* (1977) and *Steps for Astaire* (1983).

ROBERTS, PHILIP (1938–   ), born Canada, studied at the Universities of Acadia (Canada), Oxford and Sydney, and has worked as a sub-editor for Reuters news agency in London, and as a public relations consultant. In 1967–79 he taught English at the University of Sydney and since 1980 he has been a writer, now resident in the USA. Founding editor of Island Press, Sydney, 1970–79, he was poetry editor of the *Sydney Morning Herald* 1970–74, and editor of the annual anthologies, *Poet's Choice*. He began writing poetry at Oxford, where he was encouraged by Robert Graves, and has published five collections, *Just Passing Through* (1969), *Single Eye* in *Two Poets* (1971, with Geoff Page), *Crux* (1973), *Will's Dream* (1975) and *Selected Poems* (1978). Cosmopolitan, sophisticated, condensed and polished, Roberts's poetry has a musical finesse that reflects his talents as a flautist. *Will's Dream*, his most ambitious and extended work, is a sequence of poems which deftly builds up an original interior world and which features four characters, one of whom is Will, the dreamer of the sequence. The poems of *Selected Poems* and the earlier collections are taut, witty, deceptively laconic comments on a multiplicity of subjects, some of them literary. Island Press, in addition to publishing *Poet's Choice*, has produced works by Kevin Gilbert, Martin Johnston, Robert Adamson, Phillip Hammial, Andrew Taylor, Ken Bolton, Roberts himself and many others.

ROBERTS, TED (1931–   ), born Sydney, spent twelve years in advertising and sales promotion and some sixteen years as a freelance writer, mainly for television and cinema. He has written episodes for such television series as *Homicide*, *Division Four*, *Rush*, *Certain Women*, *Patrol Boat* and *A Country Practice*; plays for television, such as *Lindsay's Boy*, included in *Five Plays for Stage, Radio and Television* (1977, ed. Alrene Sykes), 'Three Men of the City', 'Wilde's Domain', 'The Amorous Dentist', 'Straight Enough' and 'The Kiss and Ride Ferry'; and feature films for cinema, *Bush Christmas* and *The Settlement*.

ROBERTS, TOM (1856–1931), born Dorchester, England, arrived in Australia in 1869. He trained as an artist in Melbourne and London. One of the famous Heidelberg School (q.v.) of painters who practised a modified form of impressionism and attempted to capture the essence of Australian light and colour, Roberts is sometimes referred to as 'the father of Australian painting'. He was one of the first to paint outback subjects; among such works are his *Shearing the Rams*, *The Breakaway*, *The Golden Fleece* and *Bailed Up*. He also painted

Opening of the First Federal Parliament of the Commonwealth of Australia, a remarkable work which hangs in the High Court of Australia in Canberra. R.H. Croll published *Tom Roberts: Father of Australian Landscape Painting* (1935), and edited *Smike to Bulldog* (1946), the letters of Arthur Streeton (q.v.) to Roberts. Peter Batey's entertainment, 'From Smike to Bulldog' is also based on the letters. Virginia Spate published *Tom Roberts* (1972).

ROBERTSON & MULLEN, see **ROBERTSON, GEORGE** (1); **MULLEN, SAMUEL**

ROBERTSON, ETHEL FLORENCE LINDESAY, see 'RICHARDSON, HENRY HANDEL'

ROBERTSON, GEORGE (1) (1825–98), born Glasgow, was a fellow-apprentice with Samuel Mullen (q.v.) in the Dublin firm of William Curry, booksellers. In 1852 the two friends emigrated to Australia (coincidentally arriving on the same day as E.W. Cole), Mullen to follow a life on the land and Robertson, after selling a case of second-hand books on the Melbourne wharf, to open a bookshop in Russell Street. By 1855 Robertson was thriving as a retail and wholesale bookseller, publisher and stationer and Mullen joined him as his assistant. In 1857 Robertson opened a London office and Mullen was sent to England to manage it only to find, on his arrival, that the job had been given to William Robertson, George's brother. From that time Robertson and Mullen were completely estranged and it was not until 1922, long after both men were dead, that the two companies, George Robertson & Co and Melville and Mullen came together as the now famous firm of Robertson & Mullen. In 1860 Robertson bought the derelict property at 69 Elizabeth Street, Melbourne, and built a magnificent new bookshop. The Elizabeth Street premises (now numbered 107) were occupied for many years by the firm of Robertson & Mullen and later by the Melbourne branch of the Sydney firm, Angus & Robertson. Robertson opened a Sydney branch in 1860 under the charge of William Maddock, a notable early Sydney bookseller to whom he sold the Sydney business in 1862. By 1875 Robertson was back in Sydney at 125 Pitt Street and later also at 361 George Street. He opened branches also in Adelaide and Brisbane. Through the Robertson bookshops passed names destined to become legendary in Australian bookselling and publishing: William Dymock, David Angus, George Robertson (2), George Philip, E.J. Dwyer and T.V. Carroll. E.A. Petherick (q.v.) was, at one time, manager of Robertson's London branch. The publisher of more than 600 titles, George Robertson produced many of the works of Adam Lindsay Gordon, Henry Kendall, Marcus Clarke, 'Rolf Boldrewood', G.G. McCrae and James Bonwick. In 1861–89 he published *George Robertson's Monthly Book Circular*, a list of new books and periodicals, sometimes with notes and short literary reviews. The Melbourne journals, *Melbourne Review* and *Tatler*, were published by him 1879–85 and 1897–98. Robertson retired from active bookselling and publishing in 1890. John Holroyd, veteran bookseller and formerly head of the rare books departments of Robertson & Mullen in Melbourne and then of Angus & Robertson in Sydney, published the biography, *George Robertson of Melbourne* (1968).

ROBERTSON, GEORGE (2) (1860–1933), born Halstead, Essex, England, was apprenticed to James MacLehose, publisher and bookseller to the University of Glasgow. In 1879 he migrated to NZ and came to Sydney in 1882. By coincidence, he found employment in the Sydney branch of George Robertson (1) (q.v.), bookseller and publisher of Melbourne, where a fellow-employee was David Mackenzie Angus (q.v.), with whom in 1885 he formed the Australian publishing and bookselling firm of Angus & Robertson (q.v.). After Angus's death in 1901 Robertson continued in partnership with Frederick Victor Wymark, a long-time employee, and Richard Thomson, who had bought Angus's share of the business; in 1907 the partnership was converted into a public company.

The firm's interest in Australiana sprang largely from George Robertson and Wymark. They collected and sold countless books, pamphlets, manuscripts, prints and maps from all over the world relating to Australia and influenced such major collectors as David Scott Mitchell and Sir William Dixson. George Robertson's evidence to a parliamentary committee in 1905 on the value of the Mitchell and Dixson collections was instrumental in the establishment of the Mitchell Library. A dominant figure among Australian publishers of his time, George Robertson was always highly esteemed and affectionately regarded by the writers whom he assisted. Henry Lawson referred to him as 'The Chief', while Mary Gilmore commented in a 1932 letter, 'I never think of you that I do not see Australia. You and she are inseparable'. A selection of George Robertson's correspondence, titled *Dear Robertson: Letters to an Australian Publisher*, was published in 1982 by A.W. (Tony) Barker, a former A & R editor. The early history of Angus & Robertson is contained in George Ferguson's *Some Early Australian Bookmen* (1978).

ROBERTSON, GILBERT (1794–1851), was a West Indian farmer who migrated to Van Diemen's Land in 1822. He entered journalism in the 1830s, edited the *Colonist* in 1832 and was proprietor of the *True Colonist* (1834–44), which was a daily, the first in Australia, for three months in 1835, and the *Horn Boy* (1834–38). Known as the 'Tasmanian Cobbett', Robertson was not only an uncompromising opponent of the lieutenant-governor, George Arthur, in the fight for press freedom in Tasmania, but also involved in controversies with fellow pressmen, R.L. Murray, James Ross and William Gore Elliston. He later settled on Norfolk Island where the memoirist, John Mortlock, worked for him.

ROBERTSON, Sir JOHN (1816–91), born London, arrived in Australia in 1822 and had a long and colourful career in NSW politics from the beginning of responsible government in 1856 until his resignation in 1886. Four times premier of NSW, he played a vital role as a land reformer and framed the famous Selection Acts of 1861. One of his supporters during this period was Charles Harpur, whom Robertson, as secretary for lands, appointed as gold commissioner at Araluen in 1859. As a result of his prominence in the land question Robertson earned such sobriquets as 'Free-Selection Jack' and, from some of his critics, 'Dingo Jack'; the *Bulletin* satirized him in 1883 as 'Rip Van Robertson'. There are periodic references to him in selection literature, particularly in the bush songs, 'The Eumerella Shore' (q.v.), 'The Old Bullock Dray' and 'The Free Selector'. Henry Lawson wrote an obituary poem for him in the *Boomerang*, ' "Jack Robertson" '.

ROBERTSON, JOHN GEORGE (1867–1933), born Glasgow, Scotland, graduated in science from the University of Glasgow in 1889. In the same year he left for Leipzig, where he studied European languages and literature, gaining his doctorate in 1892, and where he met the future novelist, 'Henry Handel Richardson' (q.v.) whom he married in 1895. After a period as lecturer at Strasbourg University, he was offered a chair in German at the University of London in 1903. A distinguished and productive scholar, Robertson was prominent in making London a centre of German studies, published numerous works on German writers and in 1905 founded the *Modern Language Review*, which he edited for four years. Robertson, who undoubtedly influenced the literary interests of his wife, directing her towards Scandinavian literature, took immense pains to leave her free for writing by protecting her from domestic and other cares. One of her

most perceptive critics, he wrote an essay titled 'The Art of Henry Handel Richardson' (1928–29), first published with *Myself When Young* (1948).

ROBINSON, GEORGE AUGUSTUS (1788–1866), born London, emigrated in 1824 to Hobart, where he established himself as a builder and manifested philanthropic concerns. In 1829 he was given the task of conciliating the Aborigines on Bruny Island and from 1830 to 1834 contacted tribes in all parts of Tasmania with a view to persuading them to join the new settlement at Flinders Island. Although the settlement was under Robinson's general superintendence, it was managed by commandants who saw themselves as gaolers. Mortality amongst the Aborigines was high, the population having shrunk from 4000 to 150 by 1835. In October 1835 Robinson took control of the settlement and attempted, unsuccessfully, to inculcate the remaining Aborigines with the Protestant ethic and nineteenth-century European village values. His failure did nothing to erode the confidence of the white settlers in their plans to 'civilize' the native tribes, and in 1838 Robinson was appointed chief protector of Aborigines at Port Phillip, where he remained for the next eleven years. His protectorship was undistinguished and his assistants condemned by Governor Gipps for inefficiency although he made several journeys to SA, NSW and the Murray Valley, which yielded valuable information about the tribes. After the protectorate was abolished in 1849, Robinson returned to England in 1852 and settled at Bath. Truganini (q.v.) assisted Robinson in contacting the tribes of Tasmania and accompanied him to Port Phillip. Robinson's Tasmanian journals and papers 1829–34 were published in 1966, titled *Friendly Mission* and edited by N.J.B. Plomley, and his career has been described by Lyndall Ryan in *The Aboriginal Tasmanians* (1981). He appears as a character in Bill Reed's plays about Truganini (1977), in Hume Nisbet's novel, *The Savage Queen* (1891), and in Robert Drewe's novel, *The Savage Crows* (1976), C.S. Ross's novel, *Dick Arnold* (1893), includes references to Robinson's work.

ROBINSON, MICHAEL MASSEY (1744–1826), lawyer turned blackmailer, arrived in NSW as a convict in 1798. His legal experience gained him appointment as secretary to the deputy judge-advocate of the Colony. Corrupt use of his office and the charge of 'promoting discords', probably by the writing of lampooning verses known as pipes (q.v.), saw him in 1805 at Norfolk Island. Pardoned in 1811, he advanced to principal clerk in the police office before he died. Under Governor Lachlan Macquarie, Robinson composed odes to celebrate the birthdays of George III and Queen Charlotte 1810–21. With one exception they were published in the *Sydney Gazette* and read by Robinson at the annual birthday ceremonies at Government House. In 1818 and 1819 he was repaid 'for his services as Poet Laureate' by a grant of two cows from the government herd, probably the first royalties to a poet in Australia. The odes, in the stilted flowery language of the public poem genre, lavished praise not only on the royal couple but also on their subjects who were energetically evangelizing the new southern land to the British way of life. The odes blatantly flattered Macquarie also, for the governor, accepting Oliver Goldsmith's opinion that a bold peasantry was its country's pride, favoured the development of peasant farming and a cottage economy and Robinson depicted the settlement in the romanticized manner of Macquarie's hopes for it. On Macquarie's resignation, Robinson lost his poetic 'office' but vented some of his spleen on Governor Sir Thomas Brisbane by celebrating in several ballads the virtues of Macquarie over his successor. Twenty-seven of Robinson's poems, including twenty royal birthday odes, were published by George Mackaness in his monograph, *Odes of Michael Massey Robinson* (1946). He appears as a character in Eris O'Brien's play, *The Hostage* (1928).

ROBINSON, ROLAND (1912–   ), born County Clare, Ireland, was brought to Australia when nine years old. After a brief schooling he began work as a rouseabout on a sheep station near Coonamble, NSW. Since then he has been boundary rider, railway fettler, fencer, dam-builder, factory-worker, ballet-dancer, gardener and golf-course groundsman. His literary interests have involved him as book reviewer and literary critic for the *Sydney Morning Herald*, editor of *Poetry Magazine* and president of the Poetry Association of Australia. During the Second World War he worked in the Northern Territory, an experience which provided contact with tribal Aboriginal life to add to his existing familiarity with detribalized Aborigines from his youthful wanderings in the bush. Strongly attracted to the Australian landscape and spirit of place long before the Jindyworobak movement and before he met its founder, Rex Ingamells, in 1944, Robinson has come to be accepted as the best and most dedicated of the Jindyworobak poets, but he is not as stereotyped as the Jindyworobak label would imply. His published verse began with *Beyond the Grass-tree Spears* (1944), twenty-one brief poems, the first of which indicates, in its opening lines, Robinson's poetic stance:

I made my verses of places where I made
    my fires;
of the dark trees standing against the blue-
    green night
with the first stars coming; of the bare plains
    where a
bird broke into running song, and of the
    wind-cold scrub
where the bent trees sing to themselves, and
    of the night
black about me, the fire dying out, and the
    ashes left.

Later volumes include *Language of the Sand* (1949), *Tumult of the Swans* (1953), and *Deep Well* (1962), the last incorporating selections from the earlier volumes and adding new poems that continued to explore his pantheistic vision of the land and its primal inhabitants, the Aborigines, and in other verses examining the 'deep well' of his own self. *Grendel* (1967), has, in addition to its Aboriginal legends, a section on the impact of white settlement that tends, especially in a poem such as 'The Pioneers', to suggest the ultimate meaninglessness of all human endeavour. *Altjeringa and Other Aboriginal Poems* (1970) is a collection of Robinson's earlier, but revised, Aboriginal poems. The first part of the volume contains translations of poems that he had gathered from the Aborigines themselves; the second part has his own poetry on Aboriginal themes. *Selected Poems* (1971), a surprisingly small collection, is made up of poems mostly in accord with the Jindyworobak movement. His eighth volume of poetry, *The Hooded Lamp*, was published in 1976 and a second *Selected Poems* (1983) was edited by M.J. Bennett and Michael Sharkey. Robinson's prose collections indicate, by their titles, his deep interest in Aboriginal lore. They include *Legend & Dreaming* (1952), *The Feathered Serpent* (1956), *Black-feller, White-feller* (1958), *The Man Who Sold His Dreaming* (1965), and *Aboriginal Myths and Legends* (1966). He has published three autobiographical volumes, *The Drift of Things* (1973), *The Shift of Sands* (1976), and *A Letter to Joan* (1978).

Rockchoppers, see **CAMPION, EDMUND**

Rocks, The, a name applied to a small harbourside area of Sydney west of Sydney Cove, is distinguished by configurations of sandstone. The area was settled early and had acquired its name by 1803. By the mid-nineteenth century, frequented by sailors and the crews of whaling vessels, it had also acquired a notorious reputation. The Rocks 'Push' of the 1890s also added to the area's colourful image and is featured in the novels, *King of the Rocks* (1900) by Ambrose Pratt and *An Outback Marriage* (1906) by A.B.

Paterson, and Henry Lawson's poem, 'The Captain of the Push'. Well-known Australians who lived in the area include George Howe, Henry Kendall, Sir Edmund Barton, Sir George Reid and Conrad Martens. The area was also visited by Joseph Conrad and Jack London, both of whom stayed at the Ship and Mermaid Hotel, which London also used as the setting for one of his short stories. The area is described in Isadore Brodsky's *Heart of the Rocks of Old Sydney* (1965) and Alan Sutherland's *The Rocks* (1965). The recent redevelopment of the Rocks area has attempted to recapture something of the atmosphere of Old Sydney.

RODD, LEWIS CHARLES (1906–79), born Sydney, was the husband of Kylie Tennant. The son of a sea captain, he describes his early years in *A Gentle Shipwreck* (1975), which is also a revealing account of life in poverty-stricken Surry Hills, Sydney, before the First World War. He subsequently became a primary school headmaster and produced a number of literary studies for use in schools as well as editing two anthologies of Australian essays: *Venturing the Unknown Ways* (1965, with Donald McLean), and *The Australian Essay* (1968). His biography of John Hope, rector of Christ Church, St Laurence (1972), is also a social history.

RODDA, PERCIVAL CHARLES ('GAVIN HOLT') (1891–?), born Port Augusta, SA, was a journalist on the *Age* before going in 1919 to the USA where he became a music critic for *Musical America*. In 1926 Rodda went to London and lived from then on in England and France, where he established a world-wide reputation as a writer of crime and mystery fiction under the pseudonym 'Gavin Holt'. His best-known creation was the criminologist, Professor Bastion, who first appeared in the novel, *Six Minutes Past Twelve* (1928), and was the chief character in a long series of books. Rodda's first novel, *The Fortunes of Geoffrey Mayne* (1919), appeared in A.C. Rowlandson's Bookstall series. Both it and *The Scarlet Mask* (1926) are stories of the Australian bushranging days. There are only incidental associations with Australia in his other novels.

RODERICK, COLIN (1911–), was born Mt Morgan, Queensland. He was foundation professor of English at James Cook University, 1965–76, editor for Angus & Robertson 1945–65, and director 1961–65, and has written extensively on Australian literature. Some of his most significant achievements are his definitive editions of Henry Lawson's work, *Collected Verse* (1967–69) and *Collected Prose* (1972). He has also edited other Lawson anthologies; Lawson's letters (1970); a selection of critical writing on Lawson (1972); and has written several biographical and critical accounts, including *Henry Lawson: Poet and Short Story Writer* (1966) and *The Real Henry Lawson* (1982). His other writings on Australian literature include three studies of fiction, the first two combining selections and commentary, *The Australian Novel* (1945), *20 Australian Novelists* (1947) and *An Introduction to Australian Fiction* (1950); a companion to Walter Murdoch's essays (1945); a lecture on the nature of Australian literature, *Suckled by a Wolf* (1968); a biographical account of Rosa Praed, *In Mortal Bondage* (1948); and the biography, *Miles Franklin: Her Brilliant Career* (1982). He also edited James Tucker's *Ralph Rashleigh* (1952) and *Jemmy Green in Australia* (1955); compiled a collection of travel writings, *Wanderers in Australia* (1949) and a collection of short stories, *Australian Round-up* (1953); and has written an account of the murderer, John Knatchbull (1963), and an historical novel, *The Lady and The Lawyer* (1955).

RODRIGUEZ, JUDITH (1936–), born Brisbane as Judith Green, was educated at the University of Queensland, where she met David Malouf, Don Maynard and Rodney Hall, with whom she is represented in *Four Poets* (1962). Married to a Colombian academic, 1964–79, she has travelled extensively and has taught literature in a number of overseas and Australian institutions; now married to Thomas Shapcott, she teaches English and Australian literature at La Trobe University. She has published five collections of verse, *Nu-Plastik Fanfare Red* (1973), *Water Life* (1976), *Shadow on Glass* (1978), *Mudcrab at Gambaro's* (1980, winner of the Golden Jubilee PEN Award) and *Witch Heart* (1982); she has illustrated some of her collections with her own lino-cuts. Rodriguez gives expression to her strong, independent perceptions in a poetry that is visually precise, heightened by original, sometimes exotic, imagery and vigorously responsive to experience.

'ROHAN, CRIENA' (DEIRDRE CASH) (1928–62), was born in Melbourne into an Irish-Catholic family to which she had the same ambivalent response of such Australian writers as Laurie Clancy, Ron Blair, Peter Kenna and Desmond O'Grady. She published two novels, *The Delinquents* (1962) and *Down by the Dockside* (1963), both of which deal with the experiences and love affairs of working-class, urban youngsters. Although they fit within the social-realist genre, they are not propagandist and are enlivened by Rohan's versatile style, which ranges from the colloquial to the lyrical, and by her lively sense of humour.

'ROLAND, BETTY' (1903–), born in the Victorian Mallee town of Kaniva as Elizabeth Maclean, later adopted her father's christian name. After leaving school at sixteen she worked as a journalist for *Table Talk* and *Sun News–Pictorial*; married in 1923; and in 1928, at a time when Australian drama was generally neglected by theatres, saw her first play, *The Touch of Silk* (q.v., 1942) produced by the Melbourne Repertory Theatre. Another play, *Morning*, produced in 1932, was published in an anthology in 1937. Her marriage failed in 1933 and she eloped with a prominent Australian communist, Guido Baracchi, to Russia, where she stayed for fifteen months working as a journalist. After returning to Australia in 1935 and joining the Communist Party, she wrote a series of political plays and sketches that were frequently performed as street theatre. Of these, 'Are You Ready, Comrade?', which won a competition in 1938 and was widely performed in theatres, is the only full-length piece. Disillusioned with communism by 1939, she abandoned political plays and became a prolific and versatile writer for radio. 'Daddy Was Asleep' (1945) is her most notable radio play, although in 1952 'Granite Peak', a striking three-act play about central Australia, was televised in Britain. Another radio serial, 'A Woman Scorned', became the basis of a popular television serial of 1983, *Return to Eden*. She has also written several children's books, travel accounts and three novels: *The Other Side of Sunset* (1972), *No Ordinary Man* (1974) and *Beyond Capricorn* (1976). *Caviar for Breakfast* (1979) narrates her experiences in Russia.

ROLFE, PATRICIA, see *Bulletin*

ROLLS, ERIC C. (1923–), born Grenfell, NSW, has farmed near Narrabri. His poems have appeared in three collections, *Sheaf Tosser* (1967), *The Green Mosaic* (1977) and *Miss Strawberry Verses* (1978). A versatile, exuberant poet with a gift for satire, wry irony and the macabre as well as for the simple nature lyric, Rolls focuses mainly on his farming and family experiences in *Sheaf Tosser* and on his memories of New Guinea in *The Green Mosaic*. Both collections demonstrate his keen interest in animals and the processes of nature. *Miss Strawberry Verses* is a collection of humorous poems for children. Rolls has also written an account of the importation into Australia and subsequent proliferation of the rabbit and other pests, *They All Ran Wild* (1969), which won the Cook Bicentenary Award for a work of non-fiction. Revised for children and titled *Running Wild* (1973), it also won the John Franklin Award. Rolls's other writings are *The River* (1974), an autobiographical essay reflect-

ing his farming experiences in the Namoi River district, *A Million Wild Acres* (1981), a natural and social history of the Pilliga forest in central NSW which won the 1981 C.J.Dennis Award and the *Age* Book of the Year Award, and *Celebration of the Senses* (1984), a partly autobiographical work which explores the joy to be gained from the five senses.

Romance of Runnibede, The, see 'RUDD, STEELE'

Romance of a Station, The, see **PRAED, ROSA**

Romantic Nineties, The, an influential volume of reminiscences and essays by A.W. Jose, was published in 1933. The most important of its four sections is the title one, in which there are brief chapters on authors, artists, editors, journals and club life of the 1890s. Jose's exuberant picture of the decade as the 'birth-years of Australian literature' helped to foster the romantic legend of the nineties (q.v.).

ROMERIL, JOHN (1945–), born Melbourne, was educated at Monash University, graduating in 1970. In 1968 he joined the theatre ensemble which was to become the Australian Performing Group and remained strongly committed to its aims and style of theatre. Most of his plays have been performed by the Group, first at La Mama and later at the Pram Factory. Six of his plays have been published, *Chicago, Chicago* in *Plays* (1970), edited by Graeme Blundell, *The Kitchen Table* and *Brudder Humphrey* in *Komos* (1973), *I Don't Know Who to Feel Sorry For* (1973), *The Floating World* (q.v., 1975), and, with Jack Hibberd, *Marvellous Melbourne* in *Theatre-Australia* (1977). Selections from *Mickey's Moomba*, produced in 1979, have also been published in *Meanjin* (1978). His unpublished plays are 'A Nameless Concern' (1968), 'The American Independence Hour' (1969), 'Mr Big the Big Big Pig' (1969), 'In a Place Somewhere Else' (1969), 'Dr Karl's Kure' (1970), 'Whatever Happened to Realism' (1971), 'Rearguard Action' (1971), 'Christie in Love' (1971), 'Mrs. Thally F' (1971), 'And the Beast' (1972), 'Bastardy' (1972), 'He Can Swagger Sitting Down' (1972), 'Waltzing Matilda' (1973), 'The Golden Holden Show' (1975), 'The Dudders' (1976, with John Timlin), 'The Radio-Active Horror Show' (1977), 'Carboni' (1980), 'The 700,000' (1980) and 'Samizdat' (1981). He also wrote the screenplay, *The Great McCarthy* (1975), an adaptation of Barry Oakley's novel, *Salute to the Great McCarthy*. In 1976 Romeril won the first Canada–Australia Literary Award.

Romeril, who has described himself as a 'community pen', is concerned to rouse Australians from what he sees as their political apathy. Confining himself mainly to 'agit-prop' (agitational-propaganda) theatre, he has written several street plays and plays for demonstrations, e.g. 'Mr Big the Big Big Pig', 'Whatever Happened to Realism', for factory tours, restaurants, children and women's liberation groups. Several of his more finished productions, such as *Chicago, Chicago* and *Marvellous Melbourne*, have been rewritten to fit the needs and demands of the acting group. Influenced strongly by Brecht, he prefers a rough, bold, abrasive, improvisational, free-wheeling, musical theatre that is collaborative in its growth, obviously political in its message and broadly humorous in its effects. He has commented of street theatre, to which he strongly adheres: 'The arsenal is limitless: the aside, the placard, the topical references... the exploiting of accidents, the songs, the dances, the tempos, the noise, the relying on contrasts, the shorthand of exaggeration, the false noses, the stock types, the stuffed bellies'. *Chicago, Chicago* and 'He Can Swagger Sitting Down' focus on alienation and violence in American society; *Mickey's Moomba* deals with American cultural imperialism; 'The Golden Holden Show' with multinationals, Liberal politics and the Holden car industry; 'Mrs Thally F' with extremes of suburban isolation; 'The Dudders' with American-Australian relations during the Second World War; 'The Radio-Active Horror Show' with the uranium industry; 'Samizdat' with repressive activities of the Queensland Police Force. 'Carboni' is an adaptation of Raffaello Carboni's account of the Eureka Stockade. Two plays in which Romeril's interest in a particular human scene merges with his political aims are *I Don't Know Who to Feel Sorry For* and *The Floating World*. The former, a part-naturalistic, part-absurdist play, explores some fundamental human needs and attitudes; the latter concentrates on the depths that underlie an Australian male stereotype, a middle-aged 'ocker'.

RONAN, TOM (1907–76), born Perth, the son of Jim Ronan, stockman and cattle-station manager, spent his childhood in the inland areas of north-west Australia. At the age of fourteen he joined his father as an apprentice stockman and subsequently worked as a rouseabout and drover and as a ship's clerk and shell-opener on pearling boats at Broome. During the Second World War he served with the AIF and in 1950–70 lived with his wife and eight children on an old property, Springvale, near Katherine. Ronan published five novels, *Strangers on the Ophir* (1945), *Vision Splendid* (1954), *Moleskin Midas* (1956), *The Pearling*

Master (1958) and *Only a Short Walk* (1961); a biography of his father, *Deep of the Sky* (1962); and two volumes of autobiography, *Packhorse and Pearling Boat* (1964) and *Once There Was a Bagman* (1966). His last collection, *The Mighty Men on Horseback* (1977), includes sketches, yarns, short stories and previously unpublished sections of *Vision Splendid* which won the 1951 Commonwealth Jubilee literary competition. Ronan, described by his publishers as having boiled 'either a stockman's billy-can or a drover's quart pot of tea by the side of almost every watercourse between Wyndham and Camooweal, and between Darwin and Oodnadatta', describes the landscape and social life of outback northern Australia from the early nineteenth century to the 1950s with an engaging impression of authenticity. His short stories, novels and autobiographies, written in a plain but vigorous prose and enlivened by his understated humour, are rich in portraits of eccentric outback types.

Rooted, a three-act play by Alexander Buzo (q.v.), was first performed in Australia in 1969 and published in 1973; it has also been staged in the USA and England. Bentley, a Sydney civil servant in his mid-twenties, is successively stripped of his home, wife, possessions, livelihood and mates by the never-seen, all-powerful Simmo. Although the situations are often farcical and the characters two-dimensional, the picture of a hollow, image-obsessed culture that emerges is serious and credible. Both Bentley, the born loser who ineffectually apes the required attitudes, owns the required technological possessions and mouths the required clichés, and the supersuccessful Simmo whose amazing feats on the sportsfield, in bed, in the pub or in the business world are constantly recounted, express the sterility of this generation's aspirations. Simmo, appropriately unseen, represents the generalized public ideal of the new, young middle class of both sexes, just as Bentley embodies its private fears.

RORABACHER, LOUISE ELIZABETH, see Anthologies

(Rosa): Love Sonnets to Mary Doyle, see **HARPUR, CHARLES**

ROSA, S.A. (SAMUEL ALBERT) (1866–1940), born Sydney, was educated in London, became a journalist in America and then returned to Australia, where he worked for the Sydney *Truth* (1901–23) and the *Labor Daily* (1923–34). An advocate of revolutionary socialism, he was expelled from the NSW Labor party and formed a short-lived socialist party.

His published fiction, *The Coming Terror: Or, the Australian Revolution* (1894), was published in 1895 as *Oliver Spence*. He was also the author of the political analyses, *Federation* (1898), *The Federal Bill Analysed* (1899), *The Invasion of Australia* (1920) and the autobiographical, *The Troubles of An Editor* (1936).

Rosella, from 'Rosehiller', a derivation of 'Rose Hill parrot', is a name given by early settlers to a beautiful and common parrot. It has also acquired a general Australian connotation, being well known as the brand name of a ubiquitous tomato-sauce, regarded by satirists such as Barry Humphries as being as representative of the Australian diet as the meat pie.

ROSKOLENKO, HARRY (1907–80), born New York, was self-educated and worked at numerous occupations including sailor, law clerk, factory-hand and patent-researcher before joining the US army in 1942. Posted to the Pacific area, he made numerous visits to Australia in the 1940s, became friendly with poets of the *Angry Penguins* group, and contributed to Australian magazines. Two volumes of his poetry were published in Australia, *A Second Summary* (1944) and *Notes from a Journey* (1947), illustrated by Sidney Nolan. With Max Harris he also edited the tenth issue of *Angry Penguins Broadsheet* and, with Elisabeth Lambert, edited an Australian issue of the American poetry magazine, *Voices* (1944). Roskolenko subsequently travelled widely and was a familiar contributor to such magazines as *New York Times Book Review*, *New Republic* and *Partisan Review*. He published novels, travel books, autobiographies and several collections of poetry, some of which reflect his experience in Australia. In 1969 he visited Australia again and in 1970 published another collection of poetry in Melbourne, *American Civilization*, illustrated by several well-known Australian artists.

ROSMAN, ALICE GRANT (1887–1961), who was born at Kapunda, SA, contributed numerous sketches, stories and poems to Australian anthologies, newspapers and magazines, including the *Bulletin*, the *Native Companion* and the *Lone Hand*. She was also associated with C.J. Dennis in the *Gadfly* and was Adelaide correspondent for the *Bulletin* 1908–11, using the pseudonym 'Rosna'. In 1911 she left for London, where she was on the literary staff of the *British Australasian* and the editorial staff of the *Grand Magazine*. She gave up journalism for full-time writing in 1927 and established an international reputation as a popular novelist, one of her novels, *The Win-*

dow (1928), becoming a best-seller. Novels which include Australian characters are *Miss Bryde of England* (1915), *The Tower Wall* (?1914), *The Back Seat Driver* (1928) and *The Sixth Journey* (1931). Rosman's mother, Alice Mary Bowyer Rosman, published a verse collection, *An Enchanted Garden* (1916).

ROSS, JAMES (1786–1838), was born and educated in Scotland and was a successful schoolmaster in England before emigrating to Van Diemen's Land in 1822. He farmed near Hobart until 1825, when he was appointed joint government printer with George Terry Howe and editor of the *Hobart Town Gazette*. In 1827 the partnership was dissolved, with Ross remaining government printer and the *Gazette* changing from a newspaper to a government information organ. Soon after, Ross founded the *Hobart Town Courier* (q.v.), which he ran until 1837; both in the *Gazette* and the *Courier* he supported the controversial lieutenant-governor of Van Diemen's Land, George Arthur, and was thus inevitably attacked by his fellow, pioneering pressmen, including Andrew Bent, Henry Melville, Gilbert Robertson, and R.L. Murray. Among other publishing activities, Ross wrote *An Essay on Prison Discipline* (1833), ran the short-lived *Hobart Town Chronicle* (1833) and the early literary periodical, the *Van Diemen's Land Monthly Magazine* (1835), and issued eight almanacs, 1829–36, usually with the *Hobart Town Almanack* as part of the title. The 1835 volume contained the first part of Jorgen Jorgenson's autobiography, and was a source for Marcus Clarke's *Old Tales of a Young Country* (1871).

ROSS, LLOYD (1901–), born Melbourne, the son of R.S. Ross (1875–1931), who was founder of the Victorian Railways Union, editor of the *Socialist* and author of *Eureka – Freedom's Fight of '54* (1914), is a graduate of the University of Melbourne. Secretary of the NSW branch of the Australian Railways Union 1938–43 and 1952–69, and public relations officer of the post-war reconstruction programme, he was a member of the Communist Party of Australia in his youth, but left the party before the Second World War. His keen interest in the labour movement and politics is reflected in the numerous articles he has written for Australian and international trade union and political journals. He has written *William Lane and the Australian Labor Movement* (1937), a classic labour history which was reprinted in 1980; and a biography of John Curtin (1977), whom he had known since childhood. Ross has also written several plays, two of which have been published, *On the Edge of the Future* in *Eight Plays by Australians*

(1934), and *The Rustling of Voices* in *Best Australian One-Act Plays* (1937), ed. T. Inglis Moore and William Moore.

Ross' Poems (1978), a collection of seventy-five poems by Geoffrey Lehmann (q.v.), is illustrated by old photographs of some of the personalities and places mentioned and by etchings of rural scenes done by Sally McInerney, 'Sally' of the poems. *Ross' Poems* traces the establishment by Ross and Olive McInerney, Lehmann's then parents-in-law, of the property, Spring Forest, near Cowra in the Lachlan Valley of central western NSW in the period just after the Second World War. Interspersed with incidents and events in the development of Spring Forest are Ross's memories of his own rural childhood. The poems present an analytical ('my laboratory is the dust where I stand') account of country life and a catalogue of country characters, including the bagman, Mr Long, who, walking all day on the western plains, sustains himself 'with a line of trees on the horizon'; Ross's father who, at eighty-seven, still rides a horse; his Auntie Bridge who, at eighty, still plants trees; and the parsimonious neighbour who sends his horses to the knackery when their working lives are over. The poems also carry Ross's country-wise reflections on such features of modern life as 'lurid newspaper headlines' that contain 'all the trash of our world'; the constant exposure to violence; the built-in obsolescence of modern machines; and the insidious attraction that the city ('the son and daughter stealer') holds for young people. The undemonstrative Lehmann style adapts easily to the flat, laconic tones of the countryman narrator but a judicious use of reverie frequently elevates the poems from an ordinary to a highly imaginative plane. Some of the poems were published in 1976 in the Poets of the Month series, as *Extracts from Ross' Poems*.

Rouge, see **Feminism and Australian Literature**

ROUGHSEY, DICK (1924–), born Langunarnji, an island near Mornington Island in the Gulf of Carpentaria, has a tribal name Goobalathaldin, meaning 'water standing on end', which has been anglicized to Roughsey (Rough Sea). His childhood was spent with the tribe in the bush before he was taken to a Presbyterian mission to be educated. After primary school education he returned to tribal life, but in the Second World War worked on Queensland cattle stations and as a deckhand on a coastal supply ship. Later, at Kurumba Lodge at the mouth of the Norman River, he met an Ansett pilot, Percy Trezise, who encouraged him to paint. He became proficient in both

the traditional Aboriginal method of bark painting and the Western method of painting in oils and has held successful exhibitions of his work in many Australian cities. Roughsey's *Moon and Rainbow: The Autobiography of an Aboriginal* (1971) is the story of his early life and the legends and customs of his people, the Lardil tribe. The book, which is profusely illustrated, presents in considerable detail Aboriginal beliefs about conception, birth, death and the life hereafter. He has also published *The Giant Devil Dingo* (1973), the legend of Eelgin, the grasshopper woman, who taught Galya the giant dingo to hunt and kill men for food. When the giant dingo is killed, the medicine man makes two small dingoes from his bones to be man's friend and helper. The book, illustrated in magnificent colour, was named the Children's Picture Book of the Year for 1973 by the Children's Book Council. The award was repeated for a similar book, *The Rainbow Serpent* (1975), which deals with a legend forming the basis of much Aboriginal tradition. Roughsey joined with Percy Trezise to produce a third legend book, *The Quinkins* (1978). In 1973 Roughsey was appointed chairman of the newly-established Aboriginal Arts Board; in 1976 he was awarded the Patricia Weickhardt Award for an Aboriginal writer.

Rouseabout, derived from 'rouse', meaning to stir from a state of apathy, sleep or inaction, was the name given to the ordinary stationhand. A common figure in Australian literature, the rouseabout is given his best-known literary embodiment in Henry Lawson's poems, 'Middleton's Rouseabout', which records the progress of the laconic, unquestioning, practical Andy, 'type of a coming nation', from stationhand to station-owner, and 'Ballad of the Rouseabout'. Two traditional songs entitled 'Rouseabout' give a complete picture of the 'Generally Useful . . . poor bloody rouseabout'; one is by an anonymous author, the other by Jim Lawson. The author of the novel, *Jackeroo* (1891), otherwise known only by his initials, P.G.A., used 'Rouseabout' as his pseudonym.

ROWBOTHAM, DAVID (1924–), born Toowoomba, Queensland, served in the RAAF in the Pacific in the Second World War and subsequently studied at the Universities of Queensland and Sydney, where he won prizes for his poetry. He has worked as a journalist, broadcaster and academic; from 1969–79 he was literary and theatre critic for the *Courier-Mail* and in 1980 became its literary editor. A prominent Queensland poet since the 1940s and a regular contributor to the *Bulletin* when Douglas Stewart was editor of the Red Page,

Rowbotham has published eight collections of poetry, *Ploughman and Poet* (1954), *Inland* (1958), *All the Room* (1964), *Bungalow and Hurricane* (1967), *The Makers of the Ark* (1970), *The Pen of Feathers* (1971), *Selected Poems* (1975) and *Maydays* (1980); a novel, *The Man in the Jungle* (1964); and a selection of short stories, *Town and City* (1956). He has also edited an anthology of verse and prose, *Queensland Writing* (1957). Rowbotham won the Grace Leven Prize for Poetry in 1964 and second prize in the Cook Bicentenary literary competition. Originally perceived as primarily a poet of the Queensland landscape, preoccupied with transience and the pattern of life in rural Australia, Rowbotham has moved in his later work towards a more idiosyncratic vision that resists categorization. Writing in a bare, physically-precise and metrically-conservative style, he often explores fundamental philosophical problems through reflection on homely objects and ostensibly ordinary themes. Included by critics and fellow writers, e.g. David Malouf, as among those who have been involved in a radical redefinition of Australian poetry, Rowbotham has also gained international attention. His *Selected Poems* and *Maydays* have been particularly praised, e.g. in the USA, for their skilful conjunction of personal, national and universal themes.

ROWCROFT, CHARLES (1798–1856), born London, son of Thomas Rowcroft, East Indian merchant and London alderman who became British consul in Peru, where he died in Simon Bolivar's uprising. After an Eton education, Rowcroft went in 1821 to Hobart Town and took up a grant of 2000 acres. He remained only four years in the colony, returning in 1826 to England by way of Brazil. In 1843 he published his first novel, *Tales of the Colonies* (q.v.), a work which was partly a description of life in the colony, partly a guide for intending settlers and partly a sensational tale of the hazards of Van Diemen's Land in its pioneer times. His second Australian novel, *The Bushranger of Van Diemen's Land* (1846), recounts the violent exploits of both white and black bushrangers in the south-east of the island. Of his other novels (nine in all) only *An Emigrant in Search of a Colony* (1851) is connected with Australia. In England, Rowcroft edited *Hood's Magazine and Comic Miscellany*. See Aboriginal, Bushranger in Australian Literature.

ROWE, JOHN (1938–), a graduate of the Royal Military College, Duntroon, has seen active service in Malaya, Kashmir, Borneo and Vietnam. He has written five novels, most of which deal with sensational political events. His first novel, *Count Your Dead* (1968), writ-

ten while he was serving with the Defence Intelligence Agency in Washington, is critical of the American role in the Vietnam War and was followed by his resignation from the army. His second, *McCabe P.M.* (1972), deals with a political crisis following the assassination of an Australian prime minister by an Aboriginal extremist. His other novels are *The Chocolate Crucifix* (1972), *The Warlords* (1978) and *The Jewish Solution* (1980).

ROWE, RICHARD ('PETER POSSUM') (1828–79), born Doncaster, England, came to Australia in 1853 and worked first as a tutor before being befriended by literary patron, Nicol D. Stenhouse (q.v.) and becoming part of the Sydney 1850s literary *coterie* that included Frank Fowler, J. Sheridan Moore, Henry Kendall, Henry Halloran and Daniel Deniehy. A regular contributor to the *Month*, the Sydney *Punch*, *Freeman's Journal* and the *Sydney Morning Herald*, Rowe published a collection of his essays and verse as *Peter Possum's Portfolio* (1858), one of the first such colonial collections; he returned to England in 1858. He published numerous books for boys, including several, such as *The Boy in the Bush* (1869), *Roughing It in Van Diemen's Land* (1880) by 'Edward Howe' and *Fred Leicester: Or, the Southern Cross and Charles's Wain* (1889), which have Australian settings. Among his best works were *Episodes in an Obscure Life* (1871) and *Friends and Acquaintances* (1871), part of his writings about the London poor. Rowe is described in Ann Mari Jordens's *The Stenhouse Circle* (1979).

ROWLAND, JOHN RUSSELL (1925–), born Armidale, NSW, joined the Department of Foreign Affairs in 1944 and has served in London, Washington, Saigon, Malaysia, Paris, Moscow and other East European countries. He was ambassador in Moscow 1965–68, and in Paris 1979–82. He has published four collections of poetry, *The Feast of Ancestors* (1965), *Snow and Other Poems* (1971), *Times and Places* (1975) and *The Clock Inside* (1979). Rowland writes an elegant, controlled poetry, which often recreates the atmosphere of other countries or celebrates the daily realities of family life. One of his best-known poems, 'Canberra in April', evokes the social and physical landscape of the national capital of the 1950s and 1960s.

ROWLANDS, GRAHAM (1947–), born Brisbane, was educated at Flinders University, SA, and at the University of Queensland. He has been an academic, freelance writer, editor and reviewer. One of the chief organizers of the Friendly Street (q.v.) poetry group, Rowlands has also edited *Dots Over Lines: Recent*

Poetry in South Australia (1980). His own publications of verse include *Stares and Statues* (1972), *Replacing Mirrors* (1975), *Poems Political* (1975), *Adam Scolds* (1976, with Grahame Pitt and Lyndon Walker) and *Dial-A-Poem* (1982).

ROWLANDSON, A.C. (ALFRED CECIL) (1865–1922), born Daylesford, Victoria, joined the NSW Bookstall Company, then owned by Henry Lloyd, as a tram ticket seller in 1883 and became owner of the company in 1897. He turned it into one of Australia's most successful book-publishing and selling ventures, publishing some 200 titles by Australasian authors and selling some five million copies, mainly through the Bookshop's eight shops and many railway bookstalls. The books, in coloured wrappers, sold for one shilling per copy, rising to one shilling and threepence per copy during the First World War, when paper was scarce and expensive, but reverting to the popular 'bob' after the war. The Bookstall series (or 'Bookstalls') include novels by Arthur H. Adams, J.A. Barry, 'Louis' Becke, Randolph Bedford, E.J. Brady, Edward Dyson, Vance Palmer, 'Steele Rudd' (q.v.), Thomas E. Spencer and A.G. Stephens. The remarkable sales of these Australian books confirmed Rowlandson's intuition that the Australian reading public was keen for local reading matter and the impact of his company on the development of Australian writing was considerable. A biographical work, *The Late Alfred Cecil Rowlandson: Pioneer Publisher of Australian Novels* (1922), has a foreword by R. Wynn and appreciative articles by A.G. Stephens and Bertram Stevens. A novel, *The Rival Physicians* (1909) by 'Paul Cupid', has been attributed to Rowlandson. Harry F. Chaplin has written two descriptive and bibliographical articles about the Bookstall series in *Biblionews* (1961).

ROWLEY, CHARLES DUNFORD, see **Aboriginal in Australian Literature**

Roxburgh, Ellen, see *Fringe of Leaves, A*

Royal South Australian Almanack and General Directory, see **Almanacs**

Rudd Family. The Rudd family's fortunes are chronicled in a series of books about selection life written by Arthur Hoey Davis under the pseudonym, 'Steele Rudd' (q.v.), the narrator of the series, who appears as a character in the seventh volume. The series began with *On Our Selection* (q.v., 1899) in which Murtagh Joseph Rudd, known primarily as Dad (see Dad and Dave), brings his family from Stanthorpe to his selection at Emu Creek on the Darling

Downs. Accompanying Dad are his wife Ellen (Mother), his sons Dan, Dave and Joe, his daughters Kate and Sarah (sometimes called Sal), and the as-yet-unnamed narrator, Steele. In the course of *On Our Selection*, which focuses on the struggle of Dad and the family to establish themselves on the selection, three further children are born: the twin boys Bill and Tom and another son, unnamed in the story in which he is born, 'The Night We Watched for Wallabies' (q.v.), but eventually christened Bartholomew. After the first few sketches, the eldest son Dan is seldom at Shingle Hut, the family home, although he reappears periodically in the Rudd family volumes along with the eldest daughter, Norah, a schoolteacher elsewhere in Queensland. Dan is the black sheep of the family and his farming experiences are the subject of *The Book of Dan* (1911).

On Our Selection is the best and most famous of the Rudd volumes. There are nine others, through which, and according in general to the sequence of publication, the subsequent fortunes of the family are traced. In *Our New Selection* (q.v., 1903), the Rudds begin to prosper: Shingle Hut is sold and Dad takes up the better holding of Saddletop, which he leaves temporarily after his election to parliament. *Dad in Politics and Other Stories* (q.v., published 1908, written 1904) records his experiences as a vociferous backbencher and the disillusionment with governments which causes him to resign his seat and return to Saddletop in *Back at Our Selection* (1906), in which there is mention of another daughter, Amelia. Meanwhile, Kate has married the neighbour, Sandy Taylor, in 'Kate's Wedding', an *On Our Selection* sketch; the struggle of Kate and Sandy to establish their selection at Sleepy Creek, which parallels the initial hardships of Dad and Mother at Shingle Hut, is the subject of *Sandy's Selection* (1904), in which Dad becomes parsimonious in his prosperity. His meanness is confirmed when Dave gets married in *Back at Our Selection* and in the later *Grandpa's Selection* (1916), by which time Dad has become Grandpa, a widower living with Joe.

The other Rudd volumes are *Stocking Our Selection* (1909), which includes the last part of *On Our Selection* (where Uncle Peter, an important character in *Sandy's Selection*, was introduced), together with a further seven stories featuring Dad in the city with Norah; *From Selection to City* (q.v., 1909), which introduces Steele as a character, the next son in line to Joe, and traces his movement from bush work into the public service; *The Book of Dan* (1911); and *The Rudd Family* (1926), by which time the Emu Creek area is known as Ruddville, Sarah and Joe have married, Bill, Frank, Eileen and Peggy are the children at home, and

Uncle Sam Rudd pays a visit. In the stage adaptation of *The Rudd Family* (1928) the Rudds become the Dicksons, using material from an earlier play. The final appearance of the Rudds in fiction occurs in the last novel, *The Green Grey Homestead* (1934), in which Dave and Joe visit the selector Dick Gall around the time in which *On Our Selection* or *Back at Our Selection* are set, and have to be hauled home by Dad.

The success of *On Our Selection* owed much to 'Rudd''s ability to write from his experience. The commercial popularity of the later books owed something to his willingness to let his characters evolve, e.g. the emergence of Dad's meanness and the development of Joe's stutter, and to vary the focus on different members of the family in succeeding volumes. Nevertheless, Dad and Dave were the most important characters in the family and in exploiting their popularity 'Rudd' made them increasingly farcical after *On Our Selection*. He was influenced by his illustrators and perhaps also by the stage and screen adaptations of his work, in which he had little part: *Grandad Rudd* (1918), adapted from *Grandpa's Selection*, and the stage version of *The Rudd Family* were his work but he made little direct contribution to the stage adaptation of *On Our Selection* (1912) starring Bert Bailey (q.v.), the sound film (1932) based on it, and the three later Rudd spin-off films. Bailey became identified with Dad, and in time Dad and Dave moved beyond the Rudd family to become comic stereotypes, notably in the Dad and Dave radio serial produced by George Edwards. In addition, there have been several versions of the Rudds, including 'Rudd''s other fictional families, the Dashwoods, the Davidsons, the Duffs (in *On Emu Creek* (1923) in which Mrs Duff is identified as Joe's daughter), the Pettigrews and the Kaytons. Among other writers to be influenced by 'Rudd' are Henry Fletcher, in his novels about the Waybacks family of which the patriarch is Dads Wayback and Dan Wayback is the equivalent of Dave Rudd; and Sumner Locke, in her novels about the Dawson family in which Mum Dawson is the counterpart of Dad. Although the first film in the series preceded the silent version of *On Our Selection* (1920), the several films (1918–37) about the Hayseed family clearly also benefited from the popularity of the Rudds.

'RUDD, STEELE' (ARTHUR HOEY DAVIS) (1868–1935), born Drayton on the Darling Downs in Queensland; he was the son of a blacksmith who in 1870 selected land at Emu Creek, where the family moved in 1875. 'Rudd' left school in 1880 and worked on local properties and shearing sheds until 1885, when he moved to Brisbane to become a clerk in the public service. In 1889 he transferred to the sheriff's office in the Justice department and was promoted to under-sheriff in 1902; he was retrenched from this position in 1904. Around 1890 he began contributing rowing skits to the Brisbane *Chronicle* under the pseudonym 'Steele Rudder' (the Christian name derives from his admiration for the English essayist, the surname from boating); 'Rudder' had been contracted to 'Rudd' by the time his first sketch about selection life, 'Starting the Selection', appeared in the *Bulletin* in December 1895. The popularity of 'Rudd''s contributions encouraged the *Bulletin* management to publish in 1899 an illustrated collection, *On Our Selection* (q.v.). In preparing the book he revised the sketches, originally about different families, so that they focused on the pioneering struggles of the Rudd family (q.v.). The success of *On Our Selection* was repeated four years later with the sequel, *Our New Selection* (q.v.).

'Rudd' believed that his identification in 1897 with his pseudonym had been influential in his retrenchment. Refusing offers on reappointment at a lower level in the public service, he opted to trade on his popularity and founded *Steele Rudd's Magazine* (q.v.), an illustrated monthly to which he was a major contributor. In 1909 he bought a farm not far from Emu Creek, where he continued to write and became prominent in local affairs. In 1912 the stage adaptation of *On Our Selection* by Bert Bailey and Edmund Duggan was a huge success, but 'Rudd' benefited little from the royalty payments. Similarly, the arrangement he made with A.C. Rowlandson of the NSW Bookstall company for later editions of *On Our Selection* and *Our New Selection* worked to his disadvantage, except in higher payments for the rights to his other books. In 1917 he moved to Brisbane and revived his magazine as *Steele Rudd's Annual* (1917–23), later *Steele Rudd's* (1924–25) and *Steele Rudd's and the Shop Assistant's Magazine* (1926–27). But although Raymond Longford's (q.v.) silent film version of *On Our Selection* (1920) and its sequel, *Rudd's New Selection* (1921), kept his name before the public, his personal and financial affairs continued to decline in the 1920s and 1930s. Major setbacks were the failure of the film version of his first novel, *The Romance of Runnibede* (1928), and the bankruptcy of the producer of the stage adaptation (1928) of *The Rudd Family*. 'Rudd''s son, Eric Drayton Davis, has written *The Life and Times of Steele Rudd* (1976) and Harry Reade, the play, 'The Execution of Steele Rudd' (1982).

A prolific contributor to his own and other journals, 'Rudd' published some two dozen works of fiction, wrote six plays based on his books (though not the script for the Bailey-

Duggan *On Our Selection*), and in addition to the three silent films based on his work there were four sound features starring Bailey as Dad: *On Our Selection* (1932), *Grandad Rudd* (1935), *Dad and Dave Come to Town* (1938) and *Dad Rudd M.P.* (1940). His most important work went into the ten volumes in which he chronicles the fortunes of the Rudd family: *On Our Selection* (1899), *Our New Selection* (1903), *Sandy's Selection* (1904), *Back at Our Selection* (1906), *Dad in Politics and Other Stories* (q.v., 1908), *Stocking Our Selection* (1909), *From Selection to City* (q.v., 1909), *The Book of Dan* (1911), *Grandpa's Selection* (1916), and *The Rudd Family* (1926). The success of the Rudd volumes, particularly the first half of the sequence, clearly influenced 'Rudd''s direction as a writer. With the exception of three novels, *In Australia* (1908), which shows the influence of Nat Gould, *The Romance of Runnibede* (1927) and *The Green Grey Homestead* (1934), and the autobiographical *The Miserable Clerk* (1926), his other books were almost a copy of the Rudd books formula, a series of sketches about families and characters working selections on the Darling Downs or visiting Brisbane. Of these, the best is *The Poor Parson* (1907), in which the central character is Duncan McClure, the subject also of a play by 'Rudd'. Of the others, *On An Australian Farm* (1910) and its sequel *The Dashwoods* (1911), *We Kaytons* (1921), and *Me an' th' Son* (1924) all chronicle the experience of countrymen and their families in the city; *The Old Homestead* (1917) centres on Abe Pettigrew, a Dad Rudd figure toiling with his family at Ironbark; *Memoirs of Corporal Keeley* (1918) traces the shearing life of a young bush worker before his enlistment and service in Gallipoli and France; and *On Emu Creek* (1923), studies the problems of an urban innocent who moves to a selection after his retrenchment from the public service.

'Rudd' was at his best when writing out of his early experiences. In one sense that generalization applies to most of his books but is particularly true of *On Our Selection*, in which the struggles of the Rudd family parallel those of his own family in the later 1870s and early 1880s. Dad, however, was not based directly on his father, and of the characters in *On Our Selection* only the rouseabout Cranky Jack (q.v.), is drawn directly from real life. *On Our Selection* and its immediate sequels succeeded also because of 'Rudd''s pictorial gifts and because the presentation of the members of the Rudd family, particularly Dad, Dave, Joe, Mother and Kate, was both rounded and unsentimental. But particularly from *Dad in Politics* onwards the dominant tone was farce, present in the earlier volumes but there both a comment on and a relief from the struggles of pioneering

life; together with the effects of 'Rudd''s illustrators and the presentation of Dad and Dave on stage, screen and radio, the later Rudd volumes helped transform Dad and Dave into stereotypes of rural yokels. The later Rudd volumes and the other sketches of Darling Downs life came finally to rely less and less on 'Rudd''s experiences than on his use of a previously successful formula. Of his later work, only *The Miserable Clerk* and *The Green Grey Homestead* have much of the strength of *On Our Selection*.

Rue Tree, The, see GILMORE, Dame MARY

RUDGE, FLORENCE (1860–?), born London as Florence Thompson, came to Australia in 1914. Under the pseudonym 'Fairelie Thornton' she published twenty collections of verse, 1922–44; nearly all are on conventional, religious themes and some were set to music and sung at church services. The titles of her collections adequately express their content, e.g. *Work for Jesus* (1923), *Heart Cheer for All the Year* (1928), *Daily Comfort* (1936) and *Peace, the Gift of Love* (1937). She also wrote several prose texts of the same religious tone, and for several years contributed the devotional page to a religious magazine, *Grit*.

RUHEN, OLAF (1911–), born NZ, pursued numerous occupations including deep-sea fishing before serving in the RNZAF during the Second World War. In 1947 he moved to Sydney, where he worked for the *Sun* and the *Sydney Morning Herald*; he resigned in 1956 to work as a freelance writer after several of his short stories had been accepted by the *Saturday Evening Post*. His extensive travels in Australia, the South Pacific and New Guinea are reflected in both his documentary and fictional writing. He has published five novels, *Naked Under Capricorn* (1958), *White Man's Shoes* (1960), *The Flockmaster* (1963), *The Broken Wing* (1965) and *Scan the Dark Coast* (1969); two collections of short stories, *Land of Dahori* (1957) and *Lively Ghosts* (1964); documentary accounts of New Guinea, *Mountains in the Clouds* (1963), of the South Pacific, *Tangaroa's Godchild* (1962), of the whale-hunters of Tonga, *Harpoon in My Hand* (1966) and of the bullock drivers of Australia, *Bullock Teams* (1980); an account of a Japanese ship wreck in the South Pacific, *Minerva Reef* (1963); a biography of Lawrence Hargrave (1977); a novel for children, *Corcoran's the Name* (1967); an account of an aspect of Australia's prehistory for children, *The Day of the Diprotodon* (1976); and a manual for writers, *Writing: The Craft of Creative Fiction* (1964). He has also edited an anthology of short stories, *South Pacific Adventure* (1966).

RULE, EDGAR JOHN, see **War Literature**

Rum Rebellion was the name given to the deposing of Governor William Bligh (q.v.) by the officers of the NSW Corps, 26 January 1808. The NSW Corps was known as the 'Rum Corps' because it had attempted, more or less successfully, to obtain the monopoly on the sale of rum in the Colony. Leaders of the rebellion were Lieutenant Colonel George Johnston, commanding officer of the Corps, and John Macarthur (q.v.). The events are recounted in H.V. Evatt's *Rum Rebellion* (1938), George Mackaness's *The Life of Vice-Admiral William Bligh* (1951) and M.H. Ellis's *John Macarthur* (1955). In many fictional and dramatic recreations of events from Bligh's life the Rum Rebellion is featured, e.g. J.H.M. Abbott's semi-historical novel, *The Governor's Man* (1919), Doris Egerton Jones's play, *Governor Bligh* (1930), Eleanor Dark's novels, *The Storm of Time* (1948) and *No Barrier* (1953), George Farwell's play, *The House That Jack Built* (1950), Brian Medlin's play, 'Governor Bligh' (1955), and Ray Lawler's 'The Man Who Shot the Albatross' (1971). Rob Inglis wrote a musical, 'A Rum Do' (1970), in which the rum trade is highlighted. See also Bligh, Sir William.

Run is a term found in Australia as early as 1804. In its earliest use it referred to a large, open and reasonably well-grassed area for grazing sheep or cattle. Originally an English dialect word, it became widely used to denote specific characteristics of the Australian pastoral scene, e.g. 'sheep run', 'cattle run'. It is found in many fictional and factual accounts of life in the colony, e.g. in Alexander Harris's *The Emigrant Family* (1849), and has been frequently used in the titles of fiction and poetry, e.g. Miles Franklin's *Ten Creeks Run* (1930) and A.B. Paterson's 'On Kiley's Run'.

RUSDEN, GEORGE ('YITTADAIRN') (1819–1903), born Surrey, England, accompanied his Anglican minister father to Maitland, NSW, in 1834. He worked as property manager in south-western NSW before two years of adventure in China 1847–49. Back in Australia, he became associated with education, publishing *National Education* (1853), an early proposal for State-directed education; he was also active in local politics and cultural affairs. An enthusiastic writer on political, religious and literary topics, Rusden published a poem, *Moyarra: An Australian Legend in Two Cantos* (1851), an account of two Aboriginal lovers who die because they transgress tribal law, and several documentary works, including *The Discovery, Survey and Settlement of Port Phillip*

(1871), *Curiosities of Colonization* (1874), and the important *History of Australia* (1883).

Rush That Never Ended, The, see **Gold**; **BLAINEY, GEOFFREY**

'RUSSELL, LINDSAY', see **STONEHOUSE, PATRICIA ETHEL**

Rusty Bugles, a play by Sumner Locke Elliot (q.v.) was first performed at the Independent Theatre, Sydney, in October 1948. Although the audience was enthusiastic, the play's 'blasphemous' language was brought to the attention of the chief secretary of NSW who temporarily banned further production. After much public debate, the play was performed again by the end of the month although some deletions were made. It was subsequently produced with great success in the other capital cities of Australia, except Brisbane, and toured NZ, with less success, in 1952. In 1964 Doris Fitton revived the play at the Independent and the New Theatre staged it successfully in 1979; it has been broadcast several times on ABC radio and was produced on television in 1965. Included in Eunice Hanger's collection, *Khaki, Bush and Bigotry* (1968), *Rusty Bugles* was also separately published in 1980.

Comprising ten scenes that convey the experiences of the protagonists over six months of 1944, it is set in a remote army camp in the Northern Territory. The action opens with the arrival of Private Rod Carson and his initiation into the monotony, discomfort and ugliness of camp life, alleviated only by the nightly game of 'swy' (two-up), the arrival of the mail, bickering, the occasional unsatisfactory and public call home, the hope of leave or of replacements. His camp-mates include Des Nolan (The 'Gig Ape'), the good-natured butt of rough-house jokes; Mac, the unpopular shirker who finally gets leave when his wife deserts him only to be held back by the dermatitis that he has been encouraging; the taciturn Ken Falcon, who eventually 'goes troppo'; the cheerful, resourceful Ot, who is granted longed-for leave only to discover that his girlfriend has married another; Chris and Ollie, the versatile youngsters who take on the role of camp clowns; the eternally-depressed Keghead Stephens; and the universally-detested, petty official, Sergeant Brooks. The play's absence of plot and its circular movement which at the close brings back the men who had vowed they would never return, emphasizes the meaningless, desultory progress of the soldiers' experience.

RUTHERFORD, JAMES, see **Cobb & Co**

Rutherford, see **STEWART, DOUGLAS**

RYAN, LES, see Shearer in Australian Literature

RYAN, LYNDALL, see Aboriginal in Australian Literature

RYAN, PETER (1923–), born Melbourne, served in New Guinea in the Second World War and subsequently worked in public relations. He has been director of Melbourne University Press since 1962. He has published a novel, *Fear Drive My Feet* (1959), which is closely based on his own experiences in New Guinea 1942–43. As one of a small group of Australian commandos who linked up with the New Guinea Volunteer Rifles under the joint title Kanga force and who stayed on in New Guinea after the fall of Lae and Salamaua to maintain contact with the indigenous people and observe and harass Japanese movements, Ryan underwent extraordinary dangers and hardships. He has also edited the *Encyclopaedia of Papua and New Guinea* (1972) and written a short biography of Judge Redmond Barry (1972).

'Ryebuck Shearer, The', see **'Backblocks Shearer, The'**

S

'Said Hanrahan', the most popular and frequently anthologized of the poems of 'John O'Brien' (q.v.), was published in *Around the Boree Log and Other Verses* (1921). The poem catches to perfection the legendary pessimism of the farmer, who sees prospects of ruin in every variation of weather. The lugubrious lament of the poem, 'We'll all be rooned', has passed into Australian folklore.

SALA, GEORGE AUGUSTUS (1828–95), born London, was a scene painter and engraver before establishing himself as a journalist with *Household Words, Temple Bar* and, most notably, the London *Daily Telegraph*. Widely travelled, he lectured and toured Australia in 1885; while in Melbourne, where his wife died and is buried, he coined the phrase 'Marvellous Melbourne' (q.v.) which soon became a popular description of the city. During his Australian tour Sala wrote for the *Argus, Australasian* and *Sydney Morning Herald* as well as for the *Daily Telegraph*. After his return to England he published *A Journey Due South* (1885) and *The Life and Adventures of George Augustus Sala* (1895), which both include Australian impressions. Sala also wrote stories, 'The Australian Nights Entertainments', purporting to be 'related by convicts at the Antipodes while lying in their hammocks after sunset'; they were published in *Chat*, the journal, in 1848.

SALOM, PHILIP (1950–), born Perth, WA, published *The Silent Piano* (1980), a book of verse which won the Commonwealth Poetry Prize (q.v.) for 1981, and *The Projectionist* (1983) which contains some long verse sequences in which the poet assumes the persona of a projectionist at the local cinema in an outback town in WA.

Salt, an army journal, published weekly, later fortnightly, in Melbourne 1941–46, included short stories, poems, articles and drawings by personnel to whom it was distributed. A book review section, 'Dustjackets Off', was a regular feature of *Salt*. Staff members included Mungo MacCallum, Frank Hardy and Ambrose Dyson.

Saltbush Bill, one of A.B. Paterson's (q.v.) best-known characters, appeared in five poems, 'Saltbush Bill' (in *The Man from Snowy River and Other Verses*, 1895), 'Saltbush Bill's Second Fight' and 'Saltbush Bill's Gamecock' (both in *Rio Grande's Last Race and Other Verses*, 1902), and 'Saltbush Bill, J.P.' and 'Saltbush Bill on the Patriarchs' (both in *Saltbush Bill, J.P. and Other Verses*, 1917). As a drover in charge of travelling sheep, Saltbush Bill sparks fear and anger in the hearts of squatters like Stingy Smith, on whose best runs his sheep always manage to stray. When his natural cunning occasionally fails him, his determination usually wins the day. Grown old and grey, respectability comes to Bill, for 'Edward Rex' appoints him a Justice of the Peace. Bill discovers in the fine print of his high office that he can charge a pound for an inquest on a fire. Over the course of a week, while Bill's sheep feed freely on a nearby run, twenty-five 'residences' in the local Aboriginal camp are destroyed by fire. With his twenty-five pounds from fees Bill is able to spend Christmas with his sister in the south. There, as loving uncle to his sister's 'little rouseabouts', he recounts, in a superb outback analogy, the drover's version of the Patriarchs. Isaac is the squatter; Jacob, his son, takes to the droving track, 'for any boy that's worth his salt will roll his swag and roam.' On his uncle Laban's run Jacob works, not for 'the speckled and spotted' animals of Genesis but, in Bill's words, for 'the roan and strawberry calves'. In the character of Saltbush Bill, Paterson incorporates many of the qualities he considered essential for survival in the rough and tumble of outback life: determination, ingenuity, a wry sense of humour and a talent for sharp practices.

Salute to the Great McCarthy, A, see **OAKLEY, BARRY**

Salzburg Tales, The, see **STEAD, CHRISTINA**

'Sam Holt', an Australian folk-song in which a bushman sardonically recalls the seamy past of a former mate, Sam Holt, who has finally succeeded as a digger and returned to a gentleman's life in England, was originally a poem, 'A Ballad of Queensland', written by G.H. Gibson (q.v.) and published in the *Bulletin* 26 March 1881. A parody on the English popular song of the 1840s, 'Ben Bolt', 'Sam Holt' passed into oral currency and was included as an anonymous composition in A.B. Paterson's *Old Bush Songs* (1905). The opening lines of 'Sam Holt'

> Oh! don't you remember Black Alice, Sam Holt –
> Black Alice, so dusky and dark,
> The Warrego gin, with the straw through her nose,
> And teeth like a Moreton Bay shark

are quoted with minor variations in Xavier Herbert's *Capricornia* (qq.v., 1938) and illustrate the racial attitudes of much of Australian folk-song and ballad. Earlier parodies of 'Ben Bolt' were written by the goldfields entertainer, Charles Thatcher.

SANDES, JOHN (1863–1938), born Cork, Ireland, and educated at Oxford, migrated to Australia in 1885 and for fifteen years from 1887 worked for the *Argus* as music and drama critic. One of the first contributors to the 'Oriel' column of the newspaper, he also used the pseudonym independently. In 1903 Sandes joined the Sydney *Daily Telegraph* and attended the London peace conference in 1919 as that newspaper's representative. After his return to Sydney in 1922 he edited *Harbour*, a monthly shipping magazine. Sandes's topical, patriotic poetry found a ready audience, especially his 'With Death's Prophetic Ear', a poem on the Boer War which was published in numerous contemporary anthologies. He published five collections of verse, *Rhymes of the Times* (1898), *Ballads of Battle* (1900), *The House of Empire* (1909), *Landing in the Dawn* (1916) and *The Escort* (1925); three adventure novels, *Love and the Aeroplane* (1910), *Designing Fate* (1912) and *The Call of the Southern Cross* (1915); and, under the pseudonym 'Dan Delaney', a group of novels mainly with bushranging themes, *Gentleman Jack, Bushranger* (1911), *For Turon Gold* (1913), *The Captain of the Gang* (1913), *A Rebel of the Bush* (1914) and *The White Champion* (1917).

Sandgroper is a colloquialism for a person from WA; according to Xavier Herbert in *Disturbing Element* (1963), it 'measured the contempt of the Easterners for the comparative infertility of the West and the social backwardness of its first settlers'. The anthology of WA writing, *Sandgropers* (1973), edited by Dorothy Hewett, is an example of the contemporary usage of 'sandgroper' in contrast to the relative obsolescence of equivalents like 'cornstalk' and 'Vandemonian'.

SANDS, JOHN (1818–73), was a famous early Australian printer and stationer who was born in Sandhurst, England; a fifth-generation engraver and printer, he came to Australia for health reasons in 1837 and set up business in Sydney. In 1852, in partnership with his brother-in-law, Thomas Kenny, he expanded into Melbourne; when Kenny retired in 1861, the firm, which had been joined by Dougal McDougall in 1860, became Sands & McDougall. After Sands's death, his widow divided the business so that John Sands Ltd, run by the Sands family, operated in Sydney and Sands & McDougall, run by the McDougall family, operated from Melbourne. Under various titles, Sands was one of the largest booksellers and stationers in Australia, and published an important series of almanacs (q.v.), directories and gazetteers covering Melbourne, Sydney, Adelaide and country areas in NSW and Victoria. In 1881 the John Sands company became the first Australian firm to issue Christmas and New Year cards. A centenary history of Sands & McDougall was compiled by H.P. Down and published in 1956.

'Sandy Maranoa, The' is a rollicking Australian folk-song (q.v.) which celebrates the life of the overlanders moving cattle to and from the Maranoa pastoral district in central southern Queensland, through which runs the Maranoa

River, named by Sir Thomas Mitchell in 1846. 'The Sandy Maranoa' was included in A.B. Paterson's *Old Bush Songs* (1905) as an anonymous composition, 'The Maranoa Drovers', but claims have been made that it was composed at the end of the nineteenth century by a young Queensland stockman, A.W. Davis.

Sandy's Selection, see **Rudd Family**

SANSOM, CLIVE (1910–81), lived in London until 1950, when he migrated to Tasmania. A speech educationalist, he was the author of seven collections of verse on religious and historical themes, *In the Midst of Death* (1940), *The Unfailing Spring* (1943), *The Witnesses and Other Poems* (1956), *The Cathedral* (1958), *Dorset Village* (1962), *Return to Magic* (1969) and *Francis of Assisi* (1981), Sansom also wrote a novel, *Passion Play* (1951), and a verse play, *The World Turned Upside Down* (1948). His poem 'The Witnesses', one of the prize-winning entries of the Festival of Britain competition, was also published in *Poems 1951* (1951). In addition, Sansom compiled anthologies of poetry for adults, including *The English Heart* (1945) and *The World of Poetry* (1959), as well as numerous anthologies of verse and plays for children.

SANTAMARIA, B.A. (BARTHOLOMEW AUGUSTINE) (1915–), born West Brunswick, Melbourne, graduated in arts and law from the University of Melbourne. Catholic activist and, from 1957, president of the National Civic Council, he has published numerous political tracts including *The Price of Freedom* (1964), *Point of View* (1969), *The Defence of Australia* (1970), *The Australian Labor Movement (1966–71): The Issue of Control* (1971). He is caricatured as Greensleeves in Barry Oakley's play, *The Feet of Daniel Mannix* (1975).

Sara Dane, see **GASKIN, CATHERINE**

Sarsaparilla, one of Patrick White's (q.v.) fictional outer Sydney suburbs, represents the materialism, ugliness and 'exaltation of the average' that he deplores. It features in his novels *Riders in the Chariot* (1961) and *The Solid Mandala* (1966), in his plays, *A Cheery Soul* (1965) and *The Season at Sarsaparilla* (1965), and in several of the short stories collected in *The Burnt Ones* (1964). In *Flaws in the Glass* (1981), White indicates the connections between Sarsaparilla and Castle Hill, where he lived 1948–63.

Saturday Club Book of Poetry, The, a Sydney magazine, was edited by Patricia Laird. First published in 1972 as an issue dedicated to Kenneth Slessor, it ran until 1977 when it was replaced by *Scopp*, a magazine that includes prose as well as poetry, also edited by Laird.

Saturday Night, a weekly magazine published in Melbourne, ran 1879–94, changing its title to *Once a Week* in 1881; in 1894 it was incorporated into the *Weekly Budget*. It included some serials and short stories.

Saturdee, a novel by Norman Lindsay (q.v.), was published in 1933, illustrated by the author. A revised version of a series of short stories published 1908–19, it forms part of his trilogy on small-town life in the 1890s that also includes *Redheap* (q.v., 1930) and *Halfway to Anywhere* (1947). The novel centres on the escapades of twelve-year-old Peter Gimble and his friends, Conkey Menders, Bullyo Peddlar, Bufflehead and others as they unremittingly pursue fun, freedom and the mysteries of the female in the face of Redheap's sleepy but repressive narrowness. Distinctive aspects include Lindsay's humorous insight into the amoral world of the schoolboy and the pretensions of the adult, his versatile characterization and zestful narrative.

Satyrs and Sunlight: Silvarum Libri, the first volume of poems by Hugh McCrae (q.v.), was published in Sydney in 1909. The first part of the title, *Satyrs and Sunlight*, was also used for McCrae's 1928 collected verse. The seventy-nine poems, mainly short lyrics, were highly regarded by the bohemian literary set of the day, of which Norman Lindsay was the centre. Poems such as 'I Blow My Pipes', 'The Satyr's Lass', 'Bacchanalia', 'Fantasy' and 'Muse-Haunted', filled with fauns and nymphs, dryads, centaurs, Bacchanals and the god Pan, all whirling and cavorting in an exultant, sensuous vitality, were a startling contrast to the homespun balladry of the previous two decades.

Savage Crows, The, see **DREWE, ROBERT**

SAVERY, HENRY (1791–1842), the first Australian novelist and essayist, was born in Somerset, England, the son of a prominent Bristol banker; his movements thereafter until his marriage in 1815 are not known with certainty, although the evidence of his strongly autobiographical novel, *Quintus Servinton* (q.v., 1831), suggests that he was educated at a grammar school and that he spent his early manhood in London. After his marriage he moved to near Bristol, where he was engaged in business as a sugar refiner until bankrupted in 1819; in 1819–22 he was editor of the *Bristol Observer* and an insurance broker. In 1822 he returned to sugar refining and soon became the dominant partner in the business, but over-reached himself financially and forged fictitious bills to meet his problems. Panicking at the prospect of detection, he fled, planning to escape to America, but was captured in dramatic circumstances at Cowes in the Isle of Wight within half an hour of his ship's sailing. Brought back to Bristol, he was advised to plead guilty but was condemned to death. Reprieved almost at the last moment, he was transported to Van Diemen's Land and arrived in Hobart in 1825.

Savery was soon involved in controversy: he was appointed to clerkships in the colonial administration and gained permission to bring his wife and child to join him, which led to accusations that he had received favoured treatment from the lieutenant-governor of the colony, George Arthur, who had to defend his actions to the Colonial Office in London. In 1827 Savery was assigned to the superintendent of the Van Diemen's Land Establishment, a development company which did not prosper; in the ensuing investigation he was exonerated of any financial malpractice. In 1828 Eliza Savery, encouraged by her husband's misleading reports of his prospects, arrived in Hobart to find him in debt; within a week he had attempted suicide, his despair possibly increased by rumours of a shipboard liaison between his wife and Algernon Montagu. When Eliza left Hobart early in 1829 Savery's debts had landed him in prison; during his fifteen months incarceration he probably wrote the sketches of Hobart life and people which were published under the pseudonym 'Simon Stukeley' in the *Colonial Times* 1829, as *The Hermit in Van Diemen's Land* (q.v.), which, when issued in book form in 1830, was the first book of Australian essays. Some uncertainty remains concerning Savery's authorship of *The Hermit in Van Diemen's Land*; there is no doubt, however, about his authorship of *Quintus Servinton*, the first Australian novel. Subtitled *A Tale Founded upon Incidents of Real Occurrence*, it records in fictional form the main incidents in Savery's life until 1829, except that Quintus's wife remains faithful to her husband and eventually secures his release. After his own release from prison, Savery underwent periods of assignment until securing his ticket-of-leave in 1832; it was temporarily withdrawn in 1833 following complaints that he had run the *Tasmanian* during the absence of Henry Melville (q.v.), who published *Quintus Servinton* and included Savery material in the *Van Diemen's Land Almanack* for 1831. For several years from 1833 Savery was mainly engaged in pastoral pursuits securing his conditional pardon in 1838, but he again overreached himself financially, again resorted to forgery, and was sent to Port Arthur after a trial presided over, iron-

ically, by Algernon Montagu. He died there early in 1842, his decline graphically described by David Burn in *An Excursion to Port Arthur in 1842* (1842).

In some respects Savery's tragic life is of more interest than his writing, but *The Hermit in Van Diemen's Land* offers a valuable picture of colonial Tasmania and *Quintus Servinton*, in addition to its autobiographical and historical significance, is of some interest in the way, as a cautionary tale, it links convict (q.v.) fiction with the convict memoirs. Again, although there is no evidence that Henry Kingsley read the novel, *Quintus Servinton* looks forward to *The Recollections of Geoffry Hamlyn* (1859) in its admiration of prudence and moderation, and in its disapproval of wilfulness and self-centredness, to which Quintus no less than Mary Hawker is victim. There have been suggestions also that William Hay was influenced by *Quintus Servinton* in writing *The Escape of the Notorious Sir William Heans* (1919), in which Savery appears as a minor character.

SAXBY, H.M., see *History of Australian Children's Literature, A*

'Say to Me Ronald!', a short story by Hal Porter (q.v.), was first published in the *Bulletin* in 1961. An amusing study of well-intentioned individuals afflicted with language difficulties and notions of good form inherited from their respective, very different cultures, it is one of Porter's most popular stories. Perrot, an Adelaide schoolteacher, has been tutoring Ronald Wee San Wat, the seventeen-year-old son of a Singapore millionaire exiled in Australia during the Second World War. Aghast when Wee gratefully presents him with a massive golf-bag, Perrot is finally persuaded in lieu to attend afternoon tea with Wee and his sisters. At their hot, over-furnished flat, Wee's well-plied whisky and the cement-like 'melting-moments' of the Misses Wee, help to frustrate the determined efforts of both sides to achieve a social success and the party rapidly degenerates into a farcical fiasco.

SAYCE, C.H. (CONRAD HARVEY) (1888–1935), born in Hereford, England, and educated in England, was a well-known architect who was resident for some time in Australia and designed some of the buildings of the University of WA. He also wrote a series of adventure novels, which have conventional plots and wooden characters but which reflect an intimate knowledge of outback localities and conditions. They are *The Valley of a Thousand Deaths* (?1920), *Golden Buckles* (1920), *In the Musgrave Ranges* (1922), *The Golden Valley* (1924), *The Splendid Savage* (?1928) and *Com-*

boman (1934). Sayce also used the pseudonym, 'Jim Bushman'.

SAYERS, C.E. (CHARLES EDWARD) (1901–80), worked on the staff of the *Age* for many years, and published four novels, *The Jumping Double* (1923), *Boss of Toolangi* (1924), *Green Streaked Ring* (1930) and *Desperate Chances* (1930); a biography of David Syme (1965); and numerous local histories. He also edited several historical and literary texts including James Bonwick's *Western Victoria* (1970) and *John Batman* (1973), 'Rolf Boldrewood''s *Old Melbourne Memories* (1969) and John Morgan's *The Life and Adventures of William Buckley* (1967).

SCANLON, HERBERT (1899–?), served in the First World War and published numerous collections of short stories, nearly all dealing with the experience of war. They include *Recollections of a Soldier's Life* (1919), *Into Turkish Harems* (?1922), *Gay Mademoiselles, Sly Digs and Wedding Bells* (192?), *In a Nutshell* (1921), *Humoresque* (1922), *Bon Jour Digger* (1922), *Triolette* (?1922), *The Vengeance of Etna* (1924), *Forgotten Men* (1927), *The Deathless Army* (1927), *Veterans of War* (1928) and *Great Short Stories* (?1932).

Scarlet Woman, see **Feminism and Australian Literature**

Scent of Eucalyptus, The, see **HANRAHAN, BARBARA**

Schindler's Ark (1982) by Thomas Keneally (q.v.), won the 1982 Booker McConnell Prize. Based entirely on facts ascertained from official documents, interviews, testimonies, correspondence and private papers, the book uses, in Keneally's words, 'the texture and devices of a novel' to tell the authentic story of the protection of thousands of Jewish lives in the Second World War by the German industrialist, Oskar Schindler (1908–74). Born in the Czechoslovakian industrial city, Zwittau, Schindler follows the German invasion into Poland, where in Cracow he establishes an enamelware factory. Within a few months he is employing 150 Jewish workers and his Emalia factory begins to develop among Jews the reputation of a haven. Arrested on several occasions for 'racial improprieties', Schindler bears a charmed life, buying and blackmailing himself out of trouble. As the Holocaust develops the Jews are gathered into vast labour camps; one such camp is at Plaszow, near Cracow. Knowing the intolerable conditions experienced by his Jewish employees in Plaszow, Schindler gains permis-

sion to build, at his own expense, a camp for them in the grounds of his Emalia factory. It becomes a relative paradise, Schindler devoting vast sums of money and practising all kinds of stratagems and subterfuges to build up its population. In 1944 Emalia is ordered disbanded and the workers scheduled for 'relocation' at the extermination camps of Gross-Rosen and Auschwitz. Schindler succeeds in having the factory, now committed to armaments, re-established at Brinnlitz in Moravia. He compiles a list of several thousand 'essential' workers; at a time when the crematoria of Auschwitz alone are consuming nine thousand victims a day it becomes a 'list of life'. In a supreme irony that immensely pleases Schindler, his new armament factory does not produce a single shell in the course of its existence. At the end of the war a bodyguard of Jewish ex-prisoners sees Schindler to safety in Switzerland. An international Jewish relief organization helps him settle on a farm in Argentina in 1949 but he returns to Germany in 1958. In 1961 he is welcomed ecstatically in Israel and declared a Righteous Person, a peculiarly Jewish honour extended to Gentiles. He is awarded the Cross of Merit by the West German government in 1966; by his own wish he is buried in Jerusalem.

Keneally's claim that the techniques of the novel are suited to the portrayal of a character of such ambiguity and events of such magnitude is validated in the work, which is a valuable contribution to the literature of the Holocaust.

SCHLUNKE, E.O. (ERIC OTTO) (1906–60), born Reefton, near Temora, NSW, lived most of his life on the family sheep and wheat property, Rosenthal, near Reefton. Schlunke's ancestors were among the group of German Lutheran settlers who came to Australia under the sponsorship of George Fife Angas and who settled mainly in the Barossa Valley of SA. An efficient and enterprising farmer, Schlunke was also a skilled writer of fiction. He published three collections of short stories, *The Man in the Silo* (1955), *The Village Hampden* (1958) and *Stories of the Riverina* (1965); the last, except for seven stories, is selected from the earlier collections. Schlunke wrote three novels, 'Rosenthal' and 'Foray on Freeling' both published serially in the *Sydney Morning Herald* in 1939, and 'Feather Your Nest' published serially in the *Bulletin* in 1954. A regionalist, Schlunke has captured in his fiction the essence of the Riverina and central-western NSW – its sunbleached expanses of wheat paddocks and sheep runs, red-brown soil, dusty townships and drily taciturn inhabitants, especially those of the old German extraction. Sardonically humorous and slyly debunking in the 'Steele Rudd' manner, Schlunke is also, in his later works, a social satirist. His notable humorous stories include 'The Cowboy from Town', 'Once a Sheep Stealer', 'The Man in the Silo' and 'The Enthusiastic Prisoner', the last one of several stories he wrote about Italian prisoners-of-war who worked as agricultural labourers in the Riverina in the Second World War. Schlunke liked to depict, as in 'Riding the Boom', 'Into My Parlour' and 'Sale of a Car Owner', the machinations of such archetypal city slickers as car salesmen, real estate agents and stockbrokers, who cheated the naive and seemingly slow-witted country folk. Beneath the ironic humour of his stories, a trace of seriousness is sometimes present, 'The Man Farther Out', for example, hinting in science-fiction style at the future problems inherent in the greedy mismanagement of the land. Schlunke's biographical novel, 'Rosenthal', has been highly commended. It tells of three generations of German-Australian farmers: Adolph Weismann, the pioneer ancestor who established Rosenthal, his son Karl and grandson Otto (Schlunke himself). It recounts their pioneer experiences, the traumas of the First World War which was an agonizing period for Germans in Australia, and their struggles to survive the boom-bust syndrome of the 1930s depression years. An authentic documentary of the effect of the rigorous creed of Lutheranism on the lives of those enmeshed in its rules and customs, 'Rosenthal' is also an absorbing study of childhood and schooling in the Australian outback. It glows, as does all Schlunke's writing, with affection for the landscape and the rural life. Schlunke's wife, Olga, lover of art, music and literature, published poems in the *Bulletin*.

Science Fiction (SF). Van Ikin concludes his introductory survey in *Australian Science Fiction* (1983) with the assessment that 'the Great Australian SF Novel is yet to be written'. For many readers and critics more basic questions are whether the terms 'Great Novel' and 'Science Fiction' are, in fact, compatible; whether SF has any place in the mainstream of literature; and, if it has, how is it to be defined, and what are its limits and extent. The 'inclusive' view, towards which majority opinion tends, accepts SF as a legitimate literary form, anticipates the ultimate birth of 'the Great Australian SF Novel', and is inclined to locate SF itself within the genre of fantasy literature.

One of the earliest Australian fantasy stories is the anonymously-authored 'Oo-a-deen', which appeared in the *Corio Chronicle and Western Districts Advertiser* (October 1847). Sated with the delights and vices of the old world, a young man comes to Australia, where he finds 'Ooadeen, the country of Mahanacumans . . . a country fair as the "land of promise" seen by the Hebrew Lawgiver from the top of Mount Pisgah'. His illicit romance with the beautiful Ooadeen maiden, Yarranee, leads to his banishment and he passes the rest of his life 'wedded in thought and memory to Ooadeen' but fails in all his efforts to find it again. 'Ooa-deen' represents one of the earliest appearances in Australian literature of the 'lost civilization' motif; confronted with this mysterious and unknown continent, writers fell to conjecturing about the possible existence in Australia's unexplored vastness of older civilizations and lost kingdoms. Speculation of mid-century became more pronounced in the final two decades of the nineteenth century, when the Lemurian legend gripped the imagination of writers the world over. 'Lemuria' had been used in the 1850s by C.L. Sclater to refer to a lost continent of prehistoric times extending from the coast of Africa to Malaysia and including Australia. Australian fantasies that embrace aspects of the Lemurian theme (white explorers, strange peoples, unknown regions and fabulous treasures) include John Boyle O'Reilly's *Moondyne* (1879), J.F. Hogan's *The Lost Explorer* (1890), Ernest Favenc's *'The Last of Six': Tales of the Austral Tropics* (1893) and *The Secret of the Australian Desert* (1896), W.H. Willshire's *A Thrilling Tale of Real Life in the Wilds of Australia* (1895), J.D. Hennessey's *An Australian Bush Track* (1896), G. Firth Scott's *The Last Lemurian* (1898), and Henry Grin's *The Adventures of Louis de Rougemont* (1899). Favenc, an explorer-writer, was particularly intrigued by the dimly-known, mysterious, tropical regions of Australia and viewed them with typical Lemurian romanticism. Firth Scott's novel discovers the lost civilization of Lemuria in the Australian desert; the two heroes, Dick Halwood and the lapsed English aristocrat, 'Yellow Hatter', trick Tor Ymmothe, queen of Lemuria, into allowing them to take a fortune in gold out of the kingdom but the 'Hatter' falls in love with the queen and seeks to return. Such stories, remote though they are from modern Science Fiction, carry occasional suggestions of advanced technical achievements, e.g. *The Last Lemurian* has a water-powered, artificial doorway guarding the entrance to the legendary kingdom.

A frequent component of the Lemurian legend is Utopianism. Fantasy literature itself is often Utopian-oriented; sometimes it depicts a Shangri-La existence in a newly-discovered paradise (as in 'Oo-a-deen'); sometimes the Utopia is the ordinary world turned into paradise by a sudden change in material fortunes, e.g. hidden treasure discovered. Robert E. Dudgeon's

Colymbia (1873), the earliest work of Australian SF published in book form, describes a Utopian submarine colony linked to a Pacific island. One of the first major works of Utopian SF actually set in Australia is Joseph Fraser's *Melbourne and Mars: My Mysterious Life on Two Planets* (1889). *Melbourne and Mars* is the story of Adam Jacobs, who comes to Australia in 1828 with his mother and convict father, has a successful business career, experiences the depression of the 1840s, and seeks to restore his fortune on the goldfields. In middle age he has persistent dreams of a second infancy and it is gradually revealed that he is living again in childhood in the Utopian civilization of the planet Mars, with its vastly superior social system. The Martian lifestyle is also presented in considerable technical detail e.g. people travel by a contraption resembling a flying fish which rises spirally and then progresses forward by giant sweeping strokes of its fins. Other Utopian-oriented works include S.A. Rosa's *The Coming Terror: A Romance of the Twentieth Century* (1894), in which a rebellious country overthrows its established authorities by the use of a poisonous gas ('Panmort') and enters into a period of Utopian prosperity; G. Read Murphy's *Beyond the Ice: Being a Story of the Newly Discovered Region round the North Pole* (1894), in which Dr Frank Farleigh, sole survivor of an Arctic expedition, is saved by members of a highly-advanced civilization in the 'Fregida' (North Pole) area and becomes indoctrinated in their ways; and W.H. Galier's *A Visit to Blestland* (1896) where a boatload of people is transported on a mysterious cloud to the planet, Blestland, where sectarian hatred and personal rivalry are non-existent.

Widely regarded as the first classic of Australian SF, Erle Cox's *Out of the Silence* (1925) is a work in which science and fantasy are in equal proportions. Alan Dundas discovers beneath his land the remnants of a highly advanced civilization, and the body, in suspended animation, of a beautiful woman, Earani. Restored to life, Earani reveals to Dundas the philosophy of her civilization and explains to him something of its ingenious gadgetry, e.g. death rays, light without heat, tablet meals, sophisticated and powerful eavesdropping devices. Although attracted to her, Dundas is appalled by the plans she unfolds to develop the world along the lines of controlled genetics. Ironically she is killed and civilization as we know it is saved by a primitive weapon (a knife) wielded by the most primitive of all passions (the jealousy of Dundas's jilted lover, Marian Seymour).

Although interplanetary travel is occasionally mentioned in earlier fiction, e.g. *A Woman of Mars* (1901) by 'Mary-Ann Moore-Bentley' and

The Germ Growers (1892) by Robert Potter, it is not until *Vandals of the Void* (1931) by J.M. Walsh ('H. Haverstock Hill') that Australian SF enters the era of spaceships, interplanetary alliances, battles in space and extra-terrestrial beings with weird physical characteristics and remarkable intellectual powers. In *Vandals of the Void*, legitimate space traffic is harassed by unknown enemies and the Interplanetary Guard is assigned to sort out the trouble. The Guards' own ships are attacked and some of the planets (Earth, Mars and Venus) are saved in an epic clash in the now-famous *Star Wars* fashion. Significant features of *Vandals of the Void* are the realistic scientific explanations of events and devices, e.g. robots and ray tubes, and the provision of a Buck Rogers type hero, Space Captain Sanders of the Interplanetary Guard. M. Barnard Eldershaw's *Tomorrow and Tomorrow* (1947), set in Australia in the twenty-fourth century illustrates the fact that literary craftsmanship rather than theme is the real prerequisite for literary acceptance. The book's chief character, Knarf, a writer of the twenty-fourth century, divides his attention between his own contemporary life and that of the early twentieth century, when the 'Australians', who had taken over from the first white 'Pioneers', had inherited the land from its original dwellers, the 'First People' (Aborigines). In Knarf's time, the errant Murrumbidgee of four hundred years earlier sits 'quiet and full between canal-like banks, tame and sure' and that fruitful land, once named 'Riverina', has been renamed the Tenth Commune. The interesting traditional aspect of the novel is its sophisticated twenty-fourth century perspective on present Australian history; its SF interest lies in the author's attempt to convey a picture of the Australian society of four hundred years. By mid-twentieth century SF was a recognizable literary commodity in Australia, with Ivan Southall's Simon Black series catering for a new generation of young SF fans and the Commonwealth Satellite Space Station stories of Frank Bryning accommodating older readers. Bryning's stories, given continuity by the presence of the female scientist, Dr Vivien Gale, and set in the twenty-first century, combine intriguing plots with highly-realistic scientific content.

In the decades 1940–60 American SF had only a limited impact in Australia. During the Second World War and through the 1950s, the Golden Age of American SF, there was, because of the dollar imbalance, an embargo on the importation of American publications into Australia which was not lifted until after 1960, by which time Australia had virtually missed out on the influence of that remarkable period of growth in the USA. It is from as late as 1975 that the current and continuing boom in Australian SF dates. In that year the 33rd Annual World SF Convention (Aussie Con) was held in Melbourne with American writer, Ursula Le Guin, as the central conference figure. The success of Aussie Con created a new climate for Australian SF; new publishing houses for SF sprang up, e.g. Norstrilia Press, Void Publications, while established presses such as the University of Queensland Press and Wild and Woolley showed increased interest; new SF magazines came into being, e.g. *Science Fiction: A Review of Speculative Literature*; writers' workshops were conducted which led to the emergence of new writers and anthologies of SF writing; and the Literature Board, which had helped fund Aussie Con, continued to give generous assistance to the publication of SF writing.

Established Australian SF writers include George Turner (q.v.), A. Bertram Chandler, Frank Bryning, Lee Harding (q.v.), Wynne Whiteford, Jack Wodhams, Damien Broderick (q.v.) and David J. Lake (q.v.). Talented new writers include Philippa Maddern, Bruce Gillespie, Van Ikin, Petrina Smith, David Grigg and John Alderson. Occasional venturers into SF, usually with conspicuous success, include mainstream writers Michael Wilding, Dal Stivens and Peter Carey. Film producer Peter Weir, with his provocative films, *The Cars That Ate Paris* (1974), *Picnic at Hanging Rock* (1975), and *The Last Wave* (1977), has also made a significant contribution in a different medium to Australian fantasy.

With William Noonan, George Turner is Australia's longest-established reviewer, critic and proponent of SF writing. He is also the creator of the SF trilogy, *Beloved Son* (1978), *Vaneglory* (1981) and *Yesterday's Men* (1982), novels that are set in the twenty-first century, after the holocaust. Turner eschews the 'apocalyptic' SF novel, 'with everybody slapped back to the caves and three-headed mutants springing up everywhere'. He uses instead the power of biological science and such forms of biowarfare as crop toxicity, defoliants, soil poisons and self-limiting insect plagues. Meticulously based on the most accurate, if speculative, science knowledge that research can produce, Turner's SF writing is also concerned to investigate the sociological implications of a science-dominated future and to probe the individual's situation in that future. Above all, he is concerned with literary standards; the SF novel should be 'a work of art, or at least of craftsmanship, in its own right'. A. Bertram Chandler, a writer of SF stories since the 1940s, is Australia's most prolific and successful writer in the traditional SF mould. Crammed with adventures on the outer rim of the galaxy Chandler's books are escapist excitement of high quality. His publications include *Rendezvous on a Lost World* (1961), *Beyond the Galactic Rim* (1963), *Into the Alternate Universe* (1964), *Space Mercenaries* (1965), *The Road to the Rim* (1967), *The Rim Gods* (1969), *Alternate Orbits* (1971) and *The Broken Cycle* (1975). One of his more unusual is the 'alternative history' fantasy of Australia, *Kelly Country* (1983), which considers what might have happened if Ned Kelly had won the siege of Glenrowan. Lee Harding, whose SF anthologies have stimulated interest in Australian SF, has written numerous novels including *A World of Shadows* (1975), *Future Sanctuary* (1976), *The Weeping Sky* (1977), *Displaced Person* (1979) and *The Web of Time* (1980). *Displaced Person*, which Harding describes as 'a schizophrenic fantasy' is a poignant story about adolescence. Teenager Graeme Drury gradually loses contact with the ordinary world around him and drifts away from family and friends into a dim, grey world, peopled only by others like himself. Its fine characterization and subtle fantasy won it the Alan Marshall Award for 1978. *The Weeping Sky*, a remarkably imaginative work, describes with brilliant visual detail the impact on a rather primitive society of the terrifying sight of the sky rent by a gaping, weeping wound. Damien Broderick (q.v.) wrote the fantasy, *The Dreaming Dragons* (1980, runner-up in the John W. Campbell Award for the best SF novel in the world) which posits a new prehistory of the human race; David J. Lake has published *Walkers on the Sky* (1976), *The Gods of Xuma* (1978), *The Fourth Hemisphere* (1980) and *The Man Who Loved Morlocks* (1981), the last being Lake's sequel to H.G. Wells's *The Time Machine*. Jack Wodham's *Future War* (1982) contains four unusual stories on the theme of the title; he is particularly acclaimed for the story, 'One Clay Foot'. Of the more mainstream writers, David Ireland's *A Woman of the Future* (1979) is largely fantasy while Stivens, Wilding and Carey have all dabbled, quite impressively, in fantasy, e.g. Carey's 'Report on the Shadow Industry', Wilding's 'The Man of Slow Feeling' and Stivens's 'The Gentle Basilisk'. Although the new SF writers discovered in recent SF workshops have not yet published substantially, their short stories have appeared in contemporary magazines and anthologies. Notable among them are Philippa Maddern's 'Inhabiting the Interspaces', 'Silence' and 'Wherever You Are'; Petrina Smith's 'In the Garden', 'They and They's' and 'Going Home'; John Alderson's 'The Sentient Ship'; Bruce Gillespie's 'A Laughing Stock' and 'Vegetable Love'; and David Grigg's, 'A Song before Sunset', 'Islands' and 'A Compassionate People'. Another emerging SF writer is Jenny Summerville whose children's SF work, *Shields of Trell*

(1984), was the 1983 *Australian*/Vogel Award winner.

Anthologies have probably done more to advance the cause of Australian SF than any individual writer or individual novel. The earliest significant anthologies are John Baxter's *The Pacific Book of Australian Science Fiction* (1968) and *The Second Pacific Book of Science Fiction* (1971). The Baxter anthologies contain stories by Harding, Bryning, Chandler, Wodhams and Broderick and by mainstream fiction writers Wilding, Olaf Ruhen, Douglas Stewart and George Johnston. Damien Broderick's *The Zeitgeist Machine* (1977) also includes fantasy fiction as distinct from pure SF in works by Wilding, Carey, Stivens, G.M. Glaskin and John Romeril. Paul Collins maintained the impetus from the 1975 Aussie Con with his Void Publications' four anthologies, *Other Worlds* (1978), *Envisaged Worlds* (1978), *Alien Worlds* (1979) and *Distant Worlds* (1981). Lee Harding combines stories from Australian and overseas writers in *Beyond Tomorrow* (1976) and *Rooms of Paradise* (1978); his best-known anthology, *The Altered I* (1976), contains the fruits of Ursula Le Guin's writers' workshop that followed Aussie Con. George Turner's anthology, *The View from the Edge* (1977) gathers together the stories and Turner's critical notes from a Monash University writers' workshop conducted by Turner, the American, Vonda McIntyre, and the English writer, Christopher Priest. In 1979 Rob Gerrand edited the anthology, *Transmutations*.

Australian SF magazines began in the 1950s with *Scientific Thriller* (1948–52), *Thrills Incorporated* (1950–52), *Future Science Fiction* (1953–55), *Popular Science Fiction* (1953–55) and *Science Fiction News* (1953–59). More substantial magazines of SF criticism and commentary began with John Bangsund's *Australian Science Fiction Review* (1966–69) which was nominated in 1967 to receive an award at the International Science Fiction Convention for the best amateur SF magazine of that year. Bangsund's magazine was incorporated into *Scythrop* 1969–71. *SF Commentary*, which began in January 1969, was collated by Harding, printed Bangsund and edited by Bruce Gillespie. *Science Fiction: A Review of Speculative Literature*, edited by Van Ikin, began in 1977, as did *The Cygnus Chronicler* edited by N.J. Angove.

The most complete account of Australian SF writing, with illustrative extracts, is *Australian Science Fiction*, edited and introduced by Van Ikin in the Portable Australian Authors series of the University of Queensland Press. Van Ikin gives a chronological survey of Australian SF and includes a bibliography. Other significant bibliographical works include S.L. Larnach, *Materials towards a Checklist of Australian Fantasy to 1938* (1950) and Graham Stone's *Australian Science Fiction Index 1925–1967* (1968).

Scobie, see **Young Man of Talent, A**

Scopp, see **Saturday Club Book of Poetry, The**

SCOTT, ANDREW GEORGE, see 'MOONLITE, CAPTAIN'

SCOTT, Sir **ERNEST** (1867–1939), born and educated in England (although he did not attend a university), worked as a journalist in London and in 1892 migrated to Australia, where he joined the staff of the Melbourne *Herald*. He was on the staff of the Victorian *Hansard* 1895–1901, and the Commonwealth *Hansard* 1901–13. In 1913, after the publication of his impressive histories, *Terre Napoléon* (1910) and *Lapérouse* (1913), he was appointed professor of history at the University of Melbourne, a position he held until 1936 when he retired as emeritus professor. His other publications include *The Life of Captain Matthew Flinders, R.N.* (1914), an important early history, *A Short History of Australia* (1916), *Men and Thought in Modern History* (1920), *History and Historical Problems* (1925) and *Australian Discovery* (1929). Scott also wrote *Australia during the War*, volume eleven of *The Official History of Australia in the War of 1914–1918* (1936). The Ernest Scott Prize, a triennial award, is granted to a scholar of Australian or NZ history.

SCOTT, MARIA J., born Maria Barney, wrote five semi-religious, sentimental and romantic novels which rely on such plot devices as substituted infants and mistaken identities and are rich in villains, usually lawyers, and saintly deaths, usually of children. They are *Annine* (1871), *Pearl and Willie* (1873), *A Many Coloured Bubble* (1874), *Not So Ugly* (1874) and *A Brother or Lover? A Sister or Bride? and the Lights and Shadows of Hazleglen* (n.d.). For her second, third and fifth novels Scott used the pseudonyms 'Mist' or 'M.I.S.T.'

SCOTT, PATRICIA ETHEL, see STONEHOUSE, PATRICIA ETHEL

SCOTT, ROSE (1847–1925), born Glendon, NSW, into a well-known Australian family, was the cousin of the book collector, David Scott Mitchell. She became involved in the women's suffrage movement in 1891 when she was appointed secretary of the Women's Suffrage League, and subsequently took a prominent part in the achievement of a number of reforms affecting women and children. President of the Women's Educational League 1902–10, Scott was also president of a local branch of the London Peace Society and international secretary of the National Council of Women of NSW, but her main influence derived from her wide circle of acquaintances, which included several leading politicians. She was also well-known to numerous Australian writers, including J.F. Archibald, Victor Daley, Henry Lawson, Louisa Lawson, Miles Franklin, A.B. Paterson, Bernard O'Dowd, E.J. Brady and Mary Gilmore. Scott wrote some verse and short stories, but had little time for literary creativity, although some of her illustrated limericks were published in the *Bulletin*. Miles Franklin contributed an account of her achievement in *The Peaceful Army* (1938), ed. Flora Eldershaw.

Scottish Martyrs was a name given to five men who, inspired by the French Revolution, became such strong advocates of parliamentary and constitutional reform that an alarmed British government subjected them to sedition trials in 1793–94 and had them transported to the infant colony of NSW. Thomas Muir (1765–99), Maurice Margarot (1745–1815), Thomas Fyshe Palmer (1747–1802) and William Skirving (?–1796) came out in the *Surprize* in 1794, and Joseph Gerrald (1760–96) arrived a year later. Although the Scottish Martyrs were well treated as political prisoners, only Margarot, who during his time in the colony was suspected both of being a government informer and of plotting rebellion, lived long enough to return to Britain. Of the others, Gerrald and Skirving died soon after arrival; Muir escaped in 1796 with the intention of making his way to America, but only reached France and died there of wounds received on the harrowing journey; and Palmer died enfeebled at Guam, en route home at the expiration of his sentence. The post-trial decline of the Scottish Martyrs meant that they made little contribution to transportation literature, although Palmer wrote an account of his and Skirving's ill treatment on board the *Surprize* after a trumped-charge of mutiny, which includes his reaction to NSW and was published in 1797 as *A Narrative of the Sufferings of T.F. Palmer, and W. Skirving, . . . on Board the Surprise Transport* (1797), and Muir wrote an account of his exile which was lost during his last years in Paris. In 1796, however, *The Telegraph: A Consolatory Epistle from Thomas Muir, Esq., of Botany Bay, to the Hon. Henry Erskine*, which was written, not by Muir but probably by a Scottish minister, George Hamilton, was published anonymously in Edinburgh. This poem, a satire relating mainly to Scottish university politics, has been claimed as the first separately-published, imaginative work set in the colony of NSW. Frank Clune wrote *The Scottish Martyrs* (1969).

'SCOTTY THE WRINKLER', see **MOUBRAY, PHILIP**

Script, Screen & Art, a monthly journal published in Sydney and concerned with film, television, art and the performing arts in Australia, began publication in 1968 and frequently includes interviews with or information on writers for the visual media.

'SCRIVENER, MARK', was a pseudonym of Marcus Clarke derived from 'Marcus Scrivener', the nickname given to Clarke by his schoolmate, Gerard Manley Hopkins.

Sea Cruise Books, see **BOLTON, KEN; COUANI, ANNA**

Sea Spray and Smoke Drift (1867) is the first collection of poems by Adam Lindsay Gordon (q.v.). The major poem of the collection is 'Ye Wearie Wayfarer'. There are several ballads, e.g. 'The Roll of the Kettledrum', and some melancholy personal poems in which Gordon regrets his youthful follies and wasted opportunities. 'Hippodromania', a poem in five parts, is an indication of the importance of horses and horse-racing both to Gordon and Australia.

SEARLE, JAMES (1938–), born Sydney, where he has practised as an architect, is the author of *The Lucky Streak* (1972), one of the plays performed at the first Jane Street Theatre season in 1966. Searle first wrote revue sketches for the Illawarra Theatre Guild and a pantomime, 'Aladdin', performed in the 1960s. His subsequent writing for theatre has included 'The First Theatre of Pollution Play' (1972), 'A Married Man' (1974) and 'The National Hero and the Daily Press'. *The Lucky Streak*, a working-class comedy set in a boarding house and dealing loosely with the subject of gambling, achieves subtle Pinteresque effects with well-worn situations and ostensibly stock characters.

Season at Sarsaparilla, The, a play by Patrick White (q.v.) first produced in 1962, was published in *Four Plays* (1965). The set is formed of the kitchens of three houses in Sarsaparilla (q.v.) belonging to the Knotts, a young couple expecting their first baby; the more affluent Pogsons, who have two daughters, Judy and Joyleen ('Pippy'); and the lower-class

Boyles. The hot weather, the imminent birth and a variety of mating rituals, echoed by the constant barking of dogs pursuing a bitch on heat, emphasize that this is the 'season' at Sarsaparilla. In the course of the play Mavis Knott has her baby; Judy Pogson rejects the romanticism of Roy Child, Mavis's brother, and accepts the 'loving-kindness' of Ron Suddards; Nola Boyle has an affair with her husband's mate; Pippy Pogson learns about life's cycle of birth, copulation and death; Roy Child abandons his teaching job for a life of adventure; and Julia Sheen kills herself after discovering she is pregnant to Mr Erbage, a local councillor. Only Girlie Pogson, for whom 'it's a man and a washing-machine that counts', remains untouched by the natural forces.

'**Secret Society of the Ring**' is one of several stories by 'Price Warung' (q.v.) about the Ring, a convict secret society which was supposed to have flourished on Norfolk Island in the 1840s; Marcus Clarke also wrote about the Ring, making Rufus Dawes one of its leaders in *His Natural Life* (1874). 'Secret Society of the Ring', originally published in the *Bulletin* in 1892, centres on the attempt by Captain Alexander Maconochie (q.v.) to weaken the power of the Ring by showing a kindness uncharacteristic of Norfolk Island commandants towards the convicts. The attempt fails when Reynell, an incorrigible convict and Ring member who has been won over by Maconochie, is condemned to death by the secret society at one of its ceremonies. The warrant to execute Reynell is given to one of his mates, Bill Felix; although Felix provokes a sentry into shooting him, his sacrifice is in vain because Reynell, who has been placed in solitary confinement by Maconochie when he learns of the sentence passed by the Ring, commits suicide before hearing news of Felix's death.

Seed, see **COWAN, PETER**

Seedtime, see *Golconda* Trilogy

Selected Poems of Henry Lawson (1918), the major edition of Henry Lawson's (q.v.) poems published during his lifetime, was the idea of the publisher, George Robertson (2). Lawson and Robertson worked together on the volume in 1917, when a number of Lawson's best-known poems, e.g. 'Black Bonnet' (q.v.), 'One-Hundred-and-Three' and 'Faces in the Street', were extensively revised. Before *Selected Poems* appeared, however, David McKee Wright (q.v.), who wrote a preface to the volume and gave it a favourable review in the *Bulletin*, made numerous further emendations which did more

harm than good to Lawson's reputation as a poet.

Selection, or **Free Selection**, were terms which after 1860 particularly referred to the choosing of a portion of land for farming purposes; the land so chosen eventually came to be called a 'selection' and the person working it a 'selector' or 'free selector'. Selection was an attempt at land reform: the extent of the squatters' (q.v.) monopoly over land tenure in Australia can be measured by the fact that in 1860 4000 squatters controlled under lease or licence 160 million acres of land from the Darling Downs in Queensland through NSW and western Victoria up to the northern part of SA, paying an average of less than a farthing an acre in rent for their runs. Agitation to 'unlock the lands' to allow greater opportunities for small scale farming grew in the 1850s, and Selection Acts to achieve these ends were passed in all the Australian colonies 1858–72; the most famous were the two Acts finally shepherded through the NSW parliament by Sir John Robertson in 1861. Essentially, the Selection Acts allowed anyone to select in designated areas a block of crown land for agricultural purposes. The size of the selection permitted varied in different colonies within limits of forty and 640 acres (16.19 and 259 hectares), as did the provisions regarding price, usually £1 per acre; method of payment; selection before or after land had been surveyed; and requirements for residence and improvements. The Selection Acts led to bitter conflict between the selectors and the squatters, who adopted various practices to strengthen their hold on the land. Two of the most prevalent were 'dummying', the employment of people to select land and then hand it over after the title was complete, as practised by Barefooted Bob in *Such is Life* (1903); and 'peacocking', the selection of choice pieces of land, for example around water, so that adjoining land was useless. In general, the selection experiment, which owed something to agrarian Utopianism, was a failure. The attempt to establish a yeomanry succeeded best in SA, but squatting interests remained entrenched in Queensland and parts of Victoria, even though in both colonies, as elsewhere, the pastoralists lost political ground. The selectors were hampered by their own ignorance and inexperience and by the vagaries of soil, climate and geography; many of them became 'cockatoo' (q.v.) farmers, barely scratching a living from the land, despised by squatters and itinerant bush workers alike, and exploited by storekeepers and middle men. An additional effect was the exacerbation of rural class tensions. The bushranging activities of Ned Kelly (q.v.), for example, can be linked with the oppression felt by selectors in north-eastern Victoria in the 1870s.

Selection has been a significant theme in Australian literature. Several Australian writers, notably 'Steele Rudd', Henry Lawson and Mary Fullerton, were from selector families; others, including Joseph Furphy and George Essex Evans, had unsuccessful stints working selections, and Barbara Baynton's first marriage was to a selector. The most extensive treatment of the experiences of the selectors occurs in 'Steele Rudd''s *On Our Selection* (1899) and other volumes in which he drew on his own experiences as he chronicled the fortunes of the Rudd family (q.v.). The selectors' grim struggle for survival, as depicted in the early Rudd books, is also mirrored in some of the stories and poems of Lawson, e.g. ' "Water Them Geraniums" ' and 'A Day on a Selection', and stories of Baynton, e.g. 'Bush Church' and 'The Chosen Vessel'. The conflict between selector and squatter is the subject of Lawson's story, 'The Bush Fire', and is featured in some of Rosa Praed's station romances; in other novels, e.g. Anthony Trollope's *Harry Heathcote of Gangoil* (1874), E.S. Sorenson's *The Squatter's Ward* (1908), and Albert Dorrington's *Children of the Cloven Hoof* (1911); in T.E. Spencer's poem, 'Moods of the Bush', and in several folk-songs, e.g. 'The Eumerella Shore' (q.v.). Among other Australian writers on the selection theme are Mary Fullerton, in poems like 'The Selector's Daughter' and in the autobiographical *Bark House Days* (1921); W.H. Traill, who established a reputation as an investigative journalist when he probed dummying on the Darling Downs in 1874 and later wrote digests of Selection Acts for the Queensland government; the balladists Will Ogilvie in 'Abandoned Selections' and A.B. Paterson in the poem 'The Free Selector's Daughter'; M. Broda Reynolds in two novels, *The Selector Girl* (1917) and *Dawn Asper* (1918); Sumner Locke (q.v.), in her sketches of Mum Dawson, and Henry Fletcher in his Wayback (q.v.) family series, which both show the influence of 'Rudd'; and Frank Dalby Davison in *Forever Morning* (1931). A fine painting by Arthur Streeton, *The Selector's Hut (Whelan on the Log)* (1890), captures the atmosphere of the selection.

SEMMLER, CLEMENT (1914–), born Mercunda, SA, joined the ABC in 1942 and worked mainly in the programmes area; he was deputy general manager 1965–77. A well-known book reviewer, he has written three studies of A.B. Paterson, of which the most significant is the biography, *The Banjo of the Bush* (1966), and has compiled a collection of Paterson's writing, *The World of 'Banjo' Pater-*son (1967). He has also written a study of Douglas Stewart (1974), and monographs on Kenneth Slessor (1966) and Barcroft Boake (1965); has published two collections of his essays, *For the Uncanny Man* (1963) and *The Art of Brian James* (1972); edited two collections of literary and cultural essays, *Twentieth Century Australian Literary Criticism* (1967) and, with Derek Whitelock, *Literary Australia* (1966); edited a collection of short stories by E.O. Schlunke, *Stories of the Riverina* (1965), a controversial account of the ABC, *The ABC – Aunt Sally and Sacred Cow* (1981), and a collection of writing by Frank Hardy, *A Frank Hardy Swag* (1982). In 1965 he was awarded an honorary D. Litt. by the University of New England.

Semper Floreat, a student magazine of the University of Queensland, began publication in 1932 and has frequently included original literary contributions and articles on Australian literature.

'**Send Round the Hat**', a story by Henry Lawson (q.v.) included in *Children of the Bush* (1902), is a celebration of mateship (q.v.). Set in Bourke, where Lawson worked some months in 1892, it focuses on 'The Giraffe', Bob Brothers, a Victorian shearer whose kindness leads him regularly to send round his hat collecting for those in distress. Among the bush workers who are 'touched' by the Giraffe are Jack Mitchell, Lawson himself, Barcoo Rot, One-Eyed Bogan and Jack Moonlight, who at the end of the story send round the hat among themselves when they learn the Giraffe is leaving Bourke to get married. Other *Children of the Bush* stories in which these characters are grouped in Bourke are 'That Pretty Girl in the Army' and ' "Lord Douglas" '.

Sentimental Bloke, see *Songs of a Sentimental Bloke, The*

'**September in Australia**', a well-known Henry Kendall (q.v.) lyric poem was published in *Leaves from Australian Forests* in 1869. The poem celebrates, in a riot of alliterative musical phrases, the coming of the Australian spring.

Serials in Australian Libraries: Social Sciences and Humanities (SALSSAH), published in four volumes by the National Library of Australia (1968–74), lists locations and holdings of periodicals in Australian libraries. It is updated by the monthly publication, *Newly Reported Titles* (1974–).

SERLE, GEOFFREY (1922–), born Melbourne, son of Percival Serle, has taught history at the University of Melbourne and Monash University. He has written two influential histories of Victoria, *The Golden Age* (1963) and *The Rush to be Rich* (1971); a history of high culture in Australia, *From Deserts the Prophets Come* (1973); and *John Monash: A Biography* (1982) which won the *Age* Book of the Year Award, the Con Weickhardt and Wilke Awards and first prize in the National Book Council awards. Joint general editor for part of the *ADB* (q.v.) he has also edited the journals, *Historical Studies* and the *La Trobe Library Journal* and co-edited, with Alan Davies, *Policies for Progress* (1954).

SERLE, PERCIVAL (1871–1951), born Elsternwick, Victoria, worked for twenty years in a life assurance office before becoming chief clerk and accountant at the University of Melbourne. Moderately successful with investments, he was able to retire in 1920 to pursue his cultural interests, although he ran a second-hand bookshop in the Eastern Market, Melbourne, in the depression years 1931–36. He was guide-lecturer at the National Galley of Victoria 1929–38, curator of the Art Museum of the National Gallery in Melbourne 1934–36, and member of the council of the Victorian Artists' Society for many years. He was also president of the Australia Literature Society 1944–46. Serle's first publication was an edition, with notes, of *A Song to David and Other Poems* (1923) by Christopher Smart, a minor eighteenth-century English poet. Serle's meticulous scholarship is evident in *A Bibliography of Australasian Poetry and Verse: Australia and New Zealand* (1925), a much-needed reference work of Australian literature at that time, to which later bibliographies were indebted. To complement his *Bibliography* he published, in collaboration with 'Furnley Maurice' and R.H. Croll, *An Australasian Anthology* (1927), a standard Australian literary work not supplanted until after the Second World War. His most significant work, laboured over for almost twenty years, was his *Dictionary of Australian Biography* (1949). It comprises more than a thousand biographical sketches of prominent Australians or people connected closely with Australia. In 1944 Serle edited the poems of 'Furnley Maurice' and in 1951 published *A Primer of Collecting*. Serle brought to all his literary work a rigorous sense of, and passion for, scholarship. A commemorative number of *Southerly* was published in 1953.

Settlers and Convicts: Or, Recollections of Sixteen Years' Labour in the Australian Backwoods, a fictional-factual account of life in the colony of NSW, in the emigrant handbook genre, by Alexander Harris (q.v.), was published in 1847 under the pseudonym, 'An Emigrant Mechanic'. The book is a lively and informative account of sixteen years of colonial adventuring. It is filled with stories of brushes with bushrangers, Aborigines, convicts, colonial police, cattle stealers, greedy squatters, and the denizens of Sydney's Rocks area. The 'mechanic' begins as a carpenter in the Five Island territory (Illa Warra), then becomes a sawyer and cedar cutter, first around the Hawkesbury River, later as far north as the Manning River. His attempts to join the squatter ranks leads him to the 'Australian prairies' of near-western and south-eastern NSW, where he discovers a good run, 'a fine tract of flats of good grass, open timbered, and stretching a good mile and a half along a creek side'. After marriage, parenthood and years of the routine but never dull life of a far-out station, the mechanic returns to England.

The book seriously examines the main problems of colonial life, commenting on land regulations, the iniquities of the convict system, the moral and religious needs of the population, and the mishandling of the Aboriginal situation (see Aboriginal in Australian Literature). It includes advice and guidance for potential emigrants, ranging from the best method of becoming a squatter to the provisioning of an up-country station. The striking quality of the landscape is expansively described, and there are graphic accounts of the perennial hazards of colonial life: bushfires, floods, snakes, attacks by blacks, and getting lost in the vastness of the bush.

Seven Little Australians, a children's novel by Ethel Turner (q.v.) was first published in 1894. The novel centres on the Woolcott family, who live in a large, rambling house on the Parramatta River, nicknamed Misrule. The family comprises Captain Woolcott, his second wife Esther and seven children who range from babyhood to early adolescence, Meg, Pip, Judy, Nell, Bunty, Baby and Esther's baby, the General. Mischievous and imaginative, the children easily influence their young stepmother and are nearly always a match for their earnest, well-meaning but stern father, whether they are engaged in daring adventures or unwisely attempting to be good. After a particularly embarrassing incident involving Pip and the adventurous, high-spirited Judy, arrangements are made for Judy to go to boarding school. While Judy is away, her elder sister Meg indulges her adolescent fantasies, making Herculean efforts to be beautiful and tight-lacing her waist. Influenced by her more sophisticated friend, Aldith MacCarfy, she half-encourages the attentions of a neighbouring young man, Andrew Courtney, although she prefers his brother Alan. She is led unwittingly into a compromising situation, which is complicated by her use of the unreliable six-year-old Bunty as messenger. Alan substitutes himself for Andrew but realizes her innocence and later becomes firmly attached to her. When Bunty lames one of his father's horses with a cricket ball, he hides in a disused shed, where to his amazement he meets Judy, who has escaped from school, walking the seventy-mile distance home. The children conceal her presence, stealing food and furniture from the house, until Bunty, under the stress of a particularly severe whipping from his father, blurts out their secret. Captain Woolcott's anger is disarmed by his discovery that Judy's lungs have been affected and she is taken home to be carefully nursed. To help her recovery, it is arranged that Esther and the children will visit Esther's parents at their station, Yarrahappini. There they enjoy the excitements of bush life and make the acquaintance of Mr Gillet, an exiled Englishman prone to episodes of alcoholism. Meg's mixed relationship with Mr Gillet contributes to her maturing. When Esther attends a ball the children are taken by bullock-cart to a picnic ground fourteen miles away and there Judy saves the baby, the General, from a falling tree but suffers a broken back. While Pip goes to get a doctor ten miles away and Mr Gillet returns home for help, Meg comforts the suffering, dying Judy. Her death deeply affects her family, although life eventually resumes an outward normality. Frequently reprinted, *Seven Little Australians* was produced as an ABC television serial in 1975.

Seven Poor Men of Sydney, a novel by Christina Stead (q.v.), was published in 1934. Set in Sydney in the 1920s, it deals with the experiences of a group of people which includes the printers, Joseph Baguenault, Tom Withers, Baruch Mendelssohn; their employer, Gregory Chamberlain; Michael Baguenault, an emotionally disturbed returned soldier; Tom Winter, a librarian; and Kol Blount, a paralysed youth. The other important characters are Catherine Baguenault, Michael's half-sister, and Fulke and Marion Folliot, bourgeois intellectuals and social reformers. Linked generally tenuously by work, friendship, interests, love or family, they are mostly alike in their oppression by poverty and their final defeat. Unconventional in structure, with little in the way of plot and few dramatic incidents, the novel is shaped by its concentration on the diverse emotional lives of its protagonists. Although the inner landscape is more important than the outer, both are expressed with poetic intensity and cumulative, impressionistic effect. The most striking individuals are the idealistic, introspective rebels and half-lovers, Michael and Catherine, whose emotional struggles end in suicide for Michael and incarceration in a mental home for Catherine. The intellectual Baruch Mendelssohn is the wisest and most balanced of the group, although he is merely one of the refracted responses to experience explored by the author and by no means her representative. At the opposite extreme to Michael and Catherine stands Joseph, their dull, unimaginative but dependable cousin, who finds a limited salvation in domesticity. Others, like Winter and the Folliots, find refuge in simplistic ideologies, or like Withers in business schemes and feuds. Kol Blount, the cripple, expresses both in his person and his moving 'In Memoriam' the frustrations and limitations of their inimical world.

SEWELL, STEPHEN (1953–), born Sydney, wrote the plays, *The Father We Loved on a Beach by the Sea*, first produced in 1978 and included in *Three Political Plays*, ed. Alrene Sykes (1980), *Traitors* (1983) first produced in Melbourne in 1979 and in London in 1980, *Welcome the Bright World* (1983) and *The Blind Giant Is Dancing* (1983). *The Father We Loved on a Beach by the Sea* contrasts a father who helplessly submits to a coercive political system and his two sons who fiercely rebel against it; both alternatives prove to have destructive effects. *Traitors*, set in Leningrad in 1927, concerns the experiences of a group of ordinary people, although its theme is the collapse of the communist ideal in the face of Stalinism. *Welcome the Bright World* concerns conflict within the family group, community and State. *The Blind Giant Is Dancing* traces the moral decay of an erstwhile man of principle through the corrupting influence of power politics. A deep, even sombre, dramatist, Sewell portrays modern man against a universal rather than a local background. He has no specific political affiliations, although his plays reflect his conviction that 'everything has a political dimension, even the family'.

SEYMOUR, ALAN (1927–), was born in Perth, and from the age of ten was brought up by his sister after the death of his parents. Educated at state schools in Perth, he spent some time as a freelance film and theatre critic in Sydney, worked for the ABC in the late 1940s and 1950s and directed operas for the Sydney Opera Group 1953–57. Since 1961 he has lived overseas, mostly in London, where he was theatre critic for *London Magazine* 1963–65. More recently he has lived in Turkey, which has led to a new play dealing with modern Turkish politics and an adaptation for the stage of *The Wind from the Plain* by the

Seymour, Alan

Turkish novelist, Yashar Kemal. A cosmopolitan and experimental playwright in the main, he has written 'Swamp Creatures' (1958), *The One Day of the Year* (q.v., 1960, published 1962), 'The Gaiety of Nations' (1965), 'A Break in the Music' (1966), 'The Pope and the Pill' (1968–69), 'The Shattering' (1973) and 'The Float' (1980). He has also written a novel, *The Coming Self-Destruction of the United States of America* (1969), and a novel-adaptation of his play, *The One Day of the Year* (1967); two radio plays, 'A Winter Passion' (1960) and 'Donny Johnson' (1965); and several television plays, 'The Runner' (1962), 'Lean Liberty' (1962), 'Auto-Stop' (1964), 'And It Wasn't Just the Feathers' (1964), 'The Trial and Torture of Sir John Rampayne' (1965) and 'Stockbrokers Are Smashing but Banks Are Better' (1965).

'Swamp Creatures', which was a finalist in the first Sydney Journalists' Club Competition and won recognition in the London *Observer* competition of 1957, has a macabre, compelling atmosphere, reminiscent of Tennessee Williams; ostensibly about two middle-aged sisters, one of whom is engaged in unnatural monster-producing experiments, the play expresses common fears of a future nuclear disaster. The play for which Seymour is best known in Australia, *The One Day of the Year*, is the least typical of his work; rejected by the Adelaide Festival's board of governors in 1959 on the grounds that its treatment of Anzac Day, the servicemen's national day of commemoration, might give offence to such groups as the RSL, it was first staged by an amateur organization, the Adelaide Theatre Group, in 1960. In 1961 it was given a professional production in Sydney, supported by the Australian Elizabethan Theatre Trust. Performed in London the same year and subsequently widely staged in Australia, the play has become almost as well known as Ray Lawler's *Summer of the Seventeenth Doll* (1957) and is popular as a school and university text. The subject of the play is not so much Anzac Day as the familiar antagonisms between generations, exacerbated in this instance by rapid social change and disparity in education. Seymour explores the opposing points of view of digger-father and university-educated son with sensitivity and insight, developing especially the pathos of the father's situation and breaking new ground in his energetic exploitation of the Australian vernacular and the inadequacies of the ocker/digger stereotype.

Of Seymour's other plays, 'Swamp Creatures', 'Donny Johnson' and 'A Break in the Music' are ostensibly set in Australia, although the first two could be set anywhere. 'Donny Johnson', winner of the 1960 Sydney Journalists' Club competition, deals with the typical experiences of a pop singer; 'A Break in the Music' draws on Seymour's family memories of Australian life in the 1930s and 1940s. Political subjects have also interested him: 'The Gaiety of Nations' has the Vietnam war as its subject, and *The Coming Self-Destruction of the United States of America* deals with American race relations. His other stage and television plays range over a wide number of countries and situations.

Shabbytown Calendar (1975), by Thomas Shapcott (q.v.), with cover design and illustrations based on the paintings of Charles Blackman, is a series of twelve sequences of poems, one for each month of the year. 'Shabbytown' is Ipswich, the Queensland city where Shapcott spent much of his early life. The poems reflect, with gentle irony for the most part but sometimes with acerbity, the barrenness of provincial life. Symbols of that barrenness range from events such as church socials, engagement parties and service club activities, to local identities such as retired schoolmasters, salesmen and shopkeepers. Victims of it include Tommy Jennings who commits suicide and the anonymous housewife who every day buys groceries, lingerie, books and magazines — 'something that might alter the world'. Shapcott also reflects on Shabbytown's influence on his own personality and character and sees the dramatic tropical climate as a factor in the eccentricity of the inhabitants' behaviour. The series contains brief memorial poems to Francis Webb and Michael Dransfield.

Shakespeare and Australia. Although there are no references to Terra Australis in Shakespeare's plays, though there are to the Antipodes (q.v.), the playwright has been enormously significant in the cultural history of Australia; indeed Shakespeare was one of the names considered for the new national capital after the creation of the Commonwealth of Australia. The first recorded performance of a Shakespearean play (*Henry IV*) took place in Sydney in 1800, and as a professional theatre developed in NSW and the other colonies from the 1830s, Shakespeare's plays were intermittently performed at benefits or other special performances in the theatres, like Barnett Levey's Theatre Royal in Sydney, that catered mainly for the melodramas, comedies and farces imported from London. Auctioneers' and booksellers' catalogues from the 1820s onwards attest to the popularity of editions of Shakespeare, and in the same decade Edward Smith Hall, like many subsequent Australian newspaper proprietors, adopted Othello's 'Nothing extenuate,/Nor set down aught in malice', as a motto for his *Sydney Monitor*.

620

Most early significant Shakespearean performers, such as Conrad Knowles, Australia's first Hamlet, and Eliza Winstanley, a notable early Lady Macbeth who went on to successes in England and America, were immigrant amateurs without prior theatrical training. One of Knowles's contemporaries, however, Joseph Simmons, claimed prior English experience and in the 1840s a steady stream of English provincial actors and actresses started to flow into the colonies, including Francis Nesbitt in 1842 and George Selth Coppin (q.v.) the following year. Coppin's main stage reputation was as a comic actor, but as an entrepreneur and manager he was prominent in arranging, particularly in the decades following the discovery of gold, the theatrical tours by American, English and other overseas performers which remained a distinctive feature of Australian theatrical history well into the twentieth century. The repertoires of these performers were by no means always focused on or even included Shakespeare, but among the established Shakespearean performers Coppin was instrumental in bringing out were G.V. Brooke in 1855, Charles and Ellen Kean (q.v.) in 1863, and Alfred Dampier (q.v.) in 1873. Other notable touring actors and actresses who presented Shakespearean programmes were Edwin Thomas Booth and Laura Keene in 1854, Barry Sullivan (q.v., arrived 1862), Charles John Mathews (1870), and George Rignold (1876). Arrivals in the twentieth century have included Oscar Asche (1909); the Old Vic with Laurence Olivier and Vivien Leigh in *Richard III* (1948) and with Robert Helpmann and Katharine Hepburn in *The Taming of the Shrew* (1955); the Shakespeare Memorial Theatre in 1950 and 1953, headed by Anthony Quayle; and its successor, the Royal Shakespeare Company, with Peter Brook's *A Midsummer Night's Dream* in 1973. Helpmann and Asche, who carried a pocket edition of Shakespeare in his swag while roaming southern NSW for some months in the 1880s, were Australian-born performers who had won a reputation overseas. Similarly, Keith Michell and Leo McKern, who both toured with Quayle, established Shakespearean reputations in England, while other actors such as Ron Haddrick and John Bell had seasons at Stratford before returning to Australia.

Many of the Shakespearean performers who visited Australia left reminiscences of their travels, e.g. Daniel Edward Bandmann's *An Actor's Tour: Or, Seventy Thousand Miles with Shakespeare* (1885) and several remained to play a significant part in Australian theatrical history, including influencing acting styles. Brooke (1855–61) and Sullivan (1862–66) had long tours encompassing several seasons and some experience in management. Brooke's leading

lady, Fanny Cathcart (q.v.), settled and matured as an actress in Australia, encouraged her brother James Cathcart to visit, and married George Darrell, who thought his melodrama, *The Sunny South*, inferior only to *Hamlet*. Alfred Dampier retained, like James Cathcart, a reputation as a Shakespearean actor even though some of his energies were directed towards adapting, producing and performing Australian material. Perhaps most significant of all was George Rignold (George Richard Rignall, 1839–1912), whose presentation of *Henry V* in 1876 (twenty-four performances) was the first long run of a Shakespearean play in Australia. After later tours of Australasia and America he was based from 1887 in Sydney, where he was a partner in Her Majesty's Theatre in 1887–95, alternated Shakespeare with melodrama and flew Henry V's standard whenever in residence at his Middle Harbour home.

Touring performers, however, have visited not only capital cities, nor have Shakespearean companies only come from overseas. Numerous reminiscences of Australians attest to Shakespearean performances in small country towns: William Walker, for example, records in his *Reminiscences* (1890) a performance of *Othello* at Windsor around 1850 when an actor named Kemble (possibly the same Henry Kemble who had vegetables and other food thrown at him by enraged audiences in Hobart in 1859) painted one side of his face black and alternated his profile to play both Othello and Iago. Towards the end of the century Dan Barry (q.v.) was a legendary outback manager who murdered Shakespeare most touring Saturday nights, and W.J. Holloway ran an Australian Shakespeare company, which starred the colonial-born actress, Essie Jenyns (1865–1920). Later still, Alan Wilkie (1878–1970), who had previously toured extensively in England and India, arrived in Australia in 1916 and in 1920 formed a Shakespeare company which toured almost non-stop in 1920–26, playing an estimated 1200 performances all over Australia. Wilkie's leading lady, Lorna Forbes, has been judged by Hal Porter as Australia's 'greatest stay-at-home' Shakespearean actress. In 1951 John Alden (1908–62), born Taree, NSW, began a decade's regular touring with a Shakespearean company. In 1958 the Young Elizabethan Players, attached to the Australian Elizabethan Theatre Trust in Sydney, and later to the Melbourne Theatre Company, began bringing Shakespeare to thousands of city and country children. These schools' companies had a home base in organizations which have also included Shakespeare in their repertoires. Similarly, in contemporary times Shakespearean plays form part of the repertoires of regional professional companies and a variety of amateur dramatic organizations. Some of the professional companies, e.g. Nimrod in Sydney, have developed a strong tradition in Shakespeare.

From early colonial days, performances of Shakespeare attracted the newspaper reviews and journal articles that are an important primary source for Australian theatre historians. A notable example of a controversial performance was Walter Montgomery's interpretation of Hamlet in 1867, which led to a spirited correspondence in the Melbourne press. *The Hamlet Controversy: Was Hamlet Mad?* (1867) reprinted the comments of David Blair, Charles Bright, R.H. Horne, Sir Archibald Michie, J.E. Neild and James Smith. All contributed to the intellectual life of Melbourne in the second half of the nineteenth century, but Neild and Smith in particular had long careers as dramatic critics and wrote some of the best Australian theatre reviews. With Blair and others they also helped in 1884 to found the Melbourne Shakespeare Society, which claimed at one time to be the largest in the world, fostered the reading and study of Shakespeare, and sponsored prizes such as an annual essay prize which Mary Grant Bruce won three times. In Sydney the Shakespeare Society of NSW was in existence 1900–?36, and published a *Shakespeare Quarterly* in 1922–24. A second Shakespearean journal was the *University Shakespeare Journal*, which was associated with the University of Adelaide's Shakespeare Society and published briefly in 1886–87; the same society also published its annual *Proceedings* for at least a decade either side of 1900. A Shakespeare Society was formed in Brisbane in 1919 and in Tasmania in the 1930s, while even a country town such as Wagga Wagga could boast in 1895 of a Shakespeare Society and in 1922 of a Shakespeare Club.

If the reviews of Shakespearean productions form part of the extensive history of Shakespearean performance in Australia, they also form part of an extensive body of Australian writing about the playwright and his work. The list of books includes editions of the plays, biographical, textual and critical studies, and bibliographies; it extends from William a Beckett's *Lectures on the Poets and Poetry of Great Britian* (1839), which had a Shakespearean component, to contemporary works published both in Australia and overseas. Among editions of the plays, the most significant are perhaps Rignold's acting arrangements of several of the plays published between 1876 and 1879; the Australasian Shakespeare, a series of seven plays published 1916–20, each edited by a different academic or educationist, including J. le Gay Brereton, A.T. Strong, T.G. Tucker and Walter Murdoch; other school series such as Oxford University Press's Austra-

lian Students' Shakespeare, General Editor J.J. Stable and the Australasian Students' Shakespeare (1936–37, edited by Murdoch and Albert Booth Taylor); the Challis Shakespeare, a series under the general editorship of G.A. Wilkes and A.P. Riemer, which began publication in 1980; and the contributions by Australians to notable series of the plays published elsewhere, such as the editions for the Arden Shakespeare (*Timon of Athens*, 1959, *The Merry Wives of Windsor*, 1971) and the New Penguin Shakespeare (*As You Like It*, 1968) by H.J. Oliver (1916–82). Among textual studies, the most important is *Stolne and Surreptitious Copies* (1942) by Alfred Hart (1870–1950), an American-born scientist and educationist who arrived in Melbourne in 1879 and was active in the Melbourne Shakespeare Society. *Stolne and Surreptitious Copies*, written in isolation from libraries and scholars overseas, although it won recognition there, is a study of the provenance of the 'bad' quartos, the pirated editions of single Shakespearean plays published before the famous First Folio of 1623. Two hundred and thirty-odd copies of the First Folio survive, one of them in the State Library of NSW's Shakespeare Tercentenary Memorial Library of Shakespeare material. The library was opened in 1923 to commemorate the tercentenary of Shakespeare's death; the quatercentenary of his birth in 1964 occasioned displays and exhibitions in libraries throughout Australia. An early bibliography, Percy Joseph Marks's *Australasian Shakespeareana* (1915), lists Australian and NZ books, journals, articles, pamphlets on and references to Shakespeare up to 1913.

There have been many biographical, critical and other studies, apart from the contributions to Australian and overseas academic journals and the addresses and lectures to Shakespeare and other literary societies. In the nineteenth and early twentieth centuries most of the Australian books on Shakespeare were by amateur scholars: doctors, clergymen, public servants, journalists, educationists, businessmen. Several focused on the authorship question, including Hugh Junor Browne, who in *The Grand Reality* (1888) presented Shakespeare's experiences in spirit life as received by a Melbourne medium and in *The Baconian Authorship of Shakespeare's Plays Refuted* (1898) gave an account of an interview with Shakespeare in which the playwright told how he had written the plays while under spirit control. The comic balladist, W.T. Goodge in *Hits! Skits! and Jingles!* (1899), reached the same conclusion more succinctly ('Who Wrote the Shakespere Plays'):

> Shakespere's the author, I'll vow,
> And nothing my faith can be shakin',
> For it would be ridiculous, now,
> If we talked about 'Lamb's Tales of Bacon'.

Other studies published in this period included the politician Sir Josiah Henry Symon's *Shakespeare Quotation* (1901) and *Shakespeare at Home* (1905), both included in his *Shakespeare the Englishman* (1929); the drama critic Austin Brereton's *Romeo and Juliet on the Stage (1662–1890)* (1890); the historian and public servant G.W. Rusden's *William Shakespeare: His Life, His Works and His Teaching* (1903); the politician Henry Gullett's *The Making of Shakespeare and Other Papers* (1905); *Shakespeare's Plays* (?1908–09) by the journalist E.H.C. Oliphant (1862–1936), who later taught Elizabethan literature in the USA; and *The True Text of Shakespeare and His Fellow Playwrights* (1923) by the businessman and philanthropist, Thomas Donovan (1843–1929), who also edited Shakespeare and presented his extensive Elizabethan library to the University of Sydney. Increasingly, however, and notwithstanding Hart's *Stolne and Surreptitious Copies*, his earlier *Shakespeare and the Homilies* (1934) and the contributions to Shakespearean studies of Eric Partridge, the major studies have come from Australian universities, many of them by academics who settled in Australia or studied overseas. A notable early example was *Shakespeare's Roman Plays and Their Background* (1910) by Sir Mungo MacCallum (q.v.) who developed the University of Sydney's tradition in Shakespearean and Elizabethan studies. Subsequent works include E.H. Sugden's *A Topographical Dictionary to the Works of Shakespeare and His Fellow Dramatists* (1925); Cowling's *A Preface to Shakespeare* (1925); A.J.A. Waldock's *Hamlet: A Study in Critical Method* (1931); J. le Gay Brereton's *Writings on Elizabethan Drama* (1948); D.R.C. Marsh's *The Recurring Miracle* (1962), *Shakespeare's 'Hamlet'* (1970) and *Passion Lends Them Power* (1976); A.P. Riemer's *A Reading of Shakespeare's 'Antony and Cleopatra'* (1968) and *Antic Fables: Patterns of Evasion in Shakespeare's Comedies* (1980); Dennis Bartholomeusz's *Macbeth and the Players* (1969); Philip Martin's *Shakespeare's Sonnets* (1972); E.A.M. Colman's *The Dramatic Use of Bawdy in Shakespeare* (1974); S.L. Goldberg's *An Essay on King Lear* (1974); Alan Brissenden's *Shakespeare and the Dance* (1981) and his edited collection of essays, *Shakespeare and Some Others* (1976); and Jane Adamson's *Othello as Tragedy* (1980).

The number of editions of the plays and studies of Shakespeare and his work lends credence to E. Morris Miller's 1940 claim that Shakespeare had dominated the Australian study of literature. The significance of the playwright extends, however, beyond the performance of his plays and the various publications about him. The statues to Shakespeare, the reports of fancy-dress balls held on his birthday in which

the guests dressed in appropriate costume, the performance of operas derived from Shakespearean themes, the names of public houses (e.g. the Shakespeare Tavern in the basement of the first theatre in Hobart), theatres (e.g. the Twelfth Night Theatre in Brisbane) and racehorses (e.g. Malvolio won the 1891 Melbourne Cup), all attest to Shakespeare's contribution to an enduring English influence on the cultural history of Australia. Finally, the response of and influence on Australian writers should be noted. An early example is Charles Nagel's burlesque *Shakespericonglommorofunnidogammoniae* (1843) in which Macbeth suggests to Othello that he should prevent Ophelia's desertion to Richard III because of her valuable property in NSW; Shakespeare also appears in several nineteenth-century pantomimes. Charles Harpur's play, *The Bushrangers*, employs Shakespearean verse and has Falstaffian characters; Harpur also wrote a poem on Shakespeare, as did James Hebblethwaite, J.B. O'Hara, David Campbell and numerous other writers. Around the turn of the century Joseph Furphy in *Such is Life* (1903) and other works consistently alludes to Shakespeare, often for comic effect; Henry Lawson in 'Mateship in Shakespeare's Rome' gives his version of *Julius Caesar* and also refers to *Timon of Athens*; and C.J. Dennis in *The Songs of a Sentimental Bloke* (1915) includes an account of a visit by the Bloke and Doreen to a performance of *Romeo and Juliet*, which is as famous in Australian literature and as funny as the Duke's rendition of Shakespeare in *Huckleberry Finn* in American literature.

Among more recent writers, Kenneth Mackenzie wrote a radio play 'The Young Shakespeare'; 'M. Barnard Eldershaw''s novel *Tomorrow and Tomorrow and Tomorrow* (1983), takes its title from *Macbeth*; Eunice Hanger's play, *Upstage* (1952), gathers together several Shakespearean heroines to compete for the title of Miss Shakespeare; the Nimrod pantomime, 'Hamlet on Ice' (1971), featured Grahame Bond, the author and star, as the ageing schoolboy Terry Shakespeare, of the hilarious *Boy's Own McBeth* (1979), set in Dunsinane Boys' School; and David Williamson wrote a much criticized Australian-idiom adaptation of *King Lear*, which was performed in 1978.

SHAPCOTT, THOMAS (1935–   ), born and educated at Ipswich, Queensland, left school at fifteen and worked as a clerk in his father's accountancy business. He completed an accountancy degree in 1961 and was a public accountant until 1978. He graduated in arts from the University of Queensland in 1967. In 1973–76 he was a member of the Literature

Board and became its director in 1983. His wife is the poet, Judith Rodriguez.

Shapcott's publications include *Time on Fire* (1961), which was awarded the Grace Leven Prize for poetry; *Sonnets 1960–1963* (1964); *The Mankind Thing* (1964); *A Taste of Salt Water* (1967), which won both the Sir Thomas White Memorial Prize for poetry and the Myer Award for Poetry; *Inwards to the Sun* (1969), which also won the Myer Award for Poetry; *Fingers at Air* (1969); a group of poems for opera, *The Seven Deadly Sins* (1970); *Begin with Walking* (1972); *Shabbytown Calendar* (q.v., 1975); *Selected Poems* (1978); *Turning Full Circle* (1979) and *Welcome* (1983). He has also published novels, *Flood Children* (1981), *The Birthday Gift* (1982), a book of 'prose inventions', *Stump & Grape & Bopple-Nut* (1981), and an experimental narrative work, *White Stag of Exile* (1984). He edited the anthologies, *New Impulses in Australian Poetry* (q.v., 1968, with Rodney Hall), *Australian Poetry Now* (1970), *Contemporary American and Australian Poetry* (q.v., 1976) and *Consolidation: The Second Paperback Poets Anthology* (1981).

Shapcott's verse reflects his interest in experimental poetic techniques, although his early poetry, as seen in *Time on Fire* and *The Mankind Thing*, is conventional in both form and theme. It is also largely autobiographical, reflecting the country boy's distaste for the garish city environment; the wakening of young love; courtship, marriage, parenthood; and a preoccupation with transience. The fourteen-part 'Two and a Half Acres', the story of the poet, his wife and child settling on their small property, is typical of this intimate, lyrical early verse. With *A Taste of Salt Water* and *Inwards to the Sun*, self-understanding ('Self's the unique toy that I grapple with') and the ultimate understanding of human nature, especially in the light of transience, become his abiding concerns and are illuminated by a wide use of mythology, history, religious and social commentary. In these volumes Shapcott's interest in innovatory techniques is illustrated, e.g. in the blank opening page of *Inwards to the Sun* ('This Blank Page . . . is where I begin to exist'), and in the experimental settings of 'Night Songs' and 'Ceremony for Cedar'. That interest is given free rein in his book of experimental verse, *Fingers at Air*. Substantial Shapcott poems of this period are 'The City of Acknowledgement', a fourteen-part ironic treatment of the life of Christ; the sonnet sequences, 'Suite of Sonnets' and 'Minotaur'; and the historically-based 'Portrait of Captain Logan'. Shapcott's best-known and most widely-acclaimed work is *Shabbytown Calendar*; 'Shabbytown' is the poet's home town of Ipswich, its 'calendar' ranging over a year from the 'mango weather' of January to the thunderstorms and Christmas bells of the following December. The course of life in the provincial town is conveyed with precision and irony. Shapcott's volume of *Selected Poems* is structured in four chronological sections from 1956 to 1976; his volume, *Turning Full Circle*, comprises eight sections of prose poems; *Welcome* contains a selection of his most important work since the *Selected Poems* and indicates a new poetic direction.

As critic, editor and anthologist Shapcott was an influential supporter of the 'New Australian Poetry' (q.v.) that sprang up in the late 1960s. In addition to being one of the most interesting of present-day poets he continues to be a major reviewer of and authority on contemporary Australian poetry as a whole. He won the Canada-Australia Literary Award in 1979.

SHARP, WILLIAM ('FIONA MACLEOD') (1856–1905), the English poet, essayist and biographer of Rossetti, Shelley, Heine and Browning, visited Australia in 1876 and travelled in NSW and Victoria. His *The Human Inheritance* (1882) contains poetry written in response to his Australian experience.

'SHARPE, LUCINDA', see LANE, WILLIAM

SHAVE, LIONEL (1888–1954), born Hawthorn, Victoria, was a Melbourne advertising agent. He wrote numerous competent but lightweight plays for stage and radio, some of which were broadcast overseas. He also published a collection, *Five Proven One-Act Plays* (1948), which comprises *A Sirius Cove*, *Red and Gold*, *That's Murder*, *The Resignation of Mr Bagsworth* and *Twelve Moons Cold*.

SHAW, BRUCE, see Aboriginal Song and Narrative in Translation; Aboriginal Writing in English

SHAW, CHARLES (1900–55), born Melbourne and orphaned early, worked at a variety of occupations in rural areas of Victoria and on country newspapers, before joining the literary staff of the *Bulletin* in the 1930s. Some of his short stories were published in two collections, *Outback Occupations* (1943) and *A Sheaf of Shorts* (1944); a popular collection of his ballads, *The Warrumbungle Mare*, appeared in 1943. Shaw also wrote the best-selling, international novel, *Heaven Knows, Mr Allison* (1952), which was subsequently produced as an American film; a mystery story, *Who Could Hate Purcey?* (1944), as well as three mystery stories under the pseudonym 'Bant Singer', *You're Wrong Delaney* (1953), *Don't Slip Delaney* (1954) and *Have Patience Delaney!*

(1954); and two novels for children, *The Green Token* (1943) and *The Treasure of the Hills* (1944).

SHAW, WINIFRED (1905–   ), born Maitland, NSW, married R.M. Taplin and was interned in Singapore's Changi prison camp during the Second World War. She subsequently lived in England. While still in her teens she published three collections of lyrical ballads which show a striking technical control, *The Aspen Tree* (1920), *The Yellow Cloak* (1922) and *Babylon* (1924).

Shearer in Australian Literature. The wool industry in Australia began with the introduction of merino sheep into the colony of NSW in 1797 and the export of merino wool from John Macarthur's (q.v.) flock to England in 1808. With the opening of new pastoral areas, central and western NSW, the Hunter Valley, the Darling Downs in Queensland, the Australia Felix districts of Victoria, thirty million hectares of grazing land became available for sheep farming. The shearing industry that sprang from this pastoral expansion developed in three phases. Prior to 1850, when flocks were relatively few in number, shearing was done either by the owner, his family and a few permanent employees, or by a small group of itinerant shearers. The simple open-air shearing process of that early period, adapted to whatever facilities of water and grass were available, is described in books of reminiscences such as *A Homestead History* (1942, ed. G.F. James), the memoirs of early squatter, Alfred Joyce in the Port Phillip District, and *Recollections of Squatting in Victoria (1841–1859)* (1883) by E.M. Curr. Peter Freeman, in *The Woolshed: A Riverina Anthology* (1980), describes an etching from an 1852 London journal, the *Leisure Hour*, which depicts an Arcadian scene with father and son kneeling on the grass taking off the fleece with knives. The few professional shearers, either 'Derwenters' from Van Diemen's Land or 'Sydneys' from NSW, were paid ten shillings per hundred sheep (thirty shillings per hundred in the labour shortages of the gold rushes, eighty-two dollars per hundred in 1981). With the spread of fencing wire over the outback in the late 1850s and 1860s, flock numbers increased rapidly, the wool clip improved dramatically and the second phase, with large numbers of professional shearers using blade shears, began. From that period sprang many of the characteristics of the shearing legend: the ragtag, itinerant army of workers, the idiosyncratic vocabulary, the colourful personalities, the strictly-observed customs and codes of conduct and behaviour, and the host of ballads and songs. Significant among contemporary accounts of the blade-shearing days is 'Rolf Boldrewood''s *Shearing in Riverina, New South Wales* (1983, first published 1870). 'Duke' Tritton in *Time Means Tucker* (1964) tells of the last blade shearing at Conimbia Station on the Castlereagh, describes the blade-shearing process and pays tribute to the blade shearers for the dramatic improvement in shearing conditions in that period. With the introduction of machines, the third phase of shearing began. The first patent for a shearing machine was granted in 1868; the first complete shearing of a flock by machines occurred at Dunlop Station, Louth, on the Darling in 1888. To accommodate machine shearing and the changed shearing process, the modern shearing shed, with its board, stands, pens and long string of workers behind the shearer, e.g. the 'pony', 'picker', 'broomie', 'skirter', 'dagboy', 'tarboy', 'wool-roller', 'classer' and 'presser', came into being. The character of the shearer and of shearing life in both the blade and early machine period is preserved in the pages of the *Bulletin* in the closing years of the nineteenth century; there is, for example, a collection of shearing terms in the *Bulletin* (1898). C.E.W. Bean's documentary, *On the Wool Track* (1910), and Tritton's autobiography, *Time Means Tucker*, are two of the major chronicles of the shearing life and lore of that time. Other works which include the shearer are Nat Gould's *On and Off the Turf in Australia* (1895) which describes the shearing at Winbar Station and a shearing strike there in 1894; and two retrospective accounts, William Hatfield's *Sheepmates* (1931), and H.M. Eastman's *Memoirs of a Sheepman* (1953), which gives the squatter's viewpoint on union shearing. Eastman's chapter, 'A Shearers' Race Meeting', displays something of the lighter side of shearing life, as does *Time Means Tucker* with its post-shearing activities such as picnic race-meetings, sprees and lively country dances.

In the creative literature of the late nineteenth and early twentieth century the shearer is a ubiquitous but never dominating presence. Shearers pass casually through much of Henry Lawson's writing but his story 'A Rough Shed' presents the harsh reality of the shearing environment while 'The Shearer's Dream' (q.v.), with the ecstatic lines

> Oh, I dreamt I shore in a shearers' shed,
>   and it was a dream of joy,
> For every one of the rouseabouts
>   was a girl dressed up as a boy

expresses, as does another Lawson poem. 'The Shearing Shed' and Frank Moorhouse's satiric story, 'The Drover's "Wife" ', the sexual deprivation of the shearer's world. Other Lawson shearing poems include the rouseabout verses,

'The Ballad of the Rouseabout', 'The Greenhand Rouseabout' and 'The Boss's Boots'; the bitter 'Out Back', which pours scorn upon the myth of the carefree, idyllic life of tramping from one 'jolly' shearing shed to another; 'Shearers', which emphasizes the mateship and camaraderie of those in the profession; and 'The Boss-Over-the-Boards', which describes something of the worker versus management syndrome. Other shearing poetry includes 'John Drayman''s nostalgic ballad, 'I Don't Go Shearing Now', whose wistful lines

> Every year I get a longing,
>   as the shearing time draws nigh,
> To saddle up and slither, and
>   to have another try
> At the game I loved so dearly

indicate the appeal of the shearing life to the Australian male. Will Ogilvie's 'Northward to the Sheds' expresses the excitement and anticipation that rise as the time for the annual migration to the sheds approaches and A.B. Paterson's 'Shearing at Castlereagh' gives shearing something of the quality of a good-natured and boisterous game where the characters combine to despatch 'another bale of golden fleece . . . branded "Castlereagh" '.

The shearer has flourished most, however, in folk-song and ballad. The best-known shearing song is 'Click Go the Shears' (q.v.), which probably dates from the 1890s or early 1900s. The song which best reflects the male world of the shearer and the mysterious appeal of mateship is 'The Banks of the Condamine' (q.v.). The shearer's incorrigible habit of boasting is reflected in such songs as 'The Ryebuck Shearer' and 'Flash Jack from Gundagai', while the supreme example of the shearer tall story is the ballad, 'Bill Brinks'. Bill, who shears 200 sheep a day and drinks with the same gusto, is given sulphuric acid by a barman who hates him. Several days later Bill reappears at the pub, demanding more of the 'new' brew and complaining (only mildly) that every time he coughs his whiskers catch fire. Incompetent shearers are pilloried in 'I'm Tomahawking Fred, the Ladies' Man', 'tomahawking' being a term to indicate that the wool appears to have been hacked off with an axe. The shearer's close analysis of the other sex is usually expressed in sheep terminology, as in the song 'The Euabalong Ball' (q.v.). Some of the toughest shearing sheds are mentioned in the song 'Goorianawa'. The legendary shearers' spree after the shed cuts out is illustrated in 'The Keg of Rum' while the practice of 'lambing down', i.e. cheating the drunken shearer on the spree by corrupt inn-keepers, is seen in 'Lazy Harry''s (q.v.). In 'The Big-Gun Shearer', one who has been lambed-down by the faraway

Sydney experts offers the advice:

> Head for the nearest wayside shack
> It's not so far when you're got to walk back.

Famous shearing personalities include blade-shearer, Jack Howe (q.v.), who shore 321 sheep in a day in 1892, and Jimmy Gibbs, whose strength and stamina were unaffected even when he was in the grip of the 'Barcoo spews'. The terminology of the shearing industry, including such picturesque expressions as 'dreadnought' (a clumsy, blundering shearer) and 'Cunnamulla Gun' (a 'flash' shearer whose big tallies only occur in a burst of wind-baggery in the Cunnamulla pub), has been discussed in the *Bulletin* article of 1898, in *The Australian Language* (1945) by Sidney J. Baker and particularly in *The Terminology of the Shearing Industry* (1965) by J.S. Gunn.

The greatest single crisis in the shearing industry was the shearers' strike of 1891, which resulted in the imprisonment of a number of shearers on conspiracy charges, produced a dramatic outburst of radicalism and republicanism, with the Eureka flag flown at the camps of the striking shearers and Henry Lawson's 'Freedom on the Wallaby' (q.v.) expressing the rage of the unionists. Accounts and analyses of the strike are given in W.G. Spence's *Australia's Awakening* (1909), Julian Stuart's (q.v.) *Part of the Glory: Reminiscences of the Shearers' Strike Queensland 1891* (1967) and in an anonymous manuscript in the Mitchell Library, 'The Shearers' Strike, January to June 1891'. The gaoling of the shearers on the conspiracy charge was the spur to William Lane's writing of the novel *The Workingman's Paradise* (1892) where the strike is part of the background. The strike is also the subject of E.S. 'Milky White' Emerson's narrative poem, 'Jock McPhail (A Tale of the 1891 Shearers' Strike)' and George Farwell's play, 'Sons of the South', and is significant also in Vance Palmer's play, *Hail Tomorrow* (1947) and Nigel Krauth's novel, *Matilda, My Darling* (1983). The title story of 'Rolf Boldrewood''s *In Bad Company* (1901) is hostile to the strikers. In the Australian film, *Sunday Too Far Away* (1975), the itinerant nature of the shearing life, its radicalism and the problems inherent in its closed male society are portrayed. The popular and frequently-staged musical play, *Reedy River* (1970), with its echoes of the shearers' strike, highlights such shearing songs as 'Click Go the Shears' and 'Flash Jack from Gundagai'. The shearer has been immortalized also in Tom Roberts's painting, *Shearing the Rams*. Patsy Adam Smith published a comprehensive historical and anecdotal account of the shearers and shearing, *The Shearers* (1982); Les Ryan, author of several authoritative textbooks on shearing, has also published a novel,

The Shearers (1975), which recreates the tough life of the shearing sheds. Written in the 1950s, it was then rejected by publishers because of its ribald but authentic language. Ryan's book also includes a valuable glossary of the shearers' idiom.

SHEARER, JILL has lived mainly in Queensland and has written some poetry and short stories for children and adults, but is best known as a playwright. She has won numerous awards and written several full-length and one-act plays; they are 'But I Won't Wear White' (1972), 'Ships That Pass' (1973), 'The Trouble With Gillian' (1974), 'Who the Hell Needs Whipbirds' (1974), 'The Job' (1974), 'Release Lavinia Stannard' (1975), *Catherine* (1976, published 1977), *The Foreman* (1976, published 1977), *The Boat* (1977), 'The Expatriate' (1978), 'Echoes' (1980), *The Kite* (1980), *Stephen* (1980), and *Nocturne* (1980). *The Boat* is included in the collection, *Can't You Hear Me Talking To You?* ed. Alrene Sykes (1978); Shearer's independent collection, *Echoes and Other Plays* (1980), includes *Stephen*, *Nocturne* and *The Kite*. A writer with an acute ear for the subtleties of dialogue, Shearer tends to favour the one-act play with an ordinary setting, into which an element of the bizarre intrudes. Her most complex play is *Catherine*, a play within a play, which moves from contemporary time to 1790 and the voyage of Catherine Crowley, mother of William Charles Wentworth (q.v.), to Australia with the Second Fleet.

Shearer's Colt, The, see **PATERSON, A.B.**

'Shearer's Dream, The', one of the poems of Henry Lawson (q.v.) which was subsequently set to music and became an Australian folksong, was written in 1901. It tells the story of a shearer who, until he wakes up and finds that he has been dreaming, imagines himself in a shed with electric fans and mahogany pens, shearing sheep that have been washed before they are shorn, and served drinks every hour by female rouseabouts who also attend to the other 'needs' of the shearers. The poem first appeared in print in a story, also titled 'The Shearer's Dream', which was included in *Children of the Bush* (1902). Mitchell and Lawson, camped for the night, listen to the song coming from an adjoining camp, although the singer is silenced before he reveals that he 'woke with my head in the blazin' sun to find 'twas a shearer's dream'; this ending, however, was revealed when the poem was published in *When I Was King* (1905). A similar Australian folksong is 'The Drover's Dream', in which the drover dreams that the bush fauna put on a concert for him until he is rudely awakened by his boss, demanding to know where the sheep have gone.

'Sheedy Was Dying', a poem by John Shaw Neilson (q.v.), published in the *Bulletin* 1901 Christmas number, records the lonely death that usually comes to drifters of the outback.

Sheepmates, see **HATFIELD, WILLIAM; Shearer in Australian Literature**

Shepherd, later replaced by the stockman, drover and jackeroo, was a familiar figure in the colonies before the introduction of fencing wire on pastoral holdings in the 1850s. The shepherd prevented the sheep from wandering, escorted them to water and fresh pastures, and protected them from depredations by blacks and dingoes. The solitary shepherd was sometimes himself the victim of marauding Aborigines, who killed him and made off with his flock. He was usually dressed in a rough serge suit tied at the waist with a leather belt; mostly bearded and long-haired, he wore a cabbage-tree hat or a less durable one made of plaited kangaroo grass. The itinerant shepherd made a rough shelter each night from branches and leaves; in more settled areas he lived in a rough slab hut with a dirt floor, occasionally with a wife and family for company but more often with a hut keeper who kept watch over the sheep at night. Detached for long periods from the company of fellow humans, the shepherd often grew erratic in behaviour, such a misfit when restored to society that he could only return to the solitude that had become part of him. Henry Kendall, himself a shepherd when a young man, planned a major poetic work, 'The Australian Shepherd', using the sheep herder as the central figure around which to weave the epic story of life in the bush. Only fragments of this work were completed, e.g. 'A Death in the Bush'. Prominent in most histories of the pastoral age, the shepherd is discussed in James Bonwick's *Romance of the Wool Trade* (1887) and is the central subject of W.R. Glasson's *Our Shepherds* (1942); the latter also contains a selection of shepherd vocabulary and slang. Artist S.T. Gill painted the well-known work, *Sleeping Shepherd*.

SHEPHERD, CATHERINE (1912–76), born Rhodesia (Zimbabwe) and educated in Wales, came to Australia in the 1920s. In the 1930s and 1940s she wrote plays and dramatic adaptations of classic novels for radio which included 'Lethe Wharf', 'Seapiece', 'Exit Socrates', 'The Flying Swan', 'I Saw the New Moon', 'Three Mile Cross', 'Sabotage', 'A Citizen of the World', 'The Valiant Tinker', 'The Heroic

Journey', 'Balzac', 'The Golden Cockerel', 'Arthur of Van Diemen's Land', 'The Hayfield', and 'The Judas Sheep'. She also wrote several stage plays, *Daybreak* (1942), and 'Jane, My Love' (1951), and a children's novel, *Tasmanian Adventure* (1964).

SHERER, JOHN (1810–?), born Edinburgh, trained as a printer and published, 1844–81, sixteen miscellaneous works which include histories, travel books, pamphlets and general reference works. He also edited the popular narrative, *The Gold-Finder of Australia: How He Went, How He Fared, And How He Made His Fortune* (1853), which was once regarded as an authentic account of Sherer's own entertaining adventures on the Australian goldfields. It has since been established that Sherer never visited Australia but derived most of his ideas for *The Gold-Finder* from S.T. Gill's *Sketches of the Victorian Goldfields* (1852) and other oral and printed accounts, and published the book to tap the lucrative English market for informative literature on the gold discoveries.

SHERMAN, PAUL (1933–), born Brisbane, has worked as journalist, high school teacher and actor. He has written short stories and poems, and the plays, *Melba*, produced 1974, published 1976, and *The Mangrove Man*, produced 1977–78 and published in *Australian Theatre Workshop One Act Plays, Series 1* (1978). *Melba*, an interpretation of Dame Nellie Melba, has a more documentary and external approach than Jack Hibberd's contemporary *A Toast to Melba* (1976). Sherman has also written the libretto of a musical, *Captain Starlight*, produced in 1964, and three unpublished plays, 'The Hero of Too' (an adaptation of David Martin's novel), 'Jungles' and 'The Murder of Gonzago'.

Shields of Trell, see **Science Fiction**

Shifting Heart, The (1960), a play by Richard Beynon (q.v.), was first produced in Sydney in 1957 after winning first prize in the 1956 Playwrights' Advisory Board competition. Set in Collingwood, a working-class Melbourne suburb, on Christmas Eve, the play deals with the fortunes of an Italian migrant family, the Bianchis: Poppa, Momma, a son Gino and a daughter Maria, who is married to an Australian, Clarry Fowler, and is anxiously waiting for the birth of her child, having previously suffered two miscarriages. Gino appears to be drawn to the local dance-hall, where he attracts the violent attentions of the local, racist youths, a fact which receives scant sympathetic attention from Clarry, despite Maria's anxiety. The Bianchis have a friendly, if noisy, relationship

with one set of neighbours, the Pratts; with their other neighbours they are in a state of warfare, Momma resorting to blocking their drains and depositing garbage over their fence. Act Two ends with Gino's death following a fight in which it is unclear whether he was aggressor or victim, although chauvinist, Australian attitudes have clearly played a part. The birth of Maria's baby is precipitated by the news and by her angry conflict with Clarry, whom she blames for the tragedy. Act Three takes place on Christmas Day. The baby is safely born and Clarry and Maria reconciled, Clarry maintaining with an inarticulate show of sentiment that his son's name will be Gino.

SHILLINGLAW, J.J. (JOHN JOSEPH) (1831–1905), born London, came to Australia in 1852 during the gold rush and held various public service appointments in Victoria. A member of the Yorick Club and of the literary society, the Cave of Adullam, he acquired a reputation as a historian, contributed to various Victorian periodicals and in 1869 took over the *Colonial Monthly*. He published six books but his most important achievement was the discovery and editing of a number of documents relating to the early history of the Port Phillip settlement, published in 1879 as *Historical Records of Port Phillip*. His personality is described in Hugh McCrae's *Story-book Only* (1948).

Shillingsworth Family, see *Capricornia*

'**Ship of Ice, The**', a long, dramatic poem by Rosemary Dobson (q.v.), won the *Sydney Morning Herald* prize for poetry in 1946 and was published in three parts in that newspaper in 1947. The ship of ice is the English schooner, *Jenny*, which lay locked in the Antarctic ice from 1823 to 1860 until discovered by a whaling vessel. 'Snap-frozen' as it were in an instant of time, the bodies of the crew had been perfectly preserved, caught for thirty-seven years in their frozen postures until released by discovery into conventional death. The poem's seven individual voices (the captain, his wife, and five of the crew) comment on the event in the light of their own personalities and philosophies of life.

Shiralee, according to D'Arcy Niland (q.v.), who wrote the novel *The Shiralee* (1955), was a particular type of swag (q.v.), one shaped like a leg of mutton, carried over the shoulder by a strap or rope, which usually balanced some other load, probably a tucker bag on the chest. The origin of the word is unknown. A film of Niland's novel with Peter Finch (q.v.)

as the swagman Macauley was screened in 1957.

'Short Shift Saturday', one of Gavin Casey's and Australia's best-known short stories, published in *It's Harder for Girls* (1942), is an account of the gulf that grows between man and woman in marriage and, on the broader level, of the even greater gulf that exists between the sexes in the male-dominated Australian society. Set in Kalgoorlie, the story is based on the different reactions of man and wife to the sight of a drunken miner being thrown out of a hotel. In the woman's eyes a drunken beast, the miner, Don Bell, is viewed more sympathetically by the husband, who knows Bell has silicosis and is soon to die. That night, in bed, the husband ponders the gulf that has grown between them over the years, 'I wanted to touch her, to make some sort of contact with her'. That gulf is seen to be due both to the Australian male habit of turning to his mates and beer 'because bars are the most cheerful places I know' and to the Australian woman's inability to cope with the ethos of masculinity and mateship that is so destructive to harmonious marital and family relationships. See also *Casey's Wife* in Casey, Gavin.

Short Story Embassy, The, see **WILDING, MICHAEL**

'Shots in the Orchard', a short story by 'Brian James' (q.v.), was first published in the *Bulletin* (1944). Typical of 'James''s ability to interpret the collective small-town mind, it concerns a domestic tragedy in the otherwise crime-free town of Templeton and the townsfolk's subsequent enjoyment and assimilation of the incident. When Enoch Rath, a despised 'shrimp' of a man, shoots both his wife and her lover, Tommy Ramsbottom, he arouses surprise and sympathy in many of his neighbours on the grounds of his courage and marksmanship. Eventually, however, Enoch's refusal to talk about the shooting and the town's long-standing preference for Tommy lose him so much support that the court's failure to hang him is regarded as a mistake. Mrs Ramsbottom, a 'poor colourless little woman' with four children, is held much to blame and leaves the district.

'SHUTE, NEVIL' (NEVIL SHUTE NORWAY) (1899–1960), born Middlesex, England, trained at first as a Royal Flying Corps gunnery officer, although he failed his final medical examination. After a brief period in the British infantry in 1918, he studied at the University of Oxford and in 1923 joined the de Havilland Aircraft Company as an engineer.

His first published novel, *Marazan*, appeared under the pseudonym 'Nevil Shute' in 1926; two earlier attempts, 'Stephen Morris' and 'Pilotage', were published after 'Shute''s death as one volume under the title, *Stephen Morris* (1961). In 1924 'Shute' left de Havilland to work on the R100 airship project, which was halted in 1930 following the disastrous crash of the rival F101 airship. 'Shute' then helped to found a new aircraft manufacturing company, Airspeed Ltd, for which he worked as managing director until 1938, when the success of his novels *So Disdained* (1928) and *Lonely Road* (1932) prompted him to turn to full-time writing. On the outbreak of the Second World War, however, he joined the Royal Navy Volunteer Reserve, and was set to work on weapons developments; in 1944 he was sent to Normandy with the invasion fleet as correspondent for the Ministry of Information. Novels that draw on his war experiences are the outstandingly popular *Pied Piper* (1942), which established 'Nevil Shute' as a household name in the English-speaking world, *Most Secret* (?1945) and *Pastoral* (1944). In 1945 'Shute' resigned from the navy and visited Burma, again as a Ministry correspondent, an experience he incorporated in his novel, *The Chequer Board* (1947). *No Highway* (1948), his next novel, returned to his experience in the aviation industry and dealt prophetically with the problem of structural fatigue in aircraft. In 1948–49 'Shute' flew his own plane to Australia in search of novelistic material, an experience which resulted in two of his best-known novels, *A Town Like Alice* (q.v., 1950) and *Round the Bend* (1951). In 1950, disappointed with the current British political scene, he decided to live permanently in Australia. Subsequent novels dealing mainly or partly with Australia are *The Far Country* (1952), *In the Wet* (1953), *Beyond the Black Stump* (1956), *On the Beach* (1957), *Requiem for a Wren* (1955) and *The Rainbow and the Rose* (1958).

'Shute' wrote twenty novels in all and an autobiography up to the year 1938, *Slide Rule* (1954). His books draw heavily on his experiences, his travels and his professional expertise, especially his knowledge of aircraft and weaponry; most of them are concerned with contemporary issues or problems and several, such as *What Happened to the Corbetts* (1939), which deals prophetically with the civilian destruction caused by bombing raids, and *On the Beach* which focuses on the actuality of a nuclear holocaust, have appealed to the common anxieties of readers. Perennially popular, his novels are characterized by naturalistic, fast-moving plots; diverse settings; credible if unexceptional characters; an easy style; serious, if old-fashioned, moral purpose and happy or optimistic endings. Several have been produced as films including *Scotland Yard Commands*, a version of *The Lonely Road* (1937), *No Highway in the Sky* (*No Highway*) (1951), *On the Beach* (1959, made in Australia), and *A Town Like Alice* (1958), which was also produced as a television serial in 1982.

'Sick Stockrider, The', a popular and well-known poem of Adam Lindsay Gordon (q.v.), was written in 1869 and published in *Bush Ballads and Galloping Rhymes* (1870). The ballad of the dying stockman, with its creed of mateship, its laconic acceptance in true bush style of whatever life and death may offer, led Marcus Clarke to assert that in Gordon's work lay the beginnings of a national school of Australian poetry. 'The Sick Stockrider' is accepted as the progenitor of the Australian literary ballad, but differs markedly in tone and language from the later bush ballads of the *Bulletin* school. See Folk-Song and Ballad.

SIDNEY, JOHN, see **SIDNEY, SAMUEL**

'SIDNEY, NEILMA' (NEILMA GANTNER) (1922–), a daughter of the prominent businessman Sidney Myer, lived in California for some years and has worked in India for Community Aid Abroad. She has published two novels, the autobiographical *Beyond the Bay* (1966) and *The Return* (1976), and two collections of short stories, *Saturday Afternoon* (1959) and *The Eye of the Needle* (1970).

SIDNEY, SAMUEL ('A BUSHMAN') (1813–83), born Birmingham, England, was baptized Samuel Solomon but throughout his career as a journalist was known as Samuel Sidney. His long-term interest was in English agriculture, but for several years either side of 1850 he was an acknowledged expert on Australian emigration. In 1847 'A Bushman''s *A Voice from the Far Interior of Australia* was published, written by Sidney from material supplied by his younger brother, John, who had spent six years in NSW. *A Voice from the Far Interior of Australia* became the initial section of the wide-selling *Sidney's Australian Hand-book: How to Settle and Succeed in Australia* (1848) by 'A Bushman', also written by Sidney, possibly in collaboration with his brother. Its success led the Sidneys to establish *Sidney's Emigrant's Journal* (1848–50), which ran as a weekly until John returned to Australia in 1849, and then as a monthly. Samuel subsequently wrote the popular pot-pourri *The Three Colonies of Australia* (1852) and a homiletic novel, *Gallops and Gossips in the Bush of Australia* (1854). Influenced by Caroline Chisholm, Alexander Harris and Robert Lowe,

he was an opponent of the theories of Edward Gibbon Wakefield, who, like him, never went to Australia, and argued that the Australian colonies were an ideal location for working-class settlement. He contributed articles on Australia to Charles Dickens's *Household Words*; his influence on Dickens, Edward Bulwer-Lytton and Charles Reade, and on the creation of an Arcadian myth about Australia, are discussed in Coral Lansbury's controversial *Arcady in Australia* (1970).

'Silkworms, The', a poem by Douglas Stewart (q.v.), was published in *Quadrant* (1957). Generally regarded as one of Stewart's finest lyric poems, 'The Silkworms' belongs, according to its author, to 'a sequence of suburban satires' inspired by his residence in a Sydney northern suburb, St Ives. The poem's opening phrase, 'All their lives in a box!', represents not only the silkworms but also their human counterparts, the suburb-dwellers. The human situation in which freedom of action and choice is limited by environment-conditioned attitudes is linked to the inertness of the silkworm's existence consequent upon generations of confinement and restriction. The poem's deliberate but restrained gravity, its measured but unemphatic tone and quiet, relaxed movement accentuate the tragic frustration of the situation it represents.

Silver Brumby, see **MITCHELL, ELYNE**

'SILVERLEAF', see **LLOYD, JESSIE GEORGINA**

SIMMONS, JOSEPH (?1810–93), born England, arrived in NSW in 1830 and in 1834 joined Barnett Levey in ownership and management of the Theatre Royal, where he also performed as an actor and was the Colony's first Macbeth. After much discord, Simmons terminated his partnership with Levey, but was once again manager, after Levey lost control of the theatre, 1835–36, and 1837–38, after Levey's death; in between, he performed in Van Diemen's Land. Simmons also managed the Royal Victoria Theatre 1838–39 and 1842. In 1843 he opened the small City Theatre in Sydney with his own company, but was forced to close after only a few weeks. Best known as a comedian, Simmons played the role of Lanty O'Liffey in Edward Geoghegan's *The Currency Lass* in 1844; he also wrote several dramatic pieces, including 'New Engagements' (1842) and 'The Duellist' (1844). He seems to have retired from the stage in 1845, although he reappeared at his benefit in 1879.

SIMMONS, SAMUEL ROWE (1871–1952), was a Melbourne printer who established two small private presses, the Argonaut Press and the Simmons Press, which published his own verse and criticism and other works, e.g. the poems of the English writer, Christopher Smart. Of Simmons's six books, the most important were *Sonnets and Other Verses* (1925), published under the pseudonym 'Oswald Gray', and *A Problem and a Solution* (1946), a textual study of Marcus Clarke's first novel, *Long Odds* (1869). A prominent member of the Bread and Cheese Club, Simmons also prepared a bibliography of Clarke which was enlarged by L.T. Hergenhan and published in 1975.

'SIMON STUKELEY', see SAVERY, HENRY

SIMPSON, COLIN (1908–83), born Sydney, worked for several years as a journalist for such Sydney newspapers as the *Daily Telegraph* and the *Sun*, the latter of which published one of his most brilliant coups, the revelation of the facts of the Ern Malley hoax. In 1947 he joined the ABC as a writer of travel documentaries and from 1950 worked as a freelance writer of well-researched and popular travel books. The best known are *Adam in Ochre* (1951), which is partly based on an Australian-American expedition Simpson accompanied to Arnhem Land in 1948, sponsored by the National Geographic Society; *Adam with Arrows* (1953) and *Adam in Plumes* (1954), both of which describe life in New Guinea; *Greece, the Unclouded Eye* (1968); and *The New Australia* (1971). Simpson also wrote a novel, *Come Away, Pearler* (1952); a biography of Charles Kingsford-Smith (1937); and contributed verse, 'Infidelities', to *Trio* (1931) with Harley Matthews and Kenneth Slessor. Vice-president of the ASA, Simpson was prominent in gaining the Public Lending Right legislation for Australian authors. He was made OBE in 1981.

SIMPSON, HELEN (1897–1940), granddaughter of a French marquis who had settled at Goulburn in the mid-nineteenth century, was born in Sydney and educated in Australia, although she left for England at the age of sixteen. She subsequently visited Australia several times, most notably in 1937 when she gave several talks for the ABC. During the First World War she worked in decoding for the British Admiralty, subsequently studied music at Oxford, and in 1927 married Denys John Browne, a nephew of 'Rolf Boldrewood'. In England she quickly acquired a reputation as a novelist, a writer of historical biography, a radio broadcaster and later a politician; in 1938 she stood unsuccessfully as Liberal candidate for the Isle of Wight. Two of her novels have Australian content, *Boomerang* (1932), winner of the James Tait Black Memorial Prize, and *Under Capricorn* (1937); and *The Woman on the Beast* (1933), a trio of fantastic novellas, includes one set in Australia in 1999. Both *Boomerang* and *Under Capricorn* have involved, highly-coloured plots, lightly-sketched but credible characters, and a lively, humorous and sophisticated narrative style. *Under Capricorn*, produced as a film by a British studio in 1949, directed by Alfred Hitchcock and starring Michael Wilding and Ingrid Bergman, is a tale of passion and misunderstanding set in colonial NSW and deals with the fortunes of an ex-convict and Irish groom, married to an aristocratic Irish lady; *Boomerang*, a more ambitious novel, relates the history of four generations of a family of French origin both in Australia and elsewhere. Simpson's other work includes a volume of poetry, *Philosophies in Little* (1921); the novels, *Acquittal* (1925), *The Baseless Fabric* (1925), *Cups, Wands and Swords* (1927), *Mumbudget* (1928), *The Desolate House* (1929), *'Vantage Striker* (1931), *Saraband for Dead Lovers* (1935), which was also produced as a film), *The Female Felon* (1935) and *Maid No More* (1940); three novels written in collaboration with Clemence Dane; the historical biographies, *The Spanish Marriage* (1933) and *Henry VIII* (1934); an account of Mary Kingsley, *A Woman Among Wild Men* (1938); and a translation of a selection from Louis-Sebastian Mercier's *Le Tableau de Paris* (1933). She also published several plays, *Pan in Pimlico* in an anthology, *Four One-Act Plays* (1923); *A Man of His Time* (1923), an interpretation of the life of Benvenuto Cellini, produced by Gregan McMahon in 1923; and *The Women's Comedy* (1926). An earlier play, 'Masks', was produced by the Sydney University Dramatic Society in 1921.

SIMPSON, MARY, born Stawell, Victoria, contributed numerous humorous sketches and short stories to the *Bulletin*, the *Australian Journal* and *Woman's Mirror* for more than two decades. Some were collected and published under the title *Tell-Tale Stories from the Bulletin* (1926), and one, 'Santa Claus', was reprinted in Nettie Palmer's *An Australian Story-Book* (1928) and George Mackaness's *Australian Short Stories* (1928). Simpson, who used the pseudonym 'Weeroona', also wrote comedies and one-act plays, e.g. *Crossing Swords with Fate* (1940), a play based on the life of Adam Lindsay Gordon.

SIMPSON, R.A. (RONALD ALBERT) (1929–), born Melbourne, studied at the Royal Melbourne Institute of Technology, taught in schools in England and Australia before his appointment in 1968 to the Caulfield Institute of Technology. Poetry editor of the *Bulletin* 1963–65, he was appointed poetry editor of the *Age* in 1969. His poetry has appeared in numerous magazines, newspapers and anthologies, in *Eight by Eight* (1963), in *Twelve Poets 1950–1970* (1971, ed. Alexander Craig) and in eight collections, *The Walk along the Beach* (1960), *This Real Pompeii* (1964), *After the Assassination* (1968), *Diver* (1972), *Poems from Murrumbeena* (1976), *The Forbidden City* (1979), and *Selected Poems* (1981). He has also edited *Poems from the Age 1967–1979* (1979). One of a group of Melbourne poets that came to prominence in the late 1950s, and included Vincent Buckley, Evan Jones, Chris Wallace-Crabbe, Alexander Craig and Noel Macainsh, Simpson has been the most consistent in his development, continuing to write an urbane, understated poetry that is more international than Australian in style. His collections include some light satires and verse on political subjects, but his preoccupations are the texture of ordinary life, the difficulties and joys of communication, both in art and with people, and the tensions between the desire for permanence and the reality of change, between aspiration and actuality. Complex but intelligible, spare and rigorous in thought and expression, often humorous and provocative, Simpson's verse has an analytical sensitivity that is often uncompromisingly directed at the self. In his later work he achieves a particularly relaxed, flexible and deceptively artless style.

SINCLAIR, JAMES PATRICK (1928–), district commissioner in the Eastern Highlands of New Guinea until 1975, has written numerous books about New Guinea and northern Australia. They include *Behind the Ranges* (1966); *The Outside Man* (1969), a biography of Jack Hides (q.v.), a New Guinea explorer and writer; *Sepik Pilot* (1971), a biography of the Australian aviator and founder of Sepik Airways, Bobby Gibbes; and *Kiap: Australia's Patrol Officers in Papua New Guinea* (1981).

SINCLAIRE, FREDERICK (1881–1954), born Auckland, NZ, studied for the Unitarian ministry at Manchester College, Oxford, where he achieved distinction. In 1908 he arrived in Melbourne, where he became prominent in the Victorian Socialist Party, co-edited the *Socialist* 1911–13 with Marie Pitt, and edited the organ of the Free Religious Fellowship, *Fellowship*, 1914–22, to which Vance Palmer, Louis Esson and 'Furnley Maurice' contributed. In 1911 he left the Unitarian ministry to further the aims of the Free Religious Fellowship, founded that year. An outspoken opponent of conscription,

he advanced his pacifist and socialist ideas and his search for a 'living theology' into the pages of *Fellowship* and other journals. In the late 1920s he left Melbourne for Perth, where he lectured in English, and was professor of English at the University of Christchurch, NZ, 1932–49. He published two collections of essays, *Annotations* (1920) and *Lend Me Your Ears* (1942). David Walker in *Dream and Disillusion* (1976) has given an account of his aspirations and their affinity with those of Louis Esson, Vance Palmer and 'Furnley Maurice'.

Singabout, the magazine of the Sydney Bush Music Club, founded 1954, was published intermittently 1956–67. Less eclectic in coverage than its Victorian equivalent, *Australian Tradition*, it comprised mainly words of songs together with articles, reviews and news items on folk music and folklore societies. Edited by John Meredith, 1957–62, *Singabout* numbered Merv Lilley and John Manifold among its contributors.

'Singapore', a poem by Mary Gilmore (q.v.), was published in the *Australian Women's Weekly* in March 1942, soon after the fall of Singapore to the Japanese forces in the Second World War. Much weakened because of wartime censorship from its original scathing indictment of corruption and ineptitude, the poem echoed the widespread belief that Australian troops in Malaya, and possibly the ultimate safety of this country, had been needlessly sacrificed to other Allied interests.

SINGER, VIOLET, see BRENNAN, C.J.

Singing Gold, The, see COTTRELL, DOROTHY

Singing to the Cattle, see ELLIOTT, BRIAN

SINNETT, FREDERICK (1830–66), born Hamburg, Germany, emigrated to Australia in 1849 because of tuberculosis, which eventually caused his death. After working as surveyor and explorer in SA he moved to journalism in Melbourne, where he helped to found and edit *Melbourne Punch*, was involved in the management of the Melbourne *Herald* and the Geelong *Daily News*, and was employed as leader writer by the *Argus* 1857–60. He returned to Adelaide in 1859 and ran the first ice works and the first evening newspaper in that city before returning to Melbourne and the *Argus* a year before his death. Sinnett wrote *An Account of the Rush to Point Curtis* (1859), based on his visit to the Queensland goldfields as *Argus* correspondent, and prepared *An Account* of the Colony of South Australia (1862) for the International Exhibition in London; but his most significant work was *The Fiction Fields of Australia* (q.v. 1856), the first extended critical essay devoted to Australian literature. His brother, Alfred Percy Sinnett, was a prominent theosophist and writer in England, and his son Percy (1859–82), who wrote under the pseudonym 'Per Se', produced the anthology, *Wattle Blossom* (1881).

Sisters Poets, see **Anthologies; Feminism and Australian Literature**

SKINNER, MOLLIE (1876–1955), born Perth, WA, was educated in England and at the age of twenty-three returned to WA, where she worked as a nurse and also tried journalism. A Quaker by religion, she later worked in the London slums and, in the First World War, in India. Her wartime experiences provided the material for her first book, *Letters of a V.A.D.* (1918), published in England under the pseudonym 'R.E. Leake'. Her acquaintance with D.H. Lawrence began in 1922; they collaborated on *The Boy in the Bush* (q.v., 1924), a story about the experiences of a young English immigrant, Jack Grant, in the WA outback of the 1880s; it was shown as a TV series in 1984. Her later books were *Black Swans* (1925), a romance set in WA in the nineteenth century, which includes a preface by Lawrence; *Men Are We* (1927), a collection of Aboriginal stories; *Tucker Sees India* (1937); *WX – Corporal Smith: A Romance of the A.I.F. in Libya* (1941); and *Where Skies Are Blue* (1946). Another unpublished novel, 'Eve in the Land of Nod', was also worked over by Lawrence. Her autobiography, *The Fifth Sparrow*, with a foreword by Mary Durack, was published in 1972.

SKIPPER, MERVYN (1886–1958), born Adelaide, was associated with the Eastern Extension Cable Co. 1902–24, and spent some time in Borneo. He was subsequently Melbourne representative of the *Bulletin* and contributed frequently to the *Lone Hand* and other journals and newspapers. While in Borneo he collected stories of the jungle, which he wove into fantasies for children and published in two collections, *The Meeting-pool* (1929) and *The White Man's Garden* (1930). Lively and humorous, the tales are told by the animals, birds, insects and plants of the jungle and reflect the natural biases, abilities and predilections of the various creatures involved. More realistic and unpredictable, if less memorable, than Kipling's *Just So Stories*, they have been translated into several European languages.

SKRZYNECKI, PETER, (1945–), born Germany, came to Australia in 1949 and has worked as a teacher. His poetry has appeared in several collections, *There, Behind the Lids* (1970), *Headwaters* (1972), *Immigrant Chronicle* (1975), *The Aviary: Poems 1975–1977* (1978) and *The Polish Immigrant* (1983). Immigrant experience in a new land is the dominant theme of Skrzynecki's gently lyrical and accessible poetry. He won a prize in the Cook Bicentenary competitions of 1970 and the Grace Leven Prize in 1972.

SKUTHORPE, LANCE (1870–1958), born Kurrajong, NSW, a legendary buckjump rider and showman, formed Australia's first professional rodeo or 'wild west' show in the 1890s and toured country towns for almost forty years. He showed his horsemanship by repeating Adam Lindsay Gordon's famous Blue Lake leap. Skuthorpe's best-known and much anthologized short story is 'The Champion Bullock Driver'; the bullocky demonstrates his talents of whip work and persuasive language by getting several panels of fencing to move of their own accord. Jack Pollard published the biography, *The Roughrider* (1962), later titled *The Horse Tamer*.

Skyline Riders and Other Verses, The, see **LAWSON, HENRY**

SLADE, ERNEST AUGUSTUS (1805–78), was an English army officer who served in Australia before returning in 1832 to Sydney, where in 1833–34 he was superintendent of the convict barracks and a police magistrate. Forced to resign because of scandals surrounding his domestic arrangements with his female convict servants, he returned in 1836 to England, where he boasted to a parliamentary committee on transportation that his improved cat-o-nine tails, if properly administered, had never failed to break the skin in four lashes. Slade is presented as the corrupt and vicious Slyde in several 'Price Warung' stories, notably 'Mr Slyde's Auction', and was the model for the seducer, Brade, in John Lang's novel, *The Forger's Wife* (q.v., 1855).

'SLADE, GURNEY' (STEPHEN BARTLETT) was a prolific writer of both children's and adult fiction. His early books were tales of adventure set in the South Seas and Australia, e.g. *Pleasure Island* (1924), *The Pearlers of Lorne: A Story for Boys* (1925), *The Fifteen Men* (1925) and *The Black Pyramid* (1926). *The Pearlers of Lorne, Lovers and Luggers* (1928) and *Captain Quid* (1937) have the pearling industry of north-west Australia as their backdrop. *Ships That Pass in the Night Clubs* (1926) is about a shipboard romance and its aftermath. He also wrote a travel book, *Through the Never Never* (1935).

SLADE, LEON (1931–), born Melbourne, has published three collections of verse, *Slade's Anatomy of the Horse* (1972), *Wilderness* (1970) and *Bloodstock Breeding* (1979). Often humorous or satiric, Slade uses colloquial diction and imagery to express his urban, contemporary themes.

SLADEN, DOUGLAS (1856–1946), born London, took an arts degree at Oxford before coming in 1879 to Victoria, where he graduated in law from the University of Melbourne. He was appointed as the first lecturer in modern history at the University of Sydney in 1883, but returned to England the following year. In spite of his brief Australian experience he was considered in England something of an Australian literary expert but his editorial judgements were not so well esteemed in Australia, for example by A.G. Stephens. Sladen's publications began with the rather ordinary verses, *Australian Lyrics* (1883) and *A Poetry of Exiles* (1883). His anthology, *Australian Ballads and Rhymes* (1888), was the basis for two similar works, *A Century of Australian Song* (1888) and *Australian Poets 1788–1888* (1888). Although unimaginative and conventional in their selection of poems, the anthologies aroused interest in England in Australian poetry (see Anthologies). His keen interest in the Australian poet Adam Lindsay Gordon (q.v.) led to his editing Adam Lindsay Gordon's *Poems* (1912) and, with Edith Humphris, the biographical *Adam Lindsay Gordon and His Friends in England and Australia* (1912). He was secretary of the Adam Lindsay Gordon Memorial Committee which was responsible for Gordon's bust being placed in the Poets' Corner of Westminster Abbey in 1934, and to mark that occasion he edited *Adam Lindsay Gordon: The Life and Best Poems of the Poet of Australia* (1934). Sladen also wrote several minor novels; edited a volume of W.M. Hughes's speeches, *From Boundary-Rider to Prime Minister* (1916); was editor of the original English *Who's Who*; and published two autobiographical works, *Twenty Years of My Life* (1913) and *My Long Life* (1939).

Slaughter of St Teresa's Day, The, see **KENNA, PETER**

SLESSOR, KENNETH (1901–71), was born at Orange, NSW, of German-Scottish ancestry. His father was Robert Schloesser, who had come to Australia as a mining engineer; his mother, the daughter of Scottish immigrants.

The family name was anglicized to Slessor in the First World War. After leaving school Slessor took up journalism, and except for a short period in Melbourne 1925–26, lived in Sydney, mainly in the eastern suburbs, often within view of Sydney Harbour, which he loved and frequently used in his poetry. He worked for the Sydney *Sun, Smith's Weekly* (editor 1935–39) and the *Daily Guardian*, and was appointed official war correspondent with the Australian army in 1940. He followed the AIF through its campaigns in Greece, Crete and Syria to El Alamein and New Guinea, then in February 1944, after disagreements with army authorities, resigned his commission. His wartime experiences provided the much-acclaimed poem, 'Beach Burial' (q.v.), and also 'An Inscription for Dog River', a savage indictment of what he saw as the delusions of grandeur of Field-Marshal Sir Thomas Blamey. He rejoined the Sydney *Sun*, staying with it as leader writer and literary editor until 1957 when he went to the *Daily Telegraph* and *Sunday Telegraph* as leader writer and book reviewer. Although he wrote virtually no new poetry after 1944 Slessor remained active in Australian literature. He compiled the 1945 anthology, *Australian Poetry*, and co-edited, in 1958, *The Penguin Book of Australian Verse*. He became in 1953 a member of the advisory board of the CLF and in 1968 a member of the National Literature Board of Review; in 1956–61 he edited the literary magazine, *Southerly*. A *bon vivant*, Slessor relished his period as president of the Sydney Journalists' Club from 1956 to 1965, which gave him considerable influence over the city's literary and journalistic scene.

Slessor's publications of verse are *Thief of the Moon* (1924), *Earth-Visitors* (1926), *Trio*, with Harley Matthews and Colin Simpson (1931), *Cuckooz Contrey* (1932), *Darlinghurst Nights and Morning Glories* (1933), *Five Bells* (1939), *One Hundred Poems 1919–1939* (1944), and *Poems* (1957), a reissue of *One Hundred Poems* with two additional poems. A further volume of Slessor's light verse (*Darlinghurst Nights* was the first) titled *Backless Betty from Bondi* was published in 1983, edited by Julian Croft. His prose was collected in *Bread and Wine* (1970). In the early 1920s Slessor was associated with Norman Lindsay and the Lindsay family as co-editor of the literary magazine, *Vision*. His early verse, especially poems like 'Earth-Visitors', 'Thieves' Kitchen', 'Pan at Lane Cove' and 'Thief of the Moon', have been dismissed as 'feverish sensuosities' and 'strained exoticism', but they reveal, even at the outset of his literary career, his superb pictorial ability and talent for creating bright, startling images. With poems such as 'William Street', 'The Night Ride' (q.v.) and 'Country Towns', Slessor abandoned the Lindsay-type surrealist landscape for the more realistic environment of Sydney and the Australian countryside, although the latter was never his favourite milieu. The most significant poem in Slessor's development as a poet is probably 'Captain Dobbin' (q.v.) from *Cuckooz Contrey*. With its interest in a romantic but realistic past, taste for poetic portraiture, and mention of 'that Captain with the sad/ And fine white face', it led inevitably to the great work, 'Five Visions of Captain Cook' (q.v.), widely regarded as the seminal voyager (q.v.) poem. 'Five Bells' (q.v.), Slessor's elegy for his dead friend, Joe Lynch, is his greatest work. The unsuccessful attempt to recapture a strong, personal memory of the dead man leads Slessor into a rueful judgement of the triumph of time over life and the seeming insignificance of human existence. Slessor's poetic silence of more than a quarter of a century, virtually from 'Five Bells' until his death in 1971, remains an unsolved mystery. Some answers have been sought in his own quoted remarks – 'I'm an extinct volcano', 'Poetry is for young men' and 'It wasn't for want of trying'. But the truth may possibly be contained in 'Five Bells' itself. In his early poetry Slessor's brilliant language and imagery run unchannelled, wasting their magic on exotica; in 'Five Bells' they are the incomparable instruments which shape the emotional and intellectual pronouncements which that poem contains. In that achievement Slessor may well have recognized both the totality, and the limit, of his poetic ambitions. The first issue (1972) of the Sydney magazine, *The Saturday Club Book of Poetry* (q.v.), was dedicated to Slessor. Herbert C. Jaffa wrote the critical and biographical *Kenneth Slessor* (1971), and Douglas Stewart, the critical memoir *A Man of Sydney* (1977).

Slow Natives, The, a novel by Thea Astley (q.v.), first published in 1965, won the Miles Franklin and Moomba awards. Set mainly in suburban Brisbane, the novel explores a series of sterile relationships, both emotional and spiritual. The Leverson family, which comprises the sensitive but bored Bernard; his equally bored but dull wife, Iris; and their precocious son Keith is the focus. Others, whose lives are also empty and whose malaise touches on theirs, include the spiritually alienated Sister Matthew and Father Lingard; Gerald Geoghegan, Iris's lover; the sexually-frustrated Miss Trumper and her severely deprived garden-boy Chookie. When Keith attempts to punish his parents for their apparent indifference by running away, he meets Chookie who is also in flight from an encounter with Miss Trumper which he interprets as rape. Their escapade ends in a car crash in which Chookie is killed and Keith loses a leg.

'SLY, CHRISTOPHER', see **NEILD, J.E.**

SMITH, BERNARD (1916–), born Sydney, art critic and professor of contemporary art and director of the Power Institute of Fine Arts at the University of Sydney 1967–77, has written several influential histories of art in Australia, which are also important as histories of ideas and cultural movements. They include *Place, Taste and Tradition* (1945), *European Vision and the South Pacific 1768–1850* (1960) and *Australian Painting 1788–1960* (1962). He has also edited *Concerning Contemporary Art* (1975) and *Documents on Art and Taste in Australia* (1975), and published a collection of his essays on art and history, *The Antipodean Manifesto* (1976). His autobiography, *The Boy Adeodatus*, was published in 1984.

SMITH, GRAEME KINROSS, see ***Australia's Writers***

SMITH, JAMES (1820–1910), born Kent, England, had a successful and varied publishing and journalistic career in England before migrating in 1854 to Australia, where he became leader writer and dramatic critic for the *Age*. He rapidly became one of the colony's most influential newspapermen and public figures. Editor of the *Leader* (1856), *Melbourne Punch* (1859), the *Australasian* (1871) and the *Evening Mail* (1881), he founded the satirical magazine, *Touchstone*, in 1869 and the *Victorian Review* in 1879. He helped establish the Garrick Club (1855), the Melbourne Shakespeare Society (1884), the Alliance Francaise (1890) and the Dante Society (1896); as a trustee of the Public Library and the National Gallery of Victoria 1880–1910, he exerted considerable influence on the cultural life of Melbourne. His own publications include the important *Cyclopedia of Victoria* (1903–05), *From Melbourne to Melrose* (1888) and *Junius Unveiled* (1909); a play, 'Garibaldi, was performed at the Prince of Wales theatre, Melbourne, in 1860.

SMITH, Sir JAMES JOYNTON, see ***Smith's Weekly***

SMITH, SYDNEY URE (1887–1949), born London, was brought to Australia in infancy and studied art at the Julian Ashton school in Sydney, where he became friendly with a group of young artists, including Norman Lindsay and Will Dyson. A pioneer of art publishing in Australia, he started the publishing house, Art in Australia, in 1916 with Bertram Stevens as co-editor. He also founded and edited the influential periodical, *Art in Australia* (q.v.), as well as *Home* and wrote and edited several books on the work of Australian artists. The Art in Australia company was sold to John Fairfax and Sons in 1934 and in 1939 Ure Smith established the firm of Ure Smith, which produced high quality publications, mostly on art and related subjects. A well-known etcher and artist, he published several collections of his etchings and drawings and also illustrated numerous works by other authors, including *Glimpses of Old Sydney* (1928) and *Old Colonial By-Ways* (1928) by Charles H. Bertie and *The Sydney Book* (1947) by Marjorie Barnard. His love of Sydney is also reflected in the anthology of literary references to the city that he illustrated and edited, *The Charm of Sydney* (1918). With Gwen Morton-Spencer he edited the magazine, *Australia National Journal* (1939–47) and its annual anthologies, *Australia Week-End Book* (1942–46). President of the Society of Artists (1921–48), and trustee and vice-president of the Art Gallery of NSW, Ure Smith also organized numerous overseas exhibitions.

SMITH, THOMAS, see 'MIDNITE, CAPTAIN'

SMITH, VIVIAN (1933–), born and educated at Hobart, Tasmania, graduated from the Universities of Tasmania and Sydney and has taught in both institutions. He has published four volumes of verse, *The Other Meaning* (1956), *An Island South* (1967), *Familiar Places* (1978) and *Tide Country* (1982), which won the NSW Premier's poetry prize. He edited *Australian Poetry 1969* and *Young Street Poets Anthology* (1983). He has published monographs on James McAuley (1965) and Vance Palmer (1971) and the critical studies, *Vance and Nettie Palmer* (1975) and *The Poetry of Robert Lowell* (1974). He also edited *Letters of Vance and Nettie Palmer 1915–1963* (1977) and wrote the poetry section of *The Oxford History of Australian Literature* (q.v., 1981).

Smith's first volume, *The Other Meaning*, reveals Tasmania as the focal point of his work. The poetry is melodious and romantically imaginative with a melancholy pensiveness. It was influenced, according to Smith, by Judith Wright and Kenneth Slessor and reflects the emphasis of those poets on the landscape and the sea, the latter of which is an 'inescapable element' for one who has grown up in Tasmania. The best of these traditional formal lyrics, e.g. 'Myth', 'Girl by Green Water', 'Bedlam Hills', 'Summer Evening', are attractive and meaningful poems reflecting both the personal inner world and the actual external in onomatopoeic language and effective imagery. *An Island South*, named for Tasmania, has Hobart in a number of titles and conveys the cold, stillness and luminosity of that wintry island. Other poems stress the poet's personal doubts and anxieties but end in affirmation, a stance that is perhaps responsible for the charge that Smith's poetry is too controlled to bite deeply. *Familiar Places* celebrates places and people that have become meaningful to the poet, Sydney ('Twenty Years of Sydney', 'Balmoral Summer') and Tuscany ('Il Convento, Batignano') joining with that first familiar place, Tasmania ('View from the Domain, Hobart', 'Back in Hobart'). *Tide Country* continues the Smith penchant for elegant, traditional verse. It contains, perhaps as a gesture to modernism, some translations of modern European poetry.

Smith's Weekly, an uninhibited Sydney newspaper which won an overseas reputation for its raciness and for the quality of its black-and-white art, was published 1919–50. It was named after Sir James Joynton Smith (1858–1943), an English-born adventurer who became a successful businessman and lord mayor of Sydney, and provided the funds which allowed Claude McKay and R.C. Packer, assisted by an ageing J.F. Archibald, to produce the first issue. Packer remained with the newspaper until 1931, Smith until 1939, and McKay intermittently until 1950; Kenneth Slessor was editor 1935–39 and editor-in-chief in 1939–40. Aggressively nationalist and somewhat racist, *Smith's* championed the cause of the digger, espoused the White Australia Policy, and was aggressively anti-communist; it rivalled the *Bulletin* with its blend of sporting and other news, satire and visual humour in which horse-racing, Dad and Dave and the Anzacs were regular subjects. Among many notable artists who drew for the journal were Cecil Hartt, George Finey, Frank Dunne, Jim Russell and Stan Cross, whose famous cartoon, 'For Gorsake stop laughing – this is serious', was first published in *Smith's* in 1933. Among its best-known writers were the sporting reporter, Jim Donald, the satirists Lennie Lower, Ronald McCuaig and Alexander Macdonald, and the political commentator, Brian Fitzpatrick. Smith's memoirs, *My Life Story*, were published in 1927, and George Blaikie's *Remember Smith's Weekly?* was published in 1966.

'SMITHY', see KINGSFORD-SMITH, Sir CHARLES

Snowball, see CASEY, GAVIN; Aboriginal in Australian Literature

Snowy River, made legendary in Australian folklore by A.B. Paterson's poem, The Man from Snowy River' (q.v.), rises in the Snowy Mountains near Mt Kosciusko in NSW and flows into Bass Strait, some 450 kilometres away, in the Gippsland district of Victoria. First explored in 1840 by P.E. Strzelecki (q.v.), who named Mt Kosciusko, the area was named Muniong (or Munyang) by geologist, W.B. Clarke, after the Aboriginal word for the region, but the name Snowy Mountains caught public imagination and was later officially adopted. The Snowy Mountains are the source of many rivers; others in addition to the Snowy are the Tumut and a major tributary of the Murray, the Swampy Plain. The spring run off from the heavy winter snows provides the water for the Snowy Mountains hydro-electric scheme which was completed in 1972. The alpine country through which the Snowy initially flows is ruggedly beautiful; its lofty grandeur influenced, and is reflected in, the poetry of Sydney Jephcott (q.v.). Elyne Mitchell (q.v.), who lived in the alpine country, draws on it for the background to her popular children's Silver Brumby series; to her book of essays, Images of Water (1947); to her experiences as a skier and climber in the area, Australia's Alps (1942); and to her work on the family property during the Second World War, Speak to the Earth (1945). Douglas Stewart's poem, 'The Man from Adaminaby', is about the drowning of the old township by the Snowy hydro-electric scheme.

Snugglepot and Cuddlepie, see GIBBS, MAY

Social Patterns in Australian Literature, see Criticism; MOORE, T. INGLIS

Society of Women Writers (Australia) was founded in 1925 with the object of drawing together women writers from a variety of fields and promoting the publication of Australian books. An honorary organization with affiliations with the Society of Women Writers and Journalists, London, it includes numerous distinguished Australian authors.

Socrates and Other Poems, see WEBB, FRANCIS

Solid Mandala, The, a novel by Patrick White (q.v.), was published in 1966. Set in pre-war and contemporary urban Australia, it is divided into four sections. The first describes the elderly twin brothers Arthur and Waldo Brown as they are glimpsed by two housewives, Mrs Poulter and Mrs Dun, from the 8.13 bus from Sarsaparilla to Barranugli (qq.v.). Shabbily dressed,

they are accompanied by their scruffy dogs and trudge along hand in hand; 'it was difficult to decide which was leading and which was led'. The second and longest section, titled 'Waldo', describes the brothers' present and past, largely as realized by Waldo's repressed, embittered consciousness. Brought to Australia from England in childhood by parents who were always inadequate in terms of their own dreams, Waldo has been dogged by resentful embarrassment at his own inadequacies and, even more, those of his father and his backward brother Arthur. Although Waldo frequently hates Arthur, they seem doomed to live side by side, sharing the same house, parents, relationships, experiences, habits, aspirations, and even the same bed. Waldo's cultural ambitions are fated to be stillborn; his promising relationship with Dulcie Feinstein, daughter of a middle-class Jewish family, comes to nothing and is surpassed by Arthur's intimacy with her, and even his dog is only technically his own. Waldo's resentment of Arthur's invasion of every area of his life and of his superior gifts of self-expression reaches a crescendo when he discovers his brother in the library, previously his own preserve, reading such spiritually important works as The Brothers Karamazov. In his anger he physically ejects Arthur and later, intolerably chafed by the yoke that joins them, plans his brother's death. The third section, titled 'Arthur', presents several of the same facts and events, although this time refracted by Arthur's more relaxed, open and perceptive consciousness. Despite his apparent slowness, Arthur, more spiritually alive than his brother, is in quest of a vision of totality that is most suggestively hinted at in the idea of the mandala as the 'dwelling of the god'. It is embodied for him most persistently in the four glass marbles that he lovingly treasures. Unlike Waldo, Arthur establishes genuine communication with Dulcie Feinstein and her family and with Mrs Poulter. His tentative vision is expressed most notably in his dance of the mandala for Mrs Poulter and in his gifts of the marbles: the golden one to Mrs Poulter, the knotted one to Waldo and the blue one to Dulcie. The whorled marble, expressive of the cloudy ambiguities of life, he keeps for himself. The novel's final section, 'Mrs Poulter and the Zeitgeist', returns to the consequences of Waldo's murderous feelings for his brother. Waldo's dead body, abandoned by the appalled Arthur and hideously disfigured by the dogs, is discovered by Mrs Poulter. Arthur, unhinged by the corrosive force of Waldo's hate, is led away to an institution.

SOLOMON, IKEY (?1787–1850), a notorious London 'fence', was first sentenced to transportation in 1810 but escaped from the prison hulks and continued to ply his trade. Arrested again in 1827, he again escaped, but his wife stood trial in his stead and was transported to Van Diemen's Land in 1828. Ikey followed her, was arrested in Hobart, sent back to England for trial and returned to Australia as a convict in 1831. Several writers about convictism traded on Solomon's notoriety and include him as a minor character in their work, e.g. James Tucker in *Ralph Rashleigh*, 'Price Warung' in *Tales of the Early Days* (1894) and 'W.T. Moncrieff' in *Van Diemen's Land* (1830).

SOLOMON, SAMUEL, see **SIDNEY, SAMUEL**

'Some Popular Australian Mistakes', see *Bulletin* Debate; Outback

Somers, Richard, see **LAWRENCE, D.H.**; *Kangaroo*

SOMERS, THOMAS, see **DAMPIER, ALFRED**

SOMERVILLE, OLIVER M. (?–1946), a Sydney poet who was acquainted with such writers as A.D. Hope, Harry Hooton, James McAuley, Harold Stewart and Garry Lyle, contributed to such periodicals as *Arna* and *Hermes* and to the collection, *The First Boke of Fowle Ayres* (q.v.). Politically and personally eccentric, he is remembered for his impact on the cultural life of the University of Sydney, e.g. by Donald Horne in his *The Education of Young Donald* (1967).

'Song of Ninian Melville, The', see *Songs from the Mountains*

Song of the Dardanelles and Other Verses, see *My Army, O, My Army! and Other Songs*

'Song of the Republic, A', was Henry Lawson's (q.v.) first published poem; a stirring appeal to the 'Sons of the South' (the original title) to bring about a new social order, it appeared in the *Bulletin* in October 1887. The circumstances of its composition, acceptance and publication are recorded in Lawson's 'A Fragment of Autobiography'.

Songs from the Mountains, Henry Kendall's (q.v.) final volume of verse, has an interesting publishing history. When first published in December 1880 it included a satirical poem, 'The Song of Ninian Melville', which heaped abuse upon the then member for Northumberland in the NSW parliament. Because the publishers feared a libel action by Melville the volume was hurriedly withdrawn, the satire

replaced by a poem, 'Christmas Creek', and the volume reissued in January 1881. Kendall's best collection, *Songs from the Mountains*, contains the autobiographical lyrics, 'Mooni' and 'Narrara Creek', and the well-known character pieces, 'Bill the Bullock Driver' and 'Jim the Splitter' (qq.v.). The dedicatory poem of the volume, 'To a Mountain', reveals Kendall's understanding and acceptance of the problems that had so embittered his early life and his new sense of self-reconciliation.

Songs of a Campaign, see **GELLERT, LEON**; War Literature

Songs of a Sentimental Bloke, The (1915), the colloquial verse narrative that bestowed on C.J. Dennis (q.v.) the title 'Laureate of the Larrikin', tells of the courtship and marriage of Bill, a larrikin of the Melbourne streets, much given to 'gettin' on the shick', and his 'ideal tart' Doreen, whose 'lurk' was 'pastin' labels in a pickle joint'. Other characters in the story, Ginger Mick and Rose of Spadgers, were used by Dennis in later volumes to continue the series. An immediate best-seller, the book went through five printings in three months and has been frequently adapted for the stage, film and television. Although it has never re-captured its first popularity and has sometimes been accused of gross exaggeration in its vernacular style and unrealistic characterization, it occupies a unique position in the folk literature of Australia. In it Dennis has immortalized, and romanticized, the city larrikin who was a feature of Australian urban life in the early part of the twentieth century.

Songs of the Army of the Night, see **ADAMS, FRANCIS**

SORENSEN, JACK (1907–49), born Kalgoorlie, WA, of mixed Danish, Irish and English heritage, was a WA boxing champion, shearer, newspaper representative and balladist whose poems appeared regularly in the *Bulletin* and in the newspapers of the WA goldfields. His publications were *The Gun of Glindawor* (1932), *The Last Shanty* (1939) and *The Collected Poems of Jack Sorensen, 1907–1949* published posthumously in 1950. *The Collected Poems*, with such segments as 'Shearing Ballads and Rhymes of the North-West', 'Goldfields Verse' and 'Songs of the Kimberleys', illustrates the themes of Sorensen's verse.

SORENSON, E.S. (EDWARD SYLVESTER) (1869–1939), of mixed Norwegian and Australian parentage, was born at Dryaaba near Casino, NSW. His life was spent in a variety of bush occupations: farming, dairying, droving, shearing and prospecting for gold. A member of the FAW, a contributor to the *Bulletin*, and an enthusiastic naturalist, Sorenson published numerous volumes of fiction interspersed with verses about the bush. His major publications were *The Squatter's Ward* (1908), *Quinton's Rouseabout and Other Stories* (1908), *Life in the Australian Backblocks* (1911), *Friends and Foes in the Australian Bush* (1914), and *Chips and Splinters* (1919).

SOUTER, C.H. (CHARLES HENRY) (1864–1944), born Scotland, came to Australia in 1879 and spent three years in the bush before returning to Scotland to train as a doctor. After a journey to China as a ship's surgeon and some years in NSW he settled in a practice in SA. He began to contribute ballads to the *Bulletin* in 1908 and published four collections of verse, *Irish Lords and Other Verses* (1912), *To Many Ladies and Others* (1917), *The Mallee Fire and Other Verses* (1923) and *The Lonely Rose and Other Verses* (1935). Souter wrote bush ballads and sea shanties as well as straightforward lyrical verse. His bush ballads, which reflect the daily life of the small farms of SA, are sensitive to the experience and idiom of a wide range of personalities, both male and female. Some of his most memorable are 'Irish Lords', 'Pump'kin Time', 'When the Missus Is Away' and 'Harvestin'. His rhythmic, suitably salty, sea shanties, such as 'What the Red-Haired Bo'sun Said' and 'Blue Peter', are less individual and distinctive but found a ready audience. His brother, D.H. Souter (1862–1935), was a long-term *Bulletin* cartoonist and book-illustrator.

SOUTER, GAVIN (1929–), born Melbourne, joined the staff of the *Sydney Morning Herald* after graduating from the University of Sydney in 1948. As a representative of the newspaper he spent 1950–51 in New York and 1968–70 in London. He has written a history of the European relationship with New Guinea, *New Guinea – The Last Unknown* (1963); a profile of Sydney, *Sydney* (1965), titled in subsequent reprints, *Sydney Observed*, illustrated by George Molnar; an account of the settlements of New Australia and Cosme in Paraguay under the leadership of William Lane, *A Peculiar People* (1968); an autobiography of his childhood in Sydney, NSW and Queensland 1939–45, *The Idle Hill of Summer* (1972); a history of the British-Australian relationship from Federation to 1919, which won the award of the Foundation for Australian Literary Studies, *Lion and Kangaroo* (1976); and *Company of Heralds* (1981). Written to mark the 150th anniversary of the *Sydney Morning Herald*, *Company of Heralds* is also a socio-historical docu-

ment, especially significant as an account of the role of the press in Australian political life; it won the 1981 award of the Foundation for Australian Literary Studies.

South-Asian Register, published quarterly in Sydney 1827–28, carried poetry, literary reviews and articles on literary subjects.

South Australia, which comprises the central southern part of the Australian continent, is the only Australian State without convict origins and was settled experimentally in 1836 after proposals for systematic colonization were initiated by Edward Gibbon Wakefield (q.v.) in 1829. In 1842 South Australia became an ordinary British colony, and in 1861 its western boundary was extended so that it became co-existent with the eastern boundary of Western Australia. In 1863–1911 the Northern Territory was under the jurisdiction of South Australia, which became part of the Commonwealth of Australia in 1901. It now advertises itself as the Festival State, which confirms the importance of the Adelaide Festival to its citizens.

South Australian Advertiser, see *Advertiser*

South Australian Chronicle, South Australian Weekly Chronicle, see *Chronicle*

South Australian Gazette and Colonial Register, see *Register*; STEVENSON, GEORGE

South Australian Magazine, the first SA literary periodical, was published as a monthly 1841–43. Founded by James Allen, a pioneering SA journalist who was associated with several early Adelaide newspapers and periodicals, it included literary articles, serial fiction and poetry.

South Australian Register, see *Register*

'**South of My Days**', published in *The Moving Image* (1946), is the poem that chiefly characterizes Judith Wright (q.v.) as the poet of the New England countryside. The poem echoes her affectionate memories of the 'clean, lean hungry country' in which she was born and grew to womanhood. It contains, too, fragments of stories from that countryside's pioneer past – drovers and bushrangers, desperate droughts and starving cattle, and the legendary coaches of Cobb & Co.

South Pacific Association for Commonwealth Language and Literature Studies, see **Association for Commonwealth Language and Literature Studies**

SOUTHALL, IVAN (1921–   ), born Melbourne, left school at the age of fourteen to work for the Melbourne *Herald* before joining the RAAF in 1942. In the same year he published at his own expense a collection of short stories for adults, *Out of the Dawn*. Posted to England, he served in Coastal Command, was awarded the DFC, and at the end of 1944 was transferred to RAAF headquarters in London as a writer in the historical section. In 1946 he returned to Melbourne and resumed work as a process-engraver, but in 1947 gave up his job in favour of casual work that would leave more time for writing. Now Australia's best-known writer of serious children's fiction, whose books have been published in numerous countries and translated into several languages, he frequently travels and lectures overseas. Southall's first nine books for children, which form a series published in 1950, centre on an incredibly courageous, resourceful and stoical airman, Simon Black (*Meet Simon Black, Simon Black in Peril, . . . in Space, . . . in Coastal Command, . . . in China, . . . and the Spaceman, . . . in the Antarctic, . . . Takes Over, . . . at Sea*). *Hills End* (1962) his next children's book, is a complete departure from his previous work and reflects a strong interest in the real-life problems, emotions and experiences of young people. The thirteen novels that follow *Hills End* have continued to explore this vein of realism; they are *Ash Road* (1965), *The Fox Hole* (1967), *To the Wild Sky* (1967), *Sly Old Wardrobe* (1968), *Let the Balloon Go* (1968), *Finn's Folly* (1969), *Chinaman's Reef is Ours* (1970), *Bread and Honey* (1970), also published with the title, *Walk a Mile and Get Nowhere, Josh* (1971), *Over the Top* (1972), also published as *Benson Boy* (1973), *Head in the Clouds* (1972), *Matt and Jo* (1973), *What about Tomorrow* (1977) and *King of the Sticks* (1979). Southall has also published several non-fiction books for young people. Much of Southall's fictional and non-fictional writing for children has links with his books he has written for adults, especially those that derive from his wartime experiences, *They Shall Not Pass Unseen* (1956), a popular history of 461 Squadron, RAAF; *Bluey Truscott* (1958), a memoir of one of Australia's most famous air aces; and *Softly Tread the Brave* (1960), an account of the work of mine disposal officers. Southall also drew on these experiences for six adventure stories for adults published in his War in the Air series 1958–60. His other writing for adults includes a biography of Godfrey Hirst, *The Weaver from Meltham* (1950) and an account of missionary work in the outback, *Parson on the Track* (1962). Some of his lectures on writing for children were collected in 1975, titled *A Journey of Discovery*. Southall has won the Children's Book of the Year Award in 1966, 1968, 1971, and 1976, the Picture Book of the Year Award in 1969; in 1971 he was awarded the British Library Association Carnegie Medal, and in 1972 the Zilver Griffell of Holland. In 1974 he received the Australian Writers' Award and in 1981 was made AM.

Southall combines an outstanding ability to identify with and to realize the thoughts, feelings and agonies of childhood and adolescence with a gift for evoking suspense in scenes of gripping action. A realist who deals frankly with contemporary and universal problems ranging from physical disability to psychological instability and emotional inadequacy, he makes few concessions to his youthful audience. His first three serious books for children, *Hills End, Ash Road* and *To the Wild Sky*, form a group in that they are all about groups of children who face disaster without adult help and with varying degrees of success; in all of them the central theme is the growth to maturity. *Finn's Folly* is an even more harrowing and probing story of disaster in which three adults are killed in a road accident, a foggy hillside is made treacherous with overturned drums of deadly cyanide and a mentally-retarded boy wanders without protection. *Chinaman's Reef Is Ours* explores love/hate relationships in a dying mining town. *The Fox Hole* concentrates on a tense drama between a frightened child and his greed-crazed uncle. *Let the Balloon Go*, which was produced as a film in 1975 and is a compelling story of a spastic boy's bid for independence, is the first of a series of studies of individual growth towards adulthood, *Bread and Honey, Josh, What About Tomorrow* and *King of the Sticks*. With *Josh, Head in the Clouds, Matt and Jo* and *Over the Top* Southall has also begun to explore a new vein of humour.

Southerly, the quarterly journal of the Sydney branch of the English Association (q.v.), was founded in 1939 under the editorship of R.G. Howarth; subsequent editors have been Kenneth Slessor (1956–62), Walter Stone (1962), and G.A. Wilkes (1963–   ). In its early years it gave coverage to English and American literature but from 1944, when Angus & Robertson (publishers 1944–71) became involved in its production, it gave increasing attention to Australian writing; from Slessor's editorship it has been subtitled *A Review of Australian Literature*. Now produced by Wentworth Press, *Southerly* publishes creative work, chiefly short stories and poetry, as well as criticism and reviews. Apart from 1960, when no issues appeared, *Southerly* has continued to play a significant part in the study of Australian literature, particularly through its contribution to the establishment of a body of criticism on significant Australian writers such as C.J. Brennan, 'Henry Handel Richardson' and Patrick White. It sponsors the H.M. Butterly–F. Earle-Hooper Award, named after two active members of the English Association, for the best *Southerly* contribution in creative writing or literary criticism by a writer who is not yet established.

Southern Australian, an early SA newspaper, was published weekly and semi-weekly 1838–51; founded soon after the establishment of the colony of SA in response to the anti-gubernatorial views expressed by George Stevenson (q.v.) in the *South Australian Gazette*; it changed its title to the *South Australian* in 1844.

Southern Cross (1), a notable constellation in the southern heavens, whose four chief stars are in the shape of a cross, was first described as a 'cross' shape by Andrea Corsali in 1517 and first officially segregated and named *Crux* by the astronomer, Royer, in 1679. Five of the stars of the constellation are represented on the flag of the Commonwealth of Australia. The Southern Cross has been frequently evoked or used as a nationalistic title.

Southern Cross (2) is the name of the flag hoisted by the rebellious diggers of the Eureka (q.v.) stockade. Raffaello Carboni in his *The Eureka Stockade* (1855) describes the flag as 'silk, blue ground, with a large silver cross, similar to the one in our southern firmament; no device of arms, but all exceedingly chaste and natural'. Len Fox (q.v.) gives an account of the flag's history in *The Strange Story of the Eureka Flag* (1963); Louis Esson called his Eureka play *The Southern Cross* (1946).

Southern Cross: A Magazine for the People, a monthly journal published in Sydney and edited in succession by Maxwell Keely and Charles Turner, ran 1898–1900. It included some general literary articles and original poetry and short stories.

Southern Cross: A Weekly Journal of Politics, Literature and Social Progress, founded and edited by Daniel Deniehy (q.v.) as a vehicle for his political and literary ideas, was published in Sydney and ran 1859–60. Apart from Deniehy (whose well-known prose satire *How I Became Attorney-General of New Barataria* was first published in the *Southern Cross* in 1860), other well-known contributors included Charles Harpur, R.H. Horne and William Forster.

Southern Lights and Shadows: Brief Notes of Three Years' Experience of Social, Literary, and Political Life in Australia was written by Frank Fowler (q.v.) while returning to England from Australia in 1858 and was published in 1859. Fowler records his experiences of life in Sydney; compares Sydney and Melbourne, to the latter city's advantage; gives a series of brief comments on the colonial press of the day; vividly describes such characters as bullock drivers, city larrikins and modish young colonial belles; trenchantly criticizes the new parliamentary system of self-government; and provides anecdotes from his country travels. Written in haste, *Southern Lights and Shadows* was undoubtedly a 'pot-boiler', pandering to the eager market in England for descriptive works on the colony. Although it was a rather mild document overall and one of the more interesting of the contemporary accounts of Australian life, its errors and exaggerations provoked some criticism and hostility in the colony. Its shortcomings are discussed in the preface to R.H. Horne's *Australian Facts and Prospects* (1859).

SOUTHEY, ROBERT, see **Convict in Australian Literature**

Sowers of the Wind, see **HUNGERFORD, T.A.G.**

Span, see **Association for Commonwealth Language and Literature Studies**

Spats' Fact'ry, see **DYSON, EDWARD**

SPEAR, R.C., see *Golden West*

SPEARS, STEVE J. (1951–), born Adelaide, studied law at the University of Adelaide before deciding to follow a career in theatre. He has published six plays, *Africa – A Savage Musical* (produced 1974), *Mad Jean* (produced 1978) and *People Keep Giving Me Things* (published with the preceding two plays in *Early Works*, 1978); *The Elocution of Benjamin Franklin* (q.v.) in *Drag Show* (1977); *The Resuscitation of the Little Prince Who Couldn't Laugh as Performed by Young Mo at the Height of the Great Depression of 1929* (or *Young Mo*) in *Theatre-Australia* (1977); and *King Richard* in *Three Political Plays* (1980), ed. Alrene Sykes. His other plays include 'Stud' (1973), 'Eliza Q' (1975), 'There Were Giants in Those Days' (1978), 'The Death of George Reeves' (1979), 'Friends of the Family' (1980) and 'When They Send Me Three-and-Fourpence' (1982). Spears has also written for radio and television and worked as an actor.

An innovative and lively playwright, Spears

is at home in a wide range of theatrical modes from vaudeville to naturalism. The protagonists of 'The Death of George Reeves' and 'There Were Giants in Those Days' are the larger-than-life cartoon-strip characters, Batman, Superman and Wonderwoman, whom Spears reveals as privately human and limited; *Young Mo* (produced in 1976), recreates the life and personality of the famous Australian comic, Roy Rene; *King Richard* (produced in 1978), part-thriller, part-farce, part-political satire, focuses on a confrontation between a convicted murderer and a State premier, which reveals their basic similarity. But Spears is best known for his one-actor play, *The Elocution of Benjamin Franklin* (first produced in 1976), a complex study of a middle-aged transvestite, which has been widely staged in Australia as well as in London, New York and San Francisco.

Spectator was the title of four Australian journals. Richard Thompson's *Spectator*, with original verse and reviews, was published weekly in 1846; the *Spectator: Journal of Literature and Art*, published fortnightly 1858–59, was edited by Cora Anna Weekes; the *Spectator*, edited by Edward Langton, contained articles on political and literary topics as well as original prose and verse and ran monthly 1865–67. In 1900–05, the *Spectator*, a WA weekly, was published and edited by R.C. Spear, carried short fiction, verse, book reviews and literary comment, and was illustrated with satirical cartoons by Ben Strange.

Speewah (Speewaa, Speewa), the home of great men and tall tales, was a mythical station in Australian folklore from about 1870 to the 1950s. Ernestine Hill places it near Swan Hill on the Murray River, but it has also been located by other writers in Queensland and the Kimberleys. Its chief character is Crooked Mick of the Speewah who, though no giant by Speewah standards, often uses Ayers Rock to 'stone the crows'. Other celebrities of the Speewah are Big Bill and Slab-face Joe. Crooked Mick features in Alan Marshall's story, 'They were Tough Men on the Speewah', in *How's Andy Going* (1956), in Julian Stuart's anecdotes in the *Australian Worker* in the 1920s, and in Bill Wannan's *Crooked Mick of the Speewah* (1956). David Campbell included a poem, 'The Speewah Picnics', in *The Miracle of Mullion Hill* (1956). The comic strip, *Speewa Jack*, written by Alan Marshall and drawn by Doug Tainsh, ran in the *Argus* 1954–57, and later briefly in the *Age*. Its central character, Speewa Jack, is noted for his tall stories, many of which relate to the goldfields and bushranging days.

SPENCE, CATHERINE HELEN (1825–1910), born near Melrose, Scotland, where she

was educated, migrated to SA with her family in 1839. She became a governess at seventeen, largely because she felt that experience as a teacher would advance her literary ambitions. In 1854 she published anonymously *Clara Morison: A Tale of South Australia during the Gold Fever* (q.v.), a novel she described as 'more domestic than exciting'. In 1856 she published, also anonymously, a second novel, *Tender and True: A Colonial Tale*. Her interest in social reform, which first expressed itself in her disaffection with the existing electoral system, began in 1858 after she had read an article by John Stuart Mill on proportional representation. In 1861 she published *A Plea for Pure Democracy*, which advocated the Thomas Hare system of proportional representation. The first novel under her own name, *Mr. Hogarth's Will*, was had been earlier serialized as 'Uphill Work' in the Adelaide *Weekly Mail* in 1863–64, was published in 1865. It was followed in 1868 by *The Author's Daughter*, which had been published serially as 'Hugh Lindsay's Guest' in the Adelaide *Observer* in 1867. Among her continuing social concerns were the removal of destitute children from institutions into normal homes and the provision of increased educational opportunities for the very young and for adolescent girls; such concerns were expressed in the articles published in the *Register* in 1878 as 'Some Social Aspects of South Australian Life'. Her social commentary, *The Laws We Live Under* (1880), became the first civics or social studies textbook to be used in Australian schools. In 1881–82 her novel, *Gathered In* (q.v.), was serialized in the *Observer* but was not published in book form until 1977. Another novel, *Handfasted*, (1984) was unpublished in her lifetime, its themes and sentiments considered too advanced for the time. In 1884 she published, anonymously, *An Agnostic's Progress from the Known to the Unknown*, an account of the way in which maturity and self-knowledge, together with her shift from Calvinism to Unitarianism, brought relief from the religious despondency of her early life. 'A Week in the Future', serialized in the *Centennial Magazine* in 1889, was probably her last fictional work, although indications of other writings exist. Her public participation in social causes then became more pronounced. She made lecture tours of the USA and Britain speaking on the inequalities of the voting system; helped to form the Effective Voting League of SA; became Australia's first female political candidate in the federal convention elections of 1897; was vice-president of the Women's Suffrage League of SA; and helped establish a SA branch of the National Council of Women. A Catherine Spence Prize for the best woman student in economics has been annually awarded at the University of Adelaide, and the SA government awards an annual social sciences scholarship in her name.

More emphasis is usually placed on her role as pioneer feminist and social reformer than on her literary achievements, but with *Clara Morison*, which Frederick Sinnett in 1856 judged 'decidedly the best Australian novel we have met with', and with *Gathered In* she made a considerable contribution to colonial Australian fiction. *Catherine Helen Spence: An Autobiography*, begun by her and completed after her death by her companion, Jeanne F. Young, was published in 1910. Jeanne F. Young also published *Catherine Helen Spence: A Study and an Appreciation* (1937).

SPENCE, W.G. (WILLIAM GUTHRIE) (1846–1926), born in the Orkney Islands, Scotland, came to Australia in 1853. A miner on the Victorian goldfields from an early age, he was prominent in labour affairs and became general secretary of the Amalgamated Miners' Association, president of the Amalgamated Shearers' Union and a conspicuous figure in the maritime strike of 1890 and the Queensland shearers' strike of 1891. He became general secretary of the AWU in 1894; in 1898 he was elected to the NSW Legislative Assembly and in 1901 to the Commonwealth parliament. Spence wrote the *History of the A.W.U.* (1911) and *Australia's Awakening: Thirty Years in the Life of an Australian Agitator* (1909), which gives an interesting if biased view of social conditions in Australia at the end of the nineteenth century. Spence also became known in bush society via a bush ballad by F.J. Murray as the owner of a mythical station, Spence's Station, as a result of attempts by rural landowners to present him to his followers as a man of property.

SPENCER-BROWNE, REGINALD (1856–1943), born Appin, NSW, served in the Boer War and the First World War, before joining the staff of the *Brisbane Courier*, of which he became associate editor. He published a series of bush and mining yarns, *Romances of the Goldfield and Bush* (1890); two collections of poetry, *Shadow and Shine* (1874) and *The Last Ride* (1875); and reminiscences, *A Journalist's Memories* (1927).

SPENCER, T.E. (THOMAS EDWARD) (1845–1911), born London, visited Australia at eighteen and returned in 1875 to settle in Sydney, where he became a building contractor and a prominent figure in industrial arbitration. He is best known for his humorous ballads, several of which, e.g. 'How McDougall Topped the Score' (q.v.), 'Why Doherty Died' and

'O'Toole and McSharry', have become familiar recitation pieces. His ballads, frequently contributed to the *Bulletin*, appeared in two collections, *How McDougall Topped the Score and Other Verses and Sketches* (1906) and *Budgeree Ballads* (1908), reprinted in 1910 as *Why Doherty Died*. He also published a novel, *Bindawalla* (1912), and short stories, most of which deal with the experiences of another popular character, a loquacious Irish-Australian lady, Mrs Bridget McSweeney, *The Surprising Adventures of Mrs Bridget McSweeney* (1906), *A Spring Cleaning and Other Stories by Mrs Bridget McSweeney* (1908), *The Haunted Shanty* (1910) and *That Droll Lady* (1911).

SPENCER, Sir WALTER (1860–1929), born Lancashire, England, became the first professor of biology at the University of Melbourne in 1887. He joined the W.A. Horn expedition into Central Australia in 1894 and met his future collaborator, Francis James Gillen (1856–1912), who for twenty years had worked with the Arunta tribes amongst whom he was accepted as an initiate. Spencer and Gillen subsequently lived with the Arunta and allied tribes for lengthy periods and were permitted to observe their sacred ceremonies, previously unwitnessed by Europeans. The results of their studies were published in 1899, titled *The Native Tribes of Central Australia*. Later they spent a year studying the Warramunga and more northerly tribes, which resulted in *The Northern Tribes of Central Australia* (1904). Spencer made further investigations after Gillen's death, visiting Central Australia in 1923 and 1924, and published a revision and extension of his earlier work with Gillen, *The Arunta* (1927). Spencer also published the *Native Tribes of the Northern Territory of Australia* (1914) and two more popular accounts of his work, with Gillen, *Across Australia* (1912) and *Wanderings in Wild Australia* (1928). The journal of Spencer's last expedition to Tierra del Fuego, where he died, was published in 1931, edited by R.R. Marett and T.K. Penniman, *Spencer's Last Journey*.

Sphinx of Eaglehawk, The, see 'BOLDREWOOD, ROLF'

Spicer, Mrs, see Wilson, Joe

SPIELVOGEL, NATHAN (1874–1956), born Ballarat, worked as a teacher in rural areas of Victoria and at Ballarat and contributed short stories, sketches and verse to the *Lone Hand*, the *Bulletin* and other newspapers. Many of his short stories dealing with Jewish life in Ballarat appeared regularly in the Jewish press and some were collected in *Selected Stories of Nathan*

Spielvogel (1956). His impressions of Europe during a lengthy visit, titled *A Gumsucker on the Tramp* (1905), ran into four printings and was followed by *The Gumsucker at Home* (1913). Spielvogel also published sketches of school life and farming, set mainly in the Wimmera district, *The Cocky Farmer* (1907); a series of sketches dealing with the experiences of an unorthodox schoolmaster, *Old Eko's Note-Book* (1930); a collection of verse, *Our Gum Trees* (1913); several brief histories of Ballarat's institutions as well as a general history of the city (1935); a popular account of the Eureka rebellion, *The Affair at Eureka* (1928); and a ballad, *The Call of the Wandering Jew* (1940).

Spinifex, the name of a creeping, salt-tolerant grass that is abundant on Australian sea shores, is also popularly used to denote the tussock grass that covers much of the inland. Sometimes used as a pseudonym by writers, e.g. Alfred Chandler and David Martin, spinifex was also used in the titles of books, especially about WA, e.g. D.W. Carnegie's *Spinifex and Sand: A Narrative of Five Years' Pioneering and Exploration in Western Australia* (1898).

Spinner (1924–27), a monthly poetry magazine, was published in Melbourne, edited by R.A. Broinowski. Numerous poets of the time, including Dorothea McKellar, Zora Cross, Mary Gilmore, Louis Lavater and 'Furnley Maurice', were contributors to the magazine, which also included brief reviews, biographical notes and photographs. Issues of the *Spinner* were also reprinted as annual volumes 1925–27, titled *Poetry in Australasia*.

Springtime in Taranaki, see **STEWART, DOUGLAS**

Springwood, a residential centre and tourist resort in the Blue Mountains area of NSW, was named by Governor Macquarie. It was the home of Norman Lindsay from 1912 until his death in 1969. The grounds of his property, which is set in ten hectares of bush, were landscaped by Lindsay himself and decorated with many of his sculptures to express his dream of an Australian Arcadia. After Lindsay died the property became part of the National Trust and in 1973 was officially titled the Norman Lindsay Gallery and Museum. The house contains a representative collection of pencil and pen drawings, etchings, watercolours, oil paintings, books, ship models and statuary, bequeathed by Lindsay to the nation.

'Sprite of the Creek, The', see **Fisher's Ghost**

SPUNNER, SUZANNE, see **Feminism and Australian Literature**

Squatter is a word which probably derived from the American term 'to squat', meaning to settle on unclaimed land without a title. The term has now gone out of general use, the modern approximation being 'grazier' or 'pastoralist'. When first used around the 1830s, squatter was a derogatory term applied mainly to convicts who settled on unoccupied land on the outskirts of the settlement. By the 1840s it was used to describe all those who grazed stock beyond the borders of the Nineteen Counties proclaimed by Governor Darling as the limits of settlement. By the end of the 1860s the squattocracy was firmly established in spite of the bitter political struggles of the 1850s and 1860s and the passing of various Selection and Land Acts aimed at producing more equable land distribution. Thereafter squatter became, and remained, something of a class term, denoting wealth and power. The squatters did not, however, succeed in fulfilling W.C. Wentworth's 1853 ambition of establishing a colonial peerage based upon 'our Shepherd Kings'; that proposal was ridiculed out of existence by Daniel Deniehy's derisive comments about a 'bunyip aristocracy'. Notable among the many squatters' memoirs and reminiscences are W.A. Brodribb's (q.v.) *Recollections of an Australian Squatter* (1883), E.M. Curr's (q.v.) *Recollections of Squatting in Victoria* (1883) and James Kirby's *Old Times in the Bush of Australia* (q.v., 1895). Notable fictional squatters include the Bractons in *The Emigrant Family* (1849), the Buckleys in *The Recollections of Geoffry Hamlyn* (1859), the Delacys in *All That Swagger* (1936), the Mazeres and Pooles in the 'Brent of Bin Bin' (q.v.) novels, Stewart of Kooltopa in *Such is Life* (1903) and the Cabells in *Landtakers* (1934) and *Inheritors* (1936).

The squatter is frequently an unpopular figure in literature. One of the earliest expressions of distaste for his greed is Charles Harpur's sonnet, 'On the Political and Moral Condition of Australia in 1845'. He is pictured as arrogant, ruthless, avaricious and miserly, the implacable enemy of the small selectors in the many selection stories of 'Steele Rudd' and Henry Lawson; of swagmen down on their luck in Lawson's stories and in poems such as A.B. Paterson's 'Waltzing Matilda'; or of travelling drovers like Saltbush Bill (q.v.) who wage ceaseless battles with squatters like Stingy Smith. In Henry Kingsley's fiction, in some of the station romances of Rosa Praed (q.v.), and in the novels of Miles Franklin, the representation of the squatter is much more favourable.

A factual account of the squatting era in

Queensland and the Kimberleys is given in Mary Durack's *Kings in Grass Castles* (1959) and in Victoria in Margaret Kiddle's *Men of Yesterday* (1961). The early development of squatting is outlined in S.H Roberts's *The Squatting Age in Australia 1835–1847* (1935); and its heyday is recalled in P.F. Gilbert's *Rural Life 1860–1890* (1971).

Squatter's Dream, The, a novel by 'Rolf Boldrewood' (q.v.), was first published as a serial in the *Australian Town and Country Journal* in 1875; radically changed, it was published as *Ups and Downs* (1878), 'Boldrewood''s first book, and republished under the original title in 1890. *The Squatter's Dream* is strongly autobiographical: the experiences of its hero, Jack Redgrave, who sells his cattle-run, Marshmead, and suffers a decline in fortune are similar to those of 'Boldrewood', who after selling his Victorian run, Squattlesea Mere, in 1861 failed on two sheep stations and was forced to go droving. In the serial version Jack wakes up to find himself at Marshmead, with the sale advertisement on the table before him unposted; in the novel version he completes the sale, buys a bigger station, fails on it, but eventually recoups his fortunes sufficiently to buy back Marshmead.

'Squeaker's Mate', see **BAYNTON, BARBARA**

STABLE, J.J., see Anthologies

'STANDBY', see **PORTEOUS, RICHARD SYDNEY**

STANLEY, OWEN (1811–50), a Royal Navy officer, commanded HMS *Britomart* in the expedition to effect a settlement at Port Essington in 1838, and HMS *Rattlesnake* in its coastal survey of New Guinea 1846–50. His name is commemorated in the Owen Stanley range of New Guinea. A significant artist, Stanley recorded the Port Essington expedition in valuable sketch-books. The original *Narrative of the Voyage of H.M.S. Rattlesnake* was edited by John MacGillivray in 1852. Marnie Bassett published *Behind the Picture: H.M.S. Rattlesnake's Australian-New Guinea Cruise 1846 to 1850* (1966); Adelaide Lubbock wrote the biography, *Owen Stanley R.N.* (1968).

Starlight, Captain, is the Byronic hero of mysterious but aristocratic origins in 'Rolf Boldrewood''s bushranging classic, *Robbery Under Arms* (1888), and the leader of the bushranging gang briefly mentioned in Adam Lindsay Gordon's poem, 'The Sick Stockrider'. The popularity of 'Boldrewood''s novel and the

dramatic adaptation of it by Alfred Dampier (1890) have led to much speculation about the model for Starlight; Dampier recorded that after stage performances of *Robbery Under Arms*, he was several times approached by men claiming to be the original. Although Frank Pearson (1837–99) had been active as the bushranger, 'Captain Starlight', in the Bourke district in 1868, it is unlikely that he was the model. 'Boldrewood', whose novel incorporates the experiences of several bushrangers and transposes them to a different historical period, himself claimed that Starlight was a composite character based partly on 'Captain Midnight' and Harry Redford (?1842–1901); a major incident in the novel, in which Starlight's gang steals a mob of cattle and 'overlands' it from Queensland to SA, parallels a similar drive in which Redford was involved in 1870. The Starlight legend is assessed in Frank Clune's *Captain Starlight: Reckless Rascal of 'Robbery Under Arms'* (1945) and in the more definitive *Starlight: The Man and the Myth* (1972) by P.H. McCarthy. A musical, 'Captain Starlight', was produced in 1964 with libretto by Paul Sherman.

Station is a term first recorded in 1815 to describe an area inland from the settlement at Port Jackson where government stock were grazed. From the 1820s it began to be accepted as any tract of land on which privately-owned sheep or cattle were grazed under the supervision of an overseer. It came into later general use to denote a large pastoral property and many compounds were formed to give additional detail, e.g. 'head station', 'back station'. The term was widely used in fictional and factual accounts of the colony, e.g. Rosa Praed's novels *The Head Station* (1885) and *The Romance of a Station* (?1889). Samuel Mossman and Thomas Banister's *Australia, Visited & Revisited* (q.v., 1853) has chapters on 'A Sheep Station' and 'A Cattle Station', as has Alexander Forbes's *Voices from the Bush* (1869); A.B. Paterson's poem, 'A Mountain Station', describes the difficulties of coping with the problems of the pastoral life. Large and well-known stations include Victoria Downs and Wave Hill in the Northern Territory; among the best-known in literature are the Elsey, of Jeannie Gunn's *We of the Never-Never* (q.v., 1908), and Billabong, in the children's novels of Mary Grant Bruce (q.v.).

STEAD, CHRISTINA (1902–83), was born and educated in Australia, but spent the greater part of her life abroad. Her mother died in 1904; her father David Stead, an eminent naturalist, Fabian socialist, and humanitarian, married for the second time in 1907 and subsequently raised an extensive family. After graduating from Sydney Teachers' College in 1921, Christina Stead taught for some time but resigned in 1924. For the next few years she worked in an office, practising severe economies in order to save her fare to Europe. She left Australia in 1928 not, as she later emphasized, to escape, but to satisfy a wandering impulse. In 1928–29 she worked in offices in London, fell seriously ill as a result of her previous privations, and wrote *Seven Poor Men of Sydney* (q.v.) as a determined effort 'to leave something behind'. In London she also met her husband, William Blake, a man of diverse gifts who successfully combined banking and Marxism as well as the writing of fiction and works on political economy. They moved to Paris in 1929 and for the next five years Stead worked as a secretary with a French bank, an experience she later put to good use in her novel, *House of All Nations*. Her first published work, *The Salzburg Tales*, appeared in 1934, followed a few months later by *Seven Poor Men of Sydney*. Her third book, *The Beauties and Furies*, a story of student life in Paris, appeared in 1936 and *House of All Nations*, written in Spain just before the outbreak of the Civil War, in 1938. The Blakes lived in the USA 1937–47. Three of her novels directly reflect her American experience: *Letty Fox: Her Luck* (1946), *A Little Tea, A Little Chat* (1948) and *The People with the Dogs* (1952). *The Man Who Loved Children* (q.v., 1940), although ostensibly set in the USA, is based on her childhood, and again in *For Love Alone* (q.v., 1944) she draws heavily on her Australian experience. Returning to Europe in 1947, the Blakes travelled widely before settling in 1953 in England, where they remained until William Blake's death in 1968. *Dark Places of the Heart* (New York, 1966), republished the following year in England as *Cotters' England* (q.v.), is Stead's only novel with an exclusively English setting. Her remaining works include a volume of four novellas, *The Puzzleheaded Girl* (1967), and the novels, *The Little Hotel* (1973), a reworking of some earlier short stories, and *Miss Herbert (The Suburban Wife)* (1976). She also wrote some uncollected short stories, edited two anthologies of short stories and translated three diverse French books into English. In 1969 Stead revisited Australia for the first time since 1928 and in 1974 returned to make it her home.

Until 1965 none of Stead's novels were published in Australia and her long absence and life of travel mitigated against her formal recognition here and elsewhere. In 1967 she was rejected for the Britannica-Australia award on the grounds that she had ceased to be Australian, although she received the Patrick White Award in 1974. The critical appreciation of her work has been fitful: from the first her novels received some discerning reviews both in Australia and overseas, but they did not win a more general following until the publication of Randall Jarrell's enthusiastic introduction to a reprint of *The Man Who Loved Children* (1965). From the beginning Stead's distinctive quality, which cannot be defined in terms of place, theory or tradition, has intrigued and challenged readers. In form, style, and subject matter her work is experimental. Immediately striking are her strong, imaginative power and range, her verbal brilliance, detachment and acute penetration of character. Her concentrated emotional intensity, interest in extraordinary passion, keen sense of the grotesque and use of fantasy have led to comparisons with D.H. Lawrence, Dostoevsky and Dickens, although her singular talent resists comparisons and categories. Both her dramatic scenes and external, physical descriptions are remarkably immediate and particular, but her approach is always inward and emotionally interpretative rather than outward and naturalistic. The irrational world of subconscious emotion is the focus of her interest, not the rational world of the senses. Firmly denying the idea of a 'necessary atmosphere', she described herself as a psychological writer for whom 'personality is a private passion'. Although she possessed firm political convictions, she remained independent of both political and literary theory, approaching her material as a detached, impartial observer, who explores rather than manipulates characters and events.

Her first published work, *The Salzburg Tales* (1934), immediately established the unusual nature of her writing. A group of diverse tales, similar in structure to *The Canterbury Tales* and *The Decameron*, it is a buoyant work which ranges from the supernatural to the legendary, romantic, macabre, naturalistic and satiric. *Seven Poor Men of Sydney* (1934) appeared an anomaly in Australian fiction of the 1930s. Lacking both a conventional plot and a central protagonist, and written in a lyrically-meditative manner, it explores the inner lives of a group of casually connected people, who live under the pressure of poverty. In *The Beauties and Furies* (1936) romantic grotesquerie gets somewhat out of hand, but *House of All Nations* (1938) shows firmer control: epic in scale, encyclopaedic in detail, cinematic in form, it is a scathing account of the world of international finance, although once again the eccentricity of private obsession rather than generalized class interest holds the foreground. Radical in her political convictions and well aware of the facts of economic exploitation, Stead consistently avoids the reductions of ideology in her fiction; instead she presents exploitation and ideology as part of the texture of life, private as well as public, meshed as intricately into family relations as into social ones. Nowhere is this more apparent than in her greatest achievement, the autobiographical *The Man Who Loved Children* (1940), an acknowledged masterpiece of twentieth century fiction. An intensely-realized, unsentimental study of a claustrophobic family, this novel revisits the bitter, frustrated and tragi-comic world of childhood, while remaining keenly sensitive to the needs and susceptibilities of its rulers, the adults. Although the emotional growth of the child Louise charts the contours of the story, sympathy is not reserved for her but extends to all the participants, even to the monstrous, egoistic father, Sam Pollit. Two other novels approach this one in significance: *For Love Alone* (1944) and *Cotters' England* (1966). Her three American novels are lesser works, although characteristically vigorous and penetrating. *Letty Fox: Her Luck* (1946), a lengthy, picaresque novel with a diverse cast of characters, takes up the theme of freedom which figures also in earlier novels; *A Little Tea, A Little Chat* (1948) is interesting for its portrait of another unpleasant male egoist, Robbie Grant; *The People with the Dogs* (1952), is a quieter work, a recreation of the mellow, communal life of an American country estate. Her last two novels, *Miss Herbert (The Suburban Wife)* (1976) and *The Little Hotel* (1973), are very different: the former a concentrated study of a commonplace personality, the latter a complex exploration of a cross-section of life casually brought together in a Swiss hotel. Ron Geering has written two biographical and critical studies of Stead (1969).

Steak for Breakfast, see 'O'CONNER, ELIZABETH'

Steele Rudd's Magazine (1904–07) was the first of several journals exploiting the popularity of the 'Steele Rudd' (q.v.) pseudonym of Arthur Hoey Davis. An illustrated monthly, it contained contributions from George Essex Evans, Victor Daley, G.A. Taylor and others as well as from 'Rudd' himself. The journal was subsequently revived as *Steele Rudd's Annual* (1917–23), *Steele Rudd's* (1924–25) and *Steele Rudd's and the Shop Assistant's Magazine* (1926–27). Although dominated by 'Rudd''s contributions, many of which also went into his books, it continued to publish other well-known Australian writers and artists.

Steelman, a character in several stories by Henry Lawson (q.v.), was reputedly modelled on a ' "commercial traveller" out of Wellington' whom Lawson met during his first visit to NZ in 1893–94; Smith, Steelman's dim-witted and naive offsider, was Lawson's conception of 'the weaker side of myself'. A travelling confidence man who survives on the sharpness of his wits, Steelman is usually triumphant, although his success is only partial in the best-known Steelman story, 'The Geological Spieler' (q.v.). A bush type and the focus for some of Lawson's best yarns and tall stories, he lacks the complexity of other recurring characters in Lawson's fiction such as Jack Mitchell and Dave Regan.

STELLMACH, BARBARA (1930–), born Queensland, has written numerous plays, which have been frequently produced. She has published *4 Australian Plays* (1973), which comprises *Dark Heritage*, a three-act drama with a theme of racism; *Dust Is the Heart*, a one-act tragedy which evokes the hardship and loneliness of the outback; *Hang Your Clothes on Yonder Bush*, an award-winning comedy; and *Legend of the Losers*, a chronicle drama based on the legends surrounding the bushranger, Frederick Ward (Captain Thunderbolt). Her other published plays are *Not Even a Mouse* (1978), a three-act thriller, and *From the Fourteenth Floor You Can See the Harbour Bridge* (1983).

STENHOUSE, N.D. (NICOL DRYSDALE) (1806–73), born Scotland, graduated from the University of Edinburgh and subsequently practised as a solicitor. A protégé of the book-collector and philosopher, Sir William Hamilton, Stenhouse became acquainted with several literary men in Edinburgh, including Thomas De Quincey, with whom he corresponded. In 1839 he emigrated to Sydney, where he set up a legal practice and became the centre of a circle which included numerous writers and intellectuals. In particular, he provided financial and moral support to Daniel Deniehy, Charles Harpur and Henry Kendall and was friendly with Frank Fowler and Richard Rowe, with whom he associated in the establishment of the periodical, *Month*. The owner of an extensive library, he also provided his friends with access to European cultural developments. He exercised a wider influence on colonial society of the 1850s and 1860s through his involvement with the Sydney Mechanics' School of Arts (president 1867–73), the Free Public Library of Sydney, Sydney College, and the University of Sydney (member of the senate, 1869–73). The Stenhouse library is now in the Fisher Library of the University of Sydney. Ann-Mari Jordens in *The Stenhouse Circle* (1979) gives an account of Stenhouse's life and his cultural milieu.

STEPHEN, HAROLD (1841–89), the son of George Milner Stephen, a lawyer, colonial administrator and convert to spiritualism, and a relation to Sir Leslie Stephen, was born in England and educated in Melbourne and Germany. Editor for a time of *Sydney Punch*, he published three volumes of short stories and novelettes, *The Golden Yankee* (1877), *Saved by a Ring* (n.d.) and *Lily's Fortune* (1886); and edited and contributed to the anthologies *Our Exhibition Annual* (1878) and *Fizz, Home-Made for Christmas Use* (1881), which both include contributions from G.G. McCrae, Henry Kendall and Henry Halloran, and *Our Christmas Budget* (1872). He also wrote an account of the colourful life of his father, *George Milner Stephen and His Marvellous Cures* (188?), and *Vagabonds and Their Dupes* (1879), a reply to 'Julian Thomas' (John Stanley James) who had earlier written an 'exposure' of spiritualism, *Mediums and Their Dupes* (1879).

STEPHENS, A.G. (ALFRED GEORGE) (1865–1933), born and educated at Toowoomba, Queensland, was in 1880 apprenticed to a Sydney printer and in 1886 admitted to membership of the NSW Typographical Association. In 1888 he returned north to take up an appointment as editor of the *Gympie Miner* after it had been taken over by supporters of Thomas McIlwraith and the Queensland Nationalist Party. Stephens became a leading member of the Gympie Literary Circle, reporting its meetings in the *Miner*. Stephens also edited and largely wrote the *Apostle*, the organ of the local secular association. In a *Miner* editorial in May 1890 on the visit of Henry George, he wrote 'Truth is not in extremes', suggesting the even-handed view of political questions characteristic of his later writings.

At the end of 1890 Stephens went to Brisbane and became sub-editor of the radical *Boomerang*, to which he contributed leaders, features, social jottings, *faits divers* and a regular column, 'The Magazine Rifler', which surveyed the latest numbers of the English and American journals. When he left the *Boomerang* in October 1891, it was in the hands of a liquidator and Stephens received the office bible in lieu of wages. He then joined the staff of the Cairns *Argus*, becoming editor by the end of 1891 and part-owner in 1892. He instituted a literary supplement and ran an essay competition as he had done on the *Miner*. Stephens himself won the prize of £25 in a competition run in conjunction with the North Queensland Separation League for his essay 'Why North Queensland Wants Separation', later published as a pamphlet in 1893. The essay criticized the control over the north wielded by Brisbane and the south, and attacked the general concepts of political and economic centralization. In 1893

Stephens finished another polemical essay on Queensland politics, *The Griffilwraith, Being an Independent Criticism of the Methods and Manoeuvres of the Queensland Coalition Government, 1890–1893*. The pamphlet attacked the coalition government of the factions led by Sir Samuel Griffith and Sir Thomas McIlwraith which had ended the two-party system in the legislature. Immediately after the pamphlet's publication, Stephens left on a trip overseas, using funds from the sale of his interest in the *Argus* at the end of 1892. He travelled in America, Canada and Europe. *A Queenslander's Travel Notes*, published on his return to Sydney in 1894, was a collection of the articles he had sent back to Australian journals and newspapers during his trip. Stephens criticized the pretensions and decorums of traditionalist Europe, and in the half of the work devoted to America used the high divorce rate, drug abuse, poverty and crime, side by side with American 'progress' and smugness at its achievements, to define what he saw as the peculiar and contrary American character. At the end of 1893 Stephens was working in Fleet Street for the *Daily Chronicle·* when J.F. Archibald offered him a sub-editorship on the Sydney *Bulletin* (q.v.), which he took up in 1894. By that time the *Bulletin* was a major inter-colonial publication, and with Archibald's return to the editorship in 1886, it entered a period of high literary consciousness. It encouraged local authors, advocated literary nationalism and promoted a distinctive model of the short story. From the time of his arrival Stephens contributed literary notices and comments, and full-scale articles by him on George Eliot, Conan Doyle, and the Brontes had appeared in July 1895. In August 1896 the first Red Page (q.v.) appeared, a full-page literary section developed from the prototype 'Books of the Day' and 'Book Exchange' columns, also on the inside front cover, which Stephens conducted from September 1894. Stephens continued his cosmopolitan interests, dividing comment among Australian, American, English and European writers. He frequently called for a greater awareness of overseas trends and standards. 'Is there a single Australian', he asked in January 1897, 'who could pass an examination in Huysmans, Maeterlinck, or Verhaeren?' Stephens's broad views on politics and his international literary tastes were consistent with his favourite critical yardstick, the concept of 'universality'. The concept recurs throughout his writings and indicates an absolute standard of critical appraisal beyond mutable and transitory criteria such as a work's national or moral value.

Stephens was, however, a nationalist critic in that he encouraged and welcomed new *Bulletin* writers as signs that Australian literature was growing toward maturity. Joseph Furphy, Shaw Neilson, Hugh McCrae, Mary Gilmore, Miles Franklin, and Roderic Quinn all acknowledged his personal encouragement and guidance, and as controller of the *Bulletin's* publishing division from 1897 Stephens saw most of these writers into print in book form for the first time. Under Stephens the *Bulletin's* publishing activities were greatly expanded, beginning with Barcroft Boake's *Where the Dead Men Lie and Other Poems* in 1897 and producing some twenty-five further volumes over the next nine years. Stephens acted as editor, literary agent and book designer. His editorship saw the publication of the classics, *On Our Selection* (1899) by 'Steele Rudd' and *Such Is Life* (q.v., 1903) by Furphy; the *Bulletin* anthologies, *The Bulletin Reciter* (1901), *The Bulletin Story Book* (1901) and *A Southern Garland* (1904); and the first volumes of verse by Will Ogilvie, Arthur Adams, Louise Mack, E.J. Brady, W.T. Goodge and Bernard O'Dowd. Stephens's role as editor of the *Bulletin's* book division alone guarantees him a place of permanent importance in the history of Australian literature.

In 1902 Stephens's own volume of poems, *Oblation*, was published privately, with illustrations by Norman Lindsay. In 1904 he saw through the press two lavish folios of the *Bulletin* artists Phil May and Livingston Hopkins, and a selection of his own essays from the *Bulletin* on social and literary topics, *The Red Pagan*, was issued in the same year under the paper's imprint. The volume expresses some of Stephens's characteristic literary attitudes, including the criterion of universality, the emotional impact necessary in great art, the sexual and racial conditioning of artistic creativity, and the correlation of artistic genius with insanity. Stephens believed that the emotive qualities of poetry derived from a 'female' species of creativity. It has been argued that this made Stephens's poetic preferences lachrymose and led to bias in his selections of the work of Daley and Neilson. His views about the psychopathological origins of artistic creativity were derived from the writings of Havelock Ellis and through the latter from Francis Galton's *Hereditary Genius* (1869) and Cesare Lombroso's *L'Uomo di Genio* (1888). These views underpinned Stephens's emphasis on biography in his criticism and sometimes precluded from high praise writers who lacked the correct racial or temperamental qualifications.

In 1906 Stephens left the *Bulletin*. Archibald had stood down as editor in favour of James Edmond in 1902, and Stephens's relations with William Macleod, its former artist and now business manager, were prickly. He had also fallen out with Henry Lawson and Norman Lindsay. Stephens had a bluff, dogmatic side

to his personality which sometimes irked acquaintances and which, according to Lindsay in *Bohemians of the Bulletin* (1965), formed the contrary to his emotional side. Stephens may also have been dissatisfied with the conditions and limitations of his role at the *Bulletin*. On 1 November 1906 the Red Page announced his departure and the establishment of his business venture, The Bookfellow, a literary bookshop named after the monthly literary magazine he had run for five issues from January 1899. In 1907 Stephens revived the *Bookfellow* (q.v.). Its files contain a high standard of discussion of Australian, English and European contemporary writers and artists. By 1907, however, the magazine and the shop were in trouble, and in June the shop's stock and much of Stephens's own library were auctioned 'without any reserve'. In 1894 Stephens had married Constance Smith; the couple now had six dependent children, and financial necessity compelled a move to NZ, where Stephens accepted an offer from his old editor, Gresley Lukin of a job on the Wellington *Evening Post*. Stephens maintained an aloof demeanour at the *Post* and in 1909 returned to Sydney, reviving the *Bookfellow* and working as a freelance journalist. The magazine lasted intermittently until 1925 and fulfilled an important literary role. It provided an outlet for Shaw Neilson, Hugh McCrae and Mary Gilmore, and as he had done at the *Bulletin* Stephens also published books under the paper's imprint. In his last years the stream of Stephens's work hardly abated. He planned future publishing projects, toured NSW and Victoria giving lectures on Australian literature, published another volume of verse, *The Pearl and the Octopus and Other Exercises in Prose and Verse* (?1911) and several pamphlets of his own poems, wrote a novel, *Bill's Idees* (1913), two plays, *The Australian Flower Masque* (1924) and *Capturing the Bushranger* (1924), and edited textbooks and anthologies for Australian schools, as well as producing significant critical studies of Henry Kendall and Christopher Brennan (1928, 1933). Rated by many as Australia's most influential pioneer man of letters, Stephens, especially through his editorial work and his steady stream of authoritative criticism, stimulated the development of Australian writing to a marked degree in the decades spanning the nineteenth and twentieth centuries. Leon Cantrell has edited *A.G. Stephens: Selected Writings* (1978) and Stephens's diary in *Cross Currents* (1981, ed. Bruce Bennett); P.R. Stephensen and Vance Palmer wrote, respectively, the biographical works, *The Life and Works of A.G. Stephens ('The Bookfellow')* (1940) and *A.G. Stephens: His Life and Work* (1941).

D.J.

649

STEPHENS, ALFRED WARD (1804–52), born Portsmouth, England, arrived in Sydney in 1829 and joined the *Sydney Gazette*. In 1831 with Frederick Stokes and William McGarvie he established the *Sydney Herald*, later the *Sydney Morning Herald*; by 1836 he was sole editor and proprietor. Under his guidance, and with Edward O'Shaugnessy as leader writer, the newspaper became an important influence in the struggle for representative government, the cessation of transportation and the more ready accessibility of land for colonists, including security of tenure for squatters. In 1839 Stephens sold the *Herald* back to Stokes and participated, with considerable ill-luck, in pastoral activities, dying a virtual pauper.

STEPHENS, EDWARD JAMES (1846–1931), born London, came to Melbourne in 1853, served an apprenticeship in the printing trade and began a lifelong career in country newspapers by establishing the *Horsham Times* in 1873. Other newspapers which he founded or held an interest in were the *Broken Hill Times*, the *Dimboola Banner*, the *Omeo Telegraph*, the *Warragul News*, the *Yarram Chronicle* and the *Nhill Free Press* and *Nhill Mail*, which both had published early poems of John Shaw Neilson. By his work in developing the provincial press in the country areas of Victoria, Stephens helped to overcome the isolation of rural communities.

STEPHENS, JAMES BRUNTON (1835–1902), born Bo'ness near Edinburgh, received a sound Scottish education, including a period at the University of Edinburgh. He was a private tutor and schoolmaster both before and after his migration to Queensland in 1866. Following the publication of several volumes of verse, and to acknowledge his growing literary stature, he was appointed to the civil service, ultimately becoming acting under-secretary to the colonial secretary in Brisbane. After the death of Kendall in 1882 Stephens became the leading literary figure of the period. He contributed both creative works and literary comment to important newspapers and journals, including the *Bulletin*; his poetry appeared in contemporary anthologies such as Douglas Sladen's *A Century of Australian Song* (1888); and he figured prominently in contemporary critical works such as H.G. Turner and Alexander Sutherland's *The Development of Australian Literature* (1898). He attempted fiction, publishing two novels in Scotland as well as *A Hundred Pounds* (1876), an Australian story; he wrote an ineffective drama, *Fayette: Or, Bush Revels* (1892); but his major successes were the poetry, *Convict Once* (q.v., 1871), *The Black Gin* (1873), *The Godolphin Arabian* (q.v.,

1873) and *My Chinee Cook* (1902). Despite the contemporary respect for him and the present-day acknowledgement of his undoubted influence on the literary scene during the two decades prior to the end of the nineteenth century, his own poetry now arouses little enthusiasm among readers and critics. He is extensively discussed in H.A. Kellow's *Queensland Poets* (1930); Cecil Hadgraft wrote the biographical study, *James Brunton Stephens* (1969). He is the poet featured in Rosa Praed's reminiscences, *My Australian Girlhood* (1902).

STEPHENS, JOHN (1806–50), born Northumberland, England, became a bookseller after leaving school. In 1832 he helped to found the influential anti-slavery journal, the *Christian Advocate*, and after further experience in journalism was engaged by George Fife Angas to write promotional material for the new colony of SA. In 1839 he published *The Land of Promise*, a second edition of the same work titled *The History of the Rise and Progress of the New British Province of South Australia*, and a pamphlet attacking the unfavourable picture of the colony presented by another writer. In 1842 Stephens emigrated to SA, where he founded the *Observer* in 1843, took over the *Register* in 1845 and printed some of the colony's first almanacs as well as his brother Edward's periodical, the *Adelaide Miscellany of Useful and Entertaining Knowledge* (1848–49) which was succeeded by his own *Stephens's Adelaide Miscellany* (1849).

STEPHENSEN, P.R. (PERCY REGINALD) (1901–65), a flamboyant and controversial figure known familiarly as 'Inky' Stephensen, was born at Biggenden, Queensland, and educated at Maryborough, where he was taught briefly by V. Gordon Childe, and at the University of Queensland, where he was a contemporary of Jack Lindsay and Eric Partridge. Elected Queensland Rhodes Scholar for 1924, Stephensen went to the University of Oxford where he was a controversial left-wing student, nearly expelled for communist activities. In 1927 he became associated with Lindsay and Jack Kirtley in the publishing activities of the Fanfrolico Press (q.v.) in London. Stephensen's version of his two years as business manager of the Press, during which he was also involved in the publication of the *London Aphrodite* (q.v.), is told in *Kookaburras and Satyrs* (1954), although other narratives of the Franfrolico days differ in detail and emphasis. In 1929 he started the Mandrake Press (q.v.), which published D.H. Lawrence; Stephensen had by this time established his reputation as an ebullient conversationalist and after one long meeting with him Lawrence wrote that next morning, 'the walls still shook'. Stephensen was also familiar with such well-known figures as Augustus John, Sacheverell Sitwell, Rhys Davies and Aldous Huxley; he is thought to have been the model for Huxley's Cuthbert Arkwright in *Point Counter Point*. The Mandrake Press had collapsed by 1931 and after struggling to support himself in England by freelance literary work, Stephensen returned to Australia late in 1932. He had already collaborated with Walford Hyden in the preparation of the biography, *Pavlova* (1931), the first of many works which he co-authored or 'ghosted', and had had published on his own account a translation of Nietzsche (1922), *The Legend of Aleister Crowley* (1930), *Harry Buckland, Master of Hounds* (1931), the prose or verse texts for three slim, illustrated satires, *The Sink of Solitude* (1928), *Policeman of the Lord* (1928) and *The Well of Sleevelessness* (1929), and a volume of short stories, *The Bushwhackers* (1929). Some of these works reveal a crusading spirit, e.g. *Policeman of the Lord* against censorship and wowserism, while *The Bushwhackers* reflects a nostalgia for Stephensen's bush childhood mixed with a social criticism of Australia.

In Australia, Stephensen worked for a year as managing director of the Endeavour Press, a book-publishing outlet of the *Bulletin*, and then established his own company, which published Eleanor Dark, 'Henry Handel Richardson' and other authors before going into liquidation early in 1935. During this period Stephensen met Xavier Herbert (q.v.), also recently returned from England, whom he helped considerably in the revision of *Capricornia* (q.v., 1938). Although the exact nature of his assistance to Herbert has been the subject of some dispute, Stephensen clearly deserves much of the credit for finally getting the book into print. An editorial essay on Australian culture published in the *Australian Mercury* (q.v.) in July 1935 brought Stephensen to the attention of W.J. Miles (q.v.), a successful Sydney businessman who encouraged Stephensen's increasing isolationism, anti-communism and anti-Semitism as well as his already aggressive nationalism and anti-Englishness. Miles published *The Foundations of Culture in Australia* (1936), an expansion of the *Australian Mercury* editorial which became a significant cultural document of the 1930s, drawing support in particular from Rex Ingamells, Ian Mudie and other Jindyworobak (q.v.) writers. Miles also employed Stephensen to write for the *Publicist* (q.v., 1936–42), an Australia First monthly which espoused the Miles line and published the work of a number of Australian authors. Although the outbreak of war caused the *Publicist* to modify its sympathies towards Germany and Japan, its views were monitored by

the government, as were the activities of the Yabber Club and the isolationist Australia First movement (q.v.), which was formally founded by Stephensen and others later in 1941. In March 1942, Stephensen was one of sixteen Australia First members arrested in Sydney and subsequently interned; he was not released until August 1945. Both Stephensen, portrayed as 'The Bloke', and Australia First, called Australia Free, are caricatured in Herbert's *Poor Fellow My Country* (q.v., 1975).

After internment, Stephensen lived in Victoria and stayed clear of literary and other controversies for several years, although he continued as a collaborator with Frank Clune (q.v.), with whom he had begun work in the mid 1930s. In 1956 he returned to Sydney to pursue a career mainly as an historical writer and researcher specializing in books on the sea. Apart from his work with Clune, for which he is accorded co-authorship status for *The Viking of Van Diemen's Land* (1954) and *The Pirates of the Brig Cyprus* (1962), he collaborated on several books with the English seamen, W.H. Jones and Sir James Bissett, and published on his own account, *Sydney Sails* (1962) and *The History and Description of Sydney Harbour* (1966). His other writings, mainly pamphlets, include *The Life and Works of A.G. Stephens* (1940), with whose career Stephensen identified; *Philip Dimmock: A Memoir of a Poet* (1958); *William John Miles* (1942); and four volumes of an edition of the poems of 'William Baylebridge' (1961). These publications make Stephensen the author, co-author, or acknowledged editor of more than twenty works, and he ghosted many more. Despite his breadth of writing, vigorous style and the historical importance of *The Foundations of Culture in Australia*, he was most influential as a literary and cultural promoter, an iconoclast who did much to put into practice his commitment to Australian writing. His assistance in the publication of *Capricornia* was the best-known example of his commitment. Craig Munro wrote *Wild Man of Letters: The Story of P.R. Stephensen* (1984).

STEVEN, ALEXANDER GORDON (1865–1923), born London, came to Australia in infancy. He studied medicine at the University of Melbourne, but was prevented by ill health from completing the course. His lyrical, introspective verse appeared in five volumes during his lifetime, *The Witchery of Earth* (1911), *Wind on the Wold* (1914), *Poems* (1918) *Revolt* (1919) and *Lures* (1923), and in a posthumous collected edition, *Collected Poems* (1925), with a foreword by Hugh McCrae.

STEVENS, BERTRAM (1872–1922), born Inverell, NSW, became a solicitor's clerk in Sydney but abandoned law to become a prolific editor of works on Australian literature and art, in which role he exerted a considerable influence on the development of Australian culture in the first quarter of the twentieth century.

Stevens's first editorial venture was John Farrell's *My Sundowner and Other Poems* in 1904. He then edited George Essex Evans's *The Secret Key and Other Poems* (1906) and *An Anthology of Australian Verse* (1906), which was revised and enlarged in 1909 as *The Golden Treasury of Australian Verse*, one of the first significant Australian anthologies (q.v.). In 1911 he edited, with a memoir, Victor Daley's *Wine and Roses*, and in 1920 an edition of the poems of Henry Kendall. His other editorial works include *The 'Bulletin' Book of Humorous Verse and Recitations* (1920), several anthologies of verse for children, anthologies of verse in collaboration with George Mackaness, and critical and illustrative art works on Norman Lindsay, Arthur Streeton, Conrad Martens, Hans Heysen and others. In 1909–11 Stevens was editor of the Red Page of the *Bulletin* and in 1912–19 editor of the *Lone Hand*. One of the founders in 1916 of *Art in Australia*, he was involved editorially in it until his death; he was also connected editorially with the journals *Commerce*, from 1918, and *Home*, from 1920.

STEVENSON, GEORGE (1799–1856), born Berwick-upon-Tweed, England, was an author and editor who produced the first issue of the *South Australian Gazette and Colonial Register* (see *Register*), published in England in 1836. He then went with the first colonists to SA to continue the *Gazette*, which had fallen foul of the government and become the *South Australian Register* by the time he withdrew from the journal in 1842. In 1845 he founded another *South Australian Gazette and Colonial Register*, from 1847 until it ceased publication in 1852 it was titled the *South Australian Gazette and Mining Register*.

STEVENSON, ROBERT LOUIS (1850–94), paid four visits to Australia during the period (1888–94) that he was based in Samoa: February-April and August-September 1890, January-February 1891 and February-April 1893. On each visit his presence was prominently noticed in Australian newspapers; in 1893 he met J.F. Archibald and visited Julian Ashton's artists' camp at Balmoral. There are Sydney Domain scenes in *The Wrecker* (1892), written partly in Australia by Stevenson and his stepson, Lloyd Osbourne. Other Stevenson publications associated with Australia are the rare collaborative work, *An Object of Pity*, printed in Sydney in 1891, and *Father Damien* (1890), a pamphlet defending the Pacific 'leper Priest',

Father Joseph Damien (1841–89), from an attack by a Honolulu missionary; the pamphlet was printed in Sydney after its publication in the *Australian Star* (1890) as 'In Defence of the Dead'. Stevenson, whose associations with Australia are the subject of a pamphlet by George Mackaness (1935) which inaugurated his Australian Historical Monographs series, had real affection for Sydney, although the poor effect it had on his constitution caused him to dub Australia the 'New South Pole'.

STEWART, DOUGLAS (1913–85), born Eltham, Taranaki Province, NZ, came to Australia in 1933, expecting to take up a position as light verse writer on the *Bulletin* staff. When that position did not eventuate he returned to NZ in 1934, visited England in 1937, then came back to Australia in 1938 to become assistant to Cecil Mann, editor of the Red Page. In 1940 he took over the Red Page and remained its editor until 1961. With the *Bulletin* change of ownership Stewart joined Angus & Robertson as literary editor. He retired from Angus & Robertson in 1971 but actively continued his own literary career, consolidating his reputation as writer and critic.

Stewart's first publications were two volumes of poetry, *Green Lions* (1936) and *The White Cry* (1939). This early poetry is characterized by a delight in the beauty and colour of the NZ landscape and by an exuberance of language. Two small books of wartime verse, *Elegy for an Airman* (1940) and *Sonnets to the Unknown Soldier* (1941), followed. The title poem of the earlier volume is in memory of Stewart's boyhood friend, Desmond Carter, who was killed in action with the RAF in 1939. Stewart's first 'Australian' book of verse, *The Dosser in Springtime* (1946), contains both lyrics and ballads. The title poem, with its humorous account of an old cave-dweller's excited arousal by the sight of a girl bathing in a creek, sees Stewart giving expression for the first time to the gently ironic and whimsical strain that became so characteristic of his later writing. 'The River' (from *The Dosser*), a poetic meditation upon the spiritual and intellectual influences of his NZ boyhood, is one of Stewart's best poems. *Glencoe* (1947) is a sequence of twenty-six ballads based on the infamous slaughter of the MacDonald clan by the Campbells in 1691. *Glencoe* has been praised for its sustained and dramatic balladry, and applauded for its theme, a protest against barbarity, cruelty and violence in any age. *Sun Orchids* (1952), in addition to numerous small nature pieces, also contains 'Worsley Enchanted', a sequence of seventeen poems based on Shackleton's Antarctic expedition of 1914. This sequence indicates, as does his verse-drama *The*

Fire on the Snow (q.v.), the attraction that Antarctic exploration and the explorer figure held for him (see Voyager). 'Terra Australis', also in *Sun Orchids*, describes a chance meeting between, and a comparison of notes by, two explorer/adventurer idealists, Pedro Fernandez de Quiros, a sixteenth-century Portuguese seaman, and William Lane, the founder of the Utopian socialist colony, New Australia, in Paraguay. That meeting allows Stewart to reflect, ironically but not too destructively, upon the way in which the idealism of the human spirit is often thwarted by the weaknesses of human nature. Commissioned in 1954 to produce a script for a projected film, *Back of Beyond*, Stewart travelled along the Birdsville Track (q.v.) and published his reaction to the desolate Australian interior in a poem sequence of that title. The sequence begins at Marree in SA, 'the corrugated-iron town/In the corrugated iron air'; describes such identities as 'The Whipmaker', 'The Afghan', 'The Dogger', and an Aboriginal rainmaker; casts sidelong glances at red desert grasshoppers, dingoes, wild mules, and bicycle lizards; and concludes, three hundred miles north, at Birdsville, an undistinguished little desert town, whose glory lies in the fact that Leichhardt and Sturt once trod its dusty street. *The Birdsville Track* (1955) also contains Stewart's customary meticulous observations on small birds, animals, flowers and landscapes. The best of these lyrical recreations of his visual and spiritual experiences in the Australian landscape are 'Brindabella', 'Spider-Gums' and 'The Snow-gum'. Stewart's final volume of poetry, *Rutherford* (1962), emphasizes, in Leonie Kramer's phrase, 'intellectual voyagers' rather than the physical explorers of earlier volumes. In the title poem the NZ atomic scientist, Rutherford, is addressed as 'the great sea-farer of science'. The most ambitious of Stewart's poems, 'Rutherford' examines the problem of man's need to extend his spirit and intellect to their fullest, even when the consequences are unforeseeable. The poem decides that man has no choice but to accept the destiny inherent in his own searching, restless human nature. 'The Silkworms' (q.v.), from *Rutherford*, is widely regarded as Stewart's finest individual poem, both for its sensitive and imaginative insight and for its perfect fusion of technique and theme. Stewart's *Selected Poems* was published in 1963, another edition appearing in 1973. *Collected Poems 1936–1967* (1967), which Stewart arranged in reverse chronological order, begins with a section, 'The Flowering Place' that includes numerous satirical and explorer poems written since *Rutherford* or unpublished in earlier volumes.

Stewart also wrote six verse dramas, four of which were intended as radio plays. *The Fire on the Snow*, his greatest literary success, deals with Captain Robert Scott's tragic expedition to the South Pole in 1912. It was performed on radio by the ABC in 1941, was published in 1944, has been produced and published in many countries, and has been studied by countless Australian schoolchildren. *Ned Kelly* (q.v.), written as a stage play during 1940, had its first performance in an abbreviated form as a radio play in 1942. It follows the affairs of the Kelly gang of bushrangers from the robbery of the Jerilderie bank to their last stand in the hotel at Glenrowan. *The Golden Lover*, first performed on radio in 1943, was published with *The Fire on the Snow* in 1944. Based on the Maori legend of the Golden Lover, the play traces a Maori eternal triangle: Whana, the 'golden lover', chief of the Maori fairy people ('the people of the mist'); Ruarangi, the cuckolded, unimaginative real-life husband; and between them Ruarangi's beautiful, wilful wife, Tawhai. On the husband's side are the conventional forces of family, tribe and traditional morality; the 'golden lover' can call on romance, passion and the lure of the forbidden fruit. Convention wins, and the play's message is that it mostly does, for 'golden lovers' are myths, no part of the world of reality. A warm and humorous play which catches the Maori character and the NZ background, *The Golden Lover* is one of Stewart's most spontaneous and pleasant works. 'The Earthquake Shakes the Land' (performed in 1946) is set against the background of the Maori Wars of the 1840s; *Shipwreck* (1947) is a play based on the bloody events that followed the wrecking of the Dutch ship, *Batavia*; *Fisher's Ghost* (1960) is a lighthearted romp around the well-known legend from colonial times (see Fisher's Ghost).

Stewart's published fiction consists of one collection of short stories, *A Girl with Red Hair* (1944), and a handful of other stories in the *Bulletin* and *Coast to Coast*. The collected stories reflect the leisurely, uncomplicated NZ of Stewart's youth and its unspoiled landscape with its poetic Maori names. The title story concerns a beautiful and sensitive young woman who has a capacity for a higher destiny than that offered by her humble background. Although trapped in a loveless marriage, she is spiritually freed by the birth of her daughter ('a girl with red hair'), seeing in the child her own symbolic rebirth. Stewart's book of essays, *The Seven Rivers* (1960), named for the seven coastal streams of his Taranaki province, is a delightful discourse on fishing, informed by Stewart's attractive wit and wisdom and memorable for its graceful, fluent prose. A selection from it, *Fishing around the Monaro*, was published in 1978.

Stewart's greatest contribution to Australian

literature, however, came from his twenty years' editorship of the Red Page, his ten years as publishing editor with Angus & Robertson, and his lifetime encouragement of Australian writers. In the Red Page, Stewart adopted encouragement and enthusiasm as his editorial philosophy, largely to counteract the apathy with which local writing was usually met. Although occasionally over-generous, he not only gave continued encouragement to established writers but accurately assessed the potential, and assisted in the development, of such major new writers as Judith Wright, James McAuley, Francis Webb, David Campbell, Rosemary Dobson and John Blight. Stewart's critical judgements on the literature of his editorial years are included in his two books, *The Flesh and the Spirit* (1948) and *The Broad Stream* (1975). His publications as anthologist and editor include *Australian Bush Ballads* (1955), *Old Bush Songs and Rhymes of Colonial Times* (1957) and *The Pacific Book of Bush Ballads* (1967), all in collaboration with Nancy Keesing; *Voyager Poems* (1960); *Kenneth Mackenzie: Selected Poems* (1961); *Modern Australian Verse* (1964), with an introduction that stresses his belief that literature should provide joy; *Hugh McCrae: Selected Poems* (1966); *Short Stories of Australia: The Lawson Tradition* (1967); and *The Wide Brown Land* (1971), Australian verse. His suggestion that there should be annual anthologies of Australian poetry and short stories led to the introduction in the early 1940s of the *Australian Poetry* and *Coast to Coast* series. His reflections on some of Australia's famous literary figures are in *Norman Lindsay: A Personal Memoir* (1975), *A Man of Sydney* (1977) on Kenneth Slessor, and *Writers of the Bulletin* (1977). In 1955–70 Stewart was a member of the advisory board of the CLF; in 1960 he was made OBE for his services to Australian literature; in 1967 he received the Sydney Myer Award for the best volume of poetry in that year; and in 1968 he received the Britannica-Australia Award in the humanities. *Springtime in Taranaki* (1983) is his autobiographical account of the first twenty-five years of his life.

STEWART, HAROLD (1916–), born Drummoyne, Sydney, studied briefly at the Conservatorium of Music and the University of Sydney, and was a member of the Australian army's directorate of research and civil affairs from 1942 to 1946, as also was James McAuley. In 1944 Stewart and McAuley perpetrated the famous Ern Malley hoax (q.v.). After the war Stewart was a journalist, lecturer, bookshop salesman and radio broadcaster for the ABC. His first books of verse were *Phoenix Wings: Poems 1940–46* (1948) and *Orpheus and Other*

Poems (1956). The poems of *Phoenix Wings*, many of them drawing on Chinese literature and culture, reveal Stewart's deep interest in the Orient, an interest that took him to visit and, from 1965, to live permanently in, Japan, where he studied under Bando Shojun, a Shin Buddhist priest and scholar at the Shinshu Buddhist University, and where he ultimately became a member of the Shinshu Buddhist sect. In Kyoto he has eked out a frugal existence by teaching English, buying and selling antiques, and publishing two very popular volumes of translations of Japanese haiku, *A Net of Fireflies* (1960) and *A Chime of Windbells* (1969).

Stewart's poetry has attracted a small but devoted following. *Phoenix Wings* and *Orpheus* have been praised for their observation and understanding of a culture other than Australian, and for the superb descriptive and narrative qualities of poems such as 'A Flight of Wild Geese' (q.v.) and 'The Ascension of Feng'. As an expatriate, his more recent work has not been well known in Australia. The haiku translations, which are accompanied by his essays on the history, philosophy and technique of haiku, have been criticized by experts on the culture and language of Japan for being too idiosyncratic in approach. The haiku, however, which allows, in Stewart's view, the achievement of 'perfection in little things', is a suitable vehicle for combining his own predilection for sensuous imagery with epigrammatic succinctness. *By the Old Walls of Kyoto*, subtitled *A Yearly Cycle of Landscape Poems*, Stewart's most recent verse (1979), is a long poem in twelve parts, which celebrates the beauty and significance of that ancient capital and cultural centre of Japan and pays Stewart's personal homage to it.

STEWART, JOHN INNES MACKINTOSH, see 'INNES MICHAEL'

STEWART, NELLIE (1858–1931) was the stage-name of Eleanor Stewart Towzey, born Sydney, who made her theatrical debut at the age of five with Charles Kean in *The Stranger*. Star or principal boy in the 1880s of numerous pantomimes and comic operas staged by the J.C. Williamson 'triumvirate', which included Arthur Garner and George Musgrove, she later formed a liaison with Musgrove, an earlier marriage having failed. Some of her most successful roles included Marguerite in Gounod's *Faust* (1888) and Nell Gwynne in *Sweet Nell of Old Drury* (1902), which was produced as a film in 1911. She was also the star in *Paul Jones* (1889), *Blue-Eyed Susan* (1892), *Sweet Kitty Bellairs* (1909) and *What Every Woman Knows* (1910). She sang at the opening of the first federal parliament in 1901; her autobiography *My Life's Story* was published in 1923. Marjorie Skill wrote the biographical *Sweet Nell of Old Sydney* (1974).

'Still Life', one of the best-known of Rosemary Dobson's (q.v.) painting poems, was first published in the *Bulletin*, 1946. It describes a painting by an unknown seventeenth-century artist of a table set for a simple, sacramental meal of bread and wine. The never-to-be-consumed meal is one of the many examples in Rosemary Dobson's poetry of the permanence of art. A belated sharer in the meal (as all are who have gazed at the painting down the centuries) the poet involuntarily reaches out to break the loaf and pour the wine that awaited the arrival of an unknown guest three hundred years ago.

STIRLING, Sir JAMES, see **Swan River Colony**

STIVENS, DAL (1911–   ), born Blayney, NSW, has worked as a bank officer, freelance journalist, a public servant and a court reporter. He served in the army education service, 1943–44, the Department of Information, 1944–49, and was press official at Australia House, London, 1949–50, when he resigned to try freelance writing. During his years in London his short stories appeared in such well-known newspapers and magazines as *Lilliput*, the *Times Literary Supplement, John o' London's* and the *Observer*, and were frequently broadcast by the BBC. In 1963 Stivens became the foundation president of the ASA, with which he has continued to work closely. An amateur naturalist, he has contributed to Australian and international natural history journals and since 1971 has made a reputation as a painter; in 1974 he held the first exhibition of his paintings, which have also been reproduced in *Art in Australia*.

Stivens's short stories are represented in numerous anthologies and have appeared in eight collections, *The Tramp and Other Stories* (1936), *The Courtship of Uncle Henry* (1946), *The Gambling Ghost and Other Tales* (1953), *Ironbark Bill* (1955), *The Scholarly Mouse and Other Tales* (1957), *Selected Stories: 1936–1968*, introduced by H.P. Heseltine (1969), *The Unicorn and Other Tales* (1976) and *The Demon Bowler and Other Cricket Stories* (1979). He has also published four novels, *Jimmy Brockett* (1951), *The Wide Arch* (1958), *Three Persons Make a Tiger* (1968) and *A Horse of Air* (1970); a book for children, *The Bushranger* (1978); a work on natural history, *The Incredible Egg* (1974); and edited *Coast to Coast 1957–58* (1958). He won the Miles Franklin

Award in 1970 for *A Horse of Air* and the Patrick White Award in 1981.

His first collection of stories, based on his experience of rural life during the 1930s depression, includes human psychological studies and stark sketches of natural life; in both Stivens reveals a keen insight into the disillusionments, frustrations and cruelties of ordinary existence. 'The Tramp' describes the unsuccessful but spirited attempt of a tramp to win a small prize of money by surviving a side-show boxing contest; 'Pearl Before Swine' evokes the inarticulate feelings of rough men in a bar at the sight of a fresh, innocent girl; in 'Mr. Bloody Kearns', a train guard, conscious of his own insecurity and of the power of the inspector, finds himself throwing a swagman off the train. In his subsequent collections, Stivens explores a range of genres and displays a distinctive comic gift, most popularly in his tall tales and cricketing stories. 'The Courtship of Uncle Henry', a richly rural tale, recounts the transformation of Uncle Henry from tractable, long-suffering swain to despotic husband; 'The Gambling Ghost' deals lightly with the relationship between Frying-Pan Fred and some ghostly gamblers, ending with Fred's own unconscious crossing of the barrier between life and death; 'The Batting Wizard from the City' describes the superhuman feats of an unknown city cricketer, faced with the menace of a local bowler known as the Demon. His tall tales recount such events as Rawhide Harry's capture of the giant groper that has run away with the farmer's plough and Cabbage-Face Ned's duel with a bushranger. Another distinctive genre that has attracted Stivens is the adult animal fable; stories such as 'The Scholarly Mouse', 'The Blue Wren' and 'The Remarkable Cockerel' are a mingling of fantasy and reality, which also probe human inadequacies, fears and failings. Characteristics of Stivens's short fiction include a comic combination of hyperbole and understatement, a deft economy of treatment and a narrative stance that is both detached and sympathetic. His novels are as diverse and experimental as his stories. *Jimmy Brockett*, set in Sydney 1905–38, is the story of a ruthless, brash, manipulating businessman who makes his fortune in boxing, newspapers and racing, rises to political eminence and ends his life lonely, bitter and malicious; *The Wide Arch* is both a murder story and a psychological drama, reminiscent of *Hamlet*; *Three Persons Make a Tiger*, an allegorical fairy-tale based on an oriental legend, satirizes aspects of contemporary life; *A Horse of Air*, Stivens's most ambitious and complex novel, is the story of a mystical search for a rare bird, the night parrot, in Central Australia, seen through the eyes of the leader of the expedition, Harry Craddock, a wealthy, amateur ornithologist, and his wife Joanna, and qualified by comments from the psychiatrist, who treats him and the footnotes of his friend who has edited the manuscript.

STOCK, RALPH (1881–?), contributed short stories and his first novel *The Recipe for Rubber* (1911) to the *Lone Hand*. He recorded his early travels in Canada and the South Seas in *The Confessions of a Tenderfoot* (1913), and a subsequent voyage to the South Pacific in a small sailing ship in *The Chequered Cruise* (1916). After war service in France, Stock was invalided to England and later sailed again for the South Seas. This journey is described in his most popular work, *The Cruise of the Dream Ship* (1921), and is also the subject of a book by his sister and sailing companion, Mabel Stock, *The Log of a Woman Wanderer* (1923). Stock also published two other novels, *Marama* (1913), a tale of the South Pacific, and *The Pyjama Man* (1913), a romance of a playwright and an unhappily-married Sydney girl; and four volumes of short stories, mostly tales of the Pacific set in Fiji and the surrounding islands and dealing with the experiences of traders, planters and beachcombers, *Tadra of the Lagoon* (1914), *Beach Combings* (1920), *South of the Line* (1922) and *Uncharted Waters* (1924).

Stockade, see **COOK, KENNETH**

Stocking Our Selection, see '**RUDD, STEELE**'

Stockwhip, a weekly free-thought newspaper established by John Edward Kelly (1840–96) in February 1875, ran until September 1876, when a court case forced Kelly to cease publication. Purchased by H.N. Montague, who changed the title to the *Stockwhip and Satirist*, the newspaper continued fortnightly from October to November 1876, when its title was changed to the *Satirist*. It ceased publication in January 1877. A vehicle for Kelly's outspoken views on politics, religion and the land question, and for his support of Sir Henry Parkes, the *Stockwhip* aimed, unsuccessfully, to avoid scurrilous personal abuse in its attacks on 'religious, social, commercial and political charlatans'. G.H. Gibson was a regular contributor of satirical poetry, and Havelock Ellis, who may also have been a contributor, mentions the newspaper in his novel *Kanga Creek* (1922). J.F. Archibald, founder of the *Bulletin*, acknowledged that his conception was influenced by the *Stockwhip*, the 'short-lived audacious Sydney weekly ... which had battled against the smug and respectable'. Margaret Woodhouse has published *An Index to 'The*

Stockwhip' 1875–1877, with a Life of John Edward Kelly, 1840–1896 (1969).

STONE, KEN, see **Hunter Valley Poets**

STONE, LOUIS (1871–1935), born Leicestershire, England, was brought to Australia in 1884 and lived for some time in Redfern and Waterloo, the poorer suburbs of Sydney that he used as the setting for his novel *Jonah* (q.v.). After combining attendance at the University of Sydney (although he did not take a degree) with training as a primary schoolteacher, he began his teaching career in 1895. He spent some years in country areas of NSW but returned permanently to Sydney in 1904. Two years later he married another teacher, Abigail Allen, who shared his musical interests. At this time he was also working on his novel *Jonah*, painstakingly gathering material for his representations of the city's life. The novel was completed in 1909, published in London in 1911 and republished in Sydney in 1933. By 1912, the effects of a debilitating nervous illness which led to his long periods of absence and early retirement in 1931 were already apparent. His next novel, *Betty Wayside*, appeared first in full as a serial in *Lone Hand* in 1914, and in book form in 1915, bowdlerized to accord with the publisher's ideas of suitable family reading. Apart from two short stories, one published in *Norman Lindsay's Book No. II* (1915) and the other in *The Australian Soldiers' Gift Book* (1917), Stone's remaining major work was a three-act play, *The Lap of the Gods* (1923). Drama appealed strongly to him as a medium and in 1920 he took the play to London in a bid to gain production. He was unsuccessful but received encouragement fom John Galsworthy and others. In 1923 the play won second place in a competition run by the *Daily Telegraph*, which also published it that year, although it was not produced until 1928, when Gregan McMahon undertook its presentation. Reviews were mixed and the production, which seems to have been inadequate, was withdrawn after one week. Another one-act play, *The Watch That Wouldn't Go*, was published in *Triad* in 1926.

Stone is chiefly remembered for his novel *Jonah*, the story of a larrikin (q.v.), Joe Jones, leader of a city 'push'. In dealing with an urban rather than a rural environment Stone broke new ground, although his lead was not immediately followed. Not the first to use the larrikin as a subject, he was the first to make him popular. Striking, naturalistic descriptions of place and incident, authentic dialogue and a well-realized array of diverse characters are the novel's distinctive attributes. Although his characters are credible and interesting, Stone's imagination is visual and dramatic, rather than analytical and novelistic; he is more concerned to render the colourful surface of life than to probe its depths. *Betty Wayside* is set in Sydney's lower middle-class suburbs Paddington and Woollahra, and deals with the emotional relationships of a woman pianist of potential genius. It is an uneven work, flawed by some weak writing and Stone's uncertain attitude to his protagonist. *Jonah* is a striking achievement but Stone, whose natural bent seems to have been dramatic, was unfortunate to be writing at a time when Australian drama lacked an audience.

Stone, Sandy, see HUMPHRIES, BARRY

STONE, WALTER (1910–81), was a well-known Australian book collector, publisher, printer, editor and bibliographer. He was educated in Orange and Parramatta, and for some years worked on an Auburn newspaper, eventually becoming editor. In 1956 he bought the Wentworth Press, which he managed with his sons. The first work he produced as a private printer, under the imprint Talkarra Press, was an edition in 1953 of one hundred copies of Dulcie Deamer's poem, *Blue Centaur*. Later, under the imprint Stone Copying Co., he produced the various bibliographies in the Studies in Australian Bibliography (q.v.) series. He was probably best known as a book collector, however, especially to other Australian bibliophiles and writers; he was a founder member, and office bearer of the Book Collectors' Society of Australia, editor of its journal, *Biblionews*, and the owner of an extensive collection of Australiana which included books, manuscripts, photographs and memorabilia of many of Australia's writers. President of the FAW and founder member and patron of the Christopher Brennan Society, he was also an office-holder of the ASA and a member of the English Association. In 1975 the National Book Council named him Bookman of the Year; in 1981 he was awarded the OAM.

Apart from numerous bibliographies in periodicals and books, and reviews, bibliographical and biographical essays in journals, Stone compiled four separate bibliographies, *Henry Lawson: A Chronological Checklist of his Contributions to "The Bulletin"* (1887–1924) (1954); *Joseph Furphy, an Annotated Bibliography* (1955); *The Books of the Bulletin 1880–1952* (1955, with George Mackaness); and *Christopher John Brennan* (1959, with Hugh Anderson). He took over the editorship of *Southerly* for a year (1962), and edited James Mudie's 1837 account of the colony of NSW, *The Felonry of New South Wales* (1964), as well as

several popular selections of Lawson and Paterson and *Treasury of Australian Folklore* (1980).

STONEHOUSE, PATRICIA, born Charlton, Victoria, contributed verse early in life to the *Bulletin* and the *Australian Journal*. She published two volumes of verse, *The Road of Yesterday* (1916) and *The Caravan of Dreams* (1923), and fifteen novels, most of which appeared under the pseudonym 'Lindsay Russell', although she also used the names 'Harlingham Quinn' or 'E. Hardingham Quinn'. They are *Smouldering Fires* (1912), *Love Letters of a Priest* (1912), *Kathleen Mavourneen* (1913), *Sands o' the Desert* (1913), *Souls in Pawn* (1913), *The Years of Forgetting* (1914), *The Eternal Triangle* (1915), *Gates of Silence* (1915), *The Interior* (1916), *The Woman Who Lived Again* (1916), *Son of Iscariot* (1916), *That Woman from Java* (1916), *The Gates of Kut* (1917), *Land o' the Dawning* (1917) and *Earthware* (1918). Stonehouse's early novels are marred by her fanatical Irish Protestant attitudes but she progressed to some competent studies of relationships. The settings of her novels include Australia, India, the Middle East, England, Ireland and Scotland.

***Storm Boy*, see THIELE, COLIN**

***Story-book Only*, see McCRAE, HUGH**

STOW, RANDOLPH (1935–), born Geraldton into a long-established WA family, was educated at the University of WA. His varied career has included periods of lecturing in English literature at the Universities of Adelaide, WA and Leeds, eighteen months of intensive travel in the USA, work on an Aboriginal mission and as an anthropologist and cadet patrol officer in New Guinea. Since 1966 he has lived permanently in England. His novels are *The Merry-Go-Round in the Sea* (q.v., 1965), *A Haunted Land* (1956), *The Bystander* (1957), *To the Islands* (q.v., 1958, rev. ed. 1982), *Tourmaline* (q.v., 1963), *Visitants* (1979) and *The Girl Green as Elderflower* (1980). He has also written an outstandingly popular novel for children, *Midnite* (q.v., 1967), and two libretti for operas with music by Peter Maxwell Davies, *Eight Songs for a Mad King* (1969) and *Miss Donnithorne's Maggot* (1974). He has also published collections of poetry including *Act One* (1957), *Outrider* (1962), *A Counterfeit Silence* (1969) and *Randolph Stow Reads from His Own Work* (1974) and has edited *Australian Poetry* (1964). Stow's work, which won recognition early, has received several prizes including the 1958 Miles Franklin Award, the Gold Medal of the Australian Literature Society in 1957 and 1958, the Britannica-Australia Award in 1966 and the Patrick White Literary Award in 1979. The seriousness of Stow's aims and the distinctive nature of his talent were obvious from the first, although his work has aroused a variety of critical reactions. His use of different narrative techniques and his mingling of realism, symbolism, myth, allegory and romance, make his fiction difficult to classify. Sensational, melodramatic plots, obsessive, even demonic, characters and imagistic prose, characterize his first two novels. Although in both the WA landscape is brilliantly rendered, Stow's method is not predominantly naturalistic but dramatic and poetically suggestive. His persistent theme, imperfectly developed in these first two novels, is general and universal: man's metaphysical isolation and his implication as oppressor and victim in a cruel system. For Stow the uneasiness of time-conscious European culture in the timeless, haunted Australian environment is a peculiarly apt metaphor of this condition. This mythopoeic concern is more apparent in his next two, more assured, novels. *To the Islands* describes the journey to death of an old missionary, Heriot, which is also a spiritual expiatory journey in which he transcends his white heritage. *Tourmaline*, a powerful exploration of the interplay of power in an isolated but representative community, is also a blend of allegory and realism. Shaped by a quasi-religious theme which draws on Chinese Taoism, it has no social message but probes the essence of the human condition. *The Merry-Go-Round in the Sea*, Stow's most popular novel in Australia, achieves several effects at once. Set in Geraldtown in the 1940s, it is an intimately-realized study of a particular boy's growth into adolescence which has also a deeper philosophical significance as an expression of transience and isolation. *Visitants*, set in Papua in 1959, has a concentrated atmosphere of mystery, touching on the other-worldly; using the divergent perspectives of a group of individuals of varying cultural backgrounds, it explores a sequence of strange, violent events. *The Girl Green as Elderflower* is a traditional romance which merges life in Suffolk of the 1960s with medieval myth. Stow's smaller volume of poetry reflects, like his fiction, his Australian experience, his feeling for landscape, his wide reading and interest in myth and folklore, his sense of dynasty and preoccupation with time, transience and isolation. Technically assured and traditional in form, his verse achieves, at its best, a simple, spare lyricism.

Strabane of the Mulberry Hills, a novel by William Gosse Hay (q.v.), was published in 1929. Set in Tasmania in 1841 it recounts the experiences of Newton Caillemont, whose letters to his solicitor friend form the substance of the narrative and who as a boy comes to stay with the owner of Strabane, Haylin Talmash. A widower, Haylin has adopted two nieces, Miss Molly and Miss Flo; their skittish conduct offends him, however, and after he becomes convinced that an attempt has been made to poison him, he orders them from the house and substitutes Newton as his heir. The rest of the novel focuses on the attempts by the sisters to repossess Strabane and their inheritance, although Newton faces the additional problem of an attack by the bushranger Martin Cash and his gang. At the end, Strabane is burnt but rebuilt and Newton returns to live there.

STRAHAN, LYNNE, see Feminism and Australian Literature; *Meanjin*

Stranger and Afraid, A, see Treelake series

STRAUSS, JENNIFER (1933–), born Heywood, Victoria, and educated at the University of Melbourne, has taught at the Universities of New England and Melbourne, and since 1964 at Monash University. Her poetry has appeared in several anthologies and numerous magazines and newspapers, and in two collections, *Children and Other Strangers* (1975) and *Winter Driving* (1981). Especially sensitive to the experience and predicament of women, she writes with wit, irony and pathos of such subjects as the passing of time, death, love and parenthood.

Stream (July-September 1931), a monthly magazine published in Melbourne, which described itself as a 'medium of international art expression', had an avant-garde outlook and published articles on overseas literary movements as well as some original poetry and articles on Australian literature. Contributors included Bertram Higgins, Edgar Holt, A.R. Chisholm, Nettie Palmer, Cyril Pearl and Adrian Lawlor.

STREET, JESSIE, see Feminism and Australian Literature

STREETON, Sir **ARTHUR** (1867–1943), born Mount Duneed, Victoria, studied art at the National Gallery School, Melbourne, and became part of the Heidelberg School (q.v.). His best works, Australian landscapes and scenes, include *Still Glides the Stream*, *Golden Summer*, *Circular Quay* and *Redfern Station*. R.H. Croll edited *Smike to Bulldog* (1946), the letters of Streeton to fellow artist, Tom Roberts; Peter Batey wrote 'From Smike to Bulldog', an entertainment based also on the letters. Lionel Lindsay wrote 'The Art of Arthur Streeton' in a special edition of *Art in Australia* in 1919; Anne Kern published *Arthur Streeton: The Man and His Art* (1981).

Streets of the Long Voyage, see DRANS-FIELD, MICHAEL

STREHLOW, T.G.H. (THEODOR GEOR-GE HENRY) (1908–78), was born at Hermannsburg, central Australia, where his father, Carl Strehlow (1871–1922), was in charge of the Lutheran mission. After graduating from the University of Adelaide, he investigated central Australian Aboriginal languages and ceremonial traditions for the Australian National Research Council 1931–34, and worked in native administration in Central Australia 1936–42 before serving with the army in the Second World War. He subsequently joined the English department at the University of Adelaide, later becoming reader in Australian linguistics. He spent long periods in central Australia 1953–65, recording Aboriginal myths, songs and sacred ceremonies. His published work includes *Aranda Phonetics and Grammar* (1944), *Aranda Traditions* (1947), *Dark and White Australians* (1957), *Songs of Central Australia* (1971), *Central Australian Religion* (1978), and two studies of Aboriginal artists, *Rex Battarbee* (1956) and *Nomads in No-man's-Land* (1961, an account of Albert Namatjira). Strehlow also wrote *Journey to Horseshoe Bend* (1969), a record of his father's desperate but unsuccessful journey to seek medical help for his fatal illness, attended by himself, then fourteen, and his mother. A moving account of a journey of extreme suffering and hardship, *Journey to Horseshoe Bend* also recreates the world of Carl Strehlow, his aspirations and achievements, which included the translation of the Lutheran catechism into Aranda, his disappointments over twenty-eight years at Hermannsburg, difficulties with the Mission Board and inability to understand the mythology of the Aboriginal people.

Stretch of the Imagination, A, see HIB-BERD, JACK

Strine, a term invented to represent the way Australians pronounce the word 'Australian', is now also used by some commentators as a synonym for Australian English (q.v.), Australian speech and the word 'Australian' itself when used as an adjective. The inventor of Strine is Alistair Morrison (q.v.) who under the pseudonym 'Afferbeck Lauder' (Strine for 'alphabetical order'), wrote *Let Stalk Strine* ('Let's Talk Australian') (1965), a satire on the elisions and transliterations of uneducated speakers of Australian English. A famous example of Strine is 'Emma Chisit', for whom the English writer Monica Dickens once autographed her novel in a Sydney store not realizing that the shopper had asked, 'How much is it?'.

Stringy-bark, the common name of a Eucalyptus with a tough, fibrous bark, is also used as an adjective meaning uncultured or poverty-stricken; thus a 'stringy-bark cockatoo' is a farmer who farms the poorest land, covered only with the drought-resistant, stringy-bark gums. In the 1920s the term also became a symbol of the bushman's capacity for improvization and endurance, pioneers of the inland being referred to as 'stringybarks'. 'Stringybark and Greenhide', one of Australia's most famous bush ballads celebrates the diverse, useful properties of greenhide and stringy-bark, 'the mainstay of Australia'. Stringybark Creek in the Wombat Ranges is also famous in Australian folklore as the place where in 1878 Ned Kelly and his gang shot the police constables, Lonigan, Scanlon and Kennedy.

'Stroke', a seven-poem sequence by Vincent Buckley (q.v.), was first published in *Quadrant* (1965). The poem describes the familiar events associated with the death of a parent: the hospital bedside, where the embarrassed visitors ('voyeurs of decay') engage in stiff, platitudinous conversation; the son's guilt over the lifetime lack of communication between himself and his father; and memories of the father in his prime compared with his present state. Belonging to the 'life studies' genre, which Buckley was one of the first Australian poets to employ, 'Stroke' conveys, in spite of its calm, almost detached phrasing, the anguish that the son feels, not simply because of the imminent death of his father, but because of the gulf between them that even at the end seems unbridgeable.

STRONG, Sir ARCHIBALD THOMAS (1876–1930), born Melbourne, the son of Herbert Augustus Strong (1841–1918), professor of classics at the University of Melbourne, was taken to England in 1883 and was educated at Liverpool, Oxford, and Germany. In 1901 he returned to Melbourne, where he edited the *Trident*; was for many years literary critic for the *Herald* and lectured in English at the University of Melbourne. In 1922 he was appointed professor of English at the University of Adelaide and was knighted in 1925. One of the founders and trustees of the Melbourne Repertory Theatre under Gregan McMahon, he was also vice-president of the Adelaide Repertory Theatre. He published three collections of conventional verse, *Sonnets and Songs* (1905), *Sonnets of the Empire* (1915) and *Poems* (1918); three collections of essays, *Peradventure* (1911), *Three Studies* (1921) and *Four Studies* (1932); *A Short History of English Literature* (1921) and a translation of *Beowulf* (1925). He also contributed the chapter on Australian literature to the first edition of the *Australian Encyclopaedia* (1925). He was chief Commonwealth film censor 1919–22.

Struck Oil is an appropriately-named play that J.C. Williamson (q.v.) originally purchased in California from Sam Smith, an itinerant Irish wood-chopper. It was expanded by Clay Greene and later revised by Williamson himself. Set in the American Civil War period, with a simple, melodramatic plot, the drama offered histrionic scope for Williamson and his wife, Maggie Moore; when they brought it to Australia in 1874, it was enormously successful, providing the financial base for Williamson's theatrical empire. The Williamsons toured with the play in India Europe, Britain and the USA, 1875–78, and frequently revived it in Australia.

Struggle for Europe, The, see **WILMOT, CHESTER**

STRZELECKI, Sir **PAUL** (1797–1873), born Poland of aristocratic background but no accompanying wealth, arrived in Australia in 1839 after a series of indiscretions and misadventures, acquiring along the way a practical knowledge of mineralogy and geology. In attempting to construct a geological map of the colony he reached the southern Alps and climbed and named Mount Kosciusko, after the Polish democratic leader, Tadeusz Kosciuszko. He later performed important geological and exploration surveys in Tasmania and returned in 1843 to England, where he published *Physical Description of New South Wales and Van Diemen's Land* (1845) for which he received the Founder's Medal of the Royal Geographical Society. He also published *Gold and Silver* (1856) to support his claim of having been the earliest discoverer of gold in NSW. Biographies of Strzelecki include B. Strzelecki's *Biography of Count Paul Edmund de Strzelecki* (1935), Geoffrey Rawson's *The Count: A Life of Sir Paul Edmund Strzelecki* (1954), H.M.E. Heney's *In a Dark Glass: The Story of Paul Edmund Strzelecki* (1961). H.P.G. Clews wrote *Strzelecki's Ascent of Mount Kosciusko, 1840* (1970). The Strzelecki Ranges of Gippsland, Victoria, are named after him.

STUART, DONALD (1913–83), son of Julian Stuart, an early *Bulletin* writer and radical of the 1890s, and brother of Lyndall Hadow, a noted short-story writer, was born at Cottesloe, WA. After a limited education he took to the bush, working as horsebreaker, drover, stockman, prospector, miner, well-sinker and fencer. He was a POW in the Second World War and in later years a prolific novelist, freelance broadcaster for the ABC in Perth, writer of numerous short stories and the federal president of the FAW. His novels began with *Yandy* (q.v., 1959), a fictional-factual account of the establishment of the Pindan Co-operative in 1946, when some 800 striking stockmen on the pastoral stations inland from Port Hedland, WA, broke the long-established system of working Aboriginal stockmen for little pay and of segregating Aborigines from whites. *The Driven* (q.v., 1961), one of the best of his outback novels, is the story of a great cattle trek across the north-west of WA in the late 1930s. *Yaralie* (q.v., 1962) uses the part-Aboriginal girl of the title to examine the problem facing people of mixed races. A succession of other novels followed, including *Ilbarana* (1971), about an Aboriginal boy, its sequel *Malloonkai* (1976), *Walk, Trot, Canter and Die* (1975), *Drought Foal* (1977), and *Wedgetail View* (1978). Stuart also wrote a six-novel autobiographical series, *The Conjuror's Years*, which begins with *Prince of My Country* (1974) and concludes with *I Think I'll Live* (1981). Stuart's *Morning Star Evening Star: Tales of Outback Australia* (1973) is a collection of short stories, colourful yarns which capture the colloquial idiom and unfailing humour, even in such hard times as the depression years, of the rough and ready outback type. A simple and direct writer, Stuart uses character rather than plot to reinforce his theme of the intrinsic worth of the individual, whatever his colour. The background to most of his fiction is the tough north-west country over which he wandered most of his life.

STUART, JOHN McDOUALL (1815–66), was a Scots-born son of an army captain; he emigrated to SA in 1838 and was a member of the inland exploration party of Charles Sturt in 1844–46. During 1852–62 he led four explorations into central and northern Australia: in 1860 he reached the centre of the continent and in 1861 made a valiant attempt, in competition with the Burke and Wills expedition, to cross Australia from south to north. The major record of his journeys is *Explorations in Australia: The Journals of John McDouall Stuart* (1864, ed. William Hardman). Stuart's life and achievements are discussed in Mona Stuart Webster's *John McDouall Stuart* (1958), T.G.H. Strehlow's *Comments on the Journals of John McDouall Stuart* (1967) and Ian Mudie's *The*

Heroic Journey of John McDouall Stuart (1968). The Stuart Range, west of Lake Eyre, and the Stuart highway from Darwin to Port Augusta commemorate his name.

STUART, JULIAN (1866–1929), born Raymond Terrace, NSW, of Scottish ancestry, worked on his parents' farm in the Hunter Valley until eighteen, then went to Sydney where in 1887 he joined the civil service. In 1 888 he went to the upper Dawson Valley in Queensland and became interested in the Shearers' Union, which had been begun by W.G. Spence in 1886 at Ballarat, Victoria. In 1890 he was at Barcaldine when the shearers' strike was brewing; in 1891 he was elected chairman of the Central Queensland Labourers' Union at Clermont. Arrested in March 1891, he was convicted of conspiracy under an old law which had already been repealed in England and sentenced to three years' gaol. On his release he went to WA, where he took up journalism, wrote radical poetry and remained active in politics. His verses were already known in the *Bulletin* under the pseudonym 'Curlew'; much of his poetry in the *Geraldton Express* and the *Coolgardie Miner* appeared under the pseudonym, 'Saladin'. In 1903–06 he edited the *Westralian Worker* and was a member of the WA parliament. He was later a clerk in the WA public service but retained his interest in the bush, the goldfields and the working class. Stuart was prominent in the halcyon days of bush balladry and radical poetry that flourished in WA newspapers at the turn of the century. His radicalism is succinctly expressed in the lines

> I am deformed by labor
> I am the working man
> Cursing the fate that holds me
> A dull-browed Caliban.

Lyndall Hadow, Stuart's daughter, published *Part of the Glory: Reminiscences of the Shearers' Strike, Queensland 1891 From the Pen of Julian Stuart* (1967). The novelist Donald Stuart was his son.

'STUKELEY, SIMON', see **SAVERY, HENRY**

STURT, CHARLES (1795–1869), born India into an East India Company family, joined the army and arrived in Australia in 1827. He achieved fame as an explorer, in particular for his discovery in 1828–30 of the Darling and Murray (q.v.) Rivers and for his leadership of a hellish journey from Adelaide into the centre of Australia in 1844–46. One of the most literate of Australian explorers, Sturt wrote *Two Expeditions into the Interior of Southern Australia* (1833) and *Narrative of an Expedition into Central Australia* (1849). Henry Kingsley's

essay 'The March of Sturt' focuses on Sturt's river journeys, which are also the subject of the novel by J.K. Ewers, *Who Rides on the River?* (1956). Jane Sarah Doudy wrote *Magic of Dawn: A Story of Sturt's Explorations* (1924); Michael Langley, *Sturt of the Murray* (1969); Daniel Brock, *To the Desert with Sturt* (1975) and Margaret Carnegie and Keith Swan, *In Step with Sturt* (1979). Max Harris wrote the poem, 'Sturt at Depot Glen', and Francis Webb, 'Sturt and the Vultures'. A modern appraisal of Sturt, together with a medical commentary by Sir Kenneth Noad, is given in Edgar Beale's *Sturt: The Chipped Idol* (1979). Sturt is commemorated by Sturt's Stony Desert, the Sturt highway and Sturt's Desert Pea, the last the floral emblem of SA.

Such is Life are supposedly the last words spoken by Ned Kelly on the scaffold; the words also form the title of Joseph Furphy's (q.v.) famous novel, although it is not known whether Furphy knew of the connection between Kelly and the expression.

Such is Life, a novel by Joseph Furphy (q.v.), was published by the *Bulletin* in 1903; details of its preparation and reception are provided in the entry on Joseph Furphy. A second 'edition', made up from surplus *Bulletin* sheets with a new title page and a preface by Vance Palmer (q.v.), was published in 1917, and an abridgement in 1937 in which Nettie Palmer had a major hand. The 1944 edition was the first to sell widely and was an important factor in the emergence of Furphy as a major figure in Australian literature.

Furphy objected to the type of colonial romance made popular by 'Rolf Boldrewood' and Henry Kingsley, whose *The Recollections of Geoffry Hamlyn* (1859) is dismissed as 'exceedingly trashy and misleading' in *Such is Life*, where an alternative history of the Buckley family (q.v.) is presented. As a result he made *Such is Life* as little in form like a conventional novel as possible and as much like the 'jumble of incident, dialogue, reflection, etc.' that he described life to be to A.G. Stephens in 1897. In this sense *Such is Life* is an experiment in realism, 'a novel based on a theory of the novel', as A.D. Hope suggested in 1945. *Such is Life* is subtitled *Being Certain Extracts from the Diary of Tom Collins*; Tom Collins (q.v.) is the principal narrator, who takes the opportunity of being 'Unemployed at last!' (the opening line of the novel) to enlarge on certain entries in his collection of diaries and thus provide his readers with a 'fair picture of Life, as that engaging problem has presented itself to me'. He decides to amplify a week's record, choosing at random the entry for 9 September

1883, when as a deputy-assistant-sub-inspector in the NSW public service he camps with a group of bullockies, including Steve Thompson, Cooper and Dixon, on the edge of Runnymede run in the Riverina; among the yarns swapped at the camp is Cooper's tale of his sister's disfigurement when kicked by a horse and her subsequent jilting and suicide. Collins recounts the events of that day and the following morning, during which he exchanges his horse for that of another itinerant arrival at the camp, and helps the bullockies avoid the impounding of their teams for foraging without permission on Runnymede grass; he then realizes that the events of the next day are not suitable material for narration. He opts instead to amplify the diary record of the ninth day of each succeeding month, a method which is followed in the next five chapters, the bulk of the novel, covering the events of October 1883–February 1884. In Chapter II he tells of his visit to the home of Rory O'Halloran; on the journey there he passes a swagman whom he chooses not to disturb in order to let him rest, only to discover next morning that the swagman has died. Chapter III focuses on the hilarious incident in which Tom loses his trousers in attempting to cross the Murray River, gets 'bushed' in attempting to get back to his camp at night, disturbs a number of travellers returning from a church picnic and eventually steals a pair of trousers at a farm after diverting the attention of the household by burning a haystack. In Chapter IV he provides assistance to the reclusive bullock-driver, Warrigal Alf Morris, whose team has strayed from the track while he is ill with a fever; Collins twice rescues them from capture by boundary riders and arranges help for Alf, who during his fever reveals something of his life and tells of four husbands who responded differently to the infidelity of their wives, asking Tom to judge which acted best. In Chapter V Tom again meets Steve Thompson, one of a number of fellow travellers whose animals are impounded for trespassing in a well-grassed paddock on Mondunbarra run; while camped overnight they recount three stories of children lost in the bush, including Thompson's tragic tale of the death of Mary O'Halloran, Rory's daughter, who perishes just before her rescuers reach her. Chapter VI finds Tom at Runnymede, where he has been waiting at the homestead for the arrival of the mail to complete his government business; he is ordered to Nyngan, which allows him to escape the advances of Maud Beaudesart, the housekeeper at Runnymede, and spends that night in the company of the disfigured Runnymede boundary rider, Nosey Alf Jones, whom Collins tells of his assistance to Warrigal Alf. At this point in the novel

Collins decides that his final proposed diary entry (9 March 1884) is also unsuitable material for narration; he chooses instead to amplify the entry for 28–29 March, the 'arbitrary departure' of dates allowing him to chronicle Nosey Alf's departure from Runnymede and to end *Such is Life* back at the station homestead, where he discovers that his ruse to undermine Maud's marriage plans by having his character blackened by an employee of Runnymede has failed.

In opting to chronicle the events of one day per month, Collins states that 'no one of these short and simple analyses [chapters in the novel] can have any connection with another'. In fact, there are a number of connections within *Such is Life*, apart from the beginning and ending at Runnymede and the several appearances of such characters as Thompson. For example, the mystery of the saddle, which Tom finds on his newly-acquired horse the morning after the swap in the first chapter, is cleared up more than two hundred pages later, when Tom realizes that it has been stolen previously from one of the Runnymede hands; the tramp, Andrew Glover, whom Tom meets just before he loses his trousers, turns up at Runnymede in the last pages of *Such is Life* and reveals to Tom, though neither recognizes the other at first, that he has been gaoled for burning the haystack; and most important of all, it emerges from the clues Tom leaves that Cooper's sister Molly is Nosey Alf in disguise, and that Warrigal Alf is the now repentant fiance, who had jilted her. The Molly Cooper–Warrigal Alf–Nosey Alf relationship, which establishes, perhaps ironically, a romantic dimension to *Such is Life*, is not realized by Tom, who fails to make similar connections between incidents elsewhere in the novel and thus lacks the intuition on which he prides himself. He also sees himself as possessing a 'limpid veracity', but reveals himself to be a polysyllabic 'windbag'. That Tom is so obviously lacking in self-knowledge has led to disagreement among commentators about the central philosophy of the novel, whether through Tom Furphy is suggesting that life is a series of decisions between alternatives, but that once a decision is made events are beyond the control of the individual until another decision is necessary. The 'unfettered alternative followed by rigorous destiny' is a pattern Tom sees operating tragically in the death of the swagman and comically in the loss of his trousers. The idea of the controlling alternative is not firmly adhered to throughout the novel, however, and Tom's responsibility for the swagman's death and for the loss of his trousers is only part of Furphy's concern to emphasize throughout *Such is Life* the 'ageless enigma' of life as suggested by the title of the novel. The relativity of .truth and the difficulty in establishing reality are part of that enigma, the recognition of which makes it necessary to accept life's ironies and ambiguities. Moreover, Furphy's relationship with Collins, like the form and themes of the novel, is itself ambiguous. Tom's inadequacies are exposed, but he has his moments of perception and is also the mouthpiece for some of Furphy's ideas, e.g. the democratic temper of *Such is Life*, as well as the vehicle for much of the humour central to the novel: for example, as self-mocking victim as in the loss of the trousers, or as an ironically unknowing character, when he fails to connect Warrigal Alf and Nosey Alf because his mind is filled with 'Ouida', the contemporary romancer. Even Tom's inflated diction, which stands in contrast to the natural idiom of such as Steve Thompson, enables Furphy not only to display his reading of Shakespeare and other authors but also to satirize the habitual swearing of so many of his bush companions.

Sugar Heaven, see **DEVANNY, JEAN**

SULLIVAN, BARRY (1821–91), born England of Irish parents, trained as a lawyer but became an actor and by 1844 was playing leading Shakespearean roles in Scotland and England. In 1862 he arrived in Melbourne, played in a variety of Shakespearean plays in Melbourne and Sydney, and managed the Theatre Royal in Melbourne 1863–66, acquiring considerable popularity as both actor and manager. He left for London in 1866 and continued his successful career, touring North America several times and appearing frequently in Ireland, until ill-health forced him from the stage in 1887. R.P. Whitworth, a Melbourne playwright, based a popular farce, 'Catching a Conspirator' (1867), on an incident from one of Sullivan's visits to Ireland; arrested as an alleged Fenian, Sullivan was forced to prove his identity by declaiming passages from Shakespeare.

SULLIVAN, MARGARET, see **MOORE, MAGGIE**

Summer of the Seventeenth Doll, an outstandingly popular play by Ray Lawler (q.v.), was first produced in 1955, published in 1957 and produced as an American film in 1960. The action, set in 1953, takes place in the faded living-room of a Victorian house in Carlton, Melbourne. The room's otherwise undistinctive furnishings are enlivened by a collection of sixteen kewpie dolls, some stuffed north Queensland birds, a variety of tinted coral and a collection of tropical butterflies. The dolls are

mementos of the years of a relationship between Roo, a cane-cutter, and Olive, a barmaid. Seventeen years earlier they, with their friends Barney and Nancy, began an unconventional arrangement in which the men spent their five-month lay-off season in the city with the girls, working in the cane-fields for the other seven months. Roo (short for Reuben) is the epitome of the bronzed Anzac, rugged and taciturn; Barney, his little mate and an inveterate womanizer, is more gregarious and articulate. For Olive, who regards the men as 'a coupla kings' compared to the 'soft city blokes' and even as 'two eagles flyin'' down out of the sun and coming south every year for the mating season', this arrangement is far superior to marriage. Nancy, however, has recently defected, exchanging the romance of the lay-off for more lasting qualities in her marriage to a bookish city man. The changed realities of the situation are more completely grasped by Emma, Olive's wiry, acerbic, unsentimental mother; its past romance and warmth by Bubba Ryan, the twenty-two-year-old girl from next door. Nancy's place in the seventeenth summer has been taken by Pearl, a prim widow who sees a chance of remarriage in the situation. The arrival of Roo and Barney insinuates further hints that this summer will be different; Roo's leadership of the gang had been successfully challenged by a younger man, Johnnie Dowd, and he had spent most of the winter in Brisbane; Barney had failed to follow him. Roo's acceptance of a city job, the inability of Pearl to join in the jollity, the unresolved tension between Barney and Roo, exacerbated by the arrival of Johnnie Dowd and the failure of the ritualistic celebrations to live up to the past, culminate in a fight between the two men and Roo's destruction of the seventeenth doll. The following morning reveals that Olive has removed all traces of her mementos; Roo, aware that he is too old for cane-cutting, proposes to settle for marriage and work in the city, but Olive angrily rejects him. He leaves despairingly with Barney, unable to respond to his mate's rallying sentiments that 'there's a whole bloody country out there—wide open before us'.

Lawler later wrote two plays to complement *The Doll, Kid Stakes* (produced 1975), which deals with the beginning of the relationship in 1937, and *Other Times* (produced 1976), which is set in 1945 and traces the impact of the war and of time on the foursome. The three plays were published as *The Doll Trilogy* in 1978.

SUMMERS, ANNE (1945–), born Deniliquin, NSW, educated at the Universities of Adelaide and Sydney, is best known as a journalist and radical feminist; in 1983 she was appointed head of the women's unit in the

Prime Minister's Department. One of the founders of the magazine, *Refractory Girl*, she has also been prominent in practical aspects of the women's liberation movement. Political correspondent of the *Australian Financial Review*, she became the first woman president of the national press gallery in 1982 and won the Walkley Award for journalism in 1976 for her report on conditions in prisons in NSW. Her polemical book, *Damned Whores and God's Police: The Colonization of Women in Australia* (1975), is an attempt to begin the process of re-analysing Australian society and history and to suggest a new framework 'in the light of the insights and assumptions of the new feminism'. Summers sees Australian women as historically imprisoned within the two stereotypes indicated by her title. Her study of both the contemporary and historical condition of women is well documented and includes some discussion of Australian women writers as well as a fresh perspective on most of the key historical and cultural studies of Australia. Summers has also compiled, with Margaret Bettison, a bibliography of writing by Australian women on general topics as well as on literature, *Her Story: Australian Women in Print 1788–1975* (1980).

Sun, a Sydney afternoon newspaper and the great rival of the tabloid *Daily Mirror* (1941–), began publication in 1910, superseding the *Star* as Sir Hugh Denison's (q.v.) first venture into newspaper ownership. Innovatively edited by Monty Grover (1910–17), it was aggressively marketed, with a motto ('Above All "for Australia" ') and a masthead (1910–76, Phoebus Apollo's seven-horse chariot before a rising sun) which became familiar to generations of Sydney readers. Denison's Sun Newspapers ran the *Sun* until 1929, when it was merged with Samuel Bennett Ltd to form Associated Newspapers; in 1953 the *Sun*, politically conservative for much of its life, came under the control of the Fairfax press. Notable editors have been Adam McCay (1917–19), Delamore McCay, Thomas Dunbabin, and B.J. Tier (1959–73); long-term staff include the actress, broadcaster and novelist, Mary Marlowe, who was theatre critic and reporter 1921–46. In modern times dominated by advertising, the *Sun* was described as early as 1929 as something printed on the back of retailers advertisements; now a weekday newspaper, it published a Saturday edition until 1974.

The *Sunday Sun* began publication in 1903 as the Sunday companion of the *Star*. Although for many years after Denison's acquisition of the newspaper it carried the title of the *Sun* and may have appeared to be its Sunday edition, it came in effect to be a separate newspaper with its own editor, e.g. Grover in 1917–20, 1921–22, and later Eric Baume and Colin Simpson; Grover introduced a 'Sunbeams' children's page which was first edited by Ethel Turner and starred Ginger Meggs (q.v.). A notable scoop by the *Sunday Sun* was its exposure of the Ern Malley hoax (q.v.) in 1944. The *Sunday Sun* incorporated the *Sunday Guardian* in 1931 and was merged with *Sunday Herald* (1949–53) to form the *Sun-Herald* in 1953. Fred Peterson was editor in 1956–76 of the *Sun-Herald*, which ran Leon Gellert's columns, 'Something Personal' and 'Speaking Personally', until 1961.

Sun: An Australian Illustrated Newspaper for the Home and Society, see **CHAMPION H.H.**

Sun News-Pictorial, a Melbourne morning daily, began publication in 1922 when the proprietor of the Sydney *Sun*, Hugh Denison, attempted to establish a Melbourne outlet for his operations. In 1925 Denison sold the newspaper to the Herald and Weekly Times company; since then the *Sun News-Pictorial* has been the morning companion of the afternoon *Herald*.

Sunday Times, founded in Perth in 1897 by F.C.B. Vosper, was WA's first Sunday newspaper. It linked up in 1901 with the Kalgoorlie *Sun*, another Sunday newspaper, established by Arthur Reid and James MacCallum. Both papers combined to initiate a period of literary activity in WA, centring on goldfields themes, both contemporary and nostalgic. C.W. Andrée Hayward alternated editorship of the papers in the period 1901–1912, and contributors included such well-known literary figures as J.P. Bourke ('Bluebush'), Alfred Chandler ('Spinifex'), Julian Stuart ('Saladin'), E.G. Murphy ('Dryblower'), T.H. Wilson ('Crosscut') and Francis Ophel ('Prospect Good'). The Christmas numbers of each paper were literary-oriented; in addition to numerous poems, sketches and short stories, they often contained literary articles. In 1910 Alfred Chandler published an assessment of Australian poetry in a ten-article series in both papers; throughout 1901–10 both papers ran 'The Bookfellow', a syndicated literary column by A.G. Stephens.

Sundowner, see **Swag**

Sundowners, The, a novel by Jon Cleary (q.v.), was published in 1952, adapted for radio presentation by Max Afford and produced as a highly successful film in 1962 starring Deborah Kerr and Robert Mitchum. Set in Australia of the 1920s, it deals with the experiences of

Paddy Carmody, a wandering drover, his wife Ida and their fourteen-year-old son Sean. Although Paddy is temperamentally committed to their wandering life, Ida yearns for a permanent home and is bitterly disappointed when their chances of buying a share in a farm are destroyed by Paddy's gambling spree. Their love survives the crisis, however. The novel also describes Sean's growth from childhood as he adjusts to changes in his relationship with his father and learns from the lives of other men such as Venneker, Bert McKechnie and Ern Bateman.

Sunny South, The, an outstandingly popular melodrama by George Darrell (q.v.) and his only extant work, first produced in 1883 and first published in 1975, was frequently revived in Australia until the 1890s. Darrell, playing the lead, took the play to London in 1884 where it seemed set for a long run had he not suffered a severe accident on stage. With its ebullient humour, vitality, and acute social observation, the play crystallizes the distinctive qualities of Australian melodrama, although its Anglophilia soon became outdated.

'SURCINGLE', see **BOAKE, BARCROFT**

Surprises of the Sun, see **McAULEY, JAMES**

Survivor, The, see **KENEALLY, THOMAS**

SUTHERLAND, ALEXANDER (1852–1902), born Glasgow, came to Australia at the age of fourteen, graduated from the University of Melbourne, and in 1877 became headmaster of a school, Carlton College. He retired in 1892 but was forced by the depression of 1892–93 into journalistic work and wrote leaders for the *Argus* and the *Australasian*. He tried unsuccessfully in 1897 and 1901 to gain election to the Victorian parliament, became registrar of the University of Melbourne in 1901 and lecturer in English following the death of E.E. Morris. He edited the first posthumous collections of Henry Kendall's poetry (1886 and 1890); wrote the manual, *Victoria and Its Metropolis: Past and Present* (1888); with his brother George, *The History of Australia* (1877); and collaborated with H.G. Turner in one of the earliest surveys of Australian literature, *The Development of Australian Literature* (q.v., 1898). He was on the editorial staff of the *Melbourne Review*, for which he wrote several significant critical articles; published *Thirty Short Poems* (1890); and wrote short stories. He also wrote on philosophic and scientific subjects, his most notable work being the pioneer study, *The Origin and Growth of the Moral Instinct* (1898).

SUTHERLAND, GEORGE (1855–1905), born Scotland, was brought to Australia in 1864, taught for some time after graduating from the University of Melbourne, but then turned to journalism. Regarded as an outstandingly cultivated and versatile journalist, he was on the staff of the *South Australian Register* 1881–1902, when he joined the editorial staff of the *Age*. With his brother Alexander he wrote *The History of Australia* (1877), and published on his own account the historical and descriptive sketches, *Tales of the Goldfields* (1880). He wrote accounts of SA in *Australia: Or, England in the South* (1886) and *The South Australian Company* (1898), as well as geographical studies and practical works on vine-growing and livestock-handling. An inventor, he patented a successful photographic engraving process and in *Twentieth Century Inventions* (1901) discussed a range of current and possible future inventions. His daughter, Margaret Sutherland the composer, collaborated with Vance Palmer in the collection, *Old Australian Bush Ballads* (1951).

SUTTOR, WILLIAM HENRY (1834–1905), born NSW, was a prominent pastoralist and member of both houses of the NSW parliament. He contributed a series of historical sketches dealing with pastoral life, gold-mining, bushrangers and Aborigines to the Sydney *Daily Telegraph*. They were subsequently collected, titled *Australian Stories Retold and Sketches of Country Life* (1887). Beverley Suttor, who was a member of the same pioneering family, published *Original Poetry* (1838) and other volumes; he has been judged as one of Australia's worst poets.

Swag was originally an English word meaning the general booty or spoils from a robbery or theft and it is still used colloquially in that sense to mean a large quantity of goods. It was applied in 1819, by James Hardy Vaux in his 'flash' vocabulary, only to stolen wearing apparel, linen and piece goods. Later in the nineteenth century the term came to be part of the vocabulary of the Australian outback meaning, according to an 1857 definition, 'portable luggage that can be carried on the person'. That meaning has persisted to the present day, although many other different words, e.g. 'matilda', 'shiralee', 'bluey' and 'drum', have been used to denote the bundle of possessions that itinerant work-seekers (and avoiders) carried from place to place. The swag, a tightly-rolled, sausage-shaped bundle, usually contained a blue blanket, hence 'bluey' for the swag itself, a waterproof sheet, spare clothes and personal odds and ends. The swag was slung over the shoulder by a piece of leather or rope and from it hung a sugar bag of food and a billy (q.v.) for making tea. Carrying the swag has been variously described as 'humping the bluey', 'humping the drum' and 'waltzing matilda'. Derivatives of swag include 'swagman' and 'swaggie', while variations of 'swagman' include 'bagman,' from the English term for a commercial traveller; 'tramp', applicable to all itinerants, especially in the depression years of the 1920s and 1930s; 'sundowner', because of the habit of arriving at a homestead or station at sundown, thus avoiding the risk of having to work for food; and 'whaler', itinerants like the *Bulletin*'s 'Scotty the Wrinkler', who travelled the inland rivers such as the Murrumbidgee, the Murray and the Darling. The profession of swag-carrying has produced a large vocabulary of associated colloquialisms, e.g. 'on the wallaby' denoting being on the track, and 'roll the swag' meaning to quit one's job. The swag and its carriers have been widely featured in Australian literature from the early colonial works of Alexander Harris, *The Emigrant Family* (1849), through and beyond the 1890s in Henry Lawson's *While the Billy Boils* (1896), *In the Days When the World Was Wide* (1896) and *On the Track* (1900), Barcroft Boake's *Where the Dead Men Lie* (1897), Barbara Baynton's *Bush Studies* (1902), John Farrell's *My Sundowner and Other Poems* (1904), John le Gay Brereton's *Swags Up!* (1928), E.P. Harrington's *The Swagless Swaggie and Other Ballads* (1957) and up to modern times in D'Arcy Niland's *The Shiralee* (1955). Among the best descriptions of the life and hard times of the swagman are Lawson's poems, 'Out Back' and 'Knocked Up', and his short story, 'Some Day'; John Shaw Neilson's poem, 'The Sundowner'; Louis Esson's poem, 'Whalin' Up the Lachlan'; 'J.P.B.''s poems about derelict swaggies, 'His Story' and 'His Last Stage'; and A.J. Boyd's sketch, 'The Swagsman' in *Old Colonials* (1882). The swag and the swagman have also been celebrated in folk-songs and ballads, e.g. 'Australia's on the Wallaby', 'Humping Old Bluey', 'Three Little Johnny Cakes', 'The Reedy Lagoon', 'The Old Bark Hut', 'The Rambleeer', 'With My Swag All on My Shoulder' and 'My Old Black Billy'. The Australian literary journal *Overland* has a page of topical comment by its editor, Stephen Murray-Smith, titled 'Swag'. The Bronze Swagman Award (a bronze statuette of a swagman, sculpted by Daphne Mayo, and a Winton opal) is awarded annually by the Winton Tourist Promotion Association for the best bush verse of the year.

Swagless Swaggie, The, see **HARRINGTON, E.P.**

SWAN, NATHANIEL WALTER (1835–84), born Ireland and educated at the University of Glasgow, came to Victoria during the gold rushes. He became acquainted with Henry Kingsley, who advised him to take up writing, and with Adam Lindsay Gordon, Marcus Clarke and Henry Kendall. A contributor to numerous colonial newspapers, he edited the *Ararat Advertiser* and the *Pleasant Creek News* and was for a time proprietor of the *Stawell News*. Three publications by Swan were issued, *Tales of Australian Life* (1875), which includes a short novel, 'Marie Denton', and short stories dealing mainly with life on the diggings; *A Couple of Cups Ago* (1885), a collection of short stories, again reflecting his experiences of the diggings and of station life; and *Luke Mivers' Harvest* (1899), a novel for which he won the *Sydney Mail* prize in 1878 and which includes some effective descriptions of the Australian landscape, although the plot is unwieldy and the characters indistinct.

Swan River Colony, the infant colony of WA, took its title from the Swan River, on whose northern banks a settlement was established in 1829. Although Captain James Stirling (1791–1865) was not the first to discover the Swan River (it was found by Willem de Vlamingh, a Dutch seafarer, in 1697) he surveyed it in 1827 and became governor of the first settlement. Literature from the infant Swan River colony comprised mainly diaries, journals, letters and memoirs; representative samples, often published much later than the events they portray, include G.F. Moore's *Diary of Ten Years Eventful Life of an Early Settler in Western Australia* (1884); J.G. Hay's *The Visit of Charles Fraser to the Swan River in 1827* (1906); Peter Cowan's compilations *A Faithful Picture: The Letters of Eliza and Thomas Brown at York in the Swan River Colony 1841–1852* (1977) and *A Colonial Experience: Swan River 1839–1888* (1978); and *The Tanner Letters: A Pioneer Saga of Swan River & Tasmania* (1981, edited by Pamela Statham). *Swan River Saga* (1975), a play by Mary Durack, recreates the experiences of Eliza Shaw, an important pioneer woman. The well-known Swan River Aboriginal, Yagan (q.v.), and the problem of white–black relationships in pioneer times, are featured in Mary Durack's *The Courteous Savage: Yagan of Swan River* (1964) and in G.F. Moore's *Diary*. Popular modern historical novels about the colony are Rix Weaver's *Behold, New Holland* (1940) and *New Holland Heritage* (1951) and Phyllis Hastings's *The Swan River Story* (1968). In its first decade the Swan River colony boasted some ten newspapers, the most significant of which were the *Perth Gazette* and the *Swan River Guardian*.

Swayne Family, The, see **PALMER, VANCE**

Swords and Crowns and Rings, a novel by Ruth Park (q.v.), was published in 1977 and won the Miles Franklin Award. Set mainly in rural Australia 1907–32, it is the story of a dwarf's quest for self-acceptance, love and dignity. Jackie Hanna is fortunate in his mother Peggy, and his stepfather Jerry MacNunn. Their determination to discount his disability supports him during his childhood at Kingsland, a small town in NSW. He is also sustained by his close relationship with Cushie Moy, his 'princess', the daughter of a local bank employee and his class-conscious wife. After leaving school the only employment available to Jackie is on a fruit farm in the High Valley country owned by Jerry's German relations, the Linzes. Oafish and brutish in the extreme, the Linz brothers treat Jackie with the same cruelty that they show to all things animate. Only Maida, their young sister, who invites herself to Jackie's bed, and Hof, the eldest brother, show any kindness. After a particularly vicious and humiliating attack by the brothers, Jackie flees home and is passionately reunited with Cushie. But he soon decides to return to the Linz orchard as a gesture of self-respect, unaware that Cushie is pregnant. Mrs Moy secretly arranges an abortion in Sydney and Cushie is dispatched to be cared for by her eccentric, promiscuous Aunt Claudie and her housemate, Iris. Cushie's humiliating experiences in Sydney strengthen her determination to break free from her dominating mother and she escapes to live with her wealthy grandmother in Balmain. Meanwhile, for Jackie, returning to the Linz farm has meant a forced marriage to the pregnant Maida. The child is stillborn but the couple find happiness on the shores of the River Dovey where Jackie works for a milk supplier, Lufa Morgan. Five years later when their son Carlie is seven months old, they are visited by Maida's embittered mother, Eva. The visit ends tragically: Maida, Carlie and Eva die during a fire, Jackie's part in the catastrophe becomes a matter of notoriety and he discovers incidentally that Maida's first pregnancy has been to one of her brothers. After some time in the outback, Jackie in 1931 learns of his mother's death and returns to Kingsland, which has been affected by the depression. The now elderly and grief-stricken Jerry MacNunn is forced to abandon the family shop and father and son take to the road, along with thousands of others, in search of work. Their journey, which is a sequence of sufferings, terminates several months later in Sydney. There Jerry recovers some happiness and dignity and Jackie learns more of the world, finally coming to terms with his

dwarfism. His odyssey is complete when chance reunites him with Cushie Moy.

S.W. Silver & Co.'s Australian Graziers' Guide, see **'BOLDREWOOD, ROLF'**; Almanacs

Sydney, the oldest city in Australia and the capital of New South Wales (q.v.), is situated on the eastern coast of the continent. It developed around Port Jackson (Sydney Harbour) and now extends northwards to the Hawkesbury River, southwards past Botany Bay (the original landing place of the First Fleet) and westwards to the Nepean River. It takes its name from Viscount Sydney, home secretary to whom Arthur Phillip reported, but was never officially named, evolving from Sydney Cove, near the present Opera House, where the first settlement was established. Very much a convict settlement in its early years, Sydney began to be laid out during Governor Macquarie's term of office; its first municipal council was formed in 1842. Overtaken briefly by Melbourne during the latter part of the nineteenth century, Sydney is now the largest city in Australia; twenty per cent of Australians live there. P. Holt edited *A City in the Mind* (1983), which includes writers' impressions of Sydney.

Sydney Delivered: Or, The Princely Buccaneer is a short farce by David Burn (q.v.) published in 1845 under the pseudonym 'Tasso Australisiatticus' but never performed. The work, which has more vitality than Burns's serious dramas, is set in Tahiti and deals with an Anglo-French confrontation, thus reflecting Burn's interest in colonial defence and general naval matters.

Sydney Gazette (1803–42), Australia's first newspaper, was first published by George Howe (q.v.); it remained in the control of the Howe family for much of its life. Significant contributors included Charles de Boos, Henry Halloran, Edward O'Shaughnessy, Michael Massey Robinson and Charles Tompson; in addition, the advertisements and notices in the *Gazette* provide valuable evidence of the literary interests and habits of the colonists during the foundation years of settlement. Mainly pro-government, the *Sydney Gazette* eventually succumbed to the competition of the *Sydney Morning Herald* and the effects of the 1840s depression.

Sydney Mail, the weekly companion to the *Sydney Morning Herald*, was published 1860–1938. Like its rival, the *Australian Town and Country Journal*, it was popular with both country and city readers, and combined general news with agricultural, pastoral, mining, sporting and literary features and included illustrations. A.B. Paterson was its Boer War correspondent, and 'Rolf Boldrewood' had his *Robbery Under Arms* serialized there in 1882–83. Its editors included W.H. Traill, F.W. Ward (1879–84), Edwin Burton (1885–98), J.P. Dowling (1895–1905) and W.R. Charlton (1905–38).

Sydney Monitor, a prominent early Australian newspaper, began publication in 1826 as the *Monitor*, its title until 1828, and ran mainly as a weekly or semi-weekly until 1841. For much of its time under the control of its founder, Edward Smith Hall (q.v.), the 'Australian Cobbett', the *Monitor* was aggressively pro-convict and anti-government in its early years, particularly during the governorship of Sir Ralph Darling. It welcomed Darling's more liberal successor, Sir Richard Bourke, although siding with James Mudie, who was contemptuous of convicts, during Mudie's disputes with Bourke in 1834. In 1835 the *Monitor* published extracts from Charles Harpur's play, *The Bushrangers* (1853), under the title 'The Tragedy of Donohoe'.

Sydney Morning Herald, the oldest surviving Australian newspaper, commenced publication as a weekly, the *Sydney Herald*, in 1831; two of its three founders, William McGarvie and Ward Stephens (qq.v.), alternated ownership during its first decade. In 1840 it became a daily and the following year was bought by John Fairfax (q.v.) and Charles Kemp, and in 1842 took its present title. In the 1840s it became established as Sydney's leading newspaper, a position retained despite competition from the *Empire* under the youthful Henry Parkes (qq.v.) and since 1879 from the *Daily Telegraph* (q.v.). From 1853, when Fairfax bought out Kemp, until 1956, when a public company was formed, the *Sydney Morning Herald* remained under the financial control of the Fairfax family. A conservative organ for most of its life, the *Sydney Morning Herald* – or 'Granny' to many of its readers since about 1850 – is, along with the *Age* (q.v.), Australia's most famous newspaper and one of the few to achieve a world-wide reputation. Its editors have included several prominent names in Australian journalism, notably John West (1854–73), Andrew Garran (1873–85), William Curnow (1886–1903), Thomas Heney (1903–18), C. Brunsdon Fletcher (1918–37), H.A. McClure Smith (1938–52), and John Douglas Pringle (1952–57, 1965–70) and its staff or contributors a number of prominent Australian writers, including S.J. Baker, C.E.W. Bean, Marcus Clarke, Leon Gellert, Charles Harpur, Montague Grover, A.B. Paterson, and

Catherine Helen Spence (qq.v.). The company publication of John Fairfax & Sons, *A Century of Journalism: The Sydney Morning Herald and Its Record of Australian Life 1831–1931* (1931) has extensive information on the first hundred years of the *Sydney Morning Herald* and on other Fairfax publications; its more recent history, and information on the activities of the Fairfax organization in radio, television and other ventures, is detailed in Gavin Souter's prize-winning *Company of Heralds: A Century and a Half of Australian Publishing by John Fairfax Limited and Its Predecessors 1831–1981* (1981).

Sydney Punch, see **Melbourne Punch**

Sydney Quarterly Magazine, published by the Sydney Quarterly Magazine club, ran 1883–92 and included some articles on literary subjects and some original poetry. J. le Gay Brereton was a contributor.

Sydney Times, see **KENTISH, N.L.**

Sydney University Magazine, the first magazine of the University of Sydney, ran for three issues in 1855, sponsored by Dr John Woolley, edited by three students, Alexander Oliver, James Stewart Paterson and William Windeyer, and assisted by Henry Parkes, then editor of the *Empire*. Surprisingly nationalistic in its social, cultural and political aims, the *Magazine* included some original verse, the first episode of a serialized novel, and essays on English literature, all contributed anonymously. Two subsequent journals, published in 1878–79 and 1885, had the same title although the 1878–79 journal edited by Joseph Sheridan Moore was not published under the auspices of the University; its contributors included Henry Kendall, Henry Halloran and Moore.

Sydney University Review, founded and administered by the University Union, ran for five issues 1881–83. According to its first issue the *Review* intended to provide 'a platform' from which Australian writers could 'express their matured thoughts' and to act 'as a nursery for aspirants to literary fame' and aspired to attract contributions from numerous eminent Australians. Some poetry by Henry Kendall, Henry Halloran, Emily Manning and C.E.W. Bean is included in its issues, although articles on education, theology, history and legal matters predominate. Articles of literary interest include W.B. Dalley's obituary essay on Kendall (December 1882) and George Knox's review of the first century of Australian verse (July 1883).

SYKES, BOBBI (1943–), born Queensland, a prominent activist for Aboriginal rights, left school at fourteen and has had numerous occupations. She was the first executive secretary of the Aboriginal Embassy erected on the lawns in front of Parliament House, Canberra, in 1972, has written and lectured widely on race relations in Australia and in the USA, Great Britain, Jamaica and NZ, and has worked voluntarily for the Aboriginal medical and legal services. She is also a member of the Australian Advisory Committee on the Environment. She has contributed to a debate with Senator Neville Bonner, *Black Power in Australia* (1975); helped Colleen Shirl Perry, one of the founders of the Aboriginal medical and legal services, to compose her autobiography, *Mum Shirl* (1981); and has published a collection of poems, *Love Poems and Other Revolutionary Actions* (1979). She was awarded the 1981 Patricia Weickhardt Award for an Aboriginal writer. See Aboriginal in Australian Literature.

SYME, DAVID (1827–1908), newspaper proprietor, was born and educated in Scotland and joined the Victorian gold rush in 1852. In 1856 he purchased a half-share in the fledgling *Age* (q.v.) newspaper from his brother Ebenezer (1826–60) and on Ebenezer's death took over the management of the journal. Under Syme for almost half a century, the *Age* supported protection and adopted a liberal radical stance. Syme also won minor repute as a political economist with the publication of *Outlines of an Industrial Science* (1876). The subject of biographies by Ambrose Pratt in 1908 and Charles Sayers in 1965, Syme was also the subject of the 1982 Daniel Mannix Memorial Lecture by the *Age* newspaper executive, Ranald Macdonald, whose lecture was published as *David Syme* (1982).

SZYMANSKI, LESZEK (1933–) was born and educated in Warsaw. In 1956 he became editor of an independent literary magazine, the *Contemporary*, which took its title from a literary group he founded. Szymanski left Poland in the 1960s and spent some time in Australia; he now lives in Los Angeles. He has published two collections of short stories, some of which are set in Australia, *Escape to the Tropics* (1964) and *On the Wallaby Track* (1967); an account of some of his experiences in Australia, *Living with the Weird Mob* (?1975); *Warsaw Aflame* (1967), a description of the German occupation of Poland; and *Candle for Poland* (1982), an account of the Solidarity movement.

T

Table Talk, an illustrated Melbourne journal established by Maurice Brodzky, who edited it until 1903, ran 1885–1939, merging with *Melbourne Punch* in 1929. Strongly literary in flavour, it carried short fiction, serials, poetry, sketches, literary and theatrical reviews, and biographical sketches.

Tabloid Story, a publishing experiment designed to provide an outlet for new short fiction, was devised in 1972 by Michael Wilding, Frank Moorhouse (qq.v.) and Carmel Kelly, joined later by Brian Kiernan and Colin Talbot; in 1975 control of the magazine passed to a group of Melbourne writers. Dissatisfied with the lack of opportunities available through the established literary magazines for short fiction that did not conform to the Lawson tradition, the founders of *Tabloid Story* developed the concept of preparing a tabloid fiction supplement ready for printing which could be offered free to an established journal; in return, the host journal would print the *Tabloid Story* issue and publish it as a supplement, supplying additional copies to the editors for distribution to subscribers and contributors. Assisted by a CLF grant, *Tabloid Story* first appeared in October 1972 in *National U*, the newspaper of the Australian Union of Students. With continuing government support, it has since been hosted by other student newspapers, e.g. *Newswit, Semper Floreat, Honi Soit, Lot's Wife, Tharunka;* by radical or fringe newspapers and little magazines, e.g. *Living Daylights, Nation Review, New Literature Review, Warringah Women's Times;* and by more middle-of-the-road journals, e.g. *Bulletin, Australian Book Review.* The fiction in *Tabloid Story* is characterized by its sexual explicitness, the radical, political and social stance of many of its writers, and its eclecticism of form and techniques, including fabulist, process and confessional stories. Among contributors to *Tabloid Story*, apart from Moor-house, Wilding, Kelly and Talbot, have been Murray Bail, Peter Carey, Laurie Clancy, Kris Hemensley, Elizabeth Jolley, Rudi Krausmann, Peter Mathers, Dal Stivens and Vicki Viidikas. Michael Wilding's selection from the first nineteen issues of *Tabloid Story*, published in 1978 as *The Tabloid Story Pocket Book*, includes an account of the magazine's evolution.

TAIT Family was involved in theatrical and concert management in Australia for many years. The family included five sons of John Turnbull Tait (1829–1902), a Scotsman who migrated to Victoria in 1862: Charles Tait (1870–1933), John Henry Tait (1871–1955), James Nevin Tait (1876–1961), Edward Joseph Tait (1878–1947) and Frank Samuel Tait (1883–1965). One of the earliest achievements of Charles, John and James was the production of a popular film, *The Story of the Kelly Gang* (1906). In 1908 John and James, guided by their brother Charles, established a concert bureau, J. & N. Tait, which rapidly expanded into theatrical management. They were later joined by their brothers Edward and Frank. In 1920 the Taits merged with the giant of theatrical management in Australia, J.C. Williamson Ltd, and were responsible for the visits of numerous world artists such as Pavlova, Paderewski, Harry Lauder and Gracie Fields; from 1920 to the 1950s they dominated the production of ballet and opera in Australia. The family's achievements were recorded in Viola Tait's *A Family of Brothers* (1971).

Taking Stock (1953), edited by W.V. Augh-terson, one-time professor of education at the University of Melbourne, is a collection of assessments of mid-twentieth century Australian society. Concerned to preserve and defend the good aspects of Australian life, *Taking Stock* examines the problems facing Australia in the second half of the century. Contributors are Aughterson, W. MacMahon Ball, W. D. Bor-rie, Robin Boyd, Donald Cochrane, Allan McCulloch, P.H. Partridge, A.A. Phillips, G.V. Portus, Geoffrey Sawer and W.H. Stanner. Phillips contributed the essay, 'Australian Literature' and Alan McCulloch, 'Australian Art'.

TALBOT, COLIN (1948–), has worked as a journalist and in radio and has spent some time in the USA. He has published two novels, *Massive Road Trauma* (1975) and *Sweethearts* (1978); a collection of his journalism, *Colin Talbot's Greatest Hits* (1977); a collection of verse, *Greek Roulette* (1973); and has compiled, with Robert Kenny, an anthology of poetry, *Applestealers* (1974). He has been a director of

Outback Press and was involved in *Tabloid Story*.

TALBOT, NORMAN (1936–), born Suffolk, England, has taught English at the University of Newcastle since 1962 and has published several collections of verse, *Poems for a Female Universe* (1968), *Son of a Female Universe* (1971), *The Fishing Boy* (1973), *Find the Lady* (1977) and *Where Two Rivers Meet* (1980). A strong supporter of the arts in the Newcastle area, he has edited four collections of Hunter Valley poets (q.v.). A colleague of the Welsh-born poet, T. Harri Jones, Talbot published the poem, *The Seafolding of Harri Jones* (1965), after Jones's death by drowning.

Tales of Mystery and Romance, see **MOOR-HOUSE, FRANK**

Tales of the Colonies: Or, The Adventures of an Emigrant was published in London in 1843 by Charles Rowcroft (q.v.) but was attributed to 'A Late Colonial Magistrate'. The preface reveals the emigrant guidebook nature of the novel: 'this book was written with the view of describing the process of settling in a new country; the precautions to be taken; the foresight to be exercised; the early difficulties to be overcome; and the sure reward, which awaits the prudent and industrious colonist.' It purports to be the journal of William Thornby, who emigrates to Van Diemen's Land, settles on a grant of land, establishes a house and farm and experiences such hazards of pioneer life as sheep stealers, bushrangers, Aboriginal attackers, floods, snakes, eagles and wild cattle. The novel also provides a prolonged account of the convict system as it operates in Van Diemen's Land. A highly popular work, *Tales of the Colonies* was translated into both French and German. See Aboriginal in Australian Literature.

Tales of the Convict System, see 'WARUNG, PRICE'

Tallangetta, see **HOWITT, WILLIAM**

Taruru: Aboriginal Song Poetry from the Pilbara, see **Aboriginal Song and Narrative in Translation**

'TASMA', see **COUVREUR, JESSIE**

TASMAN, ABEL JANSZOON (?1603–59), the Netherlands mariner and explorer, undertook between 1633 and 1649 numerous trading and military voyages for the Dutch East India Company; two of these expeditions, 1642 and 1644, resulted in important discoveries about

Australia. Tasman subsequently engaged in private trading and became one of the largest landowners in Batavia. His journal of his 1642 voyage to Van Diemen's Land and NZ was first published in England in 1694. There have been numerous biographies of Tasman, including James Backhouse Walker's (1896), and Andrew Sharp has written an account of his voyages (1968). In addition to Tasmania itself, his name has been applied to numerous geographical and other features. Tasman's achievements have been celebrated in poems by Frances Sescadorowna Lewin (1889) and by E.J. Brady (1909) and he is the hero of R.D. FitzGerald's well-known poem, 'Heemskerck Shoals' (1953). He also appears in Ernest Favenc's novel, *Marooned on Australia* (1896).

Tasmania, a heart-shaped island to the south of Victoria (q.v.), is the smallest Australian State (almost 168 000 square kilometres, including its neighbouring islands) and the only one not part of the mainland continent, from which it is separated by Bass Strait. It was discovered in 1642 by Abel Tasman, who called it Van Diemen's Land (q.v.), its name from 1803, when the first English settlement was made near the site of the present capital of Hobart, until 1855. Part of NSW 1803-25, Tasmania was granted responsible government in 1855 and remained a separate British colony until its incorporation into the Commonwealth of Australia in 1901. The significance of transportation (q.v.) in Tasmanian history from the 1820s to the 1850s explains its importance in Australian convict literature; 'Tasmania', in use from the 1820s, replaced Van Diemen's Land because of the latter's association with convictism. The early settlement of Tasmania also explains its significance in Australian press history.

Tasmanian was an early Tasmanian newspaper which had a complicated publishing history over twenty years, involving several prominent pioneering journalists. A weekly for most of its life, it was founded in 1825 by George Terry Howe in Launceston as the *Tasmanian and Port Dalrymple Advertiser*; later that year Howe moved his press to Hobart to help produce the *Hobart Town Gazette*. In 1827 he re-established the *Tasmanian* but sold it several months later to J.C. Macdougall, who in 1829 amalgamated the journal with R.L. Murray's (q.v.) *Murray's Austral-Asiatic Review* to form the *Tasmanian and Austral-Asiatic Review*. The two journals amalgamated, usually under the title of the *Tasmanian and Austral-Asiatic Review*, in 1829-33, 1834-37 and 1841-45; in 1834 and 1837-41 they co-existed in Hobart. Murray was involved in the

proprietorship either of his own *Austral-Asiatic Review* or of the amalgamated journal throughout this period; Macdougall sold his interests to Henry Melville (q.v.) in 1831 but resumed his involvement in 1838. Other journalists who wrote for or helped to edit the *Tasmanian* in one or other of its forms were Thomas Richards and Henry Savery. In 1845 the journal was incorporated into the *Colonial Times*.

Tasmanian Punch, see ***Melbourne Punch***

TATE, HENRY (1873-1926), born Prahran, Melbourne, was a successful musician, composer and music critic for the *Age* (1924-26), as well as a poet. His ideas for an individual and distinctive Australian music are contained in *Australian Musical Possibilities* (1924). His verse included *The Rune of the Bunyip (Four Grotesques)* (1910), *Lost Love* (1918) and a collected edition, *The Poems of Henry Tate* (1928).

TAYLOR, ADOLPHUS GEORGE (1857-1900), born Mudgee, NSW, was a teacher and journalist there and in Bathurst before entering politics in the early 1880s. In 1890 he became first editor of *Truth*; replaced by John Norton in 1891, he returned to the position in 1894-96. A colourful figure known by such nicknames as 'Giraffe' and 'The Mudgee Camel', Taylor was rumbustious and unstable but had a flair for investigative journalism and for the rough and tumble of colonial politics. His satire, *The Marble Man*, was published in 1889.

TAYLOR, ANDREW (1940-), born Victoria, has taught English at the Universities of Melbourne and Adelaide and took part in the first poetry readings at La Mama in 1968. His poetry has appeared in several collections, *The Cool Change* (1971), *Ice Fishing* (1973), *The Invention of Fire* (1976), *The Cat's Chin and Ears: A Bestiary* (1976), *Parabolas* (1976), *The Crystal Absences, The Trout* (1978) and *Selected Poems 1960-1980* (1982). He has also edited, with Ian Reid, the second annual Friendly Street poetry reader (1978). Influenced by American poetry, especially by Wallace Stevens, Taylor writes a difficult but powerful poetry which deals with wide-ranging, cosmopolitan themes.

TAYLOR, GEOFF (1920-), born England, grew up in Australia and served in the RAAF during the Second World War. He flew briefly on operations with an RAF squadron of the Bomber Command before he was shot down in October 1943 and spent two years as a POW. After the war he returned to Melbourne, where he has worked in journalism and advertising. His first book, *Piece of Cake* (1956), recounts his experiences as a POW and most of his subsequent novels have drawn on his knowledge of flying and of Germany. They include *The Hollow Square* (1958), *Court of Honour* (1966), *Beware the Wounded Tiger* (1971), *The Nuremburg Massacre* (1979) and *The Hour of the Octopus* (1978). He has also written three other novels, *The Crop Dusters* (1960), which focuses on the exploits of agricultural pilots; *Dreamboat* (1962), a farcical story set in the world of advertising; and *Day of the Republic* (1968), a political fantasy of the future; *Sir* (1963), a tribute to his old headmaster; a children's fantasy, *Blueberg* (1960); and *Return Ticket* (1972), an account of a return visit to Germany.

TAYLOR, G.A. (GEORGE AUGUSTINE) (1872–1928), born Sydney, first became known as an artist and cartoonist, a contributor of drawings to the *Bulletin*, the *Worker*, the *Sunday Times*, the *Referee* and the London *Punch*. A member of the Dawn and Dusk Club, and a particular friend of Victor Daley, he wrote his reminiscences of its personalities, *'Those Were the Days'* (1918), which is also valuable as a record of Sydney in the 1890s. In 1898 he launched a highly original comic paper, *Ha-Ha*, although it survived for only three issues. Subsequent periodicals that he founded and edited fared better and reflected his fervent nationalism and his numerous interests, aviation, engineering, radio technology and town planning. They include *Building*, the *Australasian Engineer*, the *Soldier*, the *Commonwealth Home* and the *Radio Journal of Australasia*. He achieved original work in aviation and radio, constructing and successfully flying in 1909 a full-size biplane, the first flight in Australia of a manned heavier-than-air machine; his son, P.G. Taylor, flew with Charles Kingsford Smith. A prolific journalist, Taylor also published several minor works of fiction, *The Christmas Swag* (1902), *The Schemers* (1914), and *There!* (1916), as well as *The Sequel: What the Great War Will Mean to Australia* (1915), his most ambitious attempt to express his political ideas in fiction. He also published two collections of verse, *Songs for Soldiers* (1913) and *Just Jingles* (1922), and a travel book, *The Ways of the World* (1922).

TAYLOR, KATHERINE ('DAVID HAMLINE') (1893–), born Kywanna, Queensland, published her first book, *Ginger for Pluck*, a children's story of station life, under the pseudonym 'David Hamline' in 1929. Her other children's stories and popular fiction include *Pick and the Duffers* (1930), *Many Years: A Story of Russia during the War and the Revo-lution* (1931), *Wards of the Outer March* (1932) which won second prize in the *Bulletin* novel competition in 1930, and *Bim* (1937).

'Teams, The', Henry Lawson's (q.v.) well-known ballad celebrating the bullock wagons that did so much to open up the country in pioneering times, was first published in 1889; it is a popular anthology and recitation piece. Renowned for their strength, the bullock teams became the subject of many tall stories, notable among which was the occasion when one team became stuck in the river and was pulled out when another team was hitched on. In the process the bends in the river were straightened. The teams were not always composed of bullocks; those made up of horses, controlled by teamsters, were equally well known. The most famous account of the feats of the horse-drawn wagons is Will Ogilvie's poem, 'How the *Fire Queen* Crossed the Swamp'.

TEGG, JAMES (1808–45) and his brother, **SAMUEL AUGUSTUS** (1813–?), sons of Thomas Tegg, publisher and bookseller of Cheapside, London, arrived in Australia in 1834 and opened a bookshop in George Street, Sydney, in January 1835. Samuel returned to England the same year but in 1836 came back to open a bookshop in Hobart. Although primarily a bookseller, James Tegg was also an active and important publisher. He published *Tegg's New South Wales Pocket Almanac and Remembrancer* annually 1836–44, and *Tegg's Monthly Magazine*, edited by himself and devoted to general literature, in 1836. In the latter's first number appeared the celebrated story of Fisher's Ghost (q.v.). Other works published by James Tegg include *Literary News*, a weekly which he edited with William à Beckett, 1837–38, and works by James Martin, Henry Parkes, William Hovell and Hamilton Hume, and J.H. Plunkett. He was also involved in the *Handbook for Emigrants* published by his father in 1839.

Samuel Augustus Tegg added a circulating library to his Hobart bookshop in 1839, opened a further bookshop in Launceston in 1844 and left Tasmania in 1847 for London. He published works by David Burn, James Bonwick and Nathaniel Kentish.

Telegraph, a Brisbane daily afternoon newspaper, began publication in 1872; it was owned by the Telegraph Newspaper Company until 1955, when it came under the control of the Herald and Weekly Times group. A number of figures prominent in journalism in Queensland, e.g. Theophilus Pugh and George Hall, and in NSW, e.g. Thomas Heney and F.W. Ward, edited the *Telegraph*; Nat Gould's first

Australian appointment was on the *Telegraph* in 1884–87.

'Tell Us About the Turkey, Jo', the title story of Alan Marshall's 1946 collection, describes the narrator's encounter with a small boy, Jimmy, and his elder brother Jo. Jimmy's delight in his brother's accounts of various disasters which have befallen himself in the past and his pride in the minor scars and bruises that resulted are interrupted by the arrival of their sister and the news that they have a new baby sister. Jimmy is unimpressed by the news and urges his brother to recount the story of 'how I got chased by the turkey'.

TEMPLEMAN, IAN, see **Fremantle Arts Centre**

Ten Creeks Run, see **'BRENT OF BIN BIN'**

'Ten Thousand Miles Away', see **'Thousand Miles Away, A'**

TENCH, WATKIN (?1758–1833), born Chester, England, entered the marine corps in 1776 and went with the First Fleet to Botany Bay. An enthusiastic explorer, he participated in expeditions which discovered the Nepean and Hawkesbury rivers and penetrated south as far as the Razorback Range fringing the Camden valley. Tench left the Colony in 1792 and continued his military career until his retirement with the rank of lieutenant-general in 1821. His valuable and lively accounts of the establishment of the Colony are *A Narrative of the Expedition to Botany Bay* (1789) and *A Complete Account of the Settlement at Port Jackson in New South Wales* (1793); they were combined as *Sydney's First Four Years* (1961), edited by L.F. Fitzhardinge.

TENISON-WOODS, JULIAN EDMUND (1832–89) born London, migrated to Australia in 1854. Ordained a Roman Catholic priest in 1857, he was appointed to Penola, SA, where he befriended Adam Lindsay Gordon. Director-General of Catholic schools in SA from 1867, he edited various religious magazines; he published some 150 scientific papers after he relinquished his parochial duties in 1883 and became a wide-ranging scientific observer and investigator of the physical world of Australia, the East Indies and Japan. Two of Tenison-Woods's most significant works are *A History of the Discovery and Exploration of Australia* (1865) and a serialized survey, 'Australian Biography', in the *Australian Monthly Magazine* 1866–67. His biography, *Life of the Reverend Julian Edmund Tenison-Woods*, by G. O'Neill was published in 1929.

TENNANT, KYLIE (1912–), born Manly, NSW, has had varied experience as journalist, publicity officer for the ABC, barmaid, church sister, reviewer and lecturer. She has frequently tried to acquire first-hand experience for her novels, including taking to the roads with the unemployed in the 1930s depression, living in Sydney's slums and with Aboriginal communities, travelling with itinerant bee-keepers and even spending a week in gaol. In 1932 she married the teacher and social historian, Lewis Charles Rodd. Her novels include *Tiburon* (q.v., 1935) which won the S.H. Prior Memorial Prize, *Foveaux* (1939), *The Battlers* (q.v., 1941), which won both the S.H. Prior Memorial Prize and the Australian Literature Society's Gold Medal, *Ride On Stranger* (q.v., 1943), *Time Enough Later* (1943), *Lost Haven* (1946), *The Joyful Condemned* (1953, published in its full form with title *Tell Morning This* in 1967), *The Honey Flow* (1956), and *Tantavallon* (1983). She has also written *Speak You So Gently* (1959), an account of life in Aboriginal co-operatives; *Australia: Her Story* (1953), a popular history of Australia; a biography of the former Australian prime minister, H.V. Evatt (1970); *Ma Jones and the Little White Cannibals* (1967), a collection of short stories; a series of plays and books for children, including *All the Proud Tribesmen* (1959), winner of the 1960 Children's Book Award; *Tether a Dragon* (1952), a prize-winning play about Alfred Deakin; and *The Man on the Headland* (1971), an account of the Diamond Head area of NSW. She has also edited three collections of short stories. A vigorous, versatile, high-spirited and witty writer, her fiction ranges from the satiric to the poetic and expresses a richly comic but sympathetic appreciation of multifarious humanity. The protagonists of her novels are usually the dispossessed and underprivileged slum-dwellers, juvenile delinquents, the unemployed, tramps and nomads of all descriptions. By no means an ideologue, she is more delighted with the spirited waywardness of her disparate outcasts than concerned to offer political or social remedies. Nevertheless, politics, education, the law and the bureaucracy are all subjected to her satiric wit. Characteristically, she affirms the value of life in the face of a clear perception of the tragedy of the human condition, a vision that is implicit in her richly suggestive descriptions of the indifferent Australian landscape, both natural and urban. A descriptive rather than a dramatic writer, she is more interested in groupings of people than in individuals and in general activity than in a single shaping action. Her prose style is flexible and expressive, moving easily from poetic suggestiveness to racy vigour. She was made AO in 1980.

Terra Australis, meaning 'the South Land', and its derivatives 'Terra Australis Incognita' (the unknown South Land), 'Terra Australis Nondum Cognita' (the not-yet-known South Land), were Latin phrases printed on maps from the earliest times to represent the concept of a great undiscovered land mass in the southern oceans. The dream of discovering Terra Australis became an obsession that haunted the sea voyagers of Spain, Portugal and England from the sixteenth to the eighteenth century. In 1568 Alvaro de Mendana discovered the Solomon Islands; in 1605 Pedro Fernandez de Quiros (see *Captain Quiros*), named the New Hebrides, in error, Austrialia del Espiritu Santo. Numerous Dutch voyagers, e.g. Jansz, Hartog, Tasman, touched, often unwittingly, upon the shores of Hollandia Nova, and English explorers William Dampier and James Cook, the latter always sceptical of the existence of a great southern continent other than New Holland, made the first significant landfalls on the Australian coastline. It was not until Matthew Flinders (q.v.) circumnavigated the Australian continent in *Investigator*, 1801–03, and reported his findings in *A Voyage to Terra Australis* (1814), that the ghost of 'a great south land', other than Australia, was laid to rest. The particular interest of 'Terra Australis' for Australian writers is evident in such poems as 'Australasia' by W.C. Wentworth, 'The Story of Abel Tasman' by Frances S. Lewin, 'The Dream of Dampier' by G.H. Supple, *Captain Quiros* (q.v.) by James McAuley, 'Five Visions of Captain Cook' (q.v.) by Kenneth Slessor; and in 'Terra Australis' poems by McAuley, Douglas Stewart and Chris Wallace-Crabbe. R.H. Major published *Early Voyages to Terra Australis, Now Called Australia* (1859).

Territory, The (1951), an *omnium gatherum* of Northern Territory history, geography, legend, tall tale and folklore, was written by Ernestine Hill (q.v.) and illustrated by Elizabeth Durack. It is a Who's Who of Territory identities: the explorers John McDouall Stuart and Ludwig Leichhardt; the first overlander, D'Arcy Wentworth Uhr, who drove cattle from Queensland to Darwin in 1872; the legendary bushman Nathaniel ('Far Away') Buchanan, who helped establish several of the early stations; the Buffalo Bill of Australia, Rodney Spencer, who shot 6000 buffaloes in three years; the horsebreaker, Jack Macleod, who is the Quiet Stockman of *We of the Never-Never* (1908); and unsung heroines such as Katie Rogers, Phoebe Farrar and Hazel Gaden, Territorian wives and mothers. Its pages are filled with fabled names: cattle stations such as the Elsey, Wave Hill, Brunette Downs, Victoria River Downs; stock routes such as the Canning, the Great North Road, the Georgina; and rivers such as the Victoria, the Ord, the Daly and the Roper. It describes significant events in the Territory's history: the construction of the overland telegraph line; the gold and diamond rushes at Pine Creek and in the Kimberleys; the early agricultural experiments with sugar, tobacco, coffee and rice; and the growth and development of Darwin, Australia's 'front gate'. It abounds in anecdote: macabre and grim, as in the Aboriginal massacres at the Barrow Creek telegraph station and at Daly River; and humorous, as in the exploits of the poddy-dodgers and brand-forgers. It concludes with an illuminating appendix of Territory phrases, which are frequently a combination of pidgin and bush colloquialisms.

Thargomindah, a small pastoral settlement on the Bulloo River in south-western Queensland, is reputedly the setting for Mary Hannay Foott's (q.v.) poem, 'Where the Pelican Builds Her Nest'. The Elliott brothers leave the district to search for better land further westward and are never seen again.

Tharunka, a student journal of the University of NSW, began publication in 1955 and has frequently contained reviews and articles on Australian literature as well as some original poetry and short stories.

'That Pretty Girl in the Army', see '**Send Round the Hat'**

THATCHER, CHARLES (1831–78), born Bristol, England, was a flautist in theatre orchestras in London before seeking his fortune on the Victorian goldfields in 1852. Failing as a digger, Thatcher became a favourite goldfields entertainer, composing and singing catchy songs with topical local subjects. After several years in NZ (1861–66) he returned to Victoria, resuming his career as an entertainer, before leaving the colony in 1869 to live again in England. Thatcher's songs, usually represented in anthologies of Australian folk-songs and ballads, were published as broadsheets in contemporary newspapers, and in such collections as *Thatcher's Victoria Songster* (1855), *Thatcher's Colonial Songster* (1857) and *Thatcher's Colonial Minstrel* (1859). Hugh Anderson (q.v.) compiled a selection of Thatcher's songs, *Goldrush Songster* (1958), and wrote the biography, *The Colonial Minstrel* (1960). In Eric Lambert's novel, *The Five Bright Stars* (1954), Thatcher engages in a singing contest with another character.

THATCHER, DICK (RICHMOND) (1842–91), brother of Charles Thatcher, was born Brighton, England. From 1871 he lived in NSW and was a journalist on the *Empire*, the *Evening News* and the *Australian Town and Country Journal*. He founded the *Upper Hunter Courier* at Murrurundi and edited the *Western Independent* at Bathurst. He edited several anthologies of stories, poems and articles, notably *Something toHis Advantage* (1875), *Thatcher's Holiday Book* (1881) and, with Grosvenor Bunster, *It Runs in the Blood* (1872). He wrote fiction, including *Mr Newcombe in Search of a Cattle Station*(1868), *A Travelled Actor* (1881) and the biographical *Life and Times of Jem Punch*(1885).

Theatre–Australia, a monthly magazine edited by Bruce Knappett, Robert Page and Lucy Wagner, was published 1976–82. It included reviews of stage productions throughout Australia, playscripts, interviews with playwrights, directors and actors, a section on film, television and radio and general theatrical news.

Theatre Board, one of the seven arts boards of the Australia Council (q.v.), was established in 1973; it receives an annual allocation, the largest given to any of the seven boards, which is distributed to support drama and dance, principally in the form of grants to companies and theatres. It has a similar structure to the Literature Board (q.v.), which also assists theatre in Australia by awarding writing grants to dramatists, by subsidizing the publication of Australian plays and by contributing to the cost of the Australian National Playwrights Conference.

Theatre Buildings in Australia to 1905 (1971), by Ross Thorne, is a detailed description, accompanied by numerous drawings, of the major theatres in Australia from the first settlement until the advent of cinema. The result of much original research, Thorne's study also focuses on historical and sociological changes and the impact of such events as the gold and mining booms on entrepreneurs, audiences and players. Thorne has also published *Picture Palace Architecture in Australia* (1976) and *Cinemas of Australia via U.S.A.* (1981).

Theatre Royal, see LEVEY, BARNETT

Theatregoer, titled *Australian Theatregoer* in the first four issues, a magazine founded and edited by F. R. Harvey, published in Sydney and concerned with live theatre in Australia, appeared at irregular intervals 1960–63. It included reviews of productions, interviews with playwrights and actors, general articles on drama, and playscripts by Australian and English dramatists. In the December–January 1961–62 issue *Theatregoer* was published with *Australian Theatre Year*.

THEODORE, E.G. (EDWARD GRANVILLE) (1884–1950), born Port Adelaide, began his political career in the mining districts of northern Queensland and was Queensland premier 1919–25 before entering federal politics. He was treasurer and deputy prime minister 1929–30 in the James Scullin Labor ministry, resigned over a mining scandal in 1930, returned to parliament after being exonerated but lost his seat in 1931 and turned to business, helping to establish Australian Consolidated Press. In 1942 Prime Minister John Curtin invited him to accept the honorary wartime post of director-general of Allied Works, which he held until the end of the war. Vance Palmer drew on his career for the central character of his *Golconda* trilogy (q.v.), Macy Donovan, and he also figures as Ted Thurgood in Frank Hardy's novel, *Power Without Glory* (1950). Irwin Young wrote *Theodore: His Life and Times* (1971).

There Is No Armour, see FOSTER, LYNN

THERRY, JOHN JOSEPH (1790–1864), born Cork, Ireland, arrived in Sydney in 1820 as the official Roman Catholic chaplain for the Colony. For the next forty years he was an influential religious and political figure, espousing the democratic cause against the entrenched privileges of the Establishment. He founded St Mary's, which became the first Roman Catholic cathedral in Sydney. Eris O'Brien published *Life and Letters of Archpriest John Joseph Therry: Founder of the Catholic Church in Australia* (1922).

THERRY, Sir **ROGER** (1800–74), born Cork, Ireland, arrived in Sydney in 1829 after being called to the English and Irish bars. He acted as attorney-general in NSW in the 1840s and served as a judge in Victoria and NSW. He also pursued a political career, although his Catholic religion aroused opposition. Generally well-regarded as a judge, Therry acquired some notoriety for his championing of the rights of Catholics and his work as a pamphleteer. He retired from the Bench in 1859, returned to England and published his *Reminiscences of Thirty Years' Residence in New South Wales and Victoria* (1863), which immediately sold out in England. A second edition was recalled after reviews in Sydney had objected to some of Therry's opinions. Valuable as commentary on contemporary personalities and customs, the *Reminiscences* are particularly interesting on transportation.

'They'll Tell You About Me' is the title of Ian Mudie's (q.v.) celebrated *pot-pourri* of Australian myth, legend, tall tales, folklore and history. In ironic, colloquial language and spiced with the good-natured *braggadocio* that has come to be recognized as the stock-in-trade of the brash Australian male, the poem is a treasure chest of such Australiana as Eureka, Ned Kelly, the Man from Snowy River, Waltzing Matilda, the Dog on the Tuckerbox, Lasseter's Lost Reef, the Sydney Harbour Bridge, and Gallipoli.

They're A Weird Mob, see O'GRADY, JOHN PATRICK

THIELE, COLIN (1920–   ), born Eudunda, SA, graduated from the University of Adelaide in 1941, and served with the RAAF in the Second World War. He taught in SA high schools 1946–56, before joining Wattle Park Teachers' College of which he was principal 1965–73 and director 1974–80. A prolific writer of verse, fiction, children's books, radio plays, historical, environmental and educational texts and an editor of verse anthologies, short stories and one-act plays, Thiele has published more than fifty books, many of which have gone into multiple reprints and popular paperback editions. A leading literary figure, especially in his own State, he is the author of numerous radio features and documentaries and has been active in the English Teachers Association of SA and in the SA FAW. He was made AC in 1977.

Thiele's strongly nationalistic poetry comprises *Progress to Denial* (1945), an elegy to a soldier killed in the Second World War, which won the W.J. Miles poetry prize; *Splinters and Shards* (1945), also largely war poems; *The Golden Lightning* (1951); *Man in a Landscape* (1960), which won the Grace Leven Prize for poetry; *In Charcoal and Conté* (1966); *Selected Verse* (1970); and *The Best of Colin Thiele* (1980), a combined selection of prose and verse. Although he has written an adult novel, *Labourers in the Vineyard* (1970), set in the Barossa Valley, and a book of short stories, *The Rim of the Morning* (1966), Thiele's most successful fiction has been for children. *The Sun on the Stubble* (1961), a story of the German immigrant farmer family, the Gunthers, was commended in both the Miles Franklin and Australian Children's Book of the Year Awards for 1962. *Storm Boy* (1963), Thiele's classic children's novel set on the Coorong (q.v.), was made into a successful film in 1976. His other significant children's books include *Blue Fin* (1969), a story of the tuna-fishing industry which was commended in the Hans Anderson Award in 1972 and was filmed in 1978; *The Fire in the Stone* (1973), a story of the opal

fields which won the Edgar Allan Poe Award in the USA; *Albatross Two* (1974), a story set on an offshore oil rig; *Magpie Island* (1974); *The Hammerhead Light* (1976); *The Sknuks* (1977), a fable for small children which won the Austrian state prize in 1979; and *The Valley Between* (1981), which won his first Children's Book of the Year Award. His environmental, historical and educational works include *Barossa Valley Sketchbook* (1968, illustrated by Jeanette McLeod); *Range without Man* (1974), on the North Flinders Ranges; *The Little Desert* (1975); *The Bight* (1976); and *Grains of Mustard Seed* (1975), a history of the SA Department of Education. Thiele also wrote the biography, *Heysen of Hahndorf* (1968).

THIRKELL, ANGELA (1890–1961), a well-known English novelist, spent some years in Australia and wrote one novel with Australian associations. The daughter of the classicist John W. Mackail, professor of poetry at Oxford, she was also the granddaughter of Edward Burne-Jones and was related to Rudyard Kipling and Stanley Baldwin. After a private education, she married James Campbell McInnes, a distinguished singer, in 1911 and had two sons, Graham and Colin McInnes (qq.v.), and a daughter who died in infancy. The marriage ended in divorce in 1917 and the following year she married an Australian captain in the AIF, George Thirkell (q.v.). After some time in Sheffield, the Thirkells left for Australia in 1920 aboard a troopship, the *Friedrichsruh*; their journey became the subject of Angela Thirkell's novel, *Trooper to the Southern Cross* (q.v., 1934), published under the pseudonym 'Leslie Parker'. In Australia they spent some time in Tasmania and then settled in Melbourne, where George Thirkell managed a works that produced motor accessories and Angela Thirkell became well-known in cultural and social circles. Her Australian friends included such prominent individuals as Dame Nellie Melba, Sir John Monash, Ernest Scott, Arthur Streeton, Thea Proctor and Sir Hubert Murray and the governor-general, Lord Forster. Prompted partly by literary ambition and partly by lack of money, she began to contribute articles and short stories to English and Australian magazines and to broadcast on radio. She detested the restrictions of her life in Melbourne, however, and although another son, Lance, was born in 1921, her marriage to Thirkell rapidly deteriorated. The situation became critical after her husband's business failed during the depression and she left permanently for England in 1929 with her sons Colin and Lance. Graham McInnes remained in Melbourne until 1934. In London Angela Thirkell recognized her true milieu and almost immediately began the writing career that resulted in thirty-five novels and made her one of England's best-known, middle-brow, lady novelists. Her years in Melbourne are memorably recorded in Graham McInnes's autobiographies, *The Road to Gundagai* (q.v., 1965) and *Humping My Bluey* (1966) and are also described in Margot Strickland's biography, *Angela Thirkell* (1977).

THIRKELL, GEORGE (1891–1959), was born into an English family that had been settled in Tasmania since 1820. After graduating B.Sc. from the University of Tasmania, he served at Gallipoli and in Europe. Three diaries that he kept at Gallipoli were referred to by the official war historian, C.E.W. Bean. During his leaves in London he became friendly with many members of the upper class, was entertained by the Countess of Strathmore at Glamis Castle, and in 1918 married Angela McInnes, who was to become the well-known novelist, Angela Thirkell (q.v.). The Thirkells left for Australia in 1920 and settled in Melbourne, where George Thirkell managed a works that produced car accessories. A son, Lance, was born in 1921 but the marriage deteriorated and Angela left permanently for England in 1929.

George Thirkell lived on in Melbourne, an increasingly pathetic figure; Lance Thirkell was educated in England and has had a distinguished career with the BBC. George Thirkell's personality has been memorably recorded in Angela Thirkell's novel, *Trooper to the Southern Cross* (q.v., 1934), where he appears as the protagonist, Major Bowen, and in Graham McInnes's autobiographies, *The Road to Gundagai* (q.v., 1965) and *Humping My Bluey* (1966), where he appears as 'Thirk'.

Thirroul, see **LAWRENCE, D.H.**

Thirty Years in Australia, a memoir by Ada Cambridge (q.v.), was published in 1903; it covers 1870–1900 and encompasses Cambridge's marriage to the clergyman, George Cross, their almost immediate departure to Australia, and their life there spent mainly in the country districts of Victoria. Written with wit, compassion, humour and candour, *Thirty Years in Australia* chronicles Cambridge's struggles to make the best of things as the wife of a 'bush parson, the sense of exile, with her for 'about seven-eighths of that long time in Australia', and the evolution of her literary career; one chapter deals with a memorable visit to Sydney in 1887, which she relished for the opportunity it gave her to meet writers and painters. The companion memoir, *The Retrospect* (1912), records her impressions and recollections of her youth when she was finally able to revisit England in 1908. She delighted

in her liberation from exile but recognized the insularity of English society.

This Night's Orbit, see **FITZGERALD, R.D.**

This Old Man Comes Rolling Home, a play by Dorothy Hewett (q.v.), was first performed in 1967 and published in 1976. Set in the 1950s in Redfern, one of Sydney's poorer suburbs, it presents a cross-section of working-class folk, bound together by their hardships and resilient humour. Central to the play are the vicissitudes within the large Dockerty family, headed by the feckless and alcoholic Laurie Dockerty, once the belle of Bundaberg, and her perpetually optimistic husband Tom. Other striking characters are Julie Dockerty, the forceful eldest daughter, Edie, the strong, practical wife of Lan Dockerty, and Don Dockerty, a young spiv.

This Vital Flesh, see 'BAYLEBRIDGE, WILLIAM'

THOMAS, EVAN HENRY (?1801–37), was born in Ireland and arrived in Hobart in 1822, the year in which his poems in the *Hobart Town Gazette* were the first to be published in the infant colony of Van Diemen's Land. In 1824 he was appointed editor of the *Gazette* by Andrew Bent, with whom he fought strenuously to preserve the freedom of the press; Thomas wrote the famous editorial referring to George Arthur, later lieutenant-governor of Tasmania, as a 'Gideonite of Tyranny', for which Bent was imprisoned for libel. After his resignation from the *Gazette*, Thomas lived mainly at Launceston, where his play, *The Bandit of the Rhine*, was published in 1835; although the first Australian play to appear in book form, no copies of *The Bandit of the Rhine* are extant. Thomas also may have had a hand in the early satire, *The Van Diemen's Land Warriors* (q.v., 1827).

THOMAS Family, well known in SA newspaper circles, included Robert Thomas (1781–1860), who was born in Wales, migrated to SA and in 1836 established, with George Stevenson, the *South Australian Gazette and Colonial Register*, later the *Register*. His second son, William Kyffin Thomas (1821–78), was connected with the paper, as were his grandsons Sir Robert Kyffin Thomas (1851–1910) and Evan Kyffin Thomas (1866–1935), the latter also editing *Diary and Letters of Mary Thomas* (1915), a record of his grandmother's life as a pioneer in SA. Evan Kyffin's son, Archer Kyffin Thomas (1906–78), ultimately became editor of the Melbourne *Herald* (1945–56), editor-in-chief of the Herald and Weekly Times

(1962–66) and chairman of Australian Associated Press (1966–68).

'THOMAS, JULIAN', see JAMES, JOHN STANLEY

THOMAS, WILLIAM GEORGE, see 'MONCRIEFF, WILLIAM THOMAS'

THOMES, WILLIAM HENRY (1824–95), born Portland, USA, worked on ships on the Californian hide trade before joining the gold rush to San Francisco. In 1851–55, during a visit which also took in Hawaii and China, Thomes worked on the Victorian goldfields as digger and storekeeper before returning to the USA to become a journalist and publisher. He used the Australian experience in two popular novels, *The Gold Hunters' Adventures: Or, Life in Australia* (1864), and its sequel, *The Bushrangers* (1865), which together established his reputation. Among his later publications were *On Land and Sea* (1883), an account of his Californian experience and the most highly regarded of his dozen or so books, and another popular novel *The Belle of Australia* (1883).

THOMPSON, JOHN (1907–68), born Melbourne, was a war correspondent in New Guinea and Java 1945–46, and subsequently made a career as a broadcaster with the ABC. He was well known as an interviewer and published a series of interviews with prominent Australian poets in *Southerly*, as well as two collections of profiles of famous Australians, based on interviews, *On Lips of Living Men* (1962) and *Five to Remember* (1964). He also published four collections of his own poetry, *Three Dawns Ago* (1935), *Sesame and Other Poems* (1944), *Thirty Poems* (1954), winner of the Grace Leven Poetry Prize, and *I Hate and I Love* (1964); edited, with Kenneth Slessor and R.G. Howarth, *The Penguin Book of Australian Verse* (1958), and *Australian Poetry 1965* (1965); and compiled *Alfred Conlon: A Memorial* (1963). One of his adopted children is the well-known Australian actor, Jack Thompson.

THOMPSON, RICHARD (1810–65), born England, was transported to NSW in 1834 for fourteen years for theft of silver. After a conditional pardon in 1842 he worked as a journalist in the Port Phillip District then on the *Australian* in Sydney. He was editor of Robert Lowe's *Atlas* 1844–45, of another weekly serving the squatting interests, the *Spectator* in 1846, and of the *Australian*, 1847–48. In 1856 he edited the *Report of the Proceedings . . . to Celebrate the Establishment and Inauguration of Responsible Government in the Colony of New South Wales*. Thompson's other

literary interests lay in supplying scripts for Sydney's theatrical activities and acting as a drama critic.

THOMPSON, TOM (1953–), born Parkes, NSW, was educated at Macquarie University and has worked as a bookshop manager and freelance journalist. Editor of Red Press publications 1978–81 and associate editor at Currency Press 1977–78, he has also edited the magazines *Dodo, Leatherjacket* and *Australasian Small Press Review*. He has published two collections of verse, *The Island Hotel Dreams* (1977) and *From Here* (1978) and one of short stories, *Neon Line* (1978). He has also co-edited the prose anthology *Island in the Sun* (1980), is co-author of two selections from the speeches of contemporary politicians, and has selected and introduced *Here's Lower* (1983), a selection from the writings of Lennie Lower.

Thorn Birds, The, a commercially-successful novel by Colleen McCullough (q.v.), was published in the USA in 1977. The novel is divided into seven chronological sections, each section covering a set period between 1915 and 1969 and highlighting a particular character from the story. The first section, 1915–17, set in NZ, introduces the Roman Catholic Cleary family who are lifted out of their struggling farming existence by Paddy Cleary's ageing sister, Mary Carson, who brings them to Australia to manage Drogheda station in north-western NSW. The remaining six sections plot the affairs of the Cleary family and introduce the two other chief characters, Mary Carson and the Catholic priest, Ralph de Bricassart. The Cleary family is headed by Fiona ('Fee'), the Protestant daughter of an important NZ pioneering family, the Armstrongs. She disgraces them by bearing a child out of wedlock and is married off to Paddy Cleary, the dairy hand on the Armstrong property. Paddy and Fiona come to love each other but Paddy is killed fairly early in the novel in a bushfire. Other male Cleary characters include Frank, Fiona's love-child, who is imprisoned on a manslaughter charge; Hal, who dies of croup as a small child; Stuart, who is killed in an encounter with a wild pig; and the other sons, Jack, Hughie, Bob, James and Patrick, who are less relevant to the story. Meggie Cleary, the only girl and perhaps the chief character interest in the novel, later becomes involved with the handsome Gillanbone parish priest, Ralph de Bricassart, who has resisted Mary Carson's infatuation with him but who advances to eminence as Cardinal de Bricassart as the result of Mary's giving Drogheda to the Church. Meggie has a child by Ralph, Dane, who becomes a priest but dies in a drowning accident.

Meggie's other child, Justine, by her husband Luke O'Neill, becomes a talented Shakespearean actress.

The backdrop to this congested, sensational and often bizarre plot, is the Australian outback, with its dramatic landscapes, vast distances, isolation, bush camaraderie, and natural hazards. The novel aroused lively literary controversy. It was labelled by its critics as a 'potboiler': crudely crafted, sensationally exaggerated, devised to cater to the florid expectations of the mass of undiscriminating readers of modern popular fiction. Its supporters see it as a vigorously-written and racy narrative. The novel was screened as a television series in 1983.

THORNBURN, HANNAH (1878–1902), was a bookkeeper and clerk when she met Henry Lawson (q.v.) around 1897. Lawson became infatuated with her, may have planned to leave his wife Bertha for her and was shattered by her death just before he arrived back from England in 1902. The subject of the poems, 'To Hannah' and 'Hannah Thomburn' (*sic*), Hannah has also been identified in such other Lawson poems as 'Ruth', 'The Lily of St Leonards', and 'Do They Think That I Do Not Know'.

THORNE, ROSS, see *Theatre Buildings in Australia to 1905*

THORNE, TIM (1944–   ), was born in Launceston, Tasmania, where he has also taught modern languages. He has published four collections of verse, *Tense Mood and Voice* (1969), *The What of Sane* (1971), *New Foundations* (1976) and *A Nickel in My Mouth* (1979). Tough, witty, technically innovative and assured, Thorne's verse focuses on contemporary ideas and problems, political issues, the tensions of city life, the experience of love and the relationship of the artist to his art.

'Those Were the Days', see **TAYLOR, G.A.**; **Nineties**

'Thousand Miles Away, A', is an Australian folk-song dating from the last decades of the nineteenth century which celebrates the overlanders travelling westwards in Queensland to muster cattle 'On the far Barcoo, where they eat nardoo, a thousand miles away'; the song was included as an anonymous composition in A.B. Paterson's *Old Bush Songs* (1905), but Charles Augustus Flower (q.v.) has been identified as the author by some writers. 'A Thousand Miles Away' is one of three folk-songs and ballads which share the same rollicking tune. The others are 'Ten Thousand Miles Away', a

London music-hall song of the 1840s and later the seamen's song in which the singer is joining his convict lover who has 'taken a trip on a government ship/Ten thousand miles away'; and 'The Old Palmer Song', in which the singer is en route to the Palmer diggings in Queensland, which opened up in 1873. The 'Ten Thousand Miles Away' tune forms the basis for the popular theme song of the 1970s television series, *Rush*.

Three Cheers for the Paraclete, see **KENEALLY, THOMAS**

Three Colonies of Australia, The, see **SIDNEY, SAMUEL**

Three Elephant Power and Other Stories (1917) is a collection of nineteen short stories and sketches by A.B. Paterson (q.v.). Best-known are the title story, 'Three Elephant Power', 'The Oracle', 'The Cast-Iron Canvasser' (q.v.), 'White When He's Wanted' and 'Done for the Double'; they reveal Paterson's capacity for capturing an authentic Australian tone.

Three Miss Kings, The, a novel by Ada Cambridge (q.v.), was serialized in the *Australasian* in 1883, and republished in book form in 1891. The first of Cambridge's novels to win her recognition in England as well as Australia, *The Three Miss Kings* is set in Melbourne at the time of the Great Exhibition of 1880 and traces the fortunes of Elizabeth, Patty and Eleanor King after they are orphaned and left with meagre incomes. Assisted by Paul Brion, the son of the family solicitor, the inexperienced sisters settle in Melbourne, where they are discovered by a leader of society, Mrs Duff-Scott, who protects them and tries to arrange suitable marriage partners. Each falls in love, though not always with Mrs Duff-Scott's choice: Elizabeth with the English visitor, Kingscote Yelverton, Patty with Paul Brion, Eleanor with Mr Westmoreland. Each, however, finds obstacles in the path towards marriage: Yelverton's religious and philanthropic beliefs are unconventional, Paul and Patty offend each other's pride, Mr Westmoreland seems interested in marrying for money. Towards the end of the novel, it is discovered by chance that the three Miss Kings are in reality the daughters of Kingscote Yelverton, the uncle of Elizabeth's suitor, and are thus heirs to the Yelverton fortune, which the younger Kingscote has been holding in trust. Her doubts already resolved, Elizabeth marries Yelverton and lives at the family seat, while Patty and Eleanor return to Australia to be married to their lovers. Although conventionally resolved, *The Three Miss Kings* offers ironic comment on class relationships in 'Marvellous

Melbourne' and chronicles the rituals of society life, including the Melbourne Cup; there is also reference to the hanging of Ned Kelly.

THRELKELD, LANCELOT, see Aboriginal in Australian Literature

THROSSELL, RIC (1922–), the son of the novelist Katharine Susannah Prichard (q.v.) and of Captain Hugo Throssell, was born in Perth. In 1943, after war service in New Guinea, he joined the Department of External Affairs and has served in the Australian legations in Moscow and Rio de Janeiro. He has also been closely associated with the Canberra Repertory Society as actor, director and writer. His published plays, several of which have won awards, are *Valley of the Shadows* (1950, first produced 1948), *Devil Wear Black* (1955), *Suburban Requiem* (produced 1955) in *Australian One-Act Plays. Book One*, ed. Eunice Hanger (1962), *The Day Before Tomorrow* (1969, first produced 1956), and *For Valour* (1976, first produced 1960 and winner of the Mary Gilmore Award of 1959). His other plays include 'Sailor's Girl' (1945), 'Epitaph for the Unborn' (1955), 'A Kiss and a Promise' (1956), 'If Thy Heart Offend' (1957), 'Legend' (1958), 'The Contemporary Approximation' (1958), 'Dr Homer Speaks' (1963, produced in 1965 with the title 'The Sweet Sad Story of Elmo and Me'), 'The Death of Damien Burr' (1965), 'The Fourth Course' (1971) and the children's play, 'South Sea Gold Bay'. Throssell has also written an informative biography of his mother, *Wild Weeds and Wind Flowers* (1975). A versatile playwright, Throssell has written satires (*Devil Wear Black* and 'Dr Homer Speaks'), naturalistic plays ('The Death of Damien Burr' and 'Legend'), and plays with a serious, polemical purpose (*The Day Before Tomorrow*, which deals with nuclear war). Particularly striking is *For Valour*, a representative study of a First World War hero's economic and personal decline after returning to Australia.

'thumbnail dipped in tar', see 'Clancy of the Overflow'

'THUNDERBOLT, CAPTAIN', see **WARD, FREDERICK**

THURSTON, ROBIN, see Feminism and Australian Literature

THWAITES, F.J. (FREDERICK JOSEPH) (1908–79), was born at Narrandera in the NSW Riverina, a region which figures prominently in his fiction and where he personally sold the first copies of *The Broken Melody* (q.v., 1930). It was followed, 1932–73, by another

thirty novels and three travel books; the best-known, apart from *The Broken Melody*, are *Broken Wings* (1934), *The Melody Lingers* (1935), *The Mad Doctor* (1935), *Rock End* (1937), *Fever* (1939), *Whispers in Tahiti* (1940) and *Shadows Over Rangoon* (1941). Thwaites published more than a dozen of these titles under his own imprint and others were published under the imprint of the Harcourt Press, named after his wife Jessie Harcourt, an actress who played the role of Sylvia Vickers in the 1926 film version of *His Natural Life*. Virtually all the novels went through several editions or impressions (one estimate calculates fifty-four reprintings of *The Broken Melody* alone) and at the peak of his popularity, 1930–60, Thwaites was possibly the largest-selling Australian author. His novels are characteristically sentimental romances in which a range of locales is covered (the Riverina, Sydney, Thursday Island and London in *The Broken Melody*, other parts of Australia as well as the East, Africa and the Pacific in subsequent novels) as his heroes and heroines win through tribulation, sometimes injury or self-inflicted disgrace, to happiness. As well as exotic settings, sensational plots and steamy covers, the successful Thwaites mixture incorporated a shrewd topicality, cumulative effect titles, e.g. *The Broken Melody, Broken Wings, The Melody Lingers*, a political and social conservatism that allowed identification with the major characters, and a tempestuous prose style.

THWAITES, MICHAEL (1915–), born Brisbane, won a Rhodes Scholarship to Oxford and served with the RNVR 1939–45. He lectured in English at the University of Melbourne for two years and was head of counter-espionage in ASIO 1951–70. Winner of the Newdigate Prize, Oxford in 1938 and the King's Medal for poetry in 1940, he has contributed verse to numerous anthologies and has published three collections, *Milton Blind* (1938), *The Jervis Bay and Other Poems* (1942) and *Poems of War and Peace* (1970). He has also written *Truth Will Out* (1980), an account of the defection of the Russian diplomat, Vladimir Petrov, in 1954. Traditional in rhetoric and theme, Thwaites's poetry reflects his commitment to the moral rearmament movement and his admiration for such poets as John Masefield.

Tiburon, a novel by Kylie Tennant (q.v.) serialized in the *Bulletin* in 1935 and illustrated by Norman Lindsay, was also published separately in the same year and awarded the S.H. Prior Memorial Prize. Set in a small NSW town in the early 1930s, it deals partly with the experiences of a young teacher, Jessica Daunt, recently posted to the town, and her love affair with Paul White, a member of the town's most despised family. The novel's more general theme turns on the conflict between the outcast unemployed and the 'respectable' citizens, especially as that conflict is illustrated in the obsession of the policeman, Scorby, with the White family. Lively and comic, *Tiburon* presents a vivid picture of the narrowness and complacency of small-town life.

Tichborne Case was a *cause célèbre* in England in the 1860s and 1870s. In 1865 a world-wide advertisement for Roger Tichborne, heir to a baronetcy, produced a Wagga Wagga butcher, Thomas Castro, probably one Arthur Orton, as the claimant. He was believed by the mother but disputed by the family; a civil action in 1871–72 led to Castro's imprisonment for perjury. The case has similarities with John Rex's impersonation of Richard Devine in *His Natural Life* (1874) and Lawrence Trevenna's impersonation of his half-brother, Lance Trevanion, in 'Rolf Boldrewood''s *Nevermore* (1892). Marcus Clarke traded further on the Tichborne name in his novel *Chidiock Tichborne* (1893), which had nothing to do with the case. The melodrama, 'Tichborne: Or, Is He Butcher or Baronet', was performed in Sydney in 1877. Eli Grup in George Darrell's *The Sunny South* (performed 1883) is a butcher's son. D. Woodruffe published *The Tichborne Claimant* (1957) and Michael Roe, *Kenealy and the Tichborne Cause* (1974).

Ticket-of-Leave System, which enabled convicts to work for wages and select their own masters before their sentences were concluded, was first instituted by Governor Phillip in 1790. The system was subject to a certain amount of abuse and dispute under Macquarie, and his successor, Sir Thomas Brisbane, published regulations for the issue of tickets in 1822 which were expanded in 1827 by Governor Darling. Ticket-of-leave holders were not allowed to leave their districts of employment and tickets would be withdrawn for misconduct. In 1832, contrary to the advice of Governor Bourke, more stringent rules, which also deprived convicts of the right to own property, were laid down by imperial Act; Bourke then granted conditional pardons, which had a long history of use during transportation (q.v.), to some prisoners instead of tickets-of-leave. The system was also used in Van Diemen's Land and was given further refinements at Norfolk Island where prisoners under Alexander Maconochie could earn tickets by gaining marks for good conduct. James Tucker's loss of his ticket-of-leave in 1844 meant he was sent to Port Macquarie, where *Ralph Rashleigh* was probably written; Henry Savery's was with-

drawn in 1833 on the grounds that he had dabbled in newspaper management. There are numerous references to tickets-of-leave in Australian convict literature, e.g. in the stories of 'Price Warung'.

TIERNEY, JOHN, see 'JAMES, BRIAN'

TIGHE, HARRY (1877–1946), born near Newcastle, NSW, lived mainly overseas from the age of seventeen, although he returned to Australia for lengthy periods. The author of sixteen novels, some of which, such as *Archie Wynward of Glen of Imaal* (1903), *A Man of Sympathy* (1908), and *The Four Candles* (1909), draw on his Australian experience, he also wrote numerous plays for the London stage. One of these, 'Open Spaces' (1927), retitled 'The Bush Fire' (1931), is set in Australia. His published plays include *Jean* (1901) and *The Atonement* (1929). His later impressions of Australia are recorded in his semi-fictional *As I Saw It* (1937).

Tilted Cart, The, see **GILMORE**, Dame MARY

Tilted Cross, The, a novel by Hal Porter (q.v.), was published in 1961. Set in Hobart 1845–46, it deals partly with the last bitter and despairing months of the life of the transported forger and suspected poisoner, Judas Griffin Vaneleigh. The character is based on Thomas Griffiths Wainewright (q.v.), although Porter slightly alters the historical facts to suggest that Wainewright's wife may have been the guilty party. Vaneleigh's life becomes involved with that of the low-born son of an actor, Queely Sheill, whose inborn Christian feelings are stirred by Vaneleigh's sufferings. Both Sheill and Vaneleigh live in the notorious and insalubrious Campbell Street, but have contact with the other, polite extreme of Hobart society when they visit Cindermead, the property of Sir Sydney Knight, where Vaneleigh is to paint the portrait of his wife, Lady Rose. There, Queely's good looks arouse the passions of both Asnetha Sleep, Sir Sydney's crippled sister, and his wife, who is currently between lovers, and the jealousy of Asnetha's black page, Teapot. Again Queely responds to his feelings of compassion, although Vaneleigh warns him that pity will beget infamy. The forces of lust, hatred, envy, despair and bitterness that secretly govern relations at Cindermead combine to trap Queely: he is unjustly arrested for theft, imprisoned, and attempts to escape with the help of his friends, Polidorio Smith and Pretty Dick. Badly injured in the attempt, he suffers a hideous operation in the criminal hospital and dies of gangrene on Christmas Eve. Life, meanwhile, continues at Cindermead in its apparently civilized manner and Vaneleigh, now seriously ill, enters hospital.

Time is Not Yet Ripe, The, a political comedy by Louis Esson (q.v.), was first performed in Melbourne in 1912 and published in the same year. Reminiscent of the theatre of Bernard Shaw and Oscar Wilde and particularly memorable for its lively heroine, Doris Quiverton, the play is a witty exposé of the unreality of political life.

Time Means Tucker, see **TRITTON, 'DUKE'**

Time of the Peacock, The, see **ABDULLAH, MENA; MATHEW, RAY**

Timeless Land, The, a novel by Eleanor Dark (q.v.) published in 1941, is the first volume of her historical trilogy. The succeeding volumes are *Storm of Time* (1948) and *No Barrier* (1953). The trilogy was reprinted as one edition in 1963 and presented as a television series by the ABC in 1980. *The Timeless Land* concentrates mainly on the first five years of European settlement at Port Jackson. Even before the arrival of the First Fleet, Bennilong and his father, Wunbula, have watched for the return of the winged boat that Wunbula had seen several years previously, the *Endeavour* captained by James Cook that had visited eastern Australia in 1770. Against a background of authentic historical events, Dark then traces the destinies and experiences of the historical, and of some fictional, characters. After the arrival of the First Fleet at Botany Bay and their removal to Sydney Cove in 1788, Bennilong and his wife, Barangaroo, and others of his tribe observe the activities of the white people with amazement and, in Bennilong's case, fascination. One of their number, the gentle Arabanoo, is captured and kept as part-guide, part-prisoner, part-friend by Governor Phillip, but dies later in the smallpox epidemic that afflicts many of the Aborigines. Among the convicts the experiences of Ellen Prentice, her husband Andrew and son Johnny are prominent; among those in authority, the experiences of Phillip, William Dawes, David Collins, Watkin Tench and Richard Johnson. Andrew Prentice escapes in 1789 and survives with the help of the inland tribes, taking an Aboriginal woman, Cunnembeillee, as wife. Later his discovery of some of the cattle that had wandered from the settlement contributes to his sense of security. After two and a half years of isolation

from the home country, the European settlers face starvation but the arrival of the *Lady Juliana* in June, forerunner of the Second Fleet, averts disaster. The *Lady Juliana* also brings the first family of free settlers, Stephen and Harriet Mannion and their six-year-old son, Patrick. Meanwhile Bennilong has become a willing captive, frequently enlivening Phillip's life with his amorous or quarrelsome exploits. Colbee, who is captured with him towards the end of 1789, escapes. By 1791 Andrew Prentice's hideout is threatened by exploring parties and by the settlement of an estate by Mannion and his convict labourers. After Harriet's death giving birth to another son, Miles, Mannion takes Ellen Prentice as his housekeeper/mistress. Andrew Prentice makes plans to move further westward but dies saving Cunnembeillee and their son in a flash flood. By a strange series of coincidences, his son Johnny inherits his secret farm. Accompanied by Bennilong and the young Immerawanye, Phillip sails for England. The epilogue describes Bennilong's return three years later with Governor Hunter after a bleak experience in England, the desertion of his second wife, Gooroobarooboolo, his inability to recover his sense of wholeness, and the growing faction fights and difficulties that threaten the new settlement.

Storm of Time, which continues the saga from 1799–1808, narrates the fortunes of the Colony under the governors Hunter, King and Bligh, as well as those of the Mannion and Prentice families. *No Barrier* picks up the action in February 1808 and covers the first five years of the governorship of Macquarie as well as the destinies of Patrick Mannion, his brother Miles, his young stepmother Connor and her second husband Mark Harvey, Johnny Prentice and his second mate Emily, and Dilboong, Bennilong's daughter. The narrative ends with the crossing of the Blue Mountains in 1813.

TIMMS, E.V. (EDWARD VIVIAN) (1895–1960), born Charters Towers, Queensland, served in both world wars and made a reputation as a writer of historical romances, some of which are set in Australia and others in Europe. They include *The Hills of Hate* (1925), *James! Don't Be a Fool* (1927), *The Cripple in Black* (1930), *Whitehall* (1931), *Conflict* (1934), *Far Caravan* (1935), *Alicia Deane* (?1932), *Ten Wicked Men* (1937), *Maelstrom* (1938), *Dark Interlude* (1939), *James! How Dare You!* (1940), *Forever to Remain* (1948), *The Pathway of the Sun* (1949), *The Beckoning Shore* (1950) and *The Valleys Beyond* (1951). The last four novels form an 'Australian saga' in historical sequence with common characters. Timms also wrote serials for radio, books for children and a biography, *Lawrence, Prince of Mecca* (1927).

TIPPING, RICHARD (1949–), born Adelaide, has lived in Balmain and worked as a freelance writer on documentary films. Editor or co-editor of such poetry magazines as *Mok* and *News and Weather*, and of the anthologies *The Friendly Street Poetry Reader* (1977) and *Poet's Choice* (1979), he has published two collections of his own poetry, *Soft Riots* (1972) and *Domestic Hardcore* (1975).

Tirra Lirra by the River, see **ANDERSON, JESSICA**

TISHLER, JOSEPH (1871–1957), born NZ but resident most of his life in Victoria, was a fanatical contributor of atrocious, but distinctive and often unconsciously funny, verse to the *Bulletin* under the pseudonym 'Bellerive'. Most of his naive, unrhythmic outpourings were printed in the answers to correspondents column over a period of forty years. *The Book of Bellerive* (1961) is a selection of his verse, edited by Douglas Stewart, who dubbed him 'Australia's Worst Poet'.

'TITUS SALT', see **EDMOND, JAMES**

'To God: From the Warring Nations', a poem by 'Furnley Maurice' (q.v.), first appeared in the *Book Lover* in 1916, with the word 'weary' in the title instead of 'warring'. It was published with the new title in *Eyes of Vigilance* (1920). The poem's theme is humanity's general guilt for war and its horror. In 1916 it met a mixed reception; its pacifist plea angered patriots, who saw it as an attack on the nation's will to fight, but it echoed the mood of the anti-war faction of the time.

To the Islands, a novel by Randolph Stow (q.v.) published in 1958 (rev. ed. 1982) won the Miles Franklin Award and the Gold Medal of the Australian Literature Society. Set in the wilderness area of north-western Australia, the novel deals with the last days of Heriot, an old, disillusioned and weary missionary, director of an Anglican Aboriginal mission for many years. Heriot's bitterness reaches a peak when Rex, the native he detests and blames for the death of his foster daughter, defiantly returns to the mission. After an encounter with Rex in which Heriot attacks him with a stone, presumably killing him, the missionary sets out into the wilderness in search of the islands, which according to Aboriginal myth are the islands of death. Justin, another Aboriginal, insists on accompanying and caring for him. Heriot's journey is both physical and spiritual, an attempt to expiate his personal and racial guilt towards the Aboriginal people. Gradually he moves towards the quietism and resignation

demonstrated by the Aborigines, thus transcending his Western tradition. Finally, Justin consents to leave him alone with his vision before the onset of death, and returns to meet the rescue party and the recovered, forgiving Rex.

Toast to Melba, A, see **HIBBERD, JACK**

Tocsin, subtitled *The People's Penny Paper*, a weekly radical Melbourne journal expressing the main socialist thinking of the day, began publication in 1897, largely under the influence of Bernard O'Dowd (q.v.). The title page carried a sketch of a bell-ringer (tocsin means an alarm bell) by Norman Lindsay. The *Tocsin* platform, published in each volume, represented a mixture of the ideas and philosophies of Henry George, Edward Bellamy, the Fabians and the emerging political Labor Party. O'Dowd's regular column in *Tocsin* was 'The Forge' by 'Gavah the Blacksmith'. The journal was known as *Labor Call* 1906–53 and from 1953 until its demise in 1961 was titled *Labor*.

TOLMER, ALEXANDER (1815–90), born England of French parents, spent some of his early years at sea and in the British cavalry, and in 1840 migrated to SA, where he became commissioner of police in 1852. In 1847 he opened up an improved mail route between SA and NSW and was responsible for a successful gold escort between Mount Alexander, Bendigo, Ballarat and Adelaide. An intemperate man, he was dismissed from the police service in 1856 and began trading in a small cutter near the mouth of the Murray. He also tried sheep-farming and made an unsuccessful attempt to win the reward for the first south–north crossing of the continent. His *Reminiscences of an Adventurous and Chequered Career at Home and at the Antipodes* (1882), is an entertaining contemporary memoir.

Tolpuddle Martyrs, see **LOVELESS, GEORGE**

Tom Thumb, see **FLINDERS, MATTHEW; BASS, GEORGE**

TOMASETTI, GLEN (1929–), born Melbourne, has travelled widely in Australia and overseas. She has written poetry, songs, radio and stage plays and works frequently as a contemporary troubadour, playing her own songs on the guitar. She has published a collection of her songs, *Songs from a Seat in the Carriage* (1970), and two novels, *Thoroughly Decent People* (1976) and *Man of Letters* (1981). Dissatisfied with the conventional rural, male version of Australian history, Tomasetti presents another less celebrated aspect of the past in *Thoroughly Decent People*; a representation of the daily family life of ordinary Melbourne people of the 1930s, it has been praised for its sociological authenticity. *Man of Letters* is a study of a certain male type, a cloistered academic whose romantic notions finally confront real experience.

'Tomb of Lt. John Learmonth, A.I.F., The', an elegy by John Manifold (q.v.) in memory of a school friend who had been captured in Crete in the Second World War and later died in a German prison camp, was first published in *New Republic* in 1945. Written while Manifold himself was involved in the German offensive in the Ardennes in 1944, the poem is both a tribute to the unpretentious quality of common human heroism as exemplified in John Learmonth's hopeless stand against the Germans in Crete and a linking of that courage to 'the old heroic virtues' that are part of Australia's past.

TOMHOLT, SYDNEY (1884–1974), born Melbourne, fought in France in the First World War, travelled widely thereafter in China, Mongolia and the Philippines, returning to Sydney in 1932. In Australia he wrote dramatic pieces and serials for radio and later became film and drama critic for the *Sydney Morning Herald*. A serious dramatist, as Bernard Shaw recognized, with a flair for atmosphere and emotional and dramatic intensity, he ranges from realism to poetic symbolism anticipating the work of Patrick White. Unlike his fellow playwrights, the physical environment interested him less than the inner, psychological one. Although he wrote at a time when Australian plays lacked a theatre and his work was only occasionally produced, either by repertory companies or on radio, he published a collection of ten one-act plays in 1936, titled *Bleak Dawn and Other Plays*. Of these *Bleak Dawn* and *Anoli the Blind* (qq.v.) are the most striking. Another drama, *Searchlights*, was included in *Best Australian One-Act Plays* (1937).

Tomorrow and Tomorrow and Tomorrow, a novel by the collaborating writers known as 'M. Barnard Eldershaw' (q.v.), was published in 1947. Marjorie Barnard (q.v.), who was the predominant author, has described the circumstances of its writing and publication in *Meanjin* (1970). Wartime conditions resulted in an abbreviated title and other excisions by an overzealous censorship, and it was not until 1983 that the novel was published in full with its complete title. The setting is divided between one day in the twenty-fourth century and several decades of the twentieth, as Knarf, a ded-

icated writer modelled on Frank Dalby Davison, reads his historically-retrospective novel to Ord, his friend and a great archaeologist. Looking back at Australia's past from his materially-secure but spiritually-torpid Utopia, Knarf describes how the First People, the Aborigines, who had lived in harmony with the land, had been succeeded by the tough-spirited Pioneers. The descendants, the Australians, had allowed themselves 'to be dispossessed by the most fantastic tyranny the world had ever known, money in the hands of a few' and had endured the Third World War, pestilence, internal subversion, the destruction of Sydney and finally total loss of sovereignty. Australia, tamed by twenty-fourth century technology and governed by a small, enlightened élite, is enjoyed by the third people. The Riverina has become the Tenth Commune as Australia has become part of a smoothly-functioning global order in which war, competition, violence, suffering and struggle are things of the past. Two-thirds of the novel are concerned with the past, especially the 1930s and 1940s, and centre on the sufferings of an Australian Everyman, Harry Munster, a poultry farmer turned Sydney truck-driver. Saddled with a lazy, selfish wife, Ally, Harry endures the privations of rural and city life, the death of a son, the indignity of unemployment during the 1930s depression, and the gradual souring of a late love affair and is finally killed in the bombing of Sydney. Thereafter the story of the past expands into a more general social panorama, though dominated by various figures from Harry's past. When invasion by foreign powers seems inevitable an underground group led by the Marxist, Sid Warren, destroys Sydney by fire. Meanwhile in the novel's present, to which the narrative returns at intervals, Knarf's idealistic son Ren has reached the culminating point of his efforts to revitalize the idea of liberty. A motion to allow public opinion some force is to be put to the people that day. Ren's friend, Sfax, has perfected a votometer which can record unvoiced thoughts and Oran, a powerful official from the Technical Bureau, has arrived to observe the experiment. Military forces stand by in case they are needed. But to Ren's dismay, apathy turns out to be the real enemy and the votometer records sixty-two per cent as indifferent to the motion.

TOMPSON, CHARLES (1807–83), born Sydney, tried farming before beginning a career in the public service, ultimately rising to be clerk of the Legislative Assembly. Tompson's chief work is *Wild Notes, from the Lyre of a Native Minstrel* (q.v., 1826). A currency lad, he was the first poet to attempt an appreciation of the beauty of the local landscape. His verse invests it with an arresting, picturesque quality and an aura of romantic sadness. One of the earliest conservationists, Tompson adopts a condemnatory tone towards the destructive effects of progress on both nature and the Aboriginal race. Although occasionally attractive with fresh and original imagery, his polished verses, heavily apostrophic, ponderous in tone and ornate in language, belong largely to the poetic tradition of the eighteenth century; *Wild Notes* was the first volume of poetry, written by a poet born here, to be published in Australia.

Torch and Colonial Book Circular, see **PETHERICK, E.A.**

'Torrents, The', see **GRAY, ORIEL**

T'othersiders was the name given to people from the eastern States of Australia by the native-born Western Australians. Used especially in the gold rushes of the 1890s, it reflected the Sandgropers' (q.v.) parochialism and suspicion of the East. A brief-lived newspaper, *T'Othersider*, was published in Coolgardie in 1897.

Touch of Silk, The, a play by 'Betty Roland' (q.v.) which was first produced in 1928, was originally published in 1942 and has been frequently revived on stage and radio. Tragedy ensues when Jeanne, the charming, homesick French wife of Jim Davidson, a shell-shocked digger, contributes in a moment of thoughtlessness to the desperate financial plight of their drought-stricken farm. Although the plot creaks in places, the unsympathetic physical and emotional environment of the bush, in which Jeanne finds herself, is evoked with oppressive effect, as is her relationship with her malevolent mother-in-law.

Touchstone, subtitled *A Saturday Journal of Criticism, Commentary, and Satire*, was published weekly in Melbourne 1869–70. Henry Kendall, who was in Melbourne, was briefly its editor; it published literary articles and reviews but its tone was largely satirical. A later weekly of the same title, with some literary content, was published briefly in Ballarat at the end of 1883, edited by 'Tom Touchstone' (Thomas Bury), and was a considerable influence on radical poet Bernard O'Dowd.

'TOUCHSTONE, TOM', see **BURY, THOMAS**

Tourmaline, a novel by Randolph Stow (q.v.), was published in 1963 and is a philosophical novel; based on the opposing ideas of Taoism and Christianity, the key to its theme is contained in Stow's sequence of poems titled '*From The Testament of Tourmaline*: Variations on Themes of *Tao Teh Ching*', published in 1966. Tourmaline is an isolated, WA mining town, a place of heat and dust, but so cut off from outer society that it is an allegorical rather than a realistic entity. Significant individuals in the town are Kestrel, the arrogant hotel owner, Deborah, his part-Aboriginal mistress, Byrne, his drunken nephew, and Tom Spring, the wise storekeeper. The narrator of the story, who also participates in the drama, describes himself as The Law of Tourmaline. One day a young man, Michael Random, half-dead from exposure in the desert, is dumped in town. Michael, who reveals himself to be a diviner, is soon regarded as the town's spiritual saviour, although both Kestrel and the quietist Tom Spring refuse their allegiance. Michael fails to discover water although he finds a gold reef, and eventually leaves Tourmaline, defeated, his place as leader filled by the bullying Kestrel. Tom Spring dies at his store although his quietist perspective lives on in his spiritual descendant, Dave Speed, the desert-dweller.

Towards the Source, see **BRENNAN, C.J.**

Tower of the Dream, The, published by Charles Harpur (q.v.) in a pamphlet in 1865, is a long poem in blank verse, interspersed with songs. Highly symbolic, the poem, which delves into the division between conscious knowledge and unconscious forces in the life of man, uses allegorical devices such as a monster, a lake, a tower and a maiden. Apart from fellow-poet Henry Kendall's obsession with it ('the greatest of Australian poems') the poem aroused little contemporary interest. More recent critical opinion sees it, and Harpur's other philosophical verse, as evidence of a wider poetic talent than the corrupt 1883 collection of his poetry indicates.

Town and Country Journal, see *Australian Town and Country Journal*

Town Life in Australia, see **TWOPENY, R.E.N.**

Town Like Alice, A, a novel by 'Nevil Shute' (q.v.), was published in 1950. Narrated by an elderly lawyer, Noel Strachan, it is an account of the experience of an English girl Jean Paget, who in 1947 at the age of twenty-seven inherits a small fortune from her uncle. Jean has grown up in Malaya and England and is working in Malaya at the outbreak of the Second World War. Just before the fall of Singapore, Jean goes to Batu Tasik near Kuala Lumpur to say goodbye to her friends, the Hollands. Captured by the Japanese, Jean is one of a group of fourteen women and nineteen children which is held prisoner for forty-five days in such severe conditions that one child dies. The group is dispatched to Singapore on foot, guarded by four soldiers. After they have been on the march for several days, one of the older women dies and they are diverted to Port Swetenham, thirty miles away, where a ship should be waiting for them. The ship does not arrive, and after a wait of eleven days and the death of another child they are ordered to walk to Port Dickson fifty miles away. For the next two months, unwanted by the Japanese army, they wander over Malaya; others of their party die, including Mrs Holland and her two elder children. They meet two Australian soldiers, Ben Leggatt and Joe Harman, who obtain medicines and soap for them. Joe Harman, a ringer from northern Australia, is drawn to Jean whom he nicknames Mrs Boong, assuming that she is married and that the child which she carries is hers. When Joe steals five chickens for Jean's group from the local Japanese commanding officer, Captain Sugamo, he is discovered and is crucified by Sugamo. Guarded now only by a sergeant, the women are sent on their way again. By August 1942 the party, now reduced to seventeen, has reached a small village called Kuala Telang, where their guard dies and where they are allowed to stay to work in the paddy fields. They remain there for three years, and are repatriated at the end of the war; Jean, discovering that both her mother and brother have died, takes up clerical work in London. When Strachan informs her of her inheritance, she decides to return to Malaya to build a well for the village which had befriended her group. In Malaya she discovers that Joe Harman has survived the crucifixion and decides to fly to Australia to find him. Meanwhile in London, Strachan is visited by Joe who is searching for Jean, having discovered that she is unmarried. Strachan sends Joe off on his return journey, refraining from telling him that Jean is already there. At Alice Springs Jean discovers that Joe is managing a station in the Gulf country, Midhurst, near Willstown. She spends several days at Willstown, where she discovers that Joe is returning from England; amazed at the general deprivation of the town, she makes plans to establish a shoe factory and an ice-cream parlour. Joe and Jean are reunited at Cairns and decide to marry. Helped in a practical way by Strachan and Joe, Jean is successful in her business ventures in Willstown and achieves fame when she rides over forty miles to get help for an injured man. After three years Joe is making plans to buy Midhurst station, Jean is the proprietor of several flour-

ishing businesses at Willstown, which she intends to transform into a town like Alice, and they are the parents of two children. *A Town Like Alice* was produced as a film in 1956 and as an Australian television series in 1980.

TOWNEND, CHRISTINE, see Feminism and Australian Literature

TOWZEY, ELEANOR STEWART, see **STEWART, NELLIE**

Tracks We Travel, The, see **Australasian Book Society**; **BEASLEY, JACK**

TRAILL, W.H. (WILLIAM HENRY) (1843–1902), born London, arrived in Australia about 1860. He worked on stations in Queensland, including a period on Maroon, where Rosa Praed was brought up, and as a public servant in Melbourne and Brisbane until the middle 1870s, when he went into journalism. In 1881 he wrote the leader for the *Bulletin* (q.v.) which led to the Clontarf libel case and the imprisonment in 1882 of its founding editors, J.F. Archibald and John Haynes. As editor and proprietor or major shareholder, Traill ran the *Bulletin* 1881–86; his regime was a period of consolidation during which he installed new machinery, developed the *Bulletin*'s political and economic philosophy, established its tradition of black-and-white art, and set it on its way to becoming the legendary 'Bushman's Bible'. Before his *Bulletin* years, Traill was proprietor of the *Darling Downs Gazette*, a reporter for the *Queenslander* and *Brisbane Courier*, and editor of the *Sydney Mail*. After his departure he edited the *Australian Star* (1887–89) and *Truth* (1893), was a member of the NSW parliament 1889–94 and engaged in pastoral and mining speculations. In his last years he worked mainly on journalistic assignments for the Queensland government, preparing, among other commissions, *A Queenly Colony* (1901).

TRAIN, GEORGE FRANCIS (1829–1904), American-born entrepreneur, spent three busy and profitable years in Victoria in the gold rush period 1852–55. He was partly instrumental in Freeman Cobb establishing Cobb & Co. (q.v.) and mooted the idea of a Melbourne-based American style of federal government for Australia. He published his autobiography, *My Life in Many States and in Foreign Lands* (1902). Clive Turnbull wrote *Bonanza: The Story of George Francis Train* (1946); Willis Thornton, *The Nine Lives of Citizen Train* (1948); and E. Daniel and Annette Potts edited *A Yankee Merchant in Goldrush Australia: The Letters of George Francis Train 1853–55* (1970).

'Tramp, The', see 'Chosen Vessel, The'

Transit of Cassidy, a novel by George Turner (q.v.), was published in 1978. Cassidy Edwards, once an arrogant star of the boxing ring, is the anti-hero. His downward course begins when he loses a challenge fight because his wife and children fail to attend. Thirteen years later, his adolescent son Mike seeks him out, but their reunion turns into a violent confrontation culminating in Cassidy's death. As Mike searches for his father a complex, many-sided picture of Cassidy emerges as we see him through the eyes of all those whom he later alienated: Paddy, his brother; Perce, his dedicated manager; Eleanor, his wife; and Jack Wild, the sports writer. Meanwhile the compassionate attitude of Rod Trelawney, who knows Cassidy best, leads Mike to a more mature understanding of his father.

Transit of Venus, The, a novel by Shirley Hazzard (q.v.), was published in 1980 and won the National Book Critics' Circle Award in the USA. The first part, titled 'The Old World', opens in southern England in the 1950s with the arrival of Ted Tice, a scientist, at the home of Professor Sefton Thrale, with whom he is to work on the siting of a large telescope. Ted, who has been on a walking tour, arrives at the house in the middle of a violent storm. At the Thrales, Caro Bell, the woman he is to love for the rest of his life, transits his destiny for the first time. Caro and her sister Grace are young Australians brought up in Sydney by their half-sister Dora, a neurotic, self-dramatizing martyr, after their parents' early death in a ferry accident. Grace is already engaged to Christian Thrale who, like his father the professor, is conventional and self-centred. Caro is about to enter government service. The sisters, indissolubly bound by their childhood experience, are dissimilar in both appearance and temperament, Caro giving the impression of a dark, strong nature, whereas Grace seems as easy-going as she is fair. Dora's emotional dependence on her sisters appears to be suddenly resolved by her marriage to a Major Ingot and departure for Portugal. Although Caro enjoys friendship with Ted Tice, she falls in love with Paul Ivory, a sophisticated young playwright. Ivory flirts with Caro but becomes engaged to a local heiress, the insipid Tertia Drage. His relationship with Caro deepens but is broken off when Tertia is made aware of the love affair and Caro realizes that the discovery will make no difference to the status quo. In distress Caro leaves abruptly for London. In the second part, titled 'The Contacts', Caro is impelled by her love to resume her affair with the now-married Paul. Ted follows her progress from a distance,

and at the same time successfully pursues his career despite his public criticism of the work of Professor Thrale. Grace becomes involved in her role of wife and mother. After some years, Tertia Ivory becomes pregnant, Paul breaks off the affair and Caro goes through a period of intense misery. Her suffering is exacerbated when Ingot deserts Dora and the ensuing financial and emotional burden falls exclusively on her shoulders, even though Christian Thrale inherits a large fortune on his father's death. In the third part, titled 'The New World', Caro meets and falls in love with an American writer and peace-worker, Adam Vail. She marries him and moves to New York, where she is happy, although Adam's daughter Josie, a victim of the protest-culture of the 1970s, makes no secret of her resentment. Ted Tice, now despairing of ever winning Caro, marries an old friend, Margaret. Christian Thrale, meanwhile, makes a brief excursion into danger by having an affair with a young typist, Cordelia Ware. Although Cordelia suffers, Christian's insensitivity shields him from pain. By contrast, Grace, at the age of forty-three, feels the anguish of a deep, unsatisfied passion when she falls in love with a young doctor, Angus Dance. The final part, 'The Culmination', brings several destinies full circle. Adam Vail dies suddenly. Then Caro discovers from a chance meeting with Paul Ivory that he had many years earlier failed to save the life of a man who was blackmailing him. Ted Tice had been made aware of his crime on the very day that he had arrived at the Thrale house to work with Sefton, but had remained silent. The discovery of Ted's integrity stirs Caro's love for him. Paul, however, grief-stricken because of his son's imminent death from leukemia, sees himself as visited with retribution for a life of evil. Later, Caro meets Ted by chance in Stockholm, they declare their love and decide to live together.

Transportation, the banishing from Great Britain of offenders against the law, was regularized by the Transportation Act of 1718; under its provisions the responsibility for carrying out the penalty of transportation fell upon the masters of the ships which carried the offenders into exile. Until the War of Independence most transportees went to the American colonies or the West Indies, but in 1784 an Act was passed which authorized the British government to select another place for the reception of convicts. In 1786, the eastern coast of New Holland (Australia), discovered by Lieutenant James Cook in 1770, was chosen; in 1787 the First Fleet left under Captain Arthur Phillip for the Colony which, on arrival, was named New South Wales, and where the government continued to maintain and employ convicts. There were strategic and commercial arguments as well as administrative and penal ones for a British settlement in the South Pacific; the relative importance of trade, defence and the problem of the prisons is the subject of *The Founding of Australia*, ed. Ged Martin (1978), and Alan Frost's *Convicts and Empire* (1980), although most contributors to the 'Botany Bay Debate', as it has come to be called, accept that the penal reason was a significant one.

About 150 000 convicts were transported to the eastern part of Australia 1787–1852, 80 000 to NSW, which ceased receiving convicts after 1840, and virtually all the remainder to Van Diemen's Land, later Tasmania, which received about 37 000 convicts after 1840. The importance of the convict experience in Tasmanian history explains why Tasmania is the setting of so much Australian convict literature. Of the other colonies, NSW incorporated Victoria until 1851 and Queensland until 1859, although Moreton Bay was a remote penal settlement in 1824–39; South Australia was founded as a separate colony in 1836 and never formally received convicts although, like Victoria, it was a place where 'Vandemonians' (q.v.) settled; and Western Australia received just under 10 000 convicts over a long period, 1829–68. The origins of the convicts are analysed in L.L. Robson's *The Convict Settlers of Australia* (1965), which, with A.G.L. Shaw's *Convicts and the Colonies* (1966) and George Rude's *Protest and Punishment* (1978), are standard studies of the convict experience. The research of Robson, Shaw and others has established a profile of the convicts at odds with the 'convict legend'. The legend, influenced by the literary treatment of transportation, is of some longevity among Australians and postulates that the convicts, 'more sinn'd against than sinning', were the victims of a repressive legal system in England and a brutal penal one in Australia, and were characteristically Irish political prisoners, English poachers, or minor offenders forced to commit crimes to feed starving families, or innocents like Rufus Dawes in *His Natural Life* (1874). All four types of convict were transported to Australia but most were urban offenders convicted at least once before transportation, whose crime was often underestimated in order to prevent trial on a capital charge. Roughly a quarter of those convicted of crimes in England in the period 1788–1840 underwent transportation.

The voyage to Australia on a convict transport, the subject of Charles Bateson's *The Convict Ships 1787–1868* (1964), could be hazardous, either because of the conditions or because of weather or war, or, less often, because of rebellion. Despite the rebellions in *Ralph Rashleigh, His Natural Life* and other convict novels, there were relatively few such insurgencies either on board ship or after landing: the seizure in 1829 of the brig, *Cyprus* (q.v.), is a notable example of the former; the Vinegar Hill (q.v.) uprising is perhaps the most famous of the latter. There is an extensive First Fleet literature, almost solely from the official side, although later convict memoirs usually incorporated an account of the voyage part of the transportation experience. Once at the colonial settlements, the earliest convicts were employed on the construction of public works or in tending government farms, but as the number of free settlers, ex-convicts and emancipists (q.v.) increased, so did the practice of assignment, the assigning of a convict to a master or masters who maintained the convict in clothing and rations. An equally common problem, and a major theme in the creative literature about transportation, was the 'lottery of assignment', a phrase used to describe the defenceless position convicts were placed in regarding the conduct of their masters. After serving part or all of their sentence convicts were eligible to receive a ticket-of-leave (q.v.), which permitted them to seek employment in a specified area, like the passes available to black workers in South Africa today, or a conditional pardon, the condition being that they remain in the colony.

During Lachlan Macquarie's term as governor the number of convicts greatly increased, partly as a result of the end of the Napoleonic Wars. Macquarie is generally recognized as having had a liberal attitude towards the acceptance of emancipists into society; although vindicated in the 1812 report of a British parliamentary committee investigating transportation, his policy aroused the ire of many settlers. In 1819–21, John Thomas Bigge (q.v.) investigated Macquarie's administration on behalf of the British government; his reports were critical of Macquarie and led to a tightening up of the 'System', as it came to be called. That many of the worst excesses of the System occurred after the Bigge investigation, during a period when the great majority of convicts (just over eighty per cent) was sent to Australia, helps to explain why so little convict, as distinct from historical, fiction deals with transportation before 1820; Thomas Keneally's *Bring Larks and Heroes* (1967) and Colin Free's *Vinegar Hill* (1978) are among the exceptions. The practice of assignment continued after 1820, but those remaining in government service were worked arduously in gangs, often engaged on the construction of roads. A variety of punishments, of which the lash was the most prevalent, awaited both assignee and road gang member, and for the more recalcitrant there were the secondary punishment centres, where reconvicted convicts were sent. Port Arthur (q.v.), where the first Australian novelist, Henry Savery, was sent after a colonial forgery conviction in 1840, Macquarie Harbour, Norfolk Island (q.v.) and Port Macquarie were the most notorious of these settlements.

During the decades after 1820 the tightening up of the System coincided with an increase in the controversy about the efficacy of transportation. The widely fluctuating views expressed included arguments that the colonies had made sufficient progress to be allowed to develop free of the convict taint; that convict labour should be retained; that transportation had failed both because crime had not declined and too many emancipists had done well; and that the System still was brutal and in need, if not of abolition, at least of reformation. Not all the combatants had first-hand experience of Australia, e.g. Richard Whately, whose attacks on transportation were sternly contested by George Arthur (q.v.), who believed in the severity of transportation and that his own colony of Van Diemen's Land should be the gaol of the empire. One of the major consequences of the controversy was the British parliamentary select committee of 1837–38, whose report, usually called the Molesworth Report after its chairman, Sir William Molesworth (1810–55), led to the cessation of transportation to NSW and to Van Diemen's Land becoming the focus of the new probation system, which abolished assignment, required a period of compulsory labour for all convicts and established a strictly regulated process by which a convict passed 'through' his sentence. The convict memoirist John Mortlock underwent the probation system. By 1846 the economic depression forced an end to the probation system. A revised system, whereby convicted prisoners would spend the first two stages of their sentence in England before coming to Australia holding a ticket-of-leave or a conditional pardon, led to strongly resisted moves for a revival of transportation to NSW. The last convicts arrived in Tasmania in 1853, although WA, chronically short of labour, continued to receive them for another decade and a half.

The effects of the convict experience on the development of Australia have been the subject of some speculation; the male ethos, anti-authoritarianism and egalitarianism, antagonism towards large pastoral landowners, and development of a harsh penal code are among the suggested legacies. Both the generalizations and their origins in the convict experience are difficult to prove; what is more certain is that most convicts stayed in Australia and thus helped to establish the ambivalent relationship of its citizens with England. Among those who stayed were several who played a pioneering role in Australian publishing and newspapers, and a number of the first creative writers. See also Convict in Australian Literature.

TRANTER, JOHN (1943–), born Cooma, NSW, graduated from the University of Sydney in 1970. In 1971–73 he was the senior Asian editor in Singapore for Angus & Robertson. In 1975–77 he was a producer in Brisbane for the ABC's radio drama and features division. Since 1978 he has lived in Sydney where he has been critic, editor and poet. Tranter's books of poetry are *Parallax* (1970), published originally as the June 1970 issue of *Poetry Australia; Red Movie* (1972); *The Blast Area* (1974); *The Alphabet Murders* (1976); *Crying in Early Infancy: 100 Sonnets* (1977); and *Dazed in the Ladies Lounge* (1979). He edited *Poetry Australia's Preface to the 70s* issue (1970) and an anthology, *The New Australian Poetry* (1979). His *Selected Poems* was published in 1982.

Tranter's early poetry is autobiographical in tone and conventional in theme and form. From the latter part of *Red Movie* onwards it becomes less personal, more abstract and obscure in theme, and experimental in technique. He describes *The Alphabet Murders* as an attempt to find both a valid reason to keep writing poetry and an understanding of what that poetry should be. With *Crying in Early Infancy* the strained attempt to convey his attitudes by means of sheer verbal effects gives way to the more effective method of allowing the poetry to enunciate its own significance. Although Tranter has, in his critical canon, attempted to evade the trap of modernism ('today's modernism is outdated tomorrow') by advocating the need for constant change ('what does not change is the need for change') his poetry itself carries many of the cliches of dated modernism. Accepted as one of Australia's significant contemporary poets he has, paradoxically, received only moderate critical esteem. Throughout the 1970s Tranter was an outspoken, even rabid, opponent of conservatism in Australian poetry. His own poetry, his editorship of such small magazines as *Transit, Leatherjacket* and the hoax issue, *Free Grass*, his anthologizing of modern poetry, and his numerous critical writings, all confirm his strong advocacy of modernism in Australian writing. His literary reviews are lucid and judicious and display, as does his poetry, wit and skill.

Trap, see **MATHERS, PETER**

Travelling North, see **WILLIAMSON, DAVID**

'Travelling Post Office, The', see **Castlereagh River**

TRAVERS, PAMELA (1906–   ), the author of *Mary Poppins* (1934) and of numerous children's books published in England, was born in Queensland and worked as a journalist, actress and dancer in the 1920s. Some of her poetry is included in *Poetry in Australia 1923* (1923), ed. Jack Lindsay and Kenneth Slessor and in *The New Countries* (1929), ed. H. Bolitho.

Treatment, The, see **KOCAN, PETER**

Tree of Man, The, a novel by Patrick White (q.v.), was published in 1956 and won the Gold Medal of the Australian Literature Society. Extending from the 1880s to the 1930s, it describes the lives of Stan Parker and his wife Amy, who clear a piece of land in NSW for a mixed farm. During the early years of their marriage the couple achieve an inarticulate but poignant and dignified communion, although their responses to experience soon begin to diverge. External crises such as floods and fire shape their lives and meanwhile other people settle nearby: the inadequate Quigley family, eventually reduced to Doll Quigley and her mentally defective brother Bub; the loquacious Mrs O'Dowd and her alcoholic husband; Mrs Gage, the postmistress whose 'queer' husband paints pictures and eventually hangs himself; and Armstrong, the butcher, who becomes a man of means. After some childless years, the Parkers have two children, Ray, a naturally vicious boy, and Thelma, delicate and reserved. Amy finds contentment in the becalmed years of child-rearing. Only her novelettish dream about a beautiful socialite, Madeleine, a visitor to the Armstrongs' property, Glastonbury, disturbs her peace; this too evaporates when Madeleine, trapped in a fire at Glastonbury which destroys her hair, is rescued by Stan. Stan, however, yearns for some transcendent fulfilment. Especially after the First World War in which he participates, he becomes withdrawn and longs to 'express the great simplicities in simple, luminous words for people to see. But of course he could not.' Many changes take place in the post-war years. Amy, divided from Stan by his reticence, has a casual affair with a commercial traveller, discovered and grieved over by her husband. Ray, who as a child has found a vent for his aimless cruelty in cutting his name in green trees and stealing birds' eggs, and in his sadistic treatment of the farm-hands, Fritz the German and Con the Greek, drifts into his destiny of petty criminal. Before he is shot dead in a club brawl he is married to a Methodist girl, Elsie Tarbutt, who has a son.

Both Elsie and the grandson become closer to Amy than her own children. Ray's later liaison with a showgirl, Lola, produces another grandson, although Amy refuses to recognize him. Thelma makes a prudent marriage with her employer Dudley Forsdyke and pursues a childless and sterile existence in the city. Doll Quigley finally does away with her infantile brother Bub and ends her life in an institution. Amy's relationship with the O'Dowds stagnates for long periods but quickens at times of crisis such as Ray's death and Mrs O'Dowd's discovery that she has cancer. Towards the end of Stan's life a mixed, ugly, suburban development overtakes their farm and it is eventually subdivided and sold up. The novel closes on the day of Stan's death. Seated in the centre of his circular garden, which is enclosed within other circles, the last circle of all being 'the cold and golden bowl of winter', Stan is accosted by a young man with a fundamentalist religious message. He is pressed into a moment of articulate illumination: 'the old man, who had been cornered long enough, saw, through perversity perhaps, but with his own eyes. He was illuminated.' Pointing with his stick to a gob of spittle, 'That is God,' he said. Both his spiritual separation from Amy and the circularity of life is emphasized by her interruption of his vision with a delighted account of her rediscovery of a wedding gift, a silver nutmeg grater. Shortly afterwards he dies, but his vision will persist in his grandson, who dreams of writing 'a poem of life, of all life'.

Treelake Series is a tetralogy of novels by George Turner (q.v.), set in the fictional Victorian town of Treelake. They comprise *A Stranger and Afraid* (1961), *The Cupboard under the Stairs* (1962), *A Waste of Shame* (1965) and *The Lame Dog Man* (1967).

Trevelyan, Laura, see *Voss*

Triad, a monthly magazine published 1915–27, was founded in NZ, transferred to Sydney and edited successively by C.N. Bayertz, Frank Morton and L.L. Woollacott, although Morton did most to sustain it. Self-consciously cultured and independent in its social attitudes, the *Triad* included reviews of literature, music, art and drama, original poetry, articles and general news of interesting events and people. Better-known contributors included Hugh McCrae, Kenneth Slessor, 'Furnley Maurice', Ethel Anderson, Randolph Bedford, Will Lawson, Mary Gilmore, Louis Esson and Cecil Mann. It was succeeded by the *New Triad*.

Tribune, the weekly newspaper of the Communist Party of Australia, published in Sydney, began publication in December 1920 titled the *Australian Communist*. Titled the *Communist* 1921–23 and the *Worker's Weekly* 1923–39, the newspaper suspended publication from May 1940 to January 1941 and resumed as the *Tribune*. In 1943 it incorporated *Forward* and in 1967 the *Guardian* (Victoria) and the *Queensland Guardian*. *Tribune* has occasionally published articles and reviews of Australian literature, especially of the socialist-realist school. Mary Gilmore wrote its socio-political column, 'Arrows' (1954–61).

Trident ran for twelve issues 1907–09, published in Melbourne and edited by Walter Murdoch, A.T. Strong, Bernard O'Dowd, B.A. Levinson, H.H. Champion and J.G. Latham. Numerous Melbourne writers, including 'Furnley Maurice' and Vance Palmer, and some of the editors contributed to the magazine.

Trist, Eadith, see *Twyborn Affair, The*

TRIST, MARGARET (1914–), born Dalby, Queensland, has written three novels, *Now That We're Laughing* (1945), *Daddy* (1947) and *Morning in Queensland* (1958), and two collections of short stories, *In the Sun* (1943) and *What Else Is There?* (1946). She writes from a feminine point of view in an understated, often lightly humorous way of ordinary domestic experience and is particularly adept at reproducing the nuances of small-town life.

TRITTON, 'DUKE' (HAROLD PERCY CROYDON) (1886–1965), born Fivedock, Sydney, was well-known as a folk-singer and source of Australian folk-songs (q.v.) and stories. Tritton had a scanty education and a series of labouring jobs before going off in 1905 with a mate, 'Dutchy' Bishop, to try his luck in the shearing sheds. The story of his four years battling round the bush was told much later as a serial in the *Bulletin* (1959) and then published as *Time Means Tucker* (1964). A simply-written, leisurely yarn of shearing, droving, fossicking for gold, swagging and odd-jobbing in outback NSW, *Time Means Tucker* is a mine of information about bush life and people in the early years of the twentieth century. John Meredith wrote the biographical *Duke of the Outback* (1983).

TROLLOPE, ANTHONY (1815–82), had been retired from the Post Office for three years when he left England in May 1871 to visit his son Frederic, who was the proprietor of a station near Grenfell, NSW. On the voyage out Trollope wrote a novel, *Lady Anna* (1874); he arrived in July 1871 and during the

next year, before travelling on to NZ, visited each of the Australian colonies, recording his impressions in a series of letters for the London *Daily Telegraph* which form the basis of *Australia and New Zealand* (1873). He made a second, briefer, visit to Australia in 1875; his letters from that journey, published in the Liverpool *Mercury*, were reprinted in *The Tireless Traveller*, ed. Bradford A. Booth (1941). Trollope's reputation as a novelist meant that he was fêted in Australasia; at Gulgong in 1871, for example, he was honoured by a luncheon presided over by Thomas Alexander Browne, 'Rolf Boldrewood'. Apart from *Australia and New Zealand*, which is a perceptive account of the colonies from an imperialist's point of view, Trollope wrote two novels with a significant Australian content, *Harry Heathcote of Gangoil* (1874) and *John Caldigate* (1879). *Harry Heathcote of Gangoil* focuses on the selector-squatter conflicts which characterized pastoral life in NSW after 1861; the squatter-hero is modelled on Trollope's son. In Garnet Walch's 1873 pantomime, *Australia Felix*, the Demon of Gloom, Kantankeros, is subjected to the Curse:

> May Trollope make you, oh! how low to grovel,
> The hero of his next Australian novel!

In *John Caldigate*, recognized as the better novel, Australia is seen as a frontier environment which is significant in Caldigate's moral development. Trollope's posthumous *Autobiography* (1883) discusses his Australian experiences, which are the subject of Marcie Muir's *Anthony Trollope in Australia* (1949). The Australian section of his *Australia and New Zealand* was republished in 1968, eds. R.B. Joyce and P.D. Edwards, while Jim Davidson, later editor of *Meanjin*, edited the parallel volume on Trollope's visit to South Africa (1973).

'TROOPER BLUEGUM', see **HOGUE, OLIVER**

'TROOPER GERARDY', see **GERARD, EDWIN FIELD**

Trooper to the Southern Cross, a novel by Angela Thirkell (q.v.), was first published in 1934 under her pseudonym 'Leslie Parker' and in 1939 as *What Happened on the Boat*. Based on her own memories of a voyage to Australia in 1920, the novel describes the experiences of a group of English and Australian passengers aboard a troop-ship, the *Rudolstadt*, returning to Australia from England after the First World War. The interest of the account owes a great deal to Thirkell's choice of narrator, Major Bowen, an Australian doctor. Cheerful, extrovert, resourceful and simple-hearted, if limited by his class and time, Bowen narrates events in a straightforward, succinct manner that is both consciously and unconsciously humorous. Some of the novel's chapter-titles indicate its tone: 'How I Got with the Diggers', 'Larry Gives Us the Dinkum Oil', 'The Digger Isn't a Bad Chap' and 'Good Old Aussie Once More'. Recently married to an English girl, Celia French, whom he frequently describes as 'a bonzer kid' or his 'little missus', Bowen narrates the circumstances of their embarkation on the unseaworthy *Rudolstadt*, once a German troop-ship and now crammed with several hundred restless diggers returning home, as well as some prisoners. At sea, troubles proliferate, compounded by ineffective commanding officers, inadequate supplies and tropical heat. Bowen describes the varying relations, the frictions and love affairs between the passengers, and interprets a range of individuals from 'Mrs Jerry', the indomitable wife of his friend, Colonel Fairchild, to Cavanagh, one of the prisoners; to Colonel Bird, the ineffective but 'white' senior doctor. Particularly useful in a crisis are the resourceful Sergeant Higgins and the padre, Father Glennie, whose Christian behaviour tempers Bowen's poor opinion of the Roman Catholic faith. At the same time he paints a vivid picture of the average digger, his sardonic, rough sense of humour, anti-authoritarianism, loyalty to those officers who have won his respect and open contempt for those who have not, his kindness and occasional cruelties. Rioting between the diggers and the local populace breaks out at Colombo, and after leaving that port the situation aboard ship becomes increasingly dangerous; the chance of mutiny is a major anxiety, the soldiers having stolen most of the officers' guns, there is insufficient water, food supplies for the children run short, the ship develops steering problems and Higgins is severely injured in a fight. At Fremantle, after a fierce brawl breaks out between the diggers and the crew, several passengers leave the ship to go home by rail. Eventually, with a guard of armed officers protecting the crew, the *Rudolstadt* limps home to Melbourne.

True Patriots All, see **Broadsides**

TRUEBRIDGE, BENJAMIN ARTHUR, see **'VREPONT, BRIAN'**

TRUGANINI (?1812–76), the last full-blooded Tasmanian Aboriginal to live on the island, assisted G.A. Robinson (q.v.), who named her 'Lallah Rookh', in his missionary activities and in his attempts to settle the Tasmanian Aborigines on Flinders Island. In 1847 she and a handful of surviving Aborigines were resettled in Oyster Bay in her tribe's traditional territory.

By 1869 she and William Lanney, 'King Billy', were the only two full bloods still alive, Lanney dying in March of that year. The Tasmanian Aborigines' story is told in James Bonwick's *The Lost Tasmanian Race* (1884) and *The Last of the Tasmanians* (1870) and in Robert Travers's *The Tasmanians: The Story of a Doomed Race* (1968). The story of Truganini's life is told in Vivienne Rae Ellis's controversial *Trucanini: Queen or Traitor?* (1976) and a film *Truganini: The Last of Her People*, recalling her last years, was made in 1976. Bill Reed wrote the three play series, *Truganinni* (1977). Gwen Harwood recalls an incident from Truganini's life in 'Looking towards Bruny' and makes a general comment on the white treatment of the Tasmanian Aborigines in 'Evening, Oyster Cove', both poems from *The Lion's Bride* (1981). The Boyer Lectures for 1980, given by Bernard Smith, were titled *The Spectre of Truganini*. There are busts of Truganini and her husband, Woureddy, by Benjamin Law (made in 1836) in the Australian National Gallery and other galleries.

Truth, one of the first Australian Sunday newspapers, was founded in Sydney in 1890 by W.N. Willis; its first editor was A.G. Taylor. In its early days *Truth* gave emphasis to sport, the theatre and mining but changed its direction after the arrival on the staff of John Norton (q.v.). Norton established its reputation in the 1890s when Henry Lawson and 'Price Warung' were prominent contributors, both as a crusader for the disadvantaged and as a muckraker with a gamey nose for sexual, criminal and political scandals. Norton was editor in 1891–92, was replaced in 1893 by W.H. Traill, who tried to make the newspaper more wholesome, and returned in 1896. S.A. Rosa took over as editor in 1906, although Norton remained owner of the newspaper from 1899 until his death in 1916, when it came under the control of his son Ezra. Under Ezra Norton, *Truth* continued to be a success by combining sport and scandal; there were editions in all the mainland States, a venture initiated by John Norton at the turn of the century. In 1958 the parent edition changed its title to the *Sunday Mirror*, which passed into the hands of Rupert Murdoch in 1960, and ceased publication in 1979.

Try Anything Once, see **CLUNE, FRANK**

TSALOUMAS, DIMITRIS (1921–), a Greek poet from the island of Leros, came to Australia in 1952, studied at the University of Melbourne and later taught modern languages and English. After moving to Australia he ceased writing poetry until 1974, but has since published several collections both in Greece and Australia. They include a selection *The Observatory* (1983), with translations by Philip Grundy, which won the National Book Council Award.

TUCKER, JAMES (?1808–?88), the probable author of the important early convict (q.v.) novel, *Ralph Rashleigh* (q.v.), and other works, was born in Bristol, England, and was said to be eighteen when convicted in 1826 of sending a threatening letter to his cousin. Sentenced to transportation for life, he arrived in Sydney early in 1827 and was sent to Emu Plains at the foot of the Blue Mountains, where he may have taken part in theatrical activities. For most of the 1830s he was in Sydney employed in the colonial architect's office; he won a ticket-of-leave in 1835 and although he lost it for drunkenness in 1839 regained it in 1840 when he went to Maitland. In 1844 he again lost his ticket-of-leave and was sent to the penal settlement of Port Macquarie, where he was engaged as a storekeeper. He was in Goulburn in southern NSW in 1849–53, probably left there for Moreton Bay, but thereafter fades from the convict records. It is now thought that he died in Sydney in 1888, although he has been linked with a James Tucker who died at Liverpool Asylum in 1866.

While at Port Macquarie Tucker seems to have initiated theatrical entertainments, and also is said to have written several literary works; manuscripts of two, *Jemmy Green in Australia* (q.v., first published 1955) and 'The Grahames' Revenge' (by 'Otto von Rosenberg'), and a novel, *Ralph Rashleigh* (by 'Giacomo di Rosenberg') have survived. The existence of these works was first noticed publicly in the *Sydney Morning Herald* in 1892, when their authorship was linked with Francis Greenway. In 1920 the manuscripts were brought to an exhibition organized by the Royal Australian Historical Society, whose president sent *Ralph Rashleigh* to London, where it was published in 1929, in a severely edited form, as a convict memoir. After patient research in 1949–51 Colin Roderick established the connections between Tucker and the manuscripts, and was responsible for the editions of *Ralph Rashleigh* and *Jemmy Green in Australia* which were published in 1952 and 1955 respectively. The case for Tucker's authorship rests on four grounds: the fact that the manuscripts are in his hand; the link between the 'Rosenberg' pseudonym and the same alias used in the letter which caused Tucker's arrest; the 1950s oral testimony of an old Port Macquarie resident; and parallels between the movements of Ralph Rashleigh in the novel and Tucker's documented experiences as a convict. Some commentators, however, notably M.H. Ellis in an exchange with Rod-

erick in the *Bulletin* December 1952–February 1953, have argued that Tucker was a copyist whose known writing, e.g. the 1826 letter, does not reveal the kind of literacy and education required of the author of *Ralph Rashleigh*. Although Ellis's claims for Greenway as an alternative seem weaker than the claims for Tucker, Tucker's own claims have not been established with complete certainty. Whatever the outcome of the authorship dispute, *Jemmy Green in Australia*, an adaptation of a 'Billy Barlow' song Tucker probably heard in Maitland, is a characteristic example of 'new chum' literature, and *Ralph Rashleigh* is an important contemporary account of the convict system.

TUCKER, T.G., see **Criticism**

TULLIPAN, RON (1917–), born into a well-known Queensland circus family, pursued numerous occupations in the outback before serving with the AIF in the Second World War. He subsequently travelled extensively and studied art in London, before returning to Australia. A socialist-realist writer, he has published numerous short stories, mainly in the *Australian Journal*, some novels which he now describes as 'entertainments', and three more serious novels. These are *Follow the Sun* (1960), which deals with the effects of changes in the sugar industry on the lives of ordinary people; *March into Morning* (1962), which won the Mary Gilmore Award and describes the inner growth of its working-class protagonist against a background of grim experiences from depression and war to flood and personal tragedy; and *Daylight Robbery* (1970), which develops the drama of a bushranging incident.

Turf, The. The first organized race meeting in Australia took place at Hyde Park, Sydney, in 1810 although it was some years later (1825) before the first turf club was formed and some years after that (1842) before the formation of the historically most important club in NSW, the Australian Jockey Club (the AJC). The same pattern for development was repeated in the other colonies: for example, in Victoria racing began in 1838 and the Victoria Racing Club (the VRC) was formed in 1864. For much of the nineteenth century these, their rival and other clubs, including many in the rural districts, held their own meetings, but gradually the administration of racing became regularized. In 1859 the AJC introduced a weight for age (WFA) scale, based on 1 August as the official 'birthday' of horses; in 1878 the *Australian Stud Book* began publication to register thoroughbred horses; and in 1912 thoroughbred horse racing, with meetings still run by individual clubs, came under the jurisdiction of the Australian Rules of Racing. Meetings of unregistered horses continued for some years on the 'pony' racecourses but such racing only survives in the picnic race meetings held in some country areas; the picnic race meeting, now usually an annual festive occasion, is a survival from race meetings 'got up' on such places as the goldfields, where sharp practices were often indulged in, e.g. the ringing in of Rainbow at the Turon Races in *Robbery Under Arms* (1888). Most thoroughbred racing is flat racing, although steeplechase and hurdle races were more popular in the nineteenth century when Adam Lindsay Gordon (q.v.) was a champion steeplechase jockey, and the Grand National Hurdle, the Grand National Steeplechase, still run in Melbourne, and the Great Eastern Steeplechase, run in Adelaide, have long traditions. Each, significantly, is a handicap race, for despite the classic races such as the AJC, Victoria and Australian Derbys and other WFA races, there is more popular interest in a number of handicap events on the Australian racing calendar. Of these, the most famous is the Melbourne Cup (q.v.), first run in 1861 and already a national day when 'Mark Twain' wrote about it in *Following the Equator* (1897) and when a Cup scene was included in the 1893 stage version of Nat Gould's novel, *The Double Event* (1891). Melbourne Cup day, with its sweepstakes and the cessation of work for the duration of the race broadcast, is the November ritual focused on in Alexander Buzo's *The Front Room Boys* (1970); it has produced an extensive literature, some of it about its two most famous winners, Carbine (1890) and Phar Lap (q.v., 1930).

The Australian passion for the turf in particular and for sport and gambling in general are commonplace observations in writings about Australian society, particularly those of visitors like 'Mark Twain', Anthony Trollope and Thomas Wood; *Cobbers* (1934), for example, contains an account of Wood's first night in Australia in the 1930s, which was spent at the 'trots'. Trotting, the racing of specially-bred horses in which the driver is pulled in a sulky by a horse using either a pacing or a trotting gait, is also popular in Australia. Some creative writers have deplored these passions, seeing in them evidence of the kind of anti-intellectualism satirized in A.D. Hope's *Dunciad Minor* (1970)

> . . . Now all the Austral Scene,
> Race-track, pub, football-ground, poker machine –
> Pleasing enough to these Yahoos, perhaps,
> To whom all books are made with bets, poor chaps!

Despite the attacks of Hope and others, including Joseph Furphy, Henry Lawson and Pa-

trick White, many Australian writers have had a personal commitment to the turf. A.B. Paterson (q.v.) is perhaps the most notable apart from Gordon, although Vincent Buckley has written several racing poems as well as a perceptive and autobiographical account of the Australian racing tradition.

The racing theme is a significant one in Australian literature, even setting aside the many literary works in which racing plays an incidental part, e.g. the racing scenes in *Robbery Under Arms*, or the news of a Melbourne Cup success which is important in the resolution of the play, *Marvellous Melbourne* (1883). The most famous novelist of the turf was Nat Gould, who spent a decade in Australia from 1884, wrote for the *Referee*, one of the many sporting newspapers which have had long lives, and moved from sports reporting to fiction in the early 1890s. He wrote more than 130 sporting novels, most of which were about racing, in which he drew regularly on his Australian experiences; he also wrote reminiscences, including *On and Off the Turf in Australia* (1895), and *The Magic of Sport* (1909). Although his reputation was perhaps larger in England, he virtually inaugurated the Australian sporting novel; his most prominent descendant was Arthur Wright (q.v.), advertised as the 'Australian Nat Gould', whose novels contain the Gould blend of sporting (usually racing) subject with elements of the detective story and the romance. Among other, but less well-known, racing novelists who briefly flourished were Leon Breaker, Robert Adam and Con Drew, while several popular novelists have written fiction either about racing, e.g. Ambrose Pratt, W.N. Willis, 'Smiler' Hales, or in which experiences both on or off the turf figure prominently, e.g. Jessie Couvreur in *In Her Earliest Youth* (1890). Racing scenes or subjects were common in the Australian melodramas of the second half of the nineteenth century and in many early Australian films.

The racing novel tradition of Gould was satirized in 'Done for the Double by Knott Gold', a story included in A.B. Paterson's *Three Elephant Power and Other Stories* (1917). Yet Paterson not only wrote a novel about racing, *The Shearer's Colt* (1936), to the Gould formula, but also is central to a second Australian literary tradition in which racing plays a significant part. Paterson is generally regarded as the leading literary balladist of his generation, and of all the *Bulletin*'s 'equestrian' balladists, who include Barcroft Boake, Will Ogilvie and 'Breaker' Morant, Paterson is the one who wrote most about horse sports, polo, as in 'The Geebung Polo Club', as well as racing. Many of his racing poems, e.g. 'Father Riley's Horse' (q.v.), 'How the Favourite Beat Us', are narratives which recount the plans for ill-gotten gain of dishonest racehorse owners, bookmakers or jockeys. Comic exaggeration, a rural setting and a sporting subject are common ingredients in these poems, which form part of an Australian tall story tradition which also accommodates the poems of 'Arthur Ferres' (J.W. Kevin) and Thomas E. Spencer, the cricket fantasies of Dal Stivens, and several Billy Borker racing yarns by Frank Hardy (q.v.). Elsewhere, Hardy is less amused about the social effects of racing. *The Four-legged Lottery* (1958) is an indictment of the effects of gambling on the individual and *Power Without Glory* (q.v., 1950) focuses on the network of corruption established by John West through his 'tote' and other gambling enterprises; gambling is also featured in Lawson Glassop's novel, *Lucky Palmer* (1949). The language of gambling has contributed significantly to Australian English, particularly in the area of informal usage, as also have racing and trotting generally: e.g. the colloquialism 'further behind than Walla Walla', meaning to be delayed or at a serious disadvantage, derives from the champion pacer of the 1930s, Walla Walla, which gave away starts of up to 260 metres behind the scratch mark. Similarly, the prominence of champions like Walla Walla or significant events in the history of the turf has produced a body of occasional verse on the subject of racing. This tradition seems to have its origins in the newspaper forecasts of the early racing tipsters of the 1840s and 1850s, although there is a racing description in Edward Kemp's satire, *A Voice from Tasmania* (1846). By the 1860s Adam Lindsay Gordon was predicting the result of the Melbourne Cup in verse narratives included in *Sea Spray and Smoke Drift* (1867). In subsequent years, racing disasters as well as triumphs have provided the occasion for comment. Two notable examples are the death of the champion hurdle jockey of the 1880s, Tommy Corrigan, which produced a tribute from Paterson, and the death of Phar Lap in the USA in 1932, which produced a series of sentimental eulogies.

If racing has made its contribution to Australian literature, the reverse has also happened. At the AJC's annual Expressway Stakes meeting, minor races are named after Australian poets, e.g. Adam Lindsay Gordon, 'Banjo' Paterson, Will Ogilvie, Mary Gilmore, Henry Kendall, Henry Lawson and Dorothea Mackellar.

TURNBULL, CLIVE (1906–75), born and educated in Tasmania, worked as a journalist on the staff of the *Mercury*, the *Argus* and the Melbourne *Herald*. His publications include two collections of verse, *Outside Looking In* (1933) and *14 Poems* (1944); several books

on Australian art; a history of the destruction of the Tasmanian Aborigines, *Black War* (1948); a biography, *Essington Lewis* (1963); a concise history of Australia (1965); and a number of biographical sketches of Australian personalities. These comprise *Bluestone* (James Brunton Stephens, 1945), *Mulberry Leaves* (Charles Whitehead, 1945), *Bonanza* (George F. Train, 1946), *Eureka* (Peter Lalor, 1946), *These Tears of Fire* (Francis Adams, 1948) and *Frontier* (Paddy Hannan, 1948). The sketches were combined as *Australian Lives* (1965).

TURNER, ALEXANDER FREDERICK (1907–), born England, came in 1925 to WA, where he worked as a bank officer in rural towns. He served in the AIF 1942–46, and subsequently worked for the ABC as drama and feature producer. Turner, whose career as a playwright for radio extended from the 1930s to the 1960s, won numerous awards for his radio and stage plays, including first prize in the 1939 Perth Drama Festival for his three-act play, *Royal Mail*. Several of his plays were published, *Hester Siding* (1937), which includes the stage plays, *Centurion, Not the Six Hundred, The Old Allegiance* and *One Hundred Guineas*, and the radio plays, *Hester Siding, All Stations, Strong Archer* and *Coat-of-Arms*, as well as some verse previously contributed to the *Western Mail* and the *Bulletin*; *Australian Stages* (1944), a verse play for radio; and *Royal Mail and Other Plays* (1944), which includes the radio plays, *Wheat Boat, Sea Power, In Thy Most Need* and *After Three*, and the stage play, *The Golden Journey*. Another of his radio plays, *Conglomerate*, is included in *Australian Radio Plays* (1946), ed. Leslie Rees. Turner's other plays include 'The Neighbours', 'Champion Bay', 'Westward Journey', 'I'm a Dutchman', 'Star at the Irwin', 'Flight from Granite' and 'Buccaneer Bay'. At first Turner wrote historical plays reflecting his English background, but he soon moved to dramas evocative of the WA landscape, such as *Hester Siding, Royal Mail* and *Conglomerate*, or of the Australian experience of war, such as *Wheat Boat*, 'The Neighbours', and 'Westward Journey'. Although his stage plays were successful, his understated, quiet, poetically-suggestive style was more suited to radio.

TURNER, ETHEL (1872–1958), was born in Yorkshire, the second child of G.W. Burwell, who died within two years of her birth. Her mother's second marriage was to Henry Turner, whose name was adopted by Ethel and her sister Lilian (see Lilian Turner) but who also died young. In 1880 Mrs Turner with her three daughters left for Sydney, where she married Charles Cope, a clerk in the NSW public service. While still in her teens Ethel, with her sister Lilian, edited a schoolgirls' magazine, *Iris*, which was superseded by the *Parthenon* and which stimulated her gift for children's fiction. Later she contributed to the *Bulletin* and, as 'Dame Durden', was responsible for the children's column of the *Illustrated Sydney News*, later incorporated in the *Australian Town and Country Journal*. Her best-known children's novel, *Seven Little Australians* (q.v.), was first published in 1894, followed by its sequel, *The Family at Misrule*, in 1895. *The Story of a Baby*, an adult novel, appeared the same year. By 1895 her reputation was well-established in Australia and her short stories were appearing regularly in Australian and English magazines. She continued to write after her marriage to the lawyer, H.R. Curlewis, later Judge Curlewis, in 1896 and eventually published twenty-seven full-length novels as well as numerous collections of short stories and anthologies of verse and fiction. Her other publications were *The Little Duchess* (1896), *The Little Larrikin* (1896), *Miss Bobbie* (1897), *The Camp at Wandinong* (1898), *Three Little Maids* (1900), *Gum Leaves* (1900), *The Wonder-Child* (1901), *Little Mother Meg* (1902), *Betty & Co.* (1903), *Mother's Little Girl* (1904), *A White Roof-Tree* (1905), *In the Mist of the Mountains* (1906), *The Stolen Voyage* (1907), *Happy Hearts* (1908), *That Girl* (1908), *Ethel Turner Birthday Book* (1909), *Fugitives from Fortune* (1909), *Fair Ines* (1910), *The Raft in the Bush* (1910), *The Tiny House* (1911), *Fifteen and Fair* (1911), *The Apple of Happiness* (1911), *An Ogre Up-to-date* (1911), *Ports and Happy Havens* (1912), *The Secret of the Sea* (1913), *Oh, Boys in Brown!* (1914), *Flower o' the Pine* (1914), *The Cub* (1915), *John of Daunt* (1916), *Captain Cub* (1917), *St Tom and the Dragon* (1918), *Brigid and the Cub* (1919), *Laughing Water* (1920), *King Anne* (1921), *Jennifer J.* (1922), *Nicola Silver* (1924), *The Ungardeners* (1925), *Funny* (1926) and *Judy and Punch* (1928). She also edited, with Bertram Stevens, *Australian Soldiers' Gift Book* (1918), and compiled, with Jean Curlewis (q.v.) her daughter, *The Sunshine Family: A Book of Nonsense for Girls and Boys* (1923). Selections from Ethel Turner's diaries 1889–1930, compiled by her granddaughter, Philippa Poole, were published in 1979.

Although Ethel Turner wrote mainly children's books, some of which such as *Seven Little Australians, The Family at Misrule, Miss Bobbie* and *Flower o' the Pine* are still read by children, she has also always attracted adult readers. Drawing on the tradition of domestic fiction established by such writers as Louisa M. Alcott and Charlotte Yonge, she invested her children's stories with specifically Australian, middle-class characteristics and values. The two

most successful of the group of novels dealing with the Woolcott family, *Seven Little Australians* and *The Family at Misrule*, are deliberately anti-heroic in tone, concerned with the activities of real children who have an engaging capacity for mischief and rebellion. The children of these novels, three sons and four daughters of an army officer who range from babyhood to young adulthood, undergo a multitude of experiences from punishments to bush picnics, love affairs to sicknesses; and both their daily, confused experience of the complicated process of growing and its overall, long-term nature are realistically expressed. All Ethel Turner's best novels show an understanding of children's interests, needs and anxieties, as well as an insight into the irritations, tension and joys of family relationships. Dealing mostly with large families and interested more in city life than in the outback, her novels frequently present parents as inadequate, negligent, tyrannical or simply absent, removed by death or separation; if trustworthy authority figures are lacking, however, the sustaining solidarity of the family emerges as a thoroughly adequate substitute. Two novels which deal in a particularly realistic and humorous way with the unheroic world of children are *The Little Larrikin* and *Miss Bobbie*; the former also reveals Ethel Turner's awareness of the hardships and evils of city life as well as her attitude to social injustice. Although she never equates money with gentility, she values good taste, education and cultivated attitudes, regarding a middle state of genteel comfort as the ideal environment, as *Fugitives from Fortune* most explicitly suggests. With the outbreak of the First World War her democratic and socialist inclinations become more pronounced; her three war novels, *The Cub, Captain Cub* and *Brigid and the Cub*, stress the disciplining effects of patriotic sacrifice on both men and women. Ethel Turner's range is limited and she has a tendency to lapse into sentimentality or melodrama, specially in her studies of older adolescents, but she has created some perennially authentic children, such as Judy, Meg, Pip and Bunty of *Seven Little Australians* and the madcap heroine of *Miss Bobbie*. Other qualities that are likely to make her best work durable are her humour, empathy with children and representative pictures of Australian middle-class life of the early twentieth century. Brenda Niall compares the fictional worlds of Ethel Turner and Mary Grant Bruce (q.v.) in *Seven Little Billabongs* (1979).

TURNER, GEORGE (1916–), born and educated in Melbourne, has become acknowledged not only as an important mainstream novelist but as Australia's best-known science fiction (q.v.) critic and a leading SF writer. In the Second World War he served in the Middle East, Africa and New Guinea. His first novel, *Young Man of Talent* (q.v., 1959), which was published the same year in New York with the title *Scobie*, was virtually unnoticed. His second, *A Stranger and Afraid* (1961), the first of a tetralogy set in a fictional small Victorian town called Treelake, also aroused little interest, although its successor, *The Cupboard under the Stairs* (1962), was widely acclaimed and shared the Miles Franklin Award for 1962. The remaining novels of the Treelake series are *A Waste of Shame* (1965) and *The Lame Dog Man* (1967). Turner's other novels are the science fiction trilogy, *Beloved Son* (1978), *Vaneglory* (1981) and *Yesterday's Men* (1982), and *Transit of Cassidy* (q.v., 1978), a mainstream novel which deals with the moral deterioration of a boxing champion. He has also edited a collection of science fiction stories, *The View from the Edge* (1977). Turner's Treelake series reveals him as a competent, conventional novelist with a flair for tailored plots, convincing characters and credible incidents. His main interest in the tetralogy is the interaction between the individual and his social environment and the effects the latter has on the psychiatric adjustment of the former. Jimmy Carlyon, the central character of *A Stranger and Afraid*, faces a moral struggle when, as district employment officer, he discovers some chicanery which also implicates his mother and other members of his family. Jimmy is also a minor character in *The Cupboard under the Stairs*, which turns mainly on the rehabilitation of Harry White after six years in a mental hospital. *A Waste of Shame* describes the self-destruction of another inhabitant of Treelake, the alcoholic carpenter, Joe Bryen. *The Lame Dog Man* returns to the fortunes of Jimmy Carlyon and Harry White with the addition of the strange destiny of an ex-convict, Teddy Johnson. In all the novels the town of Treelake exists more to provide links between the various identities than as a specifically realized entity. Turner's first novel, *Young Man of Talent*, a complex, dramatic study of a private struggle between antipathetic personalities against the background of war, is his most powerful and suggestive work. *Transit of Cassidy* shows a fine insight into adolescent experience and returns to the study of the corrosive effects of uncontrolled egoism.

TURNER, GEORGE WILLIAM, see Australian English

TURNER, HENRY GYLES (1831–1920), born London, emigrated to Victoria in 1854 and was for many years general manager of the Commercial Bank of Australasia. Well-known in Melbourne's literary circle, in 1875 he helpd

to found the *Melbourne Review*, which he subsequently edited with Alexander Sutherland. His publications include two histories, *A History of the Colony of Victoria, during the period 1797–1900* (1904) and *The First Decade of the Australian Commonwealth, during the period, 1901–10* (1911); an account of Eureka, *Our Own Little Rebellion* (1912); and, with Alexander Sutherland, *The Development of Australian Literature* (q.v., 1898).

TURNER, IAN (1922–78), born East Melbourne, had a variety of occupations including secretary of the Australasian Book Society and a turbulent political career before becoming an academic in 1964. At his death he was associate professor of history at Monash University. Active in the Australian labour movement, he wrote several books on its history; compiled *The Australian Dream* (1968), a historical collection of anticipations about Australia from the time of James Cook; and edited *Cinderella Dressed in Yella* (1969), a collection of lighthearted, irreverent children's rhymes. A fanatical follower of Australian Rules football, he was famous for his annual Ron Barassi Memorial lecture, instituted in 1967, and, with co-author Leonie Sandercock, wrote a history of the game, *Up Where, Cazaly?* (1981). After his death, friends made a selection of his essays and articles, *Room for Manoeuvre* (1982); a special number of *Overland* (October 1979) contains numerous tributes from writers and historians.

TURNER, LILIAN (1870–1956), born Yorkshire, England, came to Australia in 1881. With her better-known sister, Ethel Turner (q.v.), she edited the schoolgirl magazines *Iris* and *Parthenon* and similarly wrote extensively for children. Her first book, *The Lights of Sydney* (1896), won first prize in Cassell's novel competition in 1894, and she published a further twenty novels for children 1902–31 as well as a book of short stories, *Written Down* (1912). Her novels, written for the older teenager, reflect Australian middle-class life and concentrate on the experience of girls, particularly girls with a creative bent who have to struggle for recognition. Aware of hardship and injustice, she frequently portrays motherless families, as in *Betty the Scribe* (1906), *Three New Chum Girls* (1910) and *Anne Chooses Glory* (1928), and is adept at representing the tensions and changing relationships of family life.

TURNER, WALTER JAMES REDFERN (1889–1946), one of the best-known English Georgian poets, was born and educated in Melbourne. He left Australia at seventeen to study in Europe, served in the First World War, during which he published his first volume of poetry, *The Hunter and Other Poems* (1916), and subsequently became literary editor of the *Spectator*. Drama and music critic of other London newspapers, he was also a well-known member of London's literary circles. He published sixteen volumes of poetry, two plays, including the successful comedy, *The Man Who Ate the Popomack* (1922), and several critical works on music, painting and literature. He also published several comic, semi-autobiographical works of fiction, of which one, *Blow for Balloons* (1935) includes references to his Australian experience. Turner is the author of the familiar lines 'Chimboroso, Cotopaxi, They have stolen my heart away' often quoted in English verse anthologies.

Turtle Beach, see **D'ALPUGET, BLANCHE**

'TWAIN, MARK' (SAMUEL LANG-HORNE CLEMENS) (1835–1910), visited Australia in 1895 as part of a world lecture tour to recoup losses his publishing company had suffered; his route took him from Sydney to Melbourne, Adelaide, Ballarat, Bendigo and Tasmania. His *Following the Equator: A Journey around the World* (1897), published also as *More Tramps Abroad* (1897), includes the material republished in 1973 as *Mark Twain in Australia and New Zealand*; notable comments are the references to 'Ballarat English', which satirizes the elisions of Australian English, and the observation of the Melbourne Cup (q.v.) as a national ritual. Brian Kiernan's edition of contemporary short fiction, *The Most Beautiful Lies* (1977), also takes its title from Twain's *Following the Equator*.

XXI Poems, see **BRENNAN, C.J.**

Twenty Thousand Thieves, The, Eric Lambert's (q.v.) first novel, was published in 1951; Lambert arranged its publication himself, following the example of his then friend, Frank Hardy, with *Power Without Glory* (1950). A popular success informed by Lambert's experiences during the Second World War, *The Twenty Thousand Thieves* chronicles the experiences of an infantry battalion in the Middle East, notably their part in the defence of Tobruk and in the battle of El Alamein. The major character of the novel, its title deriving from a label given to the Allied forces by the broadcaster, Lord Haw Haw, is Dick Brett, one of the few survivors of the platoon on which *The Twenty Thousand Thieves* is focused; Brett's experiences parallel those of the author himself. While not ignoring the larrikin and racist sides of the ordinary Australian troops, the novel pays tribute to their courage and endurance in the face of the carnage and futility of war and incompetent officers like the drunken colonel, Fitzroy Orme.

'Two Boys at Grinder Bros', see **Aspinall, Arvie**

Two Fires, The (1955), a volume of poetry by Judith Wright (q.v.) written at the time of the Korean War, sees, in the title poem, mankind threatened by a nuclear holocaust. The poem reflects the uncertainty that worried people as they witnessed the brinkmanship of statesmen prepared to run unimaginable risks to achieve their objectives. Poems such as 'For Precision', 'The Man beneath the Tree' and 'Gum Trees Stripping' also show man baffled in his painstaking search for things that should come effortlessly, e.g. love and truth, and indicate that in the natural world there are modes of existence whose simplicity and completeness deflate the human ego.

TWOPENY, RICHARD (1857–1915), born Rutland, England, came to Australia in 1876 and joined the literary staff of the *South Australian Register*. In 1877 he left the *Register* and held a series of appointments connected with various great exhibitions, including those in Paris (1878), Sydney (1879) and Melbourne (1880 and 1888). He also managed private exhibitions in Adelaide and Perth (1881) and Christchurch (1882). He edited the *Telegraph* in Christchurch (1881–82), the *Daily Times* in Otago (1882–90), and in 1891, following the shearers' strike, was invited to found and edit the *Australian Pastoralists' Review*; he remained a proprietor of the newspaper until 1915. From 1896 he frequently made lengthy visits to Europe and England, where he died. Twopeny is best known for his observations on life in Adelaide, Sydney and Melbourne, *Town Life in Australia* (1883), a record that has been frequently used by later historians. Witty and urbane, Twopeny writes discerningly of regional differences within Australia and of differences between Australian and English society; topics that he discusses include houses, furniture, servants, food, dress, social relations, religion and morals, education, politics, business, amusements, newspapers and the state of Australian culture.

Two-up is an illegal gambling game in which coins are spun in the air and bets are won when the coins fall either as heads or as tails. Two-up, which seems to have emerged at the end of the nineteenth century, is regarded as Australia's national game and is traditionally played without prosecution of participants on Anzac Day. It has contributed a number of expressions to the idiom of Australian English, including 'Thommo''s, a famous two-up school in Sydney; 'come in on the grouter', to gain an unfair advantage, as when a two-up bet is withheld until a run of heads or tails seems likely to end; and 'come in spinner' (q.v.), the title of a novel by Dymphna Cusack and Florence James, originally the call which announces the tossing of the coins, now also a phrase deriding someone easily misled.

Twyborn Affair, The, a novel by Patrick White (q.v.), was published in 1979. Composed of three sections, it deals with an individual for whom sexuality is problematical. Eddie or E, the child of an eminent circuit judge, Judge Edward Twyborn and his wife Eadie, a lady with transvestite tendencies, has a male body and a female consciousness. In the first part of the novel E appears in her feminine aspect as Eudoxia Vatatzes, the young mistress of Angelos, an ageing Greek merchant from Smyrna with Byzantine imperial fantasies. The two are staying at a small French town, St Mayeul, and the time is February 1914. An Australian couple, E. Boyd ('Curly') Golson and his wife Joan, friends of the Twyborns, are also staying at St Mayeul. Joan, who has lesbian tendencies, becomes fascinated with Eudoxia and finally the threat of discovery forces the Vatatzes to leave. During their flight Angelos dies in a boarding-house, releasing Eudoxia from a relationship that had become oppressive. In the second phase of the novel E appears as Lieutenant Eddie Twyborn returning to Australia after the war, in which he has been decorated. He is reunited with his parents although they remain bewildered about the reasons for his previous sudden disappearance. Unable to establish frank links with them, he escapes by taking a job as jackeroo on a property, Bogong, owned by Greg Lushington. He makes a strong impression on everyone at Bogong: Greg Lushington feels a fatherly affection for him which he returns; Marcia, Greg's wife, takes him as her lover; Mrs Tyrrell, the manager's housekeeper, finds him as congenial as a daughter; Don Prouse, the manager, deserted husband and Marcia's ex-lover, depends on his sympathy and later responds to the latent homosexuality that Eddie's physique arouses in him. The most natural, authentic relationship seems to be the arranged marriage between an illiterate stockman, Denny Allen, and Dot, the unattractive daughter of a rabbiter, Dick Norton, who is also the incestuous father of her baby. Disillusioned by the sexual exploitation he finds in both male and female, Eddie disappears once more. Afterwards his mother learns in a letter from Marcia that her fourth son, which was possibly also Eddie's, had, like her previous three sons, died in infancy. After a gap of more than a decade, E appears as the middle-aged Eadith Trist, madam of a high-class brothel in London, partly financed by an aristocratic patron, Lord Gravenor. For Eadith, morality is a complexity that conventional attitudes cannot begin to comprehend. Gravenor loves Eadith passionately but their relationship is strained by her unwillingness to reveal the truth. Only after their last meeting when the war has intervened does she realize that he would love her 'in whatever form' she appeared. She receives news that her father is dead, learns that her mother is in London and is affectionately united with her, despite her change in sex. Persuaded by her mother to return home to Australia, she resumes her role as Eddie and hands the brothel over to Eadith's housekeeper/confidant. On the way to his mother Eddie dies in a bombing raid which also destroys the hotel where his mother is staying.

Tyranny of Distance, The, see **BLAINEY, GEOFFREY**

TYRRELL, JAMES (1875–1961), born Sydney, lived as a boy at Balmain, where his father kept refreshment rooms. In 1888 Tyrrell joined the bookselling firm of Angus & Robertson and progressed from errand-boy to manager before he left to found his own shop in 1905. He moved to Adelaide to open another bookselling business in 1910 but in 1914 returned to Sydney, where he joined J.F. Archibald in a publishing venture, Tyrrells Ltd, and founded his famous second-hand bookshop. Frequented by most of Sydney's writers and literary identities, the shop is celebrated in such poems as Henry Lawson's 'The Song of Tyrrell's Bell', Roderic Quinn's 'Tyrrell's Bookshop' and Kenneth Slessor's 'In Tyrrell's Bookshop'. Tyrrell's memoirs, *Old Books, Old Friends, Old Sydney* (1952), which include his boyhood reminiscences of Sydney and his recollections of numerous identities of the book world, are an invaluable record of Sydney's social and cultural scene in the 1890s. Individuals he recalls include the booksellers, the George Robertsons of Melbourne and Sydney, David Angus and William Dymock; the writers Henry Lawson, J.F. Archibald, C.J. Dennis, Victor Daley, Norman Lindsay and A.B. Paterson; the public figures Sir Henry Parkes, W.M. Hughes, Sir William Dixson and Cardinal Moran; and the book collector David Scott Mitchell, with whom he had frequent dealings. Tyrrell also published a compilation of Australian Aboriginal place-names (1933), a reminiscence of David Scott Mitchell (1936), and *Postscript: Further Bookselling Reminiscences* (1957), which includes the poems of James Lionel Michael as transcribed by Henry Kendall.

TYSON, JAMES (1819–98), born Narellan, NSW, was a famous pioneer pastoralist who made money as a butcher on the Bendigo goldfields in the 1850s and then bought large properties in the Deniliquin area of south-western NSW. He eventually owned more than two million hectares of land in NSW, Victoria and Queensland. A bachelor whose frugality was a by word in the outback, Tyson was nick-named 'Hungry' Tyson by the *Bulletin*; he was, however, a major benefactor of the Women's College at the University of Sydney and of the University as a whole. He is the model for Abstinens Levison in 'Rolf Boldrewood''s *A Colonial Reformer* (1890) and is commemorated in A.B. Paterson's poem, 'T.Y.S.O.N'.

U

ULLATHORNE, WILLIAM BERNARD (1806–89), born Yorkshire, England, was or-dained in 1831 and came in 1833 to Sydney, where for the next decade he was actively involved in the development of Catholicism in Australia. A fervent opponent of transportation (q.v.), he wrote *The Horrors of Transportation* (1838) and other polemical works, gave evidence before the British parliamentary inquiry into transportation in 1838, and influenced later writers about the convict system. These included 'Price Warung', who presented Ulla-thorne sympathetically as Nellathorne in several of his early stories. Ullathorne's autobiography, written in 1867 and dealing largely with his work in Australia, was published in 1891 in an expurgated form and in 1941 from the original draft, edited by Shane Leslie and titled *From Cabin-Boy to Archbishop*. A biography by Cuthbert Butler, *The Life & Times of Bishop Ullathorne, 1806–1889*, was published in 1926.

Ultima Thule, see *Fortunes of Richard Mahony, The*

UNAIPON, DAVID (1873–1967), the first Aboriginal writer to have a book published in Australia, was born at the Point McLeay mission in the Tailem Bend area of the Murray River. He was educated at the mission school and then spent most of his life in Adelaide, where he was encouraged in his writing and work for his people by the Aborigines' Friends' Association; he was awarded the Coronation Medal in 1953. Unaipon's chief work, *Native Legends* (1929), written in an elevated and somewhat archaic style, contains two stories, 'The Release of the Dragon Flies by the Fairy Sun Beam' and 'Youn Goona the Cockatoo', with two short pieces which provide some an-thropological and mythological background to the legends, and a longer piece 'Hungarrda: Jew Lizard'. The Christian virtues and values that are illustrated in Unaipon's legends are shown to be similar to Aboriginal values.

Uncle Piper of Piper's Hill, a novel by Jessie Couvreur (q.v.) published under her pseudo-nym, 'Tasma', was serialized as 'The Pipers of Piper's Hill' in the *Australasian* 1888, and published in book form a year later. Set on board an emigrant ship, in 1860s Melbourne and in up-country Barnesbury, a fictional por-trait of Malmsbury, where Couvreur lived after her marriage, the novel opens with the genteel but impoverished Mr Cavendish unwillingly en route to Australia with his wife and two daugh-ters, Sara and Margaret, where they are to join Mrs Cavendish's brother, Tom Piper, who has prospered in Australia after beginning as a butcher; also on board to take up a colonial ministry is the Reverend Francis Lidiat, whose widowed mother had emigrated to Australia, become the second Mrs Piper, but died less than a year later in childbirth. In Melbourne awaiting with Piper the arrival of the Cavendish family are George, a son by Piper's first mar-riage; Laura, his stepdaughter, Lidiat's sister; and Louisa, his daughter by the second mar-riage. George is in love with Laura but Piper warns him that he will be disinherited if their marriage takes place. On arrival in Melbourne, Lidiat's connection with the Pipers is discovered and he becomes a regular visitor at Piper's Hill, where the Cavendishes take up residence. The novel records the relationship between the two families, including Laura's rivalry with Sara, her equal in beauty, and Cavendish's dislike of the Piper patronage. Long in love with the wilful Sara though beloved by the plainer Margaret, Lidiat proposes marriage just before leaving for his Barnesbury parish; Sara rejects this proposal but accepts a second one after Piper tells the profligate George that his debts will only be paid on condition that he gives up gambling and marries one of the Cavendish sisters. Sara rethinks her acceptance when subject to a third proposal, this time from Reginald Hyde, a visiting heir to a baronetcy, and suitable pairings are effected in the aftermath of a crisis at Barnesbury, where Louisa is gravely injured while on a visit to Lidiat and Laura. Margaret's devoted nursing of Louisa opens Lidiat's eyes to her virtues, and Laura and George are reconciled after Piper withdraws his objections as a consequence of Louisa's recovery. Only Sara, her engagement to Hyde now also behind her, remains unmarried at the end of the novel.

Uncle Piper of Piper's Hill won wide praise at the time of publication, and was compared with *His Natural Life* (1874) and *Robbery Under Arms* (1888). It was subsequently criticized for the novelistic resolution of its plot and for its lack of 'Australianness', although the desiccated Cavendish is more 'Tasma''s target than the opinionated and authoritarian Piper. It remains an important early urban novel which is enlivened by the strength of its characterization, particularly the title character and his sister, and its wryly satiric observation of middle-class life.

'Uncultured Rhymer to His Cultured Critics, The' was a strongly-worded verse rebuke by Henry Lawson (q.v.) to university-trained critics of his work; it was first published in the *Bulletin* in 1897. The target seems to have been Lawson's friend, J. le Gay Brereton, although Lawson managed to convince Brereton, as Brereton's chapter in *Henry Lawson by His Mates* (1931) confirms, that he had been provoked by a review written by E.E. Morris.

Under Aldebaran (1946), the first volume of poetry published by James McAuley (q.v.), is a mixture of introspective and philosophical poems which represent, in Vincent Buckley's words, 'an affirmation of the values which give real life and real stability to society'. One of the chief poems in the volume is 'The Blue Horses', which is inscribed in honour of Franz Marc, one of the founders of the Blue Rider expressionist movement in Germany and creator of the famous painting, *The Tower of the Blue Horses*; the poem seeks to find in art a panacea for the 'malice, fraud and guile' of the modern world 'gone bad' as well as an escape for the individual to 'spaces infinite'. 'The Incarnation of Sirius' is a warning that the forces of revolution bring, not the desired changes,

but a 'bloody and aborted' vision, a world of bestiality and chaos; 'Henry the Navigator' praises men of foresight and courage who, like the Portuguese prince who 'saw no distant seas, yet guided ships', are vital to the realization of mankind's full potential; and 'The Family of Love' reflects McAuley's own incertitude and inner turmoil. Other notable poems of the volume are the epithalamium, 'Celebration of Love', and the trio, 'Terra Australis', 'Envoi', and 'The True Discovery of Australia'; the last reflects McAuley's frustration with Australian attitudes ('the faint sterility that disheartens and derides') yet his indissoluble link with the environment ('there you come home').

Under Capricorn, see **SIMPSON, HELEN**

'Union Buries Its Dead, The', a widely-anthologized story by Henry Lawson (q.v.), was written in 1893. The story, which chronicles the funeral procession and burial service for a young unionist who has drowned in the Darling River, has been cited as evidence of mateship (q.v.) among outback workers of the 1890s, but the flatness of the prose and the grim, ironic tone of the narrator establish 'The Union Buries Its Dead' as one of Lawson's most pessimistic, even nihilistic, pictures of bush life.

University of New South Wales Drama Foundation was established in 1965 in association with the Australian Elizabethan Theatre Trust (q.v.). The purpose of the Foundation was to promote the practice and study of the theatre arts in NSW, particularly through the drama organizations at the University, such as the National Institute of Dramatic Art (NIDA) and the Jane Street Theatre (qq.v.), and to administer funds for this purpose.

University Presses. There are two types of university presses in Australia. The first comprises the scholarly presses established by several Australian universities: Melbourne University Press (MUP, established 1922), University of Queensland Press (UQP, 1948), University of Western Australia Press (1954), New South Wales University Press (1961), Sydney University Press (1964), Australian National University Press (1966) and Deakin University Press (1980). These presses form the membership of the Association of Australian University Presses (established 1965), which publishes annually *Scholarly Books in Australia*; some of them evolved from a publications unit within the university (e.g. the ANU Press from the university's publication section, established in 1964). Within all Australian universities there are departments or organizations which publish material independently of the university presses, e.g. the Department of English, University of Queensland, which has published *Australian Literary Studies* since 1979, the University of Tasmania Library, and the Centre for Research in New Literatures in English (CRNLE) at Flinders University.

The second type of university press comprises the Australian branch of an overseas university press. The major example of this type is the Australian branch of Oxford University Press (OUP). In 1890 E.R. Bartholomew established an Oxford presence in Australia with biennial selling trips as representative of OUP, Hodder & Stoughton and other firms; in 1908 an OUP office was opened in Melbourne, with Bartholomew as manager until 1922, when he was succeeded by his son, E.E. Bartholomew (1922–49). Although Australian books, e.g. F.M. Robb's edition of Adam Lindsay Gordon, were published by OUP in London as early as 1912, and from the 1930s OUP published and printed educational books in Australia, it was not until after the Second World War that the Australian branch changed its orientation from sales to publishing. Frank Eyre, managing editor of the Australian branch of OUP 1950–75, has recorded its history in *Oxford in Australia 1890–1978* (1978).

Although all university presses in Australia publish scholarly, educational and more general books in a range of disciplines, they have each developed particular strengths and traditions, e.g. UQP in contemporary fiction and poetry, MUP in biography, the University of Western Australia Press in regional history, the ANU Press in Aboriginal and New Guinea studies, OUP in children's literature, lexicography, Australian history and Pacific studies. Roger McDonald (editor UQP, 1969–76), Frank Wilmot (manager MUP, 1932–42), Peter Ryan (director MUP, 1962–) and Eyre are university press employees significant in Australian literary and publishing history. Significant Australian literature series emanating from the university presses include UQP's Paperback Poets, Poets on Record and Portable Australian Authors, Sydney University Press's Australian Literary Reprints, and OUP's Australian Writers and Their Work and Australian Bibliographies.

Unknown Industrial Prisoner, The, a novel by David Ireland (q.v.), was published in 1971, and won the Miles Franklin Award. Reminiscent of the work of Gogol and Solzhenitsyn, it deals with the dehumanizing life of a vast oil refinery owned by a multi-national company called Puroil. A comprehensive representation of men caught up in a ruthless but inane system, compared to a termitary in its activity, the novel exposes the company's reliance on incompetence, avarice, self-seeking and subservience. By using a fragmented narrative structure and a multiplicity of individual perspectives, Ireland builds up an impression of a collective experience in which work and slavery are equated. Sobriquets for the characters such as the Enforcer, the Python, the Garfish and the Good Shepherd heighten the sense of confinement within work roles. The attitudes and experiences of three more fully-developed characters structure the narrative. They include the violent and confused Glass Canoe, who futilely seeks to live within the system and win its rewards; the Great White Father, who offers the workers the reliefs of alcohol and sex in his haven in the mangroves called Home Beautiful; and the Samurai, a complex figure who pursues a pattern of dedication that he finds difficult to define and justify. Although disaffection with the system is widespread, the final explosions that rock Puroil are not the result of a planned rebellion, but a haphazard amalgam of individual resentments.

Unspoken Thoughts, a volume of poems by Ada Cambridge (q.v.), was published anonymously in 1887 but withdrawn by her soon after publication; the exact reason has never been revealed, although clearly the poems which discuss religious uncertainty, e.g. the long opening poem, 'The Shadow'; sexuality, e.g. 'The Physical Conscience', 'A Wife's Protest'; and marriage, e.g. 'An Answer', 'The Fallen', might have embarrassed or offended her clergyman husband, George Cross. The later volume of poems, *The Hand in the Dark* (1913), excludes such poems and is more conventional in subject, although still informed by Cambridge's passionate concern for the underprivileged. *Unspoken Thoughts* came at a time of physical and mental stress in Cambridge's life and marks a point in her writing after which her novels take a more critical attitude towards the marriage question and social issues.

Up the Country, see 'BRENT OF BIN BIN'

UPFIELD, ARTHUR (1892–1964), born Gosport, England, arrived in Australia at about the age of eighteen, largely through the insistence of his draper parents, who were convinced that he had no intention of settling to the conventional white collar career they had planned for him. He was immediately attracted to the outback, following a variety of itinerant occupations including mule-team driver, boundary rider, opal digger, shearer, seasonal fruit-picker, and fencer. After four years in the AIF in the First World War, he resumed his nomadic outback life and began writing. His first novel, *The House of Cain*, appeared in 1928. Between then and his death he published thirty-two novels; for the last twenty-five years of his life he was able to support himself and his family solely by his writing, largely because of the popularity of his books in the USA, where he was the first foreign writer admitted as a full member of the Mystery Writers' Guild of America. Many of his novels, such as *The House of Cain*, *The Barrakee Mystery* (1929), *The Sands of Windee* (1931) and *A Royal Abduction* (1932), belong to the 'thriller' category but he includes more substantial themes in works such as *Gripped by Drought* (1932), which gives an account of the effects of a prolonged drought in western NSW; *The Widows of Broome* (1950), which deals with the death throes of the pearling industry in north-west Australia; *Death of a Lake* (1954), which is set against the effect on the environment of a lake drying up in north-western NSW; and *The Will of the Tribe* (1962), which examines contemporary racial attitudes. The background to his novels – bush lore, Aboriginal customs, the landscape, outback camaraderie – has been acclaimed more than his slow-moving plots and unexceptional prose style. Upfield's chief literary creation, and a major reason for the success of his books, is the part-Aboriginal detective-inspector Napoleon Bonaparte, usually referred to as 'Bony',

who first emerges in *The Barrakee Mystery* and is featured in most of the later novels. Bony combines the mystic intuitiveness of his Aboriginal mother with the sophisticated intelligence of his white father. Bony, based according to Jessica Hawke's *Follow My Dust!* (1957) on a well-educated part-Aboriginal Queensland tracker, Leon Wood, has been an extremely popular creation, for some readers rivalling Sherlock Holmes.

UREN, MALCOLM (1900–73), born Adelaide, moved to Perth as a boy. He worked for some years on the literary staff of the *West Australian*, served as a war correspondent during the Second World War, and was a newspaper executive with the *West Australian* group 1953–65. He also edited the *Western Mail* (1941–53), the *Broadcaster* (1942–52) and *Milady* (1948–52). He wrote numerous local histories as well as an original account of the *Batavia* wreck, *Sailormen's Ghosts* (1940); with Robert Stephens, a biography of Edward John Eyre, *Waterless Horizons* (1941); an account of Governor James Stirling, *Land Looking West* (1948); and a history of the WA goldfields, *Glint of Gold* (1948).

V

'VAGABOND, THE', see *Vagabond Papers, The*; JAMES, JOHN STANLEY

VALLIS, VAL (1916–   ), born Gladstone, Queensland, served with the AIF 1941–46, spent some time in New Guinea and taught at the University of Queensland from 1950. His poetry has appeared in two collections, *Songs of the East Coast* (1947) and *Dark Wind Blowing* (1961). He also edited, with R.S. Byrnes, *The Queensland Centenary Anthology* (1959), and, with Judith Wright, *Witnesses of Spring* (1970) by Shaw Neilson.

Van Diemen's Land was the name originally given to Tasmania in 1642 by its discoverer, Abel Tasman, in honour of the governor-general of the Dutch East Indies, Anthony Van Diemen. Although the name Tasmania was in use for the colony by the 1840s, it was not until 26 November 1855 that the new designation was officially proclaimed, principally be-

cause of the association between 'Van Diemen's Land' and convictism. 'Van Diemen's Land', used in numerous early geographical historical, descriptive and autobiographical works e.g. G.W. Evans, *A Geographical, Historical, and Topographical Description of Van Diemen's Land* (1822), was the title of 'W.T. Moncrieff''s 1830 London play, and of a well-known Irish street ballad, also regarded as an Australian folk-song (q.v.), in which a poacher laments the rigours of his life as a convict in Van Diemen's Land. The term is also the source of the word 'Vandemonian' which was applied to Tasmanians for much of the nineteenth century, and was particularly used in reference to ex-convicts from the island.

Van Diemen's Land, one of the earliest plays about Australia, was written by 'William Thomas Moncrieff' (q.v.) and first performed in London in 1830 to celebrate the arrival in Australia of William Gore Elliston and his brother. A four-act extravaganza, the play focuses on the experiences of the new settler, John Hardy, and the romantic entanglements of his children, John, who meets again his sweetheart Eliza, wrongly transported for stealing from the family home, and Amelia, who marries the 'new chum' settler, James Gooseberry. Eliza's innocence is established during the climax to the play, when Hardy is attacked by bushrangers and assisted by friendly Aborigines. In writing *Van Diemen's Land*, 'Moncrieff' exploited the reputation of Bennilong, Michael Howe, James Hardy Vaux and Ikey Solomon, who all appear as characters, often in situations which bear no resemblance to historical experience. Among other points of interest are the songs, e.g. 'The Lincolnshire Poacher', 'The Ram of Derby', which make up one of the play's several elements, and the favourable pictures presented of the Aborigines, e.g. in the marriage between Bennilong's sister, Kangaree, and Gooseberry's servant, Darby Ballylaggin.

Van Diemen's Land Gazette and General Advertiser, one of the first Australian newspapers, was published in Hobart Town in 1814. Andrew Bent assisted George Clark in the production of the newspaper.

Van Diemen's Land Monthly Magazine, see ROSS, JAMES

Van Diemen's Land Warriors: Or, the Heroes of Cornwall, The, the first book of Tasmanian verse, was published in 1827. A satire on the ineffectual attempts to capture the bushranger, Matthew Brady, it narrates the misadventures of a group of citizens who, contemptuous of the failure of Governor Arthur (q.v.) and his soldiers to capture Brady, decide to do the job themselves. In the first of the poem's three cantos, each of ten tradesmen displays his bravado in punning couplets applicable to his trade. In the second, the Tailor is elected leader and the party sets out, but has to retrace its steps when it is discovered that the gunpowder has been forgotten; when they start again and stumble across what they think to be the gang, they flee in fright. In the final canto, Snip explains that he has run away to cover the gang's retreat; they return and discharge their firearms, only to discover that the 'gang' is a herd of donkeys. The noise awakens two soldiers, who arrest Snip and his associates on suspicion that they are the bushrangers; released by a magistrate, they eventually meet Brady, who has them all flogged, relieves them of their trousers and forces them to return in shame to their homes. *The Van Diemen's Land Warriors* is a rare work, possibly because it was

suppressed. Its author, 'Pindar Juvenal', has been tentatively identified as Robert Wales, an officer of the Tasmanian courts.

Varnek, Neda, see *Golconda Trilogy*

Vashti's Voice, see Feminism and Australian Literature

Vatatzes, Eudoxia, see *Twyborn Affair, The*

VAUX, JAMES HARDY (1782–?), born Surrey, England, was transported for theft and in 1801 arrived in Sydney, where he worked as a clerk. Despite a term of trouble following his forgery of Governor King's initials, he ingratiated himself with the chaplain and magistrate, Samuel Marsden, and with King, who took him back to England in 1807. Vaux, however, became insubordinate after his sentence expired and deserted once the ship reached Portsmouth. Convicted again of theft in 1809, he was again transported and reached Sydney in 1810. In 1811 he was sentenced to twelve months' hard labour for receiving property stolen from the judge-advocate, Ellis Bent, and sent to the Newcastle penal settlement. In January 1814 he attempted to escape from the Colony, but was recaptured and returned to Newcastle. At Newcastle he wrote a slang dictionary included in his autobiography, *Memoirs of James Hardy Vaux*. The manuscript came into the hands of Barron Field, who arranged for its publication in 1819. Vaux's life continued to be as colourful as his *Memoirs*; he received a conditional pardon in 1820, the terms of which he broke in 1829, when he absconded from his employment. He went to Ireland, where he was convicted in August 1830 under the alias 'James Young' for passing forged bank notes. Transported again to Sydney, he arrived in May 1831, was recognized and sent to Port Macquarie penal settlement. In 1837 he was allowed to return to Sydney and although he was soon in further trouble and was sentenced to two years' imprisonment, he was released in 1841 and disappeared thereafter from public notice. During his career Vaux also married three times, probably bigamously. His *Memoirs*, the first full-length autobiography written in Australia, presents a fascinating, graphic picture of London's underworld; his flash vocabulary, the first dictionary compiled in Australia and a valuable glossary of London slang, has been frequently used by subsequent lexicographers of Australian English (q.v.). Vaux's life has also been the subject of drama: he appears in 'W.T. Moncrieff''s (q.v.) play, *Van Diemen's Land* (1830) and is the subject of Ron Blair's ballad opera, 'Flash Jim Vaux' (1971).

VENNARD, ALEXANDER VINDEX ('BILL BOWYANG', 'FRANK REID') (1884–1947), born Winton, Queensland, became correspondent for the *N.Q. Register*, Townsville, and the *Bowen Independent*. He published a series of booklets of bush ballads and recitations 1932–40 as 'Bill Bowyang' with such titles as *Australian Bush Recitations, Bill Bowyang's Bush Recitations* and *Old Bush Recitations Collected by Bill Bowyang*. As 'Frank Reid' he also wrote *The Fighting Cameliers* (1934) and *Toilers of the Reef* (1925), a book for children.

Venture: An Australian Literary Quarterly, edited by Rex Ingamells (q.v.), appeared for one issue only (July 1937) and was superseded by *Venture: Jindyworobak Quarterly Pamphlet* (1939–40). Ingamells's 1937 editorial, titled 'Concerning Environmental Values', was published in 1938 as part of his book, *Conditional Culture. Venture* included poetry, short stories and articles from such contributors as Leonard Mann, Max Harris, Victor Kennedy, Flexmore Hudson and Garry Lyle.

Venus Half-Caste, see **MANN, LEONARD**

Vernacular Republic, The, see **MURRAY, LES**

VERNON, BARBARA (?–1978), spent her early life at Inverell in northern NSW, apart from a period of service in the WAAAF during the Second World War. In 1959 she moved to Sydney, where she worked for several years as a freelance writer and then joined the ABC drama department, first in radio and then as a television script editor. A prolific author, she wrote radio and television plays, features, revue sketches, stage plays and children's plays. One of her stage plays, *The Multi-Coloured Umbrella*, published in *Theatregoer* (1961), won second prize in the Sydney Journalists' Club competition of 1956 and was subsequently widely produced. Her other published plays are *The Passionate Pianist* (1958), which forms part of a trilogy, *The Growing Year*, and includes 'The Bishop and the Boxer' and 'First Love'; and *King Tide Running*, written with Bruce Beaver and included in *Australian One-Act Plays: Book Three* (1967), ed. Musgrave Horner. Her other plays include 'Enough to Make a Pair of Sailor's Trousers', 'The Questing Heart', 'Naked Possum', 'Dusty Frangipanni' or 'No Picnic Tomorrow', 'Lancelot and the Lady', 'The Loquat Tree' and 'Silver Bells and Cockle Shells', and the children's plays, 'The Sleeping Planet', 'Theseus and the Minotaur', 'Hullaballo Belay!' and, with Bec Robinson, 'Swords to the Rescue'. In 1967 Vernon originated and

planned the popular television serial of the 1960s and 1970s, *Bellbird*, and subsequently published the novels, *Bellbird: The Story of a Country Town* (1970), which is based on the first twenty episodes, and *A Big Day at Bellbird* (1972), part of which was used as the script for the film, *Country Town* (1971). She also contributed to another popular television serial of the 1970s, *Certain Women*.

Verse, a bi-monthly poetry magazine published in Melbourne and edited by Louis Lavater (q.v.), succeeded the *Spinner* (q.v.) and appeared 1929–33. Although *Verse* generally published poetry that was conventional and nondescript, the magazine also attracted such contributors as 'Furnley Maurice', Frederick Macartney, Mary Gilmore, Paul Hasluck, R.H. Croll and Hal Porter.

Verses Popular and Humorous, Henry Lawson's (q.v.) second book of verse, was published in 1900, just before his departure for London. The volume included early work such as 'The Captain of the Push', and 'The Grog-an'-Grumble Steeplechase', a parody of A.B. Paterson, but most of the poems, e.g. 'The Lights of Cobb and Co.', 'The New Chum Jackaroo', 'The Uncultured Rhymer to His Cultured Critics' and 'Reedy River', had been written after the publication of Lawson's *In the Days When the World Was Wide* (1896). *Verses Popular and Humorous* was reissued several times in two parts, *Popular Verses* and *Humorous Verses*, although in the volumes published under those two titles in 1924 the selection and arrangements are significantly different.

VICKERS, BERT (1903–), born Oldbury, England, came to Australia in 1925 and worked in a variety of jobs, cook's rouseabout, shearer's cook, woolclasser and general hand, in the WA wheatbelt. After an accident while he was in the Army he occupied his time in hospital by taking a course in journalism conducted by Alan Marshall. Encouraged to write fiction by Marshall, Vickers had almost immediate success, a manuscript novel, *First Place to the Stranger*, winning a *Sydney Morning Herald* award in 1946. In spite of its success, the unpretentious but authentic account of the experiences of a young urban immigrant in the Australian bush was not published until 1956. Vickers's best novel, *The Mirage* (1955), based on the life and prospects of part-Aboriginals, is both convincing social documentary and effective fiction. His other works include *Though Poppies Grow* (1958), an account of the erosion by corruption, privilege and a growing class-consciousness, of the traditional Australian values of mateship and a 'fair go'; *No Man Is*

Himself (1970), a story of the human problems associated with life in the isolated outback as well as a further indictment of white treatment of the Aborigines; and *Without Map or Compass* (1974) and *A Stranger No Longer* (1977), two largely autobiographical works.

Vickers, Sylvia, see *His Natural Life*

Victoria, the smallest (just over 227 000 square kilometres) mainland Australian State but second only to New South Wales in population, comprises the south-eastern corner of the Australian continent and is bordered by New South Wales in the north and South Australia in the west. Originally part of New South Wales, it was known as the Port Phillip District (q.v.) until its separation in 1851 from New South Wales, with which it shares the Murray River as a border. It remained the British colony of Victoria until its incorporation in the Commonwealth of Australia in 1901. Victoria was briefly settled in 1803–04 by a party under David Collins (q.v.), and in 1826–28 the explorers Hamilton Hume and William Hovell reached Port Phillip Bay, on which the present capital, Melbourne, stands. Permanent settlement began in the middle 1830s, when John Batman and John Pascoe Fawkner (qq.v.) independently established themselves at Port Phillip, and the Hentys (q.v.) also crossed from Van Diemen's Land to settle further west at Portland Bay. After T.L. Mitchell (q.v.) reached Portland Bay overland from New South Wales in 1836, the 'Australia Felix' part of Victoria was quickly settled by squatters, who included the novelist, 'Rolf Boldrewood'. Victoria made rapid progress after the discovery of gold, and for a period in the 1880s, the heyday of 'Marvellous Melbourne' (q.v.), was the most populous Australian colony. The progress of Victoria in the decades following the discovery of gold is an important theme in 'Henry Handel Richardson''s massive trilogy, *The Fortunes of Richard Mahony* (1930).

Victorian: A Weekly Journal of Politics, Literature, Irish and Catholic Intelligence, Colonial, Foreign and General Information, published in Melbourne 1862–64, was edited by Daniel Deniehy and included poetry and prose, book reviews and theatrical notices. Contributors included Charles Harpur and R.H. Horne.

Victorian Review, a monthly magazine published in Melbourne 1879–86, was edited by H. Mortimer Franklyn. The magazine, which included literary articles, verse and fiction as well as discussions of current affairs, attracted a wide range of notable contributors, including Marcus Clarke, Catherine Helen Spence, E.E. Morris, G.B. Barton, Jessie Couvreur, Victor Daley, David Blair, Francis Adams, Edmund Finn and 'Mark Twain'. An earlier *Victorian Review* was published weekly 1860–61, and included R.H. Horne, James Smith and Charles Whitehead as contributors.

VIDAL, MARY THERESA (1815–69), born Devon, England, came to Australia with her husband in 1840 but returned to England in 1845. Her popular book, *Tales for the Bush*, first published in Sydney in 1845, has little to do with Australia. It is a series of brief, morally-edifying stories intended to instil a proper sense of Christian duty into servants and other members of the lower social classes. She also wrote *Cabramatta, and Woodleigh Farm* (1850), only the first part of which, the story 'The Cabramatta Store,' is concerned with Australia. It is set in the Nepean district of NSW and deals mainly with the minutiae of domestic life of the day, although it features some of the stock ingredients of pioneer life such as bushrangers, droughts, floods and bushfires. Her only other Australian-centred work, the novel *Bengala: Or, Some Time Ago* (1860), is set in a fictitious township, probably Penrith, NSW, where her husband ministered. *Bengala* uses the domestic and community concerns of a small colonial rural society to frame a melodramatic and romantic tale. One of the earliest women fiction writers in Australia, Mary Theresa Vidal is linked by her grandmother to the famous English portrait artist, Joshua Reynolds. Her granddaughter was the novelist Faith Compton Mackenzie, in whose autobiography, *As Much As I Dare* (1935), Vidal briefly figures.

VIDLER, E.A. (EDWARD ALEXANDER) (1863–1942), born London, where he worked in publishing, arrived in Melbourne in 1888. He edited the *Evening News* in Geelong and the *Tatler* and the *Spinner* in Melbourne; he also wrote several art monographs and books for children and edited *The Adam Lindsay Gordon Memorial Volume* (1926), *Art and Letters: Hassell's Australian Miscellany* 1921–22 (1922) and, as 'Paul Vedder', the *Dramatic Year* (1886–87). An enthusiast of Australian drama, he wrote two plays, a verse-drama, *The Rose of Ravenna* (1913) and *Pan Calls* (1926) in the series, *Australian Repertory Plays*, which he published 1925–28.

View*, see *Vista

***Viewpoint*, see Australian Writers Guild**

VIIDIKAS, VICKI (1948–), born Sydney of an Australian mother and Estonian father, left school at fifteen and worked in various occasional jobs. At sixteen she began writing poetry for reasons she termed 'therapeutic' and 'confessional', and had her first poem, 'At East Balmain', published when she was nineteen. She has published two books of verse, *Condition Red* (1973) and *Knäbel* (1978), and a volume of short prose, *Wrappings* (1974). As a result of several prolonged visits to India and the East she became interested in Indian life and the Hindu religion, an interest that is reflected in *Knäbel* and *Wrappings*.

Viidikas's aim in both poetry and prose has been to write about the realities, as she sees them, of those subcultures that conventional society regards as abnormal – drugs, crime, sexual deviance, non-conformism in general. Such subcultures are illustrated in *Wrappings*, a volume of thirty-one prose pieces, many of which are too brief to be accessible. Of the longer, particularly effective stories, 'The Snowman in the Dutch Masterpiece' describes a barren, drug-and-alcohol-filled affair in a lush apartment, and in 'The Silk Trousers', a conventional Australian girl tourist almost succumbs to the mystery of India in the guise of a repulsive monkey man. The poems of *Condition Red* and *Knäbel* are written mainly from her female experiences of love and sexuality. In her search for authenticity Viidikas has insisted that the spontaneity and immediacy of emotion, however chaotic and disturbed, should be reflected in the poetic form.

Village Hampden, The, see SCHLUNKE, ERIC OTTO

VILLIERS, ALAN (1903–82), a well-known sailor and author of more than thirty books on maritime history and affairs, was born in Melbourne. His father, Leon Joseph Villiers, was a union organizer and writer, whose poems were published in the *Bulletin*. On the staff of the Hobart *Mercury* 1924-29 Villiers combined sailing voyages of all descriptions and journalism until the Second World War, when he served in the Royal Navy; from the 1930s he was mainly resident in England. Villiers's best-known maritime adventures include his voyages in the Danish schoolship *Joseph Conrad* (1934–36), the barque *Parma* (1931) and the *Mayflower* replica (1956). He also commanded square-rigged ships for such films as *Moby Dick* (1955), *Billy Budd* (1961) and *Hawaii* (1965). Villiers published several narratives of personal voyages, such as *Falmouth for Orders* (1928), *Voyage of the 'Parma'* (1933), *Sons of Sinbad* (1940), *Cruise of the Conrad* (1937) and *The New Mayflower* (1959); general autobiograph-

ical accounts, such as *The Set of the Sails* (1949) and *Give Me a Ship to Sail* (1958); maritime histories, such as *Vanished Fleets* (1931), *The Cutty Sark* (1953) and *Captain Cook* (1967); and several books for children, of which the best known is *Whalers of the Midnight Sun* (1934).

Vinegar Hill, which took its name from the Vinegar Hill in Ireland where the United Irishmen suffered defeat in 1798, was the site of the first rebellion in Australia. In March 1804 a rising of two hundred Irish convicts from the government farm at Castle Hill was quashed at Vinegar Hill, near the Parramatta-Windsor road some forty-three kilometres from Sydney; the leader of the government forces was George Johnston, himself later a rebel in the deposing of Governor Bligh. The uprising in Thomas Keneally's *Bring Larks and Heroes* (1967) is loosely based on the Vinegar Hill episode, which is recreated in Colin Free's novel *Vinegar Hill* (1978) and Richard Butler's *Against the Wind* (1978), a novelization of the television series; R.D. FitzGerald's poem, 'The Wind at Your Door', mentions the Castle Hill rebels, although the flogging of convicts in the poem, witnessed by Joseph Holt (who was detained after Vinegar Hill), took place earlier. Vinegar Hill was renamed Rouse Hill by Governor Macquarie; so was the Sydney suburb Bellevue Hill, which was also known as Vinegar Hill for some years after 1804.

Vision (1923–24), a periodical edited by Jack Lindsay, Kenneth Slessor and Frank C. Johnson (qq.v.), was published in Sydney. It lasted only four issues but was of major importance. Jack Lindsay was the main force behind the magazine's production but its inspiration derived chiefly from Norman Lindsay, who also provided the title and contributed illustrations and essays. The editors, who looked forward to a 'Renaissance' of 'creative passion' beginning in Australia, opposed both European modernism and the nationalist strain in Australian writing. Instead, looking back to the Greeks and such European writers as Shakespeare, Byron, Burns, Villon, Browning, Rabelais and Nietzsche, they espoused a romantic, vitalist credo. The same ideas were continued in two other periodicals, the *London Aphrodite* (1928–29) and the *Australian Outline* (1933–34). Contributors to *Vision* included Kenneth Slessor, Jack Lindsay, Hugh McCrae, Adrian Lawlor, Dorothea Mackellar, R.D. FitzGerald, Dulcie Deamer, Louis Lavater, Philip Lindsay and Blamire Young. An important dispute between Jack Lindsay, Kenneth Slessor and Norman Lindsay on the circumstances of the magazine's publication and its influence later took place in *Southerly* (1952 and 1953).

Vision: A Magazine of the Arts, Science and Australiana (1963–72), published by the Adelphi Students' Library, Sydney, and edited by Bruce Skurray and others, superseded *Friends of the Glenaeon Library* (1961–63). Numerous poets contributed verse to the magazine including Joan Mas, Imogen Whyse, A.D. Hope, Martin Haley, 'Mary Lisle' and Flexmore Hudson.

Vision of Ceremony, A (1956), James McAuley's (q.v.) second collection of poetry, published after his conversion to Roman Catholicism, reflects the personal certainty and joy of faith and his confidence that its 'vision of ceremony', ritual, order and beauty, can transfigure the material world. The central poem of the volume, 'Celebration of Divine Love' (one of the 'Black Swan' lyrics), affirms that creation, 'grown timeless and distraught', can be renewed by the love of God in whom 'are all things in perfection found'. Other 'Black Swan' lyrics include 'Invocation', 'To the Holy Spirit', 'To a Dead Bird of Paradise' and 'Canticle'. 'New Guinea', subtitled 'In Memory of Archbishop Alain de Boismenu, M.S.C.', expresses both the impact of New Guinea upon McAuley and his wonder at the noble faith of de Boismenu, a faith that makes 'life become authentic'. The mythological tales of the Prometheus legend, 'The Hero and the Hydra'; 'A Leaf of Sage', a brief and highly effective rendering of a tale from the *Decameron;* and the long and discursive 'Letter to John Dryden', add variety to the volume which won the Grace Leven Prize for poetry in 1956.

'Vision of Melancholy, A Fragment, The', by 'C.S.', the first poem published in Australia, appeared in the *Sydney Gazette* 4 March 1804.

Visitants, see **STOW, RANDOLPH**

Vista (April 1946, December 1946 and a third, undated issue), the magazine of the Brisbane Catholic Readers' and Writers' Society, was edited by Martin Haley, Paul Grano and J.P. McGoldrick. Titled *View* in its first issue, the magazine included literary articles and reviews and verse; contributors included 'Brian Vrepont', James Devaney, James Picot, Peter Miles and Mary Finnin.

Vital Decade, The, see *Australian Letters*

Vivisector, The, a novel by Patrick White (q.v.), was published in 1970. The life of an eminent artist, Hurtle Duffield, from his child-

hood at the turn of the century to his death in the late 1960s is the novel's subject. Born into a large working-class family in Sydney, the son of a rag-and-bone man and a washerwoman, Hurtle is conscious at an early age of his apartness from them. He begins to spell his way through the Bible, draws on the walls and in the dust of the yard. On several occasions he is taken by his mother to her wealthy employers, the Courtneys, and becomes entranced by the splendours of their luxurious mansion, Sunningdale. He also attracts the attention of Sunningdale's mistress, the exquisite Alfreda Courtney who, with the approval of her husband Harry, buys Hurtle from his parents for £500. The purchase satisfies Alfreda's pride in her ability to recognize genius, and Harry's longing for a manly son in compensation for his having only a hunch-backed daughter, Rhoda. As Hurtle's relationships with both Alfreda and Rhoda grow in intensity, other significant experiences shape his life: a visit to Harry's property at Mumbelong, the suicide of his tutor, Mr Shewcroft, which he reproduces on the walls of his bedroom, and a tour of Europe during which he fleetingly sees Rhoda naked at the washstand. Eventually oppressed by Alfreda's near-incestuous love, Hurtle escapes to the First World War. In the succeeding years, he casts off his Courtney identity and associations and remains for a time in France washing dishes and studying art before returning to Sydney. A prostitute, Nance Lightfoot, falls passionately in love with him but commits suicide when she perceives the truth, that he is fated to use relationships for his art as dispassionately as a vivisectionist uses animals.

The next stage of Hurtle's life opens when his reputation is established and he is settled in a decaying old mansion in Flint Street, Sydney, his home for the rest of his life. Important relationships in his middle years include those with his mistress, Hero Pavloussi, the wife of a Greek shipping magnate, and with the socialite, Olivia Davenport. Olivia has figured earlier in his life as his mysterious patron, Mrs Lopez, and earlier still as Rhoda's upper-class friend Boo Hollingrake, the identity to which she finally reverts. After accompanying the intensely egoistic Hero to Greece in an abortive attempt on her part to achieve redemption, Hurtle returns to Flint Street and his life of wrestling with ultimate reality through art. Of the varied range of others who fugitively but significantly touch his experience, the most important are Maurice Caldicott, his agent who also loves him; Cec Cutbush, a grocer; Mothersole, a widower; Mrs Valkov, the mother of his last mistress; Shuard, the music critic; and Don Lethbridge, his servitor after his first stroke. Towards the end of his life, Hurtle rediscovers

Rhoda, now an impecunious old woman given to caring for the local cats, and provides her with the bottom floor of his house. His last, most serious sexual relationship is with a young pianist, Kathy Volkov, his artistic and vivisectionist equal. His final years are marked by the contrast between his eminent but bland public identity and the sordid actualities of his private struggle to express the truth of his experience. Crippled by a stroke, he fights back in a last effort to find the liberating vision of God that has obsessed him, but dies from a second attack.

Voice: The Australian Independent Monthly, published Sydney 1951–56 and titled *A.I.M.* in its first issue, was edited by Harold B. Levien. Supported by the Australian Labor Party, the WEA and socialist groups, *Voice* was mainly concerned with current affairs but also carried reviews and articles on Australian literature. Contributors included Russel Ward, Alan Marshall, Max Harris, John K. Ewers, A.D. Hope and T. Inglis Moore.

Voice from Tasmania, A, a verse satire written by Edward Kemp (q.v.), was published in 1846. The major target of the poem is the governor of Van Diemen's Land, John Eardley-Wilmot, although there are attacks on Kemp's fellow *litterateurs*, including David Burn, Nathaniel Lipscomb Kentish and R.L. Murray. *A Voice from Tasmania* has some historical interest as the first book by an Australian-born author to be published in Tasmania; the racing description included in the poem is an early specimen of the genre, preceding the better-known work of Adam Lindsay Gordon by almost two decades.

Voices of the Desert, see **FAVENC, ERNEST**

VON BRANDENSTEIN, C.G., see **Aboriginal Song and Narrative in Translation**

VON GUÉRARD, EUGENE (1812–1901), born Vienna, Austria, came to Australia in 1852, participated in the gold rushes and later, as artist, accompanied expeditions by explorers A.W. Howitt and G.B. von Neumayer. He became curator of the National Gallery of Victoria and head of its art school before returning to Europe in 1882. He published an album of lithographs, *Australian Landscapes* (1867). Marjorie Tipping edited his diary, *The Artist on the Goldfields* (1982), a collection of succinct and perceptive comments accompanied by drawings of the events described. The definitive *Eugene von Guérard* (1983), by Candice Bruce, Edward Comstock and Frank McDonald, contains fifty colour plates, von Guérard's journal,

a biography and a survey of his works, techniques and exhibitions.

VOSPER, F.C.B. (FREDERICK CHARLES BURLEIGH) (1867–1901), born Cornwall, England, emigrated at fifteen to Bolivia, where he took part in two sporadic revolutions. He arrived in Queensland in 1883 and worked as timber-miller, drover, boundary-rider and miner, before working for newspapers at Eidsvold, Maryborough, Bundaberg and Charters Towers. During the 1891 shearers' strike he was tried for sedition on the grounds of an inflammatory editorial, but was ultimately acquitted. A year later, however, his involvement in a mining strike resulted in his receiving a sentence of three months' imprisonment. By 1893 he was alienated from a large segment of the Queensland labour movement and moved to WA. He edited the Murchison *Miner*, the *Miner's Right* and, in 1894–97 when he was elected to the Legislative Assembly, the *Coolgardie Miner*. He also subsequently established and edited the *Perth Sunday Times*. Probably the most brilliant and persuasive orator on the WA goldfields, he became a powerful force in arousing opposition to the government on a wide range of issues. A member of the Australian Institute of Mining Engineers, he was one of the founders of the Geological Society of Australasia and author of *The Prospector's Companion* (1894), which was widely used on the WA goldfields in the 1890s. Few of his political pamphlets, such as his influential *A Social Armistice*, have survived.

Voss, a novel by Patrick White (q.v.), was published in 1957 and won the Miles Franklin and the W.H. Smith awards. The narrative opens in colonial Sydney of 1845, where the German explorer Voss, whose experience has affinities with that of Ludwig Leichhardt (q.v.), is preparing to cross the continent from one end to the other. For Voss the desert exists purely as a worthy challenge for his will, a place where he can rival the Almighty and wrest superhumanity for himself. At the house of one of his patrons, Mr Bonner, a wealthy merchant, Voss meets Laura Trevelyan, Bonner's niece, an intelligent, sensitive girl though outwardly a rather stiff bluestocking. Laura and Voss have only four meetings before he departs, but their relationship develops a fierce intensity. Perceiving the truth about his expedition, she challenges him in a 'wrestling' of minds and although the contest does nothing to alter his purpose Voss is already strongly influenced by her transforming power. Of the other members of his expedition, Palfreyman an ornithologist, Harry Robarts, a simple, physically-powerful boy, Frank Le Mesurier, a young, inwardly-anguished poet, and Turner, a soured cunning individual, only Palfreyman, a man of profound Christian humility, offers Voss any moral challenge at this point. After a sea trip to Newcastle the group stays at the beautiful property, Rhine Towers, belonging to the cultivated Mr Sanderson. Two new members join the expedition: a wealthy young pastoralist, Ralph Angus, and an emancipated convict, Judd. At Rhine Towers, Voss's Nietzschean will to power is slightly undermined by several softening experiences, not least his memory of Laura, and he decides to ask Mr Bonner for her hand. Before setting out into the harshest country the group stays at a squalid outpost, Jildra, where they acquire two inscrutable but apparently domesticated Aborigines, Dugald and Jackie. Side by side with the vicissitudes of Voss and his group in the wilderness, White develops Voss's intense relationship and eventual 'marriage' with Laura, conducted both by letter and by telepathy, and the events of life at the Bonners in Sydney. When Rose Portion, the Bonner's maid, is found to be pregnant, Laura participates so intensely in her experience that the birth of the child Mercy, from which Rose dies, is also hers. Meanwhile in the desert misfortunes proliferate: Voss is injured, cattle are lost or stolen, food runs short, Turner and Le Mesurier become ill, and the party is constantly dogged by watchful Aborigines. Palfreyman, speared by the blacks, dies in a Christ-like way, and Judd, Angus and Turner turn back. The severe sufferings of Voss's last days, Le Mesurier's suicide, Harry Robart's death and Voss's decapitation at the hands of Jackie, are also shared by Laura as she is consumed by a fever in Sydney. The final section of the novel is in two phases; the first, taking place two years later when Laura has become a mistress at an academy for young ladies, describes retrospectively the deaths of Angus, Turner and Jackie and the failure of a further expedition under Colonel Hebden to establish Voss's fate. The second phase, taking place several years later, narrates the contrasting fates of Laura, now headmistress of the academy and mother of Mercy, and her cousin Belle Radclyffe, mother of a large family, and the contrasting interpretations of Voss. Destined to figure in history books, regarded as a saint by the now confused Judd, and as a 'poor, twisted fellow' by Sanderson, he was, as Laura comments, a man like other men, composed of good and evil.

VOWLES, GEORGE (1844–1928), born Ipswich, became a schoolteacher in NSW and Queensland and published *Sunbeams in Queensland* (1870), the first book of verse by a Queens-

lander. H.A. Kellow's *Queensland Poets* (1930) devotes a chapter to Vowles, but his disharmonious, anglicized imitations of Romantic models have been neglected by other critics.

Voyage into Solitude, see **DRANSFIELD, MICHAEL**

Voyage of Lions, A, see **LEHMANN, GEOFFREY**

Voyage to Terra Australis, A, see **FLINDERS, MATTHEW**

Voyager. The voyager theme in Australian poetry is recognized and illustrated in Douglas Stewart's anthology, *Voyager Poems* (1968). The theme embraces all adventurers and discoverers down the centuries but it concentrates on particular voyagers such as William Dampier, James Cook and Abel Tasman, who discovered the Australian continent, or others like George Bass, Matthew Flinders, Ludwig Leichhardt and Charles Sturt, who explored it. The poetry applauds the results of their efforts – colonization and settlement – but, more importantly, emphasizes their vision, skill and courage in battling against the unknown. The voyager theme is present in early colonial literature, as titles 'Dampier's Dream', 'The Story of Abel Tasman', and eulogies on the lost explorers Burke and Wills testify, but its unusually strong appeal in this century for Australian poets is demonstrated in such poems as Kenneth Slessor's 'Five Visions of Captain Cook', R.D. FitzGerald's 'Heemskerck Shoals', William Hart-Smith's 'Christopher Columbus' and Francis Webb's 'Leichhardt in Theatre' (qq.v.).

'VREPONT, BRIAN' (BENJAMIN ARTHUR TRUEBRIDGE) (1882–1955), born Melbourne, where he eventually became a teacher of violin at the Melba Conservatorium, also lived in Queensland and WA and tried a variety of occupations, including masseur. He began publishing serious poetry late in life and in 1939 won the C.J. Dennis Memorial Prize for his poem on soil erosion, 'The Miracle'. Apart from some ephemeral writing for children, his publications are *Plays and Flower Verses for Youth* (1934), *The Miracle* (1939) and *Beyond the Claw* (1943). 'Vrepont''s best verse, simple and Wordsworthian in tone, reveals a strong but unsentimental response to nature. Surprisingly experimental for his generation, he uses some unusual, idiosyncratic forms that are clearly influenced by his musical interests.

W

WAINEWRIGHT, THOMAS GRIFFITHS
(1794–1847), was born near London and as a
young man showed both literary and artistic
talent. A contributor to the *London Magazine*,
he became known to such writers as Charles
Lamb, William Hazlitt, Thomas Hood, Thomas
de Quincey and Charles Dickens. In 1822 and
1824 he committed forgery to gain access to
his capital, which was held in trust. Later he
was suspected of having poisoned his uncle, his
mother-in-law and his sister-in-law in order to
obtain money, although the poisonings were
never proved. His forgeries discovered in 1835,
he was arrested in 1837 and sentenced to transportation for life. He arrived in Hobart in
1837 and worked at first on the roads and then
as a wardsman in Hobart Hospital. His health
declined and he was granted some freedom,
which he used to take up painting again. Finally granted a ticket-of-leave in 1846, he died
of apoplexy the following year. Forty of the
paintings he did at Hobart, which are considerable achievements, are in existence. In 1825
he published '*Some Passages' in the Life, Etc of
Egomet Bonmot, Esq.* and his collected *Essays
and Criticisms* were edited by W. Carew Hazlitt
in 1880. After his death a nefarious legend
grew up about his name, perpetuated by such
novels as Bulwer-Lytton's *Lucretia* (1853), and
Charles Dickens's *Hunted Down* (1860). This
popular version of his life also appears in *The
Criminal* (1890) by Havelock Ellis and in Oscar
Wilde's collection of essays, *Intentions* (1891),
and is perpetuated by his later biographers.
Robert Crossland's *Wainewright in Tasmania*
(1954), however, is a balanced account. In
Australian fiction Wainewright figures briefly
in Edward Dyson's *In the Roaring Fifties*
(1906) but he is given the most extensive
treatment in Hal Porter's *The Tilted Cross*
(q.v., 1961), where he appears as Judas Griffin
Vaneleigh, and in Porter's radio play, 'The
Forger', broadcast by the ABC in 1983. George
Farwell's radio play, *Portrait of a Gentleman*,
included in *Australian Radio Plays* (1946), ed.
Leslie Rees, also deals with his life.

Wake in Fright, see **COOK, KENNETH**

WAKEFIELD, EDWARD GIBBON (1796–
1862), was born in London into a Quaker
family of modest means, although his own
ambitions appear to have been grandiose. After
some success in the diplomatic service and an
earlier, short-lived marriage, from which he

acquired a substantial fortune, he abducted a
young heiress from school in 1826, married her
against her will and was sentenced to three
years' imprisonment. His experiences in Newgate transformed his life, leading to his critical
study of transportation and colonization. His
observations of prison life led to his publication
of various works on criminal justice, chief of
which was his *Facts Relating to the Punishment
of Death in the Metropolis* (1831). His *A Letter
from Sydney* (1829), written in prison, and published with Robert Gouger (q.v.) as editor,
which first expounded his ideas on systematic
colonization, caused some controversy in Sydney, where it was accepted as the work of an
Australian colonist. Wakefield further developed his colonial theory in his major works,
England and America (1833) and *A View of
the Art of Colonization* (1849). His economic,
social and political theories, which attracted
numerous adherents, played a part in the establishment of an assisted migration scheme to
NSW in 1831 and in the formation of the SA
colony in 1836. In the latter enterprise his work
The New British Province of South Australia
(1834) was particularly influential. Wakefield
was also connected with the parliamentary investigation of transportation in 1837, which
led to its abandonment. Although he never
visited Australia, he was active in the theoretical and practical aspects of the colonization of
NZ, to which he migrated in 1853 and where
he died. He also visited Canada in 1838 with
Lord Durham, the governor-general, and was a
valuable adviser to three Canadian governors,
1841–44. Of the numerous biographies of
Wakefield, the most significant are those by R.
Garnett (1898), A.J. Harrop (1928), Irma
O'Connor (1928), and P. Bloomfield (1961);
Richard C. Mills in *The Colonization of Australia (1829–42)* (1915) examines Wakefield's
achievements in colonization and colonial policy. His *Collected Works*, ed. M.F. Lloyd Prichard, were published in 1968.

WALCH, CHARLES EDWARD (1830–
1915), the son of an English major and brother
of Garnet Walch, was brought to Van Diemen's Land in 1842. Walch's father bought the
bookselling business of Samuel Tegg and renamed the firm J. Walch & Son, trading with
his eldest son, James. Charles Walch spent
some years at sea and at the Victorian gold-
diggings before entering into partnership with
his brother, James, of the bookselling firm. He

worked in London as buyer for the firm, 1854–58 and 1861. In 1859 he instituted *Walch's Literary Intelligencer and General Advertiser* (q.v.), which became a standard reference work, as did his *Walch's Tasmanian Almanack*. Walch published one semi-fictional narrative that included some verses, *The Rovers* (1884), and a collection of essays published in two parts, *The Story of Charles Edward Walch* (1908).

WALCH, GARNET (1843–1913), born Tasmania, was mainly educated in England, returning to Australia in 1860 and taking up a career of journalism. In 1873 he settled in Melbourne, where he became a member of the Athenaeum Club and of the group which included Marcus Clarke and R.P. Whitworth. Introduced to the theatre by George Darrell, he became a prolific writer of burlesques, extravaganzas, pantomimes and farces, producing about thirty works, many of them hack adaptations but contributing to the Australian stock of folk humour. One of his most characteristic is the pantomime *Australia Felix: Or, Harlequin Laughing Jackass and the Magic Bat* (1873), which celebrates things Australian with gusto. His other published plays include *Hey Diddle Diddle* (1878) and *Jack the Giant Killer* (1891). He also frequently collaborated with Alfred Dampier (q.v.) in adaptations and original productions, produced two books of verse, a life of General Gordon, and edited a range of anthologies and popular annuals, including *Hash* (1877).

Walch's Literary Intelligencer and General Advertiser, a monthly newsletter 1859–91, was published in Hobart Town and Launceston by J. Walch & Sons, which has been a significant publisher of Tasmanian material. Edited by Charles Walch (q.v.), it carried lists of new books and periodicals, articles on literary and cultural topics, literary notices and reviews and became a standard reference work.

WALES, ROBERT, see *Van Diemen's Land Warriors, The*

WALES, ROBERT, see 'Cell, The'

WALFORD, FRANK (1882–?), was educated in Sydney and tried various occupations including crocodile-hunting, buffalo-shooting, droving and fishing in northern Australia before turning to journalism. He published two booklets of verse, *Starlight and Haze* (1919) and *The Eternal Ego* (1921); a collection of short stories, *The Ghost and Albert and Other Stories* (1945); and five novels, several of which proved popular, *Twisted Clay* (1933), *The Silver Girl*

(1935), *And the River Rolls On* (1939), *The Indiscretions of Iole* (1940) and *A Fool's Odyssey* (1942). He also edited various small, shortlived periodicals, including *Walford's Weekly* (1918).

Walkabout, a monthly magazine published by the Australian National Travel Association, began publication in November 1934. It was founded by Charles Henry Holmes (1891–1981), who edited it until 1957. Consisting mainly of articles about the flora, fauna and geographical regions of Australia and neighbouring countries, *Walkabout* has frequently included informative articles by or about Australian writers. The title derives from 'walkabout', a term of European origin which originally denoted a period of nomadic wandering on the part of Aborigines. The expression 'to go walkabout' has lost much of its original racist or disparaging overtones, and is now applied to anyone who wanders the country in a leisurely manner, or to anything that has been mislaid.

WALKER, DAVID, see **Criticism; *Dream and Disillusion***

WALKER, KATH (1920–), a part-Aboriginal of the Noonuccal (Noonuckle) tribe of Stradbroke Island off the Queensland coast near Brisbane, was the first of the modern Aboriginal protest writers. She was educated only to primary school level, then at thirteen worked in domestic service in Brisbane. At sixteen she wanted to be a nurse but was rejected because she was an Aboriginal. By 1961, when she was State secretary of the Federal Council for the Advancement of Aboriginals and Torres Strait Islanders, she was deeply involved in the Aboriginal activist movement. She campaigned strenuously and successfully for the 1967 abolition of Section 52 of the Australian Constitution which discriminated against Aborigines. In her life and through her writings she has constantly sought to generate Aboriginal self-pride by emphasizing the value of the Aboriginal way of life and the innate worth of the Aboriginal people. This crusade has often led her to criticize white Australian attitudes and to demand basic Aboriginal rights. She was made MBE and is also a member of the Mark Twain Literary Society of America. Her first volume of poetry, *We Are Going* (1964), is not, as its title might imply, an indication of her resignation to the loss of Aboriginal identity. She meant it, in her own words, 'as a warning to the white people: we can go out of existence, or with proper help we could also go on and live in this world in peace and harmony . . . the Aboriginal will not go out of existence; the whites will'. Her second volume, *The Dawn Is at Hand* (1966), won the 1967 Jessie Litchfield Award. *My People: A Kath Walker Collection* (1970) reprinted the poems of the two earlier collections, together with some new poems, short stories, essays and speeches. *Stradbroke Dreamtime* (1972) is a collection of thirteen whimsical stories of her childhood and fourteen traditional stories from Aboriginal folklore or new ones in traditional form. In her best-known poem, 'We Are Going', in 'Gooboora, the Silent Pool' and in 'Last of His Tribe' her nostalgia for the lost Aboriginal past echoes the same note of loss and desolation that is present in Judith Wright's 'Bora Ring'. Her anger at white intolerance and cruelty is expressed in poems such as 'Dark Unmarried Mothers', 'Acacia Ridge' and 'God's One Mistake', but a sense of fairness compels her to admit, in 'Civilization' and 'Integration — Yes!', that some benefits have flowed to the Aboriginal from racial contact. 'Aboriginal Charter of Rights' is a straightforward declaration of the basic rights of her race, while 'Tribal Justice' and 'The Food Gatherers' idealize the Aboriginal existence of primitive times. 'I Am Proud' is her angry assertion of pride in her Aboriginal identity. She describes her poetry as 'sloganistic, civil rightish, plain and simple'. Always vigorous and deeply committed, it is more, and better, than that assessment indicates.

'WALKER, LUCY' (DOROTHY LUCIE SANDERS) (1903–), born Kalgoorlie, WA, has published novels both under her own name and her pseudonym. Chiefly romance and light fiction, they included several set in Perth, e.g. *Pepper Tree Bay* (1959) and *Monday in Summer* (1961). Other titles among her forty wide-selling novels are *Fairies on the Doorstep* (1948), *Waterfall* (1956), *Love in a Cloud* (1960), *The Man from Outback* (1964), *The River Is Down* (1967) and *The Runaway Girl* (1975).

WALKER, THOMAS (1) (1804–1886), born Leith, Scotland, came to Sydney about 1822. A merchant, banker and land speculator, Walker subsequently made a large fortune in NSW and devoted a substantial proportion to charitable projects. In 1837 he rode overland with three friends to Port Phillip, and published his journal of the trip, *A Month in the Bush of Australia* (1838).

WALKER, THOMAS (2) (1858–1932), born Lancashire, England, had a colourful and wandering career in Canada, the USA, England, NZ, NSW and South Africa before finally settling in WA. In 1874 he migrated to Can-

ada, where he set up as a spiritual medium; he was implicated in a felonious killing but escaped indictment and then worked as a spiritualist and journalist in the USA before coming to Sydney in 1877 under the sponsorship of Australian spiritualists. After a chequered career in NSW and some further wanderings overseas, during which he published a book of verse in South Africa, he abandoned spiritualism and established himself in Sydney as a secularist spokesman and populist campaigner. His second volume of verse, *Bush Pilgrims*, was published in 1885 and in the same year he enjoyed the success of his dramatization of *His Natural Life* (1874) and the production of his own play, in which he acted, 'Marmondelle the Moor'. In 1887 Walker was elected to the Legislative Assembly, where he had a vociferous career, cut short in mid-1892 when he inadvertently shot and wounded a clergyman. Convicted of being drunk and disorderly, he immediately set up as a temperance lecturer and in 1899 arrived in WA in that role. He wrote for and edited the *West Australian Sunday Times*, worked for the Kalgoorlie *Sun* and the *Kalgoorlie Miner* and in 1905 was elected to the Legislative Assembly, where he remained until 1932, successfully combining politics, farming and law. He was attorney-general 1911–16 and speaker 1924–30. Apart from some polemical works, Walker published *Felonry of New South Wales, by an Old Identity* (1891).

'WALKER, W.H.', see **RANKEN, GEORGE**

WALKER, WILLIAM (1828–1908), born Glasgow, Scotland, came to Australia in 1837. A solicitor and member of the NSW parliament 1860–69, he was appointed to the Legislative Council in 1887 and was also prominent in civic, charitable and educational affairs. He published a collection of lectures and articles, *Miscellanies* (1884), which includes his lecture, *Australian Literature* (probably 1864), the first separate work of Australian criticism. His other published works include the poem, *The Flood, 1850* (1860), *Poems Written in Youth* (1884), *Recollections of Sir Henry Parkes* (1896) and *Reminiscences* (1890). See Criticism.

WALKER, WILLIAM SYLVESTER (1846–?), who also wrote as 'Cooee', was a nephew of 'Rolf Boldrewood' and was born Heidelberg, Melbourne, and later experienced station life and mining in NSW. He spent some time in NZ, tried diamond mining in South Africa, and finally retired to Devon, England. He published two collections of short stories, *When the Mopoke Calls* (1898) and *From the Land of the Wombat* (1899), and seven novels, *Native Born* (1900), *Virgin Gold* (1901), *In the Blood*

(1901), *Zealandia's Guerdon* (1902), *The Silver Queen* (?1908), *What Lay Beneath* (1909), *Blair's Ken* (1910) and *At Possum Creek* (1915). His work is marked by superficial characterization and sensational, geographically wide-ranging, complicated plots; for the modern reader his stories have more historical than literary interest, especially in their incidental reflections of bush life.

'Walking to the Cattle-Place: A Meditation', a sixteen-poem sequence by Les Murray (q.v.), was first published in *Poetry Australia* (1972). In the opening poem, 'Sanskrit', the poet, listening to the familiar sounds of cattle nearby in the night, repeats to himself the Sanskrit words for the various stages of a cow's life and vows that for the coming day he 'will follow cattle'. In the following sequence, 'Birds in Their Title Work Freeholds of Straw', the dairy-farm children bring in the cows for the morning milking, a detested chore in 'the child-labour districts' that leads inevitably to the late morning schoolroom scene of 'children dead beat at their desks'. 'The Names of the Humble' shows the cows at eyeball range and as he watches the regular circling movement of champing jaws the poet joins the ruminants by pondering on the vast ingestion of grass by cows down the ages. If he envies the cow one thing it is her stolid, cud-chewing indifference, 'her ease with this epoch'. 'The Artery' sees the herd disturbed by a passing 'beef mob' being driven to the abattoirs where, ultimately, 'out of cool rooms they crowd into our veins'. 'Death Words' reflects on the cows' habit of stampeding at the death of one of their number. The sequence then becomes extremely complex, breaking into fragments which contain Hindu and Krishna motifs. With 'Boopis' it returns to the cows, the opening lines 'Coming out of reflections/I find myself in the earth' indicating the meditative digression of the previous verses. The long concluding poem, 'Goloka', takes its title from the cow heaven of Krishna on Mount Maru.

Labelled by Murray as 'cow' poems, the Cattle-Place verses are among his most controversial and complex. The cattle, often set against historical and allegorical backgrounds, are used to carry deeply symbolic interpretations of the actual world.

WALL, DOROTHY (1894–), born Wellington, NZ, came to Australia in 1914. Her reputation as an illustrator of children's books was established early, especially after her work for J.J. Hall's *The Crystal Bowl* (1921), a collection of nature stories, and she continued to illustrate the work of other authors during her own successful career as a writer of children's

fiction. *The Story of Tommy Bear and the Zookies* (1920), which she illustrated herself, was her first effort at authorship, but her reputation depends mainly on her series of stories about an engaging koala, Blinky Bill. *Blinky Bill the Quaint Little Australian* (1933) was followed by *Blinky Bill Grows Up* (1934), *Blinky Bill and Nutsy, Two Little Australians* (1937) and *Blinky Bill Joins the Army* (1940). Wall also wrote *The Tale of Bridget and the Bees* (1934), *Brownie, the Story of a Naughty Little Rabbit* (1935) and *Stout Fellows* (1936). Blinky Bill, a perennial favourite with Australian children and as well-known as May Gibbs's Snugglepot and Cuddlepie, has well-marked human characteristics and even clothes, although physically he is otherwise true to nature. Curiosity, a love of food, especially gum nuts, an independent spirit and an unfailing propensity for mischief lead Blinky Bill into a variety of adventures. He has been revived to suit the modern child by Carol Odell in *Let's Call Him Blinky Bill* (1970) and by Anne-Marie Willis in *Blinky Bill and the Pelicans* (1976).

Wallabadah Manuscript, The, see **Myall Creek Massacre; New England**

Wallaby, The (Wallaby Track, The), phrases frequently used in Australian writing, are based on the wallaby, the smaller species of the kangaroo. The phrase 'the wallaby track', indicating the tracks of the outback, became in the late nineteenth century shortened in conversational idiom to 'the wallaby' and the phrase 'to go on the wallaby' meant to go tramping around the country, somewhat like a swagman. The most famous usage of the term is Henry Lawson's radical poem, 'Freedom on the Wallaby' (q.v.), the same title being given by Muir Holburn and Marjorie Pizer to their anthology, *Freedom on the Wallaby* (1953). E.J. Overbury in his *Bush Poems* (1965) has a poem, 'The Wallaby Track', and the traditional songs, 'Australia's on the Wallaby' and 'The Wallaby Brigade', are well-known folk-songs. Frederick McCubbin's famous painting, *On the Wallaby Track* (1896) portrays man, wife and child boiling the billy by the side of a bush track. Nicholas Enwright's play, *On the Wallaby* (1982), recreates the 1930s depression, when many homeless men wandered the outback tracks looking for work or food.

WALLACE-CRABBE, CHRIS (1934–), born Richmond, Melbourne, was educated at the University of Melbourne. In 1961–63 he was Lockie Fellow in Australian Literature and Creative Writing at the University of Melbourne and in 1965–67 Harkness Fellow in the USA. Since 1968 he has taught English at the University of Melbourne. Wallace-Crabbe's published volumes of verse are *The Music of Division* (1959), *In Light and Darkness* (1963), *Eight Metropolitan Poems* (1963), *The Rebel General* (1967), *Where the Wind Came* (1971), *Selected Poems* (1973), *Act in the Noon* (1974), *The Foundations of Joy* (1976), and *The Emotions Are Not Skilled Workers* (1980). He has edited the poetry anthologies, *Six Voices* (1963), *Australian Poetry* (1971) and *The Golden Apples of the Sun* (1980). He has compiled a selection of critical essays by various writers, *The Australian Nationalists* (1971), and two selections of his own articles, reviews and lectures, *Melbourne or the Bush* (1974) and *Toil & Spin* (1980). He has also written a novel, *Splinters* (1981), set in Melbourne in the late 1960s, which examines the impact of the growing sense of chaos in contemporary life.

Wallace-Crabbe's early poetry in *The Music of Division* and *In Light and Darkness* is, by his own admission, 'four square and syllogistic ... written by a Lockean rationalist'. In the middle of unemphatic glimpses of the limited possibilities of life ('Ancient Historian', 'Fog at Midnight' and 'In Light and Darkness') there is a remarkable poem, 'The Wintry Manifesto', which is an affirmation of the potentialities of the here and now: 'our greatest joy to make an outline truly/And know the piece of earth on which we stand'. The early volumes also reveal Wallace-Crabbe as a poet of the Melbourne suburbs, whose chief reaction is compassion for the shabby and often bewildered participants of modern city life, tempered by gentle irony. With his third volume, *The Rebel General*, Wallace-Crabbe turned towards more public and political themes, a trend accentuated in later volumes. The title poem, a portrait of failure and futility, is the centrepiece of a group of poems titled 'Brief Lives', mostly sardonic character sketches of figures such as Noah, King David and the young concubine, Abishag. Wallace-Crabbe's changing poetic ambitions are reflected in the statement prior to the publication of *Where the Wind Came*: 'After stoical-formalist beginnings, I seek a poetry of Romantic fullness and humanity. I want to see how far lyrical, Dionysian impulses can be released and expressed without a loss of intelligence'. *Where the Wind Came* opens with the long poem, 'Blood Is the Water', which concerns a Latin-American military dictator who has engineered power through a well-planned coup; the poem examines the motives and consequences of such dictatorial seizures of power. Wallace-Crabbe's freer approach to form is evident in the prose sequence, 'Going to Cythera', where the thin line that separates poetry and prose is illustrated. His *Selected Poems*, a severe pruning of the first four vol-

umes, is unusual in its grouping of seven poems from various volumes under the heading 'Meditations'. Wallace-Crabbe saw these meditative poems as a 'recurring series', part of a 'continuous landscape of debate'. His later poetry, especially in *The Emotions Are Not Skilled Workers*, is, in spite of a sometimes debonair and breezy tone, philosophically grave, even sombre. In the long poem 'The Shapes of Gallipoli', he joins the long line of Australian poets who have satisfied their need to write on a subject rooted in Australian history. That Wallace-Crabbe could recently express greater satisfaction with 'The Shapes of Gallipoli', set though it is in 'mundane local conditions', than with 'Blood Is the Water', which is set in a 'laboriously constructed but finally metaphysical banana-republic', is a measure of his liberation from his 'stoical-formalist beginnings'.

One of the group of Melbourne University poets who emerged in the late 1950s, Wallace-Crabbe has occupied the middle ground between the mainstream of Australian poetry of the late 1940s and 1950s and the new poetry of the late 1960s. In an essay, 'The Habit of Irony: Australian Poets of the Fifties', Wallace-Crabbe expressed the view that poetry has to be partly ironic to represent 'our age and our condition'. Much of his own poetry adopts an ironic stance and is marked by an air of controlled understatement that comes with the deliberate distancing of artist from his subject.

WALLACE-CRABBE, ROBIN (1938–), born Melbourne, the brother of Chris Wallace-Crabbe (q.v.), is best known as an artist. He has published two novels, *Feral Palit* (1978), a powerful study of a city-bred man's inability to come to grips with rural living, and *Goanna* (1982), a strikingly unusual account of the spiritual odyssey of a contemporary Melbourne businessman.

WALLACE, JOHN, who also used the pseudonyms 'Aintree', 'Texas Ranger' and 'Gerald Grantham', wrote thirteen crime, mystery, racing and adventure novels 1937–42. His complicated, action-filled plots are rapidly propelled by means of his abbreviated prose style and predictable, lightly-observed characters; although several are ostensibly set in Australia, their location is really indeterminate. The titles of his novels give some indication of their subjects and tone, e.g. *Millionaire Gangster* (1937), *The Sedan Murder Mystery* (1938), *Vengeance of —— ?* (1939), *Dead 'un Wins* (1940), *Dope Runners* (1940) and *Invasion* (1940).

WALSH, J.M. (JAMES MORGAN) (1897–1952), born Geelong and educated in Melbourne, is best known as an extremely prolific writer of crime mysteries, mostly located in England. His first novel, *Tap-Tap Island* (1921), was first serialized in the Melbourne *Leader*; his second, *The Lost Valley* (1921), was a prize-winner in the C.J. De Garis competition; his third was *Overdue* (1925). After experience in auctioneering and book-selling, Walsh visited England in 1925 to negotiate with publishers, returned to Victoria but left for permanent residence in England in 1929. Pseudonyms he used include 'John Carew', 'George M. White' and 'H. Haverstock Hill'; he also wrote in collaboration with E.J. Blythe and Audry Baldwin. His first three novels, which are adventure romances, are set in New Guinea and western Victoria and he also wrote two Australian detective stories, *The Man behind the Curtain* (1927) and *The League of Missing Men* (1927). The five adventure stories that he wrote under the pseudonym 'H. Haverstock Hill', *Anne of Flying Gap* (1926), *Spoil of the Desert* (1927), *The Golden Isle* (1928), *Golden Harvest* (1929) and *The Secret of the Crater* (1930), range between New Guinea, the Northern Territory, Gippsland, WA and the South Seas.

WALSH, RICHARD, see Angus & Robertson; NEVILLE, RICHARD

WALSTAB, GEORGE ARTHUR (1834–1909), born and educated in London, migrated with his parents to Australia in 1852. After service with the Victorian mounted police and with the Indian army, he turned to journalism in 1860. Editor in 1862 of the Calcutta *Englishman*, he returned to Melbourne in 1865 and in the late 1860s was editor of the *Australian Journal*, the *Australasian Monthly Review and the Colonial Monthly*. Bankrupted in 1869, he was a public servant (1873–80) and subsequently worked on the Melbourne *Herald*. Several Walstab novels were serialized in the *Australian Journal* and the *Colonial Monthly* during 1867–69; an earlier novel, *Looking Back* (1864), won him notice in London. Perhaps more important for Australian literature were his involvement in the founding of the Yorick Club and the two chapters of *Long Odds* (1869) that he wrote in 1869 when it was being serialized in the *Colonial Monthly* and Marcus Clarke was incapacitated.

'Waltzing Matilda' is the title of Australia's most famous song. The phrase 'to waltz Matilda', meaning to carry a swag on one's travels, was in existence by the 1890s and probably derived from two German words: 'walzen', which was applied to apprentices travelling around from master to master; and 'Mathilde', a girl's name which became generic for a female travelling companion and then for a bed-roll. The song chronicles the experiences of a swagman waltzing his Matilda who has camped by a billabong or waterhole; as he is boiling his billy, a jumbuck (sheep) comes to drink at the billabong, and is captured by the swagman for food. The swagman is then accosted by the owner of the sheep, a squatter, who is accompanied by three mounted policemen; to escape arrest the swagman jumps into the billabong and is drowned near the coolibah tree shading the billabong. 'Waltzing Matilda' became enormously popular, particularly among Australian troops, has assumed the status of an unofficial national anthem, and remains the song most closely identified with Australia among overseas people. Its anti-authoritarian sentiments probably prevented its selection as the national anthem (q.v.) in a 1977 national poll (28 per cent of the vote compared with 43 per cent for 'Advance Australia Fair') although its sympathy for the underdog has been seen as characteristically Australian and as a significant reason for its continuing appeal.

The provenance and transmission of 'Waltzing Matilda' have been the subject of some dispute. The most generally accepted version is that the words were written early in 1895 by A.B. Paterson (q.v.) at Dagworth station near Winton. Paterson was on a visit to western Queensland and while staying at Dagworth heard Christina Macpherson, the sister of the owner, Robert Macpherson, play 'Craigielee', a march adapted from the Scottish song, 'Thou Bonnie Wood of Craigielea', which she had first encountered at the Warrnambool races the previous April. In putting the words to the tune Paterson drew on several experiences during his three weeks at Dagworth: the discovery while riding of a dead sheep with a forequarter missing; a picnic at Combo waterhole, near where a suicide had taken place; and the casual after-dinner use of the phrase, 'Waltzing Matilda', which took the fancy both of Paterson and Macpherson. The song was performed publicly for the first time in Winton in April 1895 and spread quickly in Queensland. A wider audience was reached after 1903 when Marie Cowan adapted Paterson's words and the 'Craigielee' tune as remembered by Macpherson to produce the version that has become the standard popular one. This audience was enlarged further by its inclusion in Thomas Wood's (q.v.) *Cobbers* (1934). Paterson, whose own 'Waltzing Matilda' was first published in his *Saltbush Bill, J.P.* in 1917, approved the adaptation, which was printed as part of an advertising leaflet wrapped around Billy Tea, and later in music broadsheet form.

The Paterson-Macpherson origin for 'Waltzing Matilda' was established by Sydney May in *The Story of Waltzing Matilda* (1944 and 1955). May found support from John Manifold, who in *Who Wrote the Ballads?* (1964) links it with the treason songs of the convicts, but alternative theories have been proposed: by Oscar Mendelsohn, in *A Waltz with Matilda* (1966), who claims that Paterson plagiarized the words from an anonymous bush song collected during the preparation of his anthology, *The Old Bush Songs* (1905), and that Harry Nathan, a Toowoomba musician, composed the music; and by Harry Pearce, in *On the Origins of Waltzing Matilda* (1971), who claims that there were originally two 'Waltzing Matildas', one written by Paterson and Macpherson which became a variant now known as the Queensland or Buderim version, and an earlier version (the popular one) in the preparation of which a Winton pianist, Josephine Pene, drew on her knowledge of the English marching song, 'The Bold Fusilier'. Richard Magoffin's *Fair Dinkum Matilda* (1973) convincingly refutes the theories of Mendelsohn and Pearce and, while correcting some of May's conclusions with new evidence, substantiates the gist of his argument. Nigel Krauth's novel, *Matilda, My Darling* (1983), set in Winton in 1895, has Paterson composing 'Waltzing Matilda' after hearing Robert 'McPhee''s story of his disturbing a swagman at the Combo waterhole, although the verse in which the swagman defies the squatter is written as a tribute to a party of shearers whom Paterson also meets during his stay. The Combo waterhole also figures in the novel as the place where the body of a unionist is discovered by a private detective sent up from Brisbane to investigate his disappearance.

Wandering Islands, The, see HOPE, A.D.

WANNAN, BILL (WILLIAM FIELDING FEARN-WANNAN) (1915–   ), born Victoria, has travelled widely in Australia and abroad and served in the Pacific with the AIF in the Second World War. His first published work was a poem, *The Corporal's Story* (1943). Now widely-known as a leading collector of and authority on Australian folklore and humour, especially of the sort of humour that was the staple of such periodicals as *Smith's Weekly* and the *Bulletin*, Wannan has compiled numerous collections of ballads, yarns, anecdotes and legends. He is also well known for his column, 'Come In, Spinner!', contributed to the *Australasian Post* 1955–78. His published work includes the frequently-reprinted collections, *The Australian* (1954), *Tales from Back o' Bourke* (1957), *Bullockies, Beauts and Bandicoots* (1960), *Hay, Hell and Booligal* (1961), *A Treas-*

ury of Australian Frontier Tales (1961), *Fair Go, Spinner* (1964), and *My Kind of Country* (1967); accounts of bushrangers, *Tell 'Em I Died Game* (1963), notorious colonial figures, *Very Strange Tales* (1962), and famous Australians, *Legendary Australians* (1974); dictionaries of humour, traditional invective and folk anecdotes, *A Treasury of Australian Humour* (1960), *Australian Folklore* (1970), *Folklore of the Australian Pub* (1972), *With Malice Aforethought* (1973), *Robust, Ribald and Rude Verse in Australia* (1972) and *Dictionary of Humorous Australian Quotations* (1974); anthologies of writing by and about the Irish in Australia, *The Wearing of the Green* (1965), and the Scots, *The Heather in the South* (1966); and a satire on Australian local histories, *Chronicles of Boobyalla* (1979). He has also edited an anthology of urban short stories, *Australian Pavements* (1964), a selection of Marcus Clarke's writing, *A Marcus Clarke Reader* (1963), and in 1952 the Melbourne periodical the *Realist Writer*.

War Crimes, see **CAREY, PETER**

War Literature. Boer War (1899–1902): Australian war literature produced by the Boer War was slight, the amount of notable writing minute. None of the verse about the war is memorable. *Ballads of Battle* (1900) by the Melbourne journalist, John Sandes ('Oriel'), *War Songs, 1899–1900* (1901) by W.H. Dawson, and *Collected Verses* (1928) by George Essex Evans, contain examples of the imperialistic verse popular at the time. Other poems in similar vein are John B. O'Hara's 'Australia's Call to Arms' and Garnet Walch's 'The Lion's Cubs', which appeared in *The Coo-ee Reciter* (1904), compiled by W.T. Pyke. In its sentimental, pro-British propaganda and old-fashioned rhetoric, Sandes's poem, 'A Call from England', is typical of the genre:

> There came a cry forth speeding o'er the
>   mighty Indian main,
> A whisper that was borne upon the breeze,
> 'Twas the voice of England calling, and
>   the words were clear and plain,
> 'Come and help me, O my children over-
>   seas . . .'

Not everything published by Sandes, however, is imperialistic. In 'Death Song of the Boers', there is a note of sympathy for the enemy's threatened way of life. Mixed attitudes are also found in the war poems of A.B. Paterson included in his *Rio Grande's Last Race* (1902). Paterson, who served as a war correspondent, ends his poem, 'Johnny Boer', on the confident note that the Boer will be made to run, but in 'On the Trek' the thoughts of the war-weary Australian soldiers return to peace-time life in rural Australia. Henry Lawson's verses are consistently hostile to the British cause and to Australian participation in the war, as the ironic 'Our Fighters (From a Worldly Point of View)' (1899) and 'The Blessings of War' (1900) indicate. Although he served in the Australian contingent to South Africa, another writer, Monty Grover, came to think as Lawson did in one of the few authentic confessional poems of the war, 'I Killed a Man at Graspan', also from *The Coo-ee Reciter*. Memories of the look in the eyes of a dead enemy soldier lead Grover to reject the traditional heroic view of war and to assert that 'If the Empire ask for me later on/It'll ask for me in vain'.

Of the personal narratives of the war, *On the Veldt* (1902) is a plain, factual account by R.C. Lewis, the officer commanding the Tasmanian Imperial Bushmen. W.T. Reay's *Australians in War* (1900) and Frank Wilkinson's *Australia at the Front* (1901) are works by Australian war correspondents, while James Green's *The Story of the Australian Bushmen* (1903) is a chaplain's account. The most sensational personal narrative of the war is George R. Witton's *Scapegoats of the Empire* (1907). It deals with the author's army life from the outbreak of the war until his release from prison in England and return to Australia in 1904, and includes an account of the events that culminated in the court-martial and execution by the British army of Lieutenants P.J. Handcock and Harry Harbord Morant (q.v.). 'Breaker' Morant, a minor poet, is said to have written the bitter lines, 'Butchered to Make a Dutchman's Holiday', a short time before his death. He is the subject, in addition to several biographical works, of the two novels, *Where Day Begins* (1911) by Alfred Johnson Buchanan and Kit Denton's *The Breaker* (1973). These are the only Australian novels on the Boer War to warrant mention, apart from A.G. Hales's *McGlusky* (1902), the first of a long series of novels narrating the varied adventures of that aggressive, eponymous hero. The most outstanding single literary work on the Boer War is J.H.M. Abbott's *Tommy Cornstalk* (1902), a personal narrative which emphasizes the initiative, independence and fighting abilities of the bushmen who were the core of the Australian mounted troops in South Africa. Honest and interesting, lucid and literate, Abbott's account expresses not only national pride but also the personal impressions and opinions of a soldier who experienced a good deal of active service and formed balanced judgements about the capabilities of the British army and the character of the Boer. Abbott returns to the subject of the war in some of the fictional sketches and stories in his *Plain and Veldt* (1903), and occasionally in his volume of journalistic articles, *An Outlander in England* (1905), especially in the chapter in which he criticizes the emphasis on 'pomp and circumstance' in Britain's army during peace-time.

First World War (1914–18). Australian poetry of the First World War began with slim volumes of patriotic and imperialistic rhetoric such as L.E. Homfray's sixteen-page pamphlet, *Australians, Awake!* (1915). Several of Homfray's poems are simply pious utterances about the troops abroad and their families at home, e.g. 'Sons of Australia' heaps scorn on those unwilling 'to fight for (their) country – or fall'. In 'List to the Call' in *The Call to Arms!* (1915), Winsome Jennings expresses similar sentiments, urging the 'shirkers' to 'Fight for Australia, the King and the Flag'. Similar volumes include *Hoisting Our Flag on the Anzac Redoubt* (1917) by George Smith ('Patrius'), *At Vancouver's Well* (1917) by Australia's chaplain-general, J.L. Rentoul, and *Troop Trains* (1917) by Alice Gore-Jones. J.O. Burns's 'For England', from *In the Dawning of the Day* (1916), Henry Lawson's 'England Yet', from *Selected Poems* (1918) and Christopher Brennan's (q.v.) 'Irish to England' and 'Kitchener' from his volume, *A Chant of Doom* (1918), are more worthwhile examples of this loyalist verse. Many of Brennan's other war poems, however, including 'A Chant of Doom' are little more than anti-German propaganda. Pride in the achievements of the Australian troops mingles with an elegiac strain in such poems as L.H. Allen's 'Gallipoli', first published in 1916 and reprinted in *Patria* (1941), Mary Gilmore's 'These Fellowing Men' from *The Passionate Heart* (1918), 'William Baylebridge''s sonnet sequence, *A Wreath* (1915), and John le Gay Brereton's 'The Dead' and 'Anzac' from *The Burning Marl* (1919). Disillusionment with war is the main mood in Mary Gilmore's 'The Measure' from *The Passionate Heart*, Brereton's 'Transports' and 'The Patriot' from *The Burning Marl*, 'Furnley Maurice''s 'To God: From the Warring Nations' (q.v., 1916) and Zora Cross's (q.v.) *Elegy on an Australian Schoolboy* (1921).

Of the soldier-poets, many were rhymesters and balladists in the popular tradition. Typical of them was Tom Skeyhill, who published *Soldier Songs from Anzac* (1915) and *A Singing Soldier* (1919). In his poem 'Shrapnel', the colloquial style and simple humour characteristic of much of this unpretentious writing are captured in his description of a shell landing nearby while he is sitting in his dug-out, chewing his Queensland bully-beef and his 'biscuit 'ard as wood':

> When, boom! I nearly choked meself,
> I spilt me bloomin' tea;
> I saw about a million stars,
> An' me dug-out fell on me.

Skeyhill, who was blinded by an exploding shell, became an international figure during the war years through his lecturing and fund-raising and subsequently recovered his sight in 1918 after an operation. Other popular soldier-versifiers are James Andrews (*Garrison Ginger*, 1919), Peter Austen (*Bill-Jim*, 1917), Norman Campbell (*The Dinki-Di Soldier*, 1918), who all wrote in imitation of C.J. Dennis's famous war poem, *The Moods of Ginger Mick* (1916), J.P. O'Donnell (*Songs of an Anzac*, 1918), F.S. McDonnell (*The History They Have Made*, 1919), William Michael McDonald (*Soldier Songs from Palestine*, 1918), and Edwin Gerard (q.v.) ('Trooper Gerardy'), whose two volumes, *The Road to Palestine* (1918) and *Australian Light Horse Ballads and Rhymes* (1919), represent the best in the popular tradition. In ballads such as 'Lofty Lane', 'Riding Song', 'North of Jerusalem' and 'Garden Post', Gerard gives vivid descriptions of desert warfare and the feelings of the Australian troopers involved. The most skilled of the soldier-poets were Leon Gellert, Frederic Manning, Harley Matthews (qq.v.) and Vance Palmer. Gellert's *Songs of a Campaign* (1917) contains some fine vignettes of the Gallipoli experience and its aftermath of illness and desolation. Manning's *Eidola* (1917) expresses the protracted agony and horror of war on the Western Front in a series of poems that alternate between the realistic and visionary modes of presentation. In Palmer's *The Camp* (1920), the long title poem offers an interesting comment on the dehumanizing effect of military training on the human spirit; but the short piece, 'The Farmer Remembers the Somme', most perfectly encapsulates the trauma of war. Matthews's best war poems are the three narratives about Gallipoli published in *Vintage* (1938) – 'The Day Before', 'Two Brothers' and 'True Patriot'. Other significant volumes of verse were Martin Boyd's *Retrospect* (1920), which contains some poems on post-war psychological problems, Reginald Godfrey's elegiac *Anzac Memorial Poems* (1925), Henry Weston Pryce's *Your Old Battalion* (1926), and Oscar Walters's *Shrapnel Green* (1931).

In 1983 an anthology of more recent poems on the war by poets too young to have been participants, was published under the title, *Shadows from Wire*. Edited by Geoff Page, the volume juxtaposes poems by nineteen poets, including Page, Les Murray, Hal Porter, Roger McDonald, Chris Wallace-Crabbe, David Malouf, John Tranter, Thomas Shapcott, Dorothy Hewett, Michael Dransfield, David Campbell, and Kevin Hart with contemporary photographs held by the Australian War Memorial to suggest some of the ironies and ambiguities now present in the modern Australian response to the First World War.

The early prose writings on the war fall into three main categories – patriotic effusions, humorous fiction and descriptive accounts. The first group includes Oliver Hogue's *Love Letters of an Anzac* (1916), the personal narrative, *Trooper Bluegum at the Dardanelles* (1916), and the sketches and poems making up *The Cameliers* (1919); E.F. Hanman's ('Haystack') personal narrative, *Twelve Months with the 'Anzacs'* (1916); Roy Bridges's volume of sketches, *The Immortal Dawn* (1917); and Mabel Brookes's novels, *Broken Idols* (1917), *On the Knees of the Gods* (1918), and *Old Desires* (1922). The humorous fiction encompasses 'Steele Rudd''s novel, *Memoirs of Corporal Keeley* (1918), Gladys Hain's volume of short sketches, *The Coo-ee Contingent* (1917) and A.G. Hales's *McGlusky's Great Adventure* (1917) and *Ginger and McGlusky* (1917). The best of the many descriptive accounts of the war include J.L. Beeston's *Five Months at Anzac* (1916), David Doull's *With the Anzacs in Egypt* (1916), F.S. Lock's ('Sydney de Loghe') *The Straits Impregnable* (1916), C.E.W. Bean's *Letters from France* (1917), H.W. Dinning's *By-Ways on Service* (1918), and T.A. White's *Diggers Abroad* (1920). The best of the early short fiction are *Saints and Soldiers* (1918) by Harley Matthews, and *An Anzac Muster* (q.v., 1921) by 'William Baylebridge'. The direct realism and simple unpretentious prose style of *Saints and Soldiers* contrast strongly with the indirectness, artifice and idiosyncrasy of style of *An Anzac Muster*, although both contain some effective humour. Of the other prose writing of the period, C.E.W. Bean's two-volume history of Gallipoli, *The Story of Anzac* (1921, 1924), is outstanding for its fine blending of historical and literary qualities. Most of the more memorable war writing belongs to the years following 1927. The volume of short stories, *Glimpses* (1928) by Eric Partridge ('Corrie Denison'), contains the story, 'A Mere Private', dealing with the experiences of an infantryman who serves in Egypt, Gallipoli and France. Partridge's personal narrative, 'Frank Honywood Private', appeared in *Three Personal Records of the War* (by R.H. Mottram, John Easton, and Eric Partridge) in 1929; and a more imaginative war narrative, 'From Two Angles', was published in the miscellany, *A Martial Medley* (1931). In 1928 A.L. McLean's unfinished personal account, *War Vistas*, and T.W. White's personal account of flying, captivity and escape from the Turks, *Guests of the Unspeakable*, appeared, followed in 1929 by A.W. Wheen's fable, *Two Masters*. The most important Australian work on the First World War, Frederic Manning's novel *The Middle Parts of Fortune* (qq.v.) was published in 1929, an expurgated version, *Her Privates We*, appearing in 1930. Manning's novel draws on his experiences as an expatriate Australian, who served with an English county regiment in France, but the nationality of his characters is less important than the universal truths which they embody. The author's Australian origin may be detected behind the portrait of his central character, but Manning's integrity and artistry are such that his novel triumphantly transcends the limitations implied by such terms as 'documentary realism' and 'national ethos'. It is, thus, a very different novel from the other well-known Australian novel on the war, Leonard Mann's *Flesh in Armour* (q.v., 1932), which is a tribute to the courage, independence and mateship of the ordinary Australian soldier. Frank Dalby Davison's hybrid narrative, *The Wells of Beersheba* (q.v., 1933), is a reconstruction in literary terms of a number of historical events associated with the Anzac Light Horse Division in Sinai and Palestine. Leslie Meller's novel, *A Leaf of Laurel* (1933), contains, in its first section, scenes relating to Gallipoli. J.P. McKinney's *Crucible* (1935), a realistic account of war experiences in France, becomes increasingly cynical as it progresses. Martin Boyd's novel, *Lucinda Brayford*, with its concluding anti-war scenes, appeared in 1946, followed in 1962 by Boyd's strongly pacifist novel, *When Blackbirds Sing*. Roger McDonald published *1915* (q.v., 1979), an historical novel set partly on Gallipoli; in the last section of *1915* the war and its traumatic effects are vividly and movingly portrayed.

Important personal accounts of the war were written by John Lyons Gray ('Donald Black'), H.R. Williams and Martin Boyd. Gray's *Red Dust* (1931), the story of his experiences as a trooper in Palestine, expresses the author's pride in the AIF and intense disillusionment with war. Similar pride is present in Williams's *The Gallant Company* (1933), while the disillusionment predominates in the war section of Boyd's autobiography, *A Single Flame* (1939), as the author traces his growing sense of isolation from his fellow officers in first the Buffs Regiment and then the Royal Flying Corps. Other interesting personal accounts were written by Ion L. Idriess (q.v.), Joseph Maxwell, E.J. Rule, G.D. Mitchell, Sir John Monash and A.B. Facey (q.v.). Idriess's *The Desert Column* (1932) deals straightforwardly with experiences on Gallipoli as well as in Sinai and Palestine, while Maxwell's *Hell's Bells and Mademoiselles* (1932) deals informally and modestly with experiences on Gallipoli and in Egypt and France. Rule, the author of *Jacka's Mob* (1933), was an officer in the same battalion as Albert Jacka, the first Australian VC winner in this war, and his book describes events on Gallipoli and in France in a direct, objective fashion. Mitchell's *Backs to the Wall* (1937) earned praise from both C.E.W.

Bean and H.M. Green. Monash's *War Letters* (1934, ed. F.M. Cutlack) give some interesting insights into the character of this intelligent and highly-educated Australian commander. A.B. Facey's autobiography, *A Fortunate Life* (1981), contains, in its short war section, some vivid memories of the author's Gallipoli experiences. In simple prose Facey recreates, in the first part of his book, the harsh conditions under which life was lived by many Australians in the years before the war and the fortitude displayed, a fortitude that helps the author and his companions to withstand the hardships and horrors encountered on Gallipoli.

Second World War (1939–45). The three outstanding Australian poems of the Second World War, written by poets who would not normally be thought of as war poets, are David Campbell's taut ballad of the New Guinea campaign, 'Men in Green' (q.v., 1943), J.S. Manifold's affectionate epitaph on a courageous soldier, who fought and died in Crete, 'The Tomb of Lieutenant John Learmonth, A.I.F.' (q.v., 1945), and Kenneth Slessor's beautiful and compassionate elegy to the drowned sailors of all nations, 'Beach Burial' (q.v., 1944). Other noteworthy occasional poems on the war include Rosemary Dobson's 'Windfall Apples', Donovan Clarke's 'Ruin Ridge', Geoffrey Dutton's 'Abandoned Airstrip, Northern Territory', Mary Gilmore's brief lyric, 'The Swallow at King's Cross', Kenneth Mackenzie's love fantasy, 'The Tree at Post 4', Leonard Mann's 'Anzac Day, 1943', Elizabeth Riddell's 'The Soldier in the Park', Douglas Stewart's sonnet sequence, 'Sonnets to the Unknown Soldier', Judith Wright's elegy, 'To A.H., New Year 1943', Russel Harte's 'Landing at Lae' and Peter Middleton's 'War in Papua'. Typical of the volumes of war verse written by mothers, wives and other relatives of Australian servicemen which appeared during the war or shortly afterwards are Gwen Bessell-Browne's *The Road to Kokoda* (1943), Joan Kinmont's *This, My Son* (1943), Nora Kelly's *1940–1942* (1944), and Coralie Clarke's *Silent His Wings* (1946). Many of the volumes written by servicemen follow the tradition of popular Australian verse. Tip Keleher's *The Digger Hat* (1942) contains a number of patriotic ballad-like pieces together with a few poems like 'Nostalgia', written in a more formal lyrical manner. Bert Beros, a Canadian who served with the AIF in the Middle East and New Guinea, first achieved fame with the sentimental title poem of his volume, *The Fuzzy Wuzzy Angels* (1943), in which he paid tribute to the loyalty, devotion, and gentleness of the native bearers during the New Guinea campaign. Most of the poems in Maurice Clough's *The Fighting 'Ninth'* (1943) and *We of the A.I.F.* (1943) are confident, patriotic and optimistic in mood. 'What War Can Give a Man' emphasizes the power of war to cement relationships between men; 'Invasion Landing', which describes an action against the Japanese, is representative of Clough's better work. David McNicoll's *Airmail Palestine* (1943) is, in the words of a contemporary reviewer: 'a pleasing documentation of the places where the A.I.F. . . . fought'. The most successful poems in Paul Buddee's (q.v.) *Stand To* (1943) are the humorous and satirical pieces. Humour is the keynote of J.F. Dettman's *Here Was Glory* (1944), a collection of colloquial pieces in the style of C.J. Dennis. The most significant volumes of serious war poetry came from civilians-turned-soldiers: Tom Inglis Moore (q.v.), Shawn O'Leary, John Quinn, Maurice Biggs, Eric Irvin, J.A. Henderson, Val Vallis, Kevin E. Collopy, Michael Thwaites and W.S. Kent Hughes. In the title poem of Moore's *Emu Parade* (1941), irritation at the trivialities of army life is succeeded by a more positive attitude towards the Allied cause, which in 'Wardens of Wisdom' bursts out in the form of satire against academics and undergraduates who believe they are 'too valuable to go and fight'. O'Leary's *Spikenard and Bayonet* (1941) is a collection of twenty short poems based mainly on the author's experiences in the Middle East and written in a variety of verse forms. Quinn's *Battle Stations* (1944) contains two good descriptive poems, 'Troopship by Day' and 'Troopship at Night', and a number of shorter pieces in which death in war is treated from different angles and with varying degrees of emotional intensity, ranging from the dirge-like effect of 'The Dead' to the over-wrought incitements to kill in 'Action'. Four of Biggs's poems in *Poems of War and Peace* (1945) were cited by the reviewer in the *Bulletin* as 'the finest group of poems turned out by any Australian in the forces'. Biggs's 'Spring Offensive, 1941', 'What the Bullets Sang' and 'Christmas, 1941' are powerful, individual statements about war. Irvin's poems in *A Soldier's Miscellany* (1945) are sensitive, reflective pieces which describe the jungles of New Guinea and other places and highlight the brief moments of physical contentment in a soldier's life. In Henderson's *The World is Wide* (1946), two of the Mediterranean poems, 'Two Desert Graves' and 'The Middle Sea', stand out because of the author's concern with the deeper issues of time and eternity. Vallis's *Songs of the East Coast* (1947) contains two poems on death in war, 'Flotsam' and 'The Gannet and the Soldier'. Kevin E. Collopy, like Henderson a member of the RAAF, included in his *The Splendid Hour* (1951) a number of sensitive and skilfully-executed sonnets which pay tribute to courage and commemorate, with pity but without bitterness, death in its various forms. His 'Night Flight over Hamburg' is a successful narrative poem. The narrative mode is also employed, but more extensively, in *The Jervis Bay* (1943) by Michael Thwaites and *Slaves of the Samurai* (1946) by W.S. Kent Hughes. The title poem in the former volume, one of the few poems dealing with naval warfare, tells in longish rhyming couplets and in dramatic fashion the story of the unequal fight between the British escort vessel, *Jervis Bay*, and the German pocket battleship, *Admiral Scheer*, during the battle of the Atlantic. Hughes's volume, an ambitious poem in thirty-one cantos, 'written at odd times, on odd scraps of paper, in many odd places', is an effective account in heroic couplets of Australian POW experience. Other, less significant writers include Robert S. Byrnes (*Endeavour*, 1954), Louis H. Clark (*Romance and Reality*, 1944), Colin Thiele (*Splinters and Shards*, 1945 and *Progress to Denial*, 1945), Eric Locke (*From Shore to Shore*, 1944), Bill Wannan (*The Corporal's Story*, 1943), T.W. White (*Sky Saga*, 1943) and, although not Australian-born, Patrick Hore-Ruthven (*The Happy Warrior*, 1943).

Three early volumes of war fiction, which appeared in 1944, were G.H. Fearnside's *Sojourn in Tobruk*, Lawson Glassop's (q.v.) *We Were the Rats* and James Aldridge's (q.v.) *The Sea Eagle*. Fearnside's stories are often little more than anecdotes, sometimes realistic and at other times in the tradition of the Australian 'tall story', such as the humorous ghost story 'A for 'Arris'; but even the realistic sketches are enlivened by the author's sense of life's ironies and oddities. The first part of Glassop's *We Were the Rats* deals with the hero's life in Australia before the war, the remainder with army life in Australia, Palestine and North Africa. The book's strength lies in its frank and realistic documentation of digger talk, attitudes and behaviour, aspects of which shocked some of the original readers and led to its being banned in 1946 and republished in revised form in 1961. *We Were the Rats* is not an anti-war novel, despite its revelation of the carnage of war, and the author pays tribute to the bravery and mateship of the Australian soldier. Glassop wrote a sequel, *The Rats in New Guinea* (1965), more in the tradition of popular war fiction. Aldridge's *The Sea Eagle* is concerned with escape through the German lines by some Australian soldiers left behind on the island of Crete after the Allied withdrawal. The author, who served as a war correspondent in many theatres of war, including Crete, concentrates on the adventurous elements of his story but does not ignore the political issues dividing the resistance fighters who help the Australians to avoid capture. *The Winds*

Are Still (1947), by John Hetherington, is the best of the escape novels set in the Mediterranean. Concerned with a group of Australian and British servicemen who are cut off behind the German lines in Greece, sheltered for a while in the home of a Greek family, and subsequently assisted by other Greek patriots, the novel has popular appeal as a story of adventure and love. But it is also a realistic account of war experiences and contains some good studies of both Allied and Greek characters. *The Twenty Thousand Thieves* (q.v., 1951) by Eric Lambert is a novel about the exploits of the Australian Ninth Division in the Middle East; its merit lies in its vivid descriptive style, seen most obviously in the Tobruk and El Alamein sections, its vigorous narrative movement and its lively cast of Australian 'type' characters, as found among the other ranks; its weakness is in its distortion of the characters of the officers. Other less significant, fictional works set in the Mediterranean area include W.H. Williams's *Bardia Blow-Up* (1959), *Benghazi Blitz* (1960) and Richard Beilby's *No Medals for Aphrodite* (1970). Beilby's novel is another escape story set in Greece and follows a similar plot line to that of *The Winds Are Still*, although at a somewhat more consistently popular level. Williams's books are little more than adventure yarns, recounting the exciting exploits of a purely fictitious group of Australian desert raiders.

Three novelists who wrote about the wartime home front were Kenneth Mackenzie (q.v.), Dymphna Cusack and Xavier Herbert. In *Dead Men Rising* (q.v., 1951) Mackenzie writes about garrison soldiers guarding Italian and Japanese prisoners of war at a camp near 'Shotley' (Cowra) in NSW. The novel's climax is based on an historical incident, an uprising by Japanese prisoners. Cusack's *Come In Spinner* (1951), written in collaboration with Florence James, and Herbert's *Soldiers' Women* (1961) both deal with war time life in Sydney, and in particular with the lives of a number of women caught up in the frenzied atmosphere of a garrison city. The former tends towards an unsentimental feminist view of woman's lot, the latter displays a predominantly male cynicism and produces effects that fluctuate between the comic, the tragic and the bizarre. Two of the outstanding novels of the war, set in the mountains and rain forests of islands in the Pacific area, are T.A.G. Hungerford's (q.v.) *The Ridge and the River* (1952) and G.R. Turner's *Young Man of Talent* (1959). The main strength of Hungerford's short novel lies in its tight form and vivid descriptive style, which re-create with immediacy and intensity the physical exhaustion and mental strain of war in the jungle and the atmosphere of the oppressive, damp jungle

itself. Also impressive is the author's skilful treatment of the inner conflicts and the relationships among the characters, which are conveyed mainly through their lively colloquial dialogue and given additional depth through brief passages of reverie and 'flash-back'. Turner, in *Young Man of Talent*, goes a good deal further than Hungerford in character development. With a psychological subtlety rare in Australian war fiction, he creates in Sergeant Peter Scobie a highly-individualized and complex character, whose considerable intellectual gifts prove to be tragic flaws in the circumstances of the wartime situation in which he finds himself. The odd relationship that develops between the educated Scobie and the primitive, almost animal-like, private soldier, Andy Payne, ends in violence and tragedy and the novel explores the degree to which the responsibility can be sheeted home to Scobie's pride, insincerity and overweening confidence.

Other, less significant, jungle warfare novels were written by Peter Pinney, Eric Lambert, Jon Cleary, V.H. Lloyd, Leonard P. Manning, 'David Forrest' (q.v.) and Ron Tullipan. Pinney's *Road in the Wilderness* (1952) is somewhat deficient in form and characterization, but includes vivid descriptions of the jungle and a realistic account of war, particularly the hardships, the diseases, the brutality of killing and the fear. Lambert's *The Veterans* (1954), an inferior sequel to *The Twenty Thousand Thieves*, contains sections condemning black-marketing and military bureaucracy in Australia and concludes with scenes set in New Guinea, where many of the veterans from the Middle East campaigns meet their death. The tone is bitterly anti-war, anti-officer, anti-army, anti-civilian and anti-American. In *The Climate of Courage* (1954) Jon Cleary also deals with Australian Middle East veterans returning to their homeland then departing for the war in New Guinea. Its final section, loosely based on an historical incident, describes the fortunes of a small group of soldiers retreating before the Japanese in New Guinea. Cleary's other war writings include a creditable volume of war sketches and stories, *These Small Glories* (1946), with settings in Greece, Crete and the Middle East and which deal with such varied topics as the brutality of war, the anguish of a lovers' separation and the joyous oddity of characters thrown up by war, such as the glass-eating hero of 'The Magnificent Czech'. Lloyd's *The Hidden Enemy* (1957) is partly realistic war novel and partly romantic tale. Describing the rescue by an Australian infantry company under Captain John Grant of a party of women marooned at a mission station during the early stages of the Japanese invasion of New Guinea, it offers a credible account of military operations within a plot in which emotions run strong and actions and motives are not always fully convincing. A more documentary kind of truth is exuded in Manning's *Assignment New Guinea* (1958), an account in fictional form of the battle against the Japanese in the Markham Valley region of New Guinea. 'Forrest''s *The Last Blue Sea* (1959), the story of a group of militia soldiers pitted against the Japanese in New Guinea, contains some vivid descriptive writing. Only in part a war novel, Tullipan's *March into Morning* (1962) opens with an account of Australia in the years of the Depression before the war and concludes with an account of Australia in the post-war years. L.H. Evers, T.A.G. Hungerford, and Hal Porter wrote novels about the Australian occupation forces in Japan after the war. All three are concerned to emphasize the moral disintegration that overtakes an army of occupation as a result, particularly, of sexual promiscuity and black-marketing. In Evers's *Pattern of Conquest* (1954) and Porter's *A Handful of Pennies* (1958) the moral issues, however, receive fairly superficial treatment. Hungerford, in *Sowers of the Wind* (1954), offers not only skilful characterization and description but also a successful embodiment of a number of significant moral themes, involving such issues as integrity, responsibility for one's own actions, guilt and conscience.

Novels about the war at sea include the purely adventurous fiction of J.E. Macdonnell (q.v.) such as *Gimme the Boats!* (1953), which portrays his popular RAN character, Petty Officer Jim Brady; Wal Watkins's toughly-written tale of a mutiny on an Australian destroyer against its martinet of a captain, *Wayward Warriors* (1970); and Jack Harvey's documentary novel of the merchant navy, *Salt in Our Wounds* (1954). Harvey's novel, which is based on his own experiences in an open boat in 1944, is the story of the hardships endured by thirty-nine seamen, survivors of a torpedoed oil-tanker who, after enduring machine-gunning by a Japanese submarine, fight for their lives in a small boat adrift on the Indian Ocean for forty-three days. Similarly documentary in style is Norman Bartlett's novel about the war in the air, *Island Victory* (1955), which details incidents befalling members of an RAAF Kittyhawk squadron during a campaign on a Pacific island in the closing stages of the war. As the author observes: 'The events in this book all happened. It is fiction only in so far as events have been rearranged in a coherent pattern'. Part of the book is concerned with the adventures of a pilot who parachutes into the jungle and travels through enemy-held territory to safety. Other documentary novels about aerial warfare mostly concern life in Britain in the RAF, such as Ray Ollis's *101 Nights* (1957),

Geoff Taylor's (q.v.) *The Hollow Square* (1958), and Olaf Ruhen's *The Broken Wing* (1965). Ivan Chapman's *Details Enclosed* (1958) and H.V. Clarke's *The Tub* (1963) are also documentary novels, the former dealing with the experiences of two Australian soldiers in POW camps in Europe and the latter with four Australian prisoners of war in the hands of the Japanese from the time of the fall of Singapore until the end of the war. Vastly different in style are Geoffrey Dutton's irreverent comic novel, *Andy* (1968), about the airforce life and amorous adventures of its hero, and John Vader's fantasy, *Battle of Sydney* (1971), about a conjectured invasion of Australia by the Japanese. 'Nevil Shute''s romantic novel, *A Town Like Alice* (q.v., 1950) contains a section set in Japanese-occupied Malaya of the war years.

Much of the non-fictional prose written about the war, e.g. books by war correspondents, belongs to the areas of journalism and contemporary history rather than to literature. It is in those categories that the writings of such outstanding Australian war correspondents as Alan Moorehead, Chester Wilmot and John Hetherington (qq.v.) should largely be placed, although occasionally a war correspondent's book such as Geoffrey Reading's *Papuan Story* (1946), through its greater concentration on events the author himself witnessed and its more personal style, may lay claim to recognition as a personal narrative. The war correspondent George Johnston also is significant, to some extent, for his *New Guinea Diary* (1943), but more particularly for his success in transmuting the raw material of his life as a war correspondent into the stuff of literature in the final section of his novel, *My Brother Jack* (1964). One of the earliest personal accounts of army life is Donald Friend's *Gunner's Diary* (1943), a frequently droll account of the author's experiences of military training in Australia, and its sequel, *Painter's Journal* (1946), which ends as the author is about to forsake his career as an undistinguished private soldier for that of a distinguished official war artist. Another early account of army life, albeit of a very different kind, is Mary Kent Hughes's *Matilda Waltzes with the Tommies* (1943), an unusual story of military service and travel by an Australian doctor who voyages to England to enlist in the RAMC because the Australian army will not accept service from women doctors. Bruce Robinson's *Record of Service* (1944) records the author's experiences as a doctor with the AIF during the New Guinea campaign. Two other early personal accounts (both 1944) are P.C. Neasbey's *Blokes I Knew* and Leslie Taylor's *So Passed My Year*, the latter describing the author's experiences as a YMCA welfare officer. Two more significant books published in 1944 were Denis Warner's *Written in Sand*, the story of the desert campaign in North Africa written by a private soldier of the Ninth Division, and the anonymous *Word from John*, a volume of letters edited by John and Richard Ackland. Although restricted by the inevitable censorship of the war years, these letters provide an interesting account of the life of an AIF officer in the Middle East and New Guinea from the time of his sailing from Australia in April 1940. Of the army memoirs published after the war, David Selby's *Hell and High Fever* (1956) effectively recounts the adventures of a group of Australian soldiers who survived the Japanese capture of Rabaul and retreated to the southern coast of New Britain, where they enjoyed a precarious freedom, full of dangers and hardships, for several months until rescued. Selby tells his story simply, vividly, modestly and without sensationalism or bitterness. Equally effective is Peter Ryan's (q.v.) impressive story of danger, hardship and fortitude in New Guinea, *Fear Drive My Feet* (1959), a personal account of the experiences of a young ANGAU officer while patrolling the isolated and rugged country bordering the Lae-Salamaua region during 1942–43, usually in close proximity to the enemy. The book, a saga of heroic conduct, ends with reflections on the folly and vanity of war. Malcolm Wright gives an account of his coastwatching and guerrilla activities in New Britain in *If I Die* (1965). Other later army memoirs include Ken Clift's *The Saga of a Sig* (1972), subtitled *The Wartime Memories of Six Years in the Second A.I.F.*, and *The Soldier Who Never Grew Up* (1976), a collection of anecdotes and stories; G.H. Fearnside's *Half to Remember* (1975); and Henry (Jo) Gullett's *Not as a Duty Only* (1976). Clift wrote about the war in unvarnished soldier's language and was a man who, in the words of one of the introductions: 'must have been a headache to his seniors at times, but after many demotions in non-commissioned ranks ... finally won his commission through sheer fighting ability'. Fearnside, author of the earlier volume of stories, *Sojourn in Tobruk* (1944), gives in *Half to Remember* some well-written reminiscences as an infantry sergeant at Tobruk and as an infantry officer in the Aitape-Wewak campaign. Gullett, grandson of Barbara Baynton, subtitled his book *An Infantryman's War* and writes effectively of his experiences, initially in the ranks in the Middle East, then, after gaining a field commission following the battle for Bardia, in Greece and New Guinea, and subsequently with the British forces in the Second Front in Europe. Airforce memoirs include Gordon Powell's *Two Steps to Tokyo* (1945), John Beede's *They Hosed Them Out* (1965), D.E. Charlwood's (q.v.) *No Moon Tonight* (1956), and Ivan Southall's (q.v.) *Fly West* (1974). Powell relates in an episodic, anecdotal fashion various experiences observed and shared as a chaplain with the RAAF on Pacific islands to the north of New Guinea. Beede and Charlwood served with the RAF's bomber command, the former as a rear gunner and the latter as a navigator. Charlwood's book is a restrained, moving and convincing account of the high losses of life and the fears, tensions and sense of comradeship among those airmen lucky enough to survive their compulsory quota of flying missions over Europe. Southall, the author of several books about the war, including the biography, *Bluey Truscott* (1958), tells the story of his own service with the RAAF 461 Squadron while flying Sunderlands during the Battle of the Atlantic.

Prisoner of war and escape stories are conspicuous among the personal narratives of the war. Early volumes which deal with the Mediterranean and European theatres of war include L.J. Lind's *Escape from Crete* (1944), Edwin N. Broomhead's *Barbed Wire in the Sunset* (1944), and John Buckland's *Adriatic Adventure* (1945). These were followed after the war by Paul Brickhill's (q.v.) *The Great Escape* (1951) and Geoff Taylor's *Piece of Cake* (1956). Brickhill, a fighter pilot shot down and captured in Tunisia, tells an exciting story of tunnelling to escape from a German POW camp. Taylor, shot down near Hamburg during one of bomber command's night raids, tells of hardship and hunger in a German POW camp until the end of the war. The hardships endured by Australian prisoners in the hands of the Germans were probably less severe than those endured by prisoners of the Japanese. The accounts by the latter group of prisoners provide the most harrowing personal narratives in Australian literature. This suffering was touched on in Graeme McCabe's brief, tersely written *Pacific Sunset* (1946), but the full picture of sadistic brutality and callous neglect on the part of the captors did not emerge until the appearance of such books as Rohan Rivett's *Behind Bamboo* (1946), Roy H. Whitecross's *Slaves of the Son of Heaven* (1951) and Russell Braddon's (q.v.) *The Naked Island* (1952). In *Behind Bamboo* Rivett tells how, after escaping from Singapore where he had been a leading member of the news staff of the Malayan Broadcasting Service, he was captured by the Japanese in Java and subsequently sent to prison camps in Burma and Siam. The third part ('Burma Railway'), the grimmest section of the book, shows the experienced journalist at work, combining personal observations and experiences with historical material consulted after his release. Roy H. Whitecross, in *Slaves of the Son of Heaven*, limits himself to describing what he experienced and witnessed in POW camps in Singapore, Burma, Thailand, Indo-China, South Malaya and Japan. It is a remarkably objective account of stoical endurance and chronic suffering occasioned by brutality, dietary deficiencies, tropical diseases, and shortage of medical supplies. In Russell Braddon's *The Naked Island* objectivity is replaced by a highly personal style reflecting the author's bitterness, not only towards the Japanese but also towards the British high command, the British civilian population of Malaya and the many officers who illustrated the pettiness, inflexibility and folly that he came to associate with the military mind. An indignant and caustic book, *The Naked Island* reflects the emotional state of its author at the time when he wrote it. A change of attitude was to appear in its sequel, *End of a Hate* (1958). Betty Jeffrey's *White Coolies* (1954) and Jessie Elizabeth Simons's *While History Passed* (1954) are both personal accounts of the suffering endured by the thirty-two Australian army nursing sisters who, of the sixty-five who escaped from Singapore on the tiny ship, *Vyner Brooke*, survived its bombing and sinking and escaped the massacre that overtook twenty-one of their original number after their landing on the coast of Sumatra. The tale of their captivity in Japanese hands is told with great restraint by Betty Jeffrey and with somewhat more emotion by Jessie Simons. Restraint also characterizes *The Rising Sunset* (1957), in which Ken Attiwill, an Australian journalist who served with the British army, tells the story of his captivity in camps in Java and Japan, and Ray Parkin's *Into the Smother* (1963) and *The Sword and the Blossom* (1968), in which the author, a survivor of the sinking of HMAS *Perth* in Sunda Strait in 1942, records his experiences as a prisoner working on the Burma–Siam railway and in Japan. Norman Carter, an Australian radio script-writer who was in Malaya at the time of its fall, tells the story of his imprisonment with members of the Australian 8th Division and how he helped to organize stage productions in camps on the Burma–Siam railway in *G-String Jesters* (1966). Significant later accounts of POW life include Kenneth Harrison's *The Brave Japanese* (1966), *The Albert Coates Story* (1977) by Albert Coates and Newman Rosenthal, and Stan Arneil's *One Man's War* (1980). Harrison, a sergeant in an Australian anti-tank regiment, was captured in Malaya and endured the hardships of POW life in several places including the Burma–Siam railway and Japan. While describing the brutality of his Japanese captors, he takes pains to acknowledge their bravery and explain the reasons for their brutality towards prisoners, but without forfeiting critical judgement as to their faults. Harrison writes

with vigor and a feeling for style. *The Albert Coates Story* is a hybrid work, part-biography and part-autobiography. In the first and third sections Rosenthal supplies details of Coates's earlier and later years; the middle section is basically Sir Albert Coates's own first-person account of his experiences as a doctor tending Australian and other prisoners of war in Japanese hands. Coates, who was senior surgeon to the AIF in Malaya, gives a terse and balanced account of events. *One Man's War*, Arneil's diary record of his captivity in Changi, Thailand and Johore, supplemented by later summary sections and pictorial illustrations, is a moving, restrained, balanced, and comprehensive account of a prisoner-of-war's life. The author, an infantry sergeant, objectively records his sufferings in Thailand, and occasionally expresses criticism of the more brutal Korean guards and Japanese officers, together with his anger at acts of incompetence by British and Australian military authorities; he also describes the times in Changi when his life was less wretched.

Three dramas about the war require mention – Sumner Locke Elliott's *Rusty Bugles* (1948), Alan Seymour's *The One Day of the Year* (1962), and John Romeril's *The Floating World* (1974). *Rusty Bugles*, originally banned by the chief secretary of NSW on the grounds of its 'blasphemous and indecent' dialogue, is a naturalistic anti-war play, whose mood alternates between earthy comedy and pity as it documents the boredom and frustrations of a group of young soldiers stationed at an ordnance depot in the Northern Territory during 1944. *The One Day of the Year*, also a naturalistic work, is a serious exploration of the significance of Anzac Day in the Australian national consciousness and the generation gap as it exists between a working-class, returned-soldier father and his university-educated son. *The Floating World* is experimental in technique; through a mixture of naturalistic and expressionistic scenes set on a cruise ship bound for Japan in 1974, Romeril at first satirizes and later evokes sympathy for his returned-soldier hero, whose memories of sufferings and indignities as a prisoner-of-war in Japanese hands and guilt as a survivor ultimately undermine his sanity.

Korean War (1950–53) and **Vietnam War** (1962–73). The Korean War generated little Australian war literature. In *Korean Diary* (1955) Frank Clune gives an informal but undistinguished journalistic account of what he saw as a UN war correspondent visiting Japan and Korea; and in such narratives as *Mig-Meat* (1960), a story of Australian jet pilots in action in Korea, William R. Bennett wrote about the war at the 'popular fiction' level. The only significant work to emerge from the Korean War was A.M. Harris's novel, *The Tall Man* (1958), which won a prize in the *Sydney Morning Herald* literary competition for 1957 under the title *No Flowering Road*. Harris's novel, the story of a mission behind enemy lines led by an Australian military intelligence agent, is both a good story and a realistic account of the dangers, hardships and brutality inherent in the Korean situation, but its success is limited by the shadowiness of the portrayal of the unnamed Australian hero, the lack of serious themes and a mechanical reliance on authorial omniscience in the sections devoted to the earlier careers of various characters.

The Vietnam War inspired a considerable amount of Australian literature, including both verse and prose, the former mainly protest poems by civilian poets and the latter mainly novels about active service written by participants. The bulk of the verse is now available in two collections: an anthology containing prose as well as verse, titled *We Took Their Orders and Are Dead* (q.v., 1971) and a special issue of the journal *Overland* (54, 1973), titled *Vietnam Voices: A Retrospect*. An introductory statement in *We Took Their Orders and Are Dead*, which was edited by Shirley Cass, Ros Cheney, David Malouf and Michael Wilding, points out that all the writers contributed to 'register their opposition to the military involvement of Australia and her American and other allies in the war in Vietnam'. A similar statement in the *Overland* issue, which was compiled by R.H. Morrison, speaks of Australia's 'shame' over her entry into the Vietnam War and describes the poems themselves as 'a record of anguish and of protest'. Poets represented include Dorothy Green, Bruce Beaver, R.F. Brissenden, David Campbell, C.B. Christesen, Dennis Davison, Bruce Dawe, Geoffrey Dutton, R.D. FitzGerald, Len Fox, Rodney Hall, Nancy Keesing, Craig Powell, Tim Thorne, John Tranter, Chris Wallace-Crabbe and Judith Wright.

One of the few impressive prose extracts in *We Took Their Orders and Are Dead* is a passage describing a Viet Cong ambush in which an American army officer meets a particularly gruesome death at the hands of an old man and a boy. This passage on the death of Major Hatton is taken from Hugh Atkinson's novel, *The Most Savage Animal* (1972), a novel of protest against the Vietnam War set partly in Europe and partly in Vietnam. The five other Australian novels about the war are set either entirely or almost entirely in Vietnam. These are John Rowe's (q.v.) *Count Your Dead* (1968), Kenneth Cook's *The Wine of God's Anger* (1968), Rhys Pollard's *The Cream Machine* (1972), William Nagle's *The Odd Angry Shot* (1975) and David Alexander's *When the Buffalo Fight* (1980). Rowe, Cook and Nagle offer

honest, critical and reasonably well-balanced insights into the political and moral issues surrounding the Vietnam War, while at the same time sustaining interest in the characters as individuals. Each also offers vivid descriptions of the kind of fighting engaged in by Australian and American troops. Rowe's novel concentrates on the American contribution to the conduct of the war, with Australian characters playing subsidiary and somewhat inglorious roles. Although Rowe raises a number of pertinent questions about Australia's motives for intervention, he devotes most of his novel to American methods of conducting military and 'civil affairs' operations. He also explores differences in national characteristics with a candour that exposed him to official disapproval, since at the time of publication he was still a commissioned officer in the Australian army. The novel reflects the author's respect for humane and civilized values and also for the traditional military virtues such as courage and honour. The narrator of *The Wine of God's Anger* is a young Australian soldier whose Catholic upbringing has led him to enlist to 'save the world from Communism' but who at the end, guilt-ridden over his involvement in the war, sits in a Bangkok bar as an army deserter. Much of the effect of the novel derives from the wry, confidential style, which conveys the narrator's initial naivety, growing mental confusion, and an ultimate sense of nightmare, expressed through the black comedy of napalm-produced mayhem during modern jungle warfare. *The Odd Angry Shot* is also narrated by a young Australian soldier, whose story is told in a style of raw realism, complete with blasphemies, indecencies and crude humour. The death and maiming caused by the war, the frantic quest for pleasure during 'rest-and-recreation' leaves, the larrikinism and defiance of petty military authority among Australian soldiers are all brought out, as are their feelings of bitterness against the Australian civilian population who show them insufficient understanding and gratitude. Also expressed is their sense of pride in their professionalism as soldiers. Covering virtually the same range of activities as *The Odd Angry Shot* is *The Cream Machine*, which suffers by comparison because of its incoherent structure and disjointed style. A more documentary kind of novel is *When the Buffalo Fight*, closely based on events that befell members of the Australian First Battalion during their tour of duty in 1965 and 1966. This novel pays tribute to the fighting ability and efficiency of the Australian troops, often at the expense of the troops of South Vietnam and the USA. Two other prose works are Ian Mackay's journalistic account *Australians in Vietnam* (1968) and Dymphna Cusack's novel *The Half-*

Burnt Tree (1969). The latter, set in Australia, deals with the unhappy life of a returned serviceman maimed and disfigured by napalm burns, but contains sections in which the brutality of the fighting in Vietnam is recalled with horror and loathing.

J.L.

Waratah is the Aboriginal and common name for a bright flowering shrub of the genus *Telopea*, which grows in NSW, Victoria and Tasmania. The floral emblem of NSW, the waratah has figured frequently in Australian writing and has been particularly popular for its nationalist cachet in the titles of anthologies, collections, periodicals and school books. In 1909 a passenger and cargo liner named the *Waratah* disappeared without trace on a voyage from Australia to England, a disaster which gave rise to numerous books and articles, as well as a poem, 'The *Waratah*: Memorial Lines', by John Howard, published separately in 1911. Henry Lawson wrote a poem 'Waratah and Wattle'; Roland Robinson in his poem, 'Waratah', describes the flower as 'resurrected flame'.

WARD, FREDERICK ('CAPTAIN THUNDERBOLT') (1835–70), a bushranger who acquired legendary status, was born at Windsor, NSW, and worked as a horse-breaker and station-hand in the Muswellbrook and Mudgee districts. In 1856 he was sentenced to ten years' imprisonment at Cockatoo Island for horse-stealing, received a ticket-of-leave four years later but was again found guilty of horse-stealing. In 1863 he escaped from Cockatoo Island with another prisoner, Frederick Brittain, probably assisted by his wife Mary Ann, a part-Aboriginal also known as 'Yellow Long'. Ward carried out a series of armed robberies in the New England district 1865–70, at first with associates and later alone or with apprentice bushrangers. His success in eluding arrest was frequently attributed to his riding skills, although the ineptitude of the police undoubtedly contributed. Ward, now known as 'Thunderbolt' or 'Captain Thunderbolt', also achieved, apparently undeservedly, the altruistic reputation of a Robin Hood and of a gallant in his dealings with his women victims. He was finally shot at Uralla, NSW. One of his apprentices, William Monckton, subsequently published *Three Years with Thunderbolt* (1905), edited by Ambrose Pratt (q.v.), and Monckton's account forms part of an alternative version of the legend by Annie Rixon, *The Truth About Thunderbolt* (1940). Jack Bradshaw, however, who claimed to be personally acquainted with Ward, questioned parts of Monckton's account in his *The True History of the Australian Bushrangers* (?1924). The Thun-

derbolt legend has been celebrated in verse, drama, ballad and fiction; it is alluded to in the anonymous *Reminiscences of Australian Early Life by a Pioneer* (1893), and drawn on by J.M. Macdonald in his novel, *Thunderbolt* (1894) and Francis Adams in his *John Webb's End* (1891); it is celebrated in the anonymous ballads, 'A Day's Ride' and 'Those Bould Bushrangers', and touched on in Judith Wright's poem, 'South of My Days'. Ward's life has also been the subject of two popular films, *Thunderbolt* (1910), and *Captain Thunderbolt* (1953), both of which present him as a folk hero.

WARD, RUSSEL (1914–), born in Adelaide and professor of history at the University of New England, has written several socio-cultural, historical accounts of Australia, of which the most influential has been *The Australian Legend* (q.v., 1958). His other writings include the histories, *Australia: A Short History* (1965, revised in 1982 as *Australia Since the Coming of Man*), *A Nation for a Continent: A History of Australia 1901–1975* (1977) and two well-illustrated and documented socio-cultural studies, with Peter O'Shaughnessy and Graeme Inson, *The Restless Years, Being Some Impressions of the Origin of the Australian* (1968) and, with Graeme Inson, *The Glorious Years of Australia Fair from the Birth of the Bulletin to Versailles* (1971); and, with John Robertson, two compilations of select documents in Australian social history titled *Such Was Life* (1969, 1980). He has also translated Edmond Marin la Meslee's *L'Australie Nouvelle* (1973) and edited *The Penguin Book of Australian Ballads* (1964).

'Ward Two', a poem sequence in eight parts by Francis Webb (q.v.), was first published in its entirety in Webb's volume, *The Ghost of the Cock* (1964), although separate parts had been published in the *Bulletin* and *Meanjin* in 1962. The sequence is probably set in the male ward of the Parramatta Psychiatric Centre, where Webb was a patient in 1962. The stark hospital setting, the poet's own well-known mental illness, and the deep compassion and sensitivity of the poem, have contributed to make it one of Webb's best-known works. In it is Webb's acknowledgement that only in the real world, even if that world is the seemingly crippled world of Ward Two, can any individual make a meaningful existence. The opening segment, 'Pneumo-Encephalograph' (a device to locate brain tumours), counterpoises the cold, clinically-beautiful, scientific apparatus of psychiatry and the human agony that has brought it into being and in the service of which it functions with magnificent precision. Other sections of the poem describe the ward's inmates through the sensitive and understanding eyes of a fellow sufferer: the moronic Harry, writing his letter; the 'Old Timer', that 'small grey mendicant man', whose wistful plea for communication melts the poet into instant compassion; the Homosexual; and the Old Women who visit the ward on Sunday afternoons. In the poem's final segment, 'Wild Honey', where the poet watches a girl combing her golden hair, the apprehension of the beauty in that ordinary everyday action brings the recognition that in 'the tiny, the pitiable, meaningless and rare' lie the stars themselves – in 'sacred dishevelment' perhaps, but the stars nevertheless.

WARDELL, ROBERT, see *Australian* (1)

Wardens of the Seas, see **BRADY, E.J.**

WARNECKE, GEORGE, see *Australian Women's Weekly*

'WARREGO, PAUL', see **WENZ, PAUL**

Warrigal, spelt 'waregal', 'warragle', 'woregal' and 'worragul', was the Aboriginal word for the dingo (q.v.) or wild dog. Colonial poets such as Henry Kendall used the term in their verse rather than the more common but less poetic 'dingo'. Kendall's poem, 'The Warrigal', carries a grudging note of admiration for the dog which, although 'fierce and fickle and strange', possesses determination resourcefulness and cunning. The word was later used to denote anything wild and savage, especially an Aboriginal. Examples of its use in this way are 'Rolf Boldrewood''s *Robbery Under Arms* (1888), where Warrigal is Starlight's Aboriginal associate, and *The Squatter's Dream* (1890), where 'warrigul devils' is used to describe the blacks. Wild horses are described as 'warrigals' or 'brumbies' in Gilbert Parker's *Round the Compass in Australia* (1892). Joseph Furphy's creation, 'Warrigal Alf' Morris, is the disguised bullock-driver in *Such is Life* (1903). The town of Warragul in western Gippsland, Victoria, derived its name from the plentiful wild dog population in the area when the settlement was formed about 1865.

Warrigal Alf, see *Such is Life*

'WARRIGAL JACK', see **FURPHY, JOSEPH**

'WARUNG, PRICE' (WILLIAM ASTLEY) (1855–1911), born Liverpool, England, was brought to Australia in 1859 and educated in Melbourne. He was an itinerant journalist 1875–90, when he settled in Sydney. His career peaked in the early 1890s, when he was the

Bulletin's most prolific contributor of short stories and was well known as a radical journalist and political commentator. After he broke with the *Bulletin*, he devoted himself to the labour and Federation movements, being editor of the *Australian Workman* in 1893 and organizing secretary of the Bathurst People's Federal Convention in 1896; in 1897 he wrote for *Truth* and thereafter lived virtually as a recluse, his decline exacerbated by ill-health and drug addiction.

'Warung''s interest in Australian history was aroused as a youth and he claimed to have spent twenty years researching the background for his stories, mainly of convict life, which were published in six series in the *Bulletin* 1890–94, and *Truth*; about half of these contributions were included in the volumes *Tales of the Convict System* (1892), *Tales of the Early Days* (1894), *Tales of the Old Regime and the Bullet of the Fated Ten* (1897), *Half-Crown Bob and Tales of the Riverine* (1898), based on his experiences at Echuca 1876–78, and *Tales of the Isle of Death (Norfolk Island)* (1898). 'Warung''s best-known work includes the imaginative reconstruction of convict Ring freemasonry in 'The Bullet of the Fated Ten' and 'Secret Society of the Ring'. His indictment of the British administrators of 'the System' paralleled his strong early support of republicanism, added valuable literary fuel to the anti-imperialist fire of J.F. Archibald, and played a significant part in consolidating the legend that the convicts were more sinned against than sinning. Some of his lesser-known comic stories are included in *Tales of the Convict System* (1975), ed. Barry Andrews, who has also written the biographical and critical study, *Price Warung (William Astley)* (1976). See Convict in Australian Literature.

Wasters, The, a play by Arthur Henry Adams (q.v.), was first produced in 1910 and published in 1914. Reminiscent of Ibsen's *A Doll's House*, the drama explores the position of women via the relationship between John Dangar, a man exclusively and wastefully dedicated to his business, and his neglected wife Baby.

Watch Tower, The, a novel by Elizabeth Harrower (q.v.), was published in 1966. After the early death of their father, Laura and Clare Vaizey find that their opportunities narrow. Their unconcerned, chronically lazy mother, Stella, removes them from boarding-school to live with her in a Sydney flat, arranges for Laura to attend business college and enrols the nine-year-old Clare in the local school. Bound by their duties at home and at school or work, the girls have no outside interests or friends and even the outbreak of the Second World

War scarcely touches them. Laura becomes increasingly useful to her employer, the businessman Felix Shaw. He is a restless individual, apparently deliberately unpleasant except with the succession of young men whose goodwill he vainly attempts to buy. When Stella abruptly decides to leave for England, Felix casually proposes marriage to Laura although their relationship so far has been a business one. He buys a beautiful house at Neutral Bay, which Laura persuades herself is a guarantee of happiness. Felix's behaviour, enigmatic and unpredictable at best, rapidly deteriorates to the level of manic violence. For Clare he comes close to the Bluebeard figurine given to him by one of his reluctant protégés, Peter Trotter. Laura, working harder than ever although now she is unpaid, desperately tries to propitiate him, frequently sacrificing Clare's feelings in the process. As she grows older, Clare, who is both participant and detached observer, becomes aware of the 'collusion' in the situation: 'There was nothing not depraved, perverted. There was no feeling of sufficient grace to earn the august name of suffering'. Nevertheless, pity for her sister binds her to their shared life. Felix, meanwhile, delights in all forms of psychological cruelty as well as physical violence and deliberately cultivates an atmosphere of uncertainty, selling both house and businesses as the mood takes him. Finally, years later, the arrival of another unfortunate protegé, a Dutch refugee called Bernard, provides Clare with such a positive experience of usefulness that she finds the spirit to abandon the Shaw household. Although she elects to find her destiny alone, she is grateful to Bernard: 'Because of him that futile, wasted, lacerated thing behind her – her life – was transmitted into an apprenticeship of infinite worth'.

Watcher on the Cast-Iron Balcony, The, the first volume of an autobiographical trilogy by Hal Porter (q.v.), was published in 1963. His early years at Kensington, Melbourne, 1911–17, are dominated by his keen, sensual, detailed awareness of his material surroundings and by his consciousness of his parents as simple fatherly and motherly essences whom he implicitly trusts. After his family moves to Bairnsdale, Gippsland, however, when he is six, he becomes far more aware of his mother's distinctive qualities, her creative vitality, humour and courage. He attends first the primary school, State School 754, and then Bairnsdale High School, where he does well, avoids sport, discovers literature, and makes a variety of friends. He suffers mild bereavements, falls in and out of love, enjoys the frequent gatherings of his mother's relations, responds insensibly to the political events of the time and profoundly to

the familiar rhythms of small-town life between the wars and the lavishness of the Gippsland landscape. By 1927 he is sixteen, a cadet reporter on the *Bairnsdale Advertiser* and anxious to escape home, which now houses six children, and experience city life. After getting a job as junior teacher in a state school at Williamstown, he leaves to spend the next crowded eighteen months teaching school children, going to the theatre, making another set of friends, studying drawing at Melbourne National Gallery and acting under the tutelage of Gregan McMahon. But an 'avalanche' of suffering begins with an unfortunate love affair with an older teacher, the involvement of two of his pupils in a fatal accident, and culminates in the sudden death of his mother which he is called home to witness.

WATEN, JUDAH (1911–), was born in Odessa, Russia, into a Jewish family which settled in 1914 in a small town in WA, where his father earned a living as a hawker. In 1926 the family moved to Melbourne, where Waten still lives. He has had a variety of occupations ranging from kitchen-hand to schoolteacher but his paramount interests have been writing and politics. In 1931–33 he visited Europe and then England, where he became involved in the Unemployed Workers' Movement, and served a three months' term in Wormwood Scrubs prison as a result of his political activities. A dedicated communist, he had a difficult relationship with the Communist Party of Australia and is now a member of the pro-Soviet segment. He was also a member of the Realist Writers group and has close connections with overseas writers, especially in the USSR. Waten began writing early but failed at first to find his true direction because of his enthusiasm for such writers as James Joyce, John Dos Passos and Michael Gold. In the 1940s, however, he turned to his childhood for inspiration and began the series of short stories that culminated in the popular collection, *Alien Son* (q.v., 1952). Prominent in many literary organizations, including the FAW, he was a member of the Literature Board 1973–74. Some of his novels have been translated into other languages and several of his stories have appeared in overseas anthologies.

Waten has written seven novels, *The Unbending* (1954), *Shares in Murder* (1957), *Time of Conflict* (1961), *Distant Land* (1964), *Season of Youth* (1966), *So Far No Further* (1971) and *Scenes from Revolutionary Life* (1982); a collection of impressions of childhood experiences, *Alien Son* (1952), and another of autobiographical essays and short stories, *Love and Rebellion* (1978); an account of a visit to the Soviet Union, which also contains some autobiography, *From Odessa to Odessa* (1969); and a brief history of the Depression years in Australia (1929–1939) in the *Australia since the Camera* series (1971). He has also written a book for children, *Bottle-O!* (1973); has co-edited two collections of short stories, with V.G. O'Connor, *Twenty Great Australian Stories* (1946) and, with Stephen Murray-Smith, *Classic Australian Short Stories* (1974); and has translated a book by the Jewish writer Herz Bergner, *Between Sea and Sky* (1946).

Waten has described his *Alien Son* cycle, a series of loosely-connected stories dealing with the experiences of a European Jewish migrant family in Australia at the time of the First World War, as 'a kind of novel without architecture'. In these plotless sketches, humour and pathos, detachment and sympathy, psychological insight and social detail blend to evoke the flavour of Jewish life. Australian society, meanwhile, perceived as alien and hostile but necessary by the older Jews, becomes more and more an exciting challenge for the children. *The Unbending*, also a study of a Jewish migrant family of the same period, retains the solidity and resonance of *Alien Son*, although here the family is presented in more detail, and Australian political themes are given prominence. Waten's representations of the strong-willed, courageous Hannah Kochansky and her romantic, eternally-optimistic husband Solomon are the most compelling of his studies of Jewish parents. Reactions to his treatment of the local political struggle have varied widely, however. *Shares in Murder* is not a detective-thriller as its title and subject suggest, but a shrewd, documentary-type exploration of human corruption and police psychology. *Time of Conflict*, the story of a young Australian's inevitable evolution into a communist, achieves a sense of felt life in the descriptions of the hero's early hardships, but some critics have found that concentration on Communist Party politics during the Second World War weakens some of the novel's fabric. *Distant Land* is a return to the Jewish migrant theme, although this time set in the Second World War period. In *Season of Youth* Waten deals with an Australian working-class boy with literary ambitions who attempts to find encouragement in the bohemian circles of Melbourne in the 1930s. *So Far No Further*, a novel with a contemporary setting, deals with the experiences of Jewish and Italian post-war migrants and the inevitable gap between parents and grown children. *Scenes from Revolutionary Life* views the 1930s depression through the eyes of a communist activist and aspiring writer.

' "**Water Them Geraniums**" ', see **Wilson, Joe**

Water under the Bridge, a novel by Sumner Locke Elliot (q.v.), was published in 1977 and produced as a television series in 1980. The celebrations following the opening of the Sydney Harbour Bridge in 1932 dominate the beginning of the story and bring together some of the various individuals whose destinies are intertwined: the wealthy Mazzini family; the unpleasant opportunist, Archie Ewers; the youthful Neil Atkins, the novel's central character; the journalist and ex-country girl, Maggie McGhee; the English teacher and critic, T.C. Shallicott; and two sisters, who seem doomed to spinsterhood in Mosman, Ila and Geraldine Flagg. Neil is drawn into the Mazzinis' orbit by the fact that he goes to school with their son Ben and is assumed to be his friend, and by his fascination with their beautiful, restless daughter Carrie. Unknown to him, his foster mother, Shasta Davies, has earlier had a serious affair with the father, Luigi Mazzini. Others are also drawn to the family: Geraldine Flagg desperately but futilely attempts to break out of suburban stagnation and form a relationship with the disturbed Ben; Shallicott, who becomes the generous Maggie's lover, is bound by a formal commitment to Honor Mazzini and dies in a plane crash on his way to keep his promise; Maggie loses first Shallicott and then Neil to the Mazzinis, although at the close of the novel in 1973 there are suggestions that she will finally win Neil. Archie Ewers, handicapped by his unconscious vulgarity, plays a peripheral role for the most part, but at one point his vengeful interference costs one of Maggie's friends, Don Brandywine, his life. The Mazzinis become a subject of national gossip when the parents are brutally attacked by an unknown assailant, Luigi dying as a result and Mrs Mazzini surviving only to lead a vegetable existence. Later, after Ben's death, it emerges that the tragedy was of their own making and that Ben, tortured by the discovery that Luigi was not his father, had been the assailant. Contrasting with the glamour, melodrama and unreality of the Mazzinis is the earthy reality of Neil's ambivalent relationship with Shasta. Dominated by her pity for the infant Neil after his parents' death, Shasta had been forced to abandon her work and her prospects of a permanent relationship to care for him. Now, in impoverished middle-age, she alienates him with her violent oscillations between oppressive care and hysterical recriminations; at the same time she holds him by her jaunty heroism, her suffering, integrity and generosity. After a long period of acrimonious separation following Neil's decision to live with Carrie Mazzini, their original relationship is reversed when she suffers a stroke. Finally, when Neil is offered an acting opportunity in

London, he is forced to leave her in a nursing home, although she contrives to have the last word. The novel closes with Neil's return to Australia in 1973 as a famous actor, his last meeting with Carrie and his reunion with Maggie.

Waterway, see **DARK, ELEANOR**

WATLING, THOMAS (1762–?), born Scotland, received a good education, especially in art. In 1788 he was charged with forgery and in 1791 was transported to NSW, where he was assigned to the surgeon-general and naturalist, John White. Letters to his aunt, which Watling had begun at Capetown and continued in the Colony and which were critical of various aspects of the administration, were published in 1794 as *Letters from an Exile at Botany-Bay*. In 1797 he was given an absolute pardon and lived for a time in Calcutta, where he earned a living as a miniature painter, before returning to Scotland. Some of his work, including landscapes, natural history drawings and studies of Aborigines, has survived in the so-called Watling Collection, held in the British Museum.

WATSON, GRANT (1885–1970), was born in London, the son of a barrister who died young. Brought up mainly by his mother, Watson was influenced by her passion for Darwinism and read biology at the University of Cambridge. Watson paid two visits to Australia, the first in 1887 and the second in 1910–11, when he was a member of a scientific expedition led by the anthropologist Alfred Radclyffe-Brown, who intended to study the marriage customs of the Aborigines in northwestern Australia. Daisy Bates and a Swedish cook, Louis Olsen, were the only other European members of the party. With Brown, Grant Watson travelled to the Upper Murchison, Bernier Island and the Gascoyne, an experience which profoundly affected his later life and turned him towards the writing of fiction. In his autobiography, *But To What Purpose* (1946), he describes the impact of the desert and the Aboriginal culture on his European consciousness. Already unsettled in his own culture by his reading of Nietzsche, Ibsen, Jacobsen, Conrad and Hardy, and dissatisfied with mechanistic explanations of the world, Grant Watson felt that his European conventions suffered 'an objective devaluation' in Australia: 'It was in a way a unique experience, not so much understood and valued at the time, but valued and partly understood *afterwards*. It had lifted me, or perhaps sunk me, above or below the orthodox horizon of vision'. From this experience sprang his interest in psychology, especially in the work of Jung and

Steiner; his fascination with what he called 'the great Shadow', the problem of evil; and his commitment to what he termed 'the philosophy of the fringe', the belief that 'in the centres of civilisation life was withering away' and that 'human life was centripetal, having its sources at the circumference, and that it drove inward towards congestion and death'.

The author of over forty books, including novels, works on natural history, essays and some poetry, Grant Watson wrote six novels with Australian settings, *Where Bonds Are Loosed* (1914), *The Mainland* (1917), *The Desert Horizon* (1923), *Daimon* (1925), *The Partners* under the pseudonym 'John Lovegood' (1933), and *The Nun and the Bandit* (1935). His collection of short stories, *Innocent Desires* (1924), includes several with Australian settings, as well as his first piece of fiction, a story titled 'Out There', which deals with European–Aboriginal relations and which he contributed to the *English Review* in 1913. *Journey under the Southern Stars* (1968) describes some of the outward events of his visit to Australia that he had dealt with earlier in *But to What Purpose*. Familiar with a number of established writers and editors such as Edward Thomas, Austin Harrison, Havelock Ellis and Norman Douglas, Grant Watson also knew Joseph Conrad, who made copious critical comments on the manuscript of *Where Bonds Are Loosed*.

Although Grant Watson was the earliest writer of fiction to deal with the Aboriginal culture without ethnocentric prejudice, *Where Bonds Are Loosed* is concerned more with relations between European characters on a remote Australian island, based on his experience of the islands of Bernier and Dorré, than with Aboriginal life. For the central character, Sherwin, however, life takes on some of the primitive freedom experienced by the Aborigines. In *The Mainland*, a sequel to *Where Bonds Are Loosed*, Grant Watson develops the theme of the challenging emptiness, the spiritual purity of the desert, and the entangling complexities of civilization. *The Desert Horizon* and *Daimon*, its continuation, engage more rigorously with the idea of solitude as either ennobling or degrading. Interwoven through the life of the central character, Martin O'Brien, is the mystical attraction of the desert, which he experienced as a child and continues to feel as an 'inner exaltation' and even as 'the core of his life'. Martin gives up his attraction to the desert for the sake of his wife Maggie, but returns to it as an old man; Maggie, aware now that the desert is not evil but is beyond good and evil and expresses the mysterious, uncomprehended, non-human part of life, follows her husband's solitary search and is reunited with him before they both die. *The Partners* deals more sparingly and ironically with a similar concept of the desert as amoral and non-human; *The Nun and the Bandit*, which has an even simpler plot and a shorter time span, develops further Grant Watson's ideas on the co-existence and co-determination of good and evil that only the desert lays bare.

Grant Watson's novels are uneven and often overweighted with ideas, although enlivened by his sensitive response to the WA landscape. Historically anomalous, they are interesting in that they foreshadow themes used by later novelists; his feeling for the metaphysical implications of the Australian desert links him to Randolph Stow and Patrick White, his sympathy for the Aboriginal culture to Xavier Herbert, and his sensitivity to the experience of women in a predominantly male environment to contemporary feminist writers.

WATSON, KATHLEEN (1870–1926), was born in Wales and came to Australia as a young woman. The author of three novels, *The Gaiety of Fatma* (1906), *The House of Broken Dreams* (1908) and *Henriette Says!* (1921), and two collections of prose pieces, *Litanies of Life* (1897) and *Later Litanies* (1913), she wrote on romantic or sentimental themes. Her favourite mood is a stoical nostalgia; her favourite subjects are ill-fated love, death, exile, loneliness, altruism and motherhood. Her *Litanies* record the individual, regretful reflections of a group of lonely women; *The House of Broken Dreams* focuses on the emotional experience of a mother whose only son seems marked for tragedy from the outset; *The Gaiety of Fatma* recounts the experiences and extraordinary charity of a Franco-Arab girl who marries a Scottish baron shortly before his death, and visits London and Scotland before devoting herself to the Algerian poor. Watson is also represented in *Melba's Gift Book* (1915).

Wattle was the popular name given to the *Acacia* genus of plants found in abundance in the Colony by the early settlers. They brought with them from England the 'wattle and daub' method of building shelters, i.e. using long pliant twigs known as 'wattles', plastered over with mud. The acacia provided a ready source of such twigs, hence were named 'wattles'. The presence of the wattle in literature is noted as early as Adam Lindsay Gordon's lines 'In the spring when the wattle gold trembles/'Twixt shadow and shine' and Henry Kendall's phrase 'yellow-haired September'. The popularity of the wattle as an Australian motif is seen in its widespread use in the titles of early Australian books of verse and anthologies, e.g. George Wright's *Wattle Blossoms* (1857), *Wattle Blossom: An Australian Annual* (1881), edited by

Percy Sinnett, and *Oak-bough and Wattle-blossom* (1888), edited by A. Patchett Martin. The wattle's acceptance as a national emblem is evident in Henry Lawson's poem, 'Waratah and Wattle', Australia's two floral emblems, and in his dire prediction that if Australian society did not become more egalitarian, 'blood should stain the wattle'. Leslie Haylen wrote the play, *Blood on the Wattle* (1948), and one of David Campbell's most memorable brief poems is 'Under Wattles'. The wattle blossom is featured on the Australian coat-of-arms.

Way Home, The, see ***Fortunes of Richard Mahony, The***

Wayback, a synonym for outback, refers to the parts of Australia remote from settlement; it has also come to refer to the inhabitants of those areas. Examples of the usage of 'wayback' include *The Wayback* (1926), Sarah Musgrave's account of pioneering life in south-western NSW, and the Waybacks, a family of unsophisticated rural folk in a series of novels by Henry Fletcher. 'Wayback' is also commonly used in Australia as an instruction to dogs working sheep and cattle, as in Merv Lilley's autobiographical *Git Away Back!* (1983).

Ways of Many Waters, The (1899), the first volume of verse by E.J. Brady (q.v.), established him as Australia's balladist of the sea. John Masefield praised the poems as 'the best yet written about the merchant sailor and the man of war's man'. Notable poems include 'Lost and Given Over', 'Tallow and Hides', 'The Great Gray Water' and the title poem, 'The Ways of Many Waters'.

We Are Going, see **WALKER, KATH**

We of the Never-Never (1908) is a factual account of thirteen months spent by the author, Jeannie Gunn (q.v.), and her husband Aeneas (1862–1903), at the Elsey cattle station on the Roper River some 500 kilometres south of Darwin. The narrative commences in January 1902 with the couple at Darwin about to travel to the Elsey, where Aeneas is to become manager. In spite of spirited attempts by the station workers to prevent an Unknown Woman ('probably a snorter') from intruding into their all-male world, Jeannie Gunn battles on horseback through the hazards of the wet season to the Elsey. 'A nice little place', the Elsey is of undisclosed extent but its front gate is seventy kilometres from the homestead. The homestead turns out to be 'mostly verandahs and promises' but in the months that follow it is made more habitable through the intermittent exertions of an itinerant bush carpenter, Johnny.

Other vexations to the 'little missus' are the Aboriginal girl servants, who quickly 'knock up longa work', and a recalcitrant Chinese cook, Sam. The narrative follows the station activities throughout the year culminating in the celebration of the Gunn's first Christmas there. The episodic plot is primarily a device to illustrate the characters, notable among whom are the Sanguine Scot, a bushman of the old type, 'full of old theories, old faiths and old prejudices', whose one fear is that the onward march of civilization will not leave 'enough bush to bury a man in'; the Quiet Stockman, 'six foot two of bone and muscle' but sparing of speech; the Dandy, 'only a dandy in his love of sweet clean clothes and orderly surroundings', and with a capacity 'for finding something decent in everybody'; the Fizzer, the outback mailman who makes his hazardous trips to the far-flung stations to give them eight mails a year; Cheon, the new Chinese cook, 'the jolliest old josser' in the territory; and the Maluka (Aeneas Gunn), 'the best boss that a man ever struck'. The idyll ends suddenly and tragically: Gunn dies of malarial dysentery in March 1903 and Jeannie Gunn returns to civilization. An affectionate portrait of life in the back of beyond at the turn of the century, *We of the Never-Never* is one of Australia's folk epics; it has sold over half a million copies and has been read by four generations of Australian schoolchildren. A film of the book was screened in 1982. The homestead site at the Elsey is now a national reserve.

We Took Their Orders and Are Dead: An Anti-War Anthology (1971), edited by Ros Cheney, David Malouf, Michael Wilding and Shirley Cass, includes work by numerous Australian poets and prose-writers and was compiled as a protest at the military involvement of Australia and the USA in the Vietnam War. The title is taken from a line of A.D. Hope's poem, 'Inscription for Any War'. See also War Literature.

We Were the Rats, see GLASSOP, LAWSON

WEARNE, ALAN (1948–), born Melbourne, has published two collections of poetry, *Public Relations* (1972) and *New Devil, New Parish* (1976). Wearne has described his verse as having moved since 1966 'from Augustan-inspired satires and squibs, via elliptical investigations of my state of mind to the field of large-scale dramatic monologues and narratives'. He is concerned particularly with individual experiences of social change and in 'Out Here', which is the centrepiece of *New Devil, New Parish* and is composed of nine dramatic monologues, he explores a wide range of relationships and social perceptions.

Weatherboard Cathedral, The, see MURRAY, LES

WEBB, BEATRICE (1858–1943) and WEBB, SIDNEY (1859–1947), the Fabian writers and social reformers, visited Australia in 1898. Their observations of Australian society proved to be surprisingly inaccurate from a sociological point of view; although they met numerous public men, politicians, educationists and writers, they appear to have been handicapped by their English preconceptions and their total ignorance of Australian issues, circumstances and history. Their Australian diary, edited by A.G. Austin and titled *The Webbs' Australian Diary 1898* (1965), is an important addition to knowledge of the Webbs rather than of Australia.

WEBB, FRANCIS (1925–73), was born Francis Charles Webb-Wagg in Adelaide; after the death of his mother in 1927 he was raised in Sydney by his paternal grandparents (Webb), from whom he gained his interest in books, music, sailing and the seas. He had a reasonably happy and trouble-free childhood and adolescence and served with the RAAF 1943–45. He trained as a wireless air gunner in Canada but did not see action in the war. In 1946 he began an arts course at the University of Sydney but abandoned it in 1947 to return to Canada where he was employed as a publisher's reader. In 1949 he went from Canada to England, where he suffered his first mental breakdown. He returned to Australia in 1950, spent the years 1953–59 in England, much of the time in hospitals in Birmingham and Norfolk, and came back to Australia in 1960. Throughout the 1960s Webb struggled unavailingly against schizophrenia and spent most of the decade in mental institutions in NSW and Victoria.

Webb's published works are *A Drum for Ben Boyd* (1948), *Leichhardt in Theatre* (1952), *Birthday* (1953), *Socrates and Other Poems* (1961), and *The Ghost of the Cock* (1964). His *Collected Poems* was published in 1969. 'A Drum for Ben Boyd' (q.v.), first published in the *Bulletin* (1946), is a long poem about the Scottish merchant-entrepreneur, Benjamin Boyd. Webb also uses an heroic figure in the poem 'Leichhardt in Theatre' (q.v.), which was published in the *Bulletin* (1947), an abridged version appearing in his second volume of poetry in 1952. That volume, *Leichhardt in Theatre*, contains some of Webb's most significant shorter verse, e.g. 'Morgan's Country', 'Melville at Woods Hole', 'Dawn Wind on the Islands', 'On First Hearing a Cuckoo' and 'A View of

Montreal'. *Birthday* (1953) takes its title from his radio verse-play 'Birthday', about the final days of Adolf Hitler in the bunker in Berlin; it also contains the sequence of poems, 'The Canticle' (q.v.), dealing with another heroic figure, St Francis of Assisi, and several fine individual pieces, e.g. 'Galston' and 'End of the Picnic'. Most of the poems of Webb's next volume, *Socrates and Other Poems* (1961), had been written in Norfolk, England, following a long period of illness and recuperation during the late 1950s. Dedicated to Dr F.W. Klinghardt, who had supervised his recovery, and to the Australian poet David Campbell, who had much to do with his subsequent return to Australia, *Socrates* contains the most mature and assured of Webb's poetry. In it, and especially in 'Poet', his new concept of the artist's function (which W.D. Ashcroft has termed 'meditative purposefulness') is apparent. *Socrates* contains Webb's chief lyric poems, e.g. 'Bells of St. Peter Mancroft' and 'Five Days Old' (q.v.), and some of his most technically-innovative and skilfully-crafted verses, e.g. 'The Yellowhammer', 'Light' and 'Mousehold Heath'. *Socrates* also includes the fourteen-verse sequence, 'Eyre All Alone' (q.v.), Webb's finest analysis of an heroic figure, in this case the Australian explorer Edward John Eyre. The ordeal through which Webb had passed in his period of illness in England is revealed in such poems as 'The Brain-washers', 'Hospital Night' and 'A Death at Winson Green'. In the title poem, a dramatic monologue by Socrates just before his death, there is an unusual and impressive air of acceptance of the order of things; it reflects perhaps one of the few brief periods of remission in the progress of the mental illness that was engulfing Webb.

> . . . I front the grieving
> Song of the long spear that is your lifted
>   voice
> And coolly read the outcome in your eye,
>   my star.

Webb's final volume, *The Ghost of the Cock* (1964), was compiled largely from his unpublished poems prior to his admission to Callan Park mental hospital in the early 1960s. The title piece is a radio verse-play in three acts, to be accompanied by the scherzos of Bruckner's ninth and seventh symphonies, in which Michael and Tobias descend to earth intending to 'ferry to eternity' the sole human survivors, a man and a woman, of a nuclear war. Accused by the surviving animal inhabitants of cruelty and selfishness, the humans are forgiven and saved only by the intercession of the cock. The last volume contains two of Webb's finest poetic achievements, 'Ward Two' (q.v.), a powerful and moving sequence set in the Parramatta

psychiatric centre, and 'Around Costessy', a sequence centred on the Norfolk village of Costessy and conveying impressions of the Norfolk countryside. In the seventh part of 'Around Costessy', i.e. 'In Memoriam: Anthony Sandys, 1806–1883', Webb again defines the function of the creative artist. Webb's long-standing attraction to music, glimpsed in the earlier 'Tallis to Vaughan Williams' in *Birthday*, is indicated more strongly in this volume in 'Gustave Mahler' and 'Brahms at Bruckner's Funeral'. The *Collected Poems*, with a preface by Sir Herbert Read, adds a section 'Early Poems 1942–1948' to those volumes already mentioned. Important among Webb's uncollected poems is 'Lament for St. Maria Goretti' (q.v.), published in *Poetry Australia* (1973).

Francis Webb has drawn his greatest commendations from fellow poets: he was posthumously given the Christopher Brennan Award by the FAW. The most-publicized estimation of him is Sir Herbert Read's judgement, that he is not inferior to Rilke, Eliot, Pasternak and Robert Lowell. Similar high opinions have come from Douglas Stewart, who believes that in his profoundly original writing Webb has created 'a new language . . . a new imagery'. David Campbell insisted that Webb 'went higher than any other poet who has ever written in Australia'. Bruce Beaver sees the 'touch of genius' in Webb's capacity to 'take the earth-bound and spiritualize it, turning it into a holy fire of music'. Other reactions to the total body of Webb's poetry have been ambivalent. The earlier poetry, in which historical figures such as Boyd and Leichhardt are represented, has been generally well-received, *A Drum for Ben Boyd* winning the 1948 Grace Leven Prize for poetry. In the later, extremely complex, poetry the obsessively religious nature of his personal response to experience, the brilliance of his language and intensity of imagery have combined to categorize him as an extraordinarily gifted, though esoteric and somewhat inaccessible poet. Something of a cult-figure since his death, Webb exercised considerable influence in the development of some of the new attitudes that spread through Australian poetry in the late 1960s and 1970s. The September 1975 number of *Poetry Australia* is a Francis Webb commemorative issue.

WEBB, JOHN, see *Bulletin*

'WEEROONA', see SIMPSON, MARY

WEIR, PETER, see Gallipoli; Science Fiction

'We'll all be rooned', see 'Said Hanrahan'

Well Dressed Explorer, The, a novel by Thea Astley (q.v.), was published in 1962 and was co-winner of the Miles Franklin Award. It is a close, chronological study of a journalist, George Brewster, a supreme egotist with an insatiable appetite for sexual adventure. A practised charmer, with as wide a repertoire of appropriate roles and emotions as of journalistic clichés, he creates general destruction by instinctively exploiting relationships. He remains, throughout, engagingly oblivious of his shallow self-absorption.

WELLS, ERNEST (1902–), a lawyer and public servant, is the author of two books for children and three novels for adults, *Hemp* (1933), *Brave Music* (1934) and *Dirk Spaanders* (1936). *Hemp*, set partly in the convict era, includes numerous colourful subjects from pirates and whaling to the Victorian gold rush; *Brave Music*, a chronicle novel, has an action-filled plot ranging from the mid-Victorian period in Australia and England to the outbreak of the First World War; *Dirk Spaanders* is a buccaneering romance set in the seventeenth century.

Wells of Beersheba, The, an account by Frank Dalby Davison (q.v.) of the Australian Light Horse in a crucial battle during the Palestine campaign of 1917, was first published in 1933 and revised in 1947. Well researched, historically accurate, and written with spare realism, the story celebrates the heroic endurance of man and beast and the united effort that underlay their achievement.

WELLS, THOMAS (1782–1833), born London, was convicted of embezzlement in 1816 and transported to the colony of Van Diemen's Land. Wells was the author of *Michael Howe: The Last and Worst of the Bush Rangers of Van Diemen's Land* (1818), the first 'general work of literature' (J.A. Ferguson) published in Australia. During five years' imprisonment for debt in the late 1820s, Wells was involved, probably as amanuensis, in the preparation of *The Hermit in Van Diemen's Land* (q.v., 1830), although some contemporary obituarists and later historians, e.g. James Bonwick, credited him with the authorship of the work.

WENTWORTH, WILLIAM CHARLES (1793–1872), son of surgeon and magistrate D'Arcy Wentworth and Catherine Crowley, a transportee, was born en route from Sydney to Norfolk Island. Educated in England, Wentworth returned to Australia in 1810 and was appointed acting provost-marshall by Governor Lachlan Macquarie in 1811. He crossed the Blue Mountains with Blaxland and Lawson in 1813 and returned to England to study law 1817–20. In 1819 he published *A Statistical, Historical, and Political Description of the Colony of New South Wales* in which he foreshadowed such radical reforms for the Colony as trial by jury and a Legislative Assembly elected on a property franchise with no exclusion of emancipated convicts from that franchise. While at Cambridge in 1823 he wrote the poem, *Australasia* (q.v.), which was a distinguished entry in the chancellor's poetry competition for that year. Returning to Australia in 1824 Wentworth began publishing, with Robert Wardell, the *Australian* (q.v.), a newspaper which gave expression to the radical political reforms espoused by himself and his emancipist followers. Wentworth was instrumental in the creation of the Australian Patriotic Association in 1835, which under his guidance was to draft a proposed constitution for NSW. A substantial land owner, he became increasingly conservative and from 1843 onwards, when he took his place as an elected member of the Legislative Council, he advanced the cause of the large pastoralist interests at the expense of small landowners. In 1852, under Wentworth's leadership, the Legislative Council demanded and received approval for self-government for NSW; Wentworth was chairman of the committee formed to draft the constitution. His proposal for a colonial peerage, dubbed by Daniel Deniehy (q.v.) 'a bunyip aristocracy', came to nothing. His active political career finished in 1861 and he returned to England to live in 1862. His biography by A.C.V. Melbourne, *William Charles Wentworth* was published in 1934.

WENZ, PAUL (1869–1939), born Rheims, France, went to school with André Gide, with whom he remained friendly. He came to Australia in 1892 after extensive travels in North Africa, South America and NZ, married an Australian girl and worked as a jackaroo and pastoralist in various parts of Australia. He finally established a station in NSW, Nanima, where he died. Although his books deal mainly with Australia, he remained a French citizen, frequently revisited his native country, and served in the French army in the First World War.

Wenz published two collections of short stories which deal mainly with his Australian experiences, *A l'autre Bout du Monde (At the Other End of the World)* (1905) and *Sous la Croix du Sud (Under the Southern Cross)* (1910); an account of his early years in Australia, *Diary of a New Chum* (q.v., 1908), the only work he wrote in English; and four Australian novels, *Le Pays de Leurs Pères (The Land of Their Fathers)* (1919), *L'Homme du Soleil*

Couchant (The Sundowner) (1923), *Le Jardin des Coraux (The Coral Garden)* (1929) and *L'Echarde (The Thorn)* (1931). His other writings are *Bonnes Gens de la Grande Guerre* (1918), *Choses d'Hier* (1919) and *Il Etait une Fois un Gosse* (1930). Wenz used a pseudonym, 'Paul Warrego', for *A l'autre Bout du Monde* and *Diary of a New Chum*.

An acute and compassionate observer of Australian outback life, particularly fascinated by the daily experience of sheep stations, Wenz describes a wide range of bush individuals in his fiction – station-hands, new chums, swagmen, boundary riders, Aborigines, Chinese cooks and, especially, children. As aware of the hardship and potential tragedy of bush life as Barbara Baynton (q.v.), and as unsentimental, he is a more openly sympathetic recorder of its burdens, limitations and griefs. His gifts of keen observation, psychological insight, irony, dramatic compassion and eloquent understatement are seen at their best in his short stories. These range from the lightly humorous, such as 'Cinquante-cinq Minutes de Retard' ('Fifty-five Minutes Late') in which the birth of a child delays a train, to the poignant, such as 'Son Chien' ('His Dog'), an account of the relationship between an old swagman and his dog, to the starkly horrific, such as 'La Hutte des Becs-Cuillers' ('The Spoonbill Hut'), the tragic story of a new chum boundary rider. Wenz's *L'Homme du Soleil Couchant*, which deals with an Englishman-turned-swagman who finally makes good as a prosperous settler, is rich in vivid, detailed descriptions of bush life and memorable minor characters. *Le Pays de Leurs Pères* concerns mainly the experiences of backblock Australian soldiers in wartime England. Although Wenz humorously exploits the social gaucheries of the Australians to some extent, he also creates a clear impression of the bushman's integrity and simplicity. *Le Jardin des Coraux*, uncharacteristic of Wenz's fiction in its narrow scope, is set mainly on an island off the coast of Queensland and combines scenes of idyllic beauty with scenes of horror and violence. With *L'Echarde*, his darkest novel, Wenz returned to the Australian bush; a tale of an unusual evil passion, it has a powerful dramatic action.

'WEP', see PIDGEON, WILLIAM EDWIN

West Australian (1879–), successor to the *Perth Gazette* (1833–79) and the *Western Australian Times* (1874–79), became a daily in 1885. Its editors have included Charles Harper, Sir John Winthrop Hackett, Sir Alfred Langler, C.P. Smith, H.J. Lambert, E.C. de Burgh, W.T.G. Richards, M.C. Uren and D.B. Smith. Literary material in the *West Australian* has

included regular columns on writers and books; its contributors have included well-known WA literary figures such as J.K. Ewers, Henrietta Drake-Brockman and Walter Murdoch.

WEST, JOHN (1809–73), born and educated in England, arrived in Tasmania as a Congregational minister in 1838. An effective and leading advocate for the abolition of transportation, he wrote *The History of Tasmania* (1852) as part of the campaign; despite its polemical zeal it is one of the best nineteenth-century Australian histories. In 1854 West became editor of the *Sydney Morning Herald*, remained with the paper until his death, and helped consolidate its reputation in Australian journalism.

West, John is the central character of Frank Hardy's novel *Power Without Glory* (q.v., 1950). A semi-fictional study of a Melbourne multi-millionaire, John Wren, the novel gave rise to a charge of criminal libel against Hardy.

West Midland Underground, The, see **WILDING, MICHAEL**

WEST, MORRIS (1916–), born St Kilda, Melbourne, graduated from the University of Melbourne in 1937 and taught in schools in Tasmania and NSW. For twelve years he was a member of the Christian Brothers order but left the order in 1939 before taking his final vows. During the Second World War he served as a cipher officer at Darwin and was also private secretary to W.M. Hughes for a brief period. His first novel, *Moon in My Pocket*, a semi-autobiographical account of a disillusioned religious, was published in 1945 under the pseudonym 'Julian Morris'. West worked as publicity officer for a Melbourne radio station 1944–45, and was managing director of Australian Radio Productions, a company he founded, 1945–54. West left Australia in 1955 to pursue a career as a writer and published two novels in 1956 to finance his venture, *Gallows on the Sand* and *Kundu*. His account of the slum urchins of Naples, *Children of the Sun* (1957), brought him wide attention and with *The Devil's Advocate* (1959) he became an international best-selling novelist. His subsequent novels, which have frequently demonstrated his knack of predicting world issues and even events, have sustained him in this position. Since 1955 West has lived in Austria, Italy, England and the USA but recently returned to Australia and in 1983 became president of the National Book Council. His other novels are *The Big Story* (1957), *The Second Victory* (1958), *McCreary Moves In* (1958, as

'Michael East'), *The Naked Country* (1960, as 'Michael East'), *Daughter of Silence* (1961), *The Shoes of the Fisherman* (1963), *The Ambassador* (1965), *The Tower of Babel* (1968), *Summer of the Red Wolf* (1971), *The Salamander* (1973), *Harlequin* (1974), *The Navigator* (1976), *Proteus* (1979), *The Clowns of God* (1981) and *The World Is Made of Glass* (1983). West has also written plays, some of which are dramatized versions of his novels, 'The Illusionists' (1955), *The Devil's Advocate* (1961), *Daughter of Silence* (1962), *The Heretic* (1969) and 'The World Is Made of Glass' (1982). Some of his novels, such as *The Shoes of the Fisherman*, *The Big Story* and *The Salamander* have also been produced as films. Awards won by West for *The Devil's Advocate* are the Heinemann Award, the Black Memorial Prize and the Conference of Christians and Jews' Brotherhood Award. West deals with serious, often religious themes, as in *The Devil's Advocate* and *Daughter of Silence*, and internationally-significant political events, as in *The Ambassador* and *The Tower of Babel*.

Westerly, a literary magazine but concerned also with historical, social and political issues, commenced publication in 1956 as a student-edited magazine of the arts union of the University of WA under the editorship of R.W. Smith. From 1963, when it was first assisted by a CLF grant, *Westerly* began quarterly publication. By contrast with its fellow journals, *Meanjin*, *Overland* and *Quadrant*, *Westerly* began with neither a commitment to a particular ideology nor a well-known editorial identity. It thus became a forum magazine, although some continuity of editorial opinion and character was achieved in the late 1960s through the presence of Peter Cowan and John Barnes, and from 1975 when Cowan and Bruce Bennett became joint editors after publication of the magazine was transferred to the English department of the University of WA. Concerned from its beginnings to propagate local, national and international interest in Australian writing and culture, *Westerly* has sought a continuing discussion of the nature and character of Australian literature, and of the need for Australian studies in universities and schools. *Westerly's* publishing preference has been mainly for fiction, e.g. it published early work by Frank Moorhouse, Murray Bail and Michael Wilding, and the Patricia Hackett Prize, awarded from 1965 onwards for the best annual contributions, usually went to prose writers. The 1960s saw greater emphasis on art and poetry. *Westerly Index 1956–1977* (1978), compiled by Linda Goldstiver, is a useful bibliographical guide. *Westerly 21: An Anniversary Selection* (1978), edited by Bennett and Cowan, is an anthology

from the magazine's first twenty-one years of publication.

Western Australia, the largest Australian State (more than 2.5 million square kilometres in area, and occupying just less than a third of the Australian continent), was possibly discovered in 1616 by Dirk Hartog. It was not part of the original claim for the eastern part of Australia made by Governor Arthur Phillip in 1788, but in 1826 British interest began with the arrival of a small penal party from New South Wales. In 1829 a permanent settlement, the Swan River (q.v.) colony, was established near the present capital of Perth and the territory west of the 129th meridian, the then western limit of New South Wales, was designated the British colony of Western Australia. Although many older West Australians were unenthusiastic about Federation (q.v.), the State became part of the Commonwealth of Australia in 1901.

Western Australian Monthly Magazine, an early periodical published in Perth, ran from October 1843 to March 1844 and included some original poetry.

Western Mail, a weekly newspaper of WA, ran 1885–1955 when it was incorporated in the *Countryman*. In 1897 the first Christmas edition of the *Mail* was published; the Christmas editions became lavish, 100 page productions with substantial literary content, including the winning entries of the *Mail's* annual short-story competition. Contributors included well-known WA literary figures, e.g. Julian Stuart, J.K. Ewers, Henrietta Drake-Brockman and Mary Durack.

WESTGARTH, WILLIAM (1815–89), born Edinburgh, Scotland, migrated to Melbourne in 1840. In Melbourne his career as an import merchant prospered and he soon began his prolific publications. In the 1840s he founded the Benevolent Society and was prominent in the Melbourne Mechanics' Institute and the Port Phillip separation movement. By 1849 he had become one of the most respected public men in Victoria, a spokesman for those of broadly liberal sympathies who opposed the conservative Anglican establishment. In 1850 Westgarth represented Melbourne in the NSW Legislative Council and headed the poll for Melbourne in the 1851 election for the new Legislative Council of Victoria. Absent in Britain in 1853–54, he was appointed on his return chairman of the commission of enquiry into the Eureka rebellion. In 1857 he returned to London, where he established a sharebroking firm and subsequently played a prominent part in the granting of colonial loans and the general promotion of the Australian colonies. Active in 1862–64 in the campaign against the continuation of transportation to WA, he also helped to found the Colonial Institute in 1869 and was one of the preliminary committee of six which founded the Imperial Federation League. In 1888 he paid a last visit to Australia and on the voyage out wrote his *Personal Recollections of Early Melbourne & Victoria* (1888), among the most outstanding pioneer reminiscences. Westgarth's other major works on Australia include *Victoria, Late Australia Felix* (1853), *Australia: Its Rise, Progress and Present Condition* (1861), *The Colony of Victoria* (1864), and *Half a Century of Australasian Progress* (1889). Described by historians of Victoria as the most outstanding sociological thinker of the colony, Westgarth was both an effective, practical man and a perceptive intellectual. His major works on Victoria are primarily informative and unpretentious, but in their questioning of circumstances and events and their discussion of social and political assumptions, they reveal his powers as an original thinker.

Westralian Worker, published in Kalgoorlie 1900–12 and in Perth 1912–51, when it was incorporated in *Australian Worker*, printed considerable radical verse in the editorial periods of Wallace Nelson (1901–03) and Julian Stuart (1903–06).

WESTWOOD, WILLIAM (?1820–46), was transported at sixteen to NSW for forgery. In 1840, after brutal treatment at the hands of his overseer, he absconded and became a bushranger in the Goulburn district; he established a reputation for politeness and became known as 'Jacky-Jacky'. In the period 1841–46 Westwood was imprisoned at, but managed to escape from, Cockatoo Island in Sydney and Port Arthur and Glenorchy in Tasmania, where he was also a bushranger. Eventually sent to Norfolk Island, he led in July 1846 a riot involving most of the prisoners on the island; he was convicted of the brutal murder of a warder and executed later that year. Westwood is often cited as an example of a convict brutalized and then broken by his treatment. He is mentioned in many bushranging and convict histories and volumes of reminiscences, e.g. by Charles MacAlister and by Martin Cash, who was on Norfolk Island but not involved in the 1846 riot. The play by Thomas McCombie and J.M. McLachlan, 'Jackey Jackey, the N.S.W. Bushranger', refused a performance licence in NSW in 1845, was staged in Geelong, Victoria, in 1853.

Wet, The, a term used to describe the rainy season in central and northern Australia from December to March, has frequently figured in Australian fiction. Novels in which the Wet plays a dominant role are 'Nevil Shute''s *In the Wet* (1953) and *A Town Like Alice* (1950), Mrs Aeneas Gunn's *We of the Never-Never* (1908), and Xavier Herbert's *Capricornia* (1938).

Whaler (waler) was the name given to that species of swagmen who travelled, not the outback tracks, but on the inland rivers. These river tramps, usually possessors of a canoe or home-made small boat in which they carried their possessions, paddled along the rivers living off the land as they went, either fish from the river or sheep from the banks. Best-known among them were the 'Murray Whalers', 'Darling Whalers' and 'Murrumbidgee Whalers', all taking their names from the main inland rivers. Henry Lawson's sketch, 'The Darling River', depicts the whaler as 'mostly a withered little old madman'. Mary Gilmore wrote 'The Song of the Waler' in *The Tilted Cart* (1923); Louis Esson wrote 'Whalin' Up the Lachlan'; and C.H. Winter ('Riverina') wrote 'The Whaler's Odyssey'. George Dunderdale wrote of the whaler in his *The Book of the Bush* (1898). A noted whaler was the *Bulletin* contributor, 'Scotty the Wrinkler' (Phil Mowbray). 'Waler' is also a word for an Australian-bred horse named after the colony of N.S.W., used extensively in the cavalry in the Boer War and the First World War.

What If You Died Tomorrow, see **WILLIAMSON, DAVID**

WHATELY, RICHARD (1787–1863), born London, was an Oxford professor before his appointment as Anglican archbishop of Dublin in 1831. A man whose main hobby was the theory and practice of boomerang-throwing, although he never visited Australia, Whately became an implacable opponent of transportation (q.v.). His *Thoughts on Secondary Punishments in a Letter to Earl Grey* (1832) provoked *Observations upon Secondary Punishments* (1833), George Arthur's (q.v.) defence of secondary punishment (the further incarceration of convicts in colonial places of confinement such as Port Arthur and Norfolk Island). Whately responded with *Remarks on Transportation . . . in a Second Letter to Earl Grey* (1834), to which Arthur replied in *Defence of Transportation* (1835), and later wrote *Substance of a Speech on Transportation, Delivered in the House of Lords* (1840); all three publications are important examples of transportation literature and influenced the anti-transportation movement.

Whately's reference to Norfolk Island as an 'Isle of Death' gave 'Price Warung' the title of his last series of convict stories (1898). David Burn, however, wrote *Vindication of Van Diemen's Land* (1840) in response to Whately's criticism of the moral tone of the colony.

WHEEN, ARTHUR (1897–1971), born Bathurst, NSW, served in the First World War, won a Rhodes Scholarship in 1920, and later became librarian at the Victoria and Albert Museum, London. His well-known short story, *Two Masters* (1929), an analysis of the moral problems posed by war, was originally published in *Hermes* (1923). Wheen also translated works of war literature, including Erich Remarque's *All Quiet on the Western Front* (1929).

When Blackbirds Sing, a novel by Martin Boyd (q.v.), was published in 1962. The fourth in a tetralogy dealing with the Langton family, the novel follows the fortunes of Dominic, who is also the subject of *A Difficult Young Man* (1962). In this novel Guy Langton's role as narrator is relinquished. Dominic leaves his wife Helena, with whom he has been happy, to join the English forces in the First World War. In England he becomes an efficient officer and drifts into an affair with Sylvia Tunstall, although later feelings of guilt alienate him from Sylvia and from the war effort. The act of killing a German soldier in hand to hand combat turns him into a pacifist. After a period in military hospital, where he is deeply stirred by the fate of a mutilated friend, Dominic returns to Australia, which he sees as the innocent hemisphere. There, however, his wife's incomprehension of his pacifist position deepens his sense of spiritual rootlessness.

'Where the Dead Men Lie', the best-known poem by Barcroft Boake (q.v.) and the title poem of his only volume of verse (1897), was published in the *Bulletin* (1891) under the pseudonym 'Surcingle'. In the poem Boake uses the contemptuous name 'Moneygrub' to denote the typical wealthy absentee landlord who lives in city luxury provided for him by the ordinary men and women of the outback; 'out on the wastes of the Never-Never', they give their lives in the one-sided struggle against poverty, privation and the harshness of the land.

'Where the Pelican Builds', see **FOOTT, MARY HANNAY**

While the Billy Boils, Henry Lawson's (q.v.) first major collection of prose, was published in 1896. The fifty-two stories of *While the Billy Boils*, generally considered Lawson's best book,

include the most significant Mitchell and Steelman yarns and several stories, e.g. 'The Union Buries Its Dead' and 'The Drover's Wife', which are central to his creation of a pessimistic bush world. *While the Billy Boils* proved to be a popular title, not merely in terms of sales for the original volume; the publisher George Robertson reprinted a number of Lawson's works under a series title, The Billy Boils, and the Lawson selection which was filmed in 1921 also bore the title, *While the Billy Boils*, as do some modern selections of Lawson's prose.

'White Australia: Or, the Empty North', see **Chinese in Australian Literature**

WHITE, CHARLES (1845–1922), the uncle of Mary Gilmore (q.v.), was born in Bathurst, NSW, and became a reporter on his father's *Bathurst Free Press*, which he edited 1884–1902. As a police roundsman in the 1860s, White reported on the activities of the local bushrangers, including Ben Hall, Frank Gardiner and John Gilbert; he remained interested in the subject and wrote *The Story of the Bushrangers* (1891–93), which later became the popular *History of Australian Bushranging* (1902). Equally important as a work of history, though less known, is his *Convict Life in New South Wales and Van Diemen's Land* (1889).

WHITE, GILBERT (1859–1933), born Cape Town, South Africa, was successively bishop of Carpentaria and of Willochra and wrote numerous theological works as well as the descriptive accounts, *Round about the Torres Straits* (1917) and *Thirty Years in Tropical Australia* (1918). He also published six volumes of verse, *Melchior and Other Verses* (1893), *Night* (1897), *The World's Tragedy* (1910), *Australia* (1913), *The Poems of Gilbert White* (1919) and *The Later Poems of Gilbert White* (1930).

WHITE, JOHN (?1756–1832), born Sussex, was chief surgeon in the First Fleet. A keen naturalist, he kept a journal in which he made notes of birds in the Colony and which he sent to a London friend, Thomas Wilson, in November 1788. It was published in 1790 as *Journal of a Voyage to New South Wales*, was immediately successful and subsequently widely translated. White also contributed drawings to *The Voyage of Governor Phillip to Botany Bay* (1789). Although his capacities as a surgeon were severely tested in the new settlement, especially after the arrival of the Second Fleet in June 1790, he kept up his naturalist interests and after October 1792 was assisted by the convict and artist, Thomas Watling. Before he left the Colony in December 1794, White received grants of land, which he retained until

1822. He died in England after further service in the RN.

WHITE, MYRTLE ROSE (1888–1961), born Acacia Vale near Broken Hill, NSW, lived in the outback for most of her life and published several popular books about her experiences: *No Roads Go By* (1932), *For Those That Love It* (1933), *Beyond the Western Rivers* (1955) and *From That Day to This* (1961). Of these, *No Roads Go By* has acquired the status of a classic; an account of the seven years she spent in an isolated area at Lake Elder between Lake Frome in SA and the NSW border with her station-manager husband and three children, the book was later described by John Flynn as one of the most potent influences on his determination to establish the Flying Doctor Service. White's books combine starkly realistic representations of the loneliness and hardships of outback life with wry humour, lively descriptions of the mischievous activities of young children and an unpretentious style.

WHITE, PATRICK (1912–   ), is a member of a family of pastoralists that has been established in Australia for three generations. Born in London, he was brought back to Australia at the age of six months and educated first at private schools in NSW and, from the age of thirteen, at Cheltenham College, England. *Thirteen Poems*, a collection privately printed in Sydney in about 1930, dates from his years at Cheltenham. In 1929 he returned to Australia, where he spent two years as a jackeroo and one reading history for entrance to King's College, Cambridge. At Cambridge, however, he decided on modern languages, a study which took him on frequent visits to France and Germany. After graduating in 1935 he moved to London where he became friendly with other artists, writers and musicians, both English and Australian. His first published novel, *Happy Valley*, appeared in 1939 but his main ambition at this time was to write for the stage. Two 'inferior comedies', as he has described them, 'Bread and Butter Women' and 'The School for Friends', were produced at Bryant's Playhouse, Sydney, in 1935; in the same year he also wrote sketches and lyrics for intimate revues staged by Herbert Farjeon at the Little and Gate theatres, London. Two short stories, 'Cocotte' and 'The Twitching Colonel', and some poetry, later included in his collection *The Ploughman* (1935), appeared in prominent London journals. In 1939 he went for an extended visit to the USA where he wrote his novel, *The Living and the Dead* (1941). He joined the RAF in 1941 and was an intelligence officer in the Middle East. Experience of the desert, coupled with a subsequent year's stay in Greece, stimulated his yearning for 'the scenes of childhood'. Demobilization left him with the alternatives of turning into what he later described as 'the most sterile of beings, a London intellectual', or of 'returning home, to the stimulus of time remembered'. After a visit to Australia in 1946 he chose the latter and returned permanently in 1948. His play *The Ham Funeral* (q.v.) was written in London in 1947 and another play that has since been lost, 'Return to Abyssinia', was performed at Bolton's Theatre, London that year. He completed the novel *The Aunt's Story* (q.v., 1948) on the 1948 sea voyage to Australia. He settled at first on a small farm at Castle Hill on the outskirts of Sydney but in 1964 moved to Centennial Park near the centre of the city.

Although White has lived a secluded life in Australia, he has occasionally made public statements on national issues such as the war in Vietnam, environmental matters and Aboriginal affairs. He was also involved in the 1972 federal election campaign that resulted in a Labor government and in the protests after its dismissal in 1975. In 1976 he withdrew from the Order of Australia in protest against some of the government's policies. He has contributed generously to Aboriginal schools, donated a collection of works by Australian painters to the Art Gallery of NSW and, with his 1973 Nobel Prize, established the Patrick White Literary Award (q.v.). White's other writings are the novels, *The Tree of Man* (q.v., 1955), *Voss* (q.v., 1957), *Riders in the Chariot* (q.v., 1961), *The Solid Mandala* (q.v., 1966), *The Vivisector* (q.v., 1970), *The Eye of the Storm* (q.v., 1973), *A Fringe of Leaves* (q.v., 1976) and *The Twyborn Affair* (q.v., 1979); the collections of short stories, *The Burnt Ones* (1964) and *The Cockatoos* (1974); the plays, *Four Plays by Patrick White* (*The Ham Funeral, The Season at Sarsaparilla, A Cheery Soul* (qq.v.) and *Night on Bald Mountain*) (1965), *Big Toys* (q.v. 1978), *The Night the Prowler* (1978), *Netherwood* (1983) and *Signal Driver* (1983); and the autobiography, *Flaws in the Glass* (q.v., 1981). His essay, 'The Prodigal Son', in *Australian Letters* (1958) is an important statement on his work and reasons for living in Australia. In 1973 White won the Nobel Prize for *The Eye of the Storm* and his other awards include the Gold Medal of the Australian Literature Society for *Happy Valley* and *The Tree of Man*, the Miles Franklin Award for *Voss* and *Riders in the Chariot* and the W.H. Smith Literary Award for *Voss*.

Although White's work received some important early appreciations in Australia it was not until the overseas acclaim of *The Tree of Man* that it began to arouse more general, if still ambivalent, interest. Ambivalence, in turn, is also a dominant feature of White's response to Australia. On the one hand critical of Australia's 'exaltation of the average', of 'the Great Australian emptiness in which the mind is the least of possessions ... and ... the march of material ugliness does not raise a quiver from the average nerves', he has emphasized the crucial link between the land and his creativity. Only in Australia could he achieve 'the state of simplicity and humility [which] is the only desirable one for artist or man'. Here he 'began to see things for the first time. Even the boredom and frustration presented avenues for endless exploration; even the ugliness, the bags and iron of Australian life, acquired a meaning'. Much of the distinctive energy, dynamism and constructive conflict of his work springs from this source. In his early fiction White's debts to the European tradition, especially to such writers as James Joyce, D.H. Lawrence, Virginia Woolf and T.S. Eliot, are easy to discover, but from *The Aunt's Story* onwards his original talent has appropriated and shaped the novel in a strikingly distinctive way. He has described his writing as a 'struggle to create completely fresh forms out of the rocks and sticks of words', a struggle that each work resolves differently. White never repeats himself, each novel creating a fresh perspective even while remaining faithful to his central preoccupations. The most immediately impressive features of his work are a protean, creative energy that releases itself in uninhibited, confident play, mordant wit, sharp clarity of observation, zestful comedy and a sure grasp of a wide variety of idioms, people, places and incidents. Particularly striking is his prophetic tone, that seems to enhance every powerfully-seized detail with transcending significance. A novelist of dualisms, White combines Swiftian satire and Blakean vision, an ability to render the everyday in all its palpable and even sordid actuality and at the same time invest it with illuminating intensity. Although he belongs to no specific creed, he has frequently described himself as a religious artist whose intention is to 'convey a splendour, a transcendence which is ... there above human realities'. Concerned above all with consciousness, his work bears witness to the immanence of all worlds in the immediately apparent one, expressed most succinctly in the epigraph to *The Solid Mandala*: 'There is another world, but it is this one'. Rational processes or a commitment to the material can only apprehend a fraction of the totality of being and both the sterile intellectual and the shallow materialist are familiar figures in his fiction. Contrasting with these are the visionary few, those who are courageous enough to explore the non-rational world and accept

the inevitable suffering and solitude that the spiritual quest brings: 'True knowledge only comes of death by torture in the country of the mind' (*Voss*). Necessarily set apart, in that their unusual openness to experience frequently appears as outward eccentricity or even madness, the saints of White's world are nevertheless bound to the rest of humanity in their frailty and capacity for evil. Failure, furthermore, is a necessary feature of the spiritual journey: 'The mystery of life is not solved by success, which is an end in itself, but in failure, in perpetual struggle, in becoming' (*Voss*). Nor does spirituality preclude the carnal or the material; the physical existence both of objects and of the self, grasped in an intensely palpable way by White's visionaries, is frequently the means to their experience of heightened, psychic awareness. Thus, objects often act as hinges between the worlds of consciousness, such as the butterflies in *Voss*, the cracks in the path or the gob of spittle in *The Tree of Man*, the glass marbles in *The Solid Mandala* and the little red-eyed hawk in *The Aunt's Story*. White is preoccupied with the complex dualisms of existence on the one hand, and with totality and the possibilities of integration on the other. He sees ambivalence as present in everything: good and evil, body and spirit, joy and suffering, love and hate, life and death, male and female, dream and actuality, time and eternity. For White's visionaries, however, in their fugitive experiences of the immanent spiritual world, the eternal co-existence of thesis and antithesis blends into a higher cosmic synthesis. The difficulties of transmitting such a vision are overcome by White's urgent, dynamically suggestive imagery and his expressive eccentricities of language and syntax. Frequently his use of uniting, mandalic symbols, such as the heavenly chariot in *Riders in the Chariot*, the glass marbles in *The Solid Mandala* and the storm in *The Eye of the Storm*, shape and complicate his fictional structures with a visionary dimension. Deliberately poetic in its effects, his work depends on the cumulation of detailed effects and is consciously indebted to the arts of music and painting: speaking of *Voss* he has said: 'Always something of a frustrated painter and a composer *manqué*, I wanted to give my book the textures of music and sensuousness of paint, to convey through the theme and characters ... what Delacroix and Blake might have seen, what Mahler and Liszt might have heard' ('The Prodigal Son').

In White's first novel, *Happy Valley*, a dark study of a small community in NSW, some of his characteristic preoccupations, such as the necessity of suffering, emerge. Although self-conscious literariness and a novelettish quality betray it as an early work, the powers of strikingly original description and interest in human motive are already apparent. *The Living and the Dead*, a conventional novel of manners set entirely in England, is a distinct advance in skill and polish and shows a confident assimilation of literary debts. Impressive for its social comedy and representation of Edwardian and post-First World War England, it lacks the cohering force of White's later positive vision and fails to resolve the problem posed by its title: how to live rather than merely exist.

It is in his third novel, *The Aunt's Story*, that White's powerful originality first firmly declares itself. Theodora Goodman, an outwardly unattractive spinster, is his first extended study of the visionary individual, bent on a solitary quest for the ultimate reality. The first section of the novel, dealing with Theodora's early life in Australia, combines an outer, representational movement with an inner, poetically suggestive one. But after Theodora is freed by the death of her mother to pursue her singular vision, the narrative becomes appropriately surreal and expressionistic, although still organically connected to the earlier section. The last brief phase of the novel takes on a sustained lyricism as Theodora penetrates to a state of total lucidity that is interpreted by witnesses as madness. In *The Tree of Man* White attempts a much broader canvas. Epic and even biblical in tone, it narrates the lives of a pioneering couple, Stan and Amy Parker, from youth to old age. White has said that he tried to suggest in this novel 'every possible aspect of life, through the lives of an ordinary man and woman. But at the same time . . . to discover the extraordinary behind the ordinary, the mystery and poetry which alone could make bearable the lives of such people'. The novel includes a representation of rural life as a felt actuality, but Stan and Amy's inner lives and especially the increasing conflict between Stan's intuitions of meaning and the outer confusion are the centre of interest. The vision that is granted to him before his death comprehends both the unity of being and the inevitable isolation of the self. *Voss* turns back to the 1840s to the experience of a German explorer who has affinities with Ludwig Leichhardt. Moving with a deft wit between the complacent materialism of colonial Sydney and the stark agonies of Voss and his followers in the desert, White transforms the explorer myth into a metaphor of modern alienation and arrogant individualism. As Voss pits himself against the desert in an act of self-deification, Laura Trevelyan, his betrothed, commits herself to a struggle for his soul. The spiritual, emotional contest between the two, conducted telepathically and culminating in their 'marriage' and mutual discovery of a higher but immanent reality, is counterpointed with actual events both in the wilderness and in Sydney.

Riders in the Chariot, White's most controversial novel, introduces a more idiosyncratic group of novels which seemed at the time to mark him to his critics as both aloofly patrician and bitterly misanthropic. Although its savage social satire and portentous tone have alienated some readers, White's virtuoso mastery of a wide range of modes and the sustained grandeur of his informing religious conception are impressive. Set in his imaginary Sydney suburbs of Sarsaparilla, Barranugli (qq.v.) and Paradise East, it is structured by a brilliant realization of the inner and outer lives of four illuminates: Miss Hare, a spinster; Mordecai Himmelfarb, a Jewish refugee; Ruth Godbold, an Australian housewife; and Alf Dubbo, a tubercular Aboriginal artist, whose painting of the heavenly chariot finally expresses the transcending vision that unites the four. Contrasting with these is a range of wittily-seized satiric creations such as the plastic ladies of suburbia, Mrs Jolley and Mrs Flack, and the perfectly assimilated Jews, Harry and Shirl Rosetree. *The Solid Mandala* has the same setting as *Riders in the Chariot* but is a more modest, relaxed and unified novel. The outwardly uneventful but inwardly dramatic lives of twin brothers, Arthur and Waldo Brown, are the centre of interest. The two brothers, yoked by genes, experiences and habit, love and hate, are also divided by their differences: the bright but neurotic Waldo forever shuts himself off from growth by his emotional solipsism, whereas the mentally-backward Arthur effectively communicates with others and pursues a transcending mandalic vision. In *The Vivisector* White treats a difficult and complex subject, the act of creation and its costs as realized from within the artist's consciousness. Hurtle Duffield, the artist-protagonist, is the vivisector who cuts up living experiences and relationships for the purposes of his art. But Hurtle also comprehends art as an avenue to a realization of the Divine Vivisector, God, and both the successive women in his life and his paintings represent stages in his quest for a perception of pure being. The quest culminates in his final attempt, disrupted by his last stroke, to paint God. As a background to Hurtle's experiences, described with uncompromising honesty, is White's most comprehensive and intimately realized picture of the changing Australian social milieu.

The Eye of the Storm moves to a study of a life which is itself conceived as a work of art. Ostensibly a conventionally structured novel, it extends White's basic preoccupations in a completely different direction. Elizabeth Hunter, once a brilliant socialite and a rich, sensual, materialistic woman, now into her eighties, is dying in her Sydney mansion, perceived as a house-shrine by the nurses and servants who devotedly revolve around her. Mrs Hunter's crucial experience, during the eye of a cyclone, of harmony between her inner, essential self and the outer void has determined the rest of her life, especially the act of dying. Flawed as she is, her strength and intense authenticity of being is communicated in varying degrees to her servants, her lawyer and to her two inauthentic children, the Princess de Lascabanes and Sir Basil Hunter. The comic brilliance of White's conception of Sir Basil, the weary actor for whom life and acting are perpetually fused, is one of the novel's highlights. *A Fringe of Leaves*, an ostensibly artless, modest novel, demonstrates once again the unpredictable nature of his talent. Ellen Gluyas, a simple farm-girl, who marries a gentleman, Austin Roxburgh, undergoes a searing but spiritually illuminating experience after her shipwreck off the Queensland coast in the 1830s. Stripped of social position, possessions and even clothes, and treated as a slave by an Aboriginal tribe, Ellen is reduced to the core of her self. Rescued later by an escaped convict, she experiences real passion for the first time. Her ordeal initiates her into a condition of spiritual harmony that yet recognizes the implication of all in 'the brutality of life'. *The Twyborn Affair*, more deliberately fractured and the least metaphysical of his works, deals extensively with the bisexual theme that also appears in earlier work. Apparently composed as three distinct novellas with three distinct protagonists, the novel eventually reveals that all three are in fact the same. The child of Mr Justice and Mrs Eadie Twyborn of Sydney is born with a dual sexual identity and appears at first as Eudoxia Vatatzes, the mistress of an old Greek; then as Eddie Twyborn, war hero and jackeroo; and lastly as Eadith Trist, madam of a high-class London brothel.

Although his novels have won the most attention, White's shorter fiction also displays his characteristic style and effects, though in a more dramatically compressed way. If he is deprived of the cumulative, complex effects of the novel, he nevertheless finds scope in the short-story form for a wide variety of tones, moods and settings. Of his two early, uncollected stories, 'Cocotte' (1940) and 'The Twitching Colonel' (1937), the latter is important for the creation of Colonel Trevellick, the first of White's unorthodox visionaries. *The Burnt Ones* (1964) brings together a group of stories published over several years. The range of the eleven stories, four of which are set in Greece and seven in Australia, extends from farce to pathos, from the surreal to the intensely psychological, from the satiric to the compas-

sionate. As the collective title indicates, most of the central figures of these stories are alienated individuals suffering from an inward malaise. In all of them, but especially in 'Down at the Dump' and 'Willy Wagtails by Moonlight', White's eye for the significant, illuminating detail, his graphically expressive powers of description and satirically-puncturing wit combine to create a virtuoso performance. Of the six novellas and stories collected in *The Cockatoos* (1974), some of which date from the 1960s, four have Australian settings or characters. Darker in tone and less enlivened by imagery than *The Burnt Ones*, they have the same general theme of alienation in the midst of bourgeois life. In all of them, simple and orthodox situations are transformed by White's ability to render both the surface tedium of life and its inner intensity.

White's plays represent a watershed in the history of the Australian theatre, initiating a period of experimental drama. After the controversial staging of his 1947 play, *The Ham Funeral*, in 1961, production of the remaining three of *Four Plays* (written from 1961–62) followed in quick succession. *The Ham Funeral*, given its date, is an extraordinary foray into an expressionistic mode in which the set and the characters become a schematic representation of the central figure's personality. Like *The Aunt's Story*, the play treats of ways of being, although the Young Man resolves his struggle to come to terms with life differently from Theodora. *The Season at Sarsaparilla* presents once again White's version of Australian suburbia, although this time with more affection. This play most effectively embodies White's characteristic movement, noted by R.F. Brissenden, between the 'individual struggling to come to terms with himself and with the universe' and 'the cyclic processes of living, impersonal, inscrutable and inescapable'. *A Cheery Soul*, an adaptation of a short story, is dominated by the striking dramatic creation of Miss Docker, a blindly self-righteous individual who alienates all those around her with her 'sin of goodness'. *Night on Bald Mountain*, the most lyrical but least successful of the plays, has an overly schematic structure that is stated rather than dramatically achieved. *Big Toys*, less expressionistic than his earlier plays and ambitious in its social and political comment, is a compressed work that draws on caricature, melodrama, parody and music to express its subject of compromise and class betrayal. In *Netherwood* and *Signal Driver* he mixes realism, surrealism, symbolism, fantasy and satire in an exploration of the themes of loneliness, alienation and the problematic nature of contemporary Australian society. Major studies of White's work include Patricia Morley's *The*

Mystery of Unity (1972), Ingmar Bjorksten's *Patrick White* (1973), Peter Beatson's *The Eye in the Mandala* (1976), William Walsh's *Patrick White's Fiction* (1977) and Brian Kiernan's *Patrick White* (1980).

White Thorntree, The, a novel by Frank Dalby Davison (q.v.), was published in 1968. Lengthy and complex, set in middle-class Sydney between the wars, it concentrates exclusively on the place of sexuality in modern culture. The story begins with the relationship of the outwardly normal couple, Norma and Jeff Mitchell, who stand at the centre of the novel, and ends with the violent deaths of Jeff and his mistress. The first book, 'Babes in the Wood', a retrospective exploration of the Mitchells' experience before marriage, includes brief sketches of the sexual history of a range of relatives and reveals an encyclopaedic knowledge of all types of sexual repression and aberration. The second book 'The Fringe Dwellers' turns its attention to the sexual life of the so-called 'abnormal' individuals, many of whom have tenuous links with the central couple. The third book, 'The Promised Land', turns on the theme that the marital happiness promised by romantic myth is an illusion. The destructive power of both sexuality and the yearning for romance is illustrated in the lives of three couples, the Mitchells, the Teasdales and the Gillespies, and in the violent ends which litter the latter part of the book. In the fourth book, 'The White Thorntree', fate seems to negligently destroy one last chance of romantic love. Although the novel concentrates narrowly on the search for sexual happiness and its inevitable frustration, it is clear that the characters are also searching for love, fellowship, purpose and meaning. The conflict between the claims of conformism and individual need is a central theme in Davison's fiction, although here his vision is at its bleakest.

White Topee, see LANGLEY, EVE

White with Wire Wheels, a play by Jack Hibberd (q.v.), was first produced in 1967 and published in *Plays*, ed. Graeme Blundell (1970). Mal, Simon and Rod, young Australian executives who live together, pursue a stereotype of the good bachelor life; beer, their hopes of promotion, cars and girls are the main topics of their scabrous conversation, the last two, assessed frequently in terms of 'performance', emerging as almost synonomous. A new girl, Helen, enters their lives soon after they have all failed in their individual relationships with girl friends. Helen, who is played by the same actress as plays the part of the other three women, is adept at male expletives, refuses to

be ignored, and, in an expressionistically realized scene, succeeds in penetrating their fragile barriers against self-consciousness. Disturbed by the experience, the three decide to get drunk at their favourite pub in the hills, 'thrash' the Valiant 'to death' and 'really write themselves off!'.

WHITECROSS, ROY H., see War Literature

WHITEHEAD, A.N., see FITZGERALD, R.D.

WHITEHEAD, CHARLES (1804–62), a neglected minor English poet, novelist and dramatist, was born in London. He earned a precarious living as a man of letters, contributed to periodicals, edited *The Library of Fiction* (1836) for the publishers Chapman and Hall, and compiled biographies of highwaymen, one of which, *Jack Ketch* (1834), aroused some interest. He also received some favourable recognition after the publication of his poem, *The Solitary*, in 1831 and one of his plays, *The Cavalier*, was performed in 1836; but his most significant literary achievement, *Richard Savage* (1842), a novel based on the life of a figure he found congenial, was virtually unrecognized. A member of the Mulberry Club and familiar with Charles Lamb and Charles Dickens, Douglas Jerrold and William Thackeray, Whitehead appears to have gradually alienated his friends because of his alcoholism. In 1857 he migrated to Melbourne, where he already knew R.H. Horne and was befriended by James Smith and J.E. Neild. In Melbourne Whitehead wrote for the *Examiner*, *Melbourne Punch* and *My Note Book*. His novel, *Emma Latham*, was serialized in *My Note Book* from February 1858 and a verse-drama, *Spanish Marriage*, appeared in the *Victorian Monthly Magazine* in July 1859. Whitehead's poverty and alcoholism which was probably in part due to his excessively shy and nervous disposition, became more extreme in Australia. In early 1862, after having been charged in court with 'lunacy, caused through drink', Whitehead applied for admission to the Yarra Bend Asylum, was refused and was eventually picked up in the streets when close to death. His death in July in Melbourne Hospital went unnoticed by his friends and their subsequent efforts to retrieve his body from its pauper's grave were unsuccessful. Whitehead's life is the subject of the English writer H.T.M. Bell's *A Forgotten Genius* (1884) and of Clive Turnbull's *Mulberry Leaves* (1945).

WHITINGTON, DON (1911–77), grew up in Tasmania and worked in his youth as a jackeroo, woolclasser and freelance journalist. He later worked on the staff of the Sydney *Daily Telegraph*, the *Sunday Mail* and the *Courier-Mail*, and early in the Second World War became head of the *Daily Telegraph*'s Canberra bureau. In 1947 he began an independent, national, weekly newsletter, *Inside Canberra*, and later instituted another newsletter, *Money Matters*, and two newspapers, the *Northern Territory News* and the *Mount Isa Mail*. Well-known to Australian federal politicians, Whitington wrote a range of guides to and accounts of federal politics as well as two novels, *Treasure upon the Earth* (1954) and *Mile Pegs* (1963), and an autobiography, *Strive To Be Fair* (1978).

WHITMAN, WALT (1819–92), the American poet, had a substantial influence on some Australian writers. He corresponded with Francis Adams but his most enthusiastic admirer was Bernard O'Dowd, who was introduced to his work by Thomas Bury, ('Tom Touchstone'), the writer of a regular column for the Ballarat *Courier* in the 1880s. In the early 1890s, O'Dowd, who was at the time the dominant spirit of the Australeum, a small group which met to discuss literary and socio-political affairs, corresponded with Whitman and received some positive, if paternalistic, encouragement; O'Dowd also delivered several public lectures on Whitman's work. Another writer, who arrived in Australia in 1888, William Gay (1865–97), was the author of two monographs on Whitman (1893, 1895). The O'Dowd–Whitman correspondence and a range of Australian commentaries on Whitman's work are collected and edited by A.L. McLeod in *Walt Whitman in Australia and New Zealand* (1964). The influence of Whitman on Australian writers is also discussed in Joseph Jones's *Radical Cousins* (1976).

Who Shot George Kirkland?, see HARDY, FRANK

Who Wrote the Ballads?, see Folk-Song and Ballad; MANIFOLD, J.S.

Whoring Around, see BRYSON, JOHN

Who's Who in Australia, a biographical dictionary of prominent Australians, has been published by the Herald and Weekly Times company since 1933. The 1933 publication covered 1933–34; since then *Who's Who in Australia* has appeared triennially, 1935–50, in 1955, and triennially, 1959–82; its editors have been Errol Knox, 1933–35, J.A. Alexander, 1938–65, J.S. Legge, 1968–77, and W.J. Draper, 1980–83. The predecessors of *Who's*

Who in Australia were the biographical dictionaries of Fred Johns (q.v.), the last titled *Who's Who in Australia* (1927); Johns sold the rights to the Herald and Weekly Times before his death. A rival *Who's Who in Australia*, published by the International Press Association, appeared in 1922, 1927 and 1929.

'WICKHAM, ANNA' (EDITH HEPBURN) (1883–1947), born London of Australian parents, came to Australia in infancy but returned to England in 1903 to pursue a literary career that saw the publication of two minor plays for girls, *The Seasons* (1902) and *Wonder Eyes* (1903) and several small volumes of personal poetry that gained her recognition in the contemporary literary scene. They were *Songs* (1913), by 'John Oland'; *The Contemplative Quarry* (1915), by 'Anna Wickham'; *The Man with a Hammer* (1916) and *The Little Old House* (1921), both under the 'Anna Wickham' pseudonym. A combined volume, *The Contemplative Quarry and The Man with a Hammer*, was published in the USA in 1921.

'Wide Brown Land, The', see Anthologies; 'My Country'

'Widgigoweera Joe', see 'Backblocks Shearer, The'

WILCOX, DORA (1873–1953), born Christchurch, NZ, worked as a teacher in NSW and with the VAD in England during the First World War. Her second husband was Australian art historian, William Moore. Some of her poems appeared in Australian magazines and in 1927 she won a *Sydney Morning Herald* prize for an ode celebrating the opening of the Commonwealth parliament. Two of her plays were published, *Commander Capston* (1931) and *The Fourposter* in *Best Australian One-Act Plays* (1937), ed. William Moore and T. Inglis Moore. She also published three volumes of poetry, *Verses from Maoriland* (1905), *Rata and Mistletoe* (1911) and *Seven Poems* (1924), although only the last collection contains poems drawn from her Australian experience.

Wild Ass of a Man, A, see OAKLEY, BARRY

Wild Cat Falling, see JOHNSON, COLIN

'Wild Colonial Boy, The', one of Australia's best-known folk-songs (q.v.), tells the story of an Irish-born bushranger (q.v.), named Jack Doolan, who terrorizes the squatters, holds up the Beechworth mail coach in the 1860s and robs Judge MacEvoy, and is eventually killed when surrounded by three troopers, Kelly, Davis and FitzRoy, to whom he refuses to surrender. Several versions of 'The Wild Colonial Boy', which is often sung to the Irish tune 'The Wearing of the Green', e.g. by Ned Kelly at Glenrowan, have survived: in some of them MacEvoy is called Macaboy, and Jack Doolan is variously Jim or John Dowling/Duggan/Dublin/Dolan/Davis. That the hero of the song always has the initials 'JD' has led many folklorists, e.g. John Meredith in *The Wild Colonial Boy* (1982) to argue that the Wild Colonial Boy was a fictitious character and that the song is an 1860s variant of the 'Bold Jack Donahoe' (see Donohoe, John) cycle of songs and ballads, which, as a result of oral transmission, acquired a new set of characters and events. The argument is strengthened by a chorus beginning 'Come along, my hearties, we'll roam the mountains high,/Together we will plunder, together we will die', which is common to versions of both ballads, and by the fact that the songs are traditionally linked in Irish folk music. John Manifold, however, in *Who Wrote the Ballads?* (1964), speculates hat there was a bushranger of the 1860s named Jack Doolan and that his experiences were celebrated by taking over the existing Bold Jack Donahoe songs. Further investigation has established a Judge Macaboy and families of Dowlings, Doolans, etc. in the Beechworth district in the 1860s, but as yet no bushranger named Doolan has emerged. Whatever the origins of the song, 'The Wild Colonial Boy' is well known overseas and is sung by John Wayne in the film, *The Quiet Man*. In Australia, its popularity is such that 'wild colonial boys' became a phrase describing the bushrangers in general, as in Frank Clune's book, *Wild Colonial Boys*, and even any Australian sharing their bravado and daring. In contrast, the heroic image of the bushranger is satirized in David Martin's novel, *The Hero of Too* (1967), in which Dick Grogan is a 'mild' colonial boy whose adventures are the subject of 'Dauntless Dick Grogan', a ballad imitation of 'The Wild Colonial Boy' which prefaces the novel. In 'Steele Rudd''s stage play, *Gran'dad Rudd* (1918), a recalcitrant cow is encouraged to give milk by a rendition of 'The Wild Colonial Boy'.

WILDING, MICHAEL (1942–), was born at Worcester, England, and studied at the University of Oxford before arriving in Australia to take up a lectureship at the University of Sydney. In 1967–68 he taught at the University of Birmingham but in 1969 he returned to Sydney, where since 1972 he has been reader in English at the University. Apart from *Australians Abroad* (1967), an anthology co-edited with Charles Higham, and *Cultural Policy in*

Great Britain (1970), co-authored with Michael Green and Richard Hoggart, Wilding's first major publications were in the field of English literature: he edited *Three Tales* by Henry James (1967), *Marvell: Modern Judgements* (1969) and *The Tragedy of Julius Caesar and Marcus Brutus* (1970) by John Sheffield, a patron of Dryden, and wrote a monograph on *Paradise Lost* (1969). Although in the last decade Wilding has continued work in the fields outside Australian literature – e.g. as editor, with Stephen Knight, of *The Radical Reader* (1977, 1982) and as author of *Political Fictions* (1980), an important study which includes discussion of D.H. Lawrence's *Kangaroo* – he has become increasingly important in Australian writing, not only as a writer of fiction but also as editor, publisher, scholar and critic. In 1971 he co-edited, with Shirley Cass, Ros Cheney and David Malouf, the anti-war anthology, *We Took Their Orders and Are Dead*. Since then he has published three collections of short stories, *Aspects of the Dying Process* (1972), *The West Midland Underground* (1975) and *The Phallic Forest* (1978), and four novels, *Living Together* (1974), *The Short Story Embassy* (1975), *Scenic Drive* (1976), and *Pacific Highway* (1982). Three of these works were published by Wild & Woolley, the alternative publishing house Wilding established in 1973 with Pat Woolley (q.v.). He was also associated in the foundation of the short-fiction magazine supplement, *Tabloid Story* (q.v., 1972–); in 1978 Wilding edited *The Tabloid Story Pocket Book*, a retrospective anthology which includes an account of the venture. His other publications include a scholarly edition of William Lane's novel, *The Workingman's Paradise* (1980) and several significant contributions to Marcus Clarke studies: a Portable Australian Authors edition (1976), a separate edition of Clarke's short stories (1983) and a critical monograph (1977).

As a writer of fiction, Wilding has often been labelled as one of the Balmain writers who gathered in that Sydney suburb from the late 1960s and documented its radical lifestyle. Yet despite the links with other inner-city writers such as Frank Moorhouse (q.v.), which extend beyond their involvement in *Tabloid Story* to each writing stories to answer the other's (Moorhouse in *Tales of Mystery and Romance*, Wilding in *Scenic Drive*), Wilding has developed in such a way as to defy categorization simply as a chronicler of the urban sub-cultural milieu, as in *Living Together*. The radicalism apparent in his publishing activities and in his revaluation of writers such as Clarke and the subjects of *Political Fictions*, finds expression also in his fiction; rejecting the realist mode, he is an experimental writer whose stories and novels, rich in allusions to literature beyond Australia, display his willingness to employ a variety of forms, e.g. fantasy, romance, fable, parable, the comic and the surreal. A major theme in his work, Bruce Clunies Ross has suggested, is the way people 'define themselves through stories, deliberately authored inventions and rumours . . . creating legends about their world'. Thus 'Hector and Freddie', a story from *The West Midland Underground* (which also contains a fictional account of Wilding's publishing activities), focuses on the power of stories to define existence, and in *The Short Story Embassy*, a fiction in which the characters are creating fiction, those characters are aware of the way they can thus structure reality. As Lazlo concludes, 'I am not going to write that I will write no more for fear that might become an irreversible state . . . The novel structures what has happened to us; with the short story we sketch our future actions'.

In *Pacific Highway*, Wilding's latest and most spontaneous work, the locale moves to the north coast of NSW, where a small community retreats into nature. Described as an attempt at 'literary ecology', the novel shows the paradoxes of mankind's response to nature by juxtaposing the attitude of the narrator's community and those who threaten its ideals.

Wild Men of Sydney, see **PEARL, CYRIL; NORTON, JOHN**

Wild Notes, from the Lyre of a Native Minstrel (1826), by Charles Tompson (q.v.), was the first volume of poems by an Australian-born writer to be published in Australia. The volume, containing the long poem 'Retrospect', together with odes, elegies, and miscellaneous verses, gives a picture of the foundation of the Colony and a description of the landscape from the well-disposed 'currency' viewpoint. Contrary to the title, the 'notes' are well-polished verses, strikingly ornate in a stereotyped, traditional style.

'Wild Rover, The', see 'Lazy Harry''s

'Wild Scotchman, The', see **McPHERSON, ALPIN**

Wild Swan, The (1930), is the most significant book of verse by Mary Gilmore (q.v.). Her favourite themes, nature, the Aborigines, wholehearted commitment to life, and love, are embodied in verse where her craftsmanship is at its best. She mourns, especially, the passing of the wild swans, which had been so beloved a feature of the landscape of her youth.

WILKES, G.A. (GERALD ALFRED) (1927–   ), born Punchbowl, NSW, foundation professor of Australian literature at the University of Sydney (1962–66), has edited numerous Australian literary texts and written several studies of Australian literature. The latter include the monographs, *New Perspectives on Brennan's Poetry* (1953), *Australian Literature: A Conspectus* (1969), *R.D. FitzGerald* (1981) and *The Stockyard and the Croquet Lawn: Literary Evidence for Australian Cultural Development* (1981). He also edited *Australian Poetry* (1963) and *Ten Essays on Patrick White* (1970); in 1963 he became editor of *Southerly*. He has also published *A Dictionary of Australian Colloquialisms* (1978), and was special Australian consultant to *The New Collins Dictionary of the English Language* (1979) and companion volumes.

WILKIE, ALAN, see **Shakespeare and Australia**

WILLEY, KEITH (1930–84), grew up in Queensland. He worked as a journalist on newspapers in Darwin and throughout Australia, as well as in New Guinea; spent some time as a professional crocodile-shooter; and, from 1979, also engaged in academic work. In 1961–63 he won three Walkley Awards for journalism. He wrote several accounts of his experiences and acquaintances in the Northern Territory and New Guinea, *Eaters of The Lotus* (1964), *Assignment New Guinea* (1965), *Crocodile Hunt* (1966), *Boss Drover* (1971), *Tales of the Big Country* (1972), *Ghosts of the Big Country* (1975), and *The Drovers* (1982); an account of Ludwig Leichhardt, *Strange Seeker* (1966); and a well-researched, detailed history of the destruction of the Aboriginal tribes of the Sydney region, 1788–1850s, *When the Sky Fell Down* (1979). He collaborated with other authors and photographers in books about Queensland and New Guinea, and with Frank Flynn in *Northern Frontiers* (1968), *Northern Gateway* (1979), and *The Living Heart* (1979). Willey also edited *News, News, News* (1982), a selection of some 300 items from newspapers over the past century.

'William Street', a brief poem by Kenneth Slessor (q.v.), published in *One Hundred Poems, 1919–1939* (1944), describes the main traffic artery that runs from the city up to Kings Cross (Sydney) as it would have appeared in all its garish flamboyance in the 1930s. The poem is part of Slessor's defence of his 'patch' – 'you find it ugly, I find it lovely'.

WILLIAMS, HAROLD ROY, see **War Literature**

WILLIAMS, JUSTINA (1916–), born Coolgardie, WA, has been a journalist on the *West Australian* and the *Daily News*, and an active supporter of radical and feminist causes over many years. Active also in the FAW, she has published two collections of poetry, *The Dreaming Vine* (1970) and *By All the Clocks* (1975); a book of short fiction, *White River and Other Stories* (1979); and two socio-political histories, *The First Furrow* (1976) and *Trade Unionism* (1978).

WILLIAMS, MASLYN (1911–), born England of Irish parents, was orphaned early and grew up in Australia, where he worked at first as a writer for film and radio. In 1940 he was appointed producer and writer to the official Services' film and photography unit and has subsequently travelled widely as a documentary film-maker. He has written several books on China, Cambodia, Papua and New Guinea and Indonesia, and four novels, *The Far Side of the Sky* (1967); *The Benefactors* (1971), published as *Dubu* in the USA; *Florence Copley of Romney* (1974); and *The Temple* (1982).

WILLIAMS, MAX, born Redfern, Sydney, where he spent a very deprived childhood during the 1930s depression, had his first brush with the law at the age of five and at the age of ten was committed to an institution for wayward boys. He spent most of the next thirty years in prison. He has contributed to *Poems from Prison* (1973) and *Australians Aware* (1975), both edited by Rodney Hall, and to *Poet's Choice*. He has also published three collections, *The Poor Man's Bean* (1975), *Hard Is the Convict Road* (n.d.) and *Baronda* (1977), and has written an autobiography, *Dingo! My Life on the Run* (1980).

WILLIAMS, RUTH (1897–), published several books for children, including *Our Friend Rodney* (1945), *Pirates' Gold* (1945), *Timothy Tatters* (1947), *Verity of Sydney Town* (1950) and *The Aboriginal Story* (1955). *Verity of Sydney Town*, set in the colony of NSW in the days of Governor Macquarie, won the Children's Book of the Year Award in 1950–51.

WILLIAMS, VICTOR (1914–), born Perth, was a farm worker and schoolteacher in WA before serving with the Australian army in the Second World War. He has written three books of verse, *Harvest Time* (1946), *Hammers and Seagulls* (1967) and *Three Golden Giants* (1977), as well as *The Years of Big Jim* (1975), a biography of Jim Healy, waterfront union official.

WILLIAMSON, DAVID (1942–), was born in Melbourne and brought up in Bairnsdale in north-eastern Victoria. After graduating in mechanical engineering, he studied social psychology and lectured in both subjects at the Swinburne Institute of Technology before becoming a success in the commercial theatre. His first full-length play, *The Coming of Stork*, the basis of the 1969 film *Stork*, was first performed at the La Mama theatre in 1970. His next two plays, *Don's Party* (q.v.) and *The Removalists* (q.v.), were also both performed in 1971 by the alternative theatre (*Don's Party* by the Australian Performing Group and *The Removalists* at the La Mama theatre) before moving on to the commercially-successful productions at the Playbox Theatre and the Royal Court theatre in London. His published plays include *The Removalists* (1972), *Don's Party* (1973), *Three Plays: The Coming of Stork. Jugglers Three. What If You Died Tomorrow* (1974), *The Department* (q.v., 1975), *A Handful of Friends* (q.v., 1976), *The Club* (q.v., 1978), *Travelling North* (1980), and *The Perfectionist* (1983). His unpublished plays include 'Celluloid Heroes' (1980). Film versions have been made of several of his plays and he has also written other scripts for film, a medium that he admires, including *Peterson, Mrs. Eliza Fraser, Gallipoli* and *Phar Lap*. He has won several awards, including part of the British George Devine Award for *The Removalists* and Awgies on three occasions. As well as receiving widespread Australian production, several of his plays have been performed in New York and London.

Raucous wit, naturalistic plots and settings, fast-moving, scatological dialogue and recognizable social types, brilliantly seized and satirized, are familiar characteristics of Williamson's plays. Writing mainly for, and of, his own affluent, educated, permissive generation, he seeks to represent what he sees as the 'awful uniqueness' of Australian life. More interested in rituals of social interaction than in individuals or issues, he has a keen eye for the power games played by any group, whether an academic department, a football club or a party. Colliding temperaments are the subject of his comedy and the hypocrisies, insecurities, defences, aggressions, betrayals and complicities that they generate. Although his subject range is narrow and his attitude comically detached, his plays have a fluid diversity of emotional tones, from the farcical to the sad. Often this emotional range is dependent on a subtext that subtly undercuts the crudities of the dialogue.

The Coming of Stork, an exuberantly crude romp about the complicated sexual adventures of one girl and a group of graduate technologists, is more concerned with farcical effects than serious comment. *The Removalists*, however, is a profound, tightly-structured exploration of the links between violence, sexuality and uniformed authoritarianism. A serious tone also underlies the comic satire of *Don's Party*, a study of middle-class, older graduates, subservient to a materialist culture they profess to despise. *Jugglers Three*, *What If You Died Tomorrow* and *A Handful of Friends*, similar in their upper middle-class settings, have a finer insight into female experience. *Jugglers Three* explores the embittered or indifferent relationships of a married couple and the wife's current and ex-lovers. *What If You Died Tomorrow*, Williamson's most autobiographical play, concentrates on one embattled evening in the life of a successful novelist, under pressure from his agent, publishers, mistress and parents. *A Handful of Friends*, subtle and finely worked, probes the intricacies of failed relationships. With *The Department* and *The Club* Williamson turns to the comic interactions of role-playing within bureaucracies, the first an academic department, the second a football club. *Travelling North* is a quieter, less satiric study of a pair of lovers who, in old age, attempt to discard their expected roles. 'Celluloid Heroes' satirizes the mores of the film industry, and *The Perfectionist* comically explores the marital limitations of a certain academic type.

WILLIAMSON, J.C. (JAMES CASSIUS) (1845–1913), Australia's most successful theatrical entrepreneur, was born in Pennsylvania, USA. He achieved some success as an actor in the USA, particularly after starring in *Struck Oil* (q.v.), with his wife Maggie Moore (q.v.). In 1874 he came to Australia with *Struck Oil* under contract to George Coppin and, on the crest of the play's success, toured England, Europe and the USA, returning to Australia in 1879 and leasing the Melbourne Theatre Royal, in 1880. Two years later he formed an association with his major competitors, Arthur Garner and George Musgrove, which was popularly known as 'the Triumvirate' and dominated Australian theatrical life. Surviving several changes of membership, the J.C. Williamson 'Firm' continued to thrive and to absorb competitive organizations, controlling theatres in Sydney, Melbourne, Adelaide and Brisbane and becoming a proprietary company, J.C. Williamson Theatres Ltd, in 1907. Although the Williamson 'Firm' generated productions and tours by overseas actors, its opposition to the avant-garde and commitment to long, profitable runs of star-studded shows tended to repress the development of local theatre. Williamson was also co-author with Bert Royle of a popular pantomime, 'Djin Djin: Or, The Japanese Bogeyman' (1895).

WILLIS, WILLIAM NICHOLAS (?1860–1922), one of the *Wild Men of Sydney* in Cyril Pearl's (q.v.) book (1958) dealing with Sydney journalism and politics at the turn of the century, was born in Mudgee, NSW, was a country storekeeper and landowner before entering politics. A member of the NSW parliament, 1889–1904, he was the founder of the radical *Truth* in 1890, and was involved in its management until 1896. In 1905 he was implicated in a political scandal over the sale and lease of land and was extradited from South Africa to stand trial; discharged, he settled in England, where he wrote several sensational novels under his own name dealing with sport, sex and crime. A further dozen works, dealing with the same subjects and written under the pseudonym 'Bree Narran' have also been attributed to Willis, e.g. *One Night* (1919), *Three Nights* (1919), and *Seven Nights* (1919).

WILLOUGHBY, HOWARD (1839–1908), born Birmingham, England, migrated to Victoria in 1857 and made a reputation as a journalist by reporting on the Maori wars in NZ in 1862–63. His examination of the convict system in WA appeared in the *Argus* and as a pamphlet, *Transportation: The British Convict in Western Australia* (1865). He was editor of the Melbourne *Daily Telegraph* (1869–77) but returned to the *Argus*, becoming its editor in 1898. Among his other publications are *Australian Pictures Drawn with Pen and Pencil* (1886), his observations on Australian life, and *Australian Federation* (1891).

WILLS, WILLIAM JOHN, see **BURKE and WILLS**

WILMOT, CHESTER (1911–54), born Melbourne, a graduate of the University of Melbourne, was a war correspondent for the ABC in Greece, Syria, Tobruk and New Guinea, and subsequently for the BBC in western Europe. He was the BBC's special correspondent at the Nuremberg trials 1945–46, and later became well known as writer and broadcaster for the BBC. He was also military correspondent for the London *Observer*. Wilmot published two books, an account of the 1941 siege of Tobruk, *Tobruk* (1944), which is based on official documents, Wilmot's own observations, and the accounts of men engaged in the fighting; and an authoritative, well-researched and highly-praised history of the Second World War, *The Struggle for Europe* (1952).

WILSON, EDWARD (1813–78), born Hampstead, London, migrated to the Port Phillip District in 1842 and took up farming. In 1848 he and J.S. Johnston purchased the Melbourne *Argus* and incorporated the *Daily News* in 1852. In those newspapers he voiced his conviction that Port Phillip should be separated from New South Wales and that transportation should cease. He published an account of his travels in Australia and New Zealand, *Rambles at the Antipodes* (1859) illustrated by S.T. Gill.

WILSON, ERLE (1898–   ), born Scotland, travelled widely before settling in Australia. He published three novels for adults, *Coorinna* (1953), *Minado, the Devil-Dog* (1955) and *Adams of the Bounty* (1958); the first two reflect his interest in animal life, the last is a treatment of the Bligh mutiny. He also wrote books for children, including *Churinga Tales* (1950), a collection of Aboriginal stories, and *Far-away Tales* (1954), a collection of South Sea legends.

WILSON, HARDY (1881–1955), born in Sydney, was a notable and influential architectural theoretician and watercolour artist. He lived for an extensive period in London and also travelled widely in Europe, the USA and China, before settling finally in Australia in 1930. A qualified architect, he abandoned his profession in 1927 to devote himself to writing and drawing and published several polemical, philosophical and prophetic works. These include two fictional narratives, a semi-autobiographical account of the wanderings and meditations of an Australian architect, *The Dawn of a New Civilization* (1929) and *Yin Yang* (1934), a Utopian fantasy. Hardy Wilson's most enduring works are *The Cow Pasture Road* (1920), which focuses on the Camden district of NSW and includes his own illustrations; *Old Colonial Architecture in New South Wales and Tasmania* (1924), a collection of finely-executed drawings; and *Grecian and Chinese Architecture* (1937).

WILSON, HELEN HELGA (1902–   ), born Mayne at Zeehan, Tasmania, spent her early years in the WA goldfields area, where her father was a mining engineer. A graduate of the University of WA, she has published several anecdotal, historical accounts of the goldfields, including *Gateways to Gold* (1969), *Westward Gold!* (1973), *The Golden Miles* (1977) and *Cyclone Coasts* (1980); seven novels, *The Golden Age* (1959), *Quiet, Brat!* (1958), *Where the Wind's Feet Shine* (1960), *If Golde Rust* (1961), *Island of Fire* (1973), *Bring Back the Hour* (1977) and *The Mulga Trees* (1980); two collections of short stories, *A Show of Colours* (1970) and *The Skedule and Other Australian Short Stories* (1979); and three of verse, *Songs of Empire* (1941), *Occasional Verse, 1942–1943* (1943), and *The Letters of Huang Hu* (1946). She has also written *Bushman Born*

(1982), an account of Tommy Windich, Sir John Forrest's guide on his 1874 journey across the WA desert, and contributed texts to several WA sketchbooks.

Wilson, Joe, is an important character in ten stories by Henry Lawson (q.v.); most of them have Joe as narrator and were written in 1900–01 while Lawson was in England. The best known and most admired of the stories are the four which comprise the Joe Wilson sequence in *Joe Wilson and His Mates* (q.v., 1901): 'The Courtship of Joe Wilson', 'Brighten's Sister-in-Law' (q.v.), ' "Water them Geraniums" ' and 'A Double Buggy at Lahey's Creek'. The sequence traces the development of the relationship between Joe and his wife Mary from the time of their courtship until, six or seven years later, Joe is beginning to prosper.

In 'The Courtship of Joe Wilson', the gawky Joe first encounters Mary Brand when he is working as carpenter with his mate, Jack Barnes, at the homestead where Mary is in service; their innocent romance is encouraged by Jack but stutters along uncertainly until Mary is insulted by a passing shearer, whom Joe fights. 'Brighten's Sister-in-Law' opens with news of the birth at Gulgong of Jim, the first child, two years after the marriage, although the main incident of the story, developed from a poem Lawson had written in 1899, takes place when Jim is rising three and Joe and Mary have just moved to a selection at Lahey's Creek. Jim has been staying with relations at Gulgong and while travelling back to the selection with his father comes down with a fever. Having experienced Jim's convulsions as a baby, Joe panics, but is guided by the vision of a woman he sees in the branches of a tree to a nearby shanty, where Jim is nursed through the fever by the shanty-keeper's sister-in-law. ' "Water them Geraniums" ' deepens the tragic mood of the series. It begins with the move to Lahey's Creek and details Mary's profound disappointment on arrival, the quarrel in which Joe's drinking problem is raised, and Joe's worry that Mary will become a 'gaunt, haggard Bushwoman' like Mrs Spicer on the adjoining selection. The second part of the story, ' "Past Carin" ' ', also amplified from an earlier poem, covers the first year or so on the selection; a second child is born but the focus of the story is Mrs Spicer, who shows the same kind of courage in adversity as the woman in 'The Drover's Wife', which has some incidents in common with ' "Water them Geraniums" ', but is eventually broken by poverty and isolation and dies 'past carin''. 'A Double Buggy at Lahey's Creek' returns to something like the mood of 'Joe Wilson's Courtship'. Joe has a good year on the selection and surprises Mary with a new double buggy, which has been provisioned by their friends and by shopkeepers in Gulgong. But just as the sentimentality of 'Joe Wilson's Courtship' is controlled by Joe's retrospective narration, so it is clear, when Joe and Mary talk 'more than we'd done for years' the night the buggy arrives, that hardship has placed strain on the marriage.

The Joe Wilson sequence has been justly admired for its controlled presentation of the process of alienation and disintegration wrought by the experience of bush life. It was Lawson's most extended piece of fiction although the order of composition of the four stories differs significantly from the chronological sequence as arranged in *Joe Wilson and His Mates*. Of the remaining Joe Wilson stories, ' "Shall We Gather at the River?" ', 'His Brother's Keeper' and 'The Story of "Gentleman-Once" ', were published in *Children of the Bush* (1902) and centre on Peter M'Laughlan, the bush missionary, reformed alcoholic and befriender of the down and outs. Joe is seventeen when he hears M'Laughlan's sermon in ' "Shall We Gather at the River?" ' and twenty-three or four in the other two stories, in which the central incident is Peter's rescue of Jack Barnes from the drink after a shearing stint, which takes place just before the time of 'Joe Wilson's Courtship'; the links with the Joe and Mary stories are not strong, however, and the choice of Joe as narrator is of little more significance than the appearance of Jack Mitchell (q.v.) on the track in 'The Story of "Gentleman-Once" '. In contrast, 'James and Maggie' and 'Drifting Apart', both published in *Triangles of Light* (1913), are later stories than those in the *Joe Wilson and His Mates* sequence. 'James and Maggie' deals with the courtship of James, Joe's brother-in-law who lives at the Lahey's Creek selection from the time of ' "Water them Geraniums" ', and Maggie Charlesworth, who lives at the home of the local squatter; and 'Drifting Apart' is almost a sequel to 'The Double Buggy at Lahey's Creek' and chronicles the estrangement and eventual reunion between Joe and Mary during a trip to Sydney and back. In the final story, 'Joe Wilson in England', included in *Rowlandson's Commonwealth Annual*, Lawson himself, rather than Joe, is the narrator, who records the reactions of the Wilsons to England, where Joe is the representative of an English wool firm. An unfinished Joe Wilson story, identified by Brian Kiernan in recently-discovered Lawson material, is included as 'Going on the Land' in his selection, *The Essential Henry Lawson* (1982).

That Lawson wrote the intensely personal Joe Wilson stories when his own marriage was under strain clearly influenced his presentation of Joe and Mary; there are further links between the Wilsons and the Lawsons in that Joe has a weakness with alcohol, that Mary is 'German in figure and walk' in ' "Water them Geraniums" ', and that in 1916 Lawson stated that 'Mrs Joe Wilson was . . . a portrait of Mrs Henry Lawson (as I idealized her then)'. It is equally clear, however, that the four major stories were informed by other experiences of Lawson (he also claimed in 1916 that Joe, at various points, was 'my uncle by marriage', 'my father and myself') as well as by a creative imagination that transformed experience into what is regarded, with *While the Billy Boils* (1896), as the peak of his achievement.

'Wind at Your Door, The', a poem by R.D. FitzGerald (q.v.), was first published in the *Bulletin* (1958). It is based on the uprising of Irish rebel convicts at Castle Hill in 1804, although the incident of the flogging depicted in the poem took place at Toongabbie in 1800. The poem has two central characters: the poet's ancestor Martin Mason, surgeon, magistrate, and seemingly-callous overseer of the brutal flogging of a convict; and the poet's namesake Morris Fitzegarrel, the stoic convict victim. In these two figures and their history, FitzGerald sees the continuing problem, on both the national and the individual level, of the Australian identity. On the general level is the problem of the nation adapting to its development from a 'jailyard'; on the personal level is the problem of individual Australians, in this case, the poet himself, adapting to both sides of their ancestry, authoritarianism and rebellion against authority. The poem indicates that the wind that blows the blood and flesh from the lacerated back of the convict, Fitzegarrel, into the faces of the bystanders will continue to blow the memory and the impact of that event, and scores of similar events, into the present and future Australian consciousness. FitzGerald's personal compromise is to accept that both the characters in the poem and others like them are equal victims. The convict Fitzegarrel also appears in Thomas Kenneally's novel, *Passenger* (1979).

Windabyne, see **RANKEN, GEORGE**

Windsor, see **Hawkesbury River**

WINDSOR, A.L. (ARTHUR LLOYD) (1833–1913), was born on the way to the West Indies, where his father's family were plantation owners. Educated in England, where he established a reputation in literary and journalistic circles, he arrived in Australia in 1863 to become editor of the *Argus*. He left that newspaper in 1865, edited the *Mount Alexander*

Mail at Castlemaine 1865–69, and became editor of the *Age* in 1872, a position he held until his retirement in 1900. He was president of the Australian Institute of Journalists in 1892; his book of essays, *Ethica: Or, Characteristics of Men, Manners and Books*, was published in 1860.

Wine and Roses, see **DALEY, VICTOR**

Winged Seeds (1950), the final novel of Katharine Susannah Prichard's (q.v.) goldfields trilogy, examines the period from the mining depression of 1936 through to the end of the Second World War. The focus increasingly moves to Sally Gough's communist grandson, Bill, his involvement with Paddy Cavan's step-daughters, Pam and Pat, who share his revolutionary sentiments, and his eventual death in a war fought against fascism. The final scene in which a kalgoorluh nut sheds its seeds as Sally and Dinny bury their Aboriginal friend, is a symbolic affirmation of the ideas expressed in the trilogy; 'the life force' which 'strives towards perfection' will ensure that seeds sown in the past for a better system come to fruition. See *Roaring Nineties The*, and *Golden Miles*.

S.B.

WINSTANLEY, ELIZA (1818–82), born England, came to Australia in 1833, making her first stage appearance at Barnett Levey's Theatre Royal the next year. A versatile, hard-working actress, she showed a particular flair for tragic roles, learning a great deal from her mentor, Conrad Knowles. She married H.C. O'Flaherty (q.v.) in 1841 and in 1846 left with him for England, where her career prospered. In 1847 she left for a successful run in the USA, often playing leading Shakespearean roles. She returned to London in time to join the company formed by Charles Kean at the Princess's Theatre in 1850, and shared in Kean's achievements for the next eight years. She turned to writing as a means of support in the 1850s when she was becoming too stout and old for the theatre. *Shifting Scenes in Theatrical Life* (1859) is her first novel in book form, although she could also be the author of 'Lucy Cooper', a short novel published anonymously in the *Illustrated Sydney News* (1854). Other novels, stories and articles followed in quick succession, often drawing on her Australian experiences. She finally abandoned her acting career in 1864, returned to Australia in 1880 and died in Sydney two years later of diabetes and exhaustion. Her Australian novels, which include *Margaret Falconer* (1860), *Twenty Straws* (1864), *What Is to Be, Will Be* (1867) and *For Her Natural Life* (1876), have more historical than literary value.

WINTER, S.V. (SAMUEL VINCENT) (1843–1904), born in the Goulburn River district of Victoria, founded the Catholic newspaper the *Advocate* in 1868 and managed it for three years before passing it to his brother, Joseph (1844–1915), who managed it until his death. In 1871 he purchased the Melbourne *Herald* in partnership with John Halfey and others, took over the editorship of the paper three years later and rapidly built up its circulation. He also founded and edited the *Sportsman* (1881) and was active in the ANA, local government and charitable organizations. Nicknamed 'Stormy' Winter, he was well known for his quick temper, his drive and vituperative powers, as well as his generosity. Fiercely committed to the Irish Home Rule movement in Victoria, Joseph published the *Irish-Australian Almanac and Directory* from 1870.

Winton, see **Literary Awards**; **Swag**; **'Waltzing Matilda'**

WODHAMS, J., see **Science Fiction**

'Woman at the Mill, The', see **DAVISON, FRANK DALBY**

Woman in a Lampshade, see **JOLLEY, ELIZABETH**

Woman of the Future, A, a novel by David Ireland (q.v.), was published in 1979, and won the Miles Franklin, the National Book Council and the *Age* Awards. A mixture of surrealistic, realistic and allegorical modes, it has a discontinuous narrative structure that renders experience in a piecemeal but composite way. Set in an unspecified time in the near future, it is the story of Alethea Hunt from conception to the age of eighteen when she disappears and, it is implied, turns into a leopard. Alethea, who does everything superlatively and who is to some extent representative of Australia, has a sense of herself as unique and as having untapped resources; she remains virginal, however much her sexual capacity is exploited. The actuality of the surrounding Australian life is degraded and ugly, however. Alethea lives in a rigid social structure, divided between the privileged serving class and the so-called Free who are condemned to a life of futility. Surreal physical aberrations match the social distortions: a man grows a coffin out of his side, some people sprout branches and leaves, a girl has a proliferation of vulvas in her armpits. Alethea's final transformation is interpreted in a visionary way that celebrates Australia's magnificent potential.

Woman Tamer, The, a one-act comedy by Louis Esson (q.v.), was first produced in 1909 by William Moore and published in 1911. Set in the Melbourne slums and coloured by a racy, underworld vernacular, the action relates the downfall of the arrogant and lazy Chopsey Ryan, who is supplanted in the heroine's affections by tough guy, Bongo Williams, just out of gaol.

Woman to Man (1949), the second volume of poems published by Judith Wright (q.v.), takes its title from the opening poem, 'Woman to Man', a delicate, sensitive, yet forthright statement of the special relationship between man and woman as sharers in the act of conception. The sequential poems 'Woman's Song' and 'Woman to Child' are equally compelling statements of woman as mother. The poet's preoccupation with time is evident in 'Letter to a Friend', 'Spring after War' and 'The Bones Speak', but echoing as they do the optimism of her earlier poem, 'The Moving Image' (q.v.), they indicate time's regenerative as well as destructive power.

Woman's Love, Mary Leman Grimstone's (q.v.) didactic and early feminist novel set among the provincial aristocracy in south-west England, was published in 1832. Although not set in Australia, *Woman's Love* was written during Grimstone's sojourn with her sister in Van Diemen's Land 1826–29 and is probably, therefore, the first novel written in Australia.

Womanspeak, see **Feminism and Australian Literature**

Women of the Sun (1984), a series of four self-contained television plays, each dealing with an episode of Aboriginal history as seen through an Aboriginal's eyes, was written by Hyllus Maris and Sonia Borg (q.v.). First screened in 1982, it won the 1982 United Nations Association of Australia Media Prize and an Awgie in 1983. Hyllus Maris, who won the Patricia Weickhardt Award in 1982 for *Women of the Sun*, is an Aboriginal rights worker, sociologist and educator.

'Women of the West, The', see **EVANS, GEORGE ESSEX**

'WONGAR, B.' ('BANUMBIR', 'BIRIM-BIR'), (SRETEN BOZIC) (1936–   ), is the pseudonym of a writer and anthropologist from Yugoslavia who came to Australia in 1960 and otherwise uses the name Sreten Bozic. Wongar's writing first appeared in 1970 and won immediate recognition and literary awards for its understanding of Aboriginal culture. His short stories, signed B or Birimbir (and later Banumbir) Wongar, appeared in such varied periodicals as *Temps Modernes* (Paris), *Atlantic Monthly*, *London Magazine* and *Australian Women's Weekly*. A collection of short stories 'from Vietnam', titled *The Sinners* and with a foreword by Alan Marshall, appeared in 1972, and another, titled *The Track to Bralgu* with a foreword by Alan Paton, in 1978. Wongar has also published a novel, *The Trackers* (1978), a play, *Balang an Village* (1973), and has contributed to the anthology, *Ethnic Australia* (1981), ed. Manfred Jurgensen. 'Wongar' is described in the publisher's note to *The Track to Bralgu* as an Aboriginal born in northern Australia in the late 1930s but educated overseas; his probable European origins were not fully disclosed until 1981 when Robert Drewe summed up in the *Bulletin* the results of a prolonged search for his identity.

WOOD, G.A. (GEORGE ARNOLD) (1865–1928), born and educated in England, was challis professor of history at the University of Sydney from 1891 until his death. His quality as an influential teacher of great personal magnetism and independent mind has been recorded by one of his students, R.M. Crawford, in his biography '*A Bit of a Rebel*' (1975). Wood's major research work was *The Discovery of Australia* (1922).

WOOD, THOMAS (1892–1950), the English composer, visited Australia 1930–32 and published a delightful record of his travels, *Cobbers* (1934), in which he printed the words and music of 'Waltzing Matilda' without realizing copyright might be involved but percipiently praised it as being 'Good enough to be the official National Anthem of Australia'. Further impressions of Australia are recorded in his autobiography, *True Thomas* (1936). *Cobbers*, which owes a great deal to Wood's gregarious qualities, includes graphic descriptions of Australian landscapes and ways of life and work, both urban and rural. Enlivened by his personal, easy style, it includes numerous original comments on the national character, language and humour and distinctive summations of regional differences. Victoria is described as having sobered down 'after a riotous youth . . . It creases its trousers and goes to Church'; Hobart 'has the air of an English country town which has shed its old houses and wandered down to the sea for a rest'; Sydney is 'an exotic: a lovely and petulant spend-thrift, going its own wilful headstrong vivid way; self-centred, yet open-hearted; absurdly vain, yet very likeable'.

WOODBERRY, JOAN (1921–), born Narrabri, NSW, was a teacher and librarian 1946–52 before joining the British Council in London as bursar 1953–58. Back in Australia she became first woman warden of Hobart Teachers' College but retired after an attack of encephalitis in 1971. Her numerous published works include children's fiction, e.g. the Rafferty series, of which *Rafferty Rides a Winner* (1961) shared the Children's Book of the Year Award for 1962. She has written a series of Tasmanian sketchbooks, compiled several anthologies, been active in the FAW and has published an early Tasmanian press history.

WOODHOUSE, MARGARET, see *Stockwhip*

WOODS, WALTER ALAN, see **HEAD, WALTER WILLIAM**

Woolcott Family, see *Seven Little Australians*

WOOLLEY, JOHN (1816–66), born Hampshire, England, was first principal and professor of classics at the University of Sydney. He arrived in Sydney in 1849 to prepare for the opening of the University in 1852. An influential educationalist, he was particularly prominent in an attempt to expand the Sydney Mechanics' School of Arts. He was also well known in literary circles and was friendly with N.D. Stenhouse, Henry Kendall, J. Sheridan Moore and Daniel Deniehy. Some of his Australian lectures were collected and published in 1862, titled *Lectures Delivered in Australia*.

WOOLLEY, PAT (1947–), born California, USA, worked as a fashion designer and singer 1966–69, and came to Australia in 1970 where she has become established as a printer, publisher and bookseller. Presses with which she has been associated include Tomato Press, Wild and Woolley, which she founded with Michael Wilding, and Redress Press. She has written on collectives, *The Art of Living Together* (1978), and has edited *The Wild and Woolley Comix Book* (1977) and *All About Grass* (1973).

WOOLLS, WILLIAM (1814–93), born Hampshire, England, came to Australia at the age of seventeen and subsequently became a schoolmaster and an Anglican clergyman. His personality is described by one of his students, 'Rolf Boldrewood', in *In Bad Company and Other Stories* (1901). Woolls was one of Australia's first essayists, his *Miscellanies in Prose and Verse* appearing in 1838. An authoritative botanist, whose work was useful to Ferdinand von Mueller, he wrote several scientific books as well as articles published in proceedings of the Linnean Society. He also published three booklets of verse, *The Voyage* (1832), *Australia* (1833) and *In Memory of R.D. FitzGerald* (1892), grandfather of the prominent Australian poet of the same name; and a sermon in memory of the novelist Caroline Atkinson (1874).

'Wooyeo Ball, The', see **'Euabalong Ball, The'**

Worker, a Brisbane labour journal, was established as a monthly but ran mainly as a weekly 1890–1974. A trades union organ, it carried labour news, political articles and reports, fiction and poetry; among prominent contributors in the 1890s were Francis Adams, John Farrell and Henry Lawson. The *Worker* emerged at a time of labour agitation in Queensland and in its early days was more strongly established than its NSW equivalent, the Sydney *Worker* which it incorporated in 1892–93. The best-known editor of the *Worker* was its founding one, William Lane, whose novel, *The Workingman's Paradise*, was serialized in the journal in 1891. Later editors included the poet and politician, Francis Kenna, and the journalist and writer, H.E. Boote.

Worker (Sydney), see **Australian Worker**

Working Bullocks, see **PRICHARD, KATHARINE SUSANNAH**

Working Papers in Sex, Science and Culture, see **Feminism and Australian Literature**

Workingman's Paradise, The, a novel by William Lane under the pseudonym 'John Miller' and subtitled, *An Australian Labour Novel*, to emphasize its openly propagandist attitudes, was published in 1892. In his preface Lane explains that the novel's purpose is to assist the fund for the unionists imprisoned for conspiracy in the shearers' strike of 1891 and to explain socialism to the world at large. The novel's title, ironically used, is a phrase taken from Henry Kingsley's novel, *The Recollections of Geoffry Hamlyn* (1859).

The novel is in two parts, 'The Woman Tempted Him' and 'He Knew Himself Naked'. Its protagonists, Nellie Lawton, a Sydney dressmaker (claimed by Mary Gilmore to be a fictional representation of her) and Ned Hawkins, a Queensland bushman, meet in Sydney in the summer of 1888–89. Nellie, an ardent socialist, introduces the naive, generous-hearted Ned to the squalor and destitution of Sydney's poorer areas: the grimy slums themselves; the sweated labour of the rag trade and restaurants; Paddy's Market, the festering sore of Sydney's poverty; the prostitutes and beggars who live off the streets and sleep in the parks; the circle of radical intelligentsia (e.g. Connie and Harry Stratton, and Geisner), where social solutions are aired in 'a medley of conversation'. Notable incidents include the recitation of F.J. Broomfield's poem 'The Vision of Labour' by the poet, Arty, thought to be modelled on Henry Lawson; Nellie's illustration of practical socialism by kissing a sleeping prostitute; and the indoctrination of young Ned by Geisner with the principles of Marxism and new unionism. The second part occurs after an interval of two years. The maritime strike of 1890 has failed, the shearers' strike of 1891 is imminent and Ned is now an active, dedicated unionist. Several stereotyped incidents, e.g. the death of a young child through deprivation and the moral ruin of Nellie's younger sister through poverty, cause Nellie to refuse to marry Ned. She vows never to bring children into the degradation and misery that constitute working-class life. Ned is inspired to confront capitalism even more strongly and returns to Queensland to implement the shearers' strike.

Woroni, a student journal of the Australian National University, began publication in 1947 and has occasionally attracted original work from poets and writers living in the Canberra region.

Wort Papers, The, see MATHERS, PETER

Wowser, defined by *The Macquarie Dictionary* (1981) as 'a prudish teetotaller' or 'a killjoy' and by C.J. Dennis as 'an ineffably pious person who mistakes this world for a penitentiary and himself for a warder', is a term of uncertain origin. It is popularly accepted to be an acronym coined by John Norton, owner of the newspaper *Truth*, signifying 'We Only Want Social Evils Remedied (or Righted)'. Alec H. Chisholm, however, has suggested that the word derives from 'rouser', a term for religious fanatics current in Victoria in the 1870s. The wowser, who has been a persistent figure in Australian cultural life but who appears to have had his heyday from the 1880s to the end of the First World War, was frequently depicted in cartoons in the *Bulletin* and other newspapers during those years. He invariably appeared bearded, wearing a small, flat hat or a gimlet and carrying the universal symbol of a wowser, an umbrella. Numerous Australian writers have inveighed against wowsers, including Norman Lindsay, C.J. Dennis, Frank Hardy, Hugh McCrae, A.D. Hope, Douglas Stewart, Dal Stivens, Geoffrey Dutton and Dorothy Hewett; others have suffered the effects of wowserism in the form of censorship. Keith Dunstan in *Wowsers* (1968) has written 'an account of the prudery exhibited by certain outstanding men and women in such matters as Drink, Smoking, Prostitution, Censorship and Gambling'.

WREN, JOHN (1871–1953), a Melbourne sports promoter and financier, was born into a poor family at Collingwood, where he ran an illegal, but highly profitable, totalizator 1893–1907. He later acquired interests in racecourses and other sporting enterprises and in 1916 took control of the interstate boxing enterprise, Stadiums Ltd. In 1915 he acquired the Brisbane *Daily Mail*. Wren, frequently accused of illegal and even criminal activities and of political manipulation, appears as the central character John West in Frank Hardy's novel, *Power Without Glory* (q.v., 1950). Hardy, charged with criminal libel (of Mrs Wren only) in 1951, was acquitted after a nine-month trial and gave an account of the writing of the novel and of his trial in *The Hard Way* (1961). Wren also appears as a character in Barry Oakley's play, *The Feet of Daniel Mannix* (1975). There are two accounts of his life, Niall Brennan's *John Wren: Gambler* (1971) and Hugh Buggy's *The Real John Wren* (1977).

WRIGHT, ALBERT and MAY, see *Generations of Men, The*

WRIGHT, ARTHUR (1870–1932), born near Bathurst, was a writer of fiction, usually with a background of horse-racing, other sports and crime. He published numerous novels and stories including *Keane of Kalgoorlie* (1907), *A Rogue's Luck* (1910), *Gambler's Gold* (1911), *Rung In* (1912), *In the Last Stride* (1914), *Under a Cloud* (1916), *Over the Odds* (1918), which contains three other stories, *The Breed Holds Good* (1918), *When Nuggets Glistened* (1918), *The Outlaw's Daughter* (1919), *A Game of Chance* (1919), *A Rough Passage* (1920), *Fettered by Fate* (1921), *A Colt from the Country* (1922), *The Squatter's Secret* (1927), *A Good Recovery* (1928), *A Crooked Game* (1928) and *Gaming for Gold* (1929). Occasionally classified with Nat Gould, Wright nevertheless lacks Gould's ease, versatility and range. His novels are characterized by simple, 'low-life' characters, straightforward if action-filled plots, rough humour and sketchily-realized Australian backgrounds. Four of Wright's novels were produced as films, *Keane of Kalgoorlie* and *Gambler's Gold* in 1911, *In the Last Stride* in 1916, and *A Rough Passage* in 1922, and he also won an award for his screenplay, 'The Loyal Rebel' (1915).

WRIGHT, DAVID McKEE (1869–1928), born Ireland, was educated in London, and at eighteen migrated to NZ, visiting Sydney *en route*. In NZ he worked on a sheep station, studied for the Congregational ministry and from 1890 contributed to many NZ journals. In 1905 he gave up the ministry to become a journalist on the *New Zealand Mail*. Four of his volumes of verse were published in NZ, *Aorangi and Other Verses* (1896), *Station Ballads* (1897), *Wisps of Tussock* (1900) and *New Zealand Chimes* (1900), and some of his poems appeared in Australian periodicals. In 1910 he moved to Sydney, where he worked as a freelance writer for the *Bulletin* and other newspapers before succeeding Arthur H. Adams as editor of the *Bulletin*'s Red Page. He continued to write prolifically in prose and verse, often using such pseudonyms as 'Pat O'Maori', 'George Street' and 'Mary McCommonwealth'. In 1918 he published his most substantial collection of verse, *An Irish Heart*, and in 1920 was awarded a prize for a poem commemorating the visit of the Prince of Wales, as well as the Rupert Brooke Memorial Prize for a long poem titled 'Gallipoli'. Wright also wrote some plays, although these, with much of his verse and prose writings, are uncollected; a prose playlet is included in the *Australian Soldiers' Gift Book* (1918). Like Victor Daley, Wright was strongly influenced by Irish history and legend, although his verse is generally thinner and less striking. Predominant characteristics of his prolific output are an indistinct but pervasive nostalgia for Ireland, visual, general imagery, firmly-handled rhythms and a generally optimistic content. An influential editor of the Red Page, Wright also edited *Poetical Works of Henry Lawson* (q.v., 1925). He was married after a long and much-publicized *de facto* relationship to the poet, Zora Cross.

WRIGHT, JUDITH (1915–), was born at Armidale, NSW, into a pastoralist family whose roots go back to the original settlement of the Hunter Valley in the 1820s. Her father, Phillip Arundell Wright (1889–1970), prominent New England pastoralist, wrote the autobiographical *Memories of a Bushwacker* (1971). She grew up on the family property, Wallamumbi, near Armidale, in the heart of the New England tablelands, and her love for that countryside, her 'blood's country', runs through much of her early poetry. Educated at the University of Sydney, she visited England and Europe 1938–39 before settling in Sydney to write. She published an occasional modest, thoughtful poem, e.g. 'The Hanging Avalanche of Days' in *Southerly* (1940), but with the entry of Japan into the war returned to help out at Wallamumbi, then badly beset by manpower prob-

lems. That homecoming, which brought the rediscovery and reassessment of her attachment to the countryside and the opportunity to think deeply about her art, led to her first intensive creative period. From the old stockman Dan's tales of the early days of the district and from the diaries of her grandfather, Albert Wright, came material that filled much of her early writing, stories that in her own words 'still go walking in my sleep'. Several fine poems about the war, 'The Trains', 'The Company of Lovers', 'To A.H. New Year, 1943', were written at this time. In 1944–48 she worked at the University of Queensland, where she met and married J.P. McKinney (q.v.), philosopher and writer. Since Wright's publication of *The Moving Image* (q.v., 1946), she has been a prolific poet, literary critic, anthologist, editor, fiction writer and active conservationist. She has received doctorates of letters from the Universities of Queensland and New England and awards for poetry, e.g. the Grace Leven Prize twice, and for literature, the Australia-Britannica Award in 1964. In 1970 she was elected a foundation fellow of the Australian Academy of the Humanities and has been a member of the governing body of the Australia Council.

Her chief volumes of poetry after *The Moving Image* are *Woman to Man* (q.v., 1949); *The Gateway* (q.v., 1953); *The Two Fires* (q.v., 1955); *Birds* (1962); *Five Senses* (1963) (one of several selected and collected volumes); *City Sunrise* (1964); *The Other Half* (1966); *Alive: Poems 1971–1972* (1973), and *Fourth Quarter and Other Poems* (1976). Her *Collected Poems 1942–1970* and *The Double Tree: Selected Poems 1942–1976* were published, respectively, in 1971 and 1978. She has written children's fiction and a book of short stories, *The Nature of Love* (1966); edited several anthologies, including *A Book of Australian Verse* (1956), and two selections of John Shaw Neilson's poetry (1963 and 1970); written monographs on Charles Harpur and Henry Lawson; narrated her family's history in *The Generations of Men* (q.v., 1959) and its sequel, *The Cry for the Dead* (1981); published a selection of her essays and reviews, *Because I Was Invited* (1975); written an important seminal book of Australian poetic criticism, *Preoccupations in Australian Poetry* (1965); and in her role as conservationist told of the battle to preserve the Great Barrier Reef from oil drilling and limestone mining in *The Coral Battleground* (1977).

The appearance of *The Moving Image* in 1946 brought a sense of excitement and anticipation to the Australian literary world; its impact was summed up in Douglas Stewart's *Bulletin* review: 'These poems promise anything, everything, the world'. The poems were acclaimed for their lyric beauty, brilliant craftmanship, and emotional honesty. The volumes following *Woman to Man*, except for the whimsical *Birds*, were received with less general enthusiasm. In them she reached beyond the easily-perceived world of the senses in a search for some ultimate reality, perception or self-knowledge. In *The Gateway*, she refers to 'the Traveller' and many of the poems of it and succeeding volumes are a record of her pilgrimage towards that reality and knowledge. Her initial view of the poet as the creative interpreter of the universe and its eternal processes of change still remains, however, at the centre of her poetry. Her recognition of 'the continuity of experience through time' leads her to accept the world as an interdependent community of all living things (human, animal, plant) and her use of nature as a stepping-stone to a deeper exploratory probing of universal human questions is still a satisfying basis from which the reader can proceed to an understanding and appreciation of her total work. In later volumes again, especially in 'Shadow' (1970), the closing section of her *Collected Poems 1942–1970*, she attacks the evils of modern society, especially its abnegation of responsibility for the brutality that daily characterizes world affairs. Australian society with its history of crimes against the land and the Aborigines is also a subject of her poetry, speeches and prose, especially in *The Cry for the Dead*. Shirley Walker wrote *The Poetry of Judith Wright: A Search for Unity* (1980).

WRIGHTSON, PATRICIA (1921–   ), born Lismore, NSW, an outstanding writer of children's fiction, has won the Children's Book of the Year Award in 1956, 1974 and 1978. Her novels are *The Crooked Snake* (1955), *The Bunyip Hole* (1957), *The Rocks of Honey* (1960), *The Feather Star* (1962), *Down to Earth* (1965), *I Own the Racecourse!* (1968), winner of the Hans Christian Andersen Award, *An Older Kind of Magic* (1972), *The Nargun and the Stars* (1973), *The Ice Is Coming* (1977), *The Dark Bright Water* (1978), winner of a special children's book award, and *Behind the Wind* (1981). The last three, dealing with the adventures of Wirrun, an Aboriginal boy, were published as a trilogy in 1983, titled *The Book of Wirrun*. She has also edited two anthologies, *Beneath the Sun* (1972) and *Emu Stew* (1976), and was editor of the influential NSW *School Magazine* (1970–75). A versatile writer, interested in fantasy or science fiction as a medium for exploration and in Aboriginal lore, Wrightson frequently tells a story that is credible, lively and engaging, but that also suggests more than surface reality. Sensitive to the real interests and anxieties of children, her subtle explorations of human relationships are neither patronizing nor pretentiously adult. Particularly striking is *I Own the Racecourse!*, a study of a boy of subnormal mentality, whose integrity and simple trust compel others to a humane, respectful acceptance of his standards and perceptions.

Wyville, see *Moondyne*

Y

Yabber (Yabba) Club was a club which met weekly in the Shalimar cafe in Sydney during the late 1930s and early 1940s. Originally formed by P.R. Stephensen, W.J. Miles and others to discuss the editorial policy of the *Publicist*, the Australia First journal, its meetings subsequently embraced literary and cultural topics. Eleanor Dark, Frank Dalby Davison, Miles Franklin, Lionel Lindsay and T. Inglis Moore were among writers 'permanently invited', and Franklin, Xavier Herbert, Harley Matthews and Ian Mudie were among writers who attended.

Yabsley, Ada, see *Jonah*

YAGAN (?–1833), a WA Aboriginal who acquired a reputation for patriotism, courage and resourcefulness, was sentenced to detention for killing a white man in 1832 but soon escaped. He was proclaimed an outlaw in April 1833 with his father, Midgigoroo, following the massacre of other whites, and was shot for the reward in July 1833 by a young shepherd, William Keates. Yagan's escapades are described in G.F. Moore's *Diary of Ten Years Eventful Life of an Early Settler in Western Australia* (1884). An extended account of his activities is in W.B. Kimberly, *History of West Australia* (1897). Mary Durack wrote *The Courteous Savage: Yagan of Swan River* (1964).

Yandy (1959), a novel by Donald Stuart (q.v.), gives a fictional account of the establishment of the Aboriginal Pindan Co-operative in WA in 1946. The station Aborigines of north-west WA, led by Winyerin, or Dooley as he is called by the white people, and assisted by the help and advice of a white man, Don McLeod, strike for better conditions and more tolerant racial attitudes. The Aborigines turn to 'yandying' for a livelihood, i.e. shaking minerals from alluvial dirt by the use of a special dish. In spite of confrontations with police and white society, the Aborigines remain steadfast. They discover the profitable mineral wolfram and begin to construct a new life.

Yaralie (1962), a novel by Donald Stuart (q.v.), is the story of a young, part-Aboriginal girl, Yaralie. After her mother's death the young girl shares with her father, a stockman-turned-prospector, an itinerant life in outback WA. They are separated when he goes south to recover from a stroke and she endures the cruelty and intolerance customarily extended to the Aboriginal. As a girl of fifteen she falls in love with young Raymond Mendoza, of Filipino extraction, and they resume the old life of prospecting. At the end of the novel Yaralie has a final meeting with her dying father and tells him of the child she is carrying, a child of mixed descent, Australian, Scottish, Aboriginal and Filipino, 'a child of the country', one who would form part of the future generations that would people the North-West. In Stuart's and the old man's words, 'They'll be the *real* people of Nor'-west, the people who know it and understand it, the way it's got to be known and understood'. The novel's strength is its compelling picture of the harsh but beautiful inland environment and the precarious existence of those who live in fragile affinity with it.

Yarra River flows (Sydneysiders believe that to be a euphemism) from Mount Baw Baw, east of Melbourne, some 250 kilometres to Port Phillip Bay. Discovered by Charles Grimes in 1803, the river was named Yarra Yarra by J.H. Wedge in 1835. On its banks, John Batman (q.v.) decided, was 'the place for a village' – the present city of Melbourne. More often the subject of derisive comments than of panegyrics, the Yarra is nevertheless an essential part of the Melbourne scene. It has given its name to the 'Yarra Banker', originally a specialist in the art of loafing, more recently a soapbox orator who harangues the passing crowds, especially on a Sunday afternoon. When the Murray River became part of the boundary between NSW and Victoria, the term 'Yarrasiders' denoted the Victorians as opposed to 'Sydneysi-

ders', who lived north of the Murray. Some of the picturesque aspects of the river are captured in Bill Beasley and Brian Carroll's *River Yarra Sketchbook* (1973).

YARRINGTON, W.H.H. (WILLIAM HENRY HAZELL) (?–1920), a clergyman with numerous literary friends, published several volumes of verse in book and pamphlet form 1880–1919. They include *University Prize Poem and Other Verses* (1880), *Coelestia* (1882), *Turning to the East* (1890), *Australian Verses* (1892), *Sonnets on Ritualism* (1901), *The Man of Principle* (?1904), and *Crossing the Mountain* (1919). He also edited the anthology, *Prince Alfred's Wreath* (1868), which includes poetry by Henry Kendall and J. Sheridan Moore. Yarrington is one of the minor targets of Kendall's satiric poem, *The Bronze Trumpet*.

Year of Living Dangerously, The, a novel by Christopher Koch (q.v.), was published in 1978, won the *Age* Book of the Year and the National Book Council Awards, and was made into a film in 1982, scripted by Koch, Peter Weir and David Williamson. It is set in Jakarta in 1965 against the backdrop of the mysterious intrigues that culminated in Sukarno's fall. Public events have strange, revolutionary effects on the lives and relationships of Guy Hamilton, an Australian news correspondent; his remarkable Chinese-Australian cameraman, Billy Kwan; and the woman they both love, Jill Bryant. Oppressive, unpredictable and latently violent, the external situation powerfully complements these suspenseful, personal vicissitudes.

YELDHAM, PETER, born Gladstone, NSW, worked as a scriptwriter for radio before leaving for England in 1956 and establishing a reputation as a writer for film and television. In 1975 he returned to Australia, where he has written such popular novel-adaptations for television as *The Timeless Land*, *1915* (qq.v.), *Golden Soak*, *Sporting Chance*, *Ride on Stranger*, *Run from the Morning* (which was also published as a book in 1980) and *All the Rivers Run*. Yeldham has also written stage plays, three of which have been produced, 'Birds on the Wing', 'Ready When You Are Darling' and, with Donald Churchill, *Fringe Benefits* (1977).

'YITTADAIRN', see **RUSDEN, GEORGE WILLIAM**

You Can't See Round Corners, a novel by Jon Cleary (q.v.), was published in 1947 and won second prize in the *Sydney Morning Herald's* novel competition of 1946. It was also produced as a film and as a television series.

Set mainly in Sydney during the Second World War, it is the story of twenty-one-year-old Frankie McCoy, who has experienced poverty in childhood, has learnt to depend on his wits and holds an inarticulate grudge against the social system. A basically weak individual who lacks self-knowledge, he drifts inevitably towards his shabby fate. Conscripted into the army, he hates the boredom and regimentation and soon deserts. After Margie, his girlfriend of seven years, rejects him in consequence, he becomes involved with another, more sexually-experienced girl, Myra. Entangled in gambling debts, he robs a shop and then inadvertently kills Myra in a fit of frustrated passion. A reconciliation with Margie leads to his apprehension by the military police, his death and the discovery of his crimes.

Yorick Club, which included most of the prominent Victorian writers of the 1860s, was founded by Frederick William Haddon in 1868 and grew from the informal meetings he held during 1867–68 at his rooms in Spring Street, Melbourne. Established 'for the purpose of bringing together literary men and those connected with literature, art or science', it included among its earliest members Adam Lindsay Gordon, Hamilton Mackinnon, J.J. Shillinglaw, Marcus Clarke, James E. Neild and George Arthur Walstab. Clarke was the Club's first secretary, although he left it soon afterwards to form a more bohemian group, the Cave of Adullam. Henry Kendall became a member during his stay in Melbourne and later literary members included George Gordon McCrae and Patrick Moloney. At first a lively and informal gathering of writers, committed to practical jokes and all-night suppers, the Yorick soon dwindled into a respectable institution. By 1871 its entry rule had been altered to include 'professional men' and the financial pressures of the 1890s caused further enlargements. The original Yorick Club was wound up in 1894. *The Yorick Club: Its Origin and Development, May 1868 to December 1910* (1911) by Thomas Carrington is an account of its history and membership, and Hugh McCrae describes some of its activities in *My Father, and My Father's Friends* (1935).

Young Desire It, The, a novel by Kenneth Mackenzie (q.v.), which was first published in 1937 under his pseudonym 'Seaforth Mackenzie', won the Gold Medal of the Australian Literature Society. An account of a year in the life of a sensitive fifteen-year-old-boy, Charles Fox, it deals with his intellectual, emotional and sexual awakening when he leaves his home and his protective mother to enter boarding school. One of the masters, an Englishman named Christopher Penworth, forms an attachment for him, although Charles remains innocent of its homosexual implications. Meanwhile, Charles has formed a stronger, idyllically-realized relationship with a girl, Margaret McLeod. The romance eventually excites Penworth's jealousy and leads to a cooling of his relationship with Charles. Penworth returns to England and at the same time Charles learns that Margaret is to leave for finishing school in Switzerland. The book ends with Charles back at school in the new year, a letter from Penworth in his hand, contemplating his past, irrevocable experiences.

Young Man of Talent, a novel by George Turner (q.v.), was published in London in 1959 and in New York the same year with the title *Scobie*. Set in New Guinea during the Second World War, it probes the fatally dissimilar personalities of three Australian soldiers: Scobie, a veteran New Guinea campaigner who has speedily risen to platoon commander and developed a taste for power; Payne, a rebel, who quickly accedes to total subservience to Scobie's superior intellect; and Tolley, a paranoid, insecure graduate from the Royal Military College, Duntroon, who arrives to take over Scobie's command. The story traces Scobie's moral deterioration as he effectively uses Payne to destroy Tolley, destroying his own humanity in the process.

Young Wife, The, a novel by David Martin (q.v.), was published in 1962. Anna Christofidou, a Cypriot girl, arrives in Sydney to marry a man she has never met, Yannis Joannides, a greengrocer. She is welcomed by Yannis, his successful but devious brother Alexis and his wife Elena, and by her future mother-in-law, Maria, who has arranged the marriage. Yannis becomes friendly with a Cypriot artist, Criton, who has come to Australia to escape his terrorist past and is drawn to Anna by her special qualities of purity and deep feeling. He later paints a picture of Ariadne rising from the sea, based on his drawings of Anna, on the wall of Yannis's shop. Anna is drawn into amateur theatricals through her family's friendship with a Professor Peter Barwing and his wife Patricia, an association that ends abruptly when Peter Barwing attempts to make love to Anna. Yannis later beats Anna when he hears something of what has happened. Meanwhile Criton becomes unwittingly involved in the political feuds of the Greek community and in a love affair with Patricia Barwing that ends in her attempted suicide. Anna intercedes unavailingly on Patricia's behalf with Criton and Patricia leaves for an extended visit to India. On her return she contributes to false rumours about the now pregnant Anna and Criton, which are exacerbated by his enemies and by Yannis's insensitive reaction to his drawings of Anna. A fight ensues between Criton and Yannis in which Criton is killed. Martin also wrote a dramatized version of *The Young Wife*, which was staged in 1966.

YOUNG, WILLIAM BLAMIRE (1862 -1935), painter and poster artist, was born England and came to Australia in 1885, when he became friendly with Phil May, the illus-

trator. Young returned to England in 1912, served in the First World War and subsequently had several major exhibitions in London. In 1923 he returned to Melbourne, where he became art critic for the *Herald*. Two of Young's one-act plays, 'Art for Art's Sake' and *The Children's Bread* (1912) were produced in Melbourne in 1911. His painting was the subject of a special number of *Art in Australia* in 1921.

Younger Australian Poets, see **Anthologies**

Z

ZILLMANN, JOHN HERMAN LEOPOLD (1842–1919), an Anglican minister, born Brisbane and resident in Queensland, published two novels which are mainly religious in tone, *In the Land of the Bunya: Or, the Convict and the Boy* (1899) and *From Old to New: Or, Mitre Versus Gown* (1901); four collections of religious verse and one of hymns; a prose meditation on the supernatural, *Two Worlds Are Ours* (1885); and two works which mingle history, description and personal reminiscence, *Past and Present Australian Life* (1889) and *Career of a Cornstalk* (1914).

ZWICKY, FAY (1933–   ), born Melbourne, began writing as an undergraduate at the University of Melbourne and has published short stories and poems in anthologies and periodicals. A concert pianist for some years before teaching English at the University of WA, she has published two collections of verse, *Isaac Babel's Fiddle* (1975) and *Kaddish and Other*

Poems (1982), winner of the NSW Premier's Award, and has edited *Quarry* (1981), a selection of contemporary WA poetry, and *Journeys* (1982), an anthology of poems by Judith Wright, Rosemary Dobson, Gwen Harwood and Dorothy Hewett. Her first collection of short stories, *Hostages*, was published in 1983. Zwicky writes an individual, emotionally-direct and densely-textured poetry which is concerned with division, conflict and dispossession, the paradoxes of experience, the ambivalences of relationships and the relation between artist and art. One of her most admired poems, 'Kaddish', is a lament for the death of her father, which is also a vivid, funny/sad evocation of life in a Melbourne Jewish family. Four of the stories of *Hostages* also draw on her youthful experience in Melbourne and evoke the pains, humiliations and enlightenments of growing up; others use a range of narrators to explore various aspects of contemporary Australian life.